May 7–12, 2011
Vancouver, BC

Association for
Computing Machinery

Advancing Computing as a Science & Profession

2011 CHI

The 29th Annual CHI Conference on
Human Factors in Computing Systems

Sponsored by:
ACM SIGCHI

Volume 3

Association for
Computing Machinery

Advancing Computing as a Science & Profession

The Association for Computing Machinery
2 Penn Plaza, Suite 701
New York, New York 10121-0701

ISBN: 978-1-4503-0228-9 (Digital)

ISBN: 978-1-4503-0267-8 (Print)

Additional copies may be ordered prepaid from:

ACM Order Department
PO Box 30777
New York, NY 10087-0777, USA

Phone: 1-800-342-6626 (USA and Canada)
+1-212-626-0500 (Global)
Fax: +1-212-944-1318
E-mail: acmhelp@acm.org
Hours of Operation: 8:30 am – 4:30 pm ET

ACM Order Number: 609111

Printed in the USA

About SIGCHI and ACM

CHI 2011 is sponsored by ACM's Special Interest Group on Computer-Human Interaction (ACM SIGCHI). The scope of SIGCHI consists of the study of the human-computer interaction processes and includes research, design, development, and evaluation efforts for interactive computer systems. The focus of SIGCHI is on how people communicate and interact with a broadly-defined range of computer systems. SIGCHI serves as a forum for the exchange of ideas among computer scientists, human factors scientists, psychologists, social scientists, designers, educators, and practitioners involved in the design, implementation, and evaluation of interactive computing systems. Nearly 5,000 professional members of the SIGCHI community work together toward common goals and objectives. Visit SIGCHI at http://www.sigchi.org.

ACM, the Association for Computing Machinery http://www.acm.org/, is an educational and scientific society uniting the world's computing educators, researchers and professionals to inspire dialogue, share resources and address the field's challenges. ACM strengthens the profession's collective voice through strong leadership, promotion of the highest standards, and recognition of technical excellence.ACM supports the professional growth of its members by providing opportunities for life-long learning, career development, and professional networking. ACM offers its 87,000 global members cutting-edge technical information through world class journals and magazines, dynamic specia linterest groups and globally recognized conferences.

Welcome from Chairs

Over the last year or so, we have been blessed with the challenge, the opportunity, and the distinct pleasure of organizing the CHI 2011 Conference on Human Factors in Computing Systems, the premier international conference for the field of human-computer interaction.

CHI 2011 takes place in gorgeous, energetic, sophisticated Vancouver BC, a city renowned for its innovation in entertainment, sustainability, accessibility, and inclusivity. The New York Times calls it, "a liquid city, a tomorrow city, equal parts India, China, England, France and the Pacific Northwest." Vancouver lays a beautiful backdrop for our conference, which boasts nearly 30 years of wonderful work.

Behind the success of the conference is our diverse community of faculty and students, of researchers and practitioners, of young and, well, also of experienced. It is a community of designers, technologists, psychologists, social scientists, biologists, artists, engineers, anthropologists, musicians; the list goes on. Wherever we are, we are always a community of near and far. Most impressively, ours is a community that cares deeply about innovating, learning, sharing, and interacting; all with the common goal of using technology to shape the way people around the world live and play.

Returning attendees will recognize the general conference format - 2 days of small intimate workshops, followed by 4 days of technical content, all surrounded by social and intellectual exchanges. In addition to the familiar venues that form the core of the conference, we have also arranged various special events, such an keynotes by Howard Rheingold and Ethan Zuckerman; invited talks by ACM SIGCHI award winners Terry Winograd, Larry Tesler, Alan Newell, and Clayton Lewis; an HCI museum exhibit hosted by Bill Buxton; and a panel celebrating Stu Card's achievements and contributions to the field of HCI.

With the record number of submissions and accepted content this year, we hope that you will utilize the print and electronic programs, but also the daily CHI Madness presentations that provide a glimpse of the day ahead. In the interest of continuing to evolve the conference to best serve our needs, we will experiment with shorter talks this year (20 minute slots for long pieces of content and 10 for shorter ones) to infuse even more energy into the program. We will also have a pretty full slate of social media applications to help you connect with other attendees and to provide you with the fullest experience possible.

It has been quite the ride, and we'd like to thank everyone involved and welcome you all to the conference. We hope that CHI 2011 inspires you reflect on the past, the present, and perhaps most importantly, the future of the people and body of work that is ACM SIGCHI. We hope you enjoy CHI 2011 in Vancouver and that you have a great time "Connecting..."

Desney Tan
CHI 2011 General Conference Chair
Microsoft Research

Bo Begole
CHI 2011 Technical Program Chairs
PARC

Wendy Kellogg
CHI 2011 Technical Program Chairs
IBM Research

From ACM SIGCHI's President and Vice President for Conferences

SIGCHI is proud to sponsor the premier annual conference in the field of human-computer interaction. Past CHI conferences have been known for being the stage of new developments and advances in HCI, and for memorable events. CHI 2011 is no exception. We are extremely grateful to the CHI 2011 Conference Chair Desney Tan, to Technical Program Chairs Bo Begole and Wendy Kellogg, and to their wonderful crew, who succeeded to build an impressive program and experience.

CHI, the conference that is organized on behalf of ACM's Special Interest Group on Computer-Human Interaction (SIGCHI) is an ideal forum for people to meet formally as well as informally, to exchange knowledge and views, to share experiences, and to learn. The CHI conference brings together professionals from research and practice; people from industry, academia, and from government; long-term veterans of HCI, young professionals and students; all in an environment designed to encourage interaction. We invite you to actively participate in that interaction: introduce yourself to people, interact with presenters and speakers, renew old friendships and make new ones.

SIGCHI is an international community of professionals who share an interest in the many diverse facets of HCI. SIGCHI is committed both to advancing the field of HCI, to facilitate exchange of information within the SIGCHI community, and to support students to enter the domain.

The CHI conference is arguably the single most visible activity of SIGCHI, but we also sponsor and support a wide range of specialized conferences in areas ranging from interactive systems design to user interface technology to computer-supported cooperative work to "intelligent" user interfaces. Visit the SIGCHI website at http://www.sigchi.org to find our conference schedule, listing upcoming as well as past conferences.

SIGCHI and ACM produce some of the most respected publications in the field. All members receive interactions, a highly-acclaimed magazine covering the broad field of HCI and user interface design. ACM Transactions on Computer-Human Interactions (ToCHI), now in its 17th year, is our flagship journal - a quarterly publication with the top-quality archival research aimed at researchers and those translating research into practice.

SIGCHI is truly an international organization, with 32 local chapters and 3 student chapters in 19 countries on 5 continents. We encourage all SIGCHI members to join their local chapter - or if there isn't one in your area, we would love to help you create one. And don't forget virtual communities! SIGCHI hosts dozens of electronic mailing lists on topics ranging from HCI and the Web, to HCI educations, to public policy and beyond. Those lists range from dozens of subscribers to thousands, and are an excellent way to keep up with the field and with friends and colleagues.

Finally, on behalf of ACM SGICHI, we again want to thank the conference committee and all of the hundreds of volunteers who make this conference possible. Their work makes this a rewarding experience for all of us.

Gerrit C. van der Veer
SIGCHI President

John "Scooter" Morris
SIGCHI Vice-President for Conferences

CHI 2011 Table of Contents

CHI 2011 Table of Contents

CHI 2011 Table of Contents

CHI 2011 Table of Contents

CHI 2011 Table of Contents

CHI 2011 Table of Contents

CHI 2011 Table of Contents

CHI 2011 Table of Contents

CHI 2011 Table of Contents

CHI 2011 Table of Contents

CHI 2011 Table of Contents

CHI 2011 Table of Contents

CHI 2011 Table of Contents

CHI 2011 Table of Contents

CHI 2011 Table of Contents

CHI 2011 Table of Contents

CHI 2011 Table of Contents

CHI 2011 Table of Contents

CHI 2011 Table of Contents

CHI 2011 Table of Contents

Engaging Youth

Session Chair: Juan Pablo Hourcade, *University of Iowa*

Tangibles

Session Chair: Patrick Baudisch, *Hasso Plattner Institute*

Groups Around the Table

Session Chair: Kenton O'Hara, *CSIRO*

Rehabilitation

Session Chair: Sunny Consolvo, *Intel Labs*

CHI 2011 Table of Contents

CHI 2011 Table of Contents

CHI 2011 Table of Contents

CHI 2010 Organizing Committee

Conference Chair
Desney Tan, *Microsoft Research*

Conference Chair Assistant
Saleema Amershi, *University of Washington*

Technical Program

Chairs
Bo Begole, *PARC*
Wendy A. Kellogg, *IBM Research*

Technical Program Chairs Assistant
Manas Tungare

Papers
Geraldine Fitzpatrick, *Vienna University of Technology*
Carl Gutwin, *University of Saskatchewan*

alt.chi chairs
Daniel Wigdor, *Microsoft*
Patrick Baudisch, *Hasso Plattner Institute*

Case Studies Chair
Manfred Tscheligi, *University of Salzberg*

Courses Chairs
Nancy Frishberg, *MSB Associates*
Regina Bernhaupt, *IRIT -- University of Toulouse*

Doctoral Consortium Chairs
Mary Beth Rosson, *Penn State University*
Saul Greenberg, *University of Calgary*

Interactivity Chairs
Jan Borchers, *RWTH Aachen University*
Lyn Bartram, *Simon Fraser University*
Sid Fels, *University of British Columbia*

Panels Chairs
John C. Thomas, *IBM Research*
Simone Barbosa, *PUC-Rio*

Poster Chair
Anthony Tang, *Georgia Tech*

Special Interest Groups (SIGS) Chairs
Ido Guy, *IBM Research*
Daphne Raban, *University of Haifa*

Student Design Competition Chairs
Stephen Brewster, *University of Glasgow*
Youn-kyung Lim, *KAIST*

Video Chairs
Michael Bernstein, *Massachusetts Institute of Technology*
Shahram Izadi, *Microsoft*

Work-in-Progress (WIPs) Chairs
Brian Bailey, *University of Illinois, Urbana-Champaign*
Mark Newman, *University of Michigan*

Workshops Chairs
Daniela Busse, *SAP Labs (Palo Alto)*
Catalina Danis, *IBM Research*

Core Communities

Communities Chair
Arnie Lund, *Microsoft*

Design Community Chairs
Scott Pobiner, *Parsons The New School for Design*
Carla Diana, *Smart Design*

User Experience Community Chairs
Elizabeth Buie, *Luminanze Consulting*
Jhilmil Jain, *Microsoft*

Engineering Community Chairs
Ruven Brooks, *Independent Consultant*
Keith Butler, *University of Washington*

Management Community Chairs
Jim Nieters, *Yahoo!*
Carola Fellenz Thompson, *Mindjet*

FEATURED COMMUNITIES

Child Computer Interaction Community Chairs
Janet C Read, *University of Central Lancashire*
Panos Markopoulos, Eindhoven University of Technology
Allison Druin, *University of Maryland*

Games and Entertainment Community Chairs
Regina Bernhaupt, *IRIT - University of Toulouse*
Katherine Isbister, *NYU-Poly*

Health Community Chairs
Gillian R. Hayes, *University of California, Irvine*
Madhu Reddy, *The Pennsylvania State University*

Sustainability Community Chairs
Azam Khan, *Autodesk Research*
Eli Blevis, *Indiana University-Bloomington*

PARTICIPATION & VOLUNTEERING

Student Volunteer Coordinators
Aaron Houssian, *Philips Research, TU/Delft*
Vicky McArthur, *York University*

Madness Chairs
Paul André, *University of Southampton*
Max L. Wilson, *Swansea University*

Social Media Chair
Cliff Lampe, *Michigan State University*

Publicity Chair
Kirstie Hawkey, *University of British Columbia*

SPONSORS, EXHIBITS, & TECHNOLOGY

Sponsors and Exhibits
Carol Klyver

Registration Coordinator
Yvonne Lopez

Design Directors
Oscar Murillo, *Microsoft*
Cole Benson, *University of Washington*

Webmaster
Lydia Chilton, *University of Washington*

Proceedings & Program Chairs
Aurélien Tabard, *IT University of Copenhagen*
Max Van Kleek, *Massachusetts Institute of Technology*
Nirmal Patel, *Georgia Tech*

Technology Liaisons
Scooter Morris, *University of California, San Francisco*
Sara Drenner, *Inuvo*

LOGISTICS

ACM Staff Liaisons
Ashley Cozzi, *Association for Computing Machinery*

CMC Staff Liaisons
Scooter Morris, *University of California, San Francisco*

Conference Logistics
Janeé Pelletier, *Conference & Logistics Consultants*

CHI 2011 Sponsors, Supporters, Champions, Contributors, & Friends

CHI 2011 Champions

Bloomberg Microsoft

ebay PayPal

NSF

Google

SAP

CHI 2011 Contributors

Autodesk

IBM Research

Graphisme, animation et nouveaux médias

GRAND

Graphics, Animation and New Media

NOKIA

event/burn

Friends of CHI

Adobe Systems, Inc.

Disney Research

FX Palo Alto Laboratory, Inc.

University of Maryland

Yahoo!

University of Michigan

The Polymath Project: Lessons from a Successful Online Collaboration in Mathematics

Justin Cranshaw
School of Computer Science
Carnegie Mellon University
Pittsburgh, PA, USA
jcransh@cs.cmu.edu

Aniket Kittur
School of Computer Science
Carnegie Mellon University
Pittsburgh, PA, USA
nkittur@cs.cmu.edu

ABSTRACT
Although science is becoming increasingly collaborative, there are remarkably few success stories of online collaborations between professional scientists that actually result in real discoveries. A notable exception is the Polymath Project, a group of mathematicians who collaborate online to solve open mathematics problems. We provide an in-depth descriptive history of Polymath, using data analysis and visualization to elucidate the principles that led to its success, and the difficulties that must be addressed before the project can be scaled up. We find that although a small percentage of users created most of the content, almost all users nevertheless contributed some content that was highly influential to the task at hand. We also find that leadership played an important role in the success of the project. Based on our analysis, we present a set of design suggestions for how future collaborative mathematics sites can encourage and foster newcomer participation.

Author Keywords
large-scale collaboration, online collaborative mathematics, online collaborative science, online communities

ACM Classification Keywords
H.5.2 Information Interfaces and Presentation: Miscellaneous

General Terms
Human Factors

INTRODUCTION
The Internet has made creative collaboration possible on an unprecedented scale: tens of thousands of people work together to consolidate knowledge (e.g. Wikipedia), or to write software (e.g. Apache and Linux). However, there have been few examples of scientific knowledge creation being done by large online groups. Tasks such as scientific discovery are difficult to carry out on a large scale for a number of reasons: they are complex, they require significant expertise and prior knowledge, and they have high coordination demands. Furthermore, professional advancement in science is typically subject to a highly developed and closed-loop reward structure (e.g., publications, grants, tenure). These factors do not align well with the open, asynchronous, independent, peer production systems that have typified social collaboration online. However, one notable exception is the Polymath Project, a collection of mathematicians ranging in expertise from Fields Medal winners to high school mathematics teachers who collaborate online to prove unsolved mathematical conjectures.

There are many reasons to believe why mathematics might be well suited for large-scale online collaboration. Mathematicians, unlike most empirical scientists, require little experimental equipment to do their work, making the asynchronous nature of online collaborations less of a deterrent. In addition, mathematical ideas transfer between mathematicians, especially between those who specialize in the same sub-field, with remarkable speed and efficiency, which might help minimize coordination costs [30].

In many ways, the deductive nature of proofs and theorems is inherently collaborative. Although proofs themselves are typically produced by a small number of primary contributors, they often rely on a rich history of prior contributions to the problem made by past mathematicians. Gian-Carlo Rotta, in reference to Wiles's proof of Fermat's last theorem describes this notion of proof as "a triumph of collaboration across frontiers and centuries [28]." This pattern is a common one in mathematics. As Luca Trevisan explains, works of "genius" in mathematics typically occur when "a large collection of 'incremental' results and 'observations' has been made, and all the pieces are there, ready to be put together [31]." These series of incremental results are often the work of a great many mathematicians sometimes spanning decades or even centuries. The mathematical "genius" is then often one who excels at putting these pieces together. According to Trevisan, massively-collaborative mathematics could re-define this idea of genius. Instead of the few who are able to "put together the zeitgeist," genius could rather "be in the union of many minds, each doing nothing more than saying what is obvious to them [31]."

In this paper we combine social science theory, with an in-depth descriptive analysis of data gathered from the Polymath Project, in order to explicate the factors that contributed

CHI 2011, May 7–12, 2011, Vancouver, BC, Canada.

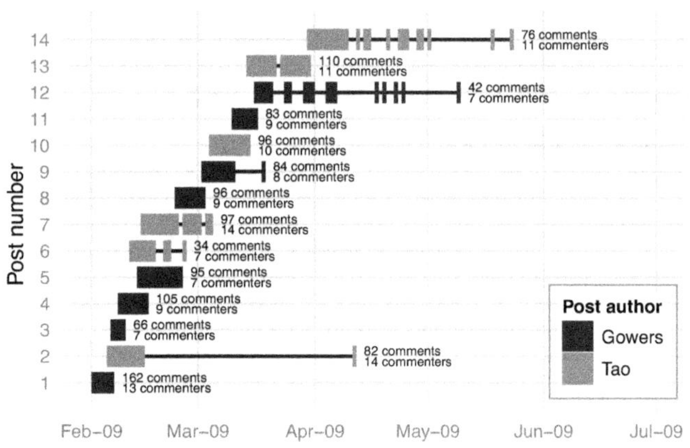

Figure 1. The time span of active comments for each blog post by blog author in the Polymath1 project. Between February and May of 2009, there were 14 blog posts by two authors, Timothy Gowers and Terence Tao. Vertical bars on the timeline indicate days of activity. During this time, a total of 39 contributors left a total of 1228 numbered comments.

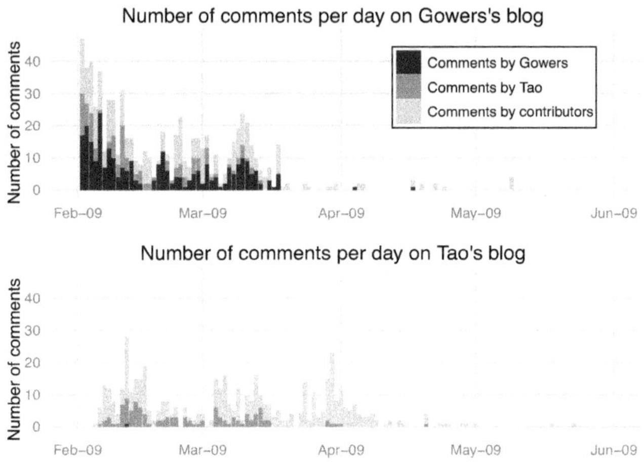

Figure 2. Number of comments per day on each blog, separated by comments from each of the two leaders, and the contributors of their blogs.

to its success. We also discuss design implications for technical tools and social structures that may promote large scale scientific collaborations in the future.

The main contributions of this work are threefold. First, we find that although a large percentage of the Polymath content is produced by small number of individuals, most participants, even those only who only contribute a few comments, nevertheless produce high quality content relevant to the ongoing task. Additionally, we examine the role of leadership in Polymath, both qualitatively and quantitatively, and find that comments from leaders have a greater effect at spurring new discussion than non-leader comments. Finally, we look at the burden that newcomers have in getting acclimated, and provide a set of design suggestions that might lessen this burden and help increase the number of sustained contributors to the project.

RELATED WORK

Although scientists have worked together for centuries [11], science is becoming progressively more collaborative, with teams increasingly dominating the production of knowledge [33]. These teams are also becoming increasingly distributed, with labs spread across continents and spanning multiple institutions [13]. However, despite the push by researchers and funding agencies to share resources and expertise across geographic and institutional boundaries [10], distributed collaborations impose high coordination costs that can have a significant negative effect on the likelihood of success [7, 8]. These costs are rooted not only in geographical distance and time differences but also in institutional culture and norms, and differences in reward structure [8].

There have been a number of notable success stories of using the Internet to crowdsource parts of the scientific research process. For example, NASAs ClickWorkers program had hundreds of thousands of volunteers classifying craters on Mars' surface, resulting in work virtually indistinguishable from expert geologists [18]. Other examples of citizen science include eBirds, a volunteer bird observation network [29]; GalaxyZoo, which has provided visual classifications for nearly one million galaxies [22]; and FoldIt, in which volunteers play an online game help scientists to predict protein folding [5]. Even science-based R&D is being crowdsourced by companies such as Innocentive, who tap into a network of more than 120,000 scientists around the world to solve problems too difficult or labor intensive for internal R&D labs; over 400 problems have been solved to date [21].

In contrast to these successes, large scale online collaboration between established scientists has been rare. The Internet has made it easier to span geographical and time boundaries, with technologies such as email, blogs, and wikis supporting asynchronous communication around the globe. However, this has led to large scale collaborative scientific successes. There are some notable exceptions, including the MIT Registry of Standard Biological Parts, which has spurred multiple scientific papers [24]; and the Gene Ontology project, which aims to provide a dynamic controlled vocabulary for biology [1]. These exceptions, however, focus on sharing and standardizing resources for individual researchers rather than supporting large scale collaborations between researchers.

In this context Polymath is truly remarkable in that it has succeeded at large scale collaboration between scientists. Understanding the principles underlying its success and how they might be improved and applied more generally is an important area of research. While there have been a few studies qualitatively describing the Polymath Project to date [2, 15]), to our knowledge ours is the first study to take a quantitative approach to investigating the project.

BACKGROUND OF THE POLYMATH PROJECT

The Polymath Project began when mathematician Timothy Gowers published a blog post with the provocative title "*Is massively collaborative mathematics possible?*" [14]. Of course, as Gowers pointed out, collaboration on a large scale is not a new phenomenon to mathematics. Hundreds of mathematicians produced over 500 publications in the second half of the 20th century in a successful collaborative attempt to the classify all the finite simple groups in abstract algebra. Although this was indeed a massive collaboration, the nature of the collaboration was quite different from what Gowers was proposing, since in the case of finite simple group classification, the larger task being solved had hundreds if not thousands of natural and predefined subtasks whose solutions were largely independent of the solutions to the others subtasks. Gowers was instead proposing to collaboratively solve a single problem that "does not naturally split up into a vast number of subtasks."

Gowers outlines three *potential* advantages for such large-scale collaborations in mathematics. First there is the role of chance in problem solving. Having more people work on a problem increases the odds that one person will get lucky and discover a great insight. Second, different mathematicians have different areas of expertise, so having a large number of contributors work on a problem creates a collective expertise that cannot be achieved by small groups of contributors. Finally, Gowers argues that different people have different characteristics, and will thus assume different roles in the problem solving process. Some contributors will be proficient at coming up with new ideas or approaches, others will perform complex calculations, still others will "fact check" the work of their piers. In short, having a large pool of people working on the problem allows for a greater opportunities for people to specialize in the problem solving process. These advantages are succinctly summarized by Gowers:

> If a large group of mathematicians could connect their brains efficiently, they could perhaps solve problems very efficiently as well. [14]

Of course there are risks to this approach too, most notably the possibility that an individual might use material being developed on the blog to individually publish a great breakthrough.

Organization of the Polymath Project

Following Gowers's initial problem proposal, the community rapidly organized itself in order to begin work on solving the problem. Contributors made use of numerous and distinct web-tools available to them to fulfill their needs. The resulting suite of tools that they assembled was highly decentralized and spread across at least 5 Internet domains. We describe these components of the Polymath Project below.

Blogs of Noted Mathematicians

The primary venue for participants to work on the Polymath problems is within the posts and comments of the personal blogs of noted mathematicians. Initial work began on Gowers's blog just days after his initial post. On February 1st, mathematician Terence Tao wrote a general post discussing Gower's initiative, and shortly after that Tao started an official post working on Polymath from his blog as well. Since then other mathematicians have also on occasion hosted Polymath work on their blogs.

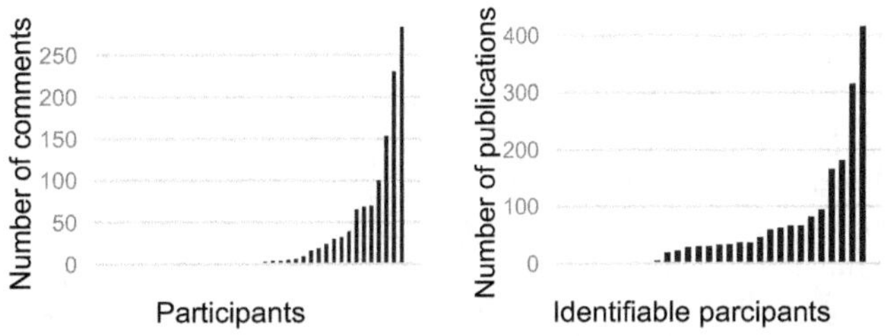

Figure 3. Right: Number of Google Scholar publications of each of 29 the users who tied their blog identity to their real names, sorted from lowest to highest by number of publications. Left: Count of numbered-comments left by the 39 users, sorted from lowest to highest by comment count.

The Polymath Wiki

A wiki for the project was created and hosted by physicist Michael Nielsen[1]. The wiki primarily serves as a clearinghouse for background material, summaries, and preliminary write-ups relevant to work being done on the blogs. Each problem the community decides to work on has its own devoted page on the Polymath Wiki page where material related to that problem is posted.

The Polymath Blog

A dedicated blog was created primarily for administrative discussions, and for high level summaries of the progress being made on the other blogs[2]. Additionally, some of the discussions about what problems the community wishes to work on are carried out on the Polymath Blog.

The Ground Rules for Participation

In many ways Gowers's proposal was an experiment. For the experiment to be a success, it would not be enough to simply prove a theorem via blog comments. It is instead, the way the problem is ultimately solved that is essential to the experiment's success. For instance, if one contributor decided to work independently from the group continuously for days and solved the problem on his own, this would clearly not be an example of massively collaborative mathematics. To minimize the chances for this type of failure, and to generally set the tone of the project, Gowers proposed a set of 12 ground rules. Many were intended to guide the nature of the comments that participants produce to maximize the chance that the experiment succeeds. Several rules explicitly discourage collaborators from working extensively on their own on the problem without discussing their progress on the blog. Additionally, there are rules that are designed to make sure the discourse remains polite and focused, while also not discouraging comments that may not be fully thought out. Finally the last ground rule specifies that any publications that result from work done on the blog will be published under a pseudonym, and will contain links to the full discourse for readers to examine.

[1] http://michaelnielsen.org/polymath1
[2] http://polymathprojects.org/

The Polymath Projects

Currently there are five official Polymath Projects (denoted by Polymath1 through Polymath5). Each of these projects focuses on a significant unsolved problem in mathematics. These five projects make up the core of the serious work being done by the group. In addition, there are also two Mini-Polymath Projects, which are intended mainly as puzzle exercises and are not serious open problems, and a wiki page dedicated to the discussion of the purported proof by Deolalikar that $\mathbf{P} \neq \mathbf{NP}$ [9]. To date, on the 5 Polymath Projects and 2 Mini-Polymath Projects, there have been over 275 unique commenters, who have left over 5000 comments containing well over 20000 equations.

POLYMATH1

In this work, our analysis will focus almost entirely on the Polymath1 project, which was the first, and to date most successful of the Polymath Projects. At the time of this writing, Polymath1 was the only project that was complete, making it a particularly appealing artifact to study in its entirety as an example of successful collaboration.

The target problem for Polymath1 was to find a combinatorial proof of the density version of the Hales-Jewett theorem, a theorem in combinatorics. Although proofs exist, they have relied on techniques from ergodic theory [12] and are non-combinatorial. There is often great value in mathematics to finding multiple proofs for one theorem. In particular, elementary proofs (ones that rely only on first principals) such as what Gowers was proposing, are often most valued for their instructiveness. As G. H. Hardy said, "the history of mathematics shows conclusively that mathematicians do not evacuate permanently ground which they have conquered once [17]."

Success from a mathematical point of view in Gowers's words would be "anything that could count as genuine progress towards an understanding of the problem." In this strict sense, Polymath1 was successful well beyond Gowers's expectations. To date there are two journal articles that have been submitted [26, 25]. Additionally, at least two new proofs of the theorem, plus new bounds on Hales-Jewett numbers were discovered. In this work we will examine whether and to what extent Polymath1 was successful in the larger sense, that is as a collaborative framework for doing higher mathematics on a large scale.

Participation and demographics

Between February 1 and May 23, 2009, there were 1555 comments written on the 14 blog posts of Polymath1. These 14 blog posts were distributed across two mathematics blogs; 8 of which were written by Timothy Gowers[3] and 6 were written Terence Tao[4]. Of the comments, 1228 were assigned a sequential and unique "comment number" by the participants so that they could be easily and succinctly referred to by subsequent comments. The comments that received a number typically were direct contributions to the proof

Previous day:	b	β	p-value
Comments by contributors	0.24	0.24	0.044
Comments by leaders	0.35	0.41	< 0.001

Table 1. The extent to which comments on the previous day spur contributor comments on the current day. Raw b-coefficient, standardized β-coefficient estimates and p-values are shown from a multiple linear regression. The two independent variables are the number of comments by the two leaders and the number of comments by the contributors on the previous day. The dependent variable is the number of comments by the contributors on the current day.

attempt, whereas comments that did not receive a number were typically administrative in nature, commenting on the process, rather directly contributing to the proof. We call these two types of comments *numbered comments* and *meta-comments* respectively.

Since we wish to study the act of proving a theorem collaboratively, we will primarily focus on numbered comments and the participants who write these numbered comments. This is not to say the meta-comments are without value. On the contrary, some meta-comments played a critical role in the organization of the discourse. Rather, we will primarily treat numbered-comments as quantitative data, and meta-comments as qualitative data.

In total 39 distinct users contributed at least one numbered comment to Polymath1. Although, this number seems small compared to the thousands of users who actively edit popular Wikipedia articles, it is large in comparison to the number of authors who traditionally collaborate on the proof of a theorem. The number of comments per user is shown in Figure 3 (left). Similar to other online content producing communities, a majority of the content is produced by a very small number of users. Indeed the top three commenters produced 55% of the comments, and the top ten commenters produced nearly 90% of the comments.

Of these 39 users, 29 linked their online profiles to their true identity (the remaining 10 were either anonymous, or we were unable to map their account to a true identity). Their range of backgrounds varies widely, from Fields Medalists winners to high school mathematics teachers, however the distribution of their backgrounds is relatively homogeneous; almost all of the participants are either university professors or graduate students in mathematics or computer science and almost all of them are male (28 male, 1 female).

What does vary fairly drastically among these 29 is their level of seniority in the higher-mathematics community as measured by number of academic publications. To measure this, we use the Google Scholar author search restricted to mathematics, computer science, engineering, and physics articles. Figure 3 (right) shows the number of Google Scholar publications for each of the 29 identifiable participants. The median number of publications is 35, and the mean is 65.2. It is also notable that there are 4 participants with 0 publications, 6 with 1 publication or less, and 8 with 5 publications or less, showing that there is a mix of well established mathematicians, and those who are early in their career.

[3] http://gowers.wordpress.com
[4] http://terrytao.wordpress.com

THE ROLE OF LEADERSHIP

Research in online content producing communities has shown that leadership can be essential to the production of high quality content [27, 23]. We find that this is also true of the Polymath1 project.

From its inception, leadership was essential to the Polymath Project. The idea was initially conceived and implemented by Timothy Gowers, a well know mathematician and Fields Medal winner. It is natural then that Gowers would take on a number of leadership duties in the Polymath1 project. In addition to setting the guidelines for participation, and selecting the problem for Polymath1, it was Gowers's intention to host the work in the comments section of his mathematics blog. This made him best positioned to be the person that guides the progress on the problem, if for any other reason than he has administrative privileges on the blog and others do not. It was Gower's role to summarize past progress and guide future progress with each new blog post.

Very soon after Gower's initial post, fellow Fields medalist Terance Tao wrote a blog post discussing Gowers's project that quickly would become a second thread to Polymath1, running in parallel to Gowers's first post (see Figure 1). Like Gowers, this naturally positioned Tao to take various leadership roles, both on his blog, and on Polymath1 in general.

Though there were certainly other participants that at various times showed leadership, Gowers and Tao were leaders in Polymath1 throughout. For this reason, we will refer to Gowers and Tao as the *leaders* of Polymath1, and we refer to the collective readership of their blogs as the *contributors*.

Blog posts summarizing progress

In a meta-comment near comment number 350, Tao proposes that every post should be limited to 100 comments. Although this proposal was out of necessity, as it allowed threads to run in parallel while still being numbered sequentially (since the numbers for a thread could be allocated in advance), there were important unforeseen consequences. Ending a thread after 100 comments allowed for the leaders to make fairly frequent summary posts, highlighting what they thought was relevant in the previous thread and guiding the contributors on the next thread. This proved to be one of the essential roles of the leaders throughout the project.

Leader comments versus contributor comments

Aside from this very important role of summarizing the progress, the leaders also made direct contributions to the proofs by posting comments. On their own Gowers and Tao were the top two commenters on Polymath1. Gowers contributed 285 numbered comments, and Tao contributed 232 numbered comments, thus in total there were then 517 leader comments, which was 42% of all numbered commented (readers contributed a total of 711 numbered comments).

Judging by volume alone, it is clear that Gowers and Tao made significant contributions to the work of the proof. However we hypothesize that their comments were themselves very important in guiding and driving the work of the contributors. To address this hypothesis, we examined whether or not the leader comments on any given day actually spurred increased contributor activity on the next day. To control for the fact that comments in general on any given day (both from leaders and contributors) could spur increased contributor activity on the next day, we compare the effects of leader comments to contributor comments. Table 1 shows the results of a multiple regression, where the two independent variables are the number of comments by the leaders and the number of comments by the contributors on the previous day. The dependent variable is the number of comments by the contributors on the current day. This shows that contributor and leader comments are both significant factors in spurring activity on the next day. However leader comments have a much greater effect on spurring new comments ($\beta = 0.41$ for leader comments, compared to $\beta = 0.24$ for contributors).

COORDINATION AND THREADING

Collaboration among many people on a task with a potentially large set of interdependencies can require a great deal of coordination. Here we look for evidence of coordination and interdependencies by examining the attempts of users to parallelize their efforts.

Threading

The decision to have a fixed number of comments (roughly 100) on any single blog post was consequential in opening the possibility of parallel blog threads (i.e. two or more blog posts with active comments). Setting a fixed number of comments per post allowed the the space of comment numbers for any post to be allocated in advance, thus maintaining a sequential numbering system on parallel posts.

At the same time, very early in the comments of the first post, parallel discussions began to develop on different possible proof approaches. Participants attempted to use the limited tools made available to them by the blog site to organize these discussions. They annotated the subjects of comments with either a thread name, or a list of relevant comment numbers. It was clear very early that there was certainly potential for some parallelism in discussing distinct approaches to the problem.

Dual threads: Gowers and Tao

This potential for parallel discussions was partially realized when Tao and the readers of his blog began working on Polymath1 in parallel to Gowers. In Figure 1, note the high degree of temporal overlap between work being done on Gowers's weblog and that being done on Tao's weblog.

Despite this overlap, it is difficult to claim that this is evidence of coordination and organization, since the work being done by Tao and his readers was related but distinctly different from the work being done on Gower's blog. Tao and his readers were trying to compute exact bounds on Hales - Jewett numbers for small dimensions, while Gowers and his readers were attempting to prove the general theorem.

In general there was little evidence of any coordination constraints between work being done across the two blogs, which allowed them to operate almost indendependently.

However, aside from the parallelism of the dual Gowers / Tao posts, there is very little evidence of any successful parallel threads despite explicit attempts to parallelize both blogs. Parallelism was attempted at least once by Gowers. He intended that post number 4 proceed in parallel to post number 3 on a separate but related topic. However, note in Figure 1 that work on post 3 ends soon after the creation of post 4, and well before the allocated 100 comments for that post. In a meta-comment on the success of threading, Gowers remarks

> Im not completely convinced that the multiple-threads idea has worked. Or rather I think it has partially worked. It seems that the upper-and-lower bounds thread was sufficiently separate that it has thrived on its own. But the experience of the other two threads was that once the 400 thread was opened the 300 thread died pretty rapidly.

Tao had some success in parallelizing his blog, as post 6 was active in parallel to each of post 2 and post 7. However, the nature of post 6 was quite different than the others, as it was designed to be an interactive "reading group" to discuss background material. Aside from this one instance, all other posts comprised one linear thread.

Although parallel threading was not as successful as the participants had hoped, there were unintended benefits to this approach. Gowers, best summarizes this: "An advantage of the multiple threads was that we had multiple summaries: I think it would be quite good to be forced to summarize more often." In this sense having multiple threads was a success, though not in the way originally envisioned.

The comment reference graph

To examine the nature of dependencies in the comments, we constructed a directed graph based on comment references. Nodes of the graph are numbered comments, and directed edges are placed from node b to node a if comment b explicitly mentions the comment number for a. There were 655 edges, 702 non-isolated vertices, and 135 weakly connected components of the comment reference graph. The mean component size was 5.2, the median was 2, and the standard deviation was 25.5. The largest component contained 299 comments. The second largest had 15 comments. This large gap in size suggests the largest component might have comprised the "main discussion" and the remaining components were side discussions.

Figure 4 shows a visualization of the structure of the comment references with respect to the 14 blog posts. The columns indicate the post number of the originating comment, and rows indicate the post number of the referenced comment. Thus the diagonal shows the number of intra-post comment references, and off the diagonal shows inter-post comment references. The size of each bar is proportional to the number of such references, and the color of the bar is according

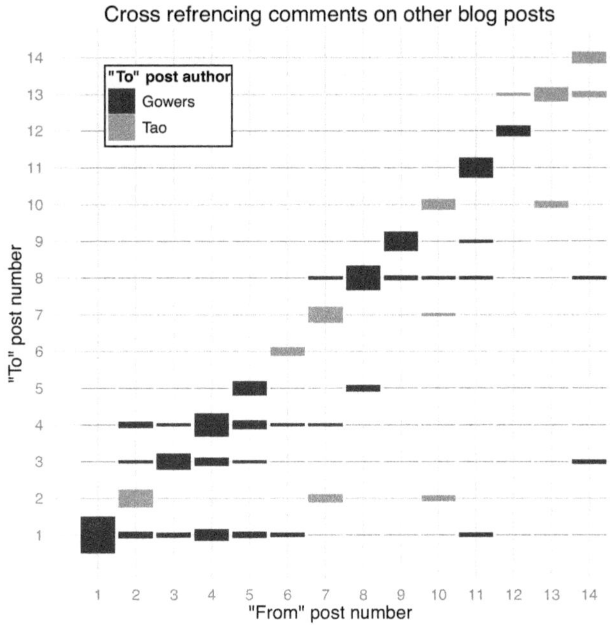

Figure 4. A visualization of the structure of the comment reference graph with respect to inter- and intra-post comment references. Along the diagonal shows the number of intra-post comment references. Off of the diagonal shows inter-post references. The size of the bars is proportional to the number of such comments.

to the originating post author. Figure 4 illustrates that there was a fair amount of comment referencing, highlighting the importance and usefulness of the sequential comment numbering scheme. Although inter-post comment references did exist, the majority of comment references were intra-post, suggesting that the discussion was largely localized and focused. This is further quantitative evidence of the linear nature of the work, perhaps suggesting that comment references might have been constrained by the linearity of the blog.

THE BURDEN TO NEWCOMERS

It has been shown that socializing newcomers is an essential component to sustaining a healthy and productive online community [4, 3]. The level of technical sophistication of the Polymath content and the pace at which progress on problems moves means that it is necessary to have measures in place to allow newcomers to quickly and efficiently get up to speed with the material.

Figure 5 shows the cumulative number of contributors to Polymath1 over time, split by the number of comments the users would ultimately contribute to the project. This figure shows that the core set of contributors started contributing to the project very early. By the end of the first week of the project, over 2/3 of the contributors who would go on to produce at least 10 comments had already joined. This could suggest that once the project started, the technical nature of the generated content made it difficult for newcomers to join. This hypothesis is supported by the meta-comments. Gowers, at one point remarks

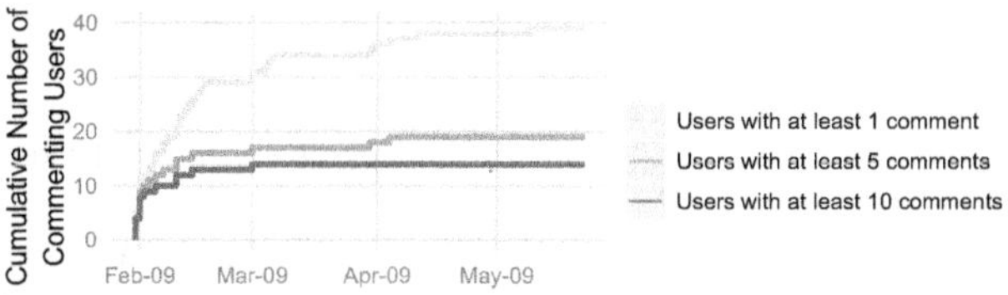

Figure 5. Cumulative number of users who join the project grouped by total number of comments.

> A number of people have commented that it is difficult to catch up with the discussion if you come to it late. We should try to start each thread in a way that makes it as self-contained as possible.

There is additional evidence that the work done on Gower's blog required a significant amount of background knowledge in combinatorics in order to participate, in contrast to the problem on Tao's blog, which was more elementary. On this issue, one participant remarked:

> Regarding the amount of background knowledge required, while on the thread here it did stray through intimidating territory, [...] on Terry's blog the arguments [...] were relatively elementary.

This burden may have discouraged a number of qualified individuals who were interested in the project from actually participating. This also may explain why there were more individuals contributing to Tao's blog. Over the course of the project 32 people contributed to Tao's blog, 20 contributed to Gowers's blog, with 14 contributing to both.

In addition to the burden of keeping up with the fast pace, and the burden of mastering the required background knowledge, an additional barrier to participation emerged from the meta-comments. One participant was discouraged by the large volume of comments that were not fully "thought out" that nevertheless required a significant amount of time to validate. Despite making some important contributions early on, he concluded his time was "better spent on problems that do not get as much attention."

All of this evidence suggests that the project could have benefited from targeted mechanisms to aid and encourage newcomers to join and continue to participate.

DOES EVERYONE REALLY CONTRIBUTE?

As we noted, there were many users who only contributed a few comments to the project. Indeed, there were 13 participants who only contributed 1 comment, and 21 participants contributed 5 comments or less. This begs the questions, did they all really contribute to solving the problem? Can one or two comments from a user who never comments to the project again really have any impact on the final solution when there are over 1200 comments in total? Perhaps all but the top few contributors were irrelevant?

To investigate these questions, we first turn to the official Polymath1 timeline[5], which was created on the wiki to highlight the comments that were important milestones to the proof. We will use the timeline to to better understand which comments were important as judged by the participants themselves. In total there were 215 numbered comments listed in the timeline, from 22 distinct users (18% of all numbered comments, 56% of all users). Out of the users who only commented 5 times or less, there were 6 comments listed in the timeline from 5 distinct users (17% of the 36 comments from these users, 23% of these users). Thus it was not uncommon for users who commented very infrequently to nevertheless have a large impact on the proof.

Comment graph centrality

Of course a comment does not need to be a milestone in the proof for it to be a meaningful contribution. For instance, imagine if someone leaves a comment that by itself is not a milestone, but it links together several other contributions in an important way. Or perhaps, the user leaves a comment that directly contributes to the the ideas of a subsequent milestone comment. To look for evidence of such contributions, we can examine the structure of the comment reference graph.

We first compute a series of graph centrality measures on each node of the comment reference graph. The centrality measures we use are: eigenvector centrality, betweenness centrality, authority score, Bonpow centrality, closeness centrality, alpha centrality, page rank, in degree, and total degree. We next compute the ranking on the vertices that is induced by each centrality measure. Finally, we aggregate the rankings by averaging them to produce a single ranking of the 1228 comments.

Figure 6 is a visualization of three variables that are essential to understanding the nature of participation and contribution in Polymath1. Each of the identifiable users are plotted according to the number of comments they contributed to to the project, and the maximum ranking of all of their comments. Additionally, the size of each point is proportional to the number of publications of that user according to Google Scholar.

There are a number of observations that one can immediately make from this Figure. First, the leadership of Gowers and Tao can be seen instantly. Not only did Gowers and Tao have the highest, and second highest number of comments respectively, they produced the second highest and third highest ranking comments respectively under our ranking method. Additionally, it can be seen that there is a third potential leader, that had the highest ranked comment, and the third highest number of comments overall. Like Gowers and Tao, in addition to being a prolific contributor, this individual took on various administrative roles in the project, including being in charge of one of the final write-ups.

In addition to observing leadership in the upper right quadrant, we can see that there are a number of contributors in the bottom right quadrant. These are individuals who were

[5] http://michaelnielsen.org/polymath1/index.php?title=Timeline

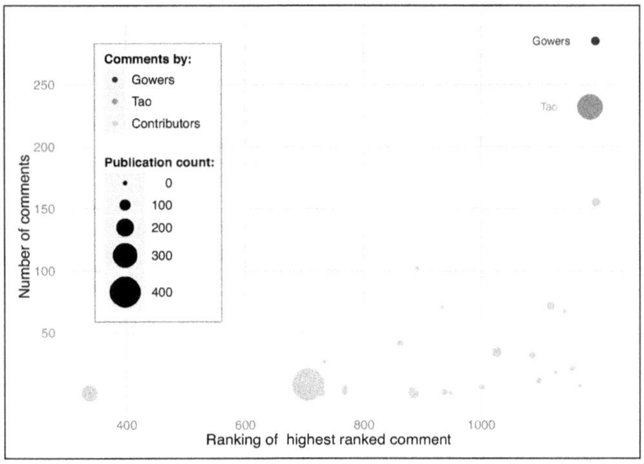

Figure 6. Here we show the ranking of the highest ranked comment for each user together with the total number of comments from that user. Points are sized proportional to the number of scholarly publications of that user (as given by Google Scholar).

not prolific contributors, but who nevertheless made significant, highly ranking comments. Finally, using the number of Google Scholar publication as a proxy for seniority, one can see that the level of seniority of the participants varies greatly. Furthermore, if you discount Tao and Gowers, it does not seem to correlate to volume or importance of contribution.

To put this finding in more precise terms, the 662 comments that received highest ranking (those above the median) were produced by 28 users. Conversely, there were only 11 users whose comments all ranked less than the median ranking. We feel this result is quite surprising given the volume of comments written by the top contributors (recall 90% of the comments were written by the top contributors).

DISCUSSION

Was Polymath1 a success? From a mathematical point of view, the answer is unequivocally, yes. In just over 6 weeks a collective group of distributed individuals accomplished some highly non-trivial mathematical feats. Whether or not the project was a success as an experiment in "massive-scale" collaboration, requires a more nuanced discussion.

Certainly, the scale of the project could hardly be considered "massive," falling short of the vision originally put forth by Gowers [15]. However, it is clear that the scale was large compared to most collaborations in higher math. It is relatively uncommon for a mathematics publication to have more than 3 authors, let alone 40. Additionally, although the core set of contributors by volume was small, we have shown that several users were still able to make important contributions to the work, despite producing a small percentage of the comments.

The ambiguity regarding the success of Polymath1 is amplified by the roles played by the two leaders. Not only were Gowers and Tao by far the top contributors to the project in terms of number of comments, but they also each undertook a significant number of administrative duties in order to guide the project to its mathematical success. Additionally, it is evident from the number of popular press articles written about Polymath, that their collective celebrity had a large role in both the publicity the project received and in the recruitment of contributors. Their involvement was so significant all throughout, that it is questionable whether the Polymath project would have succeeded without their efforts. Whether or not large-scale collaborative mathematics can succeed without such high-profile leaders is of course an open question.

Incentives for participation

In order to maintain a diverse community, incentives for participation should be such that all levels of mathematicians have incentive to participate. This may be difficult to maintain in practice unless the individuals are able to get proper academic attributions for the work they do in Polymath. There is a potentially large misalignment in incentives between the demands of a professional academic career in mathematics, and long-term involvement in the Polymath Project. This misalignment is best expressed by an anecdote told by a Polymath contributor during meta-discussion. While having a conversation about the Polymath with an offline colleague, the colleague asked "how will participants put their grant acknowledgment lines" in the final document?

This begs several other questions regarding the sustainability of long-term involvement. How do the universities that employ the participants receive attribution? Could someone justify to their university that they deserve tenure if all of their work is published collectively? Unlike work in open source software, where there are significant economic incentives at play at the heart of these communities, it's unclear that the economics of truly large scale collaborative mathematics are scalable absent the right incentive structure.

Design recommendations for encouraging newcomers

We have discussed several barriers to entry that might discourage newcomers from participating. Here we focus on three challenges: identifying the important content to read, identifying tasks to work on, and learning the required background material.

Identifying important content

We have shown that one potential problem discouraging newcomers is the large volume of content that is generated by existing users, together with the lack of any mechanisms that sort out important content from unimportant content. Although it is inevitable that newcomers must read some existing content in order to become acclimated, when so much of the work done in mathematics is validating ideas that may or may not work, participants may be discouraged by reading content that has already been invalidated by others. Newcomers may feel that they are simply replicating work that has already been done by the existing users in order to get acclimated to the project. Thus in addition to the cost associated to with reading a potentially large volume of irrelevant content, there is the added cost associated with the redundancy of this task.

We have two proposals to address this challenge. First, there should be better explicit linkage among the comments utilizing the explicit comment referencing done by the participants. For any comment, there should be automated tools that generate and display all the comments that refer to it. This might be accompanied through a visualization of the comment reference graph. This mechanism will allow newcomers to see where each comment fits into the larger body of work. Second, there should be mechanisms for users to rate the importance of each comment. Ideally this would include both a numeric rating of importance, such as a "star" mechanism, as well as a categorical importance rating where old-timers could, for example designate a given comment as "Important for getting up to speed" or "A core contribution." One might also pair socially generated ratings, with algorithmically generated ratings, such as the graph-based comment ranking that we employed in this work.

Identifying tasks to work on

Similar structural problems make it difficult for newcomers to identify tasks to work on. Research on task identification in Wikipedia suggests that automated mechanisms can significantly improve productivity [6]. The manifestation of this challenge in Polymath was outlined in Gowers & Nielsen

> A significant barrier to entry was the linear narrative style of the blog. This made it difficult for late entrants to identify problems to which their talents could be applied. There was also a natural fear that they might have missed an earlier discussion and that any contribution they made would be redundant. [15]

They suggest using a task management system similar to those in use by open source software communities. To some extent the participants attempted to use the wiki for these purposes. However, without the explicit assignments of tasks to people, this likely had little affect. We agree that a task management system would be of use here, however we strongly suggest that such a system be designed to have explicit tasks for acclimating newcomers. These tasks need not be content producing tasks, but could be administrative tasks, or even tasks designed to get the newcomer up to speed. We suspect that task assignment, or automated task suggestion might not be useful for experienced Polymath contributors, and could even discourage them, since they are more familiar with the content and their own abilities, and thus may not work well with the rigidity of a task assignment system.

Dealing with background material

Finally, it is natural that many Polymath projects will require a significant amount of background material to participate, as is often the case in communities of practice. However, this should not be so prohibitive that it precludes someone with sufficient technical abilities from participating. The community has attempted to address this issue by suggesting longer "lead times" for the start of new projects, for potential participants to research the background material. Additionally, they experimented with "reading group" blog threads. These are both temporary solutions. Ideally there would be some structural mechanism in the design of the collaborative website that deals with this issue. One approach would be to have a forum section of the website which is designed to discuss and ask questions related to background material.

This would ideally be integrated so that primary content could link and refer back to the forum in a structured way. This would help with the problem of identifying what background material should be studied to understand a given piece of primary content. For the most part, the wiki was useful as a clearinghouse for background material, however the lack of integration between the wiki and the primary content being produced on the blogs was likely prohibitive. Like comments, different pieces of background material have differing and evolving levels of importance. Tools that connect the primary content back to the secondary content and visa versa, could significantly reduce the burden of newcomers by helping them focus on what background material they need to understand most to contribute to any given area.

CONCLUSION

In this work, we examine the Polymath Project, an experiment in large scale collaborative mathematics, to better understand its successes and shortcomings as a online community and tool for open collaboration. We find that a large percentage of the content is produced by small number of individuals. However, many individuals that produce a low volume of content are still producing high quality, influential content. We also examined the role of leadership, and the burden to newcomers. Based on our analysis, we gave a set of design recommendations for encouraging newcomers.

REFERENCES

1. M. Ashburner, C. A. Ball, J. A. Blake, D. Botstein, H. Butler, J. M. Cherry, A. P. Davis, K. Dolinski, S. S. Dwight, J. T. Eppig, M. A. Harris, D. P. Hill, L. Issel-Tarver, A. Kasarskis, S. Lewis, J. C. Matese, J. E. Richardson, M. Ringwald, G. M. Rubin, and G. Sherlock. Gene ontology: tool for the unification of biology. the gene ontology consortium. *Nature genetics*, 25(1):25–29, May 2000.

2. M. J. Barany. '[b]ut this is blog maths and we're free to make up conventions as we go along': Polymath1 and the modalities of 'massively collaborative mathematics'. In *WikiSym '10: Proceedings of the 6th International Symposium on Wikis and Open Collaboration*, pages 1–9, New York, NY, USA, 2010. ACM.

3. M. Burke, R. Kraut, and E. Joyce. Membership Claims and Requests: Conversation-Level Newcomer Socialization Strategies in Online Groups. *Small Group Research*, 41(1):4–40, 2010.

4. M. Burke, C. Marlow, and T. Lento. Feed me: motivating newcomer contribution in social network sites. In *Proceedings of the 27th international conference on Human factors in computing systems*, CHI '09, pages 945–954, New York, NY, USA, 2009. ACM.

5. S. Cooper, F. Khatib, A. Treuille, J. Barbero, J. Lee, M. Beenen, A. Leaver-Fay, D. Baker, Z. Popovic, and F. Players. Predicting protein structures with a multiplayer online game. *Nature*, 466(7307):756–760, August 2010.

6. D. Cosley, D. Frankowski, L. Terveen, and J. Riedl. Suggestbot: using intelligent task routing to help people find work in wikipedia. In *Proceedings of the 12th international conference on Intelligent user interfaces*, IUI '07, pages 32–41, New York, NY, USA, 2007. ACM.

7. J. N. Cummings and S. Kiesler. Collaborative research across disciplinary and organizational boundaries. *Social Studies of Science*, (35), 2005.

8. J. N. Cummings and S. Kiesler. Coordination costs and project outcomes in multi-university collaborations. *Research Policy*, 36(10):1620–1634, 2007.

9. V. Deolalikar. P neq np, unverified claim, 2010.

10. T. A. Finholt. Collaboratories. *Annual Review of Information Science and Technology (ARIST)*, 36:73–107, 00 2002.

11. T. A. Finholt and G. M. Olson. From laboratories to collaboratories: a new organizational form for scientific collaboration. *Psychological Science*, (8):28–35, 1997.

12. H. Furstenberg and Y. Kaznelson. A density version of the hales-jewett theorem. *J. Anal. Math*, (57), 1991.

13. O. Gassmann and M. von Zedtwitz. New concepts and trends in international randd organization. *Research Policy*, 28(2-3):231 – 250, 1999.

14. T. Gowers. Is massively collaborative mathematics possible? http://gowers.wordpress.com/2009/01/27/is-massively-collaborative-mathematics-possible/.

15. T. Gowers and M. Nielsen. Massively collaborative mathematics. *Nature*, 461(7266):879–881, 10 2009.

16. C. Gutwin, R. Penner, and K. Schneider. Group awareness in distributed software development. In *Proceedings of the 2004 ACM conference on Computer supported cooperative work*, CSCW '04, pages 72–81, New York, NY, USA, 2004. ACM.

17. G. H. Hardy. Mathematical proof. *Mind*, 38(149):1–25, 1929.

18. B. Kanefsky, N. G. Barlow, and V. C. Gulick. Can Distributed Volunteers Accomplish Massive Data Analysis Tasks? In *Lunar and Planetary Institute Science Conference Abstracts*, volume 32, page 1272, Mar. 2001.

19. A. Kittur and R. E. Kraut. Harnessing the wisdom of crowds in wikipedia: quality through coordination. In *Proceedings of the 2008 ACM conference on Computer supported cooperative work*, CSCW '08, pages 37–46, New York, NY, USA, 2008. ACM.

20. A. Kittur and R. E. Kraut. Beyond wikipedia: coordination and conflict in online production groups. In *Proceedings of the 2010 ACM conference on Computer supported cooperative work*, CSCW '10, pages 215–224, New York, NY, USA, 2010. ACM.

21. K. R. Lakhani and J. A. Panetta. The principles of distributed innovation. *Innovations: Technology, Governance, Globalization*, 2(3):97–112, July 2007.

22. C. Lintott, K. Schawinski, S. Bamford, A. Slosar, K. Land, D. Thomas, E. Edmondson, K. Masters, R. Nichol, J. Raddick, A. Szalay, D. Andreescu, P. Murray, and J. Vandenberg. Galaxy zoo 1 : Data release of morphological classifications for nearly 900,000 galaxies. Jul 2010.

23. K. Luther and A. Bruckman. Leadership in online creative collaboration. In *Proceedings of the 2008 ACM conference on Computer supported cooperative work*, CSCW '08, pages 343–352, New York, NY, USA, 2008. ACM.

24. J. Peccoud, M. F. Blauvelt, Y. Cai, K. L. Cooper, O. Crasta, E. C. DeLalla, C. Evans, O. Folkerts, B. M. Lyons, S. P. Mane, R. Shelton, M. A. Sweede, and S. A. Waldon. Targeted development of registries of biological parts. *PLoS ONE*, 3(7):e2671+, July 2008.

25. D. H. J. Polymath. Density hales-jewett and moser numbers, preprint, available at arxiv.org/abs/1002.0374, 2009.

26. D. H. J. Polymath. A new proof of the density hales-jewett theorem, preprint, available at arxiv.org/abs/0910.3926, 2009.

27. J. M. Reagle, Jr. Do as i do:: authorial leadership in wikipedia. In *WikiSym '07: Proceedings of the 2007 international symposium on Wikis*, pages 143–156, New York, NY, USA, 2007. ACM.

28. G. C. Rota. The phenomenology of mathematical proof. *Synthese*, 111:183–196, 1997. 10.1023/A:1004974521326.

29. B. L. Sullivan, C. L. Wood, M. J. Iliff, R. E. Bonney, D. Fink, and S. Kelling. ebird: A citizen-based bird observation network in the biological sciences. *Biological Conservation*, 142(10):2282 – 2292, 2009.

30. W. Thurston. On proof and progress in mathematics. In R. Hersh, editor, *18 Unconventional Essays on the Nature of Mathematics*, pages 37–55. Springer New York, 2006. 10.1007/0-387-29831-2_3.

31. L. Trevisan. A people's history of mathematics. http://lucatrevisan.wordpress.com/2009/02/01/a-peoples-history-of-mathematics/.

32. H. Wickham. *ggplot2: elegant graphics for data analysis*. Springer New York, 2009.

33. S. Wuchty, B. F. Jones, and B. Uzzi. The Increasing Dominance of Teams in Production of Knowledge. *Science*, 316(5827):1036–1039, 2007.

Collaborative Creativity: A Complex Systems Model with Distributed Affect

Cecilia R. Aragon
University of Washington
Seattle, WA 98195 USA
aragon@uw.edu

Alison Williams
University of East London
London E16 2RD UK
alisonwilliams62@googlemail.com

ABSTRACT
The study of creativity has received significant attention over the past century, with a recent increase in interest in collaborative, distributed creativity. We posit that creativity in distributed groups is fostered by software interfaces that specifically enable socio-emotional or affective communication. However, previous work on creativity and affect has primarily focused on the individual, while group creativity research has concentrated more on cognition rather than affect. In this paper we propose a new model for creativity in distributed groups, based on the theory of groups as complex systems, that includes affect as well as cognition and that explicitly calls out the interface between individuals as a key parameter of the model. We describe the model, the four stages of collaborative creativity and the causal dynamics in each stage, and demonstrate how affect and interface can facilitate the generation, selection, and amplification of ideas in the various stages of collaborative creativity. We then validate our model with data from three field sites. The data was collected from longitudinal studies of two distributed groups involved in producing creative products—astrophysicists studying supernovae and the expansion rate of the universe and children creating multimedia programming projects online—and interviews with staff in a multinational engineering company.

Author Keywords
Collaborative creativity, distributed affect, distributed groups, computer-mediated communication, creativity model.

ACM Classification Keywords
H5.3. [Information interfaces and presentation]: Group and organization interfaces–Computer-supported cooperative work.

General Terms
Theory.

INTRODUCTION
Creativity is arguably humanity's supreme achievement, the subject of research in multiple domains—including, among others, psychology, computer science, economics, organizational studies, environment and planning, and small group theory. Contrary to the popular belief of the "aha" moment of insight, recent work has indicated that creativity is often a series of incremental steps to discovery [57]. As the discovery/idea is developed, it is amplified over time in its social context/milieu. Ideas that are judged to have positive value are magnified while ideas of lesser value are progressively discarded. This suggests that a dynamical systems approach similar to that used to understand the spread of innovative technologies in the market [7] or the dynamics of small groups [6] may also be applied to collaborative creativity.

Recent technological developments have led to a sudden jump in the ability of humans to collaborate across distance in many types of activity, including creative work [10], resulting in a research focus on collaborative creativity and its underlying cognitive processes [20, 53]. There is also an extensive body of work on the importance of affect or emotion in the individual creative process; and yet more recent work on the socio-emotional processes of virtual teams [53]. We apply the theory of groups as complex systems [6] to synthesize elements of these disparate but interrelated areas of research into a new creativity model.

This paper's primary contribution is a new dynamical systems model of creativity in distributed groups that includes affect as well as cognitive processes, and that explicitly calls out the interface between individuals (mediated communication) as a key parameter of the model. Our work draws upon much previous research in multiple areas, including Poincare's and Wallas' models of creativity [51, 63], Russ's work on affect and creativity [56], work on group creativity by Sawyer [57] and Tatsuno [60], Arrow et al.'s theory of groups as complex systems [6], and Hutchins' distributed cognition [28]. We were additionally influenced by Sutton and Hargadon's work on group brainstorming [59], Girotra et al.'s hybrid idea-generating model [24], Arthur's work in economics on the phenomenon of increasing returns based on assumptions of random processes and on the evolution of technology [7], Benkler's work on networks [10], work on virtual teams by Powell et al. [53], and creativity research by Amabile, Czikszentmihalyi, Harrington and others [3, 4, 16, 27].

We first provide a brief survey of creativity and virtual team research relevant to the topic of group creativity and affect as facilitated by computer-mediated communication (CMC). We define key terms, such as creativity, distributed groups, and affect. We then describe the study methodology and the background of the three creative groups to which we applied our model: astrophysicists studying supernovae and the expansion rate of the universe, children creating multimedia programming projects online, and employees in a multinational engineering company.

We next present a new, dynamical systems based theory of collaborative creativity, including the four key stages identified in the collaborative creative process. We illustrate the model's dynamics and stages with examples from our longitudinal studies of the groups. A key strength of our model is that it is based on long-term observation of real-world creative groups. Because creativity is a process that often takes place over a span of time [37] it is critical to understand the temporal aspects of group creativeness, rather than relying exclusively on single-session laboratory experiments.

Arrow, McGrath, and Berdahl argue that groups form complex dynamical systems, and thus our study of distributed creative groups focuses "not on differences in *values* of variables between distinct social entities at a given time but rather on qualitative *patterns* of dynamical variables exhibited by social entities or systems over time" [6].

BACKGROUND

Although Guilford's [26] landmark speech to the American Psychological Association led to a flowering of creativity research, much of this work continued, as it had done previously, to focus on the individual [3, 4] and the individual creative process [21, 51, 63]. By the 1990s interest in group creativity was growing, with Tatsuno's [60] organizational group process, Resnick's [55] creative learning spiral, and Sawyer's performance-based studies [57], among others, exploring what happens when creativity develops in a face to face group environment. However, with the growth of electronically-enabled distance working, researchers are now examining what happens when distributed groups of people work on projects explicitly aimed at generating a creative product [10].

Definitions and types of creativity

Within the field of creativity research there is a consensus [42] that novelty or originality and usefulness or value [11] together with development over time [37] are defining characteristics of creativity. Simonton's definition of creativity incorporates different types or levels of creativity: big-C creativity that contributes to and changes culture and history, and small-c creativity that leads to improved problem-solving in daily work and in life [58]. Simonton concludes that there is a continuous scale of creative activity on which these different types of creativity are graded; and it is this definition that we adopt, studying it across the whole spectrum from small-c to big-C creativity in the context not just of generating big-C ideas and outputs, but also of using small-c creativity to problem-solve challenges facing the group.

We adopt Edwards' and Al-Ani's [20] definition of *distributed groups* as meeting two out of the three following criteria: members occupying more than a single time zone, located in different countries, and from different cultures or speaking different languages.

Additionally, for the purposes of this paper, we utilize Russ's definition of *affect* as "a feeling or emotion as distinct from cognition" [56]. It is a more inclusive term than *emotion*. We use the term *socio-emotional* to refer to relationship-building or affect-laden communication, thought, or behavior—both in terms of content (*"My wife has just had a baby*") and of expression ("*Yayyy production!*"). Finally, we use the term *collaborative creativity* here to refer specifically to creative work carried out by distributed groups. The work of purely collocated groups is beyond the scope of this paper.

RELATED WORK

Three kinds of creative process are relevant: individual internal or cognitive creative processes, group creative processes within a team or collaborative environment, and contextual processes situating individual creativity within its wider academic and social context. We examine current work that brings together these three creative processes and look at work on affect within creativity, setting the scene for the proposed model.

Individual creative processes

While it is arguable that each person devises their own unique creative process, the individual creative process has been formalized by Wallas [63], building on Poincaré's [51] examination of his own creative thought processes. Wallas proposed four stages to creative work: Preparation, Incubation, Illumination, and Verification. This firmly established the place of conscious as well as unconscious work in the creative process, laying the foundations for other models [21, 27, 49, 64].

Affect and individual creativity

A substantial body of work, primarily in the field of psychology, exists to demonstrate the importance of affect in the individual creative process. Russ [56] describes a body of research that indicates that "affective processes influence divergent thinking abilities and transformation abilities." She specifically cites the following affective processes important to individual creativity: access to affect-laden thoughts (e.g. primary process thinking), openness to affect states (e.g. passionate involvement in a task), affective pleasure in challenge or problem solving, and cognitive integration of affective material. She has found that emotion broadens search, and that mood-relevant cognition "triggers a broad associative network" [56].

Amabile [3, 4] found that enjoyment can be taken in the creative process and that creativity is intrinsically motivating. Langley and Jones [33] developed a computational model of scientific insight and applied it to the use of analogy in creative problem solving. Martindale [41] believed that creative individuals have states of "defocused attention," where large numbers of neurons are activated simultaneously, so that the more nodes that are activated, the greater the likelihood that an analogy will be noticed between two different elements. Csikszentmihalyi [15], in his work on *flow*, found that love of the work (autotelic activities) caused one creative act to lead to others over time. Lazarus theorized in "Emotion and Adaptation" that affect plays a major role in the process of *appraisal*, or the quick determination of what action to take to survive, thus demonstrating the value of emotion in adaptation and natural selection [35]. Research by Picard into the development of computing that relates to affect and emotion has shown its relevance in the field of artificial intelligence [50]. This wide array of psychology research into the role of affect in the creative process has mainly focused on the individual rather than the group creative process.

Group creative processes

There is a substantial body of work on group creativity, variously described as collective, collaborative, or social creativity. There is a general consensus that as group creativity becomes increasingly significant in the world today, particular attention must be paid to the technologies that support collaborative creativity.

Fischer and Shipman call for careful design of technologies and socio-technical environments to support social creativity and cultures of participation [22]. Aside from the use of technological interfaces, much research on the group creative process itself has focused on verbal communication between individuals. Sawyer's studies of improvisation in music and theater focus on the value of group creativity from a linguistic and cognitive point of view [57]. Dunbar [19] studied biologists collaborating. He found that conversation was a driver of collaborative creativity as the biologists spoke, argued, and came up with analogies and collaborative insights in meetings. In a comparison of four labs, he found that the ones that used analogies in conversation came up with more important discoveries. Markman et al. [40] found, in a Lego-building experiment, that talking about their work caused the group to create richer and more complex categories. John-Steiner [30] introduced the concept of "integrative collaboration" and described the profound bonding within a group that leads to shared vision and radical innovation. Within the context of Japanese manufacturing, Tatsuno [60] described five group creative process stages (*recycle, search, nurture, breakthrough, refine*) that, while echoing Wallas' four stages of an individual creative process, are all collaborative.

Since Janis' work on *groupthink* [29], there has been an implicit assumption that groups must be less effective than individuals at creative thought. The cliché "designed by committee" has served to solidify that impression. However, recent work by Nemeth et al. [47] argues that dissent and diversity play an important role in avoiding groupthink. They cite studies showing that social inhibition also reduces creativity. Their study focuses on dissent as a stimulus of creative thought. "[D]issent, even when wrong, serves to liberate the individual from a tendency to conform" [47]. This value of dissent is echoed by a study by Uzzi and Spiro [62] on musicals and creativity, finding an optimal level of interconnection between individuals for creative success. More connections can expose a team to a wider variety of source material, but if a network moves towards complete connection, there is less diversity and conflict, and ideas may become more conventional.

In many of these studies of group creativity, examples are given of processes where affect is clearly present. Sutton and Hargadon discuss the role of affect in how brainstorming allows designers to "experience skill variety" [59]. However, in most studies, affect is usually not called out explicitly for its role as a group creative process driver.

Contextual creative processes

As well as research on individual and group creative processes, work has also been done on contextual creative processes. These examine how social, socio-political and domain environments impact on the creativity of those working within them.

Csikszentmihalyi [16] describes a domain theory of creativity in which creativity is situated in the interaction between an individual, the domain (a subject's organized body of knowledge) and the field or 'gatekeepers' of the domain. Sutton and Hargadon [59] position creative brainstorming firmly within organizational contextual processes. Harrington [27] proposes an ecological model of creativity where "acts of social creativity must be viewed as the products of a human ecosystem as well as the products of an individual or two" [27]. As early as 1990, Harrington's work identified the need for a creative process that describes and underpins what he calls *social creativity*. In this paper, we apply dynamical systems theory to construct a new model that does just that.

In his seminal work "Cognition in the Wild" [28] Hutchins introduced the concept of distributed cognition. We see this as a precursor to our theory of collaborative creativity, describing as it does cognition as a process that includes the formation of knowledge outside any one particular individual. It depicts a cognitive ecosystem (echoing Harrington [27]) where information and cognitive processes exist as interactions between individuals and between individuals and their environment. The distributed cognition framework is now used widely in multiple areas such as computer-supported cooperative work (CSCW) and computer-supported collaborative learning (CSCL).

It is interesting that the seminal event leading to this research was a crisis on a naval vessel that generated high levels of emotion and stress. Hutchins noted the emergence of collaborative cognitive processes that accumulated a combination of knowledge that did not exist within any individual human brain. However, he did not explicitly call out the emotional states that drove the collaborative problem-solving process that led to the solution of the vessel's mechanical problem and enabled them to avoid crashing into the shore. It is this area of emotional states in distributed groups that we explore in our research and present here.

Finally, from the extensive literature of team development we reference Tuckman and Jensen's work [61] as important in bringing forward the balance between the team's task and its socio-emotional needs and states. As we set out our four-stage model of collaborative creativity we refer to the five stages (*form, storm, norm, perform* and *adjourn*) in their more detailed original form [61].

METHODOLOGY

The theory developed in this paper arose out of the authors' longitudinal studies of multiple long-term collaborations exhibiting creativity across the continuum from small-c to big-C. One author works with organizations supporting their creative processes and studying in depth the physical environments necessary for organizational creativity. The other has studied scientific and technical online collaborations in detail, with a focus on distributed creative technical work. In the course of our work, we both had come to see facets of group creativity that were not fully explained by previous creative models. This research emerged from our desire to find a model that could more effectively capture the commonalities in the group creative process that we observed time and again across widely dissimilar groups, and that could lead to a deeper understanding of collaborative creativity in the networked world of today. New technologies facilitating mediated communication over distance have contributed to our work by making previously hidden content more explicit; thus the evidence driving much of our research is online from chat logs and other persistent modes of CMC. It is also supplemented by a rich data set of interview and observation.

We revisited existing data sets to derive the model we put forward in this paper, then tested and refined it within the context of the various distributed groups that we have studied closely (astrophysicists' collaboration, children creating multimedia projects online, and engineering company employees).

The groups we focus on all meet the criteria for distributed groups [20], and all possess the following key characteristic: they are performing creative technical work that requires both a degree of specialized knowledge (astrophysics, programming, or engineering) and the generation of a range of creative ideas. The astrophysicists are working all the way from small-c to big-C (e.g. trying to solve a grand challenge problem about the nature of the universe, but also needing to build novel software tools to solve practical telescope engineering problems), while the children and engineers, although not attempting foundational societal change, nevertheless exhibit boundless amounts of creativity across the small-c to big-C spectrum in their daily work. A description of the three groups and the study methodologies follows.

Scratch

Scratch [39] is a programming language developed by Mitchel Resnick's research team at the MIT Media Lab, designed to enable children to create programmable media such as games, interactive stories, animations, music and art. The Scratch Online Community (scratch.mit.edu) [45] was developed to be a source of inspirational ideas, to provide an audience for children's creations and to foster collaboration among its members.

Since scratch.mit.edu went online in May 2007, a number of "companies" or collaborative groups have been formed spontaneously on the Scratch web site by the children themselves, with the main goal of creating projects together. We studied one such company that has been relatively successful in terms of producing several finished video games which were "published" to a gallery on the Scratch web site. The company, referred to here as "Green Bear Group" (GBG), was active for over two years from 2008 to 2010, and produced seven complex, polished projects during this time.

Three children, ages 8, 13, and 15, were the "founders" of the company, and it had a membership ranging from 12 to 18 children over the period studied. The active participants in Green Bear Group have, for the most part, never met one another, live in different time zones, and do not even know each other's real names. The 8-year-old "owns" the GBG gallery and the founders collectively make decisions on company membership. The members then vote on which games to develop. Each member has a specific skill, such as art, music, programming, or storytelling, which they contribute to the game by downloading an unfinished version, editing the program, and re-uploading a new version. This process is called "re-mixing" and is iterative. Each finished GBG game has had on average 17 remixes [5].

The Nearby Supernova Factory

The Nearby Supernova Factory (SNfactory) [2] is an international astrophysics collaboration studying supernovae (exploding stars) in order to address a physics grand challenge problem about the expansion rate of the universe. The collaboration consists of about 30 members; about half of the scientists work at several different locations in the U.S. and the other half in three research institutes and universities in France. Collaboration members develop software to aid the collection and analysis of supernova data, remotely operate a telescope in Hawaii, and collaborate on scientific research and publications. The scientists are in different time zones from each other (France, California, the US East Coast) and from the telescope itself (Hawaii). Some team members have never met and come from differing cultures with dissimilar assumptions; some are not native English speakers.

Collaboration scientists use chat (augmented by a virtual assistant [52]) and VNC (virtual network computing) as their primary means of communication during telescope observation.

Multinational Engineering Company (MEC)

Interviews conducted with senior staff in the engineering company [name withheld by request] formed part of a wider post-graduate research program and focused specifically on collaborative creativity with distributed groups across the company of 80,000 employees.

Study Methodology and Group Demographics

The examples used to illustrate the model are derived from longitudinal studies of the collaborations described above. The SNfactory was studied over a period of five years, and GBG over a period of two years. Study methods were participant observation, semi-structured interviews, and chat log analysis. More detail on the studies can be found in [5].

At the end of one study period (July 2009), the SNfactory had a membership of 28 scientists, including 14 senior scientists (permanent or tenured positions), eight junior scientists (post-doctoral researchers), and six graduate students. Each level had an even distribution of personnel between the US and France, satisfying Edwards and Al-Ani's criteria for distributed groups [20].

Within MEC, separate interviews were conducted in April 2010 with two network leaders of distributed groups comprising, respectively, 150 people in 90 transglobal locations and 12 people across the three global areas of AsiaPacific, the Americas, and EMEA (Europe, Middle East and Africa).

As of July 2010, Green Bear Group had 18 members ranging in age from 8 to 17 (self-reported). 11 of the members were located in the US, three in the UK, two in Canada, and one each in Poland and India.

All quotations in this paper use pseudonyms.

THEORY

Abrahams has explored the mathematical fields of dynamical systems theory and complexity theory in the context of psychology [1]. This, along with recent work by Arrow, McGrath, and Berdahl on a theory of small groups as complex systems [6] and our observations of creative practice across three field sites, has led us to apply similar principles to the process of group creativity.

As we construct our model of collaborative creativity, we focus primarily on the nature of creative groups as open, adaptive, complex systems, and on the causal dynamics in the group that facilitate the creative process on local, global, and contextual levels. We describe the role of affect and interface in facilitating these dynamics to foster creativity, and use analogies from complex systems to develop our model. In our previous work with distributed creative groups [5], we have repeatedly observed a phenomenon akin to the physical behavior of resonance, or driven harmonic motion, where key ideas begin small and grow and are elaborated over time. We hypothesize that, as in physics—where for an impulse to be amplified and for the system to oscillate at the resonant frequency, the system must easily be able to store and transfer energy between two or more different modes (e.g. a pendulum and the case of kinetic and potential energy)—the same phenomenon can be observed as creative ideation flourishes across a distributed group. We term this process *creative resonance.*

This model of incremental development leading to apparent discontinuous growth is consistent with previous theories of the individual creative process [17, 21, 56, 57, 63].

Key ideas of our model are based on group creativity research in psychology that shows that the creative process is much less of a "spark" or "leap" and much more incremental than commonly believed [57]. The nature of dynamical systems, similarly, is that local dynamics of the incremental type plus feedback loops can lead to nonlinear/discontinuous global dynamics (e.g. the "sudden insight"). We postulate that group interactions, specifically those of affect, facilitate these feedback loops. The 'sudden leap' appears to happen in the individual creative process only because many of the incremental stages are hidden in the 'intelligent unconscious' [13]. In the group process the interface makes it overt.

Finally, we hypothesize that affective, social or technological factors may act to damp the phenomenon of resonance. These three factors are consistently identified across disciplines: Quershi and Vogel [54] working with virtual teams, identify technology, work, and social adaptation issues as key within a virtual team environment. The social psychology of creativity [3, 4] identifies social and affective inhibitors to creativity, as does the literature of creativity in collocated teams [43]. Research into virtual teams [53] identifies trust, relationship building and cohesion as key socio-emotional aspects of successful virtual teams. We hypothesize that the obverse of these aspects acts to damp creative resonance in the system: e.g. low levels of trust which lead to an inability to establish a shared knowledge base [14]; poor relationship building resulting in negative conflict [46] and consequent lack of group cohesion [61].

Technological issues include poor quality technological interfaces [65] or overly-complex ones [48]. Our finding, that group members will adapt inadequate technology to their specific needs [5], is confirmed by Majchrzak et al. [38]. We postulate that recent technological developments have both reduced the damping factors inherent in the means of communication and decreased those present in human behavior. We suggest that communicating affect between members of a distributed group increases the level of energy and engagement between them, and hence the resonance of ideas in a distributed group. "A system needs access to itself. It needs to understand who it is, where it is, what it believes, what it knows. These needs are nourished by information" [66]. The study of resonance-damping and -enhancing factors specific to distributed creative groups is an area for further research.

Our model includes four key phases of collaborative creativity: *focus,* in which the group's rationale is explored and discovered, *frame,* in which the group forms within its context, *create,* when the group does just that, and *complete,* when the final idea or ideas converge and are tested and consolidated. This model is based on our observations of distributed groups; a topic for future study may be to explore its possible application to collocated groups. While we set out our model linearly for clarity, we suggest that it in fact works iteratively within each of its four stages, and across the whole model, nearer to Resnick's spiral model than Wallas' linear one.

FOCUS is concerned with *problem-finding* (as distinct from *problem-solving*) creativity [18]: a problem, curiosity, or area for exploration emerges with greater or lesser force. Where a group is already working together *focus* typically explores an issue arising from, or impacting on, the context within which the group and its members are based. In team development terms [61] this is the first stage of *testing and dependence* in which the activity is *orientation to task.* In dynamic systems terms, a *founded group* emerges from an internal, planned context whereas when an issue or opportunity arises in a wider field a *concocted* group may form specifically to explore it within an external planned context [6]. The process is the same in each case: one person (or small node) notices an anomaly, issue or opportunity and begins an iterative process of sharing their awareness. The wider group opens to the information and builds a picture of the anomaly or issue, collaboratively determining its level of importance and urgency and hence whether or not to proceed; an *extrinsic collective goal* [57] is identified and described. For one MEC team a small issue identified in one site and then shared across the distributed group was found to be present in all sister sites: "so the awareness builds from one or two of us seeing something, discussing it, crystallizing what the problem is, [to] testing it with the extended group in an extended discussion" (MEC engineer).

FRAME describes how "a sense of family" (MEC interviewee) is created in new or existing groups, building a complex system that can deliver the extrinsic collective goal. Component parts are: behaviors, interfaces, and structures. Information and affect have begun to flow around the system in the *focus* stage, and are made explicit and consolidated in the *frame* stage; the group undergoes a process of enculturation and the establishment of group cohesion [61]. This observation is supported by studies identifying group norms of individual expertise, collective achievement, open communication and interpersonal trust [12, 31, 43] as key to a flourishing creativity. "[Never having met] we just talked as if we had known each other for 20 years. And it always happens when somebody inside the company rings up to discuss something, there's never any kind of tension or difficulty about getting going. I suppose it's because you've got this very strong shared attitude – that is what enfolds it all" (MEC interviewee). Similarly a GBG member, age 13, expressed comfort with sharing her work specifically because of her trust in other members [5].

Group members are able to share information safely and freely within the group norms, to absorb external information, data, ideas and intellectual nourishment, and at the same time to filter out potentially harmful environmental pressures. Trust is a key affective component of open systems [44, 66], building the relationships that include rather than exclude group members and the knowledge they bring. This *affective integration* is experienced as emotional as well as cognitive strength, bringing people closer together [6]. In this *frame* stage group norms are established and interfaces are built enabling affect, cognition and information to be distributed across the system. It is worth noting that trust and affective integration does not mean consensus. Nemeth et al. are clear that creative ideas are unlikely to be generated by consensual thinking, but instead "there is evidence of greater creativity in response to minority dissent" [47]. Intragroup conflict or emotional response to task demands [61] is an integral part of distributed and collocated group development. Montoya-Weiss et al. [46] find a positive impact on performance from *competitive and collaborative conflict* (as opposed to *avoidance and compromise conflict).* Framing creates a supportive affective environment within which dissent and positive conflict is encouraged and productive.

Framing is also the stage at which interfaces that facilitate affect-laden communication are set up or consolidated: collaboration relies on a free flow of information unrestricted by censorship or gatekeeping [66], requiring efficient and easy-to-use interfaces [48]. For example, the chat environment the supernova scientists used and modified was deliberately designed to have a very low barrier to entry and to facilitate communication of all types [52]. Measurements of the amount of socio-emotional or affective content in the chat room confirmed that relatively high levels were present (32% of total content, as opposed to 16% in an earlier collaboration) [5].

For an existing group *frame* is a continuation or re-energizing of an existing state; with a new group the optimum state for collaborative creativity is established at its inception during *focus*, and developed in the *frame* stage with growing group cohesion [61]. In individual group members there may be a level of resistance to or rejection of ideas as evidenced in Evans and Russell's *frustration* stage [21]. *Framing* parallels Tatsuno's nurturing stage, setting out the ethos and parameters for the ongoing collaborative creative process: creating through the social environment the possibility of "discussing offbeat ideas [...] tossed about, expanded, picked apart, and playfully combined with other ideas" [60]. Framing starts early in the process, but is consciously maintained and grown throughout the life of the group or project.

CREATE By the *create* stage the distributed group has established cohesion through open exchange of perspectives [61]. The group uses iterative, incremental ideation steps, leading to non-linear discontinuities that are experienced as ah-ha! moments of insight [57]. The group shares the raw material of ideas – cognitive information, data, experiential knowledge from internal and also unrelated fields – generating ideas randomly as this divergent [49] process opens the possibility of unexpected juxtapositions [32] in Einstein's 'combinatory play'. As yet more raw material enters the system and is shared through the affective interfaces, so it sparks yet more ideas and a systemic resonance emerges. The system becomes more able to store and easily transfer energy between two or more different storage modes, in this case from individual minds to external representations. As the relative chaos of the initial divergent thinking moves towards complexity and order we see the emergence of structure which becomes the scaffolding for attaining the extrinsic collective goal. In this process we see emerging aspects of Resnick's [55] five-stage spiral process of *imagine, create, play, share, reflect, imagine*, and Laseau's [34] iterative model of creative revision in which "the more often the information is passed around the loop [eye to brain to hand to paper], the more the opportunities for change."

The iterative process of creative revision occurs in product design: Sutton and Hargadon observed designers calling physical prototypes "solidified intellect" [59]; these external representations enabled them to easily transfer and remember creative ideas. We observed analogous processes in the groups we studied; for example, the children created intermediate artifacts on the Scratch website which they used for the same purposes (remixing). These artifacts served as both a reminder of their intellectual work and a source of positive affect. Group product creation was greatly facilitated by the ease with which the Scratch interface allowed this type of idea transfer. As the group experiences success (progress towards creative outputs, small quick wins etc.) and acknowledges it, this enhances the distributed affect in the group. The affect within the system makes the connections between ideas and between people stickier. Sawyer [57], in examining group creativity among performers, suggests that in performance, creativity consists of the parallel processes of ideation and evaluation, both processes done collectively by the group as the performance is underway.

In *create* we observed a similar (if less instantaneous) process taking place: ideas generated by individuals, then shared and built upon by the group members from the perspective of their particular knowledge bases, adding aspects of information and data that may not have been apparent to the idea's originator. Girotra et al. [24], in their comparison of the effectiveness of group structures for idea generation, also conclude that a hybrid model where individuals work both independently and then together has advantages over to group brainstorming.

Three system dynamics are at play in the *create* stage: local, global and contextual [6]. Each of these dynamics contains the key components of information, affect and norms, and interfaces. *Local dynamics* comprise interactions between group members, and how their varying needs are taken into account by the behaviors and structures of the group. Arrow et al. posit that group members have a need to 'tune' the interactions between them, focusing on *affiliation* where they develop socio-emotional links with other group members, needs for *achievement* and power where their skills in specific areas are acknowledged and encouraged, and *agreements* that cover benefit and resource needs [6]. When these local dynamics are tuned, there is a greater possibility of distributed affect creating the resonance that drives and grows ideation.

In the longitudinal study of the Scratch group, affect magnified as each group member shared their excitement about the game they were building: their productivity rate went up, and with each new version the others were excited in their turn. This is borne out by Russ who conjectures that affective experience serves as a cue for problem-finding as individuals experience "tension, pleasurable anticipation of challenge in a problem [and] the ambiguity of a situation" [56]. Csikszentmihalyi's work on *flow* explores this phenomenon in depth and links it to creativity [16, 17]. This process is enhanced where there is high horizontal differentiation in the *global dynamics* (across the group as a whole) allowing members to specialize deeply, and low vertical differentiation so that group members are not inhibited and the resonance not damped by a task-based hierarchical status [6].

Throughout the *create* stage the group is also responding to changes in its external environment. These *contextual dynamics* are mediated by the group's *frame*. Adaptation to the external environment (proximal and distal) can be either undirected (emergent) or directed (driven by goals). For example, the junior supernova scientists were constantly driven by the need to publish and establish a positive reputation in the wider astronomy community so that they could obtain a permanent research position upon leaving their postdoctoral appointment. This led to emotional content in their communication with group members, with junior scientists pressing for goals valued by the wider community, such as open data release. This is a prime example of contextual dynamics driving the end products of the *create* stage.

This stage is characterized by multiple interactions: socio-emotional interaction between people, and between people and information, mediated by the affective interfaces; interaction between ideas, driven by resonance through the system; and interaction between the three system parameters (local, global and contextual). These interactions can be visualized as spirals and feedback loops and are the point where dynamical systems processes such as bifurcation and nonlinear development occur [1]; ideas may resonate with the group, grow wildly, or be damped out.

We hypothesize that the means of communication between individuals can be likened to a physical conductor. The higher the conductivity, the less the resistance, the less the damping/dissipative force. We suggest that the information to be transferred must include the two strands of cognition and affect. Thus we have not only distributed cognition but also distributed affect. New technologies, plus a new generation growing up with the new technologies and co-evolving along with them, have, we hypothesize, led to a decrease in the resistance along these communication channels; thus the reduced resistance of the interface is a local parameter that can have profound effects on the global state. As one GBG member commented, "Scratch is simple, so that made it easy and fun to use and people kept coming back." Affect of various types will also modify the resistance, and can be considered another local dynamic parameter.

The process is about the growth of the idea, the growth of the individual through learning about themselves and others and how to work in collaboration, and the growth of the distributed group as a productive entity. So in the same way as people and technologies co-evolve, so the ideas and the group co-evolve through changing technologies. As a result the process must be seen as a dynamic one, with complex interacting subprocesses rather than simple cause and effect.

COMPLETE The resonance within the group drives the ideas from chaos towards order in the *create* phase, and as the system moves towards order the ideas converge, a final idea coalesces and other ideas fall away. In the *complete* phase the emergent idea is evaluated and, where appropriate, elaborated [57], cycling back for as long as necessary into the *create* phase. As discussed earlier, this is part of the continuous iterative process within as well as between the four stages of the model. This final phase parallels previous creative processes models as, variously, *refine* [60] *reflect* [55], *verify* [63], or *working it out* [21]. This *completing* evaluation is different from the *create* phase's synchronic interaction [57] ideation/evaluation loop; rather this evaluation is done within the external context of the group, when an idea is aligned with the extrinsic collective goal. Researchers have also identified the skills needed at this phase: Belbin [9] in his study of team roles identifies the need for a *monitor/evaluator*, Foy's [23] adaptation of Belbin calls for a *critic*, and Luther and Diakopoulos [36] identify *analyzers* 'who provide feedback and evaluation' engendering further iterative improvement loops. Foy adds the caveat that critics are best kept away from the *create* phase lest they damp the resonance and the ideas converge too early.

DISCUSSION

Our empirical observations suggest that designers of interfaces should focus on building to facilitate distributed affect across group systems, concentrating on ease of use, simple access and intuitive process. The networking tools used by MEC employees permit simultaneous document access, electronic chat logs, and voice, enabling groups of varying sizes to communicate easily at and between on-line meetings. Our observations also suggest the key role of how these interfaces are used; for example, MEC's explicit rule set for working on-line "means that people are better at waiting and listening" supported by a "careful moderated approach to chairing." This encourages strong horizontal and low vertical systemical differentiation with its resultant rise in creative resonance. It also supports the ability to engage all the group participants, an important element where distributed groups include a wide geographical area with a concomitant range of expertise, cultural perspectives and personalities.

For the children on Scratch, the primary motivating factor keeping the kids coming back to communicate on the site is, in the words of one founder, "because it's fun. We're not getting paid for this." In an interview, one GBG member said, "If one person is excited about a project, other people will see that excitement and it'll motivate them to be excited too. They'll say, this is an exciting project and I want to contribute." The sheer joy and excitement of the children in creative production is evident from the site logs.

> *Yib: Yayyy production! Sounds like this Claw Game may actually go somewhere. Now as for the name...Retro Claw Capture?*
>
> *King: Yes! Yes! It is called Retro Claw Capture, looking at the recent remixes... I'm going to add to the game today.*

The importance of feedback to the group creative process is also clear. This resonance was described by one member as "a friendly version of peer pressure." We see similar examples of creative contributions in the astrophysics projects, where a positive feedback loop encouraged members to contribute new software:

> *Kevin: Ah, OK. I made a "sooper looper" for the SNIFS processing like I did for the search automation, and at least the first part of that pipeline seems to be working.*
>
> *Sam: :)*
>
> *Kevin: Since you are at home with your roomba, I am sure you are on your mac, but I wanted to mention I made some hacks to the tightvnc unix viewer handy for summit watching. ... I can toggle the bell off and on in the menu for one! ... I can also make 1/2 and 1/3 sized thumbnails of the desktops.*
>
> *Sam: oh, nice ... I think ultravnc (for windows) had a feature like that; I always missed it on Unix and Mac.*

Kevin's pride in his work and Sam's encouragement led to the development of more novel software tools to facilitate the group's work. Conversations of this type were rampant throughout the scientists' chat logs, indicating the importance of affect in accelerating local, global, and contextual dynamics over time across a range of creative endeavors.

Affect can be hard to measure, especially in face-to-face interactions, where body language, facial expressions, and tone of voice convey a wealth of non-cognitive information. However, we suggest that with the increasing prevalence of computer mediated communication in group work, that communication of affect is both being facilitated and made more overt. At the same time, our research has shown that people can feel freer to express emotion online, and the lack of non-cognitive information can be a positive benefit: "When you can't see the body language, the ideas stand more strongly in their own right" (MEC engineer).

CONCLUSION

Our long-term work with distributed creative groups gave us the impetus to develop a new model for collaborative creativity that includes the importance of *distributed affect* and carefully designed *affective interfaces*. We built upon a large body of research in multiple domains to devise a model based on complex systems theory, a tool that has been useful in numerous areas. It is often counter-intuitive to express affect in professional circumstances, and arguably, many are wary of what designer Jean Muir called "the messy bits." In facilitating the resonance that helps drive ideas around a distributed group and in the dissent that can spur them in the first place, affect is, we posit, at the heart of the collaborative creative process. With the escalating quantity of persistent data available from online collaborations, we hope to see further study of this important aspect of group creativity.

ACKNOWLEDGMENTS

We deeply appreciate the reviewers' careful reading of our work which greatly strengthened this paper, and we thank the scientists of the SNfactory collaboration, the members of Green Bear Group on Scratch, and the MEC engineers for their time and detailed commentary.

REFERENCES

1. Abraham, F. D. *A Visual Introduction to Dynamical Systems Theory for Psychology*. Aerial Press, Santa Cruz, CA (1990).
2. Aldering, G., et al., Overview of the Nearby Supernova Factory. *Proceedings of the SPIE* (2002), 61-72.
3. Amabile, T. M. *The social psychology of creativity.* New York: Springer-Verlag (1983).
4. Amabile, T. M. *Creativity in Context.* Oxford: Westview Press (1996).
5. Aragon, C.; Poon, S., Monroy-Hernández, A., & Aragon, D. A Tale of Two Online Communities: Fostering Collaboration and Creativity in Scientists and Children. *Creativity & Cognition* (2009).
6. Arrow, H., McGrath, J. E. & Berdahl, J. L. *Small Groups as Complex Systems.* CA: Sage (2000).
7. Arthur, B. W. *The Nature of Technology*, Free Press, New York, (2009).
8. Arthur, B. W. Competing Technologies, Increasing Returns, and Lock-In by Historical Events. In *The Economic Journal, Vol. 99*, No. 394 (1989) 116-131.
9. Belbin, M. *Management Teams.* Oxford: Heinemann (1981).
10. Benkler, Y. *The wealth of networks: How social production transforms markets and freedom.* US: Yale University Press (2006).
11. Boden, M. Computer Models of Creativity. In Robert J. Sternberg (Ed.) *Handbook of Creativity.* New York: Cambridge University Press (1999).
12. Cherns, A. The principles of socio-technical design. *Human Relations*, 29(8), (1976), 783-792.
13. Claxton, G. Hare Brain, Tortoise Mind. UK: Fourth Estate (1997).
14. Crampton, C. The Mutual Knowledge Problem and its Consequences for Dispersed Collaboration. *Organization Science,* Vol. 12, No.3, (2001), 346-371.
15. Csikszentmihalyi, M. *Beyond boredom and anxiety.* San Francisco: Jossey-Bass (1975).
16. Csikszentmihalyi, M. The Domain of Creativity. *Theories of Creativity,* Mark A. Runco & Robert S. Albert (Eds.) pp.190-212. London UK: Sage (1990).
17. Csikszentmihalyi, M. *Creativity: Flow and the Psychology of Discovery and Invention.* New York: HarperCollins (1996).
18. Csikszentmihalyi, M., & Sawyer, R. K. Creative Insight: The social dimension of a solitary moment. In R. J. Sternberg & J. E. Davidson (Eds.) *The nature of insight.* MIT Press (1995), 329-363.
19. Dunbar, K. How Scientists Think: Online creativity and conceptual change in science. T. B. Ward, S. M. Smith & S. Vaid (Eds.) *Conceptual structures and processes: emergence, discovery and change.* Washington DC: APA Press (1997).
20. Edwards, H.K., Kim, J.H., Park, S., Al-Ani, B. "Global Software Development: Project Decomposition and Task Allocation" International Conference on Business and Information (2008).
21. Evans, R. & Russell, P. *The Creative Manager.* London: Unwin Hyman (1989).
22. Fischer G. & Shipman, F. "Collaborative Design Rationale and Social Creativity in Cultures of Participation", *Human Technology J.* (2010).
23. Foy, N. *Empowering People at Work.* London: Gower (1997).
24. Girotra, K., Terwiesch, C. & Ulrich, K. T. Idea Generation and the Quality of the Best Idea. INSEAD Business School Research Paper No. 2009/65/TOM (2009).
25. Gordon, W. *Synectics: The development of creative capacity.* New York: Harper & Row (1961).
26. Guilford, J. P. Creativity. *American Psychologist, 5* (1950) 444-454.
27. Harrington, D. M. The ecology of human creativity: A psychological perspective. In *Theories of creativity,* edited by M. A. Runco and R. S. Albert. Newbury Park, Calif.: Sage Publications (1990) 143-169.
28. Hutchins, E. *Cognition in the Wild.* Cambridge, Mass.: MIT Press (1995).
29. Janis, I. L. *Groupthink: Psychological Studies of Policy Decisions and Fiascoes.* Second Edition. New York: Houghton Mifflin (1972/1982).
30. John-Steiner, V. *Creative Collaboration.* Oxford: Oxford University Press (2000).

31. Katz, D. and Kahn, R. *The social psychology of organizations*. NY: Wiley (1978).
32. Koestler, A. *The Act of Creation.* New York: Dell (1964).
33. Langley, P., & Jones, R. A computational model of scientific insight. In R. Sternberg (Ed.), *The nature of creativity.* US: Cambridge University Press (1988).
34. Laseau, P. *Graphic thinking for architects and designers.* (2nd Edition) NY: Van Nostrand Reinhold (1989).
35. Lazarus, R. S. Theory-Based Stress Measurement. *Psychological Inquiry: An International Journal for the Advancement of Psychological Theory*, 1532-7965, Vol. 1, Issue 1, (1990) 3-13.
36. Luther & Diakopoulos. Distributed Creativity. In *Proc. Creativity & Cognition* (2007).
37. MacKinnon, D. W. The nature and nurture of creative talent. *American Psychologist, 17,* (1962) 484-495.
38. Majchrzak, A., Rice, R., Malhotra, A., King, N., and Ba, S. Technology Adaptation: The Case of a Computer-supported Inter-organizational Virtual Team Innovating Using a Collaborative Tool. *Information Resources Management Journal,* Vol. 13, No.1, (2000) 44-53.
39. Maloney, J., Resnick, M. and Rusk, N., Scratch: A Sneak Preview. *Second Intl Conference on Creating, Connecting, and Collaborating through Computing.* Tokyo, Japan, (2004).
40. Markman, A., Yamauchi, T., Makin, V., "The Creation of New Concepts: A Multifaceted Approach to Category Learning," in *Creative Thought: An Investigation of Conceptual Structures and Processes,* ed. T. Ward, S. Smith, and J. Vaid (Washington, DC: American Psychological Association, 1997), 179-208.
41. Martindale, C. & Hines, D. Creativity and cortical activation during creative, intellectual, and EEG feedback tasks. *Biological Psychology*, 3 (1975) 71-80.
42. Mayer, R. E. Fifty Years of Creativity Research. In *Handbook of Creativity.* R. J. Sternberg (Ed.). New York: Cambridge University Press (1999).
43. McCoy, J. M. *The Creative Work Environment: The Relationship of the Physical Environment and Creative Teamwork at a State Agency – A Case Study.* PhD Thesis, University of Wisconsin-Milwaukee (2000).
44. Meyerson, D., Weick, K. E. and Kramer, R. M. Swift Trust and Temporary Groups. In RM Kramer & TR Tyler (Eds.) *Trust in Organizations: Frontiers of Theory and Research.* Thousand Oaks, CA: Sage (1996) 166-195.
45. Monroy-Hernandez, A. and Resnick, M. Empowering Kids to Create and Share Programmable Media. *Interactions*, Mar/Apr 2008.
46. Montoya-Weiss, M. M., Massey, A. P., Song, M. Getting It Together: Temporal Coordination and Conflict Management in Global Virtual Teams. *Academy of Management Journal,* Vol. 44, No.6, (2001) 1251-1262.
47. Nemeth, C. J. & Nemeth-Brown, B. Better than Individuals? The potential benefits of dissent and diversity for group creativity. In P. Paulus and B. Nijstad (eds.) *Group Creativity*. Oxford: Oxford University Press (2003).
48. Norman, D. A. *The Invisible Computer.* Cambridge, Mass.: MIT Press (1998).
49. Osborn, A. F. *Applied imagination.* New York: Scribner's (1953).
50. Picard, R. W. *Affective Computing.* MIT Media Laboratory Perceptual Computing Section Tech Report No. 321 (1995).
51. Poincaré, H. *The foundations of science.* Lancaster, PA: Science Press (1913).
52. Poon, S., Thomas, R. C., Aragon, C. and Lee, B., Context-Linked Virtual Assistants for Distributed Teams: An Astrophysics Case Study. *CSCW 08*, San Diego, CA, USA (2008).
53. Powell, A., Piccoli, G., and Ives, B. Virtual Teams: A Review of Current Literature and Directions for Future Research. *The DATA BASE for Advances in Information Systems,* Vol. 35, No. 1 (Winter 2004).
54. Quershi, S. and Vogel, D. Adaptiveness in Virtual Teams: Organizational Challenges and Research Directions. *Group Decision and Negotiation,* Vol. 10 (2001), 27-46.
55. Resnick, M. All I Really Need to Know (About Creative Thinking) I Learned (By Studying How Children Learn) in Kindergarten. In *Proc. Creativity and Cognition* (2007).
56. Russ, S. W. *Affect and Creativity: the role of affect and play in the creative process.* NJ: Lawrence Erl. (1993).
57. Sawyer, R. K. *Group Creativity.* NJ: Lawrence Erlbaum (2003).
58. Simonton, D. K. Creativity. In C. R. Snyder, Shane J. Lopez (Eds.) *Handbook of Positive Psychology.* US: Oxford University Press (2005), 189-201.
59. Sutton, R. I. and Hargadon, A. Brainstorming Groups in Context: Effectiveness in a Product Design Firm. *Administrative Science Quarterly*, Vol. 41, No. 4 (Dec. 1996), 685-718.
60. Tatsuno, S. M. *Created in Japan.* New York: Harper & Row (1990).
61. Tuckman, B. W. and Jensen, M. A. C. Stages of Small-Group Development Revisited. *Group & Organization Studies* 2, 4 (1977), 419-427.
62. Uzzi, B. & Spiro, J. Collaboration and creativity: The small world problem. *American Journal of Sociology*, 111 (2005), 447-504.
63. Wallas, G. *The Art of Thought.* New York: Harcourt, Brace, Jovanovich (1926).
64. Ward, T. B., Smith, S. M., & Finke, R. A. Creative cognition. In R. Sternberg. (Ed.) *Handbook of Creativity.* New York: Cambridge University (1999).
65. Warkentin, M. E., Sayeed, L. and Hightower, R. Virtual Teams versus Face-to-face Teams: An Exploratory Study of a Web-based Conference System. *Decision Sciences,* 28, 4 (1997), 975-996.
66. Wheatley, M. & Kellner-Rogers, M. *A Simpler Way.* San Francisco: Berrett-Koehler (1996).

Predicting the Perceived Quality of Online Mathematics Contributions from Users' Reputations

Yla R. Tausczik, James W. Pennebaker
Department of Psychology
University of Texas at Austin
{tausczik, pennebaker}@mail.utexas.edu

ABSTRACT
There are two perspectives on the role of reputation in collaborative online projects such as Wikipedia or Yahoo! Answers. One, user reputation should be minimized in order to increase the number of contributions from a wide user base. Two, user reputation should be used as a heuristic to identify and promote high quality contributions. The current study examined how offline and online reputations of contributors affect perceived quality in MathOverflow, an online community with 3470 active users. On MathOverflow, users post high-level mathematics questions and answers. Community members also rate the quality of the questions and answers. This study is unique in being able to measure offline reputation of users. Both offline and online reputations were consistently and independently related to the perceived quality of authors submissions, and there was only a moderate correlation between established offline and newly developed online reputation.

Author Keywords
online reputation, community question-answering, information quality

ACM Classification Keywords
H.5.3 Information Interfaces and Presentation: Group and Organization Interfaces—*Computer-supported cooperative work*

General Terms
Experimentation, Human Factors

INTRODUCTION
MathOverflow (MO) is a small online community of question-answering comprised of 3470 active users. Users contribute 'research level math' questions and answers, and everyone is encouraged to participate: 'Remember, MathOverflow is run by you!' Questions like 'Can a positive binary quadratic form represent 14 consecutive numbers?' are posted and answered by community members. The members also rate the quality of the questions and answers.

The site is an example of crowdsourcing, a strategy for achieving high quality content by pooling the knowledge and effort of many people, regardless of their expertise. Wikipedia, the best known example of crowdsourcing, has been found to have a comparable number of errors as traditional encyclopedias written by experts [2]. A comparison of question and answer sites revealed that sites with a wider user base as opposed to a set of experts produced higher quality answers [4].

Many crowdsourcing communities are designed to create a level playing field, in which previous experience and reputation does not hinder contributions. Specifically, by de-emphasizing established reputation, small insights from untrained or less trained users that would otherwise go undeveloped can contribute to the body of knowledge in addition to insights from experts. Many authors have found that even within these projects, there are still major differences between contributors. One study found that power users, those who made the most contributions, had greater influence than first-time users in discussions of which news articles should make it to Wikipedia's front page [7]. An attempt to employ online crowdsourcing to solve an open mathematics problem, a project known as "polymath1", resulted in a proof of a new mathematical result but in the end far fewer individuals than hoped, almost all experienced mathematicians, actually made substantial contributions [3].

Other researchers have taken the position that it may not matter that these communities are not egalitarian. They argue that communities may benefit from combining the advantages of a wide user base and a reputation system that identifies experts and promotes their contributions. Past user behavior on Yahoo! Answers (YA), such as the number of questions answered, was found to be a significant predictor of the quality of answers [9]. Jurczyk and Agichtein present evidence and argue that metrics like high network centrality in giving answers, could identify authors with higher expertise on YA [6].

The central question is: To what extent is reputation related to the quality of contributions? By answering this question, communities can be designed to place the optimal emphasis on reputation. On the one hand, minimizing reputation may give individuals with little or no reputation the opportunity to produce high quality content. On the other hand, an author's reputation may be a good heuristic for the quality of their contributions and may make it easier to identify high quality content.

THE CURRENT STUDY

Collaborative crowdsourcing projects could be improved if there was a greater understanding of the degree to which reputation affected the perceived quality of contributions. We use behavior on MO to measure the importance of four reputation variables in predicting the perceived quality of questions and answers.

Launched in September, 2009, MO consists of 3470 active users (6280 registered accounts). About half of the users use their real names; a majority of these users are academic mathematicians. Most academic users have recognizable offline academic activity such as journal publications.

MO is unique in having a small online community that draws members from a specific offline community–academic mathematicians. The existence of an offline and online community allows us to contrast multiple forms of reputation and expertise on perceived quality of contributions. In addition, the content of the site, research level mathematics, requires extensive knowledge to make good contributions and there are quantifiable differences in the quality of the contributions. Accordingly, it is an ideal site to answer our research questions.

Both offline and online reputations reflect people's standing in the community. In this study, **offline reputation** in the academic mathematics community was measured by the number of publications the contributors had. Online reputation was measured in three ways: **MathOverflow Points (MO Points)**, **authoritativeness**, and **social connectedness**. MO Points are a feature of the software running MO and are based on the ratings of a user's past submissions; it is displayed next to the user's name. The other two measures were selected because they have been used in previous studies and are indirect measures of reputation. Authoritativeness measures how confidently a user worded his or her submission. Network betweenness centrality was measured; it is a social network analysis metric that measures social connectedness.

The one offline and three online reputation variables were regressed against two measures of perceived quality of submissions: the **net number of votes a question received** and the **net number of votes an answer received**. Registered users are encouraged to up vote a question or answer if they find it valuable and to down vote it if they do not. Next to each submission appears a box which gives the total score that it has received. In the context of research level mathematics questions it is difficult to measure objective quality because there are few judges qualified enough to evaluate the content. The perceived quality is a good approximation of objective quality because the MO users voting on the content are themselves some of the few judges who are qualified to evaluate the objective quality.

First, we examined the relationships between the four reputation variables, to test whether these measurements represent four fundamentally different kinds of reputation or if they are actually measuring the same construct. Many question-answering sites, like MO, have begun to implement online reputation systems. The impact of these systems and the relationship between newly created online and established offline reputation is unclear.

Second, we compared the different measures of reputation to see which was the best predictor of perceived quality. We compared different measures of online reputation. MO Points is a direct measure of online reputation and is a record of past achievements. There is some evidence that indirect methods of measuring reputation, like authoritativeness and social connectedness, may be better than direct methods, like MO Points, because they record social processes rather than achievements and are more proximate. For example, in analyzing communication between Enron employees it was found that social connectedness was the best predictor of actually leading projects [5].

We also compared online and offline reputation. Studies of reputation have focused on reputation created on the site. There is some doubt whether those with higher online reputation actually make better contributions; an analysis of edits to Wikipedia made by regular and one-time users showed that both could make high quality edits [1]. Few studies have assessed the importance of offline reputation directly because most communities involve anonymous users and so it is difficult to measure the level of reputation outside of the online community.

Finally and most importantly, we addressed the central research question by assessing the total contribution of reputation in predicting the perceived quality of contributions.

METHOD

Information about registered users and matched user information was collected with records of posting behavior on the MO site. MO moderators publicly post dumps from MO servers with user and post data monthly, allowing access to this publicly available data.

Perceived Quality of Questions and Answers

All posts on MO from May 1, 2010 to June 1, 2010 were downloaded. In all, 953 questions made by a single author and 1213 answers to multi-answer questions (from 422 questions) were collected. There were an average of 32 questions posted per day, each question received an average of 225 views, 3.74 votes, 2.70 comments, and 1.61 answers. The two primary perceived quality measures focused on the rated quality of questions and of answers. Users can vote on the quality of a question based on its novelty, insight, or interest. The more votes, the higher the perceived quality. Users can also vote on the quality of an answer.

User Reputation

For each author of a question or answer, four different measures of reputation were collected.

Table 1. Correlations between author reputation measures.

	(2)	(3)	(4)
offline reputation (1)	0.38**	0.06	-0.08*
MathOverflow Points (2)		0.15***	-0.06
authoritativeness (3)			0.00
social connectedness (4)			

Signif. codes: '' 0.05, '**' 0.01, '***' 0.001*

Offline reputation Sixty-two percent of users filled out personal details when they registered such as their real name, an academic or personal website, a short self-description, and a location, that allowed us to collect information about their offline reputation. Offline reputation was operationalized as the number of papers a user published in peer-reviewed mathematics journals. The number of publications for each user was collected from their academic website if provided or by searching MathSciNet (a comprehensive database of mathematics articles) using the user's name if provided. Data was analyzed using two approaches by either imputing offline reputation assuming no papers or by excluding missing values. In both cases, offline reputation was significant. Users who did not identify themselves on the site displayed different behavior: they had lower online reputation and did not participate as much. Because there was not a substantial difference in the results from using either approach and in order to preserve information on users with low identity information, the imputed measure of offline reputation was used and an additional dichotomous variable of whether offline reputation was identifiable was also included.

MathOverflow Points MO was designed to display a score for each user based on the number of votes all his or her submissions had received. This score was recorded just prior to the period in which questions and answers were collected, April 29th, 2010.

Authoritativeness The text of each question and answer were processed linguistically using the computer program Linguistic Inquiry and Word Count (LIWC) which counts the rate of word use in psychologically meaningful categories [8]. Three categories of word use were recorded based on their ability to predict existing and manipulated status in past research: total word count, first person plural, and the inverse of first person singular [11]. A composite of these was created by taking the sum of the z-score for each variable.

Social connectedness Social network analysis was performed on users' history of posting to question and answer threads just prior to the period in which questions and answers were collected, April 29th, 2010 [12]. That is an edge was created from Person A to B if B answered a question given by A, edges were weighted by the number of answers provided to questions by A. For each user, betweenness centrality was measured in this network. This has been used as a measure of social connectedness in online communities [10]. The measure of network betweenness centrality was corrected to control for the user's level of participation to separate it from MO Points.

Table 2. The relationship between author reputation and the perceived quality of questions and answers.

	number of votes per question (β)	number of votes per answer (β)
intercept	0.08	-0.01
offline reputation	0.22**	0.12***
MathOverflow Points	0.26***	0.12***
authoritativeness	0.18***	0.00
social connectedness	0.07*	0.03
missing identity	-0.24**	-0.01
lifetime of post	0.01	0.06**
lifetime of user account	0.02	-0.02
amount of math notation	-0.02	0.05*
variance explained by author reputation measures	0.40	0.07

Signif. codes: '' 0.05, '**' 0.01, '***' 0.001*

Statistical Approach

Separate analyses were conducted on which characteristics of the author predicted highly rated questions and answers. The authors varied greatly in their levels of offline and online reputation. Those that submitted answers had higher reputation scores than those who submitted questions (median values 233 versus 11 MO Points and 4 versus 2 publications).

Multi-level logistic and linear regression models were calculated to estimate the degree to which the status variables predicted the perceived quality of a question or answer. Questions were nested within authors and answers were nested within questions. A few other variables were included in the model as covariates: whether offline reputation was missing, days since the submission was posted, the number of days between the first and last day the author logged onto MO, and the amount of mathematical notation. In the model predicting the number of votes an answer received, the average number of votes per answer to the question was also included to control for the popularity of the question. Measures that were right skewed were log-transformed to correct for deviations in normality. All measures have been standardized so the magnitudes of their coefficients can be compared. Variance explained was calculated for the addition of the reputation variables to the model with covariates.

RESULTS AND DISCUSSION

Relationship between author reputation measures

There was moderate to small overlap in the four reputation variables. The strongest relationship was between offline reputation and MO Points; these two variables were moderately correlated (Table 1). Among measures of online reputation, MO Points and authoritativeness were slightly related, but neither was related to social connectedness. These results suggest that the four measurements of reputation are measuring different types of reputation.

The best predictors of perceived quality

All four reputation variables partially predicted the perceived quality of submissions (Table 2). Offline reputation and MO

Points were the best predictors. MO Points was a better predictor of perceived quality of submissions than the two other measures of online reputation, authoritativeness and social connectedness. The indirect measures were significant predictors for the perceived quality of questions only and they had lower magnitudes of effect. Of the two indirect measures, authoritativeness was more important than social connectedness. These results show that in the case of MO, direct measures of past achievements are the best predictors of the perceived quality. Achievements may be more important than social factors, like how authoritative the submission is worded or how socially connected the user is, because contributions in mathematics are more objectively quantifiable.

Both offline reputation and MO Points significantly and independently predicted the perceived quality of questions and answers. The two forms of reputation had nearly equal magnitudes of effect. MO Points was a slightly better predictor for the perceived quality of questions. The other two forms of online reputation were worse predictors than offline reputation at predicting the perceived quality of submissions. These results demonstrate that online and offline reputation are measuring different forms of reputation and one form of online reputation and offline reputation are nearly equal in contributing to the perceived quality of submissions.

Without some mathematical training it unlikely a user will be able to make a significant contribution to MO. The interesting comparison is between the first year graduate student who will have no mathematics papers and the Fields medalist who may have a hundred. These results show that some of the inexperienced students are able to develop reputation on MO and exert influence; they also show that newly developed reputation on the site does not erase the importance of long-standing reputation–the Fields medalist's submissions are still prominent. Although not visible, it is likely that the same relationship between online and offline reputation generalizes to other communities of collective action. Future research should investigate whether communities of collective action should be designed to display offline reputation as well as online reputation. Designers are faced with the problem of delicately balancing advertising user's offline reputation with the possible consequence of suppressing valuable contributions by low reputation individuals against the possible benefit of promoting valuable expertise.

Overall importance of author reputation

Overall, reputation explained a significant, but moderate percentage of the variance. Reputation variables explained about 40% percent of variance in the perceived quality of questions and only 7% of variance in the perceived quality of answers. Not surprisingly reputation seems to be important in making highly rated submissions, but the majority of variance in perceived quality must be attributable to other variables.

Counterintuitively, reputation variables were better predictors of perceived quality in questions than answers. There are two likely explanations. One, readers may be more discriminating in which questions they pay attention to and find interesting. There are far more questions to choose between than answers to a single question. Two, there is a high threshold for submitting answers. The average online and offline reputations for users submitting answers was far higher than for questions. Reputation may explain the difference between submitting and not submitting an answer, but the difference between a good and a bad answer may have more to do with a single insightful idea than overall expertise and reputation.

CONCLUSION

This study shows that multiple forms of reputation are related to the perceived quality of contributions. Which suggests that both offline and online reputation could be effectively used to identify high quality submissions, although counter intuitively reputation may be better at predicting high quality submissions when there is low barrier for entry. Two issues should be addressed in future research. One, whether there is a systematic effect of displaying an authors reputation information on the quality of content on the site. Two, separating the degree to which reputation effects actual quality of submissions and perceptions of quality above actual quality.

REFERENCES

1. Anthony, D., Smith, S. W., and Williamson, T. Reputation and reliability in collective goods: The case of the online encyclopedia Wikipedia. *Rationality and Society 21* (2009), 283–306.
2. Giles, J. Internet encyclopaedias go head to head. *Nature 438* (2005), 900–901.
3. Gowers, T., and Nielsen, M. Massively collaborative mathematics. *Nature 461* (2009), 879–881.
4. Harper, F. M., Raban, D., Rafaeli, S., and Konstan, J. A. Predictors of answer quality in online Q&A sites. In *Proc. CHI 2008*, ACM Press, 865-874.
5. Hossain, L., Wu, A., and Chung, K. K. S. Actor centrality correlates to project based coordination. In *Proc. CSCW 2006*, ACM Press, 363 – 372.
6. Jurczyk, P., and Agichtein, E. Discovering authorities in question answer communities by using link analysis. In *Proc. CIKM 2007*, ACM Press, 919–923.
7. Keegan, B., and Gergle, D. Egalitarians at the gate : One-sided gatekeeping practices in social media. In *Proc. CSCW 2010*, ACM Press, 131–134.
8. Pennebaker, J. W., Booth, R. J., and Francis, M. E. Linguistic Inquiry and Word Count: LIWC.
9. Shah, C., and Pomerantz, J. Evaluating and predicting answer quality in community QA. In *Proc. SIGIR 2010*, 411–418.
10. Sylvan, E. Predicting influence in an online community of creators. In *Proc. CHI 2010*, ACM Press, 1913–1916.
11. Tausczik, Y. R., and Pennebaker, J. W. The psychological meaning of words: LIWC and computerized text analysis methods. *Journal of Language and Social Psychology 29* (2010), 24–54.
12. Zhang, J., Ackerman, M. S., and Adamic, L. Expertise networks in online communities: Structure and algorithms. In *Proc. WWW 2007*, ACM Press, 221–230.

Why Is My Internet Slow?: Making Network Speeds Visible

Marshini Chetty[1], David Haslem[2], Andrew Baird[3], Ugochi Ofoha[1], Bethany Sumner[1] and Rebecca E. Grinter[1]

Georgia Institute of Technology[1]
{marshini, uofoha3, bsumner8, beki}
@gatech.edu

Orange Sparkle Ball[2]
david@orangesparkleball.com

Amazon[3]
baird.gatech@gmail.com

ABSTRACT

With widespread broadband adoption, more households report experiencing sub-optimal speeds. Not only are slow speeds frustrating, they may indicate consumers are not receiving the services they are paying for from their internet service providers. Yet, determining the speed and source of slow-downs is difficult because few tools exist for broadband management. We report on results of a field trial with 10 households using a visual network probe designed to address these problems. We describe the results of the study and provide design implications for future tools. More importantly, we argue that tools like this can educate and empower consumers by making broadband speeds and sources of slow-downs more visible.

Author Keywords

Home networks, broadband speed, broadband tools

ACM Classification Keywords

H5.m. Information interfaces and presentation (e.g., HCI): Miscellaneous.

General Terms

Human Factors

INTRODUCTION

With increased broadband adoption in the U.S., more households report experiencing sub-optimal internet speeds [9]. Often broadband speed varies because there are more users on larger home networks, frequently using high bandwidth media such as real-time voice and video applications [1,20-21]. Not only are slow speeds frustrating, they may indicate households are not receiving services they are paying for [26]. In the U.S., only 30% of online Americans receive "advertised" speeds, even though internet service providers (ISP) charge higher rates for faster speeds [9]. Adding to concerns over inconsistent home broadband speeds, are ongoing debates about "net neutrality" which would introduce a tiered internet service—paying fees for various types of web traffic [10]. Regardless of which side of the debate one is on, regulators, companies, and consumer groups agree that users need visibility into what performance the ISP is actually delivering for various services [17-18].

For these reasons, households require tools to help them determine their internet speed, diagnose a slow connection and take action to rectify the problem [8]. Our research goals were to make home broadband speeds visible and manageable for users and to study how this informs their thinking. To this end, we created a probe called Kermit to show householders factors causing internet slow-downs. In this paper, we describe results from a field trial of Kermit with 10 households where we also ascertained real consumers' awareness of broadband speed issues.

We have three major HCI contributions. First, we introduce a novel visual tool for home broadband management. Second, we provide insights from our field trial into how real consumers conceive of tiered internet services, broadband issues, and implications for the design of future tools. Our third contribution is showing how such tools can serve to educate and empower consumers about broadband service in general.

We begin by reviewing related work on home networking and broadband issues. We then describe Kermit's design and our evaluation methods. Finally, we discuss our results, and how tools similar to Kermit can help households better understand and manage their broadband connections. More importantly, we call for the HCI community to conduct more research on household broadband tools—to help consumers become aware of, and engage in public debates on broadband issues affecting them, such as net neutrality.

RELATED WORK

Previous studies highlight how setting up, maintaining and troubleshooting a home network is far from straightforward [11]. Not only is digital housekeeping a problem, its resolution depends on the social makeup of the home and how people rely upon each other for help, particularly when technologies fail [24]. Notably, these studies suggest that even technically knowledgeable individuals struggle with home networking. To overcome these challenges, researchers propose that visual tools might better ease the task of digital housekeeping [27].

More specifically, households often create their own make-shift visual representations of their networks (e.g., using post-it notes) because they have no unitary visualization easily accessible to them [3]. Moreover, even when information is available in router configuration pages or other equipment, it is not presented in layman's terms. Overall, household members lack conceptual models of their home networks and usable information required to manage and troubleshoot them—advocating a need for tools that provide both real-time and historical data so users can understand changes over the network's lifetime [23].

Recently, not only is managing the home network a challenge, but increased internet congestion means that households also have to deal with varying, and often slow broadband speeds. Slow speeds can be detrimental for the overall internet experience, with 2 Mbps being barely sufficient for TV quality streaming media [1,20]. Speed slowdowns can be caused by factors internal and external to the household [21,28]. Internal factors include bandwidth intensive applications choking a connection, old computing equipment causing stalls or multiple people using the internet simultaneously creating bottlenecks. External factors include the access technology itself (e.g., cable) only allowing for a maximum speed, ISPs shaping internet traffic (i.e. controlling network packets to optimize performance) or peak times when most consumers get online. With a myriad of factors involved, deciding why a connection might be slow is complicated. Moreover, inherently limited last mile access technology, network congestion and traffic shaping, mean speed variances are likely to persist [6,21].

In fact, the gap between actual and advertised speeds is large in the U.S., with overall speeds being quite low relative to other countries. To help improve offerings, in the recent National Broadband plan, the Federal Communications Commission (FCC) outlined minimum download speeds of 100 Mbps and upload speeds of 50 Mbps for all American broadband users [8]. Because of speed variances, certain countries have criticized providers for so-called "headline" speeds in their broadband package offerings. Mostly, the concern is that "up to" (e.g. "up to 1.5 Mbps") does not alert consumers that they may not attain those speeds consistently, or at all [19].

Amidst concerns over a minimum broadband speed for all, in the U.S and elsewhere, deliberations about creating tiers of internet service continue [28]. These net neutrality discussions (summarized by Jordan [16]), revolve around whether all internet traffic should be treated equally, regardless of where it is from, where it is going or its content.

Proponents of net neutrality argue that a tiered internet with slow and fast speeds would create a new type of digital divide. Opponents of net neutrality argue that tiered internet will guarantee a reasonable quality of service for real-time applications and ensure that content providers are not "free riding" on infrastructure maintained by ISPs. Already violations of net neutrality have occurred, notably with the case of Comcast, a U.S. ISP found to be shaping Bit Torrent traffic in 2007 [15]. In the most recent debates, consumer groups (such as moveon.org and Free Press) challenged the FCC for only considering big business viewpoints—such as net neutrality supporters, Google and Microsoft and opponents, Comcast and AT&T [12]. For consumers, concerns include costs falling on them, high bandwidth users being penalized, and access to certain sites being limited because of additional fees.

With these broadband debates raging on and speed variances, the need for users to be more informed is clear. Yet, there is little data on whether users are aware of the broadband issues at hand, their connection speeds, or factors influencing their internet experience.

To date, the majority of home network tools are geared towards managing and configuring devices [13]. Although broadband speed measurement tools from the FCC, M-Lab, Glasnost and popular sites such as speedtest.net exist [17-18,28], it is unclear how many households are aware of, or regularly use these tools. More importantly, these sites are not tailored to the average consumer, providing tools that are difficult to install, and results that are not easy to interpret without a technical background. Therefore, although these sites are geared towards "enhancing internet transparency", the question of how to create tools for what users desire or need to see, in a language they can readily understand, remains open. One exception to the above, and most closely related to our own work, is Home Watcher. This tool helped households identify bandwidth hogs as a first step towards understanding what visual network tools might do for a home [2].

With Home Watcher's visualization of home machines' bandwidth usage, households were able to learn more about high bandwidth users. However, users wanted more say in how they were personally represented in a network visualization. Our research builds upon the lessons learned from the Home Watcher study. Aside from presenting an alternative network visualization that allows personalization of icons [2], we also provide the estimated internet speed from the ISP. Kermit further differs from Home Watcher because we show all devices connected to the home network as opposed to computers alone; we allow users to prioritize any device's internet traffic instead of just providing a throttle function; and our tool is browser-based instead of a standalone appliance.

With our research on Kermit, not only do we offer a new prototype tool for home networking, we also provide insights into how real residential broadband consumers conceive of issues around internet speed—particularly, when more information has been made visible to them.

PROBE DESIGN

We chose to create and deploy a technology probe called Kermit to determine what households desire in a broadband visualization and management tool, to field test the

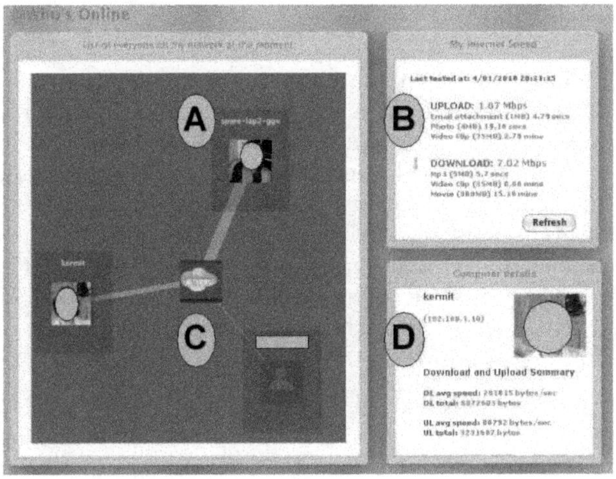

Figure 1: Screenshot of household five's "Who's Online" screen with participants' self-selected photos

prototype in a real-world setting, and to prompt users to think about how they might use a broadband tool, for our own design inspiration [14]. As such our results cover user needs and desires, improvements to the technology in its current form factor and ideas for future tools.

Our three design goals for Kermit are grounded in prior research as discussed in related work. First, we wanted to provide an estimate of the broadband connection speed to help households see if they were attaining advertised speeds. Second, we wanted to show real-time and historical information about bandwidth usage for all household devices on the home network—allowing households to identify bandwidth bottlenecks within their homes. Third, we wanted to provide households with agency to control factors influencing their internet speed.

Probe Features

For our first goal, as shown in Fig. 1B, we created the "Who's Online" screen, where we provided an estimate of the broadband upload and download speed in Mbps, every hour using our own automated speed test. We also provided a "Refresh" button so that users could do a speed test at any point if they desired.

To satisfy the second design goal, we provided a visualization of all the home computers. In this visualization, shown in Fig. 1, users' machines are depicted as little boxes linked to a central internet cloud. Each link changes from a thin to thick line in real-time based on how much bandwidth that machine is consuming, in relation to other machines on the network. The largest bandwidth user (Fig. 1A) always has the thickest line connecting it to the internet cloud with line thicknesses updated every minute. Mouse-ing over a computer icon pops up a bubble showing each machine's average bandwidth use (uploads and downloads) for the last minute. Icons gray out when users are idle for several minutes.

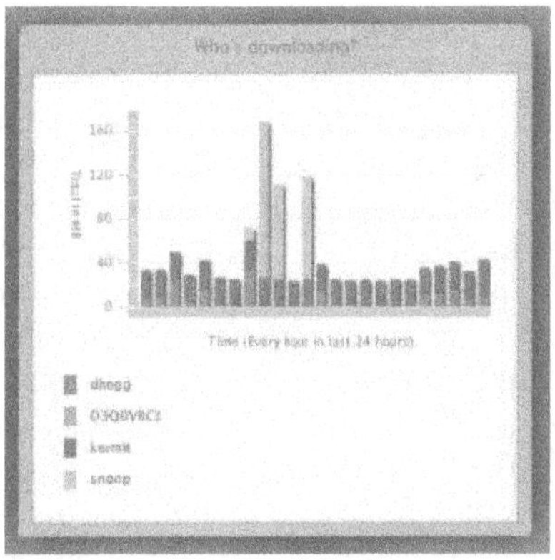

Figure 2: Household seven's download history graph for one day showing four machines usage in MB

For personalization, users can associate pictures with their home computers and change the names used to refer to computers. By default, each machine has a blue person icon (Fig. 1C) and the machine's hostname or IP address is displayed. If users choose to, they can also add a status message to any machine's icon. Double clicking on an icon brings up additional information on that machine in a computer details panel (Fig. 1D). To provide historical bandwidth information, we created the "Who's Hogging the Bandwidth" screen in a separate tab. Users can access a stacked color coded bar chart depicting all home machines uploads and downloads in two side-by-side charts, for the last 10 minutes, one hour or 24 hours. The stacked charts show at a glance which color is dominating uploads and downloads so that bandwidth hogs can be visually identified as shown in Fig. 2.

For our third design goal, users can take actions to influence their speed. Using Kermit, users can limit or prioritize the bandwidth for any machine connected to the network. To do so, a user selects and right clicks the relevant machine icon in the "Who's Online" view and chooses "Limit" or "Prioritize". Once limited or prioritized, a "Limited" or "VIP" is depicted below that computer's name. When a user unlimits or de-prioritizes a machine to return it to its former state, using the same right-click menu, this denotation is removed.

Implementation

Kermit uses data collected from a router flashed with open-source Linux based firmware called DD-WRT [4]. We use a plug-in called RFlow collector to detect packets flowing through the router and to calculate bandwidth counts for each machine, as well as their online status. Since no established methods for determining speed exist, our speed test is based on uploading and downloading a random sized file to, and from, our well provisioned server machine, hosted at a local university. We then calculate the time for the upload and download. When a user limits or prioritizes a machine, the router treats the data packets from that machine accordingly relative to other home network machines' internet traffic.

All back-end information is stored in a MySQL database and accessed using PHP. The Kermit interface was implemented using Adobe Flex. Kermit is deployed by swapping out participating households' routers with a Kermit-router and connecting our server machine to the home network. For data collection purposes, we logged only speed tests results, machines' bandwidth usage, and user interactivity with the probe. We did not collect any privacy-violating data such as urls or packet information.

Kermit Field Trial

We piloted Kermit in two households with 4 adults from December 2009 to February 2010 to ensure it was robust for a larger field deployment and to evaluate our field protocol. Our full field trial occurred between February 2010 and May 2010. We recruited 10 households in Atlanta, a major U.S. city, to participate in the study through word of mouth, snowball sampling, and email lists. We specifically sought households with a broadband connection, at least 2 computers connected to the internet and each other, and a wireless network. Each household was compensated with 100 USD gift card for their time.

We visited each home a minimum of three times during the month long study period. The first visit set the context for the study. Participants completed a basic demographic survey and a week-long diary to indicate their internet usage habits. We also performed a speed test using speedtest.net to collect data about the household's broadband speed. Semi-structured interviews covered questions around home networking roles and routines. To find out more about participant awareness of broadband issues beyond their homes, we asked them about net neutrality and their attitudes towards fee based services. Specifically, we asked participants whether they had heard of the net neutrality debates, provided an overview of the basic premise, and asked for their opinions.

In the second visit one week later, we deployed Kermit. Each household member was given a set of four tasks or "Kermit Homework" to complete for each week of a two week deployment period. All eight tasks were designed to be lightweight to allow participants to test out and reflect on all Kermit functions, for example, "Limit a computers traffic for 30 minutes" or "Who's the biggest bandwidth hog in your house today?". In the third visit, we removed Kermit and administered a final post-study survey. During our exit interview, we asked about Kermit's use as a speed and bandwidth monitoring tool for the household.

All interviews were audio-taped and transcribed, and our surveys were digitized. For the qualitative analysis, three researchers coded the data and the quotes presented in this paper are representative of broad themes of agreement grounded in our data [25]. Our qualitative data was supplemented with descriptive statistics from our surveys, internet diaries, and limited logs of usage. In this paper, we draw mainly from the qualitative data which was triangulated with our other data sources.

Participants

We interviewed 10 households with a total of 21 adult participants between the ages of 23 to 46 years and 2 teenagers aged 15 and 18. Four households comprised families with children between the ages of 2 and 18, three were households with roommates, and three were couples. Participants' occupations were varied, from graduate students, consultants, software engineers to a musician, firefighter and stay at home dad. Six of our households had at least one member with a technical background and four had no members with technical training, so our sample was slightly skewed towards the more tech-savvy user.

Eight households had cable internet, one had DSL and one had broadband through WiMax. Of our 10 households, only two were paying more than 60 USD per month for their broadband connection. In general, our cable users had faster speeds than the DSL and WiMax households. The cable users upload speed range was 2 to 4.14 Mbps and the download speed range was 11.36 Mbps to an unusually high 52.83 Mbps. Both the DSL and WiMax households reported low upload speeds of between 0.2 to 0.25 Mbps but the WiMax household had a much faster download speed of 6 Mbps in comparison to the 1.61 Mps of DSL. All of our household speeds were well below the FCC's goal speeds with the DSL speeds being the lowest.

RESULTS

We first present baseline data collected before we introduced Kermit. Namely, we discuss our participants' awareness of broadband issues, such as knowledge of their internet speed, their arguments for and against net neutrality and their attitudes towards paying for web content. We then discuss Kermit's role as a broadband management tool to visualize the home network, diagnose a slow connection, identify bandwidth bottlenecks and manage their speeds. Finally, we discuss how, although it was not our intent to design a tool for consumer rights, our participants perceived Kermit to be a technological consumer watchdog.

Awareness of Broadband Issues

Our users had very little prior knowledge about factors causing their varying connection speed. For example, households suspected internal hogs or external service providers to be the causes of slow-downs. Just under half of the respondents had never performed a speed test before. Additionally, half the participants did not know what speed they were paying for. Yet, over two thirds agreed that they would like to know their internet speed to see if they were being charged too much.

Before we introduced Kermit, we also noted a distinct lack of trust in internet service providers. For instance, a 40 year old firefighter in household two declared: "I mean it's hard to know what you're supposed to be getting. And whether or not they're actually telling the truth is a whole other story." (H2P2) and a young project coordinator told us: "Comcast offers those three different packages, three different speeds, and I don't really necessarily trust that any of them are really faster than the others." (H1P1).

Aside from speed concerns, our participants wondered if their networks were secure. For instance, the firefighter said: "That's our wireless router, and like I said, the only way I can know if anyone is on there…I can come down here. And it's got up to four [lights], and right now the only one that connected is hers. If I'm on, the second one will light up. If someone else is on, the third and the fourth." (H2P2). Similarly, a mother of three, working in insurance, pondered: "I'd like to see if someone unauthorized can get into our bandwidth usage. In other words, somebody sucking up our *air* without our knowledge." (H6P2). Next, we discuss how participants reacted to the idea of a tiered internet service.

Consumer Attitudes for Net Neutrality

More than half of our participants (57%) told us that they had never heard of net neutrality. Even of those that had, most were not entirely clear about what the debate was on or what the effects of a non-'net neutral' policy would have on them. For those that were not aware of the issues, we outlined the basic premise and asked for their opinions.

All our participants were supportive of the current policy, citing reasons such as "I support net neutrality. The internet wants to be free. Free as in speech, not as in beer." (H8P1), "I believe everybody should have the same speed across the board." (H6P1), "It's ludicrous to have to pay different things for different data." (H1P1). The project coordinator explained: "Well, for me, it would be like charging for different power stations that are all feeding into your electricity, and you have to pay a different rate based on where it's coming from locally. It should be a utility, and it should be regulated like a utility." (H1P1). His roommate, a pharmacy technician added: "That's pretty much an ingrained entitlement at this point. Like the question, 'Would I ever pay for YouTube or Google?' It's just the internet. It's free exchange of information. That would defeat the purpose." (H1P2).

Along with strong support for net neutrality, participants were wary of ISPs abusing tiered services. For instance, a mother of two and usability analyst, worried that a tiered service could shut down access to certain sites. She gave the following example: "But the things that concern me that I hear going on about net neutrality. There are some sites, especially, I think ESPN's site, for example, that are only accessible if you are with a particular ISP, and that's a problem." (H10P2). A software engineer added his take: "I think it's too prone to abuse, especially when most ISPs have a local monopoly…Yeah. I mean, they could charge too much or even flat out censor or block sites if they were able to. And since there's no competition around there's nothing really stopping them from doing that." (H9P2).

Aside from worries about abuse by ISPs, our data indicated that participants felt that tiered services could stymie the accidental discovery of new information typical of browsing the web. For instance, a therapist and step-mom in her thirties told us: "I think I'd rather be net neutral. I think it would prevent you from exploring websites that you would never go on…Right? Like, I think people are much more apt to search the web and go someplace new or different if everything is equally accessible." (H7P1).

Consumer Attitudes Against Net Neutrality

Despite the consistent support for net neutrality, our participants expressed views on the fence about the finer details. For example, participants felt that network neutrality is not sustainable because the underlying infrastructure requires maintenance and upgrades. This viewpoint is captured by a parent and software engineer, who explained: "If they ever do enforce net neutrality, no one is ever going to make an investment in improving the network. Because there is no pay off. So it's like well ok, if it is going to kill innovation, or it's…this stuff isn't free. This stuff doesn't build itself. It doesn't maintain itself. So where's that money going to come from unless the government starts subsidizing and we're just back to the same federally mandated or regulated across everything." (H10P1). He explained further, using an online streaming media company called Netflix as an example to show where a non-neutral network could be useful: "I'm a Netflix customer, I only have 1.5 [Mbps], but Netflix pays extra to deliver stuff at 6 megs to me under the hood.".

Other participants argued a tiered service may be more fair, comparing it to cable TV. For example, a self-employed thirty six year old male said: "From a consumer standpoint, it has its benefits just like cable. I never watch Nickelodeon. Why should I have to be paying for it? Even if it's not a line item, I know it's in there, and somehow I'm paying for it? I never go to MySpace. Why should I have to pay for it?" (H3P2).

Attitudes to Paying for Online Content

When asked on the survey, our participants also told us they objected to the idea of paying additional fees for the privilege of using certain sites. For instance, 70% of respondents did not want to pay a separate monthly fee for any one of the services: Google YouTube, Skype, Facebook, Flickr, or Hulu. Participants were more evenly split on whether paying a fee for a bundle of sites was acceptable with 55% of survey respondents willing to pay a fee for an inclusive package of websites. Despite these responses, participants were not entirely opposed to paying for content provision services. The following quote illustrates this: "And when it's a service like Netflix or something like that where you're getting stuff that people produced and made, and you're doing it for your own entertainment, don't have a problem." (H1P1).

A mother of two and consultant echoed this sentiment: "I mean if you wanted to access certain You Tube videos I understand charging for that. But I don't think as a whole, charging for different bundles [is ok] because the internet is kind of known as free." (H5P1). Other households felt that even switching to a pay-per-use model of bandwidth would be preferable as illustrated by a graduate student in his twenties: "I'd just prefer to just pay for my bandwidth rather than having different prices for different services." (H8P2).

What became clear before we introduced Kermit was that our participants were relatively uninformed about their broadband speed and the net neutrality debates. We found this surprising, given many were concerned about their rights with respect to the broadband service providers. Even those with technical backgrounds were not certain of what was at stake in a tiered internet service. Yet, all our participants had strong opinions about the issues once we explained the basic premise. Moreover, few were aware of or used tools available at their disposal to help protect their rights as consumers. Many did not even know how to check whether their actual speeds met the advertised ones. In essence, it became apparent that tools that make usable information about broadband speeds more visible, are fast becoming a necessity.

Kermit as a Broadband Management Tool

Now that we have discussed households' prior knowledge of broadband issues, we turn to how Kermit the probe was received. Our data revealed that Kermit was used beyond the tasks we asked our participants to undertake. Specifically, of our 10 households, eight completed the homework tasks and all provided feedback about the probe. On average, based on eight intact database logs (two were corrupted), Kermit was running in each household for 12 days on average, with a mean of 21 automated and user run speed tests per day.

During the deployment period, each household used the limits and prioritize functions for their machines at least three times each. Each household accessed the history pages for the last ten minutes activity on average seven times, for the last hour on average six times and for the last day on average five times. We found that Kermit gave participants a way to visualize their home network, allowed users to diagnose slow speeds, determine bandwidth bottlenecks, and manage their broadband connections.

Visualizing the Home Network

Generally, our data indicated that participants found Kermit easy to use with one teenager going so far as to say: "I think Nana [her grandmother] could use it." (H5P2). Participants told us they liked being able to access Kermit from any browser, as opposed to having a standalone appliance because it allowed them to check Kermit whenever they wanted.

Our findings suggest the most popular feature of Kermit was the household view of machines and networked devices in the home. Eight of our participating households changed the icons for and renamed all the machines in their network, despite only being tasked with doing this for one machine. Names were either descriptive of the machine such as "Xbox", "Small Netbook" or "iPhoney" or included the owner's name and machine type, for instance, "Matt's Desktop". Other labels were nicknames or "funny" names including "snoop" to depict an unidentified machine.

Pictures varied from personal photos of device owners to cartoon characters or famous people. Some participants changed the icon for the Kermit machine to Kermit the frog from the U.S. children's program "Sesame Street". In each case, participants chose pictures to be "funny", directly represent the person in question or a particular machine with a local household reference or inside joke. Status messages varied from expressions of emotion such as, "iHappy", to greetings (e.g., "hi") or messages about activities (e.g., "Really Choking" or "I am the great internet hawg") and finally declarations about the self (e.g., "Too Awesome!" or "The King".)

Aside from being "nifty", more interestingly, participants liked the pictures and labels because it allowed them to form a clear picture of their household's home network. In some cases, households felt more secure as the following quote illustrates: "Because you can change the pictures, you know that 'Hey, that person, that computer is not ours', 'It doesn't belong', 'It's not part of our family'" (H2P2). In fact, one of our families did discover someone else was using their wireless internet from seeing an unknown computer in Kermit when all their devices were already accounted for. In the words of the mother: "Now I know there's a little mouse on the internet. On our internet, stealing our internet." (H7P1).

In some ways, Kermit made household members feel more connected to each other as exemplified by a participant who lived with her brother: "It's kind of like a community feel. Like what is he doing? What have you been uploading? What are you downloading so much of?...But it's interesting just to see. Maybe I could make a joke to him." (H9P1). These participants saw Kermit as conversation piece.

In summary, our data indicates that participants found Kermit easy to use and understand. Households took time to personalize their representations to form a clear picture of their home network. They also used Kermit to express their identity to others in the home. For these reasons, Kermit was a precursor for an internal household social network.

Diagnosing a Slow Connection

Our data showed that Kermit confirmed for some participants that they were getting the speeds they were paying for. A male participant living with his sister said: "It did. I mean I thought we were getting pretty good speeds and it quantified and confirmed what I suspected so." (H9P2). A full time dad and home maker similarly found: "We're paying for 12 Mbps high-speed. I pay you know, 25 bucks a month. Literally 25 dollars a month. And it's a separate bill. I know, for the most part, right on the spot I've gotten 12 or better every day. So that much I do know from looking at the Kermit system." (H6P1).

Participants also learned other things about their broadband connection, such as a participant who discovered that his internet speed varied from hour to hour (H2P2). In another example, the stay-at-home father told us: "I did learn that bandwidth just isn't about uploading and downloading. It's a lot more. It's not what I do by myself, it's what everybody in the house does. And it's not just the little bit of difference that I make on my computer. It's the collective and being able to put all that together, that was really cool". (H6P1).

Even though participants learned more about their internet speed, several were confused about the types of information shown. For instance, a usability analyst was not sure about the difference between "the total pipe coming into the house" from the provider, versus what each computer was getting. She categorized the different notions of speed as such: "You had those three things so it's the household speed, what's maximally available at a given time. And then how it's been allocated. And then what my current usage of it is." (H10P2).

Additionally, participants desired more context about the quality of the speed they were getting as well as how their actual speed compared to their advertised speed. For example, a female therapist, suggested a rating system for the speed similar to the U.S. financial score of credit worthiness: "So, if you're gonna do a graphical representation, I think you also need to have a rating system for that. Kind of like your credit score. Like over 700 is really good." (H7P1). Others added that a color coded indicator or having an anchor point for the average speed would provide more context. More importantly, our data revealed that participants were not sure what recourse they would have armed with Kermit's information. Essentially, participants lacked confidence that the service provider would take action if they were alerted about the mismatch between actual and advertised speeds.

Finally, we noticed that several participants found the automatic speed tests somewhat intrusive. In particular, the tests occasionally disrupted normal browsing activities because of the need to upload and download a large file. Having the ability to more easily set the parameters of the speed test, such as how often and when they occur, would improve this aspect of a broadband management tool.

Identifying Bandwidth Bottlenecks

Participants liked the real-time bandwidth visualization to see "how much juice everyone is getting" (H2P1). A teenager in high school told us: "I found myself actually checking it while I was online to see when mommy was down here on the computer. And I'd be upstairs doing homework, to see who was using more bandwidth". A student with a design background exclaimed: "When I did the bandwidth hog test, it was me by a mile because I had five YouTube windows up and those use a lot." (H11P1). For others, the information was surprising as in the case of a parent in household six who discovered he was the biggest hog despite suspecting his son of using the most bandwidth. Participants also learned more about the bandwidth usage of different devices: "I was really, really surprised by how much bandwidth the Xbox takes relative to other things. I think it may just be that it's consistently being used, whereas other machines are sitting around a lot." (H1P1).

Our participants also suggested several improvements to the bandwidth visualization. For example, a mother of two told us: "There's nothing explicitly shown about remaining bandwidth. I mean do I have an excess right now or is everything being pegged? So something like that. Is there any to spare right now? Versus no everything is being maxed out" (H10P2). To address this concern, showing the sum of bandwidth may be better as captured by the quote: "It might be more useful if I could see the, oh, he's using up this much of the whole pie." (H9P1).

A male parent's quote encompasses a common suggestion: "If somebody is sucking up a little bit more bandwidth, maybe they need to rotate up to the top so that you see who's got the priority on sucking the bandwidth right now." (H6P1). Participants also repeatedly told us they wanted to see bandwidth use by applications (e.g., Skype versus Facebook). Such information could help them decide which applications to shut down to speed up their connection. In addition, participants suspected they could identify whether machines have been compromised. For example, high traffic on a machine may indicate that it has a virus, or someone has infiltrated the network.

Generally, participants found the historical information less useful than the real-time visualization. In some of our households, the history views displayed the Kermit server machine as the main bandwidth culprit due to a software bug—a common challenge in deployment studies. Even with this bug, all our participants were able to easily identify the bandwidth hog in the color coded stacked graphs. Some joked that Kermit was installed to do music downloads for the researchers. More seriously, our participants were still able to learn from the history views. A participating software engineer managed to identify that uploads caused significant bottlenecks: "I actually did learn something. Basically doing uploads actually greatly affects overall experience. Or basically has the biggest effect on the network in general—At least going to the internet" (H10P1). To improve this type of view, participants desired a history of internet speed and network connection drops in addition to machine's bandwidth usage, all over longer time periods.

In sum, our data suggests participants were able to learn from the bandwidth information provided. They also proposed improvements to a bandwidth display, such as knowing if there is left over bandwidth and having a history of speed tests to plan when to go online.

Managing the Connection

Our logs showed that participants made use of the limit and prioritize functions and they also spoke of using them in our interviews. In particular, they embraced the concept of prioritizing a machine's internet traffic. For example, three participants who worked primarily from home felt their machines could be prioritized during their work hours. In household two, a wife limited her husband's machine and prioritized her own because she worked from home. Similarly in household six, a father limited his son and ensured his work machine was the "VIP" because he suspected his son was using up too much bandwidth. In household seven, a business consultant working from home limited his girlfriend's machine and his son's Xbox and prioritized his own machine.

A stay at home dad told us: "I think that limiting and prioritizing are great. Having general control for just an average user is a good option, having a bit more detailed control over it for an advanced user great option as well. And there again, like I said earlier, having the option to totally cut somebody off or setting up a time restriction. And being able to throttle it down to zero for internet usage overall." (H6P1).

Even though participants used the limits and priorities, many neglected to undo those actions because they forgot they had applied them. In one example, a mother had limited her daughter's machine to slow down her time on Facebook and had forgotten about it. To remedy this situation, our participants suggested that there be a notification for the person being limited or the limiter. Moreover, participants suggested that a limit or priority should expire and provide an option to renew.

Our data revealed other improvements. For instance, participants wanted to schedule priorities and limits much like a thermostat. For example, a father of two suggested that Kermit should allow families to create different groups of machines to denote children's', parents' and household devices such as media centers. He envisioned these groups could be treated differently depending on the time of day. He talked about prioritizing a media center when the family is watching a movie and similarly, prioritizing a backup machine late at night. In fact, all of our participating parents requested that there be a mechanism to shut off access completely to the internet on a particular machine. Specifically, parents in our study wanted to control internet access and schedule when their kids could go online. Kermit was therefore seen as a tool for what Rode describes as "digital parenting" [22].

Our participants did not always know exactly what the limit and priority actions did, as highlighted by this quote: "Well, to me priority just means that your packets get sent out first. But throttling, it can either be the inverse of that, or it could be that you have a bandwidth cap or something like that." (H8P2). Participants also expressed similar confusion in our interviews about how multiple machines could be "VIP"s or prioritized or how these slots were determined in practice.

Because there was often no perceptible effect after applying a limit or priority, participants did not know how well Kermit was working. One quote from a software engineer illustrates this frustration: "I don't think prioritization was actually working or I could not observe an effect. If I was running traffic, I'd set the machine with priority, or not priority. And it was still running traffic on another machine and my responsiveness was still good". Others, who were less technically inclined, were content even with a placebo effect: "Psychologically, it's kinda nice to just click 'Prioritize my bandwidth'. And it's one more thing I can do to make my Hulu video load more smoothly." (H8P3).

In summary, participants enjoyed being able to take control of factors influencing their broadband, and the ability to prioritize machines was often viewed more favorably than the ability to limit machines. However, participants wanted more control over the parameters for setting priorities and limits. Additionally, participants desired a perceptible or visual indication that an action was having an effect.

Kermit as Consumer Watchdog

Although we did not specifically design Kermit as a tool for protecting consumer rights, our data showed participants perceived Kermit as technological consumer "watchdog". For instance, one participant in his twenties, a project coordinator at a research institute told us of the hassles of getting his service provider to fix network drops. He spent hours on the phone being shunted between the manufacturer of the router he purchased and the cable company, as they sought to determine why his network connection was not working. He complained of how his service provider always ran their own tests on his line and never picked up problems even though his network connection was faulty.

In our last home visit with him, we serendipitously observed him on a hour long technical support call. At this time, we witnessed first-hand how difficult participants find it to communicate details about the nature of their connectivity problems to their providers. The participant in question joked of the provider's typical tests which were run remotely on his machine in a standard troubleshooting call: "Apparently my computer is not complaining the way that I want it to." (H1P1). His frustration was that he could never get the ISP to respond or deal with his problem. Instead, he had to fumble through the ISP's scripted troubleshooting routines despite knowing the real nature of the problem.

For him, and other participants, having a log of network drops or a neutral speed test in Kermit would be good fuel for discussions with providers. In particular, such information would be useful for troubleshooting and protecting the consumer. He explained further: "But, you know a lot of times they'll say…you know you'll have connection issues and stuff. And you'll just call them and they'll say, "Well, I tested your connection and it's fine right now.' But, you know if it's a re-occurring problem, then if you have a log of 'Yeah, we went down at this time.' We went down at this time. We went down at this time. And there's something that keeps track of it, then I think you'd just be more likely to be able to get support if you have that. Rather than just saying, 'Yeah, my internet connection goes out all the time'." A self employed thirty six year old, also saw Kermit fulfilling this role for consumer rights so that he could say: "Hey, my software told me the system was down even though I wasn't here to [see it]" (H3P2).

Our data also showed how participants wanted Kermit to help them identify the source of internet slow-downs so that they could take appropriate actions. For instance, deciding to call their ISP in the first place, shutting down offending applications or limiting a bandwidth hog. A mother told us: "Like when [Daughter] can't get on the internet and I'm on the internet, why is she not getting on? What is there a problem with the [Cable ISP] server or is there a problem with the router or is there a problem with her computer?" (H5P1). Many of our participants also wanted to print or email a record of Kermit's collected data to their ISP to complain about their service or help the provider solve their problems.

In sum, our participants viewed Kermit as more than a tool for managing broadband connections. For them, Kermit was a trusted instrument for providing valuable information on whether they were getting advertised services.

DISCUSSION

Our study findings are applicable to HCI designers and researchers creating residential broadband management tools. First, we summarize the most important aspects of our results and discuss implications for the design of home broadband management tools. Second, we describe broader implications of our work for the CHI community.

Summary of Findings

We found participants were not aware of broadband issues which were external to their homes but have a direct effect on them. Yet, they were keen on having their rights as consumers protected at all costs. When we introduced Kermit, they were able to learn about their speed and security because it allowed visualization and personalization of their home network. Moreover, participants were able to exercise direct control over how bandwidth is used in the home. Participants particularly enjoyed the concept of prioritizing machines and found a browser based application more useful than a separate appliance. Kermit was also seen as a consumer watchdog, especially in the face of concerns around net neutrality. Finally, Kermit allowed us to elicit design inspiration for future broadband management tools.

Designing Broadband Tools for the Home

Building on the experience with Kermit, several improvements could be made for designing future household broadband management tools. First, visualizations that can handle more devices would allow for a less cluttered display as a home network grows. Second, adding more personalization options would offer users more flexibility for depicting themselves on a tool display and further scaffold understanding of a home network layout. Third, providing more context around the concepts of uploads, downloads, bandwidth and speed would help households know whether their usage is normal and if their speeds are within a defined range—for example, specifying a rating of the quality of the connection helps consumers know if their line speed is poor or excellent.

Fourth, for limit and prioritize functions, households need to perceive a visual difference to understand how their changes are taking effect and be given more control over the schedule and parameters of these limits. For example, setting a schedule of how to treat various machines at different times of day or being able to shut down internet access for certain machines totally. Fifth, for a tool similar to Kermit to fulfill its role as technological consumer watchdog, showing the speeds that a household is supposed to be receiving compared to actual speeds would be helpful. Additionally, allowing consumers to print or email historical speed test logs or network drops could be added. Moreover, tools could also show information about speeds in one's general neighborhood or for similar service providers to show household variance in service delivery.

Finally, designers need to consider how to store the massive amounts of traffic data to power such tools— perhaps it is better to offload this data into the cloud. Determining points at which the data is no longer useful, and what types of aggregate data is most appropriate for users, may pose solutions to avoid requiring significant storage capacity. One caveat is that home users may be wary of the security of this data. Moreover, these tools and speed tests need to be efficient and as unobtrusive as possible.

Empowering the Consumer in Broadband Debates

More broadly for the HCI community, the experience with Kermit suggests that households need more tools that give them a voice in broadband and internet issues extending beyond the home, for example, the net neutrality debate. Our participants told us about the lack of trust in their service providers and generally had misconceptions and concerns about the looming introduction of a tiered service. For them, Kermit was not just about viewing or controlling online activities in their homes but also having a means for collecting irrefutable proof of service mishaps, drops, or well below advertised speeds.

This genre of broadband tools falls into the realm of other technologies created for user empowerment. For example, the HCI community has recently seen a surge of research geared towards environmental sustainability to give households the ability to take control of energy and other resources in their homes. The driving force behind these applications is to encourage households to be green or lobby for change in policies in their locales around energy use [5]. Yet, Dourish, for example, discusses how HCI has not yet addressed questions of scale in sustainability research. He makes the case for tools that do not depend solely on individual motivations but also empower society to take charge of environmental issues as groups, consumers and corporations [7].

We see Kermit and other tools in this vein as potentially performing a similar function of scale for broadband issues, if the speed information data they collect can be made public to enable community level views of internet speeds in various locales, neighborhoods, and by different service providers. This information could be used by government agencies and consumer rights groups to influence internet policy. Even at the scale of individual households, these tools can educate consumers about what the issues are and what is at stake—in this case, bandwidth and speed variance and factors influencing a broadband service. With better tools, consumers are not only more informed, but also given mechanisms by which to take their own experiences into the debates.

In sum, better broadband tools could pave the way for creating a data set that can better inform internet debates and keep consumers informed about speed issues affecting them. More importantly, such tools are invaluable in the face of uncertainty around net neutrality and because the ever-increasing demand for bandwidth means speed issues are likely to persist.

CONCLUSION

Because of concerns around minimum broadband speeds to American homes, we designed and deployed a probe to show households their broadband speeds and bandwidth usage. Our probe was well received, and suggests the need for more tools that give consumers advanced control over their broadband connections. More importantly, such tools can serve as a technological consumer watchdog and can empower households to have a voice in debates around broadband speeds.

ACKNOWLEDGMENTS

We thank our participating households. This work was supported by NSF IIS-0904431, Microsoft Research and an Intel PhD fellowship.

REFERENCES

1. Akamai, *4th Quarter 2009: The State of the Internet*, 2009.
2. Chetty, M., Banks, R., Harper, R., Regan, T., Sellen, A., Gkantsidis, C., Karagiannis, T. and Key, P. Who's Hogging the Bandwidth?: The Consequences of Revealing the Invisible in the Home *CHI 2010*, ACM, Atlanta, GA, USA, 2010, 659-668.
3. Chetty, M., Sung, J. and Grinter, R.E. How Smart Homes Learn: The Evolution of the Networked Home and Household *Ubicomp 2007*, Springer-Verlag, Innsbruck, Austria, 2007, 127-144.
4. dd-wrt.com. http://www.dd-wrt.com/site/index, 2010.
5. DiSalvo, C., Sengers, P. and Brynjarsdóttir, H. Mapping the landscape of sustainable HCI *CHI 2010*, ACM, Atlanta, GA, 2010, 1975-1984.
6. Dischinger, M., Haeberlen, A., Gummadi, K.P. and Saroiu, S. Characterizing Residential Broadband Networks *SIGCOMM Conference on Internet Measurement,* ACM, 2007, 43-56.
7. Dourish, P. HCI and Environmental Sustainability: The Politics of Design and the Design of Politics *DIS 2010*, ACM, Aarhus, Denmark, 2010, 1-10.
8. Federal Communications Commission, *Connecting America: The National Broadband Plan*, 2010.
9. Federal Communications Commission, *Internet Access Services: Status as of June 30, 2009*, 2010.
10. Goth, G., The Global Net Neutrality Debate Back to Square One, *IEEE Internet Computing 14*, 4 (2010), 7-9.
11. Grinter, R.E., Edwards, W.K., Chetty, M., Shehan-Poole, E., Sung, J., Yang, J., Crabtree, A., Tolmie, P., Rodden, T., Greenhalgh, C. and Benford, S., The Ins and Outs of Home Networking: The Case for Useful and Usable Domestic Networking., *ACM Trans. Computer-Human Interaction 16*, 2 (2009), Article 8.
12. Gross, G. Consumer groups protest industry net neutrality talks *IDG News Service\Washington Bureau*, 2010.
13. Ho, J.T., Dearman, D. and Truong, K.N. Improving Users' Security Choices on Home Wireless Networks *SOUPS 2010*, ACM, Redmond, WA, 2010, Article 12.
14. Hutchinson, H., Mackay, W., Westerlund, B., Bederson, B.B., Druin, A., Plaisant, C., Beaudouin-Lafon, M., Conversy, S., Evans, H., Hansen, H., Roussel, N. and Eiderbäck, B. Technology probes: inspiring design for and with families *CHI 2003*, ACM, Ft Lauderdale, Florida, 2003, 17-24.
15. Joch, A., "Debating net neutrality," *Communications of the ACM 52*, 10 (2009), 14-15.
16. Jordan, S., "Implications of Internet Architecture on Net Neutrality," *ACM Trans. Internet Technology 9*, 2 (2009), 1-28.
17. Max Planck Institute for Software Systems. Glasnost: Bringing Transparency to the Internet, http://broadband.mpi-sws.org/transparency/, 2010.
18. New America Foundation's Open Technology Institute & The PlanetLab Consortium & Google Inc. Measurement Lab, 2010.
19. Ofcom, *UK Broadband Speeds, May 2010. The performance of fixed-line broadband delivered to UK residential consumers*, 2010.
20. Pew Internet & American Life Project, *The Broadband Difference: How online American's behavior changes with high-speed internet connections at home*, 2002.
21. Raghavendra, R. and Belding, E.M. Characterizing High-bandwidth Real-time Video Traffic in Residential Broadband Networks *WiOpt*, IEEE, Avignon, France, 2010, 597-602.
22. Rode, J.A. Digital Parenting: Designing Children's Safety *HCI 2009 - People and Computers XXIII – Celebrating people and technology*, British Computer Society, 2009, 244-251.
23. Shehan-Poole, E., Chetty, M., Grinter, R.E. and Edwards, W.K. More than Meets the Eye: Transforming the User Experience of Home Network Management *DIS 2008*, ACM, Cape Town, South Africa, 2008, 455-464.
24. Shehan-Poole, E., Chetty, M., Morgan, T., Grinter, R.E. and Edwards, W.K. Computer Help At Home: Methods and Motivations for Informal Technical Support *CHI 2009*, ACM, Boston, USA, 2009, 739-748.
25. Strauss, A. and Corbin, J., *Basics of Qualitative Research Techniques and Procedures for Developing Grounded Theory*. Sage Publications, London, 1998.
26. Sundaresan, S., DiCioccio, L., Feamster, N. and Teixeira, R., *Which Factors Affect Access Network Performance?* Georgia Institute of Technology Technical Report GT-CS-10-04, 2010.
27. Tolmie, P., Crabtree, A., Rodden, T., Greenhalgh, C. and Benford, S. Making the Home Network At Home: Digital Housekeeping *ECSCW 2007*, Springer London, Limerick, Ireland, 2007, 331-350.
28. Wallsten, S., *Understanding International Broadband Comparisons Update 2009*. Technology Policy Institute: Studying the Global Information Economy, 2009.

GridOrbit – An Infrastructure Awareness System for Increasing Contribution in Volunteer Computing

Juan David Hincapié-Ramos, Aurélien Tabard, Jakob E. Bardram
IT University of Copenhagen
DK-2300 Copenhagen, Denmark
{jdhr,auta,bardram}@itu.dk

ABSTRACT

The success of a volunteer computing infrastructure depends on the contributions of its users. An example of such an infrastructure is the Mini-Grid, a local peer-to-peer system used for computational analysis of DNA. The speed of analysis increases as more users join the Mini-Grid. However, the invisible nature of such an infrastructure hinders adoption, as it is difficult for users to participate in an infrastructure they are not aware of. This paper introduces GridOrbit, a system designed to increase user awareness, fostering contributions to this infrastructure. We designed GridOrbit using a participatory design process with biologists, and subsequently deployed it for use in a biology laboratory. Our results indicate that the number of contributors to the Mini-Grid increased with the use of awareness technologies. In addition, our analysis presents their motives and behaviors. Finally, a characterization of user interaction with GridOrbit emerged, which enabled us to understand how awareness systems can be better designed. We see GridOrbit as an example of a broader class of technologies designed to create 'Infrastructure Awareness' as a means to increase the contributions to technological infrastructures.

Author Keywords

Volunteer Computing, Infrastructures, Infrastructure Awareness, Public Displays, Ambient Displays.

ACM Classification Keywords

H.5.3 Collaborative computing

General Terms

Experimentation

INTRODUCTION

Volunteer computing is a powerful way to conduct computation-intensive data processing by harnessing computing resources from large numbers of geographically distributed individuals. The most prominent examples of volunteer computing initiatives are SETI@Home and Folding@Home[1], which seek to gain computational power by enlisting end-user computers like PCs and game consoles.

Volunteer computing infrastructures however, like other infrastructures, are often invisible to their end-users [16, 22], and this invisibility poses a fundamental obstacle to their adoption [5]. A core question is how end-users can become aware of such an invisible infrastructure, and start participating and contributing to it. Existing volunteer computing projects rely on individual and social motivations, leading to efforts in building communities, setting up competitions, and rewarding users who participate [18]. Thus, there is a substantial overhead associated with recruiting users who will donate CPU cycles 'for free', and this in turn becomes a core challenge for the scientists using the infrastructure.

In this paper, we explore the use of awareness technologies to recruit contributors to a volunteer computing infrastructure in a molecular biology research laboratory. Molecular biologists use the infrastructure to execute bioinformatics algorithms for analyzing DNA/RNA sequences of millions of bytes. This infrastructure uses peer-to-peer (P2P) technology for distributing tasks to computers within the organization. This implies that the infrastructure requires many users to participate. Thus, one central challenge is to motivate users to contribute despite the fact that only a minor part of them have the actual need of submitting tasks.

To facilitate recruitment, we aimed at increasing the visibility of the P2P grid. We engaged in a user-centered design process with biologists, which resulted in the design of a system named GridOrbit. GridOrbit displays an interactive visualization of the underlying activity in the infrastructure on public screens (see figure 3), and provides users with feedback about their contributions through notifications on their personal computers (see figure 4).

GridOrbit was designed with the hypothesis that increasing awareness of a local resource sharing infrastructure will lead to broader participation and increased contribution. We tested this hypothesis in a one-month deployment of the system. Results show that public display visualizations and personal notifications can be used for creating an awareness of an otherwise invisible infrastructure. We further show that awareness of the activity of an infrastructure through both public and personal displays supports the recruitment of new contributors. Based on this case, we expand the notion of *Infrastructure Awareness* and discuss how it can improve the adoption and thereby the value of voluntary infrastructures.

[1] http://setiathome.ssl.berkeley.edu/ http://folding.stanford.edu/

RELATED WORK

Research on the participative aspects of volunteer computing focuses on how to attract and maintain contributors. Anderson, who leads the SETI@home and BOINC projects [1], proposes the use of visualizations through a screen-saver application to give feedback about participation. He also proposes credits as a way to provide immediate gratification and foster competition through public rankings. Based on the credit system, different participant-oriented websites emerged, with features like user profiles, team formation, and public message boards. These websites serve the double purpose of attracting and maintaining contributors, and also providing "cheap customer support". Likewise, Mowbray reflects on the participative aspects of OurGrid [17], and argues that successful volunteer computing infrastructures need to build a network of human social interactions to function well. BitTorrent's faster downloads [8] or OurGrid's Network of Favors [7] also aim at maintaining existing contributors by ensuring fairness among contributors.

A different strategy to engage volunteers is to offer an "understandable and fun" game experience. With FoldIt, Cooper et al. [10] propose a multiplayer puzzle-like game that leverages human spatial reasoning ability to engage non-experts in making protein structure predictions.

Krebs studied the motivations of volunteers in a large-scale volunteer computing infrastructure [14]. In her study, users ranked pre-defined motivations, and considered intrinsic motives like solidarity, enjoyment, and supporting good causes as the most important ones to start contributing. Krebs proposes a series of improvements for volunteer computing including: (1) overview and statistics, (2) better communications about what is going on behind the scenes, (3) increased awareness, and (4) on-line communities. Similarly, Nov et al. [18] investigated the motivational and non-motivational factors impacting participant contribution. Their findings also suggest that personal motives like enjoyment, reputation and value of the project influence enrollment. However, Nov et al.'s show that these personal motives do not improve long term contribution whereas social factors do. For instance, while contribution levels decrease over time, if contributors are part of a team, their contribution levels tend to remain stable. From this study, the authors define a set of implications for the design of volunteer computing infrastructures including: (1) presenting up-to-date individual contribution levels, (2) increasing the number of channels for communicating rankings, (3) displaying contributions from other team members, and (4) providing secondary activity channels to sustain long term engagements.

Beyond volunteer computing infrastructures, the Ubicomp and CHI communities have also discussed the adoption of technological infrastructures. Here the main goal is to help users understand the infrastructures they interact with. For instance, Lim et al. studied the automatic generation of explanations for improving the intelligibility of technological infrastructures, and thus support their adoption [15]. In order to elicit the behavior of an intelligent home infrastructure, Vermeulen at al. also proposed a system to visualize the inner-workings of the infrastructure and override them if necessary [23]. Preliminary tests suggest that users value the ability to see what is happening inside the system and that this ability helps them to correct their mental models.

In a similar fashion, Chetty et al. designed the HomeWatcher to visualize the invisible usage of home bandwidth, and studied its consequences in traditional households [6]. Their findings suggest that public visualizations of shared infrastructure usage helps users to understand the technology (in terms of current capacity and availability), and, at the social level, reveal the household politics and mediate power relations. By using the HomeWatcher, users experience a better bandwidth use in the household.

Within Ubicomp, recent research have considered how a person's behavior might be changed through ambient displays. For example, Rogers et al. [21] used ambient displays to inform in playful ways about stair and elevator usage, and to induce people to use the stairs. Their findings suggest that people were not aware of their behavioral change while the logged data showed a significant difference. They conclude that ambient displays could induce positive attitudes and behavioral change in situations with multiple choices, and that this influence occurs without conscious thought.

In this paper we focus on the recruitment for a *local* volunteer computing infrastructure by raising awareness of the infrastructure within a specific organization. We argue that awareness technologies are an efficient way to provide personal and group feedback, and that this feedback fosters contribution. Our hypothesis is based on Nov et al.'s recommendations to create local communication channels [18], Krebs' increased awareness recommendation [14], and Rogers et al.'s behavioral effects of awareness displays [21].

THE MINI-GRID CASE

The Mini-Grid is a local volunteer computing infrastructure, harnessing the CPU power of contributors' desktop and laptop computers [2]. The main motivation of the Mini-Grid is to allow biologists to run computationally intensive DNA/-RNA analyses without computing clusters. Running this kind of analyses is an important part of their work, as they simulate experiments and analyze experimental results. Our biologists share their time between planing and analysis work, and lab work. Faster computation allows for more interactive analysis work, more extensive exploration, and more laboratory experiments.

Like other volunteer computing infrastructures, the Mini-Grid's main challenge lies in the recruitment of contributors. At the architectural level, the Mini-Grid is designed as a symmetric system, based on a P2P network. This means that computers can act both as contributors of CPU power and submitters of tasks. Symmetric infrastructures like the Mini-Grid and OurGrid [7] are different from traditional volunteer computing infrastructures. The ability for *any contributor to also submit tasks to the Mini-Grid* changes the assumptions of traditional volunteer computing. For example, there is no shared common goal (like the projects in BOINC), so users can join only to submit tasks and get a free-ride.

At a practical level, the usage of the Mini-Grid by molecular biologists is influenced by two factors: *(1) invisibility*, the Mini-Grid is a software component and biologists have no way to know whether other researchers are contributing to it, or if they need help. This challenge is related to Poole et al.'s argument that invisibility hinders trust and adoption, keeping users from forming correct mental models of infrastructures [19]. *(2) alternative solutions*, the Mini-Grid is a new technology and biologists already developed ways of executing computationally demanding tasks. Biologists run their tasks on high-end computers over long periods of time, or use cloud services such as the ones from NCBI[2].

Using the Mini-Grid

The Mini-Grid works as a plug-in to the CLC Workbench[3] (CLC-WB), a bioinformatics software suite. To run an analysis or simulation on the Mini-Grid, the user selects the algorithm s/he would normally use and, if the algorithm is grid-enabled[4], ticks an extra box for running on Mini-Grid. To participate contributors simply run the CLC Workbench.

Once submitted, the computational task is broken down in smaller instances distributed to executing computers over the network. Upon completion, the task's results are returned to the source. The speed at which a batch of tasks is completed thus depends on the current capacity of the Mini-Grid, i.e. the number of computers currently contributing CPU power. As more computers join the Mini-Grid, the computation time of a batch of tasks decreases.

DESIGN METHODS AND RESEARCH

To better understand how to support the adoption of the Mini-Grid, we engaged in a participatory design process with biologists from the molecular biology department of a large university [13]. The design process comprised a set of five detailed workplace studies (each lasting 2 days, top line in fig. 1) and a series of participatory design workshops (bottom line in fig. 1) over a period of one year .

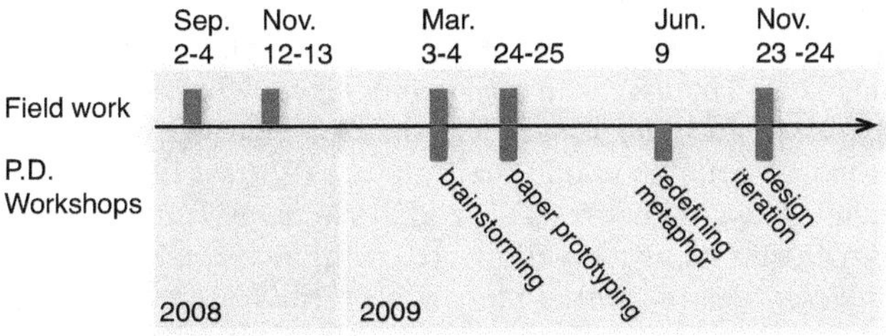

Figure 1. Field work and participatory-design workshops.

We conducted task-centered observations of biology work; place-centered observations of work in the laboratory and in the office; and artifact-centered observations focusing on the use of digital and physical research resources [4]. At this stage we worked with eight biology researchers: three PhD students, two post-docs, two lab technicians and the professor heading the group. We further documented group meetings and casual encounters between researchers. We observed three biologists in detail throughout the day; one executing simultaneous lab experiments, another moving between office space and laboratory, and a third one running experiments with hazardous materials. The observations were supplemented with contextual inquiries for selected activities like running an experiment at the bench or working with software to predict and analyze experimental results.

After the initial fieldwork, we initiated a series of participatory design workshops aimed at co-designing interactive technologies to support adoption of the Mini-Grid. During the workshops we created personas, and discussed different technologies including awareness systems and public displays.

Observations and Implications for Design

Based on our fieldwork and design workshops we summarized the implications for design in three categories: the role of awareness in sharing, the use of public and personal displays, and the Mini-Grid-related awareness information.

Sharing and Awareness

During our place-centered observations we paid particular attention to the sharing of equipment and research materials (tubes, samples, protocols). The resources within the department are a shared infrastructure which researchers rely on to pursue their research, and sharing is common among researchers from different groups. Nevertheless, to benefit from it, they have to maintain an awareness of the resources, their availability, owner, location and conditions of use. For cheap equipment, awareness is achieved through informal systems such as verbal notification or post-it notes. Equipment that is more scarce due to expense or ownership requires more complex awareness systems. Expensive equipment relies on a public booking system to enable distributed use. Genetic material is owned by individual researchers, and therefore its use by others must be negotiated.

The Mini-Grid can be viewed as a similar shared infrastructure, where computing power is a personal resource to be shared among researchers, like tubes or materials. But unlike such physical resources, computing power is not tangible, and hence cannot embody the same sharing practices. In order to benefit from the existing sharing practices, biologists should have an awareness of the Mini-Grid similar to that of the other equipment they share. Awareness technologies are good canditates to provide users with this knowledge.

Public and Personal Displays

Task-centered observations revealed that biologists are mobile when carrying out experiments. Biologists start an experiment in the office by studying the relevant literature, running simulations, and defining protocols. They then move to the laboratory to carry out the empirical work, sometimes running several experiments simultaneously, while using remote computers somewhere else in the building to process experimental data. When done, they return to the office for analyzing results and reporting.

[2] http://www.ncbi.com
[3] http://www.clcbio.com/
[4] Only the PPfold algorithm was grid-enabled during the study.

Laboratories embed different codes of conduct from and office space. The lab is regulated by safety norms requiring users to wear lab coats and gloves while working in a sterile environment. For example, researchers are not supposed to bring in their laptops or to use smart-phones while running experiments. Furthermore, objects in the room cannot be removed before being sterilized and checked for radioactivity.

These observations highlight that technologies for providing awareness to biologists need to take into consideration the specific work context. While in the office, personal displays can provide biologists with awareness of the Mini-Grid. When biologists move out of the office, public displays located in the open spaces like the lab, the cafeteria or the corridors seem more appropriate.

Awareness Cues

A central part of the participatory design process was devoted to identifying the important information cues that users could be interested in with relation to the Mini-Grid. These cues could then be displayed on the personal and public displays. We identified the following cues:

Grid Capacity – The current capacity of the Mini-Grid in terms of connected computers or available computing power. This cue would provide users with an awareness of the availability of the Mini-Grid and the need for user participation.

Grid Activity – The current activities taking place in the Mini-Grid in terms of submitted and executing tasks. This cue would help users reflect upon usage of the Mini-Grid at a given moment in time, and in the recent past.

People and Computers – The people contributing to the Mini-Grid. This cue would allow users to relate the activity on the Mini-Grid to real persons they know, thereby providing an awareness of colleagues' activity.

THE GRIDORBIT AWARENESS SYSTEM

The participatory design process led to the design of GridOrbit, a technology for providing biologists with an awareness of the Mini-Grid. Derived from our fieldwork, GridOrbit is made up by two elements for public and office spaces. The first is a public display for casual and mobile users. The second is a notification system for personal computers for the office workspace.

The GridOrbit public display

The GridOrbit public display is designed to provide the aforementioned awareness cues, and to attract passersby to the Mini-Grid to start contributing. The GridOrbit public display visualizes the locally running Mini-Grid as a cloud of computers (see figure 2). Computers currently connected are shown in color, while off-line computers are gray and progressively fade away after a week of inactivity. The tasks submitted and executed are respectively represented by green and red concentric rings, forming an aura. Their thickness depends on the number of submitted and executed tasks, with the red rings always in the center. The aim of this cloud metaphor is to convey awareness about the capacity (in terms of number of computers) and the current activity level (in terms of tasks being executed at the moment) of the Mini-Grid. It also illustrates the collective nature of the Mini-Grid as made up of these pooled contributions. Moreover, highlighting the activity in terms of auras makes it easier to understand the concepts of submitting and executing tasks.

Figure 2. GridOrbit visualizes the Mini-Grid as a cloud of computers.

When users install the Mini-Grid plug-in on their computer, they can assign a custom name to the computer, which is then displayed in GridOrbit. Users can also use the GridOrbit to attach a picture of themselves to their computer. This functionality conveys awareness about people and computers, by making the individual participants visible.

As a way to foster social interaction, GridOrbit supports posting messages to the display. Messages are associated with computers. Messages are known as Tweets and are accumulated in the TweetBox. Messages are broadcasted to all running instances of GridOrbit and can hence be read on every public display. GridOrbit analyzes the content of the messages, extracts recurrent words, and presents them through a TagCloud component, reflecting the interests of the users. By selecting a tag, users filter out the messages in the TweetBox.

For interacting with the GridOrbit public displays, we defined three interaction zones that modulate the level of detail in the information visualized; as passersby get closer to the screen, more detailed information is available. Our interaction zones are inspired by the Hello.Wall implicit interaction zones [20]. The user is in the *Ambient zone* when more than 70cm away from the display. In this zone, GridOrbit shows a cloud of computers and their auras as shown in figure 2. When the user is between 40 and 70cm away from the display (illustrated as the yellow area in figure 3B), the user is in the *Notification zone*. In this zone, GridOrbit presents the TagCloud made from the messages. When the user stands in front of the display (shown as the red area in figure 3B), s/he is in the *Interactive zone*. In this zone, touch interaction is enabled and used for looking up detailed information about each computer, looking at the TagCloud, and reading or writing messages using an on-screen keyboard. Users can also obtain information about joining the Mini-Grid, and leave suggestions on how to improve GridOrbit.

The GridOrbit notification system

To complement GridOrbit public displays, we designed a notification system to provide awareness to contributors working in their offices. The GridOrbit notification system pro-

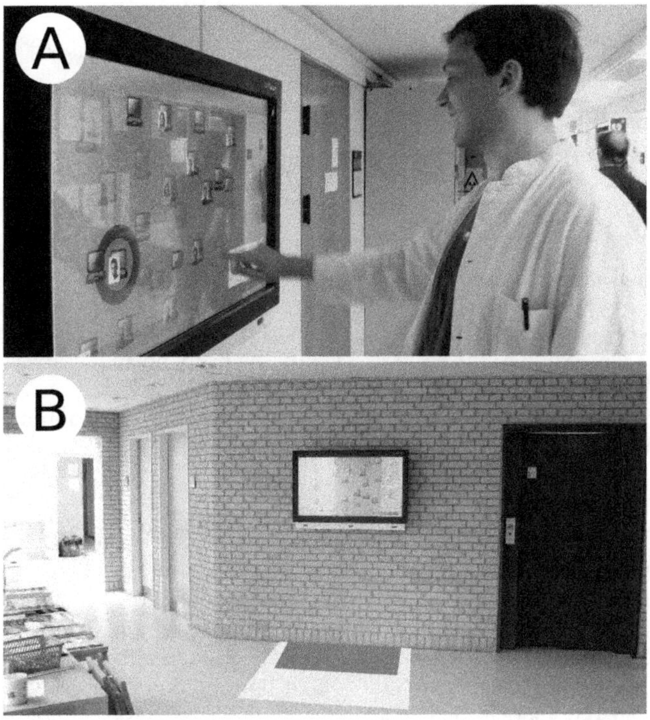

Figure 3. GridOrbit public displays are deployed at two different places on the campus; (A) across the corridor from the cafeteria, and (B) next to the elevator in the local mail area. The interaction zone is marked in red. The notification zone is marked in yellow.

vides more personalized feedback about the contributors' activity on the Mini-Grid using standard desktop notifications. Its goal is twofold. Since the Mini-Grid does not run as an always-on daemon but as a plug-in to a software suite, we wanted to remind users to contribute while in front of their computers. We also wanted to investigate if different notification strategies would lead to different level of contribution.

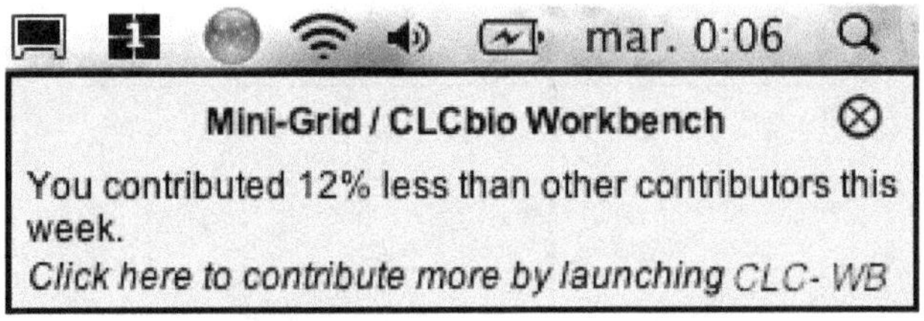

Figure 4. A message displayed by the GridOrbit notification system.

We tested two different types of feedback strategies: (i) personal and (ii) norm-activation [12]. The personal strategy promotes contribution to the Mini-Grid by notifying volunteers of their actual contributions, relying on the volunteers' reflection and call to action to contribute more. The personal strategy displayed messages such as: "*You contributed for less than XX hour(s) to the Mini-Grid this week*". The norm-activation strategy promotes contribution to the Mini-Grid by comparing the volunteer's contribution to the rest of the group, relying on the users willingness to stand out or at least not be left out of the group. The norm-activation strategy displayed messages such us: "*You contributed ZZ% less than other contributors this week*", as shown in figure 4. Messages popped-up every 20 to 120 minutes to test the impact of notification frequency on participants' contribution. The frequency changed on a daily basis and participants could not modify it, but could de-activate the notifications.

We used negative phrasing to encourage more contribution and because we wanted to have similar sentence construction in both strategies. For the personal message strategy, we measured contribution by monitoring the CLC Workbench. We used a Wizard-of-Oz technique to define the values used in the norm activation messages[5], presenting every contribution as less than the mean, even if contribution was superior to the average. In order to still be realistic, particularly toward the people who where dedicating a computer to the Mini-Grid most of the time, the values varied between 5 and 25%. These values were designed to be believable for participants with both high and low levels of contribution.

Implementation

The GridOrbit public displays are 40" touch-enabled screens enhanced with a custom designed ProximityBar for detecting the distance from the display to users standing in front of it. This ProximityBar is composed of three PING))) ultrasonic sensors controlled by an Arduino board and connected to the display via USB. The public displays run a .NET WPF standalone application which monitors the UDP control messages and captures all task related packages sent by the Mini-Grid. Relevant information is extracted from these packages, mapped into the data model, which again is bound to the UI components.

The GridOrbit notification system is implemented in Java and runs as a daemon on Linux, MacOS X and Windows. It uses a modified version of JToaster[6] for generating the notifications. The GridOrbit notification system measures contribution by monitoring when the CLC Workbench was active on a computer, hence we also used it to measure volunteers' contribution to the Mini-Grid throughout the deployment.

DEPLOYMENT

We deployed the Mini-Grid and GridOrbit in the molecular biology department of a large Danish University over a period of one month to investigate two aspects of the awareness technology: (i) What is the impact of awareness technology on the number of volunteers participating in the Mini-Grid and the number of hours they contributed? (ii) How do users relate to, and interact with, such awareness technology?

In order to measure the impact of awareness technologies on the contribution to the Mini-Grid we followed a Quasi-Experimental design [9]. We divided the deployment into three phases as illustrated in Figure 5. The first phase (10 days) served as a baseline with the Mini-Grid deployed without awareness technology; during the second phase (7 days), the GridOrbit public displays were turned on; and during the third phase (13 days), the GridOrbit personal notification sub-system was enabled on users' computers.

[5]Many variables can be used to measure contribution: CPU use, time the computer was available, contribution time effectively used, number of tasks computed, etc. These different metrics require access to low level information we did not have access to, and generate very different contribution results.

[6]http://jtoaster.sourceforge.net/

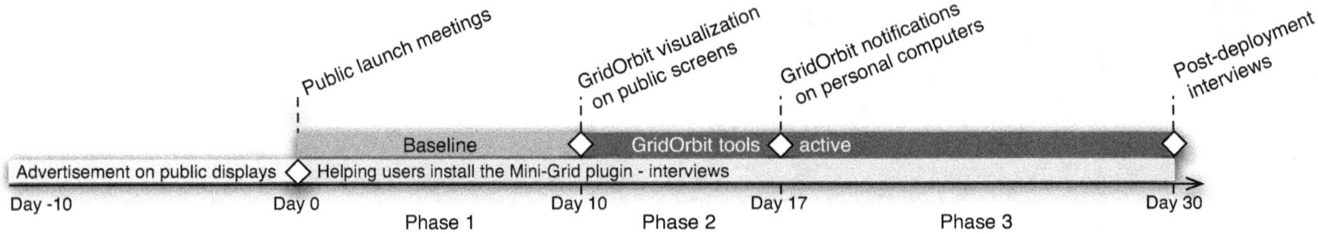

Figure 5. Timeline of our one-month deployment

The deployment started with two public meetings explaining biologists how to use the Mini-Grid. These meetings took place in the two buildings of the department. A GridOrbit public display was deployed in both buildings, which are in 15 minute walking distance of each other. Overall, 28 people attended these meetings and we gathered a list of 10 attendees interested in contributing to the Mini-Grid. After the workshop, we met with 8 of the potential participants in order to help them install the Mini-Grid plug-in and the GridOrbit notification system. Participants who joined later installed the Mini-Grid plug-in without our help, but did not install the GridOrbit notification system.

To decrease novelty effects, we turned on the public displays 10 days before the initial meetings. The displays showed an announcement of these upcoming meetings. During phase 1, the public displays only showed some background information on the Mini-Grid and information on how to join it. During phase 2 and 3, the public displays visualized the Mini-Grid and its activity. During phase 3, the personal notification system displayed messages about users' contribution to the Mini-Grid. Only the 8 initial participants had the personal notifications as it required a computer-specific set-up, and because we wanted to compare contribution with and without GridOrbit from day-0 to day-31.

Across all phases, we captured both quantitative and qualitative data. In order to study contribution to the Mini-Grid, we captured the number of computers connected, and the number of task submissions and executions per computer. To study usage patterns, we captured data on the visits and interactions with the GridOrbit public displays and the users' responses to the notification messages. Finally, we carried out semi-structured interviews with a selected group of participants when the deployment went from one phase to another (illustrated as diamonds in figure 5).

GridOrbit registers a visit when a user stands by the screen for more than 2 seconds, within either the notification or interaction zones. Users observing GridOrbit from a distance greater than the notification zone could not be tracked by the ProximityBar. An interaction is logged when the user touches the screen. GridOrbit does not identify users.

RESULTS AND ANALYSIS

At the end of the 30 day deployment, 35 different computers had contributed to the Mini-Grid at least once. The GridOrbit public displays had received 5022 visits, out of which 592 involved interacting with the screen. Researchers submitted 103 task batches to a total of 7264 individual tasks. Out of the 35 contributing computers, 8 submitted at least 1 task batch to the Mini-Grid. Finally, users posted 14 messages through the messaging functionality. Below we present results related to both the impact of GridOrbit on adoption, as well as insight into how users were using it.

Adoption Impact

We label the number of computers that installed the Mini-Grid plug-in and contributed at least once as *potential capacity*. Similarly, we label the average number of computers connected to the Mini-Grid at any given time *actual capacity*. Figure 6 shows the potential and actual capacity of the Mini-Grid. The figure shows that both potential and actual capacity increased after introducing the awareness technologies. During the first (baseline) phase, the potential capacity reached 19 computers. After introducing the awareness technologies, 16 new computers joined the Mini-Grid, increasing the potential capacity to 35. Moreover, the actual capacity was 5.33 ($\sigma = 2.66$) computers in the baseline phase. After introducing the awareness technologies, the actual capacity increased to 8.02 ($\sigma = 3.56$) computers: a 2.69 change ($p < 0.001$). This data represents a 75% increase in potential capacity, and a 51% increase in actual capacity.

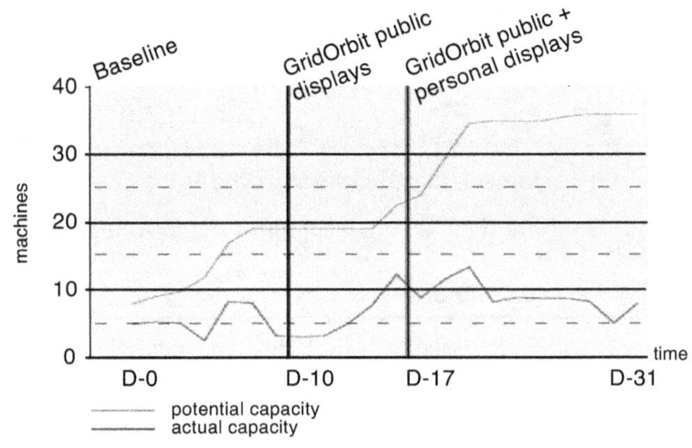

Figure 6. Potential and actual capacity as seen during the deployment.

Further analysis focusing on users logged on the personal computer shows no significant difference in actual capacity between phase 2 and phase 3. While we can observe an increase from a mean contribution time of 10h57 to 14h22 per day, the standard deviation is very high in both cases (~8h20) because of volunteers' contribution patterns: either a few hours a day or the entire 24 hours. We obtained similar results when analyzing the impact of the GridOrbit notification system's strategies on contributions. Analysis shows no significant difference in contributions resulting from the strategies.

Based on interviews and logs from personal computers with the notification system installed, we are able to analyze the contribution patterns on a per-computer basis. This analysis revealed 5 distinct ways of contributing to the Mini-Grid:

Bootstrapping Computers – Biologists involved in the project dedicated two off-the-shelf desktop computers running 24/7, to guarantee a minimal capacity.

Dedicated Secondary Computers – 3 biologists with desktop computers rarely used in their office decided to dedicate them to the Mini-Grid. Figure 7 shows an always-on mode of contribution. Interestingly, Participant 2 switched from having his computer on only during working hours to an always-on mode when GridOrbit started to display messages about the computer's contribution.

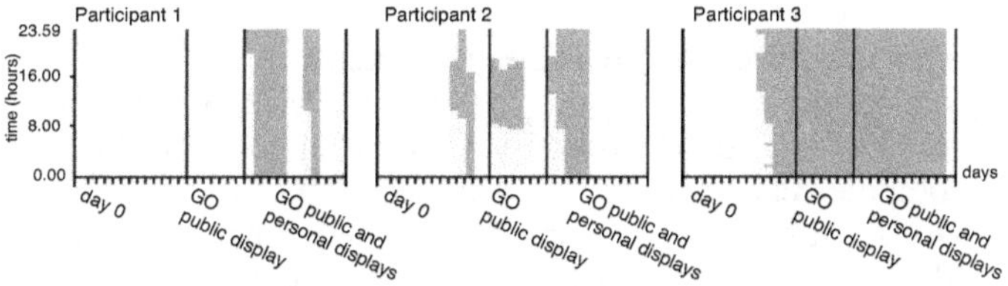

Figure 7. Contribution pattern of dedicated secondary computers, *(white is inactive; green is sharing resources.)*

Work Computers – 3 biologists installed the Mini-Grid plug-in on their office desktop computers, which they used for everyday work. Figure 8 shows a hybrid pattern; always-on when they were working in the lab and hence not using the office desktop computer (green), mixed with periods off-the-grid when working intensively in their offices (red).

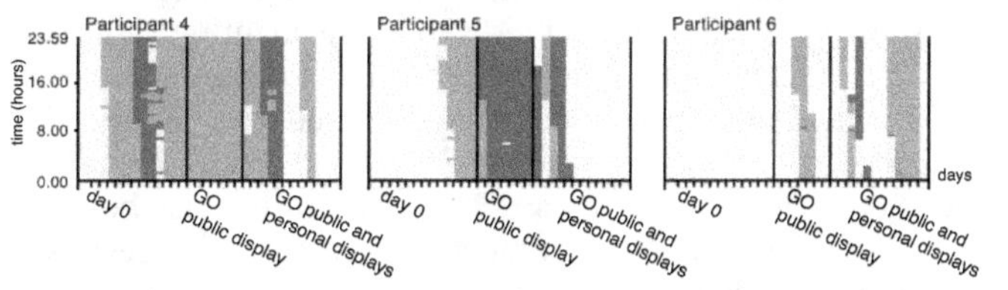

Figure 8. Contribution pattern of work computers *(white is inactive; green is sharing resources; red is active not sharing resources.)*

Intermittent use – 2 biologists installed the Mini-Grid plug-in on their laptop, i.e., main computer. Figure 9 shows a very intermittent contribution to the grid.

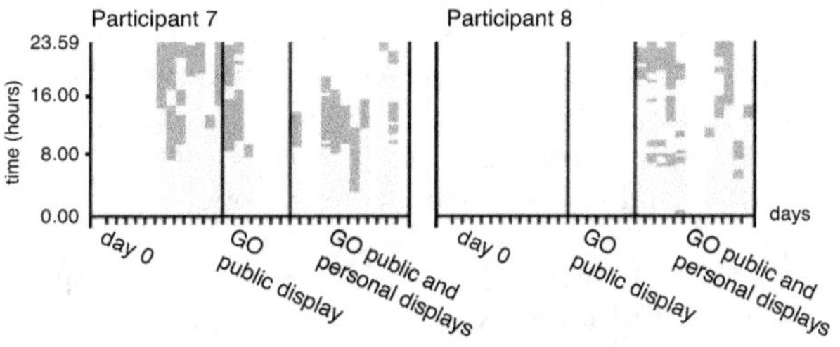

Figure 9. Contribution pattern of laptops *(white: inactive; green: sharing resources.)*

Shared Public Computers – Finally, biologists deployed the Mini-Grid on public computers, in the department library and on the desktop computers available in the different labs. During pre- and post-deployment interviews, we identified a diverse set of motivations for contributing to the Mini-Grid. For the few researchers using the Mini-Grid-enabled algorithms, getting as much computer power as possible was the primary drive. Combined with a curiosity about the power of the Mini-Grid and testing the limits of system, this led to configure several public computers. Another set of participants did not use Mini-Grid-enabled algorithms, but was interested in the potential of the Mini-Grid and thus wanted to participate and experiment with it. Finally, some participants only joined to contribute to the Mini-Grid, not benefit from it in terms of faster calculations. Being recognized as a contributor and being involved in an experimental technological project was the main drive. This recognition was reinforced when participants started to associate their own portrait to the computers displayed in GridOrbit. This feature helped more anonymous people like lab technicians to be visible as part of the research activities and projects of the lab.

Using GridOrbit

We looked into how GridOrbit was used in everyday work, particularly in terms of visits to the public displays. We examined the visitor data in relation to the interaction zones, and type of interaction. We removed outliers: visits of less than 1.5 seconds (twice the time to walk past the screen) and more than 70 seconds. In relation to the interaction zones, 39.57% of the visitors walked into the interaction zone, and 60.43% stayed in the outer notification zone. In relation to the type of interactions, only 9.87% of the users interacted with GridOrbit via touch, with an average user session lasting 17.5 seconds ($\sigma = 1.5$). Crossing these two datasets shows that 29.7% of the users who walk into the interaction zone (very close to the display) do not interact.

This data reveals three different visitor behaviors, which we label (i) *aware*, (ii) *curious*, and (iii) *explorer*. There seems to be a 60–30–10 distribution between these three behaviors in front of the public display.

We analyzed the effects of the dynamic elements of GridOrbit's visualization on the visitors' behavior. The visualization of GridOrbit changes in response to task executions, representing activity; the more tasks being executed on the Mini-Grid, the bigger the green and red auras around the involved computers are. The visualization also changes in response to potential capacity in terms of the total number of computers contributing to the Mini-Grid; the more computers contributing to the Mini-Grid, the more computers are shown in GridOrbit. The potential drawback of this visualization is that the display may be cluttered when capacity increases.

Table 1 shows the relationship (r) between the number of visitors per hour, and the visualization of activity and capacity of the Mini-Grid. The top row in the table shows that, overall, the number of visits to GridOrbit correlates positively to the activity level (auras), but negatively to the capacity (computers). The following rows show that both correlations hold true for the three visitor behaviors identified previously. The correlations are significant at the levels shown in the table, meaning both activity and capacity effectively account for variations in the number of visitors.

Visitors	Activity	Capacity
Total	$r = 0.212$ (p<0.002)	$r =$ -0.116 (p<0.1)
Aware	$r = 0.186$ (p<0.01)	$r =$ -0.135 (p<0.05)
Curious	$r = 0.202$ (p<0.005)	$r =$ -0.181 (p<0.01)
Explorer	$r = 0.133$ (p<0.06)	$r =$ -0.114 (p<0.1)

Table 1. Correlational data between visitors of GridOrbit and changes in visualizations of activity level and capacity.

We can conclude from this analysis that activity visualization seems to have attracted more visitors, whereas visualizing a higher capacity seems to have decreased the number of visitors. Thus, adopting the Mini-Grid can lead to awareness stagnation; the more users adopt the Mini-Grid, the more cluttered GridOrbit will look, which decreases the number of visitors. The efficiency of awareness technologies designed to support the recruiting of contributors may hence decrease as they start to look cluttered. Therefore, the design of infrastructure awareness visualizations should take into account issues of scaling.

DISCUSSION

To explore the participative aspect of local volunteer computing infrastructures we designed GridOrbit as a means to increase users' awareness of the Mini-Grid's activity. Our results suggest that awareness technologies increases the use of local volunteer computing infrastructures. In this section we reflect on three issues: first, the relation of our results to other studies of volunteer computing infrastructures. Second, the impact of infrastructure design on the recruitment of contributors. And third, how our experience can be expanded to support other cases of infrastructure adoption.

Recruiting and Awareness Technologies

Volunteer computing infrastructures like BOINC and OurGrid use rewards and community websites to attract and maintain contributors. We depart from these approaches by proposing awareness technologies as a way to generate genuine interest and provide users with feedback on their contributions. Our results show that, as suggested by Nov et al.'s [18] study, providing feedback on contribution and increasing the number of feedback channels are effective ways to recruit volunteers. These results validate Rogers et al's [21] *ambient influence* in a situation where a socially desired behavior is induced through ambient technologies.

While other works highlight the importance of supporting communication to sustain contribution, passersby and Mini-Grid contributors rarely used the messaging functionality on the GridOrbit public display (14 messages total). This behavior could be explained by the relatively small number of potential contributors (approximately 300 people), and the social dynamics that such a small co-located group affords. This suggests that, during the initial phases of deployment, local infrastructures like the Mini-Grid can rely on the existing social dynamics and communication channels to recruit contributors in small and co-located groups of users. In this perspective, one of GridOrbit's effects was to sustain word-of-mouth as an informal communication channel. Awareness technologies should focus on fewer and simpler features, providing awareness through ambient information visualizations.

Our conclusions on recruitment are more relevant for local groups, rather than large and distributed groups in which creating and supporting social dynamics can prove valuable as they might not already exist. Furthermore, our month-long study was too short to provide insights on the effects of long term contributions. It might be, as documented by others [18], that contribution decreases over time, and that secondary engagement channels can modulate the decrease. Another area to explore is the exposure of historic contribution/usage data, and estimated future demand for capacity.

Infrastructure Design and Participation

The Mini-Grid's design as a P2P infrastructure influenced adoption and contribution. By design, each Mini-Grid-enabled computer can both execute and submit tasks to the Mini-Grid. This feature prompted some researchers to join the Mini-Grid not only to help but also to explore how they could benefit from it. Some researchers contributed to determine whether they could improve their own algorithms with the use of the Mini-Grid.

More broadly, our study adds to the discussion [11] on how the architecture of infrastructures shapes the way people will participate in them. It is important to focus not only on how to design tools or strategies to recruit contributors, but also on how the infrastructure itself could be improved to better sustain the contribution of its participants. For instance, during our participatory workshops we identified how the Mini-Grid could be improved to be more engaging and more efficient. One improvement we discussed was to broadcast the results of a task execution. This would both increase interest and willingness to participate, and would also be a way to get results quickly for someone interested in the results of a complex task already executed.

Infrastructure Awareness

Current approaches for recruiting contributors, or solving the problems arising from the infrastructures' invisibility, aim at visualizing the infrastructure itself and providing detailed feedback about users' contributions. These approaches assume that users put all of their attention on the feedback system. Providing detailed information in the center of users' attention is ideal for learning, troubleshooting, triggering reflection, and accomplishing difficult tasks. However, it also requires effort and attention from contributors.

Our work with the Mini-Grid, GridOrbit's public displays and personal notifications explore a calmer approach (in Weiser's sense of calm technology). In this approach, which we call Infrastructure Awareness, systems provide feedback while staying on the periphery of users' attention.

Infrastructure Awareness is a feedback mechanism on properties of technological infrastructures provided in the periphery of user's attention. Feedback is conveyed through representations of the state or changes of such properties. Infrastructure Awareness Systems aim to convey this information on the periphery of users' attention by means of ambient technologies. The infrastructure awareness system can either be embedded in the infrastructure itself, or be an entirely separate system. The latter case is relevant for infrastructures that cannot themselves provide the awareness, or legacy systems that did not consider doing so.

We theoretically ground Infrastructure Awareness on Benford and Fahlén's spatial model of awareness [3]. This model uses the notions of 'nimbus' and 'focus': nimbus is what an object projects about itself, i.e. the things that can be known about an object; focus is what an user is interested in. Benford and Fahlén argue that awareness takes place when the user's focus meets the object's nimbus i.e. when the user is interested and has access to what the object projects about itself.

We modeled the problem of the invisibility of infrastructures in terms of this awareness model, as presented in figure 10A. In our model there are two obstacles to awareness: first, the user's focus (U in figure 10) does not meet with the infrastructure's nimbus (I in figure 10); and second, the infrastructure's invisibility (shown in dashed lines in figure 10) represents the users' incapacity to see the it. An Infrastructure Awareness System (IA) seeks to overcome these difficulties by extracting data from the infrastructure's nimbus and translating it into information that the user is interested in and can acquire by means of technologies like ambient displays. This is shown in figure 10B.

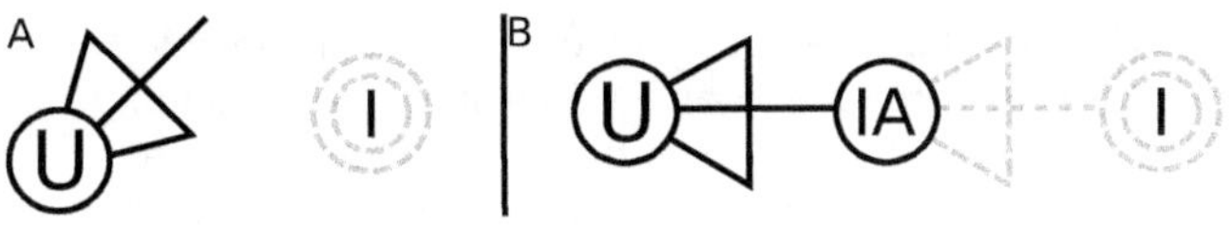

Figure 10. Infrastructure Awareness' awareness model.
(The circle represents the object's nimbus. The cone represents the object's focus and its orientation.)

In creating Infrastructure Awareness Systems, designers should not only elicit users' interests (their focus), but also which properties of the infrastructure can be acquired. Infrastructure Awareness can also be used as tool to frame participatory design activities as we describe in [13], and applied for the design of GridOrbit. Furthermore, this deployment showed how relevant Infrastructure Awareness can be for everyday and mid-term engagement with infrastructures.

Infrastructure awareness systems should support the different visitor behaviors (aware, curious, and explorer) that we observed in our deployment. While further deployments should look at the proportions with different visitors and in different situations, we speculate similar proportions can be found. To support these visitors, infrastructure awareness systems can provide information at different granularities. Peripheral feedback, achieved with representations at high levels of abstraction, can support adoption and participation. More attention-demanding feedback, achieved with representations at lower levels of abstraction (higher fidelity), can support in-depth interaction. Attention-demanding feedback could be used to support learning, troubleshooting, triggering reflection, or accomplishing difficult tasks.

CONCLUSION

We presented GridOrbit, an infrastructure awareness system designed to foster participation to the Mini-Grid, a local volunteer computing infrastructure. During our deployment, we observed that the GridOrbit public displays and personal desktop notifications led to an increase in both the total number of computers that joined the grid, and the average number of computers available at any point in time (respectively potential and actual capacity).

We identified four main motivations for biologists to join the Mini-Grid: getting analysis results faster, exploring the potential benefit of the infrastructure, being recognized as a contributor, and helping their colleagues. We also identified five contribution patterns: bootstrapping computers and secondary work computers with a 24/7 contribution; primary work computers and shared public computers with an interrupted 24/7 contribution pattern when the computers were used for other tasks; and laptops with a very intermittent contribution pattern.

Analyzing how passersby engaged with the GridOrbit public displays, we distinguished three types of visitors: aware, curious, and explorer. By looking further into visitors' interaction with the screens, we identified that visualizing activity rather than the potential capacity increased users' engagement with GridOrbit .

Reflecting on the design and use of GridOrbit, we discussed how the Mini-Grid and its awareness technologies depart from other volunteer infrastructures and their recruitment models. Because the Mini-Grid is P2P (hence symmetric) and local, it led us to foster participation through ambient technologies rather than competitions or games. This suggests that HCI researchers should not only focus on designing systems for engaging contributors, but should also consider the architecture of infrastructures as a means to shape how infrastructures are used. Finally, to generalize our work, we proposed the notion of infrastructure awareness, and defined an infrastructure awareness model extending Benford and Fahlén's spatial model of awareness.

ACKNOWLEDGEMENT

We thank N. Venkataraman, E. Andersen, Z. Sukosd and all the participants from Aarhus University. This research has been funded by the Danish Agency for Science, Technology, and Innovation under the project "PC Mini-Grids for Prediction of Viral RNA Structure and Evolution", #09-061856.

REFERENCES

1. D. P. Anderson. BOINC: A system for public-resource computing and storage. In *GRID '04: Proceedings of the 5th IEEE/ACM International Workshop on Grid Computing*, pages 4–10, Washington, DC, USA, 2004. IEEE Computer Society.

2. J. E. Bardram and N. Venkataraman. The mini-grid framework: Application programming support for ad-hoc, peer-to-peer volunteer grids. In *Proceeding of the GPC 2010 Conference.*, May 2010.

3. S. Benford and L. Fahlén. A spatial model of interaction in large virtual environments. In *ECSCW'93: Proceedings of the third European Conference on Computer-Supported Cooperative Work*, pages 109–124, Norwell, MA, USA, 1993. Kluwer Academic Publishers.

4. J. Blomberg, M. Burrell, and G. Guest. The human-computer interaction handbook. chapter An ethnographic approach to design, pages 964–986. L. Erlbaum Associates Inc., Hillsdale, NJ, USA, 2003.

5. M. Chalmers and A. Galani. Seamful interweaving: heterogeneity in the theory and design of interactive systems. In *DIS '04: Proceedings of the 2004 conference on Designing interactive systems*, pages 243–252, New York, NY, USA, 2004. ACM Press.

6. M. Chetty, R. Banks, R. Harper, T. Regan, A. Sellen, C. Gkantsidis, T. Karagiannis, and P. Key. Who's hogging the bandwidth?: the consequences of revealing the invisible in the home. In *CHI '10: Proceedings of the 28th international conference on Human factors in computing systems*, pages 659–668, New York, NY, USA, 2010. ACM.

7. W. Cirne, F. Brasileiro, N. Andrade, L. B. Costa, A. Andrade, R. Novaes, and M. Mowbray. Labs of the world, unite!!! *Journal of Grid Computing*, 4(3), 2006.

8. B. Cohen. Incentives build robustness in BitTorrent. In *Workshop on Economics of Peer-to-Peer systems*, volume 6, pages 68–72, 2003.

9. T. D. Cook and D. T. Campbell. *Quasi-Experimentation: Design and Analysis Issues for Field Settings*. Houghton Mifflin Company, 1979.

10. S. Cooper, A. Treuille, J. Barbero, A. Leaver-Fay, K. Tuite, F. Khatib, A. C. Snyder, M. Beenen, D. Salesin, D. Baker, and Z. Popović. The challenge of designing scientific discovery games. In *FDG '10: Proceedings of the Fifth International Conference on the Foundations of Digital Games*, pages 40–47, New York, NY, USA, 2010. ACM.

11. W. K. Edwards, M. W. Newman, and E. S. Poole. The infrastructure problem in HCI. In *CHI '10: Proceedings of the 28th international conference on Human factors in computing systems*, pages 423–432, New York, NY, USA, 2010. ACM.

12. J. Froehlich, L. Findlater, and J. Landay. The design of eco-feedback technology. In *CHI '10: Proceedings of the 28th international conference on Human factors in computing systems*, pages 1999–2008, New York, NY, USA, 2010. ACM.

13. J. D. Hincapié-Ramos, A. Tabard, and J. Bardram. Designing for the invisible: user-centered design of infrastructure awareness systems. In *DIS'10: Proceedings of the 8th ACM Conference on Designing Interactive Systems*, pages 302–305, New York, NY, USA, 2010. ACM.

14. V. Krebs. Motivations of cybervolunteers in an applied distributed computing environment: MalariaControl. net as an example. *First Monday*, 15(2-1), 2010.

15. B. Y. Lim, A. K. Dey, and D. Avrahami. Why and why not explanations improve the intelligibility of context-aware intelligent systems. In *CHI '09: Proceedings of the 27th international conference on Human factors in computing systems*, pages 2119–2128, New York, NY, USA, 2009. ACM.

16. S. D. Mainwaring, M. F. Chang, and K. Anderson. Infrastructures and their discontents: Implications for ubicomp. In *6th International Conference in Ubiquitous Computing. Ubicomp 2004*, pages 418–432. September 2004.

17. M. Mowbray. How web community organisation can help grid computing. *Int. J. Web Based Communities*, 3(1):44–54, 2007.

18. O. Nov, D. Anderson, and O. Arazy. Volunteer computing: a model of the factors determining contribution to community-based scientific research. In *WWW '10: Proceedings of the 19th international conference on World wide web*, pages 741–750, New York, NY, USA, 2010. ACM.

19. E. S. Poole, C. A. Le Dantec, J. R. Eagan, and W. K. Edwards. Reflecting on the invisible: understanding end-user perceptions of ubiquitous computing. In *Ubicomp '08: Proceedings of the 10th international conference on Ubiquitous computing*, pages 192–201, New York, NY, USA, 2008. ACM.

20. T. Prante, R. Stenzel, C. Röcker, N. Streitz, and C. Magerkurth. Ambient agoras: InfoRiver, SIAM, Hello.Wall. In *CHI '04: CHI '04 extended abstracts on Human factors in computing systems*, pages 763–764, New York, NY, USA, 2004. ACM.

21. Y. Rogers, W. R. Hazlewood, P. Marshall, N. Dalton, and S. Hertrich. Ambient influence: can twinkly lights lure and abstract representations trigger behavioral change? In *Proceedings of the 12th ACM international conference on Ubiquitous computing*, Ubicomp '10, pages 261–270, New York, NY, USA, 2010. ACM.

22. S. L. Star. The ethnography of infrastructure. *American Behavioral Scientist*, 43(3):377–391, November 1999.

23. J. Vermeulen, J. Slenders, K. Luyten, and K. Coninx. I bet you look good on the wall: Making the invisible computer visible. In *AmI '09: Proceedings of the European Conference on Ambient Intelligence*, pages 196–205, Berlin, Heidelberg, 2009. Springer-Verlag.

How Users Associate Wireless Devices

Ming Ki Chong[1] **and Hans Gellersen**[2]
School of Computing and Communications
Lancaster University, UK
mingki@acm.org[1], hwg@comp.lancs.ac.uk[2]

ABSTRACT
In a wireless world, users can establish connections between devices spontaneously, and unhampered by cables. However, in the absence of cables, what is the natural interaction to connect one device with another? A wide range of device association techniques have been demonstrated, but it has remained an open question *what actions users would spontaneously choose for device association*. We contribute a study eliciting device association actions from non-technical users without premeditation. Over 700 user-defined actions were collected for 37 different device combinations. We present a classification of user-defined actions, and observations of the users' rationale. Our findings indicate that there is no single most spontaneous action; instead five prominent categories of user-defined actions were found.

Author Keywords
Wireless devices, spontaneous interaction, device association, input actions

ACM Classification Keywords
H.5.2 Information Interfaces and Presentation: User Interfaces—*Interaction styles, User-centered design*

General Terms
Human Factors

INTRODUCTION
Computers, media devices and accessories now widely support wireless ad hoc networking. This enables users to establish device connections unhampered by cables, and in a spontaneous and serendipitous manner. However, before devices can transfer any data wirelessly, they are required to establish a virtual connection amongst one another, a process known as *device association*.

While protocols exist to automate device association, it is generally desired that users initiate and control the process by explicitly identifying the target devices they wish to connect (e.g., to avoid unwanted or untrusted communication).

CHI 2011, May 7–12, 2011, Vancouver, BC, Canada.
Copyright 2011 ACM 978-1-4503-0267-8/11/05...$10.00.

Figure 1. The low-fidelity acrylic prototypes we used for our user study. (Left) A situated *interactive display*. (Right, top row) A *tablet computer* and a *wireless keyboard*. (Second row) A *media player*, a *digital camera*, a *wireless microphone*, a *wireless mouse* and a *handheld projector*. (Bottom row) A *digital watch*, a *mobile phone*, a *gaming device* and *wireless headphones*.

A familiar way for users to associate devices has been to connect them via a cable. However, as devices have become wireless the user action required to connect them is no longer dictated by the communication medium. A key challenge of wireless device association is therefore to find *natural interactions* for users to establish connections. This challenge exists as wireless connections are no longer represented by a physical entity; instead, the users are required to accomplish the association task by interacting with the interface of the connecting devices.

Many techniques for wireless device association have been introduced over the last decade. A widely deployed mechanism is Bluetooth pairing which involves selection of a target device from a list of available devices (with an additional authentication procedure using PIN codes if security is required). A plethora of alternative approaches have been demonstrated in research work, some focused on simplicity of the required user action [6, 8, 23], and others on interactive authentication protocols (addressing the problem that connections can't easily be verified in the absence of wires [1, 12, 26]). This body of work shows that the association task can be implemented in many different ways, with the involved user actions including synchronous device input [7, 22], device alignment and pointing [12, 17, 23], gestural manipulation of devices [6, 8] and context capture (e.g., select a target by taking a photo [18]). However, the existing work does not shed any light on user preferences and how users would spontaneously choose to associate devices.

In an ideal setting, a naive user should be able to associate wireless devices quickly, extemporaneously, and without explicit instructions. It is therefore important to examine the types of actions that users would spontaneously perform to connect wireless devices, regardless of the technical limitations that might be posed by current hardware. To this end, we contribute an investigation of the following research question: *Based on users' intuition, what types of actions do they spontaneously produce to associate wireless devices?*

Prior to the implementation of a real system with existing devices, preliminary explorations of user-defined actions for associating wireless devices provide a valid setting for investigations. In this paper, our goal is to obtain a rich set of actions elicited by participants. We employed a *guessability study* methodology [29], where our task was to gather human actions that the participants spontaneously produce for associating wireless devices, understanding of the participants' rationale, as well as feedback from the participants about the actions they produced. Low-fidelity "plastic" prototypes of 12 types of wireless device (see Fig. 1) were used as tangible thinking aids for participants to perceive different association scenarios. To understand how users spontaneously associate wireless devices, we observed the actions and the behaviours of how the participants interacted with the artificial devices. A set of 37 device combinations (see Table 1) were selected; every participant was required to generate actions for each of the combinations. In total, over 700 actions from 18 participants were collected. Based on this data we form a charaterisation of how users want to associate wireless devices, including a classification of user-defined actions. We also report on observations of the users' rationale and discuss design implications.

RELATED WORK

Research on wireless device association has been conducted from HCI, security and ubiquitous computing perspectives. Most work to date has focussed on contribution of specific techniques which we review here to provide an understanding of the diversity of concepts that have been proposed. We then review related work on the usability of device association techniques, as well as work on eliciting input actions from users, as this is methodologically related to ours.

Techniques for Wireless Device Association

Stajano and Anderson were among the first to discuss spontaneous association of wireless devices [26]. They suggested the use of *electrical contact* between devices, as this would allow device to exchange information securely to establish an association. "Touch-And-Play" is an alternative contact-based technique, where information between devices is transferred across the human skin, so that the *tactile touch* action performed on the devices triggers an association [20]. Hinckley's *synchronous gestures* are a different touch-based pairing technique, where an association is formed when a user causes a synchronous collision event on the devices (i.e., bumping together of devices). "PhoneTouch" demonstrates this concept for associating a surface computer with mobile phones [25]. Similarly, the Bump app[1] for mobile phones is a widely used commercial solution that embraces the bumping concept for connecting devices.

An alternative to direct touch is user input on the devices to initiate an association. Standard methods in commercial products include input of the same key on both devices and display of a key on one device for entry on the other. Another direct input technique is simultaneous input on both devices, for example pressing a dedicated association button on each of the devices [22]. For devices with a touch-screen interface, Hinckley et al. [7] introduced "*Stitching*"; a technique based on pen gestures on touch-screen devices. An association is established when a user draws a continuous stroke across multiple displays.

A number of association techniques involve as user action the spatial alignment of devices. This includes pointing of one device at another, for example with an infrared beam [1, 12] or visible laser light [17] where the beam supports both the selection of a target and the exchange of information to establish and secure an association. Alternatively, an association may be triggered by the user placing devices into close proximity of each other [23], for example using RFID technology, or NFC (near-field communication).

Users can also pair devices by performing gestures with devices. Patel et al. suggested a technique for pairing a handheld device with a situated terminal, where the terminal displays a sequence of gestures that the user has to mimic with the mobile device in order to successfully associate [21] . Chong et al. introduced discrete device gestures to replace PIN code entry, for devices that do not have an interface for number entry [4]. "Smart-Its Friends" employs random gestures that a user performs while holding the devices together [8]. The user is not required to learn or mimic any specific gestures, and the association is established by the simultaneous movement patterns to which the devices are exposed. Mayrhofer and Gellersen demonstrated a secure extension of the concept, with rapid shaking employed as a random gesture with high information content [16].

Techniques that are focused on security have considered a range of so-called out-of-band channels for information exchange under the user's control. McCune et al. [18] presented "Seeing-Is-Believing", where a user aligns their phone's camera towards a visual tag of the target device, and captures a snapshot of the tag. The phone analyses the tag's information to associate with the target. Saxena et al. [24] simplified the output by using blinking patterns of LEDs instead of visual tags. Likewise, Wilson and Sarin [28] proposed "BlueTable" for associating a mobile phone with a camera-based interactive surface. An alternative for secure association is the use of biometric information. "SAfE" for instance is a system that requires users to enrol their biometrics (faces or hand grip patterns) with their devices [2].

Usability Studies on Device Association Techniques

Several researchers have compared the usability of various association schemes. Uzun et al. [27] showed results on comparing user performance between different text-based pairing schemes. They showed that the method of copying a text between devices is the most robust. Whilst, results in [10] and [13] both showed that users achieved faster average completion time when using numerical-based methods

[1] `http://bu.mp/`

than image- or audio-based methods. Kainda et al. [11] presented results on device associations in scenarios of multiple users. Their findings show, on the contrary to conventional beliefs, group scenarios are less prone to failures during an association. Group members help each other to overcome weaknesses of struggling members. Ion et al. [9] presented results that indicate people do not always use the easiest or most popular method. Instead, people prefer different methods in different situations; hence, context is a influential factor on users' acceptance of an association method.

In our study, however, instead of requesting users to compare different existing methods, we intended to solicit people's creativity, where the end result is a set of device association actions defined by users.

Eliciting Input Actions from Users

Some work from surface computing employed ordinary users to define *gestures* for a variety of input functions and activities. Wobbrock et al. [30] presented a study on designing tabletop gestures, which relies on eliciting natural gestures from non-technical users. The participants were first portrayed with the *effect* of a gesture, and then asked to perform its *cause*. Frisch et al. [5] adopted a similar methodology to elicit multi-touch and pen gestures from users for editing diagrams on a tabletop, whilst Micire et al. [19] also adopted the approach to find gestures for controlling robots. Other than surface computing, Lee et al. [15] elicited user-defined gestures for deformable displays. They presented their observation on how users interact with artificial deformable displays, using several deformable materials.

The study by Kray et al. [14] is most related to our work. Their study investigated user-defined gestures for various activities when using mobile phones, tabletops and public displays (e.g., what gestures would users perform with their phone to scroll the screen content of another device). Whereas, their work focused on finding gestures for different activities for the three selected devices, our focus is on one activity – associating assorted wireless devices.

Unlike previous studies that were limited to defining gestures (or movement-based actions), we set no such limit. Our participants had the freedom to suggest *any type of actions and technology* that they felt comfortable with for establishing wireless connections.

METHODOLOGY

In our study, we embraced the user-centred philosophy, where participants were involved as informants. This section describes the approach of our study in detail.

Selection of Devices

For a device to be connectable, it requires network capability. Here, our focus is on establishing wireless communication; thus, we are only interested in devices that have (or suitable to have) wireless connectivity.

As devices become ubiquitous, they are no longer in the conventional shape of a personal computer. Instead, ubiquitous devices could be in any shapes, with functionalities for various purposes. We need to anticipate that users may want to associate different types of devices, hence, common devices that people regularly use. To pick out those devices, we held informal discussions with our colleagues. Overall, a set of 12 types of devices were selected (see Fig. 1 for the list of the devices). The set consists of computing devices, as well as accessory devices for input and output features.

Table 1. 37 combinations of associating devices (30 pairings and 7 miscellaneous) were selected for our user study.

	Primary Devices (3 groups)		
	Mobile Phone	*Tablet Computer*	*Interactive Display*
Pairing Devices	Digital Camera	Digital Camera	Digital Camera
	Digital Watch	Digital Watch	Digital Watch
	Gaming Device	Gaming Device	Gaming Device
	Handheld Projector	Handheld Projector	Handheld Projector
	Interactive Display	Interactive Display	Media Player
	Mobile Phone	Media Player	Wireless Headphones
	Media Player	Tablet Computer	Wireless Keyboard
	Tablet Computer	Wireless Headphones	Wireless Microphone
	Wireless Headphones	Wireless Keyboard	Wireless Mouse
	Wireless Keyboard	Wireless Microphone	
		Wireless Mouse	
Miscellaneous	Mobile Phone + Handheld Projector + Wireless Headphones		
	Mobile Phone + Wireless Headphones + Gaming Device		
	Tablet Computer + Wireless Headphones + Media Player		
	Tablet Computer + Wireless Microphone + Handheld Projector		
	Interactive Display + Digital Camera + Wireless Microphone		
	Interactive Display + Wireless Headphones + Wireless Mouse + Wireless Keyboard		
	Interactive Display + Mobile Phone + Tablet Computer		

This study focused on single-user controlled device association (i.e., only one person is involved to conduct the association). The subjects' task was to suggest actions for associating various combinations of the twelve selected devices. In order to keep the study manageable, we pre-selected a set of device combinations. To extract the combination set, primary devices – a *mobile phone*, a *tablet computer* and an *interactive display* – were assigned, where each combination includes at least one primary device. The three primary devices were selected based on their mobility [3] – *mobile*, *portable*, and *situated*. In addition, we have excluded any futile or illogical device combinations (e.g. an association of a mobile phone and a wireless mouse). In total, 37 combinations (30 pairings and 7 groups of miscellaneous devices) were selected. Table 1 summarises the set of combinations.

Apparatus, Material, and Environment

Our aim in this study is to elicit what actions would users spontaneously perform for associating devices. Participants should not be misled by any pre-existing interfaces [29]. The use of real devices can influence people's selections of actions. To avoid any biases caused by the apparatus, we abandoned the use of existing devices and we also prohibited the participants using their personal devices. Instead, we fabricated alternative representations, by using low-fidelity plastic props – with minimal user interfaces – to surrogate as generic devices. The adoption of plastic props minimised influences on the subjects' mindset towards any existing commercial products. Additionally, the intention of using generic prototypes was to force the participants to be creative and imagine any additional features, functionalities and user interfaces that the devices must have to accomplish the actions that they want.

We created plastic components with abstract user interfaces that offer the similar look-and-feel to real devices. Acrylic objects were cut into sizes that resemble the selected devices (see Fig. 1). To increase visual affordance, the components were engraved with shapes that resemble the essential features of the devices (e.g., a keyboard must have alphanumeric keys; a watch must have a face and a strap; etc.). Yet, we refrained from adding brand logos to avoid users affiliating the plastic prototypes with any commercial devices.

The study took place in a quiet room to avoid distractions. Only the participant and the experimenter were present. A video camera was installed to record the study sessions. In addition to videos, the experimenter also took notes.

Participants

Eighteen paid participants volunteered; nine were female. Their age ranged from 19 to 50 (mean=26.4, *sd*=7.65). All of the participants were students from our university (15 postgraduates and 3 undergraduates). To recruit the subjects, we advertised the study through posters at our campus. As we aim to design for the general public, we recruited people with non-technical background (e.g., no computer science majors). Prior to accepting the participants, we asked the applicants to provide their background information, which was used for screening out unsuitable candidates.

Setup and Procedure

The study was conducted as a one-on-one study: one participant and one experimenter per session. Overall, 18 study sessions were recorded.

Upon arrival, the participants first took part in an introduction session, which provided an overview of the study. The subjects were then required to fill in an initial questionnaire, which captured their demographic information and their experience with using the twelve selected devices. The experimenter explained the functionalities of any devices that the subjects were not familiar with and clarified any queries. Overall, the participants were familiar with most of the selected devices, except for the handheld projector that required additional explanations.

The study began after all queries were resolved. The participants were asked to produce actions for the list of pairing combinations. The combinations were divided amongst the three primary devices into three groups (see table 1). The study followed a within-group study design. We counterbalanced the order of the subjects' exposure to the three groups using a Latin square design. In addition, we randomised the order of presenting each combination within each primary device group. Subsequently, the participants were also requested to produce actions for the remaining seven scenarios that involved multiple (i.e., more than two) devices. Similarly, the order of presenting the multiple-device combinations was also randomised.

For each device combination, the experimenter would allocate the participants with the plastic props that represented the devices. The props were intended as a thinking aid for the participants to define actions. In addition, if the participants questioned the purpose of the combination, the experimenter would suggest a simple application scenario for the participants to envision how the devices could be useful when they work together. For example, an association of a mobile phone and a handheld projector can be used for extending the display of the phone as a projection. The participants were requested to adopt the think-aloud method, where they were required to verbalise their reasoning. To avoid biasing the results, the conversations between the experimenter and the participants were restricted to clarifying queries only. No examples of the existing association methods were mentioned or demonstrated to the participants.

Once the participants had defined actions for all thirty-seven combinations, the participants answered a final questionnaire about their attitude towards self-defining actions for associating devices. After which, the participants received a small payment, and they were discharged.

RESULTS

On average, the participants spent between 60 to 90 minutes to complete a study session. In total, we have collected over 20 hours of video footage as well as written notes from the study sessions. We analysed the collected data to seek for similarities between participants. In this section, we present the results of our user study. Our results include identifying key characteristics of different user-defined actions, a classification of the actions, and qualitative results of the participants' impression on defining actions for device association.

Participants' Prior Experience

In the first questionnaire, the participants were asked to define their proficiency in using digital technology on a five-point Likert scale (1 indicates no experience, 5 represents expert), and their average was 3.75 (*sd*=0.57). In addition, we requested the participants to rate their experience with *connecting a mobile phone to another mobile phone* (mean=2.94, *sd*=1.11), as well as *connecting a computer to the wireless internet* (mean=3.94, *sd*=0.94). We also asked the participants to use the same scale to rate their experience with the twelve pre-selected devices. The participants were most familiar with using mobile phones (mean=4.67, *sd*=0.59) and digital watches (mean=4.67, *sd*=0.69), whilst handheld projectors were the least familiar (mean=1.83, *sd*= 0.79). This finding is not surprising, as handheld projectors were still relatively new in the market.

User-Defined Actions for Device Association

Our results show that the participants often re-adopt strategies; they often reuse actions that they had previously produced. This is expected, as an action that is suitable for a device combination may also be suitable for other similar combinations. Theoretically, $18 \times 37 = 666$ actions would be recorded. Nevertheless, the participants sporadically suggested multiple actions for various combinations of devices. In total, we have recorded 752 actions.

We began data analysis by looking for the key characteristic of each action defined by the participants. Our analysis consists of two iterations. During the first iteration, we went through the recorded videos and written notes to annotate every action produced by the participants. We specifically looked for uniqueness and common actions between subjects. At the end of the iteration, 36 distinguishable actions were identified. In the second iteration, we isolated on finding similarities between the thirty-six distinguishable actions, where similar actions were grouped into a category. Twelve distinctive categories of interactions were classified:

- *Audio*: a user interacts with one device to play an audio tune. The tune is then captured by the target devices to establish a device association. This scheme requires the initiating device to be capable of creating audio sound, while the accepting devices need audio capturing capability.
- *Biometric*: the associating devices individually capture a user's biometric data; if the captured data is from the same person, an association is established. Our results show that the particpants were mostly familiar with 3 kinds of biometrics – face, fingerprint, and voice.
- *Button Event*: a user performs a single or a series of button event(s) on the associating devices to establish a device connection. This scheme has a minimum user interface requirement. The devices need at least one button for users to initiate an association.
- *Device Touch*: when two or more devices form a physical contact, the devices establish an association. The physical contact of devices represents an association.
- *Drawing*: a user selects a symbol and draws the same symbol on all of the associating devices. This scheme requires the user to be able to reproduce the same symbol accurately multiple times.
- *Gesture*: a user explicitly performs a human gesture on the connecting devices to associate them. In other words, the user performs some explicit movement action near or while holding the devices.
- *Image*: one device captures an image representation of the target devices to establish an association. This requires one device to have a camera for capturing and computer vision capability for analysing the image representation of the other devices.
- *Proximity*: devices associate automatically when they are brought within a close distance of each other. Once the devices are within proximity, the devices associate without further user assistance.
- *Search & Select*: a user first searches for a list of nearby available devices (i.e., device discovery) and then selects the target devices from the list of available devices. This is the current standard approach of Bluetooth Pairing.
- *Tactile*: a user's physical tactile touch on the connecting devices initiates a device association.
- *Token*: the initiating device has a dedicated token. To associate with other devices, a user inserts the token into the target devices. Once a wireless connection is established, the token can be removed.

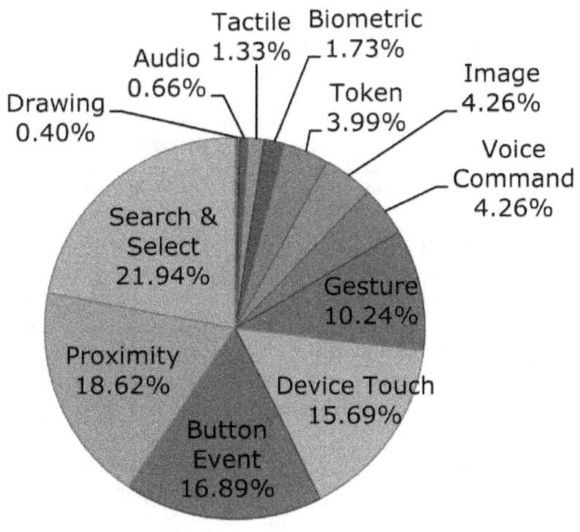

Figure 2. An illustration of the overall occurences of different types of actions (expressed in the classification categories). The diagram shows that the top five categories dominate over 80% of the overall occurrences.

- *Voice Command*: a user verbalises a command into associating devices. The devices interpret the command and associate accordingly.

The overall results of our annotation are summarised as a classification table in table 2 (see Fig. 3 for illustrations of several actions performed by the participants). In addition, the overall occurrences of each category per device combination are illustrated in table 3.

In table 2, for each action, we have indicated the number of participants that had suggested the same action (see the last column; actions that were suggested by multiple participants are highlighted in bold font). The higher the number of people suggested the same action indicates that the action is likely to be more agreeable amongst the participants.

The *search and select* action was the most suggested strategy amongst our subjects (suggested by 17 participants). This was expected, as the current customary way of connecting devices is by first searching for the available devices and then selecting the target. Our initial questionnaire results show that most of our participants had prior experience with connecting wireless devices using the conventional methods (like Bluetooth Pairing or Wi-Fi setup), which involve the search and select strategy. This is logical since our participants already had the basic knowledge of using the search and select strategy. When the participants felt there is no obvious strategy for associating a combination of devices, the participants resorted to adopt the conventional strategy.

On the contrary, the actions that were suggested by only one participant are likely to be less agreeable amongst the participants. Of all the collected actions, 9 of them were suggested by no more than one person (see table 2).

Of the twelve categories listed above, some categories occurred more often than the others. Fig. 2 summarises the overall occurrences of each category. The results show

Table 2. A classification of user-defined actions for device association. The right-most column indicates the number of participants that had suggested the same actions.

Categories	Name	Description	No. of people suggested
Audio	Play an audio	One device plays an audio tune and the other devices capture the audio.	**2**
Biometric	Face	Devices capture the user's face and associate if the captured face belongs to the same person.	**3**
	Fingerprint	Devices capture the user's fingerprint and associate if the captured fingerprint belongs to the same person.	**2**
	Voice	Devices record the user's voice and associate if the captured voice belongs to the same person.	**2**
Button Event	Asynchronous Presses	A user presses a button on one device to initiate and then presses a button on the other devices to accept.	**9**
	Dial a number	Dial the phone numbers of the target devices.	1
	Key presses pattern	Press a pattern of keys on the associating devices.	**5**
	Press a button + proximity	Press a button (e.g. an easy button) to initiate and then bring the associating devices close together.	**6**
	Press and hold + proximity	Press and hold a button to initiate and then bring the associating devices close together.	**2**
	Text entry	A user selects a textual information (e.g. a word or a phrase) and types it into the associating devices.	**4**
Device Touch	Docking	Insert one device into another directly to associate. Once associated, the devices can be undocked.	**6**
	Hanging	(Headphones + i. display only, see Fig. 3(b)) Rest the headphones on the top edge of the display.	**2**
	Physical contact	An association is formed, when the bodies of devices physically touch each other (on any location).	**7**
	Stacking devices	Stack devices on top of each other. Hence, one device's surface is touching another device's surface.	**4**
Drawing	Draw a symbol	A user draws an identical symbol on the associating devices.	1
Gesture	Clapping	A user claps near the associating devices to initiate a connection.	1
	Distinctive body movement	A user performs a distinctive body movement for the associating devices to capture (e.g. waving hands).	**2**
	Pointing by approximation	Hold one device and point it approximately towards the direction of the other devices (like shining a torch).	**7**
	Pointing with precision	Precisely align devices towards each other (like pointing a laser).	**5**
	Rotational gestures	A user performs rotational movements on the associating devices simultaneously.	1
	Shaking (synchronous)	Hold devices together in one hand and shake them rapidly for a short period.	1
	Shake a device + proximity	Shake one device near other associating devices.	**2**
	Swiping	Bring one device near the edge of another device and slide it along the edge (like swiping a credit card).	**4**
	Synchronous finger strokes	Place devices side by side and perform a pinching gesture, where each finger is on a device.	**2**
	Tapping	A user holds one device and taps it on the surface of another device.	**2**
	Throwing	A user holds a device and performs a throwing gesture (without releasing the device) towards another device.	1
Image	Barcode	One device captures a barcode of the other associating devices (i.e. barcode recognition).	**2**
	Snap a picture	Using one device to take a picture of the other associating devices (i.e. objects recognition).	**3**
Proximity	Close range	Bring devices within a very close proximity and they associate automatically.	**10**
	Dedicated zone	When a device is brought into a dedicated zone of another device, they associate (e.g. a dedicated pad).	**3**
	Specific position	Bring devices close together and place them in a relative position (e.g. side by side, top to bottom, etc.).	**8**
Search & Select	Search and select	Search for nearby devices and select the targets by their unique descriptions (e.g. name, model number, etc.).	**17**
Tactile	Human touch (asynchronous)	A user touches each of the associating devices individually (e.g. detecting the skin temperature).	1
	Human touch (synchronous)	A user touches the associating devices simultaneously.	1
Token	Dedicated token	Each device has a dedicated token. Insert token into the associating devices to connect them.	**4**
Voice Command	Voice Command	A user speaks the command into the associating devices (e.g. "device A connects with device B").	**9**

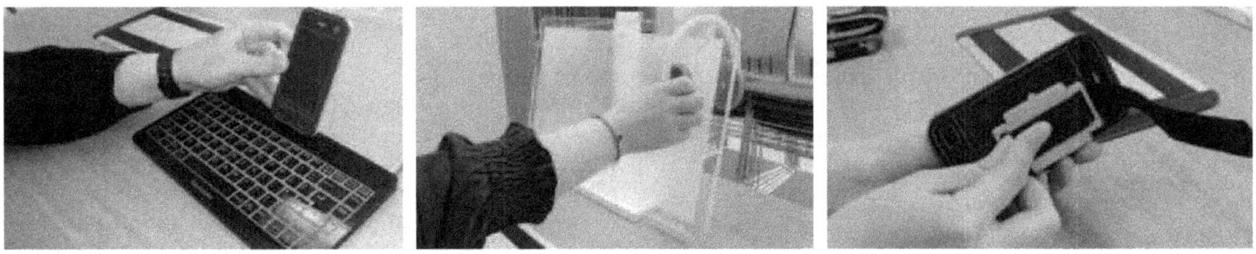

(a) Docking (b) Hanging (c) Phyical Contact

(d) Pointing by approximation (e) Snap a picture (f) Swiping

Figure 3. Example illustrations of several actions performed by the participants.

Table 3. Overall occurrences of each category per device combination (the highest value of each row is highlighted in bold font).

		The "Big" Five											
	Device Combinations	*Button Event*	*Device Touch*	*Gesture*	*Proximity*	*Search & Select*	*Audio*	*Biometric*	*Drawing*	*Image*	*Tactile*	*Token*	*Voice Command*
Mobile Phone	*Digital Camera*	1	4	2	4	**7**	-	1	-	2	-	-	-
	Digital Watch	**8**	3	-	3	5	-	-	-	1	-	-	-
	Gaming Device	4	4	2	3	**6**	-	1	-	1	-	-	-
	Handheld Projector	2	4	**5**	2	**5**	-	-	-	1	-	-	-
	Interactive Display	-	3	2	5	**6**	-	1	-	1	-	-	2
	Mobile Phone	3	3	-	5	**6**	-	-	-	1	-	-	1
	Media Player	2	2	2	**5**	4	1	-	-	2	-	-	1
	Tablet Computer	3	5	-	1	**9**	-	1	-	1	-	-	1
	Wireless Headphones	**8**	2	1	3	1	-	-	-	2	1	-	1
	Wireless Keyboard	**7**	3	-	4	4	-	-	-	1	-	-	-
Tablet Computer	*Digital Camera*	1	**7**	2	2	5	-	-	-	1	-	1	-
	Digital Watch	**5**	**5**	1	4	4	-	-	-	-	-	-	-
	Gaming Device	2	6	1	5	**7**	-	-	-	-	-	-	-
	Handheld Projector	3	4	**5**	2	2	-	-	-	1	-	1	-
	Interactive Display	1	2	4	**6**	5	-	-	1	-	-	-	-
	Media Player	**7**	5	1	3	2	-	-	-	-	-	-	2
	Tablet Computer	2	2	3	**5**	**5**	-	-	-	1	1	-	-
	Wireless Headphones	3	4	1	**5**	3	-	-	1	-	1	1	-
	Wireless Keyboard	5	**6**	-	3	2	-	-	-	-	1	1	1
	Wireless Microphone	**6**	1	1	1	4	-	1	-	-	-	2	3
	Wireless Mouse	**6**	2	3	3	1	1	2	-	-	-	2	-
Interactive Display	*Digital Camera*	-	1	3	**6**	4	-	-	-	3	-	1	-
	Digital Watch	3	2	2	**7**	5	-	-	-	1	-	-	1
	Gaming Device	2	3	2	**5**	**5**	-	-	-	-	-	1	1
	Handheld Projector	2	-	**8**	1	5	-	-	-	1	1	1	-
	Media Player	-	3	3	**5**	3	1	-	-	1	-	-	3
	Wireless Headphones	**4**	2	1	**4**	**4**	1	-	-	-	1	1	-
	Wireless Keyboard	**8**	3	-	2	1	-	-	-	-	-	3	1
	Wireless Microphone	**6**	-	3	2	1	-	1	-	-	-	1	4
	Wireless Mouse	4	1	3	**5**	4	-	1	-	-	-	2	-
Multiple Devices	*Phone + Projector + Headphones*	4	3	3	**6**	4	-	-	-	2	1	1	1
	Phone + Headphones + Gaming Device	1	6	1	5	**7**	-	2	-	1	1	1	1
	Tablet + Headphones + Media Player	5	5	1	3	**6**	1	-	-	1	1	2	-
	Tablet + Microphones + Projector	2	3	**6**	2	5	-	1	-	1	-	2	4
	Display + Camera + Microphone	3	1	1	**5**	**5**	-	1	1	2	-	2	4
	Display + Headphones + Mouse + Keyboard	2	2	3	6	**7**	-	-	-	2	-	3	-
	Display + Phone + Tablet	2	**6**	1	2	**6**	-	-	-	1	1	1	-
	Total = 752	127	118	77	140	165	5	13	3	32	10	30	32
	%	*16.89*	*15.69*	*10.24*	*18.62*	*21.94*	*0.66*	*1.73*	*0.40*	*4.26*	*1.33*	*3.99*	*4.26*

that Search & Select achieved the highest portion (with almost quarter) of the overall figure; whilst audio-based and drawing-based actions were the least suggested (both occurred less than 1% of the time). Four other categories also achieved large portions of occurrences. The sum of the top five categories – *Search & Select*, *Proximity*, *Button Event*, *Device Touch*, and *Gesture* – forms the majority (83.38%) of occurrences. This indicates that the participants found those five action categories were most obvious for device association.

Observations

In addition to annotating actions, we also observed the participants as they chose and performed actions.

Associating Multiple Devices

Within the set of actions for associating multiple (more than two) devices, a large number (75.4%) of the associations were conducted in multiple steps. Many participants chose to divide the association process into pairings of two devices at a time. This behaviour indicates that many users prefer to keep the process simple, by individually associating the least number of devices. Alternatively, this may also be explained by the mere fact that people only have two hands, so only two devices could be associated at a time. Further study is required to support these conjectures.

Distance of Proximity

From the video data, we examined the associations when proximity was applied. In general, the participants bring the associating devices within a distance of 1 to 6 inches (2.5 cm to 15cm). We also noticed that the distance of proximity between small devices is generally shorter than the distance between large devices (e.g. tablets).

Touch Regions

For scenarios based on physical contact of devices, the participants frequently placed the smaller device on the corners of the larger device. Some participants explained that they used the corner space to avoid occluding any information displayed on the larger device. Moreover, for the docking action, the participants preferred docking the bottom edge of the smaller device to the top edge of the larger device (as shown in Fig. 3(a)); like, the smaller device should be docked into the larger one, while not vice versa.

Form Factor

The shapes and sizes of devices can affect the actions produced by users. The props that we used in the study were cut from acrylic sheets. As shown in Fig. 1, many of the devices have flat surfaces. Some participants utilised this form factor to devise actions. For example, the *stacking devices* action, where the participants placed devices on top of one another.

The flat surfaces allow the devices to maintain balance and not tumble.

Selecting the Operating Device

We noticed that the participants often focus on one primary device to operate with for initiating the device association. Their selection of primary devices varies according to the association action. For select and search (which requires several steps of user interaction), we noticed that the participants prefer to operate the association with a device that has the largest output interface. This is expected, as the output requires sufficient space for displaying the list of nearby devices. Yet, on the contrary, for actions that involved agile movements (like pointing, swiping, and throwing), the participants preferred to initiate the association using the smallest (or lightest) device.

Adopting Actions from Habits

During the study, we requested the participants to give reasoning about how they derived their actions. The conversations revealed that some participants defined actions based on their habits. For example, the hanging headphones action (see Fig. 3(b)) was derived from how the participants usually placed their headsets when they are not in use. Similarly, some of the participants were familiar with giving verbal instructions, and as a result, the voice command action was elicited. Although users' habits can be derived into device association techniques, the selection of the habits is crucial. If a system is designed for a large number of users, then only habits that are common to many people are worth considering. This is because a habit of one person's may not be the habit of another person; thus, only common habits that are applicable across many people are useful.

General Feedback

The final questionnaire contained questions for understanding the participants' attitude towards self-defining actions for device association.

From the group of actions defined by the participants, we requested the participants to identify of which actions that they thought would be the easiest to describe to (or to teach) another person. The most common answers were *physical contact of devices* (mentioned 5 times), *search and select* (mentioned 4 times), *asynchronous button presses* (mentioned 3 times), and *voice command* (also mentioned 3 times). In addition, we asked the participants to explain their reasoning. The general explanations included: "the process is demonstrable"; "the interaction is natural"; "small number of steps"; "the action is direct, which implies a connection"; and "already widely adopted".

We also wanted to understand the participants' preferences of whether using self-defined actions or system-defined actions for associating devices. We gave the participants several choices, which they had to select an option. The first option was having *only one system-defined action* for connecting all types of devices; hence, one action fits all. The second option was having *several system-defined actions* for connecting devices; in other words, users have a few options of actions that were defined by the system designer. The third option was having *self-defined actions* for connecting devices. The first and the second options were each select by 4 participants, whereas 9 participants had selected the third option. Surprisingly, one participant suggested an alternative option: first see what the system offers, and then decide whether to define personal actions based on the satisfaction with the methods proposed by the system designer.

DISCUSSION

In this section, we discuss our findings and the implications of our results.

The "Big" Five Categories

As identified earlier, the top five categories – *search & select*, *proximity*, *button event*, *device touch*, and *gesture* – formed over 80% of the actions defined by the participants (see Fig. 2). Besides their dominance in overall occurences, table 3 shows that the five categories also achieved high coverage across the individual device combinations. Particularly proximity and search & select, the two categories were considered in every device combination. Further examination revealed that search & select was the most chosen option for associations that involved a mobile phone (see the boldfaced values in the Search & Select column). We conjecture that this was due to the participants' familiarity with the current Bluetooth pairing on mobile phones. Also, remarkably, for device associations that involve an interactive display, proximity was the most selected option. People recognise associations when a device is intentionally brought near a situated device. This implies that near-field technology (like RFID) is a suitable option for associating mobile devices with a situated device.

The Image Category

The image category also achieved a high coverage across different device combinations. Most of its occurrences involved a mobile phone. As many mobile phones nowadays are manufactured with a built-in camera, the participants adopted this phenomenon for pairing a mobile phone with another device. On the contrary, the image category achieved very low coverage in combinations where a tablet computer was involved. This could be explained by the fact that people are not used to using a tablet computer to take pictures.

The Token Category

Token-based association achieved moderate coverage across device combinations. However, it is remarkable that token-based association was never suggested in pairings that involved a mobile phone. As mobile phones are mostly small in sizes, it is difficult for people to envision that a mobile phone would have sufficient space to accommodate the physical size of a token. Although token-based association is widely adopted in connecting computer accessory devices (such as a dedicated USB dongle for a wireless keyboard and a wireless mouse), we found no existing research that explored the use of dedicated tokens for association of other wireless devices.

The Voice Command Category

The data in table 2 indicates that half of our participants thought of using voice command, and table 3 also shows that voice command had a high coverage across device combinations. However, the category's overall occurrences (4.26%; see Fig. 2) reveal that the strategy was one of the least adopted. Although voice command was suggested by many, the participants tended not to reuse the strategy often. The participants chose to avoid the complexity of personalising commands. The strategy requires users to think of the correct command, whilst it must also be unambiguous. Voice commands also lack protection of privacy; the technique is susceptible to eavesdropping, as it requires the commands to be broadcasted.

Handheld Projectors and Gestures

Inspections across individual device combinations in table 3 revealed gesture-based techniques were the most selected option for associations that involved a handheld projector. Many participants adopted the affordance of seeing a handheld projector as a torch, and they used the analogy of pointing a shining light onto the target to associate the devices. The affordances offered by devices can influence users' selection of device association methods.

Implications for Technology

Many of the collected actions require the devices to be within proximity of each other. Our observations also revealed that the distance of proximity varies across different users, as well as different devices. The variation of distance can cause ambiguity and a system may connect the wrong devices. To correctly associate the intended devices, the system requires technology that can recognise (or predict) the users' intention. When devices are brought close together, the system can calculate the change of contextual conditions (e.g. distance and direction) of the devices to determine whether they were intentionally brought close together for association.

Other than accuracy, the execution time cannot be neglected. Although many existing approaches provide accurate associations, they are accomplished at the expense of the execution time. Using Bluetooth Pairing for example; the device discovery phase is burdensome as searching for nearby devices requires the user to wait. This waiting period extends the execution time of the association. Device association should be as transient as possible, and choosing the right technology can reduce the execution time.

Implications for Research and Design

Some of the actions elicited by our participants are related to the methods suggested in research. In our study, proximity and device touch interactions were shown to be sensible options; yet, we found little research that explored those categories for devices association, and furthermore, token-based associations were not found at all. This indicates that what research had suggested is not always in harmony with people's mindsets.

The results presented in this paper are beneficial for situations where a system is deployed "in the wild". Designers cannot expect users to learn the instructions before operating the system. Instead, the design of the system should anticipate (and incorporate) the actions that the users would perform. Our results give insight into the types of actions that users would spontanesously produce to associate wireless devices.

As technology evolves, new interaction techniques are continuously being introduced. Users' exposure to new technology may affect their spontaneous responses in the future. As such, people's experience as well as their expectation of how to associate devices change over time. Although we show that users produce certain categories of actions for spontaneous device association, researchers and designers *should not* refrain from developing new techniques because they are not currently obvious to people. For example, although our results show that only one person had thought of *synchronous shaking* gesture (see table 2), research have demonstrated that the scheme is intuitive for associating mobile devices [16]. This paper contributes by providing information that will influence current design of device association methods, which in turn will influence how people conceptualise device association.

CONCLUSION

We have presented a study of user-defined actions for device association based on users' spontaneous responses without premeditation. Whilst previous work on device association provides insight into security and usability for a range of concrete techniques, our work complements the previous work by gaining insight into people's spontaneous preferences with abstract technology.

From the results, we learnt that there is no single category that dominates what people perceive as a suitable spontaneous action for associating devices. Instead, five dominant categories were found and, in addition, users evoked various novel interaction techniques that were not suggested in research. We have presented a classification of actions useful for analysing and characterising user interaction for device association. Furthermore, on a micro level, our results also provide understanding of users' preferences for particular device combinations.

REFERENCES

1. D. Balfanz, D. K. Smetters, P. Stewart, and H. C. Wong. Talking to strangers: Authentication in ad-hoc wireless networks. In *Proc. NDSS 2002*, 2002.
2. I. Buhan, B. Boom, J. Doumen, P. H. Hartel, and R. N. J. Veldhuis. Secure pairing with biometrics. *Int. J. of Security and Networks*, 4(1/2):27–42, 2009.
3. M. K. Chong and H. Gellersen. Classification of spontaneous device association from a usability perspective. In *Proc. IWSSI/SPMU 2010*, pages 1–7, 2010.
4. M. K. Chong, G. Marsden, and H. Gellersen. GesturePIN: using discrete gestures for associating mobile devices. In *Proc. MobileHCI 2010*, pages 261–264. ACM Press, 2010.

5. M. Frisch, J. Heydekorn, and R. Dachselt. Investigating multi-touch and pen gestures for diagram editing on interactive surfaces. In *Proc. ITS 2009*, pages 149–156. ACM Press, 2009.

6. K. Hinckley. Synchronous gestures for multiple persons and computers. In *Proc. UIST 2003*, pages 149–158. ACM Press, 2003.

7. K. Hinckley, G. Ramos, F. Guimbretiere, P. Baudisch, and M. Smith. Stitching: pen gestures that span multiple displays. In *Proc. AVI 2004*, pages 23–31. ACM Press, 2004.

8. L. E. Holmquist, F. Mattern, B. Schiele, P. Alahuhta, M. Beigl, and H.-W. Gellersen. Smart-Its Friends: A technique for users to easily establish connections between smart artefacts. In *Proc. UbiComp 2001*, pages 116–122. Springer-Verlag, 2001.

9. I. Ion, M. Langheinrich, P. Kumaraguru, and S. Čapkun. Influence of user perception, security needs, and social factors on device pairing method choices. In *Proc. SOUPS 2010*. ACM Press, 2010.

10. R. Kainda, I. Flechais, and A. W. Roscoe. Usability and security of out-of-band channels in secure device pairing protocols. In *Proc. SOUPS 2009*. ACM Press, 2009.

11. R. Kainda, I. Flechais, and A. W. Roscoe. Two heads are better than one: security and usability of device associations in group scenarios. In *Proc. SOUPS 2010*. ACM Press, 2010.

12. T. Kindberg and K. Zhang. Validating and securing spontaneous associations between wireless devices. In *Proc. ISC 2003*, pages 44–53, 2003.

13. A. Kobsa, R. Sonawalla, G. Tsudik, E. Uzun, and Y. Wang. Serial hook-ups: a comparative usability study of secure device pairing methods. In *Proc. SOUPS 2009*. ACM Press, 2009.

14. C. Kray, D. Nesbitt, J. Dawson, and M. Rohs. User-defined gestures for connecting mobile phones, public displays, and tabletops. In *Proc. MobileHCI 2010*, pages 239–248. ACM Press, 2010.

15. S.-S. Lee, S. Kim, B. Jin, E. Choi, B. Kim, X. Jia, D. Kim, and K.-P. Lee. How users manipulate deformable displays as input devices. In *Proc. CHI 2010*, pages 1647–1656. ACM Press, 2010.

16. R. Mayrhofer and H. Gellersen. Shake well before use: Intuitive and secure pairing of mobile devices. *IEEE T. Mobile Comput.*, 8(6):792–806, 2009.

17. R. Mayrhofer and M. Welch. A human-verifiable authentication protocol using visible laser light. In *Proc. ARES 2007*, pages 1143–1148. IEEE Computer Society, 2007.

18. J. M. McCune, A. Perrig, and M. K. Reiter. Seeing-Is-Believing: Using camera phones for human-verifiable authentication. In *Proc. Symp. on Security and Privacy 2005*, pages 110–124. IEEE Computer Society, 2005.

19. M. Micire, M. Desai, A. Courtemanche, K. M. Tsui, and H. A. Yanco. Analysis of natural gestures for controlling robot teams on multi-touch tabletop surfaces. In *Proc. ITS 2009*, pages 41–48, New York, NY, USA, 2009. ACM.

20. D. G. Park, J. K. Kim, J. B. Sung, J. H. Hwang, C. H. Hyung, and S. W. Kang. TAP: Touch-And-Play. In *Proc. CHI 2006*, pages 677–680. ACM Press, 2006.

21. S. N. Patel, J. S. Pierce, and G. D. Abowd. A gesture-based authentication scheme for untrusted public terminals. In *Proc. UIST 2004*, pages 157–160. ACM Press, 2004.

22. J. Rekimoto. SyncTap: synchronous user operation for spontaneous network connection. *Pers. Ubiquit. Comput.*, 8(2):126–134, 2004.

23. J. Rekimoto, Y. Ayatsuka, M. Kohno, and H. Oba. Proximal interactions: A direct manipulation technique for wireless networking. In *Proc. INTERACT 2003*, pages 511–518. IOS Press, 2003.

24. N. Saxena, J.-E. Ekberg, K. Kostiainen, and N. Asokan. Secure device pairing based on a visual channel. In *Proc. Symp. on Security and Privacy 2006*, pages 306–313. IEEE Computer Society, 2006.

25. D. Schmidt, F. Chehimi, E. Rukzio, and H. Gellersen. PhoneTouch: A technique for direct phone interaction on surfaces. In *Proc. UIST 2010*. ACM Press, 2010.

26. F. Stajano and R. Anderson. The resurrecting duckling: Security issues for ad-hoc wireless networks. In *Proc. 7th International Workshop on Security Protocols*, pages 172–194. Springer-Verlag, 1999.

27. E. Uzun, K. Karvonen, and N. Asokan. Usability analysis of secure pairing methods. In *Proc. USEC 2007*, pages 307–324, 2007.

28. A. D. Wilson and R. Sarin. BlueTable: Connecting wireless mobile devices on interactive surfaces using vision-based handshaking. In *Proc. GI 2007*, pages 119–125, 2007.

29. J. O. Wobbrock, H. H. Aung, B. Rothrock, and B. A. Myers. Maximizing the guessability of symbolic input. In *Ext. Abstracts CHI 2005*, pages 1869–1872. ACM Press, 2005.

30. J. O. Wobbrock, M. R. Morris, and A. D. Wilson. User-defined gestures for surface computing. In *Proc. CHI 2009*, pages 1083–1092. ACM Press, 2009.

ShadowStory: Creative and Collaborative Digital Storytelling Inspired by Cultural Heritage

Fei Lu[1], Feng Tian[1*], Yingying Jiang[1], Xiang Cao[2], Wencan Luo[1], Guang Li[1], Xiaolong Zhang[3], Guozhong Dai[1, 4] and Hongan Wang[1, 4]

[1] Intelligence Engineering Lab, Institute of Software, Chinese Academy of Sciences, Beijing, China
{lvfei, tf, jyy, luowencan, liguang, dgz, wha}@iel.iscas.ac.cn

[2] Microsoft Research Cambridge, Cambridge, UK
xiangc@microsoft.com

[3] Pennsylvania State University, PA, USA
lzhang@ist.psu.edu

[4] State Key Lab. of Computer Science, Institute of Software, Chinese Academy of Sciences, Beijing, China

[*]Corresponding author: tf@iel.iscas.ac.cn

ABSTRACT

With the fast economic growth and urbanization of many developing countries come concerns that their children now have fewer opportunities to express creativity and develop collaboration skills, or to experience their local cultural heritage. We propose to address these concerns by creating technologies inspired by traditional arts, and allowing children to create and collaborate through playing with them. ShadowStory is our first attempt in this direction, a digital storytelling system inspired by traditional Chinese shadow puppetry. We present the design and implementation of ShadowStory and a 7-day field trial in a primary school. Findings illustrated that ShadowStory promoted creativity, collaboration, and intimacy with traditional culture among children, as well as interleaved children's digital and physical playing experience.

Author Keywords

Storytelling, children, creativity, collaboration, cultural heritage, shadow puppet.

ACM Classification Keywords

H5.m. Information interfaces and presentation (e.g., HCI): Miscellaneous.

General Terms

Design, Human Factors.

INTRODUCTION

During the recent years, the developing world has attracted much attention in HCI research, resulting in various technologies created specifically for it, such as to facilitate education [13, 26], to assist illiterate populations [18, 24], or provide service in rural areas [16, 17]. Such efforts could potentially enhance the wellbeing of such developing societies, and reduce the technology gap between them and the rest of the world.

CHI 2011, May 7–12, 2011, Vancouver, BC, Canada.

However, the other side of the coin, which has only recently started to draw attention, is that the fast economic growth and urbanization in some of these developing countries may themselves create new social problems that did not exist before. The weakening of community ties, the overindulgence in information technology, and the loss of traditional values are just a few to mention. As the newest generation of the society, such new problems often can be most easily observed in children. For example, in today's China, especially urban regions, on the one hand children enjoy more attention, comfort, and education than the previous generations ever did, and receive ever higher expectations from their family; while on the other hand they were also reported to be more isolated, more self-centered, and lack interpersonal skills compared to their predecessors [11]. In addition, children's entertainment activities lean more and more towards electronic toys and computer games, most of which tend to simply entertain them rather than encourage self-initiated creativity as some more traditional ways of playing do [6]. These problems may have serious impacts on children's development.

Besides, as globalization penetrates the developing countries both economically and culturally, much of their local traditional culture and arts, which had been carried on for many generations, have now become less known to their younger generations, or even on the brink of disappearing. Such intangible cultural heritage has been identified by UNESCO (United Nations Educational, Scientific and Cultural Organization) as "provides them a sense of identity and continuity, thus promoting respect for cultural diversity and human creativity" [25]. How to preserve it and pass it onto future generations in the context of vast modernization is yet another challenge for the developing world.

Interestingly, what may be lacking in today's environment for children, namely space for creativity and collaboration, are indeed abundant in many traditional art forms. Taking China as an example, ancient arts such as Beijing opera or shadow puppetry combine various aspects of artistic creations (visual, musical, theatrical, etc.) and require several artists to closely work together. Thus, letting children playfully involve in such art activities could perhaps become a potential opportunity to promote creativity and collaboration among them, while at the same time increase their intimacy with their own cultural heritage. However, given the decreasing number of traditional artists fewer opportunities are now available for children to experience these arts first-hand. These arts often also require intricate skills and significant time investment to learn, creating a higher entry barrier for children to involve themselves, compared to modern entertainment technologies. Immersing children in traditional arts is not as straightforward as we may hope.

Motivated by such challenges, we propose a hybrid approach to combine the key elements and appeals of traditional arts with the convenience and immediacy of interactive technologies. We aim to create playful interactive systems for children which are inspired by traditional art forms. The goal is to capture and emulate certain experience, style, process, and skill of the original art, while at the same time significantly lower the entry barrier and higher the freedom of creation through digital technology.

For a first exploration in this direction, we take shadow puppetry, a Chinese traditional art, as our inspiration. Officially listed as a state-level intangible cultural heritage, Chinese shadow puppetry (Figure 1a) is an ancient theatre art with a reported history of over two thousand years [7]. Differing from most other forms of puppets, shadow puppets are flat articulated figures made of semi-transparent leather. These are manipulated behind and against a back-illuminated screen using a set of sticks. Sceneries, or backdrops, also made of leather, are attached to the screen. Story plots are depicted through puppet movements, narrations and conversations, as well as librettos sung by the performers, similar to those heard in Chinese operas. The special mechanism of shadow puppets results in highly unique visual styles and movement languages. Several schools of shadow puppetry developed in China, and variations of it could be found in more than 20 countries. A rich repertoire of plays and puppet designs was accumulated throughout the generations, covering traditional myth, legend, history etc. However, once a very popular folk entertainment throughout China, shadow puppetry is now becoming an endangered art. Dominance of modern entertainments, high skills required in making and performing the puppets, and lack of formal curriculum were all contributing factors. We chose shadow puppetry as the theme of our system for its playful nature, unique art style, richness in creativity and expression, deep root in traditional culture, but also its endangered status.

Inspired by this, we created ShadowStory (Figure 1b), a digital storytelling system that allows children to freely create digital puppets and perform stories using them, in a style consistent with traditional shadow puppetry. We offer simplified operations and intuitive interfaces through digital technologies; while still conserve key processes and elements of physical shadow puppetry. Digital puppets are created through pen and tablet input, using virtual tools similar to the tools for creating physical shadow puppets. Public performance of stories can be held on a projected screen and controlled by handheld orientation sensors, again emulating the atmosphere of traditional shadow puppetry plays.

Figure 1. (a) Chinese shadow puppetry. (Image by Alex Yu) (b) Three children playing with ShadowStory.

In the rest of the paper, we first overview related research, followed by an initial investigation of current children's play in urban China, and a summary of key elements in Chinese shadow puppetry. After describing the ShadowStory system in detail, we report a 7-day field trial of it in a primary school, with findings regarding how it promoted creativity, collaboration, and intimacy with traditional culture, as well as interesting interactions between physical and digital play.

RELATED WORK

Many researchers attempted to facilitate children's creativity and/or collaboration through technology. For example, I/O Brush [21] is a "magic" brush that allows children to pick up colors, textures and motions from everyday objects and use them to draw creatively; MEDIATE [15] uses visual, auditory, and vibrotactile stimuli to inspire creativity by children with autism; Tangible Flags [8] is a mobile technology to allow young children to collaboratively create presentations during field trips; and WHAT-IF [14] combines several handheld devices to create a larger information viewing surface and therefore promote collaboration among them.

Among these attempts, of particular similarity to our work are those focusing on children's storytelling activities. Fantasy storytelling play was found essential for children's development [6, 20]. In addition to accommodating almost unlimited creative imagination, fantasy storytelling offers a space for children to take different roles in their play, allowing various group interactions and collaborations to emerge and potentially be transferred into the real life. Numerous digital systems were created to support such fantasy storytelling. Many aimed to interleave digital and physical worlds. For example, StoryMat [19] and Rosebud [12] both included instrumented physical toys as index and trigger for narrated stories; Video Puppetry [2] used an overhead camera to track performances of paper puppets and translate them into digital stories; while to offer more space for creativity, both Pogo [9] and Telltable [4] allowed children to use photography to capture real-world objects as elements of their digital stories. TellTable [4] also leveraged the affordances of multi-touch tabletops to allow several children to work both collaboratively and independently. Other systems, such as StoryTable [5] and KidPad [3] went further and explicitly encourage collaboration by introducing actions that must be performed jointly by several children.

The preservation and promotion of cultural heritage has also attracted attention of many HCI researchers. For example, Ruffaldi et al. [22] created an information landscape system for digitally presenting cultural heritage content as immersive visualizations. Multicultrual Videos [10] is an interactive online museum for artists around the world to share their cultural heritage. And targeting at children in particular, Amicis et al. [1] used playful virtual environments and video games to promote the learning of history and cultural heritage among them.

Despite the rich literature listed above, to our knowledge we are the first to explore incorporating components of creativity, collaboration, and cultural heritage in the same system to promote them among children. The effectiveness of such combined approach will be demonstrated through this paper.

INITIAL INVESTIGATION ON CHILDREN'S PLAY

To further investigate the current situation and issues in children's daily play in urban China, especially relatively developed regions, we conducted informal interviews in a public primary school in Beijing. Two teachers and five pupils (aged 7-8) from the school participated. Both teachers were directors of grade-2 classes (aged 7-8), one for a class of 37 day pupils, and the other for a class of 36 boarders. The former had 4 years of teaching experience, and the latter had over 20 years of teaching experience. The interview questions focused on the children's playing habits, creativity and collaboration, as well as their familiarity with traditional culture. In addition, we observed pupils playing in the school during breaks, which helped verify the findings from the interviews.

According to the teachers' experience, there were two main issues in these children's daily play. Firstly, the children did not seem to have many opportunities for creative play. The most common game among boys was "One two three, freeze", a simple chasing game, and among girls it was "knitting flower baskets", a simple hopping game. Fantasy role playing were not commonly observed. Secondly, the children's collaboration skills tended to be lower than those of the same age several years ago. For example, when taught to play "throwing the bean bag", a dodgeball-style game between two teams, they required help from the teacher to coordinate the turn-taking between teams. Many children would simply follow the teacher's actions instead of coordinating with other teammates. These comments were confirmed through our observation of the children playing. The teachers further commented that these issues had become more apparent in the recent years, but had not yet drawn enough attention.

Three main reasons may have contributed to these issues. Firstly, much of these children's playing time was now dominated by electronic entertainment. The interviews with the pupils revealed that their forms of entertainment at home were mainly television watching, electronic toys, and computer games. For example, two boys indulged in Happy Farm (www.kaixin001.com), a popular online social game targeted mainly at young adult professionals. Such virtual content not only reduced the children's direct interaction with others, but might also pre-shape their ways of thinking and playing in the real world. Secondly, the lower birthrate today means that compared to previous generations these children had fewer playmates at home who were from the same family and of similar age. And lastly, the high expectation by Chinese parents today often resulted in many children attending various extracurricular tutorials such as music, art, or foreign languages, reducing their time to play freely. All these factors may have resulted in a decrease in children's creativity and collaboration skills.

In addition, despite the school's efforts on education about Chinese traditional arts, most pupils were not particularly familiar with them. This was again partly due to the fact the children had much of their entertainment through cartoons and computer games which were mostly westernized, whereas local arts were no longer a regular part of their daily life. In the case of shadow puppetry in particular, only one out of the 36 children in a class we asked had experienced it in person with her parents, while the majority of the other children had only seen it on television and did not know much about it.

This investigation confirmed our concerns about today's Chinese children's creativity, collaboration, and knowledge of cultural heritage. This led to our attempt to develop a digital storytelling system that aim at promoting all these three aspects among children, inspired by the ancient Chinese art of shadow puppetry and allowing children to freely and intuitively express their creativity in a collaborative setting.

ELEMENTS OF SHADOW PUPPETRY

In order to extract key elements of shadow puppetry that might be appealing to children and applicable to our system, we studied 20 classic Chinese shadow puppet plays, which involved reading scripts and watching videos of the plays, watching media interviews with the shadow puppetry artists, as well as learning to manipulate the shadow puppets ourselves. As a result, below we draw a summary of their production process, control mechanism, art style, etc.

Design and Performance Stages

Like other puppetry arts or indeed theatre arts in general, the production of a shadow puppet play consists of a design (or composition) stage and a performance stage. In the design stage, the plot of the play needs to be determined, and all characters, backdrops, music, and lyrics created or composed. The play plots most often center around traditional Chinese myths or legends that are familiar to most local audiences. Famous characters such as the Monkey King (Figure 2c) are depicted frequently, as they are in other forms of Chinese arts. In the performance stage, the performers manipulate articulated characters behind the back-illuminated screen while narrating, conversing, or singing librettos for the characters. The combination of puppetry, lighting, music, and storytelling creates a compelling experience for the audience.

Creating Puppets

Shadow puppets are made of donkey or cow leather. Such leather is light and semi-transparent, making it ideal for the back illumination used in the play to penetrate. First the outlines of the puppet parts are carved out using a pricker knife, and inner patterns carved using a set of graver knives (Figure 2a). Then the parts are painted in bright colors using special brushes, resulting in lively tints when back-illuminated (Figure 2b). Finally the parts are riveted or bound together to create the articulated puppet (Figure 2c). Making shadow puppets is a highly skilled handcraft, and a typical puppet can take an experienced artist two or three days to make. Each single puppet is unique and bears strong signature of the region and the artist.

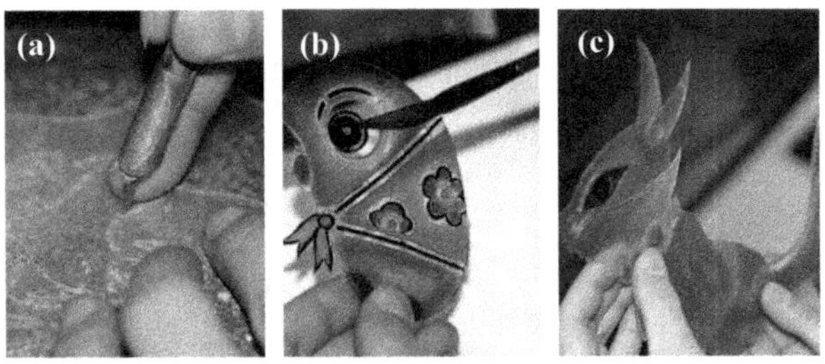

Figure 2. Creating shadow puppets. (a) Carving. (b) Painting. (c) Assembling.

Colors and Patterns

Similar to in Beijing operas, colors are used to represent personalities of the characters, e.g., black represents justice, red represent loyalty, and yellow represents duplicity. Meanwhile, various symbolic decorative patterns such as flowers, animals, and Chinese scripts are also utilized to illustrate the identity and traits of the character.

Figure 3. Shadow puppets with various colors and patterns.

Components and Manipulation

A shadow puppet is typically composed of eleven or twelve components: head, upper body, lower body (or two thighs), two calves, two upper arms, two forearms and two hands (Figure 4a). The performer manipulates the puppet using three sticks (Figure 4b). One stick is connected to the neck joint between the head and the upper body, controlling the basic movements of the character such as walking, sitting, standing up, jumping, or flying. The other two sticks are connected to the two hands, controlling the movement of the arms and hand gestures. Combining the manipulation with all three sticks, a skilled performer can make the character do a large variety of actions.

Figure 4. (a) Components of a typical shadow puppet. (b) Manipulating puppets with sticks.

Singing, Narration and Music

Besides the visual elements, singing, narration, and accompanying music also play essential roles in the performance. Bearing many similarities to those found in various forms of Chinese operas, these are not only to help the audience understand the story, to add to the atmosphere and effect, but also to synchronize the puppet movements with rhythms.

Collaboration in Performance

Collaboration is the key in shadow puppet performances. Several performers, each controlling one or several characters, need to work in precise coordination, especially for interactive actions such as shaking hands, hugging, fighting, etc. Sometimes it may also require more than one performer to control a single complex character.

As illustrated above, shadow puppetry is a composite art that combines painting, sculpting, music, playwriting, and performance, which are often mastered by the same artists. This makes shadow puppetry the fascinating art it is, but also creates very high entry barrier for would-be artists. We believe the attractiveness of shadow puppetry would make it an ideal metaphor for our system. However, in applying these elements to our system design we need devise ways to not only allow children to achieve the similar rich expressiveness, but at the same time significantly lower the complexity and skill requirement of the process, and create an environment for children to design and perform in ways that are intuitive, efficient, and familiar to them.

SHADOWSTORY: DESIGN AND IMPLEMENTATION

Based on such understanding and consideration, we designed ShadowStory, a storytelling system that allows children to use a Tablet PC to create articulated digital characters and other props in the style of shadow puppets and with similar (virtual) tools; and perform live stories together on a projection screen by controlling the characters with simple body movements through wireless handheld orientation sensors. We employed an iterative design process. An initial prototype was trialed with 3 children in a primary school. Led by observations during this initial trial, we simplified the workflow, improved usability, and ensured robustness in the final system presented below.

ShadowStory includes two interaction modes: "Design" mode, in which story elements can be created; and "Perform" mode, in which stories can be performed in public. There is also a video library of real shadow puppet plays that is available for the children to watch at any time.

Design Mode

In the Design mode, children can use a Tablet PC with pen input to create three types of story elements: characters, props, and backdrops.

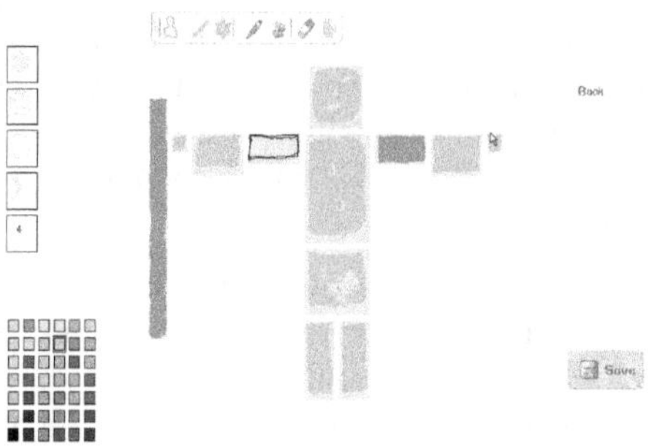

Figure 5. Interface of "Design" mode (for creating characters).

To start creating a character, the system provides an articulated template consisting of 11 required body parts: head, chest, belly, left/right forearm, left/right upper arm, left/right hand and left/right leg; and one optional item held by the character (Figure 5). Children can create these parts individually by using a "knife" tool and a "brush" tool to carve or paint on them. Similar to the physical knives used in creating real shadow puppets, two types of "knives" are provided: one for carving the outline, and one for carving inner patterns. The brush tool allows children to paint in various colors and thicknesses. In addition, several "stamp" tools allow children to directly imprint common traditional decorative patterns without efforts, such as peony, longevity, and crescents. After all individual parts are created, children can save the completed articulated character to the library to be used in performance. Such articulated characters can potentially display an abundance of actions.

To create props, which are all unarticulated, the system provides an empty grey background representing a piece of leather as used by puppet artists, on which children can use the same knife and brush tools to create simple movable objects such as animals. Similarly they can create backdrops which remain static during performance.

In addition to elements created by the children, the system also includes a library of digitized traditional shadow puppetry characters, props, and backdrops, the content of which are generally familiar to Chinese children. These can be directly used by the children in their performance, or serve as inspiring material for their own creations.

Auditory elements such as singing, narration, or music are not included in the Design mode. These are slightly more challenging for the children to compose ahead, therefore are left for the children to create in situ during the performance, should they choose to do so.

Performance Mode

After all story elements have been created, children can switch to Performance mode to act out their stories. Firstly, they should arrange the stage with elements according to their stories. They can bring in saved story elements into stage by selecting from the characters, props, or backgrounds library. Every character or prop added into the stage is automatically assigned to a pair of handheld sensors, while a backdrop brought into the stage replaces the previous one. Once the stage is set up, children can press the "perform" button to activate the handheld sensors and perform their stories, as shown in Figure 6. The performing interface is also displayed on a projection screen visible to all performers and audiences, allowing them to engage with each other similar to in the case of real shadow puppet plays.

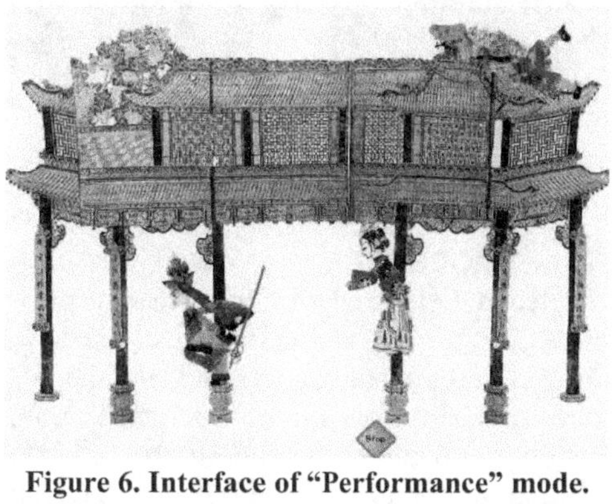

Figure 6. Interface of "Performance" mode.

As we described, manipulating a real shadow puppet requires highly skilled hand control and directly touching the puppet with sticks. To simplify the control mechanism in our system, and to free the children from standing next to the computer, we opted for using simple wireless handheld sensors instead. For each character, the controlling child holds a pair of 3D orientation sensors, one in each hand. Instead of direct manipulation on the puppet parts, the child can move the character left, right, up, and down by tilting the first sensor in the corresponding direction. Tilting the second sensor leftwards or rightwards results in the character bending the body in the corresponding direction, as if bowing or looking up. Other joints of the character automatically move accordingly to match these main movements, e.g., the arms and legs swing naturally as the character walks. Similarly, the child can move and rotate a prop using a pair of sensors. Given that one child can only control one character or prop, almost all stories need to be performed by several children collaboratively.

Children can narrate, dub, or make any sound effects as they perform. When the story is over, they can press the Stop button to finish.

Implementation

The ShadowStory hardware includes a Tablet PC, a projector, and currently six wireless WiTilt v3.0 [27] orientation sensors manufactured by SparkFun (Figure 7b). The dimensions of the sensor are 2.20 x 2.81 x 0.73", convenient for children to hold in hands. Each sensor transmits pitch, yaw, and roll angles at 50Hz via Bluetooth to the Tablet PC. For each pair of sensors used by one child, the character or prop's vertical position is linearly mapped to the pitch of the first sensor; its horizontal position is linearly mapped to the roll of the first sensor; and its bending (for character) or rotation (for prop) angle is linearly mapped to the roll of the second sensor. Additional pairs of orientation sensors can be easily added to the system should they become necessary. The ShadowStory user interface was implemented in Flash, and the communication with sensors implemented in C++.

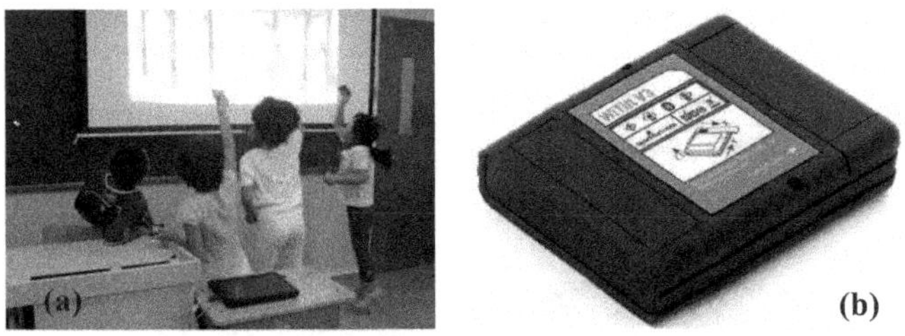

Figure 7. Hardware interface. (a) Playing with the hardware. (b) Handheld sensor (image from www.sparkfun.com).

FIELD TRIAL PROCEDURE

We conducted a field trial of ShadowStory in a primary school in Beijing for one and half weeks (7 school days) to explore how children would understand and play with it, and what interesting behaviors might emerge. The school has approximately 4000 pupils, including approximately 3600 day pupils and 400 boarders. The boarders have an activity class as a break between afternoon classes and supper.

We ran 7 trial sessions, one each day, with a grade-2 class of 36 boarders aged between 7 and 9. Each session lasted 40 minutes during their activity class. In total 14 children played with ShadowStory, comprising 5 boys and 9 girls. They divided themselves into 4 groups voluntarily. On the last day, the 4 groups gave public performances of their stories for the whole class of children.

During the sessions, one teacher (the director of the class) and three researchers were present. On the first day, before the session began, a researcher demonstrated the system usage to the children. Each group of children then practiced both the design and the performance mode with the Tablet PC and the handheld sensors for 10 minutes in total, with hands-on assistance from the researcher. Before trying performing their stories for the first time, children were again given 3 minutes to re-familiarize themselves with the handheld sensors. Most stories were rehearsed by the children through the performance mode the days before the public performance. Once the children have learned the system, the researchers and the teacher remained unobtrusive and merely observed the children's creation and performance processes. They only stepped in when occasionally children faced technical difficulties and requested assistance, such as helping rotate the screen of the Tablet PC.

We chose the classroom as the location for the field trial, firstly because it was a familiar environment that the children spent much of their day studying, playing, and socializing, so that they would behave naturally, and potentially interaction may emerge between ShadowStory and their other daily activities. Secondly, the children were already familiar and comfortable watching and using the projector installed in the classroom, which was used daily in lessons, removing the potential technology barrier. And lastly, classrooms are indeed among the main venues that we envision the system to be used in, therefore it is important to understand if it would fit within the physical, social, and organizational constraints of the classroom contexts without disrupting other activities.

Two video cameras were set up to record all activities around the Tablet PC and the projection screen respectively. All interactions on the computer, in both design and performance stages, were recorded using screen-capture software.

Throughout the period of the trials, we interviewed 10 children who played with ShadowStory, and in addition 6 children who did not but watched other children playing and performing using it. These semi-structured interviews took place in the classroom and focused on their impression of the system, sources of inspirations for plot, interactions with audience and other groups, etc.

We examined transcriptions of the interviews together with field observation notes and video recordings. Findings were organized into themes to explore commonalities and diversities in how the children played with ShadowStory.

EXPERIENCE WITH SHADOWSTORY

Children's impression of ShadowStory was unanimously positive. All the children who had played reported that they had enjoyed it very much, and those who did not play asked for opportunities to play next time. Many requests were made for us to visit the school again with the system. The design tools were found intuitive to use. During the initial introduction and practice, the use of handheld sensors was quickly understood by the children, and after a few minutes they all became proficient in controlling characters this way.

Going beyond such general evaluation of the system itself, we will now report experience regarding the three aspects we aimed to promote through the system, namely creativity, collaboration, and intimacy with traditional culture, followed by a few additional observations between digital and physical play.

Creativity

Despite the relatively short time frame available, children created 6 unique stories, some with several variations, and in addition to using traditional elements provided by the system, created 4 characters, 3 "animals" (in the form of props), and 4 backdrops. Figure 8 illustrates a few of the stories and Figure 9 illustrates some new elements created. Table 1 summarizes the characteristics of these stories. Each story had a clear, albeit simple, storyline.

Figure 8. Stills from children's stories. (a) "*Catching rabbit*". (b) "*One day at home*".

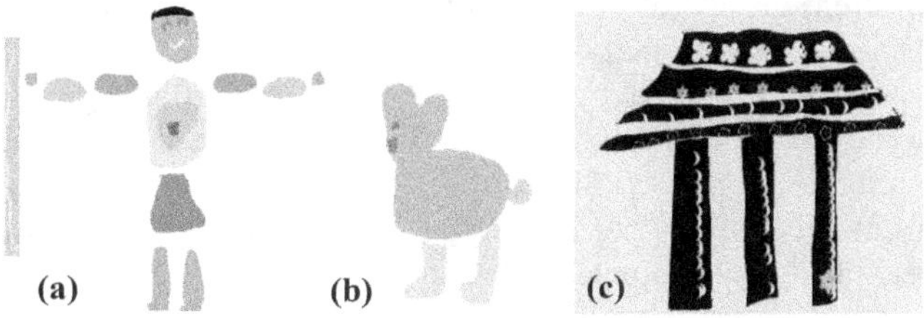

Figure 9. Story elements created by children. (a) Character. (b) Animal "rabbit". (c) Backdrop (imprinted with traditional patterns).

As shown in the table, the story plots children created were inspired by a variety of sources. Apart from inspirations from traditional myth, which we will discuss in more detail later, life at home serves as another rich repertoire for inspirations, be it realistic daily life, or stories told by family members. Even more interesting was how they blended these two sources together. For example, in the "*Catching rabbit*" story (Figure 8a), the rabbit, which was created after the pet rabbit at one child's home, was combined with traditional characters of a princess and Nezha the child deity to create a half-myth half-reality story. And in the "*One day at home*" story (Figure 8b), multiple copies of the traditional Monkey King character were used as representations of one of the children himself and his playmates, to depict them playing together on a backdrop they painted to represent his home.

Story Title	Inspiration Source	Elements Used	Number of Performers
New journey to the west	Traditional myth	Traditional	4
Story of Pigsy	Traditional myth	Traditional	3
Catching rabbit	Pet rabbit at home	Traditional + Created	3
One day at home	Daily life	Traditional + Created	2
Horse training	Story told by grandparents	Traditional	2
Go to Mongolia	Family holiday plan	Traditional	3

Table 1. Summary of children's stories.

Another interesting aspect was how the children creatively defined new performance languages to overcome the constraints in the functionalities supported by the current system implementation. For example, one story required a monk to lie down and pretend to be ill, a movement not current supported. Instead, the children decided to make him stand still against a pillar, symbolizing the lying down action – a similar style of symbolic actions are often seen in Chinese operas. Another constraint in the system was that it did not support introducing new characters or backdrops during the performance. To overcome this, in the "*Go to Mongolia*" story, the ridge of an archway was used to symbolize a Mongolian tent for their similarity in shape, and when the character rode on a horse and moved to the tent, this symbolized that the scene had now changed to Mongolia. A second example was in an early version of the "*Story of Pigsy*", where the same character was used to represent both a real and a fake Monkey King, and performed by the same boy.

In addition to these planned creations, we also observed improvisations in both the design and the performance stage. While characters were being created, many of them completely changed from what they were originally envisioned to be because of other children's suggestions. And in most story performances, much flexibility existed in the plot, and many children preferred to freely perform what they felt was appropriate to happen under the story context. For example, in the "pretending to be ill" example we mentioned, both this action and its symbolic representation were indeed suggested by a fellow performer on the fly, in order for the monk to confuse an evil witch. This type of improvisation is also commonly observed in children's fantasy play [23].

These rich creative behaviors assured us that creativity is inherent in children's minds. ShadowStory provided an opportunity for them to more easily express such creativity, and at the same time inspired by the rich repertoire of traditional arts.

Collaboration

Collaboration was inherent in the performance stage of ShadowStory, requiring multiple children to coordinate their characters to perform a coherent story. Children often explicitly talked to each other during the performance to coordinate, especially to align their characters (*"Don't move. Let's play over there!", "Wait for me! You should walk right."*) and to plan next steps (*"Let's play on the sky, and then I will get down."*). Some children might voluntarily take the role or the "director" to coordinate all performers during the performance. Collaboration was also essential in the design stage. Most of the designs and plots went through considerable evolution through group discussion and included contribution from each member. Children often helped each other when they had difficulties doing certain actions.

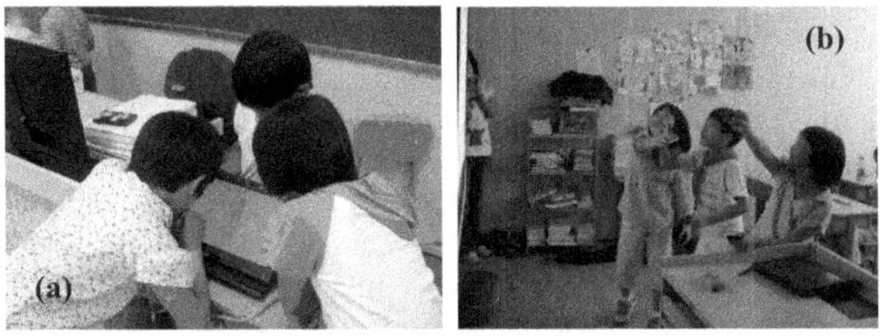

Figure 10. Collaboration during: (a) Design. (b) Performance.

Besides the above more general collaborative behaviors, there were several specific aspects we would like to detail:

Turn-taking

Although in the performance stage ShadowStory requires several children to act simultaneously, in the design stage the Tablet PC only supports one child to use at a time. This differs from multi-touch tabletop systems that allow multiple children to create independently [4], and mandates turn-taking between children.

Somewhat contrary to the findings in our initial investigation, children were very conscious of coordinating turns fairly between themselves when using ShadowStory to create story elements. We did not observe cases of one or a few children dominating the system, as was reported with some other systems [4]. Instead, many children voluntarily yielded the turn to others when they finished certain steps, such as when switching from carving to painting. This was particularly common between close friends. In other cases, the order of turns needed to be explicitly determined beforehand, sometimes using simple rules such as from the youngest to the oldest (it is customary in China for older children to yield to younger ones to show caring), and at other times using "fairer" methods such as finger-guessing games to decide when consensus could not be reached. When "unfair" turn-taking emerged, some member of the group would usually point it out and the problem was corrected. We suspect such slight difference in children's turn-taking behaviors might be attributed to cultural differences, as Asian cultures tend to emphasize more on courtesy and avoid aggressiveness, and this is solidified in the early education of children.

Assigning Roles

Given the stronger emphasis on public performance in ShadowStory as compared to some other storytelling systems, children attached more value on choosing which roles (characters) they perform in the stories, as these were considered projections of themselves. Personal feelings about the characters were the main reason of choices, for example many girls would choose pretty female characters or cute child/animal characters, while powerful male characters were preferred by boys. When conflict happened, they negotiated alternatives ("*I have chosen this one already. You can take the other girl, she's pretty, too.*"); and when some children could not make their mind, other members of the group gave suggestions. Sometimes a satisfying role assignment was even the driving factor of the plot development itself. For example, in the case of "*Story of Pigsy*", the boy who had the original idea envisioned a simple scene of Pigsy (himself) resting in the park. However when asked by other children what would be roles for them, the plot evolved and enriched to become a fight between Pigsy and a witch to feature all group members. With the only girl in the group refusing to take the role of the witch, the plot changed again to finally became a fight between Pigsy, Sandy, and Monkey King, all of which were positive characters in the original myth.

Although roles were usually explicitly assigned beforehand, sometimes the assignment may evolve during performance: one girl yielded her role of Nezha halfway in the performance because another girl thought it was cuter. Sometimes role assignments were even exchanged between different groups of children. On the final performance day, the girl who originally played Sandy in the "*Story of Pigsy*" was replaced by a boy who was not part of the group, because the other two members (boys) thought it would be more fun to play with a boy in fighting scenes. This girl instead joined another boy in the "*Horse training*" story and became a new character in the story.

Interaction with Audience

On the final day, the entire class of children was present to watch the performances. We found that the performers and the audience were mutually influential to each other. While watching the performances, the audience often thought about stories they could tell themselves. More interestingly, children in the audience who were to perform themselves were often inspired by what they saw. Ideas in earlier stories were often alluded to in later ones. In other cases, the groups who were to perform next adjusted their acting according to the audience's response: when the audience commented the story was too simple, later groups added new plots to their own stories.

Conversely, encouragement and acknowledgement from the audience were found effective for the performers to build self-confidence, especially for isolated children. There was one boy who was often isolated by other children in class activities for being "weepy". However he created an interesting story and eventually found a story partner. His performance was well received by the audience, and he started to engage more in group activities after the performance.

Given these rich collaborative behaviors observed, we feel we should be cautious about the simple conclusion of these children lacking collaboration skills. Compared to some existing games with relatively fixed rules that we mentioned, ShadowStory provided an open and creative environment that required various self-initiated collaborative behaviors but did not explicitly dictate how these should be achieved. We believe it was such opportunities that helped open up the children's potential for collaboration.

Intimacy with Traditional Culture

As mentioned previously, few children in the class were familiar with traditional shadow puppetry before the field trial. In the beginning of the trial, we also provided real shadow puppets for the children. They showed a great deal of interest and immediately tried to play with them. However they soon discovered they could not master the control of the puppets, and started randomly pulling the limbs. Before long the puppets were broken and returned to us, and the interest diminished. This clearly illustrated how the high entry barrier prevented the children from becoming more intimate with such traditional arts despite their initial interest. In contrast, ShadowStory retained the inherent appeal of traditional arts, yet eliminated the initial barrier and allowed the children to immerse in a more holistic, if simulated, experience. Through playing with the system they gained knowledge of the complete process of creating and performing shadow puppets, and experienced some of the unique skills involved, e.g., the use of virtual carving knives was found particularly attractive to many children. And mostly importantly, they could enjoy a sense of achievement through their own new creations, which would be near impossible for them with the physical form of the art. Such positive experience of initial contact could serve as a good basis to attract them to further understand the art.

In addition to shadow puppetry itself, other elements of traditional culture were ubiquitously seen in children's experience with ShadowStory. Some of these elements were already known to the children and contributed to their intimacy with the system. For example, the first two stories in Table 1 both originated from the traditional myth novel "*Journey to the West*" and featured the Monkey King and his companions. This was not only thanks to the beauty of such characters provided in the system library, but also due to the myth's extreme popularity in China. Moreover, as shown earlier children re-appropriated these traditional characters to suit their own plots, or redefined their relationship to create new plots. Children also brought their own knowledge about tradition and history into the system. For example, one boy's grandparents told him stories about post-horses used for sending urgent mails in ancient China. He was fascinated by this, and created the "*Horse training*" story about catching and training wild horses to send messages for him.

Conversely, many traditional cultural elements were introduced to the children through the system and adopted by them. For example, the children particularly enjoyed using the "stamp" tool to imprint traditional patterns on many of their creations. Although they would need later education to be able to understand the symbolic meanings of these patterns, such initial impression might plant seeds in their minds for such pursuit in the future. A similar example was that one girl sang during the performance of the "*New journey to the west*", clearly influenced by the librettos in the videos of traditional shadow puppet plays they watched.

Examples we showed here suggested that today's children are not as unfamiliar with or uninterested in traditional culture as many may believe. The question for HCI researchers is then how to design technologies to resonate with their potential interest in traditional culture and provide easy access to it. We believe ShadowStory is one successful attempt towards this direction.

Between Digital and Physical Play

Many other digital storytelling systems [4, 19] successfully combined elements from the physical and the digital worlds. Although this was not an explicit design goal of ShadowStory, we also observed interesting examples how these two worlds interleaved with each other in children's play:

Differing from many other storytelling systems, performance in ShadowStory was not based on direct manipulation but the orientations of handheld sensors, which could be controlled by wrist rotation only. Despite this, many children tried to create more direct mappings between the character's position/action and those of themselves. For example, one girl waved her own hands when the character she controlled was doing so. One boy was controlling a character to fly in the sky, and while doing so he stood on a chair so that he was also physically above other performers. Such interesting correspondence seemed to add to the engagement with the story, and blurred the boundary between digital and physical play.

Children also tried to bring elements of their physical games into the digital stories they created. For example, the action of chasing as seen in their "One two three, freeze" game became a central part in the "*Catching rabbit*" story. Conversely, plots of their digital stories were often translated into physical role playing. Again taking "*Catching rabbit*" as an example, after its performance, three girls in the group started physically acting out the plots themselves in the roles they had taken. This role playing quickly evolved into a brand-new chasing game with set rules – the game was over whenever the "rabbit" was caught, and played again with the roles reassigned. This "catching rabbit" game soon attracted many more players to join enthusiastically, including children who did or did not watch the original performance. Meanwhile, the girls who invented the game gained recognition and admiration in the class. Different from the "throwing the bean bag" game reported earlier, turn-taking in this game was handled seamlessly. Both the creativity and the collaboration promoted by ShadowStory were now translated back into the children's real world play.

CONCLUSION AND FUTURE WORK

We presented ShadowStory, a digital storytelling system for children, inspired by and capturing key elements of the traditional art form of Chinese shadow puppetry. ShadowStory was designed to promote creativity and collaboration among children, and at the same time letting children become intimate with their cultural heritage. Findings from a field trial in classroom confirmed our approach was successful in achieving these goals, and revealed many interesting behaviors regarding children's creative and collaborative play.

In the future we plan to more deeply investigate the longer-term effects of ShadowStory in promoting traditional arts and culture among children, as well as the transfer of creativity and collaboration skills from ShadowStory to the real life. We are also interested in designing other creative systems by drawing inspirations from other forms of traditional arts, and deploying them with children and/or adults.

ACKNOWLEDGMENTS

We thank the financial support from National Key Basic Research and Development Program of China under Grant No. 2009CB320804, the National Natural Science Foundation of China under Grant No. U0735004, and the National High Technology Development Program of China under Grant No. 2008AA01Z303, 2009AA01Z337. We thank the anonymous reviewers for their constructive comments. We also thank the experiment participants and puppet resource providers - Mr. Zhongbo Mao and Beijing Dragon-in-Sky Shadow Shows Club/Museum.

REFERENCES

1. Amicis, R.D., Girardi, G., Andreolli, M. and Conti, G. Game based technology to enhance the learning of history and cultural heritage. *ACE*, (2009), 451.
2. Barnes, C., Jacobs, D.E., Sanders, J., Goldman, D.B., Rusinkiewicz, S., Finkelstein, A. and Agrawala, M. Video Puppetry: A Performative Interface for Cutout Animation. *ACM Transactions on Graphics*, 27(5), 124: 1-9.
3. Benford, S., Bederson, B.B., Åkesson, K.P., Bayon, V., Druin, A., et al. Designing storytelling technologies to encourage collaboration between young children. *CHI*, (2000), 556-563.
4. Cao, X., Lindley, S.E., Helmes, J. and Sellen, A. Telling the whole story: Anticipation, inspiration and reputation in a field deployment of TellTable. *CSCW*, (2010), 251-260.
5. Cappelletti, A., Gelmini, G., Pianesi, F., Rossi, F. & Zancanaro, M. Enforcing cooperative storytelling: First studies. *ICALT*, (2004), 281-285.
6. Cassell, J. and Ryokai, K. Making space for voice: Technologies to support children's fantasy and storytelling. *Personal and Ubiquitous Computing 5*, 3 (2001), 169-190.
7. Chinese Shadow Play - Precursor of Modern Cinema. http://traditions.cultural-china.com/en/17Traditions7497.html
8. Chipman, G., Druin, A., Beer, D., Fails, J.A., Guha, M.L. and Simms, S. A case study of tangible flags: a collaborative technology to enhance field trips. *IDC*, (2006), 1-8.
9. Decortis, F. and Rizzo, A. New active tools for supporting narrative structures. *Personal and Ubiquitous Computing 6*, 5-6 (2002): 416–429.
10. Fernández, J.M. Multicultural videos: an interactive online museum based on an international artistic video database. *CommunicabilityMS*, (2008), 23-30.
11. Gao, J.Q. Psychology investigation of the generation born in 1990's and 2000's. *Journal of Changchun Education Institute, 26*, 2 (2010), 48-50.
12. Glos, J.W. and Cassell, J. Rosebud: technological toys for storytelling. *CHI*, (1997), 359-360.
13. Kam M., Kumar A., Jain S., Mathur A. and Canny J. Improving literacy in rural India: Cellphone games in an after-school program. *ICTD*, (2009), 139-150.
14. Mandryk, R.L., Inkpen, K.M., Bilezikjian, M., Klemmer, S. R. and Landay, J.A. Supporting children's collaboration across handheld computers. *CHI Ext. Abstracts*, (2001), 255-256.
15. Parés, N., Carreras, A., Durany, J., Ferrer, J., Freixa, P., Gómez, D., Kruglanski, O., Parés, R., Ribas, J.I., Soler, M. and Sanjurjo, À. Promotion of creative activity in children with severe autism through visuals in an interactive multisensory environment. *IDC*, (2005), 110-116.
16. Parikh, T.S., Javid, P. Sasikumar K., Ghosh, K. and Toyama, K. Mobile phones and paper documents: evaluating a new approach for capturing microfinance data in rural India. *CHI*, (2006), 551-560.
17. Parikh, T.S. and Lazowska, E.D. Designing an architecture for delivering mobile information services to the rural developing world. *WWW*, (2006), 791-800.
18. Prasad, A., Medhi, I., Toyama, K. and Balakrishnan, R. Exploring the feasibility of video mail for illiterate users. *AVI*, (2008), 103-110.
19. Ryokai, K. and Cassell, J. StoryMat: A play space for collaborative storytelling. *CHI*, (1999), 272-273.
20. Ryokai, K. and Cassell, J. Computer support for children's collaborative fantasy play and storytelling. *CSCL*, (1999), 63.
21. Ryokai, K., Marti, S. and Ishii, H. I/O Brush: Drawing with everyday objects as ink. *CHI*, (2004), 303-310.
22. Ruffaldi, E., Evangelista, C., Neri, V., Carrozzino, M. and Bergamasco, M. Design of information landscapes for cultural heritage content. *DIMEA*, (2008), 113-119.
23. Sawyer, R. K. Pretend play as improvisation: Conversation in the preschool classroom. *Lawrence Erlbaum Associates Publishers*, (1997).
24. Taoufik, I., Kabaili, H. and Kettani, D. Designing an e-government portal accessible to illiterate citizens. *ICEGOV*, (2007), 327-336.
25. The Convention for the Safeguarding of the Intangible Cultural Heritage. (2003). http://www.unesco.org/culture/ich/doc/src/01852-EN.pdf
26. Tian, F., Lv, F., Wang, J.T., Wang, H.A., Luo, W.C., Kam, M., Setlur, V., Dai, G.Z. and Canny, J. Let's Play Chinese Characters – Mobile Learning Approaches via Culturally Inspired Group Games. *CHI*, (2010), 1603-1612.
27. WiTilt v3.0, sparkfun.com/commerce/product_info.php?products_id=8563

Designing for Perceptual Crossing to Improve User Involvement

E.J.L. Deckers, S.A.G. Wensveen, R.M.C. Ahn, C.J. Overbeeke
Eindhoven University of Technology, Department Industrial Design,
Den Dolech 2, 5600 MB, Eindhoven, The Netherlands
{e.j.l.deckers, s.a.g.wensveen, r.m.c.ahn, c.j.overbeeke}@tue.nl

ABSTRACT
In this paper we describe our research on how to design for perceptive activity in artifacts in order for perceptual crossing between subject and artifact to happen. We base our research on the phenomenology of perception [19] and on ecological psychology [10]. Perceptual crossing is believed to be essential to share perception and thereby to feel involved in the situation [5,15]. We propose a theoretical model in which perceptive connections between user, artifact and event are presented. We designed an artifact to function as physical hypotheses [9] and show the design relevance of the model. In an experiment we investigate how the user's feeling of involvement is influenced in relation to differentiations of the proposed theoretical model. The results of our experiment show that indeed perceptual crossing between user and artifact influences the user's feeling of involvement with the artifact in their common space. We conclude with describing several design notions important for designing for perceptive activity in artifacts.

Author Keywords
Perception, Design Theory, Design, Phenomenology, Perceptual Crossing, Behavior, Interaction

ACM Classification Keywords
H5.m. Miscellaneous.

General Terms
Design, Theory

INTRODUCTION
Our research through design tradition follows the Lab approach [14] where design knowledge is generated through empirical research on theoretically inspired designed artifacts. One of the critiques on research through design [28] is the lack of formalization of the approach. Therefore we try to formalize our approach by describing the theoretical departure and the resulting design-relevant model, the design of the physical hypothesis and the testing of the hypothesis in a controlled experiment in order to generate design relevant knowledge, i.e., design notions.

For our current research on designing perceptive and expressive qualities in artifacts we looked to phenomenology of perception and ecological psychology. Especially the work of the French phenomenologist Maurice Merleau-Ponty inspired and grounded our work.

Phenomenology in HCI
Winograd & Flores (1986) introduced the relevance of phenomenology to the broader HCI community. The work of the French phenomenologist Merleau-Ponty was introduced by Dag Svanœs (2000) in "Understanding Interactivity: Steps to a Phenomenology of Human Computer Interaction" showing the importance of 'being-in-the-world' and a new understanding of interaction-as-perception. This issue has also been addressed in the work by Dourish [8] and shown to be relevant in areas of Movement & Interaction [20,22,24], Aesthetics & Interactions [4,11] and Tangible Interaction [12]. Perceptual crossing is relevant for Mediated Social Interaction [16] and Social Robotics [7,18].

Where in the referred work phenomenology is used to provide knowledge of and a better understanding of how users are acting-in-the-world, our work takes a next step. We specifically aim at providing design knowledge on how to design for new artifacts, that interact with users, in such a way that perceptual crossing and therefore the feeling of sharing a common space is possible. We move from using the theoretical background as method for analysis, to a means of inspiration and input for the synthesis of new designs.

Theoretical Departure
The question we address in our research is if and how Merleau-Ponty's work can inform design. We especially focus on his statement that "perception is inherently interactive and participatory; it is a reciprocal interplay between the perceiver and the perceived" [1,19]. Our goal is to design artifacts that are capable of perceptive activity and can engage in reciprocal interplay with the perceived. With the perceived we mean the world including the user interacting with the artifact.

Recently researchers at the Compiègne University of Technology (France) made reciprocal interplay operational for the perception between two human subjects [15]. In their work they describe two kinds of perception over time: perceiving the other as part of the environment (perceiving the body-image), versus perceiving the perceptive activity of the other perceiving me, and our common space (perceiving the lived-body). It is by switching between these two kinds of perception that it becomes possible for one subject to understand the position from which the other perceives the scene. In more simple words: I see you seeing me and you see me seeing you. Perceptual crossing between the two subjects happens. The constitution of the other subject's viewpoint is essential to get a feeling of sharing a common space: to feel involved [15].

In earlier research we set out perceptive activity in three components [5]. This way the phenomenon of perceptual crossing becomes more tangible to start the design process. The first component is the *perception of presence*. In this situation one subject perceives the other without being perceived oneself. One recognizes the possibility of the other subject to perceive: the presence of the lived-body [16]. Second, for perceptive crossing to happen one needs *perception of perceptive actions*. These actions are the exploratory movements one undertakes to perceive the other and the space. It are these perceptive actions, like looking at each other, that tell us what another subject perceives. Lastly the third component is the *perception of expressivity*. It is by perceiving expressivity of another subject that we know how this person feels or thinks about what he or she perceives. For example if someone rubs a surface to the sensitive skin of the cheek this reveals to me that the surface feels soft or pleasant.

An example will clarify the concept of perceptual crossing in subject-subject interaction. Figure 1 shows two people and their bicycles.

Figure 1. Example of perceptive activity of subjects

Both persons have perceived each other's presence, the ability of the other to perceive (the first component). The woman in the picture (person on the right) undertakes specific perceptive actions; she looks in the direction up in the tree and points in that same direction (second component). The fact she expressively points might already reveal the event is interesting to look at (third component). In reaction to her perceptive activity the man looks in the same direction, trying to perceive what she is looking and pointing at. It is her perceptive activity that makes him undertake these perceptive actions.

Theoretical Model

In figure 2 our model on perceptive connections between two subjects and an event, as in the example in figure 1, is presented. The people on their bicycles are subject 1 and subject 2. The event is up in the tree. Both subjects undertake actions to perceive the event, resulting in sensory feedback. The subjects can also perceive each other's perceptive activities, built up out of the three components described before.

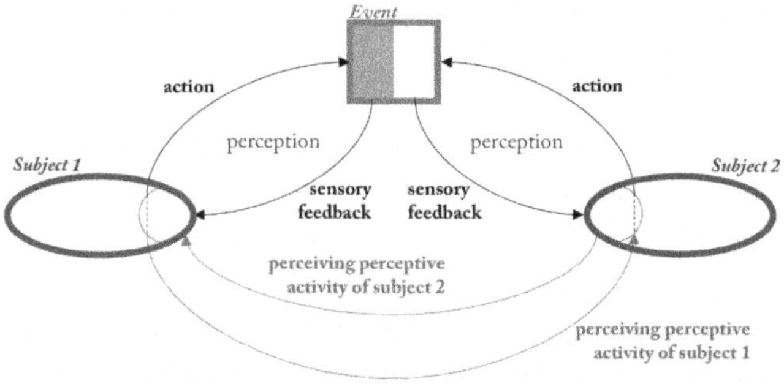

Figure 2. Model showing perceptive connections between 2 subjects and an event. The perceptive connections are presented as arrows in this model.

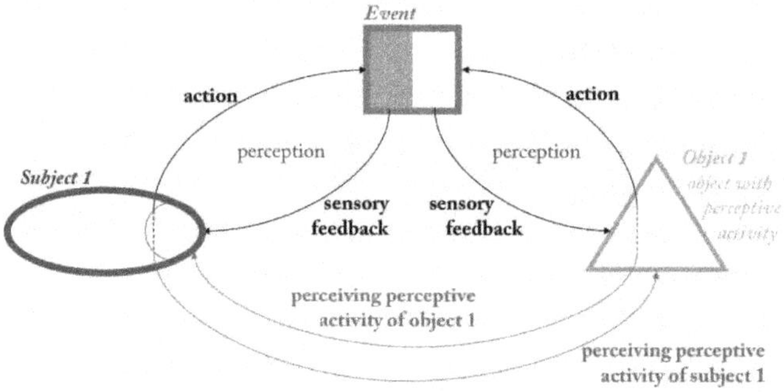

Figure 3. Model showing perceptive connections between subject, object with perceptive activity and event.

We now propose a second theoretical model (figure 3) in which we put forward the idea that one of the subjects might be an object with perceptive qualities. We question if we can design for perceptive activity in an artifact in order to make perceptual crossing between subject (user) and a designed artifact possible. By enriching the reciprocal perception between user and designed artifact hypothetically the user-involvement with the artifact in their common space will increase. In figure 3 this model on perceptive connections between subject, object with perceptive activity and event is shown.

Before discussing the designed artifact further two of the introduced concepts are summarized and defined.

Perceptual crossing: reciprocal interplay of perceiving the other as part of the environment (perceiving the body-image) and perceiving the other perceiving me (perceiving the lived-body).

Perceptive activity: Actions undertaken to perceive. These are actions that show presence, perceptive actions and expressivity.

THE DESIGNED ARTIFACT

We designed and built an artifact with perceptive activity to explore the phenomenon of perceptual crossing. This *physical hypothesis* [9] is our vehicle to explore how to design for perceptive activity in an artifact. Furthermore we use it to test the effect the perceptive activity of the artifact has on the feeling of involvement the subject experiences with the artifact in their common space. The design is therefore deliberately kept minimalist. Only by keeping the design simple, changes in the subject's feeling of involvement can be attributed to the design variables.

Based on the three components of perceptive activity and the proposed model, the following criteria apply to the design:

- The artifact should be able to detect perceptive activity, i.e. the presence, perceptive action and expressivity of the subject.
- The artifact should be able to show perceptive activity to allow for the reciprocity, where the subject is able to perceive the perceptive activity of the designed artifact.
- The artifact should be able to detect the presence of an external event. For this event we chose a piece of popular instrumental music.
- The artifact should be able to show perceptive activity relating to the event, i.e. actions that show the artifact perceives the event and an expression on this perception.

The designed artifact named PeP, i.e. 'Perception Pillar' has next to a physical body, housing the electronics, a dynamic light body. In figure 4 again the model is presented. The criteria that apply to the design are included. The direct perceptive connections between PeP and subject are given in more detail. Note that we chose our design to be sensitive to music, as the external event.

The physical body

The artifact has the shape of a purple square pillar. On each of the four sides a light sensor (Light Dependant Resistor) is attached for the detection of intentional subjects. On the topside 13 LEDs (Light Emitting Diodes) are evenly placed in a five to five grid. The square shape is deliberately picked as it gives PeP, the design, clear sides and thus makes that the subject has a clear position towards PeP.

Nevertheless the dynamic light behavior, reflected in the LED grid, overtakes this shape. When lighted in a dark room, the blue LEDS draw the subject's attention. The purple pillar now just functions as a container for the dynamic light design and the pillar fades to the background. This makes that the dynamic light body overtakes the overall form and shows perceptive activity to the subject. This light body becomes the perceptive body.

The light body

The dynamic behavior of the light body, reflected in the LED grid, is based on the interplay between the input of the four light sensors and the following properties: the **location** of the light body within the grid, the surface **size** and the **brightness** of the light body and the **direction** and the **speed** of the movement of the body.

The dynamic characteristics for the light body were determined after acting out sessions between two human subjects through active exploration in movement [13]. In the exploration one participant acts as the perceiving object, the other participant acts as the subject interacting with the perceiving object. The choice for this design tool is made explicitly, as it allows for exploration from PeP's point of view [17].

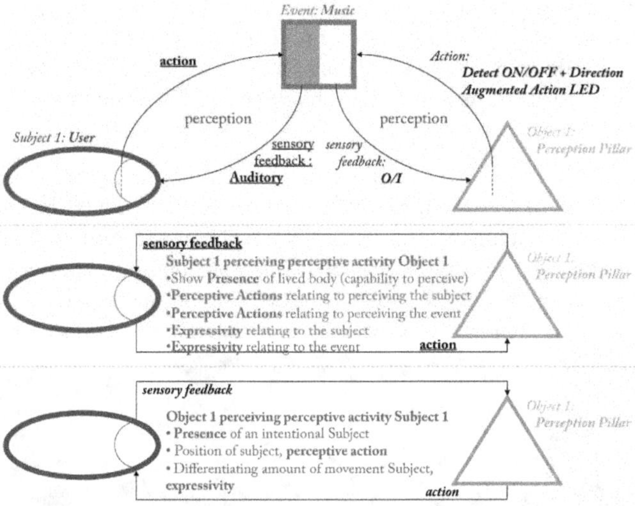

Figure 4. Model showing perceptive connections between subject, PeP (object with perceptive activity) and event and the criteria that apply to the design.

The emphasis when creating the dynamic light body lies on the algorithm that translates the input of the four light sensors into perceptive activity shown in the LEDs. The algorithm developed over time; trying several ideas and interact with the behavior that emerges. Important more general design notions that were implemented and aspects that need further consideration are part of our conclusion section. Next is a specific description of PeP's behavior.

Figure 5. PeP, perception pillar, light sensors on the four sides detect perceptive activity of the subject, grid of 13 blue LEDs shows perceptive activity of PeP.

PeP perceives its environment by means of the light sensors. When a change in this light is detected, in a conditioned setting, this movement indicates the presence of a lived-body. The light body is positioned within the grid according to an angle and a radius. The angle is depending on the side on which the movement is detected and the radius is depending on the amount of movement. PeP will focus on this movement and follow when the subject walks around. If the subject is not moving enough to be recognized as lived-body PeP returns its focus inside. Also when there is too much movement, PeP will turn back to the middle. The light body does not jump but gradually adjusts its position, moving along the sides. Before focusing on the subject the light body first exploratively moves along the side the subject is positioned. In figure 6 several interactions states between subject and PeP are shown.

PeP is, as can be seen in the model, also able to perceive an event. For this event a piece of modern instrumental music is chosen. PeP will show perceptive actions towards the music by focusing his perceptive body in the direction of the sound and will give expression by changing brightness and size: PeP will move to the beat of the music. For practical reasons we chose the reaction to music be triggered by a function within the algorithm, so PeP is not really given the opportunity to hear by means of a microphone. The limitation of this implementation is that PeP will not react to sounds the subject makes, whereas PeP is clearly able to perceive music.

EXPERIMENT

The designed perceptive activity is evaluated by means of an experiment. In this experiment the 12 participants, design students, go through five situations in which the perceptive connections between subject (participant), object (PeP) and event (music) vary. Theses situations will be discussed further below. The general hypothesis is that if perceptual crossing between the subject and object happens, the feeling of involvement of the subject increases.

In this experiment deliberately an order effect is created, to make it possible to build up the perceptive activity and give the participant the opportunity to get familiar with PeP's activity. Only subsequent situations are compared to each other analyzing the results.

Situations

The five situations we chose for the participants to go through have different conditions according to the possible perceptive connections. Four perceptive connections are evident within the test set up. The first connection is a constant, as the subject (participant) is always able to perceive (the physical) PeP, either when PeP performs perceptive activity or when PeP does not. The other three connections can vary; PeP perceives the subject or PeP does not, the subject perceives music or the subject does not, and PeP perceives music or PeP does not. A complete overview of possible connections between subject (participant), PeP and event (music) are presented in Table 1. The grey marked situations are the situations the subject goes through. In the table also the order by which the subject goes through the different situations is given. The situations will be discussed next in this order, the model per situation can be found in figure 7.

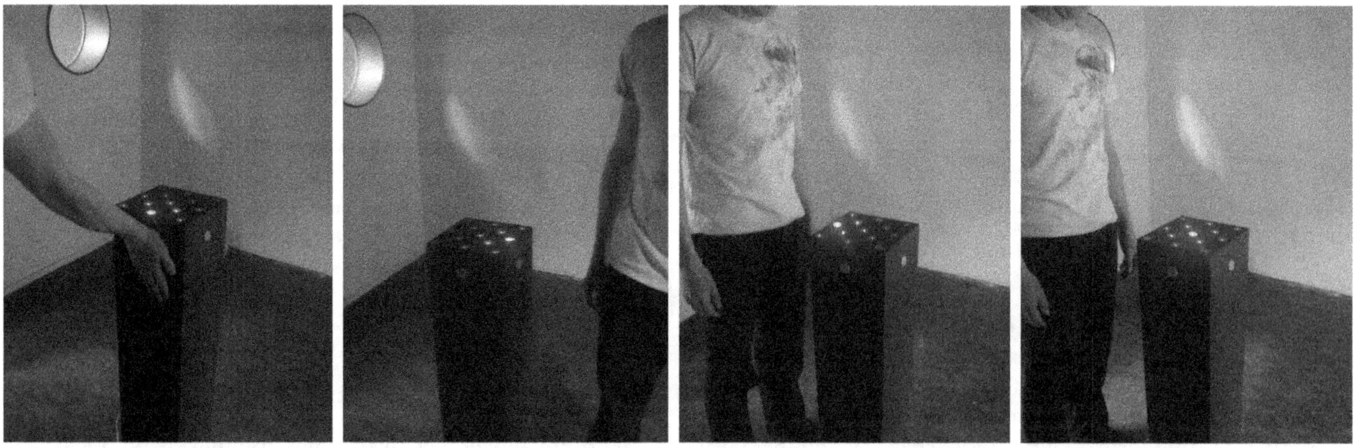

Figure 6. Several interaction states between subject and PeP. From left to right: PeP focuses in the direction of the subject and follows when the subject walks around, if the subject does not move enough the focus returns inside.

Situation 1

The subject encounters PeP, who is only able to perceive music. The subject can't hear this music and PeP does not perceive the subject. Perceptual crossing between subject and PeP and sharing the perception of music is not possible.

Situation 2

Next the subject encounters PeP who is only capable of perceiving the subject. No music is present in this situation. Perceptual crossing between subject and PeP is possible in this situation.

Situation 3

PeP perceives the subject and perceives music. The subject still does not hear the music. Perceptual crossing between PeP and the participant is possible but the participant is not able to share PeP's perception of the music directly.

Situation 4

All perceptive connections are evident. Perceptual crossing between subject and PeP and sharing perception of the music is possible in this situation.

Situation 5

Last perceptual crossing between PeP and Subject is possible but now only the subject is able to hear the music, sharing this perception is not possible.

Situ-ation	*Subject Perceives PeP*	*PeP Perceives Subject*	*Subject Perceives Music*	*PeP Perceives Music*
4	x	x	x	x
5	x	x	x	-
3	x	x	-	x
	x	-	x	x
2	x	x	-	-
1	x	-	-	x
	x	-	x	-
	x	-	-	-

Table 1. Overview of different conditions (C1 to C8) in relation to the perceptive connections between Subject (participant), PeP (designed object) and Event (music). The grey marked conditions are part of the experimental set-up

Hypothesis

As stated before the main hypothesis is that *"the feeling of involvement of the participant increases if perceptual crossing between the participant and PeP happens."* Furthermore we see how the ability to share the perception of an event in the common space influences the feeling of involvement. Hypothetically "*sharing the perception of an external event increases the subject's feeling of involvement.*" These hypotheses are based on the earlier discussed theory. The sub-hypotheses are a comparison between subsequent conditions. Summarizing the expected result is that the user-involvement in situation 2 is greater than in situation 1 and in situation 4 is greater than in situation 3 and situation 5. The comparison between situation 3 and situation 2 is somewhat different.

Measure of involvement

Involvement within the situation is measured through thirteen 7-point differential semantic scales. The list of differentials is based on a semantic exploration of the term involvement [21]. The differentials are: intense/shallow, contact/no contact, close/distant, intimate/not intimate, connected/detached, warm/cold, understanding/ignorance, familiar/unfamiliar, sharing/isolated, influential/not influential, unity/individual, associated/dissociated, and involved/alone.

Results and discussion

The results are analyzed using the chi square test for nonparametric statistics between two successive situations to see whether the observed sample significantly differs from the expected values [25]. In figure 7 the results, in which the direction of the effect is visible, are presented. In this overview also the model of perceptive connections per situation is given. The bar diagrams give an overview of all cumulated ratings of all participants. As said only successive situations are compared in which the expected values are the values of the first situation. The ratings of the second situation are considered the observed values. For all the compared situations the number of significance of, p, is smaller than 0,001. This indicates that there is a significant difference between the ratings of different situations.

Compared to situation 1 the user-involvement in situation 2 increases significantly (see figure 7). The subject is enabled in situation 2 to experience perceptual crossing with the designed object resulting in a greater feeling of involvement. In the situations 3 to 5 perceptual crossing between subject and object is possible but it differs if the perception of the event, music, can be shared or not. It is clear that perceptual crossing between the subject and object and of the event, situation 4, results in the greatest user-involvement. However we can see that although perception of the event cannot be shared in situation 5 the level of user involvement does differ remarkably to the user-involvement in situation 3. In situation 3 PeP is able to perceive something the subject does not. In situation 5 the subject is able to perceive something the object does not perceive. The fact that the subject is able to perceive the music but can't share this perception with PeP is of less influence on the subject's feeling of involvement than when he or she is not able to perceive and share the perception of the event that PeP does perceive.

The comparison between situation 2 and 3 is different from the so far discussed comparisons. In both situations perceptual crossing between subject and object is possible but in situation 3 the object perceives an event the subject does not perceive. The user-involvement decreases significantly in situation 3 compared to situation 2.

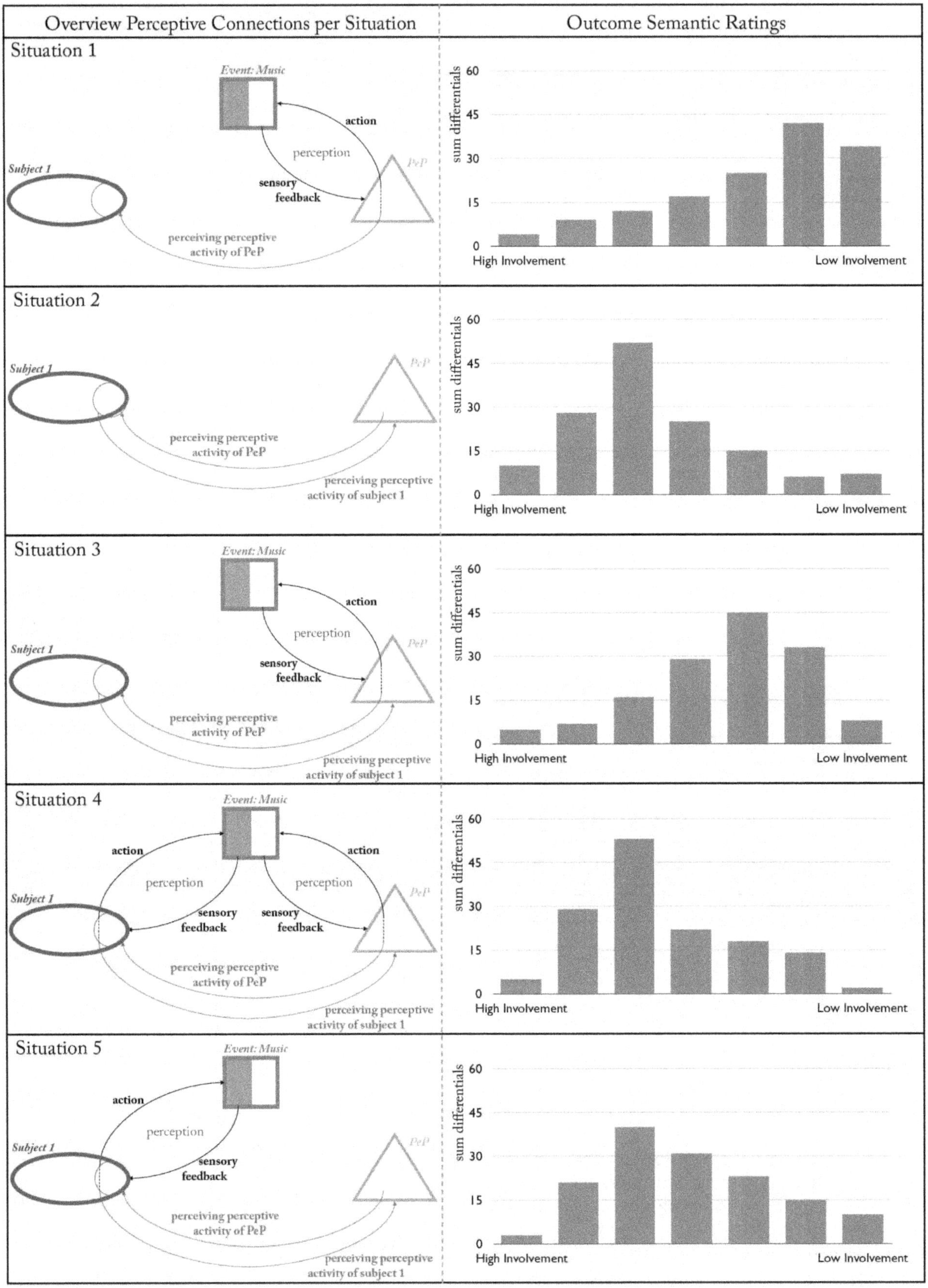

Figure 7. Left: model on perceptive connections per situation. Right: sum of differentials (n=13) over all participants (n=12) for each of the seven scales (high-low involvement)

It seems that the subject does not perceive PeP's perceptive activity as related to perceiving music. If the subject was able to relate PeP's perceptive activity to perceiving music, the subject as it were could perceive 'through' the designed artifact. It is like when we see someone dancing to music we don't hear ourselves. If indeed the subject can perceive 'through' the designed artifact the subject is able to become aware of events that the subject does not or is not capable of perceiving directly oneself. This refers back to the work of Bach-y-Rita, on sensory substitution systems [2,3]. Direct sensory mediation gives a person the ability to perceive objects and events, that one was not able to perceive by one's perceptive capabilities, in these systems. In the experimental situation described here this mediation indirectly happens through the object by means of its perceptive activity.

CONCLUSION

The experiment shows the relation between user involvement and perceptive product activity. Our hypotheses and designs are grounded in phenomenological and ecological perception theories. Recent research in this field showed the importance in subject-subject interaction of perceiving not only the other as part of the environment but also perceiving the activity of the other perceiving me [15]. To design for perceptual crossing between subject and object, we started from three components of perceptive activity; the perception of presence, perception of perceptive action and perception of expressivity to direct our designing.

Our design is an example of designed perceptive activity. PeP reacts to the activity of the subject and to music by means of a dynamic light design. Our experiment shows that indeed it is possible to design perceptive activity in an object to allow for perceptual crossing between subject and object and for sharing the perception of an event. We show that this indeed positively influences the feeling of involvement of the user.

We now end our paper with a set of design notions that need consideration when designing for perceptive activity in an artifact. The design notions will be validated in our future design research.

DESIGN NOTIONS

The first four design notions were explicitly considered in our final design of PeP. The last three notions came forward after analysis of our design and the experiment. For each notion is discussed why the notion is considered, how the notion is implemented in the current design and what the implications are for our future design and research.

Focus the Senses

Living organisms typically focus their senses, e.g. you close your eyes and turn your ear in the direction of the sound. In similar fashion, upon detecting presence, the light body in the design of PeP moves into the direction of the presence, as it detects movement, and increases in size and brightness. In living organisms action and sensory feedback are directly coupled. Challenging for future work is to couple the sensory and active parts of the design as direct as possible in the algorithm, improving the *embodiment of the sensing and acting body*.

Active Behavior Object

Living organisms act to gain sensory input on the environment, e.g. you turn your body and head to look around the room to see whether someone is there. The light body in our design also moves around, exploring the sensor sides for intentional subjects. When the body has detected presence, it will give the impression that it actively explores the subject [16]. The light body focuses in the direction of the subject and makes little movements from left to right to explore the subject. In the current design these implementations are really just an impression; by doing so the light body does not really explore. These actions should be come more than pre-programmed movements. In further work we will try to give the design its own intentions depending on the situation; *perceptually motivated perceptive activity.*

Subtleness

The actions we undertake to perceive are smooth; we turn our head in a continuous movement to look at what is behind us. This subtleness of not jumping between sides is implemented in the design. In the shape and movements of the light body, the following decisions were taken. The center of the shape is brighter than the edges. Changes happen exponentially instead of linear to create a more gradual and natural effect. All LEDs have an analogue range and can fade in and out. If the body were to move from north to south, the body moves either along west or east instead of directly jumping from north to south. In our future design we will focus on balancing the aesthetics of the behavior, electronics and physical appearance of PeP.

Reaction to external event

While interacting with another subject we build a common space in an environment. This environment influences and shapes our interaction. PeP is capable to perceive an external event, namely music. PeP focuses on the music and expresses meaning by bouncing to the beat. This addition of an event is very interesting from a designerly point of view because the question if the subject has the feeling of sharing a common space with the design can be explored. The user can be enabled, as discussed in the results section, to perceive 'through' the design.

Active Behavior Subject

In the interaction not only the designed artifact shows perceptive activity, also the subject will show explorative actions to perceive. It should be these actions that are detected by the design to further enrich the behavior. PeP is already not just sensitive to the sensor input but to the change in sensor input. In other words it compares the forgoing measurement of the sensor with the present measurement. This makes PeP sensitive to movement and holding still will result in no longer being detected as an intentional subject (lived-body) but as object in the environment (body-image). Perceptual crossing cannot longer occur and the light body looses focus. In our further research we will focus on detecting the actions by the subject in more detail and on differentiating these actions.

Contextual Noise

When one is in dialogue with someone, one's perception is focused on the person one is talking to. However this neither means there is no contextual sensory input, nor does it mean that one does not undertake any action to get other sensory input. Especially when the sensory input reaches a certain level, for example when something makes a lot of noise or moves sudden and quick one will perceive and react to this event. The design of PeP makes use of light sensors. This amount of light is changed by the presence of the subject as the subject causes a shadow to fall on the sensor. Not every side of the design is equally exposed to the light and so the effect the subject causes might differ for each sensors. Furthermore a change of light, not caused by the subject, influences the behaviour of PeP. We found that this gives a natural feel to the behaviour. However this also makes the design less controllable. One should consider this effect and weigh it to the control one has over the design.

Course of perceptions in time

In our experience of the world we are aware of bygone perception and anticipate future perception. PeP has no clue of its own perception, in other words it does not rely on history or anticipate on what could happen next. A challenge is to include this kind of learning algorithms in the design and give the design as it were an experience. The richness of actions and expressivity in relation to the subject's activity will be enhanced.

DISCUSSION

One of the most interesting points of our design is that by designing perceptive behavior the object could become an interface for more than just one function. PeP for example could not only react to music and presence of a subject but also to bygone activity or host of other events. We also think that not only the direct interaction between subject and object is interesting, also perceptive activity between objects could become recognizable and understandable to the subject. By integrating this perceptive activity of objects into the space we work and live in [6] activity between different artifacts in an environment become perceptible to the user.

Deliberately designing from the point of view that perception is inherently interactive and participatory makes that the designed object's actions express meaning to the subject. This emergent meaning we have seen in tangible approaches [9, 26].

We now move to a dynamic interface that can adapt to multiple events, in time and to multiple user(s). Here lies the interest of our future work where we are moving from designing for interaction between user and product to designing for systems of interactive products.

REFERENCES

1. Abram, D., The spell of the Sensuous: Language and Perception in a More Than Human World. Vintage Books, New York, NY, USA 1996.
2. Bach-y-Rita, P., Tyler, M.E., Kaczmarek, K.A., Seeing with the Brain, Int. J. of Hum-Comput. Int. (2003), pp 285-295.
3. Bach-y-Rita, P., Substitution sensorielle et qualia. In J. Proust (Ed.), Perception et intermodalité. Approches actuelles de la questions de Molyneux Paris, PUF (1997), 81-100.
4. Dalsgaard P., Hansen, L.K., Performing Perception-Staging Aesthetics of Interaction, Transactions on Computer Human Interaction, 15(3) Article 13, 2008, ACM
5. Deckers, E., Westerhoff, J., Pikaart, M., Wanrooij, G.v., Overbeeke, C., How Perception Gets Emotional Value Through the Use of an Object. Proc. DPPI, 2009, 104-115
6. Deckers, E.J.L., Wensveen, S.A.G., Overbeeke, C.J., PeR: Designing for perceptive qualities, Proc. DeSForM 2010, 68-70
7. DiSalvo, C. F., Gemperle, F., Forlizzi, J., Kiesler, S., All robots are not created equal: The design and perception of humanoid robot heads, Proc. DIS 2002
8. Dourish, P., Where the action is: The foundation of embodied interaction. Cambridge, Massachusetts: MIT-Press, 2001
9. Frens, J., Designing for rich interaction: integrating form, interaction, and function. Doctoral Dissertation, Eindhoven University of Technology, 2006
10. Gibson, J. (1979). An ecological approach to visual perception (Repr. 1986.). London: Lawrence Erlbaum Associates.
11. Hallnäs, L., Redström J., From use to presence: on the expressions and aesthetics of everyday computational things, Transactions on Computer-Human Interaction (TOCHI), 9/2 (2002), 106-124.
12. Hornecker E., Buur, J., Getting a grip on tangible interaction: a framework on physical space and social interaction, Proc. CHI 2006, 437-446
13. Hummels, C., Overbeeke, C., & Klooster, S., Move to get moved: a search for methods, tools and knowledge to design for expressive and rich movement-based

interaction. Personal and Ubiquitous Computing, 11/8 (2007), 677-690.

14. Koskinen, I., Binder, T. and Redström, J. Lab, Field, Gallery, and Beyond. Artifact, 2/1 (2009), 46—57

15. Lenay, C., Thouvenin, I., Guénand, A., Gapenne, O., Stewart, J., Maillet, B., et al., Designing the ground for pleasurable experience. Proc. DPPI 2007, 35-58.

16. Lenay, C., "It's so touching"; Emotional value in distal contact. International Journal of Design, 4/2 (2010), 14-26.

17. Loke, L., & Robertson, T., Studies of dancers: Moving from experience to interaction design. International Journal of Design, 4/2 (2010), 39-54

18. Marti, P., Perceiving while being perceived. International Journal of Design, 4/2 (2010), 27-38.

19. Merleau-Ponty, M., Phenomenology of Perception (Original: Phénoménologie de la perception 1945). (D. Tiemersma & R. Vlasblom). Boom.

20. Moen J., Towards People Based Movement Interaction and KinAesthetic Interaction Experiences, Proc Critical Computing: Between Sense and Sensibility 2005, ACM Press, 121-124

21. Osgood, C., Suci, G., & Tannenbaum, P., The measurement of meaning, University of Illinois Press, 1956

22. Robertson, T., The Public Availability of actions and artefacts, Computer Supported Cooperative Work 11, 3-4 (2002), 299-316.

23. Svanœs, D., Understanding Interactivity, Steps to a Phenomenology of Human-Computer Interaction, Doctoral Dissertation, NTNU Trondheim, 2000

24. Schiphorst T., soft(n): Toward a Somaesthetics of Touch, Proc CHI Extended Abstracts 2009, pp. 2427

25. Siegel, S., Nonparametic Statistics for the behavioral sciences, p249, Mc-Graw Hill, 1956

26. Wensveen, S., A Tangibility Approach to Affective Interaction, Doctoral Dissertation, Delft University of Technology, 2005

27. Winograd, T., and Flores F., Understanding Computers and Cognition: A New Foundation for Design, Ablex Publishing Corporation, Norwood, NJ, 1986.

28. Zimmerman, J., Stolterman, E. & Forlizzi, J., An analysis and critique of Research through Design: towards a formalization of a research approach. Proc. DIS2010, ACM Press, 310-319

Limits of Rereadability in Procedural Interactive Stories

Alex Mitchell and Kevin McGee
Communications and New Media Programme
National University of Singapore
Singapore
{alexm,mckevin}@nus.edu.sg

ABSTRACT
The paper investigates the limits of what authors can vary procedurally to encourage and reward rereadability in procedural hypertext fiction. Exploring these issues raises a methodological challenge: how do we study *re*-reading in the context of stories that change? We have developed an adapted form of the Piagetan *clinical interview* to do this. Using this approach, we have determined that readers, surprisingly, do *not* want to experience endless variation when rereading interactive stories. Instead, they are looking for some form of *closure*, either in terms of "understanding the story", reaching the "best ending" for the characters in the story, or finding the "most interesting" version of the story. This has implications for the design/authoring of interactive stories and interactive art and entertainment.

Author Keywords
rereadability, procedural hypertext, interactive storytelling, narrative closure, qualitative research methodologies

ACM Classification Keywords
H.5.4 Information Interfaces and Presentation: Hypertext/ Hypermedia

General Terms
Experimentation, Human Factors

INTRODUCTION
Interactive storytelling research tends to focus on the goal of creating *variability* in interactive stories – and on handling the attendant problems of narrative coherence and consistency. This focus comes from an implicit assumption that people want to re-experience interactive stories, and that variability, both as an inherent property of the system and as an expression of user agency, will form both an encouragement and a reward for repeated experiences of the work.

But a simple example highlights some problematic issues. Many people have a strong desire to rewatch M. Night Shyamalan's film *The Sixth Sense*. Many of the reasons for this can be undermined if the film dynamically changed in a number of ways. Similarly, it would frustrate the desire of many people to tell a friend, "you should watch *The Sixth Sense*" if they knew that the film would be significantly different for their friend. And for someone who wanted to rewatch the film *with* a friend who had not seen it, the experience would be even more frustrating.

These examples illustrate that the use of procedural change – variability – to encourage and reward rereading is complex and involves a number of narrative and technical constraints and challenges.

The remainder of this paper is structured as follows. We begin with a brief review of work that has attempted to understand and address these challenges. This is followed by a discussion of the research problem, and the method we have adopted to study these issues. We then discuss in detail our observations, and the implications of these observations for encouraging and rewarding rereading. We conclude by summarizing the implications of these observations for the limits of procedural rereadability in hypertext fiction.

RELATED WORK
Although there has been some work to discuss rereading from a literary critical perspective, there has been little work done to empirically study rereadability in either traditional or interactive stories.

There have been some empirical studies of rereading in non-interactive fiction. The area in which the most empirical work has been done is that of what is often referred to as "anomalous suspense": the fact that the reader/viewer still experiences some degree of suspense even when rereading/ rewatching a story [3, 4, 8].

In the field of hypertext fiction, rereadability has been seen as a key feature of the form [1, 2, 6]. In fact, Bernstein suggests that "hypertextuality is perceived through rereading and reflection" [2, p. 2], and "hypertext structure is perceived through *recurrence*... [r]ecurrence is the essence of hypertext" [2, p. 4]. It is only through repeated readings of a hypertext story that the reader can see the consequences of choices, in the variations that are a result of these choices. This notion of repetition, and the resulting juxtaposition of variations of the plot, is celebrated as a strength of hypertext. As Bernstein says, "A film must usually choose one plot or the other, but a hypertext can contrive to tell both." [2, p. 5]

Empirical studies of hypertext fiction have focused on reading, rather than rereading. Dobson and Miall have conducted a number of studies of literary hypertext [11, 13]. These studies largely involve creating a "simulated" hypertext from an existing literary short story, creating the illusion of links and choice while actually preserving the linearity and repeatability of the reading experience, for the purpose of maintaining the ability to compare reactions across subjects within the study. Taking a more naturalistic approach, Pope [17] has conducted a detailed study of readers' responses to hypertext, making use of a combination of free reading and verbal protocols, questionaires, and focus groups to access readers' responses to the works.

There has been little work to study procedural change and readers' responses to variability either in hypertext fiction or in other forms of interactive storytelling. Mitchell [14] presents the results of an initial investigation into rereadability in text-based interactive fiction, suggesting a series of motivations for rereading based on a close reading of Short et. al.'s *Alabaster*. Knickmeyer and Mateas [10] study players' responses to Mateas and Stern's interactive drama *Facade* through the use of retrospective protocol analysis. Dow et. al. [7] studied engagement and presence in several variations of *Facade* using a combination of player observation and interviews.

RESEARCH PROBLEM

As can be seen in the above review of the related work, although there has been work looking at the theoretical issues surrounding rereadability in traditional (non-interactive) stories, there has been little empirical work in this area. The majority of the empirical studies of rereading have looked specifically at the issue of "anomalous suspense". Similarly, in the area of interactive stories, although there has been discussion of the issue of rereading in hypertext fiction, there has been very little work done to study the actual experience of reading, let alone rereading, hypertext fiction or other forms of interactive stories. The few empirical studies that have looked at hypertext fiction and interactive drama have not specifically addressed either the issue of rereading, or the notion of procedural change and variability as it relates to rereading.

Since we are looking at *procedural* hypertext fiction, in which the text, and links between fragments of text, may vary procedurally between readings, to understand what techniques can be used to encourage and reward rereading, we first need to understand *what we can vary* as a reader re-encounters a text. These limitations on variability are the focus of our current study. This paper investigates ways that authors can (and cannot) use procedural variability to encourage rereading in procedural hypertext fiction.

Our initial hypothesis, based on the theoretical discussions of hypertext fiction cited above, is that readers of hypertext fiction will attempt to exhaustively follow *all* links that they find, in the pursuit of variation – and procedural changes will be rejected/accepted to the degree they violate or thwart this. Our study systematically investigates ways in which this goal can be thwarted, and how readers respond to these attempts to disrupt rereading. This highlights some of the things authors can, and cannot, vary procedurally and still maintain rereadability.

METHOD

We want to understand what people think they are doing as they read, and reread, procedural hypertext fiction, with the goal of determining the boundaries of what authors can (and cannot) do in terms of variability to maintain rereadability. Exploring these issues raises a methodological challenge: how do we study rereading in the context of stories that *change*?

Techniques have been developed for empirically investigating literary appreciation and other aspects of reading literature [3, 5, 12]. These generally involve having subjects read a traditional, static text. Those which involve interactive stories (hypertext) are careful to ensure that the text experienced by subjects is identical [13], or focus on general issues of appreciation and reader response, without focusing specifically on rereading [17].

In contrast, we want to look at how readers respond to *procedural change* in hypertext. This is problematic, as we want to be able to look at how people are behaving in a situation where the system they are interacting with is *changing* as a result of their actions. What they encounter as they read, and reread, may not be the same between subjects, or even between readings by the *same* subject. Since the text itself is changing, we need to find something else that can be held constant.

This situation is remarkably similar to a situation that Piaget was studying in children – the cognitive processes that are at work in the face of changing problems [16]. This suggests that an adapted form of the Piagetan *clinical interview* [9] would be an appropriate methodology to use to investigate rereading in procedural hypertext fiction. The clinical interview is a flexible interview in which the researcher has subjects perform tasks, and then attempts to look for contradictions in the ways that the subjects explain their actions. Starting from some standard tasks, the researcher is free to modify the tasks in response to, and to more clearly understand, the subject's reactions. The changes to the tasks that a subject is given are often carefully chosen to create cognitive dissonance, revealing the ways in which the subject is thinking. The constant factor, which the researcher is trying to uncover, is *how the subject is solving problems.*

Our claim is that, to study rereading in the context of a dynamic, procedurally varied text, we need to understand what it is that readers *think they are doing* when they reread a story - what are their expectations, and how would these expectations possibly be violated by procedural variation. This will enable us to understand what authors can (and cannot) do when designing rereadable, procedural hypertext fiction. What is actually being held constant in this situation is *what the readers think that they are doing* as they read/reread.

In our study, we adopted an approach that is very similar to the clinical interview as described above: we started with a standard task of reading two simple hypertext stories, and then varied the stories in ways which were designed to thwart the readers' desire to follow all links. By probing the readers' reactions to these obstacles to their intentions, we were able to gain insight into the thoughts and motivations underlying the readers' explanations for their actions.

The Study Design

Using a modified version of the Piagetan clinical interview, we studied the ways in which a group of 12 readers (3 male and 9 female, ages 20-24) responded to variations of two hypertext stories, focusing on what they claimed to be doing as they read, and reread, the text, and how they responded to procedural variation of the text during rereading. The subjects were drawn from an undergraduate research methods class, and the subjects were given academic credit for participating in the study.

We constructed two simple hypertext stories using HypeDyn [15], representing the two most common ways in which authors structure hypertext fiction: those where links correspond to a choice of *action* within the story, and those where the links represent a choice of *perspective*. These two approaches can be seen as representing interaction at either the *story* or the *discourse* level. Both stories provided one choice between two or more links in the first node, each link leading to a different path through the story. The first story consisted of a total of three nodes in each path, including the first node, and the second story consisted of a total of two nodes in each path, including the first node.

For each story, we had subjects first read through the story once. Immediately before the subject made the choice in the first node, we asked them *what they were doing* when making the choice. Comparisons were given to, for example, buying tickets on an online movie booking website. We then asked them to read through to the end of the story. At that point, we:

1. asked for their initial reaction to the story, and
2. asked if they want to reread, and why.

To begin to understand what they *thought* they were doing as they read, and reread, the story, we then proceeded to introduce a series of hypothetical variations on the story, based on a strategy of constantly *thwarting* their possible motivations to reread the story. The intention here was to see how they react to these attempts to thwart their motivations, with an aim to foreground those motivations. This is similar to the process of identifying cognitive dissonance in a clinical interview as a means of exposing the subject's cognitive processes.

Based on our hypothesis, people should think that they are "following different paths", with the intention to "see everything". This suggests that as long as there is another unfollowed path available, they will want to take it. We wanted to block these attempts in various ways, and see how they reacted. More importantly, we wanted to see how they would explain these reactions, and whether there would be any contradictions in their explanations.

Going into the sessions, we had the following plan for thwarting readers' intentions to follow every available path:

1. make the already-followed path enticing through a "reframing" or twist ending,
2. make the not-yet-followed path seem less "interesting" by revealing what will be seen down the not-yet-seen path,
3. procedurally block whichever path has not been followed, and
4. make it so that it is impossible to follow all paths, by repeatedly adding more links, and either promising that these links will lead to better or worse variations, or by promising that revisiting previous links will always result in different text being shown.

Although we have chosen two relatively simple stories for our study, the subsequent variations contain much more than two links, in the extreme case presenting possibly limitless links to the reader. As the variations were presented to the subjects, we asked them whether they wanted to continue to follow the new links, and how these attempts to stop them from seeing everything made them feel.

We will now discuss the results of the study.

DISCUSSION

From our study, we made the following surprising observations:

1. Although readers did want to reread to follow unfollowed links, they did not do this for long. After only a few rereadings, they came to a point where they no longer felt that it was worth continuing.
2. Readers appeared to be *trying to arrive at something* – rather than simply exploring possible variations, they were goal-oriented, looking for some form of closure, whether this was in the form of the "best ending for their character", an "understanding of what the story was about", or the "most exciting/interesting version of the story".

These observations point towards limitations on what authors can vary procedurally and still maintain rereadability.

We will now discuss the results of the study in detail, and suggest implications for what authors can, and cannot, vary procedurally in interactive stories.

Following Links – But Not For Long

Our initial hypothesis was that readers will want to follow all links as long as these links have not yet been visited. At the end of each of the stories, readers were presented with a link, labelled *reread?* At this point, we asked them if they want to reread the story, and why. We observed that readers did, indeed, want to follow unfollowed links, often giving these links priority over other, presumably more attractive but already followed links. However, after a short while, readers stopped following links.

The Desire to Follow the Unfollowed Link

For the first story, ten of the twelve subjects stated that they wanted to go back and follow the unfollowed link. The two subjects who did not want to follow the unfollowed link both stated that they didn't understand the ending of the story, and wanted to reread the same path to try to figure out what went wrong or what they had missed. For the remaining subjects, they all claimed that they wanted to follow the link that they had not followed in their first reading of the story.

For example, when subject 7 was asked if she wanted to go back and read again, she replied:

> *Subject 7*: I want to try the other option.
> *Researcher*: Oh, why do you want to choose the other option?
> *Subject 7*: Because I want to see what the ending is like.
> *Researcher*: What do you expect to see?
> *Subject 7*: I think it will be different.
> (10:50)

In the second story, all subjects said that they would indeed want to reread. One subject said that he'd actually reread the same path, as he felt the other link wasn't going to add much, and instead he wanted to see the story more clearly by rereading. All the remaining subjects wanted to read the unfollowed link.

This appears to support our hypothesis that readers will always want to follow unfollowed links. To explore this further, we set out to attempt to thwart the desire to follow unfollowed links by making use of a number of different techniques.

Reframing to Thwart the Desire to Follow Unfollowed Links

The first technique used in the story was an attempt to create a *reframing* at the end of the text. Using *The Sixth Sense* as a model, we structured the story such that the ending undermines the reader's initial reading of the story, and changes the way that the reader perceives, and feels about, the main character in the story. The first page of the story presents a scenario where the main character, at home alone, hears kidnappers breaking into the house. The choice, of whether the character should make a break for the front door or stay quiet and hide in the kitchen, leads to a second page, where in both cases he is caught by the kidnappers, although he stabs one of them in the process.

The third page reverses the reader's understanding, revealing that the police who are responding to the disturbance are concerned about a situation where a family is trying to subdue their son, who has apparently gone crazy. This reveals the kidnappers to actually be the main character's family, whom he imagines to be strangers breaking into the house. Note that both paths which the reader could take ultimately lead back to the same third page.

We intended this reframing to act as an encouragement for the reader to go back and reread the *same* passage that they had just read, as they may want to see the text a second time now that they know something they didn't originally know.

Despite the presence of the reframing at the end of the story, readers still insisted that they wanted to go back to *follow the unfollowed link*.

For example, when asked why she didn't want to re-read the first path, subject 6 said:

> *Subject 6*: If I choose the first scenario, I know what's going to happen. If I choose the first scenario, nothing's going to happen. And now for me as, like, I'll be looking at it, if I read again I want to see more stuff happening.
> (08:16)

Here, subject 6 clearly wants to see something she hasn't seen before.

Interestingly, although subject 7 had originally said that she wanted to follow the unfollowed link, when asked again later in the study, she said she would want to reread:

> *Subject 7*: The part where he grabbed the knife.
> *Researcher*: So how would that be different?
> *Subject 7*: Because a usual boy wouldn't, you know, grab the knife to murder someone.
> *Researcher*: But you didn't find it strange the first time.
> *Subject 7*: No [laughs]
> *Researcher*: Why is that?
> *Subject 7*: Um, because I thought its like self-defense, its something that's close to him and he grabbed it.
> *Researcher*: And now?
> *Subject 7*: Now I think, umm [pauses] he just wants to kill someone.
> *Researcher*: Hmm, so you think the reason for grabbing the knife is very different?
> *Subject 7*: Yeah.
> *Researcher*: Would you want to read that part again?
> *Subject 7*: Yeah! [laughs]
> *Researcher*: Ok, but previously you said that you would go back and do the different one, right?
> *Subject 7*: [nods]
> *Researcher*: So now you want to go back and read the same one again? or are you thinking that maybe he grabbed the knife in the other one as well?
> *Subject 7*: I would read through the original one that I clicked first, make sure I didn't miss out anything.
> (23:45)

Note that at this point in the study, as will be described below, the unfollowed link has been procedurally blocked, so that it *cannot* be clicked. The subject has apparently changed her mind, and now claims that she'd rather follow the previously followed, and currently unblocked, link. What is interesting here is that her justification for this preference is not that the previously followed link is unblocked, and is therefore the only available choice. Rather, she says that the unblocked, previously followed link is the more interesting choice, which contradicts her earlier response.

The researcher wanted to probe into this contradiction, to find out what the reader was thinking – why was she now saying she wanted to reread the same link? Did she still want to follow the unfollowed (and now blocked) link, or was the reframing really more enticing? To do this, he presented her with a slightly different dilemma:

> *Researcher*: So if you had a choice, if it was like this [resets system so that both links in first node are unblocked] if it wasn't blocked out when you came back, which one do you think is more interesting to do? What you just said, which is go back and read the same one again and think about the knife for example, or what about finding out what happens if he makes a break for the door?
> *Subject 7*: You mean after I read this?
> *Researcher*: Yes, so imagine you read through and came back and it wasn't blocked, so you could click on either link.
> *Subject 7*: I would click this [gestures to unfollowed link].
> *Researcher*: Even though you just said that its interesting to see that bit about the knife again and think about it?
> *Subject 7*: Yeah but I wanna know the other ending before I go back and look at the first one again.
> (25:34)

It appears that the reframing is indeed encouraging the reader to go back and reread the first link. However, when probed, subject 7 still felt that, if given the choice, following the unfollowed link was more interesting, *after* which she wanted to go back and follow the first link again.

Note that the type of dissonance present in this situation, where the subject is making a decision which appears to be in conflict with an earlier decision, is exactly the sort of occurance which forms the core of the clinical interview method. At this point, the subject's attempts to reconcile the contradiction between the current and the previous decision can reveal the underlying reasons for the subject's actions.

The use of a reframing at the end of the story was an attempt to thwart the reader's desire to follow all unfollowed links by providing a strong reason for the reader to want to go back and reread *the same version* of the story. However, subjects still wanted to follow unfollowed links, despite the change in understanding of the other path, and in the face of a desire to also reread the original path, as can be seen in the difficulty subject 7 had making a decision. This suggests that our hypothesis that following unfollowed links is the main reason for rereading still holds.

Thwarting by Revealing Outcome

A second way that we attempted to thwart the reader's desire to visit all unfollowed links was to reveal the outcome of unfollowed links *before* the link was followed. Note that this suggestion was made before the "reread?" link was clicked.

The idea behind this variation was to see how subjects responded to the possibility that they *already know* what they will see when presented with unfollowed links. If our hypothesis holds, then readers will *still* insist on following these links. In this case, we were interested in hearing their rationalization for this behaviour – if they already know the outcome, and their reason for saying they wanted to follow the unfollowed link was to find out "what happens" as a result of following that link, then why still insist on following the link, particularly in the face of the reframing, which should make the already-followed link at least somewhat tempting.

All but two of the readers claimed that they would still want to follow the unfollowed link, despite knowing what the path contained. When questioned, subjects insisted that they "wanted to see for themselves" what the path contained. They felt that it was the *details* of what happened that would be important, and that being told, in what they assumed would be a summary, was not enough.

One subject in particular stressed that the exact wording of the story might reveal information that would help her understand the story. According to subject 11:

> *Subject 11*: The way text is being written, the words they use, the description is quite important.
> (16:16)

When it was suggested that the unfollowed link would be *much less satisfying* than the original link, subjects still wanted to follow the link, again stating that they would want to "see for themselves" if it was better or worse. Interestingly, for subject 2, who was one of the two subjects who said that they would not follow the link if the outcome was revealed, he changed his mind when it was suggested that the unfollowed link would be less satisfying. He clarified that this was because he now assumed that the ending would be different – for him, it was whether or not the *ending* was the same that mattered:

> *Subject 2*: For me I'm more interested in like, the ending, the end result, like what happpens. Even though there's some variation in the process, if the end result is like the same, then I'm like, I don't really find it interesting any more since its going to be the same
> *Researcher*: What if the end result is definitely uninteresting?
> *Subject 2*: I guess then I'd follow it, since the end result is different, even though I find it boring its different.
> (25:46)

This suggests that readers do indeed feel the need to follow all links, not merely to have actually clicked on all the links, but to have actually traversed all the possible paths, and gained access to all possible information.

Thwarting by **Literally** *Blocking Choices*

The above attempts to thwart the reader's desire to follow all unfollowed links did not literally prevent the reader from following the link – instead, they attempted to either increase the reader's interest in following the previously followed link (reframing) or to make the unfollowed link less interesting (by revealing its contents). A more literal, and more clearly procedural, approach would be to actually *block* or disable the unfollowed link. In our stories, when the subject first makes a choice as to which path to follow, the system remembers which link was taken. Then, when the subject clicks on the "reread?" link to go back to the first page, the system disables whichever link was *not* previously followed.

At this point, we asked the subject how they felt. We had varying reactions, from mild frustration (subject 6) to "this is shitty!" (subject 10). All subjects except for the two who claimed that they wanted to reread the first link expressed disappointment that they were unable to follow the link that they had not yet seen. When then asked if they would instead go back to reread the first link, they still felt that this was not of interest, as they had "seen it before". Subjects seemed to have an expectation that they would be able to follow the other path, and were disappointed that this option had been removed.

For example, according to subject 2:

> *Subject 2*: So its like, I'm rereading it because I already, I don't see a need to actually correct my image because I already know this is describing kidnappers that are actually trying to help the boy because he's mentally unstable, so I'm actually rereading to see what the second option is all about, so now since the second option is actually blocked out, so I'm now like...
> *Researcher*: Would you try to follow the first link again?
> *Subject 2*: I would say on my very first thought that there's no point reading it any more.
> (16:55)

We next suggested that a *new* link would appear below the two existing links when the reader clicked on "reread?" The intention here was to see how they react to the new link, and to see if this makes up for the frustration of being unable to follow the second link. We wondered whether they would still want to go back to the second link, or would it be enough to follow *any* new link.

Subjects were somewhat less annoyed, claiming that they would, indeed, want to follow this new link, but that they were still disappointed that they couldn't follow the second link. Most said that this was because they had that second link in mind as they were reading the story, and had been planning on going back and trying it once they reached the end.

As subject 2 explained:

> *Subject 2*: At least I have some other thing to try other than what I've already chosen, but they're forcing me, I don't have the same choice as before.
> (18:32)

As a subtle variation on this technique, we suggested that the new link *replace*, rather than appear in addition to, the unfollowed link. This generally resulted in the same reaction. However, two subjects did say that this might not feel so bad, as they may not have clearly remembered the details of the unfollowed link. As subject 2 said:

> *Subject 2*: I think it will reduce the affect, because basically perhaps I won't remember the first choice, its like I'm not sure if that's the same as the first one, at least its different than trying to stay as quiet as possible.
> (21:07)

When Will They Stop Following Links?

Our initial hypothesis was that people will want to reread a hypertext *as long as there are unfollowed links.* When rereading, our hypothesis was that people are aiming for completeness, to make sure that they have seen everything and followed every link. This implies that as long as there is an unfollowed link, the reader will follow it.

The subjects' reactions to the thwarting of their attempts to follow an unfollowed link suggest that readers do indeed want to follow all unfollowed links. Even when presented with a strong reason for reading the previously followed link, with information on the contents of the unfollowed link, and when literally blocked from following the unfollowed link, they *still* wanted to follow the unfollowed link.

To investigate this further, we introduced a variation intended to make it *impossible to successfully follow all the links in the story*, by dynamically adding new links *every time* the story is reread. This means that there is no way that the reader could ever finish following new links.

We then asked subjects whether they would be interested in following these links. With the exception of the one subject who said he had no interest in following any new links, all the subjects said that yes, they would like to follow the new links, for the same reasons that they gave in the initial presentation of a second link. When we probed further, reminding the subject that each time they followed a link, another would appear, they admitted that they would "eventually" give up. When pushed as to when they would stop, they tended to give an arbitrary number, such as 5.

For example, according to Subject 4:

> *Subject 4*: If there are like 3, 5 maximum, if it goes any bigger than 5, then I'd just give up on the story.
> (18:12)

Asked to clarify how they would make this decision to stop, most subjects mentioned some variation of noticing repetition or "not getting anything new" from the links. Subject 4's explanation was as follows:

> *Subject 4*: Yes, I would go on until I get bored. If its repeating the same scenario again in different words I might get bored.
> (23:01)

The above observations show that, as we had originally hypothesized, readers do indeed want to follow unfollowed links, and do so even in the face of other techniques, such as reframing, which should make the already-followed link more enticing. Readers are frustrated when their desire to follow the unfollowed links is thwarted, for example by procedurally blocking the unfollowed link. However, as seen above, readers report that they *would* stop reading after a few iterations. This is quite different from what we originally believed.

We will now discuss our observations as to what readers claim that they are doing as they read and as they reread, and how this connects to their reasons for stopping.

Rereading to Arrive At Something

Readers tended to stop rereading, even when there were unfollowed links, which did not match our initial hypothesis. When pushed for further explanations, and coupled with what readers said they were doing as they clicked on links, it became clear that readers were *rereading to arrive at something* – a "good ending" for the main character, a clear understanding of the story, or some explanation as to "what really happened". They tended to stop either when they felt they had reached this goal, or when that goal came to seem unattainable. We will now discuss the observations that led to this conclusion.

What Do People Think They're Doing As They Are Reading?

To begin with, we need to understand what readers felt they were doing as they read the story and made choices as to which link to follow.

In the first node of both stories, readers were initially presented with two choices. As the subject was about to click on one of the links, we asked the subject how they would describe what they were about to do. In the story that presents a choice of action, readers claimed to be either choosing the "safest" option for the character, choosing the option which they felt would be "most interesting" in terms of creating an entertaining story, or choosing the option most likely to reveal more information which will help the reader understand what is happening in the story.

For example, according to Subject 4:

> *Subject 4*: I was trying to guess what would happen, I'm trying to find the perfect ending.
> *Researcher*: So how would you know when it's the perfect ending?
> *Subject 4*: It just kind of feels right, its more subjective, something rational, there's a cause to it, I hate when it so abruptly ends, there's no closure to the whole thing.
> (14:45)

In this case, the reader was trying to get some form of "good" ending and a sense of closure.

For Subject 3, the focus was more on helping the character to survive:

> *Subject 3*: I chose to remain quiet, I think its the smarter way, because they're armed [pause] it's the smarter way for the character.
> (12:26)

The second story involved a choice of perspective. The first page of the story presents a scenario where two characters, a man and a woman, are having dinner. The woman pays, and outside the restaurant the couple argue, and then drive home in silence. The reader is initially given a choice to hear what happened according to either the man or the woman.

In this story, readers described what they were doing as either choosing the person they most "identified with", choosing the person whose perspective they felt would be "most interesting" based on the context, or choosing the person they felt would add the most information to their understanding of the story.

For example, Subject 12 chose to follow the link describing the man's perspective, because she felt it would give her more information to help her understand the story:

> *Subject 12*: I saw the woman she's like paying with her credit card, and there's nothing about the guy, so yeah it makes me want to know like, maybe the fight started because he has some, uh, ideas about something and I want to find out.
> (12:30)

Readers had many explanations for making a choice between the two links in the first node of the story. However, all the explanations appear to be describing a careful choice which, rather than simply involving an attempt to "see everything", appears to be working towards a specific goal or end-point. This goal-oriented behaviour can also be seen in the subjects' descriptions of what they thought they were doing as they *reread* the stories.

At the point when the reader has already clicked on the "reread?" link, we probed them again as to what they were doing when clicking on a link, given that previously they had explained that they were either making a choice that seemed best for the main character, looking for the "best" story in terms of the dramatic impact, or trying to find out as much as possible about the story.

Some subjects continued to claim the same motivation. Others, however, responded differently. For example, one subject, who had initially claimed to be thinking about the choice from the point of view of the main character, now said he was looking for a dramatically interesting story. He claimed that it was only during that first choice that he was concerned about the fate of the character – after that, his focus shifted to exploring all the possibilities for a satisfying story, where satisfaction was defined in terms of the storytelling rather than the outcome for the character. Whether their explanation changed or remained consistent with their original motivation, all subjects described a goal that they were working towards.

Reasons For Stopping

In an attempt to clarify this situation, where subjects seem willing to follow unfollowed links, but at some point they stop, we introduced several slight variations to our procedurally added links. Our intention was to figure out if there was some "stopping condition" that the subjects were using, and if so, what this condition might be.

For the first variation, we suggested that subsequent links would be "better" than the previous link. Note that we didn't define what we meant by "better", leaving this up to the subject to interpret. All but one subject said that they would continue to follow links as long as the resulting content was "better", but that they would still stop after several clicks. Most claimed that, although we insisted the story would "get better", they felt this was not possible, and that at some point it would "become predictable" or "start repeating". Even if it could somehow get "better", they felt that this would become almost insignificant.

When probed as to what they thought we meant when we said the story was "getting better", subjects had varying responses. These responses corresponded to their explanation as to why they wanted to reread.

In the "choose action" story, except for two subjects, all said they were looking for a *more interesting story* in terms of the dramatic impact and events that happened. Of the other two subjects, one didn't want to reread, and the other continued to look for the best choice for the character. Some mentioned that they were also looking for what "really" happened, referring back to the reframing and the revelation that the man was not actually being attacked by kidnappers.

In the "choose perspective" story, subjects said they were looking for a clearer understanding of "what happened", seeing each link as providing new perspectives on the story. However, they felt that simply giving "new" information was not enough, and that they would judge whether a link was worth following by how relevant they felt the new information would be to their understanding of the story. Some felt that providing new information that further reframed the story, such as suggestions of an affair between the couple, might increase their interest, but as long as it didn't "go too far" from the original story. Similarly, they tended to judge whether a link was worth following by "how close" the new pespective was to the original scenario: the waiter's perspective was usually important (although one subject said they already had his point of view as presented in the first page), whereas the couple at the next table were not so important, and somebody passing by outside was largely unimportant.

For example, according to subject 11, if offered the waiter's point of view:

> *Subject 11*: Yes I'd like to see it, but it won't give me the true reflection of the main characters, its like a third party view.
> (17:46)

However, she still might click on it, as:

> *Subject 11*: At least I have an option to listen to one more person's perspective [pause] like it forms part of the picture, like a jigsaw.
> (18:36)

For subject 11, reading the story was like putting together a puzzle, and new links were followed as long as they seemed to contribute to that puzzle.

In all these cases, it seems that the subjects feel they will reach a point where it "can't get any better", although they resisted the suggestion that they had actually seen the "best" version. The belief that it will become repetitive suggests that they feel that although there is the *possibility* of a better version, it wouldn't be better in any significant way.

For subject 8, reading the "choose perspective" story was all about getting to know the characters clearly. When told that new links would add complications to the story, she said:

> *Subject 8*: It might change how I feel towards the man, maybe the second layer that I want to know about the guy is what the character's like, so I hear from another person then I know what the character is about [pause] it gives more room for me to think about.
> *Researcher*: What if subsequent links continue to add depth to the character?
> *Subject 8*: I think I would, would stop when I hear enough, like if I'm more interested to know about the man's character, if I'm looking for one lead in the story then I would follow that.
> *Researcher*: When is it enough?
> *Subject 8*: Like you know the man's character then ok, so he's a philanderous person, then enough to the point that I can link back to the point that I know why he doesn't want to pay, he doesn't love his wife already, then that's enough.
> (23:10)

Similarly, we suggested a variation where each subsequent link is *worse* (by the subject's own measure of "better") than the previous. In this case, subjects said they would try "2 or 3" links, to see if there were any better links, and then stop.

This series of variations suggests a change to our original hypothesis. We had originally claimed that readers would want to follow *all* unfollowed links. Although our attempt to thwart this through reframing and revealing the contents of the link did not succeed, when there were limitless unfollowed links, it became clear that subjects were *looking for the "best" link*, limited by their concept of whether the links could actually improve beyond a certain point. This was the case in both the "choose action" and the "choose perspective" stories.

IMPLICATIONS: LIMITS ON PROCEDURAL CHANGE

The observations discussed above suggest certain limits on what authors can do in terms of procedural change and variation, if the author wants to maintain rereadability. We will now summarize the findings.

Our initial hypothesis was that readers of procedural hypertext fiction would continue to follow unfollowed links, in an attempt to explore all variations. When rereading, as we had expected, readers seemed to prioritize trying to follow unfollowed links over rereading followed links. Somewhat surprisingly, this desire to follow new links remained even in the face of reframing. However, what was more interesting, considering that most discussion of hypertext suggests that readers will continue to try to follow unfollowed links, was our discovery that readers claim that they would stop following new links quite soon, after 5-6 links, even if the new links are presented as more interesting than previously read links. It appears that readers feel that, after a certain point, it is highly unlikely that new links will continue to be more interesting, even if a "best" version has not yet been found.

We also saw that readers seemed to have been trying to arrive at a particular conclusion, based on what they felt that they were doing as they made choices in the story. Readers who were convinced that they would not get any further towards this goal, either because the links seemed not to be getting "better", or because they felt that it was not possible for the links to continue to improve, felt that they would stop rereading.

This behaviour is quite different from the notion of the reader who is willing to reread an interactive story to seek out variation for its own sake, or simply to compare the new reading with previous readings. In non-interactive stories, readers tend to be looking for closure, as this is a natural part of narrative. People also tend to be fairly goal-directed. With these two facts in mind, it isn't surprising that readers tend to be goal-directed and look for closure when reading, and rereading, procedural interactive stories. This desire for closure is consistent with what Pope observed in his studies of readers of several existing hypertext fictions [17].

These findings imply that, before trying to solve the problem of procedural variation in interactive stories, researchers first need to determine *what it is that readers really want* from procedural interactive stories. Although it can be argued that readers don't know what they want, and authors innovate all the time, this does not invalidate the need to understand how people actually respond to the new forms of storytelling that are being invented. Without some attention being paid to reader response, research into interactive storytelling risks focusing too much on technological solutions to problems that may not connect with the reader's actual experience of these works.

CONCLUSION

In this paper, we have discussed our investigation, through a series of clinical interviews, of the limitations which authors face when creating procedural variations in hypertext fiction. From this study, we derive insight into what can, and cannot, be varied procedurally to encourage rereading of procedural hypertext fiction. Surprisingly, we found that 1) although readers did want to read variations on either action or perspective, they *did not want to do this for very long*, and 2) readers appeared to be *trying to arrive at something* – a sense of "what actually happened", the "best ending" for the characters in the story, or a clear understanding of the narrative.

The desire for closure is not, on its own, surprising. What is surprising is that even in the case of narratives deliberately designed to foster and support multiple perspectives (or other authorial attempts to support something other than narrative closure), readers *still* have the goal of achieving narrative closure (which can take many forms), and that they stop reading when they feel they have reached this goal.

This is very different from the commonly held belief that readers of interactive stories are looking for continued variation, a belief which drives much of the technical research in the interactive storytelling community. The problem of procedurally generating variation on repeated experiences of a work, and maintaining consistency and coherence in the face of this variation, is usually seen as a way to solve the problem of the "explosion of branches" that results from manually creating variation. Our findings suggest that this may not, in fact, be the problem that needs to be addressed. Rather, work is first needed to understand *what readers are looking for* in repeated readings of a work. Only once this is understood can we begin to address the creative and technical challenges involved in satisfying what readers want from interactive stories.

This paper makes three significant contributions. First, we have presented a methodology, based on a modified version of the Piagetan clinical interview, for studying *rereading* in the context of interactive stories that change: namely, to focus on the *goals of rereading* (rather than, say, aspects of the story that remain constant). Second, by concentrating on *what people are doing* when they reread, we have also identified an important aspect of rereading in hypertext fiction: rather than simply exploring variations, readers are trying to reach the "best story" – even when the variant versions/stories are clearly framed as "alternate" versions. Finally, based on the evidence that people are searching for the "best version", we have identified a number of surprising limitations on the kinds of procedural change that re-readers will accept. For procedural stories that involve choosing from a set of options, whether these options are presented as links in a hypertext, text to be entered via a parser, or other ways of selecting from a range of possibilities, readers expect a sense of progression towards a goal. Variations which thwart movement towards this goal, such as the generation of seemingly unrelated stories or stories which contradict previous versions, will not be accepted. This places severe limitations on the types of variation which can be created procedurally.

It should be noted that we are deliberately taking a qualitative approach to our research, as the goal of this research is to understand what people care about, and what they are doing, as they reread procedural hypertext fiction. Quantitative studies will be important as a follow up to this study to provide support for generalizing these findings.

Beyond their implications to the creation of procedural interactive stories, the contributions discussed above are relevant to the wider CHI community. For example, when searching for a particular topic in an Internet search engine, users often type in a search string, and then follow some of the links. When returning to the original search, it is possible that the results may have changed. It isn't clear how a user will react to this – will they expect to be able to follow the "next" link? What if that link is no longer the same as it was on the previous search? What if the user sends the search results to a friend, and asks the friend to look at the second link? Similarly, if a user is browsing an e-commerce system which presents customized results to the user based on both the user's previous browsing and purchasing behaviour, and the behaviour of other users of the same site, there is no guarantee that what is available on, for example, a "recommendation" page, will be the same between visits. There is even less guarantee that a user will be able to make reference to what they've seen on the web page when discussing the site with a friend.

These implications can also be extended to various forms of art and entertainment, where there are attempts to procedurally generate different kinds of content or other aspects of the artwork. If subsequent experiences of an artwork, either by the same person or by a friend, result in the generation of variant versions, how can the participants engage in any form of meaningful discussion about the resulting aesthetic experience? Even if this lack of a stable reference point *is* the intention of the artist, it is worth considering the impact of procedural variation on the participants' experience.

The issue of how people react to these types of dynamic systems, and how these systems can be studied, is something that has not clearly been addressed, and is very similar to the issues discussed in this paper. Based on our observations of how people respond to procedural change in hypertext fiction, it is clear that people have certain expectations of how these systems will behave, expectations that may not match with the assumptions that researchers and developers have made. As these types of dynamic, adaptive systems are becoming more widespread, it is important that we know both how to study such systems, and how people respond to them.

ACKNOWLEDGMENTS

This work was funded under a Singapore-MIT GAMBIT Game Lab research grant, "Tools for Telling: How Game Development Systems Shape Interactive Storytelling."

REFERENCES

1. M. Bernstein. Patterns of hypertext. In *Proc. Hypertext '98*, pages 21–29, New York, NY, USA, 1998. ACM.
2. M. Bernstein. On hypertext narrative. In *Proc. Hypertext 2009*, New York, NY, USA, 2009. ACM.
3. W. F. Brewer. The nature of narrative suspense and the problem of rereading. In P. Vorderer, H. J. Wulff, and M. Friedrichsen, editors, *Suspense: conceptualizations, theoretical analyses, and empirical explorations*, pages 107–126. Routledge, 1996.
4. N. Carroll. The paradox of suspense. In P. Vorderer, H. J. Wulff, and M. Friedrichsen, editors, *Suspense: conceptualizations, theoretical analyses, and empirical explorations*, pages 71–91. Routledge, 1996.
5. P. Dixon, M. Bortolussi, L. C. Twilley, and A. Leung. Literary processing and interpretation: Towards empirical foundations. *Poetics*, 22(1-2):5 – 33, 1993.
6. J. Y. Douglas. *The End of Books - or Books Without End? Reading Interactive Narratives*. University of Michigan Press, 2001.
7. S. Dow, M. Mehta, E. Harmon, B. MacIntyre, and M. Mateas. Presence and engagement in an interactive drama. In *Proc. CHI 2007*, pages 1475–1484, , New York, NY, USA, 2007. ACM.
8. R. J. Gerrig. Suspense in the absence of uncertainty. *Journal of Memory and Language*, 28(6):633 – 648, 1989.
9. H. P. Ginsburg. *Entering the Child's Mind: The Clinical Interview in Psychological Research and Practice*. Cambridge University Press, 1997.
10. R. L. Knickmeyer and M. Mateas. Preliminary evaluation of the interactive drama Facade. In *CHI '05 extended abstracts*, pages 1549–1552, New York, NY, USA, 2005. ACM.
11. R. Luce-Kapler and T. Dobson. In search of a story: Reading and writing e-literature. *Reading Online*, 8(6), May/June 2005.
12. D. S. Miall. Readers' responses to narrative: Evaluating, relating, anticipating. *Poetics*, 19(4):323 – 339, 1990.
13. D. S. Miall and T. Dobson. Reading hypertext and the experience of literature. *Journal of Digital Information*, 2(1), 2001.
14. A. Mitchell. Motivations for rereading in interactive stories: A preliminary investigation. In R. Aylett, M. Lim, S. Louchart, P. Petta, and M. Riedl, editors, *Proc. ICIDS 2010*, pages 232–235. Springer Berlin / Heidelberg, 2010.
15. A. Mitchell and K. McGee. Designing hypertext tools to facilitate authoring multiple points-of-view stories. In *Proc. Hypertext 2009*, pages 309–316, New York, NY, USA, 2009. ACM.
16. J. Piaget. *The child's conception of the world*. Rowman & Littlefield Pub Inc, 2007.
17. J. Pope. Where Do We Go From Here? Readers' Responses to Interactive Fiction: Narrative Structures, Reading Pleasure and the Impact of Interface Design. *Convergence*, 16(1):75–94, 2010.

Rigid Structures, Independent Units, Monitoring: Organizing Patterns in Frontline Firefighting

Sebastian Denef
Fraunhofer FIT and TU Delft
Schloss Birlinghoven
53754 Sankt Augustin
Germany
sebastian.denef@fit.fraunhofer.de

David V. Keyson
TU Delft
Landbergstraat 15
2628 CD Delft
The Netherlands
d.v.keyson@tudelft.nl

Reinhard Oppermann
Fraunhofer FIT
Schloss Birlinghoven
53754 Sankt Augustin
Germany
reinhard.oppermann@fit.fraunhofer.de

ABSTRACT
Providing firefighters working on the frontline of interventions with ubiquitous computing support remains an open challenge. Designing meaningful solutions for this complex work environment requires reflective thought and conceptual understanding of its social configuration. This paper presents organizing patterns of firefighting frontline practice as a means to inform ubiquitous computing design processes. The patterns originate from a qualitative analysis of an extensive range of user studies conducted with French and German firefighters. As the patterns show, firefighting on the frontline is based on a rigid structure that gains its flexibility through independent units whose safety is ensured by a number of monitoring activities. We conclude that the interaction between the presented patterns forms a balanced whole and needs to be recognized by ubiquitous computing design.

Author Keywords: **Ubiquitous Computing, Firefighting, Ethnography, Safety-Critical Work, Pattern Research**

ACM Classification Keywords
H.5.3 Information interfaces and presentation (e.g., HCI): Group and Organization Interfaces – Collaborative computing, Computer-supported cooperative work
H.1.2 Models and principles: User/Machine Systems – Human factors

General Terms: Human Factors

INTRODUCTION
Fighting fire is a task carried out in a hazardous and dynamic environment. The work on the frontline of an intervention requires a set of specific skills and tools. It is often conducted in buildings full of smoke, which the firefighter can only access equipped with protective clothing, breathing apparatus, and by crawling on the floor due to the heat distribution in a room—a work environment very different from everyday experiences (Figure 1).

Figure 1: Firefighter in Training Environment

Bringing the seminal work of Weiser [39] out of the offices and homes into the wild, researchers in the field of safety-critical HCI aim at providing firefighters working in such life-threatening environments with new means to better cope with their difficult tasks. Projects such as [15, 27, 36, 37] envision ubiquitous computing solutions for firefighters working on the frontline and propose to introduce navigation support, health monitoring or novel means of communication. Research funding bodies such as the European Commission additionally sponsor projects for the 'first responder of the future'. Here, projects should enhance the operational effectiveness and capability and reduce injury or loss of life of first responders by optimizing their protection equipment using sensors and means of communication or by guiding first responders in the field [13, p. 23]. Despite these promising visions and the ongoing research efforts, firefighting on the frontline, as of today, remains an activity with almost no IT support.

For the design of computing systems, the hazardous work context on the frontline poses a complex set of requirements. Some researchers stay away from the constraints of the frontline by focusing on the part of the firefighting that takes place in less restrictive environments and support command work, e.g. with mobile phones [4]. The work that specifically focuses on technology for firefighting on the frontline often focuses on certain aspects of firefighting but usually does not understand firefighting as an organizational whole. The work context is instead analyzed from a rather specific perspective focused on the requirements closely linked to the technological interest (e.g. [32]). Providing meaningful support to firefighters, however, requires design concepts that take into account the work context as a social configuration, as a living system that gains stability from a number of aspects.

As Harper et al. point out, "the bottom line is that computer technologies are not neutral—they are laden with human, cultural and social values", therefore technology design requires "reflective thought and conceptual analysis" [18, p. 57]. With promises to prevent some of the tragic accidents of the past, designing computing support for firefighters, at first sight, might be easily justified and appears positive at all times. However, the introduction of novel technology can negatively influence the social configuration, as it exists today. Technology designers have to acknowledge that firefighters already have done a great job in learning how to deal successfully with the extreme conditions. Current organization and practice are the results of long experiences, with firefighting as a profession dating back to the ancient Rome and Caesar Augustus [23]. Leveraging this experience has the potential to be highly beneficial for the design of ubiquitous computing; yet novel technology will also require transforming the existing organization.

To better understand the concepts we propose and the prototypes we are building, it is crucial to begin a reflective dialogue between users and technology designers and discuss questions such as 'Which kind of technology should we design?', 'How can we conceptualize the hypothetical and actual impact that these new technologies have?', 'How will and does ubiquitous computing interact with the existing social configuration?'

Based on extensive fieldwork with firefighters, the research presented here, aims at providing insights of firefighting practice motivated not by a pre-defined problem or technological concept but instead with the idea of studying the practice in-situ and reveal aspects that could become relevant to such reflective dialogue of ubiquitous computing design for frontline firefighting interventions.

RELATED WORK

Studies of Frontline Firefighting

The hazardous work conditions on the frontline and the sheer impossibility to access a firefighting frontline operation as a non-firefighting researcher appears to greatly limit the amount of available work.

Frequently cited, as an example of firefighting frontline practice, is Weick's analysis of the 'Mann Gulch' disaster, a firefighting incident in 1949 in which out of 16 firefighters dispatched to a forest fire only 3 survived [38]. Without direct access to the field, Weick bases his work on a novel by Maclean [28]. He applies his analytical perspective of 'sensemaking' from which reality becomes "an ongoing accomplishment that emerges from efforts to create order and make retrospective of what occurs" [38, p. 635]. While this work certainly provides an insightful perspective on the social dynamics of a team faced with a dangerous task, modern urban firefighting is certainly different. On the one side, urban frontline firefighting faces other challenges as it often takes places in densely populated building structures, on the other side, modern frontline firefighting builds on professional training and equipment, different from the 'Mann Gulch' disaster where most firefighters were indeed college students, who volunteered to fight forest fires as a summer job and never worked together before [28, p. 41].

Two other, non-scientific sources provide records of modern frontline firefighting. First, TV documentaries, in which the work is either reenacted based on the records and descriptions of real interventions [8] or is recorded at firefighting training sites [3], present a snapshot of the work on the frontline. Second, firefighting online communities publish records of frontline practice (e.g. [14, 16]). The interest of these websites is in sharing experiences among firefighters, often focusing on critical incidents. The records are numerous but lack a structure in order to be easily accessible for technology designers.

Digital Technology for the Frontline

Facing the challenge to design for firefighters on the frontline, researchers driven by HCI concerns, take a number of different approaches in conceptualizing firefighter frontline practice and in informing their designs.

Firefighting can be rationalized as an executed plan. Camp et al. [7] present their work on improving traditional, analogue radio systems, addressing the problem that channels easily get overloaded and that half-duplex systems make it difficult to pass and prioritize important information among firefighters on the frontline. Based on the structure found in firefighting guidebooks, the authors design a newly structured radio system that introduces a mixture of half and full duplex communication to better support the official hierarchy.

Other research projects use frontline firefighting more as a motivation for the need of a certain technological development and less as a real context of use. Jiang et al. [22], for example, designed a system to automatically issue warnings to teams inside burning buildings based on sensor readings. Testing the PDA-based system, firefighters were concerned about the fitness of the stylus-based interaction and stressed the point that they would prefer a system that does not solely rely on sensors embedded in buildings.

To learn about the work context on the frontline, Naghsh and Roast [32] take new technology and test the interaction with firefighters by simulating certain aspects of firefighting frontline practice in user studies. In their design, an array of LEDs is mounted to the helmet of a firefighter, displaying a 'safe' direction as computed by a robot swarm. In the study, firefighters expressed that they need reliable navigation information and that the visual display did not constitute a bearing they could trust. Reflecting on their results, the authors point to the difficulties in simulating real world conditions.

In another approach, empirical data serves as a means to identify shortcomings and to design technology to prevent them. Steingart et al. [34] conducted interviews with 60 firefighters regarding technology acceptance, existing equipment and concerns towards digital health monitoring. Based on that material Wilson et al. underline that firefighters frequently base their decisions on "guesswork" [41, p. 1]. Firefighters "guess where the safest and most effective place to enter the building is" [42, p. 103]. To decrease this level of uncertainty, the proposed system triangulates firefighters' locations with high accuracy and displays them on a map to the incident commander.

Instead of eliminating shortcomings, Denef et al. [10, 11] and Ramirez et al. [33] propose to amplify and support already existing practices. In their design of a navigation support system for frontline firefighters they present the characteristics of the work on the frontline, such as the physical nature of the job and the need for collaboration among the teams [11] and study the tools in use [10]. They propose a novel navigation system in which nodes of a sensor network, distributed by the firefighter himself, should serve him as a new orientation guide [33].

While not reaching the frontline, other work in the field of designing ICT for firefighters provides a case in which ethnographic research informed systems that are now in use. For firefighters en route to incident sites, Landgren [24] shows the collaborate efforts of the team to learn about the incident when information is scarce and incomplete. He details the different steps of a firefighting operation and suggests that verbal communication should be made persistent and visible in IT for firefighting commanders [25]. Following that line of research and making use of mobile phones as of already existing computing devices, Landgren et al. [26] introduce a system that allows emergency responders to use their mobile phones to produce on-site videos and make them available as video feeds to command center operators [21]. According to Bergstrand et al. [4] the system has been successfully introduced to three organizations, firefighters, paramedics and traffic authorities of the city of Gothenburg, Sweden.

UNDERSTANDING FRONTLINE FIREFIGHTING

Pattern Research Methodology

Seeking to form a better understanding of the firefighters frontline work, this research is guided by the works of Erickson [12], McCullough [29], and Crabtree [9] in their interpretation of Alexander's work [1, 2] to understand the configuration of environments and to guide, inspire and reflect design by means of patterns of events derived from ethnographic data that allow understanding configurations in contexts where no design exists yet.

For Alexander, any environment, any system is a configuration of interacting patterns. In this original interpretation, patterns are not primarily distinct rules or best practices as they have been introduced to the field of computer science [17], instead they are a means to learn about the configuration of a working whole. Reflecting on his original pattern approach Alexander notes: "I finally understood that all the troublesome entities, which were so important as the building blocks of nature, were not truly bounded entities but were in fact non-bounded centers: Centers of influence, centers of action, centers of other centers—centers of some kind, appearing in the seeming mass of the wholeness." [2, p. 107-108]

As intended by Alexander, patterns successfully served as a means to inform design processes in urban planning projects. Whyte [40] presents patterns of people's behavior as studied in public places of New York City that helped to evaluate urban spaces and directly impacted public policy making. Hester [19] presents the story of the publication of patterns he extracted from events happening in a small town that gave its citizens a voice in urban design discussions.

Referring to Alexander and Hester, Erickson suggests patterns for HCI as the building blocks of a lingua franca in interaction design and presents exemplary patterns of collaborative office work [12]. Rooted in ethnographic research, patterns form a bridge between designers and users and inform change processes posed by ICT. A language of patterns can be used "for discussing changes and reflecting on their possible impacts, both in terms of the activities of the organization, and in terms of the qualities of work life which its members value" [12].

McCullough points to the dynamic character of patterns in his work towards a typology of situated interactions to inform design at the intersection of architecture and ubiquitous computing. "Repeating relationships embody workable conventions. These are not rigid rules, but transformable configurations." [29, p. 55] Patterns inspire design, a pattern framework "recognizes how creativity does better with themes and variations." [29, p. 118]

In the same spirit, Crabtree et al. point to patterns of social action as a means "for structuring and presenting ethnographic fieldwork" [9, p. 265] that can make "unsupported use practices available to the design of future technological arrangements in place" [9, p. 269].

Following these writings, the research presented here understands the context of frontline firefighting as a social configuration formed by long experiences and culture that becomes accessible for technology designers in interacting patterns of human activity. Explicating patterns from ethnographic data should serve as a means for inspiration and reflective discussion of ubiquitous computing designs for the frontline of firefighting operations.

Field Studies

Data coming from a range of multi-sited, bi-national user studies forms the empirical base. Over a period of three years, 21 workshops with firefighters were organized ranging from half-day interview sessions at a fire station to three-day events at firefighting training facilities. This research was conducted with the firefighters in Paris, France at their training center and fire station in St. Denis and with the firefighters of Cologne, Germany at their local fire station and at Europe's most advanced firefighting training facility, the firefighting school of the state of North-Rhine-Westphalia in Münster, Germany that allows simulating interventions close to real world conditions (Figure 1). During the workshops at the fire station firefighters sometimes had to leave for incoming alarm calls and returned to the workshop after finishing their mission, drawing a close connection between real-world incidents and what was discussed in the workshops. In combination, the firefighting organizations provide a diverse picture of the practice. While the Paris firefighters are a military division, the Cologne firefighters are a civil organization. Procedures and tactics vary, as do the tools in use.

The studies on one side were of ethnographic nature and on the other side were technological-oriented, following the approach of research through design [44]. The following list provides an overview of the different studies.

Ethnographic Studies

- In different building structures (apartments, nursing home, basement garage), search and rescue operations were observed. After the missions, firefighters were interviewed about their experience.
- Inspired by studies on tools used in special environments (e.g. [31]) the equipment and tools used by firefighters were studied in interviews at training sites, including both formally assigned and personally chosen tools.
- In empathic exercises [43] the first author worked approximately 30 hours in firefighting gear and joined trainings like the ones repeatedly undertaken by firefighters working on the frontline. These trainings simulated different aspects of firefighting frontline practice, sometimes focusing on procedures applied inside buildings, in which researchers had to team up with professional firefighters to work in apartment buildings filled with artificial smoke to search and rescue victim dummies, and sometimes focusing on the physical conditions, in which the task was to carry heavy goods, to navigate and to extinguish real fire in environments in which the temperature raised up to 300° Celsius and breathing apparatuses became crucial as a means to protect from the surrounding toxic air.
- As part of a role-playing workshop, the first author has served as incident commander, assisted by a professional firefighter, for a simulated fire intervention with an entire brigade, starting from the incoming alarm call until the end of the operation.
- Additionally, written documents were used as input. Especially accident reports but also official firefighting regulations, official training materials and unofficial firefighting guidebooks were studied.

Ubiquitous Computing Evaluation and Design

- To understand the impact of envisioned ubiquitous computing solutions, a wizard-of-oz prototype simulating a navigation support system was tested in different scenarios. With the system the commander received an image of the location of each of his troops.
- Towards the design of a ubiquitous computing navigation system, participatory design workshops were held in the training facilities, in research labs, and at the fire station.
- As triggering artifacts [30], consumer interactive textile products were handed to firefighters to merge the expertise of firefighters with the usage experience of novel interaction techniques of those artifacts.
- Experience prototypes [5] of novel interaction techniques were designed. A prototype for visual feedback inside the breathing mask was evaluated with firefighters.
- A commercial ubiquitous computing system that allows firefighters to find comrades in cases of emergency was evaluated in a scenario where a team suddenly faces problems and has to be rescued by a backup team.

Documentation and Analysis

The studies were captured using video and audio recordings, photos, location tracking data when available and personal notes. Transcriptions were produced for audio and video materials and captured both the ongoing action and spoken words. Notes also captured informal statements made by firefighters before, during and after the studies. The data was analyzed in an open coding process, as suggested by grounded theory [35], constantly comparing findings looking for patterns. Starting from the transcripts, we identified incidents in the data, compared them and started to build categories. The focus then shifted from the comparison of individual incidents to the comparison of incidents with the already existing categories. Finally we aimed at increasing the integrity by grouping categories and reducing them as patterns. As suggested by contextual inquiry methodology [20], affinity notes and maps were used to support this process. During the analysis, critical incidents and associated interview statements of firefighters helped to understand the relation between the workshop experiences and real interventions.

PATTERNS

While the analysis process is still ongoing, the following three patterns evolved into categories that describe how firefighters organize the frontline work from different perspectives. In order to provide a condensed version of the patterns, each pattern starts with a capitalized headline, and a short summary of the problem and solution of the pattern in bold. The pattern is linked back to the studies in a list of the central aspects and selected empirical data that the pattern is based on and illustrated with a figure.

RIGID STRUCTURE

Firefighting operations face unknown, often chaotic situations. Nevertheless, firefighters have to act promptly and decisively.

Therefore, a rigid organizing structure forms the backbone of the operation. Roles are clearly defined and visible, allowing everybody to see who is in charge at different levels. Beyond fixed roles and hierarchies, the structure serves as a means for mutual responsibility and trust.

A role is assigned before starting the work. Before starting a shift, firefighters have to sign in for the role that they take during a shift. A strict handover protocol makes sure that all roles are manned and that there is no moment of ambiguity about who is serving on what role as alarms may come at any moment. A firefighter can have the qualification to serve in different functions. A lower rank commander might be able to serve in a higher rank if a superior commander is off duty or on vacation. The role is also defined by the physical and health conditions of a firefighter. Having a cold or a lack of fitness might make the firefighter unavailable from taking a position that requires work with a breathing apparatus; however, he may still serve as a medical assistant or driver in the ambulance.

Every role has its fixed place in the hierarchic overall system. Starting from the smallest unit of two or three firefighters in a team that enters a building, there is always a clear ranking of the positions to define who is subordinated to whom. Colored stripes on the shoulders and markings on the helmets (Figure 2) provide an immediate visual indication of the rank of the person and distinguish the firefighters in their otherwise similar clothing.

Along with each role comes a set of procedures and tasks. The role defines the seat in the car that the firefighter is going to take; it defines whether he is going to be on one of the teams who is engaging a burning building. For a large part of the work the crew already knows what to do. After a training situation where the crew lined up behind the car to receive their orders, as the protocol suggests, a firefighter noted that this is different in the real incidents. "Once we arrive onsite everybody seems to be gone", he said, "we already know what we have to do."

The role defines the tools that a firefighter carries. A team lead of a Cologne firefighters is for example the only one in his team who carries a radio, a team lead in Paris is the one to whom the lifeline, a rope that he carries to find the way back outside, is directly attached. While such tools are part of trained tactics, firefighters also carry tools that are not officially assigned or predefined from training but personally chosen in relation to their individual role. We found an incident commander carrying earplugs to protect from the noise and a cap to protect from the cold while standing outside, while a team lead who would engage in a burning building joked about those tools and instead

Figure 2: Helmets of firefighters with rank markings

brought shortly cut seat belts as a multi tool for carrying victims and also, as he noted, to be prepared in case one of his subordinated teammates forgets holders to fix a heavy water hose to a handrail.

Along with the role comes a set of responsibilities. A commander needs to send a person whom he often knows for many years, into an unknown, hazardous environment. Inside a building a team lead is telling the others where to stop. "If anybody [...] continues [when I say 'stop'], he will get punched on the nose. [...] imagine you go into some building [as a three man team] and all of a sudden you recognize that we are only two. I cannot look again into the eyes of the women, wives. We all know each other, after all." On the one hand a team lead is the one making the decisions in the building; on the other hand he is responsible for the safety of his colleagues. Subordinates need to trust their superiors for making safe decisions.

For firefighters the structure is the normal case. In the workshops in which researchers and firefighter jointly performed missions, firefighters quickly imposed their known structure on the newcomers. Sitting in the engine before the intervention the highest ranked firefighter in the car created the organizational structure with the following statement: "We form a three-man team as the water team. Then we have a three-man team as hose team. That means your task is to create the water supply from the water source to the pump and from the pump to the distributor; your task is to prepare the water hose for the two of us and we two will equip us with breathing mask, breathing apparatus and the other equipment and will then proceed to do the firefighting."

The structure is important beyond the operation. As firefighters stay together during night and day shifts, the fire station becomes a second home. Here, an incident commander, for his subordinated team, is not only a superior firefighter or commander, but also an advisor for issues of daily life. "I have many jobs here, sometimes I act as marriage counselor", stated an incident commander.

INDEPENDENT UNITS

As a result of the extreme conditions of the environment, frontline firefighting takes place in isolation making it very difficult to give detailed instructions from outside.

Therefore, small work units of two or three firefighters work very close with each other and only receive general missions. Detailed decisions are left to the unit itself.

In the beginning of an operation there is little information from which an engaging team could benefit from. Usually, the operation starts on the basis of scarce or incomplete information. Incident commanders are advised to learn from all the information available. Bystanders, or people in the building may be able to provide more information. Nevertheless, a lack of information remains a central challenge to the work of firefighters.

And indeed, the engaging team is also sent in a building to learn about the situation. The practice of the Paris brigade, who at the time of the study had not established radio as a standard for engaging teams, greatly relies on reconnaissance teams who engage a building without a water hose and create a path for the subsequent teams using a rope.

Orders given by commanding people leave open the detailed actions. The teams engaging a building receive orders such as this formal command: "Attack team one, engage on a life-saving mission, with CABA [compressed air breathing apparatus], with the first C-hose, on the 3rd floor, use the staircase." Here the commander follows a protocol that specifies the addressee, the mission, the equipment, the target floor and the way of access. In this case, the command specifies an operation using a breathing apparatus and thereby enacts the safety regulation for such missions and it specifies that people are possibly in danger and thereby also enacts regulations that allow to refrain from certain safety measures [6]. In a less formal way, a French incident commander issued a command to his subordinate commander: "Command post in support of CFC [Centre de Formation des Cadres]. You will send a team on the second floor, knowing that the third floor is inaccessible by windows and stairs. The fire started on the ground floor. Keep a team as backup." The subordinate then commanded the attack team under his supervision: "Your mission: Do a reconnaissance of the entire second floor and go on to the third floor if there is access to the third floor." In the German and French variations of the commands the engaging team only receives a general mission of what to do, in the first case to rescue people, in the second to perform a reconnaissance.

Once engaged, firefighters become isolated in a hazardous environment. When a team enters a burning building it has to pass a barrier of smoke, before which it has to connect its breathing apparatuses. This may be in front of the building or, in case of a high-rise building, in the floor below the actual fire.

Figure 3: A team working inside an apartment

This is especially significant for teams engaging without radio contact. Here, the only connection to the outside world is a rope and a small horn that the Paris firefighters carried to let their outside colleagues know that they should stretch the lifeline to provide a clear direction back. But also in the case of available radio devices, there is only very limited connection between the frontline and the higher levels of command. The radio devices are difficult to use with firefighting gear and a firefighter has to stop crawling in order to search for the microphone, press a button and speak. A commander said: "You can make them pretty busy when you ask them too much." Additionally, the building structure negatively impacts radio connections and talking simply wastes otherwise scarce compressed air.

This isolation allows for local decisions, for dynamic strategies. On the frontline, firefighters have room to improvise, to deviate from trained tactics, if found necessary. As an example, a firefighter on the frontline saw the shimmering light under the door of a room across the hallway. While the researcher whom he guided followed the previously trained right-hand rule, where the firefighter always follows the wall on his right, the firefighter reported later that in this case he would have deviated from the rule, as a means to find the fire faster.

The integrity of the unit is absolutely vital. For a unit, comprising usually two people, it is absolutely crucial to stay together. Repeatedly firefighters stated "the most important thing is that we two stay together", accident reports call the splitting of a team a 'mortal sin'. Firefighters continuously put effort into staying together and knowing about the other, a difficult task in this isolating environment.

MONITORING

Firefighters might face situations where sudden changes and threats put them in danger and they need immediate help. Those situations need to be recognized. Especially with INDEPENDENT UNITS it is difficult to ensure that emerging threats are identified in time.

Therefore, firefighters monitor the operation and thereby gain an understanding of what is going on now in the context of what has happened before. More than a mere procedure, monitoring means caring for others and fulfilling an expected obligation.

Before a firefighter enters a building, a monitoring process is initiated. Attached to the firefighter's breathing apparatus is a plastic tag that he inserts in a breathing control board before starting a mission. Outside the building, a firefighter is dedicated to monitor the board. He writes down the time at which the firefighter connects the breathing apparatus and the initial pressure of the compressed air cylinder. A standard bottle provides the firefighter air for about 30 minutes. With the Cologne firefighters, the board additionally features a timer (Figure 4). After each 10 minutes the firefighter at the board requests the firefighters inside the building via radio to report their current pressure left in their bottles. The standard procedure suggests the firefighters to plan 10 minutes of air as backup when scheduling a mission. Beyond the pressure check, firefighters state that the radio call serves them as a clock as they do not bring a wristwatch to the frontline.

Movement sensors in the firefighting equipment detect crucial situations. Monitoring also happens directly on the frontline. The Personal Alert Safety System (PASS) devices feature movement sensors attached to the breathing apparatus to detect when a firefighter faces problems. When he is no longer moving, the sensor triggers an audible alarm to inform colleagues. In the studies, firefighters could be observed moving the apparatus periodically as a means to avoid this alarm from being triggered when waiting for instructions.

Some monitoring activities are quite subtle. When positioned near our computer system in a control room and thereby relatively far from the position close to the building where he usually stands, a commander noted that he misses the unwinding lifeline as a means to monitor the progress of the engaging team. He said: "There is also another thing … the man who is outside who holds the lifeline … from my position, I do not see a lot … what is his progress, etc… that is also a point. I do not see how fast … two meters … I do not see two meters of rope passing. I do not know if it was two meters that he made."

Monitoring also takes place within the small units. To ensure the integrity of their unit, firefighters frequently check if their partner is doing OK. They want to stay aware of each other's condition and location. In introductions to the frontline work, researchers were told to frequently touch their partners' bodies as a means to communicate their presence. At the same time, team leaders were advised to frequently check if

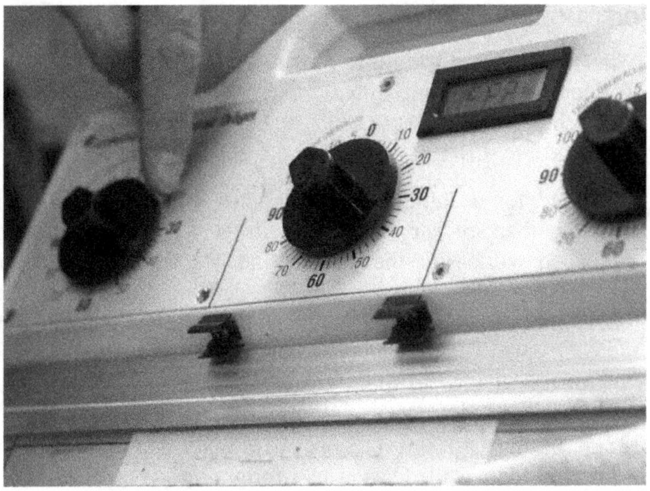

Figure 4: Breathing Control Board

their teammate is still there. In this way, firefighters are trying to be constantly aware of each other, as they need to stay close to not loose each other.

Monitoring also takes place individually, with each firefighter on the frontline. Each firefighter tries to keep track of his location. Keeping track also helps the firefighters form a mental model of the physical space that they encounter. After coming back out of an apartment, firefighters could draw a map of the building recounting their experiences step by step. Both German and French firefighters relied on counting the steps of staircases and the floors in a building and based on that information, estimate their own position and path.

Monitoring is a social process. Knowing that there is somebody outside monitoring what is going on inside, who checks time and air pressure level and knowing that there is a partner who takes care, creates a safety net that the frontline firefighter can trust. After the workshops, firefighters told stories about how they sometimes play jokes on each other in their free time but that they in contrast can rely on each other in interventions: "You might think now we're a bit crazy. But you have to know: We can have a lot of fun but when it gets serious, we can work very hard. I know I can count on everybody here when it gets serious." In the heat training exercises, where the work was done facing real fire under potentially dangerous conditions, firefighters were always alerted and immediately offered help, even if their research teammate rolled the eyes just for fun when wearing a breathing mask. While the researchers drew more attention and firefighter acknowledged that they were more cautious when entering hazardous training environments with novices, their frequent checks and continuous monitoring actions nevertheless showed, how automatically firefighters look after each other and how deep this mutual care is rooted in their practice. Fulfilling monitoring procedures is not only a task but also a means to care for a colleague and an mutually expected obligation.

DISCUSSION

The Patterns and the State-of-the-Art

Reflecting on the presented patterns in terms of existing research sets RIGID STRUCTURE and MONITORING apart from INDEPENDENT UNITS.

The need for a static hierarchy and a strict organizational structure that are part of RIGID STRUCTURE are included in published work. For the case of the Mann Gulch disaster Weick states that "what people needed was a structure in which there was both an inverse and a direct relationship between role systems and meaning" [38, p. 646] and that a "major contributor to this disaster was the loss of the only structure that kept these people organized, their role system" [38, p. 636]. MONITORING is also an activity that is, at least to a large extent, well defined in firefighting procedures. The patterns presented here, underline both aspects and puts them in a context as lived by firefighters. Additionally, the presented patterns add the notions that RIGID STRUCTURE becomes an expression of responsibility and MONITORING a means of mutual care.

What is unique about INDEPENDENT UNITS is that this concept cannot be easily found in the writings of firefighting literature. The independence of teams inside a burning building is not something initiated by human thought, by preparation or training. Instead, the isolation is enforced upon the firefighters by the hazardous work environment, the need to respond quickly and limited human resources. Here, we have the social nucleus of a firefighting operation, the smallest possible unit. Weick already showed that having at least one partner is crucial. "A partner is a second source of ideas. A partner strengthens independent judgment in the face of a majority. And a partner enlarges the pool of data that are considered." [38, p. 642] Certainly, INDEPENDENT UNITS come along with great risks. Getting lost, experiencing a threatening situation is a risk of life for a firefighter. Yet, the isolation also provides the units an open space to work in.

The Patterns as Interacting Components

Considered about understanding working wholes as assemblies of patterns, as 'pattern languages', Alexander stresses that "the links between the patterns are almost as much a part of the language as the patterns themselves." [1, p. 314] And indeed, putting the three patterns into interaction, creates a framework for understanding firefighter's frontline work: RIGID STRUCTURE provides the backbone of the operation; they form a social binding and put everybody in the position to act promptly. INDEPENDENT UNITS bring flexibility to the structure; they allow coping with a dynamic environment. The firefighter is able to act in accordance to the local situation that he faces. MONITORING spans a safety net for INDEPENDENT UNITS and helps to detect if somebody is in danger; it allows calling backup teams or additional support. In this interaction, the three patterns form a balanced whole that novel technology is confronted with.

Following Weiser's call for seamlessly networked devices, most proposed ubiquitous computing systems for firefighting operations, aim at building an overall network. Computing technology is envisioned for MONITORING, especially health conditions and locations of firefighters, and communicating them to the outer world, as parts of coordinated actions. As experienced in the workshops, such systems can decrease the current isolation of INDEPENDENT UNITS, putting previously agile teams back into the stiff lines of RIGID STRUCTURE.

One of the simulated interventions with the Paris firefighters showed for example that it is difficult to grasp the complexity of the context on the frontline as experienced by a firefighter. In the experiment, the incident commander received a digital floor plan of the building in which one team engaged. On the plan, spots marked the current positions of the firefighters. The engaging team was equipped with radio devices and thus had a direct link to the commander. With their masks covered, the firefighters' view was blocked, but it was possible to observe their actions. Problems arose as details, such as the position of furniture, are relevant on the frontline but were not displayed to the commander. A firefighter (FF1) noted: "This is why one time I had to defend myself because I often tried to follow [the walls] with my hand, but there were beds, so we were a little confused."

In the same intervention, the incident commander (IC) tried to confirm the team's position close to a door that he saw on the plan. The following dialogue shows, how they collaborated.

IC	(radio)	You find a door on your right. Is this the case?
FF1	(radio)	Yes, that's right, there is a door without … a doorframe … I do not see the door. But there is a kind of corridor.
IC	(radio)	Do you see a door on your right?
FF1		*Feels the wall with his hands. (10 sec)*
FF1	(radio)	Yes, this is a door.

Asking for the door twice, the commander insisted on his outside view and thereby made the team spent extra effort in order to map the outside information to their local experience. FF1 commented afterwards: "Even there are some doors, that are just frames, no swinging doors, but when you say: 'it is a door' we feel it directly."

In the above case, the team followed the interpretation suggested from outside, in contrast to relying on the established approach that is based on interpreting what is found on-site and collaborating within the team only to build an understanding of the situation.

The incident commanders, in different exercises, did not understand engaging teams as sources of information that provide insights from the frontline, but instead, mediated by technology, extended their range of command to the frontline. This also had negative effects, especially in cases where the commander could not track the position of the firefighters due to technical breakdowns. Following the commands from the outside, perspectives in- and outside offset and seeming clues of reference were misinterpreted. As a consequence, teams went unnoticed in circles and lost their ability to draw maps of the rooms they had scanned.

After a mission where engaging teams received outside instructions from a commander who guided them using a map, a firefighter summarized the problem showing the dilemma between trusting command and the local situation: "The main problem is that I do not see, I am sent to a building that I do not know, to look for something and my commander, he guides me, now he has no vision, nor is he where I am in the room. So he can tell me: 'go right', 'you make a left', but he does not know exactly where I am. I have confidence in him but he did not really know where he sent me."

While one certainly should not derive from these examples the understanding that outside support generally hinders the operation, it shows that with a reduction of the independence of the units, roles need to be reconsidered.

Ubiquitous Computing Design for INDEPENDENT UNITS

Computing technology can, however, also be designed to emphasize the concept of INDEPENDENT UNITS. Two computing devices found at today's firefighting frontlines, namely the PASS devices and thermal cameras, already have shown to work within the existing system.

The infrared camera is a rather bulky device and weighs an extra 1.5 kg; nevertheless, it has been shown to provide meaningful support for firefighters on the frontline. With one camera per team it is a tool that provides INDEPENDENT UNITS a new sense, directly increasing their capabilities for navigation and the search for missing people.

The PASS devices embedded in the breathing apparatus also mostly preserve INDEPENDENT UNITS. The movement sensors allow the firefighters to easily dismiss a false alarm, by shaking their breathing apparatus. Only in cases when they cannot move at all, a relatively clear indication that something has gone wrong, they cannot control the alarm. In that case the independence gets broken and the audible alarm can be heard by others and supports them in MONITORING that something has gone wrong and in tracking the team's location.

Instead of large, integrated computing systems, it is these two tools that, at least currently, provide the most valuable support on the frontline. This approach, building tools for INDEPENDENT UNITS and thereby leaving them intact, is also part of current research and can be found in the design of the navigation system presented by Ramirez et al. [33]. Instead of receiving commands where to go, frontline firefighters are envisioned to manually deploy beacons of a sensor network as a means to tag important places with new reference points and to enhance their understanding of the unknown environment.

FUTURE WORK & CONCLUSION

Based on a qualitative analysis of a broad range of user studies with firefighters we presented three patterns of the frontline practice that provide insights how firefighters organize their work. RIGID STRUCTURE, INDEPENDENT UNITS, and MONITORING have been identified as interacting components of firefighting frontline practice.

Instead of focusing on solving a particular problem by technological means, this work intended to focus on the practice first and understands the design and research of a specific problem or technology as an additional, second step. This research should therefore not be misinterpreted as a call for a particular type of technology nor does it necessarily directly allow deriving design solutions. We instead envision the identified patterns of frontline practice to become part of a dialogue between technology designers and users to discuss the potential and actual impact that ubiquitous computing systems have on firefighters' frontline work.

ACKNOWLEDGMENTS

We are grateful to the reviewers for their insightful comments and suggestions, to our colleagues at Fraunhofer FIT, to all our project partners and especially to the firefighters of Cologne and Paris for their invaluable support in this research. This work has been partly funded by the German government as part of the landmarke project (contract no. 13N9916) and the European Commission as part of the WearIT@Work project (contract no. 004216).

REFERENCES

1. Alexander, C. The timeless way of building. New York: Oxford University Press, 1979.
2. Alexander, C. The Nature of Order, Book 1: The Phenomenon of Life. Berkeley, CA: Center for Environmental Structure, 2002.
3. BBC: Fire training school - Skyscraper Fire Fighters. http://www.youtube.com/watch?v=nnVXQ_9CIAc.
4. Bergstrand, F. and Landgren, J. Information Sharing Using Live Video in Emergency Response Work. In *Proc. ISCRAM 2006*, (2006).
5. Buchenau, M. and Suri, J.F. Experience prototyping. In *Proc. DIS 2000*, ACM Press (2000), 424 - 433.
6. Bundesamt für Bevölkerungsschutz und Katastrophenhilfe Feuerwehr-Dienstvorschrift 7 (Atemschutz). Bundesrepublik Deutschland (2005).
7. Camp, P.J., Hudson, J.M., Keldorph, R.B., Lewis, S., and Mynatt, E.D. Supporting communication and collaboration practices in safety-critical situations. In *Ext. Abstracts CHI 2000*. ACM Press (2000), 249-250.
8. CBS: Rescue 911 Episode 522. http://www.youtube.com/watch?v=Km5du5rKpec.
9. Crabtree, A., Hemmings, T., and Rodden, T. Pattern-based support for interactive design in domestic settings. In *Proc. DIS 2002*. ACM Press (2002), 265-276.
10. Denef, S., Ramirez, L., and Dyrks, T. Letting Tools Talk: Interactive Technology for Firefighting. In *Ext. Abstracts CHI 2009*, ACM Press (2009), 444 - 447.

11. Denef, S., Ramirez, L., Dyrks, T., and Stevens, G. Handy navigation in ever-changings Spaces: an ethnographic study of firefighting practices. In *Proc. DIS 2008,* ACM Press (2008), 184-192.

12. Erickson, T. Lingua Francas for design: sacred places and pattern languages. In *Proc. DIS 2000*, ACM Press (2000), 357-368.

13. European Comission 4598: Work Programme 2009 Cooperation Theme 10 Security. European Commission, (2008), 40.

14. Feuerwehr Forum. http://www.feuerwehr-forum.de/.

15. FeuerWhere - Tracking Fire Fighters. http://www.feuerwhere.de/.

16. Firefighter Close Calls. http://www.firefighterclosecalls.com.

17. Gamma, E., Helm, R., Johnson, R., and Vlissides, J. Design patterns: elements of reusable object-oriented software. Addison-wesley Reading, MA, 1995.

18. Harper, R., Rodden, T., Rogers, Y., and Sellen, A., eds. Being Human: Human-Computer Interaction in the year 2020. Microsoft Research, Cambridge, (2008).

19. Hester, R.T. Sacred Structures and Everyday Life: A Return to Manteo, NC. in Dwelling, Seeing, and Designing: Toward A Phenomenological Ecology, Seamon, D., Editor. State University of New York Press, New York, NYC, (1993), 363.

20. Holtzblatt, K., Wendell, J., and Wood, S. Rapid Contextual Design: A How-to Guide to Key Techniques for User-Centered Design (Interactive Technologies). Morgan Kaufmann, 2004.

21. LiveResponse. http://www.liveresponse.eu.

22. Jiang, X., Chen, N.Y., Hong, J.I., Wang, K., Takayama, L., and Landay, J.A. Siren: Context-aware Computing for Firefighting. *Pervasive Computing*. Springer, Berlin, (2004), 87 - 105.

23. Kenlon, J. Fires And Fire-Fighters; A History Of Modern Fire-Fighting With A Review Of Its Development From Earliest Times. Young Press, 2008.

24. Landgren, J. Supporting fire crew sensemaking enroute to incidents. *International Journal of Emergency Management 2*, (2005), 176-188.

25. Landgren, J. Making action visible in time-critical work. In *Proc. CHI 2006*. ACM Press (2006), 201 - 210.

26. Landgren, J. and Nulden, U. A study of emergency response work: patterns of mobile phone interaction. In *Proc. CHI 2007*. ACM Press (2007), 1323 - 1332

27. landmarke project. http://landmarke-projekt.de.

28. Maclean, N. Young men and fire. University of Chicago Press, 1992.

29. McCullough, M. Digital ground: Architecture, pervasive computing, and environmental knowing. MIT Press, 2005.

30. Mogensen, P. and Robinson, M. Triggering Artefacts. *AI & Society 9*, (1995), 373 - 388.

31. Molotch, H. and McClain, N. Things at Work: Informal social-material mechanisms for getting the job done. *Journal of Consumer Culture 8*, 1 (2008), 35-67.

32. Naghsh, A.M. and Roast, C.R. Designing user interaction with robots swarms in emergency settings. In *Proc. NordiCHI 2008*. ACM Press (2008), 519 - 522.

33. Ramirez, L., Denef, S., and Dyrks, T. Towards Human-Centered Support for Indoor Navigation. In *Proc. CHI 2009*, ACM Press (2009), 1279–1282.

34. Steingart, D., Wilson, J., Redfern, A., Wright, P., Romero, R., and Lim, L. Augmented cognition for fire emergency response: An iterative user study. In *1st International Conference on Augmented Cognition*.

35. Strauss, A.L. and Corbin, J.M. Basics of qualitative research : grounded theory procedures and techniques. Newbury Park, Calif.: Sage Publications, 1990.

36. Tri-Sentinel. http://www.trisentinel.com/solutions.htm.

37. Ubiquitous IP Centric Government & Enterprise Next Generation Networks. http://www.efipsans.eu/.

38. Weick, K.E. The Collapse of Sensemaking in Organizations: The Mann Gulch Disaster. *Administrative Science Quarterly 38*, (1993), 628-652.

39. Weiser, M. The computer for the 21st century. *Scientific American 265*, 3 (1991), 66-75.

40. Whyte, W. The Social Life of Small Urban Spaces. Project for Public Spaces, 2001.

41. Wilson, J., Bhargava, V., Redfern, A., and Wright, P. A Wireless Sensor Network and Incident Command Interface for Urban Firefighting. In *Proc. MobiQuitous 2007*. IEEE Computer Society. (2007), 1 - 7.

42. Wilson, J., Steingart, D., Romero, R., Reynolds, J., Mellers, E., Redfern, A., Lim, L., Watts, W., Patton, C., and Baker, J. Design of monocular head-mounted displays for increased indoor firefighting safety and efficiency. In *Proc. of SPIE on Helmet-and Head-mounted Displays X: Technologies and Applications 5800*, (2005), 103–114.

43. Wright, P. and McCarthy, J. Empathy and experience in HCI. In *Proc. CHI 2008*, ACM Press (2008), 637-646.

44. Zimmerman, J., Forlizzi, J., and Evenson, S. Research through design as a method for interaction design research in HCI. In *Proc. CHI 2007*, ACM Press (2007), 493-502.

Zero-Fidelity Simulation of Fire Emergency Response: Improving Team Coordination Learning

Zachary O. Toups, Andruid Kerne, William A. Hamilton, Nabeel Shahzad
Interface Ecology Lab | Department of Computer Science and Engineering
Texas A&M University, College Station, Texas USA
{zach, andruid, bill, nabeel} @ecologylab.net

ABSTRACT

Fire emergency responders rely on team coordination to survive and succeed in high-stress environments, but traditional education does not directly teach these essential skills. Prior simulations seek the highest possible fidelity, employing resources to capture concrete characteristics of operating environments. We take a different tack, hypothesizing that a *zero*-fidelity approach, focusing on human-centered aspects of work practice, will improve team coordination learning. Such an approach promotes simulation focus by developing an *alternative environment* that stimulates participants to *engage in distributed cognition*. The costs of simulation development are reduced.

To supplement preparation for burn training exercises, 28 fire emergency response students played the *Teaching Team Coordination game* (T^2eC), a zero-fidelity simulation of the distributed cognition of fire emergency response work practice. To test our hypothesis, we develop quantitative evaluation methods for impact on team coordination learning through measures of communication efficiency and cooperative activity. Results show that participants improve cooperation, become more efficient communicators, differentiate team roles through communication, and leverage multiple communication modalities. Given the context of the study amidst the educational process, qualitative data from the students and their expert instructor supports the ecological validity of the contribution of the T^2eC zero-fidelity simulation to fire emergency response education.

Author Keywords

Zero-fidelity simulation, distributed cognition, implicit coordination, education, games, emergency response

ACM Classification Keywords

H.5.3 Information Interfaces: Group and Organization Interfaces—*Computer Supported Cooperative* [*Play & Learning*]

General Terms

Experimentation, Human Factors

INTRODUCTION

For the sake of argument and as an antidote to the fever for glitzy, high-fidelity sweeping the simulation field, we introduce a new *zero*-fidelity approach to simulating fire emergency response to teach team coordination. Prior approaches to simulation have assumed that increasing fidelity means better simulation [1]. The result is increasingly immersive, but literal, representations. They have addressed the physical conditions of fire emergency response, but not how team members work together. Team coordination saves lives in emergency response scenarios, but traditional education techniques direct limited resources at urgent needs, such as the basics of firefighting. The present research reduces the cost of simulation, with the potential to increase the scope of educational applicability, by focusing on human-centered characteristics of situated distributed and team cognition.

Our long-term goal is to develop human-centered education systems derived from work practice that are transferable across domains. The present research establishes zero-fidelity simulation as an effective method for teaching team coordination to fire emergency responders (FERs) without diminishing the value of existing simulations. Prior work developed design implications to teach team coordination from fire emergency response work practice [28] and established design implications for non-mimetic simulation by testing with non-FERs [30].

Our *principal hypothesis* is that by playing zero-fidelity simulation games, fire emergency responders will learn team coordination skills. We develop measures of team coordination based on communication efficiency and cooperative effectiveness. Communication efficiency is evaluated through a new speech/action coding scheme that quantifies the content of team communication and in-game action. Cooperative effectiveness is calculated directly from game log data.

We present an ecologically valid user study in which students at the Texas Engineering Extension Service's (TEEX) Emergency Services Training Institute Firefighter Training Academy (FTA) play the Teaching Team Coordination Game (T^2eC, pronounced "tech"). Students find the game motivating. They improve at cooperative tasks and become more efficient communicators, indicating improvement in their team coordination skills. The study validates our design implications for teaching team coordination and designing *non-mimetic* simulations, which we now call *zero-fidelity*, situating the work in the simulation literature. Depending on players' roles in T^2eC, they communicate differently. Participants employ multimodal communication to efficiently work together. They and their instructor articulate how the simulation contributes to their performance on the fireground.

Throughout this paper, we bring in the voice of expert and practitioner, Fire Chief Cary Roccaforte, Program Coordi-

CHI 2011, May 7–12, 2011, Vancouver, BC, Canada.
Copyright 2011 ACM 978-1-4503-0267-8/11/05...$10.00.

nator of the FTA. Roccaforte has spent over 20 years as a program coordinator, instructor, and/or training officer; he has 12 years of experience as a firefighter prior to that. Roccaforte works closely with his students; throughout the user studies, he provided his own observations and insights into the impact of the game on their education.

BACKGROUND: TEAM COORDINATION

The present research develops educational systems for team coordination from fire emergency response work practice. Distributed cognition forms the basis for an information-centric understanding of teams, while team cognition contributes understanding of how team members work together and share information. We provide an overview of team coordination in fire emergency response work practice to understand the roles of workers and how they communicate.

A central construct in both distributed and team cognition is the *mental model*. Mental models are the way in which individuals maintain and manipulate a representation of the functioning of an object or process in their heads [8]. The model is a form of internal simulation based on experience, enabling high-level problem solving and prediction.

Distributed Cognition

Distributed cognition holistically analyzes working environments, describing cognitive processes spread among mutual interactions of humans and artifacts over time [12]. Task-relevant information is stored in multiple forms: mental models, embedded in the environment, and derived via formulae. Those working in a distributed cognition environment move components from an original to other, workable forms, applying new forms to the situation. Workable forms are communicated through a variety of media, enabling cooperation.

Team Cognition

Team cognition theory posits implicit coordination as an efficient mode for teams. In an *explicit coordination* mode, team members communicate frequently. Wide-area communication bandwidth is limited by single-channel, half-duplex[1] radios. Further, those receiving communication expend time and cognitive effort to listen and understand. The bandwidth, cognition, and time costs of communicating are *overhead* [17, 25]. High-performance teams reduce communication overhead through *implicit coordination*: they speak less and act more [5]. Implicitly coordinating team members *share* mental models, enabling them to predict and account for each other's work [2, 19]. As team members maintain *situation awareness*, they monitor the environment and predict its future states [4]. Shared mental models combine with situation awareness, supporting implicit coordination. The present research develops the implicit coordination skills of FERs.

Emergency Response Work Practice

Fire emergency response work practice involves intense team coordination in a distributed cognition environment. It is carried out by companies (teams) of *firefighters* directed by an *incident commander* (IC) [13, 15, 21, 28]; collectively, these are FERs. Companies operate at an *incident*, where they gather, integrate, and share information to rescue victims and fight fire. The IC observes from a distance, and combines information from artifacts and deployed responders to direct the action. The communicative role of IC is an instance of situated distributed cognition.

Communication is essential in emergency response. FERs prefer face-to-face communication because it is fast and easily understood [28]. However, half-duplex radios reach all FERs at an incident. Radio is problematic because it is slow and because crosstalk, a situation in which two radio operators transmit simultaneously, results in information loss.

[1] A *half-duplex* device switches between send or receive mode, but cannot do both simultaneously.

ZERO-FIDELITY SIMULATION

We develop and validate a new theory of *zero-fidelity simulation*: learning environments that emphasize distributed cognition instead of mimicking concrete characteristics [30]. Prior simulations aspire to *high-fidelity*, capturing as much of a real-life environment as possible. There is a widely held belief that higher fidelity automatically translates to more effective learning [1, 11, 27]. Low-fidelity simulations have been shown to be effective for educating [1], but capture aspects of the real-world working environment. Some lower-fidelity simulations have addressed coordination of resources among team members without addressing the human-centered aspects of work practice [9, 14, 31]. Others take a high-fidelity approach to team education [26].

We take an alternative tack. Gagné suggests that training devices might be constructed to teach specific skills *without* a complete simulation [7]. According to Hays and Singer [11], much simulation research ignores these findings. Lave and Wenger [16] suggest that learning must be situated socially and operationally to be effective, but Reder and Klatzky [22] refute this claim in studying skill transfer. Through an extensive review of existing literature, they conclude that fully situated learning is frequently *un*necessary. They note, however, that situated learning *is* valuable in social environments. The present research develops a social context in which participants learn team coordination by engaging in distributed cognition like that of the source environment.

The present zero-fidelity simulation addresses not the concrete environment, but, instead, distributed cognition characteristics, abstracting alternative means by which participants can learn to perform tasks. Learned abilities are applied back in the target domain; prior work [7, 22] and performance studies' concept of restored behavior [24] support that this transfer of skills will be successful.

We discussed the need for zero-fidelity simulation education during a think tank with four response experts with the TEEX Urban Search and Rescue (US&R). Combined, these professionals possess over 100 years of experience in disaster response and recovery in the USA and EU. The experts were involved in the response to Hurricanes Katrina (2005), Rita (2005), and Ike (2008); the Oklahoma City Bombing (1995) and 9/11 (2001); all of the Provisional Irish Republican Army bombings in London, and the 7/7 bombings (2005). Two of the experts had played T^2eC; they cited its value for US&R operatives. The group mandated that zero-fidelity simulation's focus on how people communicate and cooperate under stress provides urgently needed educational experience, because the current practice in training fails to directly address team coordination. Meanwhile, they informed us, breakdowns in communication, not in equipment or people's understanding of how it works, are the primary source of failures in emergency response. The US&R experts indicated

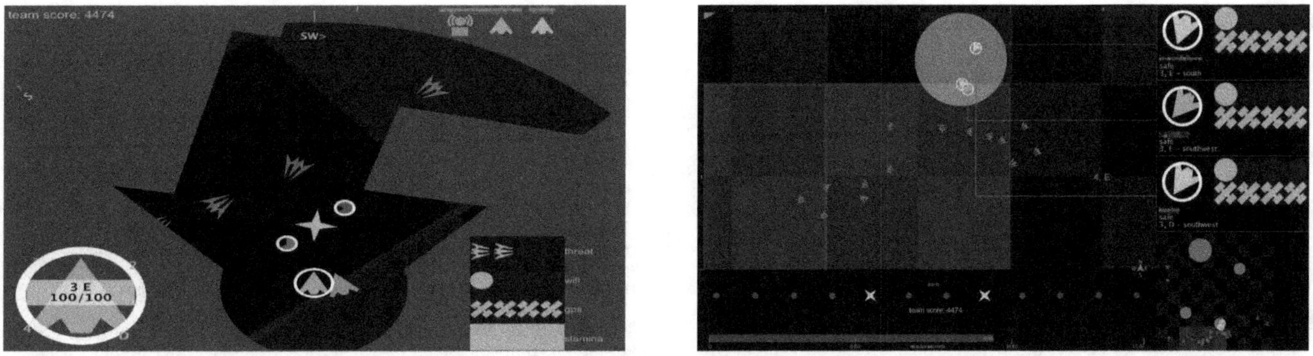

Figure 1. Screenshots from the T²eC zero-fidelity simulation (Team 5, game 8, 5'15"). Purple and orange seekers collect a cooperative goal from a base. **Seeker View (left):** The white shield around the purple avatar indicates safe status; purple cannot detect information about orange's status. Threats are nearby. **Coordinator View (right):** The main view shows the terrain with all entities; highlighted regions contain goals. Walls (visible to seekers) cannot be seen. The right column shows the status of each seeker; a mini-map is on bottom. Below the main view is the goal list (two are un-collected) and remaining time.

that T²eC fulfills a strategic hole in education that existing, expensive simulations do not, by capturing the human-centered components of practice.

Both the think tank and Chief Roccaforte discussed use of educational exercises to teach teams to cooperate. The think tank described tabletop exercises for command personnel, but indicated that the lack of stress limited their value. Similarly, Roccaforte described classroom exercises in which students practice using the radio; his concerns echoed those of the think tank. These low-fidelity simulations of team cooperation are ineffective for real world practice.

Effective zero-fidelity simulations are grounded in practice: practiced skills are based on those in real-life work. Practical grounding is essential for learning skills [22]. Zero-fidelity simulations take a place side-by-side with other forms of simulation training, such as the high-fidelity burn training simulations used in the FTA, fulfilling a complementary role.

Advantages of Zero-Fidelity Simulation

Zero-fidelity simulations have two main advantages over high-fidelity simulations: economy and focus. Zero-fidelity simulations are *economical* in that they are simpler to produce by abstracting out details that would be expensive to replicate. The present research investigates *focus* by showing the effectiveness of zero-fidelity simulations for teaching the distributed cognition of team coordination. As a point of comparison, FTA students undertake *burn training*, a high-fidelity simulation of firefighting in actual burning buildings.

Zero-fidelity simulations omit actual reality for conceptual learning. Cost is a consideration in simulators that leads designers to reduce simulation fidelity [7, 11]; zero-fidelity simulations are more economical. For example, to simulate the fire emergency response environment, we would need algorithms for and visualizations of fire and smoke, and more expensive and power-hungry processors. Instead, the present research runs with minimal system requirements. The monetary costs of running T²eC are negligible, while burn training costs over 125USD per student per term.

Focusing simulation resources on distributed cognition focuses learning. High-fidelity simulations capture as much as possible about working conditions. The characteristics addressed by zero-fidelity simulations are based on the educational program. In burn training, participants *might* engage in team coordination, but the focus is maneuvering in closed environments, manipulating equipment, and predicting fire. According to Roccaforte, the FTA extended burn exercises to provide an opportunity for students to practice communicating with the radio under stress. The FTA includes radio practice in the classroom, but the value is limited because there is neither stress nor consequences for failure.

Because there is a need for team coordination education, the present research targets the *distributed cognition* of work practice. Essential characteristics of the original environment must be incorporated, such as those that are not a part of the classroom radio exercises. For example, in fire emergency response, participants must make quick decisions while under stress, so this is a requirement for a zero-fidelity simulation.

Games as Zero-Fidelity Simulation

Games function as a form of simulation [3, 23] in which physical and social processes are carried out. Narayanasamy et al. [20] classify games and simulators: games are not primarily designed to teach skills and simulations are not intended to be fun. Zero-fidelity simulation games bridge the gap, teaching skills while entertaining, so that players are encouraged to learn, providing intrinsic motivation [18, 23]. Gagné suggests that metrics within training devices can encourage cooperation or competition [7], adding external motivation. Framing zero-fidelity simulation as a game encourages players to compete and cooperate with each other.

Salen and Zimmerman [23] describe games as consisting of rules and play. Rules restrict action, while play is freedom to move within the rules; the rules make play meaningful. They identify the *core mechanics* of a game as the set of rule-constrained actions that players take repeatedly to play.

TEACHING TEAM COORDINATION GAME

The present research studies our game design for teaching team coordination [29, 30]. Game mechanics in the virtual world are instantiated through *entities* that operate in *terrain*. Entities include seekers' *avatars*, *goals* that seekers collect, and *threats* that hunt avatars to prevent collecting goals.

Participant Roles

Because teams operate in distributed cognition environments, we identified the design implication of *distributing information* between team members to encourage communication

[28, 29, 30]. By apportioning parts of an emerging information puzzle to team members, they rely on one another to accomplish shared goals. *Participant roles* are the axis along which information is distributed, and each role has a different subset of game mechanics [30]. Information distribution is instantiated by only making some terrain components and entities visible in certain interfaces. In T^{2}eC, players on a human team take on one of two roles that are analogous to FER roles: seeker and coordinator.

Seeker players (three per team) each move an avatar in a virtual world, finding and collecting goals while avoiding threats. Seekers observe a local, high-detail perspective on the virtual world with a limited scope (Figure 1, left). The present game design differs from the design previously studied [30]: the location of threats is distributed to seekers, in addition to the coordinator; previously, only the coordinator could see threats. This change was made because information that changes quickly in a zero-fidelity simulation should be readily accessible to players, since communication is too slow to account for it. In spite of the high detail, locations where seekers are safe, *bases*, are only visible to the coordinator. Seekers are analogous to firefighters, who move through an incident to gather information and act on the environment.

The *coordinator* player (one per team) is physically isolated from the seekers and observes a limited overview of the game (Figure 1, right). The coordinator's view shows the locations of seekers' avatars and threats, as well as the general locations of goals. Some details of the virtual world can only be observed by seekers, such as walls that prevent seeker movement. The coordinator cannot directly interact with the virtual world; like an IC, she observes and communicates.

Virtual World Entities & Terrain

Seekers drive avatars in the virtual world to find and collect goals while avoiding threats. Seekers move through the terrain, circumnavigating walls and collecting and sharing information about the local environment. Threats move in the virtual world and take the seekers' avatars out of play. Once a seeker is *taken out*, reaching a *base* allows her to *come in*.

The team of T^{2}eC players collects goals to win the game. Goals are spread throughout the virtual world, and each goal requires one, two, or three seekers to collect. Cooperative goals are more difficult to collect than single-seeker goals, because players must coordinate action in the virtual world, including avoiding threats.

Virtual world terrain includes features that hinder or benefit seekers. Bases allow the seeker to rejoin the game after a threat attack. Walls impede movement.

Mixing Communication Modalities

Because the design implications for teaching team coordination recommend enabling players to dynamically mix communication modalities [28], T^{2}eC is designed to be a seamful mixed reality game. The present work, like [30], is not a mixed reality, but simulates regions in which seekers are offline. To enable mixing communication modalities, we use co-located and distributed study conditions (Figure 2).

In the *co-located condition*, seeker players sit around a table and communicate with each other face-to-face. In this condition, the coordinator is isolated and can be reached by radio.

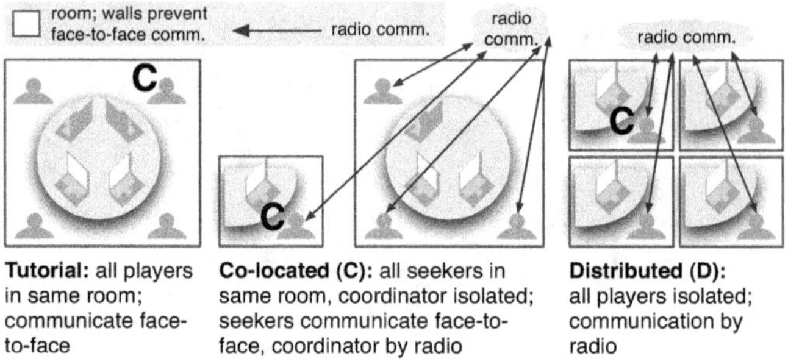

Figure 2. T^{2}eC study conditions. The coordinator is identified by a label "C". Walls indicate where face-to-face communication cannot be used.

In the *distributed condition*, all players are isolated and must communicate by radio. Because information is distributed among the players, they must communicate constantly to integrate and share it. *Communication is a core mechanic.*

TEAM COORDINATION MEASURES

We develop measures to detect changes in a team's coordination performance, as members combine communication and cooperative activity. A speech/action coding scheme, applied by researchers to assess player communication and game action, integrates communication with play. We combine the scheme with computed cooperation measures based on task performance data.

We apply the measures to audio recordings of players' communication, synchronized with game logs. For each player, we capture all speech from that player and all radio communication she hears. The audio record stores a synchronization track that links each moment of audio to a state in the game log. Game logs store all game state: locations and status of all entities and terrain. The logs allow researchers to play back game events and analyze player activity.

We employ the Coordinated Log + Audio Playback System (CLAPS) [10] to analyze data, observing game play while simultaneously listening to players' speech. The ability to synchronize multiple streams of data is essential, as the meaning of speech/action codes can only be disambiguated in the context of play. CLAPS re-creates a complete view of the gameplay experience, enabling researchers to discover critical incidents of effective team coordination.

Communication Performance: Speech and Action

Communication within a team offers insight into its ability to coordinate effectively [17]. To analyze team communication, we developed a protocol analysis coding scheme [6], grounded in prior findings of FERs' work practice and the team cognition literature. We classify each utterance as a particular type based on content and action taken in the game (Table 1). The result is a count of the number of times each player used a particular speech/action code in each game. In addition to recording content of communication, we record the modality the participant used and success or failure (crosstalk, radio interference).

The speech/action coding scheme is grounded in our prior work with FERs [28] and based on the established *anticipation ratio* measure of implicit coordination [5, 17]. The codes are analogs to observed FER practice, applied to the game. By observing game play, we discovered that some utterances overlapped multiple audio codes, showing especially efficient

code	AR	description	example
game state request ($RQGS$)	$pull$	player asks for information about the virtual world (entities, terrain), but not other players	"Where is the next goal?"
game state report ($RPGS$)	$push$	player supplies information about the virtual world (entities, terrain), but not other players	"There are threats here!"
status request (RQS)	$pull$	player asks for information about another player (including seeker status)	"Where are you?"
status report (RPS)	$push$	player supplies information about him/herself or another player, including progression toward an objective	"I'm out right now."
action request (RQA)	$push$	player asks another player to do something	"Let me know where to go next."
metacommunication	–	communication about communication, including indicating a message was heard and understood and asking for clarification	"Repeat please."
metagame	–	communication about the game itself	"How do I run?"

Table 1. Speech/action coding scheme for analyzing T²eC user study data. Each code is accompanied by its abbreviation, used throughout the Results and Analysis sections. The AR column indicates whether the code is a push, pull, or none when calculating anticipation ratio.

communication. For these, we used *hybrid codes* to mark a single utterance with two or more base codes.

Codes were applied by three researchers, so that each game was coded twice. Inter-rater reliability was calculated as the coder pairwise Pearson correlation coefficient. The average, for all coders on all codes was 0.87.

Data Subsets

In our analysis, we work with subsets of the data. For each of the five speech/action codes, the subscript $_p$ indicates a code utterance count is normalized against all the utterances by a *player*, measuring the *composition of a player's communication.* Player communication composition indicates how players are focusing the information they supply or request in play; it is how they are playing the game. The subscript $_t$ indicates that the code is normalized against the amount of *time* in a game. This allows measurement of the aggregate communication of teams, supporting *comparisons across teams.* The measure UT_t counts the total utterances for the team, normalized for the time in the game (Table 4). When a subset of the data comes from a single role, this is indicated with a bracketed subscript: $_{[S]}$ for seekers, $_{[C]}$ for coordinators.

Anticipation Ratio

Anticipation ratio (AR) measures communication efficiency in a range of teams; an improvement in communication efficiency indicates a shift toward implicit coordination [5, 17]. The implicit coordination mode reduces unnecessary communication overhead because team members become more effective at predicting each others' actions through shared mental models. Intuitively, what AR measures is that the less one needs to speak to get one's information needs met, the lower the load on cognition and communication channels.

AR measures the amount of information team members provide against that requested. *Pulling* information functions as a form of noise in the limited communication channel, burdening the team with cognitive load and reduced access to the communication channel. AR places value on *pushing* information out to the team. The function for computing AR is $push/(pull + push)$. Where $push$ is the number of utterances pushing information by part of the team and $pull$ is the number of utterances pulling information by part of the team. Other utterances are excluded.

Each speech/action code is classified as a push, a pull, or none of the above (Table 1). In practice, AR is customized using different combinations of team members, based on the team being studied. In the present research, coordinator pushes are compared with seeker pulls from the coordinator over the limited bandwidth of the radio, as described in Table 4. Because hybrid codes are more efficient, only the $push$ component of each was counted (so a $pull$ component did not penalize AR); if a hybrid was multiple $push$'s, the $push$'s were counted multiple times. The higher a team's AR, the better team members are anticipating each other's information needs. An increase in AR indicates an improvement in communication efficiency and, thus, implicit coordination.

variable	description
GC_{xS}	number of x-seeker goals collected in game, normalized against number of that type available
$cycRem$	game cycles remaining when all goals have been collected, normalized against the performance of all teams (if the team fails to collect all goals, this value is 0)
$gamePerf$	$GC_{1S} + GC_{2S} + GC_{3S} + cycRem$; $gamePerf$ directly captures the set of performance measures used in determining the end of the game, weighting the total collected goals and cycles remaining evenly
$band_{1S}$	% time all seekers alone, normalized for $cycRem$
$band_{2S}$	% time two seekers banded together (one isolated), normalized for $cycRem$
$band_{3S}$	% time all seekers banded together, normalized for $cycRem$

Table 2. Measures of team task performance.

var.	description	range
seq	ordinal value indicating the game in the sequence	1–8
cnd	game condition	$\{C, D\}$
rl	player role in game	$\{S, D\}$

Table 3. Independent variables for teams and individual players.

variable	description
$AR_{C:S(rd)}$	anticipation ratio of coordinator reports to seeker requests over the radio ($RPGS_{t[C]} + RPS_{t[C]} + RQA_{t[C]} : RQGS_{t[S]} + RQS_{t[S]}$)
UT_t	total utterances for the team, normalized for $cycRem$ ($RQGS_t + RQS_t + RPGS_t + RPS_t + RQA_t$)

Table 4. Audio data variables building on Table 1.

Team Task Performance

We directly calculate metrics of team task performance, measuring the team's ability to efficiently complete cooperative activity in T²eC. Team task performance measures are summarized on Table 2.

We calculate how many of each type of goal the seekers collect (GC_{xS}). Goals that require more seekers to cooperate ($x > 1$) are more difficult, but single-seeker goals require significant coordination. Because the game ends early when all goals are collected, the measure $cycRem$ represents time remaining; it is used to normalize other measures. We combine GC_{xS} and $cycRem$ into the unified $gamePerf$ measure.

Inspired by emergent player strategies informally observed in [30], we investigate how players band together in the virtual world. *Seeker bands* occur when one or more seekers can see each other in the virtual world. The measure $band_{xS}$ counts the amount of time x seekers were moving together in the virtual world, normalized for $cycRem$.

Burn Training Observation

Burn training exercises are qualitatively evaluated by instructors at the FTA. The exercises are commonly run with different combinations of students over two weeks. Instructors provide feedback to the students in an after-action review. For the present study, Chief Roccaforte observed the burn training exercises of participating and non-participating students, providing a qualitative account of how playing T²eC impacted their performance, supporting ecological validity.

EVALUATION METHODOLOGY

The purpose of the present study is evaluate the effectiveness of T²eC for teaching team coordination to FERs, so we work with students from the Emergency Services Training Institute Firefighter Training Academy (FTA). The FTA is an intense program in which students attend nine weeks of full-time (8+ hours per day) classes, then perform two weeks of burn training, followed by a week of exams. Many students hold outside employment while attending the school.

A total of 28 students participated in the user study, forming seven teams (three from spring and four from summer 2009). Studies were conducted prior to participants beginning burn training exercises. A self-report instrument indicated that the subject population was 14% female and that highest education was high-school or lower for 85%. The instrument also asked for years of experience in team-based situations; 46% had less than one year's experience and another 29% had 1–5 years experience. Team members selected pseudonyms for the study[2], and optionally created a team name. The teams that did select names were called calTEXANADA, Team Firestorm, Team Rainmen, and FoxtrotAndCo.

Experiment Design

We build on established experimental methods to observe team coordination in T²eC [30], using an iterated game design. We deploy the user study after-hours with the FTA students, so they engage with it as a leisure activity outside of class. This develops ecological validity, confirmed through qualitative data. T²eC supplements the course material as an enjoyable education opportunity.

Teams join for four sessions, at one-week intervals. During a session, team members play the two game conditions: co-located and distributed (Figure 2). In the first session, the team plays a tutorial, in which every team member acts as seeker, but simultaneously observes the coordinator's interface. The tutorial explains game play and controls and demonstrates information distribution. For the tutorial game, all players are co-located and can speak to each other face-to-face. It is followed by the two normal conditions.

[2] We refer to players by their pseudonyms unless that identifies them; otherwise, we use a code: <P-*teamNumber-playerNumber*>. We also identify team name, if any.

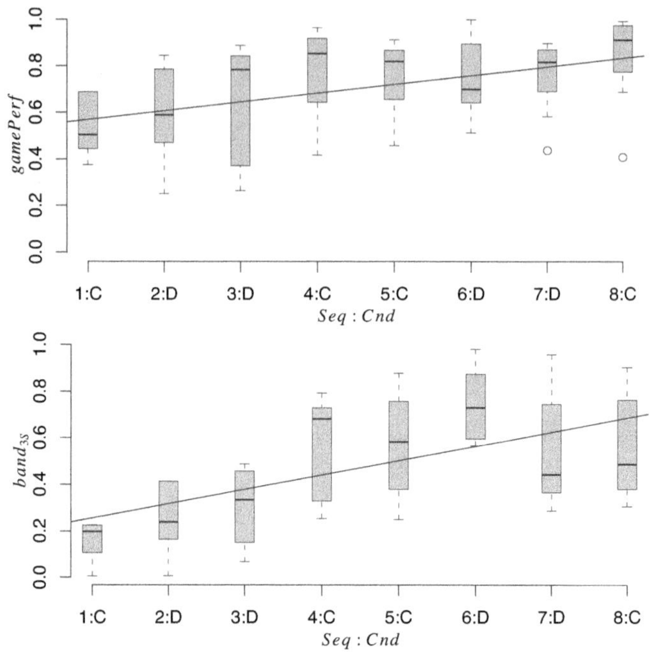

a. $gamePerf \sim seq : m = 3.29, R^2 = 0.17, p < 0.005$
b. $cycRem \sim seq : m = 6.97, R^2 = 0.07, p < 0.06$
c. $gamePerf \sim cnd : p > 0.4$
d. $band_{3S} \sim seq : m = 4.43, R^2 = 0.26, p < 0.001$
$band_{2S} \sim seq : m = -2.02, R^2 = 0.07, p < 0.05$
$band_{1S} \sim seq : m = -4.47, R^2 = 0.27, p < 0.001$
e. $band_{3S} \sim cnd : p > 0.9$
$band_{2S} \sim cnd : p > 0.8$

Figure 3. Team task performance results. Teams collect goals quicker in later games (top plot) while banding together more (middle plot).

Quantitative Analysis Methods

The dependent variables in the evaluation are team coordination measures. Independent variables (Table 3) are derived from the experiment and game designs: seq is index of the game sequence across sessions, measuring time; cnd is the condition for a game, either co-located $[C]$ or distributed $[D]$; rl is a player's role, either seeker $[S]$ or coordinator $[C]$.

We use several quantitative analysis methods for analyzing the resulting data. The first method is a linear model of how a team coordination measure changes with an independent variable. Results are presented as ($[dependentVariable] \sim [independentVariable] : m = [value], R^2 = [value], p < [value]$), where m is the slope of the regression line and R^2 is the fitness of the line. A positive slope indicates a direct relationship, while a negative slope indicates an inverse one. Where we call attention to an insignificant result, we omit the m and R^2 values and report p as greater-than.

The second analysis method is Welch's t test [32]. The t test compares the mean value of a set of samples in a pair of conditions of possibly unequal variances for a statistically significant difference between them. We report t test results as $([variable], [conditionVariable] = \{[1stConditionValue], [2ndConditionValue]\} : t(df) = [value], p < [value])$, where t is the t statistic and df is the number of degrees of freedom of the data. In this section, we use one-tailed t tests, which determine if one condition is greater (positive t) or less (negative t) than the other.

RESULTS

We report results from T^{2}eC user studies with FER students using speech/action code and team task performance measures. Team task performance compares variables derived from game logs that describe cooperative performance. Using the speech/action coding and post-study interview data, we discover changes in player communication. We compare communication data across participant roles, noting different communication styles. Finally, we discuss the ways players use different modalities to communicate with each other.

Team Task Performance

Players improved their ability to play T^{2}eC as a team through repeated sessions. They collected more goals in a shorter time (Figure 3, bottom, a.). Teams completed the game faster as they played more (Figure 3, bottom, b.). Game condition did not significantly impact performance (Figure 3, bottom, c.). Figure 3 (top) plots game performance over time, showing the increasing trend. *Cooperative task performance* improves.

Seeker band variables indicate the percentage of time during which seekers banded together. Game sequence strongly influenced the amount of time seekers banded together (Figure 3, bottom, d.). Game condition did not strongly impact seeker band formation (Figure 3, bottom, e.). Figure 3 (middle) charts the change in $band_{3S}$ over game sequence. *Seeker banding* occurs more frequently in later games.

Improved Communication Efficiency

Analysis of the data resulting from team coordination measures shows that playing T^{2}eC improved participants' communication efficiency. Increases in team anticipation ratios were observed. From the coded audio data, we computed $AR_{C:S(rd)}$: coordinator's pushes to seekers ($RPGS_{t[C]}$, $RPS_{t[C]}$, $RQA_{t[C]}$) against seekers' pulls over radio ($RQGS_{t[S]}$, $RQS_{t[S]}$). A one-tailed t test compared $AR_{C:S(rd)}$ for the first and last sessions, the result indicates an increase in AR (Figure 4, bottom, a.). Further analysis with a linear model revealed an overall increase in AR over repeated sessions (Figure 4, bottom, b. and top plot). Condition did not impact AR (Figure 4, bottom, c.). We observe that *anticipation ratio improves* through play.

Ecological Validity

Qualitative results establish the ecological validity of the quantitative findings. Participants completed the user study prior to beginning burn training. When subsequently interviewed, they noted that burn training ICs who played T^{2}eC used the radio more effectively: they were "...short, sweet, and to the point" [Boomhower] over the limited radio bandwidth. This qualitative data supports the ecological validity of the findings. According to participants, engagement in zero-fidelity simulation resulted in *increased communication efficiency* in the high-fidelity burn training simulation.

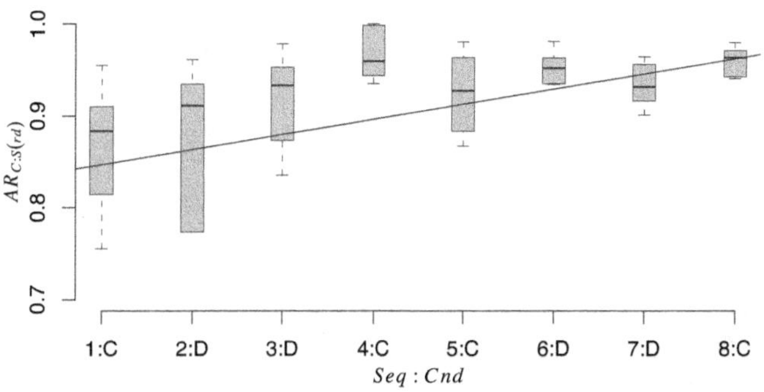

a. $AR_{C:S(rd)}, seq = \{\{1, 2\}, \{7, 8\}\} : t(12) = -2.03, p < 0.04$

b. $AR_{C:S(rd)} \sim seq : m = 2.32, R^2 = 0.09, p < 0.03$

c. $AR_{C:S(rd)} \sim cnd : p > 0.2$

Figure 4. Changes in anticipation ratio (top plots 4, b.). Coordinators get better at anticipating the needs of seekers, while seekers request less. Team members communicate more efficiently over time, improving anticipation ratio; game condition does not impact communication efficiency.

Chief Roccaforte concurred, he observed an improvement in game-playing students' ability to coordinate. According to Roccaforte, students who had played demonstrated an increased confidence in their ability to direct other FERs. They were more articulate with the radio, specifying needs more clearly than other students. Further, they demonstrated a significant capacity to organize teams, instantiating an assistant role to help track deployed firefighters, improving accountability in the field.

Differences Across Roles

The roles players took on in game (rl) impacted the composition of their utterances to other players. A one-tailed t test was performed for each type of player communication (Table 1: $RQGS_p$, RQS_p, $RPGS_p$, RPS_p, RQA_p), comparing the composition of communication by rl. Figure 5 (top) plots the percentages, clearly showing a difference in communication types favored by roles. Seekers requested game state and status more than coordinators while reporting status more (Figure 5, bottom, a.). Coordinators reported on game state and request action more than seekers (Figure 5, bottom, b.). *Communication composition is dependent on role.*

Communication Modality Use

Condition impacted total communication by seekers; a one-tailed t test showed that *seekers* communicated more in the co-located condition ($UT_{t[S]}, cnd = \{C, D\} : t(107) = 13.05, p < 0.001$). Condition did not impact total communication by coordinators ($UT_{t[C]}, cnd = \{C, D\} : p > 0.4$). *Seekers speak more when face-to-face than by radio.*

ANALYSIS

The present research establishes the value of zero-fidelity simulation for team coordination learning. The design implications of information distribution, roles for engaging participants in alternative communicative tasks, and employing multi-modal communication are validated. In the T^{2}eC user studies, we see the FER students improve their team coordination by shifting to implicit coordination. Players employ different communication styles when operating as coordinator or seeker. Rich, multimodal communication emerges through game play. Participants and instructors connect game play to practice, motivating ecological validity.

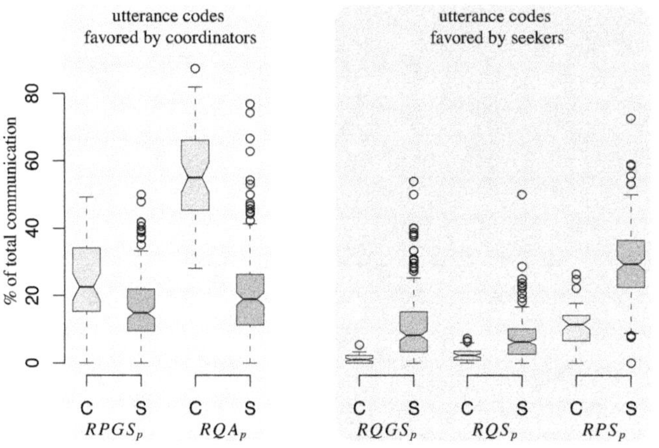

a. $RQGS_p, rl = \{S, C\} : t(172) = 11.47, p < 0.001$
$RQS_p, rl = \{S, C\} : t(213) = 7.99, p < 0.001$
$RPS_p, rl = \{S, C\} : t(197) = 14.88, p < 0.001$

b. $RPGS_p, rl = \{S, C\} : t(80) = -4.27, p < 0.001$
$RQA_p, rl = \{S, C\} : t(97) = -16.29, p < 0.001$

Figure 5. Impact of role on communication. Plot: Within each pair, coordinator data points are on left, seeker are on right. Each point represents one instance of a player in a game. Table: Positive *t-values* indicate that seekers favor a communication code, while negative values indicate that coordinators do.

Shift to Implicit Coordination

Through play in T^{2}eC, we observe an improvement in team coordination through concurrent improvement in cooperative task performance and communication efficiency.

Cooperative Task Performance

Players improve their *cooperative task performance* over time by practicing collaborative action. The design of cooperative goals in T^{2}eC requires that players work together to succeed [29]. The team's performance depends on seekers gathering at goal locations, while avoiding threats. Even single-seeker goals require coordination, such as scouts or decoys to distract threats. In spite of the difficulty of banding together, players succeed at collecting more goals in less time.

Seekers learn to *band together* in the virtual world and successfully collect more cooperative goals. There are two mechanisms for collecting goals: moving together or meeting up. The data indicate that seekers find it more effective to move together. According to Boomhower "[Team Firestorm]. . . learned pretty quick that if all three people stayed together. . . that was the easiest way to get it done." An alternative strategy, less often employed, was to locate a cooperative goal, then meet up. Moving together is difficult because the seeker view only shows what is ahead and not, for example, that a companion is following behind. Banding together means that seekers are frequently in more danger, as threats can attack the whole group.

Improving Anticipation Ratio

We find that team anticipation ratio improves through play. *A high AR indicates a shift to implicit coordination* [5]; team members actively share information while their own information needs are fulfilled. *The observed increase in participants' AR shows they learn to implicitly coordinate.* Teams reduced their communication overhead, increasing the amount of communication that informs and directs, rather than requests.

We find that one player strategy to improve AR is that team members respond with action, rather than communication. In connecting to practice, participants noted that it was essential to communicate less and that their communication efficiency increases. Ryan [Team Firestorm] noted that while responding to communication with action was essential, the game design allowed the coordinator to observe activity that an IC might not. This suggests an interesting new line of research, in which we manipulate information distribution to provide the coordinator with even less information.

Stepping into Game Roles

Prior work suggests that participant roles are an effective way to distribute information and build team coordination in zero-fidelity simulation [30]. In our study, *communication composition was dependent on role*, demonstrating that this mechanism of information distribution is effective in structuring team communication. Coordinators, who can only influence game play through radio communication, *direct* and *inform*. Seekers, who need information about the world outside of their scope, receive it from the coordinator. They *request* what they need to know. They supply one another and the coordinator with information about their own *status*.

In FER work practice, alternative perspectives and positions at the emergency incident enable different sets of action and communication. The IC has access to information through information artifacts; these enable tracking status of firefighters, like the coordinator's interface. Radio communication is available to both the IC and the firefighters. The IC directs the team, as the coordinator does. Firefighters, at the fireground, have direct access to the situation, like seekers. They know and communicate about the state of their environment and their bodies, like reporting game state and status.

We also see that seekers, but not coordinators, communicate more frequently in co-located games. These games offer more expressive power than distributed games because players communicate face-to-face, instead of only by radio. The coordinator, like the IC, cannot communicate face-to-face. This demonstrates *employing multi-modal communication*.

Multi-Modal Communication

We develop the design implication of mixing communication modalities in systems to teach team coordination, reflecting the FER practice of using face-to-face communication when possible and radio when necessary [28]. The present user study was configured to require radio for speaking to the coordinator, while seekers have the option to speak face-to-face when co-located. Throughout the user study, we observe participants using both face-to-face and radio communication.

When T^{2}eC is played co-located, seekers have the ability to speak to each other face-to-face. We observe them taking advantage of the communication modality this condition affords them. In co-located games, seekers use face-to-face communication because it is more effective and convenient, but contact the coordinator when necessary.

Multimodal communication is an instance of distributed cognition. Participants select the form of communication that best fits the situated affordances and constraints. In emergency response practice, this is critical. Participants must consider how to best share information while minding the limitations of the communication channel. Participants suggested a future line of research might go so far as to simulate even more entities vying for the limited bandwidth. Real-time stress plays an essential role in the decision-making process; information must always be shared quickly because the situation changes rapidly.

Value to Practice

Based on qualitative data gathered from interviews with FER T^2eC players and Roccaforte, we found that students connect T^2eC play with practice. Participants reported that "the rules of using a radio" were the same in T^2eC and in FER practice [Jack, Team Firestorm]. According to participant Ryan [Team Firestorm], "The key to the game was (almost) less communication, and it's the same on the fireground, too." <P-1-3> [calTEXANADA] noted that "on the fireground, there's only one radio frequency, so you have to really... key in on when they're talking to you... it really helped being able to listen for that.". Another player noted that:

> It's the learning of communication... its blanketed, it is not just with the game or with the fire service, once you learn how to communicate with a team, it just comes natural to start communicating like that. [Wilson0803[3], calTEXANADA]

The T^2eC study served to reinforce team learning in the FTA. During a reflective session, calTEXANADA appointed one of their seekers to "task force leader"[4]. The leader would direct the other two seekers on the team during the next game. Chief Roccaforte overheard the exchange; he was surprised that the team successfully applied course knowledge to organize themselves.

CONCLUSION

The present research supports the method of zero-fidelity simulation learning by evaluating the Teaching Team Coordination Game with fire emergency response students. The novel method of zero-fidelity simulation eschews the popular method of capturing the physical environment with the highest possible fidelity. While such simulations have value, the zero-fidelity approach *reduces the cost and increases the focus of education*, avoiding the need for complex algorithms and hardware to model concrete reality. Instead of capturing *all* of the target environment directly, zero-fidelity simulation design begins with understanding and re-situating distributed cognition task components in an alternative context. The results of the present study support our principal hypothesis: *by playing zero-fidelity simulation games, fire emergency responders learn team coordination skills*, indicating that zero-fidelity simulation is an effective approach to education.

In processes of distributed cognition, such as those undertaken by FERs, team members transform information, taking it from original forms into representations that facilitate sharing, displaying, speaking about, and otherwise communicating to co-located and distributed partners [12]. In distributing information, it is thus essential to vary form (embodied in the environment, a gauge, a map) as well as function (health status, waypoints) [28, 30]. Participant roles restrict the choices in the zero-fidelity simulation game; they situate players amidst the core game mechanics. Game mechanics, such as speaking to team members or moving in the virtual world, are the means through which players transform and share information. In the present research, we observe participants engaging in processes of information transformation. For example, to communicate with each other about their locations, players use the block-and-grid coordinate system shown in the interface [29]. Other information, such as plans held in the mind, must also be communicated; participants use gesture, block-and-grid coordinates, and the game's vocabulary to communicate plans and associated understanding, contributing to shared mental model formation [2, 19], and thus to situation awareness [4].

Participant students apply what they learn to their work as firefighters, supporting the ecological validity of the study. They and Roccaforte note that ICs who have played are more effective, they economize the limited communication channel, reducing communication overhead [17, 25]. Roccaforte cited improved organizational skill, clarity of radio use, and confidence in coordinating in ICs who had played. The skills of operating in a distributed cognition environment, one in which valuable information is apportioned among team members, is essential to the job. Knowledge of what to communicate, when, and how saves lives in the field.

We show that the interface design implications of information distribution, participant roles, and mixing communication modalities function as design *principles*. Information distribution and action capabilities characterize roles and drive learning. Players use information available to them, sharing it to coordinate. Players mix communication modalities based on information available, who needs the information, and the affordances of the environment. The mixing of communication modalities *leads to implicit coordination*. The teams become more effective, then apply what they learn to their work. Roles are an effective axis on which to distribute information and mechanics; participants use their roles to guide choices about communication modality. Researchers and practitioners can use these principles to develop their own zero-fidelity simulations and games.

We present experimental methods for measuring the impact of collaborative virtual worlds on team coordination. These measures may be applied to other situated contexts in which users communicate. By examining and coding communication content, we gain insight into how well a team performs. Directly computed measures can be evaluated using performance logs that track cooperative tasks in the environment.

Zero-fidelity simulations have the potential to transfer across domains. We hypothesize that a zero-fidelity simulation of the intense team coordination of fire emergency response may be effective in other contexts. This opens doors to exciting new forms of hands-on education in which participants learn human-human interaction skills essential to a number of domains. As abstracted socio-technical systems, zero-fidelity simulations educate participants in distributed cognition tasks. Future work will investigate transferability by testing T^2eC and other zero-fidelity simulations across domains, from diverse emergency responders to programming teams.

ACKNOWLEDGEMENTS

Special thanks to Cary Roccaforte and the instructors at TEEX for supporting this research. This material is based

[3]Wilson0803 is an outlier among the novice students, having had over 10 years experience in military teamwork.

[4]*task force*: "Any combination of [personnel or equipment used in an operation] assembled to support a specific mission..." [21]

upon work supported by the National Science Foundation under grants IIS-0803854 and IIS-0742947. Any opinions, findings, and conclusions or recommendations expressed in this material are those of the authors and do not necessarily reflect view of the NSF or TEEX.

REFERENCES

1. Beaubien, J. M., Parker, D. P. The use of simulation for training teamwork skills in health care: How low can you go? *Qual. Saf. Health Care 13* (2004), i51–i56.
2. Cannon-Bowers, J. A., Salas, E., Converse, S. Shared mental models in expert team decision making. In *Individual and Group Decision Making: Current Issues*, N. J. Castellan, Jr., Ed. Earlbaum, Hillsdale, NJ, 1993, 221–246.
3. Ellington, H. *A Handbook of Game Design*. Kogan Page, London, 1982.
4. Endsley, M. R. Toward a theory of situation awareness in dynamic systems. *Human Factors 37*, 1 (1995), 32–64.
5. Entin, E. E., Serfaty, D. Adaptive team coordination. *Human Factors 41*, 2 (1999), 312–325.
6. Ericsson, K. A., Simon, H. A. *Protocol Analysis: Verbal Reports as Data*, revised ed. MIT Press, Cambridge, MA, 1992.
7. Gagné, R. M. Training devices and simulators: Some research issues. *Am. Psychol. 9*, 3 (1954), 95–107.
8. Gentner, D., Stevens, A. L. *Mental Models*. Earlbaum, Hillsdale, NJ, 1983.
9. Granlund, R., Johansson, B., Persson, M. C3Fire: A micro-world for collaboration training in the ROLF environment. In *Proc. Simulation and Modelling, Simulation Theory and Practice* (2001).
10. Hamilton, W. A., Toups, Z. O., Kerne, A. Synchronized communication and coordinated views: Qualitative data discovery for team game user studies. In *Ext. Abs. ACM CHI* (2009), 4573–4578.
11. Hays, R. T., Singer, M. J. *Simulation Fidelity in Training System Design: Bridging the Gap Between Reality and Training*. Springer-Verlag, New York, 1989.
12. Hutchins, E. *Cognition in the Wild*. MIT Press, Cambridge, MA, 1995.
13. Jiang, X., Hong, J. I., Takayama, L. A., Landay, J. A. Ubiquitous computing for firefighters: Field studies and prototypes of large displays for incident command. In *Proc. ACM CHI* (2004), 679–686.
14. Kleinman, D. L., Serfaty, D. Team performance assessment in distributed decisionmaking. In *Proc. Interactive Networked Sim. for Training* (1989), 22–27.
15. Landgren, J. Making action visible in time-critical work. In *Proc. ACM CHI* (2006), 201–210.
16. Lave, J., Wenger, E. *Situated Learning: Legitimate Peripheral Participation*. Cambridge Univ. Press, Cambridge, 1991.
17. MacMillan, J., Entin, E. E., Serfaty, D. Communication overhead: The hidden cost of team cognition. In *Team Cognition: Understanding the Factors that Drive Process and Performance*, E. Salas S. M. Fiore, Eds. Amer. Psychological Assn., Wash., DC, 2004, 61–82.
18. Malone, T. W. Toward a theory of intrinsically motivating instruction. *Cognitive Sci. 5*, 4 (1981), 333–369.
19. Mathieu, J. E., Goodwin, G. F., Heffner, T. S., Salas, E., Cannon-Bowers, J. A. The influence of shared mental models on team process and performance. *J. Appl. Psychol. 85*, 2 (2000), 273–283.
20. Narayanasamy, V., Wong, K. W., Fung, C. C., Rai, S. Distinguishing games and simulation games from simulators. *ACM CIE 4*, 2 (2006), 1–18.
21. *National Incident Management System*. U.S. Dept. Homeland Security, Wash., DC, 2004.
22. Reder, L., Klatzky, R. L. Transfer: Training for performance. In *Learning, Remembering, Believing: Enhancing Human Performance*, D. Druckman R. A. Bjork, Eds. Nat'l. Acad., Wash., DC, 1994, 25–56.
23. Salen, K., Zimmerman, E. *Rules of Play: Game Design Fundamentals*. MIT Press, Cambridge, MA, 2004.
24. Schechner, R. *Between Theater and Anthropology*. Univ. Pennsylvania Press, Philadelphia, 1985.
25. Serfaty, D. E., Entin, E. E., Volpe, C. Adaptation to stress in team decision-making and coordination. In *Proc. Human Factors and Ergonomics Soc.* (1993), 1228–1233.
26. Small, S. D., Wuerz, R. C., Simon, R., Shapiro, N., Conn, A., Setnick, G. Demonstration of a high-fidelity simulation team training for emergency medicine. *Simulation Training 6*, 4 (1999), 312–323.
27. Thorndike, E. L., Woodworth, R. S. The influence of improvement in one mental function upon the efficiency of other functions (I). *Psychol. Rev.*, 8 (1901), 247–261.
28. Toups, Z. O., Kerne, A. Implicit coordination in firefighting practice: Design implications for teaching fire emergency responders. In *Proc. ACM CHI* (2007), 707–716.
29. Toups, Z. O., Kerne, A., Hamilton, W. Game design principles for engaging cooperative play: Core mechanics and interfaces for non-mimetic simulation of fire emergency response. In *Proc. ACM SIGGRAPH Video Games* (2009), 71–78.
30. Toups, Z. O., Kerne, A., Hamilton, W., Blevins, A. Emergent team coordination: From fire emergency response practice to a non-mimetic simulation game. In *Proc. ACM GROUP* (2009), 341–350.
31. Trnka, J., Granlund, H., Granlund, R. Using low-fidelity simulations to support design of decision-support systems for command and control applications. In *Proc. Distributed Media Systems* (2008), 158–163.
32. Welch, B. L. The generalization of the "Student's" problem when several different population variances are involved. *Biometrika 34*, 1-2 (1947), 28–35.

Kairoscope: Managing Time Perception and Scheduling Through Social Event Coordination

ReeD Martin
MIT Media Lab
77 Mass. Ave, Cambridge, MA 02139 USA
reedm@media.mit.edu

Henry Holtzman
MIT Media Lab
77 Mass. Ave, Cambridge, MA 02139 USA
holtzman@media.mit.edu

ABSTRACT

If everyone says time is relative, why is it still so rigidly defined? There have been many attempts to address the issue of coordinating schedules, but each of these attempts runs into an issue of rigidity: in order to negotiate an event, a specific time must be designated in advance. This model is inherently poor at accommodating life's unpredictability. Kairoscope looks at time from a human perspective, focusing on time as made up of a series of events, rather than simply a series of events in time. By removing our reliance on a fixed time system, events are coordinated socially and on the fly, without worrying about precision. This paper explores the creation of Kairoscope, rooted in ideas of time perception and aiming to reduce time-related stress, optimize time usage, and increase social interaction. The result is a socially-coordinated, constantly adapting, and highly malleable guide through time.

Author Keywords

Social Time, Agents and Intelligent Systems, Social Computing, Automated Planning and Scheduling.

ACM Classification Keywords

H.5.m. Information interfaces and presentation (e.g., HCI): Miscellaneous.

General Terms

Design, Experimentation, Human Factors, Theory.

INTRODUCTION

We never seem to have enough time. There's not enough time to cook a real dinner, to grab lunch with that friend we've been meaning to for weeks, or to work on that project with the rapidly approaching deadline. Our lives are full of events: meetings, appointments, classes, and other scheduled and unscheduled activities. With the possible exception of corporate executives, there's almost always plenty of time in between, yet schedules don't match, timings vary, and events fail to materialize. We end up spending a large amount of time planning, scheduling, coordinating, or simply thinking about our upcoming activities instead of focusing on the ones we're engaged in presently.

CHI 2011, May 7–12, 2011, Vancouver, BC, Canada.

The ancient Greeks had two words for time: Chronos (Kronos) and Kairos, represented by two gods of time. Chronos is, more or less, how we generally think of time today: a linear sequence (or chronology) of events. In this model, we become reliant on an endless linear flow of time. Kairos, although varying definitions and interpretations exist, generally refers to the "moment" or qualitative time: an idea that the only time that's important is now [1]. The concept of kairos was fundamental to the Sophists, where educated persons were described by Isocrates as "those who manage well the circumstances which they encounter day by day, and who possess a judgment which is accurate in meeting occasions as they arise, and rarely misses the expedient course of action." [2]

What if we spent less time caring about the specifics of how things will come to pass (scheduling and planning), and instead simply rest assured that they will indeed happen, freeing us to focus on the moment? This question forms the foundation of Kairoscope. Kairoscope looks at ways to remove the cognitive load of scheduling and managing time from the user, and instead relies on the combined scheduling power of participants and software. This allows a user to know that she is getting dinner with, for example, her friend John tonight at their favorite restaurant. When are they going? Why, at dinnertime, of course! (Or, more precisely, when they're both hungry and available.)

BACKGROUND

In order to understand some of the decisions behind Kairoscope, it's important to look at some of the sociological and psychological implications of how we manage and think about time today. Time perception itself can vary drastically from situation to situation: a boring class can seem to drag on forever, an exciting evening with old friends can make hours seem like minutes. But what senses are we using to perceive time?

We cannot precisely describe the passing of time without describing the events or changes in time. We experience each of these events as "present" when they occur, but the movement from experience to memory may be what allows us to construct an understanding of time having passed [3]. Ernst Pöppel describes 5 elementary time experiences: duration, non-simultaneity, order, past and present, and change or passage of time. While order is relevant to our understanding of time passing, multiple events that occur in close succession often result in incorrect memories of the order in which the events occurred. Yet an individual will often retain memories of "when" an event occurred: in the morning, on a weekend, or in the summer [4].

Philosophers debate the metaphysics of time elapsing, largely surrounding two aspects: presentism vs. eternalism, and objective time passing vs. temporal relations of precedence and simultaneity [5]. While there are differing viewpoints about how time itself passes, a human's perception of time can be considered to be grouped into 3 categories: past, present, and future [6]. This view, labeled "egocentric," is indeed indicative of how we organize events in our minds—relative to our present experience.

An individual's ability to accurately perceive the passing of time is variable, based largely on the experiences of events. Normally, this variability would prevent us from being able to effectively manage large number of events in a day, particularly when the events require coordination with others. However, with the advent of coordinated time systems, we can monitor and quantify the passing of time, based on a set of rules largely agreed upon around the world. Our time perception may be poor, but a sequence of numbers helps us quantify our understanding of time passing.

While this model is effective at creating a baseline for time agreement, it's somewhat of a brute force solution. If our ability to perceive distance were similarly poor, a parallel solution would be to have a wristband giving our precise latitude and longitude at all times, allowing us to navigate physical space by these numbers. Clearly this idea seems absurd: navigating distance without factoring in relative distances and context would not provide a true understanding of a space, and could even lead you to walking right into a wall. A clock informs you that it's 9:23, without relating this to any temporal events in your day, even forcing you to calculate your own relative event spacing and durations ("How long do I have before that 11:15 meeting?") It is no wonder we spend so much time *checking the time*.

Just as we experience our physical world from an egocentric point of view ("That building is around 10 feet from me" rather than "That building is located at 48°51'22.55 N, 2°21'39.20 E, I am at 48°51'22.15 N, 2°21'39.15 E"), it is important to consider time as relative to our present.

GOALS & MOTIVATIONS

There are three primary goals of Kairoscope that are investigated: reducing stress caused by chronic time pressure, improving time management through optimizing for time efficiency, and promoting happiness by enabling opportunities for social interaction.

Chronic Time Pressure

Time pressure has become an increasing social problem affecting quality of life, stress, and overall health of individuals in modern societies, despite increases in quality of life in a variety of other aspects, including subjective well-being [7]. A few methods of addressing this negative trend of time stress have emerged, ranging from imposing mandatory work day hour limits to simply managing one's tasks better. Countless articles have been written about "time management," often attempting to take better advantage of time by decreasing cognitive load of remembering specific tasks and due dates (such as "Getting things done" or GTD). These models inherently seek to alleviate time stress through adding an additional layer of complexity in managing one's stressors. At the same time, an untold number of articles encourage people to enjoy the "little things" in life—how can we be expected to manage everything we want to do with everything we need to do, all while slowing down and enjoying the small details?

It has been suggested that one of the primary aspects of the perception of time shortage is the direct result of feeling rushed [8]. Often it is the quantity of activities in a given day, rather than the number of hours spent in activities, that causes additional stress [9], as an individual is forced to manage and schedule each of these events. Two 3-hour meetings would generally cause less time-related scheduling stress than twelve 30-minute meetings, yet would occupy the same amount of actual time spent in meetings.

In addition, there have been a number of studies looking at our perception of time and what causes certain moments to seem as if they drag on forever, while others feel much shorter than they actually are. Mihály Csikszentmihályi describes the idea of *flow* as, "the state in which people are so involved in an activity that nothing else seems to matter. [...] being completely involved in an activity for its own sake. Time flies." [10] It's apparent that the amount of time one spends in flow can be somewhat inversely related to the amount of time pressure one feels. One of the characteristics of an individual experiencing flow is a lack of awareness of time in an absolute sense [11]. By creating a system that does not demand a continual awareness of time progression, opportunities for engaging in activities that reduce time pressure may be increased.

Optimizing for Time Efficiency

Removing the burden of time precision from individuals has the benefit of also being able to more effectively optimize time through a layer of technology. This optimization can occur in a few fundamental ways: First, events can simply be grouped together by time, with the goal of minimizing awkward gaps: situations where a time space between events is long enough to feel annoying but too short to engage in another activity in the interim.

Second, schedules become easily adaptable when one event changes or is cancelled, again limiting extra space that might occur as a result of changes. Traditionally, if an event is cancelled, one can often be left with an awkward moment in a schedule while waiting for the next event to occur. If the time precision is removed, there is more flexibility to adjust the subsequent event with potentially minimal (or no) consequences. This can allow for a 30-minute cancelled meeting to automatically bump up the following meeting if the impacts are minimal or beneficial.

Third, additional timing abilities are opened up when events aren't limited to standardized fixed durations, start, or end times: a 24-minute meeting can be accounted for just as well as a 30-minute one. One benefit of this is that it allows repetitive events to become optimized for true durations: the meeting that always runs short can now more accurately allow for subsequent meetings to begin earlier.

Finally, while not explored directly in this paper, optimizations could be performed to group events based on location, participants, or type. The abstraction of precision allows events to be grouped by concepts other than chronology.

Optimizing for Social Interaction

While optimizing for efficiency clearly can enable new opportunities, efficiency itself is not always an interesting metric, particularly when developing a system designed to affect humans. In fact, it can often be the contrary: efficiency optimizations have the potential to simply yield even *more* opportunities to pile onto one's schedule. Optimizing for social interaction provides an example of one of the benefits of such a system.

While technological advances in communication have enabled new methods of interacting, facilitated long-distance communication, and offered increased efficiency in managing large numbers of interactions, they have also shown to potentially be decreasing the number of face-to-face interactions [12]. A commonly cited complaint of mid-twenties through mid-fourties individuals in America has been a lack of unplanned ways to engage with their friends face-to-face.

Another contributing factor is the design of our cities and towns. Urban development, particularly since the inception of the automobile, has not necessarily designed with humans in mind. Our cities have seen an increase in sprawl and a higher reliance on car-based cultures. This has literally increased the physical distance between people in a city, thereby reducing many opportunities for social interaction, particularly outside of organized activities [13].

There have been numerous studies looking at overall stress levels compared with levels of social interaction and social isolation. The seminal 1976 Sidney Cobb article, "Social support as a moderator of life stress," discusses the physiological and behavioral implications of social interaction, framed within the context of social support [14]. While social interaction does not imply support, increasing social integration opportunities paves the way to stronger social bonds and support. Increased social interaction, particularly face-to-face [15], does lead to self-reported happiness levels increasing and stress levels decreasing, as well as a variety of physiological improvements. It has been shown that an increase in positive face-to-face interactions can increase cortisol and oxytocin levels [16, 17]. While Kairoscope certainly cannot create positive social interactions, it can facilitate the frequency of occurrence of interactions.

Proposed Methods

There are therefore two main methods in which Kairoscope attempts to increase social interaction. First, the model of reducing scheduling difficulty stands to also facilitate the scheduling of social events in one's life, where the burden of planning is largely alleviated on the part of each individual. "We should hang out sometime" may not be restricted to a statement which is said, and meant, but often not realized due to the weight of scheduling the actual event.

Second, Kairoscope has the ability to increase opportunities for unscheduled social interactions. As Kairoscope gains information about each individual user's schedule, the schedules can be compared within a social network to look for similar opportunities and potential overlaps. A simple example of this would be a casual coffee between friends: On Monday, Paul and Emilie decide to get coffee "later this week" at Café Flore. A group of three of their friends are already planning to get coffee on Thursday at the same café. Kairoscope can add additional probability to this time on Thursday for Paul and Emilie's coffee such that, assuming there are no other conflicts, Kairoscope will be more likely to schedule their coffee to overlap with their friends.

This lightweight approach to unspecified social opportunities increases the likelihood an interaction may occur, without adding additional stress, planning, or even requiring any interaction. Should last minute changes affect Paul and Emilie's coffee, there is no negative impact—no direct plans were ever made. This creates a sense of social serendipity, increasing the frequency individuals might encounter friends, without requiring specific plans to be made.

RELATED WORK

There is a wide body of related work in the areas of time management, schedule management, artificial intelligence planning, intelligent and load-reducing agents, and commonsense scheduling. Some particularly relevant work includes EventMinder [18] and CMRadar [19], which evaluate using agents to manage calendars and scheduling. EventMinder's goal-oriented approach seems particularly relevant in the context of Kairoscope. CMRadar is part of a larger project to help coordinate and manage users' lives, looking at the negotiations and optimization models necessary to facilitate scheduling. Maes' defining work on software agents that act on users' behalves, including "Agents that reduce work and information overload" [20] and "Learning interface agents" [21] are fundamental to the understanding of how agents can be treated as personal assistants and can learn from a user's habits and decisions. In addition, Sycara and Zeng lay out how more than one agent can interact together to negotiate and build consensus in "Coordination of multiple software agents" [22].

There has also been a reasonable amount of work done in calendar optimization agents, such as Jennings and Jackson's "Agent-based meeting scheduling: A design and implementation" [23] or Garrido and Sycara's "Multi-Agent meeting scheduling: A design and implementation" [24] which describe early agent-based scheduling agents. In addition, the more context-sensitive "Learning User's Scheduling Criteria in a Personal Calendar Agent" by Lin and Hsu show a model for learning a user's needs and desires over time, without needing to specifically ask [25]. There are also novel approaches to schedule coordination, such as Kim et al.'s "Compensatory negotiation for agent-based project schedule coordination" which looks at how agents can negotiate when each has distinct constraints and needs, weighing impacts through a model of compensation [26]. Agents that are forced to compromise, accepting less-than-ideal situations, are given compensation by other agents.

A few other scheduling projects exist, such as RhaiCAL [27] , which looks at how users can make decisions when an agent is unsure, showing scheduling implications of both options. PTIME [28] is another project, which chooses a conversation-style interaction. Within this project's context, PLIANT is a learning system used to provide "adaptive assistance in an open calendaring system" [29]. The system uses a set of minimal explicit preferences, such as "I like to have long blocks of free time," augmenting them with knowledge of how the user actually interacts, often superseding the initial preferences with learned versions.

While these models help to set the stage for Kairoscope's implementation, there are a few primary aspects of Kairoscope that stand out from the approaches that exist:

1. Kairoscope hypothesizes that the specificity of time is not relevant to managing a series of events in a user's day, and that by removing the reliance on time precision, we can both more effectively schedule and continually adjust times for events in a day, allowing users to focus less on times and more on activities.

2. Kairoscope does not assume events are always fixed. Events may have varying levels of flexibility, and that flexibility should be exposed and used to easily modify on-the-fly, to best take advantage of moments and situations as they occur.

3. Kairoscope is designed to increase social interaction by coordinating events and locations of its users socially, crowdsourcing an individual's social calendar through a social network.

An important note in the evaluation of Kairoscope is that, while it takes an agent-based approach, it does not attempt to entirely automate scheduling between users. The design of an agent-based UI is particularly important, as agents have been shown to cause reduced awareness when not properly exposed to users. Kairoscope works only within user-defined constraints, sitting between a delicate balance of a feeling of control and being overwhelmed.

DESIGN

There are five primary aspects of how Kairoscope looks at scheduling: improving ease of scheduling, coordinating between individuals and groups, supporting modifications that are constantly updating and evolving, using contextual data to affect schedules, and handling the precision of time technologically.

Ease of Scheduling

One could argue that one of the primary reasons scheduling has been less successful in the personal realm is simply that people are not dedicated enough to input every event of their lives into the calendar, often a very tedious manual procedure. This manual process often leads to key components of a user's day being absent from their calendars. For example, how often do users schedule breakfast at home?

One basic way to improve scheduling today would be to simply have every event that occurs in a person's life inputted into a schedule, and modified regularly. Kairoscope therefore has a variety of input methods: GUI-based input, text-based input, data detection in communications, and a physical input on clocks.

Schedule Coordination

It's generally accepted that time systems were invented primarily to allow for measurement and coordination. Coordination is especially important in a modern society, affecting everything from running a transportation system to managing a staff of employees at a store. While coordination is highly relevant, the time itself is less so: the only reason an employee may be scheduled to begin their shift at 3:00 PM is because another employee is scheduled to stop working at that same moment. The time itself is somewhat arbitrary, and generally chosen for clarity and simplicity.

Kairoscope employs an agent-based model for coordination, rather than relying on fixed times. Users are able to focus on the creation and maintenance of the events themselves, while the agents manage the optimal times and ensuring that each user is aware of when the event is occurring, to ensure all participants show up at the same place at the same time. This model relies on agents that are able to contact each other at a moment's notice, and agents that are able to prompt a user as needed. The majority of the interaction with users occurs when creating an event, while the agents adapt timing based on initial provided parameters.

On-the-Fly Modifications

Often, scheduling software falls apart when there are last-minute changes. Most standard calendaring systems are not real-time, and even systems that can notify each individual when another makes an adjustment frequently have no reliable way of ensuring that each user sees the change in time, or that the modifier is aware of everyone else's responses to the modification [30]. Kairoscope supports a multi-tiered model where users can adjust their own timing or the timing of an event, depending on how much time they need.

When a user wants to push back or move forward an event, they simply indicate this to the agent, which contacts the other agent, notifies it of the adjustment, and is given an affirmative or negative response. For minor adjustments, the agents may not choose to notify the user. If the updated times fall within the same levels of scheduling probabilities, without time precision, adjustments can often occur without bothering the other user. The other user may be aware of an event happening "late this afternoon," but when the agents adjust the time from 3:13 PM to 3:25 PM, the impact of the change may be minimal, and thus no notice is necessary.

Contextual Intelligence

Given the desire to have a much greater data set of timing information for each person's schedule as well as the ability to adjust rapidly on the fly, a system that looks to implement this effectively needs to use some basic contextual "intelligence" [9]. For example, to effectively schedule dinner between two individuals, it would be helpful to know when each of the individuals generally has dinner, their locations, or potentially what kinds of food they like. This can be helpful both in the initial scheduling aspect as well as the moment itself. For example, if a user is a 40-minute drive away from the restaurant she's supposed to meet a friend at for dinner, and it's currently 30 minutes before the dinner, it's very unlikely that she will be able to make the original time, and the event timing is forced to change.

While there's a broad range of contextual knowledge that could be incorporated into this system, the primary contexts Kairoscope looks at are: past timing experiences for similar events, previous events occurring at identical locations, and previous events with the same participants.

Time Precision Handled Technologically

Perhaps the most radical approach to time in Kairoscope is the decreased emphasis on specific time-system-based times. One could begin to think of time as something "understood", rather than a precise value, a bit like temperature. While we do have measuring devices and weather widgets, and occasionally it's informative to find out what today's exact high temperature is, we're generally looking to know the answer to a few basic questions: Do I need a coat? Should I wear a t-shirt or long sleeves? Do I need an umbrella? We have a pretty good sense of these needs simply by feel, although forecast can be helpful in giving us an indication of what conditions might exist in the near future.

If we apply this weather metaphor to time, one could imagine a system where it's relevant to get a "forecast" of events that will be occurring—for example, to see how busy a user's afternoon might be, and what she or he needs to do to prepare. The precise moment at which each of those afternoon events occur may be less relevant, in the same way the difference between 77° F and 79° F is not typically relevant when one is already standing outside in a t-shirt.

When scheduling precisely, we often round to a nearest hour for simplicity. We may use half-hours on occasion, or even quarter hours, but rarely would we have an event for, say, 4:13 PM. This, of course, is a direct result of how our time system splits up the day, rather than any specific lack of affinity for times that fall between integer-based hours. There's no reason coffee with a friend shouldn't be scheduled from 4:13 PM to 4:47 PM, but it's a silly notion that we'd schedule such an odd time, although in reality it's no more silly than 4:00 PM to 4:30 PM. This is especially true when one considers that frequently a coffee scheduled for the latter time ends up occurring at the former time.

IMPLEMENTATION

Kairoscope coordination uses peer-to-peer agents to manage and schedule each user's events in time. Each user of Kairoscope has an agent that represents the user externally to any other agent that wishes to schedule an event. The agent itself runs as a background process on each user's mobile device. In order to determine when events should occur, the agent is designed to use a scalable lexicon of time-based events, drawing from common knowledge until it defines a more specific set related to the individual user. Each of these agents is able to communicate in real-time with other agents to continually adapt as situations change.

The larger common knowledge information is stored in a database on a server, which each agent can query when it encounters an event that it is unfamiliar with. The server responds by delivering an XML response with additional timing information. For example, if a new user schedules a dinner with another user for Thursday (day 3 of the week, where 0 is Monday), the agent may query the server to ask what range of times a dinner might occur within:

```
getNormalTime("dinner", "Cambridge, MA", 3);
```
(Eq. 1)

The server could then respond that generally dinnertime falls between 5:35 PM and 9:42 PM.

If a user requested a dinner for some time "this week," the Kairoscope client would need to query for multiple days, as the average timing for dinner may vary during the week. Since this information is culturally, regionally, and contextually variable, aspects such as location knowledge serve to affect this information as well, and the server will respond with a closest match within a distance of the user that meets a minimum threshold of information.

Server Model

The Kairoscope server model is designed to be accessible, both as a client-API and for coordination. Scheduling an event could be tied to a specific external event timing: for example, a festival in your town can be provided timing details by the town, in the standardized XML format. This event can be referenced by agents when scheduling, allowing any changes in the event's timing to be kicked back to all agents participating in the event. Kairoscope also allows services to provide timing information through a separate tag called <kairoscope:timing> which is interpreted by a Javascript include, fetching the latest timing information, combined with any additional information from the Kairoscope server for the event. This information then replaces "at 9:30PM on Friday" with text such as "Tonight after dinner." This model allows timing changes to be reflected in real time, even should this code be in an email, avoiding the necessity for constant updates and notifications.

Should certain events not contain enough information for Kairoscope to determine correct timing, the user must be prompted. A more advanced common sense "intelligence" system could be employed to make guesses about the best time or location, although this falls outside of the scope of the current project. Kairoscope does not attempt to guess, but rather it works to fill in gaps based around the constraints provided by users.

When a request for an event is made from two individuals, their agents query the server for information about each other. Each agent is able to communicate with a variety of pre-authorized devices (e.g., physical clock devices and computers), in order to receive modifications. When incoming scheduling requests are received for new events, the agent confirms with the user that she or he is interested in making this plan, and then stores the event.

Time Fuzziness

Event definition is based on confidence levels, which are in turn based on the number of times an event has occurred in the past with similar conditions. When an event is specified, such as "dinner," Kairoscope begins by looking for any past events that match. This process begins by determining whether the agent is aware of this event or not. If it is not, it queries the server for information about the event. If it is, it will look at past behavior to predict future possibilities,

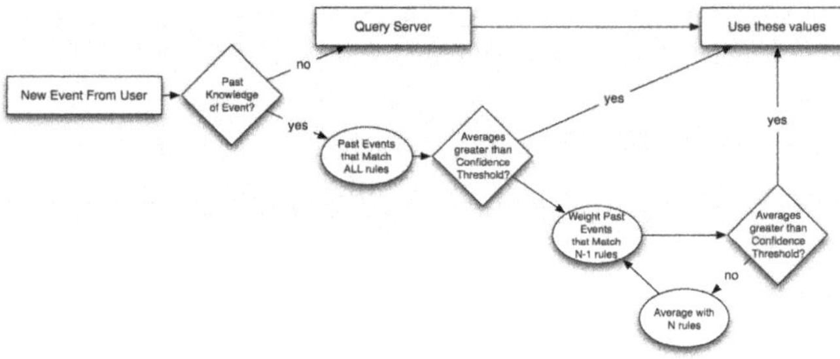

Figure 1. Flowchart for determining what confidence weights to use for understanding event constraints

assuming there is sufficient past data to draw reasonable conclusions, defined as a "confidence threshold." Kairoscope begins by evaluating whether there are events that match all rules, a limited initial set which is defined as location, people, day of week, and month.

If there is a sufficient number of events that match all four of these categories, Kairoscope will use these values to draw predictions about when this event will occur. Otherwise, an average based on the relative weight of each rule is drawn. This calculation is done by looking at an array of rules (numbered sequentially), and iterating through combinations of each, weighting them according to the order specified in the rules. A new average is calculated for each time matching an event and the rules, and is accepted if the total weighted number is greater than the confidence threshold *(fig. 1)*. In the scenarios where Kairoscope does not have an event definition, Kairoscope can attempt to add an event to a schedule with some default characteristics, allowing the user to adjust and clarify the event details as it draws near.

Stages of Scheduling

In addition to the fuzziness levels of an event's timing, Kairoscope moves through three different stages of scheduling for events, varying the fuzziness in each from vague to more precise, depending on their definition:

Stage One - Potential Times Noted

Kairoscope places every possible option on the schedule, assigning different weights to each, based on factors such as how busy the user is or how often the user tends to do that activity. For example, if a user tends to only go out to dinner on the weekend, scheduling a dinner out next week would yield a higher weighting for dinner on the weekend than during the week. Kairoscope builds a confidence table for each event, defined within the constraints given by the user, compared to knowledge of similar events in the past, normalized on the time range, adding any supplemental constraints. These confidence values K are then overlaid onto the schedule, compared with any overlapping confidence values for other events K', to determine adjusted confidence K_{adj}:

$$K_{adj} = K - ((K' \div 2) \times K) \qquad (Eq. 2)$$

Stage Two - Tentative Time Chosen

In stage two, Kairoscope has chosen a tentative time for the event, allowing the ability to indicate to the user a specific date for an event, and allows the two agents to coordinate based around an assumed time, or more importantly, a specific date. This is done in advance, varying based on individual preferences (planner vs. spontaneous). In the prototype, this is 30 hours in advance, although could be variable based on the type of event or the individuals involved.

In this stage, if an event needs to change times on the same date, Kairoscope moves the event freely within the range of possible times. However, if the event needs to change dates, a notification must be given to the user, with an indication of the reason and the possibility to re-evaluate. This is designed to give the user ample time to react to changes within the near future, providing the user the ability to plan for upcoming events with a high level of confidence. This is accomplished by evaluating each possible event's confidences for any given times within the possible time range, and optimizing for earlier events. Choosing an earlier time yields a higher rate of likelihood that the event will occur.

Stage Three - Time Scheduled

In stage three, Kairoscope isolates the precise time when the event will occur. In our prototype, this is done at the beginning of a day for events within half a day, with the remaining day events moving to stage three as they approach, in order to provide the user a clear itinerary for events during the day. While a specific time has been chosen, the time itself is not exposed to the user by default, as Kairoscope may continue to slightly modify timing as needed throughout the day up until the event itself. The purpose of the system choosing a specific time is simply to provide the user with a chronology of events that will occur. Once in stage three, Kairoscope uses basic contextual cues and manual adjustments to slightly alter event timing.

Agent Interactions

Integral to the functioning of Kairoscope is how agents communicate. Kairoscope agents have a simple XML based protocol used to convey event information, both locally for understanding a user's schedule and externally for coordination. Agents do not communicate calendar data with each other, outside of event-specific scheduling.

Event Initialization

When a user attempts to create a new event involving one or more other users, the agent sends out an initial event XML file to each other agent, requesting confirmation and updates regarding their confidences within the time constraints. Each agent submits a response, updating with their confidences for the event timing. The originating agent is tasked with managing the confidences between each agent, equally re-weighted across multiple agents.

Event Modifications

Removing time precision makes the act of changing or adjusting events more fluid. When these adjustments are initiated by a user, the agent immediately contacts any other agents whose events by also be affected. This allows each agent to respond based on their needs. For example, if pushing an event forward results in a conflicting situation for another user, the agent will push back against the desired changes. This interaction can lead to two outcomes: either the originating user decides against modifying the event or the event "pops out" of the schedule and moves into a rescheduling queue.

Events that fall into a rescheduling queue look at potential times that match with the original user request, and immediately reschedule if there is a match. If there is no match within the users' constraints, the event stays in the rescheduling queue awaiting specific feedback from the user about what to do. The user could redefine times such as "tomorrow," "later this week," or "next week."

If the event is in stage three of the scheduling process, this update is made apparent to the user. If the event is in stage two, the event may be updated without involving the user if the change does not move the event outside of a time category. An event that moves by 10 minutes in the afternoon will not inform a user in stage two, but an event that moves from afternoon to morning will trigger a notification.

Location

Location data is aggregated by monitoring the GPS location of an individual over time, stored when the location changes over a specific threshold (set at ¼ of a mile, or a 5 minute walk). Kairoscope associates these locations with events using a Markov model [31], looking for gaps or freezes in location data (shown in grey) or, more interestingly, are of a similar duration to an event (fig. 2). Kairoscope stores general location ranges associated with each event, as well as storing time between locations, to begin understanding times taken between distances, that may differ from initial predictions. Matching location data with user events can yield links between the two. Locations that do not fall within the proximate range are assumed to be separate locations. When no previous location-based time data is available for events and locations, Kairoscope can query the server for averages between the two locations.

User Interface

The interface for Kairoscope could be envisioned as an ecosystem of devices or software that can relay and input time information. For the scope of this project, a few primary interfaces were created: a physical clock, software on a mobile device, and desktop computer software. Each of these devices is capable of both displaying upcoming events and adding new or modifying existing events.

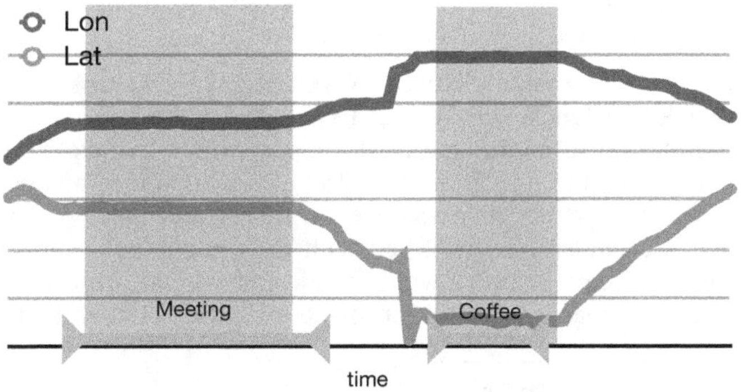

Figure 2. Graph of longitude and latitude of a user, with event and location prediction overlays.

Figure 3. Desktop Physical Clock, with haptic wheel.

Physical Clock

The clock was made by placing a screen behind existing clock hardware, to emulate the feel of a desktop clock (fig. 3). The clock simply displays the next upcoming event with a visual representation of the amount of time available before the next event. The visual representation moves from green to red as an event draws closer, alternatively as a pie chart style visual countdown for an event with a specific start time, or as a gradual fade for an event that occurs more loosely. When there are no upcoming events for a while, the clock simply displays solid green.

To interact with the clock, there is a knob on top that allows a user to view upcoming events, adjust event times, and add new events. Adding an event can be triggered by clicking and holding the knob and choosing from a selection of event types and participants. Viewing upcoming events is performed by simply rotating the knob. Adjusting an event time occurs by pushing and rotating the knob, counter-clockwise to add more time before the event, clockwise to move the event sooner. This action triggers the the agent communication described earlier, simultaneously performing this visual "rotation" on the friend's clock. The friend might then see this change and dispute it (by rotating his or her own knob back forward), or accept the adjustment.

The clock provides haptic feedback to the user when making timing adjustments through the use of a TouchSense PR-1000 knob, which is equipped with programmable detents and varying levels of friction. When user A pushes back an event that runs up against a fixed-time meeting for user B, a strong end-point is triggered, indicating that the user can not move the event past that point. Similarly, if a user has other events that occur after the one she or he is modifying that will also need re-adjusting, the friction becomes increasingly stronger. One can imagine each event having a "weight" to it, and attempting to push multiple events rapidly becomes "heavier", providing an indication as to the impacts of the modification.

The haptic feedback in the knob also becomes valuable when de-coupling an individual's schedule from an event. If a user forces timing of a fixed event, we use a "snap" feedback, simulating a 'break.' This is also shown visually on the clock, as the individual user's timing has now been dis-

Figure 4. Mobile App Interface

associated from the meeting's timing itself. This is particularly useful in situations where a user might be forced to have conflicts with a meeting. This snapping behavior is similar to, yet different from, the "bumping" behavior that occurs when a user forces an event to an irresolvable situation, landing in the rescheduling queue.

Mobile App

In addition to the physical clock interface, Kairoscope runs as a user-facing application and a background application on the computer and on an iPhone. The method of interacting with events largely replicates the interactions described with the physical clock, albeit without the haptic feedback. The visual interface closely mimics the same snapping, bumping, and end point behaviors.

The iPhone application is designed as the primary interface for interacting with Kairoscope, as it is always with the user and generally connected to the internet. The primary screen of this application shows the upcoming event, with the ability to flick upwards to reveal all upcoming events. Upcoming events are grouped by time of day (*Afternoon*, *Evening*). Each event's time is indicated as relative to the user through a visual pie chart indicating time remaining before the event occurs, just as on the physical clock (fig. 4).

Adding a new event takes the user through some basic event-related questions, "What?" "When?" "Who?" and "Where?" (fig. 5). Kairoscope begins by asking the user to indicate what type of event they are scheduling. In the implementation, these are grouped by most common event

Figure 5. 4-Step Process to Create New Event

Figure 6. Desktop Computer Interface

types and shown as a pie menu, enhancing angular memory, with the ability to see a larger list of every event type. If there is no predetermined event type, a generic event type may be chosen, requiring specification of duration.

Desktop Computer Software

The desktop computer software is similar to the iPhone app model, showing alternately a floating radial clock with the next upcoming event, a menu bar clock, or an icon in the dock indicating the same. In addition, there is a window which shows all upcoming events, and the amount of time remaining before they occur. This is accessible by clicking on any of the three Kairoscope clocks described.

While scheduling an event on the desktop has the same 4-step option as the iPhone app, one other additional ability on the desktop is to use text- or speech-based input (fig. 6). Using a slightly modified version of the Chronic natural date processing library for Ruby[1], the input is translated into usable event data, containing participants, activity, location, and time. Speech-based input is handled by MacSpeech[2] using a simple plugin to deliver the interpreted results directly to Kairoscope to parse.

EVALUATION

In order to evaluate Kairoscope, limited implementations of the system were made available to a small number of users for two sessions: a two-day period, where users were assigned specific tasks to complete, and a separate two-week period, where users were encouraged to use Kairoscope in their daily activities. The users were all users and owners of iPhone devices. This criteria was selected for simplicity of running the study and to avoid inexperience with the chosen devices being a heavily contributing factor.

In the first session, 8 users were assigned two tasks: to schedule a lunch with a friend (we played the role of the friend) and to coordinate a film night with 4 friends. The users ranged in age from 19 to 35 years, with a median age of 25. The gender mix was even: 4 males, 4 females. Each user's calendar was pre-filled with the same set of events, such that certain times would work and others would not. The participants were told to make a best-effort attempt at

[1] http://chronic.rubyforge.org/

[2] http://www.macspeech.com/

scheduling the event, but conflicts happen and not every event can be successfully scheduled. The group was split in two, half using Kairoscope, half scheduling in their preferred method, which was swapped on day two of the study. A series of conflicts and alternate timings came up during the scheduling that each user had to adapt to. In the second task, no perfect solution was available for scheduling all participants, without readjustments.

Each user was asked to fill out a brief survey before the study and after the study, asking them how the experience was. The success rate of each user in each scenario and with each method was noted. Users were introduced to the concept of Kairoscope and shown how the software worked for 20 minutes prior to each of the scenarios.

In the second session, 13 users were chosen who had previously indicated they use a scheduling program to manage events. Each of the users provided calendar data from the previous 4 weeks and completed a pre-survey about their scheduling habits and initial thoughts, one week prior to being introduced to Kairoscope directly. The users ranged in age from 20 to 57 years, with a median age of 32. The gender mix was 5 females and 8 males.

In this session, users were not given specific tasks, rather told to use Kairoscope for a two week period in their lives, and compare it to how they normally managed and thought about time. This session was designed to get initial feedback about the interface, thoughts on scheduling difficulty, a better understanding of individual levels of control and feedback, and responses to social interaction optimizations.

For Session One, 7 out of 8 participants succeeded in scheduling the lunch without using Kairoscope. Of the eight, four used only email to coordinate, two used only phone, one used both phone and email, and one used calendaring software (Google Calendar). Of the seven, four of the users cancelled another engagement without otherwise rescheduling the event with the other person, thus indicating a preference for completing the given task over another existing event. As a result, only 50% of the users successfully maintained all of the events in their schedule while adding the new lunch event.

All 8 users successfully completed the assigned task in Kairoscope. The survey results indicate that users found Kairoscope "surprisingly simple" and "it felt like an extension of my mind." When asked to rate their preference of using Kairoscope (1) vs. other scheduling means (5), the average score was 1.5, overwhelmingly preferring Kairoscope. One user, however, did note "I liked how easy it was, but I'm leery of seeing events moving on my calendar." This is the same user that currently uses Google Calendar for scheduling. When following up with the participant to clarify the concerns (no advance calendar is ever shown), the user conceded that it was largely due to having completed the task first in the standard way, so "[the user] knew it was doing things back there somewhere!" It is potentially worth noting that this user successfully scheduled the lunch, but ended up canceling another meeting and did not reschedule. The same user also mentioned some concerns over feeling a bit "out of control [...] maybe it's not so bad, and I'm just not used to it." This sort of comment is particularly of note, as this could be seen as one of the biggest challenges to the acceptance of the system. While the participants in this study did not have the opportunity to spend a long time using Kairoscope, it's not initially clear how the mentioned user's concerns might become exacerbated or eased.

Other results of note include that for the 4 participants who ended up canceling an event, each of them mentioned in their comments that they were "impressed" and "surprised" that Kairoscope was able to schedule all of the events. One user commented, "What a hassle. Makes me wonder how many things I don't do because it's such a pain to deal with, all this scheduling stuff. Ugh." Another commented "It didn't feel like I did anything. I just said...i want lunch with Reed this week, and I was done. Did I cheat?"

In the second session, 5 participants scheduled the film night without one of the friends being able to attend, 2 participants canceled another event without rescheduling to make room, and 1 participant canceled the film night altogether. The users used the same methods of scheduling as in the first task. This scenario was designed such that there was no perfect match, and even Kairoscope would be unable to find a perfect match given the constraints given. The participants would be forced to make an adjustment, regardless of the chosen time or scheduling method.

7 of the 8 users successfully completed the task using Kairoscope, with 7 moving another event to the following week, while the remaining user moved the film night to the following week. The user who had previously expressed some concern regarding levels of control commented "I appreciated that Kairoscope asked me what to do and didn't go beyond what I told [it to do]." The comments on coordinating multiple users was overwhelmingly positive, as this seems a common complaint among 6 of the participants. One of them used an online site called "Doodle" during the study to accomplish the scheduling. While initially this yielded positive results, as friends changed their availabilities it became quickly confusing and the user ultimately "spent more time doing it over email anyway."

CONCLUSION

In this paper we have introduced Kairoscope, a novel events-based approach to interacting with, experiencing, and enjoying time. Kairoscope's egocentric approach to time navigation guides users through time from their own perspectives, relative to them, and with contextual knowledge of the events that make up their lives. This paper presents a different vision of time management, questioning the premise of the human experience of time represented as a linear sequence of numbers. Through this different approach to time perception and experience, a more clear sense of time emerges, opening up new possibilities to coordinate, experience, and interact.

Certainly a premise as bold as reevaluating our representation and perception of time has a variety of potential implications, only the most basic having been explored in this paper. Future work can be categorized into: improving upon Kairoscope's scheduling and user understanding, evaluating implications of the irrelevance of time systems in human time experiences, experimenting with new ways to visualize events-based time, and exploring time malleability impacts, particularly on social interaction.

It's difficult to imagine how many potential directions for future development exist; the implications are vast. Treating time as something perceived, intimate, and human rather than quantized and systematic could indeed shift navigating events back to a core human experience, freeing us from feeling like slaves to the minutes ticking away.

ACKNOWLEDGMENTS

I would like to thank the Information Ecology group, particularly John Kestner and Matt Hirsch, for their support and ideas on this project, as well as Ned, Matt, and Agata for our initial project that served as inspiration. I also thank Pattie Maes and Henry Lieberman, who always took time to help shape the work and offer advice.

REFERENCES

1. Miller, C. R. "Kairos in the rhetoric of science" A rhetoric of doing: Essays on written discourse. Southern Illinois University Press, 1992, 310-326.
2. Isocrates. Isocrates with an English Translation in three volumes, by George Norlin, Ph.D., LL.D. Cambridge, MA, Harvard University Press; London, William Heinemann Ltd. 1980.
3. Friedman, W. J. About Time: Inventing the Fourth Dimension. Cambridge, MA: MIT Press. 1990.
4. Pöppel, E. "Time Perception," in Richard Held et al. (eds.), Handbook of Sensory Physiology, Vol. VIII: Perception. Berlin: Springer-Verlag. 1978.
5. McTaggart, J. "The Unreality of Time" in Mind: A Quarterly Review of Psychology and Philosophy: 456-473. 1908.
6. Le Poidevan, R. "Egocentric and Objective Time," Proceedings of the Aristotelian Society, XCIX: 19–36. 1999.
7. Garhammer, M. "Pace of life and enjoyment of life." Journal of Happiness Studies. 217-256. 2002.
8. Szollos, A. "Toward a psychology of chronic time pressure." Time and Society. 332-350. 2009.
9. Kahneman, D., Krueger, A. B., Schkade, D. A., Schwartz, N., and Stone, A. A. "A Survey Method for Characterizing Daily Life Experience: The Day Reconstruction Method." Science. 1776-1780. 2004.
10. Csíkszentmihályi, M. Flow: The Psychology of Optimal Experience. New York. 1990.
11. Csikszentmihályi, M. "Time's Winged Chariot: Reflections on the Psychology of Time," paper presented to the Conference on "Time pressure, Work-Family Interface, and Parent-Child Relationships." Univ. of Waterloo. 2002.
12. Sigman, A. "Decline In Face-to-Face Contact Linked to Biological Changes in Humans As Social Networking Increases" Biologist. 56(1): 14-20. 2009.
13. Mitchell, W. J., Borroni-Bird, C., and Burns, L. D. Reinventing the Automobile: Personal Urban Mobility for the 21st Century. Cambridge, Mass: MIT Press. 2010.
14. Cobb, S. "Social support as a moderator of life stress." in Toward an integrated medicine: classics from Psychosomatic medicine 1959-1979. American Psychiatric Pub. 1995.
15. Goffman, E. Interaction Ritual: Essays on Face-to-Face Behavior. New York: Doubleday Anchor. 1967.
16. Uvnäs-Moberg, K. "Oxytocin may mediate the benefits of positive social interaction and emotions." Psychoneuroendocrinology. 819-835. 1998.
17. Heaphy, E. and Dutton, J. "Positive social interactions and the human body at work: Linking organizations and physiology." Academy of Management Review vol. 33, 137–162. 2008.
18. Smith, D. A. EventMinder: A Personal Calendar Assistant That Understands Events. Master Thesis, MIT, 2007.
19. Modi, P. J., Veloso, M., Smith, S. F., and Oh, J. "CMRadar: A Personal Assistant Agent for Calendar Management." Proceedings of the National Conference on Artificial Intelligence. 1020-1021. 2004.
20. Maes, P. "Agents that reduce work and information overload." Communications of the ACM. 1994.
21. Maes, P. and Kozierok, R. "Learning interface agents." Proceedings of the National Conference on Artificial Intelligence. 459-459. 1993.
22. Sycara, K and Zeng, D. "Coordination of multiple intelligent software agents." International Journal of Cooperative Information Systems. 181-212. 1996.
23. Jennings, N. R. and Jackson, A. J. "Agent-based meeting scheduling: A design and implementation." IEEE Electronics Letters (1995), 350-352.
24. Garrido, L. and Sycara, K. "Multi-Agent meeting scheduling: A design and implementation." In Proceedings of the First International Conference on Multi-Agent Systems (ICMAS), 1995.
25. Lin S. and Hsu, J. Y. "Learning User's Scheduling Criteria in a Personal Calendar Agent." Proceeds of TAAI (2000), Taipei.
26. Kim, K., Paulson Jr., B. C., Petrie Jr., C. J., and Lesser, V. R. "Compensatory negotiation for agent-based project schedule coordination." Proceedings of the Fourth International Conference on Multiagent Systems (2000)
27. A.Faulringand & B.A.Myers. "Enabling rich human-agent interaction for a calendar scheduling agent." In Proc. of CHI-05, 2005.
28. Berry, P., Conley, K., Gervasio, M., Peintner, B., Uribe, T., Yorke-Smith, N. "Deploying a Personalized Time Management Agent" International Conference on Autonomous Agents. 2006.
29. Gervasio, M., Moffitt, M., Pollack, M., Taylor, J., and Uribe, T. "Active Preference Learning for Personalized Calendar Scheduling Assistance." In Proceedings of the International Conference on Intelligent User Interfaces. New York: Association Computing Machinery. 2005.
30. Hendler et al. "Calendar Agents on the Semantic Web." IEEE Intellegent Systems (2002), 84-86
31. D. Ashbrook and T. Starner. Learning Significant Locations and Predicting User Movement with GPS. 2002.

Practical, Appropriate, Empirically-Validated Guidelines for Designing Educational Games

Conor Linehan, Ben Kirman, Shaun Lawson
Lincoln Social Computing Research Centre
University of Lincoln, LN6 7TS, UK
{clinehan, bkirman, slawson}@lincoln.ac.uk
++44 1522 837084

Gail G Chan
Oxford Brookes University
Jack Straws Lane, Oxford, OX3 0FL, UK
gchan@brookes.ac.uk
+44 7576 347701

ABSTRACT
There has recently been a great deal of interest in the potential of computer games to function as innovative educational tools. However, there is very little evidence of games fulfilling that potential. Indeed, the process of merging the disparate goals of education and games design appears problematic, and there are currently no practical guidelines for how to do so in a coherent manner. In this paper, we describe the successful, empirically validated teaching methods developed by behavioural psychologists and point out how they are uniquely suited to take advantage of the benefits that games offer to education. We conclude by proposing some practical steps for designing educational games, based on the techniques of Applied Behaviour Analysis. It is intended that this paper can both focus educational games designers on the features of games that are genuinely useful for education, and also introduce a successful form of teaching that this audience may not yet be familiar with.

Author Keywords
Education, Educational Games, Serious Games, Games Design, Applied Behaviour Analysis, Psychology, Behavioural Psychology.

ACM Classification Keywords
K.8.0 [Personal Computing]: Games – *General;* J.4 [Computer Applications]: Social and Behavioral Sciences – *Psychology*; K.3.1 [Computers and Education]: Computer Uses in Education – *Computer-assisted instruction.*

General Terms: Design, Human Factors, Theory.

INTRODUCTION
There has recently been a great deal of interest in harnessing the motivational qualities of computer games in order to create powerful, engaging educational tools [22,49,48,46]. However, little is known about how, exactly, games achieve these motivational qualities. Furthermore, there are very few practical recommendations made on how to recreate the motivation seen in entertainment games when designing educational games. Most literature that has been published on the design of games for education is purely descriptive and discusses why games *should* be good learning tools, rather than what can be done to make sure that they *are*. Perhaps as a consequence, the majority of educational games can be described as chocolate-covered broccoli [9] neither fun, nor of educational benefit.

The intention of this paper is to provide a clear, practical framework for designing engaging game mechanics in educational games, based on the successful, empirically validated teaching methods developed by behavioural psychologists. We are motivated by the findings that whilst there is very little evidence of computer games outperforming traditional teaching methods in terms of contributing towards students successfully achieving education outcomes, there is a great deal of evidence of behavioural teaching programmes doing so. Crucially, the methods that computer games designers and behavioural psychologists have developed for teaching appear very similar to each other in many ways. Both computer games and behavioural teaching programmes are approaches to education that reject the traditional lecture format and use novel, creative methods of structuring the education process, centred on personalised instruction.

In this paper we will first introduce the argument for using games as educational tools and the problems that are inherent in doing so. We will then discuss the processes involved in designing engaging computer games, before addressing the problem of merging the disparate goals of education and game design. We will then suggest that Applied Behaviour Analysis (ABA), the method of teaching developed by behavioural psychologists, can provide a foundation for the design of educational games, while maintaining those aspects of entertainment games that are crucial to player motivation. We will conclude by providing a step-by-step guide in designing an educational game on the basis of ABA.

GAMES AS TOOLS FOR EDUCATION

Student motivation is a key predictor of successful educational outcomes [38,39]. Indeed, one of the most basic and important predictors of student achievement is the amount of time a student spends engaged in learning (or time-on-task; [1,27,20,57]). Traditional mainstream education has been criticised by many as being poor at motivating all but a small minority of learners [55]. Much criticism has been directed towards the lecture-based structure that is still ubiquitous in educational institutions today [45,48]. Critics have typically asserted that the primary advantage of the lecture format is economical rather than pedagogical [41]. What appears to be needed is a medium that provides similar cost-effectiveness as the lecture format, but with the ability to retain rather than alienate learners [41].

Video games have emerged as a technology that specialises in, and is hugely successful at, engaging and motivating users to spend time-on-task [15,22,41]. It is clear that people are highly motivated to engage in these games [48]. In addition to the apparent motivational qualities of computer games, many have commented on how learning is an essential part of successfully playing a game [22,23,30,48]. Indeed, it could be argued that all commercial games are educational, as they train players to learn the skills needed for gaining success within that game. Essentially, it seems that games designers have hit on profoundly successful methods of getting people to learn and to enjoy learning [22,30].

Given that games specialise in engendering motivation, are hugely popular and already require players to learn, it should be no surprise that the creation of games that provide some form of learning experience for the player has been proposed. Educational games appear to offer the potential to improve learner motivation, time-on-task and, consequently, learning outcomes.

Existing games are not particularly successful

While it seems apparent that games have the potential to function as valuable teaching tools, there is very little evidence that they 1) produce reliable, valid and long-lasting educational outcomes, or 2) do so better than traditional education structures. There is very little empirical work published that investigates the educational potential of games in any rigorous manner, and less still that measures the learning outcomes of games compared to other teaching methods [41]. Indeed, review articles [15,44] tend to focus on pointing out reasons why games have the potential to constitute valuable learning tools, rather than reviewing any empirical evidence.

O'Neill et al. [46] conducted a thorough review of articles published on educational computer games in the previous 15 years. They found that, despite the thousands of articles available, only 19 presented a rigorous quantitative or qualitative analysis of educational outcomes from computer games. Of those 19 articles, findings regarding the educational benefits of games were mixed, which echoes the findings of other commentators [14,24,49]. Furthermore, in cases where positive educational outcomes have been found, it is possible that these can be attributed to the instructional design of the educational programme and not to games as a medium (see [12] for a discussion on this point). O'Neill et al., conclude that, "the evidence of potential is striking, but the empirical evidence for effectiveness of games as learning environments is scant" (p. 468).

It is important to note that although reviews have pointed to a lack of convincing evidence for games as educational tools, this does not mean that there haven't been any games that have produced positive educational outcomes. For example, Lee et al. [31] found that students completed 3 times as many maths problems over 19 days using a computer game than they normally did using just worksheets. McLean et al. [43] found favourable results for games in comparison to other teaching methods, across a range of games that taught subjects as diverse as geology and biology. A randomised control trial of a diabetes-management game was found to reduce hospital visits for children aged 8-16 who played it [32]. Indeed, every month there are growing numbers of studies that demonstrate how games can facilitate learning.

However, despite this growing evidence base, it is questionable whether any greater level of understanding on how to best produce learning outcomes through game-based teaching programmes is being generated. Without a solid theoretical framework through which to design studies and interpret results, it is very difficult to differentiate which elements of a successful game were essential in producing those successful outcomes and which were not necessary.

Factors that predict effectiveness of educational games

Given the apparent consensus that games should be effective tools for education, and, further, that some studies have found positive effects for games on educational outcomes, it is surprising to discover that there have been very few concrete, empirically validated suggestions on how to design successful educational games [15,21,24,41,44,46]. In fact, a large number of factors have been suggested as potentially important, but few have been demonstrated conclusively. For example, commentators have suggested that factors such as fun [2], flow [29], engagement [30], feedback [40, 41], goals [15, 56], problem solving [23], game balance and pacing [23], interesting choices [51] and fantasy narrative [38,39], among many others are essential to the success of a game. Indeed, perhaps the most influential book in the field of educational gaming [22] mentions 36 possible ways that people *can* learn from games. What is missing is the evidence of components that *do* reliably predict successful outcomes.

One exception to this analysis appears to lie in the concept of *Intrinsic Learning* ([25]; also referred to as procedural rhetoric [8]). Intrinsic learning requires the embedding of learning outcomes of a teaching programme within the mechanics of a game. It appears crucial that the task learned in the game maps directly on to the challenge faced in the real world. Habgood [25] investigated experimentally the importance of integrating learning content with the mechanics of a game. Specifically, in two studies, he found that a game in which learning was intrinsic to game play was motivationally and educationally more effective than an almost identical game in which learning was not intrinsic to game play. Thus it appears that we have at least one coherent, experimentally verified rule for designing educational games; a successful educational game must integrate the learning with the game play mechanics, rather than as an addition to the game play mechanics.

In summary, while it may prove useful for games designers to give suggestions on game features that enhance engagement, if they are not specific enough to test empirically they are of very little use to other designers. What is necessary in order to advance the understanding of how to build successful educational games is a rigorous framework for defining parameters that can be experimentally validated. We propose that applied behaviour analysis (ABA; [13]) may form an ideal framework for both guiding the design of educational games and conducting the basic research on how to teach successfully via games.

DESIGNING COMPUTER GAMES

One of the key mistakes made by educational games designers lies in focusing too heavily on educational content to the detriment of the gameplay [25]. The reason why games have been proposed as good educational tools is that they are seen as intrinsically motivating. However, that does not mean that everything which is called a game, or looks like a game, will have those motivating qualities. Simply translating a standard textbook-style educational programme into a point-and-click computer programme, does not constitute game design. Rather, a similar approach must be taken to designing an educational game as that is taken to entertainment games.

In order to build a successful educational game, it is crucial to understand what is involved in designing a traditional computer game. From a review of the literature on game design [7,30,36,51] the following features appear important to most games:

Games typically present the player with a series of short, medium and long-term goals. Indeed, Swartout and van Lent [56] found that goals of different levels help motivate learners to continue playing.
Games typically require the player to take some actions or decisions in order to reach those goals [51].
Games typically excel at providing immediate, appropriate and specific feedback to players. This feature is at the heart of the motivation, sustained attention, learning and fun experienced by game players [36,40,41].
Games often have a complex system for presenting players with rewards for achievement.
Games methodically teach players the skills needed to meet complex challenges. Long, complex tasks are broken down into short, simple components. These components are trained individually before being chained together [22,23,30].
Generally, players are expected to demonstrate excellent performance of a skill before they can advance to using that skill in a more challenging environment. Complex tasks, then, simply require the chaining together of these previously learned simple skills.
Where games present the player with options for taking action, no one action should be obviously correct, while others are obviously incorrect [22,30,48,51].

Table 1: List of features seen in most entertainment games.

Of course, this list is in no way exhaustive, and including these seven features will not guarantee a successful game. However, these features are observed in a lot of successful entertainment games, thus implying that they are useful in the engendering and maintaining of player motivation. So, when designing educational games, it appears important to take a pedagogical approach that allows for the inclusion of those features.

INTEGRATING THE GOALS OF EDUCATION AND GAME DESIGN

In order to design successful educational games we need to adopt an educational framework that is both successful and congruent with the goals of game design. We also need a method of instruction that takes greatest advantage of the benefits that medium of computer games offer; their ability to teach in a one-to-one manner, to adapt to the performance of each individual player, to deliver timely and specific feedback to players in a controlled manner, and to motivate players of a wide range of knowledge or skill levels. We propose that Applied Behaviour Analysis (ABA), as a framework, fulfills all of these requirements.

ABA programmes, such as Precision Teaching [33,34,35], Direct Instruction [16], and the Personalized System of Instruction [28] are methods for teaching based on the findings of behavioural science. They are typically delivered on a one-to-one basis and reject the lecture format, relying on the teacher more as a coach. They are designed on the assumption that learning is maximised when high performance targets are set and teaching is focused on the individual. Indeed, unlike in traditional education, the passing criterion in behavioural education is not 40%, but typically somewhere around 90%. If the learner does not reach this stringent passing criterion, they are required to repeat the programme until they do reach it.

ABA programmes are highly successful

There has been a great deal of empirical support for the effectiveness of behavioural teaching programmes. Indeed, they have been extremely successful wherever implemented, from university modules [52] to secondary school, [45] primary school [33,34], driver education programmes [4] and challenging populations [11]. Behavioural teaching methodologies have been particularly successful as early interventions for children diagnosed with autistic spectrum disorders [37].

Despite the empirical evidence for the effectiveness of behavioural teaching methods, they have not yet been widely adopted within mainstream education in any country to date. A number of suggestions (i.e., [4,35,45,52]) have been put forward to explain this situation. For example, educators may be hesitant to adopt instructional methods that are contrary to traditional pedagogical systems or are difficult to fit into the traditional academic calendar [52]. Behavioural strategies require substantial planning, preparation of resources and training, which many educators have been unwilling to undertake [4].

One of the core barriers to acceptance, according to Lindsley [35], is the focus on repetition and discipline within behaviour methodologies and how these don't fit well with current views commonly held by educators that learning should be fun. He draws a comparison between the attitudes of educators and those who coach in athletics and the performing arts. "It is amazing that educators and the public accept the need for disciplined regular daily practice in the performing arts and in athletics, yet reject it in academics."

Crucially, computer games appear ideally suited to circumvent a large number of the factors that are holding back the uptake of these highly effective teaching programmes in mainstream education. The use of computer games require little extra training for the teacher, since a well designed game itself teaches the user how to play it. Games can be fit within the traditional academic timetable, they require no resources other than the game itself, and they motivate players to engage in exactly the type of disciplined, repetitive rehearsal that Lindsley [35] suggested as crucial to success in education.

ABA is similar in structure to games

ABA programmes, have structures that resemble computer games in important ways. For example, in a Precision Teaching programme [33,35], the teacher defines each individual target behaviour that the student needs to improve on. They also define a target frequency of that behaviour, and clearly state the rewards for reaching that target. For example, the goal may be to answer forty 12-times-tables problems in a 30 second period. The student practices the behaviour until the specified target is met. Once performance targets have been met, the student obtains the pre-defined reward and the teacher sets a new task. Students record their own performance under supervision of teachers on specially designed charts. From viewing these charts, students have constant access to feedback on their performance relative to previous sessions.

Interestingly, highly engaging games typically have clearly specified and measurable goals (such as to level-up), require a great deal of repetition of skills in order to reach that goal (fighting numerous similar enemies), are often conducted under time constraints, have clearly specified rewards for reaching the specified goal (stronger player/more weapons/access to new levels) and provide constant feedback from the game state on how successfully the player is performing. The similarities to behavioural teaching programmes are striking. In addition, successful games pay a great deal of attention to the rate in which complexity is increased over the course of game levels and to the balance and pacing of player advancement through these levels. These issues of rates, balance and pacing appear to precisely parallel the process that the behaviour analyst undertakes in defining larger programmes for students.

Has this approach to educational games been undertaken before?

Some researchers have already adapted and used games within behavioural education programmes. For example, Foxx et al. [19] adapted a commercially available board game to train social and vocational skills to developmentally delayed adults. The game contingencies increased social/vocational skills in all targeted areas. Medland and Stachnik [42] successfully used a game to improve the classroom behaviour of fifth grade students. The game reduced the dependent measures from their baseline rate by almost 99% for one group and 97% for the other. Bay-Hinitz, Peterson and Quiltich [3] used co-operative games to modify the aggressive and co-operative behaviours of young children. Cooperative behaviour increased and aggression decreased during cooperative games and these behaviours generalised to subsequent free-play sessions.

It appears that behaviour modification and teaching programmes can, and have, been delivered effectively via games. Indeed, Bay-Hinitz [3] point out that there is a practical advantage to delivering behavioural interventions via games; "instructing children in the use of particular games is a simple strategy, particularly when compared to training a teacher to carry out a specific treatment plan using contingent reinforcement for certain responses" (p. 445). However, these findings have made little impact on the field of educational games in general.

In summary, it appears that ABA programmes are both highly successful methods for teaching, and also resemble games in a number of important ways. In fact ABA programmes appear ideally suited to taking advantage of the benefits that the medium of computer games offer; they excel in teaching in a one-to-one manner, they are adaptive to the performance of each individual learner, they are based on delivering timely and specific feedback to learners in a controlled manner, and they have been used to motivate players of a wide range of knowledge or skill levels. As games and ABA programmes appear to share all of these important features, it should be possible to build games based on ABA principles without losing the motivation typically elicited by entertainment games.

ABA AND THE DESIGN OF EDUCATIONAL GAMES

In this section will attempt to explain some basic steps taken by behaviour analysts in designing educational programmes, and point out how they can be implemented in the design of educational computer games. The steps presented below should, on their own, be enough to improve the chances of games genuinely helping learners to achieve their learning outcomes. These steps can be broken into three categories; a) defining and measuring behaviour, b) recording and analysing behaviour change, c) presenting corrective feedback, and d) dynamically adapting to student performance.

Defining and measuring behaviour

Selecting and defining target behaviours

The most basic and important step in the design of any educational programme is to clearly define the intended learning outcomes of that programme. These outcomes must be defined as clearly, objectively observable behaviours, and it must be possible to provide a specific definition of when a learner has and has not reached that learning outcome. For example, rather than an outcome of 'knowledge of 12-times tables' it should be defined as, the ability to solve any twenty randomly presented 12-times tables problems in a 30 second window. This definition is testable and is possible for a computer to evaluate as correct or not.

Similarly to the concept of intrinsic learning suggested by games designers [8,25], behaviour analysts insist that the "behaviour chosen .... must be *the* behaviour in need of improvement, not a similar behaviour that serves as a proxy for the behaviour of interest, or the subjects verbal description of the behaviour" ([13], p.16). So, whether or not participants have reached a learning outcome should not be judged by their answers to a questionnaire (unless the learning outcome is to improve the learners ability to answer questionnaires). Rather, whether they have reached that learning outcome or not should be observable from the action of the player as they are playing.

Essentially, instruction should not be designed as blocks of play and tests. The play, itself, should be the behaviour that is examined. This is especially important in a computer game, where a teacher is not present to interpret behaviour. So, if the game has been designed to teach industrial chemistry, and a learning outcome is an understanding of the chemical reactions necessary for the extraction of iron from iron ore, the game should take place at the molecular level. It is not appropriate to create a game where people can throw random chemicals into a furnace, then observe the outcomes and answer a multiple choice questionnaire.

ABA programmes, like games, break complex tasks into simpler component tasks and ensure that learners can perform those simpler tasks before requiring performance of the complex skill. So, the designer must clearly define not only the ultimate learning outcome of the programme, but also the series of steps that learners must reach on their way to that goal. In this way, a hierarchy of learning outcomes is created, where knowledge of the simplest concepts and processes are taught first, and knowledge and performance are built methodically. Once the player has passed a challenge and demonstrated a knowledge of a particular concept, they are immediately presented with a more complex challenge that builds upon that newly acquired information.

Measuring Behaviour

Measurement refers to the process of assigning numerical values to observed behaviour. Above, we mentioned the importance of ensuring that the skill that is the focus of the programme is exactly the same as the skill being measured. This is particularly important when designing educational computer games, as it will allow us to automate the process of evaluation and feedback.

We must also consider the units we are measuring. In traditional educational settings it is normal to report the number of tasks that have been performed correctly and the number that have been performed incorrectly. ABA

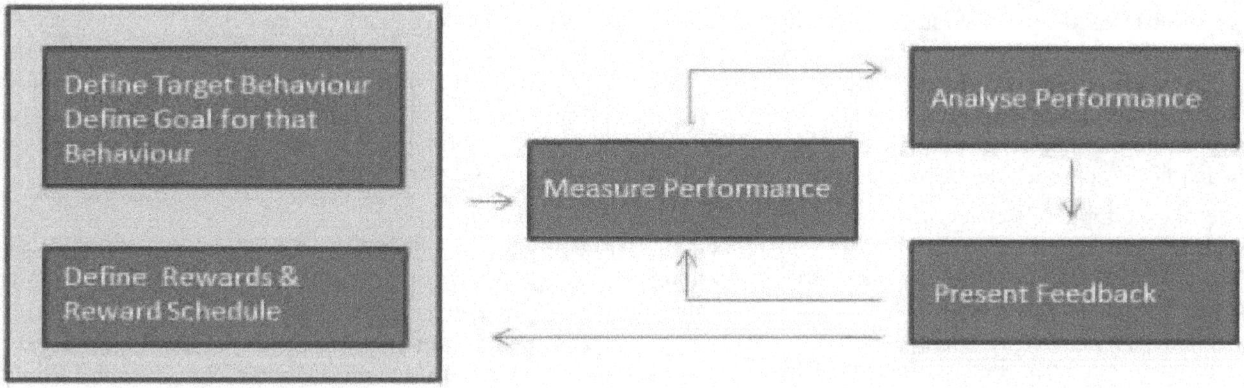

Figure 1. Diagram of the processes involved in an ongoing ABA programme.

programmes focus heavily not only on accuracy, but on temporal aspects of performance. So, tasks are typically carried out within time constraints. Behaviour analysts have found that measures which include temporal components are a more accurate method for judging how comfortable, or fluent the learner is with the material than simple measures of accuracy [13]. So, requiring accurate performance within strict time constraints is a proven method for ensuring that learners are familiar with the material, and also reflects a commonly used game mechanic.

RECORDING AND ANALYSING BEHAVIOUR CHANGE

Recording data

Closely related to the process of measuring behaviour, is that of recording those measurements in a way that is easy for both the learner and instructor to understand. Behaviour analysts record every single instance of every target behaviour. For example, in a spelling exercise, the position of each letter in a word is checked and marked whether it is correct or not. These raw data points are then entered on line graphs, called *celeration charts*, which allow both the teacher and learner to view easily any changes in the learners' performance of that behaviour. In a computer game, these data points must be recorded in a way that is easy for the game application to read and analyse.

Interestingly, the delivery of ABA programmes via computer games allows for a great deal of innovation in terms of recording and presenting data in ways that are useful for both educators and learners to understand. Celeration charts have been developed for their ease of use for the instructor, but computers have a far greater capacity for manipulating data. While it will still be essential to record every data point and present them in a meaningful way, just *how* that data is presented is open to the creativity of the game designer. For example, games typically track performance through a representation of health, lives, level, and other such metrics. This ability to present data in an engaging manner may be one of the key ways that computer games can actually improve upon existing ABA programmes.

Analysing behaviour change

The key metric used by behaviour analysts in monitoring the success of learners is the change in their behaviour over time. Essentially, once a learning outcome has been defined, the behaviour analyst continually measures the learner performing that behaviour and examines whether or not the learner is approaching that outcome.

Consider the example of a coach who is teaching a player to improve their ability to score 3-point shots in basketball. The coach will allow the player to shoot freely, marking down the number of baskets the player makes out of ten shots. The coach then instructs the player in how to improve their technique before watching them practice. Again, the coach observes and marks down on a chart how many are scored. This continues, until the player reaches their target, with the coach intervening only occasionally.

Automating the process of analysing behaviour change is simple, once the preceding steps of defining, measuring and recording behaviour have been carried out in a methodical fashion. In computer games, it may not be always possible to take a true baseline – if the taking of baseline data does not seem congruent to the game design, then performances on early attempts can be compared with performance on later attempts in order to evaluate whether change in behaviour is happening. Computer games can do exactly this type of analysis, without the need for complex machine learning algorithms.

Providing corrective feedback

Presenting feedback

Feedback is presented to learners in most educational programmes in order to give them information regarding how closely their current level of performance matches their goals. The intention is to guide the learner towards excellent performance.

The process whereby performance-related feedback alters the behaviour of learners has been referred to, by behavioural psychologists, as operant conditioning [53,54]. Through investigations of operant conditioning, behavioural psychologists have demonstrated how feedback should be presented in order to maximize the attention and motivation of learners [10]. These findings are directly relevant to the design of educational games. A brief explanation of how these concepts are currently used in games is presented below.

Positive Reinforcement describes a situation where the presentation of a stimulus as a consequence of an instance of behaviour makes that behaviour more likely to occur in that context in future. For example, gaining experience points and gold pieces for killing a goblin may make goblin-slaughter the more likely response to future goblin encounters.
Negative Reinforcement describes a situation where the removal or termination of an existing stimulus (or existing aversive condition) as a consequence of an instance of behaviour makes that behaviour more likely to occur in that context in future. Negative reinforcement is manifest in games where players are forced to re-start from the beginning of a level or stage when they die - not wanting to waste time replaying the easy parts of the same level over-and-over is a powerful motivator.
Positive Punishment describes a situation where the presentation or addition of a stimulus as a consequence of an instance of behaviour makes that behaviour less likely to occur in that context in future. For example, in modern First-person Shooter Games, running aggressively into battle with machine guns firing and little regard to tactics is typically punished by the player's' rapid death.

Negative Punishment describes a situation where the removal or termination of a stimulus as a consequence of an instance of behaviour makes that behaviour less likely to occur. For example, in role-playing games, upon the player's death they are deducted an amount of previously collected experience points.

Table 2. Explanation of how operant conditioning processes work in computer games.

Both engaging games and successful ABA programmes use these basic processes in combination in order to ensure that the game is able to provide consistent, appropriate and specific feedback to the player, and to guide them towards performing at a high skill level. When you wish a player to learn a particular skill or strategy while playing your game, it appears that adopting the following approach is useful; a) offering a variety of rewards for correct performance, b) offering persistent negative consequences for poor performance, which the player will work to avoid, and c) directly presenting negative consequences when the player does something that you do not want them to do.

Evaluating the effectiveness of feedback

In order to apply these techniques successfully, it is crucial to understand the difference between a 'reward' and a reinforcer. A reward is any stimulus given to a player on *the assumption* that it will increase the likelihood of the rewarded behaviour being repeated in future. However, simply providing game players with extra points, new items, or access to new levels is of little value unless the game actually checks to see whether the player has learned from the reward.

Behavioural psychologists continually test whether the rewards they offer produce changes in the target behaviour (i.e. learning). If the targeted behaviour does increase as a consequence of the delivery of a reward stimulus, then the game can classify that stimulus as a reinforcer, and use it later when necessary [53]. So, a reward simply refers to anything presented as a consequence of desired performance; a reinforcer is an example of one of those events that has been demonstrated to work. The same principle applies to punishers.

As there are very few (if any) stimuli that function as a reinforcer or punisher for all people at all times, it is necessary that the game should be able to evaluate the impact of the different rewards that it offers in order to evaluate whether the rewards provided by the game are ones that the player, as an individual, is personally motivated to obtain. Indeed, there should be different types of rewards that players can work for at any time and the game should include some simple way of evaluating which rewards are most reinforcing for each player.

Fortunately, behavioural psychologists have developed useful techniques for evaluating the relative reinforcing strength of different rewards, and it appears that these techniques may be ideal for use in computer games. Herrnstein [26] found that when two or more behaviour options are available, behaviour can be explained quite well via a mathematical formula that he called the 'matching law.' Understanding the matching law can help games designers create uniquely adaptive and engaging games. Herrnsteins algorithm allows us to monitor the relative attractiveness of each of the various reinforcers on offer with a given game.

Through continuously monitoring a players behaviour, a game (educational or otherwise) can automatically calculate which rewards are eliciting the most work from that player (i.e., which are most reinforcing). In an entertainment game such as *Fallout 3* [6], for example, through monitoring player activity, the game could easily identify that a given player has spent twice as much time or effort doing missions for which they will receive rare items, as those for which they receive 'karma' points. Using the Matching Law to interpret this data, the game could deduce that rare items are twice as reinforcing for that player as karma points. Thus, using this simple strategy, it is possible for games to dynamically evaluate the reinforcing strength of each of the available game rewards for each individual player player, and make adjustments to its own reward system in order to exploit this data. A similar process would be very useful for maintaining the engagement of educational games players.

Scheduling rewards

Of huge importance to educational game design is the question of how best to maintain the attention and motivation of the learner. Behaviour analysts have found that in order to maintain behaviour, we must carefully consider not only what to use as a reward, but also how and when learners should gain access to those rewards. It is not sufficient to offer a reward after every action that a user takes. Rather, in order to sustain attention over a period of time, it is necessary to manipulate either the number of responses required, or the time elapsed before reinforcement is delivered for a particular behaviour [18]. Different schedules are appropriate in different contexts, depending on the type of behaviour you wish to engender in the user. This process has been examined extensively in the behaviour analysis literature under the term 'schedules of reinforcement' [10,18]. Below are four schedules commonly used in both education settings and computer games.

Fixed Ratio schedules deliver reinforcement after every nth response. For example, FR5 schedules provide reinforcement consistently after every fifth response. This schedule produces a high, steady rate of responding with a brief pause after the delivery of the reinforcer.
Variable Ratio schedules are similar to FR schedules, with the exception that, rather than being predictable, the number of responses required for reinforcement oscillates around a mean. This type of schedule creates a high and steady rate

of responding and is typically the most economical; a lot of work can be generated by few instances of reinforcement.
A Fixed interval is a schedule where only the first response after a specified amount of time has elapsed is rewarded, while premature responses are not reinforced.
Variable Interval schedules are similar to FI schedules, with the exception that the time for which reinforcement is unavailable oscillates around a mean, rather than being predictable.

Table 3. Explanation of four different schedules of reinforcement.

Behaviour analysts use combinations of these schedules in order to motivate learners. Indeed, the literature [10,13,18] suggests that if people have a consistent history of being reinforced for their efforts, the workload required to reach those same rewards can be increased gradually over time without losing the motivational effects of those rewards. It is not necessary, or even good practice, to keep rewarding every action. Behavioural Psychologists refer to this technique as 'schedule leaning.' Indeed, the technique is also observed in computer games, where the first few tasks that a player completes are reinforced through new items, new skills and leveling-up. However, as the player progresses and spends more time playing the game, the number of actions needed to produce a reinforcer are increased.

Adapting to student performance

Both games and ABA programmes are built on the assumption that the challenges presented should be appropriate to the users' skill level. There should always be the opportunity for reinforcement, regardless of the level of ability that a learner initially demonstrates. In order to ensure that this is the case within an ABA-based educational game, that game must be able to analyse the players performance and adapt in order to consistently present appropriate challenges. This appears to be quite a challenge, but can be done quite effectively if the previous steps have been taken carefully.

Firstly, clearly defined goals, each representing components of the ultimate target behaviours, mean that present behaviour can always be compared to a relevant goal. If goals are met quickly, the player should advance at a fast pace. If goals are not met after repeated attempts, the player should be required to repeat the simpler component tasks. In this way, the player will always be striving towards achievable goals and the game will not present any challenge without providing the player with the skills required to pass it.

Secondly, as the player advances through the game at a quick pace, the game can recognize this and begin presenting rewards on a leaner schedule. The increased scarcity of rewards as the game progresses functions to sustain behaviour.

Thirdly, using the matching law, the game can evaluate the relative reinforcing strength of the various rewards on offer in the game. This information can be used in a variety of different ways, depending on what effect on player behaviour is necessary. For example, they can offer proportionally more of the more attractive rewards (adapting to individual differences), reduce the frequency of those rewards over time (leaning the schedule), or adjust the amount of work required to achieve each of the available awards, in order to ensure that players are motivated to experience each element of the game.

CONCLUSION

In this paper we have identified that while computer games appear to represent an exciting new paradigm in education, there is a lack of empirical evidence for their effectiveness. We suggest that the current lack of success of these tools is due to a lack of theoretical and methodological rigor in the design of educational games. There is a misunderstanding of the game features that must be included in educational games and the teaching methodologies that are compatible with gameplay.

We propose that Applied Behaviour Analysis (ABA), a personalised method of teaching that has been demonstrated as highly successful wherever implemented, appears uniquely positioned to take advantage of the benefits that the medium of computer games offer; their ability to teach in a one-to-one manner, to adapt to the performance of each individual player, to deliver timely and specific feedback to players in a controlled manner, and to motivate players of a wide range of knowledge or skill levels.

Finally, we have laid out some steps that are central to the design of any ABA programme. Including these steps in the design of any educational game will ensure that the game teaches in a way that has both been demonstrated as effective and is also appropriate to the medium of computer games.

ACKNOWLEDGEMENTS

This work was carried out as part of the "Leonardo" project "Learn to Lead" funded by the EU Lifelong Learning Program (http://www.learn2lead.unina.it).

The authors also wish to acknowledge informal discussions held with Bryan Roche at the National University of Ireland, Maynooth, and with Denis O'Hora and Ian Stewart at the National University of Ireland, Galway, which have been useful in formulating the ideas presented in this paper.

REFERENCES

1. Admiraal, W., Wubbels, T., and Pilot, A. College teaching in legal education: Teaching method, students' time-on-task, and achievement. Research in Higher Education, 40 (1999), 687-704.
2. Amory, A., Naicker, K., Vincent, J., and Adams, C. The use of computer games as an educational tool: identification of appropriate game types and game

The Mathematical Imagery Trainer: From Embodied Interaction to Conceptual Learning

Mark Howison
Center for Computation and Visualization
Brown University
Providence, RI 02912-1824 USA
mhowison@brown.edu

Dragan Trninic, Daniel Reinholz, Dor Abrahamson
Graduate School of Education
University of California, Berkeley
Berkeley, CA 94720-1670 USA
{trninic,reinholz,dor}@berkeley.edu

ABSTRACT
We introduce an embodied-interaction instructional design, the Mathematical Imagery Trainer (MIT), for helping young students develop grounded understanding of proportional equivalence (e.g., 2/3 = 4/6). Taking advantage of the low-cost availability of hand-motion tracking provided by the Nintendo Wii remote, the MIT applies cognitive-science findings that mathematical concepts are grounded in mental simulation of dynamic imagery, which is acquired through perceiving, planning, and performing actions with the body. We describe our rationale for and implementation of the MIT through a design-based research approach and report on clinical interviews with twenty-two 4th–6th grade students who engaged in problem-solving tasks with the MIT.

Author Keywords
Educational technology, mathematics education, embodied cognition, Wii remote, design-based research.

ACM Classification Keywords
H.5.2. [Information Interfaces]: User Interfaces—input devices and strategies; user-centered design.

General Terms
Design, Human Factors, Theory.

INTRODUCTION
Human-computer interactions can be the site of rich, transformative cognitive development, including the construction of new concepts. As mathematics–education researchers, we study this generative space by analyzing students' learning progressions as they interact with computer-based, educational technologies.

Current instructional practices in mathematics education rarely leverage the learning opportunities presented by students' body-based experiences. Yet, research into the embodied nature of mathematical cognition implicates the critical role of concrete, body-based activity in grounding mathematical concepts and solving problems [2,21,26,29]. In particular, a pilot study conducted by Fuson and Abrahamson [16] demonstrated that students' *cognitive* difficulties in understanding proportional progression (e.g., the sequence of equivalent proportions 2:3, 4:6, 6:9, etc.) coincided with their *physical* difficulty in enacting such progressions with their hands (e.g., one hand rises vertically by 2 units per time beat while the other simultaneously rises by 3, beginning from a common baseline, such as a desk).

Figure 1. **The Mathematical Imagery Trainer (MIT) in use by a 5th-grade student during a clinical interview.**

Oriented by the embodied cognition paradigm and the above research finding, we have designed, implemented, and evaluated a technology (see Figure 1) for providing students with an embodied experience from which to build understanding of the mathematical concept of proportional equivalence. Our design starts with the premise that basic mathematical concepts can be grounded [6] in dynamic imagery [36], a subclass of visual imagery (e.g., "pictures inside the head") [20], which is acquired from and encodes perceptual and motor experiences. For instance, "addition" sprouts from early experiences of stacking and grouping sets of objects together [21]. Moreover, mathematical reasoning, such as determining the angle at which a glass of water spills or inferring rules for the rotation of gears, has been found to rely on the mental simulation (or "imagined action") of dynamic imagery [37].

Plausibly, certain mathematical concepts may be difficult to learn because our everyday experience fails to provide suitable dynamic imagery. That is, students who display difficulties in learning a mathematical concept may be otherwise ready to learn the concept, except they lack a suitable image for grounding the concept. Our broad aim is to help students acquire such missing imagery from contrived experiences that rely on computational media to "phenomenalize" [30] the abstract mathematical concept in the form of a concrete, physical challenge.

To evaluate the effectiveness of our design, and in order to deepen our understanding of the apparent roles of embodied interaction in mathematical learning, we have conducted a series of clinical interviews with twenty-two 4th–6th grade students. In these interviews, we monitored students' learning trajectories as they attempted tasks involving our instructional device. Starting with an *a*mathematical situation, we introduced a sequence of activities to shift the students' initial perceptions and reasoning toward mathematically normative practices and discourse [1]. Central to our approach is a pedagogical commitment to Papert's vision of constructionist learning in which *bricolage* antecedes hypothesis [28].

RELATED WORK

Learning and Dynamic Imagery

We chose the content domain of proportionality (e.g., 2:3 = 4:6) because the learning of rational number concepts has historically been fraught with conceptual impediments (for a recent review, see [14,22]). We focus specifically on proportional *progression,* because this content lends itself to challenging physical actions, as in the pilot study mentioned previously [16]. In that study, the authors asked a classroom of 5th graders to lay both hands on the desk and then raise one hand by 2 inches per beat while simultaneously raising the other hand by 3 inches per beat. Most students maintained a constant vertical distance between the levels of their rising hands, which would correspond to a progression such as 2:3, 3:4, 4:5, etc.

This physical demonstration of non-proportional movement foreshadows the most frequently demonstrated (and lamented) student error in the mathematics-education literature: the inappropriate use of additive reasoning in multiplicative situations. Students frequently and erroneously assume that "2/3 = 4/5" because of the additive/subtractive equivalence across numerators and denominators (i.e., "4 – 2 = 5 – 3") [5]. We conjecture that students' robust confusion stems from a lack of suitable dynamical imagery in which to ground, or against which to check, their nascent understanding of proportionality [29].

Unfortunately, conjectures pertaining to hypothetical cognitive constructs raise methodological challenges. A central difficulty in evaluating the roles of imagery in mathematical reasoning has been that these psychological constructs are currently inaccessible for direct measurement. Because we cannot see people's "pictures in the head," we instead rely on indirect means of investigating imagery. For instance, to examine how procedural fluency is deeply rooted in body-based experiences, Hatano et al. [18] asked abacus users to solve arithmetic problems in the absence of an actual abacus while also performing interfering finger-tapping tasks. Performance at "mental abacus" degraded for all but the most skilled abacus users, demonstrating how arithmetic reasoning relies on simulated imagery. This finding is corroborated by a related study in which Stigler [40] found that skilled abacus users self-reported visualizing an image of a real abacus while performing mental arithmetic.

Such experimental designs are well geared for studying imagery, because the researcher can confidently identify the experiential basis of the mental operations, and especially because the experience is based on interaction with a known object. However, cross-sectional studies, such as the above, do not examine individual learning *processes*, which are important in curricular design and in investigating the emergence of conceptual understanding.

Rather than seeking out an existing physical artifact, such as the abacus, we took a more proactive approach by directly inducing an unfamiliar image and then asking students to begin reasoning with it as its mathematical meanings emerged. Prior research has not examined the initial construction of imagery from embodied experiences nor how it begins to support mathematical reasoning, moreover in a single instructional session.

Our design is inspired by the notion of reflective activity, and, in particular, the notion of learning as a reflective conversation with materials. In their analysis of design and learning, Bamberger and Schön [6] posit that learning is necessarily *knowing-in-action.* Due to limited information-processing capacity, users of our design cannot, in advance of implementing a particular "move," consider all the consequences and qualities that may eventually be considered relevant to its evaluation. The immediate corollary is that some decisions emerge organically through the user's conversation with the material of a given system; that is, the user analyzes the system, plans and executes the move, then reflects on the (oftentimes unintended) consequences of this move—a process referred to as *seeing-moving-seeing*. The term "seeing" can be interpreted as sense-making; the user makes sense of the system by using it and reflecting on his actions. In our design, we have aimed to sequence the available user actions such that the consequences of one move may lead naturally to more pedagogically desirable moves in a trajectory from naïve to mathematical reasoning.

Embodied Interaction and Tangible Interfaces

Antle, Corness, and Droumeva [4] have used embodied-interaction designs to elicit, train, and apply users' embodied metaphors as a means of developing intuitive fluency with music creation. Their work extends the classical uses of metaphor in graphical user-interface design, such as the "desktop" metaphor, to whole-body, remote-action interfaces. Working with the specific metaphor of "Music is physical body movement," they implemented a computational system that helps children understand musical concepts such as melody, harmony, and rhythm in the form of intuitive, physical analogs (cf. [15]). Whereas our work shares many similarities in its design rationale, we are targeting a different underlying cognitive mechanism: dynamic imagery pertaining to the ubiquitous conceptual metaphor of "Quantity is spatial extension" [21].

Antle et al. [3] have also studied the role that embodied metaphor can play in supporting "reasoned imagination and learning." Their conclusion after analyzing several case studies is that theoretical expectations for embodied-interaction designs often do not match empirical findings in user studies. Whereas Antle et al. investigated open-ended and imaginative uses of their designs, our study employed a protocol to funnel users' interactions toward a specific outcome. While our participants occasionally explored the interface in unanticipated ways, the protocol of goal-oriented activities constrained interactions with our design into pedagogically desirable trajectories.

Cress et al. [13] used digital dance mats in a design for improving kindergarten children's fluency with relative numerical magnitudes. Their study built on the premise, supported in the literature, that basic numeracy reliably predicts future mathematical performance. In an experimental condition, children used whole-body gesture to solve a magnitude comparison task on a number line that was projected on the floor in front of the mat. A control condition presented a similar task on a tablet PC with input from an electronic pen. In a randomized, cross-over study of these conditions, children's improvement at the magnitude comparison tasks was greater for the experimental group that used full-body motion. This result supports our rationale for choosing embodied interaction as a promising means of promoting mathematical learning among children.

Although we find Cress et al.'s experimental design—a pre-to-post-intervention quantitative assessment of learning gains—to be appropriate for their research questions, our study seeks, rather, to understand the processes between the "pre" and "post." This includes nuanced interpersonal exchanges that occur in the middle of the activities themselves. We believe that qualitative analyses of *process* rather than only *product* constitute an important complement during the development of curricular designs [35].

Marshall, Cheng, and Luckin [25] conducted a study to measure adults' learning gains on a computer-based balance beam task while controlling for the effects of manipulation and agency. Their two-by-two experimental design varied both the type of interface (tangible vs. traditional, mouse-based) and the degree of learners' agency (self-directed vs. prescribed activities with the beam). They found no significant effect for either condition, and conclude that although this finding may not apply to other learning tasks and other groups (such as young children), it is a caution against assuming without rigorous proof that tangible interfaces are more effective at promoting learning than traditional interfaces.

A controlled experiment similar to Marshall et al.'s would be crucial for comparing our tangible interface against

a. b.

Figure 2. **The MIT with IR-reflective tennis balls as hand trackers. A 5th-grade study participant "searches for green": having moved her left hand too high (see red screen in Figure 2a), she lowers it to effect a green screen (Figure 2b).**

Figure 3. **The MIT with hand-held IR emitters, which we found to be the most reliable means of hand tracking. A black matte surface on the desk helps reduce glare that can confuse the Wiimote's IR camera into seeing two IR sources. See http://tinyurl.com/edrl-mit2 for a 5 minute video clip showing the MIT in use.**

alternatives (even non-technological learning materials) to justify widespread deployment in schools. We believe that the successful design and deployment of educational technology at scale requires mixed-method assessments that include experimental designs. This approach is demonstrated by Roschelle et al.'s [32] deployment of SimCalc, a curricular design for entry-level calculus concepts that started as a design-based research effort similar to ours. We also note, however, that our instructional design encompasses more than just a tangible interface: the sequence of activities as mediated by the interviewer in our study is a critical component.

Finally, several HCI research studies have, like ours, used the low-cost Nintendo Wii remote as an input device for capturing complex hand movement and for implementing tangible or gestural interfaces. These include successful applications of hand-motion tracking for painting and drawing [23], music creation [8], and auto-racing and fencing simulation [39]. We extend those results to a new application area: mathematics education.

THE MATHEMATICAL IMAGERY TRAINER

Our instruction design leverages the high-resolution infrared camera available in the inexpensive Nintendo Wii remote to perform motion tracking of students' hands, similar to that described by Lee [24]. In our setup, an array of 84 infrared (940nm) LEDs aligned with the camera provides the light source, and 3M 3000X high-gain reflective tape attached to tennis balls can be effectively tracked at distances as great as 12 feet (see Figure 2). Lee reports that the camera has a 100 Hz refresh rate and a 45 degree field-of-view. In practice, we found the field of view to be slightly more restricted, requiring that we place the camera and LED assembly 10 feet from the student to reliably capture a 3 foot window of arm movement. We oriented the camera on its side, since we required greater resolution (1,024 versus 768 pixels) along the vertical axis.

The Wii remote is a standard Bluetooth device, with several open-source libraries available to access it through Java or .NET.[1] Our accompanying software, called WiiKinemathics[2], is Java-based and presents students with a visual representation on a large display in the form of two crosshair symbols (*trackers*). The orientation of the 22" LED display (rotated 90 degrees and aligned to table height) and the responsiveness of the trackers is carefully calibrated so as to continuously position each tracker at a height that is near to the actual physical height of the students' hand above the desk. This feature is an attempt to enhance the embodied experience of the virtual, remote manipulation [10].

We found that in some cases detection of the reflective balls was too sensitive to the rotation caused by students' natural arm movement as they lifted the balls. This motion pivots the arms about the shoulder and consequently deflects the main reflector attached to the balls away from the axis of the camera and LED array. Our solution was to replace the LED array and reflective balls with battery-powered, hand-held IR emitters that the students point directly at the Wii camera (see Figure 3). With LEDs repurposed from generic TV remote controls, these emitters have a wide enough angle of operation to robustly capture students' hand motion.

DESIGN-BASED RESEARCH

The overarching approach of our study is that of design-based research [11,12], in which theory and design co-develop iteratively. Design-based research is not a methodology per se or a type of assessment. Rather, it is a disciplinary context within which we carry out empirical studies. As designers, we have the advantage of creating the instructional as well as the experimental design. We do so because we have a conjecture as to how learning could be better, yet current learning environments are unsuitable for addressing the conjecture; therefore, we design and evaluate a novel learning environment.

In our study, empirical data were gathered by conducting interviews using the semi-structured clinical technique championed by Jean Piaget, the founder of modern cognitive-developmental research. We spread the implementation of the interviews thinly (no more than two per day), such that from day to day we would be able to

---

[1] Our software uses the WiiRemoteJ Java library, available from http://code.google.com/p/bochovj/wiki/WiiRemoteJ. A .NET library called WiimoteLib is available from http://wiimotelib.codeplex.com/.

[2] Source code is available through a BSD license at http://code.google.com/p/wiikinemathics/.

introduce changes to the materials, activities, and protocol in light of the emergence and refinement of theoretical constructs.

These rapid-prototyping changes—all motivated by the goal of optimizing the pedagogical quality and empirical utility of our subsequent interviews—were based on fieldnotes, preliminary analyses, verbal transcriptions, minutes from our team's daily debriefings, and collaborative wiki postings. Thus, both the interview protocol and the interactive affordances of the instructional materials evolved as we progressed through the pool of participants. We gradually incorporated into the protocol any activities and prompts that arose during interviews and that, in debriefing, we evaluated as eliciting "researchable moments" from the participants. These were moments in which unexpected behavior from a participant suggested new theoretical constructs that we wished to test in subsequent interviews.

There is an inherent trade-off of control for exploration in design-based research. Because we modified our protocol and even our materials over the course of the study, we cannot compare among or draw conclusions for all participants. The scientific merit of case studies emerging from design-based research is often disputed on the grounds of generalizability: regardless of how rich, systematic, and extensive they may be, our studies present only a minor collection of data points sampled from a larger universe of potential cases.

Drawing on Robert Yin's [43] work, we offer an alternative view on this criticism. Yin distinguishes two types of generalization. Statistical generalization is the (rightfully) acknowledged standard approach where researchers sample individuals from a population (people, classrooms, cultural groups) in order to generalize to the larger universe. Yet when dealing with context-dependent activities, such as learning, in a particular community, we encounter a difficulty with statistical generalization. After all, the community under investigation is one of myriad human communities, and grounds for generalization to the larger universe of cultural groups tend to fall short with appeals to statistical generalization (cf. [34])

Acknowledging the utility of statistical generalization, Yin argues for a different kind of generalization, one that he terms "analytic." In analytical generalization, the focus is not generalization to the larger population from which a sample was drawn. The target is theory, and the endeavor is to refine theoretical constructs as their utility is explored and corroborated. In our work, we have found analytic generalizability well-suited to design-based research, which is itself characterized by its reciprocal iterations of design and theory.

With this approach to generalization, theoretical considerations inform the design, and the design, in turn, is used to further develop theory. From such a perspective, our research contributes to characterizing the larger population universe not through statistical inference but by refining our theoretical understanding. As Yin emphasizes, and particularly relevant to our work, analytic generalizabilty is a natural approach when phenomena and "context" have fuzzy boundaries, which is to say, whenever one studies learning in a rich setting.

CLINICAL INTERVIEWS

Participants

The empirical data presented and analyzed in this paper were collected at a private K-8 suburban school in the greater San Francisco Bay Area (33% on financial aid; 10% minority students). In addition, we collaborated with the school principal, the head of general studies, and five mathematics teachers. Within each grade level (4th–6th), we grouped the pool of volunteering students according to three achievement levels as reported by their teachers (high/middle/low). Across these performance groups, we selected roughly equal numbers of students, balancing for gender, for a total of 22 students.

We preferred working with students whom the teachers had indicated as typically more disposed to communicate their thoughts articulately. These more verbose students were distributed almost uniformly across gender and achievement level. Whereas this bias in our selection of participants, as well as the by-and-large upper-middle-class demographics of the school, limits the generality of our conclusions, this initial stage of our research required dense real-time verbal feedback from the students as they interacted with the designed learning tools.

Protocol

Interviews took place in a quiet room within the school facility. Students participated either individually or paired with a classmate (duration: mean 70 min.; SD 20 min.).

The interviewer guided the participant through a sequence of activities by first explaining each activity and then monitoring the participant's performance and providing formative comments so as to ensure that the task was clear. The first activity was introduced with the simple instruction, "Make the screen green" (see Figure 4a—in the final protocol the screen initially bore no virtual elements at all). The background of the application is colored along a gradient from red to green depending on how close the hand heights are to the chosen a:b ratio. For instance, raising the hand trackers to 3" and 12" will turn the screen red or yellow for a 1:2 ratio (the color feedback is modulated by an adjustable tolerance control), whereas moving to 6" and 12" turns the screen green (see Figure 5). For the students interviewed in pairs, each student controlled one of the two hand-trackers.

Once the participants found an initial "green" position, the interviewer asked them to "find green somewhere else." If participants responded by "locking" the distance between their hands in a fixed interval and moving them up or down, the screen turned red. Only once they relaxed this

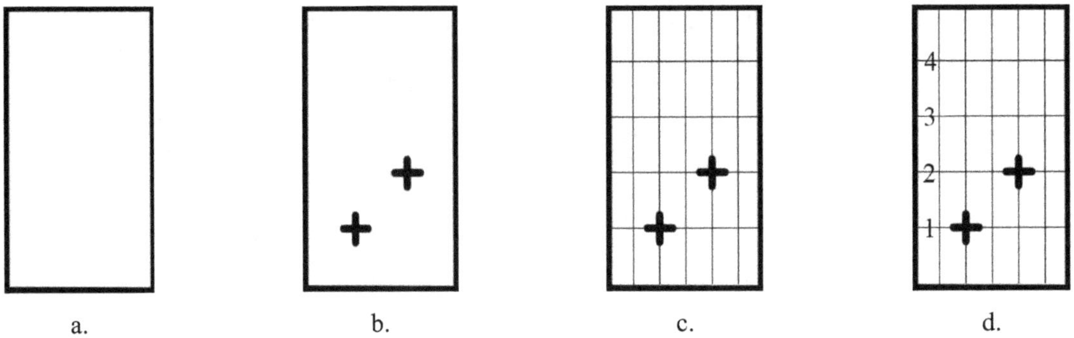

***Figure 4.* Four display configurations: (a) continuous-space mode; (b) continuous-space mode with crosshairs; (c) crosshairs with grid overlay; (d) crosshairs with grid overlay and *y*-axis numerals.**

fixed distance between their hands and attempted to adjust it appropriately would they strike green again.

In the next activity, two crosshairs appeared on the screen to track the position of participants' hands (see Figure 4b). Participants might also at this point identify and articulate a rule to the effect that, *The higher you go on the screen, the greater the distance should be between your hands.*

Next, a grid appeared on the screen (see Figure 4c). The grid bears the capacity to shift participants' attention so as to re-construe each crosshair's location as its height above the base line—a height that can be quantified in terms of discrete units (e.g., 1 and 2 units, respectively). This may encourage a "snap to grid" strategy that utilizes the grid's inherent discrete-quantity relations, for example a recursive rule for transitioning from one green spot to the next: *For every 1 box you raise your left hand, raise your right hand by 2 boxes.* Note that this hand-to-hand relation is also a covariation, just as the height-to-distance relation, above, was a covariation. However, the values of the covariation have shifted from continuous–qualitative descriptors ("higher," "greater") to discrete–quantitative values ("one," "two"). Thus, though both covariations refer to the same hand motions—the objective stimuli—the meanings and planning of this physical enactment have evolved: the latter covariation is closer to normative mathematical practice and discourse for proportional equivalence, and in line with our pedagogical goals.

In the final mode, numerals appeared to the left of the grid (see Figure 4d, previous page), potentially alleviating a need for counting the grid boxes. Specific "green" numeral pairs, such as "3" and "6" in the case of 1:2, may evoke

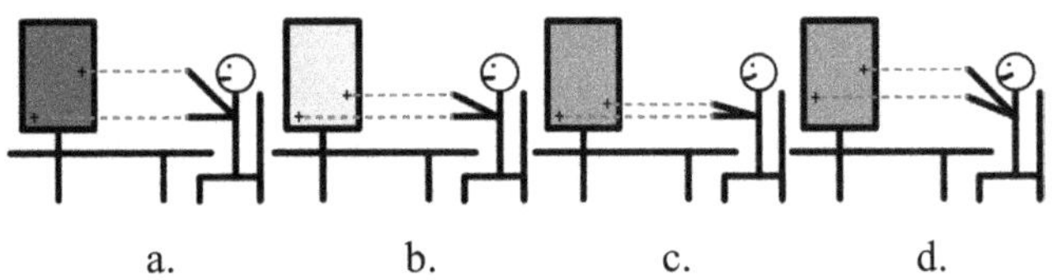

***Figure 5.* An example of continuous-space mode with crosshairs and a 1:2 ratio. A student exhibits (a) incorrect performance; (b) almost correct performance; (c) correct performance; (d) another instance of correct performance.**

basic arithmetic operations and "facts," so that students recognize that the right hand should always be double (the height of) the left hand.

The interview ended with an informal conversation, in which the interviewer explained the objectives of the study, to help participants situate the activities within their school curriculum and everyday experiences. Finally, the interviewer answered any questions participants had, such as about our technology.

Results

All students succeeded in devising, performing, and articulating strategies for making the screen green. These spontaneous strategies bore logical and linguistic structures commonly observed in mathematical discourse pertaining to proportionality. For example, some students discovered, enacted, and stated the covariation of two constant rates (e.g., the left hand rises 1 unit per the right hand's 2 unit rise). We found variations in individual participants' initial interpretation of the task as well as in their trajectory through the protocol. However, by and large the students responded to the protocol items by progressing through similar problem-solving stages, with the more mathematically competent students generating more mathematical meanings and coordinating more among the quantitative properties, relations, and patterns they noticed.

Each student started either by working with only one hand at a time; waving both hands up and down in opposite directions; or lifting both hands up at the same pace, in continuous or abrupt gestures. Students soon realized that the actions of both hands are necessary to achieve green and that the distance between their hands was a critical factor. At first, though, most students anticipated they could achieve a continuously green screen by maintaining a *fixed* distance between their hands, as they moved both hands up and down along the screen, rather than by managing a *proportional* distance between the hands. For example, one 6th grade middle-achieving male student, Penuel, referred to this relation between the hands' respective positions as a "certain distance."

> [15:32] Penuel: So it looks like... they have to be a certain distance away from each other for it to turn green.

[15:37] Interviewer: Uh-huh—

[15:37] Penuel: And if it's not a certain distance, it's not green—it's yellow or red.

Following further experimentation, Penuel proceeded to introduce another parameter into his reasoning about the distance between the hands, namely the hands' height above the desk.

[15:54] Int: Can you say anything more about the distance you're looking for?

[16:00] Penuel: I think it depends how far... how far they are from the ground.

Other students, such as Irit (5th grade; female; high achieving), realized that the fixed-interval rule was not optimal and articulated a changing-interval rule as a variant on the fixed-interval rule. (Note, below, the gentle prompt from the interviewer, who implicitly challenged Irit's assertion by drawing her attention to a phenomenal dimension she had taken to be constant.)

[19:26] Irit: Well, they are same distance, but like, away from each other. Like, uhm.

[19:35] Int: Uhm-hm?

[19:36] Irit: They're still the same distance away from each other, but they're just lower down here.

[19:45] Int: Huh... so what happens to the distance?

[19:52] Irit: Well... Oh! No, it gets shorter if you go down more, and then it gets tall...longer if you go up.

Along this same learning trajectory, another student (Liat; 6th grade; female; middle achieving) exhibited a telltale indication of conceptual development: a mismatch between her gestured actions and her verbal explanation [9,17]. Initially, Liat moved her hands in small fixed-interval gestures; the screen color would change away from green, and each time Liat would restore green with small jolting gestures. It appeared as though Liat implicitly assumed that her strategy enactment, rather than her strategy rationale, was at odds with the system (cf. [19]). Although the distance between Liat's hands was small lower down on the screen and dramatically larger farther up, she persisted in articulating her intended strategy (fixed interval) rather than her *de facto* enactment (changing interval).

[20:17] Liat: I think if I keep them apart and keep going up, it stays the same...

[20:23] Int: If you keep them apart and you keep going up it stays the same?

[20:31] Liat: It's not becoming red, but...

[20:36] Int: So... how are you thinking about keeping them apart? What is it that you are doing?

[20:41] Liat: Umm... I don't know.

Following the interviewers' prompts to "find green" farther up on the screen, Liat was finally able to generalize the rule that she had already objectively enacted.

[21:46] Liat: Oh maybe it's more... if it's farther up, then it has to be...they have to be more apart.

While most students initially located specific hand positions as stably producing green, several students also realized that there are infinitely many "green" hand-position pairs, so that in fact one can simultaneously raise both hands along respective continuous trajectories, a realization that some students articulated in terms of the hands moving at different speeds. For example, Penuel used the differing rates of his hand motions to deduce that a fixed-interval rule could not be correct and that, instead, the distance between the hands must increase with height.

[33:20] Penuel: I think the right hand has to move faster, while the left hand is kind of moving slower.

[33:41] Int: So what's going on?

[33:44] Penuel: Well, they obviously can't be at the same distance. But if I start here, and if the right one is moving, like a little faster, and it's going farther and farther away from the left hand, it will still stay green.

Another student, Siena (6th grade, female, low achieving), went on to formalize a rule for interaction in terms of both continuity and rate.

[15:13] Siena: Make the right hand go a little bit faster but... but let them both be at their own continuous pace.

The introduction of the Cartesian grid caused several students to shift their attention from the relative distance between their hands to the absolute height of their hands above the baseline. The pair Keith and Asa (6th grade, both male, high achieving) who were working with a 1:2 ratio, discovered and articulated a multiplicative relation for the heights in this way.

[30:41] Keith: Maybe it has to be double the number.

[30:44] Asa: Hmm, that's very possible. I'm going to be at one,... you're going to be at two. And then I'll be at two, and you'll be at four. And now I'm going to be at three...

[30:58] Keith: I'll be at six.

[31:38] Asa: You're totally right!

[31:39] Int: What is he right about? What is it?

[31:40] Asa: Uhm, the number has to be double.

Thus, they recast the rule "the higher, the bigger the difference" in terms of covariation between the absolute heights, that is, "for every 1 on the left, it's 2 on the right."

DESIGN ITERATIONS

Throughout our study, we iteratively modified the materials and protocol in light of new conjectures and theoretical constructs. Here, we explain the most important of these design iterations.

Passive versus active interaction

As an early prototype, we fabricated a mechanical device using rope and pulleys that physically moved participants' arms in a fixed 2:3 proportional progression, so that they could "feel" the progression. As opposed to the passive experience of hanging onto a rope, operating the MIT requires immediate agency, and so a question emerged as to how this agency should be framed, elicited, and guided. That is, what were participants to do with the MIT? What would be their task, how would they accomplish it, and what form of feedback might they receive on the quality of their performance?

Initially, we designed a task analogous to feeling the tension in the rope: participants used the hand trackers to closely follow two circular "targets" that moved in a proportional progression up the screen, with the background color indicating their accuracy. However, the first interview suggested that instead allowing "free-form" movement of the trackers was more theoretically compelling, because the ambiguity of the task better reflects what students must cope with in trying to make mathematical sense of the world around them. Figure 6 shows a schematic culminating from our brainstorming around this issue, which then formed the basis of the protocol for all subsequent interviews.

The numerical grid: scheme versus image

In later interviews, we added a new task at the point in the protocol soon after the grid and numerals were introduced (see Figure 4d). Namely, once students had expressed an *a*-for-*b* strategy—whether *b* was the increment in the right hand or the distance between the hands—the interviewer removed the grid and numerals from the display and asked students to resume searching for green.

Students' gesture and verbal utterances strongly suggest that they continued operating as though a grid were present. However, students' errors further suggested that their "mental grid" [6,13] was functioning more like a scheme [41] than as an image [20]. That is, the errors were not procedural but were expressed in imprecise magnitudes resulting in positional inaccuracies. As such, we may be witnessing the instrumental genesis of a utilization schema for proportionality [42]. In future work, we wish to better understand this phenomenon of the mind becoming equipped with mathematical instruments as the residual effect of working with objects [27], because we view it as paradigmatic of mathematical learning [33].

Overriding the hand trackers

Some students expressed a desire to force the trackers to move to precise height ratios that they inputted numerically. In response, we added a "driver" module to allow students to enter a list of heights for each tracker then animate the corresponding motion of the trackers (with corresponding background colors). In our seventh interview, a 4th grade student working with a 2:3 ratio began referring to the ratio as "one and one-and-a-half" and

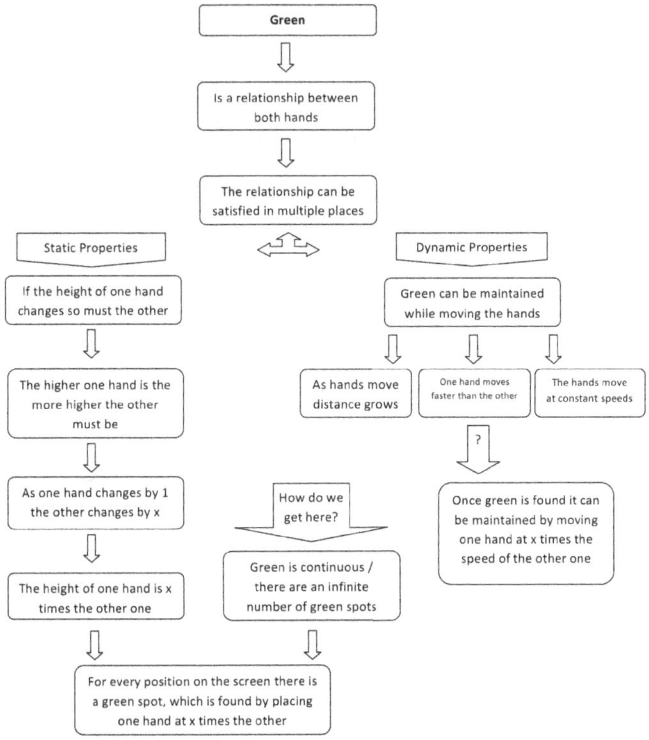

Figure 6. **"What does green mean?" — a schematic created during the design process to conjecture on students' trajectories when given the task, "Make the screen green."**

entered the sequence 1:1.5, 2:3, 3:4, 4:6 into the driver module.

The driver module was programmed to accept only integer values, and the input of a floating point value caused a runtime error! The student worked around the error by multiplying each ratio by 2 and entering the sequence 2:3, 4:6, 6:9, 8:12 instead. This left us with a designer's dilemma: should we fix the bug? Or had the bug created a "teachable moment" for exploring the decimal representation of rational numbers? Our solution was to fix the bug but add an additional switch that could "break" the input again by reverting it back to integer-only operation. This design decision mirrors the central principle of Schwartz's "Broken Calculator" [38], which has selectively disabled number or operation keys that force students to decompose and better understand arithmetic operations.

CONCLUSIONS

We have presented the rationale, design, and early results from the implementation and study of a novel educational technology. Remote manipulation, it appears, is more than just hand waving; it can be an opportunity for the mind to reflect on what the body can already do. Embodied interactions can drive both the realization and resolution of cognitive conflicts between users' implicit assumptions and their own observable enactment; and with careful guidance, these experiences can be recast in terms of emerging mathematical principles.

The interviewer played a critical role in the learning process, which we hope has not been understated. The MIT device could not stand in isolation, as an artifact separate from a knowledgeable instructor (for instance, in a museum installation). Our instructional design encompasses not only the MIT device but also an explicit protocol mediated by the interviewer. There will always need to be an educator providing similar support as the interviewer, and this is an important issue as we determine how to scale up our design to full-classroom use.

ACKNOWLEDGMENTS

The study, which followed the guidelines of the Committee for Protection of Human Subjects, was funded by a UC Berkeley Committee on Research Faculty Research Grant to the PI (Abrahamson). We thank the participant students and their consenting parents as well as the school principal, teachers, and staff for their collaboration and hospitality. We are grateful to Jeanne Bamberger for her valuable input on reflective activity; to Tobin White for his comments on our early results; and to Ricardo Nemirovsky, Paulo Blikstein, Win Burleson, and Byron Lahey for technological consultations during the development of the MIT.

REFERENCES

1. Abrahamson, D. Embodied design: Constructing means for constructing meaning. *Educational Studies in Mathematics 70*, 1 (2009), 27-47.
2. Alibali, M.W., Bassok, M., Olseth, K.L., et al. Illuminating mental representations through speech and gesture. *Psychological Science 10*, 4 (1999), 327-333.
3. Antle, A.N., Corness, G., Bakker, S., et al. Designing to support reasoned imagination through embodied metaphor, in *Proceeding of the 7th ACM Conference on Creativity and Cognition* (Berkeley CA, 2009), 275-284.
4. Antle, A.N., Corness, G., and Droumeva, M. What the body knows: Exploring the benefits of embodied metaphors in hybrid physical digital environments. *Interacting with Computers 21* (2009), 66-75.
5. Artigue, M. Learning mathematics in a CAS environment: The genesis of a reflection about instrumentation and the dialectics between technical and conceptual work. *International Journal of Computers for Mathematical Learning 7*, 3 (2002), 245-274.
6. Bamberger, J. and Schön, D. Learning as reflective conversation with materials. In F. Steier (Ed.), *Research and Reflexivity*, Sage, London, 1991, 186-209.
7. Barsalou, L.W. Grounded cognition. *Annual Review of Psychology 59* (2008), 617-645.
8. Bott, J.N., Crowley, J.G., and LaViola, J.J. Exploring 3D gestural interfaces for music creation in video games. In *Proceedings of the 4th international Conference on Foundations of Digital Games* (Orlando FL, 2009), 18-25.
9. Church, R.B. and Goldin-Meadow, S. The mismatch between gesture and speech as an index of transitional knowledge. *Cognition 23* (1986), 43-71.
10. Clinton, K.A. Embodiment in digital worlds: What being a videogame player has to teach us about learning. Paper presented at the Annual Meeting of the American Educational Research Association (San Diego CA, 2004).
11. Collins, A. Towards a design science of education. In Scanlon, E. and O'Shea, T. eds. *New directions in educational technology*, Springer, Berlin, 1992, 15-22.
12. Confrey, J. The evolution of design studies as methodology. In Sawyer, R.K. ed. *The Cambridge handbook of the learning sciences*, Cambridge University Press, Cambridge MA, 2005, 135-151.
13. Cress, U., Fischer, U., Moeller, et al. The use of a digital dance mat for training kindergarten children in a magnitude comparison task. In *Proceedings of the 9th International Conference of the Learning Sciences* (2010), 105-112.
14. Davis, G.E. Fractions, ratio, and proportional reasoning [Special Issue]. *The Journal of Mathematical Behavior 22*, 2 (2003).
15. Farber, A. and Parker, L. Discovering Music through Dalcroze Eurhythmics. *Music Educators Journal 74*, 3 (1987) 43-45.
16. Fuson, K.C. and Abrahamson, D. Understanding ratio and proportion as an example of the Apprehending Zone and Conceptual-Phase problem-solving models. In Campbell, J. ed. *Handbook of mathematical cognition*, Psychology Press, New York, 2005, 213-234.
17. Goldin-Meadow, S. and Singer, M.A. From children's hands to adults' ears: gesture's role in teaching and learning. *Developmental Psychology 39*, 3 (2003), 509-520.
18. Hatano, G., Miyake, Y., and Binks, M. Performance of expert abacus operators. *Cognition 5*, 1 (1977), 57-71.
19. Karmiloff-Smith, A. The child is a theoretician, not an inductivist. *Mind & Language 3*, 3 (1988), 183-195.
20. Kosslyn, S.M. 2005. Mental images and the brain. *Cognitive Neuropsychology 22*, 3/4 (2005), 333-347.
21. Lakoff, G. and Nuúez, R.E. *Where mathematics comes from: How the embodied mind brings mathematics into being*. Basic Books, New York, 2000.
22. Lamon, S.J. Rational numbers and proportional reasoning: Toward a theoretical framework for research. In Lester, F.K. ed. *Second handbook of research on mathematics teaching and learning*, Information Age Publishing, Charlotte NC, 2007, 629-667.

23. Lee, H., Kim, H., Gupta, G., and Mazalek, A. WiiArts: creating collaborative art experience with WiiRemote interaction. In *Proceedings of the 2nd International Conference on Tangible and Embedded Interaction* (Bonn, Germany, 2008), 33-36.

24. Lee, J.C. Hacking the Nintendo Wii Remote. *IEEE Pervasive Computing 7*, 3 (2008), 39-45.

25. Marshall, P., Cheng, P.C.-H., and Luckin, R. Tangibles in the balance: a discovery learning task with physical or graphical materials. In *Proceedings of the 4th ACM International Conference on Tangible, Embedded, and Embodied Interaction* (2010), 153-160.

26. Nemirovsky, R., Tierney, C. and Wright, T. Body motion and graphing. *Cognition and Instruction 16*, 2 (1998), 119-172.

27. Norman, D.A. Cognitive artifacts. In Carroll, J.M. ed. *Designing interaction: Psychology at the human-computer interface*. Cambridge University Press, New York, 1991, 17-38.

28. Papert, S. An exploration in the space of mathematics education. *International Journal of Computers for Mathematical Learning 1* (1996), 95-123.

29. Pirie, S.E.B. and Kieren, T. Growth in mathematical understanding: How can we characterize it and how can we represent it? *Educational Studies in Mathematics 26* (1994), 165-190.

30. Pratt, D. and Noss, R. Designing for mathematical abstraction. *International Journal of Computers for Mathematical Learning 15*, 2 (2010), 81-97.

31. Radford, L. Gestures, speech and the sprouting of signs: A semiotic-cultural approach to students' types of generalization. *Mathematical Thinking and Learning 5*, 1 (2003), 37-70.

32. Roschelle, J., Shechtman, N., Tatar, D., et al. Integration of Technology, Curriculum, and Professional Development for Advancing Middle School Mathematics: Three Large-Scale Studies. *American Educational Research Journal 47*, 4 (2010), 833-878.

33. Salomon, G., Perkins, D.N., and Globerson, T. Partners in cognition: Extending human intelligences with intelligent technologies. *Educational Researcher 20*, 3 (1991), 2-9.

34. Saxe, G.B. and Esmonde, I. Studying cognition in flux: a historical treatment of fu in the shifting structure of Oksapmin mathematics. *Mind, Culture, and Activity 12*, 3-4 (2005), 171-225.

35. Schoenfeld, A. H., Smith, J. P., and Arcavi, A. Learning: The microgenetic analysis of one student's evolving understanding of a complex subject matter domain. In R. Glaser ed. *Advances in instructional psychology*, Erlbaum, Hillsdale NJ, 1991, 55-175.

36. Schwartz, D.L. Physical Imagery: Kinematic versus Dynamic Models. *Cognitive Psychology 38* (1999), 433-464.

37. Schwartz, D.L. and Black, T. Inferences through imagined actions: Knowing by simulated doing. *Journal of Experimental Psychology 25*, 1 (1999), 116-136.

38. Schwartz, J.L. Can technology help us make the mathematics curriculum intellectually stimulating and socially responsible? *International Journal of Computers for Mathematical Learning 4*, 2 (1999), 99-119.

39. Shirai, A., Geslin, E., and Richir, S. WiiMedia: motion analysis methods and applications using a consumer video game controller. In *Proceedings of the 2007 ACM SIGGRAPH Symposium on Video Games* (San Diego CA, 2007), 133-140.

40. Stigler, J.W. "Mental abacus": The effect of abacus training on Chinese children's mental calculation. *Cognitive Psychology 16*, 2 (1984), 145-17.

41. Vergnaud, G. The theory of conceptual fields. In Nunes, T. ed. *Giving meaning to mathematical signs: psychological, pedagogical and cultural processes. Human Development* [Special Issue] *52* (2009), 83-94.

42. Vérillon, P. and Rabardel, P. Cognition and artifacts: A contribution to the study of thought in relation to instrumented activity. *European Journal of Psychology of Education 10*, 1 (1995), 77-101.

43. Yin, R.K. *Case study research: design and methods*. Sage, London, 2009.

Kineticons: Using Iconographic Motion in Graphical User Interface Design

Chris Harrison[1] **Gary Hsieh**[2] **Karl D. D. Willis**[3] **Jodi Forlizzi**[1] **Scott E. Hudson**[1]

[1]Human-Computer Interaction Institute
Carnegie Mellon University
5000 Forbes Ave. Pittsburgh, PA 15213
{chris.harrison, forlizzi, scott.hudson}
@cs.cmu.edu

[2]College of Communication
Arts and Sciences
Michigan State University
East Lansing, MI
garyh@msu.edu

[3]Computational Design Lab
Carnegie Mellon University
5000 Forbes Avenue
Pittsburgh, PA 15213
kddw@cmu.edu

ABSTRACT

Icons in graphical user interfaces convey information in a mostly universal fashion that allows users to immediately interact with new applications, systems and devices. In this paper, we define *Kineticons* - an iconographic scheme based on motion. By motion, we mean geometric manipulations applied to a graphical element over time (e.g., scale, rotation, deformation). In contrast to static graphical icons and icons with animated graphics, kineticons do not alter the visual content or "pixel-space" of an element. Although kineticons are not new – indeed, they are seen in several popular systems – we formalize their scope and utility. One powerful quality is their ability to be applied to GUI elements of varying size and shape – from a something as small as a close button, to something as large as dialog box or even the entire desktop. This allows a suite of system-wide kinetic behaviors to be reused for a variety of uses. Part of our contribution is an initial kineticon vocabulary, which we evaluated in a 200 participant study. We conclude with discussion of our results and design recommendations.

ACM Classification: H.5.2 [Information interfaces and presentation]: User Interfaces - Graphical user interfaces.

General terms: Human Factors

Keywords: Icons, kinetic, animation, GUI, look and feel.

INTRODUCTION

Graphical icons, without doubt, are a critical component of computing's successes. Their ability to convey information in a fairly universal fashion allows users to immediately interact with new applications, systems and devices [16,33]. People's ability to pick up e.g., an iPhone for the first time and successfully use a wide variety of its features is a remarkable achievement. Conversely, walking up to a command line interface offers no similar affordances. The user, even if knowledgeable with other command line systems, must essentially follow a trial-and-error approach.

CHI 2011, May 7–12, 2011, Vancouver, BC, Canada.

The content of *graphical icons* is typically pictographic (pictorial resemblance to a physical object or action) or ideographic (a visual representation of a concept). However, their visual properties can also be modified along other dimensions to convey extra information. For example, a common metaphor for an inaccessible or hidden item is a ghosted, faded or grayed-out appearance. This modification is iconographic in and of itself, and can be applied to a wide variety of "icons" (i.e., GUI elements), including files, applications, dialog boxes, title bars, drop down menus, menu items, buttons, cursors, sliders, and many more.

Highly intertwined with graphical icons is *animation*. One form of animation is changes to graphical content of an icon over time [2,3,10,14,42]. A progress bar [37] is a good exemplar – its visual state changes over time to convey the progress of an extended operation. Buttons could also depict their action with an animated sequence – a draw tool might display a small pen drawing a line, as seen in [3,10]. Many other interactions exist: an item that has become accessible could smoothly fade in [35] or highlight [32]; an afterglow could be used to convey the recentness of an interface change [6]; files that are dragged could feature a graphical motion blur [13]. The temporal staging of these animations can also be used to convey information [18].

Several non-visual iconographic forms exist, which are also powerful. Computing devices can often output sound, allowing for *auditory icons* [15,19,20]. These typically depict audio relating to real world events, objects or actions to convey meaning. For example, a ticker sound might indicate a news item has arrived; a cheer might be used for a sports-related item. Related are *earcons* [8,9,12,22], which are synthesized sounds that are easy to learn and associate meaning with. *Hapticons*, as the name suggests, convey iconic information haptically [17] (see also tactons [11]). Although almost exclusively done though vibro-tactile means at present, texture could also be used [23].

In this paper, we define a new type of iconographic scheme for graphical user interfaces based on motion. We refer to these "kinetic icons" as kineticons. A kineticon is the result of a sequence of geometric manipulations (e.g., scale, rotation, deformation, translation) applied to pre-defined regions of a graphical element over time. We call these ma-

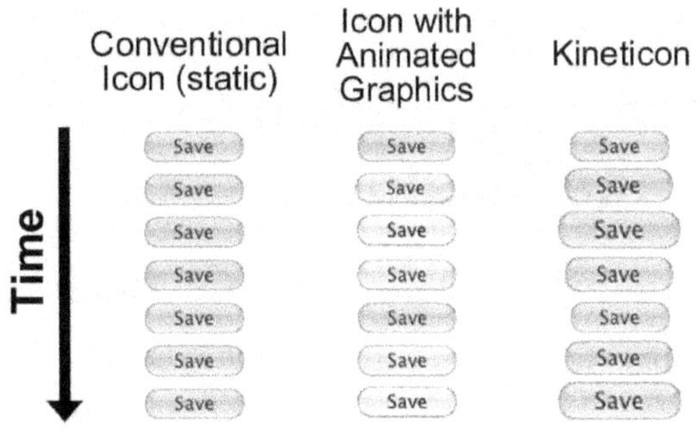

Figure 1. The appearance of a conventional icon, an icon with animated graphics, and a kineticon over time. A MacOSX save button serves as the example icon.

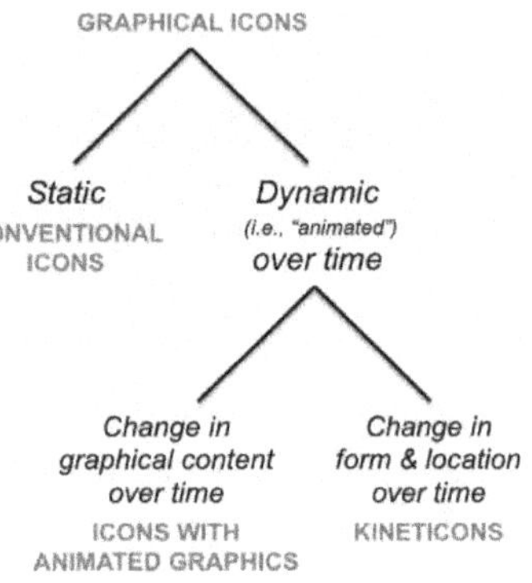

Figure 2. A taxonomic breakdown of graphical icons.

nipulations *kinetic behaviors*. The bounds of these regions (potentially one encompassing the entire element) could be defined in several ways (e.g., a 20x20 pixel region in the top left, or the top 50% of the item - similar to e.g., how CSS can define absolute or relative sizes). This content independence allows the kinetic behaviors to be applied to almost all GUI elements, including those with radically different shapes and sizes.

In contrast to static icons and icons with animated graphics, kinetic behaviors do not alter the visual content or pixels' RGBA values (i.e., "pixel-space") of an element (where as e.g., fades, blurs, tints, and addition of new graphics exclusively changes the pixel-space). Stated differently, pixels in an icon can be moved, rotated, stretched, and so on - but not altered or added to. Figure 1 illustrates the difference between a standard graphical icon, an animated icon and a kineticon. A taxonomic breakdown is provided in Figure 2.

The contribution of this work is multi-fold. Foremost, we define kineticons and clearly delineate their scope. This offers a name to an existing, but loosely applied interaction technique. This process involves carefully teasing out the difference between *icons with animated graphics* and *kineticons* (typically both referred to as "animated icons"). This distinction should help to better classify and target future research efforts. We also briefly review existing in-the-wild kineticons, before outlining the many properties of motion that make it an excellent dimension to leverage for interface design. Additionally, we review several popular sources of inspiration kineticon designs can draw upon. To illustrate and motivate our approach, we introduce eight example classes of interactions where kineticons could enhance current GUIs. We share our initial kinetic behavior vocabulary, and the results from our 200 participant user study, from which we draw many conclusions and design recommendations. Finally, throughout this process, we coalesce a wide variety of relevant work to aid future researchers.

EXISTING KINETICONS

Importantly, although we present a definition of the space, kineticons are not new. Although much previous academic work has been grossly labeled "animated", most would be considered "icons with animated graphics" – a handful would be classified as kineticons [13,29,30,43,44]. Animation in graphical user interfaces dates back more than two decades, with Baecker et al. [3] and Bodner et al. [10] pioneering its first uses.

Beyond academic work, several successful kineticons exist in production systems used today. One of the oldest and most successful kinetic behaviors is window and menu transitions – in particular, those that slide or expand the window in from a hidden or minimized state. This feature debuted as early as Windows 95, and traces its origins back to at least the first Macintosh interface (where a series of ever-larger gray rectangle outlines was used to graphically animate the opening). Overall, the most common use of kineticons at present is to aid in transitions between states, which helps to provide context and causality [14,21,41]. However, as we will see, kineticons have many more uses.

Apple's Aqua interface contains some of the most visible kineticons. For example, when an application is launching, its icon "bounces" in the dock (Figure 5, *Bounce*). A slightly different bounce effect is used when an application requires user attention (e.g., printer out of paper). Window minimization and maximization can use either a "scale" or "genie" kineticon (Figure 5, *Suck In*). Finally, if an incorrect password is entered into the login screen, the window shakes left to right (Figure 5, *Shake No*).

The latest generation of touch-driven interfaces tends to feature very rich graphics, animation and kineticons. The iPhone, for instance, employs a small, but powerful set of kineticons. Of particular note is the "wobbly" state icons assume if they are able to be dragged (Figure 5, *Rumble*). Also effective is the "zooming" effect used to transition from the home screen to an application (Figure 5, *Zoom*).

WHY MOTION?

The benefits of using motion are many and diverse. Chief among them is the ability to readily apply motion to GUI elements of different sizes. For example, a simple "wave" kineticon could be applied to something as small as a close button or file icon, to something as large as window of files or even the entire desktop. This allows a suite of system-wide kinetic behaviors to be reused for a variety of purposes. Importantly, this allows the iconic set to be smaller, since behaviors unique to toolbar items, windows menus, application icon, etc, are not necessary. It also establishes a common iconography that can be used throughout the system, potentially increasing ease of use. For example, a movable file, a movable window and a movable menu item can all use the same kinetic behavior.

Systems wishing to offer a similar suite of reusable graphical-level manipulations have two primary options: 1) provide a series of sub-icons or badges that could be added to existing icons, or 2) provide a series of whole-icon graphical manipulations. This works fairly well in practice with simple augmentations, such as superimposing a number badge or graying out an icon. Indeed, graying out a GUI element is perhaps the most widely used visual metaphor; however, the design space is very small: one state. Additionally, both of these schemes graphically change the content inside elements, which has the potential to alter (even destroy) the appearance and affordances of a GUI item.

In general, the graphic design of icons and interactive elements lies in the realm of the interface and application designer; the system typically does not know the application-level state or appearance of an element. For example, the superimposition of a "printing badge" onto an application icon might cover an application-level badge (e.g., number of buddies online). Adding additional complexity is the fact icons can be designed in numerous styles, including flat, isometric, cartoon, and photo-realistic. Superimposing a generic e.g., "printing badge" could harm the look-and-feel of an application.

Kineticons suffer less from these complications. In general, they can be applied to almost all graphical styles and operate in harmony with other dynamic visual elements. It is entirely possible to have an icon with animated content that is grayed out, and also performing a kinetic behavior. Indeed, motion can act as an additional dimension to all aforementioned iconographic schemes, adding more expressive power to interfaces. However, similar to other iconographic schemes, combining several kinetic behaviors is likely to be problematic.

Motion also has considerable psychophysical benefits. Foremost, we possess an innate understanding of how the world operates physically. Metaphors such as mass, rigidity, and inertia are readily portable to digital domains and make operations more intuitive and expressive [24]. Moreover, humans have incredibly parallelism in their visual processing and for motion in particular [5,27,47]. Not only can multiple motions be viewed and interpreted at any given instant [40], but we can perform complex grouping tasks (e.g., common fate principle in Gestalt psychology) [31]. Although humans have some ability to ignore or attend to motion, it is widely accepted that motion in interface design is attention grabbing. Thus, motion must be judiciously applied so as to minimize unnecessary distractions.

Equally impressive is our ability to perceive motion in our peripheral vision, which operates at a far lower resolution than our fovea, but has high sensitivity to motion. This potentially allows kineticons to be detected and identified with peripheral vision. This stands in contrast to graphical changes, such as overlaying the number of unread messages onto the email application icon (as seen in MacOSX). Although the eyes could detect a change has occurred, it would require a glance to read the number. Although we can only speculate, it seems likely kineticons could have implications to users with impaired vision, which typically impacts visual acuity, but not motion perception.

DESIGN

At present, GUI design is typically motivated by the iterative design process of interface designers. Researchers continue to develop ways to systematically apply design and perception knowledge to aid system builders. As an initial step in our research, we considered six popular sources for design inspiration, which we share below. Importantly, these sources can heavily leverage our innate perpetual abilities and knowledge of the world. In the same way that good graphical icons are often pictographic, kineticons can be emblematic of real-world motions.

Biological Motion

Scientists in many disciplines have researched animal and human body motion. From the ancient Greeks to DaVinci, from Muybridge to Disney, researchers in many disciplines have been fascinated with how humans stand, move, and gesture. Today, studies of motion are conducted in robotics, graphics, and biomechanics and benefit such disparate application areas as athletics, rehabilitation, ergonomics, animation, virtual training, and humanoid robotics.

The utility of employing animal and human motion is clear; even eight-month-old infants recognize and fixate longer on causal human motion than non-causal motion [28]. Recognition and understanding of human motion is core to many basic human skills, allowing us to correctly interpret non-verbal communication, to recognize friends from a significant distance, and to acquire new skills through imitation.

The most dramatic demonstration of our perceptual abilities is with light point figures. In these experiments, an actor is augmented with small lights on his shoulders, elbows, knees, ankles, and wrists. When the actor sits motionless, viewers perceive nothing more than a random constellation of disconnected elements. However, when the actor moves, viewers immediately perceive human motion, even though the actor himself is invisible [25,38]. Researchers have subsequently discovered that people are able to make quite sophisticated judgments about the motion, for example, deducing the gender of the actor [4].

Gestures

Gestures are a class of motion that is explicitly designed to convey information (where as locomotion or posture is more suggestive or causal). Robust meanings can be expressed via simple gestures such as a head nod, shoulder shrug, thumbs up, or rapid foot tapping [26,36]. For example, a single hand can either beckon or ward away and, by changing motion parameters in the gesture, the urgency of the message can also be made apparent.

Figure 3. Illustration of how MacOSX indicates drag-drop applicability (Microsoft Windows has a similar behavior). A) The user begins to drag a JPG document. B) User drags the file over the QuickTime Player application. There is no highlight because QuickTime is not able to open JPG files. C) User drags the file over the Preview application. This application can open JPG files; the blue highlight indicates the file can be "dropped" here.

Human gestures make for excellent kineticons, primarily because of our extensive training with them. Actions such as wave, shake head (i.e., no), stretching (e.g., after getting out of bed), and jumping up and down with hands flailing have immediate kinetic translations to icons. Although less visible to us, animals signal to each other in equally sophisticated ways. Gestures most familiar to us are from domesticated species, such as a dog's tail wagging.

Organic Motion

Beyond animal locomotion and gestures, there is a plethora of smaller motions inspired by organisms and organic processes, to which we are intimately familiar. For example, the blossoming of a flower, the beating of a heart, and pupils dilating. These iconic actions in nature can have very strong and particular associations that can be readily leveraged in interface design (e.g., a flower opening has strong connotations of rebirth and freshness).

Mechanical Motion

Today's GUIs have been imitating mechanical motion successfully for several decades: e.g., toggles, knobs, buttons and sliders. Designers have codified this knowledge into a set of guidelines that can be used reliably for interface design [7,24]. Furthermore, our brains have dedicated areas for processing non-biological-motions, including those of artificial or mechanical origin [38,39]. The huge number of designed artifacts in the world gives us a rich library of mechanical motions from which to draw upon. For example, the "tick-tock" of a clock hand, the unzipping of a garment, and the cyclical motion of an engine. Even now-obsolete representations, such as the motion of a steam locomotive's pistons, continue to have strong connotations.

Physics and Natural Effects

Conventional GUIs tend to rely solely on digital artifacts. The integration of a physics engine into these experiences has been shown to be powerful [1,24,46]. More importantly, it can leverage our innate perceptual abilities and extensive training with physical objects and how they behave in the real world [38,39]. We can simultaneously leverage this knowledge by borrowing motions from natural and physical effects. For example, how a leaf falls from a tree, glass shatters, paper folds, a sign blows in the wind, a swing rocks back and forth, or liquid drains from a sink.

Cartoon Conventions

Finally, cartoons and comics provide an interesting source of artistic embodiments of motion [34,45], which are typically caricatures of real-world motions. This exaggeration translates well to animation and certainly to the 2D desktop of conventional graphical user interfaces [13,29,43,44]. The canonical example is that of "squash and stretch" - defining the rigidity and mass of an object by distorting its shape during an action [13,29]. For example, when a ball hits the ground, its shape is flattened vertically. Upon leaving the surface, it squeezes horizontally, stretching upwards, as if leaping from the surface.

The fanciful content of cartoons led animators to design new motion metaphors [45], which have entered pop culture. For example, the rapid spinning of The Road Runner's legs or Superman changing outfits. Although often supplemented with motion blurs and graphical "streaks", the action can often be conveyed effectively using motion alone.

EXAMPLE USES

We now introduce and discuss a small subset of possible uses for kineticons in modern graphical user interfaces. We focus on three classes of interactions: the state of a GUI element, state changes, and finally, positive/negative events (e.g., an operation succeeded or failed). This initial set is by no means comprehensive; instead mostly illustrative.

State

There are many classes of state that a digital item can assume and are important in user interfaces; we touch on four:

Ability/Affordance of an item

Kinetic behaviors could be used to convey the abilities or affordances of a graphical element. For example, the ability to be moved (e.g., dragged with the mouse) could apply to a variety of elements, including file icons, toolbar items, menus, menu bar items, windows, and perhaps even the whole desktop (if in a multi-screen environment). A single kinetic behavior conveying "is movable" could be applied to this diverse set (the iPhone uses a rumbling kineticon to convey this affordance; Figure 5, *Rumble*). Other states might be whether an item is delete-able, edit-able, open-able, and resizable, to name a few.

One GUI operation that is particularly awkward at present is drag and drop of files onto applications. In many systems, whether the application is a possible drag-drop destination for a file is not known until the dragged object is over the application icon. If the operation is possible, the application icon highlights; if not possible, the icon is unchanged. Figure 3 illustrates this behavior. The key problem with this interaction is one has to scan over application icons in order to find an applicable opener.

Kineticons offer an immediate solution to this. When dragging a GUI element, interface elements that applicable drop-targets could exhibit a kinetic behavior with a receptive connotation. This could not only apply to application icons, but also disks, application windows (e.g., photo editor or email), and file browsers (Figure 4). Interface elements with inapplicable state can either remain motionless, or exhibit a not applicable kinetic behavior. This would allow users to effortlessly identify possible drop-targets.

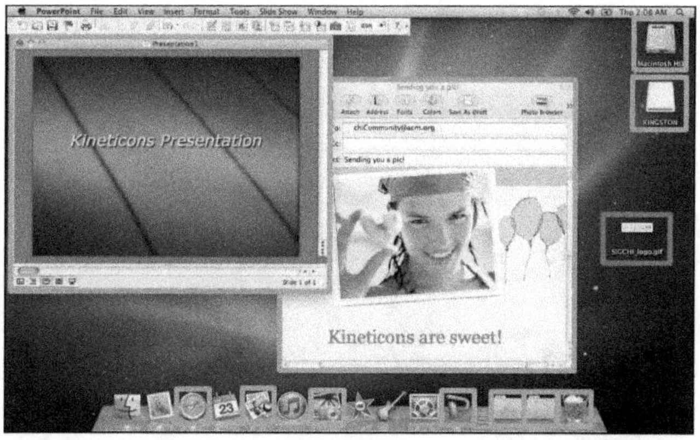

Figure 4. A user dragging a JPG file (red highlight) has numerous potential drop-targets (green highlight), including applications, the trash, folders, disks, a PowerPoint presentation and an email. These regions could be indicated to the user through subtle kinetic behaviors.

Needs Attention

An important state in interfaces is one that requires the users attention to proceed or resolve. This might occur if a location needs to be specified for a file save, the printer is out of paper, a laptop is running low on energy, a file has finished downloading, and countless other states. It need not convey a positive or negative connotation, just one of urgency. Kinetic behaviors could be used to signal users. Indeed, MacOSX uses an iconic "double bounce" kinetic behavior for this purpose - although it is limited to icons in the dock. Again, as mentioned many times previously, a "needs attention" kinetic behavior could also be applied to a save dialog, a print button, a battery indicator, and so on.

Operation is Progressing

Another common state for GUI elements to occupy is one of an operation in progress. This can occur when a file is downloading, a document is spooling to a printer, and a new application is being installed. In many cases, the duration of the processes can be computed (e.g., 10Mb file downloading at ~100kbps takes roughly 100 seconds). Kineticons could reflect the progress or speed of an operation through motion in the same way progress bars depicts it graphically. Alternatively, a progress bar could be used to convey percent-done [37], while motion is used to indicate e.g., download speed. This could allow for more ready comparison between processes and an overall greater awareness of state.

Launching and Opening

Highly related to the previous class of "operation is progressing" is launching and opening of elements. There are two key differences. First, launching and opening often has indeterminate duration. Second, it has a slightly different connotation: it is the start of a new process, with something new appearing or becoming available when launching/opening is complete. For example, a "connecting" kinetic behavior might be applied to a server share being mounted, where as a "progressing" kinetic behavior might be used when a file is being downloaded from the server.

State Changes and Events

In addition to state, such as a document being editable, there are state changes and events that could be facilitated by kineticons. We now briefly discuss four classes:

Entrance

This class can be thought of as the birth or arrival of a new item. In other words, from something not existing to existing. Instead of simply instantly appearing, the appearance of a new item can eased though kinetic behaviors. Examples include the mounting of a USB drive on the desktop, the appearance of a new application following an install, the opening of a new file browser.

Departure

This class of state change is the opposite of entrance – it is an item that transitions from existing to not existing. This might be a DVD ejecting from the desktop, a file being deleted, a dialog box closing, and a buddy logging out of an instant messenger application.

Replace/Update

This special case is two actions occurring in parallel: the end of one state and the beginning of another. As such, the transition between the two can be represented by two kinetic behaviors: *departure* of the old element, and *entrance* of the new one. Examples include the updating of an application to a new version, the replacing of one file with another, or advancing to the next slide in a presentation. Also, options available in a toolbar could update given the type of object selected in the interface.

Positive/Negative Events

The outcome of many operations and actions in user interfaces are binary – the install either succeeded or failed, the printer is available or not available, the disk had space for the transfer or did not have space. Kineticons are well suited to conveying the outcome of an event, either user-driven or application-driven [14].

MacOSX offers a paradigm example. If a password is accepted, the dialog disappears. However, if the password is rejected, the dialog shakes left to right briefly, essentially a "no" gesture (Figure 5, *Shake No)*. This behavior is highly effective – there is no reason why this kinetic behavior could not be applied to interface elements beyond a dialog box. For example, entering letters into a numerical telephone text field (interactor), attempting to open an Excel file in Adobe Photoshop (application icon), or attempting to operate an out-of-order ATM (whole screen).

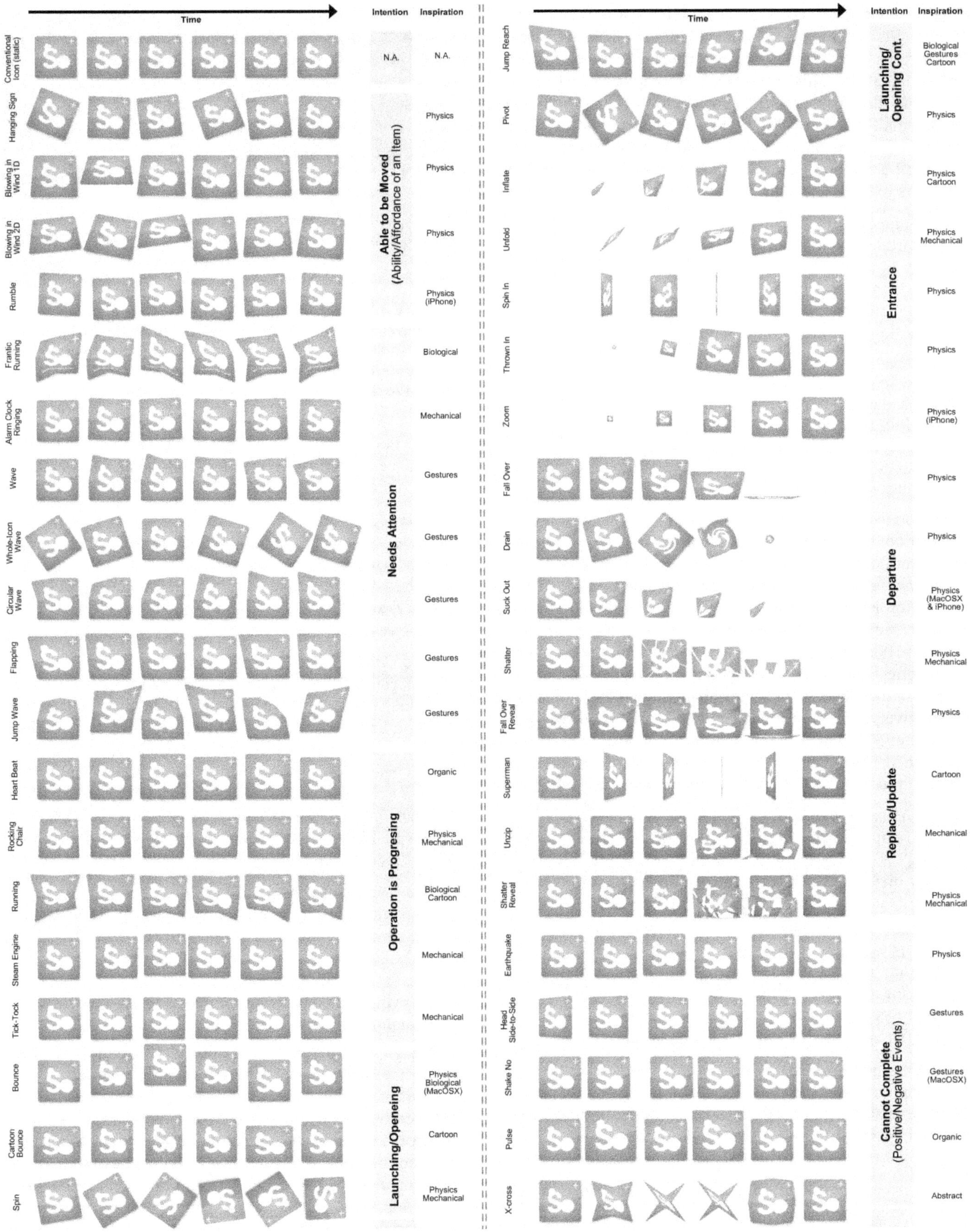

Figure 5. Our proof-of-concept kineticon vocabulary.

Figure 6. Kineticon applied to an application-style icon, menu item, dialog box, and entire desktop.

Gender	%	Age	%	Salary	%	Daily Comp. Use	%
Male	33	18-24	27	<$20k	35	<1 hr	2
Female	67	25-30	27	$20k-30k	17	2-3 hr	25
		31-40	27	$30k-$50k	24	4-6 hr	37
		41-50	10	$50k-$75k	16	6-10 hr	21
		51+	9	$75k+	8	> 10 hr	15

Table 1. The demographics of our MTurk Participants

PROOF-OF-CONCEPT KINETICON VOCABULARY

To motivate, illustrate and evaluate kineticons, we created a set of 39 kinetic behaviors. Obviously the set of possible behaviors and GUI elements to apply them to is limitless. To cover the design space with a fairly diverse set of kinetic behaviors, we created between 4 and 7 iconic motions for an interaction from each class we discussed in our Example Uses section. In some cases, we designed very specific behaviors (e.g., "able to be moved"); in other cases, very general ones (e.g., "progressing"). We also selected interactions that were conceptually similar (e.g., "progressing" and "loading") to see if well-designed kinetic behaviors could convey subtle differences. Interactions that were highly distinctive (e.g., "departure") were also included.

To aid our design process, we drew on the sources of design inspiration noted earlier. We also included five kinetic behaviors found in MacOSX and the iPhone, primarily for later discussion. Figure 5 provides an overview of our initial kineticon vocabulary. Motion is hard to convey on paper, so please also refer to the Video Figure.

USER STUDY

We conducted a user study to answer two key, high-level questions. Foremost, can motions be iconic, and recognized across users? This is a fundamental property kineticons must exhibit if they are to be useful in the design of graphical user interfaces. Our second question was whether or not kinetic behaviors can be reliably applied across different GUI elements, a key property we champion in this paper.

There are several important secondary outcomes from our study. Evaluating our proof-of-concept kineticons allows us to suggest an initial vocabulary of kinetic behaviors interface designers can employ. It also allows us to gauge how well our design intention matched the interpretations of our participants. Concurrent with this is the evaluation of current in-the-wild examples, most notably those used in Apple products. We conclude with high-level design recommendations based on our interpretations of what worked and what did not.

Setup & Measures

We applied our 39 kinetic behaviors to a generic application-style icon (Figure 5). These were rendered as movies for the purposes of the study, but are fully programmatic. We then showed this set of 39 kineticons to a three independent coders, whom (through a consensus vote) selected the best kineticon in each of our eight interaction examples. We then chose four from these (*Heart Beat*, *X-cross*, *Running and Blowing in the Wind 2D*) to be applied to three other GUI elements beyond an application icon: a menu item, a dialog window, and entire desktop (Figure 6 and Video Figure). This added 12 additional kineticon videos to our test set (51 items total).

In order to recruit a large and diverse set of participants, important for making claims of broad recognition, we conducted an online study through Amazon's Mechanical Turk (MTurk). Remote participants watched videos of the kineticons, one at a time. These videos were presented on our study's webpage through an embedded video player, which automatically started and looped.

While watching the videos, participants were asked to rate how strongly they agreed or disagreed (five-point Likert scale) with the following eight interpretations of the motions seen in the video.

1. Item is progressing with an operation.
2. Item has been replaced with a new item.
3. Item cannot complete the user's request.
4. Item is newly available.
5. Item is no longer available.
6. Item needs attention.
7. Item is opening or loading.
8. Item is able to be moved.

Each participant rated a total of ten kineticons, drawn randomly from our pool of 51 videos (the ordering of the interpretations was also randomized per participant). After completing ten ratings, participants answered a set of background questions.

Participants

Participation in this study was limited to participants residing in the US, have previously submitted at least one unit of work (MTurk HIT) and have approval ratings (previously approved tasks / all submitted tasks) greater than 80%. This pre-screening was to ensure both basic English proficiency and to minimize the number of low-quality MTurk workers. 200 MTurk workers participated in the study (67% female), who were paid $2. Most of our participants spend between 2-6 hours on their computers per day (62%). Table 1 provides a breakdown of demographics.

Statistical Analysis

To control for individual biases, participants' Likert ratings for each interpretations were standardized (into z-scores). To do this, each individual's rating had their mean rating (for that interpretation) subtracted, and was then divided by the standard deviation of their ratings (for the interpretation). When standardized, 0 means an average rating for that interpretation, +1 means a rating that is one standard deviation above the average, and -1 means a rating that is one standard deviation below the average. Ratings from twelve participants were excluded in our analyses due to zero variance (e.g., all 1s) or spending too little time on ratings (under 10 seconds).

To calculate which kineticons were rated highest for each interpretation, an ANOVA was used. The eight interpretation ratings were used as dependent variables and kineticon type (39 possibilities) was the independent variable. Tukey's HSD was then used in our post-hoc analyses to test the differences between kineticons.

To determine if kinetic behaviors were interpreted the same way across different GUI elements, we used a regression model. Interpretation ratings for the four sets (*Running, Blowing in the Wind 2D, Heart Beat, X-cross*) were analyzed, one set at a time. In these analyses, the interpretation rating was the dependent variable and the element type (application icon, menu item, dialog, desktop) and interpretation (across the 8 possible interpretations) were the independent variables. Tukey's HSD was also used here to test the differences between interpretations.

RESULTS AND DISCUSSION

We conducted several analyses to investigate different performance aspects of kineticons. We interweave this review of the results with discussion and design recommendations where appropriate. We first discuss the 39 application kineticons (Figure 5), and conclude the section with discussion regarding applicability across GUI elements.

Performance of Initial Kineticon Vocabulary

We conducted oneway ANOVA analyses on each item and found that 36 of the 39 kineticons are significantly more likely to convey some meanings than others (all at $p \leq 0.01$, except for *X-cross*, *Wave*, and *Circular Wave*). The strengths of Kineticons in a given interpretation were generally evenly distributed. To group the best performing kineticons, we define two thresholds, $\mu+\sigma$ ("best") and $\mu+2\sigma$ ("top"), based on the distribution of standardized z-scores. Additional statistically significant results are noted inline. We consider possible interpretations of the results if themes are present in the successful kineticons.

"Item is able to be dragged by the mouse"

Six kineticons operate above the best threshold: *Hanging Sign*, *Blowing in the Wind 2D*, *Blowing in the Wind 1D*, *Jump Wave*, *Jump Reach and Running*. The first three were designed to convey the ability to be moved, suggesting our designs were successful in generating the right interpretation. Moreover, these three kinetic behaviors perform strongly in only this category, suggesting a primary interpretation, which is the desirable outcome.

The high performance of the other three kineticons is curious. Unfortunately, *Jump Wave* has an additional strong interpretation of "needs attention", diminishing its benefit and utility (i.e., leading to confusion). *Running* and *Jump Reach*, however, do not have strong alternative interpretations, and join the first three as a strong indicators of "is draggable by the mouse". It is possible the reaching and running anthropomorphizations suggested to participants the icon "wanted to go somewhere", and thus was movable. A waving gesture, on the other hand, has less of a goal- or destination-oriented connotation.

"Item needs attention"

We hypothesized that most kineticons would rank highly in the "needs attention" interpretation due to motion's inherently attention-grabbing quality. However, 20 of the 39 kineticons had negative z-scores, suggesting that there is actually a spectrum of "attention-grabbing-ness". Seven kineticons yielded rankings above the best threshold: *Shake No*, *Jump Wave*, *Cartoon Bounce, Rumble*, *Whole-Icon Wave*, *Heart Beat* and *Alarm Clock Ringing*. The latter four perform well in this interpretation alone, suggesting they could be good kineticons to employ.

The two waving-inspired kineticons clearly leverage the human gesture, which typically has an expectation of attention. We intended both of these kinetic behaviors to elicit this effect, and it appears to have succeeded. *Rumble*, *Shake No*, and *Alarm Clock Ringing* have a similar vigorously shaking appearance – embodying a lot of energy and urgency. This appears to have been translated to a need for attention (the similar *Earthquake* kineticon lies just under the best threshold). The reasons for the success of *Cartoon Bounce* and *Heart Beat* are not immediately obvious.

"Item is progressing with an operation"

The *Steam Engine* kineticon is the strongest in this interpretation, surpassing the top threshold by a wide margin. Unfortunately, it also performs well in the conceptually similar "loading" interpretation. Five others exceed the best threshold: *Spin*, *Drain*, *Cartoon Bounce*, *Pivoting*, *Rocking Chair*.

The commonality between *Steam Engine*, *Spin*, *Pivoting* and *Rocking Chair* is their highly cyclical and mechanical nature, like an engine running. Moreover, these represent four of the six kineticons that exhibit this behavior - the other being *Hanging Sign and Whole-Icon Wave,* neither of which exude a strong feeling of mechanical motion.

"Item is opening or loading"

Seven kineticons perform above the best threshold. Four are kineticons we intended to convey "entrance": *Fold In*, *Inflate*, *Spin In*, and *Zoom*. Clearly our choice of the words "opening" and "loading" provided the impression of something new being instantiated, and thus appearing. Interestingly, despite a subtle, if not ambiguous difference from the "progressing with an operation" interpretation, there were only two overlapping best-performing kineticons: *Steam Engine* and *Spin*. Finally, *Frantic*, a more energetic version of *Running*, was also highly ranked.

"Item is newly available"

This interpretation was more polarizing than others, with kineticons tending to either be in strong agreement or disagreement. Consequently, ten kineticons fall above the best threshold. All five of our intended "entrance" kineticons are included in this set (*Spin In*, *Inflate*, Zoom, *Thrown In*, and *Unfold*), showing the metaphor of appearing from nothing is unsurprisingly a strong signal new availability. All four of our conceptually related "Replace/Update" kineticons also operate above the best threshold (*Fall Over Reveal*, *Superman*, *Shatter Reveal*, and *Unzip*). Although unintended, this result actually suggests the metaphors we used to signal the arrival of a new item are strong. Additionally, the *Bounce* kineticon performed well for unknown reasons.

"Item is no longer available"

This interpretation had strong results, with three kineticons in the top tier and three above the best threshold. The clear winners were the intended "departure" kineticons: *Shatter*, *Suck In*, *Drain*, and *Fall Over (*Tukey's HSD; p<.05 compared to all other kineticons, but not compared to each other). As noted subsequently, departure is viewed as similar to "cannot complete" interpretation, and consequently, *Shatter*, *Fall Over* and *Suck In* perform well in that category. *Drain*, as noted previously, is interpreted as a "progressing" kineticon. The remaining two high performing kineticons are both "Replace/Update" kineticons: *Fall Over Reveal* and *Unzip* – both of which feature a departing action. Overall, it is apparent the kineticons designs are working. However, some refinement might be needed to better separate them from the clearly different "cannot complete" interpretation.

"Item has been replaced with a new item"

Participants had very decisive reaction to this interpretation. Four kineticons operate in above in excess of the top threshold (none scored between best and top thresholds). Unsurprisingly, given the distinctive sequence of these kinetic behavior sequences (two kineticons in parallel), *Shatter Reveal*, *Fall Over Reveal*, *Superman* and *Unzip* work well (p<.05 compared to all other kineticons, but not among the four).

"Item cannot complete the user's request"

The best performing kineticon was *Shatter* (top tier). It is clear this metaphor has a strong "breaking" and negative connotation. Nine other kineticons performed above the best threshold: *Head Side-to-Side*, *Pulse*, *Fall Over*, *Alarm Clock Ringing*, *Flapping*, *Suck Out*, *Earthquake*, and *Rumble*.

Four of the five kinetic behaviors we designed with a "cannot complete" connotation were highly ranked. Interestingly, many of the behaviors intended to convey departure also ranked highly. It appears the two are linked conceptually – loosely, something that fails typically ends or disappears.

Performance of Existing Kineticons

We incorporated five kinetic behaviors found in MacOSX and the iPhone into our proof-of-concept set. Although not a comprehensive analysis, it does provide an initial gauge of whether or not in-the-wild kineticons are successful and potentially improved upon.

The *Shake No* gesture was shown to be iconic of a "cannot complete" event and "needs attention" state. This dual meaning is appropriate given its current use in MacOSX (a password entered incorrectly). *Zoom* and *Suck In* were similarly successful as entrance and departure kineticons. *Bounce* was interpreted as a kineticon conveying "newly available", which is close to the MacOSX use. However *Rumble*, used in the iPhone to signal "movability" of icons, is less strong; it only scores well as a gross representation of "needing attention" and quite poorly in its intended "is movable" interpretation.

Correlations Between Interpretations

As noted several times in the results discussion thus far, it appears several of our interpretations were related conceptually. This manifested in the data as kineticons performing well in two categories. Indeed, our earlier suppositions are confirmed statistically (Pearson's correlations). As one would expect, "cannot complete" and "departure" are negatively correlated with loading (ρ=-.21 and ρ=-.23 respectively, p<.001). "Cannot complete" is also negatively correlated with the entrance interpretation (ρ=-.24, p<.001).

There were also several positive correlations. As hypothesized previously, "progress" appears to be conceptually similar to "loading/opening" (ρ=.40, p<.001). Also correlated were: replace/update and entrance interpretations (ρ=31, p<.001), and "cannot complete" and "no longer available" (ρ=.36, p<.001).

Applicability Across GUI Elements

There were two key behaviors we wanted our GUI element sets (application icon, menu item, dialog box, entire desktop) to exhibit if associated kinetic behaviors were to be considered successful. The first was that all four GUI element types performed well in a single interpretation (i.e., not ambiguous). Secondly, we wanted low variance in the strengths of that interpretation, which would suggest that a kineticon had similar expressive power across GUI types.

Encouragingly - as we believe this is one of the key benefits of kineticons - the results are strong. The four GUI elements with the *Heart Beat* kineticon clearly convey the "need for attention". This significantly out performs any other interpretations (p<.05). *Blowing in the Wind 2D* has an equally strong and singular result with the movable interpretation (p<.05). We designed *X-cross* to be a "cannot complete" behavior, an interpretation that was correlated with "no longer available". As such, the GUI element set with *X-cross* performs best in those two interpretations (p<.05 compared to all other interpretations, but not between "cannot complete" and "no longer available").

Conversely, the *Running* kineticon, which performed well as an application icon, yielding a strong "is movable" connotation, does not seems to generalize to other GUI elements. None of the positively rated interpretations are significant from each other, primarily due to high variance in participants' estimations of the interpretation strengths.

The high level result here is that kineticons can successfully generalize across a variety of GUI elements (3 of our 4 designs). However, this does depend on the specific design employed. Even kinetic behaviors that are extremely iconic when applied to some GUI elements, could have even a reverse connotations when applied to a different item. Thus, careful testing and iterative design is a necessity.

CONCLUSION

We have presented a definition of kineticons, or motion-based icons, and placed them into a taxonomy along side conventional graphical icons and those with animated graphics. Significantly, kineticons can be applied in concert with other iconographic schemes, including other forms of animation. Moreover, we show kineticons can be applied to and reused for a variety of elements in graphical user interfaces. Our evaluation yielded an initial set of effective kinetic behaviors and let us better gauge the effectiveness of kineticons that exist in popular platforms, like the iPhone.

ACKNOWLEDGMENTS

This work was supported in part by a Microsoft PhD Fellowship and grant IIS-0840766 from the National Science Foundation.

REFERENCES

1. Agarawala, A. and Balakrishnan, R. Keepin' it real: pushing the desktop metaphor with physics, piles and the pen. In *Proc. CHI '06*. 1283-1292.
2. Baecker, R., Small, I. (1990). Animation at the interface. In: B. Laurel (Ed.) *The Art of Human-Computer Interface Design*. Addison-Wesley, Reading, MA.
3. Baecker, R., Small, I., and Mander, R. Bringing icons to life. In *Proc. CHI '91*. 1-6.
4. Barclay, C.D., Cutting, J.W., and Kozlowski, L.T. Temporal and spatial factors in gait perception that influence gender recognition. *Perception and Psychophysics* 23, 1978, 145-152.
5. Bartram, L. Perceptual and interpretative properties of motion for information visualization. In *Proc. NPIV '97*. 3-7.
6. Baudisch, P., Tan, D., Collomb, M., Robbins, D., Hinckley, K., Agrawala, M., Zhao, S., and Ramos, G. Phosphor: Explaining Transitions in the User Interface Using Afterglow Effects. In *Proc. UIST'06*.169-178.
7. Baumann, K. and Thomas, B. (2001). *User Interface Design of Electronic Appliances*, 1st Ed. CRC Press.
8. Beaudouin-Lafon, M. and Conversy, S. Auditory illusions for audio feedback. In *Proc CHI '96 Companion*. 299-300.
9. Blattner, M.M., Sumikawa, D.A., and Greenberg, R.M. Earcons and icons: their structure and common design principles. *Hum.-Comp. Interac.* 4, 1 (1989), 11-44.
10. Bodner, R.C. and MacKenzie, I.S. Using animated icons to present complex tasks. In Proc. Conf. Centre For Adv. Stud. Collab. Res. IBM Press. 1-11
11. Brewster, S. and Brown, L.M. Tactons: structured tactile messages for non-visual information display. In *Proc. Australasian User interface '04*. 15-23.
12. Brewster, S.A., Wright, P.C. and Edwards, A. An evaluation of earcons for use in auditory human-computer interfaces. In *Proc. CHI '93*. 222-227
13. Chang, B. and Ungar, D. Animation: from cartoons to the user interface. In *Proc. UIST '93*. 45-55.
14. Chatty, S. Defining the dynamic behaviour of animated interfaces. In *Proc. IFIP TC2/WG2.7 '92*. 95-111.
15. Conversy, S. Wind and wave auditory icons for monitoring continuous processes. In *Proc. CHI '98*. 351-352.
16. Easterby, R. The Perception of Symbols for Machine Displays. *Ergonomics* 13, 1 (1970), 149-158.
17. Enriquez, M.J. and MacLean, K.E. The Hapticon Editor: A Tool in Support of Haptic Communication Research. In *Proc. HAPTICS '03*. 356-362.
18. Findlater, L., Moffatt, K., McGrenere, J., and Dawson, J. Ephemeral adaptation: the use of gradual onset to improve menu selection performance. In *Proc. CHI '09*. 1655-1664.
19. Gaver, W. Auditory Icons: Using Sound in Compute Interfaces. *Hum.-Comp. Interac.* 2, 2 (1986), 167-177.
20. Gaver, W. The Sonic Finder: An Interface that Uses Auditory Icons. *Hum.-Comp Interac,* 4, 1 (1989), 67-94.
21. Gonzalez, C. Does animation in user interfaces improve decision making? In *Proc. CHI '96*. 27-34.
22. Hankinson, J.C. and Edwards, A.D. Designing earcons with musical grammars. *SIGCAPH Comput. Phys. Handicap.* 65 (Sep. 1999), 16-20.
23. Harrison, C. and Hudson, S.E. Texture displays: a passive approach to tactile presentation. In *Proc. CHI '09*. 2261-2264.
24. Jacob, R.J., Girouard, A., Hirshfield, L.M., Horn, M.S., Shaer, O., Solovey, E.T., and Zigelbaum, J. Reality-based interaction: a framework for post-WIMP interfaces. *Proc. CHI '08*. 201-210.
25. Johansson, G. Visual Motion Perception. Scientific American, 232 (1975). 76-88.
26. Kendon, A. (1988). How Gestures Can Become Like Words. In *Cross-cultural Perspectives in Nonverbal Communication*. Toronto, C.J. Hogrefe, 131-141.
27. Kolers, P. A. (1972). *Aspects of Motion Perception*. Pergamon Press Inc., New York.
28. Kosugi, D. and Fujita, K. How do 8-month-old infants recognize causality in object motion and that in human action. *Japanese Psychol. Research*, 44 (2002), 66–72.
29. Lasseter, J. Principles of traditional animation applied to 3D computer animation. In *Proc. SIGGRAPH '87*. 35-44.
30. Lee, J.C., Forlizzi, J., and Hudson, S.E. The kinetic typography engine: an extensible system for animating expressive text. In *Proc. UIST '02*. 81-90.
31. Lee, S.H., and Blake, R. Visual form created solely from temporal structure. *Science*, 284 (1999). 1165-1168.
32. Liang, J., Huang, M.J. Highlighting in Information Visualization: A Survey. In *Proc. IV '10*. 79-85.
33. Lodding, K. Iconic Interfacing. *IEEE Computer Graphics and Applications.* 3, 2 (1983), 11-20.
34. McCloud, S. (1993). *Understanding Comics: The Invisible Art*. Kitchen Sink Press, Inc., Northampton, MA.
35. McCrickard, D., Zhao Q. and Stasko, J. Exploring Animation as a Presentation Technique for Dynamic Information Sources. In GVU Technical Report, GITGVU-99-47, 1999.
36. Mulder, A. (1996). Hand Gestures for HCI. School of Kinesiology, Simon Fraser University, Technical Report 96-1.
37. Myers, B.A. The importance of percent-done progress indicators for computer-human interfaces. *SIGCHI Bull.* 16, 4 (Apr. 1985), 11-17.
38. Neri, P. Moroone, M.C. and Burr, D.C. Seeing Biological Motion. *Nature*, 395 (1998), 894-896.
39. Pelphrey, K.A., Mitchell, T.V., McKeown, M.J., Goldstein, J., Allison, T., and McCarthy, G. Brain activity evoked by the perception of human walking: Controlling for meaningful coherent motion. *Jour. Neuroscience*, 23 (2003), 6819-6825.
40. Pylyshyn, Z., Burkell, J., Fisher, B., Sears, C., Schmidt, W. and Trick, L. Multiple parallel accessing visual attention. *Canadian Journal of Exper. Psychology*, 48, 2 (1994), 260-283.
41. Shanmugasundaram, M., Irani, P., Gutwin, C. Can smooth view transitions facilitate perceptual constancy in node-link diagrams? In *Proc. GI '07*. 71-78.
42. Stasko, J.T. (1993). Animation in user interfaces: principles and techniques. In *User Interface Software*. John Wiley & Sons, New York, NY. 81-101.
43. Thomas, B. H. and Calder, P. Supporting cartoon animation techniques in direct manipulation graphical user interfaces. *Inf. Softw. Technol.* 47, 5 (2005), 339-355.
44. Thomas, B.H. and Calder, P. Applying cartoon animation techniques to graphical user interfaces. ACM Trans. *Comput.-Hum. Interact.* 8, 3 (2001), 198-222.
45. Thomas, F. and Johnston, O. (1984). *Disney Animation: The Illusion of Life*. Abbeville Press, New York, NY.
46. Wilson, A.D., Izadi, S., Hilliges, O., Garcia-Mendoza, A., and Kirk, D. Bringing physics to the surface. *Proc. UIST '08*. 67-76.
47. Wolfe, J.M., Kluender, K.R., Levi, D.M., Bartoshuk, L.M, Herz, R.S., Klatzky, R.L., and Lederman, S.J. (2006). *Sensation and Perception*. Sinauer Associates, Sunderland, MA.

Temporal Distortion for Animated Transitions

Pierre Dragicevic[1], Anastasia Bezerianos[2], Waqas Javed[3], Niklas Elmqvist[3] and Jean-Daniel Fekete[1]
dragice@lri.fr, anastasia.bezerianos@ecp.fr, {wjaved, elm}@purdue.edu, fekete@inria.fr
[1]INRIA Orsay, France [2]École Centrale Paris Paris, France [3]Purdue University West Lafayette, IN, USA

(a) Constant speed. (b) Slow-in/Slow-out. (c) Fast-in/Fast-out. (d) Adaptive speed.

Figure 1. Different temporal distortion strategies for animated transitions. Solid shapes show original positions, faded shapes show ending positions.

ABSTRACT
Animated transitions are popular in many visual applications but they can be difficult to follow, especially when many objects move at the same time. One informal design guideline for creating effective animated transitions has long been the use of slow-in/slow-out pacing, but no empirical data exist to support this practice. We remedy this by studying object tracking performance under different conditions of temporal distortion, i.e., constant speed transitions, slow-in/slow-out, fast-in/fast-out, and an adaptive technique that slows down the visually complex parts of the animation. Slow-in/slow-out outperformed other techniques, but we saw technique differences depending on the type of visual transition.

ACM Classification Keywords
H.5.1 Multimedia Information Systems: [animations]; H.5.2 User Interfaces: [Graphical user interfaces (GUI)]

Author Keywords
Animated transitions, animation, information visualization.

General Terms
Design, Human Factors

INTRODUCTION
Animated transitions, where the transformation between visual states is conveyed with smooth rather than abrupt visual changes [17], are increasingly being used in modern interaction design. For example, the photo viewer Picasa smoothly expands and collapses image galleries, the Pivot browser [25] fluidly moves visual entities during faceted browsing, and different information visualization systems use animated transitions when switching between data dimensions [10, 14], visual representations [16, 38], or when navigating in time [9, 12, 26]. Research suggests that animated transitions not only improve the aesthetics of a user interface, but also helps users to understand the underlying data [5, 16, 35]. However, there are many parameters involved in designing effective animations, including motion paths, staging, scheduling, and timing. In this paper, we focus on the latter: timing aspects of animated transitions.

Rather than having objects move or change at a fixed rate during an animation (Figure 1(a)), cartoon animators sometimes use a "slow in" or "slow out" effect [8, 18], causing more frames to be dedicated to the beginning or end of the animation (Figure 1(b)). Essentially, slow-in and slow-out *distort* time throughout the animation. Computer applications have been quick to adopt this idea [20], and many graphical toolkits (e.g., [6, 15]) and animation packages (e.g., Microsoft PowerPoint and Autodesk Maya) use a combination of slow-in and slow-out (SI/SO) as their default animation pacing. Its use has also been advocated for optimizing animations in user interfaces [2, 8, 17, 33, 38].

There are several arguments for using SI/SO, one being realism. However, physical realism is generally less crucial in graphical user interfaces than in cartoon animation. Another, more practical reason often cited for using SI/SO pacing is that it helps users to anticipate the beginning and ending of the animation. However, no perceptual studies have been performed to confirm this informal design rule. In particular, SI/SO dedicates less frames to the middle segment — effectively accelerating it – so it is not clear whether it should be used in all cases, especially when the middle animation segment is visually complex or particularly important.

In this paper, we address this lack of empirical data by comparing object tracking performance in visually cluttered animations under different temporal distortion strategies, and show how effective these strategies are for important low-level tasks. We expect our results to help improve the animated transitions used in user interfaces and information visualization systems so that they become more useful to users.

BACKGROUND

Animation is the rapid display of static sequences to create the illusion of movement. It has been extensively studied by psychologists and applied to both films and computer graphics as well as for improving user interfaces.

Perception of Movement

Perceiving and interpreting motion is a fundamental capability of human perception with deep roots in our evolution: moving objects stand out in our visual field, and the Gestalt principle of common fate states that entities moving in the same direction are seen as a unit [28]. Perception research suggests that the human visual system is capable of tracking multiple objects simultaneously [7, 30]. The actual tracking is performed by the visual system using a mechanism known as *smooth pursuit* [28]. However, many factors influence this capability, including the number of distractors, object speed, occlusions, and motion paths of the objects being tracked.

Cartoon Animation

Designing animations was an active practice long before computers, and there is a wealth of literature, tradition, and design guidelines to draw upon for designing effective animations. In particular, Johnston and Thomas presented the "12 basic principles of animation" in their seminal work *The Illusion of Life: Disney Animation* [18], discussing effective ways of making animations — particularly character animations — as realistic and as lifelike as possible.

Because most animation nowadays is done with computers, much effort has been devoted to transfering these principles to computer animation [24]. Accordingly, major computer animation packages such as 3D Studio MAX, AutoDesk Maya, and even Microsoft PowerPoint, today adopt most of the above basic principles of animation in their algorithms.

Animation in User Interfaces

Animations have been used in interactive applications since the advent of graphical user interfaces [2]. Before GUIs, programmers would animate terminal output, e.g., to show progress in a time-consuming task. In 1993, Chang and Ungar [8] as well as Hudson and Stasko [17] concurrently proposed applying cartoon animation to interfaces. Thomas and Calder [33, 34] have since further improved upon this idea.

Similarly, efforts towards evaluating animated transitions date back to the early 1990s. Gonzalez [13] performed an experiment to show that use of animated transitions in graphical user interfaces can improve the user's decision making process. Later, Bederson and Boltman [5] empirically measured the effect of animated transitions on user capability to build mental maps of spatial information. Interestingly, Tversky et al. [35] study the use of animation in graphical interfaces, and find that its use is mostly detrimental — except for congruence of motion. Building on this result, Heer and Robertson [16] present results from two user studies that emphasize the importance of animated transitions for highlighting changes between related statistical data graphics. In a similar study, Shanmugasundaram et al. [32] found that smooth transitions dramatically improved performance for memorizing graphs using node-link diagrams.

However, all of the above studies investigate the benefits of adding animation to an interactive application, whereas there exists very little work that compares the performance of different *types* of animations. Notable exceptions focus on using animations as notification mechanisms [1, 4]. In particular, we are aware of no existing work studying how temporal pacing for animation affects object tracking performance. While best practice design guidelines suggest the use of smooth animations with slow-in/slow-out extrema, no formal evaluation exists that verifies that this is indeed the optimal pacing strategy for animated transitions.

TEMPORAL DISTORTION IN ANIMATION

Computer animations can be modelled as parametric graphics with time-varying parameters (object positions, size, color, opacity, etc.). The simplest way to animate parametric graphics between two visual states is by linear interpolation, i.e., for each parameter p changing from p^0 to p^1:

$$p(t) = p^0 + t(p^1 - p^0), \quad t \in [0, 1]$$

where t is a global parameter that controls the speed and duration of the entire animation. When p is an object's position, this formulation produces trajectories that follow straight paths. If objects follow non-straight paths [18, 24], arc-length parametrization can be used instead.

On a computer screen the animation must be sampled. Assuming a constant frame rate f and given a total time T for the animation, we need $n = f \times T$ frames to complete the animation. Typical values for f are 60 Hz and typical durations of T are 0.5–1.0 seconds for transitions [16]. The pacing of an animation is defined by a list of n values of t:

$$t \in \{t_1, t_2, \cdots, t_n\}$$

Setting $t_1 = 0$ and $t_n = 1$, the increments $\Delta t(i) = t_i - t_{i-1}$ for $i \in [2, n-1]$ are left in the hands of the animation designer. Below we will discuss different strategies for determining these increments of the animation parameter t.

Constant Rate

Choosing a fixed $\Delta t = 1/(n-1)$ results in an animation with constant rate throughout its duration (Figure 2(a)). When an object's position is animated, this pacing yields a constant object velocity. In a collection of moving objects, all objects start and stop at the same time, but move with different velocities depending on the distance they must travel.

Constant rate animation has several advantages: it is easy to implement and yields predictable motion because the initial speed of an object suggests its final destination [31]. However, it also produces high accelerations and decelerations on the first and last frames, and has a mechanical look that has been referred to as the "computer signature" [20].

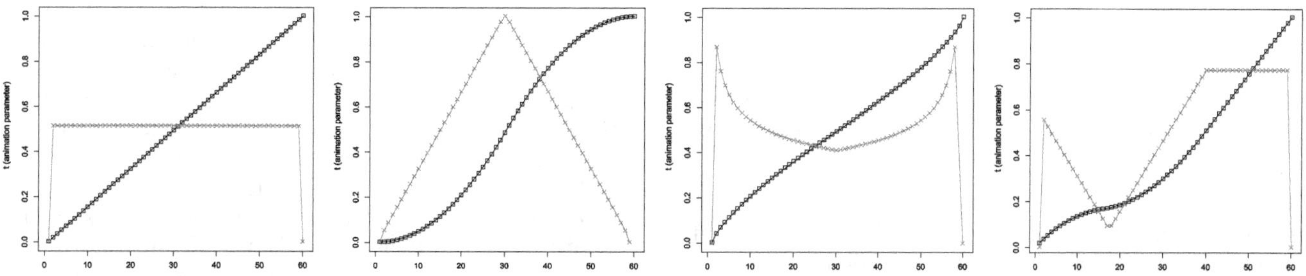

(a) Constant rate. (b) Slow-in/Slow-out. (c) Fast-in/Fast-out. (d) Adaptive rate (frame 18).

Figure 2. Evolution of the animation parameter t (black squares) and animation rate Δt (red crosses) for 4 different temporal pacing strategies in an animation consisting of $n = 60$ frames. The animation rate is normalized across all 4 techniques to allow for comparison. For adaptive speed, the technique has detected a complexity peak at frame 18. Note that all techniques except SI/SO have abrupt speed changes at the start and end.

Using a varying $\Delta t(i)$ – or equivalently, applying a transformation $t(i) \mapsto t'(i)$ to the constant pacing [17] – can be used instead in order to emphasize different parts of the animation. Below we describe some approaches to achieve this.

Slow-in/Slow-out

The concept of slow-in/slow-out (SI/SO) [18, 20] uses $t(i)$ values that devote more frames (smaller increments of t) to the endpoints of the animation, causing the motion to gradually speed up then slow down. Although many SI/SO pacings are possible, we use the following quadratic transformation of the linear pacing, illustrated in Figure 2(b):

$$t' = \begin{cases} 2t^2 & \text{if } t \leq 0.5 \\ 1 - 2(1-t)^2 & \text{if } t > 0.5 \end{cases}$$

SI/SO is a recommended animation pacing for transitions in user interfaces [8, 17, 38] and is used by default in several applications — e.g., MS PowerPoint, 3D Studio MAX and AutoDesk Maya — as well as graphical libraries like Piccolo [6] and Prefuse [15]. Beyond aesthetics, the supposed benefits of SI/SO are (i) that the gradual speed increase at the beginning of the animation helps users to start tracking an animated object, and (ii) that the decreasing speed at the end allows users to predict when an object will stop moving.

Fast-in/Fast-out

One potentially harmful effect of SI/SO is that it accelerates the middle of the animation, which can be problematic if something important occurs at this point. The middle of an animation can also be more cluttered and more difficult to follow, which happens for example when many points move from a random location to another [16]. In this case, one intuition would be to slow down the midpoint of the animation instead of slowing down its endpoints. This not only reduces object velocity, but it also smoothens object motion, which can help visually resolving cluttered animations [33].

We define fast-in/fast-out (FI/FO) animation as the dual of SI/SO, slowing down the animation in the middle as opposed to at its extrema. Again, many designs are possible but we use the following function to achieve this effect (Fig. 2(c)):

$$t' = \begin{cases} \frac{(2t)^{0.75}}{2} & \text{if } t \leq 0.5 \\ 1 - \frac{(2(1-t))^{0.75}}{2} & \text{if } t > 0.5 \end{cases}$$

Of course, this strategy has the unfortunate side effect that objects will move at their fastest speed at the beginning and end of the animation, presumably making it difficult to start and stop tracking any of them. In other words, this idea completely abandons the predictability property of SI/SO animation in favor of reducing visual complexity in the middle.

Adaptive Rate

SI/SO slows down the animation to emphasize its endpoints whereas FI/FO slows down its middle. To strike a balance between these two, we designed an adaptive technique that dynamically selects the frames with the highest visual complexity and slows down the animation around these frames. Figure 2(d) showcases this idea with one visual complexity peak at frame 18. We use an exponential function to slow down (but not completely stop) the animation around this frame. The technique is a generalization of both SI/SO and FI/FO: with peaks at the extrema or at the midpoint of the animation, the technique will reduce to the former or latter.

The remaining design parameters in this scheme are the calculation of visual complexity and the selection of peaks. For the former, complexity depends on the particular type of animated transition and the type of task. In our study, we focus on tracking points in animated point clouds, so for complexity we use a simple distance metric calculated on a per-frame basis for the constant rate animation:

$$D(t) = \sum_i \min_{j \neq i} ||p_i(t) - p_j(t)||$$

where $p_i(t)$ is the position of the point i at t in the constant rate animation. The intuition is that a frame t with low D is complex to follow because a large portion of the objects are located very close to each other, resulting in high degrees of occlusion and making single object tracking difficult.

The final step is to select a small set of frames representing visual complexity peaks, and to slow down the animation speed around these. Bear in mind that given a finite animation time T, slowing down one moment of an animation means speeding up another, so this should be done sparingly. We use a greedy scheme that keeps selecting peaks of high visual complexity (to a particular maximum) as long as they fall within a specific proximity (90-95%) of the most complex frame. This will result in at least one peak — the most complex one — being selected for slow-down. Because visual complexity often changes smoothly throughout an animation, we also enforce a minimum peak separation to avoid one portion of an animation to dominate the peak selection.

USER STUDY BACKGROUND

Here we present several decisions we made in the design of our user study, as well as some first exploration results.

Task Rationale

The goal of our user study is to determine the best way to present animated transitions in terms of temporal distortion, and we thus evaluated how accurately users understood different types of transitions under different temporal distortion schemes. Although what is exactly meant by "understanding" a visual transition is a matter of debate, a common experimental task is to have subjects track an object among others [9, 16]. This is an elementary low-level task, ensuring that if users are unable to perform it, then more complex tasks — e.g. following multiple independent objects or groups of objects — will be equally or more difficult. It is also safe to assume that many higher-level tasks will be difficult to perform if single objects cannot be tracked. For example, reading a scrollable text aloud is likely to be difficult if individual words cannot be tracked during scrolling.

Since our task is tracking an object among others, we focus on visual transitions that involve moving objects. Object translation is the most basic operation in animations. Other examples are changes in color or shape, but to keep the task simple we focused on moving objects that do not change during transitions. To further ensure that perceptual phenomena not directly related to animations such as object recognition and preattentive processing [37] will not interfere with the task, all objects were visually identical. One can assume that if an animation is effective for identical objects, it will also be effective for dissimilar objects. Arguably, in real applications users can highlight objects to facilitate tracking, but interactive highlighting is an orthogonal and complementary approach to animation: effective animations with highlighting support are preferable to poor animations with highlighting support, because they better help users follow objects that are not of immediate interest to them — hence providing context and facilitating incidental discoveries — and saves time by not requiring explicit object selection.

We therefore chose as visual transitions large sets of small objects that move from one location to another, i.e., *point cloud transitions*. This type of transition captures common visualization applications, such as scatterplot-based data exploration (e.g. [10, 12, 26]) and faceted browsing of object collections (e.g. [14, 25]). Finally, since we focus on time and not space, points move on straight paths. Although other trajectories have been proposed [10, 24], this is a simple approach that has been widely employed so far [12, 14, 25].

Datasets

We use two datasets of point cloud transitions. The first one is randomly generated. User studies sometimes involve randomly generated data (e.g., synthetic graphs [27] or images [11]) because compared to real-world data, it is easier to describe in a reproductible way, eliminates the problem of selecting unbiased case scenarios — which is challenging when real-world data is very heterogeneous — and allows for better experimental control. Since we do not know of a method for randomly generating structured point cloud transitions, we introduce such a method. We also use another set of point cloud transitions taken from a real information visualization dataset (described in the *User Study* section).

A *random point cloud* is defined by 6 parameters:

- r is the random seed,
- n is the number of points in the cloud,
- c is the amount of point clustering,
- p is the clustering power,
- s is the separation between points, and
- i is the number of iterations.

Figure 3 illustrates some values for c and s. A *random point cloud transition* is defined by the parameters above — which serve to generate the initial and final point clouds — plus the parameter m or *motion coherence* that affects how the final point indices are mapped to the initial ones (Figure 4). Details on the dataset generation are described in an appendix.

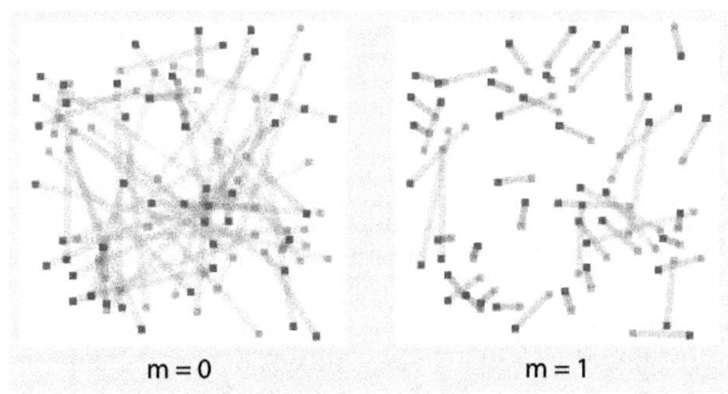

Figure 4. Two transitions between the same point clouds, one with low motion coherence (m = 0) and one with high motion coherence (m = 1). Point trajectories are shown with trails going from blue to red.

Task Difficulty

We first set out to discover what makes a point cloud animation easy or hard to follow with regards to tracking single points. We experimented with various randomly generated point cloud transitions and although we did not find any perfectly reliable predictor of task difficulty, we found that the number of object crossings strongly affected difficulty. We define *distractor count* or NDIST as the number of objects which cross the object of interest over the course of the animation. Incidentally, NDIST also captures the density of the point cloud (in denser clouds we expect more crossings), as well as the distance traveled by the target (the longer the distance, the more distractors are likely to cross the target).

Pilot Study

We conducted a pilot study investigating the traditional pacing profiles: constant speed and SI/SO. For this study we generated 100 random point cloud transitions by varying the

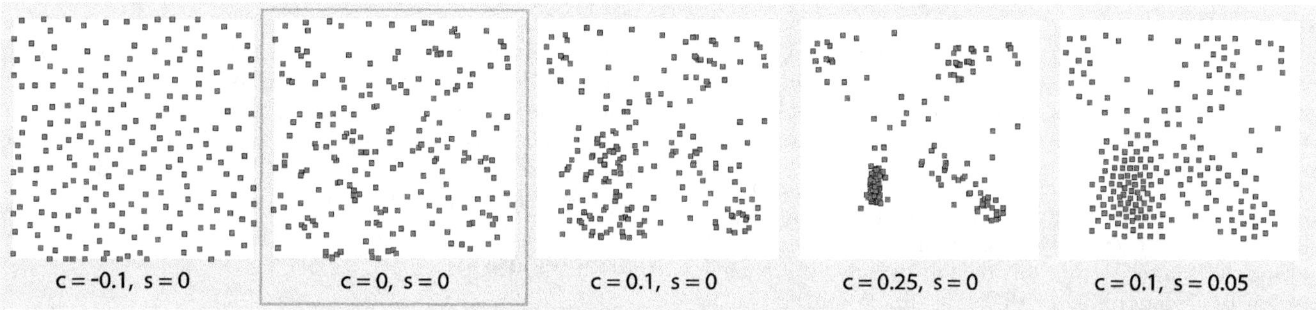

Figure 3. Examples of point clouds generated with parameter values r=0, n=200, p=-2, i=60, and various values of c (clustering amount) and s (point separation). The second point cloud shows a true pseudo-random distribution.

parameters $\boldsymbol{r}$, $\boldsymbol{n}$, $\boldsymbol{c}$, $\boldsymbol{p}$, $\boldsymbol{s}$, $\boldsymbol{i}$, and $\boldsymbol{m}$. We ensured that the generated trials had different instances of NDIST values. All animated transitions were limited to 1 second, a common duration for even complex animated transitions [16]. The task consisted of tracking a point, and was identical to the one used in the full study. Four subjects participated in our pilot.

We explored the data using ScatterDice [10] and first observed that all tasks for which all 4 users were successful using constant rate were also successfully completed by all 4 users using SI/SO. We then examined tasks for which SI/SO yielded more successful trials than constant rate. These were all tasks where the target point (i.e., the point to follow) was surrounded by other points (e.g., inside or next to a cluster) at the beginning and/or at the end of the animation. We hence postulated that SI/SO worked well primarily because it allowed users to better see what happens when the animation was the most difficult to follow. Inspired by this finding, we designed the adaptive speed technique and decided to also include the FI/FO technique (the dual of SI/SO) in the study.

Distractor Profiles

To test whether temporal distortion helps in following complex parts of an animation, we decided to explicitly include trials where animations are the most complex in the middle or at the endpoints. We thus introduce the measure *distractor profile* or DISTPROF, which captures the evolution of animation complexity in time, i.e., whether it is mostly complex at the endpoints or the middle (for a given target point to track):

$$\text{DISTPROF} = \frac{(n_1 + n_3)/2 + 1}{n_2 + 1}$$

where n_1 is the NDIST measure for $t \in [0, \frac{1}{3}[$, n_2 is NDIST for $t \in [\frac{1}{3}, \frac{2}{3}]$ and n_3 is NDIST for $t \in]\frac{2}{3}, 1]$. An animation that is mostly complex at the endpoints (e.g., the target goes from a dense cluster to another) yields DISTPROF > 1. An animation that is mostly complex at the middle (e.g., the target point goes through a dense cluster) yields DISTPROF < 1.

Error Metric

As our transitions were of fixed duration, we chose to not measure completion time but rather accuracy in tracking the target. Our *selection error* or ERROR metric is defined as:

$$\text{ERROR}(p_s, p_t^1) = \frac{err(p_s, p_t^1)}{E(err(p_i^1, p_t^1))}, \quad err(a,b) = ||a - b||$$

where p_t^1 is the position of the target in the final point cloud, p_s that of the user selection, and $E(err(p_i^1, p_t^1))$ is the expected error that would have been measured had the participant given a random answer, and is equal to the average distance of all points from the target. Thus, an average value of 1 means users guessed the answer whereas a value well above 1 could mean users were misled by the animation.

The definition of the ERROR metric is such that if the user selects the correct target, her error is 0. If she selects an object close to the target, her error is smaller than when selecting an object far from the target. Thus, good approximate selections are penalized less than completely random ones. Moreover, the normalization with the expected error ensures that in cases where most objects are close to the target, as in a tight object cluster, an arbitrary object selection within the cluster does not give too small an error.

USER STUDY

Given the above background, we designed a controlled experiment to formally evaluate object tracking performance under different temporal distortion strategies. We describe the details of this experiment in this section.

Task Generation

A *task* consists of a *point cloud transition* and a *target*, i.e., a particular point to follow. We included two task datasets (one generated, one real) with different properties in terms of structure. The generated dataset (see Figures 3 and 4) was used to ensure we could fully test the different techniques under different distractor profiles. The use of the real dataset ensured that our findings were generalizable to real life data.

Generated: We generated a set of random transitions with $\boldsymbol{n} = 200$, $\boldsymbol{c} \in [-0.25, 0.5]$, $\boldsymbol{p} = -2$, $\boldsymbol{s} \in [0, 0.05]$, $\boldsymbol{i} = 60$ and $\boldsymbol{m} \in [0, 1]$. For each of these transitions, we generated a task by randomly selecting a target point that (i) is not occluded by other points at the first and last animation frame and (ii) travels a minimum distance of 0.5 — i.e., half of the point cloud size. We then pruned tasks for which NDIST < 15 in order to further ensure that they were not too easy. We grouped these tasks into into three bins (d_e, d_m, d_o). Tasks in the first bin d_e are complex at the two endpoints (DISTPROF > 1), and we chose ones with DISTPROF $\in [5, \infty[$. In bin d_m tasks are complex in the middle ($0 <$ DISTPROF < 1) with DISTPROF $\in [0, 0.5]$. Finally, tasks in d_o are close to constant complexity (DistProf ~ 1) and we chose ones with DistProf $\in [0.8, 1.2]$. The chosen margins for the values of DistProf between bins ensures that tasks differ enough in their distractor profile. We randomly selected 12 tasks per bin and obtained a total of 36 randomly-generated tasks.

Real: The second dataset is a high-dimensional dataset of digital cameras[1] (1,038 objects and 8 dimensions per object). A point cloud transition in this dataset depicted the change between two scatterplots of different dimension pairs. To select tasks that follow the distractor profiles we wanted to explore, we generated about 800 potential tasks by combining (i) random transitions (combinations of dimensions), and (ii) random objects as targets, always ensuring that the target was not covered by other objects at the first and last animation frame. Since values for DistProf were very close to 1, we used only two bins (d_e, d_m) for which we selected the 12 tasks with highest DistProf (complexity at the extrema) and the 12 with lowest DistProf. The selected bins verified DistProf > 1.2 and DistProf < 0.8 respectively.

Procedure and Apparatus

Participants were first shown the initial point cloud. They were asked to press the Space bar to highlight the target in red. After releasing Space, the highlighting of the target would disappear (but it persisted for at least 1 second). When subjects were ready to begin the trial they pressed Space again, after which all objects were animated to their final state. Participants were then asked to use the mouse to select the target in this final state as accurately as possible.

The experiment was conducted on a desktop computer equipped with a mouse, keyboard, and a 19" LCD monitor (1280 × 1024 resolution, 60 Hz refresh). Point clouds were shown in a 800 × 800 rectangular area, with points being dark gray 16-pixel squares. Animations lasted one second.

Experimental Design and Procedure

12 participants (paid university students) were randomly assigned to one of 4 groups. Each group used all 4 techniques described in the design space section in an ordering balanced using a Latin square. Tasks were selected as described previously, and were repeated across techniques. To avoid learning, task order was randomized across techniques, and point clouds were rotated by 90° between techniques.

Prior to each technique users were given brief instructions, without explaining the implementation details of each technique, and performed a short warm-up session (2 trials) to familiarize themselves with the technique. The experiment lasted on average 45 minutes and had the following design:

	12	participants
	4	Tech (*C, SI/SO, FI/FO, A*)
	2	Dataset (*Generated, Real*)
	3, 2	DistProf (d_e, d_m, d_o)
×	12	repetitions
	2280	total trials

[1] Collected from `http://www.dpreview.com/`.

RESULTS

Trials were marked as outliers when Error was beyond 3 standard deviations from the mean for a given subject, Tech and DistProf (1% of all trials), and were removed from further analysis. The remaining trials were aggregated per subject for each combination of conditions, and followed closely the normal distribution.

Error (Figure 5)

Generated Dataset

ANOVA showed a significant effect of Tech on Error ($F_{3,33} = 35.1$, $p < .0001$). Post-hoc pair-wise means comparison (all adjustments Bonferroni) showed that *SI/SO* and *C* were significantly different from each other and from all other techniques (all $p < .01$). Mean Error was lowest for *SI/SO* (0.28), then *C* (0.49), *A* (0.63), and *FI/FO* (0.65).

A significant Tech × DistProf interaction was present ($F_{6,66} = 4.4$, $p < .0001$). Pair-wise means comparison (all $p < .05$) showed that *SI/SO* was significantly better than all other techniques across distractor profiles. However, the results differ for the remaining techniques. Specifically under the d_m and d_o distractor profile, *A* performs significantly worse than *C*, but not in the d_e distractor profile case.

Real Dataset

ANOVA on the real dataset yielded a significant effect of Tech on Error ($F_{3,33} = 17.6$, $p < .0001$). Pair-wise means comparison (all $p < .05$) showed that *SI/SO* was significantly more accurate than *C* and *FI/FO*, with no significant difference between *SI/SO* and *A*. Contrary to the generated dataset, mean Error was less for *SI/SO* (0.25), followed this time by *A* (0.32), *C* (0.39), and *FI/FO* (0.51).

A significant Tech × DistProf interaction was present ($F_{3,33} = 2.9$, $p < .05$) for the 2 distractor profiles. Pair-wise means comparison (all $p < .05$) showed that for the d_e distractor profile, the trends follow that of the main analysis (*SI/SO* not different from *A*, but better than *C* and *FI/FO*). However, for the d_m distractor profile, we found that *SI/SO* was significantly better than *A*, but not *C*.

Correct Answers (Figure 6)

Although we were mainly interested in the selection error Error, we investigated perfectly correct trials (trials where Error $= 0$) to see the percentage of correct answers per technique and distractor profile.

Error rates were relatively high compared to the many user studies that focus on completion time. This is because we only measure errors: had we measured low error rates (by giving trivial tracking tasks) we would have seen little or no difference between techniques. Note that the relatively high difficulty of our tasks is not artificial, as many graphical applications display large numbers of objects and animate them very rapidly so as not to slow users down (e.g., [25]).

Generated Dataset

The number of correct answers (303 overall) was higher for *SI/SO* (38%), followed by *C* (31%), *FI/FO* (15%), and *A*

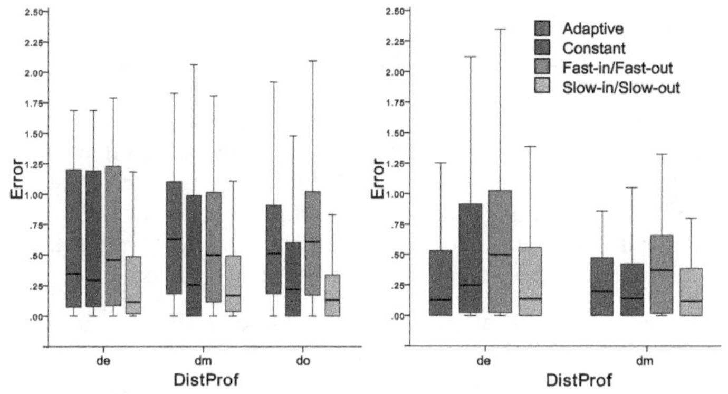

Figure 5. Mean selection error ERROR grouped by distractor profile DISTPROF for all TECH. Generated (left) and real DATASET (right).

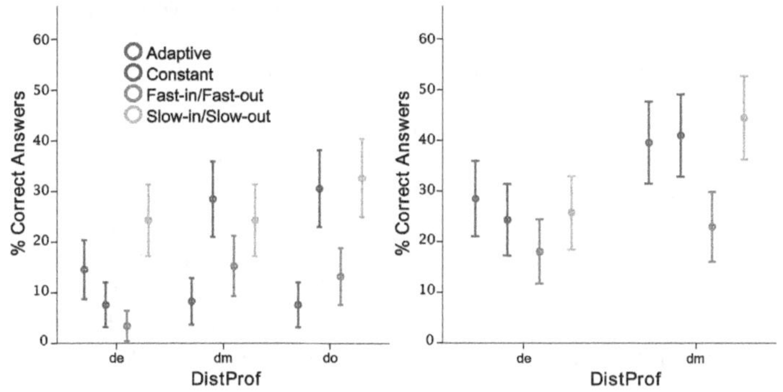

Figure 6. Percent of correct answers grouped by DISTPROF for all TECH. Generated (left) and real DATASET (right).

(14%). There was a significant effect of TECH ($F_{3,33} = 21$, $p < .0001$), with *SI/SO* and *C* having more completely correct trials than *A* and *FI/FO* (all $p < .05$). A significant TECH × DISTPROF ($F_{6,66} = 5.1$, $p < .0001$) interaction showed that this trend was not followed in the d_e distractor profile, where *SI/SO* was significantly better than *C* as well, but not *A* (all $p < .05$). By examining the correct trials in detail, we found that if a task was completed correctly in any of the techniques (303 correct trials corresponding to 17 tasks), it was also performed correctly using *SI/SO* in 95% of tasks.

Real Dataset

The number of correct answers (352 overall) was higher for *SI/SO* (36%), then for *A* (34%), *C* (32%), and finally *FI/FO* (20%). There was a significant effect on TECH ($F_{3,33} = 12.2$, $p < .0001$), where *SI/SO* had significantly more correct trials than *C* and *FI/FO*, but not *A* (all $p < .05$). No interaction effect with distractor profile was present. We further found that if a task was completed correctly in any of the techniques (352 trials corresponding to 24 tasks), it was also performed correctly with *SI/SO* in 84% of tasks.

DISCUSSION

We can summarize the results from the study as follows:

- The SI/SO animation pacing technique has better performance (i.e., significantly higher accuracy) than any of the other techniques tested for all distractor profiles;
- The other pacing techniques, while all less accurate than SI/SO, have different performance depending on the distractor profile; in particular, we see the following:
- Adaptive speed pacing works best for transitions with high complexity at the extrema of the animation (d_e), where it basically reduces to SI/SO; and
- Constant speed motion is better than adaptive speed and FI/FO for all other distractor profiles (d_m and d_o), second only to SI/SO.

In the following section, we try to explain and generalize these results. We also try to offer some recommendations for designers planning to use animation in interaction design.

Explaining the Results

There seems to be two primary and conflicting principles at work for how to effectively design the temporal pacing of linear animated motion of point clouds:

P1 **Allocate frames to endpoints:** Spend the majority of the frame budget on the beginning and end of an animation to allow users to anticipate motions; or

P2 **Allocate frames to complex segments:** Spend the frame budget on segments of an animation that are visually complex, either by calculating the complexity (adaptive) or by observing typical point cloud transitions (fast-in/fast-out).

Principle P1 has so far been the dominant approach in animation literature, practice, and tradition, whereas P2 has barely received any attention at all. One of the conclusions of the present work should be that this emphasis on the endpoints of an animation has been justified, and that a strategy based on adapting animation speed depending on frame complexity will only be successful when those complex frames happen at the animation endpoints. In other words, easing in and out of an animation seems much more important than slowing down and speeding up around frames of high visual complexity. The question is of course why this is the case.

A common explanation is that gradually accelerating and then decelerating motion aids tracking the object as well as helps the user in anticipating the beginning and ending of the animation. In particular, if the user is not expecting the animation to happen in the first place, a slow and gradual start will help the user to detect that the animation is starting and to adjust to the tracking task accordingly. In other words, *predictability* seems to be one of the key features named for slow-in/slow-out pacing, *not* that the slow movement allows users to better decipher complex parts of the animation (P2 above). To begin to find an explanation for why predictability is so dominant in this task, it is necessary to delve into the workings of the human visual system.

Human Vision and Smooth Pursuit

Voluntary eye movement can be performed in only two separate ways: *saccadic movement* and *smooth pursuit* [21, 28], where the latter is the method employed during object tracking (at least for objects moving slowly enough that catch-up saccades are not necessary [3]). Research in smooth pursuit shows that it consists of two stages [22]: *open-loop* and *closed-loop* pursuit. Open-loop pursuit is the first visuomotor response to motion and typically lasts 100 ms; it is ballistic and thus not attuned to the velocity or direction of the visual stimulus. Closed-loop pursuit then takes over until the motion ends, and is characterized by uniform pursuit gain, i.e., the ratio between angular velocity of the eye and the target is close to 1 (the target's retinal velocity is zero).

This suggests two things: First, that a slow and gradual start of an animated motion will help mitigate any inaccuracies caused by the ballistic behavior of the first open-loop response. This presumably prevents the user from losing tracking of an object in the first few instants of the animation. Second, a gradual slow-down will help the closed-loop stage in dynamically adjusting the angular velocity of the eye to maintain zero retinal velocity of the moving object. In other words, this presumably prevents the user's eye from overshooting a target as it reaches the end of its motion path.

Note that recent evidence in vision science suggests that overshooting generally does not occur, even if the motion stops unexpectedly [23], and that the eye, after a latency of about 100 ms, is capable of decreasing its velocity to zero in a constant time of 100 ms [29]. Nevertheless, overshooting the target as it stopped was a common complaint among participants for other pacing techniques than slow-in/slow-out in our experiment. We speculate that because our point clouds involved many distractor objects that often ended up in the same vicinity at the end of an animation, the final few instants of an animation were crucial for successfully distinguishing the target, and thus that the $\sim$200 ms response may cause tracking loss for abrupt stops.

It should also be noted that given the time intervals involved in smooth pursuit, i.e., 100 ms for the ballistic open-loop response, 100 ms latency for detecting motion termination, and 100 ms for slowing down the eye velocity to zero, our one-second animations are highly taxing for the visual system — around 30% of the duration of the animation is spent in visuomotor response to the motion! Nevertheless, one-second transitions remain an informal guideline for interaction design [16], and the fact that the error rate in our experiment was so low for such comparably difficult tasks attributes to the capabilities of the human visual system.

Scientific findings on smooth pursuit may also explain why principle P2 is not more significant than it is. While it is generally difficult to initiate smooth pursuit without visual stimulus [21], research shows that it is possible to continue smooth pursuit if a target is momentarily occluded [3]. This suggests that visual complexity in the form of overlapping and crossing motion paths may not be as serious a problem as we may have initially thought, and that frame budgets are better spent on the extrema of the motion.

Finally, it is possible that abrupt changes in object velocity must be avoided not only at animation endpoints, but also during the animation itself in order to facilitate object tracking. If true, this would suggest a third design principle (P3): keep velocity variations as low as possible, from which P1 (SI/SO) would simply be a consequence. This is an intriguing possibility that needs further investigation in the future.

Limitations

Our work makes a number of assumptions that may limit its broad applicability to other areas. For example, we focus on animated transitions of point clouds where each point has the same visual appearance, whereas it can be argued that in many real-world animations, the objects have a unique visual identity which would simplify object tracking. However, this is an orthogonal aspect of temporal distortion, and we think that our results should generalize to real-world tasks as well.

Another potential limitation is that our study only measured tracking of a single object, but many realistic tasks involve several objects moving simultaneously; in fact, perceptual research suggests that most humans are capable of tracking up to four or more objects at the same time [7, 30]. Our motivation here is that object tracking of a single object is clearly a task component of tracking multiple objects, so our results should give an indication of the general case. Nevertheless, more research is needed to study this in full detail.

Furthermore, recent results in vision science show that it is possible to initiate smooth pursuit even *before* the target starts to move, especially if the person knows exactly when it will start [3]. This was of course the case for our experiment, where participants initiated the transition by pressing the space bar. More research is needed to see whether unexpected animated transitions will cause different results for animation pacing on object tracking than those we observed.

Finally, given the perceptual nature of our evaluation, it would be interesting to also study these effects using a high-precision eye tracker. For example, is there an overshooting effect when an object moving at constant speed stops, and is there a marked difference for slow-in/slow-out motion?

Generalizations

Despite the above limitations, we still believe that our task and our findings are general enough to apply to a wide spectrum of interaction and visualization scenarios. In other words, our recommendation for short-duration animated transitions to show state changes in an interactive application is to use slow-in/slow-out animation pacing — not only does this result in more realistic and aesthetically pleasing motion, it also provides the high predictability necessary for reliably tracking individual objects in the animation.

It is hard to say whether our findings also generalize to other animation durations or to non-linear motion paths. They should hold for slightly different animation durations, but with very different durations we would have observed either a ceiling effect or a floor effect given our task difficulties. As for non-linear paths, animation practice suggests using them [18, 24], but our intuition suggests that this would again decrease the predictability of the motion. Future research should address this question.

Finally, it is important to note that our work has not addressed the question whether or not to use animation in the first place, but rather which pacing methodology should be chosen if animation is adopted in an interactive application. For the former question, we refer the reader to existing literature on the topic, such as that of Tversky et al. [35].

CONCLUSION AND FUTURE WORK

We have presented results from a formal user study evaluating object tracking accuracy in animated point cloud transitions under different temporal distortion strategies. These results provide solid empirical data on the use of animation for graphical user interfaces, an area that so far has largely been dominated by design principles from general animation that may not necessarily transfer to interaction design. Our findings show that slow-in/slow-out, i.e., smoothly stretching time at the endpoints of an animation, is the most accurate temporal distortion strategy, and we speculate that this is because it maximizes the predictability of the motion.

In future work, we plan to design temporal distortions that support both design principle P1 — slowing down around the endpoints of the animation — and principle P2 — slowing down around visually complex animation frames. We are also interested in mathematically optimizing temporal distortion functions similar to van Wijk and Nuij's approach to pan-and-zoom animation [36]. Finally, we would like to explore more complex time distortion schemes, such as staging animation [16] so that all objects move at the same velocity.

Animation for interaction design is a large topic, and we plan to continue to study differences between this domain and cartoon animation. For example, slow-in/slow-out is just one of Disney's 12 basic principles of character animation [18], and it would be useful to explore the other principles in equal depth as our present work. In addition, our results also open up an array of new questions on human perception that needs further investigation, including impacts of momentary occlusion, curved motion paths, and the number of distractors.

REFERENCES

1. S. Athènes, S. Chatty, and A. Bustico. Human factors in ATC alarms and notifications design: an experimental evaluation. In *Proceedings of the USA/Europe Air Traffic Management R&D Seminar*, 2000.
2. R. Baecker and I. Small. Animation at the interface. In B. Laurel, editor, *The Art of Human-Computer Interface Design*, 251–267. Addison-Wesley, 1990.
3. G. R. Barnes. Cognitive processes involved in smooth pursuit eye movements. *Brain and Cognition*, 68(3):309–326, Dec. 2008.
4. L. Bartram, C. Ware, and T. Calvert. Moticons: detection, distraction and task. *International Journal of Human-Computer Studies*, 5(58):515–554, 2003.
5. B. B. Bederson and A. Boltman. Does animation help users build mental maps of spatial information? In *Proceedings of the IEEE Symposium on Information Visualization*, 28–35, 1999.
6. B. B. Bederson, J. Grosjean, and J. Meyer. Toolkit design for interactive structured graphics. *IEEE Transactions on Software Engineering*, 30(8):535–546, 2004.
7. P. Cavanagh and G. A. Alvarez. Tracking multiple targets with multifocal attention. *Trends in Cognitive Sciences*, 9(7):349–354, 2005.
8. B.-W. Chang and D. Ungar. Animation: From cartoons to the user interface. In *Proceedings of the ACM Symposium on User Interface Software and Technology*, 45–55, 1993.
9. F. Chevalier, P. Dragicevic, A. Bezerianos, and J.-D. Fekete. Using text animated transitions to support navigation in document histories. In *Proceedings of the ACM CHI Conference on Human Factors in Computing Systems*, 683–692, 2010.
10. N. Elmqvist, P. Dragicevic, and J.-D. Fekete. Rolling the dice: Multidimensional visual exploration using scatterplot matrix navigation. *IEEE Transactions on Visualization and Computer Graphics*, 14:1141–1148, 2008.
11. N. Elmqvist, P. Dragicevic, and J.-D. Fekete. Color lens: Adaptive color scale optimization for visual exploration. *IEEE Transactions on Visualization and Computer Graphics*, 2011. To appear.
12. GapMinder, 2006. `http://www.gapminder.org/`.
13. C. Gonzalez. Does animation in user interfaces improve decision making? In *Proceedings of the ACM CHI Conference on Human Factors in Computing Systems*, 27–34, 1996.
14. Health Visualizer, 2009. `http://www.ge.com/visualization/health_visualizer/`.
15. J. Heer, Card, S. K., Landay, and J. A. prefuse: a toolkit for interactive information visualization. In *Proceedings of the ACM CHI Conference on Human Factors in Computing Systems*, 421–430, 2005.
16. J. Heer and G. Robertson. Animated transitions in statistical data graphics. *IEEE Transactions on Visusalization and Computer Graphics*, 13(6):1240–1247, 2007.
17. S. E. Hudson and J. T. Stasko. Animation support in a user interface toolkit: Flexible, robust, and reusable abstractions. In *Proceedings of the ACM Symposium on User Interface Software and Technology*, 57–67, 1993.
18. O. Johnston and F. Thomas. *The Illusion of Life: Disney Animation*. Disney Editions, 1981.
19. C. Klein and B. B. Bederson. Benefits of animated scrolling. In *Extended Abstracts of the ACM CHI Conference on Human Factors in Computing Systems*, 1965–1968, 2005.
20. D. H. U. Kochanek and R. H. Bartels. Interpolating splines with local tension, continuity, and bias control. In *Computer Graphics (SIGGRAPH '84 Proceedings)*, volume 18, 33–41, July 1984.
21. R. J. Krauzlis. The control of voluntary eye movements: New perspectives. *Neuroscientist*, 11(2):124–137, Apr. 2005.
22. R. J. Krauzlis and S. G. Lisberger. Temporal properties of visual motion signals for the initiation of smooth pursuit eye movements in monkeys. *Journal of Neurophysiology*, 72(1):150–162, July 1994.

23. R. J. Krauzlis and F. A. Miles. Transitions between pursuit eye movements and fixation in the monkey: Dependence on context. *Journal of Neurophysiology*, 76:1622–1638, 1996.

24. J. Lasseter. Principles of traditional animation applied to 3D computer animation. In *Proceedings of the ACM Conference on Computer Graphics and Interactive Techniques*, 35–44, 1987.

25. Microsoft Pivot, 2009. `http://www.getpivot.com/`.

26. MicroStrategy, 2010. `http://www.microstrategy.com/dashboards/`.

27. T. Moscovich, F. Chevalier, N. Henry, E. Pietriga, and J.-D. Fekete. Topology-aware navigation in large networks. In *Proceedings of the ACM CHI Conference on Human Factors in Computing Systems*, 2319–2328, 2009.

28. S. E. Palmer. *Vision science: Photons to phenomenology*. MIT Press, 1999.

29. J. Pola and H. J. Wyatt. Offset dynamics of human smooth pursuit eye movements: effects of target presence and subject attention. *Vision Research*, 37(18):2579–2595, Sept. 1997.

30. Z. W. Pylyshyn and R. W. Storm. Tracking multiple independent targets: Evidence for a parallel tracking mechanism. *Spatial Vision*, 3:179–197, 1988.

31. D. A. Rosenbaum. Perception and extrapolation of velocity and acceleration. *Journal of Experimental Psychology: Human Perception and Performance*, 1(4):395–403, 1975.

32. M. Shanmugasundaram, P. Irani, and C. Gutwin. Can smooth view transitions facilitate perceptual constancy in node-link diagrams? In *Proceedings of Graphics Interface*, 71–78, 2007.

33. B. H. Thomas and P. Calder. Applying cartoon animation techniques to graphical user interfaces. *ACM Transactions on Computer-Human Interaction*, 8(3):198–222, Sept. 2001.

34. B. H. Thomas and P. R. Calder. Animating direct manipulation interfaces. In *Proceedings of the ACM Symposium on User Interface Software and Technology*, 3–12, 1995.

35. B. Tversky, J. B. Morrison, and M. Bétrancourt. Animation: can it facilitate? *International Journal of Human-Computer Studies*, 57(4):247–262, 2002.

36. J. J. van Wijk and W. A. A. Nuij. A model for smooth viewing and navigation of large 2D information spaces. *IEEE Transactions on Visualization and Computer Graphics*, 10:447–458, 2004.

37. C. Ware. *Information Visualization: Perception for Design*. Morgan Kaufmann Publishers Inc., San Francisco, CA, USA, 2004.

38. K.-P. Yee, D. Fisher, R. Dhamija, and M. Hearst. Animated exploration of dynamic graphs with radial layout. In *Proceedings of the IEEE Symposium on Information Visualization*, 43–50, 2001.

APPENDIX

To generate a random point cloud from the parameters listed in the *Datasets* section (in bold here), we first initialize the random seed to $\boldsymbol{r}$ and choose $\boldsymbol{n}$ points $p_i \in \mathcal{S}$, with $\mathcal{S}$ being the unit square. We then move them using a force-directed algorithm and $\boldsymbol{i}$ iterations. The force exerted on each p_i is:

$$\vec{F}(p_i) = [\frac{1}{\boldsymbol{n}} \sum_{j \neq i} \vec{F}_C(p_i, p_j)] - \vec{F}_{SQ}(p_i) + [\sum_{j \neq i} \vec{F}_R(p_i, p_j)] + \vec{F}_{ER}(p_i) + \vec{F}_F(\vec{v}_i)$$

• $\vec{F}_C$ is the *clustering force*, defined as:

$$\vec{F}_C(p_i, p_j) = \begin{cases} f_{C_0} ||p_i - p_j||^{\boldsymbol{p}} \cdot \widehat{p_i p_j} & \text{if } ||p_i - p_j|| \geq d_{Cmin} \\ f_{C_0 min} \cdot d_{Cmin}{}^{\boldsymbol{p}} \cdot \widehat{p_i p_j} & \text{otherwise} \end{cases}$$

with:
$f_{C_0} = \frac{\boldsymbol{c}}{1000} \cdot \frac{k^2}{k - \boldsymbol{p}}$ being the force magnitude. We use $k = 7$ because it yields similar degrees of visual clustering for different values of $\boldsymbol{p}$.
$\widehat{u}$ is the unit vector $\frac{\vec{u}}{||u||}$
d_{Cmin} is the minimum distance above which the force applies. We use $d_{Cmin} = 0.1$ if $\boldsymbol{c} > 0$ and $= 0.05$ otherwise.
$f_{C_0 min}$ is the force applied below the minimum distance. We use $f_{C_0 min} = f_{C_0}$ if $\boldsymbol{c} > 0$ and $= 0$ otherwise.

• $\vec{F}_{SQ}$ is the *clustering force in an homogeneous square*, a term that prevents the whole point cloud from collapsing:

$$\vec{F}_{SQ}(p) = \iint_{p' \in \mathcal{S}} f_{C_0} \cdot ||p - p'||^{\boldsymbol{p}} \cdot \widehat{p_i p_j}$$

• $\vec{F}_R$ is the *point repulsion force* that locally reduces cluster density and point overlap:

$$\vec{F}_R(p_i, p_j) = \begin{cases} -f_{R_0} \cdot (\frac{\boldsymbol{s}}{||p_i - p_j||} - 1) \cdot \widehat{p_i p_j} & \text{if } ||p_i - p_j|| < \boldsymbol{s} \\ 0 & \text{otherwise} \end{cases}$$

f_{R_0} being the amount of repulsion. We use $f_{R_0} = 0.001$.

• $\vec{F}_{ER}$ is the *edge repulsion force* that prevents points from going past the unit square:

$$\vec{F}_{ER}(p_i) = \begin{cases} f_{ER_0} \cdot \overrightarrow{p_i \Omega} & \text{if } p_i \notin \mathcal{S} \\ 0 & \text{otherwise} \end{cases}$$

Ω is the point on $\mathcal{S}$'s edge closest to p_i. We use $f_{ER_0} = 2$.

• $\vec{F}_F$ is the *fluid friction force* that prevents points from moving too fast: $\vec{F}_F(v_i) = -f_{F_0} \cdot \vec{v}_i$, with $\vec{v}_i$ being the speed of p_i. We use $f_{F_0} = 0.1$.

To generate a transition, we first generate two point clouds $P^0 = (\boldsymbol{r}, \boldsymbol{n}, \boldsymbol{c}, \boldsymbol{p}, \boldsymbol{s}, \boldsymbol{i})$ and $P^1 = (\boldsymbol{r} + 1, \boldsymbol{n}, \boldsymbol{c}, \boldsymbol{p}, \boldsymbol{s}, \boldsymbol{i})$ with the previous method. At this point, every point of index i moves from the location $p_i^0 \in P^0$ to the location $p_i^1 \in P^1$.

We then increase motion coherence by taking two random indices i and j and swapping p_i^1 and p_j^1 if this yields a lower value of $\Delta_i + \Delta_j$. This operation is repeated $\boldsymbol{n}^2\boldsymbol{m}^2$ times.

Δ_i is the *relative motion* of the point of index i, defined as:

$$\Delta_i = \frac{\sum_{j | d_{i,j} \neq 0} \frac{(p_j^1 - p_j^0)}{d_{i,j}}}{\sum_{j | d_{i,j} \neq 0} \frac{1}{d_{i,j}}} \text{ with } d_{i,j} = (p_i^0 p_j^0)^2 + (p_i^1 p_j^1)^2$$

Tactile Brush: Drawing on Skin with a Tactile Grid Display

Ali Israr and **Ivan Poupyrev**
Disney Research Pittsburgh
4615 Forbes Avenue, Pittsburgh PA 15213, USA
{israr, ivan.poupyrev}@disneyresearch.com

ABSTRACT
Tactile Brush is an algorithm that produces smooth, two-dimensional tactile moving strokes with varying frequency, intensity, velocity and direction of motion. The design of the algorithm is derived from the results of psychophysical investigations of two tactile illusions – apparent tactile motion and phantom sensations. Combined together they allow for the design of high-density two-dimensional tactile displays using sparse vibrotactile arrays. In a series of experiments and evaluations we demonstrate that Tactile Brush is robust and can reliably generate a wide variety of moving tactile sensations for a broad range of applications.

Authors Keywords
tactile feedback, illusions, psychophysics, tactile displays.

ACM Classification
H.5.2 Information interfaces and presentation: User Interfaces --- Input devices and strategies; B.4.2 Input/output and data communication: Input/Output Devices --- Channels and controllers.

General Terms: Design, Measurement.

INTRODUCTION
The sense of touch provides rich information about the world around us. It informs us about object properties, such as texture, softness and viscosity, and provides dynamic feedback on our interactions with physical environments around us. Although tactile feedback can be a powerful modality in developing compelling, realistic and efficient human computer interfaces, current tactile technologies can produce only a small fraction of the infinite variety of tactile sensations. Designing new technologies that enhance the vocabulary of tactile "expressions" is, therefore, an important research direction in haptics and HCI.

Research in developing tactile displays can be separated into two broad categories. First is the design of actuation technologies and control techniques needed to produce a microstructure of tactile sensations, e.g., vibration [27], surface roughness [5], skin stretch [23], rotational profiles [25] and others. Second is the construction of high-order tactile percepts to communicate complex meanings, expressions and experiences, such as symbolic information, images and sounds [2, 12], alerts, messages [7] and spatial information, such as directions and shapes [35, 37]. The challenge summarized by Sherrick is "… to discover a set of tactile patterns that, like speech sounds or letters … are clearly discriminated, rapidly processed, and easily learned" [29].

This paper is concerned with the development of tactile displays capable of producing a *two-dimensional moving tactile stroke*, i.e., a high-order tactile percept. Developing such displays is important because, first and foremost, moving tactile strokes are one of the most common and rich tactile experiences [10]. Gibson listed such common sensations as stroking, rubbing, caressing, the crawling of an insect, scratching, rolling and the brushing of a leaf [17]. Combined with video and audio, the tactile stroke display can greatly enhance user experiences in a broad variety of interactive scenarios, e.g., games, movies and music.

Second, tactile strokes naturally form semantic units. Just as a brush stroke on paper, a tactile stoke "drawn" on the skin is sensed, recognized and remembered as a single unit of information [10]. By varying the speed, length, direction, location and intensity of tactile strokes, information can be communicated in a compact and efficient manner. Therefore, a tactile stroke display can be used in innovative tactile communication systems for the blind, emergency workers, vehicles operators, athletes, and many others.

Finally, although there is a long history of interest in tactile strokes [10], we are not aware of previously successful attempts to develop general purpose, scalable and compact haptic solutions to generate moving tactile strokes.

We present here Tactile Brush, a control algorithm that uses a low-resolution grid of vibrating actuators to produce high-resolution tactile strokes on skin. Tactile Brush allows interface designers to incorporate and control moving tactile strokes in a broad variety of applications using any vibrotactile actuators: from inexpensive pager motors to military-grade tactors. The algorithm is scalable and robust. It can be used on any body location, including the back, chest, thighs, hands, tongue, etc. The design, implementation and evaluation of Tactile Brush algorithm is the first major contribution of this paper.

The design of Tactile Brush is derived from rigorous psychophysical modeling of tactile illusions. The basic idea is to a) utilize the apparent motion illusion to create tactile motion sensation between vibrating actuators and b) use phantom illusion to create virtual actuators where no physical actuator is present. There has been no previous attempt to develop tactile displays by combining tactile illusions due to the limited understanding of their control mechanisms. To overcome this, we systematically measure the illusions' control space, construct their models, and validate them in psychophysical experiments. The resulting data and models not only inform the design of Tactile Brush, but provide tools to control tactile illusions that can be used beyond the scope of this work. Investigations of tactile illusions constitute the second major contribution of this paper.

Finally, we report a preliminary discussion of applications. While there are many potential uses for Tactile Brush, developing compelling visio-tactile-audio experiences was our primary goal. We synchronize moving tactile strokes with dynamic game and movie contents to add tactile feelings to drops of water, the recoil of a gun, buzzing of insects and air movement from passing cars. Although we implement the Tactile Brush system in combination with a chair, the algorithm can be utilized with tactile grids embedded into clothing, gloves, tools, sporting equipment and mobile computing devices. We believe that Tactile Brush opens a broad field for future innovative applications.

The remainder of this paper is organized as follows: in the next section we summarize the state of the art for multi-point tactile displays and their control techniques. We continue with an overview of vibrotactile illusions. We propose models to control the behavior of these illusions and outline a set of psychophysical experiments to validate them. We then combine these illusions in a general algorithm and evaluate its usability. We conclude the paper with a brief overview of example applications.

BACKGROUND AND RELATED WORK

Multi-point tactile displays, where stimuli are delivered by the simultaneous and coordinated use of multiple vibrating actuators, have a long history. In particular, sensory substitution systems for blind and deaf individuals have been an important application area of such displays. One of the earliest designs was Teletactor developed by Gault in 1927 [11]. It subdivided speech into five frequency bands and mapped them to five vibrators attached to the fingers and thumb of a user's hand. It was intended for use as a communication aid for the deaf. A number of similar systems, so-called tactile vocoders, were subsequently developed, including the Felix system and Tactaid VII [33].

With the development of reliable photo electronics a number of pictorial tactile communication systems that converted the output from an array of photo sensors into vibrations have been developed. Examples of such systems include Optohapt, developed by Geldard in 1966, using nine vibrating actuators spread across the body [13]; Optacon, using a small 24×6 matrix of vibrating pins to present images from a miniature camera to the finger [33]; and TVSS [2] and Tactile Television [9], using as many as 400 vibrating solenoids embedded into the back of a chair to display tactile images captured directly with a camera. More recently, electrical stimulation on the tongue has been used [3].

The development of schemes for encoding meanings into tactile patterns that users could learn and recognize is another important application of multi-point tactile displays. An early attempt was a Vibratese encoding schema developed in 1957 [12]. There are numerous studies that have investigated the encoding of information into tactile stimuli (e.g. [7, 24]). It was found that these schemes were quite efficient when multiple actuators were used, e.g., Tan et al. showed that an abstract coding scheme for fingerpads could resolve large amounts of information at 12 bits/sec [32].

Another class of multi-actuator tactile displays attempted to present spatial information using dense actuator arrays, such as creating static 3D shapes [20, 35], indicating directions [33] and motion [28, 37]. However, due to rapid adaptability of the human hand, static shape and pattern displays could only be used for active hand exploration and usually were not able to provide dynamic motion cues.

Most previous work on multi-point tactile displays was focused on displaying static tactile shapes or a-priory defined spatial-temporal patterns. Significantly less progress has been reported in developing displays capable of producing smoothly moving tactile stimuli. Previous research on such displays employed moving air- and water-jet stimuli, rolling wheels, sliding brushes and even moving probes glued to a user's skin (in depth survey in [10]). Although important in studies of tactile perception, none of these designs are scalable enough to result in a feasible general-purpose solution that can be used in end-user applications.

Indeed, with the rapid proliferation of digital computing technology, there has been growing interest in using multi-actuator tactile displays to enhance user experiences, improve quality and better the efficiency of interactions. Popular embodiments of tactile arrays include vests [34], chairs [2, 33], sleeves and arm bands [36], patches [31], as well as tools and mobile computing devices [37]. Because of such a diverse range of possible uses, scalability of tactile displays becomes an important issue: a tactile platform that scales across multiple embodiments will substantially benefit both research and application development. Tactile Brush is developed with such scalability in mind. We are proposing a flexible tactile platform that can be used to design a broad array of experiences for a wide range of applications, actuation technologies and embodiments.

TACTILE ILLUSIONS AS DESIGN TOOL

The design of Tactile Brush is based on exploiting vibrotactile illusions, perceptual phenomena that arise when two or more vibrotactile actuators are stimulated on the skin. Although tactile illusions have been studied for more than 200 years, they are still not well understood. Their differences are subtle, and they are often referred to by different names, leading to confusion. In this section we present two well-known vibrotactile illusions that form the basis for Tactile Brush: *apparent haptic motion* and *phantom sensation*. Both illusions share a common thread: a perception of a change in the stimuli location when time relations are manipulated [29].

Apparent Tactile Motion

Apparent tactile motion is also known as phi-phenomena. It has been studied since the early 1900s when it was observed that when two vibrotactile stimuli were placed on the skin in close proximity and their actuation times overlapped, the user would not perceive two actuators, but rather a *single actuator* moving between them [8].

Early studies of apparent tactile motion failed to produce robust movements: usually only partial movement was observed by participants [4]. As a result of this instability it was impossible to isolate control variables that would produce reliable tactile motion. It was Neuhaus who, in 1930, demonstrated that the variables producing robust apparent tactile motion were (a) stimuli *duration* and (b) *inter-stimulus onset asynchrony* (SOA), i.e., time interval between onsets of subsequent actuations [30] (Figure 1a). A number of follow-up studies confirmed Neuhaus's observations and estimated "optimal" values of SOA as functions of stimuli duration [21, 30].

It can be observed that by manipulating stimuli duration we can control the *speed* of illusionary movement. Indeed, as the duration decreases, the speed of apparent motion increases. This, however, requires adjusting SOA values to preserve the illusion. Failing to do so results in stimuli being perceived simply as a discrete sequence of vibrations rather than continuous tactile motion.

An exciting property of apparent tactile motion is that it can produce a strong and clear sensation of continuous tactile motion with just a few actuators. However, the major challenge in designing tactile displays based on this illusion is that there is still insufficient understanding of the parameter space where motion exists. Indeed, the main motivation of previous studies [21, 30] was to identify variables that control this illusion by demonstrating *an instance* of control values producing stable motion. How these values would change for different signal frequencies or directions, and how far they can deviate without breaking the illusion of motion, are not known.

Designing robust tactile displays based on apparent tactile motion requires mapping the control parameter space where the motion exists. We report the results of experiments that accomplish this in the next section.

Phantom Tactile Sensation

Phantom tactile sensation is also known as the funneling illusion and should not be confused with the phantom limb illusion discussed elsewhere. In discovering the phantom sensation in 1957, Bekesy was inspired by the working mechanism of the auditory system [6]. He observed that a simultaneous stimulation of two vibrotactile actuators placed in close proximity would create an illusory vibrating actuator located between the real actuators (Figure 1b). Unlike apparent motion, the phantom illusion is static and no motion is perceived [1].

Both location and intensity of phantom sensations are controlled by the intensities of physical actuators simultaneously. However, there is a subtle difference.

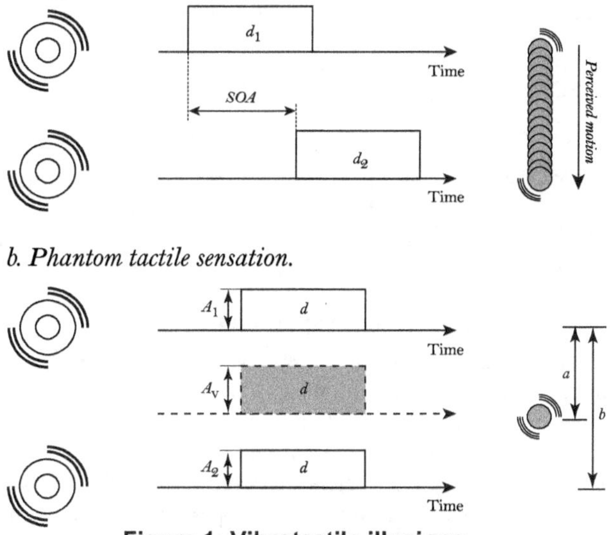

Figure 1: Vibrotactile illusions.

The *location* of the phantom depends on the *relative* intensity of physical actuators [6, 15], e.g., if their intensities are equal, the sensation will appear at a midpoint between them. However, the *intensity* of the phantom is controlled by the actuators' *absolute intensities*, e.g., increasing both in equal proportion should increase the intensity of the phantom without changing its location. The challenge here is to control both the location and intensity of the phantom *independently* by manipulating the intensities of real control actuators.

In 1970, Alles proposed linear and logarithmic relations between the intensities of phantom and physical actuators. He suggested that the logarithmic relation maintains the constant phantom intensity over the entire range of locations [1]; however, no experimental validation was reported. Recently, Seo and Choi showed that, while logarithmic relation was better for predicting the phantom intensity, linear relation was better for predicting the phantom location [28]. Therefore, currently there is no model that can accurately predict both the location and intensity of the phantom sensation.

The phantom illusion allows the placement of a virtual actuator anywhere between physical actuators, an important design element of the Tactile Brush algorithm. In this paper we propose and validate a new model for predicting both the location and intensity of phantom sensation based on energy summation theory [19, 26].

Is There a Unifying Theory of Tactile Illusions?

There are many similarities among tactile illusion theories. However, there is no consensus on a single unifying theory. Any such theory should also take into account other tactile illusions, such as saltation or "cutaneous rabbit" illusion [14], Tau and Kappa effects [18]. Thus, in the absence of such theory, in the present paper we consider all illusions to be unique and investigate and use them independently.

TACTILE BRUSH

In this section we report the design of Tactile Brush, an algorithm that allows for the generation of two-dimensional mov-

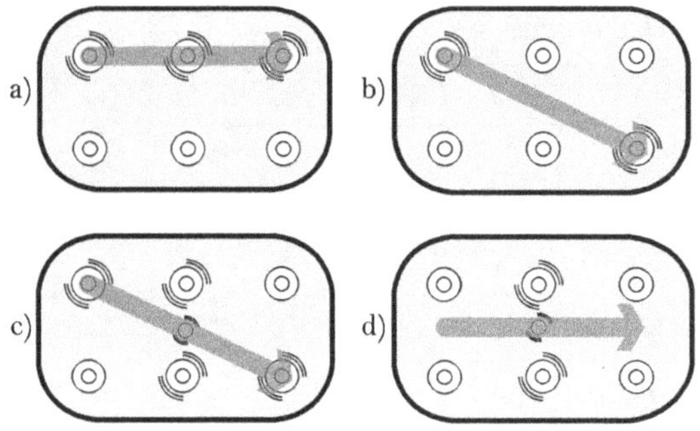

Figure 2: Basic approach.

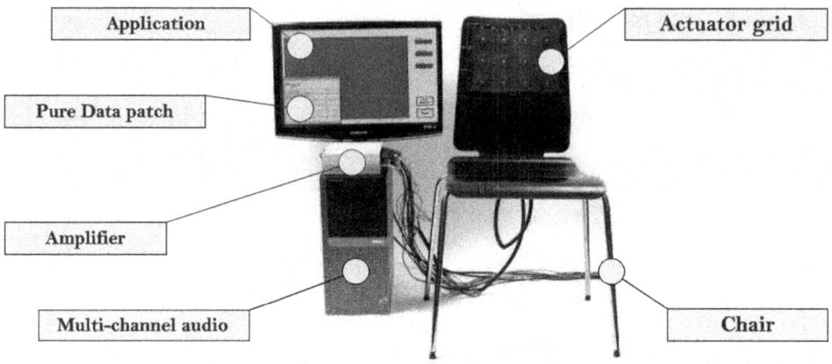

Figure 3: Tactile apparatus.

ing tactile strokes with a variety of speeds, intensities and directions using a small number of vibrotactile actuators arranged in a grid. The algorithm is constructed using two perceptual phenomena: a) apparent tactile motion and b) phantom illusions. The parameters that control these illusions are a) SOA vs. duration in apparent motion and b) actuator intensities in phantom illusion. However, the exact relations between control parameters and perceived sensations are not well understood. We cannot develop the algorithm without first determining these dependencies.

Therefore, a significant part of this section constitutes experimental investigations of illusions. We design and execute two experimental studies to gain a deeper understanding of how we can control human perception of tactile illusions. We must emphasize that these experiments are not related to actuators, hardware or the particulars of tactile apparatus design. Instead, we investigate *the underlying mechanisms of human tactile perception* using a well established, classical apparatus of psychophysics that has been used to gain insight into human perception for more than 150 years [16]. The knowledge we obtain is then applied to the design of the Tactile Brush algorithm.

Principles, definitions and challenges

We define a moving tactile stroke as a sensation that a) presents continuous motion, b) has a clear start and end, c) is perceived as a single semantic unit that cannot be subdivided, and d) can move with varying velocity [10].

To create such strokes we use apparent tactile motion illusion to produce continuous tactile motion between any two locations on the actuator grid. For example, in Figure 2a we produce a moving tactile stroke by sequentially vibrating actuators along the horizontal row. However, a difficulty arises when we attempt to generate a diagonal stroke as seen on Figure 2b. Because there is no actuator between start and end points, the apparent motion fails to produce a single tactile stroke, i.e., the user feels a gap in the middle.

To solve this problem we generate a virtual actuator by using the phantom illusion (Figure 2c). We then proceed to generate a tactile stroke using apparent motion, where *the phantom actuator is treated just like a normal physical actuator*. In other words, the Tactile Brush algorithm does not distinguish between virtual and physical actuators. In fact, we can produce tactile strokes consisting of virtual actuators only, as shown on Figure 2d.

Implementing this approach presents a major challenge: we must be able to control apparent motion and phantom illusions with a high degree of precision. Therefore, in this section we report two experimental studies that investigate the control of these tactile illusions. In the first study we measure the space of control parameters that produces robust apparent motion. In the second experiment we propose and validate a set of equations that control the location and intensity of phantom actuators. The results of these experiments were used to design the Tactile Brush algorithm as we report at the end of this section.

Tactile apparatus

We used a 4×3 equally-spaced rectangular grid of C-2 tactors (www.eaiinfo.com) with inter-tactor spacing of 63 mm (2.5″). The tactors were placed in a finely cut sheet of foam padding and glued to the back of a wooden chair (Figure 3). The choice of the chair embodiment was driven by gaming and entertainment applications presented later in the paper. The combined frequency response of tactors had slight variability across frequencies that was compensated for in the software. Each actuator on the grid was individually controlled by a multichannel audio card with tactile waveforms generated in a Pure Data (puredata.info) sound design environment. A custom control board amplified the current and voltage of individual waveforms and sent it to the actuators. Custom application software controlled Pure Data patches over UDP protocol (Figure 3).

Measuring Control Space of Apparent Motion

Stimulus onset asynchrony (SOA), i.e., time interval between subsequent actuator vibrations, is a critical control variable for apparent tactile motion illusion. When SOA is too large, the continuity of motion breaks and the user feels a series of successive stimuli. Alternatively, when SOA is too small, the stimuli collapse into a single vibration, and there is no perception of motion. Between these extremes there is an optimal range of SOA where the stimuli are perceived as continuous directional motion. This section reports on experiments measuring this optimal range of SOA.

The research question is as follows: *What are the upper and lower thresholds of SOA beyond which smooth tactile motion cannot be perceived?*

Methods

We utilized a one-interval two-alternative forced-choice (1I-2AFC) paradigm combined with one-up one-down adaptive procedures to determine SOA thresholds [22].

When measuring the *upper threshold* of SOA, the selected initial value was large enough that participants could clearly feel independent stimulation points. Participants were asked if they could feel individual "discrete" actuators. For every "yes" response the SOA value decreased until participants responded "no", i.e., they did not feel discrete actuators. At this point the SOA was increased. The change of decreasing to increasing SOA, and vice versa, is referred as a "reversal". The experiment continued until reaching the termination condition (described below).

When measuring the *lower threshold* of SOA, the selected initial value was small enough that participants felt a single vibration burst, i.e., they were not able to perceive the direction of motion. Participants were asked if they felt actuators "merged" as one. For every "yes" response the SOA value increased until participants responded "no", i.e. they could judge the direction of motion. At this point, the SOA was increased and the experiment continued until reaching the termination condition (described below).

Each experiment series started with a SOA step-size of 16-msec and, after the first two reversals, the step-size decreased to 4-msec. The experiment terminated after six reversals at the small step-size. An average SOA threshold was computed from the last six reversals.

Stimuli and Participants

The SOA thresholds were determined for five apparent motion patterns, shown in Figure 4. Three frequencies (150, 200, 270 Hz) and two durations (40- and 160-msec) at an amplitude of 20 dB above sensation level (SL) were used.

Ten participants (five males and five females; average age 25 years) were tested. They wore headphones playing pink noise and earmuffs to isolate environmental noise. Each participant completed 60 test series divided into three sessions over three days in random order.

Results

Figure 4 presents upper- and lower-SOA threshold values for two durations and five patterns, averaged across ten participants with standard error bars. A four-way repeated measures ANOVA was used to determine the significant effects of frequency, duration, pattern and thresholds.

We observe a significant difference between the upper- and lower-SOA *threshold* values ($F(1,9)=49.8$; $p<0.001$). In between there is a *region* of SOA values where participants perceived apparent tactile motion phenomena. Duration is also a significant factor ($F(1,9)=43.2$; $p<0.001$). As the duration increases, the SOA threshold also increases, increasing the entire range of reliable apparent tactile motion, see Figure 4. Frequency is also a significant factor ($F(2,18)=10.1$; $p<0.01$): as the frequency of stimuli increases, the region of SOA values producing smooth tactile motion decreases. Hence it is easier to generate apparent tactile motion with lower frequency vibrations.

Discussion

Figure 4 shows average SOA thresholds as a function of duration. As long as values of SOA are kept between these two lines, the tactile display generates continuous tactile motion across the skin. We also computed an average of the upper- and lower-SOA thresholds and fit a straight line through them. This line equation defines the near *optimal SOA control* for robust apparent tactile motion.

With this equation, generating smooth tactile motion becomes a trivial problem: as long as the time interval between subsequent actuators is computed using this equation, the user perceives smooth tactile motion. Tactile Brush algorithm uses this equation to "chain" multiple actuators in a carefully controlled vibration sequence to create tactile motion of arbitrary length.

Controlling Phantom Actuators

Phantom illusion is used in Tactile Brush to create a phantom actuator when no real actuator is present (Figure 2c). The goal is to create a phantom actuator that is indistinguishable from the real one. This section proposes and validates a model that allows "placing" a virtual actuator in the desired location and with the desired intensity.

The research question is as follows: *How do the intensity and location of phantom sensation relate to the intensities of the physical actuators that produce it?*

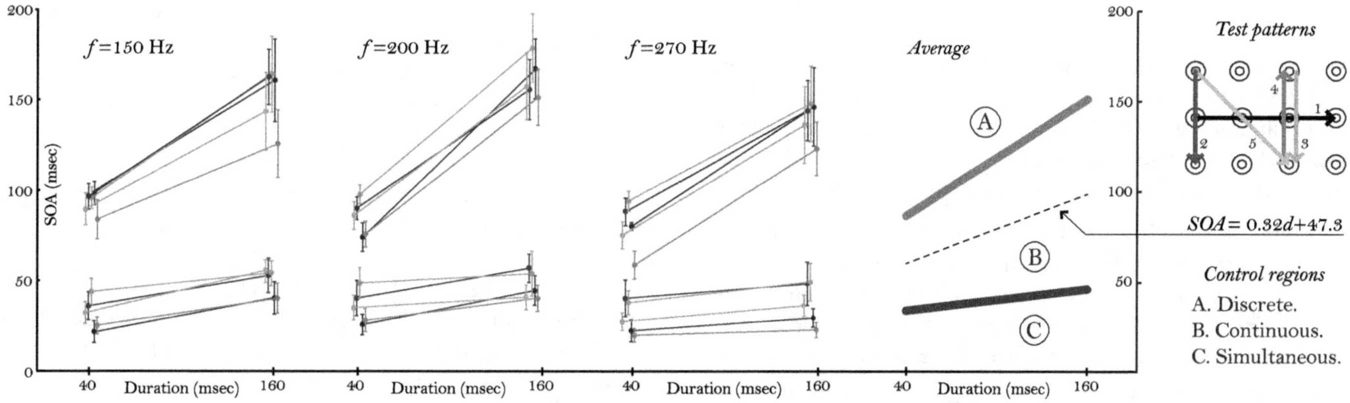

Figure 4: Upper- and lower-SOA thresholds *and* equation of optimal SOA control.

Model for Phantom Intensity

Following the energy summation model in the Pacinian channels [26], we propose that the intensity of a phantom actuator A_v is calculated as follows:

$$A_v^2 = A_1^2 + A_2^2, \qquad \text{Eq. 1}$$

where A_1 and A_2 are intensities of physical actuators (Figure 1b). This equation assumes that a) driving frequencies of physical actuators are the same and b) skin sensitivity thresholds at locations where the actuators are placed are the same, a reasonable assumption for closely-spaced actuators. This *energy model* departs significantly from the currently used linear and logarithmic models proposed by Alles [1].

We validate the energy model in experiments reported below and test the following hypothesis: *The perceived intensity of phantom sensation computed with Eq. 1 and the perceived intensity of the reference physical actuator are the same, i.e., their ratio is not different from unity or 0 dB.*

Methods

We use the classical *method of limits* [16], where we gradually increase or decrease the intensity of the phantom actuator until it matches the reference intensity generated with the real actuator. Here, *matching* means that when two stimuli differ by less than a certain threshold value, there is a complete "lack" of stimuli discrimination by the user, i.e., stimuli intensities are perceived to be equal [16].

In the case of phantom illusion, as we change the intensity of physical actuators, not only the phantom intensity but also its location may change. To control for location, we assume that the phantom location is defined only by the *relation* of the physical actuators' intensities and changing them in equal proportion would change the phantom intensity but not its location. Thus, we can control intensities of physical actuators using a single control variable α:

$$A_1 = \alpha, A_2 = k \cdot \alpha, \qquad \text{Eq. 2}$$

where a constant k defines the location of the virtual actuator. By increasing or decreasing α we can increase or decrease phantom intensity without affecting its location.

Stimuli, Participants and Procedure

Two physical actuators in the center of the first row of the tactile grid (Figure 3) were driven with 200 Hz, 110 msec stimuli. Eleven participants (six males and five females; average age 27) took part in the study.

We used a 3I-2AFC paradigm in which participants were first presented with a real left actuator, followed by a phantom actuator, and finally a real right actuator. Participants were asked to match the intensity of the phantom with real reference stimuli having intensities equal to 22 dB SL.

Participants adjusted the phantom intensity by controlling parameter α (Eq. 2). Experimental series started with the intensity substantially lower than the reference intensities. Each participant responded by gradually increasing α by 1 dB until the phantom intensity was perceived higher than the reference intensity, prompting the participant to decrease α. At this point the series was terminated and the average α from the last two trials was recorded. In the case of opposing series, the initial phantom intensity was significantly higher than the reference intensity. Participants decreased the phantom intensity by decreasing α until it felt lower that the control intensity, prompting the participants to increase α. At this point the series was terminated and the average α from the last two trials was recorded.

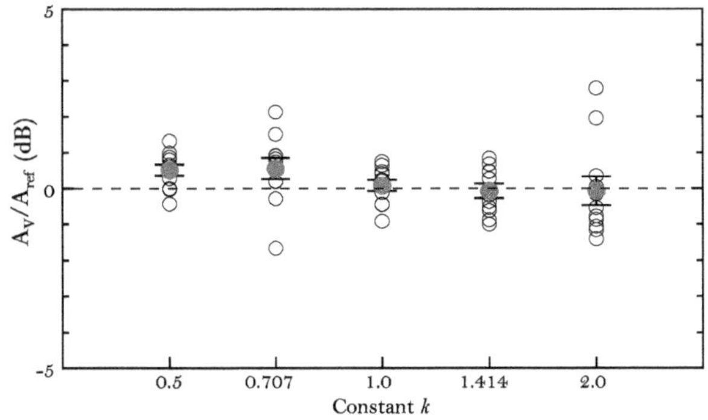

Figure 5: Ratio of the perceived intensity of phantom actuator to the intensity of reference actuator.

Each of the ascending and descending series was tested three times for five phantom locations defined by k = {0.5, 0.707, 1, 1.414, 2}. The resulting 30 series were randomly presented in one experimental session that lasted for about 15 minutes. The final matched phantom intensity was computed as the average of ascending and descending series.

Results and Discussion

All participants reported that they felt three distinct actuators. The average phantom intensity was calculated from measured α values using Eqs. 1 and 2, normalized by the intensity of the reference stimulus and plotted in Figure 5. We observe that the ratio of phantom intensities calculated with our model and intensities of reference actuators falls almost exactly on the zero dB line: averaged across locations it was 0.20 dB, i.e., a 2% variability. It was not significantly different from 0 dB ($t(54) = 1.7, p = 0.09$), thus supporting our hypothesis that the intensity of the phantom actuator can be predicted using our energy model. The importance of this result is that it allows us to accurately generate virtual actuators of a desired intensity. This plays a crucial role in the design of the Tactile Brush algorithm.

Model for Phantom Location

The energy model presented above also allows us to control the *location* of the phantom. Indeed, for any location between two physical actuators, the energy moment due to these actuators must be same:

$$\beta \cdot A_1^2 = (1-\beta) \cdot A_2^2, \qquad \text{Eq. 3}$$

where, β is the ratio of the distances a to b, see Figure 1b. Substituting Equation 3 into Equation 1, we have:

$$A_1 = \sqrt{1-\beta} \cdot A_v, \; A_2 = \sqrt{\beta} \cdot A_v. \qquad \text{Eq. 4}$$

Equation 4 computes the intensities of two physical actuators A_1 and A_2 that produce a single virtual actuator with intensity A_v at the location specified by parameter β. We will use this equation in the Tactile Brush algorithm.

The in-depth psychophysical validation of Equation 4 is beyond the scope of the present paper, however a preliminary quantitative evaluation was necessary. To this end we conducted a brief psychophysical study with three participants, comparing linear, logarithmic and energy models. Participants compared two sequences where each sequence consisted of four phantom actuators generated by one of the models, randomly selected. The models were used to calculate locations of phantom actuators to be equally spaced between the two physical actuators. The participants were required to choose the sequence where actuators were perceived to be more equally spaced. Our hypothesis was that *phantom locations computed using the energy model would be perceived as equally spaced more often than locations computed with logarithmic and linear models.*

The results showed that out of the 180 pair-wise comparison trials, participants chose the energy model 71% of the time, compared to 43% and 37% respectively for the linear and logarithmic models. These preliminary findings suggest that the energy model allows for the best phantom location accuracy.

Tactile Brush Algorithm

In this section, we design a general algorithm that uses the apparent tactile motion and phantom sensation illusions to draw continuous moving tactile strokes on actuator grids. The goal is to design a universal algorithm that treats tactile grids as a generic content-rendering platform. In particular, the algorithm must be independent from the specific mechanical and electrical properties of the tactile actuators used. The design of Tactile Brush was inspired by the evolution of computer graphics from special-purpose hardware solutions to today's universal content presentation platforms.

Definitions

We define a *rectangular* grid of *equally-spaced* tactile actuators $S = \{s_{i,j}\}$, $i = [0..m]$, $j = [0..n]$ where the distance between actuators is l (Figure 6a,b). The tactile stroke H is defined by a) starting and ending points P_0 and P_1, b) intensity I, c) frequency F, and d) the time T required to complete the stroke: $H = \{P_0 = (x_0, y_0), P_1 = (x_1, y_1), I, F, T\}$, where starting and ending points are defined in cm/inches in a coordinate system with the origin at $s_{0,0}$ (Figure 6a).

The goal is to compute a sequence Γ of physical actuators, their intensities, onset times (*SOA*), and actuation durations that will produce a *continuous* tactile stroke H:

$$\Gamma\Big|_{\eta=\overline{1,k}} = \{s^{\eta}_{i,j}, i^{\eta}, SOA^{\eta}, d^{\eta}\},$$

where k is the number of physical actuators required. The outline of the algorithm is shown in Figure 6.

Step 1: Virtual Actuation Points

Virtual actuation points $\{\lambda_i\}$ are a set of locations that will be used to compute the tactile stroke H (Figure 6b). Similar to Bezier curve control points, virtual actuation points $\{\lambda_i\}$ define stroke H independent of the tactile hardware, i.e., some λ_i would overlap with physical actuators but others would not. In the current implementation, we compute $\{\lambda_i\}$ at the intersections of tactile stroke H and the tactile actuator grid (Figure 6b). This choice of $\{\lambda_i\}$ easily maps them on the physical actuator space, as demonstrated later. Alternative mapping schemes are also possible.

Step 2: Speed of the Stroke and Timestamps

The speed v of the tactile stroke is computed by dividing its length by the stroke duration T. To complete the stroke in time T, each λ_i must reach its maximum perceived intensity in at least τ_i msec (Figure 6b), where:

$$v = \frac{|H|}{T} = \frac{\sqrt{P_1^2 - P_0^2}}{T}, \tau_i = \frac{\sqrt{\lambda_i^2 - \lambda_0^2}}{v}.$$

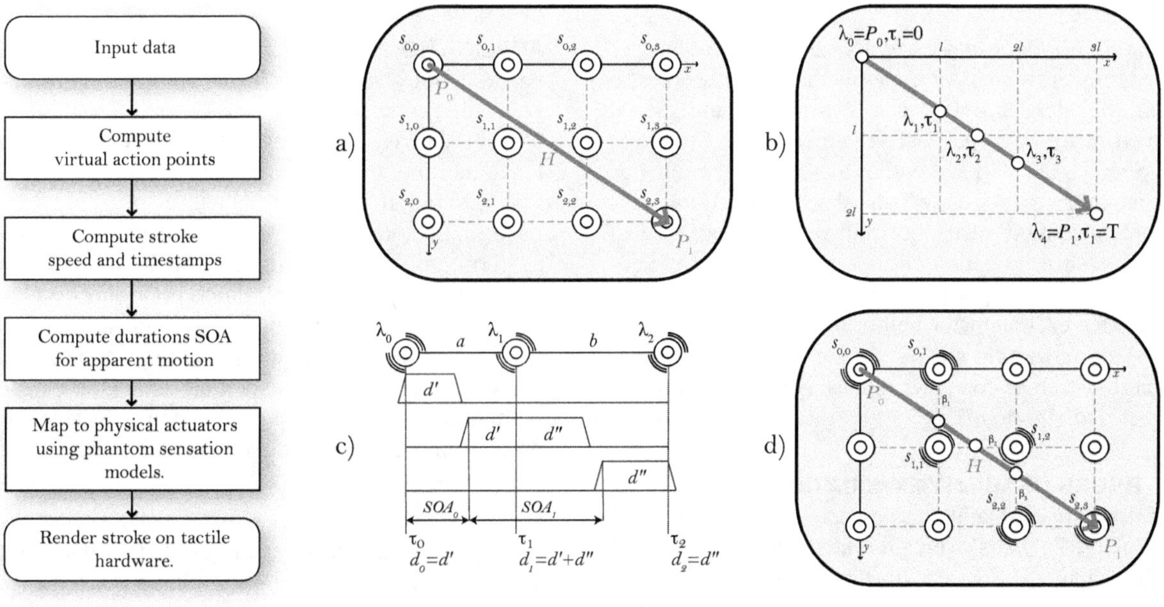

Figure 6: The Tactile Brush algorithm

Step 3: Durations and onset times for apparent motion

We produce continuous tactile motion along the path of the stroke by using apparent tactile motion illusion. However, instead of real actuators, we compute apparent tactile motion for *virtual actuation points* $\{\lambda_i\}$, i.e., for each λ_i we calculate a) vibration durations d_i and b) SOA_i. Figure 6c provides a timing diagram for a stroke that consists of three virtual actuation points. We observe several relationships between SOA_i and d_i:

$$SOA_0 + SOA_1 + d'' = T, SOA_0 + d' = \frac{a}{v},$$

and complete the system of equations by adding equations of optimal apparent motion that we obtained from the experimental studies of apparent tactile motion:

$$SOA_0 = 0.32 \cdot d' + 47.3, \quad SOA_1 = 0.32 \cdot (d' + d'') + 47.3$$

This set of equations gives us four linear equations and solution for four unknowns: two durations and two SOAs. It is trivial to extend this solution for a larger number of λ_i.

Step 4: Mapping to physical actuators

The final step of the algorithm is mapping λ_i on the physical actuator grid. When λ_i overlaps physical actuators, then $\lambda_i = s_{i,j}$. Otherwise, we consider λ_i to be a *virtual actuator*, and we find the closest pair of physical actuators that are capable of producing a virtual actuator at the λ_i location. The intensity of the physical actuators is then calculated by using the phantom location and intensity model (Eq. 4).

Algorithm Discussion

The advantage of the proposed algorithm is that it is *broadly scalable*. Since the design is based on fundamental properties of human tactile perception, the same techniques can be used on any body sites and with any vibrotactile actuator as long as the desired timings are within the actuator's capabilities. Furthermore, depending on application requirements, the algorithm can be adapted to other grid topologies, such as a honeycomb or triangular mesh, which is an interesting future research direction.

The Tactile Brush algorithm currently has some limitations. First, it can only draw *straight lines*. We have implemented a version of the algorithm that can draw open and closed curves, such as a circle, but that remains a topic for future research. Second, the start and end of a tactile stroke must be on the rectangular grid joining two adjacent actuators. This makes implementation easier but reduces the flexibility of placing tactile strokes in desired locations. Third, the algorithm currently pre-computes all of the temporal and intensity controls for each actuator before the stroke is displayed to a user. This restriction creates certain challenges in real-time scenarios, such as computer games. Developing on-the-fly tactile stroke computing is another future research directions.

TACTILE BRUSH USABILITY EVALUATION

In a brief usability evaluation participants (8 males and 4 females; mean age 29 years) were presented with three patterns (Figure 7): a diagonal stroke with three virtual actuators in the middle (1), a horizontal stroke starting and ending on virtual actuators (2), and a stroke made of virtual actuators only

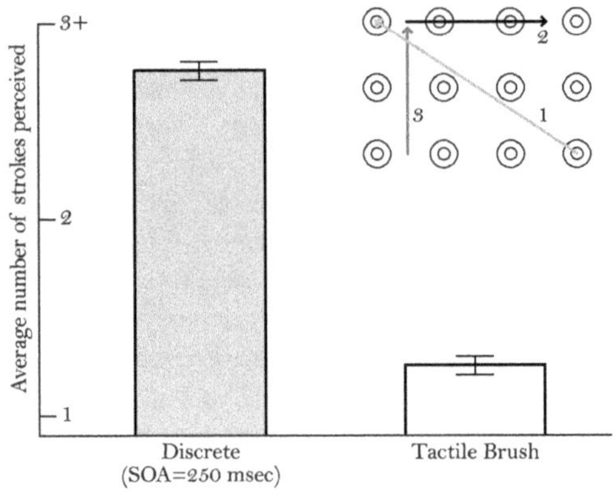

Figure 7: Tactile Brush usability evaluation

(3). The goal of the study was to validate that the Tactile Brush algorithm could produce the sensation of continuous motion.

Each stroke was presented twelve times: six times it was generated with the Tactile Brush algorithm, and six times it was a sequence of discrete tactile pulses of the same duration. Different frequencies, intensities and velocities were randomly assigned to each stroke. In each trial, the participants were asked if they felt (1) a single continuous moving stroke, (2) two strokes or (3) multiple strokes. Participants felt the stroke only once before responding. A brief training session before the experiment familiarized participants with the setup and experimental procedure.

The results of the evaluation are presented in Figure 7. They demonstrate that tactile strokes produced by the Tactile Brush algorithm were felt as single continuous strokes by most participants ($t(35)=23$, $p<0.001$). We also observed that in some cases, when participants felt two strokes, it was due to participants' posture – their backs were not touching all of the actuators on the grid. This problem can be solved by designing chairs that encourage certain user postures or using sensors to measure the actuator contact and dynamically adjusting the intensity.

APPLICATIONS

An in-depth discussion of Tactile Brush applications is beyond the scope of this paper. Indeed, Tactile Brush can be used in a variety of applications including rides and attractions, gaming and sports, aids for blind individuals, driving and navigation aids, mobile computing and many others. Each application would require specific embodiments, such as furniture, clothing, gloves and accessories, mobile devices, sporting equipment, game controllers and so on. Designing the tactile apparatus and tactile stimuli for a specific application will constitute an exciting research challenge in itself. However, we are not able to address this challenge within the confines of the current paper. Instead, we do focus on developing basic, fundamental technology that enables all these possible applications.

However, we also believe that it is important to illustrate some possible applications of Tactile Brush and indicate how the technology can be applied. Since our long-term goal is creating rich multidimensional tactile experiences for games,

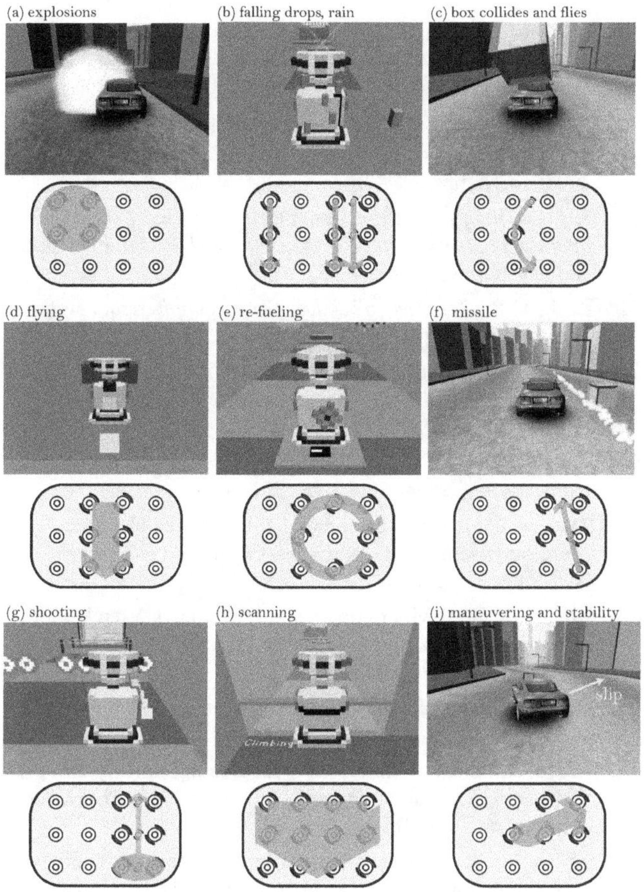

Figure 8: Applications: in game footage and sensations.

movies and location-based entertainment, we elected to develop two simple computer games and enhance them with tactile feedback using the hardware platform described earlier. Games were implemented using Unity3D game engine (http://unity3d.com/) and enhanced with stereoscopic 3D rendering mode.

In a *character control* game, the user navigated a robot through a variety of static and dynamic obstacles, such as laser rays and falling projectiles. In a *simulation game*, the user was driving a car through a simulated urban environment. The goal of designing these games was to investigate the application of tactile strokes in two popular game genres: driving simulators and role-playing games.

After reviewing a variety of existing computer games and extensive brainstorming, we identified four design strategies for combining gaming with directional tactile feedback. We discuss them in the remainder of this section.

Egocentric tactile feedback

This category includes tactile feedback that informs the user of changes in the internal state of the virtual game character. Examples include the level of health, amount of fuel or ammunition, feelings of tiredness or injury, etc. For instance, in a character control game we have implemented feedback on the amount of fuel (Figure 8e) as well as damage to the robot. In the driving game, we used tactile feedback to let the user feel the amount of tire traction and the possibility of the car skidding out of control. The goal here was to enhance immersion and state awareness by making the user feel what the virtual character "feels". In our tests users enjoyed and appreciated this feature.

Environmental tactile feedback

The tactile feedback in this category informs the user about the surrounding environment, but not interactions with objects. Examples include feeling weather (Figure 8b), oxygen levels, gravity, radiation, textures on the ground, airstreams and so on. In our demonstrations we found that, while it was effective, this type of tactile feedback required a certain amount of learning.

Tactile feedback for object interactions

This form of tactile feedback is the most direct and obvious. It simulates physical interactions between the user and game objects, other users and the environments. This category includes, but is not limited to, objects passing by closely (Figure 8f), shooting and feeling the recoil from a gun or missile launcher (Figure 8g), getting hit, feeling collisions (Figure 8a and 8c), feeling objects crawling and moving on the skin, explosions, electrocution and many others events. In the games that we have developed, these types of interactions were the most common. While they were popular and made the experience rich and enjoyable, a lot of care must be taken not to overwhelm the user.

Magic, spells and other innovative experiences

Most games are not based on reality and include many magic experiences and tools that can be expanded with tactile feedback. Examples include laser body scans (Figure 8h), an enhanced perception of free-fall or flying (Figure 8d), shrinking and growing, zooming, glowing, converging and diverging, casting spells, going through a portal and so on. This form of tactile feedback may be the most popular and easy to exploit because these mappings are artificial and the user can learn them quickly, without expecting to feel them as they do in real world experiences.

These four categories are by no means a complete list, but rather a starting point to explore the applications of complex tactile experiences enabled by Tactile Brush. Similarly, neither of the two games discussed above are the end result of this project. Instead, we provide them simply as initial examples of how the Tactile Brush technology can be used in future entertainment applications.

CONCLUSIONS AND FUTURE WORK

The Tactile Brush algorithm provides a solution for creating two-dimensional, high-resolution, continuous moving sensations on the surface of the skin. Using Tactile Brush and a few off-the-shelf tactile actuators researchers and interfaces designers can begin creating complex and rich multidimensional tactile experiences. In future research we will continue to expand the vocabulary of the Tactile Brush, design new tactile sensations and improve on existing ones. We will further explore means of combining multidimensional haptics with visuals and sound in order to deliver deep, immersive and believable user experiences. We hope that the Tactile Brush algorithm will help researchers and practitioners interested in haptics to begin experimenting with this new and exciting interaction modality.

AKNOWLEDGEMENT

We thank Disney Research for supporting this work. We are also thankful to Jan Stec for designing and developing the games used in the evaluation of Tactile Brush, Cheng Xu for helping us in conducting experiments and Mark Baskinger for designing the next generation of tactile apparatus. Finally, we thank the anonymous reviewers and CHI Associate Chair for their comments, constructive criticism and invaluable help in improving this manuscript.

REFERENCES

1. Alles, A.S., *Information Transmission by Phantom Sensations*. IEEE Trans. on Man-Machine Systems, 1970. ***11***(1): p. 85-91.
2. Bach-Y-Rita, P., C.C. Collins, F.A. Saunders, *et al.*, *Vision Substitution by Tactile Image Projection*. Nature, 1969. ***221***(5184): p. 963-964.
3. Bach-y-Rita, P. and S.W. Kercel, *Sensory substitution and the human-machine interface*. Trends in Cognitive Sciences, 2003. *7*: p. 541-546.
4. Bartley, S. *Principles of perception*. 1958, NY: Harper.
5. Bau, O., I. Poupyrev, A. Israr and C. Harrison. TeslaTouch: Electrovibration for touch surfaces. in *UIST*, 2010: ACM, pp. 283-292.
6. Bekesy, G.v., *Sensations on the Skin Similar to Directional Hearing, Beats, and Harmonics of the Ear*. The Journal of the Acoustical Society of America, 1957. ***29***(4): p. 489-501.
7. Brewster, S. and L. Brown. Tactons: Structured tactile messages for non-visual information display. in *5th Conf. on Australasian User Interface*, 2004: ACM, pp. 15-23.
8. Burtt, H.E., *Tactual Illusions of Movements*. Journal of Experimental Psychology, 1917. ***2***: p. 371-385.
9. Collins, C.C., *Tactile Television - Mechanical and Electrical Image Projection*. IEEE Trans. on Man-Machine Systems, 1970. ***11***(1): p. 65-71.
10. Essick, G.K., Factors affecting direction discrimination of moving tactile stimuli, in *Advances in Psychology*, J.W. Morley Ed. 1998, North-Holland, p. 1-54.
11. Gault, R.H., *Hearing through the sense of organs of touch and vibration*. J. Franklin Institute, 1927. ***204***: p. 329-358.
12. Geldard, F.A., *Adventures in tactile literacy*. The American Psychologist, 1957. ***12***: p. 115-124.
13. Geldard, F.A., *Cutaneous coding of optical signals: The optohapt*. Perc. and Psychophysics, 1966. ***1***: p. 377-381.
14. Geldard, F.A. and C.E. Sherrick, *The cutaneous "Rabbit": A perceptual Illusion*. Science, 1972. ***178***(4057): p. 178-179.
15. Gescheider, G.A., *Cutaneous Sound Localization*. Journal of Experimental Psychology, 1965. ***70***(6): p. 617-625.
16. Gescheider, G.A. *Psychophysics: method, theory, and application*. 1985, Hillsdale, NJ: Lawrence Erlbaum.
17. Gibson, J. *The senses considered as perceptual systems*. 1966, Houghton Mifflin.
18. Goldreich, D., *A Bayesian Perceptual Model Replicates the Cutaneous Rabbit and Other Tactile Spatiotemporal Illusions*. PLoS ONE, 2007. ***2***(3): p. e333.
19. Israr, A., J. Mynderse, G.T.-C. Chiu and H.Z. Tan. A Psychophysical Model of Motorcycle Handlebar Vibrations. in *IMECE*, 2007: ASME, pp. 1233-1239.
20. Iwata, H., H. Yano, F. Naakaizumi and R. Kawamura. Project Feelex: Adding haptic surfaces to graphics. in *SIGGRAPH*, 2001: ACM, pp. 469-475.
21. Kirman, J.H., *Tactile apparent movement: The effects of interstimulus onset interval and stimulus duration*. Perception and Psychophysics, 1974. ***15***(1): p. 1-6.
22. Leek, M.R., *Adaptive procedures in psychophysical research*. Perc. and Psychophy., 2001. ***63***(8): p. 1279-1292.
23. Luk, J., J. Pasquero, S. Little, *et al.* A role for haptics in mobile interaction: Initial design using a handheld tactile display prototype. in *CHI*, 2006: ACM, pp. 171-180.
24. MacLean, K. and M. Enriquez. Perceptual design of haptic icons. in *Eurohaptics*, 2003, pp. 351-363.
25. MacLean, K., S. Snibbe and G. Levin. Tagged Handles: Merging Discrete and Continuous Control. in *CHI*, 2000: ACM, pp. 225-232.
26. Makous, J.C., R.M. Friedman and J. Charles J. Vierck, *A critical band filter in touch*. The Journal of Neuroscience, 1995. ***15***(4): p. 2808-2818.
27. Poupyrev, I. and S. Maruyama. Tactile interfaces for small touch screens. in *UIST*, 2003: ACM, pp. 217-220.
28. Seo, J. and S. Choi. Initial study for creating linearly moving vibrotactile sensation on mobile device. in *2010 IEEE Haptics Symposium*, 2010: IEEE, pp. 67-70.
29. Sherrick, C., Vibrotactile pattern perception: some findings and applications, in *The Psychology of Touch*, M. Heller and W. Schiff Eds. 1991, Lawrence Erlbaum, p. 189-217.
30. Sherrick, C.E. and R. Rogers, *Apparent Haptic Movement*. Perception and Psychophysics, 1966. ***1***: p. 175-180.
31. Spelmezan, D., M. Jacobs, A. Hilgers and J. Borchers. Tactile motion instructions for physical activities. in *CHI*, 2009: ACM, pp. 2243-2252.
32. Tan, H.Z., N.I. Durlach, C.M. Reed and W.M. Rabinowitz, *Information transmission with a multifinger tactual display*. Perception and Psychophysics, 1999. ***61***(6): p. 993-1008.
33. Tan, H.Z. and A. Pentland, Tactual Displays for sensory substitution and wearable computers, in *Fundamentals of Wearable Computers and Augmented Reality*, W. Barfield and T. Caudell Eds. 2001, Lawrence Erlbaum, p. 579-598.
34. Vaucelle, C., L. Bonanni and H. Ishii. Design of haptic interfaces for therapy. in *CHI*, 2009: ACM, pp. 467-470.
35. Wagner, C.R., S.J. Lederman and R.D. Howe, *Design and performance of a tactile shape display using RC servomotors*. Haptics-e, 2004. ***3***(4).
36. Wong, E.Y., A. Israr and M.K. O'Malley. Discrimination of Consonant Articulation Location by Tactile Stimulation of the Forearm. in *HAPTICS*, 2010: IEEE, pp. 47-54.
37. Yatani, K. and K. Truong. SemFeel: a user interface with semantic tactile feedback for mobile touch-screen devices. in *UIST*, 2009: ACM, pp. 111-120.

A Comparative Study of Tactile Representation Techniques for Landmarks on a Wearable Device

Mayuree Srikulwong
University of Bath
Bath, BA2 7AY, United Kingdom
M.Srikulwong@bath.ac.uk
Tel: +44 1225 38 3374

Eamonn O'Neill
University of Bath
Bath, BA2 7AY, United Kingdom
eamonn@cs.bath.ac.uk
Tel: +44 1225 38 3216

ABSTRACT
Wearable tactile navigation displays may provide an alternative or complement to mobile visual navigation displays. Landmark information may provide a useful complement to directional information for navigation, however, there has been no reported use of landmark information in tactile navigation displays. We report a study that compared two tactile display techniques for landmark representation using one or two actuators respectively. The single-actuator technique generated different vibration patterns on a single actuator to represent different landmarks. The dual-actuator technique generated a single vibration pattern using two simultaneous actuators and different pairs of actuators around the body represented different landmarks. We compared the two techniques on four measures: distinguishability, learnability, short term memorability and user preference. Results showed that users performed equally well when either technique was used to represent landmarks alone. However, when landmark representations were presented together with directional signals, performance with the single-actuator technique was significantly reduced while performance with the dual-actuator technique remained unchanged.

Author Keywords
Tactile interface, tactile feedback, tactile representation of landmarks, tactile representation of direction, pedestrian navigation, wearable interface.

ACM Classification Keywords
H.5.2. User Interfaces: Haptic I/O.

General Terms
Experimentation, Measurement.

INTRODUCTION
Wayfinding can become problematic when one has to find one's way in an unfamiliar environment. Using assistive technologies can help in improving navigation performance [6]. Existing electronic navigation applications deliver information mainly through the visual and audio channels, however, there are many situations where a user's visual and auditory capacities are limited or subject to ambient interference. For example, firemen working in a burning building may have their vision impaired by smoke and their hearing may be overwhelmed by noise. Presenting navigation information via the tactile sense may be an effective alternative or complement to visual and auditory displays in such situations [6].

Research has shown that tactile navigation displays help improve navigation performance, target detection and situation awareness in many operational settings, such as aircraft piloting [4,26], vehicular driving [9,22], boat driving [25,26], pedestrian navigation [6,8,24], situation awareness [4,6], and alerts for command decision making [10].

According to May et al. [15], the two most important pieces of information that navigation guidance systems should provide are directional and landmark information. Direction plays a significant part in navigation completion while landmarks help in building spatial knowledge of the surroundings. In visual- and audio-based pedestrian navigation systems, both types of information are represented, typically as *visual icons* (e.g. arrows and graphic symbols) and as *speech.*

May et al. [15] also suggest that distance information can help provide "approaching" feedback. We did not investigate distance in this study partly because "approaching" feedback does not make sense in the lab setting and, following a more general principle, where there is a large number of factors with potential influence it is often necessary to tease them out in a series of studies, as we have done. Here, we focus on direction and landmark recognition. Distance is a factor in our current field trials but it is worth noting that May et al. [15] concluded that while distance information may play a significant part in vehicular navigation, it is not crucial in pedestrian navigation given the speed of movement.

In tactile-based pedestrian navigation systems, directional information is presented as *tactile icons*, i.e. short vibration signals [22] but there is no reported use of landmark representation in tactile displays. This absence of landmark information in tactile navigation displays may reduce their effectiveness as useful assistive tools that provide data crucial to navigation success [3,15]. This paper reports the evaluation of tactile landmark representation techniques that could work effectively in combination with tactile directional representation techniques that we have previously shown to be effective [19,20].

DESIGN CHALLENGES AND OBJECTIVES

Previous research, e.g. [8,9,19,20,24,25,26], suggests that the waist is an appropriate location for conveying tactile spatial information. In addition, it is large enough to accommodate multiple-location tactile perception compared to other areas such as the wrists, legs and head. In previous studies [19,20], we showed that a wearable device in the form of a waist belt using an point vibration technique to represent directions provided very effective tactile representation of directions for navigation tasks. This paper investigates the effectiveness of combining this technique with complementary tactile landmark representation techniques.

As we aimed to develop a tactile navigation display that can provide directional *and* landmark information, the chosen techniques to represent landmarks must work effectively and be distinguishable from a tactile technique used to represent directions. For this study, we drew on tactile display design frameworks [16] for general guidelines and suggestions; an absolute point vibration technique [22,26] for the design of directional signals; and the heuristic tactile rhythms [11,17,23] for the design of landmark signals. In addition, we assume that the use of tactile displays follows the information processing loop of the Prenav model, consisting of the processes of sensation-perception-decision-action (see [27]).

There are two main approaches to creating informative tactile stimuli: the *abstract* and *symbolic* approaches [14]. Abstract representation focuses on manipulating a stimulus' characteristics, whereas the symbolic approach focuses on the semantic association of stimuli with known metaphors. For example, MacLean et al. [12] designed 36 *abstract* stimuli by systematically varying waveform, amplitude and frequency of vibration signals, while Chan et al. [5] designed a *symbolic* tactile set in which signal patterns were associated with heartbeat and finger-tapping metaphors.

Previous research in tactile navigation (e.g. [22,26]) proposed *symbolic* mapping for the representation of directional information, involving the mapping of a limited set of cardinal and ordinal directions to their associated vibration signals. These signals have commonly been generated using one of two techniques: (1) simulation of straight-line patterns (i.e. pointing arrows) on an array of actuators, e.g. [22]; and (2) an absolute point vibration for each direction in a distributed placement of actuators around the waist, e.g. [26]. Our previous studies [19,20], investigated the performance of the two techniques and their findings underpin our choice of the symbolic absolute point vibration technique used in this paper. Nevertheless, representing direction using an abstract approach may be useful if the sizes of body contact area or device are limited (e.g. see [12]).

The representation of landmarks is even more challenging. Landmarks can be any objects or places on routes that are stationary, distinct and salient [3]. If we were to map landmarks using a *symbolic* approach, appropriate metaphors would require investigation. For example, it might be possible to draw on a shape metaphor, with each landmark signal represented by a simplified form of its shape. However, such an approach would require a different hardware layout, number of actuators and actuator placement (e.g. [1]) from the waist belt approach adopted here. In addition, the numerous landmarks studied in research projects and used in commercial systems are not systematically classified, are highly diverse and are often poorly differentiated. As a result, signal patterns for landmarks and their meaning associations are effectively arbitrary. All these constraints suggest an abstract approach to extending our tactile directional representation technique to include the tactile representation of landmarks.

The design challenges also include the creation of a usable set of tactile icons to be displayed on a device when rendering size is limited [14] and human tactile perception capacity is restricted [17]. An approach to the tactile representation of landmarks therefore requires two steps: the identification of a limited set of appropriate landmarks and the selection of appropriate representation techniques. The number of unique landmarks that could be represented is very large but both Chan et al. [5] and Gallace et al. [7] have suggested that the optimum number is seven. In a previous study [21], we identified a small set of important and generalisable landmark types based on particular navigational purposes proposed by Sorrow and Hirtle [18]: *commuting* (travelling to a familiar destination), *questing* (travelling to an unknown destination), and *exploring* the area. We use that set here.

To create a distinguishable and learnable set of *abstract* tactile stimuli, researchers [5,12,22,23] have suggested that a technique that manipulates tactile signal duration on a single actuator to create a variety of rhythms provides effective results. In this study, we employed the heuristic tactile rhythms proposed by Ternes and MacLean [23].

Another technique that may help the users of a tactile navigation system distinguish direction from landmark signals is to introduce *discontinuity*. Having motivated our objective of investigating representations of direction and landmark type with the waist belt, a technique to introduce discontinuity had to be localised to the waist area. Since any directional signal is generated on one actuator, discontinuity may be achieved by increasing the number of contact points on the body [17], e.g. using a combination of two or more actuators [11]. Although proposed, this technique has not previously been investigated, therefore, in this study we examined the use of two actuators to create unique tactile stimuli.

To summarise, this study investigated the following tactile landmark representation techniques: (1) manipulating the signal rhythms, and (2) increasing the number of body contact areas (i.e. increasing the number of actuators used to display information). In this paper, we refer to the two techniques as the single-actuator and dual-actuator techniques respectively. Both techniques for tactile representation of landmarks were presented alone and together with tactile directional signals.

EXPERIMENTAL DESIGN

The tactile display took the form of a waist belt with embedded actuators. For the set of landmarks we drew on our previous research [21]. This research suggested that the most suitable small set of landmarks for our prototype tactile landmark representation should be: mall and market, religious place, tourist attraction, public transportation, bridge, monument and memorial, and railway station. These findings corroborated the results of previous research suggesting that there are some generic landmarks that will be appropriate across different environments [2]. To represent directions, we used an established technique, generating an absolute vibration in a corresponding location on the user's body [25]. We evaluated novel tactile representation techniques for the landmarks, both alone and in combination with the directional signals.

Equipment

The main equipment for our experiment consisted of controllers, motors, and an associated switch circuit. The main controller unit was built using two 0/16/16 interface kit controllers, manufactured by Phidgets (www.phidgets.com). Vibrating points, i.e. actuators, were built using VPM2 vibrating disk motors, manufactured by Solarbotics (www.solarbotics.com). The actuators were 1 cm in diameter, which was small enough to be easily embedded in clothing. The motors were connected to the controller's digital output channels. Motor vibration was powered by a 6v battery and controlled by an additional custom-built controller switch.

The prototype was connected to an HP Compaq tablet PC via a USB port. The control software was written using the programming language Java under the Microsoft Windows environment. When the control switch and interface controllers received an input from the tablet PC, corresponding tactile stimuli patterns were generated. The system performed this by turning the output channels of the interface controllers on and off very quickly.

The wearable device consisted of 8 actuators mounted in a waist belt (Figure 1). It was worn around the participant's waist over light clothing. Following previous research, e.g. [24,26], the actuators were adjusted to account for participants' varying body shape and size, to ensure that each actuator was located in the optimum location and to avoid any bias in direction perception towards the midsagittal plane of the body (see [25]).

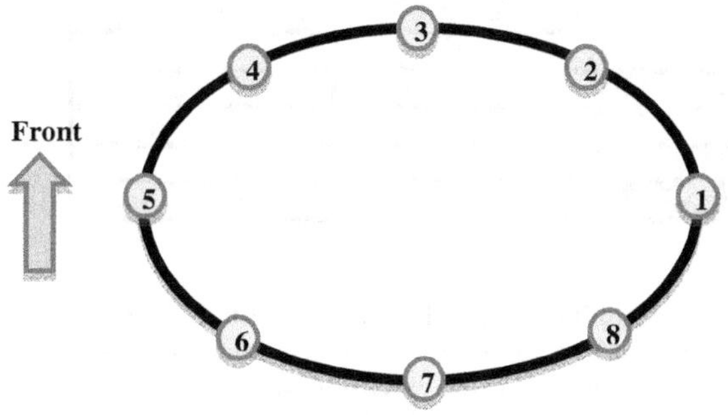

Figure 1. The Waist Belt Prototype (motor number 3 is the front centre actuator.)

Landmark Stimuli Design

The Single-actuator Technique

For the single-actuator technique, we used a set of tactile stimuli proposed by Ternes and McLean [23]. They were designed by using *eliminative heuristics and constraints,* a principled validation methodology based on perceptual optimization [23]. They have been systematically designed, tested and proved to be perceptible and distinguishable. Each signal in a set contains different *note length* and *evenness*. Rhythm is defined as a repeated monotone pattern of variable-length notes, arranged relative to a beat (4/4) and played at a set tempo, manipulated by changing the length, number, or gaps between notes [23]. Essential elements of the heuristics are that signals: (1) are monotone, (2) have a gap between successive notes, (3) have 2 second duration, (4) contain repetitions, and (5) to be perceivable must last at least 1/16 of the 500 ms interval (31.25) plus the same-length break; this signal is called an 'eighth' (1/8) note. The set contains five note lengths: 1/8 (62.5 ms), ¼ (125 ms), ½ (250 ms), ¾ (375 ms) and whole (500 ms). Each note length includes a 62.5 ms gap except the 1/8 note which has a 31.25 ms gap. Positive selection heuristics, i.e. a combination of different note lengths (including gaps between them), allows the generation of distinguishable tactile patterns. For example, a 2-second short stimulus contains a number of repetitions of ¼ notes; a 2-second long stimulus contains repetitions of ¾ notes.

The initial set of Ternes and MacLean's heuristic tactile rhythms contains 21 signals. In the original studies [23], participants experienced vibrations through their hands and a stylus. In order to make sure that these stimuli were still distinguishable when displayed on the waist area, we ran pilot sessions with four participants. Results showed that five out of 21 rhythms were clearly distinguishable (signals S1 to S5 in *Figure 2*). We further followed the positive selection heuristics by testing a combination of two of the five rhythms. As a result, signal S6 is a combination of S2 and S3; Signal S7 is a combination of S5 and S2. The final set of the most distinguishable rhythms is shown in Figure 2.

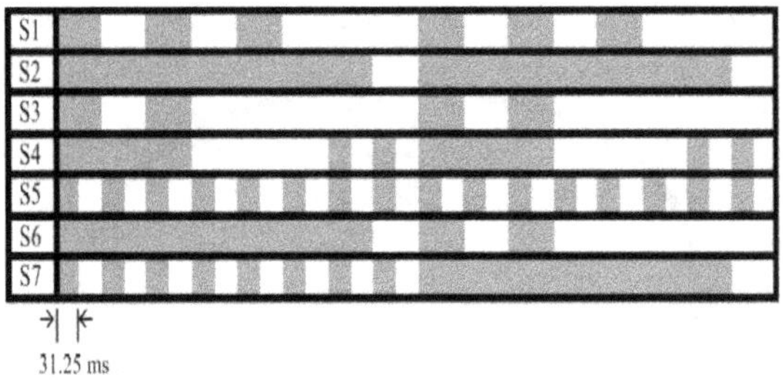

Figure 2. Single-actuator Landmark Signals. Each row represents one bar, to be represented 2 times as a 2-second stimulus. Each note contains vibration on- (grey) and off-time (white) that separates it from the next.

The Dual-actuator Technique

In contrast to the single-actuator technique which used different vibration patterns to represent different landmarks, our dual-actuator technique used the same vibration pattern for all landmarks. The pattern used was the same as that for directional signals: a 1.2 second stimulus consisting of 12 repetitions of a 50-millisecond pulse and inter-pulse. The different landmarks were represented by different combinations of actuators simultaneously providing the signal. Schiffman [17] suggested that increasing the contact area of tactile stimuli would result in better perception and distinguishability among different types of information. Loomis [11] suggested that an effective approach to this would be to use multiple contact points, however, an optimum number was not suggested. Our initial pilot testing found several possible combinations to be indistinguishable from each other. We omitted these from further study and ran pilot studies with 4 participants using the remaining combinations to find the optimum number of simultaneously activated actuators to represent our 7 landmarks. Tested alternatives included (a) pairs of non-adjacent actuators, (b) pairs of adjacent actuators, (c) three non-adjacent actuators, (d) three adjacent actuators, (e) four non-adjacent actuators, and (f) five adjacent actuators. We measured accuracy, mental demand, physical demand, temporal demand, effort, level of frustration, and both distinguishability amongst the landmark signals themselves and distinguishability from directional signals.

Results from this pilot study suggested that the best arrangement was two non-adjacent actuators. This alternative received high scores on distinguishability and accuracy performance, and low scores on mental, physical and temporal demand and effort required. It should be noted here that for the waist belt device with 8 actuators, the more actuators that were simultaneously activated, the more confused participants were.

Assuming for ease of referring to the angles that the belt is in the form of a circle, the final list of actuator pairs included: (see Figure 1 for referents of actuator numbers)

- 180° actuator pairs (3-7, 2-6, 1-5 and 4-8);
- 90° actuator pairs (1-3, 2-4, 3-5, 4-6, 5-7, 6-8, 7-1 and 8-2);
- 135° actuator pairs (1-4, 2-5, 3-6, 4-7, 5-8, 6-1, 7-2 and 8-3).

Stimuli code	Vibrated Actuator Number (see Figure 1 for reference)	Direction
B1	1	East
B2	2	Northeast
B3	3	North
B4	4	Northwest
B5	5	West
B6	6	Southwest
B7	7	South
B8	8	Southeast

Table 1. Directional Stimuli: 12 repetitions of signals at 50-millisecond pulse and inter-pulse duration.

Directional Stimuli

Following existing suggestions [22] and guidelines [16], each directional tactile stimulus involved actuation of one motor and consisted of 12 repetitions of signals at 50-millisecond pulse and inter-pulse duration, giving a 1.2 second stimulus (see Figure 3). The eight directions represented included: *east, west, north, south, southeast, southwest, northeast,* and *northwest*. Each actuator represented a direction based on its location around the participant's waist, with *north* represented by the front centre actuator (see Table 1). For details on the design, generation and use of the directional signals see [19,20].

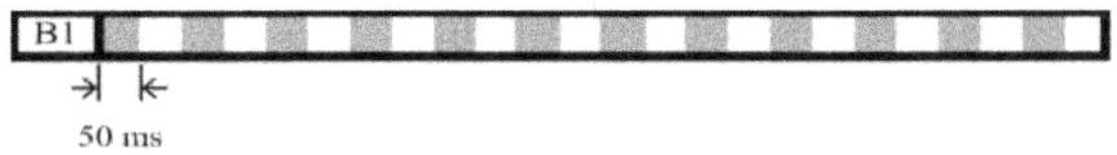

Figure 3. Direction Signals. A row represents one bar, producing a 1.2-second stimulus. Each note contains vibration on- (grey) and off-time (white) that separates it from the next.

Participants

There were 20 participants: 10 males and 10 females with an average age of 29 (SD = 4.94, range 20-40 years). None of the participants reported irregularity with tactile perception around their waist at the time of the study. Participants' average waist size was 78 centimetres (cm) (SD = 9.93, range 62-99 cm). We established from pre-test questionnaires that all participants understood the concept of "direction" and "landmark" and had no difficulties identifying them. Each of them received a 5 British pounds monetary incentive at the end of the experiment.

Experimental Conditions

Our experiment had two independent variables: representation technique (one actuator or two) and the presence or absence of directional signals. The dependent variables were response time (in ms) and accuracy performance. Response time refers to the onset of the stimulus to the onset of the response, including the movement time. The experiments were divided into two stages with five conditions (see Table 2), 2 of the stage 1 conditions being repeated in stage 2. Each participant ran all five conditions. In the first stage, we measured distinguishability, learnability and users' preferences. The first condition was a control condition in which only directional signals were presented. In conditions 2 and 4, only landmark signals were presented. In conditions 3 and 5, we presented directional signals together with landmark signals.

In stage 2, we measured the short term memorability of each type of signal. Approximately 30 minutes after participants finished conditions 2 and 4, we interviewed them and asked them to complete a set of questionnaires. They then repeated conditions 2 and 4. Both response time and accuracy performance were measured and compared with previous results. Since our focus for the study was on landmark representation rather than directional representation, we did not repeat C3 and C5 during stage 2.

Hypotheses

The vibration signals for directions are symbolically straightforward. They involve symbolic mapping of a limited set of cardinal and ordinal directions to their respective vibration signals on corresponding parts of the body. In this and other research (e.g. [26]), there was an absolute point vibration for each designated direction on a distributed placement of actuators around the waist. The representation of landmarks is more challenging. In the navigation design domain, the large set of landmarks studied in research papers and used in commercial systems are not systematically classified and differentiated. As a result, signal patterns for landmarks and their meaning associations are effectively arbitrary. Hence, it was hypothesised that *learning time required for landmark representations will be significantly longer than those for directions* (**H1**) as participants have to learn the association between the signal and what it represents.

Previous research, e.g. [13,22], has suggested that humans can recognize 4-7 abstract tactile patterns and associate them with predefined meanings. We hypothesized that *participants will be able to recognize 7 landmarks with at least 80% accuracy in at least 1 non-control condition, either in condition 2 or 4* (**H2**). Based on the same previous research, we predicted that *participants will be able to distinguish landmark from directional signals in conditions 3 and 5* (**H3**).

However, in conditions 3 and 5 where we present directional signals together with landmark signals, we hypothesised that *the presence of direction signals will reduce participants' performance in recognizing landmark patterns* (**H4**). This is due to the constraints on human memory and attention capacity [17]. In both conditions, participants had to attend to directional signals then to landmarks and then provide responses.

Condi tion	Description	Stage
C1	Direction only	1
C2	Landmark (single-actuator)	1
C3	Direction + Landmark	1
C4	Landmark (dual-actuator)	1
C5	Direction + Landmark	1
C2r	Landmark (single-actuator)	2
C4r	Landmark (dual-actuator)	2

Table 2. Experimental Conditions

While many researchers (e.g. [22,23]) have concluded that using different signal rhythms will effectively make stimuli distinguishable, the combination of two simultaneous actuator vibrations may make the iconic stimuli for landmarks unique [11,17] and clearly distinguishable from directional stimuli. With the single-actuator technique, signal patterns could be generated on an actuator that has just generated a direction signal, so participants might suffer from tactile adaptation, i.e. continued pressure stimulation that may result in a decrease of sensory experience [17]. As a result, they might fail to distinguish between different signal types. Using two actuators to represent landmarks introduces 'discontinuity' [17] that could help to make landmark signals perceptibly different from direction signals. Hence, we predicted that *the dual-actuator technique will produce better performance than the single-actuator technique when representing landmarks in a waist-belt tactile display that provides both directional and landmark information* (**H5**).

Experimental Procedures

Participants were given training to learn the signal patterns and their associations. In phase 1, each vibration stimulus was presented twice with its associated meaning, direction or landmark. Phase 2 allowed participants to memorise the signals for 4 minutes. By clicking with a stylus on direction and landmark icons on a tablet PC screen, the participant generated the associated vibration signals. In phase 3, vibration signals were generated randomly and participants had to select the associated direction or landmark icon. They received feedback for every selection that they made. Signals were repeated until the correct selection was made. In the final phase, participants were presented with vibration signals and again they selected the associated direction or landmark. In this phase, participants were given a performance score only at the end of each set. Training stopped when participants scored over 71% or had been through 4 repetitions of the entire 4-stage process.

Each participant then completed all five conditions in stage 1 and repeated conditions 2 and 4 in stage 2.

Stage 1 – Measuring learnability and distinguishability

In stage 1, we investigated whether performance with the two tactile representation techniques for landmarks differed in terms of learnability and distinguishability. The system generated tactile stimuli and participants identified perceived directions or landmarks by selecting corresponding icons on a touch screen tablet PC. We measured: perceived directions, perceived landmarks and response time.

All participants started with C1. The order of experimental conditions C2-C5 was counterbalanced. Vibration signals in all conditions were generated in a pseudo-random order. In addition, landmark associations with vibration signals were systematically shuffled. Vibration signals and meaning associations were counterbalanced amongst participants.

In the control condition C1 (direction only), participants experienced 3 repetitions of 8 directions. In C2, C3, C4, and C5, participants experienced 21 signals (i.e. 7 landmarks x 3 repetitions) for each condition. Repetitions were introduced to mitigate the possibility that participants might make correct responses by chance.

In C2 and C3, the tactile single-actuator technique was used to generate landmark signals. In C2, only landmark stimuli were generated. In C3, the system generated a random directional signal, paused for 2 seconds, and then generated a landmark signal on the same actuator.

In conditions C4 and C5, the dual-actuator technique was used to generate landmark signals. In C4, landmark stimuli were generated on pairs of actuators. Of the seven landmark signals, four were generated using the 180° distance pairs. The other three pairs were a mix of pseudo-random 90°, and 135° pairs, counterbalanced on the left and the right sides and front and back of the body. We randomized the non-adjacent pairs and sought the optimum distance that provided the best performance. In C5, the system generated a random directional signal, paused for 2 seconds, and then generated a landmark signal on a pair of actuators.

Each stimulus was presented only once. When each tactile stimulus had been generated, participants were required to indicate (as "quickly and accurately" as they could) to which direction or landmark they thought it corresponded, by selecting one of the associated icons on the tablet PC. The computer logged response time. Each session was followed by a short questionnaire capturing subjective data on distinguishability and learnability. When participants had finished all 5 conditions, they were asked to answer questions comparing the one- and dual-actuator techniques. They were also asked to reflect on their experiences with tactile communication. The final questionnaire took around 5-10 minutes to complete.

Stage 2 – Measuring memorability

In stage 2, we aimed to compare the two tactile representation techniques for their short term memorability. Stage 2 took place after participants completed distraction tasks, i.e. answering a questionnaire and discussing their experience of the experiment, approximately 30 minutes after they had been exposed to each type of landmark vibration stimulus.

Participants were asked to repeat conditions 2 and 4 in the same order that they had carried them out in stage 1. In each condition, each stimulus was presented only once. When each tactile stimulus had been generated, participants were required to indicate (1) the associated landmark by selecting an icon on the tablet PC and (2) their level of confidence in their answer on a 1 to 5 likert scale (1 being very unconfident and 5 being very confident). The computer logged response time.

RESULTS

Learnability

During training, participants learned the vibration signals and their associated meanings. Tables 3, 4 and 5 present quantitative results on learnability in terms of average number of rounds, average number of signal trials, and average training duration in each training phase.

Training phase	Direction	Single-actuator	Dual-actuator
Phase 1	1.2	1.65	1.65
Phase 2	1.05	2.40	2.05
Phase 3	1	1	1
Phase 4	1.05	2.55	2.15
Total	4.3	7.6	6.85

Table 3. Training Requirements: Average Number of Rounds.

Training phase	Direction	Single-actuator	Dual-actuator
Phase 1	10	12	12
Phase 2	15	54	61
Phase 3	8	7	7
Phase 4	8	18	15
Total	41	91	95

Table 4. Training Requirements: Average Number of Signals.

A repeated-measures ANOVA (sphericity assumed) indicated that overall training requirements for all representation techniques were significantly different: number of training rounds $F(2, 38) = 16.93$, $p < .01$, training duration $F(2, 38) = 26.07$, $p < .01$ and number of signal trials $F(2, 38) = 20.91$, $p < .01$. Statistical data for each training phase can be found in Table 6.

Training phase	Direction	Single-actuator	Dual-actuator
Phase 1	00:45	00:56	01:01
Phase 2	00:36	01:26	01:38
Phase 3	00:39	01:09	00:55
Phase 4	00:39	00:45	00:39
Total	02:40	04:17	04:14

Table 5. Training Requirements: Average Duration (min:sec).

Training phase	Duration	No of Rounds	No of Signals
Phase 1	7.03*	7.03*	2.47
Phase 2	26.49*	11.07*	19.91*
Phase 3	6.11*	*n/a*	*n/a*
Phase 4	11.89*	12.78*	10.06*

Table 6. Repeated-measures ANOVA Results for Training Requirements: * indicates that the result is significantly affected by representation technique $F(2, 38)$, p < .01.

Post-hoc pairwise comparisons (Bonferroni adjustment) indicated that training requirements for both landmark representation techniques were significantly greater than those for the directional technique in number of training rounds (both $p < .01$), training duration (both $p < .01$), and number of training signals (both $p < .01$). No significant difference was found in training duration, rounds and number of signal trials between the one- and dual-actuator techniques (all three $p > .05$). These results were congruent with our expectation that learning to associate landmark signals with their meanings should require more effort than learning directions since meaning associations for landmarks are completely arbitrary. Hence, we accept *H1*.

Performance and Distinguishability

The repeated-measures ANOVA (sphericity assumed) showed that the time to complete each condition was not significantly affected by the type of representation technique, $F(2, 38) = 1.60$, $p > .05$. However, different techniques significantly affected accuracy performance, $F(2, 38) = 3.82$, $p < .05$. Post-hoc pairwise comparison (Bonferroni adjustment) revealed that participants performed significantly better with directional identification than with both landmark techniques, (both $p < .05$). There was no difference in accuracy performance between the landmark one- and dual-actuator techniques ($p > .05$).

Prior to the study, we predicted that participants would spend more time and effort in learning landmarks with the single-actuator technique (according to *H5*). However, our results indicated that participants spent as much time and effort on either technique. Performance scores for all techniques at the end of training showed no significant difference $F(2, 38) = 2.82$, $p > .05$.

We predicted that participants would exceed 70% accuracy performance with either landmark technique. Results in Table 7 (1st row) show that participants were able to recognize landmark signals with over 80% accuracy rate for both landmark techniques. Therefore, *H2* is accepted.

We predicted that the performance of landmark signal perception would be affected by the presence of directional signals. We ran a dependent *t*-test that compared accuracy performance of C2-C3 (single-actuator technique) with C4-C5 (dual-actuator technique). With the single-actuator technique, landmark identification performance was significantly lower when directional information was present than when it was absent, $t(19) = 2.65$, $p < .05$. In contrast, with the dual-actuator technique participants were able to identify landmarks equally well whether or not directional signals were presented $t(19) = 0.32$, $p > .05$. Therefore, we reject *H4* since the presence of directional signals affected only the landmark single-actuator but not the landmark dual-actuator technique.

Description	Direction	Single-actuator	Dual-actuator
Accuracy (C1, C2 and C4)	93.75	80	82.14
Accuracy after adding direction (n/a, C3 and C5)	n/a	68.1	81.43
Accuracy after distraction (n/a, repeating C2 and C4)	n/a	77.14	83.57
Average completion time (C1, C2 and C4)	01:22	01:40	01:37
Average completion time (n/a, C3 and C5)	n/a	03:08	02:33
Average completion time (n/a, repeating C2 and C4)	n/a	00:55	01:00

Table 7. Performance Measures: Accuracy in %, Time in mm:ss.

Memorability

In order to measure the landmark signals memorability, we distracted participants with interviews and questionnaire sessions before asking them to repeat conditions 2 and 4. Raw results are presented in Table 7, 3rd row.

Paired-samples *t*-tests showed no significant difference in forgetting rates between the two landmark representation techniques. There was no significant difference in accuracy performance between repeated C2 and repeated C4, $t(19) = -0.95$, $p > .05$; no significant difference in performance between C2 and repeated C2, $t(19) = 0.64$, $p > .05$, and no significant difference between C4 and repeated C4, $t(19) = -0.51$, $p > .05$.

Subjective Measurements	Single-actuator	Dual-actuator
Distinguishable among themselves	3.55	3.55
Memorable	2.75	3.2
Associable with landmarks	2.6	2.65
Distinguishable from directions	4.25	4.5
Interference with directions	2.55	2.3

Table 8. Average Scores of Subjective Measures: n of 5 on a 1-5 likert scale, 1 being low and 5 being high.

Subjective Data and Preferences

Post-questionnaires were used at the end of each experimental condition. We gathered user's subjective data on the two landmark representation techniques on several measures. They included: distinguishability from direction signals, distinguishability amongst landmarks themselves, memorability, ease of meaning association, and the level of directional signals' interference. Participants gave ratings on a 1-5 likert scale, 1 being low and 5 being high.

The single-actuator representation technique scored lower than the dual-actuator technique in all subjective measures except for distinguishability amongst landmark signals, in which it scored equal with the dual-actuator technique (see Table 8).

Paired-samples *t*-tests showed no significant difference in all subjective measures. Specifically, there were no significant differences between the two landmark representation techniques in: distinguishability amongst landmark signals, $t(19) = 0.00$, $p > .05$; memorability, $t(19) = -1.76$, $p > .05$; association with landmarks, $t(19) = -0.15$, $p > .05$; distinguishability from direction signals, $t(19) = -1.10$, $p > .05$; and level of interference with direction signals, $t(19) = 0.84$, $p > .05$.

Based on landmark accuracy performance and the subjective measurement scores on distinguishability, we conclude that all participants were able to distinguish landmarks from directional signals in both conditions 3 and 5. Therefore, we accept *H3*.

As for subjective preference between the two landmark representation techniques, while 12 participants (60%) preferred the dual-actuator to the single-actuator technique, paired-samples *t*-tests showed no significant difference in preference, $t(19) = -0.89$, $p > .05$. Whichever technique a participant preferred, their comments and reasons were very similar and included "easy to remember and interpret", "more natural", and "easy to associate with landmarks".

If we look carefully at accuracy performance, each participant performed better with his or her preferred technique in C2 and C4. However, in C3 and C5 (when directional information was presented), performance of participants who preferred the dual-actuator technique dropped drastically when they carried out the single-actuator condition, while that of participants who favoured the single-actuator technique remained similar in both conditions. As a result, we found a significantly low overall accuracy performance score in condition 3.

Overall

Results showed that the one- and dual-actuator techniques offered almost equal support for landmark representation. To be precise, they required equal amounts of training and users performed equally well in experimental conditions in which only landmark signals were presented.

However, both direction and landmark information are crucial for navigation completion and should be provided in an operational tactile pedestrian navigation system. According to the accuracy performance results of C3 and C5 (Table 7, 3rd row), participants were able to perform significantly better with the dual-actuator technique than with the single-actuator technique when landmark signals were presented together with directional signals $t(19) = -2.63$, $p < .05$. Therefore, *H5* is accepted.

For the dual-actuator representation technique, we varied the pairs of actuators used. All the 180° actuator pairs were used by all participants. Other pairs were distributed evenly across all participants. Detailed results on the accuracy of each actuator pair are presented in Table 9.

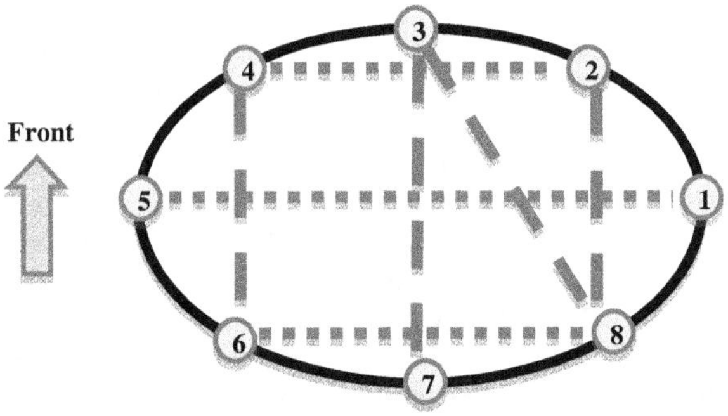

Figure 4. Best Actuator Pairs (motor number 3 is the front centre actuator). Horizontal lines show the three best pairs: 2-4, 1-5, 6-8; vertical lines demonstrate the next best three pairs: 2-8, 3-7, 4-6. The diagonal line shows the next best pair: 3-8.

Participants performed well with the actuator pairs that were vertically or horizontally aligned with their body. These pairs included the 2-4, 1-5, 6-8, 2-8, 3-7 and 4-6 pairs. The next best pair was the 3-8 pair. The actuator pairs which afforded highest performance, are shown in Figure 4. We recommend choosing these 7 pairs to represent our set of 7 landmarks in a tactile navigation aid.

We expected participants to have performed better with the other two 180° actuator pairs (i.e. the diagonal 4-8 and 2-6). However, results revealed that asymmetric or diagonal pairs did not support good performance.

Actuator Pairs	Condition 3	Condition 5	Repeated Condition 3
3-7	90.00	98.33	95.00
2-6	80.00	75.00	80.00
1-5	96.67	95.00	90.00
4-8	71.67	68.33	75.00
1-3	100.00	100.00	66.67
1-7	100.00	66.67	100.00
2-4	100.00	100.00	100.00
2-8	88.89	72.22	100.00
3-5	88.89	66.67	66.67
4-6	85.71	80.95	85.71
5-7	86.67	73.33	100.00
6-8	100.00	100.00	83.33
1-4	41.67	75.00	75.00
1-6	66.67	66.67	50.00
2-5	83.33	83.33	100.00
2-7	55.56	66.67	100.00
3-6	33.33	44.44	33.33
3-8	88.89	100.00	100.00
4-7	66.67	83.33	100.00
5-8	58.33	66.67	50.00

Table 9. Accuracy Performance (%) by Actuator Pairs (See Actuator Number Reference in *Figure 4*.

CONCLUSION

In this paper, we report an empirical study which compared two techniques to represent landmark information via the tactile channel. Our results have shown that the mapping symbology chosen to represent landmarks achieved acceptable performance. Through a device capable of presenting the information with a number of actuators, users perceived the vibration signals quite well and they were able to recognize the signals' meanings.

Compared with directional signals, participants took a significantly longer time to learn landmark signals and their associations. In the presence of directional signals, performance of landmark identification significantly dropped for the single-actuator technique and remained the same with the dual-actuator technique. With training, participants were able to distinguish landmark signals from directional signals and recognized over 80% of learned landmarks. With respect to both techniques' forgetting rates, it appeared that they were equal.

Results from our study suggest that the dual-actuator technique was better than the single-actuator technique in various ways, especially as it afforded better performance when presented together with directional signals. This is crucial to the development of a tactile pedestrian navigation system that provides both directional and landmark information.

Participants had an average response time of 4 seconds per signal across all conditions. This value is probably just about satisfactory for the intended use. Nevertheless, if these signals were to be used in outdoor urban environments, performance levels might drop since there are several other factors such as different levels of users' cognitive load and levels of noise in those environments. We anticipate that further training might help decrease response time in the lab setting, which might in turn reduce response time in applied environments. Further study is necessary to investigate whether extensive training can better the performance and the extent to which external factors such as noise might affect the results and system robustness, especially in the field.

The wearability and aesthetics of such systems will be crucial to user acceptance. Clearly our prototype, involving a notebook computer and protruding wires, allows for little meaningful evaluation of these issues. It is also worth noting that the tactile signal is brief and skin perception adapts through time so continued stimulation may lead to a decrease or even elimination of the sensory experience [17]. This may cause some missed signals in use. And as with all vibration-based systems, it is susceptible to not being perceived in high vibration environments.

Our experimental study assessed learnability and short-term memorability and we have obtained some promising results. However, based on these results, it is not possible to determine the effects of longer term use. A longitudinal study is required to address such issues.

Our next steps are to refine the tactile navigation prototype for use in field trials in an urban area. We will build on the insights from the lab-based work reported here to investigate specific applications' utility and acceptability with various users and in particular settings, for example in situations of high cognitive and visual load. Through these investigations, we will evaluate and improve the design and address user acceptability, and the performance-related benefits and challenges of a wearable tactile pedestrian navigation system.

ACKNOWLEDGMENTS

Mayuree Srikulwong's research is supported by the University of Thai Chamber of Commerce, Thailand. Eamonn O'Neill's research is supported by a Royal Society Industry Fellowship at Vodafone Group R&D. Thanks to Steve Payne for his valuable comments.

REFERENCES

1. Bach-y-Rita, P., Kaczmarek, K.A., Tyler, M.E. and Garcia-Lara, J. Form Perception with a 49-point Electrotactile Stimulus Array on The Tongue: A Technical Note. *Journal of Rehabilitation Research and Development 35*, 4 (1998), 427-430.

2. Burnett, G. *"Turn Right at the King's Head" Driver's Requirements for Route Guidance Information*. PhD Thesis, Loughborough University, UK, 1998.

3. Burnett, G., Smith, D. and May, A. Supporting the Navigation Task: Characteristics of 'Good' Landmarks. In *Proc. Annual Conference of the Ergonomics Society*, Taylor & Francis (2001), 441-446.

4. Chiasson, J., McGrath, B. and Rupert, A. Enhanced Situation Awareness in Sea, Air, and Land Environment. In *Proc. NATO HFM Symp. on Spatial Disorientation in Military Vehicles: Causes, Consequences and Cures (RTO-MP-086)*, NATO RTO (2002), 1-10.

5. Chan, A., MacLean, K.E. and McGrenere, J. Learning and Identifying Haptic Icons under Workload. In *Proc. WHC 2005*, IEEE Computer Society (2005), 432-439.

6. Elliott, L.R., Van Erp, J.B.F., Redden, E.S. and Duistermaat, M. Field-based Validation of a Tactile Navigation Device. *IEEE Transactions on Haptics 3*, 2 (2010), 78-87.

7. Gallace, A., Tan, H.Z. and Spence C. Numerosity Judgments for Tactile Stimuli Distributed over the Body Surface. *Perception 35*, 2 (2006), 247-266.

8. Heuten, W., Henze, N., Boll, S. and Pielot, M. Tactile Wayfinder: a Non-Visual Support System for Wayfinding. In *Proc. NordiCHI 2008*, ACM Press (2008), 172-181.

9. Ho, C., Tan, H.Z. and Spence, C.E. Using Spatial Vibrotactile Cues to Direct Visual Attention in Driving Scenes. *Transportation Research Part F 8: Traffic Psychology and Behavior*, Elsevier (2005), 397-412.

10. Krausman, A., Elliott, L., Redden, E. and Petrov, P. Effects of Visual, Auditory, and Tactile Cues on Army Platoon Leader Decision Making. In *Proc. ICCRTS 2005 (ARL-TR-3633)*, U.S. Army Research Laboratory (2005), 2-8.

11. Loomis, J.M. and Lederman, S.J. Tactual Perception. *Handbook of Perception and Human Performance Volume II*. John Wiley & Sons, NY, USA, 1986, 31:1-31:41.

12. MacLean, K.E. and Enriquez, M. Perceptual Design of Haptic Icons. In *Proc. Eurohaptics 2003*. http://www.eurohaptics.vision.ee.ethz.ch/2003.shtml.

13. MacLean, K.E. Using Haptics for Mobile Information Display. In *Proc.PERMID 2008*, 175-179.

14. MacLean, K.E. Haptic Interaction Design for Everyday Interfaces. *Reviews of Human Factors and Ergonomics 4*, Human Factors and Ergonomics Society (2008), 149-194.

15. May, A.J., Ross, T., Bayer, S. and Tarkiainen, M. Pedestrian Navigation Aids: Information Requirements and Design Implications. *Personal Ubiquitous Computing 7*, 6 (2003), 331-338.

16. Nesbitt, K.V. Structured Guidelines to Support the Design of Haptic Displays. In *Proc. GOTHI 2005*, University of Saskatchewan, Canada (2005), 65-74.

17. Schiffman, H.R. *Sensation and Perception: An Integrated Approach*. John Wiley & Sons, NY, USA, 1976.

18. Sorrows, M.E. and Hirtle, S.C. The Nature of Landmarks for Real and Electronic Spaces. *Spatial Information Theory (LNCS 1661)*, Springer-Verlag (1999), 37-50.

19. Srikulwong, M. and O'Neill, E. A Direct Experimental Comparison of Back Array and Waist-Belt Tactile Interfaces for Indicating Direction. In *Workshop on Multimodal Location Based Techniques for Extreme Navigation at Pervasive 2010*, HaptiMap (2010), 5-8. http://www.english.certec.lth.se/haptics/HaptiMap/proceedings_combined_final_with_frontmatter.pdf.

20. Srikulwong, M. and O'Neill, E. A Comparison of Two Wearable Tactile Interfaces with a Complementary Display in Two Orientations. In *Proc. HAID 2010* (LNCS 6306), Springer-Verlag (2010), 139-148.

21. Srikulwong, M. and O'Neill, E. Tactile Representation of Landmark Types for Pedestrian Navigation: User Survey and Experimental Evaluation. In *Workshop on Using Audio and Haptics for Delivering Spatial Information via Mobile Devices at MobileHCI 2010*, HaptiMap (2010), 18-21. http://www.english.certec.lth.se/haptics/HaptiMap/MobileHCI2010workshop_proceedings.pdf.

22. Tan, H.Z., Gray, R., Young, J.J. and Traylor, R. A Haptic Back Display for Attentional and Directional Cueing. *Haptics-e: The Electronic Journal of Haptics Research 3*, 1 (2003). http://www.haptics-e.org/Vol_03/he-v3n1.pdf.

23. Ternes, D. and MacLean, K.E. Designing Large Sets of Haptic Icons with One-actuator. In *Proc. EuroHaptics 2008 (LNCS 5024)*, Springer-Verlag (2008), 199-208.

24. Tsukada, K. and Yasumura, M. ActiveBelt: Belt-type Wearable Tactile Display for Directional Navigation. In *Proc. UbiComp 2004 (LNCS 3205)*, Springer-Verlag (2004), 384-399.

25. Van Erp, J.B.F. Presenting directions with a vibrotactile torso display. *Ergonomics 48*, 3 (2005), 302-313.

26. Van Erp, J.B.F., Van Veen, H.A.H.C., Jansen, C. and Dobbins, T. Waypoint Navigation with a Vibrotactile Waist Belt. *ACM Transactions on Applied Perception 2*, 2 (2005), 106-117.

27. Van Erp, J.B.F. *Tactile Displays for Navigation and Orientation: Perception and Behavior*. Mostert & Van Onderen, The Netherlands, 2007.

Handscope: Enabling Blind People to Experience Statistical Graphics on Websites through Haptics

Da-jung Kim, Youn-kyung Lim
Department of Industrial Design, KAIST
335 Gwahangno, Yuseong-gu, Daejeon 305-701, Republic of Korea
{jung1118, younlim}@kaist.ac.kr

ABSTRACT
Statistical graphics on the web such as a tag cloud visually represent statistical data which are generated by website users. While sighted people can scan the latest information through the dynamic changes of statistical graphics, blind people, who cannot perceive them, lose opportunities to keep up to date in this quickly-changing society. In order to enable blind people to experience socially-generated statistical graphics, we propose a new assistive device, namely, Handscope, which translates statistical graphics on websites into simple height changes of its haptic pole. We conducted a two-phase user study with blind people in order to test its usability and explore its effects on the quality of blind users' web experiences. The results show the meaningful contribution of Handscope in extending the area of blind people's web experiences.

Author Keywords
Statistical graphics, haptic, blind users, web accessibility

ACM Classification Keywords
H.5.2.User Interfaces: User-centered design. K.4.2.Social Issues: Assistive technologies for persons with disabilities.

General Terms
Design

INTRODUCTION
Handscope translates *statistical graphics* on websites into haptic expressions for blind people. Statistical graphics like a tag cloud and five-star rating visually represent *socially-generated statistical data* such as popularity of search keywords or ratings of movies and books. Statistical graphics are seemingly small graphics, but very critical for users to quickly scan and fully understand the meaning of data. In addition, in the web environment, such graphics are dynamically updated by the website users, which enhance their importance for blind people, who also want to understand social trends. The screen-reading software that most blind people are using cannot enable them to either scan the information or even recognize the existence of statistical data in some cases. In other words, blind people's low accessibility to these statistical graphics on the Internet is an obstacle for their participation in this society.

Many have studied the field of haptic data visualization (HDV) of graphics that represent statistical data such as charts and graphs [3, 4]. However, not many have attempted to translate such dynamically changing information specifically to the web environment. Although Yu et al. [5] developed audio-haptic visualization of web-based graphs, they still focused on traditional types of graphs such as line graphs, pie charts and bar charts. Also, researchers have mainly focused on inventing new modeling techniques and evaluating their accuracy and efficiency. Unlike these approaches, with quality-centered design thinking, we have more interest in designing a technically simple, but sufficiently valuable assistive device and exploring its values in design for blind people.

By designing the haptic expression system of Handscope in a very simple but sufficiently clear way to deliver numerical values, we also aimed to make it intuitively and universally understandable without high-expense devices. Since Handscope expresses only the critical information in a 1-dimensional haptic model, it is much more affordable for real users compared to existing commercialized products like PHANTOM and Novint Falcon.

HANDSCOPE: STATISTICAL GRAPHICS TO HAPTICS
Before we designed the Handscope, we conducted pre-observations of five blind people in order to better understand their current experiences of web-browsing and to extract the key design requirements for blind people.

The form of Handscope was designed to be asymmetric, so that blind people can easily determine its orientation. Also, it was designed to be used with two hands, since we discovered that most of the blind participants in our pre-observation felt more comfortable when grabbing an object with two hands because they could be sure of its form.

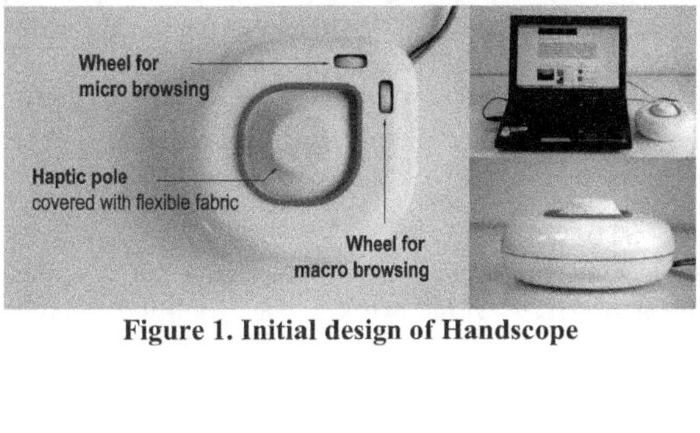

Figure 1. Initial design of Handscope

The two wheels, which are rotatable and clickable, were designed to allow users to browse web contents. The vertical wheel is for macro browsing, which is used to look through the whole structure, and the horizontal wheel is for micro browsing, which is used to see the details of each piece of content. This two-wheel system was inspired by blind users' searching steps on the interfaces they use with the screen-reading software: for macro browsing, they use the up-and-down arrow keys; for micro browsing, they use the left-and-right arrow keys (Figure 1).

If Handscope finds a statistical graphic by using the vertical wheel, which reads block elements of HTML, it vibrates to let users know of its existence. Then, blind users can examine more details by rolling the horizontal wheel, which reads inline elements. Although the algorithms for detecting statistical graphics need to be studied further, the experts we consulted were all sure of its feasibility. With the hypothesis that the algorithm is available, we performed more exploration of new values from a design perspective.

Figure 2. HDV process of a tag cloud through Handscope

Whenever the horizontal wheel is rotated, the haptic pole, which is covered with flexible fabric, moves up and down to translate the statistical data into a tangible height. The HDV process of Handscope consists of three steps: i) It loads the HTML codes of the selected statistical graphic (Figure 2-a); ii) It extracts only the statistical data and the related words. It translates the range of statistical data into the motion range of the servomotor that moves the haptic pole. After then, the words are synthesized to voice and the translated statistical data are mapped onto the angles of the servomotor in order to create different heights of the haptic pole (Figure2-b); iii) The flexible fabric is transformed depending on the haptic pole's height and it can be touched and felt underneath the user's hand (Figure2-c).

For user studies—both the pilot study and the primary user study—, we needed to provide the same statistical graphics for all the participants so that we could compare the results in equal conditions. To do so, we devised Flash prototypes, borrowing structures and contents from existing websites instead of using actual websites that are changing in real time. We used MIDAS [1], which was developed for designers to easily prototype hardware-software integrated interactive products in a Flash environment.

PILOT STUDY

For the pilot study, we first had to figure out whether our concept of HDV would work or not. If blind people can understand the meaning of the height difference, then we would not have to display all content materials as they actually look. In addition, we were interested in seeing if our design for Handscope is ergonomically appropriate.

Study Setup

A tag cloud was selected as a Flash content because it is the best example of something that blind users do not even know the existence of. We used popularly searched tags on Flickr for the content of the tag cloud. We recruited three blind people (P1-P3) who were high school students, and who were interested in different kinds of web contents. Each participant was given a short explanation about how to use Handscope and asked to do two things: 1) explore the Tag Cloud by manipulating Handscope; 2) explain how they interpreted the meaning of the height difference either through oral explanation or by using Lego bricks. The Lego kit was used as a supporting communication tool to enable blind participants to describe their thoughts visually. The whole study process for each participant was recorded with a camcorder to observe their behavior while they were interacting with Handscope.

Study Results

Two of three participants perceived the height of the haptic pole as *a representation of size or as an amount of something related to the mapped words in the tag cloud.* P1 explained the height as the size of countries and named the tallest block he built on the Lego board as 'Japan', because the words we included in the tag cloud contained names of several countries and Japan was the most popular one (Figure 3). P3 also interpreted the meaning of height as the amount of information related to each tag.

P2, on the other hand, couldn't guess the meaning until we explained the tag cloud. This reaction seemed to reflect this participant's particular style of using the Internet. She doesn't as frequently encounter visual contents as the others do. She uses the internet for reading books and listening to lectures on an audio library; the other, however, use the internet for playing games, for browsing new digital products, and even for buying products. It might have been hard for this one participant to imagine visualized-text. However, she still understood the haptic pole's taller height as the representation of bigger size or larger amount.

From the results of each participant, we determined that the meaning of the height can be understandable if a clear explanation of what the haptic pole's height represents is given so that the blind users are sure what contents they are

Figure 3. P1 created a Lego model in the user study. Heights of the blocks in each corner represent different sizes of tags

looking at and how to interpret the Handscope's display .

In addition, we observed interesting behavior through the video analysis. We used the wheel interface to enable the blind users to quickly browse the web. However, sometimes they rotated the wheels too quickly and were confused about how many steps they had skipped. This implies that discrete step-by-step browsing is important and more appropriate for blind people than continuous browsing. This also implies the importance of matching interactivity quality of a product with expressed meaning of information it delivers based on the types of users [2].

PRIMARY USER STUDY

Before we conducted the primary user study, we refined Handscope to improve its usability based on the findings from the pilot study (Figure 4). While keeping its basic structure, we refined the parts that had made participants uncomfortable or confused. We replaced the wheels with buttons so that users wouldn't lose their imaginary cursor, and assigned functions as tab buttons to go previous or next link. This was done because we discovered that macro browsing is more familiar and convenient for blind users when it is controlled with the keyboard, because the keyboard provides more various ways to look through the whole content structure by using keyboard shortcuts. When they encounter a statistical graphic, they will move their hands from the keyboard to Handscope to browse the detail information. We also modified Handscope's features in a way that users can grasp it more comfortably.

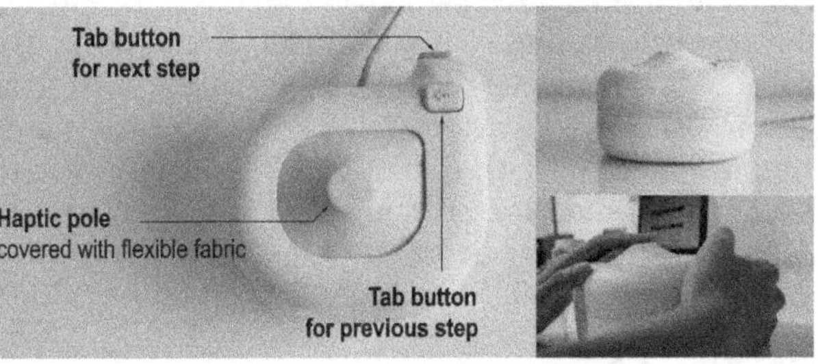

Figure 4. The refined Handscope

Regarding the flexible fabric, all participants very much enjoyed the feeling of its dynamic form changing. In addition, that unique transformation seemed to help users not misunderstand the meaning of its height. Since the pole expands as it is raised, the participants feel a larger volume on their hands compared to the case when the pole falls. Therefore, we kept this element in the second prototype.

Study Setup

In the primary user study, we aimed to explore the effects that Handscope actually had on blind users' web experiences. To determine this, we devised the experiments and Flash prototypes in two situations in order to compare the differences: with Handscope (Case A) and without Handscope (Case B).

For the contents of Flash prototypes, we selected two types of statistical graphics that contains *preattentive features* like basic shapes or colors that are instantaneously identified

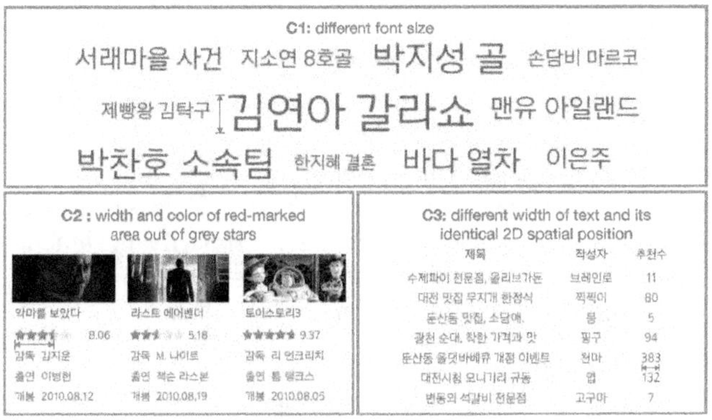

Figure 5. Preattentive features in each set of content

even after a very brief exposure; blind users, therefore, have problems to scan and understand the information when they hear those contents through the screen-reading software (Figure 5). There are two types of problematic data: i) statistical data that are eliminated in the process of HDV and cannot be delivered by auditory feedback; ii) statistical data that are recognizable even without Handscope, but are ineffectively delivered because the auditory feedback delivers them in a linear manner. For the first type, we chose a tag cloud, which represents the popularity of each search-keyword with different font sizes (C1). For the second type, we selected a five-star rating for representing average ratings of movies (C2), and aligned text, which uses the text width of the recommended numbers as a preattentive feature for scanning through the width of the numerical text (C3). The content was about good places and restaurants to visit. Flash prototypes of each portion of content were devised both for Case A and Case B. We had six Flash prototypes in total (1-A, 1-B, 2-A, 2-B, 3-A, 3-B); each participant went through all of the cases. To prevent participants from being influenced by each Flash prototype when browsing the same type in Case A and Case B, we used a different set of words for each division of content.

We recruited ten blind people who were familiar with using the internet. Five of them were high school students and the others were teachers. We explained how to use Handscope and randomly provided the six Flash prototypes to each participant, and asked a question according to the content type. For the first content type, we asked participants to select the most popular word in the tag cloud in order to explore *the effect of recognizing the statistical information on one's interpretation of the content.* For the second content type, we aimed to explore *the effects of the haptic expressions* when users were asked to select a certain piece of information after browsing the content (i.e. C2 for the movie they most want to see, or C3 for the local place they most want to go), compared to the cases in which only auditory expression was given. Since statistical data of the second content type can be delivered through auditory feedback even without Handscope, we wondered what benefits Handscope can make in such a case. That's why we asked participants to select the most preferable item, instead of directly asking them which item is the most popular one, which is a type of a decision making task resulting from the information they had gathered.

Regarding the instruction about the height of the haptic display, we didn't explain this in the case of 1-A in order to explore how participants came to understand what the height means; however, we explained it for cases 2-A and 3-A because these two cases were primarily designed to explore the effects of haptic expressions by comparing results for this situation with and without Handscope.

Study Results

Regarding the effect of having statistical graphics on a blind user's understanding of content, all the participants *correctly understood the content rather than guessing or being biased* when they read the content with Handscope (1-A). None of the participants selected the word that is actually the most popular one in 1-B, and their rationales were only based on their *individual interests*; however, in 1-A, their rationales were supported by *reliable objective data*. Six of the participants selected the correct word and two of the others selected the 2nd most popular word because they were unable to distinguish the small height difference between the 1st most popular word and the 2nd most popular one. Although the other two participants F and J selected the 4th most popular word, they actually selected the most popular word from their point of view. Participant F said, "I did understand that height means the popularity, but the top three words are related to visual materials, which we cannot see, so I selected the 4th word, which is the most popular among the remaining words."

Some reactions were quite meaningful beyond the correct comprehension of information, because these participants *expressed a will to participate in generating social statistics* when using Handscope. Participant H (3-A) said, "Why this restaurant's ranking so low? I thought it was very nice. There might be some hygienic problems that I can't see. If not in the reviews, I would like to vote for this restaurant to raise the recommended number." Participant A (1-A) also had the same opinion for one of the small-sized tags—i.e. the name of a TV drama which he thought was very popular.

Regarding the effects of haptic expressions on users' selection of an item on the web, when compared to the case B, 5 to 6 *more participants did care about statistical information* when they were able to obtain the information through Handscope. Just as in previous examples, participants mentioned their opinions about the statistical graphics that Handscope displayed in 2-A and 3-A, while most of them used the information as just a reference for their selection in Case B. In addition, 4 more participants in Case A explicitly expressed that Handscope helps them *quickly scan the content*, because its multimodal interface can deliver more than single pieces of information at the same time. In Case B, everyone attempted at least one time to skip the auditory feedback even before listening to the statistical information.

We also found that Handscope's *haptic change can emphasize certain information* through which participants may give more attention to that information. Participant J said, "It commands my attention whenever the height change is big. If I hear certain words at that time, I can remember those words better." This *attention effect* has great meaning in HDV, because the state change from one to the other within one haptic pole can be understood as one step. This implies that motion translation within one haptic pole should be considered as another haptic language and should be carefully designed in order not to be confused.

CONCLUSION AND FUTURE WORKS

Our study discovered that Handscope provides valuable benefits to their understanding of web contents the quality of their web browsing. The key implication of this result is that blind people's web accessibility can be increased with a simple haptic display, such as that which Handscope provides, instead of relying on realistic representation through advanced haptic devices.

However, Handscope still has problems with the inefficient use of going back and forth between a keyboard and Handscope although it reduced the time for scanning information by letting people use its tab buttons. In order to make the haptic model of Handscope truly and preattentively perceivable, this will be the next step to be studied.

ACKNOWLEDGMENTS

We like to thank all the participants and experts, especially, Don Norman, engineers from XVison Technology, Hyun-chul Rho and Sangjeong Lee for their insightful comments. This research was supported by Basic Science Research Program and WCU(World Class University Program) through the National Research Foundation of Korea (NRF) funded by the Ministry of Education, Science and Technology (2010-0023206 and R33-2008-000-10033-0).

REFERENCES

1. Introduction to MIDAS. http://cidr.kaist.ac.kr/mediawiki/index.php/MIDAS
2. Lim, Y., Lee, S. and Lee, K. Interactivity attributes: a new way of thinking and describing interactivity. In *Proc. CHI 2009*, ACM Press (2009), 105-108.
3. Wall, S.A. and Brewster, S.A. Tac-tiles: multimodal pie charts for visually impaired users. In *Proc. NordiCHI 2006*, ACM Press (2006), 9-18.
4. Yu, W., Ramloll, R. and Brewster, S.A. Haptic Graphs for Blind Computer Users. In *Proc. International Workshop on Haptic Human-Computer Interaction*, Springer-Verlag (2000), 41-51.
5. Yu, W., Reid, D. and Brewster, S.A. Web-based multimodal graphs for visually impaired people. In *the 1st CWUAAT*, Cambridge (2002), 97-108.

Nenya: Subtle and Eyes-Free Mobile Input with a Magnetically-Tracked Finger Ring

Daniel Ashbrook[1], Patrick Baudisch[2], Sean White[1]

[1]Nokia Research Center Hollywood
2400 Broadway, Santa Monica, CA 90404
{daniel.ashbrook, sean.white}@nokia.com

[2]Hasso Plattner Institute
Prof-Dr-Helmert Str. 2-3, D-14482 Potsdam, Germany
patrick.baudisch@hpi.uni-potsdam.de

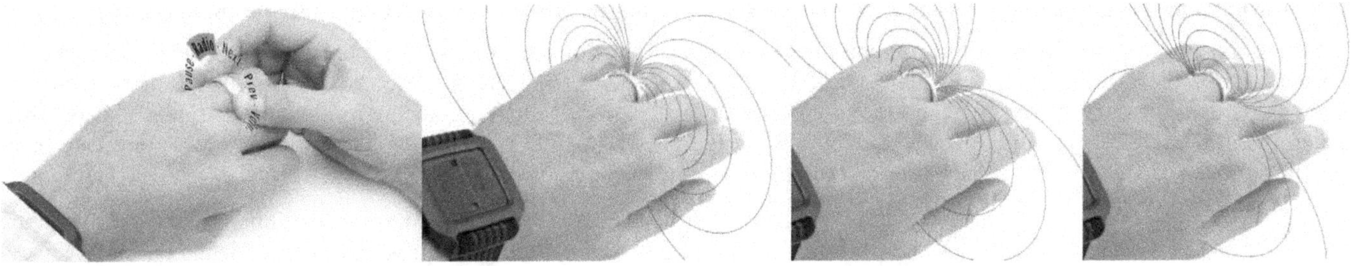

Figure 1: The *Nenya* ring. Left: twisting the ring enters a 1D parameter; here rotation is used to select the menu item "radio". Users confirm a selection by sliding the ring along the finger. Center through right: Nenya's tiny size is due to it being magnetically tracked by the wrist-worn *baselet*. The lines illustrate how the magnetic field changes through a 90° ring rotation.

ABSTRACT

We present Nenya, a new input device in the shape of a finger ring. Nenya provides an input mechanism that is always available, fast to access, and allows analog input, while remaining socially acceptable by being embodied in commonly worn items. Users make selections by twisting the ring and "click" by sliding it along the finger. The ring—the size of a regular wedding band—is magnetic, and is tracked by a wrist-worn sensor. Nenya's tiny size, eyes-free usability, and physical form indistinguishable from a regular ring make its use subtle and socially acceptable. We present two user studies (one- and two-handed) in which we studied sighted and eyes-free use, finding that even with no visual feedback users were able to select from eight targets.

ACM Classification: H5.2 [Information interfaces and presentation]: User Interfaces. - Input Devices and Strategies.

General terms: Design, Human Factors, Experimentation

Keywords: mobile, wearable, subtle, eyes-free, screen-less, finger ring, jewelry, wristwatch, one-handed, two-handed.

INTRODUCTION

Social situations present unique challenges for the usability of mobile devices. Whether asking a caller to "hang on a second" while paying at a grocery store register, letting a significant other know a meeting is running late, or updating one's location on a social network after arriving at a party, there are many situations wherein pulling out and using a mobile phone is considered inappropriate.

In this paper, we introduce the *Nenya* finger ring, a subtle, eyes-free input device designed for these types of scenarios.

THE NENYA RING

Nenya is an ordinary-looking band-style finger ring (Figure 1). Users spin Nenya for 1D input, e.g., to select an item from a menu or to specify a parameter, and commit a selection by sliding Nenya along the finger.

Unlike previously proposed input methods designed for subtle use [3,7], Nenya provides high-fidelity input; unlike earlier ring devices [8,11], Nenya is unobtrusive, small, and wireless. Nenya can be used by itself as an eyes-free input method or in combination with subtle output devices, such as haptic displays or visual output such as *eye-q* [4].

Tracking

The thin, unpowered Nenya ring is a strong permanent magnet, with the magnetic poles located on opposite sides of the ring, as shown in Figure 1. Such rings can be purchased inexpensively ($8–$20). Also shown in Figure 1 is the Nokia-developed wrist-worn wireless tracking base bracelet, or *baselet*. The baselet includes a HMC5843 3-axis magnetometer sampled at 25Hz; inspired by Harrison and Hudson's *Abracadabra* [6], we use the magnetometer to track the ring's position via magnetism. A Bluetooth radio allows the baselet to transmit ring input to the user's other devices, such as a wrist display or mobile phone.

(a) (b)

Figure 2. (a) One-handed use is more difficult, but is even more discreet. (b) We alleviate the additional friction of one-hand use by using a thin ball bearing with mounted magnets.

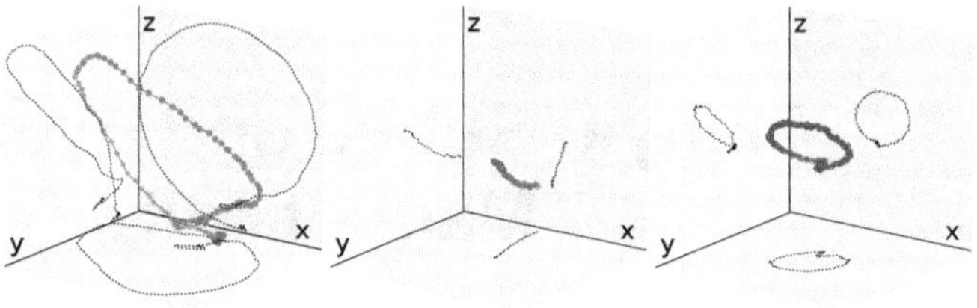

(a) (b) (c)

Figure 3: Traces of ring motion sensed by the 3-axis magnetometer. The hand points into the *x/z* plane with the palm parallel to the *x/y* plane. (a) is a full ring rotation at the base of the finger; (b) is a slide from the finger base to the middle of the finger; and (c) is a full rotation near the middle of the finger.

When users spin or slide the ring, the magnetometer in the baselet senses the change in the magnetic field. Figure 4 shows raw data for three different ring motions. In order to determine the angle relative to the finger at which the ring is being moved, our software ignores motion along the finger's length and only considers the two axes perpendicular to the finger (see the *x/z*-axis projection in Figure 4a).

To "click" users slide Nenya in the direction of the fingertip (Figure 4b, *x/y* projection), moving the ring away from the baselet. The magnetic field strength measured at the baselet thus decreases; when it falls under a threshold, the baselet detects a click.

Since the magnetometer in the baselet senses the *absolute* orientation of the ring, Nenya can be used as a *positional* input device. We leverage this ability to enable eyes-free use. We added a small disc magnet as an explicit *tactile landmark* [2], which allows users to read the ring's position by touch. Once users are familiar with a menu, they may re-enter it by turning the ring until the landmark is in the expected position. Note that more elaborate rings worn as jewelry naturally bear landmarks, such as mounted stones.

Benefits and limitations

Nenya is designed for subtle use: (1) We have achieved a **tiny form factor** by handing off all active sensing to the baselet. (2) Users operate Nenya using **small, discreet movements**. (3) While users obtain best control manipulating the ring using their opposing hand, Nenya supports even more subtle **one-handed use** (Figure 3a). (4) Nenya can be operated **eyes-free**: in contrast to earlier magnetic tracking work [6,9], Nenya fixes the movement to the finger, preventing the user from drifting. Additionally, tactile landmarks on the ring allow users to access known functions without looking. (5) Nenya is already present on the hand, making it **always immediately available and fast to access** (see Ashbrook's *microinteractions* [1]). (6) Whenever the (social) situation requires, Nenya is **instantly interruptible**. Unlike with a mobile phone, Nenya immediately leaves both hands free when the user stops using it. (7) Nenya has a **familiar appearance**: it does not look different from rings people wear for decorative purposes or as wedding rings.

Nenya does have some limitations. First, the magnetic tracking method requires users to wear the baselet. However, the sensor and radio are small enough to be incorporated into a standard wristwatch or more decorative bracelet, which will improve its attractiveness and wearability. Second, our system is currently susceptible to false positives when the user is in motion; however, more advanced pattern recognition techniques should alleviate this problem. Finally, the involved magnetism requires that users be careful not to damage objects sensitive to magnetism, such as the magnetic stripes on credit cards, and avoid getting the ring stuck on metal objects during daily use.

RELATED WORK

Our work on Nenya is related to subtle and eyes-free input and rings in particular, as well as magnetic tracking.

Subtle and Eyes-Free Interaction Technology

Work on both subtle and eyes-free input includes Electromyography (EMG), a method that supports nearly undetectable use [3]. Current versions accomplish this using multiple electrodes placed on the user's arm. Rekimoto's GestureWrist [14] is a watch band-integrated capacitive sensor that detects hand shape. Users operate it using large-scale gestures. Blaskó proposed eyes-free parameter entry through touching the surface of a wristwatch [2], but his system was more suited to discrete rather than analog input.

Rings

In 2001, researchers at IBM presented industrial design concepts of digital jewelry, including a bracelet and a ring featuring a single-button input [13]. Kim et al. created design concepts exploring the affordances of commonly worn objects, including rings, for controlling a mobile music player [10]. Functional ring form-factor devices were either wired (e.g., [8,11]) or included batteries for wireless communication and were thus bulky [12].

Magnetic Tracking

Han et al. tracked a finger-mounted magnet for handwriting input [5]. Similarly, Harrison and Hudson used a finger-attached magnet for radial and 2D input for a watch device [6], and Ketabdar et al. tracked a magnet in the space around a mobile phone [9]. Nenya's improved form factor allows subtle use due to its tiny form factor and small motions; eyes-free use based on constraining the motion of the magnet to a fixed axis around the finger; and one-handed usability as demonstrated in the second study below.

USER STUDIES

In order to determine users' ability to provide input using the ring, we performed two target selection studies. The first tested two-handed use; the second study examined one-hand use. Our goal was to explore how many targets can be fit onto a full rotation menu on the ring, and how quickly and accurately users can select from it. Both studies used the setup illustrated in Figure 5.

USER STUDY 1: TWO-HANDED USE

Participants twisted the ring with the opposing hand (Figure 1). We performed testing under both visual and auditory-only (eyes-free) feedback conditions to simulate different use cases. A questionnaire followed the study.

Task

The participants' task was to rotate the ring such that the yellow pointer shown in Figure 5 was inside the green target; the yellow pointer mirrored the ring's motion. When satisfied with their selection, participants committed by pressing a foot switch located under the desk. (This method was used rather than "pull-to-click" to separate target homing and click response times.) Upon successful selection, the red and green wedges swapped places. After 10 clicks, the screen displayed a new target configuration. We measured task time and error rate for target sizes of 45°, 60° and 90°, with distances between targets up to 180°.

Conditions

In the *visual* condition participants performed the task while looking at a screen similar to that in Figure 5. **In the *audio* condition**, no visual feedback was provided, and a computer-synthesized voice read the number of each wedge when the pointer entered it. The audio was clipped if the participant pointed to a new wedge before the current wedge's audio had finished playing. **In the *combined* condition,** participants saw both the wedge display *and* heard the synthesized voice. We included this condition, which redundantly encodes feedback, to determine if the extra feedback gave users any advantage.

Interface & apparatus

Participants wore the ring on their left ring finger and the baselet on their left wrist (Figure 1). As described earlier, the ring included a disc magnet as a tactile landmark; its position was calibrated to correspond to the direction of the pointer on the screen. Participants picked a ring from a set in US sizes from 6.5–14 (17–23mm) in ½-size steps.

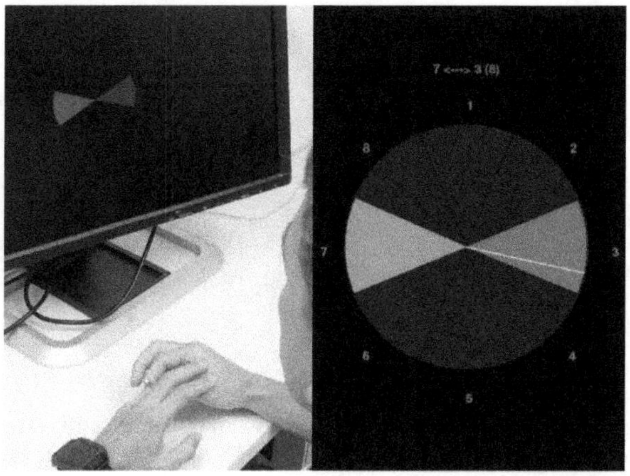

Figure 4: Participant targeting in the visual condition. The yellow pointer (in target 3) mirrors the ring's position. The target information "7 <--->3 (8)" (indicating *green target at 7, red at 3, 8 wedges total*) was shown as a memory aid for the eyes-free condition.

Experimental design

The experiment was a 3x3 within-subjects factorial design, with three wedge size conditions (45°, 60°, and 90°, corresponding to 8, 6 and 4 divisions of the circle), and three feedback conditions (visual, auditory, and combined). Each wedge size/feedback combination had eight randomly generated target start/end positions, and each combination was repeated twice, so every participant performed 144 trials overall. The feedback conditions were grouped, and after each completion of the 24 trials (all three wedge sizes x eight configurations), participants took an enforced 30-second break. The order of feedback conditions was counterbalanced across participants. Before the study, participants received 8 minutes of training per condition. All participants completed the study in 30 minutes or less.

Participants

We recruited 18 participants (10 female, two left-handed), aged 20–62 (mean 35) via an ad placed on Facebook. We rewarded each participant $100 for their time.

Results

There were no significant differences ($p < .05$) between the two visual conditions (visual and combined visual/audio); the availability of visual information may have overwritten the audio cues. We therefore combine data from these two conditions for the remainder of the analysis. A multi-way ANOVA found significant differences between the sighted and non-sighted conditions for error, movement time, and effective width. Figure 6 summarizes the results. There was a significant interaction between feedback condition and width for movement time; *post-hoc* testing showed the difference to be between all widths in the audio condition, with width (°)/time (s): 45/2.61, 60/2.21, 90/1.77. No other significant differences were found between target sizes. The distance between targets was significant, especially when the distance was large; a 180° distance took longer than shorter distances in all conditions (visual: 1.0s, audio: 2.7s).

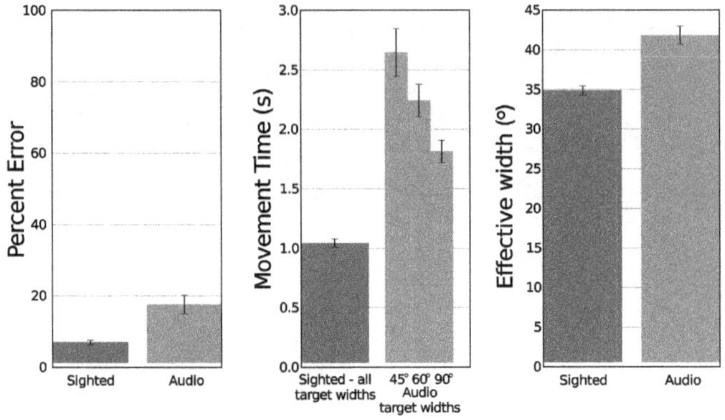

Figure 5. Study 1 error rate, movement time, and effective width for feedback conditions, with 95% confidence intervals.

We computed the *effective width* (defined as 4.133 times the standard deviation of the movement endpoints) to inform the minimum target size that we might be able to employ. The upper limit of effective width was 42° in the audio-only condition, which suggests that users can select from up to eight choices (45°) in a menu.

Although our procedure is similar to a Fitts' law-style task, we found a poor fit to the Fitts' equation (R^2=0.09). This is likely due to the non-ballistic nature of twisting the ring.

In a post-study questionnaire, participant response to Nenya was positive. Several participants expressed that they would enjoy having similar technology for personal use. We asked participants about strategies used during the audio condition. Several participants mentioned developing visio-spatial mental models, referring to "clocks," "windshield wipers," and "radio dials". Another common strategy was to simply listen for the audio cue that they were seeking, without creating a mental spatial model. Combined with a lack of edge or boundary condition for rotation, this strategy suggests that the devices could be used for both absolute and relative input.

USER STUDY 2: ONE-HANDED USE

We performed a second, exploratory study to evaluate one-handed use with a reduced number of participants. While we did not plan on performing any statistical analysis due to small number of participants, we were interested in getting a rough understanding of how single-handed use would affect performance. Participants wore the bearing-based version of Nenya (Figure 3b) on their left ring finger and manipulated it as shown in Figure 3a. The experimental setup matched our first study; however, we tested only the visual condition. We recruited a new set of eight participants (one female, all right-handed; ages 27–48, mean 35) from our institution. The study lasted about 20 minutes.

Results

Feedback from participants was weaker in this condition, and clearly pointed out that single-hand operation of Nenya is substantially harder than two-handed use. However, performance data did not appear very different. Reporting mean/std, at 8.9/10.7%, error rates were slightly higher than with two-handed use. Effective widths in contrast seem comparable, averaging 35.9/17.0°. Movement time was only marginally higher than with two-hand use (1.1/.55s).

CONCLUSIONS

Our two studies show that Nenya is usable with two hands and, with reduced performance, also with a single hand. The upper limit of effective width for the two studies (42°) suggests that users can control up to eight choices (45°) in a menu.

As future work, we plan to explore additional degrees of freedom, such as tilting the ring or moving the finger itself rather than the ring. We also plan on creating smaller versions of the baselet.

REFERENCES

1. Ashbrook, D. Enabling mobile microinteractions. *PhD Thesis,* Georgia Institute of Technology (2009).
2. Blaskó, G. Cursorless interaction techniques for wearable and mobile computing. *PhD Thesis*, Columbia University (2007).
3. Costanza, E., Inverso, S., Allen, R. and Maes, P. Intimate interfaces in action: assessing the usability and subtlety of EMG-based motionless gestures. *Proc. CHI* (2007), 819–828.
4. Costanza, E., Inverso, S., Pavlov, E., Allen, R. and Maes, P. eye-q: eyeglass peripheral display for subtle intimate notifications. *Proc. MobileHCI* (2006), 211–218.
5. Han, X., Seki, H., Kamiya, Y. and Hiziku, M. Wearable Handwriting Input Device Using Magnetic Field. *Proc SICE Annual Conference* (2007), 365–368.
6. Harrison, C. and Hudson, S. Abracadabra: wireless, high-precision, and unpowered finger input for very small mobile devices. *Proc. UIST* (2009), 121–124.
7. Hudson, S., Harrison, C., Harrison, B. and LaMarca, A. Whack gestures: inexact and inattentive interaction with mobile devices. *Proc. TEI* (2010), 109–112.
8. Iwamoto, T. and Shinoda, H. Finger ring device for tactile sensing and human machine interface. *Proc. SICE Annual Conference* (2007), 2132–2136.
9. Ketabdar, H., Roshandel, M. and Yüksel, K. Towards using embedded magnetic field sensor for around mobile device 3D interaction. *Proc. MobileHCI* (2010), 153–156.
10. Kim, K., Joo, D., and Lee, K. Wearable-object-based interaction for a mobile audio device. *Ext. Abs. CHI* (2010), 3865–3870.
11. Lam, A., Li, W., Liu, Y., and Xi, N. MIDS: micro input devices system using MEMS sensors. *Proc. IROS* (2002), 1184–1189.
12. Marti, S. and Schmandt, C. Giving the caller the finger: collaborative responsibility for cellphone interruptions. *Ext. Abs. CHI* (2005), 1633–1363.
13. Miner, C., Chan, D. and Campbell, C. Digital jewelry: wearable technology for everyday life. *Ext. Abs. CHI* (2001), 45–46.
14. Rekimoto, J. Gesturewrist and gesturepad: unobtrusive wearable interaction devices. *Proc. ISWC* (2001), 87–94.

The Haptic Laser: Multi-Sensation Tactile Feedback for At-a-Distance Physical Space Perception and Interaction

Francis Iannacci[1], Erik Turnquist[1], Daniel Avrahami[2], and Shwetak N. Patel[1]

[1]Computer Science & Engineering
DUB Group, University of Washington
Seattle, WA 98195 USA
{iannacci, erikturn, shwetak}@cs.washington.edu

[2]Intel Labs Seattle
1100 NE 45th Street
Seattle, WA 98105
daniel.avrahami@intel.com

ABSTRACT
We present the Haptic Laser, a system for providing a range of tactile sensations to represent a physical environment at-a-distance. The Haptic Laser is a handheld device that simulates interaction with physical surfaces as a user targets objects of interest (e.g., a light switch, TV, etc). Using simple computer vision techniques for scene analysis and laser range finding for calculating distance, the Haptic Laser extracts information about the physical environment and conveys it haptically through a collection of hardware actuators. Pointing the Haptic Laser around a room, for example, presents the user with information about the presence of objects, transitions, and edges through touch rather than, or in addition to, vision. The Haptic Laser extends current work on haptic touch screens and pens, and is designed to allow for haptic feedback from a distance using multiple feedback channels.

Author Keywords
Haptic feedback, ubiquitous computing, computer vision, motor control, at-a-distance interaction.

ACM Classification Keywords
H5.2 [Information interfaces and presentation]: User Interfaces. - Graphical user interfaces.

General Terms
Design

INTRODUCTION
As computing continues to move off the desktop and into the physical world, there will be an increasing need to interact with various computational systems and physical widgets at a distance. The most common scenarios for at-a-distance interaction currently include video gaming (e.g., the Nintendo Wii), and presentations where both speaker and audience want to interact with out-of-reach displays. In the future, computational abilities promise to be embedded in a wide range of objects, creating intelligent environments full of remote interaction targets.

In this paper, we present Haptic Laser, a handheld device that uses a laser pointer and a camera to extract features from the physical environment and two vibration motors, a solenoid and a servo motor to convey those features haptically. In particular, the Haptic Laser encodes the targeted region's *macro-texture* (which we define as a measure of the density of differentiable objects in the target region), the *physical distance* to the current target, and the sensations of *moving across a bump or an edge*.

Figure 2: The Haptic Laser handheld device

Unlike the Wii, which uses an infrared tracking system to detect the position of the Wii-mote relative to IR markers placed in the environment, the Haptic Laser contains both the environment analysis and the haptic feedback systems in one device. It is thus able to provide tactile feedback about uninstrumented physical environments. Rather than just presenting distance information as in existing work [2, 13], our system conveys both distance-to-target and contextual information of the targeted space.

The Haptic Laser is thus designed to enable a set of new applications in both virtual and physical domains. For interacting with *virtual* environments, the Haptic Laser can be used as a sort of self-contained Wii-mote to assist the user in pointing to objects on a large screen display. Traditional laser-pointing interaction has been shown to be significantly slower and less accurate than direct physical contact or mouse-based selection [7]. Allowing users to feel ridges, edges, and other displayed visual artifacts as they sweep the Haptic Laser across the screen is designed to improve remote targeting accuracy. For interacting with *physical* environments, the Haptic Laser can be used to experience and explore arbitrary physical spaces. This is designed to be useful for finding and interacting with devices in an intelligent environment (i.e., the haptics allow the user to feel and discriminate between physical objects from a distance) or as an assistive technology to help a low-vision, blind, or deaf-blind user understand the physical composition of a room. Like existing space perception devices, the Haptic Laser conveys the distance from the user to a targeted surface. Unlike prior work, however, Haptic Laser provides feedback about which regions might contain objects for further exploration and interaction.

RELATED WORK

Systems that provide tactile feedback for at-a-distance interaction have been the subject of much research, including the assistive technology community's work on digital walking aids for the visually impaired. These technologies have largely focused on conveying distance information, obtained through range-finding sensors, through either auditory feedback (e.g., MiniGuide [6]) or single actuator tactile feedback (e.g., TactileWand [2], Teletact [13], Haptic Torch [14], and [15]). However, these way-finding technologies are less useful for exploring a physical space because they allow only single point probing of distance, and do not convey contextual information about the space or transitions in the environment. In contrast, our technique simultaneously presents distance and a summary of the targeted region, thus communicating context without requiring point-by-point sweeping.

The work most closely related to the Haptic Laser is Fingersight [12]. While both Haptic Laser and Fingersight are camera-based and use computer vision techniques for scene analysis, the Fingersight device is limited to a single channel of information presented via vibration feedback. By using several distinct types of tactile feedback, Haptic Laser removes this limitation, enabling multiple independent channels of information to be presented simultaneously from a single device.

Significant work in at-a-distance interaction has focused on selection and control of devices in an environment (e.g., [8, 11]). Projects in this space have used lasers to help users target and interact with individual computing devices in the environment [8, 9]. Other work has investigated the ways to hold a laser-based targeting device to improve accuracy [7]. However, exploring real-time haptic feedback has been limited for these applications.

Finally, other related systems provide haptic feedback for direct physical interactions with touch screens [10], stylus-based interaction [5], and more recently for interactions with virtual objects (e.g., the Wii). While most of this work has been limited to conveying information about the virtual environment, our primary contribution is in providing haptic feedback about the physical world from a distance.

THE HAPTIC LASER EXPERIENCE

The Haptic Laser usage experience is partly built on the metaphor of a telescoping stick. Our intent is not to convey small details of the physical environment (e.g., surface texture), but rather to provide general contextual information that is useful for at-a-distance pointing tasks. Important features include the ability to feel (1) the macro-texture of the targeted region (by modulating two vibration motors), (2) a relative measure of distance to the space the user is exploring (by changing the Haptic Laser's center of mass, similar to [3]), and (3) edges or sharp transitions (by activating the solenoid).

The Haptic Laser conveys macro-texture as a sensation similar of dragging a rod across a surface. Surfaces that have a non-uniform appearance (i.e., coarse macrotexture), such as a home entertainment system, result in more intense vibration feedback than uniform surfaces such as walls or whiteboards. To convey distance, the Haptic Laser's center of mass shifts as the user explores targets at different distances. Moving from a surface that is nearby to one that is across the room results in a center-of-mass shift away from the user, a sensation modeled on a stick extending to maintain contact with a physical surface. In the case of large, abrupt changes in distance, such as the transition between a table and the floor, the device produces a recoil-like sensation. This feedback is similar to the feeling of a stick rapidly extending or retracting.

IMPLEMENTATION DETAILS

The Haptic Laser prototype consists of two main components: the computer vision and the haptic systems. To generate the experience described above in a reasonable form factor, the Haptic Laser consists of a front-mounted camera, a laser diode, 3 small motors, and a single solenoid. The power and the processing for our prototype reside on an external portable computer that is linked to the Haptic Laser through a cable. In the future, we plan to integrate both computing and power into the Haptic Laser device itself, to make it an entirely self-contained device.

Computer Vision System

The Haptic Laser is outfitted with a front-mounted camera for sensing the physical space. We selected the Sony PlayStation Eye Camera because of its fast frame rate (60 frames per second at 640x480 resolution) and relatively low cost. Once an image is captured, the computer vision system performs two primary functions: distance and macro-texture evaluation.

Distance. The approximate distance from the device to an object's surface is calculated using a red laser pointer mounted parallel to the camera. The forward-mounted laser pointer creates a high-intensity dot in the field of view of the camera, which can be tracked in software. Once the laser point is segmented from the image, the vertical sub-pixels from the image origin to the laser point, N_y, is used to calculate physical distance, D, according to:

$$D = \frac{h}{\tan(N_y \theta_r)}$$

where h is the physical distance from the laser pointer to the camera lens and θ_r is the radians per pixel constant specified for the camera. The result across all the frames are low pass filtered to eliminate spurious distance changes.

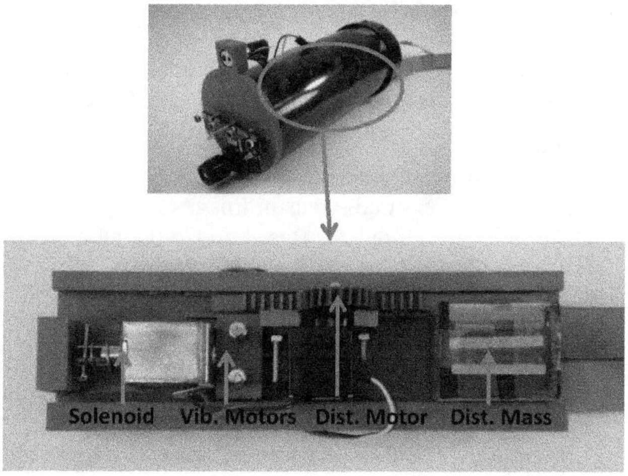

Figure 3: The internal haptic actuator components

Macro-texture. A goal of our computer vision system is differentiating potential objects of interest from their backgrounds. We have observed that many foreground objects, unlike their backgrounds, have numerous small, sharply contrasting regions (such as a laptop on a table). We define image regions with many different contrasting components as having a rough macro-texture, and we use this to identify the presence of foreground objects. The Haptic Laser determines macro-texture based on the number of connected components in an image segment. The algorithm is modified from a well-known texture detection algorithm [1] with performance improvements.

The imaging from the camera is de-noised using a Gaussian blurring and then divided into 20x20 pixel blocks. For each block, two-level adaptive histogram segmentation is used to separate the foreground from background. The group with the largest number of pixels is designated as "background."

For each block, the number of connected components of the background is calculated. If the connected component count is greater than an empirically determined threshold, then the block is considered to have a rough macro-texture. We limit the macro-texture detection search space to a small region centered on the laser point to reduce computational latency. The image search space size changes with the distance from camera to surface so that the physical search space remains a constant size.

Haptic Feedback

The feedback portion of the device is able to convey a rich set of haptic sensations to the user using three main components: two vibration motors, a solenoid, and a servo-controlled mass adjustment system (Figure 2).

Vibration Motors. The Haptic Laser uses two pager motors (maximum speed of 16,000 RPM) mounted laterally inside of the handheld device to provide macro-texture feedback. Motor speed is controlled by an 8-bit pulse width modulated signal, which is sent from a microcontroller to the base of a bipolar junction transistor (TIP31C) connected in series with each motor.

To allow perception of fine differences in vibration intensity, the Haptic Laser operates the motors at slightly different frequencies to create acoustic beats, perceived by the user tactilely as regular pulses. These beats result from the interference between the motors' vibration waves, and have a perceived frequency equal to that of the frequency difference between the motors [4]. To create this small frequency difference, we affixed an additional metal mass to each motor's rotating head. The masses for the two motors differ by 20 mg, resulting in one motor operating more slowly than the other with the same input signal. We found this produces regular beats for a given input signal, and the frequency of the beats increases as the input signal increases. Initially we attempted to maintain the frequency difference using a PID controller, but the quality of feedback suffered from slow settling times and noise.

Solenoid. A single 12V pull-type solenoid mounted with 1/8" stroke generates a recoil-like force linearly along the axis of the handheld device to inform the user of an abrupt change in distance (an edge). The solenoid is connected in series with an NPN bipolar junction transistor, and, when actuated with a single 10 ms pulse from the microcontroller to the transistor's base, the solenoid's plunger impacts the rear plastic wall of the device, maximizing the linear force returned to the user (see Figure 2). When not actuated, the solenoid is mechanically reset using a spring connected to the plunger.

Servo Mass Adjustment System. The mass adjustment system changes the handheld device's center of mass to indicate the distance between handheld device and the targeted surface. The sensation felt by the user is similar to that of telescoping stick, where the center of mass moves away from the user as the stick extends. This feedback is generated by a metal mass on a linear track running axially along the motor chassis. A small servo motor adjusts the position of the mass through a rack and pinion gear system.

Motor Control Hardware. The Haptic Laser uses an Arduino Pro 328 (3.3 volts/8 MHz) microcontroller. The tethered computer vision system sends 3-byte packets to the microcontroller via a USB serial connection. Because all three motor systems must be adjustable for each analyzed image, the communication speed between laptop and microcontroller must be at least (3 bytes x 3 packets x 60 Hz) = 4320 bps. To give the computer vision software adequate time to process the image, we chose a communication speed of 115200 bps.

Feedback Mapping Software. The Haptic Laser translates the vision system output into motor control commands. The mapping software sends a single activation pulse to the solenoid when the vision system detects an edge. Distance is mapped to the servos in the following way: distances of 1m or less are mapped to a servo position of 0°, and distances of greater than 10m are mapped to the fully extended position of 180°. Distances between these limits are mapped proportionally along the servo range of motion.

The software translates the macro-texture to a vibration motor intensity by linearly mapping the number of texture items (connected components) in the region around the center of the webcam image to the pulse width. This linear mapping is robust to noise because small changes in pulse width are nearly imperceptible to the user.

DISCUSSION AND FUTURE WORK

The Haptic Laser is designed to provide tactile feedback when exploring and interacting in a space at a distance. Through an informal evaluation, we asked a user to reflect on what he felt using the Haptic Laser in exploring parts of an unknown room, without any visual feedback. He was able to identify the large transitions, such as moving between walls and tables as well as indentifying clusters of objects, which included bundles of cables, backpacks, and books lying on a table. Although preliminary, the user was able to understand the feedback and cited the Wii experience as an analogy. We plan on investigating how the Haptic Laser's tactile feedback can improve targeting beyond that of purely vision-based targeting.

We encountered a number of technical challenges when building the Haptic Laser, including reliably and quickly detecting the laser for distance estimation. The high intensity red dot saturates the webcam's charge coupled devices, causing the dot to appear white. We were able to distinguish the laser point from true white light sources using a software filter that leaves only those sources appearing due to saturation, but bright or reflective environments still proved noisy. Additionally, the software filter was the source of substantial lag between targeting an object and feedback, since it updated the distance estimate only when the laser pointer was stable over a series of camera frames. We intend to explore other ranging technologies for more stable distance estimation, such as TDA laser ranging, and the use of optical filters.

In addition, generating robust haptic feedback was a significant challenge in hardware. The center-of-mass adjustment system was dependent on the device's weight and weight distribution. Its feedback conveyed relative distance clearly, but the prototype's weight distribution made it difficult for the device to communicate absolute distance. Future work will investigate different packaging solutions to make this feedback more robust.

The capabilities enabled by the Haptic Laser open up explorations in the field of assistive technology for individuals with limited vision. Existing solutions have focused on point-wise ranging (e.g., [2] and [6]), whereas the Haptic Laser can potentially deliver a richer experience of relationships between objects and physical transitions. We believe that the Haptic Laser could serve as a platform for investigating multi-sensation at-a-distance haptics in the physical world, thus allowing us to study which haptic feedback mechanisms are most valuable for sighted and visually impaired users in exploring the physical environment.

ACKNOWLEDGEMENTS

The authors thank Milda Zizyte for assistance in developing the hardware platform, as well as Jon Froehlich and Eric Larson for their valuable feedback and help.

REFERENCES

1. Bergman, R., Nachlieli, H. and Ruckenstein, G. Detection of Textured Areas in Images Using a Disorganization Indicator Based on Component Counts. HP Laboratories Israel, HPL-2005-175(R.1), 2007.
2. Han, Jin Woo. TactileWand: Wand for Blind – Research Work. http://bit.ly/caNAEP.
3. Hemmert, F., Hamann, S., Lowe, M., Wohlauf, A., and Joost, G. Weight-Shifting Mobiles: One-Dimensional Gravitational Displays in Mobile Phones. In *Adj. Proc. UIST'09*. (2009).
4. Kinsler, L.E., Frey, A.R., Coppens, A.B., and Sanders, J.V. *Fundamentals of Acoustics*. 4th Edition. John Wiley and Sons, Inc., 2000.
5. Lee, J.C., Dietz, P.H., Leigh, D., Yerazunis, W.S., and Hudson, S.E.. Haptic Pen: A Tactile Feedback Stylus for Touch Displays. In *Proc. UIST'04*, (2004).
6. MiniGuide, http://bit.ly/cIl0rh
7. Myers, B. A., Bhatnagar, R., Nichols, J., Peck, C. H., Kong, D., Miller, R., and Long, A. C. Interacting at a Distance: Measuring the Performance of Laser Pointers and Other Devices. In *Proc. of CHI'02*, (2002), 33-40.
8. Olsen, D. R. and Nielsen, T. Laser pointer interaction. In *Proc. of CHI'01*, (2001), 17-22.
9. Patel, S. N. and Abowd, G. D. A 2-Way Laser-Assisted Selection Scheme for Handhelds in a Physical Environment. In *Proc. UbiComp'03*, 200–207..
10. Poupyrev, I. and Maruyama, S. Tactile Interface for Small Touch Screens. In *Proc. UIST'03*, ACM Press (2003), 217-220.
11. Wilson, A., and Pham, H. Pointing in Intelligent Environments with the WorldCursor, In *Proc. Interact'03*.
12. Stetten, G., Klatzky, R., Nichol, B., Galeotti, J., Rockot, K., Zawrotny, K., Weiser, D., Sendgikoski, N., and Horvath, S.. Fingersight: Fingertip Visual Haptic Sensing and Control. *HAVE'07*, 80-83.
13. Farcy, R. and Bellik, Y. Locomotion Assistance for the Blind. In Keates, S., Langdom, P., and Robinson, P., eds.: Universal Access and Assistive Technology, Springer (2002), 277-284.
14. Haptic Torch, http://bit.ly/bDLOML.
15. Yano, H., Miyamoto, Y., and Iwata, H. Haptic Interface for Perceiving Remote Object Using a Laser Range Finder. *In Proc. WHC'09,* IEEE (2009), 196-201.

Interactive Generator: A Self-Powered Haptic Feedback Device

Akash Badshah[1], Sidhant Gupta[2], Gabe Cohn[2], Nicolas Villar[3], Steve Hodges[3], Shwetak N Patel[2]

[1]Phillips Exeter Academy
Exeter, NH (USA)
akashbad@comcast.net

[2]University of Washington
UbiComp Lab, DUB Group
Seattle, WA (USA)
{sidhant, gabecohn, shwetak}@uw.edu

[3]Microsoft Research
Cambridge, UK
{nvillar, shodges}
@microsoft.com

ABSTRACT
We present Interactive Generator (InGen), a self-powered wireless rotary input device capable of generating haptic or force feedback without the need for any external power source. Our approach uses a modified servomotor to perform three functions: (1) generating power for wireless communication and embedded electronics, (2) sensing the direction and speed of rotation, and (3) providing force feedback during rotation. While InGen is rotating, the device is capable of providing the sensation of detents or bumps, changes in stiffness, and abrupt stops using *only* power that is harvested during interaction. We describe the device in detail, demonstrate an initial 'TV remote control' application, and end with a discussion of our experiences developing the prototype and application. To the best of our knowledge, InGen is the first self-powered device, which also provides haptic feedback during operation. More broadly, this work demonstrates a new class of input systems that uses human-generated power to provide feedback to the user and wirelessly communicate sensed information.

Author Keywords
Self-powered, human-powered, force feedback, haptics, tactile feedback, user interface device, remote control

ACM Classification Keywords
H.5.2 [Information interfaces and presentation]: User Interfaces. – Input devices and strategies

General Terms
Design, Experimentation

INTRODUCTION
Haptic feedback refers to the force experienced when an object is touched or physically manipulated. It is an essential part of human interaction with physical objects, including electronic devices. Notably it provides a useful interaction channel independent of sound and vision, which are predominant in today's digital interfaces. Moreover, haptic feedback serves as a primary input modality to convey information when auditory and visual feedback may not be appropriate or available. However, with the exception of vibrating cellphone alerts, computer-controlled haptic feedback (sometimes called force feedback) it is not yet ubiquitous. Even so, other forms of haptic feedback, such as electronic control of temperature, stiffness and texture, are potentially valuable.

Figure 1: Interactive Generator is a self-powered general purpose wireless controller capable of providing haptic feedback.

Unfortunately, the electric motors, solenoids, or other electromechanical actuators employed in many force feedback systems have significant power requirements. This seems inevitable since haptic feedback ultimately relies on electrical energy to affect physical movement. This in turn, limits mobile applications where battery life is an important factor. As such, many of the haptic design schemes reported in the HCI literature require external power supplies.

The design goals of incorporating haptic feedback and reducing power consumption therefore seem inherently at odds with each other. However, this is not the case. Our system exploits unique properties of DC motors to provide rotational haptic feedback with no external power requirements. We call this system the Interactive Generator, or InGen (see Figure 1). InGen uses a modified servomotor, to act simultaneously as (1) an input sensor, detecting the speed and direction of rotation; (2) an actuator, providing haptic control for feedback such as detents (or bumps) and stiffness changes; and (3) an energy harvester, creating enough power from the interaction to operate a wireless communications link, sensory input, and force feedback system. In combination, these three features enable the device to provide haptic feedback as the user interacts with it. For example, in an application where turning a knob scrolls through a media collection, a detent sensation might indicate the movement between items in the list. Also, a change in the knob's rotational resistance from easily rotated to stiff could convey nearing or reaching the end of a playlist.

RELATED WORK

There has been substantial prior research in ultra-low power embedded devices which harvest energy in order to remove the need for replacing or recharging batteries. Many of these projects use human effort as a source of power, including hand crank flashlights and portable radios. In these devices a geared dynamo produces energy, which is stored using a capacitor or rechargeable battery, and can be used later to power the device [3]. InGen is different because the processes of power generation and device operation are tightly coupled into one action. Similar coupling has previously been explored by using piezo-electric transducers in skis and snowboards for active speed dampening [2]. Others have also looked at using a person's action for both harvesting and sensing [6]. Our work differentiates itself because we incorporate a third dimension – generating output in the form of haptic feedback.

Related to InGen's power harvesting approach is the Peppermill controller [7], which shows how a user interface device can source power from the physical effort required to interact with it. InGen takes this approach further by incorporating a mechanism that produces haptic feedback by periodically stiffening the rotary input. This is done using the same DC motor that harvests the power required to operate the device, by *selectively shorting* its two terminals. The notion of stiffening (or braking) a motor in this way is a common technique that is widely used in control systems and robotics [5]. However, the approach described in this paper accomplishes this without losing any of the stored energy so that the device stays powered even while such feedback is being generated.

In addition, detents and varying stiffness have been reproduced in several previous rotary systems, including [4]. However, to our knowledge there has been little work in the HCI community on generating these feedback patterns using motor shorting in a battery-less haptic system.

THE INTERACTIVE GENERATOR

InGen is a general-purpose handheld controller with two distinct sections that rotate relative to each other. A user holds one section in one hand while using the other hand to rotate the section relative to the first. As Figure 1 shows, the two sections are identical so that the device can be operated in either orientation. The two sections are connected with a modified servomotor. When a user turns the knob, the motor simultaneously generates power for the device and controls the stiffness with which the device may be rotated. In addition, when rotating the knob the user also turns a potentiometer, which we use to record the speed and direction of rotation with higher precision than what sensing only the motor could provide.

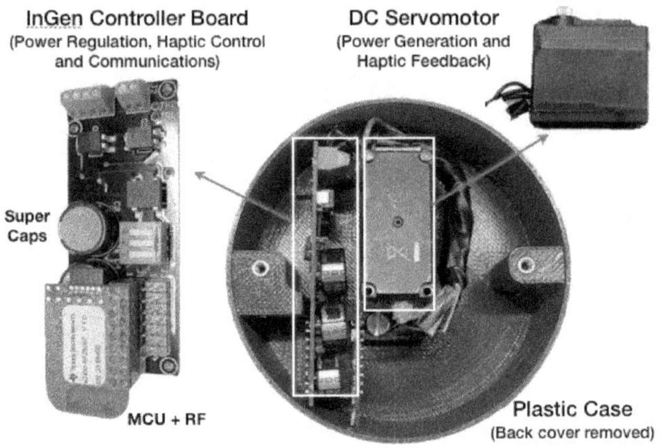

Figure 2: The internal components of Interactive Generator.

Implementation Overview

InGen has three main subsystems: haptic feedback, power generation, and sensing/communication. Figure 2 shows the various components that make up InGen.

Central to both the haptic subsystem and power generation is the geared, permanent magnet DC motor that is part of the Hi-Tec HS-625MG servomotor (see *M,* in Figure 3). A property of DC motors is that when their armature is rotated they act as generators, creating a potential difference across their terminals. The magnitude of this potential difference is directly proportional to the rate at which the armature is rotated (in rotations per minute or RPM), the strength of the magnets, and the number of turns on the armature. The last two parameters increase the cost and the size of the motor. As such, we chose to maximize RPM by using a motor with a reducing gear head.

The servomotor in InGen has a 240:1 gear ratio (for each turn of the InGen device, the motor shaft turns 240 times), which we found to give a good balance between ease of rotation, and effectiveness of power generation and braking. The internal resistance of the motor is 3.3 Ω that generates around 4.2 V when the motor is turned at a rate of 1 revolution per second (or 60 RPM). The MG variant has a metal gearbox, which we found to be essential – the plastic gearbox common to many servomotors are very fragile to fast rotations.

Generating the Haptic Feedback

As mentioned earlier, InGen uses the inherent property of dynamic *motor braking by shorting*. If the terminals of a DC motor are short-circuited while the motor's armature is rotated, the current generated by the turning motor acts to power the motor in the opposite direction. Under such conditions, the motor still turns but its stiffness greatly increases–as if a brake were being applied. The perceived increase

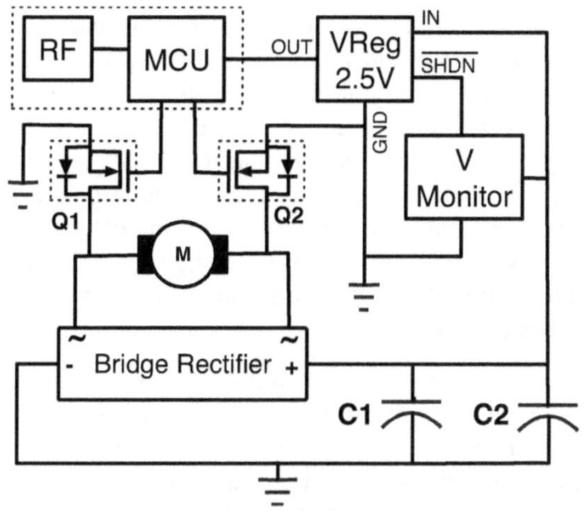

Figure 3: The InGen circuit regulates the generated power, controls motor braking (feedback), and powers the device.

in resistance felt by the user is magnified because of the torque amplification effect of using a reducing gear head.

By programmatically braking and releasing the motor, we are able to dynamically generate a variety of haptic sensations. When the braking is continuous, the device is hardest to turn – it is in its most-stiff state. If the braking is duty cycled at a suitably high frequency, the feedback can be varied continuously from very stiff to freely rotating. Braking momentarily as a user interacts is perceived as a detent or bump that can, for example, be used to indicate an item of interest as the user navigates an interface.

Digital braking control of the motor is accomplished using two IRLD024PBF N-channel MOSFETs with built-in protection diodes, which have their gates connected to the digital output pins of a microcontroller (see *Q1* and *Q2* in Figure 3). When either of the gates is driven high the drain-source channel conducts. If the motor terminal connected to the *Q1* drain, for example, is at a higher potential (i.e. when the motor is turned in a particular direction), the motor is shorted to ground through the protection diode in Q2.

Two transistors are used, so that haptic feedback for each rotational direction can be controlled independently. For example, the motor can simultaneously be stiff to turn in the one direction while being easy to turn in the other direction (i.e., when one transistor is on and the other is off).

With this configuration, it is possible to produce a variety of interesting sensations by simply changing the digital control signals. The microcontroller drives the control pins via pulse width modulation (PWM), allowing the stiffness perceived by a user to vary anywhere between very stiff and easy-to-turn. In the current prototype, we have implemented three different types of haptic feedback: detents, static stiffness, and dynamic stiffness. A detent can be provided by rapidly braking and un-braking the motor, creating the impression of a *bump* as the user turns the motor. Static stiffness can be achieved by setting the duty cycle of a pin to a specific level and maintaining it, making the motor harder or easier to turn for the user. Dynamic stiffness is produced by gradually reducing or increasing the duty cycle of braking to create an impression that the motor is becoming harder or easier to turn.

Power Harvesting

InGen uses a rectifier bridge followed by an LT3008 adjustable low-dropout linear regulator to produce a stable output voltage for the microcontroller at 2.5 V (see Figure 3). However, providing haptic feedback by shorting the motor causes a disruption in power (i.e., the power is diverted to braking the motor instead of powering the microcontroller). To overcome this, we used high energy density double layer capacitors (also known as supercaps) for power storage in the power harvesting circuitry (see C1 and C2 in Figure 3). This keeps a steady voltage supply to the circuitry even when force feedback is being applied.

Though the addition of these storage capacitors helps to maintain power, it also increases start-up latency because voltage must be accumulated before it is sufficient to power the device. That is, when the system is completely drained of power, the user needs to turn the knob for about one second before the system starts functioning. However, the higher capacitance allows the device to stay powered for five to six seconds even if there is no interaction.

We further reduce startup latency by using a MAX8211 voltage monitoring IC (see *V Monitor* Figure 3). This IC switches off all power to the microcontroller and the rest of the circuitry until there is enough power in the storage capacitors to turn on all of the hardware for a substantial amount of time. Once cut-off, the residual power in the capacitors decays over a number of hours (at least 5 hours and as much as 2 days depending on the charge on the device). When the device is used again it wakes up in less than 300 ms, because the voltage stays on the supercaps. Thus, the device becomes responsive almost instantaneously. We found that if the user interacts with it for four to five seconds the circuitry can remain powered for up to five to six seconds even after the interaction stops. After the initial interaction, the device can be interacted with instantaneously for a number of hours.

In this way, the startup latency is a concern only when the device is *cold started.* That is, the device has not been interacted with for a significant period, causing the storage capacitors to discharge completely. On other occasions such as when the device is used after a few hours of inactivity, the residual power in the capacitors plus the generated power are enough to trigger the voltage monitoring IC to turn the system on very shortly after interaction starts.

Sensing and Wireless Communication

The direction and the rate of rotation can be sensed using the DC motor by monitoring the polarity and magnitude of the voltage it produces [7]. However, the InGen has an Alps RDC803001A dual-wiper potentiometer integrated with the servomotor for sensing rotation more precisely. Using a dual-wiper device instead of the single-wiper variant (which is standard in servomotors) provides accurate position information for the full 360° of operation. The amount of power consumed by the potentiometer is insignificant compared to other components such as the wireless link. InGen's circuitry consumes on an average 52mW (104mW when wireless is active and 21mW otherwise).

The TI eZ430-RF2500 platform with a MSP430 microcontroller and integrated CC2500 radio communications was chosen primarily on the basis of low power requirements and ease of use (see *RF* and *MCU* in Figure 3). We make use of the optimized, low-power RF protocol stack called SimpliciTI for all wireless communication. To minimize power consumption, the transmit radio is only turned on briefly every 50 ms to beacon the speed and direction of interaction to the PC. The PC has a matching microcontroller and radio that is always on. To ensure that InGen receives commands sent from the PC, every 5th wake up cycle (every 250 ms), the microcontroller turns on its receiver radio and polls for command messages. A pending command is then executed before going into a low power mode again. More experimentation needs to be done to establish the ideal rate of polling, but we found that 250 ms provides a good tradeoff between interactivity and "device on" time.

EXPERIENCES WITH AN INITIAL APPLICATION

We have built a simple application to demonstrate the feedback characteristics of our prototype InGen device. This is a scrolling menu similar to a television channel guide. The rotational input can be used to scroll forward or backwards through a list of channels. As each item in the list is passed, the user feels a short detent to indicate this. On approaching either end of the list, the knob offers maximum resistance in that direction to indicate the end.

DISCUSSION AND FUTURE WORK

In this paper, we have described a number of key contributions with the development of InGen: the use of a single transducer to generate power and provide force feedback; we have detailed a fully functional handheld device that combines these characteristics with additional sensing and wireless communication; and the insights gained from building the device and using it in a simple 'TV remote control' application.

To gather some initial feedback on InGen, we conducted an informal evaluation, where we allowed various users to explore the use of InGen with our television channel guide application. We found that almost everyone was able to start up the device in a just a single rotation (< 1 sec). The start up latency did not seem to pose a problem for anyone as we had initially expected. If some users were turning the device too slowly to turn on the device, they often gradually increased their speed as a natural reaction.

The overall feedback on the haptic sensation generated by InGen was largely positive. Most indicated that they were able to easily discern the change in stiffness at the ends of the list and the detents between the channel items. However, one problem we observed was that having too many detents during the scrolling task tends to slow down the rotational momentum for some people and can eventually cause InGen to run out of power too soon. One solution is to reduce the time duration of the detent (of course, this could make the haptic feedback imperceptible). The other is to design the user interface so that the detent occurs farther apart (i.e., making the gap between items larger) or reserving the detent feedback for just special indicators in the list. More broadly, we can imagine designing for interactions with these limitations in mind and creating interfaces that encourage more rotation.

There are still some areas of improvement for future work. Although the current prototype has modest power requirements, reducing consumption would allow the device to operate longer without rotation. This could be accomplished by employing a radio technology that has lower peak power. Another area of future exploration is the integration of additional sensors, such as an accelerometer which can report the orientation in which the device is being operated, as well as push buttons that can provide additional input capabilities for an application. Similarly, other forms of output such as sound generation, which is typically low-power, merit investigation. The combination of haptic and audible feedback has been found to be quite powerful, especially in eyes-free applications [1]. We would also like to explore different form factors than the one presented in this paper. In some cases a linear version of InGen, based on an actuated mixing-desk fader, might be more appropriate than the rotary system we have built to date. We would also like to explore more applications, including gaming – imagine a fishing game where the player feels their catch struggling as it is wound in. One can also imagine using InGen to indicate snap to grid actions in a user interface. Overall, we believe that InGen provides a start for a new class of battery-less interaction devices that leverage human-generated power for both input and haptic feedback.

REFERENCES

1. Chang, A. and O'Sullivan, C. Audio-haptic feedback in mobile phones. In *Proc of CHI '05 Extended Abstracts on Human Factors in Computing System,* 2005.
2. Bianchini E., Spangler R.L. Jr., Andrus C. Use of piezoelectric devices to control snowboard vibrations. In *Proc SPIE 3329*, 106, 1998; doi:10.1117/12.316884
3. Human powered consumer electronics. http://www.freeplayenergy.com/
4. Immersion Corporation, Rotary Haptic Knob. http://www.immersion.com/markets/automotive/
5. Mohan, N., Undeland, T.M., Robbins, W.P. Power Electronics: Converters, Applications, and Design, 2nd edition, *John Wiley & Sons.*
6. Paradiso, J. A. Systems for human-powered mobile computing. In *Proc Annual Design Automation Conference*, 2006
7. Villar, N. and Hodges, S. The Peppermill: a human-powered user interface device. In *Proc. of TEI 2010.*

Security through a Different Kind of Obscurity: Evaluating Distortion in Graphical Authentication Schemes

Eiji Hayashi
ehayashi@cs.cmu.edu

Jason I. Hong
jasonh@cs.cmu.edu

Nicolas Christin
nicolasc@cmu.edu

Carnegie Mellon University
5000 Forbes, Pittsburgh, PA 15213, USA

ABSTRACT

While a large body of research on image-based authentication has focused on memorability, comparatively less attention has been paid to the new security challenges these schemes may introduce. Because images can convey more information than text, image-based authentication may be more vulnerable to educated guess attacks than passwords. In this paper, we evaluate the resilience of a recognition-based graphical authentication scheme using distorted images against two types of educated guess attacks through two user studies.

The first study, consisting of 30 participants, investigates whether distortion prevents educated guess attacks primarily based on information about individual users. The second study, using Amazon Mechanical Turk, investigates whether distortion mitigates the risk of educated guess attacks based on collective information about users. Our results show that authentication images without distortion are vulnerable to educated guess attacks, especially when information about the target is known, and that distortion makes authentication images more resilient against educated guess attacks.

Author Keywords

Educated Guess Attack, User Authentication, Graphical Authentication

ACM Classification Keywords

H.5.2 Information Interfaces and Presentation: Miscellaneous

General Terms

Security, Human Factors

INTRODUCTION

Knowledge-based authentication remains the most pervasive type of authentication system because of its simplicity and availability on almost any type of platform. One of the fundamental assumptions in knowledge-based authentication is that users can memorize secrets, e.g., passwords, shared between the users and the authentication system. However, because people have difficulty in memorizing many complicated passwords, a typical strategy is to choose simple, easy-to-remember passwords and/or reuse a limited number of passwords for many accounts, all of which undermine the security of password authentication [1, 7]. Researchers have proposed alternatives to traditional text-based passwords with the hopes of improving memorability. One such approach is image-based authentication, which leverages research in cognitive psychology that shows that it is significantly easier for users to recognize images than to remember text [9, 18]. In that respect, image-based authentication schemes (e.g., graphical passwords) are a promising alternative to text-based passwords.

However, while image-based authentication facilitates memorability, it also poses new security challenges. One of these challenges is the *educated guess attack*, where an attacker tries to guess a user's shared secrets based on knowledge about that user. Because graphical authentication tokens (e.g., authentication images) preserve more contextual information than text-based passwords, image-based authentication could actually be *less* resilient against educated guess attacks than its text-based counterpart.

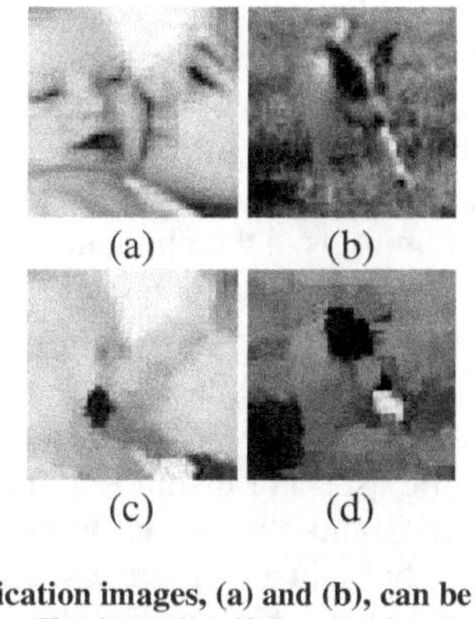

Figure 1. Authentication images, (a) and (b), can be vulnerable to educated guess attacks. For instance, if the attacker knows that users are likely to choose animal pictures as their authentication images, the attacker can guess that (b) is an authentication image (collective educated guess attack). If the attacker knows the target's wife, and sees her in (a), (a) is likely to be an authentication image (individualized educated guess attack). In contrast, if distorted pictures, (c) and (d), are used, these attacks are unlikely to work because the contextual information of the distorted pictures is obfuscated.

CHI 2011, May 7–12, 2011, Vancouver, BC, Canada.

In this paper, we investigate the security of user chosen authentication images against two types of educated guess attacks by emulating these attacks in two user studies. We also evaluate the marginal security gained against these attacks by performing image distortion, which was proposed in *Use Your Illusion* [10].

Through this investigation, we make novel contributions. First, we provide quantitative, empirical results that show that an attacker can make very accurate guesses about a user's authentication images if the attacker possesses enough information about the user. Second, we demonstrate that distorting images can mitigate educated guess attacks against recognition-based graphical authentication systems.

The rest of this paper is organized as follows. First, we discuss the two types of educated guess attacks and related work. Second, we formulate our research hypotheses, which we test in the two user studies. Third, we describe our first user study, in which we emulate educated guess attacks by asking pairs of "friends" to guess their friend's authentication image(s). Fourth, we describe our second user study using Amazon Mechanical Turk. The study evaluates whether distortion can prevent the educated guess attacks based on collective information about users. Finally, we discuss the implications of our findings.

EDUCATED GUESS ATTACKS

In educated guess attacks, an attacker tries to guess a user's shared secret (e.g., a password) based on the user's information. Most educated guess attacks can be categorized into two types, *collective educated guess attacks* and *individualized educated guess attacks* (Figure 1). The collective educated guess attack rely on knowledge about the entire population of users, while the individualized educated guess attacks rely on knowledge specific to a given user.

Collective educated guess

A lot of past work has investigated collective educated guess attacks on graphical authentication schemes [14, 21–24]. The collective educated guess attacks rely on knowledge about the entire population of users. For instance, in the context of recognition-based schemes (e.g., Use Your Illusion), if an attacker knows that most people prefer to select pictures of animals as their authentication images, the attacker could infer that pictures of animals in the challenge set (Figure 1 (b)) have a higher probability of being authentication images.

Individualized educated guess

The individualized educated guess attacks rely on knowledge about a specific user. For instance, if an attacker knows that a user has a wife and a baby and finds a picture showing a woman and a baby in a challenge set, the attacker can guess that the picture has a high probability of being one of the authentication images (Figure 1 (a)).

As described above, there has been a great deal of past work investigating collective educated guess attacks. However, there has been little work on individualized educated guess attacks against graphical authentication schemes. As such, one of the primary contributions of this paper is to quantify the risk of the individualized educated guess attacks on recognition-based graphical authentication schemes.

RELATED WORK

Based on the observation that humans are considerably better at remembering images than they are at remembering text [18], much work has been devoted to investigating graphical password authentication (e.g., [5, 11, 16]). Evaluations of these techniques have shown that graphical password authentication can achieve higher memorability, but also have some security drawbacks. We outline various schemes below, and discuss some of their strengths and weaknesses.

Recall-based schemes

Recall is one of the cognitive processes utilized in graphical authentication schemes. Recall is the ability to remember items from memory without help. For example the Draw-A-Secret scheme requires users to draw a pre-determined image on a grid in order to authenticate [11]. The drawings can provide a larger password space, and more memorable passwords than a text-based password does; however, users have a tendency to choose drawings with high symmetry and a small number of strokes [21, 22], which are analogous to choosing simple passwords in text-based authentication. An attacker can thus use collective educated guess attacks, i.e., an attacker do better than randomly guessing by trying symmetric drawings based on the knowledge that users *in general* are likely to choose specific types of drawing.

Cued-recall-based schemes

Other authentication systems rely on *cued recall*, where retrieval cues are provided to a user to aide the recall task. As an example, in the PassPoints graphical password scheme, users authenticate by clicking on points, or selecting regions, of an image that were previously chosen by the user [2, 16, 24]. In this case, the image itself serves as a cue to the regions of the image that a user must recall. This scheme however produces predictable authentication sequences. This is because users tend to choose "hot spots," i.e., regions that are often selected because they are most memorable or most obvious [23, 24]. As a result, an attacker is more likely to succeed by guessing hot spots rather than all possible positions of clicks. Again, biases common to many users biases let attackers launch collective educated guess attacks against PassPoints.

Recognition-based schemes

There is another class of graphical authentication schemes that rely on *recognition*, the ability to judge whether a person has seen an item before or not. Past work in cognitive psychology has demonstrated that humans have an impressive ability to recognize pictures they have seen before [18–20]. This body of work has also shown that they recognize pictures better than they recognize words or sentences [18].

As such, recognition is used in many graphical password schemes by asking users to select previously chosen images from a larger subset of images [4, 5].

In selecting previously chosen images, people remember images more accurately when they are contextually meaningful and when the images are generated by the individuals themselves [12]. Hence, graphical password images selected by users tend to be more memorable than assigned images. For that reason, many recognition-based graphical authentication schemes let users choose their authentication images.

For example, in PassFaces [4], users authenticate by identifying a set of faces they have previously chosen. An evaluation of PassFaces showed such authentication images are much more memorable than text-based passwords [4]. However, users are also more likely to choose faces of females belonging to their ethnic group [14], which makes authentication predictable and thus less secure. This bias toward specific faces allows an attacker to guess a user's authentication images based on the user's profile.

THWARTING EDUCATED GUESS ATTACKS

One countermeasure against educated guess attacks is to randomly assign authentication images to users, or to use abstract images [5], which are less predictable than real images. However, past work has shown that image scenes that are coherent and contextually meaningful are memorized more accurately than incoherent or abstract images [3, 8]. For instance, a picture taken on a vacation trip will be easier to memorize than randomly assigned scenery, or abstract images. As such, random assignment or use of abstract images can reduce the memorability of the authentication images.

Another alternative is to have users self-select images and assign distorted versions of these images to authenticate. Use Your Illusion [10] requires users to produce three images to authenticate. These images are assigned as authentication images after being distorted through an "oil-painting" filter, which preserves rough shape and colors, but eliminates most details. When users want to be authenticated, they are asked to identify their three authentication images from a set of 27 distorted images. Use Your Illusion relies on a finding from cognitive psychology that people's interpretations of visual input are affected by their expectations [6]. Users expect to find distorted images representing contextual information of their original photos; thus they interpret the distorted images as images with the contextual information. However, an attacker is far less likely to have these expectations, and therefore should have a much more difficult time interpreting the contextual information of the distorted images. The work [10] demonstrated that users could recognize their authentication images accurately even one month later. Nevertheless, the marginal security created by the distortion technique has not been investigated yet. As such, a secondary contribution of this paper is to evaluate the marginal security obtained by distorting images in quantitative ways.

HYPOTHESES

At a high level, we hypothesize that educated guess attacks will let an attacker guess user-chosen authentication images with a higher success rate than random guesses. In addition, we hypothesize that *Use Your Illusion* [10] will increase the security of the authentication images against educated guess attacks. In the rest of this section, we formally define five hypotheses that we tested in our user studies.

H1 (context effect): *If a recognition-based graphical authentication system lets users choose original, undistorted pictures as authentication images, an attacker can predict the images more accurately by using educated guesses than by guessing randomly.*

In H1, we hypothesize that an attacker can launch collective educated guess attacks against authentication images. We argue that original, undistorted pictures will improve an attackers ability to make guesses better than by chance, even without knowing anything about the specific user.

H2 (knowledge effect): *An attacker can make more accurate guesses about authentication images if the attacker possesses information about the user who chose them.*

In H2, we hypothesize that an attacker can launch individualized educated guess attacks against authentication images. Authentication images have more contextual information than text-based authentication images. The additional information helps users to memorize the authentication images; however, at the same time, the additional information also helps attackers guess the authentication images more accurately given user preferences. For instance, if the attacker knows that her target is a car fanatic and finds photos of cars in the challenge set, the attacker can infer that those photos have a higher likelihood to be authentication images.

H3 (distortion effect on educated guesses): *Distorted authentication images are significantly more resilient against educated guess attacks than original, undistorted authentication images.*

In H3, we hypothesize that distortion improves the security of authentication images against educated guess attacks. We argue that distorted authentication images are more difficult to interpret without knowing the original images, as distortion obfuscates the contextual information of authentication images. As a result, an attacker should have more difficulty in guessing authentication images based on the contextual information.

H4 (user biases): *Users tend to choose specific categories of images as their authentication images.*

In H4, we hypothesize that there are biases toward certain types of images among authentication images chosen by users. For instance, people could tend to choose pictures of faces because they are good at memorizing faces. Observing biases toward certain types of images among authentication images chosen by users, the attacker can make better guesses by choosing frequently chosen types of images. That is, the attacker can launch the collective educated guess attacks against authentication images. According to existing work [14, 23, 24], H4 is highly likely to be supported. However, we still want to test H4 as a baseline for the next hypothesis.

H5 (biases after distortion): *Even when authentication images are distorted, attackers still can make better guesses based on users' biases in choosing authentication images.*

In H5, we hypothesize that, even after distortion, attackers can launch collective educated guess attacks. This hypothesis is supported when, for instance, distorted images which seem like *people* are more likely to be authentication images than distractors.

USER STUDIES

We conducted two user studies to test the hypotheses defined in the previous section.

In the first user study, we tested H1 (context effect), H2 (knowledge effect), and H3 (distortion effect on educated guesses). We recruited pairs of friends as participants. We asked participants to guess their friends' authentication images. In other words, we asked participants to act as attackers and to guess authentication images of targets whom they know well. Based on the results, we evaluated whether knowing the target well helps attackers to make more accurate guesses about the user's authentication images.

In the second user study, we tested H4 (user biases) and H5 (biases after distortion). We used Amazon's Mechanical Turk to organize images into 12 categories according to their contextual information. Mechanical Turk is a web service that coordinates many users working on tasks that require human processing, such as image tagging tasks [13]. Our participants organized two sets of photos. The first set consisted of 120 photos randomly selected from Flickr.com. The other set consisted of 180 photos chosen as authentication images by the participants in the first user study. We asked the participants to categorize these two sets of photos and distorted versions of them. Based on the categorizations, we evaluated whether attackers could make collective educated guesses effectively.

USER STUDY #1: EVALUATION WITH PAIRS OF FRIENDS

For our first user study, we evaluated the security of authentication images against both individualized and collective educated guess attacks using *Use Your Illusion* as a platform. We asked participants to act as attackers and to guess their targets' authentication images. We evaluated the security based on the number of correct guesses that participants made.

Participants

We recruited pairs of friends as participants from our university. We defined "friend pair" as a pair of two persons which satisfied the following four conditions: 1) both of them had Facebook accounts; 2) both of them had "friended" each other in Facebook; 3) they met face-to-face at least twice a week; and 4) they had known each other for at least three months. In total, we recruited 30 university students (15 pairs). Nineteen participants were male and 11 participants were female. Their ages ranged from 20 to 28 with a mean age of 22.6 years old. According to a post experiment survey, the pairs had known each other for three months to six years with a mean length of 19.4 months. Also according to the post experiment survey, the pairs met each other 6.3 days a week on average.

We compensated the participants $10 USD for their participation. In addition, we paid an additional $5 USD for each correct guess they made about their target's authentication image. This additional payment gave participants an incentive to make their best guesses about their target's authentication images.

Our participants did not have deep knowledge of authentication systems. However, *Use Your Illusion* and its distortion technique are simple enough for them to understand. At first glance, it appears that the system should be more vulnerable to security experts with knowledge of the system's internals. However, for the educated guess attacks, which are essentially variants of social engineering attacks, we contend that knowledge of the target is more critical to the attack's success than technical expertise. For this reason, we asked friends rather than security experts to pose as attackers in this study.

Variables

For this user study, we had two independent variables: type of image and relationship between the attacker and target. The type of image variable was either original photo and distorted photo. In the rest of this paper, we refer to these conditions as *original* condition and *distorted* condition. Relationship between attacker and target was either friend or stranger. We refer to them as *friend* condition and *stranger* condition respectively. In the friend condition, participants were asked to guess images chosen by their partners. While, in the stranger condition, participants were asked to guess images chosen by another set of 15 participants, living in a different city, and who were not part of this experiment. This selection allowed us to avoid attackers guessing authentication images by choosing images taken in local areas, such as neighboring landmarks.

We conducted this user study in a 2×2 mixed design (Figure 1). We used a within-subject design for type of images variable, i.e., all participants tested both image types, because the amount of knowledge that an attacker had about his target varies from attacker to attacker. If an attacker tested both image types, we could minimize the effect of the variation. For relationship, we used a between-subject design, i.e., in each pair, one of the pair was chosen randomly and assigned to a friend group and the other was assigned to a stranger group. If we used within-subject design for relationship as well, participants must have tested four conditions, which could cause ordering effects, such as fatigue. Thus, to minimize the ordering effects, we used between-subject design for relationship. In other words, participants in the friend group and in the stranger group only tested the friend condition or the stranger condition, but not both (Table 1). The dependent variable of this user study is the success rates of the educated guess attacks. Using this dependent variable, lower success rates mean higher resilience to educated guess attacks.

		Relationships	
		Friend	Stranger
Image Type	Original	2× 2 mixed design	
	Distorted		

Table 1. The first user study was conducted in a 2×2 mixed design. We assigned participants to either the friend group or the stranger group. Among four combinations of conditions, participants in the friend condition tested both friend-original condition and friend-distorted condition. Likewise, participants in the stranger group tested both stranger-original condition and stranger-distorted condition.

Hypotheses

We tested H1 (context effect), H2 (knowledge effect) and H3 (distortion effect on educated guesses). We conducted the tests by comparing number of correct guesses, using a binomial test and a Fisher's exact test.

For H1 (context effect), we compared the number of correct guesses in the original condition and the expected number of correct guesses, assuming that a participant made guesses randomly. H1 was supported if there was a statistically significant difference between these two numbers

For H2 (knowledge effect), we compared the number of correct guesses in the friend condition with that in the stranger condition. In the friend condition, participants had information about their targets, whereas in the stranger condition, participants did not have information about their target. H2 was supported if there was statistically significant difference between these two numbers.

Finally, for H3 (distortion effect on educated guesses), we compared the number of correct guesses in the original condition with that in the distorted condition. H3 was supported if there was a statistically significant difference between these two numbers.

Evaluation Environment

We emulated Use Your Illusion [10] on a desktop computer (Figure 3). Images used in the emulator had the same resolution as those used in Use Your Illusion. Use Your Illusion has a setup phase and a challenge phase. During setup, the user is asked to produce three pictures as his authentication images, Then, during authentication, the system presents the user with a challenge set consisting of 27 images, including the three authentication images. The user is asked to correctly identify the three authentication images from the challenge set within three trials. The 27 images are shown as the three sets of nine images (Figure 2). However, it does not mean each set contain one authentication image. Each set can contain zero to three authentication images. When choosing the images, the user can go back and forth among the three sets.

In the original condition, all 27 images, including user-chosen images and distractors, were original, non-distorted images. In the distorted condition, all images were distorted using an oil-painting image processing filter. The filter distorts precise shape and minor colors while keeping rough shapes and major colors. Previous research showed that users can memorize the distorted images as accurately as they memorize original images for at least one month [10].

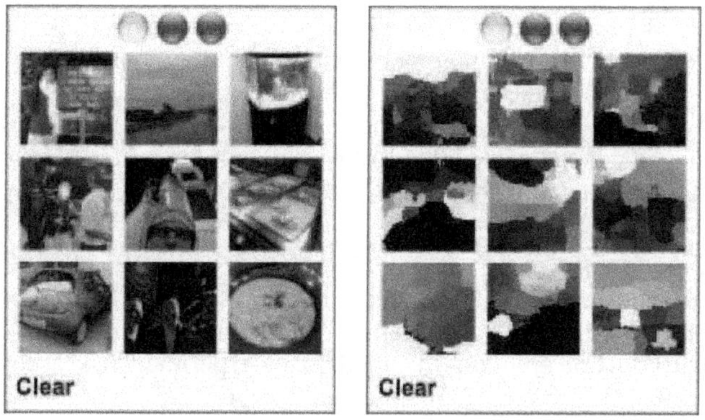

(a) Original (b) Distorted

Figure 2. Example of challenge sets. A challenge set consists of three screens showing nine images (27 images in total). The examples show one of the three screens in the original condition and the distorted condition. A user has to select 3 images correctly from the 27 images to be authenticated. Distractors are chosen from an image pool consisting of 144 images.

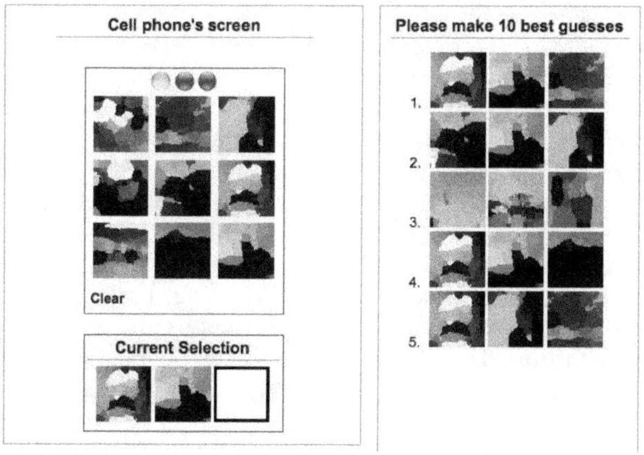

Figure 3. Use Your Illusion emulator. The top left part emulated Use Your Illusion. The right part showed combinations of images already chosen by a participant. The bottom left part showed images which a participant was currently choosing.

Procedure

This user study consisted of three phases: preparation, an experiment and a post experiment survey. The entire user study took about 40 minutes.

Preparation

Prior to our user study, we asked all participants to submit six digital photos taken by themselves. The participants could submit photos that they had already taken or took specifically for this study. In the request, we explicitly mentioned that the photos would be used as "passwords" in a graphical authentication system. Moreover, we asked participants not to talk with others about the photos they selected. Three of the photos were randomly selected and distorted using an oil-painting filter, for use in the distorted condition. The other three photos were used as is for the original condition.

In our post-survey, we asked when the participants took the photos. One participant responded he took his photos after we started this study. Other participants answered that they took their photos at least one month before we started this study. This indicated that most participants submitted photos that they had already taken.

Experiment

We conducted this experiment in an isolated room under the supervision of an experimenter. Each participant used a Use Your Illusion emulator installed on the experimenter's laptop to guess his target's authentication images.

When a participant tried to guess his target's (i.e., his friend's or stranger's) authentication images, two sets of images were given, one at a time. One of them consisted of original photos (i.e., original condition) and the other consisted of distorted photos (i.e., distorted condition). Each set consisted of three authentication images and 24 distractors. The distractors were chosen from a pool consisting of 144 images. The images in the pool were randomly chosen from photos under Creative Commons License in Flicker.com. All of the sets were manually composed ahead of time to achieve balance, and to make the two sets given to a participants mutually exclusive. Thus, each individual saw different distractors in the two conditions. The images were resized to 56×56 pixels to be used in Use Your Illusion emulator.

In the original photo set, photos taken by the target were used as authentication images after resizing. In the distorted photo set, photos taken by the target were used after resizing and distortion. The photos used as authentication images or source of authentication images were mutually exclusive.

We randomly chose half of the participants and let them start with a set of original photos, while the other half of the participants started with a set of distorted photos. After we gave one of the sets, we asked the participant to make their 10 best guesses (i.e., to choose 10 sets of three photos.) The experimenter did not give feedback whether their guesses were correct or not. After 10 guesses were made in the first set of photos, we gave another set of 27 images. Then, participants were asked to make 10 best guesses for this set.

Post Experiment Survey

After the experiment, we asked participants to answer a post experiment survey. The survey polled participants' profile, intimacy with their friends, their photo sharing through web sites and their strategy of making guesses. The survey consisted of 70 questions and took 15 minutes to complete.

Results

We considered attackers to be successful if they could correctly guess their targets' authentication images within ten trials. In Use Your Illusion, the number of trials was limited to three. However, considering the difficulty of the guessing task, we allowed attackers to choose ten different combinations of three images, so as to have more statistical power. Among these ten guesses, an attacker could not choose the exact same combination twice. Assuming that an attacker chose images completely randomly, the probability that the correct combination was included in the ten selected combinations was $P = 10/\binom{27}{3} \approx 0.003$. We used the success rate of random guess denoted by P as a baseline in the following analysis.

Table 2 shows the success rates of the attackers in each condition. Asterisks "*" in Table 2 denote statistical significance when the success rate is greater than the baseline P at significance level $p = 0.01$ based on a binomial test. The numbers in parentheses are the number of attackers who successfully guessed their targets' authentication images.

	Friend	Stranger
Original	0.53* (8/15)	0.20* (3/15)
Distorted	0.067 (1/15)	0.00 (0/15)

Table 2. Success Rates of Educated Guesses. Asterisks "*" denote that the success rates were higher (statistically significant) than success rate of random guesses. The success rate of random guesses is 0.003. Numbers in parentheses denote the number of attackers (out of 15) who made correct guesses.

As Table 2 shows, in the original conditions, the success rates were higher than the baseline ($p < 0.01$). Therefore, H1 (context effect) was supported.

These results showed that participants could guess better than chance even without any knowledge about their targets. This finding suggested that contextual information in the undistorted images themselves could help an attacker make better guesses.

In the friend-original condition, eight attackers out of 15 correctly guessed targets' authentication images. In addition, three attackers chose correct combinations in the first attempt. One of the eight attackers answered that his strategy was "[to] try to think of places my friend has been and guess those pictures." Other attackers also used similar strategies to make their guesses. These results strongly suggested that using self-selected original photos for authentication was highly vulnerable to individualized educated guess attacks. Thus, H2 (knowledge effect) was supported.

In the stranger-original condition, where attackers did not know their targets, three attackers correctly guessed their targets' authentication images. According to post surveys, these attackers chose images that had common properties. One of the three attackers said that "[he] selected the 3 photos depicting the similar content." His target's authentication images consisted of two photos of a beer can and one photo of a bottle of alcohol.

In contrast, in the distorted conditions, there was no statistical significance between the success rates of attackers and random guesses ($p > 0.01$). Moreover, in the post-survey, most of the attackers answered that they relied on random guess. Moreover, using Fisher's exact test, the success rate in friend-distorted condition was lower than in friend-original condition ($p = 0.007 < 0.01$). Thus, H3 (distortion effect) was supported.

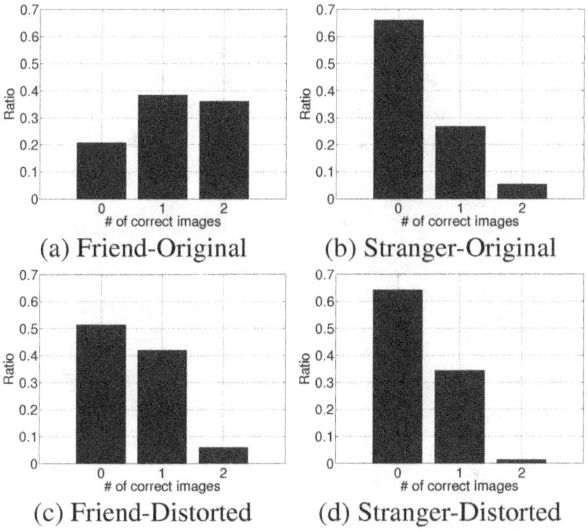

Figure 4. Partially correct guesses, showing number of correctly guessed authentication images. For example, in Friend-Original (a), 21% of all guesses by all participants in that condition had zero of the three correct images, 38% had only one of the three images, and about 36% had two images (i.e., a very close guess). The distributions were skewed to the right if participants had more accurate partially correct guesses.

Figure 4 shows distributions of partially correct guesses, which included zero, one or two authentication images. Distributions skewed to right mean that attacker made more accurate guesses. The ratios were calculated by dividing the number of partially correct guesses by the total number of guesses. As described above, in the friend-original condition, there were two attackers who chose correct combinations of three images in their first choice. According to the post survey, they were completely sure that they chose the correct combinations and that they chose images randomly for their other nine guesses to save their effort. Thus, in the analysis of partial hits, we discarded their data. Differences among the distributions in Figure 4 were statistically significant except for the difference between the stranger-original condition and the stranger-distorted condition (Table 3).

In the friend-original condition (Figure 4 (a)), the distribution was skewed to the right. This illustrates that the ratios of partial hits, which included more authentication images, are higher than other conditions. It indicates that using original images as authentication images was more vulnerable to the educated guess attack. In friend-distorted condition (see Figure 4 (c)), the ratio of guesses including one authentication image was higher than that in stranger conditions (see Figure 4 (b) and (d)). This may indicate that, even in the case where an authentication system uses distorted images, attackers have an advantage if they make guesses based on the knowledge they have about their targets. However, the effect would be small because we did not observe statistical evidence that attackers could predict authentication image better than random guesses in friend-distorted condition.

USER STUDY #2: CATEGORIZATION

In the second user study, we further evaluated the risk of the collective educated guess attacks against authentication images by testing H4 (user biases) and H5 (biases after distortion) using Amazon Mechanical Turk. We asked Amazon Mechanical Turk users to organize images into categories. Then, we compared distribution of the categorization between images chosen by users as their authentication images in the previous study, and the images randomly chosen from Flickr. If the distributions were different, attackers could launch collective educated guess attacks with knowing the distributions. If they were similar, collective educated guess attacks were not feasible even knowing the distributions.

This study consisted of two parts. In the calibration study, we asked the Mechanical Turk users to label images based on their contextual meanings in an open format. The purpose of this part was to investigate what labels they used to describe images. Then, we coded the labels to categories used in the actual study. In the actual study, we asked the Mechanical Turk users to choose one of the categories for each image based on its contextual meaning.

Calibration Study

We randomly collected 50 photos under Creative Commons license from Flickr. Then, we asked Amazon Mechanical Turk users to label each photo with one tag describing the color in the photo, and three tags describing the content in that photo. We gave participants four guidelines: 1) the color tag must denote the dominant color in the photo; 2) the content tags must describe the contents of the photo or some relevant context; 3) the content tags should include at least one noun; and 4) no tag can be longer than 25 characters. For each photo, we asked three users to label it. As a result, we obtained 450 content tags in total for 50 photos. We asked users to add the color tag to prevent the users from writing names of colors in content tags. We paid each user \$0.03 USD for tagging a photo. The task was completed in five hours by 40 unique users.

	Friend-distorted	Stranger-original	Stranger-distorted
Friend-original	$p < 0.01*$ $\chi^2(2, 273) = 49.4$	$p < 0.01*$ $\chi^2(2, 271) = 68.5$	$p < 0.01*$ $\chi^2(2, 275) = 79.0$
Friend-distorted		$p = 0.02 < 0.05*$ $\chi^2(2, 276) = 7.9$	$p = 0.02 < 0.05*$ $\chi^2(2, 300) = 7.8$
Stranger-original			$p = 0.07 > 0.05$ $\chi^2(2, 298) = 5.1$

Table 3. Results of χ^2 test among distributions of partial hit rates in the four conditions. Except for a combination of the stranger-original condition and the stranger-distorted condition, the differences are statistically significant.

The content tags were very diverse; thus, we coded them into more abstract concepts to make the categorization task in the actual study easier. Finally, as a result of the calibration, we defined 12 concepts, which were used as categories in the following study. (Table 4).

#	Category	#	Category
1	Human	7	Plant
2	Transportation	8	Building
3	Animal	9	Food
4	Insect	10	Clothing
5	Interior	11	Object
6	Landscape	12	None of them

Table 4. Category tags. One of the author coded 450 content tags collected in the calibration study.

Method

To test H4 (user biases), we compared two sets of original images. The first set is a set of images chosen by participants as authentication images in the first user study. The second set is a set of images randomly chosen from Flickr. We collected another 120 photos from Flickr using the Perl script. Because we could not prevent users who participated in the calibration study from participating the actual study, we used another set of photos to avoid possible contamination. Ideally, as the second set, we wanted to use a set of all the pictures which people in general took. However, such a set of images was not available. Therefore, we approximated the set by choosing images randomly from Flickr. By comparing distributions of categories in these two sets of images, we could test whether users were likely to choose specific categories of images as their authentication images.

To test H5, we tested distorted versions of the two sets of original images. We evaluated how distortion affects categorization of images by comparing categorization of the original and distorted images. Consequently, we used four sets of images in total:

- original baseline: 120 images randomly chosen from Flickr.com
- original user chosen images: 180 images chosen as authentication images by participants of the first user study
- distorted baseline: 120 distorted images generated from *original randomly chosen images*
- distorted user chosen images: 180 distorted images generated from *original user chosen images*

For each of these 600 images, we asked five Mechanical Turk users to choose one of the 12 categories shown in Table 4. For the distorted images, using examples, we explained that the distorted images were generated from original photos using an image processing filter. Then, we asked the users to guess the original photos of the given distorted images, and to choose one category according to their guesses. As a result, we obtained 3000 categorizations (five categorizations for each of the 600 images). This categorization task was completed by 288 unique Mechanical Turk users.

Results

Table 5 shows the ratios of category tags given to the original images. The ratio $p_i, (i = 1, 2, 3..., 12)$ is calculated as $p_i = c_i/N$ where c_i and N denote the number of ith category's tags and the total number of tags. For instance, the number in the top left cell is calculated as $153/600 = 0.26$.

Category	Baseline		Users' choice	
Human	0.26	(153)	0.26	(251)
Transportation	0.06	(38)	0.02	(21)
Animal	0.07	(39)	0.05	(38)
Insect	0.00	(0)	0.00	(1)
Interior	0.10	(60)	0.04	(35)
Landscape	0.10	(58)	0.15	(127)
Plant	0.01	(3)	0.03	(24)
Building	0.11	(68)	0.25	(218)
Food	0.09	(51)	0.04	(34)
Clothing	0.00	(2)	0.00	(1)
Object	0.17	(101)	0.13	(122)
None of them	0.04	(27)	0.03	(28)
Total	1.00	(600)	1.00	(900)

Table 5. Distribution of categories given to the original images. The numbers in parentheses stand for actual number of images in each category. The difference between the distributions of categories in the baseline and the users' choice was significant, $\chi^2(11, 1500) = 106.64, p < 0.01$.

In Table 5, the numbers in the baseline column shows categorization of photos people *take*. On the other hand, the numbers in the users' choice column shows categorization of photos participants *choose* as their authentication images. The differences between numbers in these two columns indicates participants' tendency choose or not to choose categories of images as their authentication images. Attackers can launch collective educated guess attacks by choosing the categories where the numbers for the users' choice are greater than the numbers for the baseline.

In Table 5, the difference between the distributions of categories in the baseline and the users' choice was significant, $\chi^2(11, 1500) = 106.64, p < 0.01$. Table 5 shows that the participants were less likely to choose photos of transportation and food as their authentication images. On the other hand, they were more likely to choose photos of landscapes, plants and buildings as their authentication images. This results indicates that there are biases in the user-chosen authentication images. Thus, H4 (user biases) was supported.

Participants showed stronger biases toward landscapes and buildings. One possible interpretation of these biases was that participants thought that landscape and building photos would be appropriate for their authentication images because anyone could take these photos and they seemed to be less related to their identities.

Although more studies using different sets of images would be necessary, this observation implies that an attacker can launch collective educated guess attacks based on the knowledge that users are likely to choose specific types of authentication images. In this specific case, if an attacker chooses landscape and building photos, the attacker would have better chance of guessing a user's authentication images than a random guess.

In contrast, when images were distorted (Table 6), there was no statistically significant difference between the distributions of categories in the baseline and the user chosen images, $\chi^2(11, 1500) = 18.00, p = 0.08$. Therefore, H5 (biases after distortion) was not supported. This indicates that after distortion, attackers do no have a statistically significant advantage in the collective educated guess attack even with knowing the biases shown in Table 6.

Category	Baseline		Users' choice	
Human	0.20	(120)	0.18	(166)
Transportation	0.04	(24)	0.02	(20)
Animal	0.10	(58)	0.09	(83)
Insect	0.00	(1)	0.00	(3)
Interior	0.10	(57)	0.10	(96)
Landscape	0.36	(216)	0.36	(316)
Plant	0.04	(21)	0.03	(31)
Building	0.06	(33)	0.09	(84)
Food	0.00	(4)	0.01	(14)
Clothing	0.01	(5)	0.01	(12)
Object	0.09	(54)	0.07	(61)
None of them	0.01	(7)	0.01	(14)
Total	1.00	(600)	1.00	(900)

Table 6. Distribution of categories given to distorted images. The numbers in parentheses stand for actual number of category tags given. There was no statistically significant differences between distribution of categories in the baseline and the users' choice.

DISCUSSION

Our user studies support H1 to H4, and reject H5. The first study shows that an attacker can make guesses better than random guess when authentication images are not distorted (H1: context effect), especially when the attacker knows about a target user (H2: knowledge effect). Furthermore, the study shows that using distorted images prevents these two attacks (H3: distortion effect on educated guesses). The second study illustrated that there are biased in choosing authentication images (H4: user biases), and that, with distortion, attackers have little advantage even if they know the biases (H5: biases after distortion).

These results yield a number of interesting implications. First, contextual information helps attackers as well as users. Balancing the two competing goals of resilience against attacks with ease of memorization is a critical design goal for any image-based authentication system. Our work in this paper helps quantify how well educated guess attacks can work, and offer a baseline for other image-based authentication systems.

Second, our results show that distortion is an effective technique for mitigating both individualized and collective educated guess attacks. Thus, it may be possible to apply the distortion technique to other recognition-based graphical authentication schemes. If an authentication scheme uses limited kinds of images (e.g., faces in PassFaces), users would have difficulty in recognizing their authentication images after distortion; however, if a scheme uses a wide variety of images, we could distort the images to improve their resilience against individualized educated guess attack and collective educated guess attack.

Third, we found that individualized educated guess attacks against undistorted authentication images were considerably more successful than collective educated guess attacks. To launch individualized educated guess attacks, attackers must collect adequate amount of information about their targets. However, recently, many people make personal information, such as preferences, recent activities, and personal histories, public through social networks, such as Facebook [15, 17]. As a result, it is becoming easier for attackers to collect such information. Thus, individualized educated guess attack can be one of the major threat against image-based authentication systems.

LIMITATIONS

This paper is not, and does not aim to be, a comprehensive security analysis of graphical password schemes. Instead we evaluated how a specific countermeasure (image distortion) provides resilience to a specific family of social engineering attacks (educated guess attacks). Studying resilience to other attacks, such as shoulder surfing, would require further work. Likewise, we focused on a specific authentication scheme (Use Your Illusion), and we need to caution against directly extrapolating to other graphical password schemes. Formally generalizing our results would likely require additional experimentation with a myriad of other graphical password schemes. We nevertheless believe our results are a useful contribution, in that neither security research nor cognitive science work has investigated the impact of distortion of image authentication security.

Our user studies also had limitations. As discussed in the first user study, our participants were not skilled attackers, but instead people with intimate knowledge of their targets; while we believe that the amount of knowledge about a target is the most important factor in the educated guess attacks, we need to point out that skilled attackers could launch sophisticated educated guess attacks. For instance, they could collect many photos about a target user from web services, such as Flickr, then, distort all the photos to make better guesses about the user's authentication images. Whether such attacks are practical remains an open problem, that this paper does not attempt to address.

In the second study, we used a set of photos randomly chosen from a pool of photos shared on Flickr under the Creative Commons license. We assumed that this random selection was a representative sample of pictures that people take in general. However, there would be some bias in the selected sample. For instance, private photos would not be shared under the Creative Commons license. Another possibility is that online users with knowledge of the Creative Commons license are likely to be more computer-literate than the general population. These biases are not straightforward to measure, and could have affected our analysis.

CONCLUSION

In this paper, we evaluated the security of authentication images against educated guess attacks. Our first user study showed that the original photos taken by users are vulnerable to individualized educated guess attacks if attackers have a good amount of information about the users. Moreover, even in the case when an attacker does not have any information about users, the attacker can make better guesses than random guesses based on the contextual information of the original photos. In contrast, when distorted photos are used as authentication images, attackers cannot make better guesses than random guesses even with a good amount of knowledge about target users. In our second user study, we showed that the distortion technique could mitigate the risk of the collective educated guess attacks using the biases in users' choices of authentication images.

These findings suggests that, while keeping their memorability as high as that of original photos [10], distortion technique makes *Use Your Illusion*, and potentially other recognition-based graphical authentication schemes, more secure against educated guess attacks.

ACKNOWLEDGEMENTS

This research was supported by CyLab at Carnegie Mellon under grants DAAD19-02-1-0389 and W911NF-09-1-0273 from the Army Research Office.

REFERENCES

1. A. Adams and M. Sasse. Users are not the enemy. *Communications of the ACM*, Jan 1999.
2. G. Blonder. United states patent, 1996. United States Patent 5559961.
3. G. H. Bower, M. B. Karlin, and A. Dueck. Comprehension and memory for pictures. *Memory and Cognition*, 2:216–220, 1975.
4. S. Brostoff and M. Sasse. Are passfaces more usable than passwords? a field trial investigation. In *Proc. of HCI 2000*, pages 405–424, 2000.
5. R. Dhamija and A. Perrig. Déjà vu: A user study, using images for authentication. In *Proc. of the 9th USENIX Security Symposium*, 2000.
6. W. Epstein and I. Rock. Perceptual set as an artifact of recency. *The American Journal of Psychology*, 73(2):214–228, 1960.
7. S. Gaw and E. Felten. Password management strategies for online accounts. In *Proc. of SOUPS*, 2006.
8. A. Goldstein and J. E. Chance. Visual recognition memory for complex configurations. *Perception and Psychophysics*, 9:237–241, 1970.
9. R. Haber. How we remember what we see. *Scientific American*, 222(5):104–112, May 1970.
10. E. Hayashi, R. Dhamija, N. Christin, and A. Perrig. Use your illusion: secure authentication usable anywhere. In *Proc. of SOUPS*, 2008.
11. I. Jermyn, A. Mayer, F. Monrose, M. K. Reiter, and A. D. Rubin. The design and analysis of graphical passwords. In *Proc. of the 8th USENIX Security Symposium*, 1999.
12. H. Kinjo and J. G. Snodgrass. Does the generation effect occur for pictures? *The American journal of psychology*, 6:156–163, 2000.
13. A. Kittur, E. Chi, and B. Suh. Crowdsourcing user studies with mechanical turk. In *Proc. of SIGCHI*, 2008.
14. F. Monrose, D. Davis, and M. Reiter. On user choice to graphical password schemes. In *Proc. of the 13th USENIX Security Symposium*, pages 151–164, 2004.
15. A. Rabkin. Personal knowledge questions for fallback authentication: security questions in the era of facebook. In *Proc. of SOUPS*, 2008.
16. J. B. S. Wiedenbeck, J. Waters and N. M. A. Brodskiy. Authentication using graphical passwords: Basic results. In *Human-Computer Interaction International*, 2005.
17. S. Schechter, A. J. B. Brush, and S. Egelman. It's no secret: Measuring the security and reliability of authentication via 'secret' questions. In *Proc. of the IEEE Symposium on Security and Privacy*, 2009.
18. R. Shepard. Recognition memory for words, sentences and pictures. *Journal of Verbal Learning and Verbal Behavior*, 113(1):95–121, 1967.
19. L. Standing. Learning 10,000 pictures. *The Quarterly Journal of Experimental Psychology*, 25(2):207–222, 1973.
20. L. Standing, J. Conezio, and R. N. Haber. Perception and memory for pictures: single trial learning of 2,500 visual stimuli. *Psychonomic Science*, 19(2):73–74, 1970.
21. J. Thorpe and P. van Oorschot. Graphical dictionaries and the memorable space of graphical passwords. In *Proc. of the USENIX Security Symposium*, 2004.
22. J. Thorpe and P. van Oorschot. Towards secure design choices for implementing graphical passwords. In *Proc. of the 20th Annual Computer Security Applications Conference*, 2004.
23. J. Thorpe and P. van Oorschot. Human-seeded attacks and exploiting hot-spots in graphical passwords. In *Proc. of USENIX Security Symposium*, 2007.
24. S. Wiedenbeck, J. Waters, J. C. Birget, A. Brodskiy, and N. Memon. Authentication using graphical passwords: effects of tolerance and image choice. In *Proc. of SOUPS*, 2005.

More than Skin Deep: Measuring Effects of the Underlying Model on Access-Control System Usability

Robert W. Reeder
Microsoft
Redmond, WA
roreeder@microsoft.com

Lujo Bauer
Carnegie Mellon University
Pittsburgh, PA
lbauer@cmu.edu

Lorrie Faith Cranor
Carnegie Mellon University
Pittsburgh, PA
lorrie@cmu.edu

Michael K. Reiter
University of North Carolina, Chapel Hill
Chapel Hill, NC
reiter@cs.unc.edu

Kami Vaniea
Carnegie Mellon University
Pittsburgh, PA
kami@cmu.edu

ABSTRACT
In access-control systems, policy rules *conflict* when they prescribe different decisions (ALLOW or DENY) for the same access. We present the results of a user study that demonstrates the significant impact of conflict-resolution method on policy-authoring usability. In our study of 54 participants, varying the conflict-resolution method yielded statistically significant differences in accuracy in five of the six tasks we tested, including differences in accuracy rates of up to 78%. Our results suggest that a conflict-resolution method favoring rules of smaller scope over rules of larger scope is more usable than the Microsoft Windows operating system's method of favoring deny rules over allow rules. Perhaps more importantly, our results demonstrate that even seemingly small changes to a system's semantics can fundamentally affect the system's usability in ways that are beyond the power of user interfaces to correct.

Author Keywords
access control, security, human factors

ACM Classification Keywords
H.1.2 User/Machine Systems: Human factors; D.4.6 Security and Protection: Access controls; H.5.2 User Interfaces: User-centered design

General Terms
Experimentation, Human Factors, Security

INTRODUCTION
Access-control policies must be specified correctly to ensure that authorized access is allowed while unauthorized access is denied. One obstacle to accurate access-control policies is human error; the people who author and maintain these policies—whom we call "authors" or "policy authors"—are prone to making specification errors that lead to incorrect policies [8, 16, 21].

Rule conflicts are one important area of difficulty for policy authors. Access-control policies consist of a set of rules that dictate the conditions under which users will be allowed access to resources. These rules may conflict with each other. For example, one rule may allow user u access to file f, while a second rule may deny group g, of which u is a member, access to f. Past work has shown that authors have difficulty detecting and resolving rule conflicts [16].

Usability improvements to security systems, such as access-control systems, can come from two sources: improvements to user interfaces and changes to underlying system models. User interfaces for policy-authoring systems have already received a fair amount of attention from researchers [3, 9, 14, 16, 18, 23], so we set out to improve usability in an access-control policy authoring system by varying an aspect of the underlying access-control model. Specifically, we studied the conflict-resolution method, which is the algorithm an access-control system uses for determining which rule, of a set of rules in conflict, will take precedence over others. We describe a conflict-resolution method that we expect will lead to fewer specification errors. Our method is aimed particularly at improving upon the Windows NTFS conflict-resolution method, since Windows is such a widely deployed operating system, and since it has been shown to be prone to policy-specification problems [16, 21].

We implemented our conflict-resolution method and the Windows method in a simulated Windows NTFS file system. For a policy-authoring user interface across both conflict-resolution method conditions, we used the *Expandable Grid*, which has been shown in past work to be more usable than the equivalent Windows interface [18]. An Expandable Grid (see Figure 2) is an interactive visualization that approximates Lampson's access-control matrix [15]. It displays *effective policy* resulting from an underlying set of rules and permits authors to modify effective policy directly.

We evaluated our conflict-resolution method by running a user study in which participants performed a variety of tasks using one of three different combinations of interface and conflict-resolution method: Grid with Windows conflict-resolution method, Grid with our conflict-resolution method, and Windows interface with Windows conflict-resolution method. Since two of our conditions use the same interface, we can compare the effect of just the conflict-resolution method on usability, with interface held constant. Our results show that the choice of conflict-resolution method can have a profound effect on usability. Whichever conflict-resolution method selects the intended rule for a given task by default (and thus requires no action from the policy author) is the more usable for that task. Moreover, we demonstrate that our conflict-resolution method is far more usable for tasks that require the author to take action — leading to gains of up to 78% in accuracy rates. (Of course, many considerations go into choosing an access-control model for a given usage context, so our method, while better for usability, may not be best for all contexts.)

Our results also illustrate a larger point about designing usable security systems. Designing security systems has traditionally been the work of expert security architects versed in technical arcana like access control and cryptography. The work of making a security system usable is typically pushed to usability experts after the work of the security architects is done, so that a suitable user interface can make the underlying security model usable by humans. Some researchers have suggested this "security-then-usability" approach is suboptimal; they suggest "user-centered security" in which usability is considered early on, as part of the process of designing the security model as well as the interface [1, 13, 24]. Following the logic of user-centered security, the ultimate usability of a system should be affected by both underlying model and interface. Our results provide empirical evidence that this proposition is true, at least for access-control models, and that leaving usability as an end-of-cycle, user-interface-only solution is misguided. In fact, security-model decisions made early in the development lifecycle *can* have a substantial impact on usability, even when those decisions at first appear to bear no relation to usability. We show that while the user interface is clearly an important part of a system's usability, underlying models also matter a great deal.

PROBLEM DESCRIPTION

Our objective is to find a conflict-resolution method that helps authors accurately set the policies they intend. Specifically, we want a conflict-resolution method that helps authors set policies accurately in the presence of rule conflicts.

We define an access-control policy to consist of rules, which are tuples of the form (*principal*, *resource*, *action*, *decision*). Principals may be users or groups containing users; in Windows, groups cannot contain other groups, but different groups may have overlapping memberships. Resources may be files or folders; resources are arranged in a strict hierarchy, so folders cannot have overlapping memberships. READ and WRITE are examples of actions. Decisions can be ALLOW or DENY. *Requests* to an access-control system are tuples of the form (*principal*, *resource*, *action*). A rule *matches* a request if the rule's principal, resource and action contain (or equal) the request's principal, resource, and action, respectively. Rules that match a request *conflict* if they prescribe different decisions for that request. When conflicting rules apply to a request, the conflict-resolution method comes into play to resolve the conflict. The resulting mappings of requests to decisions are known as *effective permissions*.

Conflict-resolution methods

To resolve rule conflicts, there must be a method for unambiguously choosing a decision. Most conflict-resolution methods in practice choose one of the rules in conflict to take precedence over the others. (Other methods are possible, however, such as "majority rules.") Note that it is sufficient to define these methods in terms of their behavior when exactly two rules are in conflict, because the access control system can handle cases of more than two rules in conflict by following a simple algorithm that does paired matches of each ALLOW rule against each DENY rule. This algorithm issues an ALLOW decision if any ALLOW rule wins its matches against every DENY rule, and otherwise issues a DENY decision.

While numerous methods for choosing rules to take precedence are possible, two are relevant to this paper:

- *Specificity precedence*: A rule that applies to a more specific entity (principal or resource) takes precedence over a rule that applies to a more general entity. For example, a rule that applies to a user takes precedence over a rule that applies to a group, or a rule that applies to a subfolder or file takes precedence over a rule that applies to the subfolder's or file's parent.
- *Deny precedence*: DENY rules take precedence over ALLOW rules.

These conflict-resolution methods may be used in combination. It is possible to use different conflict-resolution methods depending on whether conflicting rules differ in the principals they cover, the resources they cover, or both. It may also be necessary to resort to multiple conflict-resolution methods when one method fails to resolve a conflict. For example, when conflicting rules cover groups, but those groups are peers of each other (i.e., neither contains the other), specificity precedence cannot resolve the conflict.

Weaknesses of the Windows NTFS method

The Windows NTFS conflict-resolution method combines specificity and deny precedence. When conflicting rules differ only in their resources, specificity precedence is used. When conflicting rules differ only in their principals, deny precedence is used. When conflicting rules differ in both principals and resources, specificity precedence is used.

The Windows conflict-resolution method has two primary weaknesses we seek to improve upon. First, the use of deny precedence not only leads to specification errors, it also makes certain policy configurations impossible. Second, the Win-

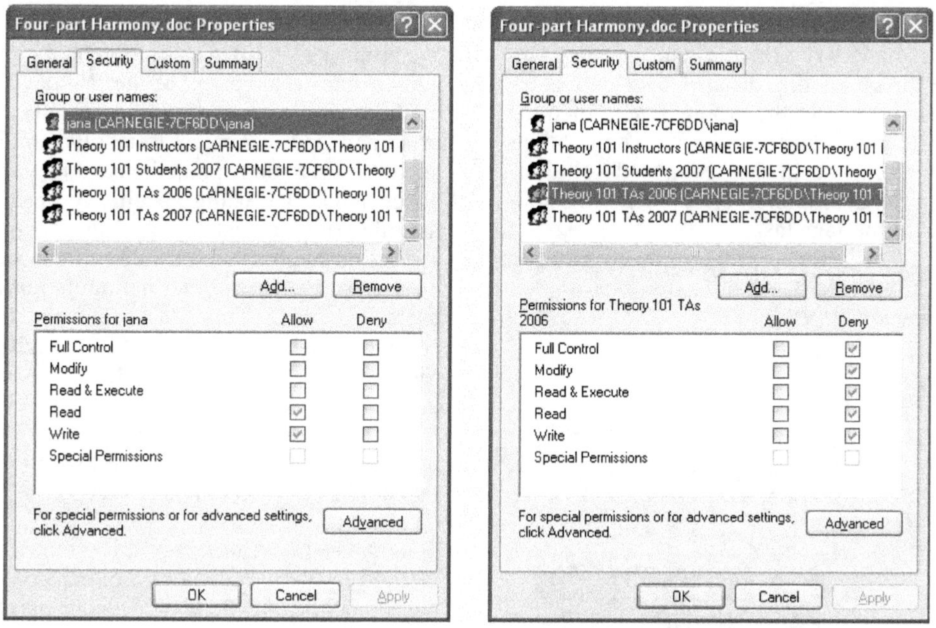

Figure 1. The Windows XP file permissions interface. The left-hand screenshot shows rules applying to Jana that appear to state that Jana is allowed to read and write the operative file, but the right-hand screenshot shows rules applying to a group of which Jana is a member that conflict with Jana's rules. If a policy author does not know that Jana is in the group and that the DENY rules take precedence, the author may have difficulty determining the effective permissions in the presence of a rule conflict.

dows behavior in the presence of a *two-dimensional conflict*, in which one rule is more specific in its principal and another rule is more specific in its resource, is likely to confuse some policy authors' expectations. We discuss each of these weaknesses below.

Deny precedence

By using deny precedence, the Windows conflict-resolution method leads to violations of *direct manipulation*, a user-interface design principle stating that interfaces should allow users to operate directly on objects or data of interest [20]. In policy-authoring interfaces, direct manipulation translates to allowing authors to change effective policy directly whenever possible.

The Jana task, one of the tasks we assigned to participants in our user study (see the "User study method" section), is a good example of where the Windows conflict-resolution method leads to violations of direct manipulation. The goal of the task is to allow Jana read and write access to a file. Jana is initially a member of two groups, one of which is allowed access to the file and the other of which is denied access to that file. Windows uses deny precedence to resolve the conflict, so Jana is effectively denied access to the file. However, many authors do not understand this; they may see only the rule allowing Jana access, and not realize that another rule conflicts with it. Even if they do notice the conflict, it is not easily resolved. There are two ways to grant Jana access: the DENY rule applying to the latter group can be removed, or Jana can be removed from the group. Direct manipulation is violated because the task cannot be completed by simply manipulating rules applying to Jana; the task requires making a change at the group level. Moreover, both potential solutions may lead to undesirable side effects. Removing the DENY rule may change policy for the other members of the group and for members added to the group in the future. Removing Jana from the group may be undesirable since it may affect Jana's permissions on other resources. The Windows conflict-resolution method provides no entirely satisfactory way to complete the Jana task.

Figure 1 shows the Windows file permissions user interface. The screenshot on the left shows the approach many participants in our study took to try to resolve the conflict; they set a rule applying specifically to Jana indicating that she can read and write the file. However, under the Windows conflict-resolution method, Jana is still denied access because of the group rule, shown in the right-hand screenshot of Figure 1, that denies access to the file. Because it is difficult to view effective permissions in the Windows interface (the display of effective permissions is buried three mouse clicks away), many authors assumed they had correctly completed the task when in fact they had not.

The Expandable Grid interface, shown in Figure 2, was designed to show effective permissions prominently and to allow the author to directly manipulate them. In the Expandable Grid screenshot shown in the figure, the cells at the intersection of "jana" and the "Four-part harmony.doc" file are red, indicating that Jana cannot read or write the file. To stay faithful to the principle of direct manipulation, an author should be able to click on the red squares to allow Jana to access the file. The author should see the squares turn green, which indicates an effective permission of ALLOW. Unfortunately, under the Windows conflict-resolution method, direct manipulation is still impossible, even in the Grid interface. Clicking on the red squares can set ALLOW rules that state that Jana can read and write the file, but the rules will not take effect until the conflicting group DENY rule is removed, or Jana is removed from the group. Even when the user clicks on them, the red squares stay red. The conflict-resolution method we propose in the "Proposed solution" section enables direct manipulation of effective permissions in the Grid interface for the Jana task.

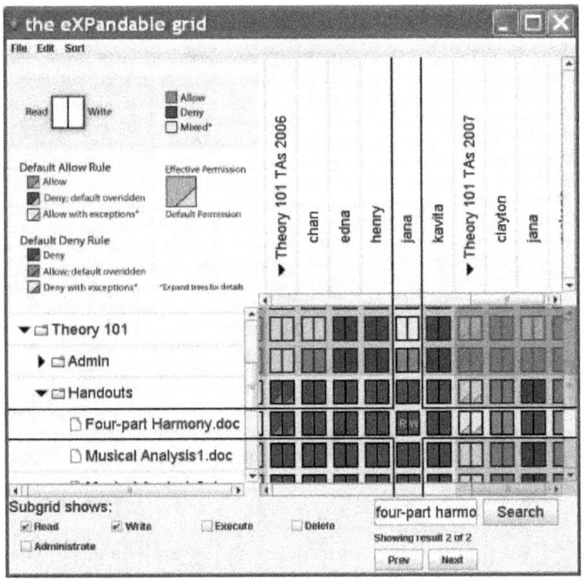

Figure 2. Our Expandable Grid interface for setting file permissions in Windows XP. The interface shows principals along the upper axis, resources along the left-hand axis, and the effective permissions applying to the principals and resources in the colored squares in the grid itself.

Two-dimensional conflicts

Besides violations of direct manipulation in the presence of rule conflicts, we seek to improve upon a second aspect of the Windows conflict-resolution method: behavior in the presence of a two-dimensional conflict. A *two-dimensional conflict* occurs when two rules are in conflict and one rule is more specific in the principal dimension (i.e., the dimension of users and groups) while the other is more specific in the resource dimension. For example, in the Lance task we describe in the "User study method" section, one rule denies Lance access to an Admin folder, but another rule allows a group he is in access to the gradebook.xls file contained in the Admin folder. Since neither rule is strictly more specific than the other, specificity precedence cannot resolve this conflict. Windows resolves such conflicts by favoring the resource dimension over the principal dimension, so the rule that is more specific in the resource dimension will take precedence. Since Windows uses deny precedence to resolve other conflicts, some authors may expect deny precedence to also resolve two-dimensional conflicts, so this aspect of the Windows conflict-resolution method is likely to be inconsistent with some authors' expectations. Moreover, some authors may expect the principal dimension to be favored, rather than the resource dimension.

PROPOSED SOLUTION

We propose a conflict-resolution method that we believe will address the weaknesses of the Windows conflict-resolution method. We propose to use specificity precedence, in both principals and resources, to resolve conflicts when possible and to resort to deny precedence only when specificity precedence fails. By using specificity precedence, we address the rule-conflict weakness in Windows in which the conflict-resolution method violates direct manipulation. Specificity ensures support for direct manipulation for rules that cover users and files. Thus, tasks like the Jana task are easily completed using the Grid with our specificity-based conflict-resolution method; clicking Jana's red squares turns them green. The rule-conflict weakness in Windows where either a group access rule has to be changed or Jana has to be removed from the group is solved by allowing a specific rule that applies to Jana to take effect.

To address the weakness of the Windows conflict-resolution method in the case of a two-dimensional conflict, our proposed method uses deny precedence for two-dimensional conflicts. Since there is no natural way to resolve such conflicts using specificity, we ensure fail safety by using deny precedence. We believe the Windows use of specificity in the resource dimension is likely to be confusing to policy authors, who may expect that deny precedence would apply in these situations. Our choice of deny precedence may or may not be confusing, but at least it is safe and, in any case, it is easily overridden by creating a rule that is equally or more specific in both resources and principals than the rules in conflict. Note that while we resort to deny precedence in two-dimensional conflicts, the fact that our method uses specificity precedence first means that overriding the two-dimensional conflict with a more specific rule is easy.

Table 1 shows the differences between our specificity-based conflict-resolution method and the Windows method. It lays out the entire space of rule conflicts with respect to the structural relations between principals and resources of the rules in conflict. In a conflict, there will be an ALLOW rule in conflict with a DENY rule. The static differences between our method and the Windows method can be seen in two of the table cells: first, where the ALLOW rule's principal is contained by (and thus is more specific than) the DENY rule's principal, but the two rules' resources are the same; second, where the ALLOW rule's principal contains the DENY rule's principal, but the ALLOW rule's resource is contained by the DENY rule's resource. However, the most significant difference between the two methods is in some of the conflicts where both methods give a DENY decision, but the author intends an ALLOW decision. Our specificity method makes these cases easier to fix than does the Windows method.

From a usability perspective, a good conflict-resolution method is one that gives the decision the author intends, or, if it cannot give the intended decision by default, makes it easy to change the policy to get the right decision. No method can always make the intended decision by default, since it cannot know the author's intention. Thus, it is on the latter point—the ease of changing the policy—that we expect our

Table 1. Table showing which rule, of an ALLOW rule and a DENY rule in conflict, will take precedence for our specificity-based conflict resolution method (S) and the Windows method (W). The table shows the relevant cases defined by the rules' principals and resources. Each cell shows which rule takes precedence and the conflict-resolution method in play: specificity in the *resources*, specificity in the *principals*, specificity in *both* resources and principals, or *deny* precedence. In the case where both rules' resources and principals are the same, there will be *no conflict*, since the more recently set rule will have overwritten the other.

		ALLOW rule's principal is ____ DENY rule's principal			
		Less specific than	Peer of	Same as	More specific than
ALLOW rule's resource is ____ DENY rule's resource	Less specific than	DENY (both)	DENY (resources)	DENY (resources)	S:DENY (deny) W:DENY (resources)
	Same as	S:DENY (principals) W:DENY (deny)	DENY (deny)	no conflict	S:ALLOW (principals) W:DENY (deny)
	More specific than	S:DENY (deny) W:ALLOW (resources)	ALLOW (resources)	ALLOW (resources)	ALLOW (both)

method to have the greatest usability gains over the Windows method. To resolve a conflict for which the conflict-resolution method is not already giving the intended decision by default, an author must (1) notice the problem; and (2) fix it. The Expandable Grid, by virtue of showing effective permissions directly, makes noticing the problem much easier than does the Windows interface, and our specificity conflict-resolution method makes fixing the problem easier by allowing user-level exceptions to group rules, instead of requiring that a user be removed from a group or requiring an entire group's permissions to change. In the Jana task, for example, both methods will result in a DENY decision, but specificity allows an author to specify an exception for Jana to the group-level DENY decision, while Windows simply does not allow such an exception, and instead forces the author to make a group-level policy change.

USER STUDY METHOD

We have argued that our conflict-resolution method should be more usable than the Windows method for tasks that require action from the policy author because our method enables direct manipulation in the Grid interface. To test this argument empirically, we ran a laboratory user study to measure the effects of conflict-resolution method on policy-authoring usability, as measured by task-completion accuracy. Our study had 54 participants, who each performed 12 policy-authoring tasks in one of three experimental conditions. Experimental conditions were combinations of interface and conflict-resolution method. We used a between-participants design, so 18 participants were in each of the three conditions. We measured accuracy for each task. The three conditions we compared were:

- the Grid interface with our specificity-based conflict resolution method, a combination henceforth called *GS*;
- the Grid interface with Windows conflict-resolution method, a combination henceforth called *GW*; and
- the Windows interface with the Windows conflict-resolution method, a combination henceforth called *WW*.

The WW condition served as the control in our study; it was the condition on which we hoped to improve. The GS condition is our best effort at improving upon WW, because GS has both the visual presentation advantages of the Expandable Grid and the expected advantages of our conflict-resolution method. The GW interface serves to help us separate the effects of the Grid as a presentation technique from the effects of the conflict-resolution method. When we observe differences between the GW and WW conditions, we attribute them to the Grid presentation (i.e., the user interface), and when we observe differences between the GW and GS conditions, we attribute them to the conflict-resolution method (i.e., the underlying model). Differences between the GS and WW conditions are the cumulative effect of the Grid presentation and the specificity-based conflict-resolution method. (Note that, while results from a fourth combination of the Windows interface with the specificity conflict-resolution method would have been enlightening, it was infeasible to implement such a combination for this study.)

We recruited 54 undergraduate and graduate students from technical disciplines (science, engineering, or mathematics) to participate in the study. Eighteen were female. Participants were all daily computer users, but had never served as system administrators. As in prior work evaluating the Expandable Grid interface [18], our participant pool was consistent with a target demographic of novice and occasional policy authors. The policy authoring population largely consists of information technology professionals with some technical education who have so many job responsibilities that access-control is an occasional activity. Other populations, like managers and staff, author policy but were out of scope for this study.

Task design

Of the 12 tasks in which each subject participated, six were designed to test the advantages and disadvantages of each of the two conflict-resolution methods, as well as the overall usability of each interface/conflict-resolution-method combination. We discuss only these six tasks here. (The other six tasks are fully reported elsewhere [17].) All tasks were based on a teaching assistant (TA) scenario, in which the participant is put in the role of a TA maintaining the file server for a hypothetical music department. The hypothetical file server contained roughly 500 principals and 500 resources. Each task is defined by its task statement (i.e., the text we presented to participants in the study) and its initial configuration, including existing access rules, group memberships, and file locations. Task statements asked participants to make changes to the initial configuration.

The tasks were designed in pairs: the Charles/Kent pair, the Lance/Adria pair, and the Jana/Pablo pair. For the Charles/Kent and Lance/Adria pairs, the tasks are structured similarly except that goals are inverted. This way, each pair of tasks has a task that favors our conflict-resolution method and a task that favors the Windows conflict-resolution method. The Jana and Pablo tasks share essentially the same structure, though they differ superficially in the specific users and files involved. We used two tasks with the same structure because this structure best illustrates the advantage of specificity precedence, and we wanted to show that any usability differences between conflict-resolution methods were due to the underlying task structure and not the superficial aspects of the task. Also, pairing the Jana and Pablo tasks gave us a fair balance of tasks: two tasks in which our conflict-resolution method completes the task goal by default (Charles and Lance), two tasks in which the Windows method completes the task goal by default (Kent and Adria), and two tasks in which neither method completes the goal by default and the author has to take action (Jana and Pablo).

The six tasks can be classified by their initial configuration. Each task's initial configuration included a rule conflict that fit into one of the rule-conflict structures shown in Table 1. The tasks only cover the three table cells corresponding to interesting rule conflict structures, i.e., those for which the two conflict-resolution methods yield different decisions or for which they lend themselves to different means of resolving the conflict. Specifically, the Charles and Kent tasks present cases where the ALLOW rule's principal is more specific than the DENY rule's principal and the resources are the same. The Lance and Adria tasks present 2-dimensional conflicts, where the DENY rule's principal is more specific, but the ALLOW rule's resource is more specific. The Jana and Pablo tasks present cases where the principals are peers of each other and the resources are the same. We describe each task pair in more detail below.

Charles/Kent

We designed the Charles task to show the advantage a specificity conflict-resolution method has over the Windows method when ALLOW rule exceptions to a group DENY rule are desired. The Charles task involves adding a user to a group; the user has several ALLOW permissions on some files, the group has DENY permissions on those files, and the goal is to keep the user's ALLOW permissions. The Charles task statement presented to participants was:

> Charles has just graduated, but is going to come back to sing in the choir with his friends.
>
> Add **Charles** to the **Alumni** group, but make sure he can still **read** the same files in the **Choir 1\Lyrics** folder that his good friend Carl can read.

In the initial configuration, there are rules stating that Charles is allowed READ access to four files in the Choir 1\Lyrics folder. These are the same files that Carl can read, so in the final state, we want Charles to be allowed READ access to the four files. There are rules stating that the Alumni group is denied READ access to the same files. When Charles is moved into the Alumni group, the group's DENY rules will apply to him, and under the Windows deny precedence, he will be denied access to the files. However, under specificity precedence, his rules are more specific than the group access rules, so he will still be allowed to read the files. Thus, specificity precedence makes this task easier, and we expected participants in the GS condition to perform better than GW and WW in the Charles task.

We designed the Kent task to show a drawback our specificity-based conflict-resolution method has when ALLOW exceptions to a group DENY rule are not desired. The Kent task was structured similarly to the Charles task, but the goal was inverted to give the advantage to the Windows conflict resolution method.

The Kent task statement presented to participants was:

> Kent was a terrible TA for Choir 1 so the instructor demoted him to the level of student. While Kent previously had permissions to read and write the attendance and gradebook files, as a student he should no longer have access to that information.
>
> Remove **Kent** from **Choir 1 TAs 2008** and add him to **Choir 1 Students 2008**. For files in the **Classes\Choir 1\Admin** folder, make sure he only has the same permissions as the other Choir 1 students.

As in the Charles task, Kent inherits a DENY permission from a group to which he is moved. This time, however, Kent is to keep the DENY permission, so we expect participants in the GW and WW conditions to perform better on the Kent task.

Lance/Adria

We designed the Lance task to test the behavior of our conflict-resolution method in the presence of a two-dimensional conflict when a DENY decision is desired. The Lance task introduces a two-dimensional conflict, in which there are conflicts in both the principals and resources. The Lance task statement presented to participants was:

> Lance was hired by the New York Philharmonic and can no longer serve as Head TA this year.
>
> Remove **Lance** from the group **Head TAs 2008**, but make sure you don't remove him from **Head TAs 2007**. Then make sure he is not allowed to access any files in the **Music 101\Admin** folder.

In the initial configuration, there is a rule stating that Lance is denied READ access to the Music 101\Admin folder, and there are rules stating that the Head TAs 2007 group is allowed READ access to the Music 101\Admin\gradebook.xls file, but that the Head TAs 2008 group is denied READ access to the file. When Lance is removed from Head TAs 2008, a two-dimensional conflict is revealed, since the rule applying to Lance on the Admin folder is more specific in its principal, but the rule applying to Head TAs 2007 on the gradebook.xls file is more specific in its resource. In the Windows conflict-resolution method, the rule that is more specific in the resource takes precedence, so Lance will be allowed to read the gradebook.xls file, but in the specificity-based conflict-resolution method, the DENY rule takes precedence, so Lance will not be allowed to read the gradebook.xls file. Since the task calls for Lance not to be allowed to access any files in the Admin folder, our conflict-resolution method requires less work to complete the task correctly, and we expected participants in the GS condition to perform best.

We designed the Adria task to test the behavior of our conflict-resolution method in the presence of a two-dimensional conflict when an ALLOW decision is desired. Just as the Kent task is similar to the Charles task with the inverse goal, the Adria task is similar to the Lance task with the inverse goal.

The Adria task statement presented to participants was:

> Adria, an Opera Instructor, was not getting along with the other instructor and left the class. You need to remove her from the Opera Instructors group. She is still a Music 101 instructor, though, and the Music 101 instructors need access to the Music 101 Lecture Notes.
>
> Remove **Adria** from the **Opera Instructors** group. Make sure she has the same permissions on the files in the **Music 101\Lecture Notes** folder as the other Music 101 instructors.

As in the Lance task, when Adria is removed from a group, a two-dimensional conflict involving another group is revealed. However, the goal is inverted in the Adria task, so that now, we expect the advantage to lie with the GW and WW conditions.

Jana/Pablo

The Jana task involves a rule conflict at the group level that must be resolved to give Jana access to a file. The Jana task statement presented to participants was:

> Jana, a Theory 101 TA, complained that when she tried to change the Four-part Harmony handout to update the assignment, she was denied access.
>
> Set permissions so that **Jana** can **read and write** the **Four-part Harmony.doc** file in the Theory 101\Handouts folder.

We expect specificity precedence to enable authors to perform better for the Jana task compared to deny precedence. Thus, we expected participants in the GS condition to outperform participants in the GW and WW conditions for the Jana task.

The Pablo task was structured similarly to the Jana task, and we expected better performance in the GS condition compared to the GW and WW conditions. The Pablo task statement presented to participants was:

> Pablo, a student in Music 101, tried to download the homework file, assignment4.pdf, but couldn't.
>
> Set permissions so that **Pablo** can **read** the file **assignment4.pdf** in the **Music 101\Handouts** folder. Make sure you don't change any other students' permissions. (Hint: If you need to, you can add Pablo to a new group or remove Pablo from a group he's already in.)

As previously discussed, the Pablo task was superficially different from Jana in the names and numbers of principals and resources involved in the task, but structurally the same.

Procedure

At the start of each study session, participants filled out a demographic survey so that we could ensure they were students in technical disciplines. Following the survey, our experimenter read instructions explaining our teaching-assistant scenario to participants. After reading these instructions, our experimenter read interface training materials. For each interface, training covered how to perform the following operations: viewing files and folders; moving a file; viewing group memberships; adding a user to a group; removing a user from a group; creating a new group; checking an access rule; checking effective permissions; creating an access rule; and searching for a file or principal. During training, the experimenter also explained that effective permissions may differ from access rules because of the way rules combine, but did not explain the precise workings of the conflict-resolution methods. After these operations had been explained to participants, the experimenter walked them through a training task. The training task gave participants practice with some of the basic operations covered during training, but did not involve a rule conflict. Participants received the same training task in all three experimental conditions. Training took about 10 minutes.

Participants then began completing tasks. Before each task, the experimenter brought up the interface in a preconfigured state tailored to each task. Task statements were then presented to participants in a Web browser on screen. Participants indicated they were done with each task by clicking a button in the Web browser. Participants were asked to think aloud while they worked on the tasks. Task order was counterbalanced across participants using a pseudo-random Latin square design to guard against ordering and sequence effects.

RESULTS

Our results are in the form of accuracy rates for each condition and task. While we also measured times-to-task-completion, we do not present them in detail due to space constraints. Time-to-task-completion data resulted in few statistically significant differences between conditions and the results that were significant corroborate the accuracy results, so the data show that the accuracy results we present here were not merely due to a time-accuracy tradeoff. Complete time-to-task-completion data can be found elsewhere [17].

Accuracy rates represent the proportion of participants in each condition who correctly completed the task. We scored a task as correct if the participant's final effective permissions matched the task goals and did not introduce any extraneous changes not called for by the task statement or otherwise required to complete the task. Tasks in which the

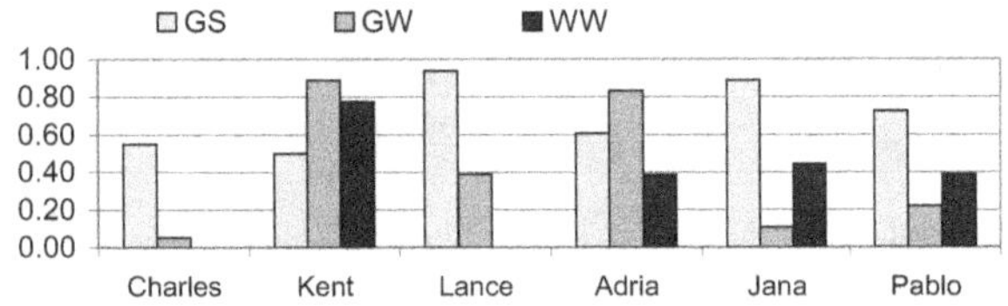

Figure 3. Accuracy results, showing proportion of participants correctly completing each task with GS, GW, and WW interfaces.

goals of the task were not met or in which the goals were met but extraneous changes were introduced were scored as incorrect. Accuracy results can be seen in Figure 3.

We conducted post-hoc task-by-task tests. Each of our tasks tested a specific hypothesis about the effects the conflict-resolution methods would have on usability, as measured by accuracy. We tested hypotheses regarding accuracy rates by using one-sided Fisher's exact tests with the null hypothesis that the difference in accuracy rates was zero. We used one-sided tests since our hypotheses are directional (i.e., we expect better performance from one condition than another). Results of all hypothesis tests of accuracy rates can be seen in Table 2.

In the Charles, Kent, Lance, and Adria tasks, one of the two conflict-resolution methods yielded the goal decision by default, so had an advantage over the other conflict-resolution method in helping participants complete tasks correctly. Thus, for those four tasks, either our conflict-resolution method or the Windows method had a natural advantage, and we expected the conditions using the advantaged conflict-resolution method in each task to lead to better performance. For the Charles and Lance tasks, in which our specificity-based conflict-resolution method had the advantage, the accuracy rate for the GS condition was statistically significantly higher than that for the GW and WW conditions, as expected. For the Kent task, in which the Windows conflict-resolution method had the advantage, the accuracy rate for the GS condition was statistically significantly lower than that for the GW condition, as expected, but the result for GS compared to WW was not statistically significant. For the Adria task, in which the Windows method had the advantage, there was no statistically significant difference between the GS condition and the GW and WW conditions. This somewhat surprising result in favor of GS is likely due to the combination of the Grid's presentation aspects, which allow authors to easily notice the discrepancy between the effective policy and their goal policy, and the ease of adding a specific rule applying to Adria to overcome the conflict with specificity precedence.

For the Jana and Pablo tasks, both conflict-resolution methods yield a DENY decision in the presence of the conflict, so we did not expect either to have an advantage by default. However, we expected the specificity-based method to make it easy to overcome the conflict by setting a specific rule allowing Jana or Pablo to access the relevant files. As we have explained, the Windows method makes it cumbersome to overcome the conflict at the group level. As expected, the GS condition led to better performance over both the GW and WW conditions in both the Jana and Pablo tasks.

In summary, we observed GS to be statistically significantly better than both GW and WW in the four tasks in which GS had the default advantage or in which there was no default advantage. In the two tasks where the default advantage went the other way, GS was statistically significantly worse compared to GW in the Kent task, and was behind GW and WW in both tasks, though not significantly so. The comparisons between GS and GW illustrate the substantial usability gains that can be had just from our conflict-resolution method; even if the Charles/Kent and Lance/Adria accuracy rates are viewed as a wash, GS gave a gain of 78% in accuracy rate compared to GW for Jana and 50% for Pablo.

DISCUSSION

We discuss three aspects of our results: comparison of the two conflict-resolution methods, broader implications for designing usable security systems, and limitations of our study.

Comparing conflict-resolution methods

Our results show that the policy conflict-resolution method underlying a file-permissions interface has a significant effect on task-completion accuracy. The precise effect of the conflict-resolution method depends on what the task goals are. If task goals are aligned with a conflict-resolution method, such that the method yields the desired effective policy by default, accuracy rates are likely to be higher than if the method requires an author to take additional action to change the decision. In the Charles, Kent, and Lance tasks, we saw that the method that yielded the correct effective policy by default led to the highest accuracy rates.

No conflict-resolution method can always yield the desired effective permissions, as we designed our inverse task pairs (Charles/Kent, Lance/Adria) to show. However, we have argued that our specificity-based conflict-resolution method is superior to the Windows deny-based method because, even in a situation where specificity is not yielding the desired effective permission, it is easy to change the effective permission with a specific rule. Contrast this to the Windows deny-precedence method, which forces an author in some conflict situations to remove a user from a group or change rules applying to the whole group. The Adria task shows a situation in which, although our specificity-based conflict-resolution method does not yield the desired decision by default, getting the task right is a simple matter of adding a rule more specific than those in conflict. The Pablo and Jana tasks further illustrate the advantage that a specificity-based conflict-resolution method has over a deny-based method in overcoming rule conflicts. Thus, our argument that specificity is more usable when the author is required to take action to fix a rule conflict is borne out by our empirical results.

While our empirical results are based on holding only one user interface, the Expandable Grid, constant across conditions, we note that a different interface could not have negated the difference in usability between the two conflict-resolution methods. No user interface can overcome the advantage of making the right decision by default; doing so would require making it easier for the author to do something than to do nothing. And no user interface can make it

Table 2. Summary of post-hoc statistical tests for significant differences in accuracy rate for Grid with our specificity-based conflict-resolution method (a_{GS}), Grid with Windows conflict-resolution method (a_{GW}), and Windows (a_{WW}). For each task, the table shows accuracy rates for the three interfaces, hypotheses tested, and p-values from one-sided Fisher's exact tests; p-values at or below the $\alpha = 0.05$ rejection threshold are shaded and highlighted in bold, indicating significant tests.

Task	a_{GS}	a_{GW}	a_{WW}	GS vs. GW hypothesis	p-value	GS vs. WW hypothesis	p-value
Charles	0.56	0.06	0.00	$a_{GS} > a_{GW}$	**0.001**	$a_{GS} > a_{WW}$	**< 0.001**
Kent	0.50	0.88	0.78	$a_{GS} < a_{GW}$	**0.014**	$a_{GS} < a_{WW}$	0.082
Lance	0.94	0.39	0.00	$a_{GS} > a_{GW}$	**< 0.001**	$a_{GS} > a_{WW}$	**< 0.001**
Adria	0.61	0.83	0.39	$a_{GS} < a_{GW}$	0.13	$a_{GS} < a_{WW}$	0.95
Jana	0.89	0.11	0.44	$a_{GS} > a_{GW}$	**< 0.001**	$a_{GS} > a_{WW}$	**0.006**
Pablo	0.72	0.22	0.39	$a_{GS} > a_{GW}$	**0.003**	$a_{GS} > a_{WW}$	**0.046**

possible to do the Jana and Pablo tasks under the Windows semantics without making a group-level change.

One concern with adopting a specificity-based conflict-resolution method is that it introduces a risk that, when setting a group-level DENY rule, the DENY rule will not apply to members of the group who already have ALLOW rules applying to them. Specifically, in a situation like the one in the Kent task, where a group-level DENY rule is meant to override any user-level ALLOW rule exceptions, specificity does not give the desired decision by default. If a policy author fails to notice the undesired ALLOW exceptions to the DENY rule, unauthorized access may be allowed. However, the Expandable Grid interface can help mitigate this issue by making it much easier for authors to see anomalies in their policies [18]. Thus, if using such an interface, the usability gains from specificity are likely worth this slight security risk for many applications. Moreover, an unusable policy model may itself be a security risk, as humans frustrated that they are unable to implement the policies they want may set policies that are more liberal than necessary [2], or circumvent access-control systems altogether [11].

Implications for designing security systems

The substantial differences in accuracy rates due to relatively small changes to the access-control model in our study are striking. Differences in accuracy rates between the GS and GW conditions were 50%, 38%, 55%, 22%, 78%, and 50% for our six tasks. In five of six cases, these differences were statistically significant. Since we held interface constant between GS and GW and only varied conflict-resolution method, these substantial differences are due only to changes in the underlying model. In real-world security system design, these kinds of details of underlying models are usually determined by security experts, who may not consider their effects on usability. Our results suggest they should, since the effects can be large, and since, as we have just pointed out, an unusable system that users circumvent is itself a security risk. Other researchers have called for "user-centered security," in which usability is a prime consideration during the design of underlying models and in which security and usability experts work side-by-side [1, 13, 24]. Our results lend empirical evidence to back up these calls for user-centered security.

Limitations

Some limitations of our study are worth noting. Our results tell us that the success of any conflict-resolution method depends largely on the requirements of the particular tasks that an author performs. Since we do not have data on the frequency with which particular tasks are performed, we cannot say conclusively that a specificity-based conflict-resolution method is always superior to deny precedence. However, our results showed that over the six tasks in our balanced set (balanced to be fair in alternating the advantage they gave to the two conflict-resolution methods) the specificity-based method was superior. We attribute its superior performance largely to the ease with which it enables authors to fix situations in which its default behavior is not what is desired.

Our study created scenarios that participants could complete within a few minutes in our lab. We were not able to recreate certain real-life scenarios in which policy-authoring may happen periodically over long periods of time. Particularly difficult to simulate in the lab are scenarios in which an author must remember the intention behind a setting that may have been made weeks or months before.

RELATED WORK

There is an extensive body of work describing formal access-control models and languages. The authors of these models and languages necessarily describe a semantics and usually address conflict resolution. The conflict-resolution methods we have discussed here have been covered in the access-control literature (e.g., [5, 7, 10]), but rarely from a usability perspective. Most of these works, as well as others in the general access-control model literature, are concerned with describing the formal aspects of their models and proving theoretical properties about them. A few of these works address ease of policy-authoring under their semantics, but none that we are aware of actually ran user studies to evaluate their semantics empirically as we have.

Others have noted that the underlying model may affect usability [22]. However, past work in policy-authoring usability has mostly focused on interface design or policy visualization [3, 4, 9, 14, 18, 19], rather than how the underlying access-control model (of which the conflict-resolution method is a part) could be best designed for usability. Papers by Fisler and Krishnamurthi [6] and by Kapadia et al. [12]

are exceptions that do address usability through underlying models. Fisler and Krishnamurthi introduce an access control model that captures information about the broader organizational context in which an access-control policy exists and uses this information to sanity check the actual policy itself. Kapadia et al. discuss a system that enables users to debug denied access errors.

CONCLUSION

We have argued that significant usability improvements can be had from an access-control conflict-resolution method based on specificity precedence compared to a method based on deny precedence. We implemented a specificity-based conflict-resolution method in a simulated Windows file system and ran the Expandable Grid interface on top of it. Our user study showed that the specificity-based method provides substantial usability gains for tasks that require a policy author to make changes to a default decision issued by the conflict-resolution method. That is, when the conflict-resolution method gets the decision wrong, specificity-precedence helps the author fix it.

More generally, our results illustrate the impact that underlying system models can have on usability. Our results strengthen the argument for user-centered security, in which usability is a prime consideration during the formative stages of security system design, and in which security and usability experts work side-by-side to ensure a security system that will work as intended when humans interact with it.

ACKNOWLEDGMENTS

This work was supported in part by NSF grants CNS-0756998 and CNS-0627513, and by CyLab at Carnegie Mellon under grants DAAD19-02-1-0389 and W911NF-09-1-0273 from the Army Research Office.

REFERENCES

1. A. Adams and M. A. Sasse. Users are not the enemy. *Communications of the ACM*, 42(12):41–46, December 1999.
2. L. Bauer, L. F. Cranor, R. W. Reeder, M. K. Reiter, and K. Vaniea. A user study of policy creation in a flexible access-control system. *ACM SIGCHI Conference on Human Factors in Computing Systems*, pages 543–552, April 2008.
3. S. Brostoff, M. A. Sasse, D. Chadwick, J. Cunningham, U. Mbanaso, and S. Otenko. 'R-What?' Development of a role-based access control policy-writing tool for e-Scientists. *Software Practice & Experience*, 35(9):835–856, June 2005.
4. X. Cao and L. Iverson. Intentional access management: Making access control usable for end-users. *2nd Symposium on Usable Privacy and Security*, pages 20–31, 2006.
5. D. J. Dougherty, K. Fisler, and S. Krishnamurthi. Specifying and reasoning about dynamic access-control policies. *3rd International Joint Conference on Automated Reasoning*, Lecture Notes in Computer Science, Vol. 4130, pages 632–646, August 2006.
6. K. Fisler and S. Krishnamurthi. A model of triangulating environments for policy authoring. *15th ACM Symp. on Access Control Models and Technologies*, p. 3–12, June 2010.
7. I. Goldberg, D. Wagner, R. Thomas, and E. A. Brewer. A secure environment for untrusted helper applications: Confining the wily hacker. *6th USENIX Security Symposium*, July 1996.
8. N. S. Good and A. Krekelberg. Usability and privacy: a study of Kazaa P2P file-sharing. *ACM SIGCHI Conf. on Human Factors in Computing Systems*, pages 137–144, April 2003.
9. P. Inglesant, M. A. Sasse, D. Chadwick, and L. L. Shi. Expressions of expertness: The virtuous circle of natural language for access control policy specification. *2008 Symposium on Usable Privacy and Security*, July 2008.
10. S. Jajodia, P. Samarati, V. S. Subrahmanian, and E. Bertino. A unified framework for enforcing multiple access control policies. *1997 ACM SIGMOD International Conference on Management of Data*, pages 474–485, 1997.
11. M. Johnson, S. M. Bellovin, R. W. Reeder, and S. E. Schechter. Laissez-faire file sharing: Access control designed for individuals at the endpoints. *2009 New Security Paradigms Workshop*, pages 1–10, 2009.
12. A. Kapadia, G. Sampemane, and R. H. Campbell. KNOW why your access was denied: Regulating feedback for usable security. *11th ACM Conference on Computer and Communications Security*, pages 52–61, 2004.
13. C.-M. Karat, C. Brodie, and J. Karat. Usability design and evaluation for privacy and security solutions. In L. F. Cranor and S. Garfinkel, editors, *Security and Usability*, chapter 4, pages 47–74. O'Reilly, Sebastopol, CA, 2005.
14. C.-M. Karat, J. Karat, C. Brodie, and J. Feng. Evaluating interfaces for privacy policy rule authoring. *ACM SIGCHI Conference on Human Factors in Computing Systems*, pages 83–92, 2006.
15. B. W. Lampson. Protection. *Operating Systems Review*, 8(1):18–24, January 1974.
16. R. A. Maxion and R. W. Reeder. Improving user-interface dependability through mitigation of human error. *International Journal of Human-Computer Studies*, 63(1-2):25–50, July 2005.
17. R. W. Reeder. *Expandable Grids: A user interface visualization technique and a policy semantics to support fast, accurate security and privacy policy authoring*. PhD thesis, Computer Science Department, Carnegie Mellon University, Pittsburgh, PA, May 2008. Available as technical report number CMU-CS-08-143.
18. R. W. Reeder, L. Bauer, L. F. Cranor, M. K. Reiter, K. Bacon, K. How, and H. Strong. Expandable grids for visualizing and authoring computer security policies. *ACM SIGCHI Conference on Human Factors in Computing Systems*, pages 1473–1482, April 2008.
19. J. Rode, C. Johansson, P. DiGioia, R. S. Filho, K. Nies, D. H. Nguyen, J. Ren, P. Dourish, and D. Redmiles. Seeing further: Extending visualization as a basis for usable security. *2nd Symp. on Usable Privacy and Security*, pages 145–155, 2006.
20. B. Shneiderman. Direct manipulation: A step beyond programming languages. *Computer*, 16(8):57–69, August 1983.
21. U.S. Senate Sergeant at Arms. Report on the investigation into improper access to the Senate Judiciary Committees computer system. Available at http://judiciary.senate.gov/testimony.cfm?id=1085&wit_id=2514, March 2004.
22. T. Whalen, D. Smetters, and E. F. Churchill. User experiences with sharing and access control. *Conference on Human Factors in Computing Systems Extended Abstracts*, pages 1517–1522, April 2006.
23. M. E. Zurko, R. Simon, and T. Sanfilippo. A user-centered, modular authorization service built on an RBAC foundation. *1999 IEEE Symposium on Security and Privacy*, pages 57–71, May 1999.
24. M. E. Zurko and R. T. Simon. User-centered security. *Workshop on New Security Paradigms*, pages 27–33, Lake Arrowhead, CA, September 1996. Available at http://www.memesoft.com/adage/.

Does Domain Highlighting Help People Identify Phishing Sites?

Eric Lin, Saul Greenberg, Eileah Trotter, David Ma and John Aycock
Department of Computer Science
University of Calgary, Calgary, Alberta, Canada T2N 1N4
{linyc, saul.greenberg, davma, aycock}@ucalgary.ca, eileaht@gmail.com

ABSTRACT

Phishers are fraudsters that mimic legitimate websites to steal user's credential information and exploit that information for identity theft and other criminal activities. Various anti-phishing techniques attempt to mitigate such attacks. *Domain highlighting* is one such approach recently incorporated by several popular web browsers. The idea is simple: the domain name of an address is highlighted in the address bar, so that users can inspect it to determine a web site's legitimacy. Our research asks a basic question: how well does domain highlighting work? To answer this, we showed 22 participants 16 web pages typical of those targeted for phishing attacks, where participants had to determine the page's legitimacy. In the first round, they judged the page's legitimacy by whatever means they chose. In the second round, they were directed specifically to look at the address bar. We found that participants fell into 3 types in terms of how they determined the legitimacy of a web page; while domain highlighting was somewhat effective for one user type, it was much less effective for others. We conclude that domain highlighting, while providing some benefit, cannot be relied upon as the sole method to prevent phishing attacks.

Author Keywords

Phishing, domain highlighting, usable security.

ACM Classification Keywords

H5.2. Information interfaces and presentation (e.g., HCI): User Interfaces. K.6.5 Security and protection.

General Terms. Security, Human Factors, Design.

INTRODUCTION

Phishing attacks are a method whereby fraudsters try to steal user's credentials – user names, passwords, bank accounts, credit card numbers, and so on – via technical means and by social engineering [6]. Typical phishing attacks involve a message (e.g., email) sent to a user, purporting to be from a legitimate entity like a bank; the message would try to convince the user to follow a URL to the phisher's web site. At this web site, the phisher visually mimics the real web site, and will save and later exploit the sensitive information sent to that fake web site by the user/victim.

CHI 2011, May 7–12, 2011, Vancouver, BC, Canada.

Figure 1. Domain name highlighting in Google Chrome (top) and Internet Explorer (bottom)

Of course, the web security landscape is not blind to phishing attacks, and consequently many methods try to thwart them. Some methods are technical ones that work under the covers, such as creation of blacklists that identify suspect phishing sites, and filtering of suspect sites by internet providers. Other methods try to help web users identify suspect sites, as discussed in the related work section. Yet in spite of these efforts to combat the threat of phishing, recent statistics paint a bleak picture of their overall effectiveness. The 2008 Gartner study [10] estimated that upwards of 5 million people in the U.S. alone were subject to financial losses due to phishing (non-financial losses also exist, but [10] did not consider these), even though safe-browsing features were used by 36% of the people surveyed. Furthermore, at least 9400 phishing attempts were identified in the month of August 2010 alone [12]. Thus phishing continues to occur, and users continue to fall victim despite efforts to deter attacks.

One problem is that a well-crafted phishing site will be visually identical to the original site. Indeed, the sole telltale sign of such a site may only be that its domain name is incorrect, something users can easily miss (e.g., [6]. The new user-centric anti-phishing method of *domain highlighting* [15] exploits this: it visually enhances the domain name portion of the web address in the browser's address bar. Figure 1 illustrates how domain highlighting is incorporated in the default interface of recent releases of Google Chrome (top) and Microsoft's Internet Explorer [15] (bottom). In both cases, the host domain is drawn in black, while the rest of the address is rendered in gray. The only visible difference between the two browsers is that Explorer does not highlight the "www" prefix.

Domain highlighting is based on two assumptions which, if correct, would make it a critical anti-phishing measure:

1. Users can recognize legitimate domain names, likely from their knowledge of the web, their expectations of what a well-formed domain name should be, and their prior experiences visiting particular web sites.
2. Users will naturally attend to the address bar as part of their normal browsing practice, where they will quickly examine the highlighted domain name portion of the address to judge the legitimacy of the web site.

We ask in this paper if domain highlighting really meets its potential. Our objective is to provide insight into the effectiveness of domain highlighting in user identification of phishing sites. We first review related work that investigates phishing security as part of interface design. We then describe our study, its methodology, and results. We identify limitations and faults with domain highlighting and its assumptions, which imply possible directions for security developers who wish to improve the effectiveness of phishing deterrents. We also identify three types of users. One type consistently cited brand, content and previous experiences with the web page as major factors of trust; a second type scrutinized the address bar as part of their evaluation; the third type was a hybrid between these two.

RELATED WORK

Much prior work on anti-phishing security focuses on its technical aspects. Yet many technical solutions are often thwarted because they expect users to understand them (most cannot), or because phishers and other spammers used social engineering methods to fool users into taking actions they would not normally do. This is why researchers are now seriously focusing on the gap between technical approaches to security *vs.* user interface design (e.g., ACM SOUPS conference focuses on user aspects of security).

Within the context of phishing and the web, the majority of attention on user-oriented security methods has been on security toolbars and visual security indicators. In general, these methods situate visuals (such as icons) on the edges of the browsing window or in the address bar that display the security status of a particular web site (e.g., whether it is SSL). Where a phishing site is blacklisted, more prominent and active notifications may be used [3].

Yet why, despite the existence of such measures, do phishing attacks continue to be effective against users? Wu et al. [18] identified many drawbacks with existing security toolbars. First, people rarely noticed them because these were located in the peripheral area of a browser. Second, users did not necessarily care about the toolbar even if they did take notice. Third, the toolbar often mis-classified sites (e.g., legitimate sites as phishing sites), which led users to mistrust the toolbar. Other visual methods were similarly ineffective: subjects typically ignored visual lock icons located at the periphery of their attention, and continued their browsing even when confronted with a blatant pop-up warnings for fraudulent certificates [2,16].

The problem is that the intuition used to develop the above visual security cues assumes that what works for protecting the technically-knowledgeable specialist must, by extension, also work for the average consumer. This is not true. When researchers examined what people actually use to form their opinion of trust, they found that non-technical people judge security primarily from the visual content of the page itself and its relevance to their own task [9,6,4]. Seldom do they consider security icons and toolbars.

Other approaches move security indicators directly into the user's field of view, although this has to be carefully done as it could affect the usability of a browser. With enhanced sign-in indicators, first-time users of a legitimate site are asked to choose an image and/or enter some personal text during login. That image and text are then displayed on all subsequent logins. If they are missing or wrong, then he or she should suspect that they have been misdirected to a visually similar but fraudulent phishing site [13].

Domain highlighting is yet another approach added to the arsenal of security indicators. To our knowledge, the actual effectiveness of domain highlighting has not been examined in detail. While our study here is somewhat similar in nature to the above-mentioned studies, it differs from them in three significant ways. First, ours is the first formal study of domain highlighting. Second, our methodology masked our interest in domain highlighting (following fraud experiment recommendations by [8]), where participants only knew that we were conducting a security study of some kind. This allowed us to evaluate domain highlighting in the context of how users may behave outside of a lab setting. Third, during a second evaluation round, we did tell people to focus their attention on the address bar, but we did not tell them about domain names or how to identify phishing sites. This allowed us to evaluate how people used their own knowledge while removing problems associated with attention as found in prior studies of security icons.

DESCRIPTION OF THE EXPERIMENT

We ask: to what extent does domain highlighting aid in identifying phishing attacks? To answer this, our study evaluates the effectiveness of domain highlighting as an anti-phishing measure, where effectiveness is measured by whether a person makes appropriate judgments of the trustworthiness of legitimate and fraudulent web sites.

Our study was a controlled experiment. 22 participants were shown 16 web pages (8 legitimate and 8 phishing pages) in randomized order[1] across two phases. In phase 1, subjects were merely asked to classify how "safe" each page appeared to be. Phase 2 repeated the exercise, except this time they were told to focus on the address bar area.

[1] We also ran a pilot study involving 7 participants to help form and debug our study. The method and results obtained in the pilot are essentially identical to those found in this full study.

Focus of Participants

Participants were *not* told or instructed about domain name spoofing, nor domain highlighting, nor that we were specifically concerned with phishing attacks. Rather, we told them that they would be involved in a study on the visual security aids as generally found in Internet Explorer 8. They were consciously aware that they were being asked to judge a web site's trustworthiness. While this sensitized them to security, it was up to them to decide what informational cues were present and how to use them to evaluate a site's legitimacy. We did this because we wanted to evaluate the effects of domain highlighting in a semi-realistic context. Had we made participants specifically aware of domain highlighting, they would likely have knowledge atypical of everyday users, and they likely would have given that feature far more scrutiny than they would normally do while browsing. In real world contexts, security concerns are secondary goals in relation to the primary goal of completing a specific task [17,10]. Our emphasis on security shifted their primary goal to security. Consequently, we expect our participants to perform better than in a typical browsing scenario where judging security is at best a secondary goal. That is, if domain highlighting performs poorly when people are asked to judge a web site's security, it would certainly perform more poorly under more routine browsing conditions. Thus our study portrays a reasonable *upper bound* on the effectiveness of domain highlighting in standard browsing environments[2].

Participants

22 participants (17 male and 5 female), recruited from the University of Calgary, were compensated with $15 cash. Ages ranged from 19-41 (mean = 27.7, σ=6.2). They comprised 10 graduate engineering students, 2 computer science graduate students, 6 science or social science students, and four university employees or previous university graduates from non-technical fields. None were trained in security. Average weekly computer usage was ~47 hours (σ=24.0, median=49). All regularly banked online, and all were familiar with Internet Explorer. 18 shopped online regularly, 2 occasionally, and 2 not at all.

Method

Each ~45 minute study, conducted in an office, was comprised of an initial interview, 2 study phases, and an exit interview. Interviews were audio recorded.

The initial interview asked about computer experience, prior use of web sites similar to those in our study, and knowledge of security concepts. We wanted to see if any prior experience would affect user performance.

In phase 1, no particular instructions were given on how to evaluate the web sites' trustworthiness. In phase 2, we asked subjects to re-evaluate the web sites' trustworthiness where we directed them to focus on the address bar area (we did not tell them what to look for in that area). If subjects changed their ratings between these two phases, then we could attribute this to their using the extra information supplied by domain highlighting in the address bar. If there was no change, then we could assume that the participant either could not recognize or could not exploit the extra information supplied by domain highlighting.

In each phase, participants were shown a series of 16 web pages representing web sites (presented in randomized order across participants) and asked to gauge how "safe" a site was on a 5-point scale. In case subjects were unfamiliar with a site, we explained generally what each site was for (e.g., online banking, social networking, shopping). For our analysis, we collapse their ratings as unsafe (1-2), unsure (3) and safe (4-5)[3]. As they did this, we asked participants to describe their rationale for their ratings as well as what visual element(s) they were currently inspecting on the web page via a think-aloud process.

In the exit interview, we explained domain highlighting and how it could help people evaluate phishing attacks. Participants were asked if they knew about this feature, whether they had noticed it[4], and were asked for their thoughts on its potential effectiveness and what could be improved.

Materials

System. We used a standard computer, Windows XP and Internet Explorer 8. The only change was to point the web browser to a proxy server, which cached and presented the spoofed domain name / URL address in the participant's web browser for the fraudulent web pages. Legitimate pages were loaded by the proxy server directly from the real location and displayed without modifications.

Web sites. We used 16 different web pages representing 16 web sites. 8 were legitimate (Table 1a), while the other 8 were simulated phishing pages that we created along with a spoofed domain name / URL address (Table 1b). As common in 'better' phishing sites, each phishing page was a perfect replica of the original site. Thus the URL, including its domain name, was the only discernible visual difference between a fraudulent and its legitimate page.

For realism, the 16 web sites in Table 1 were selected according to one or both of the following criteria.

1. *Familiarity to participant.* We wanted participants to be either familiar with the displayed site or other sites like it. Thus we selected popular sites (as described in the rightmost columns of Table 1) within our geographic region, where those sites were also representative of online tasks our target group would likely encounter during routine web browsing. If participants were

[2] Identifying domain highlighting as a study goal and instructing people on typical phishing attacks would produce a 'true' upper bound, but one likely not reachable (on average) in the real world.

[3] A 5-point rating reasonably captures a person's judgement. For the analysis, however, we assume the collapsed 3-point scale is a reasonable approximation of the likelihood of that person actually using the website.

[4] While eye-tracking could tell us if people looked at the address bar (see [16]), self-disclosure reveals what people actually looked for.

unfamiliar with a particular site as shown by the web page they saw, we described (at a conceptual level) the kind of organization hosting that site, and then presented a sample scenario illustrating the purpose of that site.

2. *Frequently targeted market sector.* The Anti-Phishing Working Group [1] names 'payment services', 'financial', 'auction', and 'retail' as heavily targeted areas, while PhishTank [12] adds social networking. As described in the right columns, most pages in Table 1a/b are login pages to sites that ask for account credentials. If our fraudulent pages were actual phishing attacks, then people entering information into them would likely incur financial misappropriation, identity theft, or both.

Phishing Domain Names / URLs. Phishers use domain name obfuscation techniques to fool people into believing that the domain name / URL in the address bar is not fraudulent. For our fraudulent sites, we crafted URLs representative of typical obfuscation techniques (see Table 1b) as listed below. While we name these methods below, the community has no consistent names for most of them.

Similar-name attacks are addresses that are similar sounding to the legitimate address. For example, the fraudulent amazon.checkingoutbooksonline.ca appears similar to the legitimate www.amazon.ca, even though the second-level domain portion is quite different (checkingoutbooksonline *vs.* amazon).

IP-address attacks display a cryptic IP address as the domain rather than the real domain name, e.g., http://192.168.111.112/login *vs.* http://www.facebook.com/login.

Letter substitution attacks substitute one or more characters in the domain name with a character that is visually similar in appearance. These can be seen as crude homograph attacks [4]. An example is 'www.uca1gary.ca' rather than 'www.ucalgary.ca' (note the number '1' instead of the letter 'l'). The user may miss this in a quick glance.

Complex URL attacks are addresses that span the length of the address bar or that may contain nonsensical characters, making interpretation of the URL difficult.

Metrics

Our primary quantitative metric used to evaluate the effectiveness of domain name highlighting was derived by comparing user ratings (safe *vs.* unsafe) to web page legitimacy (legitimate *vs.* fraudulent). This led to the measures below, illustrated in Table 2 as a matrix.

Table 1a. Legitimate web pages (Row order matches top half of Figures 2 and 3)

URL (abbreviated here with '...')	**Company / Description / Information requested**
https://www1.royalbank.com/ cgi-bin/rbaccess/...	**Royal Bank of Canada.** Bank site's log-in page. Requests user account credentials.
http://clothing.shop.ebay.com/ i.html?_sacat=11450&_nkw...	**eBay.** Online auction for posted items; browsing, purchasing and paying for various items.
http://alumni.lib.ucalgary.ca:3048/ login?url=http://proquest.umi.com/...	**UC-library.** University library login page to access online library services. Requests user account credentials that could be used to access other university services.
https://www.google.com/ accounts/ServiceLogin?uilel=3&service=youtube...	**Youtube.** Video-sharing login page. Requests user account credentials.
https://auth.me.com/ authenticate?service=...	**Mobile Me.** Login page to syncronize user devices, e.g., iPod, iPhone, iPad, and laptop or desktop computer. Requests user account credentials.
http://websms.fido.page.ca/ 2way/	**Fido.** Phone company login page for text messaging services. Requests user account credentials.
https://canada.frenchconnection.com/ login.htm?returnUrl=/...	**French Connection.** Clothes store log-in page for online shopping. Requests user account credentials.
http://www.facebook.com/ r.php?invid=10000...	**Facebook (invitation).** Social network invitation sent by another person. Requests user account credentials.

Table 1b. Fraudulent web pages (Row order matches bottom half of Figures 2 and 3)

Phishing Type	**Spoofed URL** *long URLs abbreviated here with '...'*	**Original (non-spoofed) URL** *for comparison purposes*	**Supposed Company / Description**
IP address	http://192.168.111.112/ login	http://www.facebook.com/	**Facebook.** Social network login page. Requests user account credentials.
similar	http://www.easyweb.td-canadatrust.ca/	https://easywebcpo.td.com/ waw/idp/login.htm?...	**Canada Trust Bank.** Bank site's log-in page. Requests user account credentials.
similar	http://www.meebo.webmessenger.com/	http://www.meebo.com/	**Meebo.** Login page. Requests user account credentials for multiple social networking sites.
letter	http://www.uca1gary.ca/ registrar/payment	http://www.ucalgary.ca/ registrar/payment	**UC- Enrollment.** For fee payment. Describes how to pay tuition fees, but doesn't require any personal information.
letter	http://www.paypa1.ca	http://www.paypal.ca	**Paypal.** Login page for payment of goods via bank / credit cards. Requests account credentials.
complex	http://www.amazon.ca.checkingoutbook online.ca/Golden-Mean-Annabel-Lyon/...	http://www.amazon.ca/ Golden-Mean-Annabel-Lyon/	**Amazon.** Online store for browsing and purchasing books and other items.
similar	http://login.hotmailsecure.com	http://login.live.com/ login.srf?wa=wsignin1.0...	**Hotmail.** E-mail/messaging login page. Requests user account credentials.
complex	http://login.flickr.net/ config/login?.src=flickr...	https://login.yahoo.com/config/ login?.src=flickr	**Flickr.** Photo-sharing login page that requests user account credentials.

Table 2: Measurement matrix

		Subject decision	
		Site is safe	**Site is unsafe**
Site type	**Legitimate**	Correct: safe	Wrong: unsafe
	Fraudulent	Wrong: safe	Correct: unsafe

Correct decision is the percentage of participants who correctly classified (as an average) a page as legitimate or fraudulent. It is the sum of the two measures below.

- ***Correct**: **safe*** occurs when one correctly rates a legitimate web page as safe.
- ***Correct: unsafe*** occurs when one correctly rates a fraudulent web page as unsafe.

Wrong decision is the percentage of participants who incorrectly classified (as an average) a page as legitimate or fraudulent. It is the sum of the two measures below, which are equivalent to Type I (false positive) and Type II (false negative) errors in hypothesis testing.

- ***Wrong: safe*** occurs when one incorrectly rates a fraudulent web page as safe. This is very critical factor, because this incorrect decision directly measures the vulnerability of participants to a phishing attack.
- ***Wrong: unsafe*** occurs when one incorrectly rates a legitimate page as unsafe. This means that the participant will not continue to use the page even though it was, in fact, safe to do so. While a (possibly serious) inconvenience, this error is not a security threat.

Focus

Our quantitative analyses were driven by three questions of interest.

Is there a difference in web page ratings in terms of correct decisions, wrong decisions, wrong:safe, and wrong:unsafe

1. regardless of whether or not subjects were told to pay attention to the URL address?
2. regardless of whether the page is actually legitimate or fraudulent?
3. regardless of the type of phishing method used (letter, IP-address, complex, and letter substitution attacks)?

Question 1 considers differences that happen before and after a person is told to pay attention to the URL, i.e., if they even notice and exploit domain highlighting more effectively after being told to look at that area of the page. Question 2 considers differences between measures when we compare rates on legitimate *vs.* fraudulent pages. Question 3 considers how well people can or cannot detect particular types of domain name attacks.

QUANTITATIVE ANALYSIS AND RESULTS

We use a combination of descriptive statistics plus hypothesis testing.

Hypothesis testing. Our null hypothesis is a rephrasing of Questions 1 and 2 above to state that no such difference exists between decisions over legitimate *vs.* fraudulent pages across the two phases. For hypothesis testing, we used a 2x2 ANOVA repeated measures: Phase (1 *vs.* 2) x Web Page Type (legitimate *vs.* fraudulent*)* with a threshold of $p < .05$ (with a Bonferroni correction of .0125 for post-hoc tests). We calculated frequency values (i.e., parametric proportion data) of correct/unsure/wrong decisions by averaging particular ratings across participants. As is common with proportional data in ANOVA that ranges between 0 and 1, we transformed them to arcsin values.

For correct and unsure decisions, a significant difference was found between the frequency of people's rating of Web Page Type ($F=10.24$, $p = .004$ for correct; $F=11.35$, $p = .003$ for unsure, $df=21$). That is, people rated fraudulent and legitimate web pages differently in terms of their correct / unsure frequency. There was no significant difference between the phases; the fact that they were made aware of the address bar in Phase 2 did not change these frequencies.

For incorrect decisions, an interaction effect existed for the frequency of people's ratings. Post-hoc tests revealed there was a significant difference between people's incorrect frequency ratings of legitimate *vs.* fraudulent sites in both phases ($t=-5.06$, $p=.00$ in Phase 1, $t=-3.61$, $p=.002$ in Phase 2), and between their ratings of fraudulent pages between Phases 1 and 2 ($t=3.96$, $p = .001$). However, there was no difference in people's ratings of legitimate sites between Phases 1 and 2 ($t=-.35$, $p=.73$).

The means describing these differences (and other descriptive statistics) are detailed and discussed below.

Correct *vs.* wrong decisions (Phase 1). Figure 2 is a visualization of each participant's decision data for each web page seen in Phase 1. Each column represents an individual participant, where columns are sorted by participants with the most correct results on the left. Each row represents a particular web page, with the 8 legitimate pages at the top and the 8 fraudulent pages at the bottom. For cross referencing URL and obfuscation type, row order is identical to rows in Tables 1 and 2. Each set of rows in the legitimate and fraudulent section is sorted by pages with the most correct score at the top. Green cells are correct decisions, red are incorrect, and yellow are those rated as unsure. Participant numbers are shown in the topmost row. Participant type (A, AB, or B) - explained in the qualitative results section - is shown on the bottom row.

For legitimate pages, participants rated 54% of them correctly (correct:safe), 15% incorrectly (wrong:unsafe), and were unsure of 31% of the pages. Figure 2, top, illustrates this by the moderate amount of green squares showing the correct ratings.

For fraudulent pages, participants rated 25% of them correctly (correct:unsafe), 57% incorrectly (wrong:safe), and were unsure of 18%. Figure 2,vividly reveals the high number of incorrect ratings shown in red at its bottom.

Correct vs. wrong decisions (Phase 2). Figure 3 is a visualization of how people changed their ratings of a page after they were told to attend to the address bar. White cells are those that were unchanged, or where the new rating was

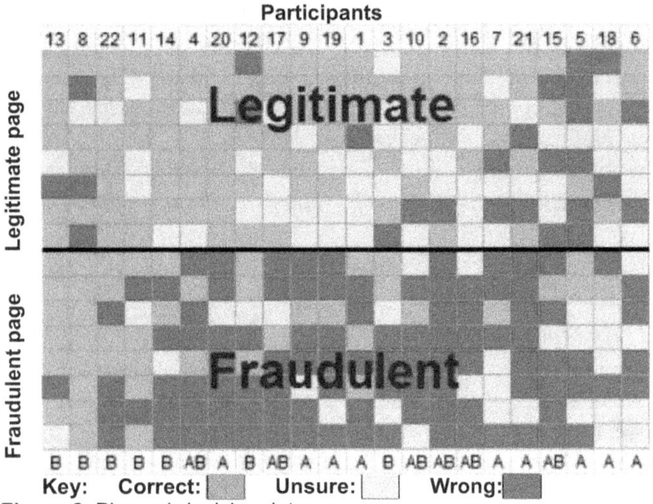

Figure 2. Phase 1 decision data.

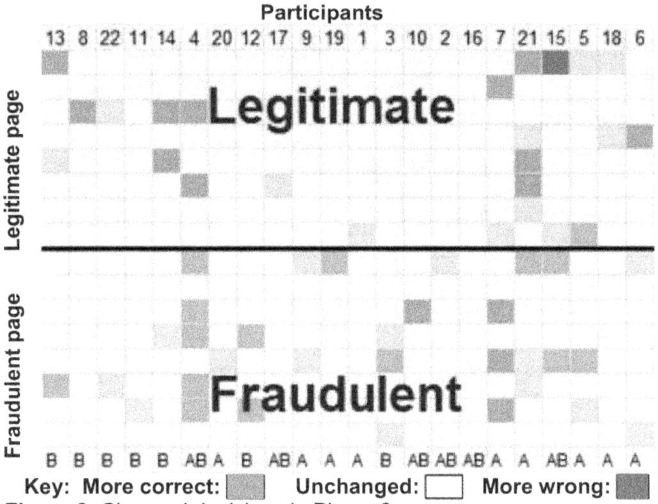

Figure 3. Changed decisions in Phase 2.

insufficient to move that page into a different safe/unsafe/unsure category. Pale green cells are page ratings that improved by one category (e.g., unsure to safe for a legitimate page, or unsure to unsafe for a fraudulent page). The dark green cells occurred when a person correctly changed their decision between safe and unsafe, while the (single) dark red cell occurred when a person incorrectly changed their decision between safe *vs.* unsafe.

For the legitimate pages, the overall percentages of ratings barely changed between Phases 1 and 2; as stated previously, no significant difference was found for legitimate pages between these phases. While changes were made, the number of incorrect re-ratings approximately equaled the correct re-ratings to produce no net gain. This can be seen visually by the balanced scattering of red and green cells in Figure 3, top.

For fraudulent pages, participants' correct ratings improved from 25 to 34% (correct:unsafe), with a decrease in incorrect ratings from 57 to 44% (wrong:safe). As mentioned, these differences were statistically significant. Unsure ratings increased from 18 to 23%. The overall gain in correct performance in re-rating these fraudulent pages can be seen visually by the predominance of light and dark green cells in Figure 3, bottom.

Discussion. Participants appeared reasonably accurate at identifying legitimate sites, where they wrongly rated only 15% of them as unsafe (the caveat is that they were still unsure of 31% of these pages). Yet their performance was effectively unchanged between the phases. We suspect that this good performance is due more to people's disposition to trust familiar-looking pages *vs.* their ability to recognize the domain name as legitimate. As we will see, this suspicion is verified in the qualitative analysis.

For fraudulent pages, participants fared poorly, where they correctly identified phishing pages only about 25% of the time. Fully 57% of these pages were incorrectly rated as safe (i.e., the wrong:safe measure), which would have put them at substantial risk of a successful phishing attack. Even when they were told to attend to the address bar, their performance only improved marginally (although it was statistically significant); fully 44% of the pages were still incorrectly rated (i.e., again as wrong:safe).

We interpret this as follows.

- Domain name highlighting is, at best, only somewhat effective at helping people identify fraudulent sites.
- Participants do not always attend to the address bar (and thus the domain name) to determine site legitimacy. If they had attended the address bar in Phase 1, we would not have found a difference between the two phases.
- However, when participants were told to attend to the address bar, they did do somewhat better – but not much better – in correctly identifying fraudulent sites.

Participant performance. As mentioned, the columns of Figures 2 and 3 are participants sorted by those with the most correct results on the left. Evident from these figures is that there is marked variation in participant performance. We will revisit this difference between participants in the qualitative analysis section, where we identify three user types and how they differ in what they look for.

Ratings by obfuscation method. While we did not use obfuscation method as a statistical factor in our analysis, we inspected our results for gross effects. The order of web pages within Tables 1a and 1b correspond with the row ordering in Figures 2 and 3. That is, both are ordered from those with the most correct ratings (top rows in each section) to the most incorrect. As evident in Figure 2, the majority of people frequently and incorrectly rated a fraudulent page as safe, regardless of the type of obfuscation method used. When people were asked to look at the address bar, people did improve the correctness of their ratings somewhat (but not that much) across all obfuscation methods. The exception is the IP-address attack (top row in the fraudulent section of Table 1b and Figures 2 and 3). More people correctly identified the IP-address attack as a fraudulent page: 9 people in Phase 1, and 14 people in Phase 2 after being told to look at the address bar.

Discussion. Legitimate web sites rarely use an IP address as a domain name. If the domain name was displayed as an IP address, this should be an obvious cue suggesting a phishing attack. Our results indicate that this is the case, but only marginally.

- IP-address attacks are still an effective phishing method. Even when participants were asked to attend the address bar, only 64% of them were able to spot the attack. That is, people either did not notice or, more likely, they did not understand the implications of seeing an IP address in the domain name.
- The other three types of phishing attacks seem equally effective at fooling people, as there is little practical difference between them in terms of people's ability to spot them. This strongly suggests that people are equally bad at judging domain name legitimacy when slightly more sophisticated obfuscation methods are used.

QUALITATIVE DATA ANALYSIS AND RESULTS

Analysis method

We used a form of open coding [14] to analyse user comments and behaviours observed during the think-aloud phases and interviews. We first identified four overarching category types of information used to form trust judgments: (a) institutional brand; (b) content as presented in the main pane of the browser; (c) input information requested, and (d) information in the address bar and other security indicators. These will be described in more detail shortly.

Within these categories, we then grouped comments into two sub-categories that asked *what* specific information they scrutinized, and *how* they used that information to form their judgments. We then looked at differences between any of these categories as described by a participant between Phase 1 and Phase 2. Finally, during our analysis, we noted that participants did not use these categories equally. Consequently, we sorted participants with similar traits into a typology as described next.

Predisposed Perceptions: A Typology of Groups

Perhaps the most interesting behavioural pattern we identified concerned the differences between people in how and when they attended different elements of the browsing interface to judge a site's legitimacy. These differences suggest a typology, where people can be (loosely) categorized as clustering along points of a spectrum in terms of how they scrutinized a mix of information covering a web page's: (a) institutional brand; (b) content as presented in the main pane of the browser; (c) input information requested, and (d) information in the address bar and other security indicators. The three types of people are briefly described below and illustrated in Figure 4, Following sections detail how each type used this information.

Type A people focus solely on information present in the browser's content pane (9 participants). This confirms prior findings on how people judge web site credibility [9, 6, 4]. Information brand as identified in the content pane was

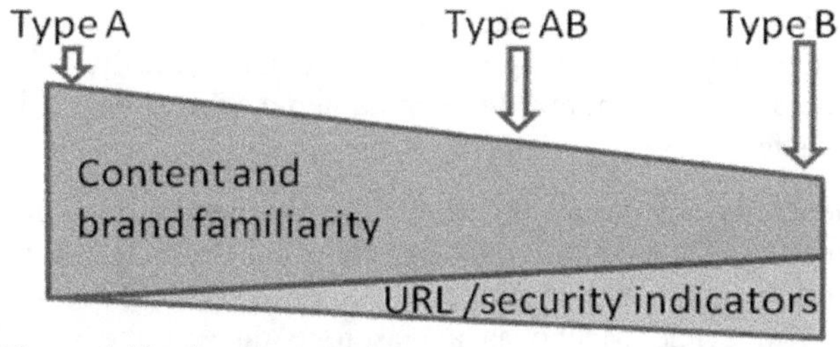

Figure 4. The typology spectrum.

critical. They did *not* consider information in the address bar. Nor did they consider other security indicators shown outside the content pane, verifying findings by [16,18].

Type B people consistently focused on the information found in the address bar, the information being requested, and other security indicators (7 participants). While they did use information visible in the content pane (e.g., to determine brand familiarity as with Type A people), it was not the sole source of their judgement.

Type AB people were a composite (6 participants). Like Type A, they relied primarily on the content pane and institutional brand. Like Type B, they sometimes considered information in the address bar and the kinds of information being requested. They were much more variable in the information they considered across pages.

Institutional Brand

A salient criterion people used for evaluating site security was the brand(s) depicted on the page. Both Type A and Type AB participants appeared predisposed to implicitly trust particular brands. The quintessential cases were financial institutions where: two people explicitly stated that banks *had* to be secure; and eight people used familiarity and/or personal experience with two banking sites (Canada Trust and Royal Bank) as their main or sole reasoning for trusting the sites. It is rather concerning that a good portion of our participants did not seem to even look at the URL, let alone correctly recognize one of them as a phishing site, for these high-risk banking pages. Other recognizable brands, such as Amazon, Google, the University of Calgary (UC), and Yahoo! were met with positive judgments, despite several of them being fraudulent. This suggests that for many users, the perception of safety and legitimacy of a site is tied heavily to their preconceived perception of the brand itself.

Type A and Type AB subjects were also often quick to identify symbols and logos associated with familiar brands. This included logos by other companies on a page, such as the Google logo on the YouTube page, the Yahoo! logo on the Flickr page, and the Apple logo on the MobileMe page. Any sign of these 'famous' and familiar big-brand logos seemed to instill these participants with a measure of (unwarranted) trust.

In contrast, the seven Type B participants showed a different pattern in their use of brand. Five mentioned brand for only two of the pages. Even when brand was mentioned, these participants never used brand as the sole category of information to form their ratings. Most Type B comments involved only a passing mention of brand, typically to say whether they recognized the brand depicted or connected to the site.

Generally, participants were also inclined to distrust particular brands or types of sites. For example, a few participants mentioned privacy issues with Facebook, YouTube and Meebo as a reason to distrust the site. If anything, participants (especially Type A and AB) showed greater caution toward social networking sites, especially if they had little or no personal experience with that site, or had heard negative things about it.

Page Content

While it is natural to interpret page content as an indicator of trust, this is irrelevant in the detection of a phishing page that replicates the look and feel of the legitimate page that results in no discernible difference. What is alarming that Type A (and sometimes Type AB) instinctively relied on this page content to determine legitimacy. In contrast, Type B participants, for the most part, were not strongly influenced by page content in their evaluations of site legitimacy: they instead spoke mostly about the content of the address and status bars.

Type A and AB participants formed their judgment around the content information as present in the main content pane of the page. They were particularly sensitive to security and legitimacy indicators within the content pane, where their presence of these indicators positively influenced their perception of that page as trustworthy. These indicators fell into three groups: security and privacy related information, the content itself, and the type of information requested. Of course, a phisher can easily spoof all this information.

Security and privacy related information. Type A and Type AB subjects were often quick to identify symbols that associate a site as being verified as 'safe' by an external authority. An example is the appearance of the Verisign logo. They also pointed out internal indicators of security, such as a "security guarantee" logo on the Royal Bank page (9 of the 15 Type A and Type AB subjects mentioned this and also rated the site as trustworthy). The presence of a virus scan advertisement was interpreted by two participants as being a positive sign of site security, and a few mentioned the option to forget user login credentials ("Remember Me") as a sign that it would be safe to enter their login information. Indirect security-related content such as an 'updated' copyright date and links to contact/support information were also frequently reported by Type A, and some Type AB participants. In fact, Type A (and some Type AB) participants frequently spoke of the security and non-security-oriented vocabulary typical found on the edges of the content pane (copyright, security/privacy links, contact info link). In these instances, links to legal, privacy and security policies implied that the site had safeguards to ensure that disclosed information would be held in the sole possession of the particular site.

The content itself. Content amount, the kind of information, and its layout within a page were also important factors contributing to Type A and AB interpretations of a site's trustworthiness (see also [4]). One notable example involved customer reviews and book information in the amazon.com product page. The amount and layout of information on that page instilled a sense of confidence in its legitimacy (because it was information-rich and professionally laid out). The customer reviews on that page instilled a sense that others had visited the site before, and that others had purchased the depicted product.

Type of information requested.

All but one of our pages requests people to enter different kinds and amounts of information. Some pages request sensitive identification information, and/or financial information, and/or unusual or excess information that could seem disproportionate to that page type. Curiously, financial information requests did not seem to warrant greater caution by participants, and most participants did not even comment on it. Type AB people made the most comments about pages that seemed to request excessive or unusual information whereas Types A and B provided fewer comments; we have no explanation for this discrepancy.

Address Bar and Other Security Indicators

There was considerable disparity between our three participant types in whether they looked at the address bar and, if they did, their technical understanding of URLs and how they could be used to inform trust judgments.

Type A people focused almost exclusively on information present in the browser's content pane, and they rarely considered information in the address bar. Even when asked to look at the address bar, most Type A people clearly had no idea about 'unusual' URLs, nor what to do with the information contained within it. Comments included "this (URL) doesn't mean anything to me" or "this (URL) doesn't change anything for me". They mentioned they were uncertain of how to interpret '.net' or '.ca' suffixes, or the 'https' prefix. Some incorrectly considered the URL length as meaningful (i.e., perceived as 'too long' or 'too short'), while others thought that certain words in the URL had positive connotations, e.g., the appearance of the word 'secure', 'deliveryaddress', the brand name, and so on. Long URLs and those containing seemingly nonsensical argument characters (even if legitimate) prompted frequent comments about what the URL meant and why it was so complex. For IP attacks (e.g., top row, Table 1b), the three Type A people who noticed the IP numbers in the domain name mentioned their suspicions, but still rated that site as trustworthy: "the URL are just numbers".

Type A people tended to use brand identity and site type to over-ride any suspicions they may have had when seeing unusual URLs. To illustrate, one subject who was judging a fraudulent bank page commented "the highlighted [domain name] part is strange… [but] banks are secure" and then rated that page as trustworthy. Another subject spotted a letter substitution attack (the '1' in 'paypa1'), yet also rated that page as trustworthy because of site familiarity.

Unlike Type A, Type AB paid more attention to URLs and to other security indicators, although not consistently. The content pane remained their primary source of information across all pages, but they did occasionally look at the URL on some pages. At least some of them seemed aware that the URL may contain security and other indicators that could be used to inform their trust judgements. For example, one said "https is more secure". Another recognized the "1" substitution attack as strong evidence of a fraudulent page. Yet Type AB people were often unsure of what to look for in the URL, and did not have a full understanding of phishing indicators. For example, 3 of the 6 Type AB people caught the "1" in the 'paypa1' domain name, but were confused as to how this should influence their ratings, i.e, they continued to trust that phishing site.

Unlike Type A and AB people, Type B participants paid heavy attention to the address bar. They knew of the security indicators built into the address bar area. They knew the URL was important to determine page legitimacy, and they consistently looked for clues in the address bar to appraise the legitimacy of the sites. For example, many of them consistently looked for 'https' and the lock icon in the URL. Some knew about the importance of the domain name, where they tried to match it with the page being displayed. For example, one person viewing the fraudulent Meebo page said "the URL is not meebo.com, and it looks phishy". While all this sounds like good news, Type B people still missed many fraudulent pages (see Figure 2). While one Type B person did correctly identify all fraudulent pages, four other Type B people missed 50% or more of the fraudulent pages.

Subjects with Type AB or Type B classifications demonstrated a marked improvement in successful identifications of phishing sites during the second phase. Contrary to Type A, these participants focused their attention more on the technical rather than superficial aspects of the address bar. Secure protocol indicators like 'https' or the lock icon were noted; the entire URL was examined, and (albeit with only a modest success rate), the obfuscation method was seen.

Perhaps surprisingly, when asked about it during the exit interview, most participants – including Type B – said they were not even aware that the domain name part of the URL was highlighted.

Correlating Type to Rating Correctness and Training

Between types and correctness of ratings. We did not statistically re-analyze our data based on these types, as our typology was determined post-hoc. However, a qualitative inspection suggests correlations between types and how correct their ratings are likely to be. Recall that the bottom row of Figures 2 and 3 indicates the participant type (A, AB, B) and that columns are sorted by participants with the most correct to least correct rating, from left to right. Not surprisingly, almost all Type B people are clustered on the left side, i.e., those with the most correct ratings. Types AB tended towards the middle, and Type A tended towards the right (least correct) side.

Between types to formal technical training. Some of our participants were trained as computer scientists and engineers. Most – but not all – of those fell into the Type B category. Similarly, most Type A people were in non-technical fields, with AB being a mix. However, this correlation was not perfect. For example, two of the nine Type A people were either computer scientists or engineers.

LIMITATIONS AND FUTURE STUDIES

Our methodology tries to balance the constraints of a laboratory study with real world validity, which introduces several limitations. Our results, while strongly indicative of real world behavior, are approximations. For example, by using real web sites, we could not easily control for people's familiarity particular sites and brands, nor with their familiarity (or expectations) of the actual URL address. Participants also knew that they were judging a web site's legitimacy, which is why we suggest this is a best case vs. average scenario. We left out other important factors that could have revealed additional nuances. One suggestion for future study could compare address bars with and without highlighting, thus providing a control comparison, i.e., to determine the marginal improvement of highlighting (if any). Another study could tease out obfuscation type as a statistical factor, i.e. to see if people do better at identifying particular obfuscation methods. A third study could incorporate user types (A, A/B, B) as a statistical factor.

CONCLUSIONS AND IMPLICATIONS

In spite of the above limitations, our study provides reasonable 'upper bounds' of how likely people are to detect phishing attacks based on domain name highlighting. That is, participants in Phase 1 were primed to judge security as their goal, and in Phase 2 they were specifically told to attend to information in the address bar. Our participants were also highly educated (although not in security), with several of them being technically knowledgeable.

What we found was that domain highlighting works, but nowhere near as well as we would like. Our participants still incorrectly rated about half to two-thirds of the fraudulent pages as safe, depending on whether they were told to attend to the address bar. For Type A users, domain name highlighting is rarely effective, as they judge a page almost solely by its content area (similar to [9, 6]). This is highly problematic, especially because we believe Type A behavior will characterize the general population, as most people are not technically sophisticated. And even Type AB and Type B people who do scrutinize address bars are at best 'hit and miss' at detecting domain name anomalies. To make matters worse, most people don't even bother to look at the address bar unless they are told to do so. Consequently, in everyday life, we expect people to be much worse at identifying phishing attacks via domain name highlighting, as they lack technical knowledge and they will be focused on their normal web browsing activities rather than security.

Two questions worth asking are: should we abandon domain name highlighing, and are there ways to improve it? We speculate on three areas for future work.

Education. Our results showed several problems that could be associated with a lack of user knowledge. First, Type A and AB people mistakenly place great reliance on the information in the content area and the brand, which can be easily mimicked by phishers. Second, Type A (rarely) and Type AB (only sometimes) attend to the address bar, likely because they do not know of its importance. Third, even if they do look there, almost all participants – even Type B – frequently miss the spoofed domain name, likely because they are unaware of the common obfuscation methods used. Alternately, they use information in the URL to form their judgement that is simply not relevant. Education would likely help [10]. People need to know that they cannot rely on the content area, that they should scrutinize the domain name, and that they should be aware of common phishing methods. As one person said: "highlighting the domain name is fine for people who normally look at the URL, but we need to reach the general population… more knowledge would help." The challenge is to find effective ways to train (likely unmotivated) users without getting in the way of their primary task [10].

Attention. When people browse, they tend to focus on the content area as it is the reason why they are browsing. Security is a secondary concern [17,10], and consequently even the most careful (and knowledgeable) may fail to scrutinize the domain name if they are immersed in their task. This makes us question if there are methods that we can use to draw people's attention to the domain name, or if we can present that information another way. Solutions here may try to make the domain name even more obvious, or draw the person's focus onto the address bar (especially if the browser can detect anything suspicious about the site), or somehow place the domain name in a portion of the page where the person is more likely to attend to it.

URL Complexity. URLs can be quite complex, and it was clear that many of our participants were confused by this complexity. This could perhaps be resolved by either presenting the domain name by itself in a dedicated area separate from the rest of the URL, or by somehow reducing complexity of the URL by (perhaps) hiding extra information in URL address.

In summary, domain highlighting gives only marginal protection and cannot be relied upon as the sole means to identify a phishing site. Still, it is worth including as it comes at almost no cost in terms of interface clutter, browser performance, and interference with a user's task. Clearly, it must be used with other anti-phishing tools, where the combination of those tools may provide better protection (although this has not yet been shown to be true).

We believe that domain name highlighting can be made somewhat more effective by making the domain name even more obvious, by drawing the person's focus onto the address bar, by reducing URL complexity, and – most importantly – by educating people about the importance of the domain name in judging web sites, and what typical obfuscation methods are used by phishers.

Acknowldegewments. This research is partially supported by NSERC and ISSNet.

REFERENCES

1. APWG (2009) Phishing activity trends report, 4th quarter. http://www.antiphishing.org/
2. Dhamija, R., Tygar, J. D. and Hearst, M. (2006) Why phishing works. *Proc ACM CHI*, 581–590, ACM.
3. Egelman, S., Cranor, L., Hong, J. (2008) You've been warned: An empirical study of the effectiveness of web browser phishing warnings. *Proc. ACM CHI*, ACM.
4. Fogg, B. Marshall, J., Laraki, O. et. al. (2001) What makes Web sites credible?: A report on a large quantitative study. *Proc ACM CHI'2001,* 61-68, ACM.
5. Gabrilovich, E. and Gontmakher, A. (2002). The homograph attack. *CACM 45*(2).
6. Jagatic, T., Johnson, N., Jakobsson, M. and Menczer, F. (2007) Social phishing. *Comm. ACM* 50(10), 94-100
7. Jakobsson, M. (2007) The human factor in phishing. *Privacy and Security of Consumer Information '07.*
8. Jakobsson, M., Johnson, N. and Finn, P. (2008) Why and how to perform fraud experiments. *IEEE Security and Privacy*, 6(2):66–68.
9. Jakobsson, M., Tsow, A., Shah, A., Blevis, E. (2007) What instills trust? A qualitative study of phishing. *Proc Usable Security, LNCS, Springer-Verlag, 356-61.*
10. Kumaraguru, P., Sheng, S., Acquisti, A., Cranor, L. and Hong, J. (2010) Teaching Johnny not to fall for phish. *ACM Trans. Internet Technol.* 10(2).
11. Litan, A. (2009) The war on phishing is far from over. Garnter, April. http://www.gartner.com
12. PhishTank (2010) Statistics about phishing activity and PhishTank usage. //phishtank.com/stats/2010/08/, Aug.
13. Schechter, S., Dhamija, R., Ozment, A. and Fischer, I. (2007) The Emperor's New Security Indicators. *IEEE Symposium on Security and Privacy*, 51-65.
14. Strauss, A. and Corbin, J. *Basics of Qualitative Research.* 2nd Edition. Sage Publications, 1998
15. Vaughan, C. (2008) Address Bar Improvements in Internet Explorer 8 Beta 1, *IEBlog*, 11 March.
16. Whalen, T. and Inkpen, K. M. (2005) Gathering evidence: use of visual security cues in web browsers. *Proc. Graphics Interface*, 137–144.
17. Whitten, A. and Tygar, J. D. (1999) Why Johnny can't encrypt: A usability evaluation of PGP 5.0. *Proc. USENIX Security Symposium*, USENIX Association.
18. Wu, M., Miller, R. C. and Garfinkel, S. L. (2006) Do security toolbars actually prevent phishing attacks? *Proc ACM CHI'2006,* 601–610, ACM.

Exploring Reactive Access Control

Michelle L. Mazurek⋆
mmazurek@andrew.cmu.edu

Peter F. Klemperer⋆
klemperer@cmu.edu

Richard Shay⋆
rshay@cmu.edu

Hassan Takabi†
hatakabi@sis.pitt.edu

Lujo Bauer⋆
lbauer@cmu.edu

Lorrie Faith Cranor⋆
lorrie@cs.cmu.edu

⋆Carnegie Mellon University
Pittsburgh, PA, USA

†University of Pittsburgh
Pittsburgh, PA, USA

ABSTRACT

As users store and share more digital content at home, access control becomes increasingly important. One promising approach for helping non-expert users create accurate access policies is *reactive policy creation*, in which users can update their policy dynamically in response to access requests that would not otherwise succeed. An earlier study suggested reactive policy creation might be a good fit for file access control at home. To test this, we conducted an experience-sampling study in which participants used a simulated reactive access-control system for a week. Our results bolster the case for reactive policy creation as one mode by which home users specify access-control policy. We found both quantitative and qualitative evidence of dynamic, situational policies that are hard to implement using traditional models but that reactive policy creation can facilitate. While we found some clear disadvantages to the reactive model, they do not seem insurmountable.

Author Keywords

Access control, Home computing, Human factors, Privacy

ACM Classification Keywords

H.1.2 User/Machine Systems: Human factors; D.4.6 Security and Protection: Access controls; H.5.2 User Interfaces: User-centered design

General Terms

Experimentation, Human Factors, Security

INTRODUCTION

Users without technical expertise are accumulating content on their home devices. Increasing network capacities facilitate sharing this data, increasing the risk of unauthorized information disclosure. Access-control mechanisms are needed to ensure these users maintain control of their data. However, providing this access control effectively is a challenge. Managing access-control policy has historically been time consuming and error-prone, even for experts [9, 16]. Non-expert home users may lack the time, patience, and experience needed to specify correctly a traditional access-control policy covering hundreds of files.

One promising solution is *reactive policy creation*. In a reactive model, resource owners are not required to determine all access-control policies a priori, but may instead do so in response to a request. If a user tries to access a resource but lacks sufficient permission, she can use the access-control system to send a request to the resource owner, who can opt to update his policy and allow the access.

Ad-hoc reactive access control is frequently used in practice. When a person finds herself unable to access a given file, she may contact the file owner to ask permission. However, in most cases reactive policy creation is not supported directly by access-control systems. Instead, users go outside the system and make requests via e-mail or telephone calls. This disconnect between traditional system affordances and user behavior motivates our study; we believe that shifting these requests from external channels to within the system may provide valuable benefits in convenience, security, oversight, and accountability.

Further, we are motivated by a prior study that suggested reactive access control might help non-technical home users more easily manage their access-control policies [10]. Participants in that study responded positively to the idea of reactive policy creation; for many, a system based on requests seemed like it would provide a greater sense of control over their data. Moreover, it fit within the familiar social convention of asking for permission. However, that study asked participants to consider a reactive system only briefly.

In this study, we set out to discover in more depth whether and how a reactive model could contribute to making access control more usable. In particular, we wanted to know whether people have specific policy needs that match better to a reactive model than a traditional model, as well as whether reactive policy creation better matches users' mental models and preferences. We also wanted to know whether

CHI 2011, May 7–12, 2011, Vancouver, BC, Canada.

responding to requests would prove so tedious or annoying that the reactive model would be impractical. For this study, we chose to focus on how well the reactive model could work for file owners; we leave examining reactive policy creation from a requester's point of view to future work.

To address these questions as realistically as possible without building an actual reactive system, we designed and executed an experience-sampling study intended to simulate the experience of using a reactive policy creation system to manage file access. Our 24 participants provided names of files they have and people they know. For one week, each participant received and responded to simulated access requests drawn at random from these lists of people and files.

We collected a rich set of data that bolsters the case for using reactive policy creation as one of the modes by which home users specify file-access-control policy. We found quantitative and qualitative evidence of dynamic, situational access-control policies that are hard to implement using traditional models but that reactive policy creation can facilitate. Our study showed that the reactive model supports many of our participants' policy creation needs, including the desire for more control and interactivity. While we found some clear disadvantages to the reactive model, they do not seem insurmountable. In fact, we found that some seemingly obvious disadvantages, such as the annoyance of receiving frequent requests, had only a minor impact on the usability of our simulated system and on user satisfaction. In the process, we captured detailed information about the policy decisions users made and how they made them. Our study also served as a very low-fidelity prototype, providing insight into effective interface design for incorporating reactive policy creation into the access-control system we plan to build.

In the remainder of this paper, we describe the methodology of our study, present an overview of our results, describe the trends we identified in more detail, discuss the limitations of our approach, review related work, and present our conclusions.

METHODOLOGY

We recruited 24 adult participants, using craigslist advertisements and fliers posted at our universities. We conducted the study in two rounds, one month apart, with 10 and 14 participants respectively. To focus on non-experts, we limited participation to those without degrees or jobs in computer science or engineering. Table 1 lists demographic information about our participants. Participants were compensated $10 for the initial briefing interview, $15 for the debriefing interview, and 25¢ for each response to a reactive request.

We encountered a large gender disparity during recruitment: the first 10 volunteers who met our requirements were all women. To counter this, we performed a second round of interviews with nine men and five women. While this may affect our results, we believe the effect is small. We discovered no major differences between the participants in the first and second round, apart from expected changes in the use of *maybe* policies, described below.

Code	*Age*	*Gender*	*Occupation*	*Household*	*Condition*	*Files*	*Requesters*
P01	23	F	marketing manager	R	pre	24	10
P02	41	F	magazine editor	A	post	24	9
P03	26	F	law student	R	pre	20	8
P04	32	F	unemployed	C	post	22	10
P05	25	F	law student, legal secretary	A	post	20	11
P06	23	F	student	R	pre	19	10
P07	24	F	graduate student	A	post	20	9
P08	43	F	unemployed	A	pre	9	9
P09	29	F	student	R	pre	26	9
P10	46	F	video producer	C	post	25	9
P11	34	M	legal assistant	F	pre	26	8
P12	23	F	student	F	post	20	8
P13	23	F	student	C	pre	19	8
P14	22	F	student	R	pre	20	8
P15	37	F	business administrator	F	post	24	11
P16	23	F	product developer	C,R	post	25	8
P17	26	M	unemployed	R	pre	21	9
P18	37	M	HR manager	F	post	22	9
P19	34	M	lawyer	C	post	14	8
P20	23	M	marketing coordinator	C,R	pre	20	10
P21	54	M	purchasing manager	F	post	20	8
P22	21	M	student	R	pre	15	8
P23	24	M	bookkeeper	R	post	23	8
P24	26	M	entertainment	F	post	26	8

Table 1. Participant demographics. For household, R indicates roommates, F families, C couples, and A participants who live alone.

Experience-sampling process

We modeled our experience-sampling study on a location-sharing study by Consolvo et al. [5]. Our study included an initial briefing interview, a request phase, and a final debriefing interview. We used two conditions: *pre*-condition participants filled out a grid representing their proactive policy during the briefing interview, while *post*-condition participants filled out this grid during the debriefing interview.

Briefing interview.

We collected lists of eight to 11 people with whom the participant might share files. Participants were required to list anyone they live with, a romantic partner if applicable, at least two family members and two friends not living with the participant, a supervisor, and at least two work colleagues or fellow students.

Participants were also asked to name files they store on digital devices. We prompted participants to think about photos, music, videos, financial files, work or school files, e-mail, and address-book information. In each category, we asked for groups of files, then one or two examples per group. We obtained 14 to 26 file names per participant.

Pre-condition participants only were then asked to define a *yes*, *no*, or *maybe* access policy for each of the file/requester combinations. We call this the *proactive* policy, because it is established before any hypothetical access attempts. The *maybe* policy indicates the participant cannot or does not want to make a decision without more information.

During the first round, participants appeared to have difficulty comprehending the *maybe* policy. To address this, we read a more detailed description of the *maybe* policy to second-round participants and asked them to provide and explain examples of *yes*, *no*, and *maybe* policy choices before completing the grid on their own. As we expected, this change led to increased use of *maybe* policies in the second round, mainly in exchange for decreased use of *no*. No other significant differences were found between the first and second rounds in the Likert questions, proactive grid policies, or reactive policies, except for a slight increase in participants who said they might use a reactive system to request files.[1] As a result, we consider the effect of conducting the study in two rounds to be small.

Request phase.

In the second phase, participants received mock file-request e-mails indicating a particular person wanted to access a particular file. The people and files were randomly selected, using a uniform distribution, from the lists provided during the briefing; combinations were not repeated. Each participant received five to 15 requests per day between 7 a.m. and 11 p.m., during a six- to seven-day period, with the exact number and timing also randomly selected with uniform distribution. All requests were simulated; none of the participants' acquaintances were contacted, nor were their files actually shared. Requests were assigned randomly to examine a broad range of requester/file combinations, including those that participants might find strange or uncomfortable.

Each request directed the participant to a website where she could select a response from seven options, as illustrated in Figure 1. The options allowed the participant to *ignore*, *allow*, or *deny* the request. *Allow* and *deny* responses could be set for that request only, all future requests from that person for that file, or all future requests from that person for that file group. The participant was also asked to supply a short explanation of her reasoning, intended specifically for the researchers and not the hypothetical requester. In the second round, participants were also able to provide an optional free-form description of additional policies they would like to create.

Participants' persistent reactive policy decisions did not feed back into requests they received later. As a result, requests could be inconsistent with participants' previous policy decisions (e.g., a participant might receive a request from someone they had previously stated they wished to allow all requests from). A more complete system would have automatically screened out inconsistent requests.

We asked participants to imagine the requests were real when responding. We asked them not to check their e-mail more often or respond sooner than they might if the requests were real, and to consider any factors that might influence their answer to a real request. During the debriefing interviews, we found that for the most part our participants immersed themselves in the system and demonstrated strong, sometimes emotional reactions to the simulated requests.

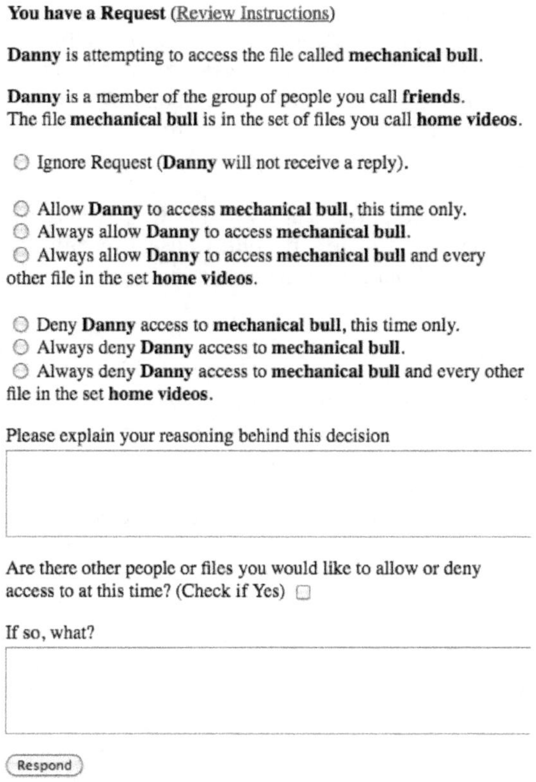

Figure 1. Sample response form.

Participants responded to 1360 of 1452 total requests sent to them. The responses represented 30% coverage of 4481 possible requester/file combinations, with minimum coverage of 19% and maximum coverage of 45% per participant.

Debriefing interview.

At the start of the debriefing interview, post-condition participants only were asked to define a proactive *yes*, *no*, or *maybe* access policy for all of the file/requester combinations they had defined in the briefing.

All participants then completed a seven-question survey. Using a seven-point Likert scale from 'strongly agree' (1) to 'strongly disagree' (7), we asked how enjoyable or convenient they found the system, and whether they would consider using such a system in real life. We also asked whether they found the number of messages they received annoying.

We then asked open-ended questions about their experience. We asked for which people and files they particularly did or did not want to use a reactive system, and how well the response options met their needs. We also asked how realistic they found the requests.

Then, we discussed in detail several individual requests, cho-

[1]All differences calculated using unpaired t-tests. Significant p-values (<0.05): Likert *use to request*, p=0.0285; proactive *no*, p=0.0296; proactive *maybe*, p=0.000284. Non-significant p-values: Likert *convenience*, p=0.983; Likert *annoyance*, p=0.741; Likert *enjoyable*, p=0.272; Likert *use to share*, p=0.788; proactive *yes*, p=0.508; reactive *allow*, p=0.0884; reactive *deny*, p=0.125; reactive *ignore*, p=0.803.

sen to provide broad coverage and include particularly interesting cases. For each selected request, participants were asked to explain why they answered as they did and whether they would choose the same answer again. Where applicable, we asked about any social awkwardness that could arise from denying or ignoring a request.

Finally, we asked participants whether they would prefer to create policy all at once, up front; to use a reactive system; or to use a combination of the two, and why.

Grid conditions.
As discussed earlier, participants were divided into two conditions. Participants in the first condition filled in a proactive access policy grid during the initial interview, while participants in the second condition completed the same grid during the debriefing. This grid allowed us to contrast the participants' proactive policies with the reactive policies created by responding to requests, and provided participants with a clear point of comparison between setting policy all at once and setting policy on a per-request basis. We used the conditions to examine priming effects on participants who were required to think through every possible person-file combination by filling out a grid before responding to requests.

In both cases, we emphasized to participants that we were not asking them to match their grid and request responses, and that changing their minds was normal and allowed. We cannot completely account for the fact that participants may have tried to match their answers to appear more consistent, but we attempted to minimize its effects.

Data analysis
We collected both quantitative and qualitative data. To evaluate participants' free-form responses to debriefing questions, we applied an iterative coding process [14, 15]. An initial fine-grained review of a subset of the debriefing survey responses resulted in an initial set of codes. Then two of the authors independently coded the participant responses. Disagreements were resolved through modification or clarification of the codes until consensus was reached.

Several participants provided no policy choice for some grid cells. To facilitate analysis, only files with complete grid policy definitions are included in this paper. One participant failed to complete an entire page of grid policy, resulting in 97% of the blank grid entries. The dropped entries account for approximately 2% of possible grid policies.

A few participants answered the same request more than once, creating 26 duplicate responses (less than 2% of total responses). In this paper, the first response provided by the participant for any requester/file combination is assumed correct and used for data analysis.

FINDINGS
In this section, we first provide an overview of quantitative results. We then discuss seven specific findings drawn both from these results and from qualitative data that we collected. The first four provide evidence that users' policy needs can be better met by reactive policy creation than by traditional models. The next three describe additional interesting, somewhat unexpected qualitative results that can guide effective design of reactive-policy-creation systems.

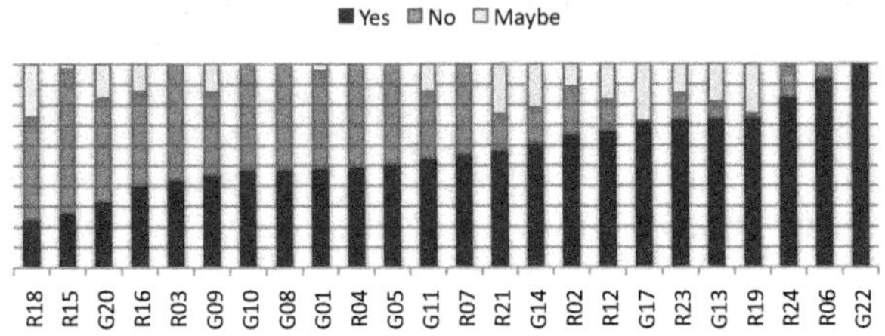

(a) Participants' proactive policies, normalized.

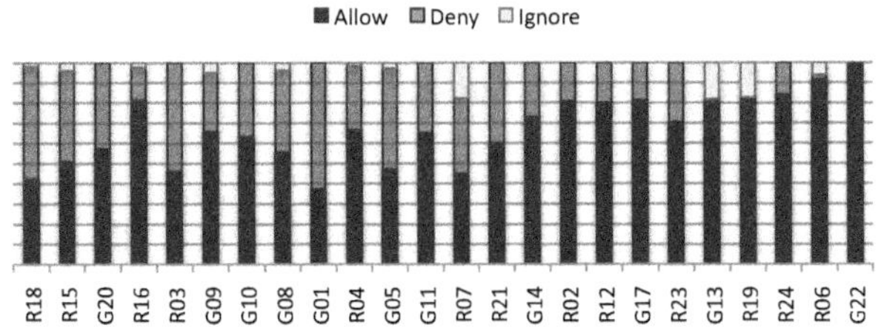

(b) Participants' reactive policies, normalized.

Figure 2. Participants' proactive and reactive policies varied widely.

Overview of quantitative results
Participants filled in a total of 4481 policy grid entries. Of these, 56% (2518) were *yes*, 34% (1518) were *no*, and 10% (445) were *maybe*. Individual choices ranged from 100% *yes* (P22) to 72% *no* (P15). Details of each participant's grid policies can be found in Figure 2(a).

Request responses showed a similar distribution, with 67% (913) *allow*, 30% (406) *deny*, and 3% (41) *ignore*. Individuals ranged from 100% *allow* (P22) to 62% *deny* (P01). Participants used *allow once* 251 times, *always allow file* 281 times, and *always allow group* 381 times. *Deny* responses were divided into 108 *deny once*, 81 *always deny file*, and 217 *always deny group*. Figure 2(b) summarizes individual participants' responses.

We also measured conflicts between participants' grid entries and their responses to requests. We consider instances where the participant marked *yes* but responded with any type of *deny*, or marked *no* but responded with any type of *allow*, as conflicts. Overall, 12% of responses resulted in conflicts, ranging from several participants with no conflicts to P08, for whom 49% of responses resulted in conflicts.

We found no significant difference in grid or response patterns between pre- and post-condition participants.[2]

[2]Differences calculated using unpaired t-tests, with p-values as follows: proactive *yes*, p=0.952; proactive *no*, p=0.972; proactive *maybe*, p=0.967; reactive *allow*, p=0.808; reactive *deny*, p=0.704; reactive *ignore*, p=0.619.

During the debriefing interviews, participants answered several Likert questions about their experiences. When asked whether they enjoyed using the system, the median response was a moderately positive 5 out of 7 (66.7% agree, 16.7% disagree, 16.7% neutral). Participants also agreed (median 6 out of 7; 66.7% agree, 12.5% neutral, 20.8% disagree) that this type of system would be convenient for them. Asked whether they found the e-mail requests annoying, participants disagreed slightly (median 3 out of 7; 25% agree, 16.7% neutral, 58.3% disagree).

We also asked participants whether they would use a similar system in real life, both to share their own files and to request files from others. Eleven participants said they probably would use such a system, nine said they might or might not, and only four said they probably would not.

In addition, we asked participants whether they would prefer reactive policy specification (represented by the request system), proactive policy specification (represented by the grid they filled out), or a combination of the two. Seven participants preferred the reactive model and 14 preferred the combination; only one preferred proactive policy alone.

During the second round, we asked participants if they would rather receive requests via e-mail, text message, phone call or other means. They overwhelmingly preferred e-mail, often in combination with text messages. A few participants asked for requests to be aggregated, either in a periodic digest e-mail or via a web-based service the participant could check at her convenience.

Policies change over time

Our results indicate that participants' file-sharing policies change relatively often, in response to a variety of factors. Reactive policy creation is better suited to express these kinds of dynamic policies than traditional access-control models. Participants demonstrated this dynamism through their proactive and reactive policy choices, including use of *maybe*, one-time decisions, and policy conflicts.

One indicator of dynamic policy was the frequent use of *maybe* in participants' policy grids, both before and after using the request system. As mentioned previously, in the second half of the study, when we clarified the *maybe* option, the use of *maybe* rose from 3% of grid entries in round one to 15% of grid entries in round two. Second-round participants used *maybe* more often at the expense of *no*; the rate of using *yes* stayed roughly unchanged. Especially in round two, participants often used *maybe* in thoughtful, deliberate ways in cases where context was important and access policy could not be entirely specified in advance. For example, P21 used *maybe* in reference to sharing financial data from his son's business with some of his co-workers. He never expected to share that file with those people, but said he might make an exception if an accountant wanted to provide financial advice. He chose *maybe* rather than *no*, planning to make an informed decision in context. P17 never used *no* in his grid, preferring *maybe* for the same reason.

Proactive *yes*, reactive *deny*	
Number of yes-deny conflicts	64
As percent of all conflicts	38.1
As percent of all responses	4.7
Proactive *no*, reactive *allow*	
Number of no-allow conflicts	104
As percent of all conflicts	61.9
As percent of all responses	7.7
Total conflicts	
Number of conflicts	168
As percent of all responses	12.4

Table 2. Conflicts between proactive and reactive policy. Most conflicts occurred when a proactive *no* decision was overturned by a reactive *allow* decision.

As with *maybe*, participants used the one-time *allow* and *deny* options to express policies that were expected to change. P10 selected *deny once* rather than *always deny* for one request because "it is within the realm of possibility that something would alter" and she would change her mind. P23 denied a work colleague access to a photo of him with friends once, after marking that combination maybe in the grid. He explained that he might grant access "maybe if we were just having casual talk at work and I mentioned something we did over the weekend."

In many cases, differences between proactive and reactive policy also indicated changing policy preferences. We found that 12% of total request responses conflicted with the participants' grid entries. Although a few of these conflicts were generated by participant misclicks in the response form, most reflect actual policy changes. Table 2 details the conflicts we observed. Interestingly, 62% of all conflicts involved answering *no* in the grid but allowing a request, regardless of whether the participant filled out the grid first or answered the request first. This provides some evidence that people will share more reactively than proactively.

P05 approved an access on her grid, but refused the same access as a request because "today he's on my blacklist." P12 said, "Some files might be consistent all the time," while others "depend on [the requester's] reasoning or might depend on my mood." P02 refused a request for a work document in progress, but later marked yes in her grid because the document had since been completed. (This is consistent with Razavi's findings about sharing patterns over document life cycles [13].)

Policies are situational

Our results indicate that participants' policies are dynamic in part because their sharing decisions depend heavily on the details of the situation at the time the access-control decision is made. Again, this context-awareness is a natural fit for a reactive model, which allows users to make decisions at the relevant time rather than a priori.

Participants frequently explained that the reason why someone wanted to access a file mattered in making policy. P04 denied a request from a friend for video of a family wedding because "there's no reason she would want to see it. ... If it had come with some kind of explanation for a reason why," then she might have permitted the access. P10 said, "Almost every answer I have is based on context." She chose to allow her husband to see an invoice from her business only once, saying she would want a reason to give him the file because he is "less careful than I am about sharing digital information." P12 used *deny once* for several requests for videos of herself practicing public speaking because "I don't really like to be recorded and on camera, but in the future if there were some really good reason, I'd allow it." She also said she might consider a request from a professor for work from a different class, but she would want a valid academic reason to share it. P08 added that if she were sending requests, she would want to supply a reason, as it seems "presumptuous" to ask without explaining.

Some participants even invented reasons for our randomly generated requests. P23 allowed a request from a friend for his sister's contact information once only, suggesting he might accept that request in an emergency. P12 guessed a friend might want to see her resume "as an example." P13 allowed a work colleague's request for a term paper she'd written on 'Feminism and Film' because "maybe he's interested in the topic and if I can help him get a broader understanding of it, then that would be good." She said an explanation of the request would help her make a better decision about a file like this one, which is "kind of personal but then kind of not."

Other examples demonstrate that this situational dependence can make it difficult to accurately specify policy ahead of time. Seeing a request helped remind P06 of ethical considerations. In reference to a request from another student for a term paper, she said, "Sharing your work with another student has potential to get you in trouble. ... At the time [when filling out the grid], I didn't think it would be an issue with me, but actually seeing, 'Matt is requesting your term paper,' the light went off, saying 'bad idea.'" In her grid, P01 allowed her work photographs to be seen by many requesters. However, when the requests were sent, she reconsidered her professional responsibilities and decided against sharing those files. P02 had the opposite reaction; she allowed a request for a sensitive file, but then said no in the grid because seeing all the people at once on the grid reminded her that information shared with one person will often be disseminated further.

Policies are also complex in other ways

Our findings indicate that many users' policy preferences are also complex in less dynamic ways.

Some participants considered factors beyond the sensitivity of the information in question when making decisions. For example, P09 denied a request from a friend for a Christmas photograph because "she doesn't celebrate Christmas and might be offended." P07 denied several requests for music when she thought the requester might not enjoy the song in question.

Two participants said they might like to grant fine-grained permissions to sections within files, not just to files themselves. P02 keeps all her passwords written down in one file; discussing a request from her teenage daughter for that file, she said that she might want to share some of those passwords with her daughter, but not others, "because someone who's younger doesn't know how to disseminate it or not." Similarly, P21 said he might want to share inventory and planning spreadsheets from his construction business with clients or vendors but redact some cost and pricing details.

Reactive policy creation fits users' interest in control

Several of our participants found a request-based system appealing because they felt it provided added control over the dissemination of their files. This finding confirms that reactive policy creation continues to fit well into users' mental models after a week of simulated exposure to it.

Six participants said they might use reactive policy creation to help them track who was accessing their files and when. P11 said he would use a system like this one to "see who is actually accessing my files" and create considered responses. P21 liked that a system like this would provide a record of "who had access to what." P02 said a reactive policy creation model would make it easier than a proactive model to start saying no if someone is abusing access privileges. P02 also never used the group options for a response, saying that she wanted to know which individual files people were accessing, even if that would mean receiving more requests. P13 added that "it makes me feel comfortable knowing what people are trying to access."

Other participants liked that the reactive policy model incorporates the idea of requesting permission. P01 said, "I enjoyed people asking for permission to see the files." P16 said she used *maybe* for certain grid entries because "sometimes I would be willing to share ... but I'd like him to ask me."

Participants also said the reactive model helped them make better decisions. P15 said answering requests "made you think"; with current systems, she often sends files or forwards e-mails "automatically, without thinking." P14 said the reactive model provides "more of an opportunity to really think about it."

Social norms influence policy choices

As a low-fidelity prototype, our study provided insight into the ways people might use a reactive-policy-creation system. Social factors played a large role in participants' reactions, as well as in the specific policy decisions they made. Understanding these influences can help designers structure a reactive system to maximize user comfort.

Many participants expressed discomfort at receiving requests they considered inappropriate, such as from friends for confidential work documents or from co-workers for financial files. Several said they were confident they would never receive such requests from real people, who would "know better."

Participants had interesting reactions to the *ignore* option.

The 11 participants who used this option applied it only 41 times, totaling only 3% of responses from all users. Seven participants told us they expected never to use this option, mainly because they found it rude not to send a reply. P01 said she wouldn't use *ignore* because she would like a reply if she sent requests. P05 said she wouldn't use *ignore* because "I don't like to live in the gray area." Others suggested that using *ignore* would only postpone the problem, as the requester would simply ask again until she received a response.

Some did see value in using *ignore*. Most commonly, *ignore* was used when the participant felt uncomfortable sharing the file but also uncomfortable denying the request outright. In many cases, this happened when a supervisor or authority figure asked for personal materials. For example, P13 felt "uncomfortable sharing personal pictures with a professor I am not close with, but I don't want to deny him access outright and make him feel uncomfortable. I figure ignoring his request will get the message across." She added that "For me, an ignore is like, 'I never want you to see it, but I don't want to talk about why.' It's just a more passive rejection for me." P06 used *ignore* to avoid saying no to her father, who had asked to see a video from her 21st birthday party that she preferred not to share with him. A few participants suggested that if they chose to *ignore* a requester, that requester might forget about the request entirely, neatly solving the problem.

Other explanations for using *ignore* included adding a delay while deciding how to answer, handling requests the participant considered too outlandish or inappropriate to deserve an answer, and handling requests for files the participant could not immediately identify. One participant used *ignore* to register her displeasure with a friend who had "made me upset that day."

We also asked participants directly if it bothered them to refuse or ignore requests, and if they worried that the requester would be upset. Most participants said they weren't bothered, saying that people who asked for inappropriate files should expect to receive a negative result. This is one area where we think the gap between experience sampling and real life has a strong impact; we expect that people might be more worried about the social consequences of denying or ignoring requests from real people. On the other hand, P06 pointed out that ignoring or denying a request is no worse within a reactive policy creation system than in any other sharing model, "just because I think eventually you have to do that anyway."

Social factors also played a role in several participants' desire to manage file access "manually," in person or otherwise outside a file-sharing system like the one we proposed. Several participants said they might not use a system like ours to request files, preferring to ask directly, over the phone or even by e-mail, rather than allowing the system to send an automated request. P07 said she would rather share in person: "I can show [this friend] this collection of music some other time when I see her on a daily basis." P10, a video producer, said she might use a request for one of her films to generate a personal interaction. She wanted to send a message with her response, saying "I'd love to share that with you. ... Do you want to watch together?" and hoping to "develop a conversation." P04 was also looking for more personal interaction, saying, "If my stepmother wants my friend's contact information, she needs to personally talk to me."

As discussed above, our participants were far more likely to say *yes* than *no* in their grids, and even more likely to accept a request than to say *yes* in the grid. Some of this may be attributable to the files being self-selected (discussed in more detail later), but it may also reflect a general social pressure to say yes when asked for something and to avoid the appearance of having secrets. In addition, as mentioned above, most conflicts between proactive and reactive policy were more permissive reactively. Taken together, these results suggest that perhaps forcing users to respond to direct requests increases social pressure to share.

People have difficulty trusting systems

Several participants were concerned about the security of our proposed system. Some worried that a system that exposed files for access via requests could be attacked, allowing unauthorized access. P08 said she would be "sort of paranoid" about exposing her files this way, in case an attacker "somehow [got] in to take other stuff" or "plant a worm on your drive. ... I would feel more comfortable if I would send it versus they go in and get it off my computer." Another participant worried that showing the existence of financial files could provide incentive for attackers to attempt to break into her system. Others were concerned that the source of a request could not be properly authenticated, and worried they might grant permission to a malicious user masquerading as a friend or co-worker. P08 suggested a spammer would "sooner or later ... hit on a name that was someone I know," and P18 asked "can someone request a file [with my friends name] and I'm giving access that I shouldn't be?"

These concerns, expressed by one quarter of participants, arose organically; in our script, we were careful to specify that "no one can access [your files] without your permission," but participants were unwilling to take our word for it, even with no real data at risk. This suggests a strong level of skepticism toward new systems claiming to provide secure data sharing. Designers of new reactive systems must take this into account and find ways to convincingly demonstrate security in order to get user buy-in.

Reactive policy specification raises specific concerns

Although we found significant evidence of the need for and popularity of reactive policy creation, we also identified specific concerns that must be carefully managed for a system based on this model to be successful. These potential problem areas include annoyance with too many messages, the possibility that users may not recognize a requested file, the need for well-chosen response options, and the potential for disclosing information via lists of requestable files.

Annoyance with requests.

We feared that even a small set of daily requests would cause annoyance and delay in answering, outweighing the possible benefits of reactive policy specification. We discovered this was not at all the case—participants expressed little annoyance and for the most part answered requests promptly. Most participants reported answering requests immediately upon receiving the e-mail. Measured request-response intervals accord with this, showing no increase in delay from the beginning to the end of the study. On a Likert scale, participants disagreed slightly with the statement "I found the e-mail requests annoying." We also asked them whether the number of requests they received was "way too many, very annoying"; "more than I would have preferred but not so many that it really bothered me"; or "a reasonable number of messages." Only one participant chose "way too many"; the rest split evenly between the other two options. Several participants indicated that although they received a lot of messages during the study, they would expect to receive many fewer in real life, limiting the annoyance. A few participants said the requests were no worse than the normal volume of e-mail they receive.

Although our ability to realistically evaluate the annoyance potential of a request-based system was somewhat limited, our impression after talking with participants is that while some frequency of requests would be intolerably annoying, our study did not reach that level. We are optimistic that a real system could maintain a tolerable message frequency. We expect that requests in a real system would decrease over time, as users grant persistent permissions or apply policy to groups of people or files and the system handles more and more situations automatically. This depends, of course, on how often users select the *always* and *always group* responses. In our study, participants selected these options more than two-thirds of the time, despite the fact that only a few coarse-grained file groups were available. P13 said she and a friend "share photos all the time," so she would allow all that friend to see all photos because it's "less of a hassle" than handling them individually. P23 also mentioned that he wished "the system after a while would have recognized" his previous choices and then sent fewer requests.

Trouble recognizing files.

The reactive policy model assumes users can make effective decisions when presented with a request for file access. This assumption breaks down if the user does not recognize the file in question. At least three participants in our study could not identify a requested file, despite the fact that we used only a small subset of their files, which we asked them to describe memorably less than a week prior to the request. We expect this problem to get worse when dealing with a user's complete set of files, some of which may not be named descriptively, over an indeterminate period of time. This problem could be mitigated by offering the user a chance to view the file in question before making a decision.

Additional response options.

We asked participants if they had ever wanted to provide a response not available on the form. The most popular suggestion was to reply asking why the file was wanted, further demonstrating the context-dependent nature of some policies. Other interesting suggestions included a "request pending" response to provide assurance the request was not being ignored, as well as an option to forward the request directly to a third party to make a decision. The forwarding option was mentioned in the context of work-related requests requiring approval from a supervisor as well as requests for address book information that should be approved by the person whose contact information was being requested.

Information disclosure via lists of files.

For a request-based system to work, requesters will likely need some information about what files or directories are available. This will by necessity leak information about what files exist, possibly including sensitive information if filenames are specific and descriptive. In a real system, we would expect to provide users with some control over file visibility; for simplicity, in this study we assigned requests randomly rather than allowing users discretion.

We asked participants how this issue would affect their interest in using this kind of system. Some participants weren't worried at all, because the files they wanted to restrict included things like tax files or calendar entries; these participants reasoned that "everyone" has files like those and so revealing their existence wouldn't be damaging.

As expected, however, many participants did express concerns. These concerns generally took two forms: worry that listing files would provide temptation for attackers to attempt to break the system security, and worry that sensitive information would be leaked as part of file and directory names. For example, P21 mentioned keeping the existence of a new resume file from a boss when searching for a new job; another participant was concerned that revealing e-mail subject lines might lead to a friend discovering a social event she hadn't been invited to. We believe these concerns can be effectively addressed by allowing users to decide which files should be visible and requestable to which people.

LIMITATIONS

It can be difficult to evaluate how well a proposed system feature will work without actually implementing the system to test it. Because of this, we put significant thought into our study design, and evaluating its success was one of our major goals. Despite the inherent limitations of experience-sampling simulation and the specific limitations of our methodology, overall we found evidence to suggest that our results can apply to reactive policy-creation systems in general.

First, although we asked participants to imagine receiving requests and sharing their files, they were aware no data was actually at risk. As a result, a participant might have refused a simulated request that in reality she might have accepted in order to avoid an awkward social situation. On the other hand, participants might have more casually accepted simulated requests than they would real ones. This problem is compounded by randomly generated requests that sometimes appeared bizarre or inappropriate, combined with our inability to tell participants why a given request was made. Several participants said they might accept requests they considered unusual or inappropriate if the requester had a good reason, which we were unable to supply. This may have reduced participants' ability to imagine the system to be real. However, based on our debriefing interviews we contend that our participants suspended their disbelief, took the requests they received seriously, and answered carefully.

In addition, our reactive response form allowed participants to explain their decisions. Participants provided reasons for 87% of responses, indicating thoughtful decision making. We also asked each participant for details about several individual responses; their detailed, reflective answers demonstrate they took the requests seriously. Participants who made policy decisions because they were angry at the requester or concerned she would not like the content, or who created justification scenarios for unlikely requests, clearly engaged with the system as though it were real.

Our decision to pay participants 25¢ per response created another potential limitation. We paid participants this way partially in order to replicate social incentives to respond to requests received from friends, family, and colleagues. The payment, however, might have induced participants to respond to more requests than they would have otherwise, or else reduced their annoyance at receiving requests. Because the payment per request was so small, we don't believe it introduced very much skew into our results. In addition, during the debriefing we asked participants directly about the annoyance of receiving requests; their frank and thoughtful replies provide at least some evidence that annoyance was not suppressed by the payment. Participants' tendency to respond relatively quickly to requests (as discussed earlier) also suggests they were motivated more by interest than payment, as they were paid regardless of when they answered.

Another possible limitation is that the requestors and files used in our study were selected by the participants. Because participants selected only a small subset of their files, it is likely they chose not to mention some of the most sensitive or private items. They also selected only a small subset of the people they know, so it is likely that some people with whom they have unique or complex relationships were left out. We tried to mitigate this by asking about a diverse variety of people and files, and by requiring each participant to supply at least one requester and file in each of several standard categories, including potentially sensitive categories like financial files and supervisors.

We asked participants to use our simulated reactive-policy-creation system for only a week. Longer use might cause behaviors and opinions to change. We believe, however, that the one-week period was enough to gain valuable insights. Observing most participants, it quickly became clear which requesters or files would result in strong policy preferences and which would be complex, dynamic, or borderline cases. Even dynamic decisions often followed similar lines of reasoning for each participant. As a result, we believe that for most participants we reached a saturation point where we had explored the majority of their policy decision space.

Our methodology only addressed reactive policy creation from the point of view of the resource owner; in future work, we hope to examine it from the requester's perspective. We also do not consider how users could view or modify existing policies created via *always* or *never* responses, which would be an important piece of a real reactive policy-creation system. A practical system would also need to consider how users could verify the source of a request.

RELATED WORK

Several prior studies investigate when and how users are willing to share personal data. Brush and Inkpen found users want individualized data and settings within shared devices [4]. Ahern et al. found that users' online photo sharing decisions are driven by concerns about security, social disclosure and convenience [2]. Participants interviewed by Little et al. expressed concern that information disclosure related to ubiquitous computing would disrupt family dynamics. Our work, also focused on personal sharing, examines how well reactive access control meets these consumer needs.

Olson et al. investigated sharing preferences related to a wide variety of personal and professional data [11]. They found that preferences can be categorized into broad groups based on trust relationships as well as the information sensitivity, but that more granular specification may also be required to handle exceptions. In this study, we explored trust relationship and file groupings in the context of a reactive model; we found that while broad groupings do often apply, exceptions remain important and meaningful.

Ackerman's study of the gap between social norms and technological possibility for information sharing in computer-supported cooperative work suggests that human information sharing relationships are fluid, nuanced, and time and context dependent [1]. In a similar result, Razavi et al. found that file sharing preferences in a personal learning space vary with document lifecycle and cannot be sufficiently expressed by static access polices [13]. The same study also demonstrated that implementing this kind of dynamic policy using traditional access controls was too labor intensive for users. Reactive policy creation supports dynamism by allowing information owners to consider requests in context, without the need to predetermine all possible policy in advance. We do not address other issues Ackerman raises, including user buy-in and the ability to gracefully change existing policy.

Early work by Lampson hints at problems with revealing the existence of files in order to validate access control, an unresolved issue in reactive policy creation, but asserts that content owners will shield files with directories that limit access to those who can know the existence of the files [8].

The closest analog to reactive policy creation may be Povey's optimistic access control scheme, which assumes that most requests are legitimate and should be granted [12]. This model relies on external administration to detect and respond to unauthorized access. Neither the reactive nor the optimistic models require content owners to predetermine complete policies; the optimistic model supports exigent circumstances more neatly, but the reactive model avoids the potential for unauthorized accesses that succeed and must be dealt with post facto.

Other prior efforts also concern non-traditional access control models. Egelman et al. designed a new model for home computer accounts, leveraging the fact that home users may not need controls as strict as those required in corporate environments [7]. Bauer et al. implemented the Grey system, which allows mobile phone users to reactively delegate authority to open locked doors [3]. We consider the reactive model in the context of security for personal and home data.

Our use of experience-sampling methodology was inspired by Consolvo et al.'s work examining location-sharing preferences [5]. The experience-sampling method was developed by Csikszentmihalyi and Larson [6].

CONCLUSION

In this study, we set out to determine if users' expressed interest in a reactive policy creation tool would hold up under simulated use of such a tool. Despite some limitations, the experience-sampling methodology we used yielded rich quantitative and qualitative data about users' access-control decisions and the factors that influence them.

Reaction to our simulated system for reactive policy creation was encouraging, if not definitive. We found evidence of access-control policies that are hard to express using existing static mechanisms, but that reactive policy creation can facilitate. Of the policies we collected from participants in our study, 21% used *maybe* or involved conflicts, and hence could not be easily expressed without a reactive policy-creation mechanism or other extension to traditional policy-creation practices. An additional 16% of policies were one-time policies, meant to be changed after a single access. These too may be difficult to define using traditional methods, and we conjecture that many of them would benefit from reactive policy creation.

We also found that when making policy decisions, people want more control and interactivity and rely on social norms, all areas where reactive policy creation can contribute to an access-control system. We found that while there are some clear disadvantages to the reactive model, they don't seem insurmountable. Overall, our results demonstrate that reactive policy creation is a strong candidate for further research and for potential inclusion in future access-control systems.

ACKNOWLEDGMENTS

This research was supported by the National Science Foundation via grants CNS-0831407 and DGE-0903659, by CyLab at Carnegie Mellon under grants DAAD19-02-1-0389 and W911NF-09-1-0273 from the Army Research Office, and by a gift from Microsoft Research. The authors thank Meghana Koushik for her help with the interviews. In memory of Niel Mazurek.

REFERENCES

1. M. S. Ackerman. The intellectual challenge of CSCW: the gap between social requirements and technical feasibility. *Hum.-Comput. Inter.*, September 2000.
2. S. Ahern, D. Eckles, N. S. Good, S. King, M. Naaman, and R. Nair. Over-exposed? privacy patterns and considerations in online and mobile photo sharing. In *Proc. CHI*, 2007.
3. L. Bauer, L. F. Cranor, M. K. Reiter, and K. Vaniea. Lessons learned from the deployment of a smartphone-based access-control system. In *Proc. SOUPS*, July 2007.
4. A. Brush and K. Inkpen. Yours, mine and ours? Sharing and use of technology in domestic environments. In *Proc. UbiComp*. 2007.
5. S. Consolvo, I. E. Smith, T. Matthews, A. LaMarca, J. Tabert, and P. Powledge. Location disclosure to social relations: why, when, & what people want to share. In *Proc. CHI*, 2005.
6. M. Csikszentmihalyi and R. Larson. Validity and reliability of the experience-sampling method. *J Nerv Ment Dis*, September 1987.
7. S. Egelman, A. Brush, and K. Inkpen. Family accounts: A new paradigm for user accounts within the home environment. In *Proc. CSCW*, 2008.
8. B. W. Lampson. Dynamic protection structures. In *Proc. AFIPS*, 1969.
9. R. A. Maxion and R. W. Reeder. Improving user-interface dependability through mitigation of human error. *Int. J. Hum.-Comput. Stud.*, 63, 2005.
10. M. L. Mazurek, J. P. Arsenault, J. Bresee, N. Gupta, I. Ion, C. Johns, D. Lee, Y. Liang, J. Olsen, B. Salmon, R. Shay, K. Vaniea, L. Bauer, L. F. Cranor, G. R. Ganger, and M. K. Reiter. Access control for home data sharing: Attitudes, needs and practices. In *Proc. CHI*, 2010.
11. J. S. Olson, J. Grudin, and E. Horvitz. A study of preferences for sharing and privacy. In *Proc. CHI*, 2005.
12. D. Povey. Optimistic security: A new access control paradigm. In *Proc. NSPW*, 2000.
13. M. N. Razavi and L. Iverson. A grounded theory of information sharing behavior in a personal learning space. In *Proc. CSCW*, 2006.
14. L. Richards. *Handling Qualitative Data: A Practical Guide*. Sage Publications, 2007.
15. L. Richards and J. M. Morse. *Readme First for a User's Guide to Qualitative Methods*. Sage Publications, 2007.
16. S. Voida, W. K. Edwards, M. W. Newman, R. E. Grinter, and N. Ducheneaut. Share and share alike: exploring the user interface affordances of file sharing. In *Proc. CHI*, 2006.

Reflecting on Pills and Phone Use: Supporting Awareness of Functional Abilities for Older Adults

Matthew L. Lee & Anind K. Dey
HCI Institute, Carnegie Mellon University
5000 Forbes Avenue, Pittsburgh, PA 15213
{matthew.lee, anind}@cs.cmu.edu

ABSTRACT

Older adults often struggle with maintaining self-aware of their ability to carry out everyday activities important for independence. Unobtrusive sensors embedded in the home can monitor how older adults interact with objects around the home and can provide objective accounts of behaviors to support self-awareness. In this paper, we describe the design and four month deployment of a prototype sensing system that tracks medication taking and phone use in the homes of two older adults. We describe two case studies on 1) how they engaged with the data by looking for and explaining their own anomalous behaviors and 2) how they used the sensor data to reflect on their actions and their own self-awareness of their abilities to remain independent. Finally, we propose recommendations for the design of home sensing systems that support awareness of functional abilities for older adults using reflection.

Author Keywords

Older adults, reflection, awareness, functional ability, aging-in-place, embedded assessment.

ACM Classification Keywords

H5.m. Information interfaces and presentation (e.g., HCI): Miscellaneous.

General Terms

Human Factors, Design.

INTRODUCTION

Many older adults strive to age in place, in the familiar setting of their own homes. As they age, older adults often experience subtle changes in their cognitive and physical abilities [1]. These changes manifest themselves as changes in their functional abilities, that is, how well they are able to carry out everyday activities such as taking medication, managing their finances, preparing a meal, or using the telephone.

However, many older adults have difficulty noticing and keeping track of these subtle changes in their functional abilities [19] and thus are unable to make the appropriate adaptations to compensate. As a result, this lack of awareness can lead to a pattern of repeated errors [6] such as taking the wrong medications, misdialing the telephone, and using kitchen appliances in unsafe ways. Not only can these errors be a hazard to safety, they can also be early signs of pathology such as Alzheimer's disease, Parkinson's disease, or other progressive neurodegenerative diseases that are considered most treatable in their early stages [12]. Often the impetus for having an individual screened for these conditions are when family members notice an unusual decline in functional abilities. Older adults, particularly those who live alone or have infrequent contact with others, can benefit from a means to stay more self-aware of the functional changes they are going through so that they are able to make the appropriate self-adaptations to continue to age in place gracefully.

Home sensing technology, or sometimes called embedded assessment technology, to monitor the well-being of older adults is a growing research area in human-computer interaction. Sensors can track how people move around in the home [2] and perform household activities [16,23]. Many of these research efforts focused on detecting problems and offering assistance to help correct them. In contrast, the focus of this work is how similar home sensing technology (and the data they collect) can be applied to provide timely and objective cues for older adults to reflect on their abilities as they age. Home sensing systems, like many ubiquitous or embedded sensing systems, can collect an overwhelming amount of data, particularly for older adults who may not be familiar with the types of detailed data that sensors can collect. Understanding what information older adults look for and then how to present this information can help designers refine home sensing systems to support reflection.

In this paper, we present a prototype home sensing system that monitors two tasks important for independence, medication taking and telephone use. We describe qualitative case studies of two older adults and how they used the data collected about their own behaviors over four months to investigate and reflect on their abilities to maintain independence. From these case studies, we provide design recommendations on how to present personal data from home sensing systems to support reflection and sensemaking for older adults to increase awareness of their functional abilities as they age.

RELATED WORK

Embedded assessment, the concept of using embedded sensors in the home to monitor the functional abilities of older adults, was introduced by Morris *et al.*, [18] and later discussed at a CHI workshop [17]. They envisioned systems that could automatically collect data to assess wellbeing, detect disease earlier, and facilitate informal caregiving. One of the main HCI challenges identified in the workshop is in understanding how to support individuals who want to manage their own health with the data collected from these systems. Since the concept was introduced, technology has made possible the development and testing of a number of prototypes of embedded assessment systems with real users, including TigerPlace [21] and EliteCare [10]. Both TigerPlace and EliteCare are independent-living facilities that use sensors such as motion and bed sensors to monitor the activities and ensure the safety of its residents. Our sensing approach is to monitor specific tasks such as medication taking and phone use that may provide earlier and more sensitive signs of cognitive or functional decline rather than overall activity levels.

In addition to research on technical systems for monitoring health in the home, there has been research in the CHI community investigating how older adults and people with chronic conditions manage their health in their everyday lives. Birnholtz & Jones-Round [3] investigated the tensions between older adults' need for security and their desire for independence. Ballegaard *et al.* [1] called for designers to not only take a clinical-centric view of health technologies but also to consider the needs of the patient and the everyday contexts in which technologies are used for self-learning. We adopt a similar non-clinical, user-centered perspective in this paper to understand the unique needs of older adults and how they make use of sensor data about their functional abilities.

We investigate how older adults use sensor data to support reflection on their own health. Li *et al.* [13] discuss a framework for how users deal with information collected about themselves (such as how they carry out everyday activities). We analyze the *reflection* and *action* stages of that framework from the perspective of the older adult for this paper. Reflection has shown to be effective for people with diabetes, for improving their sense of control and improved diet outcomes [15]. Reflection and the ensuing awareness of healthy and unhealthy behaviors for cardiac rehabilitation patients were found to be important for successful recovery [14]. In this paper, we conduct two case studies to investigate how older adults used data about how they perform everyday activities important for independence to become more aware of their abilities as they age, through reflection. Our case studies focus on the following three research questions:

1. How do older adults engage with and reflect on embedded assessment data?

2. Does reflection on embedded assessment data help older adults have a more accurate awareness of their abilities?

3. If reflection is helpful, how do we support reflection on the performance of everyday tasks important for independence to increase awareness?

In the following section, we describe our prototype sensing system and the tasks that it monitors.

SENSING SYSTEM DESIGN

We developed prototypes of a sensing system designed to monitor different activities that are important for independence and commonly used in clinical assessments [11] and deployed the system in the homes of two older adults for about six months. Our system unobtrusively and automatically monitored two everyday activities: medication/pill taking and phone use. Both sets of sensors transmitted their data wirelessly in real time to a research laptop placed out of sight behind a couch. The laptop logged the data and uploaded it every night through a modem connection to a campus server.

To monitor the pill-taking task, we developed a smart pillbox (Figure 1) that could monitor when a door was opened and how the box was manipulated. We augmented an existing off-the-shelf pillbox with snap action switches to know which doors were open. The design is similar to the MedTracker prototype [8], but our design adds an accelerometer that can monitor how individuals handled the pillbox and whether the pillbox was inverted (a common strategy to remove the pills because older adults' finger often do not comfortably fit inside the box). The electronics, including a microcontroller, a ZigBee wireless card, and a battery, are mounted in an adjacent compartment (actually a second pillbox with the dividers removed). The resulting smart pillbox is easily grasped and has an appearance nearly identical to that of a non-augmented pillbox.

Figure 1. The smart pillbox uses snap action switches to detect when doors are opened and closed. An accelerometer tracks how the box is held, shaken, or inverted.

To monitor phone use, we developed a custom circuit that we connected directly to the phone line. The circuit uses a Mitel MT8870 DTMF decoding chip to monitor what numbers are dialed, whether the phone is on or off the hook, and the length of phone calls. A computer modem monitored incoming calls and Caller ID. Both the phone sensor and modem were "invisible" in their operation to the user, as they did not affect the users' calls.

Sensing System Deployment

We deployed the smart pillbox and phone sensors for six months in the apartments of two older adults who lived alone. We replaced their pillbox with our instrumented pillbox that had the exact same size, lettering, and shape as their existing pillbox. We encouraged participants to carry on as normal and avoid being extra careful just because their activity was being tracked.

In the first two months, we continually revised and reintroduced more robust versions of the sensors, which left us with approximately four months of valid pill-taking and phone use data. Throughout the deployment, a researcher visited the apartments every two weeks to replace batteries, debug sensors, and ensure that the sensors were not getting in the participant's way. We verified the accuracy of the sensors through a combination of lab testing, field testing, and observations of use during bi-weekly visits to the apartments. On a few occasions we were unable to collect data for one or more consecutive days due to a power loss or error in the logging script. In the four months (122 days) of data, there were 15 unlogged days for Participant 1 and 16 unlogged days for Participant 2.

Case Study Participants

We recruited two older women who lived alone in their apartments through a professional connection with the management of a low-income senior apartment building. These two individuals represent a population that may benefit the most from monitoring technologies as they lack care support from a spouse or a daily caregiver. Both have an adult child who lives within an hour's drive.

Participant #1 (P1) (age 81) is a retired nurse, who is aging successfully. P1 has set in place the routines that ensure her safety in her medication taking. She prides herself in keeping up to date with the latest news and politics and overall has a generally accurate impression of her own abilities. She has mobility issues that make it difficult for her to walk up and down stairs and for long distances. Based on psychometric testing (Computer Assessment of Mild Cognitive Impairment) [22], P1 exhibits a slightly higher level of ability in attention, memory, and executive functioning compared to her peers.

Participant #2 (P2) (age 77) is an older adult who once struggled with moderate symptoms of Parkinson's disease. The disease once took away P2's ability to concentrate and control her limbs. However, she has recently started to take medication that was effective at eliminating most of her Parkinson's symptoms, resulting in her being able to walk, write, and concentrate moderately well. She admits to having a memory problem due to the lingering symptoms of the disease, but generally believes that she is pretty aware and aging well. She also does not consider herself to be an organized person, preferring clutter to putting things away. Based on psychometric testing [22], P2 exhibits a lower level of cognitive ability across attention, memory, and executive functioning compared to her peers.

After using the final version of the sensors for four months without seeing the data, each participant was presented with visualizations of data showing their own pill taking and phone use behaviors. We chose to withhold the data during the sensor deployment so the sensors could capture the participants' natural behaviors without the influence of feedback from the system.

CASE STUDY INTERVIEWS

We conducted qualitative semi-structured interview sessions with each participant in which we showed them data about their pill taking and phone use tasks to allow them to reflect on their own abilities to stay independent. The interview consisted of a researcher-guided training phase (to ensure the participants could understand the visualizations) followed by a participant-guided exploration phase. In the training phase, the researcher first showed the participant visualizations of data from a short time frame (for example, from the day or week immediately preceding the interview) and then explained what the marks, axes, and dimensions represented. The researcher refrained from making any interpretations of the data (*e.g.*, "you made a mistake here" or "you missed your pills a lot in the past month"). The researcher then tested the participant's understanding by having her describe a visualization of another day's data.

After adequately demonstrating their comprehension, the participant was allowed to guide what level of detail of the data they wanted to see. We used a think-aloud study protocol to allow the participant to express her thoughts and reflections during the interview. To understand any change in awareness, the researcher asked the participant to assess her own pill taking and phone use abilities before and after looking at the data. To understand the participant's intent for future actions, the researcher also asked questions such as "Would you do anything differently because of what you are seeing, or not?" The interviews were video recorded. The video was segmented into units of analysis that consisted of a participant's single thought or stream of related thoughts. These segments were analyzed using Grounded Theory [7] where coded segments were grouped into successively higher order categories resulting in emergent themes. In the following sections, we describe the data visualizations and the results of the analysis.

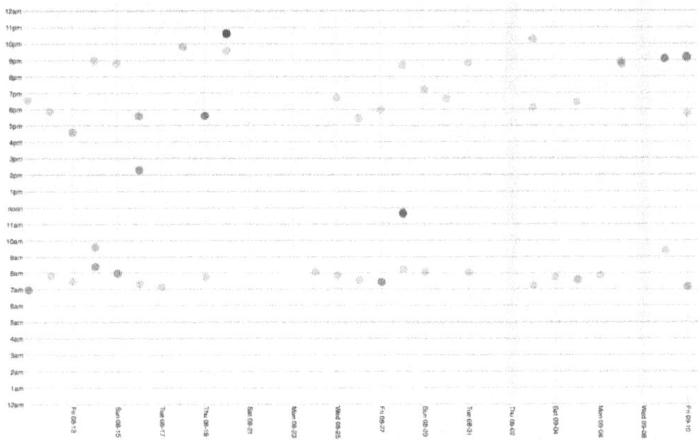

Figure 2. Long-term visualization of pill taking. The y-axis is the time of day, and the x-axis is the date. A green dot represents opening and closing a door that matches the day of the week. A red dot represents when the door does not match the current day of the week. A yellow dot indicates the door was not closed.

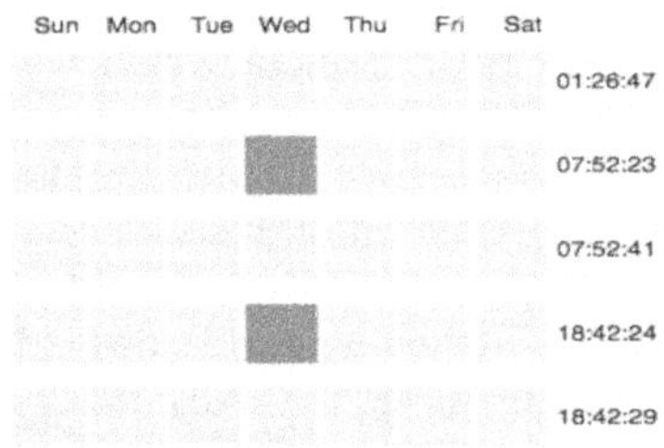

Figure 3. Short-term pill taking visualization showing pillbox door states and times for a particular day. The user opened and closed the Wed door in the morning and in the evening.

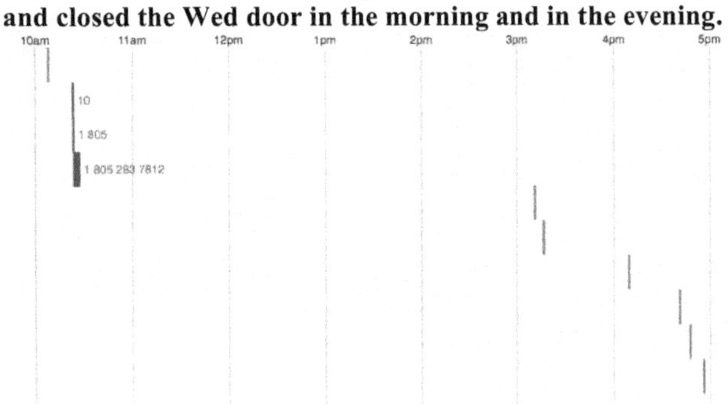

Figure 4. Detailed view of phone calls on a particular day, showing how the user misdialed twice and successfully dialed the number on the third try. The width of the bar represents the length of the call. Red indicates a misdialed number.

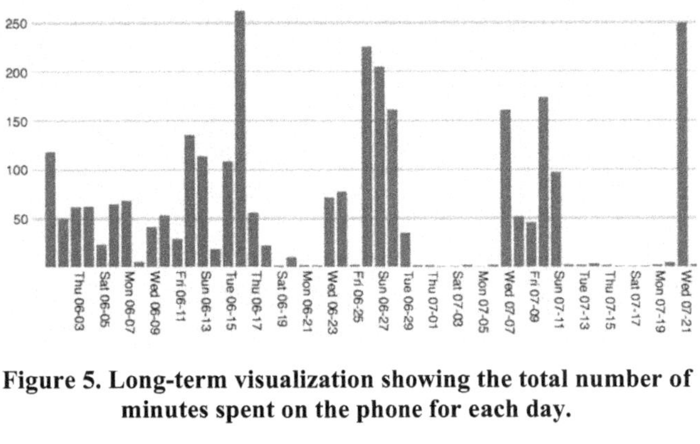

Figure 5. Long-term visualization showing the total number of minutes spent on the phone for each day.

Data Visualizations

For both pill taking and phone use, a high-level, long term view showing performance over weeks or months and a low-level, short term view showing the specific details about the task performance for one day were available.

For pill taking, the long-term visualization (Figure 2) showed the date and time of every instance when a pillbox door was opened over a user-configurable time span of a week to multiple months. Each mark's color represents whether the door was left open until the next pill taking episode (yellow) and whether the pillbox door's label matched (green) or did not match (red) the current day of the week. The green color represents the most typical "correct" sequence of pill taking, that is, opening the correct pillbox door and closing it within a reasonable amount of time, before opening another one. Dots from multiple door openings can overlap and appear in darker shades. A grayed out column represents a day that we were not able to collect data due to a system problem. The short-term visualization (Figure 3) showed how the pillbox doors were opened (dark shading) throughout a particular day.

For phone use, the long-term visualization showed the date and time of every outgoing phone call over a user-configurable time span of a week to multiple months. Each mark was colored green if the call was not misdialed and colored red if misdialed. The metric we used for marking whether a call was misdialed was if two numbers were dialed within a minute of each other and also had 70% of the digits in the first number overlap with the digits in the second number. In the short-term visualization (Figure 4), we showed them the time, length, and number of every phone call made on a particular day. Another long-term visualization of phone use (Figure 5) included the total number of minutes spent on the phone for each day over the course of a week or a few months.

RESULTS

In this section, we describe how the participants both engaged with the data by investigating it and how they reacted to the data with respect to changes in their awareness or intention to change their behaviors.

Engaging with Embedded Assessment Data

Based on the interactions with the visualizations of the task performance data we showed to the participants, we observed how they engaged with the data, what they paid the most attention to, and what other information they wanted to help interpret the data. Participants engaged in three different behaviors: looking for their mistakes in the data, investigating and attempting to explain away these mistakes, and diving down into the details of their task performance to verify their explanations.

Looking for Anomalies/Mistakes

When presented with the visualizations of the data, participants attempted to find any mistakes or anomalies in their own behavior. For example, in the visualizations depicting the states of the pillbox doors on a given day, participants would point out the door states that did not seem normal given that day or that time of day. For example, when P1 first saw the pillbox door state visualization that showed how she opened the pillbox at 7:30pm, she immediately mentioned how it showed her that she took her pills later than usual.

The visualization (Figure 2) that showed long-term pill-taking performance for a week or more highlighted only positive examples of pill taking. The graph contains a dot for every instance a pillbox door was opened. It did not contain, for example, a marking to show when the pillbox was not opened that day. The only visual indication of a missed day is the rather inconspicuous between-dot whitespace, which can be difficult to see especially because the dots do not line up closely with each other. Nonetheless, we observed that P1 and P2 did not focus on the positive examples of pill-taking but rather went to the effort of going through the whitespaces on the graph and seeing if they lined up with a particular day to find instances of missed pills. When first seeing this graph, P2 moved closer to the screen and she said,

"I'm trying to see how quickly I can tell if I missed anything. And to be honest, I have to set [sic] here and study it to see if I did."

Then she used her finger to move along a couple of days to see if a dot lined up vertically with that day. Then she noticed the block of days in the middle of the previous month with no dots, and lamented about her pill taking,

"[There are] a heck of a lot of mistakes on that graph. There're things goin' on that shouldn't be goin' on."

Generating Explanations

After identifying the anomalies in their performance in the data (such as missed pills, opening the pillbox doors incorrectly, or unusually long phone calls), participants immediately tried to think of reasons why the anomalies might have occurred. Finding a reasonable explanation, other than they made a mistake, was important for the participants to know whether they were having a problem or not. Participants used a number of information sources in addition to the pill-taking and phone use visualizations including their memory, routines, and a wall calendar.

Explaining with Personal Memory

Our participants' first natural reaction to seeing an anomaly in the data was to think back to the events of that particular day or week to find an extenuating circumstance to explain the unusual behavior. P1 was particularly good at remembering recent significant events that helped to explain anomalies in her pill taking. For example, upon noticing that many of the pillbox doors were opened out of sequence a few days earlier, she recalled that she received a new supply of heart medication and was placing them into her pillbox to fill out rest the week. In contrast, P2 was less able to recall the details of recent events. When the sensor data showed that she did not interact with the pillbox three days ago, she tried to recall what she did that day that might have explained this error. She said,

"I'm trying to think…I don't remember what I did. I tell you the truth, ever since I've had this problem with my memory, I can't remember that day at all."

P2 had difficulty remembering even recent events as a result of her Parkinson's disease. However, this problem was not isolated to P2 with her Parkinson's, but P1's difficulty in recalling events from the more distant timeframe of a couple of weeks ago also made it difficult for her to explain some apparent instances of missed pills. For example, when thinking back to a weekend three weeks prior, P1 tried to recall whether she was out of town or not. She said,

"I don't think I was away. [thinks hard for a few seconds] I wonder if I was at [my daughter's], but I'm trying to remember."

Then she thought about another instance of when she visited a friend for one night but disqualified that as a valid explanation because that visit happened during the middle of the week. Ultimately, she did not remember what happened on that weekend unassisted, but rather she went to review her wall calendar (discussed in a later section) for some cues for her memory. Even though P1 was able to recall recent experiences adequately, both P1 and P2 eventually had difficulty relying solely on their memory to recall the personal experiences important for explaining anomalies in their behaviors and had to resort to other means such as their routines.

Explaining with Routines

Without an explicit recollection of an event or circumstance that would explain why an anomaly such as a missed pill or a misdialed telephone call might have occurred, participants thought about their routines and whether the anomaly might fit within one of their many variations on their routines. For example, when noticing a few instances of taking her morning pills much later (at 9am) than she normally would have (7am), P1 reasoned that she must have slept in on those mornings. Likewise, when she noticed an instance when she opened up all the doors late on a Friday evening. To explain this anomaly, she drew on two different variations on her routines. She routinely fills her pillbox on a Saturday, but she occasionally refills the box on a Friday and this must have been what happened in this case. To explain why it was so late in the evening, she mentioned that she sometimes goes downstairs to play cards on Fridays and does not return home until after 9pm.

"I can understand that because sometimes on Fridays, not too often, I put [the pills] in for the following week. And that would be in the evening when I come back up from downstairs from what I was doing."

P2 was less able to draw on specific memories of events that might explain anomalies in her pill taking. When noticing in the data that she took her pills very late at night only two days ago, P2 reflected on one of her routine behaviors that she often falls asleep on the couch during the evening which accounts for the lateness of the pill taking.

"I fall asleep, like instantly, if I sit down and even if I'm talking to you, I'll fall asleep, and then I wake up three hours later and know now it's time for my bedtime pills and I'm going to take my pills different[ly]."

Routines and their subtle variations can provide the context to explain away anomalies in task performance data.

Explaining with the Calendar

When unsuccessful in finding either a specific circumstance or routine to explain an anomaly in the task performance, P1 referred to her calendar for hints about what happened on the day(s) of the anomaly. The most common explanation P1 used to explain days with no pillbox activity was that she was away from her apartment which she often recorded on her wall calendar. For example, P1 went to stay with her daughter for a few days in the second month of the study. For that episode, she prepared her medications and placed them in her travel pillbox that she took with her. Naturally, the pillbox instrumented for the study stayed in the apartment and sent signals indicating no activity for those days. While attempting to explain why there was no pillbox activity for that weekend, she noticed that her grandson's name was written in her calendar for that weekend and realized that he was returning from the Army and was home for a visit. Reminded of the details, she said,

"That's right, I went to [my daughter's], [my grandson] took me home with him and we had our get-together that Sunday, and I returned on Tuesday because she was working in town."

Similarly, to explain a couple of misdialed phone calls to numbers that she did not recognize, P1 wondered whom she might have been trying to call that day. She glanced at her calendar and saw a note to herself to call the senior-accessible transit organization to schedule a ride and reasoned that she was trying to call them but became frustrated at the misdialing and used the speed dial on her mobile phone instead. P2, on the other hand, did not keep her appointments on a calendar and struggled to recall what she did on particular days and had more difficulties when trying to explain anomalies. Date-specific information about circumstances from a calendar can help explain date-specific anomalies in the data.

Confirming with Details

Our sensing system could capture task performance at a fairly fine level of detail (*e.g.*, the specific time that a particular pillbox door was opened and every digit dialed for a particular phone call). We presented both a long-term view of the data usually spanning weeks or months and also allowed the participants to review the specific details of each phone or pill-taking episode in a given day. Both participants were able to understand the detailed information after it was explained by the researcher, but they expressed different interest in the detailed information. P1 was interested in knowing the details of when each pillbox door was opened and closed to make sure that she took her pill that day. She also used the details to confirm her explanations. For example, to explain why the log showed that she did not take her medications on Friday night, she remembered that she went to her nephew's party that evening and took her pills with her. She looked at the details of her pillbox interactions that day and saw that it took her 20 seconds in the morning, much longer than normal because she was moving her evening pills into her travel container. P1 also used the detailed data about what phone numbers were dialed in a particular episode of misdialing to explain that she was trying to dial her bank and that it was common for her to make mistakes with all those numbers and would have to restart the call often. In P1's case, she was able to use the detailed information collected about the tasks she performed along with knowledge of her recent events and habits to understand why anomalies occurred.

In contrast, the detailed information was less helpful for P2 for generating explanations because even though she understood the details, she could not think of the context of that interaction to explain why particular doors were opened at that time or why a particular phone call was so long. As a result, P2 was repeatedly baffled by the details the sensors recorded which challenged her self-awareness of her behaviors. With a perplexed look on her face, she said,

"I can't imagine why I would open it that way. Looking at an individual day isn't all that helpful because I don't remember what I did that day."

The value of providing low-level details of task performance to users for reflection depends on their ability to use the details to recall the context and explain their behavior.

Reactions to the Data

In addition to observing how the individuals reflected on the data and made sense of it to themselves, we found that the sensor data about their everyday performance provided the ground truth by which they could reaffirm or gain an accurate awareness of their functional abilities. After realizing the inconsistency in their routines through exploring the data, both individuals intended to "do something about it" and be more consistent to ensure safety. The participants also expressed opinions about sharing the information with members of their care network. In the following sections, we describe these themes in detail.

Supporting Accurate Awareness

Awareness of changes in functional abilities is key for successful aging, as it provides opportunities for the individual to make the appropriate adaptations to ensure she remains functional and avoid situations that threaten her safety [6]. Prior to viewing any of the sensor data, both participants P1 and P2 were confident that they performed their pill taking regularly and almost never missed their medications. P1 expressed, "I do feel confident that I always take my medications, but hopefully it will continue a few more years." P2 also expressed her confidence that she never missed her medications because "I'm afraid if I don't take them, I'll regress and my Parkinson's will start again."

However, P1 and P2 differ in the accuracy of their confidence in their pill taking routine. P1's confidence in her routine actually matches her functional abilities. She believes that she almost never missed a pill and over the four months that we monitored her pill taking, she never missed a day without opening the pillbox at least once when she was home. However, P2's pill taking routine is more erratic, showing instances of isolated days where she did not open the pillbox at all or opened up a pillbox door that did not match the day of the week. As a result, the sensor data had very different impacts on P1 and P2.

For P1, the data provided a means to affirm her accurate confidence in her pill taking, whereas for P2 the data was useful for re-assessing her own (over-)confidence in her pill taking routine. When seeing that there was a green dot almost every day indicating that she opened the correct pillbox door, P1 said

"I always feel confident that I take my medications and [the data] helps me confirm that I've taken my medicines."

She also commented that even the gaps in her pill taking shown in the data was helpful because

"I see in front of me what I do, and as long as I can confirm in my mind that I've taken my medication, that's good."

Even though P1's awareness of her abilities was relatively accurate, she was initially surprised at the variability of when she took her pills during the day and how often she misdialed the telephone. Her feelings of surprise quickly transitioned to acknowledgement, as she was able to explain the variability and the number of misdials by accounting for them in natural variations in her routines, as described in the Generating Explanations section above.

P2, on the other hand, had her confidence challenged when she saw the inconsistency and variability in her pill taking data. For example, when seeing in the data that she tended to take her morning pills anywhere between 10am and noon, she said,

"I thought I took my pills around 9:30am because I sleep late. No longer do I rise at 7am, but I never thought of it."

When seeing many gaps in her pill taking data, she remarked about her own prior confidence,

"You actually physically know that you took it that day, but no, you didn't. I hate to acknowledge that; it's just another thing that I don't want happening."

During the interview session, P2's awareness went through a transformation from being absolutely (but falsely) confident in her abilities to feeling a little shaken that she might not be as aware as she thought she was. She expressed,

"Being able to see it right in front of you, the bad things, is amazing to me. Gawd! It's making me feel really screwed up. I wouldn't have thought I did that."

Adding to P2's frustration was her inability to think of specific reasons why she might not have opened her pillbox on particular days or why she opened the pillbox doors in a strange way. At the end of the interview after she saw all the data, her prior confidence changed to concern, she said,

"I have to admit, you're not aware of the mishaps you do. You have no idea you're doing some of those dumb things you see other people do. It's just a fact of life."

Despite their different emotional outcomes, both P1 and P2 were able to use the objective and timely data collected from the sensors as "ground truth" to evaluate their own confidence in their functional abilities.

Intention to be More Consistent

Based on a newly gained awareness of their abilities to take the right pills at the right time and correctly make telephone calls, the participants resolved to be more consistent in their routines to ensure their safety and adherence to their medications.

P1, despite her relatively accurate awareness of her pill taking routine, decided she wanted to be more consistent in what time of day she takes her pills. A more consistent routine would make her feel more confident that she took them and would help her to ingrain in her brain a successful habit that will last into the future. Talking about how she will continue with her routine to move her pills from the box to the visible bowl on her counter, she said "I have to get more consistent in opening that box and putting them in [the bowl]. See, I'm so used to that routine. I keep that little black bowl on my counter for that reason." After seeing how often she was misdialing the phone, she said she wanted to buy a new phone with buttons that are easier to press so that she can be more consistent in her phone dialing and figure out whether the problem was caused by her old phone or her old arthritic fingers.

P2, after seeing the large variability and the unexplainable instances of missed pills, resolved to be more consistent and to pay more attention to her pill taking. She equated her poor pill taking performance with "messing with [her] life" because she currently is taking a "miracle" drug for Parkinson's disease and she certainly does not want to regress to a point where the Parkinson's symptoms re-emerge. She said, "I'm gonna set a time for me for my pills and try to adhere to that, say at the 11 o'clock news." She even began to question her evening medication taking routine (which is not monitored by our pillbox because her evening pillbox is a different type) and whether she was taking that properly. She considered whether or not to keep a written diary where she would check off everyday whether she performed important tasks like taking her pills.

Desire to Share Data and Potential for Misinterpretation

Both participants wanted to share their information with their family members so that others could know how well they are able to remain independent. P2 said her daughters, particularly the one who is a nurse, would want to see the data and help her mother fix any problems that might come up. Similar to previous findings [3], participants wanted to keep their information private to just their own family, close friends/helpers, and their doctors.

With sharing comes the additional risk for misinterpretation. P1 was concerned that others who would look at the data might not be able to determine whether the anomalies in the data (*e.g.*, missed or late pills or misdialed telephone) are benign or a cause for concern. She is able to look at the graphs and figure out whether the apparent missed pills are explained by being out of town or taken in some other acceptable way. She often talked about "confusing the poor little pillbox" when she does something that is not typical of routine. She explained, "I know what I'm doing, but the interpreter doesn't know why I haven't been consistent in opening the boxes right."

Data about Everyday Activities Useful as Memory Cue

Many older adults (as well as younger adults) struggle with recalling the details of events on particular dates. P1 explains how her memory is important to her:

"I worry about being able to remember things and like Sunday evening when I go to bed, I try to give myself a test to see if I can remember what I did all week, sometimes I can easily where something sparks in my head about what happened Sunday and everything comes back."

Time or a date is a typically poor memory cue [5]. Often calendars (electronic or paper) can be a good source of memory cues. However, not all events are typically recorded on a calendar. P1 found the automatically generated log of her pill taking and phone use to provide good cues to help her remember her recent summer activities. As she was explaining away the days for which she did not open a pillbox door, she fondly reminisced about the many times she travelled to her daughter's, had a visit from her grandson, and went to stay with a friend. She said, "this is good because it makes me think about some of the things I did this summer." When looking at the length of phone calls for each day of the previous month, she was reminded of when she had a long talk with a friend who was sick. P1 was able to use the sensor data, as well as her own memory and calendar, to do some "mental time travel" by mentally reliving recent events. In contrast, P2 was unable to use the sensor data to cue into her memory because she just did not remember the details of recent events at all.

DISCUSSION

From our interview case studies, we observed how the two older adults engaged with the data about how well they took their medications and used the telephone, two everyday tasks important for independence and aging in place. As more research and commercial systems for home health monitoring are being developed and marketed for older adults, the demand for principles for maximizing the usefulness and usability of these systems becomes clear. In this section, we first discuss the value these systems had for our participants and other older adults like them. Then we describe recommendations for how to improve the design of home sensing systems for older adults.

Value of Embedded Assessment for Older Adults

One of the benefits of embedded assessment proposed in [18] was that it provides objective data about performance of behavior to complement the subjective accounts from self-report and caregiver reports for older adults. We saw in our case studies that both individuals were able to use the automatically collected data about their behaviors to test their awareness of their functional abilities. When the participants were unable to explain an anomaly (*e.g.*, missed pill or misdialed phone number) in the data, they trusted that the system recorded it correctly and became aware of their mistake. The data also enabled them to reflect on not just the recent past but also on their behaviors months earlier, allowing them to see if isolated behaviors were actually more common than they realized and thus cause for concern. Thus, presenting embedded assessment data can support self-reflection, resulting in greater and more accurate awareness for older adults, a benefit both for individuals who have an accurate perception of their abilities (as in the case with P1) as well as for those whose perception is less congruent with their actual behavior (as in the case with P2). In addition to providing an objective account of their actions for supporting awareness, the embedded assessment data provided them with both the trigger as well as the specific information necessary to make adaptations to ensure their independence and safety.

An unexpected value of the embedded assessment data that we identified in this study is they can be used to support everyday reminiscence of activities and events unrelated to the particular tasks monitored much like richer cues such as photos and messages [20]. The data provides a window into the pattern of activities that active older adults perform. Deviations from the normal pattern can signify a non-routine event that may not normally be salient enough (but nonetheless meaningful and personally significant) to recall without a cue. Data about tasks around the home can provide cues for special events that older adults (and indeed younger adults) want to be able to recollect and mentally re-experience in their minds.

Design Recommendations

Based on our observations of how the older adults in our case studies explored and used the information to make sense of and reflect on their own functional abilities, we provide recommendations for designing home sensing systems that support self-reflection for older adults.

We observed that users were eager to not just look at the visualizations at a glance but actually spent the time to study them to find instances where it looked like they made a mistake. Similar to the process of finding key events in data used in intelligence analysis [4], users looked for anomalies. However, in contrast to intelligence analysis, which requires a high amount of interpretation by the analyst, anomalies in task performance can be more easily identified computationally. Thus, we recommend from a usability standpoint that *the instances of anomalous behaviors likely to be caused by the user should be highlighted or at least represented in a way that requires minimal analysis by the user.* As a negative example, the multi-month visualization (Figure 2) for pill taking only included marks where the pillbox was opened, relegating the representations of missed pills to narrow, difficult-to-notice columns of white space.

The contrasting outcomes between our two participants highlight the need for supporting better explanations of anomalous behaviors. Many older adults have difficulty remembering their recent experiences due to either neurological conditions (like P2) or simply benign declines in memory associated with aging (like P1). To be able to identify whether an anomalous behavior is acceptable or a mistake, the context of the behavior needs to be available. Thus, designers of embedded assessment systems should *provide tools to allow the user to retrieve the context of the data such as special events from calendars, people encountered that day, or to-do lists in addition to just presenting the data by itself.*

In addition to providing context for explanation, *providing the low-level details of the behavior can support a better understanding, explanation, and fixing of the behavior.* For example, seeing that a particularly long telephone number is being misdialed helps the user to understand they might have a problem with digit span memory and have to pay attention more when dialing that number. We also found that there was little demand to see the details of behaviors that were judged as "good" (such as correctly dialed phone calls or days where pills were taken). Thus designers, if faced with a shortage of resources, can focus on providing the details for the anomalous cases. For example, when a system is able to detect an anomaly in near real time, the system can increase the resolution of sampling at the cost of a temporary increase in battery or memory consumption.

The value of embedded assessment data extends beyond the individual monitored to other members in their care network such as relatives and clinicians. The users in our case studies suggested that the information be shared with their relatives so they can look after them more closely. However, users were concerned that others might misinterpret their seemingly errorful but explainable behaviors as mistakes. Therefore, designers should *allow for collaborative sharing and exploration of behavioral data or support annotation of the data before sharing with others to avoid misinterpretations.*

Study Limitations

Our case study approach provided us with a rich understanding of how our participants engaged with the data and found the data useful for building or reinforcing their awareness of their functional abilities. We acknowledge that not all older adults are similar to our participants. However, the case studies were most useful for comparing and analyzing the similarities and differences between two very different older adults, each representing a different end of the spectrum in their abilities to remain aware of their functional abilities. Even though P1, a successfully aging older adult, and P2, a struggling, less aware older adult are very different, they both benefited from the objectivity and timeliness of embedded assessment data. Also, the scope of our data collection was limited to two tasks. However, the pill taking and phone use tasks have been standardized as part of the normal battery of tasks used for functional assessments [11] and thus are likely to be most sensitive for indicating changes in cognitive and functional abilities. Furthermore, the sensors may collect false data, particularly if users purposely game the system. Our future work includes developing a suite of other task-based sensors that can monitor sleep, sitting, meal preparation, and coffee making. These sensors will monitor the entire process of the task such as from the first step of opening the pillbox to the near final step getting water from the tap to take with the pills. This study also used only researcher-designed visualizations as probes. The results from this study can serve as the first round of user-centered iterative refinement of the visualizations.

CONCLUSION AND FUTURE WORK

In this paper, we discussed how we designed and deployed a prototype home sensing system that collected four months of data about how two different older adults performed two tasks important for successfully aging in place, pill taking and phone use. We presented two case studies of how two older adults (one aging successfully and managing her awareness well, and another who struggles with maintaining consistency and awareness of her abilities) investigate their data and how they used the data to adjust or reaffirm their awareness of their functional abilities.

We found that our participants looked for and focused on anomalies in the data (*e.g.*, missed pills or misdialed phone calls) that may indicate a mistake that might be their fault. They tried their best to explain away the anomaly by thinking of an event, circumstance, or reason why that anomaly might actually be acceptable. They drew first on their own memory of events to find an explanation. Often lacking a specific explanation from their declining memories, the older adults drew next on their routines in an attempt to make the anomaly acceptable by placing it within one of their routines. They then consulted other sources of date-specific information such as calendars and diaries if they were available. Designers can support this investigation process by clearly marking the anomalies and can support the explanation process by providing the date-specific context that gives hints as to what activities might have occurred on particular days.

We also were able to validate one of most important potential benefits of embedded assessment data—that it helps older adults with managing their awareness of their functional abilities. We found that the objective data collected on her task performance allowed an older adult to adjust her inaccurate awareness of her functional abilities as well as for another older adult to affirm her accurate awareness of her abilities. As a result, they were empowered to make the appropriate adaptations to be more consistent and aware of their pill taking and phone use to safeguard their independence. Furthermore, to avoid misinterpretation when sharing performance data, designers should support joint viewing or at least allow the older adult to annotate and explain their performance.

In future work, we plan to continue monitoring our two participants as well as to include other adults with different levels of awareness and abilities. Home sensing systems have the ability to monitor behaviors seamlessly and over a very long term, and thus we plan to investigate how older adults and other stakeholders including caregivers and doctors engage with much longer-term data such as over years instead of months.

ACKNOWLEDGEMENTS

This work was supported by the Robert Wood Johnson Foundation Project HealthDesign Grant RWJ67167 and National Science Foundation ERC Grant EEEC-0540865.

REFERENCES

1. Ballegaard, S., Hansen, T. and Kyng, M. Healthcare in everyday life: designing healthcare services for daily life. *Proc. CHI 2008*, ACM Press (2008), 1807–1816.
2. Bamis, A., Lymberopoulos, D., Teixeira, T., and Savvides, A. Towards precision monitoring of elders for providing assistive services, *Proc .PETRA*, (2008), 49-56.
3. Birnholtz J. and Jones-Rounds, M. Independence and interaction: understanding seniors' privacy and awareness needs for aging in place. *Proc. CHI*, ACM Press (2010), 143-152.
4. Chin, G., Kuchar, O.A., and Wolf, K.E. Exploring the analytical processes of intelligence analysts. P*roc. CHI 2009*, ACM Press (2009), 11-20.
5. Dijkstra, K. and Misirlisoy, M. Event components in autobiographical memories. *Memory*, 14(7), (2006) 846–852.
6. Fried, L., Herdman, S., Kuhn, K., Rubin, G. and Turano, K. Preclinical disability: hypotheses about the bottom of the iceberg. *Journal of Aging and Health*. 3(2), (1991) 285-300.
7. Glaser, B.G. and Strauss, A.L. *The discovery of grounded theory: Strategies for qualitative research*, Aldine (1967).
8. Hayes, T., Hunt, J., Adami, A. and Kaye, J. An electronic pillbox for continuous monitoring of medication adherence. *Proc. EMBS*, (2006), 6400-3.
9. Hilton, K., Fricke, J. and Unsworth, C. A comparison of self-report versus observation of performance using the ALSAR with an older population. *The British Journal of Occupational Therapy*, 64(3), (2001), 135–143.
10. Kaye, J. Home-based technologies: A new paradigm for conducting dementia prevention trials. *Alzheimer's & Dementia*, 4(1), (2008), S60–66.
11. Lawton, M.P. and Brody, E.M. Assessment of older people: self-maintaining and instrumental activities of daily living. *The Gerontologist*, 9(3), (1969), 179-187.
12. Leifer, B.P. Early diagnosis of Alzheimer's disease: clinical and economic benefits. *Journal of the American Geriatrics Society*. 51(5), (2003), S281–288.
13. Li, I., Dey, A., and Forlizzi, J. A stage-based model of personal informatics systems. *Proc. CHI 2010*, ACM Press (2010), 557–566.
14. Maitland, J. and Chalmers, M. Self-monitoring, self-awareness, and self-determination in cardiac rehabilitation. *Proc. CHI 2010*, ACM Press (2010), 1213-1222.
15. Mamykina, L., Mynatt, E., Davidson, P. and Greenblatt, D. MAHI: investigation of social scaffolding for reflective thinking in diabetes management. *Proc. CHI 2008*, ACM Press (2008), 477–486.
16. Mihailidis, A., Boger, J., Canido, M. and Hoey, J. The use of an intelligent prompting system for people with dementia. *Interactions*, 14(4), (2007), 34-37.
17. Morris, M. and Intille, S. HCI challenges in health assessment. *Extended Abstracts CHI 2005*. ACM Press, (2005), 2130-1.
18. Morris, M., Intille, S. and Beaudin, J. Embedded assessment: Overcoming barriers to early detection with pervasive computing. *Pervasive Computing*, (2005), 333–346.
19. Okonkwo, O. *et al.*, Awareness of Functional Difficulties in Mild Cognitive Impairment: A Multidomain Assessment Approach. *Journal of the American Geriatrics Society*. 57(6), (2009), 978–984.
20. Peesapati, S., Schwanda, V., Schultz, J., Lepage, M., Jeong, S. and Cosley, D. Pensieve: supporting everyday reminiscence. *Proc. CHI 2010*, ACM Press, (2010), 2027-2036.
21. Rantz, M. *et al.*, TigerPlace: an innovative educational and research environment, *AAAI in Eldercare: New Solutions to Old Problems*, Washington DC, 2008.
22. Saxton, J., Morrow, L., Eschman, A., Archer, G., Luther, J. and Zuccolotto, A. Computer assessment of mild cognitive impairment. *Postgraduate Medicine*, 121(2), (2009), 177-185.
23. Tapia, E., Intille, S., and Larson, K. Activity recognition in the home using simple and ubiquitous sensors. *Pervasive Computing*, (2004), 158–175.
24. Willis, S. Everyday cognitive competence in elderly persons: Conceptual issues and empirical findings. *The Gerontologist*. 36(5), (1996), 595-601.

User-Centred Multimodal Reminders for Assistive Living

Marilyn R. McGee-Lennon[1], Maria K. Wolters[2], Stephen Brewster[1]

[1]Glasgow Interactive Systems Group,
School of Computing Science,
University of Glasgow, UK
(mcgeemr, stephen)@dcs.gla.ac.uk

[2]School of Informatics,
University of Edinburgh
Edinburgh, UK
maria.wolters@ed.ac.uk

ABSTRACT

While there has been a lot of research on the usability of reminders and alarms in the work context, the home has been somewhat neglected despite the importance of reminder systems for telecare and assistive living systems. We conducted a comprehensive mixed-methods study into the requirements for useable and acceptable reminders in the home. The study consisted of a questionnaire (N=379), 6 focus groups, and 7 home tour interviews. Our results highlight the need for highly flexible and contextualized multimodal and multi-device reminder solutions that build on existing successful strategies for remembering in and around the home. We suggest that developers of home care reminder systems should design for diversity, context, priorities, autonomy, shared spaces, and optimal care.

Author Keywords

Multimodal interfaces, personalisation, reminder systems, assisted living, telecare. focus groups, home tours, surveys

ACM Classification Keywords

H5.2. Information interfaces and presentation: User Interfaces (User Centred Design).

General Terms

Design, Human Factors.

INTRODUCTION AND MOTIVATION

People with disabilities or chronic long-term illnesses are increasingly being cared for at home in the community [5]. Home care and assistive living solutions are crucial for enabling this user group to stay active and independent for longer in their own homes [6]. Reminder systems can be an important part of the assisted living telecare package. Many service users have problems remembering information, tasks, and chores in and around the home. This can be a consequence of cognitive ageing, the conditions for which they need care, or the medications they need to take. Forgotten tasks may be as trivial as returning library books or as crucial as taking important medication. Being able to remember these tasks can be the difference between having to send people to care homes and enabling them to age in place, in the comfort of their own home.

CHI 2011, May 7–12, 2011, Vancouver, BC, Canada.

Even though many people with care needs would benefit from assisted living technology, uptake is still comparatively low [3, 9]. In order to increase adoption and ensure successful implementation of assistive living technology, we need to provide users with effective, accessible solutions that are enjoyable to use. These solutions need to be adaptable to a set of devices and interaction modalities that will depend on user needs, abilities and preferences as well as on available services and budgets.

The home is a special interaction space. Even though it is private and intimate, it is often shared with other people [11, 15]. A home is a very personal space for everybody who lives there, not just for the intended user of the system but also for a spouse, children or even visitors. This means that we need to design reminders that are both useable and acceptable to a range of direct end users, i.e. the intended recipients of reminders, and indirect users, i.e. people who can perceive the reminder message despite not being the intended recipients. Reminders need to be adapted to multiple, sometimes conflicting, stakeholder needs [17], they need to be appropriate in a variety of changing contexts and they need to accommodate a wide range of ability levels [22].

Existing approaches to reminder design only partly address these complex issues. There is a clear need for guidelines that allow designers and developers (and where appropriate end users) to create configurable and multimodal reminder systems which can rise to the challenges of home care. The systems that are discussed in the literature on alerts in the work place [26, 28], telephone-based health care reminders [2], and general reminders in the home [16] are often unimodal, and personalisation is limited to one or two parameters, such as preferred times for reminder calls. On the other hand, studies that take a wider view of design issues, such as [4, 19, 20], tend to focus more on home monitoring of frail older people than on reminding.

With the present study, we address this gap in the literature by studying reminder design using a rich mixed-methods approach in order to understand both trends and deeper social context. Themes that emerged from a survey and focus groups were cross-validated in the home. We worked with a broad range of users, including older people and people with sensory impairments. We distil our findings into six design guidelines that can be used to improve the design of future homecare systems.

DESIGNING TECHNOLOGY FOR THE HOME

Home care and assisted living pose very specific challenges for design. The key issues can be clustered around three main themes; complexity of care needs, the multi-user and multi-stakeholder nature of home care, and the need for well-defined pathways and accountability [17].

Complex and Dynamic Care Needs

Interventions for people who are cared for in the community are complex [13]. Many people require care for two or more different conditions, which may or may not be causally related. Reminder systems must be able to accommodate such holistic care plans and the team of formal and informal carers that manages them [4, 19]. Due to the potential deluge of reminders for such complex interventions, it is important to choose delivery options carefully, otherwise vital messages may be missed and the system will not be effective.

We advocate a person-centred approach to care similar to [4] where needs and preferences are regularly reviewed and stored in a format such that they can be easily communicated to relevant stakeholders including end users. To accommodate this approach, reminder systems need to be highly modular, flexible and easy to configure.

Care plans change over time not just because of new care needs but also due to changes in the available devices and services. Care provision may need to shift from people to technology because the budget for formal carers is cut or informal carers are no longer able to provide the level of care they used to give. People's beliefs and behaviours can also change. Users who were highly sceptical of technology may become advocates after having experienced the difference a well-designed system can make and vice versa. Good reminder systems need to be able to accommodate these changes.

Making reminders multimodal is particularly important given that the acuity of all sensory modalities declines with age [1], often as a consequence of the condition that caused the original care needs. For example, diabetes may lead to impaired vision and, due to peripheral neuropathy [7], to an impaired sense of touch. The number of people with both significant vision and hearing impairment is set to increase dramatically in the future, partly as a consequence of the ageing population [25]. Alerts that are based on touch and smell are particularly important for these users.

While it is tempting to use only those modalities for reminders where acuity is relatively well-preserved, it is in fact important to make reminders in all modalities as accessible as possible to people with varying abilities. For example, even though touch can function as an alert to take medication, users might not remember which medication they need to take or how many of each pill are required. This information might need to be presented graphically or sonically. Designers need to work with care professionals to devise a strategy for accommodating different levels of sensory impairment. An example for such a strategy for tasks that require dexterity can be found in [27].

Home Care is Multi-User and Multi-Stakeholder

In the home care reminder context, we define users as people who choose (or in some cases are selected) to receive reminders. Direct end users can include the person with care needs, family, friends and formal carers. For example, a system might remind all members of the household of an appointment, or it might remind the formal carer of tasks such as checking the medicine cabinet.

Stakeholders are defined as those who can directly or indirectly specify requirements and add, delete or change reminders or the information the system produces. Examples include the health and social care team that manages care, the providers of specialist housing, telecare equipment providers, informal carers such as friends and neighbours, and people who live in the same home but are not directly involved in care.

Many potential conflicts regarding reminder delivery can arise between users and other stakeholders. For example, a user may prefer auditory reminders, but due to a hearing impairment, these reminders need to be so loud that the neighbours can hear. A formal carer may have decided to use a loud beep to remind a user to lock the doors at night because this has been identified as a safety threat, but the user perceives this sound to be highly disruptive and disturbing. These conflicts need to be resolved so that the reminders remain effective while still being acceptable to the user and those sharing the home interaction space.

Pathways and Accountability

Since reminder systems are multi-stakeholder, it is particularly important to identify clear pathways for resolving any conflicts. These pathways need to include explicit mechanisms for seeking user input and validating the selected options. The different goals and needs that underpin each conflict need to be identified [8]. In resolving conflicts, clinical efficacy needs to be balanced with an acceptable user experience and institutional requirements.

Ideally, the care team should have a variety of devices, modalities and strategies at their disposal. For example, potentially disruptive auditory reminders could be delivered straight to the user's hearing aid. Disruptive beeps might be replaced by a light next to the user's bed that changes colour when the doors are locked. Finally, it needs to be clear who owns the data generated by the reminder system and who controls the system's behaviour (e.g. who is responsible for configuring the system or repairing faulty devices).

AIMS AND APPROACH

In order to inform the design of configurable, adaptable reminder systems for the home, we sought to determine

- What users need to be reminded of, i.e. the tasks they forget to do in and around the home;
- Why users need reminders, i.e. reasons for forgetting;
- What strategies are used to remember, i.e. what techniques and technologies people currently use;
- How users would like to receive reminders, i.e. the devices available and preferred by users and the modalities available and accessible to users.

Our user requirements work consisted of a full year of user engagement activities with various user panels (older adult volunteers), social work professionals, charities and groups specialising in sensory impairment, and technologists and technicians working in the area of assistive technologies. We designed a mixed methods approach including a questionnaire (to gain a wide range of views and trends), focus groups (with specific groups of older adults and adults with sensory impairments) to more fully understand trends and responses in the questionnaire data and home tour interviews (with older users in their home) to probe how social and contextual issues of living can influence the usability and acceptability of reminders in situ.

Using any one of these techniques on its own is common in HCI but each has its own well-reported problems. Surveys can be cheap to administer but often have a poor return rate. It is difficult to encourage people to answer anything but forced choice questions, and it is hard to get respondents to explain their choices. Other techniques are often required to understand quantitative response patterns.

Focus groups are a good way for HCI researchers to probe issues in more depth and to obtain feedback on prototypes. In discussion, participants will share and elaborate on stories and insights that do not fit into the boxes of a questionnaire form. It is also much easier for users to comment on reminder technology if they can see, hear and touch, and smell examples. However, what people claim they do may be different from what they actually do. An ethnographic component is needed to address this issue.

Cultural probes and in depth interviews in the home have been shown as successful ways to engage with older users [11]. In this study, we used home tours to gather a rich contextualized understanding of how people use reminders in their own homes and the social and physical context in which remembering succeeds or fails. Successful reminder strategies could be demonstrated in practice and important details could be observed and recorded (photos and audio) that might not be reported during a focus group.

The temporal sequence of the three methods was designed to support our overall research strategy. The main online data collection for the survey finished before the focus groups began, so that these results could inform the focus groups. Likewise, the home tours started after a few focus groups had already taken place. Therefore, the researcher who conducted the home tours was already highly sensitized to different reminder strategies, which made it easier to observe them in context.

Using these three techniques in combination provided a much richer understanding than any one of the techniques alone. While the survey enabled us to establish the range of preferences for devices and modalities that should be accommodated in reminder system design, the focus groups allowed us to discuss the pros and cons of different strategies in depth, and the home tours gave a vivid picture of reminder strategies people really use in their homes.

STUDY DESIGN

We included younger, middle-aged and older users with and without sensory impairments in our study because people of all ages can be stakeholders in home care systems. For example, some of our younger participants had sensory impairments or cared for people with sensory impairments. We were also interested in generational differences in reminder preferences. Since today's middle-aged users will be tomorrow's older generation, reminder solutions that would be difficult to deploy widely today might be almost universally acceptable in a decade's time.

Questionnaire

Since we wanted to explore the diversity of the design space, we chose a broad sampling strategy. Online and postal versions of our questionnaire were distributed through email, social networking sites, Web sites, local user panels, senior's forums, charities and community health partnerships across Scotland. Our sample was deliberately skewed towards older people, as they are more likely to require home care. More information about the survey can be found in [29].

The questionnaire was designed based on previously validated topics and question formats as well as in-depth qualitative work with older users on assistive technology and home care projects by the research team [3, 15, 16]. We used a balance of open ended and multiple choice questions and piloted the questionnaire with older people from our user panel. The online survey can be found at http://www.multimemohome.com/get_involved. To ensure legibility, the postal version was typeset with a large font.

We present an analysis of all 379 questionnaires (206 online, 173 postal) that had been returned by the end of July 2010. The return rate for the postal questionnaire was 19%. 13% of respondents were aged between 18 and 30 (younger group), 46% between 31 and 60 (middle-aged) and 41% were aged 61 and above (older). The ratio of female to male respondents was 2:1. 34% lived alone (older group: 51%), 2% with a flat mate or lodger, and the remainder lived with a partner or family (older group: 48%). Only 3% lived in sheltered accommodation.

Compared to the general UK population [21], our sample is highly computer literate. While only 24% of UK citizens aged 60 and above use the Internet regularly, 75% of our older sample were online (postal: 55%). Nevertheless, our older sample is just as likely to use a mobile phone regularly as the average older person (45% in our survey versus 48% UK average).

20% of respondents reported problems with their vision, 17% had hearing difficulties and 4% each had a reduced sense of touch or smell. 27% of our sample said they had problems with their memory (younger: 6%, middle-aged: 13%, older: 48%). 30% of our sample reported chronic care conditions (older: 50%, middle-aged: 18%, younger: 4%). Of the people with a care condition 24% had heart conditions including angina, 18% had mobility problems, often due to arthritis and 17% had hypertension. Other conditions included diabetes (14%), asthma/breathing problems (10%), fatigue (9%) and cancer (6%).

Focus Groups

We conducted 6 focus groups (summarized in Table 1) with older adults, assistive technology technicians and younger adults with sensory impairments over a period of three months, starting after the online questionnaire survey had gone live. This was feasible because the survey was already based on extensive previous qualitative work.

#	N	Location	User Group	Impairments
1	6	Glasgow	older users	Hearing (slight, one; severe, two)
2	5	Glasgow	younger users	Vision (one)
3	2	Edinburgh	older users	Memory (slight, one)
4	2	Falkirk	technicians	Hearing (severe, one)
5	2	Falkirk	older users	Hearing (both)
6	2	Glasgow	younger users	Deaf (both)

Table 1: List of focus groups conducted.

The focus groups were structured around the main research questions outlined above. Reminder devices and modalities were illustrated using technology probes for four of the five modalities covered in the survey – speech, non-speech audio, touch, and smell. Participants were also asked to respond to each of the research questions on 'sticky notes' and organise the resulting themes into hierarchies of importance to them. This was used to stimulate further discussion. The same researcher acted as facilitator across each focus group. An additional researcher took notes, observed and demonstrated speech technology probes.

Home Tours

We conducted seven Home Tours (summarized in Table 2) with users in their own homes. Each tour consisted of an interview and a tour of the home to capture current reminder strategies. Interview responses and the home owner's verbal comments during the home tour were recorded using a digital audio recorder and later transcribed for analysis. Photographs were taken of objects/items that were used to remember things and strategies that were used to remind people to do things. The photos were stored digitally and tagged in relation to the context of the interview and observations. More detailed information about the Home Tours can be found in [18].

#	Participants	Description
1	Mrs. M	Single older woman (76)
2	Mrs. H	Single older woman (74)
3	Mr. PL	Single man (39)
4	Mrs. R	Single older woman (89), Parkinson's, mobility, received home help
5	Mr. & Mrs. G	Husband (65) and wife (64),
6	Mr. & Mrs. L	Husband (72) and wife (72)
7	Family PC	Grandmother (65), mother (37), two children (11, 9)

Table 2: List of home tours conducted

METHOD

Statistical Analysis

Unless otherwise specified, chi-square tests were used for analysis of multiple-choice items from the questionnaire. For correlations, Spearman's correlation coefficient was used. P-values were reported at three significance levels, $p<0.01$ (*), $p<0.001$ (**), and $p<0.0001$ or lower (***).

Qualitative Analysis

Qualitative data was stored and managed using the data management software NVivo. The salient responses and themes for each of the research questions were identified and categorized using the Framework Approach [24].

RESULTS

What Do People Forget and Why?

41% of older respondents in the questionnaire said that they forgot to do certain things in and around the home often or all the time, as opposed to 32% of middle-aged and 17% of younger respondents. However, when specifying what tasks they forget, older people ticked fewer boxes than younger or middle-aged people. In particular, they were less likely to report that they forget daily chores (older: 4%, middle-aged: 14%, younger: 22%) and paying bills (10%; 32%; 42%). All age groups were equally likely to forget medications and appointments.

The most popular responses across the focus groups for the things forgotten around the home fall into five groups: chores around the house (closing windows and doors, putting out bins, unloading the washing machine), preparing to go out (remembering to take keys, umbrella, or hat), appointments, health care-related tasks (taking tablets), and ambient or place-specific reminders (what I went into a room for, where I have put something, or when to get off the bus).

The things that cause people to forget tasks were similar across all methods used. Memory problems, failing to use reminder strategies, and distractions, e.g. by phone calls or more important events, were all mentioned. People also stated that they tended to forget tasks that were not important or urgent. The only significant difference between age groups in the survey was that middle-aged people were more likely to say they were too busy (67%) than younger (48%) or older (34%) people ($p<0.0001$).

Stress, tiredness, and low mood were cited as further reasons for forgetting. Some respondents mentioned that physical problems prevented them from remembering or completing tasks. These problems were not just caused by ill health, but also by the medications people were taking.

How Do People Remember?

The highly varied strategies people claim to use can be grouped into five categories: *paper-based* (e.g., calendars), *technological and specialized* (e.g., mobile phone reminders and pill boxes), *temporal* (e.g., integration into routines), *people-based* (e.g. phone calls from friends) and *physical* (e.g., placing books to be returned near front door).

In the multiple-choice items of the survey we mainly explored paper-based and technology-based reminders. Figure 1 shows how often our respondents use six representative strategies. The other three reminder types emerged from the open questionnaire items, the focus groups and the home tours.

Paper-based methods

Calendars and diaries were the most popular, followed by to-do lists and sticky notes. In the questionnaire sample, older people were more likely to use diaries and calendars, and were less likely to set alarms or use an electronic personal organizer (see Figure 1).

While the survey revealed the central role of paper-based reminders, the home tours allowed us to fully document the complexity of such systems. Many people had multiple calendars, diaries and notebooks and complex systems for annotating them and working between them (see Figure 2(a)). This could involve one calendar for the family events and appointments and one for an individual's activities. It also included strategies for copying selected diary appointments on to the calendar while some remained in the diary only.

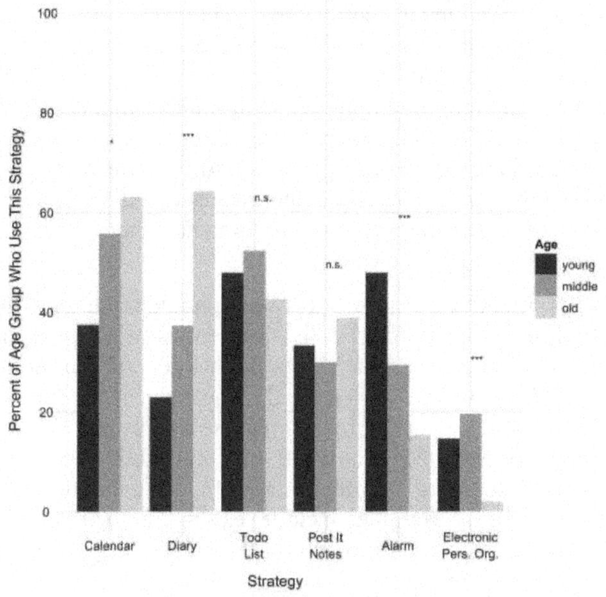

Figure 1: Reminder methods used by respondents

Diaries and calendars were used as memory aids for information about past events needed to plan future ectivities. One couple noted down when they had last replaced watch batteries so they knew when the next replacement was due, and one person recorded information gained at important medical appointments to help him manage his care.

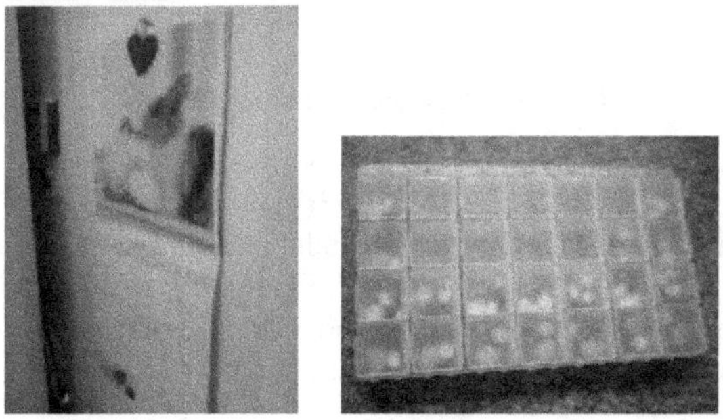

(a) (b)

Figure 2: Paper based (calendar) and specialized reminders (pill box).

Technological/specialised reminders

Technological and specialised reminders mentioned by our participants included reminders sent to themselves on their mobile phones, computer applications, timers worn on the person and specialized solutions such as pill boxes to remember to take their medication (Figure 2 (b)).

People-based reminders

Several respondents mentioned people-based strategies, such as relying on friends and family to remind them of important tasks. Several people in the survey also described serving as the main personal reminder system for a family member with dementia.

Temporal reminders

Temporal reminder strategies emerged as central throughout our research. A common strategy was to integrate tasks that would otherwise be forgotten into routines, e.g. "*I never leave the bathroom without looking at taps*" (male, 46-60, survey). This plays to older people's strengths, because this age group found it particularly easy to remember daily chores. Temporal cues could be external, such as radio programs that served as indicators of the time.

Physical reminders

The importance of a close fit between reminder strategy and daily life is illustrated by the large variety of physical reminders, which were a prominent feature of our home tours. Many people left visually meaningful or salient objects such as packaging in places where they would noticed. For example, people left out empty food packaging to remind them to log their daily food intake on their computer. Other examples include leaving library books by the door as a prompt to return them (see Figure 3(a)). Technological reminder strategies such as pill boxes were supplemented by the physical reminder of empty medication packaging near the television.

(a) (b)

Figure 3: Physical/visual reminders

Kitchen surfaces such as a fridge or a blackboard/whiteboard (Figure 3(b)) often acted as a todo list. The surfaces were used for leaving messages to other family members, detailing shopping lists and posting reminders of upcoming appointments and things to remember to take out of the house.

Physical context and spatial location even affected the reminder system used. A questionnaire respondent listed, for example, "*[a] shopping list on the freezer door. A to-do list on my mobile phone with alarms attached to the individual items [...]* " (female, 31-45, survey).

How Would People Like To Receive Reminders?

In the questionnaire, we collected extensive quantitative data on device and modality preferences. First, we asked respondents whether they would prefer to receive visual, tactile, olfactory, speech, or non-speech audio reminders. 21% of questionnaire respondents did not state any preference, 46% expressed a preference for one modality, 21% named two modalities and 12% found three or more modalities acceptable. The only significant difference between age groups was that older people were less likely to favour visual reminders (38% positive versus 60% for middle-aged and 69% for younger). Interestingly the self-reported impairment of a particular sensory modality did not affect whether the user would like to receive reminders using that modality.

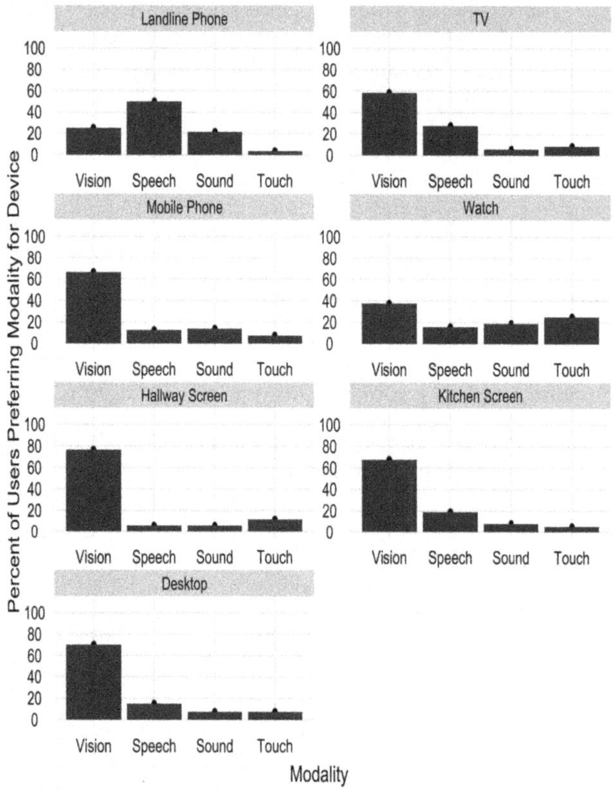

Figure 4: Modality preferences by device for people who prefer only one modality.

66% of questionnaire respondents who expressed a modality preference wanted visual reminders, 37% liked speech, 30% non-speech audio, 23% touch and 3% smell. Users who liked speech were unlikely to choose touch (Spearman's ρ=-0.41, p<0.000), and users who preferred vision were unlikely to favour non-speech audio (ρ=-0.24, p<0.01). There were also weak dissociations between speech and non-speech audio (ρ=-0.19, p<0.05) and vision and touch (ρ=-0.18, p<0.05).

Device preferences were even more varied than modality preferences. 83% of respondents expressed a preference for one or more devices. The most popular device was the mobile phone (55% of those who specified a device), followed by the desktop computers (43%), a screen in the kitchen (30%), the watch (29%), the TV (25%), the landline phone (20%) and a screen in the hallway (15%).

The main difference in device-related preferences between age groups concerned phones. 40% of our older sample wanted reminders to be delivered by landline phones, whereas fewer than 5% of younger and 8% middle-aged users favoured this mode of delivery (p<0.001). Conversely, 83% of younger and 67% of middle-aged adults, but only 32% of older adults, chose mobile phones ($p<0.001$) as a reminder delivery method. Only a third of those older people who liked reminders on landlines also wanted to receive them on mobile phones.

To investigate associations between devices and modalities, we looked at the device preferences of 174 respondents who selected only one modality for reminders (see Figure 4). For each device, we determined how many of the people who had chosen this device wanted to receive visual, haptic, spoken, or other auditory reminders. Smell was excluded because there were too few data points. The results are summarized in Figure 4. Visual reminders dominate for screens and desktops. Of the two mobile devices, mobile phone and watch, the watch shows the greatest range of desired modalities. Mobile phones, on the other hand, appear to be mainly associated with visual reminders such as text messages. Speech and sound figure prominently in reminders delivered via TV and landline.

In the qualitative component of our work, five strong themes emerged regarding the type of reminders people would find useful and acceptable: adaptability, integration, privacy, accessibility, and choice.

Adaptability to User

Users wanted a system that can be adapted to their own preferences and capabilities. "*I mean different people want different things don't they... they would need to be able to choose what suited them I suppose...*" (FG1, male, 71-85). Several survey respondents highlighted using paper calendars and diaries instead of technology, extending strategies people already successfully use. Some also wanted to receive reminders by post, when appropriate. Speech output in particular should be configurable. Individual reactions to gender, politeness, accent and length of message were very strong and varied. *"I mean I would want a short abrupt kind of message if it was an urgent matter but if it was like 'take the dog out' then the longer softer ladies voice would be nice."* (FG5, female, 71-85).

The family home tour revealed clear generational effects. The middle-aged mother discussed solutions that could exploit her mobile phone, the young children were very positive towards wearable devices and the grandmother was keen to exploit mainstream technologies such as their TVs. The youngest participant summarized the need for personalisation as follows. "*I would want it to like a hair band or a watch ... you know telling me to remember my school stuff ... but then mum could get her reminder to her phone cos she is always on that...*" *(Tour 7, Male, 9).*

Seamless Integration into Life and Home

Users wanted a reminder system to be easily integrated into their daily life and their physical surroundings. "*Maybe like a digital photo frame or something ... but it would have to look okay wouldn't it – you wouldn't want some big box in your living room...*" (FG2, male, 46-60). Successful reminder systems need to strike a delicate balance between being prominent enough to attract users' attention, but subtle enough not to be perceived as intrusive or distracting. Audio reminders, in particular, can startle or scare users if played unexpectedly.

Screens should be placed where users are most likely to see them, such as in the living room or kitchen. Many people favoured the idea of a controllable panel in the hallway. Users also liked the idea of more ambient display technologies (such as a coloured light) that act as generic reminders. "*Sometimes I just need reminding that I have to remember something you know ... so I wouldn't even need to hear 'take your pill' I would just know if I heard the bleep that I have to take my pill.*" (FG3, female, 85+).

Surprisingly, location was also an important factor for phone-based reminder systems. People were concerned that they might not be able to get to a landline phone in time or that they might not be able to hear mobile phone reminders because they did not know where their mobile was. A final aspect relevant to the theme of seamless integration was robustness. Quite a few users doubted the reliability of technology, and they were wary of the disruption that a malfunctioning reminder system was likely to cause.

Privacy in Shared Spaces

Conflicts due to privacy and shared interaction spaces were highlighted in particular during the home tours – they did not emerge as strongly in the focus group and survey components. "*I wouldn't want all my messages sent to the system so that everyone could see them. I would need to be able to pick which ones went to my phone [mobile] so that only I could see them." (Tour 7, Female, 37)*

Accessibility for People with Impairments

Many users raised concerns about usability issues such as the font size of visual reminders and intelligibility of audio reminders. However, this does not mean that people with a visual or auditory impairment would not use visual or auditory reminders, In our focus groups with people with severe hearing impaired people (including Deafness), one person said "*Some speech is okay with my hearing aid ... I mean it would depend on the volume and quality [of the speech] wouldn't it...*" (FG6, male, 18-30, Deaf). Thus, even for people with severe sensory impairment, the choice of delivery modality is not straightforward.

Choice between Diverse Modalities

Overall, modality preferences depended did not just depend on the modality itself, but also on the amount of information to be conveyed with beeps and vibration favoured for more simple alerts. Some users wanted to be able to remove reminders once the associated task had been completed while others would like a view of the history of reminders they have attended to.

Participants reacted positively to the idea of smell and tactile reminders but this may have been due to the novelty of these delivery methods. "*Yes...I mean like a horrible smell to tell me the washer [washing machine] needs emptied – that would be ideal...*". (2G5, female, visually impaired, 31-45). This illustrates the effect of technology probes – in the survey, respondents were far less likely to comment on olfactory reminders.

Why do Reminders Fail?

Reminder strategies are only effective if people can adhere to them. Adherence can be affected by health problems. For example, a person with depression may choose not to act on reminders when feeling low. A few users argued that their needs were so complex that they could not be met by a reminder system alone. For example, one older male respondent was a diabetic who sometimes forgot his insulin. Since double doses of insulin can result in complications, what this person needed was not simply a reminder to take his insulin, but also a way of monitoring that he had already taken it.

The very routines that are crucial for establishing successful temporal reminder strategies can also interfere with adherence. Participants noted that existing habits can interfere with new habits that need to be established as a response to care needs. Conversely, a lack of routines means that users lacked a temporal scaffold to which tasks and events could be attached.

Some of the respondents who did not state any modality or device preferences disliked the idea of automated reminders because this would result in an external locus of control, i.e. others having power over their lives. Others did not think they needed them, reflected in comments like "*don't feel I am in this category*" (survey, male, 85+). For these users, reminder systems were a threat to their identity and autonomy.

OUTPUTS AND IMPLICATIONS FOR DESIGN

Our methodology allowed us to develop a rich picture of the breadth and complexity of the design space involved in creating reminder solutions for people from a range of age groups and with complex care conditions. We found that if novel reminder systems are to be usable and acceptable they will need to exploit existing metaphors and strategies of reminding. Knowledge of the home and the structure of daily life is also required to ensure that that reminder systems can be seamlessly integrated into users' lives.

In this section, we synthesize our findings into a set of six design guidelines. These are intended to be used by health and social care professionals to inform their prescription and deployment of assistive technologies involving reminder systems, and by designers and technologists to produce systems that are more likely to be used and accepted in the homes of users in the future.

Design Guidelines

Designing for Diversity

Reminders need to be highly personalizable, because one size does not fit all. Phone-based solutions are a good example: Even though mobile phones are the basis of many telecare packages, less than half of the older people we surveyed used their mobiles regularly; instead, 40% of this age group wanted to receive (mostly spoken) reminders on their landline phone. This limits the extent to which mobile-phone based location-sensitive solutions like PlaceMail [12] can be deployed with the current generation of older people.

Personalisation is particularly important if users are to successfully integrate the reminders into their identity as a person with a chronic condition. For example, in their study of the mobile health management system MAHI, Mamykina et al. [13] found that each participant used MAHI in a unique way that was consistent with the way in which they approached their condition and its effect on their life. This was only possible because MAHI was sufficiently flexible. We would expect to see a similar picture for any deployed reminder system.

The associations we found between age groups and devices or modalities are tendencies, not rules. We would strongly caution against creating reminder technology packages that are mainly differentiated by the intended age group. Each person weighs the tradeoffs between modalities differently, and therefore, should be able to choose from a range of options. Age might however influence the interaction techniques that users are familiar and comfortable with and therefore find most acceptable. Since our older user group consists of people over the age of 60, their preferences provide a good estimate of the design space for accommodating the oldest old of the next decade. Technologies that are required to cater for today's older users may be all but obsolete by the time our middle-aged group might require assistive living solutions a couple of decades from now.

Many people with sensory impairments wished to receive reminders in the impaired modality. Their wishes should be accommodated as much as feasible, because reminders delivered using unwanted modalities are more likely to be ignored or switched off. Designers therefore have an obligation to provide visual, auditory, and haptic reminders that are accessible and usable even for people with mild to moderate impairments of these modalities. People who configure reminder systems (such as health or social care workers) also need to be aware of this so that modalities are not excluded from a tailor-made solution purely because of a known impairment.

In order to support multimodal multi-device reminder delivery, systems should monitor what devices are currently available and people who configure systems should monitor what the users' current needs and preferences are. If there are any significant changes, systems should be adaptable with a minimum of effort. An example of such a highly configurable system is presented in [14].

Designing for Context

Contextualization figures heavily in the successful reminder strategies that emerged from the data. Reminders are most effective when delivered at the right location, at the right time and through the right device. Systems should be configurable based on the devices that are acceptable and available to the user. There are strong synergies between location and device. For example, many people favored reminder screens at the hub of the home, which is often the kitchen [11] or the living room. These can be used to remind inhabitants of general tasks and schedules, while a screen by the front door can be used to alert people to security precautions when leaving the house, for example.

Temporal contextualization is also a powerful reminder strategy. Our results suggest that integrating tasks and reminders with a person's habits and routines is key to effective, personalized reminder solutions. Such integration requires sophisticated planning algorithms that combine knowledge of the user's schedule and habits with information about the nature and duration of the tasks that need to be supported [23]. This is also the point where data from monitoring devices like bed sensors can be integrated.

Designing for Priorities

Reminders should reflect the urgency of the task. This helps users decide whether and when to attend to the reminder. It also prevents overload, which may result in users ignoring reminders on principle. Users should be able to choose appropriate modalities depending on urgency. For example, a loud spoken reminder could warn the user that the stove needs to be switched off urgently, while ambient lights might be as a gentle reminder of an upcoming appointment.

Designing for Autonomy

Autonomy is a fundamental issue in the design of pervasive technology for healthy ageing [10]. Reminder systems should support users as autonomous agents who are in control of the system, not the other way around. For example, users should be able to silence reminders that are no longer required. Another important option are simple 'reminders to remember'. These more ambient reminders are similar to reminders that people without care needs use, which makes them potentially less stigmatizing and, crucially, support users' ability to remember tasks themselves.

Designing for Shared Interaction Spaces

As soon as other people share the home with the intended recipient of the home care reminders, issues of privacy and obtrusiveness arise. Reminders that cannot be easily interpreted by visitors provide privacy, especially if users do not want to be seen as needing care. For example, while spoken reminders are explicit, clear indicators of care needs, the meaning of non-speech sounds such as Earcons is opaque unless explained [16]. At the same time, reminders should not unduly disrupt other people living in the home. While reminders that can only be perceived by the recipient, like haptic messages, do not disrupt other members of the household, the complexity of information that can be transmitted may be too limited to be useful. It is particularly important to consult with all relevant stakeholders to ensure the right balance is struck.

Designing for Optimal Care

The guidelines detailed above need to be weighed against the imperative of delivering good care. While it is important for adoption that reminders are acceptable to the end user, guidelines may need to be violated for important tasks, such as taking vital medication.

Limitations

With this study, we aimed to scope out a design space that would reflect the needs and preferences of people without major cognitive impairments. We made this decision because (i) many chronic conditions that require home care involve at most mild cognitive impairment and (ii) telecare solutions for older people may be implemented before they are needed to ensure the systems are in place and familiar to users when they are needed. Detailed specific guidelines for adapting interfaces to people progressing through dementia can be found in [19].

It is also worth noting that our sample consisted of native speakers of English. Therefore, appropriate care should be taken when extending them to different ethnic or cultural groups.

CONCLUSIONS

The guidelines presented have emerged from a large study where a common set of research questions was investigated using three highly complementary user requirements methods; a survey, focus groups and home tours. Emergent themes were cross-validated and triangulated across all three sources of data. Including a large postal element to our survey allowed us to reach a wide range of older users with and without care needs and sensory impairments. The focus groups allowed us to target specific user groups more precisely and to obtain feedback on somewhat unusual reminder strategies using technology probes. Finally, home tours allowed us to explore reminder strategies and needs in the homes of users and to gain a richer understanding of the social and physical context that might influence what is and is not acceptable in electronic reminder systems.

The next step is to test our design guidelines in practice. To this end, we plan to evaluate different multimodal reminder strategies under controlled laboratory conditions, before implementing our findings and guidelines in a pilot reminder system that will be evaluated in longitudinal home trials with users. Throughout this empirical validation phase, we will be working with system configuration experts, health care professionals, and end users to achieve the highly flexible and adaptable assistive living reminder solutions that users both want and need.

Given our findings, we have argued that reminder systems for assistive living need to be designed for diversity, context, priorities, autonomy, shared interaction spaces, and optimal care. In order to achieve these goals, reminder systems need to be configurable to accommodate a range of needs, preferences, and impairments. Once such a system has been set up, it can then be easily adapted to changing care needs and contexts of care.

ACKNOWLEDGEMENTS

We would like to thank Karl Isaac for assisting with the focus groups, and the people who invited us in to their homes for interviews, took part in our focus groups and filled in our survey. We would also like to thank Falkirk Sensory Services Centre, Hearing Concern Scotland, the Centre for the Older Person's Agenda, and Queen Margaret University for their support. This work was funded by EPSRC (EP/G060614/1, EP/G069387/1).

REFERENCES

1. Arking, R. *Biology of Aging*. Oxford University Press, New York, NY, 3rd edition, 2005.
2. Biem, H. J., Turnell, R. W. and D'Arcy, C. Computer telephony: automated calls for medical care. *Clin Invest Med*, 26 (2003), 259-268.
3. Clark, J.S. and McGee-Lennon, M. R. A stakeholder-centred exploration of the current barriers to the uptake of home care technology in the UK. *Journal of Assistive Technology, In Press* (2011).
4. Consolvo, S., Roessler, P., Shelton, B. E., LaMarca, A., Schilit, B., and Bly, S. Technology for Care Networks of Elders. *Pervasive Computing* 3, 2 (2004), 22-29.
5. Department of Health. *National Service Framework for Older People*, London: The Stationery Office (2001).
6. Department of Health. *Building Telecare in England.* London: The Stationery Office (2005).
7. Deshpande, A. D., Harris-Hayes, M. and Schootman, M. Epidemiology of diabetes and diabetes-related complications. *Phys Therapy*, 88, 11 (2008), 1254-1264.
8. Garde, S. and Knaup, P. Requirements engineering in health care: the example of chemotherapy planning in pediatric oncology, *Requirements Engineering* 11 (2006), 265-278.
9. House of Lords Science and Technology Committee. *Ageing: Scientific aspects.* The Stationery Office, London, UK (2005).
10. Intille, S. S. A New Research Challenge: Persuasive Technology to Motivate Healthy Aging. *IEEE Trans Inf Technol Biomedicine*, *8*, 3 (2004), 235-237.
11. Leonardi, C., Mennecozzi, C., Not, E., Pianesi, F., Zancanaro, M., Gennai, F. and Cristoforetti, A. Knocking on Elders' Door: Investigating the Functional and Emotional Geography of Their Domestic Space. *In Proc. CHI 2009*, ACM Press (2009), 1703-1712.
12. Ludford, P. J., Frankowski, D., Reily, K., Wilms, K., & Terveen, L. Because I carry my cell phone anyway. In *Proc. CHI 2006*, ACM Press (2006), 889-898.
13. Mamykina, L., Miller, A. D., Mynatt, E. D., and Greenblatt, D. Constructing identities through storytelling in diabetes management. In *Proc. CHI 2010* ACM Press (2010), 1203-1212.
14. McBryan, T. and Gray, P. A Model-Based Approach to Supporting Configuration in Ubiquitous Systems, In *Proc. International Conference on Design, Specification and Verification of Interactive Systems*, LNCS 5136, Springer (2008), 167-180.
15. McGee-Lennon, M.R. and Gray, P. Including Stakeholders in the Design of Home Care Systems: Identification and Categorisation of Complex User Requirements. In *Proc. INCLUDE* (2007).
16. McGee-Lennon, M.R., Wolters, M. and McBryan, T. Auditory Reminders in the Home. *In Proc. ICAD* 2007.
17. McGee-Lennon, M.R. Requirements engineering for home care technology. *In Proc. CHI* 2008, ACM Press (2008), 1439-1442.
18. McGee-Lennon, M.R., Wolters, M. K. and Brewster, S. Designing Reminders for the Home – The Role of Home Tours. *Proc. INCLUDE* (2011), In Press.
19. Morris, M., Lundell, J., Dishman, E., and Needham, B.. New Perspectives on Ubiquitous Computing from Ethnographic Study of Elders with Cognitive Decline *Proc. UbiComp (2003)*, 227-242.
20. Mynatt, E. D., Melenhorst, A. S., Fisk, A. D., and Rogers, W. A. Aware technologies for aging in place: understanding user needs and attitudes. *IEEE Pervasive Computing (2004), 3*, 36-41.
21. Ofcom UK. Digital lifestyles - adults aged 60 and over, Report (2009).
22. Persad, U., Langdon, P. and Clarkson, J. Characterising user capabilities to support inclusive design evaluation. *Universal Access in the Information Society*, 6, 2 (2007), 119-153.
23. Pollack, M. Intelligent Technology for an Aging Population: The Use of AI to Assist Elders with Cognitive Impairment. *AI Magazine* 26 (2005), 9-24.
24. Ritchie, J. and Lewis, J. *Qualitative Research Methods.* Sage, London UK, 2003.
25. SENSE for deafblind people UK. A sense of urgency, Report, 2010.
26. Stanton, N., ed. *Human factors in alarm design*, Taylor and Francis, London UK, 1994.
27. S. Waller, P. Langdon, and P. Clarkson. Using disability data to estimate design exclusion. *Univ Acc Inf Soc*, 9 (2010), 195-207.
28. Watson, M. and Sanderson, P. Sonification Supports Eyes-Free Respiratory Monitoring and Task Time-Sharing. *Human Factors,* 46, 3 (2004), 497-517
29. Wolters, M. K. and McGee-Lennon, M.R. Designing usable and acceptable reminders for the home. *Proc. AAATE,* 2010.

Home Automation in the Wild: Challenges and Opportunities

A.J. Bernheim Brush, Bongshin Lee, Ratul Mahajan, Sharad Agarwal, Stefan Saroiu, Colin Dixon*
Microsoft Research, *University of Washington
{ajbrush, bongshin, ratul, sagarwal, ssaroiu}@microsoft.com, ckd@cs.washington.edu

ABSTRACT
Visions of smart homes have long caught the attention of researchers and considerable effort has been put toward enabling home automation. However, these technologies have not been widely adopted despite being available for over three decades. To gain insight into this state of affairs, we conducted semi-structured home visits to 14 households with home automation. The long term experience, both positive and negative, of the households we interviewed illustrates four barriers that need to be addressed before home automation becomes amenable to broader adoption. These barriers are high cost of ownership, inflexibility, poor manageability, and difficulty achieving security. Our findings also provide several directions for further research, which include eliminating the need for structural changes for installing home automation, providing users with simple security primitives that they can confidently configure, and enabling composition of home devices.

Author Keywords
Home automation, smart home, domestic technology.

ACM Classification Keywords
H.5.2 User Interfaces, H.1.2 User/Machine systems.

General Terms
Human Factors.

INTRODUCTION
Smart homes with sensing, actuation, and networked devices have been anticipated for a long time. Research and commercial versions have been built, including Mozer's adaptive house [23], Georgia Tech Aware Home [18], Orange [15], eHome [20], and MIT's House_n [17]. Although the term "smart home," with the implication that a home adapts to inhabitants [e.g., 15, 23], has caught the attention of the media and researchers, the term "home automation," defined as the capability to automate and control multiple disparate systems [21], more closely describes currently available technology. Automated homes can be seen as the stepping stones to smart homes.

CHI 2011, May 7–12, 2011, Vancouver, BC, Canada.

However, home automation itself has not been widely adopted. This adoption failure is particularly surprising because many of the devices needed to enable home automation, such as motion sensors, programmable lighting, and video cameras, have been available to consumers since the 1970s. While some automation technologies are gaining acceptance in commercial settings (e.g., motion sensitive lights), broader adoption is severely lacking with the exception of security systems installed and monitored by a service company (e.g., ADT [16]). ABI Research estimates that only 204,000 home automation systems were shipped globally in 2009 [21].

To better understand the current state of home automation and learn about barriers to broader adoption from people's long term experience of living with home automation, we conducted 14 semi-structured interviews and household tours. Our interview explored why the household had installed home automation, their experience of living with it, and how they handled guests and security considerations. We also asked participants about their interest in a set of possible home automation applications to elicit information about configuration and access control considerations.

We classified the people who have already adopted home automation in two groups: 1) Do-it-yourselfers (DIY) who have installed automation themselves and 2) Outsourced households who have outsourced the installation and management to professionals. These groups offer a rare opportunity to study the use of automation in people's own homes, in contrast to studies conducted in home laboratories [e.g., 18, 20, 26] or focused on homes that adopted automation for religious purposes [33]. To compare and contrast these two groups, we recruited both DIY and Outsourced households.

While the majority of households were quite positive about their experience with home automation, our participants' experiences also highlight four significant challenges. These are high cost of ownership, inflexibility, poor manageability, and difficulty achieving security. While the general appeal of home automation and smart homes is an open question, these challenges represent barriers that would need to be overcome before the general population could consider using home automation, a building block in many smart home visions.

We believe that some of the problems we observed will be alleviated through market competition and developing standards, but our findings also highlight problems that require further research. These include eliminating the need for structural changes for a good home automation experience, providing end-users with simple, confidence-building home security, and enabling composition of home devices. More broadly, we hope that research to overcome these barriers will enable a home technology ecosystem that allows people to easily adopt the subset of home automation technology that appeals to their household.

RELATED WORK

Visions of smart homes have long caught the attention of researchers, not to mention the popular press. Considerable effort has been put toward enabling the technology necessary for home automation. One example is the work to improve device interoperability (e.g., DLNA [9], SpeakEasy [11]).

Research related to smart homes has suggested principles of smart home control [7], outlined challenges [10, 31], and recommended approaches to controlling devices [14]. A common theme in this research has been the importance of placing people in control, thus avoiding the paradox observed by Randall [26] where control systems were so complex that people experienced a lack of control. Both [15] and [2] provide excellent overviews of smart home research over the years. Chapters in [15] explore people's conception of the home, designing for the home, and the home of the future. Bell and Kaye [2] draw from media portrayals of futuristic kitchens and smart home installations to argue that experiences and desires should be valued over efficiency.

Unfortunately, due to the relative rarity of people living with home automation, most studies have been conducted with people who have consented to reside in smart home laboratories for some period of time (e.g., Orange [26], Aware Home [18], House_n [17], Tampere [20]). Two notable exceptions are Mozer's experience living in his Adaptive House [23] which attempted to adapt to his routines using machine learning techniques, and Woodruff *et al.*'s study of 20 American Orthodox Jewish families' use of home automation for specific religious purposes [33]. Most of these households used the X10 technology and expressed that automation would not be worth having if not for Sabbath observance. In contrast, the households in our study had a range of non-religious reasons for adoption and used a diverse set of systems. Thus, our work offers an opportunity to learn from people's long-term and general use of home automation.

While not focused on home automation, a related set of research has studied home networks [e.g., 5, 12, 13, 25, 29, 30], exploring how households configure, manage, live with their home networks and manage access control for sharing data and devices [e.g., 19, 22]. Shehan and Edwards [29] described different models for addressing home networking challenges and advocated for research on exploring ways to make network management easier for people. This area of research highlights the effort necessary to manage home networks [13], the diversity across households both in terms of their technical setups and their household routines [12], the importance of planning for change, and role of the technology guru in the home [25, 28]. While we observed these behaviors in our study, we focus on use of home automation which introduces additional sensing and control into households. Grinter *et al.*'s [12] suggestion that future research should study financial considerations inspired us to explore issues of costs with our households.

STUDY METHOD AND PARTICIPANTS

Our study took place in the summer of 2010 when we conducted semi-structured visits to 14 households with home automation. We recruited households that had at least one of the following home automation systems: remote lighting control, multi-room audio/video systems, security cameras (not counting standalone professionally monitored security systems such as ADT [16]), or motion detectors. We spoke with households with a range of brands including X10, Control4, Elk M1, HAI, Creston, Lagotek, and Leviton. It was not uncommon for households to have several brands installed. Nine of our households were DIY households, while five had Outsourced their installations (see Table 1). We considered Household O1 Outsourced, because the DIY father had died recently and the rest of the family members were only consumers of the technology.

We spoke with 31 people across the 14 households: the technology *guru* of every home and typically one to two other technology *consumers*. We initially wanted households with more than one resident and achieved this for 12 of 14 households. However, recruiting households with home automation was challenging and so two households (D3, O5) with only one primary inhabitant were included, although D3's girlfriend often stayed with him. In Household D5 only the guru agreed to speak with us.

We found our households through mailing lists at Microsoft for home automation enthusiasts (8 households) and a recruiting service that found 6 households external to our organization. Households with a member that worked at Microsoft were compensated with a $50 gift card while households with external participants received a software gratuity for each participant up to four per household (max value $600 each). The majority of the households were located in the northwest United States. We also conducted four interviews using video conferencing software allowing us to interview households in North Carolina, Minnesota, and North Dakota in the USA and near Reading in the UK.

Our household visits had four main parts. First, a short technology inventory modeled on the one used by [5] to help us understand the technology installed in the household. Next, we interviewed families about their experience with home automation technology including what led them to install it, favorite and least favorite aspects of each member of the household, use by guests, how often they modify the system, and whether remote access was

	ID	Time (years)	Brands	~ Cost (USD)
DIY	D1	4	Elk M1	$5,000
	D2	2	Elk M1, Charmed Quark	$10,000
	D3	1.5	mControl, Leviton	$5,000
	D4	1	X10	$200
	D5	2	Lorax, BayWeb	$14,500
	D6	2	Control4	$50,000
	D7	5	X10 Active Home	$300
	D8	2	Lagotek	< $5,000
	D9	10	ISY-99i, Insteon, X10	$3,000
Outsourced	O1	3	HAI	Unknown
	O2	6	Creston	$60,000
	O3	2.5	Control4	$120,000
	O4	10	EIB Instabus, KNX	$13,500
	O5	2	Lagotek, AudioQuest,	$20,000

Table 1. Household Information. Number of years household has lived with automation, brands installed, and estimated cost.

enabled. While we had some specific questions, this section was semi-structured and each interview included additional discussion as we followed up on topics of interest that arose as we discussed use in each household, which varied greatly depending on the systems installed, composition of household (e.g., kids), and type of installation.

We then asked the participants to imagine a "Home Application Store" from which they could purchase applications and enabling hardware. We gave each participant a list of 17 applications, shown in Table 2, that were inspired by industry websites [e.g., 6, 9]. To understand if households had any concerns or constraints related to installing applications in their home, for each application we asked each household member if they already had the functionality, or would or would not be interested in purchasing it.

Finally, household members gave us a home tour (either in person or via web camera if remote) to show us their home automation devices in situ (e.g., motion sensors, wiring closets). We photographed the devices and asked additional questions about their installations as needed to better understand their experience. All interviews took roughly two hours and were audio recorded. Interviews were transcribed and then analyzed using the affinity diagramming technique [3].

LIVING WITH AUTOMATION

All of our participants had lived with home automation for more than a year (see Table 1), and 2 households had 10 years of experience. In this section, we describe the diversity in automation functionality across households, their use of it to augment their houses, and participants' favorite aspects: convenience, peace of mind, and control.

Diversity in Installations and Desires

One might expect the self-selected group of people interested in home automation to have installed similar

	Application	Have	Buy	Not
Con.	Ability to set 'Scenes'	24	5	0
	Centralized control of automation systems	24	4	1
Media	View computer content on TV	19	5	5
	Watch recorded TV on any TV in house	16	11	2
	View computer content on mobile phone	4	20	5
	Show mobile phone content on TV	3	13	13
	Transfer video calls between devices	0	13	15
Security/ Monitoring	Remote Access to home cameras	16	10	3
	Automatic Alerts (e.g. Stove left on)	9	18	2
	Remotely open front door	4	18	7
	Log people's use of devices	3	9	17
	Time limits across multiple devices	1	15	12
	Watch child pc use on TV	0	17	12
Environment	Thermostat that learns routines	16	10	3
	House Energy Monitor	3	23	3
	Turn devices on/off based on presence	3	20	6
	Adjust windows and shades automatically to keep house comfortable	1	24	4

Table 2. Participants' responses to a set of applications about whether they have the functionality, would be interested in buying it, or would not (N=29, two children did not answer).

functionality; however the households we interviewed had diverse installations and desires, consistent with differences previously observed in home network installations and household routines [12]. Households ranged from using X10 to control a few lights (D4) to systems with wall panels to access functionality that includes viewing cameras (O5). Example automation devices are shown in Figure 1.

Installed functionality generally fell into one of four categories: Lighting, Security, Media, or Environment. Automated lighting with programmed lighting scenes (e.g., "All Off") was the most common type of automation and was present in all but 3 households. Households with automation for security have motion sensors and/or cameras. Five households (4DIY, 1O) managed the security aspects themselves, while five households (3DIY, 2O) had professionally managed security systems in addition to their other automation systems. In fact, two DIY homes with professional security systems have additional separate motion sensors or cameras they manage themselves. Eleven households (6DIY, 5O) had media related functionality including multi-room audio (8) and/or video systems (3) and home theater systems (4). Ten households (6DIY, 4O) had environment related automation including automation to control the heating system (8) or window blinds (2).

At a high level, similar to the diversity in what functionality they had already installed in their homes, participants' interest varied across the set of applications we asked about (see Table 2). For example, not surprisingly, monitoring applications were more popular among some families with children, and universally uninteresting to the six households without. Indicating people's diverse interests, when we asked to participants to rank their top 5 favorite applications

Figure 1: Home Automation User Interfaces: remote control for lighting scenes (left), augmented light switches (center), wall panel with remote camera view (right).

from the ones they would buy, no application was ranked first by more than six people. We did find that energy conservation applications were most appealing among the applications that most participants did not already have.

Comparing Outsourced and DIY households at a high level, we generally saw that Outsourced installations were static and unchanging, while DIY households had more functionality and iteration.

Augmented Homes, Not Smart Homes

Our participants primarily used *augmentation* to add automation, closer to the vision of unremarkable computing advocated by [32] than the typical smart home vision [23]. Households left a traditional interface (e.g., light switch) available, but augmented it with additional functionality and typically the ability to be controlled remotely (see Figure 1). D9_G[1] said "the wall switches are still there and they can still be used manually. That's generally how people use them, especially [if] they come over here."

Across our households we observed two levels of automation in use, *user controlled* and *rule-based.* In user controlled automation the household member explicitly takes a single action which causes several things to happen. For example, an "All Off" lighting scene button (physical or virtual) turns off all lights in the house. In Household O4 manually arming the alarm system affected heating settings as well as lights. Triggering Household O3's theater scene included lowering automatic blinds and the projector screen, and dimming the lights.

In rule-based automation, rules trigger automation based on events or at certain times. These rules are configured by the guru or professional installer. Not all of the households we visited used rules as they definitely represented an additional level of automation complexity. Event-based rules were typically motion sensor based. For example, turning the lights on when someone walks into the bathroom. Rules triggered by timing included actions taken at sundown (e.g., turn on outside lights), at sunrise, or related to wake-up or evening routines. As we will discuss in future sections, introducing rules often introduced problems as well.

Convenience, Peace of Mind, and Control

Several household members, particularly spouses of DIYers (e.g., D2_C, D6_C, D8_C), described being initially skeptical of home automation. However, after living with it the majority of household members, with the exception of those in Household O3 and D7, seemed quite satisfied with their experience. For example, D8_C said, "At first when Bob introduced it to me, I kind of thought it was silly, but just the convenience of it, just pressing one button, I mean, it's just amazing how – just to see the whole lights on the first floor come on instantaneously." Three common themes *convenience, peace of mind,* and *centralized control* emerged for people's favorite aspects of home automation.

Thirteen participants, across both DIY and Outsourced households mentioned convenience as one of their favorite aspects, sometimes with a bit of embarrassment about laziness. D6_C said "It allows me to be lazy, honestly, because every day [before automation] I would go double check the locks, make sure all the lights are off on all the floors and make sure that everything's closed."

D6_C also felt automation gave her "peace of mind. I can track things when I'm not there and know that on your way to work that it's sort of secure and set the way you want it to be." Eleven household members similarly emphasized security as one of their favorite aspects. Household D4's primary motivation for installing automation (a set of X10 based sensors primarily on doors and windows) was for security. In Household O1, external security cameras viewable on a TV channel were the favorite of two household members.

Finally, nine participants mentioned control as a positive aspect. Five participants in Outsourced households emphasized the value of having centralized control of various devices. For example, media control that allowed displaying the same DVD in multiple rooms (O2_C) or controlling a variety of devices from an iPod (O4_C). DIYers tended to emphasize control over what automation they installed, what functionality they enabled, and

[1] Participant Ids denote household (see Table 1) and technology guru (G) or a consumer(s) (e.g., C, C1). Names have been anonymized.

knowledge about what is happening at their house. D6_G said "I like just being in control, like during the day, I get an email every time somebody comes to the door."

Not Ready For Broad Adoption

Our participants have extensive personal experience living with home automation, so we felt they were well informed to comment on the potential value of home automation for others. Given the frequent mention of eldercare as one application for smart homes, we asked participants their opinion about home automation's value to their parents or older friends. Almost universally, participants thought this was a bad idea. D8_G felt "it's just too expensive; there's no payback for the benefit you receive," while D2_G felt there was potential benefit but "[home automation] is not robust enough, I think, to be stable for the average person."

Participants' comments in response to this question, along with their responses throughout the interview illustrated four barriers to broader adoption: *high cost of ownership*, *inflexibility*, *poor manageability*, and *difficulty achieving security*. In describing these, drawing on our participants' experiences, we want to be explicit about two points. First, many of these issues we describe were not barriers to use for the households we spoke with because they were uniquely qualified (DIYers) or spent money to overcome them. Second, we explicitly do not address the question of whether home automation functionality appeals to a broader audience. The barriers we have identified would need to be overcome before the general population could even consider using it.

BARRIER 1: HIGH COST OF OWNERSHIP

The first barrier to wider adoption is the high cost of ownership of home automation, either money or time and sometimes both. We describe our participants' experience, and how little most were willing to spend on additional functionality.

Expensive in Money or Time (or Both)

As Table 1 shows, money spent by the households on home automation varied widely from about \$200 to \$120,000. Monetary cost was one of the most frequently mentioned consideration determining both the brand and amount of functionality to install. Household O2 said they had looked at higher end systems which had more capabilities, but the prices were much higher. Not surprisingly, DIY households typically spent less (\$200 to \$50,000, median \$5,000) than Outsourced households (\$13,500 to \$120,000, median \$40,000), reflecting that the DIY households paid for hardware, but not for installation or support.

However, even the hardware alone can be quite expensive. For example, individual panels to replace standard light switches might cost around \$100. DIY household D6, who spent around \$50,000, had augmented light switches and panels that could display pictures in almost every room and automated door locks. At the other extreme, Households D4 (\$200) and D7 (\$300) used very inexpensive X10 motion sensors and wall-socket plug-in controllers that are much cheaper but have more limited functionality.

Five participants mentioned cost as one of their least favorite aspects of home automation. For example, D2_G said "Costly, that's the only disadvantage." O3_C expressed "it's been expensive, heart-wrenching." Household O3, as we described later, struggled with the reliability and usability of their system and seemed particularly dissatisfied, not surprising given the amount they had spent on their system (\$120,000).

Outsourced households require an outside consultant to come when their system needs adjustment or repair. To our initial surprise, the cost of these consultant visits did not seem to concern the households as much as we expected. We then learned the visits were relatively infrequent and had a low cost relative to the initial installation cost. After initial setup, consultants were primarily called only when problems occurred. Household O4 had a consultant visit only three times over the 10 years for about \$200 each time. Household O2 had not needed a consultant in so long that they could not remember the hourly cost (either \$45 or \$65 per hour). O5_C frequently had his installer back to deal with problems but did not pay because the installer was a friend of the family who had sold him the system.

In addition to monetary cost, for DIY households the time cost currently required to install and manage home automation should not be underestimated. Frequently the guru who drove the installation had a long standing interest in automation and carefully researched which brands they installed. D8_G said "I've been following this space probably for about five years, and just waiting for something that didn't require me to be a developer [of code]." For several DIY gurus (e.g., D2, D7, D9), automation was their hobby and they described happily spending hours tweaking their systems.

Low Perceived Value of Additional Applications

For applications participants were interested in (see Table 2) we asked them about how much they would be willing to pay for them. We started asking this question after the first three interviews to learn more about how valuable the participants perceived the applications to be. While their responses are speculative, the relative value participants assigned to different applications helped us understand how desirable they were.

In general, participants did not seem to put a high value on the home automation functionality we presented, which surprised us given the amount of money and/or time they had already invested. Of the 143 times participants reported the price they would be willing to pay, 61% of the values were \$20 or less. Comments included O2_C: "Anything over \$20 it's got to be something very important to want." and D5_G: "Not more than two or three dollars, I think." In ten cases, participants were interested in the functionality only if it was free.

BARRIER 2: INFLEXIBILITY

We now describe how current installations are inflexible, often requiring a choice between a single integrated system or flexibility, as well as the need for structural changes in many installations, which limits when automation can be installed and raises concerns about moving.

Choice between Integration Ease and Flexibility

Several participants, especially DIYers did not want to be locked in one specific vendor, and expressed resistance to brands more typical in Outsourced houses (e.g., Creston, Control4, etc.) because of a perceived lack of personal control. D9_G said "But the problem with those systems is that you can't really do anything yourself." While D2_G commented "It's like the Control4 [a home automation system] stuff is, you know, integrated but [then] you're locked in to their stuff." O4_G, who Outsourced, chose to use an open standard (EIB) specifically because it meant he could buy from many vendors.

However, choosing to use multiple brands meant dealing with the challenge of integrating separate systems. D2_G commented "it's kind of a task to keep it all integrated and working." Integration difficulties caused some of the devices with network capabilities to be not connected. Eight households had some devices not get connected to their home automation system. For example, D8_G had not integrated his alarm system with his Lagotek automation system because of the cost and work involved. In his case, integrating the devices and pieces was complicated enough that it was easier to keep them separate systems.

Structural Changes Common

Perhaps one of the biggest challenges to broad adoption is the structural changes needed to install home automation. The most common trigger for installing among our participants was building or remodeling a house. Of our 14 households, nine put automation in place either during a remodel or new construction. This was seen as the ideal time to have appropriate wiring installed either by themselves or by the contractor. These changes at the structural level [27] were often complicated as builders, contractors, and even permitting agencies got involved. D6_G told us that "all the local wiring for the home automation was one of the things keeping us from getting our occupancy permit, the inspector didn't know the code very well when it came to the low voltage stuff." Frequently, the DIY gurus put in their own devices after the wiring was complete or immediately replaced standard devices installed by contractors.

In an approach more suited to broad adoption, five households (3DIY, 2O) did retrofit installations leveraging wireless to avoid wiring. D8_M described choosing his brand, "it's Lagotek, a wireless system. So it's really strong in the retrofit model and that's why we went ahead and did it." Although D8, in fact made some structural changes as well, installing Cat 5 cables for audio streaming. The other four retrofit installs had more limited functionality (e.g., the X10 installation in D7 involved only X10 wall-plugs to turn on and off devices). One participant, O5_C felt that using wireless for audio streaming was the reason it frequently stopped working. He was happy the new home he was moving into was already wired.

Given the structural changes households made, the challenge of moving was a concern. Several participants felt adding home automation would make their houses more difficult to sell. Household O4 had done the most extensive planning ahead. The guru opted to outsource even though he had the technical expertise to manage the automation. He hired a consultant to have a person available to support any new owners. O5_C described to us the challenging process of moving and reinstalling his $20,000 worth of audio equipment and other hardware to his new home.

BARRIER 3: POOR MANAGEABILITY

Living with a home automation system requires managing it. We should stress that most of the households we spoke with were well-equipped to managing their installations. However, their experience suggests challenges that would need to be addressed before broader adoption of home automation including support for the iteration necessary to customize, issues with reliability and complex user interfaces, and concerns raised by reliance on consultants.

Iteration Required

We asked households how often their home automation set-up changed. As Chetty *et al.* [5] observed for home networking there was a set of DIYers who were constantly changing their home automation set-up (D2, D3, D7, D8, D9). However, most households, even those with unchanging set-ups, described an initial period of iteration right after they installed as they customized their set-ups to their homes and household needs.

We found it particularly interesting that a few households described scaling back their initially installed functionality as they became aware of a difference between what they thought they wanted before installing automation and what functionality they actually wanted. For example, D8_G described his changing desires:

"I thought when I went into this, I'd want my alarm system integrated and I'd want these automatic features firing off in the background like, you know, I'd wake up and music is playing in my bathroom and the lights come up, you know all these Jetson type things. And the challenge with that, while they're all great, I don't live that structured of a life, not waking up into [it] every day, and I'm not going in the shower every day at the same time. And you know, I don't want to hear music all the time. So I don't think the routineness of automation is what I was really wanting."

In addition to changing desires, the challenge of creating rules that worked reliably caused iteration and scaling back. D1_G said "I came to discover that you can't really create hard rules to describe every single situation that you might want to automate." DI_G's experience is an excellent example of Edwards and Grinter's challenge of inference in the presence of ambiguity [10].

Household changes could also cause iteration. D3_G told us that he expected to change all his rules when his girlfriend moved in because they had different preferences around whether the lights should be on or off when watching TV. After the birth of their second child, Household O4 had a consultant come back to set-up a switch for turning off lights in the child's room from their bedside.

Unreliable Behavior is Frustrating

Fourteen participants explicitly mentioned problems with their current system's reliability, which typically resulted in unpredictable behavior. Four households' problems were related to rule-based automation. For example, consumers in O4 and D7 both reported the lights sometimes went off unpredictably in their homes (e.g., D7_C: "I'm sewing and the light goes out."). Participants felt rules in general were hard to debug when they did not work and so participants lived with problems or turned off the rules.

Lack of responsiveness was a related frustration. Four households described waiting several minutes for a system's response. Similarly, Household O3's central control device was extremely unreliable and finicky. O3_C commented "you have to be really, really careful ..., you have to talk to it first and do what it wants to do."

Even households not struggling with reliability emphasized its importance. D9_G said "it [home automation controller] pretty much never fails, and that was important, because otherwise it was not really helpful." He switched from using his PC as his central controller to an ISY-99i unit, with the loss of some functionality and additional expense, because his previous setup was unreliable.

Complex User Interfaces Limit Use

The augmentation strategy many households adopted, particularly for lighting scenes, aimed for a simple interface that could be used by anyone including guests. While some households were more successful than others at achieving simplicity, problems with complex user interfaces faced by participants, particularly the technology consumers, and guests illustrate that user interface challenges exist.

Eight participants mentioned complex user interfaces (e.g. Fig. 1) as one of the things they most dislike about home automation. D3_G commented he disliked "Teaching other people how to use it, the girlfriend acceptance factor is not that high." The other seven participants (3DIY, 4O) had trouble learning the user interfaces. For example, the younger brother in the household O3 mentioned that "He [his brother] spent hours trying to show me how to use it, and I still don't know how to use it."

Complex user interfaces including some augmented light switches could be confusing or even frightening to guests. Six households told us that they do not tell guests about the home automation system. Others explained problems guests experienced. O4_C1 noted people's fear: "I started explaining the panel (how to call fire department) to them and they looked in dread. People just don't want to touch it. And my own mother sat in our house in the dark, because she was scared to touch any of the controls."

Consultants (Internal or Hired) Required

To handle manageability problems, the DIY guru served as the on-site consultant, while Outsourced households relied primarily on professional consultants. In contrast to the Outsourced homes that Woodruff *et al.* [33] studied who seemed to find value in ceding control to the consultant, households we visited described downsides to being reliant on a consultant including inability to fix their own system, inability to customize, and password management.

O2_C expressed discomfort with her inability to fix their system saying: "I don't like that we can't fix it ourselves." Household O1, with the death of their guru, had a particularly challenging situation. They used the system daily, but were unsure what they would do if anything broke. O5_C also expressed his difficulty learning to troubleshoot issues.

Reliance on consultants, whom they typically only contacted for problems, also restricted households' ability to customize. O5_C also told us he would have liked to try out different scenes if he knew how to experiment with the system. While O2_C knew the brand they installed (Creston) did not restrict people from learning how to program it, she thought it was very complicated to learn how. Lastly, Outsourced households must also decide how to deal with passwords. Household O2 had explicitly decided not to share the password to their system with the consultant, while O3_C did not know the password for changing rules and assumed the consultant had it.

BARRIER 4: DIFFICULTY ACHIEVING SECURITY

During the interviews we asked participants how they managed access to their current automation functionality and what, if any, usage restrictions they would want to place on future applications they desired (see Table 2).

Presence Based Access Mostly Sufficient

Most automation functionality, (e.g., lighting, media) participants had enabled could be used by anyone physically present in the house. Because households had augmented the physical controls, when inside a house you could access the functionality using wall switches or a remote control device. The main exceptions were home security systems which always required passwords, and interfaces for writing rules, which often did. Households were also particularly concerned about remote access which we describe next.

Handle Remote Access with Care

Remote access was a double-edged sword for people. The functionality was appealing, but participants worried about introducing a security risk. Eight households currently have remote access enabled, all but one with password protection.

Households used remote access for a variety of tasks including remotely controlling lights to make a house appear occupied when no one was home, turning on heating before they arrived home, checking the state of the house using cameras, or verifying the doors had been locked.

In general, participants perceived remote access to be valuable. When asked the importance of remote access to them, participants' median response was "Important" on a 5-point Likert scale (Very Important to Very Unimportant). Remote access appealed particularly for vacation scenarios; five participants commented that it is or would be useful when they are away from home for a long time.

However, seven participants mentioned that remote access makes them concerned about security. D9_G told us that "There is a way to have the system respond to text messages… But, for security reasons, I decided not do that because anybody could send text message. So, I actually don't want to have that hooked up." O4_C who had not hooked up remote access said "I don't want software controlling my front door. I don't want it opening at random whilst I am on holiday… Once something is software controlled, it can be hacked in some way."

Even very technically savvy participants expressed concerns that enabling remote access would make their house vulnerable. D2_G had chosen not to make his automated door locks available remotely because even though it was password protected he was not 100% sure of the security. Similarly, D8_G expressed that security concerns about his wireless automation system, which was remotely accessible, were "part of the hesitancy of hooking up the alarm system" to his automation system.

Finally, the level of concern of some participants was directly related to what technology was in the house. D4_G commented "if it had cameras I would be concerned about it. But for what I have, I'm not that concerned." Similarly, D3_G, the only participant with remote access that was not password protected, was unconcerned about people accessing his system: "If you knew my port number and my IP address you could log in and turn the lights on and off."

High-Concern Devices: Door Locks and Cameras

Two devices we discussed with participants, door locks and cameras, raised the most security concerns and illustrate the tension participants felt between convenience and security. For example, two DIY households already had automated door locks. D6_G enthusiastically described remotely unlocking his front door while away on vacation (he also has a camera at his front door) to let the house cleaners in because he had forgotten to give them a new key. On the other hand, as previously mentioned D2_G had not made his automated door locks available remotely due to security concerns. He also keeps a separate password for his alarm system so that if someone steals the door access card they could not disarm the alarm system.

Cameras also raised additional security concerns for participants. Five participants described increased security restrictions being necessary for the "remote access to home cameras" application. For example, D7_G said before installing that functionality he would want "A drop dead firewall to prevent outsiders from logging in and wandering around your house visually." D9_G wanted increased security for access inside the house as he would prefer guests could not view a camera setup in his child's room.

Temporary Access Important

Participants raised the importance of being able to give temporary access to automation functionality to guests. Specific examples they shared with us included the need for babysitters to have control over media applications or grandparents staying with kids, temporarily having the same access as the parents. D8_G said "We've got my wife's parents quite often come and watch the kids. So you'd want to have the ability to delegate that." Similarly, two of the participants interested in buying the "Automatic Alerting" application wanted the ability to send the alerts to someone else temporarily while on vacation. Cisco's Valet router does provide guest access to the Internet. While a step in the right direction, the router allows Internet access only, with no access to home resources or automation.

Simple User Groups for Future Needs

For applications participants were interested in buying (see Table 2) we asked them what restrictions, if any, they would want to place on who could use the applications. Typical responses included "anyone in the house," "parents only," and "no guests." For example, not surprisingly, participants interested in logging-related applications typically felt access should be restricted to parents. For a few applications, they were very specific about wanting to limit guest access. For example, limiting guests from access to home cameras (D7), preventing guests from seeing people's use of devices in the home (D4, O2), or seeing data about the house energy monitor (O2). Occasionally, a guru also told us they would like to restrict the ability to configure an application to themselves (e.g., for automatic alerts, scenes, and setting up centralized control). Given the complex needs found for home file access control [22], we were pleasantly surprised that for times when physical presence in the home did not suffice as access control, all the restrictions our participants expressed could be handled by a small set of user groups: adult household member, child household member, guest, and technology guru.

We also asked participants if they had any concerns about the devices an application might want to access. A few participants wanted to limit the set of devices an application could access. Participants' comments suggest that having applications ask for permission, similar to methods suggested for user permissions [e.g., 1, 22], to use devices during configuration would address concerns.

IMPLICATIONS FOR HOME TECHNOLOGY RESEARCH

Our study illustrated four barriers faced by households that adopt home automation: high cost of ownership, inflexibility, poor manageability, and difficulty achieving security. The barriers existed for both types of households, DIY and Outsourced, that we interviewed, although they impact each group differently and each group has made different trade-offs to overcome them. For instance, while the Outsourced households suffer from cost of ownership primarily in terms of money, the DIYers trade-off lower monetary cost for increased time commitment. Similarly, DIYers address inflexibility with expertise, while Outsourced household tend to choose one brand.

While we believe that some of the problems we observed (e.g., reliability of individual devices, basic interoperability) will be addressed through market competition and developing standards, our findings also highlight harder problems that merit the attention of the research community. We discuss three such problems below.

Bandwidth Needs vs. Structural Changes

Requiring households to make structural changes to their homes for the best experience dramatically raises the installation cost and reduces the appeal of home automation. The primary driver for structural changes is the need for wires, either special electrical wires to power devices or network wires for reliable, high-bandwidth connections. While wireless networks have taken a huge step in the right direction; our participants' experiences with audio streaming make clear the trade-off they face between reliable bandwidth and structural changes. Continued research on reliable high-bandwidth home networks that require no additional wiring (e.g., wireless or power-line) remains critical. Emerging technologies such as 60 GHz, IEEE 802.11af and Femtocells are promising and their utility in the home environment needs investigation.

Standalone Devices vs. Home Integration

Aristotle claimed "The whole is greater than the sum of its parts," but unfortunately due to challenges with integration and manageability, several households we interviewed were forced to keep pieces of their home technology separate. This separation creates three problems: 1) each sub-system (e.g., media) must be independently managed, which can become a management nightmare; 2) it becomes difficult to add cross-device functionality such as tying changes in the home alarm state to thermostat control; and 3) careful attention needs to be paid to which devices are compatible with various sub-systems, which makes it much harder to incrementally grow the network and forces users to buy all devices in the sub-system together to ensure compatibility.

Given the diversity we saw in homes and the iteration our participants engaged in to customize their automation, ideally users would be able to organically acquire devices from a range of manufacturers, conduct lightweight experiments to understand if the functionality fits their needs (as also argued for in [24]), and reap greater benefits as they add more devices. Unfortunately existing smart home technologies do not consider this incremental growth or composability aspect [e.g., 4]. At the other extreme, device inter-operability standards allow users to buy devices from different vendors but they are insufficient alone because they provide no basis for coordinating across devices [24]. We thus see need for a more composable architecture for organizing technology in the home that includes both a basis for device coordination and incremental, vendor-independent extension of functionality.

Simple Confidence-building Security vs. Desired Functionality

Our study showed that the security and access control needs of both DIY and Outsourced households are unmet. We thus believe that research is needed to develop simple security primitives that are custom-designed for the home environment. Our work suggests that the security needs of homes, while superficially numerous, can be met with a few simple, well designed primitives that take advantage of the unique nature of the domain. For instance, proximity implies a level of trust, also noted by [19, 22], and our participants tend to think of access control in terms of a few simple groups (e.g., "parents," "kids"). We believe these provisions along with streamlined temporary access for guests would go a long way in meeting householders' needs. It would be interesting to explore whether the simplicity of using groups outweighs possible exceptions.

Our participants' choices and concerns about remote access also highlighted that households are making trade-offs between security and desired functionality. Not only must home security primitives be simple to configure, users need to be able to fully understand the implications of their security settings, so they can build confidence in them. Without this, users are likely to give up some of the convenience (e.g., remote access) for peace of mind, as we observed, or inadvertently live in insecure environments.

CONCLUDING REMARKS

Our study of long-term use of home automation illustrates why participants use automation, the diversity of use across households, and how both Outsourced and DIY households struggled, albeit in different ways. It also uncovered four barriers that need to be addressed before home automation becomes amenable for broader adoption. These are high cost of ownership, inflexibility, poor manageability, and difficulty achieving security. Most participants were positive about their experience with home automation, having addressed these barriers using a combination of expertise, effort, and money. Our findings suggest three future research problems: eliminating the need for structural change to install home automation, providing households with simple, confidence-building security mechanisms, and the ability to compose household devices. We are beginning to address these problems [8].

ACKNOWLEDGMENTS

We thank our participants for opening their homes to us.

REFERENCES

1. Bauer, L., Cranor, L., Reeder, R.W., Reiter, M.K., Vaniea, K. A user study of policy creation in a flexible access-control system. *Proc. CHI 2008*, 543-552.
2. Bell, G., Kaye, J.J. Designing Technology for Domestic Spaces: A Kitchen Manifesto. *Gastronomica 2*, 2(2002), 42-62.
3. Beyer, H., Holtzblatt, K. Contextual Design: Defining Customer-Centered Systems. Morgan Kaufmann, 1998.
4. Brumitt, B., Meyers, B., Krumm, J., Kern, A., Shafer, S.A. EasyLiving: Technologies for intelligent environments. *Proc. HUC 2000, LNCS 1927*, 97-119.
5. Chetty, M., Sung, J-Y., Grinter, R. How Smart Homes Learn: The Evolution of the Networked Home and Household. *Proc. UbiComp 2007*, 127-144.
6. Control4 home automation and control. http://www.control4.com.
7. Davidoff, S., Lee, M., Yiu, C., Zimmerman, J., Dey, A. Principles of Smart Home Control. *Proc. UbiComp 2006*, 19-34.
8. Dixon, C., Mahajan, R., Agarwal, S., Brush, A., Lee, B., Saroui, S., Bahl, V. The Home Needs an Operating System (and an App Store). *Proc. HotNets IX.*
9. DLNA. http://www.dlna.org/home.
10. Edwards, W.K., Grinter, R.E. At Home with Ubiquitous Computing: Seven Challenges. *Proc. UbiComp 2001*, 256-272.
11. Edwards, W, Newman, M., Sedivy, J., Smith, T., Balfanz, D., Smetters, D., Wong, H., Izadi, S. Using SpeakEasy for ad hoc peer-to-peer collaboration. *Proc. CSCW 2002*, 256-265.
12. Grinter, R., Edwards, W., Chetty, M., Poole, E.S., Sung, J.-Y., Yang, J., Crabtree, A., Tolmie, P., Rodden, T., Greenhalgh,C., Benford, S. The ins and outs of home networking: The case for useful and usable domestic networking. *ACM ToCHI 16*, 2(2009), 8:1-8:28.
13. Grinter, R., Edwards, W., Newman, M., Ducheneaut, N. The Work to Make a Home Network Work. *Proc. ECSCW 2005*, 469-488.
14. Hamill, L. Controlling Smart Devices in the Home. *The Information Society 22*, 4 (2006), 241-249.
15. Harper, R. (ed.) Inside the Smart Home. Springer, London, 2003.
16. Home security systems, home security products, home alarm systems - ADT. http://www.adt.com.
17. Intille, S. Designing a home of the future. *IEEE Pervasive Computing 1*, 2(2002), 80-86.
18. Kietz, J., Patel, S., Jones, B., Price, E., Mynatt, E., Abowd, A. The Georgia Tech Aware Home. *Ext. Abstracts CHI 2008*, 3675-3680.
19. Kim, T., Bauer, L., Newsome, J., Perrig, A., Walker, J. Challenges in Access Right Assignment for Secure Home Networks. *Proc. HotSec 2010.*
20. Koskela, T., Väänänen-Vaninio-Mattila, K. Evolution towards smart home environments: empirical evaluation of three user interfaces. *PUC 8*, 3-4(2004), 234-240.
21. Lucero, S., Burden, K. Home Automation and Control, ABI Research 2010.
22. Mazurek, M., Arsenault, J., Breese, J., Gupta, N., Ion, I., Johns, C., Lee, D., Liang, Y., Olsen, J., Salmon, B., Shay, R., Vaniea, K., Bauer L., Cranor, L., Ganger, G., Reiter, M. Access control for home data sharing: Attitudes, needs and practices. *Proc. CHI 2010*, 645-654.
23. Mozer, M.C. Lessons from an Adaptive House. In D. Cook and R. Das (eds.) Smart Environments: Technologies, Protocols, and Applications (pp. 273-294). J. Wiley & Sons, Hoboken, NJ, 2005.
24. Newman, M., Elliot A., Smith T. Providing an Integrated User Experience of Networked Media, Devices and Services Through End-User Composition. *Proc. Pervasive 2008*, 213-227.
25. Poole, E., Chetty, M., Grinter, R., Edwards, W.K. More than Meets the Eye: Transforming the User Experience of Home Network Management. *Proc. DIS 2008*. 455-464.
26. Randall, D. Living Inside a Smart Home: A Case Study. In: Harper, R. (ed.) Inside the Smart Home, 227-246. Springer, Heidelberg (2003)
27. Rodden, T., Benford, S. The evolution of buildings and implications for the design of ubiquitous domestic environments. *Proc. CHI 2003*, 9-16.
28. Rode, J., Toye, E., Blackwell, A. The Domestic Economy: a Broader Unit of Analysis for End User Programming. *Proc. CHI 2005*, 1757-1760.
29. Shehan, E., Edwards. W.K. Home Networking and HCI: What Hath God Wrought? *Proc. CHI 2007*, 547-556.
30. Tolmie, P., Crabtree, A., Rodden, T., Greenhalgh, C., Benford, S. Making the Home Network at Home: Digital Housekeeping. *Proc. ECSCW 2007*, 331-350.
31. Tolmie, P., Crabtree, A., Egglestone, S., Humble, J., Greenhalgh, C., Rodden, T. Digital plumbing: the mundane work of deploying UbiComp in the home. *PUC 14*, 3 (2010), 181-196.
32. Tolmie, P., Pycock, P., Diggins, T., MacLean, A., Karsenty, A. Unremarkable computing, *Proc. CHI 2002*, 399-406.
33. Woodruff, A., Augustin, S., Foucalt, B. Sabbath Day Home Automation: "It's Like Mixing Technology and Religion" *Proc. CHI 2007*, 527-536.

Creek Watch: Pairing Usefulness and Usability for Successful Citizen Science

Sunyoung Kim[1], Christine Robson[2,3], Thomas Zimmerman[2], Jeff Pierce[2], Eben M. Haber[2]

[1]Human-Computer Interaction Institute
Carnegie Mellon University
5000 Forbes Avenue,
Pittsburgh, PA
sunyoung.kim@cs.cmu.edu

[2]Mobile Computing Research Group
IBM Research - Almaden
650 Harry Road,
San Jose CA 95120
{tzim, jspierce,ehaber}@us.ibm.com

[3]Department of Computer Science
Univ. of California, Berkeley
2599 Hearst Ave.,
Berkeley, CA 94720
crobson@eecs.berkeley,edu

ABSTRACT

Citizen science projects can collect a wealth of scientific data, but that data is only helpful if it is actually used. While previous citizen science research has mostly focused on designing effective capture interfaces and incentive mechanisms, in this paper we explore the application of HCI methods to ensure that the data itself is useful. To provide a focus for this exploration we designed and implemented Creek Watch, an iPhone application and website that allow volunteers to report information about waterways in order to aid water management programs. Working with state and local officials and private groups involved in water monitoring, we conducted a series of contextual inquiries to uncover what data they wanted, what data they could immediately use, and how to most effectively deliver that data to them. We iteratively developed the Creek Watch application and website based on our findings and conducted evaluations of it with both contributors and consumers of water data, including scientists at the city water resources department. Our study reveals that the data collected is indeed useful for their existing practices and is already in use in water and trash management programs. Our results suggest the application of HCI methods to design the data for the end users is just as important as their use in designing the user interface.

Author Keywords

Citizen Science, Participatory Sensing, Mobile, iPhone.

ACM Classification Keywords

H.5.2 User Interfaces, J.4 Computer Applications: Social and Behavioral Sciences.

General Terms

Human Factors

INTRODUCTION

Citizen science is, at its core, a way of empowering people to help with large-scale scientific problems of interest to them. Typically, citizen science projects engage volunteers in data-gathering activities around a project in their natural environment (e.g., ecology, biology, astronomy, etc). This approach fulfills two broad goals: engaging and educating the public about scientific issues, and collecting data that would otherwise be difficult or impossible to obtain.

Perhaps the most successful citizen science project to date is the Christmas Bird Count (CBC), a project started over a century ago by the Audubon Society, which asks volunteers during the holidays to count the number of birds in each species they sight. The CBC is successful in two ways; it inspires the involvement of tens of thousands of volunteers, and the results, collected at thousands of sites each year form one of the most critical data sources used by ornithologists to track bird populations and distributions across the globe. Those involved in the CBC are mostly amateur birdwatchers and not full-time scientists; however, the results of their joint efforts continue to have significant scientific impact. [18]

While data collection for the CBC was traditionally done with paper forms, marked in pencil and sent by post to the Audubon Society, modern citizen science utilizes electronic communication. Web data submission is now common, and the proliferation of mobile phones in general (five billion in the world today [26]) and GPS and camera-equipped smart phones in particular (fifty million in the USA [10]) holds great promise for enhancing citizen science participation, providing a convenient means to collect and send time- and location-tagged data. Smart phones are a particularly powerful tool, combining an array of sensors paired with rich user interfaces in a personal device that is continually carried by millions of people around the world.

Previous research in citizen science and participatory sensing has focused largely on the problem of engagement; recruiting volunteers and maintaining their interest and participation [5,12,24]. Incentive structures, competition, entertainment and educational approaches have all proven successful to some extent. Yet engagement is only a partial measure of success; a citizen science project has scientific impact only when the collected data is used.

Several previous Citizen Science projects have inadvertently ignored this issue and have yet to produce any useful scientific results from the data, including NASA's Clickworkers[1] project and the Journey North project. These projects launched without scientific goals for using the data collected, and have produced no scientific results despite years of collection ([11, 22]). This problem was re-iterated by scientist stakeholders we interviewed, who observed that volunteer groups often decide to collect data that is marginally useful to the scientific community.

It seems logical to engage with scientists who need data as key stakeholders, yet they have been neglected by the design community. In our research we address this disconnect by focusing on the usability and usefulness of collected *data*, rather than just on the *interface* presented to users. We wanted our design to be driven by the scientists who need the data as well as by the volunteer groups that support their investigations. By first understanding the needs and abilities of these groups, we are more likely to build a citizen science application that is useful and usable.

In order to find suitable groups of scientists and volunteers, we met with a variety of organizations. The California Environmental Protection Agency helped us identify watershed health as a critical area that is also amenable to data gathering by average citizens. Interviews and brainstorming sessions with the California State Water Resources Control Board and the City of San Jose Environmental Services Water Resources helped us understand their priorities and needs for data. We then met with local watershed monitoring organizations to understand the capabilities and limitations of their current citizen monitoring practices.

Having assessed the data needs of the stakeholders and the abilities of volunteers we designed and developed Creek Watch. Creek Watch combines both an iPhone application and website. The iPhone application enables citizens to contribute water flow and trash data from creeks and rivers. The website, www.creekwatch.org, allows them to view contributed data, and provides scientists access to all of the collected data. We validated our design in a usability study with subjects who had no previous experience with water quality monitoring.

We then conducted an intensive user study with 10 scientists from the City of San Jose Environmental Services Water Resources team that were not involved in our earlier study and design sessions. We tested the Creek Watch interface, assessed the usefulness of data it collected, and identified potential improvements in the application and website. Overall the scientists were very pleased with Creek Watch, and are now using the data it collects. The interviews and user studies enabled us to identify what data would be useful to the scientists and the standards the data must comply with.

In the following sections we describe our series of contextual inquiries with water control boards and volunteer watershed monitoring groups. Next, we explain our design of the Creek Watch iPhone application and website, how we took the needs of these different groups and converged upon a set of data and collection standards, and our user study with members of our local water control board. We then discuss lessons for citizen science design and key implications of our work, and conclude by identifying future directions for research.

PRIOR WORK

The recruitment of citizens to participate in large scale monitoring has a long history, particularly in observing phenomena in the environment. Animal population research has been aided by citizen science in a number of ways: in addition to the annual Christmas Bird Count [18], Cornell Lab's bird monitoring program [6] attracts over 200,000 volunteers each year. A similar project exists for counting fish[2]. Technology has enhanced the participation of citizens providing communication, documentation and measurement tools. The CONE project at UC Berkeley allows volunteers to contribute to bird sighting numbers using autonomous robotic cameras deployed in birding hotspots [23]. In the Lost Ladybug Project[3] citizens submit digital photos of Ladybugs along with location and weather information.

Citizen science provides a mechanism for participants to learn about and improve their community. Participants in the GarbageWatch project contribute pictures of garbage to help figure out where to place recycling bins[4]. Urban citizens equipped with sensors track neighborhood air [13,24,27] and noise [16] pollution. Citizens in Virginia have organized a volunteer group to monitor, consolidate and share data on local stream and rivers to maintain and improve the health of the Rivanna watershed[5]. Beyond science, many cities use the non-emergency number 3-1-1 to implement a citizen service center for residents to report needed roadwork, abandoned vehicles and other neighborhood code enforcement issues [4]. On-line versions of 3-1-1 developed by several cities provide citizens the ability to digitally interact with city services [19].

The value of mobile phones as tools for citizen science has been recognized [13], with examples such as air quality [20], and the Oil Reporter service which allows volunteers to report on areas affected by the Gulf Coast oil spill[6].

Citizens' role is not just limited to data collection. Technology makes it possible for citizens to volunteer their

[1] en.wikipedia.org/wiki/Clickworkers

[2] fishcount.org

[3] lostladybug.org

[4] garbagewatch.com

[5] streamwatch.org

[6] oilreporter.org

computer and brainpower. Idle time on volunteers' home computers is being used to search for extraterrestrial life [7] and study protein folding[8]. The Galaxy Zoo[9] leverages the human brain's exceptional pattern-recognition skills, recruiting citizens to classify galaxies from photos taken by a robotic telescope. This type of citizen science is a form of crowd sourcing, wherein people can perform distributed tasks towards a greater goal [12].

Unlike prior work, an important contribution of our work is the use of HCI methods to focus on the data consumers as a stakeholder group. Much Citizen Science work from the HCI community (including [13,14,16]) has focused on projects where users are both producers and consumers, so there was no need to study separate stakeholders. While Cohn [5] considers the scientific quality of the data collected by volunteers, he does not discuss its utility to existing projects that need the data. Paxton *et al.* [21] did not explore the importance of data consumers in their design of a participatory sensing system to collect environmental data, and Cuff *et al.* [7] nicely delineated citizen sensing network infrastructure without describing the use of the collected data by data consumers.

UNDERSTANDING THE PROBLEM

We began the Creek Watch project with a discussion with the California Environmental Protection Agency of areas in which volunteers equipped with mobile devices could be empowered to help their environment. We conducted a series of interviews and brainstorming sessions with ecologists in the state agency to understand current practices and problems in environmental management. Our discussions identified the monitoring of watershed health as an ideal application of citizen science: waterways are numerous and geographically distributed, local water agencies lack the staff and resources to monitor all of them, and citizens are aware of the importance of water. While we chose to focus on waterways, the same basic issues of large geographic scope and limited resources occur in many environmental domains.

Resources and Access

Watersheds are geographically large, and monitoring all of the waterways within them would require resources that exceed most organizations. For example, the city of San Jose, California's third largest city, has over 700 miles of creeks – far too much ground for a local agency to cover, especially when creeks run through private land that officials cannot access without permission. In practice, this means many areas are never visited by officials and receive no monitoring.

However, many of these creeks run through parks and recreation areas visited by citizens every day; these citizens could perform some monitoring if the process were sufficiently convenient. Creeks that run through private land could be monitored by the land owners. As a result, watershed monitoring is well positioned to take advantage of the key potential of citizen science: there are many more people who care about the environment than just those who are professionals in the field.

Interacting Stakeholders

In addition to resource demands, environmental monitoring programs must address data standardization and sharing among stakeholders:

1. Government organizations: these organizations are responsible for enforcement of regulations pertaining to water use, wastewater discharge, and pollution, on state, regional, county and city levels.
2. Private groups: these are typically consulting companies, which work closely with these government organizations, typically funded by grants, for example by private parties to conduct evaluations for environmental permits.
3. Volunteer groups: these are typically organized on a city or county level and meet anywhere from twice-a-year to pick up trash, to monthly to monitor water quality with professional equipment.

Data sharing, re-use, and standards

Beyond collecting data, one of the biggest challenges faced by organizations is sharing data - if two groups do not gather data in precisely the same fashion (i.e. follow the same protocol), the data may be incompatible. Even for programs where collection techniques have been standardized, the problem of data sharing typically remains unsolved. Historically each government organization has maintained its own databases with poor interoperability. Currently, data is most frequently exchanged as completed reports or as spreadsheets. Recent legislation in California has mandated a state-wide system to share this data, but the system is still under development.

Getting information from private and volunteer groups can be even more difficult. Watershed volunteer groups typically aggregate data they have collected into a yearly report which is made available to government organizations as a summary document. More sophisticated groups may include a spreadsheet of the original data. Because these groups typically have a specific driving mission (e.g., searching for mercury or other toxins local to their area, tracking water flow rates which affect fish spawning, etc.), the data they collect is focused on a specific problem and may not include information that other organizations need to make further use of the data.

Our discussions with the California EPA revealed that there are over 250 organized and recognized groups in California working on watershed health [9], yet their idiosyncratic data collection and sharing practices make it likely that only a few will have their data used by others. In our work we

[7] setiathome.ssl.berkeley.edu
[8] folding.stanford.edu
[9] galaxyzoo.org

apply human-centered design methods to the design of the data collection and format to ensure usefulness by the scientists who are the primary end users of the data.

CONTEXTUAL INQUIRIES

Following on our brainstorming sessions with the California Environmental Protection Agency, we conducted a series of contextual inquiries [1] to guide the design of a citizen science mobile application for watershed health monitoring. We conducted in-depth interviews, on the phone and in the field when possible, with eleven scientists, environmental workers, and water monitoring volunteers from across seven organizations. From the government side, we interviewed four ecologists in the California State Water Resources Control Board and the City of San Jose Environmental Services Water Resources. From the private sector, we interviewed three ecologists from San Francisco Estuaries Institute (SFEI) and the Southern California Coastal Water Research Project (SCCWRP). In the volunteer sector, we interviewed three volunteers from two local groups, the Stevens & Permanente Creeks Watershed Council (SPCWC) and the Alameda Creek Alliance. We also interviewed the volunteer outreach organizers of the Water Environment Federation, an international federation of water quality experts with over 80,000 members, including most of the environmental scientists we interviewed.

The primary goal of these interviews was to identify (1) the data most needed by environmental organizations that could be gathered by citizen scientists, (2) how it would be used, and (3) how to best ensure that the data would actually be useful, including understanding the protocol and format required to make the data acceptable to the scientists. The challenge of getting useful data from citizen scientists was confirmed by our first interview subject:

> *"In the early days it was an activity to engage understanding in water quality. It didn't matter what they did as long as they did something. Then we realized no one uses the data and they aren't monitoring for things we care about." Interview #1, State Water Control Board*

Critical Data: Water Flow and Trash

Problems in watershed management are numerous and varied, including the improvement of habitats for aquatic life, water collection for drinking and irrigation, flood and erosion control, and the identification and control of pollution. The data that could help these areas are equally numerous (e.g., water flow, turbidity, pH levels, dissolved oxygen, measurements of contaminant levels, aquatic life surveys). While much of this data requires specialized measurement equipment, some very useful data requires only simple observation. We identified water flow rate as a candidate datum from our interviews:

> *"Wherever people go, if there's a creek, it would be great to get info on flow. Qualitative and quantitative: take a picture and send to a database, GPS tagged. This would be tremendous – we need data on flow." Interview #1, State Water Control Board*

Water flow data is needed by several of the stakeholders we interviewed. Water flow rate in creeks is critical to understanding the health of a watershed: these small waterways, which in aggregate hold most of the water in California, are habitat for aquatic life, a source for drinking water and irrigation, and are unfortunately also a pathway for pollution. Without an accurate picture of when and where water is flowing, it is very difficult to understand the health and capacity of waterways, making water management more difficult. Capturing water flow data using the format and protocol required by the scientists assures that this data could be used by the stakeholders. Unfortunately, water flow data available to environmentalists is spotty at best.

> *"We're not getting a lot of [flow] data. Most is generated by discharge permits: when someone has a permit to discharge [waste water] into a stream, they are required to monitor flow, so we get that information. But...there are many more places we can look then we have people or resources for. ... Flow is kind of hidden, but it's really important. What happens is when we have to get it its too late to go back in time." Interview #4, State Water Control Board*

Fortunately, flow data is easy for citizen scientists to collect. No equipment is needed to determine if water is flowing or not, and if creeks are full or low. Furthermore, people pass by these waterways all the time while walking or biking in parks and around their neighborhoods.

Each of the groups we interviewed had a different reason for wanting flow data. At the state-level, flow data is desired for water management and planning. At the city level, flow data is desired for tracking pollution. One of the local volunteer groups (SPCWC) wanted flow data to study fish spawning. One of the private consulting groups (SCCWRP) wanted flow data for clients applying for construction permits. The other (SFEI) wanted flow data for a longitudinal study of human effects on bay area water supply. To service the data needs of these different stakeholders, flow data collection must conform to standards to ensure maximum re-usability.

We also identified data concerning trash as important to our stakeholders and amenable to citizen reporting.

> *"Many of the most serious water quality problems in California are associated with non-point source pollution. ... Trash is a severe non-point source problem. Trash clogs our waterways blocking fish migration paths, impairs aquatic life and poses a threat to many beneficial uses of our creeks and streams." – Interview #1, State Water Control Board*

While many groups regularly conduct trash surveys and cleanups, there is simply too much area to cover. The

Figure 1: Creek Watch iPhone application screen shots

California State Water Resources Control Board is required by the U.S. Environmental Protection Agency (EPA) to maintain a list of waters that are considered "impaired", i.e., they are too polluted to be used for swimming, fishing, drinking, or other beneficial uses [25]. In California, trash is the second most common impairment pollutant [8].

To identify impaired waters, the state water board must collect and assess water quality data and determine if it meets standards. The process starts with stakeholders who alert the water board of locations where water quality standards may not be met. Citizens can alert state boards of pollution but need to present evidence. Photographs, tagged by location and time, provide tangible evidence of trash in waterways. Photos can help identify the type of trash (e.g., bottles, paper, car parts, and medical waste) and potential sources (e.g., individual littering, illegal dumping of landscape and construction debris). Trash occurs most frequently in sites with high public access [17], which bodes well for citizen monitoring of trash levels. The culprits for watershed pollution are often unaware of the extent to which their activities are damaging the environment.

> *"It used to be that industry was the problem. But the average resident (collectively) is now the problem. People's pesticides, car washing, dog poop, garbage that we drop it's a really big problem." – Interview #7, City of San Jose Environmental Services*

The problem of getting data on such simple measures as flow rate and trash is complicated by the fact that good news is often assumed not to be worth reporting.

> *"We have a citizen stream keeper program: people go out at least once a month to a creek to observe it ... but if they don't see anything bad they don't report, so we don't know." Interview #6, Local Water Monitoring Volunteer Coordinator*

To be successful, we concluded that our citizen science application must equally support and encourage the reporting of both problems and situations where nothing seems amiss.

We concluded from these contextual inquiries that water quality data consumers would benefit from an application that enabled citizen scientists to report on water flow and trash, and that the data needed to be collected following a protocol and format acceptable to the end users (scientists). A smart phone is ideal for collecting this data, since it is always on hand, can collect pictures and accurate location data, and can simplify submitting data to a central organization.

More advanced needs

In addition to flow and trash data, we identified several other standard measures of water quality that would be useful, such as temperature, turbidity, dissolved oxygen, and pH level. Unfortunately, for a citizen scientist to report on this data, they need to have water testing kits or more specialized equipment, complete with the training to collect data according to accepted protocol in order for this data to be acceptable for scientific studies. For example, the SPCWC volunteer group used tools ranging in price from several hundred to several thousand dollars, operated by a trained biologist, and even so would only take samples on a monthly basis due to limitations on lab time for sample analysis.

Designing an application with a focus on consumers as well as producers of the data creates a trade-off between the advanced data needs of scientists and the capabilities of citizens without specialized training or equipment. To some extent this tradeoff occurs in all citizen science projects started by domain experts (e.g., [6,18]). Working with these stakeholder groups, we were able to look at the trade-offs in a new way. We identified the importance of collecting data that complies with the format and protocol required by scientists. We pair this with the citizen's need for an easy way to collect data in a reliable and predictable way.

DESIGN & DEVELOPMENT

We designed and built Creek Watch to be a participatory creek monitoring system that allows citizen scientists to capture water flow and trash data and scientists to view and analyze the collected data. We designed the system as two parts: a data collecting iPhone application, and a data sharing and viewing website, creekwatch.org.

Data Format: Conforming to Standards

To ensure that the collected data would be usable by existing programs, we drew on the California Environmental Protection Agency's Surface Water Ambient Monitoring Program Bioassessment Standard Operating Procedures [2] and the Rapid Trash Assessment Protocol [3]. These manuals define procedures for reporting on water flow (composed of water level and flow rate) and trash levels. With consultation from the California State Water Resources Control Board, we adopted the definitions in Table 1 for Creek Watch.

Water Level	Flow Rate	Trash
Dry: No water Present	**Still**: Water is present but is not visibly flowing	**None**: no trash in the water and surrounding area
Some: Water fills less then 75% of the channel	**Slow**: Water is present but is barely moving	**Some**: A few items of trash such as cans, bottles
Full: Water reaches up almost to the top of the banks	**Fast**: Water is present and flow is easily detected	**A lot**: Ten or more items of trash

Table 1: Water observation definitions used in Creek Watch, from the California EPA's Surface Water Ambient Monitoring Program

These observations, combined with a photo of the creek, GPS location and timestamp, provide the data that water monitoring organizations most requested.

Data Collection Application

We developed the data collection tool as a mobile application for the iPhone (see Figure 1). The application contains five views divided into tabs: *Report, My data, Browse, Instructions*, and *About*. Central to the application is the data reporting view, where users can Report on a creek they are looking at using the data format described above. From the report view users can access a set of photo examples defining the different choices for each data item.

While the application attempts to immediately post reported data to the server, it can also store reported data locally on the phone when the network is unavailable (as is often the case for creeks alongside hiking trails). Users can browse through data they have uploaded as well as data that still needs to be uploaded in the *My Data* section. Users can initiate another upload attempt for any data that the application has not yet loaded. Users can also manually specify the location for a report if necessary (if, for example, the GPS on the phone could not determine the user's position) before uploading a report.

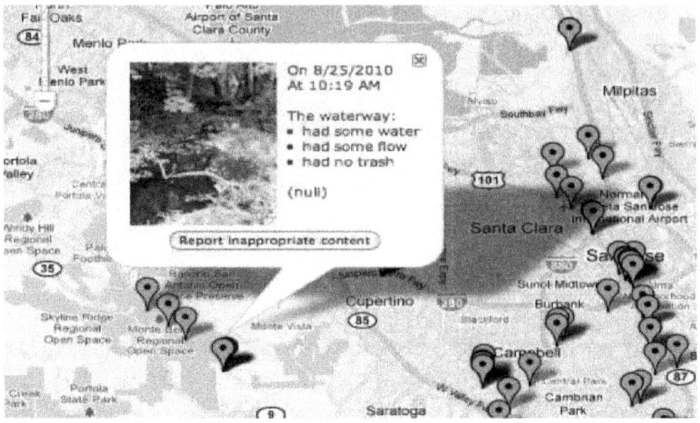

Figure 2. Map View of collected data at creekwatch.org

The *Browse* view provides a map visualization that enables users to see recent data points collected by others in their area, including photos. The *About and Instructions* views provide general information about and detailed instructions for using the application, respectively.

Data Sharing Website

The server we implemented at creekwatch.org collects data submitted by iPhones running the Creek Watch application, and presents this data in two interactive formats – a map (see Figure 2) and a table (see Figure 3).

Map-based data visualization

A map of all collected data points is the central visualization on creekwatch.org. We designed the map to enable browsing of the data by data contributors who wish to view their own and others' data. We built the visualization as a Google Maps mash-up with the Creek Watch database that displays the location of every data point as map pins, centered on the user's current location.

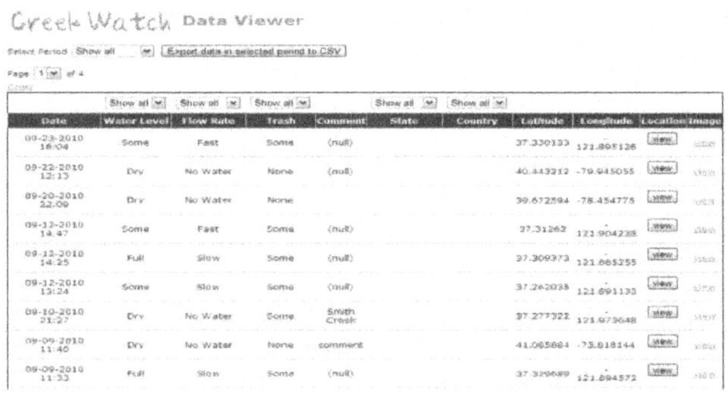

Figure 3: Table view with filters of the data collected at creekwatch.org

The detailed data collected at each location is available as a popup window with a photo of the creek, or as hover text over each pin (see Figure 2).

Table based data visualization

We designed the table view for scientists to easily work with the collected data (see Figure 3). Each column provides filters (time, location, data values), and scientists can export the filtered data to a csv (comma separated values) file for inclusion and integration with existing projects. The table view is publically available, such that anyone can manipulate and download the data in this fashion; however the intended audience is scientists in environmental management organizations.

Design process

In building Creek Watch we employed a classic iterative design process. Following our contextual inquiry interviews, we built an early version of the application to collect flow and trash data. We demonstrated this first version at an open community meeting with members of the state and local water control boards, and local volunteers. The initial feedback was positive, and we made several small changes to the workflow and appearance based on this review. Examples changes include adding an Instructions view to more clearly explain how to use the application.

Usability Study

We conducted a usability study on the user interface with four iPhone users who had no previous experience with water quality monitoring. The study was conducted in two parts: in a controlled environment in the lab, and in the field by local creeks. Our study identified some user interface glitches and workflow issues. For example, in response to our findings in this study, we employed a higher contrast between interface text and the background for easier reading in sunlight, and left more space between buttons to reduce accidental clicking. We also improved the instructions, and re-organized the application to begin with data entry, rather then with data browsing.

USER STUDY & FINDINGS

We designed and conducted a field deployment study to evaluate the effectiveness of our system at providing useful information to scientists. We recruited 10 environmental scientists in the City of San Jose Environmental Services Water Resources Department who own iPhones. The study participants included four environmental agents, three environmental outreach or volunteer coordinators, two managers, and one environmental analyst. Six participants were male and four were female. The average age was 45 years old with a standard deviation of 9.7 years. All participants had academic degrees related to environmental management or ecology. We chose to focus on environment scientists for our study participants in order to asses both the usability of the Creek Watch system and also the utility of the data it collects. None of our user study participants were involved in the brainstorming, early interviews, or design of Creek Watch. While we did work with other scientists from their departments to develop the application, for the user study we wanted to see how unbiased scientists would react. The user study consisted of three steps: a pre-study interview, a deployment period, and a post-study interview. The study lasted for 3 weeks.

Pre-study interview

The purpose of a pre-study interview was to understand the data needs and collection practices of the participants. Pre-study interview questions included:

- When you need data/information, how do you collect/access it?
- Do you share data you collect? How do you share it, and how is it used?
- How often do you participate in field work?
- What are the difficulties you perceive in water monitoring?

Each interview lasted about thirty minutes, followed by an introduction to the Creek Watch application and website. At the end of each interview we collected demographic and occupational information.

Deployment period

We asked participants to use both the Creek Watch application and the websites whenever they felt was convenient over a three week period. During this time they logged 65 data points in the greater San Jose area.

Post-study interview

The purpose of the post-study interviews was to understand both how useful our users felt this data would be and what their reactions were to using the app as a data collector. Post-study interview questions asked about the subjects' use of, opinions about, and recommendations for the Creek Watch application and website. Each interview lasted between thirty minutes to an hour. At the end of the interview, we gave participants a $10 Amazon gift coupon as compensation for their time.

FINDINGS

In our pre-study interviews, participants reinforced the lessons from our initial investigations: traditional scientific methods are expensive and don't scale. The watersheds are too vast to be monitored adequately by their small staff. Several of the participants were in the process of deploying a river monitoring system in Coyote Creek, one of the largest waterways in San Jose. The system consists of nine autonomous units, each costing approximately $8000. The units continuously measure five basic characteristics of the water but must be periodically visited to retrieve data and clean the sensors. With units this expensive, widespread deployment is not an option; most of the creeks will remain unmonitored.

While autonomous units are not the only way to measure creek health, site visits by field agents cannot provide complete coverage of the watershed either. When describing the most important difficulty he faces in his job, one of the field agents stated:

> *"Access is a problem. The big thing is we can only measure in places we can get to, resulting in data gaps."*

This access problem was echoed as the top problem by three out of the four field agents.

As our participants are both collectors and consumers of the data, our study provides insights into both aspects of Creek Watch. We therefore divide the findings from our user study into those relating to the consumption of data and those relating to the collection of data.

Data Consumption

Our participants agreed that Creek Watch provided very useful data while also providing a low barrier to entry for users. They found the trash data of particular interest. Participants saw opportunities to immediately make use of the data for existing programs in tracking watershed health:

> *"We would use this data... That's our big focus right now- trash."* (Project manager)

> *"A great tool to monitor creeks and help us identify problem areas- one of my coworkers is on creek cleanup and trash keeps coming up."* (Project manager)

> *"For our work in particular [enforcement of dumping regulations], I would be interested in the trash information- to see where folks are finding trash along the creeks."* (Field agent)

As an example, several participants commented on the particular usefulness of this data for local trash cleanup events. One of the volunteer coordinators who manages cleanup events identified the value provided by being able to easily identify "trash clusters" in the data points contributed by other users:

> *"When you get a lot of data points you can see where most of the trash is in the creeks. When groups have cleanup events, now we can find these trash areas."*

These findings were particularly interesting because during our initial contextual inquiries flow data appeared to be in greater demand than trash data. This difference in emphasis may be a reflection on the particular responsibilities of our study participants. While the scientists we interviewed during the contextual inquiry discussed longer term plans for the data's use in environmental planning, the city water board workers seemed more concerned with immediate action items. We note that the ability for a citizen science project to yield such short-term wins may increase participation in both contributing and consuming the data.

Participants did also consider flow data to be useful. One participant commented that Creek Watch was "a good way to inventory streams and maybe even keep track of the ephemeral nature of some streams and creeks." The general consensus among our participants was that flow data is useful in the long run for planning, trending and mapping. These results suggest that combining data that potential consumers can use immediately with data designed for longer-term use may increase the likelihood of success for a citizen science project by increasing the potential set of people interested in the data.

All of the participants emphasized their belief that Creek Watch would promote public engagement, increase awareness of watershed health, and provide informal science education for volunteers. One of their goals is to make city residents think more about their water and where it comes from, and twice about littering. Creek Watch provides a way for them to engage with their constituents over watershed management.

While participants were largely pleased with the desktop web interface for accessing data, they did make several suggestions for improvements. These suggestions centered on new ways to filter the contributed data. For example, a number of participants wanted to be able to easily filter the data in the table by city. Others wanted the ability to filter the data presented in the map view as well so that they could use the map view for their work.

The latter suggestion was somewhat unexpected, as in our pre-study interviews most participants agreed that they would prefer to access data in table form. However, we found in our post-study interviews that the map view was more popular for data consumption. Participants described "getting a sense of the area" by browsing photographs, as well as "finding trash" using the map view. The preferred presentation mode may depend on the intended uses, with more immediate uses (such as identifying locations with lots of trash) drawing more heavily on the map while uses that involve longer-term analysis (such as changes in flow) may rely on the table format or on the ability to download and work with the data separately.

Data Collection

All participants commented how simple and easy to use they found the application. As one participant commented:

> *"Very easy, very quick. I pull up at the creek next to the business I am inspecting and use it."*

Participants also uniformly stated that making the application as easy as possible to capture data was critical.

Five out of ten participants had friends/family members try the application out with similar results; other people found the application "simple to use," and "easy." These results suggest that, in general, volunteers without a scientific background will be able to use the application easily.

Furthermore, our study revealed that participants considered using the application fun. One example participant described how they turned using the application into a game:

> *"We played find the creek: pull over at a creek, jump out of the car, find a good vantage point, enter the data."*

Both of our participants with children of school age took their kids out to a creek to use the application and employed it as teaching tool. One participant recalled,

> *"We talked about recording only what you see and not what you think- a nice teaching moment."*

This participant was reacting to an interesting data collection phenomenon:

> *"When we went to a place that I could not see any trash, [my son] said 'some trash' because of what he knew from other times he'd seen in the area."*

We make two observations about this comment. This behavior emphasizes a potential problem with any user-contributed data: errors that occur to user mistakes, biases, etc. Because data consumers are unlikely to use any data that they do not trust, a citizen science application should thus ideally provide a mechanism to allow consumers to easily verify the data. We believe that the inclusion of pictures in the data helps provide this "check". In this case, scientists can see if the picture actually shows any trash.

Several participants requested a comment field to write down what they were seeing. This request is particularly interesting because none of these participants could think of a way that, as data consumers, they would have a use for this data. They simply "wanted to be able to add a little more data." The disparity between their desires as data collectors and as data consumers reinforces the value in studying both aspects of a citizen science application.

Five participants reported using the website to compare the data they had collected with existing data. One reported:

> *"I would occasionally browse data [on the map view]- looking where other people were making observations and checking out their photography."*

Checking data on the map "as a reference" to make sure they were taking data at least as good as their peers was a common theme. We note that this behavior presents an opportunity to seed expected use by ensuring a site has an initial set of "ideal" data points for early adopters to refer to. Previous work in this area has not highlighted this as important, perhaps because most citizen science projects started by HCI researchers (e.g., [23]) focus on widespread and/or rapid adoption by users.

Overall our participants were very pleased with Creek Watch both as data collectors and data consumers. Even after the study formally concluded they continue to use the application. Subsequent conversations revealed that two of the field agent users plan to incorporate the application into their regular data collecting practices, replacing their current pen-and-paper data collection. While we did not intend Creek Watch to primarily be used by experts in their professional data collection, we regard that adoption as validation of the usefulness of the captured data.

CONCLUSIONS AND FUTURE RESEARCH

Our goal in this research was to design a citizen science application that would provide scientists useful data as well as providing a usable interface for untrained volunteers. A key part of that process was the use of HCI methods to investigate the needs of data consumers. We worked closely with state, local, and volunteer environmental groups and employed a variety of contextual inquiry tools to determine what data they wanted and the requirements to make the data usable (e.g., format, reliability, standardization).

Those investigations revealed the following lessons that we believe generalize to other citizen science applications:

- When HCI methods are applied to the data as well as the interface, the resulting system can collect more useful data.
- Providing reliable and standardized data enables organizations beyond initial stakeholders to benefit from the data in unanticipated ways.
- New users make use of sample data to validate their collection practices, suggesting the utility of planting "seed" data
- Combining captured data that organizations can use immediately with data that provides long-term, aggregate value may increase the chance of success for a citizen science application.

Based on an initial study of Creek Watch, we believe that we have succeeded in designing a citizen science application that is both usable and useful. In addition, the collected data is already being used by the City of San Jose, including new uses that we did not originally foresee (e.g., the use of the data for trash clean up site identification and use as a data collection tool by field agents). Other water management organizations within California have expressed interest in using Creek Watch.

As next steps we are interested in exploring long-term usage patterns among data contributors and data consumers. For data contributors, we plan to examine factors such as adoption rates, sustained use, and data quality. For data consumers, we plan to explore how to improve the existing data presentation mechanisms and determine what new visualizations would significantly improve the ability to use the gathered data effectively. More broadly, much work remains in determining how best to design citizen science applications that are widely adopted and able to make an actual impact through their collected data.

ACKNOWLEDGMENTS

The authors would like to gratefully acknowledge the many scientists and volunteers who worked with us from the following organizations: the California Environmental Protection Agency, the California State Water Resources Control Board, the California State Surface Water Ambient Monitoring Program (SWAMP), The City of San Jose Environmental Services Water Resources Deoartment, San Francisco Estuaries Institute, the Southern California Coastal Water Research Project, the Stevens & Permanente Creeks Watershed Council (SPCWC), the Alameda Creek Alliance, and the Water Environment Federation division for World Water Monitoring Day. We would also like to express our particular thanks to Erick Burres from the California Water Control Board SWAMP program, to Carol Boland from the city of San Jose water control board, to Mondy Lariz and Joanne McFarlin from the SPCWC volunteer group, to the user study participants from IBM Research - Almaden, and to our user study participants from the City of San Jose Environmental Services Water Resources Department.

REFERENCES

1. Beyer, H. & Holtzblatt, K. (1988), Contextual Design: Defining Customer-Centered Systems. San Francisco: Morgan Kaufmann. ISBN: 1-55860-411-1.
2. California EPA (2010), Surface Water Ambient Monitoring Program: Bioassessment Standard Operating Procedures. swamp.mpsl.mlml.calstate.edu/ resources-and-downloads/standard-operating-procedures
3. California EPA (2004) Surface Water Ambient Monitoring Program: Rapid Trash Assessment Protocol. http://www.swrcb.ca.gov/rwqcb2/water_issues/program s/stormwater/muni/mrp/WaterBoard%20Trash%20Asse ssment%20Method%20SWAMP_v8.pdf
4. City of Knoxville (2010), Neighborhood Codes Enforcement. www.ci.knoxville.tn.us/services/codes/.
5. Cohn, J. P. (2008), Citizen Science: Can Volunteers Do Real Research? *Bioscience* 58:192–197.
6. Cornell Lab of Ornithology (2010), Mission: Citizen Science.www.birds.cornell.edu/netcommunity/page.asp x?pid=1664. September 2010.
7. Cuff, D., Hansen, M. & Kang. J. (2008), Urban sensing: out of the woods, In *Proc.* Comm. of the ACM 24-33.
8. Environmental Protection Agency 2006 Section 303(d), List Fact Sheet for California. EPA Office of Water, ,oaspub.epa.gov/tmdl/state_rept.control?p_state=CA
9. Environmental Protection Agency (2010), TMDL Program Results Analysis Fact Sheet # EPA841-F-10-002. EPA Office of Water, January 2010. www.epa.gov/waters/ doc/factsheets/303d_impaired_waters_gis.pdf
10. Gonsalves, A., (2010) Android Phones Steal Market Share. InformationWeek www.informationweek.com/ news/showArticle.jhtml?articleID=224201881.
11. Howe, J. (2009), Crowdsourcing: Why the Power of the Crowd Is Driving the Future of Business. *Crown Business*, ISBN-13: 978-0307396211.
12. Irwin, A. (1995), Citizen Science: A Study of People, Expertise and Sustainable Development. *Routledge.*
13. Kim, S., & Paulos, E. (2010), inAir: Sharing Indoor Air Quality Measurements and Visualizations. In *Proc. CHI 2010.* 11861-1870.
14. Lane, N, Miluzzo, E, Lu, H., Peebles, D., Choudhury, T., Campbell, A. (2009), A Survey of Mobile Phone Sensing. Ad Hoc and Sensor Networks. IEEE Comm. Sept 2010.
15. Luther, K., Counts, S., Stecher, K. B., Hoff, A., Johns, P. (2009), Pathfinder: an online collaboration environment for citizen scientists. In *Proc. CHI 2009,* 239-248.
16. Maisonneuve, N., Stevens, M., Neilssen, M, Hanappe, P, Steels, L. (2009), Citizen noise pollution monitoring. In *Proc. International Conference on Digital Government Research 2009,* 96-103.
17. Moore, S., Cover, M., & Senter, A. (2007), Rapid Trash Assessment Method Applied to Waters of the San Francisco Bay Region: Trash Measurement in Streams. *California Environmental Protection Agency*, www.swrcb.ca.gov/rwqcb2/docs/swampthrashreport.pdf
18. National Audubon Society (2010), Christmas Bird Count. birds.audubon.org/history-christmas-bird-count.
19. Open Plains (2010), Open 311: A collaborative effort to create an open standard for 311 services. open311.org.
20. Paulos, E., Honicky, R., & Hooker, B. (2008), Citizen Science: Enabling Participatory Urbanism. *Handbook of Research on Urban Informatics: The Practice and Promise of the Real-Time City. IGI Global 2008.*
21. Paxton, M. & Benford, S. (2009), Experiences of participatory sensing in the wild, In *Proc.* Ubicomp, *2009* 265-274.
22. Shirky, C. (2010), Cognitive Surplus: Creativity and Generosity in a Connected Age. *Penguin Press HC*, June 10, 2010. ISBN-13: 978-1594202537.
23. Song, D. & Goldberg, K.(2007), Networked robotic cameras for collaborative observation of natural environments. *Robotics Research*. Springer 2007.
24. Sukhatme, G. (2009), Air Visibility Monitoring. robotics.usc.edu/~mobilesensing/visibility/MobileAirQu alitySensing.pdf.
25. Weiner, J. F. (2010), Swimmable, Drinkable? California Coastkeeper Alliance, May 12, 2010. www. cacoastkeeper.org/news/fishable-swimmable-drinkable
26. Whitney, L. (2010). Cell phone subscriptions to hit 5 billion globally. *CNN.* reviews.cnet.com/8301-13970_7-10454065-78.html
27. Willet, W., Aoki, P., Kumar, N., Subramanian, S. and Woodruff, A. (2010), Common Sense Community: Scaffolding Mobile Sensing and Analysis for Novice Users. In *Proc. Pervasive 2010*, 301-318.

Designing Eco-Feedback Systems for Everyday Life

Yolande Strengers
Centre for Design, RMIT University
Melbourne, Victoria, 3001, Australia
yolande.strengers@rmit.edu.au

ABSTRACT
Eco-feedback systems currently frame householders as *micro-resource managers,* who weigh up the costs and benefits of their consumption, and make autonomous, rational and efficient decisions. Reporting on findings from a qualitative study of three Australian energy and water eco-feedback programs utilising an in-home display (IHD) system, this paper challenges this view. The research finds that householders consume energy and water to carry out everyday practices, such as showering, laundering and cooling, which are mediated by social, cultural, technical and institutional dynamics. The paper proposes an alternative design paradigm for eco-feedback systems premised on the realities of everyday life and identifies several design directions that emerge from this new starting point.

Author Keywords
Eco-feedback, smart meters, energy, water, sustainable HCI, consumption, demand management

ACM Classification Keywords
H5.m. Information interfaces and presentation (e.g. HCI): Miscellaneous

General Terms
Human Factors

INTRODUCTION
It is unlikely that most of us, on rising from our slumbers each morning, approach every task 'rationally' by consciously weighing up the costs and benefits of a shower, or ensuring we undertake the most efficient load of laundry. In contrast, the activities of everyday life are likely to be mediated by social and cultural understandings about how we ought to look, smell (or not smell) and feel; what we've always done or know how to do; the artifacts, technologies and resource systems which enable what we do; and institutional rules and relationships associated with resource use in the home. However, in-home display (IHD) systems, which provide householders with energy and water consumption feedback, assume that individuals will act as *micro-resource managers* in their homes. By providing householders with data regarding daily, weekly and monthly consumption in both real-time and historical formats, IHDs apply the resource management dictum: 'you can't manage what you can't measure', to the home.

Eco-feedback programs such as those utilising IHDs achieve mixed consumption reductions predominately within the range of 5–15 per cent [12]. However, eco-feedback is likely to appeal only to environmentally motivated people, and conservation benefits may wane over time [8, 12]. It is therefore surprising (and somewhat alarming) that assumptions from resource management continue to dominate the design of eco-feedback systems, particularly given that HCI has a history of designing to support everyday activities in social domains and situated contexts [1, 7, 45], rather than taking existing assumptions for granted.

Of additional concern is that resource management assumptions persist even though researchers have begun challenging them in recent studies [10, 24, 26, 31, 55], including in low-income scenarios where the cost-reflective management of resources might be expected to matter most [15]. Such assumptions are further problematic given that there is *no definitive explanation or theory* of how and why people become environmentally responsible [18]. Therefore, by starting with the 'basic assumption that home dwellers lack information and general awareness concerning household energy consumption' [31]: 244 and by assuming that this information is necessary to encourage conservation, designers of eco-feedback systems may not accurately represent how and why people consume.

Addressing these research gaps is of critical importance for eco-feedback programs given that they are likely to become a ubiquitous part of our lives. Smart meters (which link to an IHD) are being delivered in nearly every developed nation, including most of Europe, the USA, Canada, New Zealand and Australia [13]. Similarly, pervasive eco-feedback programs delivered through IPhone, Google and social networking applications, are designed to elicit informed consumption decisions [16].

Drawing on the results of a qualitative study of energy and water IHD eco-feedback programs in the Australian states of Queensland, New South Wales (NSW) and

Victoria [42], this research critiques the assumptions underpinning these programs and proposes an alternative design paradigm premised on everyday life. The paper begins by outlining the current divide between resource management and everyday life before discussing the methods used to undertake this research. Findings are divided into six sections discussing how aspects of eco-feedback are interpreted and incorporated into the energy and water-consuming practices of the home. The paper proposes several design pathways which emerge from the findings and concludes by calling for HCI designers to do what they do best: focus on everyday interactions and design eco-feedback systems to support them.

THE DIVIDE BETWEEN RESOURCE MANAGEMENT AND EVERYDAY LIFE

The content and design of eco-feedback systems draws predominantly on a resource (demand) management paradigm originating from the disciplines of economics and psychology. Demand management involves the use of financial incentives, market mechanisms, education, information feedback, efficiency measures, or other programs to modify the demand for natural resources [54]. It has emerged in part through a realization that it is unsustainable, not possible, and/or financial unfeasible to provide people with a continuing and unlimited supply of resources. In recent years, climate change, drought and other environmental issues have led to the emergence of many demand management strategies, such as eco-feedback.

Such strategies are premised on the theory of rational choice, which emerges from the view (familiar to HCI researchers) that human action is determined by purposive plans [46]. The theory of rational choice assume that individuals buy, consume or use resources in a manner that provides them with the most personal gain at the least personal cost. These consumer preferences are taken for granted without further consideration of their origins or antecedents. Calculations of utility, price and time are seen to dominate the consumption decisions of individuals [28]. Demand and supply are firmly split—the former focusing on people, and the later focusing on large technical systems.

In contrast, studies of everyday life indicate that demand for resources is highly variable, socially and culturally situated, shaped by sociotechnical systems, and the product of constantly shifting and changing expectations and practices [39, 42, 45]. Changes to everyday household practices, such as laundering, bathing, heating and cooling, are well documented in ethnographic studies. For example, from the 'dry' bodily cleaning practices of 17th century France [51] to the weekly bath of the 19th and early 20th centuries [14] and, more recently, the common daily shower [23], bathing practices have gone through periods of change and flux that do not correspond with understandings of rational action.

Similarly, studies of everyday life indicate that supply and demand are connected rather than split [40, 41, 49]. For example, when we flick a switch or turn on a tap, we are indirectly encouraged to forget about how the service is being provided to us, or what impact it might have. We are faced with 'saver-unfriendly obstacles' such as the shower, which have been designed for consumption rather than conservation [40]: 458. In treating householders as somehow separate from this socio-technical context, we fail to recognise that householders' consumption is shaped by infrastructures, technologies and institutions.

Interestingly, IHDs and other eco-feedback systems are physically located at the nexus between resource management and everyday life—at least metaphorically bridging the divide between these two realms. They have the ability to extend into the home, as well as back out again, thereby potentially facilitating new relationships between the providers and users of resources. Although IHD feedback is clearly premised on principles of rational choice (e.g. providing householders with consumption data so that they can make informed and cost-effective decisions about their consumption) it can also (quite literally) illuminate the normally invisible flows of energy and water in the home, and has the potential to engage with social and cultural dynamics. Therefore, eco-feedback systems may provide new avenues for altering the course of everyday life.

METHODS

This paper draws on qualitative research conducted with 26 Australian households from three research groups (RGs): South East Water's (SEW) EcoPioneers pilot program in Victoria (9 households); the Currumbin EcoVillage housing development in Queensland NSW (5 households); and EnergyAustralia's Dynamic Peak Pricing (DPP) trial in NSW (12 households). Throughout this paper, households are anonymously identified by their RG (EcoPioneer, EcoVillage or DPP respectively) and by number (1-28).

Methods centred on a group household interview, which where possible included children and all other household members. Interviews were conducted at the household's residence along with a household tour, during which photographs of technologies and evidence of practices were recorded to reduce self-reported action bias common with qualitative research [37]. Household visits took between one to two hours. The entire visit was voice-record and later transcribed and coded using the qualitative analysis software package NVivo.

Households were recruited using a range of methods, such as through emails sent by the program deliverers, letters sent to participants by the researcher, and 'snowballing' through contact with participating households. A broad range of household types self-selected for this study including single-person households, couples of varying ages, and families with teenage or adult children.

Data were analysed using a social practice theory framework [33, 34, 52], which viewed householders as participants in practices, rather than consumers of aggregate resources. Participants were asked if and how the IHD feedback had changed their day-to-day practices of bathing, laundering, toilet flushing, house cleaning, heating and cooling, which constitute the majority of direct energy and water consumption in Australian homes [2, 25] and OECD [30] nations.

The three RGs utilised different IHDs which had been in use by households for between one month and two years. Two of the RGs (EcoPioneer and DPP) utilised a Landys & Gyr ecoMeter IHD, which provided near instantaneous, weekly averaged and historical household consumption data for electricity (and gas and water in the EcoPioneer RG), and could be plugged into any electricity socket in the home [36; see Figure 1]. It also displayed utility tariff rates; daily, weekly and monthly consumption costs; and greenhouse gas emissions [36, 53]. Data were provided in tables and graphs. More detailed data were provided to participants through a personal website portal.

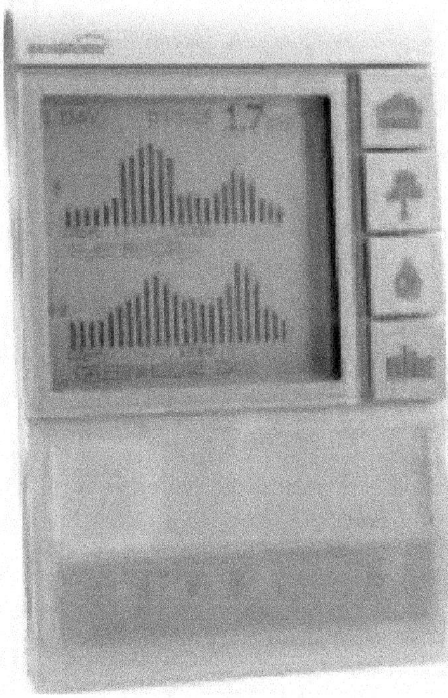

Figure 1. ecoMeter IHD displaying green traffic lights
Source: www.ecoMeter.com.au/ (an updated version of the ecoMeter is available from Landys & Gyr)

The ecoMeter also included a light-emitting diode (LED) 'traffic light' display for electricity consumption see Figure 1). A green light indicated lowest demand (for the EcoPioneer RG) or an off peak rate (for the DPP RG), orange indicated medium demand or a shoulder rate, and red indicated high demand or a DPP 'event' where the price rose between 20-40 times the off-peak rate for a four hour period.

Unlike the EcoPioneer and DPP RG participants, who volunteered to be part of a free trial, residents of the EcoVillage were contractually obligated to purchase and install an EcoVision IHD, which is described by its designers as a 'home resource management system' [17; see Figure 2]. This device provided additional feedback on solar power and energy production, rainwater usage, recycled water usage, gas usage, water level in potable water tanks, room temperature in two rooms, outdoor weather conditions, and hot water temperature.

A potential limitation of this research was the high level of reported participant environmental motivation, particularly in the EcoPioneer and EcoVillage RGs. However, as the findings below indicate, householders' environmental motivation served to highlight how IHD feedback can be limited even when 'preaching to the converted'.

FINDINGS

Converting data into meaningful information

Householders expressed difficulty in understanding data provided through their IHD, a finding reported in other eco-feedback studies [11, 24, 32]. Some householders

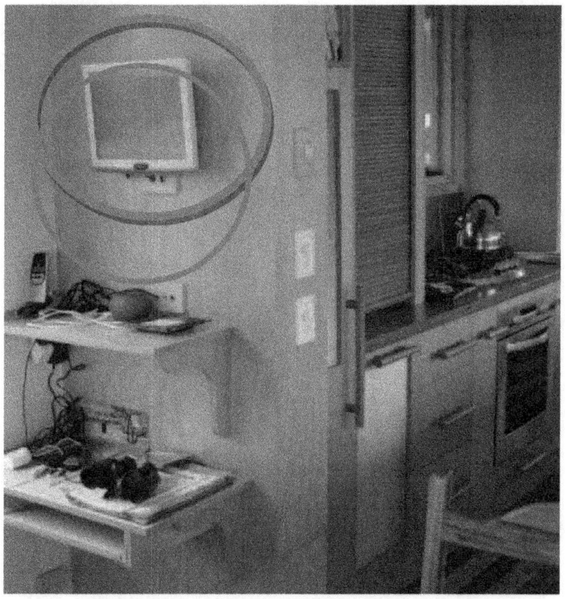

Figure 2. EcoVision IHD inside an EcoVillage household
Source: EcoVillage, 10, 25 April 2008

were unable to understand the resource language used:

> On the ecoMeter it says 2.7 tonnes per day. What is a tonne? ... What is two tonnes? There's no description (EcoPioneer, 6).

> We're pretty intelligent, but it's still googalldygook (DPP, 15).

> It says you've used so many kilowattevers (DPP, 17).

Householders could more easily translate the resource management unit of 'litres' into a meaningful unit, through analogies with buckets and bottles:

> When I see a photo of 140 litres in buckets and I think every person uses that, I think that's ridiculous. When I see 80, I think, how can I justify that? Forty—that's four big buckets of water every day! (EcoVillage, 10).

However, when householders were able to understnad their feedback, they often misinterpreted of misapplied the data. For example, because appliances such as an electric kettle, toaster, hair dryer, or oven made the IHD 'scream red' (EcoPioneer, 2; e.g. display a red light or spike in consumption), householders assumed that these appliances consumed the most electricity in the home:

> The main thing was that jug. I can't believe how much power it pulled! … It was more than the air-conditioning! (DPP, 21)

This was not necessarily true, because householders often did not use these appliances for extended periods of time. Consequently, other more ubiquitous appliances, such as the fridge, freezer or hot water service, which are in use most of time but may not cause a sharp spike in consumption, were often overlooked.

Some householders were also unclear how they could use the eco-feedback to answer questions about specific practices or appliances:

> How do you do a formula? How do you work out the answer to that question? I understand that I could read what the gas reading is, but that doesn't answer my question about which is better for the planet... having the whole house going [on gas], or just having that nasty little [electric] heater thingy that's not that warm (EcoPioneer, 1).

In other cases, householders were able to make this link:

> I have a look every morning after I make it out of the shower to see how much we use in the shower and that's how I know it's 30 litres for the two of us; 180 for the washing machine (EcoPioneer, 8).

However, as discussed below, this did not necessarily mean that householders made changes in response to this new information.

The non-negotiability of everyday practices

There was a sense of irrelevance associated with IHD feedback because it alerted householders to practices considered non-discretionary:

> I don't see the point [of the IHD] because we're now aware of which appliances create red lights and *they're all things that you need to use anyway* so …it's not like you're going to say, 'I'm wasting, so let's do something about it' (EcoPioneer, 7, emphasis added).

> It might be nice to know that the toaster is this and the kettle is this, but I don't know what I'm supposed to do about it—have cold tea? (EcoPioneer, 8)

Thus, even when householders were able to link their IHD feedback to specific practices, many dismissed this information.

Some householders believed they were already doing everything they could to reduce their impact. In these cases, the IHD feedback was deemed superfluous:

> I don't think of it at all. … We just ignore it. ... We know how we're living. As I said we have plenty of water, we're heating it as cheap as we possibly can, we've paid initial money to buy solar panels, the house is nice and warm and cosy, and we don't need *that* [pointing to IHD] to tell us how wonderful our lives are, and that we're not actually using too much water [or] electricity (EcoVillage, 13).

Due to the perceived non-negotiability of household practices and/or the seeming irrelevance of the IHD feedback, many householders discussed how they no longer used their IHDs regularly, if at all: 'The novelty wears off after a while' (EcoPioneer, 5). Similar findings are reported by Pierce et al. [31]: 247 in their study of eco-feedback systems, who conclude that the seemingly fixed nature of some practices 'point unambiguously to the fact that awareness does not imply conservation action'. Taking this argument further, this research suggests that disinterest occurs due to the *disconnection* between resource consumption data and the perceived non-negotiability of everyday practices.

Saving visible consumption, overlooking ingrained practices

Despite many practices being deemed non-negotiable by householders, there was a concerted effort to avoid waste and 'save' energy and water where possible, as reported in other studies of eco-feedback systems [24, 26, 32, 55] and thus accounting for the 5-15 per cent savings reported in most studies [12, 13]. To achieve this reduction, householders attempted to make their practices more efficient by, for example, switching from hot to cold water in the laundry:

> I used to wash in hot water to kill germs and bacteria, which is silly because if you put it in the sun it does it all for you really. … I like clean clothes when I wash them. And I suppose growing up in the UK it's just instilled in me,

> *but I've changed that now since seeing the spikes* (EcoVillage, 12, emphasis added).

In particular, householders were concerned with turning the lights off in response to IHD feedback: 'When it's red you have to go around and turn off all the lights, then it goes green and you think, "phew!"' (EcoPioneer, 9).

Householders talked about lighting a great deal during the interviews, *even though they were never directly asked about it.* However, lighting is not the largest consumer of electricity in Australian households [2], and participants could have been aware of this by correctly interpreting their IHD feedback. Gram-Hanssen [20] found a similar focus on lighting in her ethnographic study of routines, which she attributes to lighting's heightened visibility in the home, as well as its historical association with electricity usage. Several householders supported this claim: 'I was brought up in an era where leaving a light on was such a no-no that I just turn them off. I'm a shocker for that' (EcoPioneer, 8).

Householders' keen interest in lighting can also be attributed to the significant attention lighting receives in energy-saving campaigns, where it is considered a relatively easy and inexpensive practice to change [3, 48]. Consequently, lighting has become synonymous with new understandings of 'wasteful' consumption, leading householders to use this practice as a benchmark for their environmental commitment: 'Our house uses next to nothing compared to other houses. They're always leaving lights on' (EcoPioneer, 1).

IHD feedback is framed within this context, which affects householders' ability to make rational decisions. Rather than identifying the most resource-intensive practices in the home and changing them, householders interpret their IHD feedback within a normative framework about what it means to be green or sustainable, undertaking actions such as turning off appliances when not in use, buying more efficient appliances, shortening showers, washing full loads of laundry, and changing light bulbs. Shove [38]: 271 warns against this focus on visible and efficient consumption, arguing that when 'energy is in the spotlight, the services it provides are in the shadow'. In the case of IHD feedback, 'wasteful' energy and water consumption (such as leaving the lights on) is brought to the fore, while other consumption activities (like eating or cooking) silently slip into the background.

The problem with this approach is not that it does not achieve energy and water efficiencies (it clearly does), but rather that it overlooks the taken for granted practices householders engage in, and that these may change over time [39]. For example, turning off appliances at the wall does not change the practices these appliances are implicated in (although it is arguably a new practice in its own right [21]), just as installing a water-efficient showerhead is unlikely to transform the practice of showering. Therefore, eco-feedback does little to discourage the emergence of new and more resource-intensive expectations. It is unlikely, for example, to detract from an aspiration to purchase a Plasma TV or home theatre system, which may detract from the efficiency gains achieved by turning off standby power from entertainment appliances.

Acceptable and unacceptable consumption limits

In both the EcoPioneer and DPP RGs the effect of the traffic lights was the same: it contained a normative benchmark for acceptable and unacceptable electricity consumption, which in some cases applied to specific practices: 'You can see what colour it is so you can tell whether you're doing right or wrong' (EcoPioneer, 8). Traffic light feedback was therefore an important visualisation tool encouraging householders to reduce, and in some cases, increase their consumption. Thus this type of feedback has a similar role to other ambient devices, such as those developed by the Static! project, including the Power-Aware cord which illuminates electricity consumption flows into appliances [6, 22].

Several householders described traffic light feedback as a consumption limit, similar to speed limits on the road:

> It's like the speedo on a car. Years ago, people would drive at whatever speed they wanted to. But now we understand that there's a limit. Unfortunately there are repercussions in terms of driving over the speed limit. I suppose in terms of power, in terms of the cost, it should be the same. It might not come as a fine, but it will come as a cost to you (EcoPioneer, 1).

In the EcoPioneer households, this 'cost' was a moral one, encouraging householders to feel either 'good' or 'bad' about their current consumption. In DPP households, going over the 'limit' during a DPP event had both moral and financial repercussions [43]. However, participants from both RGs responded strongly to the presence of a red light, even though DPP households were being charged significantly more money for their electricity consumption during a red period, whereas EcoPioneer households were not.

The presence of a yellow or red light was the most effective form of IHD feedback, encouraging householders to reduce most of their electricity consumption, albeit for a short time—the precise outcome desired by deliverers of such schemes. Some householders described how a red light disrupted and temporally suspended *all* household consumption by creating a feeling of urgency or danger:

> If it's four red, [my daughter] will have a panic attack! … We call that redlining. … if we see the thing redlining or on three yellows we see what we can do straight away to bring it back down to green (EcoPioneer, 1).

In addition, the effect of an orange or red traffic light was only applied during specific periods of time, potentially endorsing practices undertaken at other times of the day (creating load shifting). Although load shifting is desired by electricity companies to reduce peak demand [43], it does not necessarily encourage conservation.

The effect of a traffic light could also be reversed, with the a green or orange light being seen as *approval* for existing activities. One householder described how traffic light feedback legitimised her existing practice of laundry drying: 'I was always worried about using the dryer so much, but I figure it doesn't make it scream red so it's OK' (EcoPioneer, 2). Pierce et al. [31] express similar concerns with the unintended effects of eco-feedback in their review of these systems.

Divergent interest in eco-feedback

Eco-feedback is premised on the assumption that the people interested in it are able to instigate change. The findings from this and Hargreaves et al.'s [24] study challenge this assumption, finding that consumption takes place through manipulation and debate regarding particular practices within the household. Furthermore, the householders interested in feedback may not dominate household consumption. For example, while men and children in this study were reportedly more interested in monitoring the day-to-day consumption of the household, women and teenagers were often disinterested in the feedback: 'I don't know how to use it. It's got nothing to do with me' (EcoPioneer, 7, woman)

While this research did not aim (nor does it claim) to accurately represent age or gender, other studies indicate women control and undertake the majority of cleaning activities in households, and are often more sensitive to understandings of presentability, body odour, hygiene and cosiness [19, 24, 29, 35]. For example, a mother and her children debated hair drying during an interview:

> SON: No-one uses the hair dryer anymore.
>
> DAUGHTER: Mum forces me to. … It's because she doesn't like the way it looks if I don't blow dry it.
>
> MOTHER: [Laughter] It takes about two seconds, I'm not going to stop because of that [referring to IHD] (EcoPioneer, 1).

Such issues raise an important methodological concern regarding evaluations of eco-feedback, which predominately employ survey methods [8, 53] that may inadvertently target those householders most interested in the feedback, rather than those who dominate the everyday practices of the household. The group interview method employed in this research went partway to alleviating this concern, highlighting a potential discrepancy between householders interested in analysing and managing the consumption of their household, and those who manage and/or dominate the practices within it. Had the research only focused on those householders interested in the IHD, the householders that 'don't know anything at all' (DPP, 20, woman) about this device would have been excluded, even though they were heavily involved in the day-to-day running of the household, and therefore the consumption taking place within it.

Household resource management dynamics

There was some evidence to suggest that householders act as micro-resource managers by weighing up the costs and benefits of their consumption as eco-feedback assumes:

> Sometimes I'll just glance past and have a look at what sort of rate we're on at a certain time and so forth and just to calculate how much, particularly in summer when the air-conditioning's on, how much we've used a quarter, … because I expect it to be about 100, 120, so I often look and think, we're at $80 this month so we're doing really well (DPP, 23).

In this sense, the IHD was used as a tracking device to keep households at or below a designated benchmark. It was also used to police and control 'excessive' householders: 'You could tell, like in winter, when the kids have too many heaters on—"turn the heater off!"' (RG4, 63). Householders used their IHD to regulate particular appliances and household members, predominantly young children and teenagers. In this sense, the IHD can be more accurately described as a *household* management tool.

A notable exception was found in several EcoVillage households, where this device *was* used as a resource management tool to assess whether their demand for energy and water was matching their supply: 'I quite often look at it five or six times a day to see how we're going or what we've got in the tank' (EcoVillage, 10)

In these cases, householders' role can be more accurately described as *co-managers* of supply and demand [9, 44]. Evidence of this role was rarely found in EcoPioneer or DPP households, who were dependent on resources managed by an external authority. A similar finding is reported by Woodruff et al. [55]: 316 in their study of households living in 'sustainable' homes, where participants were engaged in 'active home management' and interested in obtaining data to understand and improve the performance of their homes.

However, even within the EcoVillage RG, there was not universal acceptance of the co-management role, at least not in the sense that it required data monitoring:

> That's how I drive a car but it's not how I'd live at home. I look at monitors all day, I'm not going to come home and look at this one as well (EcoVillage, 14).

Resource management assumption	Findings from everyday life
Householders understand and respond to resource management units such as kilowatts, greenhouse gas emissions and litres.	• Householders often cannot understand resource management units. They may draw on visual analogies (such as buckets of water). • Householders are likely to change practices considered discretionary or wasteful and overlook those considered non-negotiable or taken-for-granted.
Householders will correctly interpret and analyse eco-feedback.	• Householders often misinterpret eco-feedback and/or only apply it to practices that display 'spikes' for short periods of time (like the kettle and toaster).
Traffic light feedback will 'slow down' high-consumption practices.	• Traffic light feedback can 'slow down' *and* 'speed up' consumption, potentially endorsing some practices.
Householders interested in eco-feedback have the ability to change the household's consumption.	• Householders interested in eco-feedback may not control the consumption practices in the home. This may be related to gender (with males and children more interested in data and women dominating household practices).
The efficiency gains achieved through eco-feedback will be sustained over time.	• Eco-feedback is unlikely to challenge changing expectations and aspirations in households (e.g. for central heating and cooling or plasma TVs). • Eco-feedback may have a diminishing return as new expectations emerge.
Householders behave like micro-resource managers when provided with the 'right' information.	• Householders may act as co-managers of resource supply and demand if they have their own resources to manage. • Eco-feedback can be used as a household management tool to police high consumers or track bills.

Table 2. Resource management assumptions contrasted with findings from everyday life

These findings challenge the notion of the micro-resource manager. However, they suggest that householders do engage in the co-management of their supply and demand *if they have their own resources to manage*. Similarly, householders engage in the household management of resources, but this involves dynamics that extend beyond rational decision-making processes.

DESIGN IMPLICATIONS

An alternative paradigmatic starting point

While eco-feedback is successful in reducing or shifting consumption, there are potential problems with this strategy. These can be understood as a product of the resource management paradigm dominating the design of eco-feedback programs. When contrasted with an understanding of everyday life—that is, the way people consume energy and water in order to carry out day-to-day practices—this paradigm is exposed as inadequate. Table 2 summarises the assumptions underpinning the IHD feedback programs discussed in this paper and contrasts these with household findings.

Table 2 highlights the need to rethink the role and design of eco-feedback, rather than simply 'improving' feedback within the existing paradigm. Worryingly, householders may react negatively if more 'bells and whistles' are added to IHDs to enhance and sustain consumption reductions: 'If it started making noises I would smash it with a hammer. … and I'm serious about that, it'd be out the door' (EcoVillage, 13). The following subsections provide brief examples of several design directions that emerge from this alternative starting point.

Redefining the role of eco-feedback

In re-thinking the role of eco-feedback, HCI designers can take inspiration from broader definitions of the term. One alternative form of feedback might involve 'scripting' [4] sustainable interactions into appliances and artifacts, such as making cold water wash the default setting on a washing machine. Similarly, designers of energy and water systems could attempt to reverse the 'fantasy of endless supply' [40]: 456 embedded into technologies such as the shower, by focusing on making energy and water visible. Inspiration can be taken from the Static! project [6] for less data-oriented forms of feedback.

Non-negotiable practices and changing expectations

HCI designers should be wary of immediate efficiency benefits that overlook householders' changing expectations and aspirations—a topic discussed in depth by Shove [39]. Programs and devices that specifically target non-negotiable practices or changing expectations could be developed. For example, Intille [27] reports on a study recommending when to open and close a window and turn on/off an air-conditioning unit in order to save energy associated with household comfort. This study provided practical knowledge to householders so that they could 'learn how to control the environment on their own' [27]: 76. Thus, eco-feedback might involve practical recommendations that lead to new practices which challenge taken-for-granted notions of normality.

Co-managing resources and consumption

This and other studies have found that householders with their own energy or water supply systems are more likely to co-manage their resources and consumption [5, 9, 44].

Eco-feedback can potentially assist in this regard [44, 55]. Similarly, there may be opportunities for eco-feedback to facilitate a co-management relationship between householders connected to mainstream energy and water supply systems by communicating water supply levels, progress towards electricity or greenhouse gas targets, and other resource management aims using language that is meaningful to householders. For example, IHDs could report on progress towards government targets, such as the Victorian Governments' highly successful '155' water campaign in Australia [50], which encourages households to consume less than 155 litres per person per day.

However, in pursuing these opportunities, HCI designers would do well to remember that the household management of resources involves complex dynamics and social expectations both within and beyond the household, rather than the purely rational decision-making processes of the largely fictitious micro-resource manager.

Designing for everyday life

Suchmann et al. [47]: 392 contend that 'to understand technologies ethnographically, it is required that we locate artifacts within the sites and the relations of their everyday use'. Their advice is particularly warranted in regards to eco-feedback systems, where research is required to identify *what people do in their homes*, *how people use energy and water* and *why*, within specific and locally contingent contexts and communities. Research should include those householders dominating consumption in the home, rather than those currently most interested in eco-feedback.

HCI designers can learn from the vast amount of social, cultural and anthropological research discussing how practices change in everyday life [for examples see 19, 20, 32, 39]. These studies report that practices change in relation to past experiences (e.g. growing up in a resource-constrained situation); interactions with family members and peers; and through new technologies entering and exiting the home. Such research provides new directions for eco-feedback systems, including its potential role as a facilitation tool for sharing practical knowledge about alternative ways to conduct practices (such as *how* to take a short shower, shower less or cool a home without air-conditioning), or for encouraging debate within peer networks about what is normal and necessary.

Most importantly, studies of everyday life point to the *non-environmental* focus of consumption practices [39]. This suggests that in order to alter consumption practices; it might not be useful to focus on consumption or the environment at all. For example, if the goal is to reduce water and energy usage in the laundry, one would first need to understand why people wash laundry frequently (e.g. for reasons of hygiene, brightness, freshness or presentability) [29, 39]. The aim would then be to demonstrate how these desired outcomes can be achieved with fewer resources (or to attempt the more challenging task of questioning these expectations).

CONCLUSION

The design of eco-feedback is currently framed within a paradigm of resource management, where principles of efficient and rational decision-making are applied at the household level. However, as this and other studies demonstrate [24, 32], these assumptions obscure other explanations and dynamics of household consumption.

This should not lead us to conclude that eco-feedback is ineffective—it can and does achieve significant resource reductions (and every bit surely counts). However, this approach potentially masks the practices that energy and water consumption is implicated in, legitimises those that don't 'scream red', and overlooks the rise of new resource-consuming expectations and desires—leading to diminishing returns over time as new practices take hold. Without refocusing attention on everyday life, IHDs are likely to remain limited in their scope and potential audience, appealing only to those householders interested in saving energy and water, and achieving a diminishing return over time as new non-negotiable 'needs' emerge.

In taking these findings forward, this paper has suggested that designers of eco-feedback systems must begin by studying everyday interactions and designing devices to support them—a job in which the HCI community is well-versed [45]. Framing the problem (and solution) through a paradigm of everyday life will necessitate paying closer attention to the dynamics within and between households, the practices consumption is implicated in, and shifting expectations of normality.

ACKNOWLEDGEMENTS

This research was conducted within the Australasian CRC for Interaction Design, established and supported under the Australian Government's Cooperative Research Centres Programme. The research was also supported by the Australian Housing and Urban Research Institute (AHURI). The author is grateful to the participants of this study and the anonymous reviewers of this paper.

REFERENCES

1. Abowd, G. D., Mynatt, E. D. and Rodden, T. (2002). The human experience [of ubiquitous computing]. *Pervasive Computing, IEEE*, 1(1), 48-57.
2. ABS. (2008). *Environmental Issues: Energy Use and Conservation (4602.0.55.001)*. Australian Bureau of Statistics, Canberra, Australia. [http://www.abs.gov.au].
3. ACF. (2006). *The GreenHome guide: Victorian edition*. Australian Conservation Foundation (ACF), Melbourne, VIC.
4. Akrich, M. (1992). The de-scription of technical objects. In W. E. Bijker and J. Law. *Shaping*

Technology/ Building Society. MIT Press, Cambridge, Mass. [US].

5. ATA. (2007). *The Solar Experience: PV System Owners' Survey*. Alternative Technology Association, Melbourne, VIC.
6. Backlund, S., Gyllenswärd, M., Gustafsson, A., Hjelm, S. I., Mazé, R. and Redström, J. (2006). STATIC! The aesthetics of energy in everyday things. *Proc. DRS Wonderground*.
7. Bell, G., Blythe, M., Gaver, B., Sengers, P. and Wright, P. (2003). Designing culturally situated technologies for the home. *Proc. CHI 2003*, ACM, 1062-1063.
8. Challis, C. (2004). *A Literature Review of Secondary and Smart Metering Knowledge in Managed Housing*. The Energy Savings Trust, UK.
9. Chappells, H. and Shove, E. (2004). Infrastructures, crises and the orchestration of demand. In D. Southerton, B. Van Vliet and H. Chappells. *Sustainable Consumption: the Implications of Changing Infrastructures of Provision*. Edward Elgar, Cheltenham, UK, 130-143.
10. Chetty, M., Bernheim-Brush, A. J., Meyers, B. R. and Johns, P. (2009). It's not easy being green: understanding home computer power management. *Proc. CHI 2009*, ACM, 1033-1042.
11. Chetty, M., Tran, D. and Grinter, R. E. (2008). Getting to green: understanding resource consumption in the home. *Proc. UbiComp'08*.
12. Darby, S. (2006). *The effectiveness of feedback on energy consumption: A review for DEFRA of the literature on metering, billing and direct displays*. Environmental Change Institute, University of Oxford, Oxford [UK].
13. Darby, S. (2010). Smart metering: what potential for householder engagement? *Building Research & Information*, 38(5), 442 - 457.
14. Davidson, G. (2008). Down the gurgler: historical influences on Australian domestic water consumption. In P. Troy. *Troubled Waters: Confronting the Water Crisis in Australia's Cities*. ANU E Press, Canberra, Australia, 37-65.
15. Dillahunt, T., Mankoff, J., Paulos, E. and Fussell, S. (2009). It's not all about "Green": energy use in low-income communities. *Proc. Proceedings of the 11th international conference on Ubiquitous computing*, ACM, 255-264.
16. DiSalvo, C., Sengers, P. and Hrönn, B. (2010). Mapping the landscape of sustainable HCI. *Proc. CHI 2010*, ACM, 1975-1984.
17. EcoVision. (2007). *EcoVision Solutions Pty Ltd*. EcoVision Solutions Pty Ltd, Elanora, QLD. [http://www.ecovisionsolutions.com.au/].
18. Froehlich, J., Findlater, L. and Landay, J. (2010). The design of eco-feedback technology. *Proc. CHI 2010*, ACM, 1999-20008.
19. Gram-Hanssen, K. (2007). Teenage consumption of cleanliness: how to make it sustainable? *Sustainability: Science, Practice & Policy*, 3(2), 1-9.
20. Gram-Hanssen, K. (2008). Consuming technologies — developing routines. *Journal of Cleaner Production*, 16(1181-1189.
21. Gram-Hanssen, K. (2009). Standby consumption in households analyzed with a practice theory approach. *Research and Analysis*, 14(1), 150-165.
22. Gustafsson, A. and Gyllenswärd, M. (2005). The Power-Aware Cord: energy awareness through ambient information display. *Proc. CHI 2005*, ACM, 1423-1426.
23. Hand, M., Southerton, D. and Shove, E. (2003). *Explaining daily showering: a discussion of policy and practice*. Economic & Social Research Council, UK. [http://www.sustainabletechnologies.ac.uk/].
24. Hargreaves, T., Nye, M. and Burgess, J. (2010). Making energy visible: a qualitative field study of how householders interact with feedback from smart energy monitors. *Energy Policy*, 38(6111-6119.
25. Harper, P. (2006). *Australia's Environment Issues and Trends 2006*. Australian Bureau of Statistics, Canberra, Australia.
26. Hirsch, T. and Anderson, K. (2010). Cross currents: water scarcity and sustainable CHI. *Proc. CHI 2010*, ACM, 2843-2852.
27. Intille, S. S. (2002). Designing a home of the future. *Pervasive Computing*, 1(2), 76-82.
28. Jackson, T. (2005). *Motivating Sustainable Consumption: a Review of Evidence on Consumer Behaviour and Behavioural Change*. Centre for Environmental Strategy, University of Surrey, a report to the Sustainable Development Research Network, Surrey, UK.
29. Kaufmann, C. (1998). *Dirty Linen: Couples and their Laundry*. Middlesex University Press, London, UK.
30. OECD. (2002). *Towards Sustainable Household Consumption? Trends and Policies in OECD Countries*. Organisation of Economic Co-operation and Development (OECD), France.
31. Pierce, J., Fan, C., Lomas, D., Marcu, G. and Paulos, E. (2010). Some considerations of the (in)effectiveness of residential energy feedback systems. *Proc. DIS 2010*, ACM, 244-247.

32. Pierce, J., Schiano, D. J. and Paulos, E. (2010). Home, habits, and energy: examining domestic interactions and energy consumption. *Proc. CHI 2010*, ACM, 1985-1994.
33. Reckwitz, A. (2002). Toward a theory of social practices: a development in culturalist theorizing. *Journal of Social Theory*, 5(2), 243-263.
34. Schatzki, T. R. (2002). *The Site of the Social: a Philosophical Account of the Constitution of Social Life and Change*. The Pennsylvania State University Press, Pennsylvania, USA.
35. Schwartz Cowan, R. (1989). *More Work for Mother: the Ironies of Household Technology from the Open Hearth to the Microwave*. Free Association Books, London, UK.
36. SEW. (2007). *Reference Guide: Eco-Pioneer Trial*. South East Water (SEW), Melbourne, VIC.
37. Shipworth, M. (2000). *Motivating Home Energy Action: a Handbook of What Works*. Australian Greenhouse Office, Canberra, Australia.
38. Shove, E. (1997). Revealing the invisible: sociology, energy and the environment. In M. Redclift and G. Woodgate. *The International Handbook of Environmental Sociology*. Edward Elgar Publishing, Cheltenham, UK.
39. Shove, E. (2003). *Comfort, Cleanliness and Convenience: the Social Organisation of Normality*. Berg Publishers, Oxford, UK.
40. Sofoulis, Z. (2005). Big water, everyday water: a sociotechnical perspective. *Continuum: Journal of Media & Cultural Studies*, 19(4), 445-463.
41. Southerton, D., Chappells, H. and Van Vliet, B. (2004). *Sustainable Consumption: the Implications of Changing Infrastructures of Provision*. Edward Elgar, Cheltenham, UK.
42. Strengers, Y. (2008). Smart metering demand management programs: challenging the comfort and cleanliness habitus of households. *Proc. OZCHI 2008*, ACM, 9-16.
43. Strengers, Y. (2010). Air-conditioning Australian households: a trial of Dynamic Peak Pricing. *Energy Policy*, 38(11), 7312-7322.
44. Strengers, Y. (in press). Beyond demand management: co-managing energy and water consumption in Australian households. *Policy Studies*.
45. Suchman, L. (1987). *Plans and situated actions. The problem of human-machine communication.* Cambridge University Press, Cambridge, UK.
46. Suchman, L. (2007). *Human-machine reconfigurations: plans and situated actions.* Cambridge University Press, Cambridge, UK.
47. Suchman, L., Blomberg, J., Orr, J. E. and Trigg, R. (1999). Reconstructing technologies as social practice *American Behavioral Scientist*, 43(3), 392-408.
48. SV. (2009). *You have the power. Save energy.* Sustainability Victoria, Melbourne, Australia. [http://www.saveenergy.vic.gov.au/].
49. Van Vliet, B., Chappells, H. and Shove, E. (2005). *Infrastructures of Consumption: Environmental Innovation in the Utilities Industries*. Earthscan, London [UK].
50. VictGov. (2009). *Save Water Target 155*. Victorian Government, Melbourne, Australia. [http://www.target155.vic.gov.au/home].
51. Vigarello, G. (1988). *Concepts of Cleanliness: Changing Attitudes in France since the Middle Ages*. Cambridge University Press, Cambridge, UK.
52. Warde, A. (2005). Consumption and theories of practice. *Journal of Consumer Culture*, 5(2), 131-153.
53. Wetherall, B. (2008). *Draft Report of the EcoPioneer Pilot Program*. South East Water, Melbourne, Australia.
54. Wilhite, H., Shove, E., Lutzenhiser, L. and Kempton, W. (2000). The legacy of twenty years of energy demand management: we know more about individual behaviour but next to nothing about demand. In E. Jochem, J. Sathaya and D. Bouille. *Society, Behaviour and Climate Change Mitigation*. Kluwer Academic Publishers, [The Netherlands], 109-126.
55. Woodruff, A., Hasbrouck, J. and Augustin, S. (2008). A bright green perspective on sustainable choices. *Proc. CHI 2008*, ACM, 313-322.

BeeParking: Feedback Interfaces for Collective Behavior Change

Silvia Gabrielli, Alessandra Sabatino, Jesus Munoz, Michele Marchesoni, Oscar Mayora
Ubiquitous Interaction Group, CREATE-NET
Via Alla Cascata 56/D – 38123 Trento - Italy
name.surname@create-net.org

ABSTRACT

Recent years have seen a growing interest for the study of feedback interfaces to support behavior change in different research areas, from personal healthcare and wellbeing, to energy saving and proenvironmental sustainability. While HCI design has been primarily inspired by behavior change models that best fit individual change, less attention has been deserved to test their validity in the context of collective behavior change, where interdependencies between people's choices and behaviors matter, as in the shared use of limited resources or public goods. We discuss some relevant directions to fill this gap, based on the iterative design of BeeParking, a feedback display aimed to induce more cooperative use of a parking facility within a work environment.

Author Keywords

Interaction Design, Feedback Interfaces, Persuasive Computing, Behavior Change.

ACM Classification Keywords

H5.m. Information interfaces and presentation (e.g., HCI): User Interfaces, Prototyping.

General Terms

Theory, Experimentation.

INTRODUCTION

Research in HCI and Ubiquitous Computing has recently devoted much attention to the design and study of feedback interfaces to change human behavior, mainly with the goal of encouraging healthy living, self-management strategies [2, 9], or inducing more sustainable consumption behaviors [5]. In some application fields the design of feedback technology can properly be informed by individualistic strategies for persuasion [4], as well as by relevant theories of human decision-making [6]. However, when it comes to support behavior change (BC) in fields where interdependencies between individuals' choices and actions have social consequences and play a main role, like the common use of public goods, spaces, facilities in the physical or digital world [5, 8, 10], a collective perspective might be more appropriate to apply. Previous work in cross-cultural psychology has shed light on relevant differences in personality, attitudes and behavior of Western (more individualistic) culture vs Eastern (collectivist) culture [11]. These findings have also informed the design of collectivism-focused strategies for serious games technology to be effectively deployed within Eastern communities of young people [7]. More work is however needed to support the design of feedback interfaces able to motivate people's move (at individual and group level) from opportunistic to altruistic behavior, since this might bring important benefits to collectivity.

From a theoretical viewpoint, understanding BC as a stage-based, longitudinal process is helpful, since it enables a better focus on key drivers and effects of human motivation/action at different points of time of a persuasive intervention. This is also a main reason why the Transtheoretical Model of Change (TTM) [13] is considered a milestone approach in the area of persuasive technology [14]. However, due to its origin in health psychology (e.g., individual-based addiction research) this model needs to be combined with more domain-relevant theories when designing for collective BC. Theories or models from evolutionary biology and psychology might be useful here [3, 12, 15], since they provide complementary knowledge, including concepts from game theory and dynamics, to understand the evolution of collective mechanisms, such as human cooperation and competition.

In this paper, we present an initial attempt to combine these complementary perspectives during the iterative design of BeeParking, a feedback display aimed to encourage more effective and cooperative use of limited parking spaces in a work environment. We first introduce the theoretical approach that inspired our work; then we describe the design of the BeeParking prototype and its longitudinal testing in the field. Finally, we present an analysis of our empirical findings aimed to inform future models and feedback solutions for collective BC.

DESIGNING FOR COLLECTIVE BEHAVIOR CHANGE

According to the Transtheoretical Model of Change [13] and previous applications of this model in [14], there are at least three sequential phases of BC that should be supported by feedback technology: Raise awareness, Support complex changes, and Maintain sustainable routines. Of course, if a feedback interface is expected to be used by several persons, who are at different steps of BC, the system should be able to support the three phases in parallel. In the following we combine the three phases of this model with relevant mechanisms proposed by evolutionary biology [12] to explain the dynamics of cooperative behavior from a more collective perspective.

Raise awareness (P1): a person's choice regarding the use of shared resources is often made from a self-centered, opportunistic perspective, without paying much attention to possible effects of this choice on other users. A feedback interface raising awareness about these effects (e.g., how far one's behavior is affecting others' behavior) might help users to achieve better coordination, cooperation and more effective use of a limited resource. When repeated encounters between the same individuals are likely, feedback technology might play the role of stimulating BC through direct reciprocity [12], a form of cooperation where a person decides to pay a cost for another person, with the founded expectation that the recipient of the benefit will give back the favour at the next round.

Support complex changes (P2): this phase is concerned with encouraging people who are already aware or prepared to change, to enact the new behavior in order to reach a more desirable condition. In a cooperation setting, this would mean for instance that a feedback technology should be able to promote a shift from direct to indirect reciprocity [12, 15], where individuals' choices to cooperate are not only dependent on direct exchanges between donors and recipients, but also mediated by more complex social factors, such as reputation building and consideration. A feedback interface keeping track of and showing relevant behaviors patterns over time, might support the emergence of this more complex form of BC.

Maintain sustainable routines (P3): once the desired BCs have been achieved there is the need of sustaining them in the long-term, since relapse to previous behaviors has often been reported [14]. Feedback interfaces should be designed to engage users in the new behaviors and easily turn them into stable routines. As cooperators form networks or communities where reciprocity among members provides an advantage, emphasis on this evolutionary achievement that differentiates the community from non cooperative external groups or individuals might turn out useful to maintain the new behaviors in the long term.

BEEPARKING STUDY

We designed the BeeParking feedback interface as part of an exploratory study whose main goals were to: 1) better understand which role a feedback display could play as a support to collective BC in daily car parking routines of a group of employees, sharing a same but undersized parking area, 2) identify key requirements and features of the tool designed to best inducing an evolution of cooperation processes among participants, across the three phases mentioned above.

In the early stages of this study we conducted qualitative in-situ observations to better understand the daily parking routines of employees working in three different departments of a research centre (about 60 people in total). From anedoctal interviews with employees and direct observations in the parking area it was clear that there was a peak of car arrivals in the garage each morning from 9.30 to noon. Due to the limited space available and the particular parking slots configuration, each day at least 10 cars had to be parked irregularly in the central corridor, often obstructing emergency exits or other regularly parked cars. Most of the interviewees reported to find the current parking situation very stressful; some had come up with the solution of arriving at work earlier in the morning and to avoid moving their car over lunch break for the fear of not finding any parking space available then. The building receptionists had pinned up on walls several warnings, inviting drivers who had parked irregularly to leave a note on their car with contacts details. Very few people did so, and this was causing further inconvenience in the shared use of the parking facility.

The BeeParking Feedback Interface

We conducted brainstorming sessions to come up with ideas for the design of a new feedback technology solution able to promote more cooperative behavior among colleagues in the use of the parking area. We were aware of the importance of finding a solution that would be well accepted by users from both a functional and an aesthetic point of view.

The concept eventually chosen was based on the zoomorphic metaphor [1] of bees-beehive, since bees communities are generally held in high regard for their social nature and reputation for diligence (their organization has often been proposed as an ideal model for human society).

Beelike plastic keys, each enhanced with an iButton chip[1], were planned to be assigned to the users of the parking facility as identification devices. A beehive-like feedback interface, located at the building entrance, was meant to enable a user who had been compelled to park irregularly and block someone else car, to automatically notify the driver of the obstructed car.

---

[1] http://www.maxim-ic.com/products/ibutton/

Figure 1: A participant touching with her bee-key the beehive cell N.33 to notify her obstruction of a colleague's car

This was made possible by simply touching with her bee-key the relevant iButton probe placed at the centre of each beehive cell, showing the number assigned to the colleague's car (Figure 1). Once touched, the iButton probe led would light up and the system (based on an Arduino, communicating through a wireless connection with a Java program operating on a database) would send the command to deliver an email notification to both the author and recipient of an obstruction, informing about its occurrence and exchanging relevant contact details among the interested parties. A dedicated iButton probe on the beehive interface was used, instead, to signal the end of a block, which would automatically switch off the relevant cell led and notify by email the interested colleague that his car's exit was now free. Employees passing by the interface on their way to coffee breaks or other transfers might have the chance of getting a cue on the current situation in the parking area.

We proceeded with a rapid prototyping of this concept and quickly started deploying and testing it in situ with an initial group of 24 colleagues who had promptly answered to our invitation. The main objective of deploying this mid-tech prototype in the field was to start collecting longitudinal feedback from users, through observations, weekly interviews and log data, on the way this feedback interface was able to support collective BC in the daily parking routines of participants, and the evolution of cooperation mechanisms over time. The longitudinal evaluation set up was also meant to provide insights on how to extend the BeeParking features, increase their efficacy and derive further design implications for feedback technology to support collective BC. At the time we are writing BeeParking has been in usage for about 15 weeks. Below we provide a brief report of the main findings derived from our analysis of the log data (amount and type of blocks notified), from weekly interviews and participant observations collected over the system usage, which were informed by the collective BC approach proposed.

The Barter Stage

Of the 172 blocks found in the system logs we analyzed which pairs of participants were involved and day/time of each block/unblock to derive typical variations in BeeParking usage patterns over the 15 weeks. In the first two weeks of the study four participants stood out for behaving like early adopters, showing full trust and enthusiasm for the features offered by the new system. They used to park their car in such a way to leave some space available for possible irregular parking by colleagues, placing the number assigned to their car in highly visible positions on the car's window (so as to facilitate possible obstructions). By contrast, the remaining participants tried to take advantage of the potential benefits offered by BeeParking, while reducing as far as possible any eventuality of paying a cost. They were happy to use the system in case of need (irregular parking), but in the other cases preferred to keep somehow hidden their car number (thus discouraging any potential block by other drivers). When interviewed for explanation of this behavior some participants mentioned concerns regarding the possible need of leaving the building in a hurry and having troubles in resolving a block situation. As expected, over the first two weeks most of the blocks notified occurred between the same pairs of colleagues, mainly participants sharing the same office or office floor. Direct reciprocity (P1) was a main motivator of system use at this stage, with pairs of colleagues arranging to swap parking space in the garage (e.g., after lunch break) by using the BeeParking notification mails. Also, the early adopters played an important role in stimulating the other participants to act more cooperatively (e.g., by inviting them to stick their car number in a more visible position in the car window).

Reputation Concerns at Work

In the later weeks of the experimentation the system logs showed a larger number of participants using BeeParking, with a wider mix of people involved in the daily obstructions notified through the system. We also observed an increase of gossiping activity around the system (e.g., by means of jokes, comments made by participants and other colleagues at lunch break, near the BeeParking display or in their offices), mostly centered on reporting novel effects of the system introduction on parking habits of the facility's users. Attention was paid on learning who was using the system in a proper and altruistic way, as well as who was not. Several participants put some effort on trying to learn/guess the correct matching between BeeParking car numbers and their correspondent owners (some said to better inform their choices on who to block once more alternatives were available in the garage). This shows a more complex form of cooperative behavior, based on indirect reciprocity (P2). During inteviews participants said there was an amusing aspect in using BeeParking: it offered a further excuse for having some chats with colleagues working in different building areas with whom they rarely had the opportunity to interact (e.g., newcomers). More generally, there was a main emotional benefit provided by the system to users. It had contributed to turn the blocking behavior, mostly experienced as individually stressful and unfair to others (e.g., associated to negative feelings like wasting of time for parking, late arrival, sense of guilt, etc.) into a more socially acceptable and shared behavior, now regulated by the BeeParking system/community rules.

The Influence of Participants' Group on Neighbours

So far, the BeeParking experimentation is involving a group of 24 participants within the overall number of colleagues (of the same and neighbour research centres) that are sharing the parking facility. According to evolutionary models of cooperation, this situation might lead to strengthening reciprocity among members of the participants' group, possibly to the detriment of non participants. Qualitative findings from our study interviews support this expectation: e.g., a member of the participants' group proposed to reserve an area of the parking facility to the BeeParking experimentation, as a way of better differentiating from other users of the facility not taking part to the study. By contrast, a colleague from the non participants' group expressed preference for extending usage of BeeParking to all users of the parking facility. Interestingly, BeeParking had a BC effect also on some colleagues not involved in the experimentation: once they blocked a car with the BeeParking number, instead of leaving their business card with contacts on the car window, as was usual before, they preferred to look for the car driver's name (e.g., by asking to participants or system support guys) reach his office and notify the block in person. Early notification of obstructions by blockers (through any available means) is becoming the standard rule followed by colleagues of the research centre, thanks to the BeeParking intervention and the way it raised discussions (including gossiping) around parking behavior in the facility.

We realized that the aesthetics and methaphorical qualities of our feedback interface were effective means for attracting interest and further participation in the system usage. Some participants developed a strong commitment towards BeeParking, showing signs of personalized use and appropriation of the materials delivered (e.g., attaching original neck strings to bee-keys and car numbers), as well as creative thinking and reflection over its features refinement (e.g., making the system accessible also from smarphone applications, through QR Code technology).

CONCLUSION

This paper has provided insights on how to better approach design for BC in application fields where interpersonal dynamics and their evolution play a main role. It has presented the iterative design of BeeParking, a feedback interface aimed to support more cooperative use of a parking facility in a work environment. The analysis has shown how knowledge about dynamics of cooperation mechanisms, such as reciprocity, founded on TTM and evolutionary biology/psychology, can inform the design of feedback displays and support longitudinal analyses of behavior change at individual and group level. As future steps, we will extend the number of users and features of BeeParking, and carry on its longitudinal evaluation, to further validate the collective BC approach described.

REFERENCES

1. Bush, D.J. Body Icons and Product Semantics. In Vihma, Susann (Ed.) *Semantic Visions in Design.* Helsinki, Finland: University of Art and Design Helsinki Press. 1990
2. Consolvo, S., et al. Activity sensing in the wild: a field trial of ubifit garden. *Proc. CHI'08*, 2008, 1797-1806.
3. Dunbar, R.I.M. Gossip in Evolutionary Perspective. *Review of General Psychology*, Vo 8, N.2, 2004, 100-110.
4. Fogg, B.J. *Persuasive Technology: Using Computers to Change What We Think and Do*. Morgan Kaufmann Publishers, San Francisco, CA, 2003.
5. Froehlich, J., Findlater, L., Landay, J..The Design of Eco-Feedback Technology. *Proc. CHI'10*, 2010, 1999-2008.
6. Kahneman, D.. A perspective on judgment and choice: Mapping bounded rationality. *American Psychologist, 58*, 2003, 697–720.
7. Khaled, R., Biddle, R., Noble, J., Barr, P., Fischer, R. Culturally Aware Persuasive Technology: Collectivism Focused Strategies. *Proc. of the 7th AUIC Conf.*, 2006.
8. Lakhani, K. R., & von Hippel, E. How open source software works: "Free" user-to-user assistance. *Research Policy, 32*(6), 2003, 923-943.
9. Maitland, J., Chalmers, M. Self-Monitoring, Self-Awareness, and Self-Determination in Cardiac Rehabilitation. *Proc. CHI'10*, 2010, 1213-1222.
10. Mankoff, J., Matthews, D., Fussell, Susan, R. Johnson, M. Leveraging social networks to motivate individuals to reduce their ecological footprints. *Proc. HICSS'07*, 2007, 87-96.
11. Markus, H.R., Kitayama, S. Culture and the Self: Implications for Cognition, Emotion, and Motivation. *Psychological Review*, Vo 98, N.2, 1991, 224-253.
12. Novak, M.A. Five Rules for the Evolution of Cooperation. *Science*, Vo. 314, December 2006, 1560-1563.
13. Prochaska J., DiClemente C. Toward a comprehensive model of change. In Miller WR, Heather N, eds. *Treating additive behaviors: processes of change.* NY: Plenum, 1986, 3-27.
14. Riche, Y., Dodge, J., Metoyer, R.A. Studying Always-On Electricity Feedback in the Home. *Proc. CHI'10*, 2010, 1995-1998.
15. Sommerfeld, R.D., Krambeck H.J., Semmann, D., Milinski, M.. Gossip as an alternative for direct observation in games of indirect reciprocity. *Proc. Natl. Acad. Sci.* U S A. 104(44), 2007, 17435-40.

GreenHat: Exploring the Natural Environment Through Experts' Perspectives

Kimiko Ryokai[1], Lora Oehlberg[2], Michael Manoochehri[1], Alice Agogino[2]

[1]School of Information
University of California, Berkeley
Berkeley CA 94720 USA
kimiko@ischool.berkeley.edu

[2]Department of Mechanical Engineering
University of California, Berkeley
Berkeley CA 94720 USA
{agogino, lora}@berkeley.edu

ABSTRACT

We present GreenHat, an interactive mobile learning application that helps students learn about biodiversity and sustainability issues in their surroundings from experts' points of view, before participating in unfamiliar debates about their familiar surroundings. Using the interactive location-sensitive map and video on a smart phone, GreenHat simulates how experts go about making observations in the field and encourages students to actively observe their environment. We present our design process, our initial prototype, report the results from our preliminary evaluation, and discuss ongoing work.

Author Keywords

Mobile learning, sustainability, biodiversity, location-based information, expert perspectives

ACM Classification Keywords

H5.1. Information interfaces and presentation: Multimedia Information Systems-Artificial, Augmented, and Virtual Realities.

General Terms

Design

INTRODUCTION

One of the primary challenges in scaffolding novices to become experts is helping them first develop a "professional vision" – being able to see the world from an expert's perspective [5]. Goodwin identifies the practices of *coding*, *highlighting*, and *producing and articulating material representation* as ways that participants build and contest professional vision. However, in situated contexts where experts are not present to identify the appropriate coding, highlighting, and articulation of material representations, mobile learning systems have the potential to assist students in adopting these expert points of view.

We present GreenHat, a mobile learning system that aims to help students engage with the natural environment with multiple expert perspectives (landscape architecture and conservation biology). By connecting these experts' analyses with the students' everyday landscapes, students can look at their environment from a new perspective, and develop their opinion on location-sensitive controversial conservation issues. Mobile technologies can support the development of expert perspectives by prompting novices with context-relevant information, interactively engaging the student with multiple forms of information and inquiry, and connecting their mobile experiences with the greater community discussion.

CHI 2011, May 7–12, 2011, Vancouver, BC, Canada.

BACKGROUND AND RELATED WORK

Sustainability and increasing ecological awareness is of increasing interest to the interaction design community [2]. Previous work on sustainability in interaction design has focused on leveraging social networks to promote ecologically friendly action [7], or enabling citizen science by using cellphones as a mobile sensing platform [9]. While these projects promoted ecological awareness and engaging citizen scientists data, they were not necessarily used to foster debate around sustainability issues.

The NatureTalk aimed to enhance creativity by helping children capture, geo-tag, and explore sound [8]. Researchers have also developed paper-based mobile tools for field biologists [11]. However, these interfaces are much more explorative in nature, and do not necessarily assist a novice in adopting an expert point of view.

Figure 1: In preliminary tests, students learned about contextually relevant sustainability issues using GreenHat.

Situated cognition theory argues that knowledge cannot be separated from the context in which it is situated – abstract knowledge is not fully understood until it is applied in context [3].

THE GREENHAT

The GreenHat system consists of GreenHat Mobile, an application that runs on a GPS-enabled Smartphone (e.g. Android, iPhone), and GreenHat Web View, a website that aggregates data from multiple users. Previous user needs research on Mobile Learning applications [6] has identified three core needs: *Capture*, *Access*, *Connect*. The features of the GreenHat system address the three main need categories.

- *Capture*: Using GreenHat Mobile, students document observations in the field through text, photos, and audio capture. In addition to automatically-generated time and location metadata, students can add tags to group information. Users' past tagging activity can also be used by GreenHat Mobile to suggest additional content.
- *Access*: At any point, the student can query GreenHat Mobile for more information and request GreenHat Mobile to alert them when they are near interesting opportunities to learn about biodiversity. As the student continues to use the system, GreenHat Mobile prompts further mobile exploration by highlighting locations tagged with commonly used terms.
- *Connect*: Using GreenHat Web View, collaborating students can view a common map that marks where each student has been, their observations at those locations, and frequently used tagging terms. This view enables collaborators to start conversations centered around each others' field work.

GREENHAT DESIGN PROCESS

In order to understand the specific issues of sustainability and biodiversity on campus, the design team first gathered and studied material available through the campus' existing online resources (e.g., an interactive campus map describing the history and biodiversity of the creek that runs through the campus). The design team then took a tour of the campus with experts, including a conservationist biologist and a landscape architect, and conducted interviews and discussions with these experts. Based on insights we gained from the tour and interviews and from mobile learning literature, we developed the following design features for GreenHat.

Simulating the Way an Expert Sees the World: Observe the Environment from Experts' Perspectives

While the design team was in the field with the experts, we noticed that the experts looked at the familiar environment differently from us and noticed things that we usually would not about the familiar places [5]. The expert's physical demeanor and engagement with the environment were different from ours while we walked on the forest paths on campus together. For example, the expert carefully looked around the ground as we walked together (e.g., identifying native oak seedling sprouting where they could be damaged from human traffic), looked up on the trees (e.g., identifying non-native ivy overtaking the light that the oak tree should get), looked around the shrubs (e.g., identifying non-native squirrel species). While being in the same environment, the experts' eyes and bodies were everywhere, noticing things and asking critical questions about the environment. What, then, is it like to experience this familiar environment from an expert's perspective? What exactly are the experts noticing? What kinds of questions are they asking? What kinds of observations are they making? It is this kind of perspective shift in actively observing one's environment we wanted to simulate in our mobile learning application. While experts' availability is limited, mobile devices have the potential to provide information "on demand" for learners even in the absence of experts [10]. Based on literature on expert vs. novice learning [3], our goal is to simulate an experience for the learner as if s/he is taking a walk with experts on the field.

Our design solution was to use a location-sensitive smart phone and have the device point at points of interest in situ as experts may. We curated the content of the experts' tour and delivered their teachable moments on students' mobile phones in a combination of video, images, and an interactive map. The information resolution moved from a macro view to a micro view. The campus map first indicated their current location and guided students to a specific area (Figure 2, left). Once the student reached their destination, the phone initiated a video of the expert discussing an issue specific to the area (Figure 2, right). This not only showed the expert pointing at specific trees and area, but also demonstrated how the experts go about making observations in the field.

Figure 2: Screenshots from GreenHat prototype. The left shows the interactive location-sensitive map, and the right shows experts' demonstrative videos with key concepts in text.

Utilize the Local Resource: Discover Unfamiliar Debates about Familiar Places

In contrast to in-class or desktop learning environments, mobile learning is a multi-sensory experience (e.g., the movements, noises, air, temperature, shadows, and even the smell of the outside environment, etc.). Learning about nature in nature is powerful, but as our conservation biology expert commented, "one does not need to hop on a bus to Yosemite to learn about biodiversity." Students spend a significant amount of time traveling through various places on campus where there is nature (e.g., commuter trails, paths in between classes, outdoor meeting places, etc.). We agree with the expert that there are plenty of opportunities to provide situated learning on biodiversity right in students' back yard. And, in fact, learning in familiar places make conservation issues even more personal to the student. For example, the students may learn that the beautiful forest they usually enjoy sitting in is filled with non-native species that are actually a fire hazard to the nearby buildings. Presenting evidence and facts in the familiar physical environment to the learner provides a unique learning experience.

Our design solution is to provide video of experts' presenting evidence by pointing at specific physical locations, at the same location. This actively engages the students in making observations in the field (e.g., with reference to images of native/exotic species on mobile phone). Discussions at the physical familiar location allow students to build on their personal knowledge and experience. As the students visit various familiar locations on campus, they are introduced to additional unfamiliar complex issues and debates. Our mobile learning tool engages the students with these topics by challenging them in situ with debate questions, and asking them to providing both their opinion and evidence.

Present Multiple Perspectives

We wanted to avoid having biased or polarized views by supporting pluralism in perspectives. For example, a nature conservationist may have a mission to restore the landscape with native plants, but what constraints might the landscape architect have? Are there solutions that satisfy both perspectives? To help the students explore variety of possible solutions by considering multiple perspectives, we designed the following four-step inquiry to engage the students in the topic. At each stop, 1) GreenHat asks the student to respond to a multiple-choice question about a controversial sustainability issue in their immediate surroundings (e.g., should we cut the eucalyptus trees?) 2) The student then watches videos of "experts", one conservation biologist and one landscape architect, each presenting their insights on that area. As the videos play, a list of "key ideas" is displayed next to the video. 3) The student is again asked to respond to the controversial question, this time adding the thought process behind their response. 4) The students can also view what other students have said.

Mobile and Beyond / Reflect

We connect the mobile learning experience with the students' existing desktop learning experience. Learning "on the go" provides unique opportunities for the students to make observations in situ and discover relevant facts. However, certain behaviors such as typing long notes or browsing large collections of digital library resources are not ideal on a mobile device with a small screen and keyboard. Our goal is to support uniquely "mobile" learning experiences, but at the same time not limit the experience to mobile devices only. After the trip, the students may reflect and expand on their activities by visiting their personalized online map on a web interface. This web interface also allows them to explore relevant keywords, edit their entries, browse and comment on others' entries, and visit relevant online resources.

Based on literature on mobile learning as well as our previous NSDL mobile learning research [6], interaction design on mobile device must be engaging but relatively short. Once at the desktop, we provide a web forum for the students to expand on their mobile learning experience. In the web interface, students can view the history of their activities made with their mobile device (i.e., map of explored areas, images, comments, etc.) as well as entries made by others in the community.

IMPLEMENTATION

The GreenHat Mobile prototype was implemented using the Android G1 Dev Phone [1], which features an 8cm (3.17in) 480x320 pixel touch screen, a slide-out QWERTY keyboard, a built-in GPS receiver, and Wi-Fi capabilities. The prototype software was written in Java using the Android Software Development Kit. Participant responses where saved directly to an SQLite database on each device.

EVALUATION

In order to investigate the mobile learning situation offered by GreenHat, we compared two groups, 1) a group using GreenHat Mobile outside, and 2) a group using GreenHat's four-step inquiry running on a desktop. A total of 19 undergraduate and graduate students participated in our study. Twelve students have participated in the GreenHat Mobile group. Each participant spent approximately one hour and a half exploring the campus with GreenHat Mobile. To record their experience, experimenters "shadowed" the participants with video cameras and field notes. After the tour, the experimenters asked a set of open-ended questions such as "How was the experience of learning about Strawberry Creek?"

Seven students participated in the GreenHat Desktop condition, where they had access to all the same digital material as the GreenHat Mobile condition (e.g., expert videos, campus map, key concepts in text) but received these materials on the desktop computer in a room. In both conditions, the students have explored 5 different locations on the campus, following the 4-step inquiry.

RESULTS

We have looked at both the students' answers to the controversial questions (multiple choice) and the reasoning behind their answers (their written responses to the "Why?" question). The two groups were equally diverse in their answers and reasoning behind their answers. For example, both groups equally agreed on the answer to some questions (e.g., for the question, "Which landscaped space, North vs. South Lawn, is more sustainable?" 84% "North Lawn" 16% "South Lawn" for the Mobile condition 77% "North Lawn" 33% "South Lawn" for the Desktop condition), and similarly disagreed to some questions (e.g., for the question "Transplant or pullout the seedling out of place?" 41% "Transplant" and 59% "Pullout" in the Mobile condition and 50% "Transplant" and 50% "Pullout" in the Desktop group). Despite the disadvantage of typing on the small keyboard, the Mobile group wrote as much as the Desktop group with a standard-sized keyboard (the average length of written responses was 24.14 words for the Mobile and 26.6 words for the Desktop).

More Contextual Evidence

While the students' responses to the questions were equally diverse in both Mobile Learning group and Desktop Learning group, the Mobile Learning group seemed to give more contextual evidence in their responses. For example, a student in Mobile condition wrote, *"The lawn seems more functional on this side and* ***further removed from the bustle of students walking to and from class.****"* (providing his observation in the environment). Another student in Mobile condition wrote, *"I actually like hearing the sound of the creek and being able to sit on the grass and see the creek at the same time."* (taking her personal experience into account). These types of comments from personal observation were not seen in the desktop condition. In describing their answers, the desktop group tended to quote the video, e.g., "[...] because the video said [...]"

Seeing the World through the Expert's Perspective.

Some of the connections the students made with their environment happened outside of the prompts made by GreenHat in the Mobile group. As they walked between locations on campus with GreenHat, some students voluntarily pointed out the specifics of the environment they just learned to observe (e.g., "Oh, that's the ivy I just learned about!" pointing at the non-native ivy species found outside of the previous area). The Mobile students during the post-study interview described that they would now look at their campus differently. Some students described that they have "learned to be more skeptical" and questioning what they see.

Personal and Multiple Perspectives

The students in the Mobile Learning group reported that the experience of going through their campus and learning about debates on sustainability and biodiversity was "personal." They described that it would not be the same experience if they had learned about the same issue at a desktop, as they would not be as "immersed in the environment" as they were. For example, the students learned that the design of a particular creek side garden with lawn is highly un-sustainable (due to pesticides and energy to run lawn mowers). However, at the same time, they were there on a nice sunny day to observe their fellow students enjoying the green lawn during breaks. They were pushed to consider multiple aspects of the design challenge.

Technical Issues and Future Work

The GPS reception at some locations was not as good as we had originally anticipated due to "urban canyons." Some prompts by GPS were not precise, occurring earlier or later than we designed. In such cases, the combination of the map, images, and videos of experts pointing at specific objects in the location were helpful in guiding the students.

Students reported that some of the videos seemed too long for mobile learning. We plan to edit the videos so that they can be viewed in smaller chunks and also allow the students to save the point where they paused their video and continue watching it later.

We are currently expanding the application to include the mobile location-sensitive search, as well as an interface to digital libraries [4]. This will allow the student to engage with a broader community of experts, experiencing their surroundings from an even greater set of experts and curated resources.

CONCLUSIONS

GreenHat invited students to explore complex issues of sustainability and biodiversity presented at various physical locations in their familiar environment. Our preliminary evaluation of GreenHat prototype showed that having access to multiple experts' perspectives in the physical environment, i.e., how the experts would look at and interrogate the very environment the students stand, encouraged the students to actively observe the physical environment and provide more contextual evidence in forming their responses. Mobile technologies can support the development of expert perspectives by prompting novices with context-relevant information, interactively engaging the student with multiple forms of information and inquiry, and connecting their mobile experiences with the greater community discussion. We contribute the design of mobile learning experience that takes advantage of access to multiple experts and context-sensitive information in the learner's immediate physical environment.

ACKNOWLEDGEMENTS

We thank Jennifer Wang, Ian Leighton, Christy Pratt, Elizabeth Goodman, Tim Pine, Danielle Christianson, and Arielle Simpson for their help and insightful discussions. We thank Google for providing Android phones. This research was supported by NSF Grant #0840790.

REFERENCES

1. Android SDK. Google, Inc. http://code.google.com/android
2. Blevis, E. "Sustainable Interaction Design: Invention & Disposal, Renewal & Reuse". Proc. CHI 2007 (2007).
3. Brown, J.S., Collins, A., Duguid, P. "Situated Cognition and the Culture of Learning." Educational Researcher, pp. 32-42.
4. Engineering Pathway. http://www.engineeringpathway.com/; also SMETE.org http://www.smete.org/
5. Goodwin, C. "Professional Vision". American Anthropologist, Vol. 96, No. 3 (Sep., 1994), pp. 606-633.
6. Hey, J., Sandhu, J., Newman, C., Hsu, J., Daniels, C., Datta, E., Agogino, A.. "Designing Mobile Digital Library Services for Pre-Engineering and Technology Literacy." International Journal of Engineering Education, Vol. 23, No. 3, pp. 441-453, 2007.
7. Mankoff, J., Matthews , D., Fussell, S.R., Johnson, M., "Leveraging Social Networks To Motivate Individuals to Reduce their Ecological Footprints", Proc. of International Conference on System Sciences 2007.
8. Ohashi, Y., Makoto A. "Nature talk: a proposed audible database system for environmental learning". 2006 Conference on Interaction Design and Children, pp. 167-168
9. Paulos, E., Forth, M., Satchell, S., Kim, Y., Dourish, P., & Choi, J. (2008, in press). Ubiquitous Sustainability: Citizen Science & Activism. In Proc of Ubicomp '08 Workshops.
10. Trondsen, E., Vickery, K. "Learning on Demand". Journal of Knowledge Management, 1997.
11. Yeh, R., Liao, C., Klemmer, S., Guimbretière, F., Lee, B., Kakaradov, B., Stamberger, J., Paepcke, A.. "ButterflyNet: a mobile capture and access system for field biology research", CHI 2006.

Telling Calls: Facilitating Mobile Phone Conversation Grounding and Management

Sukeshini A. Grandhi
Natural Media and Engineering, HumTec
RWTH Aachen University
Aachen, Germany
grandhi@humtec.rwth-aachen.de

Richard P. Schuler and Quentin Jones
Department of Information Systems
New Jersey Institute of Technology
Newark, New Jersey, USA
rps22, qjones@njit.edu

ABSTRACT
Current cell phone designs are limited by the information a caller can provide to the receiver at the time of a call. As a result callers are handicapped in effectively negotiating interaction commitment from the receiver, and perhaps more importantly, receivers are unable to make informed call handling decisions. To examine the nature of this information gap we 1) developed *Telling Calls,* a mobile phone application which allows users to provide and receive information such as what the call is about and the circumstances of the caller under which it is being made, and 2) conducted a qualitative field study (36 users) and a quantitative field study (30 users) of *Telling Calls* use. Together these studies provide insights on how additional caller generated information shared at the time of call handling effectively improves the process of negotiating interaction commitment, and establishing common ground.

Author Keywords
Communication, Management, Grounding, Outeraction, Availability, Response, Interruption, Design, Cell phone.

ACM Classification Keywords
H5.2. Information interfaces and presentation (e.g., HCI): User Interfaces, User Centered Design

General Terms
Design, Theory, Human Factors, Experimentation.

INTRODUCTION
Conversations often consist of multiple messages exchanged over an extended period of time through multiple communication media [28]. As a result, people put considerable effort into coordinating the initiation, re-engagement and (re) scheduling of their conversations. Communication specifically aimed at reaching out to others in patently social ways to coordinate and enable conversation in the immediate or distant future is termed as outeraction [21]. For example, sending an email or text message to coordinate, negotiate or schedule a phone conversation. It has been estimated that 34 to 64 percent of SMS text messages [11,17,27] are for coordinating future social interactions as are a similarly sizable proportion of Instant Messages (IM) [21].

The choice of media for conversation and outeraction appears to be largely based on the different affordances [23] offered by various technologies for different conversation styles [30]. Telephone communication affords synchronous '*focused conversations*' [30], where conversants engage in cadenced turn-taking, in which tone, lapses and changes in rhythm inform the parties of emotional and mental states. On the other hand, IM being near synchronous affords '*opportunistic lightweight conversations*' by presenting user availability information that allows for plausible deniability, which in turn enables parties to manage the timing and depth of their interaction commitment [21]. SMS being asynchronous allows for communication on the go that also affords reduced interaction commitment for the receiver while restricting the amount of detail the sender can provide about the conversation. As a result, both IM and SMS are popular tools for outeraction, which is often used to obtain interaction commitment for focused phone conversations. Apart from studies of IM [21], studies of SMS show that 31% of the messages were used for planning and was primarily used as a method to switch between a variety of communication media such as Facebook and phones [2].

There are however numerous occasions where individuals simply wish to engage directly in focused telephone conversations, without performing outeraction through another media such as IM or SMS first. For this reason, impromptu incoming calls from individuals are generally understood as an expression of a caller's clear intent to engage in immediate media rich communication. When this occurs, due to the synchronous nature of phone calls, the receiver is tasked with making a call handling decision (i.e., answer or ignore) as a response to the immediate interaction commitment desired. Unfortunately, these decisions are often based on very limited information (typically caller ID). This situation can be disadvantageous to both parties, with incoming calls being accepted because the receiver assumes incorrectly that they are important or incoming calls being ignored because the receiver assumes incorrectly that they are unimportant. In this paper we explore the nature of this receiver side information deficit, regarding the call content and the caller context. More specifically, we examine how reducing the receiver's information deficit while supporting caller's aim of engaging in immediate media rich communication, could afford different conversations styles and outcomes for both callers and receivers.

To support our exploration of call-receiver information gap regarding caller context and call content and its relationship with call handling decisions, we developed, *Telling Calls*, a mobile phone application. It allows users to receive calls that display not only the standard Caller ID information, but also caller generated information such as why the call is being made and under what circumstances. Using *Telling Calls* we explored: 1) what information people like to know when receiving calls; 2) what information receivers are likely to use to make call handling decisions, 3) what information callers like the receiver to know prior to making call handling decision and 4) how the provision of additional call information impacts on associated phone conversations.

Drawing on prior research on media affordances, communication styles, negotiation and initiation of conversations, we present our design rationale for *Telling Calls* and findings from two field studies of *Telling Calls* use.

BACKGROUND

In this section we begin reviewing literature that provides understanding of how different conversation styles, coordination and negotiation are managed across and within various communication media and guide this discussion to how these processes are managed with in phone calls.

Woodruff and Aaoki [29] differentiate between three styles of conversations: 1) *focused conversations* where participants engage in continuous conversational turn taking as long as the communication channel is open, 2) *bursty conversations* that occur with multiple sequences of turn taking on and off within a open communication channel and 3) *intermittent conversations* that occur with long lapses within a single sequence of turn taking. Individuals wishing to engage in focused conversations first need to obtain an attentional contract from the recipient [21]. Negotiating interaction commitment is a specific kind of coordination where grounding is important to establish a shared understanding between the two parties that will allow for conversation engagement.

In establishing common ground [5] for communication, people use many disparate media for their communication. Gergle et al. [10] found that using persistent chat and shared visual spaces were beneficial and supportive of the communication and coordination process. Nardi et al [21] observed that IM users negotiated availability in IM as a means to establish common ground for focused phone conversations. Wiberg and Whittaker [29], developed *Negotiator* for lightweight negotiation of receiver's time of availability for focused telephone conversations. However, as noted in the introduction a planned or delayed focused conversation as a result of media-switching is not always desired. The challenge that this research addresses is how to improve the process of negotiating interaction commitment and establishing common ground for impromptu phone conversations.

One of the ways in which IM and other awareness/presence systems provide common ground for interaction negotiation is by presenting to potential communicators information about the receiver's current context through the provision of status information [3,20]. Such status information has also been found to influences the decision of callers. De Guzman et al. [8] found that caller's estimate of the receiver's task and physical availability were the most important factors in deciding whether to place a call. Avrahami et al. [1] studied the effectiveness of providing the caller with contextual information by measuring the degree of agreement between the receivers' desires and callers' decisions. They found that callers with information, such as, mobile phone ringer state, location, and presence of people around the receiver, made more accurate decisions. A number of applications have been built that expand the ability of individuals to share status information with callers either manually or semi-automatically as derived by sensors and calendar information. For example, *live addressbook* and *Lilsys* display location, availability and user generated free-form messages to indicate one's availability for incoming communication requests [3,20]. *Calls Calm* [24] allows phone users to display key information of their situation to enable callers to appropriately time their calls. These studies are important since they inform us about how to support callers' decisions making based on receivers context information. However, they do not inform us about receivers' information needs or how to support their call handling decisions. In this paper we address this disparity in the research by exploring how the provision of information about the caller and the call content can help receivers make impromptu call handling decisions.

In addition to the limited information provided to call receivers, current phone designs afford a limited range of responses, mainly, that of accepting or rejecting the call. Subsequently, researchers have attempted to find methods to fill these gaps. Based on caller ID, *Taming of the Ring* [25] allows phone call receivers to respond through pre-recorded voice messages by the touch of a button such as "hold" or "will call back soon after my meeting" based on who the call is from. Nelson et al. [22] extend the use of pre-recorded response options in *Quiet Calls* by enabling receivers to listen silently to the caller without vocalizing a response. Bayesphone analyses desktop activities, calendar information and pre-compiled user preferences to decide if calls should be allowed when the user is in a meeting [14].

Very few commercial or research phone applications have design characteristics that provide the receiver with information about what the call is going to be about or other contextual information other than who it is from. Commercial products such as the *Google Voice* enable callers to screen similar to an answering machine and decide to intercept and accept the call. Milewski [19] studied call screening via answering machine and found that information such as call content, emotional impact and urgency of the caller provided receivers with rich information to make call answering decisions.

Research in the area of interruption management has made reference to two categories of **information that can affect receivers' decisions**: 1) Interrupter related information which comprises factors such as who the interruption is from, his or her activity, location, and the nature of relationship with people in the location [4,7,18] 2) Interruption content information which comprises factors such as what the interruption is about (analogous to subject fields in emails), how long it may last and its urgency/importance [13,19]. Investigation of call handling decisions by [9] found that the following information was unknown and highly desired: subject (or call reason), location of the caller, activity of the caller, the caller's estimated call length, people the caller is with, the urgency and importance of the call, and the caller's mood. Apart from these studies that allude to the utility of information for call receivers, we are not aware of any systems or evaluations that have systematically explored the potential utility of providing the receiver with information beyond Caller ID, in terms of what the call is about or under what circumstance it is being made.

RESEARCH QUESTIONS

In this paper we explore how to address the information gap that currently confronts individuals trying to make impromptu call handling decisions, while supporting callers' aim of engaging in immediate media rich focused conversation. We do this through a combination of interaction design and software development, accompanied by qualitative and quantitative field studies. The studies collectively addressed the following research questions with respect to caller context and call content information: 1) what information do receivers like to know when receiving impromptu calls; 2) what information do receivers use to make impromptu call handling decisions, 3) what information do callers want the receivers to know prior to making call handling decision and 4) how does the provision of additional call content and caller context information impact the resulting phone conversation.

TELLING CALLS

Our interaction design and development efforts focused on instantiating a system that would act as a platform for our qualitative and quantitative research into facilitating mobile phone conversation grounding and management. Our goal was to supplement the phone call process and not to replace it or drastically alter it. Instead, we hoped to design a system that aided both callers and receivers of mobile phone calls by providing callers with the ability to provide additional call content and caller context information that could help receivers make better call handing decisions.

Telling Calls was developed for use with devices available to us as part of an NSF supported mobile community system test-bed. The work described here was carried out using AT&T Tilt smartphones running Windows Mobile 6 (Note, the targeted device was a Windows Mobile 6 phone and at the time the primary input was the stylus, the iPhone and Android styles of touch input were not yet common). These phones have a touch screen and include a slide-out keyboard enabling the use of touch gestures, stylus based input and typing. For ease of use we designed our data entry interface primarily for thumb input. Based on our initial usability studies we also provided thumbable access to previously entered text for reuse and quick entry of text. Unable to rely on our test-users having high-speed data plans we used the Short Messaging System (SMS) to transfer data between the caller and receiver's *Telling Calls* clients.

Application use was centered on a single UI that was edited and sent by the caller and then presented as a static display to the receiver just before or at the arrival of the incoming call. A shared visualization was chosen to help with grounding [10] as was the simple mix of visual/icon and text based fields. We also wanted to support both the callers and receivers ability to review the information sent or received as a common ground for future coordination or re-engagement and hence designed a call history feature that stored information sent or received in the same

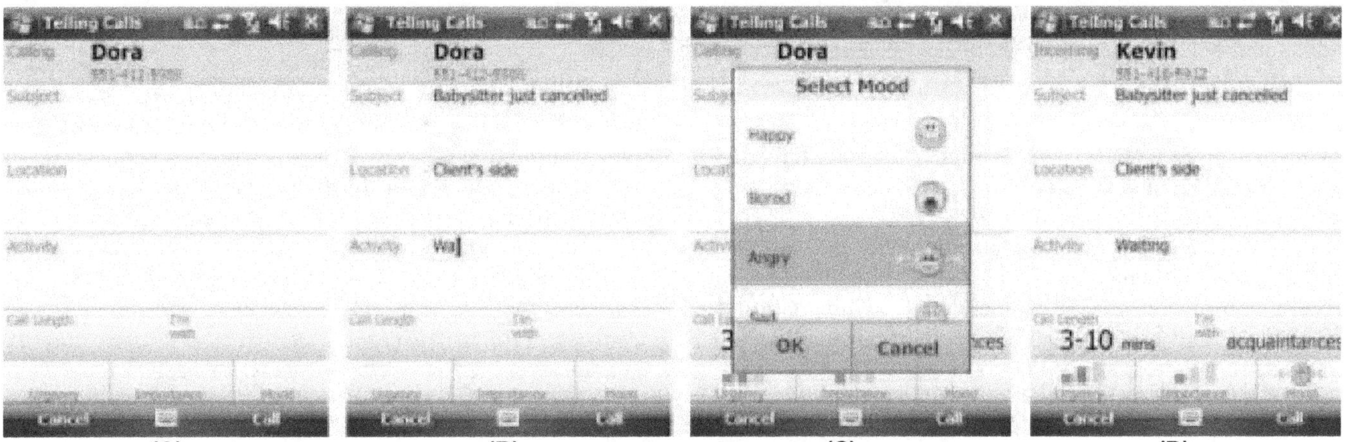

(A) (B) (C) (D)

Figure 1. Caller's interface (A, B, C) and Receiver's interface (D).

visualization. The interaction is as follows: The caller selects a contact they wish to call, which brings up the editable caller interface (Figure 1. A). The caller then fills out any of the various fields deemed appropriate for the call and then presses the Call Button (Figure 1. B and C). The receiver's phone then alerts her/him of the incoming call and displays the receiver UI (Figure 1. D).

The fields of the main UI were as follows: 1) Caller - This was generated by the standard caller ID feature of the phone. 2) Subject, location, and activity are text entry fields of up to 50 characters. Data entry for these fields is supported by a drop down list of previous entered text which could be reused. 3) Call length, urgency, importance and mood are implemented as buttons that present the caller with a scrollable list of choices to select from (illustrated in Figure 1. C). The list choices were: *Call Length:* none (i.e. no value), less than 3 minutes, 3-10 min, 10-20 min, and more than 20 minutes.*"I am with"*: none, alone, mutual friends, mutual acquaintances, friends, and acquaintances. *Urgency & Importance* (implemented separately): none, low, medium, and high, and *Mood*: a range that was inspired from popular IM clients with choices such as happy, crabby, bored, and angry.

QUALITATIVE USER STUDY

To gain an understanding of how *Telling Calls* and the additional call content and caller context information that it allows the caller to present at the time of call handling, impacted on 1) the process of negotiating interaction commitment, and 2) the gaining of common ground, we conducted an interpretive field study [16].

Method

Participants

Groups of 2-3 participants, who regularly called each other using AT&T mobile phones, were recruited for the study through convenience and snowball sampling techniques. This approach allowed us to provide participants with an AT&T Tilt Smartphone for use with his/her own SIM cards and service plan. In total, 37 individuals were interviewed as part of this study. Eighteen of our interviewees used *Telling Calls* with one or two friends, 16 with their romantic partner, and 5 with one or two family members. The gender of the participants was fairly balanced, with 46% being female. Participants were a mix of working adults and students many of whom held part-time jobs and were mobile phone users for more than 3 years.

Procedure

Semi-structured interviews were conducted both before and after participants used *Telling Calls* for 1 to 2 weeks. In the post use interviews logs of *Telling Calls* were used as interview aids. The interview questions focused on three issues: 1) the influence of *Telling Calls* on participants call receiving process; 2) the influence of *Telling Calls* on participants call making; and 3) what participants liked and disliked about the application.

Results

We recorded 785 minutes of semi-structured interviews, which were transcribed. From our analysis using the interpretive principles outlined in [16,26] several themes emerged which are illustrated through representative quotes below with the names changed to preserve participants' anonymity.

Influence of Telling Calls on Call Receiving Process

All participants reported at least one of the following two ways in which *Telling Calls* influenced their call receiving process: 1) As a response decision aid; and 2) As a conversation setting aid.

Telling Calls as a Response Decision Aid

Participants reported that *Telling Calls* was helpful in reducing their uncertainty about a call, which in turn influenced their call handling decisions. Matt, commented on information provided to him by his mother. *Matt: I know her very well. I could almost deduce everything from the location and activity. I knew if she was in the supermarket shopping that – this would be a quick call and that it was probably something important.*

Apart from reducing uncertainty, participants also reported how *Telling Calls* helped them ignore or answer the calls knowing the reason for the call and realizing that the call could wait in light of their current task. Victor a full time working male talked about how he ignored a call from his partner while driving knowing the call could wait. *Victor: The other day, she was waiting for me to pick her up. She gave me a call. I didn't have a hands free <set> on and I didn't want to pick the call up for the fear of getting a ticket. And I saw all the information <on Telling Calls> - she was finished at the gym and was waiting at so and so location. So, I knew what it was about and I was heading there, so <I thought> it's okay if I let this call go.*

Participants also reported how *Telling Calls* was also used to answer calls that would have been otherwise ignored Accounts such as that of Pia, a graduate student, with regards to a call from her boyfriend were typical. *Pia: If I can afford to, I pick it up....otherwise, I like to ignore calls in the morning. This one time he had just got an email. He just got a reply from a company <where he applied for a job> that said that he didn't make it. I had to pick it up, yes.*

Telling Calls as a Conversation Setting Aid

Participants also reported how they used the application to set the stage for the conversation with the person calling them. Some changed their style of conversation, based on the information they received, while others used the information as an icebreaker. Tim, graduate student explained how, when talking to his girlfriend, his conversation was based on what she had entered in the subject line. *Tim: The thing is that most conversations are not so urgent. We just chat. So we chat with the aim of the chatting. You're just there to kill the time. So the conversation (...) <is set > for example based on her mood*

<sent through the application> here, I adjust my mood to fit hers.

Victor talked about how he altered his conversation style with his girlfriend, based on the information such as who she was with, when calling him. *Victor: So, based on that <who she was with>, you know, the call would go from being an intimate call to just a casual call - based on who she was with. (...) once she said that she was with an acquaintance and I didn't know for sure if this call was on speaker but then I was careful and I ended the conversation saying, "Hey, you know what? Let me give you a call back later or maybe you can call back when you're free." I mean, I chose my words carefully.*

Influence of Telling Calls on Call Making Process

Participants reported using varied information items when placing calls. In particular they reported on how *Telling Calls* allowed them to set the tone of the conversation either intentionally or unintentionally. The type of information callers presented to their call partners was dictated by the nature of the relationship.

Kent, when talking to his intimate friend Kelly, explained the choice of information he provided when making calls. *Kent: "I always entered subject location and activity. Yeah I felt that those were the important information. So I would always enter the subject and then the location as to what I was doing. The call length - I thought was unnecessary. Sometimes I entered who I was with, but sometimes I figured that was a given depending on the activity but I would always enter the mood I was in, but definitely not the urgency or the importance, only if it was really important.*

Dawn, an undergraduate student, used the application with her roommate Dora, with whom she speaks often on the phone to coordinate meetings and activities, used all fields while calling, so that she could provide maximum information and receive an effective response in return. *Dawn: Yea, I chose to use all of it. (...) to let her know more information about what I want to tell her. Then when she picked up the phone she just tells me the answer right away instead of me asking her again.*

Pam mentioned that providing urgency level and subject through the tool, prompted her boy friend to respond immediately to her phone call. *Pam: For example, this afternoon, I had to pay my fees and it was through credit card (...) I really didn't know and it was a huge amount and I didn't want to take that chances. So, I called him with this information <subject, urgency>, he was like 'okay, good, you told me...in another 10 seconds, I would have left for the gym'. So having said that, providing the higher urgency level influenced him to answer it right away.*

Participants also reported how *Telling Calls* enabled them to steer the conversation in the direction they intended or set the tone of the conversation. Kent explained how polite, initial, 'small talk' was eliminated with the application when calling a friend he usually called to coordinate 'hanging out together'. *Kent: It made the conversation go faster. There wasn't like that preliminary, where are you, what are you doing? (...) you know that stuff, the small talk that happens in the beginning, that was all eliminated, it was: I'm calling you for this reason, this is what I'm doing, this is where I am"*

Dustin explained how calling his mother eliminated the usual questions as to the subject of the call from her. *Dustin: The conversation usually, I felt like it was already in the conversation. As though there was no introduction. Like hi or why are you calling kind of. So it was (...) right into the conversation (...) based off either what the Subject <field> said or usually based on the subject we had a conversation.*

Yami explained that her boyfriend would open the conversation with the information she sent across, when he picked up her calls. *Yami: Oh, when I call him, yes, I will fill out these blanks <fields> and when he picks it up he will say - hey this is interesting. I know why you called me. I know how important this conversation is. And how your mood is now – it was at the time.*

Pam stated that what she revealed in her mood set the conversation mood with her boyfriend. *Pam: You know, because sometimes even without knowing what I'm going through he would just snap <at me> like I do too. So at least when he knows – that I said sad <in the mood field>, as soon as he picked up the call, he was like, "Why? Why are you sad? What happened?"*

Bob also spoke of an experience similar to Pam's, when he was feeling down, and called his friend Roger, a fellow undergraduate student. *Bob: I just put crabby and I'm like I was crabby on emotion. And we started talking over that.*

Likes and Dislikes of Application Interface

While the aim of the field study was not to assess *Telling Calls'* design with respect immediate usability and adoption, we report here on the reaction of users to the application as it helps us understand the information sharing process. The vast majority of participants reported frustration with not having the ability to use the tool with contacts who were not part of the study.

Adam: Yes, I can tell you a story in that. This guy was calling me and I didn't pick up that call. I was thinking like maybe – I didn't want to talk – he may be talking about some office stuff. I thought I will go home and then call him. And then Bob called and revealed through his phone <Telling Calls> that he was with this guy and that they wanted to go to NY clubbing. Then I called that guy back.

Pia: Yes, <I missed the tool> like a billion times...whenever somebody left me a message and I had to go and listen to my voicemail – I always thought it could have been nice if I had at least two parts of the tool, the subject and the mood.

Participants expressed different reactions to using the application, based on the role they played as a caller or a receiver. In general, participants preferred using the application to receiving as opposed to making calls. Many commented on the effectiveness of *Telling Calls* compared to regular voicemails and text messages. The frustrations of being a caller were related to the time and effort it took to enter information before making the call. This was not surprising given that our research prototype design focused on receiver's call handling based in information received.

Kevin: "Uh, I liked uh, when my friend called me and I can see uh his mood or importance but when I use this tool to call him, I don't like to type the words....I want to talk to him, I don't want to type a long time."

Tim: Yes the thing is (...) I liked I it more when I was the receiver than the caller because I can know everything without providing anything.

The record of a *Telling Call* was also valued. *Pia: I think another advantage <of Telling Calls> is that when I missed a call, I don't have to – or the other person too - they don't have to leave a message. We could just see what the call was about and call back.*

Participants also compared *Telling Calls* interface with that of text messaging, to highlight its advantages. Participants spoke about the ease of sending chunks of information, using fewer words than in a regular text message, as well as additional information shared, that made *Telling Calls* attractive.

Emi: Well if you're tired and drunk, you don't really want to type on the keyboard. Less words. Because of the way that it was broken up into different categories - like there was the mood, subject etc. So it's like if you're feeling sick, instead of writing the words - I feel sick today or I have the flu - you just have that green face show up.

Farah: Because here <in Telling Calls> subject, activity, location - you already had it broken down to the different fields. You know... you are really leaving out words. So it really is much quicker.

Greg: For text message, you have write down a whole sentence. For this one, just a few words. For example, just write location: classroom. That's it. You don't need to write down any subject. Just classroom and that's it. It lets you understand easier too.

Lata: <Telling Calls> basically is like one word or two words or at max, three words under the appropriate category. And everything mostly is selecting it. And, you know if I say lab in location, it makes sense. But text <messaging>, if I just say lab, what will a person understand? So, <this is a> very crisp way of giving information – and making the other person understand what you're trying to tell them. And that is good.

Participants also expressed the ease with which information was processed when received using *Telling Calls*, and valued the established categories to share information.

Emi: When I'm receiving it is kind of more focused - chunked pieces of information ...

Yami: So if he sends text message, he can't tell whether the text message is important or urgent. You will not know whether he is happy or not.

EXPERIENCE SAMPLING STUDY OF CALL HANDLING

The goal of the second study reported here, were:
1) To quantify the frequency and type of information callers wish to convey through *Telling Calls*. Such information should inform designers about information conveyance requirements, 2) Test if *Telling Calls* helped reduce the information gap that currently confronts individuals trying to make impromptu call handling decisions; 3) test if reducing information gap, influenced call handling decisions; and 4) if reducing information gap improved the quality of call handling decisions and increased grounding for conversations. These tests were operationalized through the following 3 hypotheses:

H1: When callers using *Telling Calls* provide receivers with additional information it reduces uncertainty about the call.

H2: The ratio of the number of information items that influence call response decision because they are unknown to number of items that influence call response decision because they are known will be higher without *Telling Calls* than with *Telling Calls*.

H3: The more information items known to the receiver the more accurately they will be able to predicted value of taking the call (PVC).

Method

Participants

Fifteen participant pairs (30 subjects), who were university students with existing AT&T mobile phone accounts, were recruited for the study through a university wide email announcement. Fourteen percent of the participants were employed full time and 24% part-time and the remaining 62% were unemployed. All participants were experienced users of mobile phones. Seventy-nine percent (79%) of the participants classified their study partners as friends, 14% as family, and 7% as spouse/partners.

Procedure

All subjects were given an AT&T Tilt smartphone running Windows Mobile 6 to use for 2 weeks, with their own SIM cards and service plans. In order to capture participants' experience regarding the utility of *Telling Calls in situ*, we used experience sampling methodology (ESM) [6]. The ESM survey was incorporated into *Telling Calls*, and when appropriate survey questions would pop up on the phone at the end of each call made or received using the application only with study participants.

In order to reduce order effect, the assignment of participants to handle calls under the two conditions (Regular Calls and *Telling Calls*) was counterbalanced. Participants of Group 1 started without the *Telling Calls* application (Regular Calls), and later switched to condition 2 where they used the *Telling Calls* application to handle calls. Participants of Group 2 started with handling calls using the *Telling Calls* application, and later switched to Condition 1 where they handled calls without the *Telling Calls* application (Regular Calls).

The survey questions varied in content, based on whether the call was incoming or outgoing. In this paper we focused on responses to the incoming calls, which were differentiated as a) answered calls, and b) ignored calls (missed intentionally). The survey was triggered and administered in the following situations: a) immediately after the end of an outgoing call, b) after the end of an incoming call that is answered, and c) immediately after the subject hits the ignore/silence button for an ignored call. If the survey was not to be answered immediately by the subject, the survey was programmed as a pending incomplete survey, for access and completion within 24 hours.

The ESM survey questions presented to call receivers varied, according to the call handling outcomes, namely, missed (unintentional), ignored (intentional), or answered. The survey questions addressed:

1) Which of the eight information items (caller, subject, location, activity, call length, urgency, importance and caller mood) they knew when they received the call.
2) Which items influenced their call response. They were also asked if not knowing any information item influenced their decision to answer or ignore the call. For example, did they ignore a call because they did not know what the call was about, or did they answer the call in order to find out?
3) Accuracy of the respondents predicted value of taking the call (PVC): Participants were asked how worthwhile they thought the call was both before they answered/ignored it (and after they answered it) and after they answered it, on a scale of 1-7, with 7 being worthwhile and 1 being worthless. They were also given a choice to report if they did not, or could not, evaluate the call's worth, before answering/ignoring the call. These perception values of the call, before and after a answering, were used to calculate the accuracy of the PVC.

Results

Due to minor software glitches, a total of 1628 ESM questionnaires were recorded as having been sent out, for the 1714 calls made as part of the study. Of these 1416 (93%) of the ESM survey questions were completed. Table 1 provides the distribution by call type. Tables 2 and 3 address which and how many information items were provided by callers through *Telling Calls*.

Hypothesis Tests

Hypotheses 1 through 3 all examine intentional calling handling decisions. As a result, our analysis is based on 268 Regular Calls (253 answered + 15 Ignored after seeing caller ID), and 131 *Telling Calls* without software glitch (129 answered and 2 ignored after seeing the incoming *Telling Calls* display). Of the 131 *Telling Calls*, 118 had one or more information item provided by the caller.

H1: When callers using Telling Calls provide receivers with additional information, it reduces uncertainty about the call.

Call Type	Regular Calls (N=914)	Telling Calls (N=502)
Answered	253 (28%)	173 (34%)
Ignored after examining caller information	15 (2%)	4 (1%)
Ignored without examining caller information	27 (3%)	18 (4%)
Missed Unintentionally	114 (12%)	59 (12%)
Outgoing	505 (55%)	248 (49%)

Table 1: Call type distribution

Information Items	Provided (N=248)
Subject	182 (73.4%)
Location	188 (75.8%)
Activity	129 (52.0%)
Call Length	109 (44.2%)
Who Caller Is With	111 (44.8%)
Urgency	121 (45.4%)
Importance	121 (48.8%)
Mood	122 (49.2%)

Table 2: Information Item Provision

No. of items Provided	Frequency (N=248)
0	23 (9.3%)
1	39 (15.7%)
2	14 (5.6%)
3	32 (12.9%)
4	20 (8.1%)
5	21 (8.5%)
6	16 (6.5%)
7	33 (13.3%)
8	50 (20.2%)

Table 3: Number Information Items Provided

As shown in Table 4 receivers reported knowing a call information item more when it was provided through *Telling Calls*, than with Regular Calls. The relatively lower uncertainty of information items with *Telling Calls* was further reduced when a particular item was provided.

H1 was tested by comparing certainty of information knowledge (when reported to be known) for three cases 1) Regular Calls 2) *Telling Calls* where information was received, and 3) *Telling Calls* where information was not received. As the number of Regular Calls per person ranged from 6 to 49, and the number of *Telling Calls* per person ranged from 1 to 49, the data was analyzed at the participant level, rather than at the call level. Responses were aggregated by the total number of calls per participant (30 participants), in the Regular Calls and the *Telling Calls* conditions. Wilcoxon's Signed–Rank test for two related samples showed that uncertainty was significantly less for *Telling Calls* for all information items when received. Further, with the exception of Activity information, no significant difference was seen in people's reported certainty of information item, when information was not received in *Telling Calls* and Regular Calls. Table 5 summarizes these results.

	Regular Calls (N=268)	**Telling Calls Info. Received**	**Telling Calls Info. Not Received**
Subject	29.5%	70.7% (N=99)	40.6% (N=32)
Location	26.9%	70.9% (N=103)	25.0% (N=28)
Activity	14.2%	58% (N= 69)	12.9% (N=62)
Call Length	3.4%	52.5% (N= 61)	7.1% (N=70)
Who Caller is With	6.7%	42.6% (N=61)	5.7% (N=70)
Urgency	7.1%	55.4% (N=56)	6.7% (N=75)
Importance	7.5%	50.0% (N=64)	10.4% (N=67)
Mood	11.2%	52.4% (N=63)	2.9% (N=68)

Table 4: Certainty of information received

	Regular Calls vs. *Telling Calls* with Info.	**Regular Calls vs. *Telling Calls* No. Info.**
Subject	Z= -3.66, p<.000, N=23	Z= -1.1, p<.273, N=4
Location	Z= -3.71, p<.000, N=23	Z= -1.6, p<.109, N=4
Activity	Z= -3.18, p<.001, N=15	Z= -1.48, p<.014, N=7
Call Length	Z= -3.31, p<.001, N=14	Z= -1.60, p<.109, N=3
Who Caller Is With	Z= -2.86, p<.004, N=11	Z= -1.45, p<.148, N=4
Urgency	Z= -3.47, p<.001, N=16	Z= -0.37, p<.715, N=4
Importance	Z= -3.41, p<.001, N=16	Z= -1.84, p<.066, N=4
Mood	Z= -3.12, p<.002, N=13	Z= -0.45, p<.655, N=2

Table 5: Wilcoxon's Signed-Rank Test for uncertainty in Regular vs. Telling Calls

H2: *The ratio of the number of information items that influence call response decision because they are unknown to number of items that influence call response decision because they are known will be higher without Telling Calls than with Telling Calls.*

Consistent with the Hypothesis H2, Wilcoxon's Signed-Rank test showed that, for each caller, the ratio of unknown to known information items that influenced call response decisions were significantly higher in Regular Calls than in *Telling Calls* (Z=-2.133, p<0.033, N=20). Thus, with *Telling Calls* the influence of the unknown information was less on call handling decisions, than in Regular Calls

H3: *The more information items known to the receiver the more accurately s/he will be able to predicted value of taking the call (PVC).*

We excluded 44 answered *Telling Calls* where information was not received due to technical failure. Among the 382 answered calls (253 Regular Calls and 129 *Telling calls*), PVC was reported to be 'could not evaluate' for 1 call and 'did not evaluate' for 13 calls. For the remaining 368 calls, accuracy of the PVC was calculated by taking the absolute value of the difference between the value perceived before answering the call, to the value perceived after answering and ending the call. Consistent with hypothesis H3, a positive and significant correlation was found between the number of information items known, and the accuracy of PVC for all calls (Spearman's Rho= 0.121 p≤0.02, N= 369). This correlation was significant for *Telling Calls* in isolation (Spearman's Rho= 0.184 P≤0.040, N= 125), but not significant for Regular Calls analyzed in isolation (Spearman's Rho= 0.106, P=0.100, N= 244) as hypothesized.

DISCUSSION AND CONCLUSION

The results from the two field studies provided significant insight into how to alternative information exchange mechanisms could facilitate mobile phone conversation grounding and management. The data collected from the semi-structured interviews as well as usage statistics provide insights on what information callers are interested in providing, what information receivers are interested in knowing for call handling decisions and how both parties use this information to ground a conversation.

It was seen that a variety of information was used in placing *Telling Calls* (Tables 2 and 3) based on the data from the interviews as well as the ESM study. Receivers welcomed the additional information and used it to help them make their decision to answer the call (as indicated by Hypothesis 2). However, in our interviews we did not find a consistent set of fields that were used by all users. Call length, urgency, and importance tended by used under specific circumstances, such as when the caller felt that the receiver would need additional information to convince him/her to answer or to steer the call in a particular direction. They also tended to use the fields that were important to their decision making at time the call was coming in, e.g., while at work or driving using the urgency field to determine to answer or not. We also learned that receivers were able to use one or two fields of data to infer a great deal of information about the incoming call. This was influenced by the nature of caller-receiver relationship. For example knowing location informed participants about the call length and subject. Mood was primarily used by pairs who were in a romantic relationship or comprised of female-female friend relationships. Further, it is seen that routine and stable information was of no use, or even interest to receivers such as location information from someone not usually mobile or call length information from someone who only made short calls. However, they often desired and used dynamic call information, this is consistent with previous studies on people's social information needs [15]. While relationship type had an impact on the type of information shared, it did not impact on the overall utility for receivers of additional call information. It would be interesting to further explore the nuances of information sharing choices based on relationships in future studies.

Perhaps most importantly, the qualitative study illustrated how information provided by the caller through *Telling Calls*, helped call recipients make call handling decisions by reducing uncertainty as to what the call was about and establishing common ground. This was verified by the first two hypotheses tested in the ESM study where 1) Wilcoxon's Signed–Rank test showed that uncertainty was less when a Telling Call item was displayed as opposed regular calls (Table 5); and 2) that user used their greater certainty derived from information provided by the caller to make their call handling decisions (H2). More importantly, Table 5 shows that there was no statistically significant difference between Regular Calls and *Telling Calls*, when information was not provided in *Telling Calls*. This rules out any artifact effect one may fear to find, and confirms that it is the provision of explicit information that is important in reducing uncertainty.

Further participants reported that they would use the data provided by the caller as the basis for the subsequent conversation. This is an important finding because it highlights that it is possible to provide conversation grounding support for calls through *Telling Calls*. Interestingly, this applied both to callers who felt they were able to more efficiently direct the conversation in the desired direction and receivers who felt that they understood more clearly how the conversation was expected to proceed. This was particularly the case with the conveyance of emotional information or where a short focused conversation was desired. For example, changing the initial greeting response to sound more professional when answering a call from someone who indicated they are at work and are around other people or softening their tone to someone in distress. We did not see any evidence of manipulation and abuse of call information fields, probably because the study was between individuals who had established levels of interpersonal trust. Further studies exploring this issue of trust among less close relationships would be of value. The quantitative study also supported the notion that *Telling Calls* helped users make more accurate call handling decisions by helping ground the process of negotiating interaction commitment. This was seen from the results of our third hypothesis test that showed how the caller supplied information through *Telling Calls*, helped users more accurately predict the value of engaging in a conversation. We believe that together these findings highlight the ability of *Telling Calls* to efficiently help parties gain common ground.

We found that users liked the persistence of the information from the call history and likened it to how they would similarly refer back to text messages and IMs. But interestingly they viewed *Telling Calls* as a much more efficient way initiate interaction commitment than text messages because the information was already broken into separate fields. They reported that it was necessary to type in much fewer words as a caller and as a receiver were able to quickly scan the separate fields that they were interested in. This is an important finding since it highlights the utility of this type of system versus using standard text messaging or IMs for the outeraction process.

Apart from usage statics and interview responses that indicated that participants liked using *Telling Calls*, it was further highlighted when most subjects reported wanting to use it on occasions to call non-study participants. However, they also reported that they preferred using the system as a receiver than a caller. The reason for this was reported to be their dislike of the effort required to input information when making calls. This brings to light the effort-benefit conflict for callers [12,19], who, on one hand, value the increased chance of having effective and focused conversations and, on the other hand, need to make an effort ahead of time by filling in the appropriate information to enable them. The implications for designers are to consider alternate forms of input styles and minimizing the burden of data entry. Further, designers should also consider automatic capture of caller information, such as location and activity using sensor technology, minimizing the user burden of providing such information.

To summarize, in this paper we explored how to facilitate mobile phone conversation grounding and management. We did this by designing and testing a mobile phone application that allowed callers to provide call information to receivers. We found that this new affordance helped callers steer conversations in the desired direction. It also helped receivers make more satisfactory call handling decisions and adapt their initial responses to calls based on the provided information. We also found making a history of what a phone call was about available helped to ground future conversations. Our findings are important because they highlight the need for the exploration of alternative designs for mobile phone conversation management.

ACKNOWLEDGEMENTS

This research was partially supported by the National Science Foundation Grant NSF CNS 0454081 and DST 0534520. The opinions expressed are those of the authors and may not reflect those of the NSF.

REFERENCES

1. Avrahami, D., Gergle, D., Hudson, S. E., & Kiesler, S. (2007). Improving the match between callers and

receivers: A study on the effect of contextual information on cell phone interruptions. Behaviour & Information Technology, 26(3), 247-259

2. Battestini, A., Setlur, V., and Sohn, T., (2010). A large scale study of text-messaging use. Proceedings of MobileHCI , pp. 229-238.
3. Begole, J. B., Matsakis, N. E., and Tang, J. C.: "Lilsys: Sensing Unavailability"; Proc. CSCW '04, ACM Press, New York, USA (2004), 511–514
4. Bentley, F. R., & Metcalf, C. J. (2008). Location and activity sharing in everyday mobile communication. Proc. CHI '08 (EA) (pp. 2453-2462). ACM Press.
5. Clark, H. H. & Brennan, S. E. (1991). Grounding in communication. In L. B. Resnick, R. M. Levine, & S. D. Teasley (Eds.). Perspectives on socially shared cognition (pp. 127-149).
6. Csikszentmihalyi, M., & Larson, R. (1987). Validity and Reliability of the Experience Sampling Method. Journal of Nervous and Mental Disease, 175(9), 526–536.
7. Dabbish, L. A. (2006). Coordinating Initiation and Response in Computer-Mediated Communication. Unpublished PhD Dissertation, CMU.
8. De Guzman, E. S., Sharmin, M., & Bailey, B. P. (2007). Should I call now? Understanding what context is considered when deciding whether to initiate remote communication via mobile devices. In C. G. Healey & E. Lank (Eds.), Proceedings of Graphics Interface 2007 (GI 2007) (Vol. 143-150).
9. Grandhi, S. A., Schuler, R. P., & Jones, Q. (2009). To answer or not to answer: that is the question for cell phone users. CHI '09 (EA). ACM Press.
10. Gergle, D., Millen, D. R., Kraut, R. E., & Fussell, S. R. (2004). Persistence Matters: Making the Most of Chat in Tightly-Coupled Work. Proc. CHI'04 (pp. 431-438). ACM Press.
11. Grinter, R. and Eldridge, M. Wan2tlk?: everyday text messaging. Proc. CHI'03 (pp. 441-448). ACM Press.
12. Grudin, J. (1987). Social evaluation of the user interface: Who does the work and who gets the benefit? In H. Bullinger & B. Shackel (Eds.), Proc. INTERACT'87, 2nd IFIP Conference on Human-Computer Interaction (Stuttgart, FRG) (pp. 805-811). Stuttgart, North-Holland, Amsterdam.
13. Ho, J., & S., I. (2005). Using context-aware computing to reduce the perceived burden of interruptions from mobile devices. Proc. CHI'05 (pp. 909-918). ACM Press.
14. Horvitz, E., P., K., R., S., Apacible, J., & Subramani, M. (2005). Bayesphone: Precomputation of context-sensitive policies for inquiry and action in mobile devices. Proceedings of 10th International Conference (UM 2005) (Vol. 251-260). Berlin: Springer-Verlag.
15. Jones, Q., Grandhi, S., Whittaker, S., Chivakula, K., & Terveen, L. (2004). Putting Systems into Place: A Qualitative Study of Design Requirements for Location-Aware Community Systems. Proc. CSCW 2004. ACM Press.
16. Klein, H. K & Myers, M. D. (1999). A Set of Principles for Conducting and Evaluating Interpretive Field Studies in Information Systems. MIS Quarterly, 23(1), 67-95.
17. Ling, R. The Sociolinguistics of SMS: An Analysis of SMS Use by a Random Sample of Norwegians. In Mobile Communications. 2005, 335-349.
18. McFarlane, D. C & Latorella, K. A. (2002). The scope and importance of human interruption in human-computer interaction design. Human-Computer Interaction, 17(1), 1-61.
19. Milewski, A. (2006). Interruption Management and Telephone Call Screening. International Journal of Human Computer Interaction, 20(1), 19-33.
20. Milewski, A.E. and Smith, T.M., Providing Presence Cues to Telephone Users. Proc. CSCW 2000 (pp. 89-96)
21. Nardi, B. A., Whittaker, S., & Bradner, E. (2000). Interaction and outeraction: Instant messaging in action. Proc. CSCW 2002 (pp. 79-88). ACM Press.
22. Nelson, L., Bly, S., Sokoler, T., (2002). Quiet Calls: Talking Silently on Mobile Phones. Proc. CHI'02: (pp. 174-181).
23. Norman, D.A. (1988). The Psychology of Everyday Things. New York: Basic Books.
24. Pedersen, E. R. (2001). Calls.Calm: Enabling Caller and Callee to Collaborate. Proc. CHI'01 (EA). ACM Press.
25. Pering, C. (2002). Taming of the ring: context specific social mediation for communication devices. Extended Proceedings of CHI 2002 (pp. 712-713).
26. Pratt, M. G. (2008). Fitting oval pegs into round holes: Tensions in evaluating and publishing qualitative research in top-tier North American journals. Organizational Research Methods, 11(3), 481-509.
27. Schiano, D., Elliott, A., and Bellotti, V. A Look at Tokyo Youth at Leisure: Towards the Design of New Media to Support Leisure Outings. Computer Supported Cooperative Work (CSCW) 16, 1 (2007), 45-73.
28. Whittaker, S., Jones, Q., and Terveen, L., Contact management: identifying contacts to support long-term communication, Proc. CSCW 2002
29. Wiberg, M., & Whittaker, S. (2005). Managing availability: Supporting lightweight negotiations to handle interruptions. ACM Transactions on Computer-Human Interaction (TOCHI), 12(4), 356-387.
30. Woodruff A., and Aoki. P.M., "How Push-to-Talk Makes Talk Less Pushy." Proc. GROUP 2003

Deep Shot: A Framework for Migrating Tasks Across Devices Using Mobile Phone Cameras

Tsung-Hsiang Chang *
MIT CSAIL
vgod@mit.edu

Yang Li
Google Research
yangli@acm.org

ABSTRACT
A user task often spans multiple heterogeneous devices, e.g., working on a PC in the office and continuing the work on a laptop or a mobile phone while commuting on a shuttle. However, there is a lack of support for users to easily migrate their tasks across devices. To address this problem, we created Deep Shot, a framework for capturing the user's work state that is needed for a task (e.g., the specific part of a webpage being viewed) and resuming it on a different device. In particular, Deep Shot supports two novel and intuitive interaction techniques, *deep shooting* and *deep posting*, for pulling and pushing work states, respectively, using a mobile phone camera. In addition, Deep Shot provides a concise API for developers to leverage its services and make their application states migratable. We demonstrated that Deep Shot can be used to support a range of everyday tasks migrating across devices. An evaluation consisting of a series of experiments showed that our framework and techniques are feasible.

Author Keywords
Multi-device environment, mobile interaction, camera, computer vision, task migration.

ACM Classification Keywords
H5.2 [Information interfaces and presentation]: User Interfaces: Input Devices and Strategies, Interaction Styles.

General Terms
Design, Human Factors

INTRODUCTION
The landscape of personal computing has shifted from one computer per user to multiple heterogeneous devices per user [7]. To carry out an everyday task, such as finding a restaurant for dinner, a user often switches from one device to another according to the situation. For example, a user has looked up the directions to the restaurant on her PC at home but then redoes the search on her phone for navigation in her car. A recent study found that this and other common tasks, such as email and web browsing, were the source of the most frustration while switching between different devices [12].

Figure 1. A user takes a picture of the screen of her computer and then sees the application with the current state on her phone. Our system recognizes the application that the user is looking through the camera, automatically migrates it onto the mobile phone, and recovers its state.

The lack of tool support for migrating tasks across devices has also been pointed out by several previous studies. A survey [18] conducted in 1997 showed that 62.9% of people stated they transferred information for completing a task on other devices "by hand", i.e., reading a text string on a display and typing it on another computer. A non-trivial number of people transferred data through shared files, FTP, or emails. Surprisingly, a more recent study in 2008 [7] showed that people were still using these old-fashioned mechanisms plus emerging cloud services (e.g., Google Docs) to transfer information across devices. Although cloud services and ubiquitous access to the Internet seem to be an antidote, the study found people were still frustrated as they have to manually reconstruct their work state, e.g., opening and locating the part of a PDF article that was viewed on the previous computer to continue reading. Furthermore, moving between heterogeneous devices (e.g.,

* This work was conducted during an internship at Google Research.

a PC and a mobile phone) amplifies the task resumption overhead due to various contextual and resource constraints [2,3,12].

Prior work made substantial progress in providing more integrated user experience for task migration across devices (e.g., [8,15,16,19]). However, existing solutions are insufficient in two ways. First, prior work primarily focused on infrastructure for transferring data across devices, not user interaction. Compared to moving data or application windows around on a single computer by drag-and-drop, there is no similarly easy method for cross-device migration. Secondly, existing tools are mostly document-centric with little support for recovering a work state [2,3]. Manually recovering a work state requires users to deal with many details that can distract them from the task that they want to resume.

To address these issues, we present Deep Shot, a framework that supports task migration by allowing users to transfer not only documents but also application states across devices using a mobile phone camera. Deep Shot provides two novel camera-based interaction techniques, *deep shooting* and *deep posting*. These two techniques allow seamless and intuitive migration of user tasks from one device to another by one uniform operation: taking pictures.

Deep shooting allows a user to capture and to persist the *deep information*, i.e., the information behind the raw pixels, such as application states, with a camera-like mobile phone application in a single click (see Figure 1). The captured work state can be resumed immediately on the mobile phone, opened later, or migrated to another device with deep posting, which pushes deep information to a device with a camera as well.

To support deep shooting and deep posting, we created a framework, Deep Shot, for application developers to easily incorporate these techniques into their applications. It includes two key ideas. First, Deep Shot uses robust computer vision algorithms to identify what portion of the screen the user is looking at through the camera. We conducted two experiments to show the feasibility of this technology. Second, Deep Shot requires the applications to encode the deep information as Uniform Resource Identifiers (URIs) so that a task can be resumed even using different applications, such as viewing a Microsoft Outlook contact's information with a native Android application.

We make the following contributions in this paper:

- Deep shooting and posting: two novel techniques for pulling and pushing a task (information or application states) using a mobile phone camera.
- Deep Shot: a framework for developers to easily make their application states migratable across devices.

In the rest of the paper, we first clarify our motivation using a running example in which a user searches for a restaurant and discuss how Deep Shot supports this task by allowing a user to easily migrate the task across devices. Next, we discuss the design of our framework, and implementation details. We also show how developers can leverage our framework to enable deep shooting and posting in their applications. We then discuss the range of scenarios that Deep Shot can address. Finally, we describe an evaluation of our techniques and framework, and conclude with related and future work.

MOTIVATION

Here we discuss why it is important to address task migration across devices. Let us assume a user, Bob, is searching for a restaurant for dinner on Yelp at home. Bob has read several reviews of a restaurant on his desktop computer. He decides to try one restaurant and clicks on the map on the review page to read the driving directions. Everything is going smoothly until he needs to leave home and move the directions to his mobile phone for navigation in his car. How can Bob open the same region of the map on his phone?

Bob could manually type the restaurant's address or name and search on the phone. Or he could click "Link" on Google Maps to get a bookmarkable URL of the current region, and email that URL to himself so that he can look for the email and open the URL in it on his phone later. These approaches generally require the user to perform two steps: 1) *inspecting* the internal state of the application, e.g., the URL, and 2) *copying* it by hand or via a temporary medium, e.g., a file or an email, from one device to another.

The inspecting step varies widely depending on the applications. In a web page or web application, the Uniform Resource Locator (URL) on the address bar often represents the application state that a user intends to transfer. However, in many web applications using Ajax, the URL no longer represents the current state of the application. A user is often required to perform extra steps to retrieve the real "bookmarkable" URL, such as what Bob would do in Google Maps. However, many Ajax and desktop applications do not have a URL that represents what the user is viewing and working on. Tools have been developed to overcome this problem by recording the commands needed to return a page [10]. However, a desktop application's state is generally inaccessible by end users.

The copying step requires a user to either manually re-enter the information on another device, e.g., when transferring a small piece of information such as a short URL or the name of a landmark, or understand and deal with low-level operations such as how to save information in files and use file transferring software.

Anecdotally, people often take a picture of a particular region of interest (ROI) on the monitor using a camera, which is generally available on modern mobile phones. This method utilizes the camera as a physical tool to directly inspect and copy the information at the same time. In Bob's scenario, he could capture the portion of the map he needs in one simple step, i.e., taking a picture. This method is simple, independent of the application the user is using, and avoids many of the hassles of manual inspection and copying. However, it is limited in that information being transferred is encoded in raw pixels and will not allow a user to perform further interaction, e.g., panning or zooming a map.

DEEP SHOOTING & POSTING

Inspired by the picture-shooting metaphor above, we designed and implemented deep shooting and posting, two novel techniques that are as simple to perform as taking a picture, but copy *deep information* behind the raw pixels of the captured region, that is, the application state.

With deep shooting (see Figure 1), Bob can copy a specific region of the map displayed on his computer's screen to his mobile phone by simply taking a picture of it with the phone's camera. The same region is then shown on the phone automatically. More importantly, the captured map remains interactive on the mobile phone. In other words, Bob can pan the map to see the area that is not originally captured by the camera, or zoom in to see more details of the streets.

Based on the picture captured with deep shooting, our system automatically identifies the captured area on the screen and the front-most application containing that area. Our system then pulls information from the application and sends it to the mobile phone that took the picture. The information is encoded as a URI, which has been accepted as a standard way to launch applications on contemporary mobile operating systems such as Apple iOS and Android. Therefore, the user can view or manipulate the extracted information on the mobile phone with native applications.

As a complement to deep shooting, deep posting allows a user to push information from a mobile phone to another device. Let us assume Bob has opened the restaurant review page on his mobile phone to write a review, but soon decides he would rather continue this task on his desktop computer, where it is easier to type. To do so, Bob aims the mobile phone camera at the computer screen with the review page still shown on the phone. Once deep posting is activated (e.g., via a hot-button on the phone), the review page becomes semi-transparent so that the user can see through it and know which part of the screen he is targeting at. Based on the screen region as seen through the camera, once Bob confirms, deep posting identifies the intended computer screen and automatically opens the same review page on it.

Deep posting employs the same mechanism as deep shooting in identifying the target computer screen and the specific region on the screen that the user sees through the camera. However, unlike the deep shooting, deep posting does not need to identify which application the user is looking at, since the application for handling the information being posted may not be running.

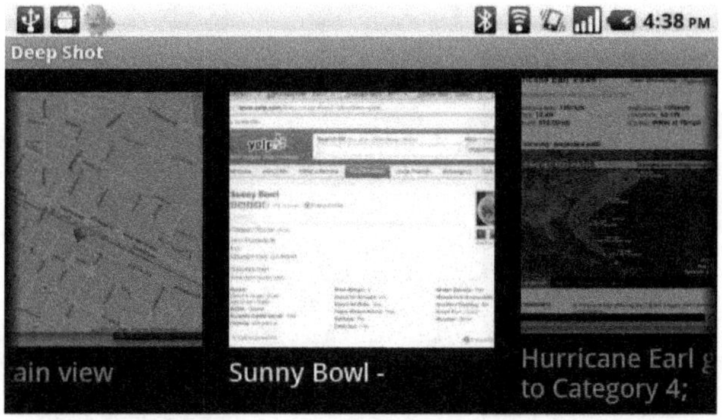

Figure 2. The Deep Shot gallery allows a user to quickly launch an application with a previously captured work state. A user can flip left or right on the touch screen to browse the gallery.

The deep shooting application running on the mobile phone maintains the history of deep shots that a user has taken. Similar to browsing photos in a photo gallery application, a user can browse all of his deep shots (see Figure 2). Each shot in this gallery shows the title and the thumbnail of the captured application. With the gallery, a user can directly launch a desired application with its captured state on the phone. The gallery provides a simple interface for users to manage their tasks and switch between them.

Currently, the Deep Shot framework is designed for migrating tasks across personal devices. Thus, before using deep shooting or posting, a user needs to log into a remote server with the user's credential on each personal device, and the credentials can be stored in the devices thereafter. Therefore, this authentication step only needs to be performed once for each device. We will discuss the possibilities of eliminating the authentication process in the Future Work section.

THE DEEP SHOT FRAMEWORK

To support deep shooting and posting, we designed the underlying Deep Shot framework with two goals in mind. First, from the user's perspective, deep shooting and posting should be as easy to use as taking a picture with an ordinary camera. Therefore, the user should not have to do any network configuration beforehand nor pair any devices to use Deep Shot. Second, from the developer's perspective, the Deep Shot framework should be easy to integrate with her applications. Developers should not need to worry about the communication between devices nor understand how to detect what portion of screen the user is looking at through the camera.

To achieve these goals, we have to carefully choose the technologies for the link layer and the network layer. Many options exist for the link-layer technologies, such as IrDA, USB, FireWire, Ethernet, Bluetooth and WiFi. We chose WiFi/Ethernet for their ubiquity on almost all devices and then we can utilize the standard TCP/IP stacks. For the network layer, device discovery and association are still challenging obstacles today. Since we want to focus on migration across personal devices, we decided to base our

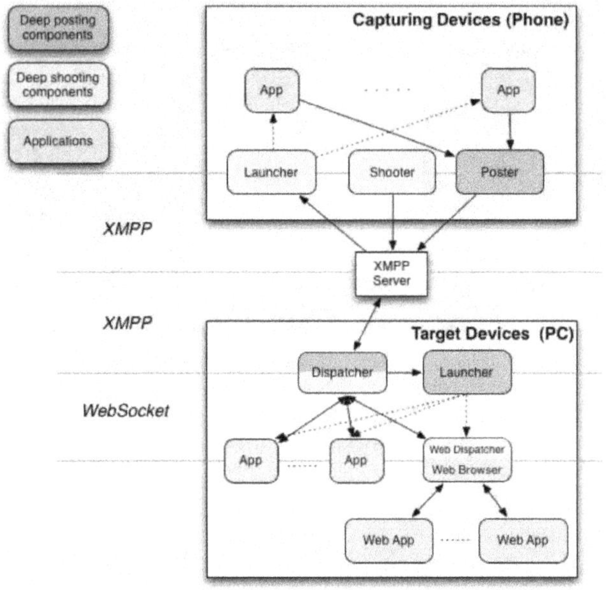

Figure 3. The system architecture of Deep Shot. Solid lines represent direct messages between components, whereas dotted lines represents the launching signal sent from the launcher.

framework on an instant messaging (IM) architecture, which was previously used in cross-device infrastructures such as PIE [16]. Thus, we can build on top of standard TCP/IP and avoid the problems of dynamic IP addresses, private IP addresses behind Network Address Translation (NAT) gateways, and firewalls that block connections from the outside. However, this architecture requires an authentication step before using our system. Fortunately, authentication only needs to be performed once for each device and does not add any cost for using Deep Shot thereafter.

We chose Extensible Messaging and Presence Protocol (XMPP), also known as Jabber, for our IM protocol. One reason is that XMPP supports logging in with the same user account from multiple different devices. A user account with a device has a unique identifier of the form "user@server/device." This allows users to set up all of their devices with the same user name. Since XMPP can list all of a user's presences across devices, users do not have to manually add their devices into their contact list. Also, the size of a XMPP message is not limited, which means we can send relatively large data, e.g., a JPEG photo, through a typical message packet without hacking the protocol.

System Components

Deep Shot's architecture is shown in Figure 3. The pink components are required for deep posting, whereas the yellow ones are required for deep shooting. There are five roles in our system: a *shooter,* a *poster,* a *dispatcher, launchers* and *applications (apps)*. The shooter and the poster only run on a *capturing device*, e.g., a mobile phone equipped with a camera. The dispatcher runs on a *target device*, which accepts a deep shooting or posting request from a capturing device. The launchers run on both sides of the system. On the capturing device, the launcher launches mobile applications to recover a work state captured by deep shooting, whereas on the target device it launches desktop applications to present a work state that is posted by deep posting.

Protocol Design

Here we describe the protocols between each pair of system components. To simplify the design of our protocols, the messages exchanged among all components are structured and encoded in the JavaScript Object Notation (JSON) key-value pairs. Besides, all binary data, e.g. images, are encoded in Base64 so we can include them in standard XMPP messages.

Deep Shooting: Shooter-Dispatcher Protocol

Once a user uses the shooter to take a picture of the region of interest on a computer monitor, an XMPP message with the picture and a subject *deepshot.req* indicating a deep shooting request is sent to each available device.

When the dispatchers running on the target devices receive the request message, they immediately take a screenshot of the entire screen of their devices. Each dispatcher then matches the picture it receives against the screenshot. The matching algorithms locate the region that the user was looking at through the camera. Then the dispatcher sends a new message with the x-y coordinates of the corners of the region and the central point of the region to the front-most application overlapping the center point, through a WebSocket connection.

After the application has handled the message and returned a response, the dispatcher inserts the application name, and the thumbnail of the matched region on the screenshot. Both are useful for browsing the deep shooting history on the capturing device. Finally, the dispatcher sends the response to the shooter via the XMPP server.

Deep Shooting: Application-Dispatcher Protocol

The dispatcher is designed as a daemon that always runs in the background on all personal devices. The dispatcher has the user's credentials, so it is always connected to the XMPP server. Therefore, any device can obtain the availability of any other device from the XMPP server.

The dispatcher communicates with each application using a dedicated WebSocket connection. WebSocket is a new protocol that supports full-duplex and bi-directional communication over a TCP socket. We choose WebSocket for two reasons. First, it is being standardized by the IETF and W3C, and modern browsers already support WebSocket. Thus, we can easily implement a browser extension as a second-level dispatcher for web applications. Second, since the traditional TCP socket is the most pervasive inter-process communication (IPC) mechanism, and WebSocket is a simple extension of TCP sockets, traditional desktop applications can support it easily.

Each time an application that supports Deep Shot is launched, it registers itself with the dispatcher through a

WebSocket connection on a TCP port. A registration process starts after the standard WebSocket handshaking. The application sends out a registration message with its name. If the dispatcher accepts the registration, it returns an OK message, or else it returns a decline message indicating the reason and closes the connection. To support deep posting, an application sends the command "accept *URI_SCHEME*", which indicates what types of URI schemes it accepts. For example, an email client can register the "mailto:" scheme, and a web browser can register the "http:" and "https:" schemes. Once the registration is completed, this WebSocket connection should be kept persistent until the application is closed so the dispatcher can proactively notify the application when a request is coming.

Once an application has dealt with the dispatcher's request, it replies with a message consisting of at least a URI that encodes the state of the application or the information to expose. If needed, the application can attach offline resources or files in the response message. Each attached file is stored in a JSON structure with the file name and the content of the file.

Deep Shooting: Dispatcher-Launcher Protocol

After the dispatcher receives a reply message from the application, it routes that message with a subject "*deepshot.resp*" back to the capturing device that sent out the request.

On the capturing device, a launcher waits for the "*deepshot.resp*" messages. Once a response message arrives, the launcher decodes the message and writes all attachments to the storage on the device. Finally, it opens an appropriate application that handles the URI replied from the target device to recover the work state and resume the task flow.

Deep Posting Protocol

The deep posting protocol is based on the same foundation we used in deep shooting, including JSON structures and XMPP communication. The key role in our system for deep posting is the *poster* that runs on a capturing device. The poster accepts requests from the applications that support our Deep Shot framework. The posting requests should consist of at least a URI representing the internal state of the application.

Once the poster receives a posting request from an application, it opens the camera and overlaps the screenshot of the application on the viewfinder so that a user can see the target device and the information to post at the same time. After the user has confirmed the target device through the viewfinder, the poster creates a "*deeppost.req*" message with the picture taken by the camera and the request from the application. Finally, this message is sent to all available devices, in the same way as deep shooting.

After the dispatchers running on the user's other devices receive the "*deeppost.req*" message, each of them runs the same vision algorithm used for deep shooting to match the picture taken by the user against its screenshot. If a dispatcher finds a match, it routes the request to the launcher.

As we mentioned before, applications register the types of URI schemes they support. The deep posting launcher requires this information to launch an appropriate application for the given URI in the request. Each application may register multiple URI schemes. If a URI scheme can be accepted by multiple applications, the launcher either opens a dialog so the user can choose an application or just launches a previously specified default application.

Screen Matching Algorithms

Once a device receives a Deep Shot request, it takes a screenshot of the entire monitor. It then extracts visual features from the screenshot and the picture taken by the camera, using a computer vision algorithm, Speeded-Up Robust Features (SURF) [4]. SURF is robust against scaling and rotation, and faster and more robust than Scale-Invariant Feature Transform (SIFT), another popular feature extraction algorithm.

We use SURF to detect the key points, which are represented by feature vectors, on the screenshot and on the picture respectively (see Figure 4). We then compute the cosine similarity between each pair of key points and find the nearest neighbor for each point. Finally, with the paired key points, a homography (the perspective transformation between two planes) can be calculated to find the projective plane on the screen image. Thus, the region of the screen that the user sees through the camera can be located.

Content and State Encoding

A migration process of an application consists of transferring not only its content but also its states. With our framework, developers can store arbitrary offline content, e.g., files, as an attachment in a Deep Shot request and encode the application states into a URI. A URI is the key element to resuming a work state in Deep Shot. A URI can be application independent. For instance, "content://contacts/15" opens a contact manager to show the person with the id 15; "geo:*latitude,longitude*" shows the given location in a map application; and "document://chi2011.pdf/3" represents the third page of the file "chi2011.pdf". Furthermore, developers can append the zoom level, the scrolling position, and all necessary information of this document to the URI as needed. We do not limit the length of a URI so arbitrary states of an application can be encoded.

Recently, some application frameworks such as Three20 (http://three20.info) have started to support URL-based navigation in traditional applications. Mobile operating systems such as Android and iOS also support launching applications with standard URIs (e.g., http:, tel: and geo:). Deep Shot allows applications to create their own URIs,

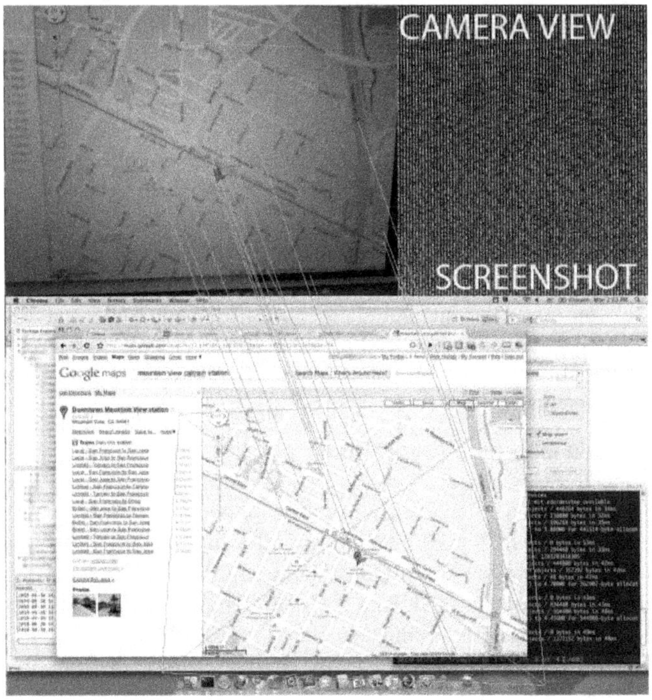

Figure 4. The screen matching algorithms match the picture (at the top) against the screenshot (at the bottom) and find a projective plane (the orange convex) on it.

although it is advisable to be compatible with public standards.

Bootstrapping with a Default Responder

To handle the work state of various applications, the Deep Shot framework, needs to be integrated into those applications by their developers. To deploy such a framework, we need to address how to bootstrap its usage when application developers have not yet adopted the framework. Therefore, we implemented a default responder in the dispatcher to handle the case in which the target application does not support Deep Shot.

If the application that the user is taking a photo of is not registered with the dispatcher, the default responder replies the screenshot of the entire screen to the capturing device as well as the coordinates of the matched region. Therefore, users can acquire a clear version of the screen, i.e., without any noise and distortion caused by the physical camera. They can also zoom in to see more detail and pan to other parts of the screen that were not in the original picture. In addition, as the dispatcher takes the screenshot, it also detects clickable URLs and information of interest such as phone numbers or addresses, using the operating system's accessibility API. These metadata are also transferred along with the screenshot, so the user can tap on a URL or a phone number on the screenshot to launch a browser or dial the number directly.

Supporting Web and Desktop Applications

Deep Shot is a general framework that supports traditional desktop applications as well as web applications. We discuss how Deep Shot supports these two kinds of applications in this section.

Most modern web applications are written in JavaScript and run inside a web browser, while their data are stored on remote servers. To further bootstrap the Deep Shot framework and support this kind of application, we created a *web dispatcher*, implemented as a Google Chrome browser extension, which has three important features.

First, the web dispatcher acts as a second-level dispatcher. It routes messages from the first-level dispatcher to the appropriate web page and sends reply messages back (see Figure 3).

Second, the web dispatcher is a default responder for all web applications that do not support Deep Shot. If the web dispatcher gets a request asking for data from a site that does not register itself with Deep Shot (discussed in a later section), it will only return the URL to that site as a default response. The URL on the address bar often maps to the state of the current web application. However, some Ajax applications do not have this property or hides their real URL on purpose. Fortunately, the last feature of our dispatcher addresses this problem.

Last, the web dispatcher can inject a script into a web application that allows Deep Shot to extract the application's state, without the application knowing about Deep Shot. This is possible because, as a browser extension, the web dispatcher is capable of injecting any content into any web page from the browser.

In addition to web applications, desktop applications could be more difficult to migrate since their developers need to make additional effort to encode the application states into a URI. Fortunately, most mobile versions of a desktop application are simplified and only provide the key features on the mobile devices. This means the developers do not need to encode the complete state of their applications, but can focus on a small set of key states. For example, the key states of a word processor may only consist of the cursor position, the zoom level, and the scrolling position of the document. The other states, such as the view mode and the toolbar's style, could be unimportant because the mobile word processor does not have these adjustable features.

IMPLEMENTATION

We implemented Deep Shot to support both deep shooting and posting. On the mobile side, we chose the Android platform and implemented the system in Java on a Google Nexus One phone. On the other side, we implemented the dispatcher and the launcher in Python on a laptop computer. We also set up a XMPP server using Jabber on a Linux machine. Besides disabling the message size limit in Jabber's default configuration, we did not modify Jabber.

DEVELOPING DEEP SHOT EXTENSIONS

To minimize the effort for developers to incorporate Deep Shot into their applications, we created a Java library that implements the dispatcher-application protocol and hides the WebSocket connection inside the library.

The library has a DeepShot class that has one public method, `void addListener(Listener listener, String app_name, String[] accepted_uris)`, for applications to register themselves to listen to Deep Shot requests. The `Listener` interface has only one method, `DeepShot.Response onShot(DeepShot.Request req)`, where the `Response` contains a URI and optional file attachments, and the `Request` contains the four corner points and the center point of the ROI. Deep posting also has a similar API, `void post(DeepPost.Request req)` in a class DeepPost, where `DeepPost.Request` contains a URI and optional file attachments.

For web developers, we also provides a JavaScript function, `DeepShot.addListener(listener)`, from a browser extension, so web developers can simply hook their web applications into Deep Shot. For example, Google Maps does not show the URL of the current region of the map in the address bar. To extract the real URL of the current map, we inject the following script:

```
if(window.DeepShot){
  DeepShot.addListener(function(request){
   return {"uri": document.getElementById("link").href};
  });
}
```

With this script, even if Google Maps does not support Deep Shot, users can still use deep shooting to open any computer map on their phone.

SCENARIOS

In this section, we illustrate four typical scenarios that can be accomplished by deep shooting and posting.

Scenario 1: Taking information to go (PC to mobile phone)

This is the classic scenario that motivated us to develop deep shooting. People usually work on desktop computers or laptops at work or home. Before moving to another place, they may look up the information related to that place on their computers. However, as the information may be hard to remember, they often write down the information on a piece of paper or look up the same information again on their mobile phones. In this scenario, people can take the information with them using deep shooting. For example, people could carry a part of a map or the address of the next meeting place so that they do not need to look it up again. People could even capture a YouTube video being played and later resume watching the video from where they left off on a mobile phone.

Scenario 2: Viewing or saving mobile phone content on PCs (mobile phone to PC)

People generate various kinds of lightweight information on mobile phones, such as photos, contacts, or unfinished readings. For lightweight tasks, such as transferring a photo in a phone to a PC so that more people can see it, using existing software tools for syncing up mobile phones with PCs is cumbersome (e.g., a user might need to plug in the cable and find the right folder). With deep posting, users can simply aim their camera at the target computer monitor with the photo still shown on the mobile phone. The photo will be automatically transferred and opened on the target monitor. Deep posting also allows an application to post information at a specific position and size, as seen through the camera, on the target screen, e.g., a Post It application, which cannot be achieved by Bluetooth-based sync tools.

Scenario 3: Using mobile phones as a bridge between PCs (PC to PC via a mobile phone)

USB flash drives are widely used to share files among computers. People are used to saving the information they want to share as files onto a USB drive, and then taking the drive to another computer. In this kind of scenario, deep shooting can be used to extract information from an application (e.g., running on an office PC) and automatically transfer it to a mobile device. The user can then take this mobile device to a home PC and post the extracted information or work states onto it with deep posting.

Scenario 4: Sharing content between mobile phones (mobile phone to mobile phone)

Although it is still rare to share information between multiple personal mobile devices, it is common to share information between mobile phones owned by different people. Researchers have developed techniques to address this need. For example, bumping is a synchronous gesture to connect two mobile devices [9]. Although the current Deep Shot framework does not support communication between multiple users' devices, deep shooting and posting can be used to locate the devices as well as the region of information to share across multiple users. For example, a user could take a picture of a contact displayed on another person's mobile phone with deep shooting, and then the full contact information would be automatically transferred to our phone. This scenario potentially requires a different authentication mechanism though.

USABILITY ANALYSIS AND TECHNICAL EVALUATION

We analyze and evaluate this work from three perspectives. From a user's perspective, we analyze the interaction model and the usability of deep shooting and posting. From a developer's perspective, we analyze the usability and the utility of the API that we provide for developers. Lastly, from a technical perspective, we evaluate the performance of our framework and the feasibility of using a camera to locate a region on a monitor.

Interaction Model and Usability Analysis

Traditional GUI applications on PCs provides an action such as "send this to ..." in their menus to let users send local files to remote devices. However, we argue this model is less intuitive than the deep shooting and posting. For the same task of migrating applications across devices, in the traditional model, a user would need to select the source application, the data of interest, and the target device from a list of names or identifiers in multiple steps with a GUI, which can distract the user from the task. In contrast, deep

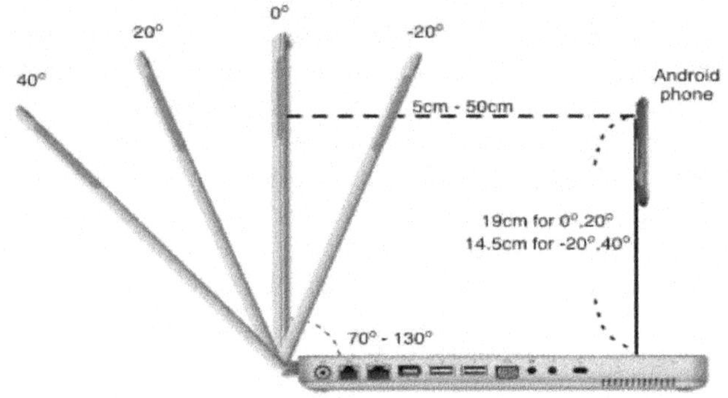

Figure 5. The setup of the reliability experiment.

shooting and deep posting adopts an old technique—taking pictures using a camera—to simultaneously identify the source device, the data to transfer, and the target device, all in one action of taking pictures of computer screens, which is just as easy as doing so of the real world. This is consistent with the informal feedback we collected from users.

Since there is no extra step beyond taking pictures, the learnability and the memorability of our techniques are as good as using ordinary cameras on mobile phones. The efficiency of our techniques is related to two factors. One is the steps performed by the user, and the other is the performance of our system in terms of speed and accuracy. To do a deep shooting or a deep posting, a user needs to perform three steps: launching our application on a phone, locating the target window on a device through the viewfinder, and pressing the shutter. These steps are exactly the same as taking a picture using a camera application on a phone. Therefore, our techniques are as fast as taking a picture from a user's perspective. The other factor, the speed and accuracy of our system, will be discussed later from the technical perspective. Finally, because the steps a user needs to perform are minimized, the type of error that may occur is taking a wrong region on the screen. However, the user can simply discard an incorrect capture and redo the procedure. In addition to user errors, our system may have errors while matching pictures against screenshots. We will examine this kind of error with a controlled experiment in the following sections.

Usability of Our Framework

As a framework, we provide a simple but powerful API that consists of two functions for developers. One is for an application to register itself with our system, and the other is to respond when a capture event occurs. We argue that these two functions are easy to use for developers who are experienced in event-driven programming.

A potential difficulty with incorporating Deep Shot into an application is to identify what components and information are located in the given region of interest. Fortunately, modern operating systems already include this functionality, known as hit testing, in their accessibility APIs. Developers may use these APIs to determine which component is hit given any point on the screen.

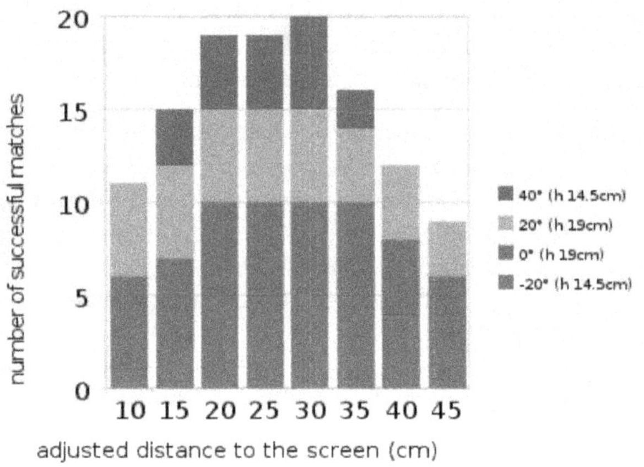

Figure 6. The results of the reliability experiment. The total number of trials for each setting is 20.

Technical Evaluation

Finally, we evaluate our system from a technical perspective. We set up two experiments to explore whether using a camera to locate a region on a monitor is feasible in terms of speed and accuracy. The first experiment was to test the speed of our system, and the second one was to test the accuracy of our image-matching algorithm.

Experiment 1: Speed Performance

We used a laptop, a 15-inch MacBook Pro with a high-resolution 1680×1050 monitor as the target device, and a Nexus One running Android 2.2 as the capturing device that takes 512x384 pictures. The capturing device was held by the experimenter at a distance of 20 to 40 cm and a pitch angle of ±20° so that about ⅓ of the screen could be seen through the viewfinder.

We tested four target applications: photos (from Google Street View), short textual information (from Yelp.com), long textual article with a few images (from CNN.com), and maps (from Google Maps). For each application three photos were taken using deep shooting under the setting described above.

The average time of the whole procedure across 12 trials (3 pictures for 4 applications) was 7.7 seconds (SD 0.3 seconds). By examining the average time of each step, we found the network transmission occupied about 50% of the total time, while the rest processing time was spent on the target device (34%) and the capturing device (16%). The transmission caused a significant portion of the latency because our current implementation attaches raw images captured by the camera in the messages and these messages were routed via an external server. As a result, we can significantly reduce the latency of our system by improving the transmission efficiency, e.g., using only visual features instead of the entire image and not using a third-party server. We will discuss the possibilities in the Future Work section.

Experiment 2: Reliability

In this experiment, we wanted to test the accuracy of our image-matching algorithm under typical conditions for taking a picture of a screen as well as extreme conditions that are not so common. Our experimental setup is shown in Figure 5. We used a 15-inch MacBook Pro laptop so that we could easily adjust and measure the pitch angle of the screen. We tested four pitch angles for the screen with respect to the phone: −20°, 0°, 20°, and 40°. The laptop shows a full-screen browser (Google Chrome) with a web page of the most popular local restaurant on Yelp, which is a typical webpage consisting of text and images. An Android phone, Google Nexus One, was tied to an L-square ruler that is perpendicular to the floor. The height of the camera, which was measured from the surface of the laptop keyboard to the center of the camera lens, was fixed at 19 cm while the pitch angle was 0° or 20°, and 14.5 cm while the pitch angle was −20° or 40°. These height settings allowed the camera to focus around the same target on the screen, namely the name of the restaurant. We set the phone in front of the screen with a distance of 5 to 50 cm, as measured from the screen shaft to the camera lens. Finally, for each pitch angle, we took five pictures for every 5 cm between 5 cm and 50 cm, which resulted in a total of 200 pictures. This experiment was conducted in an office with ceiling fluorescent lights.

We used the algorithm mentioned before to match each picture against the screen displayed on the laptop. If the center of the matched region overlapped the expected region on the screen, it was considered as a successful match.

The results of this experiment are summarized in Figure 6. The chart shows the number of successful matches for each adjusted distance to the screen, instead of the distance measured to the screen shaft. Because the screen was tilted, we adjust the distance to the shaft by adding $h \tan \theta$, where h is the height of the phone and θ is the pitch angle. With this adjustment, we only show the results between 15 cm and 40 cm where all the settings have valid measurements.

The experiment showed that the matching algorithm was highly robust with a 97% success rate, when the camera was parallel to the monitor and the distance between them ranged between 10 and 40 cm. This range is sufficient to cover everything from a small region, such as a restaurant's name, to the entire screen (see Figure 7). Even when the camera was tilted, taking pictures in the range of 20–30 cm was still robust (96.7% success). The accuracy significantly decreased when the camera is too close to (< 10 cm) or too far (> 40 cm) from the screen, but these conditions are uncommon as users can seek the appropriate size of the target through the camera. The results of this experiment showed that using a camera with our algorithm was robust enough to locate a region on a monitor.

RELATED WORK

Several research projects have addressed the issues of migrating information across devices. Remote Clip [15] is a simple way to share information via a synchronized clipboard across multiple personal computers. However, this technique is only feasible for copying textual or selectable objects. Pick-and-drop [18] is a direct-manipulation technique to pick up an object on a computer and drop it on another. Hyperdragging [17] is a technique like drag-and-drop that transfers information across devices. However, these two techniques require special, uncommon devices (pen devices and augmented tabletops) so they cannot be easily deployed to the real world. Some tools [6,21] allow users to control applications remotely. In contrast, Deep Shot allows users to interact with the same content via native applications running on a local device, which eliminates the need to have a constant network connection.

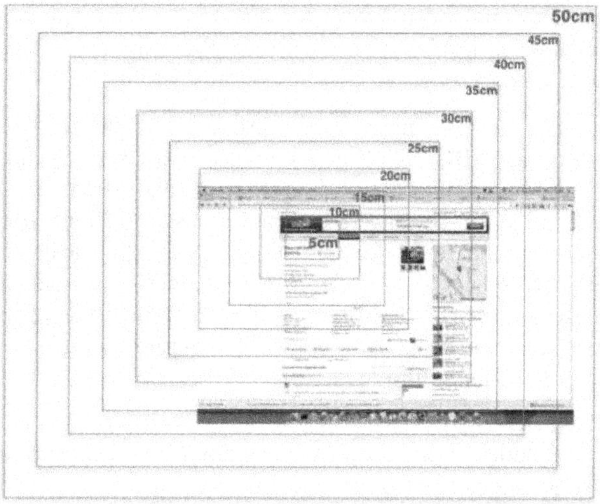

Figure 7. The regions the camera sees with a distance 5 to 50 cm away from the screen while the monitor is parallel to the phone.

Associating physical tags or bar codes to digital files is also a way to migrate information. Want et al. [22] describes using RFID tags to link physical objects to network services. Android phone users can install an application by scanning a QR code. The downside of these techniques is that they require special tags or codes that can only be read by machines. On the other hand, techniques such as [5,13, 14] based on only visual features have been proposed. Compared to these previous techniques, we used similar feature matching algorithms. However, these techniques only focused on file transfer or document manipulation for certain applications. In contrast, Deep Shot provides an extensible framework that enables an arbitrary application to migrate not only its content but also its runtime states across devices using a mobile phone camera.

PIE [16] is a general infrastructure for developers to create multi-personal-device services, which focuses on low-level mechanisms for sending information, commands, or events across devices. Device ensembles [19] also provided a viewpoint on how multiple devices communicate from the low-level link layer to the high-level application layer. In contrast with these projects, our framework provides a high-level and unified way for developers to extend their applications and for users to invoke the migration using a mobile camera.

Recently, researchers have proposed Activity-Based Computing (ABC) [2,3], which considers a user activity as the basic computational unit. From the broad perspective of ABC [12], an activity can span across different users, devices, applications, and situations. Deep Shot deals with three major challenges in ABC: activity suspend and resume, activity roaming, and activity adaption, but we only focus on a subset of activities: single user, single application, and multiple devices.

CONCLUSION AND FUTURE WORK

We conclude by discussing the limitation of Deep Shot and possible extensions for future work.

Multiple users: Our current system finds possible target devices from a list of the user's online devices. It is easy to add other users' devices into the user's "friend list," so that they can be notified when a capture event happens. However, this would add extra effort of managing the device list. A possible solution is to replace the XMPP layer with a local service discovery protocol, such as Apple Bonjour, and broadcast the request to local devices.

Transmitting visual features instead of pictures: In the current implementation, we send pictures directly in a request, which raise privacy concerns since the devices that receive the request can "see" the pictures, especially for a multiple-user environment. Therefore, a possible solution is to extract the visual features directly on the capturing device and only send the feature vectors in a request. This could dramatically speed up the performance and also prevent malicious request sniffers. In addition, this could enable *real-time matching feedback* on the target screen, so users can be confident that the matching is successful and also know which region of the screen will be captured.

Limitation on feature matching: Feature matching may not work in some scenarios. For example, nothing can be extracted and matched if a user intends to capture a blank region. However, we can assume that no valuable information exist in this area and simply show the photo she took back to her. A more common problem is unfocused photos, although this could be solved with the real-time matching feedback we mentioned above.

This paper presented two novel interaction techniques, deep shooting and deep posting, to migrate a task across devices and a robust and extensible framework to support them called Deep Shot. We demonstrated that Deep Shot is reliable and feasible to support a range of everyday tasks migrating across devices using one simple gesture.

ACKNOWLEDGEMENT

We thank the anonymous reviewers, Rob Miller, and James Lin for their suggestions and feedback, and LaDawn Jentzsch for narrating our demo video.

REFERENCES

1. Bandelloni, R. and Paternņ, F. Migratory User Interfaces Able To Adapt To Various Interaction Platforms. *International journal of human-computer studies,* 2004.
2. Bardram, JE. Activity-Based Computing: Support For Mobility And Collaboration In Ubiquitous Computing. *Personal and Ubiquitous Computing,* 2005.
3. Bardram, JE., Bunde-Pedersen, J., and Soegaard, M. Support For Activity-Based Computing In A Personal Computing Operating System. *Proc. CHI '06.*
4. Bay, H., Tuytelaars, T., and Van Gool, L. SURF: Speeded Up Robust Features. *Proc. CVIU,* 2008.
5. Boring, S., Altendorfer, M., Broll, G., and et al. Shoot & Copy: Phonecam-Based Information Transfer From Public Displays Onto Mobile Phones. *Proc. Mobility '07.*
6. Boring, S., Baur, D., Butz, A., and et al. Touch Projector: Mobile Interaction through Video. *Proc. CHI* '10.
7. Dearman, D and Pierce, JS. "It's On My Other Computer!": Computing With Multiple Devices. *Proc. CHI '08.*
8. Google Chrome to Phone. http://code.google.com/p/chrometophone.
9. Hinckley, K. Synchronous Gestures For Multiple Persons And Computers. *Proc. UIST '03.*
10. Hupp, D. and Miller, RC. Smart Bookmarks: Automatic Retroactive Macro Recording On The Web. *Proc. UIST '07.*
11. Karlson, A., Iqbal, S., Meyers, and Tang, J. Mobile Taskflow in Context: A Screenshot Study of Smartphone Usage. *Proc. CHI '10.*
12. Li, Y., and Landay, J. Activity-based prototyping of ubicomp applications for long-lived, everyday human activities, *Proc. CHI'08.*
13. Liao, C., Liu, Q., and et al. Pacer: Fine-grained Interactive Paper via Camera-touch Hybrid Gestures on a Cell Phone. *Proc. CHI '10.*
14. Liu, Q., McEvoy, P., and Lai, C.-J. Mobile camera supported document redirection. *Proc. MM '06.*
15. Miller, RC and Myers, BA. Synchronizing Clipboards Of Multiple Computers. *Proc. UIST '99.*
16. Pierce, J. and Nichols, J. An Infrastructure For Extending Applications' User Experiences Across Multiple Personal Devices. *Proc. UIST '08.*
17. Rekimoto, J. Pick-And-Drop: A Direct Manipulation Technique For Multiple Computer Environments. *Proc. UIST '97.*
18. Rekimoto, J and Saitoh, M. Augmented Surfaces: A Spatially Continuous Work Space For Hybrid Computing Environments. *Proc. CHI '99.*
19. Schilit, B and Sengupta, U. Device Ensembles. Computer, IEEE Computer Socity, 2004.
20. Tang, J., Lin, J., and et al. Recent Shortcuts: Using Recent Interactions To Support Shared Activities. *Proc. CHI '07.*
21. Tan, DS., Meyers, B., and Czerwinski, M. WinCuts: manipulating arbitrary window regions for more effective use of screen space. *Proc. CHI '04.*
22. Want, R, Fishkin, K, and Gujar, A. Bridging Physical And Virtual Worlds With Electronic Tags. *Proc. CHI '99.*

Eyes-Free Multitasking: The Effect of Cognitive Load on Mobile Spatial Audio Interfaces

Yolanda Vazquez-Alvarez and Stephen A. Brewster
Glasgow Interactive Systems Group, School of Computing Science
University of Glasgow, Glasgow, G12 8QQ, UK
{yolanda, stephen}@dcs.gla.ac.uk www.gaime-project.org

ABSTRACT
As mobile devices increase in functionality, users perform more tasks when on the move. Spatial audio interfaces offer a solution for eyes-free interaction. However, such interfaces face a number of challenges when supporting multiple and simultaneous tasks, namely: 1) interference amongst multiple audio streams, and 2) the constraints of cognitive load. We present a comparative study of spatial audio techniques evaluated in a divided- and selective-attention task. A podcast was used for high cognitive load (divided-attention) and classical music for low cognitive load (selective-attention), while interacting with an audio menu. Results showed that spatial audio techniques were preferred when cognitive load was kept low, while a baseline technique using an interruptible single audio stream was significantly less preferred. Conversely, when cognitive load was increased the preferences reversed. Thus, given an appropriate task structure, spatial techniques offer a means of designing effective audio interfaces to support eyes-free mobile multitasking.

Author Keywords
Multitasking, audio interfaces, eyes-free interaction, cognitive load, divided-attention task, selective-attention task.

ACM Classification Keywords
H.5.2. User Interfaces: Evaluation, interaction styles.

General Terms
Design, Experimentation, Human Factors.

INTRODUCTION
How much multitasking are mobile users exposed to in their daily lives? Imagine a typical morning for David as he commutes to work: *David is travelling on the New York City subway system on his way to work and listening to music on his phone, as he always does. While David is in transit, his boss Stephen tries to call him but, as there is no underground cell phone coverage, he leaves a voice mail. As David leaves the station at his usual destination, he listens to the voicemail while his favorite music is still playing. He finds out he has to reschedule a meeting with his boss. He then decides to pause his music and starts interacting with his calendar using an audio menu as he keeps on walking. As he starts browsing through his appointments to find a free slot, Stephen calls him back. While taking to Stephen, David browses his calendar and finds a suitable time later on the day for their meeting. The call ends and David continues listening to his music while making his way to the office.*

An audio interface like the one illustrated in our example makes eyes-free interactions possible while on the go when visual attention is compromised or the mobile device is out of reach, and enables the user to interact with his mobile devices purely through sound. The extent to which such an audio-only interface is desirable depends on how we deal with cognitive load and multiple streams of information. In our example, we have differing levels of both. From a notification of a voice mail, which might be delivered at the same time David listens to music, to a multitasking extreme of listening to music during a phone call while rearranging a meeting and walking the streets of New York. All of this without getting run over by a yellow cab. How should an audio interface be designed to deal with these competing requirements? In this paper, we consider basic strategies for the presentation of multiple audio streams and examine their usability under varying cognitive load.

Presentation of multiple audio streams
When multiple tasks are supported purely by audio, users must be able to direct their attention selectively to each individual audio stream representing a task. However, when performing multiple tasks at once and conveying them through audio simultaneously, masking of information (i.e. both audio streams are audible and easily confused with each other) occurs as the audio streams overlap. Spatial audio has been used in previous research [1, 2] as a successful technique to segregate multiple audio streams by placing each audio stream at a different location around the user's head, mirroring how humans perceive sounds in real life [3]. What is not yet clear is what spatial audio design might be the most effective for supporting multiple audio streams and how much, if at all, the spatialization of the streams might contribute to an increase or decrease of the user's cognitive load when engaged in a number of simultaneous tasks. Thus, an important issue is how to design audio inter-

faces that will effectively enable users to interact with simultaneous, and often continuous, audio streams whilst at the same time preventing these streams from interfering with each other. This paper presents an evaluation of different spatial and non-spatial audio techniques in such a multitasking scenario.

The importance of cognitive load

Different attention demands impose different amounts of cognitive load on the user. When David is listening to the voicemail left by Stephen, he is focusing attention on the voicemail audio stream while monitoring his music (a selective-attention task). However, when David is talking to Stephen while interacting with his calendar using an audio menu to find a suitable time for their meeting, David is dividing his attention between both audio streams (a divided-attention task). The first task results in less cognitive load, and the second in higher cognitive load. Cognitive load has been described as the amount of mental re-sources needed to perform a given task [4]. As tasks add up, the mental resources needed increase and cognitive load rises. Previous research by Marentakis and Brewster [5] investigating pointing efficiency in deictic spatial audio displays, showed that increased cognitive load resulted in reduced pointing efficiency. Shinn-Cunningham [6] and Best [7] have also investigated how perceived spatial separation of sources and consistency in source locations influences performance on selective- and divided-attention tasks. They found that performance was better when sources were perceived at different locations instead of the same location. However, she adds that "*further experiments are necessary to determine whether spatial attention influences performance differently when competing sources differ from one another in more natural ways*".

When designing audio interfaces it is critical to consider the attention demands expected from the user. This affects the attention required to monitor the information being relayed by the stream and also the attention required to monitor the spatial location of the stream. Spatial audio offers the ability to foreground and background audio streams, for example, moving an audio stream to the side (we will term this *spatial minimization* [8]), while a second stream is played from the front. Spatial minimization could help users alter focus between streams. Thus, when designing mobile audio interfaces to support multitasking, how would different auditory techniques, spatial or non-spatial, perform under different user attention demands? In this paper we quantify the effect of cognitive load on a number of spatial and non-spatial audio techniques during selective- and divided-attention tasks involving user interaction. Our research question was: Are spatial audio techniques able to efficiently support both divided- and selective-attention tasks?

METHODS

Forty-eight participants (26 males, 22 females, aged 18 to 53 years) were recruited. All were native speakers of British English, reported normal hearing and were right-handed. Participants were split equally into two groups: divided- and selective-attention in a between subjects design.

Stimuli

Participants listened to two different streams: one continuous and the other user activated. In the selective-attention group, the continuous stream was a piece of classical music taken from Mozart's Sonata for two pianos K448 in D Major. This specific music piece has been frequently used in spatial-temporal reasoning research. The sonata was divided into different fragments: one for the training session and four others were used in the four different conditions. These fragments were all mono, 16-bit and sampled at 16kHz, and approximately 1.5 minutes long. The participants were told they would have to answer a question on the audio menu tasks to ensure selective attention. In the divided-attention group, the continuous stream was a podcast selected from the BBC Radio 4 programme 'From our own correspondent'. Five different podcasts with a similar journalistic format were chosen. One podcast was used for training the participants and the rest were used in four different test conditions. They were all mono, 16-bit and sampled at 16 kHz, and narrated by a male speaker. In order to ensure divided attention participants were asked to monitor the podcast and told they would have to answer questions on content *as well* as a question on the audio menu tasks. In order to retain coherence, and to allow enough audio material to pose content questions before, during and after the audio menu tasks, the podcasts were longer than the classical musical streams (3 minutes). Our aim was to generate a low cognitive load for the selective-attention group by using classical music, and a high cognitive load in the divided-attention group by using speech.

The user-activated audio stream was a hierarchical audio menu with synthesized audio items. It consisted of a three-item top level: music, appointments and current time. The 'music' item included three items in two different sub-levels: 1) previous track, current track and next track, 2) the song title for each of the items. The 'appointments' item included three items in three different sub-levels: 1) Monday, Tuesday and Wednesday, 2) the times for the appointments, 3) appointment information. The 'current time' item only had one sub-level with time information, (for more details see [8]). All the audio items were mono, 16-bit, sampled at 16 kHz, and were spoken by a female RP voice. All the audio menu items were different for the different conditions. Both the continuous and user-activated streams were normalized to 70% of the audio dynamic range, which equals to a normal conversation typically 60-70dB.

Procedure

Each group was tested in four different conditions: 1) *Baseline*: The continuous stream was paused or *interrupted* while the participant was interacting with the audio menu, 2) *Concurrent*: The continuous stream played while the participant was interacting with the audio menu, 3) *User-activated spatial minimization*: The continuous stream was

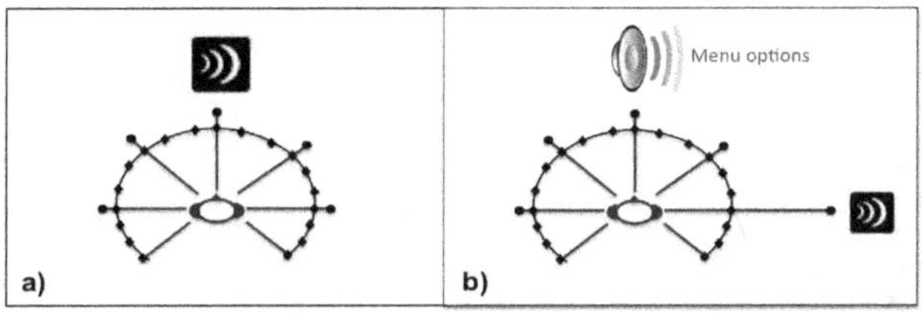

Figure 1. (a) Single continuous stream. Black filled circles show different azimuth locations. (b) User-activated spatial minimization: stream moved from front to right.

located at the origin (0° azimuth) 1m away from the listener in the frontal horizontal plane (see Figure 1), and moved to the right hand-side (90° azimuth) and out to 2m away from the listener when the participant was interacting with the audio menu, and 4) *Fixed spatial minimization*: The continuous stream was fixed to 90° azimuth and 2m away from the listener for the entire duration of this condition.

In all four conditions, participants performed three tasks using a hierarchical audio menu: 1) Finding the next music track title, 2) Checking an appointment for Tuesday, and 3) Finding the current time. The audio menu was always presented at 0° azimuth (in front of the user's nose) and always 1m away in the frontal horizontal plane. All four conditions were tested in the same randomized order in both the divided- and selective-attention groups. Participants were tested in a static lab environment seated on a chair holding the mobile phone in an upright position wearing a pair of headphones. The study was run on a Nokia N95 8GB using the built-in HRTFs and the JAVA JSR-234 Advanced Multimedia Supplements API to position the audio sources. The audio was played over a pair of DT770 PRO – 250 OHM Beyerdynamic headphones.

Participants completed two training sessions before the test conditions. First, a training session was devoted to familiarizing the participants with the audio menu structure in their own time. The second training session used the concurrent condition to familiarize the participants with listening to a continuous audio stream while interacting with the audio menu. For each test condition, participants listened to a continuous audio stream and after approximately 1 minute, the user was prompted with a 25-ms sine wave beep at 1500 Hz to start interacting with the menu and complete the three tasks described previously in any order. To initiate this interaction, the participant pressed the central navigation key on the phone. The arrow keys on the phone were used to browse the menu items. Once the tasks were completed and the audio menu was exited by pressing the central navigation key again, the user continued listening to the continuous audio stream until it was over. A NASA-TLX subjective workload assessment was completed, and, once all four conditions were completed, participants were instructed to rank them in order of preference: '1' being most preferred and '4' the least. The experiment took 30-45 minutes in total. Participants were allowed to rest between conditions.

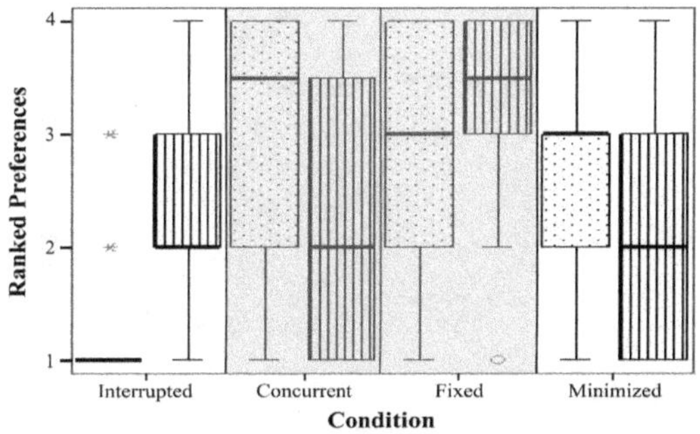

Figure 2. Box plots present ranked preferences per condition and attention group: divided-attention (dotted) and selective-attention (striped). The boxes contain the middle 50% of the data, the horizontal bold black lines show the median and the points outside are suspected outliers. The grey shaded conditions showed no significance.

RESULTS

Ranked Preferences

Figure 2 shows a stacked count for the order of preference for the four conditions compared in the divided- and the selective-attention groups. A non-parametric Kruskal-Wallis for different conditions per attention group showed there was a significant difference in the medians ($\chi 2$ (7, N=192)=61.810, $p<0.001$). Mann-Whitney tests with Bonferroni correction showed a significant difference between the interrupted conditions by group, and also between the user-activated spatial minimization conditions by group. Users' preference for interrupting the continuous stream significantly decreased (two-tailed $p<0.0001$, total 1st preferences dropped from 20 to 4) and preference for spatially minimizing the continuous stream significantly increased (two-tailed $p = 0.008$, total 1st preferences increased from 2 to 8) when the streamed source was classical music.

Overall Workload

Raw overall workload was calculated from the NASA-TLX questionnaires completed after each condition. A repeated-measures ANOVA with condition type as a within-subjects factor and attention group as a between-subjects factor showed a significant main effect for condition type ($F(3,96)=9.786$, $p<0.001$) and attention type ($F(1,32)=48.284$, $p<0.001$). There was also an interaction between attention and condition type ($F(3,96)=4.34$, $p < 0.01$). As expected, perceived overall workload was significantly higher in the divided-attention group (mean=51.71) than in the selective-attention group (mean=21.33). *Post hoc* Pairwise Comparisons with Bonferroni correction for condition type showed that perceived overall workload during the interrupted condition was significantly lower ($p<0.015$) than in the rest of conditions for the divided-attention group. No significant differences were found between conditions for the selective-attention group (see Figure 3).

Performance

Total time taken to complete the audio menu tasks was also computed. A repeated-measures ANOVA with condition type as a within-subjects factor and attention group as by-

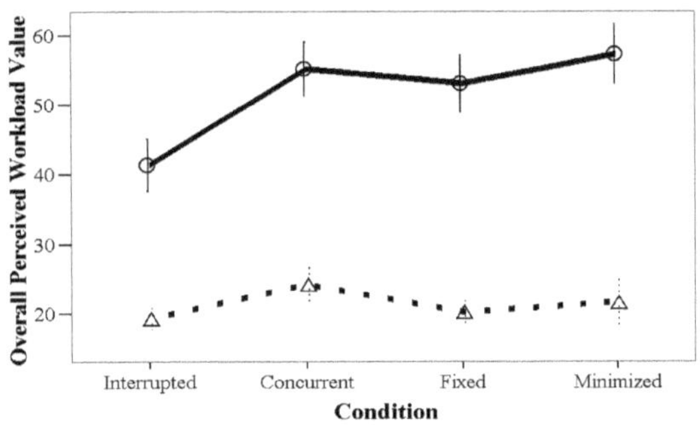

Figure 3. Overall perceived workload per condition and attention group: divided-attention (solid line) and selective-attention (dotted line). Error bars show SD of Mean ± 1.0.

subjects factor showed a significant main effect for condition type ($F(3,96)=5.45$, $p<0.005$) and attention type ($F(1,32)=7.21$, $p<0.015$). There was also an interaction between attention an condition type ($F(3,96)=2.89$, $p<0.050$). Task completion times were significantly higher (mean= 41.76 secs) for the divided-attention group than for the selective-attention group (mean=32.03 secs). *Post hoc* Pairwise Comparisons with Bonferroni correction for condition type showed that task completion times for the interrupted condition were significantly lower ($p<0.05$). Also, *Post hoc* Independent samples T tests across attention type showed that task completion times were significantly higher for the concurrent condition ($t(46)=2.640$, $p<0.050$) (mean=43.95 secs) and the minimized condition ($t(46)=2.73$, $p<0.05$) (mean=47.42 secs) for the divided-attention group than for the same conditions for the selective-attention group (concurrent: mean=32.31 secs; minimized: mean=33.53 secs). See Figure 4.

DISCUSSION AND CONCLUSIONS

As we might expect, users do not like being put under cognitive load. Participants in this study reported higher workload and took longer to carry out tasks in the divided-attention group. Furthermore, listening to concurrent audio increased the effect of load. The use of spatial techniques had a neglible impact on reducing this effect (although there was a tendency to prefer minimization compared to the other concurrent conditions). In the selective-attention group however, preference results were significantly reversed for interrupted and minimization conditions. This shows that users disliked having the continuous stream interrupted when not under load, and using spatial techniques to separate the continuous stream from the user-activated menu was preferred.

Addressing our research question, we can say that the spatial minimization technique presented in this paper offers an effective means of presenting and interacting with multiple audio streams simultaneously in a selective-attention scenario. However, spatialization techniques were not as effective in the divided-attention task, in which the interaction benefited significantly from the interruption of the continuous stream. In a mobile spatial audio interface design in which interrupting the streams is not an option, it should be noted that, even in this extreme cognitive load scenario, participants were able to carry out the tasks, although at a reduced ability.

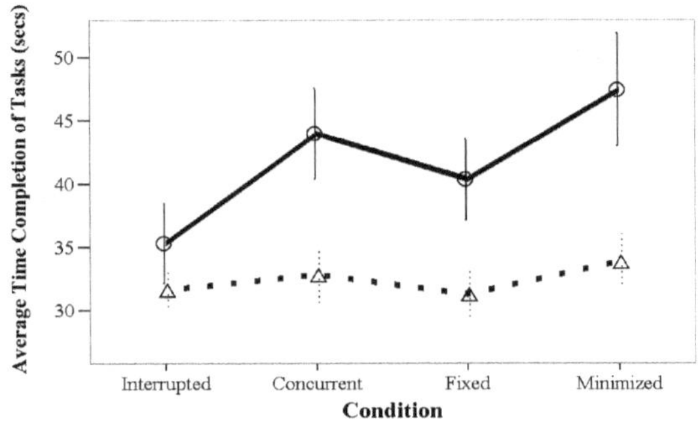

Figure 4. Mean task completion times per condition and attention group: divided-attention (solid line) and selective-attention (dotted line). Error bars show SD of Mean ± 1.0.

These results suggest a mixed design of audio techniques would be required within our initial usage example. Concurrent streams should be used to play the voicemail notification with spatial audio being used to help separate the information streams. Also, when David decides to access his calendar eyes-free, he could continue listening to the music spatially minimized, as this will not disrupt his task efficiency. It would be nonetheless important to allow him to interrupt his menu interaction at anytime while navigating the streets of New York on foot.

REFERENCES

1. Schmandt, C., and Mullins, A. AudioStreamer: exploiting simultaneity for listening. In Proc. CHI 1995, ACM Press (1995), 218-219.
2. Walker, A. and Brewster, S.A. Spatial audio in small screen device displays. Personal Technologies 4, 2 (2000), 144-154.
3. Bronkhorst, A.W. The cocktail party phenomenon: a review of research on speech intelligibility in multiple-talker conditions. Acustica 86 (2000), 117-128.
4. Draycott, S.G., and Kline, P. Validation of the AGARD STRES Battery of Performance Tests. Human Factors 38, 2 (1996), 347-361.
5. Marentakis, G. and Brewster, S.A. A comparison of feedback cues for enhancing pointing efficiency in interaction with spatial audio displays. In Proc. Mobile-HCI 2005, ACM Press (2005), 55-62.
6. Shinn-Cunningham, B.G. and Ihlefeld, A. Selective and divided attention: extracting information from simultaneous sound sources. In Proc. ICAD 04, (2004).
7. Best, V., Ihlefeld, A. and Shinn-Cunningham, B.G. The effect of auditory spatial layout in a divided attention task. In Proc. ICAD 05, (2005), 17-22.
8. Vazquez-Alvarez, Y. and Brewster, S.A. Designing Spatial Audio Interfaces to Support Multiple Audio Streams. In Proc. MobileHCI 2010, ACM Press (2010), 253-256.

FeedLack Detects Missing Feedback in Web Applications

Andrew J. Ko and Xing Zhang
The Information School | DUB Group | University of Washington
{ajko, xingz2}@uw.edu

ABSTRACT

While usability methods such as user studies and inspections can reveal a wide range of problems, they do so for only a subset of an application's features and states. We present FeedLack, a tool that explores the full range of web applications' behaviors for one class of usability problems, namely that of missing feedback. It does this by enumerating control flow paths originating from user input, identifying paths that lack output-affecting code. FeedLack was applied to 330 applications; of the 129 that contained input handlers and did not contain syntax errors, 115 were successfully analyzed, resulting in 647 warnings. Of these 36% were missing crucial feedback; 34% were executable and missing feedback, but followed conventions that made feedback inessential; 18% were scenarios that *did* produce feedback; 12% could not be executed. We end with a discussion of the viability of FeedLack as a usability testing tool.

Author Keywords

Feedback, program analysis, static analysis, JavaScript.

ACM Classification Keywords

H.5.2. Information interfaces and presentation.

General Terms

Human Factors, Algorithms

INTRODUCTION

Sometimes computers ignore us. We click save buttons, but often do not know if our documents are saved; we click on links in web pages, but are taken nowhere; we submit forms, but do not know if the site is broken, or simply slow to respond. Software that appears to ignore user input violates a basic principle of effective user interface design: for every user input, software should produce a corresponding output that explains how the system responded to the input.

The importance of this principle is reflected in the methods we use to detect feedback problems. For example, Nielsen's Heuristic Evaluation [16] focuses evaluators on feedback, stating that "The system should continuously inform the user about what it is doing and how it is interpreting the user's input." Inspection techniques such as the Cognitive Walkthrough [4] have evaluators confirm that the result of taking some action results in visible feedback. Task-based usability testing [16] can also reveal missing feedback in prototypes of widely ranging fidelity.

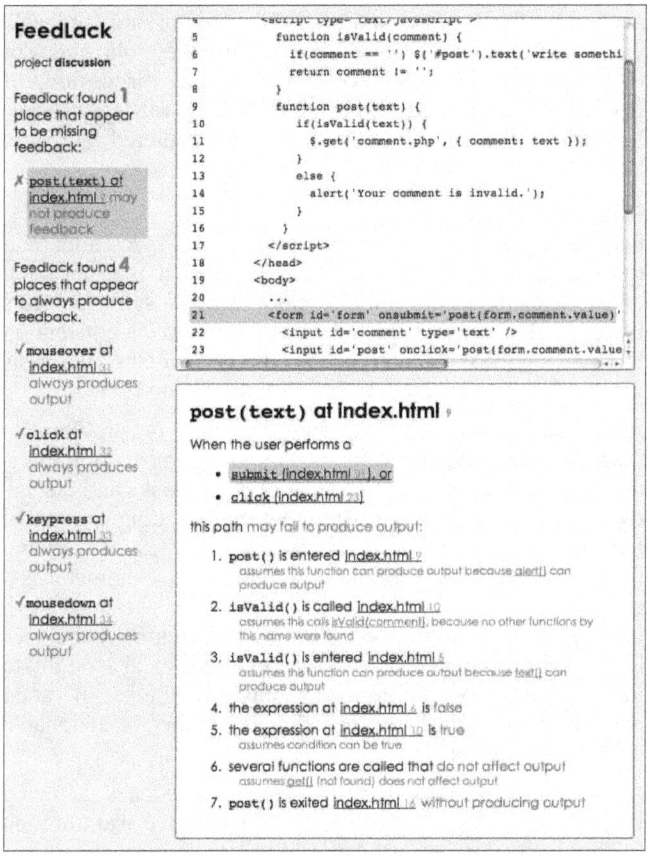

Figure 1. By analyzing paths from input, FeedLack found that function `post()` does not produce feedback upon success.

While these empirical methods are quite effective at detecting feedback issues, they often overlook problems in outside the scope of the tasks selected by evaluators [14]. Moreover, because they require users, these methods operate at a slower pace than other forms of software testing such as unit and regression testing, which run on the order of minutes and hours, not weeks. This disparity in scope and speed means that feedback issues and other usability problems can easily escape notice as code is readied to deploy.

To address this problem, we present *FeedLack*, a tool that automatically detects missing feedback in web applications. It does this by verifying that all paths originating from user input produce some form of output. To illustrate, consider the FeedLack warning in Figure 1. FeedLack has found that when the user submits the form (lines 22 and 23) and its comment is considered valid (line 10), the application provides no feedback about success or failure. It found this by enumerating all of the paths from form submission and reporting the single path that lacked output-affecting code.

In the rest of this paper, we describe FeedLack's analysis in detail. We then present an evaluation of FeedLack on a corpus of 330 web applications ranging from small personal web pages to sophisticated applications such as calendars, visualizations, and games. Of the 129 that contained JavaScript input handlers and did not contain syntax errors, 115 were successfully analyzed, resulting in 647 warnings; 36% of these were legitimate, reproducible scenarios that needed feedback, while another 34% were missing feedback, but would likely not be confusing because they followed user interface conventions. We end with a discussion of FeedLack's limitations, its generalizability to other platforms, and the viability of its role in user-centered software engineering processes.

RELATED WORK

Feedback has been a central topic in HCI research and practice for several decades. Ensuring that it is timely and understandable is one of the major heuristics in Nielsen's Heuristic Evaluation [16], it is a foundational concept in Norman's gulf of evaluation [17], and it is much of the basis for the cognitive account of direct manipulation [9].

Empirical methods for detecting missing or problematic feedback come in several forms. One of the most common is usability testing, in which evaluators devise tasks and engage representative users to attempt them. Such testing can reveal feedback issues in user interface prototypes of varying fidelity. There have been several attempts to automate data capture and analysis aspects of usability testing [10], including remote usability testing [6] and logging techniques [13]. For example, recent work by Akers et al. sought to identify usability problems by analyzing logs of undo commands from real use, revealing a number of actionable usability problems [1].

Another approach to detecting missing feedback is using inspection methods. For example, the Cognitive Walkthrough [4] has evaluators ensure that each action is not only visible and apparent, but that the result of user actions produces visible feedback. These techniques are powerful in their ability to assess both the quality and presence of feedback.

The approaches most closely related to FeedLack are automated analyses of the user interface source code. For example, basic HTML validators are capable of finding feedback problems, in that malformed HTML may often not render properly or at all. JSLint (http://jslint.com) also finds common JavaScript defects that may cause silent failures in web browsers. Other validation tools have been developed to assess the accessibility of web sites against government guidelines; for example, the Functional Accessibility Evaluator (http://html.cita.illinois.edu/iitaa.php) checks web sites against several hundred accessibility rules by inspecting the structure and content of HTML. Similarly, Mahajan and Shneiderman explored automated consistency checking tools, evaluating the consistent use of vocabulary, capitalization, type face, and color in user interfaces [15].

Considering program analysis more generally, there is a long history of verification research focusing on software qualities other than usability. For example, a recent system by Artzi et al. [2] executes and analyzes PHP programs to find scenarios that generate malformed HTML, based on a standard HTML validator. Other recent program analysis and testing-based approaches detect scenarios that may lead programs to crash [8], hang [5], leak memory [18], or expose security vulnerabilities [7]. Our work complements these approaches by analyzing a program's feedback.

DESIGN AND IMPLEMENTATION

The goal of FeedLack is to find control flow paths through web applications that begin with some user input but fail to produce any change to the web page's appearance (evaluating the *quality* of that feedback, for example, whether it was timely, visible, or comprehensible, is out of scope). To do this, FeedLack finds all functions that handle user input, explores all paths through these functions, and identifies which of these paths lack output-affecting code.

We divide our discussion of this analysis into ten steps:

1. Identifying and naming functions
2. Generating function control flow graphs (CFGs)
3. Propagating type information
4. Resolving function calls
5. Identifying output-affecting statements
6. Identifying input-handling functions
7. Enumerating paths through input handlers
8. Expanding paths through input handlers
9. Identifying output-lacking paths
10. Clustering output-lacking paths

A major decision underling these steps was whether to use *static* analysis (analyzing code without executing it), *dynamic* analysis (analyzing executions of code), or a combination of the two. Static analyses have the benefit of verifying properties of a program independent of its inputs, considering the full breadth of a program's behaviors. They can also be much less precise, however, because they must make assumptions about what inputs and program states are actually possible or likely. Dynamic analyses avoid such limitations by using real inputs, but in doing so, sacrifice breadth. Some analyses combine static and dynamic information [2]. We decided on a pure static analysis FeedLack, primarily to complement the empirical nature of usability methods. We chose not to use dynamic information to avoid the need for complex testing configurations. For example, by using only static information, FeedLack can analyze the feedback of server transactions (e.g., creating user accounts and changing passwords) without communicating with a real server.

In the rest of this section, we describe the static analyses in the 10 steps above in detail. We use the example in Figure 1 to illustrate these steps.

Step 1: Identifying and Naming Functions

FeedLack requires as input a folder containing all of the JavaScript and HTML files necessary to run the client-side user interface of the web application. It does *not* require server-side code, even when such code is responsible for generating feedback, since client-side scripts are the only scripts capable of *presenting* feedback to users.

The first step in FeedLack's analysis is to find JavaScript code. It looks in three places: (1) JavaScript source files ending in ".js", (2) `<script>` tags in HTML, and (3) attribute values that compile as JavaScript without parsing errors (as in `<div onclick="alert('error')>"`). All code is parsed using the Rhino JavaScript parser (`http://www.mozilla.org/rhino/`), generating a set of abstract syntax trees (ASTs).

From the ASTs, FeedLack identifies nodes representing JavaScript functions. Because the names of functions are particularly important for exploring paths through JavaScript functions, FeedLack makes extensive efforts to find the names by which a function is referred by considering the contexts of the function's declaration and uses. JavaScript allows developers to declare functions in a variety of contexts, including standard declarations (`function open() {...}`), inside object literals: (`{ open: function() {...}}`), as local variables (`var open=function() {...}`), or as arguments (`enable(function() {...})`). In the first three cases, the names can be extracted quite easily; in the last case, no name is extracted. However, because functions can be used as values, they can take on multiple names. For example, the function `open` in the examples above might be assigned to properties as in `element.onclick = open`, enabling a developer to call it as `element.onclick()`. As described in Step 3, FeedLack analyzes the assignments and references to variables, detecting additional names by which functions can be referred in the process.

As part of this naming process, FeedLack also classifies functions as one of four kinds, to help later determine what functions a call might invoke in Step 4. Functions that are declared at the script level are classified as `GLOBAL` and are presumed to be reachable from any function. Functions declared in object literals or assigned to a property (as in `this.open=function() {...}`) are classified as `OBJECT` functions and are presumed to be reachable only by calls on objects. Functions declared inside of functions are classified as `LOCAL` and are presumed to be reachable only from within the function, unless FeedLack finds references to these functions in function calls or return statements (meaning the function can escape the local scope). In these cases, the local function is given the type `CALLBACK`. All other functions are given the type `CALLBACK` and are not considered in determining what functions a call might invoke.

The above classifications exploit well-documented patterns in how developers use JavaScript functions [19], but they do not cover all possible uses. Our hope was that detecting these patterns would be sufficient for detect missing feedback, with the understanding that they would be one source of false positives in FeedLack's warnings.

Step 2: Generating Control Flow Graphs of Functions

The next step in FeedLack's analysis is to convert each function's AST into a control flow graph (CFG), representing the flow of execution through the function. FeedLack uses these throughout its subsequent analyses.

To create a function's CFG, FeedLack starts with the function's AST, which is made of nodes representing tokens in the program. Each type of node is responsible for adding outgoing edges from itself to its child nodes in a way that represents the potential paths through the node. For example, an addition (`+`) node, which has left and right operand nodes, evaluates left to right; therefore, the `+` node adds an outgoing edge from itself to the left operand and then an outgoing edge from the left operand to the right operand. Similarly, an `if` node adds an outgoing edge to its `expression` node, and then two outgoing edges from the expression: one to the `then` path and one to the `else` path. This is illustrated in Figure 2, which shows the two paths through the conditional in `post()` from Figure 1 (omitting literals, which do not affect control flow).

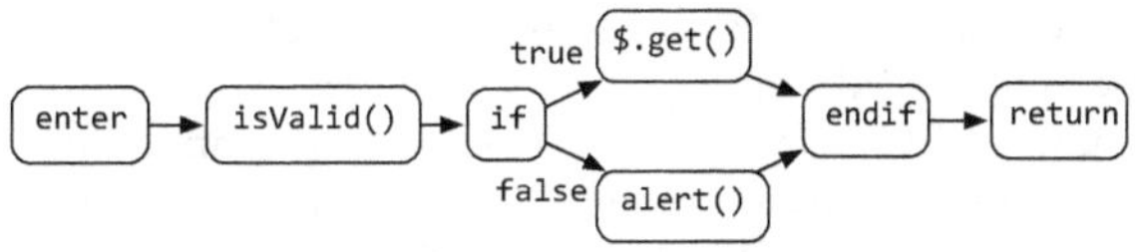

Figure 2. The CFG for `post()` in Figure 1, omitting literals.

FeedLack handles the full range of JavaScript language constructs in the same way. For example, FeedLack accounts for some runtime errors, adding edges for possible divide by zero errors on division nodes and null pointer and undefined runtime errors on object property expressions. By the end of CFG creation, FeedLack has constructed a directed acyclic graph representing the potential paths through a function for all functions in the provided source code (except for outgoing paths from function calls, which are considered later).

One decision in constructing CFGs is how to handle loops, since paths through loops can be infinite in length. FeedLack treats loops as conditional blocks, assuming that loops execute either zero or one times. This simplification was applied because FeedLack's analysis of feedback is conservative: if there's any way to produce output through the loop, then it assumes that way is feasible. This is nevertheless another source of false positives.

Step 3: Propagating Type Information

The next step is to propagate type information through each function. FeedLack needs type information to increase confidence in which functions a call might invoke (Step 4) and to identify code that might affect output (Step 5). Of course, because JavaScript is a dynamic and weakly typed language, there are few guarantees about what functions and properties are valid for any given expression at runtime (for example, even if the expression `element.innerHTML` is known to produce a string, the `innerHTML` property may have been deleted at runtime or `element` may not point to an element).

FeedLack does several things to infer the possible types of variables and properties despite the potential for imprecision. FeedLack infers the types of expression ASTs, propagating type information along data flow edges. For example, to infer the type of the `+` node in `var msg="Hello"+subject`, it inspects the possible types of its two children and determines that it may produce a string. The same type propagation on the assignment in this expression would determine that the type of `msg` is a string. FeedLack also documents all W3C DOM API types, enabling it to determine, for example, that `document.getElementById('home')` returns an `HTMLElement`.

To determine the possible types of variables and object properties, FeedLack explores the paths through the function's CFG using a depth-first search, storing the type information of expressions assigned to variables and properties by name. When this search finds a reference to a variable or property, it propagates the type information previously assigned to the reference. (This process handles local variables, but does not propagate type information for function arguments or function returns; this occurs in Step 4).

To determine the possible types of object expressions (e.g, the `el` in `el.style`), FeedLack gathers the names accessed on each identical object expression and looks for DOM API types and object literal declarations (from Step 1) that contain at least two matching property names. For example, if a function contained the expressions `el.style`, `el.innerHTML`, and `el.onclick`, FeedLack would look for types that have the names `style`, `innerHTML`, and `onclick` and find `HTMLElement`. The type with the most matching names (and in the case of a tie, the most widely used type in the program), is added to the possible types of the object expressions.

Step 4: Resolving Function Calls

After type information is propagated through each function, FeedLack's next step is to resolve all function calls in the program to the functions they might invoke. For each call, it determines the name of the function called and first checks if there are any `LOCAL` functions (as defined in Step 1) in the scope of the call. If there are not, FeedLack checks the calling context to determine whether the call is on an object (e.g., `object.run()`) or not (e.g., `run()`). If the call is on an object and object expression has type information, the function search is limited to the known functions of the expression's possible types. If no functions are found or there is no type information, FeedLack searches *all* `OBJECT` functions for functions with matching names. If the call is not on an object, FeedLack searches all `GLOBAL` functions for matches. If there are no matching names, the failure is noted so that this can be mentioned in FeedLack warning.

After resolving all calls, FeedLack uses the resolved functions to further propagate type information. It propagates the types of arguments sent to functions to each call's resolved function's parameter locals. It also propagates the types of return statements' expressions to the call itself. Lastly, FeedLack repeats Step 3 to further propagate this new type information throughout the program.

FeedLack does not resolve calls to `apply()` and `call()` or calls on arrays (e.g., `object[getFunction()]()`). While this is a source of false positives, prior work has shown that 81% of JavaScript calls only ever invoke one function and that less than 3% have more than two targets [19].

Step 5: Identifying Output-Affecting Statements

With the type information from the previous steps, FeedLack's next step is to search all functions for statements that affect output. FeedLack considers two kinds of statements output. The first are assignments to W3C DOM properties that affect the appearance of page, such as `className` and `id` (which may change the appearance of an element via CSS), `innerHTML`, which explicitly modifies the HTML inside of an element, and a variety of other properties such as `style`, `textContent`, and so on. Some assignments also cause the browser to navigate to a new URL, including assignments to `document.location` and `window.location`.

The second kind of statement considered output includes W3C DOM calls that can affect the appearance of a page. These include functions such as `appendChild`, `setAttribute`, on `HTMLElements` and calls to global functions such as `alert()` and `open()`. In addition to these native calls, FeedLack also accounts for the jQuery and Prototype APIs, recognizing calls such as `$('#home').hide().css('color', 'blue')`.

It should be noted that the statements above do not always affect output. For instance, the statement `el.style.color = 'blue'` only has an effect if the element's color was not already `'blue'`. Similarly, a call to `removeChild()` may fail if the child provided is not found. Because FeedLack is a static analysis, it cannot verify these side effects.

Step 6: Identifying Input Handling Functions

After identifying input, FeedLack's next step finds functions that handle user input. FeedLack considers the full range of input events originating from mice and keyboards, including `click`, `mouse down/up/over/move/enter/out/wheel`, `key down/up/press`, `cut`, `copy`, `paste`, `contextmenu`, `error`, all seven JavaScript drag events, and `href` attributes (which are sometimes used to handle clicks on links). FeedLack ignores events related to focus and element property change events, under the assumption that feedback is not expected for these events since they are not explicitly user invoked.

FeedLack looks for three kinds of input handling code. First, it looks for any tag with input handling attribute values that parse as JavaScript code without errors (as in `onclick="goHome()"`). Each inline script is treated as an input handling function. We include `<input>` tags with a `type` attribute equal to `submit`, `image`, `button`, `checkbox`, or `range` and `<button>` tags with a `type` attribute equal to `submit` or `button` because users expect them to provide some feedback beyond that provided by the control itself. However, we exclude `<input>` tags with type `password` or `radio` as input, assuming their intrinsic feedback is adequate. (We treat checkboxes and radio buttons differently because radio buttons explicitly label each possible mode, whereas the meaning of a checkbox with a static label can be ambiguous).

FeedLack also looks for assignments to object properties that represent input handling functions. For example, the expression `getElementById('home').onclick=goHome;` assigns the function `goHome` to the `onclick` attribute of the element returned by the `getElementById()` function.

FeedLack also looks for event binding calls that represent input handlers, including the W3C and Internet Explorer `addEventListener()` and `attachEvent()` calls as well as jQuery and Prototype event binding APIs (as in `$('#home').click(goHome)` and `$('#home').observe('click', goHome)`), respectively. Functions passed to these calls are also treated as input handling functions.

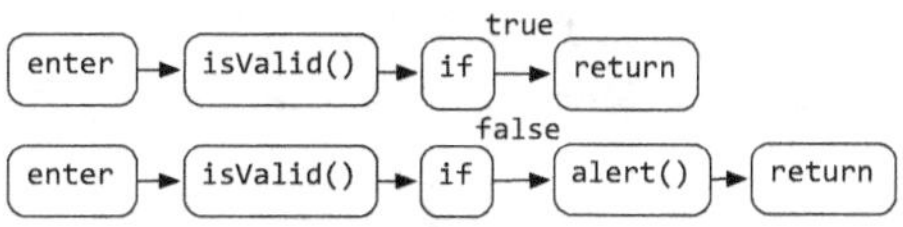

Figure 3. The two paths through `post()` in Figure 1. The first path skips the conditional's `true` block since it lacks output affecting assignments and calls.

Step 7: Enumerating Paths Through Input Handlers

Having identified the program's set of input handlers, FeedLack's next step is to find all paths through each handler. FeedLack uses a depth-first search through each function's CFG, adding each visited node to a list. At each node with multiple outgoing edges, FeedLack duplicates the set of existing paths through the function and then recursively explores each edge. Figure 3 shows the two paths through function `post()`, derived from the CFG in Figure 2. Because FeedLack's analyses are memory intensive, it represents paths as sequences of both nodes and other paths, reusing path leading up to decision points.

To simplify FeedLack's warnings, the above algorithm includes two special cases. First, FeedLack only includes calls, returns, and conditionals, and output-affecting assignments. All other program events such as expressions and non-output affecting assignments are excluded, limiting paths to control flow events. Second, FeedLack only explores *output-affecting* blocks; these are that contain at least one output-affecting call or assignment, where all functions a call might invoke are recursively inspected for output-affecting code. For example, the first path in Figure 3 omits the code within the `true` case of `post()`'s conditional because FeedLack determined that `$.get()` does not affect output.

These special cases have two rationales. First, because conditional blocks can double the number of paths through a function, this simplification mitigates the growth of the number of paths through a function. Second, and perhaps more importantly, this limits FeedLack's warnings to blocks that could possibly affect output, assuming that any block that *cannot* affect output is not one that the developer intended to affect output, and therefore not of interest.

Step 8: Expanding Paths Through Input Handlers

After generating paths through each input handling function, the next step is to replace the calls in these paths that might affect output with all possible paths such calls may result in. This process expands the scope of paths through a single input handling function to the scope of the whole program.

```
function ExpandPaths(function, callstack)
  if callstack contains function, return {}
  push function onto callstack
  let expandedPaths = {}
  let paths = paths through function
  for each path p in paths
  |  add ExpandCalls(p, callstack) to expandedPaths
  pop callstack
```

```
function ExpandCalls(path, callstack)
  let expandedPaths = {[]}
  for each node n in path
  |  append n to all paths in expandedPaths
  |  if n is a call
  |  |  let newPaths = {}
  |  |  let functions = functions call could invoke
  |  |  for each function f in functions
  |  |  |  if f contains > 1 output-affecting statement
  |  |  |  |  let paths = ExpandPaths(f, callstack)
  |  |  |  |  if |paths| x |expandedPaths| < 1 million
  |  |  |  |  |  for each path p in expandedPaths
  |  |  |  |  |  |  for each path q in paths
  |  |  |  |  |  |  |  let r = append q to copy of p
  |  |  |  |  |  |  |  add r to newPaths
  |  |  if newPaths != {}, expandedPaths = newPaths
  return expandedPaths
```

Figure 4. FeedLack uses `ExpandPaths` and `ExpandCalls` to convert the paths through a function into all possible paths from the function through the program, focusing only on calls that can invoke functions containing output-affecting code.

We list the two algorithms that achieve this in Figure 4. `ExpandPaths` iterates through each path through an individual function, converting each individual path into multiple paths with the function `ExpandCalls`. `ExpandCalls` iterates through each node in its given path, resolving calls with the results from Step 4. For each function resolved that contains an output-affecting block (as defined in Step 7), `ExpandCalls` creates new paths to represent all possible paths through all possible functions called. `ExpandCalls` does *not* expand calls to jQuery and Prototype API functions recognized as output-affecting, nor does it attempt to resolve functions passed to `call()` or `apply()`; these latter calls are assumed to affect output to avoid false positives.

An example of the result of `ExpandPaths` appears in Figure 5, showing the paths through the `onclick` handler in Figure 1. These paths show how the two paths through `post()` (in Figure 3) and the two paths through `isValid()` result in four paths through the `onclick` handler. Four identical paths (not shown) are generated for the `onsubmit` handler in Figure 1.

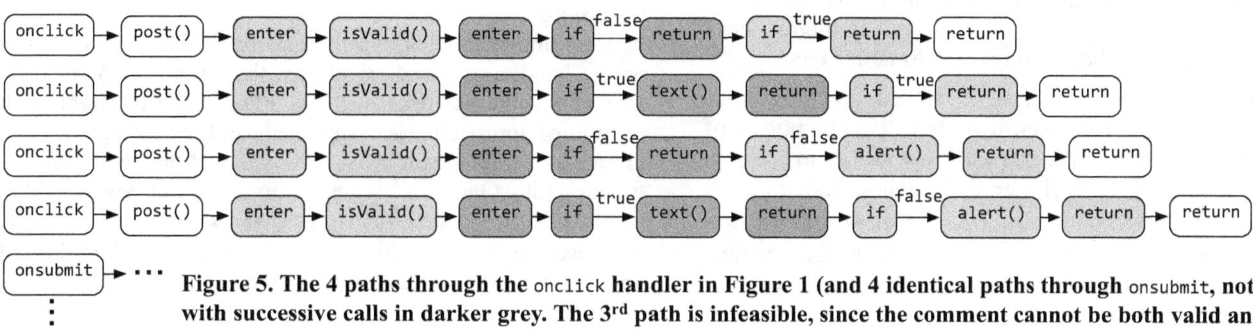

Figure 5. The 4 paths through the `onclick` handler in Figure 1 (and 4 identical paths through `onsubmit`, not shown), with successive calls in darker grey. The 3rd path is infeasible, since the comment cannot be both valid and invalid.

Limiting call expansions to only those functions that could possibly affect output is a critical part of minimizing "path explosion," or the phenomena of path analysis growing exponentially. Also note that `ExpandPaths` and `ExpandCalls` maintain a call stack of functions visited. This allows the algorithm to identify recursive calls, meaning that FeedLack assumes each recursive call occurs once (a similar assumption to that made for loops). Of course, there are cases were neither of these measures are enough to avoid path explosion. Therefore, we empirically derived a limit of one million paths by testing FeedLack on several applications with a Java process allocated 2 GB of RAM.

Finally, it is also important to note that `ExpandPaths` assumes a single thread of execution. JavaScript does allow developers to spawn threads with `setInterval()`, `setTimeout()`, and `AJAX` calls, but FeedLack does not consider the functions they call as output-affecting, requiring the input handling thread to produce feedback itself. This is because they introduce the potential for feedback delays: even if a timeout is supposed to start immediately upon calling, stutters in the network or operating system can cause delays. For example, in addition to AJAX calls producing feedback when they succeed or fail, threads invoking AJAX calls must present feedback while the call is pending.

Step 9: Identifying Output-Lacking Paths

The result of the previous step is a set of paths through each input handing function, some of which contain output-affecting statements, some of which do not. FeedLack groups these paths by the HTML tags and input events from which they originate, eliminating groups of paths that contain at least one handler that always produces output. This accounts for tags that have multiple handlers for similar events, one of which is responsible for output. FeedLack then iterates through the remaining paths, selecting ones that do not contain output-affecting statements. For example, in Figure 5, the only path lacking output-affecting code is the first one; this results in the two paths from the `onclick` and `onsubmit` handlers in Figure 6.

Step 10: Clustering Output-Lacking Paths

There are a number of reasons why presenting output-lacking paths directly to FeedLack users would be unnecessarily complex. For instance, some handlers reuse functions that are responsible for providing feedback (as in the case of `post()` in Figure 1); presenting separate handlers with intersecting paths as distinct would be redundant. Moreover, intersecting paths often share a *critical sequence*. For example, the two paths at the top of Figure 6 hinge upon two particular conditionals. This is an opportunity to highlight these commonalities, rather than require users to notice them.

To identify these commonalities, FeedLack groups output-lacking paths into *path clusters*. It starts with an empty set of path clusters, `Clusters`. Then, for each output-lacking path `P`, FeedLack considers each cluster in `Clusters`, and for each path `C` in each cluster, computes the number of nodes that `P` and `C` have in common. FeedLack remembers the smallest intersection of each cluster, and chooses the cluster with the largest minimum intersection. If there are no clusters, FeedLack creates a new cluster and adds P. The result is a set of path clusters, where all paths in each cluster have at least one node in common. For example, the two paths at the top of Figure 6 are clustered into one single path cluster.

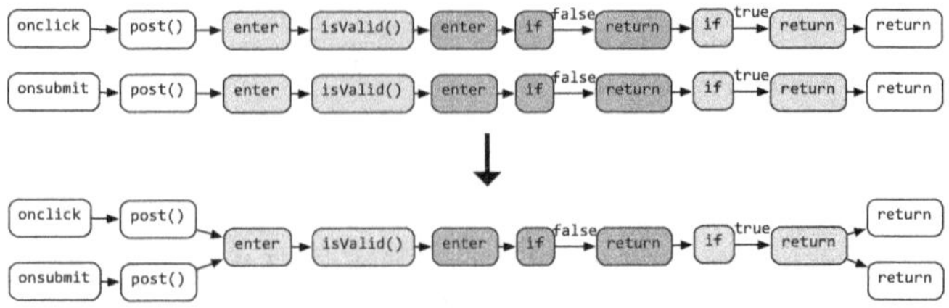

Figure 6. The two output-lacking paths from Figure 5, grouped into a path cluster with two routes to `post()`.

Next, FeedLack identifies the longest sequence of nodes that appears in all paths in a cluster; we call this the *critical sequence*. FeedLack takes the first path in the cluster and numbers each of its nodes from 1 to the number of nodes in the path, also adding each node in the path to a list representing the critical sequence. Then, it iterates through the remaining paths in the cluster, removing all nodes from the intersection list except those also contained in the remaining path. It then takes the final intersection and orders it using the numbers from the first path.

For the final step, FeedLack iterates through all paths in the cluster and identify all paths leading to and from the critical sequence. For example, the path cluster in Figure 6 has to paths leading to the critical sequence and two paths from it. FedLack then presents path clusters as these three parts. Figure 1's warning, for example, lists the two input handlers and the critical sequence; the outgoing paths were omitted since they only included function returns. More complicated paths can have several outgoing paths; for example, FeedLack will often select the conditional of a `switch` statement as a critical sequence and then enumerate the various cases the `switch` might select.

EVALUATION

There are many aspects of FeedLack to evaluate, ranging from the feasibility and legitimacy of its warnings to the understandability of its warnings to developers and usability engineers. In this paper, we focus specifically on FeedLack's *true and false positives* (paths that FeedLack believes are missing output). We do not assess its *false negatives* (paths FeedLack believes provide output but do not), primarily because of the sheer number of negative paths generated by the analysis (there were generally two orders of magnitude more negative paths than positive paths).

Sampling

In sampling web sites, we focused on sites with JavaScript input handlers, avoiding those that used rich internet application frameworks such as Flash or Silverlight. Our sampling approach was stratified and opportunistic and aimed at retrieving at least 300 applications with diverse functionality. One class of applications we chose were highly trafficked sites listed on `http://www.alexa.com`, including sites used for photos, videos, and shopping. Another class of applications included the smaller sites used frequently by the 2nd author, including those of schools, student organizations, restaurants, churches, and government. We also searched the web for "HTML 5 demo" and "HTML 5 application," resulting in several sites that used the `<canvas>` tag for output. Finally, we sampled applications from projects on Google Code (http://code.google.com/hosting/) with live demos.

To obtain the client-side source for these sites, we thoroughly exercised all interactive elements in the page to ensure that all source code for the page was downloaded and then used Google Chrome's page archiving feature to save the HTML and JavaScript source. For the Google Code projects, we downloaded the latest source for the project. The result of this process was 330 web applications and their source code.

Applying FeedLack to the Sample

Next, we ran FeedLack on these 330 web applications. All 330 applications were analyzed in less than 1 minute on a 2 GHz MacBook Pro with a Java process given 2 GB of RAM.

Of the 330 applications, 89 had syntax errors that FeedLack's JavaScript parser could not overcome (including unsupported unicode characters and missing semicolons). Of the remaining, 112 lacked JavaScript input handlers. Of the remaining 129, there were 14 that caused out of memory exceptions. We found two underlying reasons for these exceptions. In 12 applications, there was a function with anywhere from 26 to 119 sequential output-affecting conditionals, causing FeedLack to generate trillions of paths. In the other two cases, FeedLack ran out of memory while clustering tens of thousands of warnings.

In the remaining 115 applications, FeedLack identified 6,887 input handling sites, 6,362 (92%) of which FeedLack believed successfully produced output on all paths. We did not analyze these handlers for true negatives (paths that FeedLack believed produce output but do not) because of the sheer number of paths that would need to be tested manually.

Of the 115 applications, 33 resulted in no FeedLack warnings, leaving 82 applications with at least one output-lacking path to verify. Table 1 shows descriptive statistics about these applications. The average app had 2 HTML files, multiple JavaScript source files, dozens of input handlers, and several hundred JavaScript functions. To get a sense of the functionality in our sample, we categorized each as one of the 7 categories from http://versiontracker.com. As shown in Figure 7, most were games, productivity apps, design tools, or developer tools, including interactive visualizations, calculators, action games, calendars, educational lessons, graphic design tools, photo management tools, social networking apps, web storefronts, and note taking apps.

	min	mean	max
# HTML files	1	2	54
# JS files	0	5	20
# HTML handlers	0	20	278
# JS handlers	0	10	63
# JS functions	6	623	2,176
# JS statements	67	6,678	25,567

Table 1. Aggregate statistics about file, input handler, function and statement counts in our sample of applications.

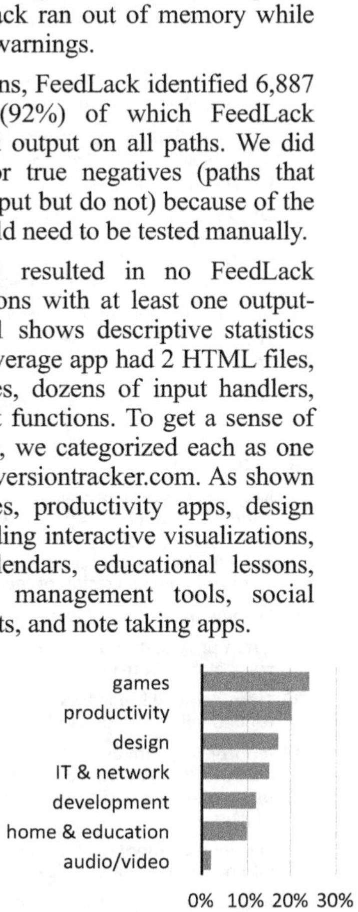

Figure 7. Distribution of application types in our sample.

Applying FeedLack to the remaining 82 applications resulted in 647 output-lacking paths. To evaluate each path, we began by attempting to execute it through manual testing of the live web site (we primarily used Firebug breakpoints, attempting to execute each step the path). If the path was *not* executable, we diagnosed the source of infeasibility in FeedLack's reasoning. If the path *was* feasible, we noted whether the path provided feedback, and if so, diagnosed the cause of the false positive. If it did *not* provide feedback, we described the missing feedback in detail for later analysis. The 1st author then classified each path as one of the following:

- **infeasible** paths, which could not be executed.
- **output-producing** paths, which *did* produce feedback.
- **output-missing** paths, which did *not* produce feedback, but did not lead to confusion about application state.
- **output-deserving** paths, which did *not* produce feedback, causing confusion about application state.

To choose between the last two categories the first author applied widely-used conventions for GUI components to make these decisions. For example, buttons that appeared disabled and did not produce feedback were classified as output-missing; buttons that appeared enabled but did not produce feedback were classified as output-deserving. Similar conventions were applied to other interactions.

Results

Frequencies of warning types appear in Table 2, separated by input event. Of all paths, 12% were infeasible and 18% produced feedback despite FeedLack's warning; 34% did *not* produce feedback but did not appear to need it; and finally, 36% of warned paths lacked feedback and needed it. There was a significant relationship between the kind of input event and warning category ($\chi 2(n{=}647, df{=}42){=}261, p{<}.001$). For example, `click`, `href`, and `mousedown` events were more likely to be warned and were less likely to be false positives than `href`, `mouseover` or `mousewheel` events.

	infeasible		output-producing		output-missing		output-deserving		TOTAL	
click	24	12%	31	16%	69	35%	76	38%	200	31%
href	2	4%	24	43%	3	5%	27	48%	56	9%
mousedown	5	9%	8	15%	30	57%	10	19%	53	8%
mousemove	2	4%	4	8%	22	46%	20	42%	48	7%
mouseup	0	0%	3	6%	13	27%	33	67%	49	8%
mouseenter	0	0%	1	100%	0	0%	0	0%	1	0%
mouseover	2	4%	20	43%	18	39%	6	13%	46	7%
mouseout	5	17%	3	10%	13	45%	8	28%	29	4%
mousewheel	5	71%	2	29%	0	0%	0	0%	7	1%
keypress	21	53%	0	0%	8	20%	11	28%	40	6%
keydown	3	7%	1	2%	19	42%	22	49%	45	7%
keyup	7	20%	0	0%	15	43%	13	37%	35	5%
cut/paste	0	0%	2	100%	0	0%	0	0%	2	0%
multiple	2	6%	15	42%	13	36%	6	17%	36	6%
TOTAL	78	12%	114	18%	223	34%	232	36%	647	

Table 2. The frequency of warning categories by input event; `multiple` represents paths invoked by multiple input event types. Percentages represent the proportion of the cell to its row; total percentages are relative to all warned paths.

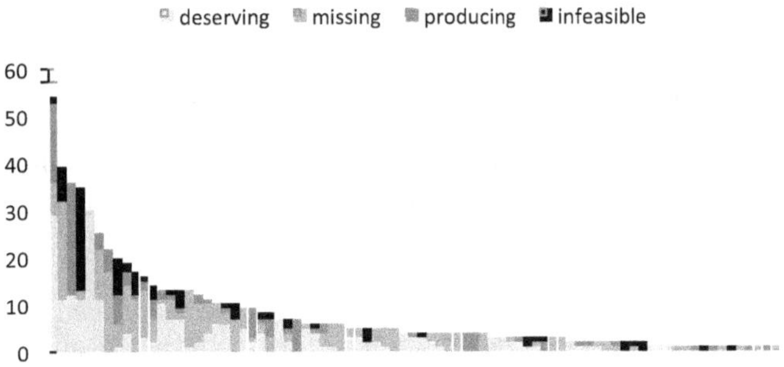

Figure 8. Warned paths per app by category, sorted by decreasing per-app total (excluding apps with no warnings).

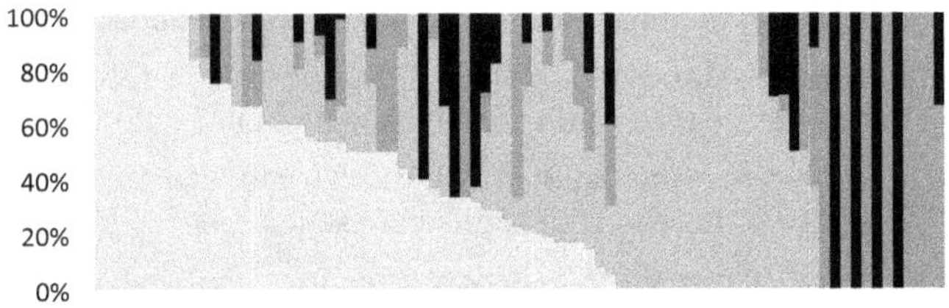

Figure 9. Proportions of warning types per app, sorted by output-deserving warnings (excluding apps with no warnings).

We show the distribution of each of these warning category per application in both absolute counts (Figure 8) and as proportions (Figure 9). Figure 8 shows that the number of warnings in our data ranged anywhere from 1 to 55 and that the number of output-deserving paths was rarely over 10 for an individual application. Figure 9 shows that FeedLack detected at least one output-deserving path for 50 of 115 applications. Therefore, if a team were considering testing a deployed web app with FeedLack, there would be roughly a 43% chance that it would detect at least one problem, if not more (the likelihood of detecting missing feedback on an app in development may be higher, but this was not studied) .

In the rest of this section, we consider each warning category individually. To begin, the 12% of **infeasible** arose from several distinct sources, listed in Table 3. Most of these stemmed from imprecision in FeedLack's call graphs, its lack of data flow analysis, and the impossibility of specific inputs. However, some infeasible warnings revealed unhandled error conditions that were impossible to reach in the current version of the application.The 18% of **output-producing** paths came from several distinct sources (see Table 4). Most came from unresolvable calls, which were assumed to not produce feedback. Many of these could have been due to incomplete archiving of an application's source code.

The 35% of **output-missing** paths were also false positives. As seen in Table 5, they primarily concerned code that was never intended to provide feedback. The most common scenario identified were interactive situations in which users would not expect feedback, such as auto-completing text fields that showed no results when empty. Most of the other handlers tracked mouse clicks for web analytics or time-delayed interactions. Although we considered these negligible, there may be some warnings that others might assess differently. For example, a privacy-sensitive site might actually want to tell users each time their clicks are tracked or explain to users why buttons are disabled.

#	description
26	**Multiple conditions** checked in separate functions that could not be simultaneously true. For example, one function in a calculator had a special case for the `1/x` button; FeedLack reported several paths from non-`1/x` buttons through the `1/x` conditional block.
21	**Infeasible calls**. For example, one application had several calls to a function named `insert()`, but FeedLack mistakenly resolved these calls to functions named insert() that were not reachable at runtime.
11	**Unreachable handlers**, such as abandoned or unfinished code that was never attached to HTML elements. One common source was jQuery expressions that returned empty sets.
10	**Impossible values** in sequences of conditionals that checked for one of from a set of values. For example, one function handled the display of two popup dialogs; if the `id` argument passed by the caller was not one of these two `id` strings, no output would occur, but there were no calls that passed an `id` other than these two strings.
7	**Hidden controls**, where the input that would have led to no feedback was not possible because the control was not visible. For example, in one warning, a cancel button had no effect when the progress dialog containing it was hidden.
3	**Unreachable error cases**, such as exceptions and errors with output-lacking else cases. We were unable to cause these errors.

Table 3. Causes of infeasible warnings.

#	description
54	**Unresolved calls**, where FeedLack could not find matching functions for a call that ultimately produced output. Some of these functions may not have been archived in our sampling.
20	**Undetected multiple handlers** on the same HTML element, at least one of which always produced output. For example, in several cases, an `onclick="return false;"` attribute was added to an HTML element, but a jQuery handler was also added.
12	**Overlooked native output**, such as assigning `window.location.hash` a new value to navigate to a new URL and jQuery extensions.
8	**Timers with imperceptible delay**. Uses of `setInterval()`, `setTimeout()`, and `clearInterval()` with no delay were effectively behaved explicit calls.
8	**Output-affecting state**, where applications modified state that was later used by a timer to affect output. For example, one handler changed the value of a `paused` variable which was inspected in an animation loop to halt feedback.
7	**Inadequate type inference**, causing FeedLack to overlook output (e.g., FeedLack overlooked changes to text area's `value` property when it was the only property referred to on an object expression).

Table 4. Causes of output-producing warnings.

#	description
61	**Negligible modal interaction states**. For example, many popup dialog handlers would hide a popup when clicking on a page body, but would have produced no feedback when the popup was already hidden. These were scenarios where the visual state of the page removed an expectation of feedback.
50	**Web analytics handlers** only intended capture click information.
46	**Event propagation handlers**, coordinating with other handlers to track mouse button states and keyboard event consumption.
32	**Time-delayed behaviors**, such as custom tooltip and link-preloading functionality intended only to appear after a mouse dwell.
14	**Ignored keystrokes**, where nothing in the user interfaces suggested that these keys would provide feedback. These were often unhandled else cases of switch statements that handled a limited set of keys.
14	**Disabled elements**, which had handlers, but provided no feedback when styled to appear disabled or inactive.
5	**Inactive in-progress animations**, such as clicked images that were inactive while animating to full screen, but active before and after.

Table 5. Causes of output-missing warnings.

#	description
41	**Hidden modal behaviors** including buttons and other controls that only produced output when the application was in a particular state. For example, in a chess game, the check mate game over state prevented any further input, but there was no message to indicate that the check mate state had been reached.
36	**Inactive command buttons appearing enabled**, including copy, cancel, load, and other commands. In these cases, the buttons were disabled, but did not appear so.
34	**Ignored keystrokes** in keyboard-driven applications. For example, in one game, the character was controlled by one of seven letter keys; if some key other than these was typed, there was no feedback that the key was not accepted. In other cases, keys that had some conventional behavior had no effect. For example, on a library search page, the enter key failed to submit a query.
32	**Dead links**, similar to those found by web site validators.
31	**Count-limited repeated inputs**, where actions that were invoked repeatedly (e.g., firing missiles in a shooting game) ceased after some number of clicks without explanation.
20	**Silent error conditions**, such as failed checks for particular browsers or keyboard layouts, that provided no feedback on failure.
19	**Missing hover feedback** where hovering or dragging over particular targets would provide no change in output. For example, a calendar application's event resize interaction supported spanning days but did not visualize the days spanned.
10	**Delayed feedback**, including behaviors that took some action, but provided feedback through a `setTimeout()` or `AJAX` call, pausing or lagging the UI for several seconds without intermediate feedback.
9	**Silent state changes**, including controls meant to change state, but when clicked, provided no feedback about the success of the change. One app had a save link that did not indicate success or failure.

Table 6. Causes of output-deserving warnings.

The last 35% of **output-deserving** paths all lacked feedback and violated the conventions of common GUI interactions. As shown in Table 6, the most common warnings involved modal behaviors in which input events only had an effect when the application was in a particular state, but that state was not visible. Other common problems included ignored keystrokes, dead links, silent error conditions, and missing selection feedback on items that appeared selectable.

DISCUSSION

The results of our evaluation show that FeedLack can detect a variety of significant feedback problems while also detecting several places in web application code potentially in need of error handling code. In our discussion, we consider FeedLack's limitations and generalizability in detail.

Prospects for Reducing False Positives

While FeedLack's false positive rates are high, they are comparable to the 50% rates reported for the widely used static analysis tool FindBugs [3]. Nevertheless, there may be ways to eliminate some false positives. For example, many of the sources of false positives were related to inadequate type inference and call graph precision; this could be improved by using more sophisticated type inference analyses (e.g., http://doctorjs.org/). Similarly, there were many kinds of input events with high false positive rates; `mousedown`, `mouseover`, `mouseout`, and `keypress` events, and handlers invoked by multiple input events, were least likely to require feedback. Were these omitted from FeedLack's analyses, most warnings would have been output-deserving. Of course, omitting these warnings would also omit some true positives; this is a tradeoff inherent to any defect detection analysis.

Issues that FeedLack Cannot Detect

First and foremost, FeedLack cannot detect issues with the *quality* of feedback. To be sure, many of the scenarios that FeedLack identified as providing feedback were still confusing. Output was often so far away from the source of input, there was no perceptible change; detecting such problems might require modeling of the location and appearance of HTML elements on screen. Moreover, much of the output produced had a weak conceptual connection to the input that caused it (in one application, clicking a save button caused a mysterious icon to appear, apparently indicating success). Without further research on feedback verifications like FeedLack, analyzing the semantic correspondence between input and output still requires the talent of experienced usability engineers.

FeedLack cannot find all missing feedback in web applications. For example, there are many things that can cause a JavaScript input handler to halt or stall, including references to undefined properties, unresolvable functions, memory errors, uncaught exceptions, infinite loops, slow algorithms and a variety of other runtime issues. While these are outside of FeedLack's scope, there are complementary approaches to detect these problems [2,11,18].

Another feedback issue that FeedLack cannot detect is the *absence* of input handlers on any HTML element that might appear to handle input but does not. For example, most web site's logos navigate to the site's home page, but some site's logos do not have these links. There is no obvious way for a machine to know which elements should have handlers (moreover, verifying that elements have handlers at all is complicated further by the flexibility of runtime binding).

FeedLack also overlooks situations where an application assigns an output-affecting property a value that is equivalent to its old value. For example, there are many cases where an element might be assigned an equivalent `class`, meaning the user would experience no visible change in the web page. More generally, applications might redirect users to the same page they were on already, or web servers might return dynamically-generated but identical web pages, again leading to situations where the application appears not to respond.

Making Sense of FeedLack Warnings

One major aspect of FeedLack we have yet to evaluate is to what extent usability engineers and software developers can actually understand FeedLack's warnings. We were able to comprehend the warnings (even the unfamiliar code of the 82 applications in our sample), but this does not mean that it would be easy for users without significant knowledge of FeedLack's analyses. Given that FeedLack report paths through code and not actions on a concrete user interface, usability engineers may have challenges understanding and triaging these issues. Future work might involve converting FeedLack's warned paths into concrete actions on the web application UI, better enabling testers to assess the warnings.

Generalizing FeedLack to Other Platforms

Few of FeedLack's algorithms are particular to the web; most of the work necessary to adapt FeedLack to other platforms is identifying input-handling and output-affecting statements, and creating language-specific CFGs. One possible challenge, however, comes from the extent to which user interface event handling and output is *declarative*. It is simple in JavaScript and HTML to detect UI controls and changes to their behavior, because most APIs require users to declare those changes explicitly. In many statically typed imperative languages, however, creating a UI button requires several lines of instantiation, configuration, and event listening code, as do customizations to these controls. Tracking these customizations, especially across procedures and subclasses, could prove difficult, although prior work has had some success on object-oriented UI toolkits [12].

CONCLUSIONS AND FUTURE WORK

We have presented FeedLack, an analysis for automatically detecting missing feedback in web applications. We have demonstrated that FeedLack can detect significant feedback issues in real web applications, as well as presented an analysis of its false positives and limitations. While FeedLack is not a replacement for usability testing or expertise, it may be an effective supplement to empirical approaches to detecting feedback issues, much like HTML validators and other software verification tools.

Our results also suggest several directions for future work. We want to explore the utility of FeedLack alongside other forms of software testing and verification by deploying it into a real web development team. Part of this deployment could involve tracking feedback issues over successive versions of web application UIs, and adding explicit support for suppressing known false positives. There may also be ways to extend FeedLack to support accessibility analyses, checking to see not only whether applications provide feedback, but that the feedback it provides is compatible with screen readers and other accessibility tools.

More generally, we would like to explore the automatic detection of other usability problems beyond feedback, such as issues with graphic design consistency, recognition vs. recall problems, confusing error messages, and support for cancel and undo. We believe that tools that tie usability concerns to code are a key part of integrating the work of usability engineers with the rest of a software team.

ACKNOWLEDGEMENTS

This material is based in part upon work supported by the National Science Foundation under Grant Number CCF-0952733. Any opinions, findings, and conclusions or recommendations expressed in this material are those of the author(s) and do not necessarily reflect the views of the National Science Foundation.

REFERENCES

1. Akers, D., Simpson, M., Jeffries, R., & Winograd, T. 2009. Undo and erase events as indicators of usability problems. *ACM Conf. on Human Factors in Computing (CHI)*, 659-668.
2. Artzi, S., Dolby, J., Tip, F., & Pistoia, M. 2010. Practical fault localization for dynamic web applications. *Int'l Conf. on Software Engineering (ICSE)*, 265-274.
3. Ayewah, N., Pugh, W., Morgenthaler, J. D., Penix, J., & Zhou, Y. 2007. Evaluating static analysis defect warnings on production software. *ACM Workshop on Program Analysis For Software Tools and Engr.*, 1-8.
4. Blackmon, M. H., Polson, P. G., Kitajima, M., & Lewis, C. 2002. Cognitive walkthrough for the web. *ACM Conf. on Human Factors in Computing Systems (CHI)*, 463-470.
5. Bodden, E. & Havelund, K. 2008. Racer: effective race detection using AspectJ. *Int'l Symposium on Software Testing and Analysis (ISSTA)*, 155-166.
6. Bruun, A., Gull, P., Hofmeister, L., & Stage, J. 2009. Let your users do the testing: a comparison of three remote asynchronous usability testing methods. *ACM Conf. on Human Factors in Computing Systems (CHI)*, 1619-1628.
7. Godefroid, P., Levin, M.Y., & Molnar, D.A. 2008. Automated whitebox fuzz testing. *Network Distributed Security Symposium (NDSS)*.
8. Hovemeyer, D. & Pugh, W. 2004. Finding bugs is easy. *ACM Conf. on Object-Oriented Prog. Systems, Languages, and Applications (OOPSLA)*, 132-136.
9. Hutchins, E. L., Hollan, J. D., & Norman, D. A. 1985. Direct manipulation interfaces. *Human-Computer Interaction 1*(4), December, 311-338.
10. Ivory, M. Y. & Hearst, M. A. 2001. The state of the art in automating usability evaluation of user interfaces. ACM Computing Surveys 33(4), December, 470-516.
11. Ko, A.J. & Wobbrock, J.O. 2010. Cleanroom: Edit-time error detection with the uniqueness heuristic. *IEEE Symposium on Visual Languages and Human-Centric Computing*, to appear.
12. Ko, A.J. & Myers, B.A. 2008 Debugging reinvented: asking and answering why and why not questions about program behavior. *Int'l Conference on Software Engineering (ICSE)*, 301-310.
13. Lecerof, A. & Paterno F. 1998. Automatic support for usability evaluation. *IEEE Trans on Software Engineering (TSE)* 24(10), October, 863– 888.
14. Lindgaard, G. & Chattratichart, J. 2007. Usability testing: what have we overlooked? *ACM Conf. on Human Factors in Computing Systems*, 1415-1424.
15. Mahajan, R. & Shneiderman, B. 1997. Visual and textual consistency checking tools for graphical user interfaces. *IEEE Trans. on Soft. Engr. 23*(11), 722-735.
16. Nielsen, J. & Molich, R. 1990. Heuristic evaluation of user interfaces. *ACM Conf. on Human Factors in Computing Systems,* 249-256.
17. Norman, D.A. 1988. *The design of everyday things*. New York: Doubleday.
18. Novark, G., Berger, E.D., & Zorn, B.G. 2009. Efficiently and precisely locating memory leaks and bloat. *ACM Conf. on Programming Language Design and Implementation (PLDI)*, 397–407.
19. Richards, G., Lebresne, S., Burg, B., & Vitek, J. 2010. An analysis of the dynamic behavior of JavaScript programs. *SIGPLAN Notices 45*(6), June, 1-12.

Entity-Linking Interfaces in User-Contributed Content: Preference and Performance

Xiao Dong*, F. Maxwell Harper, Joseph A. Konstan****

*Industrial and System Engineering
University of Minnesota
Minneapolis, Minnesota, USA
dongx080@umn.edu

**Computer Science and Engineering
University of Minnesota
Minneapolis, Minnesota, USA
{harper, konstan}@cs.umn.edu

ABSTRACT

The ability to embed links to other resources in user generated content can help authors create more useful and usable content. A variety of interfaces have emerged for entity-linking at popular online sites; such interfaces vary in the way that entity linking is initiated (in-band or out-of-band with respect to the message creation), the timing of entity resolution (interrupting or deferred), and the method of resolving the entity (auto-completion or search). Four interfaces mimicking popular entity linking websites were developed and tested. Results showed that out-of-band initiation (e.g., a link button) was faster to learn, but that in-band initiation performance improved with familiarity. Deferred search was disliked and led to worse performance. And auto-completion was generally preferred to search interfaces.

Author Keywords

Entity reference, user generated content, cross linking.

ACM Classification Keywords

H5.m. Information interfaces and presentation (e.g., HCI): Miscellaneous.

General Terms

Experimentation, Performance, Design.

INTRODUCTION

Increasingly, the modern Web is made up of user-generated content – sites like Facebook, Flickr, and Wikipedia are driven by user contributions. Matching this trend is the increasing diversity of entity types, both on-site media such as photos, videos, or web pages, and real-world entities such as people, places, and external things such as movies. For user-generated content to take full advantage of the power of the Web, users must be able to embed links to such entities in the content they generate; these entities must be recognized so they can be used to connect readers to the right pages or information. For example, a Facebook user referring to a friend in a status update is able to create a clickable link that points to that friend's Facebook page; a Wikipedia user editing an article is similarly able to insert links to other articles.

We became particularly interested in the challenge of entity-linking as we were developing an online question-and-answer (Q&A) forum for the MovieLens movie recommending site. It is critical for both questions and answers contributed to this forum to be able to link to specific movies both to enable users to click through when reading the Q&A and to display movie-related information and recommendations alongside the posts. There are several reasons why movie linking is a particularly challenging entity linking problem. First, the entity (movie) has a single canonical name which users may not be familiar with. For example, the movie a user think of as "Star Wars" may actually be "Star Wars: Episode IV-A New Hope (1977)". In this case "Star Wars" is an ambiguous reference that could refer to any of eight different movies (the six "Star Wars" films, plus the animated "Clone Wars" and a documentary). Second, the same movie title may appear in multiple years. For example, "Pride and Prejudice" has versions from 1940 and 1995, and "Titanic" has versions from 1953 and 1997. Also, canonical names typically move leading articles to the end of a title. For instance, the movie "The Godfather" is in the database as "Godfather, The". Given these challenges and the fact that the motivation of user asking or answering a question is primarily directed towards the question rather than towards movie linking, we were particularly interested in finding interfaces that would be easy to use and easy to use successfully because we feared that a difficult-to-use interface would lead the user to simply bypass the movie linking entirely. Given this goal, we set out to investigate the strengths and weaknesses of the most common entity linking interfaces found online today. To our knowledge no one has conducted a study comparing them.

Researchers have looked at general questions of usability of and user satisfaction with interactive web pages. Lowry et al. [12] studied how perceived interactivity of e-commerce websites affects users' satisfaction about them. They found that if users expected higher interactivity but the website did not provide it, user satisfaction was jeopardized. Sicilia et al. [15] studied the differences between an "interactive" Web site and a "non-interactive" Web site, finding that the interactive Web site leads to more information processing and higher user favorability toward the Web site. Similarly, studies have found that Web usability is increased with the incorporation of dynamic Web technologies (Ajax). Kasemvilas and Firpo [10] compared the usability of blogs with and without Ajax technology. They measured both preference and performance as indicators of blog usability. While there is no clear result on preference, they found that performance on the Ajax blog was worse for first-time use, but better for subsequent use. Kluge et al. [11] studied Ajax-based auto-completion search in a trip planner site. They found evidence that auto-completion has advantages in terms of both satisfaction and efficiency. However, a counter-statement on these dynamic web design element was argued by Nielsen [14]. He expressed his concern on "rich" internet UIs (e.g. Ajax shopping carts) because, if not designed well, they confuse users more than they help.

Besides these general web usability issues, there are specific challenges associated with incorporating *named entity linking* interfaces into Web sites. To incorporate a link into their post, users must interrupt their typing to search for and select entities. Modern interfaces have adopted a variety of approaches to mitigate this interruption: some use hot-keys to trigger a search window, which others add a button to the interface that users click to start the search procedure. However, it is unclear which of these interfaces is best from the perspective of user preference and performance.

One proposed solution is to automatically recognize and resolve links to such named entities. Drenner et al. [5] developed such an automated movie linking system. They found some success, but also found significant challenges due to users referring to movies using shorthand and due to movie titles that had to be placed on stop lists due to their common use as English terms (e.g., "Big" and "It"). These drawbacks led us to explore manual rather than automated linking. Even so, other researchers have used combination of algorithm classifier [8] and machine learning approaches [13] to increase success in automatic recognition of named entities. Cucerzan [4] reported on an entity recognition system for Wikipedia that used various techniques, including category information, to achieve high recognition rates. We recognize that there are opportunities to consider contextual information (including, for example, the surrounding terms and the movies already linked) to better support automatic recognition in movie linking, but we leave that as a problem for future work.

We surveyed popular websites to identify different styles of entity referencing for our movie linking problem. Twelve websites (Facebook, Flickr, Last.fm, Livejournal, Wikipedia, Twitter, Blogger, Google docs, Amazon, Threadless, LibraryThing, Engadget) which include some forms of entity linking function were included in the review. During the review, we found nine dimensions that were useful for comparing these interfaces:

- Type of entity being linked to (e.g., people, product, document)
- The context of entity linking (e.g., status message, photo, article post)
- Can links be made to targets that don't exist yet?
- The way to initiate a linking process (e.g., special characters, button)
- The sequence of steps for linking (e.g., action first, target first)
- The interface to complete the link (e.g., dialog window, auto-complete popup)
- The way to narrow down the result (e.g. auto-complete, search)
- Dose entity linking requires mark-up characters
- The appearance of the link after creation (e.g. hyperlink, plain text)

We found that Facebook, Wikipedia, Flickr, and Amazon interfaces spanned the different interaction styles and thus were good representatives to study. Of the nine dimensions, we identified three that seemed most critical to user experience.

Initiation Method. Is the linking initiated by an explicit *out-of-band* action separate from typing the user's text content (e.g., selecting an "insert link" button), or is it initiated *in-band* as part of the typed message?

Resolution Timing. Is the link to the entity resolved immediately, *interrupting* the user's completion of the message, or is it *deferred*, allowing the user to finish the message first, but putting resolution out of the immediate context?

Narrowing Method. Is the resolution performed though a *search* interface (where the typed name is sent to a search engine and candidate entities are ranked and returned) or an *auto-complete* interface (where candidates are shown and narrowed as keystrokes are typed)?

As we evaluate designs at different points in the design space, we look at both user preference and performance. We also consider whether the level of prior user experience is a moderating factor. We therefore explore the following three research questions:

- How does the entity linking initiation method of an entity-linking interface (out-of-band vs. in-band) affect user preference and performance?
- How does the resolution timing of an entity-linking interface (interrupting vs. deferred) affect user preference and performance?
- How does the narrowing method of an entity-linking interface (search vs. auto-complete) affect user preference and performance?

We next introduce the movie linking interfaces we implemented and studied. Then we present the design and results of our lab study, followed by a discussion of the implications and limitations of the results for interface design. We conclude with a discussion of the generalizability and recommendations for future work.

MOVIE LINKING INTERFACES

We developed four prototypes that mimic four entity-linking styles we identified in our survey. Each experimental interface also includes brief instructions, a text box for typing the user comment, and a preview area. Our interfaces all supported linking to a single entity type: movies from the MovieLens database of over 15,000 titles.

Facebook-style

On Facebook's status sharing box, users can type "@" followed by the name of their friend to insert a link to his/her profile page [6]. An auto-filtered friend list pops up that dynamically responds to user input. This interface is an in-band, interrupting interface with auto-completion.

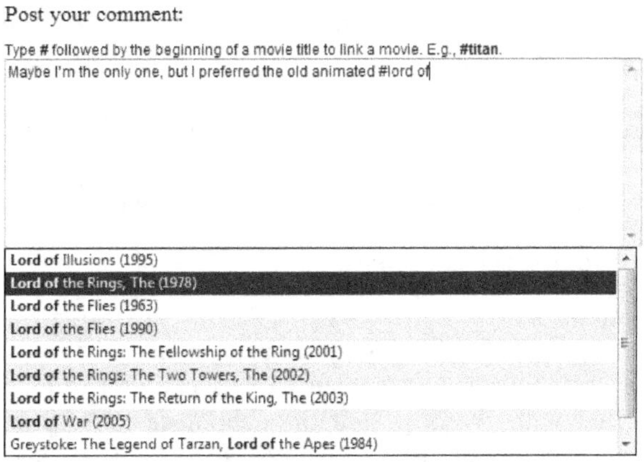

Figure 1. Facebook-style interface for linking movies

In our adaptation of this interface, whenever users want to insert a link to a movie, they can press "#" to tell the interface that the following input text is going to be a movie name. Once users start typing after "#" key, a movie list shows up below the text box as shown by Figure 1. The movie list is filtered as users type, using an Ajax auto-complete interface. If there is no match with the user's input, the movie list will disappear. When inserting a link, users can choose to complete the whole movie name or select from popup movie list. Movie selection can be done with either keyboard (UP, DOWN arrows and ENTER key) or mouse (Scroll, Point, and Click).

Wiki-style

On Wikipedia, page authors can insert a link to another page within Wikipedia by enclosing the page name in double square brackets ("[[ ]]"). There is no Ajax search as users type. Instead, a search is performed when a "show preview" button is pressed. Thus this interface is also in-band, but it has deferred resolution based on search.

In our adaptation of this interface, users can type brackets ("[ ]") to enclose the movie title (or key words from it) when composing a forum post. Multiple movie references can be added with multiple pairs of brackets. The search and match for movies is deferred until users press the "preview" button. The search results are presented in an inline drop-down list where users can browse and select the one they want to insert, as shown in Figure 2. If only one match is returned the drop down list will be replaced by the link to the movie. "Movie not found" is shown if there are no matching results. A selection in the dropdown list triggers an update in the text box to replace the keywords within brackets with the selected movie name.

Flickr-style

When browsing photos, Flickr supports adding tags such as links to a person [7]. It is done by selecting "Actions-> Add a Person", which activates a pop-up frame with an Ajax auto-complete search widget. This interface has out-of-band initiation, but then resolves the entity reference through real time interruption and auto-complete.

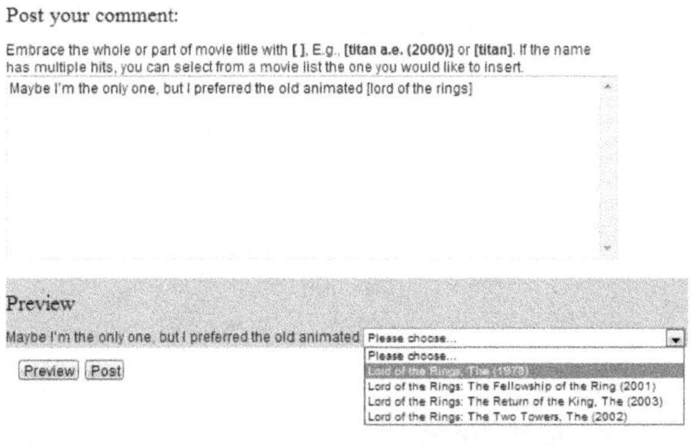

Figure 2. Wiki-style interface for linking movies

In our adaptation of this interface, we put a button ("Insert a movie") on top of the input text box. When users click this button, a pop-up frame appears with an Ajax auto-complete search widget (Figure 3). This widget works the same as the Facebook-style list. The movie list is filtered as the user types, and the movie list disappears if no match is found for the user's input. The use of keyboard and mouse are both enabled to select a movie from the list.

Amazon-style

In Amazon's product comments, a link to another product can be added using a button labeled "Insert a product link" [1]. That button opens a pop-up frame with a search box where users search for the product. The user types a search phrase, and then clicks a button to initiate the search. Search results are displayed below the search box in the popup window. This interface is also out-of-band with real-time interruption, but has search-based resolution.

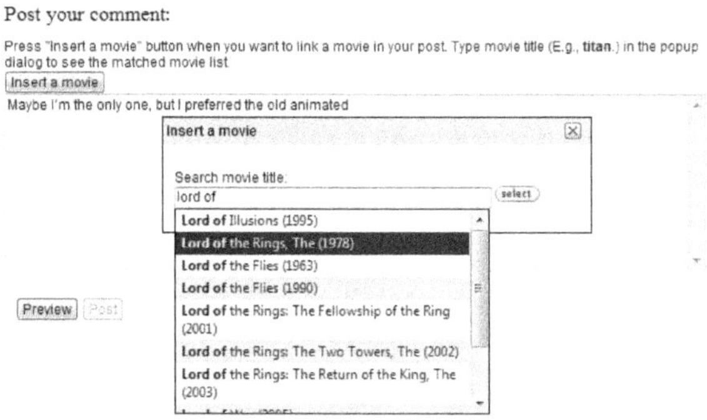

Figure 3. Flickr-style interface for linking movies

In our adaptation of this interface, a button initiates movie linking (identical to the Flickr-style interface). After the users presses the button, a frame pops up where they can type movie keywords to search for movies as shown in Figure 4. Users can press the "select" button in front of a movie to select that movie for insertion into their post. "Movie not found" is shown if there were no matching search results.

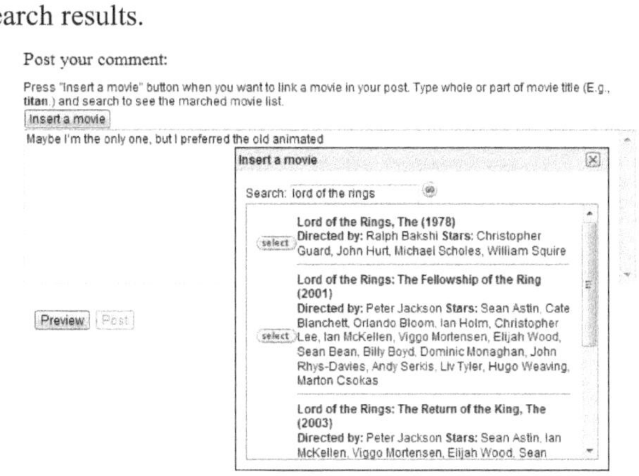

Figure 4. Amazon-style interface for linking movies

Table 1 shows the interfaces and their placement along our three design dimensions. Other possible combinations of these dimensions are either uncommon on current websites or simply do not make sense. For example, we have not seen cases of out-of-band initiation (such as a button) coupled with deferred search.

We used special markup in the text box to identify resolved movie links. The inserted movie link is shown as "[movie] Movie Title [/movie]" in the text box for all interfaces except for Wiki-style which is shown as "[Movie Title]". It is shown as an actual hyperlink in the preview. Users can mouse over it to pop-up director and cast information.

The search mechanisms for these prototypes can be categorized into two types: "prefix plus" search and "keyword" search. The search-based interfaces (Wiki-style and Amazon-style) used "keyword" search where user's input was parsed into keywords which were then searched using "AND" criteria to find movies containing all of the keywords. Auto-complete interfaces (Facebook-style and Flickr-style) used "prefix plus" search where the user's input was first taken as a string to search for movies with the same prefix. These were listed first in the result set. A keyword search was also run, and movies matching the keywords were listed after the prefix-matching movies. This design is based on observations of common practice. We understand that presentation of search results can affect user's preference and performance. Hyvönen and Mäkelä argued that semantically organized search results can present logical reasoning of user input and help user more when he is not accurate about his search keyword [9]. Amin et al. [2] conducted two studies investigating organization strategies (Alphabetical, Group and Composite) of auto-completion search results. They found Group and Composite organization help users search faster, and are easier to understand and to use than Alphabetical. However our main focus was on styles of interface, thus for both types of searching, no alphabetical or chronological sorting was used. Matching movies are displayed according to their position in the MovieLens database.

Interfaces	Initiation	Timing	Narrowing
Facebook-style	in-band	interrupt	auto-complete
Wiki-style	in-band	deferred	search
Flickr-style	out-of-band	interrupt	auto-complete
Amazon-style	out-of-band	interrupt	search

Table 1. The placement of interfaces on design dimensions

EXPERIMENTAL METHOD

Participants

16 subjects (13 male, 3 female) participated in this study. All of the subjects were students at university of Minnesota, recruited with flyers posted throughout campus. Subjects had an average age of 24 years (SD=2.94). Their average computer and Internet use experience was 12.31 years (SD=3.03) and 10.19 years (SD=1.97). We asked subjects "How often do you actively participate in online discussion forums?" with a response scale from "every day" through "never." Nine subjects responded "Every day" or "Once every 2-3 days"; they were categorized as experienced. Seven subjects responded "Once a month", "Less than once a month", or "Never"; they were categorized as inexperienced. No subjects responded "Once a week" or "Once every two weeks," confirming that we had a bimodal distribution with a clear separation of experience.

Experimental Design

This lab study was conducted as a series of one-on-one sessions between an *interviewer* (one of the authors) and a *subject*. These sessions were recorded on video for subsequent analysis. See Figure 5 below:

Procedure

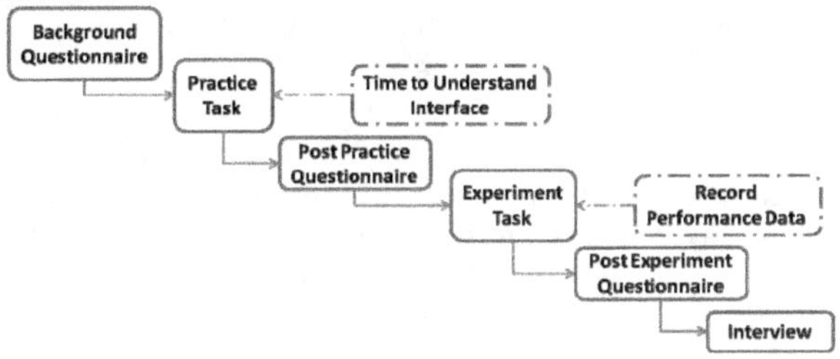

Figure 5. An overview of the experimental session

In each session, the interviewer introduced himself and the purpose of the study, asked the subject to sign a consent form, and then asked the subject to complete a questionnaire about his/her experience using online forums.

The subject's first task – known as the *practice task* – was designed to familiarize the subject with each of the experimental interfaces and to collect data on initial impressions and learnability. The interviewer introduced the idea of movie linking and showed an example of movie linking on the MovieLens Web site. The subject was then asked to insert a movie link to "*Lord of the Rings: The Fellowship of the Ring (2001)*" into a simulated discussion forum using each of the four experimental interfaces. The order of interfaces shown to subjects was counter-balanced. The subject was instructed to insert the movie link as quickly as possible without writing anything else. Once the subject completed the *practice task*, he or she was asked to fill out a post-practice questionnaire, which asked about their initial impressions of each of the interfaces.

The interviewer then asked the subject to begin the *experimental task*, a longer trial where the subject attempted a sequence of movie linking tasks. For each experimental interface, the subject saw four consecutive Web pages, with each page instructing the subject to finish one task in task booklet. It required the subject to write a fictional forum post of the following form: "*I like to watch: movie link 1 and movie link 2*" where, in the task booklet, movie links were shown as movie posters to avoid introducing bias towards a particular form of movie title. The subject was asked to complete 16 trials (4 for each interface style), for a total of 32 movie linking actions. The 32 movies were preselected to control for the *length* and the *ambiguity* of the movie title.[1] The orders of movies within conditions were randomly shuffled for each subject. Between subjects, we balanced the order in which the four interfaces were used to control for order effects. At the end of the study, the interviewer informally collected the subject's final feedback on the different interfaces, and gave the subject a $10 gift card.

RESULTS

In this study, we report on both subjective and objective data. For subjective preferences, we rely on subjects' responses to survey questions. For objective outcomes, we reviewed video capture of the experimental session to evaluate the time to complete different part of tasks, and to measure when and where errors occurred.

Subjective Preferences

We asked subjects to rate their preferences for each interface after the practice task, and again after the experimental task. Subjects rated their *preferences* by answering the question "How do you rate this interface overall?" and mark their answers on a 7-point Likert scale. Figure 6 summarizes the results:

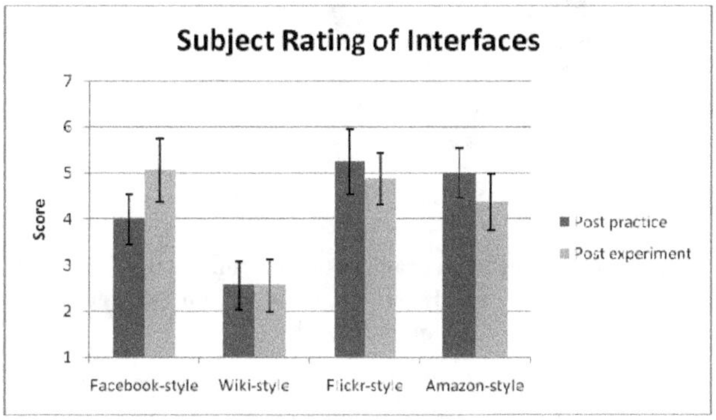

Figure 6. Subjects' average preference scores for each interface after completing the practice task, and again after completing the experimental task

We used repeated measures with *style of interface* as a within-group factor to analyze post practice and post experiment rating data. Post-hoc Bonferroni multiple comparison is employed to investigate pairwise differences. We only report statistically significant differences.

The Wiki-style interface was rated the worst in the post-practice questionnaire ($F_{(3,45)}$=14.511, p<0.001[2]; post-hoc stats: Wiki-style vs. Facebook-style, p=0.001; Wiki-style vs. Flickr-style, p=0.001; Wiki-style vs. Amazon-style, p<0.001); subjects' perceptions did not improve after the experimental task ($F_{(3,45)}$=18.069, p<0.001; post-hoc stats: Wiki-style vs. Facebook-style, p<0.001; Wiki-style vs. Flickr-style, p<0.001; Wiki-style vs. Amazon-style,

[1] Longer movie titles potentially require more typing than shorter titles. More ambiguous titles potentially require more disambiguation in the search results (e.g., "star wars" is ambiguous, as there are several movies in the MovieLens database that contain these two words in the title).

[2] All ANOVAs performed in this study were two-tailed tests.

p=0.001). Two of the interfaces exhibited a significant change in user preference after the experimental task. Users came to rate the Facebook-style interface significantly higher (t=3.597, p=0.003) and the Amazon-style interface significantly lower (t=2.298, p=0.036), based on paired sample t-tests. There were no significant differences between the two surveys for the Wiki-style or Flickr-style interfaces.

We also measured users' subjective rating of *ease of use* and *learnability* on 7-point Likert scales (Figure 7). The Wiki-style interface was the least easy to use of the four ($F_{(3,45)}$=13.458, p<0.001; post-hoc stats: Wiki-style vs. Facebook-style, p=0.001; Wiki-style vs. Flickr-style, p<0.001; Wiki-style vs. Amazon-style, p=0.001) and the most difficult to learn ($F_{(3,45)}$=19.841, p<0.001; post-hoc stats: Wiki-style vs. Facebook-style, p=0.001; Wiki-style vs. Flickr-style, p<0.001; Wiki-style vs. Amazon-style, p=0.002).

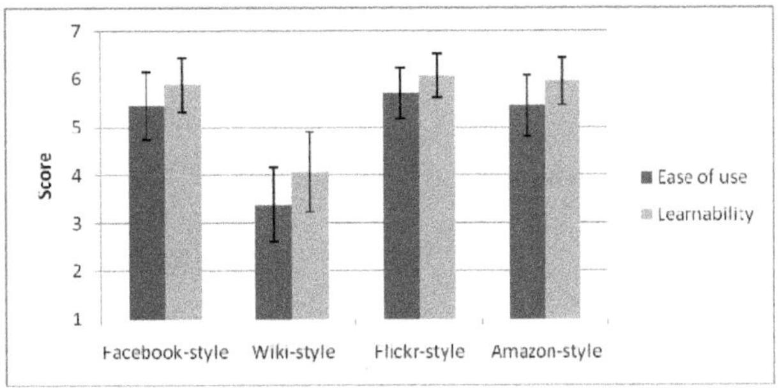

Figure 7. Subjects' average ratings about ease of use and learnability for each interface, from the post-experiment questionnaire

To better understand whether users with different levels of familiarity with online systems express different preferences for these interfaces, we compare the responses of *experienced* users with *inexperienced* users. We tested the differences using a repeated measure with one within-group factor (*style of interface*) and one between-group factor (*online forum using experience*). In the post-practice questionnaire, there was an interaction effect between experience level and interface type ($F_{(3,42)}$=2.787, p=0.050), showing that compared to experienced users, inexperienced users learned to prefer the Flickr-style and Amazon-style interfaces more but learned to prefer the Wiki-style interface less. This interaction effect did not occur in the post-experiment rating scores. See Figures 8 and 9 for details:

We obtained a confirmatory measure of user preferences using a question that asked subjects to rank the four interfaces from best to worse. Overall, the top-ranked interfaces were: Facebook-style: 53%; Flickr-style 34%; Amazon-style: 13%; Wiki-style: 0%. The bottom-ranked interfaces were: Wiki-style: 75%; Amazon-style: 12.5%; Facebook-style: 6.25%; Flickr-style 6.25%.

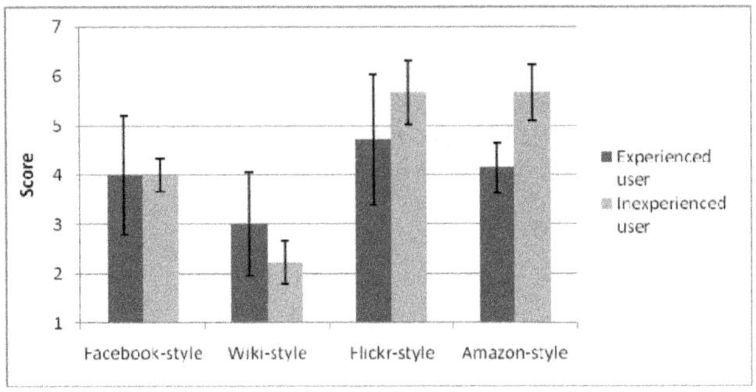

Figure 8. Subjects' average preference scores for each interface, by level of experience with online forums, from the post-practice questionnaire

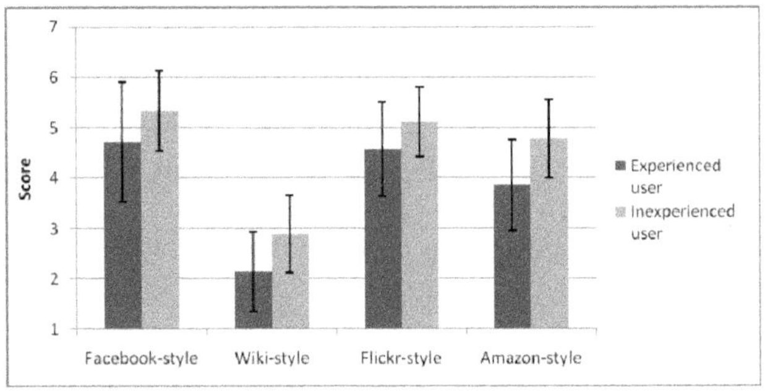

Figure 9. Subjects' average preference scores for each interface, by level of experience with online forums, from the post-experiment questionnaire

Performance

During the *practice task*, *Time to understand interface* was measured by looking at the time between the interface completely loading and the first user action to initiate movie linking. A repeated measure test was used with *style of interface* as a within-group factor. We found statistically significant differences among the interfaces ($F_{(3,45)}$=3.112, p=0.035). The Wiki-style interface had the slowest times, on average, though we only find a statistically significant difference between it and the Amazon-style interface – the fastest interface to understand on average (Wiki-style vs. Amazon-style, p=0.012). See Figure 10 for more details about overall results, and Figure 11 for the data broken out by user experience with online forums.

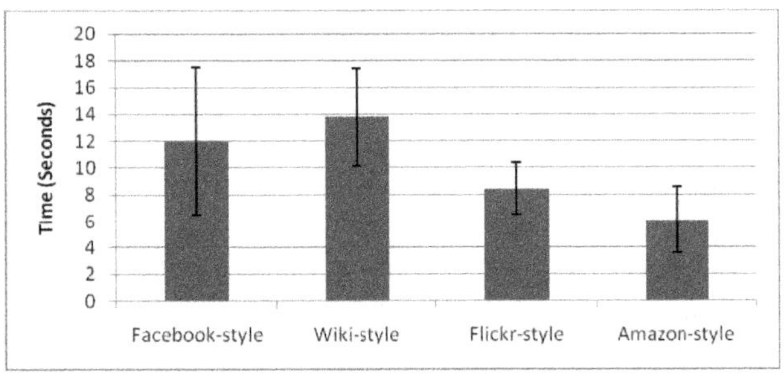

Figure 10. Average measured values of "time to understand interface" across the four interfaces

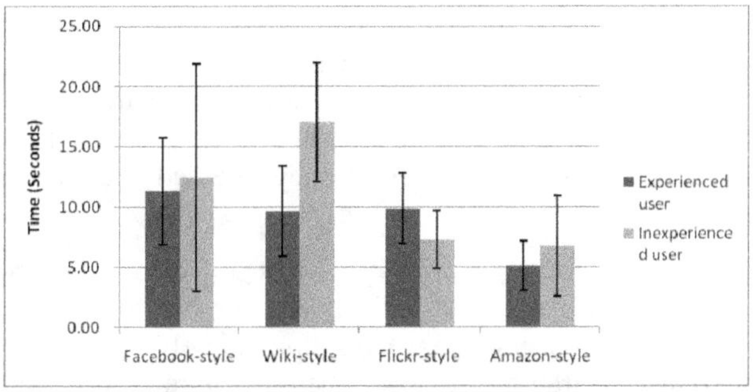

Figure 11. Average measured values of "time to understand interface" across the four interfaces, by subjects' experience using online forums

During the *experimental task*, *Time to insert movie link* was measured as the time spent between first action to initiate movie linking and the completion of movie link insertion. We controlled for the *length* and *ambiguity* of movie titles in the *experimental task*, as we hypothesized that longer and more ambiguous titles would require more time. We found that this was indeed the case: on average, linking the longest and most ambiguous titles took the most time ($F_{(3,45)}$=11.149, p<0.001). However, we found no statistically significant interaction effect between the type of interface and the length or ambiguity of the movie being linked. Thus, none of the four interfaces especially thrived or faltered in the presence of more difficult entities.

To determine the main effects between interface type and time to insert movie link, we used a repeated measure test with *style of interface* as a within-group factor. There were statistically significant differences among the interfaces in *time to insert a link* ($F_{(3,45)}$=16.272, p<0.001). The post-hoc pair wise comparison shows that Wiki-style interface took the longest time (Wiki-style vs. Facebook-style, p<0.001; Wiki-style vs. Flickr-style, p=0.003; Wiki-style vs. Amazon-style, p=0.056) while the Facebook-style interface took the least time (Facebook-style vs. Flickr-style, p=0.030; Facebook-style vs. Amazon-style, p=0.063). See Figure 12 for details. There is a trend that experienced users take less time than inexperienced users across all groups, but this effect is not statistically significant. See Figure 13 for details.

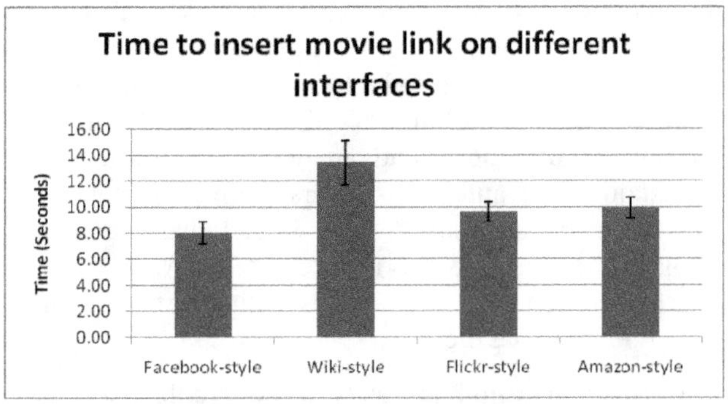

Figure 12. Average measured values of "time to insert movie link" across the four interfaces

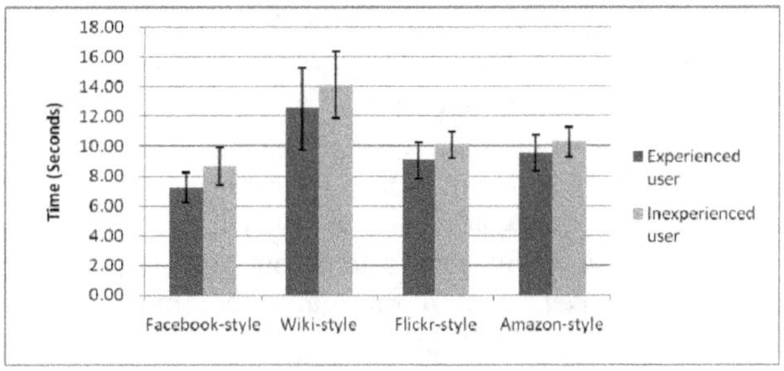

Figure 13. Average measured values of "time to insert movie link" across the four interfaces, by subjects' experience using online forums

To investigate whether subjects experienced a learning effect through the experiment, we examine the average time taken per movie link across the experimental task. Subjects inserted 8 movie links for each interface; the following figures (14 and 15) show the average time taken by users to insert these movie links at each step. For experienced users, there is no evidence of a learning effect - the time taken to insert a movie depend more on the particular trial than on the subjects' amount of experience with that interface in the experiment. On the other hand, inexperienced users show a dramatic decrease in time taken after their first trial using the Wiki-style interface ($F_{(7,56)}$=2.152, p=0.053).

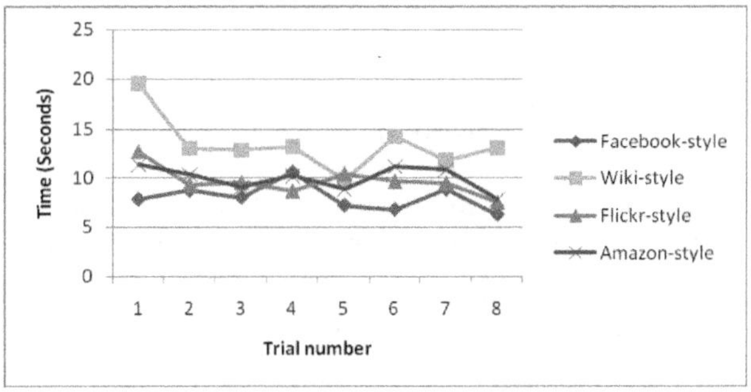

Figure 14. Average time spent on each trial for different interfaces

In this study, we also recorded the time subjects spent on each aspect of the movie linking process. Previewing the post took a mean time of 6.84 seconds (SD=12.20), 27.5% of total time (Mean=24.86, SD=13.51). The preview times for different interfaces were: Facebook-style: 3.28; Wiki-style: 15.85; Flickr-style: 6.42; Amazon-style: 2.12.

Error analysis

We measured *error rate* by dividing the number of incorrectly specified movie links by the total number of movie links in the task. The error rates for each interface were: Facebook-style interface, 1.56%; Wiki-style interface, 0.78%; Flickr-style interface, 0%; Amazon-style interface, 0.78%. These rates are very low, perhaps evidence that the interfaces we chose were reasonable.

Web interfaces often include a "preview" feature, perhaps to encourage care in posting. To investigate whether the preview feature affects error rates in the movie linking tasks, we measure the *error rate before preview*. Results show before preview error rates range between 0% and 20% (Facebook-style interface, 3.91%; Wiki-style interface, 19.53%; Flickr-style interface, 7.03%; Amazon-style interface, 0.78%). Note that the Amazon-style interface already had a very low error rate before preview, since this interface has users search for and select movies before hitting the "preview" button.

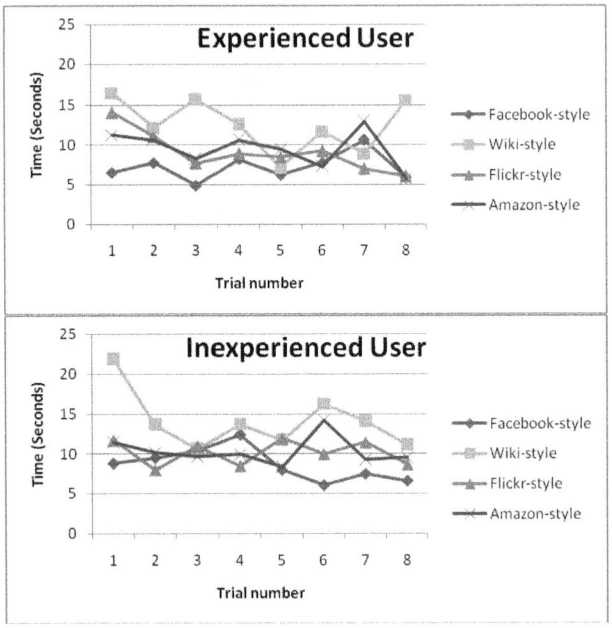

Figure 15. Average time spent on each trial for different interfaces, by subjects' experience using online forums

We identified how and where errors can occur in the movie linking process through careful review of the video recordings of subjects' tasks. Here the *error* is defined differently than above when we computed error rates – it is counted as an *error* here if, during movie linking, modifications need to be made on existing input to successfully insert a movie link.

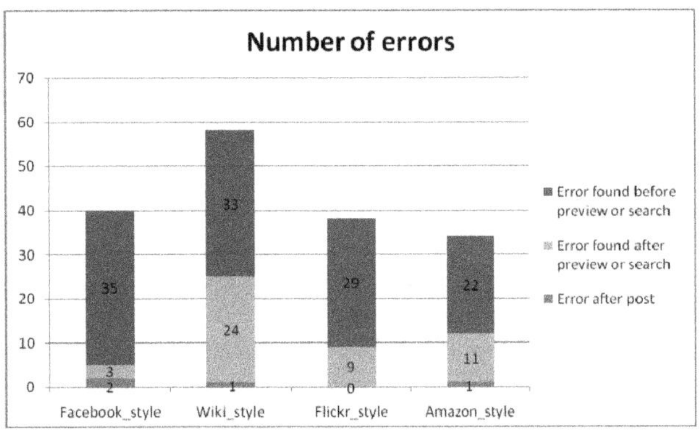

Figure 16. Total number of errors (across all subjects) during the experimental task

Figure 16 shows an overview of how many errors each interface had and when the errors occurred. This figure collapses errors from before and after the search for the Amazon-style interface. It is clear that users recovered from most errors themselves before they pressed the preview button.

Table 2 classifies errors by type. Most self-recovered errors were typos. There are actually two types of typos: one is recognized by users themselves immediately; the other is found after search or preview, when movie reference search result is unexpected. At that point users would have to navigate back and find the typo. We cannot and probably need not do anything about the first type of typos but we find evidence that real time auto-complete search can effectively reduce the second type of typos.

Error types	Facebook	Wiki	Flickr	Amazon
Forget to type #, [or press button BPS	10	5	3	2
Typo BPS	23	27	25	20
Other errors BPS	2	1	1	0
Forget to type #, [or press button APS	0	3	4	0
Typo APS	0	14	0	8
Other errors APS	2	7	5	4
Errors after post	2	1	0	1

Table 2. Number of errors classified by type in the movie linking process, across all subjects. BPS stands for "before preview or search"; APS stands for "after preview or search"

DISCUSSION

In this section, we discuss our research findings with respect to our research questions, and offer design implications for system developers.

Initiation Method: In-Band vs. Out-of-Band

Our first research question was to determine the effect of in-band vs. out-of-band designs on entity linking preferences and performance. In our study, we had Flickr-style and Amazon-style interfaces which used the out-of-band initiation action to separate movie linking from typing the user's text content. To compare, we had Facebook-style and Wiki-style interfaces which used in-band initiation with special characters ("#" and "[ ]"). We found that out-of-band button initiation has advantages for first-time use, but no sustained advantage as users gain experience. The impact of in-band initiation with special characters is more complex: the Facebook-style interface showed increasing performance and user preferences with practice, while the Wiki-style interface did not.

Out-of-band initiation is easily discoverable and learned. Buttons, our canonical example of an out-of-band control, are intuitive and common enough to understand immediately. Taken as a group, subjects preferred the out-of-band interfaces over in-band interfaces. In particular, less experienced users expressed stronger preferences for this type of interface. Various user comments suggest that out-of-band initiation was intuitive and that subjects were familiar with button controls: "I am familiar with this one;" "This is a very common interface;" "Button is a clear command, very fool-proof".

However the drawback of using out-of-band initiation is very clear: every time users insert a movie, the flow of composing a forum post is interrupted and more effort is needed. They need to move their hands away from keyboard and use mouse to click the button. This can be an explanation of why the user preference for Amazon-style interface fell off significantly and Flickr-style interface had the tendency to fall off after more experience using it.

To contrast, in-band initiation with special characters ("#" and "[ ]") was not as intuitive for first-time use. By looking at when and where errors occurred, we see that there were many cases where subjects forgot to type these special characters. However, the Facebook-style interface showed the greatest increase in user preference ratings between the first survey and the second survey. Subjects told us in the post-experiment interview that the Facebook-style interface is easy to learn and get used to. Also, this interface was the fastest for inserting movie links. Likely, this is partly because this interface only requires the keyboard, and not the mouse. While the Facebook-style interface showed this learning process, Wiki-style interface still took the most time to insert movie links and is least preferred. However, based on user feedback, and our own subjective assessment of user performance, we believe that the Wiki-style interface suffered not because of the use of bracket characters, but due to its deferred resolution timing.

Design recommendations

- Use out-of-band initiation (e.g., a button) when designing for one-time use, or when optimizing for new users.
- Use in-band initiation (e.g., typing "#") when designing for repeated use, or in situations where speed matters.

Resolution Timing: Interrupting vs. Deferred

In research question two, we investigate whether entity resolution (e.g., choosing a movie to insert) is better accomplished on the spot via interruption or deferred until after the user has finished composing the post. Out of four interfaces, the Wiki-style interface is the only one that used deferred resolution.

The Wiki-style interface was the bottom performer in terms of both user preferences and performance. The Wiki-style interface is the only interface that exhibited a learning effect (Figure 7, 14, and 15), especially for inexperienced users. In contrast, subjects performed well on the other interfaces without training. Wiki-style interface also had the largest number of errors in the movie linking process and did a poor job of helping users to correct typos – there were still one third of the typos found after the search.

One limitation of this study is that we studied user performance using artificial tasks. We may therefore underestimate the benefits of deferred entity resolution, since our tasks lack serious comment-composition thought and immersion. Bailey and Konstan [3] found that presenting peripheral tasks can worsen performance (time, error rate) in primary tasks and increase annoyance. The Wiki-style interface may reduce such performance degredation and annoyance, since users can just type it and forget it, coming back to make changes later if needed. Other researchers (Völkel et al. [16]) have invested effort into improving the linking syntax to create semantically meaningful search results. However, from our experience with creating movie linking interfaces, the Wiki-style deferred resolution is not a good design choice.

Design recommendation

- Use interrupting interfaces to allow users to complete the linking process immediately. The only exception to this rule comes when the design must keep distractions at a minimum during the act of composition.

Narrowing Method: Search vs. Auto-Complete

In research question three, we study the differences between search and auto-complete for narrowing and selecting a named entity. The Facebook-style and Flickr-style interfaces use auto-complete, while the Wiki-style and Amazon-style interfaces use search. Again, we believe that the Wiki-style interface is punished by its use of deferred resolution, so we limit this discussion to search and auto-complete in the context of real time interruption.

Auto-complete interfaces are somewhat more difficult to learn, according to our data, but result in overall faster data input. User preferences were split between these two classes of search interfaces. In terms of ease of use and learnability, there were no differences among the three interfaces. In terms of overall preference, there is a slight overall preference towards auto-complete interfaces, though this effect did not emerge until after the experimental task.

Subjects commented that auto-complete was convenient - they can start typing and see what they get from the list. They deemed the auto-complete interactions to be more dynamic and interactive than the search alternative.

Error analysis suggests that real time auto-complete interfaces excel at resolving errors such as typos earlier in the interaction. With search interfaces, subjects found nearly one third of the typos after the search action.

Design recommendation

- Use auto-complete search rather than traditional full-page-load search. The only exception to this rule comes when designing for one-time use, as traditional search is more easily learned.

Other design factors

Our results show that the preview feature affects error rates in the movie linking tasks. While the overall error rates were quite low, users found and corrected many errors on the preview screen. We therefore find that preview is a useful technique to reduce error rates. This is especially true in deferred interfaces, where initial error rates may be much higher than in interruption-based interfaces. The trade-off is time (27.5% of the total forum composing time) for improved error rates (which drop from 7.81% before the preview to 0.78% after the preview). Preview is useful for both auto-complete and search interfaces.

Design recommendation

- Incorporate a preview screen to reduce error rates in named entity linking interfaces.

CONCLUSION

In this paper we reported on a lab study of named entity linking interfaces – methods for inserting links in user-generated content to an external system entity (e.g., a movie). We implemented four interfaces commonly found in modern systems, named after the site of inspiration: Facebook-style, Wiki-style, Flickr-style, and Amazon-style. We found that in-band linking - where users type a special character to initiate an AJAX search interface - required more practice but offered better performance. Our example of a "traditional" linking interface, using a button to pop open a search window (Amazon-style), was preferred by new users and users who were less experienced using online services. We found that the wiki style of deferring linking to a future step was not well-liked by our subjects, nor did it lead to competitive performance results.

This study has certain limitations that should inform the user of the results. The tasks used were intentionally de-contextualized, and allowed for pair wise comparisons of certain interface features, which may not generalize to tasks with higher percentage of thinking or writing. The experimental interfaces could have been extended further to cover all combinations of the design dimensions detailed in Table 1. Doing so would have allowed a full analysis of the effects of, and interactions between, the factors of interest.

As with any controlled experiment, questions of generalisability can be raised and could be addressed through further longitudinal and field research. Other studies might examine the possibilities for novel linking interfaces. For instance, some problems might be better solved through drag-and-drop or intelligent entity inference. In the meantime, we hope our results are informative to systems designers implementing entity linking systems to create better-connected, richer online communities.

ACKNOWLEDGMENTS

We gratefully acknowledge the participation of all the subjects. This work was supported by the National Science Foundation, under grant IIS-0812148.

REFERENCES

1. Amazon: What are product links? http://www.amazon.com/review/guidelines/product-links.html
2. Amin, A. et al.. Organizing Suggestions In Autocompletion Interfaces. *Proc. ECIR 2009*, 521-529.
3. Bailey, P. B., and Konstan, A.J. On the need for attention-aware systems: Measuring effects of interruption on task performance, error rate, and affective state. *Computers in Human Behavior* 22, (2006), 685-708.
4. Cucerzan, S. L. Named Entity Disambiguation Based on Wikipedia Data. *Proc. EMNLP-CoNLL 2007*, 708-716.
5. Drenner, S.et al. Insert movie reference here: a system to bridge conversation and item-oriented web sites. *Proc. CHI 2006*, 951-954.
6. Facebook: Tag Friends in Your Status and Posts http://blog.facebook.com/blog.php?post=109765592130
7. Flickr: People in Photos http://www.flickr.com/help/people/
8. Florian, R., Ittycheriah, A., Jing H., and Zhang T. Named entity recognition through classifier combination. *Proc. CoNLL 2003*, 168-171.
9. Hyvönen E., and Mäkelä E. Semantic autocompletion. *Proc. ASWC 2006*, 739–751.
10. Kasemvilas, S., and Firpo, D., Effects of AJAX Technology on the Usability of Blogs. *Proc. HCII 2009*, 45-54.
11. Kluge, J., Kargl, F., and Weber, M. The Effects of the AJAX Technology on Web Application Usability. *Proc. WEBIST 2007*, 289-294.
12. Lowry, P. B. et al. A Theoretical Model and Empirical Results Linking Website Interactivity and Usability Satisfaction. *Proc. HICSS 2006*, 123-132.
13. Milne, D., and Witten, I.H. Learning to link with Wikipedia. *Proc. CIKM 2008*, 509-518.
14. Nielsen, J. Web 2.0 Can Be Dangerous... http://www.useit.com/alertbox/web-2.html
15. Sicilia, M. et al. Effects of interactivity in a Web site. *Journal of Advertising* 34, (2005), 31-45.
16. Völkel, M. et al. Semantic Wikipedia. Proc. WWW 2006, ACM Press (2006), 585-594.

Bricolage: Example-Based Retargeting for Web Design

Ranjitha Kumar **Jerry O. Talton** **Salman Ahmad** **Scott R. Klemmer**
Stanford University HCI Group
Department of Computer Science
{ranju,jtalton,saahmad,srk}@cs.stanford.edu

ABSTRACT
The Web provides a corpus of design examples unparalleled in human history. However, leveraging existing designs to produce new pages is often difficult. This paper introduces the *Bricolage* algorithm for transferring design and content between Web pages. Bricolage employs a novel, structured-prediction technique that learns to create coherent mappings between pages by training on human-generated exemplars. The produced mappings are then used to automatically transfer the content from one page into the style and layout of another. We show that Bricolage can learn to accurately reproduce human page mappings, and that it provides a general, efficient, and automatic technique for retargeting content between a variety of real Web pages.

Author Keywords
Web design, examples, retargeting, structured prediction.

ACM Classification Keywords
H.5.4 Information interfaces and presentation: Hypertext/ Hypermedia - Theory.

General Terms
Algorithms, Design, Human Factors

INTRODUCTION
Designers in many fields rely on examples for inspiration [17], and examples can facilitate better design work [22]. Examples can illustrate the space of possible solutions and how to implement those possibilities [2, 3]. Furthermore, repurposing successful elements from prior ideas can be more efficient than reinventing them from scratch [12, 21, 14].

The Web provides a corpus of design examples unparalleled in human history: by 2008, Google had indexed more than one trillion unique URLs [1]. However, we hypothesize that this rich resource is underutilized for design tasks. While current systems assist with browsing examples and cloning individual design elements, adapting the gestalt structure of Web designs remains a time-intensive, manual process [22, 10].

CHI 2011, May 7–12, 2011, Vancouver, British Columbia.

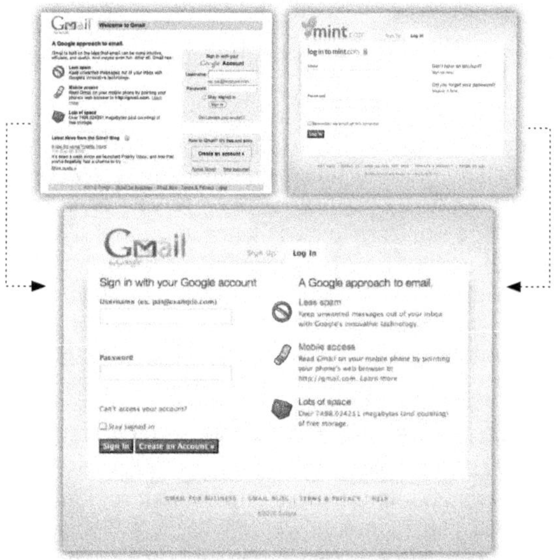

Figure 1. Bricolage computes coherent mappings between Web pages by matching visually and semantically similar page elements. The produced mapping can then be used to guide the transfer of content from one page into the design and layout of the other.

Most design reuse today is accomplished with templates [13]. Templates use standardized page semantics to render content into predesigned layouts. This strength is also a weakness: templates homogenize page structure, limit customization and creativity, and yield cookie-cutter designs. Ideally, tools should offer both the ease of templates *and* the diversity of the entire Web. What if *any* Web page could be a design template?

This paper introduces the *Bricolage* algorithm for transferring design and content between Web pages. The term "bricolage" refers to the creation of a work from a diverse range of things that happen to be available. Bricolage matches visually and semantically similar elements in pages to create coherent mappings between them. These mappings can then be used to automatically transfer the content from one page into the style and layout of the other (Figure 1).

Bricolage uses structured prediction [7] to learn how to transfer content between pages. It trains on a corpus of human-generated mappings, collected using a Web-based crowdsourcing interface, the *Bricolage Collector*. The Collector was seeded with 50 popular Web pages that were decomposed into a visual hierarchy by a novel, constraint-based page segmentation algorithm, *Bento*. In an online study, 39 participants with some Web design experience specified correspondences between page regions and answered free-response questions about their rationale.

These mappings guided the design of Bricolage's matching algorithm. We found consistent structural patterns in how people created mappings between pages. Participants not only identified elements with similar visual and semantic properties, but also used their location in the pages' hierarchies to guide their assignments. Consequently, Bricolage employs a novel tree-matching algorithm that flexibly balances visual, semantic, and structural considerations. We demonstrate that this yields significantly more human-like mappings.

This paper presents the Bento page segmentation algorithm, the data collection study, the mapping algorithm, and the machine learning method. It then shows results demonstrating that Bricolage can learn to closely produce human mappings. Lastly, it illustrates how Bricolage is useful for a diverse set of design applications: for rapidly prototyping alternatives, retargeting content to alternate form factors such as mobile devices, and measuring the similarity of Web designs.

THE BENTO PAGE SEGMENTATION ALGORITHM

To transfer content between Web pages, Bricolage first segments each page into a hierarchy of salient regions that can be extracted and manipulated. The page's Document Object Model (DOM) tree, which describes the page's content, structure, and style, provides a convenient starting point for this segmentation [18].

Existing page segmentation algorithms begin by partitioning the DOM into discrete, visually-salient regions [4, 5, 19]. These algorithms produce good results whenever a page's DOM closely mirrors its visual hierarchy, which is the case for many simple Web pages.

However, these techniques fail on more complex pages. Modern CSS allows content to be arbitrarily repositioned, meaning that the structural hierarchy of the DOM may only loosely approximate the page's visual layout. In our 50-page corpus, we found disparities between the DOM and the visual layout an average of 2.3 times per page. Similarly, inlined text blocks are not assigned individual DOM elements, and therefore cannot be separated from surrounding markup. In practice, these issues render existing segmentation algorithms poorly suited to real-world Web pages.

This paper introduces Bento, a page segmentation algorithm that "re-DOMs" the input page in order to produce clean and consistent segmentations. The algorithm comprises four stages. First, each inlined element is identified and wrapped inside a `<span>` tag to ensure that all page content is contained within a leaf node of the DOM tree. Next, the hierarchy is reshuffled so that parent-child relationships in the tree correspond to visual containment on the page. Each DOM node is labeled with its rendered page coordinates and checked to verify that its parent is the smallest region that

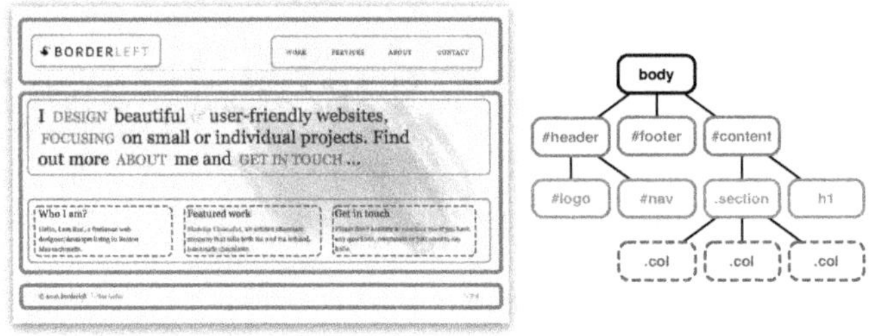

Figure 2. *Left:* The colored boxes illustrate Bento's segmentation. *Right:* Bento's output tree and associated DOM nodes for this page.

contains it. When this constraint is violated, the DOM is adjusted accordingly, taking care to preserve layout details when nodes are reshuffled. Third, redundant and superfluous nodes that do not contribute to the visual layout of the page are removed. Fourth, the hierarchy is supplemented to introduce missing visual structures. These structural elements are added by computing horizontal and vertical separators across each page region and inserting enclosing DOM nodes accordingly, similar to VIPS [4]. At the end of these four steps, all page content is assigned to a leaf node in the DOM tree, and every non-leaf node contains its children in screen space (Figure 2).

Bento is available as a web service and a BSD open-source C++ library at `http://hci.stanford.edu/bento`.

COLLECTING AND ANALYZING HUMAN MAPPINGS

Retargeting Web pages is closely related to automatic document layout and UI generation. In these domains, the state-of-the-art is constraint-based synthesis [18, 11], which begins with the designer building an abstract data model for each individual class of designs. While this strategy works well in highly-structured domains, the heterogeneous nature of the Web makes model construction impracticable.

We hypothesized that a more general retargeting scheme could be produced by training a machine learning algorithm on human-generated mappings between pages. To this end, we created the Bricolage Collector, a Web application for gathering human page mappings from online workers. We deployed the Collector online, and analyzed the produced mappings to understand how people map Web pages.

Study Design

We selected a diverse corpus of 50 popular Web pages chosen from the Alexa Top 100, Webby award winners, highly-regarded design blogs, and personal bookmarks. Within this corpus, we selected a focus set of eight page pairs. Each participant was asked to match one or two pairs from the focus set, and one or two more chosen uniformly at random from the corpus as a whole. The Collector gathered data about how different people map the same pair of pages, and about how people map many different pairs. We recruited 39 participants through email lists and online advertisements. Each reported some Web design experience.

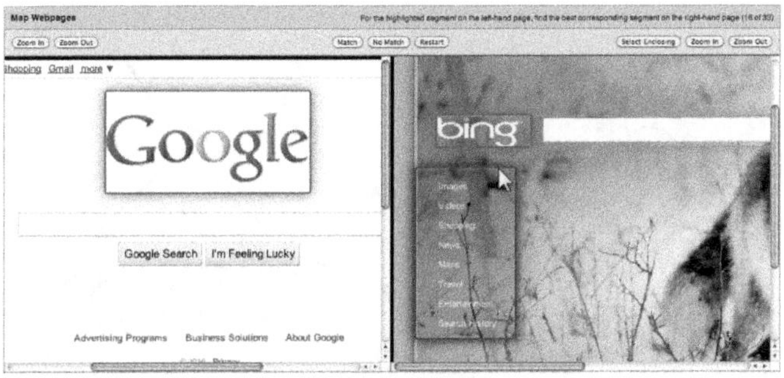

Figure 3. The Bricolage Collector Web application asks users to match each highlighted region in the *left* (content) page to the corresponding region in the *right* (layout) page.

Procedure

Participants watched a tutorial video demonstrating the Collector interface and describing the task. The video instructed participants to produce mappings for transferring the left page's *content* into the right page's *layout*. It emphasized that participants could use any criteria they deemed appropriate to match elements. After the tutorial, the Collector presented participants with the first pair of pages (Figure 3).

The Collector interface iterates over the segmented regions in the content page one at a time, asking participants to find a matching region in the layout page. The user selects a matching region via the mouse or keyboard, and confirms it by clicking the MATCH button. If no good match exists for a particular region, the user clicks the NO MATCH button. After every fifth match, the interface presents a dialog box asking,"Why did you choose this assignment?" These rationale responses are logged along with the mappings, and submitted to a central server.

Results

Participants generated 117 mappings between 52 unique pairs of pages: 73 mappings for the 8 pairs in the focus set, and 44 covering the rest of the corpus. They averaged 10.5 seconds finding a match for each page region (min $= 4.42s$, max $= 25.0s$), and 5.38 minutes per page pair (min $= 1.52m$, max $= 20.7m$). Participants provided rationales for 227 individual region assignments, averaging 4.7 words in length.

Consistency

We define the consistency of two mappings for the same page pair as the percentage of page regions with identical assignments. The average inter-mapping consistency of the focus pairs was 78.3% (min $= 58.8\%$, max $= 89.8\%$). 37.8% of page regions were mapped identically by all participants.

Rationale

Participants provided rationales like "Title of rightmost body pane in both pages." We analyzed these rationales with Latent Semantic Analysis (LSA), which extracts contextual language usage in a set of documents [8]. LSA takes a bag-of-words approach to textual analysis: each document is treated as an unordered collection of words, ignoring grammar and punctuation. We followed the standard approach, treating each rationale as a document and forming the term-document matrix where each cell's value counts the occurrences of a term in a document. We used Euclidean normalization to make annotations of different lengths comparable, and inverse document-frequency weighting to deemphasize common words like *a* and *the*.

LSA decomposes the space of rationales into semantic "concepts." Each concept is represented by a principal component of the term-document matrix, and the words with the largest projections onto the component are the concept's descriptors.

For the first component, the words with the largest projections are: *footer*, *link*, *menu*, *description*, *videos*, *picture*, *login*, *content*, *image*, *title*, *body*, *header*, *search*, and *graphic*. These words pertain primarily to visual and semantic attributes of page content.

For the second component, the words with the largest projections are: *both*, *position*, *about*, *layout*, *bottom*, *one*, *two*, *three*, *subsection*, *leftmost*, *space*, *column*, *from*, and *horizontal*. These words are mostly concerned with structural and spatial relationships between page elements.

Structure and Hierarchy

Two statistics examine the mappings' structural and hierarchical properties: one measuring how frequently the mapping preserves *ancestry*, and the other measuring how frequently it preserves *siblings*.

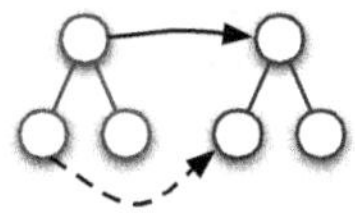

We define two matched regions to be *ancestry preserving* if their parent regions are also matched (see inset). A mapping's degree of ancestry preservation is the number of ancestry-preserving regions divided by the total number of matched regions. Participants' mappings preserved ancestry 53.3% of the time (min $= 7.6\%$, max $= 95.5\%$).

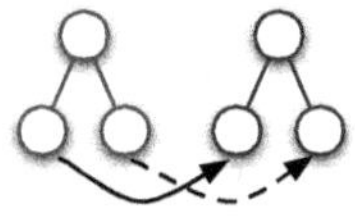

Similarly, we define a set of page regions sharing a common parent to be *sibling preserving* if the regions they are matched to also share a common parent (see inset). Participants produced mappings that were 83.9% sibling preserving (min $= 58.3\%$, max $= 100\%$).

COMPUTING PAGE MAPPINGS

The study's results suggest that mappings produced by different people are highly consistent: there is a "method to the madness" that may be learned. Moreover, the results suggest that algorithmically producing human-like mappings requires incorporating both semantic and structural constraints, and learning how to balance between them.

Prior work in mapping HTML documents presents two distinct approaches. The first ignores structural relationships between DOM nodes and maps elements irrespective of their locations in the pages' visual hierarchy [16]. The second uses tree-matching techniques [20], which strictly preserve hierarchical relationships: once two nodes have been placed in correspondence, their descendants must be matched as well [28, 24, 27]. The results from our study suggest that neither extreme is desirable.

Bricolage introduces a novel optimization algorithm which flexibly balances semantic and structural constraints. The algorithm connects the nodes of the two page trees to form a complete bipartite graph, and for each edge, assigns a cost comprising three terms. The first term measures visual and semantic differences between the corresponding page elements, the second penalizes edges that violate ancestry relationships, and the third penalizes edges that break up sibling groups. Determining the best page mapping then reduces to finding a minimum-cost matching of the constructed graph. Bricolage uses structured prediction to learn a cost function under which the set of exemplar mappings are minimal [7].

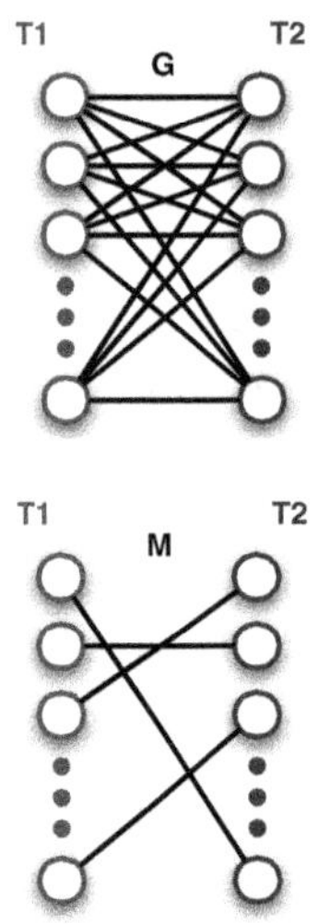

Formally, given two page trees with nodes T_1 and T_2, we construct a complete bipartite graph G between $T_1 \cup \{\otimes_1\}$ and $T_2 \cup \{\otimes_2\}$, where $\otimes_1$ and $\otimes_2$ are *no-match* nodes. These two no-match nodes enable the model to track which nodes in one tree have no counterpart in the other. We then define a page mapping M to be a set of edges from G such that every node in $T_1 \cup T_2$ is covered by precisely one edge. In this paper, given a tree node m, $M(m)$ denotes its image (*i.e.*, its counterpart in the other tree). The algorithm assigns a cost $c(e)$ to each edge $e \in M$, and aggregates them to compute the total mapping cost $c(M) = \sum_{e \in M} c(e)$. Bricolage then searches for the least-cost mapping $M^\star = \operatorname{argmin}_M c(M)$.

Exact Edge Costs

We define the cost of an edge $e \in T_1 \times T_2$ to be the sum of the visual, ancestry, and sibling costs

$$c(e) = c_v(e) + c_a(e) + c_s(e).$$

For the edges in G connecting tree nodes to no-match nodes, we fix the cost $c(e) = w_n$, where w_n is a constant no-match weight. The edge between the two no-match nodes is assigned a cost of 0 to prevent it from influencing the final mapping.

To compute $c_v([m, n])$, the algorithm compares visual and semantic properties of m and n by inspecting their DOM nodes. The *Learning the Cost Model* section describes this computation in detail.

The ancestry cost $c_a(\cdot)$ penalizes edges that violate ancestry relationships between the pages' elements. Consider a node $m \in T_1$, and let $C(m)$ denote the children of m. We define the *ancestry-violating children* of m, $V(m)$, to be the set of

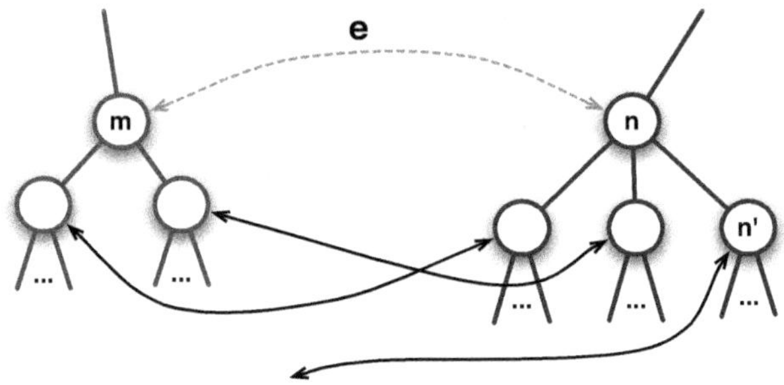

Figure 4. To determine the ancestry penalty for an edge $e = [m, n]$, Bricolage counts the children of m and n which induce ancestry violations. In this example, n' is an ancestry-violating child of n because it is not mapped to a child of m; therefore, n' induces an ancestry cost on e.

m's children that map to nodes that are not $M(m)$'s children, *i.e.*,

$$V(m) = \{m' \in C(m) \mid M(m') \in T_2 \setminus C(M(m))\},$$

and define $V(n)$ symmetrically. Then, the ancestry cost for an edge is proportional to the number of ancestry violating children of its terminal nodes

$$c_a([m,n]) = w_a\,(|V(m)| + |V(n)|)\,,$$

where w_a is a constant ancestry violation weight (see Figure 4).

The sibling cost $c_s(\cdot)$ penalizes edges that fail to preserve sibling relationships between trees. To calculate this term, we first define a few tree-related concepts. Let $P(m)$ denote the parent of m. Then, the *sibling group* of a node m is the set comprising the children of its parent: $S(m) = \{C(P(m))\}$. Given a mapping M, the *sibling-invariant subset* of m, $I(m)$, is the set of nodes in m's sibling group that map to nodes in $M(m)$'s sibling group, *i.e.*,

$$I(m) = \{m' \in S(m) \mid M(m') \in S(M(m))\}\,;$$

the *sibling-divergent subset* of m, $D(m)$, is the set of nodes in m's sibling group that map to nodes in T_2 not in $M(m)$'s sibling group, *i.e.*,

$$D(m) = \{m' \in S(m) \setminus I(m) \mid M(m') \in T_2\}\,;$$

and the set of *distinct sibling families* that m's sibling group maps into is

$$F(m) = \bigcup_{m' \in S(m)} P(M(m')).$$

We define all corresponding terms for n symmetrically, and then compute the total sibling cost:

$$c_s([m,n]) = w_s \left(\frac{|D(m)|}{|I(m)||F(m)|} + \frac{|D(n)|}{|I(n)||F(n)|} \right),$$

where w_s is a constant sibling violation weight. The two ratios increase when siblings are broken up (*i.e.*, their images have different parents), and decrease when more siblings are kept together (see Figure 5).

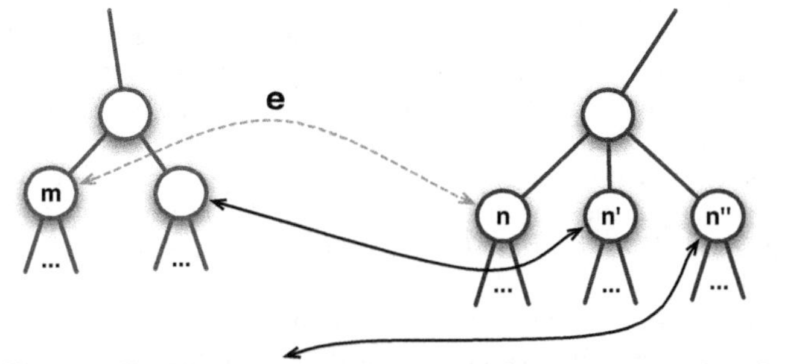

Figure 5. To determine the sibling penalty for an edge $e = [m, n]$, Bricolage computes the sibling-invariant and sibling-divergent subsets of m and n. In this example, $I(m) = \{n'\}$ and $D(m) = \{n''\}$; therefore, n' decreases the sibling cost on e and n'' increases it.

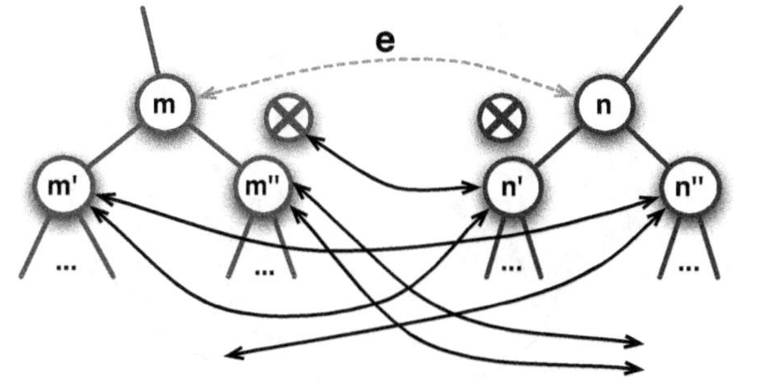

Figure 6. To bound $c_a([m, n])$, observe that neither m' nor n' can induce an ancestry violation. Conversely, m'' is guaranteed to violate ancestry. No guarantee can be made for n''. Therefore, the lower bound for c_a is w_a, and the upper bound is $2w_a$.

Bounding Edge Costs

While this cost model balances semantic, ancestral, and sibling constraints, it cannot be used to search for the optimal mapping $M^\star$ directly. Although $c_v([m, n])$ can be evaluated for an edge by inspecting m and n, $c_a(\cdot)$ and $c_s(\cdot)$ require information about the other edges in the mapping.

While we cannot precisely evaluate $c_a(\cdot)$ and $c_s(\cdot)$ *a priori*, we can compute bounds for them on a per-edge basis [6]. Moreover, each time we accept an edge $[m, n]$ into M, we can remove all the other edges incident on m and n from G. Each time we prune an edge in this way, the bounds for other nearby edges may be improved. Therefore, we employ a Monte Carlo algorithm to approximate $M^\star$, stochastically fixing an edge in G, pruning away the other edges incident on its nodes, and updating the bounds on those that remain.

To bound the ancestry cost of an edge $[m, n] \in G$, we must consider each child of m and n and answer two questions. First, is it *impossible* for this node to induce an ancestry violation? Second, is it *unavoidable* that this node will induce an ancestry violation? The answer to the first question informs the upper bound for $c_a(\cdot)$; the answer to the second informs the lower.

A node $m' \in C(m)$ can induce an ancestry violation if there is some edge between it and a node in $T_2 \setminus (C(n) \cup \{\otimes_2\})$. Conversely, m' is not *guaranteed* to induce an ancestry violation if some edge exists between it and a node in $C(n) \cup \{\otimes_2\}$. Accordingly, we define indicator functions

$$\mathbf{1}_a^{\mathcal{U}}(m', n) = \begin{cases} 1 & \text{if } \exists [m', n'] \in G \text{ s.t. } n' \notin C(n) \cup \{\otimes_2\} \\ 0 & \text{else} \end{cases},$$

$$\mathbf{1}_a^{\mathcal{L}}(m', n) = \begin{cases} 1 & \text{if } \nexists [m', n'] \in G \text{ s.t. } n' \in C(n) \cup \{\otimes_2\} \\ 0 & \text{else} \end{cases}.$$

Then, the upper and lower bounds for $c_a([m, n])$ are

$$\mathcal{U}_a([m,n]) = w_a \left(\sum_{m' \in C(m)} \mathbf{1}_a^{\mathcal{U}}(m', n) + \sum_{n' \in C(n)} \mathbf{1}_a^{\mathcal{U}}(n', m) \right),$$

and

$$\mathcal{L}_a([m,n]) = w_a \left(\sum_{m' \in C(m)} \mathbf{1}_a^{\mathcal{L}}(m', n) + \sum_{n' \in C(n)} \mathbf{1}_a^{\mathcal{L}}(n', m) \right).$$

Figure 6 illustrates the computation of these bounds. Pruning edges from G causes the upper bound for $c_a([m, n])$ to decrease, and the lower bound to increase.

Similarly, we can bound $c_s([m, n])$ by bounding the number of divergent siblings, invariant siblings, and distinct families: $|D(\cdot)|$, $|I(\cdot)|$, and $|F(\cdot)|$. Let $\bar{S}(m) = S(m) \setminus \{m\}$ and consider a node $m' \in \bar{S}(m)$. It is possible that m' is in $D(m)$ as long as some edge exists between it and a node in $T_2 \setminus (\bar{S}(n) \cup \{\otimes_2\})$. Conversely, m' cannot be guaranteed to be in $D(m)$ as long as some edge exists between it and a node in $\bar{S}(n) \cup \{\otimes_2\}$. Then, we have

$$\mathbf{1}_D^{\mathcal{U}}(m', n) = \begin{cases} 1 & \text{if } \exists [m', n'] \in G \text{ s.t. } n' \notin \bar{S}(n) \cup \{\otimes_2\} \\ 0 & \text{else} \end{cases},$$

$$\mathcal{U}_D(m, n) = \sum_{m' \in \bar{S}(m)} \mathbf{1}_D^{\mathcal{U}}(m', n),$$

and

$$\mathbf{1}_D^{\mathcal{L}}(m', n) = \begin{cases} 1 & \text{if } \nexists [m', n'] \in G \text{ s.t. } n' \in \bar{S}(n) \cup \{\otimes_2\} \\ 0 & \text{else} \end{cases},$$

$$\mathcal{L}_D(m, n) = \sum_{m' \in \bar{S}(m)} \mathbf{1}_D^{\mathcal{L}}(m', n).$$

The bounds for $|I(m)|$ are similarly given by

$$\mathbf{1}_I^{\mathcal{U}}(m', n) = \begin{cases} 1 & \text{if } \exists [m', n'] \in G \text{ s.t. } n' \in \bar{S}(n) \\ 0 & \text{else} \end{cases},$$

$$\mathcal{U}_I(m, n) = 1 + \sum_{m' \in \bar{S}(m)} \mathbf{1}_I^{\mathcal{U}}(m', n),$$

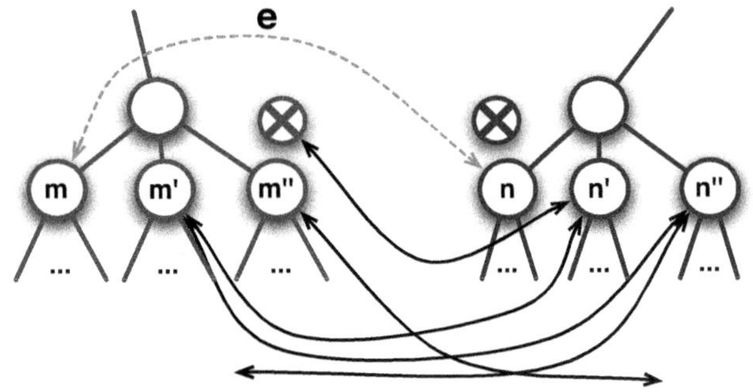

Figure 7. To bound $c_s([m, n])$, observe that m' is guaranteed to be in $I(m)$, and m'' is guaranteed to be in $D(m)$. No guarantees can be made for n' and n''. Therefore, the lower bound for c_s is $w_s/4$, and the upper bound is $3w_s/4$.

and

$$\mathbf{1}_I^{\mathcal{L}}(m', n) = \begin{cases} 1 & \text{if } \forall [m', n'] \in G,\ n' \in \bar{S}(n) \\ 0 & \text{else} \end{cases},$$

$$\mathcal{L}_I(m, n) = 1 + \sum_{m' \in \bar{S}(m)} \mathbf{1}_I^{\mathcal{L}}(m', n).$$

For all nonzero sibling costs, the lower bound for $|F(m)|$ is 2 and the upper bound is $\mathcal{L}_D(m, n) + 1$. All remaining quantities are defined symmetrically. Then, upper and lower bounds for $c_s([m, n])$ are given by

$$\mathcal{U}_s([m, n]) = \frac{w_s}{2}\left(\frac{\mathcal{U}_D(m, n)}{\mathcal{L}_I(m, n)} + \frac{\mathcal{U}_D(n, m)}{\mathcal{L}_I(n, m)}\right)$$

and

$$\mathcal{L}_s([m, n]) = w_s\left(\frac{\mathcal{L}_D(m, n)}{\mathcal{U}_I(m, n)\,(\mathcal{L}_D(m, n) + 1)} + \frac{\mathcal{L}_D(n, m)}{\mathcal{U}_I(n, m)\,(\mathcal{L}_D(n, m) + 1)}\right).$$

Figure 7 illustrates these computations.

With bounds for the ancestry and sibling terms in place, upper and lower bounds for the total edge cost may be trivially computed as $c_{\mathcal{U}}(e) = c_v(e) + \mathcal{U}_a(e) + \mathcal{U}_s(e)$ and $c_{\mathcal{L}}(e) = c_v(e) + \mathcal{L}_a(e) + \mathcal{L}_s(e)$.

Approximating the Optimal Mapping

To approximate the optimal mapping M^*, we use the Metropolis algorithm [23]. We represent each matching as an ordered list of edges M, and define a Boltzmann-like objective function

$$f(M) = \exp\left[-\beta\, c(M)\right],$$

where β is a constant. At each iteration of the algorithm, a new mapping $\hat{M}$ is proposed, and becomes the new reference mapping with probability

$$\alpha(\hat{M}|M) = \min\left(1, \frac{f(\hat{M})}{f(M)}\right).$$

The algorithm runs for N iterations, and the mapping with the lowest cost is returned.

To initialize M, the bipartite graph G is constructed and the edge bounds initialized. Then, the edges in G are traversed in order of increasing bound. Each edge is considered for assignment to M with some fixed probability γ, until an edge is chosen. If the candidate edge can be fixed and at least one complete matching still exists, it is appended to M, the other edges incident on its terminal nodes are pruned, and the bounds for the remaining edges in G are tightened.

To propose $\hat{M}$, we choose a random index $j \in [1, |M|]$. Then, we re-initialize G, and fix the first j edges in M. To produce the rest of the matching, we repeat the iterative edge selection process described above. In our implementation, we take $\gamma = .7$ and $N = 100$; β is chosen on a per-domain basis, based on the size of the trees.

LEARNING THE COST MODEL

While this mapping algorithm can be used with any visual and semantic cost model and weights w_n, w_a, and w_s, Bricolage seeks to learn a model that will produce human-like mappings. It employs a feature-based approach to compute the visual and semantic cost $c_v(\cdot)$ between nodes, and trains the weights of these features and those for the no-match, ancestry, and sibling terms.

Edge Features

The algorithm computes a set of visual and semantic properties for each node in the page trees. Visual properties are computed using a node's render-time appearance, and include attributes like width, font size, and mean RGB values. Semantic properties take Boolean values, computed by attribute tests such as "is an image" or "is contained in the header." The Appendix gives a full list of these properties.

To compute an edge's total cost, the algorithm first calculates the difference between each property for m and n, and concatenates these values—along with the exact ancestry and sibling costs and a Boolean no-match indicator—into a feature vector $\mathbf{f}_e$. Given a set of weights $\mathbf{w}_f$ for each visual and semantic feature, the edge cost is then computed as $c(e) = \bar{\mathbf{w}}^T \mathbf{f}_e$, where $\bar{\mathbf{w}} = \langle \mathbf{w}_f, w_a, w_s, w_n \rangle$.

Given a mapping M, the algorithm assembles an aggregate feature vector $\mathbf{F}_M = \sum_{e \in M} \mathbf{f}_e$ to calculate $c(M) = \bar{\mathbf{w}}^T \mathbf{F}_M$. Training the cost model then reduces to finding a set of weights under which the mappings in the training set have minimal total cost.

Generalized Perceptron Algorithm

To learn a consistent assignment for the weight vector $\bar{\mathbf{w}}$ under which the set of exemplar mappings are minimal, Bricolage uses the generalized perceptron algorithm for structured prediction [7].

The perceptron begins by initializing $\bar{\mathbf{w}}_0 = 0$. In each subsequent iteration, the perceptron randomly selects a pair of page trees and an associated human mapping M from the training set. Next, using the current weight vector $\bar{\mathbf{w}}_i$, it computes a new mapping $\hat{M} \approx \operatorname{argmin}_M \bar{\mathbf{w}}_i^T \mathbf{F}_M$. Based on the resultant mapping, a new aggregate feature

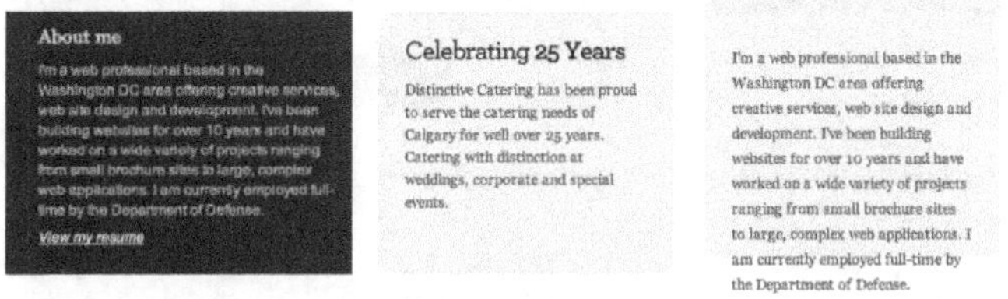

Source Target Synthesized

Figure 8. A current limitation of the content transfer algorithm illustrating the challenges of HTML/CSS. The target page's CSS prevents the bounding beige box from expanding. This causes the text to overflow (synthesized page). Also, the target page expects all headers to be images. This causes the "About Me" header to disappear (synthesized page). An improved content transfer algorithm could likely address both of these issues.

vector $\mathbf{F}_{\hat{M}}$ is calculated, and the weights are updated by $\bar{\mathbf{w}}_{i+1} = \bar{\mathbf{w}}_i + \alpha_i \left(\mathbf{F}_{\hat{M}} - \mathbf{F}_M\right)$, where $\alpha_i = 1/\sqrt{i+1}$ is the learning rate.

The perceptron algorithm is only *guaranteed* to converge if the training set is linearly separable; in practice, it produces good results for many diverse data sets [7]. Since the weights may oscillate during the final stages of the learning, the final cost model is produced by averaging over the last few iterations.

CONTENT TRANSFER

Once a cost model is trained, it is fed to the matching algorithm, which uses it to predict mappings between any two pages. Bricolage then uses these computed mappings to automatically transfer the content from one page into the style and layout of another. In its segmented page representation, page content (text, images, links, form fields) lives on the leaf nodes of the page tree. Before transferring content, the inner HTML of each node in the source page is preprocessed to inline CSS styles and convert embedded URLs to absolute paths. Then, content is moved between mapped nodes by replacing the inner HTML of the target node with the inner HTML of the source node.

Content matched to a no-match node can be handled in one of two ways. In the simplest case, unmatched source nodes are ignored. However, if important content in the source page is not mapped, it may be more desirable to insert the unmatched node into the target page parallel to its mapped siblings, or beneath its lowest mapped ancestor.

This approach works well for many pages. Occasionally, the complexity and diversity of modern Web technologies pose practical challenges to resynthesizing coherent HTML. Many pages specify style rules and expect certain markup patterns, which may cause the new content to be rendered incorrectly (Figure 8). Furthermore, images and plugin objects (*e.g.,* Flash, Silverlight) have no CSS style information that can be borrowed; when replaced, the new content will not exhibit the same visual appearance and may seem out of place. Lastly, embedded scripts are often tightly coupled with the original page's markup and break when naïvely transferred. Consequently, the current implementation ignores them, preventing dynamic behavior from being borrowed. A more robust content transfer algorithm is required to address these issues and remains future work.

RESULTS

We demonstrate the efficacy of Bricolage in two ways. First, we show several practical examples of Bricolage in action. Second, we evaluate the machine learning components by performing a hold-out cross-validation experiment on the gathered human mappings.

Examples

Figure 10 demonstrates the algorithm in a rapid prototyping scenario, in which an existing page is transformed into several potential replacement designs. Creating multiple alternatives facilitates comparison, team discussion, and design space exploration [9, 15, 25]. Figure 11 demonstrates that Bricolage can be used to retarget content across form factors, showing a full-size Web page automatically mapped into two different mobile layouts.

Figure 9 illustrates an ancillary benefit of Bricolage's cost model. Since Bricolage searches for the optimal mapping between pages, the returned cost can be interpreted as an approximate distance metric on the space of page designs. Although the theoretical properties of this metric are not strong (it satisfies neither the triangle inequality nor the identity of indiscernibles), in practice it may provide a useful mechanism for automatically differentiating between pages with similar and dissimilar designs.

Machine Learning Results

To test the effectiveness of Bricolage's machine learning components, we ran a hold-out test. We used the 44 collected mappings outside the focus set as training data, and

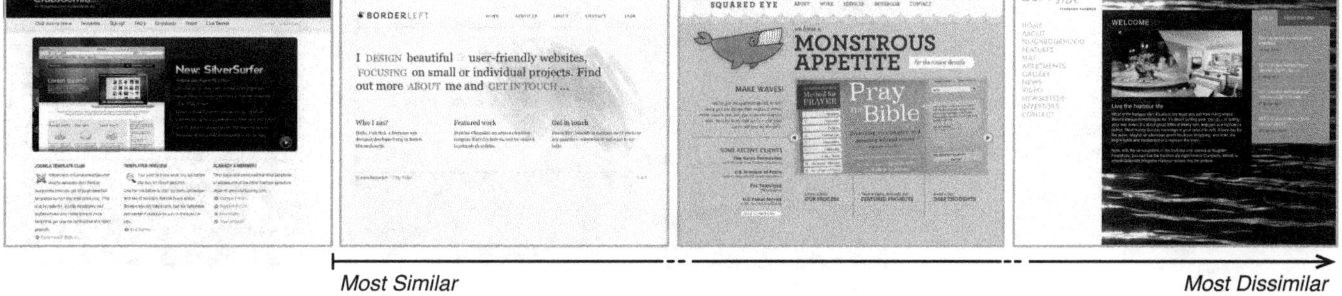

Figure 9. Bricolage can be used to induce a distance metric on the space of Web designs. By mapping the leftmost page onto each of the pages in the corpus and examining the mapping cost, we can automatically differentiate between pages with similar and dissimilar designs.

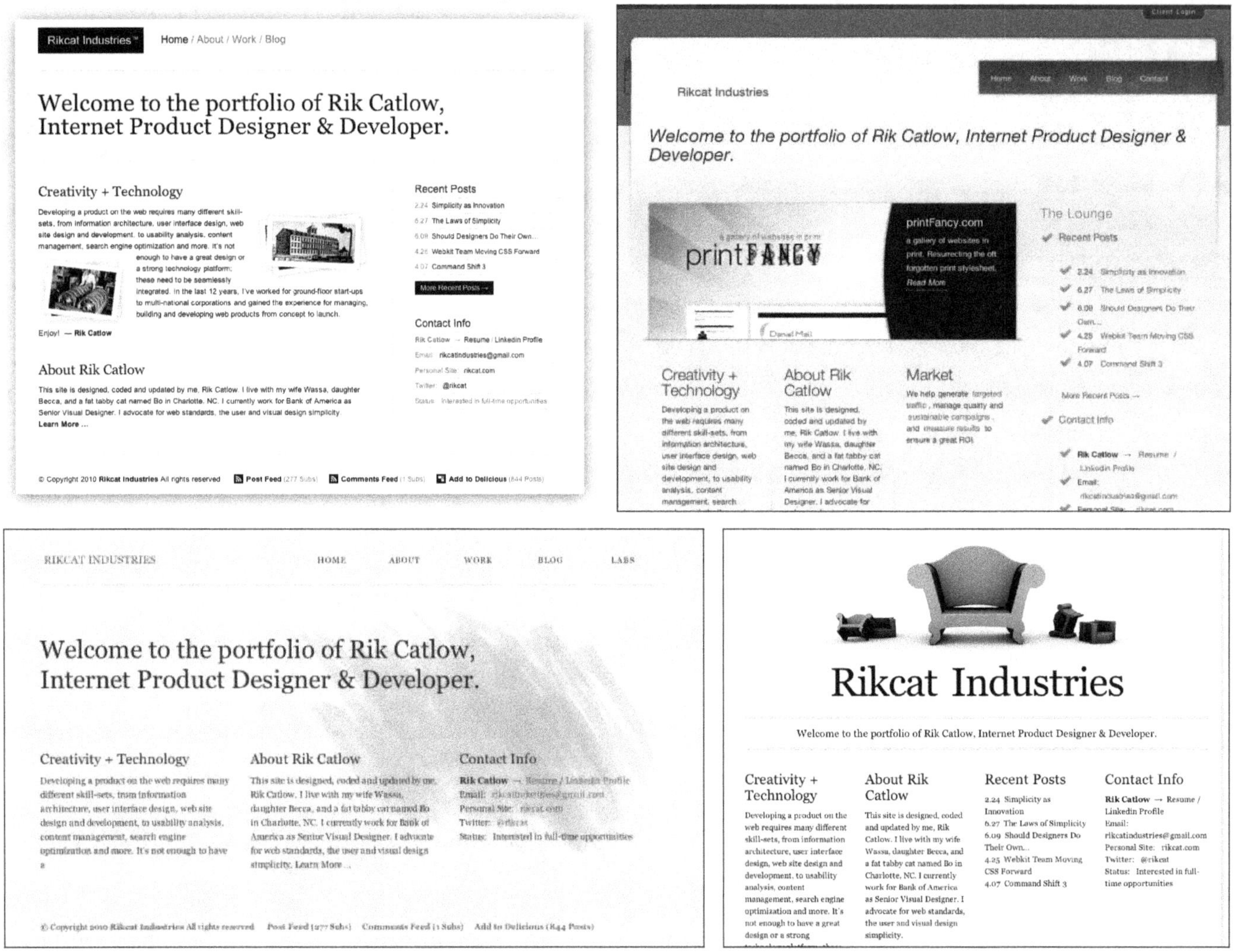

Figure 10. Bricolage used to rapidly prototype many alternatives. *Top-left:* the original Web page. *Rest:* the page automatically retargeted to three other layouts and styles.

Figure 11. Bricolage can retarget Web pages designed for the desktop to mobile devices. *Left:* the original Web page. *Right:* the page automatically retargeted to two different mobile layouts.

the mappings in the focus set as test data. The perceptron was run for 400 iterations, and the weight vector averaged over the last 20. The learned cost model was used to predict mappings for each of the 8 focus pairs. Table 1 shows the comparison between the learned and reference mappings using three different metrics: average similarity, nearest neighbor similarity, and percentage of edges that appear in at least one mapping.

The online mapping experiment found a 78% inter-mapping consistency between the participants. This might be considered a gold standard against which page mapping algorithms are measured. Currently, Bricolage achieves a 69% consistency. By this measure, there is room for improvement. However, Bricolage's mappings overlap an average of 78% with their nearest human neighbor, and 88% of the edges generated by Bricolage appear in some human mapping.

This structured prediction approach was motivated by the hypothesis that ancestry and sibling relationships are crucial to predicting human mappings. We tested this hypothesis by training three additional cost models containing different feature subsets: visual terms only, visual and ancestry terms, and visual and sibling terms. Considering only local features yields an average nearest neighbor match of 53%; mapping with local and sibling features yields 67%; mapping with local and ancestry features yields 75%. Accounting for all of these features yields 78%, a result that dominates that of any subset. In short, flexibly preserving structure is crucial to producing good mappings.

IMPLEMENTATION

Bricolage's page segmentation, mapping, and machine learning libraries are implemented in C++ using the Qt framework, and use Qt's WebKit API in order to interface directly with a browser engine. Once a cost model has been trained, Bricolage produces mappings between pages in about 1.04 seconds on a 2.55 Ghz Intel Core i7, averaging roughly 0.02 seconds per node.

The corpus pages are archived using the Mozilla Archive File Format and hosted on a server running Apache. For efficiency, page segmentations and associated DOM node features are computed and cached for each page when it is added to the corpus. Each feature has its own dynamic plug-in library, allowing the set of features to be extended with minimal overhead, and mixed and matched at runtime. The Bricolage Collector is written in HTML, Javascript, and CSS. Mapping results are sent to a centralized Ruby on Rails server and stored in a SQLite database.

CONCLUSIONS AND FUTURE WORK

This paper introduced the Bricolage algorithm for automatically transferring design and content between Web pages. Bricolage's major algorithmic insight was a technique for capturing the structural relationships between elements, and using an optimization approach to balance local and global concerns. This work takes a first step towards a powerful new paradigm for example-based Web design, and opens up exciting areas for future research.

Metric	*Cost Model*	*%*
Average Similarity	c_v c_a and c_s	68.7
	c_v and c_a	65.8
	c_v and c_s	59.1
	c_v alone	44.6
Nearest Neighbor	c_v c_a and c_s	77.7
	c_v and c_a	75.1
	c_v and c_s	67.0
	c_v alone	53.2
Edge Frequency	c_v c_a and c_s	87.9
	c_v and c_a	84.5
	c_v and c_s	81.4
	c_v alone	64.4

Table 1. Results of the hold-out cross-validation experiment. Bricolage performs substantially worse without both the ancestry and sibling terms in the cost model.

The current prototype employs thirty visual and semantic features. Adding more sophisticated properties—such as those based on computer vision techniques—will likely improve the quality of the machine learning.

Future work could extend example-based design to other domains. The current Bricolage implementation is HTML specific. In principle, the retargeting algorithm can be applied to any document with hierarchical structure such as slide presentation and vector graphics files. With richer vision techniques (along the lines of [26]), the Bricolage approach might extend to documents and interfaces without accessible structure.

Finally, an important next step is to create a retargeting design tool that allows both novice and experts to more creatively use examples. Observing how people use such a tool will provide valuable research knowledge about the role examples can play in amplifying creativity.

ACKNOWLEDGEMENTS

We thank Tim Roughgarden for helpful discussions about the matching algorithm; Chuong Do for helpful discussions about structured prediction techniques; Amy Jang for implementing machine learning features; Juho Kim and Kanya Siangliulue for helping prototype the Bricolage Collector; Mira Dontcheva and the reviewers for their helpful comments. This research was supported in part by NSF Grant IIS-0745320.

REFERENCES

1. Alpert, J., Hajaj, N. We knew the web was big... [online]. 2008. Available from: `http://goo.gl/RtmG` [cited 14 January 2011].

2. Brandt, J., Guo, P. J., Lewenstein, J., Dontcheva, M., Klemmer, S. R. Two studies of opportunistic programming: interleaving Web foraging, learning, and writing code. *Proc. CHI* (2009), ACM, pp. 1589–1598.

3. Buxton, B. *Sketching User Experiences*. Morgan Kaufmann, 2007.
4. Cai, D., Yu, S., Wen, J.-R., Ma, W.-Y. VIPS: a vision-based page segmentation algorithm. Tech. Rep. MSR-TR-2003-79, Microsoft, 2003.
5. Chakrabarti, D., Kumar, R., Punera, K. A graph-theoretic approach to Webpage segmentation. *Proc. WWW* (2008), pp. 377–386.
6. Chawathe, S. S., Garcia-Molina, H. Meaningful change detection in structured data. *Proc. SIGMOD* (1997), ACM, pp. 26–37.
7. Collins, M. Discriminative training methods for hidden Markov models: theory and experiments with perceptron algorithms. *Proc. EMNLP* (2002), ACL.
8. Deerwester, S., Dumais, S. T., Furnas, G. W., Landauer, T. K., Harshman, R. Indexing by latent semantic analysis. *Journal of the American Society for Information Science 41*, 6 (1990), pp. 391–407.
9. Dow, S. P., Glassco, A., Kass, J., Schwarz, M., Schwartz, D. L., Klemmer, S. R. Parallel prototyping leads to better design results, more divergence, and increased self-efficacy. *ACM TOCHI 17(4)* (December 2010), pp. 1–24.
10. Fitzgerald, M. CopyStyler: Web design by example. Tech. rep., MIT, May 2008.
11. Gajos, K., Weld, D. S. SUPPLE: automatically generating user interfaces. *Proc. IUI* (2004), ACM.
12. Gentner, D., Holyoak, K., Kokinov, B. *The Analogical Mind: Perspectives From Cognitive Science*. MIT Press, 2001.
13. Gibson, D., Punera, K., Tomkins, A. The volume and evolution of Web page templates. *Proc. WWW* (2005), ACM, pp. 830–839.
14. Hartmann, B., Wu, L., Collins, K., Klemmer, S. R. Programming by a sample: rapidly creating Web applications with d.mix. *Proc. UIST* (2007), ACM.
15. Hartmann, B., Yu, L., Allison, A., Yang, Y., Klemmer, S. R. Design as exploration: creating interface alternatives through parallel authoring and runtime tuning. *Proc. UIST* (2008), ACM.
16. Hashimoto, Y., Igarashi, T. Retrieving web page layouts using sketches to support example-based web design. *2nd Eurographics Workshop on Sketch-Based Interfaces and Modeling* (2005).
17. Herring, S. R., Chang, C.-C., Krantzler, J., Bailey, B. P. Getting inspired!: understanding how and why examples are used in creative design practice. *Proc. CHI* (2009), ACM, pp. 87–96.
18. Hurst, N., Li, W., Marriott, K. Review of automatic document formatting. *Proc. DocEng* (2009), ACM.
19. Kang, J., Yang, J., Choi, J. Repetition-based Web page segmentation by detecting tag patterns for small-screen devices. *IEEE Transactions on Consumer Electronics 56* (May 2010), pp. 980–986.
20. Kim, Y., Park, J., Kim, T., Choi, J. Web information extraction by html tree edit distance matching. *International Conference on Convergence Information Technology.* (2007), pp. 2455–2460.
21. Kolodner, J. L., Wills, L. M. Case-based creative design. *In AAAI Spring Symposium on AI and Creativity* (1993), pp. 50–57.
22. Lee, B., Srivastava, S., Kumar, R., Brafman, R., Klemmer, S. R. Designing with interactive example galleries. *Proc. CHI* (2010), ACM.
23. Press, W. H., Teukolsky, S. A., Vetterling, W. T., Flannery, B. P. *Numerical Recipes: The Art of Scientific Computing*, 3rd ed. Cambridge University Press, New York, NY, USA, 2007.
24. Shasha, D., Wang, J. T.-L., Zhang, K., Shih, F. Y. Exact and approximate algorithms for unordered tree matching. *IEEE Transactions on Systems, Man, and Cybernetics 24*, 4 (1994), pp. 668–678.
25. Talton, J. O., Gibson, D., Yang, L., Hanrahan, P., Koltun, V. Exploratory modeling with collaborative design spaces. *Proc. SIGGRAPH ASIA* (2009), ACM Press.
26. Wattenberg, M., Fisher, D. A model of multi-scale perceptual organization in information graphics. *Proc. INFOVIS* (2003), pp. 23 –30.
27. Zhang, K. A constrained edit distance between unordered labeled trees. *Algorithmica 15*, 3 (1996).
28. Zhang, K., Shasha, D. Simple fast algorithms for the editing distance between trees and related problems. *SIAM J. Comput. 18*, 6 (1989), pp. 1245–1262.

APPENDIX

The Bricolage prototype uses the following DOM properties as features in the learning.

The visual properties include: *width*, *height*, *area*, *aspectRatio*, *fontSize*, *fontWeight*, *meanColor*, *numLinks*, *numColors*, *numChildren*, *numImages*, *numSiblings*, *siblingOrder*, *textArea*, *wordCount*, *treeLevel*, *verticalSidedness* (normalized distance from the horizon of the page), *horizontalSidedness* (normalized distance from the midline of the page), *leftSidedness* (normalized distance from the left border of the page), *topSidedness* (normalized distance from the top border of the page), and *shapeAppearance* (the minimum of the aspect ratio and its inverse).

The semantic properties include: *search*, *footer*, *header*, *image*, *logo*, *navigation*, *bottom* (if the node is in the bottom 10% of the page), *top* (if the node is in the top 10% of the page), *fillsHeight* (if the node extends more than 90% down the page), and *fillsWidth* (if the node extends more than 90% across the page).

HyperSource: Bridging the Gap Between Source and Code-Related Web Sites

Björn Hartmann, Mark Dhillon, Matthew K. Chan
Computer Science Division
University of California, Berkeley, CA 94720
bjoern@cs.berkeley.edu, {mark.dhillon, mattkc7}@gmail.com

ABSTRACT

Programmers frequently use the Web while writing code: they search for libraries, code examples, tutorials, and documentation. This link between code and visited Web pages remains implicit today. Connecting source code and browsing histories might help programmers maintain context, reduce the cost of Web page re-retrieval, and enhance understanding when code is shared. This note introduces HyperSource, an IDE augmentation that associates browsing histories with source code edits. HyperSource comprises a browser extension that logs visited pages; an IDE that tracks user activity and maps pages to code edits; a source document model that tracks visited pages at a character level; and a user interface that enables interaction with these histories. We discuss relevance heuristics and privacy issues inherent in this approach. Informal log analyses and user feedback suggest that our annotation model is promising for code editing and might also apply to other document authoring tasks after refinement.

ACM Classification: H.5.2 [Information Interfaces and Presentation]: User Interfaces – GUIs.

General Terms: Design, Documentation

Keywords: code editors, browsing history, edit wear

INTRODUCTION

When programming, developers spend a significant amount of time outside their Integrated Development Environment (IDE) and inside their Web browser. In a lab study by Brandt, programmers spent 19% of their time on the Web [3]; in Goldman's field study, 23% of Web pages visited in temporal proximity to code edits were development-related [4]. Work-related uses of the Web include finding libraries and source code examples, consulting online documentation, forums, and question-and-answer sites, and managing project-related communication in software forges.

Despite this strong connection between Web browsing activity and code production, today's IDEs and browsers remain largely unaware of each other. We hypothesize that *making the connection between source code and visited pages explicit can benefit programmers* in multiple ways. First, for maintenance of one's own code, access to previously consulted resources can help re-establish context and shorten the time spent re-retrieving previously used resources (a common pattern in Web browsing [10]). Second, for code shared between developers, relevant Web resources can help project newcomers understand design decisions and become productive faster.

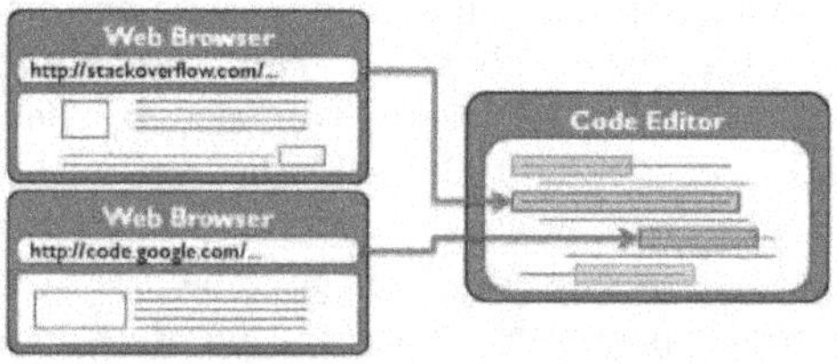

Figure 1: HyperSource associates Web pages visited by programmers with subsequent code edits.

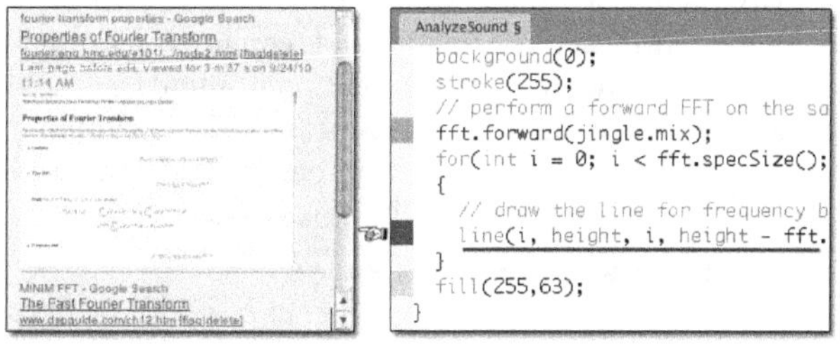

Figure 2: Web history (L) associated with the current line of code (R). Gutter highlights provide scent.

To investigate these potential benefits, we developed *HyperSource*, an augmented IDE that associates browsing histories with source code edits (Figure 1). Conceptually, HyperSource builds upon *read* and *edit wear* [5] by collecting and showing sets of Web pages that were read while code was edited. HyperSource enables this association via a source document model that attaches metadata to text at the character level. Annotations are maintained through subsequent document edits (insertions, deletions, copy, cut, paste, undo and redo). As programmers navigate their source, a panel inside the IDE displays associated Web histories and enables interaction with them (Figure 2). HyperSource builds on previous work in aggregating relevant information artifacts for software developers (Mylar [6]) and on tools that integrate web information sources into the IDE for code documentation (CodeTrail [4]) and code examples (BluePrint [2]).

The main contribution over prior work is *an architecture that implicitly collects visited pages and associates them with lines of code that developers subsequently write.*

SHARING ANNOTATED CODE WITH HYPERSOURCE

Joe, a Computer Science student, is writing a visualization of Web server logs for his student organization. As he writes his code, he discovers a bug in a drawing library. An online forum post suggests a counterintuitive workaround. As he consults these Web pages, their URLs are tracked inside his IDE and attached to subsequent code edits.

The following semester, Jan, another member of the club, has been tasked with changing Joe's code to add richer visualizations. She is initially confused by the drawing code since it does not match the library's official documentation. Because Joe wrote the code with HyperSource, Jan can select the confusing statement and see links to the original forum posts Joe consulted. She thus uncovers the rationale for Joe's code and can complete her task.

HYPERSOURCE ARCHITECTURE

Tracking and visualizing visited pages requires four components: a browser extension that captures visited Web pages; an augmented editor that can manage captured pages; a source document data structure that maintains associations between code and web pages; and a user interface that enables interaction with this history.

Browser Extension Captures Pages

Whenever a user loads a new page in her web browser, a HyperSource browser extension collects the URL, title, and a thumbnail image of the rendered page. This page record is then sent to the IDE using inter-process communication. User interactions with the page in the browser may indicate that a page is especially relevant: our extension intercepts *copy events* that place page content on the system clipboard and marks corresponding pages as *copy sources*. In addition, the extension adds a button to the browser UI which sets an *explicit bookmark* flag.

Our prototype is written as an extension to the Google Chrome browser in JavaScript and uses XML-HTTP requests to communicate with the IDE. When the IDE is not running, no information is recorded.

IDE Stores and Associates Visited Pages With Code

The HyperSource IDE receives page visit data from the web browser and attaches it to the currently open document. We have implemented HyperSource for two open source IDEs: *Processing* [1], an editor for a Java dialect focused on multimedia programming; and *jEdit*, a universal text editor with support for multiple languages. In each case, the IDE runs an additional server thread that services requests from the browser extension.

What rules should guide the association of pages to code? HyperSource models user behavior as a cycle of alternating edit and browse phases: code is annotated with the set of pages viewed just prior to the current set of edits (Figure 3). This model is operationalized using a finite state machine (Figure 4): during browsing, visited pages are added to a

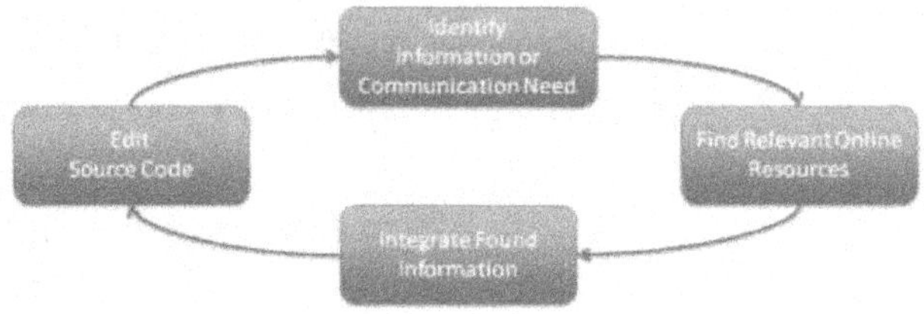

Figure 3: The underlying model of user interaction.

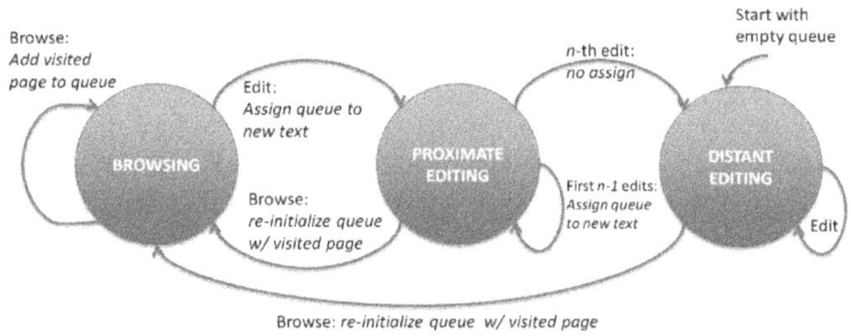

Figure 4: State machine that implements the model.

queue; when the user edits code, all pages in the queue are assigned to new characters. When the user switches back to browsing, the queue is cleared, then filled again. This model does not decide whether browsing is code-related or not; that decision is based on heuristics described below.

Early prototype testing suggested that *edit locality* matters: not all edits that follow browsing are related to collected pages. To model locality, HyperSource assumes that edits that occur in temporal proximity to browsing are the most relevant; therefore, only the first n edits are annotated with visited pages. Based on pilot studies, we currently use n=2, ignoring whitespace. This is a conservative choice: users may have to search more, but are less likely to see annotations in irrelevant locations.

Source Document Tracks Associations Over Time

To maintain the link between source code sections and visited pages, HyperSource tracks associations at the character level. After Web pages are assigned to code, subsequent code edits may insert or remove text, duplicate text through copy and paste, and reverse previous operations through undo and redo. HyperSource maintains associations between characters and pages with *position tracking* (using *Java Swing Positions*): each character is identified by a position object that describes its location throughout the document's lifecycle. While the absolute offset of a character changes, its position object remains the same. Position objects have to be updated after every edit (Figure 5).

Figure 5: Character offsets change across edits; position tracking maintains associations.

HyperSource writes a shadow file to disk for every regular source file. It shares name and directory with the source file, but has a separate extension (`.hypersrc`). Both files are written during a save operation. Use of the shadow file is optional: collaborators can still read the original source file. If collaborators edit that source file without HyperSource, shadow and source file lose sync. Differencing algorithms could be used to re-sync the shadow file.

History View Provides Scent and Details

The user interface to HyperSource provides *information scent* [8] about which code sections have associated pages; and it provides methods to filter, view, and manage pages. Analogous to the way many IDEs indicate breakpoints, Information about which text contains linked pages is shown on a line-level in a sidebar (Figure 2). The number of items for a line is encoded in highlight saturation and brightness. Clicking on any line sidebar brings up a detailed view of the relevant web history. This view enables users to display complete or filtered results, and toggle between display styles to show page thumbnails, or increase display density with text-only links. In addition to viewing line items, user can also view all items in the text span of the current selection. When viewing text selections, the view panel updates automatically as the document cursor moves through the source document. While HyperSource associates pages to individual characters, the user sees annotations for lines or active selections. The granularity of tracking annotations is fine; the granularity of interacting with annotations is under user control.

FILTERING & PRIVACY

HyperSource addresses the shortcoming that today's tools do not capture the semantic connection between browsing and coding. However, care has to be taken that automatic, implicit capture does not lead to an inverse problem of capturing too many, potentially unwanted, links. Not all visited Web pages should be logged and displayed, for two main reasons: some pages might not be relevant to the programming project (they represent noise, not signal); and sharing of logged pages might expose confidential or private information to others. We discuss possible approaches to guard against these challenges.

Maximizing signal-to-noise ratio can be approached through techniques for estimating the relevance of individual pages and then tailoring the display of logged pages to emphasize important pages and de-emphasize or hide unimportant pages. HyperSource currently uses a set of heuristics based on user actions to coarsely segment pages into two classes. Pages are deemed relevant if:

❶ text was copied from the page into the source document;
❷ the developer marked the page in the browser extension;
❸ the page was the final page visited before editing.

To address privacy and confidentiality concerns, certain pages should not be logged in the first place. To prune the set of logged pages, HyperSource offers three filtering mechanisms: a blacklist of domain names; a "clear buffer" action that empties the internal queue; and widgets for individual log item removal. An additional approach, reserved for future work, would be to attempt to automatically classify pages as programming-related, irrelevant, or private through analysis of page content features.

USER EXPERIENCES WITH HYPERSOURCE

We conducted 3 informal procedures to understand benefits and challenges of the HyperSource annotation mechanism.

Data Collection Through a Programming Competition

To understand how users visit web pages while coding, we organized a competition in which participants wrote a music visualization program in the Processing IDE in two hours. Four undergraduate Computer Science majors participated. The competition approximates end-user programmers' patterns of opportunistically learning to use new libraries [4]. It has two limitations: First, time pressure may have led participants to adopt different behaviors. Second, results will not generalize to professionals who work with the same set of technologies on a daily basis.

On average, participants visited 37 web pages (min: 26, max: 49); of which 23 were unique (min: 15, max: 30). Predictably, page visits included search engines and standard reference pages for the provided libraries. However, logs also contained pages on musical scales, frequency tables, discussions of color spaces and third party tutorials. Capturing these less obvious sources is a benefit of HyperSource over automatic documentation recommenders [6]. Associations were clustered on relatively few lines: 7 out of 141 lines of code were annotated on average (min: 5/102, max: 9/177). The relatively low number of highlighted lines suggests that browsing occurs in a small number of thematic chunks; and that association highlights can serve as useful indicators of "interesting" code sections.

Comparing Source Understanding

To assess how useful annotated source documents can be, we compared how participants answered questions about code with and without HyperSource. We manually constructed two HyperSource-annotated source files based on the music visualization code. These files likely overestimate the utility of our tool as we did not add irrelevant links. However, they can provide baseline data whether the approach benefits users. A set of four new participants reviewed each file and answered questions about the code for 15 minutes per file. Questions focused on the meaning of function calls, parameters, and the rationale for design choices in the code. Participants completed one task with HyperSource and one without. Afterwards participants reflected in writing on the two conditions.

Three participants explicitly commented that HyperSource helped them understand the unfamiliar code faster: *"It was much easier to answer the questions with the annotated URLs"*; *"a valuable tool to accelerate the process of reading code."* Two commented that the links provided the right starting point for understanding which set of sites were consulted, but that they still explored other (non-captured)

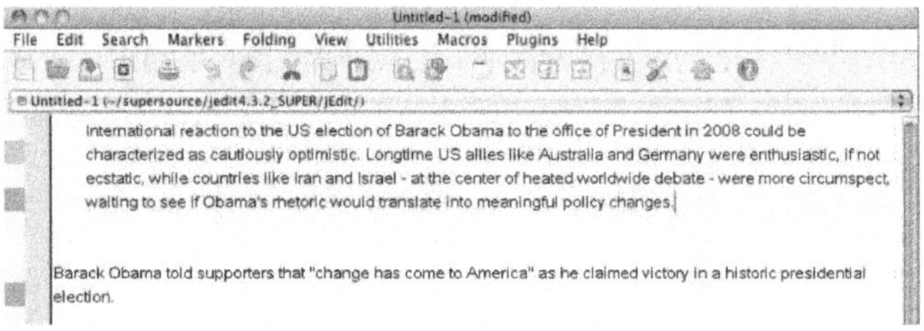

Figure 6: Part of an essay written in jEdit + HyperSource.

pages based on that starting set. One participant pointed out that programming is a very keyboard-centric activity and that tools like HyperSource must therefore be accessible without relying on (slow) mouse interactions.

Writing an Essay With Automatic Reference Tracking

Writers of prose may also benefit from HyperSource. To inform our intuition about domains beyond programming, we asked an undergraduate English student to write an essay about international media reception of the Obama presidency in jEdit. This task required visiting many diverse web resources. Figure 6 shows an intermediate stage of this task, with multiple annotated lines of text.

To our surprise, the final document contained few such annotations. We hypothesize that writing prose is fundamentally about *re-writing*: our participant frequently edited and rephrased entire sentences. HyperSource associates web pages with individual characters; if those characters are removed from the document, e.g., through replacement of a sentence, the associations vanish as well. This suggests that more sophisticated tracking algorithms may be needed.

TRACKING MORE THAN WEB PAGES

HyperSource associates relevant information from sources external to a code document with regions within that code document. This principle can be generalized beyond web pages. Developers may also have to change their underlying system configuration for their project, *e.g.*, by editing system variables, or changing file permissions. Such tasks are frequently accomplished through shell commands.

We investigated whether capturing and associating shell command histories could be useful by implementing a custom version of the Bourne-Again Shell (`bash`). Our implementation hooks into the history mechanism: whenever an executed command line is added to the bash history, the command is also sent to a HyperSource editor. This experiment yielded two insights. First, a project-specific command line history can provide valuable context about actions previous developers took outside the IDE. Second, terminal commands have *weak locality* — they are not strongly related to specific code sections. It may therefore be more appropriate to associate command line histories with the directories in which the commands were executed.

RELATED WORK

CodeTrail [4] most closely matches our motivation: It automatically selects and attaches documentation to projects using known documentation sites; opens attached documentation in a browser; and enables users to manually bookmark URLs at the file level. HyperSource differs in focus: it tracks all visited Web pages implicitly and attaches web histories to specific sections of code. HyperSource also introduces a novel user interface for showing and interacting with annotations. Blueprint [2] incorporates interactions for finding and integrating example code directly into the IDE. In contrast, with HyperSource developers continue to use their Web browser.

Better code search engines, *e.g.*, Mica [9], integrate search for documentation and example source. Such tools are not aware of the developer's IDE. HyperSource is also related to research that records Web browsing activity, *e.g.*, ActionShot [7]. We might leverage insights on session summarization from this research. Finally, HyperSource is related to task-oriented development tools such as Mylar [6], that aggregate information from disparate sources.

FUTURE DIRECTIONS: RECOMMENDATIONS

In future work, we plan to investigate the additional benefit that can be realized by mining a collection of HyperSource-annotated source documents for *code-directed collaborative filtering*. We believe that analyzing the code structure of annotated lines and the URLs attached to those lines can yield useful recommendations which URLs are frequently visited for certain types and methods. Validating this intuition will require a larger deployment of HyperSource.

REFERENCES

1. Processing 1.0. http://processing.org/.
2. Brandt, J., Dontcheva, M., Weskamp, M., and Klemmer, S.R. Example-centric programming: integrating web search into the development environment. *Proceedings of CHI 2010*, ACM (2010), 513-522.
3. Brandt, J., Guo, P.J., Lewenstein, J., Dontcheva, M., and Klemmer, S.R. Two studies of opportunistic programming: interleaving web foraging, learning, and writing code. *Proceedings of CHI 2009*, ACM (2009), 1589-1598.
4. Goldman, M. and Miller, R.C. Codetrail: Connecting source code and web resources. *Journal of Visual Languages & Computing 20*, 4 (2009), 223-235.
5. Hill, W.C., Hollan, J.D., Wroblewski, D., and McCandless, T. Edit wear and read wear. *Proceedings of CHI 1992*, ACM (1992), 3-9.
6. Kersten, M. and Murphy, G.C. Mylar: a degree-of-interest model for IDEs. *Proceedings of AOSD 2005*, ACM (2005), 159–168.
7. Li, I., Nichols, J., Lau, T., Drews, C., and Cypher, A. Here's what I did: sharing and reusing web activity with ActionShot. *Proceedings of CHI 2010*, ACM (2010), 723-732.
8. Pirolli, P. *Information foraging theory: adaptive interaction with information.* Oxford University Press, 2007.
9. Stylos, J. and Myers, B.A. Mica: A Web-Search Tool for Finding API Components and Examples. *Proceedings of VL/HCC 2006*, IEEE Computer Society (2006), 195–202.
10. Teevan, J., Adar, E., Jones, R., and Potts, M.A.S. Information re-retrieval: repeat queries in Yahoo's logs. *Proceedings of SIGIR 2007*, ACM (2007), 151-158.

Item Sampling for Information Architecture

Craig S. Miller
DePaul University
Chicago, IL
cmiller@cs.depaul.edu

ABSTRACT
When creating a taxonomy for information architecture, practitioners or design participants typically work with a sample of content items to form categories that allow users to successfully navigate to desired information, commands, or items. In order to examine how sample selection affects the coverage of the desired taxonomy, computer simulations were conducted that models the process of sample selection. The simulations reveal how the number of categories, the distribution of items in the taxonomy and the method of selection affect the coverage of a sample at various sizes.

Author Keywords
Information architecture, card sorting

ACM Classification Keywords
H.5.0 Information Interfaces and Presentation: General

General Terms
Design, Human Factors, Theory

INTRODUCTION
When developing a navigable information space or information architecture (IA), IA practitioners must devise a taxonomy. That is, they must design a system of categories consisting of content items so that users can successfully select a category that efficiently leads to what they are seeking. When creating a taxonomy, practitioners must work with a reasonable sample of content items to identify the categories. Often IA professionals turn to users and ask them to sort content items into candidate categories. Called card sorting (or more specifically *open* card sorting), this process involves users who organize content items, often displayed as cards, into categories where they would expect to find them. With its increasing practice, instructions for conducting a card sort have appeared (e.g. [2, 3, 4, 5, 6]). In addition, card sorting has been used as a methodology in other fields under alternate names including data sorting and pile sorting [1].

CHI 2011, May 7–12, 2011, Vancouver, BC, Canada.

Whether information architects organize content items themselves or ask users to do so, an important question involves the number of content items that must be considered to create valid categories. An application may contain hundreds, thousands or even tens of thousands of content items. Fully considering all of them is not possible and thus a workable sample of items is required. While it is easy to work with a small sample, doing so runs the risk of missing content items that would belong to an additional category. Despite the risk, there is no principled guidance on the number of content items (often represented as cards) that should be used. Informal recommendations vary. Rosenfeld and Morville [4] indicate that 20 to 25 is usually sufficient. Kuniavsky [2] writes that 52 (size of a standard card deck) is a good balance between having enough to make good categories and not having too many to make it difficult for participants. Finally, Spencer and Warfel [6] recommend between 30 and 100 while acknowledging that there is "no magic number."

Through analysis and use of computational simulations, this article examines the issues for creating an effective sample of cards. A major goal is to provide practical advice on the number of cards needed for reasonably covering all of the categories that would appear in the desired taxonomy. At the same time, simulation results will offer realistic expectations for categories that might be missing in the sample of cards so that practitioners can plan for possible expansion. Finally, the analysis leads to principles including tradeoffs for establishing what makes a good sample.

CONSIDERATIONS
Perhaps the first consideration in creating a sample of cards is to keep the size workably small. A workable number can depend on the amount of content on each card, the domain expertise of the sorters and the time available for each sort. While it may not be possible to create a predictive formula based on these factors, this constraint can be reasonably determined with a couple of pilot sorts or even based on prior experience under similar circumstances. In fact, much of the recommended sample sizes appear to be based on what is a workable number for the participants.

While finding a workable size is not difficult, determining a sample size that effectively covers the categories in the desired taxonomy is much more difficult. The problem is that the practitioner receives no immediate feedback on what might be missing. The so-called missing categories may not emerge until after the information architecture has been designed or new items are added. In the worst case, missing categories may never be discovered and new items are ineffectively forced into categories that are already present.

This article presents an approach that estimates the likelihood of missing categories based on results from computer simulations. For each simulation trial, a sample of cards is taken so that their probability of being selected reflects how content items are actually distributed in a taxonomy. With each trial, the simulation determines whether the probabilistically determined sample represents all categories. By repeating the simulation many trials, we can reliably predict the probability that all categories are represented for a specific sample size (i.e. number of cards in the deck) given a specified distribution among categories. An advantage of simulations is that they are based on precise, explicit assumptions and can be easily replicated. Moreover generalizing their results to practical cases can be done by assessing the extent to which a practical case matches the assumptions. Finally, simulations have the convenience of running many trials in order to obtain high statistical reliability.

RANDOM SAMPLES

We first consider creating a sample by randomly choosing the content items for the sample. Later, we will consider the benefit of choosing items that represent likely categories.

Uniformly distributed categories

Using a random sample, let us first consider taxonomies where content is uniformly distributed across their categories, that is, where each category has approximately the same proportion of content items. Perhaps not likely in practice, a uniform distribution offers an ideal case. Everything else being equal, a uniform distribution provides the most effective means for filtering out unwanted content (on average) when a category is successfully chosen. Also, the uniform distribution provides the case where a sample is most likely to cover all the categories. In effect, the assumption of uniform distribution gives us a best-case scenario. In the next section, a more likely distribution will be addressed.

Computer simulations were conducted to determine how often a set of cards would represent all of the categories in taxonomies with various numbers of categories. The simulations assumed a uniform distribution across categories and accordingly simulated category membership by randomly assigning a category to each card in the sample. Sets of simulations were run for card samples ranging from 30 cards to 100 cards and for taxonomies ranging from 6 categories to 16 categories. Each simulation set ran for one million trials, which produces a 95% confidence interval well within half a percent of the observed proportion.

For each simulation set, Figure 1 shows how likely a card set would cover all categories. For example, with 50 cards, an IA practitioner could expect full coverage at least 80% of the time for a 12 category taxonomy. Seeing simulation results at nearly 1 (100%) for 8 and 6 categories, the practitioner could be very confident that the sample of 50 would cover all cards if the ultimate taxonomy contains closer to 8 cards.

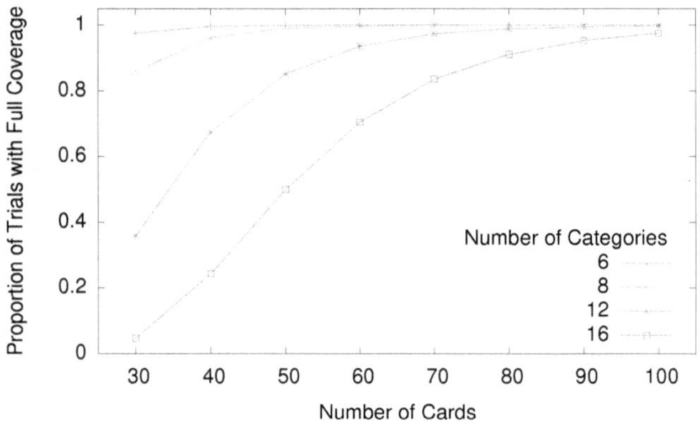

Figure 1. Proportions for uniformly distributed categories

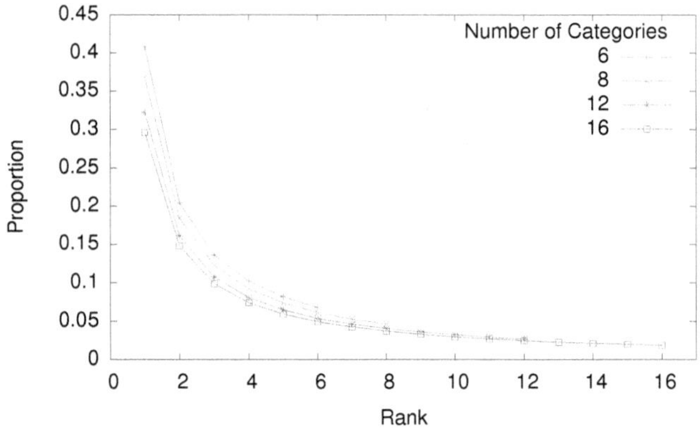

Figure 2. Zipf distributions

Successful use of the simulation results requires an estimate of the number of categories that would appear in the desired taxonomy. In some cases, the number of categories might be limited by display constraints. For cases where the ultimate number of categories is difficult to determine, a large estimate would at least produce a conservative estimate on high likely the sample would cover all categories. The use of pilot sorts will later be discussed for checking coverage.

Zipf-Distributed Categories

Many if not most taxonomies used for information architecture do not conform to a uniform distribution. To account for more naturally occurring distributions, we consider the Zipf distribution, which has been useful for modeling the distribution of naturally occurring frequencies including word frequencies [7] and which has been noted as a likely distribution in the context of other data sorting applications [1]. Figure 2 shows Zipf distributions for various numbers of categories. Note that the categories with the highest frequencies constitute the bulk of the items followed by a long tail of many categories, each with far fewer items.

Figure 3 shows the distribution among categories for five online web sites that represent a variety of applications including a general directory to web pages (Google Directory), directories to digital media or applications (Directory to Apple iPhone Applications and a directory to Podcasts), an eCommerce site (J&R) and a directory to journals (Di-

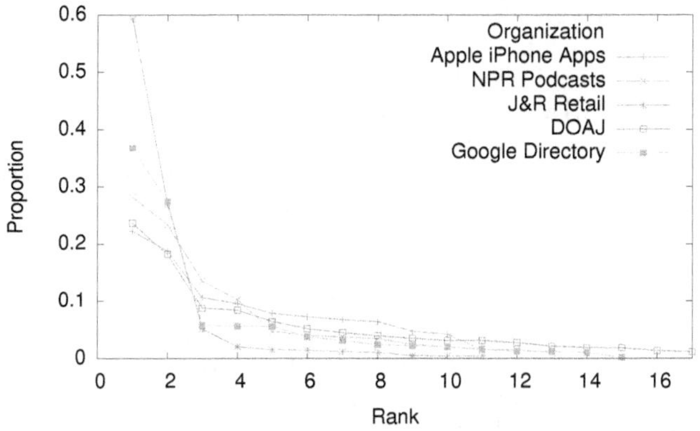

Figure 3. Distributions for actual web categories

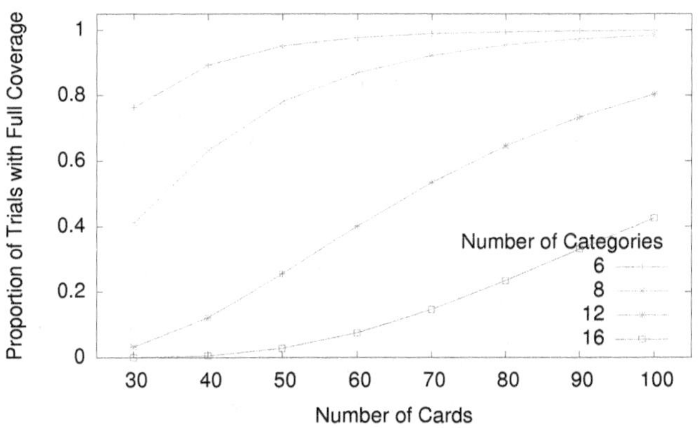

Figure 4. Proportions for Zipf distributed categories

rectory of Open Access Journals). Consistent with the Zipf distribution, these taxonomies are characterized with a few high-frequency categories followed by a longer tail of low-frequency items. By conforming to these these characteristics, the Zipf distribution makes a good approximation for many taxonomies for information architecture.

Simulations were repeated for taxonomies assuming a Zipf distribution. Figure 4 presents the results of these simulations. Compared to the results based on a uniform distribution, the results based on the Zipf distribution have substantially lower proportions for covering all of the categories. For example, a sample of 60 cards would cover a uniformly distributed taxonomy of 12 categories approximately 90% of the time. However, the 60-card sample would cover a Zipf-distributed taxonomy of 12 categories only 40% of the time. The difficulty in covering Zipf-distributed taxonomies is due to the low-frequency categories, which are much less likely to appear in a random sample of cards.

INFORMED SELECTION

The previous simulations assumed a random sample of cards. Random sampling has the benefit of imposing no systematic bias on the sample. Moreover, it does not require any knowledge or expertise in selecting items for the sample of cards. However, there are times when an IA practitioner has some knowledge of the domain and is confident enough to deliberately choose a sample in order to increase the likelihood that

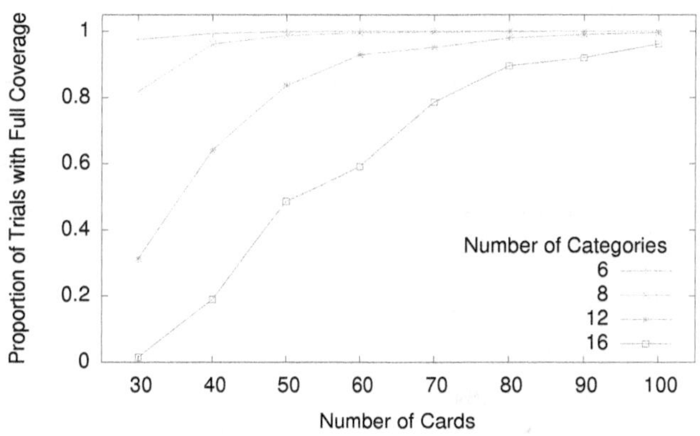

Figure 5. Proportions for expert-selected card sets

all categories are represented. In this section we examine the benefit of informed selection under plausible conditions.

An informed selection requires the use of *prospective* categories, which are the IA practitioner's informed guess of the categories that would eventually appear in the desired taxonomy. With prospective categories, the practitioner can then select content items so that all prospective categories are represented. Successfully choosing items to represent the categories in the desired taxonomy thus depends on the practitioner's ability to identify prospective categories and judge category membership for the content items.

To consider the effectiveness of informed selection, simulations were conducted that mimicked informed selection under plausible conditions. As with the previous simulation, content items were assigned to the "correct" category using a Zipf distribution. A practitioner's ability to guess categories of content items was then modeled by assuming that a practitioner can guess the actual category of a content item half of the time. The "incorrect" guesses were then modeled by having the simulation guess one of the other categories according to the Zipf distribution.

The selection procedure involved considering an item for inclusion by "guessing" its category. As long as each guessed category had less than an equal share for the desired sample size, the item was included in the sample. Otherwise, it was tossed out. Because the sample size was usually not a multiple of the number of categories, assigning guessed categories was completed before a full sample was created. The rest of the sample was completed by adding items without any informed selection. For example, creating a sample of size 30 involving 8 categories would include 3 items per guessed category plus 6 items taken from the Zipf distribution.

As with previous simulations, the coverage of correct categories can be checked for each trial. Figure 5 shows the simulation results for informed selection. Comparing to the previous simulation, informed selection generally provides a better coverage of the desired categories, assuming the IA practitioner can successfully identify and classify for the right categories half the time.

Additional experimentation revealed that informed selection generally favors random selection for covering categories provided that an item is correctly assigned to an appropriate category at least 20% of the time. Performances below 20% yielded coverages that were worse for informed selection than for random selection. It should also be noted that these comparisons assume that mistaken assignments are not systematically biased towards specific categories, in which case, informed selection could produce coverages that are much worse than random selection.

RECOMMENDATIONS

The simulations reveal that an effective size for a sample of content items can depend on the category distribution, the number of categories in the desired taxonomy and, for informed selection, the ability to guess likely categories and classify content items into them. Despite these considerations, it is nevertheless possible to make an informed decision on the size of the sample and how to select items for the sample. For example, 50 randomly selected cards will generally be adequate to represent a taxonomy with 8 or fewer categories when assuming the common Zipf distribution. Increasing the sample size may be warranted if it appears that more categories are needed. Alternatively, informed selection will successfully reduce the size needed for the sample provided that the practitioner can successfully identify most of the items for the desired taxonomy. In this case, simulations reveal that a sample of 30 will fully represent a taxonomy of 8 categories more than 80% of the time.

For cases where little is known about the desired taxonomy, pilot card sorts are recommended. The results from a few pilot card sorts can be used to estimate the number of categories, verify the distribution, and assess the practitioner's ability to make informed selections. Once assumptions have been verified, the simulation results can then be used to revise the samples if any changes are needed.

Of course, pilot results by themselves cannot be used to verify adequate coverage of the desired taxonomy. As previously noted, it is always possible that needed categories are not represented in the sample. However, using the simulation results, a practitioner can ask how likely might there be categories missing from the results. Using the number of categories from the pilot sort, the practitioner can check the graph for the point representing the next higher number of categories. With a high proportion, the practitioner can be more confident that all categories are covered. For example, if a randomly selected card sort with a sample size of 50 yielded 10 categories, the practitioner can then check the likelihood of coverage in the case that the desired taxonomy actual has 12 categories. In this case, the coverage for 12 categories with 50 cards is not likely (26%), which suggests using a larger sample or making informed selections for creating the sample. In contrast, if a pilot sort produced 7 categories with 70 cards, the IA practitioner could be much more confident that all categories are represented.

Some guides to card sorting suggest giving card sort participants the option of placing an item in more than one category [5]. At first glance, it may seem that this practice would improve the chances of a sample representing the entire taxonomy since multiple placements could potentially cover more categories. However, it is not likely that a participant would want to place a card in a second category if it were not already represented by content items. In this case, the analysis and simulation results of this article equally apply to card sorts where items may belong to multiple categories.

In addition to guidance on creating samples, the simulation results provide some helpful expectations for what the sample might include. For example, they reveal that it is generally not possible to guarantee that all categories will be represented. At best, it is possible to know that full representation is highly likely. In the absence of a guarantee, practitioners may need plans on how to accommodate additional categories should they later emerge. Also note that the simulations counted a card sample successful if all categories had at least one card, which means that some categories may only be represented with only one card in the sample. The practitioner should keep this in mind and may want to inform card-sorting participants that a category with only one card is a possibility.

In addition to detailed results, the analysis and results of this article lead to some general principles. First, the presence of Zipf-distributed categories make it less likely that low frequency categories will be represented in a sample. Second, taxonomies with a larger number of categories require a larger sample size in order to fully represent categories in the taxonomy. Third, with knowledge of the domain and users, an informed selection of content items for the sample improves the likelihood that the sample represents all categories in the desired taxonomy.

REFERENCES

1. A. P. M. Coxon. *Sorting data: Collection and analysis*. SAGE Publications, Thousand Oaks, CA, 1999.

2. M. Kuniavsky. *Observing the user experience: A practitioner's guide to user research*. Morgan Kaufmann, San Francisco, CA, 2003.

3. C. Paul. A modified delphi approach to a new card sorting methodology. *Journal of Usability Studies*, 4(1):7–30, 2008.

4. R. Rosenfeld and P. Morville. *Information Architecture for the World Wide Web*. O'Reilly & Associates, Sebastopol, CA, second edition, 2002.

5. D. Spencer. *Card Sorting: Designing Usable Categories*. Rosenfeld Media, New York, NY, 2009.

6. D. Spencer and T. Warfel. Card sorting: a definitive guide. `http://www.boxesandarrows.com/view/card_sorting_a_definitive_guide`, 2004. Accessed December 23, 2010.

7. G. K. Zipf. *The Psycho-Biology of Language*. Houghton Mifflin, Boston, MA, 1935.

When Designing Usability Questionnaires, Does It Hurt to Be Positive?

Jeff Sauro
Oracle Corporation
1 Technology Way, Denver, CO 80237
jeff@measuringusability.com

James R. Lewis
IBM Software Group
8051 Congress Ave, Suite 2227
Boca Raton, FL 33487
jimlewis@us.ibm.com

ABSTRACT
When designing questionnaires there is a tradition of including items with both positive and negative wording to minimize acquiescence and extreme response biases. Two disadvantages of this approach are respondents accidentally agreeing with negative items (mistakes) and researchers forgetting to reverse the scales (miscoding).

The original System Usability Scale (SUS) and an all positively worded version were administered in two experiments (n=161 and n=213) across eleven websites. There was no evidence for differences in the response biases between the different versions. A review of 27 SUS datasets found 3 (11%) were miscoded by researchers and 21 out of 158 questionnaires (13%) contained mistakes from users.

We found no evidence that the purported advantages of including negative and positive items in usability questionnaires outweigh the disadvantages of mistakes and miscoding. It is recommended that researchers using the standard SUS verify the proper coding of scores and include procedural steps to ensure error-free completion of the SUS by users.

Researchers can use the all positive version with confidence because respondents are less likely to make mistakes when responding, researchers are less likely to make errors in coding, and the scores will be similar to the standard SUS.

Author Keywords
Usability evaluation, standardized questionnaires, satisfaction measures, acquiescent bias, System Usability Scale (SUS)

ACM Classification Keywords
H5.m. Information interfaces and presentation (e.g., HCI): User Interfaces–Evaluation/Methodology.

General Terms
Experimentation, Human Factors, Measurement, Reliability, Standardization, Theory

INTRODUCTION
Designers of attitudinal questionnaires (of which questionnaires that measure satisfaction with usability are one type) are trained to consider questionnaire response styles such as extreme response bias and acquiescence bias [17]. In acquiescence bias, respondents tend to agree with all or almost all statements in a questionnaire. The extreme response bias is the tendency to mark the extremes of rating scales rather than points near the middle of the scale. To the extent that these biases exist, the affected responses do not provide a true measure of an attitude. Acquiescence bias is of particular concern because it leads to an upward error in measurement, giving researchers too sanguine a picture of whatever attitude they are measuring.

A strategy commonly employed to reduce the acquiescent response bias is the inclusion of negatively worded items in a questionnaire [1], [2], [17]. Questionnaires with a mix of positive and negatively worded statements force attentive respondents to disagree with some statements. Under the assumption that negative and positive items are essentially equivalent and by reverse scoring the negative items, the resulting composite score should have reduced acquiescence bias.

More recently, however, there is evidence that the strategy of including a mix of positively and negatively worded items creates more problems than it solves [4]. Such problems include lowering the internal reliability [25], distorting the factor structure [19], [23], [22] and increasing interpretation problems with cross-cultural use [29].

The strategy of alternating item wording has been applied in the construction of most of the popular usability questionnaires, including the System Usability Scale (SUS) [6], SUMI [11], and QUIS [7]. The ASQ, PSSUQ and CSUQ [12], [13], [14] are exceptions, with all positive items.

The System Usability Scale is likely the most popular questionnaire for measuring attitudes toward system usability [14], [30]. Its popularity is due to it being free and short—with 10 items that alternate between positive and negative statements about usability (odd items positive, even items negative). It has also been the subject of some recent investigations [3], [15] [8], [9], which makes it a good candidate to manipulate to study whether the benefits outweigh the potential negatives of alternating item wording. The ten traditional SUS items are shown in Exhibit 1.

1. I think that I would like to use this system frequently.
2. I found the system unnecessarily complex.
3. I thought the system was easy to use.
4. I think that I would need the support of a technical person to be able to use this system.
5. I found the various functions in this system were well integrated.
6. I thought there was too much inconsistency in this system.
7. I would imagine that most people would learn to use this system very quickly.
8. I found the system very cumbersome to use.
9. I felt very confident using the system.
10. I needed to learn a lot of things before I could get going with this system.

The response options, arranged from the left to right, are Strongly Disagree (1) to Strongly Agree (5).

Exhibit 1: The System Usability Scale (SUS).

The proper scoring of the SUS has two stages:

1. Subtract one from the odd numbered items and subtract the even numbered responses from 5. This scales all values from 0 to 4 (with four being the positive response).
2. Add up the scaled items and multiply by 2.5 (to convert the range of possible values from 0 to 100 instead of from 0 to 40).

Previous research on the SUS

Much of the research applied to the design of rating scales for usability attitudes comes from disciplines other than usability, typically marketing and psychology. In other fields, items can include more controversial or ambiguous topics than is typical of system usability. Although many findings should still apply to usability questionnaire design, it is of value to the design of future usability questionnaires to review research related specifically to the analysis of rating scales used in usability—especially the SUS.

Bangor et al. [3] analyzed a large database of SUS questionnaires (over 2300) and found that participants tended to give slightly higher than average ratings to most of the even numbered statements (negatively phrased items 4, 6, 8 and 10), and also tended to give slightly lower than average ratings to most of the odd numbered statements (positively phrased items: 1, 2, 3, 5 and 9). This suggests participants tended to agree slightly more with negatively worded items and to disagree slightly more with positively worded items (from this point on, referred to as positive and negative items). The magnitude of the difference was modest, with the average absolute deviation from the average score of .19 of a point and the highest deviation on item 4 ("I think that I would need the support of a technical person to be able to use this system.") – a deviation of .47 of a point.

Finstad [9] compared a 7-point version to the original 5-point version of SUS and found users of enterprise systems "interpolated" significantly more on the 5-point version than on the 7-point version; however, there was no investigation on the effects of changing item wording. Based on difficulties observed with non-native speakers completing the SUS, Finstad [8] recommended changing the word "cumbersome" in Item 8 to "awkward" – a recommendation echoed in [3] and [15].

In 2008 a panel at the annual Usability Professionals Association conference entitled "Subjective ratings of usability: Reliable or ridiculous?" was held [10]. On the panel were two of the originators of the QUIS and SUMI questionnaires. As part of the panel presentation, an experiment was conducted on the effects of question wording on SUS scores to investigate two variables: item intensity and item direction (for details see [21]). For example, the extreme negative version of the SUS Item 4 was "I think that I would need a permanent hot-line to the help desk to be able to use the web site."

Volunteer participants reviewed the UPA website. After the review, participants completed one of five SUS questionnaires -- an all positive extreme, all negative extreme, one of two versions of an extreme mix (half positive and half negative extreme), or the standard SUS questionnaire (as a baseline). Sixty-two people in total participated, providing between 10-14 responses per condition. Even with this relatively small sample size the extreme positive and extreme negative items were significantly different from the original SUS ($F(4,57) = 6.90$, $p < .001$) and represented a large effect size (Cohen $d > 1.1$).

These results were consistent with one of the earliest reports of attitudes in scale construction [27]. Research has shown that people tend to agree with statements that are close to their attitude and disagree with all other statements [24].

By rephrasing items to extremes, only respondents who passionately favored the usability of the UPA website tended to agree with the extremely phrased positive statements—resulting in a significantly **lower** average score. Likewise, only respondents who passionately disfavored the usability agreed with the extremely negatively questions—resulting in a significant **higher** average score.

The results of this experiment confirmed that extreme intensity can affect item-responses towards attitudes of usability, so designers of usability questionnaires should avoid such extreme items. Due to the confounding of item intensity and direction, however, the results do not permit making claims about the effects of alternating positive and negatively worded items.

Advantages for alternating question items

The major impetus for alternating scales is to control acquiescent response bias (including the potential impression that having only positive items may lead respondents to think you want them to like the system under evaluation – John Brooke, personal communication, 8/2010). The alternation of positive and negative items also provides protection against serial extreme responders – participants who provide all high or all low ratings – a situation that could be especially problematic for remote usability testing. For example, when items alternate, responses of all 1's make no sense. When items do not alternate, responses of all 1's could represent a legitimate set of responses.

Disadvantages for alternating question items

Despite the potential advantages of alternation, we consider three major potential disadvantages.

1. **Misinterpret**: Users may respond differently to negatively worded items such that reversing responses from negative to positive doesn't account for the difference. As discussed in the previous section, problems with misinterpreting negative items include creating an artificial two-factor structure and lowering internal reliability, especially in cross-cultural contexts.

2. **Mistake**: Users might not intend to respond differently, but may forget to reverse their score, accidentally agreeing with a negative statement when they meant to disagree. We have been with participants who have acknowledged either forgetting to reverse their score or commenting that they had to correct some scores because they forgot to adjust their score.

3. **Miscode**: Researchers might forget to reverse the scales when scoring, and would consequently report incorrect data. Despite there being software to easily record user input, researchers still have to remember to reverse the scales. Forgetting to reverse the scales is not an obvious error. The improperly scaled scores are still acceptable values, especially when the system being tested is of moderate usability (in which case many responses will be neutral or close to neutral).

A researcher may only become aware of coding errors after subjecting the results to internal reliability testing and obtaining a negative Cronbach's alpha – a procedure that few usability practitioners routinely practice. In fact, this problem is prevalent enough in the general practice of questionnaire development that the makers of statistical software (SPSS) have included it as a warning "The [Cronbach's alpha] value is negative due to a negative average covariance among items. This violates reliability model assumptions. You may want to check item codings" [26].

We are able to estimate the prevalence of the miscoding error from two sources. First, in 2009, eight of 15 teams used the SUS as part of the Comparative Usability Evaluation-8 (CUE-8) workshop at the Usability Professionals Association annual conference [18]. Of the eight teams, one team improperly coded their SUS results. Second, as part of an earlier analysis of SUS, we [15] examined 19 contributed SUS datasets. Two were improperly coded and needed to be recoded prior to analysis.

Considering these two sources, three out of 27 SUS datasets (11.1%) had negative items that weren't reversed. Assuming this to be a reasonably representative selection of the larger population of SUS questionnaires, we can be 95% confident that miscoding affects between 3% and 28% of SUS datasets. Hopefully, future research will shed light on whether this assumption is correct.

Despite published concerns about acquiescence bias, there is little evidence that the "common-wisdom" of including both positive and negatively worded items solves the problem. To our knowledge there is no research documenting the magnitude of acquiescence bias in general, or whether it specifically affects the measurement of attitudes toward usability.

The goals of this paper are to determine whether an acquiescence bias exists in responses to the SUS, and if so, how large is it? Does the alternating wording of the SUS provide protection against acquiescence and extreme response biases? Further, does its alternating item wording outweigh the negatives of misinterpreting, mistaking and miscoding?

METHODS

We conducted two experiments to look for potential advantages and disadvantages of reversing items in questionnaires.

Experiment 1

In April 2010, 51 users (recruited using Amazon's Mechanical Turk) performed two representative tasks on one of four websites (Budget.com, Travelocity.com, Sears.com and Bellco.com). Examples of the tasks include making reservations for a car or flight, locating items to purchase, finding the best interest rate and locating store hours and locations.

At the end of the test users answered the standard 10 item SUS questionnaire. There were between 12 and 15 users for each website.

In August 2010, a new set of 110 users (again recruited using Amazon's Mechanical Turk) performed the same tasks on one of four websites tested four months earlier. There were between 20 and 30 users for each website. The testing protocol was the same except the new set of users completed a positive-only version of the SUS as shown in Exhibit 2. Note that other than replacing "system" with "website", the odd items are identical to those of the standard SUS but the even items are different – worded positively rather than negatively.

1. I think that I would like to use the website frequently.
2. I found the website to be simple.
3. I thought the website was easy to use.
4. I think that I could use the website without the support of a technical person.
5. I found the various functions in the website were well integrated.
6. I thought there was a lot of consistency in the website.
7. I would imagine that most people would learn to use the website very quickly.
8. I found the website very intuitive.
9. I felt very confident using the website.
10. I could use the website without having to learn anything new.

Response options appeared from the left to right anchored with Strongly Disagree 1 to Strongly Agree 5.

Exhibit 2: A positively worded SUS questionnaire.

Results of Experiment 1

Both samples contained only respondents from the US, with no significant differences in average age (32.3 and 32.2; $t(81) = .04$, $p > .95$), gender (57% and 56% female; $\chi2(1) = .003$, $p > .95$) or highest degree obtained (63% and 59% with college degrees $\chi2(3) = 1.54$, $p > .67$) and prior experience with the sites (63% and 54% had no prior experience $\chi2(1) = 1.17$, $p > .27$).

The internal reliability of both versions of the questionnaires was high and nearly identical. For the original SUS questions with 51 cases Cronbach's alpha was .91. For the positively worded SUS with 110 cases Cronbach's alpha was .92.

To look for an overall effect between questionnaire types, we conducted a t-test using the scaled SUS scores, the average of the evenly numbered items, and the average of the odd-numbered items. The means and standard deviations appear in Tables 1-3.

Questionnaire	Mean	SD	N
Normal SUS	73.4	17.6	51
Positive SUS	77.1	17.1	110

Table 1: SUS Scaled scores for four websites (p > .20).

Questionnaire	Mean	SD	N
Normal SUS	3.25	.70	51
Positive SUS	3.21	.66	110

Table 2: Even number items for four websites (p>.74).

Questionnaire	Mean	SD	N
Normal SUS	2.62	.79	51
Positive SUS	2.97	.75	110

Table 3: Odd numbered items (p < .02).

The difference between questionnaires was not statistically significant for scaled SUS scores ($t(95) = -1.25$, $p > .20$) or for the average of the even items ($t(92) = 0.33$, $p > .74$). There was a significant difference for the odd items ($t(93) = -2.61$ $p < .02$) – the items not changed between versions of the questionnaire.

There was a statistically significant difference between the odd and even-numbered items for the original SUS questionnaire ($t(98) = 4.26$, $p < .001$) and the all positive SUS questionnaire ($t(214) = 2.60$, $p < .02$), suggesting the even items elicit different responses than the odd items in both questionnaires. Furthermore, a repeated-measures ANOVA with odd/even as a within subjects variable and questionnaire type as a between subjects variable revealed a significant interaction between odd/even questions and questionnaire type (F (1,159) =32.4, p < .01), as shown in Figure 1.

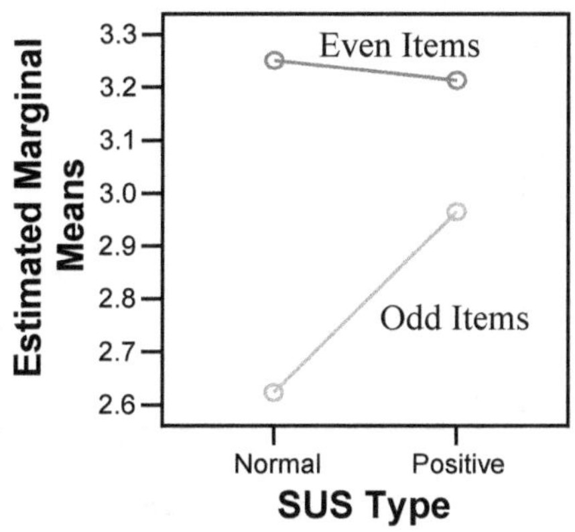

Figure 1: Even/odd by n/positive interaction from Experiment 1 (asynchronous data collection).

Acquiescence Bias

To assess acquiescence bias, we counted the number of agreement responses (4 or 5) to the odd numbered (consistently and positively worded) items in both questionnaires. The mean number of agreement responses was 3.2 per questionnaire for the standard SUS (SD = 1.67, n = 51) and 3.69 for the positive version (SD = 1.46, n = 110). The positive questionnaire had a slightly higher average number of agreements than the standard, although the difference was only marginally significant (t(86) = -1.82, p > .07.

Extreme Response Bias

To measure extreme response bias, we counted the number of times respondents provided either the highest or lowest response option (1 or 5) for both questionnaire types for all items. The mean number of extreme responses was 3.45 for the standard SUS (SD = 2.86, n = 51) and 4.09 for the positive version (SD = 3.29, n = 110), a nonsignificant difference (t (111) = -1.26, p > .21).

Mistakes

We used two approaches to assess the magnitude of the potential mistake problem. First, we looked for internal inconsistencies within questionnaires by comparing the number of times respondents agreed (responses of 4 and 5) to negatively worded items and also agreed to positively worded items (responses of 4 and 5)—an approach similar to [28]. We considered a questionnaire to contain mistakes if there were at least 3 responses indicating agreement to positively and negatively worded items or 3 responses with disagreement to positively and negatively worded items. We found 3 such cases (5.8%, 95% CI ranging from 1.4% to 16.5%).

Our second approach was to examine responses to the most highly correlated negative and positive item which, according to [3]'s large SUS dataset were items 2 and 3 (r = -.593). The correlation between those items from this experiment was also high and significant (r = -.683, p <.01, n = 51). For this assessment, we counted the number of times respondents provided a response of a 4 or 5 to both items 2 and 3. There were 18 such cases (35.3%, 95% CI ranging from 23.6% to 49.1%).

Experiment 1 Discussion

The overall SUS scores between the standard and all positive versions of the SUS were not significantly different, which suggests that changing the wording of the items in this way does not appear to have a strong effect on the resulting SUS measurements. There was no difference in the even numbered item averages (the ones changed in the positive only questionnaire). However, the odd-numbered item averages (the ones NOT changed in this experiment) were significantly different, with slightly lower scores for positive and slightly higher scores for the negative versions of the items.

To say the least, we did not expect this result, and found it difficult to explain. In examining the difference by website, the bulk of the differences came from two of the four websites (Travelocity.com and Sears.com). Investigating systems in the wild can be tricky because researchers have no control over the timing of system changes (for example, see [20], reanalyzed in [16]). It is possible that changes to the websites somehow affected only the odd numbered questions, but that is pure speculation. To minimize the potential confounding effects of website changes and item wording, we conducted another experiment with the questionnaires tested simultaneously rather than asynchronously. We also planned for a larger sample size to increase the power of the experiment.

Experiment 2

In August and September 2010, 213 users (recruited using Amazon's Mechanical Turk) performed two representative tasks on one of seven websites (third party automotive or primary financial services websites: Cars.com, Autotrader.com, Edmunds.com, KBB.com, Vanguard.com, Fidelity.com and TDAmeritrade.com). The tasks included finding the best price for a new car, estimating the trade-in value of a used-car and finding information about mutual funds and minimum required investments. At the end of the study users randomly completed either the standard or the positively worded SUS. There were between 15 and 17 users for each website and questionnaire type.

Results of Experiment 2

Both samples contained only respondents from the US. There were no significant differences in average age (32.3 and 31.9; t(210) = .26, p >.79), gender (62% and 58%

female; $\chi2(1) = .38$, $p > .53$) or highest degree obtained (58% and 63% with college degrees $\chi2(3) = 4.96$, $p > .17$) and prior experience with the sites (64% and 66% had no prior experience, $\chi2(1) = .144$, $p > .70$).

The internal reliability of both questionnaires was high – Cronbach's alpha of .92 (n = 107) for the original and .96 (n = 106) for the positive.

To look for an overall effect between questionnaire types, we conducted a t-test using the scaled SUS scores, the average of the evenly numbered items and the average of the odd-numbered items. The means and standard deviations appear in Tables 4-6.

Questionnaire	Mean	SD	N
Normal SUS	52.2	23.3	107
Positive SUS	49.3	26.8	106

Table 4: SUS Scaled scores for seven websites (p > .39).

Questionnaire	Mean	SD	N
Normal SUS	2.30	1.04	107
Positive SUS	2.15	1.09	106

Table 5: Even number items for four websites (p>.27).

Questionnaire	Mean	SD	N
Normal SUS	1.88	.97	107
Positive SUS	1.79	1.11	106

Table 6: Odd numbered items (p > .54).

The questionnaires were not statistically significant for scaled SUS scores ($t(206) = 0.85$, $p > .39$), the average of the even items ($t(210) = 1.09$, $p > .27$), or the average of the odd items ($t(206) = 0.60$, $p > .54$).

There continued to be a statistically significant difference between the odd and even-numbered items for the original SUS questionnaire ($t(210) = 3.09$, $p < .01$) and the all positive SUS questionnaire ($t(209) = 2.32$, $p < .03$).

In contrast to Experiment 1, a repeated-measures ANOVA with odd/even as a within subjects variable and questionnaire type as a between subjects variable indicated no significant interaction between odd/even questions and questionnaire type ($F(1, 211) = .770$, $p > .38$), as shown in Figure 2.

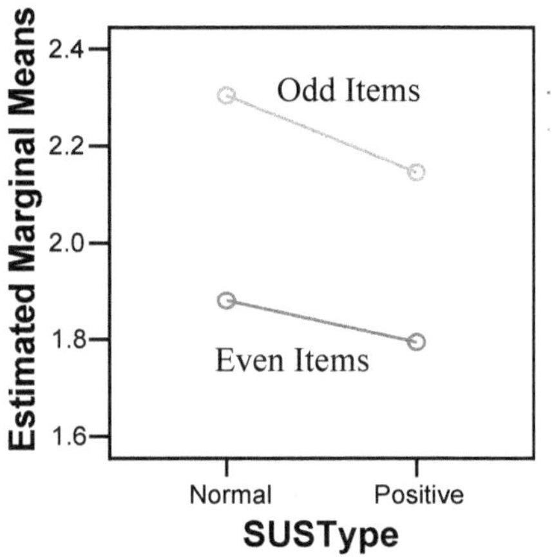

Figure 2: Interaction plot between odd/even questions and questionnaire type show no significant difference by questionnaire type (synchronous data collection).

Mistakes

As in Experiment 1, we assessed (1) the magnitude of mistaken responses: internal inconsistencies in at least 3 questions, and (2) the consistency of responses to items 2 and 3. We found 18 of the 107 original SUS questionnaires contained at least 3 internal inconsistencies (16.8%, 95% CI between 10.8% and 25.1%) and 53 questionnaires with inconsistent responses for items 2 and 3 (49.5%, 95% CI between 40.2% and 58.9%).

Acquiescence Bias

To assess acquiescence bias, we counted the number of agreement responses (4 or 5) to the odd numbered (consistently and positively worded) items in both questionnaires. The mean number of agreement responses was 1.64 per questionnaire for the standard SUS (SD = 1.86, n = 107) and 1.66 for the positive version (SD = 1.87, n = 106). There was no significant difference between the questionnaire versions ($t(210) = -.06$, $p > .95$).

Extreme Response Bias

To measure extreme response bias, we counted the number of times respondents provided either the highest or lowest response option (1 or 5) for both questionnaire types for all items. The mean number of extreme responses was 1.68 for the standard SUS (SD = 2.37, n = 107) and 1.36 for the positive version (SD = 2.23, n = 106), a nonsignificant difference ($t(210) = 1.03$, $p > .30$).

Factor Analysis of the Questionnaires

Finally, we compared the factor structures of the two versions of the SUS with the SUS factor structure reported in [15], based on the large sample of SUS questionnaires collected by [3] (and replicated by [5]). The key finding from the prior factor analytic work on the SUS was that the SUS items clustered into two factors, with one factor containing items 1, 2, 3, 5, 6, 7, 8, and 9, and the other factor containing items 4 and 10.

As shown in Table 7, neither of the resulting alignments of items with factors exactly duplicated the findings with the large samples of the SUS, and neither were they exactly consistent with each other, with discrepancies occurring on items 6, 8, and 9. Both the original and positive versions were consistent with the large-sample finding of including items 4 and 10 in the second factor. The original deviated slightly more than the positive from the large-sample factor structure (original items 6 and 8 aligned with the second rather than the first factor; positive item 9 aligned with the second rather than the first factor).

Items	Original Factor 1	Positive Factor 1	Original Factor 2	Positive Factor 2
1	**.784**	**.668**	.127	.300
2	**.594**	**.832**	.555	.437
3	**.802**	**.834**	.375	.488
4	.194	.301	**.812**	**.872**
5	**.783**	**.826**	.243	.362
6	.319	**.815**	**.698**	.230
7	**.763**	**.734**	.322	.467
8	.501	**.776**	**.688**	.404
9	**.599**	.619	.518	**.661**
10	.193	.419	**.865**	**.811**
% Var	35.9%	47.8%	32.7%	29.4%

Table 7: Two-factor structures for the standard and positive versions of the SUS (synchronous data collection)

DISCUSSION

The results of Experiments 1 and 2 were reasonably consistent, other than the bizarre outcome in Experiment 1 in which the unchanged items had significantly different values as a function of the SUS version (standard vs. positive). Because that finding did not replicate in Experiment 2, it was very likely a consequence of having collected the data asynchronously. It could be that the websites changed or the type of users who participated were in some way different.

In almost every way, the data collected in Experiment 2 with the standard and positive versions of the SUS were similar, indeed, almost identical. There were no significant differences in total SUS scores or the odd or even averages. Cronbach's alpha for both versions was high (> .90). The differences in the factor structures (both with each other and in comparison to published large-sample evaluations) were very likely due to the relatively small sample sizes. There was little evidence of any differences in acquiescence or extreme response biases between the original SUS questionnaire and the all positive version in either experiment.

Using the more conservative of the two estimation methods for mistaken responses, there were 3 out of 51 from Experiment 1 and 18 out of 107 in Experiment 2 for a total of 21 out of 158 questionnaires which contained at least 3 internal inconsistencies. This would suggest 13.3% (95% CI between 8.8% and 19.5%) of SUS questionnaires administered remotely contain mistakes. For miscoding errors, three out of 27 SUS datasets (11%; 95% CI between 3.0% and 28.8%) were improperly coded resulting in incorrect scoring.

We did not find any evidence for a strong acquiescence or extreme response bias. Even if strong evidence were found, the recommendation by [4] to reverse scale responses instead of item wording would not correct the problems of mistakes and miscoding. The data presented here suggest the problem of users making mistakes and researchers miscoding questionnaires is both real and much more detrimental than response biases.

CONCLUSION

There is little evidence that the purported advantages of including negative and positive items in usability questionnaires outweigh the disadvantages. This finding certainly applies to the SUS when evaluating websites using remote-unmoderated tests. It also likely applies to usability questionnaires with similar designs in unmoderated testing of any application. Future research with a similar experimental setup should be conducted using a moderated setting to confirm whether these findings also apply to tests when users are more closely monitored.

Researchers interested in designing new questionnaires for use in usability evaluations should avoid the inclusion of negative items.

Researchers who use the standard SUS have no need to change to the all positive version provided that they verify the proper coding of scores. In moderated testing, researchers should include procedural steps to ensure error-free completion of the SUS (such as when debriefing the user).

In unmoderated testing, it is more difficult to correct the mistakes respondents make, although it is reassuring that despite these inevitable errors, the effect is unlikely to have a major impact on overall SUS scores.

Researchers who do not have a current investment in the standard SUS can use the all positive version with confidence because respondents are less likely to make mistakes when responding, researchers are less likely to make errors in coding, and the scores will be similar to the standard SUS.

REFERENCES

1. Anastasi, A. (1982). *Psychological testing* (5th ed.). New York: Macmillan.
2. Anderson, A. B., Basilevsky, A., & Hum, D. P. J. (1983). Measurement: Theory and techniques. In P. H. Rossi, J. D. Wright, & A. B. Anderson (Eds.), *Handbook of Survey Research* (pp. 231-187). New York, NY: Academic Press.
3. Bangor, A., Kortum, P. T., & Miller, J. T. (2008). An empirical evaluation of the System Usability Scale. *International Journal of Human-Computer Interaction, 6*, 574-594.
4. Barnette, J. J. (2000). Effects of stem and Likert response option reversals on survey internal consistency: If you feel the need, there is a better alternative to using those negatively worded stems. *Educational and Psychological Measurement, 60(3)*, 361–370.
5. Borsci, S., Federici, S., & Lauriola, M. (2009). On the dimensionality of the System Usability Scale: A test of alternative measurement models. *Cognitive Processes, 10*, 193-197.
6. Brooke, J. (1996). SUS: A quick and dirty usability scale. In P.W. Jordan, B. Thomas, B.A. Weerdmeester & I.L. McClelland (Eds.), *Usability Evaluation in Industry* (pp. 189-194). London, UK: Taylor & Francis.
7. Chin, J. P, Diehl, V. A., & Norman, K. (1988). Development of an instrument measuring user satisfaction of the human–computer interface. In *Conference on Human Factors in Computing Systems* (pp. 213–218). New York, NY: Association for Computing Machinery.
8. Finstad, K. (2006). The System Usability Scale and non-native English speakers. *Journal of Usability Studies, 1*, 185–188.
9. Finstad, K. (2010). Response interpolation and scale sensitivity: Evidence against 5-point scales. *Journal of Usability Studies, 5(3)*, 104-110.
10. Karn, K., Little, A., Nelson, G., Sauro, J. Kirakowski, J., Albert, W. & Norman, K., (2008) Subjective Ratings of Usability: Reliable or Ridiculous? Panel Presentation at the Usability Professionals Association (UPA 2008) Conference Baltimore, MD.
11. Kirakowski, J., & Corbett, M. (1993). SUMI: The Software Usability Measurement Inventory. *British Journal of Educational Technology, 24*, 210–212.
12. Lewis, J. R. (1995). IBM computer usability satisfaction questionnaires: Psychometric evaluation and instructions for use. *International Journal of Human–Computer Interaction*, *7*, 57-78.
13. Lewis, J. R. (2002). Psychometric evaluation of the PSSUQ using data from five years of usability studies. *International Journal of Human-Computer Interaction, 14(3&4)*, 463-488.
14. Lewis, J. R (2006). Usability testing. In G. Salvendy (Ed.), *Handbook of Human Factors and Ergonomics* (3rd ed.) (pp. 1275-1316). New York, NY: John Wiley.
15. Lewis, J. R., & Sauro, J. (2009). The factor structure of the System Usability Scale. In M. Kurosu (Ed.), *Human Centered Design, HCII 2009* (pp. 94–103). Berlin, Germany: Springer-Verlag.
16. Lewis, J. R. (2011). *Practical speech user interface design*. Boca Raton, FL: Taylor & Francis.
17. Nunnally, J. C. (1978). *Psychometric theory* (2nd ed.). New York, NY: McGraw-Hill.
18. Molich, R., Kirakowski, J., Sauro, J., & Tullis, T., (2009) Comparative Usability Task Measurement Workshop (CUE-8) at the UPA 2009 Conference in Portland, OR.
19. Pilotte, W. J., & Gable, R. K. (1990). The impact of positive and negative item stems on the validity of a computer anxiety scale. *Educational and Psychological Measurement, 50*, 603–610.
20. Ramos, L. (1993). The effects of on-hold telephone music on the number of premature disconnections to a statewide protective services abuse hot line. *Journal of Music Therapy, 30(2)*, 119-129.
21. Sauro, J. (2010). That's the worst website ever!: Effects of extreme survey items. www.measuringusability.com/blog/extreme-items.php (last viewed 9/23/2010).
22. Schmitt N., & Stuits, D. (1985) Factors defined by negatively keyed items: The result of careless respondents? *Applied Psychological Measurement, 9(4)*, 367-373.

23. Schriesheim, C.A., & Hill, K.D. (1981). Controlling acquiescence response bias by item reversals: the effect on questionnaire validity. *Educational and Psychological Measurement, 41(4)*, 1101–1114.
24. Spector, P., Van Katwyk, P., Brannick, M., & Chen, P. (1997). When two factors don't reflect two constructs: How item characteristics can produce artifactual factors. *Journal of Management, 23(5)*, 659-677.
25. Stewart, T. J., & Frye, A. W. (2004). Investigating the use of negatively-phrased survey items in medical education settings: Common wisdom or common mistake? *Academic Medicine, 79(10 Supplement)*, S1–S3.
26. SPSS. (2003). *SPSS for Windows, Rel. 12.0.1*. (2003). Chicago, IL: SPSS Inc.
27. Thurstone, L. L. (1928). Attitudes can be measured. *American Journal of Sociology, 33*, 529-554.
28. Weijters, B., Cabooter, E., & Schillewaert, N. (2010). The effect of rating scale format on response styles: the number of response categories and response category labels. *International Journal of Research in Marketing*, 27, 236-247.
29. Wong, N., Rindfleisch, A., & Burroughs, J. (2003). Do reverse-worded items confound measures in cross-cultural consumer research? The case of the material values scale. *Journal of Consumer Research, 30*, 72-91.
30. Zviran, M., Glezer, C., & Avni, I. (2006). User satisfaction from commercial web sites: The effect of design and use. *Information & Management. 43*, 157-178.

Synchronous Remote Usability Testing - A New Approach Facilitated By Virtual Worlds

Kapil Chalil Madathil
Clemson University
110 Freeman Hall Clemson SC 29634
mchalil@clemson.edu

Joel S. Greenstein
Clemson University
110 Freeman Hall Clemson SC 29634
iejsg@clemson.edu

ABSTRACT

This study proposes a new methodology for conducting synchronous remote usability studies using a three-dimensional virtual usability testing laboratory built using the Open Wonderland toolkit. This virtual laboratory method is then compared with two other commonly used synchronous usability test methods: the traditional lab approach and WebEx, a web-based conferencing and screen sharing approach. A study was conducted with 48 participants in total, 36 test participants and 12 test facilitators. The test participants completed 5 tasks on a simulated e-commerce website. The three methodologies were compared with respect to the following dependent variables: the time taken to complete the tasks; the usability defects identified; the severity of these usability defects; and the subjective ratings from NASA-TLX, presence and post-test subjective questionnaires. The three methodologies agreed closely in terms of the total number defects identified, number of high severity defects identified and the time taken to complete the tasks. However, there was a significant difference in the workload experienced by the test participants and facilitators, with the traditional lab condition imposing the least and the virtual lab and the WebEx conditions imposing similar levels. It was also found that the test participants experienced greater involvement and a more immersive experience in the virtual world condition than the WebEx condition. These ratings were not significantly different from those in the traditional lab condition. The results of this study suggest that participants were productive and enjoyed the virtual lab condition, indicating the potential of a virtual world based approach as an alternative to the conventional approaches for synchronous usability testing.

Author Keywords

Synchronous remote usability testing, remote usability testing, virtual worlds.

ACM Classification Keywords

User interfaces, human factors, usability testing

General Terms

Human factors, experimentation, performance

INTRODUCTION

Usability studies on software interfaces analyzing how users interact with computer applications began in the early 1980's [5, 22]. At this time, several usability evaluation methodologies evolved, the most common one being laboratory-based testing. This methodology, usually conducted in a lab equipped with audio and video recording capabilities, involves a test facilitator and participant in front of a one-way mirror with the application developers watching and recording the participant's completion of the tasks assigned. User performance is then evaluated based on parameters such as speed, accuracy and types of errors. These quantitative data are combined with subjective information obtained through verbal protocols [10], critical incident reporting [7], and user satisfaction surveys [6]. Traditionally, usability evaluation has been conducted during the final stage of the design process, the cost and time requirements associated with it being significant. To address this issue, the early 1990's witnessed research developing alternative cost-effective usability evaluation methods and the inclusion of usability as a product attribute early in the design process. These results led to the development of such methodologies as heuristic evaluation [19], discount usability testing [17], cognitive and usability walk-throughs [15, 3], formal usability inspection [17] and heuristic walk-throughs [21].

The emergence of high speed internet technologies has resulted in the concept of the global village and next generation products addressing its needs. In such a scenario where usability evaluators, developers and prospective users are located in different countries and time zones, conducting a traditional lab usability evaluation creates challenges both from the cost and logistical perspectives. These concerns led to research on remote usability evaluation, with the user and the evaluators separated over space and time. The development of the Internet has enabled usability testing to be conducted remotely, with significant cost savings [13]. However, remote testing may lack the immediacy and sense of "presence" desired to support a collaborative testing process. Moreover, managing inter-personal dynamics across cultural and linguistic barriers may require approaches sensitive to the cultures involved [8]. Other disadvantages include having reduced control over the testing environment and the distractions and interruptions experienced by the participants' in their native environment [8].

The use of three-dimensional (3D) virtual world applications may address some of these concerns. Collaborative engineering was redefined when these worlds integrated high fidelity voice-based communication, immersive audio and data-sharing tools [9]. In addition, such 3D virtual worlds mirror the collaboration among participants and experts when all are physically present, potentially enabling usability tests to be conducted more effectively when they are located in different places. Virtual world applications are relatively new and as a result have been the focus of limited research. To address this need, this study compared the effectiveness of synchronous usability testing in a 3D virtual usability testing lab built using the Open Wonderland toolkit with traditional lab usability testing and WebEx, one of the commonly used tools for remote usability testing. The results of usability tests employing the three methodologies were compared based on qualitative and quantitative measurement of the work performed and feedback from the participants forming each team.

RELATED WORK

The research conducted by Hammontree *et al.* [11] on interactive prototypes at Sun Microsystems and Hewlett Packard is one of earliest studies to analyze the potential of remote usability testing. They used window/application sharing, an electronic white board, a computer-based video conferencing tool and a telephone to support the remote usability test. The shared windowing tools and telephone supported the remote think-aloud evaluations. The shared window facilitated the observation of the user interactions remotely. The researchers anticipated an improvement in the quality of tools designed to support remote collaborative work.

Remote testing, which facilitates evaluations being done in the context of the user's other tasks and technology can be either synchronous or asynchronous [20]. The former involves real time one-on-one communication between the evaluator and the user, while the latter involves the evaluator and user working separately. Synchronous usability testing methodologies involve video conferencing or employ remote application sharing tools such as WebEx. Asynchronous methodologies include automatic collection of user's click streams, user logs of critical incidents that occur while interacting with the application and subjective feedback on the interface by users. Numerous tools are available to address the needs of both these approaches. For example Microsoft NetMeeting, WebEx, WebQuilt and IBM Lotus Sametime support online screen sharing and collaborative capabilities for synchronous remote usability evaluation.

Numerous studies have been conducted comparing the effectiveness of synchronous remote usability testing methodologies. In an early such study, Hartson *et al.* [13] compared traditional lab usability testing to desktop video conferencing using Kodak's server pages as the interface to be tested. In the remote approach, a telephone connection was used to facilitate voice communication and subjective questionnaires were emailed to the remote users. The results of their study suggested that remote evaluation using video conferencing is feasible, producing similar results to the traditional lab approach.

Tullis *et al.* [24] conducted a study in which remote tests were conducted at the participant's work location without real-time observation. In the remote approach, an email was sent, including a link to the website, explaining the purpose of the study. The participants used two windows, the first one presenting the task to be performed and the second the prototype application to be tested. User actions were automatically recorded and analyzed. Users were also provided with a subjective questionnaire to rate the difficulty of each task. The data analyzed included successful task completion rates, task completion times, subjective ratings and identified usability issues. The results of the study indicated that the task completion time and task completion rate from the remote and traditional approaches were similar.

To identify the differences in the qualitative experience from the participant's and facilitator's perspective, Brush *et al.* [4] compared synchronous remote usability testing with conventional in-lab testing using a plug-in for the integrated software development environment Eclipse as the interface to be tested. The remote method was facilitated using a Virtual Network Computing based screen sharing program with the audio communication being established through a phone connection. The study revealed that there were no significant differences in the number of usability issues identified, their types and their severities. The participants felt that their contributions to the redesign of the interface were approximately the same in both conditions.

Thompson *et al.* [23] compared a traditional and remote approach to identify appropriate tools and methodologies for efficient and effective remote testing environments. In the remote approach, Microsoft NetMeeting and Snag-it were used, with the former providing the screen sharing capability and the latter the screen capture capability. A speakerphone was used to communicate with the remote participants. Both the remote and the traditional lab participants were asked to perform the same five search and shopping functions. The results suggested that there were no significant differences for time on task and number of errors. More recently, Andreasen *et al.* [1] compared the synchronous remote testing approach, with the traditional lab approach and concluded that remote synchronous method is as effective as the traditional lab method.

Although the results for the two approaches appear to be similar, the disadvantages of remote studies include loss of control over the participant's test environment, limited visual feedback, session security issues, ease-of-use issues and connection and system performance issues [2]. Dray *et al.* [8], suggest that "building trust with remote evaluations can be a real challenge", especially in international remote testing, where the interpersonal dynamics of the evaluation must be managed across cultural and linguistic barriers.

HYPOTHESES

To compare the effectiveness of the online usability testing technologies WebEx and a virtual laboratory with traditional lab usability testing, the following null research hypotheses were tested.

Hypothesis 1:

There will be no significant differences in the number and severity of usability defects identified in the three environments.

Hypothesis 2:

There will be no significant differences in the time taken to complete usability test tasks in the three environments.

Hypothesis 3:

There will be no significant differences in the participants' subjective experience in the three environments.

Hypothesis 4:

There will be no significant differences in the preference of facilitators for the three usability test methodologies.

The synchronous usability testing process involves extensive interaction between the test facilitator and the test participant, as the participant performs the test tasks and thinks aloud. In the virtual lab, the facilitator and participant can see one another's avatars as they interact with the in-world applications, perhaps enhancing their sense of interpersonal interaction.

EXPERIMENTAL SETUP

Participants

Forty-eight college students familiar with Internet applications were recruited. The 12 test facilitators, 10 males and 2 females between the ages of 24 and 40, were required to have taken at least one course in usability while the remaining 36, consisting of 22 males and 14 females between the ages of 23 and 35, served as usability test participants. These 36 were equally divided among the three environments, 12 in a traditional lab usability test, 12 in a remote usability test using WebEx and the remaining 12 in a remote usability test using a virtual lab. The 12 test facilitators were paired with one participant in each of the environments. Thus, each test facilitator monitored three sessions, one in a traditional lab, one in WebEx and one in a virtual lab.

Testing environments

The independent variable of this study was the usability test methodology, examined at three levels: the traditional usability laboratory, the web-based meeting tool WebEx, and the virtual usability testing lab. The traditional lab usability environment consisted of a participant and a test facilitator physically located together in a lab to perform the usability test. The traditional lab usability test environment included a table, six chairs, one computer, and other supplemental materials, such as pens and paper, as shown in Figure 1. The WebEx environment provided a web browser for the participant and facilitator to share. The WebEx setup is shown in Figure 2. Two computers were provided, one for the usability test participant and the other for the test facilitator. The participant and facilitator were physically separated in different rooms. The virtual lab environment, which had a similar setup as of WebEx, consisted of a virtual usability testing laboratory equipped with an integrated web browser that can be shared, as shown in Figure 3. Using these tools, the participants and facilitators can interact with a web application and record their concerns with the design of its interface. In addition, the team members can use text and audio chat tools to communicate through their avatars. Two computers were provided, one for the usability test participant and the other for the test facilitator. The participants and facilitators were physically separated in different rooms.

Tasks

An E-commerce web application modeled after Amazon.com was developed with usability flaws deliberately embedded. This application was developed using php and deployed on an Apache Tomcat web server running the Windows XP operating system with a MySQL database providing the data tier. All test participants, regardless of the test environment, performed the following tasks on the website:

1) Your watch is not working, and you want to buy a new Swiss watch. After checking the price, add the watch to your cart.

2) Winter is over, and you heard that there are good deals on North Face jackets. Look for a North Face jacket and add two to the cart.

3) One of your friends is a fan of Dan Brown's novels. Find Dan Brown's latest novel "The Lost Symbol" and add it to the cart.

4) Look in the shopping cart and change the quantity of Swiss watches to two.

5) Check out.

EXPERIMENTAL DESIGN

The study used a mixed experimental design, with the test facilitators observing the test participants' interactions with the web interface in a within-subjects design and the test participants experiencing the test environment in a between-subjects design. The experiment was counterbalanced, such that two test facilitators conducted the usability test session first with the traditional lab method, then with WebEx and finally with the virtual lab environment and two test facilitators conducted the usability test sessions in each of five remaining possible orders.

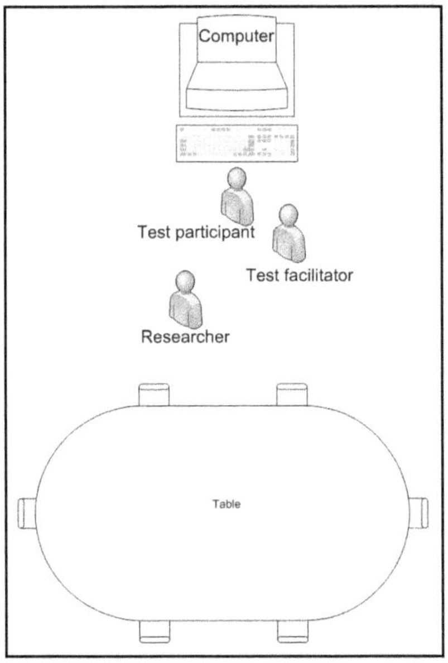

Figure 1. Traditional lab setup

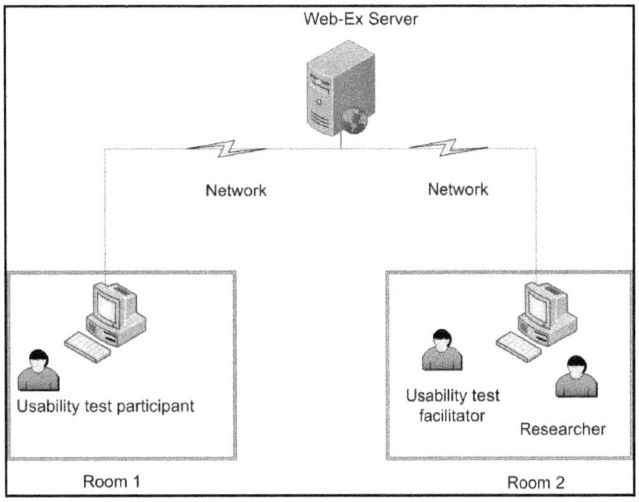

Figure 2. WebEx setup

Procedure

The facilitators and test participants employed the following procedure in all test environments. Initially the usability test facilitators were trained to conduct a usability test. Steve Krug's usability test demonstration video [14] was used for this purpose, as well as to refresh the facilitators' memories of the material in the usability testing class that they had taken.

At the beginning of each test session, the researcher greeted the test facilitator and the participant in a classroom and gave them a brief overview of the study. Then, the test facilitator was asked to read and sign a consent form and to complete a pre-test questionnaire, asking for their basic demographic information.

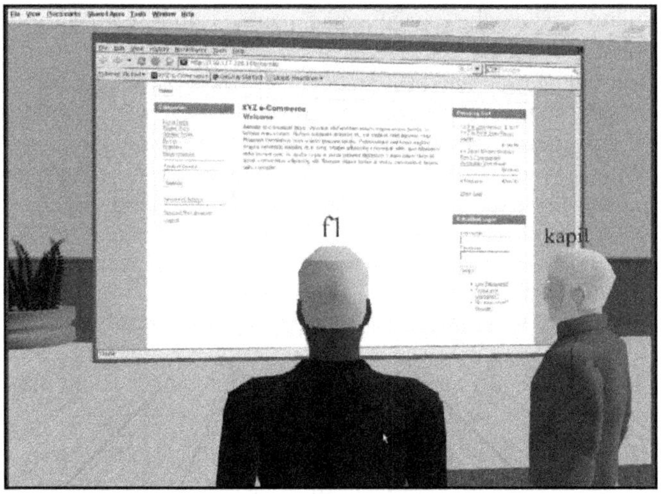

Figure 3. Virtual usability testing environment

The test participant was also asked to read and sign a consent form and to complete a pre-test questionnaire to obtain their basic demographic information and their experience with relevant Internet technologies. Next, the facilitator was provided a list of tasks to be performed, including instructions on the tasks the participant would be asked to complete while using the web interface.

The facilitator and participant were then taken to their respective usability testing rooms and given a brief training session of approximately ten minutes to acquaint them with the environment. The test facilitator used Steve Krug's test script [14] and gave the participant a sample task to familiarize him/her with the nature of the web application to be used during the test session. Next, the facilitator interacted with the participant as in a typical usability test session, asking him/her to complete the individual tasks. The researcher was co-located with the facilitator and recorded the time taken for each task using a stop watch. During each task, the test participant was asked to detail his/her concerns while interacting with the interface in a prospective think-aloud session. The researcher recorded the concerns raised and Camtasia, the screen capture software, was used to record all screen and audio activity.

Upon completing the final task, the participant and test facilitator completed the NASA-TLX workload assessment instrument [12] and the presence questionnaire [26]. The test participants also completed a post-test subjective questionnaire composed of three sections concerning their satisfaction with the usability testing methodology. The first section assessed the quality of the test environment. The user satisfaction portion evaluated perceived ease-of-use while performing the tasks, including how comfortable and confident participants felt in conducting the usability task and detecting the usability defects. The section on the quality of the collaborative usability test methodology assessed the perceived level of presence and co-presence in the test environment. The participants ranked each metric using a 7-point Likert scale, ranging from 1 (Strongly Disagree) to 7 (Strongly Agree). The questionnaire also contained a section for written comments. Upon completion of this questionnaire, the participants were de-briefed by the researcher. The time taken for each session was approximately one hour. Once the test facilitators completed the three sessions in the three environments, they completed a post-test questionnaire assessing their satisfaction with the three usability testing methodologies and they were de-briefed.

Separately, a heuristic evaluation was individually conducted by three people who had experience conducting usability evaluations. During this analysis, the severities of the problems were also rated. Nielsen's severity rating scale [16] was used as the basis for this rating. This scale ranges from 0 to 4, with 4 indicating a catastrophic defect.

Dependent variables

The three usability test methodologies were compared using objective and subjective measures. The objective measures consisted of the task completion time, the number of defects identified and the defects' severity. The subjective measures consisted of the subjective data from the NASA-TLX, presence and the post-test questionnaires completed by both the test participants and test facilitators. The data for the number of defects identified were obtained from the observations of the usability test facilitator and analysis of the video recording of the test session. The severity of each defect was obtained from the heuristic evaluation data provided by the usability experts.

The data collected were classified into two sets:

1. Dataset of test participants, which consisted of 36 datasets, 12 for each condition.

2. Dataset of test facilitators, which consisted of 12 datasets, each across all the three conditions.

The evaluation of each dataset was conducted by performing a thorough walkthrough of the videos and analyzing the NASA-TLX, the presence and the post-test subjective questionnaires. The usability test facilitator datasets were analyzed based on the data from the post-test questionnaires.

SPSS 17.0 was used to analyze the data. Initially, a normality test was conducted to determine whether the data followed a normal distribution. All of the data satisfied this test. The data were then analyzed using a one-way ANOVA with a 95% confidence interval to determine the presence of significant differences, if any, among the test environments. If the null hypothesis of an ANOVA was rejected, the results were then subjected to a post-hoc least significant difference (LSD) test to determine the locus of the significant differences.

RESULTS

In this section, the three usability testing environments are compared with respect to the time taken to complete the tasks; the usability issues identified; the severity of these usability issues; and the subjective ratings from the NASA-TLX, the presence and post-test subjective questionnaires.

Objective Measures

Time taken to complete the task. The time taken to complete the task was measured from the time the task was given to the participants to the time they completed it.

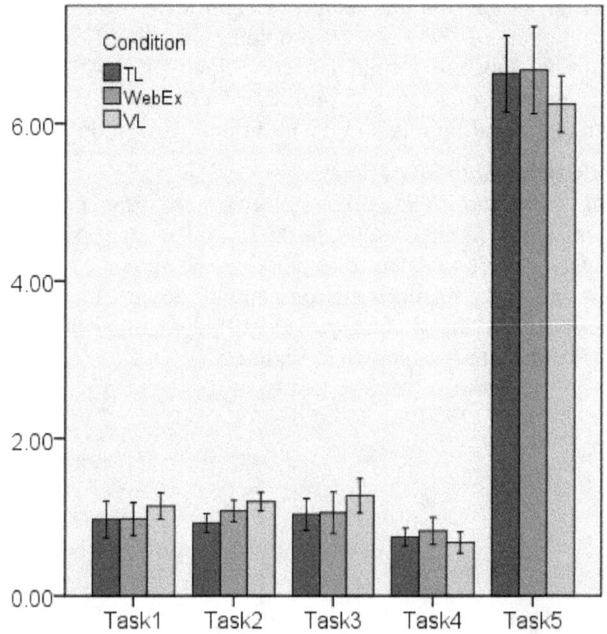

Figure 4. Mean time taken to complete the tasks (in minutes)

The effect of the usability test environment on the task completion time was not significant. The mean task completion times for the five tasks are presented in Figure 4.

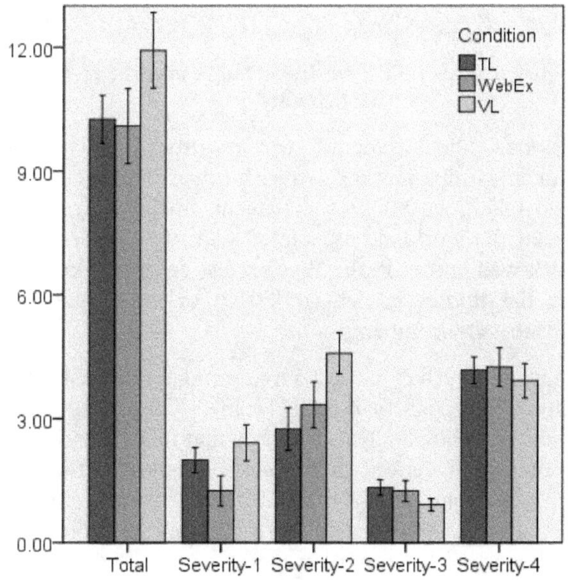

Figure 5. Problems identified in each condition

Number of usability problems identified. The mean numbers of usability problems identified are presented in Figure 5. The effect of usability test environment on the total number of usability problems identified was not significant, F (2, 33) = 1.406, p=0.260. The effects of test environment on the number of Severity 1, 3 and 4 problems identified were also not significant.

Severity 2 defects identified. The effect of test environment on the number of Severity 2 problems identified was significant, F (2, 33) = 3.222, p=0.050. Subsequent post-hoc analysis reveals that there is a significant difference in the number of Severity 2 problems identified for the traditional lab and virtual lab conditions (p = 0.018). A larger number of severity 2 problems were identified in the virtual lab condition than in the traditional lab condition.

Test participants' experience

Total Workload. The effect of test environment was significant, F (2, 33) = 4.00, p=0.028. Subsequent post-hoc analysis reveals that the total workload experienced in the traditional lab testing environment is lower than that experienced in the WebEx (p = 0.010) and virtual lab (p = 0.055) conditions, as shown in Figure 6.

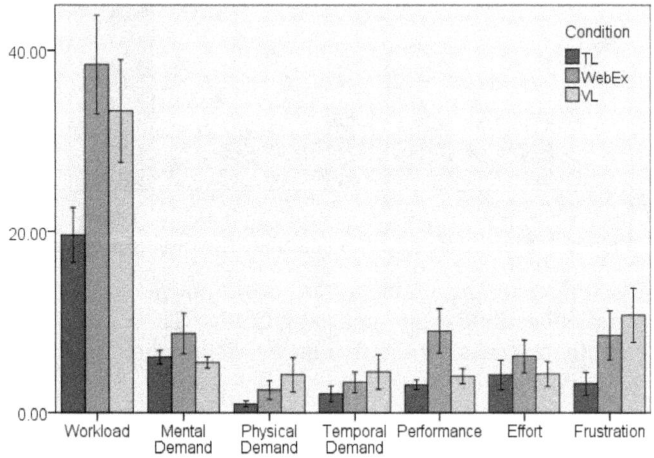

Figure 6. NASA-TLX workload indices for the test participants

Performance. The effect of test environment on the performance component of workload was significant, F (2,33) = 4.317, p=0.022. Subsequent post-hoc analysis reveals that the workload associated with the performance of the task was higher in the WebEx test environment than in either the traditional lab (p=0.010) or the virtual lab (p=0.028) test environments.

Frustration: The effect of test environment on frustration level approached significance, F (2,33) = 2.557, p=0.093. Subsequent post-hoc analysis suggests that this effect is due to differences between the traditional lab testing and virtual lab testing environments (p = 0.035). These results suggest that frustration was lower for the traditional lab condition than for the virtual lab condition.

No significant differences were observed for the NASA-TLX subscales of mental demand, physical demand, temporal demand and effort.

Presence Questionnaire:
The effectiveness of a virtual environment is to some extent dependent on the sense of presence experienced by its users [26]. The presence questionnaire categorized the overall usability testing experience into subscales of involvement, sensory fidelity, adaption/ immersion and interface quality.

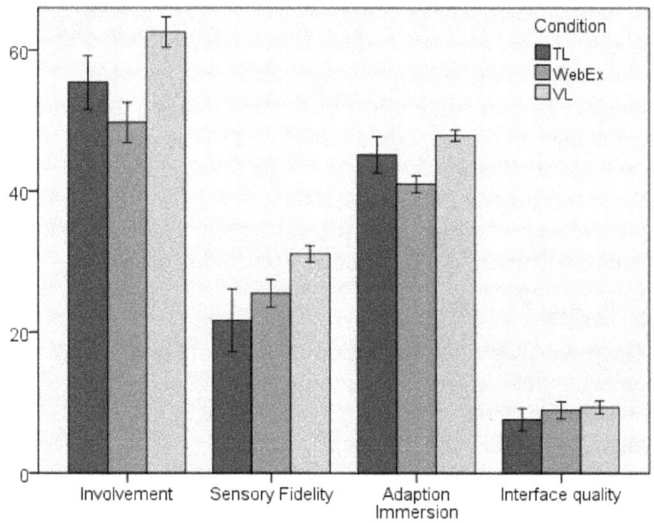

Figure 7. Presence metrics for the test participants

Involvement. The effect of test environment on involvement was significant, F (2, 33) = 4.529, p = 0.018. Subsequent post-hoc analysis reveals that there is a significant difference between the WebEx and virtual lab testing conditions (p = 0.005). Test participants experienced a lower level of involvement in the WebEx condition than in the virtual lab condition, as shown in Figure 7.

Adaption/Immersion. The effect of test environment on adaption/immersion was significant, F (2,33) = 4.145 p=0.025. Subsequent post-hoc analysis reveals that there is a significant difference in adaption/immersion for the WebEx and virtual lab (p=0.007) testing conditions. Participants achieved a higher level of immersion in the virtual lab environment than in the WebEx environment.

The subscales of sensory fidelity and interface quality did not show any significant differences.

Subjective rating.

The subjective rating questionnaire totaled 15 questions, 4 asking about the naturalness of the environment, 5 asking about the satisfaction with and ease-of-use of the usability testing methodology and 6 questions on the quality of the usability test methodology. The mean value was calculated for each of these categories.

User satisfaction and ease-of-use: The effect of the test environment on user satisfaction and ease-of-use was significant, F (2,33) = 3.715 p=0.035, as shown in Figure 8. Subsequent post-hoc analysis revealed that the traditional lab test environment scored higher in user satisfaction and ease-of-use than the WebEx (p=0.044) and virtual lab (p=0.015) test environments.

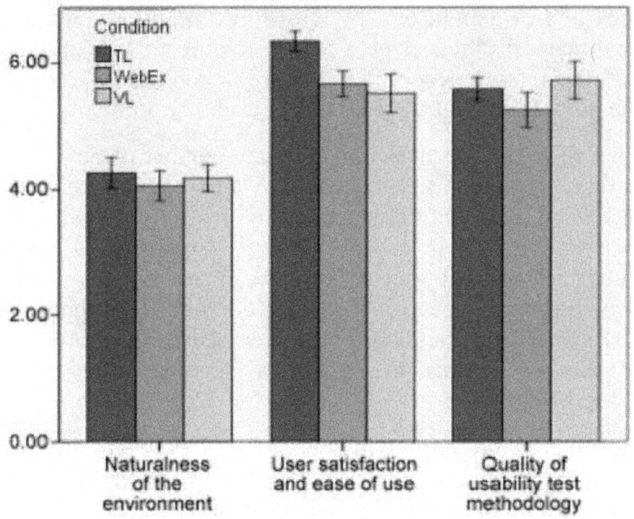

Figure 8. Subjective ratings by the test participants

The scales of naturalness of environment and quality of usability testing methodology did not show any significant differences.

Test facilitator's experience

Workload: The effect of test environment on the total workload experienced by the test facilitator was significant, Wilks' Lambda =0.461, F (2, 10) = 5.843, p=0.021, as shown in Figure 9. Subsequent post-hoc analysis reveals that the total workload experienced in the traditional lab condition is lower than that experienced in the WebEx (p=0.015) and virtual lab conditions (p=0.007).

Physical Demand: The effect of test environment on physical demand placed on the test facilitator was significant, Wilks' Lambda =0.485, F (2, 10) = 5.306, p=0.027. Subsequent post-hoc analysis reveals that the physical demand experienced in the traditional lab testing environment is lower than that experienced in the WebEx (p=0.008) and virtual lab (p = 0.023) conditions.

Effort: The effect of test environment on the effort exerted by the test facilitator was significant, Wilks' Lambda =0.445, F (2, 10) = 6.241, p=0.017. Subsequent post-hoc analysis reveals that facilitators exerted less effort in traditional lab testing environment than in the WebEx (p=0.026) and virtual lab conditions (p=0.050).

Frustration: The effect of test environment on the frustration experienced by the test facilitator was significant, Wilks' Lambda =0.429, F (2, 10) = 6.6, p=0.014. Subsequent post-hoc analysis reveals that facilitators experienced less frustration in the traditional lab testing environment than in the WebEx (p=0.035) and virtual lab (p=0.003) conditions.

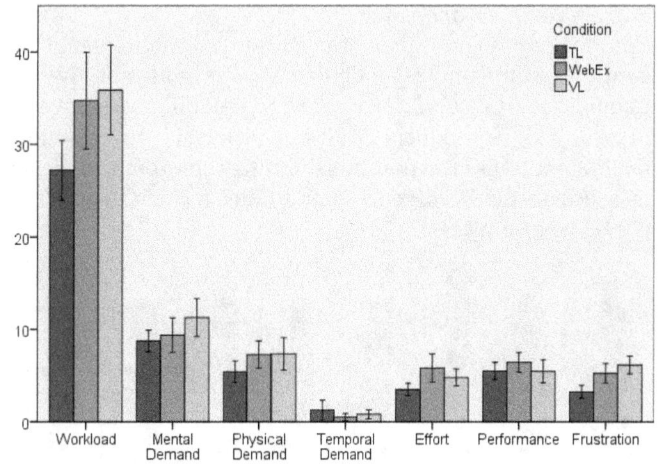

Figure 9. NASA-TLX workload indices for the test facilitators

The NASA-TLX subscales of mental demand, temporal demand and performance did not show any significant effects for the test facilitators.

Presence Questionnaire

Involvement. The effect of test environment on involvement of the test facilitators was significant, Wilks' Lambda =0.213, F (2, 10) = 18.468, p=0.000, as shown in Figure 10. Subsequent post-hoc analysis reveals that facilitators experienced a lower level of involvement in the WebEx condition than they did in the traditional lab (p=0.004) and the virtual lab (p=0.000) testing environments.

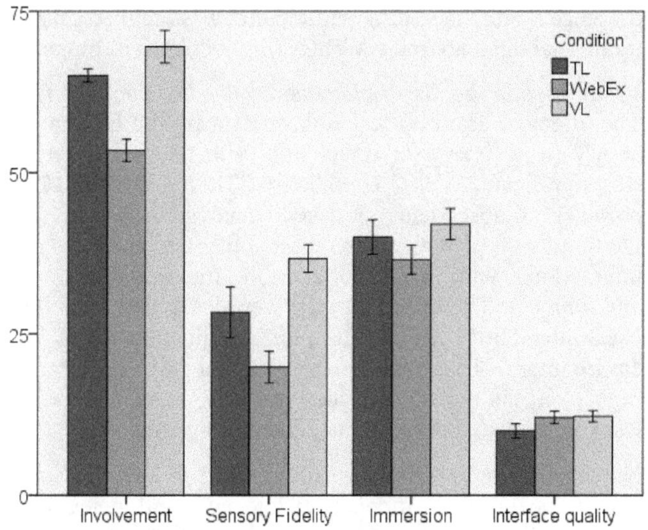

Figure 10. Presence metrics for the usability test facilitators.

Sensory Fidelity. There was a significant effect of test environment on the sensory fidelity experienced by the test facilitators, Wilks' Lambda =0.155, F (2, 10) = 27.194, p=0.000 as shown in Figure 10. Subsequent post-hoc analysis suggests that the experience of sensory fidelity was lower for the WebEx condition than it was for the virtual lab (p=0.000) condition.

The subscales of immersion and interface quality did not show any significant effects for the test facilitators.

Subjective Questionnaire

Ease of use: The effect of usability test environment on ease of use for the test facilitators was significant, Wilks' Lambda =0.162, F (2, 10) = 25.78, p=0.000, as shown in Figure 11. Subsequent post-hoc analysis reveals that facilitators found the traditional lab test environment easier to use than the WebEx (p =0.006) and the virtual lab (p= 0.001) environments.

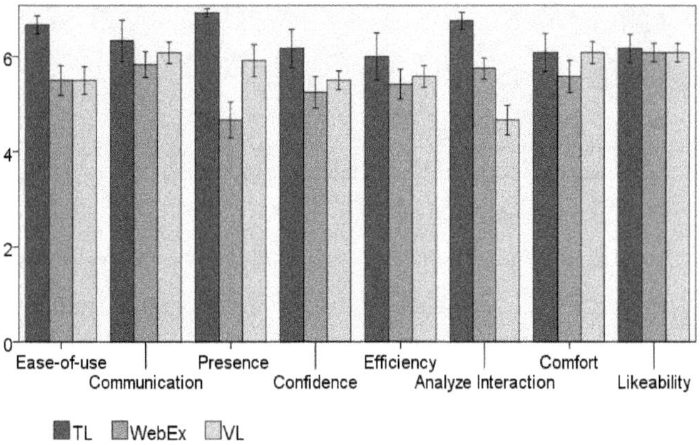

Figure 11. Subjective metrics for the usability test facilitators.

A strong sense of presence with the test participant: The effect of usability test environment on the facilitators' sense of presence with the test participant was significant, Wilks' Lambda =0.178, F (2, 10) = 23.10, p=0.000. Subsequent post-hoc analysis reveals that the facilitators' sense of presence with the test participant was higher in the traditional lab than in the WebEx (p=0.000) environment.

Ability to analyze user interaction with the web interface. The effect of usability test environment on the facilitators' ability to analyze user interaction with the web interface was significant, Wilks' Lambda =0.221, F (2, 10) = 17.66, p=0.001. Subsequent post-hoc analysis reveals that facilitators felt they were best able to analyze user interaction with the interface in the traditional lab environment. They felt that they were least able to analyze user interaction with web interface in the virtual lab environment. The WebEx environment was rated more highly on this metric than the virtual lab environment, but less highly than the traditional lab environment.

No significant effect was observed for the scales of communicability, confidence, efficiency, comfort level and approach likeability.

DISCUSSION

One of the initial research questions was to identify whether there were any objective differences in the effectiveness of the three evaluation approaches, the traditional lab approach, the WebEx approach, and the virtual lab approach, in collecting usability data. Though no significant differences were identified for the time taken to complete the tasks, the mean time for the first three tasks was slightly higher in the virtual lab condition, perhaps because of the learning process the participants experienced as they began working with this novel environment. No differences were identified for the total number of defects identified and the number of Severity 3 and Severity 4 defects identified across the three environments. These results are consistent with those of Hartson *et al.* [13] for the conduct of a synchronous usability test in different settings. Similarly, the studies conducted by Brush *et al.* [4] found no significant differences between the traditional lab condition and the remote synchronous testing condition in terms of the number, types and severities of usability problems.

The effect of test environment on the number of Severity 2 defects was significant. More Severity 2 defects were identified in the virtual lab condition than in the traditional lab condition. It is not clear why the participants in the virtual lab condition identified more minor usability defects than the participants in the other conditions. Perhaps the novelty of the virtual lab condition increased the motivation of the participants to detect and mention even minor usability issues.

Significant differences in total perceived workload were observed for the three conditions. The NASA-TLX scales, used to determine the total perceived workload, indicate that the participants experienced the least workload in the traditional lab condition. This result could have been due to the co-location of the test facilitator with the test participant during the preparatory stages as well as during the test. In the WebEx-based approach, test participants experienced some difficulty during the preparatory session figuring out how to operate the system. In addition, there was a time delay while the remote session loaded. Though this delay was short, participants complained that they did not know what was happening other than that there was a message displayed explaining that the session was loading. For the virtual lab-based testing, participants clicked on a button to launch the session and soon were transitioned to the virtual world. For both of the remote testing environments, the participants were required to perform a series of button clicks on an interface supporting the remote infrastructure to begin the session.

Significant differences were also found for the performance and frustration subscales of the NASA-TLX. The test participants felt their performance was poorer in the WebEx environment than in the traditional lab and virtual lab environments. They experienced more frustration with the virtual lab environment than with the traditional lab environment. The participants using the virtual lab environment appeared to be frustrated primarily by its slow response to the inputs of the test participants and test facilitators. Nonetheless, a number of test participants using the virtual lab environment commented that they enjoyed moving around inside the virtual usability testing laboratory and interacting with the shared web browser using their avatars.

The NASA-TLX workload indices suggest that the total workload experienced by test facilitators was also lower in the traditional lab environment than in the two remote testing environments. Significant differences were also observed for physical demand, effort and frustration subscales. Test facilitators felt that physical demands, effort, and frustration were higher for the two remote testing environments than for the traditional lab environment. This may be due to the lower initial setup required for the traditional lab condition. It took time for the test facilitators to become acquainted with the remote testing environments. In addition, the high level of physical demand in the WebEx and virtual lab conditions might also be due to the higher level of interaction with the computer required in these environments during the study. The relatively slow response times of the web browser to user inputs in the remote testing environments may also have led to increased levels of frustration for the test facilitators.

For the test participants, significant differences were observed for involvement and immersion on the presence questionnaire. Involvement was higher in the virtual lab environment than in the WebEx environment. For the test facilitators, involvement was higher in the virtual lab and traditional lab conditions than in the WebEx condition. The level of immersion experienced by the participants was also higher in the virtual lab condition than in the WebEx condition. These results may be due to the multisensory immersive experience provided by the three-dimensional virtual lab as well as its use of avatars to represent the test participant and facilitator.

The subjective ratings provided by the test participants in the final subjective rating questionnaire revealed significant differences in terms of user satisfaction and ease of use. User satisfaction and ease of use were higher for the traditional lab methodology than for the remote testing environments. The test facilitators also rated the ease of use of the traditional lab environment higher than that of the remote test environments. Interestingly, however, some of the test participants in the traditional lab environment commented that they felt some pressure to avoid making mistakes while being observed by a test facilitator. None of the participants in the remote testing environments expressed this concern.

Test facilitators felt that they were best able to analyze the user's interaction with the web interface in the traditional lab environment. They felt they were least able to analyze the user's interaction in the virtual lab environment. This may be the result of a deficiency in our implementation of the virtual lab using the Open Wonderland toolkit. Mouse movements made by the test participant within a browser were not visible to the test facilitator in the virtual lab environment.

One of the challenges of remote usability testing is the recruitment of security-conscious participants. These participants, or the organizations employing them, may consider allowing others to access their computers to be a security risk [25]. Remote testing using a virtual lab requires only that participants interact with their web browser. The test facilitator cannot view any information on their computers that is not displayed within the browser. WebEx addresses this concern by allowing its users to selectively share applications on their computers. Another difficulty encountered in remote usability testing is the need to install a client application to enable screen sharing and chat functionalities [25]. WebEx requires that users install either an ActiveX control or a Java applet on the computer at each end of the conference to enable screen sharing. The virtual lab methodology relies on Java applets to achieve these functionalities. As a result, there is no need for the users to install a program to enable these functionalities. In addition, remote usability testing with the virtual lab and WebEx retains the inherent advantages of synchronous remote usability testing, including significant savings in travel time and cost, reduced turn-around time for user-centered iterative product development, recruitment of geographically dispersed participants and the ability for geographically distributed product development teams to participate in a real time study.

CONCLUSION

This study proposed a new methodology for conducting a synchronous remote usability test using a three-dimensional virtual world, and empirically compared it with WebEx, a web-based two-dimensional screen sharing and conferencing tool, and the traditional lab method. One of the most important findings of this study is that the virtual lab method is as effective as the traditional lab and WebEx-based methods in terms of the time taken by the test participants to complete the tasks and the number of higher severity defects identified. Interestingly, participants appeared to identify a slightly larger number of lower severity defects in the virtual lab environment than in the traditional lab and WebEx environments.

Test participants and facilitators alike experienced lower overall workload in the traditional lab environment than in either of the remote testing environments. Both the test participants and test facilitators experienced a higher level of involvement in the virtual lab condition than in WebEx condition. Moreover, this method supports recruitment of geographically distributed, diverse participants who can remain in their native work environments. Given that it generates usability test results comparable to those of traditional lab testing, remote usability testing in virtual world appears to be a viable alternative to the conventional lab testing approach. The primary disadvantage of testing in the virtual lab environment was the delay the participants experienced while interacting with the interface. The significance of this study is that the synchronous remote usability testing using virtual lab provides similar results as of the traditional lab method and in some respects it works better than the conventional approaches.

ACKNOWLEDGEMENT

Thanks to Nicole Yankelovich and Jordan M. Slott for the advice and helpful comments.

REFERENCES

1. Andreasen, M. S., Nielsen, H. V., Schroder, S. O. and Stage, J. What happened to remote usability testing? : An empirical study of three methods. In *CHI '07: Proceedings of the SIGCHI conference on Human factors in computing systems.* (San Jose, California, USA). ACM, New York, NY, USA, 2007, 1405-1414.
2. Bartek, V. and Cheatham, D. Experience remote usability testing, Part 2, http://www-106.ibm.com/developerworks/web/library/warmusts2.html.
3. Bias, R. Interface-walkthroughs: Efficient collaborative testing. Software, IEEE, 8, 5; (1991), 94-95.
4. Brush, A. J. B., Ames, M. and Davis, J. A comparison of synchronous remote and local usability studies for an expert interface. In *CHI '04: CHI '04 extended abstracts on Human factors in computing systems.* (Vienna, Austria). ACM, New York, NY, USA, 2004, 1179-1182.
5. Card K, S., Moran P, T. and Newell, A. *The Psychology of Human-Computer Interaction.* CRC, 1986.
6. Chin, J. P., Diehl, V. A. and Norman, K. L. Development of an instrument measuring user satisfaction of the human-computer interface. In *CHI '88: Proceedings of the SIGCHI conference on Human factors in computing systems.* (Washington, D.C., United States). ACM, New York, NY, USA, 1988, 213-218.
7. del Galdo, E. M., Williges, R. C., Williges, B. H. and Wixon, D. R. An Evaluation of Critical Incidents for Software Documentation Design. Human Factors and Ergonomics Society Annual Meeting Proceedings, 30(1986), 19-23(5).
8. Dray, S. and Siegel, D. Remote possibilities?: International usability testing at a distance. interactions, 11, 2 (2004), 10-17.
9. Erbe, H. -H. and Müller, D. Distributed Work Environments for Collaborative Engineering. Information Technology For Balanced Manufacturing Systems, (2006), 131-140.
10. Ericsson, K. A. and Simon, H. A. *Protocol Analysis: Verbal Reports As Data,* The MIT Press, Cambridge, MA, 1985.
11. Hammontree, M., Weiler, P. and Nayak, N. Remote usability testing. interactions, 1, 3 (1994), 21-25.
12. Hart, S. G. and Stavenland, L. E. Development of NASA-TLX (Task Load Index): Results of empirical and theoretical research. In Hancock, P. A. and Meshkati, N. eds.*Human Mental Workload.* Elsevier, 1988, 139-183.
13. Hartson, H. R., Castillo, J., C., Kelso, J. and Neale, W. C. Remote evaluation: The network as an extension of the usability laboratory. (1996), 228-235.
14. Krug, S. *Rocket Surgery Made Easy: The Do-It-Yourself Guide to Finding and Fixing Usability Problems.* New Riders Publishing, Thousand Oaks, CA, USA, 2009.
15. Lewis, C., Polson, P. G., Wharton, C. and Rieman, J. Testing a walkthrough methodology for theory-based design of walk-up-and-use interfaces. (1990), 235-242.
16. Nielsen, J. Severity Ratings for Usability Problems. http://www.useit.com/papers/heuristic/severityrating.html (2007).
17. Nielsen, J. Usability inspection methods. (1994), 377-378.
18. Nielsen, J. and Mack, R. L. *Usability inspection methods.* John Wiley & Sons, Inc, New York, NY, USA, 1994.
19. Nielsen, J. and Molich, R. Heuristic evaluation of user interfaces. In *CHI '90: Proceedings of the SIGCHI conference on Human factors in computing systems.* (Seattle, Washington, United States,). ACM, New York, NY, USA, 1990, 249-256.
20. Scholtz, J. Adaptation of Traditional Usability Testing Methods for Remote Testing, Proceedings of the 34th Annual Hawaii International Conference on System Sciences (HICSS-34)-Volume 5, 2001.
21. Sears, A. and Jacko, J. A. *The Human-Computer Interaction Handbook: Fundamentals, Evolving Technologies and Emerging Applications, Second Edition (Human Factors and Ergonomics).* CRC,1997.
22. Shneiderman, B. *Software psychology: Human factors in computer and information systems.* Winthrop Publishers, Cambridge, MA, 1980.
23. Thompson, K. E., Rozanski, E. P. and Haake, A. R. Here, there, anywhere: Remote usability testing that works. In *CITC5 '04: Proceedings of the 5th conference on Information technology education.* (Salt Lake City, UT, USA). ACM, New York, NY, USA, 2004, 132-137.
24. Tullis, T., Fleischman, S., McNulty, M., Cianchette, C. and Bergel, M. An Empirical Comparison of Lab and Remote Usability Testing of Web Sites. In *Usability Professionals Association Conference.* (Florida, USA),2002
25. Vasnaik, O. and Longoria, R. Bridging the Gap with a Remote User. In *Usability Professional Association.* (Colorado, USA). , 2006.
26. Witmer, B. G. and Singer, M. J. Measuring Presence in Virtual Environments: A Presence Questionnaire. Presence: Teleoperators and Virtual Environments,7,3(1998), 225-240.

Representing Users in Accessibility Research

Andrew Sears
Information Systems Department
UMBC, Baltimore, MD
asears@umbc.edu

Vicki L. Hanson
School of Computing
University of Dundee, Dundee, Scotland
vlh@computing.dundee.ac.uk

ABSTRACT

The need to study representative users is widely accepted within the human-computer interaction (HCI) community. While exceptions exist, and alternative populations are sometimes studied, virtually any introduction to the process of designing user interfaces will discuss the importance of understanding the intended users as well as the significant impact individual differences can have on how effectively individuals can use various technologies. HCI researchers are expected to provide relevant demographics regarding study participants as well as information about experience using similar technologies. Yet, in the field of accessibility we continue to see studies that do not appropriately include representative users. Highlighting ways to remedy this multifaceted problem, we argue that expectations regarding how accessibility research is conducted and reported must be raised if this field is to have the desired impact with regard to inclusive design, the information technologies studied, and the lives of the individuals being studied.

Author Keywords

Accessible computing, accessibility, disabilities, older adults, inclusion, representative users.

ACM Classification Keywords

H5.2. Information systems: Information interfaces and presentation: User interfaces.

General Terms

Experimentation, Human Factors.

INTRODUCTION

User abilities play an important role in determining how an individual interacts with information technologies (IT). As a result, human-computer interaction researchers describe study participants so studies can be replicated and others can determine the extent to which results generalize to new situations. In most cases, this would involve providing basic information such as age and gender as well as a description of the participants experience with relevant technologies.

CHI 2011, May 7–12, 2011, Vancouver, BC, Canada.

As a general rule, HCI researchers and practitioners recognize the need to include representative users in usability studies and controlled experiments. This is even more important when the intended users are expected to have a unique set of abilities or experiences which may affect how they approach and perform a given task. For example, when studying a new interaction device designed for use by surgeons, one may question the validity of results obtained when studying university students. While this may be acceptable for a preliminary study, understanding the efficacy of the proposed solution when used by surgeons would require additional studies with surgeons.

When it comes to accessibility work focusing on needs of disabled or older users, however, it is still common to conduct research with participants that are not representative of the intended users. The most common example may be to use blindfolded sighted users in place of individuals who cannot see when studying solutions intended for blind users.

This paper explores these and related issues. We argue that non-representative users may be acceptable for preliminary evaluations, but studies seeking publication in archival venues should include representative users. We discuss the importance of including representative users, even when one may expect non-representative users to interact with a given system in the same way as the intended users. We also discuss issues such as dealing with a small N, combining data from different groups of users, the importance of a control group, and challenges associated with selecting and describing study participants such that others can determine when results can be generalized to new situations and how to replicate studies.

We cite articles which illustrate the points being discussed or solutions suggested. However, we do not cite specific articles as examples of the problems being highlighted as our goal is not to criticize any specific research. Rather, our goal is to highlight important issues and, in the process, to spur discussion within the research community and consideration of these issues during review processes.

REPRESENTATIVE VS. NON-REPRESENTATIVE USERS

The use of non-representative users is often justified, explicitly or implicitly, because of difficulties associated with recruiting representative users. The US National Institute of Health does not accept a lack of diversity in a particular geographic region as sufficient justification for excluding certain segments of society from a study. Similarly, we argue that convenience or the lack of convenience is not an adequate justification for studying individuals that are not representative of the intended users.

There are two common scenarios where non-representative users are included in studies seeking to provide insights regarding the use of IT by individuals with disabilities. In one scenario, individuals are placed in a situation designed to simulate the disability being studied. Examples include using blindfolded sighted users, special glasses that distort an individual's vision, noise-dampening headphones to remove audio input, or simply turning off the display. The second scenario involves studies involving activities which would appear to be unaffected by the disabilities of the intended users. Examples include using individuals without disabilities when studying brain-computer interfaces, or speech-based interactions, when the intended users have physical disabilities that, in theory, would not affect the use of the technologies. For example, the intended users may have disabilities that only affect their hands while the technology may not require the use of one's hands.

However, the literature reveals numerous studies that clearly demonstrate that studying non-representative users can lead to inaccurate conclusions or missed insights. For example, Sears et al. [13] studied the use of a hands-free speech-based solution for generating text including users with and without physical disabilities that made it difficult to use traditional input devices such as the mouse and keyboard. While the text generation tasks did not depend on any physical interactions, and the overall text entry rates were similar, an analysis of both satisfaction with the experience as well as the processes employed identified significant differences. Individuals with physical disabilities interrupted their dictation more often to correct errors, resulting in their use of a very different set of commands. Had the system been modified based on data gathered from individuals without physical disabilities, the focus would have been on a set of commands and interaction strategies not best suited for the target population.

Similarly, studies have confirmed important differences between individuals who are blind and those who are sighted when tasks are completed without visual feedback [6, 16]. For example, Ferres, Lindgaard, & Sumegi [4], studied the use of natural language for conveying information about graphs. They presented information to both blind and sighted participants using only audio information -- neither saw the graphs. While the two groups were comparable on error rates and response times in the task, the two differed in their strategies for using the natural language software. The blind participants used twice as many commands, checked the starting point more often, and used different navigation strategies. Given that the eventual goal of the work is a tool for blind users, these performance differences provided important information about how to refine the development of their tool. This is information that would have not been available had only sighted participants been tested.

We suggest that using non-representative users may be appropriate for preliminary evaluations of new technologies or interaction solutions. It may also be possible to study non-representative users if earlier research has investigated the impact of doing so and the implications are adequately addressed. However, as a general rule, research which has progressed beyond being a preliminary evaluation of a new idea should be expected to include representative users. In particular, for archival publications, whether journal articles or conference papers, we argue that research which claims efficacy for disabled or older individuals should include representative users and the results obtained from these users should be appropriately analyzed.

DEALING WITH A SMALL N

It can be challenging to recruit individuals with disabilities for research studies. This may be due to the very limited number of truly representative users (e.g., individuals with ALS) or challenges finding representative users (e.g., a lack of organized groups to facilitate recruiting participants with certain disabilities in many regions). In addition, it can be challenging to bring individuals with disabilities into a specific location for laboratory testing. Testing of remote users [1, 9] and other innovative solutions may help future researchers recruit and test the needed representative users. By and large, however, it is still the case that finding participants is often a challenge, making it unlikely that a study on accessibility and IT will include the same number of individuals as a traditional HCI study.

To compound this problem, the individuals who serve as the focus of accessibility research tend to vary more than the participants in traditional HCI studies with regard to their abilities, experiences, and use of accommodations with IT. As a result, traditional statistical techniques may be difficult to apply even if numerous participants can be recruited. Alternative approaches are required. This may involve alternative designs for experiments which focus on maximizing the impact of the results obtained from a limited number of participants including the use of repeated measures designs and single-subject experiments [2, 11, 12, 14]. Also, one must ensure that underlying assumptions are satisfied when applying traditional statistics, otherwise non-parametric analyses may be more appropriate.

COMBINING TWO OR MORE GROUPS OF USERS

Including multiple user groups is ideal when there is a desire to formally explore similarities and differences between two or more groups of individuals. As a result, it is not uncommon to see studies that include one group of individuals who are representative of the intended users and a second group of participants which can often be described as standard HCI study participants (i.e., college students). In some cases, participants in the two groups will be matched for age, education, or other relevant factors. While studying multiple groups of individuals is ideal for studying group differences, in some cases there is a different motivation for using multiple groups: combining the data from the different groups to produce a larger N so traditional statistical analyses can be applied. The way in which this is justified, however, and the conclusions that are drawn can lead to significant concerns.

Often, the groups are first analyzed individually based on a subset of the available data. Sometimes this preliminary analysis focuses on demographics and user characteristics, but it may also focus on factors such as overall task completion times and error rates. Assuming this preliminary analysis does not identify a significant difference between the groups, the data are then combined and analyzed. The problem is that failure to identify a significant difference does not imply that groups are equivalent. Further, surface-level similarities (e.g., success rates) can often hide important differences in how tasks are performed [3, 4]. This, combined with earlier observations regarding unexpected differences between individuals with and without disabilities, raises serious concerns regarding the validity of this approach. These concerns are magnified if, as is often the case, the number of representative users is substantially smaller than the number of non-representative users.

THE IMPORTANCE OF CONTROL GROUPS

Some studies report results only from representative users completing various tasks with one or more technologies, reporting on the results of these experiences. This can produce valuable information when comparing two or more technologies, providing a better understanding of which technology is more effective for this particular group of individuals. It may also be appropriate when the interventions being tested are not relevant to the general population such as an intervention designed specifically to address the needs of autistic children in a classroom setting [7]. The concern is when these conclusions are then attributed to the fact that the participants were drawn from a particular group. For example, numerous articles report on studies with older adults, asserting that the results are due to the fact that the participants were older adults even though the same results may have been obtained if younger users had participated. Lack of a control group makes these assertions about the influence of age problematic.

SELECTING AND DESCRIBING STUDY PARTICIPANTS

In HCI studies, participant selection is typically based on task requirements and participant descriptions are typically limited to age, gender, and perhaps some information about computing experience, experience using the Internet, or other relevant background information.

When studying accessibility, researchers need to carefully consider their target audience and determine how important characteristics of the disabled or older user population that represents the target audience will be described. Age of onset may be a critical factor. For example, studies have confirmed performance differences between individuals born blind and those who lost their sight later in life [6].

At present, common approaches include simple statements indicating that the participants were drawn from the population of intended users, such as individuals with visual impairments or older adults, or a description based on a medical diagnosis, such as a confirmation that the participants all have cerebral palsy. The challenge is that these definitions are often ambiguous. For example, the term "visually impaired" covers a range of potential vision loss and interaction experiences, and the abilities of older adults can vary dramatically. Even when recruiting from one location, such as a "school for the blind", some students may use screen magnification while others use screen readers and this choice is not always obvious based on an individual's degree of vision loss [15].

Medical diagnoses provide valuable information, but they also raise privacy related concerns and often they do not provide sufficient information in the context of accessibility research. Some diagnoses do correspond to a well-defined set of capabilities. For example, certain spinal cord injuries result in clearly defined physical capabilities. However, it is more common that medical diagnoses result in ambiguity with regard to an individual's capabilities. Examples include macular degeneration, muscular dystrophy, Parkinson's, and many other conditions that change with time. These diagnoses provide information about the types of difficulties an individual is likely to experience, but no information about the extent of these difficulties at the time of the study. Other conditions, even the seemingly well-defined concept of being legally blind, may be static such that an individual's abilities remain largely constant, but important information is still missing. For example, in the US, Canada, and much of Europe, being legally blind means that even with the best possible correction available, an individual has a visual acuity equivalent to 20/200 or less in the better eye. As a result, a legally blind individual may have some residual vision, and they may also be able to see well enough to use screen magnification software.

Some articles discuss user abilities in more detail. Often, these descriptions use assessment mechanisms derived from the medical community which can be time consuming and difficult to administer. As a result of such difficulties, self-report assessments are sometimes used. Researchers may state that participants did not have any known cognitive disabilities or that participants self-reported sign language use or self-reported normal or corrected-to-normal vision. However, discrepancies are common when comparing self-reported assessments of abilities and assessments provided by an independent third party [8, 10].

At times, researchers will describe participants by discussing their capabilities with regard to the technologies being studied based either on self-reported information or observations of the participants using relevant technologies.

For example, studies of users with motor disabilities may report whether the participants typically use a mouse, keyboard, or trackball when interacting with computers [5, 15]. These descriptions may be based on information provided by the participants, or as a result of observing the participants as they use the technologies. Such descriptions shift the focus to the participants' abilities, background, and experience. Combined with medical or other assessment information, such a description of user capabilities is extremely important in helping other researchers understand the extent to which study results can be generalized.

CONCLUSIONS

In sum, the literature shows that effective accessibility research requires the inclusion of representative users. Control groups should be included as necessary so the observed effects can be attributed to the factors of interest. We encourage the use of alternative study designs and appropriate methods for analyzing results when the number of participants is limited or variability within the participants is substantial. Data from separate groups should be analyzed separately unless rigorous tests are conducted to confirm the appropriateness of combining the groups. While there is no definitive solution at this time, we also encourage researchers to consider more comprehensive descriptions of study participants.

Finally, we encourage reviewers and editors to consider these issues as they decide if, and where, results should be published. While preliminary evaluations of new technologies may be conducted with non-representative users, it is important that the resulting claims do not go beyond what the data support. Just as with our early example of technologies for surgeons, to be able to state that a technology is usable and useful for disabled or older users, the technology needs to be tested with the target audience. For accessibility research to have the desired impact, advancing our understanding of the issues, leading to the development of more effective solutions, and improving the lives of the individuals being studied, we must expect appropriate testing with representative users.

ACKNOWLEDGMENTS

We would like to thank Armando Barreto, Jinjung Heidi Feng, Amy Hurst, Enrico Pontelli, John Richards, and Shari Trewin for valuable feedback on earlier drafts of this paper. The writing of this paper was supported by a Royal Society Wolfson Merit Award to the second author and by RCUK EP/G066019/1 "RCUK Hub: Inclusion in the Digital Economy" and EPSRC grant EP/G002118/1.

REFERENCES

1. Bigham, J. and Cavender, A. Evaluating existing audio CAPTCHAs and an interface optimized for non-visual use. In *Proc. CHI 2009,* ACM Press (2009), 1829-1838.
2. Dijkers, M. When the best is the enemy of the good: The nature of research evidence used in systematic reviews and guidelines. Austin, TX: SEDL (2009).
3. Fairweather, P. How older and younger adults differ in their approach to problem solving on a complex website. In *Proc. ASSETS 2008,* ACM Press (2008), 67-72
4. Ferres, L., Lindgaard, G., and Sumegi, L. Evaluating a tool for improving accessibility to charts and graphs. In *Proc. ASSETS 2010,* ACM Press (2010), 83-90.
5. Gajos, K., Wobbrock, J., and Weld, D. Improving the performance of motor-impaired users with automatically-generated, ability-based interfaces. In *Proc. CHI 2008,* ACM Press (2008), 1257-1266.
6. Heller, M. Picture and pattern perception in the sighted and the blind: the advantage of the late blind. *Perception 18*, 3 (1989), 379 -389.
7. Hirano, S., Yeganyan, M., Marcu, G., Nguyen, D., Boyd, L., and Hayes, G. vSked: Evaluation of a system to support classroom activities for children with autism. In *Proc. CHI 2010,* ACM Press (2010), 1633-1642.
8. Huenerfauth, M., Zhao, L., Gu, E., and Allbeck, J. Evaluating American Sign Language generation through the participation of native ASL signers. In *Proc. ASSETS 2007*, ACM Press (2007), 211-218.
9. Petrie, H., Hamilton, F., King, N., and Pavan, P. Remote usability evaluations with disabled people. In *Proc CHI '06*, ACM Press (2006), 1133-1141.
10. Price, K., and Sears, A. The Development and Evaluation of Performance-Based Functional Assessment: A Methodology for the Measurement of Physical Capabilities. *ACM Trans. on Access. Comput.*, *2*, 2 (2009), 31 pages.
11. Shinohara, K., and Tenenberg, J. Observing Sara: A Case Study of a Blind Person's Interactions with Technology. In *Proc. ASSETS 2007,* ACM Press (2007), 171-178.
12. Schlosser, R. The role of single-subject experimental designs in evidence-based practice times. *FOCUS*, 22 (2009), 1-8.
13. Sears, A., Karat, C-M., Oseitutu, K., Karimullah, A., and Feng, J. Productivity, satisfaction, and interaction strategies of individual with spinal cord injuries and traditional users interacting with speech recognition software. *Universal Access in the Information Society, 1* (2001), 4–15.
14. Stevens, R., and Edwards, A. An approach to the evaluation of assistive technology. In *Proc. ASSETS '96*. ACM Press (1996), 64-71.
15. Trewin, S., Laff, M., Hanson, V., and Cavender, A. Exploring Visual and Motor Accessibility in Navigating a Virtual World. *ACM Trans. on Access. Comput., 2*, 2 (2009), 35 pages.
16. Walker, B. and Mauney, L. Universal Design of Auditory Graphs: A Comparison of Sonification Mappings for Visually Impaired and Sighted Listeners. *ACM Trans. on Access. Comput. 2*, 3, (2010), 16 pages.

Democratising Technology: Making Transformation using Designing, Performance and Props

Ann Light
Sheffield Hallam University
Sheffield, S1 1WB, UK
a.light@shu.ac.uk

ABSTRACT

This study of personal transformation is offered as HCI increasingly seeks to change behavior with persuasive products. Performance-derived improvisation methods were used to inspire a sense of agency with ICT in people marginalized from digital design. A case study of an older person's experience shows the techniques supporting her to reconceive her response to technology. In particular, we analyze how using a 'prop' as a design artifact allows her to imagine new possibilities and take a more assertive role.

Author Keywords

Older people, performance, confidence, behavior change.

ACM Classification Keywords

H5.m. Information interfaces and presentation (e.g., HCI): Miscellaneous.

ACM General Terms: Design, Human Factors.

INTRODUCTION

This is an account of how a project to encourage confidence with technology made its impact [7]. Based on work with older people, the project's goal was to help people articulate their values and ideas about the future in the context of ubiquitous computing development. This study shows how a transition was inspired. It does so at a time when interest in behavior change has been growing, but when HCI's tools of change are largely seen in terms of products (eg [5,7]), not ways of working. By contrast, our research team used performance methods to inspire design thinking, and with it, a desire to behave in new ways. This paper briefly introduces the motivation and methods of the project before giving a detailed analysis of one person's participation and her transformation as her sense of agency increases.

Fig 1: Vi puts on the glove that will become her interface

Background to the Study

The *Democratising Technology* (DemTech) project worked with older people to devise a means of inspiring a confident attitude to digital tools. Five community groups cooperated with a team of performance artist, media artist, interaction design researcher and social scientist. Together, we devised techniques, packaged as a participatory workshop, to encourage a sense of agency and the confidence to speak about nascent technologies in people such as the elderly [3] who are habitually left out of design discussions. Through iterating the content of workshops, we built up an effective sequence of techniques for use with people who are nervous of, or indifferent to developments in computing so that their opinion on the social impact of these tools could be shared. To develop workshop material, we recorded and analyzed video of the methods in use, revising our processes and repeatedly trying versions of the exercises with new groups, gathering feedback and conducting evaluation. (The full development process is reported in [10] and the final workshop process is available for use [9]).

Evaluating methods for making change is not easy and we devoted considerable planning time to this aspect [10]. Tests such as revisiting participant accounts of future tools and collecting a qualitatively different depth of engagement show the impact of the techniques on *attitude* [8]. Our volunteers included those with severe memory loss and this affected the success rate, but the methods resulted in some success for most of our participants. Further, [8] also relates how several participants are still pursuing their workshop ideas for sustainable technology more than 18 months after working with us. So, we also substantially changed some participants' *behavior*. What has not been reported to date is *how* the workshop techniques achieved this impact.

The description that follows comes from further analysis of video data collected to assess our workshops, conducted specifically to look at group interactions. It explores the meaning of movements [6] and the choice of language [13], tracing the trajectory of objects over time and the use of grammatical constructions in verbal exchanges as we focus on how *one* person thinks about the tools she uses. We choose to focus on one person in the group to reflect the uniqueness of each path and the person-centeredness of the approach. This focus also reflects the rareness of watching a discernible *change in consciousness*. We share the analysis here for the insight it gives into how the methods worked, and to show that tools of self-discovery can lead to change quite as well as products designed to persuade or influence.

Background to the Research

The project sought a method for inspiring people who do not see themselves as part of the digital future to consider the values they would like to see in new systems. It became a collaboration with several groups of older people, since a major digital divide corresponds with age. In Britain, just one in three retired people use the internet [12]. The divide extends more broadly: products are designed without thought to ageing people [3] and what participatory design research exists, where older people are not only tested as potential users but involved in the design process (eg [4]), is still mostly to address design pertaining to ageing, rather than drawing on their long life experience more generally. So, older people made an appropriate and diverse sample to work with. We solicited volunteers from London's East End where many older people left school young, worked manually and never encountered computers professionally.

Our methods derive from performance, which is used with older people (eg [11]) and has a flourishing tradition in design futures work (eg [2]). We distinguish, here, between performance for show and performing a fictional act. DemTech did not involve audience; it used improvisational methods to experiment with change, after Weaver [14], and relied on experiential learning through participation, unlike most uses of drama in design [11].

Shifting between 'real' and 'practice' situations is a powerful way to suggest potential and support empowerment (cf Theatre of the Oppressed changing legislation in Brazil, [1]). Our goal was to find a person-centred methodology to learn what people would create when responding to an unfamiliar set of possibilities on their own terms. So we used minimal cues, working without scenarios, prototypes or other directive tools [8], and starting with individuals' interests, explored through the use of fantasy and props.

THE WORKSHOP PROJECT

Exercises were led by performance artist (L), accompanied by researcher (A). Sections below feature transcriptions of the interactions recorded during the workshop process. Our interest is primarily in Vi's choice of language and gesture, so we kept transcription simple, recording word and action.

Vi

Vi Davis signed up to help develop DemTech techniques as part of the group she regularly attends and helps run, based in a day care centre in east London, UK. Her group was asked if we could involve them in research activities using drama. Subsequently, those members who were interested joined the research sessions that ran over three consecutive weeks. Vi, a fit 71-year-old, stayed active in the project throughout its life and participated in the final public symposium. We use an account of Vi's participation as a case study to reveal how she positions herself with respect to technology and design, how this changes, and how different exercises and props functioned as support.

A First Assessment Exercise

We began work with Vi and her group (averaging 8 people) with an exercise called *Timelines*, which we used to assess participants' life experience and encourage people to reveal how they saw the relation between people, things and time before our intervention. *Timelines* required each person to record memorable events and associated objects on paper that they had marked out with their chosen life-points. Once the past was populated, they were asked to put markers in for the future. Then people were encouraged to talk about an event and object from their life. We used this to collect data about background, experience, and beliefs before doing creative work together. Other exercises followed. These are introduced in sequence.

Vi's Attitude at Outset

Here is an early exchange between L and Vi, during the *Timelines* exercise, when participants were asked to focus on the future. Note the sardonic quality of her comment:

L: Can you think of something in the future, that you, or anybody might like to do, that we can't do right now?
Vi: I don't know what I wanna do. I have enough trouble finding out what I am doing for the week.

Later, as part of the same exercise, Vi is asked to talk about an object associated with a memorable event in her past. She chooses to talk about bombs:

Vi: I was put into a big school for the duration of the war, but when I was seven we was bombed out. Three bombs fell in the playgrounds; we had three playgrounds and each was bombed. That night every window crashed in. We was put down in the cellar for the night and the next morning we had people coming along in cars, and they was taking two or three children at a time, knocking on people's doors: 'would you take this child in? would you take this child in?'

This section is characteristic of how Vi constructs her sentences at the start of the workshop. Most sentences avoid attribution of agency: 'bombs fell', 'each was bombed', 'every window crashed', 'we was put'. War was a vivid and frightening experience for Londoners in the Blitz and Vi is remembering these events with child's eyes. Children often experience being required to do things and Vi's description of being hawked around by strangers is an extreme version of this lack of self-determination. In common with other participants, Vi tells a story in which things happen and happen to her, but in which choice and self-determination are not present, either in content or grammatical structure.

Developing a Fantasy Persona

L developed the next exercise, *fantasy personas*, to find people's creative voices and it is used widely (eg in prisons [10]). Participants devise a persona through incremental steps, such as choosing an object the persona might use, making a gesture in the style of their persona, and so on. At this point, Vi has picked up a long glove from a table full of waiting objects. L instructs the group to:

L: Tell the story of your object from the point of view of your character.
Vi: Well, my…this glove has found a most beautiful owner. She's a.. dancer; she does exotic dancing. She travels the world (and therefore so do I). I'm looked after very much, so, I've stroked many a fine face.

Vi's account switches between the voice of the glove and that of the new character as she embellishes the story. She creates a rich image without preparation, which is L's intention. L uses this technique to encourage participants to improvise: we learn about the persona as Vi does.

Creating future technologies

The fantasy persona acts an opening to thinking about the future differently. In this section, we rejoin Vi when L asks the group to imagine what their character will be doing in 100 years' time. Vi has christened her persona *Talullah*, and she has evolved into a showgirl-courtesan. Talullah, Vi says, 'being the type of girl she is, would be trying to buck the system'. Interestingly, Vi has created a persona who is more sure of herself than Vi. Talullah is assertive and has clear agency: she teases men and bosses chauffeurs. L asks Talullah to describe an invention she would own and again she uses the glove as prop and hook for inspiration:

L: If I could ask you, Talullah… a 100 years from now, you are bucking the system … if this [the glove] could be some kind of invention that would help you be or do the things you need to do, a 100 years from now, what would it be?

Vi: [taking glove and stroking it] It would be a mirror [pause] into somebody's soul [pause] so that if ever anybody came in, I would know whether they was going to be good to me or.., so that anybody I did come in contact with, because we are so much advanced, I'd be able to tell as soon as that person, like you can read, to a certain extent, people as you see them, but you'd be able to do it more so.

Vi has invented a 'mirror into somebody's soul', largely through being put on the spot and having to draw on ideas that come to her fast. Her increasingly jumbled sentences show her thinking on her feet about its nature. But the idea is clear and simple and comes quickly, though it has no special association with the glove. Rather it seems born of a desire to protect the vulnerability of her persona.

To deepen the creative work, A interviews each person in role, stressing elements such as how a human-network interface might work. She does so to encourage a more detailed, perhaps more technical, answer:

Vi: It was one of my private friends and, […] he brought sort of a, a, a glove with him and he went: when you put that glove on, then it will show you a picture. […] within your own mind - though that person didn't change - but with your own mind something happened. You know and it was like this halucination and you could see that that person was a caring person. […] [puts on glove] so you can see that, through this person's eye, through this glove. [reaching out, wearing glove]..As soon as you shook hands, once you had contact… [touches A's hand] as soon as you have contact… [lifts and replaces hand on A's hand]
A: Ooh!
Vi: Can you feel it?
A: Does that mean you can see into my soul?
Vi: I can.

Fig 2: "I can see into your soul…"

If we read this account carefully we can see creative work happening. The glove/present becomes the tool, but at first it merely enables Talullah to make images in her mind. Then, as Vi continues, she puts on the glove and the nature of the glove inspires both a gesture and a new interpretation of the tool. Donning the glove, she stretches out her hand toward the interviewer. As soon as she reaches out, the interface becomes obvious to her; the tool relies on touch to gather information. Suddenly, the action is no longer reported, but in the moment, in the room.

Last attitudes – symposium, interview

Vi elects to talk at the public symposium that ends the project; an action which is, of itself, indicative of increased confidence in dealing with the idea of technology. She describes being involved in the project:

Vi: When [L] mentioned 'technology', I thought: 'Oh, I don't want to know. I can't do with technology at my age.' But [L] said it's not necessarily that, it's more to do with art work, it's more expression, it's more how you feel […] all of a sudden I became a daring lady [mimes a glove up her arm]. I put my feathers round me [mimes a boa] and I can just imagine myself in this role [slight shimmy]. […] With regards to technology, we've asked the grant to give us a laptop. Not that I'm any good at all at it. But I thought if we got a laptop, it would make it easier for people to learn.

Vi's account of the research captures key areas: her initial misgivings, the 'daring lady' it unleashed and a more decisive approach to digital tools. It is hard to appreciate the significance of the laptop but it marks Vi branching out.

We hear her familiar self-deprecating style, but again Vi's vocabulary turns positive/active on Talullah's appearance: 'I put my feathers'… 'I can just imagine myself'. We are not suggesting we can determine Vi's sense of agency from her use of linguistic constructions. But we can spot patterns and notice how her speech changes according to what she is doing or talking about: Talullah is a liberating creation.

Our last glimpse comes courtesy of a national newspaper journalist: 'Asked what she derived from the experience of engaging with design, Vi […] spoke of regaining her identity. The mother of three and grandmother of six said: "We went in as old people and came out as people with our own thoughts and agendas."' (Sarah Womack, Social Affairs, Daily Telegraph). Even allowing for the halo effect of press attention, we see a transition between her sardonic first comment and the final, self-actualized, comment here.

ANALYSIS: THE DARING LADY AND THE GLOVE

Vi's positioning of herself as old and technophobic is by no means unique [3]. Vi, like other participants, is alert to how people of her age are viewed by younger generations. She is self-conscious about the idea of 'technology' and her lack of engagement with it. Through the mechanism of creating a bold *alter ego*, she is able to leave this positioning behind and play with (im)possibilities. Without any reference to galvanic skin resistance or touch-based sensors, she comes up with a device that is plausible while fantastical, and can reveal to her the designed nature of 'things'.

Like Vi, the glove takes on a role. Vi chooses the glove from a range of objects on the table in front of the group, including other mundane small items such as hats, scarves, a cane, balls and pens. Tracing the glove shows it functioning in many ways. It behaves as a:

- prop(erty), used to develop character
- probe, to elicit Vi's values and desires for the future
- design(ed) artefact, helping to reveal the "designed" therefore "designable" nature of tools and systems
- sketch, functioning as physicalized concept of Vi's tool
- and form, with interfaces stressing kinds of connection.

Without interaction with the glove, Vi might have created something different, or nothing at all. It plays a part: giving her the glamor to create Tallulah, then the means to enact her system as she works out what it might be. It gives her something to fiddle with. And its form finds an echo in the talk she gives at the symposium, where she mimes a glove as she describes her 'daring lady', showing its importance.

In working through these shifts, we are able to go beyond the analysis of [8], which discusses the outcomes of using the techniques, to begin to identify precise components and their role in *why* it worked. It is difficult to justify claims about how change is created, especially when the people studied are not articulate designers but 'non-adopters', with values and views that often resist a discursive engagement. Here, in the detail of the text and action, we see a transition taking place that we can point at: it is embodied. This mix of fantasy and embodiment is key and we offer the method as inspiration for making change from within, supported by exercises that allow people's interests and values to surface and the artful use of everyday objects.

ACKNOWLEDGMENTS

The team of Lois Weaver, Pat Healey and Gini Simpson; Vi Davis; the AHRC/EPSRC for funding and our collaborators.

REFERENCES

1. Boal, A. Legislative Theatre: using performance to make politics. Routledge, London, 1998.
2. Boess, S.U. Rationales for role playing in design. Proc. DRS'06 2006.
3. Clarkson, J., Keats, S., Lebbon, C. and Coleman, R. (eds), Inclusive Design: design for the whole population, London: Springer-Verlag. 2003
4. Dickinson, A. and Dewsbury, G. Designing computer technologies with older people. Gerontechnology, 5, 1 (2006) 1-3.
5. DiSalvo, C. Sengers, P. and Brynjarsdóttir, H. Mapping the landscape of sustainable HCI, CHI'10, 2010
6. Farnell, B., Moving Bodies, Acting Selves. in *Annual Review of Anthropology*, 1999, 341-373
7. Fogg, B.J. A Behavior Model for Persuasive Design, Persuasive'09, 2009
8. Light, A., Simpson, G. and Weaver, L., Healey, P.G. (2009) "Geezers, Turbines, Fantasy Personas: Making the Everyday into the Future" Proc. C&C'09, 2009
9. Light, A., Weaver, L., Healey, P.G. and Simpson, G. Democratising Technology: A Method, DVD and website. Details at: http://www.demtech.qmul.ac.uk.
10. Light, A., Weaver, L., Healey, P.G. and Simpson, G. Adventures in the Not Quite Yet: using performance techniques to raise design awareness about digital networks, Proc. DRS'08, 2008
11. Newell, A.F., Carmichael A. and Morgan M. & Dickinson A., Methodologies for The use of theatre in requirements gathering and usability studies, IwC 18, 5 (2006) 996-1011.
12. Oxford Internet Survey, 2009: www.oii.ox.ac.uk/microsites/oxis/
13. Potter, J., Wetherell, M., Discourse and social psychology: Beyond attitudes and behaviour, London: Sage, 1987
14. Weaver, L. Doing Time: A personal and practical account of making performance work in prisons. In: Applied Theatre Reader (eds), T. Prentki and S. Preston, London: Routledge, 2008.

Post-Deployment Usability: A Survey of Current Practices

Parmit K. Chilana[1,2], Andrew J. Ko[1], Jacob O. Wobbrock[1], Tovi Grossman[2], George Fitzmaurice[2]

[1] The Information School | DUB Group
University of Washington
Seattle, WA 98195 USA
{pchilana, ajko, wobbrock}@uw.edu

[2] Autodesk Research
210 King St. E
Toronto, ON Canada M5A 1J7
{firstname.lastname}@autodesk.com

ABSTRACT

Despite the growing research on usability in the pre-development phase, we know little about post-deployment usability activities. To characterize these activities, we surveyed 333 full-time usability professionals and consultants working in large and small corporations from a wide range of industries. Our results show that, as a whole, usability professionals are currently not playing a substantial role in the post-deployment phase compared to other phases of user-centered design, but when they do, practitioners find their interactions quite valuable. We highlight opportunities in HCI research and practice to bridge this gap by working more closely with software support and maintenance teams. We also raise the need to understand what might be called 'usability maintenance,' that is, the process and procedures, by which usability is maintained after deployment.

Author Keywords

Post-deployment usability, usability practices

ACM Classification Keywords

H5.2. Information interfaces and presentation: User Interfaces - *evaluation /methodology*.

General Terms

Human Factors.

INTRODUCTION

A key component of user-centered design (UCD) and usability engineering is the commitment to usability principles throughout the analysis, design, implementation, and deployment phases [5, 6]. While upfront user research and prototyping are crucial to designing user-centered products, learning from users in the deployment phase about their *actual* use of the product is also valuable [5, 6]. However, prior works [4, 8] have suggested that this "ideal" UCD process across all four phases rarely happens in practice: most companies invest heavily only in upfront UCD methods. Our literature review indicated that research on usability practices has largely centered on upfront UCD methods, with little work substantiating how usability is actually practiced in the *post-deployment* phase.

Given that most software companies invest a major portion of their budgets on maintaining software [3] and providing technical support[1] *after* a software has been released, understanding the UCD practices in the post-deployment phase is critical for identifying opportunities and challenges in supporting a product's overall usability.

To better understand the state of post-deployment usability activities in industry, we surveyed usability professionals in North America and abroad. We received 333 responses from Usability professionals working in large and small corporations representing a variety of industries. Our key findings suggest that the role of usability appears to diminish in the post-deployment phase and usability professionals are rarely involved in postulated post-deployment activities [5] such as usage logs analysis, customer support logs analysis, benchmarking, and *in situ* usability testing. However, respondents also indicated that when they were involved, they found significant value in interactions with support.

This paper is the first to provide empirical evidence through a large-scale survey about the current state of post-deployment usability. In this regard, it complements prior surveys of usability practitioners [2, 8] that have focused on upfront usability activities. Our results further provide an impetus for the HCI community to better align UCD with software support and software maintenance activities that play a critical role in supporting the overall user experience.

THE SURVEY INSTRUMENT

Our survey consisted of 16 multiple choice and open-ended questions. We began by asking respondents about their demographics, such as job title, experience, company size, industry, and location. Next, we asked questions about direct involvement in the 4 different phases of UCD and asked respondents to specify their particular pre-deployment and post-deployment activities. We devised categories of activities based on previous surveys [7, 8] and recommendations in UCD/usability lifecycle guidelines [5]. We also asked respondents about their interactions with software support and software development teams in the post-deployment phase. Lastly, we gave respondents a chance to share their stories about post-deployment usability activities.

We distributed the survey online during the summer of 2010. We advertised on 15 different usability-related mailing lists

[1] http://www.supportindustry.com/2009supportmetrics.html

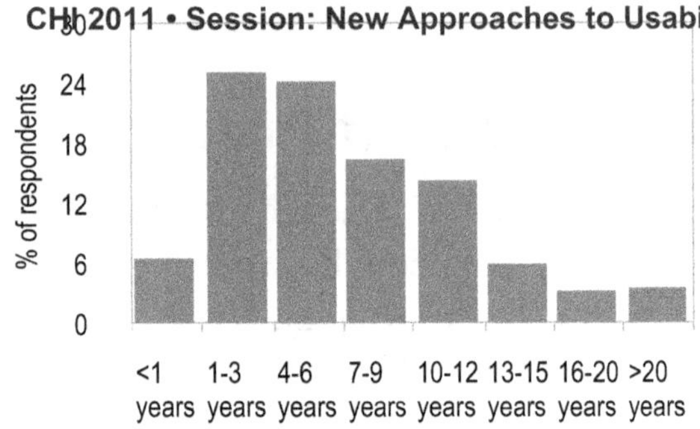

Figure 1: Distribution of respondent's experience.

Job title	%
User Experience Designer	18.3%
Interaction Designer	15.6%
User Experience Researcher	8.4%
User Experience Manager/Director	5.1%
User Researcher	4.5%
Information Architect	4.2%
Usability Professional	3.3%
Usability Engineer	3.3%
Interface Designer	3.3%
Product Designer	3.0%
User Experience Architect	2.7%
Usability Specialist	2.4%

Table 1: Top 12 job titles

Organization	%
Large Corporation (> 1000 employees)	48.7%
Small Corporation (< 100 employees)	16.1%
Medium Corporation (100-1000 employees)	15.2%
Usability Consulting Firm	7.0%
Design Agency	4.4%
Non-profit Organization	1.9%
Educational Institution	1.6%
Self-Employed/Freelance	1.5%
Government or Military	1.3%
Startup	0.9%
Advertising Agency	0.6%

Table 2: Respondents' organizations

and discussion and alumni lists of major HCI training programs. We also made use of social networking sites such as *LinkedIn* and *Facebook* to advertise our survey in professional discussion groups. In some cases, we personally contacted team leads in large corporations and consulting groups and asked them to encourage their employees to participate in our survey. The respondents were offered a chance to participate in a $50 gift card drawing.

DEMOGRAPHICS OF RESPONDENTS

The survey was targeted at anyone who identified as a usability or a User Experience (UX) professional. Our respondents listed a variety of job titles and represented various design and usability roles. Table 1 shows the top 12 job titles of our respondents. Most of the respondents (78.8%) were full-time employees, 17.1% were contractors and the remaining were part-time or temporary employees or self-employed.

Figure 1 shows the range in years of experience our respondents had in the usability field. About a quarter (25.2%) of the respondents fell in 1-3 years range while another quarter (24.3%) were in the 4-6 years range. They represented organizations of all sizes, with the majority being from large corporations (Table 2). These organizations specialized in a variety of software, hardware, and web applications, including e-commerce sites, operating systems, online search, computer-aided design tools, social networking sites, government sites, among others. We received the largest number of responses (83.8%) from North America, followed by Asia (6.3%) and Europe (6.0%).

POST-DEPLOYMENT USABILITY

We now describe responses related to survey questions that explored different facets of post-deployment usability.

One question we asked was *In which phases of development are you directly involved in some capacity?* The responses to this are shown in Figure 2. Among our respondents, 76.1% said that they were regularly (**always** or **usually**) involved in the user research phase. The majority of respondents (87.7%) said that they were regularly involved in the design phase. The involvement appeared to decrease in the implementation phase, but 69.2% of the respondents reported being regularly involved. Only 50.9% of respondents reported involvement in the post-deployment phase. Overall, the level of involvement of our respondents differed significantly across the 4 phases of development ($\chi^2_{(3, N=333)}$=219.9, $p<.0001$).

Our next question was, *Please describe your main role <u>after</u> a product that you helped design has been deployed.* Responses are shown in Figure 3. We asked respondents to select all options that best described their role after a product had been deployed. It appears that most of the respondents (70.3%) started working on another product and/or the next version of the current product (69.1%). Only 23.1% of respondents said that they were involved in conducting benchmark tests while 33.0% said that they monitored feature data for the deployed product.

Next, we asked respondents about the usability-specific activities that they engaged in both *before* and *after* a product was deployed. The activities and the comparison of responses are shown in Figure 4. Almost all usability activities appeared to drop after a product had been deployed. The only significant increase was in the use of satisfaction surveys ($\chi^2_{(1, N=333)}$=95.2, $p<.01$). Also, note that 12.0% of the respondents selected not applicable (N/A) for the post-deployment phase.

Our next question was, *How often do you interact with support specialists (i.e., product support, customer support) after a product has been deployed? (via email, phone, or in-person meetings).* Responses are shown in Figure 5.

Close to a quarter (23.4%) of our respondents reported never interacting with support specialists after deployment, while

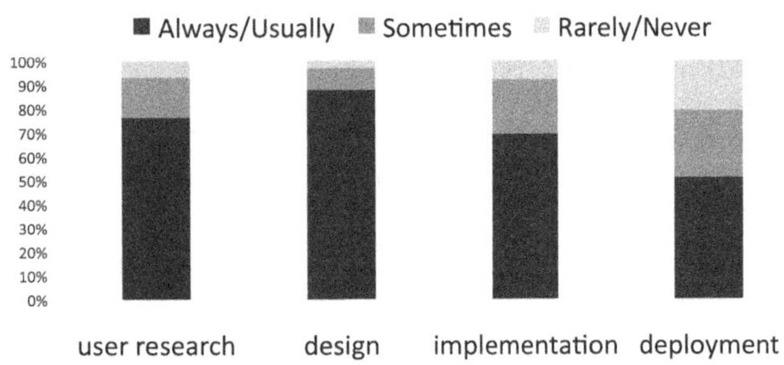

Figure 2: Usability involvement in different phases of development.

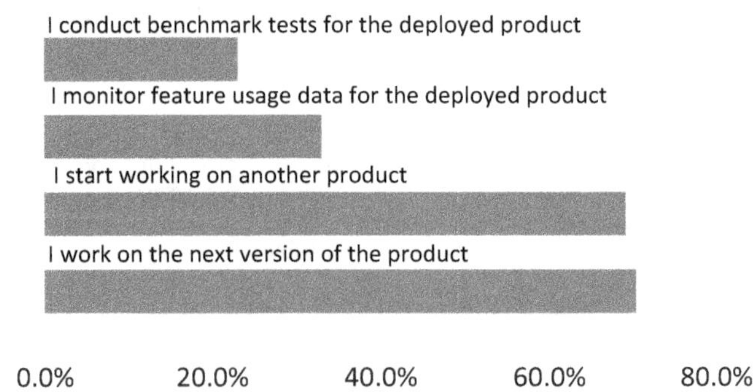

Figure 3: Main role of respondents after deployment.

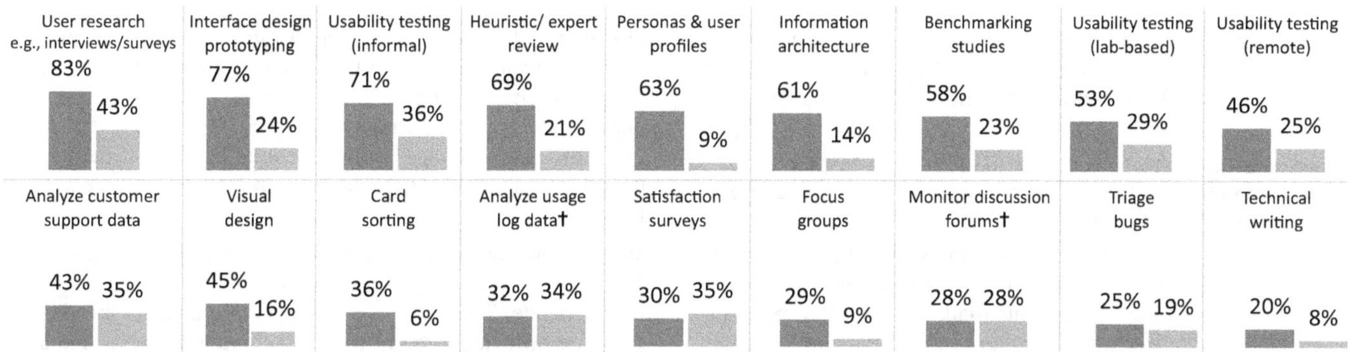

Figure 4: Proportion of respondents' indicating involvement across a range of activities. Dark bars represent the pre-deployment phase; lighter bars represent the post-deployment phase. All pre/post differences were significant (p<.05), except those indicated by (†).

another 30.2 % only interacted once in a while. Another 10.6% of the respondents said that they were not sure about their level of interaction. Among the 6.3% of respondents who talked to support specialists every day, about a third (33.3%) were from small corporations.

We also asked respondents to list where the support specialists were located in their organizations (Table 3). About half of the respondents (49.8%) said that support specialists were located on the same floor as the usability professionals or within the same building. A quarter of the respondents (23.1%) were not sure where support specialists were located.

The next question we asked was, *How often do you interact with software developers after a product has been deployed? (via email, phone, or in-person meetings)*. These results appear in Figure 5. Compared to support specialists, usability professionals appeared to have a more regular interaction with software developers after a product had been deployed ($\chi^2_{(1, N=333)}$=71.7, p<.0001). Among our respondents, 24.9% said that they interacted with developers every day and another 18.0% said they interacted a few times a week. Still, about 30.0% of respondents did not appear to have much interaction with developers (never or only once in a while).

In terms of location, 56.5% of the usability professionals said that developers were located on the same floor as them and 39.0% said that developers were in the same building (Table 3). This difference was significant compared to the relative location of usability professionals and support specialists ($\chi_{(5,N=333)}$=67.8, p<.0001). It appears that software developers in general were more collocated than support specialists and this could be one reason why usability professionals had more of an interaction with developers overall. However, closer

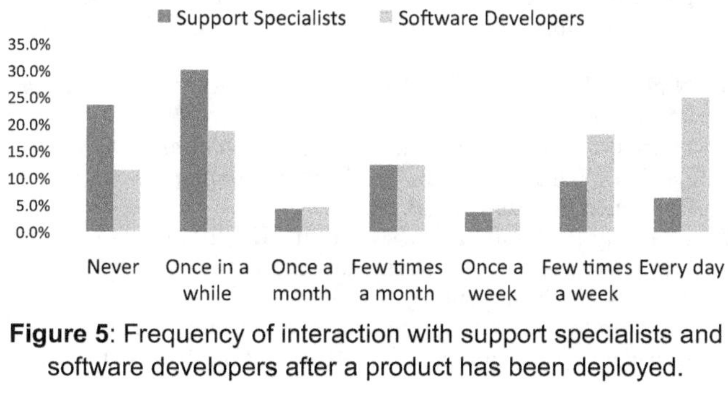

Figure 5: Frequency of interaction with support specialists and software developers after a product has been deployed.

examination reveals that of the respondents who talked to developers every day or few times a week, 35.7% said that developers were located in another office at another location. This finding suggests that there are factors other than location that could underlie the difference in interaction among usability professionals and software developers versus support specialists.

Perspectives on Post-Deployment Usability Activities

We also asked respondents to reflect on their role in post-deployment usability in free response questions; there was a 51.8% average response rate for the two questions. We used respondents' comments to begin to understand some of the trends that we observed in the quantitative findings.

First, we filtered responses based on comments from respondents who said they were always involved in the post-deployment phase to see what type of activities they engaged in. Respondents described activities such as monitoring current usage, benchmark studies, satisfaction surveys, user testing, and having informal contact with users, consistent with Figures 3 and 4. However, some respondents were still not satisfied with their level and type of involvement in the post-deployment phase:

> We get good feedback, but we don't work directly with customers, so it's hard to understand their specific pain points. I have a suspicion that there are minor irritations that don't ever get reported because people just don't think it's worth the effort to write to customer service. Without direct customer usability research, I don't exactly know what those are.

Next, we filtered responses based on comments from respondents who said they were never or rarely involved in the post-deployment phase. One prevalent response was that usability professionals tried to be more heavily involved upfront to prevent post-deployment issues. Another response

Location	Support Specialists	Software Developers
Same floor as me	25.7%	56.5%
Same building as me	25.7%	39.0%
Another office at a different location	38.4%	34.9%
I'm not sure	23.5%	7.9%
In an office, but I work remotely	7.6%	7.6%
In the office where I consult	5.1%	5.7%

Table 3: Location of support specialists and software developers in the organization, relative to the respondents

was that usability professionals did want to be more involved in post-deployment usability but the hindrance came from organizational cultures and perceptions about the role of usability:

> Involve us! Don't think we're just there to run a test for you--reach out to us and share your concerns for deployment and give us feedback after it's deployed.

Even when there was interest in sustaining usability throughout the lifecycle, it appears that product delivery schedules and resource constraints made it difficult to practice usability after deployment. Another challenge stemmed from organizational structures because in some cases customer support and software maintenance groups operated in silos, unaware of each other's activities.

DISCUSSION AND CONCLUSION

Our survey findings have several implications for post-usability research and practice, especially from the perspectives of software support and software maintenance.

The Software Support Perspective

The before/after findings of usability activities showed that only 34.8% of respondents appeared to leverage customer support data in the post-deployment phase, even less than the pre-deployment phase (Figure 4). Furthermore, over 50% of respondents never or rarely talked to support specialists. Since support specialists are at the front lines of directly interacting with end-users and helping them troubleshoot or learn about product features, it is possible that usability practitioners are missing several opportunities for learning about user experience from the field. As today's systems are becoming more complex and enabling idiosyncratic customizations, it is likely that the role of support will continue to be integral in supporting and evolving user experience. Thus, our survey findings highlight the need for the usability community to consider ways in which customer support data can be leveraged more effectively to guide iterative design tasks.

The Software Maintenance Perspective

The software engineering community has long recognized that software maintenance and evolution are an inevitable part of the software development life cycle [3]. Software developers spend most of their time triaging and fixing bugs. Only 18.9% of usability professionals said that they are directly involved in helping triage bugs, and about 30.0% of respondents never or rarely talked to software developers after a product had been deployed. Since a number of bugs that arise in the post-deployment phase are potential design and usability bugs [4], there is opportunity for exploring how usability professionals can play a more influential role in the bug triaging process.

Are usability professionals *really* doing user-centered design?

Our results show that, as a whole, the role of usability in current practice appears to diminish after a product has been deployed. This finding is somewhat troubling given that iteration and user feedback have been advocated as core components of all phases in UCD and the usability engineering lifecycle [1, 5, 6]. Given the increased uptake of usability in industry, it is not a surprise that the value of getting upfront design into organizations has paid off. However, despite sincere intentions in tackling potential usability problems upfront, we know from current industry practices that a number of issues emerge in the post-deployment phase (hence, the large software maintenance costs [3] and software support costs). Thus, post-deployment usability may be the next frontier in translating research into practice.

We propose that within the field of usability, there needs to be focus on "usability maintenance," paralleling software maintenance. The goal of usability maintenance should be to enhance post-deployment user experience based on the actual use of a product and provide ongoing support for usability principles of learnability, efficiency, memorability, recovery from errors, and satisfaction. As discussed above, we can start further studying and inventing opportunities for support and maintenance teams to interact with usability practitioners.

Limitations and Future Work

This survey provides the basis upon which future work can investigate industry practices in the post-deployment phase in more depth and devise new methods or guidelines. We generalize the survey findings with some caution since the survey was only distributed in English and respondents were largely from North America. However, since our respondents represented a variety of usability-related positions and a range of organizations of different sizes and specializations, it is possible that these results would hold globally. Our study currently provides an aggregate, quantitative view of usability practices, but in future work, we hope to tease out the effect of organizational cultures, usability positions, and differences between large and small corporations. It would also be interesting to complement these survey findings with observations of interactions among usability professionals and support specialists and software developers. Lastly, it is likely that in some cases pre-deployment activities on one version of a product can be considered post-deployment activities on the previous one and in future work we hope to shed light on such nuances. Together, we hope these perspectives will reveal new opportunities for usability maintenance.

REFERENCES

1. Gould, J. and Lewis, C. Designing for usability: key principles and what designers think. *Comm. ACM 28*, 3 (1985), 300-311.
2. Gulliksen, J., Boivie, I., and Göransson, B. Usability professionals—current practices and future development. *Interacting with Computers 18*, 4 (2006), 568-600.
3. Lehman, M.M. and Belady, L.A., eds. *Program evolution: processes of software change*. Academic Press, Inc., 1985.
4. Nichols, D., McKay, D., and Twidale, M. Participatory Usability: supporting proactive users. *Proc CHINZ (2003)*, 63-68.
5. Nielsen, J. The Usability Engineering Life-Cycle. *Computer 25*, 3 (1992), 12-22.
6. Norman, D.A. and Draper, S.W. *User Centered System Design; New Perspectives on Human-Computer Interaction*. Lawrence Erlbaum, 1986.
7. Usability Professionals Association. UPA 2009 Salary Survey. http://www.usabilityprofessionals.org/usability_ resources/ surveys/2009salarysurvey_PUBLIC.pdf.
8. Vredenburg, K., Mao, J., Smith, P., and Carey, T. A survey of user-centered design practice. *ACM CHI* (2002), 471-478.

Collaboration Personas: A New Approach to Designing Workplace Collaboration Tools

Tara Matthews, Steve Whittaker, Thomas Moran, Sandra Yuen
IBM Research - Almaden
San Jose, California, USA
{tlmatthe, sjwhitta, tpmoran, syuen}@us.ibm.com

ABSTRACT
The success of social computing has generated a host of workplace collaboration tools. However, adoption of these tools by entire groups is a major problem. One reason for the adoption problem is a lack of methods for considering collaborative groups in technology design. Even when designing *collaboration* tools, designers often employ methods that focus on *individuals*. This leads to tools that are not well targeted at the groups who will use them. To solve this problem, we propose the notion of *collaboration personas*, which are empirically derived descriptions of hypothetical groups, including details that inform the design of collaboration tools. Collaboration personas differ from individual personas in having (1) *multiple, inter-related individuals* playing specific roles; (2) a focus on *collective goals* and elaboration of individual goals that affect the collective goal; and (3) new attributes that characterize *collaborative aspects* of the group's work. We contrast collaboration personas with other design approaches and provide examples of how they can be used to design new collaborative tools that better meet the needs of typical groups.

Author Keywords
Office, workplace, collaboration, design tools, personas.

ACM Classification Keywords
H5.3. Group and Organization Interfaces.

General Terms: Design

INTRODUCTION
Recent years have seen the emergence of a multiplicity of workplace collaboration tools. Collaborative groups now face complex decisions about whether to use Facebook-style social networking tools; tools for sharing files, bookmarks, and tags; wikis; community tools; team-space tools; and so on. The complexity of these decisions often leads groups to adopt tools that are not optimized for their particular type of collaboration [13,17]. Furthermore, despite this proliferation of tools, one tool is often not enough to satisfy all the collaboration needs of a single group [1,17]. As a result, groups often cobble together multiple tools to serve their collaboration needs. Using multiple tools for collaboration adds complexity to members' lives, when they already have limited time to learn about and access these tools. These factors lead to an *adoption* problem, which is demonstrated by the continued use of email to share files, discuss projects, and coordinate tasks, instead of dedicated collaboration tools [22].

CHI 2011, May 7–12, 2011, Vancouver, BC, Canada.

A possible reason for the adoption problem is the typical technology design processes used to create these tools. Even when designing *collaboration* tools, designers often employ methods that focus on *individuals*, leading to tools that are not well-targeted at the groups who will use them. For example, personas are a commonly used design tool [6,21], but they sketch the qualities and goals of an *individual* rather than a team. Though techniques exist for understanding collaboration, such as ethnography, these are time consuming and unlikely to be performed for every product development effort. Furthermore, we lack methods for translating the understanding gained through user studies into reusable design tools for collaboration.

To address this design problem, we propose the notion of *collaboration personas*. Collaboration personas are *empirically derived* descriptions of hypothetical groups of people with specific qualities, goals, and needs realized through collaborations with each other. They are derived from empirical studies and a typology and framework describing distinct types of collaborations [17]. By considering the specific *interactional* properties of different types of collaborations (roles, interdependence, etc.), collaboration personas can improve tool adoption by helping designers create better targeted collaboration tools.

Our contributions in this paper are (1) proposing the novel concept of a collaboration persona, which is significantly different from an individual persona, and (2) presenting and motivating a set of collaboration personas that represent collaboration needs in modern enterprises.

RELATED WORK
The concept of a *persona*, introduced by Cooper [6], is a hypothetical archetype of an actual user, describing that person's goals, aptitudes, and interests. Personas are intended to avoid the problem of designers, developers, or stakeholders invoking the "elastic user" who can be bent and stretched to suit the needs of the invoker. Cooper estimates that each design problem will require between 3 to 12 personas. Many practitioners and researchers have found personas to be use-

ful in design, helping to better focus designs, allocate development resources, and contribute to product positioning and sales [6,7,11,21].

Given other design methods available, why personas? The closest alternative is participatory or cooperative design, which involves the design team interacting with future users throughout the design process [22]. Though they share many of the same goals, participatory design is primarily useful for small development teams designing for a specific or homogeneous group of users. Personas can be useful where participatory design is not effective, e.g., for large development teams and diverse user populations.

Scenario-based design creates a story with a setting, actors who have goals or objectives, and a sequence of actions and events [4]. Similarly, task analysis aims to formally represent user tasks [12]. The critical difference between personas and scenarios or task analysis is that the latter methods are not *generative*. Scenarios and tasks tend to capture key properties of specific situations. However, they do not enable designers to think about new situations.

CSCW patterns describe regularities in the organization of collaborative work practices, often focusing the role of specific artifacts [16]. They are useful complement to collaboration personas, since they can be included in the personas to describe how members of the group interact around their artifacts. Collaboration personas can provide context for CSCW patterns, by describing which roles are involved with a pattern and what part it plays in their larger project or ongoing collaboration. The key differences are that collaboration personas focus on the interactions of specific roles in a group, and describe the group in a way that it is easier for designers to relate to than an abstract model [11].

Methods for gathering data about users are an excellent complement to personas. Contextual design focuses on understanding users through field research, and communicating that data with flow, sequence, artifact, and cultural models [2]. Ethnographies also are a good (though expensive) source of data for personas. However both ethnography and contextual design have a critical limitation in capturing a concise but actionable representation of requirements data. In contrast, specific, concrete personas can address this challenge by bringing the data from contextual inquiry and ethnography to life for designers to use.

Personas have some drawbacks. It is difficult to verify that a persona accurately reflects user data [5] and challenging to pick the right personas [5,11]. It can also be difficult to initially convince a development team to use personas [21]. Despite these drawbacks, personas continue to be a popular method because of their power to engage designers and help them reason about user behavior.

DESIGNING FOR COLLABORATION: INDIVIDUAL PERSONAS ARE NOT ENOUGH

Our goal in this work was to design collaboration software for groups working in medium to large companies. Personas are the standard approach used to design software products within our company, in addition to providing the general benefits outlined above. We therefore started by following standard human-centered design processes involving personas, as outlined in [8,21]. Briefly, personas are created from data collected among user populations relevant to the design problem [7,8,21]. The data is analyzed to identify patterns of behavior which lead to categories of users. These categories are prioritized by the development team and product stakeholders. Finally, personas are fleshed out from the high-priority user categories with attributes from user data that are important to the design problem. Of particular importance in creating generative personas are the goals that underlie the behavioral patterns defining each user category [10].

Our first step was to study a sample of employees from a large company in a range of job types, to see how they collaborated. Our study is fully described in [17], but we briefly summarize here. The company was large, globally distributed and offered a complex array of technology products and services. We interviewed 21 employees drawn from hardware, software, sales, services, human resources, marketing, and communications. We used a semi-structured procedure to learn about participants' collaborations and their roles in the collaborations. We defined collaborations as activities in which people worked or interacted with others to achieve a work objective. Collaborations could also include activities that had more indirect effects on work, such as interactions in communities of practice.

We analyzed our interview data using open coding and thematic analysis. We then categorized interviewees into roles and their collaborations into types. This involved identifying behavioral and demographic variables that described each role and collaboration type.

The next step was to select our personas. Persona literature encourages designers to select one primary persona [6], perhaps a few [21]. But it also discourages putting personas in groups because it is a better use of scarce user experience team resources to create a broader set of personas representing variance in the user population [8]. At this point, we ran into our first problem when designing for collaboration:

- *Problem 1*: Which persona should we pick out of an entire group?

Not only did we discover that there were very different collaboration *types*, it was also obvious that people had different, but complementary *roles* within each collaboration type. In contrast to traditional personas where user types are independent, we discovered the importance of groups where the *interrelations* between people were critical. We therefore needed a cast of characters who comprised our collaborative group, each playing a different complementary role and providing specific expertise to the group. Characterizing each role and how they interrelated was critical to our understanding of how a collaboration tool would be used. As an example, D., a Cross-Brand IT Architect, describes the various roles on a particular dynamic project team:

On the client side, there's a project manager... [External Company] is the contractor that is doing the development, so they have a project manager and a development team... On the [customer] side, there's all the normal support people you'd have over there for infrastructure, hardware, software, networks, security, you know, the whole nine-yards... There is an overall project manager, from [our company], that keeps the task plan and leads the calls both internally and with the customer. There are sales and technical leaders for hardware and software, which I'm the software one. Then we have lots of technical specialties that we bring to bear here. Java, mainframe, Java on the mainframe. (Laughs.) Different [proprietary] technologies, database technologies. There are a lot of the technical specialties that we're employing. Then there's the whole sales team...

- *Lesson 1*: Design for collaboration requires (a) multiple inter-related people who participate in the same group, and (b) elaboration of multiple *roles* within a group with different people contributing complementary expertise.

The next step in traditional persona design is to flesh out attributes that are important to the design problem. One critical attribute is the persona's *goals*. The literature argues that persona goals should be stable over time so that they can generalize to different scenarios [6,8,21]. However, our interviews revealed that individuals have many goals, some of which are not relevant to the group's main goal.

- *Problem 2*: What persona goals are critical when designing for collaboration?

Our interviews revealed that participants had multiple, diverse goals. For collaboration, the important goals were those that contributed to the group, i.e., that overlapped across members. Focusing on individual goals only seemed to be relevant insofar as these related to group objectives.

In interviews, when asked what the group's goals were, participants would describe a goal that all members were working toward. For example, one team was put together to *win a customer sale*. Certain individual goals mattered in this case. In particular, subject-matter experts pulled into the team were motivated to lend their expertise so they could *claim the revenue brought in by the sale*. They were personally motivated to do a good job to *build their reputation and increase their access to future sales opportunities*.

- *Lesson 2*: Design for collaboration requires (a) focusing on the collective goals of individual contributors and (b) elaborating individual goals that affect the accomplishment of this collective goal. Elaborating representative tasks makes these goals more concrete.

Finally, we realized that our individual personas did not capture critical aspects of the collaboration. More specifically, purely individual personas omitted a group's *work style*, which comprises the interactive aspects of the group.

Individual personas usually include a variety of attributes that describe the individual, depending on the needs for a particular product [21]. Some common ones are basic details (e.g., name, photo), personal information (e.g., age, fears, personal goals), job information (e.g., typical tasks, professional goals, title, responsibilities, working environment descriptions), technology usage (e.g., skill levels with relevant technologies, technology attitudes), and consumer information (e.g., relationship with your product, market size) [6,21]. These attributes are not enough to describe collaborating groups, which include dynamics that should be considered in design [9,18].

- *Problem 3*: Individual personas overlook critical aspects of collaboration. How can we characterize interaction processes that are critical to collaborations?

Critical to understanding collaboration is what we refer to as *group work style,* i.e., the ways in which group members interwork. We categorized work style into three categories based on prior literature [15]. The first two were based on a core work deliverable, the third on communication:

- Deliverable pooling: members work independently until it is time to combine their work toward the group goal.
- Deliverable co-creating: members work closely together to collectively create work deliverables.
- Communication-focused: the focus is on interaction; members work independently and do not rely on other members to complete their work deliverables. This interaction may be focused on maintaining a relationship or on sharing information.

D., a Software Services Director, describes how her dynamic project team collaborates by pooling work:

"There are people who create individual documents and tools and processes and those pieces and parts are pulled together to make an overall project."

G., a Software Development Lab Manager, describes how his stable project team co-creates deliverables:

We're working on a shared document, but the input to that has come from lots of individual elements that members of the working group have created and contributed. The work group leader, who is not me, has been the point of integration of the content... We've been using email as the primary mechanism to... comment on the documents and the content as it's being created... So people will send around a draft copy of the report and people will mark that up.

For pooling and co-creating, many of our participants' activities involved coordinating with others to achieve collective goals. Coordination could involve recruiting people to staff a dynamic team, negotiations to ensure that group members were clear about collective objectives, status updates, awareness, discussing work dependencies and so on.

Also critical to collaboration is *management style*. This includes whether there is a leader and how decisions are made. For example, we found that certain collaborative groups had a democratic management style, where decisions were made by consensus. This led to long discussions and inefficiencies, according to J., an Engineer:

...There are some things like a tactical roadmap that are too complex for democracy. Maybe this would have been better as a dictatorship. So a lot of different opinions, the compromise was

> *satisfying everyone and the need to do something wasn't urgent. Not like the customer deals that I am working on now... No with the roadmap... we do not talk about the roadmap for next year... we talk about it for 3 years, and its too much discussion and not enough decisions. This was in addition to my main duties.*

In addition to work style and management style, understanding collaboration requires information about organizational relationships among members, geographic distribution, and current tool usage. A persona must include these for it to be useful in collaboration tool design.

- *Lesson 3*: We need to add new attributes to personas that characterize *collaborative* aspects of a group's work.

What then can we conclude from applying existing persona approaches to collaborations? One repeated observation is that the *group* rather than the individual is the important organizational unit. Focusing on groups rather than individuals reveals the presence of different roles, how different roles interlock, how collective rather than individual goals are crucial, and how work style and management style facilitate effective group functioning. Groups rather than individuals are the critical unit of analysis, and our design approach needs to better reflect this.

We therefore propose a new design concept, *collaboration personas,* that is focused on *groups* as opposed to individuals. We illustrate this new approach with an example of a dynamic project team persona. In our interviews, dynamic project teams were the most common, mission-critical collaboration type relevant to the products we are designing.

COLLABORATION PERSONA EXAMPLE: A DYNAMIC PROJECT TEAM

Collaboration personas are precise descriptions of hypothetical groups with specific roles, goals, work style and management style. In this section, we use in-depth data on 13 real dynamic project teams from a study presented in [17] to develop an entire dynamic project team persona, explaining why content is included as we go.

The persona consists of several sub-sections, each detailing a specific attribute of the group. The *goals* help us understand *why* the group does what it does. *Members* tell us *who* share these collective goals. *Tasks* are one instantiation of the goals, helping us understand *what* the group does. *Work style* and *tools* show *how* they accomplish the goal, detailing specific ways that specific members interact, how they are managed, and what tools they currently use. Collectively, these sub-sections illustrate certain *collaboration needs*, and these are made explicit in their own sub-section. In the discussion, we explore how this content gives collaboration personas predictive power in the design process.

One key aspect of personas is that they should be *memorable.* Within most of the persona sub-sections, narrative details are provided to improve memorability and to help designers "get to know" the group. To help us craft these narratives, we borrowed particularly evocative descriptions of typical attributes of the group type from raw interview data (e.g., "lead cat herder" to describe a committee leader).

Goals

Both specificity and generality are important for personas. A defining characteristic of the personas approach is that individual personas include *very specific* information to avoid people invoking the "elastic user" who can be bent to suit edge cases or one's own beliefs [6]. Specific information also enables personas to be a powerful behavior predictor, since they facilitate the internalization of user models [10]. At the same time, personas need to include stable goals that can be generally applied in multiple scenarios.

This balance of specificity and generality is more challenging for collaboration personas. *Lesson 2* instructs us to focus on collective group goals. However, goals for groups formed to handle an objective are tied to a particular collaborative effort, introducing a problem of goal generality. For example, our dynamic project team persona is defined by the specific objective they are working on: winning a specific customer sale. The team was formed to accomplish that objective. This means that even the people and roles chosen to be on the team are defined by the specific objective. Thus, the objective is inherently tied to a particular context making it different from the types of goals included in individual personas. This blurs the line between personas and scenarios.

However, while the dynamic project team is an example of a group formed for a particular purpose, other types of groups have goals that are independent of a particular project objective. Groups with longer life spans such as communities or stable teams, tend to have general goals, that are more similar to the goals of individual personas

Despite sometimes having a more specific goal than individual personas, collaboration personas are more general than scenarios. Scenarios are concrete descriptions of how people accomplish particular tasks [4]. Collaboration personas set the stage for a group of people with a collective and potentially time-bounded goal to enact various scenarios. How exactly they accomplish even the most specific goals is sketched out at a high level. Also, the way a group does something *now* does not preclude them changing, e.g., if a new tool were introduced or a wrench thrown in their path by their customers or management.

Thus, collaboration personas can include specific goals that are representative of other goals the same type of team could address. These goals should not preclude the team doing different tasks or using different tools/features.

Group goal

This group of Global Corp sales professionals was formed for a single, temporally-bounded purpose: addressing a customer need to make a sale. The customer, Rainbow Bank, has put out a request for proposals (RFP) describing a technical need for which they are accepting bids. Jeff and Quan, Global Corp's client relationship leaders for Rainbow Bank, have decided they have the time to respond and can provide a quality response. They need to pull together a rock star team to prepare a proof of concept demo and request for proposal (RFP) submission. Jeff already has a great relationship with Rainbow Bank's CIO and feels optimistic about their chances to win the sale by showing that Global Corp products will improve Rainbow Bank's operations:

- The team was formed to address a customer opportunity with Rainbow Bank. The ultimate goal is to close the sale.

Member goals

All members are aligned around a single goal—making the sale—since all sales employees are evaluated on the revenue they bring in. Each member is also motivated to improve his/her reputation as a good team member and strong expert in their areas, since this increases the number of sales opportunities they are asked to contribute to in the future (and also the revenue they bring in).

- Each member wants to ensure that their duties are fulfilled.
- As future dynamic team membership relies on reputation and expertise, each member wants to be helpful to team members and prove themselves as knowledgeable in their area. If they lack knowledge relevant to their area, they will seek help from their professional networks and communities of practice.

Typical tasks to accomplish the goal are also included. These are important to add concreteness, so that anyone presented with this collaboration persona can understand what the group needs to do to accomplish the goal. The tasks should be high-level enough that they make it possible to walk the collaboration persona through various scenarios.

Group tasks

- The team needs to develop a solid proof of concept demo and request for proposal (RFP) submission. The proposal consists of a presentation and a document describing Global Corp's best solution to the client's requirements.
- If Global Corp's proposal is accepted by Rainbow Bank, a pilot will need to be deployed and maintained on-site at the bank.
- The team needs to carry out extensive discussions and negotiations with the client, which tends to require several months.
- Throughout the project lifespan, customer questions and requests need to be addressed in a timely fashion.

Members and Roles

Lesson 1 tells us to include *multiple people* playing interlocking roles and providing different expertise. A group can comprise many people, but personas are labor intensive to create. Thus it is not feasible for design teams to fully specify each individual within a collaboration persona. Persona literature argues that details should be carefully limited to those relevant to the product being designed or that make the persona a generative tool, i.e., a tool to predict behavior in different situations [8,10,21]. For a collaboration persona, it is sufficient to include only member details that directly pertain to their participation in the group. At minimum, this should include an individual member's name, role (including organizational details when appropriate), expertise, and goals that affect their group participation (see the "goals" section above for member goals). Sometimes select details about an individual's attitudes or skills may be relevant (e.g., that someone is a technology champion).

The presentation of members should also include a description of whether they are stable or dynamic. Stable group members remain for the group's entire lifespan. Dynamic members come and go depending on the group's need for their expertise. Other candidate information to include, depending on the product needs, is a description of the geographic distribution of members and their organizational relationships (both are included in the example below).

Members & roles

Members are either from the Sales division of Global Corp or the customer, Rainbow Bank. The team consists of a stable leadership sub-team, which comprises the original client relationship group (Jeff and Quan), and provides an importantly consistent point-of-contact for the customers (Sophie and Marie). However, these stable members do not have the range of expertise needed to close the sale alone, so it is critical to reach out and recruit other dynamic members with that expertise on an 'as needed' basis. Hence, this team is incredibly dynamic and flexible.

Most members are already trusted by the leadership team, and are recruited because of previous working relationships. A few members have not worked together previously, and are recruited by referral. People with particular expertise (e.g., brand specialists, subject-matter experts) are brought onto the team to contribute their expertise, e.g., to deliverables or to customer discussions. These dynamic members will only stay as long as they are needed.

Members are related by a matrix organization, so the team does not have a name or formal organizational identity. All members of the group work in different sites across three countries: the United States, Germany, and France. Global Corp is based in the United States and Rainbow Bank is based in France.

Leaders (stable):

- Jeffrey Thompson (Global Corp, Coverage Sales Rep): Rainbow Bank relationship leader for all software and hardware sales. Needs to be aware of all Rainbow Bank opportunities and is involved in any that include multiple products.
- Quan Lee (Global Corp, Coverage Technical Sales Specialist (TSS)): Technical leader for all software and hardware sales to Rainbow Bank. Needs to be aware of all Rainbow Bank opportunities and is involved in any that include multiple products.

Global Corp members (dynamic):

- Diane Stallman (EfficientWorker Sales Rep), Hans Strohbach (FastServer Sales Rep), and Wendy Liu (BestMiddleware Sales Rep): Handle sales related to their specific brands. Once introduced to a new client, they will maintain the management relationship pertaining to their brand's products.
- Brian Worther (EfficientWorker TSS), Hannah Bergmann (FastServer TSS), and Mateo Badillo (BestMiddleware TSS): Handle customers' technical issues related to their specific brands. Once introduced to a new client, they will maintain the technical relationship pertaining to their brand's products.
- Helen Johnson (Delivery Services): Works with the customer's IT specialists to deploy technology at customer sites.
- Tamam Srour, Elke Schmidt, and Stella Herbert. (Subject Matter Experts or SMEs): SMEs are recruited by members to provide expertise. Involvement ranges from answering a question to joining the team for a period of time to help with development or customer discussions.

Rainbow Bank members (stable):

- Sophie Bessette (CIO): The Rainbow Bank person who makes technology purchasing decisions.

- Marie Simon (IT Specialist): Rainbow Bank's technical person in charge of helping Sophie decide what the right technology is to purchase, issuing the RFP, and deploying new technology.

Work Style

Lesson 3 argues for introducing new attributes that characterize the group's work style. Since certain tasks demand specific expertise, we stipulate who will do the major group tasks and how they will work together (specifying pooled, co-created, or communication focused work).

Group work style

Work is highly collaborative and Global Corp sales people work closely with Rainbow Bank to define requirements. Production of the proposal and demo are the result of co-creation, with SMEs contributing elements to both, in line with their areas of expertise, and the core team unifying and critiquing the results of their work.

Because of their dynamicism and the RFP deadline, the team is high-energy and fast-moving. They quickly react and adapt to new customer requests and questions.

- The RFP response presentation and document will be co-created by the coverage sales rep and brand sales reps.
- The demo will be co-created by the coverage technical specialist and brand technical specialists.
- The final RFP response and demo will be pooled together by the entire team before being presented to the customer.
- A deployed pilot will be co-created by delivery services and the demo creators. Then the pilot will be deployed by delivery services and Rainbow Bank IT specialists.
- Additional requirements will be co-created by the Rainbow Bank members and the Global Corp leaders.
- Updates to the pilot will be co-created by technical specialists from both Global Corp and Rainbow Bank.

The next persona sub-sections are current tool use and collaboration needs. Several attributes of a dynamic project team—its focus on a core work deliverable, the dynamic nature of its personnel, and its work style combining pooling and co-creating—lead to specific collaboration needs. For example, dynamic members need to be found, recruited, and on-boarded. The team in this example is client focused, which also introduces collaboration needs, like maintaining communication with the customer.

Our example team currently addresses these collaboration needs with specific tools, which are discussed in the persona. The key objective of collaboration personas is to design tools that effectively address collaboration needs. Our persona captures representative tools used now, but also provides clear information about the frustrations and pain points experienced with those tools. We also characterize the team's more general technology attitudes.

Current Tools and their Problems

The team is somewhat old fashioned in their use of current technology, partly because they are just too busy to try and learn new tools. They rely on conference calls, email, and more conference calls. Occasionally, they use instant messaging for quick communication and to guarantee a response. They share information via email, but this is often frustrating as key information is buried in emails or attachments that are "somewhere" in people's inboxes.

Another problem is that dynamic members, who are coming and going, need an easy way to get up to speed with core project materials. They've tried to solve this problem by setting up a repository to share files, but Jeff is frustrated since he feels like he is the only one adding files and is constantly nagging others to do so. Most of the time, people just send around files as email attachments. This is compounded by not having a repository that works across organizational boundaries, so when they share with customer members, they are forced to use email.

Conference calls are frustrating: slides for meetings are often sent via email minutes before, and the group has trouble co-creating without a good tool to interactively share materials in real time.

Collaboration needs

- Easily and securely share materials (e.g., documents, demo code) with internal and external members.
- Find and recruit trustworthy people, who have specific expertise and good reputations.
- On-board new members, i.e., get them up-to-speed on necessary client information and the status of the project.
- Capture outputs and required knowledge from dynamic members who have completed their tasks for the group.
- Co-create materials, e.g., the RFP document and demo code.
- Maintain awareness of members' task status.
- Keep an open communication channel with the customer.

Other Attributes

So far our collaboration personas have included only attributes that are essential to behaviorally distinguishing collaborative groups. However, a key property of individual personas is that these need to be concrete, memorable, and distinct [21]. Two important attributes discussed in prior literature are a name and photo [6,21]. Collaboration personas should also have a name when appropriate. One dilemma is whether the team should be named as its members would refer to it (in this case our example might be called "Rainbow Bank RFP Team") or with a name memorable and meaningful to the development team (our example might then be called "The Dynamic Sales Team"). We recommend a combination approach: "Rainbow Bank RFP Team (a dynamic sales team)."

A photo for a group is more challenging than for an individual persona, though valuable for all the same reasons. The best approach would be to have one photo per member as well as photos of the appropriate members interacting on the main group tasks. We exclude photos in this paper due to space constraints.

Other attributes could be supplied to help development teams explore characteristics that are important within their specific user population. For example, these could include national culture, corporate culture, certain skills or expertise, technology adoption tendencies, how well group members get along, and so on.

COLLABORATION TYPES

To illustrate collaboration personas, we have discussed a single example based on dynamic project teams. However, the standard individual personas approach involves preliminary user research to identify *categories of users* based on user roles, goals, or market segments (which can be defined by any attributes of interest to stakeholders) [21]. Our research identified other *collaboration types* that are distinguished by collaboration-specific behaviors [17]:

1. **Dynamic project team.** A group of people, where some members stay the same but most members come and go during the life of the project, working closely together toward a common deliverable that is a job related focus for its members.
2. **Stable project team.** A group of people, where most members stay the same, working closely together toward a common deliverable that is a job related focus for its members.
3. **Committee.** A group of people working closely together toward a common deliverable that is secondary to most members' main job focus.
4. **Client-supplier relationship group.** A stable group of people from both client and supplier who communicate on an ongoing basis to ensure the supplier meets the needs of the client.
5. **Community.** A group of people with similar job functions or a shared interest, who come together to exchange knowledge, information, best practices, and possibly to spark new collaborations.
6. **Professional relationships.** A professional relationship focused on communication between two individuals, typically with minimal formality or structure. Common purposes for professional relationships include mentoring, finding collaborators, building one's reputation, and/or getting answers and feedback

Consistent with the collaboration personas approach, our study revealed four main attributes that distinguished collaborative behaviors, leading to the types above (see Table 1 for how these attributes apply to collaboration types):

- their *goals* (which can be objective-, interest-, or relationship-oriented; and core or secondary to most members' job responsibilities),
- whether *personnel* are stable or dynamic,
- their *work style* which can involve pooling work, co-creating, or communication around relationships or information sharing, and
- their *leadership style* (having designated leader(s) or being democratically run).

Table 1. Collaboration types and their distinguishing dimensions.

	Goal	Personnel	Work Style	Leadership
Dynamic project team	Core deliverable	Dynamic	Pooling & Co-creating	Designated leaders
Stable project team	Core deliverable	Stable	Pooling & Co-creating	Designated leaders
Client-supplier relationship	Core relationship	Stable	Communication-focused	Designated leaders
Committee	Secondary deliverable	Stable	Pooling & Co-creating	Democratic
Community	Secondary interest/role	Stable &/or Dynamic	Communication-focused	Designated leaders
Professional relationships	Secondary relationship	Dynamic	Communication-focused	N/A

So far we have presented examples from a single type of collaboration, the dynamic project team. We now present examples from other team types to illustrate further aspects of the collaboration personas approach. The examples show how the approach generalizes to different collaboration types, and how key differences between collaboration types can be represented in different collaboration personas.

Other Examples of Collaboration Personas

In this section we include short sections from some of the other collaboration types—client-supplier relationship group, community, and committee—that illustrate their differences. We exclude stable project teams and professional relationships due to space constraints; stable teams are well-documented in the literature [10] and client-supplier relationship group shows the key aspects of a collaboration that is communication-focused toward a relationship. To save space, most of our examples relate to the people from our dynamic project team persona. Also, note that the examples below are not fully elaborated—they are snippets chosen to illustrate main differences.

Client-Supplier Relationship Group

Client-supplier relationship groups are different from project teams in their main work *goal.* This focuses on maintaining a critical work relationship with the client (see "group goals" in the example below). This goal affects the *work style*: interaction centers around communication between the client and supplier since there are no concrete deliverables to work toward (see "group work style" below). However, when new engagement opportunities arise, the relationship leader on the supplier's side will want to take action by initiating a dynamic project team. These goals and work style lead to "collaboration needs" focused on communication and awareness.

Our example below is the stable client-supplier relationship group that initiated our dynamic project team persona: it comprises the Global Corp leaders (Jeff and Quan) and the Rainbow Bank delegates (Sophie and Marie).

Group name: Rainbow Bank - Global Corp Relationship Team

Group goals

- Maintain a positive relationship between Global Corp (supplier) and Rainbow Bank (client).
- Ensure Rainbow Bank's needs related to Global Corp solutions are being met.

- Identify new solutions, or upgrades to existing solutions, that Global Corp can offer Rainbow Bank to improve their business (i.e., opportunities for new sales to Rainbow Bank).

Group work style
- Jeff will regularly ask Sophie about Rainbow Bank needs and inform her of relevant new Global Corp offerings.
- Marie will sporadically contact Quan with technical questions regarding Global Corp technology.
- Jeff and Quan will regularly, informally communicate to keep each other aware of sales leads.
- When new opportunities arise, Jeff and Quan will meet to decide whether to pursue it and to plan the initiation of a dynamic project team to go after it.

Collaboration needs
- Keep open communication channel between client and supplier.
- Maintain awareness of client changes that open sales prospects.

Community

Communities are very different from project teams because they are not focused on core work deliverables. Instead, communities are focused on the exchange of ideas and best practices (see "group goals" in the example below). This affects their *work style*: members work independently and come together mainly to share information (see "group work style" below). Because of this independent work style, multiple sections of the persona are broken down by role (sponsors, members, and community leaders): work style (see example below) member goals, group tasks, tools, and collaboration needs (not shown due to space constraints).

Our example is the Financial Industry Community in which many members of our dynamic team persona participate.

Group name: Financial Industry Community (a.k.a. "Financial")

Group goals
The financial industry is a large source of income for Global Corp, who develops servers for storing financial data and software for managing the data. It is critical to keep employees up to date on Financial-relevant information, technology updates, process changes, and so on. Due to Global Corp's highly matrixed organization, employees work on projects across departmental boundaries. Financial-focused employees cannot always turn to peers in their own department with Financial-related questions or requests. Thus, those who work with the financial industry form a loosely-knit community of practice who need to manage their own knowledge repository and educational programs.

- Allow Global Corp employees to share information, Q&A, and best practices related to the financial industry and clients.
- Connect workers for networking, social, awareness, and project opportunities (in particular, the large number of dynamic project teams that work on solutions for Financial customers).

Group work style *(Note: we exclude the section on roles due to space constrains, but the roles are also listed here.)*
Financial is an active and successful community. It has nearly 200 members, with a relatively small number of active members (about a dozen) contributing most of the content. Members work almost entirely on their own projects, mainly sharing outcomes, knowledge gained, and best practices with the community. Members are active in responding to others' questions, too—usually someone can find the time to contribute. Sometimes members will collaborate. This typically happens when a member is part of a dynamic team that needs someone with specific financial industry expertise and they use the community to find such an expert. Participation in the community is often seen as "career enhancement," since it opens the door for future beneficial collaborations.

- *All members*: (1) Independently consume shared content. (2) Some independently contribute content to the community's shared space. (3) Some will discover others and initiate friendships or collaborations.
- *Community leaders* co-create materials and co-organize events for the community.
- *Sponsors* meet with community leaders to assess progress.

Committee

Committees are the only collaboration type that has a democratic *management style* (see "members & roles" and "work style" below). The effect on committees' *work style* is that they are discussion-oriented and consensus-driven. This often proves less than ideal for producing a deliverable since it can lead to inefficiencies (see "work style" below).

Group name: Global Corp Services Dept. Promotion Committee

Group goal
- Identify outstanding performers within the Services Department and make decisions about who to promote.

Members & roles.
- *Leader*: Lucille Boltz (Services Dept. VP). Lucille is the "lead cat herder." As this title hints, she must use her charismatic personality to wrangle decisions out of sub-committees and manage decision deadlocks when the full committee meets.
- *Members*: Tony Maldonado, Diana Rios, Chen Liu, Stacy Burke, Jose Vega, Blake Norman. Each member is a manager representing a group within the Services Department.

Group work style
The group is run as a democracy, i.e., it is consensus-driven. With the set of personalities assembled, consensus is often hard to come by and debates tend to be drawn out. All members are incredibly busy, so Lucille initiates the process long before decisions are due. Members live around the world, so all collaboration happens on the phone and via email. They follow this process once per year:

- Independently, each member identifies promotion candidates from their department and ensures that the committee has a promotion application for each candidate.
- The members split up into three sub-committees of two people each. Each sub-committee reviews a set of candidates and puts forth recommendations to the full committee. Sub-committee pairs pool what they know about each candidate and work very closely in meetings to make decisions.
- Sub-committee members present their recommendations and the entire committee discusses in order to whittle the list of candidates down. Long debates ensue and the group often falls behind schedule. If no consensus can be reached over a particular candidate, the group will vote. Lucille mediates the votes.

DISCUSSION

We have developed a new, empirically motivated design approach to address adoption problems with collaboration tools. We believe that collaboration personas can transform the design process for collaboration tools. In the following, we discuss how collaboration personas differ from individual personas in what makes them generative, when and how to create new collaboration personas, and design implications that collaboration personas highlight.

Distinguishing Collaboration and Individual Personas

Collaboration personas are better suited to support design for collaboration than individual personas because they model distinct types of collaborating groups. In particular, they (1) include multiple inter-related personas playing different *roles* in the same group; (2) focus on the *collective goals* of individual contributors and elaborate *individual goals* that affect the accomplishment of this collective goal; and (3) introduce new attributes to personas which characterize *collaborative aspects* of the group's work.

Personas work because they evoke our human ability to create and use unconscious *models* of other real and fictional people [10]. These models are generative, i.e., they enable us to predict how the modeled person would feel or act in different situations [10]. Abstract methods, like scenarios and task analysis, do not evoke the same empathetic thinking [7,10]. The attributes that are most critical to creating a generative persona are *goals*, because they are the primary drivers behind behavior [7,10]. Their full predictive quality comes from helping designers internalize a holistic model of the persona. This requires enough detail to enable designers to feel they "know" the persona [10].

Collaboration personas, in contrast, cannot completely rely on goals to provide the crux of their predictive power. We have found that the dimensions in Table 1—personnel dynamicism, work style, and management style—are particularly important for describing major differences in collaborative behavior. Reasoning about these attributes can help designers predict how groups will react to new technology. As with individual personas, the predictive power of collaboration personas is fully realized with enough concrete details to enable designers to build a complex, internal model of the group with which they can engage. This is why we included narratives at the beginning of most persona sections describing aspects of the group's personality, such as their "old fashioned" technology attitudes or that the members were identified by the leaders as "rock stars." In future work, we plan to make our personas even more concrete by scripting example dialogue from key interactions, something that is uniquely possible with collaboration personas since they include multiple members.

When and How to Create New Collaboration Personas

The four dimensions in Table 1 model differences in collaborative behavior, defining a minimal set of collaboration personas—i.e., one for each of the six types defined above. Other dimensions, such as national culture or technology attitudes, could lead to many more collaboration personas, although we would not expect these to dramatically change the *types* of collaboration. The importance of other dimensions is dependent on the design problem and population being designed for.

The collaboration dimensions listed in Table 1 also help us determine how to create new collaboration personas that are specific enough to work as personas but general enough to enact various scenarios. We should be able to create a new collaboration persona of the same collaboration type (e.g., a second dynamic project team) that has all the same behavioral attributes (e.g., focused on creating a core work deliverable, with dynamic personnel, etc.) with the same associated needs (e.g., ability to co-create, finding and onboarding personnel, etc.), with a *different specific goal.* In other words, there are a sizable number of specific goals that would be accomplished in the similar ways. For example, another dynamic project team might have a goal to *produce content for an online news website.* This goal works as long as it is a core work deliverable for members, dynamic members are asked to contribute, members need to work closely together, and there are designated leaders.

Design Implications of Different Collaboration Personas

The goal of personas is to guide design. Collaboration personas therefore need to capture the characteristics of different types of groups in ways that will allow developers to generate new designs. Here we illustrate how different personas lead to very differently designed collaborative tools.

The dimensions in Table 1 represent the main differences in collaborative behavior and also in tool needs. With regard to goals, deliverable-focused groups (stable and dynamic project teams, committees) need tools that support co-creating and pooling work. They will also need to closely coordinate activities around deliverables, such as project management tools. In contrast, communication-focused groups (client-supplier relationship groups, professional relationships, communities) need a variety of communication channels, ranging from a rich open channel for client requests to unobtrusive broadcasts for community news.

A critical aspect of groups with dynamic personnel (dynamic project teams, communities) is that SMEs are recruited as needed. Often, members recruit through personal connections, but expertise location and dedicated social networking tools would also help. Groups need ways to bring dynamic members up-to-speed when they begin. These needs are not critical in groups with stable personnel.

Finally, groups that are not a primary work focus for workers (committees, communities, professional relationships) need help mitigating challenges of attention overload and motivation. These collaborations need to provide value and motivate participation, without overloading members.

Researchers could have drawn these implications from abstract models of the collaboration types. However collaboration personas bring these implications to life and make them concrete for product developers and stakeholders. Also, collaboration personas enable designers to predict how the group that is central to their design might react to specific new technologies. For example, would the Dynamic Sales RFP Team welcome a new tool to co-create documents? Given the time constraints of the group, combined with the fact that dynamic members are only part-time focused on this project, and that the team as a whole is old-fashioned with regard to technology, such a tool must be incredibly easy to learn and set up. When might this team use an SME location and recruitment tool? It could be invaluable if it made it easier to maintain their responsiveness with the customer, given the mission-critical nature of finding specific expertise quickly and the unpredictability of what Rainbow Bank might ask for. These examples illustrate how a precise, detailed collaboration persona can help designers reason about collaboration tool design.

Another way to identify design implication comes from analysis of each collaboration persona, comparing the disparity between collaboration needs and pain-points experienced by the group. For example, our dynamic team persona describes difficulties the team experience in sharing information and recruiting new members. In contrast, our committee experienced difficulties in making decisions.

CONCLUSION

We have introduced and motivated a new design tool: collaboration personas. This shifts the design focus away from *individuals* to *groups,* to address recurrent problems with the design of collaboration software. Ultimately we believe that the most stringent test for any persona is how well it enables designers and developers to design and evaluate potential new technology. In future work, we intend to implement and evaluate the designs collaboration personas have helped identify.

REFERENCES

1. Balakrishnan, A., Matthews, T., Moran, T.P. (2010). Fitting an activity-centric system into an ecology of workplace tools. *Proc. of CHI*, 787-790.
2. Beyer, H., Holtzblatt, K. (1998). *Contextual design.* Morgan Kaufmann.
3. Bødker, S. (2000). Scenarios in user-centred design – Setting the stage for reflection and action. *IWC, 13*(1), 61-75.
4. Carroll, J.M. (2000) Five reasons for scenario-based design. *IWC, 13*(1), 43-60.
5. Chapman, C.N., Milham, R. (2006). The personas' new clothes: Methodological and practical arguments against a popular method. *Proc. of HFES.* 634-636.
6. Cooper, A. (1999). *The inmates are running the asylum: Why high-tech products drive us crazy and how to restore the sanity.* Sams Publishers.
7. Cooper, A., Reimann, R. (2003). *About face 2.0: The essentials of interaction design.* Wiley Publishing.
8. Goodwin, K., Cooper, A. (2009). *Designing for the digital age: How to create human-centered products and services.* Wiley Publishing.
9. Grudin, J. (1994). Groupware and social dynamics: Eight challenges *for* developers. *CACM, 37*(1), 92-105.
10. Grudin, J. (2006). Why personas work: The psychological evidence. In J. Pruitt and T. Adlin (eds.) *The persona lifecycle: Keeping people in mind throughout the product design,* 642-664. Morgan Kaufman.
11. Grudin, J., Pruitt, J. (2002). Personas, participatory design and product development: An infrastructure for engagement. *Proc. of the Participatory Design Conference.* 144-161.
12. Hackos, J., Redish, J. (1998). *User and task analysis for interface design.* John Wiley and Sons.
13. Holtzblatt, L., Damianos, L., Weiss, D. (2010). Factors impeding wiki use in the enterprise: A case study. *Collective Intelligence Workshop at CSCW.*
14. Jackson, A., Yates, J., Orlikowski, W. (2006). Corporate Blogging: Building community through persistent digital talk. *Proc. of HICSS*, 80-89.
15. Kraut, R., (2003). Applying social psychological theory to the problems of group work. In J.M. Carroll (ed.) *HCI models, theories and frameworks: Toward a multidisciplinary science.* Morgan Kaufman, 325-356.
16. Martin, D., Sommerville, I., (2004). Patterns of Cooperative Interaction: Linking Ethnomethodology and Design. *ToCHI, 11*(1), 59-89.
17. Matthews, T., Whittaker, S., Moran, T., Yuen, S. (2010). The new organizational ecology: Symbiotic relations between collaborations. Under review.
18. McGrath, J.E. (1984). *Groups: Interaction and performance.* Prentice-Hall.
19. Millen, D.R., Feinberg, J., and Kerr, B. (2006). Dogear: Social bookmarking in the enterprise. *Proc. of CHI*, 111-120.
20. Preece, J., Maloney-Krichmar, D. (2003). Online Communities. In J. Jacko, A. Sears, A. (Eds.). *Handbook of Human-Computer Interaction*, Lawrence Erlbaum Assoc. 596-620.
21. Pruitt, J., Adlin, T. (2006). *The persona lifecycle: Keeping people in mind throughout the product design.* Morgan Kaufman.
22. Schuler, D., Namioka, A. (1993). *Participatory design: Principles and practices.* Lawrence Erlbaum Assoc.
23. Whittaker, S. (2005). Supporting Collaborative Task Management in Email. *HCI, 20*, 49-88.

From Garments to Gardens: Negotiating Material Relationships Online and 'By Hand'

Elizabeth Goodman and Daniela K. Rosner[†]
School of Information, UC Berkeley
Berkeley, CA 94720 USA
{egoodman,daniela}@ischool.berkeley.edu

ABSTRACT

From home improvement to scrapbooking, leisure activities performed "by hand" increasingly involve digital tools. In turn, software and devices to support handwork are proliferating. We use data from an observational field study of gardening and knitting to examine relationships to information technology. Handwork experiences of patience, effort, sensation, and cleverness can shift with the introduction of new tools. Our participants' attachment to these experiences made them sensitive to the potential consequences of introducing new tools. Digital tools were sometimes rejected and other times woven into handwork activities. In response, we propose three metaphors for handwork practice —extending, interjecting, and segmenting—as a resource for moving beyond the binary opposition of digital and physical practices.

Author Keywords

Handwork, craft, knitting, gardening, design theory.

ACM Classification Keywords

K.4.0 Computers and Society: general.

General Terms

Design, Human Factors.

INTRODUCTION

You can't hammer a nail over the Internet

—*Economist Alan Blinder, Princeton Affairs,* quoted in [6]

Over the last decade, information technologies (IT) designed to engage leisure handwork pastimes such as gardening, cooking, and textile crafts, have proliferated. A host of online communication tools help promote in-person gatherings[1] through social networking tools, discussion forums, and blogs. While these online resources extend pre-digital means of disseminating craft knowledge, such practices cannot be achieved solely online. Just like hammering a nail, muscular effort and dexterity are still unavoidable elements of making objects by hand. These new technologies prompt us to ask: *How and why do people integrate IT into leisure handwork activities?*

This paper explores the interplay between digital and hand tools in leisure handwork to examine the incorporation of new tools and materials. It describes an in-depth, observational study of two handwork groups: knitters and gardeners. We compared these activities (instead of, say, cooking and car repair) because both are extremely common leisure pastimes that require long term commitment to a single project or goal, have significant participation in online support forums, yet produce very different kinds of activities.

Studies of contemporary leisure handwork have examined both instructional [31] and creative [33] online activity. However, these studies often treat newer digital tools separately from traditional "hand tools." This paper combines the two in order to inform and inspire the design of computational tools that are sensitive to the diverse material practices of handwork.

CHI 2011, May 7–12, 2011, Vancouver, BC, Canada.

Fig 1. Community gardener cuts flowers as a gift.

BACKGROUND

At its simplest, "handwork" refers to manual manipulation of material objects by hands or hand-driven tools [6]. Historically, craft scholarship has treated handwork as a product of an individual's reflective consciousness and manual dexterity [1]. The processes of handwork often seem richly *embodied,* bridging mind and senses through effortful

† Authors are listed in alphabetical order.

1 Several craft & DIY social networking sites (e.g., Instructables.com, Ravelry.com) launched between 2005 and 2007, as did the social gardening site MyFolia.com.

physical manipulation [6]. Handwork processes often feel pleasurably tangible, stimulating multiple senses at once. Manual production involves accepting uncertainty and the 'thrill of avoiding failure' [6, 24] – unlike the predictable replication of "idealized" [24] forms desired by industrial production. The outcomes of handwork rely upon bodily skill [29]: trained senses, informed judgment, manual dexterity. Beginners and experts differ noticeably. Finally, handwork demands attention. With no mechanically automated processes, projects require consistent human care to make progress. Thus, despite its name, "handwork" almost always requires the full use of the human body.

Leisure handwork touches on questions of embodiment that have lately preoccupied human-computer interaction research, such as *thinking through doing, performance, visibility of collaborative tools, risks and uncertainty in physical co-presence,* and *thickness of practice* [14]. As an everyday hobby, leisure handwork also focuses attention the pleasures of hard work under the right circumstances (e.g., cooking, [10]). While a popular object of online discussion [16], handwork can also challenge our assumptions about what digital technologies should do [20].

Studies of handwork and digital technology

Studies of contemporary handwork have largely pursued three themes. First, many scholars have explored the relationship of human skill and effort to automation. Proponents of "traditional" handwork often focus on survival and popularity in the face of new technologies [12, 16, 20, 33]. Handwork often appears as an example of cultural heritage: the durability of shared memories in material objects. For example, the public exhibition of traditionally patterned African-American quilts can turn the quilts into sites of nostalgia, celebration, and defiance [28]. Emphasis on handwork's survival can take a moral tone, praising individual "makers" and "how people consume and interpret the handmade" [17]. While some argue that the conduct of skilled handwork exists in opposition to information work [6, 29], others celebrate the social and economic opportunities provided by the introduction of new communication technologies to otherwise isolated groups [17, 21].

Second, a small but rich literature explores the use of digital tools for sharing instructions, illustrations, and handwork-related messages. Online groups share expertise, exchanged feedback, and form a respected audience in which people present themselves as skilled, creative artisans [12, 32]. Wood et al. [34] explored the creation of online video resources for "bridging the gap" between novice and expert craft practitioners. Others address motivations for online craft activity [16]. These studies largely emphasize how participation in online groups recreates and extends interactions present in pre-digital counterparts.

A third area of literature follows the contestation of "originality" and "creativity" as valued qualities in handmade objects. Pre-industrial handwork groups often shared patterns, colors, and techniques [18]. Modern notions of personal authorship and unique creative identities devalued such collective aesthetics [1]. After the advent of the Internet, research has studied the struggle of both online [12, 16, 33] and co-located [13] handwork groups to evaluate personal skill when myriads of handwork patterns, examples, and tutorials are widely available online.

In terms of methods, however, these studies share one characteristic: they study online handwork social groups and co-located handwork social groups separately (e.g. [12]). There has been little attention thus far to the integration of IT into handwork-centered groups.

TWO STUDIES OF HANDWORK

We performed an in-depth, observational study of knitting circles and gardening groups for three central reasons. First, these two forms of handwork share several features that help us explore handwork and embodied action: both are sites of sensory interaction that cannot fully take place online. They rely on manual skill and dexterity that affect quality and aesthetic detail; and they both require learning to manipulate a diverse set of materials and hand tools. Second, the knitting circle and the community garden have very different characteristic activities that shed light on how people integrate a range of materials and tools. Third, each activity has begun to involve digital information technologies (social networking sites, discussion forms, email) in the coordination of their work. As we will see, these qualities let us consider how people work out relationships to IT through embodied interactions with material.

Method

Forty-six participants (13 gardeners; 33 knitters) were recruited through emails to knitting and gardening mailing lists, posts on Ravelry.com (a social networking site for knitting), and in-person recruitment at knitting circles and gardens. By sampling from handworkers who use online tools, we aimed to ensure we observed online activity, in-person social interaction, and the use of traditional hand tools. There were almost equal numbers of men and women among the gardeners, though all but three knitters were female. Participants ranged in age from early 20s to mid 80s, though most were in their 30s. They varied widely in expertise and orientation: from an award-winning dahlia grower to a "newbie" knitter still struggling with a basic sockinette stitch. They were largely middle income, and most had college degrees. Occupations included software engineer, orchid grower, retired state employee, comic book illustrator, teacher, and nurse.

Our approach to fieldwork drew from interpretive design strategies, such as generative scenarios [3]. During interviews, both knitters and gardeners were asked to imagine integrating an experimental technology into their handwork practice. In this way, we hoped to prompt reconsideration of taken-for-granted technologies (such as automatic irrigation, or digital cameras) by confronting participants with actual experimental technologies currently in development. Thirteen of the knitting interviews were conducted in context of initial field trials with Spyn [27], an experimental tool for annotating knitted objects with data about their creation. The garden interviews included a pre-scripted verbal presentation of two technology scenarios ready aloud by the interviewer. The first concerned a familiar technological situation: installing an automated watering system in their garden plot. The second was deliberately provocative: a speculative proposal for a "gardening robot" (based on current robotics agendas for agriculture [15]) that could perfectly perform monotonous physical chores, such as weeding. Introducing an experimental object (Spyn) and provocative gardening scenarios was intended to promote reflection on the implications of new digital tools for existing notions of effort, skill, and learning.

Interviews lasted approximately one to two hours and took place in a variety of locations: 29 at knitting locations (cafes or homes), four over instant messenger with remote participants (in Holland, Britain, Canada, and the Northeast United States), five at "Hillside Garden,"[2] eight at six other gardens, and one with a park volunteer in his park. Three of the interviews were with group coordinators or other group leaders. Our interview questions focused on the activities, and tools supporting established knitting and gardening practices. We also asked about the motivations for handwork activity, the discovery and use of online resources, and participation in social activities around handwork.

Interviews were complemented by participant observation over three months at monthly park workdays, four knitting circles, and other garden and knitting group events, including textual analysis of a year of park mailing list messages.

Relevant interviews and fieldwork were reviewed and transcribed by the authors; the authors met frequently to discuss the material and draw out relevant themes. The themes were iteratively revisited and revised based on discussions. The notes and transcripts were then organized and recoded based on these themes and emergent theoretical frames.

MAKING HANDWORK MEANINGFUL

Participants' projects, such as making sweaters or caring for a rosebush, often required continuing human effort and attention over months and years. In the moment, tasks such as tatting lace or plant pruning plants often required careful placement of hands and delicacy of touch. For this reason, many participants saw handwork as a healthy complement to office work, like physical exercise or meditation.

Korelle (gardener): As much as I love the city, there are some times when I need to get out, or I want a little retreat in the woods or you know something like that. And I think having a garden really helps.

Knitters also described their rhythmic motion as "therapeutic" and "meditative." For three knitters, knitting was a "direct replacement" for smoking. "*It slows me down,*" Rebecca explained. But working with plants and fibers, as we expected, resulted in different patterns of engagement over time.

Knitting does not require a specific time commitment: projects progressed intermittently or in long or short stretches, as the knitter desired. Like idly puttering (or pottering) [30] in homes, periods of knitting were often *residual* —time leftover from other tasks and often unplanned [36]. Knitting often takes place while attention is elsewhere —at meetings or while watching television. It is not tied to a specific place: people knit at home, while waiting for transit, en route, or in organized "knitting circles" that provide support and companionship while knitters worked on individual projects. Knitting, in this way, differs from other types of handwork (e.g., pottery or wood working) in what sociologist Eviatar Zerubavel calls *temporal flexibility* [36]. For Rebecca, a librarian, knitting during boring work meetings reinforces an unstructured, uncalculated sense of time. "*I can take a year or two or a week or two depending.*"

Gardening is far less flexible. Rooted in particular places and yearly cycles, it exhibits what Zerubavel calls *temporal symmetry* [36]. Gardeners cannot rush their harvests; they follow the seasons and the times of plant germination. After following directions for preparing soil, sowing seeds and watering, gardeners wait for visible results – sometimes over weeks and months. And unlike textiles, gardens could not be left untended for long. Summertime garden visits could last more than an hour — so gardeners, unlike knitters, had to free time from work or family responsibilities.

Through observing, manipulating, and reacting to handwork materials, participants developed long term relationships with the people and things around them. Knitting and gardening, of course, rely on different materials: plants and soil make different demands on humans than yarn and needles. So it is unsurprising that knitting and gardening follow markedly different spatial and temporal patterns. However, we found striking similarities in how knitters and gardeners explained why they did what they did.

Sensory sensitivity

Gardeners often mentioned the importance of putting their "*hands in the soil,*" sometimes even lowering their face to the ground to smell it.

Dana (gardener): My college degree is that I was a biology major [...]. And when I worked, I worked in research labs, so I did experiments. <pauses> So I like doing experiments, and I like trying things. And in a way, my garden, I do a little bit of experimenting. You know, I observe what happens, what, you know <pauses> I just observe.

Noticing and interpreting changes in her plants was important to Dana's sense of accomplishment. The knowledge she sought was particular and situational—attending to the plants that grew well in her plot, or patch of land. Both knitters and gardeners described learning through "*experimentation*" and "*trial and error.*" Building knowledge was intimately tied to working with the conditions at hand.

The pleasures of handwork were often described in sensual and emotional terms: the "impressive" giant dahlias grown by Gerald; Ellie's "yummy" sock yarn; Korelle, who was

[2] This and all following names of individuals and locations are pseudonyms.

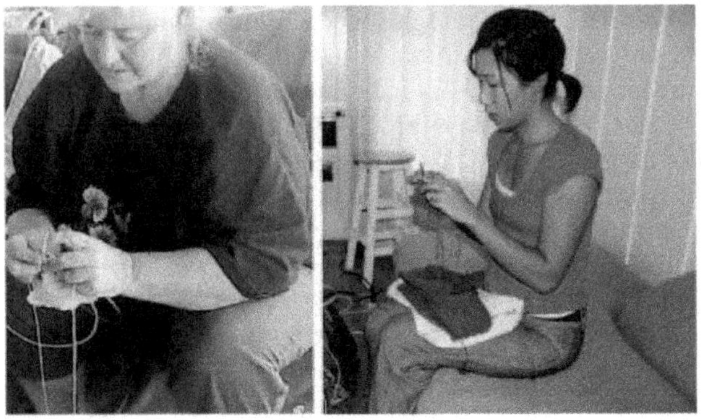

Fig 2. Knitting a washrag and baby sweater, two participants found difficult stitches require concentration.

"nuts for purple vegetables!" One gardener linked gardening to *feeling*, not thinking. She preferred not to plan her summer garden too far in advance of the growing season, explaining that gardening should be "*visceral, physical, intuitive*." For another knitter, the pursuit of sensorial novelty was almost acquisitive: "*You want to taste, try, touch the newest colors, mixes*." In this way, participants described their relationship to handwork in terms of "urges" or "hankerings" – bodily needs satisfied by physical action. Thus, as Karl, a longtime gardener, said, "*a virtual garden will do nothing for you*."

Virtuous effort

In many cases, however, participants felt that the difficulty and the effort required to produce anything "by hand" demonstrated honesty and responsibility.

Maple (knitter): It is an honest way to live, it is tangible. You can't lie with yarn. And you can't shortcut.

For Maple, manual labor itself produced virtue. Maple's motto was: "*Honest effort in, honest sweater out*." The honesty of the maker, she felt, was proven by the imperfections (and beauties) of the sweater, which revealed that it was made without mechanical shortcuts.

Gardeners' constant need to weed, water, mitigate pests, and prune was similarly described in moral terms. Iris, a graduate student, felt "*very guilty*" when school kept her away from her plot, shares with a less active older couple: "*I feel it's a moral responsibility to tend your garden*." Mark, a garden coordinator, condemned neglectful garden members: "*There's a concept of a 'flako,' and to me that's the worst thing you can be. When you commit to something, you do it*." Mark and Iris, like others, treated community gardening as a voluntary commitment both to fellow gardeners and to the plants themselves.

Cleverness

Learning to produce something by hand can be seen as a type of "special" knowledge or talent—"*the 'wow, clever me' aspect of the crafting thing*" as one knitter described. "*I doubt I would feel as clever if it on[l]y took 10 minutes*," another knitter explained.

Janus: In some ways I feel knitting is almost a secret society in that it is often only knitters who understand the work that has gone into producing something.

For Janus, part of gaining cleverness was learning how to read expertise from completed objects. It may be impossible, as Maple said, to "lie with yarn," but learning to decode the language of stitches and needles also took work.

Community gardeners similarly admired – or criticized – style and skill. With gardens packed into small urban lots, they worked near each other. As Iris said:

There's this kind of approach to gardening as a like reflection of you, like a profile. [...] Is it an artistic, creative endeavor? Is it a production line?

Longtime garden members like Iris could even deduce patterns of gifting or teaching between gardeners by observing the movements of a specific variety of flower, or a certain brand of plant trellis, from one plot to another.

Patience

At Hillside Garden, Mahon's chayote squash vine is flourishing in an explosion of leafy green. But Mahon is unhappy. It has produced no fruit for two years. He considers uprooting it, but decides to give the plant a "reprieve" for a year. As his fellow Hillside gardener Dana said, "Wasting one year on a tomato crop is not a bad thing."

Like Mahon and Dana, gardeners thought in terms of months and years. Korelle, for example, typically received seed catalogues in January, ordered by March, and planted in May. Knitting also demanded patience, but of a different sort: sustained dedication to a single task. Following a complicated shawl pattern demanded full attention. Unlike gardeners, knitters did not wait – they kept busy. As Rebecca said: "*It's not unusual for me to knit a whole sweater and take it apart, or to knit something really slowly*."

Handwork as resistance

Karl (gardener): There's not a lot of room for technology in the garden, and that's what makes it beautiful... It's like you just follow the simple laws of nature and let the insects do the work. It's like they're your employees, you know. I just think the garden should be a place where you can get away from technology.

Karl's comment illustrates a widespread, though not universal, framing of handwork in opposition to industrial technology. Knitters and gardeners often described their work as an act of resistance – to "speedy technology," "factory farms," or a "throw away culture." They often associated qualities they disliked, such as dependency, disconnection, and emotional emptiness, with IT.

Although they sought information online, participants actively discouraged the perception of "dependency" on digital information. "*It's not like [...] I have to look at Ravelry or else I don't know how to do something*," said another knitter. "*It's just a helpful little thing*."

Julia (knitter): I mean if the shit hit the fan—excuse my language—where would we be? If I didn't have an iPhone, could I make it around the city? Probably not... And it scares me sometimes. So things like gardening and knitting bring me a little bit back to earth, you know? Teaches you to appreciate how lazy we've become.

In contrast to the positive language of "effort" used to describe manual labor, Julia suggests that her phone makes her not just "lazy" but somehow adrift. She needs to be connected "back to earth." Notably, she introduces this complaint by imagining a world without her iPhone. The iPhone becomes a marker of dependence and vulnerability, something countered by growing food or making one's own clothes.

Similarly, Iris used images of disconnection in conjunction with an imagined introduction of digital technology. Standing amidst her bean plants, she rejected both the idea of installing automatic irrigation, and the speculative scenario of the "magic" gardening robot that could weed her plants for her. *"I don't want to be cut free,"* she said. *"I might want to be informed, but I want to have an engaged relationship."*

Common engineering heuristics recommend "designing out" dirty, difficult, or dangerous manual work [25]. But rather than happy liberation from dirty and boring labor, being "cut free" from watering and weeding implied to Iris an unwelcome separation from a desired relationship. To be "informed," however, might be acceptable. Iris' varying visions of being "informed," "engaged," and "cut free" suggests the complicated relationship between notions of disconnection, dependence, and human control implicated in deciding to automate versus searching online. To be "engaged" is to commit to the material details of making objects oneself – whether bean plants or alpaca yarn.

Some saw the importance in the knitting circle and the community garden in reinstating the "humanity" of face-to-face communication (as opposed to computer-mediated-communication). Yali, a knitter, described knitting circles as "real life," and online interactions as insufficient to let people "laugh out loud and be heard." Yali was not alone in feeling the importance of "being heard." Faced with the possibility of a "weeding robot" that could reduce the amount of time people spent in the garden, Gerald linked anxieties about computer-mediated communication to mechanical automation:

You don't have to have any emotion in an email, or in an Evite, or texting – they don't know if you're pissed off or whatever. When you actually speak to people, it's different. So one... I don't see how [robots] would work in this garden and two, I would vote against anything robotic here.

Earlier, Gerald had praised the garden's email list – which he said made the garden "work." Yet with the introduction of the magic garden robot scenario, the reliance on email begins to trouble him. These common scenarios of technology introduction or disappearance often spurred reconsideration of previously taken-for-granted digital technologies. Reconsidering accepted technologies often led participants to a discussion of loss: of Julia's navigational skill, or Gerald's feeling of emotional connection. These losses are rendered as a disconnection from the traditional social and material relationships produced in handwork. In turn, participation in knitting circles or community gardens becomes a way to reinstate lost skills and emotions.

Karl's metaphorical exile of "technology" to *outside* the garden, or Yali's placement of "real life" *within* the knitting circle suggests at the very least ambivalence about the compatibility of some familiar online activities within handwork activities. If designers of computational tools for handwork wish to honor the priorities of handworkers like Karl, Yali, Julia, and Gerald, the positioning of handwork as resistance to certain forms of "technology" seems to present a dilemma. Yet, as we will see in the next section, participants routinely interwove digital technologies (such as email lists and websites) into handwork projects.

INTEGRATING INFORMATION TECHNOLOGY

Discussions of activities that entwine both digital tools and human bodies often fall back on an understood shorthand terminology of "digital" or "virtual" versus "physical" or "in-person" actions. The handwork groups studied accomplished their activities both in-person and online, and through software and hand-tools. We have addressed the defining of handwork in opposition to varying types of "technology." Participants understood that distinction as meaningful while still relying on digital tools.

Working with materials

The integration of screen-based digital information into tasks requiring full attention and two hands was a prominent feature of handwork experience (see Fig 1). Participants usually engaged with certain websites or applications *purposefully*, often to accomplish bounded tasks and interventions with material.

Learning how

Iris (gardener): It is very precise. Information is very important in gardening. It's not hazy. I mean, you gotta know – you have to plant this week.

Iris and other gardeners wanted detailed knowledge of the local garden environment: weather patterns, soil conditions, even typical pest infestations. But few gardeners in this study regularly visited gardening websites. One garden kept a few faded, ragged paper print-outs of "how to" web pages in their greenhouse. Nor did we see any obvious computer equipment in gardens. Instead, specific projects – such as growing tobacco or okra – prompted initial online information searches. Later, gardeners might return to a website to cope with a specific problem, such as a failing rosebush. Some occasionally visited the blog of a local gardening journalist.

The problem was that instructions online might not match local soil and weather conditions. Instead, gardeners in the variable climates of the Bay Area (fog, sun, and mixture) adapted instructions by closely observing plants and reasoning about what they saw. Most gardeners tried to solve their problems through observation, with only rare appeals to help from senior members of their garden.

Several knitters, on the other hand, performed online searches alongside handwork. Executing intricate patterns and unfamiliar stitches pulled them back multiple times an hour to a given online reference – occasionally staring at the screen in between concentrating on their hands. Expert knitters make hundreds of stitches per hour. Replicating knitting patterns can mean counting every single stitch. Depending on the pattern, a second's loss of attention could lead to a calculation mistake undermining days of work. These different temporal and spatial patterns of online instruction use occurred in the context of the material relationships participants had with the objects they made.

Documenting sensory interactions

For many, verbally describing color, pattern alterations, and garment fit was difficult. Knitters often resorted to associative metaphors such as "scrumptious" or "luscious" yarns. Gardeners might praise a flower as "intense," or criticize a tomato that "tastes like nothing." Photographs often served to document and convey these tangible attributes. Several knitters used annotated digital images to manage large collections of yarns, and information about unfinished work and pattern alterations. All the gardeners preserved seeds in bundles of paper seed packets, sometimes brought with them to their gardens to share. Illustrated with images of mature plants (often photographs) and pre-printed with cultivation instructions, the commercially produced paper packets performed much the same function as knitters' annotated digital images.

Working with people

As contemporary handworkers, knitters and gardeners used digital means to produce and maintain lasting relationships with other people (as suggested by previous studies, e.g. [13,23]). But the two groups had some differences.

Creating and crossing group boundaries

When Ellie "got a hankering" to knit, she recalls, she looked online for a "Chicks with Sticks" meeting. Without a specific desire for education or friendship, she just wanted to talk about knitting. Eventually, she got a part-time position at a knitting store. While working, she laughingly tells a patron whose daughter, a "fourth-generation knitter," was returning from college: "She's going to be putting in a couple hours here because she needs to get in touch with the yarn!"

"Getting in touch with the yarn" means more than doing some shopping. It also entails participating in a local group of knitters. In working at the shop, coordinating with groups on Ravelry.com, and continuing attendance at a knitting circle, Ellie developed object- and technique-focused relationships with an evolving group of knitters. Handwork was thus "object-oriented": conversation revolved around techniques and aesthetic choices, and participants described other people largely through reference to the type of objects they made and how they produced them. She did not treat this "community" as a tightly-knit, well-bounded entity. Rather, people moved in and out of Ellie's daily life, online and offline, as she and they pursued engaged relationships with the yarn.

For many gardeners, the sight of a tidy and well-tended garden was the "community" they desired:

Mark (garden coordinator): You don't ever have to see [other gardeners]. If gnomes or leprechauns are doing the work in the middle of the night, we don't care.

Mark sends gardeners with weedy, dried-out plots a warning email and a letter. If two weeks pass without visible improvements, Mark expels them from the community garden. This happens once or twice a year. Most participants felt they did not permanently "own" their plots; they described themselves as temporarily "renting."

So the word "community garden," as geographer and community garden coordinator Mary Beth Pudup writes [23], may be less accurate than "organized gardening projects." For many community gardeners, membership did not imply communal values. Many participants reported only rarely talking in-person to fellow garden members. Dana, for example, spends ten or more hours each week in the summertime at Hillside, but rarely speaks to fellow gardeners. Korelle, uncomfortable at quarrelsome in-person meetings, prefers email discussions for decision-making. Mary, during her interview, was still upset about a recent fight that had split the garden into two camps. And Iris knew the names of only three of the more than 30 other garden members.

However, unlike the knitting groups, the gardening groups also used digital tools to expand the sphere of their influence outside the boundaries of personal projects. For the coordinator of Corona Gardens, two small community spaces in a neighborhood notorious for violence and poverty, the purpose of the garden blog and email list is not just to communicate with garden members. They all live on the same block, and see each other in-person frequently. Another purpose is to share uplifting "good news" about the garden and the neighborhood with outsiders – to rally support for the garden and local civic activism outside of their small group of neighbor-gardeners. The blog thus serves not as a way to facilitate individual relationships to the garden but rather as collective action directed at political and economic change in the garden's vicinity.

Similarly, only half of the 108 messages to the park volunteer mailing list in 2009 concerned group activities. The rest almost exclusively asked for participation in neighborhood urban planning— from "town hall" meetings on the renovation of a local hospital to soliciting volunteers for a meeting with the mayor about urban green space concerns.

Knitting and gardening groups used similar tools to find and maintain membership in handwork groups. However, the groups generally used those tools to pursue different types of membership. Membership in knitting groups was "object-oriented," with conversations revolving around personal techniques and aesthetics, as well as the organization of temporally coordinated individual activities. Membership in gardening groups was "place-oriented," revolving around enforcing plant upkeep responsibilities and inviting collective commitment to the surrounding neighborhoods.

Coordinating activities

For almost every community garden studied, as well as the park volunteers, garden upkeep was coordinated mainly through email. Like Mark, many gardeners cared more about managing chore schedules and shared garden supplies than teaching techniques or building friendships.

Gerald: Before email, how did this garden work? We didn't use to see each other, but now, with email, we talk to each other fairly regularly.

For Gerald, email "talk" easily replaced in-person conversation. What it often meant to have a garden "work" also seemed place-oriented: to have fertilizer purchased, common areas cleaned, and vandalism repaired. It was not friendship or even liking.

Email contact was important because many garden members had very different routines. Retirees and students came when they chose, often during weekdays; working people and families on weekends. Emails shared news, scheduled chores, reported task completion, or helped make urgent decisions. Gardeners feared – often from experience at other gardens – that without active recruitment to group "work days" their gardens would turn into weed-filled empty lots. For example, the park mailing list had a membership of 65 – but only about five people regularly showed up for the monthly park gardening days.

While knitters coordinate joint activities less frequently, several used online networking sites (Ravelry.com in particular) to arrange specific events. *Yarn Swaps* (yarn exchanges) and *Knit-Alongs* (in which a group of knitters follow the same pattern at the same time) were common prompts for online interaction. Knitters posted messages Ravelry.com forums to recruit other knitters to try out and evaluate new or altered patterns. Online groups organized participation in mass events ("Stitches West 2010") or themed projects ("10 Shawls in 2010"). Digital tools thus helped to initiate and coordinate communal activities at the same time, if not the same place.

Documenting and sharing work

Both knitters and gardeners used digital media to record their progress and distribute their artifacts to others. As we discussed earlier, for those who could interpret them, effortful artifacts such as textiles and plants acted as entry tickets to the "secret society" of expertise. For both knitters and gardeners, photography was one way to find more people to appreciate their skill.

For some knitters, sharing their work online seemed prompted by feelings of cleverness. Thus posting documentation took place at varying intervals of time —"*in fits and spurts*" based on events within the project:

Louise (knitter): I finish a project and I remember to take a picture and I remember to put it up.

Many, like Louise, valued their participation in websites such as Ravelry, but visited the sites only at critical moments during the project. Personal blogs and online forums provided knitters and gardeners with resources to "*showcase*" their ongoing handwork activities. Members of Ravelry.com used online means to echo traditional knitting circle interactions. They posted "*before and after*" photos of completed projects; asked and gave advice about choosing patterns, techniques, or yarns; and kept track of ongoing, finished or disregarded projects.

As such, digital photographs allowed knitters to "keep" sweaters they had already given as gifts, and gardeners to preserve ephemeral flowers. Those photographs then served as "calling cards" showcasing aesthetic taste and handwork skill — as with one gardener, whose first email to an author included multiple unasked-for plant photographs. Evocative images also cemented bonds with relatives and friends. Gerald emailed photographs of his prized dahlias "almost weekly" to family who lived far away. He had promised flowers to his niece for her wedding bouquet, and wanted her to see them grow. Visually rich digital imagery conveyed the multisensory pleasures of handwork (texture, pattern, color), while making unique, ephemeral, or bulky goods more portable and durable.

DESIGNING FOR HANDWORK TEXTURES

As discussed earlier in this paper, studies of handwork often conceptually and methodologically separate "digital" activities and groups from "physical" ones. While this scholarly separation does seem to echo participants' presentation of handwork as separate from "technology," it presents a dilemma for the design of new kinds of digital handwork tools. On the one hand, participants' stated beliefs suggest resistance to new digital or machine tools. On the other hand, we witnessed extensive integration of both hand-tools and software to establish and sustain a feeling of connection with other people and the material objects of their handwork practice. The integration of online and offline tools supports the physical, emotional and social relationships that make handwork meaningful. These relationships unfold through embodied commitments to handwork.

Given this integration, "digital" and "physical" may not be the most salient conceptual and methodological framework for studying handwork. Indeed, recent work by STS scholars such as Jean-François Blanchette [4] has problematized distinctions between the *material* and *immaterial*, arguing that *digital material*—from the application interface to the network stack—is structured by a host of functional constraints. Following this analytic perspective, we found that analyzing the "digital" in isolation from the "physical" does not adequately describe the significance people find in handwork, and thus can unnecessarily limit the scope of design exploration. We propose *studying handwork activities as unified pursuits that exhibit textures of tool use.*

The concept of *texture* has recently been offered in multiple disciplines as a metaphor for the processes and products of design and creative practice. Media scholar Erica Robles and interaction designer Michael Wiberg [26] recently proposed the term *texture* as a way to describe the connection between traditional architectural materials and digital interfaces for interaction design, as well as surface and compositional form. They define texture as "the feel, appearance, or consistency of a surface"—that which allows us to experience an environment as a "meaningful whole." A texture, then, is the unified effect of combining different materials.

Anthropologist Tim Ingold describes the experienced world as an ever-changing texture [11]. Making, for Ingold, "is a practice of weaving." The notion of a finished object is much less important than the "textility" or "tactile and sensuous knowledge" with which artists and makers improvise reactions to the changing world. Ingold's emphasis on making as a process of embodied knowledge unfolding through improvisational actions resonates strongly with our observations of knitters and gardeners. We extend this design metaphor to describe handwork as a "meaningful whole" for participants. Its importance emerges from a series of interactions with different kinds of groups, spaces, materials, and tools.

Drawing on our fieldwork, we describe some characteristically patterned engagements with the materials of handwork that produce knitting and gardening as distinctively textured activities.

Extending

One of the most visible patterns of engagement is that of extension, in which direct, embodied handwork interactions occur as the handworkers attend to other stimuli, such as having a friend read a book aloud to a knitting circle or watching television while knitting. These *extensions* of knitting mediated knitters' everyday interactions with needles and yarn. By contrast, gardeners in this study did not tend to accompany planting, weeding, and watering with additional sensory interactions. Some gardeners listened to gardening advice radio shows in their homes, but none brought music players, televisions or reading material to the garden itself; few brought friends or cell phones. For many, even imagining installing a computer screen in the garden was unacceptable. The absence or presence of extending behaviors follows the differences we found between the rhythms of knitting and gardening activities: gardening required its own demarcated spaces and times, while knitting was more flexible.

Designing for extension

Controlling the extension of sensory activities was critical to our participants' sense of engagement. As such, it presents new opportunities for creative combinations – or isolation. Tools to engage these extensions might consider the role of ritual in handwork processes. Many gardeners, like Karl, insisted upon the garden as a space removed from mass media, whereas many knitters took pleasure in knitting during their favorite television shows. Extension also suggests possibilities for improvisational creativity. Accompanying media (like podcasts) suggest new projects and techniques at the moment in which handworkers are already engaged in creative labor. Experimental tools, such as Spyn [27], enable knitters to layer puzzles or stories onto handwork while knitting. The experience of gardeners suggests a challenge to designers: how might devices and services engage with handworkers according to their own rhythms? How might "just in time" creative prompts enable new meaningful ways of the hand?

Interjecting

Gerald gardens with his partner, Daniel. When Daniel sees the first spring bud, he immediately calls Gerald on his mobile phone. "It's a bud, it's a bud," exclaims Gerald, imitating Daniel's excited phone calls. "It's like a baby's coming."

Immediate needs for information or coordination prompt brief switches from one activity (such as watering plants) to another (such as talking to a friend on the phone). Carried in pockets or bags, digital phones and cameras were routinely taken to the garden. Used briefly, they were not rejected by gardeners as alien "technology." When Daniel called Gerald, or when Louise snapped a picture to document a knitting project, they *interjected* a tool into an activity – then withdrew it. *Interjection* involves the brief use of an external tool (sometimes a camera or mobile phone, other times a website, book, or magazine) during handwork activity. *Interjection* also takes place when an email message, tweet, or conversation briefly focuses attention on handwork; and then the handworker returns to non-handwork activities. Here it is the bounded, momentary character of the activity that matters. Unlike extension, interjection is experienced as a departure from one activity to focus on another.

Designing for interjection

New tools might enable a range of purposeful interjections into handwork activity. For example, how else might Gerald learn about the new buds in the garden besides getting a phone call from Daniel? Interjections could involve not only getting information but also fulfilling participants' desires to connect with a recipient or keep someone informed of their progress. The Botanicalls DIY soil moisture sensor[3] is a customizable kit that helps home gardeners remember to water their plants by sending Twitter messages when the soil is dry. Botanicalls digitally *interjects* brief plant reminders into non-gardening places and times. It does not automate watering; instead, it recalls potentially neglectful, inexpert gardeners back to their plants. New tools for beginners as well as experts might produce brief yet satisfying connections with people and material that help keep handworkers connected to the objects of their craft – even when the objects are far away.

3 http://www.botanicalls.com/

Segmenting

Kyla had many worries. Among them was her alcohol consumption, for which she was getting weekly counseling. "It is a little war with myself about being perfect and not being good enough," she explained. "It's weird. I can kind of feel it physically in me. I can kind of feel it in this one [knitting] project. It's not going well. I don't know how to resolve that feeling." She decided to digitally document a sweater she had made and given to her son some time ago. Unlike her current knitting, this sweater was "perfect."

The metaphor of *segmenting* suggests that activities affecting the objects of handwork can take independent trajectories. Though Kyla's "perfect" sweater was long completed, she was able to repurpose digital documentation of its making to recapture a feeling of mastery – and then circulate it to her online audience. Documentation and production efforts, separated widely in space and time, created both handwork objects and human relationships. Recall Gerald's weekly email exchanges with his niece, as she plans her wedding and he sends her images of the flowers for her bouquet. Knitters often posted documentation of knitting projects to Ravelry.com long after they had been completed and given away as gifts. The notion of segmenting suggests that handwork activities need not be continuous – and that they take place within relationships of pride, love, and regret.

Designing for segmentation

We have discussed how the activities of documentation and knitting can *segment* time between different types of activities and materials. The LilyPad Arduino integrates computation into sewing projects [5] through a similar process of *segmentation*. Programming the LilyPad and hand attaching it to fabric *segment* time between laptop and textile. As with the gardeners who moved between group email lists and plant care, we can think of LilyPad users as dividing their time between different genres of activity: planning and writing code, designing textile patterns and stitching them, looking for instructions and documenting outcomes. Designing for segmentation can help object relationships develop in "fits and spurts" over space and time.

Handwork texturing as aesthetic experience

Extending, *interjecting*, and *segmenting* describe characteristic interwoven patterns of tool use that further develop Wright et al's [35] notion of aesthetic experience as "*an engagement of a concerned, feeling, self acting with and through materials and tools*." Within handwork, emotional and sensory engagements are critical to how people know, see, and act. The unfolding of handwork activity creates what McCarthy and Wright [19] might call the *tensions* and *cumulative patterns* of aesthetic experience. Textures are thus cumulative: they build up as handwork relationships temporally unfold. Textures can also be built upon *tension*, as we saw in Gerald's attachment to the email list that makes the garden efficiently "work," and his fear of losing the emotional connection of face-to-face contact. We can think of the texturing of handwork as the creation of aesthetic life experiences.

Treating handwork as a textured whole undermines the rationale for a methodological or conceptual binary opposition of digital and physical interactions within handwork. It can also prompt productive exploration of the possibilities for supporting the aesthetic experience of handworkers. Designers cannot assume constant use or consistent adoption of new technologies and tools. Handwork tool use, whether of software or hand tools, instead weaves into and between ongoing periods of non-use. How can we design tools that respond to the long cycles and rhythms of inactivity, contemplation, and anticipation? The interplay not just between different kinds of tool use, but also between modes of engagement and disengagement, and intensity and calm, become important resources for design.

CONCLUSION

As Malcolm McCullough has suggested,

We must look very closely at craft. As part of developing more engaging technology, as well as developing a more receptive attitude toward new opportunities raised by technology, we must understand what matters in traditional notions of practical, form-giving work" ([20]:19).

Participants described their handwork as part of an interpretive framework opposing manual aspects of handwork to technologies such as email and robotics. They valued the development of patience, cleverness, effort, and sensory sensitivity through sustained engagements with handmade objects, often in handwork groups. They frequently defined their values in contrast to negative characteristics associated with "technology" – in particular, notions of dependency, disconnection, and emotional absence.

Yet overall, knitting and gardening relied upon many different tools and interactions, digital tools among them. By tracing the relationships to IT and hand tools enacted during handwork, we witnessed the interweaving of digital technologies with traditional hand-manipulated tools to build and sustain these significant relationships. We propose three metaphors of *extension, interjecting,* and *segmenting* as part of a principled design agenda for handwork and other domestic leisure practices. Platforms such as the LilyPad Arduino exemplify how engagement with digital tools designed for handwork can change people's relationships to the materiality of the objects they make.

However, while handwork is an exciting area for design exploration and engagement, it presents some critical questions to designers. How might a professional gardener's pursuits differ from our subjects? What obstacles might a carpenter or car repair technician encounter while working with email? Engaging with additional types of handwork could suggest different textures of tool use that present new challenges. In following handwork from online to hands-on interactions with people and materials, we have tried to convey the importance of embodied practice to understanding what makes different types of handwork meaningful sites of group membership, affective attachment, and skill production.

ACKNOWLEDGMENTS

We thank our participants, reviewers, and colleagues. This research was funded by a National Foundation Graduate Fellowship and an Intel Corporation PhD Fellowship.

REFERENCES

1. Adamson, G. 2008. *Thinking Through Craft.* Oxford: Berg.
2. Armstrong, A. and Hagel, J. 2000. The Real Value of Online Communities. In *Knowledge and Communities*. Eds. Lesser E.L., et al. Newton, MA: Butterworth-Heinemann.
3. Bødker, S. 2000. Scenarios in user-centred design--setting the stage for reflection and action. *Interacting with Computers*. 13(1): 61-75.
4. Blanchette, J.-F. A Material History of Bits. (in preparation). Retrieved on January 10, 2011 from http://polaris.gseis.ucla.edu/blanchette/papers/materiality.pdf.
5. Buechley, L. and Hill, B. M. 2010. LilyPad in the wild: how hardware's long tail is supporting new engineering and design communities. In *Proc. DIS '10*. ACM Press, 199-207.
6. Crawford, M.B. 2009. *Shop Class as Soulcraft: An Inquiry into the Value of Work.* London: Penguin Press.
7. Dormer, P. 1997. The language and practical philosophy of craft. In *The Culture of Craft*, P. Dormer (ed.). Manchester: Manchester U P.
8. Francis M. and Hester R.T. 1990. The Garden as Idea, Place, Action. Pp 7-20 in *The Meaning of Gardens.* Eds. M. Francis and R.T. Hester. Cambridge, MA: The MIT Press.
9. Greenhalgh, P. 1997. The language and practical philosophy of craft. In *The Culture of Craft.* Ed. P. Dormer. Manchester, UK: Manchester University Press.
10. Grimes, A. and Harper, R. 2008. Celebratory Technology: New Directions for Food Research in HCI. In *Proc. CHI 2008*. ACM Press, 467-476.
11. Ingold, T. 2010. The textility of making. *Cambridge Journal of Economics*. 34(1): 91-102.
12. Johnson, J. S., H*awley, J. 2004.* Technology's impact on creative traditions: Pieceful co-exist*ence in quilting. Clothing and Textiles Research Journal,* 22(1/2), 69-78.
13. Johnson, J. S., Wilson L. E. 2005. "It Says You Really Care": Motivational Factors of Contemporary Female Handcrafters. *Clothing and Textiles Research Journal.*
14. Klemmer, S.R., Hartmann, B. and Takayama, L. 2006. How bodies matter: five themes for interaction design. In *Proc. DIS '06*. ACM Press, 140-149.
15. Kitchen, N.R. 2008. Emerging technologies for real-time and integrated agriculture decisions. *Computers and Electronics in Agriculture.* 61(1): 1-3.
16. Kuznetsov, S. and Paulos, E. 2010. Rise of the Expert Amateur: DIY Projects, Communities, and Cultures. In *Proc. NordiCHI '10*. ACM Press, 295-304.
17. Levine, F. and Heimerl, C. *Handmade Nation: The Rise of DIY, Art, Craft, and Design.* Princeton, NJ: Princeton Architectural Press, 2008.
18. Lucie-Smith, E. 1983. *The story of craft: the craftsman's role in society.* Prentice Hall.
19. McCarthy, J. and Wright, P. 2004. *Technology as Experience.* Cambridge, MA: MIT Press.
20. McCullough, M. 1996. *Abstracting Craft: The Practiced Digital Hand.* Cambridge, MA: MIT Press.
21. Minahan, S., & Cox, J. W. 2007. Stitch' n bitch—Cyberferninism, a third place and the new materiality. *Journal of Material Culture*, 12(1): 5-21.
22. The National NeedleArts Association. 2007. The State of Specialty NeedleArts 2007: Executive Summary.
23. Pudup, M.B. 2008. It takes a garden: Cultivating citizen-subjects in organized garden projects. *Geoforum*. 39(3): 1228-1240.
24. Pye, D. *The nature and art of workmanship.* 1995. London: Herbert Press.
25. Repperger, D. and Phillips, C. 2009. The Human Role in Automation. In *Springer Handbook of Automation.* Ed. S.Y. Nof. Berlin: Springer-Verlag.
26. Robles, E. and Wiberg, M. Texturing the "Material Turn" in Interaction Design. In *Proc. TEI '10*. ACM Press, 137-144.
27. Rosner, D. K., Ryokai, K. 2009. Reflections on Craft: Probing the Creative Process of Everyday Knitters. In *Proc. C & C* '09. ACM Press, 195-204.
28. Scheper-Hughes, N. 2003. Anatomy of a Quilt: The Gees' Bend Freedom Quilting Bee. *Anthropology Today.* 19(4):15-21.
29. Sennett, R. 2008. *The Craftsman.* New Haven, CT: Yale University Press.
30. Taylor, A., Wyche, S. and Kaye, J. 2008. Pottering by design. In *Proc NordiCHI '08*. ACM Press, 363-372.
31. Torrey, C., Churchill, E., McDonald, D. 2009. Learning How: The Search for Craft Knowledge on the Internet. In *Proc. CHI'09*. ACM Press, 1371-1381.
32. Torrey, C., D. W. McDonald, B. N. Schilit and S. Bly. 2007. How-To Pages: Informal Systems of Expertise Sharing. In *Proc. ECSCW '07*. Springer, 391-410.
33. Turner-Rahman, G. 2008. Parallel Practices and the Dialectics of Open Creative Production. *Journal of Design History*. 22(4): 71-386.
34. Wood, N., Rust, C., and Horne, G. 2009. A Tacit Understanding: The Designer's Role in Capturing and Passing on the Skilled Knowledge of Master Craftsmen. *International Journal of Design* [Online] 3:3.
35. Wright, P., Wallace, J., and McCarthy, J. 2008. Aesthetics and experience-centred design *ACM TOCHI.* 15(4): 1-21.
36. Zerubavel, E. 1992. *Hidden Rhythm.* Berkeley, CA: U. of California P.

Persona Cases: A Technique for Grounding Personas

Shamal Faily
Oxford University Computing Laboratory
Wolfson Building, Parks Road, Oxford UK
shamal.faily@comlab.ox.ac.uk

Ivan Flechais
Oxford University Computing Laboratory
Wolfson Building, Parks Road, Oxford UK
ivan.flechais@comlab.ox.ac.uk

ABSTRACT

Personas are a popular technique in User-Centered Design, however their validity can be called into question. While the techniques used to developed personas and their integration with other design activities provide some measure of validity, a persona's legitimacy can be threatened by challenging its characteristics. This note presents Persona Cases: personas whose characteristics are both grounded in, and traceable to their originating source of empirical data. This approach builds on the premise that sense-making in qualitative data analysis is an argumentative activity, and aligns concepts associated with a Grounded Theory analysis with recent work on arguing the characteristics of personas. We illustrate this approach using a case study in the Critical Infrastructure Protection domain.

Author Keywords

Personas, Grounded Theory, Design Rationale, Critical Infrastructure Protection

ACM Classification Keywords

H.5.2 User Interfaces: User-centered design

General Terms

Design, Human Factors, Security

INTRODUCTION

Personas represent archetypical users, and embody their needs and goals [5]. Essentially, personas are behavioural specifications, embodying the salient characteristics of a class of stakeholders a design needs to serve. They were proposed as an antidote to the bias of software developers who, without explicit guidance about an unseen user community, may build systems appealing to their own interests. Yet, personas are a paradox. A behavioural specification of sorts, their most endearing characteristic is that they do *not* look like specifications; they have names, jobs, feelings, and goals they want to fulfil, sometimes irrespective of the purpose a system was designed for. But what happens when a stakeholder challenges a persona? A developer may be unhappy about some system feature which directly appeals to some aspect of a persona. One way the developer can argue his case is by refuting some aspect the persona, weakening its legitimacy, and calling into question other characteristics of the persona as well. Chapman & Milham argue that, as fictional artifacts, personas cannot be falsified and, therefore, disproved [4]. They further argue that appealing to the rigorous use of interviews and ethnographic research also fails to validate personas, as specific examples of data cannot be provided to prove their accuracy.

Although Chapman & Milham argue that interviews and ethnographic approaches are not sufficient to validate data-driven personas, these are considered necessary by the two dominant approaches for building personas. In the first of these approaches, behavioural patterns are identified based on how interviewees cluster around particular behavioural variables elicited from the empirical data [5]. In the second, factoids are culled from the empirical data, before a group-based affinity diagramming exercise is carried out to induce behavioural clusters [3]. In both cases, sense-making activities are used to induce behavioural clusters upon which narrative descriptions of personas are written.

The data analysis associated with affinity diagramming is analogous to the qualitative data analysis approaches used in social-science inquiry. A standard methodology used for such analysis is Grounded Theory [6]: an inductive research method driven by sensitising research questions. However, rather than culling factoids directly from data, Grounded Theory involves coding data transcripts to elicit concepts relating to these questions. Moreover, although both approaches induce emerging themes from data, Grounded Theory also involves drawing out relationships between thematic concepts, creating memos with insights from this analysis, and preparing papers describing the theory resulting from the analysis; Corbin et al. [6] suggest that this latter act of writing clarifies thinking and elucidates breaks in logic. Finally, Grounded Theory is also supported by Computer Aided Qualitative Data Analysis tools; these can manage large data-sets, and support theory development by managing codes, memos, and automatically visualising emerging conceptual relationships.

Faily & Fléchais demonstrated how Grounded Theory could be used to develop a theory from which personas were derived [7]. Although the validity of their personas was obtained by integrating them into the design of secure systems, the problem of validating personas remains. Even though the

Grounded Theory artifacts were available during the building of the personas, they were not once the personas were used in practice to elicit requirements in focus groups. This semantic gap between Grounded Theory artifacts and persona narratives became problematic when questions were raised about characteristics of one of the personas in this study; this subsequently led to the creation of a new persona.

Recent work [9] has examined how Toulmin's work on developing practical arguments [11] can be aligned with the characteristics of personas. This work suggests that a characteristic is analogous to a *claim* being made as part of an argument, and a proposition reflecting an assumption about this characteristic may act as *grounds* of evidence, or a *warrant*: a rule of inference describing how the grounds contribute to the claim. The origin of a warrant's assumption is the *backing* knowledge for believing the claim, and assumptions may also be used as *rebuttals*, which challenge the validity of the claim. Finally, a *modal qualifier* indicates the degree of certainty about the claim.

If treating a persona characteristic as a defensible argument reduces the gap between empirical data and personas, aligning these claims with the argumentative discourse associated with Grounded Theory models may close it. To this end, this note presents the *Persona Case:* a persona whose characteristics are both grounded in, and traceable to their originating source of empirical data. We present an overview of this technique, before illustrating how it was used in a case study. We conclude by discussing further findings from this work, and suggest further directions for research.

APPROACH

Our approach for developing Persona Cases is driven from a Grounded Theory model; this model constitutes a collection of thematic concepts, and a set of relationships between them. The model is induced using data elicited from interviews or ethnographic research. Our approach does not prescribe guidance for applying Grounded Theory, nor does it prescribe the use of any specific qualitative data analysis tool. Nevertheless, the use of a software tool with some form of visualisation support is important. In addition to helping identify related themes as analysis progresses, visual models open the analysis to scrutiny when the results of analysis are reviewed by other team members.

Step 1: Summarise propositions

The first stage involves identifying the most salient thematic concepts, and eliciting propositions associated with them. These concepts are selected based on the most grounded and networked concepts in the Grounded Theory model of core themes; these represent the key themes that the Persona Case being developed needs to explore. The propositions are based on the quotations associated with each of these selected themes. These propositions are factoids because while accepted as fact by the participants, these may not always be established. For example, the quotation: *"The worst thing that could happen on a sewage site is that it would flood something"* could be reworded as the proposition *"The worse case scenario on a sewage site is a flood"*.

Step 2: Argue characteristics

The next stage involves enumerating and arguing each relationship in the Grounded Theory model. This involves succinctly describing the claim (or claims) justifying each relationship; this claim represents a potential characteristic of a persona. To justify this characteristic, propositions are selected as its grounds or warrant, and the modal qualifier will be associated with this based on the analyst's confidence in this relationship. Propositions which may rebut this characteristic are also recorded here. Such a rebuttal might arise if there is debate or disagreement about some aspect of the Grounded Theory model. Also associated with each characteristic is the type of behaviour the characteristic represents; these types are based on behavioural variable types in [5], which will be one of Activities, Attitudes, Aptitudes, Motivations, or Skills.

Step 3: Write persona narratives

The final stage involves writing a supporting narrative for each section characterised by the behavioural variable types. This narrative should be commensurate with the elicited persona characteristics and, as such, act as supplemental validation of the personas; if a commensurate narrative cannot be written then the characteristics and propositions should be reviewed in line with the Grounded Theory model. There may be a number of reasons why a narrative cannot be written to be consistent with the elicited characteristics. One reason is that not all characteristics may be relevant because they cover poorly grounded themes, or the characteristics are not relevant to the context of analysis. In this case, it is reasonable to omit characteristics if incorporating them leads to the persona becoming more elastic. Another reason is that multiple personas may be needed to reflect the elicited persona characteristic. In this case, characteristics should be sorted into natural groupings using affinity diagrams; these characteristic groups will then form the basis of separate personas.

RESULTS

Case Study

Information security officers at Critical Infrastructure organisations need to contend with a drive for increased automation, decreasing budgets, ageing infrastructure, and the threat of terrorism. It is, however, a well known problem that situating security controls that users find unusable will lead to ignored or compromised security [2]. We undertook joint work with a UK water treatment company to develop an information security policy to provide guidance to staff working at water treatment plants. To aid in this process, personas were used to voice their concerns during the development and revision of the policy. One of these personas, Barry, was pre-developed and represented a roaming technician working within a particular geographic region associated with a plant; the process for developing Barry is described in [7].

Using the Persona Case technique, a second persona was developed, Rick, to represent a plant operator. We visited 4 different water-treatment works and held in-situ interviews with plant operators and related stakeholders; interview questions dealt with the nature of work undertaken, including

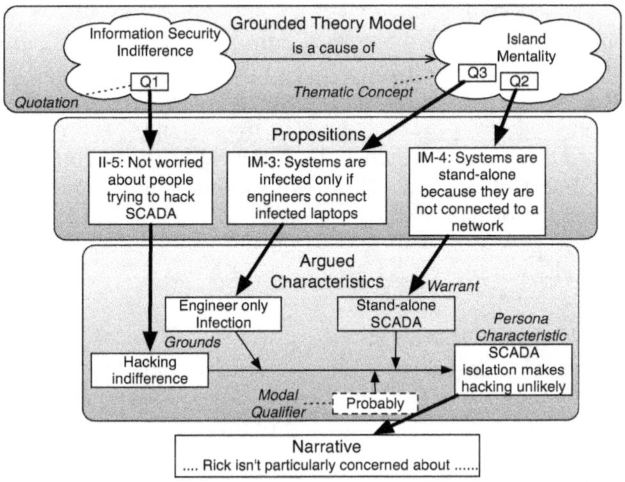

Figure 1. Contribution of Grounded Theory to Personas

what plant operators were responsible for, who they worked with, and how they obtained help if necessary. Plant operators were also asked about important artifacts and activities, and the sort of problems they often face. In total, 6 interviews were held, and each interview lasted approximately an hour.

Following the interviews, the transcripts were subject to a Grounded Theory analysis; this analysis was supported by the ATLAS.ti software tool [10]. Following an exercise of open and axial coding, 243 quotations were associated with approximately 200 initial thematic concepts; these concepts were eventually refined down to 61. Conceptual relationships were visually modelled in one central model (containing the most networked and grounded concepts), and 4 submodels. These were based on process impact, work routine, information security indifference, and site knowledge. By applying our approach, Rick was developed on the basis of 32 persona characteristics (11 Activities, 7 Aptitudes, 11 Attitudes, 3 Motivations). Each characteristic reflected a conceptual relationship, and underpinning these were 126 propositions associated with 34 concepts.

In the following sections, we describe how this approach was used to derive the following paragraph from Rick's Attitude section:

Rick isn't particularly concerned about people trying to hack into the SCADA system he uses. "The only way the SCADA will get infected", Rick says, "is by an instrument tech plugging a virus infected laptop into it".

Summarise propositions

A spreadsheet was used to catalogue propositions derived from quotations associated with the selected thematic concepts. Each proposition contained two components: a sentence containing the proposition itself, and a phrase acting as an abstract for this sentence. In our example, the paragraph of interest was derived from the following three quotations, Q1, Q2, and Q3; these quotations were coded with the *Information Security Indifference* (Q1), and *Island Mentality* (Q2, Q3) concepts:

- Q1: *Am I worried about people that want to hack my system? No, not really.*
- Q2: *Of course, security has always been an issue. Predominantly, what you'll find is that our systems are stand-alone, and they are not connected to the network. If they are then, in very limited cases, there could be an island network where a screen over here is looking after a site 8 miles up the road.*
- Q3: *If they work on a system and didn't have that, if they had to bring in their laptop with a cable and connect it in then, yes, if some guy infected their own laptop by doing other things, this could infect your own work. That's the only thing that could get infected because it's linked to all the other systems.*

As Figure 1 illustrates, the propositions representing Q1, Q2, and Q3 are *Not worried about people trying to hack the SCADA systems*, *Systems are stand-alone because they are not connected to a network*, and *Systems are infected only if engineers connect infected laptops* respectively.

Duplicate or superfluous quotations were omitted from this step. Examples of such quotations included plant shift-specific comments, and references to clean or waste water treatment operations out of scope for this study.

Argue characteristics

A sheet was added to the previously created spreadsheet to argue each association between the thematic concepts. Each row in this sheet represented a relationship, with columns for the characteristic claim being made, the behavioural variable type, grounds, warrant, backing, model qualifier, and possible rebuttals. The modal qualifier was subjectively assigned based on the grounding of the underlying quotations; the greater the grounding, the more confident the qualifying noun was. Table 1 describes the components supporting the persona characteristic *SCADA isolation make hacking unlikely*.

Table 1. Characteristic argument example

Relationship	*Information Security Indifference* is a cause of *Island Mentality*
Characteristic	SCADA isolation make hacking unlikely
Behaviour Variable Type	Attitude
Grounds	II-5, IM-3
Warrant	IM-4
Backing	Island Mindset concept
Qualifier	Probably
Rebuttal	None

Like the previous step, not all relationships were included in this analysis. Reasons for omission included a lack of grounding, and relationships which were grounded in overly site-specific data. Another reason was that the analysis itself led to new insights into the Grounded Theory model which, when investigated further, rendered a relationship superfluous.

Write persona narrative

Information about personas, including its narrative and characteristics, were stored in the CAIRIS (Computer Aided Integration of Requirements and Information Security) tool [1]; this tool supports the argumentation model presented in [9]. The spreadsheet contents were imported into CAIRIS, and persona characteristics automatically generated from these. Rick's validating narrative text was entered into CAIRIS, and associated with the generated persona characteristics.

Applying the Persona

Both personas were used to help elicit policy requirements. In total, 102 policy requirements were elicited, and these were placed in context by describing how the personas participate in 5 different work activities, e.g. fixing broken instruments and resolving reservoir water-level warnings. However, the Persona Case was found to be particularly useful when used in focus groups. On one occasion, a domain expert challenged a policy of disabling USB access to plant workstations by suggesting that Rick might bring letters or other documents into work with him. However, when Rick's characteristics and supporting elements were reviewed, it was found that this behaviour would be atypical; adding this constraint would not negatively impact Rick's working practices.

DISCUSSION AND CONCLUSION

The data used to derive Rick was sufficiently homogeneous that a single persona encapsulated most of the characteristics elicited. To explore the scaleability of this technique with more heterogeneous data, we used it to derive personas from a larger Grounded Theory model, containing 300 quotations and 90 thematic concepts; this model was a product of a published Grounded Theory analysis of Security Culture [8]. Despite the model's size, a similar number of characteristics, 31, were yielded; the breakdown of these characteristics were 6 Activities, 3 Aptitudes, 14 Attitudes, 6 Motivations, and 2 Skills. However, the characteristics were sufficiently diverse that, following an affinity diagramming exercise of the characteristics, 3 different personas were elicited. These personas represented a clinical researcher (Claire), an application developer (Tom), and a system administrator (Matt).

Although Claire, Tom, and Matt were not used in any subsequent design activities, discussions with stakeholders from the study in question suggest that the personas were accurate archetypes of their respective user communities. These findings suggest the re-use potential for other Grounded Theory models towards the design of personas. For example, existing theories about privacy for different domains might be easier to digest by software developers in the form of a persona than a conceptual model and accompanying discourse. These extensions do not, however, guarantee that a Toulmin model is the best bridge between all possible qualitative models and User-Centered Design artifacts. Further research into applicable techniques from the Design Rationale community should be examined to determine their applicability.

In conclusion, this note makes a number of contributions towards more grounded personas. First, we make the case that personas *can* be independently validated, by using argumentation as a bridge between Grounded Theory and personas. Second, we have presented a step-by-step approach for developing personas which is both traceable to its empirical data, and well argued. Third, we validate our approach using a real world case study of contemporary interest. Finally, we have presented some consequences and opportunities afforded by our work for future research.

ACKNOWLEDGEMENTS

The research described in this paper was funded by EPSRC CASE Studentship R07437/CN001. We are very grateful to Qinetiq Ltd for their sponsorship of this work.

REFERENCES

1. CAIRIS web site. `http://www.comlab.ox.ac.uk/cairis`, January 2011.
2. Adams, A., Sasse, M. Users are not the enemy. *Communications of the ACM 42* (1999), 41–46.
3. Beyer, H., Holtzblatt, K. *Contextual design: defining customer-centered systems*. Morgan Kaufmann Publishers Inc., San Francisco, CA, USA, 1998.
4. Chapman, C. N., Milham, R. P. The persona's new clothes: Methodological and practical arguments against a popular method. *Proceedings of the Human Factors and Ergonomics Society 50th Annual Meeting* (2006).
5. Cooper, A., Reimann, R., Cronin, D. *About Face 3: The Essentials of Interaction Design*. Wiley, 2007.
6. Corbin, J. M., Strauss, A. L. *Basics of qualitative research : techniques and procedures for developing grounded theory*, 3rd ed. Sage Publications, Inc., 2008.
7. Faily, S., Fléchais, I. Barry is not the weakest link: Eliciting Secure System Requirements with Personas. *Proceedings of the 24th British HCI Group Annual Conference on People and Computers: Play is a Serious Business* (2010), BCS-HCI '10, British Computer Society, 113–120.
8. Faily, S., Fléchais, I. Designing and aligning e-science security culture with design. *Information Management and Computer Security 18*, 5 (2010), 339–349.
9. Faily, S., Fléchais, I. The secret lives of assumptions: Developing and refining assumption personas for secure system design. *HCSE'2010: Proceedings of the 3rd Conference on Human-Centered Software Engineering* (2010), Springer, 111–118.
10. Muhr, T. *User's Manual for ATLAS.ti 5.0*. ATLAS.ti Scientific Software Development GmbH, Berlin, 2004.
11. Toulmin, S. *The uses of argument*, updated ed. Cambridge University Press, 2003.

When the Implication Is Not to Design (Technology)

Eric P. S. Baumer
Information Science Department
Cornell University
ericpsb@cornell.edu

M. Six Silberman
Bureau of Economic Interpretation
six@economicinterpretation.org

ABSTRACT
As HCI is applied in increasingly diverse contexts, it is important to consider situations in which computational or information technologies may be less appropriate. This paper presents a series of questions that can help researchers, designers, and practitioners articulate a technology's appropriateness or inappropriateness. Use of these questions is demonstrated via examples from the literature. The paper concludes with specific arguments for improving the conduct of HCI. This paper provides a means for understanding and articulating the limits of HCI technologies, an important but heretofore under-explored contribution to the field.

Author Keywords
Design, non-design, reflective HCI, sustainability

ACM Classification Keywords
H.5.2 Information Interfaces and Presentation: Miscellaneous

General Terms
Design

AN EXPLOSION
"HCI is bursting at the seams" [26, p. 88], expanding to tackle evermore complex problems in evermore diverse domains, including healthcare [8], education [32], religion [35], environmental sustainability [4, 12], and many others. However, with all the excitement and expansion, there has been relatively little reflection about where and when *not* to apply technology, and arguments that technological interventions might *not* be appropriate for every situation are quite rare. There are certainly cases where information technology has been less than beneficial (e.g., [8]). Such work often examines the details of failure (e.g., [14]), but rarely concludes that the technology itself was out of place or inappropriate.

We argue that just as the HCI community looks for situations that may be amenable to technological interventions, the community should similarly and simultaneously work to develop a reflective awareness for situations in which computational technologies may be inappropriate or potentially harmful. Put concisely, just as much as we value design implications, we should similarly value the implication not to design.

The remainder of this paper lays out three specific, concrete ways of articulating when technology[1] may be inappropriate, by presenting three questions to be asked during technology design and implementation: Is there an equally viable low-tech or no-tech approach to the situation? Might deploying the technology result in more harm than the situation the technology is meant to address? Does the technology solve a computationally tractable problem rather than address an actual situation? One of these questions is adapted from previous work critiquing the perspective that technology is a panacea, readily applicable to ameliorate any ostensibly negative situation [2]. This paper both builds on that work and concretizes it by illustrating how each of these questions may be applied, specifically to work in sustainable HCI.

Much recent work has explored how HCI technologies can be used to enact environmental sustainability [6, 12, 13, 19, 36]. However, it is not obvious that the complex conditions associated with unsustainability—including environmental, political, social, historical, economic, and other factors—are best addressed with computing technology. This concern is compounded by a relative lack of engagement in HCI with the question of what sustainability actually means [10, 30]. We suggest cautious and critical consideration as to whether technological intervention is the most appropriate means of fostering environmental (or any other kind of) sustainability. This paper provides specific ways to talk and think about whether a given technological intervention is appropriate in a given context. While we focus here on sustainability, this sensibility applies broadly to HCI.

ARTICULATING THE VALUE OF ABSENCE
This section suggests three specific questions to help articulate when, how, and why a technological intervention might be inappropriate, providing examples from the literature to illustrate each. We focus on sustainability but include other examples to demonstrate the questions' broader application.

Low-tech or No-tech
Could the technology be replaced by an equally viable low-tech or non-technological approach to the situation? Many problems technology designers attempt to address existed, and were addressed, before the advent of their favored technologies. For example, while a PDA application may enable "smart" grocery lists (e.g., [24]), some combination of pencil, paper, and phone calls to or from co-habitants could be just

[1] Although potentially broadly applicable, this paper focuses specifically on computational and information technology.

as effective. This is not to say that nothing is learned from the system design and development, but rather to question the need for such a system in the first place[2]. Two detailed examples, both from a recent panel about food and sustainability [18], will demonstrate the point further.

One suggestion involved using temperature sensors to map the relative warm and cool parts of a personal garden to aid in plant distribution (tomatoes go in the warmer spots, greens in cooler spots). While such data-driven gardening may seem appealing, gardeners have been making such decisions and optimizations for hundreds of years. Even if productivity increased, the sensors would require additional effort in development, testing, deployment, and maintenance. Furthermore, sensors that break or cease to function after exposure to the elements (and may contain numerous toxic chemicals) will need to be disposed of. This question of disposal goes beyond sensors and gardens; it applies to any computational technologies designed for ostensibly environmentally-friendly uses [4, 19]. Rather than the technological solution of sensor nets, we might explore a social solution, e.g., asking the advice of other gardeners. Those in the geographic vicinity may have experience with annual weather cycles, rainfall patterns, and soil composition, as well as possess other local knowledge. This social approach may have the additional benefit of creating a community of involved, invested gardener-citizens—potentially ones who, rather than spending time tweaking sensors in their lettuce beds, might engage in civic action toward environmental ends.

A second suggestion at the same panel involved connecting producers to consumers, e.g., enabling consumers of coffee to provide feedback to the coffee growers on just how good their coffee is. Such connections could be enabled through camera phones, public touchscreen displays, and other ubicomp technologies. However, they could also be enacted through postcards, letters, polaroid photographs, or any number of low-tech solutions (although without the immediacy of digital communication). Furthermore, this intervention skirts the issue that the mutual alienation of producers and consumers is a relatively novel phenomenon, itself enabled largely by modern transportation and communication technologies. The issue at hand, then, is less whether the person who grows my coffee knows if I like it, but whether drinking coffee from beans grown halfway around the world on a daily basis is sustainable in the first place. If not, it may be worth asking why we imagine that adding accoutrements—social, digital, or otherwise—to a transnational economy will make it more sustainable. This point raises the question of what issue the technology actually addresses, discussed further below.

[2]The ambiguity of "need" has troubled sustainability discourse since the definition of sustainable development as "meet[ing] the needs of the present without compromising the ability of future generations to meet their own needs" [7]. In 1996, for example, then-VP for Environmentally and Socially Sustainable Development at the World Bank Ismail Serageldin wrote, "this definition is philosophically attractive but raises difficult operational questions. The meaning of 'needs' is fairly clear for the poor and starving, but what does it mean for a family that already has two cars, three televisions, and two VCRs? And yet it is precisely this latter type of family that will consume more than 80 percent of the world's income this year" [29]. This question remains unexplored in sustainable HCI.

Doing More Harm Than Good

Does a technological intervention result in more trouble or harm than the situation it's meant to address? While technology designers and builders may see opportunities everywhere, computational technologies may at times be more disruptive or harmful than the circumstances they are meant to improve. For example, Wyche et al. [35] describe a design concept for a PDA-like system enabling church-goers to take notes during religious services and then easily refer to those notes later. Although informed by existing note-taking practices and the desire to refer to notes after the fact, the design was met with hesitation by study participants, who thought that operating computer-like technology during services might disturb the "inner stillness" that accompanies mindful worship. Although Wyche et al. do not make a significant point of it, this finding is an important contribution, in that it furthers our understanding of exactly where and how computational technologies may be inappropriate.

Returning to sustainability, there is no shortage of mobile phone applications designed to promote sustainable behaviors, such as eating local foods [22] or taking the bus [13]. However, these apps do not address the fact that the proliferation of mobile phones, and computing devices in general, is itself environmentally problematic. Not only are there difficulties in disposing of these devices' toxic materials, but environmental damage is also done extracting those materials, not to mention the energy and resource consumption associated with data centers and other infrastructure required to make "smart" phones "smart." This is not to say that encouraging people to, say, take the bus is necessarily bad. Nor is it an argument that we should not attempt to use information technologies to encourage such behavior. Rather, we want to suggest that protecting the environment through the proliferation of many novel computational devices may be contradictory. One might consider other approaches, such as educational programs, informational panels, or community outreach. Such activities may not resemble traditional HCI research; it's important to know where computational technologies are inappropriate—where the bounds of our field lie—and this may be one of those instances.

Computational Transformations

Does a technology solve a computationally tractable transformation of a problem rather than the problem itself? "It is tempting, if the only tool you have is a hammer, to treat everything as if it were a nail" [21, p. 15]. Computational research on sustainability often uses computational methods to approach environmental problems, e.g., modeling biodiversity [15]. Such work uses simplifications to create computationally tractable representations of natural and social systems, but grappling with complexity is central to dealing with the challenges of unsustainability [30]. For example, 18th century efforts at calculating and deriving "maximum sustainable yield" from lumber forests ultimately led to nutrient-poor soils, disease-ridden forests, and failed crops, due to simplifications that did not represent such factors as the roles of birds, fungi, and rotting deadwood [27].

Work in sustainable HCI often relies on similar reductions in complexity to transform real-world situations into problems amenable to computational intervention. Carbon calculators provide an illustrative example. A user of such a calculator may note that driving a hybrid gasoline-electric vehicle will result in lower carbon emissions than driving a standard internal combustion engine vehicle. However, the astute user may also wonder about the disposal of the batteries used in hybrid cars, and whether the additional pollution from the battery will outweigh the benefits from reduced emissions. In fact, they are different kinds of environmental damage and are not commensurable. Such complexities are beyond the application at hand, which simply calculates carbon emissions. Furthermore, the calculator does little to encourage the user to consider alternative possibilities, e.g., forgoing the purchase of a new car and instead buying a bicycle and/or a public transportation pass. But what if the user lives in an area where biking is not feasible at certain times, or where public transportation is scant or nonexistent? These are the kind of larger, systemic issues to which we believe the questions suggested here can help draw attention.

DISCUSSION

This paper is not a critique of specific projects. It is a reflective look at the fundamental goals and approaches of our field. We have used well known work to argue the potential value of not using technology. The approach argued for here resonates with some recent work, both in the context of sustainability and with respect to technology design broadly.

The questions of low-/no-tech solutions and whether a technology may do more harm than good are reminiscent of "zensign" [32], the notion that the features omitted from an application or system may be just as important as the features included. While this approach has much to offer design, our point is not about including or omitting specific features from a system but about whether the system should be built at all. The question of computational transformations resonates in some ways with arguments about moving beyond the scale of individual choices [10, 12]. Technology designers should attend not only to how computational systems represent such larger factors–cultural, political, societal, governmental, etc.–but also to which factors are not represented. Our argument also resonates with Toyama's [34] about the limits of ICT4D.

From Solutions to Problems

An important process in design is to explore the solution space, i.e., to investigate the realm of possible approaches that will satisfactorily address a given problem. Conversely, one may explore the problem space, i.e., consider different approaches to defining and framing the very problem being addressed (cf., [9]). The three questions posed here move progressively from a focus on the solution space (e.g., considering non-technological approaches to a situation) to a focus on the problem space (e.g., noting that computational transformation may result in addressing a different problem), thus highlighting an alternative approach to technology design.

Beyond Problems

Framing current situations as problems and technological systems as solutions is common in HCI: What problem does your system solve? Has another system solved this problem before? Is your solution better than previous ones? On one hand, these questions can be helpful in assessing a research program's progress towards its agreed-upon goals. On the other, this framing can be misleading. A problem implies a solution, where a solution eliminates a problem. For some situations, e.g., certain questions of how to make interfaces more usable, this framing is effective. However, the problem of making usable interfaces is not entirely analogous to the problem of helping users develop environmentally sustainable behaviors. Unsustainability is not a problem to be solved, but a complex and multifaceted condition with which we must grapple [16, 30]. This is not to say that unsustainability is a "wicked" problem (cf. [1, 25]); rather, we argue that framing unsustainability as a *problem* misses the nature of the situation and misguides our attempts to address it.

Rather than imagining that technology design offers solutions to the problems of unsustainability, we suggest thinking of design as an intervention in a complex situation. This framing provides at least two advantages. First, it highlights the fact that no single, simple solution will enable us to live sustainably. Second, it encourages attending to the complex ways technological interventions reconfigure the situations into which they are introduced. This is not simply a matter of understanding how technology impacts a situation; technologies are used, adopted, and repurposed in ways neither totally determined by the technology itself nor by the context in which it is used [19, 20]. Rather, the point is to understand the complex interactions between technology and the context of use. For example, the problem-solution framing requires some metric or set of metrics (e.g., miles traveled, tons of carbon emitted, watts of energy used) that can be used to compare two alternative solutions objectively to determine which is more sustainable. Such metrics, however, cannot fully capture the complexities of environmental sustainability (cf. the hybrid car example above) or the ways in which real people constitute and enact sustainability in their daily lives. Nor can metrics fully capture the lived experiences of healthcare, religion, education, or any of the highly complex domains in which HCI technologies are developed and deployed. While this paper focuses on environmental sustainability, this shift—from problems and solutions to situations and interventions—could beneficially be applied in numerous areas of HCI research and practice, and resonates with work in the "third wave" of HCI research (e.g., [5, 17, 28]).

ARGUMENTS FOR PRACTICE

So now what? On one hand, we believe that drawing attention to the trends highlighted here can in itself constitute a significant contribution. On the other, we are practical people and realize that HCI is a largely practical field. Therefore, we conclude with a number of implications for the practical conduct of HCI work, demonstrating how the perspective advocated here could be applied in a variety of situations.

Value the Implication Not to Design. In addition to presenting design implications from their studies, or not [11], researchers should consider potential implications not to design, areas where computing technology might seem applicable, but where results suggest it may be inappropriate (e.g., [35]).

Explicate Unpursued Avenues. Part of the argument here is

that we need to build a deeper understanding of where, how, and why HCI technologies are and are not appropriate. Thus, when discussing a system, presenting the final design alone may not be as informative as accompanying it with prototypes and abandoned alternatives, along with descriptions and justifications for why those directions were not pursued. This is not meant as an additional requirement for papers, but rather an argument for a different kind of paper.

Technological Extravention. Another benefit of framing computational technologies as interventions into complex systems is that it suggests exploring the results of *removing* a technology from a system. Studies of technological "extravention" might provide a new way to understand the complex connections between technology and practice (and society, culture, politics, history, etc.) (e.g., [23]).

More Than Negative Results. This paper might be seen as an argument for publishing failed systems of all sorts. "We built this technology, but people hated it and didn't use it." This result is not particularly useful *per se*. What would be useful is an explication of exactly where, how, when, and why a system failed, not to mention critical consideration of what it means to fail (e.g., [14]). Furthermore, even with "positive" results, the implication may not be that the technology being studied should be adopted or proliferated widely.

Don't Stop Building. This paper is not an argument against technology in general. "Being skeptical about technology does not mean rejecting it" [33, p. 4]; we have ourselves built computational systems (e.g., [3, 31]). The argument here is that when we do build things, we should engage in a critical, reflective dialog about how and why these things are built. The questions presented in this paper offer one set of techniques for engaging in such dialog. This approach can help HCI to do more by doing less, i.e., to have a more significant and beneficial impact while building fewer systems by intervening only where computational technologies are particularly apt. Therefore, HCI researchers and practitioners should keep building, but should also attend both to situations in which computing is appropriate and to those in which the implication is *not to design*.

ACKNOWLEDGMENTS

We thank Greg Elliott, David H. Nguyen, Lilly Irani, Marisa Cohn, and Julka Almquist for helpful conversations, and Phoebe Sengers for comments on an earlier draft.

REFERENCES

1. Aoki, P.M., R.J. Honicky, A. Mainwaring, C. Myers, E. Paulos, S. Subramanian, A. Woodruff. A vehicle for research. *CHI '09*: 375-84.
2. Baumer, E., B. Tomlinson. Questioning the technological panacea. *alt.chi '07*.
3. Baumer, E. P. S., et al. "America is like Metamucil": critical and creative thinking about metaphor in political blogs. *CHI '10*: 1437-1446.
4. Blevis, E. Sustainable interaction design. *CHI '07*: 503-12.
5. Bødker, S. When second wave HCI meets third wave challenges. *NordiCHI '06*: 1-8.
6. Bonanni, L., M. Hockenberry, D. Zwarg, C. Csikszentmihalyi, H. Ishii. Small business applications of Sourcemap. *CHI '10*: 937-46.
7. Brundtland, G., et al. *Our Common Future*. Oxford, 1987.
8. Chen, Y., M. E. Atwood. Challenges of mobile clinical system design. *HICSS '10*.
9. Cross, N. *Designerly Ways of Knowing*. Springer, 2006.
10. DiSalvo, C., P. Sengers, H. Brynjarsdóttir. Mapping the landscape of sustainable HCI. *CHI '10*: 1975-84.
11. Dourish, P. Implications for design. *CHI '06*: 541-50.
12. Foth, M., E. Paulos, C. Satchell, P. Dourish. Pervasive computing and environmental sustainability. *Pervasive Comp.* **8**(1): 78-81, 2009.
13. Froehlich, J., T. Dillahunt, P. Klasnja, J. Mankoff, S. Consolvo, B. Harrison, J.A. Landy. UbiGreen. *CHI '09*: 1043-52.
14. Gaver, W., J. Bowers, T. Kerridge, A. Boucher, N. Jarvis. Anatomy of a failure. *CHI '09*: 2213-22.
15. Gomes, C. Computational sustainability. *The Bridge* **39**(4): 5-13, 2009.
16. Greer, J. M. *The Long Descent*. New Society, 2008.
17. Harrison, S., D. Tatar, P. Sengers. Three paradigms of HCI. *alt.chi '07*.
18. Hirsch, T., P. Sengers, E. Blevis, R. Beckwith, T. Parikh. Making food, producing sustainability. *CHI '10*: 3147-50.
19. Huh, J., L.P. Nathan, S. Silberman, B. Tomlinson, P. Sengers, D. Busse. Examining appropriation, re-use, and maintenance for sustainability. *CHI '10*: 4457-60.
20. March, W., M. Jacobs, T. Salvador. Designing technology for community appropriation. *CHI '05*: 2126-7.
21. Maslow, A. *The Psychology of Science*. Harper, 1966.
22. McLeod, B. *Locavore*. Enjoymentland, 2010.
23. Morowati, T. Interventions for the overly connected. NYU ITP MS Thesis, 2007.
24. Newcomb, E., Pashley, T., Stasko, J. Mobile computing in the retail arena. *CHI '03*: 337-44.
25. Rittel, H., M. Webber. Dilemmas in a general theory of planning. *Policy Sciences* **4**: 155-69, 1973.
26. Rogers, Y. New theoretical approaches for HCI. *Ann. Rev. Inf. Sci. and Tech.* **38**: 87-143, 2004.
27. Scott, J.C. *Seeing like a state*. Yale Univ Press, 1998.
28. Sengers, P., K. Boehner, N. Knouf. Sustainable HCI meets third wave HCI: 4 themes. CHI 2009 workshop.
29. Serageldin, I. Sustainability as opportunity. *Brown J. of World Affairs* **3**(2): 187-203, 1996.
30. Silberman, M.S., B. Tomlinson. Toward an ecological sensibility. *CHI '10*: 3469-74.
31. Silberman, M.S. et al. Sellers' problems in human computation markets. *Proc. HCOMP '10*: 18-21.
32. Tatar, D., J.-S. Lee, N. Alaloula. Playground games. *DIS '08*: 68-77.
33. Thackara, J. *In The Bubble*. MIT Press, 2005.
34. Toyama, K. Can Technology End Poverty? *Boston Review*, Nov/Dec 2010.
35. Wyche, S., P.M. Aoki, and R. Grinter. Re-placing faith. *CHI '08*: 11-20.
36. Xiao, J., J. Fan. PrintMarmoset. *CHI '09*: 109-12.

Utility of Human-Computer Interactions: Toward a Science of Preference Measurement

Michael Toomim[1], Travis Kriplean[1], Claus Pörtner[2] and James A. Landay[1,3]
University of Washington, dub Group Microsoft Research Asia[3]
Computer Science & Engineering[1], Economics[2]
{toomim,travis,landay}@cs.washington.edu[1], cportner@u.washington.edu[2]

ABSTRACT
The success of a computer system depends upon a user *choosing* it, but the field of Human-Computer Interaction has little ability to predict this user choice. We present a new method that measures user choice, and quantifies it as a measure of *utility*. Our method has two core features. First, it introduces an economic definition of utility, one that we can operationalize through economic experiments. Second, we employ a novel method of crowdsourcing that enables the collection of thousands of economic judgments from real users.

ACM Classification: H5.m. Information interfaces and presentation: User Interfaces.

General Terms: Design, Economics, Experimentation

INTRODUCTION
The CHI research community grew from the need to understand *discretionary use* of computer interfaces [5]. Discretionary use—the free choices that people make about which interfaces to use to accomplish their tasks—has always been central to our field. And today, people have increasingly more choices in computing.

Unfortunately, the measures used by the CHI research community—time-on-task, the number of errors, and subjective interpretations of think-aloud and survey reports—only indirectly predict whether an interface will be preferred over other alternatives. We usually do not directly measure user *choice* itself. This means that our formative and summative research methods are somewhat misaligned with our values of supporting discretionary use. This limits the CHI community's ability to effect meaningful change in the world.

Industry, on the other hand, has developed a valuable technique to measure user choice: A/B testing [15]. Unfortunately, A/B testing is out of reach for most researchers and small developers because it requires a large up-front investment and an existing userbase to deploy.

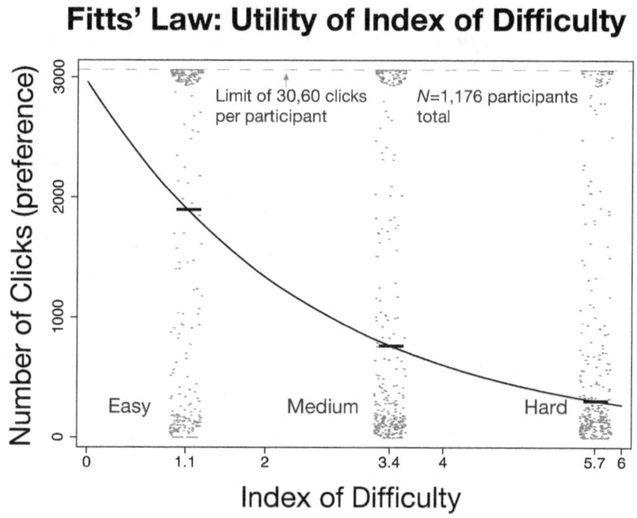

Figure 1. Fitts' law models the *time* required to click a widget of a size and width—our technique can model how much people *prefer to use* a widget. Participants were assigned one of three index of difficulty conditions. Each point is the number of clicks a participant completed before quitting (points jittered to show spread). Participants *preferred* big buttons to small buttons ($p < 0.10$). Participants were allowed a maximum of 3,060 clicks each. The regression line accounts for this maximum using a Tobit analysis.

Our goal is to help researchers and practitioners measure choice itself. We want to make the evaluation of choice and preference accessible and inexpensive. Grudin [6] and Malone [17] demonstrated early on that preference measurements can yield useful design insights. Few others have extended this work ([2]). We want to take this concept to the next level. We propose (1) a science—language, methods, and tools—for discovering, describing, and sharing knowledge about user preference and (2) evaluation techniques that practitioners can use to guide and justify an evidence-driven design process.

In this paper, we take some first steps towards establishing the language, methods, and analytical tools for evaluating choice and preference of different tasks and interfaces. The core technique we introduce is a semi-automated method for posting different interfaces and tasks to a crowdsourced labor market, such as Amazon's Mechanical Turk. These labor markets are websites where anyone can post a small task for someone else to accomplish for a small price. Our method is to create thousands of such tasks that systematically vary the interface, the price, and instructions. We then observe how many workers choose to complete the tasks, and how many times they do so. With this data, we can apply various analytical techniques to characterize user preferences for the given interfaces and tasks.

We can gain a quantitative handle on user preferences by analyzing the dynamics of the discretionary completion of tasks. Consider the classic Fitts' Law experiment [16]. Fitts' Law models the difficulty of target acquisition as a function of target size and distance. To test our methodology, we ran a study online to determine how target size and distance affect *preference*. We posted the standard Fitts' law task to Mechanical Turk, asking workers to click back and forth between a rectangle that switched sides on the screen. Our experiment manipulated the task's index of difficulty, by changing the size of rectangle and distance from cursor. We expected users to *prefer* easy tasks to difficult tasks, and in fact the data displays this trend (see Figure 1). That is, the degree a Mechanical Turk user prefers a Fitts' law task is inversely proportional to the time it takes to use it. With further experiments, one could learn if this preference result generalizes, and perhaps produce a general law of user preference with respect to task-completion time. Such a law would be useful knowledge for designers.

To be more precise, we are proposing that our method enables researchers to measure differences in *net utility* of some classes of interfaces and tasks. HCI often defines usability and utility as separate quantities: usability is the ease and efficiency of the interface apart from its function, and utility is the "usefulness" of its function [18]. However, both values influence user choice, and in fact they can be difficult to separate in practice.

In this paper, we bring the concepts of usefulness and usability together under the *Economic* definition of utility. **In Economics, utility is the degree to which a person prefers a particular choice amongst options [23].** We can infer it from user behavior: when a user chooses to use system A instead of B, it is said that *Utility*(A) > *Utility*(B). Utility encompasses all factors of function and usability that affect preference and use, and measures their net impact on user behavior (Figure 2). Economic utility quantifies aggregate user preference.

To quantify the utility difference of two interfaces, we vary the wage we offer, and find the amount that compensates for a difference in use between the two interfaces. If a user has no preference between being paid 25¢ for using system A over being paid 50¢ to use system B, then we can describe the difference *Utility*(A)–*Utility*(B) = *Utility*(25¢). That is, system A provides a measure of 25¢ more utility than system B. This is a *money-metric of utility*, a number representing the value of an interface change that can be compared across interfaces and situations, providing a lingua franca for communicating results.

This paper contributes the foundational first steps toward a net utility measurement. We define utility, an economic

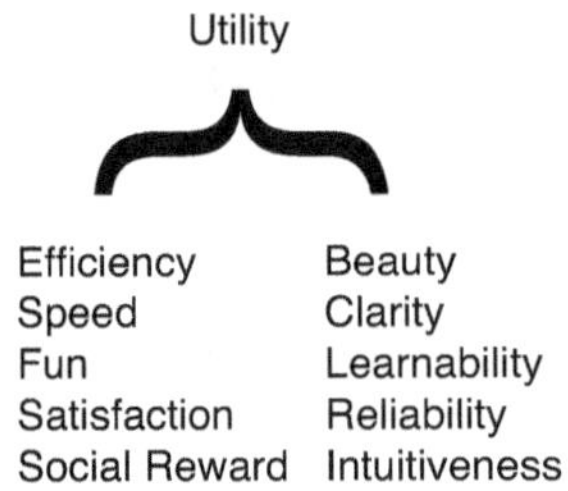

Figure 2. Utility is a summative descriptor of users' decisions of use. Many lower-level factors affect a user's choices of use. Utility aggregates the effects of all lower-level factors into a single number.

concept, in terms applicable to HCI. We show how to measure the difference in utility between two interfaces: by controlling for variables on Mechanical Turk, analyzing the data, and producing a money metric of utility. We present two utility measurement case studies conducted with our method that measure the utility of interface variations in (1) aesthetics & feedback and (2) efficiency. We believe that the further development of utility measurement methods will be able to help align the research community's focus on discretionary use with its toolset, and enable a more scientific understanding of the degree to which our interface improvements are *valued* and motivate *use*.

Using Mechanical Turk facilitates these first steps, but also has acute limitations. First, it is difficult to generalize results from Mechanical Turk to other contexts. We discuss this issue in more depth later. Second, a worker on Mechanical Turk does not complete a task for the same reason a normal user would. For instance, a father gets a particular utility sharing photos with his daughter on Facebook that is lost when we ask a Mechanical Turk worker to complete the same task. Thus, we cannot measure the value of a goal; what we *can* measure is the "cost" of an interface for completing the task, and in particular the difference in utility between two interfaces. Finally, we have yet to calibrate or validate the quantities of our measures, such as the money-metric. In this paper, we only show that their values follow our intuitions on what they should look like.

The rest of the paper is organized as follows. First, we delve deeper into the history of HCI to further motivate the importance of establishing a science for measuring and applying knowledge of interface utility. Second, we give more detail on our method for measuring differences between interfaces and how it can be achieved on Mechanical Turk. This involves (1) defining in greater detail net utility and the money-metric, (2) identifying strategies for running an interface auction and its implication for study design, and (3) detailing factors that can be controlled for on Mechanical turk in order to obtain a more accurate measurement. Third, we describe our two case studies, developing a repertoire of techniques for analyzing data as we present the cases. We conclude with a discussion of the scope of our technique's abilities and limitations as compared to other techniques, and how to develop these techniques further in the future.

HCI IN HISTORY: FROM EFFICIENCY TO UTILITY

Users have not always been able to choose their interfaces, as Grudin describes in his histories of HCI [5]. Most interfaces through the 1970s were designed for paid operators of

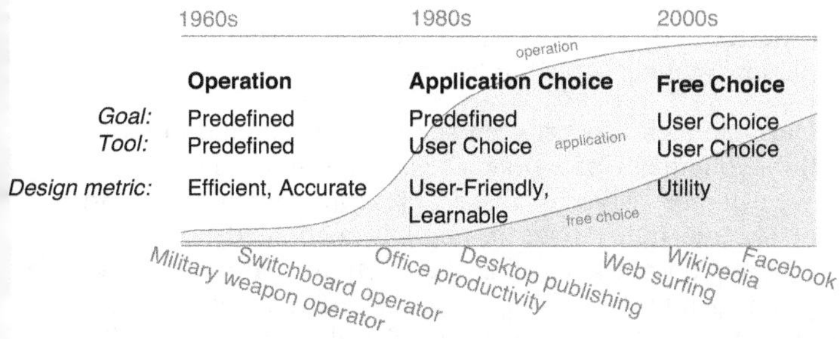

Figure 3. Three phases of choice in HCI. (1) The first user interfaces were designed for fixed tasks, in fixed industrial processes. Users had little choice in their use. (2) In the 1980s, we developed commodity software that users could choose to apply (or not) to tasks of office work. (3) Today's Internet, mobile, entertainment, and persuasive software provides users with entirely new tasks to choose from, not just tools. These interactions must have high utility to motivate use.

large, expensive machinery, such as pilots in an airplane cockpit or nuclear power plant operators in a control room. They obtained mandatory, paid training to learn an interface. A successful system design needed to be performant, efficient, reliable, and little else. It was not until the 1980s that *discretionary use* became common: a technical writer that needed to type a document could choose whether to learn a document typesetting system or use a simpler typewriter. For the first time, user interfaces needed to be easy to learn, or "user-friendly," or users would reject them in favor of alternatives.

The trend has continued, and in fact has sped up rapidly (Figure 3). The Internet makes it easier for users to find and try new software to apply to their tasks. There are more options available to choose amongst, and the ubiquity of computers has given us the option to apply computing to more parts of our lives. Moreover, a new class of computing involves choosing not only a tool to apply to a task, but often the *task itself*. For instance, web surfers constantly choose new interesting pages to surf. Users today routinely choose optional and voluntary tasks, such as maintaining blog entries, sending and accepting friend requests, creating LOLcats and editing Wikipedia articles—tasks which did not even exist two decades ago. And some software is designed specifically to give new goals to users: video gamers *pay money* to find compelling tasks to spend their time on; consumers purchase persuasive products, such as Nike+ iPod, hoping to influence their choices in life; Human Computation and Crowdsourcing applications find ways to wrap tasks like image labeling [22] and protein folding [3] within fun, high-utility games. Simply put, there is a growing, market of interfaces being chosen by (and created) to accomplish a myriad of tasks, each vying with competitors for the real scarcity of the information age: attention [20].

In acknowledging the importance of user choice, industry is increasingly prioritizing metrics of *use* in design. Industry wants their systems to be used, to be desired, popular, to get page views, sales, have millions of active users, reach critical mass, and achieve network effects. It does not make sense for Facebook to optimize the time-on-task for the task of browsing a friend's News Feed. Indeed, when a designer makes an interface fun or valuable, time-on-task should *increase*. Rather, Facebook evaluates features by deploying them and seeing if they obtain and sustain *use*. Amazon, Google, and Yahoo test all important changes with A/B testing, which tells them how their interfaces will affect real user *choices*. Websites measure success in hits, page views, ad clicks, user posts, and monthly active users: all measures of *use*, and the result of *utility*.

The nature of computer use has transformed with the rise of free choice computing, but HCI's methods and metrics have remained relatively static. Our community is not engaged with *choice* in computing. Without studying choice, preference, utility, and real-world use, the field of HCI will become increasingly irrelevant to practice.

METHOD FOR UTILITY MEASUREMENT

In this section, we give more detail on our method for measuring net utility and how it can be achieved on Mechanical Turk. We (1) define in greater detail net utility and the money-metric, (2) identify strategies for running an interface auction and its implication for study design, and (3) detail factors that can be controlled for on Mechanical turk in order to obtain a more accurate utility measurement.

Our approach to measuring the utility of an interface is to determine the *compensating wage differential* between different tasks and computer interfaces. This economic theory dates back to Adam Smith, who defined it as the additional amount a worker must by paid to convince him to do a job that is unpleasant, risky, or otherwise undesirable [21]. Our method determines the desirability or undesirability of an interface to achieve a task by observing how many workers choose to use it at different amounts of pay.

As is standard in contemporary Economics, we generally define utility as an *ordinal* measure: it describes an ordering of preference, but not the strength of preferences. This assumes very little about a user's preferences, only that he has them, and that they are not *e.g.* circular, preferring A to B, B to C, and C to A. (A complete list of assumptions can be found in [23]).

We model user choice as follows. A user finds value in completing a *task*, but to do so he must take actions on a computer *interface*, a process with its own cost or value. These values also depend upon the user's demographic, psychological, social, moral and physical *context*: the variables that determine who he is, what he knows, what he wants, and what situation he is in. All together, we say that utility is a function of three parameters:

$$Utility = f(task, interface, context)$$

Utility experiments can vary any one of these parameters to measure its effect on user choice. For instance, the *context* could theoretically be manipulated by switching to a different labor market, by augmenting or manipulating the labor market with particular community or social dynamics, by surveying workers and controlling for their demographics, or by introducing labor market mechanisms into existing user populations. Consider the task of modifying a wiki page. The value of editing it will change depending on whether that wiki page is part of Wikipedia, Conservapedia, or your research group's homepage; editing each has different meaning to you, has a different community that maintains it, has different visibility through PageRank, etc. Similarly, we might hold the interface and context constant, *e.g.* editing the HCI page on Wikipedia, while the *task* is manipulated (adding a category tag vs. reverting vandalism vs. correcting a spelling error). In this paper, we primarily show how to vary and study the *interface*, which is the easiest of the three variables to study on Mechanical Turk.

Auction Techniques

Our preference measurement technique begins with determining how much you must pay people to convince them to use an interface for a task. This is essentially an auction.

There are many auction techniques one might use. Horton and Chilton [8] measured a worker's *reservation wage*—the wage below which she will not do a task—by starting with a high wage and incrementally reducing it until the worker quit. This tested a rational model of worker behavior, elucidating many interesting aspects of Mechanical Turk as a labor market. Their style of auction could theoretically be used for interface preference measurement, but it is unfortunately biased by strong observer effects: the sequence of declining prices workers are paid has a significant effect on when they decide to stop, and thus changes the "reservation wage" the method calculates. Horton and Chilton's initial experiments found a significant effect of this pricing style on the results, but did not find a significant effect of the Fitts' law index of difficulty condition that they studied—something our technique detects.

Ben-Bassat *et al.* [2] used a traditional second-price auction to determine user preference for interfaces, implemented in a traditional face-to-face laboratory study. Participants provided an explicit money bid for each interface. However, asking a person to explicitly reason about an interface's price inherently alters their process of choice. For instance, the subjects in their study bid extra for *efficient* interfaces, but not for *highly-aesthetic* interfaces. As we will show, our technique detects strong effects for aesthetics. We hypothesize that even if subjects preferentially *choose* pretty interfaces in practice, they may not reason that this is a valid quantity to pay for when asked to reason about it, and bid only for efficiency.

These two auction techniques assume a significant degree of *rationality* of the participants. Our technique's key difference is that it does not ask workers to choose a price. We simply present a worker with a job at a price and observe their behavior. A user chooses to complete a task at a given price, or not. If they choose to complete the task, we observe how much work they do before boredom or other factors reduce the net utility of the task below their other options, and they stop. We then aggregate this data. Holding task and context constant, a data point in utility space is (interface_id, worker_id, wage_compensation_per_completion, number_of_completions).

Our approach is a between-subjects design, and minimizes the explicitness of workers reasoning about their choices. We call jobs "Mystery Tasks," presenting them as a surprise or a game rather than an explicit auction (detailed later). Workers do not know that their activities are being aggregated to infer net utility. This technique is simple, direct, and requires few assumptions. The downside is that it requires a large amount of data, because every completed job provides only one bit of information: whether the user accepted the job, or not. Luckily, obtaining this amount of data is feasible with Mechanical Turk.

MAKING IT WORK IN MECHANICAL TURK

To make our auction work, we had to overcome a number of challenges on Mechanical Turk that would bias the results and compromise their integrity as a measure of net utility. In this section, we first overview the software framework implementing the utility methodology, then describe a couple of the specific problems it helps solve, and finally detail a few outstanding problems that need to be addressed in future work.

Overview of Software Framework

We have automated most of the experimental method. An experimenter first implements a user interface for a task using HTML, JavaScript, Flash, Java, or any other technology embeddable into webpages. She can define a set of experimental *conditions* (a pairing of interface and task), and parameterize the interface for each condition, for instance implementing multiple button widths or interaction styles that she would like to test. She then tells our software to run a study with the interface and task, declaring which conditions she would like to run, and how many workers she would like to receive utility judgements from (this determines how much she will spend on Mechanical Turk). Our software automatically creates hundreds to thousands of jobs on Mechanical Turk and randomly assigns workers to the prescribed conditions. Workers complete jobs interacting directly with the experimenter's web application embedded in an IFrame on the Mechanical Turk website. Our software logs to a database how many workers look at the task, and how many jobs each completes, along with the workers' interactions, worker IDs, geographic locations, and their randomly-assigned pay and interface conditions. The software then applies micro-econometric analyses to the data, computes a money-metric, and produces graphs to explain the results. It also geolocates IP addresses and tracks local time of day for workers automatically, which make it possible to observe differences in utility across regions and time of day. We implement our system in the fantastic web2py web programming framework.

Specific Problems Addressed by Framework

The framework addresses a number of issues that anyone who wants to use our method for running utility auctions on Mechanical Turk need to address. We describe four such problems and solutions here.

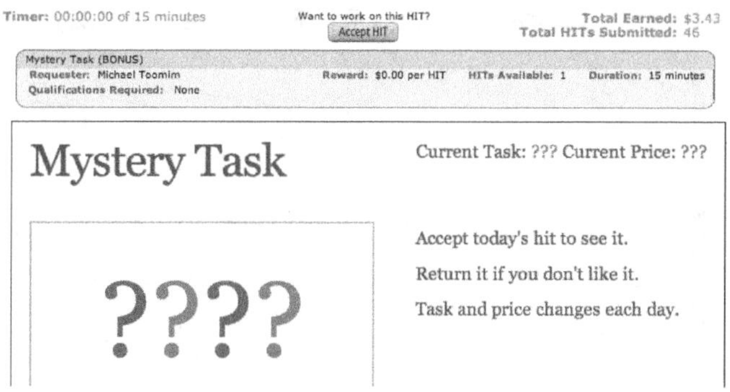

Figure 4. Until a user accepts a Mystery Task, they do not know the type of task or how much it pays. This allows us to log the percentage of users who *see* the task vs. *accept* it, and dispatch a different experimental condition and price to each worker.

Implementing multiple conditions.

We want to measure the varying work done per condition, so we need to post multiple conditions of jobs. However, if we post them all at the same time, workers will only consider completing the best, highest-priced job. If, on the other hand, we change the price over time, we have to control for the other factors that change over time, such as worker populations and market conditions, and have to control for the increases in experience and boredom that occur with workers who happen to remain on Mechanical Turk during multiple phases of the conditions. Our solution is to post all conditions to Turk simultaneously, but allow each worker to see only one of the many conditions. Mechanical Turk itself does not support this, but we were able to implement a novel workaround using Mechanical Turk's *bonus* and *IFrame* APIs. We will describe this below.

Selection bias.

The second problem is that the rate of work depends on how many workers *find* a job in the first place. We want to measure a job's inherent labor completion rate, but other factors confound the rate. For instance, we were able to get a 12x increase in work rate by modifying a job so that it appeared on the Mechanical Turk front page for workers who do not change Amazon's default search settings. Our solution is to measure the number of people who look at our jobs, separately from the number who complete them, so that we can measure instead the *proportion* of those that complete tasks out of those who consider tasks. Unfortunately, Mechanical Turk does not tell us how many people look at our task listings, since they appear in a large list of search results on the Mechanical Turk server.

Luckily, we can solve the multiple conditions and selection bias problems with one technique. Our solution is to post each job as a "Mystery Task," with a listed pay of $0.00, and a description that tells the worker she must preview the job to see the task and how much it actually pays (Figure 4). When the worker opens a Mystery Task, Mechanical Turk opens an IFrame (using the externalQuestion API) to our web server, which tracks that the worker has *seen* our task. Our framework is then able to initialize an appropriate interface, task, and price that instantiates an experimental condition. If the framework has not yet seen the worker's ID, the price is randomly assigned, and sticks with them for subsequent jobs. Our jobs pay entirely in *bonus*, a Mechanical Turk feature that allows employers to pay a worker a discretionary amount beyond the initial payment. The randomization of condition and pay is hidden from the worker, who is not told that there are multiple conditions available behind the scenes. Unfortunately, Mechanical Turk does not provide external webservers with the worker's ID when she previews the job, only when she accepts it, so we display the page in Figure 4 for a previewing worker until she accepts the job. This set of techniques removes all condition-specific information from the job description listings, which we cannot control on a per-user basis, and gives us control over every step in a participant's process of choice.

Lopping off the long tail of job completions.

Some small proportion of workers will continue to complete the same job *ad infinitum.* However, this does not necessarily yield more interesting data for informing utility analysis (see e.g. later section on survival analysis). Our framework allows the experimenter to set a parameter for the maximum number of jobs (*e.g.,* 50) any single worker can complete. This reduces the cost of the study if the experimenter is not interested in the utility of doing a job more than a certain number of times in a row. It also makes it less worthwhile for a worker to try to cheat by programming a script to parse the webpages and perform tasks automatically.

Temporal Market Price Fluctuations.

The market clearing price on Mechanical Turk can change over time because of an increase in jobs or workers. Labor supply is sensitive to short term fluctuations like time of day and day of week, as well as longer term boom and bust of the Turk economy. This can create problems for analyzing the results of utility studies conducted over a longer period of time, as well as problems comparing studies conducted at different times. To control for this, we can post a baseline control condition (answering CAPTCHAs for 1¢) along with the experimental conditions. Note that the data we present in this paper has not been controlled for in this way.

CASE STUDIES

We applied our method in two case studies, to verify that it detects significant differences in utility that we would expect. The first study is the Fitts' Law study, which we summarized in the introduction. Its purpose is to measure the utility of *time-on-task*, a factor that HCI routinely measures. The second study, on the other hand, measures the utility of two user interface factors that HCI has had a difficult time quantifying because they do not affect efficiency: aesthetics and feedback. As we describe the studies, we will also present a repertoire of techniques that are useful for analyzing and communicating about the data produced by utility measurement.

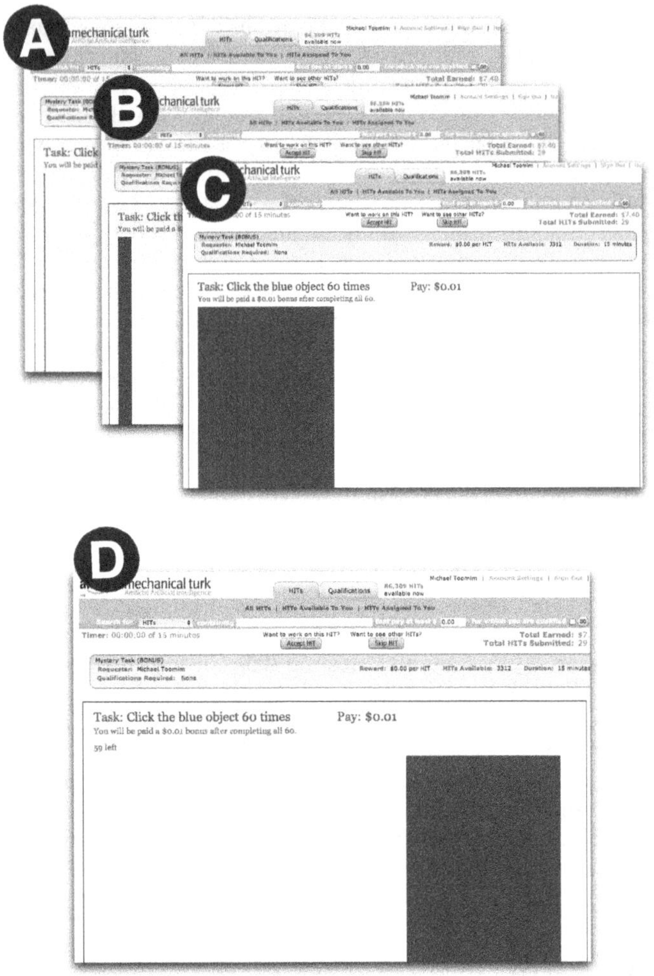

Figure 5. Screenshots of the Fitts' law task. Subjects clicked on a blue rectangle 60 times. We created three variations of bar width and the distance it moved: hard (a), medium (b), and easy (c). Each time they clicked on the bar, it moved to the opposite side of the screen (d).

These case studies demonstrate that utility measurement can apply to a range of factors—both those that we measure today, and those that we do not—and that it replicates our existing design knowledge and achieves statistically significant results.

Utility of Efficiency: Testing Fitts' Law

To get a baseline understanding of the relationship between utility and HCI's existing metrics, we studied the utility of *efficiency* in a Fitts' law task.

Study design and execution.

We implemented a traditional Fitts' law task in JavaScript, where the user must click back and forth between rectangles on the left and right sides of the screen (see Figure 5). We parameterized the task with three conditions of bar width and distance, or *indices of difficulty*. The conditions as `[width, distance]` were `[300px, 700px]` for the easy task, `[30px, 870px]` for the medium, and `[3px, 897px]` for the hard. We posted 22,190 jobs to Mechanical Turk, recruiting 1,176 distinct workers, at six prices: 1¢ through 6¢. Our software automatically crossed the six prices and three experimental conditions to create eighteen conditions total. Each job required 60 clicks to complete, giving us time-to-click data on 1,331,400 clicks. We set an upper limit of 51 jobs, or 3,060 clicks, per worker. The study took 5 hours 15 minutes to complete, and cost $970.

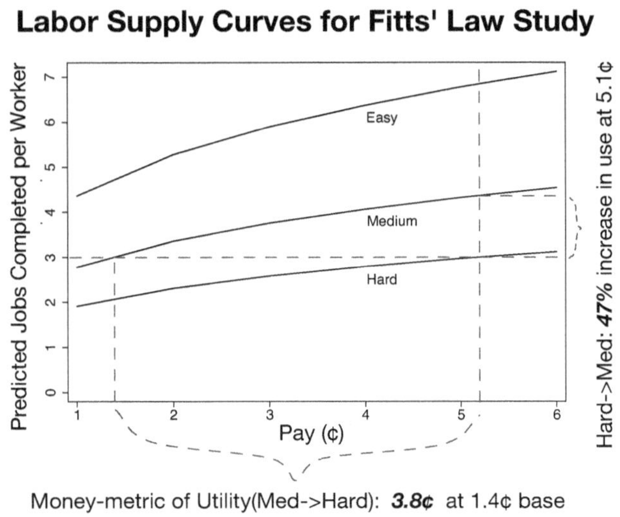

Figure 6. We paid six different prices (1-6¢) for each of the three experimental conditions: a total of eighteen conditions. By regressing on the number of jobs completed in each condition, we estimate these labor supply curves. Holding pay constant, we can quantify the effect of an interface on *use*. Holding the number of jobs constant, we can compute a *money-metric*: the amount of pay required to obtain the same amount of work between two interfaces. For 3 jobs, the utility of Medium over Hard is equivalent to 3.8¢ per 60-click job. (This data is filtered to U.S. workers.)

Analyzing the data.

Now that we have a database containing the choices of hundreds of workers completing the Fitts' law task at different prices, we would like to answer a set of questions. How much use occurs in the different conditions? How much money is this difference in use worth to users? How does utility vary over time; for instance, what is the difference between novice utility and expert utility? On the converse, how quickly do users bore of the task? And how does use vary with user context, such as a user's geographic location or local time of day? Here we define two analytical techniques that can help make sense of choice data.

Creating a Labor Supply Curve. The labor supply curve predicts the amount of use that a particular interface and degree of incentive (pay) will produce. It is a plot of the number of jobs completed at each price for each condition. We estimate the labor supply curve using a Tobit regression model [4]. The Tobit model takes into account the upper limit of 51 jobs per worker, known as "censored" data.

Figure 6 shows the predicted labor supply curves for the Fitts' Law study. In this example, we filtered to workers

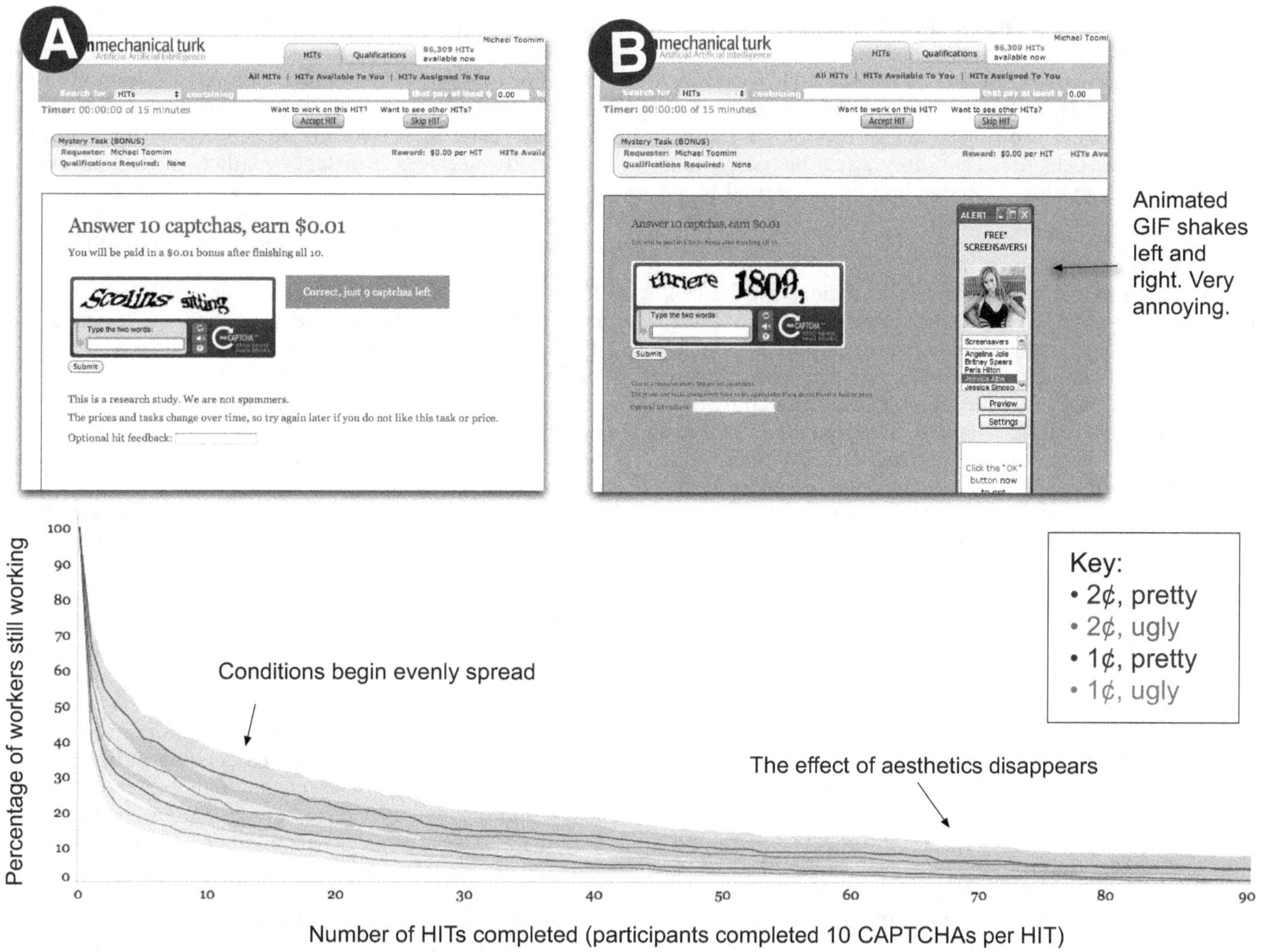

Figure 7. *Survival graph for the Aesthetics & Feedback study.* We made two interfaces for answering CAPTCHAs: one "pretty" (a), one "ugly" (b), but identical in behavior. The *survival graph* shows how many workers made it through how many tasks, for each of our four experimental conditions. The shaded regions are 95% confidence intervals. At the far left, 100% of these workers looked at the task, but only 10% to 40% completed 10 tasks (100 CAPTCHAs). Note that the *pretty* and *ugly* lines are separated at the left, but converge toward the right. This suggests either that the utility effect of aesthetics fades over time, or that the types of users who complete many CAPTCHAs are more concerned with pay than aesthetics.

from the United States (31% of the total data). As expected, workers do more work if they are paid more money. Furthermore, the curve shows they prefer the conditions in the order easy > medium > hard. These differences are significant at $p = 0.03$ from easy to medium, and 0.07 from medium to hard. In Figure 1, we can see this preference ordering even clearer. There is an inverse relationship between task difficulty and utility for Fitts' law tasks. These results are qualitatively the same for Indian workers (44% of the data), but the data show they respond much more strongly to both pay and index of difficulty than Americans. Our data can also be used to quantitatively predict the amount of work, within error bounds, that will be produced given the variables of interface, context, and incentive (pay).

Computing a Money Metric: the Compensating Wage Differential. We can also infer the amount of money an interface variation is worth: the money metric of utility. To derive the money metric, we measure the horizontal distance between two curves—the change in pay that makes them equivalent. Note that this *compensating wage differential* will generally increase with the base pay rate, as the curves spread apart. We demonstrate calculating the money metric graphically in Figure 6. With a base pay of 1.4¢ (producing 3 jobs, or 180 clicks per worker for the medium difficulty condition), we would need to pay 3.8¢ more to achieve the equivalent work rate in the hard condition.

In conclusion, our efficiency case study showed that utility can capture an existing metric: *efficiency*. Users prefer clicking efficiently-designed targets. Labor supply curves predict the amount of use an interface will get. By calculating a money-metric, we can quantify the magnitude of the utility differences across conditions, and reason and hypothesize about them in terms of the *lingua franca* of utility: dollars and cents.

Utility of Aesthetics & Feedback: CAPTCHAs

This second study demonstrates that we can measure the utility of two particularly elusive quantities in HCI: *aesthetics* and *feedback*. These quantities are elusive because they do not make an interface slower to use, or otherwise affect the user's actual behavior. They only affect his perception of the interface and his understanding of its internal process.

Study design and execution.

We experimented with two interface variations for the task of answering CAPTCHAs. One interface had a clear, minimalist design, and the other had gaudy colors, small fonts, and a distracting animated GIF advertisement (Figure 7A & B). Both tasks had the same instructions and wording, required 10 CAPTCHAs to be completed per job, and took the same amount of time to complete. The *pretty* condition implemented an elegant animated countdown reminding the user how many CAPTCHAs they had left, and the *ugly* condition only told them when they had completed all 10. We posted 15,000 jobs to Mechanical Turk, with one 10-CAPTCHA task per job. Workers were paid either 1 or 2 cents, for a total of 4 conditions. 1,270 workers completed our jobs, and the entire study cost us $388. In this study we did not limit the number of jobs a worker could complete.

Survival Analysis.

Our between-subjects auction method collects a binary choice for a user, over time until he quits. One intuitive way to represent this data is with a *survival function* [14]: a function $S(t)$ that represents the probability of a user "surviving" t tasks before quitting. Analysis starts by preprocessing the data to identify how many tasks each worker completed. Then we group data by condition and price, and plot a graph of the percentage of users who continued to use the interface after N jobs. If a line is higher in the survival graph, it means more workers completed more tasks. We compute 95% confidence intervals using Wilson's estimate [24], since survival data is binomial. When the study ends, it artificially stops, or *censors* the work of some users who might otherwise have completed more tasks. We label those users as *censored* and account for them statistically using standard survival analysis techniques.

The survival graph for the CAPTCHA experiment is shown in Figure 7. The confidence intervals for each line are shaded. The survival analysis shows how use changes over time. We can see that all four conditions are spaced apart roughly equivalent for the first 20 tasks, but for work done at 80 tasks, the top two lines (2¢) and bottom two lines (1¢) converge. This means that price dominates the utility for workers who acquire more experience with the task, and aesthetics is primarily important for those who are inexperienced. Or, those who stick with the task are more resilient to aesthetic quality.

We also estimated the effect of aesthetics on labor supply, as we did with the Fitts' law study. The results show that the effect of aesthetics and feedback is substantial: all else equal, the *pretty* style of the interface produces 58% more use. This is statistically significant at $p = 0.02$.

SCOPE, LIMITATIONS, & FUTURE WORK

We view our technique as just one point in the space of *preference measurement*, along with A/B testing and techniques that have not yet been invented. Our technique has two key features. (1) We measure behavior for controlled tasks and interfaces in a labor market, instead of experimenting with real users on a production website like A/B testing. (2) We vary pay, artificially manipulating a user's motivation, and from it infer a money metric of utility.

These unique aspects separate it from A/B testing. Interfaces to be A/B tested must be developed and tested to production quality and deployed to a real userbase. This constrains applicability in most companies, and indeed A/B testing is often limited to optimizing small variations in an existing UI—*i.e.*, for late-stage designs. Our techniques can be used to obtain quick feedback for early-stage design decisions. Furthermore, A/B testing is adept at answering "what" users will do for a particular website, but not "why." [15] By paying users, we have more discretion to ask them survey questions to elicit "why," and we also gain the ability to test abstract interfaces and tasks—such as our Fitts' law interface—to isolate factors and remove confounds of real-world websites. Future researchers can replicate and extend the results, in the same labor market, by copying and re-running the study's source code. This lets us develop and validate scientific models that generalize across concrete website instances. And by calculating utility in terms of money, we create a language to compare interfaces, tasks, and contexts and create generalizable knowledge. In summary, our techniques fill a niche in early-stage and generalizable interaction studies.

Mechanical Turk & Other Labor Markets

Although it is common to expect that Mechanical Turk workers are somehow "different" from normal computer users, the demographic data actually show workers to be remarkably representative of the Internet population. A substantial portion of workers have bachelors, masters, and PhD degrees, for instance [9,19]. Workers use Turk not just to make money, but also to have fun and spend free time, and avoid boring or distasteful tasks similarly to other Internet users [12]. We encourage the skeptical reader to investigate this data. In fact, Mechanical Turk's population is much more diverse and ecologically valid than the small-sample college populations commonly employed in HCI and Psychology research. Our Fitts' law study recruited workers from 32 countries in five hours. Moreover, the setting of use for Turk workers—*e.g.* at home, at work, at a cafe, watching TV, on one's own hardware—is often more naturalistic than a laboratory. Furthermore, we can survey workers for demographic or other information, and store it in a database with their worker-id. This allows us to examine the effect of *context* in a study, for a variety of personal characteristics, without additional experimental effort.

Yet at a higher level, our techniques are by no means limited to Mechanical Turk. In fact, there are more than ten alternative crowdsourced labor markets in current deployment [10], and we expect more to develop in the near future. Each market has different characteristics. Some markets even "pay" users with non-monetary incentives. For instance, the company CrowdFlower deploys micro-tasks through gaming company Zynga, which rewards game players with upgraded "cows" in the game FarmVille in exchange for doing small pieces of work.

Finally, we expect that our techniques could be used without a labor market at all, by finding other ways to recruit users. Facebook or Google could run utility experiments by recruiting their own users through advertisements, and paying them small amounts on PayPal. Researchers could run a custom ad campaign in this way, targeting a subpopulation. Going one step further, our economic methods could in theory be applied within A/B tests themselves, creating *utility-augmented A/B tests*. For instance, Amazon might offer randomly-selected users the opportunity to discuss a product within an experimental social system in exchange for a few cents of store credit, and thus combine many of the benefits of a traditional A/B test with many of the benefits of economic utility analysis. Indeed, it is important to remember that our existing research techniques are all biased and limited, but with time we have learned how and when to trust them. We believe the crowd enables the future of HCI evaluation.

However, when we assume we can replace a user's existing goals with money, we run into a number of potential hurdles. First, we cannot measure the value of their existing goals—only the cost (or value) inherent to the process of using the interface itself. This is a significant limitation, and difficult to get around in theory without data from actual use of the real system (*e.g.* a utility-augmented A/B test). Second, the researcher must be careful to avoid situations where the use of a money incentive adversely effects one's decision process, as has been recorded in Behavioral Economics [1]. Third, the researcher's freedom in defining the labor market worker's goal with an interface comes with the difficulty of *enforcing* it. To do so, the researcher might employ quality measurement, which we will describe next.

Quality measurement. Many computer tasks, such as writing articles, blog posts, and authoring presentations, are *open-ended.* The quality of results is difficult to verify with a computer. We have not yet studied such tasks, because we need to know which tasks were completed successfully so we can determine who to pay. The standard technique on Mechanical Turk is to post the result of tasks back to Mechanical Turk as new "reviewing" tasks, having workers review the work of other workers. This is the basis of a growing body of quality-assurance techniques used on Mechanical Turk [11]. We hope to implement this technique in our software framework. Moreover, this will enable us to study the relationship between quality and utility. High quality articles are often more difficult to write, and likely to cost more. But we can measure, for instance, whether writing on a topic of personal interest to the worker results in both higher quality *and* lower cost utility.

Cheating. Related to quality measurement is preventing cheaters and spammers on Mechanical Turk from abusing our experiments for money. Quality measurement will be critical for open-ended tasks, to prevent workers from submitting garbage results. It is also possible for someone to write a browser script to automate the submission of tasks without doing them himself. Our aesthetics task used CAPTCHAs to guard against automation, and our Fitts' law task recorded the time of each click, of which we ran simple data analyses to validate they looked human. Furthermore, we generally set a limit, such as 50 tasks, on the amount of work a worker can do. This way, even a script would make at most a dollar for its author, reducing the incentive to writing scripts.

Macroeconomic analysis. Analogous to how we are building a microeconomic analysis of user interfaces, we also imagine that future work might be able to build a *macroeconomic* analysis of entire systems, such as Wikipedia. This could attempt to answer questions such as "What is the net utility of the billions of Wikipedia edits?" analogous to "What is the GDP, or net economic output of the billions of products produced in the United States?" The path to studying this would involve first measuring the labor supply curves for users editing Wikipedia articles given different levels of pay, and exploring the different conditions—article subject, user background, education, and personality—that affect these curves. Then, by comparing these "editing costs" in to the actual amount of article editing taking place on Wikipedia, we could infer the net motivation that must be present on Wikipedia to produce the edits. We are interested in investigating where this general chain of reasoning—connecting studies relating the cost of using an interface to its use, and comparing this to actual use on a website—will allow utility studies to infer the intrinsic value of Internet user behaviors, and not just the costs of their actions.

Uniting game design and HCI. Game design and HCI often seem to pursue different metrics. HCI strives to make interactions usable, and game design strives to make them fun. HCI wants tasks to be fast, and game designers want users to spend more time on tasks. However, both fields strive for their interfaces to have high utility, and we may be able to bring the fields closer together, in common pursuit of a single metric. We note that utility is a combination of *value* and *cost*. A user often wants to achieve a goal that has some value, but in order to do so, must complete a process with a computer interface, a task with some *cost*. HCI has focused on reducing this cost, and game design has focused on increasing value. We are interested in learning how to design value into existing interfaces, rather than just reducing cost. For instance, we are currently running a utility study where we turned the traditional Fitts' law task into a video game by adding a scoreboard and graphics. By measuring the effect of these game conditions on utility, we can analyze the interaction between game mechanics and user interface costs within the same evaluative framework.

CONCLUSION

This paper presents a way to crowdsource the evaluation of utility, or the study of preference. We argue that utility measurement is necessary to make HCI relevant to free choice in computing.

In the future, we hope this class of methods will enable HCI to build a science of the human motive in computer interactions. By using the same labor marketplaces, scientists will have the equivalent of the same laboratories for interface utility studies. This would make their studies reproducible. A researcher could share her code with another researcher, who could then re-run the study and reproduce prior results, or alter the study and build on previous insights. Running studies on Mechanical Turk is cheaper and faster than traditional lab studies, as has been explored by Kittur *et al.* [13], Heer and Bostock [7], and a growing number of others.

We believe utility studies will also benefit design *practice*. Designers will be able to experiment with new interfaces and evaluate their use without building infrastructure and critical mass in a userbase. They could break up a complicated interaction into pieces, and estimate the motivation required of users for each subcomponent. This may allow practitioners to develop and test large social systems in modules, evaluating each part incrementally, before building critical mass, with greater certainty of success.

In this paper, we present just one possible method for preference measurement, using one particular labor market, and one set of economic analyses. However, preference measurement is a much larger space. In it, we can vary the user population (*e.g.* labor market, real website users), the incentive and goal structure (*e.g.* pay or no pay, real website user goals or artificial paid goals), and the experimental methods for determining value (*e.g.* auction techniques). We believe this space of investigation—understanding and designing for user preference and choice—is the future of HCI research and practice. By shifting our evaluation techniques to questions of *what people will choose to use*, we can better align our methods with our community's values.

ACKNOWLEDGEMENTS

We thank Google for a research grant that funded this work, and the anonymous reviewers for their excellent feedback. Hal Varian provided support and guidance. Lydia Chilton and Rob Miller generated early economic ideas. Jon Froehlich helped edit. Neema Moraveji and Jeffrey Heer were supportive kindred spirits. Brought to you by the letter G.

REFERENCES

1. Ariely, D. *Predictably Irrational: The Hidden Forces That Shape Our Decisions*. HarperCollins. 2008.
2. Ben-Bassat, T., Meyer, J., and Tractinsky, N. Economic and Subjective Measures of the Perceived Value of Aesthetics and Usability. *in ACM Transactions of Computer-Human Interaction*, 13 (2). 2006. 210–234.
3. Cooper, S., Khatib, F., Treuille, A., Barbero, J., Lee, J-H., Beenen, M., Leaver-Fay, A., Baker, D., Popović, Z. & Foldit players. Predicting Protein Structures with a Multiplayer Online Game. *Nature* 466, 756-760.
4. Greene, W.H. *Econometric Analysis*. Macmillan. 1990.
5. Grudin, J. Utility and Usability: Research Issues and Development Contexts. *Interacting with Computers*, 4, (1992) 209–217.
6. Grudin J. and Wang Laboratories. Adapting a Psychophysical Method to Measure Performance and Preference Tradeoffs in Human-Computer Interaction. *in Proc. INTERACT (1984)*. 737–741.
7. Heer, J. and Bostock, M. Crowdsourcing Graphical Perception: Using Mechanical Turk to Assess Visualization Design. *in Proc. CHI 2010*. (2000)
8. Horton, J.J. and Chilton, L. The Labor Economics of Paid Crowdsourcing. *in Proc. ACM Electronic Commerce 2010*. (2010)
9. Ipeirotis, P.G. Analyzing the Amazon Mechanical Turk Marketplace. *New York University Report no. CeDER-10-04*. 2010.
10. Ipeirotis, P.G. The Explosion of Micro-Crowdsourcing Services. http://behind-the-enemy-lines.blogspot.com /2010/10/explosion-of-micro-crowdsourcing.html.
11. Ipeirotis, P.G. Provost, F. and Wang, J. Quality Management on Amazon Mechanical Turk. *In Proceedings of KDD-HCOMP* (2010).
12. Ipeirotis, P.G. Why People Participate on Mechanical Turk, Now Tabulated. http://behind-the-enemy-lines.blogspot.com/2008/09/why-people-participate-on-mechanical.html
13. Kittur, A.; Chi, E. H. ; Suh, B. Crowdsourcing user studies with Mechanical Turk. In Proc. CHI 2008, ACM Press (2008). 453–456.
14. Klein, J.P. *Survival Analysis*. Springer, 2003.
15. Kohavi, R.. Practical Guide to Controlled Experiments on the Web: Listen to Your Customers not to the HiPPO. *in Proc KDD 2007*. (2007)
16. MacKenzie, S. Fitts' Law as a Research and Design Tool. *in Human-Computer Interaction (HCI)*, 1992 7(1), 91–139.
17. Malone, T.W. Heuristics for Designing Enjoyable User Interfaces: Lessons from Computer Games. *in CHI 1982*. ACM Press (1982)
18. Nielsen, J. *Usability Engineering*. Morgan Kaufmann, 2001.
19. Ross, J., Irani, L., Silberman, M.S., Zaldivar, A. and Tomlinson, B. Who are the Crowdworkers? Shifting Demographics in Mechanical Turk. *alt.chi '10*, ACM Press.
20. Simon, H.A. Designing Organizations for an Information-Rich World. in Martin Greenberger, Computers, Communication, and the Public Interest, Baltimore, MD: The Johns Hopkins Press (1971).
21. Smith, A. An Inquiry into the Nature and Causes of the Wealth of Nations. *London: Methuen and Co., Ltd.*, ed. Edwin Cannan, 1904.
22. Van Ahn, L. and Dabbish, L. Labeling Images with a Computer Game. *in Proc. CHI 2004*. ACM Press (2004)
23. Varian, H.R. *Microeconomic Analysis*. Norton, 1984.
24. Wilson, E. Probable Inference, the Law of Succession, and Statistical Inference. Journal of the American Statistical Association. 1927. 22: 209–212.

Informing Decisions: How People use Online Rating Information to Make Choices

Stelios Lelis, Andrew Howes
Manchester Business School
The University of Manchester
Booth Street West, Manchester, M15 6PB, UK
{Stylianos.Lelis, Andrew.Howes}@mbs.ac.uk

ABSTRACT
In this paper we investigate how people use online rating information to inform decision making. We examine whether a theory of searching for information to discriminate between alternative choices can explain behavior, and we contrast it to the normative theory. Partly in accord with the theory, findings from a controlled experiment suggest that in an environment dominated by positive reviews, such as the World-Wide Web, people gather more information for the best alternative under consideration, and they take more time to inspect reviews of lower rating. We discuss the theoretical and experimental implications, and propose a bounded optimal account of the way in which people acquire information in service of decision making.

Author Keywords
User modeling, information search, decision making, online consumer reviews, e-commerce.

ACM Classification Keywords
H.1.2 Models and Principles: User/Machine Systems – Human Information Processing; H.3.3 Information Storage and Retrieval: Information Search and Retrieval – Selection process.

General Terms
Human Factors, Experimentation, Theory.

INTRODUCTION
People sometimes search the World Wide Web so as to inform decision making. They use the web to help choose clothes, movies, vacations, and even homes. They choose which stocks to invest in, and which healthcare treatments to adopt. To make these decisions, people collect information about alternatives and engage in a process of comparison that is then terminated with a choice.

Choice information search presents an important Human-Computer Interaction (HCI) design challenge. It has been known for many years, for example, that simply designing e-commerce sites so that they present a logical organization of products, with meaningful link labels, is insufficient to support critical aspects of the user's task. Rather, what is needed is functionality that allows user's to bring the details of alternative products into close temporal and/or spatial proximity so that they can be contrasted [18, 20]. It is also known that choice tasks can be supported through web sites that encourage the propagation of word-of-mouth, experiential, information [5]. Indeed, systems for providing reviews, ratings, and information about what others' also liked have become pervasive [17], while some studies of how people search reviews have been conducted [16].

In parallel with the proliferation of exciting design work, HCI research has made substantial advances in understanding the ways in which people navigate the web for information. Information Foraging Theory (IFT) [23], for example, has substantially advanced our understanding of how people search information using computer systems. IFT explains user behavior in general search tasks, for example how people locate articles relevant to a topic in a large collection of documents. IFT predicts that a patch of information (for example a set of documents) should be left, so as to exploit another, when the rate of within patch gains diminishes below the expected average rate of gain. However, Pirolli and Card noted [23] "information foraging is usually a task that is embedded in the context of some other task, and the value and cost structure of information foraging are consequently defined in relation to the embedding task". More generally, it might be the case that the embedding task has substantial consequences for the information search strategy.

The Bayesian Satisficing Model (BSM) [6] and SNIF-ACT [7] also offer substantial and rigorous explanations of information search in HCI. BSM [6] has been applied to explain information seeking in a map navigation task. BSM successfully explained when participants stopped gathering information and made a choice of a route. SNIF-ACT [7] has been applied to explain when people stop evaluating links in a web page and either follow a link or backup a page, and successfully predicted user navigation behavior. Through a deep mathematical analysis of optimal behavior, complemented with empirical investigation, BSM and SNIF-ACT offer significant insights into when computer users stop gathering information, and/or evaluating links on a web page.

In the current paper, we report models that are inspired by the rigor of IFT, SNIF-ACT and BSM but which aim to complement them with analysis of choice information search. We are concerned with how information search is shaped by expectations about the value of information in embedding tasks, particularly embedding tasks that involve discriminating between choices. We distinguish between expectations about the utility of alternatives and expectations about the value of information, and examine how the former guide the latter. We are particularly interested in the effect of prior expectations concerning the utility of the choices on which alternative people decide to find out more about. To make the contrast to existing work clear: when searching for information about which digital camera to purchase (a preferred choice A or an alternative B), we can (1) just search efficiently for more information about A and B and not worry about the choice between them (e.g. as modeled by IFT) (2) choose whether to get more information about 'both A and B' or stop and act (e.g. as modeled by BSM), (3) decide whether to look for information about the stronger, currently preferred choice A, or its weaker alternative. Here we focus on this latter situation. We refer to the effect of *prior utility* on choice information search.

In addition, we complement our interest in understanding whether people search for information about preferred products with understanding how they use product ratings. For example, a review site may contain two reviews for a particular camera, one with 5 stars and the other with 2 stars, and we might ask which review should a consumer read first? In the marketing literature there is evidence that people place more weight on negative information (the 2 star review here) than positive in their decisions [13, 15]. However, the evidence about whether people prefer to seek positive or negative information and the explanation of their preferences is limited [26]. In this literature the positivity or negativity of information is called *valence*, and in the current paper we adopt the same term.

The goal of this paper then is to examine the effects of (1) prior utility and (2) review valence on choice information search. We first review theoretical questions concerning the value of information in choice tasks. Subsequently we develop a new theory of searching for information to discriminate between alternatives, and contrast it to the normative theory of information search. The review and theory development take Optimal Experimental Design (OED) [21, 22] as a point of departure. Finally, we describe an empirical study designed to test both theories. The study uses an ecologically motivated product purchasing task that focuses on online consumer reviews search, and which is amenable to formal analysis.

RELATED WORK

The Value of Information in Decision Making

There are many explorations of theories of the value of information as explanations of choice information search [2, 8, 26]. These studies have largely focused on the normative definition of the value of information known as the Expected Value of Sample Information (EVSI) [8, 24]. As with all theories of the value of information, the starting point for EVSI is Bayesian inference. It is assumed that people have prior beliefs about the utility of alternatives in choice, and that these prior beliefs guide the estimations of the value of information about the alternative. Where EVSI is distinctive, is in the idea that the value is the utility that would be gained by improving the decision. EVSI is defined as the expected gain in choice utility obtained by a likely choice reversal.

A number of studies of choice information search have examined whether people's information gathering actions conform to the predictions of EVSI [8, 26]. Hagerty and Aaker [8] examined information gathering actions in alternative-by-attribute matrices. They found that in three-alternatives-by-seven-attributes choices EVSI correctly predicted what information participants collected in 19.3% of the cases. Although this is a three-fold increase compared to random selections, it also suggests that EVSI cannot offer a comprehensive account of information search. Simonson, Huber and Payne [26] also examined information search behavior in alternative-by-attribute matrices. They measured participants' prior beliefs about alternatives and the certainty with which the beliefs were held, and they examined the acquisition order of information items. They found that, in accordance with EVSI, information concerning prior beliefs that are more uncertain is acquired earlier in the search process than information concerning more certain prior beliefs, and information about alternatives with high prior utility is acquired earlier compared to information about alternatives of low prior utility. Yet, they also observed an effect that cannot be explained by EVSI; that information concerning prior beliefs that are less favorable is acquired earlier in the search process than information concerning more favorable prior beliefs, especially for alternatives of lower utility. The access of information with negative-valence (i.e. less favorable) about inferior alternatives is not predicted by EVSI, or by an extension of EVSI with the value function of prospect theory [14], because this information cannot reverse the choice, while information with positive-valence about inferior alternatives can. In summary, these two studies [8, 26] offer partial support for EVSI as a model of information search in decision making.

In this article we explore an alternative theory of the value of information, the Discriminating Information Value (DIV). The theory is motivated by recent findings suggesting that people collect information to increase the discrimination between the alternative choices. Harvey and

Bolger [9] examined choice information search between apartments in alternative-by-attribute matrices. In these studies participants were remunerated according to a points system; the system attached a point score in each alternative and participants were awarded the points of the alternative they chosen. The studies were designed to examine whether, rather than using EVSI, participants collected information in an attempt to maximize the point score of the chosen apartment or, perhaps, to provide a basis on which alternatives could be eliminated. The authors found that neither premise offers a comprehensive account of information gathering actions, but rather that people collect information to increase the discrimination between the alternatives. In this article we explore this possibility. Below we describe the Discriminating Information Value (DIV) theory, and we also contrast it to EVSI - the normative theory. We contrast DIV to EVSI because we expect that, even if DIV cannot fully explain information search, the comparison will reveal the relative advantages of the discriminating search strategy.

THEORY DEVELOPMENT & PREDICTIONS

In this section we first describe the theory of the discriminating information value. Subsequently we deploy the theory to generate predictions about the preferences for which alternative to seek information, and the value of processing an information item (a review in our task) as a function of its valence. In addition we outline the predictions of EVSI, the normative theory.

Discriminating Information Value

In operationalising the value of information as the extent that it discriminates between alternatives we follow Optimal Experimental Design (OED) theories of the value of information [21, 22]. In OED theories the value of a question's usefulness is defined as the expected usefulness, given current knowledge of the possible answers. Each question is an information gathering action, and in our task the action is the one of obtaining and processing a review about an alternative in a choice scenario. We assume the rating of the review as the outcome of the information gathering action, or, in OED terminology, as the answer to the question. In a binary choice between alternatives i and j we define the Discriminating Information Value (DIV) of a rating r for alternative i, as the extent that it increases discrimination between the expected utilities of the two alternatives.

$$DIV_i(r) = \left|E(U_i \mid r) - E(U_j)\right| - \left|E(U_i) - E(U_j)\right| \quad (1)$$

Where $E(U_i)$ and $E(U_j)$ are the expected utilities of the two alternatives, and $E(U_i|r)$ is the expected utility of the alternative i after obtaining a review of rating r.

The value of processing one review for alternative i, the DIV of the alternative, is the sum of the values of processing a review of rating r across all ratings for this alternative, weighted by the probability of obtaining the rating r for alternative i, $p_i(r)$ [21].

$$DIV_i = \sum_r p_i(r) \cdot DIV_i(r) \quad (2)$$

Now that we have stated the definition of DIV, we should see how it is estimated in order to generate the theory's predictions. To do that we should firstly define the prior beliefs about the proportions of alternatives' ratings, and derive alternatives' expected utility.

Let the decision maker hold beliefs about the proportion of alternative's i ratings, $\theta_{i,r}$, where r stands for rating. We assume that the beliefs follow a Dirichlet distribution with known parameter vector ($\alpha_{i,1}$, …, $\alpha_{i,R}$), where R is the number of possible ratings. The $\alpha_{i,r}$ terms can be seen as the number of times that a review of rating r has been obtained for alternative i and are called the prior strengths. $\nu = \Sigma_r\, \alpha_{i,r}$ is the total prior strength.

Given the prior beliefs, the utility of alternative i is given by the formula

$$U_i = \sum\nolimits_r u_r \cdot \theta_{i,r} \quad (3)$$

Where u_r is the utility assigned to rating r, and is defined as the utility that the decision maker would obtain when experiencing an alternative of which all reviews are of rating r. The expected utility of alternative i is given by [1].

$$E(U_i) = \frac{\sum_r (\alpha_{i,r} \cdot u_r)}{\sum_r \alpha_{i,r}} \quad (4)$$

The DIV of each alternative and its ratings are estimated by projecting the processing of one more review for the alternative and are given by Equations (1) and (2). When a rating r is obtained the posterior beliefs of the proportion of ratings still follow a Dirichlet distribution with the rth component of the parameter vector increased by one [4]. Therefore, the projected expected utility of the alternative after obtaining a review of rating r, $E(U_i|r)$, is given by Equation (4) with the updated beliefs. The probability of occurring a rating r, $p_i(r)$, is given by the Dirichlet distribution of prior beliefs. The calculation of the ratings' and alternative's DIV then follows.

Predictions

DIV predicts the value of processing a review for each alternative, and the value of processing a review as a function of the review's rating (valence). To develop DIV's predictions we assume ratings with values from 1 to 5, and take into consideration the distribution of review ratings in the WWW. Consumer reviews about products are highly positive, resulting in negatively skewed or J-shaped distributions of ratings per product [12], with average ratings greater than four [3]. Hu et al [12] analysis suggests that bimodal J-shaped distributions are the most common when all products are considered, and that negatively

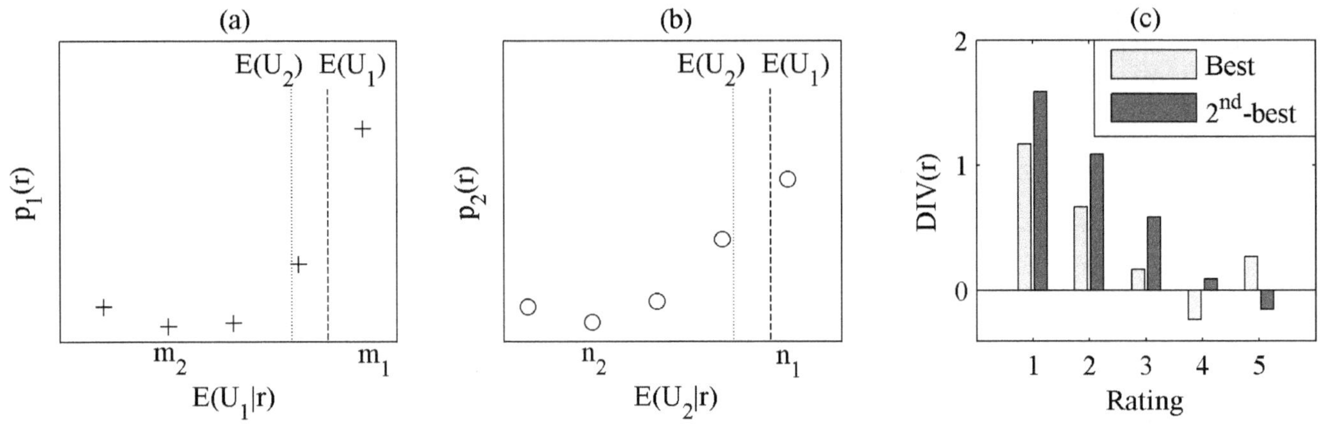

Figure 1 (a) Distribution of the posterior expected utility of the best alternative, $E(U_1|r)$. (b) Distribution of the posterior expected utility of the second-best alternative, $E(U_2|r)$. (c) Discriminating information value of each rating, DIV(r) for both alternatives.

skewed distributions are equally common for products with high average rating. Consequently in the development of the predictions below we utilize J-shaped distributions with average rating larger than 4.

Preference for which alternative to seek reviews

Let a binary choice and one of the alternatives being better than the other, i.e. having a higher expected utility. Is there a preference for which alternative to seek information? To examine this we performed a simulation exercise to determine whether the information value of processing a review for the best alternative is higher than the information value of processing a review for the second-best. In the simulation we assumed that u_r, the utility assigned to each rating, is r. Alternatives' prior beliefs were initialized by firstly utilizing the hypergeometric distribution[1], and subsequently modifying ratings' occurrence probability so as to result in J-shaped distributions. The number of successes in the hypergeometric distribution was varied from 86 to 90 out of 100 for the best alternative and from 81 to 85 for the second-best. Subsequently 0.1 and 0.04 was subtracted from the probability of the 4- and 3-star ratings occurrence respectively, and 0.07 was added to both the probability of 1- and 5-star ratings occurrence. This procedure resulted in J-shaped beliefs with expected value larger than 4. Further we initialized the total prior strength of the beliefs to integer values from 1 to 10.

The simulation results showed that in 82.4% of the cases the DIV for information about the best alternative is higher than the DIV of the second-best. There are two things to note about this percentage. First, obtaining a review for the best alternative is not always of higher value than obtaining a review for the second-best. Thus, depending on prior beliefs and total strength (i.e. the number of reviews that have been obtained), reviews of both alternatives can be of value. Second, the percentage is higher than 50%, demonstrating that in most of the cases obtaining a review for the best alternative is of higher value than obtaining a review for the second-best. We have verified that the percentage is similar for other J-shaped, and for negatively skewed distributions. Consequently, the DIV theory predicts that, when the prior beliefs are J-shaped or negatively skewed with expected value larger than 4, there is a higher preference to obtain reviews for the best alternative than the second-best.

To demonstrate why DIV predicts that people will have a higher preference to obtain reviews for the best alternative consider a choice scenario with J-shaped prior beliefs and average rating larger than 4. A positive 5-star rating for the best alternative increases discrimination, while the same rating (5-star) for the second-best alternative decreases discrimination. This is because a 5-star rating increases the excepted utility of the best alternative, shifts it further away than the utility of the second-best and therefore increases discrimination. On the other hand, a 5-star rating for the second-best alternative decreases discrimination because it shifts its expected utility closer to the utility of the best alternative. Figures 1a and b illustrate this. They show the distributions of the posterior expected utility, $E(U|r)$ of the best and second-best alternative respectively (the leftmost point of the distribution is the expected utility of the alternative when obtaining a review of rating one, the next to the right a review of rating two, etc.). The prior expected utilities of the alternatives, $E(U_1)$ and $E(U_2)$ are also depicted. A 5-star rating for the best alternative increases the discrimination from $E(U_1) - E(U_2)$ to m_1-$E(U_2)$ (Figure 1a), while a 5-star rating for the second-best alternative decreases it to n_1-$E(U_1)$ (Figure 1b). On the other hand a moderate or negative rating for the second-best alternative

[1] The hypergeometric distribution describes the number of successes in a sequence of n draws without replacement from a sample of m objects, among which k are considered a success and m-k a failure. For $n = 4$ the hypergeometric density function has 5 values (0, 1, …, 4 successes), and for high k relatively to m the shape of the distribution is negatively skewed.

increases discrimination more than when it is obtained for the best alternative. Consider a 2-star rating for the second-best alternative. It considerably reduces its expected utility, shifts it further away than the utility of the best alternative, and increases discrimination from $E(U_1) - E(U_2)$ to $E(U_1) - n_2$ (Figure 1b) A 2-star rating for the best alternative also increases discrimination but only to $E(U_2)$-m_2 (Figure 1a). Note that for some of the moderate ratings of the best alternative the discrimination may be decreased, while it is increased when the same rating is obtained for the second-best alternative, for example the 4-star rating in Figure 1.

Consequently, as Figure 1c, which depicts the DIV of each rating for both alternatives, also illustrates, the DIV of negative and moderate ratings is higher for the second-best alternative, while the DIV of positive ratings is higher for the best alternative. However, positive ratings are very common, while negative and moderate ratings are rare. Thus, the DIV of the best alternative is generally higher, because the larger increases in discrimination for the best alternative realized by obtaining a positive rating, generally overshadow when taken in average, the larger increases in discrimination for the second-best alternative realized by obtaining a negative or moderate rating, because positive reviews are considerably more likely.

We also performed the simulation we described above for EVSI to examine the theory's prediction for which alternative to seek information. The simulation results showed that in 81.8% of the cases the EVSI for information about the best alternative is higher than the EVSI for information about the second-best. Consequently, and similarly to DIV, in a choice scenario EVSI predicts that people will obtain more reviews for the best alternative.

Value of processing a review according to rating

Here we examine the information value of processing a review as a function of a review's rating. We restrict the discussion, and therefore the predictions, to 4- and 5-star ratings, and distributions with expected value larger than 4.

DIV predictions: For the best alternative under consideration DIV predicts that reviews of 4-star rating are of lower information value than reviews of 5-star rating. This is because a 5-star rating increases the excepted utility of the best alternative and therefore discrimination, while a 4-star rating decreases the utility of the best alternative, shifts it closer to the expected utility of the second-best, and therefore decreases discrimination (see also Figure 1a). For the second-best alternative DIV predicts that reviews of 4-star rating are of higher information value than reviews of 5-star rating. This is because a 4-star rating decreases the excepted utility of the second-best alternative and therefore increases discrimination, while a 5-star rating increases the utility of the second-best alternative, shifts it closer to the expected utility of the best, and therefore decreases discrimination (see also Figure 1b).

EVSI predictions: Before developing the predictions of EVSI about the value of processing a review as a function of a review's rating let us recall the definition of EVSI. EVSI is the expected gain in choice utility obtained by a likely choice reversal. This would imply that if a rating does not reverse the choice it has zero EVSI. Nevertheless, as Chater et al. [2] noted, it is possible that the information may not immediately reverse the choice, but when combined with later information, it might do so. Consequently, a rating that brings the expected utilities of the two alternatives closer, thus making a future reversal more likely, has a higher value than a rating that increases the difference between the expected utilities of the two alternatives, thus making a future reversal less likely.

For the best alternative under consideration EVSI predicts that reviews of 4-star rating are of higher information value than reviews of 5-star rating. A 5-star rating for the best alternative increases its expected utility, does not reverse the choice, and makes a future reversal less likely. On the other hand a 4-star rating decreases the expected utility of the alternative and may reverse the choice. If it does reverse the choice it has a positive information value. Yet, even if it does not reverse the choice it makes a future reversal more likely than a 5-star review. This is because it shifts the expected utility of the best alternative closer to the one of the second-best (see also Figure 1a).

For the second-best alternative EVSI predicts that reviews of 4-star rating are of lower information value than reviews of 5-star rating. Note that a 4-star rating decreases the expected utility of the alternative, does not reverse the choice, and makes a future reversal less likely. On the other hand a 5-star review increases the expected utility of the second-best alternative and may reverse the choice. If it does reverse the choice – which is the case in Figure 1b – it has a positive information value. Yet, even if it does not reverse the choice, it makes a future reversal more likely than a 4-star review. This is because it shifts the expected utility of the second-best alternative closer to the one of the best.

To summarize, the two theories give contradicting predictions about the value of processing 4- and 5-star reviews. For the best alternative DIV predicts that 4-star reviews are of lower information value than 5-star, while EVSI predicts that 4-star reviews are of higher information value than 5-star. For the second-best alternative DIV predicts that 4-star reviews are of higher information value than 5-star, while EVSI predicts that 4-star reviews are of lower information value than 5-star. Finally, note that the predictions are the same for J-shaped and negatively skewed distributions with expected value larger than 4, as they are independent of ratings' occurrence probabilities.

EXPERIMENT

To test the predictions and contrast the two theories we conducted an experimental study of how human preferences

	Alt. 1	Alt. 2	Alt. 3
Price	75	81	87
LCD Size	2.5	2	2.25
Digital Zoom	4	2	3
Battery Life	275	225	175
Weight	170	200	230
Dimensions	8.5×2.0×5.3	9.4×2.4×6.2	9.0×2.2×5.8
Note. The remaining attributes and their values were: Resolution: 7 mega-pixel; Optical zoom: 3×; Battery type: Proprietary Lithium; Memory Type: Compact Flash Card; Supplied card: 32MB; Red eye reduction: Built-in; ISO Levels: Auto, 50, 100, 200, 400; Video: Yes;			

Table 1. An example of alternatives' attribute values.

are shaped by prior utility and valence. The experiment used a digital camera choice task with high ecological validity, in which participants were first exposed to attributes information and then reviews. We used multiple levels of differences between alternatives attribute values in order to ensure that the results are robust to these differences.

The Task

The task involved a choice between three alternative digital cameras[2]. Participants were initially exposed to information about alternatives' attribute values. Subsequently, they were free to read consumer reviews for each camera, and the number and order of reviews obtained for each alternative, and the time they took to read each review, were measured.

Each participant performed a practice task, followed by two experimental tasks. The practice task involved a choice between three mega-pixel cameras, and the experimental tasks involved choices between five and seven mega-pixel cameras. In each task participants were first presented with attribute information in a single web page, and when they indicated that they had obtained as much information as they wanted, they were forwarded to another web page listing consumer reviews about the alternatives. While in this page participants could not go back to the page presenting alternatives' attributes and obtain more information.

Specific instructions were given to the participants. They were instructed to imagine that they needed to purchase a digital camera and select one that was suitable. They were told that they could take as much time as they wanted in order to inspect information and make their choice. Finally, and as a motive to engage with the task, they were informed that one of them, randomly selected, would be awarded one of the digital cameras s/he would choose.

Design and Materials

The attribute information was presented in a single web page, with layout very similar to the 'Compare Products' pages of real web sites like, for example, Epinions.com. To enhance the ecological validity of the study, choice alternatives were described in addition to features with a fictitious name and a camera picture. The pictures were randomly selected for each trial from a pool of ten camera images. The ten images were of similar looking compact digital cameras, downloaded from amazon.co.uk and processed to remove any brand information. Camera names, pictures, and order of presentation, were randomized for each choice.

Each alternative was described with fourteen attributes, and the values of six of them were randomized resulting in a large number of different choice sets. The randomization was performed so as to give multiple levels of differences between alternatives attribute values. As a result in some of the choices one alternative was better than the other two, while in others the three alternatives were more or less similar in terms of attribute values. This was done in order to make sure that people's preference for which alternative to obtain more reviews is robust to these differences. Table 1 shows an example choice scenario.

After inspecting the attributes information participants were free to read consumer reviews for each alternative. They were forwarded to another web page. In this page they were presented in a structure similar to the attributes web page, and in one column for each alternative, with its name, picture, and a numbered list of its reviews in the form 'Review 1', 'Review 2', etc. To access a review participants should place the mouse pointer over the text 'Review x' and the review opened automatically in a pop-up window. A delay of two seconds was introduced between placing the

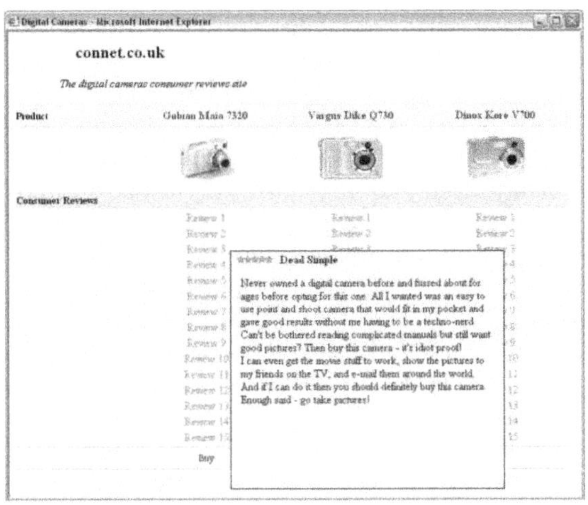

Figure 2. The reviews web page with one of the reviews being displayed.

---

2 Choices between three alternatives were utilized in the experiment although the reported theory describes opinion search in binary choices. The third, inferior in terms of ratings alternative, was introduced so as to increase the ecological validity of the task

	Ratings				
	Subset 1	Subset 2	Subset 3	Subset 4	Subset 5
Best	5, 5, 4	5, 5, 4	5, 5, 4	5, 5, 4	5, 5, 4
Second-best	5, 4, 4	5, 4, 3	5, 5, 3	5, 5, 2	5, 4, 4
Worst	5, 4, 1	5, 3, 2	5, 4, 2	5, 4, 1	5, 4, 1

Table 2 The subsets that alternatives' ratings were grouped.

pointer over the review link, and the review being displayed. Figure 2 depicts the web page with one of the reviews opened.

There were 15 reviews for each alternative. The ratings of each alternative's reviews were the same in all choices. Alternatives were firstly assigned ratings and then reviews according to the assigned ratings. Three sets of review ratings were utilized, and each set was assigned to one of the alternatives. The means of the ratings sets ranked them as best, second-best and worst. The distribution of ratings was similar to the type of distributions obtained for real products in the World Wide Web; i.e. were negatively skewed or J-shaped. The best and second-best ratings' sets were negatively skewed, and the worst set was J-shaped – reflecting the statistics of the environment reported earlier. The sets were assigned to alternatives as follows. In the choices where one of the alternatives had better attribute values than the other two, the best set was assigned to this alternative, and the other two alternatives were randomly assigned one of the second-best and worst sets. In the choices where attributes were more or less similar for all attributes, the three sets were randomly assigned. Below I refer to the three alternatives as best, second-best and worst as prescribed by the rating sets that was assigned to it.

Six sets of reviews according to alternatives' ratings were constructed; two for each alternative. Each set contained 15 reviews, which were selected so as not to contradict each other. Each alternative's sets of reviews were randomly, and separately for each participant, assigned between the two tasks that s/he made. So as to maintain ecological validity we sampled reviews from amazon.co.uk. The reviews were selected according to specific criteria. The criteria were that the review (i) had a length between 100 and 150 words, (ii) did not mention attributes different to the ones of our fictitious products, (iii) did not mention specific characteristics of other reviews, (iv) did not mention Amazon, (v) did not mention that the camera comes with extras such as case, camera dock etc., (vi) did not compare the reviewed camera to competitors, or describe the choice between two cameras, and (vii) did not extensively review the video capability. No further control was exercised on the sample. Further, a total of 90 reviews was used (44 5-star and 28 4-star), so as to minimize any effects of idiosyncratic reviews on the dependent variables. After sampling, some reviews were slightly edited for spelling, and brand and model names were replaced by the fictitious ones.

The order of review ratings was semi-randomized, and the order of reviews was fully randomized. This was done so as to (i) avoid any effects of sequential, highly positive, or negative ratings, (ii) equally position reviews of all ratings throughout the search process in order to control for the effect of fatigue on the dependent variables, and (iii) position full reviews in various stages of the search process so as to further control for the effects of fatigue and idiosyncratic reviews. The set of ratings for each alternative were grouped into subsets of mean rating similar to the average of the whole set (see Table 2). The order of subsets was held constant, yet the order of ratings within each subset was randomized. This procedure resulted in a large number of different ratings orders for each alternative. After determining the order of ratings, the full reviews were randomly selected according to their rating from each alternative's set of reviews.

Finally choice (five or seven mega-pixels), and order of differences between alternatives' attribute information were counterbalanced across participants.

Participants

Twelve members of a large UK university's community volunteered to take part in the experiment and were paid £5 for their participation. The participants were recruited by a posting an add to the university's web site. After the completion of the study, the incentive for engaging with the task was administered, and a randomly selected participant was awarded one of the digital cameras s/he chose. Since the digital cameras used in the experiment were fake, we awarded a camera with features similar to the one the randomly selected participant chose.

Results

Below we first provide an analysis of participants' preference for which alternative to seek reviews, followed by an analysis of the average time they took to inspect reviews of 4- and 5-star rating, which is an estimate of the value of processing a review according to rating.

Preference for which alternative to seek reviews

To examine participants' preference for which alternative to seek reviews we consider two dependent variables; the number of reviews participants acquired for each alternative, and the acquisition priority of each alternative's reviews. Figure 3a shows the number of reviews participants acquired per alternative. An analysis of variance (ANOVA) was conducted using alternative (best, second-best, and worst) as the within-subjects variable. The

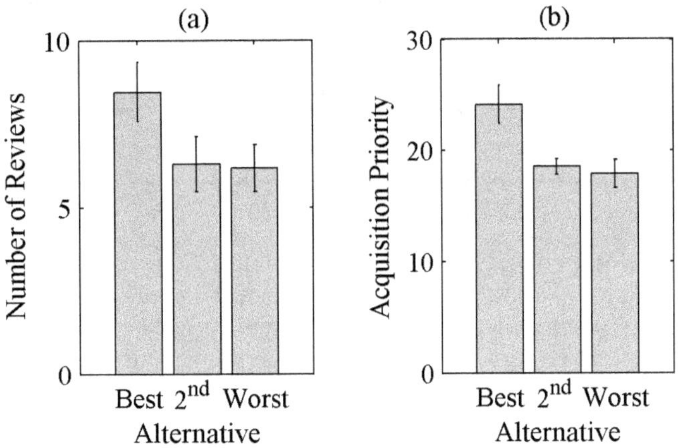

Figure 3. (a) The number of reviews participants acquired per alternative. (b) Alternatives' acquisition priority. Error bars represent standard errors of the means.

analysis revealed a significant effect of alternative, $F(2,36) = 9.7$, $MSE = 4.1$, $p < .001$. As Figure 3a illustrates participants obtained more reviews for the best alternative than for the second-best and the worst. The planned comparisons between the number of reviews participants obtained for the best and the other two alternatives were tested by performing pair-wise two-tailed *t*-tests. The *t*-tests show that the differences between the best, and the second-best and worst alternatives are significant ($t(23) = 3.78$, $p = .001$; and $t(23) = 4.41$, $p < .001$ respectively, two-tailed).

The acquisition priority (AP) is a measure of the order of reviews processing. It summarizes how early or late in the search process reviews about each alternative are acquired. AP is the measure described in [26], updated with the total number of information items (reviews) in our task (45), the number of alternatives (3), and the number of reviews that each participant acquired. The larger the value of AP the earlier the reviews about this alternative are acquired. Differences between the value of AP were tested with a one-way ANOVA using alternative (best, second-best, and worst) as the within-subjects variable. The analysis revealed a significant effect of alternative, $F(2,22) = 5.56$, $MSE = 25.6$, $p < .05$. As Figure 3b illustrates, the best alternative has the largest AP while the second-best and the worst alternatives have relatively equal. That is, participants obtained reviews for the best alternative earlier than for the second-best and the worst. The planned comparisons between the AP of the best and the other two alternatives were tested by performing pair-wise two-tailed *t*-tests. The *t*-tests show that the differences between the best and second-best, and the best and worst alternatives are significant ($t(11) = 3.17$, $p < .01$; and $t(11) = 2.32$, $p < .05$ respectively).

Time to inspect reviews per rating

To examine the value of processing a review according to its rating, we consider the average time participants took to inspect reviews of each rating. The analysis was done separately for each alternative. Only 4- and 5-star reviews were examined.

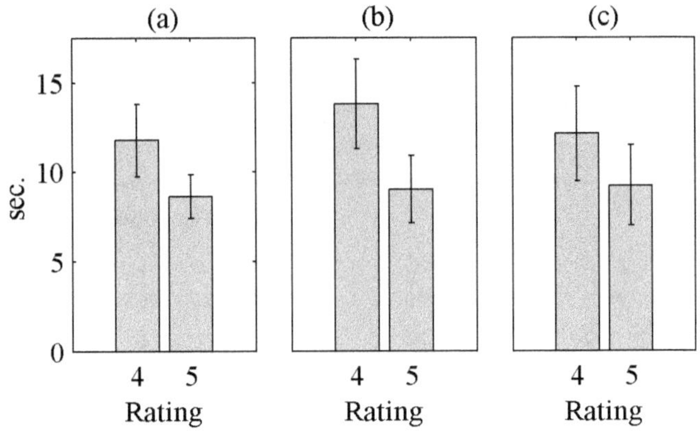

Figure 4. The average time participants took to inspect each review per rating for (a) best, (b) second-best, and (c) worst alternative. Error bars represent standard errors of the means.

For the best alternative a one way ANOVA was conducted using rating (4, 5) as within-subjects variable. The analysis revealed a significant main effect of rating, $F(1,11) = 5.05$, $MSE = 11.8$, $p < .05$. As Figure 4a illustrates participants took more time to inspect 4-star than 5-star reviews.

For the second-best alternative a one way ANOVA was conducted using rating (4, 5) as within-subjects variable. One participant who did not obtain a 5-star review was removed from the analysis. The effect of rating is significant, $F(1,10) = 17.2$, $MSE = 7.3$, $p < .01$. Participants took on average more time to inspect 4-star than 5-star reviews, Figure 4b.

Finally, a one way ANOVA was conducted for the worst alternative using rating (4, 5) as within-subjects variable. Two participants who did not obtain a 4- or 5-star review were removed from the analysis. The analysis revealed a significant effect of rating, $F(1,9) = 26.8$, $MSE = 1.57$, $p = .001$. As Figure 4c illustrates participants took more time to inspect 4-star than 5-star reviews.

GENERAL DISCUSSION

In this paper we have addressed the question of how people use rating information, found on many e-commerce web sites, in order to support choice information search tasks. We described how the Discriminating Information Value (DIV) theory made a number of predictions about user' behavior and we showed how results of an empirical study provide some evidence in favor of DIV. First, in an environment dominated by positive reviews, such as the World-Wide Web, participants gathered more information for the best alternative under consideration. Second, participants took more time to inspect reviews with lower ratings for inferior alternatives.

However, we also found evidence that is counter to DIV's predictions: when evaluating the best alternative, participants took more time to inspect reviews with 4-star ratings than reviews with 5-star ratings. In fact, the experimental results suggest that people have a tendency to take more time to inspect a review with lower rating irrespective of the ranking of the alternative. This, in turn, suggests that for participants, if not for the DIV theory, the lower the rating of a review the higher its information value.

Further analyses of the implications of the data for the normative theory of information search (EVSI) were conducted. In contrast to DIV, we found that EVSI could explain why participants took more time to inspect 4-star than 5-star reviews for the best alternative – because it increases the chance of a response reversal. However, EVSI did not explain why participants had the same preference, for 4-star over 5-star reviews, when evaluating an inferior alternative. Therefore, neither EVSI nor DIV offers an explanation of participants' information gathering preferences in the experimental choice task.

In sum then, while the results show unequivocal effects of beliefs about prior utility and of rating value on choice information search, the direction of the effects does not support existing theoretical accounts. The findings therefore present a considerable challenge to explanation, a challenge that we start to address in the following section.

Alternative Explanation

In order to introduce a new approach to understanding choice information search we take a step back and reframe the problem as a problem of bounded utility maximization [10, 11, 19, 25, 27]. Bounded utility maximization assumes that individuals adapt rationally to a utility function given constraints imposed by their cognitive abilities and their experience. Bounded utility maximization radically differs from normative accounts of behavior, by taking into account cognitive and task constraints. For example, the normative account of choice information search, EVSI, is only normative if temporal information constraints are ignored. We need a theory that is optimal given the constraints experienced by users.

The constraints experienced by users include time. Users have limited time to process information, and they trade-off time for choice utility. A means to reduce the time effort of choice is to simplify the decision by increasing the discrimination between alternatives (DIV). On the other hand a means to increase choice utility is to search for information that may reverse the choice (EVSI). From this perspective we can see that EVSI and DIV are not in competition, but rather that they can each contribute toward solving the utility maximization problem in different ways. The balance between them may be quantified and studied by examining the maximization of the difference between the choice utility and the cost (as expressed in time or cognitive effort) of making the choice. Of course the balance selected by a user will depend on cognitive constraints (e.g. limitations of short-term memory), and on a range of constraints that include aspects of the web site design such as the cost of retrieving reviews from different products and with different ratings.

Here we briefly sketch how DIV and EVSI might work together to explain the results of the reported experiment. DIV predicts that reviews of lower rating are of higher value for inferior alternatives because they largely increase discrimination. In effect these lower ratings decrease the utility of the alternative considerable, and allow the decision maker to eliminate it from further consideration and save information processing costs and time. On the other hand, EVSI predicts that reviews of lower rating are of higher value for the best-alternative because they significantly reduce its utility and have the potential to reverse the choice, therefore saving utility. That is, processing less favorable information for all alternatives results in gains; it reduces the costs of processing information and time effort (as exemplified by DIV), and increases the choice utility (as exemplified by EVSI). Therefore, it appears that both theories have advantages in explaining review processing, and together contribute to the understanding of why people take more time to inspect less favorable reviews.

Design Implications

As we have said, it is critical that web site designs are sufficiently flexible to allow people to easily compare alternative choices, whether the choices are between health plans ,holidays, or financial investments [20]. Supporting comparison involves supporting low cost of access to the most useful information when it is needed. To the extent that the reported study reveals the information that participants find most useful in choice information search, it could form the basis of research aimed at informing design. For example, the results of the study suggest that in an environment dominated by positive information, such as the World-Wide Web, people will prefer to process more information for the best alternative, and that they will prefer to process negative information about all alternatives under consideration. These findings suggest that any interface that reduces the cost of access to information about higher utility products and to negative reviews will make it easier for people to make choices. There may be ways to take advantage of these ideas in single vendor sites, as well as on product comparison sites, and product forums.

Limitations

Further experimentation is required to ascertain whether the results are replicated with more participants and to ascertain whether they generalize beyond the sample student population.

CONCLUSION

The research reported in this paper extends previous work in the following ways: It developed an OED theory of the discriminating value of information in decision making, and examined whether people gather information to discriminate between alternatives. Contrary to earlier findings [9], it suggests that people do not collect information merely to discriminate between alternative choices. In addition, by contrasting the theory to the normative account of information search (EVSI), it offers a descriptive, yet formally justified, explanation of users' preference to obtain less favorable information in environments dominated by positive information, such as the World-Wide-Web. Finally, building on its theoretical and experimental insights, it paves the way for the development of a promising theory of information search in choice tasks.

ACKNOWLEDGMENTS

This work was supported by a PhD Fellowship Award to the first author from the School of Informatics and Manchester Business School at the University of Manchester.

REFERENCES

1. Bernard, J.-M. Non-parametric Inference about an Unkown Mean using the Imprecise Dirichlet Model. *ISIPTA 2001* (2001).
2. Chater, N., Crocker, M.J. and Pickering, M.J. The rational analysis of inquiry: the case of parsing. In Oaksford, M. and Chater, N. eds. *Ratuional Models of Cognition*, OUP (1998), 441-568.
3. Chevalier, J. and Mayzlin, D. The effect of Word of Mouth on sales: Online Book Reviews. *Journal of Marketing Research 43*, 3 (2006), 345-354.
4. DeGroot, M. *Optimal Statistical Decisions*. McGrow-Hill (1970).
5. Dellarocas, C. The Digitization of Word of Mouth: Promise and Challenges of Online Feedback Mechanisms. *Management Science 49*, 10 (2003), 1407-1424.
6. Fu, W.-T. and Gray, W. Suboptimal tradeoffs in information seeking. *Cognitive Psychology 52* (2006), 195-242.
7. Fu, W.-T. and Pirolli, P. A Cognitive Model of User Navigation on the World Wide Web. *Human-Computer Interaction 22*, 4 (2007), 355-412.
8. Hagerty, M. and Aaker, D. A Normative Model of Consumer Information Processing. *Marketing Science 3*, 3 (1984), 227-246.
9. Harvey, N. and Bolger, F. Collecting information: Optimizing outcomes, screening options, or facilitating discrimination? *The Quarterly Journal of Experimental Psychology 54A*, 1 (2001), 269-301.
10. Howes, A., Lewis, R. and Vera, A. Rational Adaptation Under Task and Processing Constraints: Implications for Testing Theories of Cognition and Action. *Psychological Review 116*, 4 (2009), 717-751.
11. Howes, A., Vera, A. and Lewis, R. Cognitive constraint modeling: A formal approach to reasoning about behavior. In *Proc. CogSci 2004*, Erlbaum (2004), 595-600.
12. Hu, N., Pavlou, P. and Zhang, J. Can Online Reviews Reveal a Product's True Quality? Empirical Findings and Analytical Modeling of Online Word-of-Mouth Communication. In *Proc. EC 2006*, ACM Press (2006), 324 - 330
13. Huang, J.-H. and Chen, Y.-F. Herding in Online Product Choice. *Psychology & Marketing 23*, 5 (2006), 413-428.
14. Kahneman, D. and Tversky, A. Prospect Theory: An Analysis of Decision Under Risk. *Econometrica 47*, 2 (1979), 263-291.
15. Lee, J., Park, D.-H. and Han, I. The effect of negative online consumer reviews on product attitude: An information processing view. *Electronic Commerce Research and Applications 7* (2008), 341-352.
16. Lelis, S. and Howes, A. A Bayesian Model of How People Search Online Consumer Reviews. In *Proc. CogSci 2008*, Cognitive Science Society (2008), 553-558.
17. Li, X. and Hitt, L. Self-Selection and Information Role of Online Product Reviews. *Information Systems Research 19*, 4 (2008), 456-474.
18. Lohse, G. and Johnson, E. A Comparison of Two Process Tracing Methods for Choice Tasks. *Organizational Behavior and Human Decision Processes 68*, 1 (1996), 28-43.
19. Malloney, L. and Mamassian, P. Bayesian decision theory as a model of human visual perception: Testing Bayesian transfer. *Visual Neuroscience 26* (2009), 147-155.
20. Miles, G., Howes, A. and Davies, A. A frameowrk for understanding human factors in web-based electronic commerce. *Int. J. Human-Computer Studies 52* (2000), 131-163.
21. Nelson, J. Towards a rational theory of human information acquisition. In Oaksford, M. and Chater, N. eds. *The Probabilistic Mind: Prospects for Bayesian Cognitive Science* OUP (2008), 143-163.
22. Oaksford, M. and Chater, N. Optimal data selection: Revision, review, and reevaluation. *Psychonomic Bulletin & Review 10*, 2 (2003), 289-318.
23. Pirolli, P. and Card, S. Information Foraging. *Psychological Review 106*, 4 (1999), 643-675.
24. Raiffa, H. and Schlaifer, R. *Applied Statistical Decision Theory*. Division of Research, HBS (1961).
25. Russel, S.J. and Subramanian, D. Provably bounded-optimal agents. *Journal of Artificial Intelligence Research 2* (1995), 575-609.
26. Simonson, I., Huber, J. and Payne, J. The Relationship between Prior Brand Knowledge and Information Acquisition Order. *Journal of Consumer Research 14*, 4 (1988), 566-578.
27. Vera, A. and Howes, A. A constraint satisfaction approach to predicting skilled interactive performance. In *Proc. CHI 2004*, ACM Press (2004), 121-128.

Oops, I Did It Again:

Mitigating Repeated Access Control Errors on Facebook

Serge Egelman
National Institute of Standards and Technology
Gaithersburg, MD
serge.egelman@nist.gov

Andrew Oates
Google, Inc.
Cambridge, MA
andrewoates@gmail.com

Shriram Krishnamurthi
Brown University
Providence, RI
sk@cs.brown.edu

ABSTRACT
We performed a study of Facebook users to examine how they coped with limitations of the Facebook privacy settings interface. Students graduating and joining the workforce create significant problems for all but the most basic privacy settings on social networking websites. We therefore created realistic scenarios exploiting work/play boundaries that required users to specify access control policies that were impossible due to various limitations. We examined whether users were aware of these problems without being prompted, and once given feedback, what their coping strategies were. Overall, we found that simply alerting participants to potential errors was ineffective, but when choices were also presented, participants introduced significantly fewer errors. Based on our findings, we designed a privacy settings interface based on Venn diagrams, which we validated with a usability study. We conclude that this interface may be more effective than the current privacy settings interface.

Author Keywords
Privacy, Social Networks, Access Control, Policy Authoring

ACM Classification Keywords
D.4.6 Security and protection, H.5.2 User Interfaces

General Terms
Security, Human Factors, Experimentation, Design

INTRODUCTION
Once the realm of system administrators, even novice users are now expected to author access control policies. When using social networking websites, users may configure their profiles so that only certain people can view private information. As users share content, erroneous access control policies can have profound privacy consequences, especially when there are disconnects between the policy author's mental model of what the policy *should* say and how the system *actually* evaluates the policy. These "semantic errors" are much harder to detect than syntactic errors because they result in technically valid policies. Research suggests that policy authors are least likely to create semantic policy errors when they use natural language to specify the policy [3]. However, due to various factors, allowing policy authors to use natural language whenever they specify access control policies is simply not practical. While access control mechanisms have proliferated over the course of forty years, research on the interfaces that a human uses to author policies has only just begun. The Computing Research Association (CRA) has gone so far as to list giving "end-users security controls they can understand and privacy they can control for the dynamic, pervasive computing environments of the future" as one of the top four grand challenges in information security and assurance [4].

We present a study of how Facebook[1] users create, detect, and resolve semantic access control errors. The current interface creates opportunities for policy ambiguities—situations where a policy could be interpreted in different ways based on a parser's predefined semantics. When left undetected, policy ambiguities can transform into semantic errors. We contribute to the literature on access control interfaces by empirically evaluating the effectiveness of corrective feedback during policy authoring; we show when feedback can and cannot minimize policy errors. We identify rudimentary-but-useful scenarios where it would be impossible to correctly configure Facebook's privacy settings. Finally, we present and evaluate a new interface to help users visualize effective permissions on social networking websites.

We first present related work on privacy and online social networks. Next, we present an experiment where participants altered their privacy settings to fit realistic scenarios that exploited work-play boundaries. We examined whether participants noticed ambiguities and whether they corrected those ambiguities using two different types of feedback. Finally, we designed a privacy settings interface using Venn diagrams so that participants could better visualize how their work networks and social networks overlapped. In our second experiment, participants created significantly lower error rates in half of the scenarios, and equal error rates in the other scenarios. Finally, we discuss participants' Facebook privacy behaviors and the limitations of our experiments.

[1]Products are identified to specify the experimental procedure adequately. This is not intended to imply recommendation or endorsement by the National Institute of Standards and Technology.

CHI 2011, May 7–12, 2011, Vancouver, BC, Canada.
Copyright 2011 ACM 978-1-4503-0267-8/11/05...$10.00.

BACKGROUND

Social networking websites allow users to post personal information to share with their friends, while the users rely on access control settings to prevent the data from being shared with unintended parties. In 2005, Gross and Acquisti mined the Carnegie Mellon network on Facebook. They found that "90.8% of profiles contain an image, 87.8% of users reveal their birth date, 39.9% list a phone number (including 28.8% of profiles that contain a cellphone number), and 50.8% list their current residence [9]." Young and Quan-Haase performed a study in 2009 and found that 64% of study participants had restricted their profiles to friends [22]. Because social networking websites are primarily used to stay in touch with existing friends, rather than to form new online relationships [12, 11], we would expect users to limit the private information they expose to complete strangers. Indeed, boyd and Hargittai found that in 2010, 98% of their study participants had previously modified privacy settings [2].

Strater and Lipford performed a study of 18 Facebook users and found that over 72% of their participants took an "all or nothing" approach to privacy: they made their profiles either completely open or restricted them to only their friends. Only five participants used fine-grained controls to restrict access based on relationships and the type of information that was to be accessed [16].

As online communities evolve, controlling information on social networking websites has become a lot more complicated than restricting access to friends. Binder et al. performed a survey of Facebook users to examine how differing social spheres interact and found that privacy concerns were directly correlated with the number of family members a user had friended [1]. Stutzman and Kramer-Duffield found that some Facebook users went so far as to create a second profile to share with their "real" friends [17]. Skeels and Grudin conducted a survey of corporate Facebook users to examine how they managed privacy settings when social networks consisted of both friends and coworkers. They found that many respondents had so many problems changing privacy settings that many resorted to censoring their content rather than configuring privacy settings. In fact, many respondents complained about not being able to divide their Facebook friends into groups, oblivious to the fact that such a feature existed [14]. Access control concerns are only increasing as social networking tools become more and more accepted within the workplace [19, 6, 13, 5, 15, 21].

Researchers have proposed alternative privacy settings interfaces for social networking websites. For instance, Watson et al. proposed AudienceView, which allows users to configure settings while viewing effective permissions [20]. Tootoonchian et al. proposed Lockr, which is based on access control lists [18]. We are unaware of proposed interfaces designed around the interplay between overlapping social networks. Likewise, tools have been proposed to help users understand policy semantics through change-impact analysis [8], as well as to minimize semantic errors by asking users clarifying questions [7], we are unaware of usability studies that have been performed on these techniques.

FEEDBACK AND GUIDANCE

In our first experiment, we examined how often Facebook users detected semantic errors when specifying access control policies (i.e., privacy settings). Additionally, we examined how they went about correcting these errors and whether certain types of feedback would help them specify the correct policies. We performed a laboratory study on 33 participants who performed tasks on Facebook that were likely to lead to semantic errors in their access control policies.

Methodology

From May 26 to June 1, 2010, we conducted a laboratory experiment where we recruited Facebook users in the Brown University community. Since over 25% of Facebook users are in the 18-24 age group [10], we believe our sample is representative of an important demographic of Facebook users.

We recruited participants using flyers posted around campus as well as ads on Facebook. We directed potential participants to an online screening survey designed to establish Facebook usage and their affiliation with Brown. So as to not prime participants, we asked several subterfuge questions about their usage of several other social networking websites. Our experimental tasks required participants to have an existing *brown.edu* email address so that they could join the Brown network on Facebook if they were not already members. We invited only those participants who had been using Facebook for six months or more to schedule a time to visit our laboratory on campus. Because we wanted this study to be realistic with regard to how Facebook users might behave outside of the laboratory, at no time did we instruct participants on using Facebook's privacy settings.

When participants arrived at our laboratory, we first asked them questions about their Facebook usage. This survey contained questions about how often they posted various types of content (e.g., status updates, photos, links, etc.) and the size of their social networks. Next, participants performed four different tasks using their real Facebook profiles. They were instructed to role-play the following scenario:

> *You graduated from Brown and are now working at a local startup called "Conglomi." We will ask you to perform tasks using Facebook that you might do while you are at work. As a first step, the experimenter will help you install a Facebook app in order to help us collect data during the experiment. No personal data will be used and the app will be removed at the end of this study. This app will add you to the Conglomi network on Facebook, so that you can interact with coworkers. In addition to this, the app will also send you friend invitations from a few of your coworkers.*

Next, we gave participants a handout listing their fictitious coworkers and indicating which Facebook networks each coworker was a member of, as well as which of the coworkers were friends with them on Facebook. The Facebook app that participants installed was used solely for data collection purposes. Unbeknownst to participants, their connections were being intercepted by our proxy server so that we could

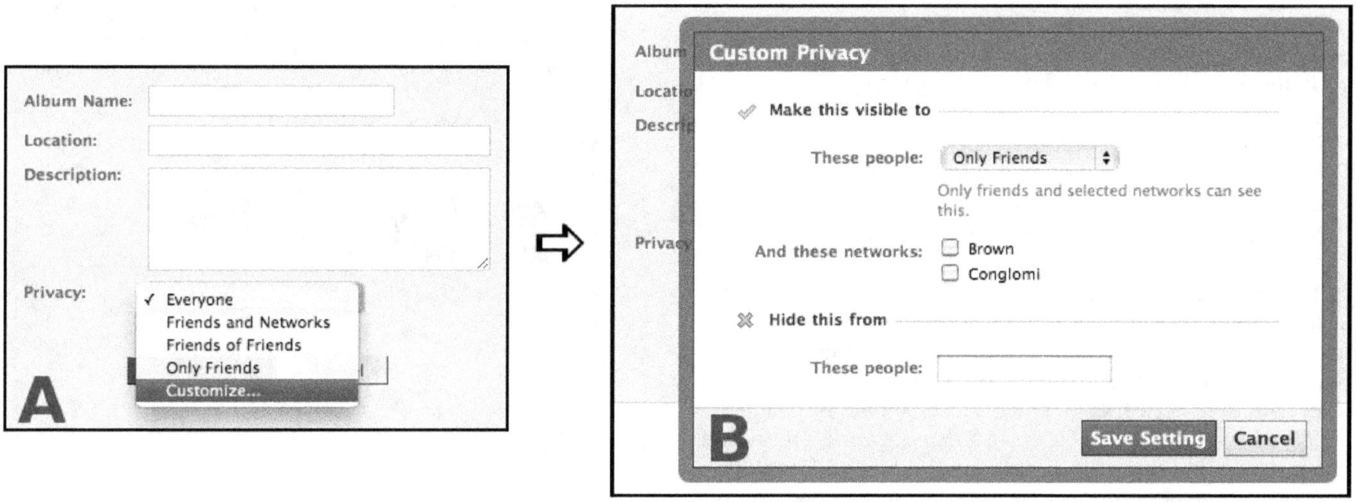

Figure 1. The default Facebook privacy settings interface. Users can use the interface on the left to share content with all Facebook users, only friends, friends and networks, or friends of friends (A). If users choose to "customize" their privacy settings, the interface on the right appears (B).

automatically add the coworkers and the Conglomi network to their profiles without actually modifying any data stored on Facebook. We also used the proxy to alter the privacy settings interface based on our experimental conditions.

Once participants added the app, we instructed them to check their email to confirm their friend requests. Five friend requests were generated by our software and appeared to come from Facebook, although in reality participants' friend lists and networks were never altered. After this, we gave participants a set of four tasks to complete using Facebook:

1. **Tag A Photo**— Browse through the photos that either you or one of your friends has uploaded to Facebook. Tag someone in one of these photos.
2. **Party Scenario**— Last Friday all of your coworkers stayed at work until midnight because of a deadline. However, some of your friends from Brown University were throwing a party at the same time. You told your coworkers that you were feeling sick so that you could leave work early in order to attend the party. You could be fired if anyone at work finds out that you were at the party. One of your friends from the party has just asked you to upload your photos. Please do so, while being aware of your concerns. You want to share the photos with as many friends and other people who may have attended the party, but with none of your coworkers.
3. **Comment on A Photo**— Browse through the photos that either you or one of your friends has uploaded to Facebook. Leave a comment on any one photo.
4. **Recruitment Scenario**— As a small Providence-based business, your manager understands that its important to recruit Brown alumni. You have recently been put in charge of coordinating a recruiting event with other Brown alumni who also work at Conglomi. At the last planning meeting, you took several photos that you want to share with the other planners. However, these photos should only be shared with the other planners (i.e., Conglomi employees who are Brown alumni). If these photos were disclosed outside of the planning group, you could get fired.

The tagging and commenting tasks were chosen solely as a buffer between the photo uploading tasks. In the photo uploading tasks, we provided participants with photos in a directory on the laboratory computer. These two tasks were intentionally designed to exploit ambiguities in Facebook's existing privacy settings interface (Figure 1). We randomized the order in which participants performed these two tasks.

We asked participants to allow friends and classmates to view the party photos, but to deny access to users in the Conglomi network, regardless of their potential Brown network membership or friend status. We created this task to examine participants' reactions to an ambiguity in the Facebook privacy settings interface: Facebook defaults to allowing rather than denying access. Specifically, when a network is not selected for sharing, members of that network may still be granted access due to other network memberships. For instance, in Figure 1B, while the Brown and Conglomi networks are not selected, members of these networks who are friends with the user will be granted access.

As written, the party scenario was impossible to complete using Facebook's existing interface because an entire network cannot be explicitly denied access. While Facebook allows the user to deny access to a specific list of people (Figure 1B), the user can only name existing friends (i.e., a user cannot enter non-friends or entire networks in this box). If a study participant granted access to friends plus the entire Brown network, there would be no way of denying access to non-friends in the Brown network. Thus, we considered it "correct" if participants only granted access to friends, and then explicitly hid the photos from the friends who were also affiliated with Conglomi. While these photos would be hidden from members of the Brown network who were not friends with the participant, this would be the only way of guaranteeing the photos would be hidden from all members of the Conglomi network. In order to do this, participants had to perform the following steps:

1. Select "Customize" (Figure 1A).
2. Leave default of "Only Friends" (Figure 1B).
3. Do not select any networks (Figure 1B).
4. Name the five coworkers to hide from (Figure 1B).

In the recruitment scenario, we asked participants to grant access to only those people in both the Brown and Conglomi networks—the intersection. Facebook's existing interface may also be ambiguous to some users because while they can select multiple networks to which access should be granted, Facebook will parse this as users in *either* network—the union. For instance, in Figure 1B, if both the Brown and Conglomi networks are selected, users may not understand whether this represents the union or the intersection of the networks. We wanted to determine whether this limitation of the interface was clear to participants. For the participants who understood that the task was impossible, we were curious how they would attempt to complete it.

The only way around this limitation is to manually specify the name of every desired individual who should have access. However, Facebook only allows friends to be specified in this manner. Thus, we considered it correct if participants granted access to only the two friends who were members of both the Brown and Conglomi networks. This errs on the side of denying access to Facebook users who are not at the intersection of the Brown and Conglomi networks, but comes at a cost of also denying access to some users who should have access—and do not because they are not friends with the participant. Participants needed to perform the following steps to accomplish this:

1. Select "Customize" (Figure 1A).
2. Change "Only Friends" to "Specific People" (Figure 1B).
3. Name the two coworkers in box that appears (Figure 1B).
4. Do not select any networks (Figure 1B).

We consider these two limitations "policy ambiguities," since without having prior knowledge of the system's semantics, the user has no way of knowing how Facebook will parse these policies. We designed two experimental conditions to automatically detect the latter type of ambiguity: the difference between "default allow" and "default deny" policies. That is, when access is granted to one of two networks, did the participant intend to explicitly deny access to members of the second network, or should access be granted solely based on membership in the first network? We decided not to include logic to detect the second ambiguity, the difference between the union and intersection, because we were concerned with overwhelming participants by asking for too much input regarding their policy ambiguities. We included the recruitment scenario to examine whether the automatic detection of *some* ambiguities would prime participants into manually locating additional—more relevant—ambiguities. The study conditions were as follows:

Figure 2. The privacy warnings in the two experimental conditions. In the *Warn* condition (A), participants were warned of an ambiguity without given any guidance. In the *Choose* condition (B), participants were given a choice to help them disambiguate.

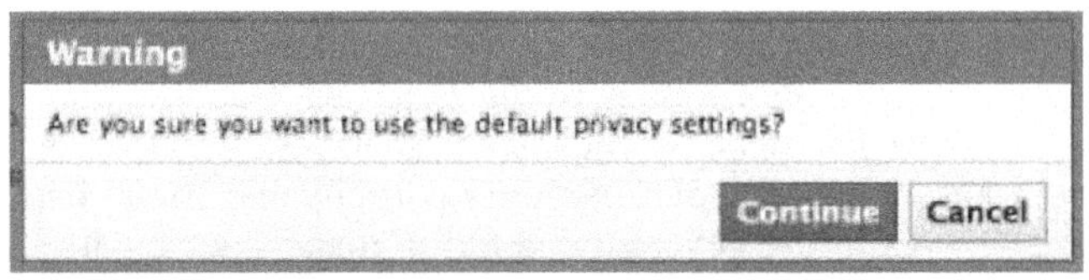

Figure 3. All participants saw this prompt if they neglected to change the privacy settings from the default of sharing with everyone. Clicking "cancel" allowed them to return to the settings interface and specify a custom access control policy, whereas clicking "continue" confirmed that they wanted to share the content with everyone.

- **Control**— Participants used a privacy settings interface provided by our proxy that exactly mimicked the existing Facebook interface (Figure 1).
- **Warn**— Participants used the same initial interface as those in the *Control* condition. However, when a policy ambiguity was detected at the time that participants tried to save their changes, a warning was displayed (Figure 2A).
- **Choose**— Participants used the same interface as those in the *Warn* condition. However, when an ambiguity was detected, participants were given options to help clarify the ambiguity (Figure 2B). When participants chose to either allow or deny access to the users depicted in the dialog box: their pictures were either superimposed with red Xs or green boxes.

Regardless of condition, we required all participants to alter settings using the "customize" interface in Facebook (Figure 1B). Under the defaults, if a participant neglected to alter the privacy settings, she would grant access to all Facebook users—and we would not yield data on the usability of the privacy settings interface. Thus, we created a prompt so that if participants attempted to share a photo album without changing the default settings, they were asked if this was their intention (Figure 3). Thus, we collected data on how many participants would have used the defaults to grant access to all of Facebook, as well as how they changed the settings after being explicitly primed to do so.

In the experimental conditions, when an ambiguity was detected, a warning showed a list of Facebook users who would be affected because they were members of both a network that was selected and a network that was unselected.[2] If the participant did nothing, these users would be granted access. For those in the *Warn* condition, this warning offered participants the option to go back and edit their settings before saving, but did not offer any other guidance. On the other hand, those in the *Choose* condition were explicitly asked whether to allow or deny access to these specific users.

For instance, if a participant selected Brown but left Conglomi unselected, it may be unclear to the participant what permissions should apply to members of both networks. That is, by not selecting Conglomi, did the participant intend to explicitly deny access to members of Conglomi? Or did she intend to grant access to all members of the Brown network regardless of their other networks?

We directed participants to an exit survey after they completed the experiment. We asked them if they had previously modified their Facebook privacy settings, if they had previously encountered scenarios similar to those in this study, how they overcame Facebook's limitations in those scenarios, with whom they intended to share photos during this study, how confident they were that those people had access, and how confident they were that no one else had access.

Analysis

We collected information about our 33 participants' ages, genders, education levels, and nationalities. We found no significant differences between the randomly assigned conditions with regard to demographics. Overall, our youngest participant was 18, while our oldest was 24 ($\mu = 20.39$, $\sigma = 1.54$). Ten of our participants were female, and the remaining 23 were male. Six of our participants were graduates of Brown, while 27 were students. Finally, thirty of our participants were from the US, two were European, and one was Indian.

In the rest of this section we present participants' task performance during the party scenario and the recruiting scenario. We explain how participants coped with Facebook's limitations, how providing automatic feedback helped participants clear up access control ambiguities, and how in certain cases, providing feedback worked to participants' detriment.

Party Scenario

We asked participants to modify permissions so that friends and classmates could view the uploaded photos, so long as these individuals were not members of the Conglomi network. Before participants in the experimental conditions had the opportunity to see any feedback regarding policy ambiguities, we observed that a third of participants across all of the conditions (11 of 33) correctly set the permissions. Of the 22 who initially made errors, those errors fell into two categories: "over-sharing" such that unintended users were granted access (17 of 22), and "under-sharing" such that intended users were denied access (5 of 22).

[2]We considered the list of "friends" to be a network.

Party Scenario	Control		Warn		Choose	
N	13		11		9	
Correct at start	5	38%	3	27%	3	33%
Saw feedback			7	64%	8	89%
Correct at end	5	38%	2	18%	8	89%

Table 1. The number of participants who correctly set permissions during the party scenario before any feedback was displayed, who saw feedback in the experimental conditions based on ambiguity detection, and who correctly set permissions after seeing the feedback.

Without feedback, participants erred on the side of data leakage; seventeen participants authored policies that would have resulted in unintentionally sharing with members of the Conglomi network. In all but two cases, these errors were due to ambiguities in the interface that we predicted and detected in our experimental conditions. Specifically, fifteen participants chose to restrict the photos to their friends and members of the Brown network, making sure that the Conglomi network was not selected. Unbeknownst to them, members of the Conglomi network who were either friends or members of the Brown network still had access. Eight of these participants went so far as to explicitly type the names of their Conglomi friends who should be denied access. This, however, had no effect on the members of the Conglomi network who were also members of the Brown network, but not friends. Thus, this specific ambiguity accounted for 68% of the errors we observed during the party scenario.

In our experimental conditions, participants were prompted when this ambiguity was detected and they were given the opportunity to change their settings. Using Fisher's exact test with the Holm-Bonferroni correction, we found that the feedback in the *Choose* condition was extremely helpful during this task (Table 1): participants used it to remove significantly more errors than those in the other conditions ($p < 0.0247$ vs. *Control*; $p < 0.0055$ vs. *Warn*). When alerted to the presence of the ambiguity and given immediate feedback on how it could be clarified, all five participants who would have specified the wrong policy were able to understand and correct their errors before the policy took effect.

The interface in the *Choose* condition detected ambiguities and suggested ways of clarifying them, whereas the interface in the *Warn* condition only detected the ambiguities and left it up to the user to determine how to correct them. The purpose of this was to separate the effect of the feedback from the effect of the guidance. A total of seven participants in this condition were prompted because their policies contained predictable ambiguities. Four of these participants chose to continue without making any changes to their policies, whereas two others made changes that did not correct the errors. The seventh participant initially set

Recruitment	Control		Warn		Choose	
N	13		11		9	
Correct at start	7	54%	4	36%	5	56%
Saw feedback			4	36%	2	22%
Correct at end	7	54%	5	45%	6	67%

Table 2. The number of participants who correctly set permissions during the recruitment scenario before any feedback was displayed, who saw feedback in the experimental conditions based on ambiguity detection, and who correctly set permissions after seeing the feedback.

the correct permissions, but after seeing the feedback about an ambiguity—the fact that friends were selected but both networks were unselected—he opted to erroneously select both the Brown and Conglomi networks. Thus, providing feedback without guidance did nothing to help six participants and prompted one participant to introduce an error into a previously correct policy. When comparing the performance of those who viewed feedback between the two experimental conditions, those in the *Choose* condition introduced significantly fewer errors than those in the *Warn* condition ($p < 0.002$ for Fisher's exact test).

Recruitment Scenario

In the recruitment scenario, we asked participants to alter permissions such that only members of both the Brown and Conglomi networks—the intersection—could view the photos. As explained in the Methodology Section, this task was impossible to complete using Facebook's existing interface because a user cannot specify the intersection of two networks, only the union. In the party scenario, when participants in the experimental conditions selected one network but not the other, they were prompted about users in both networks. In the recruitment scenario, this feedback was less helpful because it did not necessarily help them accomplish the task; they needed to grant access to *only* these users.

Before participants in the experimental conditions saw any feedback, we found that a total of sixteen participants across all three conditions (48% of 33) specified the correct permissions (Table 2). Of the seventeen incorrect policies, two of them were due to under-sharing (12% of 17), while the remaining fifteen were due to over-sharing (88% of 17). We observed that this data leakage tendency was likely attributable to the ambiguous interface: ten of the total errors (59% of 17) were due to participants selecting both the Brown and Conglomi networks. Indeed, we predicted that participants might be confused as to whether the system would interpret multiple selected networks as the intersection instead of the union.

We discovered that the presence of feedback in the experimental conditions did little to help participants correct their policies: one participant in each of the two conditions used the feedback to correctly remove policy errors. In this scenario, because the ambiguity detection focused on overlapping networks, feedback was only displayed when participants were on the verge of specifying an incorrect policy; participants who correctly specified individual friends, or incorrectly specified all of their networks, never saw feedback. Thus, for the six participants who saw the feedback, four in the *Warn* condition and two in the *Choose* condition, it could only help them. Of course, this was not a statistically significant improvement over the *Control* condition.

Lessons

We found that without relevant feedback, participants would have introduced errors into their privacy policies a majority of the time. When participants introduced errors, these errors were more likely to result in sharing with unintended parties (data leakage) rather than denying access to authorized users. Our data show that when ambiguities were detected and relevant guidance was offered (e.g., the *Choose* condition), users took the time to edit their privacy settings. However, when relevant actionable guidance could not be offered (e.g., the *Warn* condition), users were just as likely to transform a correct-ambiguous policy into an incorrect-unambiguous policy. This leads us to conclude that providing post hoc information about potential policy ambiguities is only likely to be effective when concrete guidance can be offered.

After the experiment, we asked participants how Facebook's privacy settings could be improved. Twenty participants (61% of 33) said something about wanting more fine-grained controls; examples included:

- *Not enough options*
- *There should be options for specific intersections and unions of groups*
- *It was not specific enough to keep certain people from having access to pictures and info*
- *Ability to restrict access to individuals with multiple characteristics*

The second most common complaint regarding Facebook's privacy settings interface was that it was overly complicated and offered too many options (24% of 33):

- *It's a little confusing*
- *It is sometimes unclear exactly who has access*
- *It's not great not to know for sure if there are other hidden options that I might have missed*
- *Looking at who to share the photos was confusing*

In short, users wanted more control with fewer options. These complaints hint at a much larger problem: the interface that Facebook provides for modifying privacy settings is simply inappropriate for all but the most basic privacy settings.

VENN DIAGRAMS

In our second experiment, we designed a new interface for specifying access control settings in Facebook. We created this interface as an attempt to completely eliminate the two types of ambiguities we discussed earlier. We reasoned that the act of specifying an access control policy on Facebook is a matter of indicating how the intersections of a user's networks should be granted access. We based our design on a visual metaphor with which study participants would likely be familiar: Venn diagrams. In this section we describe our usability study of this new privacy settings interface.

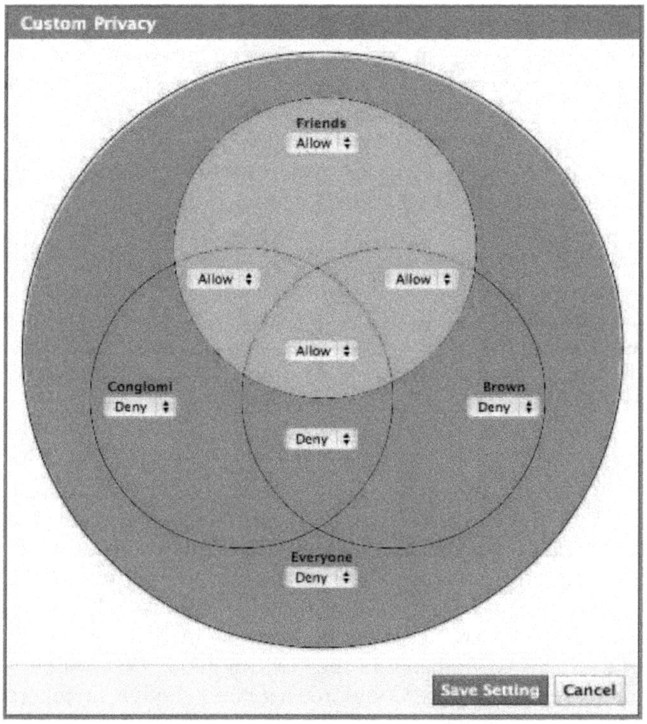

Figure 4. Venn diagram permissions interface for Facebook.

Methodology

In our second experiment, we examined whether a Venn diagram may help users to better visualize effective permissions for overlapping networks (Figure 4). Each network—friends, Brown, and Conglomi—was depicted as a set. For each subset, participants could select "allow" or "deny" from a drop-down box, which caused the selected subset and all the nested subsets to change permissions. The color of each subset also changed to reflect the effective permissions: red for deny, green for allow.

We conducted a usability study to evaluate this interface from June 2-15, 2010. We followed the methodology and recruiting procedures from the first experiment, with two notable changes. First, we created two between-group conditions:

- **Control**— Participants used a privacy settings interface identical to the current Facebook interface (Figure 1).
- **Venn**— Participants used the Venn diagram interface to "customize" settings (i.e., Figure 4 replaced Figure 1B).

Second, we used the following four tasks:

1. **Reunion Scenario**— Last week you returned from a reunion event at Brown. You had a great time seeing a lot of old friends and took lots of pictures. You decide to upload some of these photos to Facebook in order to share them with your friends and other people affiliated with Brown.
2. **Recruitment Scenario**— As a small Providence-based business, your manager understands that its important to recruit Brown alumni. You have recently been put in charge of coordinating a recruiting event with other Brown alumni who also work at Conglomi. At the last planning meeting, you took several photos that you want to share with the other planners. However, these photos should only be shared with the other planners (i.e., Conglomi employees who are Brown alumni). If these photos were disclosed outside of the planning group, you could get fired.
3. **Work Scenario**— You just got a new office at work and are anxious to post pictures of it to show all your coworkers. You decide to upload some of these photos to Facebook in order to share them with people affiliated with Conglomi.
4. **Party Scenario**— Last Friday all of your coworkers stayed at work until midnight because of a deadline. However, some of your friends from Brown were throwing a party at the same time. You told your coworkers that you were feeling sick so that you could leave work early in order to attend the party. You could be fired if anyone at work finds out that you were at the party. One of your friends from the party has just asked you to upload your photos. Please do so, while being aware of your concerns. You want to share the photos with as many friends and other people who may have attended the party, but with none of your coworkers.

The recruitment and party scenarios were identical to the ones in the first experiment. We designed the reunion and work scenarios in order to easily be completed using Facebook's existing interface and to not mention consequences for incorrect permissions. We did this in order to confirm that our new Venn diagram interface was at least as effective as the existing Facebook interface. The order in which participants performed the tasks was pseudo-randomized using the Latin squares method. After performing these tasks, participants completed an exit survey identical to the one used in the first experiment.

Analysis

We found no significant differences between the randomly assigned conditions with regard to demographics. Overall, our youngest participant was 18, while our oldest was 42 ($\mu = 20.42$, $\sigma = 3.74$). Our 40 participants were evenly split in terms of gender. Seven of our participants were graduates of Brown, while the remaining 33 were students. Finally, 80% of our participants were from the US, 10% were from Asia, and the rest were scattered.

We found that when using our Venn diagram interface, participants made equal or fewer errors in all four scenarios. In this section we first present our results for the more trivial tasks—the reunion and work scenarios—and then we present our results for the tasks that required more complex settings—the recruitment and party scenarios.

Trivial Tasks

In the reunion scenario, we asked participants to grant access to "friends and other people affiliated with Brown." We intended them to allow access only for people who were either friends or members of the Brown network. However,

	Control		Venn	
Reunion	9	45%	9	45%
Work	4	20%	14	70%
Party	8	40%	18	90%
Recruitment	10	50%	12	60%

Table 3. The number of participants who correctly set permissions during the four scenarios in the experiment. Significantly more participants in the *Venn* condition set the correct permissions for the work and party scenarios.

during the experiment we realized that this wording could also be interpreted to mean "friends from Brown as well as others from Brown." Thus, we also considered it correct if participants granted access to only the Brown network. To correctly perform this task using the existing Facebook interface, participants needed to do the following steps:

1. Select "Customize" (Figure 1A).
2. Select the Brown network (Figure 1B).

We found that only nine participants in each condition (45% of 20) correctly set permissions during the reunion scenario (Table 3). In the *Control* condition, five people erred by over-sharing—granting access to unintended people—while six people denied access to the Brown network, limiting access to friends. In the *Venn* condition, six participants over-shared the photos, while the remaining five erroneously denied access to intended recipients. Of the 22 people across both conditions who set incorrect permissions, 18 of them did so because they chose a preset option (e.g., "friends," "everyone," etc.) rather than launching the custom settings interface. Overall, we were surprised that a minority of participants in each condition set the correct permissions. This may have been due to participants not paying attention to the specific task; the lack of stated consequences may have caused some to over-share, while those who under-shared may be habituated to only sharing content with friends.

In the work scenario, we asked participants to simply share content with the entire Conglomi network. To correctly perform this task using the existing Facebook interface, participants needed to perform the following steps:

1. Select "Customize" (Figure 1A).
2. Change "Only Friends" to "Only Me" (Figure 1B).
3. Select the Conglomi network (Figure 1B).

Participants in the *Venn* condition were significantly more likely to perform this task correctly than those in the *Control* condition ($p < 0.0036$ for Fisher's exact test). Only six participants in the *Venn* condition made mistakes, whereas fourteen participants in the *Control* condition produced erroneous policies. The errors in the *Control* condition were the direct result of the interface's default settings: ten participants over-shared by neglecting to change the default in Step 2 from "Only Friends" to "Only Me." This had the effect of sharing the photos with the union of the Conglomi and friend networks, rather than only the Conglomi network. Participants in the *Venn* condition did not make this mistake because the interface defaulted to denying everyone access.

Complex Tasks

In our first experiment, we examined two impossible scenarios: denying access to an entire network and specifying the intersection of two networks. We designed the interface in the *Venn* condition directly around these limitations, so that users could visualize exactly which subsets of their friends and networks would be granted or denied access.

In the party scenario, we asked participants to grant access to friends and members of the Brown network, while denying access to anyone affiliated with Conglomi. As written, this task was impossible for participants in the *Control* condition. Instead, these participants could grant access to friends and then deny access to coworker-friends using the steps outlined in the methodology for the first experiment.

We found that participants in the *Venn* condition made significantly fewer errors than those in the *Control* condition ($p < 0.002$ for Fisher's exact test); twelve participants made errors in the *Control* condition compared to only two in the *Venn* condition. Only one of these erroneous policies resulted in under-sharing—the participant opted to share with no one. No participants in the *Control* condition explicitly granted access to the Conglomi network, though members of this network were inadvertently granted access through their memberships in the Brown network. This over-sharing was the most common mistake in the *Control* condition, and accounted for 83% of the errors.

Of the two participants who made errors in the *Venn* condition, one never saw the custom interface because he shared with "Only Friends" (Figure 1A). The second participant mentioned that some of her "work friends are in Brown" and so she denied access to the entire Brown network, rather than just the intersection with the Conglomi network.

In the recruitment scenario, we asked participants to grant access to the intersection of the Conglomi and Brown networks. Like the first experiment, this task was impossible using Facebook's existing interface. Instead, users in the *Control* condition were able to complete this task by manually granting access to people at the intersection of their three networks: friends, Brown, and Conglomi.

Once participants in the *Venn* condition viewed the custom interface, they could correctly set permissions with a single mouse click. Despite this, we were surprised to find no significant differences between the two conditions. Eight people made mistakes in the *Venn* condition, whereas ten people made mistakes in the *Control* condition. The mistakes in the *Venn* condition stemmed from five participants over-sharing by simply allowing the entire Conglomi network (63% of 8), and three other participants under-sharing by denying access to the intersection of the three networks (37% of 8). In the *Control* condition, 90% of the errors were due to over-sharing. A third of these were from participants selecting both the Brown and Conglomi networks, believing that this would represent the intersection and not the union. We repeatedly observed participants making this same mistake in the first experiment due to the ambiguous interface.

DISCUSSION

We examined two techniques to help users minimize access control errors on Facebook. In our first experiment, we observed that providing users with feedback about potential policy ambiguities was only effective when specific guidance could be offered. Without guidance, users were significantly less likely to prevent errors, and in some cases, introduced errors where none previously existed. In our second experiment, we introduced a Venn diagram interface to help users see how their networks overlapped. Overall, users of this interface introduced 55% of the errors that those using the existing Facebook interface introduced. In this section we present data on participants' privacy behaviors outside of this study, as well as limitations and future work.

Privacy Behaviors

During the six tasks spanning the two experiments, we found that participants were more than 3.5x as likely to over-share than to under-share when they created access control policy errors. In order to gauge how pervasive this problem is outside of the laboratory, we asked all 73 participants in both experiments several questions about their regular Facebook usage and privacy settings.

All of our participants had used Facebook for over a year, and 90% of them had used it for more than two years. In order to examine the potential for information leakage, participants showed us their profiles so that we could examine the number of photos in which participants were tagged ($\mu = 526.32$, $\sigma = 353.11$), networks they had joined ($\mu = 1.77$, $\sigma = 0.51$), and applications that they had installed ($\mu = 50.17$, $\sigma = 90.77$).[3]

We asked participants how and why they modified their privacy settings and found that twenty of them (27% of 73) specifically mentioned changing their settings in response to media reports of Facebook changing the defaults. These results are similar to findings by boyd and Hargittai [2]:

- *Infrequently, usually only when my friends inform me that Facebook has altered the default privacy settings*
- *When Facebook is updated I double check that it is still set on only friends*
- *Every time I hear a privacy change has been made*

Despite the high potential for data leakage and perceptions of constantly changing privacy settings, six participants stated that they had never modified their privacy settings prior to this study (8% of 73). Twenty-eight participants (38% of 73) mentioned that they simply restricted their profiles to friends. The remaining 46 participants used other strategies to keep their information private, several mentioned going out of their way to block coworkers or family members:

- *Everyone could see everything except my dad*
- *I blocked my employer from viewing pictures of me*
- *Blocked students I work with from viewing my photos*
- *Limited profile for adults/relatives who had friended me*

[3]We did not collect data on applications during the first experiment.

Limitations and Future Work

Detecting ambiguities and providing users with guidance on how to prevent semantic errors was effective in certain cases, though it can be counterproductive when specific guidance cannot be offered or it is not helpful. In response to these findings, we designed and tested a new interface that allowed users to visualize how privacy settings applied to their overlapping networks. When we asked participants in our second experiment to rate the interface they used on a 5-point Likert scale, they rated the Venn diagram interface significantly higher than the control, both overall ($t_{38} = 3.08$, $p < 0.004$), and in terms of ease of use ($t_{38} = 3.10$, $p < 0.004$). One might be concerned that the ease of use imparted by the Venn diagram solution may only apply to computer science majors. However, 92% of our participants were from outside the computer science department. At the same time, further study is needed to determine if Venn diagrams are intuitive to Facebook users without a college education.

A Venn diagram interface is also only usable if participants have three or fewer overlapping sets (i.e., two networks plus a list of friends). Of the 73 participants across both experiments, we observed that 20 (27%) belonged to only one Facebook network, 50 belonged to two networks (69%), and three belonged to three networks (4%). Taking the 95% Confidence Interval (CI), this implies our solution is usable by at least 88% of our target demographic. Gross and Acquisti analyzed data from a 2008 Facebook dump of the entire Carnegie Mellon network (following their 2005 study [9]).[4] Of the 6,404 viewable profiles, 5,591 were members of two or fewer networks. This indicates a 95% CI of over 86%.

We chose to not directly compare the techniques in the two experiments because the experimental procedures differed. Further study is needed on the effectiveness of a privacy settings interface that offers both a Venn diagram visualization and post hoc guidance. Finally, the ambiguities that we examined were far from a complete list of the shortcomings in Facebook's privacy settings interface. We also believe that the lack of realism and consequences in our study tasks impacted the effort participants exerted in setting the correct permissions (likely indicating an upper bound for the error rate). A longitudinal study is needed to determine how participants cope with complex privacy scenarios in real life, how those situations can be automatically detected, and what types of feedback are most effective at minimizing errors.

ACKNOWLEDGMENTS

This work was supported by NSF grants CT-0830945 and CNS-0627310. The first two authors were affiliated with Brown University when this research was performed.

REFERENCES

1. J. Binder, A. Howes, and A. Sutcliffe. The problem of conflicting social spheres: Effects of network structure on experienced tension in social network sites. In *CHI '09: Proceedings of the 27th International Conference on Human Factors in Computing Systems*, pages 965–974, New York, NY, USA, 2009. ACM.

[4]Private communication on November 17, 2010.

2. d. boyd and E. Hargittai. Facebook privacy settings: Who cares? *First Monday*, 15(8), August 2010.

3. C. A. Brodie, C.-M. Karat, and J. Karat. An empirical study of natural language parsing of privacy policy rules using the SPARCLE policy workbench. In *SOUPS '06: Proceedings of the Second Symposium on Usable Privacy and Security*, pages 8–19, New York, NY, USA, 2006. ACM.

4. Computer Research Association. CRA Conference on Grand Research Challenges in Information Security & Assurance, 2003. http://archive.cra.org/reports/trustworthy.computing.pdf.

5. J. DiMicco, D. R. Millen, W. Geyer, C. Dugan, B. Brownholtz, and M. Muller. Motivations for social networking at work. In *CSCW '08: Proceedings of the 2008 ACM Conference on Computer Supported Cooperative Work*, pages 711–720, New York, NY, USA, 2008. ACM.

6. J. M. DiMicco and D. R. Millen. Identity Management: Multiple presentations of self in Facebook. In *GROUP '07: Proceedings of the 2007 International ACM Conference on Supporting Group Work*, pages 383–386, New York, NY, USA, 2007. ACM.

7. K. Fisler and S. Krishnamurthi. A model of triangulating environments for policy authoring. In *SACMAT '10: Proceeding of the 15th ACM Symposium on Access Control Models and Technologies*, pages 3–12, New York, NY, USA, 2010. ACM.

8. K. Fisler, S. Krishnamurthi, L. A. Meyerovich, and M. C. Tschantz. Verification and change-impact analysis of access-control policies. In *ICSE '05: Proceedings of the 27th International Conference on Software Engineering*, pages 196–205, New York, NY, USA, 2005. ACM.

9. R. Gross and A. Acquisti. Information revelation and privacy in online social networks. In *WPES '05: Proceedings of the 2005 ACM Workshop on Privacy in the Electronic Society*, pages 71–80, New York, NY, USA, 2005. ACM.

10. iStrategy Labs. Facebook demographics and statistics report, January 2010. http://www.istrategylabs.com/2010/01/facebook-demographics-and-statistics-report-2010-145-growth-in-1-year/.

11. A. N. Joinson. Looking at, looking up or keeping up with people?: motives and use of facebook. In *CHI '08: Proceedings of the 26th International Conference on Human Factors in Computing Systems*, pages 1027–1036, New York, NY, USA, 2008. ACM.

12. C. Lampe, N. Ellison, and C. Steinfield. A face(book) in the crowd: Social searching vs. social browsing. In *CSCW '06: Proceedings of the 2006 20th Anniversary Conference on Computer Supported Cooperative Work*, pages 167–170, New York, NY, USA, 2006. ACM.

13. C. Lampe, N. B. Ellison, and C. Steinfield. Changes in use and perception of Facebook. In *CSCW '08: Proceedings of the 2008 ACM Conference on Computer Supported Cooperative Work*, pages 721–730, New York, NY, USA, 2008. ACM.

14. M. M. Skeels and J. Grudin. When social networks cross boundaries: A case study of workplace use of Facebook and LinkedIn. In *GROUP '09: Proceedings of the 2009 International ACM Conference on Supporting Group Work*, pages 95–104, New York, NY, USA, 2009. ACM.

15. C. Steinfield, J. M. DiMicco, N. B. Ellison, and C. Lampe. Bowling online: social networking and social capital within the organization. In *C&T '09: Proceedings of the 4th International Conference on Communities and Technologies*, pages 245–254, New York, NY, USA, 2009. ACM.

16. K. Strater and H. R. Lipford. Strategies and struggles with privacy in an online social networking community. In *BCS-HCI '08: Proceedings of the 22nd British HCI Group Annual Conference*, pages 111–119, Swinton, UK, UK, 2008. British Computer Society.

17. F. Stutzman and J. Kramer-Duffield. Friends only: examining a privacy-enhancing behavior in Facebook. In *CHI '10: Proceedings of the 28th International Conference on Human Factors in Computing Systems*, pages 1553–1562, New York, NY, USA, 2010. ACM.

18. A. Tootoonchian, K. K. Gollu, S. Saroiu, Y. Ganjali, and A. Wolman. Lockr: social access control for web 2.0. In *WOSN '08: Proceedings of the 1st Workshop on Online Social Networks*, pages 43–48, New York, NY, USA, 2008. ACM.

19. T. Turner, P. Qvarfordt, J. T. Biehl, G. Golovchinsky, and M. Back. Exploring the workplace communication ecology. In *CHI '10: Proceedings of the 28th International Conference on Human Factors in Computing Systems*, pages 841–850, New York, NY, USA, 2010. ACM.

20. J. Watson, M. Whitney, and H. R. Lipford. Configuring audience-oriented privacy policies. In *SafeConfig '09: Proceedings of the 2nd ACM Workshop on Assurable and Usable Security Configuration*, pages 71–78, New York, NY, USA, 2009. ACM.

21. A. Wu, J. M. DiMicco, and D. R. Millen. Detecting professional versus personal closeness using an enterprise social network site. In *CHI '10: Proceedings of the 28th International Conference on Human Factors in Computing Systems*, pages 1955–1964, New York, NY, USA, 2010. ACM.

22. A. L. Young and A. Quan-Haase. Information revelation and internet privacy concerns on social network sites: a case study of Facebook. In *C&T '09: Proceedings of the 4th International Conference on Communities and Technologies*, pages 265–274, New York, NY, USA, 2009. ACM.

Integrating User Feedback with Heuristic Security and Privacy Management Systems

Prashanth Ayyavu
School of EECS
Oregon State University
Corvallis, Oregon, 97331, USA
ayyavu@eecs.oregonstate.edu
+1-541-740-1115

Carlos Jensen
School of EECS
Oregon State University
Corvallis, Oregon, 97331, USA
cjensen@eecs.oregonstate.edu
+1-541-737-2555

ABSTRACT
Tools aimed at helping users safely navigate the web and safeguard themselves against potential online predators have become reasonably common. Currently there are two families of tools; heuristics analysis tools that test websites directly using automated scripts and programs, and community based tools where users rate websites and write reviews for the benefit of others. In this paper we examine the relative strengths and weaknesses of each technique, whether these techniques are compatible, and how community feedback can be combined with heuristic-based evaluations. In order to do this we conduct a large-scale comparison of the ratings of heuristic and community based tools, and explore novel methods for abstracting key information from user comments, which could be used to add context and nuance to heuristic based ratings. We find that heuristic and community based ratings are highly complementary, and can be combined to potentially guide users to make more informed decisions.

Author Keywords
Safe surfing tools, User feedback, User comments, Usable privacy, Usable security, Social navigation

ACM Classification Keywords
H5.m [Information interfaces and presentation (e.g., HCI)]: Miscellaneous

General Terms
Security

INTRODUCTION
Safe web-surfing tools, designed to help users identify potentially dangerous and malicious websites, are becoming commonplace. Today, most web-browsers and search engines incorporate some safe surfing features, but standalone or plug-in systems are still the norm. Some well-known safe surfing tools are Web of Trust (aka. WOT) [34], Alexa [1], McAfee's SiteAdvisor [20] and Norton's SafeWeb [25]. Perhaps for this reason, tools such as these are gaining market share, as people look for help in making decisions with respect to online privacy and security management [11]. Many users lack the confidence, skill, or time to make careful security decisions on their own due to either a lack of interest and/or understanding of the technical details of web security [11, 14].

There are two major types of safe surfing tools: Heuristic analysis based tools, and community based or end-user rating based tools. Heuristic analysis tools in essence scan websites for previously identified exploits, techniques or technologies that experts have identified as potentially problematic for users privacy or security. Most antivirus or anti-spam software follows this strategy, though anti-spam tools often include some element of machine learning to allow them to adapt to changing trends. Community based tools are those where the community in essence scores and reviews websites, giving other users advice on whether a website is safe or not.

One shortcoming of heuristic analysis tools is that they can only advise users about the technical foundations and behavior of a website. For instance: Is the web server patched for the latest known vulnerabilities? Is the website vulnerable to known types of attacks? Are downloads infected with viruses or other malware? Does the website engage in drive-by downloads? Does the website associate with those who do? Etc. These analysis techniques, though very sophisticated and useful, do have some inherent shortcomings. Heuristics cannot be used to determine whether a website's plain text privacy policy is desirable or even lawful (one could evaluate a P3P policy though), whether the company follows said policies or engages in other dubious practices not directly linked to their website (such as unwanted telemarketing or credit card fraud). It is also difficult to accurately classify the content of websites, such as whether the content is for adults only, or whether the content is credible or reliable.

Using word of mouth, or user ratings and feedback to determine whether to visit a website is not a novel concept,

CHI 2011, May 7–12, 2011, Vancouver, BC, Canada.

and a great number of rating sites and systems exist today. These services depend on building a community of reviewers with both a broad set of interests (to ensure broad coverage) of sites, as well as good knowledge of security and privacy issues (to ensure that reviews are accurate and informative). In addition, the rating site must be engineered in such a way as to promote and encourage insightful reviews rather than allowing the site reviews to revert toward the mean.

One of the chief problems associated with this approach is determining the reliability of user ratings. The problem is that most users are not terribly good at evaluating security or privacy risks, and are quite likely to be biased by factors as a sites' visual design or name recognition. Some users are more thorough and knowledgeable and can be trusted to do a good job of analyzing sites while others cannot. The challenge is identifying which is which, and ensuring that the good reviewers carry more weight than those of the uninformed or biased. Previous research has looked into some of the problems associated with these systems, and how to increase the reliability of the user ratings for such systems [13].

A problem associated with both approaches is generating ratings or recommendations that are simple for end-user to understand, and which are at the same time convincing. Sites that rely on numeric ratings are easier to interpret (a low score is less desirable than a high-scoring site for instance), but how much worse is a 4 from a 5 on a 10-point scale? If categories are used, how much risk is associated with visiting a "risky" website, and what am I at risk from? These are issues that heuristic systems often have difficulty addressing. On the other hand, community based systems often suffer from too much data (e.g. hundreds of paragraph long user reviews), or mismatched scales (e.g. is everyone rating on the same scale?) This is a well-known problem for sites like Amazon, and can be corrected for if reviewers score enough items. From our experience, we know that many end-users do not rate a large number of websites.

In this paper we seek to determine the reliability and compatibility of these two techniques: heuristic evaluation and community based reviews. In other words, we seek to determine:

- RQ1: How much conflict is there between heuristic and community-based ratings?
- RQ2: How stable are community-based ratings when compared to heuristic-based ratings?
- RQ3: When disagreements occur, are these due to different rating criteria, or to disagreements and inaccuracies in applying these criteria?

To try and answer these questions, we chose to focus on the ratings and the techniques employed by McAfee's SiteAdvisor, one of the leading heuristics-based tools, and Web of Trust, a leading community-based rating system. We chose these because they are quite popular, and because they are at the cutting edge of their respective approaches.

In this paper, we also explore an approach for extracting high-value community data based around identifying key words from reviews, and organizing these into dictionaries. These dictionaries may then be used to extract meaning and context for community-based ratings.

The rest of this paper is organized as follows: First we give a brief overview of the most relevant literature on both community and heuristic based rating techniques and systems. We then give a description of both McAfee SiteAdvisor and Web of Trust, our methodology and data collection practices, followed by our results, and finally or interpretation of these results, conclusions and future work.

RELATED WORK

Heuristic techniques use filters to find and respond to known risks and potentially risky behaviors. In this case, heuristics refer to simple rules and patterns. This may take the form of simple keyword searches, or much more sophisticated scans of software signatures, resource use, or memory footprint. Many online tools, including anti-virus [19, 24], anti-spam [20, 21], anti-phishing [23, 33], anti-spyware [6, 30], popup-blockers [35, 4], and firewalls [2, 17] use heuristics to identify potential computer based risks. Most of these systems however, treat their particular heuristics or approaches as trade secrets.

Two examples of such systems are described in more detail: Brightmail [8] is an advanced antispam and email security solution provided by Symantec. Brightmail is based on many heuristic based rules learnt from user reported spam mails. SpamAssassin [29] is an Apache project that serves as a mail filter meant to eliminate Spam. It uses a wide variety of local and network tests to identify spam signatures. The testing mechanisms include header and text analysis, Bayesian filtering, DNS blocklists and collaborative filtering.

All heuristic based tools have their own problems. One significant disadvantage with SpamAssassin and most heuristic based tools is that authors of heuristics are forever playing catch-up to the authors and discoverers of exploits. The more public a "fix" is, the quicker spammers etc. are to move to a new system and the easier it is for them to verify whether their new solution evades current filters [37]. Therefore previous research has concluded that complete automation of security decisions through the use of machine based testing is unreasonable and inefficient [12].

The wide adoption of the Internet has given people the power to publish and access a large wealth of information. Many users provide ratings for things like movies, shopping experience, business experience, websites etc. A wide range of research has been done on the use of such rating mechanisms or recommendations, and how they can be used successfully and efficiently [18, 9, 3, and 10]. Ratings for products and services published on the Internet are increasingly important, as they allow users to harvest the wisdom of the community in making decisions [9]. Using community data like user feedback is not a new idea - word of mouth and acquaintances have long been valued sources for information, and many studies have shown the efficiency of peer based community data [13]. Online reviews are a major information source for consumers [16].

Social navigation is the practice of using information from other people, exploiting social practices and behavior, to help users attain their goals. Researchers have applied social navigation systems to many diverse domains [22, 31]. Social navigation is also potentially useful in online security management [13]. In such an approach one collects data from many users and aggregates it in order to generate recommendations. It has been theorized that through proper presentation and screening, this data can help users make better decisions related to online privacy and security [13].

This approach is not without its problems however. Careful screening is necessary to avoid problems like herding behavior and information cascades. In an area where most users have relatively little technical knowledge (as in online security and privacy), it is important to make sure that knowledgeable voices are promoted and weighted differently. Previous research has addressed these issues and provided ways to mitigate these problems [13].

Due to the inherent noise present in most community data, it is important to normalize the ratings of different users to the same scale [18]. Ratings providing some review rationale are also seen as especially valuable. Explanations provide many benefits, from improving user satisfaction to increasing user confidence to helping users make better decisions by matching their concerns and expectations with different reviewers [28]. These comments and feedback help users make more reliable and correct decisions [7, 15].

At the same time, reading a large number of user comments and feedback is not always feasible or desirable. Reviews may be associated with a number of ratings or tags, which can facilitate clustering, analysis, searching, or filtering. Tags have become popular with many websites such as Delicious, Flickr, and Amazon. Tags provide both factual and subjective descriptions [26].

METHODOLOGY

In order to examine our research questions we had to conduct two connected experiments: The first being a large-scale data collection and analysis of website ratings, done over time, and a smaller, more in-depth analysis of user comments and heuristic ratings of a subset of websites.

For the first experiment our goal was to gather a broad statistical base with which we could determine whether there are significant differences in terms of the quality, focus, and stability of the ratings given by MSA and WOT for a website. This required us to gather multiple data sets.

We decided to examine sites that came from the list of top trafficked websites as published by Alexa [1]. In order to cover a wider range of websites we removed all duplicate domains. For example, the inclusion of www.google.com excluded sub-domains like www.mail.google.com and www.google.co.in. Many websites are reviewed by a small number of users, and their ratings are thus inherently unstable.

In order to account for this, WOT provides a popularity rating for each website. While the formula used to derive the popularity rating is proprietary, WOT says this rating reflects their level of confidence in their rating. All sites in our sets have a minimum popularity rating of 3 out of 5. For the second experiment we also had to filter out any website which had comments which were not in English as this complicated our text analysis. Finally, we had to filter out websites not reviewed by both MSA and WOT.

McAfee's SiteAdvisor (MSA) performs extensive and frequent heuristics-based evaluations of websites. These evaluations include tests for phishing, infected downloads, spam, drive-by-downloads, e-commerce vulnerabilities, browser exploits, popups, etc. Each site is then grouped into one of a number of risk categories: Safe, caution, risky, and untested. Each category is associated with a color, used to give users quicker, at-a-glance information (see Figure 1).

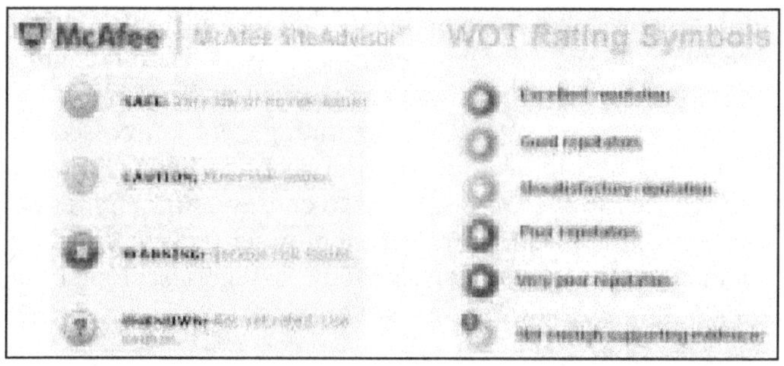

Figure 1: At-a-glance security & privacy indicators

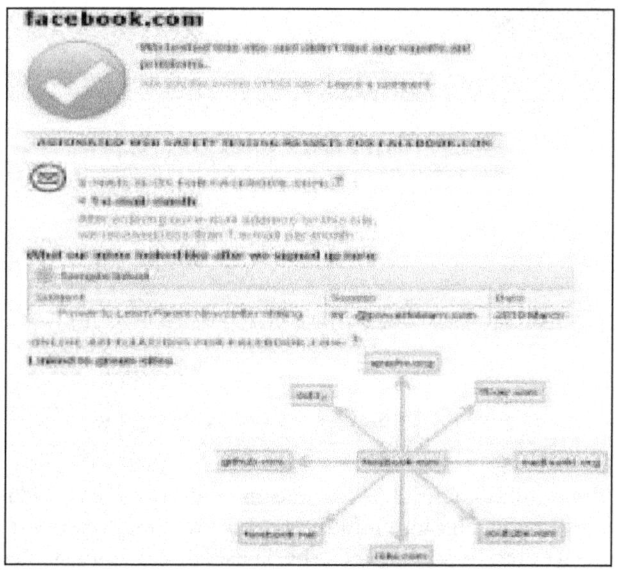

Figure 2: McAfee SiteAdvisor site review page

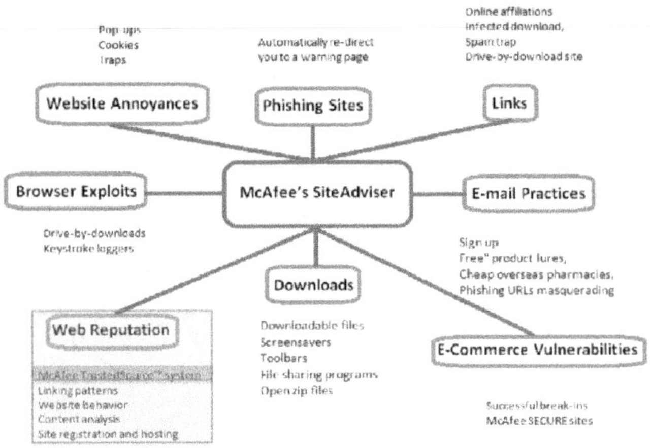

Figure 3: McAfee SiteAdvisor decision-making model.

Furthermore, a detailed site report is available describing the type of site, results of email tests, downloads tests, and online affiliations (see Figure 2). These tests are updated regularly. As seen in Figure 3, McAfee injects some reputation into its model through its McAfee TrustedSource™ system.

Web of Trust (WOT) is a community based safe surfing tool where users rate websites based on four factors: Trustworthiness, vendor reliability, privacy, and child safety. Users can post comments tagged as "good", "bad", or "reference or other". These ratings are processed by WOT and a composite reputation score is given for each site. These ratings are displayed to end-users through either a site warning (see Figure 4), or a browser plug-in. Sites are grouped into one of 5 reputation categories: Excellent, good, unsatisfactory, poor, and very poor (see Figure 1).

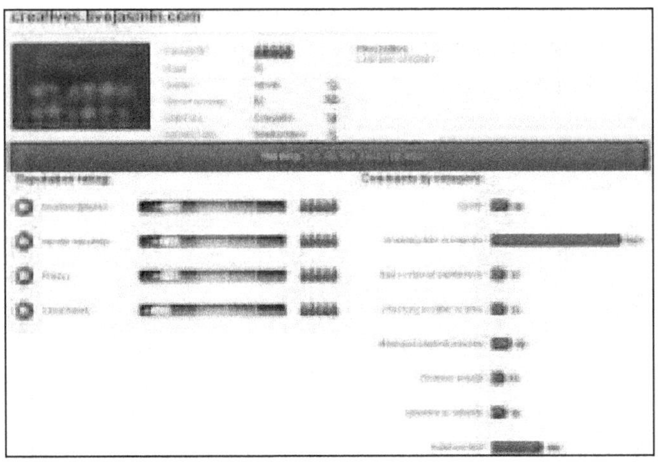

Figure 4: Web of Trust site review page

WOT encourage users to give a numerical score for a site as well as a textual feedback in the form of comments. This data can be much more informative than a numeric score, as it exposes the reasoning and criteria used for arriving at said score. At the same time, this unstructured data is difficult to process, both for users as well as the system. Users are often looking for thumbs up or thumbs down recommendation when visiting a website, not to read 20-30 reviews. Unfortunately, this unstructured data is often crucial to understanding ratings. Someone who arrives at an adult site while looking for adult content is likely to rate said site differently from someone who is surprised to arrive at the same site through a misleading link or search. Therefore, effort has to be put into extracting as much valuable information from comments, while filtering out the noise as efficiently as possible.

For our first experiment we collected reports for 20,000 websites on May 2010. These reports were collected from WOT and MSA, thus sites had to be reviewed by both services. Of these 20,000 websites, 18,650 met this criterion. These 18,650 sites were selected based on traffic, geographic representation, and topical distribution. Next, we gathered data on the top 10,000 trafficked sites, as specified by Alexa on July 2010 [1], from WOT and MSA.

For our second experiment, our goal was to collect data to determine how closely aligned the review criteria of heuristic and community-based review sites were, and what value one technique could add to the other. This required a careful analysis of user comments, thus forcing us to look at a smaller data set. Given that we were primarily interested in understanding why disagreements emerge, we carefully constructed three data sets to examine this question.

Set A: Set of websites rated as 'good' or 'safe' by both SiteAdvisor and Web of Trust.

Set B: Set of sites with conflicting rating between SiteAdvisor and Web of Trust.

Set C: Set of sites rated as 'poor' or 'risky' by both SiteAdvisor and Web of Trust.

We sampled from the list of top 10,000 websites, as listed by Alexa in June 2010. We filtered this list according to a set of selection criteria (listed below). Because of this filtering, the samples ended up being of different sizes, but roughly comparable.

Set A consisted of websites which were rated as 'Excellent' or 'Good' by WOT and 'Safe' by MSA. All sites in this set have a minimum of 100 user comments, and 90 % of these tagged as 'Good' in WOT. We had 82 websites in Set A.

Set B consisted of 97 websites where MSA and WOT were in disagreement. All sites in this set had a minimum of 5 user comments in WOT. We further divided this set into two according to the nature of the disagreement. B1 consisted of the 47 websites that were rated 'Good' by WOT and 'Risky' by MSA. B2 consisted of the 50 websites rated 'Poor' by WOT and 'Safe' by MSA.

Set C consists of websites that were rated as 'Poor' or 'Very poor' by WOT and 'Risky' by MSA. There were a totally of 54 sites in Set C. All these sites had a minimum of 5 user comments in WOT.

After the sets were identified, we collected all WOT user comments for these sites. The number of comments differed from site to site. Overall, the number of comments for Set A was higher than for the sites in Set B and Set C.

RESULTS

Starting with RQ1: How often are there conflicts between heuristic and community-based ratings? We used the first data set, containing 18,650 websites to examine this issue. We first filtered out the websites which did not have a 'good' or 'bad' rating with both WOT and MSA. In other words, we removed the sites for which MSA or WOT were unsure about. Table 1 gives an overview of the different sets.

Table 1: System discrimination

System	Set	Sample Size	% of sample
WOT	Good	16,968	90.79%
	Bad	1,722	9.21%
MSA	Good	18,062	96.64%
	Bad	628	3.36%

As we see from Table 1, the vast majority of sites in our sample were seen as safe, or 'good'. This is not surprising as we sampled from top websites. If a significant number of these sites were engaging in dubious behavior, they likely would be punished by users and quickly find their way out of the rankings.

More interesting, we find that WOT users seem more selective in evaluating websites, finding more faults (9.21% of sites found to be 'bad' by WOT users compared to 3.36% by MSA). We performed Pearson's chi-square test to check whether the difference is statistically significant or not. We found that these differences were highly significant (χ^2=543.466, $p<0.0001$, DF=1). This is important when we consider the risks associated with Type I and Type II errors, as we will in the discussion section of this paper.

The sum difference does not tell the whole story however. Two review systems might arrive at the same number of 'bad' sites, yet disagree on which sites are 'bad'. Therefore the next step is to determine the amount of disagreement between these sources. Table 2 gives an overview of the degree of disagreement in our sample.

Table 2: Degree of mismatch between WOT and MSA

Input set	Sample Size	Mismatch MSA/WOT	# Mismatch
Rated "Good" on WOT	16,968	2.06%	350
Rated "Bad" by WOT	1,722	81.54%	1,404
Total	**18,690**	**9.38%**	**1,754**

A mismatch occurs when either WOT says the site is 'good' while MSA says it is 'bad', or when MSA says a site is 'good' and WOT says it is 'bad'. What we found was quite surprising: MSA very rarely disagreed with WOT users when these claimed that sites were safe (only 2.06% of cases), whereas MSA claimed that 81.54% of the sites WOT users considered to be unsafe were safe. This is a surprising degree of disagreement, the roots of which we will explore when discussing RQ3.

Turning to RQ2: How stable are community-based ratings when compared to heuristic-based ratings?

To answer this question we turn to the second data set, based on the top 10,000 sites in July 2010. We compared this list to the 18,690 sites we collected in May of the same year. From this list we found an overlap of 5,743 sites, the remaining 4,257 sites were either not part of our original set or were being reexamined by MSA. What we were looking for was how many websites had gone from one rating to another (ie. from 'good' to 'bad' or vice versa). This means that we were not interested in sites that got additional reviews if these were consistent with prior reviews.

As we can see in Table 3, we found surprisingly few changes over the two-month period. Doing a Pearson's chi-square test, we do find that there was a statistically significant difference in terms of the rate of change between WOT ratings and MSA *(χ^2= 31.208, $p<0.0001$, DF=1), however, at least for top websites, this rate of change is very small.*

Table 3: Stability of site ratings

Data	# of sites	# of sites changed	% change
WOT	5,743	34	0.59%
MSA	5,743	1	0.02%

Finally, RQ3: When disagreements occur, are these due to the use of different rating criteria, or are they due to disagreements and inaccuracies evaluating the same criteria?

In order to tackle this question, we turn to our second experiment, where we analyzed a smaller set of sites in greater detail and extracted rating rationales from the many user comments. In total we collected 12,677 user comments from the 233 websites evaluated in this smaller experiment. Of these, 7,158 comments were related to sites in Set A, 4,688 comments were related to sites in Set B, and 831 comments were related to sites in Set C.

We can confirm after this analysis that the quality, focus, and accuracy of user comments varies wildly. User comments differ in quality and reliability, as well as what users choose to focus on in their review. Reviews of a website often include contradictory statements. Therefore, these comments need filtering and normalization before comparisons can be made.

WOT allows its users to categorize their comments when they post them. Reviewers can categorize a comment as 'Good', 'Bad', or 'Other'. Of the 12,677 user comments, 7,453 comments were tagged as 'Good', 4,691 comments were tagged as 'Bad', and 533 comments were tagged as 'other'. Each of these categories were tagged with terms like 'adult', 'spam', 'viruses', etc. (see Figure 4).

Table 4: Site reviews

Data	# of reviews	Good reviews	Bad reviews
Set A	7,158	86.70%	9.80%
Set B	4,688	24.18%	70.43%
Set C	831	14.07%	82.67%

Based on the chi-square test result we obtained (*Pearson's chi-square test, χ^2=5501.475, $p<0.0001$, DF=2*), the difference in ratio of good to bad reviews between Sets A, B, and C was statistically significant. This means that as we'd expect disputed sites get more bad reviews than 'good' sites, and 'bad' sites get the most bad reviews. Interestingly, 'good' sites are more likely to get reviews than the 'bad' sites. Part of the reason might be due to sites in Set A being the most popular in terms of visitor numbers while Set C sites were the least popular.

We used our own filter and tag cloud algorithm to organize and visualize the most common words in user comments. Our algorithm uses an English dictionary to filter and process the comments. The English dictionary was used to help identify words and variations of words for clustering. This algorithm was used to identify a set of high frequency words, based both on the total number of times a word appeared, as well as how many comments it appeared in overall. This was done to ensure that repeated use of a word in a single post would not skew results. To ensure that no important words were missed, we compared our results to those of 3 online tag clouding websites Wordle [36], Artviper [5], TagCrowd [32]. We used these online services to build clouds, which we used to identify key "non-words" that we needed to grandfather into our English dictionary, like 'NIX4KIDS'. 'NIX4KIDS' is not an English word, but many reviewers used the term in their comments related to adult sites.

We did a separate analysis for the tags in the good reviews and the bad reviews. This was done to identify words that were uniquely associated with positive and negative reviews, as opposed to generally popular words. We of course looked for modifier words, like 'not' before doing this filtering. We also tagged technical words, but left them in their respective good and bad dictionaries.

A word was included in our "Good" dictionary if it met the following 3 conditions:

1. At least 0.5% of the total comments contained the word
2. At least 0.75% of the good comments contained the word
3. The rate of use of the word in good comments should be at least 0.5 percentage points higher than that of the bad comments.

The same rules were followed for the "bad" dictionary:

1. At least 0.5% of the total comments contained the word
2. At least 0.75 % of the bad comments contained the word.
3. The rate of use of the word in bad comments should be at least 0.5 percentage points higher than that of the good comments.

The statistical limits were set after some experimentation, but this would likely benefit from more rigorous study, especially as the sets grow.

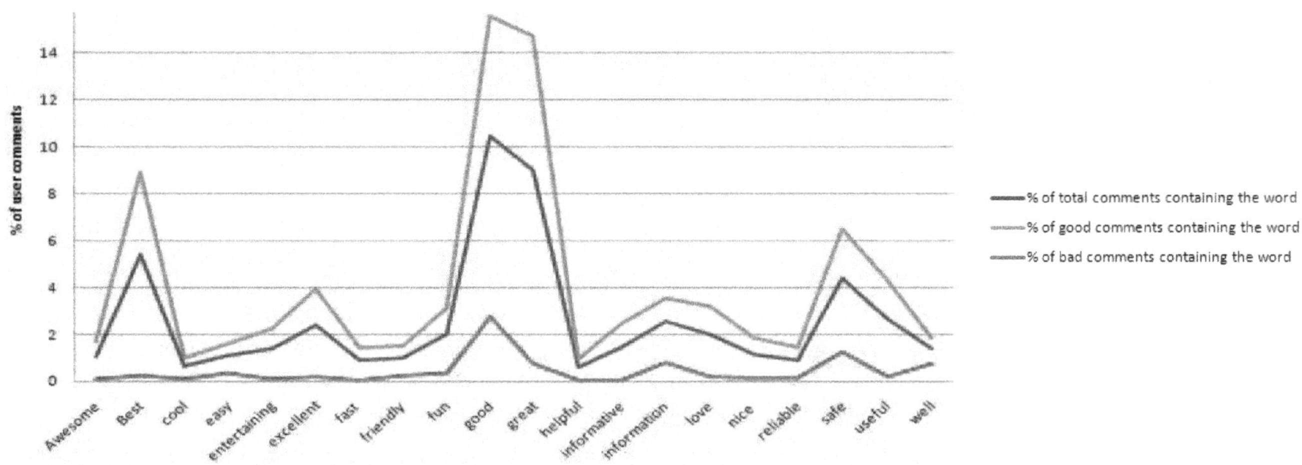

Figure 5: Construction of the 'Good' dictionary

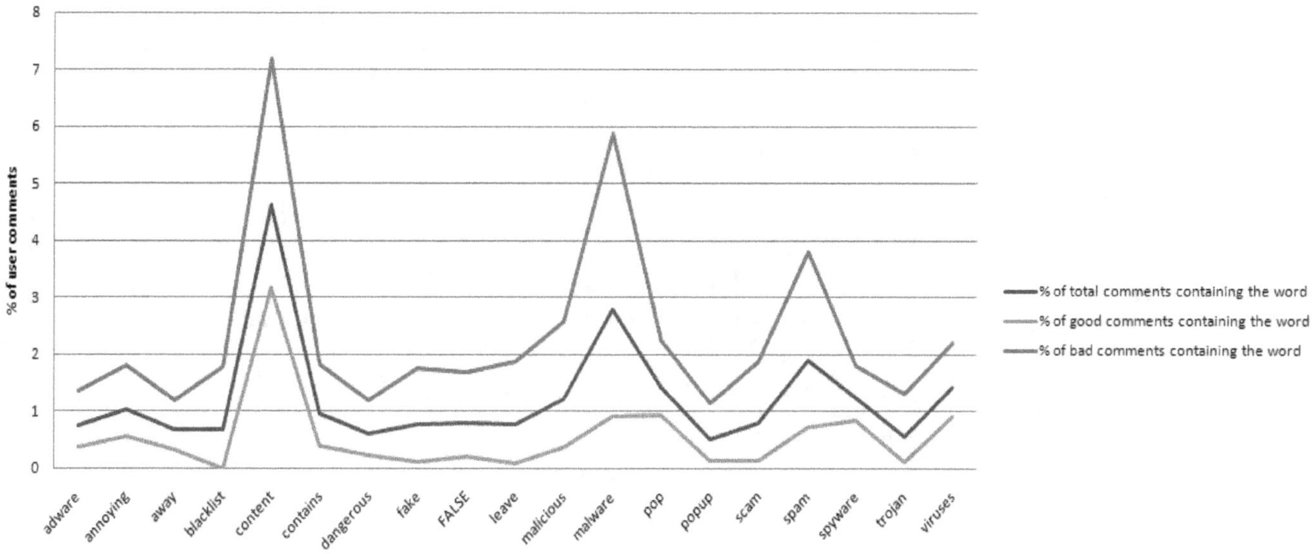

Figure 6: Construction of the 'Bad' dictionary

There were many websites with adult content in our three data sets. Adult content can sometimes be controversial. For someone looking for adult content, finding it is a good thing. Finding adult content when one is not looking for it is often undesirable. Adult words can therefore be both positive and negative, and can sometimes be used as both in the reviews of the same site. We therefore decided to build a special dictionary of adult words.

We calculated the number of user comments classifying a site as an 'Adult site'. There were naturally more adult websites in Set B and in Set C compared with Set A (see Figure 7). We defined a site as an adult site if at least 50% of comments stated that the site contained adult contents.

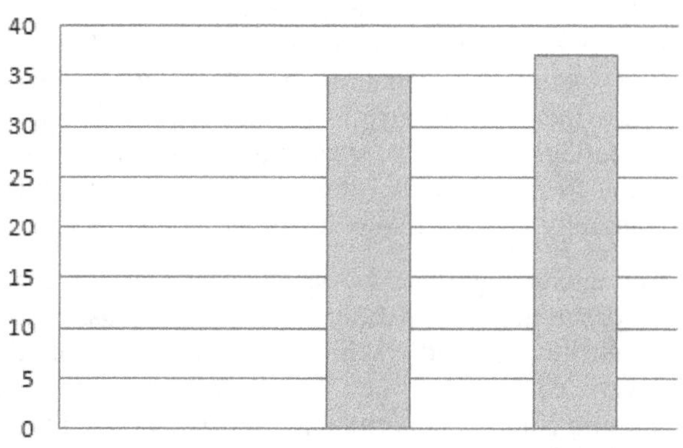

Figure 7: % of adult sites in the three samples

The dictionaries we ended up with contained the following words:

Good dictionary: Awesome, Best, Cool, Easy, Entertaining, Excellent, Fast, Friendly, Fun, Good, Great, Helpful, Informative, Love, Nice, Reliable, Safe

Bad dictionary: Adware, Annoying, Away, Blacklist, Content, Dangerous, Fake, False, Leave, Malicious, Malware, Popup, Scam, Spam, Spyware, Trojan, Virus,

Adult dictionary: Adult, Pornography, Children, Explicit, NIX4KIDS, Sex

The exact content of these dictionaries is affected by the small sample sizes in this part of the study. With a larger sample size, both the content and the size of these dictionaries would likely change. Idiosyncratic words and classifications (such as the word 'Content' being in our 'Bad' dictionary) would be less likely.

Looking at these dictionaries, we notice that a large number of the words in the bad dictionary are technical terms, and represent technologies and techniques that would have been sought out by MSA. Examples include "Adware", "Malware", "Spam", "Spyware", "Trojan", and "Virus". Thus looking back to our research question, we must conclude that there is some overlap in the rating criteria, but looking at Figure 6, we see that except for the terms "Malware" and "Spam", these terms were not outstanding features of the bad dictionary.

When we look at the content of the comments in Set B, we see that the most important 'bad' word is 'content' (as in contains), and most of the disagreements with the MSA ratings (where MSA has declared the site safe), are due to either the presence of adult content, or undesirable practices not related to technology. Looking at Figure 8, we can see how the sites in Set B were truly a mixed bag, and adult content was very prevalent. We therefore conclude that while there is some overlap between the rating criteria of WOT and MSA, it is not the only source of disagreement, and that user comments add a significant amount of data in the form of tags of unsavory content and business practices.

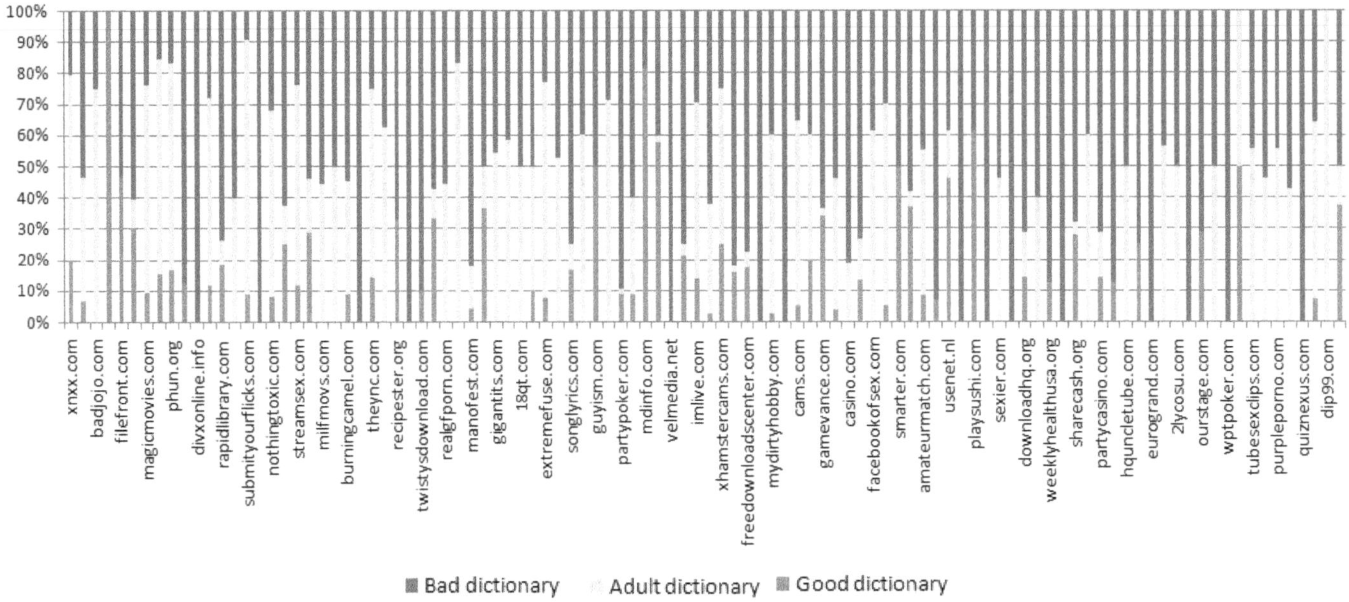

Figure 8: Classification of websites in Set B using dictionaries

DISCUSSION

The sampling decisions in our experiments were based on the goals of the experiments. Experiment 1 was done to study the focus and review criteria of MSA and WOT and the causes of disagreements between the two, thus we wanted as large a sample as possible. However, the second part of that experiment was aimed at analyzing how stable MSA and WOT ratings were over time. In order to determine whether the ratings were stable, some time had to pass. However, if too much time was allowed to pass, chances are that the site's practices would change, thus triggering a justified change in rating which might have confounded our study. We decided to study sites over a period of 2 months, deeming this to be an acceptable compromise. This decision means that for this part of the experiment we lost a significant number of sites from our sample set at this point. We realize however that not all will agree with this definition of stability, or with our concerns that site-evolution might taint our stability findings. We do recognize that the loss of sites at this step in the process is problematic, and if we were to redo this study, we would have looked for ways to avoid such a loss of data.

For our second experiment we were interested in determining what differentiated 'good' sites from 'bad', which required us to review user comments. Unfortunately, while it was relatively easy to find examples of popular well-reviewed 'good' sites, it was considerably harder to find examples of 'bad' sites. There exists no directory of such sites, so we were forced to resort to trial and error as well as a certain amount of random chance to find enough sites for sample sets B and C. This meant that we had a much harder time collecting data for 'bad' sites, both in terms of the sample sizes as well as the number of reviews available for each sample. It is therefore important that the reader not look to our dictionaries as the authoritative list of what defines a 'good' or 'bad' site, but rather as a proof of concept for how to extract such knowledge from user comments. Further study should in any case be done to determine what acceptable and useful thresholds should be for inclusion or exclusion into a dictionary, as well as determining what the most useful dictionaries for this application might be. While we think our three dictionaries ('good', 'bad', and 'adult') are useful, there might be room for more (a 'technical' dictionary perhaps?)

One of the most important findings from this study is the low rate of change of ratings (less than 0.6% over 2 months for WOT), both for MSA and WOT. At the same time, the total amount of disagreement between MSA and WOT was less than 10% over more than 16,000 websites. One of the main criticisms of community based rating systems has been that there is no guarantee that they will result in reliable ratings, or that these ratings will be stable. As we have seen from this study, those criticisms are not fair for all community-based rating systems.

Another interesting finding was the fact that WOT users were more critical of websites than MSA was, marking more websites as 'bad'. While this study did not try to objectively determine which rating was most correct, if such a thing could be determined objectively, when there is risk for fraud of privacy invasions, it might be better to play it safe. In this sense, encouraging WOT users to mark up sites which are borderline or dubious is probably a good idea.

People are generally poor at evaluating risk and technology, but good at evaluating the social, legal, and intangibles. Therefore, it might be wise to construct a separate dictionary of technical terms, and use this to carefully evaluate the reliability of technical claims users make about sites.

Our work to date has been limited to a relatively small sample of sites. More importantly, the bulk of these sites have been selected from the most popular sites on the Internet. To validate the scalability and generalizability of this work, and our tag extraction approach, we should extend our research to cover a larger set of sites, spanning a greater set of topic areas, and engaging in a wider set of business practices. This means of course, identifying a set of relatively obscure sites as well, as they are more likely to be engaging in unsavory or dubious behavior.

Rather than relying on lists and ratings to do this, we instead propose to develop a browser plug-in that will record more realistic browsing patterns. This plug-in can of course also be used to provide feedback to users, which would allow us to determine whether the combined data is more successful at spurring user to action, or helping them make the right decisions.

In the work we have done to date, we have not done any research to determine the error rates of either MSA or WOT. We know that at least some of the disagreements between the two must be due to faulty information with one of the two review systems. While it is easy to assume that MSA will be more accurate when looking for security and technology-specific privacy threats, this is a hypothesis that should be tested. Understanding how big a disconnect there is, or how big the false positive and false negative rates are would be an important contribution to our understanding of the value of user ratings.

Another future step is to examine how dictionaries should be weighted (how bad is the inclusion of an 'adult' word in a 'good' site), and if and how words should be weighted within dictionaries. This is an important next step when one considers how to practically combine heuristic data, which tends to generate a numerical or categorical score, and community feedback, which is inherently verbose and qualitative. Each word in a dictionary may be assigned a weight or numerical score depending on its relationship with user reviews and comments about that specific website. In fact each dictionary itself may have a numerical score for a specific type of website.

In this paper we have demonstrated how this approach can be used to potentially deal with morally ambiguous content such as adult sites. This is just one example of many areas of the World Wide Web where a certain amount of context needs to be applied in order to give users more nuanced and useful warnings and recommendations. This same approach might be useful when dealing with other troublesome dimensions like security, privacy, business practices, etc. where different users are going to have different concerns with regards to different websites and contexts.

User comments and feedback have their own problems, like information cascades, herding behavior, incorrect comments, misusing of community data etc. These problems are not addressed in this paper, but have been described eloquently in [13], which also shows some successful mitigating measures for them. In the future, it would be interesting to examine whether mitigating behaviors such as those described in [13] are naturally occurring in some of the community sites such as WOT, whether administrators promote them, or whether these communities have developed their own norms and techniques to avoid these pitfalls.

CONCLUSION

Users were found to be more discriminating than heuristic-based systems, at least for the sample used in our study. This may be an indicator of a higher false positive rate with community-based systems, or it may be evidence that users have access to more meaningful information (again, at least for this sample), or that user are more risk-averse than heuristic-based systems give them credit for.

User ratings and heuristic-based systems are both relatively stable, and do not change significantly over short periods of time (though user ratings change more rapidly than heuristic-based reviews). Given the low rate of change, we cannot determine how much of the change is due to genuine change in the site policies, and how much is due to shifting opinion.

Our results show that information abstracted from user comments may add value in terms of additional data to the evaluation and communication of risk to users by automatically analyzing large numbers of user comments. This may help people in at-a-glance digesting large volumes of user feedback easily. Previous research has shown that users are influenced by user feedback; this abstracted form of that information in form of dictionaries may add sufficient nuance to the heuristic machine based testing systems like McAfee SiteAdvisor and Norton SafeWeb.

ACKNOWLEDGEMENTS

We wish to thank our colleagues in the HCI group at the School of EECS, Oregon State University for their support and help in preparing the paper. We'd also like to thank Web of Trust and it's users for giving us access to their data for this study. Finally, we'd like to thank our reviewers for thoughtful feedback and suggestions on how to improve this paper.

REFERENCES

1. Alexa., http://alexa.com
2. AlpineLinux., http://www.alpinelinux.org/wiki
3. Amatriain, X., Pujol,J.M., Tintarev,N., Rate it Again: Increasing Recommendation Accuracy by User re-Rating. *RecSys'09, October 23–25, 2009,* , New York, USA.
4. AOL explorer., http://www.aol.com/
5. Artviper., http://www.artviper.net/texttagcloud/
6. Avira., http://www.avira.com/en/pages/index.php

7. Bilgic, M., and Mooney,R.J., Explaining recommendations: Satisfaction vs. promotion. In *Proceedings of Beyond Personalization Workshop, IUI, 2005*. San Diego, California, USA
8. Brightmail., http://www.symantec.com/business/products/family.jsp?familyid=brightmail
9. Chen, M., Singh, J.P., Computing and Using Reputations for Internet Ratings. *EC'01, October 14-17, 2001,* Tampa, Florida, USA.
10. Dellarocas, C., Immunizing Online Reputation Reporting Systems Against Unfair Ratings and Discriminatory Behavior. *EC'00, October 17-20, 2000,* Minneapolis, Minnesota.
11. Dourish, P., Grinter, R., Delgado de la Flor, J. and Joseph, M. Security in the Wild: User Strategies for Managing Security as an Everyday, Practical Problem. Personal and Ubiquitous Computing, 8 (6). 391-401.
12. Edwards, W.K., Poole, E.S. and Stoll, J., Security Automation Considered Harmful? *In Proceedings of the IEEE New Security Paradigms Workshop 2007*, (White Mountain, New Hampshire, 2007).
13. Goecks, J.,Edwards, W.K.,and Mynatt, E. D., Challenges in Supporting End-User Privacy and Security Management with Social Navigation. *Symposium On Usable Privacy and Security (SOUPS) 2009, July 15-17* 2009, Mountain View, CA, USA.
14. Gross, J. and Rosson, M.B., Looking for Trouble: Understanding End-User Security Management *in 2007 Computer Human Interaction for the Management of Information Technology*, (2007), ACM Press, 10.
15. Herlocker, J., Konstan, J., and Riedl, J., Explaining collaborative filtering recommendations. *In Proceedings of the ACM Conference on Computer Supported Cooperative Work, 2000*. CHI Letters 5(1).
16. Hu, N., Pavlou,P.A., Zhang, J ., Can Online Reviews Reveal a Product's True Quality? Empirical Findings and Analytical Modeling of Online Word-of-Mouth Communication. *EC'06, June 11–15, 2006,* Ann Arbor, Michigan, USA
17. Ipfire., http://www.ipfire.org/en/index
18. Jin, R., Si, L., A Study of Methods for Normalizing User Ratings in Collaborative Filtering. *SIGIR'04, July 25–29, 2004*, Sheffield, South Yorkshire, UK.
19. McAfee., http://www.mcafee.com/us/
20. McAfee SiteAdvisor., http://www.siteadvisor.com/
21. McAfee SpamKiller., http://us.mcafee.com/root/product.asp?productid=msk
22. McNee, S., Kapoor, N. and Konstan, J.A., Don't Look Stupid: Avoiding Pitfalls when Recommending Research Papers. *In 2006 Conference on Computer-Support Cooperative Work (CSCW 2006)*, (2006), 171-180.
23. Mozilla Firefox anti-phishing., http://www.mozilla.com/en-US/firefox/phishing-protection/
24. Norton., http://us.norton.com/index.jsp
25. Norton SafeWeb., http://safeweb.norton.com/
26. Sen, S., Lam, S.K., Rashid, A.M., Cosley, D., Frankowski, D., Osterhouse, J., Harper, F.M., and Riedl,J., tagging, communities, vocabulary, evolution. *In Proceedings of the ACM 2006 Conference on CSCW*, Banff, Alberta, Canada, 2006.
27. Sinha, R., and Swearingen, K., The role of transparency in recommender systems. In *CHI '02: CHI '02 extended abstracts on Human factors in computing systems*, pages 830–831, New York, NY, USA, 2002. ACM.
28. Vig, J., Sen, S., Riedl, J., Tagsplanations: Explaining Recommendations Using Tags. *IUI'09, February 8 - 11, 2009*, Sanibel Island, Florida, USA.
29. Spamassassin., http://spamassassin.apache.org/
30. SpyBot., http://www.safer-networking.org/en/index.html
31. Svensson, M., Höök, K., Laaksolahti, J. and Waern, A., Social Navigation of Food Recipes. *in 2001 Conference on Human Factors in Computing, (2001)*, 341-348
32. Tagcrowd., http://tagcrowd.com
33. Untangle., http://www.untangle.com/
34. Web of Trust., http://www.mywot.com/
35. Webroot popup washer., http://www.webroot.com/En_US/consumer-products-spysweeper.html
36. Wordle., http://www.wordle.net/create
37. Zdziarski, J.A., Ending spam: Bayesian content filtering and the art of statistical language classification.

Pairing Devices for Social Interactions: A Comparative Usability Evaluation

Ersin Uzun
Palo Alto Research Center
ersin.uzun@parc.com

Nitesh Saxena
Polytechnic Institute of New York University
nsaxena@poly.edu

Arun Kumar
Polytechnic Institute of New York University
aashok01@students.poly.edu

ABSTRACT
When users wish to establish wireless radio communication between/among their devices, the channel has to be bootstrapped first. The process of setting up a secure communication channel between two previously unassociated devices is referred to as "Secure Device Pairing". The focus of prior research on this topic has mostly been limited to "personal pairing" scenarios, whereby a single user controls both the devices. In this paper, we instead consider "social pairing" scenarios, whereby two different users establish pairing between their respective devices. We present a comprehensive study to identify methods suitable for social pairing, and comparatively evaluate the usability and security of these methods. Our results identify methods best-suited for users, in terms of efficiency, error-tolerance and of course, usability. Our work provides insights on the applicability and usability of methods for emerging social pairing scenarios, a topic largely ignored so far.

ACM Classification Keywords
H.5.m Information Interfaces and Presentation: miscellaneous

General Terms
Experimentation, Security, Human Factors

INTRODUCTION
Increasing proliferation of personal gadgets (including PDAs, cell-phones, headsets, cameras and media players) – equipped with wireless communication (e.g., Wi-Fi, Bluetooth) – continuously opens up new services and possibilities for ordinary users. There are many usage scenarios where two devices need to "work together." In commonly occurring, so called *personal* communication scenarios, both devices are controlled by a single user (Alice). Examples include communication between Alice's Bluetooth headset and her cellphone, her PDA and a wireless printer, or her laptop and a wireless access point. On the other hand, *social* communication scenarios, whereby two different users (Alice and Bob) control their respective devices, are also rapidly emerging. Examples include communication between Alice's and Bob's PDAs/laptops/cell phones for social or professional reasons, such as sharing files and music, exchanging digital business cards, multi-player games, messaging, chatting or collaborative applications.

The surge in popularity of wireless devices, however, brings about various security risks. The wireless radio communication channel is easy to eavesdrop upon and to manipulate, raising the very real threats, notably, of so-called *Man-in-the-Middle* (MitM) or *Evil Twin* attacks. To mitigate these attacks, secure communication must be first bootstrapped, i.e., devices must be securely "paired" or initialized.

One of the main challenges in secure device pairing is that, due to sheer diversity of devices and lack of standards, no global security infrastructure exists today and none is likely for the foreseeable future. Consequently, traditional cryptographic means (such as authenticated key exchange protocols) are unsuitable, since unfamiliar devices have no prior security context and no common point of trust.

One valuable and established research direction in secure device pairing is the use of auxiliary – also referred to as "out-of-band" (OOB) – channels, which are both perceivable and manageable by the user(s) of the devices. An OOB channel takes advantage of human sensory capabilities to authenticate human-imperceptible (and hence subject to MitM attacks) information exchanged over the "in-band" wireless channel. OOB channels can be realized using acoustic, visual and tactile senses. Unlike the in-band channel, the attacker can not remain undetected if it actively interferes with the OOB channel, although it can eavesdrop upon it.

For pairing methods based on OOB channels, some degree of human involvement is essential. Usability of the pairing process thus becomes extremely important. We observe that a large majority of existing device pairing methods are proposed by security professionals without giving much emphasis on their usability. Although a few methods have been tested for usability, the testing is done in isolation or with a limited focus on only "*personal pairing*" scenarios.

Motivation
Application domain for secure pairing methods is not limited to personal settings. Two users may wish to exchange files, digital business cards or play games. The main advantage of using Bluetooth or WiFi in such scenarios is that no

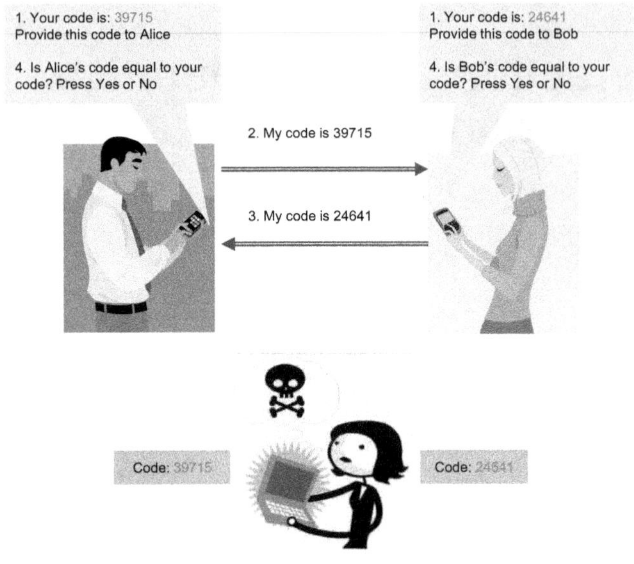

Figure 1. MitM attack scenario for social pairing based on numeric comparison: adversary is executing an instance of pairing with Bob's device and another instance with Alice's device [Step 1: Bob's and Alice's devices show their respective numeric codes as a result of pairing processes; Step 2-3: Bob and Alice exchange their respective codes via OOB communication; Step 4: Bob is asked to compare his code with the one provided by Alice, and Alice is asked to compare her code with the one provided by Bob, and accordingly accept or reject the pairing (in this case, both should be rejecting to prevent the attack)]

infrastructure is needed and *ad hoc* communication can take place without any extra cost to the users. For this reason, social scenarios have been emerging rapidly and are already quite popular, especially, in developing countries. Secure pairing is a natural way to prevent any eavesdropping and/or malicious intervention during intended communication.

Many personal pairing methods have been proposed. A personal pairing method could be directly used in a "*social pairing*" scenario, only if one of the users operates both devices. However, this might not always be desirable or feasible, as discussed below.

- PERSONAL DEVICES: Devices, such as mobile phones, are personal items regarded as extended self-identities of their bearers [9]. For example, users – especially in Asian countries – tend to personalize the exteriors of their phones to make them look unique and representative of their own selves [9]. Thus, users might become nervous or uneasy when asked to share their phones with others.
- SECURITY AND PRIVACY OF DEVICES: Sharing of phones, especially with strangers, might raise security and privacy concerns [14]. For example, Alice might become concerned that Bob would somehow read her emails or delete her folders when she hands over the phone to him for pairing. In fact, as the survey results of our study show (discussed later), majority of users understand such security and privacy implications and are not willing to share their devices with others, even temporarily, during the pairing process. To counter this, pairing application can be executed by Alice in a locked state prior to sharing the phone with Bob, as discussed in [21]. However, this requires Alice to unlock the phone after receiving it back from Bob, thus increasing overall user burden. Physical security might also deter users from sharing their phones. For example, Alice might be concerned that Bob would drop her new and expensive phone and damage it.[1]
- CONTEXT: Even when users are willing to share their phones, the underlying physical and social situation – where the pairing takes place – might not be conducive for phone sharing. For example, Alice and Bob may not be in very close proximity, e.g., sitting across a table in a conference room. Alternatively, users may not be comfortable with holding, using or even being seen with another person's device. An expensive and fragile-looking device (or a highly personalized one with flashy covers and stickers) may easily trigger discomfort. Moreover, taking responsibility for the pairing and interacting with an unfamiliar device in the process can be bothersome, as any failure may result in embarrassment.

For aforementioned reasons, the problem of social pairing can not be simply reduced to personal, one-user, pairing. In fact, social pairing presents unique challenges of its own. First, it is not clear whether personal pairing methods are suitable (and to what extent) when applied in a social pairing scenario. In fact, participation of two users makes the secure pairing process more complicated and potentially error-prone.[2] As an example, to achieve social pairing based on numeric comparison [34] (see Figure 1), an additional layer of interaction between Alice and Bob is needed to compare numbers displayed on their respective devices. Furthermore, not all personal pairing methods are applicable if each device is controlled by a different user. For example, a pairing method that requires both devices to be shaken simultaneously [22] is not suitable for social pairing.

To summarize, there is a pressing need to evaluate applicability, performance and usability of pairing methods suitable for social setting, which is the focus of our paper. Such a study is essential to identify most suitable pairing method(s) for everyday users.

BACKGROUND

Over the recent years, a number of pairing methods have been proposed. They operate over different OOB channels, use different cryptographic protocols and offer varying degrees of usability. All these methods have been proposed in the context of personal pairing and some parts of the following discussion about these methods are adopted from Kobsa et al. [16], a paper that focuses on usability in personal pairing. However, the focus of this paper is social pairing, not personal pairing, and we discuss the applicability of these methods to the social pairing scenarios in Section "Study Preliminaries".

[1]Another extreme possibility is theft of devices. However, it is quite unlikely that a user will indulge in social pairing with someone she does not trust.

[2]On the other hand, unlike personal pairing, devices taking part in social pairing are not usually constrained in terms of input/output interfaces. This simplifies the process to a certain extent.

The initial attempt to address the device pairing problem in the presence of MiTM attacks was "Resurrecting Duckling" [33]. It requires standardized physical interfaces and cables. Although it was appropriate in the 1990-s, this is clearly obsolete today, due to the greatly increased diversity (and decreased size) of devices and the requirement of a physical equipment (i.e., a cable) which defeats the purpose and convenience of wireless connections.

"Talking to Strangers" [1] was another early method, which relies on infrared (IR) communication as the OOB channel and requires almost no user involvement, except for initial setup. Moreover, it has been experimented with user (unlike many other methods), as reported in [2]. However, this method is deceptively simple since IR is line-of-sight and, setting it up requires the user to find IR ports on both devices – not a trivial task for many users – and align them. Also, despite its line-of-sight property, IR is not completely immune to MiTM attacks. Another drawback is that IR has been largely displaced by other wireless technologies (e.g., Bluetooth) and is available on few modern devices.

Another approach involves image comparison. It encodes the OOB data into images and asks the user to compare them on two devices. Prominent examples include: "Snowflake" [6], "Random Arts Visual Hash" [27] and "Colorful Flag" [5]. Such methods, however, require both devices to have displays with sufficiently high resolution and applicability is limited to high-end devices, such as: laptops, PDAs and cell phones. These methods are based on the protocol proposed in [1] which was reviewed earlier. A more practical approach, based on Short Authenticated Strings (SAS) protocols [26, 19], suitable for simpler displays and LEDs has been investigated in [29].

More recent work [24] proposed the "Seeing-is-Believing" (SiB) pairing method. In its simplest instantiation, SiB requires a uni-directional visual OOB channel for one-way authentication: one device encodes OOB data into a two-dimensional barcode which it displays on its screen and the other device "reads it" using a photo camera, operated by the user. At a minimum, SiB requires one device to have a camera and the other – a display for uni-directional authentication and both devices to have a camera and display for bi-directional authentication. Thus, it is not suitable for small or low-end devices. From the user's perspective, SiB is a relatively undemanding pairing method as user actions amount to taking a photo of a barcode.

A related approach, called "Blinking Lights" has been explored in [30]. Like SiB, it uses the visual OOB channel and requires one device to have a visual receiver, e.g., a light detector or a video camera. The other device must have at least one LED. The LED-equipped device transmits OOB data via blinking while the other receives it by recording the transmission and extracting information based on inter-blink gaps. The receiver device indicates success/failure to the user who, in turn, informs the other to accept or abort.

Quite recently, [28] developed a pairing method based on synchronized audio-visual patterns. Three proposed methods, "Blink-Blink", "Beep-Beep" and "Beep-Blink", involve users comparing very simple audiovisual patterns, e.g., in the form of "beeping" and "blinking", transmitted as simultaneous streams, forming two synchronized channels. One advantage of these methods is that they require devices to only have two LEDs (one of which is to ensure synchronization) or a basic speaker.

Another recent method is "Loud-and-Clear" (L&C) [7]. It uses the audio and/or visual OOB channels along with MadLib phrases which represent the digest of information exchanged over the main wireless channel. There are three L&C variants: "Phrase-SS", "Phrase-DS" and "Phrase-SS". In the first one, user compares two displayed phrases and in the last one, two vocalized ones. The middle one requires the user to compare a displayed phrase with its vocalized counterpart. Minimal device requirements include a speaker or a display on each device and the user either accept or abort the pairing based on the outcome of the comparison. i.e., whether the phrases are the same. As described in [7], L&C is based on the protocol of [1]. In this paper, to reduce the number of words in the MadLib sentences, we use the L&C variant based on SAS protocols [26, 19]. The third variant of L&C, "Phrase-DD," simply involves displaying the sentences on two devices, which the user is asked to compare.

Some follow-on work (HAPADEP [32]) considered pairing devices that – at least at pairing time – have no common wireless channel. HAPADEP uses pure audio to transmit cryptographic protocol messages and requires the user to merely monitor device interaction for any extraneous sounds or interference. It requires both devices to have speakers and microphones. To appeal to more common setting (one where a common wireless channel is available), we employ a HAPADEP variant, we call "Over-Audio." This variant uses the wireless channel for cryptographic protocol messages and the audio – as the OOB channel. In it, only one device needs a speaker and the other – a microphone. Also, the user is not involved in any comparisons.

An experimental investigation [34] presented the results of a comparative usability study of simple pairing methods for devices with displays capable of showing a few (4-8) decimal digits of OOB data. In the "Compare-Confirm" or "Numeric-Compare" approach, the user simply compares two 4-, 6- or 8-digit numbers displayed by devices. In the "Select-Confirm" approach, one device displays to the user a set of (4-, 6- or 8-digit) numbers, the user selects the one that matches a single such number displayed by the other device. In the "Copy-Confirm" approach, the user copies a number from one device to the other. The last variant is "Choose-Enter" which asks the user to pick a "random" 4-to-8-digit number and enter it into both devices. All of these methods are undoubtedly simple, however, as [34] indicates, Select-Confirm and Copy-Confirm are slow and error-prone. Furthermore, "Choose-Enter" is insecure since studies show that the quality of numbers (in terms of randomness) picked by the average user is very low.

The approach Button-Enabled Device Authentication (BEDA) [31] suggests pairing devices with the help of button pressing, thus utilizing the tactile OOB channel. It has has several variants: "BEDA-Blink", "BEDA-Beep", "BEDA-Vibrate" and "BEDA-Buttons". In the first three variants, respectively, the sending device blinks its LED (or beeps or vibrates) and the user synchronously presses a button on the receiving device. Each 3-bit block of the SAS string is encoded as the delay between consecutive blinks (or beeps or vibrations). As the sending device blinks (or beeps or vibrates), the user presses the button on the other device thereby transmitting the SAS between the devices. In the BEDA-Buttons variant, which can work with any PAKE protocol (e.g., [3]), the user simultaneously presses buttons on both devices and random user-controlled inter-button pressing delays are used as the means of establishing a common secret.

A very different OOB channel was considered in "Smart-Its-Friends" [8]: a common movement pattern is used to communicate a shared secret to both devices as they are shaken together by the user. A similar approach is taken in "Shake Well Before Use" [22]. Both techniques require devices to be equipped with 2-axis accelerometers. Although some recent mobile phones (e.g., iPhone) are equipped with it, accelerometers are not common on other devices.

There are also other methods involving technologies that are relatively expensive and uncommon. To summarize a few. [15] suggested using ultrasound as the OOB channel. A related technique uses laser as the OOB and requires each device to have a laser transceiver [23]. Other methods require Near Field Communication technology and devices to be touched with each other. However, the hardware needed for these methods are not readily available in many current devices and are not expected to be ubiquitous soon.

Recently, comprehensive and comparative studies of different personal pairing methods have been introduced in [12, 16] and [18]. In [18], authors selected 13 pairing methods that they deemed practical and comparatively investigated the security and usability of them. [16, 12] also conducted similar studies and all these studies indicate that Numeric-Compare out-performed other methods in terms of efficiency, security and usability. They also show that all methods involving manual comparison of SAS data yielded non-zero error rates in most cases. Unlike the work we present in this paper, these studies evaluated methods suitable for personal pairing. As we discuss later, our results stand in contrast to the results of all these prior studies. Most recently, [11] and [25] looked into the group pairing setting. However, [11] included only one group consisting of 2 users and [25] experimented with groups with at least 4 users. Both papers evaluated different sets of methods from the current paper and their focus was pairing methods geared for larger group sizes (more than 2 users). Another study [10] examines user attitudes and behaviors while pairing devices under different contexts, and is complementary to the current paper.

STUDY PRELIMINARIES

Methods Tested

There is a large body of prior research on secure device pairing. All of these methods were proposed in the context of a personal pairing setting.

There are more than twenty methods, counting variations, in the literature. However, some of them have very limited use cases due to requiring both devices to be controlled by the same user during the pairing (e.g., accelerometer-based methods such as [22]) or requiring hardware not ubiquitous among wireless devices. Some methods have stronger assumptions about the OOB channel and require it to be confidential (e.g., BEDA-Buttons variant of [31]). Notice that secret OOB channels are hard to achieve in real-life since a close-by attacker can easily eavesdrop on any human perceptible channel (e.g., by shoulder surfing).

We believe that it is very difficult to test all available methods in one single study and hope that our results yield meaningful comparative usability metrics. Obstacles, such as varying security assumptions about the OOB channel among different methods and possible user fatigue from including too many methods would undermine study results. Consequently, we have to cull the number of methods down to a more manageable number, eliminating those that are obsolete, deprecated based on prior evaluations or unrealistic due to their OOB assumptions. Of course, we also eliminated any methods that are limited to personal pairing only. The following methods are excluded from our study:

- Resurrecting-Duckling [33]: obsolete due to physical equipment, i.e., cable, requirement.
- Talking-to-Strangers [1]: obsolete since IR ports are not secure against MitM attacks and IR has become uncommon.
- Choose-and-Enter [34], Copy [34], BEDA-Buttons [31]: requires a secret OOB channel and/or performed poorly in prior evaluations.
- Beep-Beep [28]: performed poorly in prior evaluations due to user annoyance and high error rate.
- Blink-Blink [28], Image Comparison [6, 27, 5]: do not extend well to the social pairing setting, since two devices need to be placed adjacent to each other or temporarily exchanged between users.
- Seeing-is-Believing [24], Blinking Lights [30]: require photo or video cameras on devices and do not extend well to the social pairing setting due to the need for close proximity between the devices; also cameras are not ubiquitous interfaces except for mobile phones.
- BEDA-Vibrate [31]: vibration is not a common interface, except for mobile phones; also it is hard for one user to sense the vibration on another user's device, making this method unusable in a social pairing setting.
- Smart-its-Friends [8], Shake-Well-Before-Use [22]: requires one user to hold and control both devices and thus do not extend to social pairing scenarios.

- Ultrasound- [15] and laser-based [23] methods: requires hardware capabilities not common across devices.

Remaining methods, namely **BEDA-Beep**, **BEDA-Blink**, **Beep-Blink**, **Over-Audio**, **Numeric-Compare**, **Phrase-DD**, **Phrase-DS**, **Phrase-SS** and **Copy-Confirm**, have been included in the study. These were selected based on their suitability for social pairing scenarios. We had to slightly modify certain methods to standardize OOB assumptions and security level. In particular, we updated all methods to be based on a SAS protocol for better efficiency and unified security assumptions. This resulted in a slightly changed user interaction in BEDA-Beep, BEDA-Blink and Over-Audio methods.

Test Devices and Implementation

In a personal pairing setting, one of the devices might be interface-constrained. For example, a headset, being paired with a cell phone or an access point being paired with a laptop, are constrained devices (with no display, keypad). On the other hand, both devices participating in a social pairing scenario are "personal" devices (such as PDAs, cell phones, laptops) and are usually not constrained. These devices are generally equipped with at least a display and a keypad.

We wanted to simulate, as closely as possible, common social pairing scenarios. To this end, for our entire study, we used two Nokia cellphones models:[3] N73 and E61, as test devices. Our test devices have all the features and interfaces needed for the tested methods, such as a display, keypad, speaker, microphone and Bluetooth.

For methods that involve beeping, we configured a general-purpose speaker for use as a beeper. A picture of a bright LED displayed on the screen to simulate a blinking LED (Utilizing the whole screen rather than an LED is an obvious choice for social pairing).

To achieve a unified software platform, we used the open-source comparative usability testing framework developed by Kostiainen, et al. [17][4] that provides basic communication primitives between devices as well as automated logging and timing functionality. However, we implemented separate user interfaces and simulated functionality for all tested methods.

For all methods, we kept the theoretical security level constant [5]. We also tried to keep all user interfaces similar, while applying same design practices, i.e., safe-default selection prompts, clear instructions, simple language and so on. In all tests, Bluetooth was used as the wireless radio channel and the initial rounds of the underlying cryptographic protocol running over the Bluetooth channel is omitted. Instead, our implementation supplies devices with synthetic SAS strings to realistically simulate normal and MiTM attack scenarios.

[3]For N73 specs, see: `www.nokiausa.com/A4409012`, and for E61 – `europe.nokia.com/A4142101`.

[4]The same framework was also utilized by [34, 18, 16] to implement and test various pairing methods.

[5]we used SAS string length of 15 bits for all methods, which provides reasonable security for many applications[35]

USABILITY TESTING DETAILS

Having implemented all selected social pairing methods on a common platform, we set out to evaluate and compare social pairing methods (identified previously) with respect to the following factors:

1. *Efficiency*: time to complete each method
2. *Robustness*: how often each method yields false positives (rejection of a successful pairing instance) and false negatives (acceptance of an unsuccessful pairing instance). Following the terminology introduced in [34], we refer to the former category as *safe errors* and the latter – as *fatal errors*.
3. *Usability*: how each method fares in terms of user burden (i.e., ease-of-use perception), successful task completion and personal preference.
4. *User Interactions*: how two users interact in order to perform steps involved in each method.

Study Participants

We recruited 40 participants. At any given point, two participants had to be present to complete the tests. The study lasted over a period of more than two months. Each pair of participants was chosen very carefully as we required them to have varying trust relationships with each other, ranging from being strangers, to acquaintances to close friends. Each pair was briefed on the estimated amount of time required to complete the tests. Participants were mostly young (18-29 years old) university students both at undergraduate and graduate level. Thus, our study represents only the first step towards identifying methods suitable for the broad cross-section of user population.

We prepared two questionnaires: *background* – to obtain user demographics and *post-test* – for user feedback on methods tested. None of the participants reported any physical impairments that could interfere with their ability to complete given tasks. The gender split was: 65% male and 35% female. Also, prior to testing, we collected information on whether the participants knew each other and if so, how well.

Trust between participants: Among 20 subject pairs, 5 have not met before (were complete strangers), 5 were close friends, and the remaining 10 were friends or colleagues who did not consider each other as close friends. In order to gain some insight into the trust relations and acceptable interaction between subject pairs, we asked them whether they would consider temporarily handing their device to the other person in order to initiate a secure connection that they can later use to exchange files, messages or play games. We also asked their reasoning and concerns related to answers.

Not surprisingly, all 5 pairs that have not met before said they would not consider any physical exchange of devices as part of an acceptable interaction. The two main concerns were: the security of the device and the data it stores as well as the unpleasant social situation it may create. On the other hand, 4 out of 5 pairs of close friends did not state any privacy concerns and indicated that they do not mind exchanging their devices during pairing. Among 10 pairs acquaintances, 6 expressed serious concerns about any physical device exchange and considered it unacceptable; their reasonings were similar to those of the first group.

Based on observed trust relations and concerns expressed by our subjects, we conclude that any method that needs physical exchange of devices is unacceptable in many scenarios where the owners *do not know each other very well*. Moreover, it may still be problematic in some situations where owners know each other Among 8 pairs who were not reluctant to exchange devices, the relationship between the users played a strong role. Surprisingly, 5 among 8 pairs only considered friends as the acceptable social group to temporarily exchange devices and even excluded family members. The remaining 3 considered both family and friends as acceptable. However, we believe that the observed strong tendency to share devices with friends (rather than with the family members) was perhaps due to a somewhat biased sampling of our subjects, i.e., mostly single college students.

Testing Process

We created 9 test cases. They were designed such that the attacks occur probabilistically, meaning that the user does not encounter both "no-attack" and "under-attack" scenario for each method but encounters either with a 50% chance. This prevented users from expecting one no-attack and one under-attack test case for each method and reduced the number of tests. The order of tests presented to the user was counterbalanced for learning effect using the Latin Square design. During the experiments, test devices are set to have their keypad lights, Bluetooth interfaces and screen-backlights always on and their screensaver functionalities were disabled.

Our study was conducted in a variety of campus venues including: student laboratories, cafés, student dorms, classrooms, office spaces and outdoor terraces. This was possible since test devices were mobile, test set-up was more-or-less automated and only minimal involvement from the test administrator was required.

After giving a brief overview of our study goals, we asked the participants to fill out the background questionnaire to collect demographic information. Both participants in each test jointly filled out the questionnaire. After a short interview about the relationship between each pair of subjects, they were given a brief introduction to cell-phone devices.

Each pair of users was given two devices (one per user) and asked to follow on-screen instructions in completing each task. Users were closely watched to observe whether they exchanged devices during the tests.

User interactions were observed by the test administrator and timings were logged automatically by the testing framework. After completing the tasks, each user-pair jointly filled out the post-test questionnaire, where they provided feedback on tested methods and also indicated whether they found any particular test to be difficult or problematic. They were also given a few minutes of free discussion time, in order to offer comments to the test administrator.

Test Results

For each method, completion times, errors, actions and the playcount, i.e., number of trials before successful pairing was established, were automatically logged by the software. Collected data is summarized in Table 1.

Method	Avg. time* (in seconds)	Fatal error rate	Safe error rate	Avg. # of trials until success
BEDA-Beep	40.43 (se[+]=4.57)	**0.00**	0.14	1.14
BEDA-Blink	96.00 (se=21.9)	**0.00**	0.10	2.20
Beep-Blink	45.10 (se=5.46)	0.09	0.11	1.20
Over-Audio	18.75 (se=2.74)	**0.00**	**0.00**	1.13
Numeric-Compare	12.50 (se=4.75)	**0.00**	0.10	N/A
Phrase-DD	11.44 (se=1.43)	**0.00**	**0.00**	N/A
Phrase-DS	21.45 (se=5.96)	**0.00**	**0.00**	N/A
Phrase-SS	38.71 (se=16.0)	**0.00**	**0.00**	N/A
Copy-Confirm	17.00 (se=2.72)	0.17	**0.00**	N/A

*Completion time in normal (non-attack) test cases

[+]se=standard error of the mean

Table 1. Summary of Logged Data

We also observed user interactions while each pair of users was performing the various steps involved in each method. In general, we observed that subjects often decided the outcome of pairing based on mutual agreement, which, we believe, may have helped reduce errors in most comparison-based methods. We did not, however, observe any significant effect of the closeness of the relationship between the participants on their interactions during the pairing process. Observed interactions for each method are summarized below. (Assume Alice is pairing her device A with Bob's device B)

• BEDA-Beep: The user responsible for pressing the button (Bob) would listen carefully the beeping on the other device (A) and synchronously press any button on B. In most cases, the user of the beeping device (Alice) moved closer to Bob within a distance of about 1-2 feet so that he could clearly hear the beeping sound. Alice was also noticing if Bob was synchronizing the beeping with the button press. Once finished with this phase, Bob verbally notified Alice to accept or reject the pairing, based on the result shown on B.

• BEDA-Blink: The user of the blinking device (Alice) would show her device to the other user (Bob) who would press the button in synchronization with blinking. Users were again 1-2 feet apart. Once finished with this phase, Bob verbally notified Alice to accept or reject the pairing, based on the result shown on B.

• Beep-Blink: After starting the pairing process, both Alice and Bob compared the blinking/beeping on their own device with the beeping/blinking on the other device. This required the two users to be within touching distance of each other so that both could watch the flashing screen and listen to beeping of respective devices. At the end, both users accepted or rejected the pairing, based on their mutual judgement of whether blinking/beeping was synchronized.

• Over-Audio: In this method, the role of the two users was "passive." Alice's device would start to play an audio clip that encoded a bit-string and Bob's device would automatically record it. After the audio transfer, Bob would (ver-

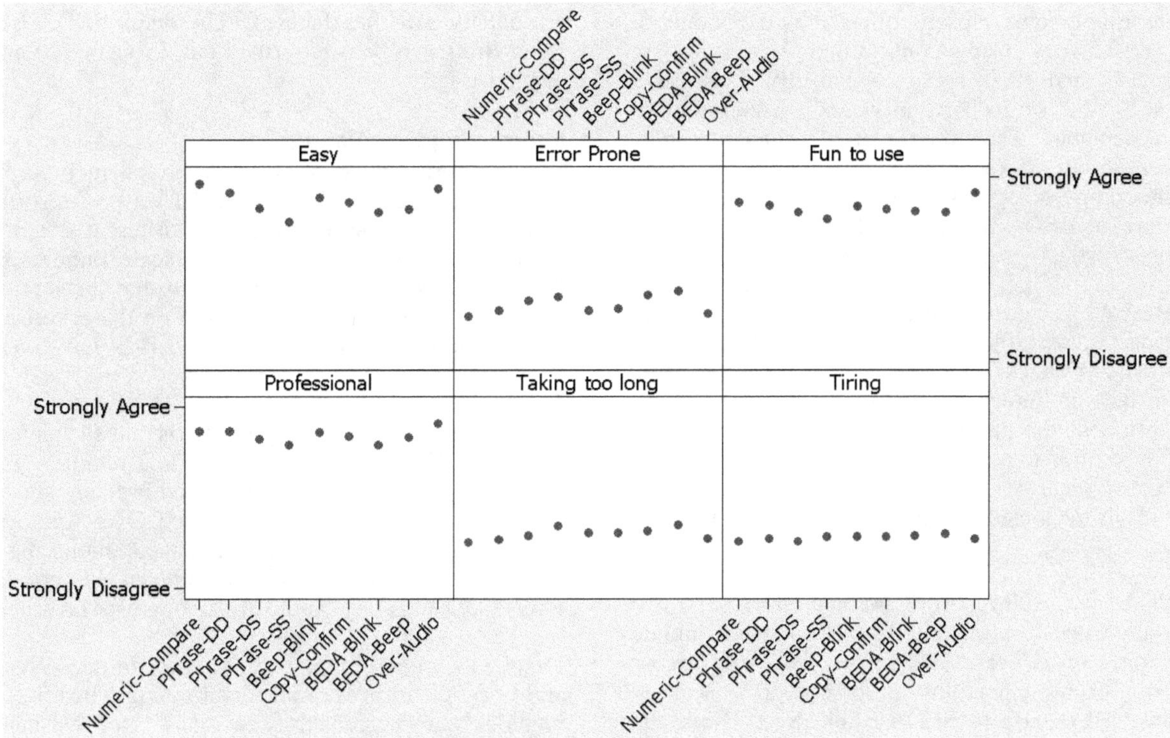

Figure 2. Means of all user ratings for the tested methods

bally) tell Alice to accept or reject depending on what his screen indicated.

• Numeric-Compare: In this method, both Alice and Bob either spell out or show the number displayed on the screens of their devices, compare the two and mutually accept or reject the pairing. Most subjects in our pool preferred to spell out displayed numbers.

• Phrase-DD: Similar to Numeric-Compare, both Alice and Bob either spell out or show the sentence displayed by their devices, compare the two and accept or reject the pairing, based on mutual agreement. Again, most test participants preferred to spell out the displayed phrase.

• Phrase-DS: This method involves the user (Alice) listening carefully to the sentence spelled out by the device of other user (Bob) and then comparing it with the sentence displayed on the screen of her device, and vice versa. For this to take place, Bob would bring his device near (about 1-2 feet) Alice's device, in order for her to be able to hear the spoken sentence. Both participants mutually accepted or rejected the pairing, following a short discussion.

• Phrase-SS: This method involves both devices vocalizing a sentence. When the devices "speak", both users would lean toward them in order to hear clearly. After listening, they would determine whether the sentences matched. Participants then accepted or rejected the pairing on their respective devices, after verbally confirming with each other.

• Copy-Confirm: Alice would either read out the number displayed on A or directly show the screen displaying the number to Bob. After inputting the number into his device, Bob would verbally notify Alice to accept or reject, depending instructions on B's screen. We observed that participants preferred to read out the number and a few also showed it to the other user after spelling out.

Finally, through the post-test questionnaire, we solicited user opinions about all tested methods. Each user-pair rated each method on a 6-level Likert scale[20]. Ratings included: *easy to use, professional, fun to use, tiring, takes too long to complete, and error prone*. Means of all user ratings are graphed in Figure 2.

INTERPRETING RESULTS

We now attempt to interpret the results of our study. We first consider various mechanical data, i.e., time to completion and error rates. Then, we analyze perceived qualitative aspects of the methods based on collected user ratings. We finalize our interpretations by looking at all measures combined with principal component and cluster analyses.

Interpreting Time and Error Results

Our results, summarized in Table 1, prompt a number of observations

Completion time: The logical way to interpret the completion time is by looking at it under normal circumstances, i.e., when no active or passive attacks occur. Thus, we only considered the no-attack test cases while calculating average completion time. Based on this performance metric, tested methods fall into three speed categories: fast (less than 20 secs), moderate (between 20 and 30 secs) and slow (more than 30 secs). The fastest method is Phrase-DD at 11.44 secs for a successful outcome, closely followed by the Numeric-Compare at 12.5 secs. Copy-Confirm and Over-Audio are next, taking 17 and 18.75 secs, respectively. Phrase-DS comes in at 21.45 secs; its performance is considered moderate and acceptable. The slow category includes the rest, ranging from Phrase-SS (38.71 secs) to BEDA-Blink which takes a whooping 96 secs. The differences between completion times for BEDA-Blink and all other methods were found to be statistically significant at 5% level.

Error Rates: As discussed in earlier, *fatal errors* have a significant impact on security of pairing since they can result in successful MiTM attacks. On the other hand, *safe errors* do not constitute an immediate security threat but can cause user annoyance as the pairing process has to be repeated. However, in addition to poor usability, safe errors may eventually influence security because high levels of user annoyance may result in careless behavior that can, in turn, cause fatal errors.

Most methods, fare well reporting no fatal errors. The two exceptions are Copy-Confirm and Beep-Blink that exhibited fatal error rates of 17% and 9%, respectively, which constitutes a significant vulnerability in the context of security applications. BEDA-Beep, BEDA-Blink, Beep-Blink and Numeric-Compare methods all yield higher than 10% error rates. However, this was for safe errors considered not security-relevant. However, as discussed above, safe errors are indication of poor usability and may eventually adversely impact security.

Timing and Error Rates: Looking at timing and error results together, it (fortunately) appears that the fastest method is also one of the error-free methods. Taking both factors into account, the best overall method is clearly Phrase-DD, followed by Over-Audio and Phrase-DS. Although Numeric-Compare is also quite fast, there is little motivation for using it over Phrase-DD. The reason is simple: both require the same hardware (basic displays) and Phrase-DD offers lower error rates and takes about the same time as Numeric-Compare. (This also confirms our intuition that users are better at interpreting phrases than numbers). Thus, if both devices are equipped with decent quality displays, Phrase-DD is a clear winner.

Using similar reasoning, Over-Audio and Phrase-DS appear to be the best choices if the audio channel can be utilized. However, Over-Audio needs a microphone on one device and a speaker on the other. Phrase-DS can also be used in scenarios where one device has a speaker. Although Phrase-SS is also error-free, it is relatively slow compared to Phrase-DS. Thus, there is no good motivation for Phrase-SS over Phrase-DD or Phrase-DS.

Although BEDA-Beep, BEDA-Blink and Beep-Blink have lower hardware requirements and work on devices with most basic interfaces, they take too long to complete. They usually require more than one trial to achieve successful pairing and Beep-Blink also yields very high fatal error rates. Considering that devices taking part in social scenarios have reasonably good interfaces, BEDA-Beep, BEDA-Blink and Beep-Blink can be safely ruled out, in favor of Phrase-DD or Phrase-DS.

Interpreting User Ratings

We now turn our attention to the graph in Figure 2, that summarizes user opinions collected via post-test questionnaires. Users are asked to rate six different statements for each method on a 6-point Likert scale ranging between "Strongly Disagree" and "Strongly Agree." The rated statements for each method were based on the criteria: $\{$*Easy, Professional, Fun to Use, Tiring, Taking Too Long, Error Prone*$\}$.

Not surprisingly, Numeric-Compare is ranked among the easiest methods due to its fast timing and familiarity to most users as it has already been deployed in many personal devices. As expected, Phrase-DD and Over-Audio also received very high ratings and are ranked among the easiest, most fun to use and professional methods. Numeric-Compare, Phrase-DD and Over-Audio are among user favorites.

Despite their poor timing and/or high error rates, Beep-Blink and Copy-Confirm are ranked surprisingly positively. Both methods were perceived as easy and error-resistant. Considering Copy-Confirm had a very high fatal error rate and rated as one of the least error-prone methods, we conclude that users who committed a fatal error were clearly not aware of it. Also, judging from the high error rates of both Copy-Confirm and Beep-Blink, users' perception of security may be far from reality. This contradiction can also be easily observed in Phrase-DS and Phrase-SS, although in the other direction. These two methods are ranked among the most error-prone, however, they yield 0% error-rate in our tests.

BEDA-Beep, BEDA-Blink, Phrase-DS and Phrase-SS are considered relatively hard, error prone, taking long time to complete, less professional and less fun to use. Relatively low user ratings for BEDA-Beep and BEDA-Blink agree with the long completion timings and high error rates observed in our tests. However, user perception was deceptive about Phrase-DS and Phrase-SS, especially, in terms of how error prone they are.

	Easy	Tiring	Professional	Long	Fun
Tiring	-0.343				
Professional	0.693	-0.266			
Long	-0.445	0.817	-0.293		
Fun	0.666	-0.318	0.737	-0.378	
Error-Prone	-0.425	0.722	-0.358	0.749	-0.361

$p < 0.01$, for all correlations

Table 2. Cross-Correlation of User Ratings

Observed Correlations: As can be seen from Figure 2, there is some observable, and statistically significant, correlation among user ratings for various usability measures. The cross correlation of user ratings for usability measures is given in Table 2. Correlation coefficients ranging from -0.3 to -0.1 and 0.1 to 0.3 are generally regarded as small, -0.5 to -0.3 and 0.3 to 0.5 as medium, and coefficients larger than 0.5 and smaller than -0.5 as high [4]. In line with observed high coefficients, our results show that methods rated easy are generally also rated as fun to use and professional.

Moreover, methods rated as taking too long were perceived as tiring and error-prone. Observed medium correlation coefficients also show that methods perceived to be easy, professional or fun to use are unlikely to be rated as error-prone, tiring or taking too long.

Principal Component and Cluster Analysis

Since most of our usability measures are correlated, looking at them as a whole is important. To this end, we performed principal component analysis for all usability measures.

Our analysis showed the first two components, i.e., PC1 and PC2, have eigenvalues more than 1, i.e., explaining more variance than one original variable [13], and they collectively explicate more than %64 of the variance. Factor loadings of PC1 and PC2 are given in Table 3.

PC1 factors positive usability measures (such as, user ratings for easiness, fun to use or professionalism; higher values indicating better usability) as negative and other measures as positive. Thus, lower PC1 scores for a method indicate better usability. On the other hand, PC2 factors in time and safe error rates much more than PC1. Thus, a very high PC2 score may be an indication of usability problems.

	PC1	PC2
Task Completion Time	0.088	0.484
Safe Error	0.033	0.461
"Easy" Rating	-0.422	0.216
"Error Prone" Rating	0.407	0.183
"Fun to use" Rating	-0.365	0.414
"Professional" Rating	-0.402	0.346
"Taking too long" Rating	0.442	0.262
"Tiring" Rating	0.396	0.336

Table 3. **Factor Loadings of PC1 and PC2**

Figure 3 shows mean values of PC1 and PC2 scores for all methods. Three observed clusters (using the Euclidian distance and average linkage method) based on principal components are also superimposed on *Figure 3*. The figure indicates that two methods, BEDA-Blink and Phrase-SS, are different from other methods and form their own clusters. This is mainly due to the significantly longer completion times of BEDA-Blink and lower user ratings for Phrase-SS. Overall, methods can be partitioned into two clusters, with good and poor usability. The former (shown with red colors in Figure 3) include Numeric-Compare, Over-Audio, Phrase-DD, Beep-Blink and BEDA-Beep. The rest (highlighted green, blue or orange in Figure 3) exhibit poor overall usability.

Among methods in the "good usability" group, BEDA-Beep takes at least twice as much time to complete and thus shows least similarity to all other methods in this group. Despite its good usability, Beep-Blink exhibits high fatal rates and suffers from robustness problems. Among the remaining three, Numeric-Compare had the highest "safe error" rate and Over-Audio took the longest.

Final Inferences and Recommendations

Our overall conclusions are as follows:

- Comparison-based pairing methods over the visual channel are preferred by users. Among those, we recommend Phrase-DD over Numeric-Compare as the former yields lower (in fact, no) errors. Since displays are ubiquitous on personal devices in social scenarios, Phrase-DD is a clear winner in terms of speed, robustness and user preference, as well as universal deployability.

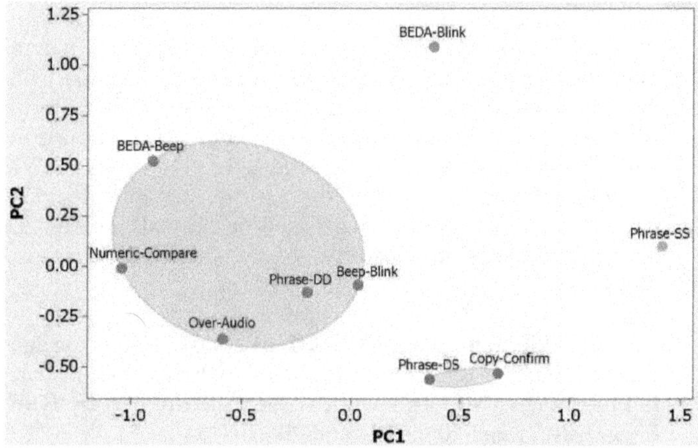

Figure 3. **Method scorings and clusters based on PC1 and PC2**

- Among methods over the audio channel, Over-Audio was the user favorite. Phrase-DS yielded low completion timing and no errors while Phrase-SS was slow and error-free, however, both performed poorly compared to Over-Audio when all usability measures are taken into account. On the other hand, Over-Audio needs a microphone on one device and a speaker on the other. If devices lack required hardware for Over-Audio, we believe that Phrase-DS is still an acceptable choice.
- Beep-Blink and Copy-Confirm produced high fatal error rates in our tests and thus we do not recommend using them.
- BEDA-Beep and BEDA-Blink demonstrated poor completion time performance. They usually take more than one trial for successful completion and too long to complete. User ratings for these methods are also relatively low and we do not recommend using them.
- In general, we recommend Phrase-DD for social pairing. Phrase-DD can be complemented with Over-Audio or Phrase-DS, depending on available hardware.

CONCLUSIONS

In this paper, we presented an experimental evaluation of prominent device pairing methods that can be used in social pairing scenarios. First and foremost, our survey results confirmed our belief that a majority of users are considerate about the security and privacy of their personal devices and they may not be willing to hand-in their devices to other users, even temporarily to perform the pairing process. This means that a social pairing method can not be simply reduced to personal pairing.

The results of our usability study show that one simple method, Phrase-DD, is quite attractive overall, being both fast and error-tolerant as well as user-friendly. It naturally appeals to social pairing scenarios where devices have appropriate quality and size displays. Slightly slower methods,

Over-Audio or Phrase-DS, can seamlessly inter-operate with Phrase-DD, for wider deployment and for scenarios where one device has a speaker. The fact that phrase comparison turned out to be the most suitable method for social pairing is in contrast to personal pairing where numeric comparison was a winner (as shown by the studies of [18, 16, 12]). We also observed that, in general, the test subjects often decided the outcome of social pairing based on mutual agreement, which, we believe, may have helped to reduce errors in most of our comparison-based pairing methods.

Acknowledgments: We thank A.J. Brush, Amy Karlson and Stuart Schechter for discussion related to their work on sharing of phones [14]. This work is supported in part by NSF Cybertrust grants #0831397 and #0831526.

REFERENCES

1. D. Balfanz et al. Talking to strangers: Authentication in ad-hoc wireless networks. In *Network and Distributed System Security Symposium (NDSS)*, 2002.
2. D. Balfanz et al. Network-in-a-box: How to set up a secure wireless network in under a minute. In *USENIX Security*, pages 207–222, 2004.
3. V. Boyko, P. MacKenzie, and S. Patel. Provably secure password-authenticated key exchange using diffie-heilman. *Eurocrypt*, 2000.
4. J. Cohen et al. *Applied multiple regression/correlation analysis for the behavioral sciences*. Erlbaum Hillsdale, NJ, 1983.
5. C. M. Ellison and S. Dohrmann. Public-key support for group collaboration. *ACM Transactions on Information and System Security (TISSEC)*, 6(4):547–565, 2003.
6. I. Goldberg. Visual key fingerprint code. `http://www.cs.berkeley.edu/iang/visprint.c`, 1996.
7. M. Goodrich et al. Loud and clear: Human-verifiable authentication based on audio. In *International Conference on Distributed Computing Systems (ICDCS)*, 2006.
8. L. Holmquist et al. Smart-its friends: A technique for users to easily establish connections between smart artifacts. In *Ubicomp*, 2001.
9. S.-J. Hong, K. Y. Tam, and J. Kim. Mobile data service fuels the desire for uniqueness. *Communications of the ACM*, 49(9), 2006.
10. I. Ion et al. Influence of user perception, security needs, and social factors on device pairing method choices. In *SOUPS: Symposium on Usable Privacy and Security*, 2010.
11. R. Kainda, I. Flechais, and A. Roscoe. Two heads are better than one: Security and usability of device associations in group scenarios. In *SOUPS: Symposium on Usable Privacy and Security*, pages 1–13, 2010.
12. R. Kainda, I. Flechais, and A. W. Roscoe. Usability and security of out-of-band channels in secure device pairing protocols. In *SOUPS: Symposium on Usable Privacy and Security*, 2009.
13. H. Kaiser. The application of electronic computers to factor analysis. *Educational and psychological measurement*, 20(1):141–151, 1960.
14. A. K. Karlson, A. B. Brush, and S. Schechter. Can i borrow your phone?: understanding concerns when sharing mobile phones. In *CHI '09: Conference on Human factors in computing systems*, 2009.
15. T. Kindberg and K. Zhang. Validating and securing spontaneous associations between wireless devices. In *Information Security Conference (ISC)*, pages 44–53, 2003.
16. A. Kobsa, R. Sonawalla, G. Tsudik, E. Uzun, and Y. Wang. Serial hook-ups: A comparative usability study of secure device pairing methods. In *SOUPS: Symposium on Usable Privacy and Security*, 2009.
17. K. Kostiainen and E. Uzun. Framework for comparative usability testing of distributed applications. In *Security User Studies: Methodologies and Best Practices Workshop*, 2007.
18. A. Kumar et al. Caveat emptor: A comparative study of secure device pairing methods. In *IEEE Pervasive Computing and Communications (PerCom)*, 2009.
19. S. Laur and K. Nyberg. Efficient mutual data authentication using manually authenticated strings. *Conference on Cryptology and Network Security (CANS)*, 2006.
20. R. Likert. A technique for the measurement of attitudes. *Archives of Psychology*, 66:68–71, 1932.
21. Y. Liu, A. Rahmati, Y. Huang, H. Jang, L. Zhong, Y. Zhang, and S. Zhang. xshare: supporting impromptu sharing of mobile phones. In *MobiSys '09: Conference on Mobile systems, applications, and services*, 2009.
22. R. Mayrhofer and H. Gellersen. Shake well before use: Authentication based on accelerometer data. *Conference on Pervasive Computing (Pervasive)*, 2007.
23. R. Mayrhofer and M. Welch. A human-verifiable authentication protocol using visible laser light. In *IEEE Conference on Availability, Reliability and Security*, 2007.
24. J. M. McCune, A. Perrig, and M. K. Reiter. Seeing-is-believing: Using camera phones for human-verifiable authentication. In *IEEE Symposium on Security and Privacy*, 2005.
25. R. Nithyanand et al. Groupthink: usability of secure group association for wireless devices. In *Ubicomp*, pages 331–340, 2010.
26. S. Pasini and S. Vaudenay. Sas-based authenticated key agreement. In *International Conference on Theory and Practice of Public-Key Cryptography (PKC)*, 2006.
27. A. Perrig and D. Song. Hash visualization: a new technique to improve real-world security. In *International Workshop on Cryptographic Techniques and E-Commerce*, 1999.
28. R. Prasad and N. Saxena. Efficient device pairing using "human-comparable" synchronized audiovisual patterns. In *Applied Cryptography and Network Security (ACNS)*, 2008.
29. V. Roth et al. Simple and effective defense against evil twin access points. In *ACM Conference on Wireless Network Security (WiSec)*, pages 220–235, 2008.
30. N. Saxena et al. Extended abstract: Secure device pairing based on a visual channel. In *IEEE Symposium on Security and Privacy*, 2006.
31. C. Soriente, G. Tsudik, and E. Uzun. Beda: Button-enabled device association. In *International Workshop on Security and Privacy in Spontaneous Interaction (IWSSI)*, 2007.
32. C. Soriente, G. Tsudik, and E. Uzun. Hapadep: Human-assisted pure audio device pairing. In *Information Security Conference (ISC)*, pages 385–400, 2008.
33. F. Stajano and R. J. Anderson. The resurrecting duckling: Security issues for ad-hoc wireless networks. In *Security Protocols Workshop*, 1999.
34. E. Uzun, K. Karvonen, and N. Asokan. Usability analysis of secure pairing methods. In *Financial Cryptography and Data Security*, pages 307–324.
35. S. Vaudenay. Secure communications over insecure channels based on short authenticated strings. In *International Cryptology Conference (CRYPTO)*, 2005.

Experiencing Security in Interaction Design

Niels Raabjerg Mathiasen
Aarhus Universitet
Aabogade 34, 8000 Aarhus C, Denmark
nielsm@cs.au.dk

Susanne Bødker
Aarhus Universitet
Aabogade 34, 8000 Aarhus C, Denmark
bodker@cs.au.dk

ABSTRACT

Security is experienced differently in different contexts. This paper argues that in everyday situations, users base their security decisions on a mix of prior experiences. When approaching security and interaction design from an experience approach, tools that help bring out such relevant experiences for design are needed. This paper reports on how Prompted exploration workshops and Acting out security were developed to target such experiences when iteratively designing a mobile digital signature solution in a participatory design process. We discuss how these tools helped the design process and illustrate how the tangibility of such tools matters. We further demonstrate how the approach grants access to non-trivial insights into people's security experience. We point out how the specific context is essential for exploring the space between experience and expectations, and we illustrate how people activate their collections of security experiences rather than deploying *one* security strategy in all situations.

Author Keywords

Design tools, Security, Experience.

ACM Classification Keywords

H5.m. Information interfaces and presentation (e.g., HCI): Miscellaneous.

General Terms

Design

INTRODUCTION

In the last decade it has become clear that IT security and privacy are not exclusively about protocols, encryption and bug fixing. It is necessary to bring on broader perspectives that include human-computer interaction. While clever protocols, complex cryptography and critical computing have lead us a long way down the road to security, we now face new challenges. More and more papers address usability of IT security or HCI in a security context. There is a tendency to strive to model users' behavior [13, 19], even though the idea of modeling users and their behavior has been criticized in general in the HCI community. Initially the goal was to help, encourage or even force upon users the underlying model of security mechanisms. Websites often enforce or encourage their users to utilize strong passwords. However, people leave sticky notes on monitors with the strong (and hard to remember) passwords [1]. Popular historical accounts [22] as well as recent discussions [13, 14, 19] point out that IT artifacts should be shaped to fit users' needs and not the other way around. While the last two decades of research in HCI has strongly emphasized the relevance of actively involving future users in design, such approaches have not yet reached the security area where researchers still strive to model user behavior [13,14,19]. While we agree that IT artifacts in general should be designed to fit the need of users, we find the idea of conceptual modeling as basis for design somewhat outdated in general [3], and accordingly, we suggest an approach that actively involves users in the design process.

CHI 2011, May 7–12, 2011, Vancouver, BC, Canada.

In [15] we proposed a tool for collecting and analyzing user experiences in situations where participants behaved securely. This was based on storytelling over time and inspired by McCarthy & Wright's approach to experience [16]. While these immediate stories helped target situations where users handled security, they were not complete enough to fully analyze why users acted as they did, and collecting user stories as we did is but a first step in such analysis. Basically we propose that the needs of the users develop with their experience, individually and as a community.

In the security domain, users' anticipated behavior is often captured as security policies, set at one time and place and enforced at another. We show that these time and place gaps are incompatible with the way people make sense of technology and propose that security is negotiated with the user him- or herself and with others through an ongoing sense making process, where experience is anticipated and reflected on. We observe and prompt for security practices and strategies that everyday people deploy, and we target the development of new ones, leading to more or less experience of security.

In this paper we introduce the project context and exemplify the challenges of this kind of research. We then proceed to address some hallmark issues and develop our participatory and experience-driven design approach, before we move on to two design processes introducing Prompted exploration workshops and Acting out security. Findings from the two design processes serve as the empirical basis for analyses of these design activities with respect to methods, security and experience. We proceed to draw conclusions on designing for secure IT experience.

PROJECT CONTEXT AND RESEARCH METHOD

The work reported in this paper is part of the ITSCI project, a four-year project that bridges between competencies in cryptography, mobile computing and HCI. As a driver for testing out new technologies, designs and methods, we iteratively design a mobile digital signature solution.

Our research approach is grounded in the action-oriented participatory design research tradition (see e.g. [12]). This approach has been strongly influenced by Schön's thinking [21] with respect to reflection in action, and is further inspired by various approaches, not least ethnomethodology, grounded theory, and Latourian studies of science; research traditions, which have made their way into HCI through the emergence of CSCW. This particular approach to understanding the practices of design and use of computer applications joins a wide attempt uniting micro-sociological studies of human practice [9].

McCarthy & Wright [16] carefully outlines a number of possible research strategies for research of, in and through experience-centered design referencing many of these same approaches and more. They are in particularly discussing e.g. how interviews may be used to access experience in research and design, relating to Schön's ideas of the relationship between reflection and action. This relationship is particularly interesting when the practice we study is a design practice: When we do design it is also research, and when we do research it is also design. Being serious about participation as a research approach has consequences: It is difficult to stand back and reflect; one does not entirely get to choose the problems to work with, and thus one finds little help to reduce the complexity of these problems.

The aim of the project is to replace an existing solution, where citizens may request a digital signature from the municipalities, in order to be able to login, authenticate, encrypt/decrypt and sign their interaction with governmental institutions. This solution is installed on a single PC, and can be used from that PC and has proven to be difficult to install for many people. Furthermore, the digital signature is activated in different manners as can be seen in this example experience from one of the authors: The author has used her digital signature for a long while to handle her taxes and in relation to the municipal services she acquired, when a new service got introduced. At a governmental health care website she would find information about her records from doctors and hospitals, etc. Out of curiosity she tried to activate this service and failed. The hotline service told her that she had not installed the digital signature correctly. This was indeed confusing since it had been working with other services for years. But, as the hotline representative phrased it: “We are not these other services!” While this was quite possibly true, and the website had been developed in a different organizational setting, it was not very obvious for the citizen/user that as a result, the digital signature needed to be installed and work differently.

USABLE SECURITY

“Security has always been an important quality factor in many types of interactive systems (...). However, there is also a common (but false) belief that security is only related to the software systems functionality and that it can be designed independently from usability, which only relates to the UI component. In fact, the term UI and the way usability is defined are perhaps major underlying obstacles that explain such erroneous conceptions. Indeed, it gives the impression that the UI is a thin layer sitting on top of the “real” system and that usability can be conceived independently from the other quality factors.” [2]

In continuation of this, [2] proposes that a more comprehensive conception of usable security should include both process-related and product-related characteristics. In this paper we primarily focus on the process and how it is related to the product. In order to pursue this relationship further, the remainder of this section will, however, focus on product-related issues pertaining to the technological products and their use.

Security decisions are always part of an activity

In everyday life it is rare that people do activities solely for the purpose of becoming more secure. Security decisions or assessments are most often sub-activities of the other activities. Working out a proper IT security configuration for an IT artifact is no natural part of everyday life. Instead most IT security decisions are part of another activity with another purpose (e.g. communicating with friends via an IM-client or signing up a kid for daycare at the municipalitiy website). When analyzing these use situations it is not possible to solely look at the IT security tasks or decisions (e.g. typing in a password or remembering to log out) without including the context and the purpose of the overlying activities. Still, experiences from one activity with integrated security tasks influence the experience of dealing with IT security in another activity (McCarthy & Wright [16]). Accordingly, it is necessary to focus on relevant prior experience when investigating and designing for the experience with IT security.

Feeling secure

Traditionally the aim of usable security has been to encourage, enforce or help people act securely. This narrows down the focus of design and evaluation and tends to neglect that not only should IT artifact and data be securely handled, it is equally important that users are feeling secure. Feeling secure when they are secure, that is, and besides other usability concerns it is essential to explore and convey this distinction in design so as to train users' gut feelings and their ability to be suspicious in the right situations [15].

Difficult access to relevant base of experiences

As with all encounters with technology, users have prior similar experiences that they draw on when they make sense of security dependent technology [6]. What is characteristic to the security domain is that, both at design time and at use time, it can be difficult to discover and get access to such similar experiences that will or could be activated when picking up a particular new technology. Users themselves may not know which experiences they utilize as a base for a security assessment, and it is not trivial to find a way to prompt people to trigger the right experiences from their past. In the security domain, use in situations where security is really at stake, is infrequent and unpredictable, and hence it is challenging to assess the technological design in use-like settings. Putting people in a situation were they perceive the same threats and risks as they would in real situations, can be unethical or impossible. Lab studies, etc., that happen in artificial settings are not likely to trigger the relevant experiences.

DESIGN APPROACH

In [15] we point out that being secure by behaving securely towards a security dependent technology, and feeling secure and experiencing a secure interaction are two quite different elements of IT security: It is indeed possible to act securely and not feel secure and *vice versa*. It is indeed a fundamental part of e.g. phishing attacks, and hoax mails to make recipients feel secure so as to act insecurely. The ultimate design goal is obviously to make users both act securely and feel secure. Braz et al [2] talk about balancing security and usability, and with inspiration from [16] we propose to focus on secure or security experience.

McCarthy & Wright [16] describe experience as an ongoing process. Instead of starting points and end points, the dynamics lies between resistances and releases. Individuals have build up cumulations, conservations, tensions and anticipation through prior experiences, which fold and shape the present experience. Cumulation addresses what happens when prior experiences are parts of a process where later parts are about to be experienced. When it comes to IT security, an expectation may be that a login procedure will lead to access to some confidential information or restricted services, which again will be followed by a logout procedure that cuts off further access. Conservation happens when a series of rich experiences is remembered as a less rich memory. A person may remember a web self-service as secure, without remembering which specific experiences made it feel secure. When a person has encountered a series of experiences pointing in one direction and another series pointing in another, McCarthy & Wright talk about tensions. A tension may exist between what is experienced as effective and as suspicious when working with security-related IT artifacts. McCarthy & Wright describe anticipations as a form of unconscious expectations that, if they are met, fold into the present experience without further notice and, if they are not met, lead to reflections. For instance, anticipations are met as long as what is expected to be confidential is experienced as confidential. Likewise, experiences of a breach in the confidentiality will lead to reflection about the technology or the handling of it. McCarthy & Wright's framework also includes four threads for analyzing the anatomy of an experience and six sense making processes for analyzing how people make sense of an experience. This paper reports on methods for granting access to prior experiences. Thus the empirical findings below are analyzed as activations of prior experiences via the four concepts introduced above.

This set of concepts emphasizes how we prepare for experiences, and digest them by placing them into patterns of past experiences while telling the experiences to ourselves and to others. Addressing security technology as experience means addressing important elements of use context, the connections between security and the use, the history of the technology in general and of the specific use in particular. By emphasizing experience we focus on understanding how users negotiate security decisions, bring out experience through recounting of stories and prepare themselves for action. From this perspective, security cannot be seen in isolation from time, place, emotions, experiences, purpose of the interaction or other actors, etc. All of these are discussions that need to be developed further in order to fully utilize the experience framework in designing for security.

In order to design for a better experience of security we have been inspired by participatory design techniques in general and McCarthy & Wright's [17] suggestions for tools in particular. We wanted to focus on the ongoing dialog among users, and to focus more on actual needs and already invented strategies. McCarthy & Wright mention as examples of methods: probes [15], experience prototyping [17] and fictional inquiry [7]. Whereas McCarthy and Wright originally (in [16]) had a quite individual focus in their approach to experience, our approach is, in accordance with their newest work, more focused on interpersonal experience and its foundation in cultural practices.

In [15] we illustrated how initial cultural probing was utilized to get to how everyday users understand security, not as threats, but as everyday experience. In everyday media, IT security tends to be framed as a struggle between software engineers and malicious hackers. The solutions mentioned are almost always purely technical. In [15] we point out that in everyday life and when people are telling the story in-situ, they tend to focus more on actual needs and worries and they describe their already invented strategies for dealing with IT security. Security is decided on through an ongoing dialog with one-self and others. In the current work we seek to get to and deal with a richer understanding of such experiences and better tools that may be applied to design for usable security.

Bødker & Christiansen [4] and McCarthy and Wright [16] both point out that human acting is situated between the space of experience and the horizon of expectation [21]. To fully work with experience in relation to design of something new, it is essential to understand this space of experience, as well as to explore the possibilities beyond the current horizon of expectation [4]. Experience prototyping [17] is similarly targeting both the understanding of existing experience and the exploration and communication of design ideas.

Our inspiration from participatory design leads back to Greenbaum & Kyng [10] and beyond, where fundamental ways of carrying out workshops with future users were presented along with examples of the tools to support such workshops, e.g. prototypes, mock-ups and situation cards.

Halskov & Dalsgaard [11] use inspiration from Schön [21] as well as from Greenbaum & Kyng [10] to develop a design approach based on inspiration cards. These inspiration cards are used in workshops with designers and users to help draw on earlier experiences as well as to catch the uniqueness of the current design setting. McCarthy and Wright [17] point out how, when used in a participatory design setting, such situation cards are activated by the participants of a workshop, hence focusing the process and how it is made relevant to users. Inspiration cards are one way in which theoretical concepts and research findings may be brought into the design process so as to provoke new ideas and reframe the ways in which users reflect upon their past experience [4]. Activating such theoretical concepts in design help users revisit and reconsider their past and, hence their future possibilities. In the following we look in further detail at how security issues may be seeded with this perspective in mind.

In our attempt to address security in design, we are looking for tools that may help users negotiate security policies and measures, bringing out experience through recounting of stories and enactment of situations, for users in collaboration. Thus, the tools need to help participants bring out experiences, provoke new ways of understanding security and assist in an exploration of possibilities, together in groups.

In the following we present our two different approaches to addressing secure experience in design: Prompted exploration workshops and Acting out security. As described above these were used when developing a prototype of a mobile digital signature. Initially the mobile cultural probing [17] provided a rich description of the users' experience of security in an everyday life context. Then two groups of potential future users participated in the design of the prototype through Prompted exploration workshops, and finally a group of users got to try out the prototype through Acting out security.

PROMPTED EXPLORATION WORKSHOP

Prompted exploration workshops were developed to engage future users in the design process and help these participants articulate their actual experiences of security. We carried out two such workshops that we report from below.

Motive

These workshops were set up to focus on people's prior experience with security, and signing possibilities and problems. By prompting the discussions through a number of inspiration cards the aims were to get people to tell stories about their experiences with signing.

Method

The methodological inspiration for the workshop was Ehn & Sjögren's situation games [8], Mogensen & Trigg's [18] and Halskov & Dalsgaard's [11] elaboration of situation cards. Participating users of Prompted exploration workshops and researchers worked together through brainstorming, design discussions and sketched possible design solutions, based on scenarios and design problems presented at the beginning of the workshops. These helped users understand and connect with the intended use situation. A number of discussion themes were presented to help participants trigger the relevant prior experience and frame the discussion.

Each discussion theme consisted of a title, a short description and everyday examples. The chosen themes were: *Implicit security*, *Security negotiation*, *Social navigation*, *Motivated security*, *Tangible security*, *Proportional security* and *Feeling secure*. See figure 1for examples of the themes and how they were presented. The idea of these themes were to clear-cut and somewhat overstate previous research findings from our own work or from literature. This way of outlining the themes were both a matter of making them pedagogically accessible to everyday users, and a matter of probing and provoking their past experiences and current assumptions regarding how IT security may be addressed in design [5,16].

Participants

The intended users of a mobile digital signature are more or less everybody. We decided to invite groups of possible users who already knew each other:

The participants of the first workshop worked professionally with typesetting of paper forms for municipal casework. They knew each other from their union even though they did not work together. Besides being potential users of the mobile digital signatures, the digitalization of services connected to digital signing was a potential threat to their jobs.

Senior citizens from a local senior citizens community formed the second group. With their lifelong experience of different payments methods (e.g. cash, credit, checks and credit cards) and authentication in digital as well as non-digital context, and with a limited experience with digital artifacts

More and more information only exist in electronic versions while applications, agreements, transactions, contracts and commitments still have to been signed by one or more people. Please design a digital signature that fits your everyday life? You may already know solutions that are tied to a single PC, and your challenge is to come up with a mobile solution. Please describe the physical design and the necessary procedure that users have to go through if they want to sign a document.

Table 1 Design problem definition (Figure 2)

in general, their perspective was anticipated as different from the first group.

Rationale

We wanted to avoid the framing of security as a struggle with malicious hackers, while setting the stage for design discussions that were focused on actual use and actual needs. We intended to activate insights from usable security literature and our previous work in the discussion, in a way that the participants could get inspired to activate their security experiences, and thereby articulate their needs and design suggestions in a better way.

Action

Each workshop lasted for three hours. At first, a researcher introduced the IT security domain. Secondly, the six discussion themes were presented along with examples from everyday life that explained the scope and the essence of the discussion theme. Each participant was handed out a sheet of paper with the themes. The design task (Fig. 2) was introduced, and subsequently the participants spent their time in two groups of 3-4 participants. At the end, each group presented their work to the other group. Each group was assisted by a researcher who answered questions regarding technological possibilities, and challenged some of the assumptions of the participants. The group work and the final presentations were video-recorded for further analysis.

Tangible Security
As human beings we trust tangible things. We know that if we got our car keys in our hands it is less likely that someone else is driving our car. We know that if we firmly push down a door handle and the door does not open, it is locked. But things like passwords and key stores are just not as tangible. Can IT security be tangible?
Proportional Security
"Take not a musket to kill a butterfly". Still that is what happens in IT security. Front doors are normally locked with a rather sophisticated lock that keep strangers out, while restroom doors have simple locks, which only purpose are to tell other people that the restroom is occupied. Strong and complex security is often required to accomplish even simple tasks when it comes to IT.
Social Navigation
When people make sense of what is secure or appropriate it is common to look at what others have done. For instance one may choose a crowded restaurant in favor of an empty one when searching for nice restaurant in a foreign city. Or when strolling through a forest, one may choose to follow a path instead of just wandering between the trees. Such traces and wear do not necessarily show up in IT. Can traces and wear in your design help the users?

Table 2 Three example discussion themes translated into English (Figure 1)

Below we focus on the workshop with the senior citizens. The participants were split in two groups: Ann, Alice and Andrew in group A, and Brenda, Bridget and Barbara in group B. Group A drew from their experiences the suggestion that users would feel secure if they had to use a dedicated website, each time they wanted to utilize their digital signature. Thus the users only had to trust this website instead of trusting an IT security device or their mobile phone. In this proposal, users could only access their digital signature when borrowing a computer connected to the Internet. Group B focused on utilizing people's personal mobile phones combined with dedicated terminals to be placed at the point of signing. The rationale behind their solution was to have a fast and smooth transaction and make it easy for users to document and prove what they have or have not signed. The two groups came up with quite different designs and the underlying rationales resulted in interesting discussions and explanations doing the final presentations.

In the following we illustrate the many discussions through examples from the workshop.

In the introduction to the presentation of Group B's design, Bridget activated her past experience with her first debit card and made the straightforward claim that technology that is hard to use, may trigger unnecessary worries about security. Nobody questioned this, and the assumption provided the participants with a common ground for design.

When my son and his wife went to the States they bought parking, hotels and everything on-line. I wouldn't dare to do that. I once bought tickets to the concert hall (via their website) and it worked out well, and my husband asked, "Do you think they will believe us?" "They're gonna have to" I answered.

Table 3 Translated transcript of Ann's monologue.(Figure 4)

Later, while discussing the quality of Group A's design, Ann talked about a need for a receipt. She needed a way to prove that she bought some goods in a different store, than the one she was currently in. She explained how she worked around the problem by having her husband wait outside a shop with some goods. Receipts continued to be a hot to-

A1: Now you can check-in yourself via mobile phone or the web.
B2: No, it's in the airport at a screen.
A1: No, it's also at your mobile phone – I saw it in a commercial.
B2: But I don't have a mobile phone that can do all that.

Table 4 Translated transcript of dialogue between Ann (A1) and Bridget (B2) (Figure 5)

pic for the rest of the afternoon. For instance Bridget talked out loud a dialogue with herself while the others listened carefully. She activated two parallel strategies of use by stating that she always asked for the receipt while also claiming that she always required a plastic bag with shops logo, so that others would see that she paid for the goods. She did not seem to have a clear strategy, yet she appeared to find the issue important, which can bee seen from the experiences that she brought up. Even though the participants of the workshop all agreed that it was important to receive a receipt when paying, Ann brought up the issue of how people handle receipts in quite a different way: some people are like herself while others are asking the clerk to throw away the receipt after paying. In this manner, relations to others, even an abstract person referred to as "somebody", become influential in the participants' ongoing sense making dialogue.

In a defense of Group B's solution, a dedicated website, Ann included others in her sense making of online shopping. She talked out loud about her son's travel arrangements, her own actions, her husband's thoughts and her expectations to the local concert hall staff (see Fig. 4). She seemed to be between not buying anything online at all and buying things online on a regular basis. Instead of giving a precise statement, her insights pointed towards the cumulation of experiences that she activated when deciding whether or not to buy online.

This was not the only time that experiences were voiced in order to make sense of something. Through a dialogue at the very end the participants made sense of what one could achieve with a mobile phone (due to Group B's design). First, Ann brought up self check-in at airports, as something that would be possible with a mobile phone. Bridget questioned this, possibly because she had not been able to make this work with her own mobile phone. Ann referenced to an experience she had with an airline's commercial promoting check-in on the go. Finally, Bridget releases this tension by concluding that it is not all about what the airline made technically possible, it was also about what her mobile phone would support (Fig. 5).

Sometimes the prior experiences served to frame discussions of hypothetical situations. For instance Ann, Alice and Andrew discussed if stores would be ready to put up terminals that would allow customers to sign or pay. They imagined the dialogue that would take place, and discussed this rather concretely, even though they were discussing a hypothetical situation.

What did we learn

In the following we summarize the lessons learned from the workshop as regards the process as such, security, specifically the security themes, and the activation of experience in the processes.

The process

In both workshops, people were quite concerned with IT security, which is illustrated by the fact that a lively debate of arguments and experience sharing started even before the introduction. The design work in groups made these rather eager discussions more focused, more detailed and more concrete, such as when the group discusses payment by mobile phone. When the groups presented their work to each other, the proposed solutions were scrutinized through sophisticated and well-articulated questions from the other group (For instance the discussions of receipts). Even after the video recording ended, the discussion carried on and from that we understood that IT security in general and digital signatures in particular were highly relevant to the participants, and also that the activities of the workshop helped them discuss these topics. At the end of each workshop, participants stated that the workshop had been exciting without being prompted for it.

The participants had started addressing important issues of security early on, and the discussion themes mainly helped set the stage for these discussions. This may be because it took a fair amount of work to actively use the themes, and the participants were more eager to get to the design task. Also, the discussion themes may not have been tangible enough, in contrast to the experiences of [10] where the discussion themes were put on individual cards. In the two versions of the future Prompted exploration workshop we did not train the participants in using the discussion themes for argumentation and inspiration. This is an area for future development of the method, as it is indeed a challenge to make the themes more accessible in the design process.

For the time being we can only speculate if a different format would have helped providing a more active role for the themes, and issue that is to be addressed in future research.

Security themes

Of the six discussion themes (see list above), the two first themes (*Proportional Security* and *Tangible Security*) presented in Fig. 1 were the most frequently activated in the groups.

Tangible security was the most popular discussion theme in the workshops. Participants found that using the mobile digital signature should be tangible. For instance in the discussions about receipts, the participants argued that it should be easy to determine whether or not a person had signed something and this preferably in a tangible way.

Also the discussion theme, *Proportional Security* kept coming back in design discussions. For instance in the discussions of whether dedicated terminals should be in place at any location where people would need to sign.

The discussion theme *Social Navigation* (see Fig. 1) was well received by the participants at first. However, we have not been able to find any examples were the discussion theme played a role in design or argumentation. One possible reason for this is that the particularly abstract nature of social navigation made it hard to grasp. To design for social navigation, it is necessary to clarify the time gap between the creation of traces and wear and the utilization of them. Moreover, design for social navigation requires that the notion of other users is included in descriptions. An obvious last possibility is that the two groups did not find social navigation relevant for the mobile digital signature design case.

Experience

Our findings above illustrate that it is possible to get access to participants' specific experiences trough their monologue and dialogue with each other.

Experience comes in different types. In Group B a participant concluded that "everybody was suspicious" while thinking of the introduction of debit and credit cards. She did not activate actual prior experiences; instead her experiences were conserved, as "everybody was suspicious". In the example of receipts, we saw that for Ann and Bridget to have a secure experience of shopping, it did not suffice to be able to prove that they had paid in the event that they were accused for stealing. They wanted others to be able to determine at a distance that they had paid for the goods they were carrying; hence avoiding the risk that someone would question their honesty.

The participants often demonstrated that they possessed a set of prior experiences that served as a base for making security decisions, rather than a clear strategy (or policy). For instance, Ann and Bridget had their own set of stories, which were activated, when claiming that receipts were important. We also saw how Ann's set of experiences regarding the security of buying tickets online was built up: First she was likely not to do it. Then her son succeeded in buying everything for his trip online, after which she herself bought tickets for a concert even though her husband questioned this. This questioning made her worry even though, in the end, it worked out well. All of these experiences formed the base that she activated when deciding whether or not to buy online. Moreover, we saw how Ann and Bridget together piled up experiences in order to make sense of how one could sign or pay securely with a mobile phone. They started out with a tension between their idea of self check-in for flights via a mobile phone and the fact that none of them actually tried it. By piling up experiences, the tension was released when they agreed on that some mobile phones probably could do it but that their mobile phones could not.

We also saw how a notion of others played a significant role in the participants' stories. Even though the stories mostly included specific people like *my husband*, *my son* or characters from a commercial they also relates to others. In the examples above the participants refer to the ones who threw away their receipts and shop-owners in general (referred to as *they* or *somebody*).

ACTING OUT SECURITY

We have developed Acting out security in order to capture future users' experience of security, the ongoing dialog of making sense of security, and the activation of prior experiences of security.

Motive

Participatory design workshops give access to activation of experience and inform brainstorming and initial design. Similarly enactments may give access to users' ongoing dialog in encounters with technology. To explore this we prototyped a mobile phone application and a point-of-sales application for a café.

Method

Participants enact situation from their everyday life in a real context. The only difference from a real situation is the introduction of new technological artifacts. The technological artifact either replaces another artifact or offers new features of the situation. The situation should be so familiar that no instructions or directions would be required, besides instructions regarding the handling of the new technology artifact. Empirical data comes from video recordings of the enactment, observations and post-enactment debriefing.

Participants

Four regular café guests and a bartender volunteered to participate. The guests frequently went to the café where the enactment took place and the bartender worked there.

Rationale

Normally guests are paying at a café using cash or credit cards. By installing our application on their mobile phone, they would be able to utilize their mobile phone and mobile digital signature as payment form. As with any other encounters with new technological artifacts, people try to make sense of the technological artifact by utilizing their prior experiences with similar technology [16], and the purpose of this enactment was to gain insight into these prior experiences. In this case, prior experiences included experiences with some of the above-mentioned forms of payment. Moreover, the method was set up to grant access to users' ongoing dialog with themselves and others.

Action

The enactment took place during normal opening hours at the café and other customers were present (For situation see Fig. 6). Two participants had the application installed on their own mobile phones; the two others borrowed mobile phones with the application preinstalled. A tablet PC worked as point-of-sales software in parallel with the café's normal cash register. The application made it possible to pay for beverages and snacks by using the mobile digital signature to sign the text: "I, [name], accept to pay [amount] for [list of beverages and snacks] to [name of the café]". In this café customers paid when they ordered. Accordingly, all participants made several transactions during the 3 hours of acting out session.

When a café guest placed an order, the bartender prepared the beverage or snack and placed it on the counter. Afterwards he selected the order on the tablet PCs and pressed the "proceed to payment" button. Then he handed over the tablet PC to the customer. The text to sign was on the screen (see above) and a list of nearby mobile phones by name of the owner. In this case, the list would show the name of the café guest and other guests nearby. The café guest verified the list of beverages and snacks and the amount to pay. Then she selected her name on the list and typed her pin-code. The pin-code and her name were verified on a remote server. The text to sign was sent via Bluetooth to her phone. Her mobile phone would vibrate, flash the screen, and the text would show up to prompt the customer to acknowledge or decline. When acknowledged, the phone sent back the signature and the tablet PC showed, that the transaction was complete and successful. After this the café guest would leave the tablet PC to the bartender, and the transaction was complete in seconds.

The participants who used the application on their own mobile phone handled this seamlessly, based on their past routines of unlocking the keypad and homing onto the acknowledging soft-key. The participants with borrowed mobile phones were initially struggling a bit with the handling of the mobile phone. However, these issues faded away. The bartender also quickly learned how to handle the point-of-sales application.

The bartender's second and a participant's first transaction were carried out with almost no verbal negotiation. The bartender looked at the participant, who said the name of a drink and that was it. In the situation there was no need for negotiating the payment, the payment form or the process. It just happened. Both the bartender and the participant relied on their prior experiences of point-of-sales technology and their prior experiences with other payment forms.

Figure 1 The café setting

These experiences were cumulated into the procedure that actually happened and their anticipations where met. Even though the bartender and the participant agreed to exchange a drink for a certain amount of money, they never talked about it. The participants were prompted to sign a commitment to pay for the beverages and snacks they ordered. Most participants read through the whole text during their first transaction. At their second transaction they spotted the pattern of the text and it seemed that they only looked at the price before acknowledging. Accordingly, they made use of a combination of their experiences with other payments forms, other café visits and their experiences from the last transaction.

For simplicity, the point-of-sales application had a hardcoded list of snacks, beverages and prices. One of the participants nonetheless asked for a drink, which was not on the list. This first led to confusion before the bartender and the participant negotiated, how to put it on the bill as a snack with the same price. When the mobile phone prompted the participant to sign a statement including the snack instead of the drink, she simply did so.

Late in the session, a friend of one of the participants came into the café. The participant offered her friend a cup of coffee and lent her phone to her friend. She whispered the pin-code in her ear and the friend went to the bar and ordered a cup of coffee. The bartender served the coffee, selected coffee on the tablet PC and handed it over to the "new participant" without further comments. She chose her friend's name on the list, took a moment to remember the pin-code, and entered it. Her friend's phone woke up in her hand, she struggled a bit with the basic handling of the phone as this was new to her, and finally she acknowledged the purchase, and handed back the tablet PC. From the debriefing we understood that it is not rare for the participants and their friends to lend somebody their credit card and pin-code, even though banks do not approve of this behavior. Past experience of lending each other's credit card clearly inspired this behavior, since we did not instruct the participants that lending out the digital signature was allowed. Because the participants anticipated lending out the mobile phone and the pin-code as normal they never got to reflect on it before we prompted them in the debriefing.

What did we learn

Based on these examples we move on to summarize what we learned about the process, security and experience through acting out security.

The process

The examples illustrate that we got access to quite advanced security behavior through only a few hours of enactment. The specific findings have strong implications for design, e.g. if the design had prevented lending out the digital signature, it would not have satisfied the needs of the users, and we would not have gotten access to the anticipation of the experience of lending out the credit card.

As described above, most transactions proceeded without handling problems. In our prototype implementation we focused on stability and usability. The participants activated prior experiences with IT security and credit cards. The smooth handling made it possible for the participants to activate prior experiences relevant to buying in a bar instead of activating experiences relevant to handling technology (e.g. how to type a pin-code). We return to the importance of these experiences below.

Since the realization of the hi-fi prototype was rather time consuming, it would be interesting to explore enactments with even lower fidelity prototypes to see if they would give similar access to the security dialogue and the actual relevant experience.

Security themes

It is indeed a very open issue what it means to do things in a secure manner. As we see in the examples, this is negotiated in every situation. In the enactment we saw how one of our participants and her friend found, that a secure way to buy a cup of coffee might include revealing a pin-code and lending out a personal mobile phone. Even though the participants afterwards (at the debriefing) told us, that it was a common thing to do, this was indeed a surprise to us. However, in this kind of setting such behavior was considered secure and negotiated from situation to situation.

Experience

With the applications working properly and the participants able to handle them, an opportunity was open to study how the technology blended into the experience of being at a café, purchasing beverages and snacks via mobile phone.

Through all the successful transactions, the participants' expectations, in terms of cumulation of how such a transaction would proceed, seem to fit what actually happened and was experienced in the situation. We did not find any incidents were participants or the bartender were confused or felt unsecure. However, buying beverages and snacks in a café is but one setting that this prototype is intended for. The café setting is in some ways special because all transactions end with the exchange of either a snack or a beverage. In addition, as the sharing of pin-codes indicates, it may be special because it is a setting of sharing, friendship and happiness.

In settings where customers buy services that will be carried out or delivered later, such as online ticket sale, the customers' cumulation might contain different acknowledgement steps, which may not end before the vacation trip is completed, or the concert is over with [17]. Accordingly, on the one hand, we have seen that the prototype manages to satisfy our participants' cumulation. On the other hand, however, it is not evident that the success scales to other settings, which are less social, less friendly or with a less tangible or immediate purchase delivery.

Another way in which prior experiences are activated, according to McCarthy & Wright [16], is as anticipation. One of the transactions was carried out in almost silence. The participant's prior experiences with café visits made her anticipate that simply mentioning the name of a drink was enough. Likewise, the bartender anticipated from his prior experiences that serving the drink would lead to the participant paying without further notice. The different ways prior experiences can be activated relates to space of experience and horizon of expectations [4,20] in that anticipation reflects the horizon of expectation and cumulation, the space of experience.

SECURE EXPERIENCE AND HOW TO DESIGN FOR IT - DISCUSSION

It is a common element of both kinds of design activities that they prompt non-trivial experiences that we did not anticipate. These experiences are surprising, and we find it unlikely that we would have seen them without some sort of activities like the ones this paper describes.

The way in which the participants bring security experiences into the action and discussions tells us that they don't have only one security "policy". Rather they have access to constellations of different ways of approaching security that is dependent on both their experiences and their expectations to the situation that they are in, or imagine to be in.

Collaboration and sharing, even as a monologue, seem important in bringing out experience in the workshops. At the same time, Ann's monologue illustrates that such experiences are fundamentally shared. In [16], experience is addressed very much at an individual level. In our approach, however, participants share storytelling and experience where they prompt each other to get to the general and cultural practices that are part of these everyday security experiences.

Our examples demonstrate that security cannot be separated from the activity in which it is situated. The enactment in the café provided a very specific context where security was part of a happy and friendly experience; in contrast to other contexts that may be less social and nice. The users in this situation were feeling secure despite their partially insecure behavior. However, the case also illustrates that this kind of enactment (only) gives access to very specific and situated experience. Based on what happened we know more about a richer set of security issues in this kind of context, and not e.g. in less friendly settings.

We have pointed out that indeed the very immediate and tangible outcome of the purchase of drinks in a café gives a rather different framing than e.g. on-line ticket purchase, due to the temporality of the experience and the cumulation that is taking place. This is one place where the experience framework needs to be explored and developed further in general, and with respect to security.

The advanced state of the prototype supported access to very specific and situated experience. However, it is still an open question if similar insights could be gained with less elaborate prototyping.

Through the two approaches, and not least the discussion themes, we have managed to frame and explore security in a manner that was not focused on villains and threats. This allowed access to security experiences where the role of collaboration with others came out more clearly that what often is the case in the IT security discourse.

Prompted exploration workshop and Acting out security have helped provide tangibility and prompt non-trivial experience, hence they have provided ways of accessing security experience. They emphasize the importance moving beyond hands-on experience [10] in this kind of design. Seeding the workshops with theoretically informed inspiration cards helped stage the discussions and change the participants' expectations, hence opening new opportunities. The eagerness and motivation and the fact that participants felt excited about participating, showed us that the topics were relevant to them and that they felt their participation mattered.

PERSPECTIVE

In their work on designing for usability and security, Braz et al [2] propose to work on these two issues separately through scenarios and ideal solutions, bringing the designs together at the end as a compromise. Such an approach is in starch contrast to the path that we have taken where we have target a richer understanding of the space of secure experience and security experience in design. However, we hope to have illustrated that the issues really cannot be separated at a level where they can meaningfully be designed for independently.

In terms of participatory design, our project has been facing a challenge that is shared with many interaction design projects currently, namely that its users are people at large in everyday situations, and not workers solving a particular task, or on groups working with a collection of applications [3]. We have not tried to deploy our tools in such more well-defined settings, but based on our past experiences in the area of participatory methods, we believe that the proposed methods will have an even easier deployment here, and that they would help focus on IT security in such settings as well. However, it is also the case that our set of tools potentially helps widen the set of participatory tools for non-work settings.

CONCLUSION

We have presented Prompted exploration workshop and Acting out security as tools to design a mobile digital signature for everyday people. We reported how the utilization of these tools helped the design process and have illustrated how the tangibility of such tools matters. The approach has granted access to non-trivial insights into people's security experience and shown how these are activated in activities where security is at stake. We have pointed out how the specific context is essential for exploring the space between experience and expectations, and we have illustrated how people activate their collections of security experiences rather than deploying *one* security strategy in all situations.

ACKNOWLEDGEMENT

ITSCI is a project financed by the Danish Strategic Research Council (NABIIT).

REFERENCES

1. Adams, A. and Sasse, M. A. Users are not the enemy. *CACM 42*, 12 (1999) 40-46.
2. Braz, C., Seffah, A., & M'Raihi, D.. Designing a Trade-Off Between Usability and Security: A Metrics Based-Model. In *Proc. INTERACT 2007*, LNCS 4663 (2007), Part II, 114 – 126.
3. Bødker, S. When second wave HCI meets third wave challenges. *Proc. NordiCHI 2006*, ACM (2006), 1-8.
4. Bødker, S. and Christiansen, E. Scenarios as springboards in design. In Bowker, G., Gasser, L., Star, S.L. & Turner, W. (eds.), *Social science research, technical systems and cooperative work*. Erlbaum (1997), 217-234.
5. Bødker, S. & Christiansen, E. Designing for ephemerality and prototypicality. Proc. DIS 2004 (2004) 255 - 260.
6. Bødker, S. and Klokmose, C.N. (in press). The Human-Artifact Model. *Journal of HCI* (2011)
7. Dindler, C. and Iversen, O. S. Fictional Inquiry - Design Collaboration in a Shared Narrative Space, *Journal of CoDesign 3(4)* (2007), 213-234.
8. Ehn, P. and Sjögren, D. From System Descriptions to Scripts for Action. In [10] (1991) 241-268.
9. Engeström, Y. and Middleton, D. (Eds.). *Cognition and Communication at Work*, Cambridge University Press (1996), 130-158
10. Greenbaum, J. and Kyng M. (eds.). Design at Work: Cooperative Design of Computer Systems, Hillsdale NJ: Lawrence Erlbaum Associates (1991).
11. Halskov, K. and Dalsgaard, P. The emergence of ideas: the interplay between sources of inspiration and emerging design concepts. *CoDesign: International Journal of CoCreation in Design and the Arts 3(4)* (2007), 185 – 211.
12. Lampson, B. Privacy and security. Usable security: how to get it. *CACM 52(11)* (2009). 25-27.
13. Landau, S. Privacy and security. A multidimensional problem. *CACM 51(11)* (2008). 25-26.
14. Kyng, M. *Users and Computers - A Contextual Approach to Design of Computer Artifacts*. DAIMI PB-507 (1995).
15. Mathiasen, N. and Bødker, S. Threats or threads: from usable security to secure experience, *Proc. NordiCHI 2008*, Society for Industrial and Applied Mathematics, (2008). 283-290.
16. McCarthy, J. and Wright, P. *Technology As Experience*. MIT Press (2004).
17. McCarthy, J., and Wright, P. *Experience-Centered Design. Designers, Users, and Communities in Dialogue*. Morgan & Claypool (2010).
18. Mogensen, P., and Trigg, R. Artifacts as triggers for participatory analysis. In *Proc. PDC 1992* (1992), 55-62.
19. Norman, D.. The Way I See It. When security gets in the way. *interactions 16(6)* (2009), 60-63.
20. Ricoeur, P. *Time and Narrative*, Volume 3. Chicago, University of Chicago Press (1988).
21. Schön, D. *The reflective practitioner*. Temple Smith (1983).
22. Whitten, A and Tygar, D. Why Johnny Can't Encrypt – A Usability Evaluation of PGP 5.0. In Cranor, L. & Simson, G. (eds). *Security and Usability: Designing Secure Systems that People Can Use*, O'Reilly (2005), 679-700.

Building Sensitising Terms to Understand Free-play in Open-ended Interactive Art Environments

Ann Morrison
Department of Architecture, Design and Media Technology
University of Aalborg, Denmark
PO Box 159, 9100 Aalborg
ann.morrison@acm.org

Stephen Viller
School of Information Technology & Electrical Engineering
The University of Queensland
St Lucia, QLD 4072, Australia
viller@acm.org

Peta Mitchell
School of English, Media Studies, and Art History
The University of Queensland
St Lucia, QLD 4072 Australia
peta.mitchell@uq.edu.au

ABSTRACT

In this paper we introduce and discuss the nature of free-play in the context of three open-ended interactive art installation works. We observe the interaction work of situated free-play of the participants in these environments and, building on precedent work, devise a set of sensitising terms derived both from the literature and from what we observe from participants interacting there. These sensitising terms act as guides and are designed to be used by those who experience, evaluate or report on open-ended interactive art. That is, we propose these terms as a *common-ground* language to be used by participants communicating while in the art work to describe their experience, by researchers in the various stages of research process (observation, coding activity, analysis, reporting, and publication), and by inter-disciplinary researchers working across the fields of HCI and art. This work builds a foundation for understanding the relationship between free-play, open-ended environments, and interactive installations and contributes sensitising terms useful for the HCI community for discussion and analysis of open-ended interactive art works.

Author Keywords

Free-play, open-ended, interactive installation, common-sense language, sensitising terms, sensitising guides.

ACM Classification Keywords

H5.m. Information interfaces and presentation (e.g., HCI): Miscellaneous.

General Terms

Human Factors

INTRODUCTION

Feltham et al describe play as a "predominantly open-ended activity with fluid rules of engagement" favouring self-determination and freedom, where game-playing favours competition and ambition ([12] p.63). The emphasis of our research is on free-play, which we define as non-narrative, non-competitive, and without logical ending point. The so-called plot of the play continually evolves in order to keep the play alive [8]. As such, free-play is activity that is constantly rejuvenated, as it is co-constructed and co-authored by its participants and is free from predetermined order or meaning [7, 8, 22].

CHI 2011, May 7–12, 2011, Vancouver, BC, Canada.
Copyright 2011 ACM 978-1-4503-0267-8/11/05....$10.00.

This paper is framed within the context of three specific open-ended interactive art installations. These open-ended works are free-form in that they provide an abstract yet *embodied* experience that requires their audience to actively construct their own meaning from direct experience with the works. As we have noted, these are non-narrative works, with no prescribed meanings, guidelines or rules to drive the interaction. Neither is there a ready character role for the participant to adopt nor a linear storyline to become engaged in; rather, the participants discover their own motivations and meaning and invent their own interpretations [20].

Games and play have become an important area of research in HCI, with much research generated that examines play within a variety of situations and audiences, with most research focusing on narrative-based, game-type scenarios, and interactive artefacts. Very little research exists on free-play, except in regard to children's open-ended play, and much less research again exists on situated activity in open-ended interactive installation works. In addition, missing from the literature is a discussion of works that set out to provoke play-experimentation-exploration and enable a process of uncovering and meaning-making that encourages initiative on the part of the participants.

We present here a set of sensitising terms that were initially derived from the existing literature and research on play. As Blumer states, sensitising concepts give "the user a general sense of reference and guidance in approaching empirical instances... and suggest directions along which to look" ([6], p.7). To distill sensitising concepts *to use as guides*, to *suggest directions to look* at the related work on play builds sensibly on precedent work. To then use the *guides* as lenses to look through, [4] adds to their usefulness and increases the possibility that they are styled in a *ready-to-use* format. Whether a sensitising concept survives from beginning to end of the process "depends on where the data take us; emergent concepts may supplement or displace them altogether" ([23] p.301). We applied, combined, dropped, added, refined and amended these sensitising terms on a case-by-case basis to prime them for use for studying participant activity in three chosen works. The terms were designed to assist in the research, analysis, and understanding of interactions in open-ended art works to use as a common language between participants (the general public), for researchers to better understand, code, analyse, discuss, and describe what participants are doing and for inter-disciplinary researchers to use to communicate effectively. As such, these terms need to exhibit a kind of "intersubjective verifiability" or communicability. That is, they need to be both simple enough and evocative enough to offer themselves as a common-sense, common-ground, and above all practical language to each and all of the groups involved in the construction of meaning in these spaces—the artists, the participants, and the researchers. Further coverage is found in "Situated play in open-ended interactive art environments" [19].

In building the sensitising terms to act as guides, we seek to discuss, in more meaningful detail, the kinds of activities people engage in when they interact with open-ended works. As we aim to develop a language that is useful for discussion across multiple disciplines that can also act as a code for analysis (as well as for communicating the results of that analysis), then language becomes doubly useful. If the language can also be useful for participants to unpack and better understand their own experience, as well as for communication with others while in the experience and afterwards, then the usefulness increases yet again. Experiences in an interactive art work are sometimes 'outside of usual life' and can be *heightened* experiences and consequently, people are motivated to communicate with others about these experiences while in them, and often immediately after. The benefit for the artist is in having a useable language and a different set of perspectives to view their work from. These terms or *guides* as language we are developing straddle disciplines. The emerging language (or terms) can act in the same way as a set of boundary objects that fit across the disciplines. Boundary objects—objects that sit between the interfaces of various communities of interest or practice—work because they contain sufficient detail to be comprehensible to more than one of the parties involved and act in a translation or mediation role between the disciplines [30]. The most useful boundary objects often take the form of tangible objects [14], but may also take the form of vocabulary and operate to uncover, test, and push boundaries between fields of practice[16], while also maintaining coherence across intersecting worlds.

The remainder of the paper is structured as follows. After summarising related work, we describe and define the sensitising terms and the process for arriving at the initial terms from the literature and the emergent terms from application. We then describe and analyse participation in three substantial open-ended interactive art works—*Autonomous Light Air Vessels* (ALAVs), *Drafting Poems: Inverted Potentialities*, and *Books of Sand*—that were part of an extensive exhibition at the Interactive Art Program, ACM Multimedia 2006. We also describe the process of defining, testing, and honing the sensitising terms as we analysed participation in these works in order to observe, describe and understand the nature of interaction in open-ended art works. By doing this, we distill initial and emergent terms related to play in order to begin foundational work for the development of a set of common-sense sensitising terms to better describe the situated work of interaction with open-ended works.

RELATED WORK: OPEN-ENDED INTERACTION AND ACTIVATED PARTICIPATION IN HCI RESEARCH

As discussed, 'play' has become a key object of study in HCI over recent years, and has spurred a reconsideration of the dominant concept of 'work.' The growth of research into recreational computing—computing outside workplace environments, including broader cultural and inter-disciplinary applications of computing—feeds into an expanded meaning of what we now understand by the term 'user experience' [4]. Crabtree et al. discuss the importance of considering play as a kind of interaction work and its relevance to Computer Supported Cooperative Work (CSCW) [10]. With the changes in computing use brought about by more widely available access and changes in robustness of ubiquitous computing devices, play and computing (and the situated work this involves) is an important addition to HCI. Moran & Anderson anticipated this progress in their much earlier CSCW research [19], with their emphasis on informal interaction in workaday environments and in the everyday use of mundane technologies. Nonetheless, HCI's interest in play has largely been in regard to narrative-based games that have outcomes and end-points that can more easily be judged as successful or not. Where play is addressed in HCI literature, it tends to be examined either in regard to works with close-ended narrative structures [4, 10, 11] or where free-play is discussed it is largely in relation to children's play in social groups and with artefacts [2, 17, 22]. These are significant studies that provide important background for this paper, particularly where they apply already-established theories of play. However, they also point to two gaps in the HCI literature: first, a gap in relation to open-ended adult interaction in non-narrative based interactive installation (spatial) works, and second, a lack of an overarching framework or language for free-play.

In addition, we argue for a broader understanding that includes the artist's intent (missing and acknowledged as a gap from much HCI evaluation of art works [13]) and the important free-play experiences open-ended interactive art environments afford their participants [8]. Broadly speaking, an open-ended work is one that meets Carse's criteria for an infinite game, as defined in the following section. The artist's intent behind the work is often to create activating and/or exploratory experiences for participants, an aspect largely ignored in HCI evaluations.

IDENTIFYING SENSITISING TERMS FOR FREE-PLAY

We develop an initial vocabulary of sensitising terms for understanding free-play in open-ended interactive art environments. These initial terms derive from research that has been broadly influential to the body of work on play and has contributed key terms that have been taken up and circulated in subsequent research. In addition, we explore philosophies of open-ended works and free play, and from this process derive specific ideas that feed into, support and define a new set of sensitising terms.

Over the last several decades, research on the nature and function of play has increased dramatically across a broad array of disciplines, including sociology, psychology, game theory, and education. Play is of interest to animal behaviourists studying the adaptive advantages of play [3], to developmental psychologists studying the cognitive and social skills that children learn through play [26, 32], and to sociologists studying the way play fits into larger social needs [25]. In the social sciences, early research into play was often delegated or discussed as something children do, and notably as the *work* of children [24]. Piaget's *Play, dreams, and imitation* provides some of the earliest systematic work on play, and continues to act as a touchstone for research into play across the social sciences as well as to much of the HCI research on play. Piaget [26] argued that in play children construct knowledge by a process of assimilation. That is, they fit new experiences into their existing schema, as in the case of a stick becoming a symbolic representation of a sword. Vygotsky [32] in continuing this work, argued that the pretend situation of play creates an imaginative dimension and promotes abstract ideas and verbal thinking. Further, Vygotsky maintained that the toys and gestures with which children play are significant social and cultural artefacts through which children learn social rules and culture. Children's tendency towards play, or playfulness, has been linked to creative thinking skills [17] with research indicating a disposition towards creativity in later life [9].

Parten [25] classified play into various roles including those of: (1) *onlooker*: where a child *observes* others playing and while they may engage in conversation, they do not engage in doing, and focus is on the children at play; (2) *parallel play*: when children play alongside each other with little direct interaction; (3) *associative play*: playing with others without organisation of play activity; initiating or responding to interaction with peers, and (4) *cooperative* play: coordinating one's behavior with that of a peer, and a sense of belonging to a group emerges. Associative and cooperative play roles represent higher levels of interaction where children play together on joint activities and coordinate their actions [25].

Smilansky [28] developed Piaget's work [26] on how children consolidate and extend their prior learning by practicing learnt aspects in their play activities [26], and provided criteria for understanding *dramatic play* The most useful categories for this project include (1) make-believe: play behaviors or speech dialogues and materials or toys substituted for real objects; (2) verbal make-believe: for actions and situations: verbal dialogue takes the place of body movements; (3) interaction: more than one person participates in pretend play episodes; (4) verbal communication: verbal dialogue is exchanged between the players and takes the place of body movements. Embodied interaction can occur through bodily gestural interaction or verbal dialogue. Interaction and verbal communication involve social dynamics in play [28, 29].

Huizinga [15] and Caillois shifted the focus of play from child development to a broader understanding of *ludology* as the foundation of culture. In *Man, play, and games*, Caillois [7] provided a typology of game play, identifying four patterns of play—*agon*, *alea*, *mimicry*, and *ilinx*—which operate on a spectrum that extends from *ludus* (formal, rule-bound game play) to *paidia* (an anarchic state of spontaneous, improvisational form of free-play that is unrestricted and without rules or meaning). More recently, theorists working specifically with free-play-like activities included Carse [8], who distinguished between finite and infinite games (and play), where finite games are played to be won, but an infinite game is played for the purpose of continuing the play.

Paidia, Infinite play, Free-play

For Carse an infinite game features six characteristics that could equally apply as a definition for an open-ended work: (1) an endlessly open outcome; (2) play is dramatic with no scripted conclusion; (3) players do not oppose the actions of others but initiate actions of their own in such a way that others will respond by initiating their own; (4) players allow others to do what they wish in the course of play with them; (5) the length of the game is determined by itself; and (6) the rules continually change to prevent anyone from winning and to bring as many people as possible into play.

Carse views infinite play as the more profound and emotionally evolved activity. A successful open-ended work could facilitate that players initiate actions of their own in such a way that others will respond by initiating their own actions, that the rules continually change to continue the play and to draw others into the play.

Further, Nachmanovitch [22] argues for the profound nature of improvisation and free-play and identifies two types of free-play: *Lila*, a state of divine play, where participants take delight and enjoyment at the simplest of things; and *Bricoleur/ Bricolage* where participants potter about and in the spirit of improvisation, add spontaneously into the play whatever is at hand in the environment. The idea of play—particularly the "meaningless" free-play of Caillois's *paidia,* Carse's infinite play, with no purpose or end-point, or Nachmanovitch's divine state of *lila*—is not always a natural fit within a competitive western society.

Player types and styles

Bartle [1] defined players as types who *played* with different goals in mind. For the purposes of this research, *achievers*, *explorers,* and *socialisers* prove useful terms to consider for understanding free play activity. *Achievers* would always be looking for where things are and what to do. *Explorers* would seek in a similar way, so these two terms could be conflated. An open-ended work is potentially less of an information space, however some players may have more of a *speculative* approach, looking at the engineering behind the functions of the work and thinking about what else might be possible and/or what works approach things in a similar fashion. *Socialisers* are often the lifeblood of an interactive art experience, interacting and playing with strangers, through the medium of the work and/or about the work.

Dow [11], building on descriptive models of play behavior including Bartle's work [1], names different *player styles* in interactive narrative works. Dow includes the styles (1) *engager:* fully engages with the experience physically, socially, and emotionally; and (2) *observer*: (as with Parten's onlooker): does not interact (or speaks and uses gestures infrequently), watches play unfold. Dow [11] and Bartle [1] caution about typecasting players or styles, since players often change focus [11]. However, Bartle suggests that most players have a primary style, and will only switch to other styles as a (deliberate or subconscious) means to advance their main interest [1].

Initial sensitising terms

We developed the initial sensitising terms from the above literature on play and show the initial set in Table 1. We have outlined above some of the most important concepts we considered when selecting the initial terms. We needed to identify terms that would capture the emergent and evolving play and interaction styles required from participants when interacting in open-ended environments. We understood that open-ended environments do not encourage fixed styles of play. While not all the terms discussed above were selected for the initial set of sensitising terms, the ideas presented feed into and/or were merged with other terms. The sensitiser terms began as a larger batch of ideas and concepts that was gradually refined to form this first initial version (Table 1). The terms were produced in an iterative process of research, design, implement, and reflect. We merged duplicated or similar ideas, erased those that did not apply and grouped potential terms into useful categories for analysing free-form play for the situated instances of use we foresaw could occur in open-ended interactive installations. As this was to some degree unknown territory, we included the already-known free-play terms from play literature, such as Caillois's *paidia,* Carse's infinite play, and Nachmanovitch's divine states of *lila* and *bricolage.* Terms were tested for usefulness by, for example, writing up video analysis code systems, or check lists for observation. Many were systematically removed from the list where they proved redundant, subsequently often triggering more

Terms for sensitiser guides compiled from literature	
Observer	Watcher and/or active or non-active observation; often noted with participants at an early stage in approaching the work. [11, 25]
Embodied play	Bodily interaction with others through gesture, body poses, moving around others [28, 29]
Verbal play	Speech with others in the spirit of play, speech that supports the imaginary world of play/ the environment (Smilansky, 1968; Smilansky & Shefatya, 1990; Parten, 1933)
Associative play	Spontaneously initiates or responds in interaction to the initiations of others (Parten, 1933)
Cooperative play	Coordinates with others activities, often forms of role play emerges, for example participants may take turns (Parten, 1933)
Parallel play	Plays alongside others with little direct interaction with others (Parten, 1933)
Lila play	*Lila divine play*: achieves highly optimised state [22] similar to *flow* state with loss of conscious awareness of self and/or time/circumstances
Bricolage play	*Bricoleur*: plays spontaneously with whatever is at hand [22]
Paidia play	*Paidia*: wild, free anarchic play, without rules or 'meaning' (Caillois, 1962)

Table 1: Initial sensitising terms from play literature

apt terms, which were added. In addition, later in-situ participant observation prompted many sensitiser term ideas (Table 2).

In order to make this work accessible and more easily deployable for other research, we systematically drew together the most-used sensitiser guide terms (Table 1) and, following analysis of the interactive works, the emergent common-sense terms (Table 2). The aim was to produce a language that could be used by all those who engage in the process of experiencing, evaluating, or reporting on open-ended interactive art. That is this common-ground language is intended for use by 1) participants in describing their experience of the art work; 2) researchers across the various stages of the research process (observation, coding activity, analysis, reporting and publication); and 3) inter-disciplinary researchers working across the fields of HCI and art. By making sense of everyday talk and action, common sense understandings are produced in a society, and, mutual objective grounding of social facts is accomplished [31]. This research is sparked by an interest to work with 'common sense' as a tool to devise a useful language, "located in our everyday situated actions, such that our common sense... is the product of our interaction" [31] p. 77.

THE ART WORKS

The evaluation presented here is of three open-ended interactive art works that were part of an exhibition of twelve works presented at the Interactive Art Program at ACM Multimedia Conference, 2006. The works were:

(1) *Autonomous Light Air Vessels* (ALAVs), by Nikhil Mitter and Jed Berk, (2) *Drafting Poems: Inverted Potentialities* by Eitan Mendelowitz and (3) *Books of Sand* by Mariano Sardon. We now briefly describe each work, before describing the exhibition, the evaluation methods, analysis and findings.

Figure 1. a. ALAVS at the site (©2005-2006. Jed Berk & Nikhil Mitter.) b. Participants feeding the ALAVs. (Image by jed eye roam: Creative Commons).

(1) *Autonomous Light Air Vessels* (ALAVs)–also referred to as blimps or balloons by exhibition participants—are networked functioning objects that fly in the air, built by Nikhil Mitter and Jed Berk, from Art Centre College of Design, Pasadena [5].

ALAVs continually bump gently into people, walls, and objects as they roam about. They make an audible soft sound when left alone for too long, (a mobile phone vibrates against the thin membrane of the ALAV) and require input from people in the form of interactive electronic feeding—their hunger level is indicated by a blue light on their suspended LED (Figure 1). A three-step feeding process switches the LED lights between blue and red. ALAVs interact with people, and each other, and exhibit flocking type behaviour (spinning together and calling back and forth) between themselves and propelling themselves towards each other as they fly about the space.

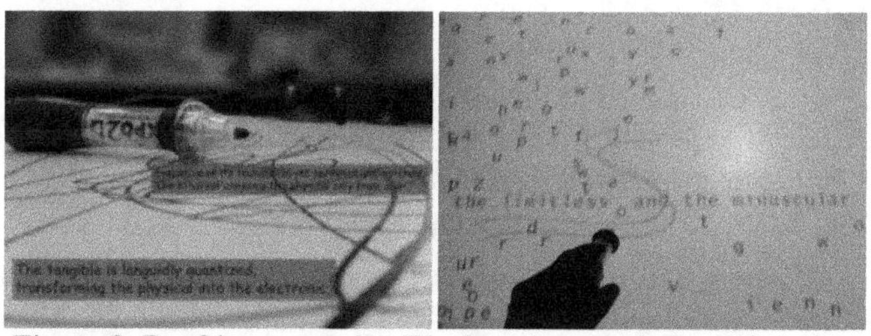

Figure 2. Drafting poems: a. The input pen and examples of phrases. b. The pen in action on the glass top surface. (Images from artists own site and by author at exhibition).

(2) *Drafting Poems: Inverted Potentialities* by Eitan Mendowitz of University of California, Los Angeles works with the idea of an AI aesthetic, building from algorithmic poetry traditions to create meaning by gathering data from participants' sketches on the glass-table top.

The gathered statistics feed into a probabilistic text generation system—an AI system named *The Poet*—that then creates poetic phrases. Users interact with a pen (a dry eraser marker) on an interactive white board (a Mimio). They either draw and add to, or erase markings already on the table. A mix of letters move around on the table, repelled by and attracted to each other, and the input pen, (Figure 2) forming phrases in response to user input. All text objects are tagged with information relative to the user's pen, including the pen's location. In this way, for example, short sentences are produced when the user draws a short line. In addition, as another example, in response to inactivity or delayed input, the work displays words and phrases on topics such as loneliness and despondency. In turn, when input is fast, the work displays related phrases such as *speed* or *sampling error* [18].

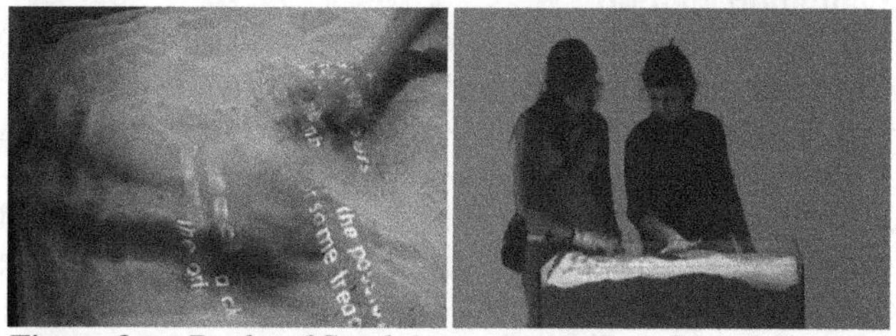

Figure 3. a. *Books of Sand* shows movement of hands in sand and text b. two people using the interactive space. (Images from exhibitions and artists own sites).

(3) *Books of Sand,* by Mariano Sardon of Universidad de Tres de Febrero, Buenos Aires is an interactive installation that streams snippets of the work of the 20th-century Argentinian writer Jorge Luis Borges.

The work itself resembles a glass sandbox. When users touch and move the particles of sand as an interactive surface (Figure 3), projected codes and phrases drawn from websites that contain Borges's work rise up in response to the movement of their hands. The words and phrases are projected onto the users' hands and onto areas of the sand. The concept fits into the idea of an infinite work with never-ending possibilities for interaction. The work presents as an interactive dynamic structure that acts as a complex emergent and unpredictable system, echoing the complex, paradoxical nature of Borges's writing. The work itself is inspired by Borges's 1975 short story "El libro de arena," or "The Book of Sand," which tells the story of a book whose pages change with every reading, In Sardon's words, Borges's imagined "book of sand" is "a countless array of pages numbered at random each time it is opened, never the same. The writing is impossible to follow and only reveals fragments of itself as the pages slip uncontrollably through the reader's eager fingers." [27].

THE EXHIBITION EVENT AND THE STUDY

An estimated four hundred people attended ACM Multimedia 2006, and about half of these attended the Interactive Arts Program exhibition opening. Between 70 and 150 of ACM attendees returned for a second visit. The Interactive Arts Program exhibition was open to the public, but the majority of the audience and participants in this study were researchers and artists presenting their work at ACM Multimedia. This multimedia community of practice comprised a mix of academic and industry researchers including artists, engineers, and technologists working around computer vision, graphics, and image processing.

For this study an expert group giving informed feedback was more useful than novice users learning about interactive works [21].

The exhibition covered several floors, accessible by lifts or stairs. Data collection methods comprised sessions of observation, face-to-face discussions, and written questionnaires. These sessions took place at the exhibition-opening event, and during two subsequent return visits to the venue.

Evaluation Method

We interacted with and/or directly observed around 60 people interacting with the works and each other on opening night and on return visits to the exhibition. In addition, we conducted informal discussions with open-ended questions, both in situ during the opening and at subsequent gallery visits, and off site, for instance after the opening, over conference dinners, and at future gatherings and meetings. Further, we gathered 25 formal questionnaires for this exhibition. Ten were from female participants and 15 were from male participants, with ages ranging between 22 and 65 years. Eighteen of the 25 made regular (more than 3) gallery visits each year, and 21 worked in Information Technology or a related or technical field. Questions included, for example, the following: Which work/s did you: 1) Find the most enjoyable? Why? 2) Spend most time with? Why? 3) Play most with? Why?

Detailed reporting from questionnaires and face-to-face discussions is omitted from this paper, largely for reasons of space. Data obtained from these approaches confirmed our observation findings, which for the purposes of this research we found to be richer. We do add instances of data from questionnaires and interviews where relevant.

FINDINGS

In this section, we report on the observed behaviour of participants and the implementation (and expansion) of the sensitising terms where they emerge. The main findings can be summarised as: 1) the participant's experiences were affected by what the work afforded (for example, the different physical constraints of the works led to different types of gestures being used) and 2) the sensitising guides proved valuable tools to use as a common-sense language to better understand and discuss the modes of participation we observed from participants.

We outline and describe below the sensitising terms we found we consistently used to discuss, observe, code, analyse, and/or report the participant experience. We first discuss for each work in turn the nature of interaction we found, including work-specific terms that emerged through the analysis process. We then present the terms, identified in Table 1, that were useful across all three art works. Finally, we define further terms that emerged through data collection, analysis, reporting, and discussion and proved useful to discuss all three art works.

ALAVs

The ALAVs were situated on the entry level to the gallery and were contained within a large open space. In this, at times crowded environment, the ALAVs propelled themselves about, bumping into people and things. The standard response exhibited by participants bumped into by an ALAV was to gently pat or *bat* at the ALAV, and to move it on its way. People *batted* the ALAVs in the same way as they might *bat* a balloon, often just away from themselves, as well as towards others and then a free-play game between those that were bumped into would spontaneously erupt. Depending on the trajectories the ALAVs took, more people might be bumped into and join in with those already participating. If the ALAVs continued to move/ be *batted* into the same area, then the *batters* maintained interest and stayed alert to the play. If the ALAVs moved out of likely *batting* range, then people either returned to their former activities or went in pursuit of the ALAVs. If these same people noticed that the ALAVS came within *batting* range again, then they would automatically join in, often reaching out to *bat* the ALAV without waiting to be bumped into, and, for example, deliberately changing the ALAV trajectory path. A strong sense of camaraderie developed among the ALAV *batters*. Conversations were interrupted with small discussions about the ALAVs erupting, and much smiling and general *goodwill* was evident around the ALAV activity.

For the majority of the participants, *batting* and interacting with others was the total experience of their participation with ALAVs. Instances of *embodied play* (interacts with gestures, body poses etc. with others [29]), *associative play* (spontaneously initiates or responds in interaction with others [25]) and *cooperative play* where participants coordinated with others and types of role play emerged [25], were observed. Participants played socially through interacting with the ALAVs demonstrating an interaction style we named (an emergent sensitising term) *situated social play* [20]. Similar interactions can be witnessed with video recordings of interactions with Andy Warhol's *Silver Clouds,* 1996, available widely on the Web.

Other participants, however, became involved at a deeper level with the ALAVs. These participants sought more information, often from the artists or from other more involved participants in order to actively 'feed' the ALAVs (Figure 1b). They learnt how to do this either through observation and imitation, or having obtained instruction. Most then assumed roles as 'carers' of the ALAVs and noticeable bonds between fellow-feeders formed. Many questions and conversation revolved around an interaction style we named *speculating* (an emergent sensitising term)—in this case, speculating on how the ALAVs worked. Participants often collaboratively speculated until they *comprehended* how the ALAVs worked—an interaction style that also emerged as a sensitising term. We found instances of *situated social play* through the work that included *verbal, embodied, associative,* and *cooperative play,* as well as an interaction style we named *interactive play* (an emergent sensitising term) (directly engaging and actively playing with the work), *speculation* and *comprehension*. The ALAVs certainly delighted people, and participants appeared charged (perhaps in a state of *lila)* from their play interactions with them and other participants.

Drafting Poems

An informal, shifting community emerged around this work, and individuals and groups of people tended to linger around the glass-topped drafting table. Participants appeared comfortable approaching and interacting with *Drafting Poems*, whose mode of interaction is based on broadly common and everyday learned actions—in this case, using a pen and eraser on a writing surface. Participants also appeared comfortable *handing over* the pen or eraser to the next person, and judging by observation and participant feedback, interaction with *Drafting Poems* was straightforward and its mode of use was unambiguous. The manner in which each participant drew on the glass top, however, produced markedly different results, and consequently most people experimented with how to create different effects. As with the ALAVs, *Drafting Poems* prompted many discussions that revolved around *speculation* on how the installation worked. Participants both espoused and tested theories, trying their own experiments or attempting to emulate the results of another. Participants and observers used *deictic gestures* to point to words, the pen, the eraser and/or movement of words on the display. People were often sensual in their actions, building and/ or erasing phrases with flowing motions. Others were more overtly performative with a larger-than-life-ness to their gestures.

We observed that people actively participated with the work. They would actively engage in *interactive play, embodied play* and/or, *observe* and/or discuss others' activities (*verbal play*). The behaviour was much like that found at a board game, where a limited number of players can be active at any one time (there was only one pen and one eraser), but where many people could be involved with the 'moves'. Unlike players in a board game, these participants could agilely exchange roles and were not confined to set durations or roles of play. *Interactors* also engaged in *associative* and *cooperative play* and people socially interacted through the work (*situated social play)*. Participants also commented on the results themselves, with outbreaks of laughter or exclamations of surprise. Humour or self-deprecation about responses was common, with participants stating for example: "I only got sad words, what does it mean?" or "I can never catch the letters, they move too fast and then they mock me with phrases about speediness" and similar.

Books of Sand

We observed that, as with *Drafting Poems*, participants gathered around the *Books of Sand* installation, exhibiting *verbal, embodied, associative* and *cooperative* play. The interaction here—with the sand and projection—was different to *Drafting Poems,* in that the participants interacted with random phrases, whereas at *Drafting Poems,* their motion could affect which phrases emerged. The interactivity subsequently took on a different quality with *Books of Sand.*

Again, this was a work where participants appeared rapidly to understand what to do with the installation and how to interact with it. As with the ALAVs and *Drafting Poems*, *Books of Sand* relied on simple, everyday manual motions. In this work, a participant simply moves their hand above or in the sand, which causes words to be projected onto their hands. Consideration of and moving around the hands of others sharing the same space seemed to occur naturally.

There is a sensual quality to a work that requires participants to interact by moving their hands around in or above a pile of sand. With this work, the participants' gestures became sensual, more considered, and slower in pace. This was for a variety of reasons. The gestures generally required finer motor actions: to move one's hands in any other way would have disrupted the work in a contained space. Participants needed to coordinate and negotiate around each other's hands (while in motion) to avoid bumping into each other. Moreover, it would have been physically difficult to move fast, and/or with large gestures with hands in the sand within the confines of the glass box. In reading the uncovered words or phrases, the work gained a contemplative quality. As with many works, only a limited number of people could fit around the work and be active in it at any given time (in this case 3 or 4 people, depending on the size of the people and how comfortable they were in being in close proximity with others; this is something that the participants self-managed). Participants and observers used *deictic gestures* to point to words and phrases in the projections, often pointing while reading aloud. Participants appeared to be mesmerised by the work to some degree, although they still entered into dialogue and exclaimed or repeated phrases or words as they appeared on top of their hand.

Participants engaging directly with the work (the *interactors*), took time to read the words and appeared to enjoy the sensuality of the sand and the aesthetic visual presentation of letters projected onto the top of their hands. In addition, conversations with others began easily since, as they had with *Drafting Poems*, the words and phrases, as well as the ways to interact, generated conversation and *speculation.* People gathered in the space around the work and waited their turn, or discussed, while observing others, and *comprehended* the work. People engaged in *verbal* and *embodied play,* they socialised with others through the work (*situated social play*), and they generally participated in *associative* or *cooperative* play with others at the work at the same time. Although this work generated discussion, most participants appeared to be quieter, more reflective, and more sensually engaged when observing and interacting with the work.

Emergent sensitising terms from participant observation	
Situated social play	Participants engage with others through the work. Forms of play that take place ***with*** others and ***through*** the work. Participants may gesture towards the work and/or discuss the work, so social communication is mediated through the work as a proxy. While this category could easily be shortened to *social,* the emphasis of social through the work may be lost by doing so. *Situated social* play can occur by verbal, embodied, associative and/ or cooperative play—even with *lila* and *paidia* play.
Interactive play	*Active interaction mode,* where *interactors,* (the participants) actively engage with the work through the modalities afforded by the work. The *interactors*—are engaged and invested in their interacting (they are beyond 'just looking'). The interactors were often spurred on by verbal play and the interjections of others to try new or different ways of interacting. *Interactive play* can occur through verbal, embodied, associative and/ or cooperative play—even with *lila* and *paidia* play.
Speculative play	Participants actively figure out how something works—both the conceptual and the technological aspects of the work—with testing and debating various theories; often done in collaboration with others/strangers. *Speculative play* can occur through verbal, embodied, associative and/ or cooperative play, even with *lila* and *paidia* play.
Comprehension	A stage or mode where participants attain *getting* the work, (conceptually and/or technically); *speculation* is complete. There were often several stages involved in achieving a general comprehension of the work.
Participants switched easily between, *observation, speculation* and *comprehension* or *interaction* as states of engagement and play	

Table 2: Emergent terms from application of sensitiser guides after observation and analysis of participation

Summary of findings

Across the three works, we observed that participants interacted with the works with varying degrees of embodied interaction. In interacting with *Books of Sand*, participants often used slow, sensual hand gestures, exhibiting fine motor control, particularly when more than one participant was active at a time. Participants interacting with *Drafting Poems* also exhibited fine motor control while experimenting with interacting at a variety of speeds and levels of intensity and using *deictic* gestures to interact with the work and other participants. In interacting with the ALAVs, participants used hand gestures, full body gestures (leaping to catch and pass on the blimp) and/or fine gesture movements for feeding or *batting* the blimp.

Overall, the works inspired conversations and discussions, and resulted in people experimenting, speculating, and freely playing within them. Importantly, the pen, the sand and the balloon/blimps, are familiar-enough and readily understandable interactive objects. That is, we know what to do with them and how to make them work. The gestures required to interact with the artworks replicate everyday manual activities common to most people. Because participants have already learnt what to do with similar tools, and because these tools provide the primary interaction access point into the works, it follows that the works enable ready access to their participants.

From the questionnaires and oral interviews, participants reported that the aesthetics attracted them to the works, and that they chose works as favourites. Additionally, there was a generally positive response to conceptual difficulty; for example, participants commented that "[the] difficulty [of the work was] not necessarily bad" and that "difficulty wasn't the reason to not stay" and continue interaction.

The sensitising guides provided a useful focus for observation, data collection, analysis, evaluation, reporting, and discussion of participant activity, and they provided a common-sense language to discuss the interaction work of free-play.

We can draw four main conclusions here:

(1) Familiar-enough interactive artefacts enabled easy entrance and an overall simplicity of use.

(2) Participants interacted with the works through varying degrees of gesture and/or movements of their full bodies, in an effort to interact with what the works afforded.

(3) Most participants were involved in some form of *situated social play* through the work at the exhibition.

(4) The sensitising terms proved useful to identify, analyse, and discuss detailed modes of interaction (see Table 2).

DISCUSSION: SENSITISING TERMS IDENTIFY ACTIVITY MODES

A number of key sensitising terms were repeatedly identified as useful across all three works. Significantly, these highlighted or pointed to social acts of observing and playing with others around and through the open-ended works. The predominantly used terms comprised a mixture of terms identified in the literature and terms emergent upon application. We compile here the initial commonly used and the emergent terms.

Literature-derived sensitising terms used for all works

1. *Observation*
2. *Verbal play*
3. *Embodied play*
4. *Associative play*
5. *Cooperative play*

A predominant activity mode identified in Table 1 was the *observer* role. However, as with all roles (and as signaled by Bartle [1] and Dow [11]), we found participants switched agilely between identified modes of play and participation. Other initial sensitiser terms that we found occurred across all three installations were *verbal play* (speech with others in the spirit of play) [25, 29], *embodied play* (interaction with others through gesture and body poses) [29], and *associative play*, whereby a participant spontaneously initiates or responds in interaction with others [25]. Additionally, when play became more established and ongoing, *associative play* changed into *cooperative play*, where participants coordinated with others and types of role play emerged [25].

Emergent sensitising terms used for all works

In addition to the initial terms, we also found a number of sensitising terms emerged from our grounded analysis of people's interactions with all three open-ended works. These are listed below and detailed in the individual analyses and Table 2:

1. *Situated social play*
2. *Interactive play*
3. *Speculative play or speculation*
4. *Comprehension*

Further, we often observed deictic gesturing as a mode of interaction, where participants used fine-muscle hand movements in smaller confines, pointing towards displays or interactive objects in the interactive spaces

Sensitising terms focus the analysis and discussion

The most consistently used of the sensitising guides throughout were the terms *embodied play, verbal play*, and *observation.* The emergent common-sense terms that were most frequently adopted across all three art works were the terms *situated social play, interactive play, speculation* or *speculative play* and *comprehension.* The term *bat* was a term used to describe activity specific to interaction with the ALAVs, a situated instance of use, which may be useful for other gesture-based works that use flying objects. Less frequently used in this context (but useful nonetheless, particularly to social and group work) were terms such as *associative* and *cooperative play*. *Lila* arose in one instance, and was often indicated by what appeared to be heightened states of play with all three works. We can say that participants joined into the spirit of play (which infers by its very nature working with whatever is at hand—acts of *bricolage*).

The three interactive art installations are open-ended non-narrative works that engage their participants in some form of free play, explorative play, or *paidia,* with the work and require their participants to play freely with their physicality (the artefact nature). However, there are orchestrated moves that the works set up, a set of prescribed movements or activities that trigger the works. These are not entirely 'open' spaces for interpretation, rather they are scoped to enable certain activities and hopefully allow the player's imaginative response to more abstract meanings. An aim is for participants to play freely with others, initiate actions that allow others to do the same and to bring as many people as possible into the play. In order to generate a successful experience, participants need to be able to interact autonomously and have some kind of motivation to act there. So as to determine this purpose, many participants *observe, interact* and appear to try to *comprehend* the works, to *speculate* some kind of theory that they then test and subsequently continue to adapt from what they find in their testing and/or speculating. Open-ended interactive works require conceptual thinking on the part of the participants. The sensitising terms proved useful in identifying these characteristics and interaction styles. From batting around ALAVs, running fingers in the sand with *Books of Sand* and chasing words in *Drafting Poems,* the works acted in varying degrees to activate their participants in their exploration of the works.

Regardless, these sensitising terms need to be used with a caveat of understanding their own situatedness. That is, the terms need to be applied on a case-by-case basis, and understood in terms of the larger discussion, both from the broad inter-disciplines from which these terms derive [20], and as they emerge and adapt by in-situ use.

The sensitiser terms portrayed (Tables 1 & 2) are those that were most often used and useful for priming observation, analysis and discussion (what to look for when observing people) throughout the study. These common-sense sensitising terms are terms that were either identified in the initial sensitiser guide terms (from play literature) and/or that emerged as being the most useful terms (and the most used) to describe the participant's observable interaction with the open-ended installation works (what it is that people did there). That is, these common-sense terms proved useful to better describe the finer detail and stages of engagement and interaction observed while watching participants at various levels and degrees of engagement with the works. The level of engagement deepens for the participants as we drill down into the table. The first stage is usually *observation* (Table 1) and most, but not all participants, who engage for any length of time go through all of the stages that comprise what it is that people do when interacting with open-ended interactive works.

CONCLUSION

In this paper we have discussed the nature of free-play in open-ended interactive environments in the context of three interactive multimedia installations. The perceived frivolity of the area has restricted study relative to other areas in HCI research. Better understanding here is increasingly important, however, as everyday interactions with technology leave behind more structured workflows and enter the more spontaneous, open-ended, exploratory and informal workaday world of ubiquitous computing.

To help establish further research into this area, we introduced a set of sensitising terms, derived from the literature on play and emergent from grounded application, which can act as a lens on people's interactions in open-ended environments. We have found that these sensitising terms were useful for observing, recording, analysing, reporting, and discussing participation and free-play in these situated open-ended interactive art installation works. The same terms can also be used by the participants who interact with the work; and discuss their interaction with each other, strangers at the work, the artist and/or the researcher. The sensitising terms can then be employed as a common-ground language for use to communicate meaningfully between inter-disciplinary researchers. Our intention is that these terms can be used for further analysis of embodied interaction in open-ended environments, and to build the foundation for a common-sense language that through reflection, application and use, allows the continual addition of new common-sense terms for use as sensitising guides that are applicable in specific and broader contexts.

The work and methods reported here provides a foundation for future work to establish a stronger understanding of the language to describe—and relationship between—free-play, open-ended environments, and design for technologies that support engagement, as ubiquitous technologies become more prevalent in our everyday lives.

ACKNOWLEDGMENTS

We thank the generous input from artists, participants and reviewers and acknowledge support from Australasian CRC for Interaction Design (ACID) and HitLab NZ.

REFERENCES

1. Bartle, R. (1996) *Hearts, clubs, diamonds, spades: Players who suit muds.* Last accessed june 16, 2010. http://www.mud.co.uk/richard/hcds.htm#ret2.
2. Bekker, T., Sturm, J., Wesselink, R., ,Groenendaal, B., and Eggen, B. Interactive play objects and the effects of open-ended play on social interaction and fun, *Proc. ACE 2008*, ACM Press (2008), 389-392.
3. Bekoff, M. and Byers, J.A., A critical reanalysis of the ontogeny of mammalian social and locomotor play: An ethological hornet's nest, in *Behavioral Development: The Bielefeld Interdisciplinary Project* 1981, New York: Cambridge University Press, 296-337.
4. Benford, S., Giannachi, G., Koleva, B., and Rodden, T., From interaction to trajectories: Designing coherent journeys through user experiences, *Proc CHI 2009*, ACM Press (2009), 709-718.
5. Berk, J. and Mitter, N., Autonomous light air vessels (ALAVs), *Proc MULTIMEDIA 2006*, ACM Press (2006), 1029-1030.
6. Blumer, H., What is wrong with social theory. *American Sociological Review, 18*, (1954), 3-10.
7. Caillois, R., *Man, play and games*. London: Thames and Hudson, 1962.
8. Carse, J., P *Finite and infinite games: A vision of life as play and possibility*, Ballantine Books, 1987.
9. Clark, P.M., Griffing, P.S., and Johnson, L.G., Symbolic play and ideational fluency as aspects of the divergent cognitive style in young children. *Early Child Development and Care, 51*, (1989), 77-88.
10. Crabtree, A., Rodden, T., and Benford, S., Moving with the times: IT research and the boundaries of CSCW. *CSCW,14,* 3 (2005), 217-251.
11. Dow, S., *Understanding user engagement in immersive and interactive stories*. Georgia Institute of Technology, 2008, http://hdl.handle.net/1853/26468.
12. Feltham, F., Vetere, F., and Wensveen, S., Designing tangible artefacts for playful interactions and dialogues, *Proc. DPPI '07* ACM Press (2007), 61-75.
13. Höök, K., Sengers, P., and Andersson, G., Sense and sensibility: evaluation and interactive art, *Proc. CHI 2003*, ACM Press (2003), 241-248.
14. Hornecker, E. and Buur, J., Getting a grip on tangible interaction: a framework on physical space and social interaction, *Proc. CHI 2006*, ACM Press (2006), 437-446.
15. Huizinga, J., *Homo ludens: A study of the play-element in culture*. Boston: Beacon Press, 1955.
16. Lee, C., Boundary negotiating artifacts: Unbinding the routine of boundary objects and embracing chaos in collaborative work. *CSCW 16,* 3 (2007), 307-339.
17. Lieberman, J.N., *Playfulness: Its relationship to imagination and creativity*, Academic Press, 1977.
18. Mendelowitz, E., Drafting poems: Inverted potentialities, *Proc. MULTIMEDIA 2006, ACM Press* (2006), 1047-1048.
19. Moran, T.P. and Anderson, R.J., The workaday world as a paradigm for CSCW design, *Proc. CSCW '90*, ACM Press (1990), 381-393.
20. Morrison, A., *Situated play in open-ended interactive art environments*. University of Queensland, 2010.
21. Morrison, A., Mitchell, P., and Viller, S., Evoking gesture in interactive art, *Proc. HCC '08,* ACM Press (2008), 11-18.
22. Nachmanovitch, S., *Free play: Improvisation in life and art*. USA: Tarcher, 1991.
23. Padgett, D.K., Coming of age: Theoretical thinking, social responsibility, and a global perspective in qualitative research, in *The qualitative research experience,* 2004, Wadsworth/Thomson Learning.
24. Papilia, D. and Olds, S., *A child's world.* 1990, New York: McGraw-Hill.
25. Parten, M., Social play among preschool children. *Journal of Abnormal and Social Psychology, 28*, 2 (1933), 136-147.
26. Piaget, J., *Play, dreams and imitation in childhood.* New York: Norton, 1962.
27. Sardon, M., Books of Sand, *Proc. MULTIMEDIA 2006,* ACM Press (2006), 1041-1042.
28. Smilansky, S., *The effects of sociodramatic play on disadvantaged preschool children*. John Wiley, 1968.
29. Smilansky, S. and Shefatya, L., *Facilitating play: A medium for promoting cognitive, socio-emotional and academic development in young children*. Psychosocial & Educational Publications, 1990.
30. Star, S.L. and Griesemer, J., Institutional ecology, 'translations' and boundary objects: Amateurs and professionals in Berkeley's Museum of Vertebrate Zoology, 1907-39. *Social Studies of Science, 19*, 3 (1989), 387-420.
31. Suchman, L., Human-machine reconfigurations: Plans and situated actions. 2nd ed. New York: Cambridge University Press, 2007.
32. Vygotsky, L.S., Play and its role in the mental development of the child, in *Play: Its role in development and evolution*. Basic Books, New York, 1976.

Evaluating the Benefits of 3D Stereo in Modern Video Games

Tad Litwiller
University of Central Florida
Department of EECS
4000 Central Florida Blvd.
Orlando, FL 32816, USA
tad.litwiller@knights.ucf.edu

Joseph J. LaViola Jr.
University of Central Florida
Department of EECS
4000 Central Florida Blvd.
Orlando, FL 32816, USA
jjl@eecs.ucf.edu

ABSTRACT
We present a study that investigates user performance benefits of 3D stereo in modern video games. Based on an analysis of several video games that are best suited for use with commercial 3D stereo drivers and vision systems, we chose five modern titles focusing on racing, first and third person shooter, and sports game genres. For each game, quantitative and qualitative measures were taken to determine if users performed better and learned faster in the experimental group (3D stereo display) than in the control group (2D display). A game experience pre-questionnaire was used to classify participants into beginner, intermediate, and advanced gameplay categories to ensure prior game experience did not bias the experiment. Our results indicate that although participants preferred playing in 3D stereo for the games we tested, it does not provide any significant advantage in overall user performance. In addition, users' learning rates were comparable in the 3D stereo display and 2D display cases.

Author Keywords
3D stereo, video games, evaluation, user performance and experience

ACM Classification Keywords
H.5.m. Information interfaces and presentation (e.g., HCI): Miscellaneous, K.8.0 Personal Computing: General – Games.

General Terms
Experimentation, Measurement, Performance

INTRODUCTION
3D stereo is making a huge push in the entertainment industry. With 13 3D movies released in 2009, 25 released in 2010, and 32 scheduled to come to theaters in 2011, as well as new television stations broadcasting entirely in 3D, movies and television are clearly pushing the technology. As the technology has started to become more available to consumers, game designers and hardware makers have started to take notice. For example, "The U-DECIDE Initiative" was an online survey run by Meant to be Seen, an advocate group for 3D stereo technology, that sought to determine consumers interest in 3D stereo gaming. The survey concluded that the overwhelming majority of users want game developers to natively support 3D stereo in their games [10]. Research has also shown that 3D stereo can be beneficial to user performance in certain, isolated tasks in the context of virtual reality and 3D user interfaces [2,6,14]. However, to the best of our knowledge, there has been little, if any, work that explores whether 3D stereo benefits a user playing video games in terms of performance and learning. Understanding these benefits could provide useful information to help understand and improve upon ways to increase motivation to play games. This motivation is important to game developers in the commercial sector, but, more importantly, it is important in the serious games domain where we can make use of these technologies to potentially improve learning in education-based games, training in military simulations, and obesity reduction and physical activity in exercise-based games.

To explore this question, we present a study investigating whether user performance and learning are enhanced when using 3D stereo over a traditional 2D monitor in modern video games. In our work, we define learning as becoming more proficient at the game and the tasks associated with the game. We analyzed several video games that are best suited for use with commercial 3D stereo drivers and vision systems (iZ3D and NVIDIA 3D Vision) and chose five modern titles including Left 4 Dead, Resident Evil 5, Flatout: Ultimate Carnage, Madden NFL 2008, and Major League Baseball 2K9 as a representative sample of modern video games. In choosing the games, we sought to have them spread across video game genres as well as have games that included tasks that, in our judgment, may benefit from 3D stereo. To evaluate player performance, we collected both quantitative data based on the tasks associated with each game and qualitative data based on post-questionnaires to gage user perception of their performance. We used between subjects design where the control group played the games using a 2D monitor and the

CHI 2011, May 7–12, 2011, Vancouver, BC, Canada.

experimental group played with a 3D stereo display. We also used a modified version of Terlekie and Newcombe's Video Game Experience survey [15] to classify participants into beginner, intermediate, and advanced categories to ensure prior game experience did not bias the experiment.

RELATED WORK

There has been a significant amount of work on the topic of the benefits of 3D stereo, especially in the virtual reality and 3D user interface communities, with mixed results [2,6,14]. Much of the research to date has focused on simple, isolated tasks in virtual environments, and there has been very little research involving more complex tasks and richer graphical environments, such as games. Menendez and Bernard have hypothesized that stereoscopic viewing would benefit a user in a flight simulation environment, but have yet to test the hypothesis [11]. Another study has concluded that binocular viewing in the real world as well as in virtual worlds may benefit the user over monocular viewing. While 3D stereo has been shown to be useful for depth ordering of objects in a virtual world, it may be impossible to measure how accurate a user's perception of 3D stereo is [13]. Research has also been conducted that looks into how shadows and stereo enhance user's perception of 3D. Positioning and resizing tasks were given to users with shadows on and off and with stereo and mono viewing. The researchers concluded that stereo viewing is more effective than shadows based on accuracy and speed with which users completed the tasks [6]. Stereo has also been found to help users playing a game in which they eliminate targets by moving objects into defined zones. The game was still a simple task of moving a cursor to a target in the virtual world that contains objects that needed to be maneuvered. To simplify the task only one object was present during the experiment [3]. This is still quite different from playing a modern video game, in which there is a lot more happening on screen and a lot more visual stimulus.

Other work has looked at benefits of 3D stereo and sought to separate the interaction technique from the stereo. In these studies, the interaction technique was found to be significant while stereo was not [9]. However, this finding has been somewhat contradicted by Teather and Stuerzlinger, who presented different positioning techniques that were dependent on the input devices used. They found that stereo was beneficial for accuracy in the tasks they presented to users, but not speed [14].

Specific work on comparing 3D stereo to 2D displays has also been done. However, very simple tasks were used to measure performance and other factors such as head tracking were included in the research. One of the more common display configurations used for this type of research is called Fish Tank Virtual Reality, where there is a desktop system with a stereoscopic display and head-tracking [2]. Arthur, Booth, and Ware used this setup to conduct experiments that compared viewing conditions of stereo display versus non-stereo display with head-tracking. In one such study, users thought that head-tracking created more compelling 3D perception than stereo viewing alone. Although head-tracking had better results in both user perception and performance in a tree tracing task, 3D stereo did show significant benefits over normal viewing [2]. While these types of studies have concluded that head-tracking produced better results than 3D stereo alone, we wanted to focus this study specifically on 3D stereo because it is more readily available to consumers.

Research has also been conducted on how well users perform with different types of 3D displays. Grossman and Balakrishnan looked at volumetric displays and concluded that for the simple tasks that were presented to users, 3D stereo always helped over simple perspective and although volumetric displays were more helpful for simple scenes, there was no benefit over normal 3D displays in more complex scenes [4]. Fully immersive virtual environments have also been shown to be more effective than stereoscopic desktop environments for certain tasks. In comparing a real world scenario of oil well path editing, researchers found that a fully immersive environment, such as a CAVE, was more effective than a stereoscopic desktop environment [5]. A similar study showed results that also suggested the immersive environment provided benefits to the user in analyzing data; however, it also concluded that users were more comfortable using the interaction techniques on the desktop environment [1]. Work has also been done that concluded users could identify targets better in an immersive 3D virtual world than with a desktop system [12]. Stereo has been shown to increase the size and amount of abstract data that can be viewed and understood, and the benefits were only increased with a higher resolution stereoscopic display [17]. We used a desktop setup for viewing the games in stereo on a 3D TV with a 1080p resolution. While some of the research may suggest that 3D stereo on different display types may be more effective, the desktop setup of a 3D TV with a computer and 3D glasses is more readily available for home use.

Many questions about the effectiveness of 3D stereo exist as the technology is far from perfect. It has been shown that depth perception tends to be underestimated by users in virtual environments [8], and also that for some selection tasks in 3D space, a one-eyed 2D cursor can be more beneficial than a 3D cursor [16]. While it may show some benefits depending on the task presented, it has also been shown to increase some negative symptoms as well. Stereoscopic viewing can have negative consequences and symptoms, such as additional eyestrain and simulator sickness. We wanted to see whether this trend of increased symptoms while viewing in 3D would also hold true while playing a game in stereo on a 3D TV, and we wished to see whether any of the benefits of 3D stereo that have been shown in virtual reality environment for simple tasks will translate to improved performance for users playing modern video games.

SELECTING THE GAMES

In order to look into possible benefits that 3D stereo provides to modern video games, we wanted to get a good sample of different game genres. We also wanted to make sure the games we used were highly rated for their use of 3D stereo. The technology we had available were iZ3D monitors and the NVIDIA 3D Vision kit, which are both products currently on the market. Both of these technologies provided a list of modern games that were compatible with the technology. We looked through both lists and picked 21 games that were rated highly for their use of 3D Stereo by both NVIDIA and iZ3D. We then played through sections of the 21 games in 3D stereo, taking notes about how they looked, any glitches that occurred, and any tasks we thought may benefit from 3D stereo. From our analysis, we decided to first remove the real-time strategy games as the 3D was not very convincing and it did not seem like any advantage could be gained in that genre. Based on our analysis, we felt a first person shooter, a third person shooter, a racing game, and sports games would be the most appropriate genres to explore. Of the 21 games that we tested, we found Left 4 Dead, Resident Evil 5, Flatout: Ultimate Carnage, MLB 2K9, and Madden NFL '08 performed the best in terms of visual quality and had tasks that we felt could benefit from 3D stereo.

Left 4 Dead is a first person shooter by Valve. Although we did not expect to see any difference in the shooting aspect of the game due to cross hairs being displayed on screen, which make aiming easier by just placing the cross hairs over the target, we wanted to explore the genre to see if 3D stereo may improve performance by helping with navigating the world or providing better sense of which enemies are closer and thus pose a more imminent threat.

Resident Evil 5 is a third person shooter by Capcom. It provided a mode in which the user is required to shoot with a bow and arrow that did not provide any cross hairs on the screen. This made targeting an enemy more difficult as the user is required to aim the arrow in 3D space. Third person perspective also adds to the aiming difficulty as the aiming is no longer only in the center of the screen as it is with first person shooters. We hypothesized that the added depth cue provided by 3D stereo may help the user with accuracy.

Flatout: Ultimate Carnage is a racing game by Empire Interactive. Although we did not expect to see any performance difference in racing games, we wanted to explore the possibility that the added depth perception of 3D stereo could aid maneuvering the course or help in judging corners.

MLB 2K9 is a major league baseball game by 2K Sports. In the baseball game we wanted to see if 3D stereo would help the user better judge where the ball was located in space as it came from the pitcher toward the batter in order to swing the bat at the appropriate time. We thought that the added depth perception could help users' timings when hitting the ball.

Madden NFL '08 is a football game by EA Sports. There was a punting mini-game in Madden that required the user to aim an arrow in 3D space to kick the ball in a desired direction toward a target. Because the aiming of the arrow was free in 3D space, we thought that 3D stereo may boost the user's performance in successfully hitting the targets.

USER STUDY

To explore whether there are any performance benefits to using 3D stereo with the video games we selected (discussed in the previous section), we conducted a usability evaluation where participants played each game using a 2D display (control group) or with a 3D stereo display (experimental group). We examined both quantitative metrics based on each game's goals and tasks and qualitative metrics based on whether participants preferred playing the games in 3D and whether they perceived any benefits. Based on our analysis of the games, we hypothesized that users would prefer playing in 3D stereo because it would provide a more engaging experience. However, there would not be any significant performance improvements in overall performance or in learning since the games were not specifically designed with 3D stereo in mind.

Participants and Equipment

Forty participants (30 males and 10 females ranging in age from 18 to 36 with a mean age of 23.15) were recruited from the University of Central Florida. We ranked the participants based on a modified version of Terlekie and Newcombe's Video Game Experience survey [15] that was used as a pre-questionnaire in which they answered questions about their previous gaming experience. Of the 40 participants, 9 were ranked as beginners, 23 as intermediate, and 8 as advanced. The experiment duration ranged from forty-five minutes to an hour and a half depending on how long the participants took to complete the tasks presented to them in the games and how much time was spent on the questionnaires. All participants were paid 10 dollars for their time.

The equipment used for the study consisted of a quad-core desktop PC with an NVIDIA GTX 260 graphics card and a Samsung 50 inch DLP 3D HDTV display, using the NVIDIA 3D Vision kit for the3D stereo gaming as can be seen in Figure 1. We decided to use the NVIDIA 3D setup over the iZ3D monitors because early pilot testing showed the NVIDIA solution had higher stereo quality with limited ghosting. In addition, the iZ3D monitors had variables that would need to be setup differently for each game and each user, where as the NVIDIA solution worked seamlessly with the games. The Xbox 360 Controller for Windows was used as the input device for the games.

Figure 1: *The experimental setup.*

Experimental Task

The participants were tasked with playing through sections of the five games that we selected. For each game, they were presented with a task specific to that game and a goal for completing each task.

Left 4 Dead. Participants had to finish the first section of "The Apartments" level. The goal was to finish the level as fast as possible. They were given three attempts with a goal of making it through the level faster each time. In the mode used for this experiment, there were three AI controlled teammates moving through the level with the participant.

Resident Evil 5. The task participants were given for Resident Evil 5 was to eliminate as many zombies as possible. The participants were instructed that the only weapon they could use was the bow-and-arrow. The moderator kept track of the time and the participants were given six minutes to play the game. They were told that deaths did not count against them.

Flatout: Ultimate Carnage. Participants were given a goal of finishing a lap in one minute and fifteen seconds. We determined that this was a challenging, but attainable goal through our time playing the game. They were given five attempts to reach the goal.

Madden NFL '08. Participants took part in a punting mini game. They were given five attempts to reach the goal of a gold medal, a score of 900 points. There were three zones in the targets they were aiming for: a 50 point zone, a 100 point zone, and a 200 point bull's eye. Each attempt consisted of six kicks to reach the desired point total.

MLB 2K9. Participants' tasks in this game were to hit 20 home runs in as few swings as possible during a home run derby. Participants controlled two hitters, both a right and left-handed batter that alternated every three outs. The pitcher would throw the ball and the participant would have to time the swing correctly to hit a home run.

Design and Procedure

Since the focus of our study was on user performance and the ability to learn to play the games dependent on whether participants were using the 2D display or 3D stereo, we chose a between subjects design. The independent variable was display mode (2D display or 3D stereo display) and the dependent variables were the various scoring metrics used in each game. A between subjects design was chosen over a within-subjects design in order to eliminate the bias and learning effects that would have followed from the subjects being exposed to the games in both 2D display and 3D stereo conditions. With a within subject design, the participants would have already been exposed to the games in a prior condition and we would not have been able to isolate their performance specifically for the 2D display and 3D stereo modes. We rejected this approach given it would have doubled the length of the study without providing much additional benefit in terms of quantitative data collection, making between subjects the better design choice. We did want to get some additional information about the use of 3D stereo in video games for those who played the games in the 2D display condition. Thus, we chose to have those participants who were in the 2D display condition, pick one game to try in 3D stereo to gather their reactions.

In order to group the participants into experience levels based on the pre-questionnaire data, we scored the questionnaire by assigning points to each question. Particular questions were given more points based on how the results fit within the context of our experimental setup. For example, participants who were familiar with the Xbox 360 controller or whose favorite games were first and third person shooters were considered to have a higher experience level. We then used the raw scores from adding up the points for each question to group the participants into the appropriate category. Both the quantitative and qualitative data was explored collectively as well as according to the three groupings.

Summary of Metrics	
Left 4 Dead	• Time for each run • Number of kills for each run • Kills per second
Resident Evil 5	• Accuracy • Number of Player deaths
Flatout	• Time for each attempt • Number of crashes • If a shortcut was attempted
MLB 2K9	• Number of swings taken to reach 20 HRs • Number of swings missing the ball
Madden '08	• Score for each attempt • Number of kicks hitting each target zone • Number of kicks missing target

Table 1: *Summary of Metrics.*

Quantitative Metrics

For each game, we tracked quantitative data that we felt was a good indication of how well the user performed. A summary of the quantitative metrics can be viewed in table 1.

Left 4 Dead. We collected times for each attempt at the level as well as the number of kills for each run. The number of kills could differ from run to run because there were three AI controlled friends helping the user in the game by shooting enemies, and the number of enemies spawned would change based on how long it took to get through certain areas of the level. We also looked at the ratio of kills per second.

Resident Evil 5. We tracked each shot the participant fired in Resident Evil 5, so we had the ability to look at the overall accuracy as well as the accuracy over the course of the participant's time playing the game. We also decided to break up the number of shots into thirds so we could track the participant's accuracy at the beginning, middle, and end of the gaming session. The number of deaths was also tracked.

Flatout: Ultimate Carnage. The time for each lap attempted was recorded along with the number of crashes, and whether or not a short-cut (i.e., a specific corner in the lap) was attempted.

MLB 2K9. The quantitative data we were tracking for MLB 2k9 was the total number of swings needed to reach 20 home runs. Each swing was tracked, so we also looked at the number of misses, both early and late.

Madden NFL '08. We recorded the score for each attempt, as well of the number of kicks that hit each section of the target and the number of kicks that missed the target completely.

Postgame Questions	
Q1	To what extent did the game hold your attention?
Q2	How much effort did you put into playing the game?
Q3	Did you feel you were trying your best?
Q4	To what extent did you lose track of time?
Q5	Did you feel the urge to see what was happening around you?
Q6	To what extent did you find the game challenging?
Q7	How well do you think you performed in the game?
Q8	To what extent did you feel emotionally attached to the game?
Q9	To what extent did you enjoy the graphics and the imagery?
Q10	How much would you say you enjoyed playing the game?
Q11	Were you disappointed when the game was over?
Q12	Would you like to play the game again?

Table 2: *Postgame Questionnaire. Participants answered these questions on a 7 point Likert scale after playing each game.*

Qualitative Metrics

Our initial approach for the qualitative aspects of the study was to provide each participant with a post-questionnaire after they played all 5 games. From early pilot studies, we determined that we should reduce the number of qualitative questions and give the survey after each game rather than one larger questionnaire at the end of playing all the games. After playing each game, participants filled out a short, 12 question survey that was based on an immersion questionnaire from Jennet et al. [10] (see Table 2) aimed at gathering their ideas on how involved or immersed in the game they became. The questions were the same for each game and responses were measured on a 7 point Likert scale (1 = most negative response, 7 = most positive response). An additional 11 question survey was also given to participants in order to gather their opinions on how playing the games in 3D stereo affected their experience (see Table 3). These questions included whether they preferred to play the games in 3D stereo and whether 3D stereo helped or hurt their performance when playing the games.

Procedure

The experiment began with the participant seated in front of the computer and the moderator seated to their side. Participants were given a standard consent form that explained the study and what they would be asked to do. They were then given a pre-questionnaire that focused on their gaming experience. Participants were then presented with the games, in random order. Half the participants played the games in 2D display mode (control group) and half played in 3D stereo (experimental group). The moderator would present the game and give instructions to the participant as to what they needed to accomplish in the game and what their goals were. After each game, the participant filled out a post-questionnaire with questions about their experiences with the game. If the participants played the five games in the 2D display group, they then selected one game to play in 3D stereo. Thus, all participants were given a final post-questionnaire about their experiences with the 3D stereo display.

3D Stereo Questions	
Q1	3D stereo improved the overall experience of the game.
Q2	I would choose to play in 3D stereo over normal viewing.
Q3	I felt that stereo enhanced the sense of engagement I felt.
Q4	3D stereo is a necessity for my future game experiences.
Q5	What would you be willing to spend on a 3D stereo device?
Q6	Did 3D stereo help you perform better in the games?
Q7	Which games did it help you in?
Q8	How did it help you in those games?
Q9	Did 3D stereo hurt your performance in the games?
Q10	Which games did it hurt your performance in?
Q11	How did it hurt you in those games?

Table 3: *3D Stereo Questionnaire. Participants responded to statements 1-4 on a 7 point Likert scale. Questions 5-11 were multiple choice and open ended questions to gauge the users' perceptions of the effects of 3D stereo.*

RESULTS AND ANALYSIS

To analyze the performance data, we used independent sample t-tests to look for significance between groups. We also wanted to see whether there was learning taking place in the form of gameplay improvement. We looked at the improvement in the performance measures for each game from the first user run to their last run using a repeated measures ANOVA. Finally we wanted to look at the participant's perception of their performance through the post questionnaires. To analyze this Likert scale data, we used the Wilcoxon Signed Rank test. For all of our statistical measures, we used $\alpha=0.05$.

Left 4 Dead

There was a significant difference in average time ($t_{37} = -2.626$, $p < 0.05$) and average kills per second ($t_{37} = 2.334$, $p < 0.05$). The 2D display group was actually faster in this game with a mean completion time of 214.36 seconds ($\sigma=116.73$), compared to 329.14 seconds ($\sigma=152.74$) for the 3D stereo group. In addition, participants had significantly

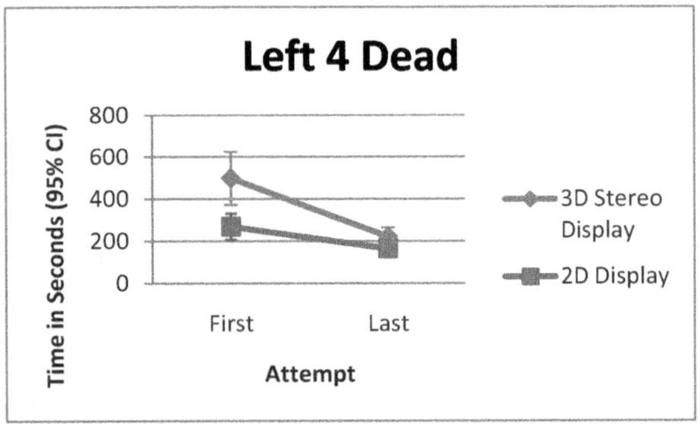

Figure 2: *Left 4 Dead Improvement. This graph shows the improvement in times from the first to the last run.*

more kills per second for the 2D display group as well with a mean of 0.204 ($\sigma=0.063$) kills/sec to the 3D stereo display group's mean of 0.155 ($\sigma=0.066$). There was no statistical difference in the average number of kills ($t_{37} = -0.981$, $p = 0.333$). After looking at the overall average of the three runs, we decided to look at the third and final run in an attempt to remove some of the experience factor, as by this time everyone would have knowledge of the level and the controls. We thought that this might be a good judgment of raw performance for the two groups. As we had originally expected for Left 4 Dead performance, there was no statistically significant difference in the completion times ($t_{37} = -1.89$, $p = 0.067$) or number of kills ($t_{37} = -0.268$, $p = 0.79$) for the last attempt.

When isolating the three gamer ranks, the beginner group and the advanced group showed no differences for any of the statistics. However, the 2D display group performed significantly better for participants in the intermediate rank for worst time ($t_{10.48} = -2.875$, $p < 0.05$), best time ($t_{21} = -2.432$, $p < 0.05$), average time ($t_{11.37} = -3.021$, $p < 0.05$), average kills per second ($t_{21} = 2.351$, $p < 0.05$) and the third attempt's kills per second ($t_{21} = 2.29$, $p < 0.05$).[1]

Because 22 out of the 40 participants had played Left 4 Dead previously, we separated the participants based on whether or not they had played the game. This resulted in no significant differences for any of the metrics. Since this result is what we originally expected, previous game experience may have affected the overall performance statistics.

Participants significantly improved their times between the 3 runs for both 2D display ($F_{2,17} = 16.64$, $p < 0.05$) and 3D stereo display groups ($F_{2,18} = 14.00$, $p < 0.05$). This shows that there was some learning taking place between runs for both groups. The 3D stereo display group improved their time from 499.54 ($\sigma=281.42$) seconds to 220.82 ($\sigma=97.90$) seconds while the 2D display group improved their run. time from 269.09 ($\sigma=141.38$) to 164.64 ($\sigma=87.08$) seconds. This translates to a 55.8% improvement for the 3D stereo display group compared to a 38.8% improvement for the 2D display group (see Figure 2).

When broken down based on the gamer ranks, the beginning 3D stereo display ($F_{2,3} = 8.448$, $p = 0.059$), beginning 2D display ($F_{2,1} = 17.59$, $p = 0.166$), the advanced 3D stereo display ($F_{2,3} = 4.452$, $p = 0.127$), and the advanced 2D display ($F_{2,1} = 0.586$, $p = 0.679$) participants showed no significance in improving their times, while the intermediate 3D stereo display ($F_{2,8} = 10.88$, $p < 0.05$) and 2D display ($F_{2,11} = 13.99$, $p < 0.05$) groups appeared to show the same results as the overall learning. As with the overall learning rates, the intermediate 3D stereo display group appeared to outpace the intermediate 2D display group by about the same amount with a 57.8% improvement in time compared to the 2D display group's 38.7% improvement.

Participants in the 3D stereo display group who had not played the game previously saw a significant improvement in their times ($F_{2,11} = 13.72$, $p < 0.05$) from 610.16 ($\sigma=255.44$) seconds to 257.16 ($\sigma=91.83$) seconds ($\sigma=91.83$), a 57.8% improvement. The 2D display group who had not played the game previously showed no statistically significant improvement between runs ($F_{2,16} = 7.92$, $p = 0.112$). For participants who had previously played the game, both the 3D stereo display group ($F_{1.04,6.26} = 6.10$, $p < 0.05$) and the 2D display group significantly improved their times ($F_{2,13} = 12.18$, $p < 0.05$).[2] The 3D stereo display group saw a 47.86% improvement with their average time improving from 294.07 ($\sigma=211.02$) to 153.33

[1] For worst time and average time, Levene's test for equality of means was significant so a correction was used.

[2] The 3D stereo display group's test violated the sphericity assumption, therefore, we applied a Greenhouse-Geisser correction.

seconds while the 2D display group improved from 258.25 (σ=136.12) to 148.16 seconds (σ=60.94), a jump of 42.6%.

There were not many statistically significant differences in the qualitative data. Overall, the game was found to be significantly more challenging ($Z = -2.394$, $p < 0.05$) for the 3D stereo display group ($\bar{x}$=4.90, σ=1.25) than the 2D display group ($\bar{x}$=4.05, σ=0.89). This would be in line with the overall average time being worse for the 3D stereo display group. For those participants that had played the game before, the game significantly held the attention more ($Z = -1.981$, $p < 0.05$) for the 3D stereo display group ($\bar{x}$=6.86, σ=0.38) than the 2D display group ($\bar{x}$=6.2, σ=0.86). The same trend was seen for participants in the advanced rank where the game significantly held the attention more ($Z = -2.049$, $p < 0.05$) for the 3D stereo display group ($\bar{x}$=6.8, σ=0.45) than the 2D display group ($\bar{x}$=6.0, σ=0.00).

Resident Evil 5

Contrary to what we expected to see in Resident Evil 5, there was very little difference between the groups. There was no overall difference in the number of player deaths ($t_{38} = -0.62$, $p = 0.539$) or accuracy ($t_{38} = 0.024$, $p = 0.981$). This also held for the beginner player deaths ($t_7 = -0.743$, $p = 0.482$) and accuracy ($t_7 = -0.779$, $p = 0.461$) as well as the intermediate group's player deaths ($t_{21} = 0.206$, $p = 0.839$) and accuracy ($t_{21} = -0.617$, $p = 0.544$). While there was also no difference ($t_6 = -1.067$, $p = 0.327$) for the advanced group in player deaths, the group did show a difference ($t_6 = 2.794$, $p < 0.05$) in accuracy, but it was the opposite of the difference we thought we may see. The 2D display group displayed a higher accuracy of 71.8% compared to that of the stereo 3D group at 59.2%.

In order to test for improvement in accuracy throughout the participant's time playing the game, we divided each user's attempted shots into the first, second, and third group of shots, with each grouping of shots being equal in number for the participant. We then looked at the accuracy change from the first third to the second third to the last third. There were no significant differences found for either the 2D display ($F_{2,18} = 0.898$, $p = 0.425$) or the 3D display group ($F_{2,18} = 0.651$, $p = 0.533$) in the changes of the user's accuracy over the course of their time playing the game. This trend held for each gamer rank, both 2D display and 3D stereo display groups.

The only difference found for the qualitative data for Resident Evil 5 was in the group that had not played the game before. In this group, there was a difference ($Z = -2.104$, $p < 0.05$) for the question about how much they enjoyed playing the game. The 2D display group actually rated that they enjoyed playing the game more ($\bar{x}$=5.33, σ=1.54) than the 3D stereo display group ($\bar{x}$=4.41, σ=1.32).

Flatout: Ultimate Carnage

As we expected from this genre, in all of the quantitative data that we tracked for Flatout, which included average time, average time in runs without a crash, number of crashes, and best time, there were no differences found between the 3D stereo display and 2D display groups overall or at any experience level.

From looking at the difference in times from the first attempt through the fifth attempt, there did appear to be significant learning taking place in both the 2D display ($F_{2.85,51.26} = 12.35$, $p < 0.05$) and 3D stereo display groups ($F_{1.72,29.29} = 5.85$, $p < 0.05$).[3] As with Left 4 Dead, the rate of learning did look to be slightly higher in the stereo group who improved their time from 90.47 (σ=12.54) seconds to 81.49 (σ=5.51) seconds, compared to an improvement from 88.71 (σ=5.44) to 82.36 (σ=4.44) seconds for the 2D display group. The 3D stereo display group showed more improvement with a 9.93% gain compared to a 7.16% gain for the 2D display group (see Figure 3). When broken down by game ranks, the only significance shown in learning was for the intermediate 2D display group ($F_{4,9} = 20.55$, $p < 0.05$) who improved their time by 6.20%.

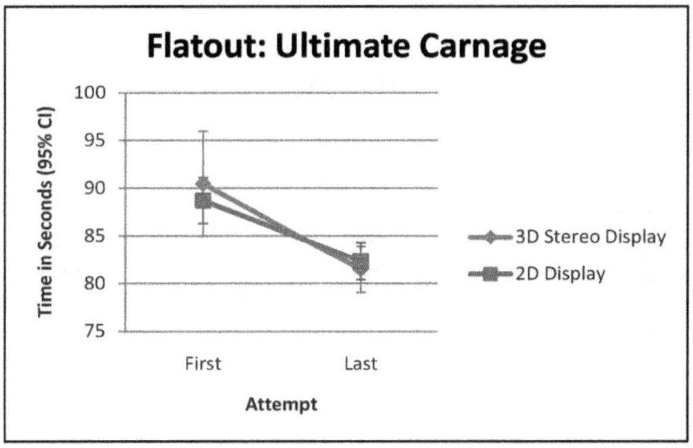

Figure 3: *Flatout: Ultimate Carnage Improvement.*

Like the previous games, there was not much difference in the answers received for the qualitative questions. The only differences came when divided into the 3 game ranks. For the intermediate rank, the 3D display group put significantly more effort ($Z = -2.35$, $p < 0.05$) into the game ($\bar{x}$=6.5, σ=0.73) than the 2D display group ($\bar{x}$=5.77, σ=0.73). In addition, the 3D display group gave significantly higher ratings ($Z = -2.344$, $p < 0.05$) for trying their best ($\bar{x}$=6.6, σ=0.70) than the 2D display group ($\bar{x}$=5.85, σ=0.80).

MLB 2k9

As we expected due to the task being more of a timing task than a spatial 3D task, there was no significant difference in the performance data for missing early ($t_{38} = 0.214$, $p =$

[3] For these tests, the sphericity assumption was violated, therefore, we applied a Greenhouse-Geisser correction.

0.832), missing late (t_{38} = -0.908, p = 0.370), outs (t_{38} = -0.141, p = 0.889), and total number of swings (t_{38} = -0.593, p = 0.556). This trend held across the gamer ranks as well.

Similar to what we did for Resident Evil 5, we broke the swings into thirds to evaluate the presence of any learning that may have been happening. Overall there did not appear to be any improvement as far as the number of home runs from the first third of the swings to the last third for either the 2D display ($F_{2,18}$ = 1.878, p = 0.182) or 3D stereo display groups ($F_{2,18}$ = 1.277, p = 0.303). There was significant improvement for both groups, 2D display ($F_{2,18}$ = 8.078, $p < 0.05$) and 3D stereo display ($F_{2,18}$ = 7.811, $p < 0.05$), when we looked at the number of swing-and-misses in each third. This time, the non-stereo group had a slight advantage in the improvement as they went from 3.6 to 2.0 misses while the 3D stereo group dropped to 3.0 misses from 4.2. This translated to a 44.4% improvement for the 2D display group compared with a 28.6% improvement for the 3D stereo display group (see Figure 4). When broken down by gamer ranks, however, the intermediate stereo 3D participants were the only group that exhibited this learning ($F_{2,8}$ = 5.954, $p < 0.05$) on the number of misses decreasing throughout their swings with a 26.3% improvement.

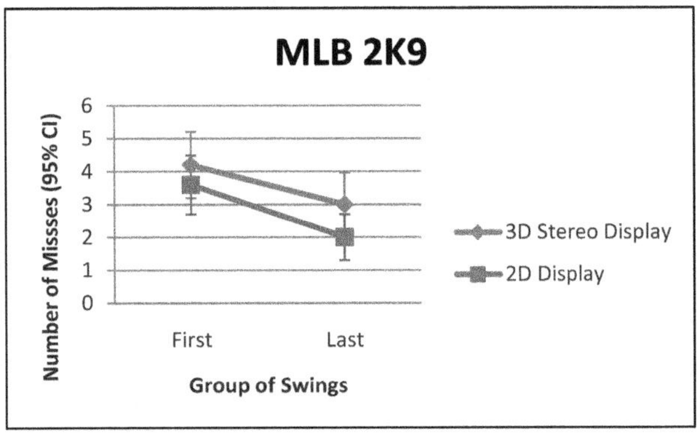

Figure 4: *MLB 2K9 Improvement.*

In line with what we have seen in other games, there was not much difference in the user's responses to the qualitative questions. The only significant difference (Z = -0.488, $p < 0.05$) was seen for the intermediate rank, where the 3D stereo display group was less likely to be distracted by what was happening around them ($\bar{x}$ =1.70, σ=0.67) than the 2D display group ($\bar{x}$ =2.85, σ=1.34).

Madden NFL '08

Going against what we expected to see from the task in Madden, there was no difference between the groups in number of kicks that missed the target (t_{38} = 0.64, p = 0.526), the number of 200 point target hits (t_{38} = -0.534, p = 0.597), 100 point target hits (t_{38} = -0.337, p = 0.738), 50 point target hits (t_{38} = 0.525, p = 0.603), best score (t_{38} = -0.858, p = 0.396), worst score (t_{38} = -0.135, p = 0.893), or average score (t_{38} = -0.62, p = 0.539). This held across the gamer ranks when broken down, there was no difference.

Overall, there did appear to be some learning happening when we looked at the difference in the user's score from the first try to the fifth and final try for both the 2D display ($F_{4,13}$ = 4.604, $p < 0.05$) and 3D stereo display groups ($F_{4,12}$ = 3.495, $p < 0.05$). As with Left 4 Dead and Flatout, the 3D stereo group demonstrated a more drastic change in this game as their scores grew to 406.25 (σ=297.7) from 171.87 (σ=146.02), a 136.4% improvement, while the 2D display group demonstrated a 103.2% improvement, increasing their score from 185.29 (σ=189.37) to 376.47 (σ=222.28) (see Figure 5). The only group that demonstrated significant improvement when isolated was the intermediate non-stereo group ($F_{4,8}$ = 4.53, $p < 0.05$). They made a 170% improvement as the increased their score from 170.83 (σ=151.44) points to 470.83 (σ=187.64).

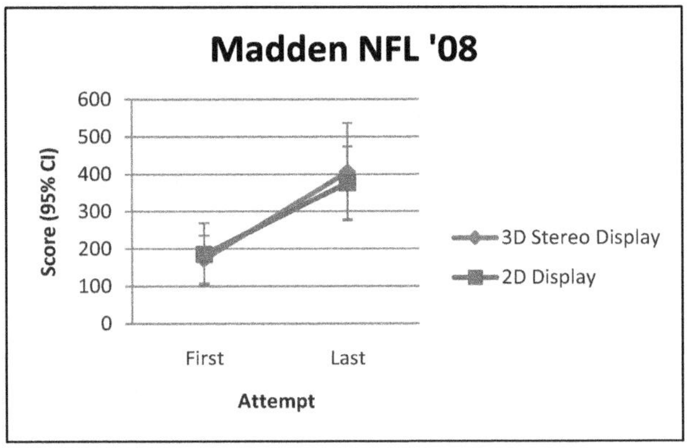

Figure 5: *Madden NFL Improvement.*

Madden NFL '08 actually did show some differences in the qualitative section. Overall, the 3D stereo display group gave significantly higher ratings (Z = -2.279, $p < 0.05$) for trying their best ($\bar{x}$ =6.05, σ=1.15) than the 2D display group ($\bar{x}$ =5.2, σ=1.20). The 3D stereo display group was also significantly more likely (Z = -2.337, $p < 0.05$) to want to play the game again ($\bar{x}$ =4.1, σ=1.41) than the 2D display group ($\bar{x}$ =2.95, σ=1.73). There were no differences for beginning users, but there were differences on 7 questions for intermediate users. The 3D stereo users had a more favorable view of the game (Z = -2.37, $p < 0.05$) in responding that the game held their attention more ($\bar{x}$ =5.3, σ=1.7) than the 2D display group ($\bar{x}$ =3.9, σ=1.38), they were more likely (Z = -2.337, $p < 0.05$) to lose track of time ($\bar{x}$ =4.6, σ=0.84) than the 2D display group ($\bar{x}$ =3.2, σ=1.63), enjoyed the graphics (Z = -2.5, $p < 0.05$) more ($\bar{x}$ =4.6, σ=1.07) than the 2D display group ($\bar{x}$ =3.2, σ=1.59), and were more likely (Z = -2.04, $p < 0.05$) to want to play the game again ($\bar{x}$ =4.5, σ=1.51) than the 2D display group ($\bar{x}$ =2.4, σ=1.56). For advanced users, there was a difference (Z = -2.037, $p < 0.05$) for 1 question in which the 3D stereo display group responded that they enjoyed the graphics and imagery more ($\bar{x}$ =4.4, σ=0.89) than the 2D display group ($\bar{x}$ =2.66, σ=0.58).

Stereoscopic 3D Questions

Three people from the 2D display group who played the five games in non-stereo then played one game in 3D stereo thought that the stereo provided them an advantage. Of the 20 participants in the 2D display group, four chose to play Resident Evil 5. Of those four people, two thought that the stereo 3D helped them. The other person who thought that stereo helped was one of the five people who chose to play Flatout: Ultimate Carnage. Of those same people who played in non-stereo, seven thought the technology hurt their performance when they got the chance to replay a game in stereo. Three of the seven participants who thought the technology hurt them were playing Left 4 Dead and another three of the participants were playing Flatout. The remaining participant who thought 3D stereo hindered their performance was playing Resident Evil 5.

Of the participants from the 3D stereo display group that played all the games in stereo, 10 of them thought that it gave them an advantage in at least one of the games, while seven of them thought that it hurt them in at least one of the games. In this group, nine participants thought the technology helped them in Left 4 Dead, eight thought so in Resident Evil 5, five felt it benefited their performance in Flatout, and another 5fivefelt the same in MLB 2K9. In the same group, three felt it hurt them in Left 4 Dead, three more participants felt it hurt their performance in Resident Evil 5, and another participant thought it hindered them in MLB 2K9. No participants from the 3D stereo display group thought that 3D hurt their performance in Flatout, and no participants thought that it helped or hurt them in Madden NFL '08.

Despite the fact that 3D stereo did not seem to impact performance and had very little impact on how the participants rated their experience with the games, the participants still preferred to play in 3D stereo. As part of the questionnaire relating to the stereoscopic aspect of the study, participants responded to four statements on a 7 point Likert scale (1 = Strongly Disagree, 7 = Strongly Agree). Participants agreed that 3D stereo improved their experience ($\bar{x}$ =5.13, σ=1.40), they would choose to play video games in 3D stereo over the 2D display ($\bar{x}$ =5.13, σ=1.47), and that it enhanced the sense of engagement they felt ($\bar{x}$ =5.58, σ=1.11). Although preferred, participants responded that it was not a necessity ($\bar{x}$ =3.85, σ=1.51).

DISCUSSION AND FUTURE WORK

Although there seemed to be a few tasks in these games in which participants could gain an advantage from added depth perception (e.g., tasks like hitting a baseball and aiming an arrow in 3D space), the quantitative data showed that 3D stereo did not provide any significant performance benefits to the user. One reason is that current video games are adapted to work with 3D stereo, but not built to take advantage of 3D stereo in terms of game mechanics and user interface. Additionally, with almost every game on the list of the best games in 3D stereo, there were settings that needed to be adjusted to maximize the 3D aspect or reduce artifacts that it would create. Most of the games needed shadows to be turned off as they would not be rendered correctly with 3D stereo enabled. Work has shown have that while not as beneficial as stereo, other depth cues such as shadows can increase the benefits for some 3D tasks [6]. Even with the settings tuned the way they were requested, some games still had noticeable glitches at times. Left 4 Dead would periodically create a flash effect in which the screen would go really bright if a light caught the camera the wrong way, which was hard on the eyes.

Another factor may have been the controls. Studies have shown that the interaction devices can have a significant impact on user performance [9]. This factor was most evident in the beginner group of participants, as it appeared that a lot of times they were struggling much more with manipulating the controls than anything that was being viewed on the screen. In addition, the controller used in our study was a standard Xbox 360 controller. Other controllers that provide 3D spatial input such as the Playstation Move or Microsoft's Kinect device could provide users with control mechanics that are more conducive to performing game tasks in 3D stereo.

One possible reason we did not see the benefits that other research has shown with 3D stereo may be that in video games, the tasks are not as cleanly isolated and evident. There is much more going on in the environment and the scenes are much more complex with a significant amount of animations than most previous research on the topic. Left 4 Dead and Resident Evil 5 are the two notable examples from our study.

We did see some differences start to show up when we looked at the possible learning effects taking place in the games. It was clear that learning occurred in most of the games for users regardless of whether they were viewing in 3D stereo or not. What is interesting in these results is that in three of the games, the learning that occurred was greater for users viewing in 3D. Thus, it is possible that 3D stereo may help users in learning the game environments or tasks in the games. Similar results have been shown by other research in which it was determined that 3D stereo allowed users to grasp larger, more complex scenes with more understanding [17]. In those studies, the benefits were only increased as the resolution of the display increased. We were running the study on a 3D TV in 1080p with 120Hz refresh rate. 3D TVs are starting to come out now with 240 and 480Hz refresh rates, so more benefits may occur as display technology advances allowing for more detail to be shown as well as motion on the screen to be cleaner.

As for the qualitative data, we had thought we would see more of a difference in the responses for the 3D stereo group. We assumed this based on previous work in which user preference was clearly for 3D stereo such as the U-Decide initiative released my Meant to be Seen 3D [10]. Overall, it did not appear that the user's perception of their performance was affected by 3D stereo as there were not very many instances where any of the qualitative data was found to be statistically different between the 2D display and 3D stereo display groups. One reason for the difference might be because of the relatively short time that our users played each game. With such short play times, it may have been difficult for them to become immersed in the game whether or not they were viewing it in stereo.

Research that has studied the benefits of 3D stereo has compared it to normal viewing as well as viewing with head tracking [2]. An important area for future work is to explore how head-tracking with and without 3D stereo affects user performance and learning with modern video games. From our results, we also postulate that if games are designed with 3D spatial tasks in mind (e.g., users must actually move in 3D space), 3D stereo could provide performance benefits, especially if 3D spatial input devices are used. We plan to explore this idea in future studies.

CONCLUSION

We have presented a study exploring whether 3D stereo provides performance benefits to users playing modern video games. Overall, the results showed that 3D stereo did not provide any significant advantage in performance over a 2D display and learning rates were comparable between display modes for the games we tested. Our qualitative data suggests that there was not much difference in perception of the gameplay experience between the 3D stereo display group and the 2D display group. Despite these results, participants indicated that they preferred playing the games in 3D stereo over playing on the 2D display. Our study indicates that the status quo for video games that make use of 3D stereo does not provide any additional user performance benefits. This means that game developers will need to develop new strategies for game interaction and potentially game narrative if they want to have 3D stereo provide any performance benefits to gamers. It remains to be seen if user performance gains can be made with games specifically designed for 3D stereo coupled with 3D spatial interaction.

ACKNOWLEDGEMENTS

This work is supported in part by NSF CAREER award IIS-0845921 and NSF Awards IIS-0856045 and CCF-1012056. We wish to thank the anonymous reviewers for their valuable suggestions.

REFERENCES

1. Arns, L., Cruz-Neira, C., and Cook, D. The Benefits of Statistical Visualization in an Immersive Environment. In *Proceedings of the IEEE Virtual Reality* (1999). VR. IEEE Computer Society, Washington, DC, 88.
2. Arthur, K. W., Booth, K. S., and Ware, C. Evaluating 3D task performance for fish tank virtual worlds. *ACM Trans. Inf. Syst.* 11, 3 (1993), 239-265.
3. Fujimoto, M. and Ishibashi, Y. The effect of stereoscopic viewing of a virtual space on a networked game using haptic media. In *Proceedings of the ACM SIGCHI international Conference on Advances in Computer Entertainment Technology* (2005). ACM, New York, NY, 317-320.
4. Grossman, T. and Balakrishnan, R. An evaluation of depth perception on volumetric displays. In *Proceedings of the Working Conference on Advanced Visual interfaces* (2006). ACM, New York, NY, 193-200.
5. Gruchalla, K. Immersive Well-Path Editing: Investigating the Added Value of Immersion. In *Proceedings of the IEEE Virtual Reality* (2004). VR. IEEE Computer Society, Washington, DC, 157.
6. Hubona, G. S., Wheeler, P. N., Shirah, G. W., and Brandt, M. The relative contributions of stereo, lighting, and background scenes in promoting 3D depth visualization. *ACM Trans. Comput.-Hum. Interact.* 6, 3 (1999), 214-242.
7. Jennett, C., Cox, A. L., Cairns, P., Dhoparee, S., Epps, A., Tijs, T., and Walton, A. Measuring and defining the experience of immersion in games. *Int. J. Hum.-Comput. Stud.* 66, 9 (2008), 641-661.
8. Jones, J. A., Swan, J. E., Singh, G., Kolstad, E., and Ellis, S. R. The effects of virtual reality, augmented reality, and motion parallax on egocentric depth perception. In *Proceedings of Applied Perception in Graphics and Visualization* (2008). ACM, New York, NY, 9-14.
9. McMahan, R. P., Gorton, D., Gresock, J., McConnell, W., and Bowman, D. A. Separating the effects of level of immersion and 3D interaction techniques. In *Proceedings of the ACM Symposium on Virtual Reality Software and Technology* (2006). ACM, New York, NY, 108-111.
10. Meant To Be Seen. The U-Decide Initiative. http://www.mtbs3d.com/findings.shtml, 2010.
11. Menendez, R.G.; Bernard, J.E., "Flight simulation in synthetic environments," *Aerospace and Electronic Systems Magazine, IEEE*, vol.16, no.9, pp.19-23, 2001.
12. Pausch, R., Proffitt, D., and Williams, G. Quantifying immersion in virtual reality. In *Proceedings of the 24th Annual Conference on Computer Graphics and interactive Techniques* (1997). ACM Press/Addison-Wesley Publishing Co., New York, NY, 13-18.
13. Treadgold, M., Novins, K., Wyvill, G., and Niven, B. What Do You Think You're Doing? Measuring Perception in Fish Tank Virtual Reality. In *Proceedings of the international Conference on Computer Graphics* (2001). IEEE Computer Society, Washington, DC, 325.
14. Teather, R. J. and Stuerzlinger, W. Guidelines for 3D positioning techniques. In *Proceedings of the 2007 Conference on Future Play* (2007). ACM, New York, NY, 61-68.
15. Terlecki, M.S. & Newcombe, N.S. How important is the digital divide? The relation of computer and videogame usage to gender differences in mental rotation ability. *Sex Roles (2005)*, 53, 433-441.
16. Ware, C. and Lowther, K. Selection using a one-eyed cursor in a fish tank VR environment. *ACM Trans. Comput.-Hum. Interact.* 4, 4 (1997), 309-322.
17. Ware, C. and Mitchell, P. Reevaluating stereo and motion cues for visualizing graphs in three dimensions. In *Proceedings of Applied Perception in Graphics and Visualization* (2005). ACM, New York, NY, 51-58.

Target Assistance for Subtly Balancing Competitive Play

Scott Bateman[1], Regan L. Mandryk[1], Tadeusz Stach[2], Carl Gutwin[1]

[1]University of Saskatchewan
Saskatoon, Saskatchewan, Canada
<firstname.lastname>@usask.ca

[2]Queen's University
Kingston, Ontario, Canada
tstach@cs.queensu.ca

ABSTRACT

In games where skills such as targeting are critical to winning, it is difficult for players with different skill levels to have a competitive and engaging experience. Although several mechanisms for accommodating different skill levels have been proposed, traditional approaches can be too obvious and can change the nature of the game. For games involving aiming, we propose the use of target assistance techniques (such as area cursors, target gravity, and sticky targets) to accommodate skill imbalances. We compared three techniques in a study, and found that area cursors and target gravity significantly reduced score differential in a shooting-gallery game. Further, less skilled players reported having more fun when the techniques helped them be more competitive, and even after they learned assistance was given, felt that this form of balancing was good for group gameplay. Our results show that target assistance techniques can make target-based games more competitive for shared play.

Author Keywords

Game design, game balance, target assistance, competition.

ACM Classification Keywords

H.5.3 Group and Organization Interfaces: CSCW.

General Terms

Algorithms, Design, Experimentation, Human Factors.

INTRODUCTION

Many kinds of video games, such as shooting or driving games, involve competition between two or more players. In these games, success is based on motor-control skills such as aiming or steering – and for the game to be evenly matched, players' skill levels must be roughly equal. If one player is far more skilled than the other, the game will not be competitive and will be less fun to play. Because many games rely on competition as means to provide fun, finding ways to provide an evenly-matched contest is desirable.

Several approaches have been used to address imbalance between players of different skill levels. Techniques in real-world games include handicaps in golf, extra points given to a player at the start of a score-based game, or explicit disadvantages such as playing with one's wrong hand in tennis. Methods in video games include automatic 'catch-ups' in racing games to bring slower players back into the action, differential capabilities (e.g., restricting a player to weaker weapons), or score-based changes (e.g., "fatboy mods" make successful players easier to shoot).

The fact that skill-accommodation mechanisms have been invented in so many different contexts shows that balancing for differing skill levels is an important concern for game designers. However, there are still problems with traditional mechanisms. First, they are often too obvious to players – it is often clear that one player has been given an advantage to make up for a lack of skill. This can lead to feelings of artificiality [8]; and many players do not want to win a game only because of an advantage. Second, traditional accommodation mechanisms can change gameplay – such as when players have different weapons, or must achieve different objectives; in these cases, two people can end up playing different individual games rather than one shared game. Third, traditional methods are usually static – they are defined and set before the game. If the accommodation is incorrectly calculated (e.g., the weaker player receives too few initial points), the game can remain unbalanced.

Overcoming these problems could improve group play for users with different skill levels. In this paper we present the idea of using *target assistance* to accomplish these goals for games that involve aiming and shooting. Target assistance techniques – such as area cursors [20], gravity [5], or sticky targets [7] – have been shown to improve targeting performance (e.g., [5,7,20,22,33]). Target assistance has been seen in games before – to reduce variance in game controllers, or as a way to cheat in online shooter games. The techniques have not previously been used to balance different skill levels, but since they can be applied differentially to different players, they hold considerable promise for these situations. Target assistance can also solve the problems of traditional balancing mechanisms: they are often minimally perceptible [22]; they need not change the basic interactions with a game; and they can be changed adaptively, scaling assistance as needed.

To test the usefulness of target assistance as a balancing technique, we carried out a controlled experiment with pairs of differently-skilled players in a simple shooting-gallery game. The experiment compared the effectiveness of three techniques (area cursors, target gravity, and sticky targets) for balancing player performance, and also examined the perceptibility of the techniques, the ways in which they altered game mechanics, and the degree to which they affected players' sense of fun. Techniques were tested in both a static mode – providing a fixed amount of assistance to the weaker player – and an adaptive mode – where assistance is scaled based on the current score differential.

Our study showed that games were more balanced with area cursors and target gravity than when no technique was used. These techniques reduced the average score differential from 47 points with no technique to less than 10 points, and the static versions resulted in the weaker player winning about half the games. The study also showed that the target assistance techniques were not perceived by the players, did not affect player ratings of fairness, and improved the sense of fun for assisted players while not affecting the fun had by non-assisted players. After we revealed that one player had been assisted, 22 of 24 participants agreed that balancing the game benefits group gameplay.

Our study is the first to show that target assistance can be an effective tool for improving competition in situations where players have different skill levels. Our results provide game designers with new tools that can extend the enjoyment of shared gaming to a much wider audience.

RELATED WORK: TARGET ASSISTANCE

The goal of target assistance is to help users select on-screen targets quickly and accurately. The underlying principles of aimed movement are well understood. In particular, Fitts's Law [13] states that targeting difficulty is predicted by the *index of difficulty (ID)*, which is calculated based on the size of the target (its width) and its distance from the starting location (its amplitude) [21]. Selecting a target involves three phases [24]: a ballistic motion, a corrective phase, and a final acquisition phase where the pointer is moved into the target and the selection action is performed. Assistance techniques have been directed at all of these phases and can be organized into three groups: manipulation of amplitude, width, or both (see review in [4]). We briefly review this work to provide the basis for our investigation into target assistance in video games.

Amplitude Manipulation

One class of techniques reduces targeting time by reducing the distance between the pointer and target. Some techniques move targets closer to the cursor [6]; the decision about which targets to move is determined by a command gesture or by the initial movement of the cursor. Other techniques warp the cursor to the target by predicting the end location of the targeting motion [3]. Both methods work well for large displays, but prediction of the final position of a moving cursor remains a problem [4].

Width Manipulation

A second class of techniques increases the target width in visual space or motor space. Visual expansion makes the target appear bigger (e.g., using a fisheye lens), which can help users determine whether their pointer is on the target; however, visual-space expansion can make users think that targets are larger in motor space than in reality, leading to errors. Increasing the target size in both visual and motor space still leads to problems, such as occlusion [23].

When the space between targets is not used for other purposes, the effective area of targets can be increased by enlarging the size of the target or the activation size of the cursor. The area cursor technique [20] increases the size of the cursor, from a single point to a larger square area. This effectively increases target size – a target may be selected when any part of the cursor's square intersects any region of the target. A major drawback of area cursor is the problem of the cursor intersecting multiple targets; it cannot determine which is the intended target. DynaSpot addresses the major drawbacks of area cursor by only increasing the area of the cursor at higher movement speeds, and reducing it to a single point for slower, more precise targeting [9].

Another approach is to allow the cursor to make selections even when it is not within a target. Bubble Cursor maps every point in the display to the closest target, allowing selection regardless of the actual cursor location [14].

A third approach for increasing width, called 'sticky targets' or 'pseudo-haptics,' changes the control-to-display ratio of the input device when the cursor is over a selectable target [7]. The user must move the pointing device farther to achieve the same cursor movement, effectively increasing the motor space of the target. Sticky targets can improve aiming time in both 1D [7, 22] and 2D [33] tasks. User perception of CD manipulation is not strong – low to moderate levels of the effect are rarely noticed [22].

Manipulating both Amplitude and Width

A third class of techniques changes both the size of the targets and their distance. Some CD-manipulation techniques alter the cursor position throughout the targeting motion [18,33], rather than just over the target.

'Force fields' [2] and 'target gravity' [5] are two such approaches. The techniques warp the cursor by increasing motions toward the target, and motions away are decreased. A similar technique leaves 'magnetic dust' around windows and widgets as they are used. Dust accumulates over time and frequently used interface elements become more attractive [18]. The TractorBeam technique for distant pointing on tabletop displays compared increasing target width and decreasing target distance (by snapping to the target). Users performed equally with both techniques [28].

RELATED WORK: GAME BALANCING TECHNIQUES

Flow is a balance between anxiety and boredom [10], and is an important part of game design. To achieve optimal flow, games must balance challenge and skill [12]. If a game is too easy, players may become bored. Conversely, if a game is too hard, players may become frustrated. In this section, we explore game play balancing and player balancing.

Game Play Balancing

Competition is a contest between two or more players, and has been shown to be a motivating factor for participating in multiplayer video games [32]. To maintain flow, competition between players must be balanced – that is, players of equal skill and experience have an equal chance of winning [1]. If a player or group has an advantage, opposing players may have to perform at a higher level than the advantaged players, and may be incapable of winning the game. If unbalanced game elements are exploited, the advantaged player may no longer be challenged, and the disadvantaged player may quickly become frustrated [26]. Therefore, balancing game elements is an important aspect of video game design that has been recognized in industry, where simulations and extensive play testing are often used to uncover potentially unbalanced game elements [15].

Player Balancing

Although games often provide optimal game play balance, it can be difficult to balance the differences between players [1]. In video games, players have varying skill, experience, tactics, and reaction time [30], and because many games reward skill, novices can have difficulty playing against experienced players. We review three common approaches for addressing the differences between players below.

Matchmaking

Grouping players by their abilities is one technique used to adjust competition. For example, ranking and ladders are often used in sports and traditional games (e.g., squash and chess). Similarly, many multiplayer online games track performance to match players and balance teams [26]. TrueSkill assesses player skill based on a number of game outcomes using Bayesian networks and the Elo chess scoring system, and has been widely used in games such as *Halo 2* [16]. A limiting factor of matchmaking is that it requires a measure of player skill, which can be difficult to determine when players initially join a game [35].

Asymmetric Roles

Providing unique tasks is another approach for addressing skill differences. Many team sports include several roles requiring different skills. For example, positions in American football differ between roles; the quarterback's job is to handle the ball on every offensive play, while an offensive lineman may play many games without ever touching the ball. Asymmetric roles can also be found in video games. Some multiplayer games (e.g., *Alien Swarm)* require players to fill several roles to succeed (e.g., Officer, Special Weapons, Medic, and Tech). Asymmetric roles allow players with different skill sets to play together; however, a team may be limited by the performance of the weakest member. Further, the use of asymmetric roles does not address the situation of competitive play.

Difficulty Adjustment

Difficulty adjustment is a popular way to support different skill levels in video games – many games allow a choice of difficulty setting. Adaptive difficulty adjustments alter game elements in real-time based on performance [17].

Adaptive difficulty adjustment has been applied in various game genres for single and multiplayer games. A version of the classic *Pong* game was implemented to support play among children and parents of different skill [19]. Players' racquet lengths, movement speed, and incoming ball speed were adjusted based on performance. Generating game content (e.g., in-game obstacles and enemies) based on the ability of the player is another approach [29]; for example, *Infinite Mario* provides endless new game levels that are suitable for a player's ability (www.marioai.org).

Many arcade-style racing games include "catch-up" or "rubber band" systems that provide advantages to a losing player. For example, in *Mario Kart* trailing players receive items that give them a greater chance of capturing the lead [26]. The "fatboy" modification of *Unreal Tournament* adjusts the size of a player's avatar, increasing its width based on the number of kills scored. This makes successful players easier targets than losing players.

Adaptive difficulty adjustments have several potential limiting factors. For example, the "catch-up" effect that occurs in *Mario Kart* can lead to a sense of frustration as more experienced players begin to feel cheated [26], and scaling game difficulty based on a player's progress can result in the player losing their sense of achievement [8].

RELATED WORK: TARGET ASSISTANCE IN GAMES

Games involving aiming tasks often include some form of computer-supported target assistance. Many FPS console-games include target assistance in order to address the lack of precision when aiming with a thumb-stick on a gamepad [25]. Alternatively, third-party software called "aimbots" have been developed to provide target assistance for many FPS games [34]. These systems are often considered as "cheats" by serious gamers [31], as they may provide an unfair advantage. Common approaches for target assistance include: reticule magnetism and target lock-on.

Reticule magnetism, like the sticky target technique, works by adjusting the control-to-display ratio during targeting; as the reticule (cursor) passes over a target, it moves more slowly. This technique is common in FPS console games (e.g., the *Halo* series), as it can be difficult to make fine aiming adjustments using a gamepad or thumbstick [27]. Reticule magnetism can, however, lead to unexpected acceleration of the cursor. As a player moves off of a target, friction is no longer applied, causing the cursor to swing rapidly in the direction they are being moved [25].

Locking a player's cursor onto potential targets is another form of target assistance in games (similar to the Tractor Beam technique [28]). For example, pressing a button on the gamepad will lock the cursor onto nearby enemies in games such as *The Legend of Zelda: Twilight Princess.* A potential downside of target lock-on is that the cursor may lock onto an unintended target as they attempt to aim.

STUDY

To understand how target assistance can balance play, we studied three target assistance techniques applied statically or dynamically, in a two-person shooting gallery game.

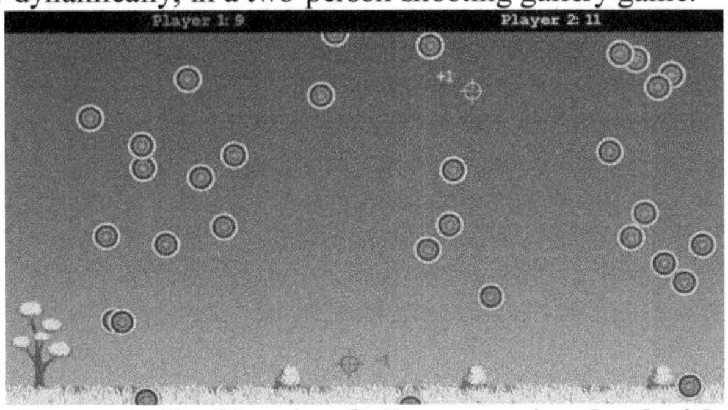

Figure 1. The Shooting Gallery game in a level with moving targets. Player 1 has missed and Player 2 has hit.

Apparatus

We designed a simple shooting-gallery game where the goal is to score points by shooting on-screen targets with a Nintendo Wii Remote (Wiimote). A cursor (crosshairs) is displayed for each player (colored yellow or red) at the absolute position reported by the Wiimote. Players score a point for shooting a target and lose a point for each miss. Targets are shot by placing the centre of the cursor (a 1px point) over any region of the target and pressing the trigger. Sound feedback identifies hits and misses. Visual feedback shows hits and misses with a '+1' or '-1' at the shot point for one second, in the same colour as the player's cursor (see Figure 1). We created five game levels that varied the size, movement, speed, and time of appearance of the targets. The goal was not to fully enumerate the space of target behaviours, but to create several interesting levels of increasing difficulty. The game was built using C# and XNA 3.1 with a screen refresh rate of more than 60 fps. The system ran on a Windows 7, Intel Core 2 Duo machine and a Dell 42-inch, 1024x768 plasma screen. Participants sat on a couch or stood approximately 250cm from the screen.

Techniques Chosen for the Comparison Study

We chose three techniques that have been considered in prior target assistance research: sticky targets that change effective target width when the cursor is on the target [7, 22,33]; target gravity that attracts the cursor towards targets [5]; and an area cursor that increases the size of the affected area when a shot is taken [20]. These techniques were selected because we felt they would improve performance, yet offer low perceptibility. Further, because these techniques do not fundamentally change the on-screen appearance of targets or the cursor (e.g., visual expansion) or the way that targets are selected (e.g., bubble cursor) they may be widely applicable in real-world video games.

We tested these techniques using both static and adaptive target assistance. The static approach provided a constant level of assistance, while the adaptive approach adjusted the assistance depending on the difference in score.

The Sticky Targets Technique

Target stickiness was applied when the cursor was over a target by changing the CD ratio of the input: the lower the ratio, the stickier the target. For example, a ratio of 0.4 meant that a movement over a target would result in only 40% of the normal on-screen cursor movement.

A previous study of sticky targets with the Wiimote found that the accumulated difference between cursor position and Wiimote position from passing through sticky targets could lead to increasing 'cursor drift' [5]. While not a problem for player performance, the infrared light source could become out of range of the Wiimote camera after accumulated cursor drift. To side-step the issue, our implementation returned the cursor to the position it would have otherwise reached had it not passed through a sticky target. This design choice resulted in the cursor rapidly accelerating off targets when exited or shot, and has also been described in observations of cursor magnetism in practice [25].

The Target Gravity Technique

Target gravity [5] is similar to the 'force field' technique [2]; but instead of restricting a target's attraction to a limited range, all targets provide an attractive force. Because target gravity is inversely proportional to the square of the distance between the cursor and target, the influence of a target decreases rapidly at greater distances.

Our gravity effect is calculated as follows. For n targets, let $p_1, p_2,..p_n$ be the positions of the targets with radii $r_1, r_2,..r_n$. Let p_0 represent the true position of the cursor (i.e., without any gravity effect applied), and let p_w be the warped position. Let G be the 'gravitational constant' (i.e., weight multiplier). Then, for each target $i=1..n$, compute the target weight with Equation 1. Finally, compute the warped position of the cursor using Equation 2.

The warped position is a weighted average of the true cursor position and the positions of each target. The weight for the cursor position is fixed at 1.0. Manipulating G changes the strength of the gravity effect, and bigger targets provide more gravity (this formulation is similar to previous work in virtual world interactions [11]). Target gravity has been shown to improve performance using a Wiimote [5].

$$w_i = \frac{Gr_i^2}{|p_0 - p_i|^2 + 1}, \text{ with } w_0 = 1 \quad (1) \qquad p_w = \frac{\sum_{i=0}^{n} w_i p_i}{\sum_{i=0}^{n} w_i} \quad (2)$$

The Area Cursor Technique

Our area cursor implementation is closely related to the original implementation [20], but in order to minimize perceptibility the physical size of the cursor remains consistent. Further, our technique does change how targets are selected or how the appearance of intersected targets, like newer related techniques [9,14]. However, like the newer techniques we use a circular activation area. The effect was imperceptible to the users before shooting. After shooting it would be possible for them to perceive the increased activation area.

Choosing Levels of Assistance Techniques

We conducted a pilot study to determine the levels of static assistance and upper limits for adaptive assistance. Eight participants tested 10 levels of each technique and rated how noticeable the assistance was on a 10-point scale.

We chose technique levels that combined performance improvement with low perceptibility. For the static levels we chose: area cursor, an area 52px in diameter; sticky targets, a CD-ratio of 0.2; gravity, a gravitational constant of 2.0. We also chose the upper limits of the adaptive assistance techniques. For sticky targets, a CD-ratio of less than 0.1 could make fast moving targets unselectable; the CD manipulation would slow the cursor too much to keep pace. A gravity constant greater than 6 could make it difficult to reach all targets, because the force exerted by closely-spaced targets was too strong to overcome. No upper limit was observed for the area cursor technique, although large area cursors could allow multiple targets to be hit with a single shot.

Adaptive assistance used the following algorithm. If the assisted player's score was greater than or equal to the unassisted player, then provide no assistance. Otherwise, give 10% of the static level for each point the assisted player trails the non-assisted player. For example, if the assisted player trailed by two points using the gravity technique, the resulting gravity coefficient would be .4 (i.e., 10% x static level x score difference = 10% x 2 x 2).

Task

Participants were tested in pairs and were told that they would be competing in a shooting gallery game where we were testing new "controller algorithms" for the Wiimote. Participants were *not* told that the algorithms gave assistance. We highlighted that we wanted their experience to be like a game with a friend, and they were free to speak to one another. They were asked to try and win each game, to have fun, but not to worry if they didn't win.

Player skill level was determined by an individual game. While one participant played the individual game, the other completed a demographics questionnaire in a separate room. The experimenter used a combination of score and completion time in the individual games to choose which player received assistance during competitive play.

The competitive play portion consisted of a series of games. Game 1 was a control condition; no assistance was given and players were told that this was the "normal algorithm". Games 2-4 presented the static assistance techniques (using a Latin square ordering across groups). Game 5 was another control game. Games 6-8 presented the adaptive techniques (using a Latin square ordering). Game 9 was a final control.

Each game started with a practice level, where the players could get accustomed to any differences in the controller algorithms. The game then randomly presented the five levels of play. A transition screen was presented between each level so that players could take a break, and see their scores. After each game the experimenter would announce the final score on the final transition screen to ensure participants were aware of their performance.

After each of Games 2-9, players answered a survey where they reported on their experience with the "controller algorithm." After the experiment, players were given another questionnaire that asked for their impressions of the game, their performance and the performance of their partner. The experimenter then revealed that the controller algorithms gave assistance to just one of them, and that the goal was to keep the game competitive and to make it more fun. They were told which player received assistance, and that this decision was based on their individual games. A final survey solicited their opinions on game balancing.

Participants

We recruited 24 players (14 male) who were undergraduate students (15), graduate students (6), or university staff (3). Participants were paired with a participant whom they did not know (9 groups), or with a friend (3 groups). Players selected for the assistance condition scored significantly lower (avg: 273.5) scores than non-assisted players (avg: 315.7) in the individual game ($t = -3.87$, $p<.001$).

Of the 12 assisted players (4 males, mean age 26.7), half reported not typically playing video games, with the rest spending under 3 hours per week. They rated their expertise with the Wiimote an average of 1.75 (sd=0.75) on a 7-point scale (1-novice, 7-expert), and five reported having played a shooting-gallery type game before. Of the 12 non-assisted players (10 males, mean age 24.3), all but one played video games regularly (three spent under 3 hours/week, and eight spent 4 or more hours). Non-assisted players rated their Wiimote expertise an average of 4.7 (sd=1.5) on a 7-point scale and all had previously played shooting-gallery games.

Data Analyses

All data were analyzed separately for assisted and non-assisted players. Performance data were gathered from computer logs and analyzed with one-way ANOVAs. Post-hoc tests were conducted using Tukey's HSD. Survey results were analyzed using Friedman's ANOVA for related samples; pairwise comparisons used Wilcoxon Signed Ranks Tests for 2-related samples; correlations used Spearman's rho. For all tests, α was set at 0.05. We conducted a series of planned comparison tests.

RESULTS

Targeting Performance

As players competed in groups, we examined performance at the individual level and relative to their partner.

Did the hit ratio change when one player was assisted? Hit ratio was calculated as the number of successful target hits divided by the total number of shots for an entire game. Hit ratio did not change for non-assisted players when their partner was provided with assistance ($F_{6,77}$=.225, p=.967). For assisted players, there was a significant effect of technique on hit ratio ($F_{6,77}$=26.3, p<.001). Post-hoc tests showed that area cursors (both static and adaptive) yielded the best hit ratio (all p<.04), and that static gravity was better than sticky targets and no assistance (all p<.02), and adaptive gravity was better than no assistance (p=.038). There were no differences between the static and adaptive versions of any of the techniques (all p>.30). See Figure 2.

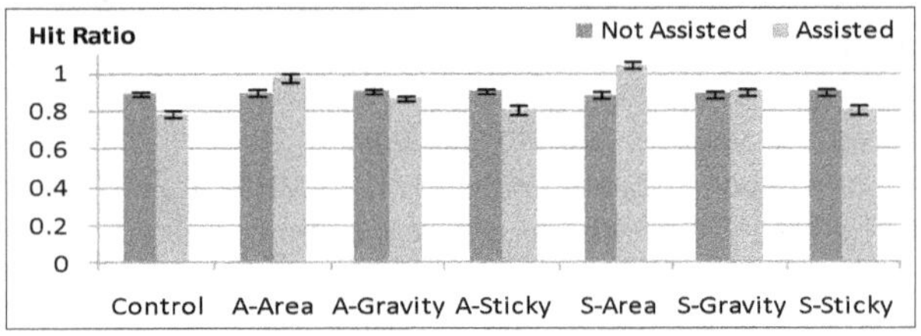

Figure 2: Mean hit ratio (±SE) by technique for assisted and non-assisted players. A-Adaptive, S-Static.

Was game score closer between the players when one was assisted? Game score was a combination of target hits (+1) and misses (-1). Although a sign of individual performance, it is linked to the performance of a player's partner, as a partner hitting more targets would result in fewer targets available for a player to hit. Game score is the measure that was shown to the participants as they played the levels.

To answer our question, we calculated the difference in score between competitors after each game, and conducted a one-way ANOVA with assistance type as the factor. The difference in game score was significantly affected by assistance type ($F_{6,77}$=11.2, p<.001). Post-hoc tests showed that area cursors resulted in a smaller game score difference than sticky targets or no assistance (all p<.002). Static gravity yielded less difference than sticky targets or no assistance (all p<.006), and adaptive gravity produced less difference than no assistance (p=.039). See Figure 3.

Were there learning or ordering effects? We used the final scores in the three competitive control games to test for learning effects. No significant differences were found between control game scores for assisted ($F_{2,22}$=.797, p=.463) or unassisted ($F_{2,22}$=1.66, p=.213) players, suggesting that there was no important learning effect as the study progressed. Therefore, comparisons between static and dynamic techniques should not be biased by ordering.

How did assistance type affect the number of games that were won by the assisted player? We counted the number of games won by the assisted player. Chi-squared tests showed no difference between the number of games won and lost by the assisted player using static area cursor (8/12 won, χ^2_1=1.3, p=.248) or static gravity (5/12 won, χ^2_1=0.3, p=.564). All others had significant differences between the number of won and lost games (adaptive area cursor: 1/12 wins, no assistance: 2/36, all others: 0/12 wins, all p<.004).

Taken together the performance results show that assisting one player boosts their hit ratio, while not affecting the hit ratio of the non-assisted player. This boost in hit ratio evens the score between the players when using the area cursor and gravity techniques. Although the scores were closer when using area cursor and gravity (for both adaptive and static) than with no assistance, this only resulted in assisted players winning games with static techniques.

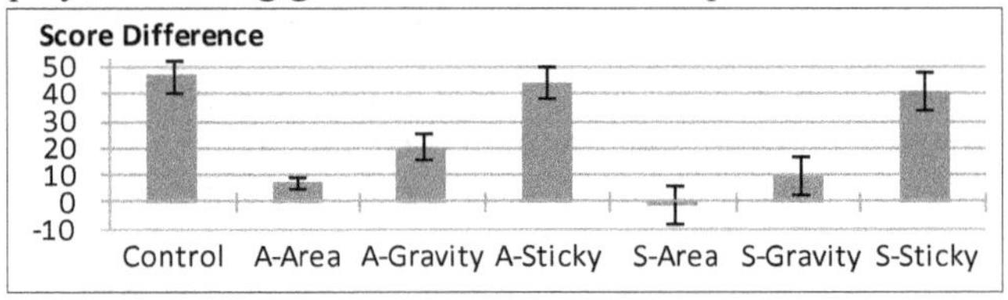

Figure 3. Mean score difference in points (unassisted–assisted) by technique. A-Adaptive, S-Static.

Perceptibility of Assistance Techniques

After each game, we asked users whether they noticed a difference in the controller algorithms compared to the normal case (4-point scale; lower-less noticeable). We also asked players about the difficulty of aiming, their perceived performance and the perceived performance of their partner after each game on a 5-point scale (lower-worse).

Did participants notice differences? There were no differences in the noticeability ratings between controller algorithms, for either assisted players (χ^2_7=6.6, p=.469) or non-assisted players (χ^2_7=6.8, p=.446). For example, there was no difference between static sticky targets and adaptive sticky targets. See Table 1.

	Noticeability (1-4)		Difficulty (1-5)	
	Not Assisted	Assisted	Not Assisted	Assisted
Control	2.6 (0.15)	2.1 (0.18)	3.2 (0.22)	2.4 (0.15)
A-Area	2.1 (0.26)	2.3 (0.26)	2.9 (0.23)	3.8 (0.21)
A-Gravity	2.3 (0.23)	1.9 (0.19)	2.8 (0.22)	3.1 (0.23)
A-Sticky	2.7 (0.31)	2.0 (0.28)	3.0 (0.30)	2.1 (0.26)
S-Area	2.6 (0.26)	2.5 (0.26)	2.8 (0.35)	3.6 (0.19)
S-Gravity	2.4 (0.26)	2.5 (0.34)	2.8 (0.27)	3.7 (0.14)
S-Sticky	2.4 (0.34)	2.4 (0.29)	3.7 (0.28)	2.3 (0.25)

Table 1. Mean noticeability and difficulty ratings ±SE. Lower is less noticeable/more difficult. A - Adaptive, S - Static.

Did players report differences in the difficulty of the techniques? Non-assisted players did not report differences in the difficulty of the controller (χ^2_7=8.8, p=.264), while assisted players did (χ^2_7=48.1, p=.264). Pairwise tests showed that the sticky technique was perceived as more difficult than area cursor or gravity for both the static and adaptive versions (all p< .02), that no assistance was more difficult than area cursor or gravity for the static techniques, and that no assistance and adaptive gravity were more difficult than adaptive area cursor (all p< .02). There were no differences between the static and adaptive versions of any of the techniques. See Table 1.

Did assisted players think they performed better when there was assistance provided? Assisted players noticed the change in their performance compared to the normal base case (χ^2_7=47.2, p<.001). They thought that they performed better with area cursors and gravity than with sticky targets or no assistance for the static techniques (all p<.01), and better with area cursors than sticky targets, gravity, or no assistance for adaptive techniques (all p<.05). In addition, adaptive gravity was perceived as resulting in better performance than adaptive sticky (p=.03). There were no differences between the static and adaptive versions of any of the techniques. See Table 2.

Did players notice the difference in their partner's performance? Non-assisted players did notice the change in their assisted partners' performance (χ^2_7=38.9, p<.001). They felt that their partner played better when provided with both area cursors and gravity over sticky targets and no assistance for both the static and adaptive techniques (all p<.05). There was no perceived difference between the static and adaptive versions of any of the techniques. Assisted participants did not think that their partners performed differently depending on the assistance they received themselves (χ^2_7=7.0, p=.430). See Table 2.

	Performance (1-5)		Partner's Performance (1-5)	
	Not Assisted	Assisted	Not Assisted	Assisted
Control	3.3 (0.19)	2.3 (0.16)	2.3 (0.20)	3.3 (0.14)
A-Area	2.7 (0.19)	3.9 (0.19)	3.6 (0.26)	3.3 (0.19)
A-Gravity	2.8 (0.21)	3.2 (0.24)	3.0 (0.21)	3.3 (0.19)
A-Sticky	3.6 (0.23)	2.2 (0.27)	2.2 (0.24)	3.2 (0.21)
S-Area	2.5 (0.36)	4.1 (0.19)	3.8 (0.25)	3.0 (0.17)
S-Gravity	2.8 (0.25)	3.8 (0.22)	3.5 (0.2)	3.2 (0.17)
S-Sticky	3.9 (0.26)	2.2 (0.35)	2.7 (0.23)	2.9 (0.23)

Table 2. Mean ratings ±SE for player performance and partner performance. Lower is worse. A - Adaptive, S - Static

Did participants without assistance think that their own performance changed when their partners were given assistance? Although the performance of non-assisted players didn't change, their performance relative to their competitor did. Non-assisted players noticed this change (χ^2_7=19.6, p=.007). They thought their own performance was better when their partner was assisted using sticky targets than with area cursor or gravity for both the static and adaptive techniques (all p<.03). There were no differences between the static and adaptive versions of any of the techniques. See Table 2.

Taken together, these results related to perceptibility and performance change suggest that assisted players attributed the difference in score to their own improvement, not to their partners playing poorly or to changes in their control mechanism, while non-assisted players perceived both an improvement in their partner's performance and a decrease in their own performance.

User Response to Game Balancing through Assistance

We asked the players how much fun it was to play the game after each assistance technique was used, at the end of the experiment, and after revealing that we were assisting one of the players, all on a 5-point scale.

Did participants rate their fun differently after playing with different assistance techniques? Players who were provided with assistance rated their fun differently after games, depending on what kind of assistance was provided (χ^2_7=29.7, p<.001). For the static techniques, area cursor and gravity were rated as more fun than sticky targets or no assistance (all p<.03). For the adaptive techniques, area cursor was perceived as more fun than any other technique (all p<.04). There were no differences between the perceived fun of any of the static or adaptive techniques. Players who did not receive assistance did not rate their fun differently after games where their partner was provided with assistance (χ^2_7=6.9, p=.439). Taken together, these results are interesting as play experience was strengthened for those receiving assistance, while not being weakened for those who weren't. See Figure 4.

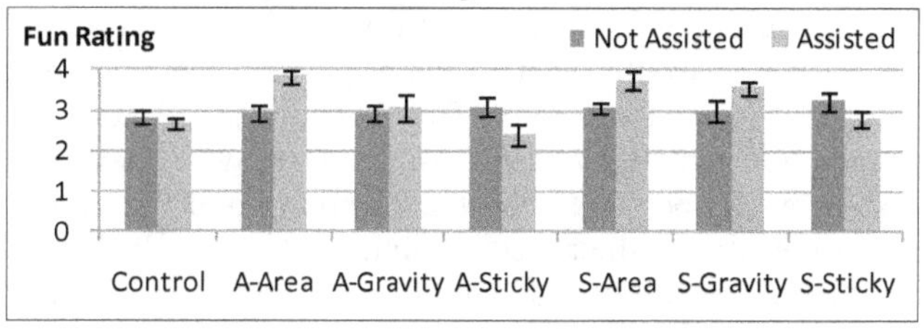

Figure 4. Mean fun ratings (±SE) (lower is less fun) by technique and player. A-Adaptive, S-Static.

Did players' performance affect how much fun they had? Fun ratings for each game were significantly related with game score differential for assisted players (p<.001, ρ=.379), but not for non-assisted players (p=.058, ρ=.194). Assisted players reported having more fun, the closer the score was in a game, but this did not come at the expense of non-assisted players' perception of fun.

Did players' ratings for fun change after finding out that there was assistance provided in the game? Neither assisted nor non-assisted players changed their ratings of fun after finding out that assistance was provided (Z=1.0, p=.257, Z=-1.1, p=.317 respectively).

Did participants think that it is fair to provide assistance to one player? Before revealing that assistance was provided, all assisted players felt that the games were fair, while 10 non-assisted players agreed. Two non-assisted players felt that games were unfair because previous experience could provide an advantage, and that fairness may have depended on how the algorithms were assigned. After finding out that one player was assisted, most non-assisted players felt that it was fair (2-No, 10-Yes). Non-assisted players commented that: it would broaden the demographics of their opponents (e.g., playing against grandmother or kids); it is better for casual gamers; and it would be more fun. Dissenting players felt that it would not be a true competition, but that it would be OK to provide assistance when playing against children. Assisted players were more split in their opinion (7-No, 5-Yes). Assisted players who thought it was fair commented that: it would improve the competition; it would increase the challenge for the better player; and that it would increase the fun. Those who thought it was unfair commented that: it doesn't give you an idea of your actual ability; the win doesn't count if you are being helped by a computer; it may not be as much fun for the better player; and the scores would be meaningless. Some assisted players commented that although there would be benefits to the group experience, it would be through unfair means.

Do players think that balancing benefits the group? Players agreed that balancing the game by providing assistance to one player can improve the experience for the group (11-Yes, 1-No for both assisted and non-assisted players). Comments included that it would: improve the competition; allow people of multiple ages and skill levels to compete together; provide a greater challenge to better players; be less frustrating for less-skilled players; and be more fun.

Would players want to know if one player was assisted? Most players would want to know (8-Yes, 4-No for both assisted and non-assisted). Those who wanted to know commented that: they would want to know if they were beaten by the person, or by the computer and the person; and to evaluate their actual ability. Those who didn't commented that: it would benefit the social aspect of games to not know; and it might ruin the experience if they did.

DISCUSSION

There are six main results from the comparison study.

- Two of the target-assist techniques (area cursors and gravity) significantly improved player performance, and significantly reduced score differences in the game.
- There was no significant difference between static and adaptive versions of the techniques, but the static versions did allow weaker players to win more often.
- Players did not notice differences between the controller algorithms (although they did notice better performance).
- Assisted players reported having more fun as games became more competitive, but this did not come at the expense of perceived fun of the non-assisted players.
- Players reported the game as being 'fair', and did not change their assessment after learning about assistance.
- After learning about the targeting techniques, assisted players' opinions were less favorable than non-assisted players, but both groups felt that assistance could benefit the group play experience.

Explanations for Results

Why did the techniques work (or not work)?

All of the assistance techniques have been effective in prior work, but only area cursors and gravity were beneficial here. One reason is that stickiness may be less useful in situations with moving targets, since the user must be on top of the target for the technique to take effect. Target gravity has an effect wherever the cursor is on the screen (and so avoids this problem), and area cursors allowed players to hit targets simply by being close. A second problem with sticky targets was that when leaving a target, the cursor had to jump to return to its actual location. This means that if the player moved through distractor targets en route to the desired target, the cursor could appear to skip. Area cursors were particularly good at improving performance because players could hit multiple targets at once. Although a success in our game, this could be a limitation in other games where users must pick out targets that are close to other objects that should not be hit.

Why did players not notice the assistance?

Players did not notice differences in the various "controller algorithms", but did notice when they (or their partner) performed better. As in previous work, it appears that people do not easily perceive target assistance [22otice when they (or their partner) performed better. As in previous work, it appears that people do not easily perceive target assistance [22]. There are three reasons. First, the effects of the techniques (if set up correctly) are subtle, and do not dramatically change the visible behavior of the on-screen objects. Second, noise in the input device hides some of the effects of the techniques: there is already some jitter in the way that the cursor tracks the motion of the Wiimote, and it is difficult for users to tell exactly where they are pointing with the device. Third, the player's attention is strongly focused on the game, not on the motion of the cursor, which reduces their ability to notice the effects of target assistance.

Which is better: static or adaptive assistance?

There was no significant difference in the effect of static or adaptive techniques on game scores or hit ratios, although static techniques allowed the weaker player to win more games than the adaptive techniques. This does not mean that adaptivity is a poor design, but rather highlights the differences between the approaches; pointing to the importance of considering the game outcome and the score differential. The adaptive techniques adjusted with each shot fired, meaning that as the score difference between players approached zero, the technique's strength also approached zero. This resulted in close games where the unassisted player won as opposed to games played with the static techniques where the assisted player also won. For situations where game outcome should be balanced (e.g., parents playing with children), it may be best to use static techniques or to change the adaptive techniques to allow for varied game outcome. For situations where the goal is to have close play, but still reward the stronger player with more wins, adaptive techniques may be more suitable.

Generalizing the Results

Here we consider whether the value of target assistance can be realized with other players, input devices, and games. First, our results suggest that the target assistance techniques will work with a wide variety of players, with a wide variety of skill differentials. In our study, we had some pairs who were closely matched, and others who were very far apart (overall the stronger player scored 15.5% higher than the weaker player in the individual game). The question for players with larger differentials are whether the maximum assistance value will be enough to bridge the gap, and whether an adaptive compensation algorithm will react quickly enough to maintain a reasonable balance. We believe that these issues can be easily addressed (e.g., as discussed below, multiple techniques could be applied in situations where there is a large difference).

Second, there is also reason to believe that these results will transfer to games using other input devices. For some devices (such as game controllers), target assistance is already being used, and our techniques should work for with little need for adjustment. For other devices, particularly those that are more precise (like a mouse), the techniques may be more perceivable (e.g., when a small vertical movement of the mouse results in a diagonal cursor movement). However, the attentional demands of games are likely to hide these effects in most cases.

Third, there is considerable opportunity to apply our results in other types of shooting games, although designers will have to adjust the techniques to suit a particular game. For example, first-person shooters could easily adopt these balancing techniques, but would have to ensure that the semantics of the game are not changed (e.g., a sniper rifle would be a poor match with an area cursor, as sniper rifles do not hit multiple targets). Game semantics, however, could be used as an additional resource for balancing techniques: for example, weapons with a wider spread of damage could be a natural fit for area cursors; spread radius could change based on the amount of assistance desired.

In addition, target assistance (or the basic ideas behind these techniques) could also be used in other game genres. In particular, the gravity technique could possibly be applied to driving games, giving weaker players better 'centre-line gravity' than stronger players. We plan to study the perceptibility of this technique in future work – but it is likely to be much less perceivable than the 'catch-up' adjustments that are currently used in some games.

Design Issues and Lessons for Designers

This study provides several lessons and raises several issues for designers wishing to employ target assistance.

- The main lesson for designers from this work is that target assistance techniques work very well as a balancing mechanism: they are able to compensate for widely different skill levels, without being overly noticeable. The techniques can be used immediately to improve the accessibility and competitiveness of shared games.
- For moving-target games, designers should first consider area cursors and target gravity. Area cursors were best at balancing games, but can only be used effectively in situations where hitting multiple targets is not a problem. Target gravity was also successful, and can work in situations with small targets. Sticky targets were not effective, and although they may be useful in other game genres, they seem to have too many drawbacks to be recommended for use in shooting games.
- It is possible for the techniques to be combined in situations where extra assistance is required. Although we did not test this, it seems clear that gravity and area cursors could both be applied to a player's controller. This would allow either a higher level of assistance – or perhaps more importantly, would allow the levels of each technique to be lowered, reducing overall perceptibility.
- It is extremely important that the values for the techniques (e.g., the maximum amounts of gravity or stickiness) be carefully chosen. The techniques can become highly obvious if these values are too high (e.g., the cursor becomes stuck to a target, or moves in the opposite direction to the player's arm movement).
- The parameters of the adaptation algorithm should also be carefully chosen. These should be matched both to the length of the game (so that the adaptive algorithm can have a reasonable effect before the game ends) and to the desired outcome (e.g., whether a designer wishes to give a boost to the weaker player, or to equalize the game).
- An important design issue is whether to reveal that target assistance is being used. Our participants were divided on whether they wanted to know about the techniques, it may be safest to make this a setting that players can see (although it need not be made obvious in the game itself). In some games that are expressly designed for casual use, or for walk-up play in public settings, designers could choose to add the technique without informing players – but in these cases, it will be important to ensure that the levels chosen for the techniques will keep the assistance below the perceivable level for most players.

CONCLUSIONS AND FUTURE WORK

Video games are an increasingly popular form of entertainment that are played by people of many different skill levels. In this paper we addressed the problem of skill imbalance using target assistance techniques, which have not previously been used for this purpose. Our study of three different techniques showed that target gravity and area cursors can balance competition between players of different abilities. We found that by making the game more competitive, less-skilled players report having more fun, and that this does not adversely affect the experience of the more skilled players. Target assistance techniques are particularly well suited for this application because they can be applied without being noticed by players, and need not change game mechanics.

In future work, we will investigate the application of similar techniques in other game genres, such as first-person shooters and driving games, to test whether our results generalize to other situations. Second, we will refine our adaptive algorithms to see if game outcomes can be more tightly controlled, and to see if technique combinations (e.g. gravity + area cursor) can provide stronger assistance with lower perceptibility. Finally, we will further investigate the real-world requirements of assistance techniques through longer-term testing, and testing with specific player types with larger differences in skill, such as teenagers and grandparents.

ACKNOWLEDGEMENTS

We would like to thank Stephen Damm for his work in implementing the experimental system. This research was supported by NSERC.

REFERENCES

1. Adams, E. *Fundamentals of Game Design*. New Riders, 2010.
2. Ahlström, D., Hitz, M., and Leitner, G. An evaluation of sticky and force enhanced targets in multi target situations. *Proc. NordicCHI*, (2001), 58-67.
3. Asano, T., Sharlin, E., Kitamura, Y., Takashima, K., and Kishino, F. Predictive interaction using the delphian desktop. *Proc. UIST '05, (2005)*, 133-141.
4. Balakrishnan, R. "Beating" Fitt's law: virtual enhancements for pointing facilitation. *IJHCS*, 61, (2004), 857-874.
5. Bateman, S., Mandryk, R., Gutwin, C., Xiao, R. Targeting-Assistance Techniques for Distant Pointing with Relative Ray Casting. Technical Report 2009-03, Dept. of Comp. Sci., Univ. of Saskatchewan, 2009.
6. Baudisch, P., Cutrell, E., Robbins, D., Czerwinski, M., Tandler, P. Bederson, B., and Zierlinger, A. Drag-and-Pop and Drag-and-Pick: Techniques for Accessing Remote Screen Content on Touch- and Pen-operated Systems. *Proc. Interact 2003*, 57-64.
7. Blanch, R., Guiard, Y., Beaudoin-Lafon, M. Semantic pointing: improving target axquisition with control-display ratio adaptation. *Proc. CHI '04*, 519-525.
8. Bostan, B., and Öğüt, S. Game challenges and difficulty levels: lessons learned From RPGs. In *International Simulation and Gaming Association Conference*, 2009.
9. Chapuis, O., Labrune, J., and Pietriga, E. DynaSpot: Speed-Dependent Area Cursor. *CHI'09*, 1391-1400.
10. Csíkszentmihályi, M. *Flow: The Psychology of Optimal Experience*. Harper and Row, 1990.
11. Elmqvist, N. and Fekete, J-D. Semantic Pointing for Object Picking in Complex 3D Environments. *Proc. GI*, 2008, 243-250.
12. Falstein, N. Understanding fun – the Theory of Natural Funativity. In *Introduction to Game Development*, Rabin, S. (ed.), 71-98. Charles River Media, 2005.
13. Fitt, P. M. The Information Capacity of the human motor control system in controlling the amplitude of movement. *J. Exp. Psychology, 47,* (1954), 381-391.
14. Grossman, T. and Balakrishnan, R. The bubble cursor: enhancing target acquisition by dynamic resizing of the cursor's activation area. *Proc. CHI '05*, 281-290.
15. Hanson, B. Game balance for massively multiplayer games. In *Massively Multiplayer Game Development*, Alexander, T. (ed.), 30-48. Charles Rive Media, 2003.
16. Herbrich, R., Minka, T., and Graepel, T. TrueSkill(TM): A Bayesian skill rating system. In *Advances in Neural Information Processing Systems*, 20, 569--576, 2007.
17. Hunicke, R. The case for dynamic difficulty adjustment in games. In *Proceedings of Advances in Computer Entertainment Technology*, vol. 265, 429-433, 2005.
18. Hurst, A., Mankoff, J., Dey, A. K., and Hudson, S. E. 2007. Dirty desktops: using a patina of magnetic mouse dust to make common interactor targets easier to select. *Proc. UIST '07*, 183-186.
19. Ibáñez-Martínez, J. and Delgado-Mata, C. From Competitive to Social Two-player Videogames. *Proc. Workshop on Child, Computer and Interaction*, 2009.
20. Kabbash, P. and Buxton, W. The "Prince" Technique: Fitts' Law and Selection Using Area Cursors. *Proc. CHI '95*, 273-279.
21. MacKenzie, I. S. Fitts' law as a research and design tool in human-computer interaction. *HCI, 7*, (1992), 91-139.
22. Mandryk, R. L., and Gutwin, C. Perceptibility and Utility of Sticky Targets. *Proc. GI '08*, 65-72.
23. McGuffin, M., and Balakrishnan, R. Acquisition of Expanding Targets. *Proc. CHI 2002*, 57-64.
24. Meyer, D., Smith, J., Kornblum, S., Abrams, R., Wright, C. Optimality in human motor performance: ideal control of rapid aimed movements. *Psych. Rev*. 8, (1988), 340-370.
25. Nelson, D. Fire Control. *Game Developer*, 16(11), 2009.
26. Newheiser, M. Playing Fair: A Look at Competition in Gaming. *Strange Horizons*. www.strangehorizons.com /2009/20090309/newheiser-a.shtml, accessed June 2010.
27. Onyett, C. Shadowrun Interview. *IGN*. http://pc.ign. com/articles/740/740187p1.html, accessed June 2010.
28. Parker, J.K., Mandryk, R., Nunes, M.N., and Inkpen, K. TractorBeam Selection Aids: Improving Target Acquisition for Pointing Input on Tabletop Displays. *Proc. INTERACT '05*, 80-93.
29. Pedersen, C., Togelius, J. and Yannakakis, G. Modeling Player Experience for Content Creation. IEEE Trans. Comp. Intell. and AI in Games, 2 (1), 54-67, 2010.
30. Sweetser, P. and Wyeth, P. GameFlow: a model for evaluating player enjoyment in games. *Computers in Entertainment*, 3, 3-3, 205.
31. Thompson, C. What Type of Game Cheater Are You? Article on *Wired.com*. Retrieved August, 15, 2010.
32. Vorderer, P., Hartmann, T., and Klimmt, C. Explaining the enjoyment of playing video games: the role of competition. *Proc. Entertainment Computing'03*, 1-9.
33. Worden, A., Walker, M., Bharat, K. and Hudson, S. Making computers easier for older adults to use: area cursors and sticky icons. *Proc. CHI '97*, 266-271.
34. Yeung, S., Lui, J., Liu, J., and Yan, J. Detecting cheaters for multiplayer games: theory, design and implementation. *Proc. IEEE CCNS 2006*, 1178-1182.
35. Youssef, A. and Cossell, S. Thoughts on adjusting perceived difficulty in games. *Proc. Australasian Conference on Interactive Entertainment*, 1-4, 2009.

Data Cracker: Developing a Visual Game Analytic Tool for Analyzing Online Gameplay

Ben Medler
Georgia Institute of Technology
Atlanta, GA
benmedler@gatech.edu

Michael John
Electronic Arts, Inc. (EA)
Redwood City, CA
MJohn@ea.com

Jeff Lane
Great Northern Way
Vancouver, BC, Canada
jefflane@post.harvard.edu

ABSTRACT

Game analytics is a domain that focuses on the systems and methods used to analyze game-related data. In this paper we present how a visual game analytic tool can be developed to analyze player gameplay behavior. Our tool, Data Cracker, was built for monitoring gameplay in Dead Space 2, the latest game in the Dead Space franchise. We use Data Cracker as a case study to inform a larger discussion of designing a visual game analytic tool while working with a game team. Our design approach focuses on increasing the data literacy of a game team. This means getting an entire team interested and involved with game analytics. We found that building our tool during the early game development cycle, creating multiple early visual prototypes and branding the tool to the Dead Space team caused more team members to become interested in our tool. Increasing interest in analytics is also a means, we argue, for changing the common occurrence within the game industry to disband teams after a game is released. Instead, we promote the creation of "live" teams which stay attached to a game long after it is release in order to continue the analysis process. Additionally, we discuss the barriers one might face when developing game analytic tools, such as prejudice against analytics or the technical issues involved when collecting large data sets. All of these examples are presented as insights we gained while coupling analytic tool design to game development.

Author Keywords

Game analytics, visual analytics, information visualization, team communication, game design, player behavior.

ACM Classification Keywords

K8.0. General: Games; H5.m. Information interfaces and presentation (e.g., HCI): Miscellaneous.

General Terms

Design

INTRODUCTION

Analytics is currently a hot topic within the game industry, driven in part by the extensive use of web-style analytics by the social gaming powerhouses [2, 20], but adoption of analytics in mainstream games tends to be more cocktail conversation than actual ongoing use. Game analytics is a domain that focuses on the systems and methods used to analyze game-related data (also referred to as game telemetry) and therefore can be a large area to cover. Analyzing a game's financial records, development progression and software metrics can all be considered game analytics. Instead, we refer to the type of game analytics which influences how games are designed by analyzing players, an area of analysis that is very prominent among industry professionals [17, 21, 23, 42] and academic researchers, with a good overview in [27]. Monitoring player behavior means logging in-game events, or metrics, such as when a player begins a level or performs an action like jumping while in the midst of gameplay [24]. From a game design point of view, behavior data is useful for determining how players are actually playing a game in their natural environment, versus other evaluation methods like self-reporting surveys or controlled play tests.

We have developed a visual game analytic tool, Data Cracker, in order to explore how visual game analytic practices based on player behavior analysis can augment the game design process and seek to use the tool as a case study to instigate a wider discussion of game analytics. Data Cracker is a prototype system built at Electronic Arts (EA), one of the world's largest game publisher/developer, as part of the company's initiative to provide its game studios with analytic tools. In the past many EA studios have built analytic tools for analyzing player data but have typically been focused on recording metrics for monitoring financial prosperity. Only a few visual systems built at EA track player behavior and with a few notable exceptions, prior to development of the Data Cracker, these had largely been side projects initiated by various EA employees who built the systems outside of their normal duties. As a response, the Data Cracker initiative is a formal attempt at EA to innovate and create best practices for building game analytic tools. However, development of Data Cracker was more than an experiment to determine how to best develop a game analytic tool, it was a chance to explore the difficulties that can arise when inserting analytic tools into a creative process such as game design.

Data Cracker was built by the authors while employed by EA for an internal EA game studio Visceral Games and deployed to monitor player behavior from the game Dead Space 2 (DS2) [45], the sequel to the critically acclaimed game Dead Space [44]. Our team worked directly with the DS2 multiplayer team in order to help monitor online multiplayer gameplay. This is the first time that a multiplayer component has been offered in a Dead Space game, which is one reason way Visceral's DS2 team was eager to use a tool for analyzing player gameplay behavior. Through our interaction with the DS2 team and the development of Data Cracker we gained many insights related to working with an external game team in addition to the best practices we discovered related to developing a visual game analytic tool. This joint effort format between a game development team and an analytic team will likely continue at EA making the insights we gained valuable for future analytic projects.

In this paper we present the insights gained from working with the DS2 team and how the design of the visual game analytic tool Data Cracker shifted as the game, and team, shifted. We begin with a review of other game analytic systems and relate them to the field of visual analytics which revolves around the exploration of data through visualization. In the past, EA teams would typically analyze data using spread sheets, or hastily created web-based visualizations. With Data Cracker we provide the DS2 team with multiple visualizations that help them explore their data from a different perspective and makes data analysis much more accessible. Next, we describe DS2's multiplayer gameplay and present the final Data Cracker architecture. Using our development cycle as a case study informs the subsequent discussion of important guidelines for implementing a visual game analytic tool as part of a game team's development process. This includes covering the production methods we found necessary to build Data Cracker along with the technological and human barriers we faced when working with a team during their development cycle. Finally, we critique our game analytic insights gained from this project in order separate the idiosyncrasies of our situation from game analytics at large. This will help other game teams gauge how our insights may or may not apply to their game or development process.

DEFINING VISUAL GAME ANALYTICS

Perhaps the most predominant examples of visual game analytic tools are the services available for games built on the Flash platform. Mochibot [26], Nonoba [28] and Playtomic [29] are three examples of visual analytic services Flash developers can use to monitor player gameplay behavior. In the past, earlier services like Mochibot were used to determine the number of users loading a particular game, which justified ad revenue for game developers who placed ads in their games. These analytic services have expanded now to include features such as player achievements, micro-transactions systems and player behavior tracking through monitoring gameplay events. However, these systems are only available for games built on the Flash platform and act as basic analysis systems similar to other, offline, visual analytic tools like Tableau [39] or Spotfire [37].

Shifting to the PC and console platforms, Zoeller [49] presented an example of a developer-facing visual analytic tool, SkyNet, used by the game developer Bioware. This system focuses on the game development process by monitoring developer behavior rather than players. Bug tracking, software metrics and social networking features are combined to create an online-portal where developers can both stay in touch with one another and have consistent access to their game's development status. While many features in SkyNet use spreadsheets to represent data, visual callouts such as color-coding important information are used, in addition to other visual graphs, to display information such as the number of bugs filed and fixed. Heat maps are also used to denote where crashes occur in a game's space, even giving developers the option to click on the map in SkyNet and be transported to the location within the game environment. SkyNet is an example of how visual game analytics can be used to monitor other game-related data, such as the developer behavior and software metrics. Data Cracker, in contrast, is used to analyze the player's experience, both during development (e.g. player testing and beta tests) and after the game is released.

Beyond a single game studio's tools, user research groups at larger game publishers also use game analytic systems for analyzing player behavior. Microsoft's TRUE system [17] is one example. TRUE is a game analytic system built for both user testing and beta testing games. When used for user testing, the system can record player metrics, capture their video output and prompt players with surveys to gauge their attitude. Collecting both video recordings and player attitudinal data help inform the behavior metrics which could otherwise be misleading without proper context. However, video and attitudinal data is only collected within an onsite lab-based setting. When TRUE is used to capture data from beta testers it essential performs in the same way as Data Cracker, only logging player metric data. Additionally, TRUE has means of visualizing the data that is collected and has proved useful for game designers when making decisions on how to alter a game's mechanics. In order to expand on systems like TRUE we seek to bolster the uniqueness and life cycle of game analytic tools on top of features like video recording and data visualization. As we discuss in the following sections, branding tools for specific game teams and promoting data literacy are needed to further advance game analytics.

Stepping away from game analytics for a moment, two other larger areas devoted to visualizing and analyze data include visual analytics [40] and information visualization [3, 6, 8, 41, 46]. These growing research areas explore the advantages of visualizing data [46] which include enhancing a person's: comprehension of large datasets, perception of emergent properties, ability to find problems within datasets, and capability to form hypotheses. "Vision is not only the fastest and most nuanced sensory portal too the world, it is also the one most intimately connected with cognition," [6] which is why we feel that visual analytics is an important area to pursue when providing game analytic tools for developers.

Visual game analytics is also a way to provide greater universal usability [36] and data literacy for members of a game team. From interacting with the DS2 team we found that if analytic tools can be created to provide greater accessibility to more members of the game team those tools become significantly more useful in advancing design discussions amongst the team. Providing visualized examples of gameplay data is less intimidating than handing a game developer a spread sheet of numbers. While there may be specific personal qualities that make someone adept at becoming data analysts [6] there are certainly examples of how "casual" information visualization can increase a person's literacy of data analysis and allow further reflection [30] that can be beneficial for game teams.

DS2 GAMEPLAY & DATA CRACKER'S ARCHITECTURE

In this section we describe the type of gameplay found in Dead Space 2 and the architecture behind Data Cracker. This information provides context to our discussion of design insights and procedures for working with the DS2 team in the next section.

Dead Space 2 Gameplay

Dead Space 2 multiplayer gameplay is based in the third-person shooter genre and places two asymmetric teams against each other in battle, the human security forces verses an alien team known as the necromorphs (necros). Matches between these two teams consist of two rounds where one team plays as the humans first, the other team as the necros, and these teams switch sides in the subsequent round. Humans and necros are asymmetric teams because each side has their own unique abilities and different goals for winning. For example, the human team has a series of objectives (holding a position, turning on a machine, gathering components) that they must complete within a given timespan, while the necro team attempts to stall the human team until time expires. This makes balancing these two teams a subtle and very challenging task for the game's designers because the diversity of abilities can make one side more powerful than the other causing an unfair game.

These and other differences between the teams affected what Data Cracker needed to monitor. The human security team uses an assortment of projectile weapons (i.e. guns) as their primary weapons and each team member has the ability to heal one another with health packs. Humans can take multiple weapons with them into each match which makes monitoring which weapons they choose an important factor. Moreover, players on the necro team must choose from four different classes with fixed abilities and weapons. For instance, the class known as the Pack is fast, lightly armored and only has a short-ranged, melee attack. Necromorph players thus cannot switch between different weapons while playing and instead are forced to choose one of the four classes each time they are killed (before they respawn and re-enter gameplay). Additionally, players gain experience for performing actions during play, some only available for either humans or necros, which lead to further rewards. Normally, gathering data about these various distinctions happens through play testing a limited population, which can be time consuming and difficult to analyze in a statistically significant way. However by recording data telemetrically, data from hundreds of thousands of games can be analyzed.

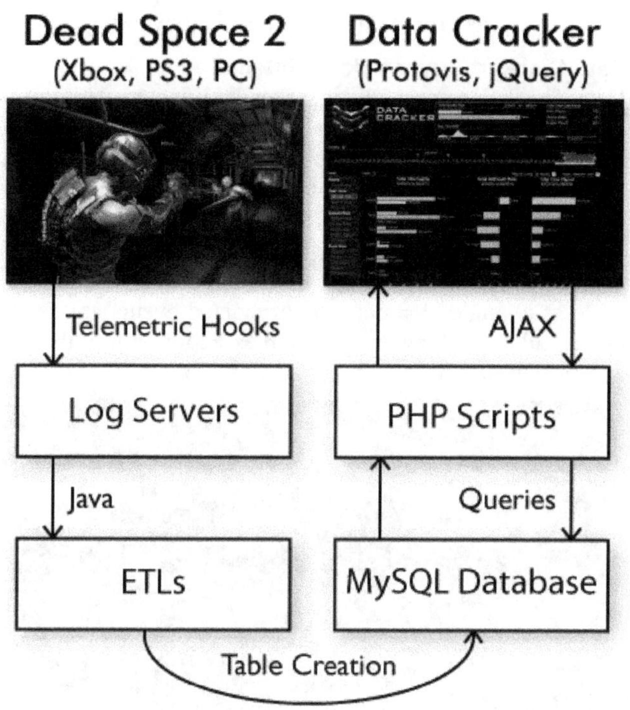

Figure 1. The Data Cracker architecture combines both server-side systems analyzing data from Dead Space 2 and a client-side web interface for data visualization.

Recording Players

Player events from DS2 multiplayer matches are recorded to monitor how each team is behaving and allows designers to balance the human and necromorph teams. Recording events in DS2 works by adding telemetric "hooks" or functions into a game's code which send event data to a separate server location whenever an event in the game is triggered. The basic data format that is sent by a hook in Dead Space 2 includes: an anonymous unique user identifier; region information; event identifiers such as an event's name and type; a timestamp of when the event occurred both on the local machine and on the server; and, finally, specific information about the event which are often represented using key-value pairs (i.e. a variable name and its value). In DS2 these key-value pairs hold information related to:

- Identifying when unique matches start and end.
- When the human team completes objectives.
- The position of players as they traverse the play area.
- When players equip weapons or classes.
- How much weapon damage players inflict on other players.
- When players are killed by or kill another player.
- When players respawn after being killed.
- Whether a team wins or loses a match.
- How much experience each player gains from a playing in a match.

After events are logged, the server-side portion of Data Cracker begins organizing the collected player data.

Data Cracker Server-side Architecture

Data Cracker uses a client-server architecture (Figure 1), processing event logs from DS2 on the server-side and presenting a visual analytic tool on the client-side. The server portion organizes and aggregates events together into data formats required for the client-side analysis tool. Beginning with raw text logs containing recorded player events from DS2, each event is stored within a MySQL table as a single element. The organized events are used to create additional aggregated tables representing the data and is similar to an online analytic processing (OLAP) system [5]. OLAPs aggregate large datasets along a single measurement, creating a separate list of multiple dimensions to query the measurement against. In DS2, each weapon type found in the game is an example of a measurement and two dimensions that are created include how long players held a weapon during a match and the amount of damage a weapon caused during a match. Even though each individual weapon event is stored in one table, additional aggregated weapon tables are created as a pre-process to ease the burden of later analysis and improve responsiveness of the tool.

The processes through which these aggregated tables are created are called Extraction, Transformation, Loading (ETL) processes. ETLs "are pieces of software responsible for the extraction of data from several sources, their cleansing, customization and insertion" into databases [43]. ETLs in Data Cracker create aggregated tables, often representing averages and totals, that are separated by day. We found that aggregating based on single days was detailed enough for the DS2 team to gain insight from the data (however this process can be duplicated using shorter or longer time frames). The aggregated data produced by the ETLs are stored in separate MySQL tables which are directly referenced by the client-side website.

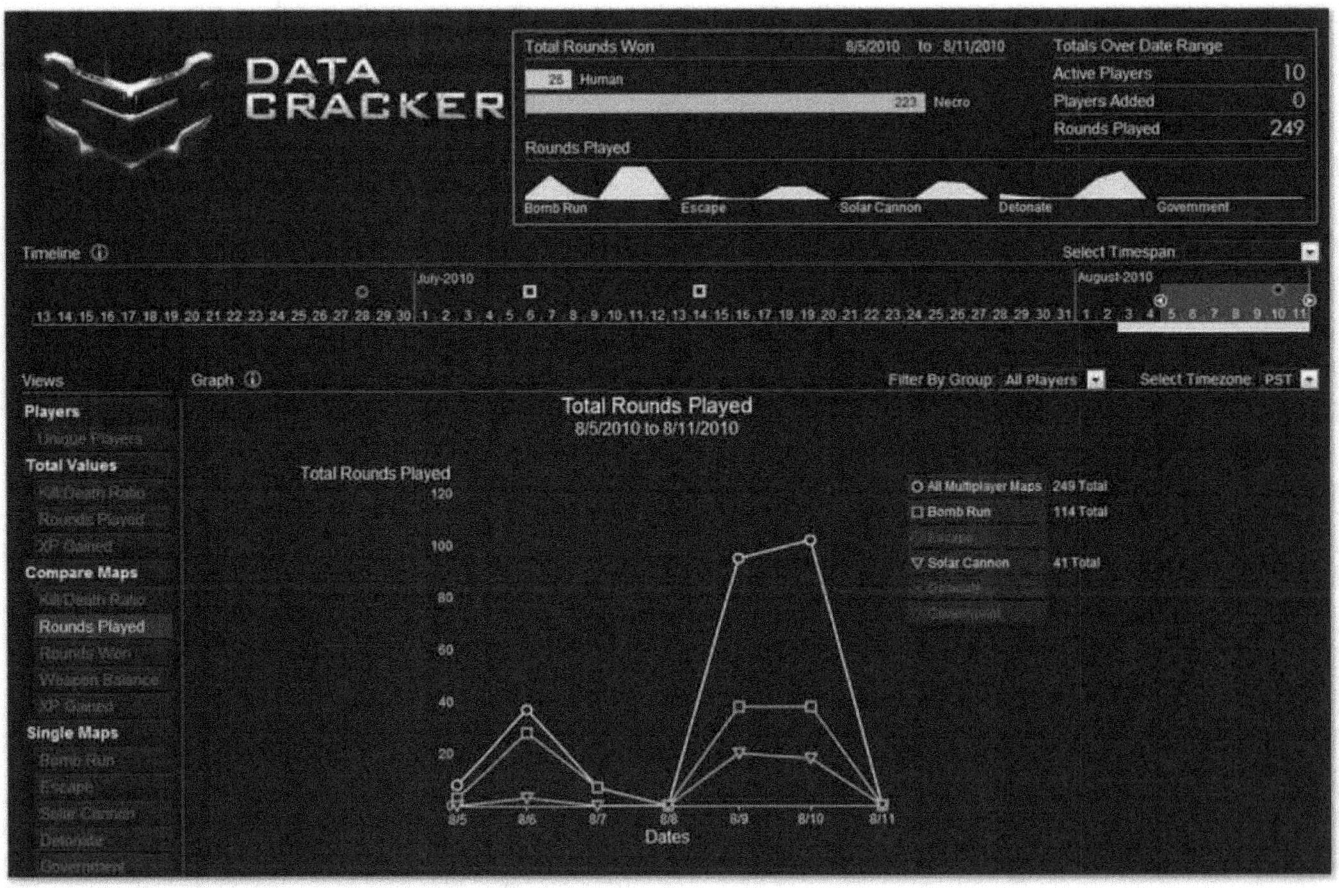

Figure 2. Screenshot of the Data Cracker client-side website.

Data Cracker Client-side Website

The client-side website (Figure 1 and 2) is an online visual analytic tool designed using a user-centered approach. Our team worked alongside the DS2 multiplayer team as they developed their gameplay, regularly meeting to design and test the tool (we go into further detail about the design of the tool in the next section). Data Cracker's client-side website visualizes the aggregated data created by the server ETLs using Protovis [31] and jQuery [14], both javascript libraries that run on the client's machine. Queries are served by AJAX calls to PHP scripts which grabs data from the aggregated tables in the MySQL database.

The basic interface and feature layout of the tool includes:

The **Summary Graphs** at the top of the page show overview values about the collected player gameplay data. This includes how many players have been tracked, how many matches have been played, the winning percentages of the human and necro teams and the number of matches played on each map in the game across time. These summary graphs change whenever the user changes the time frame they are viewing using the timeline.

The **Timeline** is an interactive selection table that displays the range of days which are currently being analyzed. When users click and drag across a range of days every graph in Data Cracker alters itself to display data from that time frame. Once a date range has been selected it can also be dragged to encompass other dates, giving users the ability to always view a fixed number of days (such as a week's worth of data). Data Cracker also allows user to mark events on the timeline, such as acknowledging when a new patch was released for the game, which may affect how a user should interpret data from that time period.

The **Main Graph** area displays the graphs built for analyzing player gameplay data. These graphs display data related to: unique/total users being monitored, kill/death ratios, number of rounds played and won, experience points gained by players, weapon statistics, and objective completion rates. Following the Shniderman visualization mantra of "overview first, zoom and filter, then details-on-demand," [35] each data area, for example number of rounds played, has an overview graph which display the total values for the current date range selected. Users can then navigate to more detailed graphs which allow them to zoom and filter the data, for instance data can be separated based on a specific map. Some graphs also offer details-on-demand through the ability to sort values or only displays values as users interact with the graph. Finally, each graph displays a title, its date range and, if necessary, its axes/key values so that screenshots of graphs can be taken and added to gameplay reports, which are often created by game development teams.

GUIDELINES FOR DEVELOPING A VISUAL GAME ANALYTIC TOOL

Working with the Dead Space 2 team brought to light many important design factors about visual game analytic tool development. In this section we list a number of insights we gained from our development process, each one discussing specific features that should appear within a game analytic tool or how the development process should be structured. Insights are broken into three categories: production, functional and game team integration. Production insights revolve around the goals and development procedures used to build Data Cracker. These production insights are the most novel in comparison to the other game analytic systems covered. Functional insights highlight the actual features and interaction capabilities of the tool while game team integration insights focus on our interactions with the DS2 game team. These insights are perhaps less novel, and more apparent to seasoned analytic tool developers, but are listed in order to reaffirm their necessity while developing a game analytic system.

Production Insights

Create analytic tools in parallel with game development

Commonly, analytic tools are created after a dataset, or the procedure for creating that dataset, is finalized. Building a tool for investigating airline ticket ordering [22], housing prices [48], document analysis [16], or network structures [7] can rely on the datasets being produced in a standard manner (e.g. airline ticket data will not suddenly change formats). However, in these investigative cases analytics tool are used to gain insight from data in order to make decisions which will not affect the data's content [16]. Someone analyzing documents for security threats will not alter the contents of those documents. Metric analysis of player behavior in games, in contrast, can be used as a powerful extension of the traditional design process of iteration and refinement, altering the very nature of the data players can produce. For example, the DS2 team continually added new telemetric hooks and altered mechanics like the types of weapons available in the game, altering the data produced along with those gameplay changes. The consideration and specification of the telemetric data format became a positive feedback loop for the game's design team during this iterative process. Having access to gameplay data forced them to quantify their experiential expectations of each gameplay alteration.

Developers therefore can benefit from analytic tools not only after a game is released, where the tools may benefit the creation of patches to make gameplay alterations, but as soon as a team begins testing their gameplay, which generally happens very early in the development cycle. For example, during the DS2 beta test the team was able to use our tool to find an exploit players were using involving a particular weapon called the javelin gun. Using Data Cracker to review the weapons usage percentage and damage dealt the team was able to tweak the weapons power to balance gameplay. At the same time players were also complaining online that the necro team was too weak in multiplayer matches. The DS2 team was able to verify these complaints using Data Cracker and subsequently knew how much to tune the necro class' health and damage by analyzing the values visualized by the tool.

Produce early visual prototypes

Just like with game development prototyping [32], presenting the graphs and analytic features of a tool early is vital to help communication between the analytic team and the game team. Each graph produced for Data Cracker was first prototyped and discussed in our weekly meetings with our DS2 team contacts. The entire process, from events being triggered to visualizing the data, was discussed at our meeting as we prototyped each graph through the development process. Giving the DS2 team high fidelity prototypes that functioned and displayed real data helped the team understand how the tool would be beneficial to them once completed. We also used prototypes to win arguments about adding certain features or what data should be collected. For example, after presenting our graphs for analyzing player experience points gained during matches we were able to show that the points needed to be separated by team type in order to show inequities between the human and necro teams, even though experience points are only awarded after matches where a team had played as both sides. Prototypes brought out these types of situations in our discussions with the DS2 team: thinking of different ways of interpreting the data and what might be missing from our analysis.

Build for a Broad Audience

Building a game analytic tool during a game development process means the data being collected could affect a large number of members on a game's team. Designers and producers may have to change the game's mechanics which affects programmers who have to code the mechanics and artists who have to create content related to the mechanics. Giving the power to analyze game data to each of these groups during the development process can help teams communicate changes more effectively.

Early game analytic tools should thus be designed with the expectation that a broad audience will use them, not just a set of "superusers" who intuitively understand the game's underlying structure. This means providing tiers of analysis, or ways that users of different levels can access the data. With Data Cracker we achieve this by providing graphs that visualize the same set of data but offer different levels of interaction. For example, users can view one graph that shows the total number of rounds played, a second graph that breaks down the total rounds played by map and the win percentage for each team, and a third set of graphs for each map breaking down the percentage of human teams that completed that map's series of objectives. Game producers may only wish to view the total number of rounds played while a game designer may want to know how often teams are completing a certain objective on a specific map.

Performing usability tests on tools are also invaluable in proving and iterating the tool's broad accessibility. We conducted tests both internally with multiple members of the DS2 team and with outside EA employees to gauge how quickly they could understand the interface and features. As a result we added features such as help icons that explain graphs to users and help indoctrinate team members who had never used our tool before. We also focused on using simple visualizations methods like bar graphs and line charts which can decrease data interpretation errors [11]. Certainly, as tool development continues, features that dive deeper into the data can be added but continuing to support the earlier broader features will keep a team focused on the benefits of using analytics.

Brand a tool to a particular team

Data Cracker could have been visually designed in a generic fashion so any game's data could be connected to the tool and analyzed. Other data visualization software takes this approach [37, 39] and offers users a common interface no matter what data is being analyzed. However, for Data Cracker we took a different approach and branded the tool specifically for Dead Space 2.

The main reason for designing the tool in such a way was to make sure that the DS2 team knew that this was their personal tool. Bateman et al. [1] found that users find charts and graphs that are visually embellished (with "unnecessary" visual elements) to be more enjoyable and help with retention. While most of the graphs in Data Cracker are not embellished with extreme graphics, certain DS2 symbols were added to mark Data Cracker as a DS2 tool. First, the term "Data Cracker" was actually decided upon because there is a term called 'Planet Cracking' that plays a major role in the lore of the Dead Space franchise. Second, the title graphic for Data Cracker also uses artwork from DS2 depicting the main character and other DS2 artwork is used throughout the tool. Third, the color scheme used in the tool is the same color scheme used in DS2. For instance, a certain shade of blue is often associated with 'safety' in the game and is used to depict the human team's data, while red symbolizes 'distress' and used to show data associated with the necro team. Finally, we also made use of DS2 artwork when ever creating material describing or promoting the tool. Each of these examples works to create a common identity for Data Cracker that links it directly with the DS2 team.

Encourage "live" teams

As the final insight into producing a game analytic tool, it is important to encourage the game team to create "live" teams which will incorporate analytic tools into the development process. A live team is a portion of a game development team that supports a game after it is released. Often times supporting a game after release refers to customer service representatives or development team that create patches or extra downloadable content (DLC). Alternatively, when referring to live teams in relation to game analytics it means a team that continues to analyze the game after release and develop further tools. Their duties should go beyond finding bugs to fix. Live teams should monitor gameplay for months after the game is released keeping track of the ebb and flow of player experiences, altering tools as required. Analysis reports should be created detailing how players are reacting to the game's mechanics and should be shared with other teams creating DLC or working on games within the same genre. Game teams are often dissolved after a game is released which is one leading cause for why game analytics has been slow to take off, there is no one around after the game is released to analyze player reactions. By promoting live teams which stay active after a game comes out it ensures that analytic tools are properly used and have a greater impact on future games produced.

Functional Insights

Aggregate data for quick analysis

Query time is often a big problem when dealing with large datasets where searching through each element can be time consuming [5]. DS2 could have upwards of hundreds of thousands of players after the game is released, each of which is reporting their behavior events back to EA's servers. The common practices of OLAP [5] and ETL processing [43] were implemented in Data Cracker in order to get around this problem. For example, one set of graphs shows how many matches were played on the different multiplayer maps available. The calculations to add the total matches played on every map, each day would have been extremely costly to perform multiple times. As a result, an ETL was produced that added the total matches played on every map, each day and placed in a separate table. Data from thousands of events are combined into a single element making querying and visualization much faster while still leaving those events intact, within another table, for other systems to access or data mine.

Use time-based queries

Time emerged as a key dimension for almost all the gameplay analytics we came across for DS2. In most cases, time provides the key added dimension to give context to gameplay data which has been the case for other game analytic systems [17]. For the Data Cracker tool, the importance of time as a data dimension is why the timeline is the highest-order interactive element of the tool (affecting all graphs in the tool), and why it received the most attention in terms of usability. Our initial designs included two text boxes that marked the start and end dates of the time frame shown on each individual graph. This eventually changed to a single set of boxes that governed the time frame for all graphs in the tool because the DS2 team wanted to compare different graphs within a single time period without having to set each graphs time frame individually. After more iterations, the time frame was shown on an interactive timeline making it easier to select a date range, move the range to different dates, as well as mark the timeline with key events that could affect the interpretation of the data (e.g. when downloadable content, DLC, is added to the game and may affect player behavior).

Debug the game and data hooks with the tool

The creation of telemetric hooks to track player behavior is a software process requiring the use of an API and as such is as prone to error as any other part of the software. Insuring that event hooks accurately represent player behavior is a key part of the analytic system development process [15]. Having game analytic tools functioning early within the development cycle allows another avenue to debug both the metric system and the game. At one point during Data Cracker's development, for instance, we started receiving additional weapon related events from players who had already completed a match, events that should not have been occurring. When we reported this to the DS2 engineers it was found that the game was creating multiple copies of each player and each was sending telemetry data. The engineers were quickly able to rectify the mistake thanks to our tool. If that data had been allowed to persist our aggregated calculations would have been skewed, affecting how the data was to be interpreted.

Create functionality to deal with legal Issues

When game companies collect player data they have to follow different rules depending on the geographic location of the player. Compliance with these rules is extremely important in the current climate where online privacy is heatedly being debated [4, 19]. EA, for instance, cannot collect data from players in over 100 different countries. In North American countries like the U.S., Canada and Mexico users must agree to a Terms of Service document in order for the company to track data. Other countries have an opt-out policy where data is collected by default but can be turned off by the player. Procedures within an analytic system must be in place to handle these different geographic categories.

Another legal issue surrounding recording player data is keeping the player's identity safe. An event tracking system has to know which unique user an event is coming from in order to maintain an accurate depiction of the events that took place in a game. However this must be stored in such a fashion that the identifier (in our case, an integer) does not identify the player personally. Data Cracker, working in concert with EA's centralized online infrastructure, maintains compliance with both the geographic and identity related restrictions.

Game Team Integration Insights

Meet with an interdisciplinary team

Interdisciplinary teams are a necessity within the game industry as much as they are within other design and media professions [18]. Game analytics too is an interdisciplinary practice and each game development discipline use analytics for different purposes [25]. While developing Data Cracker we regularly met with a team consisting of the lead programmer, producer and designer on the DS2 multiplayer team. Each was invested in the tool differently. Our main programmer adding the telemetric hooks into the game needed to know what data we wanted to collect and voiced his own opinions on what data was possible to collect. The lead producer and designer were more interested in how the tool was going to help them balance the game's mechanics. Meeting with an interdisciplinary team meant we were both able to make relevant design choices that supported multiple members while also promoting the transfer of game analytic knowledge between the members themselves. This helped bypass common interdisciplinary team communication barriers [9] by allowing our DS2 team members to understand how the tool functioned and everyone's analytic needs.

Prepare for analytic prejudices

Collecting player data is certainly not a new concept and EA already had an entire infrastructure built for monitoring player events. One persistent problem, however, was many game teams incorporated data collection but never analyzed the data. Understandably, these meant some Dead Space 2 team members were skeptical about our promise to provide a tool that would make use of player data, because they had seen how ineffective previous efforts had been. This type of prejudice against a new procedure or technology is common in other research. Herbsleb et al., for example, had similar experience while adding an instant messaging technology to a distributed team [12]. In our case, this prejudice made development difficult because we relied on the team to provide us with the necessary gameplay information and telemetric hooks that sent a player's data to our server. In order to get around this opposition we create example scenarios of how each data point would be used and how they would inform the team. For example, showing how increased fidelity of the experience point data would offer a better picture of which team, humans or necros, were achieving certain experience point events more often.

Anticipate the effects of game design changes

Development of Data Cracker was happening at the same time as the DS2 multiplayer gameplay was being developed: if the gameplay changed, the analytics had to change. Weekly meetings with our DS2 contacts were essential and kept us informed about changes to the gameplay. Most of these changes were cosmetic (e.g., maps or weapons being added or taken out) and only affected how certain data points were labeled. However, at one point the DS2 team limited human players to only two weapons and were forced to choose one specific weapon. This radically altered how often players switched weapons and the variety of weapons they had to choose from during play. Analyzing weapon data had to change as a result and while the graphs didn't change visually the interpretations of the graphs changed. Tracking those interpretation changes was vital for keeping the team updated about our progress and, in the future, would help anyone attempting to analyze DS2 data with our tool as well.

Update the team regularly

While staying connected to the DS2 multiplayer team helped us keep track of gameplay changes it was also important to stay connected with the DS2 team as a whole. Simple ways of doing this was to talk with other DS2 team members whenever possible and to participate on internal email lists, generally acting like a fellow team member. The other major way we connected with the DS2 team at large was distributing a weekly data analysis report that covered the progress of Data Cracker and interesting information we gleaned from analyzing DS2 player data. Like Data Cracker, these weekly reports were DS2 branded, often incorporating artwork from the game, and were designed to look handmade to distinguish them from standard analysis reports that game teams receive from marketing or management departments. Each issue had a certain theme based on an important feature added to Data Cracker or a specific anomaly we found in the data that week. One weekly issue focused on the Fourth of July holiday weekend, for example, where no data was logged from DS2, meaning everyone successfully stayed away from the office. We often received comments that these reports kept people interested in the tool even if they were not affiliated with the DS2 multiplayer team or DS2 in general.

DISSCUSSION

Data Cracker has been in service since August 2010. There are current plans to continue iterating on the design of the tool and to provide each team within Visceral Games with their own version. The tool has already proved useful by helping find bugs in DS2's multiplayer environment, allowing analysis of player tests and through our efforts in promoting the tool has caused other EA teams to begin designing their own analytic systems. The DS2 single player team has also used the Data Cracker's systems and web services to create complex analytics for their in-house play tests, over and above our work. While Data Cracker has been a useful tool for the DS2 team, further critiques and evaluations are required to understand how game analytics combines with the game development process.

Our insights reflect the design properties we focused on while building Data Cracker: accessibility, branding and longevity. An entire game team should have access to analytic tools throughout the game development process. Systems like TRUE seem to be particular to only user research teams [17]. We instead argue each game team must have basic data literacy skills and be able to use analytic tools as the amount of data games collect and use increases [24]. One way to raise data literacy is through branding tools for specific teams. The Skynet system [49] is an example that demonstrates how a tool can create a community around game analytics. With Data Cracker, we sought to bring a semblance of that community feature by branding our tool to the DS2 team which boosted the team's interest in the tool. Finally, analytic tools should be built to work across the entire development process. Analytics should represent a reliable means of testing a game and live teams can be created to handle the analysis of data after a game is released. A regular occurrence in the game industry is to dissolve a team after completing a game. However, the new industry emphasis on supporting games after their release (with DLC, patches and online player dossier systems [25]) demands live teams as necessary for post-release content development.

There are also limitations to some of the insights we presented. First, building a tool for broad audiences and aggregating data would not be ideal for developing data mining analytic tools. Data mining player events would require different methods [47] and would likely be built for users with special analytic or statistics training [6]. Second, creating branded systems and establishing "live" teams may create significant cost overhead that game studios are not prepared to invest. While we argue that game analytics are vital, worth the initial investment, others question the over-zealous use of metric-driven design [10, 13].

In contrast to the limitations of our insights, there are a number of avenues where our insights can be expanded upon in the future. Data Cracker was built to promote data literacy among development teams and as their literacy rises developers will be prepared for more robust analytic systems. Adding in data mining functionality for more automatic analysis, such as player modeling [33], could increase the complexity of the available analysis that a tool provides to developers. Other visual representations can be added as well. For instance, player events happen within a hierarchy (organized by map, level, play session, etc.) and graphs such as sunbursts [38] or treemaps [34] work well for displaying hierarchical data. Finally, there has been an increase in recent years in the number of game analytic systems that are provided to players instead of only game developers [25]. Future game analytic systems may combine developer-facing and player-facing systems with each audience given different analytical functionalities.

CONCLUSION

Data Cracker is a tool for monitoring player behavior by tracking and organizing in-game player events. The tool was built using a client-server model where ETLs are used to aggregate data on the server-side and a client-side game analytic website visualizes the collected data with a series of interactive graphs. Similar systems have been built before, such as the TRUE system [17], but unlike other game analytic tools our design approach for building Data Cracker was to increase the Dead Space 2 team's data literacy. As digital games increasingly utilize player data for gameplay and as part of their development process it is not enough to design for small subsets of "superusers" who understand the importance of data analysis. Therefore we set out to build an analytic tool for monitoring player behavior that is accessible to an entire game team.

The insights we gain from our design and development process were split into three separate categories: production, functionality and game team integration. Through our production process we found that building our tool in parallel with the game development cycle and having early visualization prototypes familiarized the DS2 team with Data Cracker. We used tiers of analysis to lay out visualizations offering different levels of detail so team members were not inundated by too much data at once. Branding the tool to Dead Space 2 also helped identify the tool as part of the DS2 team and created further interest. For Data Cracker's functionally we built a system that aggregated data across different dimensions including time, in-game maps and gaming platform. This meant the tool was quick to respond to queries further lowering the barrier for team members to access their data. The tool had to also follow a number of legal requirements since a broader audience would have access to potentially sensitive data. Finally, we had to maintain communications through our interactions with the game team. Initially we were met with prejudice against analytic tools and had to watch out for unexpected changes made to the game that affected our tool's functionality. We were able to minimize these problems by continually meeting with an interdisciplinary team working on DS2 to present functional prototypes that showed the effectiveness of the tool and determine if any game changes would affect the design.

The insights into designing these tools and working with game teams which we present in this paper are only the beginning to what is capable within the domain of game analytics. As a domain that is still growing game analytics shows great potential when used to augment the game design process. It is now possible for game designers to support their design intuitions with quantitative measurments, allowing for quicker iterations during the development cycle. Analytic tools can monitor millions of players after a game is released giving developers data they never had the capabilities of accessing. Developers need to continue to discuss their analytic processes and pursue creating permanent "live" teams within their company to work as tool developers and gameplay analysts.

ACKNOWLEDGMENTS

The authors would like to thank Scott Probst, Simon Cooper and the entire Dead Space 2 multiplayer team for their support of this work.

REFERENCES

1. Bateman, S., Mandryk, R. L., Gutwin, C., Genest, A., McDine, D. and Brooks, C. Useful Junk? The Effects of Visual Embellishment on Comprehension and Memorability of Charts. *In Proc. CHI 2010*. (2010).
2. Caoili, E. *Zynga Chooses Tableau For Data Visualization, Analysis*. Gamasutra. (2010) http://www.gamasutra.com/view/news/28408/.
3. Card, S., Mackinlay, J. and Shneiderman B. *Readings in Information Visualization: Using Visualization to Think*. Morgan Kaufmann (1999).
4. Carvin, A. *Debate Continues Around Facebook Privacy Changes*. NPR (2010). http://www.npr.org/blogs/alltechconsidered/2010/04/29/126394012/npr-listeners-react-to-facebook-privacy-changes
5. Chaudhuri, S. and Dayal, U. An overview of data warehousing and OLAP technology. *ACM SIGMOD Record*, 26, 1 (1997), 65-74.

6. Few, S. *Now You See It: Simple Visualization Techniques for Quantitative Analysis*. Analytics Press (2009).
7. Freire, M., Plaisant, C., Shneiderman, B. and Golbeck, J. ManyNets: An Interface for Multiple Network Analysis and Visualization. *In Proc. CHI 2010*. (2010).
8. Fry, B. *Visualizing data*. O'Reilly Media (2008).
9. Haythornthwaite, C. Knowledge Flow in Interdisciplinary Teams. In Proc. System Sciences 2005, IEEE (2005).
10. Hecker, C. Achievements Considered Harmful?. *GDC 2010*. (2010).
11. Heer, J. and Bostock, M. Crowdsourcing graphical perception: using mechanical turk to assess visualization design. *In Proc. CHI 2010*. (2010).
12. Herbsleb, J., Atkins, D., Boyer, D., Handel, M., and Finholt, T. Introducing instant messaging and chat in the workplace. In Proc. CHI 2002, ACM Press (2002), 171-178.
13. Jamison, P. *FarmVillains*. SF Weekly (2010). http://www.sfweekly.com/2010-09-08/news/farmvillains/.
14. jQuery. http://jquery.com/.
15. Kaner, C. and Bond, W. Software Engineering Metrics: What Do They Measure and How Do We Know? Software Metrics Symposium, IEEE (2004).
16. Kang, Y., Gorg, C. and Stasko, J. Evaluating Visual Analytics Systems for Investigative Analysis: Deriving Design Principles from a Case Study. *In Proc. VAST 2009*. (2009).
17. Kim, J., Gunn, D., Schuh, E., Phillips, B., Pagulayan, R. and Wixon, D. Tracking real-time user experience (TRUE): a comprehensive instrumentation solution for complex systems. In Proc. CHI 2008, ACM Press (2008), 443-452.
18. Kim, S. Interdisciplinary Cooperation. In Laurel B. (Ed.) The Art of Human-Computer Interface Design (pp. 34-44). Addison-Wesley, Reading, MA, (1990).
19. Kincaid, J. *This Is The Second Time A Google Engineer Has Been Fired For Accessing User Data*. Techcrunch (2010). http://techcrunch.com/2010/09/14/google-engineer-fired-security/.
20. Kontagent. http://www.kontagent.com/.
21. Lazzaro, Nicole (2007). The 4 Most Important Emotions of Game Design. *GDC 2007*. (2007).
22. Liu, Z., Stasko, J. and Sullivan, T. SellTrend: Inter-Attribute Visual Analysis of Temporal Transaction Data.*In Proc.Infovis 2009*. (2009).
23. Ludwig, J. Flogging: Data collection on the high seas. *Austin GDC 2007*. (2007).
24. Medler, B. Generations of Game Analytics, Achievements and High Scores. *Eludamos – Journal for Computer Game Culture*, 3, 2 (2009), 177-194.
25. Medler, B. and Magerko, B. Analytics of Play: Using Information Visualization and Gameplay Practices for Visualizing Video Game Data. Parsons Journal for Information Mapping, 3, 1 (2011). (in press).
26. Mochibot. http://www.mochibot.com/.
27. Nacke, L., Drachen, A., Kuikkaniemi, K., Niesenhaus, J., Korhonen, H., Hoogen, W., Poels, K., IJsselsteijn, W., and Kort, Y. Playability and Player Experience Research. *In Proc. DiGRA 2009*. (2009).
28. Nonoba. http://nonoba.com/.
29. Playtomic. http://playtomic.com/.
30. Pousman, Z., Stasko, J., and Mateas, M. Casual Information Visualization: Depictions of Data in Everyday Life. *IEEE Transactions on Visualization and Computer Graphics*, 13, 6 (2007), 1145-1152.
31. Protovis. http://vis.stanford.edu/protovis/.
32. Rollings, A. and Morris, D. *Game Architecture and Design: A New Edition*. New Riders (2004).
33. Sharma, M., Ontañón, S., Mehta, M. and Ram, A. Drama Management and Player Modeling for Interactive Fiction Games. Computational Intelligence, 26, 2 (2010), 183-211.
34. Shneiderman, B. Tree visualization with tree-maps: 2-d space-filling approach. ACM Transactions on Graphics, 11, 1 (1992), 92-99.
35. Shneiderman, B. The eyes have it: A task by data type taxonomy for information visualizations. *IEEE Visual Languages*, (1996), 336– 343.
36. Shneiderman, B. Universal usability. *Communications of the ACM*, 43, 5 (2000), 84-91.
37. Spotfire Professional. http://spotfire.tibco.com/
38. Stasko, J. and Zhang, E. Focus plus context display and navigation techniques for enhancing radial, space-filling hierarchy visualizations. In IEEE InfoVis, (2000), 57-65.
39. Tableau Desktop. http://www.tableausoftware.com/
40. Thomas, J. and Cook, K. *Illuminating the Path: The Research and Development Agenda for Visual Analytics*. IEEE Computer Society (2005).
41. Tufte, E. *The Visual Display of Quantitative Information*. Graphics Press (1983).
42. Valve Corporation. Steam & Game Stats. http://www.steampowered.com/v/index.php?area=stats
43. Vassiliadis, P., Simitsis, A. and Skiadopoulos, S. Conceptual modeling for ETL processes. *In Proc. 5th ACM Workshop on Data Warehousing and OLAP*. (2002).
44. Visceral Games. *Dead Space*. [PC], USA: Electronic Arts. (2008).
45. Visceral Games. *Dead Space 2*. [Xbox360], USA: Electronic Arts. (2011).
46. Ware, C. *Information Visualization: Perception for Design*. Morgan Kaufmann (2000).
47. Weber, B. and Mateas, M. A Data Mining Approach to Strategy Prediction. IEEE CIG Symposium, (2009).
48. Williamson, C. and Schneiderman, B. The Dynamic HomeFinder: Evaluating Dynamic Queries in a Real-estate Information Exploration System. *In Proc. of R&D in Information Retrieval*. (1992). 338-346.
49. Zoeller, G. Development Telemetry in Video Games Projects. *GDC 2010*. (2010).

Ceci N'est Pas Une Pipe Bombe: Authoring Urban Landscapes with Air Quality Sensors

Stacey Kuznetsov[1], George Noel Davis[2], Jian Chiu Cheung[2], Eric Paulos[1]

Human-Computer Interaction Institute[1]
Carnegie Mellon University
Pittsburgh, PA, USA
{stace, paulos}@cs.cmu.edu

School of Electrical and Computer Engineering[2]
Carnegie Mellon University
Pittsburgh, PA, USA
{gnd, jccheung}@andrew.cmu.edu

ABSTRACT

Our work explores the convergence between participatory sensing, political activism and public expressions. Unlike prior research, which focuses on personal sensing, we present low-cost, networked air quality sensors, designed to be repositioned across public landscapes by communities of citizen stakeholders. Our GPS-enabled sensors report dust, exhaust, or VOC's (volatile organic compounds), along with temperature, humidity and light levels to a website that visualizes this data in real time. The sensors can be attached to a variety of surfaces serving as research probes to demarcate ('tag') public spaces with environmental concerns. We deploy our fully functional system with four urban communities- parents, bicyclists, homeless and activists, positioning our system as a tool for studying and supporting community togetherness and public activism. Our findings highlight community sharing of the physical sensors and dialogues surrounding the collected data.

Author Keywords

Political computing, urban computing, participatory sensing

ACM Classification Keywords

H5.m. Information interfaces and presentation (e.g., HCI): Miscellaneous.

General Terms

Design

INTRODUCTION

"Objects become things, that is, when matters of fact give way to their complicated entanglements and become matters of concern."
–Bruno Latour

A range of technologies and methods enable non-experts to collect and share environmental data through participatory sensing [3, 29, 35]. We ask how low-cost and widely available sensors can be leveraged as instruments of environmental and political change. How can citizen-collected data become a point of reflection, a tool for taking action, and a matter of public *concern*?

Participatory sensing is inspired by a history of bottom-up initiatives- from neighborhood watch campaigns to political revolutions- these movements empower stakeholders to act as agents of change. Recently, DIY (do it yourself) methods and low-cost technologies resulted in new tools for data collection, including sensor-enabled mobile phones and hand-held monitors [*e.g.,* 7] or sensors deployed on moving vehicles [2]. Despite the success of existing strategies for personal participatory sensing, there has been little exploration of important related concepts of sensor ownership, public authorship, expressions and community sensing strategies. This paper directly confronts, questions, and explores these concepts by introducing a new sensing paradigm: rather than belonging to a particular person or space, our low-cost modular sensors can be moved, left and placed throughout public spaces by various stakeholders.

Sensing as a mode of expression

We challenge the conventional notion of sensors as passive instruments of data collection. The act of placing a sensor, particularly one with politically or environmentally loaded content such as air quality, can be an overt and public act. The mere presence of such a sensor can project a statement or concern about a place, and the resulting sensor data can be broadcast within and across communities to provoke and transform perceptions, usage, and labeling of space. We explore these ideas by developing a system of networked movable sensors as tools for bottom-up community data collection and expression in the public sphere (Figure 1).

PRIOR WORK

Prior participatory sensing projects have enabled non-experts to monitor air quality with handheld monitors [7]

Figure 1. Exhaust sensor attached to fire hydrant near busy street (top left); map of exhaust data gathered by parents (top right); dust, exhaust and VOC sensors attached to bridge (bottom left); VOC sensor on park railing (bottom right).

cellphones [16] and sensors installed in private homes [22]. Air quality sensors have also been deployed on moving surfaces such as street sweepers [2], bicycles [14], robots [21] and pigeons [6], or in bounded spaces [5, 19]. Drawing from HCI work that explores the intersection between technology, art and politics [7, 9 12, 15, 17, 18,], we position our system of movable sensors as an approach for supporting community expressions and activism.

Expressions across public surfaces

Numerous technologies facilitate public engagement and authorship: Pushpin Computing [27] is a platform for computation and visualization, DataTiles [31] and Siftables [28] are programmable tile displays; 'Light Bodies' [32] are distributed interactive light nodes. We apply the flexible and modular design paradigms of past systems to the design of our public place-based sensors. Similar to LED Throwies [16], our sensors can be attached to a range of public surfaces to express and monitor environmental concerns. Unlike prior public visualizations of air quality, including wearables WearAir [23] and CO2RSET[1], the spatially-fixed pollution e-sign [20], or the municipally-installed and Air de Paris Balloon[2], our movable sensors serve as a community resource for grassroots air quality monitoring.

Community engagement and the creation of 'publics'

We explore participatory sensing as an approach for sustaining and supporting cohesive *publics* [8] –groups of people that are affected by an issue, working towards alleviating a common problem. Latour and Weibel's *Making Things Public* addresses the mechanisms by which ideas are broadcast into the public sphere, exposing the complex interplay between technology, art, space and people that fosters the creation of 'assemblies' [24]. Recent HCI literature explores design principles for supporting and creating publics [10] as well as opportunities to engage with and empower specific communities [11, 12, 25]. We present a public sensing system as a tool for monitoring and expressing community concerns. We previously explored this space through the use of sensor probes- non-working sensors that simulate the measurement of exhaust, smog, pathogens, chemicals, dust and noise, distributed to stakeholders from communities of parents, students, bicyclists, and homeless [withheld]. Participants were asked to place, leave, and move the probes throughout public spaces as if they were real sensors, and our findings suggest environmental sensing as a tool of community togetherness, engagement and activism. In this paper we re-affirm, challenge and augment these findings through the deployment of a working system with four communities of urban stakeholders.

PUBLIC PLACE-BASED SENSING

Our sensors, measuring exhaust, VOC's (volatile organic compounds), or dust, report air quality along with humidity, temperature and light levels to our central website in real time (Figure 1). Integrating commercially available sensors with off-the-shelf components, the exhaust sensors respond to gases emitted by vehicular traffic and diesel engines, VOC sensors detect compounds originating from paints, solvents or pesticides and dust sensors measure particulate matter (pollen, smoke, *etc.*). These factors are of serious public health concern within the geographic region of our study: our city was rated as one of the worst in the United States in terms of air quality and exposure to exhaust, dust or VOC's can lead to chronic respiratory illnesses, including asthma, bronchitis, inflammation or cancer [1, 4]. The sensor case is outfitted with a mounting magnet, hang strap, and carabineer, affording easy attachment to public surfaces. Measurements are displayed on a community website (not the unit itself) to facilitate *community* rather than *individual* use of the sensors.

Research objectives

To gain insights into community appropriations of public place-based sensing, we deployed our system with four groups of urban stakeholders: bicyclists, parents and their children, homeless people, and activists. Each group, consisting of four to seven participants, was asked to share three air quality sensors (VOC, exhaust, and dust), placing and leaving them throughout the city over the course of one week. A website displayed community-collected data on a comment-enabled map and interactive graphs. Our findings address questions such as, 1) how do different stakeholders interact with shared technical resources; 2) how do issues of authorship, anonymity and security affect sensing in public spaces; 3) which spaces afford curiosity about specific environmental factors across different communities; and 4) what design principles leverage participatory sensing as a platform for city-wide grassroots activism?

SYSTEM

We designed and built a system of networked air quality sensors entirely from off-the-shelf parts. We intentionally chose low-cost and low-precision sensors to develop DIY (do it yourself) technology that can be re-created by non-experts without high-end calibration procedures. Our sensors provide relative rather than absolute (PPM, *etc.*) values, and the visualization enables comparison of VOC, and exhaust levels across different times and locations. Rather than focusing on scientifically precise values, our initial goal is to highlight variability across time and space.

Sensors

Our sensor circuit is supported by a custom PCB board that can be populated with exhaust, VOC, and/or dust sensors from Figaro[3]. In order to highlight specific air quality concerns and spatial affordance, every deployed unit was outfitted with a single sensor (exhaust, dust or VOC) and our participant groups received one of each. In addition, all units include a dual function temperature/humidity sensor and a light sensor. Input is processed by an Arduino[4] mini

[1] http://itp.nyu.edu/shows/spring2008/co2rset/

[2] http://aerophile.com/

[3] Figaro sensors. http://www.figarosensor.com/

[4] Arduino microcontroller. http://www.arduino.cc

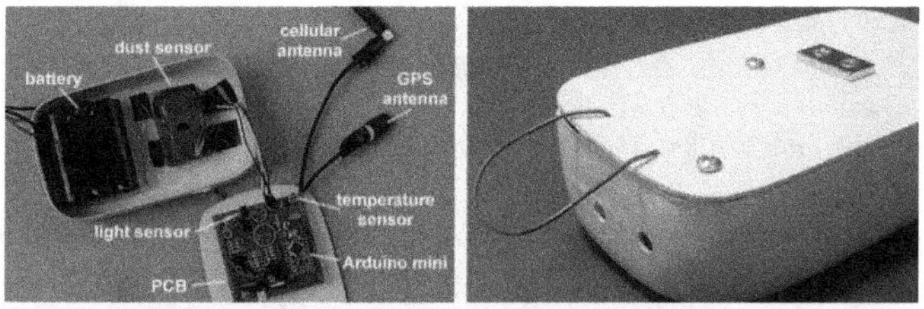

Figure 2. Exhaust sensor in case, with parts labeled (left), and back of sensor case with magnet and strap (right).

microcontroller, which interfaces with a Telit GSM/GPRS module[5] to send time-referenced sensor data along with the unit's GPS coordinates as an SMS message. Units are powered by rechargeable 6600mAh lithium batteries and enclosed in custom vacuu-formed polystyrene cases (4.0cm x 6.5cm x 13cm, Figure 2). Units are branded with our university name and logo on the front, and contact information and sensor description on the back. Small holes in the case allow for air circulation and light inside the units, and although several deployments encountered significant rain, sensor functionality was not affected.

Maximizing battery life

Our units function continuously for up to ten days by supporting three power modes: full power (300 mA) with sensors powered on and GPS/SMS transmitting, standard mode (40-100 mA) with sensors powered on and the GPS transmitter off, and low power mode (1 mA) with the system in sleep mode. During sleep mode, continuous sampling from a tilt sensor is processed to determine whether a unit is being physically moved (picked up, walked, biked or driven with). When movement is detected, units power up to full mode, transmitting GPS coordinates and sensor data every five minutes. However, if left static, units remain in sleep mode, changing to standard mode once every 30 minutes to sample sensor data and store it locally. The units then send the data in bulk every 5 hours.

Backend

Data from the units is sent as a comma-delimited SMS message to an e-mail address that is polled by cron-job. Since we did not calibrate the air quality sensors, all dust, exhaust and VOC values are scaled to a range between 1 (lowest) and 100 (highest) for consistency. Data is inserted into an SQL database, with separate tables for each of the studied communities. Consequently, participants can access sensor placements and data collected by their community.

Interface

Our front end, developed in php and javascript, leverages the Google Maps API[6] and with Google Chart Tools[7] to render data geographically (on a map) and temporally (through a series of interactive graphs).

Map

The map shows sensor placements as varied-size dots (sized according to air quality levels), connected chronologically

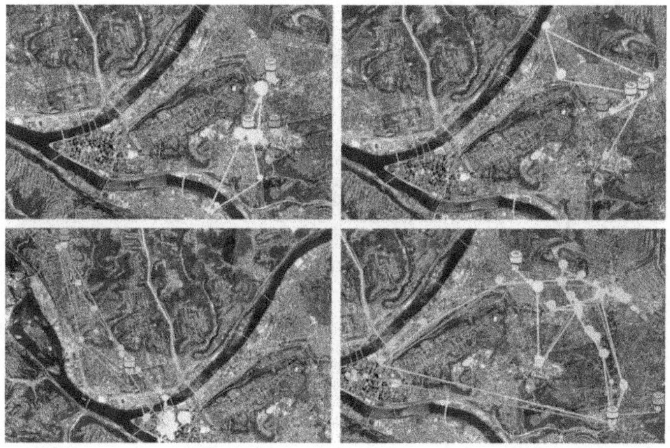

Figure 3. Sensor placements by bicyclists (top left), parents (top right), homeless (bottom left, and activists (bottom right)

with a line to illustrate the unit's path. Different sensors (dust, exhaust and VOC) are represented with different colors and can be toggled on and off, allowing users to track the units individually. Clicking or mousing over each location activates a tabbed info window (Figure 3, bottom). The default 'Overview' tab shows the latest data from the corresponding location: exhaust, dust or VOC value on a color-coded gauge along with temperature and humidity. Other tabs include temperature, humidity, air quality, and light data from the location as static line graphs. In addition, the map supports geo-referenced comments.

Graphs

The right side of the website contains interactive graphs showing data from all three sensors in the default 'Overview' tab, and from individual sensors along with temperature and humidity data under the 'VOC', 'exhaust', and 'dust' tabs. A draggable scale bar along the bottom allows zooming into parts of the graphs, and clicking on a point activates an info window over the corresponding location on the map. The 'Comments' tab contains a feed of all community comments, and clicking on a comment activates also the corresponding location.

DEPLOYMENT

Sensor units (12 in total) were deployed with four urban communities (22 participants). We selected the following communities to gain insight into how a range of urban stakeholders approach public sensing:

- *Bicyclists/students* are a young demographic with similar educational backgrounds, traversing a range of spaces with vested interests in roads, parks and traffic
- *Parents* form an older group occupying spaces that revolve around children (schools, playgrounds, etc) as well as work (office, etc.) and friends (theatres, malls, etc)
- The *homeless* are a low-income, nomadic community, with socio-political perspectives that lead to unique appropriations of technology, often overlooked by mainstream HCI literature [26]

[5] Telit. http://www.telit.com
[6] http://code.google.com/apis/maps/index.html
[7] http://code.google.com/apis/charttools/index.html

- *Activists* are a tighter-nit community who view themselves as agents of change and may have insights into spaces that facilitate or hinder their desired outcomes

In selecting these four communities, we hope to capture feedback from participants spanning diverse age groups, interests, urban spaces, social and economic backgrounds.

Methods

Each group completed a preliminary interview exploring community concerns as well as activism, roles and attitudes in public spaces. Participants were also asked to draw a community map showing locations they considered 'healthy', 'unhealthy', etc., on transparencies overlaying a map of Pittsburgh, along with spaces where they would like to monitor and publically broadcast air quality. Communities were then presented with three air quality sensors (labeled *dust*, *VOC*, and *exhaust*) and introduced to the website with a walkthrough of basic features. All participants had access to a computer during the study, including the homeless who used a shared desktop that we donated to the shelter. Groups were instructed to move, place and leave the sensors throughout the city as they preferred, over the course of one week, photographing each location (with personal cameras or a provided disposable). We encouraged participants to leave the sensors for longer periods of time, emphasizing that they were not expected to return them. We did not suggest a minimum number of placements or uses of the website, recommending that participants do 'what feels natural' for their group. After one week, participants returned for an informal wrap-up (group) interview discussing their experiences with our system. In addition, we observed participants' use of our website for 5-10 minutes to evaluate our interface. Each participant was compensated $10 for the initial interview and another $25 for completing the entire week-long study.

RESULTS

All sensors (except for 2, see 'parents') functioned as intended over the course of the study. Overall, participants enjoyed the project ("*It was fun*", parent), were impressed with our system ("*this is awesome*", homeless) and wished the study was longer ("*I wish we had more time [to place sensors]*", bicyclist). Most participants did not use the comment feature ("*I didn't really notice it, plus I wouldn't know what to say*", bicyclist). We now detail our findings, referencing data from participants in particular groups as: B, bicyclists; P, parents; H homeless; and A, activists.

Bicyclists/Students

We recruited four commuter bicyclists (1 female, age early 20's) through local bike forums. Participants are students who have been friends for several years, and three are neighbors (with two living together), such that they see each other at least a few times a week. Participants voiced individual concerns ranging from bike hazards ("*the roads are so messed up, it's dangerous to ride*", B1), to personal safety as affected by "*drug dealers, violence and vandalism behind my house*" (B3), and the homeless:

> "*There was a hobo sleeping our my porch once and... we also found recently... there's a building [across the street]- I think a hobo made it his home and it's just like a huge room with an old furnace and there's all this stuff of the hobo's. Yea, that's probably the biggest concern I have right now.*" (B2)

When asked to converge on a mutual concern, participants identified urban development, because "*we all use the city pretty heavily*" (B3), including the quality of streets, parks, and green-spaces, as well as economic and environmental disparities across the city. Participants agreed that street art was an effective approach for improving urban space ("*I think street art is like a way of art, and I see it personally as a way of doing that*", B2) and they have previously contributed to grassroots expressions including graffiti ("*by a shitty wall that could kinda use something to beautify the area*", B1), guerrilla gardening, and murals. They also discussed future plans to 'add' bike lanes to the city:

> B1: *We haven't done it yet, but we're strongly considering doing this. Just like finding areas that need a bike lane real bad*
>
> B4: *And just spray-painting it on.*
>
> B1: *Yea, just going in at night a making a big stencil of the bike think that's like kinda stretched out a little bit and just putting on some orange jackets and like just doing it.*

Sensor use and placement

Bicyclist/student participants split up the sensors for the week such that everyone had access to a sensor, without particular preference for the type of sensor they used:

> "*[B4] lives all the way in south Oakland, and we live very close to each other so, we figured [B4] should definitely get one and then I took one, and these two live together, so they took one.*" (B3)

B3 and B4 (roommates) shared the dust sensor, keeping it in their backyard for most of the week. B4 also left the dust sensor overnight on a bridge near a public library:

> "*You know the factory that's like right behind the library... yea so I wanted to know what that is, so I guess I was just curious if that would somehow affect the dust sensor in any way, so I kinda like pointed it towards that. And it's also right next to the park*" (B4)

B2 carried the exhaust sensor ("*I kinda just took it with me as I went on journeys, just to spread it around*") placing it on a busy street near a thrift store ("*I thought it would be interesting to leave it for two days, just to get a dependence of time, if it goes up and down*", B2), post office, and park. B1 did not attend the final interview but kept the VOC unit at what others identified as his friend's house on the map.

Data exploration

Participants used the website a few times during the week (B3 and B4 viewing it together), as tool for tracking where they had been rather than exploring air quality:

> "*I was more interested in what you guys were doing, like your movements, not exactly the data, I didn't look into it. I just wanted to see where you guys had been.*" (B2)

Tracing their movements, participants noted that the data made them to want to move around more, "*making a web around the city*" (B4). They initially felt that the air quality graphs looked "*very busy*", but became more interested in the data after a brief tutorial of the zoom feature ("*I do like the graphs now that I know how to use this [zoom]*", B4). Participants focused on re-occurring peaks in exhaust and VOC data ("*I didn't think that there'd be such a distinct hump [in exhaust data] at rush hour, that's cool*", B4; "*oh wow, that's [VOC peak] really early in the morning*", B2).

Expressions and activism

To avoid loosing sensors early in the study, participants first concealed their placements (*"I kinda wanted to get it back, so I kind of like hid it on the other side"*, B4). However, later in the week, B2 placed the exhaust sensor more overtly to explore "*the social aspects of the study*":

> "*The last time I placed it, I definitely wanted it to be found. I didn't wanna loose it early, 'cause then I thought I wanted to kinda take it around a few places but at the end I just wanted to see what would happen*" (B2)

Others were also curious about the whereabouts of the exhaust sensor ("*I wonder what they're doing with it or why they decided to take it*", B3). Participants indicated that they would place the sensors in more visible locations if they displayed the data, especially as a graph over time or in comparison to other locations such as parks:

> B4: *If it had that on it, then I would put it in really visible places as opposed to kinda tucking it behind a corner*
>
> B2: *Then you're making a statement*
>
> B4: *Cause then you're trying to say something*

Participants indicated that they would want to show their data to students- particularly environmentalists who could interpret and present it more concisely to the general public.

Parents

Three parents (1 female, ages 30's-50's) and their four children (1 female, elementary school ages) participated in the study. Participants have been friends for several years, meeting at neighborhood functions, children's play-dates and activities. Participants bike (P1), walk (P2) and drive or take buses (P3), and a shared concern involves roads and transportation. Specific issues range from streets that are not bike-friendly to a "*lack of an attractive mass transit and the shrinking amounts of mass transit*". When asked how their community could work towards resolving these issues, participants deferred to other groups:

> P1: *There is a bike advocacy group- and they work intimately with city planning department. It's the mayor's office frankly, that stalls things... somehow things don't get done in quick fashion*
>
> P3: *I get the feeling that that's something that a public works would do... I don't think those people are not on board-*
>
> P1: *They don't care*

Parents also noted a lack of a pressing need: " *[changes] cost a little bit of money and there's not like pressing need because we don't see the negative results*" (P3).

Sensor use and placement

Parents took turns using the sensors: each having all units for 2-3 days, and handing them off to the next person ("*we divided 7 [days] by 3 [families]*", P1). While parents tended to decide on locations, their children physically placed most sensors (on trees, street poles, *etc.*) and photographed the placements. P2 had the sensors first, using all three together to "*get readings from all 3 and then you can compare*":

> "*First I put it in our yard, and then I thought, OK let's put it in a more public space, so I chose to put it in front of the Rite Aide [pharmacy near her house].*" (P2)

An employee noticed the sensors and contacted the police, who in turn summoned the city bomb squad. Even though sensors were labeled with text detailing them as a locally approved research project, they were confiscated. Although the police were not initially sympathetic, we negotiated resuming the study and returned sensors to participants the same day, after several discussions with local authorities. During the interruption, batteries dislodged from the main board of two units (VOC, dust). However, participants continued to use the sensors, initially not realizing that two were broken. P3 and his children attached them to telephone poles using a ladder and nails:

> "*I wanted to basically be close to the river. We went further down and there were the factories and the robotics center, and the 43rd concrete center [factory]. There's also some foot traffic 'cause you can get to the river trail from there so there's a lot of dog walker.*" (P3)

P1 was interested in collecting more data ("*I was really going for the data, so I hung it in different places based on my interpretation of the study*", P1), placing the exhaust sensor at a street intersection and a bus stop; the dust sensor by his house and in a public park in a "*meadow rife with pollen and plants"*; and the VOC sensor in an alley, by a dumpster at a paint factory ("*we went inside [the paint factory] and we explained what it is we were gonna do.*")

Data exploration

Parents tended to check the website daily at the beginning of the study, but were later disappointed by the non-working sensors: "*I stopped checking once I found out things were not functioning properly*" (P1). Parents were especially interested in placements chosen by others in their group, and less concerned with the data, "*particularly because I never saw a high reading anywhere, so it didn't seem like the reading itself would be interesting*" (P3). Participants did notice higher exhaust values in some neighborhoods ("*where you [P3] put it, was higher*", P1). P3 was also interested in temperature data but could not find out "*when the hottest time of the day is*".

Expressions and activism

P2 was most disappointed by the police interruption, as she wanted others in her group to use the sensors ("*I hope I can pass it on*"). P3 felt 'amused' and 'sad':

> "*It seemed so funny that it happened so quickly... [it] makes me a little bit sad because I guess that's how people view*

Figure 4. Photographs of participant sensor placements: dust sensor attached to bridge by bicyclist (left), participant's daughter attaching VOC sensor to street pole (middle), and exhaust sensor outside a children's hospital placed by activist (right).

> *themselves as being good citizens now, and reporting terroristic threats, when if they had half a brain, they would think the Rite Aide in Pittsburgh is not a big target."* (P3)

Parents discussed the need for permission in various spaces:

> P1: *I wonder if they [Rite Aide] owned it [the space] or not.*
>
> P2: *Well, I didn't think of it in that way, because we can go park in their space so I thought we could do this... I thought, 'it's my neighborhood'. If I put it on the street that would've been municipal property maybe...*

Conversely, P1 explicitly asked for permission to place the VOC sensor at a paint factory (*"there was a moment when he was concerned... maybe he didn't want us to find some dirt on him or something"*). Participants were concerned with visibility, wanting people to "*see it [sensors] or be interested in it*" (P2), while at the same time avoiding sensor loss ("*I didn't want them to be taken, but I wanted them to be in a place that's open*", P3; "*I purposely hung it higher up, but it was completely visible*", P1). They suggested cameras to record public reactions to the sensors, to "*see what people actually do*":

> P1: *...how many people actually mused over these things...*
>
> P3: *Yea, I think that's what P2 was referring to. It would be interesting to actually see some camera action on that.*

Parents were hesitant to share their data: they did not know "*what it means before showing it... at what levels does health become impaired*" (P1), and wanted to gather "*more data, collected in a more... scientific experiment*" (P3).

Homeless

We recruited five male participants (ages mid 40's-60's) from a local shelter. The shelter offers a shared dormitory, a common 'TV' area and shower facilities for a maximum of 60 days per person per year. Occupants range from people who temporarily lost housing, to individuals traveling through the state, or living in different shelters across Pittsburgh over the past decade. Consequently, some of our participants are new to the shelter while others have known each other for years, and their routines vary greatly:

> "*When we leave here, everybody has some type of business to go to, to get up outta here, you know what I mean? To better their lives, and once all that is accomplished, then the park is... our meeting place, everyone comes through the park to get here.*" (H1)

The park serves as a group meeting place and lunch spot, but participants tend to visit a range of public spaces alone:

> *"I'm all over the city of Pittsburgh, outside and in smaller boroughs. I stop at the parks, talk to people, and then by 5-6 o'clock I'm back here [at the shelter]."* (H5)

Participants were in agreement about the common issues affecting their group, including inability to find jobs (*"If you work a union job, it's not what you know, it's who you know"*, H1), lack of affordable housing, and a poor (low-paying) recycling program (*"In San Diego, they pay $1.80 per pound of aluminum cans"*, H3). When asked if they would consider pursing actions to resolve these concerns, participants felt resigned and powerless:

> H1: *The five of us couldn't change our legislation if we wanted to.*
>
> H2: *Couldn't change anything.*
>
> H1: *If we would rally and sit outside, they would find some way to either lock us up, have somebody come along and discourage us, or call us in.*

Sensor use and placement

Although participants discussed specific locations (parks, street intersections, waterfront, *etc.*) to place the sensors, they did not coordinate a strategy for the study. Instead, individuals took whatever sensor was available as they left the shelter ("*whoever was up first got one, and I ended up with this one, I was the last one out the door*", H4). H4 '*ended up*' with the VOC sensor, placing it in a tree in the park frequently visited by the homeless for the entire week:

> *"I didn't know if they ever spray for pesticides or if they have any chemical agents on the grass- the fertilizers."* (H4)

H3 and H5 shared the exhaust sensor, placing it at street intersections and bus stops throughout the downtown area.

> *"I put it on the main drag, like where all the bus traffic is... I thought it'd be a good spot 'cause usually when I'm standing, waiting for the bus, I could smell the exhaust fumes."* (H5)

The dust sensor was taken by H1 along with the group's disposable camera. Our website shows this sensor moving extensively throughout the north side of the city, but its particular whereabouts remain unknown as H1 disappeared from the shelter and did not attend the final interview.

Data exploration

Participants accessed the website several times. Since the shelter controlled computer access to prevent illicit, participants explored the data together. They appeared to fluidly navigate the website, clicking on peak graph values to locate corresponding points on the map. However, sharing a computer made data individual exploration difficult (*"I have to sit there to figure out what I'm looking at but he'd just keep moving it [the website] around"*, H2) and participants were mostly interested in their own sensor (*"I just looked at mine"*, H5). Overall, participants were surprised to see low/moderate readings from the sensors:

> *"I was expecting it to be higher, cause the exhaust you know... it's not one bus, it's several buses are passing or stopping there. So I was expecting it to be like off the chart."* (H3)

Participants did not comment on the dust sensor (which disappeared), and generally did not discuss the data with each other (*"I tried to discuss it with them but I get nowhere with them"*, H5).

Expressions and activism

H4 wanted to avoid drawing attention to himself and the VOC sensor he placed in the park: *"somebody may have asked me, like you know, this isn't your property this is private property."* H3 and H5 placed the exhaust senor in visible spots near bus stops: *"right in [front of] everybody, where the buses pull up, right near the post, boom it's there"* (H3). While H2 did not use the sensors, he also indicated wanting to draw attention to them:

> *"I woulda put it up somewhere where it would be visible to everyone so if they read on the back of it, they woulda know the website and stuff like that, and got more data off that if they went to the computer and seen that. And they would've probably moved [the sensors] themselves... and so that could be moved around like- just having more people into it."* (H2)

Participants did not feel compelled to act on the data (*"there's really not much you can do about"*, H5), and H3 also pointed out that sensor values were not high enough to *"pursue anything"*. If given the opportunity to broadcast the information, they collected the homeless suggested showing it downtown (*"because that's where everybody has a tendency to cluster"*, H4), as well as to college campuses:

> *"College students are the future of this country. They're the future bosses, the fortune 500 companies, congressmen, senators, congress women, mayors, whatever... they need to know a lot of this stuff, better to get knowledge of it now than when a student becomes a senator, or whatever."* (H3)

Activists

We recruited a community of six activists (2 female, ages 20's-30's) who recently moved to Pittsburgh, but have known each other through an anarchist network, coordinating and meeting at various activist events over the past 3-4 years. Participants share a strong dislike for the police, as well as public spaces that do not afford gatherings (lack of open, accessible space). Broader issues fall under the umbrella of capitalism, oppression, and hierarchy (*"we actually do have a list that we've all agreed on"*, P3).

> *"There's not so much action that you take against those really broad overview things. It's more like tackling really specific, often local issues that relate to those... focusing on realistic actual things that are affecting people's lives."* (P5)

The group has previously worked to combat eviction, police brutality, gentrification, poverty and military recruitment. Participants were hesitant to disclose specific tactics, but examples range from door-to-door work, *"cooking food and serving it to people for free"*, to rallies and lockdowns (physically preventing people from accessing buildings).

Sensor use and placement

Participants decided on a set of placements for each sensor and took turns moving them to these locations within the group, based on individual routines and schedules. For instance, P1 placed the exhaust sensor in a tree in a park, and P3 and P5 retrieved it the following day, placing it on a street pole near a children's hospital. The VOC and dust sensors were initially at P2's house. The VOC sensor was then moved *"by a door in an alley, near the iron workers apprenticeship"* for a few days and then brought to an urban community farm collective (*"to see how much fertilizer and stuff is in the space where they grow food"*, P6). The dust sensor was moved between a busy downtown square and a public park. Participants tended to check on their sensors (*"I'd pass by it several times a day to see if it's still there"*, P4), and most locations were motivated by finding contrast:

> *"I think a lot of it was going for the contrasts.., to compare what we perceived would be really high with something that would be pretty low."* (P2)

Unlike other groups, activist planned to keep using sensors after the study, for instance to test air quality on the river (*"we should rent some kayaks and just take them [sensors] out for a day and paddle around"*, P1).

Data exploration

Most participants looked at the website once or twice during the study, and tended to remember some specifics (*"It was about 40 [VOC] at my house"*, P2; *"[exhaust] was higher at the children's hospital"*, P5; *"I thought there'd be more dust on the street", P1)*. Participants commented on micro-level data for different areas:

> *"Whenever they put out air quality alerts, it's like a blanket thing... But if you're like way outside of Pittsburgh up on a hill, it's probably not as bad as at the bottom of the valley, downtown. Being able to see the actual nuances of that difference is really important."* (P3)

Participants also liked being able to compare data from different locations simultaneously (*"I do like how you can hold one [info window] open and then sort of compare"*, P3*)*. The graphs were considered less useful, as participants skimmed different tabs (*"I looked at each one to see what the pattern was"*, P6). Participants wanted to know the scale for the data (*"does 100 mean that you're literally breathing in nothing?"*, P1), and see data from all sensors along the same graph ("*three lines on one graph*", P6). Longer-term data was also of interest: "*I'm curious if the level of pollution goes down in the winter*" (P1), *etc.*

Expressions and activism

Participants chose visible sensor placements and were not intimidated by '*suspicious*' looks unless police was involved ("*I'm sort of used to doing ridiculous things in public, but I'd wait for a cop car to go around the block*", P1). They discussed the study with the farm collective:

> "*It was pretty cool just to explain to people what was going on with it. Like we went down to [the farm collective] and we were like 'Look, you've been trying to get an idea of what's in your air for like years now and now we have a way for you to check it and it's free. Do you want to check your air quality?' And they were like sure, that sounds good.*" (P3)

Individuals from the urban farm collective reportedly wanted to use all three sensors for longer periods of time ("*they wanted all three [sensors] there for like an extended period of time to get some long-term data, P4).* Participants also discussed the study with each other and their friends:

> "*A lot of the people that I talked to were really into it... I think if there were a lot of sensors around the city and this website up... a lot of people would want to check it.*" (P2)

The group wanted to share their data with people from the neighborhoods where they placed the sensors ("*the people who live and work around those areas- people who spend a lot of time there*", P3), as well as other activist groups *("if there is a group of people that could do something about the air quality")*, and those most affected (e.g., "*I want iron workers to know what they're inhaling*" P1). Participants also wanted to broadcast the information at the children's hospital:

> "*By the children's hospital, I really wanted that like a display board, like look- 'it's a children's hospital, how much toxic stuff is in front of and on the side of this space.' People who bring their children to the hospital should know that*" (P6)

While participants initially did not want to pursue action based on the data ("*there's not much I can do about it*", P2) in general, they wanted to identify specific causes:

> "*It would be interesting to see who bears the most responsibility for that and then if you can sort of specifically get a group of whoever's contributing disproportionately or the most to the problem, then you can start doing something about it. Like a campaign or something like that*". (P3)

DISCUSION AND LIMITATIONS

We intentionally chose low-end sensors and did not pursue precise calibration procedures, positioning our system as a tool that can be implemented by non-experts. Consequently, our website visualizes relative measurements across time and space (values ranging between 1-100), and all four groups commented on the scale, wanting to know "*what it means*", how harmful the levels are for their health, *etc.* However, lack of absolute values did not deter participants from exploring, reflecting on, and reacting to the data. The homeless focused on individually-collected data ("*I just looked at mine*"), expecting it to be "*off the chart*". Other groups were interested in comparisons: bicyclists looked for a "*dependence of time*", tracking "*humps*" that correlated to rush hour; parents and activists compared locations ("*[exhaust] was higher at the children's hospital*", "*where [P3] put it, was higher*", *etc.*) Moreover, participants, especially activists, wanted a longer-term deployment. Battery life is an inevitable constraint for physical systems, and future work can explore different power sources (solar panels, casing that allows battery recharging, *etc.*), as well as related research questions: what happens during prolonged deployment? Do sensors become convivial tools?

Community concerns, activism and sensor use

Bicyclists and parents split the sensors (per person or by days of the week) using them independently and tracking each others' placements on the website. These uses reflect approaches for addressing group concerns: bicyclists prefer independent acts (graffiti or murals) to "*beautify the area*", while parents defer to "*advocacy groups*" for changes in urban development, roads, *etc.* The homeless are a community by circumstance rather than choice, with each person having "*some type of business to go to, to get up outta here*". Participants' sentiments of powerlessness and resignation ("*the five of us couldn't change our legislation if we wanted to*") in response to mutual concerns (housing, jobs, *etc.*) echo their lack of coordinated 'strategy' for sharing the sensors: each person took and checked data from whatever sensor was available. Conversely, the activist community revolves around group action- free food distributions, rallies, lockdowns, *etc.,* to resolve issues from a "*list that we've all agreed on*" (capitalism, oppression, *etc.*). Consequently, they adopted the study as a *conjoint practice,* moving communally-shared sensors and discussing data as a group. Our findings highlight a range of group appropriations and interpretations of our system, and we emphasize adoptions of sensing systems as reflections of community structures, values and concerns.

DESIGN IMPLICATIONS

It's not a bomb!

To varying extents, our study exposed all four groups to issues of security, privacy and authority. Participants navigated tensions between authorship and theft, placing sensors "*higher up but completely visible*" or entirely concealing them in trees or "*behind a corner*". From asking for permission and explaining the study, to placing sensors covertly ("*somebody may have asked me*"), to assuming ownership of space ("*it's my neighborhood*"), to ignoring '*suspicious*' looks or defying authorities altogether ("*until a cop car goes around the block*"), communities reflected on notions of private, public, and authorized space. For parents, these tensions were explicitly foregrounded by a police intervention, ("*people view themselves as being good citizens... [by] reporting terroristic threats*").

Although our sensors were clearly branded, in a post 9-11 world, homemade DIY objects that would have previously been considered interesting, provocative, or eccentric are almost immediately perceived as threatening. Increased surveillance as encouraged by the Department of Homeland Security warning to "*be vigilant, take notice of your surroundings, and report suspicious items or activities to local authorities immediately*"[8] has shaped and constrained artistic, academic and whimsical endeavors over the past decade (for instance, the Boston Bomb Scare [33]).

Our experience with the police reveals interesting considerations for public sensing: while theft and vandalism were major concerns across all four groups, the only sensors damaged during the study were due to police intervention; and despite suspicious glances and police presence, participants continued to pursue overt and public sensor placements- near hospitals, factories, bus stops, *etc.* We cite these findings not as reflections on law enforcement, but as points of engagement with issues of perceived safety, privacy and expressions. Participatory sensing places new tools in the hands of ordinary citizens, inevitably exposing the general public to unfamiliar technologies and contexts. The boundary between 'evocative' and 'threatening' remains unexplored, and the police (an under-studied community in HCI) may offer valuable insights for this domain. While we readily carry personal electronics and talk of a ubiquitous computing future, publically-placed technologies and sensing is fraught with a myriad of challenges – namely those embedded within a culture of fear. Future research can focus on design factors such as enclosure shape, color, texture, and sensor legibility to lessen such public concerns.

Broadcasting and sharing sensor data

Our earlier work [withheld] with probes suggested sensor data as a 'social currency'- a potential for communicating concerns within and across communities of stakeholders- and findings from the deployment of our fully functional system suggest a range of opportunities for visualizing this information. On one level, our participants were interested in data within their own groups: from tracking where their friends put sensors to comparing measurements between neighborhoods, or exploring trends over time, stakeholders expressed a need for community-specific interfaces. For groups such as bicyclists, personal devices can present geo-referenced community data, while more independent stakeholders (*e.g.*, homeless) might prefer information from their individually-placed sensors, and tighter-knit groups (activists) could adopt visualizations that engage them as a group, facilitating data exploration as a *conjoint practice*.

Moreover, participants' desire to broadcast sensor data to other communities reveals a space for engagement between and among different social groups. For instance, while the presence of '*hobos*', raised safety concerns for bicyclists/students, the homeless considered students to be the "*future of this country*" and a receptive audience for sensor data. How would students' perceptions of '*hobos*' change if data collected by the homeless was projected to a university campus, and vice versa? Instances of group sharing might be welcomed (the farming collective wanted all three sensors) or rejected (a paint salesman "*didn't want us to find some dirt on him*"). Digital spaces can make intentions and consequences more transparent, empowering groups to collaborate towards desired outcomes. Such technologies can serve as instruments of persuasion for community concerns, linking people through their actions [13] as opposed to comparisons of individual behaviors.

Sensors as instruments of change

Our system enabled communities to engage with space and express their concerns through the placement of sensors: some spaces afforded similar questions across participants (exhaust levels at street interactions and bus stops, pollen measurements in parks, dust near factories, overall air quality at participants' homes, *etc.*), while others inspired unique interpretations (VOC's by an iron apprenticeship, pesticides in a park, exhaust by a thrift store, *etc.*). Whether to explore the '*social aspects'*, inspire interest of "*people musing over these things*", or to broadcast air quality in front of a children's hospital with "*a display board"*, and bring "*more people into it"*, participants wanted to use sensors to reach the general public and transform space.

We emphasize sensing *beyond* hardware, and the inclusion of stakeholders in sensor appearance and interaction design. Groups such as homeless, for instance, may prefer inconspicuous casing to avoid attention during the act of placement, with the ability to remotely trigger a display that broadcasts data to the general public; other communities may build visualizations to target specific stakeholders (neighbors, iron workers, *etc.*) or track social aspects. More broadly, there appears to be a large opportunity for open source platforms to empower communities to create visual and material form factors, altering output modalities based on context. In doing so, groups could further leverage sensors as tools of engagement with and transformation of space. We note, however, that as any instrument, sensors can have unforeseen and unwanted outcomes: for instance, devaluing neighborhoods or small businesses through tampering with sensors to artificially manipulate readings (*e.g.,* intentionally pumping exhaust into a sensor in a strategic location). Future systems must take these potential unintended consequences into account, for example by making visualizations and functionality transparent to direct stakeholders, policy makers and the general public.

CONCLUSION

We introduced a novel system of air quality sensors, designed to be left and moved throughout public spaces. Our fully-functional sensors report air quality along with weather and light data to a server that displays it on a public website in real time. Our deployment with four groups of stakeholders- parents, bicyclists, homeless and activists, supports our system as a tool for community expressions and activism. Our findings reveal design opportunities for

[8] http://www.dhs.gov/files/reportincidents/counterterrorism.shtm

environmental data as a social currency and physical sensing systems as instruments of change.

ACKNOWLEDGEMENTS

We thank our participants for their feedback. We thank Will Odom and our anonymous reviewers for their time and help with this work. Financial support for this research was provided in part by the Vira I. Heinz Endowment.

REFERENCES

1. American Lung Association. City Rankings 2010: Most Polluted Cities. http://www.stateoftheair.org/2010/city-rankings/
2. Aoki, P. M., Honicky, R. J., Mainwaring, A., Myers, C. Paulos, E. Subramanian, S. Woodruff, A., A vehicle for research: using street sweepers to explore the landscape of environmental community action. *ACM SIGCHI 2009.*
3. Burke, J., Estrin, D., Hansen, M., Parker, A., Ramanathan, N., Reddy, S., Srivastava, M.B. Participatory Sensing. *WSW at Sensys*, 2006.
4. Coalition for Clean Air. Pollutants & Health Effects. http://www.coalitionforcleanair.org/
5. Cuff, D., Hansen, M., Kang, J. (2008). Urban Sensing: Out of the Woods. *Communications of the ACM* 51, 3.
6. Da Costa, B., Hazegh, C., Ponto, K. Pigeon blog. http://www.pigeonblog.mapyourcity.net
7. Da Costa, B., Philip, K., *Eds*. (2008) Tactical Biopolitics, Art, Activism, and Technoscience. *MIT Press,* 2008
8. Dewey, J. The Public and Its Problems. NY: Holt, 1927.
9. Dieter, M. (2008) Processes, Issues, AIR: Toward Reticular Politics. *Australian Humanities Review*, Is. 46.
10. DiSalvo, C. (2009) "Design and the Construction of Publics." *Design Issues (MIT) 25, no. 1.*
11. DiSalvo, C., Boehner, K., Knouf, N. A., Sengers, P. "Nouring the Ground for Sustainable HCI: Considerations from Ecologically Engaged Art." *CHI'09. Boston*, 2009. 385-394.
12. DiSalvo, C., Light, A., Hirsch, T., Le Dantec, C. A., Goodman, E., and Hill, K. (2010) HCI, communities and politics. *CHI EA '10.*
13. Dourish, P. 2010. HCI and Environmental Sustainability: The Politics of Design and the Design of Politics. DIS 2010
14. Eisenman, S. B., Miluzzo, E., Lane, N. D., Peterson, R. A., Ahn, G., and Campbell, A. T. 2009. BikeNet: A mobile sensing system for cyclist experience mapping. *ACM Trans. Sen. Netw. 6*, 1, 2009.
15. Gaver, B., Dunne, T., Pacenti, E. 1999. Design: Cultural probes. *interactions* 6, 1
16. Graffiti Research Lab. Throwies. http://graffitiresearchlab.com/?page_id=6 (accessed January 30, 2010).
17. Hirsch, T. Tripwire (2006) http://web.media.mit.edu/~tad/htm/tripwire.html
18. Hirsch, T. and Henry, J. 2005. TXTmob: text messaging for protest swarms. In CHI '05.
19. Honicky, R., Brewer, E. A., Paulos, E., and White, R. 2008. N-smarts: networked suite of mobile atmospheric real-time sensors. *In Proc. of ACM SIGCOMM*, 2008.
20. Hooker, B., Gaver, W.W., Steed, A., & Bowers, J. The Pollution e-Sign. Workshop on Ubiquitous Sustainability. *Ubicomp*, 2007.
21. Jeremijenko, N., Arnold, J. J., Kavesh, W. Feral Robotic Dogs. 2009. http://www.nyu.edu/projects/xdesign/feralrobots/
22. Kim, S. and Paulos, E. 2010. InAir: sharing indoor air quality measurements and visualizations. *SIGCHI '10.*
23. Kim, S., Paulos, E., and Gross, M. D. 2010. WearAir: expressive t-shirts for air quality sensing. *TEI '10.*
24. Latour, B. and Weibel, P. (eds.) Making Things Public: Atmospheres of Democracy, *MIT Press., 2005.*
25. Le Dantec, C.A., Christensen, J. E., Bailey, M., Farrell, R.G., Ellis, J. B., Davis, C. M., Kellogg, W. A., Edwards, W. K. "A Tale of Two Publics: Democratizing Design at the Margins." *In Proc of. DIS* 2010.
26. Le Dantec, C. A., Edwards, W. K. 2008. Designs on Dignity: Perceptions of Technology Among the Homeless. *In Proc. of CHI'08.*
27. Lifton, J, Seetharam, D., Broxton, M., Paradiso, J. Pushpin Computing System Overview: A Platform for Distrbuted, Embedded, Ubiquitous Sensor Networks. *Pervasive,* 2002.
28. Merrill, D., Kalanithi, J., Maes, P. (2007) "Siftables: Towards Sensor Network User Interfaces." *In Proc. of TEI'07.*
29. Paulos, E., Honicky, R.J., Hooker, B. Citizen Science: Enabling Participatory Urbanism. *Handbook of Research on Urban Informatics: The Practice and Promise of the Real-Time City*, 2008.
30. Rana, R. K., Chou, C. T., Kanhere, S. S., Bulusu, N., and Hu, W. (2010). Ear-phone: an end-to-end participatory urban noise mapping system. *ACM/IEEE IPSN '10.*
31. Rekimoto, J., Ullmer, B., Oba, H. "DataTiles: A Modular Platform for Mixed Physical and Graphical Interactions." *SIGCHI'97*. Seattle, WA, 1997.
32. Seitinger, S., Taub, D. M., and Taylor, A. S. (2010) Light bodies: exploring interactions with responsive lights. *TEI'10.*
33. Smalley, Suzanne; Mishra, Raja (2007-02-01). Froth, fear, and fury. *The Boston Globe.*
34. U.S. EPA.Volatile Organic Compounds. http://www.epa.gov/air/emissions/voc.htm
35. Willett, W., Aoki, P., Kumar, N., Subramanian, S., Woodruff, A. (2010) Common Sense Community: Scaffolding Mobile Sensing and Analysis for Novice Users. *Pervasive'10*

Second-Hand Interactions: Investigating Reacquisition and Dispossession Practices around Domestic Objects

James Pierce, Eric Paulos
Human-Computer Interaction Institute, Carnegie Mellon
5000 Forbes Avenue, Pittsburgh, PA, USA
{jjpierce, paulos} @ cs.cmu.edu

ABSTRACT
We present a qualitative study of *reacquisition*—the acquisition of previously possessed goods—involving in-depth interviews with 18 reacquirers within or nearby Pittsburgh, PA, USA. Based on critiques of sustainable consumption and our findings, we reframe technology consumption as acquisition, possession, dispossession and reacquisition. We present four reacquisition orientations describing our participants' motivations and practices: casual, necessary, critical, and experiential. We then present a range of findings including issues with work, time and effort involved in reacquisition, and values and practices of care and patience associated with invested reacquirers. We conclude with implications for designing technologies to support current reacquisition practices, as well as broader opportunities for HCI and interaction design to incorporate non-mainstream reacquisition practices and values into more mainstream technologies.

Author Keywords
Sustainability, consumption, reacquisition

ACM Classification Keywords
H5.m. Information interfaces and presentation (e.g., HCI): Miscellaneous.

General Terms: Design, Theory

INTRODUCTION
Growing concerns over sustainability have prompted a substantial area of research within the CHI community related to product durability and re-use [2,6,15,16,17,18,23,30] and sustainable consumption more generally (e.g., [31]). Motivated and informed by these concerns, we report a qualitative study of individuals engaged to some significant degree in acquiring used or second-hand goods rather than new goods from firsthand retail sites.

While we cover a range of topics and issues, specific research questions guiding our investigation include: What motivates reacquisition, i.e., the acquisition of used items? What processes, practices, experiences and values are involved in reacquiring used items versus acquiring new items? What role does the type of technology being (re)acquired play (e.g., computer versus furniture)? What role do technological tools, services and environments play in reacquisition (e.g., Craigslist versus thrift store)?

In this paper we reframe the consumption of durable goods as involving acquisition, possession, dispossession and reacquisition. This reframing is motivated both by critiques of sustainable consumption which point out that durable goods are not actually metabolically consumed, and our participants who show us that goods often circulate within and across multiple contexts of use and ownership.

Our study uncovers a great richness and diversity of practices, experiences and values related to reacquisition. We frame the value of studying reacquisition in terms of two goals: (i) designing for or with communities of reacquisition and (ii) designing from communities of reacquisition. The former is concerned with improving reacquisition as it is currently practiced through the design of interactive products as well as technological tools, services and environments. The second goal is based on the idea that we can learn much from the processes, practices, and values of invested reacquirers; and we can apply these understandings when designing technologies for more mainstream communities. We argue for the value of looking at invested reacquirers as potential experts in sustainable, ethical and meaningful consumption of and with technology. This perspective shares much in common with arguments for studying non-uses of technology [25], studying non-mainstream even marginalized communities for sustainability (e.g., [7]), and various challenges to values of ease and efficiency in technology design (e.g., [3,4,10,12,26,29,30]).

In what follows we present: (i) related consumption literature and our reframing of consumption, (ii) key findings from our qualitative study of reacquisition, and (iii) implications for HCI and interaction design.

CONSUMPTION LITERATURE
The demand and impact of firsthand goods
The enormous negative environmental impacts associated with the manufacture and disposal of vast amounts of consumer electronics and other goods have been widely

CHI 2011, May 7–12, 2011, Vancouver, BC, Canada.

discussed [2,8,10,16,18,30]. Attention has been drawn not only to the high rate of consumption of new goods but also the high rate at which still functioning goods are disposed of prematurely [2,8,16,18,29]. Reliable figures on the durability of goods are scarce, yet a 1998 UK study of over 800 households reported that 1/3 of discarded appliances were still functional, respondents usually replaced rather than repaired appliances they deemed repairable, and respondents tended to have negative attitudes toward obtaining used appliances [8]. The potential for second-hand markets to decrease demand for new goods has been observed in a number of cases, including used clothing, cars and books [28]. Economic models have predicted second-hand markets can reduce demand for new goods [28]. All this suggests the importance and potential of designing to support the use and re-use of durable goods as a matter of sustainability.

Second-hand consumption studies

One of the most substantial treatments to date of second-hand consumption is Gregson and Crewe's book *Second Cultures,* a series of ethnographic studies of vintage shopping and other types of second-hand consumption in England [14]. Other empirical and theoretical work on second-hand consumption includes investigations of second-hand clothing [24], transfer of ownership at garage sales and auctions [19], and the concepts of disposal and waste in modern society [20]. However these works have tended to overlook issues specific to newer technologies, including products as well as services and sites of second-hand consumption (e.g., eBay, Craigslist). Within HCI a number of recent works have recently investigated durability and re-use as a matter of sustainability [2,6,15,16,17,18,23,30].

THEORIZING ((UN)SUSTAINABLE) CONSUMPTION

While even a basic overview of theoretical approaches to consumption is well beyond the scope of this paper we nonetheless note some important approaches to consumption including (post-)structuralist and Marxist oriented approaches (e.g., [1]), anthropologically oriented approaches (e.g., [9,22]), and sociological approaches based on theories of practice (e.g. [5,27]). While we find these approaches useful and draw on them throughout our work, we also find that prior approaches remain relatively uncritical of the concept of consumption as a material practice. As argued by design theorist Tony Fry, academic literatures as well as design and policy approaches tend toward a conceptually problematic notion of consumption:

> [T]he very notion of consumption itself, as an economic and socio-cultural practice, is mobilized unproblematically. It is the fact that people do not metabolically consume that is at the heart of the problem. Consumption as an economic category is incommensurate with it as an ecological category. No matter the way in which products are acquired and used or whether consumption is thought and theorized as an economic activity, the fact is that all durable products at the end of useful life have not been consumed. The residual materials of land fill, waste dumps, junk yards, plus the content of our attics, cellars, sheds and garages all testify to the truth of this claim [10, p. 192].

Recent works within HCI echo such criticisms [2,6,15,16,17,18,23,30], as well as works outside of HCI (e.g., [8,29]). However here we wish to take more seriously the claim that the very notion of consumption may be flawed and *"the rhetoric of sustainable consumption either knowingly or unknowingly legitimates the unsustainable."* [10, p. 193].

Reframing the consumption of durable technology

Drawing on recent critiques of sustainable consumption, we reframe consumption of potentially durable material goods in terms of the **acquisition**, **possession**, **dispossession** and **reacquisition** of a particular material object[1]. This reframing parallels Huang and Truong's investigation of mobile phone acquisition, ownership, disposal and replacement [16]. By explicitly re-interpreting consumption as involving (re)acquiring, possessing and dispossessing we consider more seriously and explicitly the ways in which technologies can and do circulate within and across multiple contexts and temporalities of use and ownership; rather than being "consumed", a notion which may tend to obscure the fact that technologies continue to endure beyond initial moments of purchase, use and ownership—be it in the hands of another or in a landfill.

Our qualitative study focuses on reacquisition, the notion that a material object may be acquired as something that has been previously possessed, typically knowingly as such. While our reframing of consumption is based in large part on theoretical and critical considerations it is importantly also a result of working to understand and name what we observed in our study. Our participants show us ways that goods are reacquired and recirculate, or else fail to do so. Moreover these individuals may be said to teach us ways of re-acquiring, possessing and dispossessing that depart in interesting, even radical ways from the acquisition of the not-previously-acquired and the possession of the not-previously-possessed (i.e., firsthand consumption). We now turn to our qualitative study.

METHODS

We conducted an ethnographically informed qualitative study from June-August 2010 in and nearby Pittsburgh, Pennsylvania, USA consisting of in-depth interviews with 18 individuals that reacquire (previously possessed) goods. These individuals also dispossessed goods and in some cases also significantly engaged in reselling goods. Prior to these interviews we conducted approximately 20 hours of observation work that included informally conversing with

---

[1] We use the term *dispossession* to refer to the act, process or practice of discarding, giving away or otherwise "shedding off of domestic and personal objects" [20, p. 5]. We use the term *reacquisition* to refer to the acquisition of an object that has been previously possessed, i.e. "used" or "second-hand".

reacquirers and resellers at locations including thrift stores, vintage stores, yard and sidewalk sales, flea markets, and, on a number of occasions, people reacquiring items that had been discarded in streets, alleys and dumpsters.

In-depth interviews were conducted with 18 participants from distinct households. The primary inclusion criterion for participation was some significant degree of involved and/or routine reacquisition of goods. We sought to recruit a fairly diverse range of people within this population, which we knew from our observation work and prior literature was indeed diverse. All participants were currently residing within or nearby the city of Pittsburgh, Pennsylvania. Participant ages ranged from early 20s to 70s; 11 were female and 7 male. 7 participants were recruited in-person at sites including a local vintage/resale store, a flea market, a sale of used items in a parking lot, and a witnessed reacquisition of an item left outside of a home for taking. The remaining 11 participants were recruited through ads posted to Craigslist. Despite efforts to recruit diverse ethnicities most of our participants were Caucasian; the exceptions were one Asian participant (Jun) and one African-American participant (Samantha).

One and sometimes two ~1-2 hour interviews were conducted per participant. Interviews were audio recorded and conducted at the participant's home and/or site of selling second-hand goods. All participants were offered $10 compensation. Home tours were conducted in most cases during which participants described and explained their various possessions. Participants also were asked to describe and when possible demonstrate reacquisition and dispossession practices in certain ways (e.g., describing how a particular item was reacquired; showing us lists of things they planned to obtain; demonstrating use of eBay and Craigslist with the computer). Photographs were taken of each participant' possessions and homes during these visits.

Interviews were open-ended and the direction of each conversation varied with the participant. However we designed a framework of topics that were covered with each participant. This allowed for a level of comparative analysis to be conducted across participants. The topics covered were: *sites*—where participants (re)acquire items; *objects*—what types of things they (re)acquire; *processes & practices*—the mental, physical, material and symbolic processes involved in (re)acquisition; *values & motivations* for (re)acquiring; comparisons of *new & used items*; comparisons of *digital & non-digital items*; comparisons of *virtual & physical sites of (re)acquisition*; and comparisons of *the self to others* within and outside one's social circles in terms of above topics.

Our study resulted in the collection of hundreds of pages of field notes and approximately 1000 pages (300,000 words) of interview transcripts. Analysis of the data was an ongoing process throughout the study. Field notes were reviewed immediately following an interview or observation period and tentative insights and themes noted in reflective field logs and memos [13]. A more thorough analysis of all data was conducted at the conclusion of the study using an iterative process of searching for emergent patterns and themes [21]. All transcripts were closely read and reread—in conjunction with a review of field notes and photographs—while highlighting, commenting on and reorganizing text.

Two important limitations of our work should be noted. The first is the limited number of participants and interviews conducted. The second is the great diversity of participants interviewed. Together, these limit both the depth and reliability of our understandings of particular individual's experiences and practices, and the extent to which our findings can be generalized to other groups. We intend to address these limitations in future studies.

FINDINGS

The first and second-hand distinction

We find that central to understanding the practices, experiences and values of reacquisition is the distinction between firsthand acquisition and reacquisition—the acquisition of goods that have been previously possessed. Across all participants and regardless of social position, those engaged in reacquisition consistently defined themselves, their values, their practices and their things with respect to reacquisition in terms of an oppositional—at times even resistant—relation to those of firsthand acquisition. For some this was manifested through attempts to minimize this distinction; for others, it was explicitly highlighted, even embraced. This is consistent with Gregson and Crewe's interpretations of second-hand selling and shopping [14]. Further, we argue, wholly aligned with Gregson and Crewe, that the distinction between firsthand and second-hand—between acquisition and reacquisition—cannot be ignored as it often provides the very conditions within which value is created by those engaged in social and cultural practices of reacquisition.

While all of our participants share a common practical and reflective understanding of the firsthand and second-hand distinction—in some cases, an oppositional relationship core to their identity, in others, apparently much less so—it is crucial to make clear the heterogeneous nature of our participants in terms of how they (and we) view their selves, their values, their practices and their things. We found the various worlds of reacquisition and dispossession that we were drawn into to be rich, varied, complex and highly nuanced. This presents distinct challenges in how best to present our findings, requiring us to omit interesting and relevant discussions. As such, we focus here on issues most relevant to our aims of understanding reacquirers in order to design for/with them and to design from them.

Reacquisition orientations

While we anticipated that our participants represented diverse groups, we were nonetheless struck by the great diversity of viewpoints and practices described by our participants. In order to give an overview of this diversity and categorically begin to make sense of it, we outline four *reacquisition orientations*. While the orientations are not mutually exclusive, each participant has been associated with one and sometimes two primary orientations. (Note that pseudonyms have been used for all participants.)

1. Casual reacquisition. For casual reacquirers, reacquisition is primarily seen to be a cheaper alternative to the otherwise more desirable conventional retail acquisition. Participants engaging in casual reacquisition are characterized by a lack of speech reflecting a strong commitment to or opinion of reacquisition. They often have difficulty or do not feel the need to explain their practices in detail or distinguish them strongly from firsthand acquisition. For casual reacquirers, reacquisition enables them to possess everyday goods that otherwise would be financially prohibitive, even well outside their means. Casual reacquirers tend to desire to minimize the distinction between new goods acquired firsthand and used goods reacquired second-hand. For casual reacquirers, the *"regular store"* with *"new things"* is in almost every way preferably aside from the price difference.

2. Necessary reacquisition. Necessary reacquirers tend to approach reacquisition as much more of a necessity, a constant struggle to obtain goods they deem necessary or essential. While several participants with extremely low incomes tended toward necessary reacquisition (including casually-, experientially- and critically-oriented reacquirers), an orientation toward reacquisition as foremost a financial necessity is most clearly evident in the case of Joan. In Joan's words, she *"had everything"* and now has *"nothing"* owing to a recent divorce and personal injury. She describes deeply resenting now having to shop at thrift stores and charity outlets, not having money or credit cards, the embarrassment and distress at her daughter and others thinking she is *"cheap"*, and the strong desire to once again be able to shop for *"new things"* at *"expensive stores"*. Although Joan represents our only participant characterized foremost as a necessary reacquirer, we nonetheless believe this is an important orientation to consider as other participants tended also toward necessary reacquisition and there are likely many more who represent this distinct orientation. (Note the economic recession in the U.S. at the time of our study is likely of particular relevance here.) Further, this orientation offers a corrective to the notion suggested by many of our participants that reacquisition is primarily an enjoyable and meaningful practice or activity.

3. Critical reacquisition. For critical reacquirers, reacquisition is very consciously and reflectively bound up with considerations of social, political, economic, ethical and/or environmental concerns. Critical orientations were most salient among younger participants who may be identified with strong oppositions to the status quo, exhibiting even counter-cultural orientations. For example, John—a 33 year old who does various sound engineering work for films—describes himself and his social circle as *"independent"*, *"curious"*, "*shar*[ing] *a healthy defiance of authority"* and interested in *"learn*[ing] *how to do... things that everyone's forgotten how to do*", like growing food, operating a letter-press and making musical instruments. For John (re)acquiring goods involves strong political, social and moral considerations, such as where and how a product is made and the working and living conditions of those that actually manufacture and produce it.

4. Experiential reacquisition. For experiential reacquirers reacquisition is strongly appreciated for its positive experiential or aesthetic qualities—both in terms of the processes of re-acquiring and the products of reacquisition. For example, Tanya—a 30-something year old who was very recently laid off from her job as development director for a non-profit organization—engages in reacquisition to renovate and decorate an old house she lives in and plans to resell. This a profitable yet intrinsically enjoyable activity for Tanya, and the second time she has done this. Although she expresses strong ethical views on reacquisition these tend to be described in terms of an aesthetic sensibility for objects and materials, and the joys and skills of re-acquiring and re-using things. This is the case rather than having critical basis in, for example, environmental values, which she made clear did not inform her ethical views and practices.

In the remainder of this paper we commonly distinguish *casual reacquirers* from *invested reacquirers,* the latter being those of a primarily experiential or critical orientation. In what follows we present findings focused on the processes and products of reacquisition and dispossession.

Work, effort, and time: Difficulties of re-acquiring. A clear distinguishing aspect of reacquisition is that it is often discussed by participants as requiring more work, time and effort than acquiring new things at firsthand retail stores. Most casual participants described instances in which they were open to buying used items, even preferred a used item in some ways, yet constraints on time and effort (but usually not direct cost of purchase) caused them to seek these items through more conventional retail outlets. In fact all participants mentioned such issues with reacquisition as, at least at times, requiring increased work, time and effort, which in many cases caused them to resort to purchasing something from a firsthand retail store. Invested participants typically felt conflicted about purchasing new products or felt obligated to strongly rationalize such purchases. Thus we see that the practices of re-acquiring are often fraught with distinct challenges that may make firsthand acquisition appear more seductive, convenient, accessible, even necessary. However for invested reacquirers this involved process of re-acquiring is itself often a source of value.

Skill, satisfaction, discovery: Value through re-acquiring. All of the invested reacquirers we interviewed emphasized ways in which the *process* of reacquiring was an important, intrinsically valuable experience, sometimes apparently more so than the actual object reacquired. However, it is important to note that most casual and necessary reacquirers also suggested this perspective at times. For invested reacquirers this valuable experience of reacquisition was often described as a primary motivation for reacquiring. This was made clear through comparing the experience of reacquiring at thrift stores, flea markets, *"trash piles"*, etc. to the experience of shopping at firsthand retail stores. For example, Bob describes the importance of the *"the chase"* and *"the search"* in his love of flea markets and yard sales:

> I'm surprised you haven't asked the question: If you're going and looking and spend all this time looking wouldn't it be easier to *just buy the damn thing*? ... It's part of the search. The chase is half of it...you won't find that at Wal-Mart at all. There's no such thing as search and find in those places. It's categorized. No—that doesn't even enter into department stores. (Bob, 70s, retired toolmaker).

Here we see how the ways in which Wal-Mart has been designed for and experienced as *"categorized"* and usable has rendered the experience of shopping boring and unexciting for Bob. The involved and skilled processes of searching and hunting are, for Bob, clearly experientially superior in important ways to *"just buy*[ing] *the damn thing"*, where acquiring is apparently simply a means to the end of an acquired object. We find great importance in this recurring idea that a "well designed" experience that minimizes work, effort and frustration can be resisted as inferior and running counter to the value derived from thrift stores, flea markets and finding things on the street, experiences which may be considered poorly designed or not designed. To illustrate this point further we present a description given by Tanya, whom we met earlier, of her experience of eBay compared to flea markets and thrift stores.

> **Tanya:** eBay is kind of different to me because there's a lot of— it's *too much* work almost. There's *so much* and it's *so huge*. The experience of looking through page after page after page, you know, vintage ashtrays, for example. It's not as satisfying as going to the flea market and *handling* them. You know what I mean? So no, I don't care for eBay so much.
>
> **James:** I think so... tell me a little bit more about that...
>
> **Tanya:** I mean, where's the satisfaction in typing in, "I want a blue—I want a *turquoise* blue vintage ashtray with a dolphin", and three of them pop up. Is there any satisfaction in that?
>
> **James:** So what's the experience of going to a thrift store?
>
> **Tanya:** You might have to go for two years and finally, when you find that blue vintage ash tray with dolphins, which is not something I'm looking for, but, I mean, when you find it you feel like: "I got it."
>
> **James:** So you're not gonna go on eBay and buy one?
>
> **Tanya:** No. I'm not. ... I'm sure if I went on eBay right now I could find enough pressed tin [something she is actively looking for] to put pressed tin in every room of [my] house, but then there's no *joy* in that.

Throughout our discussion with Tanya, and other invested reacquirers, resistance to mainstream, predetermined, categorized and usable sites of (re)acquisition come up as well as a tendency toward embracing work as rewarding, pleasurable and meaningful. The multiple and conflicting notions of work at play here are, we argue, a crucial point. Interestingly Tanya describes eBay as being *"**too much** work almost"* compared to continuously hunting for a particular object at a thrift store or flea market where *"[y]ou might have to go for two years"* to finally find it. Tanya uses the term *"work"* in different ways throughout our discussion, one use being to indicate something intrinsically enjoyable yet underrated:

> Yeah, it's definitely work and—but I think work is underrated. I think people want to *consume* and *possess* and not—maybe the reason why America is so throw-away, everything is so ridiculously disposable, is that they're not enjoying—they're enjoying the wrong thing or they're looking for satisfaction in objects relative to, not the experience of [acquiring] it, but *having* it.

While expressing strong ethical opinions concerning work and (re)acquisition—about how one ought to live and work—Tanya also expresses that she is in a unique, even privileged position that is not shared by most, suggesting a very different understanding of *"work"*:

> Could you—could *I*—drag four kids around a flea market so that I found whatever it is that [my friend with kids is] going shopping for? Probably not. You know what I mean? ... I realize I have the luxury of time that most people might not. So no, I don't think everybody could do it.

These tensions among how one does live, how one can live, and how one ought to live were acknowledged by many invested participants. While emphasizing the importance and value of reacquisition—typically with an emphasis on positive experience and/or political critique—invested participants also often felt that they occupied a niche, even privileged, position (despite often having low incomes).

Still we see clear evidence, even from casual reacquirers, of the potential value in very different ways of going about (re)acquiring that resist the easy route and embrace work, skill, surprise and, as we will see later, patience, openness, and care. Acknowledging, understanding and incorporating these types of perspectives in HCI research and design is important as they run counter to many commonly accepted notions of work, usefulness and usability.

Quality, reliablity, hygiene: Shortcomings of the reacquired. All participants drew fairly clear boundaries separating things they could not or would not acquire used. Issues of safety, cleanliness and hygiene often played a strong role. For instance, even many invested reacquirers refused to acquire used underwear, linens, towels, bedding, mattresses or food (although we did encounter exceptions for *each* of these items). Such issues have been discussed previously in terms of *divestment rituals* whereby people desire and work to remove previous traces of use and ownership [14]. While the removal or divestment of negative histories from second-hand goods is an important and recurring theme with reacquired goods, we will focus in the remainder of this section on issues with the reacquisition of second-hand electrical and digital technologies because of their direct relevance to HCI and recent concerns with the durability/disposability of such technologies.

Overall, participants tended to perceive newer technologies—especially the newest digital consumer products—as lacking durability. Invested reacquirers in particular often had strong opinions about quality, particularly the perceived lack of quality of many newer products. Commonly cited issues with used digital products included: lack of perceived durability and reliability; lack of a guarantee or warranty; lack of availability of used products; and relatively high cost and/or risk. However, these issues were often not felt to be as relevant when re-acquiring more traditional technologies such as furniture, where it was often felt one had a stronger ability to judge quality and reliability.

Issues also arose of a lack of engagement and transparency with technology—of an inability to understand or intimately relate to the inner workings and operation of devices (see, e.g., [4,29]). Kristy, a self-described anarchist and community organizer, feels conflicted about her acquisition of a new Apple computer in relation to her values of social equity and sustainability. These issues are apparently not simply abstract ethical or political issues but are also intimately linked to Kristy's direct experience of use:

> The computer relationship feels much more dependent. [**James:** Dependent?] That I need it and want it… I'm totally dependent on a bicycle, too, but I can also *treat* it. My bicycle has a name and I, like I think it's a person because I'll be like "Mindy, why are you doing this to me? Why is your tire flat? Come on," just like "Oh, Mindy, I take such good care of you…" … I'll talk to it like that because I know how to fix it. So it's like more of a *relationship*. [**James**: You don't talk to your computer?] No, and this is more like a need or a use, an addiction or something. I would really feel compromised if this broke. I don't have the money to replace it [computer] or fix it or anything. (Kristy, 20s)

This suggests the importance of products that are not only technically durable but also perceptually durable and facilitate relationships of repair, maintenance, and dispossession for reacquisition by others.

We conclude this section by bringing in the importance of social and cultural contexts to understanding people's perceptions of and interactions with (re)acquired objects, and drawing on sociological investigations of consumption (e.g., [5,27]). This point is perhaps most salient with Katie. Katie explained most of her possessions—many if not most of which she reacquired—as largely a factor of her current *"life position"*: a 20-something year old student renting an apartment; a *"temporary situation"*. Katie described most of her possessions as temporary: *"at this point in my life these are temporary purchases. I don't plan on having them forever"*. These *"temporary purchases"* were contrasted with *"grown up purchases"*, notably the new bed and television she recently acquired, and the *"really nice dinette set"* she someday hopes to obtain when she is married. Katie's story highlights the importance of social acceptability in reacquiring, owning, using and perhaps especially displaying to others used goods. Critical or experiential reacquirers tended to describe reacquired goods as a source of pride and meaning, having a social circle of similar values and practices. In contrast casual and necessary reacquirers often desired to minimize the "second-handedness" of reacquired possessions, even resenting them as such.

Quality, uniqueness, history: The value of the reacquired. We conclude this section on reacquired and dispossessed objects by noting some recurring themes related to possessing the reacquired. In contrast to the divestment rituals [14] discussed previously we find many examples of reacquired objects having value precisely because they have been used and owned previously and are consequently thought to be *"unique"*, authentic, *"interesting"*, *"original"* or possessing *"character"* (relationships that can often be understood as the reacquirer positioning or distinguishing himself or herself as exhibiting refined, even elitist taste in the sense articulated by Bourdieu [5]). In many cases, the real or imagined history, story or biography of an object was a source of value rather than something to be eliminated or divested. Gregson and Crewe have described these types of relationships as *investment rituals* [14]. In other cases the meanings and attachments to reacquired objects is strongly related to processes of re-use, reappropriation and remaking from reacquired materials and objects, described by Gregson and Crewe as *alteration rituals* [14] and Odom et al. as *augmentation* [23]. For example, Laura described deep attachment and care for her and her husband's engagement rings and *"candidate"* rings that they finely crafted from common found objects such as paper clips (Figure 1). Such findings are interesting and important, and essential to understanding reacquisition and the possession of the repossessed. However we forego a more thorough treatment of such issues, many of which have been discussed in prior work cited, and instead move to focus in on several themes more specific to invested reacquirers.

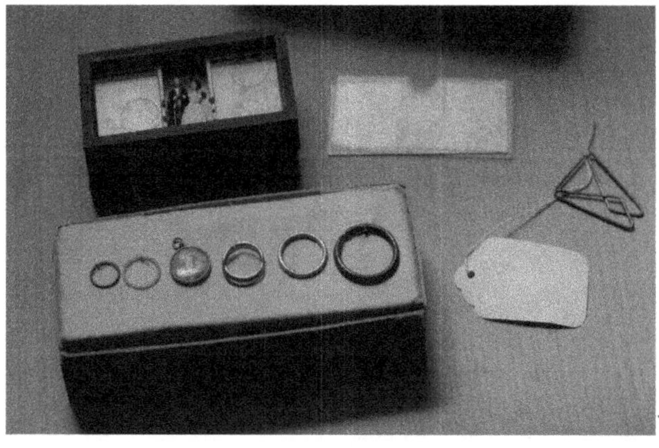

Figure 1. Laura carefully displays her and her husband's engagement rings and candidate rings they constructed from re-used everyday objects.

Departures from firsthand acquisition

We conclude this section with two themes that appear quite unique to invested reacquirers, suggesting interesting departures from mainstream acquisition.

Patience, openness and faith in things. As discussed previously, reacquisition often implies additional work, time and effort—although generally whether this is seen as negative or positive and the particular ways this is experienced can vary dramatically. Delving deeper into these issues we find that the experiences and practices of invested reacquisition are often characterized by notions of patience and openness. Laura, a 30-something year old artist, exemplifies this characterization. Laura lives with her husband, a carpenter, on a limited income, although she described this as a choice more than a necessity. She relies on reacquisition for most of her everyday possessions. Throughout our discussions, Laura described having an *"open"* relationship to things and circumstances:

> I *really* have faith that things will just *turn up* when you need them. So I've never felt like I have to have a lot of money to have stuff. Because I've always been, kind of, proven the opposite. I've never earned that much money, and I've always had everything I needed.

Even though Laura had recently moved into a new home 3 months prior from England, she exhibits extreme patience in populating her home with common items:

> There was nothing that we couldn't live without really… We didn't have a sofa for long time. ... [M]y experience has been that when I need something, if I know I need them, I'll find it. So, I've kinda learned then to know what I need and kinda have this list with me. 'Cause I think it's just—a lot of it is just perception. And if you're kinda thinking 'I need a sofa' then one will come to you, because it will be on your mind, when you're going around your everyday life. So in the end we got a sofa from a friend who was moving out.

Invested reacquirers similarly describe being patient—often a process of learning to be patient and resisting *"object envy"* (Tanya), *"retail therapy"* (John) and other characterizations of the to-be-resisted seductions of firsthand retail:

> If I need something, I don't just go out and buy it. ...I basically live without it for a while and then it comes, it finds a way to materialize. (Kristy, 20s)

> I'm patient. … You keep your eyes out. You have your list in the back of your mind as to what you want or what you need. (Bob, 70s).

We interpret such reacquisition dispositions as characterized by being patient, surrendering complete control, deeply reflecting on what one needs and wants, and accepting, even embracing reacquisition as a continual openness to one's context and circumstances. This disposition stands in stark contrast with the control, immediacy and reliability often associated, at least ideally, with firsthand acquisition.

Care of things, self and others. A deeper understanding of our invested participants' relationships to material things may be achieved through the notion of *care*. Here we are referring to an understanding of care as discussed by Tony Fry, which has its basis in the concept of care developed by Heidegger: *"as an instinctual mixture of concern, anxiety and practice over what is essential for our survival. Such a form of care directs us to act carefully by taking care of ourselves, of how and what we make, plus the manner of use of all we use."* [11, p. 82]. We find such a notion of care suggested in recurring types of speech exhibited by invested participants:

> [I]f it can be salvaged it is worth salvaging. (Tanya, 30s)

> If I had to get rid of it I would give it a good home someplace. (Bob, 70s)

Importantly notions of care were evidenced in observed practices and participants' explanations of these practices. For example, John and Kristy (as well some of their friends) had designated specific areas of their homes for collecting things they no longer needed, which they encouraged others to reacquire. John referred to these areas as *"give-away pile*[s]*"*, Kristy as her *"free pile"*. While we did come across deeply cherished things that were cared for as ones own (e.g., Laura's engagement rings, Figure 1), we also found many examples of care for objects as temporary possession that recirculate. For example, Kristy casually describes *"cycling back"* items she no longer needs and Joe describes a strong desire to get things he *"rescues" "in the hands of someone who could use 'em"*. While many invested reacquirers spoke in ways suggesting objects as constantly in circulation rather than permanently in possession, some participants also expressed what we interpret to be a care for things that recognizes, even respects, that a thing's being, as with a person's, at some point comes to end:

> But this is the chair I was talking about that I might not be able to save. … [The "damage"] may be too significant to—[pauses] I might not be able to save it. (Tanya, 30s, invested home renovator and decorator)

> I don't want to throw it away…if I know somebody can use that, it's just worth hanging on to [to try to sell, "toss in" on a deal, or give away]. But eventually if it's just something that's one man's trash and another man's treasure, well, sometimes it's just trash. (Joe, 50s, flea market seller)

IMPLICATIONS FOR HCI AND INTERACTION DESIGN

Based on our findings we discuss implications for HCI and interaction design with a focus on designing for sustainable and experientially desirable reacquisition and dispossession.

Designing for and with communities of reacquisition

We are hesitant to offer general design recommendations for designing for communities of reacquisition. Indeed, our participants suggest to us that often the very value they derive is dependent on reacquisition *not* being experienced as a "(well) designed" experience. For example, recall Tanya's and Bob's positive experiences of shopping at disorganized flea markets as being superior to the easier, more organized, more designed experiences of eBay or department stores. Further our study is focused on individual "consumers" of second-hand goods much more so than the retailers and other groups involved in selling and trading second-hand goods. Additional studies investigating the retail side of second-hand goods would be a useful complement to our study as means to inform design. Nonetheless, with these caveats in mind we offer some opportunity areas for interaction design and HCI based on common problems articulated by participants, problems which we feel are most pertinent to designing for those casual or financially restricted reacquirers that may be considered as not having the time, motivation or resources to reacquire as they might like.

Simplifying reacquisition of the dispossessed. Reacquisition is hard work, often requiring a great deal of time and effort and leading to frustration, disappointment and failure. Interactive technologies can play important roles in simplifying these processes. For example, adding on online component (e.g., ads, searchable databases, recommender systems) to second-hand stores could help avoid fruitless hours spent searching for particular items. Such systems could help shoppers determine if the right size, color, product type, etc. is currently available or notify them when an item is available. In-store and mobile phone versions should be considered, as many who reacquire out of financial necessity may not have easy access to Internet or computers. Connecting reacquirers to modes of transport is also crucial as many participants described enormous difficulties not only locating things but then also findings means of moving large items.

Simplifying dispossession for reacquisition. Related to improving the availability of reacquired items is simplifying the processes of dis-possessing for reacquisition. Digital technologies offer many opportunities to more easily connect people who are looking to get rid of things with those who are looking to (re)acquire things, helping avoid the unfortunate case when dispossessed objects are taken to landfill or forgotten in attics rather than being reacquired, as our work continuously shows us that *every thing potentially has value in the right context.*

Guaranteeing possession of the reacquired. A significant barrier to reacquiring many dispossessed goods is that people perceive them as potentially unreliable, unclean or unsafe and not worth the risk of reacquiring. This suggests, for example, the importance of systems of guarantee and warranty, as well as products themselves that can digitally record histories of possession, maintenance and repair.

Designing from communities of reacquisition

We find that invested reacquirers in particular often appear to live less materially intensive lives: They often own and (re)acquire less; they often resist (re)acquiring things, especially new things, even things that others would feel they need immediately; they often reflect on what they do and do not need and want; they rarely "throw things out" but rather carefully dis-possess things to others. Importantly these lifestyles were typically felt by participants to be "better" ways of living, and also often had very little if anything to do with values explicitly related to "the environment", "being green" or "sustainability." This suggests that much can potentially be learned from such individuals and communities that can be applied to design for more mainstream communities. We articulate several perspectives on legitimizing and promoting reacquisition as mainstream, sustainable and experientially desirable acquisition.

Redesigning objects for reacquisition. We came across many issues with the lack of perceived quality and durability of reacquired goods, particularly newer electronic and digital products. Many of these issues of durability and disposability have been discussed previously in the context of sustainable interaction design [2,15,16,17,18,23,30]. However here we highlight their significance specifically in terms of reacquisition and the importance of designing products that are not only capable of being possessed durably but also dispossessed and reacquired with care. A specific issue our findings help bring into focus is how the design of technologies affects the persistence of products not only with a single owner but also across multiple contexts of use and ownership. When designing sustainable technologies of and for reacquisition consideration should be given to issues related to perceived quality, safety and hygiene; the ability to maintain and repair an object; and care for and openness toward objects.

Recoding the reacquired and reacquiring. While constructing more durable products is important, at the same time this focus may obscure the fact that many, if not most, of our things *are* durable, are thrown out prematurely, are not metabolically consumed, and, crucially, that *every thing* potentially holds value in the right context. Our participants help us see that perceptions of durability and acceptability are to many extents matters of social and cultural perception (see also, e.g., [5,27]). Throughout our work we see many successful as well as failed examples of objects of reacquisition being successfully *recoded* as valuable, unique, clean, acceptable, normal, etc.—for example, when an object suddenly acquires value when it is removed from an attic and placed in the window of an upscale vintage shop; or an object found in the trash is "rescued" and brought into someone's home. A classic example of *recoding* is Marcel Duchamp's "readymades". Readymades were ordinary commercial products such as a snow shovel, a urinal and a bicycle wheel that were (re)presented as art thus transforming their meaning and value. These artworks demonstrate how the meanings of an object can be utterly transformed without changing the material object itself, but by changing the context in which it is interpreted (see also [10] on recoding). What these examples suggest is an approach to sustainable interaction design that has less to do with redesigning material technologies themselves than with redesigning how we think about and relate to those technologies already made (through the redesign of, e.g., interactive media, services, systems and environments). This opens up a space for designing to *recode the reacquired.*

Making space for reacquisition: Materially, spatially and symbolically relocating reacquisition to the center. Consider that the act of reacquiring items that have been "thrown out" on the curbside or in the dumpster literally requires reacquiring what is designated as trash by the space it occupies (e.g., "dumpster diving", "trash-picking"). This is in contrast to the careful designation of objects for reacquisition in John's *"give-away pile"* or Kristy's *"free pile"*. Similar can be said for other marginalized sites such as yard sales, flea markets and thrift stores. This material, spatial and symbolic marginalization of reacquisition raises the design challenge of literally and symbolically *making space for reacquisition at the center* or mainstream. For example, consider making space for repair and maintenance of digital products at an "Electronics Co-op"—perhaps within the space of a firsthand site like the Apple Store or Best Buy (a proposition we recognize is fraught with challenges and contradictions)—where people can repair, customize, share, and re-use digital parts and products. In important ways virtual spaces such as eBay, Craigslist and Freecycle are already making space for reacquisition at the center. In other ways these spaces could be interpreted as promoting increased material (re)acquisition as they exist in addition to rather than in place of firsthand retail. An analogy to an observed practice would be literally making space for *more* acquisition by throwing something out of the home. This suggests that *displacing sites of firsthand acquisition* may present a distinct challenge for interaction design in terms of reducing the manufacture, acquisition and overall demand of new technology products as a matter of sustainability.

Recirculation and shared use. Our participants present numerous "challenges in practice" to single owner/user models of technology. We see how firsthand goods become second-hand goods as they recirculate across different contexts of use and ownership. Despite expressing great love and care of objects, invested participants often described having an *"easy come, easy go relationship to things"* (Laura) or *"not getting attached* [to things]*"* (Joe). Recirculation and shared use represent very different contexts for sustainable consumption in the context of digital technology, even suggesting deemphasizing possession/ownership to focus on *usership* and *non-usership.* For example, there are many opportunities to explore digital technologies to support the shared use of products ranging from hand tools to automobiles.

Reacquisition values and technology. In line with various concerns with values and technology (e.g., [4,26,29]), we argue that as designers and researchers we should constantly be asking questions such as: How are we currently designing technology in relation to durability or disposability, care or a lack thereof, patience or immediacy? How are we currently marginalizing reacquisition while privileging firsthand acquisition? We see time and again how invested reacquirers often embrace work, patience and care involved in routine daily practices, at times even displaying resistance to ease, immediacy and flexibility[2]. These findings echo approaches within HCI that challenge values of ease and efficiency, such as designing for reflection, ambiguity, enjoyment and everyday creativity [3,12,26,30]. Such perspectives should be employed and built upon to explore ways of promoting reacquisition and dispossession that are *less* materially intensive and *more* experientially satisfying and meaningful. Based on our study, *patience* and *care* are two values we believe are worth stronger consideration in the design technology.

CONCLUSION

We have reframed the consumption of durable technologies as acquisition, possession, dispossession and reacquisition. We presented 4 reacquisition orientations and other findings from our study. Based on our work we have highlighted a number of opportunities for designing technologies to support current reacquisition practices, including simplifying reacquisition of the dispossessed, simplifying dispossession for reacquisition, and guaranteeing possession of the reacquired. An equally important contribution of our work is to more broadly inform how HCI and interaction design can lead the way in designing future sustainable contexts for technological (re)acquisition and dispossession.

ACKNOWLEDGEMENTS

We are grateful to our study participants for sharing their time and stories. We also thank Sara Kiesler for her instructive comments on an early draft of this paper, and the anonymous reviewers for their insightful comments. Financial support for this work was provided in part by National Science Foundation Grant #IIS- 1018340.

REFERENCES

1. Baudrillard, J. (1968). *The system of objects*. Verso.
2. Blevis, E. (2007). Sustainable interaction design: invention & disposal, renewal & reuse. *Proc. CHI '07.*
3. Blythe, M., Overbeeke, K. Monk, A. & Wright, P. eds. (2004). *Funology: from Usability to Enjoyment.* Kluwer.
4. Borgmann, A. (1984). *Technology and the character of contemporary life*. University of Chicago Press.
5. Bourdieu, P. (1984). *Distinction: A social critique of the judgment of taste.* London: Routledge.
6. Buechley et al. (2009). DIY for CHI: methods, communities, and values of reuse. *CHI '09 E.A.*

[2] Such practices often appear to have the engaging character of "focal practices" as described by philosopher of technology Albert Borgmann. These practices may also at times be interpreted as practical resistance to the device paradigm articulated by Borgmann. See [4].

7. Brynjarsdóttir, H. & Sengers, P. Ubicomp from the Edge of the North Atlantic: Lessons from Fishing Villages in Iceland and Newfoundland. *Ubicomp '09 workshop.*

8. Cooper, T. (2008). Slower Consumption Reflections on Product Life Spans and the "Throwaway Society". Journal of Industrial Ecology, *9*(1-2):51-67.

9. Douglas, M. & Isherwood, B. (1979). *The world of goods: Towards an anthropology of consumption.* Basic books.

10. Fry, T. (2009). *Design futuring.* Berg.

11. Fry, T. (1994). *Remakings.* Envirobooks.

12. Gaver, W., Beaver, J.,& Benford, S. (2003).Ambiguity as a resource for design. *Proc.* CHI *'03.* 233-240.

13. Glaser, B. & Strauss, A. (1967). Discovery of grounded theory: strategies for qualitative research. Sociology Press.

14. Gregson, N. & Crewe, L. (2003). *Second-hand cultures.* Berg.

15. Hanks, K., Odom, W., Roedl, D., and Blevis, E. (2008). Sustainable millennials: attitudes towards sustainability and the material effects of interactive technologies. *Proc. CHI '08.* 333-342.

16. Huang & Truong. (2008). Breaking the disposable technology paradigm: opportunities for sustainable interaction design for mobile phones. *Proc. CHI '08.*

17. Huh, J., Nathan, L. P., Silberman, S., Blevis, E., Tomlinson, B., Sengers, P., & Busse, D. (2010). Examining appropriation, re-use, and maintenance for sustainability. In *Ext. Abst. CHI '10.* 4457-4460.

18. Huh, J., Nam, K., & Sharma, N. 2010. Finding the lost treasure: understanding reuse of used computing devices. In *Proc. CHI '10.* 1875-1878

19. Lastovicka, J. & Fernandez, K. (2005). Three paths to disposition: The movement of meaningful possessions to strangers. *Jour. Cons. Research, 31*(4):813-823.

20. Lucas, G. (2002). Disposability and Dispossession in the Twentieth Century. *Jour. Material Culture, 7*(1):5–22.

21. Miles, M. B. & Huberman, A. M. (1994). *Qualitative Data Analysis.* Thousand Oaks, CA: Sage.

22. Miller, D, ed. (1998). *Material cultures: Why some things matter.* University of Chicago Press.

23. Odom, W., Pierce, J., Stolterman, E., & Blevis, E. (2009). Understanding why we preserve some things and discard others in the context of interaction design. *Proc. CHI '09.*

24. Roux, D. & Kourchia, M. (2006). I am what I wear?: An exploratory study of symbolic meanings associated with secondhand clothing. *Advances in cons. research, 33*:1-7.

25. Satchell, C. & Dourish, P. Beyond the user: use and non-use in HCI. *Proc. OZCHI '09.*

26. Sengers, P., Boehner, K., David, S., & Kaye, J. (2005). Reflective design. *Proc. Critical Computing.*

27. Shove, E. (2003). *Comfort, cleanliness & convenience: the social organization of normality.* Berg.

28. Thomas, V. M. (2003). Demand and dematerialization impacts of second-hand markets: Reuse or more use? *Journal of Industrial Ecology, 7*(2): 65–78.

29. Verbeek, P-P. (2005). *What things do: philosophical reflections on technology, agency, and design.* Penn. State

30. Wakkary & Tanenbaum. (2009). A sustainable identity: the creativity of an everyday designer. *Proc. CHI '09.*

31. Woodruff et al. (2008). A bright green perspective on sustainable choices. *Proc. CHI '08.*

Practices in the Creative Reuse of e-Waste

Sunyoung Kim & Eric Paulos
Human-Computer Interaction Institute, Carnegie Mellon
5000 Forbes Avenue, Pittsburgh, PA, USA
{sunyoung.kim, paulos}@cs.cmu.edu

ABSTRACT
E-waste is a generic term embracing various forms of electric and electronic equipment that is loosely discarded, surplus, obsolete, or broken [27]. When e-waste is improperly discarded as trash, there are predictable negative impacts on the environment and human health. Existing e-waste solutions range from designing for reuse to fabricating with eco-friendly decomposable materials to more radical critiques of current practices surrounding capitalism and consumerism. Complementary to theses efforts, this paper presents an accessible reuse framework that encourages creativity while maintaining personal ownership of e-waste. Through a series of online surveys of existing personal e-waste stockpiling behaviors combined with observational studies of existing reuse practices, we developed a *design reuse vocabulary: materials, shapes, and operations* to enable wide ranging and creative reuse of obsolete electronics by everyday people. We operationalized this vocabulary and evaluated its legibility and usefulness. As a result, we derived a novel *reuse composition framework: reuse as-is, remake, and remanufacture* designed to be accessible and to have broader impact in encouraging creative reuse across a wide range of e-waste types beyond those specifically used in our study. We believe these frameworks will be a catalyst for the creative reuse of e-waste.

Author Keywords
Sustainability, e-Waste, DIY, reuse, creativity

ACM Classification Keywords
H.5.m. Information interfaces and presentation (e.g., HCI): Miscellaneous.

General Terms
Human Factors

INTRODUCTION
Seventy-seven percent of the 1.5 million Apple's iPhone 4 sales on the first day of launch in June 2010 were upgrades purchased by existing iPhone owners [22]. Economically speaking, Apple has been successful in building a recurring revenue stream from a growing base of loyal customers. Environmentally speaking, on the other hand, the launch of iPhone 4 accelerated the creation of e-waste. In just a single day, most of those fully functioning and relatively state-of-the-art mobile phones suddenly became of little to no use: migrating into desk drawers, storage bins, and garages. While we have heard this story before [14], the sheer volume and acceleration of e-waste beyond mobile phones are staggering. More importantly, these e-waste practices significantly exacerbate environmental pollution leaving behind environmentally hazardous byproducts [26].

Electronic equipment is a ubiquitous part of modern living across the US and other developed countries. We cohabitate with electronics in a comfortable symbiosis; we watch television in our homes, listen to music on the go, and work and play on laptop computers. Americans own approximately 24 electronic products per household [5], and Europeans and Oceanians are similar: owning 26 and 22 items respectively [2,5]. Meanwhile, our relationship with electronic products is short lived; Americans replace their mobile phones every 17.5 months [13], and laptop computers every 3 years [11] on average. Such rapid change in technology resulted in a fast-growing surplus of e-waste. Approximately 30 million computers in the US and 100 million phones in Europe become obsolete or outdated each year turning into e-waste [31].

While purchasing trends follow the *replace and discard* pattern [6] by rapidly replacing old products with new ones, electronics itself does not follow this same behavior. Rather than immediately throwing things away, people often hold onto obsolete electronics [10]. For example, three-quarters of all computers ever purchased in the US remain stockpiled in storerooms, garages or basements of homes, and up to 75 percent of obsolete cell phones are stockpiled in drawers [19,30]. We posit four primary factors contributing towards this e-waste behavior:

1. **Lack of information:** information on how to properly recycle obsolete electronics is often unavailable.
2. **Burden in action:** time and location challenges for transporting e-waste are a significant barrier to proper discarding and recycling action for many consumers.
3. **Attachment or emotions**: non-technical barriers such as attachment theory [29] often play an important role in preventing individuals from relinquishing ownership of

CHI 2011, May 7–12, 2011, Vancouver, BC, Canada.

the objects even if the product's life span approaches a natural end [3].

4. **Restrained ideas**: while many individuals may indeed desire to reuse obsolete electronics in new ways, there is no accessible mechanism to easily discover, use, and invent intuitive and realistic ideas for reusing electronic objects to creative ideas beyond disposal and recycling.

These four factors emerged out of our own early internal research brainstorming sessions about e-waste. The first two factors were derived based on existing practices by governments and organizations, which try to build an infrastructure to reduce e-waste. The third factor came from the classical framings of attachment theory. The last factor was derived from our experiences with attachment theory, second hand cultures, and DIY communities. This fourth factor forms the basis of our research hypothesis and design opportunity.

The first two challenges above are currently being addressed by governments, manufacturers, retailers and non-profit organizations who have put significant effort into making information available and facilities accessible in order to encourage recycling e-waste. In this paper, we focus on the second two reasons for stockpiling e-waste: attachment or emotion, and lack of ideas, or access to ideas if any, about what to do with e-waste besides discarding. Particularly, our work attempts to make a contribution through two mechanisms: (1) the development of *a design reuse vocabulary* to characterize e-waste reusing patterns, and (2) a more generalizable *reuse composition framework* to inspire everyday designers to creatively reuse e-waste.

In the next section, we explain our goals in this work. Then, we provide a review of previous works in issues related to sustainability in the HCI community. Next, we describe the design of a series of field studies and key findings from data analyses. Then, we propose a subsequently evaluated reuse design vocabulary. We present a generalizable reuse composition framework for enabling and inspiring creative reuse of e-waste. Finally, we conclude by discussing the key implications of this work.

GOALS

The overarching long-term goal of this work is to find ways to facilitate latent resources such as e-waste, and to prolong the longevity of use in electronic products by its creative reuse. To tackle this problem as HCI researchers, we have three practical goals in this paper. First, we want to acquire baseline understanding of e-waste stockpiling behaviors, especially to answer why people keep end-of-life electronics instead of discarding them. Secondly, we aim to understand the existing creative reuse practices of e-waste within environmental activists and Do-It-Yourself (DIY) communities. Lastly, from these understandings regarding e-waste stockpiling and reusing cultures, we aim to develop a simple design strategy that can inspire everyday people to reuse domestic e-waste creatively and actively. We plan to derive high-level scaffolding patterns for the general e-waste reuse patterns from low-level properties regarding reuse practice patterns.

RELATED WORKS

Over the past several years, the HCI community has started to discourse the role of interaction design in sustainability. Blevis introduced the term Sustainable Interaction Design, proposing a rubric for understanding the material effects of particular interaction design cases in terms of forms of use, reuse, and disposal [3]. Since then HCI practitioners have begun investigating environmental sustainability within HCI from a variety of perspectives: exploring the material and behavioral challenges of sustainability in relation to interaction design [18]; taking account of sustainability as part of the material design of products [17]; helping elevate individuals to have a powerful voice in society, act as citizen scientists; and learn and lobby for change worldwide [21]. Our approach is to help promoting users to actively reappropriate domestic e-waste for creative reuse.

Wakkary *et al.* broadened the role of users and their identity from a mere consumer to a creative everyday designer by introducing the concept of design-in-use [24]. In their work, they claimed that people appropriate and adapt artifacts in the creative and sustainable ways in their everyday experience, which generates a set of design principles that can prompt sustainable interaction design. Our work is similar to their concept of design-in-use in that we also regard a user as an entity to elongate the useful lifespan of an artifice by creative reuse and reappropriation. While *design-in-use* took an ethnographic approach to understand everyday experience in the homes, we drew similar inspiration from Wooduff *et al.* research into informing everyday design practices through an exploration of existing green activists [28]. However, unlike their work, we focused specifically on the reuse of e-waste.

Huh *et al.* researched the adoption practices of used personal digital assistants (PDAs) with eBay users who bought used PDAs to explore reuse of outdated computing products [15]. In a similar vein, there are many programs and organizations to collect obsolete electronics to reuse creatively or to give away refurbished electronics to disadvantaged people all over the world [1,23]. While recycling is a prevalent method to dispose e-waste properly, its practice is actually in direct conflict with the known cultural practices of ownership and attachment theory [29]. The challenge was to develop complementary strategies for appropriate e-waste reuse for individuals who have desires to retain their ownership of e-waste regardless of its usefulness and functionalities. An important part of our approach is to focus on the existing practices of the creative reuse of e-waste in everyday life. The key insight is that such existing reuse practices provide for continued ownership of e-waste – one of our primary goals.

Factors besides the physical form and design of the object play another vital role in e-waste practices. Huang and Truong found out the importance of context in how people replace and dispose of their mobile phones through a field study of mobile phone ownership, replacement and disposal practices [13]. Further, Dourish argues for a broader rhetoric surrounding environmental HCI research and scoping that takes into account significant political and cultural contexts of environmental practices [8]. While we agree that context is a crucial factor that determines the lifespan of our relationship with various consumer electronics, the focus of this paper is on the everyday design of e-waste. [25].

METHODS

We performed three different studies in this work: a Mechanical-Turk based survey, an online community observation, and a customized online survey. First, to understand the variety and personal perceptions of e-waste found in homes, we conducted an online survey using Amazon's Mechanical Turk (AMT)[1]. AMT is an online labor market where people are paid small amount of money to complete small tasks called Human Intelligence Tasks (HITs). Online AMT "workers" previewed our HIT, completed the survey voluntarily, and got paid 25 cents for each successfully completed HIT. Second, we conducted an observational study across three Do-It-Yourself online communities to understand the current practices surrounding the creative reuse of e-waste. We studied publicly available online DIY communities where we reviewed and collected items posted on the community websites and blogs in the US such as Instructables[2], Craftster[3], and Etsy[4]. From the first two studies we developed a candidate reuse design vocabulary. Lastly, we evaluated this vocabulary within individuals in various online communities such as DIY communities, environmental activists and mothers groups. The following sections further detail our methods, studies, and findings.

UNDERSTANDING E-WASTE IN HOMES

A fundamental component towards our understandings of patterns and practices regarding accumulation and reuse of e-waste is the study of domestic e-waste life and co-habitation. In this section, we describe two separate studies that were conducted to understand patterns of e-waste stockpiling behaviors and practices of e-waste reuse.

AMT Online Survey: Accumulation of e-Waste

This survey was designed to collect data on e-waste that individuals currently live with in their homes. The purpose of this survey was to acquire a baseline understanding of the types of unused electronics stored in homes and insights into the rational and personal attachment towards their e-waste. We were particularly interested in why some electronics that had reached the end of their usable lives were stockpiled in homes rather than discarded or recycled. By understanding both the types of collected e-waste and the reasoning behind keeping it, we expected to gain a baseline understanding of e-waste stockpiling behaviors.

The survey participants were asked to complete a simple task of photographing unused electronic objects in their home in its surroundings, uploading it to AMT, and answering a series of questions about the object including:

- A title/label for the photo
- What is this? (Inviting them to tell a personal story or provide a description of a pictured object)
- How long have you kept it without using it?
- Why don't you use it anymore?
- Why do you still keep it even if you don't use it anymore?
- Is this waste? (With a four point scale of acceptable answers: Yes, definitely waste; likely waste; likely not waste; definitely not waste)

In order to prevent influencing participants' perspective on obsolete electronics in their homes, we did not use the term *e-waste* or *waste* except in the last question in this survey. Our survey was not presented or framed as a study of electronic waste or waste in general.

In total, we received 179 responses over 14 days from AMT users in the United States with 41 responses filtered out for image duplicity or quality issues – plagiarized or unrecognizable images, or those with unrelated text. In the end, we analyzed 138 answers from 61 unique users (4.4 responses per user on average) with a 58% Male / 42% Female gender breakdown. The age range was 20 - 59 years old with 32 years being the average (11.6 SD).

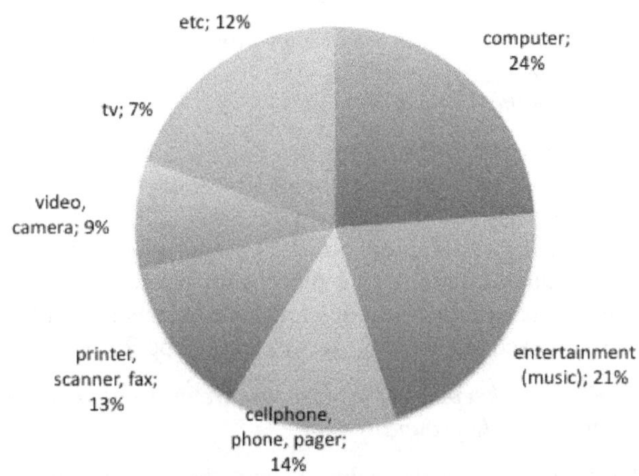

Figure 1. Proportions of e-waste by the types of electronics

The types of obsolete electronics kept in homes are analogous across households. Nearly three-fourths (71%) of all reported e-waste fell into one of only four electronics categories: computer and computer accessories (24%, *e.g.*, modems, mice, and routers); entertainment electronics

[1] Amazon Mechanical Turk, http://www.mturk.com

[2] Instructables, http://www.instructables.org

[3] Craftster, http://www.craftster.org

[4] Etsy, http://www.etsy.com

(21%, *e.g.*, video game consoles, CD players, and cassette tape players); phones (14%, *e.g.*, landline phones and cell phones); and printer/fax products (13%). (See Figure 1)

Not surprisingly, changes in technological media (e.g., CDs to mp3 players or desktops to laptops) and significant drops in retail prices (39% and 22.2% respectively) were two main reasons for why our survey participants stopped using an old but fully working products and purchased new ones. Meanwhile, only 25% of participants answered that they replaced existing electronics with new products because of broken or non-functioning issues:

> *"Buying a replacement ink cartridge was more expensive than buying a new printer. So we bought a new printer instead of refilling my old one. That still prints in pink so we might need to print lots of pink things sometime."*

Most participants had high expectations or anticipations that they would want or need to use the obsolete electronics in the future. Almost half (48%) of the participants answered "possibility for future use" as a main reason for keeping unused electronics instead of throwing them away:

> *"It [the CD player] is still in good working condition and I may have use for it in the future since I still own CDs."*

> *"I always think that I will start playing this game again. But eventually the day never came."*

However, as we evidenced in the previous quote, many participants also showed their contradicted thoughts between their expectation and anticipation of future use:

> *"I would like to use it later. But I know it would never happen. But I still hope to use it."*

11% of obsolete electronics are kept due to sentimental reasons, and 7% are kept because of a lack of knowledge or available resources to properly dispose of the electronics:

> *"There are special, environmentally friendly disposal procedures for computers and we've been too lazy to research them. We don't want to toss it the wrong way."*

One significant finding from this survey is that answers to the "Is this waste?" question were almost evenly distributed across alternatives (definitely yes: 34%; likely yes: 28%; likely not: 19%; definitely not: 19%). This wide distribution of individual values people place onto unused electronics opens up design opportunities for these objects to be reused or re-purposed since the owners express hope for reuse:

> *"Why am I keeping it? Just in case we ever get beans that aren't already ground!"*

These findings could be biased and these results are not generalizable because of the small size of user pools who are registrants on a particular website (AMT). In spite of the small sample size and possibly biased set of participants, the results still revealed some interesting insights about the characteristics of e-waste stockpiled in homes and residual values on e-waste. First, e-waste is considered different from generic waste; in fact, most obsolete electronics are not regarded as "waste". Second, much e-waste is still functioning or has either material or emotional value. Lastly, people showed a contradiction between their expectations or desires and the anticipation of e-waste for the future use of their e-waste. This sheds light onto the desire to utilize e-waste, and, at the same time, the lack of knowledge or methods for the reuse of e-waste.

Figure 2. Pictures of e-waste uploaded: desktop computers, printers, and electronics junk drawers from top to bottom

Online Community Observation: Reuse of e-Waste

Next, we collected the photos of redesigned e-waste posted to online communities. The purpose of this observation was to understand the current practices of how environmental activists and Do-It-Yourself (DIY) enthusiasts have reused obsolete electronics in creative ways. Throughout the observation of these current practices of redesigning e-waste, we developed our initial *design reuse vocabulary*. This vocabulary was derived in part from extracting various patterns of material use, e-waste forms, and reuse operations that were prevalent across these communities. We reviewed over 400 hundred unique photos with accompanying instructions for reusing various objects within three major DIY community websites hosted in the United States such as Instructables, Craftster, and Etsy. We selected 58 of these that were derived directly from electronic products.

DESIGN REUSE VOCABULARY

The combination of insights and data collected from our online survey and observation framed the choices for *design reuse vocabulary*. After examining the photos and instructions collected from our online observations, we defined three primary properties of e-waste redesign patterns based on the original properties of the object [4]: materials, shapes, and operations. To be clear, our vocabulary is not exhaustive but rather presents a novel reframing of the problem of how to inspire, enable, and encourage personal, novel reuse of e-waste.

We developed the reuse vocabulary from the previous two studies we conducted. In the first study, we examined the collected photos to extract an initial set of the vocabulary. Then, we iteratively refined the vocabulary within the colleagues in our research group. In the second study, participants were asked to provide extra keywords if the vocabulary we provided was not sufficient. Finally, we consolidated all the keywords into the reuse vocabulary.

Material Properties

Material properties refer to the physical characteristics of the primary construction material of e-waste. We derived 20 keywords to capture a range of material properties we observed in our studies.

- Transparent/transmissive
- Opaque
- Porous
- Impermeable
- Smooth
- Rough
- Fragile
- Stiff/rigid
- Reflective
- Absorbing
- Thin
- Thick
- Heavy
- Light
- Soft/malleable
- Hard
- Sharp
- Dull
- Duplicable
- Decomposable

Shape Properties

Shape properties refer to the quality of a distinct object or body in having an external surface or outline of specific form or figure. From our observations, we derived 7 keywords to describe shape properties.

- Block/rectangular
- Hollow
- Complex
- Spherical/circular/round
- Concave
- Symmetric
- Curved

Operation properties

Operation properties are the methods or means that people apply to the artifact for reappropriation. From our studies and observations, we derived 21 keywords to describe operation properties to be applicable to e-waste reuse.

- Attach
- Bend
- Break
- Burn
- Cut
- Engrave
- Fill
- Fold
- Fuse
- Glue
- Hollow
- Lean
- Melt
- Paste
- Paint
- Sand
- Screw/unscrew
- Scratch/scrape
- Smash
- Solder
- Stack

EVALUATING THE DESIGN REUSE VOCABULARY

We conducted another survey collecting personal experiences of e-waste reuse. The purpose of this survey was to verify the design reuse vocabulary presented previously. The evaluation was conducted by asking individuals to apply the vocabulary to their own experiences of e-waste reuse. In this survey, participants were asked to complete a task of photographing the object in their home, uploading it to our customized survey, and answering a series of questions about the photographed object including:

- A title/label for this photo
- What is this? (Inviting them to tell a personal story or provide a description of this piece)
- What was it originally?
- Why did you remake this object?
- How did you remake this object?
- Apply three sets of vocabulary to this object.

For the last question, we provided sets of vocabulary in three categories; material properties of the object, shapes of the object, and techniques applied for reuse. Participants were asked to select relevant keywords from a given set of vocabulary about the photographed object. If there was no relevant keyword in a given set, they were asked to add their own keywords to describe their experience.

In total, we received 55 responses over 14 days with 13 responses filtering out for duplicity and quality issues such as images plagiarized or unrecognizable. In the end, we analyzed 42 answers from 40 unique users with 99.5% Male/ 0.5% Female gender breakdown. The age range was 18 - 63 years old with 27 years being the average (9.02 SD). We received relatively small number of responses (55 in total before filtering out) in spite of the large number of media we posted our survey on (3 DIY community websites, 8 distribution mailing lists, and 2 hackers' community websites). This directly reflects the current trend of rare e-waste reappropriation or the lack of knowledge about how to reuse it. Lastly, participants were asked to add extra keywords if they found anything missing from our design reuse vocabulary.

We found a great gender bias among the participants of this survey; only two participants (0.5%) were females while the rest (95.5%) were males. There could be two possible reasons of such an enormous gender bias; registrants in the community websites or mailing lists where we distributed our survey may be male dominant. Or, practices of remaking or redesigning electronics may be prevalent for males. We claim that the gender bias might be due to high inclination that males are more responsible for and much interested in disassembling, hacking, and playing with electronic than females. The conventional wisdom is that electronics are thought to require special skills or techniques while non-digital artifacts do not except dexterity, which is not always true. Moreover, since the survey has distributed to female-dominant communities as well such as mailing lists for moms and housewives, the chances that the gender bias might be due to the gender characteristics in communities are low.

Findings

We evidenced that participants easily and actively applied the operational design vocabulary we created to their redesigned objects. In total, 456 keywords were applied to 42 objects (11.4 keywords per object on average).

Material Properties

It was not surprising that keywords that could represent hardware's material properties such as *stiff, hard, heavy, thick, impermeable and decomposable* were used frequently with electronic objects. However, we were surprised to also find frequent usage of properties more closely associated with glass such *smooth, transparent, fragile, light, reflective* and *opaque*. An obvious explanation for this is the common integration of glass into the screens of electronics. Besides 20 keywords provided, 3 keywords were additionally proposed for material properties by participants such as *light-emitting, luminescent* and *brittle,* but nothing was significant except the fact that all keywords represent additional properties for glass properties.

Shape Properties

The most commonly used shape properties were *hollow* and *curved.* With cases and enclosures being an integral part of consumer electronics, the choice of *Hollow* is not surprising. Similarly, the industrial design trend of curved surfaces for enclosures is a likely contributor the common use of *Curved. Symmetric* represents one of the electronics' characteristics; electronics have accessories or components that are symmetric in shape such as floppy disks or keyboard keys. Beside 7 keywords provided, 1 keyword was additionally proposed for shape properties, *retro.*

Operation properties

Various keywords were applied to the objects frequently that could represent various simple operational property which do not require special skills such as *attach, screw, glue, cut, bend, paint, fill, fold* and *stack.* One keyword that represents a complicated operation, *solder,* was also frequently used but not as often as simple operation properties. Besides 21 keywords provided, 13 keywords were additionally proposed by participants for operation properties, which include wide range of operations from simple keywords such as *tape, stitch* and *polish* to complicated ones such as *drill, hack, melt, program, saw* and *silicon.* Especially, complicated operations were commonly proposed across different participants; *drill* was applied 8 times and *hack, melt and programming* were applied *3 times per each.*

REUSE COMPOSITION FRAMEWORK

While we were able to gain insight and value from the development and evaluation of the design reuse vocabulary, a more important goal of our work was to develop a generalizable mechanism for encouraging and enabling everyday designers to reuse e-waste creatively. We focused specifically on the *operation properties* from our studies to develop a higher-level abstraction of e-waste reuse patterns from the lower-level reuse design vocabulary. We use the term *reuse composition framework* to describe this higher-level abstraction. We classified the type of e-waste reuse into three categories from reuse design vocabulary: *Reuse As-Is, Re-make*, and *Remanufacture*. This new higher-level abstraction is the basis of our reuse composition framework which we detail further by demonstrating its usage when various reuse techniques are combined with other properties derived from our reuse design vocabulary. This framework could be a good measure to probe the reusability of e-waste before recycling or discarding it. We hope this framework will become a catalyst for everyday designers to reuse stockpiled e-waste creatively and actively.

First, we define *Reuse As-Is* as the use of e-waste for other purposes then originally designed by simple operations such as removing off or adding some parts without any expertise in manipulating electrical parts. Second, we define *Re-make* as changing the functions or features of e-waste with medium level of expertise in either crafting or manipulating electrical parts. Lastly, we define *Remanufacture* as complete reconstruction of e-waste with high level of expertise in both crafting and manipulating electrical parts. In what follows, we present a series of everyday design operations intended to help facilitate and promote the overall potential for E-waste reuse and product lifespan while still maintaining personal ownership of the E-waste. The goal is that such everyday design operations can be generalized and readily applied to a wide range of e-waste beyond those specifically used in our study.

Reuse As-Is: Aesthetics

When its appearance is aesthetically pleasing, electronics were often used as-is for other purposes than originally designed without much restructuring. In some cases, the electric parts are removed from the piece to hollow so that it can be used as a case or a holder:

"The Apple g4 Cube is a joy to service/take apart, you click down on the handle, and pull the whole computer assembly right out of the case. Put that aside you can still use the computer, without the shell."

Figure 3. First row: a USB drive, pushpins, a necklace, and a key chain made of keyboard. Second row: a walk-man soap dish, electric Halloween pumpkins, and VHS notebook covers. Third

row: an iPod shuffle Altoids case, a Mac tissue holder, and an Apple G4 tissue box.

Characters or patterns printed on the surface of artifices were also good pieces for reuse (*e.g.*, characters on a keyboard). One interesting thing is that the majority of redesigned e-waste classified in this category is Apple products like an iPod shuffle, iMac, or Apple G4, which contain a high degree of industrial design form elements. One result is that the these aesthetics in design play a role not only in prompting the original desire for the object but also serves as valuable components in its reuse. 17% of photos uploaded from the second online surveys, and 23% from online observations were classified in this category:

"It is small, slim, slick. Perfect for Altoid or TicTac case. Isn't it cute?" (See the bottom left photo in Figure 3)

Reuse As-Is: Transparent & Hollow

A *transparent - hollow* pair is one of the most frequently selected keyword pairs for material and shape properties. *Transparency* is selected when the body of the electronics consisted of glass or transparent plastic materials in part or on the whole. *Hollow* was selected when the electric parts can be dismantled from the body to utilize only the body part. Light bulbs were the most popular artifices that people easily remake for creative reuse such as a plant pot, a vase, snowballs, and an ornamental piece (see the photos at the top in figure 3). Computer monitors are another type of electronics in this category that people often reused with creativity; we received two photos of fish tanks made out of old CRT monitors. 17% of photos uploaded from the second online survey, and 20% from online observations were classified in this category:

"I took the case of a G4 Cube, removed the computer (a simple step) and added a plexiglass bottom. Silicon and a few small brads later I had an aquarium." (See the bottom right photo in Figure 4)

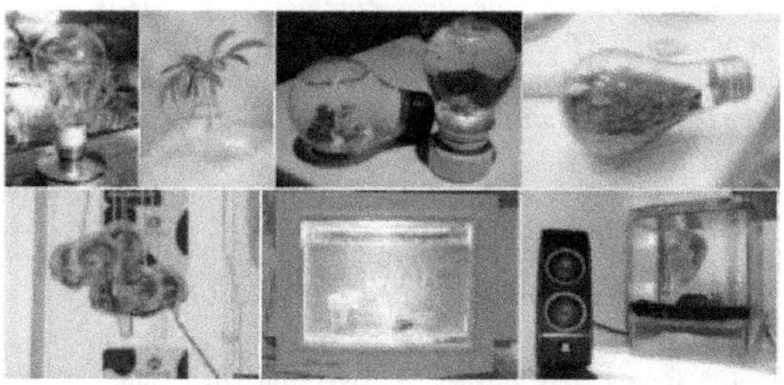

Figure 4. Light bulbs redesigned for various purposes above, and iMac speaker lights and monitor fish tanks from left to right below

We also evidenced that people are often inspired by the ideas of others when developing their own ideas for e-waste reuse.

"Someone posted his light bulb vase on a blog. It looked simple and pretty." (See the top photos in Figure 4)

"I had seen others on the Internet make a fish tank out of an old monitor and thought it was really neat. It is geek chic." (See the last two photos at the bottom in Figure 4)

Reuse As-Is: Block & Attach

When the shape of electronics is *symmetric* or *rectangular*, *assembly* was often applied to reuse for other purposes than originally designed. Most electronics are made of plastics or similar stiff materials in a rectangular shape making it is rigid and easy to *stack*, *attach*, or *assemble*. Depending on the size of the electronics and the number of pieces used, different forms and functions are made from the same piece. For example, ringing 2 floppy disks become a notepad, stitching 5 floppy disks becomes a pencil holder, and tying multiple floppy disks becomes a bag. These practices did not require any expertise either. 12% of photos uploaded from the second online surveys, and 15% from online observations were classified in this category:

"I drilled holes in the floppy disks so that they could be knotted together with twine or zip ties. These were then glued to a canvas backing and the whole thing was stitched together." (See the second photo in Figure 5)

"Overall, I thought it a waste to spend money to buy something that I could make a substitute with stuff I am going to get rid of. I thought of assembling old computer components that I am too much of a packrat to get rid of." (See the right-most photo in Figure 5)

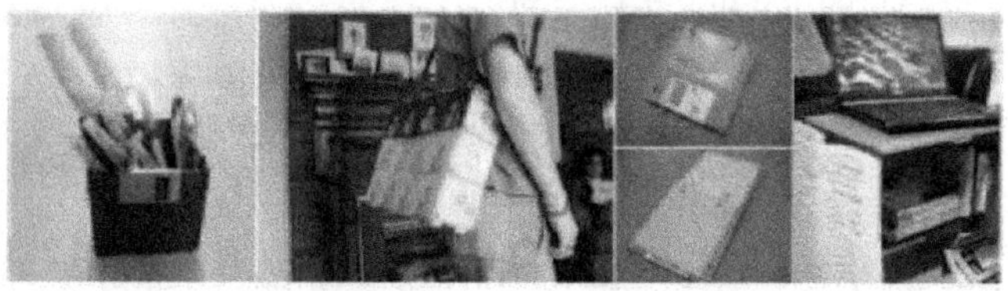

Figure 5. A floppy disk penholder bag notepad, and a laptop desk made of keyboards and a scanner from left to right

Re-Make: Circular - Cut

The unique metallic color and shape of flat circular parts in electronics such as a hard drive and CDs were often inspiration for the creation of art or ornamental pieces. In some cases, the metallic flat surfaces were used for the base of an object. The basic operation properties applied to the circular electronic parts were *attach*, same as the one in *Reuse As-Is: Block & Attach*. Circular objects differ from rectangular ones in that additional advanced operation properties were applied altogether with *attach* such as *solder*, *screw*, and *etch*. 16% of photos uploaded from the second online surveys, and 13% from online observations were classified in this category:

"I had old hard drives lying around wanting to get rid of. I dissembled it and glued parts together to use as a candleholder."(See the second photo in Figure 6)

"I found this platter at a flea market. Not knowing what to do with it, I bought it for $20 anyways because it was such a cool piece. After sitting in my basement for a

while, it became apparent that the best use would be to make a coffee table." (See the third photo in Figure 6)

Figure 6. An artificial flower, a candleholder, a coffee table, and disk clocks from left to right

Re-Make: Complex & Attach

PDAs, laptops, and other similar electronics are what people tend to retain the ownerships the most due to the original monetary values [20]. At first glance, people might think it very difficult, if not impossible, to repurpose obsolete PDAs or laptops. However, we got a few obsolete PDAs and laptops repurposed as digital picture frames. Plastic parts (or casings) were dismantled, and then the monitor was attached on a picture frame. While not requiring much expertise in manipulating electronic parts, it needs elaborate crafting skills to dismantle and assemble parts to reappropriate electronics in this category. In some cases, a basic level programming skill is applied too. For example, one participant reprogrammed the digital picture frame as a clock to show time in words (see the right-most photo in Figure 7). 12% of photos uploaded from the second online surveys, and 15% from online observations were classified in this category:

"It was an old PDA and I thought I should use it for something rather than just let it sit around unused. I removed some unnecessary parts, and mounted the PDA on the back of the frame."

"I made a very simple wood frame to accommodate the dimensions of my old laptop, and reconnected the video and power cable. I use a simple slide viewer or the screen saver to run the pictures in the frame."

"It was originally a digital photo frame, but unfortunately of very poor quality that was basically unsuitable for displaying images. Rather than throw it away, I decided to re-purpose it in a way that it could be of some use."

(See the photos in Figure 7)

Figure 7. Digital photo frames made of an old PDA and a laptop, and a word clock from left to right

Remanufacture: Reform

Form factors are good clues for creative reappropriation. For example, shape and thickness of a CD case might be suitable for a portable speaker, and the size of an empty inkjet cartridge might be appropriate for a handheld flashlight to utilize the form factor. 7% of photos uploaded from the second online surveys, and 12% from online observations were classified in this category:

"I made a portable speaker in a CD case for my iPod without spending even a penny. Now I can carry this portable speaker anywhere you like. I can even put my iPod inside the CD case when it is not in use."

Figure 8. A palm pilot display for Roomba, an inkjet cartridge flashlight, a videotape USB hub, and a portable speaker in a CD case from left to right

Remanufacture: Hacking

There were some serious expert hacking and programming works among the data we collected. These works typically required some level of expertise in manipulating electronics and/or mechanic parts. Obsolete electronics were totally dissembled, parts from different pieces were reassembled, and a piece with total new functionality was created as a final product. Many pieces in this category were more for hobbies or fun by experts rather than for practical uses by everyday users. 15% of photos uploaded from the second online surveys, and 9% from online observations were classified in this category:

"I replaced the horizontal sync with an audio input instead of a video input and left the vertical sync with video input. This is a fully functional oscilloscope with a positive and negative input. It works like a commercial oscilloscope and didn't cost me penny! " (See the first photo in Figure 9)

"The body was an Apple Airport wireless access point. The wheels/motors came from an early-series Roomba vacuum cleaner. The undercarriage is a set of wheel-mounts made from ShapeLock[5] thermoplastic screwed into the wall-mounting bracket that came with the Airport." (See the third photo in Figure9)

Figure 9. A monitor oscilloscope, a can phone, a self-moving robot, and speakers for an MP3 player from left to right

DISCUSSION

We believe that this work has several implications. Primarily, it provides insights, mechanisms, and framings for enabling people to more easily find creative reuse ideas for their obsolete e-waste. We discuss other insights from our work below.

[5] *ShapeLock* is an ultra-high molecular weight low temperature thermoplastic. http://www.shapelock.com

The Role of Aesthetics Plays in Reuse As-Is

The physical appearance of a product has a profound effect upon the way in which it is perceived [7]. Therefore, aesthetics is often used to differentiate products from the competition and stimulate consumption. Particularly in mature market segments, where products are often indistinguishable from each other on a technical basis, investing in product form may increase market share and profitability. In this work, we evidenced the important role of aesthetics along the entire lifetime of the product, from purchase to reuse. When the life span of the original functionality is over, products with higher quality design seem to be better suited as candidates for reuse. This insight should serve as motivation for industrial product designers and interaction designers of electronic objects.

Sharing Experiences Can Encourage Reuse of e-Waste

Sharing is an effective mechanism to trigger positive behaviors [9]. We evidenced the power of sharing in this work as well where we observed individuals inspired by the creative reuse of others. For example, a CRT monitor fish tank, keyboard artifacts, and light bulb casings are widely known reappropriation practices spread via sharing ideas, all of which are practical in use and pleasing in appearance. However, with limited resources outside of hackers' and DIY communities to publicize and discover these ideas, there is almost certainly a significant design opportunity to further sharing creative e-waste reuse ideas. One challenge is how to make such information widely sharable, publicly available, and easily accessible. While online forums and websites exist to share experiences and instructions in reuse, the majority of those communities focus on crafting non-digital artifacts. These communities also focus specifically on electronics for hacking and building experiences. None of these communities are solely focused on the design of e-waste for reuse. Beyond sharing, we will need further work to understand the needs of browsing, searching, using and contributing to community collected reuse ideas. Such online resources will also need to be diligent in their focus on e-waste.

Appropriate Disposal & Recycle Mechanism is Still Needed.

It is not always safe to handle electronic products. In many cases, dismantling electronics require extra safety precautions (*e.g.,* high voltage circuits and unstable batteries technologies). Thus, special steps are required when dismantling electronics for e-waste reuse. We evidenced that the majority of e-waste reuse focuses solely on the exterior properties of e-waste. This is encouraging since it may mean that a significant amount of e-waste reuse can occur while avoiding a range of hazardous dismantling procedures. This also means that e-waste reuse would not require advanced electronics skills and knowledge – avoiding even basic operations such as soldering. Our reuse composition framework is designed primarily to inspire creative reuse of everyday e-waste. As such it serves more to extend product lifetime rather than focus specifically on product redesign to avoid toxins and hazardous chemicals. It also does not serve directly to improve the recyclability of products. However, we argue that it provides an extremely valuable secondary contribution – that of e-waste awareness. By inviting broader participation by others into the creative reuse of e-waste, our approach consequently has the effect of promoting awareness of e-waste, its use, mis-use, and reuse. It a sense our approach is positioned to celebrate e-waste in ways that have the potential to elevate e-waste to a more participatory, active, and useful role in the everyday lives of individuals. The strategy is to leverage everyday design and grassroots efforts as mechanisms to motivate a new cultural awareness of e-waste and potentially a new appreciation and awareness of the importance and role of e-waste in environmental health.

CONCLUSION

The overarching long-term goal of this work is to find ways to facilitate latent resources such as e-waste, and to prolong the longevity of use in electronic products by its creative reuse. As a practical goal for this paper, we aimed to develop a simple design strategy that can inspire everyday people to participate in the creative reuse of e-waste. To that end, we acquired a baseline understanding about domestic e-waste stockpiling behaviors and e-waste recreation practices from a series of surveys and observational studies. Through a baseline understanding of current e-waste culture, we developed *a design reuse vocabulary* that consists of three primary properties: materials, shapes, and operations. The design reuse vocabulary captures a range of low-level properties that can be readily integrated into e-waste reuse practices. We evaluated and validated this design reuse vocabulary through another series of survey studies. Drawing for the results of those studies, we developed *a reuse composition framework,* which consists of three degrees of manipulation: reuse as-is, remake, and remanufacture. The reuse composition framework generalizes the practices of e-waste reuse, and provides a scaffolding mechanism for non-experts to reuse e-waste. We believe these frameworks could be a catalyst for everyday people to reuse the vast quantities of e-waste creatively and in meaningful ways – namely by allowing continued product attachment. Furthermore, we claim that the active engagement in doing and experiencing such e-waste reappropriation can lead to greater awareness of the problems and solutions regarding e-waste.

Our work has contribution to the field of HCI research for environment and sustainability in three ways. First, we identified a range of issues surrounding the secret life of our cohabitation with e-waste. Second, we developed a design reuse vocabulary that could easily be applied to e-waste by non-experts to promote product reuse and extend product lifetimes. We view this as an interim goal of solving the more general wicked problem [12] of e-waste in our culture and environment. Lastly, we came up with a simple design strategy to be accessible and to have broader impact in encouraging creative reuse across a wide range of e-waste types beyond those specifically used in our study. We are hopeful that our work can motivate future research in HCI regarding the importance of e-waste.

ACKNOWLEDGEMENT

This work is sponsored in part by the Vira I. Heinz Endowment. The authors would like to thank the anonymous reviewers for their constructive comments and feedback. The authors would also like to thank members of the Living Environment Research Group.

REFERENCES

1. Alameda County Computer Resource Center, http://www.acccrc.org, 2010 Septempber.
2. Australia Environmental Protection Agency (2005), Household Electrical and Electronic, *Waste Benchmark Survey 2005*.
3. Blevis. E. (2007), Sustainable interaction design in HCI. In *Proc. CHI 2007*, ACM Press, 503-512.
4. Alexander, C., Ishikawa, S., Silverstein, M., Max J. I. Fiksdahl-King and Angel, A. (1977) Pattern Language. *Oxford University Press*, New York.
5. Consumer Electronics Association (2008), Market Research Report: Trends in CE Reuse, Recycle and Removal, April 2008.
6. Cooper, T. (2005), Slower Consumption Reflections on Product Life Spans and the "Throwaway Society". *Journal of Industrial Ecology, 9(1-2):* 51-67.
7. Creusen M. E. H & Jan P. L. Schoormans (2005), The Different Roles of Product Appearance inConsumer Choice, *Journal of Product Innovation Management 22(1):* 63-81.
8. Dourish. P. (2010), HCI and environmental sustainability: the politics of design and the design of politic, In *Proc. the 8th ACM Conference on Designing Interactive Systems*, 1-10.
9. Fogg, B. J. Grudin, J. Nielsen, J. & Card, S. (2002), Persuasive Technology: Using Computers to Change What We Think and Do, *Science & Technology Books*.
10. Gregson, N. Metcalfe, A. & Crewe, L. (2007), Identity mobility and the throwaway society. *Environment and Planning D*: Society and Space 2007, 25 No. 4:682–700.
11. Heimbuch, J. (2010), Consumers In Emerging Markets Outpace Americans in Buying Electronics, Especially Greener Gadgets, *Science & Technology 2010*.
12. Horst W.J. Rittel and Melvin M. W. (1973), Dilemmas in a General Theory of Planning. *Policy Sciences*.
13. Huang, E. M. & Truong, K. N. (2008), SUSTAINABLY OURS-Situated Sustainability for Mobile Phones. *Interactions-New York*, 2008. 15(2): 16-19.
14. Huang, E. M. & Truong, K. N. (2008), Breaking the disposable technology paradigm: opportunities for sustainable interaction design for mobile phones. In *Proc. CHI 2008*, ACM Press, 323-332.
15. Huh, J., Nam, K. and Sharma, N. (2010) Finding the Lost Treasure: Understanding Reuse of Used Computing Devices, In *Proc. CHI 2010*, ACM Press, 1875-1878.
16. Makezine http://www.makezine.com, 2010 August
17. Mankoff J. C., Blevis, E., Borning, E., Friedman, B., Fussell, S. R., Hasbrouck, J., Woodruff, A. and Phoebe S. (2007), Environmental sustainability and interaction, *Ext. Abstracts CHI 2007*, ACM Press, 2121-2124.
18. Nathan L.P. Blevis E. Friedman B. Hasbrouck J. & Sengers P. (2008), Beyond the hype: sustainability & HCI. *Ext. Abstracts CHI 2008*, ACM Press, 2273-2276.
19. National Safety Council Electronic Product Recovery and Recycling Baseline Report. Washington D.C.
20. Odom W., Pierce J., Stolterman E., and Blevis E. (2009), Understanding why we preserve some things and discard others in the context of interaction design. In *Proc. CHI 2009*, ACM Press, 1053-1062.
21. Paulos E. Forth M. Satchell S. Kim Y. Dourish P. and Choi J. (2008), Ubiquitous Sustainability: Citizen Science & Activism. In *Proc* Ubicomp '08 Workshops.
22. Piper Jaffray Companies, http://www.piperjaffray.com/ 2010 June.
23. Solid Waste District http://www.solidwastedistrict.com 2010 August.
24. Wakkary, R. & Tanenbaum, K. (2009), A sustainable identity in HCI. In *Proc. CHI 2009*, ACM Press. 365-374.
25. Wakkary, R. & Maestri, L. (2007), The resourcefulness of everyday design. In *Proc. Creativity and Cognition 2007*, ACM Press, 163-172.
26. Widmer, R., Oswald-Krapf H Sinha-Khetriwal D et al. (2005), Global perspectives on e-waste. *Environmental Impact Assessment Review 2005*; 25; 436-458
27. Wikipedia, http://en.wikipedia.org/wiki/Citizen_science 2010 10.
28. Woodruff, A., Hasbrouck, J. and Augustin, S. (2008), A bright green perspective on sustainable choices, In *Proc. CHI 2008*, ACM Press, 313-322.
29. Verbeek, P. P. (2005), What Things Do - Philosophical Reflections on Technology, Agency, and Design. *The Pennsylvania State Press*.
30. US Environmental Protection Agency, Municipal Solid Waste Generation Recycling and Disposal in the United States: Facts and Figures for 2007, 2008.
31. US Environmental Protection Agency (2007), Fact sheet: Management of Electronic waste in the US 2007.

A Phenomenology of Human-Electricity Relations

James Pierce, Eric Paulos
Human-Computer Interaction Institute, Carnegie Mellon
5000 Forbes Avenue, Pittsburgh, PA, USA
jjpierce@cs.cmu.edu

ABSTRACT
This paper investigates the philosophical question of how we can experience energy with the aim of informing the design of future ways of experiencing energy by means of technology. Four human-technology relations formulated by philosopher of technology Don Ihde are presented. Each is then developed in the context of electrical interactive technologies. In conclusion these human-electricity and human-technology relations are employed in order to interpret current work related to energy and sustainability within HCI and point to future work in these areas.

Author Keywords
Design theory, sustainability, phenomenology, energy

ACM Classification Keywords
H5.m. Information interfaces and presentation (e.g., HCI): Miscellaneous.

General Terms
Design, Theory

INTRODUCTION
This paper proposes and investigates the question: In what ways can we experience energy—particularly, in what ways can we directly experience the presence of electrical energy itself? While this question and the method of inquiry employed are philosophical, the motivation and aim of the inquiry is *designerly*. The primary contribution of this work is to outline a theoretical framework for (i) understanding ways that we do and do not currently experience energy by means of technology and (ii) *designing* future ways of experiencing and interacting with energy. This goal is itself motivated by a recent surge of activity and concern within the CHI community with issues related to energy consumption and sustainability. Within HCI there has been a specific focus on designing energy—particularly electricity—to be more visible [4], even tangible [1,8] with a primary goal of promoting more sustainable consumption.

However this paper argues what is needed are more theoretically robust frameworks for understanding how these various designs mediate human action, perception and experience. Indeed the origins of this work can be traced to the authors' own difficulties in understanding key differences among the diversity of designs and approaches in this area.

In order to help make sense of current work in this area as well as point to areas for future work, concepts formulated by prominent philosopher of technology Don Ihde are presented. Ihde's four *human-technology relations* are summarized and then developed specifically in the context of electrical technologies.

Two additional contributions of this work can be articulated. The first is the importing of valuable literature from philosophy of technology for the CHI community, literature whose value extends beyond the immediate focus here on electricity and sustainability. Indeed some of this literature has already been engaged with in the context of HCI, notably in the works of Daniel Fallman (e.g., [3]) as well as others (e.g., [2,6,10,11]). The second contribution is to illustrate how within HCI such theory can productively be integrated and built upon to address concerns within our field but which have been neglected outside of HCI.

The remainder of this paper is structured as follows. First the phenomenological approach taken here is described. Next Ihde's four human-technology relationships are presented. Each of these relations is then developed with respect to electricity. In conclusion a discussion of some existing energy and sustainability work within HCI interpreted through these concepts is presented.

A NOTE ON METHODOLOGY
The approach employed here has its basis in phenomenology. In oversimplified terms, phenomenology has been described as an analysis of human experience. Phenomenological approaches share a common goal of understanding the "lived experience" of human beings, and an assumption that knowledge is embedded in our everyday world and cannot be reduced to numbers or statistics. This work draws primarily on the postphenomenological approach of Don Ihde [5]. Leading philosophy of technology historian Carl Mitcham has described Ihde's approach as a "pragmatic phenomenology" influenced by American pragmatism [7]. A number of examples will be presented in what follows, many of which are drawn directly from the authors' personal experiences.

HUMAN-TECHNOLOGY RELATIONS
Drawing on both electronic and non-electronic examples, Ihde's four human-technology relations will be introduced

[5, p. 72-123]. Ihde describes these relations as descriptions of the human experience of "the various ways in which I-as-body interact with my environment by means of technologies." (p. 72). These human-technology relations are: *background relations*, *embodiment relations*, *hermeneutic relations* and *alterity relations*. While the relations can be viewed as distinct modes of experiencing one's world by means of technology, they also represent points on a continuum ranging from complete withdrawl of an object (background relation) to complete presencing of an object (alterity relations).

Let us begin with embodiment relations. Embodiment relations are characterized by a "partial symbiosis" of a person and a technology during which the technology-in-use is "embodied" and becomes "perceptually transparent" (p. 86). An excellent example of an embodiment relation is the skilled use of a kitchen knife for chopping. Here the knife becomes an extension of one's hand while chopping, and the knife itself "withdraws" and is hardly noticed. Another example given by Ihde are eyeglasses, where one looks *through* rather than *at* the technology. An embodiment relation may thus be described as a relation *through* a technology.

Next we have hermeneutic relations, which involve reading a technology. Ihde's analysis emphasizes the materiality of the technology being "read" and the world being referenced. Ihde uses the example of a thermometer to emphasize the phenomena of "reading" the coldness of the outside environment. Hermeneutic relations are characterized by a "semi-opaque" connection between the technology (thermometer) and the referent(s) (the temperature, "the cold") (p. 86). This relation may thus be described as one *with* or *towards* a technology.

Next we have alterity relations. Here the *objectness* of technology comes fully into presence, but it is also more than this. An alterity relation is one characterized by a relation to a "technological other", which is a "quasi-other", something "stronger than mere objectness but weaker than the otherness found within the animal kingdom or the human one" (p. 100). Alterity relations can be seen in the ways individuals sometimes lovingly anthropomorphize their possessions, as evidenced by the names people sometimes bestow on their cars or bicycles. Many "automatic" or "intelligent" computer systems such as automatic teller machines, video games or in-car GPS systems are also often experienced as quasi-others. Ihde gives the example of a spinning top:

> [O]nce "deistically" animate through either stick motion or a string spring, the now spinning top appears to take on a life of its own. ... It traces unpredictable patterns along it pathway. It is an object of *fascination*. (p. 100).

Alterity relations may thus be described as a relation *to* a technology.

Finally we have background relations, which are understood as a "present absence", as something not directly experienced yet which gives structure to direct experiences (p. 109). Many automated, electronic and digital technologies are experienced as the present absence of a background relation. For example, the use of a gas furnace in the basement remains largely in the background of one's experience while nonetheless continuing to shape that person's experience by providing a warm and comfortable environment.

Importantly, the experience of *electricity itself* may be said to tend toward a background relation. We now turn to consider what it might mean to experience electricity more directly by means of embodiment, hermeneutic and alterity relations.

HUMAN-ELECTRICITY RELATIONS

We will now develop each relation with a focus on electricity itself. Our concern will be with what Ihde describes as "the *ratio* of the objectness of the technology and its transparency in use" (p. 108). Specifically the focus will be on the ratio of the objectness of *electricity itself* to the material technology that may be said to use, contain, create or exist by virtue of electricity.[1] As discussed by Ihde, the ratio of the presence to absence of a material technology can vary even via an embodiment relation. For example, one may feel the presence of embodied eyeglass on the face, or catch them out of the corner the eyes. Such may also be the case with electricity.

Let us begin again with embodiment relations, this time considering our experience *through electricity* and the ways in which electricity may nonetheless be present *to* us via embodiment relations. Consider first the difference in how one may relate through a power drill that is "on" and being powered with electricity versus one that is "off" and not being powered by electricity. While the experiences of drill when "on" and "off" are quite different, nonetheless in both states one can embody the drill: positioning it while "off"; drilling while "on". However, when drilling, a *breakdown* can occur if the drill suddenly loses power and ceases to operate, thus breaking the embodiment of the drill. But now consider a more gradual way this might occur. One is using a power drill as the battery slowly loses its charge—as it "dies", to use a colloquial expression—and the torque

[1] We are largely setting aside the question of whether or in what sense electricity itself should be considered a material technology. Instead we proceed with an assumption that electricity depends in some important and essential way on material technologies without engaging in the details of these dependencies. We then argue that we can in some significant sense *experience* (and also *design to experience*) electrical energy as something distinctly more or less material/immaterial and dependent/independent from (other) material technologies.

begins to diminish. As this happens one still continues drilling, understanding that the drill's energy is almost gone and he or she must drill carefully and quickly.

In this instance we see that the objectness of electricity itself presences more strongly. This relation is one in which an *electricity-technology*—that is, an electrical device that is actively using electricity—is embodied yet the electricity itself is experienced in a way tending toward an alterity relation *to* electricity. We will refer to such relations as being *through electricity to that electricity*. That is, the relation is foremost a relation *through* electricity but also importantly one tending toward a relation *to* electricity—specifically the electricity that is contributing to the embodiment relation *through* the electricity-technology. Such a relation thus exhibits a higher presencing of the objectness of electricity than is generally experienced via embodiment relations with an electricity-technology.

Consider now hermeneutic relations with electricity. The first example is the use of a laptop computer. Here we read text, images and sounds with the computer (as an electricity-technology), which are at once light and sound energies converted from electrical energy. However, we can consider a more direct experience with electricity to be reading the battery meter icon on the laptop. In this case electrical energy is being converted in order to refer to itself, specifically the "amount of itself" available. We can describe such relations as relations *with electricity to that electricity*. In other words, it is foremost a relation *with* an electricity-technology but also importantly a relation *to* the electricity that is, in a sense, referencing itself via the hermeneutic relation. Such a relation thus exhibits a strong presencing of the objectness of the electricity.

There is another way we may experience a hermeneutic relation with electricity that is of particular relevance to HCI, especially with respect to "eco-feedback" technologies [4]. Consider a home energy monitor display device that displays the electricity consumption of specific devices or the entire home, either in real-time or as aggregated analytics of data. Reading the display could be an example of a hermeneutic relation with an electricity-technology (the computer) in which what is being referred to is electricity. However, this situation may differ from a relation with electricity to *that* electricity (e.g., the battery meter icon on the laptop) in that the electricity being referred to in the case of the home energy monitor is experienced as an energy that is more removed from the immediate electricity-technology being read.

Yet a third relevant hermeneutic relation is the relation to electricity without electricity, e.g., the monthly paper-based utility bill (read under sunlight rather than an electrical lamp!). Thus we see three distinct ways in which "energy monitors" can amplify our experience of electricity by referring to it via hermeneutic relations.

Finally, consider alterity relations *to* electricity. We see signs of this potential when we look *at* a power drill, laptop computer or flashlight that is power-less and has no available electrical power to draw on. We often refer to this as a "dead" device or appliance. In this case we may look at these technologies *as* material technologies, specifically technologies that are without electricity and thus unable to operate (i.e., to be embodied or hermeneutically read). Consider when one's mobile phone is nearly depleted of charge but it is needed to make a phone call. One holds the phone as an *other*, wondering how it can be charged, perhaps even yelling at it verbally. A deeper, more qualitatively positive relationship to electricity as a quasi-other may occur when interacting with Energy Mementos, a series of design artifacts that explore the idea of emotional attachment to energy itself [6]. For example, the Shake-light Bottle is a small glass bottle that can store and activate small amounts of personal energy. Shaking the bottle generates small amounts of electricity that are stored chemically using a small rechargeable battery. The electrical energy generated can be kept and perhaps given to another person as a "gift of energy". Removing the cap of the bottle activates the stored energy as a unique pattern of glowing light corresponding to the patterns in which it was generated. One person described this Energy Memento as follows:

> I think of it like...special little energy...cuz this is like energy that is not a part of that big amorphous grid...It's like, *in my hand*. [8, p. 188].

We can describe such relations as relations *to electricity*, i.e., foremost a relation to electricity but also a relation to the associated material technology.

INTERPRETING HCI / DESIGN ENERGY APPROACHES

In conclusion the ideas presented are employed in order to help differentiate and understand current design approaches aimed at reducing energy consumption or otherwise promoting sustainable behaviors with respect to energy consumption. The human-technology and human-electricity relations discussed and developed here will be used to categorize popular as well as emerging design approaches related to sustainability and energy, particularly electricity. Specifically seven relevant relations discussed are summarized.

Background electricity relations

An example here would be an appliance engineered to operate more efficiently independently of how people interact with it. This is the "efficient technology" approach common in engineering.

Hermeneutic relations *with* electricity *to other* electricity

This relation is characteristic of many "eco-feedback" or "energy monitoring" technologies (see, e.g., [4]). One uses an electricity-technology that refers to electricity that is experienced as other than or outside of the immediate context of the hermeneutic relation that is referencing the electricity.

Hermeneutic relations *with* electricity *to that* electricity

The main example used here was the battery life icon on a laptop computer. Here an electricity-technology is referencing specific electricity: the electricity that is doing the referencing. The real-time feedback of the gas mileage in Toyota Prius vehicles is a related example. Here the electricity-technology of the in-car feedback display is referencing the energy that is making possible both the hermeneutic relation with the feedback display and the embodiment relation through various components of the car (e.g., steering wheel) or the car as a whole.

Embodiment relations *through* electricity *to that* electricity

The main example presented here was the use of an electric power drill that slowly loses charge while one is drilling, thus presencing the electricity while largely maintaining the embodiment relation. Many "ambient energy awareness" technologies may tend toward this relation (see, e.g., [1]), as does the example of the in-car mileage display. However, we can consider designing stronger embodiment relations through electricity to that electricity in order to encourage conservation, increase aesthetic engagement, and more. For example, "hand-powering" electrical devices can open up new possibilities for relating through electricity to that electricity.

Alterity relations *to* electricity

The main example was the Energy Memento. Here we see how someone may directly relate to energy itself as a thing, or in Ihde's terms, a "quasi-other". Relating *to* electricity itself is noteworthy in that it is quite different from the ways in which we currently typically experience electrical energy. Emerging microgeneration technologies such as hand-powered devices, wind farms, and domestic solar panel open up new, largely uncharted territories for explicitly designing for alterity relations to energy itself. (See also the design concepts presented in [1,8]).

Human-electricity-technology relations in general

Designing for electricity conservation or other "sustainable interactions" with respect to the use of electricity-consuming devices and systems need not directly presence or refer to electricity. For example, prior work discusses ways of "scripting" more efficient interactions with everyday appliances such as changing default settings and making certain interface options more prominent in order to encourage energy conservation (e.g., [9]). One need not consciously relate to electricity in order to instinctually use a default setting or prominent interface option, for example.

Human-technology relations *without* electricity and electricity-technologies

Reducing the consumption of and demand for energy does not require directly employing electricity-technologies. Indeed, technologies such as kitchen knives (vs. automatic food processor), bicycles (vs. automobiles), and traditional musical instruments (vs. electrical instruments and stereo systems) are often less reliant on electricity in their immediate context of use. Thus designing engaging and sustainable relations through, with and to non-electrical technologies is yet another way to promote more sustainable consumption of energy.

CONCLUSIONS

Building on Ihde's four human-technology relations this paper has outlined three human-electricity relations and some additional variations on them. The primary aim has been to show that these human-electricity/technology relations are not only of theoretical interest but also can be useful in the design and evaluation of technologies. One way this has been demonstrated is by showing how the concepts presented can delineate areas of existing work as well as point to areas for future work. In the future we believe these ideas can be applied in many other ways to the design of particular technologies, as well as to technologies related to energy construed more broadly than electricity.

ACKNOWLEDGMENTS

Financial support for this work was provided in part by National Science Foundation Grant #IIS- 1018340.

REFERENCES

1. Backlund, S. et al. (2006). Static! The aesthetics of energy in everyday things. *Proc. of DRSIC.*
2. Dourish, P. (2001). Where the action is: The foundations of embodied interaction. MIT Press.
3. Fallman, D. (2003). Mediated reality through glasses or binocular? *International Journal of Human-Computer Interaction*, *15*(2):265–284.
4. Froehlich, J., Findlater, L., & Landay, J. 2010. The design of eco-feedback technology. *Proc. CHI '10.*
5. Ihde, D. (1990). *Technology and the lifeworld: From garden to earth.* Indiana University Press.
6. Kocaballi, B., Saunders, R. & Gemeinboeck, P. (2010). Enabling new forms of agency using wearable environments. *Proc. DIS '10.*
7. Mitcham, C. (2006). "From Phenomenology to Pragmatism: Using Technology as an Instrument." In Selinger, E. (ed.), Postphenomenology: A Critical Companion to Ihde. SUNY.
8. Pierce, J. & Paulos, E. (2010). Materializing energy. *Proc. DIS '10.*
9. Pierce, J., Schiano, D., & Paulos, E. (2010). Home, habits and energy: examining domestic interactions and energy consumption. *Proc. CHI '10.*
10. Pierce, J. (2008). Material awareness. *EA CHI '08.*
11. Winograd, T. & Flores. (1986). *Understanding computers and cognition: a new foundation for design.* Ablex.

I'm the Mayor of My House: Examining Why People Use foursquare - a Social-Driven Location Sharing Application

Janne Lindqvist, Justin Cranshaw, Jason Wiese, Jason Hong, and John Zimmerman
Carnegie Mellon University
5000 Forbes Avenue, Pittsburgh, PA 15213, USA
{janne.lindqvist,jcransh,jwwiese,jasonh,johnz@cs.cmu.edu}

ABSTRACT
There have been many location sharing systems developed over the past two decades, and only recently have they started to be adopted by consumers. In this paper, we present the results of three studies focusing on the foursquare check-in system. We conducted interviews and two surveys to understand, both qualitatively and quantitatively, how and why people use location sharing applications, as well as how they manage their privacy. We also document surprising uses of foursquare, and discuss implications for design of mobile social services.

Author Keywords
foursquare, mobile computing, social computing, check-in, privacy, location based service, uses and gratifications

ACM Classification Keywords
H.5.m Information Interfaces and Presentation (e.g., HCI): Miscellaneous

General Terms
Human Factors, Design

INTRODUCTION
For the past 20 years, researchers have being proposing a wide range of location sharing systems. With the increasing diffusion of GPS and Internet-enabled smartphones, many of these research ideas are finally being adopted by consumers.

We can broadly categorize [30] location sharing applications as *purpose-driven*, where people explicitly request another person's current location (e.g. AT&T FamilyMap, Glympse, Verizon Family Locator), and *social-driven*, where people broadcast their location to "friends" in their social networks. Examples of social-driven applications include, for example, BrightKite, Dodgeball (discontinued), foursquare, Gowalla, and Facebook Places. While purpose-driven location sharing applications have not yet achieved critical mass in any system, the same is not true for social-driven applications. In particular, as of December 2010, foursquare claims to have over 5 million members [1]. This critical mass of users provides researchers with an excellent opportunity to investigate how people really use these systems and how people have appropriated them to meet their own needs.

While foursquare has features that distinguish it from other services, it is not yet clear which factors contribute to its popularity. For example, foursquare positions itself simultaneously as a mobile game, a way of exploring cities, a way of telling friends where you are, and a way of tracking where friends have been and who they have been co-located with [1]. Both its popularity and that of other location services raise many questions: What value drives people's use of these systems? How have users appropriated these systems, inventing new purposes for them to serve? Understanding these and related questions can offer valuable insights into real-world usage and can reveal design opportunities for new services and new applications.

Past work [5, 11, 22, 25, 30, 31] has found that privacy is a barrier to adoption of location sharing services. Current systems also face this challenge; however, it seems that for a large number of people, privacy concerns have not kept them from experimenting with and adopting this emerging technology. To gain some insight into this, we also investigated the kinds of privacy concerns people have with foursquare, and what strategies they take to manage their privacy.

In this paper, we present the results of three studies examining location sharing: (i) interviews (N=6) with early adopters to investigate how they use these systems and the value they construct through their use; (ii) a survey (N=18) qualitatively examining foursquare usage patterns and privacy concerns; and (iii) a survey (N=219) quantitatively probing questions about foursquare usage patterns.

This paper makes two primary research contributions. First, we show how and why people use foursquare, both qualitatively and quantitatively. Minor contributions include identifying surprising uses of foursquare, finding out where people do or don't check-in, showing differences between newcomers and longer-term users of foursquare, and the usage of foursquare to meet new people. Second, we investigate what privacy concerns people have and how they manage those concerns. Even though we found some new issues with respect to location privacy, we suggest that our participants are comfortable in managing their privacy.

THE FOURSQUARE CHECK-IN SERVICE

Foursquare describes their service as a "mobile application that makes cities easier to use and more interesting to explore. It is a friend-finder, a social city guide and a game that challenges users to experience new things, and rewards them for doing so. Foursquare lets users 'check in' to a place when they're there, tell friends where they are and track the history of where they've been and who they've been there with" [1]. Foursquare has clients for smartphones such as iPhone, BlackBerry, Palm, and the Android platform.

Foursquare lets people connect to friends, which are equivalent to the concept of friends on other online social networks. Users can check-in to locations to say that they are currently there. When doing a check-in, foursquare examines the user's current location and shows a list of nearby places. Users can also register new places.

When a user checks in to a place, a check-in notification is by default pushed to their foursquare contacts. People can choose to be notified of all check-ins by their contacts. At the time of the check-in, users can also decide if they want to check-in off-the-grid, in which the check-in is recorded by foursquare but not shared with contacts. These private check-ins still count towards gathering points, badges or mayorships (these are described below). People can also connect their foursquare account to other online services, such as Facebook and Twitter, and have their check-ins be announced on these services. Users who have checked-in to a place can also see who else has recently checked-in ("Who's here"). Users can also allow local businesses to view check-ins to their location.

The game aspect of foursquare offers virtual and tangible rewards for check-ins. Virtual rewards come in the forms of points, badges, and mayorships visible in one's public profile. Badges are awarded for a variety of reasons, e.g. for starting to use the service, checking-in on a boat, checking-in with 50 people at the same time, or checking-in at a special event. Mayorships are awarded to a single individual for having the most check-ins in a given place in the past 60 days, where only one check-in per day is counted. Some companies offer discounts for mayors of a place, for example, some coffee shops offer discounts on coffee.

Foursquare also enables social recommendations through tips, a small snippet of text associated with a place. Tips are intended to suggest possible activities for that place.

RELATED WORK

Foursquare's predecessor was Dodgeball, which was created by a co-founder of foursquare. Dodgeball was an SMS based check-in service, and was limited to major cities. Humphreys reports on a set of interviews about Dodgeball [15, 16], finding that Dodgeball provided mobile social connectivity and possibilities for "casual social congregation". However, in contrast to foursquare, the Dodgeball service didn't have game mechanics or other incentives for check-in integrated, and only offered limited information about people's check-ins due to limitations of SMS.

Ludford et al. studied people's willingness to share their locations in Sharescape [24], a place sharing system. They found that people didn't want to share "private" places such as residences and workplaces. In contrast, our work shows that such places are shared by a subpopulation interested in the gaming aspects of foursquare. The P3-systems project studied design requirements for location-aware community systems [19]. The authors found that such systems should support ad-hoc interactions with friends, family, colleagues, and strangers; show if a public resource is being used; facilitate task coordination; and help people avoid others. We saw that foursquare supports many of these features and we quantitatively report how they are used in a widely deployed system. There have also been field studies of location sharing applications. For example, Connecto [5] let users annotate their locations, and the location was shared continuously unless users disabled sharing. A two-week study of Connecto found that users used place naming as a way of social storytelling. Users also protected their privacy by vaguely defining their location. Rhub [14] also let people annotate place names by reporting their location using SMS such as "@pub". A user study of Rhub across 18 months with 150 users found that it was used mainly for coordination but not chat. Finally, Social Serendipity studied Bluetooth device encounters for social matching [12].

Our work in this paper is based on a classic two-part procedure established in marketing research for studying uses and gratifications [10]. We contribute to the research community's increasing understanding of how and why people use social media (for example, [3, 6, 18, 21]). These and other studies informed our research design, however, we note that foursquare's usage as a mobile social network and check-in service fundamentally differs from the usages of the above services, and therefore we naturally found different (even non-anticipated) uses for foursquare.

There has also been a great deal of work examining privacy issues in human-computer interaction. Iachello and Hong offer a survey of privacy [17]. There have been multiple studies regarding privacy and social media. For example, privacy on the Facebook online social network has been studied from many angles [13, 20, 29]. Our work is more closely aligned with studies on privacy in location sharing applications. Past work has examined many aspects of this problem. For example, some projects have examined how people set privacy policies [25, 31]. Other work has examined what people would share and with whom [11, 22], studied deployed research systems [5, 27], or examined the differences between purpose-driven request-based systems and social-driven broadcast systems [30]. Our work builds on this rich literature and contributes new findings about privacy concerns in a widely deployed system, as well as how users manage their privacy.

Finally, we note that safety, security and coordination of everyday life has been studied in the context of mobile phones in general [23]. Foursquare and other mobile social applications enable people to coordinate and inform about their safety without explicitly calling or sending SMS to people.

INTERVIEWS WITH EARLY ADOPTERS OF LBS

We started our work by investigating location based services (LBS) broadly to find out what kind of services besides navigation people have adopted. Specifically, we wanted to understand what LBS people used, what value they found in these applications, and instances of appropriation.

We conducted semi-structured interviews with 4 men and 2 women that were early adopters of LBS, ranging in age from 21 to 38. We refer to these participants as A1-A6. We recruited participants through Twitter, BrightKite and Loopt, and screened participants to only include iPhone users, to maintain homogeneity across applications and because, at the time, the iPhone platform offered the most options for LBS. Participants had been using their iPhones for an average of 7.9 months. Participants were given a $15 gift card.

Our participants used a number of location based applications, the majority of which were location sharing applications. Other applications included those for finding shops and restaurants, and travel planning applications.

We asked participants about their rationales for selecting specific applications, their experiences of use, and their perspectives on how they would most like to leverage location information themselves. The interviews were first processed in a round of open coding, where the data was conceptualized and coded. Following this we identified key themes across the open codes, which represented distinct topics from the interview data.

Interview Findings and Themes

Although we had a number of findings, we focus only on the check-in services, which all of our interviewees used.

Personal tracking - Participants A1, A3, and A5 expressed that they found value in using these applications to see where they have been in the past. A3 used a check-in service, and said that manually checking in is particularly important to him, as opposed to an automatic check-in system, because it provides a way for him to curate his location history and express what places he's been to that he felt were important.

Intimate sharing at a distance - A1 and A3 were involved in a long-distance relationship. They found value in checking-in as a way of maintaining a sort of passive awareness of each other. A2 had a desire for his significant other to use a check-in service for the same reason, but she was not willing to try. A5 had a very different take, saying his significant other was the only person who routinely checked in, but it was not useful "because I know where he is".

Discovery of new people - A1 expressed interest in meeting new people who shared her interests and were close by, "even if I'm busy." A2, A3, and A4 all shared experiences of having actually interacted with new people simply because they were nearby.

Running into friends - A2, A3, and A5 all shared experiences of running into friends who they didn't know were nearby because of their mutual use of a check-in service. A2 told a story of a friend who happened to be in the same neighborhood, so they grabbed a cup of coffee to catch up. Some situations were more functional. A5 was in a nearby city one afternoon for work and was planning to grab lunch alone. However, when he saw that a friend had checked in nearby, it prompted him to get in contact, and they ended up having lunch together.

Gaming aspect - At the time of the interviews, foursquare had only recently been launched. Participants A3 and A5 mentioned the gaming aspects of foursquare as reasons that they and their friends use it. For example, A5 mentioned a specific situation where he took a foursquare mayorship from somebody else that he knew personally.

Seeing where friends have been - A1, A4, and A5 expressed interest in seeing where friends had been, even if they cannot interact. A1 mentioned going to a shop after seeing one of her friends checked-in there the day before. A5 describes following updates of his friend's whereabouts as the friend took a trip through Thailand.

Routine vs non-routine places - Participants expressed reluctance to check-in at home, work, and other places that one might expect them to be at. One participant said that checking in signifies that "this place is interesting." Participants also said that being at new, unique, unusual, or non-routine places was often a reason to check-in, and that simply by arriving there they were reminded to check-in. Both A1 and A2 cited arriving at airports as a very distinct trigger to check-in. Furthermore, while the departing airport was an interesting place to check-in, the destination airport was more important, as it told their friends where they would be and sent a signal to friends in that area that they may be available to meet.

Potentially private places - A1 shared that she made it a point not to check-in when arriving at some private places, such as a friend's apartment. Her reasoning was that, while she did not mind if one of her contacts knew she was at the apartment, she wanted to protect her friend by not revealing the location of the apartment to others, who might have not had access to that information otherwise.

At large events - A3 told about being at the "South-by-Southwest" (SXSW) conference where foursquare was first announced. He said he checked in "everywhere", much more frequently than he would otherwise. He said this was "exciting" for him, and that he was trying to be as clear as possible to as many of his friends as possible about where he was, in case they wanted to meet up.

In summary, from the interviews, we saw several repeated themes from early adopters of location based services, for example, using these services as a game, offering awareness to friends, seeing where friends were, and using check-ins to meet with existing friends. We chose to probe these issues more deeply with surveys, focusing on foursquare, since it had a larger set of active users than other services.

SURVEY 1: QUALITATIVE USES OF FOURSQUARE

The goal of the first survey was to delve broadly into why and how people used foursquare, soliciting qualitative free-form responses. The goal of the second survey was to dive more deeply as to why and how people used foursquare, focusing on quantitative results. We modeled this approach on uses and gratification studies in marketing research [10], though we did not restrict our questions and analyses only to uses and gratifications. We discuss the first survey below.

Method

We solicited users through craigslist postings and flyers at Carnegie Mellon University campus. We compensated participants with a $5 gift card. For craigslist postings, we chose 20 largest US cities, 10 college towns in the US, and three major metropolitan areas in Canada. The survey included 55 questions, and we first asked our participants four open-ended questions, regarding benefits and drawbacks of using foursquare. We organized results into major themes below.

Participants

We received 25 responses (24 from craigslist) but excluded 7 because their public profiles revealed they had never checked-in. Of the 18 remaining participants, 9 were female and 9 were male, which is an acceptable division since foursquare claims that their male-female ratio is close to 60%-40% [9]. 7 were students, and occupations for the rest varied from casino employee, educator, and organic farmer, to software developers and managers. Two of our respondents were from Ontario, Canada, the rest were from the US. We refer to the participants in this study as B1-B18. The participants' activity on foursquare is shown in Table 1.

Activity	Min	Max	Mean (stdev)	Median
Days Out	11	276	94 (82)	55
Check-Ins	16	1201	300 (296)	242
Badges	0	32	14 (8)	12
Mayorships	0	29	8 (8)	4
Friends	1	48	18(15)	15

Table 1. Participant activity on foursquare in Survey 1

Results and Discussion

Foursquare Design Goals

Our first two questions asked why people used foursquare, and what they thought the benefits of using foursquare were. Many of foursquare's stated design goals were repeatedly listed as reasons, suggesting that foursquare is succeeding in achieving its design goals.

For example, 14 participants mentioned friends as the main benefit, in terms of sharing with friends where they are going and what they are doing. One participant mentioned discovering new places as the primary benefit. Aspects of location history were also described, e.g. keeping track of restaurants and bars to make it easier to go there again.

The designed features and game mechanics of foursquare also appealed to our survey participants. Three participants mentioned fun, though interestingly, three other participants described foursquare as just "something to do", especially when bored. Five participants mentioned earning points, badges, and mayorships as motivation for participating.

Discounts were mentioned by 5 of our participants. Two participants mentioned tips from other users as useful, using these tips to avoid going to places with bad reviews. Participant B9 commented that his check-in at San Diego Comic Con earned him a Superman badge, plus a mini superman flashlight by showing the badge at a specific booth. Participant B6 remarked that foursquare benefited business for promotional purposes. Badges had also motivated participants to discover new places. One participant shared "There are location-specific badges that motivate me to go to new places", and another one "In order to earn badges I have gone to shops in San Francisco that I had not visited previously."

Finally, one theme that echoes a result from our interviews is discovering new people. Participant B18 said, "[foursquare] allows me to see what other users are in the same places as me." Participant B2 saw it as a benefit to "discover real facts about customers of the places. And, maybe too, know some new people."

Privacy Concerns with foursquare

Our third survey question asked about drawbacks of using foursquare, and the fourth question was about privacy. Since privacy was featured strongly in the answers to the third question, we combine the discussion of these two questions.

Six participants mentioned privacy as a drawback. There were the usual concerns about stalkers and strangers. However, when asked more specifically about their privacy concerns, 10 of our participants seemed comfortable with using the service. Roughly, half of the participants had privacy concerns, the other half did not.

Focusing on the half that did not have privacy concerns, many of them seemed to have a good mental model of how foursquare worked, and were able to use foursquare's existing privacy controls to manage what was shared with others. For example, participant B4 explained: "I do not have my home address linked to my account. I doubt I am interesting enough to be stalked." Some participants had only real-life friends as their foursquare friends. Three participants didn't link to Facebook or Twitter and therefore didn't have concerns. Participant B15 also said she didn't have concerns because she didn't share every check-in. Two participants went even further and stated that if you have privacy concerns you shouldn't be using services such as foursquare, Facebook or Twitter in the first place.

Focusing on the other half that did have privacy concerns, there seemed to be misalignment in terms of how people understood foursquare, as well as what privacy controls people could use. For example, Participant B4 was concerned that strangers might be able to track you. B4 and B16 mentioned the threat of stalkers. B5 remarked, "everyone knows where you are when you check in somewhere." Participant B11 wasn't sure he understood the existing privacy controls, and

B14 was concerned that somebody who she doesn't want to reveal her location to would nevertheless be able to see it.

Why People Don't Check-In

People had many interesting and surprising reasons for deciding not to check-in. Self-representation issues emerged, as they have for other location sharing systems [11, 25, 27, 31]. For our participants, one form of self-representation was to not check-in to fast food restaurants. Participant B1 explained "[I don't check-in to] Fast food. It's embarrassing to be seen there." Participant B3 shared, "McDonald's and the like... Because I don't need to remember it and I'm not totally proud to have said I was there." Participant B4 "Checking in at fast food restaurants too often is embarrassing.", and finally participant B9: "I never check in to fast food restaurants like McDonalds, Burger King, Taco Bell, etc. I don't think anyone would be impressed by that sort of check in." To a lesser extent, we saw similar decisions to not check-in for doctors and banks. In contrast, one of our participants shared that she is mayor of a McDonalds.

Other self-representation issues also emerged. Two participants did not want to check-in to places if they found it boring. B17 doesn't always check-in to his house "because it gets boring." Participant B11 expressed similar feelings: "I don't check-in at work. It seems like a boring place to check-in to. I go there everyday."

One interesting variant of privacy was regarding spam and interruptions. Participant B3 stated "Privacy, too much spam on my Facebook wall if it's integrated". This participant also said that spam was a reason not to check-in to a place, saying "because I don't want it cluttering my Facebook wall". We note that foursquare offers the possibility to opt-out of sharing check-ins with friends, Twitter, and Facebook.

To a large extent, these findings suggest that there would be many social challenges to having automatic check-in systems, in addition to technical challenges in correctly identifying which of several nearby places one is at. Furthermore, while fast food was a concern for several of our participants, we can generalize this notion by stating that there are places where specific subpopulations would be embarrassed to say they were at, but that this is not universal. For example, there are many people who would be embarrassed to check-in to a strip club, but a quick perusal of foursquare shows that there are also people who actively check-in to these locations.

Surprising Uses of foursquare

Some uses of foursquare we discovered were not part of explicit design goals of foursquare, and have not been documented in previous research literature on location sharing.

For example, one participant was concerned about her safety, she said: "I have stopped checking in at home after reading about someone having a close call with a stalker. I also check in at a location as I leave that place, instead of at the time I arrive." Another participant mentioned a similar use, saying that he often checked in when he got home to let his friends know he had returned safely. We note that similar issues have been discovered with the safety of social disclosure in online and mobile photo sharing [2].

People also mentioned other reasons for checking in at either one's own home or at other people's homes. Three participants said that they used check-ins at their own home as a signal for availability. This finding is in line with a study by Anthony et al. [4], where people wanted to share their locations when they were bored and wanted to be with friends.

Three participants said that they checked-in to their own home and friends' homes because they wanted to become mayor of that location. Participant B17 said that he is a mayor of his house, his mother's house and grandparents' homes (explaining that he's the only one using foursquare at those places). Even more interestingly, he was also the mayor of his friends' houses (who also used foursquare) because they don't check-in at home.

These check-ins at people's houses introduce potential physical security risks. The web site pleaserobme.com pushed an awareness campaign in 2010 about how check-in services and certain kinds of tweets make it easy for everybody to know when a person is not at home. Foursquare offers categories for places, one of which is "home." Furthermore, foursquare offers a public search of places, making it possible to search for terms like "house" and "home". In some cases, place names unwisely include the street address of the home. We do note, however, that there have not yet been any documented cases of such abuses or criminal activities. Thus, there is a tension between the benefits of foursquare, where people either want to win mayorships of as many locations as possible or signal their availability to their friends, and physical security of private homes.

SURVEY 2: QUANTITATIVE PROBING OF FOURSQUARE

For the second survey, we decided to dig deeper into several of the themes we saw in the interviews and the first survey. Due to space, we focus only on five themes: 1. why people use foursquare, 2. where they check-in, 3. usage of foursquare by newcomers versus longer-term users, 4. privacy, and 5. meeting new people.

We received 219 participants by posting flyers near Carnegie Mellon University (3), advertising on a local newsgroup (3), asking people to share on Facebook (4), requesting participants of survey 1 to advertise to their friends (5), as "tips" on foursquare (6), and through Twitter (90 from a retweet campaign initiated by a social hub we contacted, and 108 from a retweet campaign initiated by foursquare). Participants were placed in a raffle for three $75 gift certificates.

The majority of our participants were from the US (158), with Europeans (46) being the second largest group. Our participants were predominantly male (157, 72%), with 62 females (28%). The ages of participants were distributed as follows: 18-23: 26, 24-29: 77, 30-35: 69, 36-41: 23, 42-47:13, 48-53: 6, 54+: 5. Again, foursquare claims that the gender ratio of its users is close to 60% male and 40% female [9], so our participant pool was biased towards males.

Activity	Min	Max	Mean (stdev)	Median
Days Out	1	1136	138 (121)	401
Check-Ins	1	3310	578 (613)	613
Things Done	0	393	19 (40)	7
Badges	0	96	17 (13)	14
Mayorships	0	141	12 (16)	7
Friends	0	2250	65 (165)	34
Tips	0	104	8 (14)	3
To-Dos	0	350	5 (26)	0

Table 2. Participant activity on foursquare in Survey 2

The activity of our participants on foursquare at the time of the survey is shown in Table 2. We asked participants to log into their foursquare accounts, so they could view their profiles and report accurate data.

The majority of our participants (102) used an iPhone to access foursquare, with Android and BlackBerry as a distant second and third (46 and 39 respectively). The majority of our participants (143) had started using the service during the year 2010, while only 45 participants had used the services for 3 months or less. 67 participants had used the service since 2009, of which four had started using the service the same month it was launched. About a quarter of participants used other location sharing services, including Gowalla, Google Latitude, and Loopt.

Our survey started with a question "why did you initially join foursquare", and allowed to select multiple options from a randomized list. 94 started because of friends, 144 were just curious, 127 thought it sounded like fun. Interestingly, only 29 participants stated starting because of the possibility of getting discounts, and 33 listed also answered "Other", in which they included "promotion of business", "tracking spending" and "I think I was the first user in Austria ;)".

Why People Use foursquare

Based on our interviews and qualitative survey, we asked questions organized into 19 items on a 5-point Likert scale. We also presented other questions about usage that were not suitable to be asked as Likert scale questions and we present those findings later.

We used the principal components method with varimax rotation for exploratory factor analysis [28]. The purpose of this method is to find a small number of variables that account for most of the variance in the original items. By examining eigenvalues and scree plot, we concluded that five factors would represent the data sufficiently. The five factors represent 68% of the variance, and Cronbach's alphas clearly exceed the commonly used criterion of 0.7. We note that Factor 4 is only loaded by two variables, however, both variables substantially exceed the critical values for statistical significance. As suggested by Stevens [28] we considered values exceeding critical values: $2 \times 0.182 = 0.364$ for this sample size (~200), to be statistically significant. Application of these criteria led to identification of 5 factors, which we discuss below.

Factor 1: Badges and fun (Cronbach's alpha 0.87)		
Survey Item	Item Mean (stdev)	Loading
I pay attention to the badges that I earn	4.16 (0.93)	0.85
I pay attention to the badges that others earn	3.70 (1.08)	0.77
I am proud of the badges I have earned	3.94 (1.00)	0.86
I check in because I like getting badges	4.02 (1.00)	0.87
I think foursquare is fun	4.22 (0.73)	0.62
I consider foursquare to be a game I play with my friends	3.66 (1.06)	0.72

Factor 1, which accounts for the most variance overall, is clearly focused on badges, a novel innovation of foursquare's game aspect. The loaded items indicate that one's own badges as well as other's badges are important. Factor 1 also indicates that collecting badges contributes to the perceived fun of foursquare. It also emphasizes that foursquare is also a game you play with your friends and badges are a form of self-representation.

Factor 2: Social connection (Cronbach's alpha 0.88)		
Survey Item	Item Mean (stdev)	Loading
I use foursquare to let other people know that I am available to hang out.	3.48 (1.09)	0.66
Foursquare helps me keep in touch with my friends.	3.32 (1.10)	0.82
Foursquare is fun because my friends are using it.	3.67 (1.01)	0.77
I use foursquare to coordinate with my friends.	2.69 (1.08)	0.69
I often check into a place at the same time as my foursquare friends.	3.37 (1.20)	0.70
I pay attention to other people's check-ins.	3.74 (0.85)	0.53
I consider foursquare to be a game I play alone.	3.02 (1.20)	-0.46

Factor 2 is linked to social connections as well as different ways of using foursquare to interact with friends. Note also that there is significant negative loading with the item "game I play alone" in Factor 2. We discuss other aspects of social connectivity below, in particular meeting new people through foursquare.

Factor 3: Place discovery (Cronbach's alpha 0.87)		
Survey Item	Item Mean (stdev)	Loading
I use foursquare because I can get discounts and special offers.	3.30 (1.14)	0.5
I have found a good tip about a place by using foursquare.	3.74 (1.07)	0.71
Foursquare has motivated me to go to new places.	3.81 (1.06)	0.78
I have discovered new places from my use of foursquare.	3.68 (1.07)	0.82
I use foursquare to keep track of places I have visited.	3.90 (0.98)	0.40

Factor 3 is comprised of items that highlight foursquare's incentive mechanisms for frequently visiting and discovering new places. Note that the items "discounts and special offers" and "keep track of places" have substantially less loading than the other items, and the first item has also smaller item mean compared to the other items in the factor.

Factor 4: Keeping track of places (Cronbach's alpha 0.88)		
Survey Item	Item Mean (stdev)	Loading
I use foursquare to keep track of places I have visited.	3.90 (0.98)	0.73
I use foursquare because I can get discounts and special offers.	3.30 (1.14)	-0.62

Factor 4 is bipolar and loaded by only 2 items. It clearly indicates that keeping track of places does not overlap with the motivation for getting discounts and special offers.

Factor 5: Game with yourself (Cronbach's alpha 0.88)		
Survey Item	Item Mean (stdev)	Loading
I consider foursquare to be a game I play alone.	3.03 (1.20)	0.76
I pay attention to other people's check-ins.	3.74 (0.85)	0.43
I use foursquare because it gives me something to do when I am out.	3.49 (1.08)	0.39

Factor 5 shows that foursquare can also be used as a game you play alone, echoing a comment in the first survey: "just something to do when I'm bored". The second and third items do not heavily load the factor, though they do satisfy the statistical significance criterion established above. We speculate that foursquare might also have use for "eavesdroppers," people that don't check-in but desire to know where others are [15]. Foursquare's check-in off-the-grid feature allows this kind of "eavesdropping" without sharing check-ins with others, while still allowing playing foursquare as a game and collecting points.

Where People Check-In

We next examine where people check-in. Figure 1 shows a bar chart that displays frequency of logins for various places. Restaurants and bars are fairly popular places to check-in at. This finding is not too surprising, given the above discussion of the factor analysis.

Interestingly, most participants never check-in at a school. On the other hand, our participants were predominantly older than typical college students. Foursquare's demographics also differ from other social media, which have become popular first among young teens [7]. However, the lack of mobility among young teens and the relatively high cost of smartphones may account for this finding.

We also saw that most people do not check-in when seeing a doctor. More interesting, however, was the bimodal distribution of check-ins for home and work. Note that for homes, the majority of people say that they never check-in, but there are many people who check-in 1-2 times a day. Checking in at work has a somewhat similar distribution, with many people checking in 1-2 times a day.

Results from Survey 1 can account for this finding. There are many people who are concerned about privacy, and hence manage part of their concerns by never checking in at home. On the other hand, there are many people who are interested in gaining as many points, badges, and mayorships as possible, and check-in everywhere.

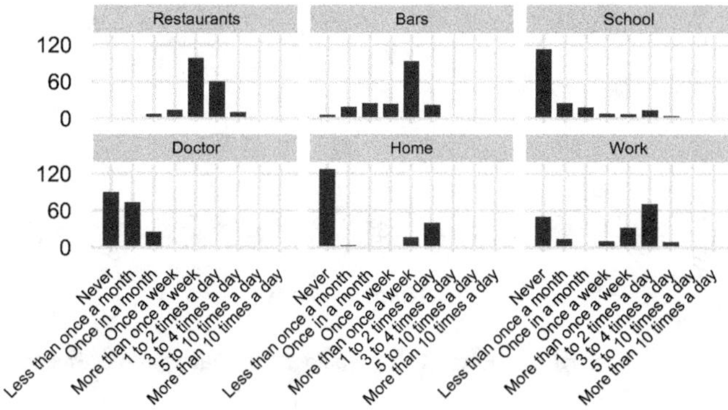

Figure 1. Distribution of how often users check in to a number of specific locations. "Home" and "Work" exhibit a bi-modal distribution.

Newcomers vs Longer-term Users of foursquare

In this section, we examine a few differences between people just starting to use foursquare versus those using it for a longer term. Note that foursquare was launched in March 2009, so longer-term use is a relative term here.

Figure 2 (Top) shows the relative effects of the five factors based on the number of days the participants have used foursquare. Recall, the number of days was obtained by asking to find the date of their first check-in in their foursquare profile. Also, this analysis is cross-sectional and does not show how an individual user's motivations change over time, but rather shows people in different stages of foursquare use.

Figure 2 (Top) shows an increase in Factor 1 in the first 200-300 days of use with a slow decline afterwards. Factor 1 is associated primarily with badges. This result suggests that badges are an important motivation for using foursquare initially but declines in importance over time. In contrast, Factor 2, which is associated with friends, and Factors 3 and 4, which are associated with places, steadily increase in importance over time. Factor 5, which is associated with the gaming alone aspect of foursquare, changes little over time. One possible explanation for these findings is that the novelty of badges wears off after prolonged use, but the social aspects, and the place discovery aspects of the service do not.

However, Figure 2 (Bottom) shows that Factor 1 is still an important motivator for using foursquare even after a person has many badges. This suggests that there are users to whom badges are a continual motivating factor. To a weak extent, this discrepancy might indicate a possible check-in fatigue after some of the novelty effects of foursquare have worn off. However, Figure 2 (Bottom) suggests that this is mitigated among users who are motivated to obtain many badges.

Managing Privacy in foursquare

We had several questions regarding privacy in foursquare. First, we will present an overview of the statistics, and then discuss some interesting findings. 163 (74%) participants had recognizable photos in their public profile, while only 10 had no photo and the rest 46 had a non-recognizable photo. Participants also shared contact information with their friends,

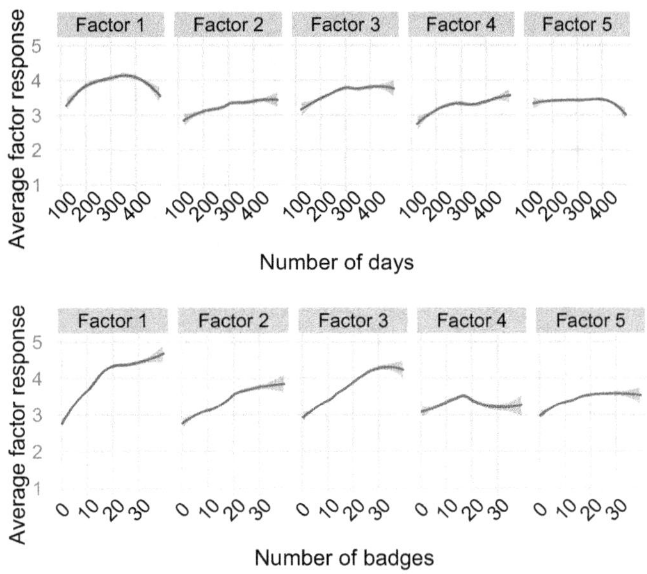

Figure 2. ***Top*****: Shows the average of survey responses for each factor as a function of how long the user has been using foursquare.** ***Bottom*****: Shows the average of survey responses for each factor as a function of the number of badges the user has. Notice the diminishing importance of Factor 1 with respect to number of days, yet no such change occurs with respect to number of badges.**

with over 70% of people sharing phone number, email address, or links to their Facebook or Twitter profile. The majority of participants (187) also allowed themselves to be seen in the "Who's here" listings and 193 let local business see that they had checked-in to a venue. 142 (64%) of our participants linked their foursquare account to Twitter, while 114 (52%) linked it to Facebook. However, only 40 participants (18%) tweet about their check-ins and even fewer 23 (11%) allow foursquare to post their check-ins to their Facebook walls. To some extent, this may be due to concerns about spamming their friends, as discussed in Survey 1.

Badges and mayorships are considered important enough to be broadcast to the world or shared with Facebook friends: 83 participants (38%) tweet about receiving mayorships and 98 (44%) tweet about receiving a badge, while 48 (21%) automatically post mayorships to their Facebook walls and 53 (24%) share receiving a badge.

We also saw a new finding we had not seen in the interviews or Survey 1. In Survey 2, 128 participants (58%) said they had friends that they had not met in person. This is a surprising finding, especially given that people have often expressed concerns about stalkers in previous research literature. One possible explanation of this finding is that people friend others who they see going to cool and interesting places, to help themselves find new places to go to. In this sense, these "friends" are more like followers in Twitter. Another possible explanation is that people are interested in just friending everyone, sort of as a display of popularity. In Survey 2, the average number of friends was 66.5 (stdev = 167.0), thus, there is no conclusive evidence.

Following up on the point about stalkers, we found only small evidence of concerns. In total, 9 participants expressed concerns about stalkers (7 male and 2 female). Again, this finding may be due to the fact that our participants are early adopters, but it also suggests that people felt in control of what was shared with whom.

We also saw further evidence of people checking-in for safety purposes. We probed this question in the second survey, and found that 29 of our participants (17 male and 12 female) sometimes check-in when they are leaving a place for safety purposes. A significant number of participants 71 (32%) also said they used foursquare to verify that someone has safely arrived at a destination.

Meeting New People Through foursquare

One aspect of location sharing applications that has not been much explored before in the scientific literature is meeting new people. Meeting new people is something that was mentioned by our interviewees and by participants of our first survey. This is not an unexpected use, but is something that can only now be studied due to the scale of foursquare.

66 (30%) of our participants had met new people with the use of foursquare and 3 participants had even used foursquare for the purpose of dating or developing a romantic relationship. 37 participants (17%) had gone to talk to new people and 30 participants (14%) have been approached by unknown people. These findings indicate that the "Who's here" feature can serve as a mobile social serendipity tool.

Although we have evidence that some foursquare users do indeed meet new people through the system, we did not probe these uses with Likert scale questions and therefore cannot compare them to factors described earlier.

DESIGN IMPLICATIONS

There are several design implications that we discovered. Clearly, designing a location sharing application as a game motivates users to share their location. Our study shows that foursquare users find utility in receiving more "points", be it in the form of check-ins on their public profile or new badges they receive. Further, having multiple value propositions seemed to be an effective strategy. It allowed users to start with badges and fun, and continue with social aspects as the users built their social network. Similar multi-value strategy have been seen, for example in Wikipedia [8], where rights and responsibilities grow with increased participation, although these tend to be more in the social structure of Wikipedia rather than in explicit features of the service.

Check-in services are particularly suited to address security and privacy issues in location sharing because user action is required every time information is shared. Systems that operate in this way can help with a variety of concerns. Furthermore, some privacy concerns arise from being at home or work. This suggests that it may be useful to treat residences differently than other places due to potential privacy risks, for example, by making places marked as "home" not publicly visible and limiting who can check-in to those places.

Even further, since 58% of our participants had foursquare friends that they had not met before, it would be useful to have an easy way to separate real friends from followers, for example, for enabling sharing some check-ins only to your real friends.

Finally, our results show that people have varying, even non-designed, uses that could be explicitly designed into future systems. Examples of these include checking-in for safety purposes and signaling availability when at home.

DISCUSSION

Through interviews and two different surveys, we examined how and why people use foursquare, as well as how people manage privacy concerns. We found many reasons as to why people use foursquare, including elements of fun, exploration, and coordinating with friends. From this perspective, foursquare is succeeding in its stated design goals.

We also saw some uses of foursquare that are well aligned with the existing research literature. These uses include, for example, signaling availability to friends, using the history of places you go as a form of presentation of self, and coordinating with friends.

We also found some unexpected uses of foursquare, for example people who were very active in the gaming aspect of foursquare and would check-in at other people's homes, as well as people who used foursquare with safety in mind or for safety purposes, either by checking-in as they were leaving a place, or checking-in when they arrived at a place.

Somewhat surprisingly, the majority of users had few privacy concerns. This can be expected, because the participants of our studies have already chosen to adopt foursquare, thus, there is a sample bias. However, given the large numbers of people who have signed up for foursquare, we now have more insights into the range of privacy concerns people have with a large-scale location sharing application, as well as into how they manage these concerns.

The most obvious way of managing one's privacy is choosing not to check-in to a place. In our studies, we saw that people chose not to check-in to places for several reasons, including places that they would be embarrassed to be seen at (e.g. fast food restaurants), places that they felt were not interesting or often visited, and places perceived as sensitive (their own home or other people's homes). Some people also opted not to connect their foursquare account to other social media sites, and for those that did, some chose not to broadcast every check-in, possibly due to a desire not to spam their friends with updates.

Surprisingly, we found that over half of our participants had people that they didn't personally know as foursquare friends. We speculate that these "friends" are more like Twitter followers, and are simply interested in knowing where interesting people go. It is not clear to us whether the other half of participants simply refused these kinds of connections.

Limitations and Further Work

The self-reporting nature of our studies is a fundamental limitation. For example, if we would have access to histories of foursquare users, we could draw usage patterns that are not possible with survey data. Our quantitative analysis is also limited by the findings of the qualitative studies: if we did not capture a usage of foursquare, our second survey would not probe into it. Further limitations come from the self-selective nature of our users: in interviews we received our participants from advertisements on social network cites, in survey 1 mostly through craigslist postings and in survey 2 mostly through Twitter re-tweets.

It is also an open question how well foursquare users manage their privacy compared to how well they think they manage it. It may be that users perceive themselves as consciously managing their own privacy, while having concerns that others do not, as seen in previous studies about Facebook [13]. It may also be that some users are simply unaware of potential risks, like the ones presented by pleaserobme.com.

Finally, we studied only foursquare, which is still a rapidly evolving service. This may limit the generalizability of our findings. We captured a snapshot of early adopters and presented results of why and how they use foursquare, and how they manage privacy concerns. When foursquare is adopted by early majority and late majority users [26], we maybe able to see different patterns of use and concerns. For example, we did not find that discounts and special offers would be a strong motivator for checking in, but if more businesses adopt foursquare as well, this factor could change.

CONCLUSIONS

We presented the results of three user studies of foursquare. The first study was a series of semi-structured interviews to understand the uses of location based services. Informed by this study, we chose to probe how and why people use foursquare, a popular social-driven location sharing application, through a classic two-part survey study. In particular, we focused on what motivations people had for using foursquare, where they used foursquare, some comparisons of newcomers vs longer-terms users, and how people managed privacy concerns.

Our findings support those of past studies of location sharing applications, and also introduce some new findings regarding surprising uses as well as how people manage their privacy. The results of our paper can inform the design of social software, and also offer some insights into how to build better mobile social applications.

ACKNOWLEDGMENTS

We thank the participants to our studies for making this research possible. We thank Naveen Selvadurai and Jon Steinback of foursquare and Chris Messina, and everybody who re-tweeted, for publicizing our survey. Janne Lindqvist is supported by Academy of Finland, and the foundations Emil Aaltosen Säätiö and Tekniikan Edistämissäätiö. Jason Wiese is supported by a Google scholarship.

REFERENCES

1. About foursquare. http://foursquare.com/about. Referenced January 12, 2011.
2. Ahern, S., Eckles, D., Good, N.S., King, S., Naaman, M. and Nair, R. Over-Exposed?: Privacy Patterns and Considerations in Online and Mobile Photo Sharing. In *Proc. CHI'07*. ACM Press, 2007. 357-366.
3. Ames, M. and Naaman, M. Why We Tag: Motivations for Annotation in Mobile and Online Media. In *Proc. CHI'07*. ACM Press, 2007. 971-980.
4. Anthony, D., Henderson, T. and Kotz, D. Privacy in Location-Aware Computing Environments. *IEEE Pervasive Computing*, 6(4), 2007. 64-72.
5. Barkhuus, L., Brown, B., Bell, M., Sherwood, S., Hall, M. and Chalmers, M. From Awareness to Repartee: Sharing Location within Social Groups. In *Proc. CHI'08*. ACM Press, 2008. 497-506.
6. boyd, d.m. Friendster and Publicly Articulated Social Networking. In *Ext. Abstract CHI'04*. ACM Press, 2004. 1279-1282.
7. boyd, d.m. Why Youth (Heart) Social Network Sites: The Role of Networked Publics in Teenage Social Life, 2007. MIT Press. 119-142.
8. Bryant, S.L. and Forte, A. and Bruckman, A. Becoming Wikipedian: transformation of participation in a collaborative online encyclopedia. In *Proc. GROUP'05*. ACM Press, 2005. 1-10.
9. Carr, A. Foursquare's Business Chief on Revenue Plans, Google AdWords, and Why Marketers Shouldn't Delay on Geo-location. FastCompany. http://www.fastcompany.com/1675626/.
10. Churchill, G. A Paradigm for Developing Better Measures of Marketing Constructs. *Journal of Marketing Research XVI*, 1979. 64-73.
11. Consolvo, S., Smith, I.E., Matthews, T., LaMarca, A.,Tabert, J., and Powledge, P. Location Disclosure to Social Relations: Why, When, & What People Want to Share. In *Proc. CHI'05*. ACM Press, 2005. 81-90.
12. Eagle, N. and Pentland, A. Social Serendipity: Mobilizing Social Software. *IEEE Pervasive Computing*, 4(2), 2005. 28-34.
13. Gross, R. and Acquisti, A. Information Revelation and Privacy in Online Social Networks. In *Proc. WPES'05*. ACM Press, 2005. 71-80.
14. Heyer, C., Brereton, M., and Viller, S. Cross-channel Mobile Social Software: an empirical study. In *Proc. CHI'08*. ACM Press, 2008. 1525-1534.
15. Humphreys, L. Mobile Social Networks and Social Practice: A Case Study of Dodgeball. *Journal of Computer-Mediated Communication*, 13(1), 2008. 341-360.
16. Humphreys, L. Mobile social networks and urban public space. *New Media & Society*, 12(5), 2010. 763-778.
17. Iachello, G. and Hong, J.I. End-User Privacy in Human-Computer Interaction. *Foundations and Trends in Human-Computer Interaction*, 1(1), 2007. 1-137.
18. Joinson, A.N. 'Looking at', 'Looking up' or 'Keeping up with' People? Motives and Uses of Facebook. In *Proc. CHI'08*. ACM Press, 2008. 1027-1036.
19. Jones, Q. and Grandhi, S.A. P3 Systems: Putting the Place Back into Social Networks. *IEEE Internet Computing*, 9(5), 2005. 38-46.
20. Lampe, C., Ellison, N.B., and Steinfield, C. Changes in Use and Perception of Facebook. In *Proc. CSCW'08*. ACM Press, 2008. 721-730.
21. Lampe, C., Wash, R., Velasquez, A., and Ozkaya, E. Motivations to Participate in Online Communities. In *Proc. CHI'10*. ACM Press, 2010. 1927-1936.
22. Lederer, S., Mankoff, J.C., and Dey, A.K. Who Wants to Know What When? Privacy Preference Determinants in Ubiquitous Computing. In *Ext. Abstracts CHI'03*. ACM Press, 2003. 724-725.
23. Ling, R. *The Mobile Connection: The Cell Phone's Impact on Society*. Morgan Kaufmann, 2004.
24. Ludford, P., Priedhorsky, R., Reily, K., and Terveen, L. Capturing, Sharing, and Using Local Place Information. In *Proc. CHI'07*. ACM Press, 2007. 1235-1244.
25. Patil, S. and Lai, J. Who Gets to Know What When: Configuring Privacy Permissions in an Awareness Application. In *Proc. CHI'05*. ACM Press. 101-110.
26. Rogers, E.M. *Diffusion of Innovations*. Free Press, 5th edition, 2003.
27. Smith, I.E., Consolvo, S., LaMarca, A., et al. Social Disclosure of Place: From Location Technology to Communication Practices. In *Proc. Pervasive'05*. Springer-Verlag, 2005. 134-151.
28. Stevens, J. *Applied Multivariate Statistics for the Social Sciences*. Lawrence Erlbaum Associates, 2002.
29. Stutzman, F. and Kramer-Duffield, J. Friends Only: Examining a Privacy-Enhancing Behavior in Facebook. In *Proc. CHI'10*. ACM Press, 2010. 1553-1562.
30. Tang, K., Lin, J., Hong, J.I., Siewiorek, P. and Sadeh, N. Rethinking Location Sharing: Exploring the Implications of Social-Driven vs. Purpose-Driven Location Sharing. In *Proc. UbiComp'10*, 2010. 85-94.
31. Tsai, J.Y., Kelley, P., Drielsma, P.H., Cranor, L.F., Hong, J.I., and Sadeh, N. Who's Viewed You?: The Impact of Feedback in a Mobile Location-Sharing Application. In *Proc. CHI'09*. ACM Press. 2003-2012.

In the Best Families: Tracking and Relationships

Clara Mancini*, Yvonne Rogers*, Keerthi Thomas*, Adam N. Joinson†, Blaine A. Price*, Arosha K. Bandara*, Lukasz Jedrzejczyk*, Bashar Nuseibeh*•
*Department of Computing, The Open University, UK
†School of Management, University of Bath
• Lero, University of Limerick, Ireland
C.Mancini@open.ac.uk

ABSTRACT
A growing body of research has been exploring the use of control mechanisms to address the privacy concerns raised by location-tracking technology. We report on a qualitative study of two family groups who used a custom-built tracking application for an extended period of time. Akin to sociological breaching experiments, the study focuses on the interferences between location tracking and relationship management. We analyze the tensions that can arise between affordances of the technology and uses that the *contracts* between family members legitimize. We describe how, by fostering misperceptions and 'nudging' behaviors, location-tracking technology can generate anxieties and conflicts even in close relationships. We discuss their vulnerability to the overreaching effects of tracking, against which the use of mechanisms such as location-sharing preferences and feedback may not be socially viable.

Author Keywords
Location-based technology, location tracking, family contract, family relationships, privacy

ACM Classification Keywords
J.4 Social and Behavioral Sciences: sociology; K.4.1: Public Policy Issues: privacy

General Terms
Experimentation, human factors

INTRODUCTION
In recent years an increasing number of location-based applications and services have become available and have been introduced into a variety of social contexts. Concomitantly, the use of location tracking has been the focus of much investigation within mobile HCI research, especially with regards to the potential implications for sensitive aspects of people's lives. Many studies have sought to identify and address the privacy concerns raised by the use of location-tracking technology, mainly looking at how it is used within loose social networks. There has been little research investigating how location-tracking technology impacts upon social relationships and dynamics within more tight-knit groups, such as families.

Our work is concerned with how location-tracking technology can affect close relationships, in particular within families. What constitutes a family is debatable (see [15]); here, we refer to a nuclear unit including a father, a mother and their children, and to an extended unit also including other relatives, such as grandparents or children's partners. Such units are characterized by social dependencies, spanning from economical co-operation to emotional attachment, and complex social dynamics that modulate those dependencies. The way in which location-tracking technology can interfere with family dynamics has been explored between particular household members [4]. We are interested in exploring the effect of this technology on the relationships between all members of the nuclear family and others who may join it at some point. In particular, our focus is on how location-tracking technology can impact upon the way family members negotiate the mutual accountabilities that explicitly or implicitly define their relations; what it means to be a family and the trade-offs that being a family involves.

To investigate how different individuals and relationships can be affected we conducted a qualitative user study of a network of participants from two sizeable family groups. They comprised a close nucleus including mother, father and children together with partners and friends who had become more closely part of the family unit. The families used a custom-built location-sharing application that was installed on their mobile phones for a period of three weeks. The application provided high frequency automatic location updates using both textual and visual information. An experience sampling method was used to elicit the participants' reactions during the study, together with extensive face-to-face individual interviews at the end.

The contribution of our work is twofold. First, we provide an in-depth analysis of the dialectic interplay between the use of tracking technology and the social roles, norms and practices in a close family group. Second, we show how the introduction of location-tracking technology into what might be considered 'safe' environments can generate tensions between the features of the technology and the behaviors relationships may legitimize. Our study shows how such technology can support the fulfillment of *family contracts* but also trigger detrimental anxieties and inner conflicts. Finally, we discuss how close family members may feel it is legitimate to keep a close eye on one another, while feeling reluctant to assert boundaries. This can make them particularly vulnerable to the effects of pervasive tracking practices, against which control mechanisms such as location-sharing preferences and feedback, may not be socially viable.

BACKGROUND

Tracking

Tracking is hard-wired in us. Its exercise was once essential to our survival and we still practice it for various purposes, such as conservation, eco-tourism, hunting, military operations, espionage, etc. In the physical world, this is a hazardous enterprise, in which exposure may have serious consequences. It is also a complex biosemiotic activity [6], which requires the skillful recognition of visual, auditory, olfactory and tactile signs left behind by a living target. It is an intrinsically voyeuristic activity, as the tracker eventually sets eyes on and contemplates the object of his quest, if only for the brief empowering moments that precede a strike. Those close moments can be so gratifying that they may be all a tracker seeks, when from the safety of his vantage point he 'captures' the motions of another's life, coming closer to the reality of their identity.

As a voyeuristic act, tracking objectifies the person who is being tracked, therefore placing itself outside any social interaction. However, the practice of tracking still takes place within a network of social relationships and its significance is determined with respect to the *contracts* defining those relationships. By this term we refer to the unique combination of social rules, norms and practices determining the set of explicit or implicit *expectations* that define the relationship between two *individuals* in a wider *social context*. These are informed by each individual's set of values and beliefs, and regard their own obligations, responsibilities, rights and inclinations towards others, as well as the others' obligations, responsibilities, rights and inclinations towards them. Moreover, these expectations determine the way in which individuals manage their own social boundaries and observe the social boundaries of others (see [16,8]).

Schoeman [17] argues that we are inherently "*social beings whose stake lies in life with others*" not as a mean to other ends, but as an *end to itself*. It is in relation to our dependence on others that privacy can be understood. For Schoeman, privacy affords us social freedom, not by granting us autonomy from society, but by allowing us to participate in a variety of associations, within which we can find safe spaces for self-expression. By restricting access to the ones outside those spaces, privacy enables us to relate in meaningful ways to the ones inside. In other words, privacy is deeply socially embedded and so too is privacy violation, which, therefore, is not without social consequences. Tracking is intrinsically prone to violating privacy, as it can easily bypass the system of boundaries set up within family contracts to modulate and maintain relationships, exposing them to undesirable states. Provided tracking remains a resource intensive and hazardous enterprise, it is only viable in response to significant demands or in prediction of significant benefits, but what happens when tracking another can be safely done at the click of a button?

Location-aware research

The impact of location-aware technology on people's privacy has been studied extensively. Some of these studies have used hypothetical scenarios to explore people's location-privacy attitudes (see, [1,2,7,13,24]), identifying a number of determining factors, for example, one's relationship with the person requesting their location [7,13] or their immediate context at the time of the request [1]. Other field studies have looked at the use of mechanisms such as feedback or location-sharing preferences to regulate access [10,22]. Generally, there has been a tendency to focus more on the point of view of the person being tracked, not taking into account that tracking and being tracked constitute the reversible roles of the same phenomenon and that both roles need to be studied dialectically to understand how tracking really affects people. Moreover, there tends to be a presumption that participants are fundamentally in control, as they are allowed to share their location with others actively and selectively by accepting or declining location-disclosure requests or by setting up ad hoc location-sharing policies. However, members of close relationships may not feel at liberty to take such a pragmatic approach to boundary management.

Another body of research, investigating the use of location-tracking technology in the wild, includes studies that are characterized by the reciprocity between trackers and tracked: participants play both roles or both the point of view of the tracker and the tracked are taken into account. For example, Troshynski *et al.* [21] and Shklovski *et al.* [19] have studied the effects that the use of tracking devices respectively have on parolees and parole officers in Californian prisons. The authors found that not only the lives of the parolees, as one would expect, but also the lives and roles of the parole officers were profoundly affected, as they spent increasing amounts of time interacting with and reacting to the technology instead of interacting with the parolees. Others, however, found that the use of location-aware technology can foster a sense of connectedness and serve co-ordination functions in cohesive groups. For example, a study by Barkhuus *et al.* [3] looked at how the use of the status and location-sharing application Connecto afforded small groups of friends both practical and psychological advantages by allowing them to share a combination of location and profile abstraction. Similarly,

Brown *et al.* [5]'s Whereabouts Clock allowed families to co-ordinate their activities while fostering a sense of reassurance, connectedness and belonging. Boesen *et al.* [4] also found that location-tracking applications could be used for benign purposes such as ensuring or reassuring oneself about the safety of family members. However, the authors also found other ambiguous and questionable uses, such as curiosity, bordering on voyeurism, and even surveillance. They note how the surveillance afforded by tracking technology has the potential of undermining the very trust work that is necessary to maintain domestic relationships.

Much research has suggested that the relationship between two people is the most important factor in determining when tracking is perceived as socially acceptable [9,15,16]. But what are the elements that modulate the reactions and interactions within those relations with respect to location-sharing? On the one hand, tracking is in itself an objectifying activity sitting outside social interaction but, on the other hand, it is a social practice taking place within a network of relationships, entailing roles and dynamics. By affording tracking, new mobile technologies can generate unprecedented tensions between an innate self-preserving drive, and an intrinsic inclination for relatedness. The aim of our study was to investigate how location-tracking technology brings out and affects these tensions.

FIELD STUDY

The field study comprised two family groups of respectively 7 and 5 participants. Each group was asked to use a custom-built location-tracking application installed on their mobile phones for a period of three weeks and through four different phases, each lasting 5 days. During each phase participants were allowed or asked to do different things such as remaining exposed, carrying out tracking tasks on other participants or using location-sharing preferences.

Methodology

Technology

A custom-built location tracking application, Buddy Tracker [12], was used in the study. The tracking functions were accessible via the application's interface (see Figure 1). They included a map displaying simultaneously the location of all group members, a description of each member's individual profile with textual information about their current address, and a link to an interactive map application displaying their geographical position. Other features included: feedback notification similar to those in IMBuddy [10] and location-sharing preferences similar to those in Locyoution [22]. Notification that a participant had looked-up someone's location was delivered in real time via a text message. An aggregated feedback mechanism allowed users to see who had accessed their profile, location or location history, and view on a map where both tracked and tracker were each time. Location-sharing options included time-sensitive, coarse-grained visibility settings (e.g., becoming invisible for a few hours) and peer-to-peer coarse or fine-grained settings (e.g., allowing a particular group member to see one's location only at city level). Accurate location updates were automatically provided every 10 minutes. Because the user interface was a web application, features could be instantly activated or deactivated and system usage could be monitored via a web-based administration panel.

Figure 1. Three screens from Buddy Tracker: Main menu (Left); Individual Profile (Center); All on Map (Right)

Participants

We solicited participants through word-of-mouth, mailing lists, and social networking sites and recruited two families of experienced iPhone users who were not related to each other or to us. The choice was based on their composition, cultural differences, and diversity of mobility patterns: we wanted to observe many instances of tracking behavior in socio-culturally different groups for whom tracking could be a worthwhile exercise and meaningful activity.

The first group (**F1**) was a South African family who had relocated to England two years ago after suffering an abduction and an armed robbery. They consisted of a married couple in their fifties, their three daughters and the partners of the two older daughters. The husband, a lawyer who worked locally, and his spouse, a housewife, lived in Milton Keynes, in Buckinghamshire, with their youngest daughter, who was in her late teens and attended high school. The middle daughter, in her early twenties, lived and attended university in Sheffield. Her boyfriend of six months, in his late twenties, lived in London and worked as a restaurant manager. The eldest daughter, in her mid twenties, worked in London for a law firm and lived with her long-term partner, who was in his early thirties and worked in London as a financial advisor. In South Africa, where crime levels are high and abductions frequent, it is common for families to use tracking technology for security purposes. This family had also done so but none of them had used it after relocating to England, prior to the study.

The second group (**F2**) was a British family who lived in Daventry, a small town in Northamptonshire, England, and consisted of a married couple, their son and younger daughter, plus a family friend and housemate of the son. Husband and wife, both in their forties, worked locally, the former as a company director, the latter as a social worker. They lived with their younger daughter, who was in her early twenties and worked as a nurse and child caretaker at various locations out of town. The older son, in his mid twenties, was a PhD student and lived in Daventry with his long-term friend, also in his mid twenties, who worked as a business consultant at various locations around the country. None of them had ever used tracking technology prior to the study.

Schedule

During the three weeks of the study, the participants were asked to carry and keep their phone on at all times, in order to be always traceable by the other members of their group. All participants were monitored to ensure they were connected and active. The overall period was divided into four phases, each 5 days long. In **Phase1**, participants familiarized themselves with the application by freely tracking their co-participants. In **Phase2**, participants were asked to locate a particular co-participant at various times depending on when the latter appeared to be in a location of interest or far away. Each member of F1 was asked to do this 2 times a day, making a total of 10 tracking tasks for each. The location tracking tasks were provided via text messages manually sent to them from the administration panel. This intervention was introduced so as to enable us to observe emotional and behavioral reactions, when tracking others under external pressure. Specifically, we were interested in whether the participants would feel uncomfortable by having to track a co-participant they would have not otherwise tracked at a particular time. In **Phase3**, each member of F1 was given four further tracking tasks. In this phase we also introduced tracking feedback to observe how the participants would react. Would the translucency [9] afforded by this new feature make them hesitant about tracking others? Would it discourage them from any less-than-benign uses of the technology? Without pre-warning, all participants started receiving real-time feedback notifications. Every time they were located by a co-participant, they would be alerted by text and told what location information about them had been requested; they could then view the location of the tracker and their own at the time of the request. The feature was enabled throughout the remainder of the study. Finally, in **Phase4**, members of F1 were given 3 other tracking tasks. In this phase the participants were also provided with location-sharing preferences that allowed them to blur or hide their location completely for up to two hours at a time. This was in addition to the real-time feedback notifications. Given the opportunity to prevent others from seeing their whereabouts, would they now use the location-sharing preferences to hide from other family members? This phase enabled us to observe how participants would use and react to the introduction of various privacy settings on the location-tracking application. Among the other tracking tasks, we asked the participants of F1 to change their location-sharing preferences three times: 1 time we asked the partner of the first daughter of F1 to reduce his visibility to city level (and he complied) and 2 times we asked the first daughter of F1 to make herself invisible (however, she made herself invisible 3 times and 1 time extended her invisibility beyond her given task).

Data collection

We collected participants' reactions both during the study and at the end. During the study, we used experience sampling, sending instant requests to the participants' mobile phones, upon each tracking event. Every time a participant tracked a co-participant, the system would send them a text message asking them to follow a link and fill an online questionnaire accessible via their phone. This included three pre-defined multiple-choice questions and a request for a memory phrase to help them remember the specific episode during the debriefing interview [14]. The sampling form contained the following text: "You have just done X (e.g., tracked Y): 1) What made you want to do X? 2) Is what you found what you expected? 3) How do you feel about it?" Additionally, there was a text box for a memory phrase. The experience sampling data was to be used as mnemonic trigger during interview.

At the end of the study, participants individually took part in extensive debriefing interviews, which lasted between one and two hours. The materials used during the interviews included: 1) the experience sampling forms they had submitted, 2) the print-outs of the maps outlining their daily trajectories for the duration of the study, 3) the records of the activities they had undertaken as trackers and those they had undergone as tracked. They were asked detailed questions about all the data they had generated. The questions aimed at exploring their *reasons for*, *feelings about* and *context around* their tracking behavior.

FINDINGS

Participant		Total	Ph1	Ph2	Ph3	Ph4
F1	Father	36	1	3	16	16
	Mother	88	13	19	24	32
	Daught1	21	2	6	8	0
	Daught2	49	12	5	21	10
	Daught3	50	24	7	13	6
	Part D1	73	8	23	11	31
	Part D2	42	2	15	14	11
F2	Father	97	93	2	0	2
	Mother	194	122	23	22	27
	Son	51	26	18	1	6
	Daught1	33	28	4	0	1
	Friend S	47	47	0	0	0
Total:		781				

Table 1: Summary of tracking events for all participants

We recorded a total of 1092 unique tracking events on the participant's mobile phones, of which 305 were compound events (a participant looking at a co-participant's current address and then looking at their location on the map) .We recorded 5 changes to location-sharing preferences, 2 of which were compound (a participant prolonging their invisibility). The combined total of single and compound tracking events was 781, none of which was accidental. Table 1 summarizes the single and compound tracking events produced by the two families in the different phases of the study. As the data shows, participants of F1 didn't always carry out the assigned tasks (for example, in Phase2 the father of F1 only produced 3 tracking events, as he missed some of the tracking requests).

Qualitative findings

The findings from the interviews reveal a complex interplay between a) the participants' personal set of values and beliefs, b) their perception of the family contracts defining their relationships, and c) their assessment of their and others' motivations for tracking. We describe these in terms of values and beliefs, family contracts and motives, describing an interplay that we might call a 'morality of tracking'.

Morality of tracking

Values and beliefs. Unsurprisingly, we found that the participants' sets of values and beliefs informed their general attitudes towards location tracking technology. For example, the two mothers manifested very different attitudes towards location tracking, in particular towards their children.

The mother of **F1** commented that, compared to South Africa, she found England very safe and did not feel that tracking her children was needed: *"Like if they were in South Africa and I was living here I would worry more...but here they are safe...nothing happens here so I'm crossing the line. I do it because I can and that's not good enough"*. However, the mother of **F2** commented that, doing social work in the rehabilitation of young offenders, she was aware of how many dangerous people there are out there, especially driving on the road. Therefore she found herself frequently checking on her adult children to make sure they had made it to their destination safely: *"I'm a big worrier and especially since my son moved out and if my daughter goes out because I know what people are like on the road and I just know what it could be like...I think it's alright checking on them"*. The two participants' different personalities and experiences had apparently led to different outlooks on the appropriateness of location-tracking.

Again, the mother of **F1** commented how, unlike partners, children have a life of their own and as a parent she ought to respect that: *"I think I would feel bad checking on the kids because I do feel that is overstepping a privacy line...I think mummy can't know everything about children...I would only check on the kids in an emergency"*. Quite differently, the mother of **F2** commented that their children were aware of and accepted the fact that she was a protective mother: *"It's not to go in their space, I mean both of them have said any time I can phone them or text them"*. This shows how different views on parenting also influenced the participants' outlook on location-tracking.

Another example is that of the eldest daughter of **F1** and her partner, who had very different views on location-tracking technology. She felt very uncomfortable about the whole idea of tracking, whether she was tracking or being tracked: *"I must say I don't feel very comfortable with this technology so I don't like using it very much at all"*. Whereas her partner had no problem with it; he was very enthusiastic about the technology and what it could achieve: *"Makes me feel closer to her and 99% of the time I know exactly where she is anyway, because we are speaking or standing next to each other, so that is nice"*. This was partly motivated by his propensity towards technology in general, which the eldest daughter did not share.

These findings suggest that all participants recognized that while there were privacy boundaries to be observed, the configuration of those boundaries varied for different participants, depending on personality, experiential and cultural factors such as country of origin, profession or gender.

Family contracts. The participants' perception of what was entailed by the family contracts defining the various members' relationship with each other played an important role in assessing their motivations for and determining their use of the technology. Participants clearly distinguished between the meaning of tracking those whom they defined as 'parent', 'child', 'partner', 'sibling' or 'friend'. Their attitude varied with the accountabilities and responsibilities they felt towards each co-participant. The mother of **F2** used the tracker almost exclusively towards her children, rather than her husband, as a way of fulfilling her maternal role: *"I felt good about it because even though they've got mobiles and I can get hold of them at any time...with this I was looking where they were without disturbing them...because* [my son] *doesn't live at home anymore, it's reassurance that I know he's in a certain area"*.

Each of the older sisters of **F1** felt more inclined to using the technology to track the younger one/s, as they felt more protective towards her/them: *"I feel more protective of* [my youngest sister] *than I do for* [my other sister], *I feel as though I am entitled to know what she is up to, more than with* [my other sister], *because I know* [my other sister] *is grown up, she'll be fine, she's running her own life"*. Likewise, the young males of **F1** also used the tracker more protectively towards their partners than the other way round: *"I looked and I saw that she was at home, I knew that she was safe, it was nice"*.

However, for the son of **F2**, tracking his younger sister was not part of the contract he had with her. He felt less comfortable about tracking her than he did about tracking his mother: while he assumed that a mother should always be there for her children and hence could be legitimately tracked at all times, tracking his sister encroached on her independence: *"I feel I shouldn't check on her so much, as she is her own person and I ought to respect her independence"*. This was symmetrical to how the mother felt legitimized in tracking her children to ensure their safety, symmetry that reflected what in this group looked like a family culture. The mother of **F2** drew the line between tracking her own children and her son's friend: *"I thought I was really naughty...what am I doing checking on him, he is not even my son"*. That was not part of her social deal with him.

Interestingly, as the relationship between co-participants developed, their contracts with each other underwent unspoken revisions. Concomitantly, their attitude towards tracking the other also changed. As the mother of **F1** became acquainted with the recent partner of her daughter, her feelings about tracking him became more ambivalent. Prior to their acquaintance she did not feel motivated to look up his location, but at the same time felt perfectly comfortable in doing so. Following their acquaintance she felt more motivated to protectively check on him, but at the same time started feeling uncomfortable about entering his space uninvited: *"Quite honestly I wouldn't have known he was sick, I wouldn't have cared, but because he spent the weekend here and he tried so hard not to be sick and he was polite and charming and helpful so he really went out of his way...I looked where he was, because if he was at home I probably wouldn't have texted but because I saw he was at work I texted to say I hope you are better...it felt a little uncomfortable* [though]".

One participant confessed that they had no problem tracking one co-participant following an episode in which they had breached their trust, hence the social deal between them. As a result of that episode, the participant deemed the co-participant no longer deserving of boundary observation and was checking on them to catch them at fault: *"I feel because* [they] *have shown in the past that* [they] *are not trustworthy, that kind of*[they] *started it and it means I can check up on* [them] *and not feel too bad...*[they] *are unlikely to do what* [they] *say they do so anything you see* [on the tracker] *is probably just going to confirm that"*.

Overall, these findings indicate that within their family contracts participants tended to feel varying levels of motivation and responsibility towards each other, which proportionately translated into either a sense of entitlement to entering others' personal space or concern over crossing boundaries. Outside of these contracts, there tended to be no motivation or responsibility towards others and therefore neither there was sense of entitlement or concern. However, if others breached a contract, there remained (negative) motivation but not responsibility, and there was sense of entitlement but not concern, which permitted behavior of a more predatory nature.

Motives. We found a connection between the way in which participants felt about tracking and the way in which, within their set of values and beliefs and with respect to their own family contracts, they assessed their motives for checking on others. These included protection, care, connection, reassurance, co-ordination, curiosity, surveillance and execution (when participants were carrying out a given task). Some of these are consistent with the findings of previous studies (e.g., [11]). We focus on how they fit in the dynamics of close social relations, when they are seen as compatible with those relations and why.

At times, participants looked at a co-participant's location with the intent of protecting them from potential harm and, because that intent was seen as honoring their social deal with the co-participant, they deemed that acceptable. For example, the mother of **F1** once tracked her youngest daughter hoping to be able to spare her the reproaches of the sisters for being late: *"They were asking where is she and the sisters sometimes do have words between each other so I thought I would try and find her and tell her to move it. I was trying to save a fight between the sisters"*.

Other times, participants used the tracking application to offer some form of care and support to their loved ones, which was also seen as a way of fulfilling their contract each other. For example, the eldest daughter of **F1** once looked at her younger sister's location knowing that she was unwell and unable to take a phone call because she was studying: *"So it was kind of like I wish I was there with her because I could bring her tea...when you're sick you want people to look after you, you want them to be there but you know that was the next best thing I could do and I knew she was trying to study so I wasn't going to call her and disturb her"*.

Participants might also track a co-participant to bridge physical distance between them and feel closer, as the partner of the eldest daughter of **F1** did several times with no concerns: *"So I was already checking on her, I'd only just arrived at the airport and I was already missing her"*.

However, tracking a co-participant with the intent of reassuring oneself evoked mixed feelings and was assessed accordingly: reassuring oneself that a loved one is safe was seen as a caring but self-serving act; similarly, reassuring oneself that everyone is where they are expected to be and that everything is in order was seen as self-gratifying and not always acceptable. For example, the father of **F1** one night, when his youngest daughter went to a party, checked on her to reassure himself she was safe: *"I saw that she was still at the party and not somewhere else... I felt reassured that she was in no riskier place than I expected...this would be a prime example of where I would have difficulty with that* [kind of tracking]*"*.

Reassuring oneself that one still occupies a certain rank in the social scale of another was seen as altogether dangerous. The mother of **F1** once looked at her eldest daughter's location from whom she had been waiting for a phone call to reassure herself that the daughter had not forgotten about her: *"I would have been very disappointed if I had seen her back in her office...that she had not found two minutes to phone me...that would be almost like checking on a spouse...if it was a spouse it puts the seed in your mind, so I think it can be a very destructive tool"*.

Curiosity was seen as a non-legitimate motive, having no other aims than the voyeuristic intent to take a peak in someone else's personal life, as the mother of **F2** was well aware: *"I think it is not good when someone is just being nosey, that's not right, just looking to be nosey"*. Tracking was seen as socially questionable when carried out as a voyeuristic act, which could easily turn into surveillance. Typical example was that of the participant (mentioned earlier) who checked on a co-participant out of mistrust expecting to catch them at fault: *"I was checking on* [them]*...if the tracker had shown* [them] *anywhere else* [other than where I expected them to be] *I would have gone ah! My worst suspicions are confirmed"*.

Quite differently, the intent to co-ordinate one's movements with another to save time and work seemed to have no emotional or social implications and was clearly seen by everybody as a legitimate motive for tracking. For example, the father in **F1** reported: *"If I am going to be picking her up from university and I want to check where she is so that I am not too early or too late I don't have a problem with it, because it is part of an interaction between the two of us and it is leading to that interaction"*.

Sometimes when participants were carrying out a tracking task they felt completely detached. In those instances, they delegated responsibility for that action altogether and didn't even need to assess its legitimacy: *"It was easier to* [check on others] *when I was asked to do so...I didn't feel it was my responsibility...it wasn't me doing it, I was just carrying out a task"*.

These findings suggest that participants found their motives for tracking others acceptable or even commendable when they saw them as honoring their contracts with them. However, when their motives could not be justified with respect to these, the participants felt a degree of discomfort. Yet, there were times in which they could have abstained from using the tracking application but chose not to. There were also times in which they could have prevented others from tracking them but did not. The reasons for this seemingly contradictory behavior are discussed in the next section.

Liabilities of tracking

Often participants noted feeling uncomfortable about tracking and being tracked via the mobile technology. Their concerns pertain to how the location awareness application can afford or interfere with *social interaction*, on the one hand, and *'a-social' action*, on the other. In this context, by social interaction we mean behavior that is intended and can be accounted for as an exchange between two subjects. By 'a-social' action we mean behavior that cannot be legitimately accounted for as an exchange between two subjects; instead, this is behavior that objectifies the other and sits outside the bounds of social interaction, as is the case with voyeuristic or predatory uses of tracking technology. We examine the participants' concerns with respect to both social and 'a-social' aspects.

Social interaction. As tracked, one of the participants' main concerns was the possibility that their behavior might be misinterpreted on the basis of location information alone. They felt that, if they did not appear to be where they were expected to be, or if they did not appear at all, others might jump to conclusions about their behavior. The partner of the elder daughter in **F1** reported an incident: *"She was really sick one night and I was at home...*[she could not see me on the tracker] *and she was ringing me to say she can't sleep, and I didn't answer my phone coz my battery was flat and I remember the next day she said what happened why did you turn your phone off and I said my phone wasn't off, my battery was flat"*. Equally, participants were concerned about the possibility that they might make unexpected discoveries about the location of others and not being able to refrain from making assumptions, as the elder daughter from **F1** reports from the same incident: *"There was one night...I know he had gone out and I wanted to know where he was, so that I could know if he was at home and I could phone or if he was still out and wouldn't answer his phone, so I looked him up but it said it was last tracked four hours ago which was when he left work. So I thought oh did he turn his phone off...or did he turn the tracker off and why did he do that because I knew he was going out, and so then and also I was ill so I start thinking so why didn't he tell me? Who is he with? And why is he there? And that was the thing"*.

Likewise, because of their concern about how others would see them, some participants felt unable to stop others from tracking them. Of all the participants, only one (the eldest daughter from **F1**) ever made spontaneous use of the location-sharing preferences, and only twice. A number of participants said that they did not or would not have used the location-sharing preferences because others would have questioned why they felt they needed to hide: *"No I didn't use the privacy settings because if I had they could have asked me why did you hide your location, have you got something to hide?"*. The same preoccupation made some participants reluctant to take advantage of the translucency afforded by the real-time feedback. Some related that they would prefer not to receive real-time notification when someone checked their location, because that would make them question others' motives: *"I would prefer not to know, because otherwise I would have to start asking myself why they are checking on me...have I done something wrong...are they after something?"*. When they were not worried about others' perception of them, some participants were concerned about letting others down: *"At times I'd rather* [my mother] *didn't track me...but I wouldn't use* *privacy preferences* [as] *I know that would hurt her feelings"*.

These comments suggest the tracking technology triggered concerns and anxieties about the participants' ability to maintain good relationships: these could have been affected by the perceptions and expectations that the use of the technology triggered in them and others.

'A-social' action. Both trackers and tracked seemed to be aware of and uncomfortable with the voyeuristic aspects of tracking. Trackers were most uncomfortable when tracking was just motivated by curiosity without a justifiable purpose, yet some found it difficult to resist the temptation of tracking others: *"I don't think it makes me a better person checking up on people...I think what drives these questions is never really a positive thing "; "it is not my place* [to check on people] *and I know that, so I try and stay far out of it as I possibly can because it's none of my business at all, but this* [technology] *makes it a little bit too easy, doesn't it, you are only human"*. Others found it even addictive: *"It's quite addictive...I got used to using it a lot and now that the study is over I really miss it"*. As they started receiving real-time notifications, these participants realized that their co-participants must be getting notifications, too. Some commented that it made them think twice about tracking others again. However, the event data does not indicate that this had a significant impact on their behavior.

Some participants were clearly uncomfortable when they were shown the printouts of the maps outlining their daily trajectories: not only was this evidence of the fact that we had been tracking them, it was also placing them in a self-voyeuristic position that made them aware of their potential vulnerability: *"Even seeing my life all laid out on a map, if I cannot remember a place I went to and I can't explain, it's really uncomfortable"*. Even though they had nothing to hide and even though where they had been or what they had done was not significant, some felt that they would have to be able to offer their co-participants (for example, to their wives) an explanation that they did not have: *"It might be I've done nothing wrong but I might have not done enough right. I thought you were at the office but it took you long enough to get there. Well I got lost, didn't do anything wrong. Well why did you get lost? Well it doesn't matter"*.

These comments indicate participants concerns about how tracking technology was at times able to push them into acting as voyeurs or even predators, just as it was making them vulnerable to other's voyeurism or predation.

DISCUSSION

Our findings illustrate a dialectical interplay between what location-tracking technology may afford and what family contracts, in terms of their social roles and relations, may allow or require. The participants' set of values and beliefs informed their perception of what the social obligations defining their relationships with others entailed. This substantiated the way in which participants assessed their motivations for tracking their co-participants and their co-participants' motivations for tracking them. Our analysis has shown how the technology can disrupt people's lives and how this interference might be managed. We have done so primarily by taking the point of view of the tracker rather than the tracked: in this active role participants found themselves compelled to reflect much more on what they were doing. This is consistent with findings by Wagner *et al.* [24], who report that people demonstrate more awareness and attention in making decisions that could affect others. Overall, our research raises a number of questions that we formulate in the following sections.

Margins of tacit misunderstanding

Within nuclear families extended by one or two members, our study has highlighted how the use of tracking technologies can interfere with the fulfillment of family contracts and generate social tensions. One such tension is the way in which social contracts change within a family. For example, as children grow up into teenagers and beyond their privacy status changes [16], which requires adjustments in how the contract between them and their parents is managed. Similar adjustments may be required as others, for example the partners of the adult children, join the family and start developing a relationship with the parents. Tracking technologies may make explicit what would otherwise remain implicit, unspoken or dealt with in other ways, which may cause anxieties or even conflicts.

But by rendering more explicitly one's assumptions about the mutual accountabilities that define one's relationships with others, the technology reduces the *margin of tacit misunderstanding* that sometimes allows relationships to work smoothly. For example, while one of our participants said that she thought her mother would be always thrilled to be tracked by her, the mother said that she would find that disturbing. The often delicate understandings that need to build up gradually and seamlessly between parents and their growing children, or between natural and acquired members of the family group, may be compromised as a consequence of an increased access to what the person is doing when out of sight. These concerns are reflected by the findings of a study, in which half of the interviewed parents stated that they had discounted using tracking technology with their children [23].

Extremes of accountability

There are trails in our daily life that we cannot explain and that may be completely insignificant. However, their representation via a tracking device objectifies and gives them significance, seemingly calling for an extraordinary degree of accountability [19]. This generates anxieties, especially within close relationships, in which people may feel under greater pressure to account for things they simply cannot account for. Moreover, location-based awareness applications can be very tempting, allowing people to indulge in behaviors that they would not have had, by luring them to becoming more voyeuristic. It also generates a conflict between what people do out of weakness and what they can morally justify. They may be tempted to manage this conflict, for example, by expanding the range of responsibilities supposedly entailed by their social roles in order to justify their propensity for tracking others. But doing so puts further pressure on their relationships with other members in the group and on the individuals partaking in them. How the adoption of such tracking technology might affect the way in which people reason about what is remarkable or unremarkable within the representations of theirs and others' movements made possible by it is an important question that needs further investigation.

Tracking technology may also serve or even foster a reduced sense of accountability. Schoeman [17] observes that when others (or aspects of their lives) are not relevant to us we are not motivated nor legitimated to encroach on them, which affords them a measure of privacy. However, our findings indicate that, while there might not be motivation to encroach, there may not be concern about it either. This opens up possibilities for less benign forms of tracking. Moreover, consistently with Boesen *et al.* [4]'s findings that tracking is sometimes motivated by lack of trust, our findings suggest that, where a breach of a contract is perceived, tracking technology can easily turn the other into fair game and become an acceptable avenue for an objectifying drive. It seems that temptations to follow socially de-constructive impulses may be engendered by tracking technology in what are otherwise socially constructive environments. This propensity to switch easily from social to a-social covert actions, without recourse to any negotiation within a family contract, needs more consideration than it has previously been given.

Impressions of reality

As noted, the incompleteness of the information provided by the tracking technology triggered the participants' concern that others might misperceive their behavior or that they might misperceive the behavior of others. The problem of signaling and interpreting social meaning via digital artifacts has been studied in other domains [18], but our findings suggest that it should be focused on more closely in this domain, too. As a medium, location-tracking technology presents important biosemiotic issues that ought to be addressed. By this we mean an approach that analyses the production, action and interpretation of signs in the biological realm. The exercise of tracking through the impoverished representation provided by location-tracking technology currently available [19] is far removed from the skilful biosemiotic activity of physical tracking and raises concerns for both the tracked and the tracker. While physical tracking and the use of tracking technology may differ in many ways, they share a fundamental aspect: they both entail approaching (in more ways that one) another from a vantage point prior to any interaction. Before any communication can be established, the tracker is drawn to making inferences about the tracked based on whatever signals they can interpret in whatever way. Indeed, our participants would often make inferences about their co-participants' behavior or circumstances based on the position of a dot on a map, as if the signs and assumptions that triggered those inferences could be relied upon. What is it about a dot on a map that triggers in us such an *impression of reality*? How could tracking devices provide us with the information we need not to make wrong assumptions, without causing us even greater exposure? These are questions that future research should address.

Closeness versus control

Other important questions concern the intricate socio-cultural elements that may influence the morality of tracking. There seems to be a widespread assumption, in the current research trends on location tracking and privacy, that if people are offered easy and sophisticated enough controls over location-sharing options and sufficient translucency on others' action, this would go a long way in resolving the privacy issues raised by this technology. However, our findings indicate that within close relationships such a rational approach to privacy management may simply not be viable.

As Schoeman [17] reminds us, "*we understand ourselves as proper objects of moral and social manipulation, by ourselves and by others*" and this is particularly true within close-knit connections, such as family relationships, in which many more aspects of our lives are relevant to those with whom we belong. The more stakes one has in a relationship, the more one has to lose; the more one has to lose, the less one can act as an autonomous agent. Within close social groups, location-tracking technology could, therefore, paradoxically make users more vulnerable than they would be within less cohesive groups. We suggest that future research should focus on investigating further the interplay between culture, social contracts and the use of location-tracking technology within different cohesive social groups. We need a much better understanding of what is socially viable for people to do when using such location awareness applications in order to protect themselves from the overreaching power of others.

CONCLUSIONS

Our research has investigated the way location tracking can affect and perturb relationships within closely related groups. We conducted a user study using a technology intervention akin to a sociological breaching experiment. Our detailed analysis showed the possible interplays that can emerge between location-tracking technology and social dynamics in relationships characterized by mutual dependencies, such as those found within families. Our approach uncovered and articulated a breach between what tracking technology can afford and what social contracts within close knit group may legitimize, with the anxieties and inner conflicts that may pressurize relationships as a result. Our findings suggest that the use of control mechanisms such as location-sharing preferences and feedback may not be compatible with the delicate and subtle dynamics on which certain social relationships are based. New tracking technology needs to be designed based on a better understanding of the complex interplay between technological affordances and social dynamics in a variety of social groups.

ACKNOWLEDGMENTS

We are indebted to the participants who took part in the study for their invaluable contribution. We thank all our reviewers for their generously thoughtful comments. This work is funded by the EPSRC grant EP/F024037/1 and SFI grant 03/CE2/I303_1.

REFERENCES

1. Anthony, D., Henderson, T., Kotz, D. (2010). Privacy in Location-Aware Computing Environments. *Proc. IEEE Pervasive Computing*, vol. 6, no. 4, pp. 64-72
2. Barkhuus, L. and Dey, A. (2003). Location-Based Services for Mobile Telephony: a Study of User's Privacy Concerns. *Proc. INTERACT '03*. Zurich, Switzerland: IOS Press, pp. 709 -712.
3. Barkhuus, L., Brown, B., Bell, M., Sherwood, S., Hall, M. and Chalmers, M. (2008). From awareness to repartee: sharing location within social groups. *Proc. CHI'08*. Florence, Italy: ACM Press, pp. 497–506.
4. Boesen, J., Rode, J. Mancini, C. (2010). The Domestic Panopticon: Location Tracking in Families. *Proc. UbiComp '10*. Copenhagen, Denmark: ACM Press.
5. Brown, B., Taylor, A., Izadi, S., Sellen, A., Kaye, J., and Eardley, R. (2007). Locating family values: A field trial of the whereabouts clock. *Proc. UbiComp'07*. Innsbruck, Austria: ACM Press, pp. 354–371.
6. Conesa-Sevilla, J. (2008). Thinking in Animal Signs. *The Trumpeter*. vol. 24, pp. 116-125.
7. Consolvo, S., Smith, I.E., Matthews, T., La Marca, A., Tabert, J., and Powledge, P. (2005). Location Disclosure to Social Relations: Why, When, & What People Want to Share. *Proc. CHI'05*. Portland, OR: ACM, 2005, pp. 81-90.
8. Dourish, P. and Palen. L. (2003). Unpacking privacy for a networked world. *Proc. CHI'03*, Ft. Lauderdale, FL: ACM Press, pp. 129–136.
9. Erickson, T. and Kellogg, W.A. (2000). Social translucence: an approach to designing systems that support social processes. *TOCHI*, vol. 7, pp. 59-83.
10. Hsieh, G., Tang, K.P., Yong Low, W., Hong, J.I. (2007). Field Deployment of IMBuddy: A Study of Privacy Control and Feedback Mechanisms for Contextual IM. Krumm, J. *et al.* (Eds.): *UbiComp2007*, LNCS 4717, pp. 91-108.
11. Iachello, G., Smith, I., Consolvo, S., Chen, M., Abowd, G.D. (2005). Developing Privacy Guidelines for Social Location Disclosure Applications and Services. *Proc. SOUPS'05*. Pittsburgh, PA: ACM Press.
12. Jedrzejczyk, L., Price, B. A., Bandara, A. K., Nuseibeh, B. (2010). On the impact of real-time feedback on users' behavior in mobile location-sharing applications. *Proc. SOUPS '10, pp. 14-16.*
13. Lederer, S., Mankoff, J. and Dey, A.K. (2003). Who Wants to Know What When? Privacy Preference Determinants in Ubiquitous Computing. *Proc. CHI'03*. Ft. Lauderdale, FL: ACM Press, pp. 724-725.
14. Mancini, C., Thomas, K., Rogers, Y., Price, B.A., Jedrzejczyk, L., Bandara, A.K., Joinson, A.N., and Nuseibeh, B. (2009). From Spaces to Places: Emerging Contexts in Mobile Privacy. *Proc. UbiComp'09*, Orlando, FL: ACM, 2009, pp. 1-10.
15. Martin, B. (1984). 'Mother Wouldn't Like it': Housework as Magic. *Theory, Culture and Society*, vol. 2, no. 2, pp.19-36.
16. Petronio, S. (2002). *Boundaries of Privacy: Dialectics of Disclosure.* Albany, NY: State University of New York Press.
17. Schoeman, F.D. (1992). *Privacy and Social Freedom.* Cambridge: Cambridge University Press.
18. Shami, N.S., Ehrlich, K., Gay, G., Hancock, J.T. (2009). Making sense of strangers' expertise from signals in digital artifacts. *Proc. CHI'09*. Boston, MA: ACM Press, pp. 69-78.
19. Shklovski, I., Vertesi, J., Troshynski, E. and Dourish, P. (2009). The commodification of location: dynamics of power in location-based systems. *Proc. UbiComp'09.* Orlando, FL: ACM Press, pp. 11-20.
20. Stacey, J. (1997). *In the Name of the Family: Rethinking Family Values in the Postmodern Age*. Beacon Press.
21. Troshynski, E., Lee, C. and Dourish, P. (2008). Accountabilities of presence: reframing location-based systems. *Proceedings CHI'08*. Florence, Italy: ACM Press.
22. Tsai, J.Y., Kelley, P., Drielsma, P., Cranor, L., Hong, J., Sadeh, N. (2009). Who's Viewed You: The Impact of Feedback in a Mobile Location Sharing System. *Proc. CHI'09*. Boston, MA: ACM Press.
23. Vasalou, A., Oostveen, A-M., and Joinson, A.N. (in review). Location sharing in the family. Paper currently under review.
24. Wagener, D., Lopez, M., Doria, A., Pavlyshak, I., Kostakos, V., Oakley, I., Spiliotopoulos, T. (2010). Hide and Seek: Location Sharing Practices with Social Media. *Proc. MobileHCI'10*. Lisboa, Portugal: ACM Press.

Opportunities Exist: Continuous Discovery of Places to Perform Activities

David Dearman[1], Timothy Sohn[2], Khai N. Truong[1]

[1]Department of Computer Science
University of Toronto
Toronto, ON M5S 3G4, Canada
{dearman, khai}@cs.toronto.edu

[2]Nokia Research Center
955 Page Mill Road
Palo Alto, California, 94304, USA
tim.sohn@nokia.com

ABSTRACT
A rich cognitive map of a space can enhance the individual's experience within the space. However, cognitive maps develop gradually through repeated experience; and because of this, on-demand mobile search services (*e.g.,* Google Maps, Yelp) are often used to compensate for missing knowledge. In this work, we developed and evaluated a context-aware place discovery application called Opportunities Exist to assist in the acquisition of spatial knowledge and meaning. The application differs from traditional search in that places are discovered using an activity (*e.g.,* drink coffee, sit in the sun) and the discovery process runs continuously, maintaining a history of places the user can perform her activities as she goes about her day. We conducted a 4-week deployment in two North American cities. The results show that users were able to discover new places to perform their activities in familiar spaces and learned to associate new activities with familiar places. In addition, participants leveraged the application to perform activities opportunistically, and used continuous place discovery as an opportunistic reminder of routines they wanted to break out of or resume.

Author Keywords
Activity, activities, Opportunities Exist, mobile, location-aware, continuous discovery, search

ACM Classification Keywords
H5.m. Information interfaces and presentation (e.g., HCI): Miscellaneous.

General Terms
Human Factors, Experimentation, Design

INTRODUCTION
An individual's cognitive map influences her ability to perform her daily activities [11]. The route she walks to work and the espresso bar she visits en route are activities influenced by spatial knowledge, and her ability to recall and sense meaning from the spaces. Spatial knowledge and meaning are not innate; they are gradually acquired with repeated experiences with a space [5, 16, 21]. Furthermore, the depth of meaning that an individual can sense from a space is influenced by the legibility or visibility of the space's meaning [18]. For example, a non-descript building does not visually convey the activities (or meaning) associated with the space, but the smell of baking bread wafting from an open window does suggest meaning for the place. Through personal experience—influenced by context—an individual can learn the activities she may perform in space, thereby assigning meaning to the space [1, 10, 14]. A community center is a place rich with many meanings; it can be a daycare in the day, a bingo hall at night and an electoral polling station every four years. The nature of an individual's experience with the community center is what defines its meaning [19], but dependent on the context in which it is experienced and the depth of its meaning may not be immediately obvious.

The acquisition of spatial knowledge and meaning (especially in new spaces) can enrich an individual's experiences in a space or place [9, 18]. However, a cognitive map develops gradually with repeated experience, meaning an individual will often have fragmented knowledge for the spaces she travels. Mobile information services (*e.g.,* Google Mobile, Yelp) are often used (on-demand) with varying degrees of success to compensate for this missing knowledge. Studies of mobile information needs [3, 7, 15, 22] show that individuals want greater access to location-information that is relevant to their activities and the spaces they frequently visit. Questions such as *"Where can I get mozzarella cheese closest to my route home?"* and *"What is something interesting to do around here?"* demonstrate the need for context-aware technologies that help with the acquisition of spatial knowledge and meaning in familiar spaces.

To assist in the acquisition of spatial knowledge and meaning, we developed Opportunities Exist, a context-aware place discovery application. Opportunities Exist differs from traditional on-demand search (*e.g.,* Google Maps) in that:

- Place discovery is achieved using specific activities (*i.e.,* ride bike) instead of generic keywords (*i.e.,* bike) that may associate alternate intentions to the object (*e.g.*, buy, repair, and tune). This method allows the user to find obvious and non-obvious places by conceptualizing what normally requires two steps (determine the types of places where an activity can be performed and then search to identify the existence/location of these places) as a simple expression of activity.

- The places discovered for an activity are relative to the user's current and future locations. The application maintains a list of activities and continues the discovery process as the user goes about her day—retaining a history of places that she can reflect upon.

We conducted a 4-week deployment of Opportunities Exist in two large North American cities. The results of the deployment show that:

- Continuous discovery of places to perform an activity helped participants acquire spatial knowledge and meaning for familiar spaces. Participants discovered new places in familiar spaces to perform their activities and learned to associate new activities with familiar places—activities they did not previous know could be performed at these places—exposing hidden meaning.
- Participants' use of the application led to changes in their spatial behaviour, enabling them to perform activities opportunistically. Continuous discovery of places to perform an activity provided opportunistic reminders and greater awareness of routines they wished to break or resume, and assisted in the decision making process.

Informed by the results, we discuss opportunities to support activities by highlighting places that have similar meaning, enabling the coordination and execution of activities within a family or social group, and allowing for opportunistic discovery of meaning without explicitly defining it.

RELATED WORK

A cognitive map is defined by Downs and Steas [11] as the process *"an individual acquires, codes, stores, recalls, and decodes information about the relative locations and attributes of phenomena in his everyday spatial environment."* The acquisition, organization and application of spatial knowledge and meaning (one's cognitive map) has a strong impact on an individual's ability to perform her daily activities—where an activity, in this paper, is an action that can be accomplished in a place (*e.g.*, drink a coffee, sit in the sun). A cognitive map is not innate; spatial knowledge and meaning is gradually acquired through repeated experiences [5, 6, 16, 21]. For example, an individual who recently moved to Manhattan will have greater difficulty navigating the city than a New Yorker who has lived in the city for 20 years. However, 20 years of residency does not mean the New Yorker knows everything there is to know about Manhattan.

An individual discovers the meaning of a space by experiencing the space. However, a space is never experienced in isolation; the experience is relative to the individual's surroundings, the events that lead to the experience, and previous experiences in the space [18]. In addition, the ability to discover meaning is influenced by its legibility and visibility [18]. For example, buying a hotdog from a street vendor when walking through a local park, or stopping to smell baking bread wafting from an open window are experiences (or activities) that an individual can use to assign meaning to a space. But, on a rainy day the hotdog vendor may not setup in the park or the building may close its windows to keep the wind out. An individual experiencing the park or walking by the building on the rainy day will undoubtedly associate different meaning with these spaces. The context in which an individual experiences a space will define the meaning she assigns to the place [1, 10, 14]. With respect to activities, they can be temporal, as in the example of the community center. Even though people following spatially and temporally reproducible patterns [12], repeated experiences with a space does not imply that an individual will know all the activities she can perform in the space, meaning is often hidden and may not be immediately obvious.

The greater an individual's spatial knowledge and meaning for a space, the richer her experiences will be in the space [9, 18]. If an individual knows that two espresso bars (kitty corner to one another) both make a good latte, but only one sells cupcakes, then the individual (assuming she likes cupcakes) can have a richer experience in the space. Unfortunately, an individual's cognitive map will always have gaps regardless of how often she frequents a space [11, 21]. Mobile information services (*e.g.*, Google Mobile, Yelp) compensate for missing location-based knowledge by allowing an individual to supplement her knowledge on-demand, but these services vary in terms of success. Location-based reminder systems [2, 13, 23] allow an individual to associate meaning or action with a location (*e.g.*, remember to buy postage stamps), but the reminder is only accessible in the location defined by the user. However, studies of mobile information need [7, 15, 22] and mobile search [3, 4] show that individuals want greater access to context-aware services on-the-go to support their activities and indirectly their cognitive map. In this work, we leverage activities (as opposed to traditional keyword search) as the search grammar to facilitate the discovery of places. Work by Dearman and Truong [8], and Shanahan *et al.* [20] have explored methods to identify the activities (*i.e.*, meaning) that can be performed in a place. In particular, we build upon the work of Dearman and Truong who use community authored content as a knowledge source for activities that can be performed in a place, for places on a city scale [8]. We believe that the use of community authored content can help discover non-obvious places where an activity can be performed, because the activity-place association is derived from the expression of personal experience.

OPPORTUNITIES EXIST APPLICATION

Opportunities Exist is a mobile application that is designed to assist the mobile user by gradually discovering places

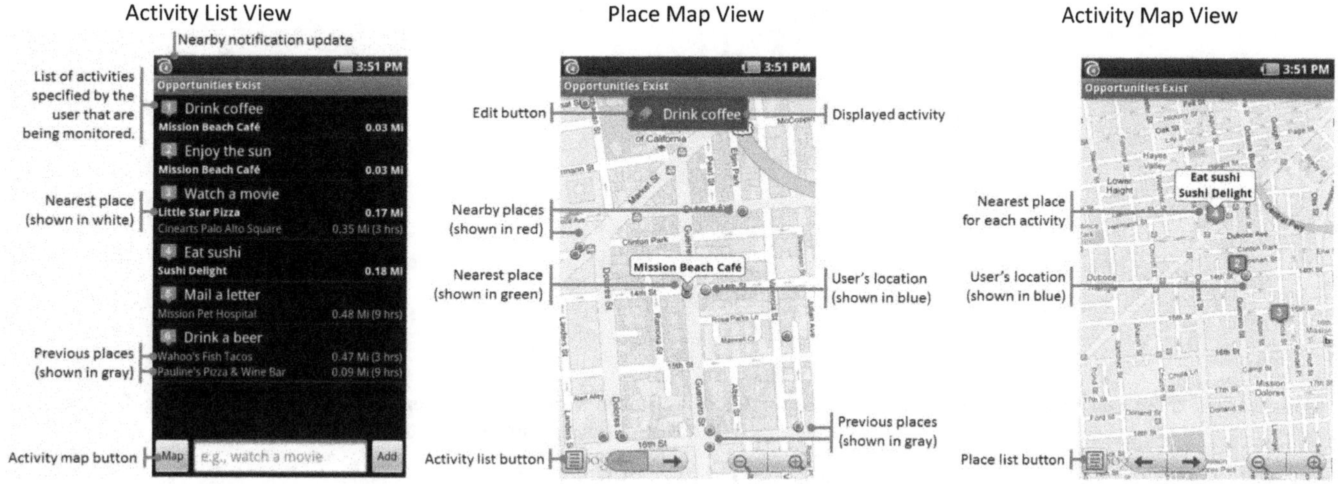

Figure 1. The interfaces for Opportunities Exist; excluding the place list view. The activity list shows all the activities entered into the application sorted by the nearest potential place; this is the default view. The place map shows the location of potential places to perform a specific activity. The activity map shows the location of the nearest potential place for all the activities.

where she can perform her activities, near her current location and all future locations she will visit. Unlike a traditional location-based search service (*e.g.*, Google Mobile, Yelp) that allows the user to conduct on demand searches with keywords, Opportunities Exist performs on demand and continuous discovery of places where the user can perform her activities. For example, if a user wants to acquire knowledge about *"places to ride a bike?"* or where there is *"something interesting to do around here?"* she can use the intended activities (*i.e.*, *ride bike*, *do something interesting*) not generic key phrases (*e.g.*, *bike*, *community center*, or *interesting places*).

High-Level Design

Opportunities Exist facilitates the acquisition of spatial knowledge and meaning over time in spaces where a mobile user travels. The application—which runs continuously on the user's mobile device—maintains a list of activities that are of interest to the user (Figure 1). The type of activities can include to-do items that the user wants to perform, casual activities the user may be interested in, or activities the user already performs but wants to learn more places to perform the activity. The intent is to help the user discover opportunistic places to perform her activities, with respect to her current location. The *activity list* view (Figure 1) presents the activity and place information in a glanceable list format. The short history of places helps the user identify the availability of places to perform the activity in previously traveled spaces.

As the user goes about her day, the application continuously searches for places (centered on her current location) where she can perform her list of activities. The application maintains a record of all the discovered places so the user can review the places (in the spaces she had been) at a later time. The search process is continuous, updating at set intervals, and requires no additional input from the user.

Implementation Details

An activity is articulated by a user as a grammatically natural verb-noun pair. For example, if the user is looking to discover places where she can drink a coffee, she could enter *drink a coffee*, *buy a coffee*, or *purchase a latte*. Similarly, if the user is interested in places where she can relax in the sun, she could enter *relax in the sun*, or *enjoy the sun*.

Opportunities Exist consists of a Web-service implemented as a Tomcat servlet (*OpportunityService*) and a native client (*OpportunityClient*) implemented as an Android mobile phone application. The *OpportunityClient* runs continuously while the mobile phone is on and starts automatically on boot-up. The user enters an activity string (*e.g.*, relax in the sun) into the *OpportunityClient* which is sent to the *OpportunityService* to be parsed[1] to identify the verb (*i.e.*, relax) and noun (*i.e.*, sun). The verb-noun pair is returned to the *OpportunityClient* and stored locally on the user's device.

The *OpportunityClient* uses the activity (as a verb-noun pair) and the user's current location to identify potential places to perform the activity by querying a location-based activity service (*ActivityService*) implemented by Dearman and Truong [8]. Dearman and Truong's evaluation of the *ActivityService* revealed a mean precision up to 79.3% and recall up to 55.9%; as a result, false positives do occur, and we do not attempt to identify and remove them. The query to the *ActivityService* is constrained to within 1 Km of the user's location, and limited to the 10 nearest places. The *OpportunityClient* continuously queries the *ActivityService* at an interval defined by the user—set to 5 minutes increments between 10 and 60 minutes. The *OpportunityClient* stores all the places returned by the *ActivityService* for 96 hours.

The interface for Opportunities Exist is comprised of four primary views (Figure 1): the *activity list* (the default view),

---

[1] http://nlp.standord.edu/software/tagger.html

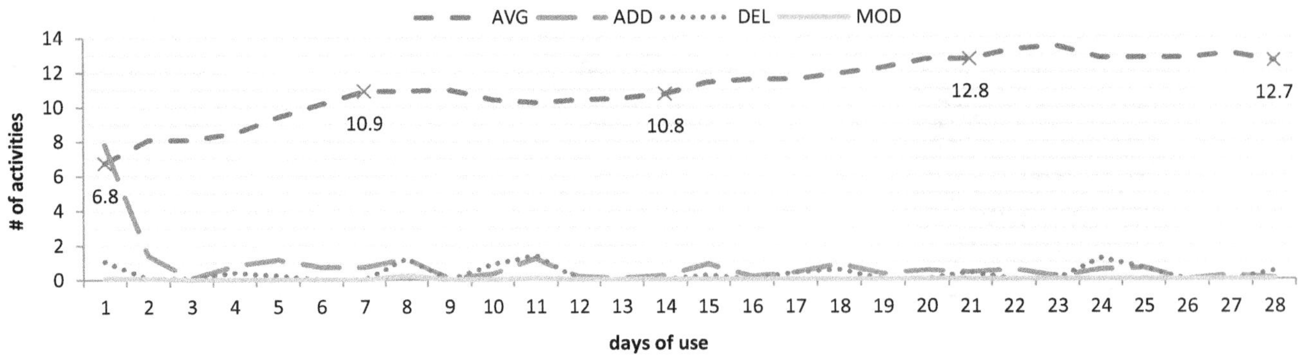

Figure 2. The average (AVG) number of activities a participant entered into their list over the course of the 28 days. In addition, the average number of activities added (ADD), deleted (DEL) and modified (MOD) on a given day.

the *activity map*, the *location map*, and the *location list*. The *activity list view* presents the user with a scrollable list of the activities she has entered into the application. The activities are ordered (top-down) by their relative distance from the user's current location to the closest potential place to perform the respective activity. In addition to the nearest potential place, a short list of up to two historic nearest potential places is also shown. The *activity map view* is a simplified map visualization of the *activity list view*—only the nearest potential place for an activity is shown on the map. Touching the activity/place marker enables a balloon popup that shows the activity and place name. Touching the balloon popup brings up a window that shows additional contextual information: address, telephone number, a link to the place's Yelp reviews, and an option to mark the activity is *wrong* for the place. The *location map view* displays all the places maintained by the application for an activity. This view is accessed by pressing an activity in the *activity list view*. The nearest (green), nearby (red) and history places (grey) are indicated with different colour markers (Figure 1). Touching a marker brings up a window containing additional contextual information for the place. In this view, we implemented functionality so the user can add a new place for the activity, which is then reflected in the *ActivityService*. The *location list view* is a textual listing of all the places for the respective activity. The places are ordered (top-down) by relative distance from the user's current location.

USER STUDY

We conducted a 4-week deployment of Opportunities Exist in two North American cities; San Francisco, California and Toronto, Ontario. We chose these cities because dense metropolitan areas are well supported by the *ActivityService*. The purpose of the deployment was to identify how the application could assist daily activities and evaluate if continuous place discovery could assist in the acquisition of special knowledge and meaning. We did not collect a baseline metric (*e.g.,* Google Maps mobile) with which to compare the application because 1) prior research has shown that implicit location-based search constitutes a small percentage (~15%) of mobile searches [4] and 2) the application's intent is to complement traditional on-demand search by satisfying a different need.

Participants

Twelve participants were recruited though a posting on Craigslist—1 female and 11 male. Three participants were recruited in Toronto and nine in San Francisco. Participation was open to anyone 18 years or older who lived in either city and owned an Android mobile phone with an active data plan. We attempted to maintain a balance in recruitment between the two cities; however, it was significantly more difficult to find Android users in Toronto.

The majority of participants were between 20 and 29 years of age: 18-19 (1), 20-29 (6), 30-39 (3), 40-49 (2). The types of Android mobile phones owned by the participants varied (*e.g.,* Nexus One, Motorola Droid, HTC Hero, G1). All participants were experienced and frequent users of mobile search services such as Google Mobile and Yelp.

Procedure

Each participant installed Opportunities Exist from the Android Market Place and used the application for 4 consecutive weeks. The application was installed during an initial interview that was conducted in-person with a member of the research team. During the initial interview, we introduced the application as a *tool that discovers where activities can be potentially performed* and provided a detailed walkthrough of its interface. We emphasized that the process of discovering places is achieved using activities structured as verb-noun pairs. At the end of the interview, we encouraged participants to add up to five activities to ensure they understood how to structure an activity as a verb-noun pair. Participants chose activities they frequently performed or wanted to know more about; we did not provide activities.

Every seven days, we conducted a 30-minute phone interview with each participant. The phone interview followed a semi-structured format exploring the participant's use of the application. The interviewer probed how the participant used the application and specific instances when it was useful and not useful.

Every three to four days (twice a week) we sent the participants a system generated online survey that listed all their activities with a matched place. We listed each activity at least twice; matched with one randomly chosen *closest place* and one randomly chosen *nearby place*. In the case that no places existed for an activity, the activity was not shown in the survey. In addition, the survey generator randomly selected a small number of activities and matched it with a random place that the application did not discover for that activity. For each match, we asked three questions: *Did the application discover this place for this activity?* (Yes, No, Maybe); *How confident are you this activity can be performed at this place?* (5 point Likert scale: 1—Not confident; 5—Confident); and, *Indicate your prior awareness for this place and activity* (chosen from a list of five possible responses and one *other* response).

At the end of the fourth week, we conducted an in–person exit interview. The exit interview followed a semi-structured format, probing the participant's reason to add each activity and the usefulness of the application for each activity. We compensated each participant $100 (CDN or USD depending on their locale) after the exit interview.

RESULTS AND OBSERVATIONS

All participants (12) completed the 4-week deployment. Participants entered 273 activities, 265 of which were correctly articulated as a verb-noun pair; the other eight entries were articulated as a keyword (*e.g.*, coffee, thrift store) and not as an activity, so no results were provided by the *ActivityService*. For the purpose of the analysis we will only discuss the 265 valid activities. The average number of activities entered by a participant was 22.1 (*SD*=10.1, *min*=9, *max*=38). At any given time the average number of activities in a participant's list was 11.1 (*SD*=3.8, *min*=0, *max*=21). The average number of activities in a participant's list grew from 6.8 on day 1 to 12.7 on day 28 (Figure 2). The majority of activities (201/265) were classified by participants as long term/recurring activities, such that there was no immediate need to perform the activity. Sixteen activities were classified as immediate and 48 were both immediate and long term/recurring. The average number of daily interactions with the application was 4.8 (*SD*=2.7, *min*=1.8, *max*=12.9).

The 20+ hours of participant interviews were fully transcribed and rigorously analyzed using open-coding by two coders. The points of discussion below are derived from the open-coding analysis and exemplar quotes are used to reinforce our findings. We do not differentiate between the Toronto and San Francisco participants in the analysis because the disparity in the recruitment for the locales resulted in negligible differences.

How Participants Structured Their Activities

The types of activities participants entered into the application were as unique as the participants. Activities include but are not limited to: *buy groceries*, *drink coffee*, *eat steak*, *recycle cans*, *buy used clothing*, *withdraw money*, *make a bonfire*, and *play pinball*. The 265 activities represent 209 unique verb-noun pairs, 35 of which were entered by one or more participant. The activities were more variable in the choice of noun (176 different) than verb (38 different). Although we argued that articulating an activity as a verb-noun pair is grammatically natural, participants struggled with the grammar and granularity they should use to define their activities, and in some cases showed influence of traditional search behavior.

Multiple Activities Can Express a Single Intent

Traditional on-demand search services (*e.g.*, Google Mobile, Yelp) typically involve multiple iterations of a query as the user refines their need [17]. With Opportunities Exist, the discovery process is both on-demand and continuous; meaning the process of refining an activity can be considerably longer. If no places were discovered or the places were wrong, participants were unsure if the activity they entered was *"working right"*, or if they just needed to give it time. To cope with the uncertainty, participants used three methods to achieve greater coverage for their activity:

- *Vary the verb* – change the verb to use a synonym or similar word, but keep the same noun (*e.g.*, T3 entered both *get iced tea* and *drink iced tea*).
- *Refine the noun's specificity* – enter multiple activities changing the specificity/granularity of the noun (*e.g.*, S5 entered both *eat vegan* and *eat tofu*).
- *Broaden the activity* – redefine the activity to be more generic (*e.g.*, to find an ATM, S1 entered both *withdraw money* and *deposit money*, later changing *withdraw money* to *visit a bank*).

These coping methods resulted in participants having at least two activities in their list at the same time for the same intent: the 265 activities represented 174 unique needs.

Defining an Activity as an Action or Place

Participants articulated the majority of activities (217/265; 81.9%) in terms of the *action* (*e.g.*, drink a beer) they were interested in, but some activities (48/265; 18.1%) were articulated in terms of a *place* (*e.g.*, find a bar) where they could perform the action. We envisioned that participants would define their activities in terms of the *action*, not the *place*. An activity that was defined as the *action* were rated as significantly more useful (*median*=4, *M*=3.57, *SD*=1.43) than an activity defined as the *place* (*median*=3, *M*=2.71, *SD*=1.62), $F(1,263)=13.63$, $p<0.001$.

Conditional Operators and Activities

Although Opportunities Exist is not a traditional search service, participants still wanted to apply traditional search operators to the activities. We instructed participants in the initial interview that conditional operators would not work, however three participants still tried: *buy records or music*; *eat a meal for under $4*; and, *eat dinner not Asian*.

Recognition of Place and Associated Activities

Analysis of the twice-weekly survey data shows that participants were able to correctly recognize and associate their activities with places the application discovered. They correctly recognized 70.2% of the *closest places*, 58.5% of the *nearby places*, and incorrectly recognized 36.3% of the *wrong places* we injected (Table 1). This result suggests that participants can recognize an activity with respect to a place (by name) and that recognition is higher for the *closest places* which were displayed beneath their respective activity on the

Group	Yes N (%)	No N (%)	Maybe N (%)	Total
Closest	610 (70.2)	111 (12.8)	148 (17.0)	869
Nearby	431 (58.5)	115 (15.6)	191 (25.9)	737
Wrong	57 (36.3)	56 (35.7)	44 (28.0)	157

Table 1. The relative percentage of closest, nearby and wrong activity-location pairs that were presented to participants in the twice-weekly survey that they indicated they were shown by the application (Yes), not shown by the application (No), or were not sure (Maybe).

default *activity list view*, rather than the *nearby places* which required the participant to navigate to the *location map view* or *location list view*.

Participants rated their confidence on the ability to perform the activity at the matched place greater for the correct places (the combined *closest* and *nearby places*: *median*=4, M=3.71, SD=1.54) than the *wrong places* (*median*=2, M=2.32, SD=1.53), $F(1,1092)$ = 43.30, $p<0.001$. The majority of places that participants recognized as discovered for an activity and they were confident (*somewhat confident* or *confident* combined) the activity could be performed at the place, were familiar and already known for the activity (Table 2: 349/650; 53.7%). However, many of the places were new (201/650; 30.9%) or the place was familiar but not already known for the activity (55/650; 8.5%). The twice-weekly survey responses show that participants were able to discover new places in the spaces they visited, and associate new activities with familiar places.

The Usefulness of Opportunities Exist

Participants found Opportunities Exist useful in a variety of ways. For each activity a participant entered, we asked the participant (in the exit interview) to rate the usefulness of the application for this activity (5-point Likert scale: 1-not useful; 5-useful). We did not define useful; the definition was left open to the participants' interpretation. The average usefulness of the application for an activity was 3.42 (SD=1.50) with a median usefulness of 4 (somewhat useful). All (12) of the participants found the application useful (Likert scale: 5) for three or more of their activities (Figure 3: M=7.42, SD=5.57, *max*=21) and somewhat useful (Likert scale: 4) for two or more of their activities (Figure 3: M=4.75, SD=2.93, *max*=12). In the weekly and

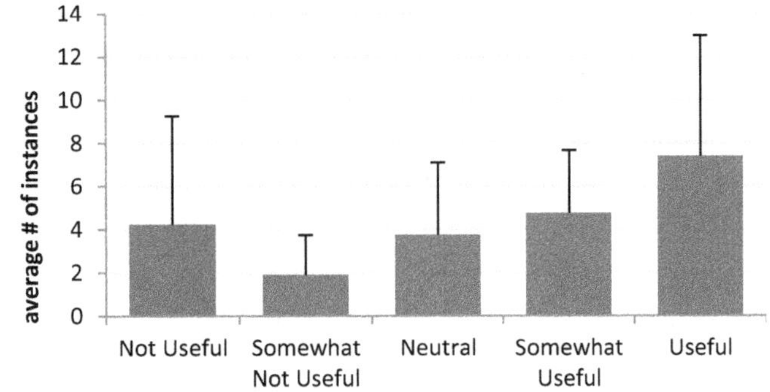

Figure 3. Average number of instance for each usefulness rating and the standard deviation.

Awareness Responses	*N (%)*
Already aware of the place and that the activity can be performed here	349 (53.7)
Not aware of the place and that the activity can be performed here	201 (30.9)
Already aware of the place, but not that the activity can be performed here	55 (08.6)
Forgot about the place, but was reminded	32 (4.9)
Forgot the activity can be performed here	10 (1.5)
Other – None of the above	3 (0.5)

Table 2. Responses from the twice-weekly survey for the participants' awareness of the location and activity. The data presented is only for places they successfully recognized and were confident the activity could be performed at the place.

exit interviews, participants disclosed a variety of ways they found the application useful. In the remainder of this section, we will discuss how the application was useful for spatial knowledge and spatial behaviour.

Knowledge: Discover New Places in Familiar Spaces

All (12) participants commented that the application was useful by helping them discover new places in familiar spaces; confirming the findings of the twice-weekly survey. The places the application discovered were always centered on the participants' location and therefore relative to the routes they travel. Participants S3 and S6 discussed that even near their home and work—both very familiar spaces—they discovered a new place to perform an activity and performed the activity at this place:

[S3—buy stamps] *"I did find some new places...one right next to me...Jenson's Mail. It is in an area where Safeway is which is where I do some of my shopping so it was like whoa, I didn't know I could go here...the other post office is like 4 miles away. I ran out so it was perfect timing."*

[S6—play soccer] *"It did help me find Columbus Park ...I've probably been to that soccer field like 5 times [since discovering it]...it is small enough that a lot of people don't go there but big enough that you can get a game going. The area is really familiar, it is right next to work, but I guess it was a street I've never been up. It is really easy to pass by."*

The experience of participants S3 and S6 highlight the discontinuity in spatial knowledge even in familiar spaces. Being familiar with a space does not mean an individual possesses full knowledge of the places within the space. The application was able to assist their spatial knowledge by discovering new places along a path less travelled.

Knowledge: Associate a New Activity with a Familiar Place

A minority of participants (4) commented on one or more experiences when the application helped them associate a new activity with a familiar place. Participant S3 discussed that for *play basketball* the application showed him a familiar local sports complex that he previously thought *"was only for soccer"*, but discovered that *"there is basketball there too."* Similarly, participant T3 who was interested in learning about new local music venues discussed that he is *"aware of the Gladstone Hotel, but not as a concert venue."* Even though S3 and T3 were familiar with both places, they had not previously associated the place with the respective activities. The application was able to assist them by revealing meanings that they were not aware of previously.

Knowledge: Discover New Places in Unfamiliar Spaces

Three participants commented on one or more experiences when the application helped them discover a new place in an unfamiliar space; a place they would not have discovered otherwise. Participant S9 who had just moved to the American city a week prior to starting the deployment epitomized this sentiment. S9 commented that the application *"pointed me to places I was not aware of, literally places that are across the street from me. Needing to do laundry and realizing there was a place across the street…it was very helpful."* Participant S6 who was house hunting in a new neighbourhood discussed an experience when the application discovered a place where he could take his three year old son to *have a bowl of soup*:

"Last weekend while we were out house hunting, Noah was complaining that he was hungry…so we just checked out the 'have a bowl of soup' [an activity already on his list] and sure enough there was a Boulangerie nearby. We just wandered over and Noah got his soup."

In these unfamiliar spaces, participant S9 and S6 possessed little spatial knowledge to inform their spatial decisions. The application was able to assist the participants by providing the spatial knowledge and meaning they could use to make a decision and perform their activity.

Knowledge: Random Place and Activity Discovery

The majority (8) of participants found the application not useful for one or more activities (Figure 3: M=4.25, SD=5.03, max=13) and somewhat not useful for one or more activity (Figure 3: M=1.92, SD=1.83, max=6). In both instances, no place was discovered or the places discovered were *"completely wrong."* However, four participants found a silver lining, identifying a place that was interesting albeit wrong for the activity:

"… with 'eat Mexican' it gave me a cheese steak shop. I researched it on Yelp and it had some good reviews and it was close to home. It is now on my radar."

Participant S3 did not find a place to *eat Mexican* using the application, but in sifting through the seemingly random places he was able to discover a new cheese steak shop. The application, although not useful for the intended activity, was able to assist the user find a place to perform an activity they had not thought to add to the application.

Behaviour: Break Out or Get back into a Routine

Two participants commented that the ability to discover places in their current space and the spaces they visit (without effort) helped them break out of a routine. Participant T3 was reminded that he can buy his fruits, vegetables and produce in Kensington Market—a small neighbourhood comprised of many small markets—rather than the large box store he currently frequents:

"It was actually useful for 'buy fresh fruit' and 'buy meat', two things that I always do…at Metro and I feel like I should try to branch out and find local little fruit stores or butchers. [It] reminded me that I can go to Kensington Market and do that, so I go to Kensington Market a lot more [now]…"

Similarly, two participants commented that the breadth of places (familiar and unfamiliar) they were able to discover through the application inspired then to get back into a routine. Participant S1 is an avid reader, but he indicated that this activity had fallen by the wayside recently:

"I'm a big person on reading. So I usually check out the library, but I don't go to the library as often as I used to in the past, and I would like to get back into that."

He entered *visit the library* as an activity, since he associates the library with reading books. The majority of places discovered for this activity were *"not new libraries"*, but given his reasoning the places do not need to be new, but rather reminders of reading. Participant T3 discussed that since he moved to Toronto (2 years prior) he has not been to many live concerts:

"I like live music and I don't see enough of it now…I know Toronto has a really good [music] scene…I'm hoping by suggesting places it'll encourage me to…do more of that."

In the exit interview, T3 discussed that although his intent was to go see more live concerts, he had yet to get back into the routine, *"[it] increased my awareness of concert venues in my city, and made me more aware of how few concerts I go to nowadays, which has in turn made me eager to get back into the habit of seeing live music more regularly."*

Whether the participant was looking to break out of a routine or get back into a routine, the abundance of places they were able to gradually discover with the application acted as opportunistic reminders of their desire. The continuous discovery of places ensured that the reminder was not a one-off, but rather repeated for the duration of the activity. In the case of participant T3, the application did not help him get back into a concert routine, but it did make him more aware of how important this routine is to him.

Behaviour: Assist in Choosing an Activity

One participant (S6) revealed that the application was not only useful for discovering places to perform his activities, but based on the relative distance of places (from his location) the application helped him choose what to have for lunch. S6 entered *eat pizza*, *eat sushi* and *eat tofu* into his activity list at the same time; three activities for food he enjoys eating. He would use the application at lunchtime to help him choose what he will eat for lunch that day:

"It was a good way for me to not have to come up with ideas for places to go or eat. I would take a look at it. It would say pizza or sushi or tofu and based on wherever it told me then that is what I'm going to eat that day."

Whichever activity had the closest place would be where he would eat lunch. This novel use of the application assisted S6 by using distance to make a decision for him.

Behaviour: Advocating for a Place of Activity

It was a common sentiment that adding a place for an activity required too much effort. Even still, four participants did add 25 new places into the *ActivityService* (*M*=2.1, *SD*=4.2, *min*=0, *max*=14) with participant S8 adding more than half (14/25; 56.0%). In the exit interview, he commented that his intent was to disseminate knowledge for a cause he supports—worker owned businesses:

"The point of this [activity] was…to add my own knowledge to the database. I've worked for worker owned business and I support them…it is something uncommon but for someone who is new in town then they might want to [know]."

S8 did not add *support worker owned businesses* to discover places, or add a single place he liked; he was advocating for a cause by adding a collection of places. The application supported his behaviour, and through his action he was able to associate new meaning with places that others who also support worker owned businesses may find useful.

Activity, Place and Expectations

When participants entered an activity it was often the case that they had a type or quality of place in mind where they would like to perform the activity. The majority (8) of participants commented that the places disclosed for one or more of their activities, albeit *"technically correct"* did not fit what they had envisioned. For example, participant T1 was looking to discover places to *play soccer* and one of the places he recalled the application discovered was a small inner city park called Trinity Bellwoods Park. He commented in the exit interview that *"… you can play soccer here, but it is not a soccer place. [I] was more thinking a pickup type place where you can join a game."*

Similarly, participant S1 sought to discover places where he could *withdraw money* and *deposit money*: He recalled an experience with a new place discovered by the application:

"I needed money one day…I was able to locate an ATM perfectly fine… it's not like [a] major bank's ATM, it's more one of those ATMs that are located within stores or supermarkets. I kind of wanted more of a bank institution versus…one of those stand-[alone] ATMs."

The application did help T1 and S1 discover new places to perform activities, but in both instances the place did not match their expectations. Participant S9 commented that for *buy a book* the majority of places the application discovered were libraries, *"while completely accurate… libraries [are]…not what I would consider a traditional place to buy a book…I think it leads people to think about [places and activities] they wouldn't normally think about."* It may be the case that he can buy a book at one of the libraries, but the fact that he was presented with libraries made him think more generically about places where he could get a book, not just *buy a book*. Similar to how the application helped some participants associate new activities with an already familiar place, the mismatch between expectations and discovered places can lead to a reevaluation the activity's intent and how it relates to different places.

A Place can Have Many Meanings

The application was not developed to accentuate the fact that a place can have multiple meanings. Three participants commented on the importance of being able to explore the intersection of activities and places. Participant S9 commented on how he entered *sit in the sun* and *sit in the park* in an attempt to see how the activities are related:

"I wanted to see how much they would overlap…'sit in the sun' turned up the car wash, 'sit in the park' did not. It did a great job in differentiating the intent of the activity. Being able to combine activities 'wash my car' and 'sit in the sun' and have it look at the intersection of those two and return that set of results, that would be supremely useful. Then I can choose the car wash not only on the location…but I can park my butt in the sun and bake while my car is baking."

Participant S9 had to enter both activities separately because the application does not handle conditional operators (*e.g.,* OR, AND). Similarly, participant S4 tried to apply the *OR* operation with *buy records or music*, highlighting the importance of this functionality.

Recalling Place Names

It was difficult for all 12 participants to recall the names of places discovered by the application. In the weekly and exit interview, participants commonly recalled a place in terms of its space (*e.g.*, a street name or neighbourhood): *"…there's one in Chinatown and there's another right outside Chinatown."* When we asked participant S5 to list places the application discovered for *get a coffee*, he commented that *"… if I go to Bell there are places I can get a coffee … in the area."* He added that he is able to recall the activity for the *"… area rather than specific spots in the area."* It was not that their spatial knowledge grew to include a specific place; rather they were able to associate new meaning with a space—a space that can serve as a cognitive anchor around which spatial knowledge will develop [6].

The Depth of Meaning for a Place

The majority of participants (11) did mark at least one place as wrong for the associated activity (*M*=16.3, *SD*=13.7, *min*=0, *max*=37). A total of 195 places were marked as wrong. Despite the ease with which a place could be indicated as wrong (in contrast to adding a place), participants were hesitant to mark a place as wrong unless they were completely sure the activity was wrong for the place. Unless the participant was intimately acquainted with a place, as discussed by S1, it was difficult to know the types of activities a place can support only by its name:

"I think San Francisco is well known for the mom and pop shops…and I have absolutely no idea what they are. I mean…in order to find out what XYZ shop is, I have to actually go in there. It's not like Wal-Mart [or] Walgreens where it's pretty obvious…"

Participant S13 commented that even after experiencing a space her understanding of the space may not include *"... other [activities] that another individual had experienced there"* and that some activities may not seem appropriate for a place, but it is *"possible they might have like a weekly or monthly meeting or something that I don't know about."* Participants were able to recognize that the activities that can be performed in a place are not restricted to only their experience and that activities are not always obvious.

Sharing Activities and Places

The primary usage of the application was personal, but in several instances it was advantageous for the participant to share a place with a partner or friend. Participant S13 shared the location of the Embarcadero YMCA with her partner so her partner could *go swimming*, but she also shared the location of a place to *buy Polaroid film*, so her partner could perform the activity for her:

"I know you will be rolling through this neighbourhood a little bit later. Here is this sort of place that it says I can...we can buy Polaroid film. It you get a minute, stop by and see if there is Polaroid film. I can't remember the name of the place in the Castro because, I, you know, rely on the application to keep this information for me. I texted her the address...I would know her route and I would say, hey it pointed me to this spot. I have to go this way, if you get a minute check this place out... We do [this] a lot...I hear of a place and I'm not near the neighbourhood so we would send each other to check it out."

Some activities do not need to be performed personally—the end result of the activity is more important than the experience. If an individual cannot perform an activity in their current space, it is possible that her social network (including weak ties) may be more opportunistically positioned to perform the activity for the individual. However, leveraging these people requires knowledge not only of their current location, but routes they frequently travel, and the ability to alert the person they can assist.

DISCUSSION AND OPPORTUNITIES

The results emphasize the utility of using activities and continuous search to assist in the acquisition of spatial knowledge and meaning. In this section, we distill the salient findings, and implicitly discuss research and design opportunities for technology that assists spatial behaviour.

Rethinking the Value of a Place

Participants were able to discover new places to perform their activities within familiar spaces and associate new activities with already familiar places. However, we observed that some places—albeit technically correct for the activity—did not match the participants' expectations. The mismatch between expectations and discovery meant that some places were not useful, but in some cases it led the participants *"to think about [places and activities] they wouldn't normally think about."* In the case of S9, he was looking for places to *buy a book* and the application discovered libraries. The libraries did not match his expectations, but made S9 think more generally about places where he could *get* a book, not just *buy* a book. Similar to how participants found new meaning in familiar places, places that are counter to expectations can lead people to reevaluate the intent of an activity and how a place relates to that intent.

Opportunistic Behaviour Needs Knowledge before Action

The continuous search functionality of the application and the persistence of discovered places ensured that participants did not have to actively search for places in every space they visited. Rather, they could quickly glance at their mobile phone to determine the opportunities their current space offers and prior opportunities in the spaces they had visited. Participants reported minimal behaviour change; however, the majority of activities reflected the participant's casual interest which did not necessarily need to be performed within the 4-weeks of the deployment. Participants commented that although they did not go to many of the places, the places are *"now on [their] radar"* for when it is convenient or the need arises. When participants did report behaviour changes, the changes were opportunistic. They leveraged the activities and the places discovered as opportunistic reminders of a routine they wished to break out of, a routine they wished to get back into, and as to assist in the decision making process.

The Meaning of a Place can be Ambiguous

Many of the places the *ActivityService* discovered for an activity were false positives. We did not attempt to identify and remove false positives because they will always occur on some level and we wanted to explore their influence. Participants did recognize the value of indicating a place as *wrong*, but they were cautious to do so because they were uncertain of a place's meaning. Inversely, if they were unsure if the activity was wrong, they would be equally uncertain the activity is correct. The meaning of a place is defined by the individual's experience with the place [1, 10, 14] and with activities that are conditional [19] the meaning of space may not be obvious; even when the individual is in the space. The inability to associate meaning with a place and trust in this meaning can have a negative impact on an individual's cognitive map: she could learn a wrong place believing it is correct, or dismiss a correct place believing it is wrong. However, ambiguous and erroneous places can be leveraged to suggest alternate activities an individual may find interesting and help her discover meaning in spaces she may not think to look, or look for.

Activities can be Related Spatially and Temporally

Participants often defined a single intent as multiple activities, primarily because they were unsure if the activity they entered was *"working right."* The problem with multiple entries is that it made the activity list longer and depending on the places discovered the activities were not always proximally close in the listing. The application needed to support this behaviour providing the ability to associate activities and highlight the similarity and differences between activities. Knowing how an activity, or multiple activities relate to one another can allow for better places to be chosen (*e.g.,* a place where the person can perform multiple activities) or places that are proximally close so multiple activities can be performed in sequence.

CONCLUSION

Spatial knowledge and meaning is not innate; it is gradually acquired with repeated experiences with a space [5, 16, 18, 21]. In this work, we presented Opportunities Exist, a context-aware place discovery application that differs from traditional on-demand search (*e.g.,* Google Maps) because place discovery is achieved using a simple expression of activity (*i.e.,* drink coffee, sit in the sun, smell baking bread). In addition, the application continues the discovery process as the user goes about her day—retaining a history of places that she can reflect upon. We conducted a 4-week deployment in two North American cities to evaluate Opportunities Exist. The results show that participants were able to discover new places in familiar spaces to perform their activities and learned to associate new activities with familiar places—activities they did not previous know could be performed at these places. Use of the application led to the opportunistic performance of activities, and continual place discovery was used to provide opportunistic reminders and awareness of routines the participants wished to break or resume, and to assist in their decision making process.

REFERENCES

1. Agre, P.E. Changing places: contexts of awareness in computing. *Human-Computer Interaction 16*, 2 (2001), 177-192.
2. Brown, P.J. The stick-e document: a framework for creating context-aware applications. *Electronic Publishing* 8, 2 & 3 (1996), 259-272.
3. Church, K., Neumann, J., Cherubini, M. and Oliver, N. The "map trap"?: an evaluation of map versus text-based interfaces for location-based mobile search services. In *Proc. WWW 2010*, ACM Press (2010), 261-270.
4. Church, K. and Smyth, B. Understanding the intent behind mobile information needs. In *Proc. IUI 2009*, ACM Press (2009), 247-256.
5. Cohen, S.L. and Cohen, R. The role of activity in spatial cognition. In *The development of spatial cognition,* R. Cohen, Eds. Lawrence Erlbaum Associates, Hillsdale, NJ, 1985, 199-224.
6. Couclelis, H., Golledge, R.G., Gale, N. and Tobler, W. Exploring the anchor-point hypothesis of spatial cognition. *Journal of Environmental Psychology 7*, 2 (1987), 99-122.
7. Dearman, D., Kellar, M. and Truong, K.N. An examination of daily information needs and sharing opportunities. In *Proc. CSCW 2008*, ACM Press (2008), 679-688.
8. Dearman, D. and Truong, K.N. Identifying the activities supported by locations using community-authored content. In *Proc. Ubicomp 2010*, ACM Press (2010), 23-32.
9. Dey, A. Understanding and using context. *Personal and Ubiquitous Computing 5*, 1 (2001), 4-7.
10. Dourish, P. Seeking a foundation for context-aware computing. *Human-Computer Interaction 16*, 2 (2001), 229-241.
11. Downs, R.M. and Stea, D. Cognitive maps and spatial behaviour: process and products. In *Image and environment: cognitive mapping and spatial behavior,* R.M. Downs and D. Stea, Eds. Aldine, Chicago, IL,, 1973, 8-26.
12. Gonzalez, M.C., Hidalgo, C.A. and Barabasi, A-L. Understanding individual human mobility patterns. *Nature 453* (5 June 2008), 779-782.
13. Griswold, W.G., Shanahan, P., Brown, S.W., Boyer, R., Ratto, M., Shapiro, R.B. and Truong, T.M. ActiveCampus: experiments in community-oriented ubiquitous computing. *Computer 37*, 10 (2004), 73-81.
14. Harrison, S. and Dourish, P. Re-place-ing space: the role of place and space in collaborative systems. In *Proc. CSCW 1996*, ACM Press (1996), 67-76.
15. Heimonen, T. Information needs and practices of active mobile internet users. In *Proc. Mobility 2009*, ACM Press (2009), 1-8.
16. Herman, J.F. Children's cognitive maps for large-scale spaces: effects on exploration, direction, and repeated experience. *Journal of Experimental Child Psychology 29*, 1 (1980), 126-143.
17. Kamvar, M., Kellar, M., Patel, R. and Xu, Y. Computers and iPhones and mobile phones, oh my!: a logs-based comparison of search users on different devices. In *Proc. of WWW 2009*, ACM Press (2009), 801-810.
18. Lynch, K. *The image of the city.* MIT Press, Cambridge, MA, 1960.
19. Nardi, B.A. Studying context: a comparison of activity theory, situated action models, and distributed cognition. In *Context and consciousness: activity theory and human-computer interaction.* MIT Press, Cambridge, MA, 1995, 69-102.
20. Shanahan, P. and Griswold, W.G. Inferring the everyday task capabilities of locations. In *Proc. of LoCa 2007*, Springer (2007), 157-174.
21. Siegel, A.W. and White, S.H. The development of spatial representations of large-scale environment. In *Advances in child development and behavior,* H.W. Resse, Eds. Academic Press, New York, NY, 1975, 9-55.
22. Sohn, T., Li, K.A., Griswold, W.G. and Holland, J. A diary study of mobile information needs. In *Proc. CHI 2008*, ACM Press (2008), 433-442.
23. Sohn, T., Li, K.A., Lee, G., Smith, I., Scott, J. and Griswold, W.G. Place-Its: a study of location-based reminders on mobile phones. In *Proc. Ubicomp 2005*, Springer (2005), 232-250.
24. Stevens, A. and Coupe, P. Distortion in judged spatial relations. *Cognitive Psychology 10*, 4 (1978), 422-437.

Location Visualization in Social Media Applications

Minna Pakanen[1], Jussi Huhtala[2], Jonna Häkkilä[2]

[1]Intel and Nokia Joint Innovation Center / CIE
P.O. Box 1001, 90014 University of Oulu, Finland
firstname.lastname@cie.fi

[2]Nokia Research Center
Yrttipellontie 10, 90230 Oulu, Finland
firstname.lastname@nokia.com

ABSTRACT
Location sharing applications are becoming increasingly popular in social media and for use on mobile devices, yet little research has focused on their user interface design. In this paper we describe our method of charting and creating comparable designs, and present a survey-based study of 106 social media users on their preferences regarding location indicators. Our paper contributes in proposing a methodology for visual element evaluation purposes, and reveals results, e.g., that users preferred simple indicators such as points or pins for their own location, and friend location indicators to include the corresponding name.

Author Keywords
Location sharing, social media, user interface design.

ACM Classification Keywords
H5.m. Information interfaces and presentation (e.g., HCI): Miscellaneous.

INTRODUCTION
Social networking sites have quickly become some of the most popular Web content for many users. For example, Facebook and Youtube are reported to have 550 million and 480 million active users, respectively (status in September 2010) [3]. Mobile phones are used to connect people. These devices are equipped with multimedia functionalities and an Internet connection, and it is evident that social media applications are increasingly being used within the mobile communication domain. Mobile phones can also easily feature positioning techniques, such as GPS. The popularity of social media applications featuring location sharing has also grown during the past few years. Today, users can share their own location and see other people's locations with applications such as Google Latitude.

Research on mobile applications using location information has existed for over a decade, and has focused primarily on tour and museum guides [9], reminders [5], advertisement [1] and navigation [7]. The emphasis of the research has been on technology and experimentation with a specific setup, and thus has typically been system- or application-specific. Methodologically, the role of graphical user interface (GUI) design has often been neglected or else has played a minor role in most research.

The limited research on mobile UI design for navigation applications suggests some UI design guidelines. In [7], May et al. reveal that mobile pedestrian way-finding applications should support navigation based on visible landmarks instead of relying only on distance information. Puikkonen et al. [8] examine indoor navigation applications and emphasize that special attention should be paid to consistency between the real world and map design, as indoor map design cannot rely on implicit descriptions of visual design elements as do outdoor maps (such as green for fields, gray for roads, etc.).

In this paper, we address the current practices and the challenges of location information visualization of people in mobile devices, concentrating especially on location sharing applications and social media. We investigated a large number of existing designs, recreate the most common types of indicators and evaluate them with a survey of real users of applications. Our research seeks to gain understanding of users' preferences and thus to offer insight to researchers as well as UI designers working on the area of mobile social media applications.

METHOD OF STUDY
We developed a method for designing visual elements. The methodology consists of three steps: background study, design phase and evaluation phase (Figure 1).

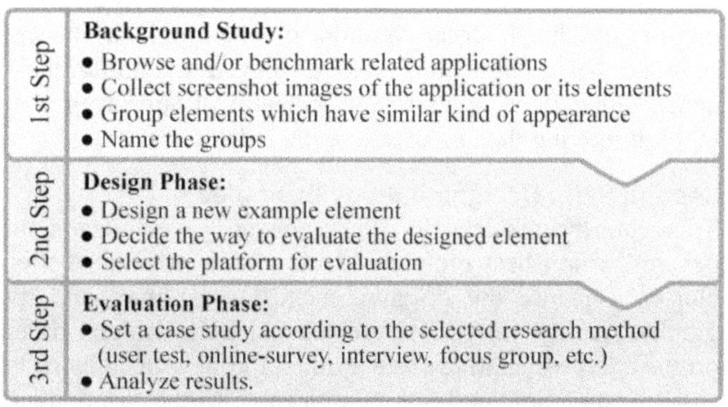

Figure 1. The steps of the method.

First Step: Studying Existing applications
We started benchmarking the designs by browsing through the most popular location sharing applications, complemented with examples made for research purposes. After

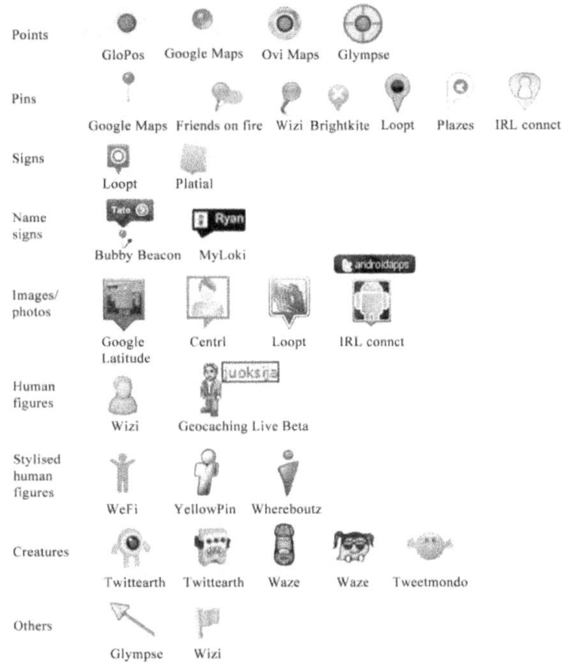

Figure 2. Original location indicators.[2]

the screenshots of applications were collected, we grouped them based on their design characteristics. Points, pins, signs, nametags, images/photos, human figures, stylized human figures, creatures and others emerged as the main clusters. Figure 2 illustrates an example of a cluster of designs categorized by their appearance [2].

Typically, the user's own location was marked differently than the locations of her friends. Some applications used entirely different indicator designs while some (e.g., Loopt, Geographica and Google Latitude) changed only the indicator's color [10]. In some applications, location indicators show the status of the user. For example, in IRL Connect indicators show both the user's social status and the social media being used. In many applications (e.g., Loopt) different icons were used depending on whether the mobile or the Internet version of the application was running. Many indicators also displayed the individual's name, either floating above the indicator or appearing after tapping/moving the cursor above the indicator.

Second Step: Designing Study Examples

To create the material for the user study, we selected the designs which best represented the characteristics of their cluster. Because the original images were small and the graphic quality varied, we created our own designs based on these representatives. We wanted the new designs to be easily comparable and less recognizable to the respondents to avoid preconceptions. A single designer redrew the designs in the same size and style and with more uniform colors. The aim was to create a neutral, consistent set of graphics which users had not seen before but also to retain the main concepts of each example. Because some of the original designs were originally intended for use on 3D maps instead of conventional maps, we decided to use a plain background for all the indicators in the study. With these principles in mind, we created two sets of location indicators. The first set of contains indicators that represent the user's own location (Figure 3), and the second set of indicators denote a friend's location (Figure 4).

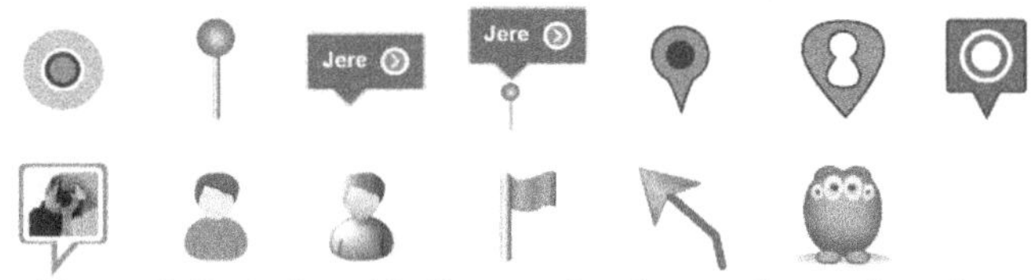

Figure 3. Redesigned indicators for the user's own location.

In the second set, two designs containing textual or pictorial content related to the friend's location were included (Figure 4).

Figure 4. Redesigned indicators for a friend's location.

Third Step: Evaluating Designs by Users

A user study was conducted via a Web survey that contained a total of 20 questions. Here, we concentrate on responses to questions related to previously-used applications and to users' opinions about our suggested designs (Figures 3 and 4).

The invitation e-mail was sent to the mailing lists of three Finnish universities; a total of 106 users of location sharing applications responded to the survey. Approximately half of the respondents were students in different fields of study. The respondents' ages varied from 20 to 59 years and 77% of them were male. Responses to background questions revealed that the participants had collectively used a total of 20 different location sharing applications and 7 navigation applications. The majority of respondents had experience using several different mobile social media applications, map applications and car navigators. Most of them (63%) had used Google's applications, and Latitude was the most commonly used (54%). The second most commonly used application provider was Nokia (17%); its Sports Tracker application was the second most popular overall (9%).

Our designs were introduced to the users, who were then asked to select three designs from those listed in Figure 3 which they preferred for representing their own location. The respondents also had to explain their choices. Participants were then asked to look at the designs indicating a friend's location (Figure 4) and to select the three that they would most like to see on their own mobile device.

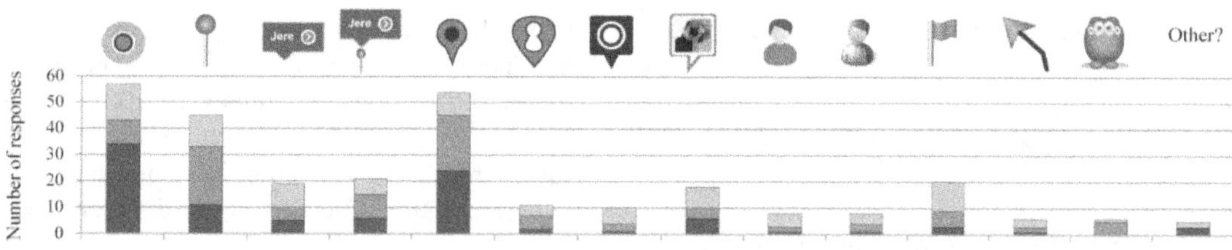

	A	B	C	D	E	F	G	H	I	J	K	L	M	N
The Best	34,7%	11,2%	5,1%	6,1%	24,5%	2%	1%	6,1%	1%	1%	3,1%	1%	0%	3%
2nd Best	9,4%	22,9%	5,2%	9,4%	21,9%	5,2%	3,1%	4,2%	2,1%	3,1%	6,3%	2,1%	5,2%	0%
3rd Best	14,9%	12,8%	9,6%	6,4%	9,6%	4,5%	6,4%	8,5%	5,3%	4,5%	11,7%	3,2%	1,1%	2,1%

Figure 5. Preference ranking of the own location indicator designs.

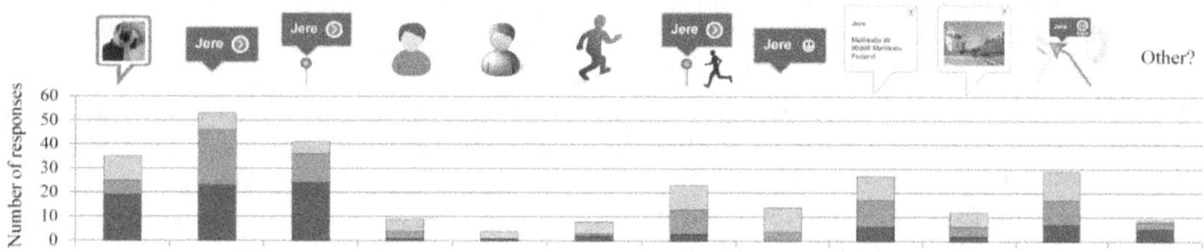

	O	P	Q	R	S	T	U	V	W	X	Y	Z
Most Important	20,4%	24,7%	25,8%	1,1%	1,1%	2,2%	3,2%	0%	6,4%	2,1%	7,5%	5,3%
2nd Important	6,9%	26,4%	13,8%	3,4%	0%	1,1%	11,5%	4,6%	12,6%	4,6%	11,5%	3,4%
3rd Important	11,9%	8,3%	6%	6%	3,6%	6%	11,9%	11,9%	11,9%	7,1%	14,3%	1,1%

Figure 6. Preference ranking of the friend location indicator designs

FINDINGS

The distribution of participants' preferred designs for the user's own indicator is presented in Figure 5. To weight the primary choices we analyzed the results using Borda count [6], which assigned a three-point value to the participant's the first choice, two points to the second choice, one point to the third, and zero to all other possible choices. The data of seven participants was removed because their answers were incomplete.

A non-parametric Kruskal-Wallis test [4] indicated significant differences between the sums of calculated points ($\chi2(13) = 279.9883$, $p < 0.001$). A simple red point (A) received the highest number of points in the Borda count (134); 35% of the respondents rated it the best alternative to represent the user's location. The second highest was a Google-type pin (E), which received 123 points and 25% of the first-place vote. Third was the simple pin (B) with 89 points and 11% of the votes. Separate pairwise comparisons between the three most popular designs (A, B and E) revealed that only the difference between A and B was statistically significant ($\chi2(1) = 6.3352$, $p < 0.05$). All three alternatives had similarly eye-catching colors that were easy to locate on a map.

The respondents had the following comments regarding alternative A: *"It is the most familiar from You-Are-Here maps"; "The indicator is either exactly on the location (A) or it shows clearly where the location is (E and C)".* Those who preferred alternative E liked it for its sharp tip, which pointed at the exact location, and because it was perceived to be more visible on a map due to its colors and round upper part. Alternative B was selected because it showed the exact location and did not block the view of the map.

There were also several comments relating to the mobility of the person and design of the indicator: *"The point [A] is easy to transform into a different symbol when the user is moving"; "If the user is moving, the point [A] should be animated to flash or pulsate".* In addition, criticism was presented: *"Pins show immobile location"* (B and E).

Not surprisingly, the user's own photo or name was not as important: *"I know who I am and where I am".* A name and a photo were perceived to indicate someone in the third person, and was not a natural way for users to refer to themselves.

The results for participants' favorite designs for a friend's location indicator are presented in Figure 6. This set of indicators also had significant differences between the design preferences ($\chi2(11) = 154.4215$, $p < 0.001$). The nametag with information button (P) received a total of 122 points and had 25% of the first-place votes. Second was the nametag with an information button and a pin underneath (Q), which received 101 points and 26% of the first-place vote. Third was the friend's photo (O) with 79 points and 20% of the votes. Pairwise comparisons did not reveal significant differences between these three designs.

The participants explained that the nametag (i.e., options P and Q) was the most important feature, especially if there was a possibility of finding more information about the user by tapping an information button. Respondents thought that a photo of the user would not work well without a name, because a photo was inevitably quite small and sometimes too unclear to be recognizable. One respondent wrote: *"A photo can be a lot of fun, but it requires a lot from the mobile device's screen to be able to recognize who is in it".*

DISCUSSION

Regardless of whether indicators were being used to mark the user's own location or a friend's, respondents wanted the location information to be precise. They preferred indicators that were informative, small and did not block the view of the map or other location indicators.

In many existing location sharing applications, locations are indicated by a photo or image of the person of interest (e.g., Google Latitude and Friend View Beta (discontinued)). In these applications, the friend's name typically pops up when the photo is tapped. However, in our survey we found that in social media applications, users did not wish to see their own image on a map but preferred a simple point or a pin. The point (Figure 5A) was chosen as the best option, in part because of its consistency with You-Are-Here Maps and because it clearly indicates the individual's precise location. Pin-like indicators show location clearly, but on the other hand, they were perceived to be too immobile for a moving user; this is an interesting finding relevant to mobile UI design.

Even if our preference ranking does not clearly indicate that a photo is not favored as a friend indicator, many comments suggested that a photo is often too small or too unclear to be recognizable. A nametag with an information button was popular with respondents because it provided essential information in a clear manner and allowed the user to easily obtain more information if desired. Our findings suggest that UI designs could use the friend's name to make the photo more understandable.

Whereas we believe that our results provide useful insight for researchers on the field, we also recognize limitations of the chosen method. In this study we aimed to reduce the bias caused by different visual factors by redrawing the icons. We still cannot assure that the quality of the resulted designs is absolutely constant, as the interpretation process as well as the artistic decisions during the design process may favor simpler designs. Moreover, using a white background differs from real use, where the indicators are typically placed on a map. Although this is a methodological limitation, the approach was nonetheless chosen to improve the comparability and consistency of the designs, as the background map styles also vary across applications.

We acknowledge that our evaluation of user design preferences was not conducted in a "real-life" application context, this limiting the validation of the results. However, the method was chosen based on our motivation to chart the design space and to reach larger number of participants than what would have been possible in a field study. To strengthen the validity of the results, the study was conducted using participants with experience using location based applications. The answers in the survey are based on perception of – not on interaction with – the indicators. In future research, it would be beneficial to see how users experience the indicators under different use situations.

CONCLUSION

In this paper we have addressed the current practices and the challenges of location information visualization in mobile devices, especially for location sharing applications and social media. We have described a method for comparing UI designs, and created location indicator designs based on those used in existing social media applications. These were assessed in an online survey of 106 social media users with earlier experience using location sharing services. Our findings indicate that designers of location sharing applications should favor precise, space-saving indicators such as points and pins, and should include name titles for friends.

REFERENCES

1. Aalto, L., Göthlin, N., Korhonen, J., Ojala, T. (2004). Bluetooth and WAP Push Based Location-Aware Mobile Advertising System. *Proc. MobiSys 2004,* 49–58.
2. Detailed information about the reference designs: www.casmteam.com/location_visualization
3. Google Ad Planner top 1000 sites (July 2010) www.google.com/adplanner/static/top1000/
4. Kruskal, W. H., Wallis, W. A. (1952). Use of ranks in one-criterion variance analysis. *Journal of the American Statistical Association 47* (260): 583–621
5. Ludford, P. J., Frankowski, D., Reily, K., Wilms, K., Terveen, L. (2006). Because I Carry My Cell Phone Anyway: Functional Location-Based Reminder Applications. *Proc. CHI 2006.* 889–898.
6. The mathematics of voting: Democratic symmetry. The Economist, page 83, Mar. 2000.
7. May, A., Ross, T., Bayer, S., and Tarkiainen, M. (2003). Pedestrian navigation aids: information requirements and design implications. *Personal Ubiquitous Comput. 7,* 6 (2003), 331–338.
8. Puikkonen, A., Sarjanoja, A.-H., Haveri, M., Huhtala, J., Häkkilä, J. (2009) Towards Designing Better Maps for Indoor Navigation – Experiences from a Case Study. *Proc. MUM 2009.* Article 16, 4 pages.
9. Raptis, D., Tselios, N., Avouris, N. (2005). Context-Based Design of Mobile Applications for Museums: A Survey of Existing Practices. *Proc. MobileHCI 2005.* 153–160.
10. Sagoo, K.P. and Rhee, Y. (2006). Real-Time Spatial Socializing through Mobile Device. *Proc. MobileHCI 2006.* 267–268.

When Are Users Comfortable Sharing Locations with Advertisers?

Patrick Gage Kelley, Michael Benisch, Lorrie Faith Cranor, Norman Sadeh
Carnegie Mellon University
[pkelley, mbensich, lorrie, sadeh]@cs.cmu.edu

ABSTRACT
As smartphones and other mobile computing devices have increased in ubiquity, advertisers have begun to realize a more effective way of targeting users and a promising area for revenue growth: location-based advertising. This trend brings to bear new questions about whether or not users will adopt products involving this potentially invasive form of advertising and what sorts of protections they should be given. Our real-world user study of 27 participants echoes earlier findings that users have significant privacy concerns regarding sharing their locations with advertisers. However, we examine these concerns in more detail and find that they are complex (e.g., relating not only to the quantity of ads, but the locations and times at which they are received). With advanced privacy settings, users stated they would feel more comfortable and *share more information* than with a simple opt-in/opt-out mechanism.

Author Keywords
location-based sharing, advertising, privacy, expressiveness

ACM Classification Keywords
H.5 Information interfaces and presentation (e.g., HCI):

General Terms
Experimentation, Human Factors

INTRODUCTION
In February 2010, the House of Representatives Subcommittee on Commerce, Trade, and Consumer Protection held a joint hearing on commercial location information. In chairman Bobby L. Rush's opening statement, he said:

> "To some extent, location-based services can be viewed as a sub-category of behavioral tracking in that they can quickly, and cheaply, tell advertisers more than contextual advertising ever could about someone's preferences, habits, and patterns." [10]

With intelligent mobile devices growing in popularity, it is possible for future ads to commonly be targeted based on one's location. Google's and Apple's recent purchases of AdMob and Quattro Wireless are examples of two major technology companies pushing into mobile and location-based advertising.

Additionally, as location-sharing continues to grow as a social phenomenon (e.g., the recent launch of Facebook's Places again moves this trend towards the mainstream), we are already beginning to see location-based coupons being offered to users. Foursquare, a popular mobile location-sharing application, is currently leading this push by allowing small businesses and national chains (e.g., Starbucks) to offer recurring, frequency-based, and loyalty-based coupons to over three million users [8]. Businesses that register with Foursquare are also given access to personally identifiable information about users that visit their locations, such as the names of the most recent and frequent visitors.

As this commercial landscape expands, we ask what types of privacy settings should be given to users to encourage broader adoption? While location-sharing with friends, family members, and members of social networks has been studied in great detail by researchers [1, 3, 7, 9, 11], the controlled sharing of location information with advertisers is largely unstudied.

In this paper, we present an empirical investigation of peoples' attitudes towards location-sharing with mobile advertisers. By analyzing three weeks of location audits combined with survey responses, we show that users' strong privacy concerns may hinder the adoption of systems leveraging this potentially invasive form of advertising. However, we also find that advanced privacy settings may help alleviate some of these concerns.

RELATED WORK
Many research groups have developed location-based services, including PARC's Active Badges [15], Barkhuus's Active-Campus [1], Intel's PlaceLab [5], Carnegie Mellon's Locaccino [11], and Burghardt's Mobile PET work [3]. While much of this work was hampered with adoption and technical issues in its infancy, more recent work has successfully investigated deployed systems where users' locations are queried in the real world. These systems, and their commercial counterparts, have almost always included some sort of privacy module, since even in early wireless advertising efforts it had been reported that participants had privacy concerns regarding location-based advertising [4]. Yet, while this module was always present in discussions [6], it has normally been regarded as a simple "opt-in" or "opt-out" mech-

CHI 2011, May 7–12, 2011, Vancouver, BC, Canada.

anism. Even in focused consumer inquiries, the discussion is largely centered on whether or not users would be willing to opt-in [13, 14].

More recently, some systems have begun to provide more privacy protective measures than simple opt-in mechanisms, including: per-person settings, granularity/resolution control, invisibility modes, and even time and location based rules. A survey of 89 commercial location-sharing applications showed that, in 2009, more than half had some form of privacy control, with varying levels of complexity [12]. However, in all of these commercial and research applications the privacy controls protect users from their friends, not the companies themselves or advertising partners. The bridge between applying advanced privacy mechanisms for location-sharing with friends, family members, and social networks has not been considered for location-sharing with advertisers. Our work unifies these two bodies of work, investigating when consumers and advertisers would benefit from these advanced privacy mechanisms.

METHODOLOGY

In November 2009, we conducted a study requiring users to carry a Nokia N95 smartphone equipped with our location-tracking software, and use it as their primary phone for three weeks. Once a day, users were required to visit our web application where they were asked whether or not they would have been comfortable sharing each location they visited with a number of pre-defined groups, one of which was advertisers. For a complete description of the methodology and technology used in executing this user study (including screen shots of the web application) please refer to our PUC publications [2].

Users were recruited with fliers and newsgroup postings within our university community. They were required to have an AT&T or T-Mobile phone contract, and an unlimited data plan (or the ability to obtain one). We compensated participants $30 for their participation and an additional $20-$30 to reimburse their data plan expenses. While we had 111 people fill out our pre-study survey, only 27 users completed the study (due to ineligibility and drop-outs).

Each time a user visited our web application, it iterated through his or her recent locations in order, and it displayed each location on a map. For each location it then asked, "Would you have been comfortable sharing your location **during this time span** with Advertisers?" (where "during this time span" was replaced with the actual time the user visited the location). Users could then respond "Yes, during this entire time," "No, not during any of this time," or "Yes, during part of this time…." Users completed these questions for each location at which they spent more than 15 minutes. If a user visited a location at two different times on the same day, it was audited separately for each visit.

RESULTS

Our results are broken into two sections: a summary of user-reported information from the pre- and post-study surveys, and a quantitative analysis of users' daily audits concerning sharing their locations with advertisers.

Survey Results

Our study included 27 participants (20 male, 7 female), all part of our university community (15 undergraduates, 10 graduate students, 2 staff members). While our users tended to be young (average age was 22.9), more tech-savvy, and most reported daily use of Facebook, we believe this community is representative of early adopters of the technologies that are likely to expose them to location-based advertising.

General Privacy Concerns

Our post-study survey sought to capture users' attitudes relating to two topics: general privacy concern and concerns related specifically to advertising. A summary of user responses related to general privacy concerns can be found in Figure 1. Overall, users report strong concerns across the six questions we asked. The strongest response was in regards to corporate information exchange, we stated: "Online companies should never share personal information with other companies unless it has been authorized by the individuals who provided the information," and 19 users responded with a 7 on a 7-point Likert scale, a strong agreement.

Privacy Concerns Regarding Advertisers

Our pre-study survey contained one question related specifically to advertisers, asking participants to "rate how comfortable you would be if **advertisers** (e.g., in order to send you promotions or coupons) could view your location," either always, at user-specified times, or user-specified locations. On a 7-point Likert scale, where 1 was labeled "Not comfortable" and 7 was "Fully comfortable," users reported an average of 2.6 for constant sharing, 3.6 at specified times, and 4.3 at specified locations. Both time and location specifications made users significantly more comfortable ($p < 0.01$ for both, paired t-tests, time: $t = 3.11$, $df = 24$; location: $t = 4.28$, $df = 24$) and location was significantly more comforting than time ($p < 0.01$, $t = 2.98$, $df = 24$).

Our post-study survey contained a few additional questions related to advertisers. The first asked "how bad" it would be if a user's location was disclosed to advertisers when they did not want it to be, and also the reverse (i.e., a non-disclosure when disclosure was wanted). On a 7-point Likert scale, where 1 was labeled "Not bad at all" and 7 was "Very, very bad," participants reported an average discom-

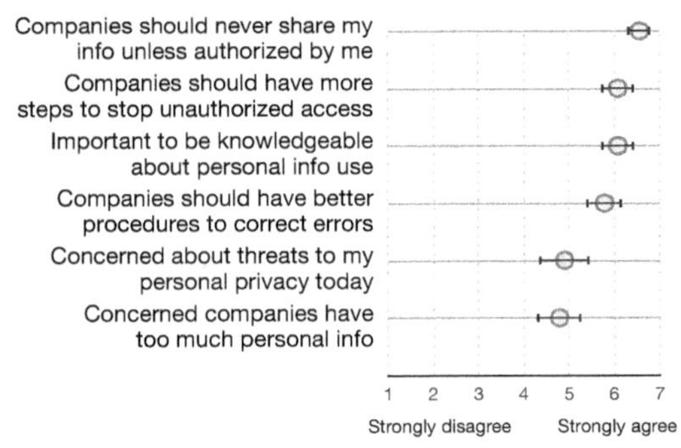

Figure 1. User responses about privacy concerns after the three week study. Answers were reported on a 7-point Likert scale, from 1 (Strongly disagree) to 7 (Strongly agree). Averages and 95% confidence intervals are shown.

fort level of 1.67 for mistakenly not-disclosing, and an average discomfort of 4.74 for mistakenly disclosing a location. These results suggest that, as expected, a missed opportunity is only a minor concern to our users, whereas disclosing a privacy-sensitive location to advertisers has a significantly higher cost.

We also asked users what the most important factors would be in allowing advertisers access to their locations. The results from this question, again on a 7-point Likert scale from "Not important" to "Very, very important," are displayed in Figure 2. From the reported responses, a user's location and the quantity of ads received mattered significantly more than the brand of the advertiser and time of day.

Quantitative Results Based On Location Audits

With over 7,500 hours of audited locations, we sought to quantify when users would be willing to share their real locations with advertisers, and how complex their preferences are regarding this sharing.

In general, users were significantly more willing to share their locations on weekdays from 9:00am–5:00pm (average of 47.5% time shared from 9:00am–5:00pm compared to 35.8% at other times). They were also significantly more willing to share their second and third most visited locations than their most visited location, which was likely their homes (average of 29% time at first most visited, compared to 55% and 41% at second and third most visited locations).

For the remainder of the analysis, we will compare the following six privacy-setting mechanisms based on the percentage of time our users would have shared under each:

- *Opt-in* – the most common privacy-setting. It simply allows a user to opt-in or opt-out of sharing with advertisers.
- *Time* – slightly more complex than Opt-in. A single rule specifies a time span during which a user is willing to share his or her location (e.g., between 8am-5pm).
- *Time with weekends (Time+)* – a modification of Time that allows specification of rules applying to weekdays only, weekends only, or both.

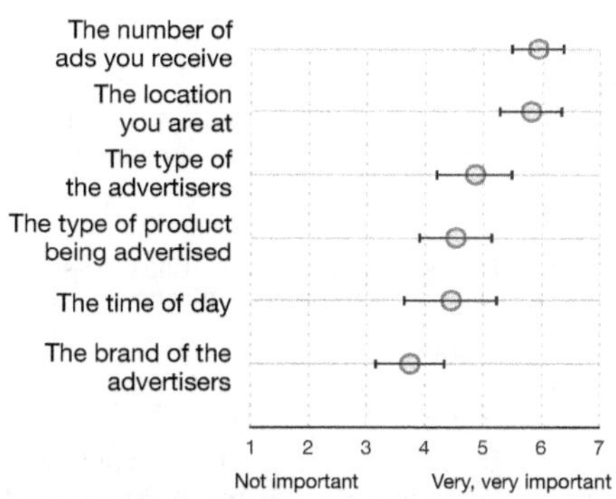

Figure 2. User responses on qualities of advertisers that would impact their future location-sharing decisions. Answers were reported on a 7-point Likert scale, from 1 (Not important) to 7 (Very, very important). Averages and 95% confidence intervals are shown.

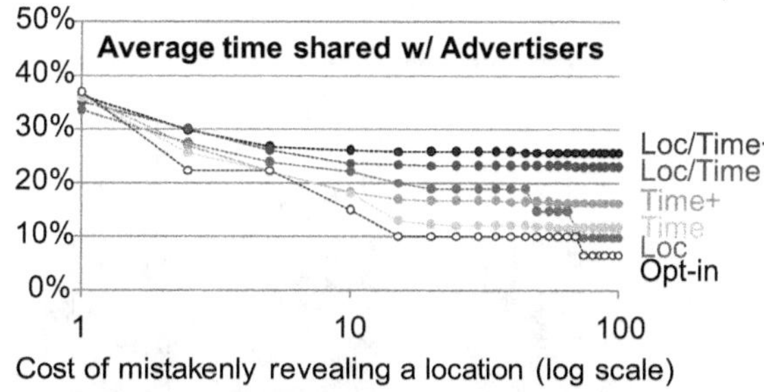

Figure 3. The relationship between percentage of time shared with advertisers under different privacy-setting mechanisms as the cost of mistakenly revealing a location increases.

- *Location (Loc)* – allows a user to give access to their location when they are in a pre-specified area. A single rule is defined by a latitude/longitude rectangle.
- *Location and time (Loc/Time)* – allows for rules that are combinations of Loc and Time rules (e.g., "grant access from 3pm-7pm when I am at location A or B.")
- *Location and time with weekends (Loc/Time+)* – modifies Loc/Time rules to apply to weekdays, weekends, or both.

Using the detailed privacy preferences we collected, we calculated the most accurate possible set of rules, or *policy*, for each subject, under each of the different privacy-setting mechanisms. In order to account for differences between subjects, we calculated the policies under varying assumptions about the cost associated with revealing a private location, which we denote as c, and the maximum number of rules users would be willing to specify.

The most accurate policy is the one that reveals as much time possible, while minimizing the amount of time mistakenly revealed. The relative weights assigned to time correctly revealed and mistakenly revealed are determined by c. A small value of c, such as $c = 1$, is equivalent to the assumption that our users would have been equally comfortable with a mistaken reveal as a correct reveal. A larger value of c, such as $c = 100$, is equivalent to the assumption that our users would always err on the safe side and protect private locations by restricting their policies to never reveal them.

We report the average time shared with advertisers for each of the privacy-setting mechanisms under different values of c in Figure 3. Here we see that as the cost of mistakenly revealing a location increases, the policies become more restrictive and the average time shared decreases. Yet, more complex privacy-setting mechanisms, such as Loc/Time+, resist this decrease, and allow policies that maximize the amount of time shared while preventing high-cost mistakes.

For even moderate values of c, such as $c \geq 15$, more complex mechanisms, such as Loc/Time+ and Loc/Time, result in nearly three times as much sharing as Opt-in, and this difference is statistically significant ($p < 0.05$ for Loc/Time+ and $p < 0.1$ for Loc/Time):[1] This substantial increase in

[1] All of the statistical tests in this section are two-sample independent t-tests with unequal variances.

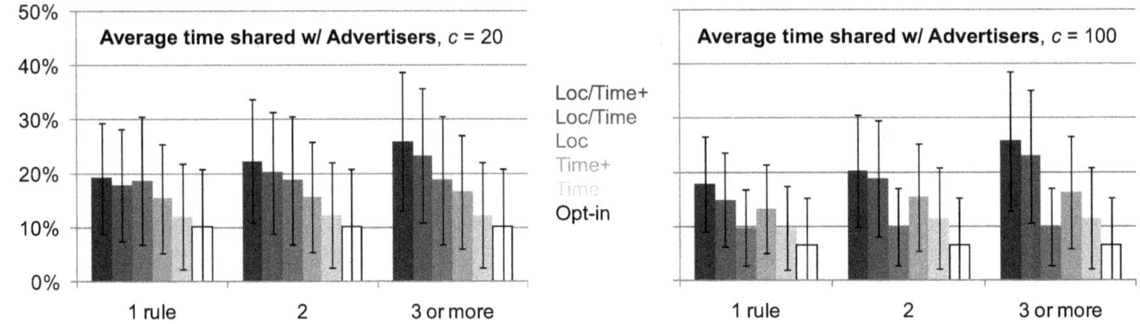

Figure 4. The percentage of time a user would share their location with advertisers under different privacy setting mechansisms, given a limited number of user-specified rules.

sharing with large values of c is particularly relevant, as our subjects reported being very concerned about sharing locations marked private with advertisers in our post-survey.

Additionally, we find that the increases in sharing from more complex setting types can be realized, even if users are only willing to make a small number of rules. As displayed in Figure 4, with $c = 20$, we see a substantial increase in the percentage of time a user would share his or her location under more complex mechanisms with only a single rule. With two rules the differences between the complex mechanisms, Loc/Time+ and Loc/Time, and Opt-in are statistically significant ($p < 0.05$) and marginally significant ($p < 0.1$), respectively. And, as the cost of mistakes increases, the increase in sharing under more complex mechanisms with small numbers of rules is even more dramatic. For example, when $c = 100$ we see an almost three times increase in sharing over Opt-in with a single Loc/Time+ rule, and this increase is statistically significant ($p < 0.05$).

CONCLUSION

Location-based advertising has the potential to fund the growth of future mobile computing systems. Our results suggest that users' strong privacy concerns may hinder this potentially invasive form of advertising, as early efforts reach the market. We also find that advanced privacy settings may help alleviate some of these concerns, making users more comfortable with location-based advertising.

We presented an empirical investigation showing that users' privacy preferences with regards to sharing locations with advertisers are complex. Our survey findings and analysis conducted on over 7,500 hours of location audits, allowed us to characterize these privacy preferences in detail. We find that if users are given only an opt-in/opt-out mechanism, a large percentage will not be able to specify their true privacy preferences, and may simply stop sharing entirely. These findings suggest that designing future systems with more complex privacy settings, that are also usable, will benefit all parties, increase sharing, and place more control in the hands of users.

ACKNOWLEDGMENTS

This work has been supported by NSF grants DGE-0903659, CNS-0627513, CNS-0905562, CNS-1012763 and a Siebel Scholarship. This research was also supported by CyLab at Carnegie Mellon under grants DAAD19- 02-1-0389 and W911NF-09-1-0273 from the Army Research Office. Additional support has been provided by Nokia, France Telecom, Google, and the CMU/Portugal ICTI. The authors would also like to thank the Locaccino team.

REFERENCES

1. L. Barkhuus and A. Dey. Location-based services for mobile telephony: A study of users' privacy concerns. In *INTERACT*, pages 702–712, 2003.
2. M. Benisch, P. Kelley, L. Cranor, and N. Sadeh. Capturing location-privacy preferences: Quantifying accuracy and user-burden tradeoffs. In *Journal of Personal and Ubiquitous Computing*, 2011.
3. T. Burghardt, E. Buchmann, J. Müller, and K. Böhm. Understanding user preferences and awareness: Privacy mechanisms in location-based services. In *OTM*, pages 304–321, 2009.
4. E. Gratton. M-commerce: The notion of consumer consent in receiving location-based advertising. *Canadian Journal of Law and Technology*, 1(2):59–77, 2002.
5. J. Hightower, A. LaMarca, and I. E. Smith. Practical lessons from place lab. *IEEE Pervasive Computing*, 5(3):32–39, 2006.
6. B. Kolmel and S. Alexakis. Location based advertising. In *Mobile Business*, 2002.
7. C. Mancini, K. Thomas, Y. Rogers, B. A. Price, L. Jedrzejczyk, A. K. Bandara, A. N. Joinson, and B. Nuseibeh. From spaces to places: emerging contexts in mobile privacy. In *Ubicomp*, pages 1–10. ACM, 2009.
8. C. C. Miller and J. Wortham. Technology aside, most people still decline to be located. `http://www.nytimes.com/2010/08/30/technology/30location.html`.
9. D. H. Nguyen, A. Kobsa, and G. R. Hayes. An empirical investigation of concerns of everyday tracking and recording technologies. In *UbiComp*, pages 182–191. ACM, 2008.
10. B. L. Rush. Statement by the Honorable Bobby L. Rush, chairman. `http://energycommerce.house.gov/Press_111/20100224/Rush.Statement.2.24.2010.pdf`.
11. N. Sadeh, J. Hong, L. Cranor, I. Fette, and P. Kelley. Understanding and capturing peoples privacy policies in a mobile social networking application. *Journal of Personal and Ubiquitous Computing*, 13(6):1–14, 2009.
12. J. Tsai, P. Kelley, L. Cranor, and N. Sadeh. Location-sharing technologies: Privacy risks and controls. In *TPRC*, 2009.
13. M. M. Tsang, S.-C. Ho, and T.-P. Liang. Consumer attitudes toward mobile advertising: An empirical study. *International Journal of Electronic Commerce*, 8(3):65–78, 2004.
14. R. Unni and R. Harmon. Perceived effectiveness of push vs. pull mobile location-based advertising. *Journal of Interactive Advertising*, 7(2), Spring 2007.
15. R. Want, V. Falcão, and J. Gibbons. The active badge location system. *ACM Transactions on Information Systems*, 10:91–102, 1992.

Typing on Flat Glass: Examining Ten-Finger Expert Typing Patterns on Touch Surfaces

Leah Findlater,[1] Jacob O. Wobbrock,[1] Daniel Wigdor[1,2]

[1] The Information School
University of Washington
{ leahkf, wobbrock }@uw.edu

[2] Microsoft Research
Redmond, WA
dwigdor@microsoft.com

ABSTRACT

Touch screen surfaces large enough for ten-finger input have become increasingly popular, yet typing on touch screens pales in comparison to physical keyboards. We examine typing patterns that emerge when expert users of physical keyboards touch-type on a flat surface. Our aim is to inform future designs of touch screen keyboards, with the ultimate goal of supporting touch-typing with limited tactile feedback. To study the issues inherent to flat-glass typing, we asked 20 expert typists to enter text under three conditions: (1) with no visual keyboard and no feedback on input errors, then (2) with and (3) without a visual keyboard, but with some feedback. We analyzed touch contact points and hand contours, looking at attributes such as natural finger positioning, the spread of hits among individual keys, and the pattern of non-finger touches. We also show that expert typists exhibit spatially consistent key press distributions within an individual, which provides evidence that eyes-free touch-typing may be possible on touch surfaces and points to the role of personalization in such a solution. We conclude with implications for design.

Author Keywords

Touch-typing, multi-touch input, tabletop computing.

ACM Classification Keywords

H.5.2. [Information interfaces and presentation]: User interfaces—input devices and strategies.

General Terms

Human factors, design, experimentation.

INTRODUCTION

Touch surfaces have become pervasive, most commonly in the form of mobile phones, and increasingly as larger tablets and interactive tabletops (e.g., Apple iPad and Microsoft Surface). Unlike their mobile phone counterparts, tablets and tabletops are large enough to accommodate ten-finger text input. Despite the importance of text entry on these devices, however, common methods for entering text pale in effectiveness compared to typing on a physical keyboard [2,12]. Indeed, text entry has been called out as a major deficiency of tabletops in multiple studies (e.g. [3,25]), potentially detracting from sustained use [22,32] and even leading users to alter their linguistic style [32]. Physical keyboards have been proposed as a solution for tabletop interaction [10], which, although useful, highlights the failings of current software-based methods.

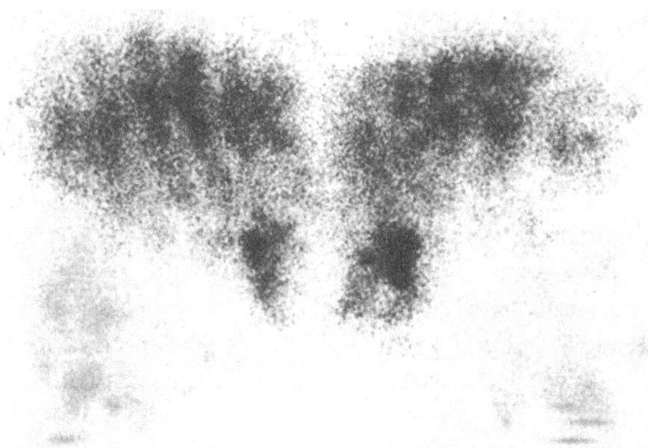

Figure 1. Finger (blue) and non-finger (yellow) touches in the unrestricted typing condition, showing space between hands, separate left and right space bar areas, and evidence of forearms and heels of the hands resting on the screen. (N = 20)

A major challenge of typing on flat surfaces is the lack of tactile feedback, not just in the physical perception of key depressions but also in the ability to feel the home row [2]. As a result, users must visually attend to the keyboard at all times. Inadvertent touches occur frequently on tabletops [25], which makes touch screen keyboards vulnerable to spurious input, especially from the user's arm or palm. However, touch screen keyboards also offer rich potential for customization and adaptation because they are software-based. Despite this potential, commercial implementations of ten-finger keyboards have largely mimicked the traditional QWERTY keyboard (e.g., Apple iPad, Microsoft Surface, Canesta keyboard [24]). Research approaches include adaptive keyboards [5,11] and wearable keyboards [6], but have not yet offered high performance text input.

In this paper, we examine typing patterns that emerge when expert users of physical keyboards touch-type on a flat surface (Figure 1). Our aim is to inform future designs of touch screen keyboards, with the ultimate goal of supporting touch-typing with limited tactile feedback. We employed a technique evocative of a *user-defined interface* (e.g., [33]): we asked 20 touch-typists to enter phrases using an interactive tabletop under three conditions: (1) with no visual keyboard and no feedback, then (2) with and (3) without a visual keyboard, and with some feedback. We were interested in questions such as: What will the distribution of key presses look like if users are given no visual constraints when typing? Will the centroids for each key follow the layout of a standard rectangular keyboard? Will certain keys have a larger spread of hits? By using vision algorithms to detect hand contours, can we identify differences among users in key-to-hand mappings?

Our findings have implications for the design of static and personalized touch screen keyboards. Based on finger touch data, we show that a curved keyboard with a gap between the hands is a more natural representation of actual typing patterns on flat surfaces than a standard rectangular keyboard. We also show that some keys are more difficult to hit consistently than others, suggesting those keys should be made larger (e.g., keys assigned to the little fingers). Typing patterns varied widely among users, but finger placement per key was highly reliable within an individual: with a simple classification approach using centroids of the key hit points, we classified key presses at 90% accuracy in a condition where there was *no visual keyboard*.

This paper contributes a formative study of unconstrained typing patterns on a flat surface, and an empirical basis for future development of ten-finger flat-surface keyboards. We also show that expert typists exhibit spatially consistent key press distributions within an individual, which provides evidence that eyes-free text input may be possible on touch surfaces and points to the role of personalization in such a solution. Finally, we also contribute design implications for both static and personalized touch screen keyboards.

RELATED WORK

Adding to the techniques mentioned in the Introduction, we discuss text entry for large multi-touch devices, virtual keyboard work in general, and physical keyboards.

Tabletops & Text Entry

In 2007, Hinrichs et al. [12] surveyed text entry techniques for tabletops, dividing the space into external methods (e.g., physical keyboards) and on-screen methods (e.g., virtual keyboards). Most of the on-screen methods were for small, mobile touch screens and none supported ten fingers. Hinrichs et al. [12] also offered evaluation criteria for tabletop text entry, such as the need for rotatability, on-screen mobility, and support for multi-person interaction. In an observational study of tabletop use, Ryall et al. [25] offered another general finding that has implications for typing: the difficulty of distinguishing between intentional and inadvertent touches of fingers, hands, and arms.

Complementing our work, recent research has focused on tactile feedback to support tabletop text entry. Weiss et al. [31] proposed a silicon keyboard overlay that could potentially support eyes-free typing; no evaluation has yet been reported. McAdam and Brewster [17] studied distal tactile feedback during text entry and found that feedback on the wrist or upper arm improved typing speed. None of the previous work has studied ten-finger typing patterns, at most reporting speed, error rates, and subjective feedback.

Virtual Keyboards

Virtual keyboards provide a temporary allocation of screen space for text entry. Solutions using a mouse, eye-trackers, or other assistive technologies have been studied for accessible text entry (e.g. [16,28]). For the broader community, studies have largely focused on stylus or direct-touch interfaces. Although findings described in this section are highly relevant to ten-finger typing, there will be differences in biomechanics and efficiency because most of these techniques support a single point of input.

Past research has examined key positioning and size. Sears et al. [27] found that smaller keys reduced text entry speed and increased errors. However, later work by MacKenzie and Zhang [21] found that, although a smaller keyboard increased errors compared to a larger one, there was no reduction in speed. This is in keeping with the application of Fitts' law to performance optimization of virtual keyboards [38].

Researchers have also explored relaxing the requirement to precisely hit each key. Kristensson and Zhai [14] proposed a method whereby the overall geometric shape formed by all of the hit points for a word is considered in linguistic matching. This approach was expanded on by Rashid and Smith [23] to enable typing without a priori determining the position of the keyboard, albeit with an extremely high error rate. Gunawardana et al. [9] proposed a method to expand or contract key areas for each press based on linguistic models, building on previous work by Goodman et al. [7] and Al Faraj et al. [1]. In similar work, Himberg et al. proposed adaptation through the movement of individual keys [11]. Alternatives to tapping a virtual QWERTY keyboard have also been proposed, including alternate key layouts [15,20,35,37], gestures [30], and methods that enable users to stroke between keys [13,36].

Physical Keyboards

The first practical typewriter was introduced in 1874 and touch-typing gained prominence a few decades later due to performance advantages and reduced fatigue over hunt-and-peck typing [4]. The development of touch-typing expertise requires extensive training [4], with skilled typists reaching speeds of 60 WPM or higher [8].

Previous work on common typing errors serves as the basis for some of our own analysis. Errors include misstrokes, which result from inaccurate finger movement, omissions, insertions, and interchanging of letters in the text [8]. Substitution errors, where one letter is substituted for another, occur most commonly in the same row or column, and can even be homologous (mirror-image position on the opposite hand) [8]. In a survey of typing studies, one relevant finding Salthouse [26] reports is that different fingers result in different error frequencies.

STUDY OF SKILLED TYPISTS

To observe unconstrained typing patterns on a flat surface, we asked skilled typists to enter text under three conditions:

1) no feedback and no keyboard (*unrestricted* typing),
2) asterisk feedback and no keyboard,
3) asterisk feedback and a visible keyboard.

The two conditions without a visible keyboard (1-2) captured natural typing patterns without the user adapting to a particular virtual form factor. In the *unrestricted* condition (1), participants were unaware of spurious and missing touches, which allowed for the most natural typing possible, mimicking an ideal touch-typing keyboard. In the *feedback* conditions (2-3), output was in the form of asterisks for each non-space touch. The asterisks allowed users to avoid spurious touches and ensure touches registered with the device without causing changes in pose and finger placement by showing which key they had hit. Feedback was also necessary to create a 1:1 mapping between touch events and letters in the presented phrase in the *asterisk feedback, no keyboard* condition (2), since there was no underlying model of key locations.

Participants

Twenty skilled touch-typists (8 female) ranging in age from 20 to 44 ($M = 29.3$) participated in our study. All participants regularly used a rectangular physical keyboard (not a split or "natural" keyboard). We evaluated typing expertise with a physical keyboard typing test at the start of each session using *TextTest*, a text entry evaluation tool [34]. Participants typed twenty phrases, randomly selected from the MacKenzie phrase set [19] (the same phrase set as used for the experimental tasks). Mean typing speed was 85.0 WPM ($SD = 19.4$) with a mean corrected error rate of 2.5% ($SD = 1.5$) and a mean uncorrected error rate of 0.1% ($SD = 0.2$). Only two participants had experience with an interactive table, but all participants had used a touch screen mobile phone. Participants were compensated $30.

Apparatus

Participants sat at a Microsoft Surface table, which ran the experiment software. The Surface API reported touch events, which served as the input signal. In addition, our software processed raw images provided by the Surface to extract additional information about the participant's hand placement. We computed the convex hull of each hand using custom vision algorithms and Emgu CV, an open source C# wrapper for the OpenCV library.[1]

Figure 2 shows a screenshot of the experiment software, with the presented phrase at the top of the screen, a rectangular text input area, and the "Next phrase" button, which allowed participants to advance through the task. The application was coded in C# .NET 3.5. The system recorded logging data with millisecond timestamps. For the physical typing test, an external 22" monitor (1680×1050 resolution) and rectangular keyboard were used.

[1] http://www.emgu.com and http://opencv.willowgarage.com

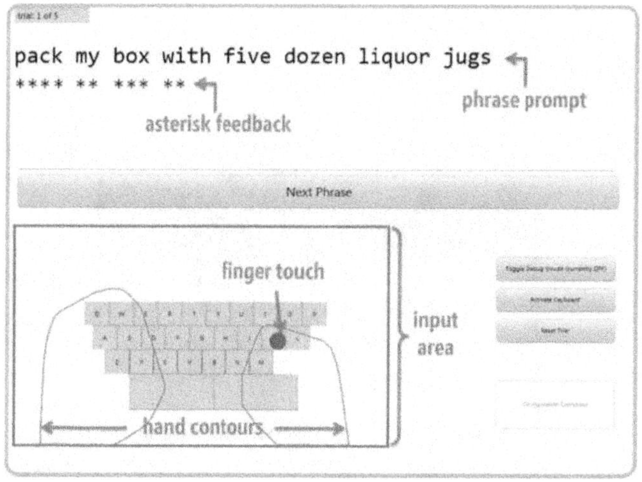

Figure 2. Task interface, showing the *asterisk feedback, visible keyboard* condition. Hand contours and finger touch point are for illustration only and were not displayed to users.

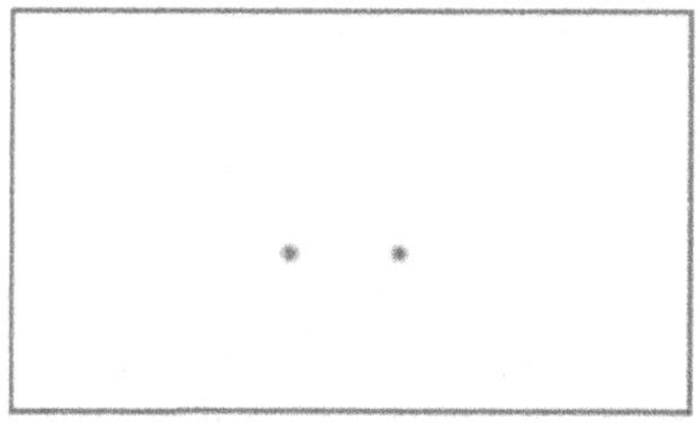

Figure 3. Input area at start of a trial in the *unrestricted* and *asterisk feedback, no keyboard* conditions. Red dots indicate where to place thumbs based on per-user configuration.

Typing Interfaces

A short *configuration step* was required at the start of each condition: participants placed their hands in a comfortable position within the input area (Figure 2) and the system recorded the (x,y) locations of the thumbs, and used them to place the keyboard. Participants could place their hands anywhere within the input area for this configuration step. The input area was inactive at the start of each trial.

Condition 1: Unrestricted (No Feedback, No Keyboard)

The goal of this condition was to observe how expert typists position their hands and fingers on the screen and type without the constraints of a visual keyboard layout or issues with touch-input recognition errors. We were interested in studying hand and finger placement, such as whether participants would rest their fingers on the home row during trials. Participants used the interface shown in Figure 2, except that the input area was *completely* blank and *no feedback* was provided on typing input (i.e., no asterisks). Participants were instructed to, "type comfortably and naturally, but also quickly and accurately, as you would normally do on a regular keyboard."

To maintain a degree of consistency across trials, two red dots appeared at the start of each trial, where the participant's thumbs had been during the configuration step (Figure 3). Participants placed their hands in the input area with their thumbs over the red dots and requested that the

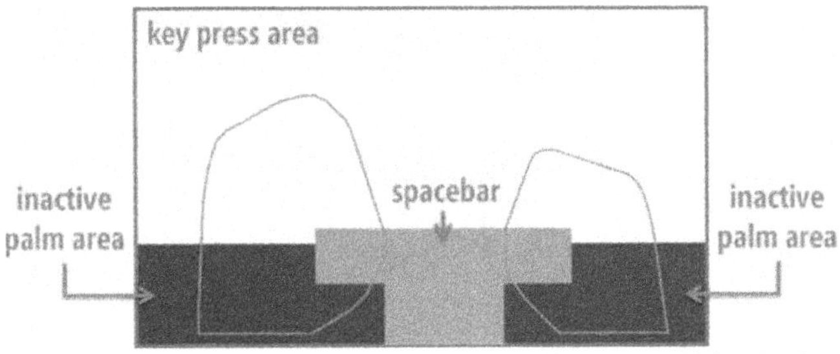

Figure 4. The *asterisk feedback, no keyboard* condition had inactive areas and a T-shaped spacebar that were not visible.

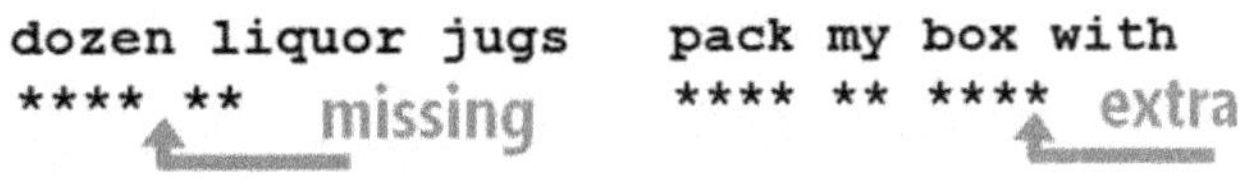

Figure 5. Sample *asterisk feedback*, showing input errors.

experimenter activate the keyboard. The experimenter did so by pressing a button on the right of the screen, causing the red dots to disappear and the input area to turn light blue. The participant entered the phrase by touch-typing on the flat-glass surface. No backspace was provided, but participants could request to restart the trial if they felt they had committed typing errors.

Conditions 2 & 3: Asterisk Feedback

The goal of the *asterisk feedback* conditions was to collect an input stream that could be reliably processed and mapped to user intention. Accurately labeled touch events were necessary to evaluate typing patterns in detail.

Condition 2: Asterisk feedback, no keyboard. Similar to the *unrestricted* condition, this condition presented only a blank input area to participants. Again, based on the location of the thumbs during the configuration step, two red dots appeared at the start of each trial to guide participants to consistent hand placement across trials (Figure 3); the dots disappeared after input area activation. Although only a blank input area was shown to users, unlike the *unrestricted* condition, an underlying keyboard model disambiguated spacebar presses, letter key presses, and all other touches. This allowed spacebar presses to be properly labeled as spaces and key presses as asterisks for the visual feedback. Figure 4 displays elements of the underlying input model that were *not* visible during the test: (1) a T-shaped spacebar area was placed based on the location of thumbs during the configuration step, such that the intersection of the T was at the midpoint between the thumbs, and (2) inactive areas on either side of the spacebar, to reduce spurious key presses from palms or forearms. The simple heuristic used to place the spacebar was enough that the hidden spacebar worked for most participants without having to reconfigure the location of the thumbs.

Condition 3: Asterisk feedback, visible keyboard. This condition presented a rectangular QWERTY keyboard (Figure 2). Key size and placement were based on the touch screen keyboard provided by the Microsoft Surface. Keys were 0.9" in width and height, slightly larger than a physical keyboard (0.75"). We confirmed the use of the larger size based on feedback during early pilots that 0.75" was too small. The space key was taller (by 1.5 times) than the other keys, as is common on physical keyboards. The keyboard was placed such that the center of the spacebar was positioned at the mid-point of the thumb location during initial configuration. This positioning was meant to place the keyboard most comfortably for each user.

Instructions in both *asterisk feedback* conditions were to type comfortably and naturally, but with an emphasis to place fingers accurately and to correct errors. As such, a backspace gesture was provided as a right-to-left swipe (> 0.5") anywhere on the right half of the keyboard, we used the gesture instead of a backspace key to avoid hand drift while correcting errors. Participants were instructed to ensure their asterisks and spaces lined up with characters in the presented text before advancing to the next trial (Figure 5). The ambiguity of the asterisks often made the precise location (i.e., character index) of an error difficult to identify, especially if participants typed quickly. Participants were asked to delete the *entire* word containing an extra or missing character if they were uncertain about the exact location of the error. This obviously affected text entry speeds but gave us the ability to infer users' intention, which is critical for the purposes of our study.

Rather than having the experimenter activate the keyboard as was done in the *unrestricted* condition, participants activated the keyboard themselves by briefly placing 10 fingers on the screen then removing them. This action allowed participants to situate their fingers on home row (whether or not a visible home row existed), and was meant to reduce inadvertent touches at the start of a trial. To provide feedback on the activation, the input area turned orange when all 10 fingers were detected, and blue once the fingers were lifted. Because the goals of the *asterisk feedback* conditions were not the same as for the *unrestricted* condition, the inconsistency in activation method did not affect the quality of collected data.

Experiment Design

We used a within-subjects, single-factor design (*typing interface*). The *unrestricted* condition was always presented first so that participants would not be biased by experience with input errors on the touch screen or by the layout of the visual keyboard. The *asterisk feedback* conditions were counterbalanced, with participants randomly assigned to orders. As such, we treat data from the *unrestricted* and *asterisk feedback* conditions separately.

Procedure

Study sessions were designed to last 1.5 hours. Participants completed a questionnaire to collect demographic information and experience with touch screens, followed by the physical keyboard typing test. Participants then completed 5 practice phrases and 40 test phrases with each of the three typing conditions. Opportunities to rest were provided midway through the test blocks. To cover all letters in the alphabet, half of the phrases in the test set consisted of two pangrams: *the quick brown fox jumped over the lazy dog* and *pack my box with five dozen liquor jugs*, while the remaining phrases were randomly selected from the MacKenzie phrase set [19]. The random phrases and pangrams were intermixed. For each condition, the thumb configuration step was done once for the practice phrases and redone before the test phrases to allow participants to adjust their hands if they wished. Finally, feedback questionnaires were administered.

Exploratory Questions

The three conditions were designed to answer different questions. We summarize the most salient here.

Unrestricted Typing

1. How fast can users type on a flat surface when they assume their input is accurate?
2. How many finger and non-finger touches occur and where do they occur?
3. How do the number of finger touches compare to the length of the presented text?

Asterisk Feedback, Visible Keyboard and No Keyboard

1. How fast will users type with a visible keyboard versus no keyboard? How many errors will they commit?
2. Is the emergent keyboard layout based on actual key presses different between the two conditions in terms of curvature and distance between hands?
3. Do some keys have greater *x*- or *y*-axis deviation than others? Are such findings systematic by row or column?
4. Do key-to-hand mappings follow the touch-typing standard (T, G, B to left hand and Y, H, N to right hand)?
5. Are key press locations for each key consistent? How reliably can we classify key presses based on the observed centroids of key presses?

Data and Analysis

Across all participants, we collected 50,289 labeled key presses from the *asterisk* tasks, and 27,830 unlabeled finger touches in the *unrestricted* condition. In addition, on every touch *down* event (as opposed to *moved* or *up* events), we processed the raw image and recorded the convex hull around each hand. Due to a technical problem, only the left hand convex hull was recorded for the first 8 participants—this was remedied for the remaining participants.

Although we asked participants to correct all errors in the *asterisk* conditions, the ambiguity of providing asterisks as output meant that uncertainty remained in the labeling. Expert typists recognize between 40-70% of their own typing errors by feel and without visual feedback [26], which means that errors likely remained in the data due to the ambiguous visual feedback we provided. Clear cases of mislabeled key presses can be identified: for example, typing E then M instead of the opposite. To account for these mislabelings, we removed outlying points for each key that were more than three standard deviations away from the mean in either the *x* or *y* direction (1.8% of instances).

We used repeated measures ANOVAs and paired two-tailed *t*-tests for our analyses. All *post hoc* pairwise comparisons following the ANOVAs were protected against Type I error using a Bonferroni adjustment. Reported fractional degrees of freedom (*dfs*) are from Greenhouse-Geisser adjustments. When parametric tests were not appropriate because the data violated the assumption of normality, we applied non-parametric equivalents, such as the Wilcoxon signed-rank test. We report significant findings at $p < .05$.

RESULTS

We examine the *unrestricted* typing condition before exploring the *asterisk feedback* conditions in more depth.

Unrestricted Typing: No Keyboard, No Feedback

Our goals were to learn how quickly users can type on a flat surface when they assume their input is accurate, and to observe the pattern of touches, especially those that were not the result of user-intended actions. The mean number of reset trials per user was 20.8% ($SD = 9.9$). Figure 1 shows finger and non-finger touch points for all participants.

Typing speed was 31% slower than the physical keyboard. We calculated WPM following MacKenzie [18]:

$$\text{WPM} = \frac{|T| - 1}{S} \times 60 \times \frac{1}{5}$$

where T is the final transcribed string and S is the elapsed time in seconds, in our case, from first to last finger touch in a trial. For reset trials, we discarded input from before the reset. This measure provides an indication of the speed that users could achieve on a flat surface under ideal conditions. Participants typed an average of 58.5 WPM ($SD = 18.0$), with a range of 31.3 to 92.7 WPM. Although mean WPM was 31% slower than the physical keyboard, it is still almost 25 WPM faster than the predicted expert typing speed of a stylus-based QWERTY keyboard [37].

Fingers often rested on the screen, especially at the start of a trial. At the start of each trial, participants placed their hands in preparation for typing, with most participants resting at least some fingers on the screen, as if on the home row (fingers down at start: $M = 5.08$, $SD = 2.94$, range: 0 to 10). We also compared the number of finger touches *after* the trial start to the length of the presented text. There were slightly more finger touches than expected (ratio of finger touches to length of the presented text: $M = 1.07$, $SD = 0.07$), indicating that participants sometimes rested their fingers on the screen or brushed them inadvertently against it. However, looking at occurrences where three or more fingers were down simultaneously, we found that only five participants exhibited this behavior more than once (for those five: $M = 0.45$ occurrences per trial, $SD = 0.48$). These results demonstrate the need to support fingers resting on the home row between text entry sequences, but not necessarily during a sequence.

Hand and arm position varied. Fewer than half the participants ($N = 7$) consistently rested their hands on the screen, while the remaining participants rested their forearms on the edge of the table and hovered their palms. These behaviors resulted in more than one non-finger touch per word (per trial: $M = 8.24$, $SD = 4.41$). As Figure 1 shows, however, finger and non-finger touches were highly segmented, suggesting that a simple approach of creating an inactive area under each palm should be highly effective at filtering non-finger touches (see Discussion for details).

Asterisk Feedback Conditions

From the *unrestricted* typing condition, we learned that users can type quickly on a flat surface if they assume their feedback is correct. With the *asterisk feedback* conditions we can conduct a more detailed analysis of typing patterns using the 1:1 correspondence between touch events and presented text. The *no keyboard* condition provides data to most directly support touch-typing (i.e., eyes-free) on a flat surface. We compare the *no keyboard* and *visible keyboard* conditions in terms of emergent keyboard shape, the spread of hits for individual keys, key-to-hand mappings, and how accurately finger touches can be classified as specific keys. Figure 6 shows key presses for all participants.

Mean trial time was 17.8 seconds ($SD = 5.0$) with the *visible keyboard* and 18.7 seconds ($SD = 5.4$) with *no keyboard*. Participants reset on average 8.1% of trials ($SD = 9.7$) with *no keyboard* and 4.7% of trials ($SD = 5.0$) with a *visible keyboard* (a Wilxocon signed-rank test was not significant: $z = 1.45$, $p = .147$). Analyses in this section are done on the text entered after a reset, if one occurred.

On average, 81.4% of key presses fell within the bounding box of their corresponding key for the *visible keyboard* condition ($SD = 12.4$). This number may seem low, but it is not surprising given that participants were provided only with asterisks and spaces as feedback. We revisit the reliability of key presses later, in the Classification section.

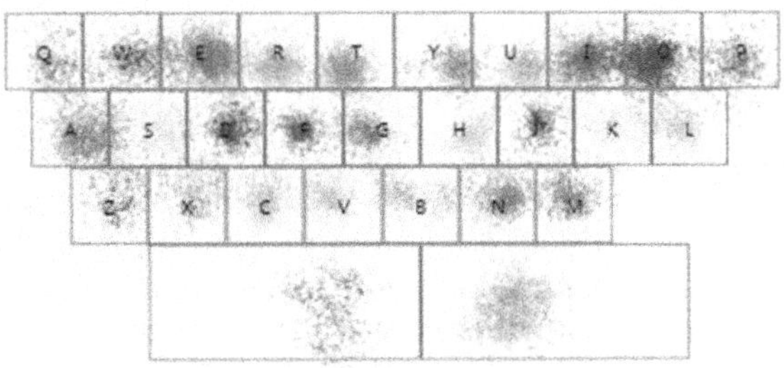

(a) *visible keyboard*

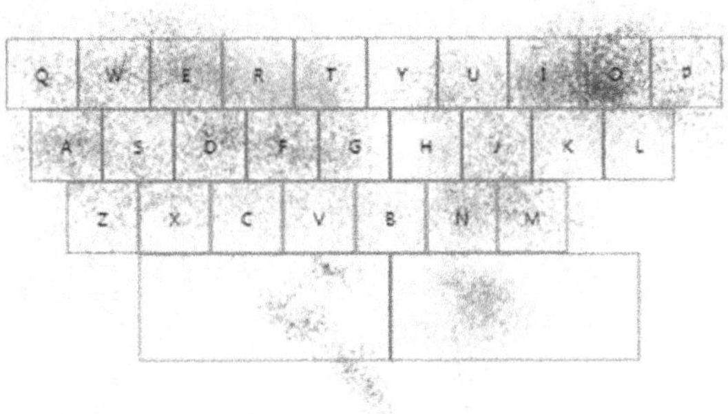

(b) *no keyboard* (overlay is for illustration only)

Figure 6. All key presses in *asterisk feedback* conditions, colored by key label. Each participant's data is translated to the same midpoint between F and J. The *visible keyboard* shows more consistency across users than *no keyboard*. ($N = 20$)

Typing Speed and Errors (Keystrokes Per Character)

Although the main goal of the *asterisk feedback* conditions was not to measure typing speed and errors, we analyze them for completeness. We calculated WPM as for the *unrestricted* condition, with elapsed time as the first to last key press per trial. The average WPM was similar across conditions: 27.5 ($SD = 7.8$) with the *visible keyboard* and 28.1 ($SD = 9.6$) with *no keyboard*. This difference was not statistically significant ($t_{19} = 0.43$, $p = .669$). That participants were slower in these trials than in the *unrestricted* typing condition is unsurprising, given the emphasis on accuracy and the presence of feedback.

To quantify errors, we calculated the keystrokes entered per character (KSPC) ratio [29]:

$$\text{KSPC} = \frac{|IS|}{|T|}$$

where IS is the input stream (including backspaces) and T is the transcribed string. Recall that participants had been asked to delete the entire word containing an error if there was uncertainty about where the error had occurred. As a result, KSPC was relatively high for both conditions: on average, 1.26 ($SD = 0.02$) for the *visible keyboard* and 1.29 ($SD = 0.03$) for *no keyboard*. Since we counted backspace gestures as key presses for this analysis, 13.0% and 14.5% of typed keys were corrected in the *visible keyboard* and *no keyboard* conditions, respectively. Overall, the similarity of the two conditions indicates participants were not significantly hindered by having no visual keyboard to reference.

Overall Keyboard Shape

We were interested in the overall keyboard shapes that would emerge when users were given a visual reference versus having no visual constraints (similar to touch-typing). For this analysis, we calculated key centroids for each participant. Since participants could place their hands anywhere in the input area to type, we normalized the centroids so that each participant's centroids were centered around the midpoint between their observed F and J key centroids (F and J often provide small raised bumps on a physical keyboard, and thus are used to place the hands). Centroids across all participants are shown in Figure 7.

Emergent keyboard shape is more arched in the 'no keyboard' condition than the 'visible keyboard' condition. We examined whether having no visual constraints would result in a more anatomical keyboard layout. Comparing the angles between each neighboring pair of keys in all rows

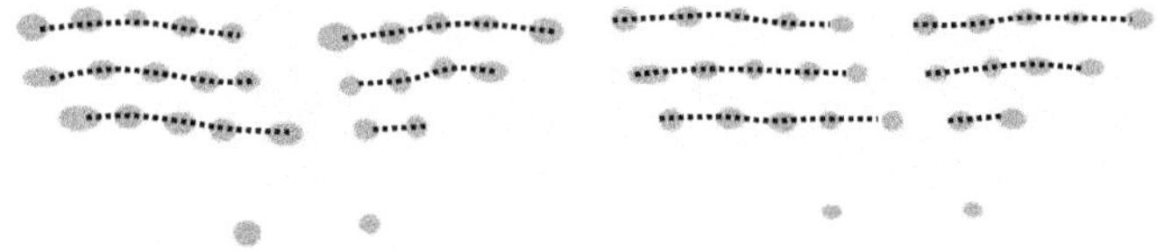

(a) *asterisk feedback, no keyboard* **(b) *asterisk feedback, visible keyboard***

Figure 7. Centroids of key hits with contour ellipses of two standard deviations in x and y directions. Bezier curves fitted to the centroids illustrate curvature. Each participant's data is translated to the same midpoint between F and J keys. ($N = 20$)

(except for the split between hands at T-Y, G-H, and B-N) provides an estimate of the deviation from a straight line for that row, where an angle of 0° would be perfectly horizontal. The mean absolute angle between each pair of keys in the *no keyboard* condition was 9.9° compared to the *visible keyboard* condition at 5.4° (significant difference: $t_{19} = 7.35$, $p < .001$). Thus, a curved keyboard design should best support touch-typing.

Distance between hands is greatest in the 'no keyboard' condition. We computed the average distance between the rightmost keys of the left hand and the leftmost keys of the right hand (between pairs T-Y, G-H, and B-N). On average, there was 1.12" of space between the hands in the *visible keyboard* condition ($SD = 0.19$") and 1.41" of space with *no keyboard* ($SD = 0.42$"), a difference that was significant ($t_{19} = 4.17$, $p = .001$). The mean distance in the *visible keyboard* condition is more than the 0.9" of space between visual key centers ($t_{19} = 5.30$, $p < .001$). This result shows that users are most comfortable typing with a gap between their hands. Even with a visible keyboard, the underlying key press model may need to take this gap into account.

Hit Point Deviations per Key

Where the keyboard shape analysis examined centroids of key hits, a more detailed examination of the spread of hits per key allows us to identify individual keys that may benefit from an increase in size. We first calculated the standard deviation of hits for each key per participant in *x*- and *y*-directions. We then grouped the 26 letter keys by finger and row, since previous research has shown these factors can affect error rates [4]. For example, the Q, A, Z, and P keys were grouped as *little* finger. For each of *x*- and *y*-direction standard deviation, we ran a repeated measures ANOVA with the following within-subjects factors: *typing input* (*no keyboard* vs. *visible keyboard*), *row* (bottom, middle, top), and *finger* (little, ring, middle, index).

Overall, hit point deviations were greatest in the 'no keyboard' condition. There was a main effect of *keyboard* for both *x*- and *y*-directions (*x*-direction: $F_{1,19} = 10.77$, $p = .004$; *y*-direction: $F_{1,19} = 39.28$, $p < .001$). These results reflect the pattern evident in Figure 6, that there was a smaller spread of hits for each key when participants were given visual constraints compared to when they were not.

The little finger resulted in the greatest horizontal spread of hits. There was a main effect of *finger* on *x*-direction deviation ($F_{1.6,31.1}=5.79$, $p = .011$). Pairwise comparisons showed the keys assigned to the little finger had significantly greater *x*-direction deviation than the ring ($p = .033$) and middle fingers ($p = .024$), while comparison to the index finger was only a trend ($p = .075$). No other significant main or interaction effects were found on *x*-direction deviation. This finding suggests that keys pressed with the little finger should be widest.

Bottom row keys, especially with 'no keyboard', resulted in the greatest vertical spread of hits. All main and interaction effects were significant for *y*-direction deviation, so we examine the highest-order effect in detail: a three-way interaction of *keyboard* × *finger* × *row* ($F_{2.8,34.3} = 5.70$, $p = .002$). Significant pairwise comparisons (at $p < .05$) showed differences were stronger with *no keyboard*: the bottom row resulted in greater *y*-direction deviation than the middle and top rows for the little and index fingers, and just the top row for the ring finger. With the *visible keyboard*, this pattern held, but was only significant with the index finger. These results suggest that making the keys in the bottom row taller may improve accuracy. For completeness, the other significant effects were: *finger* ($F_{3,57} = 17.88$, $p <$ .001), *row* ($F_{2,38} = 16.11$, $p < .001$), *keyboard* × *finger* ($F_{3,57} = 4.65$, $p = .006$), *keyboard* × *row* ($F_{1.3,23.7} = 5.59$, $p = .021$), and *finger* × *row* ($F_{1.3,3.7} = 6.96$, $p = < .001$).

Key-to-Hand Mappings

The keyboard shape analyses showed that participants were most comfortable with a gap between their hands. Although the most obvious split would be based on the standard key-to-hand mapping for touch-typing (i.e., left hand: T, G, B and keys to the left; right hand: Y, H, N and keys to the right), an analysis of actual key-to-hand mappings indicates that even skilled typists have idiosyncrasies in this respect.

Spacebar use is predominantly by only one thumb. Almost all participants used only one thumb for the spacebar (right: 14 participants; left: 4 participants), replicating previous results with a wearable keyboard [6]. There was no relationship between handedness and thumb choice.

Middle keys were often shared between hands. Based on the 12 participants for whom we logged complete hand contour data, we checked within which hand each key press occurred. Some participants used the opposite hand or alternated hands for the B, H, and Y keys (e.g., right hand for B key). Excluding potential noise from mislabeled data when there were few (< 5) key presses from a participant using the opposite hand, we saw the left hand accounted for 16.7% of Y presses (3 participants) and 5.2% of H presses (1 participant), while the right hand accounted for 11.4% of B presses (4 participants). In 0.15% of cases, the center of the touch point was offset such that it fell between the hand contours; half of such cases occurred with H.

Key Press Classification

The analyses presented above provide insight into how keyboard layout and key size may be improved to support touch-typing patterns on a flat surface. In this section, we assess the reliability of key hit locations to evaluate how accurate the modified designs could be. We perform simple distance-based classification of key presses, both within a participant, and between a participant and the group's average. Again, the *no keyboard* condition offers the closest representation to eyes-free touch-typing.

User-dependent key press classification is highest with the visible keyboard, yet still 90% with no keyboard. Using 10-fold cross-validation, we calculated the centroid of key presses for each training subset of the data, and classified the remaining key presses based on the closest centroid. Key strikes were relatively reliable for both keyboard conditions, although more so for the *visible keyboard*. Mean classification accuracy was 90.0% (*SD* = 5.4%) for *no keyboard* and 96.7% (*SD* = 3.7%) for the *visible keyboard*. The range was from 75.5% to 97.5% for *no keyboard* and 87.0% to 99.8% for the *visible keyboard*. On the whole, subjects were consistent within themselves, repeatedly hitting the same places for the same keys.

Classification accuracy per letter is shown in Figure 8. Keys in the bottom row were the most difficult to classify with *no keyboard*, which follows our earlier result that bottom row keys had the highest *y*-direction deviation. The U, I, J, and K keys were also relatively difficult to classify in both keyboard conditions. This finding requires more investigation, but may be related to hand displacement that could occur after a backspace gesture with the right hand.

Incorrect classifications most often occurred as adjacent keys in the same row. Based on the classification results, we created confusion matrices for each condition. Overall, most incorrect classifications were adjacent keys, vertically or horizontally, with most occurring in the same row (67.7% with the *visible keyboard* and 54.8% with *no keyboard*). Examining whether misclassifications occurred to the left, in the same column, or to the right, results were more evenly split: only 20.7% and 30.9% occurred in the same column for the *visible keyboard* and *no keyboard* conditions, respectively. With the *visible keyboard* condition, the most frequent misclassifications were J→K (4.0% of instances), L→K (3.4%), O→I (2.6%) and U→I (2.6%). The most frequent misclassifications in the *no keyboard* condition were B→V (7.6%) and V→B (7.5%). The predominance of same-row errors in the data, suggests that participants found it easier to reliably hit keys in the vertical direction than horizontally.

User-independent classification lowers accuracy by 19.5% in the 'no keyboard' condition. We calculated the average of key centroids for all users, translated so they were centered on the midpoint between the F and J keys. We then classified each user's input based on the average centroids. The classification accuracy dropped from the user-dependent analysis to, on average, 93.1% (*SD* = 8.1%) for the *visible keyboard* condition and 70.5% (*SD* = 15.2%) for the *no keyboard* condition. The large drop in accuracy from the user-dependent classification for the *no keyboard* condition indicates that some degree of personalization is necessary for eyes-free touch typing.

Summary of Major Results

In the *unrestricted* typing condition, users were able to achieve fast typing speeds (59 WPM) when they assumed their input was correct. Extra finger touches were largely constrained to between typing sequences, while non-finger touches were spatially segmented from the finger touches. With *asterisk feedback*, the keyboard shape in the *no keyboard* condition was more curved and had a greater gap

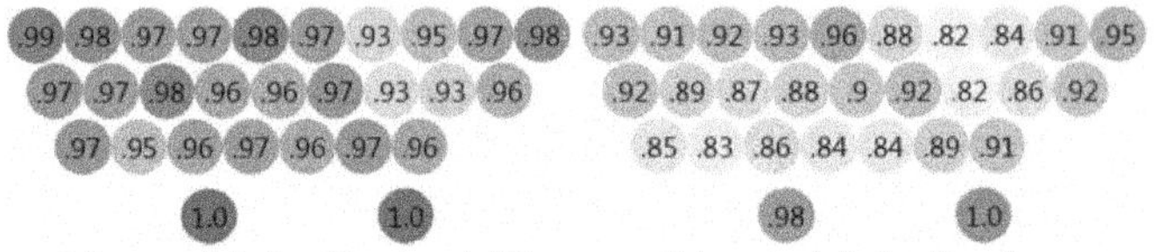

(a) *asterisk feedback, visible keyboard* **(b) *asterisk feedback, no keyboard***

Figure 8. User-dependent classification accuracy per key, showing difficulty with bottom row with *no keyboard*. (N = 20)

between hands than the *visible keyboard* condition. There was a larger spread of hits per key with *no keyboard* than the *visible keyboard*. However, key presses could still be classified with 90% accuracy in the *no keyboard* condition using a simple user-dependent classification method. Finally, some keys were pressed with both hands, and bottom-row keys and keys associated with the little fingers had the greatest hit point deviations.

DISCUSSION

Our goals were to identify typing patterns that could improve ten-finger, flat-surface keyboards, and to investigate the feasibility of touch-typing on flat surfaces.

Design Recommendations

Inactive palm area. To filter spurious hand and arm presses, three columns of space may be used, centered horizontally at the midpoint between thumbs and extending downward. The left and right columns are inactive, while the middle column may be used for input (including the spacebar). Using 4" columns, this simple heuristic would eliminate 95% of non-finger touches in the *asterisk feedback* conditions, and impact only 0.2% of finger touches.

Spacebar width. Spacebar hits in our visualizations suggest the spacebar should be narrower and taller than a traditional spacebar. Reducing the size of keys where possible has the potential to reduce spurious touch points. Thus, we recommend a spacebar extending from the middle of C to the middle of M for a keyboard of the size tested here.

Keyboard curvature. Rather than arranging each row of keys straight across, the *asterisk feedback, no keyboard* condition demonstrates that rows should be arched, more representative of relative finger lengths and reach.

Space between hands. Ten-finger keyboards should allow for a gap between hands. When no constraints were imposed on hand placement (*asterisk feedback, no keyboard*), the average distance between the centers of the rightmost keys on the left side of the keyboard and the leftmost keys on the right side of the keyboard was 1.41".

Relative key sizes. The keys assigned to the little finger and the bottom row keys had greater *x*- and *y*-direction deviation in key press locations, respectively, than other keys. These keys should be relatively larger.

Key-to-hand mappings. Keys in the middle of the keyboard, especially B, H, and Y, are sometimes typed with either hand. This finding is relevant to split keyboard designs, or designs that place keys relative to hand locations. Crossover was especially common with the B and Y keys, which could potentially be placed on both sides of a split keyboard.

In general, a more ergonomic layout should improve input accuracy over a rectangular one. In the *asterisk feedback, visible keyboard* condition, only 81.5% of key presses occurred within key bounds. However, key press classification based on the emergent key centroids for all users was almost 12% higher.

We did not explore different visual designs, but the visual affordances of the keyboard would affect typing patterns. Many of the recommendations listed here could be implemented with or without a visual affordance. For example, allowing for space between the hands could mean the underlying keyboard model adjusts key centers away from the middle of the keyboard, but it does not necessarily mean that a visual gap must appear. Future work should explore what the best visual affordance, if any, will be for each design recommendation, and how user behavior changes with respect to visual changes in the keyboard.

Towards Touch-Typing on Flat Surfaces

The goal of this study was not only to identify design recommendations for current whole-hand touch screen keyboards, but also to explore the feasibility of eyes-free touch-typing on a flat surface. In the *unrestricted* typing condition, where participants were not aware of input errors, mean typing speed was 59 WPM. This number is indicative of speeds that novice users could achieve with an ideal ten-finger touch screen keyboard, and performance should improve with use. The *unrestricted* condition was slower than the physical keyboard, which we speculate may be due to differences in the mechanics of the two setups (i.e., flat surface vs. raised keyboard) and to previous negative experiences with touch screens, which could have made some participants initially hesitant. Again, with more practice these effects should decrease.

Key press classifications from the *asterisk feedback, no keyboard* condition also point to the potential for touch-typing on a flat surface. With no visual constraints, classification accuracy with a simple user-dependent model was 90%. While 90% is hardly perfect, it could be improved through more sophisticated classification schemes. Language modeling would also improve performance further (e.g., [7,14,30]). Word-level correction approaches should be particularly effective here: such approaches require clean segmentation between words, and the spacebar was the easiest key to classify.

Personalization will most likely be a key element of any flat surface keyboard that allows for touch-typing. We observed many individual differences in terms of spacing between hands, size and shape of key press distributions, and key-to-hand mappings. Underscoring these findings, user-dependent key press classification was about 20% more accurate than user-independent classification for the *asterisk feedback, no keyboard* condition. This disparity suggests that if we want to allow users to type without frequently looking at the keyboard (as in that condition), the underlying model will need to adapt to each user.

Limitations

The conditions studied here provided either no feedback or masked feedback to users. While this decision was necessary to achieve our goals, providing users with unmasked text output would certainly impact behavior, allowing users to adapt their typing patterns to create more accurate output if necessary. We plan to explore methods to improve input accuracy, such as intelligently identifying spurious touch points or using a pressure sensitive surface. Further study is needed on how close experienced users will come to achieving the ideal speeds seen in the *unrestricted* condition. We predict that in real typing tasks users will achieve speeds somewhere between the *asterisk feedback* conditions and the *unrestricted* condition.

Our participants only included expert touch-typists, which is a critical user group to study if the goal is to design the most efficient text input methods possible. Although the *no keyboard* conditions are not directly applicable to novice typists, the resulting design recommendations may still improve performance for those users; for example, the observed differences in hit point deviations per key may be reflective of basic human motor performance. Future work will need to confirm the degree to which the *visible keyboard* findings also apply to novice typists.

Finally, we required users to place their hands consistently at the start of each trial to reduce noise from potential hand drift over the course of the study. Without this requirement, we would expect a decrease in the reliability of key press locations. Detecting the location of the user's hands and adjusting the keyboard if needed may be a useful approach for mitigating this issue. Language modeling could also be used to offset this projected decrease in accuracy.

CONCLUSION

We have investigated the unconstrained typing patterns of 20 expert typists on a flat surface. Our results demonstrate that typing patterns differ when users are provided with a visual keyboard compared to no visual affordance, yet key press locations remain relatively reliable within an individual. Design recommendations emerging from this study should improve the effectiveness of static touch screen keyboard designs. But our vision is to design keyboards that will allow users to touch-type on a flat surface. The results presented here should encourage researchers to pursue this goal, and indicate that an effective solution will require an element of personalization. Future work should apply the design recommendations here, and investigate the potential to which touch-typing on flat surfaces can be achieved.

ACKNOWLEDGMENTS

The authors thank Andrew D. Wilson and Jon Froehlich for their help and feedback. This work was supported in part by the National Science Foundation under grant IIS-0811063, NSERC, Microsoft Surface, and Intel Labs.

REFERENCES

1. Al Faraj, K., Mojahid, M., and Vigouroux, N. 2009. BigKey: A Virtual Keyboard for Mobile Devices. *Proc. HCII*, 3-10.
2. Barrett, J. 1994. Performance effects of reduced proprioceptive feedback on touch typists and casual users in a typing task. *Behaviour & Information Tech. 13 (6)*, 373-381.
3. Benko, H., Morris, M. R., Brush, A.J.B., Wilson, A.D. 2009. Insights on Interactive Tabletops: A Survey of Researchers and Developers. *Microsoft Research Technical Report MSR-TR-2009-22*. March, 2009.
4. Cooper. E. (ed.). 1983. *Cognitive Aspects of Skilled Typewriting*. Springer-Verlag, New York, NY.
5. Go, K., and Endo, Y. 2007. CATKey: customizable and adaptable touchscreen keyboard with bubble cursor-like visual feedback. *Proc. HCII*, 493-496.
6. Goldstein, M., Book, R., Alsiö, G., and Tessa, S. 1999. Non-keyboard QWERTY touch typing: a portable input interface for the mobile user. *Proc. CHI'99*, 32-39.
7. Goodman, J., Venolia, G., Steury, K., and Parker, C. 2002. Language modeling for soft keyboards. *Proc. AAAI'02*, 419-424.
8. Grudin, J.T. 1984. Error patterns in skilled and novice transcription typing. In *Cognitive Aspects of Skilled Typewriting*, W. E. Cooper (ed.). New York: Springer-Verlag, 121-143.
9. Gunawardana, A., Paek, T., and Meek, C. 2010. Usability guided key-target resizing for soft keyboards. *Proc. IUI '10*, 111-118.
10. Hartmann, B., Morris, M. R., Benko, H., and Wilson, A. D. 2009. Augmenting interactive tables with mice & keyboards. *Proc. UIST '09*, 149-152.
11. Himberg, J., Häkkilä, J., Kangas, P., and Mäntyjärvi, J. 2003. On-line personalization of a touch screen based keyboard. *Proc. IUI'03*, 77-84.
12. Hinrichs, U., Hancock, M., Collins, C., Carpendale, S. 2007. Examination of text-entry methods for tabletop displays. *Proc. Tabletop 2007*, 105-112.
13. Kristensson, P. and Zhai, S. 2004. SHARK^2: a large vocabulary shorthand writing system for pen-based computers. *Proc. UIST '04*, 43-52.
14. Kristensson, P. and Zhai, S. 2005. Relaxing stylus typing precision by geometric pattern matching. *Proc. IUI '05*, 151-158.
15. Langendorf, D.J.: Textware solution's Fitaly keyboard v1.0 easing the burden of keyboard input. *WinCELair Review*, February 1998.
16. Lankford, C. 2000. Effective eye-gaze input into Windows. *Proc. ETRA '00*, 23-27.
17. McAdam, C., Brewster, S. 2009. Distal tactile feedback for text entry on tabletop computers. *Proc. BCS-HCI'09*, 504-511.
18. MacKenzie, I.S. 2002. A note on calculating text entry speed. http://www.yorku.ca/mack/RN-TextEntrySpeed.html.
19. MacKenzie, I.S., Soukoreff, R. W. 2003. Phrase sets for evaluating text entry techniques. *Ext. Abstr. CHI '03*, 754-755.
20. MacKenzie, I.S., Zhang, S. X. 1999. The design and evaluation of a high-performance soft keyboard. *Proc. CHI '99*, 25-31.
21. MacKenzie, I.S., Zhang, S. X. 2001. An empirical investigation of the novice experience with soft keyboards. *Behaviour & Information Technology*, *20*, 411-418.
22. Morris, M.R., Lombardo, J., Wigdor, D. 2010. WeSearch: Supporting Collaborative Search and Sensemaking on a Tabletop Display. *Proc. CSCW 2010*, 401-410.
23. Rashid, D. R., Smith, N. A. 2008. Relative keyboard input system. *Proc. IUI'08*, 397-400.
24. Roeber, H., Bacus, J., Tomasi, C. 2003. Typing in thin air: the Canesta projection keyboard—a new method of interaction with electronic devices. *Proc. CHI '03*, 712-713.
25. Ryall, K., Forlines, C., Shen, C., Ringel Morris, M., Everitt, K. 2006. Experiences with and Observations of Direct-Touch Tabletops. *Proc. Tabletop 2006*, 89-96.
26. Salthouse, T.A. 1986. Perceptual, cognitive, and motoric aspects of transcription typing. *Psych. Bulletin 99(3)*, 303-319.
27. Sears, A., Revis, D., Swatski, J., Crittenden, R., Shneiderman, B. 1993. Investigating touchscreen typing: the effect of keyboard size on typing speed. *Behavour & Information Technology 12(1)*, 17-22.
28. Shein, F., Hamann, G., Brownlow, N., Treviranus, J., Milner, M. and Parnes, P. 1991. WiViK: A visual keyboard for Windows 3.0. *Proc. RESNA '91*, 160-162.
29. Soukoreff, R. W. and MacKenzie, I. S. 2001. Measuring errors in text entry tasks: an application of the Levenshtein string distance statistic. *Proc. CHI '01*, 319-320.
30. Tinwala, H., & MacKenzie, I. S. (in press). Eyes-free text entry with error correction on touchscreen mobile devices. *Proc. NordiCHI 2010* (to appear).
31. Weiss, M., Wagner, J., Jansen, Y., Jennings, R., Khoshabeh, R., Hollan, J. D., and Borchers, J. 2009. SLAP widgets: bridging the gap between virtual and physical controls on tabletops. *Proc. CHI '09*, 481-490
32. Wigdor, D., Penn, G., Ryall, K., Esenther, A., Shen, C. 2007. Living with a Tabletop: Analysis and Observations of Long Term Office Use of a Multi-Touch Table. *Proc. Tabletop 2007*, 60-67.
33. Wobbrock, J.O., Morris, M.R., Wilson, A.D. 2009. User-defined gestures for surface computing. *Proc. CHI '09*, 1083-1092.
34. Wobbrock, J.O. and Myers, B.A. 2006. Analyzing the input stream for character-level errors in unconstrained text entry evaluations. *ACM TOCHI 13(4)*, 458-489.
35. Zhai, S., M. Hunter, and B.A. Smith. 2000. The Metropolis Keyboard—an exploration of quantitative techniques for virtual keyboard design. *Proc. UIST 2000*, 119-218.
36. Zhai, S. and Kristensson, P. 2003. Shorthand writing on stylus keyboard. *Proc. CHI '03*, 97-104.
37. Zhai, S., Smith, B.A., Hunter, M. 2002. Performance Optimization of Virtual Keyboards. *Human-Computer Interaction 17(2&3)*, 229 - 269.
38. Zhai, S., Sue, A., Accot, J. 2002. Movement model, hits distribution and learning in virtual keyboarding. *Proc. CHI '02*, 17-24.

CHANTI: Predictive Text Entry Using Non-verbal Vocal Input

Adam J. Sporka
Department of Computer Graphics and Interaction
Faculty of Electrical Engineering
Czech Technical University in Prague
Prague, Czech Republic
sporkaa@fel.cvut.cz

Torsten Felzer
Institute for Mechatronic Systems
Technische Universität Darmstadt
Darmstadt, Germany
felzer@ims.tu-darmstadt.de

Sri H. Kurniawan
Department of Computer Engineering
University of California Santa Cruz
Santa Cruz, CA, U.S.A.
srikur@soe.ucsc.edu

Ondřej Poláček
Department of Computer Graphics and Interaction
Faculty of Electrical Engineering
Czech Technical University in Prague
Prague, Czech Republic
polacond@fel.cvut.cz

Paul Haiduk
Department of Psychology
Technische Universität Darmstadt
Darmstadt, Germany
haiduk@psychologie.tu-darmstadt.de

I. Scott MacKenzie
Department of Computer Science and Engineering
York University
Toronto, ON, Canada
mack@cse.yorku.ca

ABSTRACT

This paper introduces a text entry application for users with physical disabilities who cannot utilize a manual keyboard. The system allows the user to enter text hands-free, with the help of "Non-verbal Vocal Input" (e.g., humming or whistling). To keep the number of input sounds small, an ambiguous keyboard is used. As the user makes a sequence of sounds, each representing a subset of the alphabet, the program searches for matches in a dictionary. As a model for the system, the scanning-based application QANTI was redesigned and adapted to accept the alternative input signals. The usability of the software was investigated in an international longitudinal study done at locations in the Czech Republic, Germany, and the United States. Eight test users were recruited from the target community. The users differed in the level of speech impairment. Three users did not complete the study due to the severity of their impairment. By the end of the experiment, the users were able to enter text at rates between 10 and 15 characters per minute.

Author Keywords

Human-computer interaction, assistive technology, scanning, ambiguous keyboard, predictive text entry, non-verbal voice input, user study

ACM Classification Keywords

H.5.2 Information Interfaces and Presentation: User Interfaces—*Input devices and strategies (e.g., mouse, touchscreen)*

General Terms

Design, Experimentation, Human Factors, Measurement, Performance.

INTRODUCTION

Interacting with a computer often requires entering text in one form or another, especially when the computer is a communication aid; for example, in the context of Internet chat or email. The standard input device for text entry is the manual keyboard. It seems perfect for this task, since it can generate a large number of input signals – typically over 100 – accommodating all of the characters of the Latin alphabet, Arabic numerals, punctuation and special characters, as well as function keys and modifier keys – at the same time, on a single device. Some experienced typists are even able to enter text with a keyboard faster than they can utter text aloud. However, on second thought, it must be acknowledged that the manual keyboard is *not* perfect – if it were, it would be usable by everybody.

Unfortunately, persons with physical disabilities are often unable to operate a standard keyboard. Therefore, to fully utilize modern communication technology, alternative input methods are needed to enter text. Depending on the type and severity of the disability, the number of different input signals may be very limited. Sometimes everything has to be conveyed with a single touch of a button – the actuation of a single switch.

The alternatives in the minimalist case are based on *scanning* or *indirect* text input. Instead of directly entering a character, the user accepts "suggestions" highlighted by the software, which cyclically moves the highlight through a set of options – persisting on each for a *scan delay* τ (between 0.5 s and 2.0 s), before moving on [20, 2].

The shortcoming of scanning systems is that they are comparatively slow – hardly a true alternative. The scanning-based solution QANTI [6] – the predecessor of our current approach, described below – is a step in the right direction, yet it still does not compete with other input methods.

For users who can speak, *speech recognition* might be a faster alternative for text entry. However, the voice of many persons with physical disabilities is subject to conditions such as dysarthria, so producing the same vocal output (with tolerable variations) for the same word is often impossible. As a consequence, no computer really "understands" such users, applying ordinary speech recognition. "Non-verbal Voice Interaction" (NVVI), involving humming or whistling [24], is a possible answer.

This paper presents the software system CHANTI, for "voCally enHanced Ambiguous Non-standard Text Input". The tool attempts to accelerate the QANTI "Scanning Ambiguous Keyboard" [15] by using NVVI, thus allowing users to select (normally scanned) items *directly*.

The remainder of the paper is organized as follows. After reviewing NVVI, the CHANTI system is introduced, detailing the program structure and ideas behind the software. The usefulness of the system was investigated in an evaluation involving eight participants from three countries and with different levels of speech impairment – all belonging to the target population. The study organization, individual sessions, and overall results are presented and discussed. The paper concludes with a brief summary and a quick look to the future.

RELATED WORK

Non-verbal Voice Interaction

Non-verbal voice interaction (NVVI) is based on interpretation of non-verbal sounds produced by the user, such as humming or whistling. Various acoustic parameters of the sound signal (pitch, volume, timbre, etc.) are measured over time and the data stream is interpreted as an input channel. A formal description of NVVI is given, for example, by Poláček et al. [18].

Watts and Robinson [24] propose a system where the sound of whistling triggers the commands for OS UNIX. Igarashi and Hughes [12] used non-speech sounds to extend the interaction using automated speech recognition, pointing out that non-speech sounds are useful to specify analog (numeric) parameters. For example, the user could produce an utterance such as "volume up, *aaah*". In a response, the system would increase the volume of the TV for as long as the user held the sound of "*aaah*".

An emulation of the mouse device and its use as an assistive tool is described by Sporka et al. [22] and Bilmes et al. [4]. NVVI has been successfully employed as an input technique for gaming, as described by Sporka et al. [21] (Tetris) and Hämäläinen et al. [10] (platform arcade games for children).

NVVI has also been used as a means of artistic expression. A live performance designed and described by Levin and Lieberman [14] involved real-time visualization of voice, both speech and non-speech sounds. Depending on the sound the performing artists were producing, the system rendered non-figural patterns on a screen located behind the artists. Samaa Al-Hashimi created Blowtter [1], a NVVI-controlled plotter. Another system where non-verbal sounds are used to control a process of drawing is described by Harada et al. [11].

NVVI allows realtime control, unlike automatic speech recognition where the system waits for completion of an utterance. The language independence inherent in NVVI may simplify cross-cultural deployment. NVVI may thus enhance the class of applications controllable via the input acoustic modality.

Keyboard Input Methods

In an *ambiguous keyboard*, a single key is associated with more than one character of the alphabet, while a *dictionary* is checked for candidates matching a sequence of keys [16, 3].

A well-known example is the phone keypad, where most keys are associated with 3 or 4 characters. When used with dictionary-based disambiguation, the intended word appears in about 95 % of all cases for English [19]. If there is more than one matching candidate, the user scrolls through a list to select the desired word. The list typically not only contains *exact* matches, but also words extending (or *completing*) the entered key sequence; i.e., the software tries to *predict* which word the user intends to enter.

In a *scanning keyboard*, the keys are cyclically highlighted. The user selects the currently highlighted key by actuating the dedicated switch. Typically, a small number of options is presented at a time. If the space of options is larger, it must be hierarchically subdivided and the user needs to make a number of selections to reach the desired option.

A *scanning ambiguous keyboard* (SAK) is a combination of the two methods. It brings together the advantages of scanning (i.e., text entry using a single input key) and ambiguous keyboards (ideally demanding only one keystroke per character, although using less keys than characters).

QANTI, the predecessor of CHANTI

QANTI [6] is an implementation of a SAK, specifically targeted for persons with physical disabilities who are unable to utilize a standard keyboard. It was developed as a fully implemented system, rather than as a proof-of-concept prototype.

An exhaustive parameter search by MacKenzie and Felzer [15] identified a layout with four virtual keys as the most favorable (demanding the smallest number of scan steps per character for a given dictionary). Three virtual keys, each covering about one third of the alphabet, are used to produce a *code sequence*, while a fourth virtual key moves the focus to a frequency-ordered list of candidate words.

SAKs work only with dictionary words, so a separate mechanism is required to add new entries to the dictionary (see below).

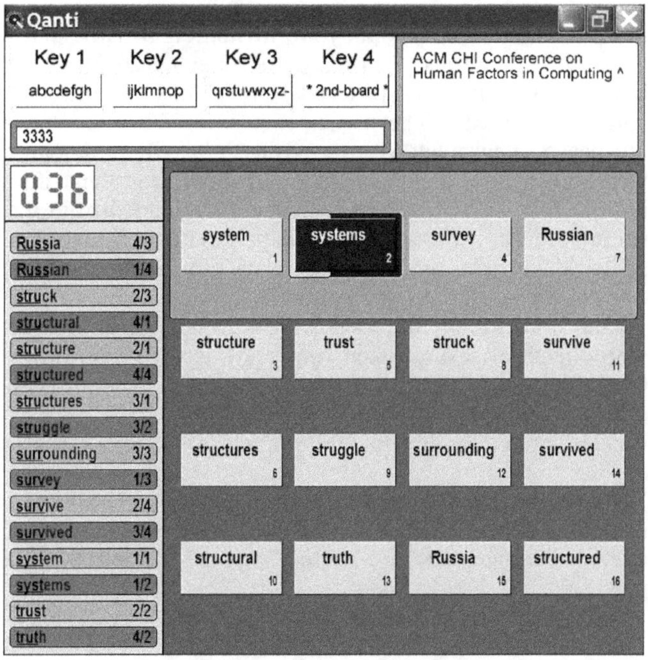

Figure 1. QANTI in candidate selection mode.

This is the basic concept of QANTI (see fig. 1 for a screenshot). To enter a word, the user first produces a code sequence with the help of the four linearly scanned virtual keys in the *sequence selection area* (top left of the screen). While the sequence is entered, a list of candidate words is constantly updated with the 16 most frequent candidates displayed both in the bottom left area of the screen (in alphabetical order) and on the buttons of a large 4×4 board on the bottom right (in frequency order). QANTI supports English and German as default languages. The dictionary may be user-extended.

Once the desired word appears, the user changes to *candidate selection mode*, where the 16 buttons are scanned in a *row-column* fashion. Having selected the candidate, the user chooses among 16 finalization options shown on the buttons of the row-column scanning board. The options determine the way the selected candidate is rendered into the entered text (top right area of the screen), for example, turning the first character into a capital letter, or appending a space, comma, or period at the end.

For initiating selections, QANTI supports *intentional muscle contractions* [8] as an input signal. This feature emphasizes

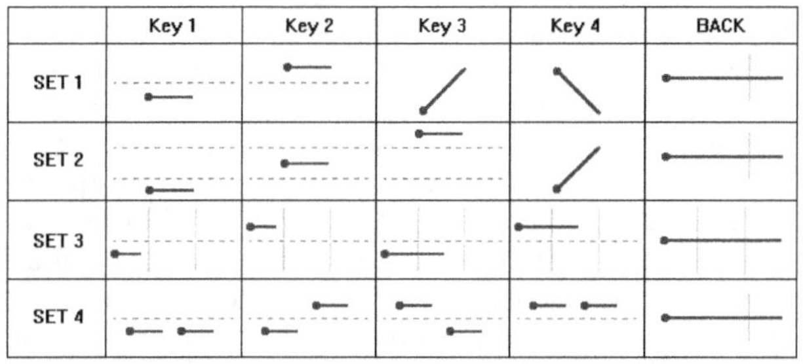

Figure 2. NVVI gestures used with CHANTI. Dark thick lines are pitch profiles over time. Horizontal dashed lines are user-specified pitch thresholds. Vertical solid lines are duration thresholds.

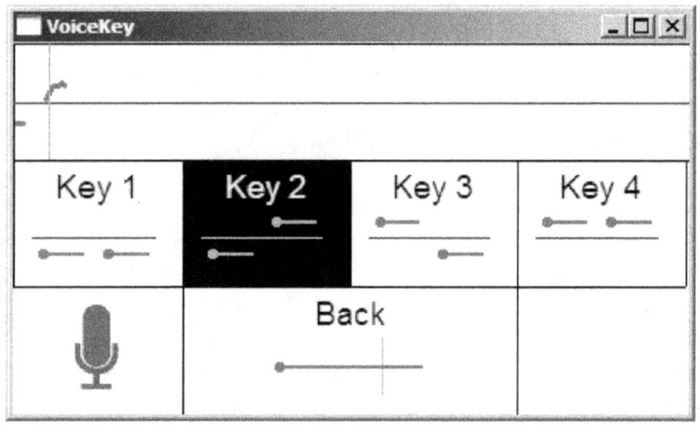

Figure 3. VoiceKey. The user has just produced a gesture G2. Upper part is the detected pitch profile. Lower part shows available gestures to produce.

the target group, since it suffices to merely issue tiny contractions of a single muscle of choice, and thus requires a minimum of physical effort. As a consequence, even someone with a very severe disability can enter text reasonably fast, provided that one muscle (e.g., the brow muscle) can be reliably controlled (also [7]).

QANTI becomes a ready-to-use system through its menu mode. When the user applies a special mechanism involving the fourth virtual "sequence key", the buttons of the 4×4 board are re-labeled, giving access to several higher-order menu functions. In this mode, the user has the choice to correct errors (either in the entered text or in the current code sequence), to enter line breaks, to configure the scan delay, or to copy the entered text to the clipboard or to disk.

One menu option invokes an ordinary (non-ambiguous) onscreen scanning keyboard, offering a total of 64 virtual keys. This "Full Keyboard" allows the user to enter arbitrary character sequences – in particular non-dictionary words (e.g., proper names) – by adhering to a three-step scanning scheme [9] (with the 64 keys arranged in four groups with 16 buttons each). The menu also includes an add-to-dictionary feature for new words.

THE CHANTI SYSTEM

Design of CHANTI

CHANTI combines the philosophy of QANTI and NVVI. CHANTI is built on a scanning-based tool (maintaining the hierarchy in the space of options presented to the user), but accepts NVVI gestures for directly selecting items. The structure of the user interface is close to that of QANTI in that text is entered word-by-word. Words are selected from a vocabulary. Each word is ambiguously entered as a code sequence. After a code sequence is specified, the user disambiguates the selection by choosing the word from a list of candidates corresponding to the entered code sequence. Various functions, such as simple editing commands and character-based virtual keyboards for entry of out-of-vocabulary words are available through a menu.

As opposed to QANTI, where the interaction is performed by a single switch activated in specific time slots to make a selection, CHANTI is controlled exclusively by NVVI gestures which are directly assigned to the choices. This provides faster access to the individual choices, compared to the scanning approach in QANTI.

An NVVI gesture is a tone or a sequence of tones with defined characteristics, such as pitch, pitch inflection, or duration, produced by the user. There were four different sets of gestures, equivalent in function, from which the user may choose. There are four NVVI gestures in each set, *Key 1* through *Key 4* (used either to enter a code sequence or advance in the menu) and the *BACK* gesture to reverse the effect of the last gesture produced. This gesture can be used multiple times (multi-level undo). The gestures *Key 1* through *Key 4* correspond to the four keys of QANTI. All gestures are shown in Figure 2.

NVVI has been implemented by VoiceKey (Figure 3), a standalone program that recognizes gestures produced by the users and communicates them to the main application of CHANTI. Other features of the acoustic signal (volume, timbre) were not used in this setup.

The structure of the user interface of CHANTI is shown in Figure 5. Initially, CHANTI awaits either one of the gestures *Key 1*, *Key 2* or *Key 3* to commence entering the code sequence (Fig. 4a) or *Key 4* to enter the menu. When a code sequence is entered, the gesture *Key 4* initiates candidate word selection mode (Fig. 4b). The user then needs to produce two gestures: One selects a row, the other selects a column. Subsequently, the user chooses a finalization option (Fig. 4c). The user may also choose to clear the code sequence and start over by selecting the "Delete Sequence" command in the candidate word selection or finalization option modes.

The menu allows the execution of simple commands (insert a space, remove the last character, remove the last word, insert a new-line character) and access to special modes. These are character-based virtual keyboards. The available characters on these keyboards are organized in a matrix. The user selects a desired character by specifying coordinates using the gestures (similar to selecting candidate words).

Items "Start Test" and "Stop Test" were included for the experiment to start and stop data collection.

THE STUDY

The Study Organization

The purpose of the study was to gauge the first impression of CHANTI, how users would adapt to CHANTI over time, and whether they would be willing to accept CHANTI as their typing tool (and for which type of text).

Since we aimed at studying users' insights, we organized the study as longitudinal and qualitative. Generally, participants were asked to use CHANTI for minimum of 30 minutes each day, over the course of 7 days.

For participation in the study we invited eight participants from three countries: Germany, the Czech Republic, and USA. This allowed us to test CHANTI in three different language contexts. The participants covered a range from no speech impairment to severe dysarthria. All participants were screened for being able to produce NVVI gestures during the Day 1. Three participants were excluded from the study because of the severity of their dysarthria which prevented them from producing the NVVI in required resolution or extreme fatigue even after very short exposure to the system. In Germany the users were recruited via interviews with clients of several local healthcare institutions. In the Czech Republic the users were recruited in cooperation with a local association of paraplegic people. In USA the user was recruited through personal contact.

We used the same dictionaries for English and German as used in QANTI. The Czech dictionary was based on a frequency dictionary compiled at the Charles University in Prague [23].

The sessions were outlined as follows:

- Day 1 — System set-up and pre-test interview: The participants were asked how they use the information and communication technology (ICT) as well as about their specific disability-induced problems relating to text input. The participants' assistive technology was discussed. The participants were screened for their sufficient ability to control their voice and trained in using NVVI (see below) and then determined which set of gestures was best for them.
- Day 2 — The participants' capacity to use NVVI was checked. The session continued with the first exposure to CHANTI and first-impression interview.
- Days 3 through 6 — Continued exposure to CHANTI: Participants were asked to begin writing using CHANTI. Their performance was measured on example phrases, between 5 and 15 words per phrase. These phrases were randomly selected from a text file. Separate collections of phrases were assembled for English, German, and Czech.
- Day 7 — Last day of exposure to CHANTI. A post-test interview took place, in which the participants were asked about their overall experience using CHANTI, and what they considered the strong and weak points of the interaction.

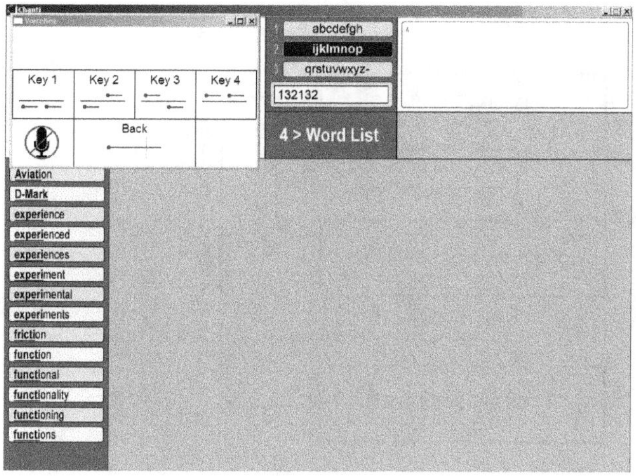

a) part of the code sequence entered

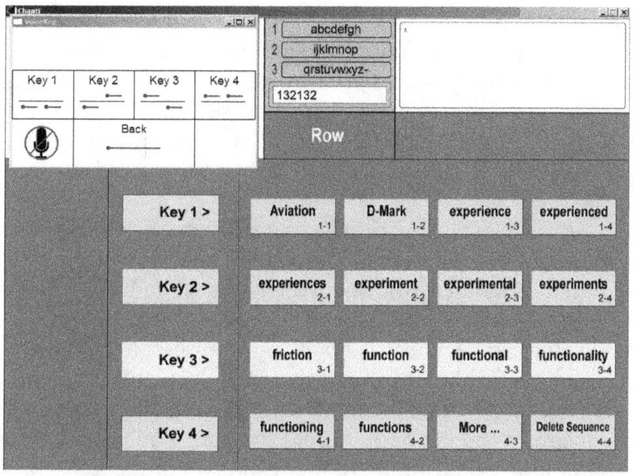

b) selecting a word from the candidate list

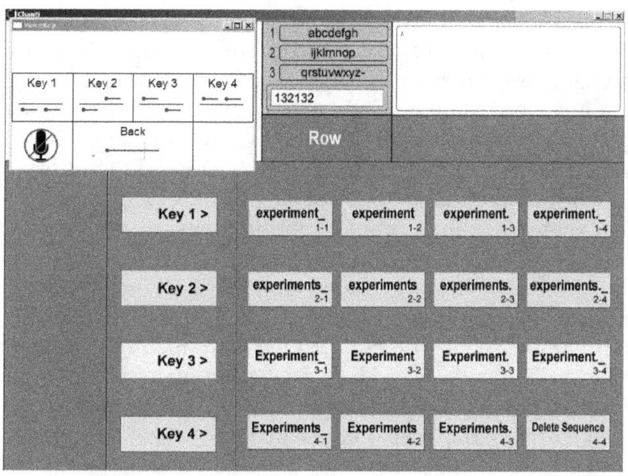

c) selecting how the word should be finalized

Figure 4. Illustration of CHANTI in various stages of operation.

NVVI Training

It is known that training is needed for proper use of the NVVI modality [21]. For this purpose we developed a simple training module which generated a random sequence of gestures and then prompted the users to produce the gestures one-by-one. The users were considered ready for the study if they were able to produce 15 gestures out of 16 without a mistake.

Participant 1

Miloš[1] is 30 years old. He is quadriplegic since birth. He is an IT specialist in a small company based in Prague. On his request, his participation was remote. The interviews were conducted over the telephone and e-mail.

He is able to use a desktop computer while sitting at his desk by a mouth-held stick through which he can type on the keyboard as well as move the mouse. When laying in bed, his laptop is suspended on a platform above him, allowing him to use the stick to type on the keyboard as well as operate a small tablet that emulates mouse control. Apart from the Sticky Keys utility available in Microsoft Windows, he uses no other assistive technology. He reports typing as fast as 100 CPM. He spends 10 hours per day using a computer. He frequently uses shortcut keys. He likes exploring new technologies and interaction techniques.

Miloš is able to use the system tools of the machines he administers through a remote desktop facility. He frequently uses Microsoft Word, composes the HTML and PHP code, edits music, etc. He does not use social networks such as Facebook. He uses the ICQ instant messaging network for quick exchanges of short messages, rather than for extensive chatting. Regarding the use of computers, he feels no disadvantage against other users.

However, he relies on the help of others in hardware-related problems, including switching the machine on. He reports problems using the mouth-held stick on capacitive-sensing devices, such as touchpads or touch switches. He is willing to invest time in training new assistive devices and solutions. He reported having spent three months training for tablet use.

Interaction with CHANTI

Miloš was using CHANTI in Czech. Miloš was eager to participate in the test. He spent 12 hours using CHANTI over 7 days, which was well over the limit set by the design of the experiment. He spent about two hours testing all the sets and deciding which set of gestures to use. ("I was trying hard to find out which set would be best for me.") Finally he opted for gesture set #1 (see Fig. 2). He felt that these gestures were the easiest for him to produce and yielded the lowest error rate. He reported that gesture set #2 was the most difficult to use. ("It was not easy to precisely hit those three separate tones.")

When using CHANTI to write unconstrained text, he noticed that the dictionary was not complete (the Czech dictionary contained only about 30,000 word forms) and tried composing words letter-by-letter, which he found very slow.

[1]The participants are represented by fictional names to protect their privacy.

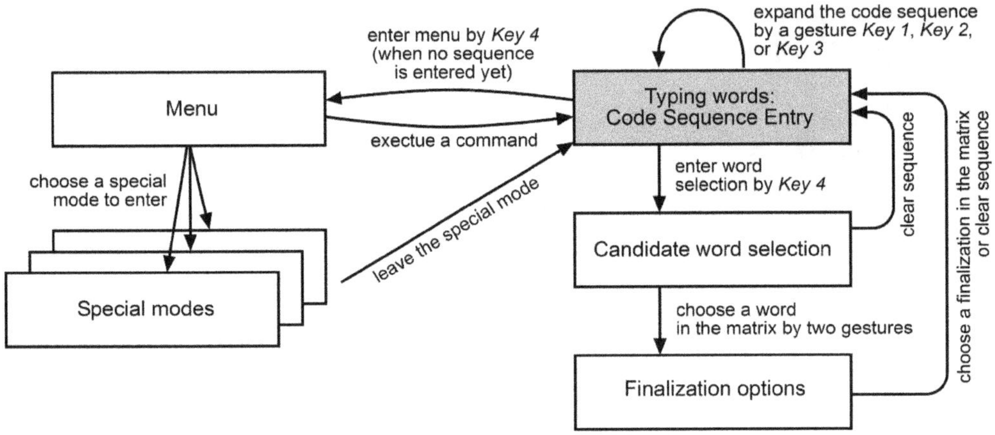

Figure 5. CHANTI user interface state diagram. The initial state is grey.

Initially, his median performance using CHANTI was about 5 CPM. The median performance over his later trials, measured using the internal test facility, was about 15 CPM (with in-vocabulary words only).

He found the structure of CHANTI simple, yet versatile. He liked the fact that it can be controlled by only five distinct voice gestures. He found CHANTI a useful tool for somebody who can not use other means of control. However, he found typing using CHANTI too slow for his needs.

Participant 2

Petr is 19 years old. He is quadriplegic since an accident two years ago. He is a senior-year high-school student who spends typically 2 to 4 hours at a computer daily. He uses the computer to access study materials, to communicate with friends over e-mail, to access the telephone and watch movies. He relies on other family members to assist him daily with the hardware setup.

He uses head motion tracker SmartNav4 by NaturalPoint which emulates a mouse and Click-N-Type software that emulates a keyboard. The device is based on tracking a reflective dot placed on the user's forehead. He is able to type at about 30 CPM using this setup. His performance is generally better when using a head rest or laying in bed. However, he reported that he can not use glasses, as the reflection distorts the output from the device.

He reported limited experience with eye tracking technology, but had tried the system introduced by Fejtová et al. [5]. He was vaguely aware of breath controllers but he was not aware of other methods of the text input, including the use of the mouth-held stick.

Interaction with CHANTI

Petr was using CHANTI in Czech. Petr reported that he found the system easy to learn and that he was able to learn to use the system rather quickly. "I only need to remember the ranges of letters for individual gestures, so that when producing gestures I would be too far off the range."

Throughout the experiment, Petr used gesture set #4. He acquired a "steady rhythm" producing gestures, roughly at the rate of 50 to 60 gestures per minute which he would interrupt when making a decision, such as selecting a word from the list. In such moments he would vocalize his thoughts in a soft voice, so as not exceed the volume threshold.

He used CHANTI in various locations with different acoustic qualities (kitchen, living room, office). He was visibly frustrated when acoustic interferences resulted in an undesired behavior of CHANTI. These interferences included background noises (he was not using a noise-cancelling headset) or a long reverberation of the room, causing the system to register longer tones than actually produced. However, he was aware of the need for calibration and requested it when he felt that it would improve the responses of the system.

He finds that the system would be best used for writing short text messages. ("I would not want to write a whole novel using this.") However, he pointed out that since the Czech language uses an extensive system of declension and conjugation, a word often needed to be specified until the very last letter, since only the ending of the word would determine the desired word form. This somewhat decreased the utility of the word prediction method used by CHANTI as opposed to English and its much simpler morphology.

His median typing rate was about 6 CPM on the first day of the data collection and about 10 CPM in the last day. He reported that in general he liked the input method but he felt frustrated when the word he was attempting to write was not in the dictionary and instead he had to type the word letter-by-letter using the virtual keyboard.

He expressed his wish to use the system again. He reported that he would use the system as an alternative to his current assistive technology when he gets tired moving his head. He and his caretaker were interested in a production-level implementation of the system.

Participant 3
Gabriele is 45 years old. Since her thirteenth birthday she has Friedreich Ataxia (FA). She used to work as an IT professional in university administration. She frequently wants to use a computer for education, entertainment, or gaming.

Due to the progressing symptoms of FA, she has significant problems using a keyboard. This keeps her from using a computer for communicating via chat or email. Typing one sentence can take up to fifteen minutes. Medium speech problems still make it impossible for her to use regular voice recognition. She immediately liked the idea of software that makes text entry more practicable for her.

Interaction with CHANTI
Gabriele was using the German version of CHANTI. Gabriele decided that gesture set #1 was the easiest and most efficient for her. The symptoms of Friedreich Ataxia also heavily affect breathing and therefore speech and humming. She needed three hours before she was proficient enough with the training tool. The large amount of unintended input was frustrating for her: Not being able to switch the microphone off, she constantly produced input, for example, by coughing. It took her four days of intense practice with the experimenter before starting the first session.

Furthermore, she could hardly create humming sounds short and strong enough. The difficulty for Gabriele was to control her sound and breathing. While trying to make a short hum (*Key 1*, *Key 2* in gesture set #1), she could not control the timing. VoiceKey is designed to allow the program to interpret a humming sound as either *Key 1* or *Key 2*. The hum has to be shorter than half a second, otherwise the program performs a *BACK* operation.

On the second day of the experiment, we prolonged the time threshold to 700ms. This meant that Gabriele was able to get *Key 1* and *Key 2* correct more often, but a longer time threshold also meant that she had to hum longer to perform a BACK key. A longer hum is more exhausting and also bears the danger of unintended inputs because of the difficulty to hold a tone for longer time (eventually the program would then rate a long hum as either *Key 3* or *Key 4*).

On average, she made 154 corrections for a sentence with 60 characters during the first day of the experiment and did not exceed 2.5 CPM. She felt she would constantly improve. At the end of the experiment, the number of corrections dropped to 47 per 60 characters.

She only reached 5 CPM after the last session. This was mainly due to the number of corrections she was forced to make. In addition, her low typing rate was caused by a symptomatic eyes dysfunction, which complicates perception of information displayed on different parts of the screen. She would have preferred a bigger screen instead of the 14.1" notebook display used in the experiment. She indicated a willingness to continue practicing and working with the software on her own.

Participant 4
Rolf is 39 years old and has been diagnosed with Friedreich Ataxia at the age of 15. He uses a wheelchair since 1988, and he has considerable motor problems, which also affect his voice. Rolf is with a small software company and mostly works from home. His work requires him to use a computer for up to 8 hours every day, and despite the fact that his disease has progressed quite far, he is still able to use a standard keyboard and mouse (albeit at a modest typing rate of 15–30 CPM, depending on the time of day).

Due to his vocal difficulties, he is unable to use ordinary voice recognition software. He *is* able to communicate verbally, but the variations in his speech are too large for a computer program – he already tried several possibilities (mostly causing frustrating experiences). In addition, impaired fine motor control makes it difficult for him to use head/eye trackers.

Rolf is very motivated to find an assistive tool allowing him to interact with a computer at a rate comparable to an able-bodied person. When he was asked about being a participant in the CHANTI evaluation, he immediately accepted the invitation, gladly saying: "This could help me a lot".

Interaction with CHANTI
Rolf was using CHANTI in German. Rolf also decided for gesture set #1, even though producing ascending or descending gestures was not easy for him. Nevertheless, he indicated that this profile worked best for him, for example, as far as timing is concerned. When using CHANTI for the first time, the participant needed almost 1000 seconds for a sentence with just 64 characters (entry rate: 4 CPM). The main reason for this was the heavy need for error correction (e.g., the *BACK* gesture) to take back erroneous selections.

However, the participant's results gradually improved. During the test week, Rolf spent more than 2 hours per day practicing with the program, and he was finally able to reach peak rates of 12 CPM. He reported that he liked the look of the program, and the colors. Besides, he commented: "At the beginning, I spent a lot of time looking for the intended word – later, I started to remember the position of the candidates, at least for frequent words; I'm sure I can beat my 'manual lower bound' of 15 CPM with longer practice".

Participant 5
Sarah is a 32 years old graduate student. She is paraplegic due to a sporting accident that happened when she was 18. She was also diagnosed with thyroid problem, which made her suffer from a symptom similar to carpal tunnel syndrome last year.

Before last year, Sarah did not use any assistive system. However, because of her thyroid problem, since last year she had been using on and off speech recognition software and screen reader (to read out the information so that she can lay down while working without looking at the screen). She spends 6-10 hours a day with her computer on weekdays, although she usually does not use her computer on weekends and holidays. She uses various computer applications, including social networking (Skype occasionally), email (almost all the time), and Facebook (occasionally). She develops C programs as a part of her graduate work.

Interaction with CHANTI

Sarah was using the English version of CHANTI. Sarah is a quick learner. She went from a median speed of 3.9 CPM on day one with a median correction of 16 out of 32 characters (50%) in her first session to a median of 12.3 CPM on the fourth day with a median of 5 corrections out of 27 characters (19%). It should be noted that on her fifth day, she was not feeling well, and while in the first trial on Day 5 she managed 15.15 CPM with only 3 corrections out of 28, her performance deteriorated quickly within minutes, possibly due to her thyroid problem, to 8.5 CPM and then down to 7.6 CPM with 16 corrections out of 24 characters.

We interviewed her at the end of her first day, and the day after her fifth session (she could not communicate effectively at the end of her fifth session). Her first impressions of the system were quite positive. She stated, "After a while I was able to get more of the hang of it. I find it easiest, more convenient to use the Full Keyboard in CHANTI." She did, however, complain about some of the key arrangements, stating that it was not intuitive for her that the shift key was in the bottom right quadrant of the full keyboard. She was using gesture set #1.

In her final debriefing, she made several remarks, which are summarized below:

- "Sometimes when using the word completion method of typing, the word I was looking for would never show up in the window. It was frustrating to have to delete each letter and then go to the full keyboard to type it up."
- "After a short while I felt that I was starting to memorize certain common inputs such as the space and I also felt I was becoming more proficient in writing, i.e., I was coming up with quicker ways of typing and looking for more efficient ways."
- "I also found it a little difficult with punctuation. I was hoping when using the word completion interface that when typing '`I'm`' that I could type '`Im`' and when choosing the word that I meant that one of the options would be '`I'm`'."

When we asked her very specific questions, such as whether the system helped her to do her work, she provided many constructive criticisms that we can take home and use for further refinement of the system. The remarks are summarized below:

- On whether the system helped her to do her work, she said, "I found myself editing a lot of my typing and believe it could be made a bit more intuitive or perhaps have more functionality to help with short cuts."
- When asked about the on-screen real estate, she stated, "I would like to resize some of the keyboard windows so that I can see some screen space where I might be doing other work."
- On whether the system provided sufficient contextual help, she answered, "I found myself guessing as to what action to take to get the end result I wanted. Or sometimes I would choose some menu options believing that option would be available and when it wasn't I would go back."
- On menu arrangement, she thought it took a lot of steps to return to the main menu at times and sometimes she had to click on *DONE* or *BACK* to go back to the main menu which was not intuitive for her.

She did have several positive comments about the system. She thought that for most part the design was consistent, intuitive, and quite easy to learn, and she had fun playing with it. She said she would definitely use the system again on her own if she could get a copy of the system.

DISCUSSION

Most users were satisfied with CHANTI and would use the method on their own if given the possibility or their condition worsened so that they were not able to use their present technology. All participants who were able to use the NVVI notably improved their performance using CHANTI over the course of the experiment (see Table 1). The peak performance of the users was typically between 10 and 15 CPM. This is comparable to QANTI [6]. In fact, Rolf also participated in an earlier study evaluating QANTI – he reached around 12 CPM there as well.

Effects of the speech impairment. Though pitch-driven NVVI, as used by CHANTI, does not require the articulation of facial muscles as in speech interaction, the users still need to promptly control their breathing and vocal folds. In our study we identified a "threshold of applicability" of NVVI: 3 participants out of 8 were not able to complete the first session (and therefore did not participate further). They had severe problems producing NVVI sounds due to their speech impairment induced by ataxia. The other two ataxic participants, Gabriele and Rolf, were able to produce NVVI sounds. While Rolf reached the performance similar to participants with no speech impairment, Gabriele frequently needed to correct malformed NVVI gestures, and this limited her performance at 5 CPM. Clearly, her speech impairment was more severe than that of Rolf. Gabriele was on the borderline of the target group. In particular, her speech problems caused a lot of frustration at the beginning (before she was able to proceed with the first test session), which almost made her decline participation in the experiment.

The NVVI threshold of applicability is lower than that of automatic speech recognition (ASR), as evident by Rolf's participation. Rolf reported that he could not use any system of speech recognition for interaction with the computer due to a different quality of his speech that was not compatible with the current ASR engines. Rolf represented "an ideal target group" of NVVI; i.e. the people who are able to speak but who cannot use the ASR as NVVI is more robust to speech

Table 1. Overview of the Results.

Participant (country and language)	Disability, condition	Dysarthria	Typical type rate (without CHANTI)	Mean type rate on first day*	Mean type rate on last day*	Gesture set	Would use CHANTI again?
Miloš (CZ)	Congenital malformation	No	100 CPM	14 CPM	21 CPM	#1	no
Petr (CZ)	Quadriplegia (accident)	No	30 CPM	6 CPM	12 CPM	#4	yes
Gabriele (DE)	Friedreich ataxia	Yes	very low	very low	5 CPM	#1	yes
Rolf (DE)	Friedreich ataxia	Yes	15—30 CPM**	4 CPM	11 CPM	#1	yes
Sarah (US)	Paraplegia (accident), thyroid problem	No	0—150 CPM	5 CPM	11 CPM***	#1***	yes

* Including the time spent on any corrections
** Depending on current condition
*** Sarah was using the *Full Keyboard* mode. Her peak performance was 16 CPM but during her last session the condition deteriorated and reached 8 CPM after an attack.

impairments than the ASR. NVVI thus expands the range of applications of the vocal modality in assistive technologies by an important margin.

The capacity to speak in a person can change notably over a short period of time and thus the performance of NVVI can vary, as documented by Sarah's participation on the last day: Sarah started out with typing rate of 16 CPM but during the session her condition worsened rapidly and her performance dropped to 8 CPM.

Language model. While NVVI is intrinsically language independent, CHANTI is by design intended to be used in the context of a specific language. When exploring the potential of CHANTI, Sarah and Miloš found the dictionary limited. Both users tried the Full Keyboard mode whereby any string could be typed. Miloš found the method very slow and would use it only to write a specific out-of-vocabulary word while Sarah switched to this method entirely. Her choice could be compared to switching off the predictive text entry method T9 available on mobile telephones. In Kurniawan's study [13] the participants were not using T9 as they found it distracting especially because of the incorrect predictions and subsequent recovery.

To fully accommodate the Czech language and its complex morphology, the method of the word selection should be changed. For example, the nouns could be selected in their basic form and the desired case could be chosen only in the next step. This would effectively reduce the size of the dictionary and thus the need for extensive browsing of the list of candidates.

CONCLUSION

When mentioning the acoustic modality for text entry, very often the automatic speech recognition (ASR) is mentioned as an example of the assistive technique suitable for this task. However, not all motor impaired people can use ASR due to the speech impairments that accompany their motor disability. This study has shown that the NVVI is a viable acoustic modality for text entry even for some of those who are not capable of speech intelligible by the ASR due to conditions such as ataxia.

In this paper we presented CHANTI, a method for text entry based on a combination of QANTI, a one-switch predictive text entry method, and non-verbal vocal input (NVVI). The main goal of the presented study was to see how users learn using CHANTI during their initial exposure to the system.

CHANTI did not outperform some assistive text input techniques in terms of the type rate: By the end of the experiment, the users were able to enter text at typical rates between 10 and 15 characters per minute.

However, CHANTI uses standard off-the-shelf hardware with no modifications needed for the system to run and therefore is inexpensive to deploy. As suggested by one participant, CHANTI can be used as an alternative system for specific conditions, such as when taking rest from the current assistive tool.

Future work

For languages with complex morphology (which includes the Czech language), the prediction mechanism should be more informed by the grammar of the target language so that the user may more optimally perform the disambiguation of the candidates. Also, the finalization options should be language dependent. The function of adding custom words to the dictionary should be enabled in CHANTI.

In the design of the study we were following the methodology described by Mahmud et al. [17] who reported that the performance of the use of NVVI reached a plateau by day 5. We did not detect a similar pattern in our data. A continuous study mapping the learning curve should be therefore carried out to determine the typing rate of this method in experienced users.

The focus of this study was on testing of the main principle of CHANTI. For this reason, some functions (such as adding new words to dictionary) were omitted for reasons of simplicity and should be implemented before CHANTI is made available for practical use.

ACKNOWLEDGMENTS

This research has been partially supported by the Ministry of Education, Youth and Sports of the Czech Republic (research program MSM 6840770014), and an EU/FP7 project VitalMind (IST-215387).

We are grateful to all our participants and their caretakers for their involvement in the study.

REFERENCES

1. S. Al-Hashimi. Blowtter: A voice-controlled plotter. In *Proceedings of HCI 2006 Engage, The 20th BCS HCI Group conference in co-operation with ACM, vol. 2, London, England*, pages 41–44, September 2006.

2. M. Baljko and A. Tam. Motor input assistance: Indirect text entry using one or two keys. In *Proc. ASSETS 2006*, pages 18–25. ACM Press, 2006.

3. M. Belatar and F. Poirier. Text entry for mobile devices and users with severe motor impairments: handiglyph, a primitive shapes based onscreen keyboard. In *Proc. ASSETS 2008*, pages 209–216. ACM Press, 2008.

4. J. A. Bilmes, X. Li, J. Malkin, K. Kilanski, R. Wright, K. Kirchhoff, A. Subramanya, S. Harada, J. A. Landay, P. Dowden, and H. Chizeck. The vocal joystick: A voice-based human-computer interface for individuals with motor impairments. Technical Report UWEETR-2005-0007, University of Washington, 2005.

5. M. Fejtová, J. Fejt, and L. Lhotská. Controlling a PC by Eye Movements: The MEMREC Project. In K. Miesenberger, J. Klaus, W. Zagler, and D. Burger, editors, *Computers Helping People with Special Needs*, volume 3118 of *Lecture Notes in Computer Science*, pages 623–623. Springer Berlin / Heidelberg, 2004. 10.1007/978-3-540-27817-7_114.

6. T. Felzer, I. S. MacKenzie, P. Beckerle, and S. Rinderknecht. Qanti: A Software Tool for Quick Ambiguous Non-standard Text Input. In *Proc. ICCHP 2010*, pages 128–135, Berlin, Heidelberg, 2010. Springer-Verlag.

7. T. Felzer and R. Nordmann. Speeding up hands-free text entry. In *Proc. CWUAAT'06*, pages 27–36. Cambridge University Press, 2006.

8. T. Felzer, R. Nordmann, and S. Rinderknecht. Scanning-based human-computer interaction using intentional muscle contractions. In *Proc. HCI International 2009*, pages 509–518, Berlin, Heidelberg, 2009. Springer-Verlag.

9. T. Felzer and S. Rinderknecht. 3dscan: An environment control system supporting persons with severe motor impairments [Poster Proposal]. In *Proc. ASSETS 2009*, pages 213–214. ACM Press, 2009.

10. P. Hämäläinen, T. Mäki-Patola, V. Pulkki, and M. Airas. Musical computer games played by singing. In G. Evangelista and I. Testa, editors, *Proceedings of 7th International Conference on Digital Audio Effects, Naples, Italy*, pages 367–371, 2004.

11. S. Harada, T. S. Saponas, and J. A. Landay. Voicepen: augmenting pen input with simultaneous non-linguisitic vocalization. In *Proceedings of the 9th international conference on Multimodal interfaces*, ICMI '07, pages 178–185, New York, NY, USA, 2007. ACM.

12. T. Igarashi and J. F. Hughes. Voice as sound: using non-verbal voice input for interactive control. In *UIST '01: Proc 14th Annual ACM Symp on User Interface Software and Technology*, pages 155–156, New York, NY, USA, 2001. ACM Press.

13. S. Kurniawan. Older people and mobile phones: A multi-method investigation. *Int. J. Hum.-Comput. Stud.*, 66(12):889 – 901, 2008.

14. G. Levin and Z. Lieberman. In-situ speech visualization in real-time interactive installation and performance. In *Proc. 3rd Intl. Symp. on Non-Photorealistic Animation and Rendering*. ACM, 2004.

15. I. S. MacKenzie and T. Felzer. SAK: Scanning Ambiguous Keyboard for Efficient One-Key Text Entry. *ACM Transactions on Computer-Human Interaction (TOCHI)*, 17(3):11:1–11:39, 2010.

16. I. S. MacKenzie and K. Tanaka-Ishii. Text entry with a small number of buttons. In I. S. MacKenzie and K. Tanaka-Ishii, editors, *Text entry systems: Mobility, accessibility, universality*, pages 105–121. Morgan Kaufmann, San Francisco, 2007.

17. M. Mahmud, A. J. Sporka, S. H. Kurniawan, and P. Slavík. A comparative longitudinal study of non-verbal mouse pointer. In *Proceedings of INTERACT 2007, Rio de Janeiro, Brazil; Lecture Notes in Computer Science (LNCS) vol. 4663, Part II.*, pages 489–502. Springer-Verlag Berlin Heidelberg, 2007.

18. O. Poláček, Z. Míkovec, A. J. Sporka, and P. Slavík. New way of vocal interface design: Formal description of non-verbal vocal gestures. In *Proceedings of CWUAAT 2010. Get page range and stuff.*, 2010.

19. M. Silfverberg, I. S. MacKenzie, and P. Korhonen. Predicting text entry speed on mobile phones. In *Proc. CHI'06*, pages 9–16. ACM Press, 2000.

20. R. C. Simpson and H. H. Koester. Adaptive one-switch row-column scanning. *IEEE Transactions on Rehabilitation Engineering*, 7(4):464–473, 1999.

21. A. J. Sporka, S. H. Kurniawan, M. Mahmud, and P. Slavík. Non-speech input and speech recognition for real-time control of computer games. In *ASSETS '06: Proc. 8th Intl. ACM SIGACCESS Conf. on Computers and Accessibility*, pages 213–220, New York, NY, USA, 2006.

22. A. J. Sporka, S. H. Kurniawan, and P. Slavík. Whistling user interface (u3i). In *8th ERCIM International Workshop "User Interfaces For All", LCNS 3196, Vienna*, pages 472–478. Springer-Verlag Berlin Heidelberg, June 2004.

23. Ústav Českého národního korpusu FF UK. Český národní korpus: Srovnávací frekvenční seznamy. http://ucnk.ff.cuni.cz/srovnani10.php Retrieved 6 January 2011, 2010.

24. R. Watts and P. Robinson. Controlling computers by whistling. In *Proceedings of Eurographics UK*, 1999.

AirStroke: Bringing Unistroke Text Entry to Freehand Gesture Interfaces

Tao Ni, Doug A. Bowman, Chris North
Department of Computer Science, Virginia Tech
Blacksburg, VA
{nitao, bowman, north}@vt.edu

ABSTRACT
In this paper, we explore the opportunity of bringing unistroke text entry to freehand gesture interfaces. Using existing text entry methods directly in such interfaces is impractical because of the differences between freehand gestures and traditional forms of input. To address this problem, we consider the design constraints of text entry methods using freehand gestures, and present AirStroke, a new technique based on a reengineering of the well-known unistroke technique Graffiti. Using Graffiti's alphabet, AirStroke takes advantage of the richer input capabilities of two-handed freehand gestures by providing combined mode selection and character entry with one hand, as well as word completion with the other hand. A longitudinal study suggests that AirStroke has competitive speed and accuracy to unistroke methods based on stylus input.

Author Keywords
Text entry, freehand gesture input, unistroke, Graffiti.

ACM Classification Keywords
H5.2 [Information interfaces and presentation]: User Interfaces. - Graphical user interfaces.

General Terms
Design, Experimentation.

INTRODUCTION
Freehand gestures (i.e., bare hand interaction in free space or mid-air) have been expected to deliver "casual" and natural yet powerful interaction, especially in non-desktop scenarios where mice and keyboards are not appropriate or available [10, 11]. Researchers have explored the use of freehand interaction for technologies such as large displays [10], virtual reality [2], and curved surfaces [1].

Previous research offers freehand gesture techniques for pointing and clicking [10], window management [11], and interacting with immersive data [1]. However, research on text entry, a fundamental interaction task in many applications, using freehand gesture input is rare.

Since numerous text input methods have been developed for other types of interfaces, it appears straightforward at first glance to adapt existing methods to freehand gesture input. Most of them, however, were developed for very different input devices such as keyboard, mouse or stylus. It is not certain if they are applicable to freehand text entry, since freehand gesture input is different from traditional input devices in several respects:

(1) There is no explicit "button" to trigger *discrete* events, and similarly, there is no explicit *out-of-range* delimiter, which is important for segmenting continuous gestures [7].

(2) Freehand pointing precision is lower than that pointing with a mouse or gesturing on a stable surface with a pen [10], and varies with the distance between the user and the display [9, 10]. Since freehand interactions involve relatively unconstrained user movement, *distance-independent* [9] techniques are preferable.

(3) Freehand gestures involve more muscles than keyboard or stylus interaction and thus can cause more fatigue [2]. Therefore, freehand interactions should avoid gestures that require high precision over a long period of time [2].

In this paper, we explore the opportunity of bringing unistroke text entry to freehand gesture interfaces. To do so, we first examine existing methods from the literature, and discuss the difficulties of using them with freehand gestures. Given the constraints, we present our design and implementation of a freehand gesture text entry method called AirStroke, and report on a longitudinal study of its speed and accuracy.

AirStroke is built upon Graffiti [3], a well-known unistroke method, but it is more than simply using Graffiti in mid-air. Rather, AirStroke takes advantage of the richer input capabilities of two-handed freehand gestures by providing combined mode selection and unistroke character entry with one hand, as well as optional word prediction and completion with the other hand.

EXISTING TEXT ENTRY METHODS
Traditionally, text entry methods have taken two primary forms: button-based and stroke-based. Button-based methods rely on one or more discrete buttons to enter characters, such as touch-typing on a QWERTY keyboard, Multitap on a 12-button cell phone keypad, and Morse code-like methods with only one button [7]. Shoemaker et al. discussed

mid-air text entry methods using a Wiimote [9], based on several variations of virtual keyboards.

Even without physical "buttons" on our hands, we may simulate button clicking via gestures (e.g., AirTap [10] or pinch [1, 11]) for virtual touch-typing. However, such a method typically involves large and frequent arm movements, causing fatigue over time. For example, the Pinch Keyboard [2] uses pinch gestures to select characters from a virtual keyboard. But since a hand can form only a limited number of pinches, users have to move their hands around to navigate to different parts of the keyboard. Pinch Keyboard reached an input speed of only about seven words per minute (wpm) after 30 minutes of training.

Other text entry methods are stroke-based, which are primarily used for stylus-based user interfaces. Well-known character-level methods such as Graffiti [3], Unistrokes [3], and EdgeWrite [14] require users to make a distinct gesture for each character. Word-level methods like Cirrin [6], QuikWriting [8], and SHARK [4] allow users to enter an entire word or sentence in a continuous gesture without lifting the pen from the surface.

Although they are faster than character-level methods, word-level text entry techniques seem problematic for freehand gesture input. They require users to access each letter within a word from certain visual alphabet layouts (e.g., a stylus keyboard in SHARK), making them *distance-* and *visibility-dependent* [9]. They may therefore be less suitable for freehand interactions that involve relatively unconstrained user movement [9]. Also, their strokes tend to be rather long and lack similarity to Roman letters [14], making them difficult for novice users to learn. In contrast, character-level methods require making a simple stroke to enter a character, and only the *relative* positions of the points in this stroke are calculated for recognition. They do not require pointing to any *absolute* location on a display.

Finally, we note that vision-based hand gesture recognition for text input has been explored, but with a focus on effective tracking algorithms (e.g., Liu et al. [5]) rather than designing a complete and useful technique and validating its user performance.

DESIGN OF AIRSTROKE

Based on our survey and analysis of existing methods, we believed that a character-level unistroke method would be a reasonable starting point to explore freehand text entry. However, naïvely using such a technique in midair is not sufficient; there are several issues we need to consider:

Choose a proper *delimiting* gesture: we may define a specific gesture as a delimiter, but it must be unambiguous, simple, and precise to perform [1].

Avoid extra gestures for *mode switching*: many unistroke methods require special "modifier" gestures to change input mode (uppercase, number, punctuation, etc.), but they slow users down and may cause higher error rates. Our goal was to avoid such extra gestures and promote more efficient mode switches and text entry by taking advantage of the richer input capabilities of freehand gestures.

Support *word completion* and *prediction*: As fatigue is always a problem in freehand interactions, it is beneficial to integrate word completion and prediction [12, 14] into a method, while not altering existing character-level strokes.

The core idea of AirStroke is to use one hand for simultaneous mode selection and character-level text entry, and the other for optional word completion. This approach can be equally applied to any character-level unistroke method, such as Jot, Unistrokes, or EdgeWrite, but currently AirStroke is based on Graffiti's alphabet.

Character-Level Input

Previous research has indicated that *pinch gestures* can be a robust delimiter [1, 11]. To enter a character, therefore, users pinch their thumb to another finger (Figure 1b), make a stroke (Figure 1c), and "unpinch" to commit the character (Figure 1d). As a hand can form different pinch gestures, we can assign them to distinct modes. Like previous text entry methods, AirStroke has four typical modes: *lowercase*, *uppercase*, *number*, and *punctuation*, which are activated by pinching the thumb to the index, middle, ring, and pinky fingers, respectively.

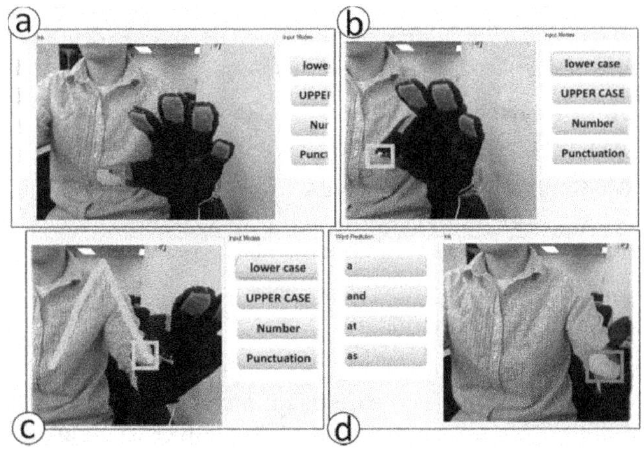

Figure 1: A user enters lowercase letter 'a' with AirStroke.

Graffiti users have to make a special "modifier" gesture to switch a mode, and then make another one to exit. To enter a comma, for example, takes three strokes. By using different pinch gestures for different modes, AirStroke "shortcuts" this process.

Word Completion

In Figure 2, the user has entered the letter "t" (Figure 2a), and a list of four candidate words beginning with "t" is displayed (Figure 2b). If the user sees the desired word in the list, he can use one of the four pinches on the *left* hand to select it and auto-complete this word (Figure 2c). When a SPACE is entered (automatically entered in word completion), context-dependent predictions for the next word are offered (Figure 2d). The user is always free to stroke character-by-character without ever selecting a word, and the list is continuously updated with the current prefix. Since different hands perform the stroke and word completion, they do not interfere with each other. Erroneous completions can be corrected with a "word-level" backspace stroke (i.e., backspace in uppercase mode). This removes the completed suffix and restores the prior characters [12].

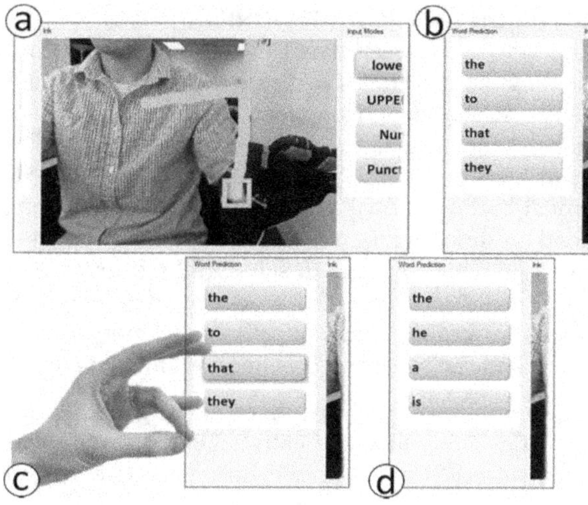

Figure 2: A user enters "that" with word completion.

Although four words in the completion list may seem to be a small number, research has shown that this provides a good coverage of common English words [12]. Also, a short list does not require as much visual search as a longer one. Importantly, words are always shown in the same order. Due to the proprioceptive feedback afforded by pinch gestures, this could allow for improvement through memorization and motor repetition.

We did consider using only one hand for both character entry and word completion. For example, Wobbrock et al. presented an in-stroke scheme [14] that uses a "subgesture" (e.g., a pigtail) to initiate word completion. However, we found this approach problematic for the Graffiti recognizer, because a subgesture causes misrecognition of characters.

Implementation

We implemented AirStroke with a Logitech webcam and a pair of Fakespace PinchGloves™. The fingertip of the right hand's thumb was painted green (Figure 1), and we used a simple color filtering and blob detection algorithm to track its movement. The PinchGloves were used for detecting pinch gestures.

We used an open-source Graffiti recognizer [7], whose alphabet differs slightly from the commercial release. AirStroke's word completion and prediction component is based on EdgeWrite's implementation [12].

Figures 1 and 2 show AirStroke's GUI, which consists of a video image with an overlay of the current stroke, visual menus showing the available modes and word completion list, and visual feedback for the user's pinch gestures.

STUDY: SPEED, ACCURACY AND LEARNING

We conducted a study to assess text entry performance with AirStroke. Our goal was not to compare AirStroke to other methods, since freehand text entry has been under-explored and it was difficult to identify an obvious baseline technique. Rather, our goal was to obtain data to validate whether AirStroke offers competitive speed and accuracy with known (non-freehand) methods, and to find out how AirStroke user performance changes over time.

Four participants (two females) were recruited from the local campus. Two of them had prior experience with Graffiti on PDAs, but none were active users of Graffiti.

We conducted our study over multiple short sessions. The evaluation was within-subjects, with two independent factors being *interface* (AirStroke *with* and *without word completion*), and *session*. Each session had two blocks, in which a participant warmed up by transcribing two phrases before testing on a set of eight phrases using one interface. Interface orders were counterbalanced in each session. Phrases were transcribed in an unconstrained fashion [13]. Participants were encouraged to proceed quickly and accurately, and were required to correct errors as they went. We measured mean session *speed* (wpm) and *corrected error rates* (%) for the test phrases—uncorrected error rates [13] were not available since our procedure made sure that each transcribed phrase was error-free. Sessions were separated by at least one hour but by no more than one day.

We used TextTest [13] to administer our study, which generated phrases and logged performance data.

Results

Over two weeks, a total of 20 sessions per participant were completed. We conducted two-way repeated-measures ANOVAs for *speed* and *corrected error rates*, respectively.

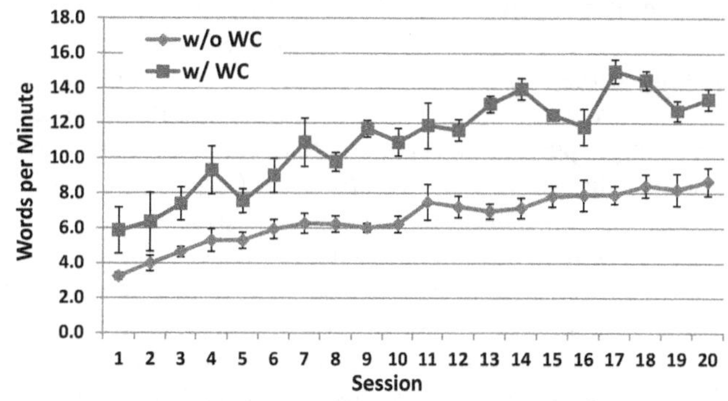

Figure 3: Text entry speed over 20 sessions (wpm).

Speed: There was a significant main effect of *interface* on text entry speed ($F_{1,3}$ = 440.48, p <. 001). As Figure 3 shows, AirStroke with word completion (WC) was significantly faster than AirStroke without WC (μ = 11.0 wpm vs. 6.5 wpm), since participants entered fewer characters for most phrases when using WC. There was also a significant main effect of *session* on speed ($F_{19,57}$ = 18.43, p < .001). Learning effects were obvious in that participants' text entry speed increased over time with both interfaces, as they became more familiar with AirStroke. Furthermore, there was a significant interaction effect between *interface* and *session* ($F_{19,57}$ = 3.73, p < .001), indicating that learning was faster in AirStroke with WC. We believe this was because users were learning at both the character level and the word level; while they were faster in entering individual characters, they were also able to scan the word completion list and perform pinches more quickly.

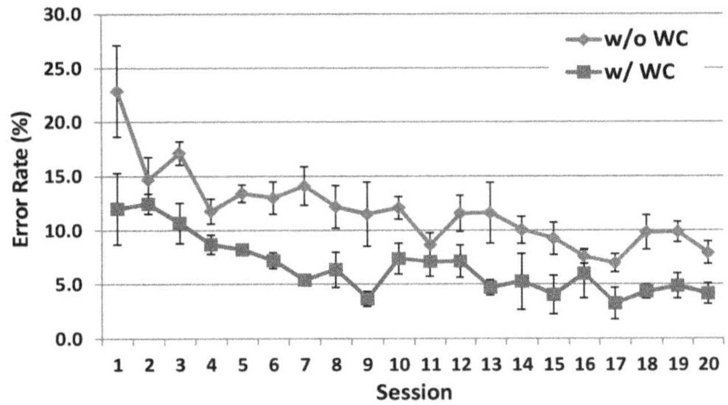

Figure 4: Corrected error rates over 20 sessions (%).

Error rate: There was a significant main effect of *interface* on corrected error rate ($F_{1,3}$ = 140.33, p = .001). As Figure 4 shows, AirStroke with WC had a significantly lower error rate than AirStroke without WC (μ = 6.6% vs. 11.8%). With WC, participants entered fewer characters, and thus committed fewer errors in proportion. There was also a significant main effect of *session* on error rate ($F_{19,57}$ = 9.01, p < .001). There was no significant interaction effect between *interface* and *session*, indicating that with both interfaces, errors decreased over sessions at a similar rate.

Compared to previously reported data, character-level AirStroke alone was slower (for these users) than Graffiti on a PDA (11.4 wpm [3]) or EdgeWrite (11.8 wpm [12]). We believe that the slower speed for AirStroke (6.5 wpm without WC) is due to the larger hand movements required for making strokes in mid-air and the lack of a supporting surface. With word completion, however, AirStroke offered text entry speed and accuracy that are competitive with existing (non-freehand) unistroke methods. As shown in Figure 3 and 4, participants achieved over 13 wpm with word completion in later sessions, while maintaining an error rate below 5%. These results demonstrate that AirStroke is a solid freehand text entry method that is applicable to real usage scenarios, as well as a good starting point and baseline for further investigation of freehand text input.

Participants commented that AirStroke was "*error prone and frustrating at first*" (P1), but as they practiced, they "*memorized gestures better*" (P4), and "*were able to [write most letters] subconsciously*" (P4). Also, word completion was "*very convenient for long words*" (P1). However, participants also commented that without word completion, "*I just had to focus on getting a letter right*" (P2), and that the WC interface required more cognitive effort. This is understandable, because participants had to switch their attention among multiple parts of the AirStroke GUI. Over time, however, participants found WC less distracting. For example, one cited that he was able to "*remember when a desired word popped up after writing one letter*" and "*perform both [character entry and word completion] almost in parallel*" (P3). In addition, although some participants reported early arm fatigue, they were "*not tired at all*" (P3) later since they "*became more confident and took more relaxed postures*" (P1).

CONCLUSION AND FUTURE WORK

In summary, our research has laid the groundwork for understanding the constraints of text entry with freehand gestures. We surveyed previous text entry methods and discussed specific difficulties with naïvely using them with freehand gesture input. By developing AirStroke, a fully-functional technique that takes advantage of two-handed freehand gesture input, we identified design issues and proposed possible solutions to successfully overcome difficulties. Finally, we provided evidence in a longitudinal study that AirStroke offers competitive text entry speed and accuracy, and can serve as a baseline for future exploration.

As future work, we plan to further investigate this design space by designing new text entry techniques and comparing them to AirStroke. We will also integrate AirStroke with a motion tracking system that tracks 3D positions and allows for "anywhere, any direction" freehand text entry.

REFERENCES

1. Benko, H. Beyond flat surface computing: challenges of depth-aware and curved interfaces. *Proc. MM '09*, 935-944.
2. Bowman, D.A. et al. Novel uses of pinch gloves for virtual environment interaction techniques. *Virtual Reality*, 6(3), 122-129.
3. Castellucci, J. and MacKenzie, S. Graffiti vs. unistrokes: an empirical comparison. *CHI '08*, 305-308.
4. Kristensson, P. and Zhai, S. SHARK^2: a large vocabulary shorthand writing system for pen-based computers. *UIST '04*, 43-52.
5. Liu, Y. et al. Hand-gesture based text input for wearable computers. *ICVS* '06, 8.
6. Mankoff, J. and Abowd, D. Cirrin: a word-level unistroke keyboard for pen input. *UIST '98*, 213-214.
7. Ni, T. and Baudisch, P. Disappearing mobile devices. *UIST '09*, 101-110.
8. Perlin, K. Quikwriting: continuous stylus-based text entry. *UIST '98*, 215-216.
9. Shoemaker, G. et al. Mid-air text input techniques for very large wall displays. *GI '09*, 231-238.
10. Vogel, D. and Balakrishnan, R. Distant freehand pointing and clicking on very large, high resolution displays. *UIST '05*, 33-42.
11. Wilson, A. D. Robust computer vision-based detection of pinching for one and two-handed gesture input. *UIST '06*, 255-258.
12. Wobbrock, J. and Myers, B. From letters to words: efficient stroke-based word completion for trackball text entry. *Assets '06*, 2-9.
13. Wobbrock, J. and Myers, B. Analyzing the input stream for character-level errors in unconstrained text entry evaluations. *TOCHI*, 13(4), 458-489.
14. Wobbrock, J. et al. In-stroke word completion. *UIST '06*, 333-336.

Sampling Representative Phrase Sets for Text Entry Experiments: A Procedure and Public Resource

Tim Paek, Bo-June (Paul) Hsu
Microsoft Research
One Microsoft Way, Redmond WA 98052 USA
{timpaek | paulhsu}@microsoft.com

ABSTRACT
Text entry experiments evaluating the effectiveness of various input techniques often employ a procedure whereby users are prompted with natural language phrases which they are instructed to enter as stimuli. For experimental validity, it is desirable to control the stimuli and present text that is representative of a target task, domain or language. MacKenzie and Soukoreff (2001) manually selected a set of 500 phrases for text entry experiments. To demonstrate representativeness, they correlated the distribution of single letters in their phrase set to a relatively small (by current standards) corpus of English prior to 1966, which may not reflect the style of text input today. In this paper, we ground the notion of representativeness in terms of information theory and propose a procedure for sampling representative phrases from any large corpus so that researchers can curate their own stimuli. We then describe the characteristics of phrase sets we generated using the procedure for email and social media (Facebook and Twitter). The phrase sets and code for the procedure are publicly available for download.

Author Keywords
Text entry, experiment, sampling, relative entropy.

ACM Classification Keywords
H.5.2. Information interfaces and presentation: Evaluation / methodology.

General Terms
Experimentation.

INTRODUCTION
Text entry experiments evaluating the effectiveness of various input techniques often employ a procedure whereby users are prompted with natural language phrases which they are instructed to enter as stimuli. Although it may seem more "natural" to have users enter whatever phrases come to mind, the variability engendered by spontaneous text production poses a threat to the internal validity of experimental conclusions [10, 7]. It is difficult, for example, to claim that one input technique performed better than another if participants using one or the other technique just happened to produce longer, more complicated phrases. To preserve internal validity, researchers typically control text production using pre-selected phrases as stimuli.

For stimuli, many researchers utilize the MacKenzie and Soukoreff (2001) phrase set [9], which contains 500 phrases that are intended to be moderate in length, easy to remember and representative of general English. In order to demonstrate representativeness, MacKenzie and Soukoreff correlated the distribution of single letters in their phrase set to the letter frequencies reported in tables by Mayzner and Tresselt [12]. Unfortunately, the letter frequencies derive from a dated corpus containing publications (newspapers, magazines, and books) prior to 1966, which may not reflect the style of text input today. Furthermore, the vocabulary size is about 20,000 words, which is relatively small by today's standards. Indeed, with the phenomenal growth of the Internet and advances in computational natural language processing, organizations such as the Linguistic Data Consortium (LDC) [8] offer researchers publicly accessible corpora of considerably larger scale for a plethora of tasks, domains and languages. For example, through LDC, Google has published a web corpus of 5-grams from a corpus of approximately 1 trillion tokens [4]. The Microsoft Web N-Gram Services [15, 13] even allows researchers to programmatically access word popularity on the Internet.

In this paper, we propose a procedure for sampling representative phrases from any large corpus so that text input researchers can curate their own stimuli for tasks, domains and languages they wish to target using publicly accessible resources. The procedure is based on grounding the notion of representativeness in terms of information theory. This paper consists of three contributions. First, we explain the mathematical concept of relative entropy and discuss how it relates to representativeness. Second, we propose an information-theoretic procedure for sampling representative phrases from a large corpus. Third, we describe the characteristics of phrase sets we generated using the procedure for email and social media (Facebook and Twitter).

ENTROPY AND REPRESENTATIVENESS
Information theory was developed in the 1940s by Claude Shannon [14] as a method to quantify "information" and determine the mathematical limits of signal processing

tasks such as data compression and reliable transmission through a noisy communication channel. The basic measure of information in the theory is *entropy*, which is computed for a random variable X over a discrete set of symbols χ (e.g., characters) with probability distribution $p(x)$ as:

$$H(X) = -\sum_{x \in \chi} p(x) \log_2 p(x)$$

The logarithm can be any base, but with log base 2, the resulting value is measured in bits. While entropy is often explained as the lower bound on the number of bits it would take to encode an outcome of X, or as the expected uncertainty of X, it can also be viewed in terms of the *Twenty Questions* game. If χ is the set of English characters, and we are given 20 yes/no questions to ascertain characters in sequence (e.g., "Is the next character a vowel?"), then entropy measures how many questions on average are needed to identify each character with total certainty [11]. In other words, $H(X)$ measures the size of the search space consisting of possible values of X and their probabilities.

We can leverage entropy to quantify and compare the "representativeness" of samples of phrases with respect to a source corpus. Suppose $p(x)$ and $q(x)$ are probability distributions of random variable X over the same set of English characters χ. In particular, let $p(x)$ be the probability distribution for a sample of a corpus, and $q(x)$ be the probability distribution for the source corpus itself. The difference between these probability distributions can be measured by *relative entropy*, or the *Kullback-Leibler divergence*:

$$D(p||q) = \sum_{x \in \chi} p(x) \log_2 \frac{p(x)}{q(x)}$$

The relative entropy is always non-negative and $D(p||q) = 0$ only when the distributions are identical. Hence, the more representative the sample distribution $p(x)$ is of the source distribution $q(x)$, the closer the relative entropy will be to zero. Note that we must be careful about interpreting relative entropy; although it may appear to be a distance metric, technically it is not because $D(p \parallel q) \neq D(q \parallel p)$ and it fails to satisfy the triangle inequality [2].

For representativeness, MacKenzie and Soukoreff (2001) [9] compute the correlation coefficient between two normalized letter frequencies. However, this approach essentially treats the frequencies as two random variables and measures the linear dependence between them. For comparing probability distributions, relative entropy constitutes a more mathematically principled method.

Perplexity

Related to relative entropy is the concept of cross-entropy. Suppose we have a true probability distribution $p(x)$ that generates some data and we wish to produce from that data a model distribution m that approximates p. To have as accurate of a model as possible, we need to minimize the relative entropy $D(m \parallel p)$, but of course we do not know p. Fortunately, cross-entropy allows us to still compare m with competing models.

By treating language as a stationary and ergodic (see [5] for more details) stochastic process consisting of a sequence of symbols $(X_i) \sim p(x)$ drawn from p, the *cross-entropy* between the empirically observed sequence (X_i) and a model m is given by:

$$H(X_i, m) = -\lim_{n \to \infty} \frac{1}{n} \log_2 m(x_1\, x_2 \dots x_n)$$

If n is sufficiently large, we can drop the limit and approximate cross-entropy as:

$$H(X_i, m) \approx -\frac{1}{n} \log_2 m(x_1\, x_2 \dots x_n)$$

Because $H(p) \leq H(p, m)$, the cross-entropy provides an upper bound on the true entropy of p. Hence, the more accurate m is, the closer the cross-entropy will be to the true entropy. This provides a way to compare which model of p is better without having to know p: just pick the model with the lowest cross-entropy.

To make cross-entropy easier to interpret, researchers in statistical natural language processing often utilize perplexity, which is just:

$$perplexity(X_i) = 2^{H(X_i, m)} = m(x_1\, x_2 \dots x_n)^{-\frac{1}{n}}$$

Perplexity is the default measure of *n-gram* language models [11], which predict a set of symbols (e.g., words, characters, grammatical constituents, etc.) based on the history of previous symbols. Just as entropy provides a measure of the size of a search space, the perplexity of a language model expresses the average branching factor of the prediction search space – in particular, the average number of equi-probable symbols that can follow any given symbol. By building language models for a particular task, domain or language, the lowest perplexity we can obtain for the language model tells us how difficult the prediction task is for that task, domain or language. For example, a coin flip has a perplexity of 2 whereas a die roll has a perplexity of 6. Predicting what word follows any previous two words (i.e., trigram language model) for the Wall Street Journal has a perplexity of 170 [5]. We report the perplexities of language models we learned for our email and social media corpora in the last section.

SAMPLING PROCEDURE

Given the information-theoretic concepts we discussed in the previous section, we can now propose a procedure for sampling representative phrases from a large corpus. For text entry experiments, because the most significant point of differentiation is the mechanism to enter characters, words and phrases [9], we have geared our procedure towards text entry of characters. However, it should not be difficult for researchers to adjust the procedure to whatever units of input they are examining. In addition, because

Fitt's Law is commonly invoked in many character entry experiments, we have focused the procedure on obtaining representative character *bigrams* (2 character sequences) to capture distances typically travelled between keystrokes. Finally, like MacKenzie and Soukoreff [9], we sought to procure phrases of "moderate length" – about 4 words, though this can be easily adjusted as well. While we did not attempt to select phrases that were "easy to remember", which was manually done in [9], as a future direction, we could explore using entropy for selection as well, especially in light of prior research demonstrating a correlation between entropy rate and reading comprehension [6].

The procedure operates as follows:

1. Obtain a large corpus of interest. Many corpora can nowadays be obtained online for a wide variety of tasks, domains and languages (e.g., [8]).
2. Clean the text to remove any undesired portions of text (e.g., MIME encoding for emails, punctuations, etc.).
3. Collect all word 4-grams (4 word sequences) from the text, keeping around duplicates as separate entries. To adjust the phrase length, change the n-gram order n to the desired number of words.
4. Randomly generate an index number between 1 and the total number of 4-gram entries.
5. Find the 4-gram at the generated index and store this as a phrase for sample phrase set S_i.
6. Repeat steps 4-5 until M sample phrase sets of the desired size (e.g., 500 in [9]) are obtained.
7. Using the source corpus C, for each sample phrase set S_i, compute the relative entropy $D(S_i \parallel C)$ (see equation in previous section) of the character bigram distributions.
8. Select the sample phrase set S^* with the lowest relative entropy:

$$S^* = \underset{S_i}{\operatorname{argmin}}\, D(S_i \parallel C)$$

Note that steps 3-5 can also be performed efficiently using *inverse transform sampling* [3]. Furthermore, the number of sample phrase sets S_i that researchers may wish to collect depends on how much time they can devote to collecting candidates for computing relative entropy. For the three phrase sets we discuss next, we selected the best from among 100 samples.

In using character bigrams, it is worth remembering that n-grams only provide an empirical estimate of the true probabilities. While using higher order n may allow better modeling of the underlying distributions, it requires more data for estimation. Furthermore, larger samples may be required to achieve reasonable representativeness.

THREE PHRASE SETS

Using the procedure described in the previous section, we generated phrase sets for email and social media. The source corpus for the email phrase set is the Enron Email Data Set, a subset of which can be publicly accessed at [1], containing approximately 517,431 Enron employee emails from 1999 to 2002. For social media, we tapped into public feeds from Facebook and Twitter. For Facebook, we collected the subset of status update messages on August 15, 2010 marked as English, for a total of 295M words across 18.7M messages. For Twitter, we collected all tweets on September 1, 2010 marked as English, yielding a total of 164M words across 12.6M tweets.

	Enron	Facebook	Twitter
# unique unigrams	102	8,609	7,864
unigram perplexity	30.70	28.05	33.36
# unique bigrams	8,281	125,657	95,659
bigram perplexity	21.26	19.97	24.50
# unique word 4-grams	84M	239M	126M

Table 1. Characteristics of the Enron Email, Facebook and Twitter corpora used to generate phrase sets

In order to demonstrate the importance of using the procedure to find representative phrases, in Figure 1, we plot the mean and standard deviation of the relative entropy over various phrase set sizes on the Enron corpus, computed over 100 random samples. As shown, the average relative entropy decreases as we increase the phrase set size, since there are less quantization effects due to sampling. Whereas the standard deviation for large phrase set sizes are negligible, it is quite significant for smaller phrase set sizes. In other words, it is much more important to make sure that a sample phrase set is "representative" of the source corpus when there is a small number of phrases (e.g., 500) than when there is a large number (e.g., 10K). We suspect that most text entry experiments only utilize a small number of phrases.

Table 1 reports the characteristics of the three corpora. Looking at the number of unigrams, or unique characters, the reason why Facebook and Twitter has over 7000 is due to the inclusion of non-English text. Despite the greater number of unigrams, if we look at the perplexity, predicting the next character in social media is at just about the same level of difficulty (about 30) as in email. Similarly, email and social

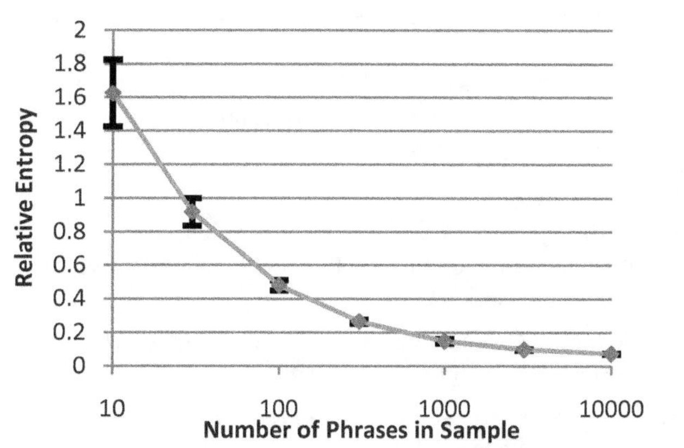

Figure 1. Relative entropy decreasing as the number of phrases in the sample increases on the Enron corpus.

Enron	Facebook	Twitter
just let me know	I'm lonely and I'm	waitin on your call
world's most liquid trading	there LOL. I learned	NOW FOLLOWIN >> @
We have the power	what im gonna do	you could win a
only 20% of stocks	that I spend with	Bout to get my
administration's national energy policy	text them to me	checked...n forwarded also..!! :)
market dipped sharply right	make things work (:	am not even kidding
the late House Speaker	of pics I have	happy hour with a
because it was your	creeppiest dream.. EVER o.o...	me. Take me, free
and penchant for double-burgers,	don't even do that	little bit of fun
happy to exploit any	me and my fam	wan go home! i

Table 2. Sample phrase sets from the Enron Email, Facebook and Twitter corpora.

media have about the same bigram perplexity; on average, predicting the next character given its previous character has a branching factor of about 20. For generating the phrase sets, we had a lot more uniq 4-grams to sample from in the Facebook corpus (239 million) than in the other corpora. Table 2 presents sample phrases from the three corpora. Note that in generating the phrase sets, we may not have fully scrubbed the text of all offensive language. For Facebook and Twitter especially, this is a difficult problem due to the variety of creative ways in which users express profanity. We recommend that researchers manually inspect the phrase sets and remove any undesirable text. Phrase sets of varying sizes for all three corpora and sample code for the procedure are publicly available for download at http://research.microsoft.com/phrasesets/.

CONCLUSION

In this paper, we presented a procedure for sampling representative phrases from a large corpus so that text input researchers can curate their own stimuli targeting specific tasks, domains and languages. The procedure relies on measuring representativeness as the relative entropy between the probability distributions of the sample phrase set and the source corpus. Researchers can modify the procedure to obtain phrase sets of the desired unit of input, word length, etc. We applied the procedure to create three phrase sets for email and social media, and discussed their perplexities. The phrase sets and code for the procedure are available as a public resource.

REFERENCES

1. 2001 Topic Annotated Enron Email Data Set. http://www.ldc.upenn.edu/Catalog/CatalogEntry.jsp?catalogId=LDC2007T22
2. Cover, T. M. and Thomas, J. A. *Elements of Information Theory*. Wiley-Interscience, 1991.
3. Devroye, L. *Non-Uniform Random Variate Generation*. Springer-Verlag, 1986
4. Google Web 1T 5-Gram Corpus. http://www.ldc.upenn.edu/Catalog/CatalogEntry.jsp?catalogId=LDC2006T13
5. Jurafsky, D. and Martin, J. *Speech and Language Processing, Second Edition*. Prentice Hall, 2009.
6. Keller, F. The entropy rate principle as a predictor of processing effort: An evaluation against eye-tracking data. *Proc. of EMNLP* (2004), 317-324.
7. Liebert, R. M. and Liebert, L. L. *Science and Behavior: An Introduction to Methods of Psychological Research*. Englewood Cliffs, NJ, Prentice Hall, 1995.
8. Linguistic Data Consortium. http://www.ldc.upenn.edu
9. MacKenzie, I. S. and Soukoreff, R. W. Phrase sets for evaluating text entry techniques. *Extended Abstracts of CHI 2003*, 754-755
10. MacKenzie, I. S. and Tanaka-Ishii, K. *Text Entry Systems: Mobility, Accessibility, Universality*. Morgan Kaufmann, 2007.
11. Manning, C. and Schütze, H. *Foundations of Statistical Natural Language Processing*. MIT Press, 1999.
12. Mayzner, M. S. and Tresselt, M. E. Table of single letter and digram frequency counts for various word-length and letter-position combinations, *Psychonomic Monograph Supplements I* (1965), 13-32.
13. Microsoft Web N-Gram Services. http://research.microsoft.com/web-ngram
14. Shannon, C. E. *The Mathematical Theory of Communication*. University of Illinois Press, 1949.
15. Wang, K., Thrasher, C., Viegas, E., Li, E. and Hsu, P. An overview of Microsoft Web N-gram corpus and applications. *Proc. of NAACL-HLT* (2010), 45-48.

Enhancing Physicality in Touch Interaction with Programmable Friction

Vincent Lévesque[1], Louise Oram[1], Karon MacLean[1], Andy Cockburn[2], Nicholas D. Marchuk[3], Dan Johnson[3], J. Edward Colgate[3], Michael A. Peshkin[3]

[1] University of British Columbia, Vancouver, BC Canada, {vlev,olouise,maclean}@cs.ubc.ca

[2] University of Canterbury, Christchurch, New Zealand, andy@cosc.canterbury.ac.nz

[3] Northwestern University, Evanston, IL USA, {colgate,peshkin}@northwestern.edu

ABSTRACT

Touch interactions have refreshed some of the 'glowing enthusiasm' of thirty years ago for direct manipulation interfaces. However, today's touch technologies, whose interactions are supported by graphics, sounds or crude clicks, have a tactile sameness and gaps in usability. We use a Large Area Tactile Pattern Display (LATPaD) to examine design possibilities and outcomes when touch interactions are enhanced with variable surface friction. In a series of four studies, we first confirm that variable friction gives significant performance advantages in low-level targeting activities. We then explore the design space of variable friction interface controls and assess user reactions. Most importantly, we demonstrate that variable friction can have a positive impact on the enjoyment, engagement and sense of realism experienced by users of touch interfaces.

Author Keywords

Haptics, tactile feedback, touch screen.

ACM Classification Keywords

H5.2. [User Interfaces]: Interaction Styles, Haptic I/O.

General Terms

Design, Experimentation, Human Factors, Performance.

INTRODUCTION

As recognition of the impact of emotion on design grows [19], designers seek natural, realistic and organic [26] means of interaction. In 1983, Shneiderman [29] observed the 'glowing enthusiasm' resulting from graphical user interfaces that allowed users to directly manipulate objects. The iPhone's success suggests a similar role of engagement and delight, presumably through the directness and realism of touch interfaces. This is driving renewed research interest in interaction metaphors using touch (e.g. [4,12]).

However, touch interactions with most current devices are 'flat' – all interface objects still *feel* like the same plastic or glass, so any physical realism must be communicated through visual and auditory illusions. Tactile effects are generally limited to clicks and buzzes that can convey a great deal of information [16] but lack realism.

This paper examines design possibilities and outcomes when touch interactions are enhanced with variable surface friction. We use a Large Area Tactile Pattern Display (LATPaD) [17,32] which creates a friction-reducing 'squeeze film' of air on a touch sensitive display's surface through imperceptible high-frequency vibrations (Figure 1). The prototype consists of a glass plate with bonded piezoelectric actuators atop an LCD screen. A 57x76 mm touchscreen is created with laser-based measurement of finger position. Friction effects are produced by varying vibration amplitude in response to finger movements.

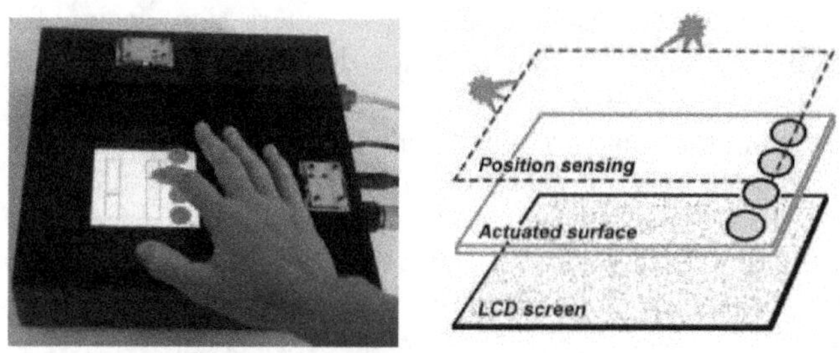

(a) (b)

Figure 1. (a) Picture and (b) illustration of components of the Large Area Tactile Pattern Display (LATPaD).

The ability to vary friction raises interaction possibilities which are interesting from both performance and emotional standpoints. Activities such as pointing and dragging may become more efficient: high friction objects might 'grab' the finger, reducing overshoot and errors, while low friction surfaces should ease sliding movements and reduce finger judder. Emotionally, variable friction may increase perceived realism and subjective satisfaction. In this paper, we report experiments measuring both effects. The specific contributions of our work are as follows:

1. Performance data showing that variable friction can improve performance in touch interactions;
2. Qualitative and quantitative evidence that friction enhanced widgets can positively impact users' emotional response to touch interactions;
3. An exploration of friction-enhanced interface design.

After providing background, we describe two studies (S1-2) examining the impact of variable friction on target selection performance, without and with surrounding distracters; S3 characterizes the effect of friction on biomechanical control. We then present design concepts exploiting variable friction and examine users' subjective responses (S4). Finally, we discuss our findings and conclude.

BACKGROUND

Issues grounding our approach range from past work to our own hypotheses on the value of variable friction.

Touch Interaction Without Tactile Feedback

Buxton et al.'s 1985 analysis of touchscreen limitations still holds: signaling while pointing requires pressure and virtual widgets need haptics [5]. Recent systems have exploited non-feedback touch to address issues like 'fat finger' occlusion, accuracy and the need to feel edges. Roudaut et al. identified these concerns for target acquisition on small touchscreens and proposed zoom techniques for thumb-based selection [27]. Physical metaphors have inspired new, more fluid gestures [25]. Others have elaborated strategies for particular control actions: Potter et al. attributed high accuracy of 'lift-off' selection to its continuous nature [22]. Increasing the tactile feedback available during this contact stream could be even more beneficial.

Tactility in Mobile Devices and Touchscreens

There are now many examples of interaction design for tactile feedback in touch-surface devices, e.g. [15,23], as well as research and commercial instantiations based on technologies such as piezo- or solenoid-actuated screens. Nearly all rely on vibration. An interesting alternative is electrovibration, which produces sensations of friction or vibration using periodic electrostatic forces [3]. Vibrations can also be applied with passive [24] or actuated pens [10].

While most efforts have layered tactile feedback atop a normal GUI (e.g. tactile overlays on soft keyboards that indicate key proximity and presses [13]), it is arguable that greater benefits are possible for interactions designed *around* taction. Pokespace relies on forces for its gesture set, and found reduced visual demand in augmented widgets tested in a similar manner to our Study 4 [30].

Generally, speed and accuracy have improved when haptics is included in pointing tasks [1,6,7]. This result is nuanced, however: in absence of knowledge of user's destination, feedback may also be encountered for non-target elements, which can introduce obstructions and slowdowns [6,14,20]. Furthermore, user preference does not always follow targeting utility [31].

Theoretical Arguments for Variable Friction

Illusions can be exploited to improve the performance or immediacy of a passive touch interaction. Synchronous sound and graphics can suggest absent tactile feedback. Users "feel" auditory clicks [8]; Apple's iPod took this illusion mainstream. But it fails when the earbuds are out, and lacks the useful physical constraint of a real click. Likewise, visuo-haptic effects such as 'sticky widgets', a manipulation of mouse control-display gain, can improve selection performance by curtailing overshoot in the closed-loop phase of motion and enlarging the motor space [2]. Variable friction may further improve performance by making the finger *actually* stick to the target.

Touch interfaces are also subject to the biomechanics of finger sliding on glass, which produces asymmetric stick-slip [18]. 'Judder' is greatest in the distal direction ('north') where friction acts to bend the finger, opposed by extensor muscles. Bending reduces contact angle, increasing the force required to maintain movement ('stick'), then the finger springs forward ('slip'). Proximal or sideways dragging is resisted skeletally with a relatively constant contact angle. Lowering friction should reduce judder for even distal movements.

Variable Friction Devices: the LATPaD

The LATPaD varies the friction felt by the fingertip at the touch surface. Its operating principle, a squeeze film of air produced by 26 kHz piezo-actuated vibrations, lowers the friction coefficient of a glass surface from ~1.0 to ~0.15. Unpublished experiments indicate that the just-noticeable-difference in friction is about 30-40%; thus the LATPaD's dynamic range provides several distinguishable friction levels. Other models demonstrate this effect on larger and smaller plates of arbitrary shape and a range of materials.

Still in early development, our prototype has several limitations. The piezo actuation is compact, but the optical position sensing uses a larger housing. The piezos produce audible noise when active. The vibrational mode used produces nodes where friction reduction is weaker (here, 2 narrow strips parallel to the longer screen axis). Development continues, focusing on these issues. Within 2-3 years, programmable friction is expected to be deployable in a form factor similar to current touchscreens with uniform feedback and no audible noise.

A Design Space for Variable-Friction Touch

These and other works (e.g. [28]) demonstrate that while entrancing, current touch technology leaves usability gaps: it is hard to accurately point, select and drag, to select and enter text, and to achieve drag & drop functions. The illusion of physicality, with both its utility and aesthetic, disappears with the withdrawal of image or sound.

In ongoing work, we are defining the design space where variable friction offers value by filling these gaps. This space is structured around dimensions of (1) rendered effects (e.g. impact, edges, stiffness) and (2) communicated information (e.g. selection support and confirmation, functional availability, spatial navigation). It has guided the design of Study 4, by indicating both the extent of the space to be sampled and opportunities within it.

STUDIES 1-3: FRICTION PSYCHOPHYSICS

S1-S3 were conducted in one session and studied the effect of variable friction on target selection and finger motion.

Study 1: Target Selection Without Distracters

S1 concerns the speed and accuracy of target selection with and without variable friction. Based on the theoretical ability of variable friction to halt the finger on target, we hypothesize:

H1. Variable friction across the surface, with high friction over the target, will improve selection speed and accuracy.

A secondary consideration is the overall level of friction during targeting. Any benefit of varying friction could be explained solely by faster inter-target movement caused by the more slippery surface, rather than by differential friction at the target. The study controls for this effect, leading to the second hypothesis:

H2. There will be no significant difference between selection speed and accuracy when using a constant low level and a constant high level of friction.

Selection modality: lift-off. Friction only matters during sliding surface contact. Thus traditional Fitts' Law [9] 'tapping tasks', where most or all movement occurs above the surface, are unlikely to be influenced by friction effects; we therefore analyzed drag-based selections that are issued when the finger lifts off the surface. This is a common modality on touch devices, particularly when targets are small (e.g., sliding text entry on the iPhone). Furthermore, a lift-off selection modality has been seen to be more accurate than others for touch input in some contexts [22].

Direction. We controlled for movement direction (north, south, east and west), with the aim of revealing movement dynamics rather than testing a specific hypothesis.

Procedure

Participants were given written instructions on how to interact with the LATPaD. They then tried the device for one minute by rubbing a finger across a checkerboard with high and low friction. They were given the exact procedure for each of trials, which consists of the following steps:

1. *Initial state.* A thin blue 'control' line and a red 'target' line appear on the display.
2. *Acquire control line* by touching and remaining stationary on it. For any movement off the control line or off the surface, the trial is repeated.
3. *Free control line and begin.* After holding for 0.2 second, an audible beep is heard and the control line is freed to move. The clock starts on movement.
4. *Drag control line over target.* The target turns green to confirm the over-target state, and in some conditions friction changes over the target.
5. *Lift-off to select* by raising the finger off the target. The target turns back to red briefly and the control line disappears until the next trial.

Participants completed 30 training selections with a 36 pixel (5.62 mm) wide target (data discarded). Ten were completed with each interface condition with the same order of exposure as for experimental trials (below). To reduce any possible influence of the LATPaD's audible sound, participants listened to white noise through Direct Sound Extreme Isolation EX-29 headphones throughout.

Each participant then completed 336 experimental trials (96 discarded) covering three factors: *interface*, *direction*, and *target width*. The three levels of interface were constant high friction (*HF*), constant low friction (*LF*) and variable friction (*VF*). In *HF* and *LF*, LATPaD oscillations were always turned off or maximally on, respectively. In *VF*, friction was high (LATPaD off) over the target, but low (maximally on) everywhere else. We did not test inverse variable friction (low over the target and high elsewhere) as it does not offer the psychophysical advantages of 'finger trapping' promised by *VF*. The four levels of direction were north (*n*), south (*s*), east (*e*), and west (*w*); and the four levels of width were 6, 12, 24, and 48 pixels (0.94, 1.87, 3.74 and 7.49 mm). The device was physically rotated when changing direction axis (*n/s*, *e/w*) so that movement remained within an optimal friction region. Movement amplitude was always 225 pixels (35.1 mm). The control and target lines were shifted slightly towards the *n* or *w* side of the screen to avoid interference from the raised screen rim. Figure 2 shows the interface for north-direction selections for the four widths.

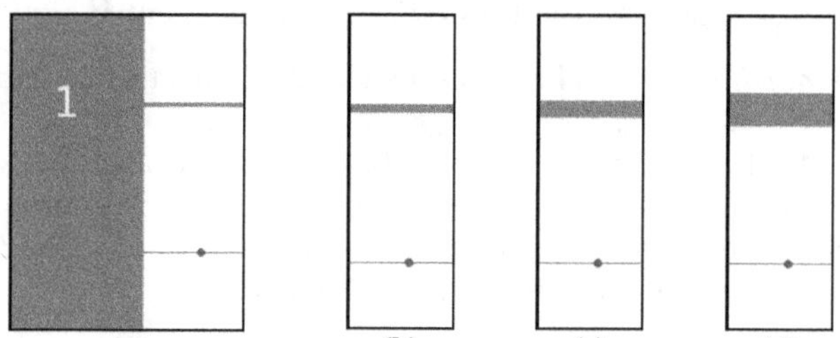

(a) (b) (c) (d)

Figure 2. Target acquisition task for S1 in the *North* direction: (a) entire screen for first interface with width of 6 pixels, and partial screen with widths of (b) 12, (c) 24 and (d) 48 pixels.

The experimental trials (target acquisitions) were administered as blocks of 14 trials, each block sharing a direction axis (*n/s*, *e/w*), interface level (*LF*, *HF*, *VF*) and target size (6, 12, 24, 48). The first 4 trials of each block were discarded to allow for strategy adaptation. Initial direction was randomized for each block, then alternated on the direction axis. Blocks sharing a direction axis were administered consecutively to minimize physical device rotation; then grouped by interface level to allow questionnaire assessment. Block sets were counterbalanced such that all combinations of 2!=2 direction axis orderings and 3!=6 interface level orderings were used for one participant. Finally, block target size was randomized within same-interface sets. A total of 24 blocks (2 direction axis × 3 interface levels × 4 target sizes) were administered.

After each of the 6 sets, participants were asked to comment on the interface used and respond to 5-point Likert-scale questions (strongly disagree to strongly agree): "I performed well / needed to concentrate to accomplish the task / felt confident in my ability to hit the target / felt frustrated / enjoyed interacting with the touchscreen." After completing all trials, participants were asked to rank the interfaces ('ties' permitted) and for final comments. Interface was referred to by order of appearance, reinforced with a numerical label on the side of the display during use.

Participants

Twelve participants (6 female) were recruited from a local university: aged 19-48 (mean 29.4), all right-handed.

Design and Analysis

Dependent measures are analyzed using a 3×4×4 repeated measures analysis of variance for the factors *interface* ∈ {*HF, LF, VF*}, *direction* ∈ {*n, s, e, w*}, and *target width* ∈ {6, 12, 24, 48 pixels}. The dependent measures are selection time, number of errors, time between entering the target and lifting off it, and number of overshoots. We also analyze the goodness of fit to Fitts' Law models (coefficient of determination) and subjective responses.

Results

In summary: variable friction (*VF*) improved targeting performance over *HF* without compromising accuracy, thus we accept *H1*. The constant low friction conditions (*LF*) produced similar results as *HF*, so we also accept *H2*.

Acquisition time. There was a significant effect of *interface* ($F_{2,22}$=6.89, p<.01), with *VF* fastest (mean 921 ms, s.d. 324), then *HF* (mean 990, s.d. 344) and *LF* (mean 1002, s.d. 341); see Figure 3. Posthoc comparison using Bonferroni correction confirms differences between *VF* and both *HF* and *LF* (p<.05), but not between *HF* and *LF*.

As anticipated, there was a significant main effect of *width* ($F_{3,33}$=82.2, p<.001); but there was also a significant *interface×width* interaction ($F_{6,66}$=3.85, p<.01). Figure 3 suggests that *VF* performance deteriorated less rapidly across increasing Index of Difficulty than the other conditions. This explanation is supported by the Fitts' Law analysis, which showed strong models for all conditions (R^2>0.98). The lower slope for *VF* corresponds to an Index of Performance (reciprocal of the slope) of 7.26 bits/s, which is higher than either *HF* (5.07) or *LF* (5.74). There was no significant main effect of *direction* ($F_{3,33}$=1.8, p=.17), with means of 943, 960, 996 and 984 ms for *n, s, e* and *w* movement respectively.

Accuracy. Analysis of count of trials per block containing an error shows no significant effect of *interface* ($F_{2,22}$=0.74, p=0.49), with similar means of 0.82 errors with *VF*, and 0.7 and 0.81 for *HF* and *LF* respectively. The relatively high error rate is due to the use of small targets, and as expected, there is a significant effect of *width* ($F_{3,33}$=53.9, p<0.001), with errors increasing from 0.14 errors per block with 48-pixel targets to 1.8 with 6-pixel targets. There was a significant effect of *direction* ($F_{3,33}$=10.0, p<.01) with the *s* movement being the most error prone (1.2 errors per block) and *n* being the least (0.4). Importantly, however, there was no *interface×width* ($F_{6,66}$=1.13, p=0.36) or *interface×direction* interaction ($F_{6,66}$=1.16, p=0.34).

Source of VF performance advantage. There are several possible explanations for the performance advantage with variable friction: users may move more quickly, resulting in a shorter target approach; they may respond more quickly to the over-target state, resulting in a shorter dwell time over the target; or variable friction may 'trap' the finger on the target, reducing overshoot. To understand which of these are at play, we conducted three more one-way ANOVAs (Figure 4) with dependent variables of approach time (from initial movement to last target border entry), dwell time (from last target border entry to lift-off), and entry count (number of times the target border was entered).

This revealed a significant effect for approach time ($F_{2,22}$=5.69, p<0.05) with *VF* faster (mean 634 ms, s.d. 268) than either *HF* (690, 283) or *LF* (706, 276). Neither dwell time ($F_{2,22}$=1.0, p=0.38) nor entry count ($F_{2,22}$=0.87, p=0.43) varied significantly, although *VF* had the lowest mean in both. Consequently, it seems that the largest effect of target acquisition with *VF* is that it increases users' confidence in moving towards the target, allowing them to approach more quickly without compromising ability to stop abruptly on the target and select it accurately [14].

Subjective results. Participants were asked to rank each interface condition after both *e/w* and *n/s* trial blocks. *VF* was ranked 1st 58.3% of the time, 2nd 29.2%, and 3rd 12.5%, producing a significant difference (Friedman χ^2=9.5, p<.01); mean rankings were 1.5, 2.0 and 2.1 for *VF, LF,*

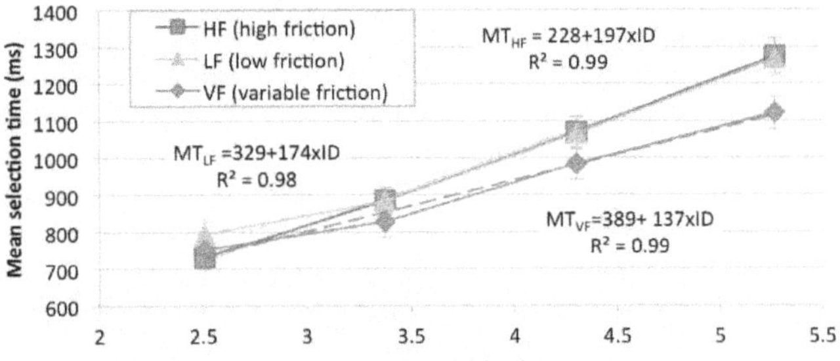

Figure 3. Results and Fitts' law models for interfaces (S1).

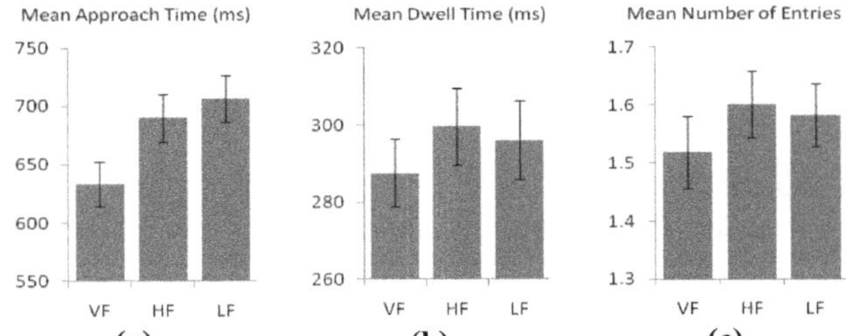

Figure 4. (a) Approach time, (b) dwell time, and (c) number of target entries as a function of the interface condition (S1).

and *HF*. Questionnaire responses (Table 1) show that mean ratings for *VF* were most appreciative in all five questions, but only significantly so for enjoyment.

	VF	LF	HF	χ^2_r	Sig
Performance	3.9 (0.7)	3.7 (0.8)	3.5 (0.7)	2.3	=0.31
Concentration	3.2 (1.0)	3.7 (1.0)	3.5 (1.0)	3.4	=0.18
Confidence	4.0 (0.7)	3.5 (0.8)	3.7 (0.6)	2.8	=0.25
Frustration	1.8 (0.7)	2.0 (0.8)	2.2 (0.8)	2.3	=0.31
Enjoyment	4.2 (0.7)	3.8 (0.8)	3.6 (0.8)	5.8	=0.05

Table 1. Mean (st. dev.) questionnaire responses, with 1= strongly disagree, and 5 = strongly agree (S1).

Study 2: Target Selection With Distracters

Previous work has demonstrated that tactile feedback can negatively influence performance in the presence of distracter targets [6]. This is a critical limitation, as most practical deployments will involve distracters. Therefore we tested the hypothesis that:

H3. Variable friction will not adversely affect targeting performance in the presence of distracter targets.

Procedure, Apparatus and Participants

The 12 participants from S1 proceeded immediately to S2. The task was identical to S1 but the space from the control line to the target and beyond was populated with distracters of the target's width. All distracters produced the same visual and tactile effects as the target, i.e. highlighted green to indicate over-target state, and presence of friction effects. Distracters were otherwise black.

Distracter density is an important variable for *H3*, so three levels of distracter separation were used: 5, 20, and 40 pixels (Figure 5). Targets and distracters were 24 pixels in width. The number of distracters placed before the target varied from 1 to 3; one distracter was always behind the target. We tested only one direction axis, and selected *n/s* for a greater range of biomechanical effects.

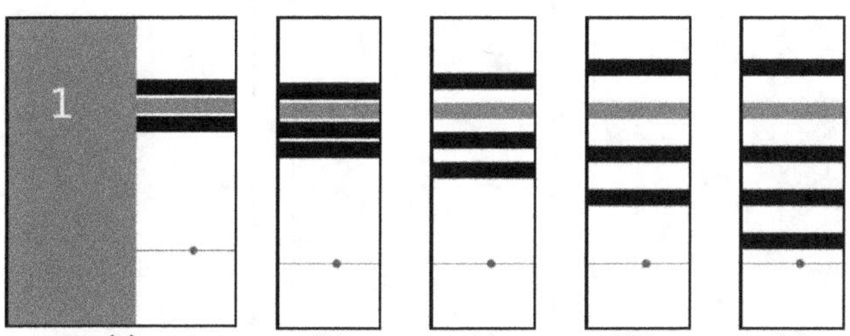

(a) (b) (c) (d) (e)

Figure 5. Target acquisition task for S2 in the *n* direction: (a) entire and (b-e) partial screen for first *interface* with 1 to 3 pre-target distracters and a *separation* of 5, 20 and 40 pixels.

A block held twenty-two target selections (trials); three blocks were performed per interface condition. The direction (*n*, *s*) was initially randomized for each block and then alternated. The number of distracters and their spacing were selected randomly for the first four trials (discarded). To prevent memorization of the tactile pattern leading to the target and its use as an aid, the remaining 18 trials cycled randomly through all 3×3 combinations of distracter number and spacing in each direction (*n*, *s*). Interface order and subjective responses were controlled as for S1.

Design

The same dependent measures as S1 are analyzed in a 3×2×3×3 repeated measures analysis of variance for *interface* ∈ {*HF, LF, VF*}, *direction* ∈ {*n, s*}, *distracter spacing* ∈ {5, 20, 40 pixels} and *number* ∈ {1, 2, 3}.

Results

In summary: the results show no effects of *interface* (main or interactions) for dependent measures of time or errors, thus we accept *H3*.

Performance. A four-way ANOVA showed a significant effect of *distracter spacing* on acquisition time ($F_{2,22}$=13.3, p<.01), with mean of 908, 892 and 874 ms for 5, 20 and 40 pixel spacing respectively. There were no significant main effects or interactions involving interface for either task time or errors. Mean times were similar (900, 892, 882 ms for *VF, HF, LF*; $F_{2,22}$=0.26, p=0.78), as were per block error rates (0.16, 0.22, 0.19; $F_{2,22}$=0.71, p=0.5). S1 trials (zero distracters) with *n/s* directions and 24-pixel targets were also compared to S2 (1, 2 or 3 distracters). A three-way ANOVA for factors *interface*, *direction* and *number of distracters* revealed no significant effects.

Subjective results. The participant's interface rankings were similar to S1: a significant preference for *VF*, but non-significant responses to other questions.

Study 3: Constant Velocity Dragging

To characterize physical effects occurring at friction borders, we conducted a third shorter study with the same participants immediately after S2. Participants tried to achieve a target drag velocity in repeated bidirectional strokes across the display by following an audible metronomic tempo. We tested two speeds (50 / 100 mm/s, or 320.5 / 641.0 pixels/s), and both orientations (*n/s, e/w*). Friction patterns (not shown visually) were produced in the middle of the strokes, including constant levels, step changes, and single or sequential pulses with the same extent, number and separation as S1 and S2's targets and distracters. Each participant performed 168 trials in six blocks. The first six trials of each block were discarded to allow speed adjustment. The order of patterns was randomized within blocks and each pattern shown once.

Results

Finger position and velocity trajectories were plotted against friction state and inspected visually for all 1584 trials. An effect of variable friction is clear in many trajectories. Figure 6 shows the best examples, where a step increase or decrease in friction leads to a temporary deceleration or acceleration of the finger. This suggests that finger velocity is affected at least under certain conditions. A sticky target with variable friction may therefore be truly sticky. This effect may in other cases have been reduced by stick-slip of the fingerpad or finger pressure, or masked by the low spatio-temporal data. A quantitative analysis is beyond the scope of this paper, but currently underway.

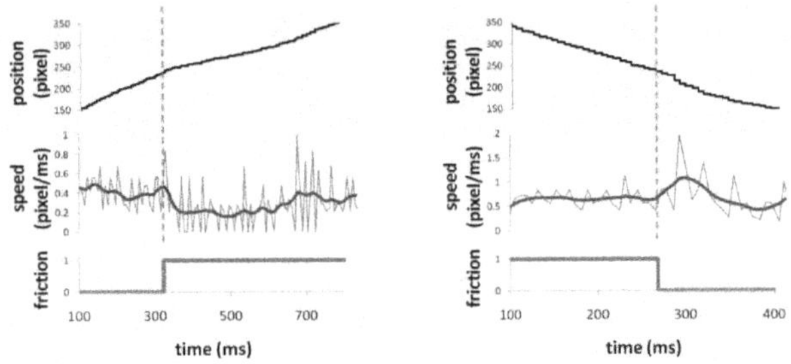

(a) (b)

Figure 6. Selected S3 results: (a) deceleration after increase in friction (P2, *e*), (b) acceleration after step decrease (P4, *n*).

STUDY 4: DESIGN EXAMPLES AND USER EXPERIENCE

We explored interface design for variable friction interfaces in an iterative process, beginning with glass etched prototypes, then exemplar designs, which finally led to a study to establish their emotional and subjective impact.

Demonstration Applications and Study Tasks

Four exemplar widgets were designed to provide good coverage of tactile sensations and of communication functions that variable friction might support.

Alarm Clock. Users set the alarm time using wheel widgets and the alarm sound using a combo box (Figure 7a-c). The wheels produce strong ticks by abruptly increasing friction as items near their center (Figure 7d). The combo box produces similar ticks but with friction peaks between targets (Figure 7e). The *Alarm Clock* study task involved setting the time and sound to a value displayed at the bottom of the screen.

File Manager. File, folder and recycle bin icons are arranged in a 3×4 array (Figure 8a); target icons enlarge 20% when a file hovers over them (Figure 8b-c). Initially low, friction increases abruptly over folders and oscillates at 37.5 Hz over the recycle bin, producing a bump and buzzing respectively (Figure 8d). The *File Manager* study task involved moving eight files labeled 1 to 3 into folders.

Game. The game consists of bouncing a ball against a round cursor around the finger and breaking bricks (Figure 9a-c). Some require multiple hits to be broken; others produce special effects - releasing a second ball or making the ball bounce erratically. The ball is launched by compressing a spring, with gradual increase in friction to simulate resistance (Figure 9a, d). For ball impact (Figure 9b, e), friction abruptly increases as the ball nears the cursor. Erratic bouncing (Figure 9c) produces the friction oscillation used on the *File Manager* recycle bin. The Game study task was to play the game, with ten difficulty levels.

Text Editor. Words are selected by dwelling with a cursor extending above the finger, avoiding occlusions. While dragging a word, collisions with adjacent words result in visual compression up to 30%, after which words remain fixed (Figure 10a). A word swaps with its neighbor when the cursor reaches a position where it can be relocated. Swiping left or right flips pages (Figure 10b). When dragging within a line, friction increases with compression, and drops abruptly after a swap, creating a popping sensation (Figure 10c). When dragging between lines, friction effects fade in and out across lines, with a brief friction pulse in-between. Page swaps trigger a tick via an abrupt increase in friction. The *Text Editor* study task consisted of 'fixing' sentences by reordering words within pages – e.g. "the store grocery sells yellow tomatoes green bananas red lettuce and eggplants purple."

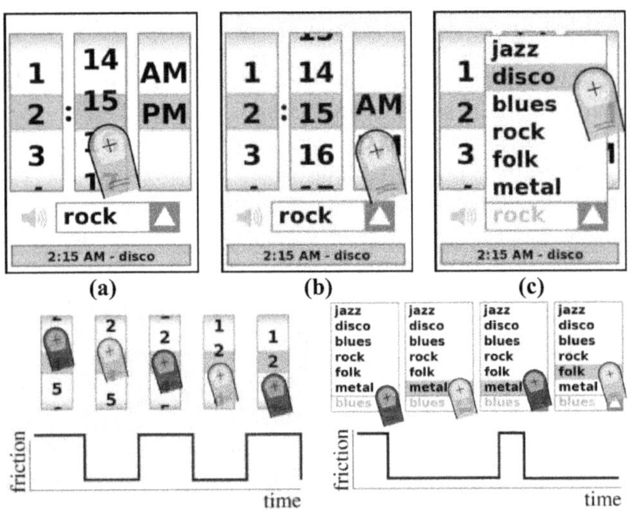

Figure 7. Alarm Clock: (a) hour and minute wheels, (b) AM/PM wheel, (c) sound combo box and friction patterns while selecting (d) hour and (e) sound. The finger color changes from light blue to dark red as friction increases.

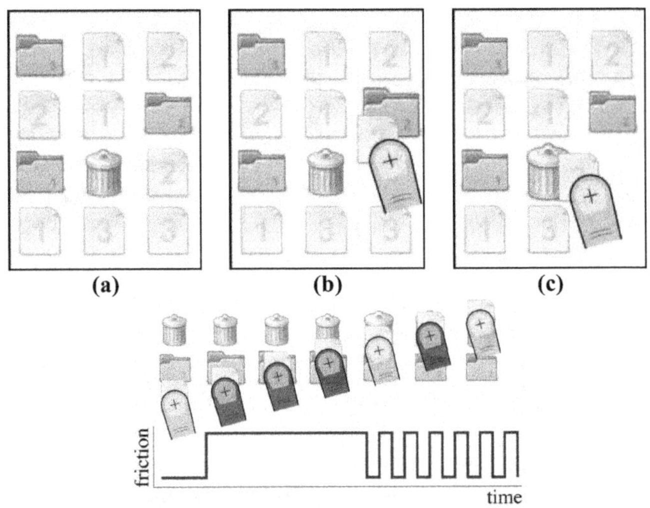

Figure 8. File Manager: (a) initial screen, moving a file into (b) a folder or (c) recycle bin, and (d) friction patterns while over a folder or bin. The finger color changes from light blue to dark red as friction increases.

Experimental Procedure

Participants interacted with each of the four applications twice, with and without variable friction. Each interaction was limited to 2 minutes to provide exposure without boredom. Each application was presented first for ¼ of the participants, and the order of the other applications was randomized. Half of the participants experienced all applications first with variable friction, the other half without. Participants were instructed to focus on experience rather than performance.

A User Engagement Scale (UE1-10) was used after each condition (twice per application; with and without friction). A tactile feedback questionnaire (TF1-7) was completed after each interaction with variable friction (once per application feature). Once both friction conditions were completed with an application, a comparison questionnaire (C1-5) was administered, followed by a short interview (I1-3). This procedure was repeated for all four applications, and followed by a final questionnaire (F1-2). The User Engagement Scale used a 7-point Likert scale and all others a 5-point scale (strongly disagree to strongly agree).

The User Engagement Scale (UE1-10) was adapted from a validated 31-question questionnaire developed to assess six aspects of engagement: Focused Attention, Perceived Usability, Aesthetics, Endurability, Novelty and Felt Involvement [21]. Ten of the 31 questions were adapted, spanning all aspects:

UE1. I was absorbed in my interaction task.
UE2. I felt in control of my interactive experience.
UE3. I found this application confusing to use.
UE4. I liked the visual and tactile effects used in this application.
UE5. This application appealed to my visual and tactile senses.
UE6. I would recommend this application to my friends and family.
UE7. I would have continued to interact with this app. out of curiosity.
UE8. I felt interested in my interaction task.
UE9. This interactive experience was fun.
UE10. I felt involved in this interaction task.

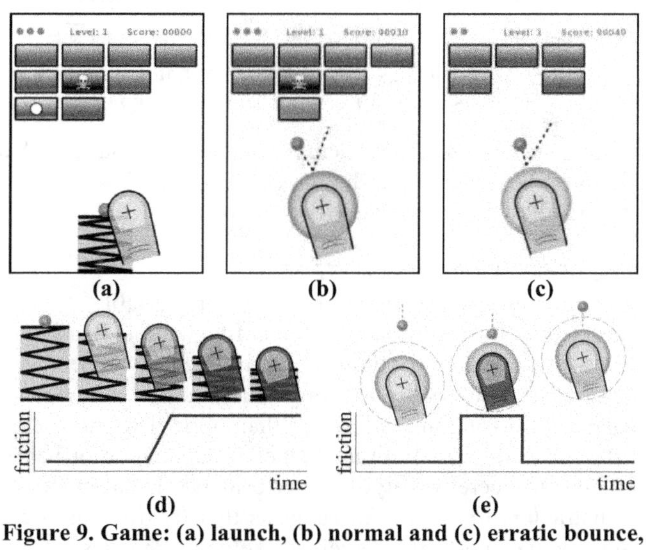

Figure 9. Game: (a) launch, (b) normal and (c) erratic bounce, and friction patterns during (d) launch and (e) bounce. Low friction shown as a blue finger, high friction red.

The tactile feedback questionnaire (TF1-7) was completed for the main tactile features of each application: hour/minute wheel, AM/PM wheel and sound combo box for *Alarm Clock*; folders and recycle bin for *File Manager*; launcher, normal and erratic bounce for *Game*; movement within or between lines and page swapping for *Text Editor*. Participants were asked if they noticed the feature, and if so rated whether the tactile feedback was (TF1) weak, (TF2) natural, (TF3) informative, (TF4) annoying, (TF5) matched the visuals, (TF6) felt good, and (TF7) was preferred.

The comparison questionnaire (C1-5) asked if tactile feedback (C1) was preferred, (C2) made the task easier to perform, (C3) the application more enjoyable, (C4) the interface more realistic and (C5) made them more confident. Interview questions (I1-3) asked participants (I1) to describe the sensations, (I2) what they liked and didn't like about the tactile feedback, and (I3) how they would improve it. The final questionnaire (F1-2) asked (F1) if participants would turn this type of feedback off on their phone, and (F2) if tactile feedback improved their experience.

Participants

The data for eight participants were rejected due to protocol irregularities and hardware or software complications that may have affected subjective responses. The remaining twelve participants (6 females) were aged from 19 to 38 (mean 24.3). Eleven were students, only four from engineering and computer science. Ten used touchscreen phones or music players once a week or more. None participated in S1-3.

Results

The participants' comments and questionnaire responses demonstrate that friction can improve the subjective experience of touch interactions. They also provide insights into potential negative effects, which need to be addressed by design. We begin with interview responses and comments, and then report questionnaire results.

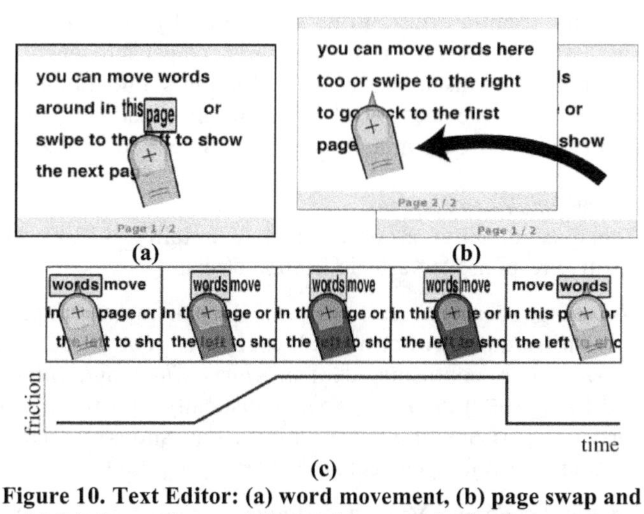

Figure 10. Text Editor: (a) word movement, (b) page swap and (c) friction patterns while moving a word. The finger color changes from light blue to dark red as friction increases.

Interview Responses

Several comments show that variable friction enhanced the participant's sense of realism: ***"When I was moving the words against something, I could feel something squeeze back."*** (P3, Text Editor); ***"I knew I was actually touching it."*** (P2, File Manager); ***"It feels [...] as if turning the wheels."*** (P11, Alarm Clock).

Comments also show that variable friction increased awareness of the system state, some suggesting a reduced dependence on vision: ***"I think it gives me accuracy, [...] if I closed my eyes I would be able to predict the amount of scrolling that I do."*** (P5, Alarm Clock); ***"Feel more informed ... when I am moving on the line I can feel each word."*** (P11, Text Editor); ***"For the garbage bin it's like oh ah don't do it."*** (P3, File Manager).

Importantly, several comments showed that participants liked the friction effects: ***"This is nice... it makes things a lot more interesting."*** (P3, Game); ***"I liked the sensation while I am rolling"*** (P8, Alarm Clock).

Nine of the twelve participants were predominantly positive in their comments about variable friction for one (1), two (3), three (4) or four (1) of the applications. The remaining three were predominantly negative or neutral. Negative words used to describe variable friction included "*unpleasant*", "*weird*", "*creepy*", "*annoying*" and "*itchy*". The tactile feedback was often described more neutrally using physics-related terms such as *"resistance"*, *"friction"*, *"slippery"* and *"sticky"*. Negative comments were often aimed at the limitations of the applications but also suggested potential pitfalls of variable friction such as *"[getting] in the way of trying to move"* (P8, File Manager) or inducing fatigue through overuse (P3, Alarm Clock).

Interestingly, there was little cross-participant consistency in assessing which applications and effects were positive additions. Similarly, participants differed in their assessment of feedback strength, with two stating that stimuli were too weak and one too strong. This suggests a need for friction effects to be very carefully designed and customizable by end users. A majority of participants also spontaneously discussed variable friction's integration in commercial devices and voluntarily shared their impressions for 5-15 minutes after experiment completion.

Questionnaire Responses

The questionnaire responses tend to amplify the overall positive response to variable friction effects.

User Engagement Scale (Table 2). Responses for variable friction were positive or neutral, except for control (UE2) in *Alarm Clock*, confusion (UE3) in *Alarm Clock* and *Game*, and liking (UE4) in *Game*; none statistically significant. Of forty comparisons (4 applications × 10 questions), variable friction received better scores in 30: χ^2=9.0, p<.005.

Tactile Feedback. Marked differences were found in the noticeability of friction effects, with only 25% noticing the

	Clock		Files		Game		Text	
	HF	*VF*	*HF*	*VF*	*HF*	*VF*	*HF*	*VF*
UE1. Absorbed.	**4.7 (1.2)**	**4.9 (0.9)**	**4.8 (1.2)**	**5.4 (1.2)**	**5.6 (0.9)**	**5.8 (0.6)**	5.1 (0.8)	5.1 (1.2)
UE2. Control.	5.3 (0.8)	5.1 (1.3)	5.6 (0.7)	5.6 (0.9)	**4.9 (1.2)**	**5.3 (0.9)**	**4.0 (1.7)**	**4.8 (1.9)**
UE3. Confusion.	2.0 (1.2)	2.3 (1.3)	1.7 (0.8)	1.7 (0.9)	1.8 (0.9)	2.2 (1.2)	**2.5 (1.4)**	**2.3 (1.6)**
UE4. Liked.	**4.4 (1.3)**	**5.0 (1.3)**	**4.9 (0.9)**	**5.4 (1.4)**	4.7 (1.7)	4.5 (1.6)	**4.5 (1.7)**	**5.1 (1.5)**
UE5. Appeal.	**4.2 (1.3)**	**5.3 (1.1)**	**4.1 (1.5)**	**5.5 (1.0)**	**5.1 (1.1)**	**5.7 (0.8)**	**3.8 (1.5)**	**5.2 (1.3)**
UE6. Recommend.	**4.2 (1.4)**	**5.0 (1.4)**	**4.1 (1.4)**	**5.0 (1.6)**	5.0 (1.3)	5.0 (1.5)	**4.7 (1.7)**	**4.9 (1.8)**
UE7. Curious.	**4.0 (1.9)**	**4.9 (1.5)**	**3.6 (1.7)**	**4.6 (1.9)**	5.6 (1.5)	5.6 (1.6)	**4.2 (1.9)**	**4.9 (1.8)**
UE8. Interested.	**4.3 (1.7)**	**5.2 (1.5)**	**4.6 (1.5)**	**5.0 (1.5)**	**5.8 (1.0)**	**5.7 (1.0)**	**4.7 (1.5)**	**5.4 (1.6)**
UE9. Fun.	**4.2 (1.6)**	**5.0 (1.7)**	**4.2 (1.6)**	**4.7 (2.0)**	**5.6 (0.8)**	**5.7 (1.0)**	**4.4 (1.8)**	**5.0 (1.5)**
UE10. Involved.	**4.6 (1.6)**	**5.3 (0.8)**	**4.6 (1.4)**	**5.7 (1.0)**	**5.2 (1.2)**	**5.7 (0.7)**	**4.3 (1.8)**	**5.5 (0.8)**

Table 2. Mean (and s.d.) for the User Engagement Scale [1-7]. Rating pairs favorable to *VF* are bold.

rapid pulse on page swap, but all noticing wheel effects. Weak noticeability is explained by rare use (recycle bin, page swap) or subtlety (launcher). Means for 67/77 contribution assessments of friction effects made by each participant reflected positive opinions (χ^2=40.7, p<.0001). Negative assessments were most common in *Game*.

Comparison. Table 3 shows that all but one of the 20 direct comparisons favors variable friction: χ^2=14.4, p<.001. None of the participants expressed a strong preference for constant high friction in any of the questions.

	Alarm Clock	*File Manager*	*Game*	*Text Editor*
C1. Preference	3.7	4.0	3.3	4.0
C2. Ease	3.5	3.1	2.8	3.3
C3. Enjoyment	3.4	3.8	3.6	3.9
C4. Realism	4.1	3.3	3.7	4.0
C5. Confidence	3.7	3.7	3.2	3.9

Table 3. Mean ratings [1-5] and distribution of answers (1 bottom - 5 top) for comparison questionnaire.

Final Questionnaire. Participant responses suggest that friction effects would not be turned off (mean 2.4, s.d. 1.0) and that they improved the experience (mean 4.1, s.d. 0.5).

DISCUSSION AND NEXT STEPS

We first investigated performance for variable friction effects and found measurable benefits without harm. S1 shows that variable friction (high on target, low elsewhere) significantly improves targeting performance. S2 verifies that variable friction is no worse than normal friction when distracters are present, crucial since pseudohaptic or haptic targets can decrease targeting performance in the presence of distracters [6,14,20]. S3 suggests that friction variations cause actual, not only perceived, velocity changes: unlike pseudohaptic and vibrotactile aids, friction slows the fingertip. Yet movement time does not rise, even with distracters, because approach stages are faster (S1-2).

We then focused on user *experience*, not performance [11] – engagement, enjoyment, directness, perceived utility – and found through our S4 application samples that variable friction can enhance the emotional aspect of using a touch interface. This approach freed us to explore many design concepts and highlights what may ultimately be the most crucial factor in improving upon passive touch interfaces.

In the following we reflect upon generalizing these results to real-world use and understanding their value.

Hardware Factors

The LATPaD is currently a bulky prototype. However, the critical components for producing variable friction are the small, thin piezoelectric actuators visible in Figure 1a and there are no major barriers to miniaturizing the technology to the scale of current mobile devices. Rendering non-uniformities are also expected to be resolved in the near future, and were successfully avoided in our S4 designs.

Performance in real-world target acquisition

The LATPaD's variable friction effects are only felt when sliding against the display surface; S1-2 therefore used dragging tasks to maximally expose participants to the effects of interest. The lift-off selection used here is common on mobile devices, including the iPhone's text entry keypad. However, when approach occurs in the air, friction effects would only be felt during the final acquisition. This has been shown to reduce targeting performance with pen-based vibrotactile feedback [24]. We need to better understand how variable friction can benefit other selection modalities, but feel that first analyzing the most effective interaction for friction was appropriate.

Variable Friction Versus Vibrotactile Feedback

Vibrotactile (VT) feedback can provide selection performance improvements similar to variable friction, at least in single target conditions [24]. Variable friction and VT actuators, however, produce sensations that are very different. Friction tends to feel more natural and provides continuous feedback during sliding; vibrations are ideal for discrete clicks and textures, including tapping confirmation [23,24]. Variable friction can physically alter finger velocity, whereas VT can communicate a larger range of informative sensations [16], even without sliding. These two tactile modalities are complementary and in theory can be produced with the same actuators.

Theoretical Design Space for Variable Friction

The exemplar applications and widgets examined in S4 were developed through an iterative design process, and were successful in generating subjective responses. We took guidance both from the beginnings of our design space and from our intuition and iterations. We will refine this beginning with a taxonomy of variable friction sensations and their mapping to interactive widgets. This includes examining generalizations of our current set of widgets to other uses. For example, the *Alarm Clock* wheel was among the most popular, and we will examine how it can be deployed in support of related uses, such as scrolling. We will also investigate interaction techniques that minimize the use of low friction and hence actuator activation and power consumption, such as reduced friction on targets.

Towards Variable Friction Design Heuristics

In its infancy, the design of interactions with tactile feedback is prone to naive uses and excesses. We hope to launch a discussion of best practices for variable friction, extending a design space with heuristics such as these:

Sliding not tapping. To be effective, friction-augmented interfaces must work around the notion of sliding, with appropriate metaphors and visual representations. The *Text Editor*, for example, associated friction with word compression to give meaningful feedback during dragging.

Shaping friction to increase expressiveness. To compensate for the limited human sensitivity to friction variations and the current display range, expressiveness can be enhanced by varying friction 'attack', modulating it to create textures and patterns, and tying sensations to visual representations.

Stop only for a purpose. Some users felt that friction variations seemed occasionally to slow them down. Strong feedback should have an equally strong purpose.

Nice not strong. We tend to maximize tactile signal strength to ensure feedback is felt and performance improvements are measurable; but this can lead to unpleasant sensations.

CONCLUSION

Programmable friction displays vary the friction felt while sliding against a touch sensitive display. Through a series of studies and design explorations, we have demonstrated the strong potential of programmable friction interfaces. Most importantly, participants preferred our exemplar designs to traditional touch interactions and reported a variety of positive effects, including increased engagement, a sense of realism and reduced dependence on vision. In addition, our examination of programmable friction showed significant performance advantages for drag-based selections and no adverse effects when distracter targets are present.

This is the first analysis we are aware of for interaction with variable friction displays. These quantitative and qualitative results show exciting possibilities; the technology is on a development path 2-3 years from commercial realizability. There is great potential for more investigation: further performance analysis, design exploration and then deployment in mobile handhelds and laptop touchpads.

REFERENCES

1. Akamatsu, M. and MacKenzie, I.S. Movement characteristics using a mouse with tactile and force feedback. *Int. J. of Human-Computer Studies 45*, 4 (1996), 483-494.

2. Balakrishnan, R. "Beating" Fitts' law: virtual enhancements for pointing facilitation. *Int. J. of Human-Computer Studies 61*, 6 (2004), 857-874.
3. Bau, O., Poupyrev, I., Israr, A., and Harrison, C. TeslaTouch: Electrovibration for Touch Surfaces. In *Proc. UIST 2010*, ACM (2010).
4. Benko, H., Wilson, A.D., and Balakrishnan, R. Sphere: Multi-Touch Interactions on a Spherical Display. In *Proc. UIST 2008*, ACM (2008), 77-86.
5. Buxton, W., Hill, R., and Rowley, P. Issues and techniques in touch-sensitive tablet input. In *Proc. SIGGRAPH 1985*, ACM (1985), 215-224.
6. Cockburn, A. and Brewster, S. Multimodal feedback for the acquisition of small targets. *Ergonomics 48*, 9 (2005), 1129-1150.
7. Dennerlein, J.T., Martin, D.B., and Hasser, C. Force-feedback improves performance for steering and combined steering-targeting tasks. In *Proc. CHI 2000*, ACM (2000), 423-429.
8. DiFranco, D.E., Beauregard, G.L., and Srinivasan, M. The effect of auditory cues on the haptic perception of stiffness in virtual environments. In *Proc. Haptics Symposium 1997*, ASME (1997), 17-22.
9. Fitts, P.M. The information capacity of the human motor system in controlling the amplitude of movement. *J. of Experimental Psychology 47*, 6 (1954), 381-391.
10. Forlines, C. and Balakrishnan, R. Evaluating tactile feedback and direct vs. indirect stylus input in pointing and crossing selection tasks. In *Proc. CHI 2008*, ACM (2008), 1563-1572.
11. Greenberg, S. and Buxton, B. Usability evaluation considered harmful (some of the time). In *Proc. CHI 2008*, ACM (2008), 111-120.
12. Hancock, M., Carpendale, S., and Cockburn, A. Shallow-depth 3d interaction: design and evaluation of one-, two- and three-touch techniques. In *Proc. CHI 2007*, ACM (2007), 1147-1156.
13. Hoggan, E., Kaaresoja, T., Laitinen, P., and Brewster, S. Crossmodal congruence: the look, feel and sound of touchscreen widgets. In *Proc. IMCI 2008*, ACM (2008), 157-164.
14. Keyson, D.V. Dynamic cursor gain and tactual feedback in the capture of cursor movements. *Ergonomics 40*, 12 (1997), 1287-1298.
15. Li, K.A., Baudisch, P., Griswold, W.G., and Hollan, J.D. Tapping and rubbing: exploring new dimensions of tactile feedback with voice coil motors. In *Proc. UIST 2008*, ACM (2008), 181-190.
16. MacLean, K.E. Foundations of Transparency in Tactile Information Design. *IEEE Transactions on Haptics 1*, 2 (2008), 84-95.
17. Marchuk, N.D., Colgate, J.E., and Peshkin, M.A. Friction measurements on a Large Area TPaD. In *Proc. Haptics Symposium 2010*, IEEE (2010), 317-320.
18. Moscovich, T. Contact area interaction with sliding widgets. In *Proc. UIST 2009*, ACM (2009), 13-22.
19. Norman, D. *Emotional Design: Why We Love (or Hate) Everyday Things*. Basic Books, NY, NY, USA, 2004.
20. Oakley, I., Brewster, S., and Gray, P. Solving multi-target haptic problems in menu interaction. In *Proc. CHI 2001*, ACM (2001), 357-358.
21. O'Brien, H.L. and Toms, E.G. The development and evaluation of a survey to measure user engagement. *Journal of the American Society for Information Science and Technology 61*, 1 (2009), 50-69.
22. Potter, R.L., Weldon, L.J., and Shneiderman, B. Improving the accuracy of touch screens: an experimental evaluation of three strategies. In *Proc. CHI 1988*, ACM (1988), 27-32.
23. Poupyrev, I. and Maruyama, S. Tactile interfaces for small touch screens. In *Proc. UIST 2003*, ACM (2003), 217-220.
24. Poupyrev, I., Okabe, M., and Maruyama, S. Haptic feedback for pen computing: directions and strategies. In *Proc. CHI 2004*, ACM (2004), 1309-1312.
25. Ramos, G. and Balakrishnan, R. Fluid interaction techniques for the control and annotation of digital video. In *Proc. UIST 2003*, ACM (2003), 105-114.
26. Rekimoto, J. Organic interaction technologies. *Communications of the ACM 51*, 6 (2008), 38-44.
27. Roudaut, A., Huot, S., and Lecolinet, E. TapTap and MagStick: improving one-handed target acquisition on small touch-screens. In *Proc. AVI 2008*, ACM (2008), 146-153.
28. Schiphorst, T., Motamedi, N., and Jaffe, N. Applying an Aesthetic Framework of Touch for Table-Top Interactions. In *Proc. TABLETOP 2007*, IEEE (2007), 71-74.
29. Shneiderman, B. Direct Manipulation: A Step Beyond Programming Languages. *Computer 16*, 8 (1983), 57-69.
30. Smyth, T.N. and Kirkpatrick, A.E. A new approach to haptic augmentation of the GUI. In *Proc. ICMI 2006*, ACM (2006), 372-379.
31. Swindells, C., MacLean, K.E., Booth, K.S., and Meitner, M.J. Exploring affective design for physical controls. In *Proc. CHI 2007*, ACM (2007), 933-942.
32. Winfield, L., Glassmire, J., Colgate, J.E., and Peshkin, M. T-PaD: Tactile Pattern Display through Variable Friction Reduction. In *Proc. World Haptics 2007*, IEEE (2007), 421-426.

Surfpad: Riding Towards Targets on a Squeeze Film Effect

Géry Casiez[1,3,4], **Nicolas Roussel**[3], **Romuald Vanbelleghem**[3] & **Frédéric Giraud**[2,3,4]
[1]LIFL, [2]L2EP, [3]INRIA Lille & [4]University of Lille, France
gery.casiez@lifl.fr, nicolas.roussel@inria.fr, frederic.giraud@polytech-lille.fr

ABSTRACT
We present *Surfpad*, a pointing facilitation technique that does not decrease target distance or increase target width in either control or display space. This new technique operates instead in the tactile domain by taking advantage of the ability to alter a touchpad's coefficient of friction by means of a squeeze film effect. We report on three experiments comparing *Surfpad* to the *Semantic Pointing* technique and constant control-display gain with and without distractor targets. Our results clearly show the limits of traditional target-aware control-display gain adaptation in the latter case, and the benefits of our tactile approach in both cases. *Surfpad* leads to a performance improvement close to 9% compared to unassisted pointing at small targets with no distractor. It is also robust to high distractor densities, keeping an average performance improvement of nearly 10% while *Semantic Pointing* can degrade up to 100%. Our results also suggest the performance improvement is caused by tactile information feedback rather than mechanical causes, and that the feedback is more effective when friction is increased on targets using a simple step function.

ACM Classification Keywords
H.5.2 [Information interfaces and presentation]: User interfaces - Graphical user interfaces.

General Terms
Design, Performance, Experimentation, Human Factors

Author Keywords
Pointing facilitation, target-aware, control-display gain adaptation, squeeze film effect

INTRODUCTION
Pointing is a fundamental task of modern human computer interfaces and has been extensively studied by the HCI research community. Fitts' law has proven to be one of the most robust and widely adopted models in this area [29]. It expresses the movement time to acquire a target of width W at a distance D as a linear function of the index of difficulty $ID = \log_2(\frac{D}{W} + 1)$.

Numerous techniques have been proposed that attempt to beat Fitts' law, i.e. to make virtual pointing easier than it is in the physical world [5]. Most of these techniques attempt to decrease D, to increase W, or both. Most of them are also inherently target-aware [34]: they take advantage of some knowledge about the size and position of the targets and sometimes modify them. In cases where pointing involves the indirect control of a visual cursor, some techniques operate by dynamically adapting the control-display gain $CDgain = V_{\text{cursor}}/V_{\text{device}}$ [12]. Other techniques supplement the visual display with auditory or haptic feedback. Yet despite their demonstrated efficiency in simple configurations, most target-aware pointing techniques are difficult to use in practice. One of the key problems that affects them in real-life situations is the potential interferences caused by intervening targets on the way to the primary one (distractors), a problem that is still largely understudied.

In this paper, we present *Surfpad*, a pointing facilitation technique that does not decrease D or increase W in either control or display space. This new technique operates instead in the tactile domain by taking advantage of the ability to alter the coefficient of friction of a particular touchpad, the STIMTAC [9], by means of a squeeze film effect (Figure 1). We report on three experiments comparing *Surfpad* to the *Semantic Pointing* technique [10] and constant control-display gain with and without distractor targets. Our results clearly show the limits of traditional target-aware CD gain adaptation in the latter case, and the benefits of our tactile approach in both cases. Our results also suggest the performance improvement is caused by tactile information feedback rather than mechanical causes, and that the feedback is more effective when friction is increased on targets using a simple step function.

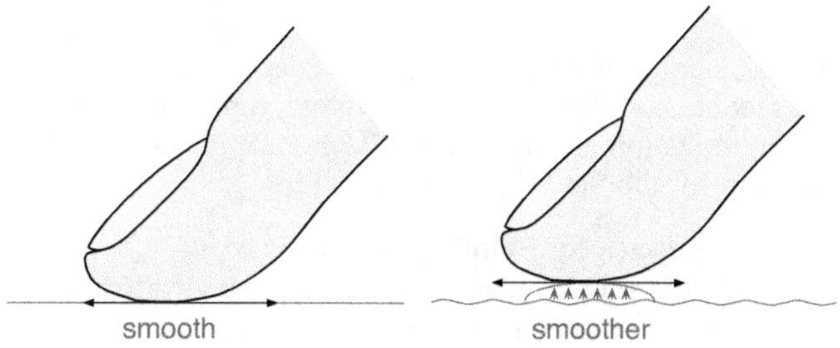

Figure 1. The squeeze film effect: controlled vibration of a surface creates an air film which reduces its coefficient of friction.

The paper is organized as follows. After reviewing related work on pointing facilitation techniques and haptic feedback, we describe the STIMTAC device and our *Surfpad* technique. We then describe our three experiments. We conclude with some directions for future work.

RELATED WORK

A detailed review of pointing facilitation techniques can be found in [5]. As explained, most of these techniques are target-aware and involve the reduction of target distance, the increase of target width, or both. In what follows, we briefly discuss the most relevant examples, focusing on the use of a haptic modality and the impact of distractors.

Reducing D and Increasing W

Different methods have been proposed to reduce target distance. *Drag-and-pop* [7], for example, temporarily brings potential targets closer to the pointer. Other techniques use endpoint prediction to make the cursor automatically jump over empty spaces and potential distractors [19, 4]. The *ninja cursors* [25] reduce D in yet another way by attaching multiple cursors to the same device and using knowledge about the targets to resolve pointing ambiguities.

Different methods have also been proposed to increase target width. *Expanding targets* [27], for example, dynamically grow to provide a larger area to interact with at the focus of attention. Expansion usually occurs in visual space, but sometimes also in control space (more on this below). Research has also shown that the W term of Fitts' law can apply to the width of the cursor, rather than that of the target, which led to the design of different *area cursors* [23, 35, 18].

A problem with the above techniques is that they are often visually distracting because of the displacement, growing or shrinking of objects. Other techniques have been proposed that preserve the display by operating only in control space. Described as *semantic pointing* [10] or using a stickiness or force field metaphor, these control space techniques operate by adapting the CD gain [35, 14, 10] or warping the cursor [31, 14, 13, 1, 21]. The CD gain is typically reduced when the cursor is over targets or approaching them, thereby expanding them in control space. Warping the cursor additionally supports trajectory adjustments in any direction.

A particular case of CD gain adaptation is described in [24], where it is not used to reduce D or increase W but to create a "cursor-catching effect". By requiring more movement effort to leave than to enter the target centre without increasing the total amount of effort to enter and leave the target area, the proposed *dynamic cursor gain* preserves the pointing task's index of difficulty. CD gain adaptation can be seen as a feedback mechanism in this context, rather than a Fitts' law optimization enabler, an approach that was also used to successfully simulate haptic percepts [26].

Haptic Feedback for Pointing Facilitation

Following the ISO standard [30], we use the term *haptic* to refer to two different types of feedback: *tactile* feedback (information received through nerve receptors in the skin) and *kinesthetic* feedback (information sensed through movement and/or force to muscles and joints). Haptic feedback has long been used as an assistive technology for disabled users, or to supplement the visual modality in teleoperation systems and virtual environments. But researchers have also investigated its potential for facilitating routine target acquisition in graphical interfaces.

Discrete $2D$ pointing tasks have received the most attention [3, 2, 24, 28, 16, 22]. But reciprocal $1D$ pointing [13], reciprocal $2D$ pointing and crossing [17], steering [11, 15], as well as ecological tasks [28, 15, 13], have also been studied. The device used for these studies is typically a haptic-enabled mouse. Other devices include a customized trackpoint [11], stylus [17] or trackball [24], a force-feedback joystick [22] and a 6DOF haptic device [28]. Feedback is provided by either exerting a force on the device to constrain its movement [2, 24, 28, 15, 16, 22] or by moving or vibrating a small part of it [3, 2, 11, 13, 17]. In [17], the haptic mechanism was used to confirm the selection of the target. In all the other studies, it was used to provide feedback about the cursor's relative position to the target, or tunnel, during the selection movement.

Haptic feedback has mostly been evaluated against "normal" pointing, i.e. pointing with no additional feedback indicating the cursor is over a target or has been selected. All the above studies showed it can improve users' targeting performance in this context by reducing the overall movement time [2, 11, 15, 16, 22, 13, 17], the time to stop after entering the target [3], or the error rate [28]. Some studies suggest that tactile feedback might be particularly effective at reducing selection times for small targets at the cost of higher error rates, although the reasons for the additional errors remain unclear [2, 13]. It has also been suggested that tactile feedback does not aid in direct input configurations [17].

Moving and vibrating parts of haptic devices usually generate audible sounds that one might want to filter out during experiments [13]. Comparisons of tactile and auditory feedback indeed showed similar positive effects on target acquisition [3, 13]. Tactile feedback has also been compared to visual feedback [3, 11] and CD gain adaptation [13], and researchers have investigated whether these different modalities can combine in a positive way [3, 2, 11, 13]. As Cockburn and Brewster put it, "some do while others do not" and the actual result depends a lot on the nature of the task: a promising technique poorly applied to a simple ecological task can damage interaction by distracting users from it [13].

Most of the devices we mentioned were based on simple and well-tested electromagnetic technologies (e.g. solenoids, voice coils, or vibratory motors with an offset mass). The problem with these technologies is that the haptic sensations they support are rather coarse. Yet recent advances in haptic technologies offer significant promise for extending their use in HCI in general, and pointing facilitation in particular, by supporting more subtle sensations. Recent works on friction reduction are particularly interesting in this context.

While most tactile feedbacks rely on active stimulation using pin-based arrays, Watanabe & Fukui proposed a method to create a smoother feeling on a surface by applying ultrasonic vibration with only a few micrometers amplitude [32]. The perceived feeling, caused by a *squeeze film effect* (Figure 1), has been used recently to simulate bumps and holes [33]. Electrovibration has also been shown to support similar sensations [6]. In contrast to traditional vibrotactile approaches, devices based on these technologies provide information passively, acting as *texture displays* [20]: they do not transfer energy to the user but modify how energy is dissipated within the contact area by a user-initiated friction process.

Impact of Distractors

Target-aware pointing techniques tend to work best on sparse layouts. For intrinsic reasons, many of them do not scale well to situations where multiple potential targets are closely packed together [5]. In real-world applications however, locally dense clusters of potential targets emerge for various reasons [8]. Surprisingly, although the problem is clearly identified in the literature, little research has been done to systematically evaluate the impact of distractors on existing techniques or design new ones that take them into account.

Among the studies of control space techniques and haptic feedback we discussed, a few took distractors explicitly into account – although in limited ways. One variable of the experiments described in [24] and [35] was the presence or absence of a single distractor along the target path (multiple distractors were actually used to make sure one would always be on the path when needed). In [22], one condition involved a distractor located at 180, 90, 0 or -90° relative to the task axis. The second experiment described in [16] displayed 13 targets arranged in a cross shape and required the user to randomly move from one to another, all the others acting as potentially avoidable distractors. The second experiment described in [13] is one of the very few that evaluated the impact of multiple distractors on a control space technique (*sticky targets*) and tactile feedback in a simple ecological task (menu selection). Results from all these studies suggest a negative impact of distractors on movement time, error rate, or user satisfaction. All the authors recommend further investigation.

STIMTAC AND THE SURFPAD TECHNIQUE

Previous research has clearly demonstrated the potential of control space techniques and haptic feedback for pointing facilitation. Yet, the impact of distractors on these techniques remains largely unknown. At the same time, recent advances in haptic technologies offer significant promise for supporting a wider range of sensations and thus more subtle bare-hand interactions. All these elements contributed to our initial motivation for the *Surfpad* technique, which relies on a particular device, the STIMTAC [9].

STIMTAC

The STIMTAC is a touchpad-like device based on the squeeze film effect described above. The tactile plate is made of 36 piezoelectric cells bonded on a $79\ mm \times 49\ mm$ copper–beryllium plate. This monomorph structure constitutes a mechanical resonator excited by a $40\ V$ sinusoidal voltage provided by a $0.5\ W$ power supply (to reduce power consumption, the device can be configured so that it vibrates the plate only if finger contact is detected). The overall design results in a compact and lightweight form factor that

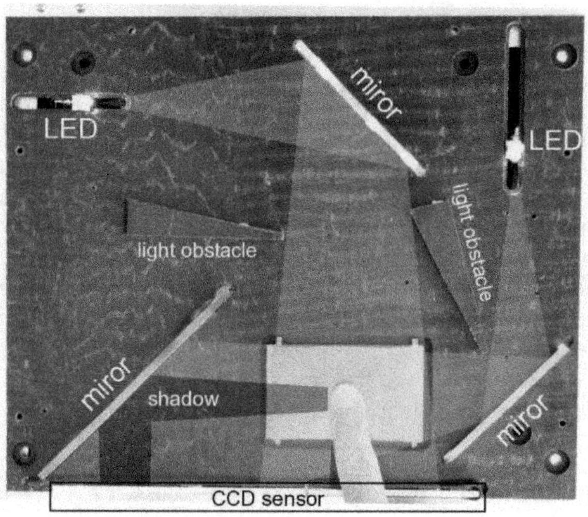

Figure 2. Picture of the STIMTAC device with its shell removed. The shell has only one opening for the tactile surface.

allows free exploration of the tactile surface (Figure 2). The plate is coated with a thin plastic layer to make finger contact more comfortable. It vibrates at the ultrasonic frequency of $28.55\ kHz$ and thus emits no perceptible noise during operation. Since the frequency is outside skin mechanoreceptors' bandwidth, users do not feel the vibration. Instead, they feel its effect on tribological contact mechanisms: the touchpad feels more slippery as one raises the vibration amplitude. The device is typically configured for a maximum amplitude of $1\ \mu m$ which can reduce friction up to 50% depending on surface preparation (e.g. cleaning the surface also affects its coefficient of friction).

Traditional touchpad sensors are incompatible with the squeeze film effect due to the relatively high voltage and frequencies (a resistive sensor would damp the vibrations and a capacitive one would be perturbed by the electric field). A custom-made optical sensor is thus used to locate the user's finger. The sensor was built from two white LEDs, three mirrors and a linear $200\ dpi$ CCD array. An on-board DSP computes the centroids of two shadow images created by the user's finger and sends them on a serial line as absolute (x, y) coordinates at a rate of $120\ Hz$. The final resolution of the sensor is $170\ dpi$ due to optical constraints and post-treatments. The serial line allows to specify the desired coefficient of friction by controling the amplitude at a rate up to $120\ Hz$ using a 7-bit encoded integer between 0 (no squeeze film effect, maximum friction) and 127 (maximum amplitude, maximum effect, minimum friction).

The Surfpad Technique

Tactile feedback through the STIMTAC builds on the relative displacement that exists between a fingertip and a surface when a user is probing for friction. A user moving a finger on the switched-off plate will find it hard, smooth, and not sticky. But, because of its high level of friction, the skin will be stretched laterally, which will become obvious at any direction change. Once the squeeze film effect is activated, the surface retains its original properties but with the reduced friction, the skin becomes less stretched. The sensation can approach the feeling of touching a silk scarf. If the effect is disabled while the finger is moving, the increased amount of friction will be quite noticeable.

Considering these new possibilities, we were excited to investigate ways in which they could be used for pointing facilitation. Influenced by the related work, we started with the idea of designing a target-aware technique. As we saw, many of these techniques operate by modifying the mechanics of motion around targets in the virtual world (for control space techniques) or in the physical one (for haptic techniques). The purpose of the modifications is to facilitate pointing and the desired result is to slow down the cursor or guide its movements. In fact, existing techniques can be thought of as increasing the friction of specific objects.

The STIMTAC can only reduce friction. In order to increase it on specific objects, one needs to decrease it everywhere else. The technique we propose originates from this figure-ground reversal in pointing facilitation: instead of slowing down the cursor around targets, why not facilitate its movement on the background? While most target-aware techniques tend to ignore the background, ours is background-aware. A surfing metaphor seemed appropriate, the low friction background corresponding to the ocean, the objects to the shore, and the finger-controlled cursor to the board.

The *Surfpad* technique uses the programmable squeeze film effect of the STIMTAC to reduce the touchpad's coefficient of friction at all times except when the cursor is over a target. We have implemented it in two ways. Similar to traditional sticky targets, *Surfpad*Π uses the following step function:

$$\mathit{Surfpad}\Pi(x) = \begin{cases} 0 & \text{\textit{maximum friction if over a target}} \\ 127 & \text{\textit{minimum friction otherwise}} \end{cases}$$

Instead of a step function, *Surfpad*Ω uses the Ω bell-shaped mixing function defined in [10] to avoid discontinuities in the amount of friction.

EXPERIMENT 1: SURFPAD

The goal of this first experiment is to investigate the effect of *Surfpad* on performance in a pointing task and compare it to target-aware CD gain adaptation and constant CD gain in the absence of distractors. We used the *Semantic Pointing* technique [10] for target-aware CD gain adaptation as it is well documented and considered as a reference in this domain.

Apparatus

The STIMTAC device described in the previous section was used as the input device for all the techniques to eliminate extraneous intra-devices differences such as ergonomics, size and sensitivity. We used a 15" LCD display at a 1280 × 800 pixel resolution. The experiment was coded in C++ and OpenGL. The frequency of the visual and haptic renderings were 60 Hz and 120 Hz respectively.

Task

We used a reciprocal one dimensional pointing task (Figure 3). Each trial began after the previous target was successfully selected and ended with the selection of the current target. After a target was successfully selected, it turned grey and the next one (on the other side of the screen) turned green. If a participant missed a target, a sound was heard and an error was logged. Participants had to successfully select the current target before moving to the next one, even if it required multiple clicks. The pointer was not constrained to screen bounds to avoid using the edges to facilitate target acquisition. Participants used the left `Ctrl` key on a keyboard with their non-dominant hand to select targets. After each block of trials, a cumulative error rate was displayed and a message encouraged participants to conform to an approximately 4% error rate by speeding up or slowing down.

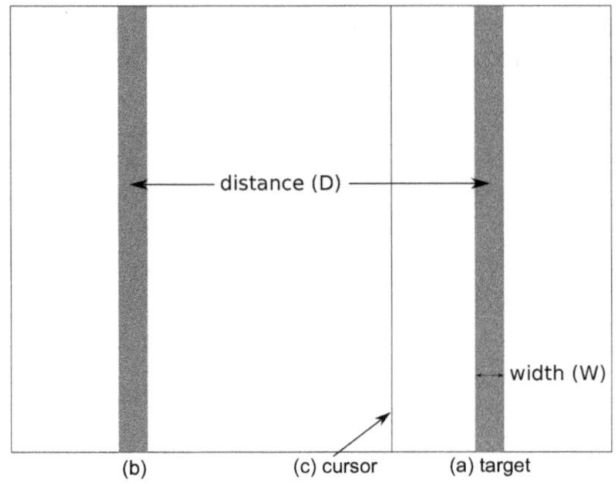

Figure 3. Experimental display. Targets were rendered as solid vertical bars equidistant from the center of the display in opposite directions along the horizontal axis. The target to be selected was colored green (a), and the previous one gray (b). The cursor was represented by a one-pixel-thick vertical black line (c).

Participants

Twelve unpaid volunteers with a mean age of 28.9 ($SD = 7.0$) served in the experiment (9 male and 3 female, 10 right-handed and 2 left-handed).

Design

A repeated measures within-subjects design was used. The independent variables were the technique used (TECHNIQUE) and the target distance (DISTANCE) and width (WIDTH). DISTANCE was evaluated with three levels (D_L = 100 mm, D_M = 50 mm, D_S = 25 mm) and WIDTH as well (W_L = 4.136 mm = 16 pixels, W_M = 2.068 mm = 8 pixels, W_S = 1.034 mm = 4 pixels)[1]. The index of difficulty thus ranged from 2.8 to 6.6.

The techniques were constant CD gain with no actuation of the STIMTAC (*Control*), constant CD gain with full actuation of the STIMTAC (*Control-*), *Semantic Pointing* using the Π step function (*SemPoint*Π), *Semantic Pointing* using the Ω mixing function (*SemPoint*Ω), *Surfpad*Π and *Surfpad*Ω. For *Semantic Pointing*, we chose to quadruple the size of targets in motor space as this was reported by Blanch et al. as yielding the best performance [10]. But while they had set their baseline CD gain to 1, we instead used one of 2 for all techniques to reduce clutching[2] with the largest distance considering the dimensions of our input surface.

[1] All distances and sizes are given in display space.

[2] Clutching consists in temporarily breaking the link between the physical device and the virtual pointer.

Participants had a few minutes to get used to the device in the *Control* condition before starting the experiment. They then completed 4 successive BLOCKS of trials for each TECHNIQUE. Each BLOCK consisted of 27 trials: 3 repetitions of the 9 DISTANCE×WIDTH combinations. The DISTANCE and WIDTH were presented in descending order. The presentation order of TECHNIQUE was counterbalanced across participants using a Latin Square design. Participants were encouraged to take a break every 9 trials. The experiment lasted approximately 50 minutes.

In summary, the experimental design was: 12 participants × 6 TECHNIQUE × 4 BLOCKS × 3 DISTANCE × 3 WIDTH × 3 trials = 7,776 total trials.

RESULTS

The dependent variables were the error rate, the movement time, the approaching time, the stopping time, the click time and the clutch time.

Error Rate

Targets that were not selected on the first attempt were marked as errors. Participants emphasized speed over accuracy with an overall error rate of 6.5%. A repeated measures ANOVA showed a significant effect of WIDTH on error rate, the latter increasing as target width decreases ($F_{2,22}$=24.3, $p<0.001$; W_S : 10.9%, W_M : 4.6%, W_L : 3.0%). There was also a significant effect of TECHNIQUE on error rate ($F_{5,55}$=7.06, $p<0.001$). Post-hoc analysis showed significant differences between *SemPoint*Π and all the other techniques ($p<0.012$; *Control* : 6.4%, *Control-* : 8.6%, *SemPoint*Π : 3.4%, *SemPoint*Ω : 5.0%, *Surfpad*Ω : 7.6%, *Surfpad*Π : 6.0%).

Movement Time

Movement time is the main dependent measure and is defined as the time taken to move from a target to the next one and click on it. Targets marked as errors were removed from the timing analysis. We also considered trials at least three standard deviations away from the mean for each TECHNIQUE×DISTANCE×WIDTH condition as outliers and removed them from the data analysis (1.6% of the trials).

A repeated measures ANOVA showed that the presentation order of TECHNIQUE had no significant effect or interaction on movement time, indicating that a within-participants design was appropriate. We also found no significant effect or interaction for BLOCK indicating there was no presence of a learning effect.

A repeated measures ANOVA showed a significant effect of TECHNIQUE on movement time ($F_{5,55}$=14.2, $p<0.001$). Pairwise comparisons showed no significant difference between *Surfpad*Ω and *Surfpad*Π (p=0.09), but while *Surfpad*Π was significantly different from all the other techniques ($p<0.03$), *Surfpad*Ω was only significantly different from *SemPoint*Π and *SemPoint*Ω ($p<0.009$). No significant difference was found between *SemPoint*Π and *SemPoint*Ω, but significant differences were found between these variants and the others techniques ($p<0.008$). No significant difference was found between *Control* and *Control-*, but significant differences were found between these two techniques and the others ($p<0.012$)

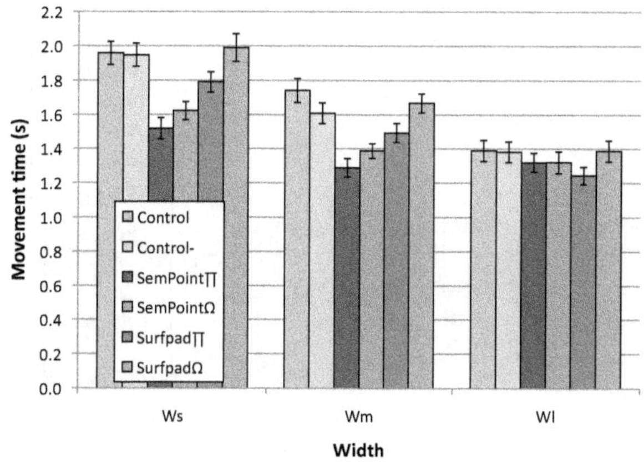

Figure 4. Mean movement time for TECHNIQUE and WIDTH. Error bars represent 95% confidence interval.

except *Surfpad*Ω (*Control* : 1.58s, *Control-* : 1.58s, *SemPoint*Π : 1.29s, *SemPoint*Ω : 1.31s, *Surfpad*Ω : 1.57s, *Surfpad*Π : 1.44s).

As predicted by Fitts' law, there was significant main effects of DISTANCE ($F_{2,22}$=106.4, $p<0.001$) and WIDTH ($F_{2,22}$=57.6, $p<0.001$) and a significant DISTANCE×WIDTH interaction ($F_{4,44}$=7.4, $p<0.001$). More interestingly, we also observed a TECHNIQUE×WIDTH interaction ($F_{10,110}$=11.2, $p<0.001$, Figure 4). Subsequent pairwise comparisons showed significant differences between the techniques as WIDTH gets smaller. For W_L, there was no significant difference between techniques except between *Surfpad*Π and *Surfpad*Ω (1.34s vs. 1.17s, p=0.032). For W_M and W_S, we observed similar patterns. There was no significant difference between the two control conditions and no significant difference between *SemPoint*Π and *SemPoint*Ω. We found a significant difference between *Surfpad*Π (1.39s) and *Surfpad*Ω (1.55s) for W_M (p=0.03), but not for W_S. For W_M and W_S, *Surfpad*Π, *SemPoint*Π and *SemPoint*Ω significantly improved movement time compared to the two control conditions ($p<0.05$). On these target sizes, *SemPoint*Π and *SemPoint*Ω were significantly better than *Surfpad*Π ($p<0.02$).

To better understand the effects observed on movement time, we split it in three parts: *approaching time*, *stopping time* and *click time*. As we noticed participants clutching during the experiment, we also analyzed the corresponding time.

Approaching Time

Approaching time is the time between the beginning of the movement and the instant the target border is crossed. There was a significant main effect of TECHNIQUE ($F_{5,55}$=7.9, $p<0.001$), DISTANCE ($F_{2,22}$=229.2, $p<0.001$) and WIDTH ($F_{2,22}$=17.5, $p<0.001$) on it as well as significant TECHNIQUE×WIDTH ($F_{10,110}$=18.6, $p<0.001$) and DISTANCE×WIDTH ($F_{4,44}$=11.4, $p<0.001$) interactions. Pairwise comparisons showed significant differences between the techniques in a trend similar to the one observed for movement time. In particular, *SemPoint*Π, *SemPoint*Ω and *Surfpad*Π showed a significantly lower approaching time compared to the two control conditions ($p < 0.05$). Pairwise comparisons showed that approaching time increased with larger target distances and smaller target widths.

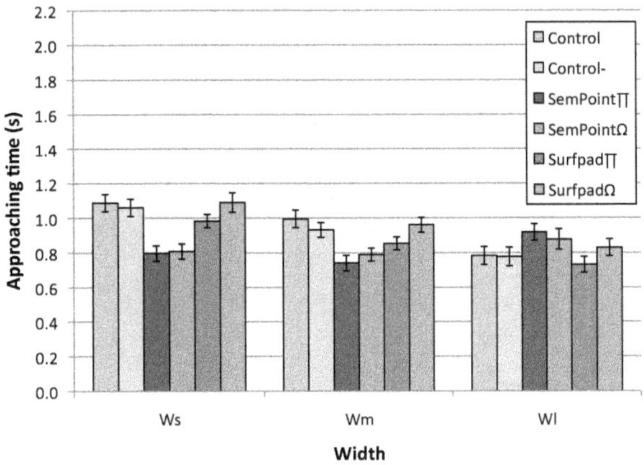

Figure 5. Mean approaching time for TECHNIQUE and WIDTH. Error bars represent 95% confidence interval.

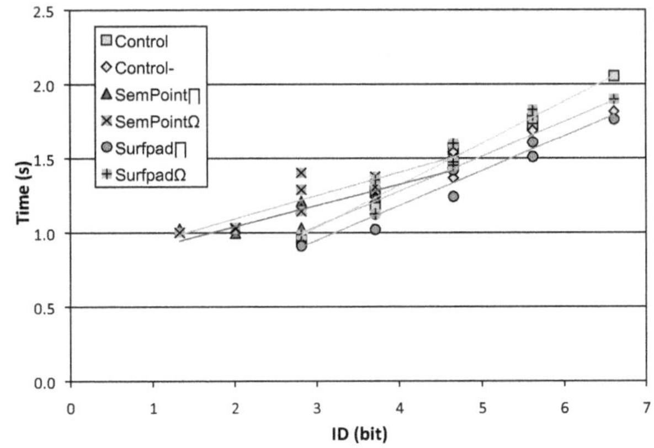

Figure 6. Fitts'law regression for each TECHNIQUE. IDs were computed in visual space for *Control*, *Control-*, *SurfpadΩ* and *SurfpadΠ* and motor space for *SemPointΠ* and *SemPointΩ*.

More surprisingly the TECHNIQUE×WIDTH interaction exhibited a different behavior for *SemPointΠ* and *SemPointΩ* for W_L with a significantly higher approaching time compared to *Control*, *Control-* and *SurfpadΠ* ($p<0.008$, Figure 5). This result might explain why no significant difference was found for the movement time on W_L between the *Semantic Pointing* variants and the two control conditions.

Stopping Time

Stopping time is the time between the first crossing of the target border and the stopping of the cursor. We observed a significant main effect of TECHNIQUE on it ($F_{5,55}$=3.7, p=0.038; *Control* : 0.44s, *Control-* : 0.44s, *SemPointΠ* : 0.34s, *SemPointΩ* : 0.34s, *SurfpadΩ* : 0.41s, *SurfpadΠ* : 0.36s). Pairwise comparisons showed significant differences ($p<0.05$) between the *Semantic Pointing* variants and the control conditions as well as *SurfpadΩ*. We also observed significant differences between *SurfpadΠ* and the two control conditions ($p<0.02$). These results might partially explain the significant differences observed for the movement time.

We also found a significant main effect of WIDTH ($F_{5,55}$=20.1, p=0.001) on stopping time, the latter increasing with smaller widths. Pairwise comparisons showed significant differences between W_S and the two other widths (W_S = 0.48s, W_M = 0.36s, W_L = 0.33s; $p<0.004$).

Click Time

Click time is the time during which the pointer remains still before the button is pressed. We observed significant effects of TECHNIQUE ($F_{5,55}$=9.9, $p<0.001$) and WIDTH ($F_{2,22}$=210.4, p=0.001) on it. Pairwise comparisons showed significant differences between the *Semantic Pointing* variants and the other techniques (*SemPointΠ* = 0.15s, *SemPointΩ* = 0.16s, *Control* = 0.20s, *Control-* = 0.19s, *SurfpadΠ* = 0.21s, *SurfpadΩ* = 0.19s; $p<0.02$). This result might explain the significant difference observed between the *Semantic Pointing* variants and *SurfpadΠ* for the movement time. There were significant differences between the widths, the click time increasing as the target width decreases (W_S = 0.24s, W_M = 0.18s, W_L = 0.13s; $p<0.001$).

Clutch Time and Number of Clutches

Clutch time is the total time the finger is lifted during a trial. There was a significant effect of DISTANCE ($F_{2,22}$=10.2, p=0.003) on it. Pairwise comparisons showed that it increases with larger target distances, with significant differences between all distances (D_S=0.018, D_M=0.045, D_L=0.147; $p<0.034$). There was also a significant effect of DISTANCE ($F_{2,22}$=6.2, p=0.014) on the number of clutches. Pairwise comparisons showed significant differences between all distances (D_S=0.36, D_M=0.58, D_L=1.73; $p<0.05$). Although not significant, we observed that the clutch time increased with target width (W_S=0.057s, W_M=0.062s, W_L=0.079s).

Fitts' Law Analysis

We ran a Fitts' law analysis on movement time removing trials where an error or clutching occured. For *SemPointΠ* and *SemPointΩ*, we computed the index of difficulty in motor space, as suggested in [10]. We aggregated the data for each target width and distance, producing a total of 9 points for each TECHNIQUE. As shown on Figure 6, we obtained good regression fitness for *Control* ($MT = 0.185 + 0.283\,ID$, $r^2 = 0.98$), *Control-* ($MT = 0.339 + 0.235\,ID$, $r^2 = 0.90$), *SurfpadΩ* ($MT = 0.295 + 0.258\,ID$, $r^2 = 0.92$) and *SurfpadΠ* ($MT = 0.247 + 0.234\,ID$, $r^2 = 0.93$), but reduced regression fitness for *SemPointΠ* ($MT = 0.756 + 0.142\,ID$, $r^2 = 0.84$) and *SemPointΩ* ($MT = 0.781 + 0.156\,ID$, $r^2 = 0.79$). These last two results are mainly explained by the outlier point (D_L,W_L) for which we have the highest amount of clutching.

DISCUSSION

The experiment compared six techniques with the same baseline CD gain. No significant difference was found between the two control conditions. Our results show that *SurfpadΠ* and the two *Semantic Pointing* variants significantly improve performance by 8.8% and 17.7% respectively, compared to the control conditions. *SurfpadΩ* did not result in any significant performance improvement compared to the control conditions. Results also show that these differences can be explained by a significant decrease in approaching time and stopping time for *SurfpadΠ*, *SemPointΠ* and *SemPointΩ* compared to the control conditions, and a significant decrease in click time for *SemPointΠ* and *SemPointΩ* compared to the other techniques.

Mechanical Effect or Information Feedback?

Our results do not show any significant difference between *Control* and *Control-* for movement time, approaching time, stopping time or click time. This inclines us to conclude that the friction reduction provided by the full actuation of the STIMTAC does not help to achieve faster movements.

The approaching time is significantly lower for *SemPoint*Π and *SemPoint*Ω than for the control conditions. As the step function and the bell-shaped mixing function operate only in the close vicinity of the targets, we assume this is the consequence of an anticipation phenomenon already observed in the use of *expanding targets* [27].

The approaching time is also significantly lower for *Surfpad*Π than for the control conditions. As friction reduction does not help to achieve faster movements, we assume this is also caused by anticipation of some later perceivable effect. Since the approaching time for *Surfpad*Ω is not significantly different from the control conditions, the perceived effect must be inherent to the Π function and incompatible with the Ω one.

Our results show a significantly lower stopping time for *Surfpad*Π compared to the control conditions. We hypothesize two reasons for this: (H1) a mechanical braking effect related to the friction increase, or (H2) tactile information feedback, i.e. a cognitive response to the perception of this increase. Although Π and Ω differ, their integral is the same[3]. From a mechanical perspective, the braking effect of H1 should also be observed with *Surfpad*Ω, which was not the case. H1 is also contradicted by the fact that *Surfpad*Π is more efficient on small target sizes where it should be more difficult to take advantage of a mechanical effect. We thus favor the second hypothesis, H2, which is also supported by previous evidence that the addition of tactile information can reduce response times by providing a confirmation without the need for visual attention [3, 17].

Target Size Matters

We observed a significant interaction between target sizes and techniques on movement time. Compared to the two control conditions, the mean movement time for target sizes W_M and W_S is reduced by 8.8% for *Surfpad*Π and 17.7% for the *Semantic Pointing* variants. Yet the three techniques fall short for W_L although according to Blanch et al., *Semantic Pointing* reduces the index of difficulty in motor space independently of target width [10].

Although clutching remained limited, we hypothesize that the slightly higher amount of it observed for W_L may have disrupted finger movements. Further experiments are required to validate this hypothesis. Still, the more pronounced effect of *Surfpad*Π as target width decreases agrees with results from previous work on tactile feedback [2].

EXPERIMENT 2: ANTI-SURFPAD

Results from Experiment 1 suggest that the performance improvement observed with *Surfpad*Π is the result of information feedback provided by the sudden increase of friction when the cursor crosses the target border. This second experiment was designed to better understand the nature of this feedback. We wanted to investigate if it can also be provided by a sudden decrease of friction. We call this condition *Anti-Surfpad*Π: the friction is minimal if the cursor is over a target, and maximal otherwise.

The apparatus and task for this experiment were the same as in the first one. The techniques were *Control*, *Surfpad*Π and *Anti-Surfpad*Π. Nine participants with a mean age of 27.3 (SD=4.7) took part in the experiment (8 male and 1 female, 8 right-handed and 1 left-handed).

A repeated measures ANOVA showed a significant main effect of TECHNIQUE ($F_{2,16}=17.8$, $p<0.001$) and a significant TECHNIQUE×WIDTH interaction ($F_{4,32}=4.4$, $p=0.02$) on the movement time. Significant differences were found between the three techniques (*Control*=1.60s, *Anti-Surfpad*Π=1.82s, *Surfpad*Π=1.49s; $p<0.007$). The significant interaction showed that *Anti-Surfpad*Π increased the movement time for all target widths ($p<0.05$). *Surfpad*Π significantly improved performance compared to *Control* and *Anti-Surfpad*Π for W_S and W_M ($p<0.009$). However, the difference with *Control* was no longer significant for W_L.

A repeated measures ANOVA also showed a significant main effect of TECHNIQUE ($F_{2,16}=17.8$, $p<0.001$) on stopping time with significant differences between all techniques (*Control*=0.46s, *Surfpad*Π=0.39s, *Anti-Surfpad*Π=0.60s, $p<0.01$). We again hypothesize two reasons for this: (H3) a negative mechanical effect stronger than the information feedback, or (H4) counter-effective information feedback. Further experimentation is needed to validate these compatible hypotheses.

EXPERIMENT 3: DISTRACTORS

In Experiment 1, we showed that *Surfpad*Π and the *Semantic Pointing* variants significantly improve the movement time compared to the two control conditions, especially for small target sizes. The goal of this third experiment was to investigate the impact of distractors on the *Surfpad* and *Semantic Pointing* techniques.

As we found no significant difference between *SemPoint*Ω and *SemPoint*Π in Experiment 1, we decided to focus on *SemPoint*Ω which is the implementation described in [10]. We also decided to focus on *Surfpad*Π since it showed significant differences with the control conditions in Experiment 1 while *Surfpad*Ω did not show any. *Surfpad* and *Semantic Pointing* will thus refer to *Surfpad*Π and *SemPoint*Ω in this section. Lastly, as we found no significant difference between *Control* and *Control-*, we decided to focus on *Control* which corresponds to the default state of the STIMTAC.

Apparatus and Task

We used the exact same apparatus as in Experiment 1 and 2. The task was also the same except for the presence of distractors evenly spaced between the two opposite clickable targets (Figure 7).

Participants

Twelve unpaid volunteers with a mean age of 28 ($SD = 9$) served in the experiment (10 male and 2 female, 9 right-handed and 3 left-handed).

[3]Friction depends on control input nonlinearly for variable friction devices. In the case of the STIMTAC however, the non-linearity is negligible. The difference between the integrals of *Surfpad*Π and *Surfpad*Ω is below 1%.

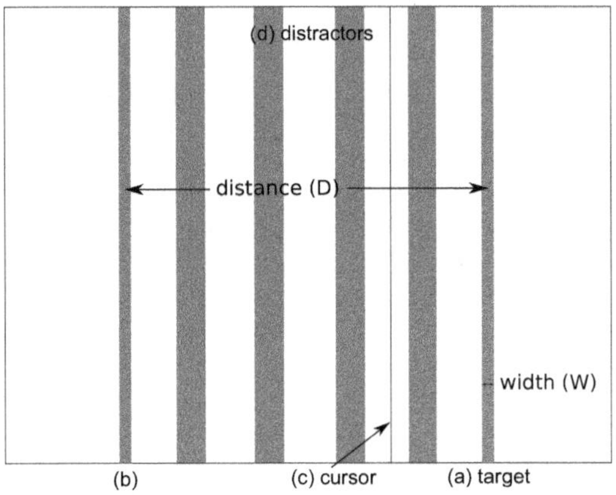

Figure 7. Experimental display. Targets were rendered as solid vertical bars equidistant from the center of the display in opposite directions along the horizontal axis. The target to be selected was colored green (a) and the last target gray (b). The cursor was represented by a one-pixel-thick vertical black line (c). Distractors (d) were evenly spaced between the targets (a) and (b) and were also colored gray.

Design

A repeated measures within-subjects design was used. The independent variables were TECHNIQUE, target width (WIDTH) and distractor density (DENSITY). TECHNIQUE was evaluated with three levels (*Control*, *Semantic Pointing*, *Surfpad*), WIDTH with two levels (W_L = 4.136 mm = 16 pixels, W_S = 1.034 mm = 4 pixels) and DENSITY with 6 levels (0, 1, 2, 4, 8, 12). The distractors were evenly spaced between the extremum targets with a size equal to W_L across all conditions. We used this width and these densities for distractors as they are representative of buttons size and densities in toolbars or menus. The target distance was kept constant to 100 mm to allow evaluating the different distractor densities while keeping a reasonably small amount of clutching.

Participants had a few minutes to get used to the device in the *Control* condition before starting the experiment. They then completed four successive BLOCKS of trials for each TECHNIQUE. Each BLOCK consisted of 36 trials: 3 repetitions of the 6 DENSITY × 2 WIDTH combinations. The WIDTH was presented in descending order and the DENSITY in ascending order. The presentation order of TECHNIQUE was counterbalanced across participants using a Latin Square design. Participants were encouraged to take a break after every 6 trials. The experiment lasted approximately 35 minutes.

In summary, the experimental design was: 12 participants × 3 TECHNIQUE × 4 BLOCKS × 2 WIDTH × 6 DENSITY × 3 trials = 5, 184 total trials

RESULTS

The dependent variables were the error rate, the movement time, the clutch time and the overshooting distance. They were computed the same way as in Experiment 1.

Error Rate

A repeated measures ANOVA showed a significant effect of WIDTH ($F_{1,11}$=96.3, $p<0.001$) on error rate with significant difference between W_S (10.2%) and W_L (1.9%) and an overall error rate of 6.1%.

Movement Time

Targets marked as errors were removed from the timing analysis. Trials at least three standard deviations away from the mean for each condition were considered as outliers and also removed from the data analysis (1.5% of the trials).

A repeated measures ANOVA showed that the order of presentation of TECHNIQUE had no significant effect or interaction on movement time, indicating that a within-participants design was appropriate. We also found no significant effect or interaction for BLOCK indicating there was no presence of a learning effect. As predicted by Fitts' law, a repeated measures ANOVA found a significant effect of WIDTH ($F_{1,11}$=199.4, $p<0.001$) on movement time with the smaller width increasing the movement time.

There was a significant main effect for TECHNIQUE ($F_{2,22}$ =119.1, $p<0.001$) and DENSITY ($F_{5,55}$=67.8, $p<0.001$) and a significant TECHNIQUE×DENSITY interaction ($F_{10,110}$=92.6, $p<0.001$) on movement time (Figure 8). Pairwise comparison showed significant differences ($p<0.001$) between all techniques: 2.1s for *Control*, 2.9s for *Semantic Pointing*, and 1.9s for *Surfpad*. It shows that *Surfpad* improves performance by 9.5% compared to *Control* and 52.6% compared to *Semantic Pointing*. *Semantic Pointing* deteriorates performance by 38.1% compared to *Control*.

Subsequent pairwise comparison for the significant TECHNIQUE × DENSITY interaction showed that the degradation of performance for *Semantic Pointing* increased with DENSITY. No significant difference between techniques was found for density 0, but we found significant differences ($p<0.04$) between *Control* and *Surfpad* for densities greater than 1. Significant differences ($p<0.03$) were found between DENSITY levels for *Semantic Pointing* except between 0 and 1 (p=0.16), and 2 and 4 (p=0.07). No significant difference was found between DENSITY levels for *Control* and *Surfpad*.

Clutch Time

A repeated measures ANOVA showed a significant main effect of TECHNIQUE ($F_{2,22}$=64.4, $p<0.001$) and DENSITY ($F_{5,55}$=164.4, $p<0.001$) and a significant TECHNIQUE×DENSITY interaction ($F_{10,110}$=121.9, $p<0.001$) on clutch time. Pairwise comparison showed significant differences ($p<0.001$) between

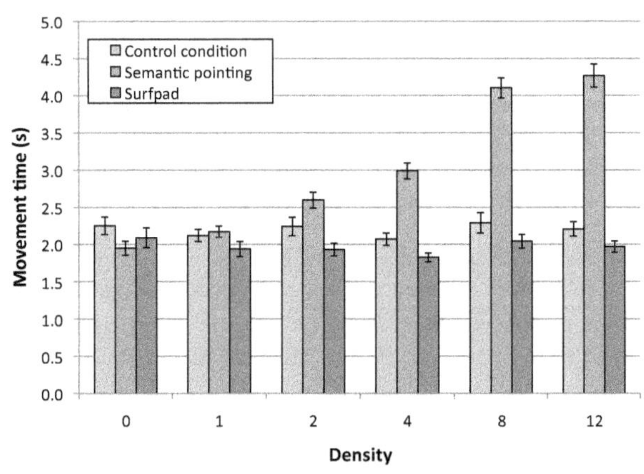

Figure 8. Mean movement time for TECHNIQUE and DENSITY. Error bars represent 95% confidence interval.

Semantic Pointing (0.59s), *Surfpad* (0.12s) and *Control* (0.15s). No significant difference was found across DENSITY for *Surfpad* or *Control*, but we found significant differences ($p<0.003$) between the following density groups for *Semantic Pointing*: (0,1): 0.28s, (2): 0.42s, (4): 0.54s, (8,12): 1.02s (Figure 9).

Overshooting Distance

We define overshooting as the distance traveled past the extend of the target. A repeated measures ANOVA showed no significant main effect or interaction on the overshooting distance. The mean overshooting distance was equal to 1.7 mm (SD=4.8 mm) and the 90th percentile was equal to 4.8 mm. The 90th percentile for overshooting was equal to 3.7 mm in Experiment 1 and 3.4 mm in Experiment 2. Considering this relatively small overshooting distance, users' strategy to acquire the target was probably not to overshoot the target and then correct to select it.

User Feedback

Most of participants comments on *Semantic Pointing* concerned the clutching required to move the pointer, especially when the number of distractors becomes important. Participants did not spontaneously comment on distractors for *Surfpad*. After debriefing, they explained they did not feel disrupted in their movement by the tactile feedback on distractors. Participants were also asked which technique they would use. Eleven chose *Surfpad* and one chose *Control*.

DISCUSSION

We compared *Surfpad* to *Control* and *Semantic Pointing* in the same conditions as in the first experiment with additional control on the density of distractors. Our results show that *Surfpad* significantly improves the movement time by 9.5% compared to *Control*, independently of the density of distractors. In contrast, we showed that *Semantic Pointing* significantly degrades the movement time compared to *Control* with a rate related to the density of distractors (from 22.4% for density 2 to 100% for density 12). Results show that the significant increase in clutching for *Semantic Pointing* compared to *Surfpad* and *Control* can be held responsible to its significant increase of movement time.

In the worse case scenario for *Semantic Pointing*, the distance to the target gets fully covered with distractors: the

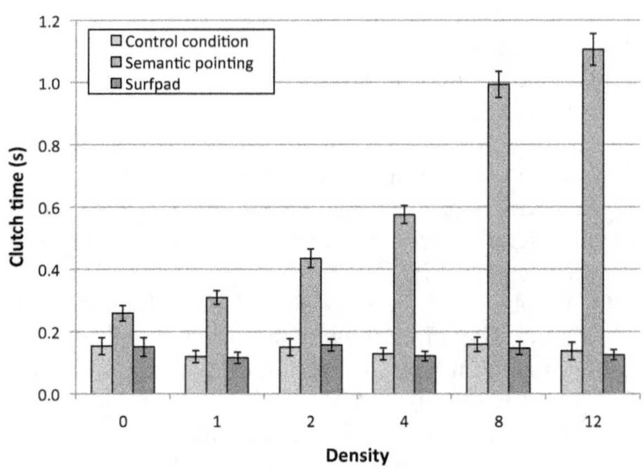

Figure 9. Mean clutch time for TECHNIQUE and DENSITY. Error bars represent 95% confidence interval.

indices of difficulty in motor and display spaces become equal (considering there is no overlapping between distractors), but the distance in motor space gets multiplied by the scale factor. Such a situation typically occurs in hierarchical menus [13]. If the device operating range is set to cover the entire display surface without clutching, multiplying the distance by the scale factor in motor space will inevitably lead to clutching and a deterioration of performance.

There was no negative effect of distractors on *Surfpad* which still showed a significant improvement of 9.5% on movement time compared to *Control* in their presence. This reinforces our belief that the *Surfpad*Π implementation mainly provides information feedback and little or no mechanical effect. Participants did not make any negative comment on the tactile feedback associated to distractors. This makes *Surfpad* a good alternative to *Semantic Pointing* and probably target-aware CD gain adaptation in general, especially for limited workspaces where clutching is likely to occur in presence of distractors.

CONCLUSION AND DIRECTIONS FOR FUTURE WORK

We presented *Surfpad*, a new pointing facilitation technique based on STIMTAC, a tactile touchpad that supports friction reduction. *Surfpad* preserves the nominal coefficient of friction of the touchpad when the cursor is on targets but reduces it in all other places. We reported on three experiments comparing it to *Semantic Pointing* and constant CD gain. Our results show that *Surfpad* leads to a performance improvement close to 9% compared to unassisted pointing on small targets without distractors. It is also robust to high distractor densities, keeping an average performance improvement of nearly 10% whereas the performance of *Semantic Pointing* can degrade up to 100% due to increased clutching caused by distractor expansion in motor space. Our results also show that *Surfpad* needs to be implemented using a step function (*Surfpad*Π) to improve performance.This implementation provides a sudden reduction in the amount of friction when the pointer crosses the target border which, we hypothesize, results in an information feedback that helps users reduce the approaching and stopping times.

Surfpad's robustness to distractors is particularly novel. This characteristic has exciting implications since it no longer requires the careful determination of targets to enable a pointing facilitation technique. Our prototype STIMTAC device can be easily carried for demonstrations, but it is still too large to incorporate in a mobile computing device such as a laptop. New prototypes are being developed which use more compact sensing techniques. Once the size is reduced, its low power consumption (0.5 W) makes it feasible to use in place of a conventional laptop touchpad. However, the tactile feedback it provides is intrinsically mono-touch. The extension to multi-touch will be addressed as future work.

Acknowledgments

This work was supported by the ANR project n°ANR-09-CORD-013 "InSTInCT".

REFERENCES

1. D. Ahlström, M. Hitz, and G. Leitner. An evaluation of sticky and force enhanced targets in multi target situations. In *Proc. of NordiCHI'06*, 58–67. ACM.

2. M. Akamatsu and I. S. MacKenzie. Movement characteristics using a mouse with tactile and force feedback. *IJHCS*, 45(4):483–493, 1996.
3. M. Akamatsu, I. S. MacKenzie, and T. Hasbrouc. A comparison of tactile, auditory, and visual feedback in a pointing task using a mouse-type device. *Ergonomics*, 38(4):816–827, 1995.
4. T. Asano, E. Sharlin, Y. Kitamura, K. Takashima, and F. Kishino. Predictive interaction using the delphian desktop. In *Proc. of UIST'05*, 133–141. ACM, 2005.
5. R. Balakrishnan. "Beating" Fitts' law: virtual enhancements for pointing facilitation. *IJHCS*, 61(6):857–874, 2004.
6. O. Bau, I. Poupyrev, A. Israr, and C. Harrison. Teslatouch: electrovibration for touch surfaces. In *Proc. of UIST'10*, 283–292. ACM, 2010.
7. P. Baudisch, E. Cutrell, M. Czerwinski, D. C. Robbins, P. Tandler, B. B. Bederson, and A. Zierlinger. Drag-and-pop and drag-and-pick: techniques for accessing remote screen content on touch- and pen-operated systems. In *Proc. of Interact'03*, 57–64. IOS Press, 2003.
8. P. Baudisch, A. Zotov, E. Cutrell, and K. Hinckley. Starburst: a target expansion algorithm for non-uniform target distributions. In *Proc. of AVI'08*, 129–137. ACM.
9. M. Biet, F. Giraud, and B. Semail. Squeeze film effect for the design of an ultrasonic tactile plate. *IEEE Transactions on Ultrasonic, Ferroelectric and Frequency Control*, 54(12):2678–2688, 2007.
10. R. Blanch, Y. Guiard, and M. Beaudouin-Lafon. Semantic pointing: improving target acquisition with control-display ratio adaptation. In *Proc. of CHI'04*, 519–526. ACM, 2004.
11. C. S. Campbell, S. Zhai, K. W. May, and P. P. Maglio. What you feel must be what you see: Adding tactile feedback to the trackpoint. In *Proc. of Interact'99*, 383–390. IOS Press, 1999.
12. G. Casiez, D. Vogel, R. Balakrishnan, and A. Cockburn. The impact of control-display gain on user performance in pointing tasks. *Human-Computer Interaction, Taylor and Francis*, 23(3):215–250, 2008.
13. A. Cockburn and S. Brewster. Multimodal feedback for the acquisition of small targets. *Ergonomics*, 48(9):1129–1150, 2005.
14. A. Cockburn and A. Firth. Improving the acquisition of small targets. In *Proc. of HCI'03*, 77–80. BCS, 2003.
15. J. T. Dennerlein, D. B. Martin, and C. Hasser. Force-feedback improves performance for steering and combined steering-targeting tasks. In *Proc. of CHI'00*, 423–429. ACM, 2000.
16. J. T. Dennerlein and M. C. Yang. Haptic force-feedback devices for the office computer: Performance and musculoskeletal loading issues. *Human Factors*, 43(2):278–286, 2001.
17. C. Forlines and R. Balakrishnan. Evaluating tactile feedback and direct vs. indirect stylus input in pointing and crossing selection tasks. In *Proc. of CHI'08*, 1563–1572. ACM, 2008.
18. T. Grossman and R. Balakrishnan. The bubble cursor: enhancing target acquisition by dynamic resizing of the cursor's activation area. In *Proc. of CHI'05*, 281–290. ACM, 2005.
19. Y. Guiard, R. Blanch, and M. Beaudouin-Lafon. Object pointing: a complement to bitmap pointing in GUIs. In *Proc. of GI'04*, 9–16. CHCCS, 2004.
20. C. Harrison and S. E. Hudson. Texture displays: a passive approach to tactile presentation. In *Proc. of CHI'09*, 2261–2264. ACM, 2009.
21. A. Hurst, J. Mankoff, A. K. Dey, and S. E. Hudson. Dirty desktops: using a patina of magnetic mouse dust to make common interactor targets easier to select. In *Proc. of UIST '07*, 183–186. ACM, 2007.
22. F. Hwang, S. Keates, P. M. Langdon, and P. J. Clarkson. Multiple haptic targets for motion-impaired computer users. In *Proc. of CHI'03*, 41–48. ACM, 2003.
23. P. Kabbash and W. Buxton. The "prince" technique: Fitts' law and selection using area cursors. In *Proc. of CHI'95*, 273–279. ACM/Addison-Wesley, 1995.
24. D. V. Keyson. Dynamic cursor gain and tactual feedback in the capture of cursor movements. *Ergonomics*, 40(12):1287 – 1298, 1997.
25. M. Kobayashi and T. Igarashi. Ninja cursors: using multiple cursors to assist target acquisition on large screens. In *Proc. of CHI'08*, 949–958. ACM, 2008.
26. A. Lécuyer, J.-M. Burkhardt, and L. Etienne. Feeling bumps and holes without a haptic interface: the perception of pseudo-haptic textures. In *Proc. of CHI'04*, 239–246. ACM, 2004.
27. M. J. McGuffin and R. Balakrishnan. Fitts' law and expanding targets: experimental studies and designs for user interfaces. *ACM ToCHI*, 12(4):388–422, 2005.
28. I. Oakley, M. R. McGee, S. Brewster, and P. Gray. Putting the feel in 'look and feel'. In *Proc. of CHI'00*, 415–422. ACM, 2000.
29. R. W. Soukoreff and I. S. MacKenzie. Towards a standard for pointing device evaluation, perspectives on 27 years of Fitts' law research in HCI. *IJHCS*, 61(6):751–789, 2004.
30. J. B. F. van Erp, K.-U. Kyung, S. Kassner, J. Carter, S. A. Brewster, G. Weber, and I. Andrew. Setting the standards for haptic and tactile interactions: ISO's work. In *Proc. of EuroHaptics'10*, 353–358. Springer.
31. K. van Mensvoort. What you see is what you feel: exploiting the dominance of the visual over the haptic domain to simulate force-feedback with cursor displacements. In *Proc. of DIS'02*, 345–348. ACM.
32. T. Watanabe and S. Fukui. A method for controlling tactile sensation of surface roughness using ultrasonic vibration. In *Proc. of ICRA'95*, 1134–1139. IEEE.
33. L. Winfield, J. Glassmire, J. E. Colgate, and M. Peshkin. T-pad: Tactile pattern display through variable friction reduction. In *Proc. of World Haptics Conf.*, 421–426. IEEE, 2007.
34. J. O. Wobbrock, J. Fogarty, S.-Y. Liu, S. Kimuro, and S. Harada. The angle mouse: target-agnostic dynamic gain adjustment based on angular deviation. In *Proc. of CHI'09*, 1401–1410. ACM, 2009.
35. A. Worden, N. Walker, K. Bharat, and S. Hudson. Making computers easier for older adults to use: area cursors and sticky icons. In *Proc. of CHI'97*, 266–271. ACM, 1997.

Understanding Touch

Christian Holz and Patrick Baudisch
Hasso Plattner Institute
Potsdam, Germany
{christian.holz, patrick.baudisch}@hpi.uni-potsdam.de

ABSTRACT

Current touch devices, such as capacitive touchscreens are based on the implicit assumption that users acquire targets with the center of the contact area between finger and device. Findings from our previous work indicate, however, that such devices are subject to systematic error offsets. This suggests that the underlying assumption is most likely wrong. In this paper, we therefore revisit this assumption.

In a series of three user studies, we find evidence that the features that users align with the target are *visual* features. These features are located *on the top* of the user's fingers, not at the bottom, as assumed by traditional devices. We present the *projected center model*, under which error offsets drop to 1.6mm, compared to 4mm for the traditional model. This suggests that the new model is indeed a good approximation of how users conceptualize touch input.

The primary contribution of this paper is to help understand touch—one of the key input technologies in human-computer interaction. At the same time, our findings inform the design of future touch input technology. They explain the inaccuracy of traditional touch devices as a "parallax" artifact between user control based on the top of the finger and sensing based on the bottom side of the finger. We conclude that certain camera-based sensing technologies can inherently be more accurate than contact area-based sensing.

Author Keywords

Touch input, targeting, generalized perceived input point model, experiment.

ACM Classification Keywords

H5.2 [Information interfaces and presentation]: User Interfaces. Input devices & strategies.

General Terms

Design, Experimentation, Human Factors.

INTRODUCTION

Current touch technologies, such as *capacitive touchpads* [7] and *FTIR* [11], sense touch by observing the *contact area* between finger and device. These devices are thereby based on the implicit assumption that the contact area encodes the information about the desired target in the first place, i.e., that *users* somehow use the contact area to encode which target they are trying to refer to, e.g., by touching the target with the center of the finger contact area.

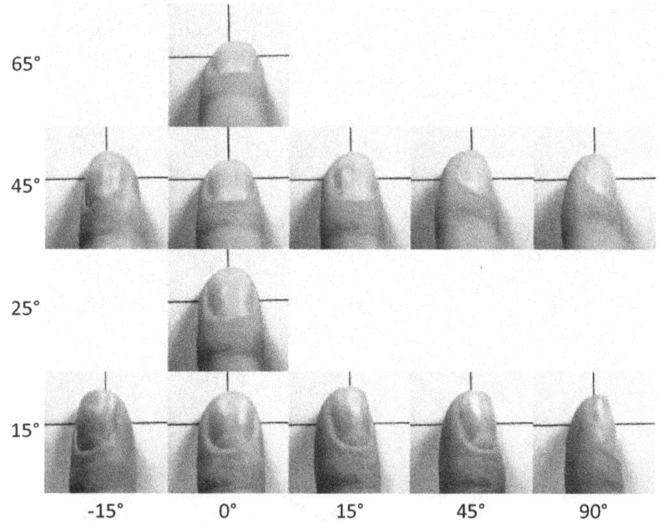

Figure 1: A study participant targeting crosshairs using different finger angles. Can you guess how this user is conceptualizing touch, i.e., what geometric relationship between finger and crosshairs the user is trying to maintain independent of how the finger is held? Our findings suggest that users indeed target as suggested by this illustration, i.e., by aligning finger features and outlines in a hypothesized top-down perspective.

Our recent findings seem to put this assumption into question. While the "contact area model" is clearly plausible on a macroscopic scale, our earlier findings with very small targets indicate that touch input on such devices is subject to systematic error offsets (*generalized perceived input point model* [12]). In fact, as much as two thirds of the overall inaccuracy of touch seem to be caused by these effects. When users target with an almost horizontal finger, for example, the target position measured by a capacitive touch device is off by as much as several millimeters—on small screens devices this is a substantial effect. In our earlier studies, the size and direction of the error offset was affected by a range of parameters, including finger posture measured in roll, pitch, and yaw [12].

In the aforementioned paper, we compensated for this effect using an elaborate schema of *corrective offsets* (user- and finger-posture specific position adjustments). The existence of these systematic offsets, however, raises much deeper questions. In particular, the existence of these offsets seems to indicate that the assumption these devices are built on, i.e., that users target based on finger contact area, *is wrong*.

So if users do not touch targets based on contact area, how *do* they target? How do they decide whether a finger is "on target" or whether it requires corrective moves? In this paper, we are attempting to answer this question.

UNDERSTANDING TOUCH

In order to help us specify what we are trying to find out, Figure 2 illustrates the general concept of touch input: users communicate a 2D target location to a touch device. As users acquire a target with their finger, such as the shown crosshairs (a), they effectively translate the 2D target location into the 6D posture of their finger (6D = 3D rotation + 2D position + pressure). (b) Due to the lack of a better term, we will refer to this 2D-to-6D mapping as *the user's mental model of touch*, in the traditional sense of a user's mental model of the way an object operates [15], but with the "object" being the user's own finger.

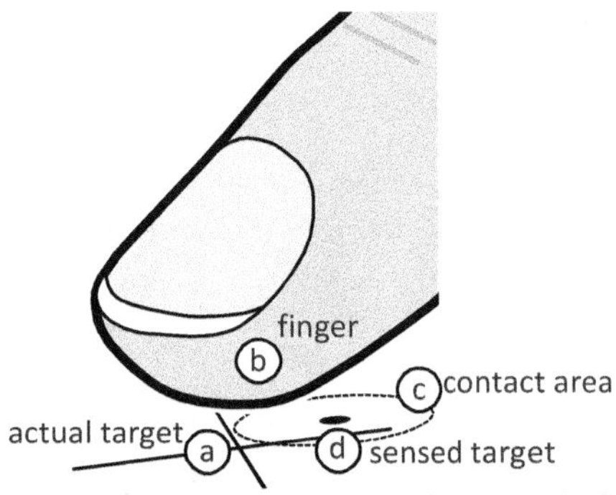

Figure 2: When acquiring a target, here marked with 2D crosshairs (a), users effectively translate the 2D position of the target into a 6D position of their finger. On traditional touch devices, the finger leaves a contact area (c), which is observed by the touch pad and reduced to its 2D centroid (d).

The objective of any touch input device is to *invert this translation*, i.e., to reconstruct the 2D target location from this 6D finger posture. We will refer to this 6D-to-2D mapping as *the device's conceptual model.* Perfect reconstruction is achieved if and only if the mapping implemented by the touch device is indeed inverse to the 2D-to-6D mapping implemented by the user, i.e., if the device's conceptual model matches the user's mental model.

Current touch devices implement this back-translation as illustrated by Figure 2c and d: They observe the 2D contact area between finger and pad (c) and reduce it to its centroid (d). As explained earlier, however, our previous findings indicate that this *contact area model* is not correct, i.e., it *does not* reconstruct the intended input position accurately. Apparently, users do *not* aim by pointing using the center of the contact area.

Note: throughout this paper, we will use an apparatus similar to Figure 2, i.e., *crosshairs* marking the target. In our previous studies, crosshairs performed indistinguishably from a dot target [12], which suggests that the influence of crosshairs onto users' mental model of touch is reasonably small.

An example and preview of findings

As a preview of our analysis, take a look at the sequence of images shown in Figure 1. They show a user (Participant #7 from User Study 1 presented in this paper) targeting a pair of crosshairs with different finger angles. Looking across the sequence of images, we may already catch some indication of what mental model of touch this user adheres to. Certain geometric relationships between finger and crosshair seem to remain—independent of what finger posture the experimenter makes this participant assume.

The participant shown in Figure 1 is a particularly good representative of the new model of touch we propose and which we call the *projected center model.* This model says that users align certain *visual* features with the target. In the shown example, it is the horizontal center of the finger outline and the vertical center of the fingernail that the user is aligning with the target.

We chose the specific viewpoint of this image sequence with intent: even though the user's head was actually located to the bottom left of the picture during these trials, our findings suggest that users imagine this top-down perspective during touch input. Based on this perspective, they decide whether their finger is on target or whether it requires adjustment.

Under the projected center model, the error offsets of the contact area model effectively disappear (they drop to 1.6mm, compared to 4mm for traditional, contact area-based sensing), suggesting that the projected center model matches users' mental model of touch very closely.

The projected center model also explains why capacitive touch input devices are inaccurate: devices based on the contact area touch model sense features located at the *bottom* of the users' fingers, while users target based on features located *on the top/along the sides* of their fingers. The inaccuracy of touch on traditional touch devices is therefore an artifact of the parallax between the top and bottom of a finger.

Approach

In the remainder of this paper, we present a series of studies that validate the reasoning outlined above.

Many models in HCI are created by measuring a feature and fitting a function to it. Unfortunately, we do not know yet what feature to measure or even what modality (sense of touch, vision, and so on). This forces us to take a more general approach to the problem: "(1) *Guess* the law (or model in our case), (2) compute the consequences, and (3) compare the computation to experiment/observation. If it disagrees with experiment it is wrong [6]."

In this paper, we apply these three steps as follows: (1) Before we attempt to guess mental models, we narrow down the search space. We conduct a series of interviews and then consider only the subset of models that are based on features mentioned by participants. (2) The consequences we predict are that models that match the user's mental model will feature error offsets approximating zero. (3) We conduct a series of pointing studies. We measure error offsets as the average distance between the sensed input location and the actual target location for the respective user (cf. offset in our previous work [12]).

Since our primary goal is to understand touch, we require the remaining error offsets of a good candidate model to be small. Only when the remaining offsets get reasonably close to zero can we argue that the tested model indeed corresponds to the actual mental model of the respective user and thus contributes to an explanation of touch.

Procedure

We proceed in four steps.

Step 1—Interviews: We interview users to learn how they (think they) target using touch input, i.e., what features they try to align with the target.

Step 2—Model creation: Based on participants' input, we create a set of 7×7 candidate models. User input inspires us to focus on models based on a top-down perspective.

Step 3—Filtering models: We conduct two pointing studies in which we determine error offset for all candidate models under different variations of finger and head postures. We eliminate models with large offsets, as they indicate a poor representation of participants' mental models. We keep 2×3 candidate models.

Step 4—Final evaluation: We conduct a final pointing study using the combined set of independent variables from the studies in Step 3 (finger and head position) to determine the error offsets and thus the "fit" of the remaining models.

Contribution

We primarily make a scientific contribution. With *scientific* we mean: an attempt to understand an *underlying*, not directly observable mechanism—in our case touch input, one of the key technologies in human computer interaction. In particular, we explain why current touch devices are inaccurate by challenging the common assumption that touch input is about the contact area.

Still, essentially as a side effect, our findings have implications on engineering in that they inform the design of better touch input technology. They suggest that devices that observe the outline or "projection" of a finger have the potential to offer better touch precision than devices based on contact area.

RELATED WORK

The work presented in this paper is related to touch input, targeting aids, impact of finger posture on touch precision, and modeling users' input behavior.

Touch technologies and determining contact points

A wide range of touch technologies determine the input coordinates based on contact area (e.g., *capacitive sensing* [7]). Most optical technologies have adopted the same approach, such as *frustrated total internal reflection* (*FTIR*, e.g., [11], [19]). Wang and Ren examined participants' input precision on such an optical system [21].

Camera-based systems, such as the *Digital Desk* [22], typically cannot see the contact area and have therefore adopted a visual model. The *Visual Touchpad* uses two cameras to identify the user's fingertips and determine finger yaw [13]. Agarwal et al. used stereo cameras above the user's hands and trained a classifier to recognize fingertips and accurately determine when the user is touching or hovering their finger above the surface [1]. *LucidTouch* centers the contact point in the outline at a fixed offset from the fingertip [23]. *PlayAnywhere* observes fingers from above with a camera mounted at an angle and derives touch input from the distance between the user's fingers and the shadows they cast [24].

Targeting aids

The inaccuracy of touch has been attributed to the *fat finger problem* [20], i.e., the softness of the fingertip in combination with the fact that the finger occludes the target. A series of targeting aids alleviate the problem by enlarging the target, e.g., *TapTap* [18] (see also [2]) and *Dual Finger Stretch* [4]. Others avoid occlusion altogether by introducing an offset between finger and target, e.g., *offset cursor* [16], *shift* [20], *cross-lever* and *precision handle* [2], as well as the use of *styli* [17]. *Back-of-device interaction* [3] avoids occlusion by moving the user's finger to the device's back.

Modeling pointing

Modeling cursor-based target acquisition has a long tradition. *Fitts' Law* models the targeting time for one-dimensional targets [8]. Grossman and Balakrishnan's *probabilistic pointing* models two-dimensional target acquisition under visual control [10]. Both models assume that users can see target location and pointer, a requirement not fulfilled by touch on targets that are small enough to be occluded by the user's finger.

Early Models of Touch and the Role of Finger Posture

While touch systems traditionally reduce contact areas to a point [21], more recently researchers have proposed considering the entire contact area as input, such as *Shapetouch* [5] and *Sliding Widgets* [14].

Several researches suggested that the angle between the user's finger and the device might impact pointing. When designing the *shift* technique, Vogel and Baudisch [20] included a correction to compensate for parallax. Forlines et al. noticed that touching a target located across a tabletop results in a flat finger angle and thus a larger contact area, which leads to an offset input location [9]. Wang and Ren find that finger posture and motion impact the size of the contact area [21]. We generalized these findings in our previous work on the *generalized perceived input point model* [12].

To illustrate the error offset problem faced by devices based on the contact area model we reprint an extract of the data from this paper (see Figure 3). All 12 participants (each one shown as one column) repeatedly acquired a target on a touchpad under varying finger roll and pitch angles. Contact point distributions are shown as 65% confidence ovals each one of which represents a different roll/pitch condition. While ovals were small, they were *offset* with respect to each other, which implied the need for the aforementioned corrective offsets. Only for Participant #3 (dashed outline) ovals align, suggesting that this was the only person the targeting behavior of whom was appropriately described by the contact area model.

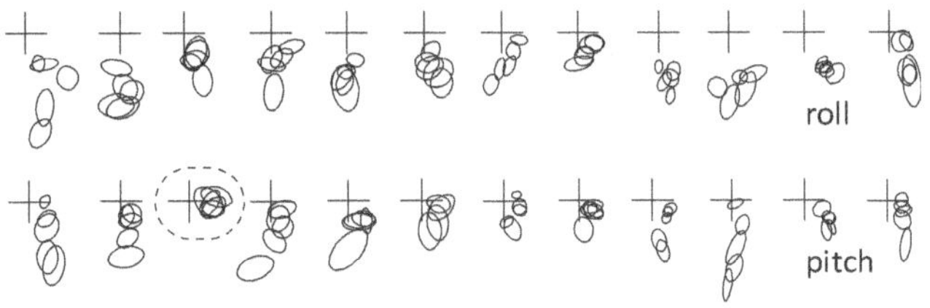

Figure 3: (from [12]) The aggregated contact locations of different finger postures are offset with respect to each other.

STEP 1: USER INTERVIEWS: PARTICIPANTS REFLECT ON THEIR TARGET ACQUISITION STRATEGIES

The purpose of this study was to learn more about users' mental models by means of an interview. While users are known to have limited ability of rationalizing low-level activities, our goal was to create a selection of *potentially* relevant models and elements that could be used to form a list of *candidate* models. We did not worry about incorrect models at this stage, as we would eliminate these in subsequent steps of our process.

Figure 4: Before being interviewed, participants acquired targets printed on a sheet of paper.

Task & Procedure

In order to help participants become aware of their mental models of touch input, participants started by repeatedly acquiring a target. As shown in Figure 4, the target was marked by crosshairs drawn on a sheet of paper and each participant acquired it 50 times. Participants were instructed to place their finger such that it would "acquire a tiny button located at the center of the crosshairs if the paper was a touch screen".

In order to help participants investigate their own mental models in more detail, participants acquired the target using the five finger postures shown in Figure 5, i.e., combinations of finger pitch and roll. All participants completed this part of the study in 10 minutes or less.

After they had completed the trials, we interviewed participants about the strategies they had used to acquire the target and based on what criteria they had decided when their fingers were "on target". We were careful not to use any terms that could bias their answer, such as "contact area", "fingertip", "finger nail", and the like. If they, however, did mention "contact area", we asked participants to draw the contact area in four figures showing stylized fingers top-down held at four different angles.

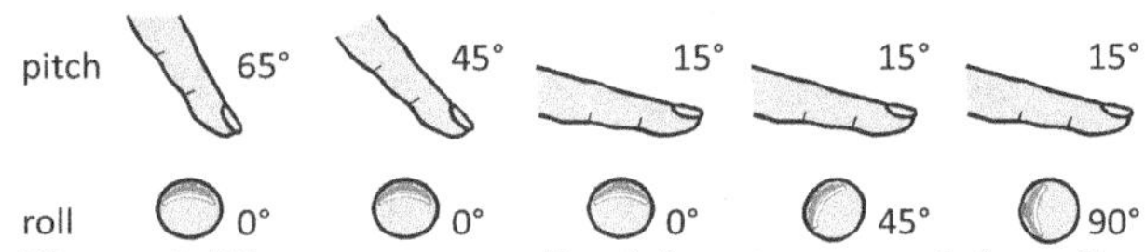

Figure 5: Finger postures. Participants assumed these five different combinations of finger pitch and roll, and then acquired the target.

Participants

We recruited 30 participants (5 female) from our institution. All participants were between 19 and 29 years old.

Results

When asked to verbalize their "targeting procedure", most participants hesitated. 4 participants insisted that they could not explain their behavior and "just touched the target intuitively without giving it too much thought".

6 participants stated right away that their experience with mobile touch-screen devices had shaped their input behavior. While two of them understood how such devices determine input coordinates, they all stated to aim based on experience with the device. They all said that the device had "taught" them how to touch small buttons over time.

Contact Area: 26 participants said that they considered contact area to be relevant to their targeting strategy. 24 of them stated that they imagined the contact area between their finger and the crosshairs and centered it on the target during the trials. One said:

> "I could not see the contact area, so I imagined where it should be located. Then I chose the center of it and positioned it on the target. That's all."

Participants' drawings of contact areas in the four figures supported our assumption that they cannot fully rationalize their behavior. Most drawings largely clashed with reality; while for a finger at a flat angle (15° pitch) the contact area extends fairly far towards the user's palm, participants always drew it too small. Similarly, for a rolled finger (90°), participants drew the contact area too large and mostly centered inside the finger, whereas in fact it is mostly offset horizontally and rather short.

Three participants mentioned a special version of contact area; they claimed to touch the target with the part of the finger that "comes down first". Five other participants explained to place their finger such that it applied the maximum amount of pressure to the target.

Visual Feedback: 13 participants reported that they positioned their finger using *visual control.* They stated that they mentally connected the crosshairs under their finger and tried to move their finger such that the target was always located under the same position inside their finger.

One said:

> "I can see my fingertip and imagine where the cross-hairs intersect. So I can visualize the bottom of my finger and always position it at the same location."

Nine participants explained that they positioned the finger, such that the target was located at a certain distance from the edge of their fingernail. Four other participants said they imagined a virtual 3D point inside their finger, which they repeatedly sought to position directly above the target. Two other participants said that they "projected" a feature in their finger down to the table and then aligned it with the target. This is an interesting observation, because such a projection is a comparably complex 3D operation that requires users to take head parallax into account.

Two participants described their targeting strategy as "cheating". Both had a visible spot on their fingernail that they vertically aligned with the target whenever finger roll was 0°. For roll different from 0° they still aligned the spot with the horizontal line of the crosshairs.

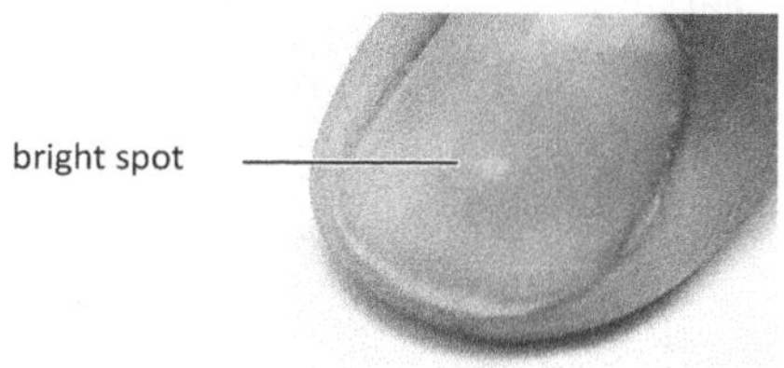

Figure 6: One participant targeted by placing a bright spot on his nail over the target.

Discussion

While the study allows proposing a wide range of possible models that explain how participants targeted, such as models based on a camera that tracks with the user's head, we decided to make an educated *guess* and limit our search for candidate models to those based on features that users can perceive *visually* and *from directly above*. This seemed plausible given that thirteen participants mentioned visual features and six of them mentioned some sort of vertical projection.

As discussed earlier when stating our 3-step approach, whether or not our intuition was right would have to be determined in the following pointing studies. If the model should perform poorly, our guess would turn out to be wrong and we would have to come back and restart the process with another model (note how this is different from phenomena that lend themselves to direct observation, in which case the interviews themselves would have already answered the question).

STEP 2: PICKING CANDIDATE MODELS

We constructed the following two (families of) candidate models (1) contact area, which had produced a good fit for one user in our previous study [12], shown as Participant #3 in Figure 3 and (2) models based on features of human fingers that are visible from above. We implemented this by tracking users' fingers using a camera placed *directly above* the crosshairs on the touchpad.

Figure 7 shows a series of features that we found to be visible from above. We classified them as *horizontal features* if they might help determine the finger's horizontal position and *vertical features* if they might help determine the finger's vertical position; some features, such as the corner of the fingernail are both (e.g., nail left and nail groove). Note the three-dimensional nature of the finger, which causes features, such as *outline center* to refer to the outline of the skin for some levels of finger roll and to the outline of the nail for other levels of finger roll.

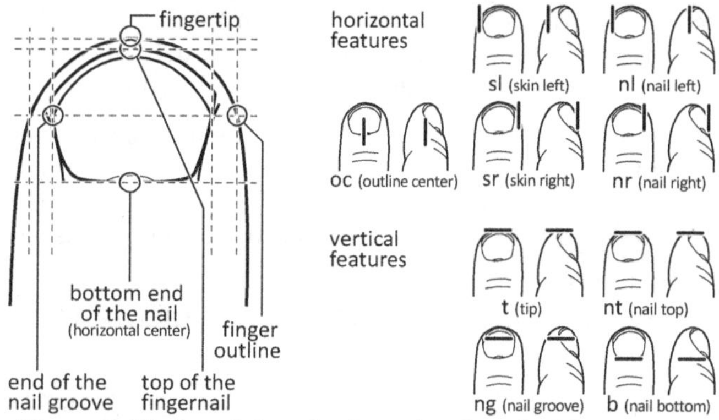

Figure 7: We found these *horizontal* and *vertical features* to be detectable and used them to construct candidate models.

In theory, users' mental models might combine any number of features in arbitrarily complex ways. We felt, however, that the effortlessness of touch pointing suggests that only simple models are truly plausible. We therefore only included models that use a single feature (such as "nr" for the mental model of users who aim relative to the right edge of their nail) and models that refer to the center point between two features, such as "sl|sr" for the mental model of users who aim relative to the center point of the finger's outline, i.e., between "*skin left*" and "*skin right*".

We will refer to terms such as "nr" or "sl|sr" as *half models*, because it takes two of them to describe the mental model of a user—one for *x* and one for *y*. To avoid the overhead of evaluating the cross product of *horizontal* and *vertical features*, however, we keep these two classes of features and models separate throughout most of this paper and will not combine them until the final study.

Figure 8 lists the horizontal and vertical half models that we created from the respective features shown in Figure 7.

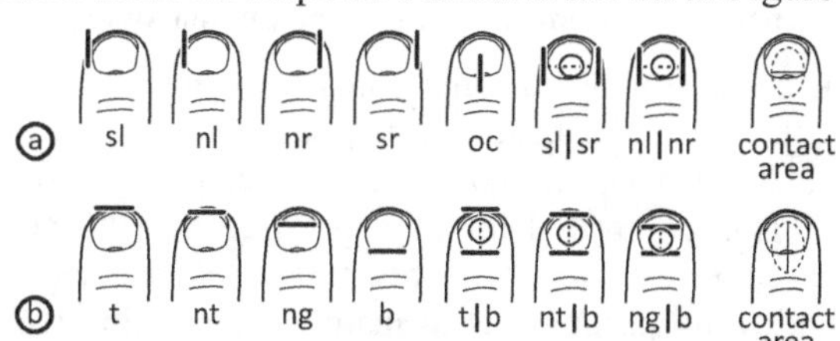

Figure 8: (a) 7 horizontal half models based on the features in Figure 7, plus the contact area based model. (b) 7 vertical half models (+ contact area based).

The idea behind a half model, such as "nail right" was not necessarily that participants would place this specific point over the target, but *some* point that is located at an offset from this feature. To include this concept, we complemented all half-models with a single user-specific *offset* (unlike our previous approach [12], which allowed for one offset *per finger angle*).

STEP 3: ELIMINATING MODELS

Next we eliminated those (half) models that did not match the mental models of any users. In order to do so, we conducted a pointing study. Using a camera above the target, we recorded participants as they repeatedly acquired a target on a capacitive touch pad. We then tried to "explain" the observed data using each of our half models and eliminated all half models that did not fit any participants.

To keep the overall number of repetitions manageable, we broke this study down into two individual studies. The first study tested twelve combinations of roll and pitch; the second tested only four combinations of roll and pitch, but varied head position in addition.

STEP 3A: ELIMINATING MODELS USING ROLL&PITCH

Task

Participants repeatedly acquired a crosshair target located on a touchpad (Figure 9). During each trial, participants first touched a 1"×1" "start" button located 2" left of the target. Participants then assumed the finger angle for the current condition with their right index finger and acquired the target. Participants committed the touch interaction by pressing a footswitch. This recorded the touch location reported by the touchpad, triggered the camera to take a picture, played a confirmation sound, and completed the trial. Participants did not receive any feedback about the location registered by the touchpad.

Figure 9: Participants acquired a crosshair target located on a touchpad and committed input using the footswitch.

We took the following four measures to minimize the impact of other potential factors. First, participants kept their head in a fixed position above the touchpad, as shown in Figure 9. This controlled for parallax. Second, the crosshairs marking the target extended beyond participants' fingers, allowing participants to maintain a certain amount of visual control during targeting. Third, the use of a footswitch to commit input allowed us to avoid artifacts common with other commit methods, such as inadvertent motion during take-off. And finally, participants were told to use as much time as necessary and that task time would not be recorded. Fourth, participants rested their elbow on the adjacent table (Figure 9) to preclude fatigue.

Note that there was no need to include distracter targets. Distracters have a major effect on *adaptive* input techniques, but not on unmodified touch.

The purpose of using crosshairs was to reduce noise, thus helping us observe the underlying mental models more clearly. While the use of visible crosshairs may in theory impact participants' targeting behavior, we did not observe any such effect in our studies.

Independent variable: finger posture

As shown in Figure 10, we used the same combinations of finger pitch and finger roll as we did in previous work [12]. However, we dropped the 90° pitch condition, because the camera located directly above the pad could not capture the participant's nail in this condition (Figure 9).

Procedure

Overall, participants performed a sequence of 12 angles × 2 repetitions totaling 24 trials. The order of pitch-roll combinations was counterbalanced across participants. Then participants filled out a post-study questionnaire. All participants completed the study in 15 minutes or less.

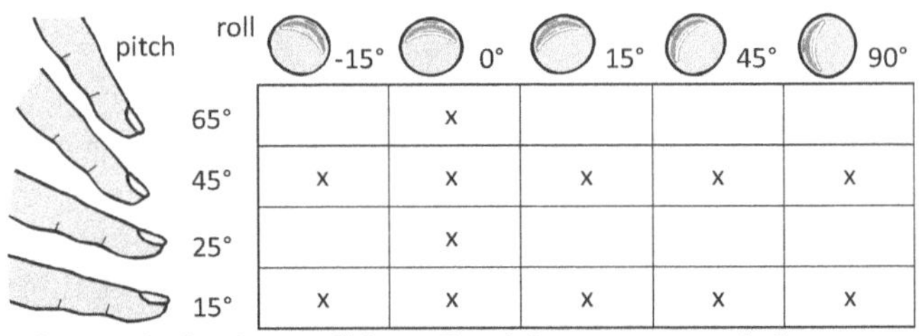

pitch \ roll	-15°	0°	15°	45°	90°
65°		x			
45°	x	x	x	x	x
25°		x			
15°	x	x	x	x	x

Figure 10: Study conditions. Participants assumed these combinations of finger pitch and finger roll during the study.

Apparatus

The study apparatus recorded contact area using a capacitive touch pad and captured a picture of the participant's finger using an overhead camera. The capacitive pad was a 6.5" × 4.9" *FingerWorks iGesture*; the camera was a *Canon EOS 450D*, capturing participants' fingers at 140dpi. Participants committed trials using a *Boss FS-5U* footswitch. All components were connected to an Intel Core 2 Duo machine running Windows XP.

Participants

We recruited a new set of 30 participants (10 female) from places around our institution. Participants were students from a range of different disciplines and were between 20 and 32 years old. We offered a €20 incentive for the most accurate participant.

Data preparation

During a pilot study, we attached markers to participants' fingers in order to allow for automated tracking. However, participants mentioned that the markers distracted them and some participants had started to include them as features into their targeting model. We therefore dropped the markers and instead annotated visual features in the photographs by hand.

Results

Vertical half models

Figure 11a shows which vertical half models produced the best fit (i.e., the lowest error offsets) for how many participants. We consider a half model to produce the best fit if the systematic offsets produced by this half model for each condition have the smallest distance from the center of mass of all error offsets produced by that model, across all half models.

No single model offers the best fit for all users, suggesting that different users may have *different* mental models. The half model t|b, i.e., the vertical center of the fingernail performs best here—it offered the best fit for 9 participants. It is followed by ng|b a slightly different version of the vertical center of the fingernail, with another 6 participants. As expected based on [12] (see also Figure 3), the contact area model offers the best fit for a very small number of participants, here only 1 out of 30.

Figure 11b shows how well different subsets of vertical half models combined fit the data. Bars represent the average vertical error offset if participants' data is processed using only the respective half models. The red bar on the left represents the error offsets produced by the capacitive baseline condition contact area.

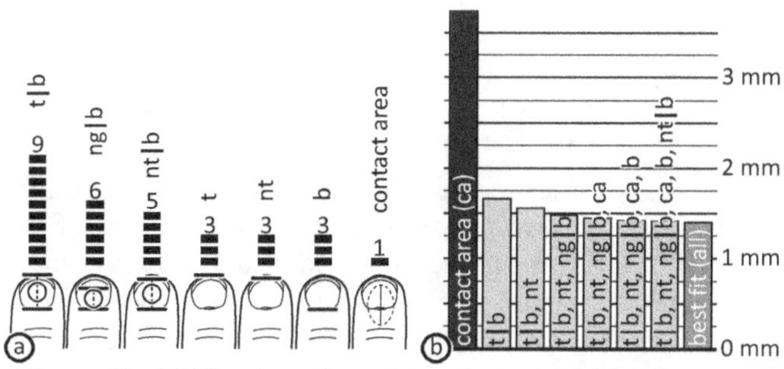

Figure 11: (a) Number of participants for which each vertical half model produced the lowest error. (b) Error produced when using only a subset of the half models to analyze participants. Switching from the model contact area to t|b reduces error offsets to 44%; using all models listed in (a) reduces the error to 37% compared to the contact area model.

The green bar on the right in Figure 11b represents the error offsets produced if every participant's input were processed using their personal best-fit model from Figure 11a; the switch to the best fit model reduces the error offsets by about 63%. We will refer to this best-fit case as "*per-participant models*" in the remainder of this paper.

Some of the half models listed as best fit model are similar. As a result it may not be necessary to maintain all of them. The gray bars in the middle of Figure 11b show how error rate increases if we drop some of the half models. We see that dropping all but three models (t|b, nt and ng|b) incurs a penalty of only 5% compared to using all vertical half models. Dropping all models but t|b incurs a penalty of 18.5% over the best-fit case. The contact area model alone, however, leads to large error offsets (averaging 3.75mm across participants).

Horizontal half models

Figure 12a shows the corresponding data for the horizontal half models. The half model oc (center of the finger outline) produced the lowest error for over a third of the participants (11 of 30). The contact area model offered the best fit for 5 of the 30 participants.

The benefit of using per-participant models is only a factor of 1.4 and, thus, by far not as large as in the vertical case (Figure 12b). This is a result that we expected based on our previous results [12], because of the smaller horizontal extent of clusters in Figure 3. Horizontal error has always been smaller, thus there is less potential for improvement.

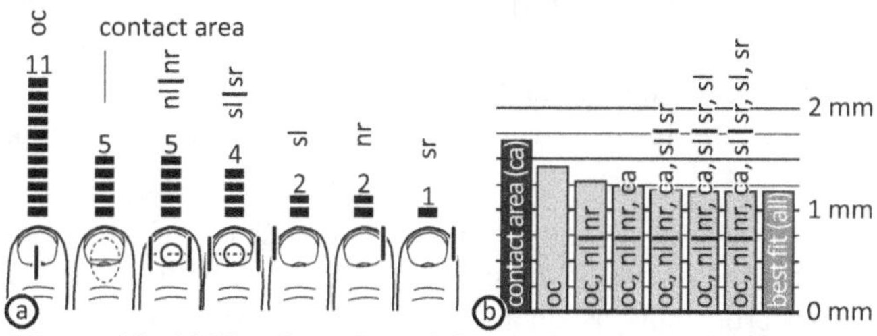

Figure 12: (a) Number of participants for which each horizontal half model produced the lowest-error offsets. (b) Using per-participant half models reduces the error offsets on average to 84% compared to using merely the contact area model.

Discussion

These findings suggest that the horizontal half-model nl (Figure 12a) and the vertical half-model ng (Figure 11a) can be eliminated, as they did not produce a best-fit for any participant. However, we will postpone the decision until we have seen results of the next study.

STEP 3B: ELIMINATING MODELS: HEAD PARALLAX

In contrast to the study in Step 3a, we added head parallax as an independent variable in this study. Again, the purpose of this study was to eliminate candidate half models.

Task

The task was the same as in the previous study, except that in addition to assuming a specific finger posture, participants also assumed one out of four predefined head positions (Figure 13).

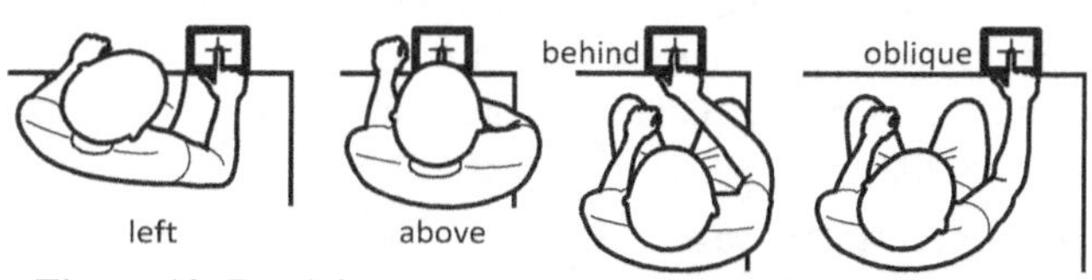

Figure 13: Participants acquired the target from these four different head positions.

Procedure

Overall, each participant completed a sequence of 2 pitch angles (15° and 45°, see Figure 10) × 2 roll angles (0° and 45°) × 4 head positions (Figure 13) × 2 repetitions = 32 trials, in four blocks, one for each head position. Finger angles as well as head positions were counterbalanced across participants. Participants filled out a post-study questionnaire. All participants completed the study in about 20 minutes.

Participants

We recruited a fresh set of 12 participants (5 female). All participants were between 19 and 24 years old. Similar to the previous study, we encouraged participants to be accurate throughout all conditions. Again, we offered a €20 incentive for the most accurate participant.

Apparatus

The apparatus was the same as in the Study 3a (Figure 9).

Results

Vertical half models

As in the previous study, the half models describing the vertical center of the fingernail together (t|b and nt|b) produced the best fit for half of all participants (6 of 12, Figure 14a). The contact area model, in contrast, never produced the lowest-error offsets for any participant in this study.

Again, we can reduce the number of half models without sacrificing too much precision; keeping only the vertical model t|b incurs a penalty of 6.5% over using all vertical half models. It still reduces the error of the contact area model by a factor of 2.5.

As shown in Figure 14b, the use of per-participant best-fit half models reduced the error offsets to 1.8mm, from 5mm of the contact area model to 40% of that value.

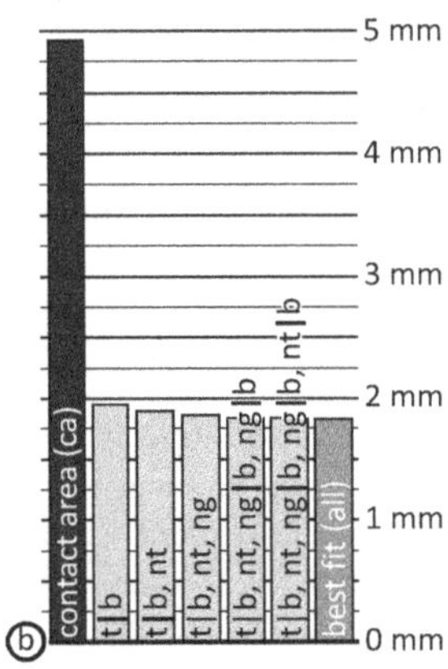

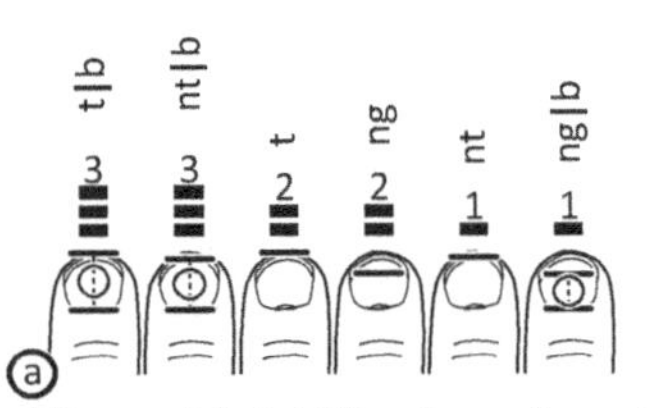

Figure 14: (a) Number of participants for which each vertical half model produced the lowest error. (b) The mean error of input drops to 39% when using t|b instead of contact area.

The contact area model incurs even bigger error offsets than in the previous study (5mm compared to 3.75mm). This suggests that the contact area model is sensitive to changes in head parallax, but more data is required to know for sure.

Horizontal Half models

As in the previous study, the horizontal half model oc produced the best fit for the largest number of participants (7 of 12, see Figure 15a). Compared to the previous study, the capacitive half model produced the best fit for a similar fraction of all participants (here 1 of 12, compared to 5 of 30).

As in the previous study, the use of per-participant half models produced only a moderate reduction of error offsets over the contact area model (about 15%).

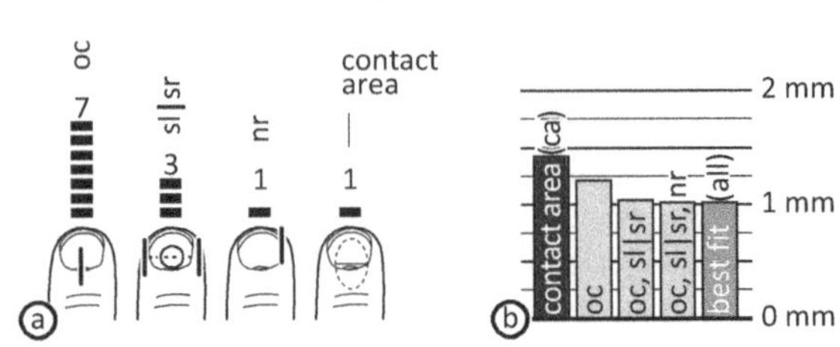

Figure 15: (a) Number of times each of the horizontal models produced the lowest-error offsets per participant. (b) The average error produced by the horizontal best-fit models sinks to 72% compared to contact area. The three horizontal half models oc, sl|sr, and t|b alone account for this improvement.

Discussion

Figure 16 lists the remaining candidate half models. We obtained this list by eliminating all models that did not produce at least one best fit in either one of the two studies. In addition, we eliminated all models the addition of which would have decreases error only marginally—the benefits of including nr, ng|b, and nt|b in the last study, for example, were less than 1%. However, we did maintain the two halves of the contact area model as well as the model *t* (absolute distance from the fingertip, which also only reduced error by less than 1%): both have been implemented in products and related work, so we wanted to see how they do in the final study.

Figure 16: The remaining candidate models.

If we take a closer look at the three remaining horizontal half models, we notice that all of them are versions of the center of the finger outline, only sampled at different locations, i.e., at the bottom of the nail (oc), at the location of the nail grooves (sl|sr), and at the horizontal center of the contact area.

The three remaining vertical half models describe the target location either in relation to the fingernail (t|b) or as an offset for the top of the fingertip (t and nt).

STEP 4: EVALUATING THE MODELS

The purpose of this final study was to evaluate the remaining half models. We could not re-use the data from the previous studies, because we had already used this data for learning and eliminating the very same half models. More importantly, though, participants had performed only few trials per condition; thus the data did not allow us to distinguish error offsets from random noise (i.e., spread by the fat finger problem [12]).

In this final study, we addressed this by increasing the number of repetitions to 4 trials per condition and two blocks. Aggregating these eight trials substantially reduced fat-finger noise and thus revealed the systematic error offsets we were looking for more clearly. These offsets provided us with a more reliable estimate sense of how far a change in mental model could reduce offsets and thus how closely the respective models were actually matching participant's mental models of touch.

Task

The task was the same as in the previous study (3b); we included all 12 levels of finger pitch and roll from Study 3a and all head positions. To keep the number of repetitions per participant manageable, we subdivided the roll/pitch variables between subjects, as shown in Figure 17.

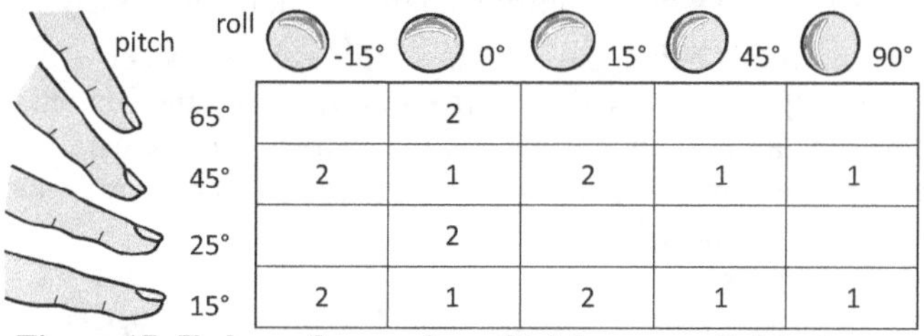

pitch \ roll	-15°	0°	15°	45°	90°
65°		2			
45°	2	1	2	1	1
25°		2			
15°	2	1	2	1	1

Figure 17: To keep the number of trials per participant manageable, we ran roll/pitch between subjects. The table shows the assignment of conditions to the two groups.

Study design

Each participant completed 6 combinations of finger angles (Figure 17) × 4 head positions (Figure 13) × 2 blocks × 4 repetitions = 192 trials. All participants completed the study in 40 minutes or less. Participants filled out a questionnaire afterwards.

Apparatus

The apparatus was the same as in Study 3b (Figure 9).

Participants

We recruited a fresh set of 12 participants (6 female) from places around our institution. All participants were between 21 and 32 years old. As in the previous studies, we encouraged participants to be accurate and offered a €20 incentive for the most precise participant.

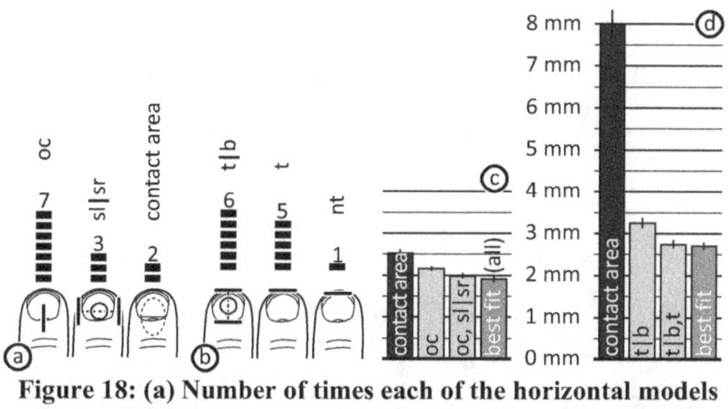

Figure 18: (a) Number of times each of the horizontal models produced the lowest error. (b) Same for the vertical models. (c) Using the best-fit horizontal half models instead of contact area reduces the error by 15%. (d) Vertical per-participant models reduce the error produced by contact area by 60%.

Results

The final study did not produce anything unexpected as the performance of the participating half models was similar to the previous two studies. As shown in Figure 18a, both oc and sl|sr produced the best fit for 5 of the 12 participants; t and t|b produced the best fit for 5 participants each. While the use of all three horizontal half models yields only 15% less error in offsets (per-participant models), vertically, per-participant models reduce the error offsets substantially by 60%. t|b alone reduces error offsets by a factor of 2.5 compared to contact area (Figure 18b).

Merging Models

Finally, we rejoined half models into full models. Figure 19 shows which half models went together well: the combination oc & t|b produced the best overall fit for 4 of the 12 participants, followed by oc & t, sl|sr & t|b, and contact area & t|b for another 2 participants each.

vertical half models \ horizontal half models	oc	sl|sr	contact area
t|b	4	2	2
t	2	1	
nt	1		
contact area			

Figure 19: Number of times a combination of half models together produced the best fit for a participant.

Figure 20 shows error offsets for the eight full models from Figure 19. A one-way ANOVA with participant as a random variable found a significant main effect of model on error offsets (F_7=38.662, p<0.001). Post-hoc t-tests using Bonferroni correction found that all six other models and the per-participant best-fit aggregate produced significantly lower error offsets than contact area (all p<0.003).

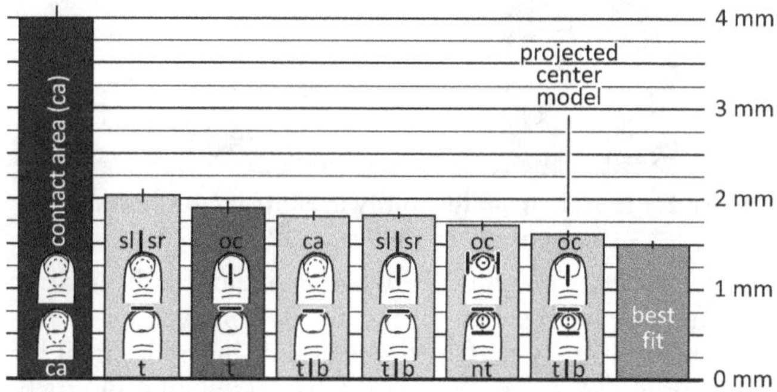

Figure 20: Remaining offset for the full models from Figure 19 compared to contact area model (+/- std. error of the mean).

The best individual model was oc & t|b. It says that participants target by placing the horizontal center of their finger outline and the vertical center of fingernail over the target. In the introduction to this paper, we already referred to this model using the name projected center model and the images shown in Figure 1 are best explained using this model.

In summary, the projected center model performed best out of all the models tested. Under the projected center model, the large systematic offsets of 4mm observed by the contact area model shrink down to 1.6mm, an improvement by a factor of 2.5. At the same time, the remaining offsets are close enough to zero to suggest that this model approximates participants' mental model indeed well.

This is the main finding of this paper.

IMPLICATIONS FOR ENGINEERING

Switching to an engineering perspective for a moment, we might be interested in how devices built on these different models will perform, as this might inform which models to base future devices on.

So far, we have discussed models based on systematic offsets, as that is a good metric for testing the quality of mental models. To answer questions about device performance, we add the other error variable, i.e., spread, back in. The resulting *minimum button sizes* for 95% reliable touch input are shown in Figure 21. These values specify how accurately a device based on the respective model can be expected to perform.

The chart shows that devices based on the projected center model allow users to acquire targets of 4.9mm with 95% accuracy, compared to 7.9mm target size for the corresponding contact area model (8.6mm in [12], corrected for yaw to match conditions in this paper). In terms of target surface this difference amounts to a factor of 2.6. This means that a device implementing the projected center model could pack 2.6 times more targets into the same screen space or, alternatively, that a device could be reduced to less than half its size and still allow users to operate it reliably.

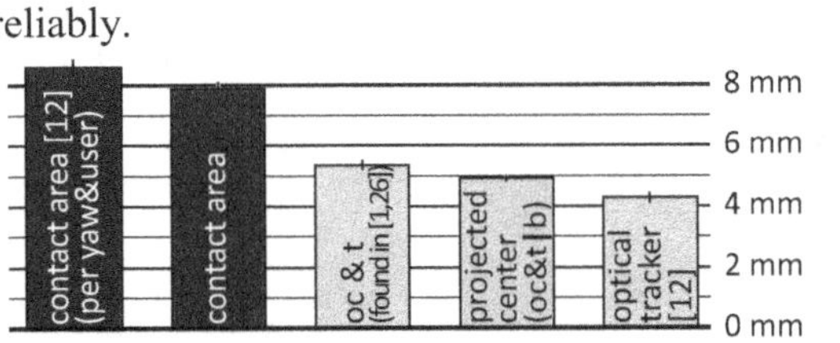

Figure 21: Results from this study in contrast to results of our previous studies in [12].

For reference, in Figure 21 we also included the 4.3mm minimum target size that we previously achieved by attaching retro-reflective markers to the users' finger and tracking using an optical tracking system [12]. Based on 600 repetitions of training data, it removes all known offsets, so that this model can be considered a current lower bound for touch accuracy. In comparison, the 4.9mm minimum button size of the *calibration-free* projected center model gets surprisingly close.

High-precision input with a much simpler device

In order to implement the projected center model a device needs to be able to reliably locate a user's fingernail, which is technically challenging.

Figure 21 points out an alternative. At 5.35mm minimum button size, the oc & t model does not quite reach the 4.9mm of the projected center model. However, it is comparably easy to manufacture, as this approach only requires locating finger outlines in a camera positioned above the target, namely the outlines of the sides and the top of the finger. This approach has already been explored in a number of research prototypes, such as *CSlate* [1] and *LucidTouch* [23]. Our findings thus suggest that this track of engineering, combined with sufficiently accurate cameras, could be a more promising approach to high-precision touch sensing than the currently more widely available devices based on contact area.

CONCLUSIONS

In this paper, we conducted an exploration of users' mental models of touch. Our primary contribution is scientific. The fact that under the proposed projected center model the error offsets found by our previous work essentially disappear suggests that this model is likely to closely match how users proceed while acquiring a target on a touch device.

On the other hand, our findings suggest that systems that track fingers using cameras from above have the potential for substantially better pointing accuracy than capacitive sensing as currently implemented, even simpler devices that track fingers based on finger outline alone.

REFERENCES

1. Agarwal, A., Izadi, S., Chandraker, M., and Blake, A. High Precision Multi-touch Sensing on Surfaces using Overhead Cameras. *Proc. Tabletop '07*, 197-200.
2. Albinsson, P. Zhai, S. High precision touch screen interaction. *Proc. CHI '03*, 105-112.
3. Baudisch, P. and Chu, G. Back-of-device interaction allows creating very small touch devices. *Proc. CHI '09*, 1923-1932.
4. Benko, H., Wilson, A. D., and Baudisch, P. Precise selection techniques for multi-touch screens. *Proc. CHI '06*, 1263-1272.
5. Cao, X., Wilson, A. D., Balakrishnan, R., Hinckley, K., and Hudson, S. E. Shapetouch: Leveraging contact shape on interactive surfaces. *Proc. Tabletop '08*, 129-136.
6. Feynman, R. The Messenger Series. Lecture 7: Seeking New Laws. *BBC Science&Nature.*
7. FingerWorks SDK, http://fingerworks.com
8. Fitts, P.M. 1954. The information capacity of the human motor system in controlling the amplitude of movement. *Journal of Experimental Psychology*, 47, 381-391.
9. Forlines, C., Wigdor, D., Shen, C., Balakrishnan, R. Direct-touch vs. mouse input for tabletop displays. *Proc. CHI '07*, 647-656.
10. Grossman, T. and Balakrishnan, R. A probabilistic approach to modeling two-dimensional pointing. *TOCHI* 12, 3(2005):435-459.
11. Han, J. Y. Low-cost multi-touch sensing through frustrated total internal reflection. *Proc. UIST '05*, 115-118.
12. Holz, C. and Baudisch, P. The Generalized Perceived Input Point Model and How to Double Touch Accuracy by Extracting Fingerprints. *Proc. CHI '10*, 581-590.
13. Malik, S. and Laszlo, J. Visual touchpad: a two-handed gestural input device. *Proc. ICMI '04*, 289-296.
14. Moscovich, T. Contact area interaction with sliding widgets. *Proc. UIST '09*, 13-22.
15. Norman, D. The Psychology of Everyday Things. *Basic Books,* 1988.
16. Potter, R., Weldon, L., Shneiderman, B. Improving the accuracy of touch screens: an experimental evaluation of three strategies. *Proc. CHI '88,* 27-32.
17. Ren, X., Moriya, S. Improving selection performance on pen-based systems: a study of pen-based interaction for selection tasks. *TOCHI*, 7(3):384-416.
18. Roudaut, A., Huot, S., and Lecolinet. E. TapTap and MagStick: Improving One-Handed Target Acquisition on Small Touch-screens. *Proc. AVI '08*, 146-153.
19. Smart Tables, SmartTech. http://www.smarttech.com
20. Vogel, D. and Baudisch, P. Shift: A Technique for Operating Pen-Based Interfaces Using Touch. *Proc. CHI '07*, 657-666.
21. Wang, F. and Ren, X. Empirical evaluation for finger input properties in multi-touch interaction. *Proc. CHI'09*, 1063-1072.
22. Wellner, P. Interacting with paper on the DigitalDesk. In *Commun. ACM* 36, 7 (Jul. 1993), 87-96.
23. Wigdor, D., Forlines, C., Baudisch, P., Barnwell, J., and Shen, C. Lucid touch: a see-through mobile device. *Proc. UIST'07*, 269-278.
24. Wilson, A. D. PlayAnywhere: a compact interactive tabletop projection-vision system. *Proc. UIST '05*, 83-92

Magic Desk: Bringing Multi-Touch Surfaces into Desktop Work

Xiaojun Bi[1,2], Tovi Grossman[1], Justin Matejka[1], George Fitzmaurice[1]

[1]Autodesk Research, Toronto, ON, Canada
{firstname.lastname}@autodesk.com

[2]University of Toronto, Toronto, ON, Canada
xiaojun@dgp.toronto.edu

ABSTRACT

Despite the prominence of multi-touch technologies, there has been little work investigating its integration into the desktop environment. Bringing multi-touch into desktop computing would give users an additional input channel to leverage, enriching the current interaction paradigm dominated by a mouse and keyboard. We provide two main contributions in this domain. First, we describe the results from a study we performed, which systematically evaluates the various potential regions within the traditional desktop configuration that could become multi-touch enabled. The study sheds light on good or bad regions for multi-touch, and also the type of input most appropriate for each of these regions. Second, guided by the results from our study, we explore the design space of multi-touch-integrated desktop experiences. A set of new interaction techniques are coherently integrated into a desktop prototype, called Magic Desk, demonstrating potential uses for multi-touch enabled desktop configurations.

Author Keywords

Multi-touch, TableTop, Desktop Work

ACM Classification Keywords

H5.m. Information interfaces and presentation (e.g., HCI): Miscellaneous.

General Terms

Human Factors, Design

INTRODUCTION

In recent years, multi-touch displays [8, 10, 37] have received a great deal of attention, both in the research community, and in consumer devices. The research literature has shown numerous benefits of multi-touch input, such as increasing the bandwidth of communication between human and computers [16] and its compatibility to control multiple degrees-of-freedom [23]. Because of its unique affordances, research in multi-touch applications generally involves a standalone touch sensitive device, sometimes with peripheral displays [36], with a custom designed UI optimized for touch [39]. Less explored is how multi-touch could be integrated into our current desktop experience.

Unfortunately, along with its advantages, touch input suffers from certain known problems. Text entry is cumbersome [14], and the "fat finger" problem limits the precision of touch input [9]. With the existence of such challenges, it is hard to imagine that our mouse and keyboard devices, which provide precision input, could be completely replaced by multi-touch surfaces. Instead, we foresee that *future computing environments will be a blend of keyboards, mice and touch devices.*

With the release of Microsoft Windows 7, which supports multi-touch [24], and the commercial availability of multi-touch monitors [7] and laptop displays [6], the industry has already moved in this direction. But, this begs the question: is a vertical display monitor the right way to integrate multi-touch into the desktop experience? Other planar regions for touch input include the areas on the desk surrounding the mouse and keyboard. To integrate touch into the desktop experience successfully, it is crucial to understand the properties of different touch regions and their relationships with the devices we already use.

In this paper, we provide two main contributions, to advance our understanding of the integration of multi-touch and desktop configurations. First, we systematically investigate users' single and multi-touch input abilities on the potential touch regions in a desktop computing environment, including the vertical display monitor. The vertical display performed poorly in both one- and two-hand touch tasks, showing that the main option commercially available today might in fact be the worst one. Second, guided by the study results, we explore the design space of multi-touch integrated desktop experiences, with the design and implementation of a set of interaction techniques, such as an enhanced task bar and multi-functional touch pad. All of the techniques were coherently integrated into a desktop prototype called Magic Desk (Figure 1).

Figure 1. Working on the Magic Desk.

RELATED WORK

Ergonomic Studies of Physical Desktop Tables

Constrained by the lengths of human arms and rotation angles of joints, a user's "reach" heavily impacts how a table can be used: it dictates the space available for interaction. Anthropometrical research has determined where the user is able to reach when sitting in front of a horizontal table [13].. Hedge [13] also proposed a model predicting maximum comfortable reach (i.e., the Zone of Comfortable Reach or ZCR) Scott et al. [29] further revealed different types of usage within the reachable area: space near the body was usually used for working while space further away was used for storage. In a desktop computing environment, the existence of mice and keyboards will probably affect the accessibilities of various touch regions. Specific studies investigating the interplay between keyboard/mouse and various touch regions are required.

Studies of Digital Tabletop Usage

Numerous researchers have explored how tabletop devices could facilitate daily desktop work. Morris et al.'s study [22] showed that though an additional stylus-enabled display provided extra screen real estate, shortcomings included complicating window management, and overhead related to input device switching. Wigdor et al. [35] reported on the experience of an individual who exclusively used a DiamondTouch table for office work. Hancock and Booth [11] investigated menu selection on horizontal and vertical display surfaces, leading to a menu placement strategy for a tabletop display. We complement these high-level studies by systematically assessing the human's interaction abilities in the different touchable regions.

Touch-enhanced Devices and Environments

We classify this research into the following three categories:

1) Using an interactive tabletop

A sizeable amount of research has explored interacting on a digital tabletop. Some important examples include Krueger et al. [17], who explored interacting with virtual objects using users' live images; the Digital Desk [15], which enabled users to interact with paper documents; the InteractiveDESK [2], which responded to users' operations on real objects (e.g., keyboards, digital pens) on a desktop to reduce workload; Rekimoto et al. [26, 27], who implemented an augmented surface allowing users to interchange digital information among various objects; and, Wu et al. [39], who studied using various multifinger and whole hand gestures. More recent work has looked at bringing physical simulation into touch-screen interaction [38]. Common among these foundational research projects is that they utilize the interactive tabletop as a standalone input platform, and do not consider the integration of multi-touch with a desktop configuration.

2) Touch enabled desktop devices

Recently, there has been substantial work augmenting common desktop devices with touch functionality. Multi-touch desktop screens are now commercially available and the Window 7 OS supports multi-touch input. Block et al. [3] introduced the Touch-Display Keyboard, in which graphical output and input are extended across the keyboard's surface. The Mouse 2.0 [32] and the Apple Magic Mouse [1] allow users to perform multi-finger gestures on the surface of the mouse. Yang et al. [40] further augmented a mouse with an interactive touch sensitive display. While these explorations are all promising, the surfaces they provide for touch are non-planer and have limited space. In contrast, we will be exploring combinations of planar multi-touch surfaces with traditional input devices, to support traditional, larger-scale, multi-touch interactions.

3) Combinations of desktop devices and touch surfaces.

The Pebbles project [21] explored an enhanced PC computing environment with a touch-screen mobile device, but the device had limited input space and only provided single point input. The Bonfire system [15] enhanced mobile laptop interaction by projecting interactive displays on both sides of a laptop keyboard, however the implementations were focused more on augmenting the surrounding environment, rather than supporting desktop activities. Hartmann et al. explored a combination of mice and keyboard input with a multi-touch surface [12]. They focused on interactions among co-located groups around a large table. We focus on enhancing a single person's desktop work.

In summary, there has been a large amount of research on touch enhanced tables and environments, but we are unaware of any which systematically investigates the integration of multi-touch technologies into a desktop environment.

EXPERIMENT

In a traditional desktop environment, where a user sits in front of a desk and input is performed with a mouse and keyboard, the planar regions available for touch input include the entire space surrounding the keyboard and mouse. However, in terms of commercial availability, multi-touch is typically constrained to the vertical display monitor.

With little current understanding of the benefits or drawbacks of using the planar regions surrounding the keyboard, and how these regions compare to a multi-touch vertical monitor, we are motivated to investigate the effect that touch region has on interaction capabilities. In addition, we investigate the transition cost when a user changes input channels from a keyboard or mouse to any of these regions, and effects on fatigue.

Touch Regions

The main independent variable for the study is the touch region: top (*t*), bottom (*b*), left (*l*), and right (*r*) regions of the desk surface, and the vertical screen (*s*) (Figure 2).

To determine reasonable sizes for these touch regions, we surveyed 20 daily computer users on their normal seating and keyboard positions. Results showed that 95% of users put the keyboard centered in front of their body. The mean distance between the bottom edge of the keyboard and center of their bodies was 17cm with a standard deviation of

5.3cm. The mean distance between the user's eyes and the screen was 68cm with a standard deviation of 10.5cm.

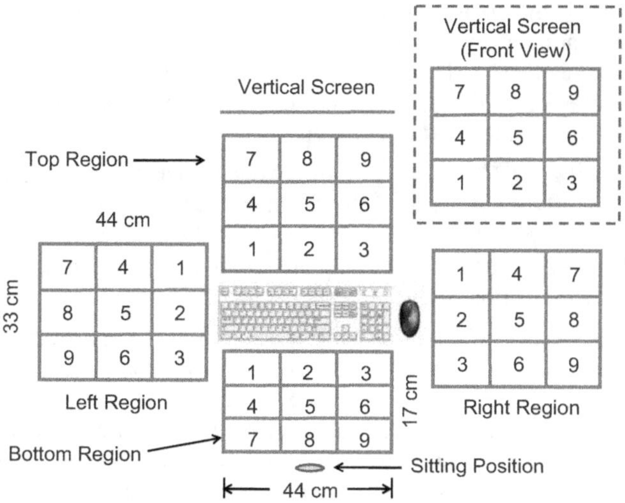

Figure 2. Experiment touch regions (top view). A front view of the vertical screen is illustrated in the top-right corner.

According to Hedge et al's [13] model, the Zone of Comfortable Reach area (ZCR) on a table is a spherical shell centered on each shoulder, the radius of which is the asromion to grip distance. Guided by the size of a regular keyboard (45 X 16cm) and a normal human arm's length (75cm), we used a 44 x 33 cm rectangle for the top, left and right regions, which would cover more than 90% of the ZCR area in these regions. Constrained by the sitting distance, we set the size of the bottom region to 44cm x 17cm.

The size of the vertical screen was also 44 x 33 cm, which is a reasonable size for a monitor. The distance between the screen and the center of the body was fixed at 68cm, which was the average eye-screen distance from the survey. Given the average human arm length of 75 cm, most users can comfortably touch the screen from such a position. On the right side we offset the screen from the keyboard by 8cm to leave room for the mouse, since we felt it would be impractical to have a multi-touch device right beside the keyboard, where it would get occluded by the mouse.

Figure 3. A participant performing the experiment in left (a), bottom (b), and screen (c) conditions.

Apparatus

We used a 21" multi-touch enabled screen with a resolution of 1600 x 1200 to simulate each of the touch regions. For the *l*, *r*, *t*, and *b* regions, the screen was placed horizontally on the table, and the keyboard and mouse were raised to the same plane as the screen (Figure 3). In the *s* condition, the monitor was titled 10 degrees backwards (Figure 3). A standard 101-key keyboard, 44cm wide, and 16cm deep, was used.

Task Positions

We further divided each region into a 3x3 grid of cells (Figure 2). The height and width of each cell was one third of its region's height and width. We numbered the cells in the row/column closest to the keyboard with #1, 2 and 3, while cells in the furthest row/column with #7, 8, and 9.

Tasks

We designed three tasks, as abstractions of the type of gestures that might be performed with multi-touch.

Gesture Task. This task represents a simple single finger gesture. Initially, a start circle, gesture direction line, and objective line (80 pixels wide) appeared on the touch screen (Figure 4a). The center of the starting circle was in the center of one of the 9 cells, and the direction of the gesture line was either up, down, left or right. The distance between the center of the starting circle and the objective line was 125 pixels. A participant had to touch the starting circle with one finger and move to cross the objective line. The widget turned white when the circle was touched (Figure 4b), and gold when the finger crossed the objective line, indicating completion of the task (Figure 4c). If the user failed to cross the target line, the gesture would need to be repeated.

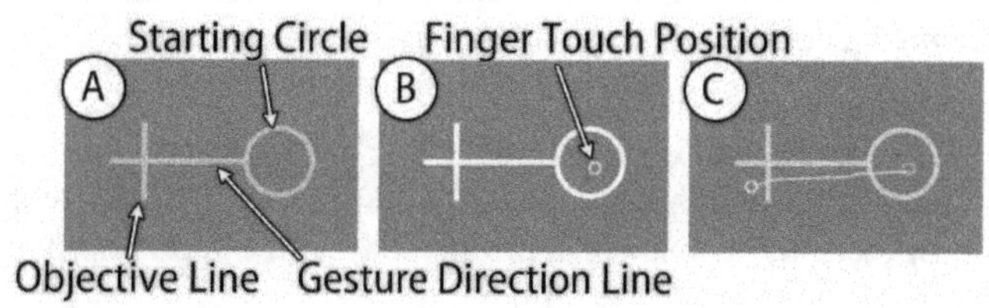

Figure 4. Gesture Task.

One-Hand Docking. This task was designed to represent a one-handed, multi-finger task. Initially, one small green square (150 by 150 pixels) and one large yellow square (250 by 250 pixels), appeared on the screen (Figure 5a). The participants were asked to dock the green square by moving, rotating, and scaling it to cover the yellow square (Figure 5b). The borders of both squares turned gold when the green square was successfully docked (Figure 5c). The participant could manipulate the green squares with commonly used manipulation gestures: translate by dragging it with one or more fingers, scale by moving two fingers apart/together, and rotate by rotating the fingers. Participants were only allowed to use one hand, either left or right, during this task.

The task position was controlled by placing the yellow square in the center of one of the 9 cells. The initial distance between the centers of the green and yellow squares was 500 pixels. The relative offset angle of these two squares was randomized.

Two-Hand Docking. This task was designed to investigate performance of two-handed tasks. Participants performed the same docking task (Figure 5) but had to use one finger from each hand.

Figure 5. Docking Task. The small white circles in pictures show finger positions.

Hand Positioning for Start and End of Each Task

To test the transition costs between devices, we considered two common desktop configurations of our hands:

Keyboard+Keyboard: In this mode, the trial begins and ends with both hands on the keyboard, when the user simultaneously presses the F and J keys with their left and right hands respectively.

Keyboard+Mouse: In this mode, the participant begins and ends the trial with one hand on the keyboard and one hand on the mouse. The participant would simultaneously press the F key with their left hand and the mouse left button with their right hand to start and end a trial.

For both the *gesture* and *one-hand docking* conditions, users could use either hand to complete the task. An experimenter recorded which hand was used for each task.

Participants

Ten subjects (4 female, ages 18~35) participated in the study, three of whom were left-handed. All worked with computers more than 5 hours per day and naturally operated the mouse with the right hand.

Design

We used a within-subject, full-factorial repeated measure design for all the experiments. Each participant first performed all trials for the *gesture* task, followed by the *one-hand docking*, and finally the *two-hand docking* task.

For each task, the independent variables were *touch region* (*l, r, b, t, s*), *grid cell* within a region (1~9), and *start-end position* (keyboard+keyboard and keyboard+mouse). The orders of the touch regions were counterbalanced using a Latin Square. Half of the participants performed the tasks with keyboard+keyboard mode first, followed by keyboard+mouse mode. For each start-end position within a region, the participant performed tasks in three blocks with each block having 9 trials. Within each block, each grid cell value appeared exactly once, in random order. The design resulted in a total of 270 trials per task, for each participant. Prior to formally starting each task, participants performed three warm-up trials to become familiar with the task. After completing each of the three tasks, each participant rated the five regions according to their overall feelings.

Measures

Completion Time. The *completion time* consisted of *switch forward*, *execution*, and *switch back* times. *Switch forward* time is the elapsed time between the trial start action and when the first finger contacted the touch region. *Execution* time is the elapsed time between the first finger contact and the moment the participant's fingers finally leaves the experiment area. The *switch back* time is the time elapsed between removing the hand from the touch surface and performing the end trial action.

Number of Clutches. A "clutch" occurs when a participant lifts all fingers off of the surface, and then proceeds to touch the surface again. Since a trial does not end until it has been successfully completed, this measure might provide indication of the difficulty level of the task.

Fatigue Level. To measure muscle fatigue, participants were asked to rate fatigue level after each block (from 0-no fatigue to 7-very fatigued). A 5-minute break was enforced between regions to increase the likelihood that each region began with a 0 fatigue rating. Since our goal was to measure how fatigue level changed as time progressed in a touch region, no break was taken within each region.

Results

We performed a factorial repeated measure ANOVA on each task independently.

Gesture Task

Completion Time. The mean *completion time* (all in ms) for the 5 regions were 2009.3 (*b*), 2162.8 (*l*), 2428.2 (*r*), 2286.0 (*s*), and 2094.6 (*t*) (Figure 6). ANOVA showed that region had a significant main effect on *Completion Time* ($F_{4,36}$ = 6.107, $p<0.05$). Pairwise mean comparison were significant for *b* X *r*, *b* X *s*, *t* X *r*, and *t* X *s* (p<0.05).

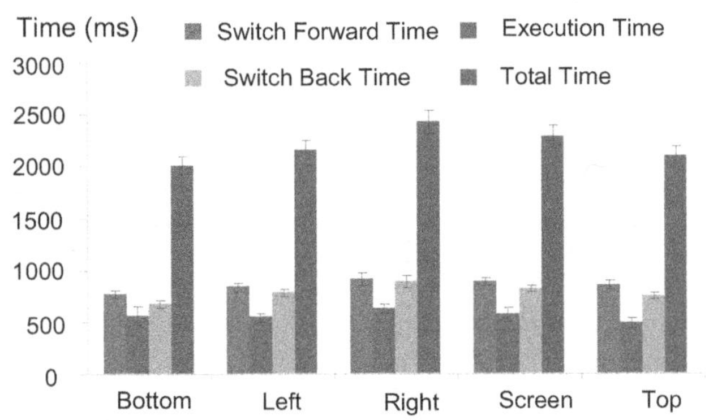

Figure 6. Completion time for Gesture Tasks.

ANOVA showed that region had significant main effects on both *switch forward* ($F_{4,36}$ = 4.910, $p< 0.05$) and *switch back* Time ($F_{4,36}$ = 7.586, $p< 0.05$), but not *execution* time ($F_{4,36}$ = 1.041, p = 0.399), indicating that the differences in completion time were mainly from the switching procedures. *Grid Cell* also had a significant main effect on completion time ($F_{8,72}$=5.75, $p<0.05$). No significant main effect was observed for *start-end position* on *completion time*. ANOVA showed a significant *Region* × *Grid Cell* interaction on *completion time* ($F_{32,288}$=18.9, $p<0.05$), but not for *Region* ×*Start-end Position* or *Start-end Position* × *Grid Cell.*

Figure 8a visualizes the mean *completion time* of each grid cell. In the *t*, *l* and *r* regions, the completion times were shortest in the cells closest to the keyboard/mouse (i.e., *grid cells* #1~#3), and increased as the distance from the keyboard/mouse grew. In the *b* region, completion times were more uniform.

Number of Clutches. No significant main effect of region on *number of clutches* was observed. The means were 0.233(*b*), 0.126(*l*), 0.239(*r*), 0.157(*s*), and 0.122(*t*), indicating that most of the time users could successfully perform the gesture task on the first stroke. Similarly, ANOVA did not show significant main effects of *start-end position*, or *grid cell* on *number of clutches*.

Fatigue Levels. We specifically investigated the average fatigue level across all the three blocks. ANOVA did not show a significant main effect of *region*, *start-end position*, or *grid cell* on average fatigue, with means of 0.6(*b*), 0.8(*l*), 0.7(*r*), 1.0(*s*), and 0.5(*t*). All participants reported that *gesture* tasks were easy to perform and they felt little fatigue.

Hand Usage. All the participants performed *gesture* tasks with their left hands on the *l* region, and right hands on the *r* region. Participants performed gesture tasks with their right hands for 67%, 71% and 82% of trials in *b*, *t* and *s* regions respectively. They commented that they preferred to perform tasks with their dominant hands.

One-Hand Docking

Completion Time. As shown in Figure 7, the means of *completion time* were 3138.9 (*b*), 3453.5 (*l*), 3860.8 (*r*), 3929.3 (*s*), 3553.2(*t*). ANOVA showed that region had a significant main effect on *Completion Time* ($F_{4,36} = 7.390$, $p<0.05$). Pairwise mean comparison showed significant differences for *bXl*, *bXr*, *bXs*, *bXt*, and *lXs* ($p<0.05$). A significant *Region* × *Grid Cell* interaction ($F_{32,288}=23.1$ $p<0.05$) was observed, but not for *Region ×Start-end Position* or *Start-end Position* × *Grid Cell*. In contrast to the gesture task, significant main effects were found for region for *Switch Forward* ($F_{4,36} = 3.433$, $p<0.05$), *Execution* ($F_{4,36}=5.025$, $p<0.05$), and *Switch Back* time ($F_{4,36}=4.585$, $p<0.05$). ANOVA also showed a significant main effect of *grid cells* on completion time ($F_{8,72} = 4.63$, $p<0.05$). As shown in Figure 8b, the effect of region on the *one-hand docking* task was similar to the gesture task. Users performed uniformally well across the *b* region, and *completion times* in the *t*, *l* and *r* regions were shorter in the cells closest to the keyboard or mouse (i.e., *cells* 1-3), and increased as the cells became further away. The mean completion time in the *s* condition was the longest among the five tested regions (Figure 7). ANOVA did not show a significant main effect for *start-end position*

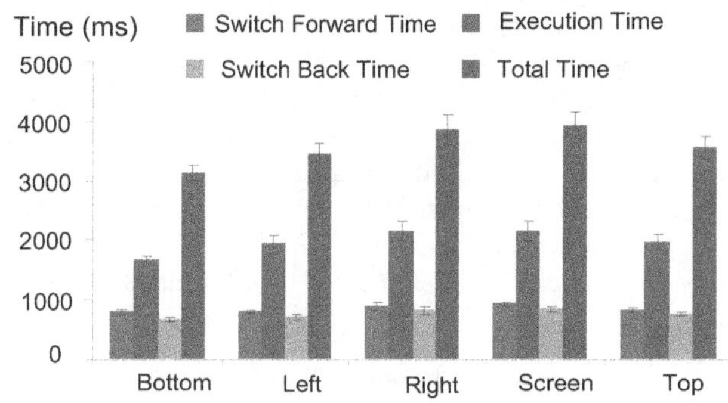

Figure 7. Completion time in one-hand docking.

Number of Clutches. Region had a significant main effect on the *number of clutches* ($F_{4,36} = 5.197$, $p<0.05$), with means of 0.31(*b*), 0.50(*l*), 0.48(*r*), 0.65(*s*), and 0.52(*t*). Pairwise mean comparison showed significant differences for *bXl*, *bXr*, *bXs*, *bXt*, *lXs*, and *rXs*, indicating that users clutched least often in the bottom region. ANOVA did not show significant main effects for either *start-end position* or *grid cell* on *number of clutches*. A Significant *Region* × *Grid* interaction ($F_{32,288}=12.1$ $p<0.05$) was observed, but not for *Region ×Start-end Position* or *Start-end Position* × *Grid Cell.*

Fatigue Levels. No significant main effect of *region*, *start-end position* or *grid cell* on average fatigue level was observed. Means were 1.3(*b*), 1.8(*l*), 2.4(*r*), 2.0(*s*), 1.6(*t*), and 8 of the 10 participants commented that it was simple and easy to perform these tasks and did not feel fatigued.

Handedness. All participants performed *one-hand docking* tasks with left hand on the *l* region, and right hand on the *r* region. They performed one-handed docking tasks with right hand for 75%, 77% and 82% of trials in *b*, *t* and *s* regions respectively.

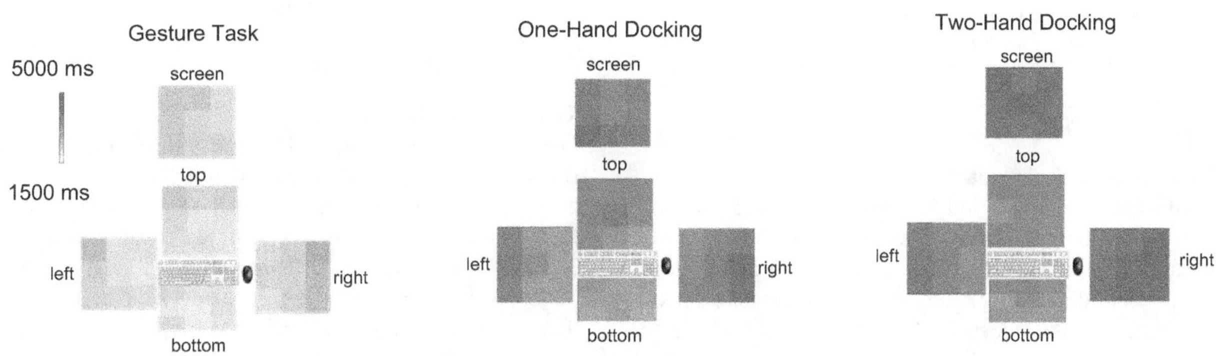

Figure 8. Mean Completion Time per cell in a region.

Two-Hand Docking

Completion Time. The means of *completion time* (ms) were 3538.5(*b*), 4004.8(*l*), 4590.2(*r*), 4434.6(*s*), 3687.4(*t*) (Figure 9). ANOVA showed that region had significant main effects on *completion time* ($F_{4,36}$ = 16.191, p <0.01), *switch forward* ($F_{4,36}$ = 21.389, p<0.01), *execution* ($F_{4,36}$ = 5.685, p<0.05), and *switch back time* ($F_{4,36}$ = 17.992, p<0.05). For completion time, pairwise mean comparison showed significant differences (p<0.05) between every pair of regions except *b*X*t*, *l*X*s*, and *r*X*s*. ANOVA also showed a significant main effect of *grid cells* on completion time ($F_{8,72}$=3.27, p<0.005). No significant main effect was observed for *start-end position* on *completion time.* ANOVA showed a significant *Region* × *Grid Cell* interaction on *completion time* ($F_{32,288}$=23.6, p<0.05), but not for *Region* ×*Start-end Position* or *Start-end Position* × *Grid Cell.*

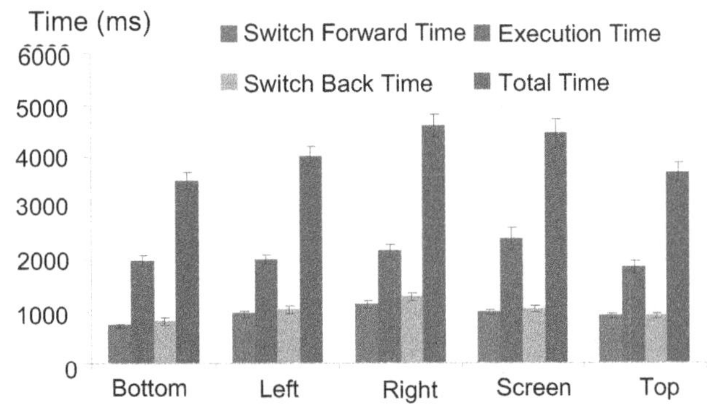

Figure 9. Completion time in two-hand docking.

Number of Clutches. No significant main effect of *region*, *start-end position* or *grid cell* on the number of clutches was observed ($F_{4,36}$ = 1.744, p=0.162), with means of 0.39 (*b*), 0.31(*l*), 0.38(*r*), 0.55(*s*) and 0.29(*t*).

Fatigue Levels. Different from both *gesture* and *one-hand docking* tasks, touch region had a significant main effect on average fatigue level ($F_{4,36}$ = 3.18, p<0.05), with the *t* being the least fatiguing and right being the most fatiguing region. The means of average fatigue level were 2.2(*b*), 2.6(*l*), 3.2(*r*), 2.7(*s*), and 2.0(*t*). Pairwise mean comparison showed significant differences for *b*X*r*, and *t*X*r*. 6 out of the 10 participants reported that they disliked performing the two-handed docking task in the right region because they had to rotate their waists significantly to complete the task. No significant main effect was observed for either *start-end position* or *grid cell* for fatigue levels. A Significant *Region* × *Grid* interaction ($F_{32,288}$=10.4, p<0.05) was observed, but not for *Region* ×*Start-end Position* or *Start-end Position* × *Grid Cell.*

Overall Subjective Opinions

Participants rated each region according to their overall satisfaction after completing all the tasks. The three tasks were classified into two categories: one-handed tasks (gesture and one-hand docking) and two-handed tasks (two-hand docking). For the question, *"Are the tested tasks easy to perform in each region (0:very difficult, 4:very easy)?"*, ANOVA showed that there was a significant main effect of region on rates in the two-handed tasks ($F_{4,36}$ = 7.075, p<0.05), with the *b* and *t* regions being the easiest and the right region being the worst. The mean rates were 3.2(*b*), 1.9(*l*), 1.4(*r*), 2.7(*s*) and 3.2(*t*). No significant main effect was observed for regions on one-handed tasks. These results are consistent with *completion time* results: it is easier to perform two-handed tasks in the *b* and *t* regions.

IMPLICATIONS OF RESULTS

One-Handed Tasks

As expected, users performed one-handed tasks the fastest in zones close to the keyboard or mouse (i.e., *grid cells* 1-3) due to the short travel distance. The entire *Bottom* region performed particularly well in both the gesture and one-hand docking task: the mean completion time of most grid cells in bottom regions is faster than the average completion time of every other region. Some users commented that it was easier and more comfortable to touch in the *bottom* region by just withdrawing a hand back than reaching it out to make contact in the other regions. Additionally, since the reachable area in the bottom region is smaller than those in other regions, the average hand traveling distance is shorter, which also contributes to the faster completion times. One problem with the bottom region is occlusion of the display caused by the user's hands. Two participants reported this occurring. These problems could be alleviated by designing occlusion-aware interfaces [33].

Given the relative prevalence of touch sensitive monitors, we believe it is a very important result that users performed one-handed tasks poorly on the screen, where mean completion time was the longest in one-hand docking and second longest in the gesture task. We argue that lifting arms up from the desk surface to the monitor leads to a greater switching cost, and operating in the air could lead to poor performance. Six out of ten participants reported that performing tasks on the vertical surface was more difficult than on the horizontal surface because they could not rest their arms while performing the tasks.

In summary, the study reveals the users' capabilities of performing one-handed tasks:

- Users perform one-handed tasks efficiently in zones close to keyboard or mouse.
- Users perform one-handed tasks generally well across the entire *bottom* region.
- The vertical *screen* is a poor region for performing one-handed tasks.

Two-handed Tasks

Overall, the results show that users performed two-handed docking tasks quickly, and felt less fatigue in the bottom and top regions than in the other three regions. We argue that this may be due to ergonomic issues. In the right and left regions, users had to rotate their torso for two-handed tasks to get both hands over to one side of the keyboard. This body rotation might lead to muscle fatigue and poor performance. Similar to one-handed tasks, users commented that operating on the vertical screen required holding their hands in the air, which caused fatigue.

Based on these results, we draw the following conclusions about the users' abilities to perform two-handed tasks:

- The best zones for performing two-handed tasks are the *bottom* and *top* regions.
- Users perform two-handed tasks poorly in the *left*, *right* and *screen* regions, and these regions also caused increased levels of fatigue.

Summary

In both one- and two-handed tasks, some of the results are within our expectation. For example, zones close to the keyboard and mouse are good for one-handed tasks, and the top and bottom suit two-handed tasks well. In doing this study, we validated such expectations, and in addition, provided a quantitative analysis and in-depth understanding of each zone. Specifically, we have captured the precise magnitude of effects by each region and its 9 grid cells.

In addition, the study also reveals some interesting findings. First, the bottom region suits both one- and two-handed interaction very well. Second, the vertical screen is less efficient for touch interaction. This is a particularly important finding, given that touch screen computers are becoming more prevalent [6, 7].

COMBINING MULTITOUCH AND DESKTOP WORK

Implementation

Guided by the study results, we designed and implemented a set of interaction techniques integrating multi-touch input with a mouse and keyboard to facilitate desktop work. Our purpose is to demonstrate example interactions and usages, and in particular, demonstrate how different regions within the desktop environment can be used for touch, and how such interactions can be guided by our study results.

The interaction techniques are coherently integrated into a desktop prototype, called Magic Desk (Figure 1, Figure 10). We demonstrate our new techniques in an environment which has all five planar touch surfaces available. The current system was implemented on a Microsoft Surface with a Dell Multi-touch display. A QWERTY keyboard and wireless mouse are used, and have tags so that their position and orientation can be recognized by the surface.

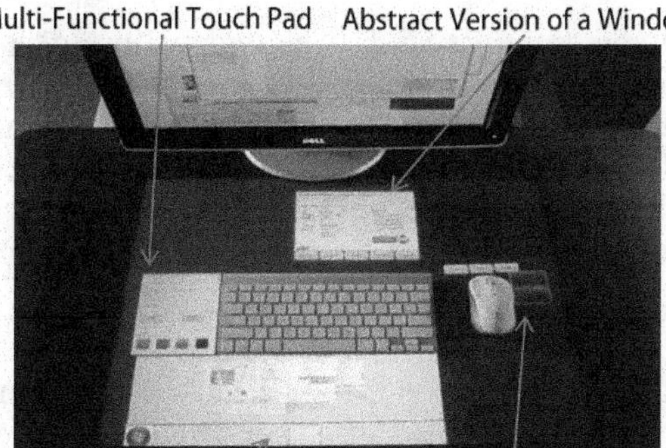

Figure 10. The Magic Desk components.

Enhanced Window Management and Task Bar

As users process increasing amount of digital information, they desire more flexibility of managing windows, such as moving/resizing multiple windows simultaneously, and arranging multiple windows to form a semantic layout [4]. To enhance the flexibility and increase the input bandwidth of managing windows, we designed an enhanced task bar (Figure 10), allowing users to simultaneously manage multiple windows directly with two hands.

Thumbnails of open windows are displayed in the enhanced task bar and the location and sizes of these thumbnails conveys the spatial location and sizes of open windows on the monitor. Since the Enhanced Task bar has a wider aspect ratio than the vertical computer screen, overlapping windows are spread out more horizontally and thus are more accessible for manipulation. Moreover, the following operations are enabled:

Resize. Moving fingers apart (or together) on the thumbnails enlarge (or shrink) the corresponding windows.

Maximize/Restore. Double tapping on the thumbnail maximize/restore the corresponding window.

Minimize/Restore. Flicking the thumbnail down minimizes the corresponding window and sends the thumbnail to a bottom strip. Flicking the thumbnail up from the bottom region restores the window.

Implications from the Study. As the enhanced task bar technique involves a rich set of two-handed operations, we suggest placing this component at either bottom or top region. In the current Magic Desk system, the enhanced task bar is coupled to the bottom edge of the keyboard.

Multi-Functional Touch Pad

Two-handed interaction has been shown to be beneficial in certain interaction tasks, such as controlling multiple-degrees-of-freedom [18]. By designing a multi-functional touch pad on the left side of the keyboard, we enable such interaction paradigm in a desktop work environment: the right hand interacts with the mouse while the left hand uses the touch pad. We implemented the following functions:

Controlling multiple degrees of freedom. The mouse is used to select a target, while the left hand fingers control additional degrees of freedom (e.g., rotating and scaling a geometric object) (Figure 11a).

Adjusting Control-Distance Gain of a mouse. Through the mouse speed region on the touch pad (Figure 11b), users can move their fingers apart to increase the CD gain and together to reduce it. This can be done in parallel to a mouse operation task with the right hand.

Controlling a secondary cursor. A secondary cursor controlled by the left hand on the touch pad is introduced to work in parallel to the primary cursor operations. Using a relative mapping, the user can move the secondary cursor, that is constrained within a tool palette, to select different tools, while controlling the main cursor on the canvas to draw graphics (Figure 11c).

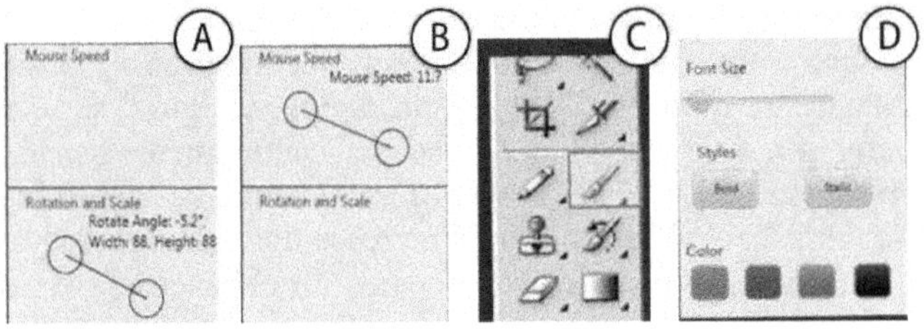

Figure 11. The content on Multi-functional touch pad for (a) rotating and scaling an object, (b) controlling mouse speed, (c) a secondary cursor for selecting drawing tool, and (d) a customized tool palette. The circles in (a, b) show finger positions.

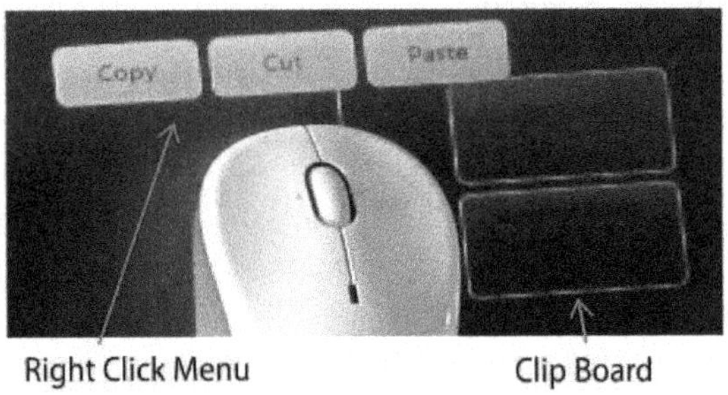

Figure 12. Digital Mouse Pad.

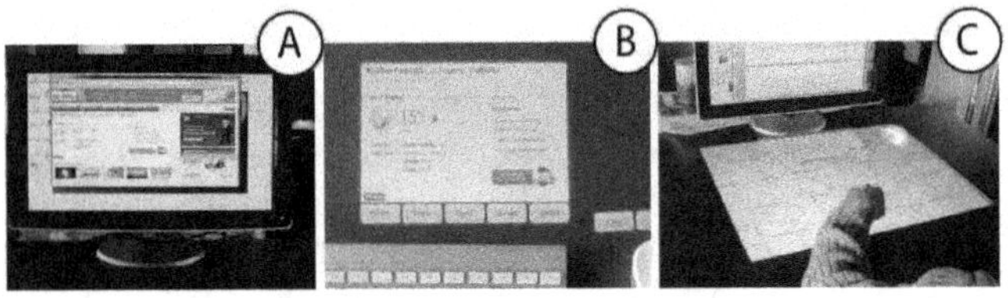

Figure 13. (a) A weather forecast window in full-version on the screen. (b) The abstract version of the same window on the table. (c) After a keyboard and mouse were pushed away, a map application automatically expanded to fill the entire desk.

Customized tool palette. The multi-Functional touch pad can also serve as a repository for storing commonly used UI elements. For example, Figure 11d shows a touch pad with touch buttons and sliders for a text editing program. To add a new element to the palette, a user duplicates it from the monitor by flicking it down with a single finger. The flicked element then animates to the touch pad. Dragging an undesired element out of the palette removes it.

Implication from the Study. All of the interactions on the multi-functional touch pad are one-handed. More specifically, most interactions are performed with the left hand while the right hand is operating the mouse. According to the experiment results, the optimal region for left-hand operations is the rightmost area of the left region. Therefore, the touch pad is coupled with the left edge of the keyboard.

Digital Mouse Pad

The digital mouse pad (Figure 12) is designed to augment mouse operations. The right-click mouse menu is persistently visualized on the digital mouse pad, and the user can trigger commands by directly touching the corresponding button. A multi-item clipboard is also visualized next to the mouse. Users can directly tap the content on the clipboard to paste it at the location of the cursor. Bringing the common commands on the digital mouse pad allows users to quickly access them, albeit it might require users switch eye-gazing position from the screen to the table. However, as users are familiar with the locations of menus on the digital mouse pad, this switch cost might be reduced. An alternative is to display virtual representations of users' hands on the screen, so that they do not have to look at the table during the interaction.

Implication from the Study. The experiment results indicated that the region close to the right side of the keyboard is one of the high-performing zones for one-handed tasks. UI elements (e.g., right-click menus and clipboard) on this region can be easily accessed.

Continuous Workspace

The touch regions on a desk can be combined with the touch screen to provide a continuous work space. The continuous workspace supports the following operations:

Adapted window content. Users can freely drag windows between displays using fingers or a cursor to take advantage of the extra display surfaces. Since interaction focus is usually located on the monitor, applications on the tabletop mostly play a supportive role in displaying peripheral information [10]. Thus, windows shift from full versions on the screen Figure 13a) to abstract versions on the interactive table (Figure 13b) to allow users to absorb the most useful information with a simple glance.

Adapted UI layouts. UI elements within a window are rearranged to be close to the keyboard (Figure 13b), because these areas are best for performing one-handed direct touch. The UI elements are also enlarged to suit touch interaction.

Full Tabletop Interaction. Using the entire desk for interaction may be well-suited for specific tasks such as previewing images, navigating maps, and annotating documents. When the keyboard is moved out of the way, the window on the horizontal table will automatically expand to fill the entire desk. The horizontal table now becomes a full multi-touch display, on which users can freely pan and zoom displayed pictures with fingers (Figure 13c). Placing the keyboard back to the center of the desk returns the table to the standard mode.

Implications from the Study. The minimal use of touch on the main monitor was driven by its poor results from the study. Instead, touch for the vertical screen was only used to send content to the horizontal surface. In addition, the adapted UI layouts were guided by our finding that touch regions should be made as close to the keyboard as possible.

Informal User Feedback

We asked each of six users to freely and extensively try the interaction techniques on the table for 40 to 50 minutes In general, they commented that interaction techniques were easy to learn and use. The most popular features were the enhanced task bar technique for managing windows, the continuous workspace for dragging windows continuously across regions, and detecting the keyboard position to enable full tabletop interaction. No major problems were observed..Although these sessions were meant for initial feedback, they did give us a sense that the integration of multi-touch into the desktop environment may be welcomed by users.

POSSIBLE ENABLING IMPLEMENTATIONS

Our implementation of Magic Desk was carried out on a Microsoft Surface, which allowed us to prototype interactions within each region surrounding the keyboard. However, one could imagine numerous other configurations supporting one or multiple regions of multi-touch interaction (Figure 14). Figure 14a shows the scenario where the entire tabletop is both display and touch capable. Figure 14b, c and d illustrate how a subset of the touch and display regions could be reproduced by using auxiliary devices. For example, a multi-touch tablet, such as an iPad, could be placed next to the keyboard (Figure 14b). This would support interactions such as our Multi-Functional Touch Pad. Additionally, an ultra-thin, multi-touch display pad, possibly implemented by layering a transparent UnMousePad [28] on top of an e-ink display, could be positioned below the keyboard (Figure 14c), thus enabling enhanced task bar techniques. An additional touch-tablet device could be positioned underneath the mouse to support digital mouse pad operations (Figure 14d). Since the mouse would sit on top of the display, the display could be positioned next to the keyboard, possibly mitigating some of the negative effects associated with the right region in our study, which was displaced from the keyboard to leave room for the mouse.

DISCUSSION AND FUTURE WORK

Some desktop users tend to clutter desk space with various physical objects such as paper documents. To cope with cluttered desk space, we suggest using automatic occlusion reduction [33], adaptive layout [33], freeform display representation [5], or customized tabletop widget [19] techniques. These physical artifacts [2, 15, 30] could also be virtually augmented with multi-touch surfaces.

These cluttered desks can be considered as subsets of the complete multi-touch enabled desktop (Figure 14a): only parts of the entire desk would be available for touch interaction. Our observation study indicates that most users have some spare real-estate in at least one of the regions we studied. (e.g., many users seldom cluttered the bottom region). Touch interaction techniques could be implemented in these areas. In addition, technology development could in turn affect users' behaviors. It is possible that users may adapt their workplaces to create room for supplementary multi-touch surfaces, thus benefiting from the proposed interaction techniques.

A related issue is the potential problem of false touch activations, potentially from the hands resting on a touch enabled surface. Many multi-touch systems, such as the Microsoft Surface, already have finger detection libraries, and can ignore non-finger input. This worked sufficiently in our implementation, but warrants further investigation.

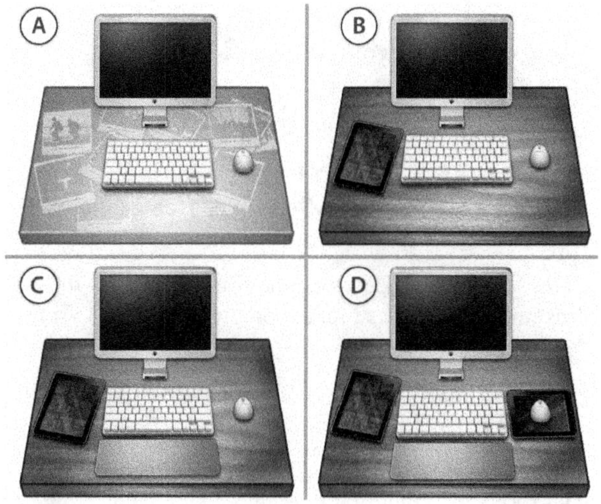

Figure 14. Potential configurations for multi-touch desktop computing. a) The entire table is a multi-touch display surface. b) A multi-touch tablet is placed next to the keyboard to be used as an additional input device. c) The addition of a multi-touch display pad below the keyboard. d) An additional touch display is placed under the mouse.

CONCLUSION

In this paper, we explored both theoretical and practical issues related to integrating planar multi-touch surfaces into a desktop computing environment. We systematically studied user's touch input abilities and transition costs between keyboards/mice and the five planar touch regions via controlled experiments. Guided by the study results, we explored the design space of a multi-touch integrated desktop environment, by designing and implementing a set of interaction techniques utilizing planar touch regions with a mouse and keyboard to facilitate desktop work. All the interaction techniques were coherently integrated into a desktop prototype called Magic Desk. The system demonstrates various possibilities of integrating multi-touch with a mouse and keyboard in desktop work.

REFERENCES

1. Apple Magic Mouse. http://www.apple.com/
2. Arai, T., Machii, K., Kuzunuki, S. and Shojima, H. (1995). InteractiveDESK: a computer-augmented desk which responds to operations on real objects. *ACM CHI Poster* 141-142.
3. Block, F., Gellersen, H., and Villar, N. (2010) Touch-Display Keyboards: Transforming Keyboards into Interactive Surfaces. *ACM CHI.* 1145-1154
4. Bi, X., Balakrishnan, R. (2009) "Comparing Usage of a Large High-Resolution Display to Single or Dual Desktop Displays for Daily Work". *ACM CHI.* 1005~1014
5. Cotting, D. and Gross, M. (2006) Interactive environment-aware display bubbles. *ACM UIST* 245-254.
6. Dell Latitude XT2 Tablet PC Touch Screen http://www.dell.com/tablet?s=biz&cs=555

7. Dell SX2210T Multi-Touch Monitor http://support.dell.com/support/edocs/monitors/sx2210t/

8. Dietz, P. and Leigh, D. (2001) DiamondTouch: a multi-user touch technology. *ACM UIST.* 219-226.

9. Forlines, C, Wigdor, D., Shen, C., and Balakrishnan, R. (2007) Direct-touch vs. Mouse Input for Tabletop Displays. *ACM CHI.* 647-656

10. Han, J. Y. (2005). Low-cost multi-touch sensing through frustrated total internal reflection. *ACM UIST.* 115-118.

11. Hancock, M. and Booth, K. (2004). Improving menu placement strategies for pen input. *Graphics Interface* 221-230.

12. Hartmann, B., Morris, M. R., Benko, H., and Wilson, A. D. (2009). Augmenting interactive tables with mice & keyboards. *ACM UIST.* 149-152.

13. Hedge, A., Anthropometry and Workspace Design, in *DEA* 325/651. 2002, Cornell.

14. Hinrichs, U., Hancock, M., Collins, C., and Carpendale, S. (2007) Examination of Text-Entry Methods for Tabletop Displays. *Tabletop.* 105-112.

15. Kane, S. K., Avrahami, D., Wobbrock, J. O., Harrison, B., Rea, A. D., Philipose, M., and LaMarca, A. (2009). Bonfire: a nomadic system for hybrid laptop-tabletop interaction. *ACM UIST.* 129-138.

16. Kin, K., Agrawala, M., and DeRose, T. (2009). Determining the benefits of direct-touch, bimanual, and multifinger input on a multitouch workstation. *GI.* 119-124

17. Krueger, M. W., Gionfriddo, T., and Hinrichsen, K. (1985). VIDEOPLACE—an artificial reality. *SIGCHI Bull.* 35-40.

18. Kurtenbach, G., Fitzmaurice, G., Baudel, T., and Buxton, B. (1997). The design of a GUI paradigm based on tablets, two-hands, and transparency. *ACM CHI.* 35-42.

19. Leithinger, D. Haller, M. (2007) Improving Menu Interaction for Cluttered Tabletop Setups with User-Drawn Path Menus. *IEEE TableTop*, 121-128

20. Matthews, T., Czerwinski, M., Robertson, G., and Tan, D. (2006). Clipping lists and change borders: improving multitasking efficiency with peripheral information design. *ACM CHI.* 989-998

21. Myers, B. A. (2001). Using handhelds and PCs together. *Commun. ACM* 44, 11, 34-41

22. Morris,M. Brush, A.J., and Meyers, B. (2008) A Field Study of Knowledge Workers' Use of Interactive Horizontal Displays. *TableTop.* 105-112

23. Moscovich, T. and Hughes, J. F. (2008). Indirect mappings of multi-touch input using one and two hands. *ACM CHI.* 1275-1284.

24. Multi-Touch in Windows 7. microsoft.com/windows

25. Pinhanez, C., Kjeldsen, R., Tang, L., Levas, A., Podlaseck, M., Sukaviriya, N. and Pingali, G. (2003) Creating touch-screens anywhere with interactive projected displays. *ACM MULTIMEDIA.* 460-461.

26. Rekimoto, J. (2002) SmartSkin: an infrastructure for freehand manipulation on interactive surfaces. *ACM CHI.* 113-120.

27. Rekimoto, J. and Saitoh, M. (1999) Augmented surfaces: a spatially continuous work space for hybrid computing environments. *ACM CHI.* 378-385.

28. Rosenberg, I. and Perlin, K. (2009). The UnMousePad: an interpolating multi-touch force-sensing input pad. *SIGGRAPH.* 1-9.

29. Scott, S.D. (2003) Territory-Based Interaction Techniques for Tabletop Collaboration. *ACM UIST Companion.* 17-20.

30. Steimle, J., Khalilbeigi, M., and Mühlhäuser, M. (2010). Hybrid groups of printed and digital documents on tabletops: a study. *ACM CHI EA.* 3271-3276.

31. Ullmer, B. and Ishii, H. (1997) The metaDESK: Models and prototypes for tangible user interfaces. *ACM UIST* 223-232.

32. Villar, N., Izadi, S., Rosenfeld, D., Benko, H., Helmes, J., Westhues, J., Hodges, S., Ofek, E., Butler, A., Cao, X., and Chen, B. (2009). Mouse 2.0: multi-touch meets the mouse. *ACM UIST.* 33-42

33. Vogel, D. and Balakrishnan, R. (2010). Occlusion-Aware Interfaces. *ACM CHI.* 263~272

34. Wellner, P. (1993) Interacting with paper on the DigitalDesk. *Communications of the ACM*, 36 (7), 87-96.

35. Wigdor, D., Penn, G., Ryall, K., Esenther, A., Shen, C., (2007). Living with a Tabletop: Analysis and Observations of Long Term Office Use of a Multi-Touch Table. *TableTop.* 60-67.

36. Wigdor, D., Shen, C., Forlines, C., and Balakrishnan, R. (2006). Table-centric interactive spaces for real-time collaboration. *AVI.* 103-107.

37. Wilson, A. D. (2005) PlayAnywhere: a compact interactive tabletop projection-vision system. *ACM UIST.* 83-92.

38. Wilson, A. D., Izadi, S., Hilliges, O., Garcia-Mendoza, A. and Kirk, D. (2008) Bringing physics to the surface. *ACM UIST.* 67-76.

39. Wu, M. and Balakrishnan, R. (2003) Multi-finger and whole hand gestural interaction techniques for multi-user tabletop displays. *ACM UIST.* 193-202.

40. Yang, X., Mak, E., McCallum, D., Irani, P., Cao, X. Izadi, S. (2010). LensMouse: Augmenting the mouse with an interactive touch display. *ACM CHI.* 2431-2440.

Benefits of Matching Domain Structure for Planning Software: The Right Stuff

Dorrit Billman*[+]
dorrit.billman@nasa.gov

Lucia Arsintescu*[+]
lucia.arsintescu-1@nasa.gov

Michael Feary[+]
michael.s.feary@nasa.gov

Jessica Lee*[+]
jessica.c.lee@nasa.gov

Asha Smith*[+]
asha.h.smith@nasa.gov

Rachna Tiwary*[+]
rachna.tiwary@nasa.gov

*San Jose State University Research Foundation (SJSURF)
[+]NASA Ames, Moffett Field, CA 94035-1000

ABSTRACT

We investigated the role of domain structure, in designing for software usefulness and usability. We ran through the whole application development cycle, in miniature, from needs analysis through design, implementation, and evaluation, for planning needs of one NASA Mission Control group. Based on our needs analysis, we developed prototype software that matched domain structure better than did the legacy system. We compared our new prototype to the legacy application in a laboratory, high-fidelity analog of the natural planning work. We found large performance differences favoring the prototype, which better captured domain structure. Our research illustrates the importance of needs analysis (particularly Domain Structure Analysis), and the viability of the design process that we are exploring.

Author Keywords

Complex work domains, planning, aeroastronautics.

ACM Classification Keywords

H5.2. [Information interfaces and presentation]: User interfaces – *evaluation/methodology*.

General Terms

Design, Experimentation, Human Factors, Performance.

I. INTRODUCTION

Building useful software depends on understanding what is needed. Work applications typically consist of a bounded domain and set of required functions. If these are identified and if software enables meeting these needs, the software will be useful. Multiple methods may be used to identify needs (e.g., Cognitive Work Analysis, Contextual Design), and such methods typically precede formal requirements specification. This paper reports on one approach to needs analysis. This is part of a larger research agenda of developing tools and methods: we aim to reduce costs of the information needed to ensure good human-system integration, particularly in high-risk domains [11,12].

Our approach to needs analysis focuses on capturing the abstract structure of the work domain; we refer to the product of such an analysis as a Domain Structure Analysis (DSA). Our approach contrasts with task analyses that capture the specifics of tasks carried out within the existing configuration of tools and procedures. Our goal is to identify high-value, low-cost information useful for design and evaluation. A Domain Structure Analysis (DSA) can guide design and evaluation of software to support work in the analyzed domain.

This paper reports an initial demonstration of the value of our approach to needs analysis, in a complex socio-technological domain: the planning work of one International Space Station (ISS) Mission Control group, Attitude Determination and Control Operator (ADCO). (*ADCO* refers to the group or an individual.) We run through a demonstration of the role of domain structure analysis from design through evaluation, "in miniature" for a limited scope of work. The logic of our demonstration is as follows: 1) We provide an example domain structure analysis. 2) We illustrate how the analysis can be used to select and design software by providing high-level constraints on key properties of the design. 3) We show how the analysis supports evaluation (as well as design) by assessing how well a candidate design matches the domain structure, and by making performance predictions based on the match. 4) We report a study that evaluated two planning tools, tested the predictions, and found dramatic performance differences as predicted.

The paper starts by setting the context for ADCO planning work. Then we report our research on the value of domain structure analysis; the focus of the paper is our experimental evaluation. Finally, we reflect on what this study suggests about needs analysis, our approach, and its role in producing useful and usable software.

CHI 2011, May 7–12, 2011, Vancouver, BC, Canada.
Copyright 2011 ACM 978-1-4503-0267-8/11/05....$10.00.

II. ADCO WORK: FLYING THE SPACE STATION

ADCO controls the attitude (yaw, pitch, & roll) of the ISS. The operators monitor and command attitude real-time and also develop plans in advance of real-time operations. They are responsible for maintaining an efficient flight attitude during quiet phases of flight and for maneuvering into different attitudes for activities such as docking and undocking of vehicles or to support various tests. Supporting these activities means carrying out detailed sequences of actions that switch among mechanisms of controlling and applying force: the thrusters on the Russian capsules currently docked with the ISS, the momentum management system (large gyroscopes which can transfer torque), and in rare circumstances the space shuttle. These mechanisms and commanding software move the ISS to the appropriate attitude.

ADCO closely cooperates with Russian counterparts, to develop detailed plans supporting these activities. While the technical complexity of these operations requires good planning, the required international cooperation imposes an even greater need for accurate, detailed planning well in advance of execution.

The following characteristics of ADCO planning relate it to other work domains: 1) **High-Risk & Safety Critical**. The ADCO planning domain is part of a safety-critical, high-risk domain [10,15,18]. The planning functions help decouple [18] aspects of the system thus protecting real-time operation: ADCO intensively checks plans, identifies potential threats, and builds contingency plans. Planning favors reuse of old, safe plan components rather than exploration of less tested but possibly more optimal plans. 2) **Products are Plans**. The ADCO planning domain is information work and the products are represented in documents. ADCO gathers, integrates, and approves the information making up a plan. (*Plan* refers to both the abstract information and its expression in a particular document.) Planning documents select different information, for different users. 3) **Not Real-Time Control.** The ADCO planning domain is not subject to strong time pressure. There are planning deadlines, but in normal circumstances, the planning activity is not heavily driven by the real-time dynamics of unalterable, extrinsic, physical events. Indeed, the point of planning is to remove time pressure from decision making, thus allowing more successful execution. 4) **Complex Socio-Technical Domain**. Technically, the ISS is unique, changing, intensively modeled, yet incompletely understood. ADCO planning aims to ensure that planned activities are well away from technical constraints on how the ISS flies. ADCO draws information from several engineering support groups rather than conducting detailed engineering work internally. Social rather than technical constraints are the primary drivers of planning difficulty: when information becomes available from another group, or when others need ADCO products.

Current planning software evolved incrementally to serve a variety of the planning needs. Our research group became involved with the ADCO group because of their desire to improve the planning tool used to build and revise plans, particularly, the plan documents used in joint planning with their Russian counterparts.

Our observation, discussion, and document-gathering focused on this part of the planning process. We developed some understanding of the communication flows; however, our focus (of both analysis and experiment) is the operations done by an individual to build and revise the planning documents used to communicate with the Russian counterparts. Further, this is the aspect that key operators thought most needed improvement.

III. NEEDS ANALYSIS

Our Process & Comparison to Other Approaches

We began our needs analysis with task analysis [8,20] at a quite specific level; we shifted focus to capturing the relatively high-level functions, far removed from low-level, button-pressing. Our approach diverged further from task analysis as we saw that many tasks should disappear or change dramatically with better-designed tools. Although a high-level analysis of tasks [14] aims to avoid over-specificity, even a high-level task characterization seemed tied to current practices. It was difficult to identify the boundary between necessary tasks and those driven by history or limitations in current tools. (We suspect that in highly routine and proceduralized domains it may be easier to identify the functions, while analyzing the "declarative" information structure may be more tractable in open, generative, information work.)

We shifted to identifying the structure and constraints on ADCO planning. We sought to identify necessary elements both of the process of planning, and of the product, namely, the ADCO plan. A critical observation was that the ADCO planning work is primarily a matter of producing documents, appropriately vetted and with appropriate content. The primary constraints concern the required properties of the plan. Requirements on the product seemed to be a particularly important, clear guide to what is needed from planning software: it must support building and editing correctly structured plans. Our focus was on identifying the fundamental structure required in a plan, rather than constraints on its detailed content.

We are similar to Cognitive Work Analysis (CWA) [3,9,19,21] in prioritizing stable, structural aspects of the domain over tasks, but we diverged from CWA concerning the nature and source of constraint. For CWA, constraints are fixed and external to the work: the chemical plant operator does not re-engineer the size of the chemical tanks. For information work, rather than lying outside the work, the "constraints" or structure may be very much part of the work, constructed by the work activity, expressed in the work product, and changeable or negotiable as part of the

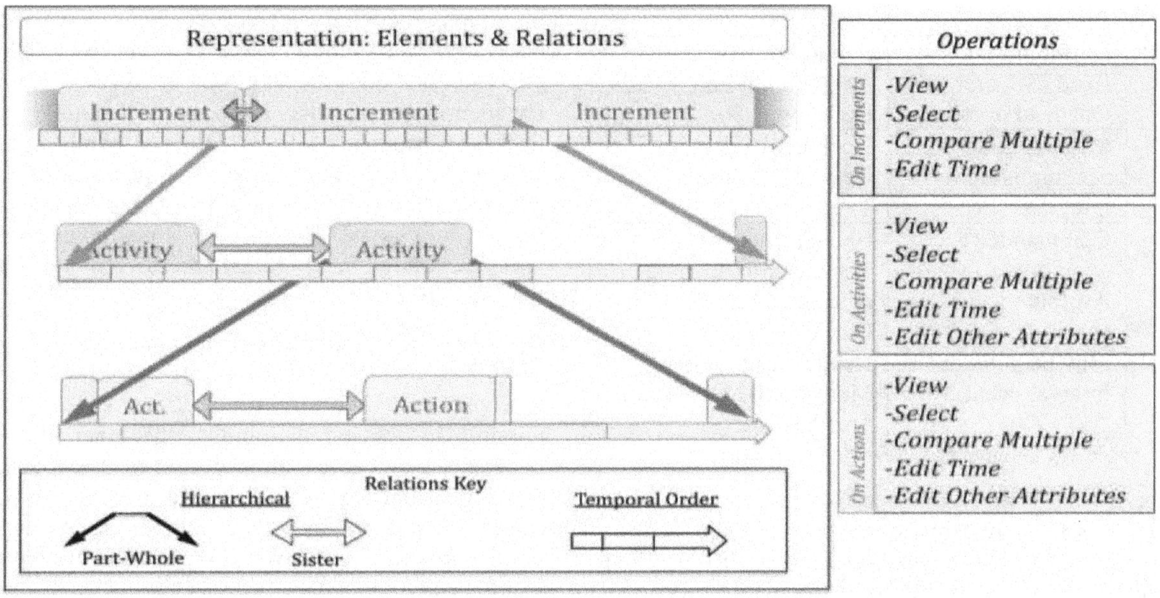

Figure 1. Schematic of the Domain Structure Analysis: Representations and operations in the ADCO planning domain. Increment, Activity, and Action elements are organized by Hierarchical (Part-whole, Sister) and Temporal (Order, contiguity) relations. Operations on these elements that are used by ADCO are shown on the right.

analysis of work products, in order to identify domain structure.

Ontology-based approaches also focus on identifying structural, "declarative" information about the work domain, and our approach is most similar to this [4,5,13]. Ontologies have been developed for information work domains, in which the structure and constraints are defined within the work, rather than outside its boundaries.

Contextual Inquiry (CI) [1] generates information about the needs that software should address. CI emphasizes gathering information about users, but also gathers information about structure or constraints, for example, in the artifact models. CI's emphasis on user observation may be most effective in less technical information work, where the domain structure can be easily understood by an observer adopting the role of a mentee [7].

We provide an example Domain Structure Analysis, for the ADCO planning domain. We believe this form of needs analysis will prove most directly applicable to 1) information work 2) for which accurate, novel, problem solving rather than speeded performance is paramount 3) and that is safety-critical or otherwise benefits from a very accurate design. This paper focuses on the product of analysis, not the process, which we continue to change significantly. Additional information on the method used here may be found in [2], but development is ongoing.

Need Analysis Results: Structure of the ADCO Domain.

A domain structure analysis identifies the organization of the work domain. The structure is expressed in terms of its elements and their relations; in addition, the operations on the domain are identified. For an information-work domain such as ADCO, domain structure is specified by the structure of ADCO plans. ADCO plans compose events into a part-whole hierarchy organized linearly in time. Primary operations on the plans and plan components are viewing, selecting, and editing. An overview of the high-level organization is shown schematically in Figure 1. The elements, relations, and operations from which the structure is built up are summarized in Table 1, and the plan elements described in Table 2.

The plan elements and types were not explicit prior to our analysis. Providing an explicit, external, representation of key concepts known implicitly by domain experts is a frequent, desirable outcome of many forms of work analysis. In our case, initially there was no general and standard term referring to *Activity*, to mark its importance as more than a series of Actions. Rather, events were often referred to very specifically, in two ways: 1) references were made to a specific docking mission (activity) or specific docking maneuver (action) in ways that glossed their relationship and 2) events were often referred to in terms of a particular format (e.g., "the UAF file") rather than the event it represents, which may appear in multiple formats and documents. The construct of *Increment* was explicit, both outside and within ADCO. Increments are the largest element for planning in ADCO, spanning the period between arrival and departure of ISS crew (i.e., from the

Elements	Increment, Activity, Action
Relations	part-whole {part-of: contains; sister} temporal{prior to: after; contiguous: gapped}
Operations	View, Select, Compare, Edit Time, Edit Other Attribute

Table 1. Components of the Domain Structure: Representation (Elements and Relations) and Operations.

Element	Description	Examples
Increment	Duration for a fixed ISS crew. One lead operator.	3+ months between Arv-Shuttle: Launch 129 Dpt- Soyuz 20.
Activity	Mission goal accomplished by integrated events	Docking, Undocking, Relocate, Reboost, Thruster Test
Action	Commanded operation. Attribute values specify parameters. May be point or interval event.	Change Attitude: Maneuver to docking attitude Change Control: Handover to Russia; Momentum Managemt; Free Drift

Table 2. Elements of the Domain Structure

Shuttle or Soyuz). One ADCO lead is assigned to each increment. Actions were explicit; however, *types* of actions as well as *types* of activities were not explicit but identified through study of documents and discussion with experts.

The temporal properties of plans are defined in terms of the three elements. All elements have both a relative temporal ordering and an absolute time value. Early in planning, events may have only relative time established or be assigned estimated times. Events at the same level are disjoint and do not overlap. Increments and Activities have durations. Some Action types have durations and others are specified as a point in time.

An action belongs to one of a small number of types, and is specified in terms of attribute values. Key attributes include start and stop times, action type, the attitude attained or maintained (yaw, pitch, and roll), and the control mechanisms used at the beginning and end of the action.

To summarize, ADCO plans consist of structure built from Increments, Activities, and Actions. The important relations between these elements come from the part-whole hierarchy (part-within-whole and sister-to-sister), and the temporal structure (including order and separation of elements). This plan structure represents events as compatible both with how people often think about events and future/planning [22] and with how these specific plans are executed. Note that this plan structure is not the only possibility. For example, in some domains plans might be appropriately represented as regulating several continuous flows. In those cases, the plan need not decompose into temporally separated, internally structured hierarchical elements.

IV. DOMAIN STRUCTURE AND SOFTWARE DESIGN

Rationale

We claim that software that matches, or aligns with, work domain structure will function better than software that does not. While a software system that does match can be defeated by bad execution, we believe a mismatching system is unlikely to be effective, whatever the details of its execution. We used the domain structure to develop prototype, planning software (called NEW) that does a better job fitting the constraints specified by the domain structure than does the LEGACY software currently in use. By identifying the key function as planning (rather than form- or document-editing on the one hand, or engineering on the other), we selected a planning framework available at NASA Ames, SPIFe (Scheduling and Planning Interface for Exploration) [16] with time-line representation. This was configured and modified to provide hierarchical representation of Increments, Activities, and Actions.

NEW was designed to cover the plan revision functions of LEGACY. (NEW did not cover the process of sending and receiving edited files to the Russians.) All revision tasks possible in one are possible in the other, but with very different cost. The resulting design of NEW also supports "for free" functions beyond those provided by LEGACY. Specifically, work thinking about or designing a plan is better supported by NEW; in the current system, operators would need to do these functions "in the head" or with tools outside LEGACY. We mention this to fill out the 'big picture' view of the functionality of the two systems.

High-Level Comparison of Software-to-Structure Match

Figures 2A & 2B illustrate the difference in match for the NEW and LEGACY systems. Each shows the three key elements, the part-whole and temporal relations, and the operations on element, which were identified in the DSA. The left panel shows that only a subset of the elements and relations are supported for LEGACY. Representation of high-level structure is impoverished: no Increment representation, no relationships between Activities, and few operations on Activities. Further, representation of Activities and all temporal relations are minimal. The right panel summarizes the match provided by the NEW prototype. All the elements and relations are represented, and almost all the operations. Comparing the information architecture and interaction design of the two systems, and how each system aligns with the domain structure can flesh out this high level characterization.

Figure 3 shows the primary window of the LEGACY system, used by ADCO to build and revise plans. The plan for an activity is represented in a UAF (unified ACR file), which is the file that lists the ACR's (actions) making up the UAF; each ACR represents an action in the activity. LEGACY acts as a form editor of UAF files. The upper left panel displays and edits metadata about the activity represented in the open UAF file. The lower left panel is a view-only window displaying the descriptions of about two actions (ACR's); the active action is highlighted. The upper right panel displays the active action, allowing the user to change the action's status and to move through the file by selecting the next or previous actions. The bottom right panel is the primary work area for editing the plan. It displays the attribute values for the selected action and allows the user to type in or select values for each of the action's attributes. When finished editing one action, the user saves that action to the buffer displaying the UAF; when finished editing one activity, the user saves the UAF to the file system. Aspects of managing versions and file names are handled automatically.

Mapping the representation and operations available in LEGACY to the abstract domain structure shows up its limitations. First, it provides no explicit representation of an increment, of multiple activities, or of relations between activities. The resulting lack of context means little support is provided for understanding or interpreting activities or their component actions. We lack detailed observation, but broadly LEGACY is used to integrate information determined other ways, rather than aiding in conceptual planning or checking. The interpretive work of the user takes place in the head or with other tools. Elements that are not represented cannot be operated on. In addition, though activities are minimally represented (as files), inside LEGACY files can only be selected or saved: it is not possible to edit an activity as a unit. For example, when an activity or set of activities slips, e.g., due to a delayed launch, the times of each action must be individually changed. This is a major frustration point. ADCO operators report trying to build their own calculators that will at least derive the values needed when times are offset by some increment. Second, there is no visual representation of time. While real numbers are indeed ratio scale as needed to appropriately represent time, representation only as text rather than also in an analog, perceptual representation means that understanding or changing time relations is a high-effort cognitive calculation rather than one supported by perception [6,23]. In sum, representation of the overall structure is very incomplete and representation of structure components (e.g., temporal relations) is far from ideal.

We illustrate how LEGACY is used with a typical revision task, of the sort used in our study: shift the time of the docking maneuver in a Soyuz docking activity an hour later. 1) Using LEGACY'S browsing window, navigate through the file system to find the file for the correct activity. 2) Select the file to open the edit window in Figure 3. 3) Scroll through the file to find and select the intended action. 4) In the edit panel change the Start Time and End Time to an hour later. 5) Click the Revise-ARC button in the lower right panel to enter the action; then click the Generate-UAF button in the lower left panel to save the activity file.

Figure 4 shows the window of NEW. An increment is represented as a plan, activities are expandable hierarchical events in a plan, and actions are component events. 1) The top tool bar includes functions such as zoom and undo. 2) The left panel displays the available plans, selectable by clicking. 3) The central panel provides timeline views of an increment. The top two colored time-lines are relevant to

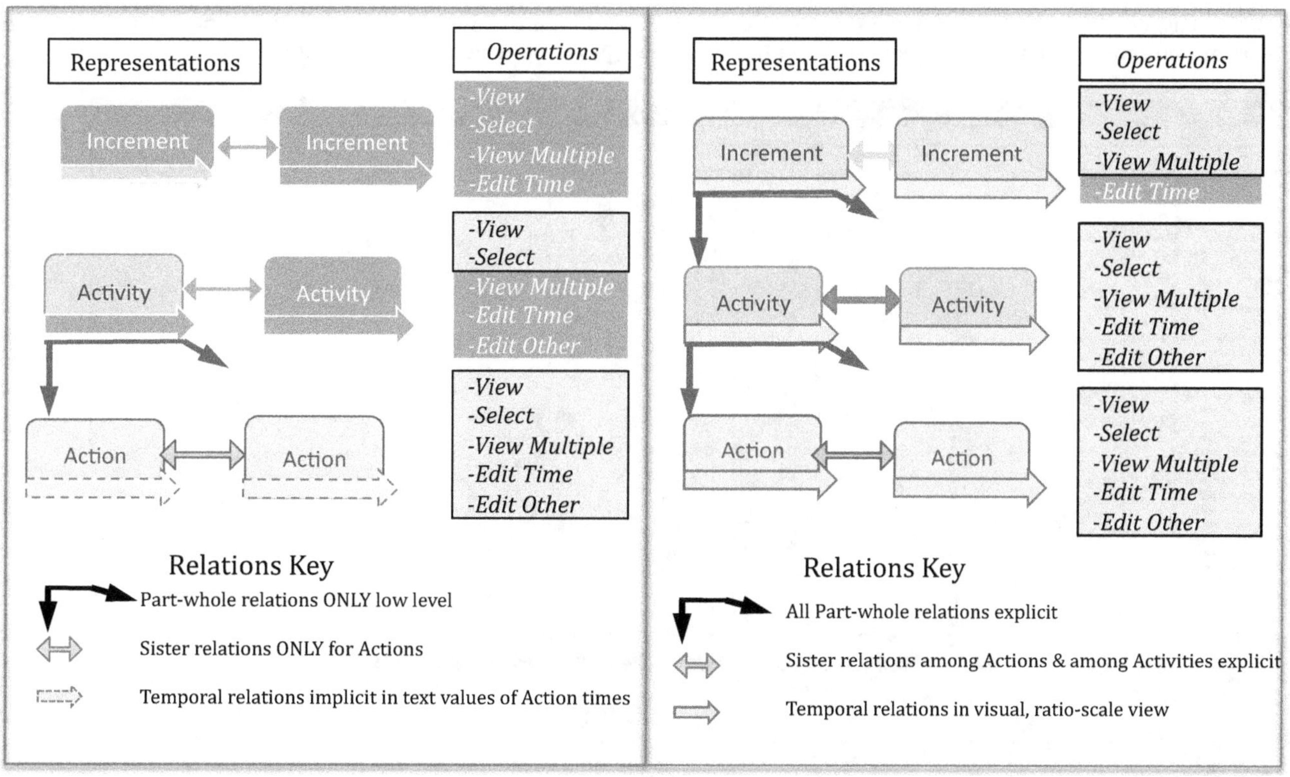

Figure 2. LEGACY system represented in Left Panel, and NEW system represented in Right Panel. Dimmed representations or operations show structure in the domain that is not expressed in the software. The NEW system provides much better match to domain structure than does the LEGACY system.

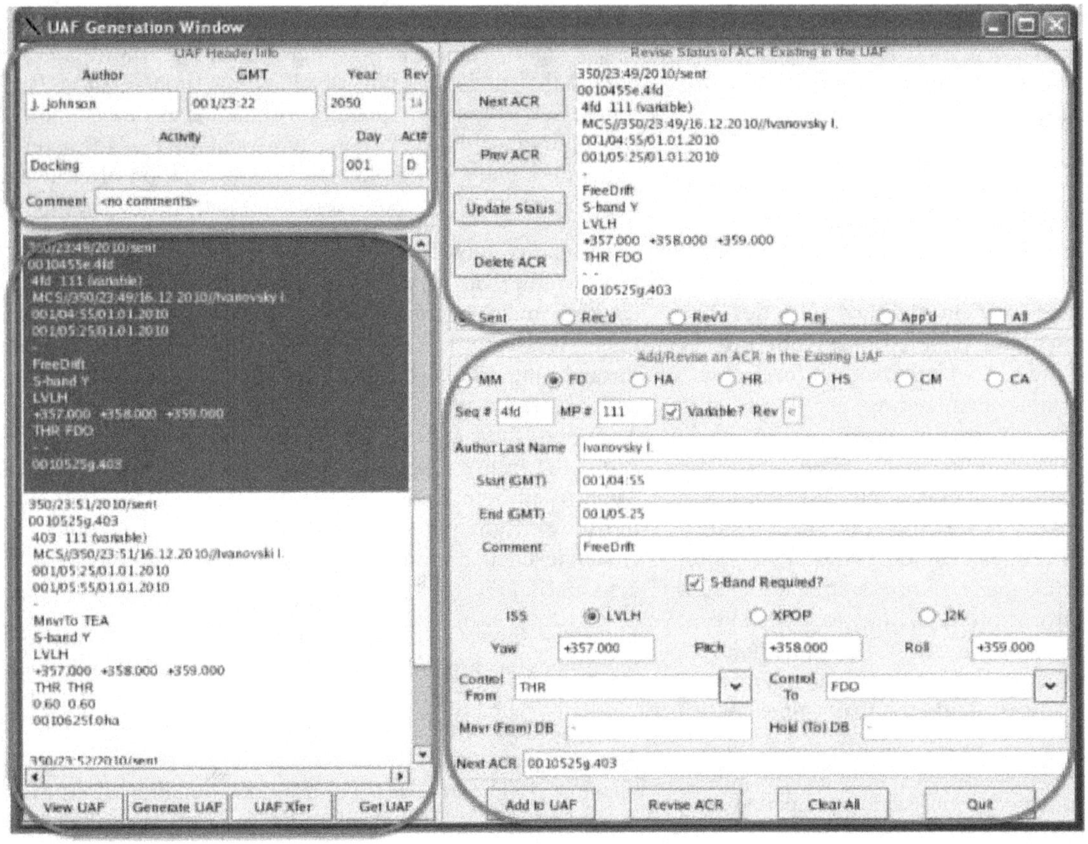

Figure 3. Screenshot of LEGACY system showing the four main function panels for editing plans. (The Actions attribute values shown here are invented, do not reflect a real event, but illustrate the types of individually possible values .)

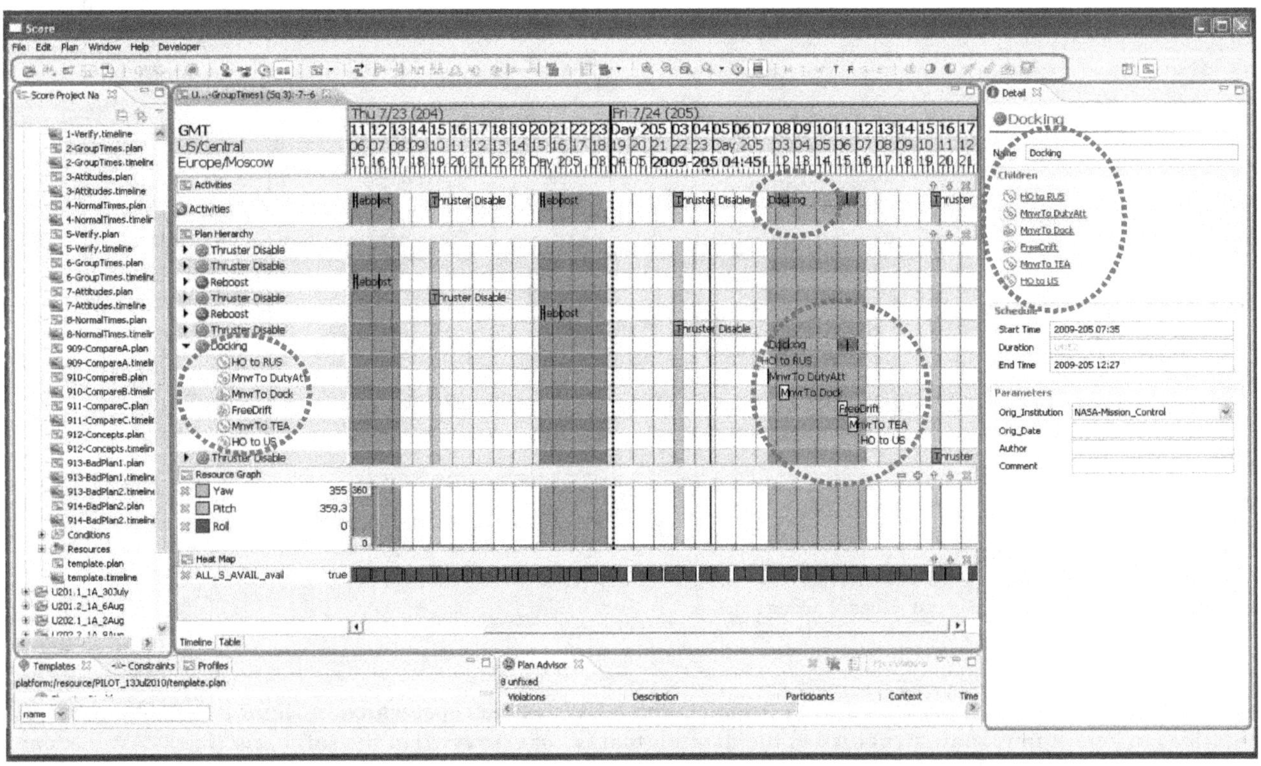

Figure 4. Screenshot of NEW system, showing the four main function panels for editing plans outlined in red. Dotted circles show 4 of the 5 repesentations of Activities

the tasks reported here. The top, *Activities* time line, summarizes events at the activity level. The second, *Plan Hierarchy* time line, provides two ways of accessing actions from activities: a) the list on the left expands the row to list the actions; b) the activity name within the timeline can be clicked to expand to show the component actions. The duration of activities and actions is indicated by their display size in the timeline. Actions and activities can be dragged and dropped to new times; a text field displays the precise time of the current start point to guide dropping. (Implementation issues limited the ease with which events could be precisely dropped.) 4) The right, Details-Edit panel allows display and edit of the attribute values of a selected event. For a selected activity, its component actions, time information, and meta-data are displayed. For a selected action, the engineering data (attitude, control, mass properties index, etc) and meta-data are displayed. In addition, collections of actions can also be selected and edited: if a constant value, say an updated Mass Properties Index, is needed for all selected actions, this can also be set through the Details Editor.

The following steps illustrate how to shift the time of the docking maneuver in a Soyuz docking activity an hour later in NEW. 1) Scan the increment plan for the intended activity, and if needed, double click on the Activity in the timeline or list at the left to open it. 2a) Drag and drop the intended action in the timeline one hour later OR 2b) Click-select the intended action, then type in the new start and end time in the Details Edit Panel. [3) Plans are automatically updated over an editing session and saved at the end of an editing session.]

Mapping the representation and operations of NEW's information architecture and resulting interface to the abstract domain structure shows the high-level correspondence. Increments are represented as Plans, setting the period displayed in the timeline. Activity and Actions have four parallel representations; Activity has an additional representation, in the *Activities* timeline. Four of the representations of activities are circled in dotted turquoise. The fifth, available for Actions as well, is a view that appears with tooltip rollover. The tooltip display (not shown) can be used to compare values of a second event with the values of a selected event, shown in the Details Edit Panel. NEW includes some additional functions not relevant to this report. In sum, the overall domain structure with all its elements and almost all relations is represented, and represented in a way that allows relationships to be quickly identified.

Predictions

The comparison of interaction designs with the domain structure generates two types of predictions. First, if one design provides better overall match than another, we predict better overall performance with the better matching system (particularly when the points of match of one system are a subset of the match points of the other). LEGACY provides a proper subset of the matches provided by NEW. Better overall match should enable tasks to be accomplished with fewer operations and should provide a more coherent model of the work domain, thus enabling better overall performance in NEW than in LEGACY. Second, the mapping identifies the locus of match or mismatch; the locus of differential match should predict the locus of greatest performance difference. Differences in representations and operations are greatest at the level Activity. In contrast to NEW, LEGACY provides only implicit representation of Activities (as a file), and no editing operations can be done at the Activity level. Rather, changes must be made individually to each action that requires a change. Further, LEGACY does not enable viewing at an Increment level or of any time span larger than one activity, thus preventing seeing an Activity in context. Thus, we predict that operations at the level of Activity will be particularly disadvantaged in LEGACY vs NEW.

We conducted a lab study comparing performance using NEW vs LEGACY. This study focused on revising plans, included a variety of tasks, and took two days. Tasks were designed both to represent the types of editing normally done by ADCO and to assess predicted differences between systems. This paper reports Day 1 data for one editing task. Preliminary analysis of the remaining edit data is consistent with the pattern of findings reported here.

V. EXPERIMENT METHOD

Participants

Participants were technical students and thus rough surrogates for ADCO trainees. The design was between-subjects with nine LEGACY and eight NEW condition participants. Degree of expertise varied within and was matched between conditions. Each condition included 3 graduate students in aerospace engineering and 1 doctoral student in another physical science, with upper level undergraduates in science or engineering as the remaining participants.

Materials & Tasks

To build the plan content used in the experiment, we reconstructed the series of events of one as-flown increment from ADCO documents. The content of our plans exactly matched the actual plan, with the following exceptions designed to make it easier for our users: 1) we divided that increment into 3 smaller, "mini-increment" plans, 2) we compressed the timing between activities, 3) we regularized the timing and naming of actions within activities. In addition, for users of LEGACY, we tried to make the file directory structure as clear, simple, and best matched to task demands as we could.

Revision of times and attitudes in response to updated information forms the bulk of actual ADCO editing tasks. Our experimental tasks also focused on time and attitudes. Our goal was to have our users engage in tasks typical of ADCO plan revision work and that also might best reveal differences between systems.

Procedure

Participants began with training about the ADCO domain, studying text and diagrams and answering questions. After roughly an hour of ADCO training in the lab, participants were trained for roughly a half hour on their respective tool (less time on the simpler LEGACY). The tool training was interactive and included "now you do it" actions for all of component functions needed. After training, the participant did two blocks consisting of 4 core editing tasks, including Group Times. After these two blocks, users did a variety of more conceptual tasks. They returned for a second day, repeating and extending tasks from Day 1. This paper reports Day 1 Group Times data.

The 12-item Group Times Task required users to reschedule the times of four different collections of events: of an activity, of several adjacent actions within an activity, of an action, and of several adjacent actions spanning activities. Table 3 details this structure. Presentation was blocked in an effort to make it easier.

We predict different patterns of difficulty in NEW vs APU. In NEW changing time of an Action or an Activity will be comparable and fast, because the user can operate on a single element. Changing the time of a group of actions, within or between activities, will be slower. In APU, changing the time of a single Action will be much faster than changing the time of an Activity. Time to make a change will be primarily a function of number of actions to change, with some cost of switching Activities.

VI. EXPERIMENT RESULTS

Differences in Overall and in Pattern of Performance

Performance on Group Times items was better in NEW than LEGACY, with average times of 59 seconds (SE=8.6) versus 124 seconds (SE=8.2) per trial. We anticipated that users would work as slowly as needed to be accurate, but in fact error rates were high at 13% for NEW and 27% for LEGACY. We did analyses with and without error responses, with and without dropping outliers, aggregating and separating blocks. We got very similar results.

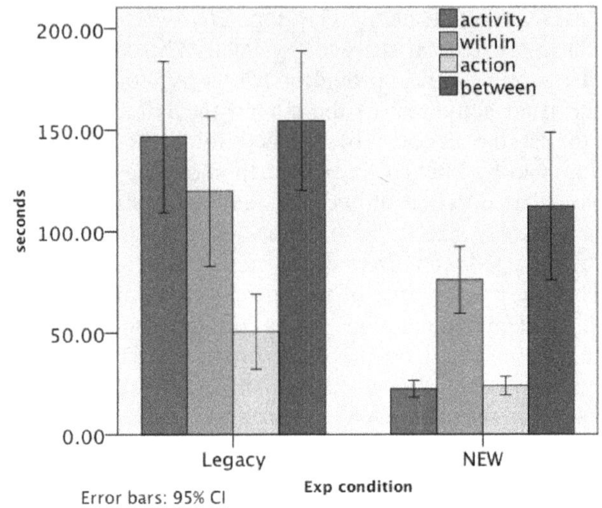

Figure 5. Response time in seconds for the LEGACY and the NEW conditions, on the 4 Group Times item types: shift an Activity, shift Actions within an Activity, shift an Action, and shift Actions spanning Activities.

Analysis with errors dropped, outliers included, blocks pooled are reported, from a 2 (condition) x 4 (item type) MANOVA.

The first question was whether overall performance was better for participants who used NEW versus LEGACY. LEGACY users took twice as long, and the condition effect on time was strong, $F(1,26)=23.20$, $p<.001$. Overall greater ease in NEW is mirrored in error rates half that of LEGACY, as well.

The second question is whether the pattern of performance differs between conditions as predicted. Response times are shown in Figure 5. The condition by item type effect is also strong, $F(1.9,50.10)=9.9$, $p<.001$, Greenhouse-Geisser adjusted. Main effect of Item type is also strong $F(1.9,50.10)=32.43$, $p<<.001$,Greenhouse-Geisser adjusted. Most importantly, the relative difficulty (measured by time) of the item types is very different, in the predicted pattern. For LEGACY changing the time of a whole activity is much slower (156 sec) than changing the time of a subset of actions (119 sec), $t(14)=2.46$, $p=.02$; while for NEW the reverse holds, with 23 sec. to change an activity and 76 secs for a subset of actions within an activity $t(14)=-6.39$, $p<.001$. Further, changing an activity takes the same time as changing an action in NEW, but is much harder than an action in LEGACY.

	Activity			**Actions in Activity**			**Action**			**Actions across Activity**		
trial	1	2	3	4	5	6	7	8	9	10	11	12
Block 1	6	2	5	4	2	3	1	1	1	6	5	3
Block 2	5	2	8	4	2	4	1	1	1	5	4	5
Ave #Act	4.67			3.17			1			4.67		

Table 3. Group Times Items: *Activity* trials shift an activity. *Actions-in-Activity* shift a subset of actions in an activity. *Action* shifts one action. *Actions-across-Activities* shift consecutive actions running across activities. Cell values are number of actions in each item to be shifted, with average for each type of trial listed below. Trial shows item order.

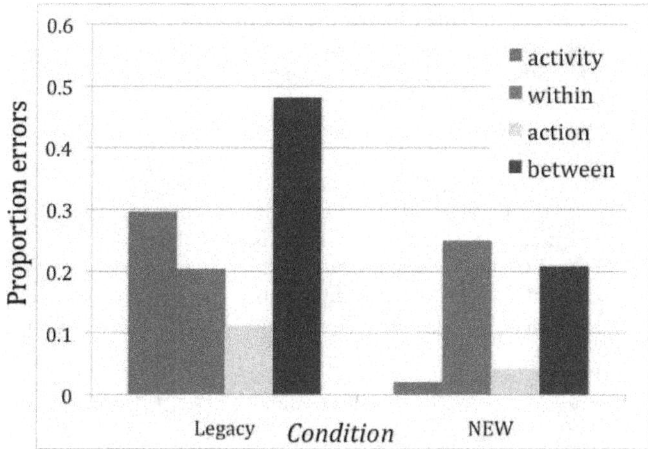

Figure 6. Proportion errors for the LEGACY and the NEW conditions, on the 4 Group Times item types: shift an Activity, shift Actions within an Activity, shift an Action, and shift Actions spanning Activities.

The error data divided by activity type and condition, in Figure 6, show the same, predicted pattern as the response times. Average times when error data were included were very slightly longer than with errors excluded.

Results Summary

We found overall faster, more accurate performance for participants using the system that better matches the domain structure (NEW), than for the system with poor match (LEGACY). Most importantly, we found the differential patterns of performance predicted by DSA-match: NEW was (equally) fast shifting Actions and Activities, and slower when multiple individual actions within an activity had to be selected; LEGACY was slow shifting Activities, faster when only a subset of Actions in an Activity needed to be changed, and, broadly, performance was faster the fewer actions to move. This NEW advantage depends on the availability of the Activity element.

Match to domain structure predicted clear, substantial impact on usefulness and usability, both overall and in determining where points of relative ease or difficulty will be encountered. In turn, this suggests the value of prioritizing domain structure analysis in conducting a needs analysis. The study provides initial evidence that the DSA approach is worth further development.

Our approach a) identified/created systems with large differences in match to DSA and b) identified specific performance patterns based on the differences in matching. Support for these predictions provides one step in supporting the claim that DSA distinctively contributes to building better systems.

From a practical perspective we found that time needed for editing tasks of the sort done by ADCO was cut in half and errors comparably reduced with the NEW system. These dramatic differences in performance are important, and we hope they will contribute toward building better tools for ADCO.

VII. CONCLUSIONS

Implications

The research we reported here illustrates how DSA can guide the whole development cycle. We ran through the cycle, in miniature, from needs analysis through design, development, and evaluation. A domain structure analysis identifies domain organization and the elements and relations composing that organization. An explicit, external, shared representation of this information is critical to develop successful software. Interaction structure of a candidate design can be matched to the DSA; alternative designs can be compared for extent and locus of how each matches to the DSA. Match and mismatch can generate predictions about performance, which can be tested in the target domain or in analogs that preserve domain structure.

When we carried out this cycle, we found large differences, predicted by DSA match, in an experimental analog of ADCO planning work. If validation accumulates, DSA could be applied to novel design problems without resorting to empirical test of predictions.

Relation to Prior Research

We share with many researchers the recognition that some form of Needs Analysis is critical to guide the design and/or evaluation of software and other socio-technological systems. Several interrelated approaches have been proposed, which prioritize different types of information yet overlap considerably, e.g., task analysis may reveal information about domain ontology through the objects and agents involved in the tasks. We believe Domain Structure Analysis can be efficiently and explicitly derived and is particularly valuable for high-stakes, safety-critical, problem-solving information work.

Our empirical evaluation compared a legacy system to one designed to match the DSA, and found dramatic advantages as predicted by DSA match. The study was ambitious in that it sought evidence about the overall design process and resulting system. A similar goal motivated an empirical comparison of systems with displays that provided better and worse match to the information needs in process control, e.g. [17] cited in [3]; here the intent was to support ecological interface design and the work analysis that motivates it. Because the systems compared and the process of developing them may differ in many ways these system-wide comparisons cannot uniquely specify the reason for a found benefit: multiple explanations for a supported prediction are possible. In contrast, studies which vary an isolated aspect of match to domain structure can make more precise claims about the limited aspect investigated.

Our approach compared a heuristic pair of applications: a legacy system and a novel system that was feasible to construct from pre-existing components. Heuristic comparison is feasible in circumstances where assessing minimally contrasting sets of applications is not.

Limitations

Our goal is to assess whether system performance improves from better match to the DSA. The support from this study is tempered because other differences between systems might have contributed. We did not sample multiple designs that matched versus violated the DSA, nor did we assess minimally contrasting pairs. In a more ideal –and very expensive study-- the effect of match to domain structure would be assessed by testing multiple designs with high versus low match to DSA. Further, our study did not investigate relative effectiveness of different approaches to needs analysis. Nor have we explored whether and when a domain structure analysis may provide a sufficient needs analysis and when it must be integrated with other information. Additional investigation is called for.

Finally, a practical limitation concerning the ADCO domain must be noted. The DSA addressed a limited scope of work: that carried out by one individual. However, communication, information exchange, and negotiation are critical parts of ADCO planning work. While the prototype we developed is a very promising basis for software redesign, an extended Domain Structure Analysis for the larger scope of work would be required prior to designing a prototype adequate for actual planning.

Future work

Our underlying motivation is to understand how the process of needs analysis can be made as efficient as possible. The foundational step is understanding what information is important, in what contexts. Based on this, we are working to convert this understanding to technology. For example, we are exploring how analysis of documents might bootstrap building a characterization of domain structure; we are also exploring how hypothesized domain-structure might best be represented. We are aware of the costs, as well as the value, of needs analysis for design and evaluation. By understanding needs analysis we hope to identify most efficient methods and tools, and to reduce the burden of these effective needs analysis methods.

ACKNOWLEDGMENTS

We thank Erin Reed and Tarik Ward, the ADCO's who worked with us, taught us, and checked materials; and Steven Hillenius, Melissa Ludowise, Mike McCurdy, and the SPIFe development team for help with the software. We thank Space Human Factors Engineering for funding.

REFERENCES

1. Beyer, H., and Holtzblatt, K. Contextual Design: Defining Customer-Centered Systems. San Francisco, CA: Morgan Kaufmann (1998).
2. Billman, D., Feary, M., Schreckenghost, D., & Sherry, L. (2010) Needs Analysis: The Case of Flexible Constraints and Mutable Boundaries. In *Proc. CHI 2009*, ACM Press pp. 4597-4612.
3. Burns, C. M., & Hajdukiewicz, J. R. (2004). Ecological interface design. Boca Raton, FL: CRC Press.
4. Butler, K.A, Jiajie Zhang, J., Esposito, C., Ali Bahrami, A. Ron Hebron, R., & David Kieras. Work-Centered Design: A Case Study of a Mixed-Initiative Scheduler. In *Proc. CHI 2007*, ACM Press (2007).
5. Butler & Zhang (2009) Design models for interactive problem-solving context & ontology, representation & routines. In *Proc. CHI 2009*, ACM Press pp. 4315-4320.
6. Card, S. K., Mackinlay, J. D., & Shneiderman, B. (1999). Information visualization: Using vision to think. San Francisco, CA: Morgan-Kaufmann.
7. Chilana, P.K., Wobbrock, J.O., & Ko, A.J. (2010) Understanding Usability Practises in Complex Domains. In *Proc. CHI 2010*, ACM Press pp. 2337-2346.
8. Diaper, D. & Stanton, N.A. (2004) *The Handbook of Task Analysis for Human-Computer Interaction*. LErlbaum Associates, Mahway, NJ.
9. Elliott, G., Crawford, J., Watson, M., Sanderson, P., & Naikar, N. (2000). Knowledge elicitation techniques for modeling intentional systems with Cognitive Work Analysis. *Proceedings of the Fifth Australian Aviation Psychology Symposium.*
10. Ellis, S. R. (2000). Collision in Space. Ergonomics in Design: The Quarterly of Human Factors Applications, 8(1), 4-9.
11. Feary, M., Sherry, L., Polson, P., and Fennel, K. (2003) Incorporating Cognitive Usability into Software Design Processes. In Harris, D., Duffy, V., Smith, M., and Stephandis, C. (Eds.), *Human-Centered Computing: Cognitive, Social, and Ergonomic Aspects*, Volume 3, Lawrence Erlbaum, Mahweh, NJ, p. 427-431.
12. Feltovich, P. J., Hoffman, R. R., Woods, D., and Roesler, A. (2004). Keeping It Simple: How the Reductive Tendency Affects Cognitive Engineering, *IEEE Intelligent Systems*, May-June, IEEE Computer Society Publications Office, Los Alamitos, CA, p.90-95.
13. Johnson, H., & Johnson, P. (1991). Task knowledge structures: Psychological basis and integration into system design. Acta Psychologica, 78, 3-26.
14. Kieras, D. E. (1996). Task analysis and the design of functionality. In A. Tucker (Ed.) *The Computer Science and Engineering Handbook (2nd Ed)*. Boca Raton, CRC Inc.
15. Leveson, N. (1995) Safeware: System Safety and Computers. Addison-Wesley, New York, NY, USA.
16. McCurdy, M. (2009) Planning Tools for Mars Surface Operations: Humn-Computer Interactions Lessons Learne. IEEE AC.
17. Moradi-Nadimian (2003). Cited in Burns, C. M., & Hajdukiewicz, J. R. (2004). Ecological interface design. Boca Raton, FL: CRC Press.
18. Perrow, C. (1984). Normal Accidents: Living with High-Risk Technologies. New York: Basic Books, Inc., Publishers.
19. Rasmussen, J., Pejtersen, A. M., & Goodstein, L. P. (1994). Cognitive systems engineering. New York: Wiley.
20. Schraagen, J. M., Chipman, S. F., & Shalin, V. L. (2000). Cognitive task analysis. Mahwah, N.J.: L. Erlbaum Associates.
21. Vicente.K. (1999). *Cognitive Work Analysis: Toward Safe, Productive, and Healthy Computer-based Work*. LErlbaum Associates, Mahway, NJ.
22. Zacks, J. M. T., B. (2001). Event structure in perception and conception. Psychological Bulletin, 127, 3-21.
23. Zhang J. (1996). A representational analysis of relational information displays. *International Journal of Human-Computer Studies*, 45, 59-74.

Developmentally Situated Design (DSD): Making Theoretical Knowledge Accessible to Designers of Children's Technology

Tilde Bekker
Department of Industrial Design
Eindhoven University of Technology
P.O. Box 513, Den Dolech 2, 5600 MB
Eindhoven, The Netherlands
m.m.bekker@tue.nl

Alissa N. Antle
School of Interactive Arts & Technology
Simon Fraser University
250 -13450 102 Avenue, Surrey, B.C.
V3T 0A3 Canada
aantle@sfu.ca

ABSTRACT
There is a wealth of theoretical knowledge about the developmental abilities and skills of children. However, this knowledge is not readily accessible to designers of interactive products. In this paper, we present the requirements, design and evaluation of developmentally situated design (DSD) cards. DSD cards are a design tool that makes age specific information about children's developing cognitive, physical, social, and emotional abilities readily accessible for designers. Initial requirements were elicited through interviews with design practitioners and students. The cards were evaluated through a design-in-use study in which design students used the cards to address three different design problems. Our analysis of observational notes and post-design interviews revealed how the cards' characteristics enabled different kinds of uses including framing, orienting, inspiring, informing, integrating and constraining. We conclude with a discussion of possible refinements and an analysis of the strengths and weaknesses of our approach.

Author Keywords
Interaction design, design cards, design tools, design methods, child development, child-computer interaction.

ACM Classification Keywords
H5.m. Information interfaces and presentation (e.g., HCI): Miscellaneous; H.1.2 [User/Machine Systems]: Design.

General Terms: Design

INTRODUCTION
This paper describes the development of a card-based design tool to support designers in taking into account children's abilities and skills during various phases of the design process. It is assumed that designers need to apply knowledge about users in design approaches such as user-centred design [31] and participatory design [28]. They can do this in various ways. They can involve users as participants or they can use analytical methods or tools that contain knowledge about users. These two approaches are complementary. For example, in early design, users can be involved in a participatory design session and/or designers can apply design principles based on empirically generated knowledge, such as the principles for user interface design [29]. In the evaluation phase, a user interface design can be evaluated by having users interact with the interface using a think-aloud method [25] and/or it can be evaluated by having experts apply a usability inspection method such as cognitive walkthrough approach [20]. Many existing analytical tools and methods can be used fairly generically, but do not include specific knowledge about children.

Designers must understand and consider children's developmental abilities and limitations to ensure that products are appropriate for the intended age group [3, 6]. There are some design methods that facilitate the consideration children's developmental abilities in the design process. For example, the Nielsen Norman Group have developed as set of design guidelines for websites for children [16]. SEEM is a usability inspection method that can be used to evaluate computer games for children [4]. However, few of these approaches are based on knowledge about children's developmental stages, ages and abilities. Another issue is that existing methods are usually only usable in one phase of the design process (e.g. evaluation) rather than making information about child development available throughout the design process. An exception is Antle's child-based personas [1].

In this paper we begin by describing how we established the need to bring developmentally specific knowledge about children into the design process. We did this by interviewing design practitioners and design students about their approaches when designing with children. We translated their needs into specific requirements for a design tool. A design tool can take many forms from a software application that specifies type and placement of interface elements (e.g.

ECLIPSE direct manipulation tool [12]) to non-computation materials that can inspire and inform design concepts (e.g. IDEO Methods Cards [19]). Based on prior work using cards in design (e.g. [17, 18, 21]), we decided to develop a card tool. We present our initial design of the DSD cards which are a set of 42 cards (14 developmental concepts x 3 age segments) that can be used in a variety of design activities. We evaluated the cards through a design-in-use study in which designers used the cards in three design cases which included concept development brainstorming and interface redesign for different children's age groups and classes of products. We present our analysis of how the characteristics of the cards enable certain kinds of uses which are ubiquitous in different design practices. We also present suggestions for the refined design of the DSD cards, and a discussion of strengths and weakness of our approach.

RELATED WORK

User Centred Design (UCD) involves iterative cycles of analysis, design and evaluation throughout the entire design process [31]. One key aspect of UCD is the recommendation to focus early on users and tasks [15]. Similarly, a principle for UCD practice for children is that there is no design that fits all, but rather design should be driven by knowledge of the target users [22]. The abilities and skills of children are different from adults' and change as children age and develop. Designers following a UCD approach for children require developmentally situated information about children in order to understand how to design for use that is "challenging but attainable for most children of a given age range, flexible enough to respond to inevitable individual variation, and consistent with children's ways of thinking and learning" [8, (p.161)].

While it is possible and desirable to design iteratively working with child participants (e.g. [11]) or informants (e.g. [26]), this does not guarantee that designs will be developmentally appropriate. Analytical methods that complement participatory approaches are needed.

Analytical design methods are based on theoretically and/or empirically derived knowledge. There is a wealth of theoretical information about child development. However, largely this information is dense, abstract and thus not accessible or usable for designers [1]. Sutcliff provides two requirements for theoretical knowledge to be applicable in design. First, the complexity of the theory has to be hidden from the designer. Second, knowledge has to be generalized so it can be used in a wide range of contexts [30]. In particular, knowledge about children's cognitive and physical skills and abilities, and emotional and social needs and abilities is important to ensure developmentally situated design [1]. What are needed are methods or tools which can be used to make theoretical knowledge about children's needs, skills and abilities accessible to designers.

There are various design methods and tools that facilitate incorporation of theoretical knowledge about users in the design process. For example, a Cognitive Walkthrough is a usability inspection method intended to introduce a theoretical model of how users learn through exploration of a problem (i.e. a new user interface) into a code walk through method [10]. The problem is that most of the most common analytical design methods (i.e. those taught in design and HCI schools) are not specific to children. A second problem is that despite many efforts to develop and market UCD tools, current studies show that the industry is still dominated by tools that do not support the activities and work styles of designers [7]. Rogers suggests that making theoretical knowledge easier to use requires a focus on the process of design [24]. What is needed is a child-specific design tool that makes theoretical knowledge accessible to designers *and* is developed to support how designers work in practice.

Developmentally Situated Design (DSD)

There are few child-specific methods or tools that can be used to facilitate developmentally situated design (DSD). However, there are several design frameworks that aim to incorporate theoretically derived information on child development into the design process. For example, the Child-Tangible-Interaction (CTI) Framework provides general concepts taken from developmental cognition which may be relevant for designers of tangible user interfaces for children [2]. CARSS (Context, Activities, Roles, Stakeholders, Skills), is a learner-centered design framework specifically for child learners [14]. Gelderblom presents ten lessons for designing for 5 to 8 years olds derived from theoretical and empirical research [13]. The benefit of these frameworks is that they provide theoretically derived concepts and considerations that may inform design. However, there are no methods or tools associated with them that can support designers to incorporate these ideas into the design process.

In the context of an industry design project, Antle describes and analyzes a method for creating and using child-personas in design [1]. The approach incorporates theoretical knowledge on the abilities and needs of children as well as and context specific design parameters into child-persona profiles. These profiles are then a tool that be used throughout the design process much like adult personas, as described by [9, 23]. However, the resultant child-personas contain information that is specific to a single design problem, and thus do not provide for reuse. We build on Antle's work in [1] with the development of the DSD card tool.

Cards as Design Tools

One approach that has been used to make conceptual knowledge from design frameworks both accessible and reusable in design is cards. Cards, like Post-it® Notes, are small which means that information must be presented simply and concisely. Their form enables a variety of uses, reuse (through their robust form), and supports a flexible hands-on approach to bringing conceptual information into design. Several design researchers have explored this approach. For example, Hornecker presents cards and a card brainstorming exercise that transforms her conceptual tangible interaction framework themes into a tool for creative dialogue during design [18]. She describes a card game which can be used to provide the structure for using the cards in an early design phase. Lucero and Arrasvuori created *PLEX Cards* to communicate a framework about designing for playfulness [21]. They chose cards over other formats (e.g. poster, projection of PowerPoint slides, handouts) because they found that the affordances of cards brought the content *into* the design process better than the other formats. Halskov and Dalsgård present domain and technology cards and a method for using them called the Inspiration Card Workshop [17]. They provide a good overview of other research that has used cards as design tools.

Another approach is to use cards that contain information about user research methods. IDEO published a deck of 51 Methods Cards that represent diverse ways that designers can understand the people they are designing for [19].

We suggest that card sets are a *form* of design tool that can be used to make conceptual information accessible to designers and can be used to support designers how they work in practice.

INTERVIEWS WITH DESIGN PRACTITIONERS AND STUDENTS

To empirically validate the need for making theoretical information accessible and usable for designers and to gather input for the design of the DSD card tool we conducted interviews with design practitioners and design students both in person and using Skype.

Interview Method

We decided to interview both experienced design practitioners and design students to get a diverse perspective on possible use of theoretical knowledge in designing for children. The interview consisted of 20 open-ended questions asking about use of knowledge about children in their design practices, possibilities for improving future design practice by making knowledge more accessible and requirements for a possible card tool. The interviews took between 30 minutes and 1 hour. The participants were asked to focus on a single recent design project when answering their questions. The interviews were audio recorded and subsequently analyzed to search for evidence about the need for a DSD approach to design, as well as to gather insights and information related to requirements and potential uses for a DSD card tool. We looked for repeated themes as evidence for validation and to inform requirements, as well as using our own experience as designers to identify important and useful card requirements from the interview responses.

Participants

A total of six design practitioners and six design students participated in the study. The design practitioners had an average experience of 10 years of designing products for children. The design students were Master's and Ph.D. students who had an average experience of working on two design project for children. The participants worked in different countries, including Canada, Europe and the United States. They worked on a wide variety of projects, including websites, exhibit design, educational computer games, online games, intelligent toys, and communication products.

Results of Interviews

All interviewees felt that their design practice could be improved by a tool that made developmentally specific knowledge about children accessible in design. The interviews also provided information about a variety of design practices in which a DSD tool could be used, the ways that cards might be used in each practice, and characteristics of the cards that would contribute to the effectiveness and reuse.

Child-Design Practice Needs DSD

The participants described very diverse design practices in terms of the intended target users, the number of people working on a design team, the number and variety of stakeholders in a project, the technologies used in the project and the length of the projects. During these practices they applied different kinds of knowledge about children taken from a wide range of domains including: social psychology, learning theory and marketing theory. For example, one practitioner used the broad theory of Constructivism to loosely inform his design for an interactive museum exhibit. Another practitioner used the concept of the Zone of Proximal Development to inform specific design features in a web based learning activity. They also used more experience-based information such as observations of children, visits to stores where products or toys for children were sold, and knowledge gleaned from other designers to inform all aspects of their designs.

Overall the interviewees felt that they would benefit from having easy access to information about the developmental stages of children during a design project. This would be complementary to some of the information they were already using. Several people mentioned that there was often a need for in-depth knowledge about a specific topic as well as easy accessible overviews of broad developmental topics. In some cases the interviewees felt that having a quick access to developmentally specific information might speed up the design process or that it might prevent them from making incorrect design decisions.

Less than half the interviewees had used explicit descriptions of the target user group (e.g. personas, user profiles) in their design practice. What they wanted was not a user profiling tool but a more flexible tool that would bring specific bits of information into their design process for a project. They also mentioned specific topics that they would be interested in including knowing about: play styles for different age groups, how children develop their sense of humor; and how children's interest in fantasy and more real-life topics develops over time.

Possible Uses of DSD Cards

Interviewees were largely positive about the idea of using DSD cards. They expressed many uses for such a set of cards designed to make theoretical knowledge about children accessible. For example, they gave the following possible ways the DSD cards could be used: in brainstorming to provide inspiration, to shift direction, or provide a starting point; as part of requirements elicitation; to inspire and inform early design concept development; as heuristics; as part of a design brief; to identity design constraints; as part of design guideline documents; to create personas; to understand tradeoffs through comparisons about how different designs meet different needs or skill levels; to inform specific design decisions; to redesign a user interface by providing information and focus on what to change; in design evaluation to identify the constructs and capabilities to evaluate; in a user study with children to support questioning about what they like and dislike about a design.

Based on Antle's previous work [1], we had initially thought that the cards might be used primarily to create personas that could be used in different projects. An important insight from talking to design practitioners and students was that the cards could be used much more widely than in the context of persona or user profile creation.

We also developed a more detailed understanding of how a card tool might be useful in relation to communicating with different stakeholders that participate in a design project. For example, the card tool could be used to bring a new team member up to speed about abilities of and assumptions about the user group. It could also be used to communicate design rationale for design decisions to clients in ways that were more credible than just talking. The cards could also be used to have (older) children discuss their abilities and interests.

Characteristics of the DSD Cards

The interviews also revealed suggestions about card characteristics that might make them usable in design practice. The cards should provide simple and up-to-date information. It would be useful if the source of the information was clear, so that more detailed information could be found easily and that the credibility of the information was evident. The cards should provide information about all aspects of child development including: cognitive, social, emotional, and physical development. Multiple team members should be able to easily and quickly use the cards. The tool used to create the cards should be open source, so that other people can contribute relevant knowledge.

Summary of Interviews

Design practitioners and design students do use knowledge about users in design. They use it both early in the design process to decide on global design decisions, and to make more detailed design decisions later. They do not always make explicit user profiles or descriptions of children for their projects. However, they would like easy access to information about developmental abilities of children and are interested in using a card tool that provides information about children's capabilities and interest. They indicated that such a card tool has the potential to be useful during the various design activities including: brainstorming, planning an evaluation session, presenting a design to a client or discussing a design with children users.

They suggested that such a tool would be complementary to the approaches they now use in design practice. Benefits of such a tool would be that it could be used as an inspiration source, it could speed up the design process, it could provide easy access to information during design activities with various stakeholders, and that it could prevent incorrect design decisions.

REQUIREMENTS FOR THE DSD CARD TOOL

Based on our literature review, our own experiences in designing and teaching about designing for children, and the results of the interviews, we developed with an initial set of requirements for the cards:

1. The cards should contain information about *cognitive, social, emotional* and *physical* development of children. These developmental categories should be easily distinguishable (e.g. by colour coding them).
2. Since most computational applications are designed to support and augment children's abilities, the cards should provide information about what children are *practicing* rather than what they can already do.
3. The information should be made accessible by writing it in layman's terms, focusing on the underlying concepts of development rather than describing complete developmental theories.
4. The information about abilities, skills and needs should also be made accessible through text and illustrations of children using both every day and computer-mediated activities and products.
5. The cards should be designed to be flexible enough that they can be used in variety of design activities and with different design methods [18].
6. The cards should be designed to facilitate collaboration [5].

THE DESIGN OF THE DSD CARDS

Based our goal to make theoretical knowledge about children accessible, usable and reusable in a wide variety of design practices and suggestions taken from the practitioner interviews, an initial design for a set of DSD cards was created (Figure 1). We started with sketches and iterated variations until we settled on a design that fit our goals. We worked with a graphic designer to formalize our design in a digital format and then created a sample set of 42 cards (available at www.antle.iat.sfu.ca/DSD).

Figure 1: Example card.

The main design rationale for the cards is described below. The four main developmental card types are colour coded to be easily recognizable: cognitive (blue), social (red), emotional (purple) and physical (green). The main category is followed by a sub-header describing the topic subcategory. The front of the card contains a textual description of the ability or skill children are practicing stated abstractly. For example, for the *Cognitive* category and has a topic subcategory *Reasoning and Logic skills: Instructions* for 7-9 age group, and the text is: "Practicing following a small sequence of instructions to achieve a task." Two pictures on the front show children engaged in this practice; one from everyday life, and one using an interactive product. The back of the card contains textual descriptions, presented as quotes from a girl and a boy, that concretely exemplify a way that a child can practice this skill in an everyday context. The descriptions include the activity, with whom they do it, what artifacts are involved, and where it takes place. For example, "She likes to make art projects with her two best friends on the dining room table." The bottom of the card shows the age range the information applies to.

The topics that are addressed by the initial card set are:

Cognitive: reasoning and problem solving: instructions, reasoning and logic skills: problem solving, reading, information processing and working memory.

Emotional: emotion expression, emotion regulation, emotion understanding.

Social: self-esteem, perspective taking, friendships.

Physical: locomotion, manipulation (gross), manipulation (fine) and stability.

These topics are not meant to be inclusive of all relevant topics, but rather to provide a sample of topics that we believe, based on our experience as designers, are important. In our experience, these topics may be relevant to specific types of children's interactive products or applications (e.g. gross motor skills for whole body interaction) or applicable to a wide variety of products (e.g. reasoning and problem solving: instructions) and thus would be appropriate to use to evaluate our card design.

Conceptual information for the cards was distilled from content in various textbooks on children's cognitive, social, emotional and physical development, from psychology and design journal articles on each specific topic, and from our own research publications. Examples were brainstormed and came largely from our in depth experience of working with children in both professional and non-professional life. At this stage content has not yet been validated through external review.

DESIGN-IN-USE STUDY

The purpose of the user study with design students was to evaluate the potential of a DSD tool based on our initial design of the card tool. Specifically, we wanted to examine in detail how designers would use the cards during different design activities. By examining how designers used the cards based on the cards' characteristics (content, presentation, form) we could evaluate our design and identify areas of improvement.

Study Design and Method

We combined an observational with an interview-based method. We conducted two similar studies at our universities (SFU in the Vancouver area of Canada and TU/e in Eindhoven, The Netherlands).We observed pairs or trios of design students doing three different design activities, one early concept development brainstorming task and two later stage redesigns of an existing solution. The design students first received an explanation about the DSD cards, and about the specifics of the first design case. They were told they could choose for themselves which cards to use. The cards were given to the students sorted by overall category and by age. They worked on the first design task for 30 minutes, followed by a short interview including questions about how they used the cards, what information was missing, and suggestions for changes. We then repeated this procedure for the second design case. In each location, we ended with a group discussion in which they were asked ten open questions. The questions probed how the cards might be useful in other design activities and asked for suggestions for changes. During the design tasks we observed how they used the cards, and noted down comments they made while using the cards. We recorded the interviews and took notes.

Participants

A total of nine design graduate students (Masters or Ph.D.) participated in the user study, four at SFU and five at TU/e. Six students were male, and three were female. Six students worked in pairs and three in a trio, and all groupings had worked together previously. The students had a background in either Industrial or Interaction Design, and had all worked on design projects for children before.

Design Cases

We chose three design cases that we expected would have different design foci based on the design goal, kind of product, target age range and relevance of cognitive, social, emotional and physical developmental abilities of children. The first design case was an initial concept development of a tangible user interface to support 10 to 12 year old boys in sharing a sense of connectedness. The second case was a redesign of an older children's multi-touch tabletop game about sustainability to make it accessible for children of all ages. The third design case was a redesign of a simple adult online game to make it suitable for children aged 7 to 9 years.

One design case focused on a broad age group (case two), and two design cases focused on a narrow age group. The cases were chosen to examine the potential of the cards in early (concept development) and late stage (redesign) design activities. They also cover a broad range of product categories (tangible, tabletop, and web) so that the design students needed to consider different abilities. For example the first design case is focused on social-emotional needs. In each location, each group did the concept development design case, and one of the two redesign cases (based on the availability of the interface to be redesigned).

Results of the Design-in-Use Study

We analyzed our observational notes and interview responses for each design case. Each of us reviewed the data individually, and then compared our findings to look for commonalities and omissions. We identified behavioral patterns about how the designers used the cards to inform their design activities. For example, in design case two (redesign for broad ages) we both noticed that several times designers picked up two cards for the same concept and different age categories and compared children's abilities between age groups. We found that designers used the information about users both for developing a deeper understanding of the users (empathy) and for triggering new product ideas (inspiration). We found the following patterns of behavior related to how the designers used the cards based on the type of design activity and the characteristics of the cards. We group these by theme to demonstrate how the cards can be used to make developmental theory accessible in a variety of design activities and different projects.

Overall Uses and Feedback

The content provided by the DSD card tool was judged to be relevant for design. Participants mentioned that the topics for the four card categories needed to be extended, as we had explained in the introduction of the study. They made some suggestions for topics that they would be interested in, such as social play styles for different age segments.

Overall, the participants were satisfied with the manner in which the information was presented on the cards. They felt that the information on the front, which explains what abilities and skills children are practicing, was complementary to the information about specific examples of such activities in daily lives of children on the back of the cards.

The participants had many ideas about how to change the form of the cards. A more sturdy material for the cards would improve the cards' tangible properties. The card size and format was good for holding them, positioning them on the table and showing them to others. Some participants felt that a different shape, such as a hexagon shape would provide more opportunities to explore and show relationships between cards.

Orienting Team Members

Some students sorted through the cards to determine which cards were relevant for the design task in order to orient themselves to category topics and specific children's abilities as they selected a focus for the design problem. We observed that they initially did this individually but then used the cards to orient their team member(s). The cards' form supports this kind of collaboration by providing a tangible reference that designers use to come to a shared understanding of the nature of the design task (Figure 2). This is similar to the finding that cards were used as an orienting tool in brainstorming [18]. However, using the cards to orient each other was not limited to early concept development activities. It was observed in all the design cases.

Framing and Reframing the Problem Space

In all three design cases, we saw instances where the cards supported framing and reframing of the problem [27]. For example, at the beginning of the design case about redesigning the multi-touch tabletop game for younger children, one designer framed the problem narrowly. He sorted and grouped only the blue cognitive cards on the table and said "*We need to change the cognitive aspects ... that's the focus.*" However, the second designer picked up the green physical cards (Figure 3) and said "*You're thinking cognitive but it's a touch interface ... also manipulation. I'm going to grab this. There's manipulation gross and fine ...we need to think about this too.*" In this case, having the physical category of cards alerted the designers early on about the importance of considering not only age specific cognitive abilities but motor skills, reframing the problem more broadly.

Some groups systematically sorted through the stack of cards and selected which cards they thought were relevant to the design problem (framing) using the topics (i.e. simple concepts) but later came back to other topics by browsing discarded cards (reframing). For example in one case, the pair first divided the cards and each took two categories. They selected relevant topics, and discussed how they might be relevant (framing). Later on they looked back at the cards that were initially rejected to look for other topics that provided new angles (reframing). This type of activity was enabled because the cards can be sorted, categories were colour coded, and topics were simply and clearly stated near the top of the cards.

Figure 2: Orienting each other to key theoretical concepts or specific abilities through a common card reference.

Figure 3. Reframing the problem by considering physical cards (green) in addition to cognitive (blue).

Inspiration and Idea Generation

The text in the speech bubbles provides example activities that children enjoy and engage in. This can function as a source of inspiration. Since there are both girl and boy speech bubbles the cards were used for inspiration in the boys' only design case and more generally for all children in the other cases. The pictures were also good as a source of inspiration because the speech bubble text is very short and may be slightly ambiguous. Designers mentioned that keywords related to the pictures would enhance the interpretation of the pictures, although this might reduce their inspirational value by constraining interpretations.

Comparing Information

The cards can be used to compare abilities in different age categories and in this way inform design (Figure 4).

The front of the cards gives indication of abilities through text and an image. The back of the cards can be to determine what kind of actions and activities children are practicing. For example, in the multi-touch tabletop game redesign for younger children, the two designers were comparing several cognitive cards by looking at the photographs on the front and back for the same topics but different ages.

One designer held up the reasoning and problem solving: instructions cards for the 5 - 6 and 7 - 9 year olds and said, "*I'm trying to understand the difference between age groups – surely older can do what younger can do so target younger.*" The other designer then said, "*But we need to think about, to make sure that the older kids won't get bored.*" The cards were used for comparing what children in different age segments could do to ensure that the design met children's needs based on concrete information.

Figure 4. Comparing the same topic for two age categories.

Expanding the Design Space

We saw various instances where participants combined cards from different categories to examine new possibilities (Figure 5). Often participants first go through all cards of one category to examine their relevance to the design problem. However, later in the sessions participants often explore combining cards from different categories (e.g. social and physical) to examine how this might inform design decisions.

Figure 5. Combining different categories.

Counter to our expectations that they might only consider the most obvious categories; almost all groups examined cards from all three or four categories for each design task. Combining different categories and topics supports designers to expand the design space by finding relationships between different cards. For example, the pair of students designing a tangible solution to support boys in feeling connected game up with a new design idea by combining the physical card of locomotion with an emotional card about expressing emotions.

Integrating with Other Design Materials

The physical nature of the cards; their small form and ease of handling supports designers to use them in an integrated fashion alongside other design materials. For example, they can be placed spatially on a sheet of paper where a designer is sketching out an interface design. We observed that designers used them in this way as a constant reminder about specific considerations represented by the card(s). The ability to place the cards virtually anywhere enabled the information on the cards to be referred to in the location where they are relevant. In contrast, consider a text book on child development that would have to be opened to specific pages for each design consideration. The cards provide a way of distributing and integrating information *into* the design process through their material form. They can be easily grouped, moved, flipped over etc. as needed to inform design.

Constraining the Design Solution

The cards can be used to help designers constrain the design solution by determining what children are not (yet) able to do. The text about skills children practice is concrete and provides opportunities for determining constraints. For example, in the multi-touch tabletop game redesign for younger children, one designer said, *"I'm trying to understand the parameters ... No fine motor skill – not concerned with that. If they can use scissors and draw numbers they can use the user interface. They can't read – don't need that. Can follow simple step by step instructions. Need this."* In this way he used went through a subset of the cards one by one to constrain what the design needed to address.

Post-Design Task Interviews

When asked how they might you use these cards in other design cases, the design students mentioned many of the uses for the cards that were the same as those that the design practitioners had mentioned including: ideation, communicating with clients, evaluation heuristics and a tool to work with older children. They also confirmed that the cards could be used to expand a design or constrain a solution, reframe by considering new factors, and provide concrete information as observed above. When asked how they would change the card design, they said it would be useful if you could quickly see the difference between the cards of different age segments, for example through colour coding or a tab-structure on the side of the cards. They felt the speech bubbles on the back were very useful to get a feel for the lives of children of a particular age, but would like to see more diverse examples of activities on the cards. For example, the physical cards mostly show examples related to physical games, but can be extended to other kinds of activities such as interacting with products.

When asked for suggestions for the tool redesign, the students expressed that they wanted aids to help explain how to use the cards (e.g. instruction sheet for each design case), an overview of the complete card set, and more information about relationships between cards. For example, how children's (social) ability of perspective taking is related to how their (cognitive) skills develop in reasoning and abstract thinking. They stated that would like to have references to other sources of information in case they wanted more in-depth explanations. They were interested in being able to have a quick overview of how children develop over time (from one age segment to the next), for example in a table format. They suggested that there should be some way to customize the cards for a specific design problem. They suggested the idea of blank cards so they could add cards with information specifically relevant for their design project.

Summary of Design-in-Use Study

Our study provides evidence that the DSD card tool was usable in all three design exercises. We suggest that it has the potential to be useful in wide range of design contexts. The study limitations were the short time taken to explain the information structure of the cards, the limited time for each design case and that the design cases represented only two types of activities (early and late stage).

RE-DESIGN OF CARD TOOL

Based on the results of the design-in-use study we determined the following suggestions for changes to the DSD card tool and usage:

- Complement pictures that illustrate the activities that children practice with keywords covering important concepts related to the abilities children are practicing.
- Provide a quick-start guide that explains different ways in which the cards can be used in different design activities, such as brainstorming, presenting designs and evaluating designs.
- Provide an instruction leaflet to explain the underlying structure of the cards.
- Provide an overview document that lists all card categories and sub categories.
- Provide a document that provides an overview of how children develop over time for each of the card tool's sub categories.
- Provide a method to link between different cards when designers combine the information from these cards for a specific design solution.
- Add questions to the cards to help designers think about how to apply the information to the design process.
- Make the difference between the abstract activity that children practice (on the front of the card) and the concrete examples of the activities (on the back) more clear and consistent.
- Add a graphical element to enable designers to quickly find the cards related to a specific age segment.

- Make the examples in the speech bubbles more diverse to cover a wider range of activities of children.

We intend to use this list to redesign the DSD card tool. Some of these revisions may result in complementary materials in forms other than cards. Future design-in-use studies will guide the development and evaluation of the card-set (and possibly complementary materials).

DISCUSSION

Design and Development of the Cards

The iterative design process in which we have combined theoretical knowledge from literature resources with practice-based knowledge from design practitioners and design students has resulted in a hands-on card-based tool that provides designers with knowledge about abilities of children in different age segments. The design-in-use study provided more detailed design insights about the *content*, *presentation* and *form* of the cards. Both studies informed our thinking about possible *uses* of the card tool. The *content* of the tool was informed by information about specific cognitive, emotional, social and emotional topics that should be covered. The design of the *presentation* of the cards was validated. Designers liked the inclusion of text and pictures about activities that children practice when developing skills and abilities, and the two quotes by children that provide concrete examples of the contexts in which children practice these skills. The visual and textual information provides a good combination of knowledge and inspiration for designers. The card physical *form* facilitated handling, sharing, organizing, sorting, and other ways of using them that supported different ways of informing design during two design activities.

Using the Cards in Design Practice

Unlike several previous card tools that were designed specifically to provide inspiration early in the design process (e.g. [17, 18, 21]) the DSD tool can be used in different design activities (concept development, redesign) at both early and late stages in the design cycle as illustrated in our design-in-use study.

The DSD cards simplify and summarize what is sometimes complex conceptual information in order to make it accessible to designers. The danger of this approach is that concepts may be misunderstood or misapplied. The theory of perceptual affordances as put forward by J.J. Gibson and then adopted and adapted in HCI is a classic case of this over simplification. One way to rectify this is to find a way to link summary information on cards to more detailed explanations taken from primary sources. We leave this to future work.

Hornecker suggests that most theory inspired design frameworks are descriptive, explanatory and rhetorical and that they would be more productive if they were also generative [18]. By making the DSD cards more generic, we have not provided any specific mechanisms (e.g. questions) or methods (e.g. game structure) which would support generative use. There is a trade-off here between using tool presentation and form to support specific versus generic design activities. It may be difficult to do both. We also leave this to future work.

Many participants in both studies suggested that the cards should be customizable to the specifics of the design problem, or use illustrations that were familiar to the designers. While it is possible to provide editable cards and blank card templates, supporting this functionality would require a software application which is beyond the scope of this work.

One limitation of the card tool is that it outlines specific abilities of children rather than providing information on broad theories which may be used to inform design as suggested by several design practitioners in our initial interviews (e.g. constructivism in museums).

CONCLUSIONS AND FUTURE WORK

The DSD card tool provides designers with a flexible design tool that makes theoretical knowledge about child development accessible to designers *and* is developed to support how designers work in practice. As such it is a complementary to other materials and to methods that are based on involving children in the design process.

We intend to develop the cards further by extending the number of cards for each category, and by checking with a wider range of design projects whether some theoretical topics need to be added. We will further optimize the examples provided on the cards to provide a diverse view of what children's world looks like at different phases in their life. In the future, we may examine whether to extend the cards with a digital tool that provides an up-to-date link to literature resources for each card, and/or explore how other formats (e.g. poster, handouts) may complement cards. We have not examined how the DSD cards would be used by professional designers under real life constraints but we hope that the DSD cards will improve child-computer interaction research and design practice by enabling designers to incorporate accessible and reusable knowledge about child development into projects through the design process.

ACKNOWLEDGMENTS

This research was funded in part by a SSHRC International Opportunities Fund Development Grant (Canada). We appreciate the thoughtful comments and suggestions made by the reviewers and the two associate chairs. Thank you.

REFERENCES

1. Antle, A.N. Child-based personas: Need, ability and experience. *Cognition, Technology & Work, Special Issue on Child Computer Interaction: Methodological Research 10* (2008), 155-166.
2. Antle, A.N. The CTI framework: Informing the design of tangible systems for children. In *Proc. TEI 2007*, ACM Press (2007), 195-202.

3. Baumgarten, M. Kids and the internet: a developmental summary. *Computers in Entertainment 1*, 1 (2003), 1-10.
4. Bekker, M.M., Baauw, E. and Barendregt, W. A comparison of two analytical evaluation methods for educational computer games for young children. *Cognition, Technology and Work, 10*, 2 (2008), 129-140.
5. Brandt, E. and Messeter, J. Facilitating collaboration through design games. In *Proc. Conference on Participatory Design,* ACM Press (2004), 121-131.
6. Bruckman, A., and Bandlow, A. HCI for kids. In Jacko, J., and Sears, A. (ed.) *Handbook of Human–Computer Interaction*, Lawrence Erlbaum, New Jersey, 2002, 428-440.
7. Campos, P. and Nunes, N. Towards useful and usable interaction design tools: CanonSketch, *Interacting with Computers 19*, 5-6 (2007), 597-613.
8. Clements, D.H. Computers in early childhood mathematics. *Contemporary Issues in Early Childhood 3*, 2 (2002), 160-181.
9. Cooper, A. *The Inmates are Running the Asylum.* SAMA, Indianapolis, IN, USA, 1999.
10. Dix, A., Finlay, J., Abowd, G.D. and Beale, R. *Human Computer Interaction*, Pearson Education Limited, Harlow, England, 2004.
11. Druin, A. The role of children in the design of new technology. *Behaviour & Information Technology 21*, 1 (2002), 1-25.
12. England, D. A user interface design tool. *SIGCHI Bulletin 19*, 2, (1987).
13. Gelderblom, H. and Kotzé, P. Ten design lessons from the literature on child development and children's use of technology. In *Proc. IDC 2009,* ACM Press (2009), 52-60.
14. Good, J. and Robertson, J., 16 (2006) 381-413. CARSS: A framework for learner-centered design with children. *International Journal of Artificial Intelligence in Education, 16* (2006), 381-413.
15. Gould, J.D. and Lewis, C. Designing for usability: Key principles and what designers think. *Communications of the ACM 28*, 3 (1985), 300 - 311
16. Group, Nielson Norman. *Usability of Websites for Children: Design Guidelines for Targeting Users Aged 3–12 Years* (2010). Available at http://www.nngroup.com/reports/kids/.
17. Halskov, K. and Dalsgård, P. Inspiration card workshops. In *Proc. DIS 2006*, ACM Press (2006), 2-11.
18. Hornecker, E. and Creative idea exploration within the structure of a guiding framework: the card brainstorming game. In *Proc. TEI 2010*, ACM Press (2010), 101-108.
19. IDEO, IDEO *Method Cards: 51 Ways to Inspire Design.* William Stout Architectural Books, Palo Alto, CA, USA, 2003.
20. Lewis, C.P., Wharton, C. and Rieman, J. Testing a walkthrough methodology for theory-based design of walk-up-and-use interfaces. In *Proc. CHI 1990*, ACM Press, (1990), 235–242.
21. Lucero, A. and Arrasvuori, J. PLEX Cards: a source of inspiration when designing for playfulness. . In Proc. *Fun and Games 2010,* ACM press (2010), 28-37.
22. Markopoulos, P. and Bekker, M.M. Interaction design and children. *Interacting with Computers, 15*, 2 (2003), 141-149.
23. Pruitt, J. and Adlin, T. *The Persona Lifecycle: Keeping People in Mind Throughout Product Design.* Morgan Kaufmann, New York, NY, USA, 2006.
24. Rogers, Y. New theoretical approaches for human-computer interaction. *Annual Review of Information, Science and Technology 38* (2004), 87-143.
25. Rubin, J., and Hudson, T. *Handbook of Usability Testing: How to Plan, Design, and Conduct Effective Tests.* John Wiley & Sons, Inc, New York, NY, 1994
26. Scaife, M. and Rogers, Y. Kids as informants: telling us what we didn't know or confirming what we knew already? In Druin, A. (ed.) *The Design of Children's Technology*, Morgan Kaufman, NY, USA, 1998.
27. Schon, D.A. *The Reflective Practioner.* Perseus, 1983.
28. Schuler, D., Namioka, A. *Participatory Design: Principles and Practices*. Erlbaum, Hillsdale, NJ, 1993.
29. Shneiderman, B. and Plaisant, C. *Designing the User Interface*. Addison-Wesley, NY, USA, 2010.
30. Sutcliffe, A. On the effective use and reuse of HCI knowledge. *ACM Transactions on Computer-Human Interaction 7*, 2 (2000), 197-221.
31. Vredenburg, C., Isensee, S. and Righi, C. *User-Centered Design: An Integrated Approach.* Prentice-Hall, Upper Saddle River, NJ, USA, 2002.

A Spreadsheet-Based User Interface for Managing Plural Relationships in Structured Data

Eirik Bakke, David R. Karger, and Robert C. Miller
MIT Computer Science and Artificial Intelligence Laboratory
32 Vassar Street, Cambridge, MA, USA
{ebakke,karger,rcm}@mit.edu

ABSTRACT
A key feature of relational database applications is managing *plural* relationships—one-to-many and many-to-many—between entities. However, since it is often infeasible to adopt or develop a new database application for any given schema at hand, information workers instead turn to spreadsheets, which lend themselves poorly to schemas requiring multiple related entity sets. In this paper, we propose to reduce the cost-usability gap between spreadsheets and tailor-made relational database applications by extending the spreadsheet paradigm to let the user establish relationships between rows in related worksheets as well as view and navigate the hierarchical cell structure that arises as a result. We present Related Worksheets, a spreadsheet-like prototype application, and evaluate it with a screencast-based user study on 36 Mechanical Turk workers. First-time users of our software were able to solve lookup-type query tasks with the same or higher accuracy as subjects using Microsoft Excel, in one case 40% faster on average.

ACM Classification Keywords
H.5.2 Information Interfaces and Presentation: User Interfaces—*Graphical User Interfaces (GUI)*

General Terms
Design

INTRODUCTION
Structured data is everywhere, and information workers need to manage it. On the storage side, the problem has largely been solved through the advent of relational databases; an off-the-shelf relational database management system will serve as a back-end for any database application. Yet, a back-end alone provides no user interface, and the database community has called for more work to be done on the front-end side of the application stack [1].

Certain kinds of database applications may be useful to a large number of people and organizations. For these, high-quality free or commercial GUI implementations are likely to be available. Examples include Personal Information Managers (PIMs), Customer Relationship Management (CRM) software, and business accounting software. Other applications are far more domain-specific, and have to be developed from scratch, possibly by an organization's IT department or an external consulting firm. Real-world examples range from cultural venue and event management systems[1] to software used by Norwegian immigration authorities to manage applications for political asylum[2].

When the effort required to either adopt or develop a new *tailor-made* relational database application is too high, information workers instead turn to a general and more familiar tool: the spreadsheet. One survey [7] shows that "sorting and database facilities" are the most commonly used spreadsheet features, with 70% of business professionals using them on a frequent or occasional basis. In contrast, less than half use "tabulation and summary measures such as averages/totals"—one of the design goals of the original VisiCalc spreadsheet—or more advanced features. Furthermore, spreadsheet users "shun enterprise solutions" [8] and "do not appear inclined to use other software packages for their tasks, even if these packages might be more suitable" [2]. Presumably these ostensibly suitable software packages include specialized database applications; after word processors, database software is the second kind of software most commonly encountered by spreadsheet users, with 60% of spreadsheet users reporting some use of them [7].

Once it is established that spreadsheets are being used for database tasks, we should ask what functionality is lost when we compare them to corresponding tailor-made relational database applications. In this paper we focus on the ability to maintain *plural* relationships—one-to-many and many-to-many—between different kinds of entities in a dataset, a key feature of any relational database application [3]. The world of tailor-made database applications has seen some fairly standard user interface paradigms for viewing and editing such relationships, see Figure 1. The user retrieves records using a *search form*, views results in a *table view*, and edits or views the details of individual entities in a *record view*. We consider two aspects of these user interfaces to be crucial to their relationship management capabilities. First, they can provide the user with joined views of related ta-

[1]E.g. `http://us.artifax.net`
[2]Unique Flyktning by Visma AS. `http://www.visma.com`

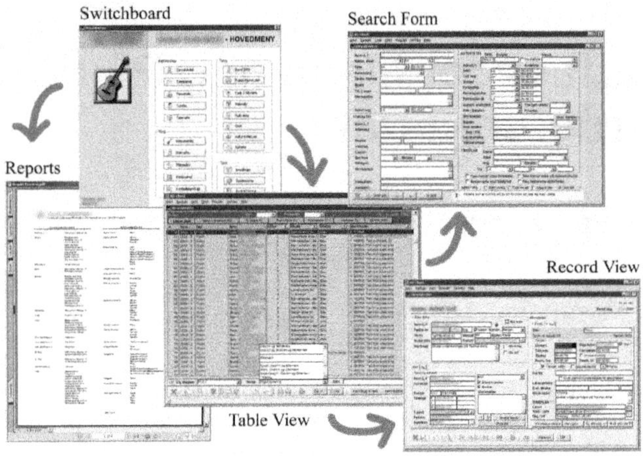

Figure 1. The stereotypical user interface of a database application made with FileMaker, Microsoft Access, or similar software development tools. (Screenshots from a Norwegian software system for public music schools.)

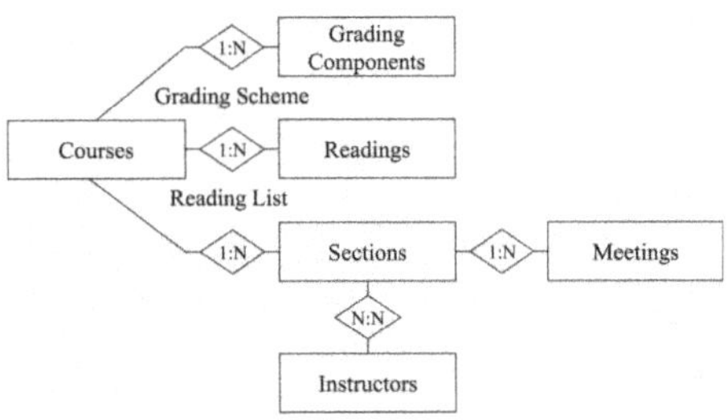

Figure 2. Simplified schema of an academic course management system (Entity-Relationship diagram).

bles in the database. Second, tailor-made interfaces are not restricted to simple tabular views, but can expose relationships in a hierarchical fashion. For instance, a record view for a single entity can itself contain tab rows or miniature table views—*subforms* or *portals*—to represent multiple, independent sets of entities related to the main entity through plural relationships. Note that in tailor-made applications, these views are hard-coded for the particular schema in question. Hard-coded views may sometimes offer significant usability benefits in terms of learning and efficiency, since they make many decisions on the user's behalf and may be fine-tuned for specific tasks. However, they are not an option in general-purpose interfaces.

As a running example, we consider the schema of an academic course management system, see Figure 2. Here, each Course entity has multiple Sections (lectures, precepts, labs, etc.), each Section has multiple Instructors, and so on. A tailor-made interface might expose many different views of the underlying data, for instance, "a list of sections by instructors, each section showing its associated course," or "a list of courses, each course showing its reading list, grading scheme, and sections, each section showing its meetings and assigned instructors." Both of these views are hierarchical, since they call for lists contained within lists. The first view could just as easily be displayed as a flat table, like that returned by a simple join query in SQL. This is not the case for the second view. Since the second view involves parallel joins on multiple independent relationships, i.e. Grading Scheme and Reading List, such joins would produce an extremely large number of rows of redundant data. Whenever we wish to represent an entity together with related entities from two or more plural relationships, hierarchical views become a necessity.

Hierarchical views can often be represented in spreadsheets using clever formatting tricks, e.g. indentation, skipped cells, or comma-separated lists. However, this strategy has a number of problems. First, such views must be manually created and, if more than one view of the same data is desired, kept in sync with the original data. Second, the strategy does not generalize well, with the sheet structure quickly growing unwieldy as relationships fan out and cascade. For instance, while a comma-separated list in a cell might be easy enough to maintain, a list of lists is not. Third, when the data representation deviates from the standard tabular format, also known as first normal form (1NF), key spreadsheet features such as sorting, inserting, charting, filtering, or even simple navigation between individual units of data become hard or impossible to apply correctly.

Because traditional spreadsheet UIs provide no easy way to create joined views of related tables, it becomes impractical to follow good practices of schema normalization, which call for tables of redundantly represented data to be decomposed into multiple smaller ones. This in turn exposes all the usual problems associated with managing improperly normalized data, i.e. insertion, update, and deletion anomalies [5].

While spreadsheets may be inadequate for managing multiple related tables of data, they are great for managing individual ones. Spreadsheets afford a large range of streamlined facilities for working with any data that can be arranged in a grid of cells, including multiple selection, copy/paste, find/replace, undo/redo, inserting and deleting, extending data values, sorting and filtering on arbitrary fields, navigating and selecting cells with the keyboard, and so on. Tailor-made database UIs seldom reach this level of sophistication, due to the limited resources available to develop an application for only one schema. When it comes to general editing tasks on tabular data, spreadsheet systems have an advantage even over most tailor-made applications.

In this paper, we propose to reduce the cost-usability gap between spreadsheets and tailor-made relational database applications by extending the spreadsheet paradigm to let the user establish relationships between rows in related worksheets as well as view and navigate the hierarchical cell structure that arises as a result. Implementing this idea, we present Related Worksheets, a spreadsheet-like desktop application which provides relationship editing facilities similar to those often developed with tools like FileMaker or Microsoft Access, but which work from a single generic user interface rather than requiring a new one to be developed for every conceivable database schema. Unlike in a regular spreadsheet, the user can model complex database schemas

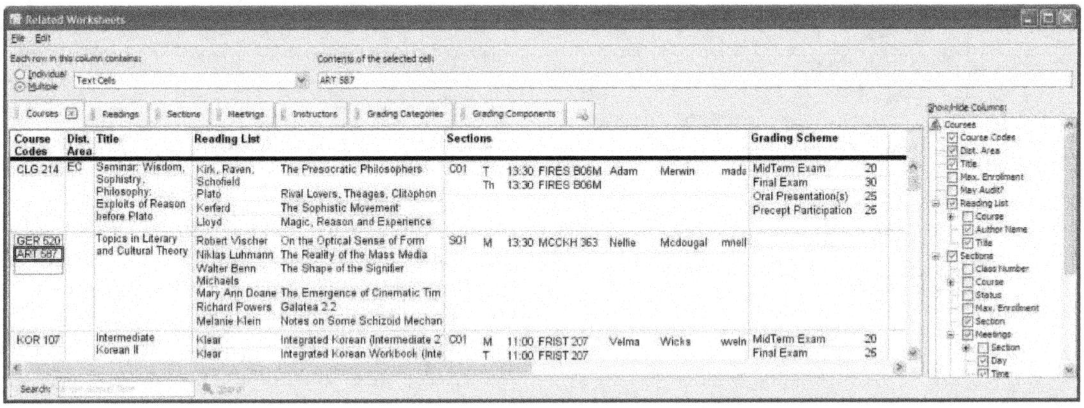

Figure 3. A particular hierarchical view of a dataset with the schema shown in Figure 2, as presented by the Related Worksheets system.

in their proper normalized form without losing the ability to view and edit related data in one place, ensuring long-term managebility of the data. Figure 3 shows one of the hierarchical views mentioned earlier, as handled by the Related Worksheets system.

We evaluate our system with a screencast-based user study on 36 Mechanical Turk workers. First-time users of our software were consistently able to solve lookup-type query tasks with the same or higher accuracy as subjects using Microsoft Excel, in one case 40% faster on average.

RELATED WORK

Visual tools for development of tailor-made database applications first emerged in the 1980s, and have since become a standard genre of office productivity software on par with spreadsheets, word processors, and presentation software. These tools provide visual form designers, wizards, and such to help speed up the development process. Among the first such tools were 4th Dimension[3] (1984) and FileMaker[4] (1985); Microsoft Access[5] appeared later (1992). Some of the newer applications in this category, such as Intuit Quickbase[6], AppForge [11], and App2You [6], have brought usability improvements on the application developer's side, in particular with respect to how well the development environment manages to hide technical details such as join queries, foreign key relationships, and the underlying relational schema. For instance, the application design processes of both AppForge and App2You are form-driven rather than schema driven, that is, the systems use the forms designed by the developer to derive the underlying relational schema rather than requiring them to be defined explicitly upfront. AppForge also has a flexible visual interface for defining updatable hierarchical views. However, these systems are application builders rather than general data manipulation tools: a new application must be built for every schema, and the actual applications produced are just as schema-dependent as any other tailor-made database application. Furthermore, neither project attempts to create a spreadsheet-like environment; these are purely form- and widget-based user interfaces.

There is an increasing tendency among commercial spreadsheet applications to encourage users to organize data in simple, flat tables like those found in a relational database. Microsoft Excel[7], Google Docs[8], and Apple iWork Numbers[9] all encourage the creation of explicit table areas in order to make table-related features such as sorting, filtering, summation, and form generation possible or more reliable.

For relational databases, Query-by-Example [12] is the standard example of a schema-independent visual query language. It inspired many of the standard search interfaces that are found in tailor-made database applications today, although these simpler interfaces typically omit features crucial to the expressiveness of the original language. QBE always retrieves flat tables, and cannot produce hierarchical views.

The concept of *pivot tables*, pioneered in Lotus Improv (1993), exists today both in spreadsheets like Microsoft Excel as well as Online Analytical Processing (OLAP) tools such as Tableau [9] (formerly Polaris) and Oracle Business Intelligence Discoverer[10]. Pivot tables are interactive user interfaces for producing cross-tabulated views of data, that is, views showing data points grouped and aggregated in categories along two axes. While interfaces like Tableau may hide adjacent duplicate data values or organize axis headings hierarchically, both the input and output of a pivot table interface is a flat table of values. Thus, these systems do not provide hierarchical views.

PrediCalc [4] approaches the problem of maintaining consistency between multiple tables in a spreadsheet when the items in the tables are related by plural relationships, including the case where there are temporary or partial inconsis-

[3]http://www.4d.com
[4]http://www.filemaker.com
[5]http://office.microsoft.com/access
[6]http://quickbase.intuit.com

[7]http://office.microsoft.com/excel
[8]http://docs.google.com
[9]http://www.apple.com/iwork/numbers
[10]http://www.oracle.com/technetwork/developer-tools/discoverer

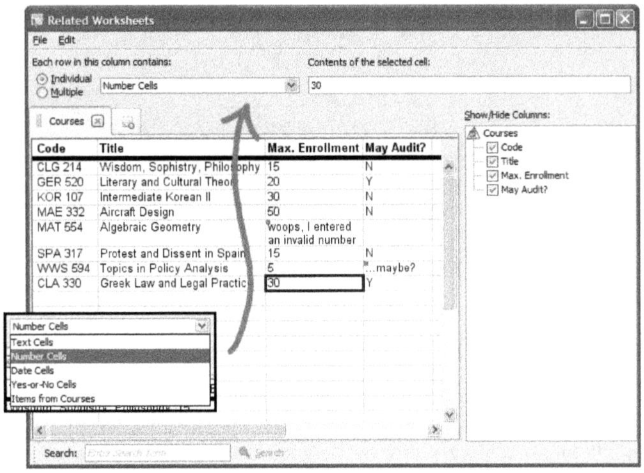

Figure 4. Related Worksheets after creating a new worksheet, entering some simple tabular data, and setting non-text preferred data types for two of the columns. Some of the values entered do not conform to their columns' data types, and have been marked with a red warning box by the software.

tencies in the constraints. It does not, however, extend the structure of the spreadsheet itself beyond two-dimensional cell grids, and thus does not support hierarchical views.

In IceSheets [10], cells in a worksheet can recursively contain entire new worksheets, allowing data to be addressed and organized in a hierarchical fashion. However, the content of the hierarchy is static, and must be built manually by the user. Moreover, the system has no concept of joins or relationships. This makes the system unsuitable for the kind of database tasks we are interested in.

THE RELATED WORKSHEETS SYSTEM

Related Worksheets is a desktop application which, in its initial state, appears largely like a regular spreadsheet. The user can create, open, and save documents known as *workbooks*, and each workbook contains a number of infinitely sized *worksheets* that can be created and selected through a row of tabs. Empty worksheets start out looking like those of Excel or any other spreadsheet application, and can be navigated and edited using standard mouse and keyboard commands—click cells to select, navigate cells with arrow keys, type to edit, drag to resize columns, etc. Since our system's novel features depend on the creation of multiple worksheets, and since worksheets are referred to by name in various parts of the user interface, we force the user to create and name every worksheet explicitly. At startup, we show a blank welcome tab with an instruction on how to create a new worksheet.

Like Google Docs and Apple iWork Numbers, we intend the user to populate each worksheet with a single table of items under a designated row of column headers. Thus, the first row of each worksheet is automatically formatted as a heading, with a bolded font and a thick border underneath, as well pinned to remain visible at the top of the worksheet view during vertical scrolling of the rest of the worksheet. Columns can be renamed at any time by editing the contents of their respective header row cells, and can be deleted or moved left or right.

In our system, each column in a worksheet has an explicit preferred data type associated with it. The user may change this type at any time using a drop-down menu in the toolbar area. If the value of a cell does not conform to its column's selected data type—e.g. text in a Number column or an invalid date in a Date column—the cell is rendered with a red warning box similar to those used by PrediCalc and Excel to indicate other kinds of inconsistencies. See Figure 4. The user is always free to keep the default Text type, which accepts any primitive value.

The system's weak form of type checking serves to allow temporary inconsistencies. For instance, it is possible to paste data from Excel without first having to set the appropriate column types, and the data type of existing columns can be changed without special conversion semantics. The type checking functionality applies not only to primitive data types, but also to reference types and column cardinalities, which we discuss next. In the header row, cells always behave as they would in a Text column.

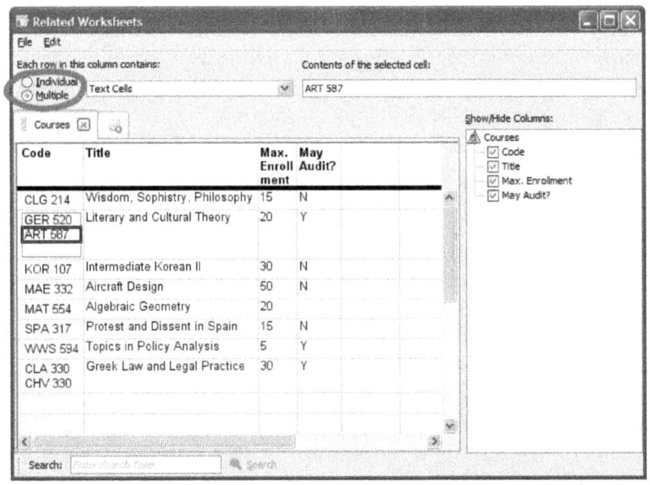

Figure 5. Related Worksheets after the Code column has been set to allow multiple inner cells and some additional course codes have been entered. The outer cell containing the currently selected inner cell is rendered with a blue border, and with one extra blank inner cell as an affordance for adding additional entries.

In addition to a preferred data type, each column also has a preferred cardinality, selected by a pair of radio buttons next to the data type drop-down. Columns preferring *individual* cells per row behave just like columns in a traditional spreadsheet; this is the default. The *multiple* cardinality, however, indicates that the column accepts multiple cells per row. This situation is illustrated in Figure 5. It now becomes necessary to distinguish between *outer* and *inner* cells; in general, outer cells are defined by the intersection of a row and a column, while inner cells are contained within outer cells. Data values are contained in inner cells, and the cursor moves left/right/up/down between the inner cells that are visible on the screen at any time. Outer cells are always rendered to show the contents of each of their non-blank inner

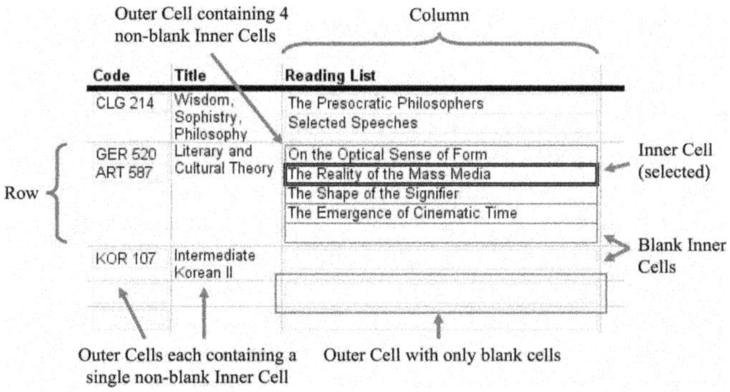

Figure 6. Terminology for describing worksheets in the Related Worksheets system.

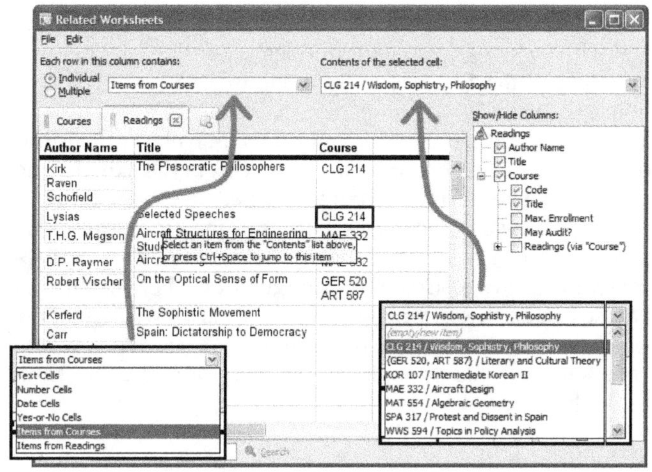

Figure 7. Related Worksheets after adding a new worksheet with data. The Course column has been set to contain references to the Courses worksheet by selecting Items from Courses as the column's preferred data type. Reference values for cells in this column can now be selected from a drop-down list (right) that shows one entry for each row in the Courses table.

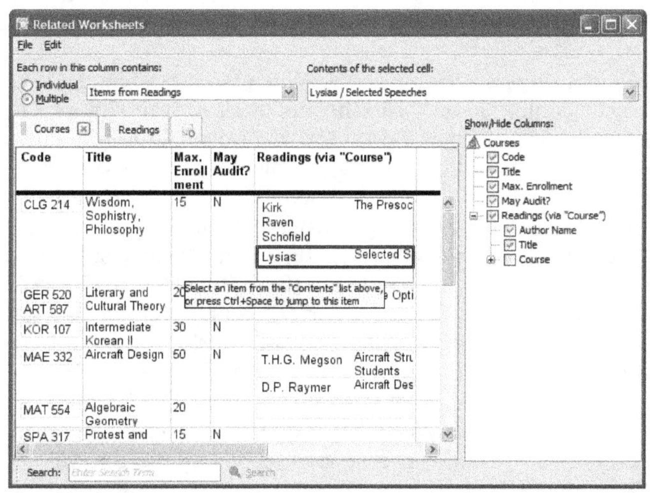

Figure 8. Related Worksheets showing the reverse reference column that was automatically created in the Courses table when the Course column of the Readings table was set to refer to the former. By pressing Ctrl+Space, the user can teleport between the cursor location selected here versus that of Figure 7.

cells, and always with at least one inner cell visible, even if blank. In columns of multiple cardinality, a light gray border is added around inner cells as a visual indicator of the special behavior of these cells. When the cursor enters such a cell, the border is highlighted in blue, and an extra blank inner cell is rendered within the same outer cell as an affordance to enter additional values. See Figure 6. Thus, to add values to a cell of multiple cardinality, the user first moves the cursor to an existing value in the list, then to the new blank cell that appears at the end. Additional blank cells will appear as the user fills the previous ones with values, or disappear again as the user deletes the last value in the list.

Besides the primitive column data types, our system provides reference types. For each worksheet in the open workbook, including the currently selected one, a reference type Items from <worksheet to be referenced> is available in the column data type drop-down, below the standard primitive types. Each inner cell in a column of such a type is allowed to contain, instead of a primitive value, a reference to a row in the target worksheet specified by the column type. When the cursor enters an inner cell in a reference column, the user can select a reference value from another drop-down list. This drop-down shows one entry per non-blank row in the referenced worksheet, plus an option to reset the cell to its default empty state. Note that unlike a relational database, our system does not have a concept of primary or foreign keys. Instead, rows are assigned an internal identifier on first use, and subsequently referenced using this identifier. This is completely transparent to the user.

As an example, suppose the user is modeling an academic course management system like that of Figure 2. In two separate worksheets, the user may have created tables of Courses and Readings, respectively, and now wishes to establish a relationship between the two in order to maintain a reading list for each course. The user can do this by creating a column Course of type Items from Courses to the Readings worksheet. This column will then contain, for each reading, the course containing the reading in its reading list, and the user can select the appropriate course from the reference selection drop-down. See Figure 7. Alternatively, the user can create a column of type Items from Readings in the Courses worksheet—we will explain this symmetry later. Note that *creating* a column simply means making use of a new empty one, like in a regular spreadsheet.

When an inner cell in one worksheet contains a reference to a row in another, a representation of the referenced row is itself rendered within the referencing cell. This representation is a recursive selection of columns from the referenced row, and can be configured through the Show/Hide Columns tree of checkboxes, similar to the Schema Navigation Menu found in AppForge. For instance, in Figure 3, each row in the Courses worksheet contains a list of references in the inner cells of the Sections column to the rows of the Sections worksheet. Each section reference is then rendered just like the corresponding row would be in the Sections table, except with some otherwise visually distracting borders removed, and with some of its columns hidden according to the user's selection in the Show/Hide Columns tree. Since each section also has a list of references to Meetings as well as to Instructors, this process is applied recursively until primitive values are rendered in the base case. Effectively, the user is able to perform arbitrary nested joins on the relationships between the worksheets, starting from any given worksheet as a base table. Each worksheet has its own recursive Show/Hide Columns configuration. For instance, a course can be shown with its full title when viewed under the Courses worksheet, while only showing its six-letter course code when viewed through several levels of references from the Instructors worksheet.

The entries in the reference selection drop-down are string representations of each potential target row, also built from the fields selected to be visible in the Show/Hide Columns tree, including nested ones, or whatever portion of the string there is horizontal space enough to display. Though not implemented in our prototype system, users should be able to pick items from this drop-down list by typing the first letters of this string representation, using a combo box instead of a list box.

Relationships are bidirectional. When the user creates a reference column in one worksheet in order to maintain a relationship with another worksheet, a corresponding reference column is automatically created in the referenced worksheet, referring back to the original worksheet. For instance, if each Reading is assigned to a Course, then each Course has a set of Readings. When the type Items from Courses is selected for the Course column of the Readings worksheet, this automatically creates a corresponding column of type Items from Readings in the Courses worksheet. See Figure 8. The column name Readings (via "Course") is only an initial default and, as for any other column, can be changed at any time. Like any other column, a reverse reference column can be hidden from the view using the Show/Hide Columns tree. Deleting a reverse reference column deletes the original referencing column as well. Note that the system itself makes no distinction between what we have been calling *forward* and *reverse* reference columns; we are merely using these terms to distinguish between the columns explicitly created by the user versus those automatically made available in the other direction.

By setting the cardinalities of a related pair of forward and reverse reference columns, the user can choose between one-to-one, one-to-many, many-to-one, and many-to-many relationships. By default, an automatically created reverse reference column is set to have the multiple cardinality, resulting in a one-to-many relationship if the forward reference column was of the individual cardinality, or a many-to-many relationship if the forward reference column was of the multiple cardinality. Our system models many-to-many relationships directly, without an intermediate join table, as long as no attibutes are required on the relationship itself. This is an important usability feature, as the concept of join tables is abstract and may make little sense to a spreadsheet user that does not have experience designing relational database schemas.

For the purposes of selecting columns to display in the Show/Hide Columns tree, forward and reverse references can be followed indefinitely. For instance, it is possible to show, for each instructor, the courses taught by that instructor (via the Sections worksheet), then for those courses, what other instructors teach the course, then for those instructors, the complete set of courses taught by those instructors, and so on. Infinite recursion is avoided by expanding the Show/Hide Columns tree lazily and hiding, by default, columns that have already been instantiated as an ancestor in the tree. Like any other column, these can be shown or hidden again by checking or unchecking the appropriate checkbox in the tree.

While references are rendered recursively and the user can easily see across many cascading and parallel relationships simultaneously, the cell cursor moves across the top level only. This was a design decision made to keep the interface simple, in particular to keep cursor behavior similar to that of a regular spreadsheet interface. As a consequence, in order to edit a particular value, whether it be a primitive or a reference, the user must first select the worksheet that contains that value directly, that is, the worksheet that contains the value in one of its inner cells. For instance, in Figure 7, it is not possible to edit the course code or title of a course without first switching to the Courses worksheet tab. This is analogous to restrictions often found in FileMaker-style database applications. However, generalizing a standard idiom often found in the record views of such applications, we introduce a *teleport* feature to simplify navigation across related entities in different worksheets.

The teleport feature allows the user to quickly jump between multiple related worksheets via the references that exist between them. With the cursor located on a cell containing a reference to a row in another worksheet, the user can press Ctrl+Space to switch to the related worksheet, with the cursor placed on the inner cell containing the corresponding reverse reference in the referenced row. After teleporting, the user is free to move the cursor around in the newly selected worksheet, for instance to edit values that were previously too deep in the hierarchy to select with the cursor, or even to teleport another degree away from the original worksheet. To get back to the original point, the user can move the cursor back to the original reverse reference that was selected after the teleport, and teleport again. Consequently, teleporting twice without changing the cursor location will always lead back to the original cell. We believe a regular set of back/forward buttons, not implemented in our prototype, would complement the teleport feature well.

As an example of the teleport feature, consider the situation in Figure 7. A user who wishes to edit the title of the course CLG 214 can press Ctrl+Space to get to the state shown in Figure 8. The user can now move the cursor to and edit the cell containing the Wisdom, Sophistry, Philosophy primitive value. When done, the user can move the cursor back to the cell containing the Lysias / Selected Speeches reference and teleport to get back to the original location in Figure 7.

We provide a simple search feature accessible from a search bar similar to that found in the Mozilla Firefox[11] web browser. By entering a text string and clicking the Search button, the cursor will move to the next cell whose string representation contains the search term. The string representation is the same as that used by the reference selection drop-down item, minus separator characters; it contains the primitive values of all the columns that have been recursively selected for display in the Show/Hide Columns tree.

In the process of setting up a sample database for our user study, we implemented two special data normalization commands that are likely to be of general utility. The Detect References command replaces each value in a column with a reference to a row in a target worksheet that contains the value in question in its first visible column (as selected in the Show/Hide Columns tree), if a unique such row exists. This is typically used to convert a column of primitive values to a column of reference values, for instance after having imported two flat tables related through a foreign key relationship from a relational database. The other command, Replace References, works oppositely; it replaces each reference value in a column with the value of the first visible column in the referenced row. This command has uses beyond undoing the work of a previously invoked Detect References command; in particular, it can be used as a step to convert the join tables commonly found in relational database schemas into directly supported many-to-many relationships.

USER STUDY

To evaluate our system, we conducted an online user study using Amazon Mechanical Turk[12] and the User Study Console, a Java-based tool we developed to allow test subjects to stream timestamped recordings of their computer screens to our server with a minimum of effort. The User Study Console would also automatically download and open sample spreadsheets we had prepared as well as allow the user to submit changed versions of these in exchange for a confirmation code to be pasted into the Mechanical Turk HIT (Human Intelligence Task, a survey form). Depending on the stage and parameters of the experiment, sample spreadsheets would be opened in either Microsoft Excel, assumed to be already installed on the user's computer, or in our own Related Worksheets application, distributed as part of the same Java Web Start executable.

Our study was a between-subjects design in two stages. The first stage was a recruiting task offered to the general population of Mechanical Turk workers, intended to let us select a group of workers who (1) were willing and able to successfully run the User Study Console on their machines, (2) happened to have Microsoft Excel or a compatible spreadsheet application installed, (3) had demonstrated good faith in solving an otherwise unrelated spreadsheet task, and (4) had provided us with answers to some background and demographic questions. We offered $0.25 for workers to launch the User Study Console, make a chart based on sample data we provided in an Excel spreadsheet, and fill in a survey. The survey included questions about gender, age, occupation, previous spreadsheet experience, and previous experience with Microsoft Access, FileMaker, or other database software, if any.

[11] http://www.mozilla.com/firefox

[12] http://www.mturk.com

Courses(Course, Distribution Area, Title, Max. Enrollment, May Audit)
Readings(Course, Author Name, Title)
Sections(Class Number, Course, Status, Max. Enrollment, Section)
Meetings(Section Class Number, Day, Time, Place)
Instructors(First Name, Last Name, Email)
Grading Components(Course, Grading Category, Percentage)
Instructors-Sections(Instructor Name, Section Class Number)
Cross-Listings(Crosslisted Course Code, Primary Course Code)

Figure 9. The normalized schema as it appeared in the Excel version of the tasks. Primary keys that participate in foreign key relationships are underlined, foreign keys are double-underlined.

In the second stage of our experiment, Mechanical Turk workers with complete and technically unproblematic submissions for the recruiting task were divided randomly into two groups of equal size, and invited by e-mail to do a longer follow-up task, worth $3.00. Workers in the control group would be instructed, like before, to launch the User Study Console and solve tasks using a Microsoft Excel spreadsheet that we provided. Workers in the treatment group would, on the other hand, be instructed to use the Related Worksheets application. The tasks and instructions in the two main forms were identical except in the description of the tool used to solve the tasks. No actual instructions were provided on how to perform the tasks, neither in the Excel nor the Related Worksheets versions of the experiment.

The actual database tasks modeled in our user study were based on the course management system example introduced earlier. The data was a subset of an actual course database, containing 37 courses and related entities.

In the Excel version of the tasks, the database was represented as a set of normalized relations, each stored as a table in its own worksheet. See the Introduction for a discussion of why this particular mapping is a natural one for our investigation. We used natural rather than surrogate primary keys, e.g. course codes in the form "KOR 107," to identify the various entities involved. The full normalized schema of the database is shown in Figure 9. For the Related Worksheets version of the task, we imported the same normalized database tables into our system as individual worksheets, converted foreign key columns into reference columns using the Detect References and Replace References operations mentioned earlier, and made default selections in the Show/Hide Columns tree corresponding to what we believed would be seen in a real course management system. In particular, the Courses worksheet was shown with all fields and subfields fully expanded, excluding reverse reference columns (each course showing its reading list, grading scheme, sections, meetings, instructors, etc.). Each of the other worksheets were shown with all of their immediate

#	*Description*
1	Find a course that is taught by Harry Morrill.
2	In the course "MUS 105: Music Theory Through Performance and Composition," what percentage of the final grade is derived from the Midterm Exam?
3	Find a course that satisfies the "LA" (Literature and the Arts) distribution area, with a lecture (meetings belonging to a section denoted "L01") that starts after noon (after 12.00).
4	What is the e-mail address of the instructor who teaches "KOR 107: Intermediate Korean II"?
5	Who teaches the precept section of "HIS 383: The United States Since 1920" that meets on Wednesdays at 10am?

Table 1. Tasks given in the user study.

fields visible, and some selection of important identifying subfields for each related entity (e.g. course code, distribution area, and course title whenever a course was referenced). Effectively, it would not be necessary for a user to show additional columns or subcolumns to solve the tasks given, though depending on window size and screen resolution, it might have been necessary to scroll horizontally or hide some columns to see the desired information.

The exact tasks given are listed in Table 1. The actual instructions given to users also specified the exact form expected of the answers and gave an example of a correctly specified answer. These tasks are lookup (read-only) tasks of the kind we would imagine to be frequently performed on a real-world course management database. We originally included a number of update tasks as well; however, these uncovered a number of discoverability bugs that would have to be fixed before realistic update performance could be measured.

After the expiration of the main task, we reviewed workers' submissions and associated screencasts, log files, and uploaded spreadsheet files. We graded each of the tasks on a pass/fail basis, and manually estimated the amount of time spent on each task using video frame timestamps and observations of the subjects' actions.

RESULTS

The recruiting stage of the study yielded 52 subjects, screened from submissions by 64 distinct Mechanical Turk workers. The subjects were divided randomly into two groups of 26 subjects each, and invited to participate in the main part of the study. Of these, 18 recruits from the Excel group and 18 recruits from the Related Worksheets group completed the main task. An additional 4 recruits from the Excel group and 4 recruits from the Related Worksheets group started doing a few of the tasks, but soon closed the User Study Console and never submitted a response. The remaining recruits never opened the User Study Console during the second part of the study.

Of the 36 subjects participating in the main part of the study, 25 were male (69%). Subjects were between 19 and 48 years of age, with first, second, and third quartiles at 26, 30, and 35 years, respectively. 16 subjects (44%) described having some prior experience using "database software such as FileMaker or Microsoft Access." Most users had significant previous spreadsheet experience; Table 2 shows the levels of typical spreadsheet use as reported by subjects themselves. The subjects' self-reported occupations are categorized in Table 3.

	"How often do you typically use spreadsheet software?"	*N*
1	Never	1
2	Once a year or less	1
3	A couple of times per year	1
4	A couple of times per month	12
5	A couple of times per week	5
6	Almost daily	10
7	Multiple times per day	6
	Total	36

Table 2. Number of subjects reporting particular levels of previous spreadsheet experience. The numbers to the left are used to calculate averages in Table 3.

Occupation	*N*	*Average spreadsheet experience*
Student, business/finance	2	6.0
Student, mechanical engineering	1	4.0
Student, unknown	1	2.0
Teacher	2	4.0
Business administration	5	5.6
Business process outsourcing (BPO)	3	6.0
Homemaker	5	3.2
Programmer	8	5.8
Other IT	3	5.0
Other technical	5	5.6
Other non-technical	1	4.0
Total	36	5.1

Table 3. Number of subjects and average levels of previous spreadsheet experience by occupations reported. Averages are based on the 7-step scale in Table 2.

Of the subjects who submitted a response to the main task, the number who passed each task is shown in Table 4. The average times taken to complete each task, for subjects who solved each task in question correctly, are shown in Figure 10. Due to intermittent network problems, 5 screencasts from the Excel group and 2 screencasts from the Related Worksheets group were incompletely streamed and could not be used for timing measurements.

Using uploaded screencasts and event logs, we summarized the features used by subjects during the study. This data is

	N	Task # 1	2	3	4	5
Excel	18	18	18	14	17	12
RS	18	18	18	14	17	15

Table 4. Number of subjects who solved each task correctly.

	Excel			Related Worksheets		
Feature	*n*	*N*	*n/N*	*n*	*N*	*n/N*
Search	13	17	76%	9	17	53%
Mark Rows	3	15	20%	2	17	12%
Filter	11	15	73%			
Sort	1	15	7%			
Teleport				8	18	44%
Show/Hide Columns				3	17	18%

Table 5. Number of users observed to make use of specific features or techniques during the user study.

shown in Table 5. Some features are found in both Excel and Related Worksheets, others are specific to one system. Except for the teleport feature, the numbers are based on manual review of the screencast videos; the number of data points is slightly less than the total number of users due to some incomplete screencasts. The teleport command was invoked 1, 1, 2, 5, 5, 7, 12, and 13 times by each respective user. Of the Related Worksheets subjects making use of the search feature, 3 discovered it only after having progressed about halfway through the study. Of the Excel subjects making use of the filter feature, 3 did not use the search feature at all. "Mark Rows" refers to subjects visibly working to keep track of rows in a worksheet; this was done in various ways by different users. Two Excel users colored marked rows yellow with the highlighting tool, one of these also at one point wrote down the primary keys of marked rows in an external text editor. A third Excel user marked rows by typing an "x" in the first empty column available next to the table. Two Related Worksheets users marked rows as well; these both used an external editor. It is possible that some subjects may have taken notes on paper as well.

DISCUSSION

For each submission we watched the screencasts and measured the time taken to solve each task. We then, for each task, applied Welch's unpaired two-tailed t-test to the times taken to complete the tasks by those subjects who got them right only. Only Task 4 showed a statistically significant ($p<0.05$) improvement in the Related Worksheets case; it was 41% faster than Excel. Task 5 showed a 31% improvement, but was not statistically significant ($p=0.09$). In all other cases the results were insignificant.

The different tasks can be analyzed in terms of the joins involved and tables traversed in the normalized database schema used in the Excel version of the database in each case. It is useful for this purpose to refer back to the Entity-Relationship diagram that was shown in Figure 2.

For Task 2, only the primary key is needed from the Courses table, and the answer can be found by looking at the Grading Components table. This makes the task simple in both Excel and Related Worksheets. We believe the fact that subjects spent a relatively large amount of time on Task 1 compared to, for instance, Task 4 to be due to the learning time needed to get acquainted with the database and, in the case of the Related Worksheets group, the software itself. For Task 4, we saw a large performance gain for subjects using our system versus those using Excel. We can attribute this to the manual join that must be done between the Sections and Instructors-Sections tables followed by the lookup in the Instructors table in the Excel case. In the Related Spreadsheets case, solving the task was a simple matter of finding the course in the Courses worksheet, which showed all related entities in one place. Task 3 is harder than Task 4, since there are both multiple meetings per section as well as multiple sections per course; in Task 4, only a single lookup was required in the Instructors table. To solve Task 3 in Excel typically requires the user to keep track of numbers of several sections to look for in the Meetings table while browsing the Sections table. In Related Worksheets, one can simply browse for the appropriate course, though since we do not provide any filter-like capabilities, the user must manually look through the entire list of courses. Task 5 involved the Sections, Meetings, and Instructors-Sections tables. Since there is often only a single instructor per section, the task is simpler than Task 3. Like in Task 4, we see indications of a performance advantage among users using the Related Worksheets application over those using Excel. While not statistically significant, it seems that the advantage is large but slightly smaller than that of Task 4. This effect could potentially be due to Excel users getting more familiar with the manual process of joining tables.

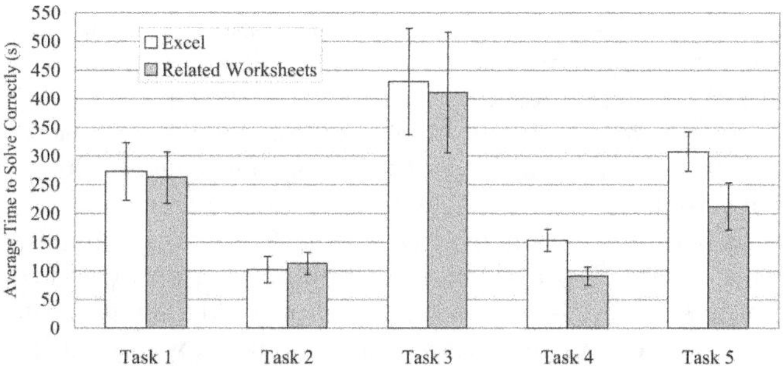

Figure 10. Timing measurements for the user study. The error bars show the standard error of the mean.

The most frequently used feature in both the Excel and the Related Worksheets version of the tasks was search, available in both systems. Typically, users of both systems would use a combination of searching and manual browsing—scrolling back and forth, switching between worksheets, and scanning the data visually—to complete the tasks. This was anticipated: the chief advantage of the Related Spreadsheets system is, in this context, the relevancy of the information seen on the screen at any time. Using a Firefox-style search interface may have put us at a disadvantage due to limited discoverability; only 53% of Related Worksheets users tried searching, vs. 76% of Excel users.

Among the Excel users, we were surprised to find that just about as many subjects made use of the filter feature as made use of the search feature. The filter feature allows the user to restrict rows shown in a table to those containing specific values selected from a drop-down menu above each column. Subjects used the filter feature both to search for specific rows in each table and to mark multiple rows of potential interest for later review. Since the drop-down list provided by the filter feature is always sorted, users could quickly locate a specific item in an otherwise unsorted table, without using the search feature. As mentioned, three users even made extensive use of the filter function without making use of the search feature at all. Given these observations, we consider a filter feature to be an important potential addition to future versions of our interface.

Users sometimes found it necessary to temporarily mark rows of interest in order to solve tasks involving more than a single join between tables; see our earlier observations. Two Related Worksheets users wrote down primary keys in an external editor, despite this not being necessary for completing the tasks in our system. We assume these users must have believed it would be faster to approach the problem in the same way as they would in a standard spreadsheet rather than spending time learning how the hierarchical views worked.

In the Related Worksheets version of the tasks, it was not necessary to modify the Show/Hide Columns configuration, since we had already provided reasonable defaults. Most users thus rightly ignored the feature. A few subjects used the Show/Hide Columns configuration, along with column resizing, to hide unnecessary data from view. The teleport feature was tried by 8 of the 18 Related Worksheets subjects; at least 5 of these subjects seemed to make productive use of it throughout the progression of the study, indicating significant potential value in this feature.

FUTURE WORK

In future work, we plan to incorporate a more expressive visual query language that allows a larger class of hierarchical views to be built by the user, including the ability to apply sorting, filtering, formulas, and aggregation functions. Furthermore, the system should be able to render these hierarchical views using a selection of different layout configurations beyond the simple tabular one, for instance to emulate the record views that are ubiquitous in FileMaker-style applications. Finally, the system should provide a more flexible interface for storing and organizing views themselves. Future evaluation should include a comparison with tailor-made UIs, and also investigate other classes of tasks such as schema creation and more complex querying.

CONCLUSION

We have presented Related Worksheets, a spreadsheet-like application that lets the user establish relationships between rows in related worksheets as well as view and navigate the hierarchical cell structure that arises as a result. These features make the system well-suited for database tasks. A user study on 36 subjects found that first-time users of our system were able to solve lookup-style query tasks with the same or higher accuracy as subjects in a control group using Excel, in one case 40% faster on average.

ACKNOWLEDGEMENTS

We thank Paul Grogan and Phumpong Watanaprakornkul for their help designing and implementing the original Related Worksheets prototype.

REFERENCES

1. Abiteboul, S., Agrawal, R., Bernstein, P., Carey, M., Ceri, S., Croft, B., DeWitt, D., Franklin, M., Molina, H. G., Gawlick, D., Gray, J., Haas, L., Halevy, A., Hellerstein, J., Ioannidis, Y., Kersten, M., Pazzani, M., Lesk, M., Maier, D., Naughton, J., Schek, H., Sellis, T., Silberschatz, A., Stonebraker, M., Snodgrass, R., Ullman, J., Weikum, G., Widom, J., and Zdonik, S. The Lowell database research self-assessment. *Commun. ACM 48*, 5 (2005), 111–118.
2. Chan, Y. E., and Storey, V. C. The use of spreadsheets in organizations: determinants and consequences. *Information & Management 31*, 3 (1996), 119–134.
3. Chen, P. P.-S. The Entity-Relationship model—toward a unified view of data. *ACM Trans. Database Syst. 1*, 1 (1976), 9–36.
4. Kassoff, M., and Genesereth, M. R. PrediCalc: a logical spreadsheet management system. *The Knowledge Engineering Review 22*, 03 (2007), 281–295.
5. Kent, W. A simple guide to five normal forms in relational database theory. *Commun. ACM 26* (February 1983), 120–125.
6. Kowalzcykowski, K., Deutsch, A., Ong, K. W., Papakonstantinou, Y., Zhao, K. K., and Petropoulos, M. Do-It-Yourself database-driven web applications. In *CIDR* (2009).
7. Pemberton, J. D., and Robson, A. J. Spreadsheets in business. *Industrial Management & Data Systems 200*, 8 (2000), 379–388.
8. Raden, N. Shedding light on shadow IT: Is Excel running your business? Tech. rep., Hired Brains, Inc., January 2005.
9. Stolte, C., Tang, D., and Hanrahan, P. Polaris: A system for query, analysis, and visualization of multidimensional relational databases. *IEEE Transactions on Visualization and Computer Graphics 8*, 1 (2002), 52–65.
10. Whitmer, B. C. Improving spreadsheets for complex problems. Master's thesis, Brigham Young University, August 2008.
11. Yang, F., Gupta, N., Botev, C., Churchill, E. F., Levchenko, G., and Shanmugasundaram, J. WYSIWYG development of data driven web applications. *Proc. VLDB Endow. 1*, 1 (2008), 163–175.
12. Zloof, M. M. Query-by-Example: A data base language. *IBM Syst. J. 16*, 4 (1977), 324–343.

Variation in Importance of Time-on-Task with Familiarity with Mobile Phone Models

Shunsuke Suzuki, Victoria Bellotti[†], Nick Yee[†], Bonnie E. John[‡], Yusuke Nakao, Toshiyuki Asahi, Shin'ichi Fukuzumi

NEC Corporation
1753 Shimonumabe,
Nakahara-ku, Kawasaki-shi,
KANAGAWA 2118666 JAPAN
s-suzuki@cb.jp.nec.com

[†]Palo Alto Research Center
3333 Coyote Hill Road,
Palo Alto, CA 94304 USA
{Victoria.Bellotti,
Nicholas.Yee}@parc.com

[‡]Carnegie Mellon University
5000 Forbes Avenue
Pittsburgh, PA 15212 USA
bej@cs.cmu.edu

ABSTRACT
We studied the extent to which time-on-task is correlated with perception of usability for people who are familiar with a phone model and for those who are not. Our controlled experiment, conducted in Japan, correlated subjective usability assessments with time-on-task for expert and novice users on three different mobile phone models. We found that the correlation between perceived usability and time-on-task is stronger when participants are more familiar with the phone model. While not significant when initially inspecting a new phone model, a negative correlation between time-on-task and perceived usability becomes significant with as little as an hour's time doing tasks on the unfamiliar phone. This suggests that designing the UI to make time-on-task as short as possible may not have much effect on the purchase decision, but as experience increases, it may increase the loyalty of existing users.

Author Keywords
mobile phone, usability metrics, time on task, expertise.

ACM Classification Keywords
H.5.2. Information interfaces and presentation: User interfaces – Evaluation/methodology; Benchmarking.

General Terms
Measurement.

INTRODUCTION
Usability is one factor affecting a mobile phone purchase [8]. Usability can be measured both objectively and subjectively. Objective usability measures (e.g., time on task, hereafter ToT) can be useful in the design process because they can detect superior designs before deployment.

CHI 2011, May 7–12, 2011, Vancouver, BC, Canada.

On the other hand, subjective measures (e.g., satisfaction) seem to relate to more nebulous concepts, (even when arrived at objectively through factor analysis, e.g., [13]), and may be more difficult to reliably improve. But for each user in the store (with no time to conduct a thorough usability test) subjective, rather than objective, usability assessment will drive the purchase decision. Knowing the relationship between the two kinds of usability measures may help a user interface (UI) designer determine when to pay attention to one measure more than the other depending on the circumstance.

Previous studies provide conflicting results. For example, in meta-analyses of a wide range of products, Hornbæk and Law [7] found weak correlations between satisfaction and objective measures at the test level (each test included several tasks) (r=0.164~0.196), but, when looking at the individual task level, Sauro and Lewis [15] found moderately high correlations between them (r=|0.44~0.51|). Frøkjær et al. concluded that effectiveness, efficiency, and satisfaction were independent, in an experiment using the X Window System [3]. One confounding variable that these studies did not investigate is familiarity, one of the most important ways in which users vary. We might guess that familiarity would strongly impact usability assessments, e.g., users are likely to be less sensitive to inefficiencies when they have no experience and are generally overwhelmed by the strangeness of a new system.

Other work has considered familiarity, albeit in a small range. For instance, Seebode et al. [17], studying a wall-mounted multi modal system with people who had "attended a previous evaluation study with an earlier system version" (which they termed experts) and people who had had "no prior experience with the system" (novices). They found significant correlations between ToT and the AttrakDiff questionnaire's scores of pragmatic quality [6] for both familiarity levels ($r_{experts}$=-0.627, $r_{novices}$=-0.548), but the only other significant correlations were between number-of-trials to pragmatic quality for experts and between ToT and product attractiveness for novices.

In work on mobile phones with consideration of familiarity,

Quin and Tran [12] collected System Usability Scale (SUS) ratings [1] after one block of nine tasks and after three blocks of the same nine tasks (which they termed *extensive practice*). They found significant correlations between the SUS ratings and ToT and %success, before and after extensive practice ($r_{ToT\text{-}before}$=-0.33, $r_{ToT\text{-}after}$=-0.32, $r_{\%success\text{-}before}$=0.51, $r_{\%success\text{-}after}$=0.33). However, the familiarity that this work considered is also in a small range.

We add to this body of work by collecting usability perception data from a larger range of familiarity, from people who have only explored a particular phone model for 3 minutes (similar to trying out a phone at a store), to those people after attempting to accomplish 17 common tasks, to people who have owned that particular model for at least 3 months and know how to do the tasks.

EXPERIMENT

In our experiment (Figure 1), participants performed 17 tasks on one of three phone models (between-subjects design) and answered 19 survey questions to assess its subjective usability [13,14] before and after the tasks.

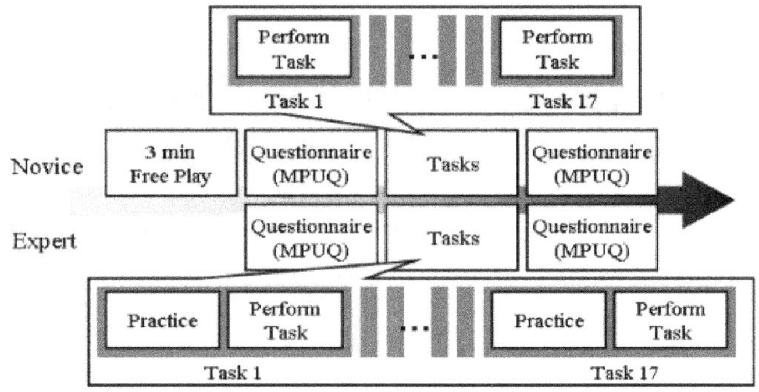

Figure 1. Experiment procedure of novice and expert participants.

Phone Models

To represent the diversity of modern mobile phones, we selected three models (Figure 2) that differed markedly in their form and interaction style. Model A, a common type of phone in Japan, flips open, has a screen, four direction keys, function keys, and a numeric keypad. Model B was a smart phone with a vertical layout similar to that of Model A, but it has a stylus-activated touch screen and rotates to provide a pull-out QWERTY keyboard. Model C, also a smart phone, has a finger-activated touch screen, distinctive interaction styles for finger touch, and, other than a hardware "home" key, all keypads and task-specific buttons are displayed on the screen.

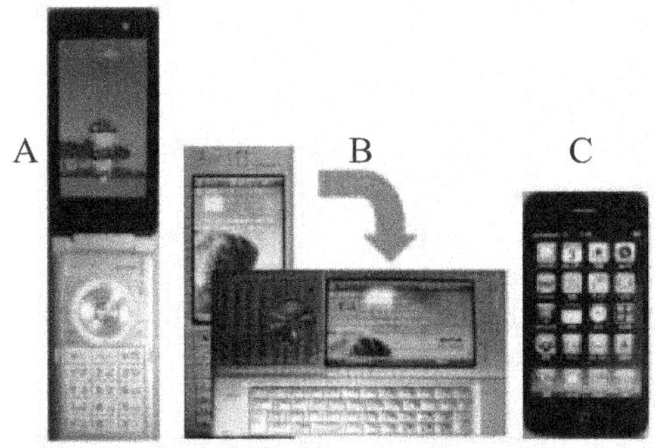

Figure 2. Phone models used in the experiment.

Participants

A total of 129 participants took part in the experiment. Because [18] reported significant differences in users' performance between extremely similar phone models, we defined an *expert* as someone who had (1) owned the exact phone model being tested for at least three months, (2) used calling and mail features at least once a day, (3) used the camera and web browser more than once a month, and (4) used the contact list, alarm clock, and calculator more than once since purchasing the phone. We defined a *novice* as someone who had never owned this model or any other phone by the manufacturer of the tested model. We recruited experts and novices with each model through an independent agency that conducted interviews to identify people with particular model ownership and our defined levels of expertise, relatively balanced for age and gender. Table 1 shows the numbers of each group.

		Expert			Novice		
Model	Age/Gender	M	F	All	M	F	All
A	18-30	4	4	8	2	5	7
	31-50	5	4	9	5	5	10
	51-70	2	3	5	3	2	5
	All	11	11	22	10	12	22
B	18-30	2	4	6	3	4	7
	31-50	9	3	12	5	4	9
	51-70	2	0	2	3	2	5
	All	13	7	20	11	10	21
C	18-30	5	4	9	4	3	7
	31-50	4	5	9	5	4	9
	51-70	3	1	4	4	2	6
	All	12	10	22	13	9	22
All	All	36	28	64	34	31	65

Table 1. The numbers of participants in each group.

Tasks

Although each phone can do tasks unique to its design, we did not want specialized tasks to influence the participants' subjective usability ratings. Therefore, we chose common tasks for all phones. Furthermore, to choose tasks that were common to general mobile phone users, we created a draft list of tasks using the following criteria. (1) Tasks used in the research that established the subjective usability questionnaire [13, 14] and did not violate the other two criteria. (2) Any task using functions appearing in the top 10 of any of five surveys of mobile phone functions used by people in Japan [4,5,9,10,11]. (3) Any task that was reported as common by more than 50% of Japanese respondents in [4,5,9].

We further refined the tasks list by examining results from a pilot experiment and questioning an additional 23 users of these particular mobile phone models. We chose 17 common tasks (plus one task to demonstrate the experiment procedure). The tasks involved phone calls and the contact list, mail, internet searching, the alarm clock, the camera, the calculator, and ring tone setting (demonstration task).

Procedure

To simulate the situation in which a potential purchaser would try a demonstration phone in the store to determine whether or not to buy a particular model, we asked novice participants to freely interact with the phone for three minutes, then fill out the survey (see Figure 1). Expert participants answered the survey questions without the short free play since they could rely on memory of their own familiar model, which we assumed they would do when making a decision about whether to continue to use their own model (or similar model) or to purchase a new model with a radically different UI.

Novice participants were then given a brief statement of each task and performed the task in any way they could, exploring the interface that was new to them. If they did not complete the task within five minutes, the experimenter stopped them, set the phone into the correct initial state for the next task, and gave them the next task.

Following Card et al.'s procedure with expert text-editing [2], experts performed each task using a specific efficient method. To establish these methods, we observed, interviewed and surveyed owners of each model and composed the sequence of steps most users took to do each task. Experts practiced the prescribed method until they could complete it without error before we collected data. To remove error recovery time, the experts repeated a task if they committed an error during its performance. We recorded time on task for all error-free tasks.

All participants then answered the subjective usability survey again to determine if more extensive experience (in the case of the novices) and recent experience (in the case of the experts) would influence subjective usability ratings.

Subjective Usability Assessment

To measure subjective usability, we used a revised Mobile Phone Usability Questionnaire (MPUQ) [13] designed to measure comprehensive usability specifically for mobile devices (similar to the AttrakDiff's pragmatic quality). The MPUQ started as a set of 72 items, shortened to 28 with later research [14], and now contains 23 items as a result of a replication study (Y. S. Ryu, personal communication). We eliminated 4 additional items that were not pertinent to Japanese mobile phone users. Participants answer each item by marking on a form the extent to which they agreed or disagreed with the statement on a scale of 1 (= strongly disagree) to 5 (=strongly agree).

RESULTS

For time on task (ToT, Figure 3), experts were faster than novices ($F[1,128] = 170.68$, $p < .001$). Participants were also slower on Model B than the other two models ($F[2,128] = 3.81$, $p = .03$, post-hoc comparison $p < .05$). For MPUQ (Figure 4), experts perceived their models as more usable than novice ($F[1, 166] = 41.26$, $p < .001$). Participants also perceived Model B as less usable than the other two phone ($F[2,166] = 31.81$, $p < .001$, post-hoc comparison $p < .05$). No interactions were significant.

To investigate the correlation between these two measures, we calculated a standardized score from the average ToT of the 17 tasks, capped at five minutes. For the MPUQ score, we used the weighted factor score of the 19 questions. We then examined correlations between the MPUQ scores and the standardized ToT within Familiarity (Expert/Novice) levels and each Trial (Before-/After-Task). As shown in Table 2, ToT was negatively correlated with MPUQ scores, except for novices before the task. In other words, when participants had more than three minutes of experience with a phone, shorter times meant higher usability scores.

Fisher's Z-tests revealed a significant difference between the coefficients for novices and experts before doing tasks ($p < .05$), but only a marginally significant difference after doing tasks ($p < .10$). To examine the correlations before and after doing tasks, we conducted Steiger's Z-tests, revealing no significant differences within either group.

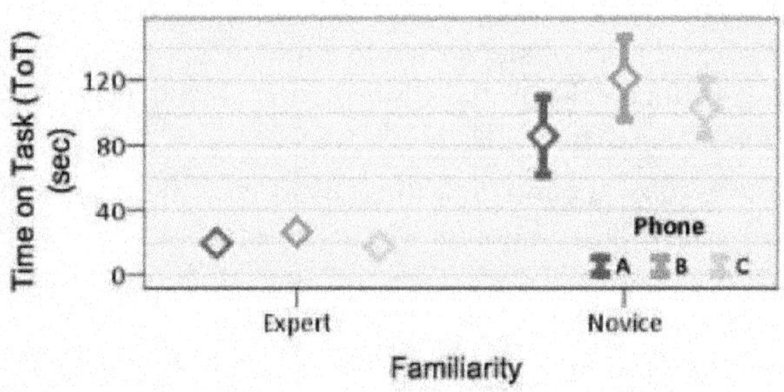

Figure 3. Average time-on-task (ToT) in seconds, by familiarity for all phone models (95% confidence bars).

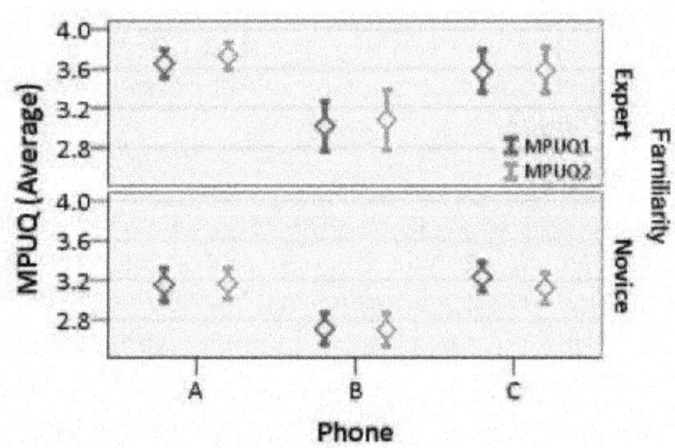

Figure 4. Average MPUQ score by phone for experts and novices, both before completing tasks and after (95% confidence bars). An MPUQ score of 3.0=neutral.

Familiarity	MPUQ Trial	Correlation between MPUQ Scores and ToT	N
Novice	Before-Tasks	-.169	65
	After-Tasks	-.263*	65
Expert	Before-Tasks	-.549**	64
	After-Tasks	-.534**	64

Table 2. Correlations (Pearson's r) between MPUQ scores and ToT (p<.01, *p<.05) for the two MPUQ trials for two familiarity levels.**

DISCUSSION AND CONCLUSION

Our results agree with Quinn and Tan [12] that there is a relationship between ToT and perception of usability on mobile phones. However, familiarity with the phone greatly affected this relationship. For people new to a phone model, the perception of usability after three minutes of free play with a phone (similar to what potential buyers might do in a store) did not significantly correlate with their subsequent ToT. This means that subjective usability of potential buyers is determined by factors stronger than how quickly they would be able to do tasks on the phone. However, ToT becomes a significant factor in perception of usability after only a short amount of task-directed use. These results are in agreement with both Seebode et al.'s novices [17] and Quinn and Tan's correlations before extensive practice [12], both of which had similar familiarity with the tested systems as our novices after doing tasks.

The significantly stronger correlations for experts than for novices (also found in [17]) indicate that ToT's influence on perception of usability increased with increased familiarity. We note, however, that the expert's ToT is related to the efficiency of methods designed into the phone (i.e., the number of steps), while a novice's ToT is probably more influenced by the information scent provided by button and screen labels.

These results suggest that those who care about efficiency or discoverability should try to become skilled with an unfamiliar model *before* committing to a purchase. For mobile phone designers, it may be best to design for discoverability (to shorten ToT for novices) to keep new customers happy in the days following a purchase, and for efficiency to increase the perception of usability in the long-term (a factor in brand loyalty and referrals [16]). However, to attract a buyer in the first place, other factors are more important than the perception of usability, perhaps marketing, branding, appearance, etc.

REFERENCES

1. Brooke, J. SUS: A 'quick and dirty' usability scale. In P. W. Jordan, B. Thomas, B. A. Weerdmeester, and I. L. McClelland (Eds.), *Usability Evaluation in Industry* (pp. 189-194), Taylor & Francis, London, (1996).
2. Card, S. K., Moran, T.P. and Newell, A. *The Psychology of Human-Computer Interaction.* Lawrence Erlbaum Associates, Hillsdale, NJ (1983).
3. Frøkjær, E., Hertzum, M. and Hornbæk, K. Measuring usability: are effectiveness, efficiency, and satisfaction really correlated? In *Proc. CHI 2000*, ACM Press (2000), 345-352.
4. Goo Ranking: Ranking of functions used commonly on a mobile phone. (2005), Retrieved September 17th, 2010, http://ranking.goo.ne.jp/ranking/065/mobile_use/.
5. Goo Ranking: Ranking of functions used commonly on a mobile phone besides call and email. (2008), Retrieved September 17th, 2010, http://ranking.goo.ne.jp/ranking/065/cellular_phone_function/.
6. Hassenzahl, M., Burmester, M. and Koller, F. AttrakDiff: Ein Fragebogen zur Messung wahrgenommener hedonischer und pragmatischer Qualität. In J. Ziegler and G. Szwillus (Eds.), *Mensch & Computer 2003: Interaktion in Bewegung* (pp.187-196), B.G. Teubner, Stuttgart, (2003).
7. Hornbæk, K. and Law, E.L. Meta-Analysis of correlations among usability measures. In *Proc. CHI 2007*, ACM Press (2007), 617-626.
8. Karjaluoto, H., Karvonen, J., Kesti, M., Koivumäki, T., Manninen, M., Pakola, J., Ristola, A. and Salo, J. Factors affecting consumer choice of mobile phones: Two studies from Finland. *Journal of Euromarketing 14*, 3 (2005), 59-82.
9. My Voice: Functions used commonly on a mobile phone. (2008), Retrieved September 17th, 2010, http://www.myvoice.co.jp/biz/surveys/11601/index.html.
10. Nikkei BP: Which functions used commonly on a mobile phone? (2008), Retrieved September 17th, 2010, http://pc.nikkeibp.co.jp/article/column/20080919/1008086/.
11. Oricon: Functions used mainly on a mobile phone. (2009), Retrieved September 17th, 2010, http://life.oricon.co.jp/64543/full/#rk.
12. Quinn, J. M. and Tran, T. Q. Attractive phones don't have to work better: Independent effects of attractiveness, effectiveness, and efficiency on perceived usability. In *Proc. CHI 2010*, ACM Press (2010), 353-362.
13. Ryu, Y. S. Development of usability questionnaires for electronic mobile products and decision making methods, Doctoral Dissertation, Virginia Polytechnic Institute and State University, Blacksburg, VA, (2005).
14. Ryu, Y. S., Suh, T. and Kim, H. S. Revising the mobile phone usability questionnaire (MPUQ): An item response theory approach. In *Proc. Society of Marketing Advances 2008*, (2008), 235-236.
15. Sauro, J. and Lewis, J.R. Correlations among prototypical usability metrics: evidence for the construct of usability. In *Proc. CHI 2009*, ACM Press (2009), 1609-1618.
16. Sauro, J. Does better usability increase customer loyalty? Measuring Usability article. Retrieved on September 19th, 2010, http://www.measuringusability.com/usability-loyalty.php.
17. Seebode, J., Schaffer, S., Wechsung, I. and Metze, F. Influence of training on direct and indirect measures for the evaluation of multimodal systems. In *Proc. Interspeech 2009*, (2009), 300-303.
18. Suzuki, S., Nakao, Y., Asahi, T., Bellotti, V., Yee, N. and Fukuzumi, S. Empirical comparison of task completion time between mobile phone models with matched interaction sequences. In *Proc. HCI International 2009*, Springer (2009), 114-122.

Some Like it Hot? Thermal Feedback for Mobile Devices

Graham Wilson, Martin Halvey, Stephen A. Brewster
School of Computing Science, University of Glasgow,
Glasgow, United Kingdom G12 8QQ
gawilson@dcs.gla.ac.uk, {first.last}@glasgow.ac.uk

Stephen A. Hughes
SAMH Engineering, 1 Leopardstown
Drive, Blackrock, Dublin Ireland
stephenahughes@gmail.com

ABSTRACT
Thermal stimulation is a rich, emotive and salient feedback channel that is well suited to HCI, but one that is yet to be fully investigated. Thermal feedback may be suited to environments that are too loud for audio or too bumpy for vibrotactile feedback. This paper presents two studies into how well users could detect hot and cold stimuli presented to the fingertips, the palm, the dorsal surface of the forearm and the dorsal surface of the upper arm. Evaluations were carried out in static and mobile settings. Results showed that the palm is most sensitive, cold is more perceivable and comfortable than warm and that stronger and faster-changing stimuli are more detectable but less comfortable. Guidelines for the design of thermal feedback are outlined, with attention paid to perceptual and hedonic factors.

Author Keywords
Thermal feedback, mobile interaction, non-visual feedback.

ACM Classification Keywords
H5.2. User Interfaces: Haptic IO

General Terms
Design, Human Factors

INTRODUCTION
Modern mobile devices are almost uniformly moving towards interfaces based on physical interactions such as multitouch and 3D spatial input through gestures. Although the use of haptic feedback has received a lot of attention, this has mostly been through the vibrotactile actuators built into most phones. There has been very little work in HCI on other aspects of the touch sense, in particular the thermal aspects, which we focus on in this paper.

There are many potential uses for thermal feedback; the following usage scenarios provide some potential examples:

"Jo is travelling to a meeting on the train. She is carrying a mobile device with personalised travel apps. Before her train arrives she has a drink near the station. After some time, her device begins to slowly warm up indicating that her train is nearing the station. She finishes up and heads for the train. As she boards the train, thermal feedback provides information regarding proximity to her seat; the device gets warmer as she moves towards the seat and colder as she moves away. This non-visual feedback would mean that she doesn't need her ticket to hand to check seat numbers as she walks down the train."

"Ted is in the library. He receives a text message and his phone vibrates in his pocket, but the rumbling of the phone off the seat disturbs people close by. Ted takes out his phone, slightly embarrassed he sets his phone to give him just thermal notifications. Now all messages, etc. will be private only to Ted. As one particular message is received his phone cools, indicating that an important message has been received. He leaves the library to check his message"

These examples illustrate the numerous potential uses for thermal feedback. It can act as an alternative non-visual notification channel for situations that are too bumpy or noisy for vibrotactile and audio feedback. It can augment both visual and non-visual feedback to add an extra richness to the interaction experience. In addition, thermal output is also entirely private; in contrast, vibrotactile feedback can sometimes still be heard or felt by others.

Much work has examined the underlying characteristics of human thermal perception and this is not the focus of this paper. Fundamental HCI research needs to be conducted to properly judge the merits of thermal feedback as a practical display method. It is necessary to understand the stimulus characteristics (e.g. intensity and rate of change) that are most effective for arousing sensation in the user. We focus on designing structured feedback for HCI that produces detectable stimuli using hardware designed for use with mobile devices. Two studies were conducted to test how well users could detect warm and cool changes in thermal sensation presented to the hand and arm; one study focused on sitting and the other walking around an indoor environment. Note that in this paper we use the terms 'warm' and 'cool/cold' (e.g. in 'warmth/cold perception') to refer to *warming* or *cooling*: increases or decreases in temperature.

BACKGROUND
Temperature Perception
The human skin rests in a relatively small 'neutral' homeostatic thermal state, ranging from around 28°C up to a maximum of 40°C when in all but the most extreme environmental conditions [12, 22]. The size of this neutral zone is relatively constant across individuals at around 6-8°C, but due to individual differences in thermal sensitivity, the relative position of each individual's neutral zone varies

(e.g. 30-36°C, 28-34°C, etc.). Within the neutral zone there is no discernable thermal sensation [12], i.e. there is no sensation of warmth or cold, and *adaptation* (where the sensation of thermal neutrality returns after heating or cooling the skin to a different temperature) only occurs within this range [22]. Outside of this range a constant sensation of warmth (above) or cold (below) is perceived [15]. Jones & Berris [12] suggested that slow changes in thermal stimulation within the neutral zone are difficult to detect. Therefore, for thermal stimuli to be reliably detected the skin must be presented with temperatures out-with this zone or changes in thermal stimulation must be rapid. There are significantly (approximately 30x) more cold than warm receptors [22] and the speed of cold perception is faster than warmth perception. Kenshalo [13] suggests that cold perception has a more immediate onset whereas warm sensations grow slowly before 'blooming'.

Thermal *just noticeable differences* (JNDs) refer to the minimum amount of change (warming or cooling) from current skin temperature that is required for that change to be detected, and are similar to tests of just noticeable differences in other perceptual modalities. For example, a JND of 1.5°C means any change of less than 1.5°C cannot be felt and, in general, the smaller the JND, the more salient the stimulus. JNDs are measured from a set baseline temperature and are inextricably linked to both this starting temperature and the rate of change (ROC) of the stimulus. At low rates (up to 3°C/sec) the size of both warm and cold JNDs decrease as ROC increases, with the most dramatic decrease occurring from ~0.01°C/sec to 0.3°C/sec. Above 3°C/sec (up to ~7°C/sec) JNDs then begin to increase again, with this being attributed to the conduction velocities of thermal receptors [2, 20] as well as reaction and cognition time [8]. This suggests that stimuli become more salient as ROC increases; however, above a set speed, even if salience increases, the ROC 'overtakes' reaction time so that further increases in stimulation have occurred by the time the participant could react. As the skin adapts to the warm or cool extremes of the neutral zone, warm and cold JNDs, respectively, decrease and decrease more as the stimulus intensity approaches the heat/cold pain thresholds (~45°C and 11-15°C respectively [11, 22]). In other words, we become more sensitive to thermal changes if they move the skin closer to pain thresholds. Conversely, warm and cold JNDs increase as the skin is cooled and warmed respectively. From this, and other evidence, it is clear that the thermal sense is more sensitive to *changes* in temperature, rather than absolute temperature itself.

Thermal sensitivity is not uniform across the body; there are marked variations between different locations as well as between different skin types. Glabrous skin (hairless skin as found on the fingertips or palm) is generally less sensitive to changes in thermal stimulation than non-glabrous, hairy, skin, with JNDs being generally larger on glabrous skin due to skin thickness [8, 20]. The thenar eminence (the bulbous region of the palm adjoining the thumb) has higher sensitivity than the rest of the palm [7], but is still not as sensitive as non-glabrous skin on the hand [8]. In general, thermal sensitivity is best on the head and trunk but worse towards the extremities [2, 7].

The JNDs mentioned above were achieved in tightly controlled laboratory settings with users who often have many hours of training making fine judgments on small changes in thermal stimulation. It may well be that these levels of accuracy do not hold in more realistic, and particularly, mobile settings. Higher rates of change and/or higher stimulus intensities may be required to produce detectable stimuli in these circumstances. For example, Nakashige *et al.* [18] found that not all users could detect changes of +3.9°C or -3.3°C at a rate of ~1°C/sec when the palm of novice users was stimulated in less controlled settings.

Thermal Feedback in HCI

In their summary of thermal perception and the design of thermal feedback for virtual material discrimination in VR, Jones & Berris [12] summarized what they saw as the "desired features" of a thermal display. These were based on both VR research and psychophysical evidence and indicate the range of control a system would need to have to make full use of the thermal sense. They recommend using stimulus temperatures of 22-42°C and employing higher rates of change to maximize detection of stimuli. However, they also suggest a thermal interface should be capable of heating and cooling resolutions of 0.001°C and 0.002°C respectively to mimic the subtle differences in the thermal conductance of different materials. These features are extremely precise, and necessarily so for VR applications, but this level of accuracy may not be necessary or even perceivable for mobile thermal feedback.

Wettach *et al.* [23] designed a Peltier-based thermal feedback apparatus for mobile devices and tested users ability to differentiate three different stimulus temperatures (32°C, 37°C and 42°C). Initially error rates were around 65%, although this number dropped to 25% after long-term training. None of these temperatures would normally be considered 'cool' and so this study suggests that individuals can identify varying degrees of warmth, not simply a change from one temperature to another. This was only an initial study, however, if users can only distinguish these three relatively disparate temperatures at 75% accuracy, it is unlikely they will be able to differentiate stimuli at the resolutions suggested by Jones & Berris [12].

Other work looking at thermal feedback in HCI has been more abstract, often focusing on emotional communication, given the inherent affective quality of thermal sensations, compared to vibrotactile or even auditory output [22]. Gooch [4] found that adding thermal feedback to remote, PC-mediated communication increased feelings of 'social presence'. Nakashige *et al.* [18] accompanied photographs of warm and cold scenes (food such as soup and ice cream, and environmental examples like fire and snow) with either warm or cold feedback. A small informal study indicated that the foods appeared more appealing when accompanied by the corresponding temperature and a small number of users reported an impression of a "loving home" from the warm soup. Iwasaki *et al.* [10] suggested a system that could be used to convey emotional information to another user through augmentation of an existing mobile phone. Lee and Lim [17] discussed existing preconceptions about the meaning or significance of thermal sensations in general and found that users did not treat sensations as binary (i.e. warm and cold) but as a continuum, They also found that sensations were almost meaningless without context but were a very unobtrusive form of feedback. They also found that cold stimuli were generally less preferred than warm.

Figure 1: Microcontroller and Peltier stimulators used in the experiments.

Recently, Kushiyama and colleagues [16] have developed thermal display technology utilizing Peltier elements and Narumi *et al.* [19] developed a contextual/ambient thermal display for more mobile scenarios. Neither piece of technology has been tested experimentally but both hold promise for future use. Thermo-pict [16], in particular, stands out as it has the opportunity to provide patterns of thermal stimulation not possible with more limited hardware, including thermal tactile 'pictures' and visible displays.

There are huge differences in feedback design requirements between the highly accurate and articulate thermal interfaces used in VR to represent real materials and the much lower resolution, "warm-or-cold" designs of affective computing. There are many potential uses for thermal feedback in HCI but more work needs to be done on how to design and structure feedback so that it is comfortable, perceivable and suitable for use in a variety of real-world static and mobile settings. As such, we ran two evaluations to identify characteristics of stimulus presentation that would be well suited for use in thermal feedback design for mobile HCI.

EVALUATIONS

We developed a custom microcontroller board that could independently drive four Peltier heat pumps (see Figure 1). Peltier heat pumps allow for a high level of control over temperature output and also allow for both heating and cooling from the same pump. Each Peltier device could be independently controlled over USB, with the temperature set anywhere within the operating temperatures of -20°C to +45°C, accurate to 0.1°C. The Peltiers themselves were bonded to circuit boards with a heat sync bonded to the other side. Safety mechanisms on the board prevented the Peltiers from becoming hotter than 45°C and cut off all power and input if the thermistor detecting the Peltier output became electrically or physically disconnected. For our study we used two Peltiers. Using two instead of one gave a larger stimulus area and meant that we would need lower intensity output to produce detectable sensations [22]. We chose not to use more than two as this would have required too large an area of skin for mobile use.

Static Indoor Evaluation

The initial investigation looked at how well users could detect thermal stimuli while sat at a desk in an indoor usability lab. The Peltier board was controlled over USB from a MacBook Pro running a Pygame interface. User input to the Pygame GUI was received via a mouse.

Stimuli

A neutral starting temperature of 32°C was chosen as this is within the defined 'neutral zone' of thermal sensation [12, 22] and has been used in other studies [5, 14]. The skin was adapted to this temperature before each trial session and was returned to it between each stimulus presentation. Two different rates of stimulus change (ROC) were used: 1°C/sec and 3°C/sec. Previous work has shown that 1°C/sec should be adequate to produce detectable sensations in ideal situations [2, 14, 20]. Other work suggests it may not always be large enough [18] so a higher rate was also included. Not only will this comparison indicate which is the more useful ROC, in terms of producing detectable sensations, but also it would allow for comparison of power requirements, which will need to be balanced with perception performance when being considered for mobile use.

	Warm		Cool	
Intensity	**1°C/sec**	**3°C/sec**	**1°C/sec**	**3°C/sec**
1°C	33°C	33°C	31°C	31°C
3°C	35°C	35°C	29°C	29°C
6°C	38°C	38°C	26°C	26°C

Table 1: Stimuli by intensity, direction and ROC.

Three different stimulus intensities were used: 1°C, 3°C and 6°C. From previous findings, 1°C changes were detectable at rates of change equal to and below those used here, but again in ideal laboratory conditions [2, 14, 20], whereas 3°C was perceivable in a less controlled desktop situation [18]. Wettach *et al.* [23] and Lee and Lim [17] suggest that users were able to differentiate varying degrees of intensity and so a stronger intensity of 6°C was introduced to investigate user responses to varying intensities. As thermal perception is a bipolar sense, both warming and cooling stimuli were used, employing each intensity change in both directions from 32°C neutral. Therefore a single stimulus consisted of warming or cooling at a set intensity (1°C, 3°C or 6°C) at one ROC (1°C/sec or 3°C/sec), for example, warming 3°C at 1°C/sec (see Table1). The temperatures were well away from the cold and heat pain thresholds. Each stimulus in this set was delivered twice, giving a total of 24 stimuli presented at each location (3 intensities x 2 directions x 2 rates x 2 presentations, see Table 1 for details).

As our interest is in using thermal feedback for mobile interaction we selected four body locations that are used to either hold, transport or interact with a mobile device, or locations that could potentially be used for mobile device interaction. The fingers and palm of the hand are the most logical choices, as mobile phones are held against the palm and gripped with the fingers. The thenar eminence (the bulbous area of skin adjoining the thumb) was chosen specifically over the central palm itself due to its apparent increased sensitivity to thermal stimuli compared to the palm [11]. The dorsal surface (hairy skin) of the forearm was chosen partly as it has differing thermal sensitivity to both the thenar eminence and the fingertips [6] but also as it is conceivable that a watch or wrist band could be worn which contains thermal elements. Finally, the upper arm is already used for MP3 players. Such a device could include thermal feedback through skin contact in the same way as one worn around the wrist.

Participants

Fourteen participants (9 male, 5 female) aged 21 to 57 (mean=29.2 years) took part in the evaluation, all studying or working at the University. All were right-handed and paid £6 for participation, which lasted just over an hour.

Variables

For this study we were interested in identifying what stimuli produce detectable sensations from a neutral base temperature, i.e. which stimuli were noticeable and so would be best suited for use in thermal feedback design. The independent variables were: *Rate of change, Stimulus intensity, Direction of change (warm or cool)* and *Body location*. The dependent variables were: *Stimulus detection* (if one was perceived), *Detection time* (how long after the initiation of a stimulus that it was detected), *JND size* (distance in °C from neutral when the stimulus was felt), *subjective intensity of stimulus* and *subjective comfort of stimulus*. We recorded user subjective reports of the intensity of the stimulation (a 7-point Likert scale from "Very Cold" up to "Very Hot") and the comfort level of the stimulus (a 7-point Likert scale from "Very Uncomfortable" up to "Very Comfortable") similar to others used before [1, 3].

Environmental temperature influences skin temperature [9, 12] and so is an important factor to consider as particularly high (>25°C) or low (<=15°C) environmental temperatures can cause the skin temperature to shift from the neutral zone. We did not have the facilities to run the experiment in a climate-controlled room and therefore recorded room temperature and humidity during each trial and compared results against these data. It should be noted, however, that the skin under the Peltier was always adapted to the neutral 32°C between trials (and measured to ensure it was so).

Procedure

The task was split up into 4 conditions based on the location of stimulation, with all participants taking part in all conditions in a counterbalanced order and the ordering of stimuli was random. The participant was sat at a desk upon which there was a computer monitor and mouse. For the fingertip and thenar eminence conditions, the Peltier stimulator lay on the desk in front of the seated participant, facing up so that the users could lay their finger/hand on the stimulator, supported by a padded rest (see Figure 2 left). For the forearm and upper arm conditions, the stimulator was held against the arm with an elastic fabric strip secured with Velcro pads. The stimulator was held between this strip and the skin (see Figure 2 right).

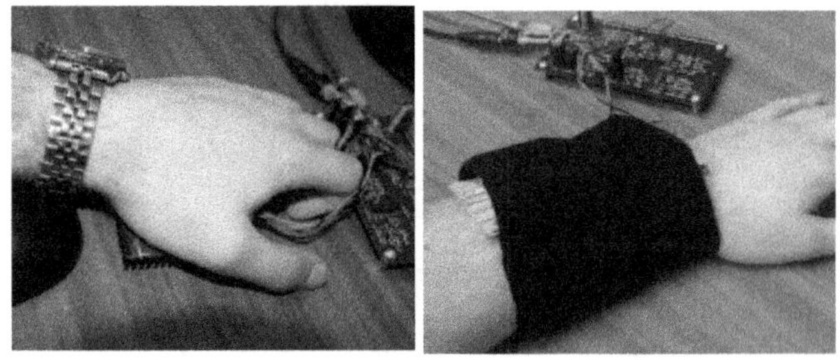

Figure 2: Stimulator sites for thenar and forearm conditions.

The stimulator was contacted with the skin of the non-dominant hand/arm (by resting on top or via the elastic strip) at the beginning of each condition and remained in contact for the duration of that condition. Green [6] found that participants reported higher intensity perceptions when they were in contact with a stimulator between successive stimuli, compared to removing their hand from the stimulator in between trials. At the start of each condition the stimulators were set to the neutral starting temperature of 32°C for one minute so as to adapt the skin to this temperature. After the adaptation period all 24 stimuli were presented in random order. A stimulus presentation comprised of 10 seconds of stimulus followed by a return to the neutral temperature and 20 seconds of adaptation. There were no visual or auditory cues as to when stimuli were presented. Participants were instructed to click the mouse button as soon as they felt a change in thermal stimulation, in any direction and at any intensity. Once this occurred, the temperature of the Peltiers was taken as the temperature that was detected, and the time elapsed since the initiation of the stimulus was taken as the time-to-detection. At this point, 2 Likert scales appeared on screen asking the participants to rate the stimulus felt in terms of *intensity* (from "very cold" to "very hot") and *comfort* (from "very uncomfortable" to "very comfortable"). They then clicked on a submit button and another stimulus was presented after the 20 seconds of adaptation. If the participant clicked the mouse button before the full 10 seconds of stimulation had passed, the Peltiers were immediately returned to neutral and the rating scales were presented.

Results

Environmental Temperature

During the experiment, room temperature ranged from 20.5°C to 25.3°C with an average of 23.6°C. Humidity ranged from 42% to 67% with an average of 48.5%. Perceptual research has shown that, at room temperatures of 15°C to 25°C, skin temperature sits at neutral temperatures of 30°C to 35°C. So the neutral starting temperature used here would have been close to overall skin temperature, producing no sensation of warm or cool.

Number of Detections

A multi-factorial repeated-measures ANOVA showed a significant effect of body location on the number of thermal detections produced ($F_{3,39}$=3.073, p<.05). *Post hoc* pair-wise Bonferroni-corrected *t*-tests showed the thenar eminence ($\bar{x}$ =87.5%) produced significantly more detections than the fingertips ($\bar{x}$ =75.5%) but non-significantly more than the forearm ($\bar{x}$ =79%) and upper arm ($\bar{x}$ =78.5%).

There was a significant effect of stimulus intensity on the number of detected stimuli ($F_{2,26}$ = 84.623, p<.001). Bonferroni-corrected *t*-test comparisons showed a significant difference between the numbers detected from all stimulus intensities. The number increased as the intensity increased with means of 53%, 90.5% and 97% for 1°C, 3°C and 6°C intensities (see Figure 6 'S' columns). There was no significant effect of ROC or direction of change on the number of stimuli detected. Both warm ($\bar{x}$ =79%) and cool ($\bar{x}$ =81.5%) stimuli produced similar numbers of detections.

Time-to-Detection & JND Size

The time-to-detection and size of JND are directly related and so are considered together. Friedman's analysis of variance by ranks showed location had a significant effect on both time-to-detection (χ^2 (3)=24.71, p<.001) and JND size (χ^2 (3)=41.65, p<.001). Wilcoxon *T* comparisons showed that the finger produced significantly longer times (median=3.22s) than the thenar (median=2.54s; *T*=3672, p=.001), forearm (median =2.68s; *T*=3205, p<.001) and upper arm (median=2.50s; *T*=2988, p<.001). Similarly, Wilcoxon pair-wise comparisons showed that all locations had significantly different JND sizes from each other (p<.05) with the finger (2.9°C) having the largest, compared to thenar (1.9°C), forearm (2.2°C) and upper arm (2.25°C). Significant effects of direction of change showed that warming stimuli were detected significantly slower (median=2.91s) than cooling stimuli (median=2.46s) (*T*=15,643, p <0.001) and, consequently, warm JND size was significantly larger (median=2.80°C) than cold JND size (median=1.85°C) (*T*=8327.50, p<.001).

Stimulus intensity also had a significant effect on time-to-detection (χ^2 (2)=63.01, p<.001; see Figure 3). Wilcoxon *T* comparisons showed significant differences in the time-to-detection between all stimulus intensities: 1°C vs. 3°C (*T*=2906, p<.001), 1°C vs. 6°C (*T*=1638, p<.001) and 3°C vs. 6°C (*T*=9419, p<.01). The amount of time decreased as the intensity increased with median values of 3.67s, 2.59s and 2.30s for 1°C, 3°C and 6°C intensities. Friedman's analysis also showed a significant effect of stimulus intensity on JND size (χ^2 (2)=261.27, p<.001). Wilcoxon comparisons showed that all intensities were significantly different from each other (p<.001) with median JNDs of 1°C, 2.7°C and 3.75°C for intensities of 1°C, 3°C and 6°C respectively.

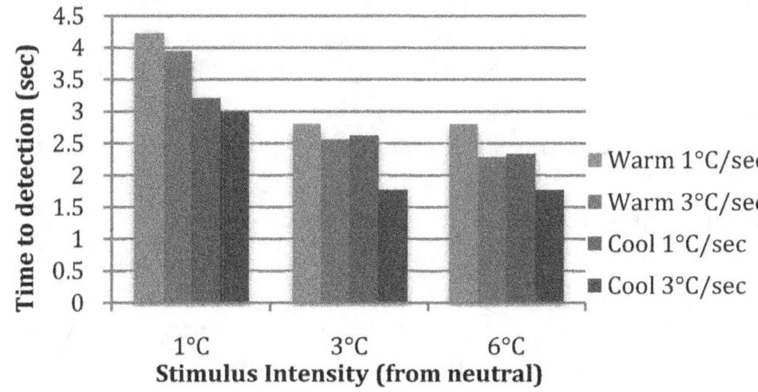

Figure 3: Median detection time at each intensity and rate of stimulus change.

Finally, rate of change significantly affected the time-to-detection (*T*=12,461, p < .001) and JND size (*T*=8213.50, p<.001). The higher ROC (3°C/sec) produced a significantly lower time (median=2.43s) than the lower rate of change (1°C/sec; median=3.04s) while the lower ROC had significantly lower JND size (median=1.90°C) than the higher ROC (median=3.00°C).

Subjective Stimulus Intensity

Intensity ratings ranged from 0 to 3, where 0 denoted "Neutral" and 3 denoted "Very Intense". A Wilcoxon *T* test showed a significant effect of ROC on subjective stimulus intensity (*T*=3935, p<.001). The higher ROC produced significantly higher ratings of intensity (median=1.5) than the low rate of change (median=1.00). There was also a significant effect of direction of change (*T*=7263.50, p<.001) as warm stimuli were rated as significantly more intense (median=1.5) than cold stimuli (median=1.0).

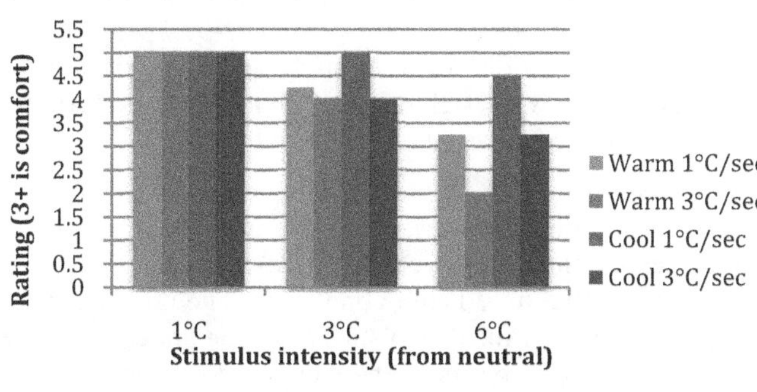

Figure 4: Median subjective comfort ratings at each intensity and rate of change. Rating of 3+ indicates comfort.

A Friedman's ANOVA showed a significant effect of stimulus intensity on perceived stimulus intensity (χ^2 (2)=160.742, p<.001). Wilcoxon *T* comparisons showed that all three stimulus intensities were significantly different from each other (p<.001) with median ratings of 1, 1.5 and 2 for intensities of 1°C, 3°C and 6°C respectively.

Subjective Stimulus Comfort

ROC had a significant effect on subjective comfort (*T*=8775, p<.001) with the higher rate of change (3°C/sec) producing significantly lower ratings of comfort (median=4.0) than the lower ROC (1°C/sec, median=4.50). A Wilcoxon *T* also showed a significant effect of direction of change on reports of comfort (*T*=8922.50, p<.001). Warm stimuli had a significantly lower average comfort rating (median=4.0) than cool (median=4.5), see Figure 4. Friedman's analysis of variance by ranks showed that stimulus intensity also had a significant effect on subjective comfort (χ^2 (2)=48.46, p<.001). Wilcoxon *T* comparisons showed significant differences in subjective comfort between all stimulus intensities: 1°C vs. 3°C (*T*=2107.50, p<.001), 1°C vs. 6°C (*T*=1500.50, p<.001) and 3°C vs. 6°C (*T*=4343.50, p<.001). Ratings of comfort decreased as the intensity increased, with median values of 5.0, 4.0 and 3.0 for 1°C, 3°C and 6°C respectively.

The results of this study show that the thenar is the most sensitive area with the arm locations slightly less so and the fingers the least sensitive. Increasing the rate of change or stimulus intensity makes the stimulus more salient, as it is more quickly detectable and more likely to be detected, but this comes at the expense of subjective comfort. In order to validate these results and also to understand how being mobile influenced stimulus detection, we carried out a follow-up evaluation using similar apparatus and stimuli but with users walking around an indoor environment.

Mobile Indoor Evaluation

For this study, the Peltier microcontroller was connected to an Ultra Mobile Personal Computer (UMPC) running Windows XP, which was carried by each participant in a backpack (see Figure 5). All commands were sent to the UMPC via Bluetooth from a Nexus One phone held in the user's dominant hand, which displayed the experimental interface; these commands were then sent to the Peltier microcontroller over USB via this UMPC. Fourteen participants (10 Male, 4 Female) aged 23 and 41 (mean=30.2 years) took part in the evaluation, all were studying or working at the University. All were right-handed and were paid £10 for participation, which lasted just over an hour.

Procedure

The same stimuli and variables were used as in the static indoor evaluation. However, in this experiment the *bodily location* variable only had 3 conditions. The dorsal surface of the forearm and the dorsal surface of the upper arm were also used in this experiment, as they are common locations where people place devices e.g. a watch on the wrist or an MP3 player on the upper arm. In place of the thenar and fingertips locations, the Peltier devices were placed in the palm of the hand of each participant to simulate holding a mobile phone (and the fingertip condition had poorer performance in the static experiment). The task was split into 3 conditions based on location of stimulation, with all participants taking part in all conditions in a counterbalanced order and the ordering of stimuli was random. Each participant walked around a triangular route in an indoor office environment. For all conditions, the stimulator was held against the arm with an elastic fabric strip secured with Velcro pads. The stimulator was held between this strip and the skin (see Figure 5). The stimulator was contacted with the skin of the non-dominant hand/arm at the beginning of each condition and remained in contact for the duration of that condition. The order and duration of the stimuli were presented in the same manner as the indoor static experiment. Participants were instructed to press a button on the phone screen when they felt a change in thermal stimulation, in any direction and at any intensity. Once this occurred, the temperature of the Peltiers was taken as the temperature that produced the sensation, and the time elapsed since the initiation of the stimulus was taken as the time-to-detection. At this point the same 2 Likert scales as were used in the static experiment appeared on screen and the procedure continued as in the static experiment.

Figure 5: Stimulator locations for forearm and upper arm.

Results

Unfortunately due to issues to do with the external thermistors on the Peltier devices not all conditions were completed for all users. Moisture from skin caused the Peltier devices to stop working when it came into contact with thermistor; this issue was remedied by placing tape over the external thermistors, this still allowed the thermistors to function as normal. As a result 662 out of 1008 stimulations were submitted to the participants. This was taken into account when calculating all of the statistics related to the mobile study. Despite this, statistical tests were still run to compare the results from the static and mobile conditions to empirically test how mobility affected thermal perception.

Environmental Temperature

Room temperature ranged from 20.2°C to 25.9°C, with an average of 21.8°C, and humidity ranged from 39% to 69%, with an average of 48.9%. As with the static experiment the neutral starting temperature used here was close to overall skin temperature, producing no sensation of warm or cool.

Number of Detections

Friedman's analysis of variance by ranks was used to analyse the effect of intensity of change and body location on the number of stimuli detected. Intensity of change was found to have a significant effect on the number of thresholds produced (χ^2 (2)=134.105, p <0.001). *Post hoc* Wilcoxon *T* comparisons showed significant differences in the number of detection between all stimulus intensities: 1°C vs. 3°C (T = 6837.0 p<0.001), 1°C vs. 6°C (T=9100.0 p<0.001) and 3°C vs. 6°C (T=2251.5 p<0.001). Wilcoxon pair-wise comparisons were also used to determine the effect of ROC and direction of change. There was no significant effect of ROC, bodily location or direction of stimulation. The number of stimuli detected increased as the intensity increased with means of 28.44%, 69.68% and 85.78% for 1°C, 3°C and 6°C intensities respectively (see Figure 6). As can be seen, the users are not able to detect as many stimuli as in the static condition but the patterns of detection were approximately the same. When compared with the static results Mann-Whitney U comparisons showed that mobility significantly affected the number of stimulus detections (U=313515.5, Z=12.049, p<.001), with more detections in the static conditions compared with mobile.

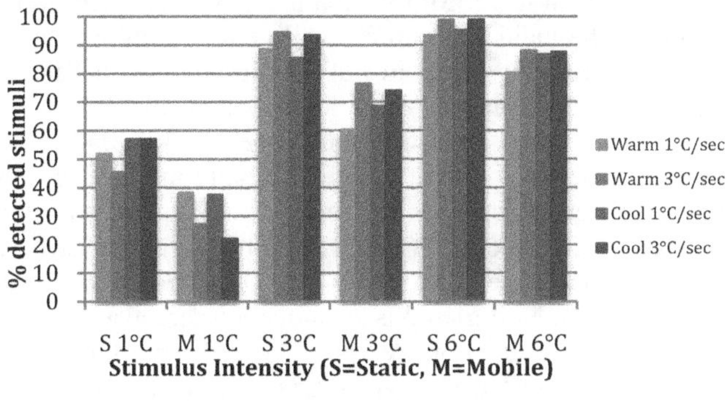

Figure 6: Percentage of stimuli detected at each intensity and rate of stimulus change for both static and mobile studies.

Time-to-Detection and JND Size

Friedman's analysis of variance by ranks was used to analyse the effect of location and stimulus intensity on the average time-to-detection. Location did not have any significant effect, however stimulus intensity did have a significant effect on time-to-detection (χ^2 (2)=36.102, p<.001). Wilcoxon T comparisons showed significant differences in the time-to-detection between the smallest intensity and the two larger stimulus intensities: 1°C vs. 3°C (T=1687.5, p<.001), 1°C vs. 6°C (T=1844.5, p<.001), but not between 3°C and 6°C. The amount of time decreased as the intensity increased with median values of 3.74s, 3.07s and 2.95s for 1°C, 3°C and 6°C intensities respectively. Wilcoxon T tests were used to analyse the effect of rate of change and direction of change on time-to-detection. Rate of change significantly affected the time-to-detection (T=12,472, p < .001): the higher ROC (3°C/sec) produced a significantly lower time (median=2.96s) than the lower ROC (1°C/sec; median=3.35s). A significant effect of direction of change (T=6105.5, p < .001) showed that warming stimuli were detected significantly slower (median=3.28s) than cooling stimuli (median=2.94s).

As stated earlier, time-to-detection is linked directly to the size of JND. A Friedman's ANOVA showed a significant effect of intensity on the size of JND (χ^2 23)=79.993, p<.001). *Post hoc* Wilcoxon pair-wise comparisons showed that all intensities differed significantly from each other (p<0.001) Median JND sizes were 1°C (1°C intensity), 2.3°C (3°C intensity), and 4°C (6°C intensity). Friedman's analysis of variance by ranks showed no significant effect of location on the size of JND. Wilcoxon T comparisons showed a significant effect of rate of stimulus change on JND size (T=14047.5, p<0.001): 1°C/sec had significantly lower JND size (median=1.90°C) than 3°C/sec (median=3.00°C). A further Wilcoxon T also showed a significant effect of direction of change on JND size (T=6820, p<0.001). Warm stimuli produced significantly larger JNDs (median=3.1°C) than cold stimuli (median=2.1°C).

When compared with the static results a U comparison also showed that time-to-detection was significantly affected by mobility (U=33452, Z=7.330, p<.001), with mobile detections taking significantly longer than static detections. As threshold size and time-to-detection are interlinked, the size of threshold was also significantly affected by mobility (U=69784.0, Z=11.440, p<.001), again with a greater threshold size for mobile in comparison with static.

Subjective Stimulus Intensity

As with the static evaluation intensity ratings ranged from 0 to 3, where 0 denoted "Neutral" and 3 denoted "Very Intense". A Friedman's ANOVA showed a significant effect of stimulus intensity on perceived stimulus intensity (χ^2 (2)=160.742, p<.001). Wilcoxon T comparisons showed that all three stimulus intensities were significantly different from each other (p<.001) with median/mean ratings of 1/1.09, 1/1.47 and 2/1.95 for intensities of 1°C, 3°C and 6°C respectively. A Friedman's ANOVA showed no significant effect for body location. Similarly, Wilcoxon T tests revealed no significant effect for either stimulation direction or rate of change of intensity.

Subjective Stimulus Comfort

A Wilcoxon T test revealed that ROC had a significant effect on subjective comfort (T=7364.5, p<.005) with the higher ROC (3°C/sec) producing significantly lower ratings of comfort (median=4 mean = 3.63) than the lower ROC (1°C/sec, median=4 mean = 3.99). A Wilcoxon T test also showed a significant effect of direction of change on reports of comfort (T=6408.5, p<.001). Warm stimuli had a significantly lower average comfort rating (median=4 mean=3.52) than cool stimuli (median=4 mean = 3.89). Friedman's analysis of variance by ranks showed that stimulus intensity also had a significant effect on subjective comfort (χ^2 (2)=412.703, p<.005). Wilcoxon T comparisons showed significant differences in subjective comfort between 1°C and 3°C (T=1405, p<0.05) stimulus intensities and 3°C vs. 6°C (T=5712, p < 0.001) stimulus intensities. Ratings of comfort decreased as the intensity increased, with median values of 4 (mean =4.1), 4 (mean =4.06) and 3 (mean =3.4) for 1°C, 3°C and 6°C respectively. A Friedman's analysis of body location also revealed a significant effect on subjective comfort (χ^2 (2)=9.968, p<.01). Pair wise Wilcoxon T tests revealed significant differences between the back of the forearm and upper arm conditions (T=39911.5, p<0.005) and between the forearm and palm of the hand conditions (T=3466.5, p<0.01), there were no differences between the upper arm and palm of the hand condition. The median values of the subjective comfort were 4 (mean = 3.63), 4 (mean =3.95) and 4 (mean = 3.71) for the arm, forearm and hand respectively.

DISCUSSION

In order to put these results into context for thermal feedback design for HCI, we will discuss each measure's significance in terms of suitability for use in feedback, either in terms of optimal sensitivity (for body location) or perceivability (for stimulus characteristics ROC, direction of change and intensity). Unless otherwise made clear, all relationships/effects refer to both mobile and static results.

Comparison of Static and Mobile

The results from the mobile study were very similar to those in the static, and as such they go some way to validating both the results themselves as well as the feedback recommendations that arise from them (see this section and Design Recommendations). In general, stimuli were more difficult to detect when mobile, with lower detection rates and slower detection speeds. However, despite the lower absolute values, the static and mobile values changed in very similar patterns. Indeed it was found that mobility significantly affected stimulus detection rates, with far fewer being detected while the user was mobile. We also found that time-to-detection was significantly slower when mobile, compared to static detections. As threshold and time are interlinked the size of threshold was significantly larger for mobile in comparison with static, meaning a larger amount of change occurred before detection.

Another prominent difference between the two studies is the minimal effect body location had on all experimental measures during the mobile study. During the static experiment, body location significantly affected the number of stimuli detected, the time-to-detection and the size of JND, but *not* subjective comfort or intensity. One reason for this difference may be the omission of the finger condition in the mobile study as, comparing the results for the three non-finger conditions in the static study, measures of both number of detections and time-to-detection were very similar. The JND sizes for all locations were significantly different; however the fingertip still performed the worst of all areas. Therefore, it may have been the fingertip performance that skewed the static results. The other important difference between the mobile and static environments was the finding that neither direction of change or rate of change significantly affected subjective intensity while mobile, whereas they both did while stationary. This is discussed in more detail below. Aside from these findings, all other variable relationships/effects were the same across both mobile and static studies and are discussed below.

Location Sensitivity

The measures that relate most to judgments of 'sensitivity' here are the *number of detections*, the *time-to-detection* and the *size of JND*. A higher number of detected stimuli, a faster detection or a smaller JND size are all indications of higher sensitivity. Considering these measures only, the thenar eminence was shown to be the most sensitive location. In all measures in the static study it performed outright best or equal best with high detection rates, low detection speeds and small JND sizes. For the mobile condition the palm was most sensitive, in terms of number of stimuli detected. Both arm conditions performed very similarly to each other, suffering slightly lower detection rates and larger JNDs than the thenar and palm but had roughly equal detection speeds. The finger performed worst out of all locations in all three of these measures. The epidermis of glabrous skin, particularly that on the pads of the fingers, can be up to 5x thicker than that of hairy skin (for example on top of the arm) which increases delay in the thermal stimulus reaching thermoreceptors [24]. Overall detection rates were somewhat lower for the mobile study than when static. Although the hand was more sensitive and both arm locations were roughly equal in both environments, the detection rates were some 10-20% lower when mobile, at 60-65%. Using more intense stimuli when mobile increased detection rates (see Figure 6), up to 86%. From these results we recommend the thenar eminence as the optimal location for thermal feedback, however, in mobile situations where contact with precisely the thenar is not practical, the palm is recommended. Non-glabrous arm locations are also suitable for stimulus presentation. As the volar/glabrous skin on the forearm is suggested to have comparable sensitivity to the thenar [7, 11] this location will also be highly suitable. The fingers are the least suitable location due to low accuracy and slow response time. When the user is mobile stimuli will be more difficult to detect and so more intense feedback is necessary to increase likelihood of detection.

Stimulus Perception

The three measures used for determining location sensitivity are also used to determine how perceivable a stimulus is. However, thermal feedback is said to have an inherent hedonic element [22] and perception often varies from veridical (true) stimulation [21, 22] so it was useful, if not necessary, to also use measures of subjective intensity and comfort in our considerations of a stimulus' suitability for use in thermal feedback. Recall that intensity values here run from 0 (neutral) to 3 (very strong) and comfort ratings ranged from 0 (very uncomfortable) up to 6 (very comfortable) with a neutral value at 3. We therefore considered any rating of 3 or above as indicating acceptable comfort levels for feedback design.

Rate of Stimulus Change

Previous research has suggested that stimulus detection is heavily influenced by the rate of stimulus change, with higher rates of change producing more noticeable stimuli [2, 5, 8, 14]. This position was only partly supported by the results here, as, although the high ROC (3°C/sec) produced a significantly faster time-to-detection, both rates produced equal numbers of detections, which suggests higher ROC did *not* produce more noticeable stimuli. Given the lower detection times, it seems that ROCs over 1°C/sec do not affect *if* a stimulus is detected as much as *when* it is detected. The faster time suggests that faster-changing stimuli are more salient, or more *immediately* salient, and so thermal interactions that are time-critical would be recommended to use faster ROC to bring attention to the event more quickly. We also found that the high ROC produced significantly larger JND sizes and was significantly less comfortable than the low ROC. Some work has shown that JND size decreases as ROC increases up to about 3°C/sec at similar body locations [2] so this result is slightly puzzling. Further, the high ROC felt subjectively more intense than the low ROC in the static setting, but not while mobile. Temporal summation would cause faster changes in a small amount of time to be perceived as being more intense [22] which would explain both the higher intensity ratings while stationary as well as the lower comfort ratings (due to higher intensity). Why the high ROC was not more intense and yet still less comfortable in the mobile condition is unclear. In terms of feedback design, it appears that increasing the rate of change brings no benefit to stimulus detectability, and reduces stimulus comfort; however it can be used to reduce detection time and to potentially increase subjective intensity of the stimulus.

Direction of Change

In almost all measures, cold stimuli were more perceivable than warm stimuli. Although they produced a roughly equal number of detections, cold stimuli were faster to detect, produced smaller JNDs and were more comfortable. Cold perception has been found to be faster than warm [12, 20], producing smaller JNDs [14], and this was also found here. These three factors (time, JND and comfort) make cold stimuli particularly appealing for feedback design as they require less power to produce a detectable amount of change and are detectable sooner, compared to warm stimuli. Warm stimuli were reported as more subjectively intense than cold during the static condition but not while mobile. The human neutral thermal zone is around 28-40°C [12, 22], however the relative proximity of heat-pain and cold-pain to this area is not equal (45°C and 15°C respectively [20, 22]). It therefore takes more cooling to feel cold-pain than it does warming to feel heat-pain. In this study, the highest temperature used (38°C) was closer to heat-pain than the coldest temperature (26°C) was to cold pain [22]. Therefore, as the warm stimuli here were closer to painful levels, it may well be that these felt more intense than cold stimuli. What this means for feedback design is that care must be taken not to use too hot stimuli, as these may be too intense. Not surprisingly, these more intense warm stimuli also felt less comfortable. Further, more extreme cold will be necessary to produce equally intense stimulations as intense warmth, requiring disproportionately more power.

Stimulus Intensity

Here "intensity" refers to the maximum amount of change from neutral, set at 1°C, 3°C and 6°C. Although most research on thermal perception focuses on the rate of change rather than the 'end-point' intensity, we chose to control and manipulate stimulus intensity here, as we were interested in designing structured feedback for HCI, and so wished to indentify set stimulus characteristics that produce detectable stimuli. Previous psychophysical work has suggested that 1°C stimuli are highly detectable at lower rates of change than those used here [5, 14], although we hypothesised that such a low intensity may not be suitable for less controlled experimental situations with less highly trained users, which seems to be the case here. The results showed that increasing intensity significantly increased the number of stimuli detected, and as can be seen from Figure 6, detection rates for 1°C stimuli were very low, compared to those of 3°C and 6°C. Therefore, it seems that 1°C changes are not suitable for thermal feedback due to the low detection rate. Increasing stimulus intensity also significantly increased JND size and significantly reduced time-to-detection. The significant reduction in time-to-detection was mainly limited to between 1°C and 3°C intensities, which would suggest that the extra power required to push further change to 6°C would be wasted, purely in terms of speed of detection. Perhaps unsurprisingly, each intensity felt significantly more intense than those beneath it. This is a useful finding as it suggests that, in agreement with Wettach *et al.* [23], participants can differentiate at least some discrete levels of warmth and cold, not simply detect dichotic 'warming' or 'cooling'. This is an important result for feedback design as it suggests intensity can be used as a design parameter or event mapping. It also means that, although the extra power required for more intense stimuli does not bring about faster detections, it can produce stimuli of perceptually distinct intensity, with increased likelihood of detection.

DESIGN RECOMMENDATIONS AND CONCLUSIONS

From the results we have highlighted several interesting and important factors that should be considered when designing thermal feedback both in general and for mobile devices.

The thenar eminence is the optimal location for feedback, but non-glabrous arm locations are also suitable. In measures of 'number of stimuli detected', 'time-to-detection' and 'size of JND' the thenar eminence either performed outright best or equal best showing it to be the most sensitive area. Similarly, the palm was superior when mobile. Although the forearm and upper arm suffered lower overall detection rates than the thenar/palm, they both performed well on measures of 'time-to-detection' and 'JND size' indicating suitability. The fingers performed poorly on all measures, showing them to be slow and inaccurate in thermal perception.

1°C/sec and 3°C/sec changes are suitable, even necessary, but power-requirements must be considered. Both rates of change produced approximately equal numbers of detectable stimuli, with the best detection rates when using 3°C and 6°C stimuli. Each has its own advantages, however. 1°C/sec changes are slower and require a larger change to detect but feel less intense and so feel more comfortable. Therefore, low rates of change may be best suited to ambient displays. 3°C/sec changes, however, are much faster to detect but sacrifice a degree of comfort without any benefit in likelihood of detection. Faster changes may be necessary when mobile, as they will increase likelihood of detection.

Warm and cold stimuli are both suitable for use. Although both warm and cold stimuli are equally detectable, cold stimuli are faster to detect, require less change to detect and are more comfortable as they feel less intense. Warm stimuli should be used carefully or more subtly as they are generally less comfortable and feel more intense. A potentially problematic effect of using Peltier-based apparatus for producing cold feedback is that of heat sinking. As the skin side cools, the other warms, which could then potentially increase the temperature within the housing/body of the device. Drawing heat away from this side of the Peltier would be necessary for safe and effective use.

Intensity or 'end-point' can be used as a parameter for feedback design as different intensities are perceptually different. This would allow for many levels of warm and cold to be used for event semantics, e.g. priority for messages, proximity for GPS or download status. 1°C intensities are best avoided despite their low power costs and high comfort level, due to high levels of missed stimuli and slow detection speed. Finally, high intensities are best used at lower rates of change, as this will minimise discomfort.

Further work will study thermal perception of the same stimuli when a user is in a more realistic outdoors environment, as it is necessary to understand how environmental factors influence perception. In conclusion, this paper presented two studies, which investigated how well users were able to detect warm and cold stimuli presented to four locations on the hand and arm with a view to identifying features of stimulus presentation that would be well suited for use in thermal feedback design for HCI. Simple guidelines for design of feedback based on our results are outlined, with attention paid to perceptual and hedonic factors as well as more practical concerns such as power requirements.

ACKNOWLEDGEMENTS

This research has been funded by the Industrial Members of MobileVCE (www.mobilevce.com), with additional financial support from EPSRC grant EP/G063427/1.

REFERENCES

1. Cherycroze, S. Painful Sensation Induced by a Thermal Cutaneous Stimulus. *Pain*, 1983. 17(2): p. 109-137.
2. Claus, D., M. Hilz, I. Hummer, and B. Neundorfer. Methods of measurement of thermal thresholds. *Acta Neurol Scand*, 1987. 76(1): p. 8.
3. Gagge, A., J. Stolwijk, and J. Hardy. Comfort and Thermal Sensations and Associated Physiological Responses at Various Ambient Temperatures. *Environ Res*, 1967. 1(1): p. 1-20.
4. Gooch, D. An Investigation into Communicating Social Presence With Thermal Devices. *MSc Dissertation*, 2009: p. 1-390.
5. Gray, L., J. Stevens, and L. Marks. Thermal Stimulus Thresholds - Sources of Variability. *Physiol Behav*, 1982. 29(2): p. 355-360.
6. Green, B.G. Temperature perception on the hand during static versus dynamic contact with a surface. *Atten Percept Psycho*, 2009. 71(5): p. 1185-1196.
7. Hagander, L., H. Midani, and M. Kuskowski. Quantitative sensory testing: effect of site and skin temperature on thermal thresholds. *Clinical neurophysiology*, 2000. 111(1): p. 5.
8. Harrison, J. and K. Davis. Cold-evoked pain varies with skin type and cooling rate: a psychophysical study in humans. *Pain*, 1999. 83(2): p. 123-135.
9. Hirosawa, I., H. Dodo, M. Hosokawa, S. Watanabe, K. Nishiyama, and Y. Fukuichi. Physiological Variations of Warm and Cool Sense with Shift of Environmental-Temperature. *Int J Neurosci*, 1984. 24(3-4): p. 281-288.
10. Iwasaki, K., T. Miyaki, and J. Rakimoto. AffectPhone: A Handset Device to Present User's Emotional State with Warmth/Coolness. *BIOSTEC 2010*, 2010: p. 1-6.
11. Johnson, K., I. Darian-Smith, and C. LaMotte. Peripheral neural determinants of temperature discrimination in man: a correlative study of responses to cooling skin. *Journal of Neurophysiology*, 1973. 36(1): p. 24.
12. Jones, L.A. and M. Berris. The Psychophysics of Temperature Perception and Thermal-Interface Design. In *HAPTICS '02*, Orlando, FL, 2002.
13. Kenshalo, D. Somesthetic sensitivity in young and elderly humans. *Journal of Gerontology*, 1986. 41(1): p. 11.
14. Kenshalo, D., C.E. Holmes, and P.B. Wood. Warm and Cool Thresholds as a Function of Temperature Change. *Perception & Psychophysics*, 1968. 3(2A): p. 4.
15. Kenshalo, D. and H. Scott. Temporal course of thermal adaptation. *Science*, 1966. 151(1): p. 2.
16. Kushiyama, K., T. Baba, K. Doi, and S. Sasada. Thermo-Pict neo. *SIGGRAPH 10*, 2010: p. 1-1.
17. Lee, W. and Y.K. Lim. Thermo-Message: Exploring the Potential of Heat as a Modality of peripheral Expression. In *CHI 10: Extended Abstracts*, Atlanta, GA, 2010. ACM Press.
18. Nakashige, M., M. Kobayashi, and Y. Suzuki. "Hiya-Atsu" media: augmenting digital media with temperature. In *Proc. of CHI '09*, Boston, MA, 2009.
19. Narumi, T., T. Akagawa, Y.A. Seong, and M. Hirose. Thermotaxis. *SIGGRAPH 09*, 2009: p. 1-1.
20. Pertovaara, A. and I. Kojo. Influence of the rate of temperature change on thermal thresholds in man. *Exp Neurol*, 1985. 87(1): p. 7.
21. Stevens, J. and L.E. Marks. Spatial Summation of Cold. *Physiology and Behaviour*, 1979. 22(1): p. 7.
22. Stevens, J.C., *Thermal Sensibility*, in *The Psychology of Touch*, M.A. Heller and W. Schiff, Editors. 1991, Lawrence Erlbaum: New Jersey.
23. Wettach, R., C. Behrens, A. Danielsson, and T. Ness. A thermal information display for mobile applications. In *Proc. of MobileHCI '07*, Singapore, 2007. ACM Press.
24. Whitton, J. and J. Everall. The thickness of the epidermis. *British Journal of Dermatology*, 1973. 89: p. 10

HeatWave: Thermal Imaging for Surface User Interaction

Eric Larson[1], Gabe Cohn[1], Sidhant Gupta[2], Xiaofeng Ren[3], Beverly Harrison[3], Dieter Fox[2,3], Shwetak N. Patel[1,2]

[1]Electrical Eng., [2]Computer Science & Eng.
UbiComp Lab, DUB Group, Univ. of Washington
Seattle, WA (USA)
{eclarson, gabecohn, sidhant, shwetak}@uw.edu

[3]Intel Labs Seattle
Seattle, WA (USA)
{xiaofeng.ren, beverly.harrison, dieter.fox}
@intel.com

ABSTRACT
We present HeatWave, a system that uses digital thermal imaging cameras to detect, track, and support user interaction on arbitrary surfaces. Thermal sensing has had limited examination in the HCI research community and is generally under-explored outside of law enforcement and energy auditing applications. We examine the role of thermal imaging as a new sensing solution for enhancing user surface interaction. In particular, we demonstrate how thermal imaging in combination with existing computer vision techniques can make segmentation and detection of routine interaction techniques possible in real-time, and can be used to complement or simplify algorithms for traditional RGB and depth cameras. Example interactions include (1) distinguishing hovering above a surface from touch events, (2) shape-based gestures similar to ink strokes, (3) pressure based gestures, and (4) multi-finger gestures. We close by discussing the practicality of thermal sensing for naturalistic user interaction and opportunities for future work.

Author Keywords
Cameras, thermal imaging, gestures, user interfaces, surface interaction, computer vision

ACM Classification Keywords
H.5.2. [**Information interfaces and presentation**]: User interfaces—*input devices and strategies*. I.5.4 [**Pattern recognition**]: Applications—*computer vision*.

General Terms
Algorithms, Design, Experimentation

INTRODUCTION AND MOTIVATION
Human-computer interface design has significant interest in natural interaction–i.e., systems that do not rely upon mediated interaction through devices such as a mouse, keyboard, or stylus. This has in part been reflected by the popularity in touch screens and surface-based systems [1, 5, 12, 22, 29, 34]. In an attempt to avoid instrumentation on users, objects, and surfaces (e.g., using RFID tags, visual glyphs), camera and imaging technologies have gained significant popularity for surface and gesture interaction. This has also largely been due to the decreasing costs, versatility, size and portability of modern cameras. Traditional (RGB) cameras have seen considerable use in the HCI community for detecting hand gestures, touch points, and object recognition [7, 12, 33, 34]. The introduction of depth cameras or pixel-mixed devices (PMDs) provides a mechanism for 3D reconstruction and depth segmentation for user interfaces [2]. However, the use of RGB and depth cameras in HCI is limited by the type of information that can be extracted from a scene, and the speed at which information can be extracted. For instance, inaccuracies or gaps in gesture detection often result if hand motion is too fast (using typical camera frame rates and real-time processing).

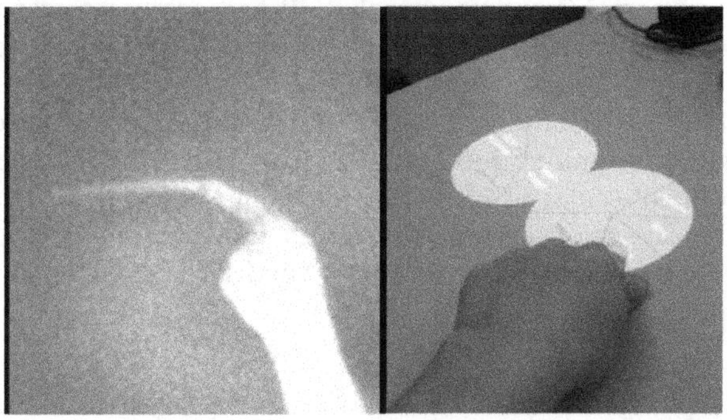

Figure 1: A thermal imaging driven projected marking menu application using the residual heat traces on a tabletop

Thermal imaging, which provides a pixel-level thermograph of anything that is in its field of view (e.g., Figure 1), has largely been under-explored in the user interface community. Recent maturation and advances in solid-state imaging technology and embedded systems have made thermal imaging more practical for consumer use in terms of size, cost and software access to video data.

In this paper, we critically examine the role of thermal imaging as a new sensing solution for enhancing user surface interaction. In particular, we demonstrate how thermal imaging and well known computer vision techniques can make segmenting and detecting certain routine interaction techniques possible in real-time and complement or simplify algorithms for traditional RGB and depth cameras. Example interactions include (1) distinguishing surface touch or target selection from hovering over surface, (2) shape-based gestures similar to ink strokes, (3) pressure based gestures, and (4) multi-finger gestures (enumerated in Figure 3). We demonstrate these in two prototype applications: (1) a pressure-aware drawing application that supports multi-touch and multi-user interactions, (2) a marking menu application using thermal traces as the "ink stroke" menu selection method (Figure 1). Both examples demonstrate the feasibility of real-time thermal traces for UI design.

In the following sections, we briefly discuss the technique of thermal imaging, how it differs from standard IR-based cameras, and the advantages gained by using thermal imaging to complement traditional RGB and depth cameras for surface user interactions. Next, we discuss the related work in surface interaction and thermal imaging, followed by details of our real-time computer vision approaches for extracting meaningful information from our thermal camera, and a collection of interaction techniques they support. Finally, we propose some challenges and future applications of thermal imaging that extend beyond surface interaction.

THERMAL IMAGING

Thermal imaging is a technique for *passively* constructing a high resolution heat map of objects appearing in a scene without using an external illumination source. This is accomplished by measuring the quantity of far-infrared (F-IR or long-wavelength infrared, LW-IR) radiation emitted by any object. Plank's law describes that the wavelength of the peak of electromagnetic radiation from any object is inversely proportional to its absolute temperature. Objects that we interact with on a daily basis are near room temperature and radiate mostly in the F-IR spectrum (Figure 2). Furthermore, the quantity of thermal, or black-body radiation, emitted by an object is directly proportional to the fourth power of its absolute temperature, as given by the Stefan-Boltzmann law [15]. Therefore, by measuring the quantity of radiation emitted in the F-IR spectrum, a thermal sensor can produce a thermographic image of anything in its field of view (e.g., Figure 1).

It is important to note that thermal imaging differs from the more well-known "IR imaging" techniques used in the HCI community. Infrared light detection and night vision devices use what is called *reflected* infrared and operate in the *near*-infrared (N-IR) spectrum. These approaches require an illumination source in order to reconstruct an image. N-IR is employed in some fairly recent interactive tabletop surfaces [11, 34] and depth cameras. Figure 2 shows the visible and infrared spectra and differentiates N-IR from F-IR. Note that we do not utilize N-IR in the present work.

Earlier sensors found in thermal imaging cameras employed a gas filled lens and required refrigeration sources. Advances in semiconductor technology have enabled the development of arrays of silicon-based bandgap detectors and photo-resistive detectors, which allow for 2D imaging planes similar to traditional CCD cameras. Thermal cameras are becoming popular for home energy auditing applications, which has created a demand for portable thermal cameras that continue to reduce in size and cost.

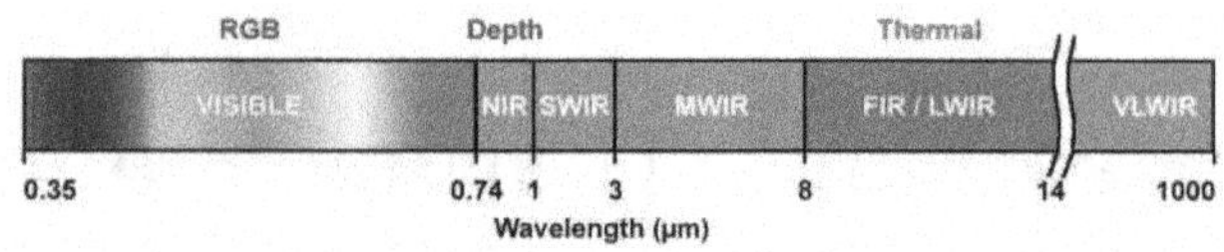

Figure 2: Infrared and visible light spectrum. Thermal imaging operates in the far-infrared (F-IR) band.

ADVANTAGES OF THERMAL IMAGING

Thermal imaging provides several distinct features that address some of the challenges faced by traditional RGB and depth cameras, and enables new applications which are difficult using traditional imaging technologies. Additionally, we believe that thermal imaging can be combined with RGB and depth to provide more robust systems for surface interactions in a variety of natural settings.

First, images produced by thermal cameras are independent of illumination and are far less susceptible to changes in light intensity than traditional RGB cameras or many IR-based depth cameras. RGB cameras do not work well in low-light scenarios, and obviously fail in complete darkness. Since thermal sensing works independently of the visible light spectrum, it works equally well in low- and no-light situations as it would under normal indoor lighting. Furthermore, thermal sensing works in direct sunlight, where some IR depth cameras do not work because their own IR illumination source is washed out by the sun. Additionally, thermal sensing is not confounded by constantly changing light sources and therefore can be used with projected systems without any special considerations.

Second, thermal sensing can detect unique features including short-lived heat transfer from one object to another, which are undetectable with traditional RGB and depth cameras. These features can be used to support a variety of user interaction techniques (Figure 3). For example, using the heat transferred from a user's hand to the surface, multiple touch points can easily be extracted as well as complicated gesture shapes. Moreover, the amount of heat transfer between the finger and the surface can indicate the *pressure* with which the user touched or grasped the object or surface. Lastly, since the transferred heat dissipates over time, a history of a user's interactions is captured in the form of residual heat traces even after the interaction is done.

Third, thermal imaging provides a distinct mechanism for easily segmenting hands (or other body parts) from the background and is independent of scene complexity, colors, and textures (i.e., it easily distinguishes heat-generating sources from inert objects, surfaces, and backgrounds). Traditional RGB sensing and algorithms rely upon computer vision techniques such as background subtraction, color and texture matching, contour detection, and/or optical flow to find target objects of interest. However, many of these features fluctuate due to changes in illumination, pose or position, and color (e.g., a person wears different clothes or color differences between skin tones). These fluctuations often make it difficult to reliably segment a person from a scene, an object from the hand that grasps it, or gestures from a scene or surface. Moreover, "warm object" segmen-

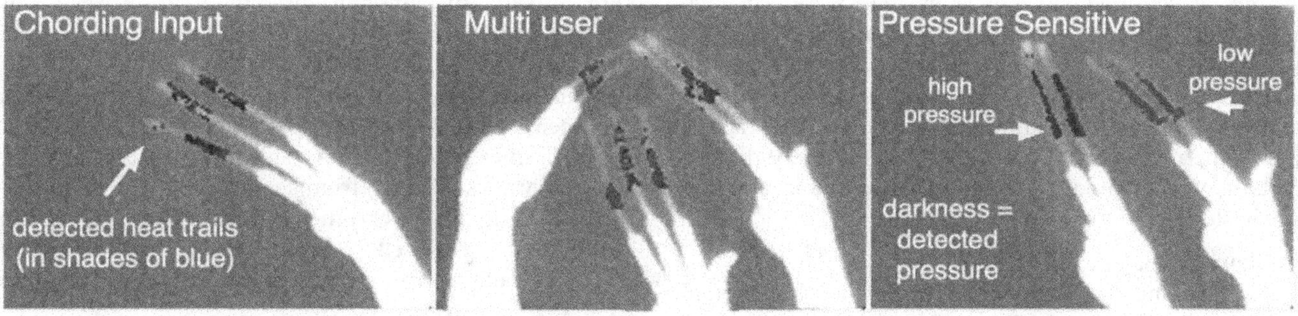

Figure 3: Top down thermal camera views of several surface interactions. Detected heat trails are shown in blue from our real-time algorithm from a single frame of video. Detected pressure differences classified by our real-time algorithm are shown using darkness of blue shades.

tation can be done easily on a real-time, frame by frame basis using well known thresholding methods, such as Otsu's method [24]. Since thermal sensing only needs a single frame for segmentation (i.e., no background image or motion from previous frame), pose and motion issues are less significant than in RGB or depth based systems.

In summary, we believe that thermal imaging provides the following added benefits over traditional imaging:

- Thermal imaging works independently of the light source and is robust to dark or sunlit environments
- Heat traces left behind enable accurate determination of hovering vs. touching without requiring under-mounted cameras or an instrumented surface Heat signatures allow for pressure-aware interaction
- The heat signatures of individual hands allow for multi-touch and multi-user discrimination
- Segmentation of people and body parts is significantly easier and faster than traditional RGB or depth

RELATED WORK

We organize the related work into three broad sections: (i) surface and gesture interaction which uses instrumented surfaces, involving traditional, depth, and thermal cameras, (ii) prior work using traditional IR sensing in the HCI community, and (iii) the use of thermal imaging in other areas of research.

Surface and Gesture Interaction

Camera-based gesture and touch detection in prior work can be roughly categorized by the type of camera sensor used: RGB, depth, and thermal. To enable multi-touch interfaces using RGB cameras [4, 12, 37] there has been substantial work in image segmentation that tracks and identifies various body parts [20]. Typically these systems use skin color matching, edge or contour detection, and motion tracking to segment fingers and hands [12]. More recently, N-IR depth cameras have also been applied alone or in concert with RGB for gesture detection and tracking [2, 8, 11, 22, 34].

Using thermal imaging, some of the initial interaction work comes from Iwai and Sato [9, 10]. They use a behind-the-surface thermal camera and rear projection for drawing upon a translucent paper surface. Users can draw with warm or cool objects in contact with the paper (such as their hands, warm water, or a hairdryer). The application deals primarily with interactive painting on a special paper, but does not investigate the problem of hand segmentation, tracking, or gesture recognition.

The work of Oka *et al.* [23] and Sato *et al.* [31] combines RGB and thermal imaging for hand segmentation and fingertip tracking to drive a gesture recognizer. They use the trajectory of extracted finger tips as input to a hidden Markov model to identify one of six different gestures. The method used does not detect finger contact with the surface, but instead makes use of the fingertip motion (whether touching a surface or in-air). The authors note that their system lags when more than one hand is used, and that their methodology may not scale well beyond tracking a few finger tips. Even so, they are able to use extracted fingertips and in-air gestures to drive an overhead projected user interface. Such a system, combined with the system we propose, could provide a pervasive vocabulary for in-air and touch gesturing.

Beyond tracking fingertips, previous work in RGB and depth imaging has attempted to identify touch pressure (for example, using finger deformation and changes in the cuticle coloring to infer how hard a finger is pressing on a surface [21]). With thermal imaging one can use not only the shape deformation of the finger but also the size and heat of the touch spot left behind to infer the pressure a user exerts on a surface (as we describe later).

Traditional IR Sensing in HCI

Aside from depth cameras, IR sensing (using N-IR) is a popular technique for surface and gesture-based interaction [8, 22, 34]. The advantage of N-IR imaging is the ability to use commodity cameras as the sensor. IR-based sensing typically requires an external illumination source, which dictates its range. A number of projects in the HCI community have used IR for tabletop interaction by detecting hand gestures using an under mounted camera and illumination source [8, 22]. Others have employed a similar approach on vertical semi-transparent surfaces [11].

IR sensing has also been used for fingertip detection and gaze tracking because the retro-reflective properties of these objects allow IR-filtered cameras to easily discern their appearance [32]. Others have used structured IR light patterns for object tracking applications [18]. As we have pointed out, IR imaging differs from thermal imaging; however, many of the computer vision techniques used in IR-based solutions parallel those that would be used in thermal imaging with minimal modification. The added value of thermal imaging is its ability to passively discern objects in view without an illumination source in addition to the hysteretic information it offers.

F-IR Thermal Imaging

Thermal imaging has largely been used for military and surveillance applications [36], where the heat signature produced by the human body is used to track individuals in arbitrary environments and conditions. Thermal imaging has also been used in hospitals and border crossings to identify individuals with a fever within a crowd of people using face temperatures [30].

The miniaturization and decreasing costs of thermal imaging cameras have more recently enabled a number of civilian applications. For example, in energy audits air filtration and insulation problems can be quickly identified by scanning the indoor space. Home inspectors have also extended the use of thermal imaging to look for hot spots near the electrical infrastructure to uncover potential arcing problems or overloaded circuits. Thermal scans of circuit boards can identify potential failure points from heat dissipation problems. The automotive industry has also used thermal imaging for similar applications, especially when temperature analysis needs to be conducted at a safe distance.

Beyond its commercial use, researchers have looked at using thermal imaging for a number of affective computing applications, such as detecting and classifying anxiety based on the minute changes in the thermal signature of one's face [13, 14, 25, 26]. Using well known techniques from the medical literature, changes in anxiety can be correlated to the blood flow on various parts of the face, such as at the forehead and cheeks. Others have extended the use of thermal imaging to infer emotional states exhibited by individuals and have used that information to enhance a user's gaming experience by altering a game's difficulty based on these sensed parameters [38]. Thermal imaging has also been used for illumination-invariant facial recognition [16].

HARDWARE

There are currently a variety of thermal cameras commercially available, and their cost varies based on the required thermal sensitivity and resolution. For instance, at the time of publication, thermal imaging cameras with super-cooled, sealed components that "see through walls" such as those used by law enforcement, cost just under 100,000 USD. HVAC auditing and general purpose thermal cameras are currently around 5,000 USD–which was the price of depth cameras less than one year ago (mass production of depth cameras for home gaming systems has recently decreased their cost significantly). As thermal sensing also gains popularity, the capabilities of these devices will surely increase while the costs decrease.

For our experimentation, we used the RazIR NANO, which contains an un-cooled Focal Plane Array (FPA) micro-bolometer sensor with 160x120 pixel resolution [28]. The thermal sensor is tuned for wavelengths in the IR spectrum between 8 and 14 μm, and captures data at a maximum rate of 30 frames per second. As an artifact of the sensor, the thermal values captured from an object of fixed temperature will drift slightly over time, and therefore a periodic re-calibration is required. We developed software to remove the effects of this drift in real-time, as described later.

Although the RazIR NANO thermal camera has an on-screen user interface and can perform some signal processing on-board, we have done all processing on an external computer using a data feed over USB. The data collected from the feed represents the raw values from the camera's analog-to-digital converter. Our algorithms operate in real-time on the 8 most significant bits of the raw data.

SOFTWARE IMPLEMENTATION

Thermal imaging has many potential applications when used independently or in conjunction with other sensors such as RGB and depth. In this work, we have focused on developing software for one of the more interesting and unique aspect of thermal imaging: the detection and extraction of heat traces. Heat traces are the residual heat left behind on a surface due to the heating of that surface by another warmer object, such as a human hand. Since traditional RGB and depth cameras cannot see signals like heat traces, there has been no other work in developing software to extract such features. This section describes our approach, using Open CV [3] on streaming thermal imaging data and demonstrates how these features can be robustly extracted in real-time using standard computer vision algorithms. Figure 4 shows the step by step processing of the algorithms with callout images for each process.

Noise Filtering

The raw thermal images returned from our camera are fairly noisy from the thermal and scattering noise around the micro-bolometer sensors in the camera. To suppress this noise we apply smoothing in both the spatial and temporal domains. We first apply a 5 pixel by 5 pixel median filter within each video frame. Then, for each pixel, we apply a 5 frame low-pass, finite impulse response (FIR) filter to smooth the signal in time.

Background Calibration

In order to accurately detect heat traces, it is extremely important to model the background signal level–there is slight drift in the hardware sensor over time and surface temperatures may change over time. For these reasons, we compute the mean background image dynamically (a moving average filter) whenever we detect that a human hand is not present in the image.

Hand Segmentation

In order to segment the hand from the image in real-time, we use Otsu's method of thresholding [24]. In this approach, second order statistics of the gray-level histogram

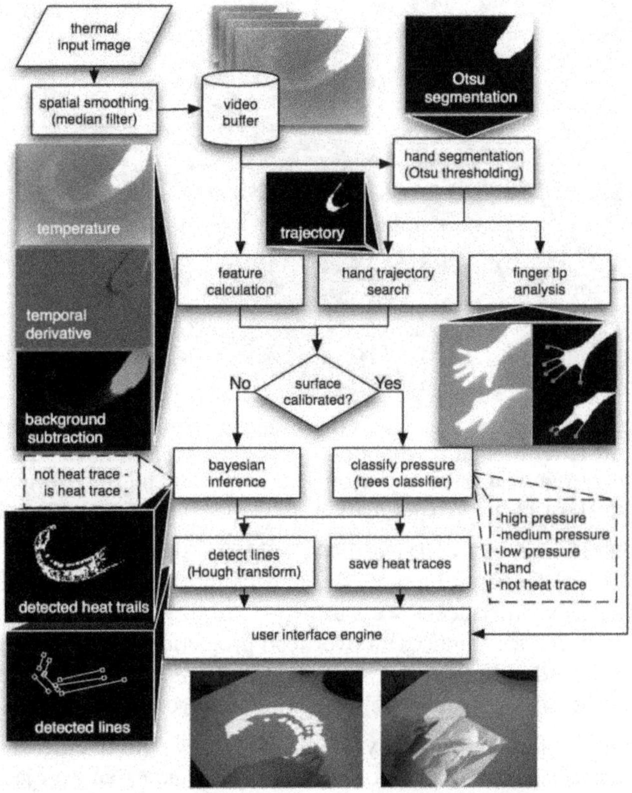

Figure 4: Flow diagram for real-time algorithm processes with callout images at each step. All callouts are captured and rendered from actual data in a real-time application.

are used to maximize the separation of pixel gray levels between two classes. This is ideal in thermal sensing because a hand's temperature is almost always distinct from the background, even when the background temperature is not uniform or has temporarily changed due to touching. This type of thresholding is widely used in computer vision applications and is highly optimized. For our image resolution, the operation takes a fraction of a millisecond. An example of segmentation is shown in Figure 4.

Fingertip Extraction

We use the segmented image of the hand together with well known morphology operations to extract multiple fingertips in a scene. We first apply a thinning operation to the binary segmented image, resulting in a skeletization of the fingers. We then iteratively apply a hit-and-miss transform to the image with a rotating, 3x3 structuring element of endpoints at each possible angle. The result tells us the endpoints of each finger. The simplicity of this extraction technique is made possible by the robust segmentation that thermal sensing provides. Ako *et al.* [23] use a more complicated form of fingertip extraction that also accounts for trajectory. However, we found endpoint extraction to be efficient and robust, especially because we only use the extracted fingertips for refining the search space in which we look for heat traces. This type of extraction is difficult using depth cameras because "thinning" is sensitive to the outline of the segmented object. Depth cameras tend to be noisy around the edges of a hand (where thermal is not) and may require further de-noising before finger extraction is possible. An example of fingertip extraction is shown in Figure 4.

Uncalibrated Heat Trace Detection

A heat trace is created when an object warmer than the background surface heats the surface enough to leave evidence of its presence. Over time, this heat trace will disappear and the surface returns to the background temperature. Figure 4 shows smoothed data in which the background has been subtracted and identifies the region corresponding to the heat decay. When the finger simply hovers over the surface, there is no heat transfer or decay, but when the finger touches the surface the heat decay is very distinctive.

We constrain our search space by "ANDing" together hand segmentations within the past one second of video (30 frames) and subtracting the current hand segmentation. In this way, we only look for heat traces in pixel locations where the hand has recently traveled. This reduces the search space significantly, and thus drastically decreases computational complexity.

We frame the detection of heat traces as a Bayesian estimation problem. In particular, we observe the likelihood of a pixel being part of a heat trace given three features: smoothed temperature, temporal derivative, and background subtracted temperature. The temporally smoothed temperature and derivative are calculated over five frames using FIR filters. This 5-frame buffering results in a system latency of 166 ms (1/6th of a second), which can be considered real-time for most interactive applications.

The likelihood distributions are assumed i.i.d. and assumed to follow a Rayleigh distribution based on empirical observations. That is, each feature is modeled well using a distribution with a single tail and the product of all these distributions is a good model of the overall posterior heat trace probability. Prior distributions are assumed to be uniform. Mathematically this is denoted,

$$P(h_p = 1|\mathbf{x}) \propto \prod_{f \in \boldsymbol{F}} \frac{x_{p,f} - \mu_f}{\sigma_f} e^{-(x_{p,f}-\mu_f)^2/2\sigma_f^2}$$

where h_p denotes whether pixel "*p*" is or is not a heat trace, $x_{p,f}$ denotes the value of feature "*f*" at pixel "*p*." $\boldsymbol{F}$ is the set of all features. Each feature variance and mean threshold, σ_f and μ_f, are selected empirically using histograms of collected heat traces. When the probability of a pixel being a heat trace, $P(h_p|\mathbf{x})$, surpasses a global threshold, we classify the pixel as a heat trace. We found this single model to work well for a variety of surfaces and users (i.e., an out of the box working system).

In addition, we allow the system to be calibrated and adapted to each user or surface. Unlike the Bayesian system, the calibrated system attempts to classify heat traces into more than one class based on the pressure with which the user pressed on the surface (i.e., the amount of heat transferred to the surface).

Calibrated Heat Trace Classification

The calibration process consists of three stages. During each stage the user "draws" a line on the surface at increasing pressures. We save features (temperature, derivative, background subtracted temperature, and background temperature) around the trajectory of the moving fingertip using the Bayesian estimate to extract pixels that are part of a heat trace. In this way, the Bayesian estimate is used to bootstrap the training of a more complicated classifier. This is done for each pressure the user wishes to calibrate. For example, these steps can be repeated for "light", "moderate", and "hard" pressure stroke calibration.

We then train the system to identify the pressure of each heat trace using a C4.5 tree classifier [27], as implemented by Weka [35] (training is less than one second, on average). We found a number of algorithms implemented in Weka to perform well on a test set of 20,000 detected heat trace pixels. We chose the tree classifier because it provided 96% accuracy on a 10-fold cross validation of the test set and runs quickly enough to assess pressure in real-time. The test set had five classes: High, medium, and low pressure, hand and background.

In addition to pressure, this method can be used to calibrate to different surfaces. To test this hypothesis, we calibrated to four different materials and asked a user to trace a fixed projected "S" eight times on each of the four materials (32 strokes). After the experiment, we superimposed the detected traces on top of each other for each material, resulting in a set of images where brightness denotes how often a heat trace was detected on the material surface. Drawing speed, temperature of the finger, hand and surface were not controlled (similar to what one would expect in real use). The superimposed image results are shown in Figure 5. Brightness denotes classification accuracy: bright yellow is 100% correct and completely black (false negatives) is 0% detection. There were no false positives detected. Notice that paper (best), table top laminate (second best), and wooden surfaces have easily detectable traces, and that plastic is the most difficult surface to detect traces upon. Based on this initial evaluation, we hypothesize that less heat is transferred to the plastic than other materials.

Line Detection

Although heat trace detection can be used to detect arbitrary shapes and gesture patterns, it is useful to detect when heat traces are collinear. We focus on lines because detected lines can be used for chording style gestures and as input to many applications such as marking menus. To detect line gestures we buffer detected heat traces into a single image for the past one second. We then apply a binary Hough transform [6] to the buffered image to reveal heat traces that are collinear. The buffered image provides a binary history of where a user has placed ink strokes with their hands and can be used with other transformations to fit arbitrary curves and circles, not just lines.

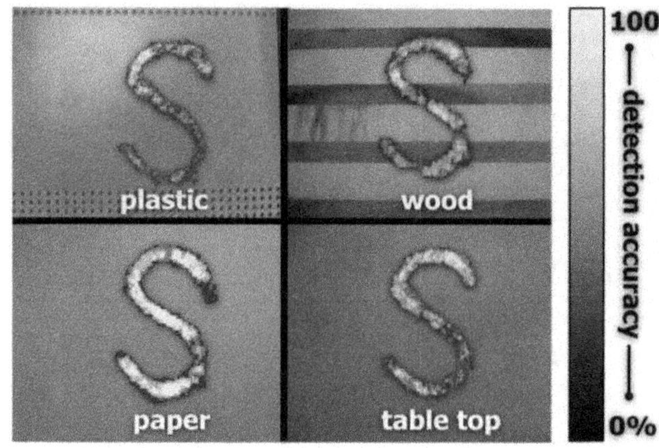

Figure 5: Heat traces (overlaid images) from a user tracing the letter S eight times on each of four materials. Each trial's detected heat trace is projected and overlaid on the previous trial. Brightness denotes accuracy.

PROTOTYPES AND INTERACTION TECHNIQUES

To test the usefulness of thermal features as driving input for user interfaces, we built two prototype applications. Each application uses an overhead projection system and an overhead-mounted thermal camera to transform an arbitrary surface into a multi-touch user interface (see Figure 6).

The system ports easily to different tables and other flat surfaces. Conversion from camera coordinates and projected coordinates is achieved using a four point calibrated homographic transform (i.e., a known mapping of four points in each space). No other instrumentation is necessary and the camera and projector can be placed at many different orientations to the surface and each other.

The first application is a multi-user and multi-touch drawing application that displays arbitrary gestures made by the users, and alters the brightness of displayed colors based on the pressure with which each user draws using three pressure levels. The second application uses line gestures for image manipulation. Images are chosen using marking menus [17], then once the images are displayed they can be translated, rotated, and scaled using thermal lines. The two applications are designed to demonstrate that thermal traces can be used as a plausible substitute for multi-touch screens and can drive typical user interfaces in real-time with naturalistic interactions. Images from interactions with each application can be seen in Figure 6.

User Interface Engine

For the drawing application no additional feature processing is necessary—it uses the unaltered heat trace locations and their corresponding pressure as the sole driving inputs. The touch positions are projected onto the surface, with their brightness representing applied pressure.

The marking menu and image editing application uses the extracted fingertip locations and heat traces (as detected by the Hough transform) as driving input. The steadiness of the fingertip is used to detect finger-down events. When a detected fingertip has been stationary for 500 ms, a marking menu is displayed at the fingertip location. After this, a

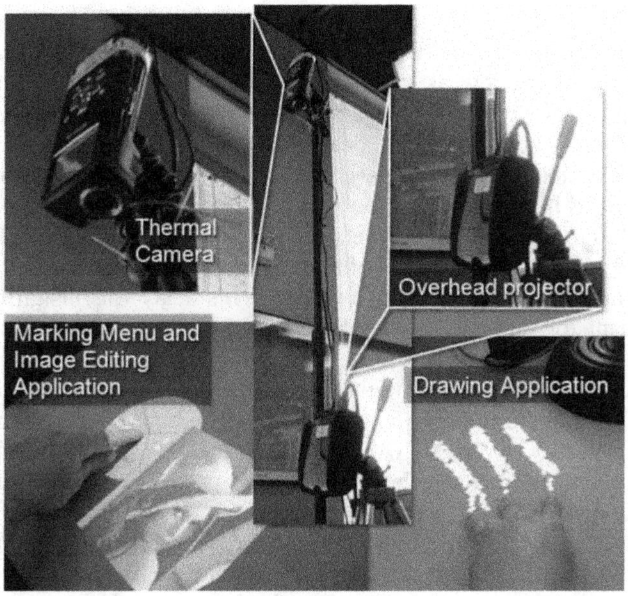

Figure 6: Example thermal camera setup with overhead projector running two prototype applications.

series of lines can be drawn by the user. The angle of the detected lines controls which sub-menu is displayed and the subsequent selections. As with any marking menu, the user can draw a line and pause to bring up another menu or, alternatively, can draw multiple lines in a single motion to navigate several menus at once. Once the user selects an image to open, they can move and scale the image using a combination of one, two, and three finger gestures. The interactions are: a single line drawn on the image translates the image; two fingers moving inward or outward from the image scales it; and three fingers in a sweeping motion dismisses the image from the surface.

We found these inputs and extraction methods to be easily implemented and the applications were straightforward additions to the system. The prototype applications provide proof of concept for systems that detect and use arbitrary gestures—using nothing more than a binary Hough transforms on detected heat traces and simple fingertip tracking.

DISCUSSION AND ANALYSIS

Although thermal imaging provides a number of advantages over traditional RGB and depth imaging solutions, there are clearly some differences and challenges. Many of the challenges with thermal imaging, such as reflection and occlusions have analogous problems in RGB and depth imaging, but there are also challenges that are unique to thermal imaging, such as surface temperature and material type. Additionally, applications driven by heat traces must be designed to minimize the effects of these limitations, but still provide an intuituve interface.

Robustness of Algorithm

In addition to the Bayesian estimation and the calibrated classifier described in this paper, we experimented with several additional methods for extracting the heat traces from a surface. These methods included temperature thresholding, change in temperature thresholding, decay template matching, hidden Markov models (HMMs), and non-probabilistic finite state machines. All of these algorithms could be tuned to work quite well in specific situations, but none of them were able to work well over a wide range of scenarios (with the exception of the HMM, which worked extremely well but was computationally too intensive to run in real-time without optmization or parallelization). The Bayesian approach described in this paper appears to be highly robust, and works well for all of the scenarios that we have tested. In addition, the approach can be used to as a bootstrap for more complicated classifiers like the C4.5 trees implemented in this paper.

Robustness of Features

During our examination of thermal imaging, we determined that the residual heat traces after touching a surface provide significant value for differentiating between hovering and touching, which is clearly a challenge for top mounted RGB cameras and can be problematic with depth cameras (e.g., noisy data due to light, reflections, or depth sensor resolution). However, two factors impact the decay rate and hence ease of detection for heat traces: material type and dwell time. Decay rate varies greatly depending upon the surface material (from a few hundred milliseconds up to five or six seconds) but can be addressed using the calibration sequence presented. Wooden and drywall surfaces exhibit the slowest decay rates due to their thermal properties and, thus, are the easiest materials to classify heat traces upon. On the other hand, metal surfaces exhibit the fastest thermal dissipation, with traces typically disappearing after only a few frames. This confounds our algorithm in many scenarios and we still consider metal surface heat trace extraction to be an open problem.

Additionally, the dwell time (i.e., how long surface contact lasts) impacts the amount of heat transfer and the size of the heated region (heat spreads). For many gesture based interactions, dwell time is not significant; however, one can easily imagine gestural vocabularies or situations where this would need to be taken into account. Our interaction techniques thus far have been fairly independent of dwell time - that is, most gestures only require the user to press the surface quickly. However, extracting reliable pressure estimates becomes more difficult with gestures that have a large variance in dwell time.

Challenges Unique to Thermal Imaging

Unlike RGB and depth cameras, the computer vision algorithms for thermal imaging must account for residual heat traces that may linger for a significant amount of time. Therefore, continually computing/updating the background model is important to avoid false positives. Similarly, it is possible for the surface to heat up due to the interaction and thus make it harder to segment out the hand if the surface temperature nears that of the hand, but we found this to be extremely rare in our experimentation where the surface was at about 20° C. Note that maintaining a background model is only important for detecting heat traces. Hand segmentation and tracking remains robust in a variety of environments and backgrounds.

Challenges with all Computer Vision Approaches

Similar to RGB and depth, occlusion is an issue for thermal imaging. Since our system relies on the heat traces left by finger contact, these traces are only visible when the finger moves away from the contact points (i.e., heat traces underneath the hand are undetectable). An angle mounted camera helps alleviate problems with occlusions when the hand covers the heat traces. Furthermore, there is an unavoidable delay in the detection of lift (mouse-up) events, and it is not possible to detect touch-down (mouse-down) events. Note that this is distinct from the algorithm processing lag of 166 ms.

An interesting solution to extracting touch-down and touch-up events with an overhead system is to use a metallic surface. Metallic surfaces tend to reflect F-IR waves (i.e., you can see thermal reflections on smooth, polished surfaces but the reflections are invisible to the user). These reflections could be used to indicate hover distance or indicate when a surface is touched (i.e., when the reflection and object meet, similar to the Wilson "shadow touching finger" approach [34]). There is a tradeoff, of course, between the reliability of extracting heat traces from polished surfaces and touch-down extraction because the reflection may be directly over the heat trace. This tradeoff is in contrast to depth cameras, which are known to have significant problems with shiny or reflective surfaces.

Limitations in Using Heat Trace Input

In our ongoing tests of multi-touch thermal drawing interfaces, it is rare that parts of the hand are not segmented correctly or heat traces are not detected. One exception occurs when someone with very cold hands uses the system. For instance, someone who was holding a cold drink moments before interacting. When this occurs, the finger tips are about the same temperature as the table top and segmentation severs a portion of the finger tip. Because we use segmentation to constrain the search space for heat traces, some heat traces are missed. Also, after long periods of being in contact with the table top (about 5-10 minutes of continual interaction) the finger tips begin to cool down and the table top begins to heat up, potentially confounding heat trace identification. The heating of the surface is magnified when many users interact. We found that letting the surface cool for about 10-20 seconds is sufficient to reset the background model and to let the fingertips return to natural temperature (alternatively users can also rub their hands together). This suggests for applications that require sustained and continuous finger strokes from the user (such as drawing and gaming applications) that thermal imaging alone may not be appropriate as an input method. Lastly, we found occlusion was not a factor for drawing applications because users almost always pull their hands away from the surface after marking a line or curve to see the visual representation, revealing the heat trace.

Our marking menu application was ideally suited for thermal line input and we were able to drive menus with selections as narrow as 15° fairly easily. Moreover, translation and scaling of images is easily interpreted from the detected lines in near real-time. The longest delay comes from line detection because our algorithm requires buffering of detected heat traces. The buffering process adds an additional 200 ms delay onto the delay in heat trace detection, resulting in an average delay of about 400 ms between drawing a line and reaction by the interface. This delay was insignificant for our example application but could be limiting for applications that require faster driving inputs, such as gaming. For image manipulation, one limitation is when the user tries to move an image towards the camera because the hand moves directly over the heat trace path. One outcome of this is that interface feedback may appear "jerky" and delayed since we can only process segments of the heat trace that are unoccluded. We have anecdotally noticed that drawing with an index finger alone tends to naturally offset the hand orientation and thus the heat trace is less often occluded. More occlusion seems to occur with multi-finger chording-style manipulations. More investigation is required but this does suggest that gesture design choices can be optimized to reduce potential problems while preserving reasonably intuitive interaction.

Challenges not Present for Thermal Imaging

In general, varying lighting conditions did not pose any problems in extracting gestures. For instance, we observed similar system algorithm behavior across indoor, outdoor, and dark environments. This is encouraging since thermal imaging may be a viable option for use in arbitrary environments. Even more encouraging is that images projected on a surface with a digital projector also do not interfere with hand/finger segmentation. This is because the IR emitted from the projector's light source is in the N-IR band, and does not extend to the F-IR spectrum.

ADDITIONAL APPLICATIONS AND FUTURE WORK

This paper describes our initial exploration of thermal imaging as a means for detecting gestural input on surfaces to support interaction. We have additionally started investigating a wider range of possible applications, some of which are briefly described below. At present, we have collected data to illustrate the viability of each of these ideas.

Distinguishing Multiple Users

We have found that multiple users have different thermal gradients on their hands (Figure 7a). Although these gradients can change over long time intervals (e.g., coming inside from a winter's day), we believe the overall hand "heat signature" may remain unchanged for the duration of a session. Using these thermal differences among the hands of multiple users, we believe that we can uniquely identify several users within an interactive session. This would allow customized multi-user interaction on arbitrary surfaces without the need for instrumenting the surface or the users. In addition, this algorithm would not use the angle of approach, enabling users to move freely around the surface.

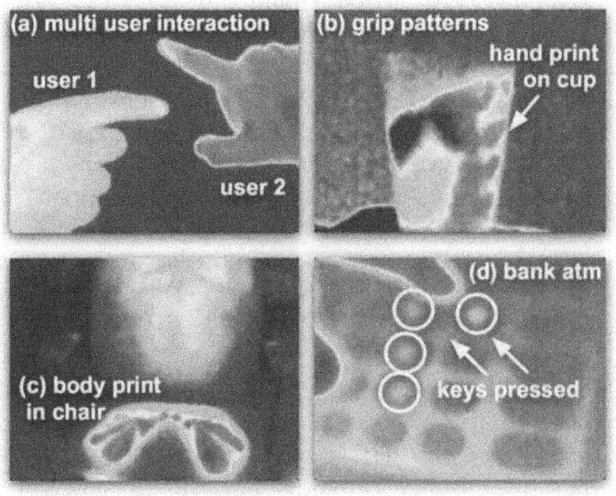

Figure 7: Additional applications of thermal imaging. Thermal data variations are mapped to different colors.

Grip Patterns

Colleagues in our lab are conducting research in personal robotics where a roving robot with a robotic arm can pick up, move or manipulate objects. A key element of this work is to understand how the robot can best grip everyday objects. Thermal imaging could help train robots about grip methods by identifying the exact positions of contact between an object and a human hand. The human hand leaves heat traces on objects, and these traces clearly show all of the points of contact between the object and the hand (Figure 7b). We plan to apply the thermal image grip patterns as a means of training robots how to grasp arbitrary objects.

Object Interaction

Similarly to the grip patterns discussed above, thermal imaging can be used to determine the points of contact between objects and any part of the human body. Figure 7c shows the heat pattern left in a chair as a result of a person sitting. This information can be used to determine elements of posture and provide feedback whenever a user stands up. Additionally, points of contact could be used to determine which chairs, household areas, and objects are used most within a space or even when these are used (e.g., eldercare or medical rehab applications).

In-Air Gestures

Since thermal imaging makes human bodies and body parts easily distinguishable from scene elements, we can easily detect and track airborne gestures and movements. We plan to continue this work, developing real-time algorithms to robustly segment and track people and airborne gestures on non-planar surfaces, arbitrary objects, and in scenes where the user stands in front of the camera.

Determining Surface Material

Our current implementation is designed to work on surfaces that are made from a variety of materials. We believe that thermal imaging can be used to identify the surface material based solely on its thermal properties. For example, each material will dissipate heat at a different rate, and the spatial spread of the initial heating point will also be different. We imagine a system in which the user would simply touch the surface (which would likely be part of a training or calibration procedure) and the system would detect and measure the spatial and temporal properties of the surface. Using a database of such parameters, the surface material could potentially be determined. This would provide mobile surface interaction systems with additional context regarding which surface the user is interacting with.

Security

The concept of heat trace detection also has interesting security ramifications. For instance, thermal heat trace detection can be used to view a password or bank PIN that a user types on a keyboard or keypad. A residual heat trace is left behind on the keys even *after* the password has been entered. Figure 7d shows the heat traces on the keys of an actual bank ATM.

CONCLUSION

We have described how thermal imaging technology can complement or augment more traditional RGB or depth cameras for surface gesture interaction. Thermal imaging is more robust under circumstances where RGB or depth would fail and thus could provide more robust solutions for the variability that occurs in natural settings. We have demonstrated that well-known computer vision techniques can provide good models for extracting the heat traces that human interaction with surfaces (and objects) leaves behind in real-time. We also demonstrated this approach on a variety of different surfaces and offered a technique for surface calibration. We have demonstrated several traditional user interface techniques can be driven in real-time based on thermal heat trace input. Finally, we have outlined a number of interesting new opportunities beyond gesture-based surface interactions where thermal imaging provides unique data to enable new applications.

ACKNOWLEDGEMENTS

We would like to acknowledge Ryder Ziola for his advice and help in the extension of this work to include an overhead projected system.

REFERENCES

1. Arai, T., Machii, K. and Kuzunuki, S. Retrieving electronic documents with real-world objects on InteractiveDESK. In *Proc. of UIST '95*. New York: ACM Press, 1995, pp. 37-38.
2. Barras, C. Microsoft's body-sensing, button-busting controller. *New Scientist: Technology*. 7 Jan 2010.
3. Bradski, G.; Kaehler, A. (2008), Learning OpenCV: Computer Vision with the OpenCV Library
4. Cohen, C.J., Beach, G.J. and Foulk, G.A. Basic hand gesture control system for PC applications. In *Proc. of AIPR '01*. IEEE Computer Society, 2001, pp. 74.
5. Dietz, P. and Leigh, D. DiamondTouch: A multi-user touch technology. In *Proc. of UIST '01*. New York: ACM Press, 2001, pp. 219-226.
6. Duda, R. and Hart, P "Use of the Hough Transformation to Detect Lines and Curves in Pictures," *Comm. ACM*, Vol. 15, pp. 11–15, Jan., 1972

7. Felzenszwalb, P., McAllester, D., and Ramanan, D. A Discriminatively Trained, Multiscale, Deformable Part Model. In *Proc. of IEEE CVPR '08*, 2008.
8. Hilliges, O., Izadi, S., Wilson, A.D., Hodges, S., Garcia-Mendoza, A., Butz, A. Interactions in the air: adding further depth to interactive tabletops. In *Proc. of UIST '09*. New York: ACM Press, 2009, pp. 139-148.
9. Iwai, D. and Sato, K. "Heat Sensation in Image Creation with Thermal Vision", *ACM SIGCHI International Conference on Advances in Computer Entertainment Technology* (ACE2005), pp.213-216, Jun. 2005.
10. Iwai, D. and Sato K, "Limpid Desk: theoretical papers of transparent projection of Mixed Reality", *IPSJ*, vol.48, no.3, pp.1294-1306, 2007.
11. Izadi, S., Hodges, S. Taylor, S., Rosenfeld, D., Villar, N., Butler, A., Westhues, J. Going beyond the display: a surface technology with an electronically switchable diffuser. In *Proc. of UIST '09*. New York: ACM Press, 2009, pp. 269-278.
12. Kane, S., Avrahami, D., Wobbrock, J.O., Harrison, B., Rea, A.D., Philipose, M., LaMarca, A. Bonfire: a nomadic systems for hybrid laptop-tabletop interaction. In *Proc. of UIST '09*. New York: ACM Press, 2009.
13. Khan, M.M., Ingleby, M., and Ward, R.D. Automated Facial Expression Classification and affect interpretation using infrared measurement of facial skin temperature variations. *ACM Trans. on Autonomous and Adaptive Systems,* 2006.
14. Khan, M.M., Ward, R.D., and Ingleby, M. Classifying pretended and evoked facial expressions of positive and negative affective states using infrared measurement of skin temperature. *ACM Trans. on Applied Perception,* 2009.
15. Kittel, C. and Kroemer, H. *Thermal Physics*. 2nd ed. New York: W.H. Freeman, 1980.
16. Kong, S.G., Heo, J., Boughorbel, F., Zheng, Y., Abidi, B.R., Koschan, A., Yi, M., and Abidi, M.A. Multiscale Fusion of Visible and Thermal IR Images for Illumination-Invariant Face Recognition. *International Journal of Computer Vision,* 2007.
17. Kurtenbach, G. The Design and Evaluation of Marking Menus, Ph.D. Thesis, Department of Computer Science, University of Toronto. May 1993.
18. Lee, J., Hudson, S., Summet, J., and Dietz, P. Moveable interactive projected displays using projector based tracking. In *Proc. of UIST '05*. New York: ACM Press, 2005, pp. 63-72.
19. Letessier, J. and Bérard, F. Visual tracking of bare fingers for interactive surfaces. In *Proc. of UIST '04*. New York: ACM Press, 2004, pp. 119-122.
20. Manresa, C., Varona, J., Mas, R. and Perales, F. Hand tracking and gesture recognition for humancomputer interaction. *Electronic Letters on Computer Vision and Image Analysis*, 5 (3), 2005, pp. 96-104.
21. Marshall, J., Pridmore, T., Pound, M., Benford, S., Koleva, B. Pressing the Flesh: Sincing Multiple Touch and Finger Pressure on Arbitrary Surfaces. In *Proc. of Pervasive '08*. Berlin: Springer-Verlag, 2008, pp. 38-55.
22. Microsoft Surface. http://www.microsoft.com/surface
23. Oka, K., Sato, Y. and Koike, H. "Real-time tracking of multiple fingertips and gesture recognition for augmented desk interface systems." *IEEE Computer Graphics and Applications*. Vol. 22, No. 6, pp. 64-71, 2002.
24. Otsu, N, "A threshold selection method from gray-level histograms". *IEEE Trans. Systems, Man, and Cybernetics.* 9: 62–66, 1972
25. Pavlidis, I., Dowdall, J., Sun, N., Puri, C., Fei, J., and Garbey, M. Interacting with human physiology. *Computer Vision and Image Understanding,* 2007.
26. Puri, C., Olson, L., Pavlidis, I., Levine, J., and Starren, J. StressCam: non-contact measurement of users' emotional states through thermal imaging. In *Proc. of CHI '05,* 2005.
27. Quinlan, J. R. C4.5: Programs for Machine Learning. Morgan Kaufmann Publishers, 1993.
28. RazIR. NANO Thermal Camera, http://raz-ir.com/raz-ir-nano-thermal-infrared-camera.html.
29. Rekimoto, J. SmartSkin: an infrastructure for freehand manipulation on interactive surfaces. In *Proc.of CHI '02*. New York: ACM Press, 2002, pp. 113-120.
30. Saletan, W. Heat Check: Swine flu, body heat, and airport scanners. http://www.slate.com/id/2217148/, 28 April 2009.
31. Sato, Y., Kobayashi, Y., and Koike, H. "Fast tracking of hands and fingertips in infrared images for augmented desk interface," *Proc. 2000 IEEE International Conference on Automatic Face and Gesture Recognition* (FGR 2000), pp. 462-467, March 2000.
32. Tanriverdi, V. and Jacob R.J.K. Interacting with eye movements in virtual environments. In *Proc. of CHI '00*. New York: ACM Press, 2000, pp. 265-272.
33. Wellner, P. Interacting with paper on the DigitalDesk. *Communications of the ACM, 36* (7), 1993, pp. 87-96.
34. Wilson, A. D. PlayAnywhere: a compact interactive tabletop projection-vision system. In *Proc. of UIST '05*. New York: ACM Press, 2005, pp. 83-92.
35. Witten, I. and Frank, E.: "Data Mining: Practical machine learning tools and techniques", 2nd Edition, Morgan Kaufmann, San Francisco (2005).
36. Wong, W.K., Tan, P.N., Loo, C.K., and Lim, W.S. An Effective Surveillance System Using Thermal Camera. In *Proc. of International Conference on Signal Acquisition and Processing,* 2009.
37. Wu, M. and Balakrishnan, R. Multi-finger and whole hand gestural interaction techniques for multiuser tabletop displays. In *Proc. of UIST '03*. New York: ACM Press, 2003, pp. 193-202.
38. Yun, C., Shastri, D., Pavlidis, I., and Deng, Z. O' game, can you feel my frustration?: improving user's gaming experience via stresscam. In *Proc. of CHI '09,* 2009.

AnglePose: Robust, Precise Capacitive Touch Tracking via 3D Orientation Estimation

Simon Rogers
srogers@dcs.gla.ac.uk

John Williamson
jhw@dcs.gla.ac.uk

Craig Stewart
craig@dcs.gla.ac.uk

Roderick Murray-Smith
rod@dcs.gla.ac.uk

School of Computing Science, University of Glasgow, G12 8QQ, Scotland, UK

ABSTRACT

We present a finger-tracking system for touch-based interaction which can track 3D finger angle in addition to position, using low-resolution conventional capacitive sensors, therefore compensating for the inaccuracy due to pose variation in conventional touch systems. Probabilistic inference about the pose of the finger is carried out in real-time using a particle filter; this results in an efficient and robust pose estimator which also gives appropriate uncertainty estimates. We show empirically that tracking the full pose of the finger results in greater accuracy in pointing tasks with small targets than competitive techniques. Our model can detect and cope with different finger sizes and the use of either fingers or thumbs, bringing a significant potential for improvement in one-handed interaction with touch devices. In addition to the gain in accuracy we also give examples of how this technique could open up the space of novel interactions.

Author Keywords

particle filter, touch, capacitive, mobile, probabilistic

ACM Classification Keywords

H.5.2 Information Interfaces and Presentation: Input devices and strategies (e.g., mouse, touchscreen)

General Terms

Algorithms

INTRODUCTION

Touch sensing has rapidly become a major method of interacting with computing devices, especially mobile phones. However, a few minutes of use of even the most expensive touch phones makes clear that there are problems with the use of thumbs, as needed for single handed interaction [13], and that even with fingers, users must adjust their tapping behaviour to suit the constraints of the current sensor signal processing technology. This is because the current devices' sense of touch is impoverished compared to the quality of information that could be captured. Most capacitive touch devices can measure one or more points of contact; but fingers are not points floating in space. The pose of the finger engaged in touching contains much salient information – from static indications of grip (left hand or right hand? portrait or landscape? thumb or index finger?) – to dynamic motions involving twisting or levering. Enhanced touch sensing has been demonstrated elsewhere ([8, 20]), but such methods rely on additional non-mobile (and quite complex) sensing. In this paper we demonstrate rich pose detection using very low-resolution capacitive sensors and sophisticated probabilistic inference to extract every bit of information from the sensors.

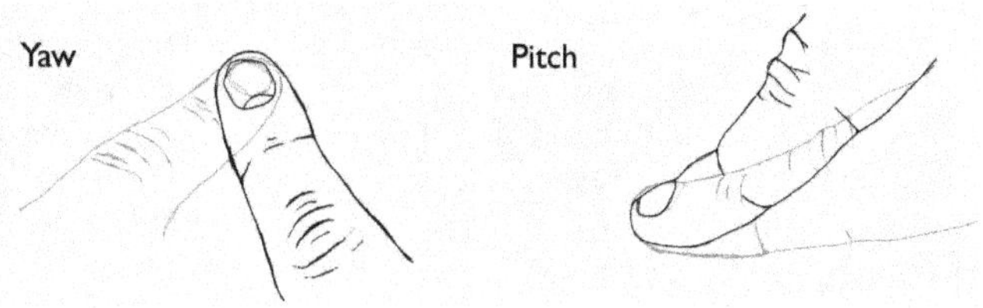

Figure 1. Yawing and pitching of the finger while the position of the intended contact point remains unchanged.

We extend the particle filtering work described in [16] to do real-time tracking of finger angle – both pitch and yaw – using a probabilistic model of the form of the finger as it appears to the sensor. Additionally, this model automatically adapts to the small but significant variation in gross finger shape among the population. The ability to infer these user- and touch-specific variables in real time allows the system to more accurately deduce the intended touch point. Experiments in [8] demonstrated that varying pitch and yaw led to consistent variation in *sensed* touch location for the same *intended* touch location. By explicitly modelling these characteristics, we demonstrate how it is possible to improve the accuracy of pointing. These improvements open up the use of smaller devices and denser control layouts, both as a result of increased accuracy in determining intended touch points, and because a range of new interaction techniques based on finger angle detection can be implemented. This technique works with multiple points of contact using small, coarse sensor arrays.

The models in our system are fully probabilistic, and provide distributions over finger parameters. When the sensing is insufficient to reliably determine the position or orientation of the finger, the distribution naturally represents the increasing uncertainty. Applications using these methods can degrade gracefully in a range of ways, from simply ignoring very noisy inputs to gradually handing over autonomy to the system as control quality decreases. This handover of control, is referred to as the "H-metaphor" in [4], as a metaphor for the relation between a horse and rider, and is explored in the context of touch sensing in [16]. The availability of meaningful uncertainty estimates is one of the major advantages of this approach to touch interaction.

Current mobile touch technology exhibits reasonable accuracy in stationary settings with two-handed use. Performance rapidly deteriorates when interacting one-handed or while mobile. The ability to infer full finger pose with well-calibrated uncertainty estimates offers potential improvements in such scenarios. Improving the accuracy in tasks such as typing on small onscreen keyboards whilst walking would substantially improve the usability of many current mobile devices.

Literature

A number of papers have used sensing of finger positions using a range of technologies to explore novel interaction mechanisms. Rekimoto and colleagues' *Presense* [14] system used capacitive sensing to infer finger position above a conventional keyboard, and explored its use for previews and gestures. Alternatives to capacitive sensing in the literature include magnetic sensing [7], and vision systems [12]. [8] investigates the reliability of touch input using fingerprint scanners, and demonstrated consistent offsets ascribable to variations in pitch, yaw and roll. [10] reviews single-handed interaction. [11] describe problems with multitouch gestures. [17] discusses techniques for one-handed data entry, and [6] expands on this. [18] shows how finger rolls could be distinguished from slides, and provides a range of interaction techniques. [1] discusses dual finger techniques for precise selection, and their *SimPress* method used finger rocking detection to activate certain interaction mechanisms. Work on pen-based interaction, such as [5] is also relevant, given the ready availability of proximity measures in many pen input systems.

Particle filtering, the algorithm used in this work for probabilistic tracking, is described extensively in the literature. Particularly relevant and accessible is the work of Isard and Blake [9], who used particle filters for visual tracking. The technique is described more comprehensively in [15, 2].

THE MODEL

Key to our approach is the development of an explicit model of a finger in contact with the sensor array. The model describes the finger position, the size of the contact area and the finger's pitch and yaw and we can infer each of these parameters in real time. This is made possible by the fact that capacitive proximity sensors (such as those shown in Figure 5) detect parts of the finger that are not in physical contact with the array – they detect the *image* of parts of the finger which

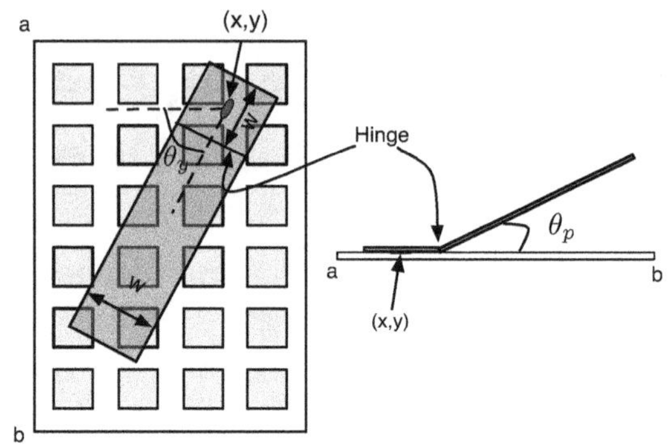

Figure 2. The finger model. The finger is represented by a hinged rectangle, here shown over a 6×4 sensor array.

are not touching the sensors. With our relatively small sensors, this gives a vertical range of approximately 15mm.

In our work, the finger is modelled as a hinged rectangular surface. This can be seen in Figure 2. The model is described by 5 parameters that we shall collectively describe as $\boldsymbol{\theta}$. These five parameters correspond to $x, y, w, \theta_y, \theta_p$, as shown in Figure 2. These are (respectively) the estimated intended contact point, the finger width, the angle of yaw and the angle of pitch. All of these parameters are inferred by the system and in our experiments, the intended touch point is taken as (x, y), the center of the $w \times w$ square. Because of the size of the finger relative to the size of our hardware, we assume that the rectangle is infinitely long although an additional parameter could be used. This model gives the system the ability to infer a broad spectrum of different touch types (i.e. left/right handed users through different yaws, different finger sizes through different values of w, one- or two-handed operation through combinations of all parameters). It is possible to imagine more sophisticated models for a finger that would be suitable in this case – the model described here is relatively crude. For example, one may wish to encode more of the physical constraints on finger positions by modelling the jointed action of the finger. It is important to note that the inference framework that we describe does not preclude any such model and is certainly not unique to the model we have chosen.

ORIENTATION TRACKING

Our implementation allows for real-time tracking of the finger pose $[x, y, z, w, \theta_y, \theta_p]$ as touch is not a static process. It seems reasonable to assume that if we knew the values of $\boldsymbol{\theta}$, they would vary within a particular touch operation (as the finger approaches the sensors and then leaves) and across several touch operations (it is unlikely that a human can perfectly reproduce a particular movement). In addition, the characteristics of the touch (and therefore the values of $\boldsymbol{\theta}$) vary depending on *where* the user is touching. As an example, consider holding a touch-screen mobile phone in the right hand and using the thumb of the same hand to touch the top left of the screen and then the bottom right. The size of the contact area (the skin in contact with the sensors) and the thumb angle will be different in both cases. To further complicate matters, different users will add an extra dimension of variability to the problem (as shown in [8]). The parameters within $\boldsymbol{\theta}$ obviously vary over time as the finger pose varies, and so they must be inferred in real time from the current state of the sensors.

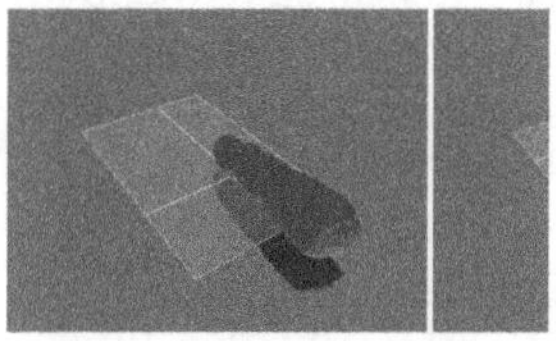

Figure 3. Finger pose estimation, with the contact point and orientation of the finger estimated in real-time.

Figure 3 shows a visualisation of the finger pose using our filter implementation. The pose compared with the actual and estimated sensor readings is shown in Figure 4. The finger angle estimation has some non-linearity in the estimated pitch angle due to the simplificiation of the finger into a flat hinged surface, but still varies monotonically with actual pitch angle. The filter gives the full distribution over the position and angles; as the finger is removed, the distribution expands as the sensing loses the ability to resolve the finger accurately. The angle estimation loses some accuracy towards the edge of the sensor array because there is insufficient coverage to distinguish different poses, but the increasing variance of the filter distribution makes this clear. The model is general enough to easily cope with multi-touch interaction, simply by introducing additional parameters to estimate (although the physical size of the hardware platform makes it hard to test multitouch beyond 2 contact points). Figure 4(d), (e), (f) shows the system estimating the orientation and position of two fingers simultaneously.

The availability of these degrees of freedom has obvious potential for designing new interfaces; effectively there is a now a joystick everywhere on the touch surface. The orientation estimation also directly improves the estimate of the finger position, because the model is a better approximation of the configuration of the the finger than orientation-less models. We anticipate that we can also improve touch interaction performance for dynamic gestures, such as distinguishing taps (which inherently involve some fingertip motion, which can be falsely interpreted as a dragging motions). Thus, the conventional 2D tracking accuracy should be improved by jointly tracking all the parameters of the model.

Inference

To infer the finger pose from the sensor values, we need a theoretical sensor model: what will the sensor "see" when the finger is in a given pose. In other words, a model that will allow us to predict $\mathbf{c}$ (the vector of sensor values) from $\boldsymbol{\theta}$. Comparing the theoretical values of $\mathbf{c}$ with the true value would allow us to rank candidate values for $\boldsymbol{\theta}$ or use more sophisticated methods (as we shall describe below). In this work, we use a method loosely based on the equation for the capacitance of a 2-plate capacitor where the plates overlap with an area A and are separated by a distance of D by a medium with dielectric constant ϵ: $C = \frac{A\epsilon}{D}$. Broadly speaking therefore, the capacitance is proportional to the overlap area and is inversely related to the distance. Given $\boldsymbol{\theta}$ and the size and position of the individual sensors, we can easily compute the area of overlap between the finger rectangle and each sensor. It is equally straightforward to compute the height of the finger rectangle above any position within a sensor (assuming that the rectangle is indeed above this position). Because the height will vary across each particular sensor, we use a single value for each sensor, computed at its centre. If the overlap for sensor i is A_i (expressed as a proportion of total sensor area, $0 \leq A_i \leq 1$) and the height of the centre is given by h_i, we compute the theoretical capacitance of sensor i (z_i) as: $z_i = A_i h_i^{-2}$ where h_i is clipped at a minimum value of 1 to ensure $0 \leq z_i \leq 1$, and compatibility with the sensor output values. h_i is squared to compensate for the nonlinear shape of the finger (it tends to get steeper) and proved to give far superior empirical results to using h_i. Much like the finger model, this sensor model is quite crude and could be improved. However, as we demonstrate later, it gives excellent empirical performance.

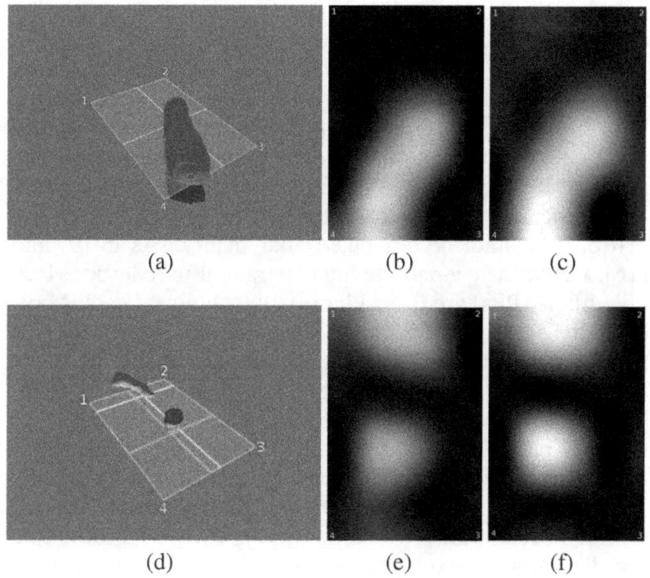

Figure 4. The finger pose (a), as shown in the visualisation, along with (b) the mean of the values the particle filter expected to observe – that is the average of the sensor "image" for each particle, given its current location and orientation, and (c) the the sensor values the that were actually observed. Values are interpolated from the 6×4 grid to more clearly show the finger shape. The numbers indicate the orientation. (d), (e) and (f) show the same visualisation for multitouch interaction.

The particle filter

Whilst it would be possible to use an optimisation routine to find an optimal value of $\boldsymbol{\theta}$ for each $\mathbf{c}$, we follow [9] and [16] and adopt a *probabilistic* approach. Rather than a single value of $\boldsymbol{\theta}$, we will work with a probability density. In particular, $p(\boldsymbol{\theta}|\mathbf{c}, \Delta)$, the density of $\boldsymbol{\theta}$ given the current sensor readings ($\mathbf{c}$) and any other necessary parameters (grouped together in Δ). The two principle reasons for this are a) that the probabilistic approach provides us with far more information than simply optimising $\boldsymbol{\theta}$; information that can be used by the current application to, for example, assist in the handover of autonomy ('H-metaphor'; see [16] for more discussion) and b) the tools exist to allow us to *track* the density, in real-time rather than having to re-optimise each time the sensors change. This reuse of information is important given that fingers move, but probably not very far within the sampling period of the sensors (which might be ca. 15-20ms). Due to the nature of the theoretical sensor model, the density $p(\boldsymbol{\theta}|\mathbf{c}, \Delta)$ cannot be computed analytically. As in [9] and [16], we will use a particle filter to track it in real time. Particle filters (PFs) are from a family of techniques known collectively as Stochastic Monte-Carlo techniques (SMC; see [2]). Particle filters use a set of samples (*particles*) from the density as a proxy for the actual density at a particular time. Given S particles at time t, the filter produces a set of S particles at time $t+1$ by sampling from the population at t with probability proportional to how good the particles are – how well their theoretical sensor values agree with the actual values – and modifying them according to a pre-determined model of how we anticipate the finger (and hence $\boldsymbol{\theta}$) changing – in other words a model of the dynamics of the finger. At any time instant, these particles can be passed to the current application as a proxy for the full density (as in [16]) or can be used to compute expectations. For example, if a single value of $\boldsymbol{\theta}$ is required, the particles can be used to compute the mean of $p(\boldsymbol{\theta}|\mathbf{c}, \Delta)$. Similarly, if one is interested in the covariance of the elements of $\boldsymbol{\theta}$, this is also easily computed.

1. Initialise particle population

The first step, is populating the filter with a set of S particles. In the absence of any sensor information (and because we have to start with something), these are drawn from a prior density, $p(\boldsymbol{\theta})$. The form of this density should reflect our belief in the poses that are possible. Although in reality there are clear physical relationships between the elements of $\boldsymbol{\theta}$ we assume independent priors on the different elements, $p(\boldsymbol{\theta}) = p(x, y)p(w)p(\theta_p)p(\theta_y)$. It is important to realise that this does not imply that the elements will be independent in the *posterior* density $p(\boldsymbol{\theta}|\mathbf{c}, \Delta)$. For example, we shall see that there are clear dependencies between the position (x, y) and the two angles.

2. Particle weighting

Given a current population of S particles, $\boldsymbol{\theta}_1, \ldots, \boldsymbol{\theta}_S$, they are assigned *weights* representing how closely the particles expected sensor values match the true sensor values. For each particle (say $\boldsymbol{\theta}_s$), we compute its implied theoretical sensor value for each of the C sensors using the equation for the sensor model. This results in a vector $\mathbf{z}_s = [z_{s1}, \ldots, z_{sC}]^T$. Each $\mathbf{z}_s$ is then compared with the true sensor values $\mathbf{c} = [c_1, \ldots, c_C]^T$ $(0 \leq c_i \leq 1)$ to produce a weight value $\widetilde{w}_s$ according to a Gaussian likelihood:
$\widetilde{w}_s = K \exp\left\{-\gamma \sum_{i=1}^{C}(z_{si} - c_i)^2\right\}$ with precision (inverse variance) γ and normalising constant K. The Gaussian likelihood suffices as a simple and tractable measure of similarity. Finally, the weights are normalised so that they sum to 1 over the complete particle population: $w_s = \frac{\widetilde{w}_s}{\sum_{t=1}^{S} \widetilde{w}_t}$.

3. Particle re-sampling

Once the particles have been weighted according to their quality, they can be used to create a new generation. The new generation consists of two types of particle: R random particles (drawn from the prior $p(\boldsymbol{\theta})$, as in step 1 above) to ensure that the system can track very rapid changes and $(S - R)$ re-sampled from the current population. For each of these $(S - R)$ particles, a particle from the previous generation – say $\boldsymbol{\theta}_s$ – is chosen with probability w_s and then modified to become a particle in the new generation – say $\boldsymbol{\theta}_{s'}$ – according to some density $p(\boldsymbol{\theta}_{s'}|\boldsymbol{\theta})$. This density encodes our belief in how the finger moves, and again here we make the prior assumption of independence: $p(\boldsymbol{\theta}_{s'}|\boldsymbol{\theta}) = p(x_{s'}, y_{s'}|x_s, y_s)p(w_{s'}|w_s)p(\theta_{ps'}|\theta_{ps})p(\theta_{ys'}|\theta_{ys})$. Once the particle population has been re-sampled, the system returns to the particle weighting step (step 2) using the new current sensor input.

Particle generations

An additional feature of the filter that we use in our experiments is the *generation* of a particular particle. Randomly produced particles (either at step 1 or as one of the R random ones in step 3) are given a generation of 0. When a particle is re-sampled, its generation is incremented. We use the average generation within the population to signal a press operation - as the finger is temporarily stationary, the average generation will be gradually increasing.

The model requires the choice of several densities; priors and movement models. Rather than being a weakness, this is a strength of the proposed approach. Take for example the prior probability on particle position $p(x, y)$. There will often be information available to us from the current application that can inform this choice – the position of targets, buttons or links. Movement models are harder to pin down but it is worth remembering that all we are interested in is how far the finger is likely to move in a very small time instant. As such, we have found that Gaussians with very low variance are suitable for all parameters. This is not to say that more realistic models (such as the minimum jerk model of Flash and Hogan [3]) could not be used – the only restriction on the choice of these densities is that we can sample from them.

EXPERIMENTS

To determine the enhancements that better pose tracking can provide, we ran two experiments using the particle filter model described above. In these experiments, we sought to determine whether the pose information could be used to improve the accuracy of targeting; in other words whether the system could better interpret where users had *intended* to touch. Our hypothesis is that our pose estimating particle filter will yield higher accuracy – the estimated touch point will be closer to the intended touch point – than naive interpretation of the sensors. We did not conduct a formal study of people's ability to directly control the pitch and yaw of their fingers, partly because of the difficulty in reliably controlling such an experiment (as described in [8]), and partly because if orientation tracking works well, this will be directly reflected in the improvement in targeting accuracy. Two experiments were performed, both intended to determine targeting accuracy on a simulated numeric keypad. Participants were asked to touch marked points on a keypad layout (see Figure 5). The data from these touches was captured, and the test algorithms were run on this data to obtain the estimated touch points. The system used in the experiments gave participants no feedback as to how either of the algorithms being tested interpreted the touch; this ensured that an entirely fair and blind comparison of the algorithms could be made.

The first experiment involved participants "entering" a sequence of digits by touching marked points on a flat surface, firstly with their fore-finger with the device resting on the table, and secondly with their thumb while their hand gripped the sensor in a phone-shaped case.

The second experiment involved participants entering sequences of four digit groups (as in PIN entry for unlocking the device, a task often done single-handedly when users are engaged with other tasks), again on the flat, marked surface. The tasks in this experiment were performed with the thumb only, and with two different sizes of target grid. The total size of smaller target grid was smaller than most participants thumbs.

Hardware

For experimental testing, an SK7 sensor pack from SAMH Engineering[1] was interfaced to the SK7-ExtCS1 capacitive sensor array (see Figure 5). This array is a capacitance-to-ground (loading mode) touch sensor with 24 individual sensing pads in a 6 × 4 layout. This is in contrast to the row-column sensors on many touch controllers. This has the advantage of having a sensitive region which extends further from the pads at the cost of reduced XY resolution. The sensitive region measures 52mm×34mm. Each pad is 7mm×7mm with a 2mm gap between sensors. The capacitance to ground on each pad is sampled at 5kHz with 16-bit resolution and then low pass filtered and decimated. A no-touch and full-touch level that are measured as part of an initial calibration are applied to the data and the resulting signals are sent to the PC as 8-bit resolution signals at 60Hz using a USB connection.

A plexiglass sheet of 2mm thickness was attached to the top side of the board with clear double-sided sticky tape, to ensure the absence of air bubbles. On to this sheet a 3×3 grid of target points was marked, at the junctions where four capacitive pads meet. This pad measured 22mm×22mm. A smaller 3×3 grid of 10mm×10mm was also laid out inside for testing extremely small target sizes. These grids are visible in Figure 5). The entire board was mounted a 40mm thick foam block and placed inside a plastic enclosure shaped like a mobile phone. This additional material made it possible to hold the assembly with the hands at the rear of the experimental hardware unduly interfering with the capacitive sensing. The surface of the board was smooth and featureless. The targets were only marked on visually.

Filter details

The details of the particular densities and parameters of the filter used in the experiments are given below: The sensor space is modelled as a 60 × 90 discrete grid (1 grid division = 0.67mm). All values given below correspond to this coordinate system. We used a total of $S = 1000$ particles, of which 20 percent were randomly sampled at each iteration and the remaining were re-sampled from the previous population. The individual components were defined as follows:

$$p(x, y) = \sum_{j=1}^{J} \frac{1}{J} \mathcal{N}_x(\mu_{xj}, 1)\mathcal{N}_y(\mu_{yj}, 1) \quad (1)$$

$$p(w) = \mathcal{U}_w(10, 20) \quad (2)$$

$$p(\theta_y) = \mathcal{U}_{\theta_r}(0, \pi) \quad , \quad p(\theta_p) = \mathcal{U}_{\theta_e}(0, \pi/2), \quad (3)$$

where $\mathcal{U}(a, b)$ is a uniform density between a and b, $\mathcal{N}(\mu, \sigma^2)$ is a Gaussian (normal) density with mean μ and variance σ^2 and Equation 1 describes a J component mixture where J denotes the number of buttons whose centres are defined by μ_{xj} and μ_{yj}. Note that elevation is restricted to be between 0 (finger flat) and $\pi/2$ (finger vertical). Also, as the users were only using the device in the upright orientation, the angle of rotation was restricted to be between 0 and π (the finger cannot approach from the top of the device).

We also assume prior independence across movement models. The individual movement models were all Gaussian densities, centred on the previous particle value with small variances. These gave excellent performance across a wide range of users. The precision of the Gaussian likelihood was set at a relatively high value of 1×10^5 although varying this made little difference to the results. In our experiments, we use the posterior average (the mean of $p(\boldsymbol{\theta}|\mathbf{c}, \Delta)$) computed after the weighting step and before the re-sampling step as:$\bar{\boldsymbol{\theta}} = \sum_{s=1}^{S} w_s \boldsymbol{\theta}_s$.

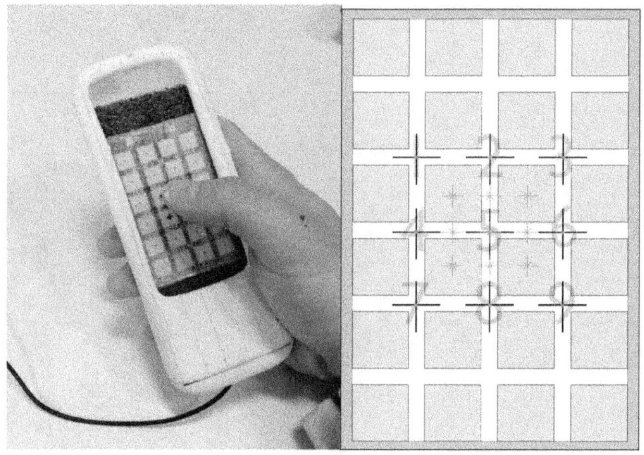

Figure 5. Left: the hardware used in this study. The 24 capacitive proximity sensors are clearly visible. Right: Experimental grid, shown to actual scale. The larger grid is marked with large dark crosses, smaller grid with small light stars.

Experiment 1

Data was captured from 10 participants, 9 male, 1 female, aged between 20 and 41, all members of the local Computing Science Department. Subjects used their dominant hand for all tasks: eight of the subjects were right-handed (used their right index finger and thumb) and two (subjects 5 and 7) were left-handed (left index finger and thumb). All

[1] http://code.google.com/p/shake-drivers/

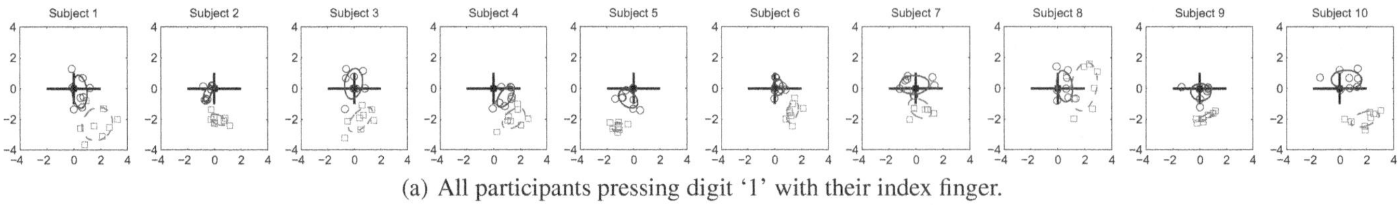

(a) All participants pressing digit '1' with their index finger.

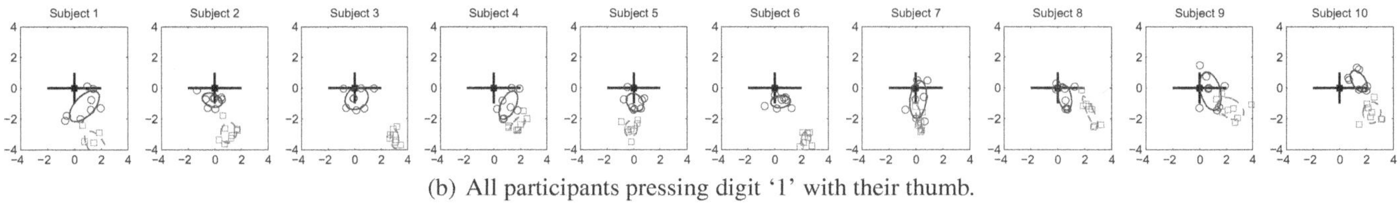

(b) All participants pressing digit '1' with their thumb.

Figure 6. Results of ten participants touching digit '1' with their index finger. Blue circles show the model output and red squares the result of sensor interpolation. Axes are labeled in millimetres. Notice the consistent bias below and to the right for all subjects except those who are left-handed (5 and 7).

had some familiarity with touch screen devices. Users were not requested to touch in any particular manner and were free to touch however they felt comfortable. Diversity in touch styles was evident whilst observing the users and can be clearly seen in Figure 6. Each participant was asked to treat the dots marked on the larger 3×3 grid (shown to scale in Figure 5) as a numeric keypad in telephone layout, containing only digits 1 through 9. In each session, participants had to enter a pseudo-random sequence of digits. During the trial, the participant heard a numeral and were then asked to place their finger on the appropriate point until they heard a beep ($\approx$ 100ms after touching). The touch location was taken at the same time as the beep was heard. The use of audio cues is intended to remove any effects from dividing visual attention. The users received no feedback as to how the system interpreted their press.

This continued until 90 digits had been entered. Each participant completed this experiment twice, once using their forefinger with the device resting on a desk and once with their thumb whilst holding the device in the same hand (as shown in Figure 5). The system logged both the model output ($\boldsymbol{\theta}$) and the location determined by an interpolation of sensor centres: if $\mathbf{r}_i$ is the (x, y) location of the ith sensor, and $\widetilde{\mathbf{c}}$ is the vector of sensor values normalised so as to sum to 1, the interpolated position is given by: $\mathbf{d} = \sum_{i=1}^{C} \widetilde{c}_i \mathbf{r}_i$. This was chosen as a baseline for comparison because the conventional technique of finding the centroid of a blob on a binary thresholded sensor image would be unreasonably inaccurate on our low resolution grid. In the second experiment (below) we show that interpolation provides a reasonable approximation to the accuracy of state-of-the-art technology (the iPhone).

Figure 6 shows an example of the results obtained. The top row shows the data for all users pressing digit '1' with their index finger and the lower row shows them all pressing digit '1' with their thumbs. The units on the axis are millimetres. In each panel, the squares show the result of interpolation and the circles the position inferred by the model.

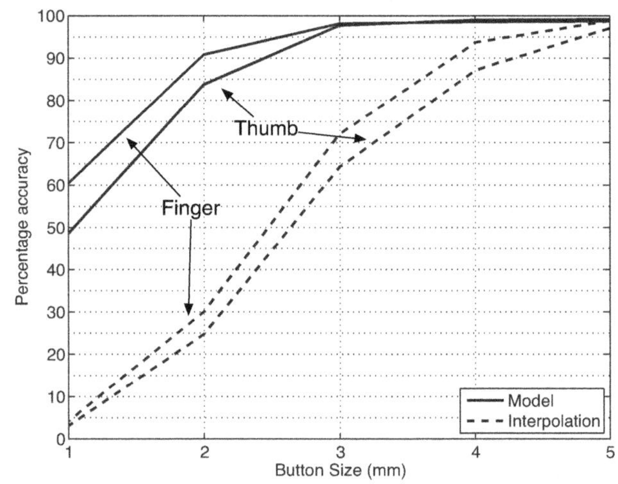

Figure 7. Percentage accuracy versus virtual button size (radius of a circular button). The model provides greater than 95% accuracy for buttons of size 3mm for use with either thumb or forefinger.

Two things are immediately obvious. Firstly, there is a great diversity amongst users (from left to right) and across finger/thumb for individual users (top to bottom). This confirms the observations in [8]. Secondly, the model provides a far more accurate position estimate than interpolation.

The improvement provided by the model is best quantified by computing the implied minimum button size that each method can tolerate. Assuming that buttons are round, with a particular radius, we can compute accuracy (percentage of times the touch would have been within the correct button) for a range of radii across all digits and subjects. The results are shown in Figure 7. The solid lines correspond to the model (for finger and thumb respectively) and the dashed lines to interpolation. The improvement offered by the model is clear: for both finger and thumb, 95% accuracy is achievable for a button with radius 3mm (note that because users sometimes entered the wrong digit, our accuracy estimates are likely to be conservative). This com-

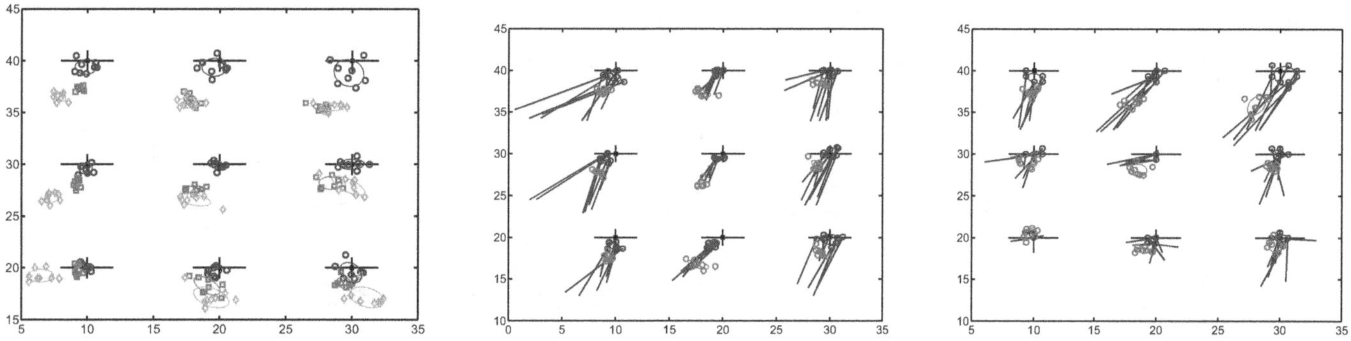

Figure 8. (a) Comparison with an implementation of a previous particle filter approach (green diamonds) for one representative user. Their model assumed that a finger could be represented as a point, as such a consistent bias is present. (b) and (c) Angles inferred for subject 5 when using finger (b) and thumb (c). Lines show projection of finger rectangle onto sensor plane (shorter lines correspond to greater pitch). This subject is left-handed. In (b) the lines are of a consistent length – when the device is on the table, the finger makes contact in roughly the same manner for each digit. In (c), the restrictions in movement caused by one-handed operation are clearly visible with pitch varying dramatically across the array.

pares very favourably with the results presented in [8] where a sensor radius of approximately 3mm (they show diameter of $\approx 5.4 \pm 1.4$mm) was achieved, when correcting for controlled pitch, roll and yaw variations. Note that interpolation gives values of approximately 70% and 65% at 3mm for finger and thumb respectively. Our results suggest that the interpolation can achieve approximately 95% accuracy for sensors of radius 5mm. This is significantly better than the value of approximately 7mm presented in [8] and is likely due to some of the extreme pitch, roll and yaw angles that the users were asked to perform in that study. The improvement that we see is a direct consequence of the explicit finger model. When a user performs a touch, parts of the their finger towards the hand will cause a response from the sensors. This response will naturally pull the interpolated value away from the intended touch location. By modelling this additional signal, our approach is able to automatically correct for this deviation.

Figure 9 plots the mean squared error for the model and interpolation across all right handed subjects. It is clear that the most consistent improvement is to be had (points further from the line $y = x$) when the users have to reach further to the target. Hence, the biggest overall improvement is for the thumb reaching across to the digit 1 with high improvements also seen for other digits towards the top and left of the grid. The smallest improvement is for those digits towards the bottom and right (9,7,6,3), where little of the thumb would be over the sensor area. The pattern for left-handers is similar (swap 1 for 3, 4 for 6, 7 for 9 etc) but not shown for space reasons.

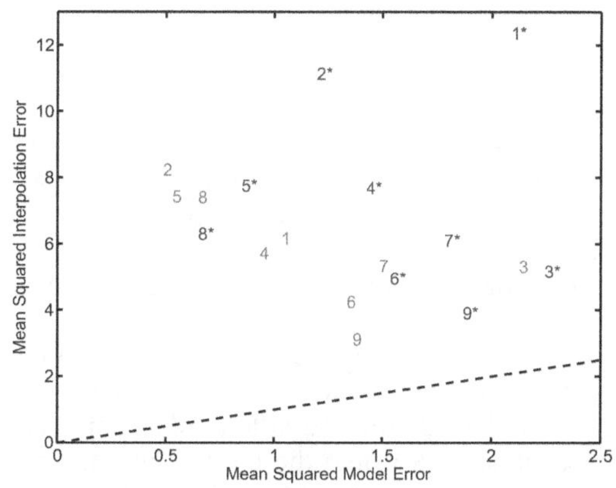

Figure 9. Mean squared error for model and interpolation across right handed participants (note the asymmetric axis scales) for each digit and thumb/forefinger. Plain (red) numbers correspond to the finger, numbers followed by a '*' (blue) correspond to thumb. Points above the $y = x$ line describe an improvement for the model over interpolation.

Experiment 2

The second experiment involved a more realistic data entry task, where participants were asked to enter a sequence of four digit numbers, again consisting of the digits 1 through 9 only. The hardware, particle filtering code and physical set up was identical to the first experiment.

The experiment consisted of two tasks, the first performed on a keypad of dimensions 18mm×18mm as in the first experiment (large grid in Figure 5), and the second performed on a grid of 10mm×10mm (small grid in Figure 5). The task was performed with the dominant thumb only, with the sensor held in the same hand in the phone-shaped case shown in Figure 5. Participants heard each four digit sequence read by a synthetic voice. Each time a touch was registered, the participants heard a beep. After four touches, the next four digit sequence was heard. This continued for 36 four digit groups (144 total digits). No feedback on the interpretation of the touches was given. 6 participants took part in this part of the study, 1 female, 5 male. 5 were right-handed and 1 left-handed, and again the tasks were performed with dominant hand only.

iPhone version

To determine whether our alternative (linear interpolation) algorithm was unreasonably poor compared to state-of-the-art commercial touch sensing, we replicated our experiment on a standard iPhone 3GS as accurately as possible. Raw sensor values are not accessible on this platform so we used

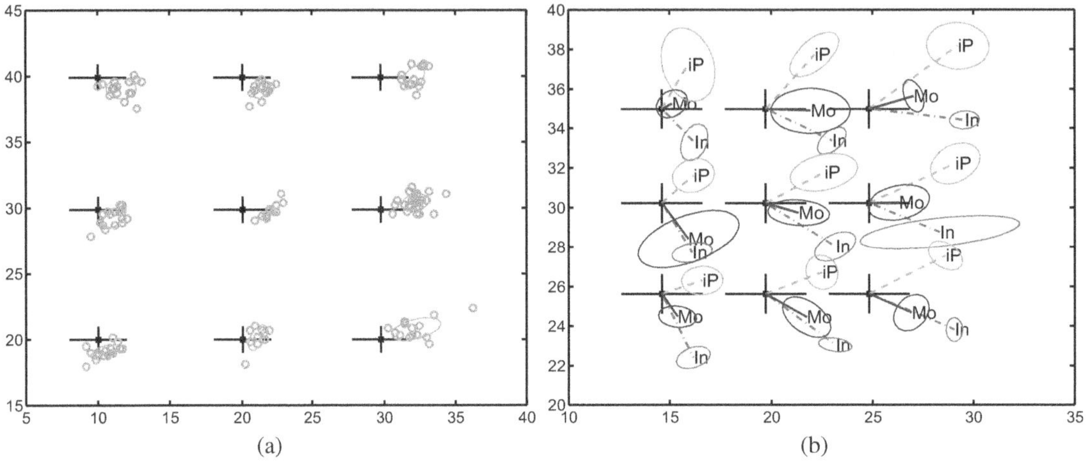

Figure 10. Comparison with the data from the iPhone (axes labeled in millimetres). (a) Raw iPhone data for subject A using their thumb on the large grid. Model and interpolation values not shown as too many points overlap. (b) Subject B using their thumb on the small grid. For clarity ellipses rather than raw data shown. Comparison of contact points for the model (Mo), Interpolation (In) and iPhone (iP). Here the model performs consistently better than both alternatives.

the contact point returned by the API and we took precautions to avoid the effect of any context sensitive target heuristics. An application which displayed an exact, to-scale image of the target grid was implemented. This was not an implementation of our particle filter but rather a test to ensure that our interpolation baseline wasn't unfairly inaccurate. The application followed an identical experimental protocol: users again held the device in their dominant hand and heard four digit sequences, whereupon they had to press on the target with their thumb and hold until a beep was heard. This was conducted for both the coarse and the fine target grid. 36 sequences were again used for each grid. The reported touch points on the iPhone were logged, and subsequently converted from pixels to mm. This gives a baseline measure of the accuracy of a high-resolution capacitive sensing system with post-processing. The results of this are shown in Figure 10. In general the iPhone performance was substantially better than the interpolation algorithm, but was not nearly as good as the pose tracking particle filter.

Although these are very preliminary results with a very small test population, it is worth noting that our system generally outperforms the iPhone, despite having a very coarse sensing array. The large sensor pad size in our hardware also makes hover tracking out to 15mm or more feasible.

DISCUSSION

The filter model clearly performs well in tracking the intended finger location with relatively coarse sensing hardware. The results indicate that the performance is much better than simple weighted interpolation of sensor locations in terms of accuracy. Although looking at plots of touch points for individual users would suggest a simple offset would give high accuracy, in reality the offsets between sensed and intended touch points vary across individuals and contexts. The pooled variance in touch location for the interpolated model is much larger than that given by our pose-tracking model. The model copes easily with the variation in digit width and orientation caused by using the device one-handedly.

Whilst in our experiments we have concentrated on touch events, the dynamic tracking performance compares competitively with the particle filter of [16], which does not model full finger pose. It is difficult to perform a rigorous comparison with the iPhone (due to differing hardware and lack of access to raw sensor values) but in the best comparison we were able to do, the accuracy achieved by the model exceeded that of the iPhone.

NEW INTERACTION POSSIBILITIES

We now explore more innovative interaction mechanisms based on finger pose dynamics – effectively giving users a subtle, context-sensitive joystick.

Rolling Context Menus Touching a surface to select an option is direct and intuitive but is limited by the size of the touching object. The initial finger position narrows down the range of options, but a secondary interaction method could open up controlled by pitch and bearing changes. For example, in Figure 12(a) we show a rolling context menu, which is controlled by changes in bearing. These techniques are similar to methods proposed in [6], but benefit from the ability to refine selection based on finger pose, rather than position in [6], or roll in [18].

Occlusion As the filter tracks the whole finger with a relatively high degree of accuracy, there are straightforward ways of automatically avoiding the common issue of finger occlusion. The work described in [19] could be enhanced with the knowledge of the orientation of the finger. Text could wrap around the "shadow" of the finger, adapting as the orientation changes.

Hidden Flaps The emotional content of messages passed between people changes the way such messages are opened. We suggest an interaction style where users conceal the message with their hand and reveal it carefully by levering the cover with their hand to expose the message (see Figure 12(c)). Secret messages passed between classmates are hidden from view and unfolded discreetly.

High-precision pointing The sensed finger contacts can be

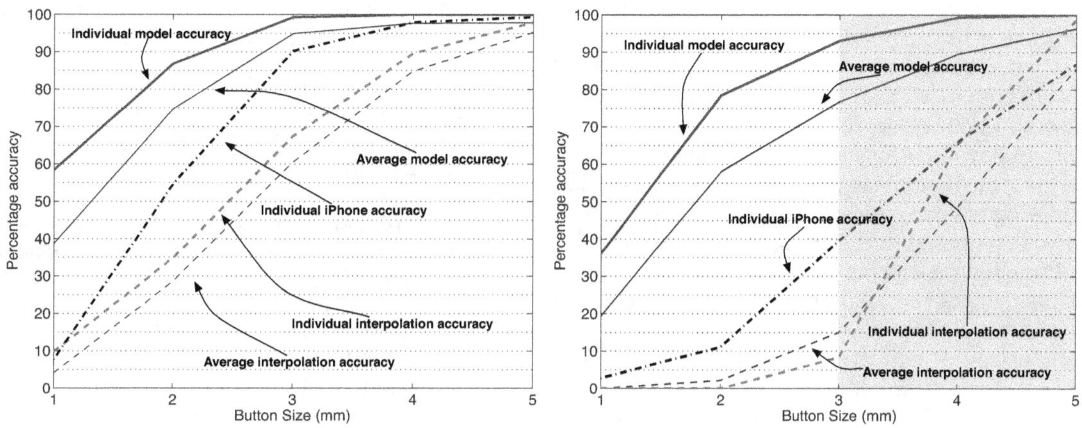

(a) (b)

Figure 11. Effective button sizes for experiment 2. (a) Accuracy as a function of button size for the large grid. Shown are the average curves for the population as well as the specific performance for user A and the same users performance on the iPhone (data from Figure 10(a)). (b) As (a) but for the small grid and also showing the individual performance for subject B (iPhone data as per Figure 10(c)).

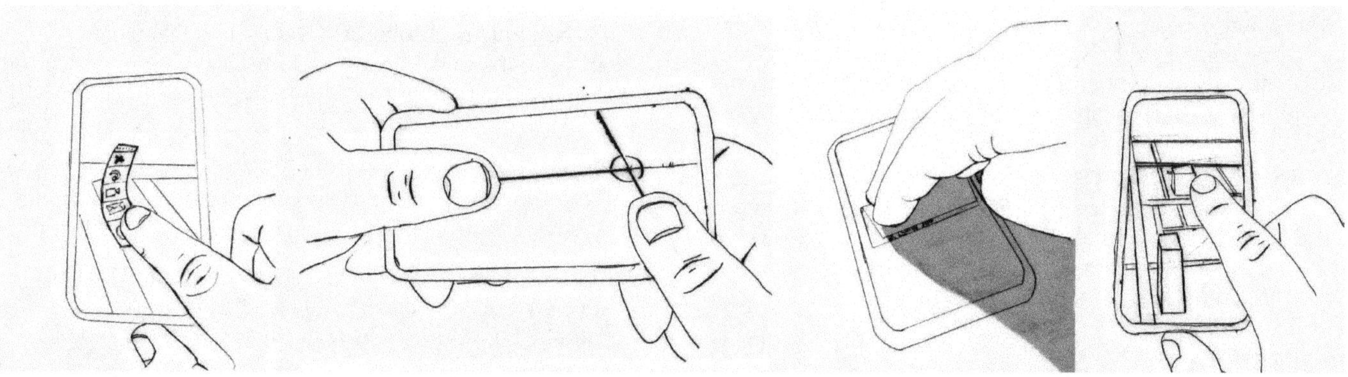

Figure 12. Interaction concepts using tilt-sensitive touch sensing on mobile devices. Left-to-right: (a) Rolling context menus; (b) High-precision bimanual pointing; (c) Peeking through message flaps using whole hand pitch angle detection; (d) 3D map navigation.

virtually "extended" like chopsticks emanating from the finger tips, similar to the work presented in [21]. The interaction techniques suggested in [20] for table-top interaction could be adapted for devices with capacitive touch screens. Figure 12(b) illustrates the concept.

CONCLUSIONS

Conventional touch sensing hardware is quite capable of extracting rich information about the pose and movement of fingers above and in contact with it. Our approach explicitly formulates a model of the finger and estimates the pose using probabilistic particle filtering. The model clearly encodes the assumptions about the physical nature of the fingers and the sensors, and is easy to extend to different contexts. This approach allows the extraction of additional degrees of freedom from the input, beyond simple 2D contact points. The probabilistic nature of our model results in meaningful uncertainty estimates as sensing degrades. It also makes for a consistent framework for integrating uncertainty from higher levels of the interface with and as a result the values measured by the sensor can be interpreted in the context of the entire interaction, from electrical and biomechanical constraints to inference about complex intentions. The potential uses for increased precision and additional degrees of freedom are numerous; we have identified several concepts which could be implemented on small-screen devices.

We have experimentally demonstrated that properly estimating finger pose with both pitch and yaw is both feasible on low-resolution capacitive sensor arrays, and significantly improves targeting performance when 2D target positions are estimated. The estimate of the point a user *intended* to touch can be improved using more complete knowledge of how the finger is posed in space. These targeting improvements mean that devices can have dense control layouts using only cheap and readily available electronics. The limitation on device size is not human finger size, but the crude interpretation of capacitive arrays in existing technologies. We have shown that buttons densely packed at a spacing of 4mm can be made usable with a sensor grid with a resolution of 6×4 pads in an overall area of 34mm×55mm; even smaller layouts are possible if coupled with appropriate secondary interaction mechanisms, such as the rolling context menus. This size of button is equivalent to that required for a QWERTY keyboard on a small touch screen and improving accuracy here could have substantial usability benefits particularly when, for example, only one hand is available or the user is walking. Our hardware comprised a small number of long range capacitive sensors in contrast to the fine row-column style prevalent in current devices. Our investigation suggests that a shift towards the type of hardware that we have used could offer significant accuracy advantages at very low cost. Heterogenous sensors composed of a spectrum of coarse long-range sensors through ultra-fine but short range sensors with regular or irregular shapes can easily be used with our algorithms, unlike conventional approaches. Such sensor arrays represent a simple way of extracting detailed 3D pose information across the entire surface of a device. Our current implementation runs on a desktop system and has not been optimised for mobile technology. We expect that an efficient fixed point implementation could easily run on modern smartphones at low CPU cost.

These probabilistic models demonstrate that by simply modelling the problem in terms of the expected measurements given known constraints, surprising amounts of relevant information can be extracted even from crude sensors. Wider use of these techniques in HCI could dramatically extend the capabilities of existing and yet-to-be-imagined hardware.

ACKNOWLEDGEMENTS

This work was supported by EPSRC grant EP/E042740/1, the PASCAL2 Network of Excellence, and by a fellowship from the Scottish Informatics and Computing Science Alliance (SICSA).

REFERENCES

1. H. Benko, A. D. Wilson, and P. Baudisch. Precise selection techniques for multi-touch screens. In *CHI '06:*, pages 1263–1272. ACM, 2006.
2. A. Doucet, N. de Freitas, and N. Gordon, editors. *Sequential Monte Carlo Methods in Practice*. Springer, 2001.
3. T. Flash and N. Hogan. The coordination of arm movements: an experimentally confirmed mathematical model. *J. Neuroscience*, 5(7):1688–1703, 1985.
4. O. Flemisch, A. Adams, S. R. Conway, K. H. Goodrich, M. T. Palmer, and P. C. Schutte. The H-Metaphor as a guideline for vehicle automation and interaction. Technical Report NASA/TM 2003-212672, NASA, 2003.
5. T. Grossman, K. Hinckley, P. Baudisch, M. Agrawala, and R. Balakrishnan. Hover widgets: using the tracking state to extend the capabilities of pen-operated devices. In *CHI '06:*, pages 861–870. ACM, 2006.
6. T. J. Gunn, H. Zhang, E. Mak, and P. Irani. An evaluation of one-handed techniques for multiple-target selection. In *CHI '09*, pages 4189–4194. ACM, 2009.
7. C. Harrison and S. E. Hudson. Abracadabra: wireless, high-precision, and unpowered finger input for very small mobile devices. In *UIST '09*, pages 121–124, New York, NY, USA, 2009. ACM.
8. C. Holz and P. Baudisch. The generalized perceived input point model and how to double touch accuracy by extracting fingerprints. In *CHI '10*, pages 581–590. ACM, 2010.
9. M. Isard and A. Blake. Contour tracking by stochastic propagation of conditional density. In *ECCV*, pages 343–356, 1996.
10. A. Karlson, B. Bederson, and J. Contreras-Vidal. Understanding single-handed mobile device interaction. In *Handbook of Research on User Interface Design and Evaluation for Mobile Technology*, pages 86–101. IGI, 2007.
11. M. A. Nacenta, P. Baudisch, H. Benko, and A. Wilson. Separability of spatial manipulations in multi-touch interfaces. In *GI '09:*, pages 175–182. Can. Inf. Proc. Soc., 2009.
12. T. Niikura, Y. Hirobe, A. Cassinelli, Y. Watanabe, T. Komuro, and M. Ishikawa. In-air typing interface for mobile devices with vibration feedback. In *SIGGRAPH '10*, pages 1–1. ACM, 2010.
13. P. Parhi, A. K. Karlson, and B. B. Bederson. Target size study for one-handed thumb use on small touchscreen devices. In *Mobile HCI'06*, pages 203–210, 2006.
14. J. Rekimoto, T. Ishizawa, C. Schwesig, and H. Oba. Presense: interaction techniques for finger sensing input devices. In *UIST '03:*, pages 203–212, 2003.
15. B. Ristic, S. Arulampalam, and N. Gordon. *Beyond the Kalman Filter: Particle Filters for Tracking Applications*. Artech House, 2004.
16. S. Rogers, J. Williamson, C. Stewart, and R. Murray-Smith. Fingercloud: uncertainty and autonomy handover incapacitive sensing. In *CHI '10*, pages 577–580. ACM, 2010.
17. A. Roudaut, S. Huot, and E. Lecolinet. Taptap and magstick: improving one-handed target acquisition on small touch-screens. In *Proc. AVI '08*, pages 146–153. ACM, 2008.
18. A. Roudaut, E. Lecolinet, and Y. Guiard. Microrolls: expanding touch-screen input vocabulary by distinguishing rolls vs. slides of the thumb. In *CHI '09*, pages 927–936. ACM, 2009.
19. D. Vogel and R. Balakrishnan. Occlusion-aware interfaces. In *CHI '10*, pages 263–272. ACM, 2010.
20. F. Wang, X. Cao, X. Ren, and P. Irani. Detecting and leveraging finger orientation for interaction with direct-touch surfaces. In *UIST '09*, pages 23–32, 2009.
21. H. Wyss, R. Blach, and M. Bues. iSith - Intersection-based Spatial Interaction for Two Hands. In *3D User Interfaces, 2006*, pages 59 – 61, 2006.

TouchCuts and TouchZoom: Enhanced Target Selection for Touch Displays using Finger Proximity Sensing

Xing-Dong Yang[1,2], Tovi Grossman[1], Pourang Irani[3], George Fitzmaurice[1]

[1]Autodesk Research
210 King St. East, Toronto,
ON, M5A 1J7 Canada
{firstname.lastname}@autodesk.com

[2]Dept. of Computing Science
University of Alberta, Edmonton,
AB, T6G 2E8 Canada
xingdong@cs.ualberta.ca

[3]Dept. of Computer Science
University of Manitoba, Winnipeg,
MB, R3T 2N2, Canada
lastname@cs.umanitoba.ca

ABSTRACT
Although touch-screen laptops are increasing in popularity, users still do not comfortably rely on touch in these environments, as current software interfaces were not designed for being used by the finger. In this paper, we first demonstrate the benefits of using touch as a complementary input modality along with the keyboard and mouse or touchpad in a laptop setting. To alleviate the frustration users experience with touch, we then design two techniques, *TouchCuts*, a single target expansion technique, and *TouchZoom*, a multiple target expansion technique. Both techniques facilitate the selection of small icons, by detecting the finger proximity above the display surface, and expanding the target as the finger approaches. In a controlled evaluation, we show that our techniques improve performance in comparison to both the computer mouse and a baseline touch-based target acquisition technique. We conclude by discussing other application scenarios that our techniques support.

Author Keywords
Touch input, target expansion.

ACM Classification Keywords
H5.2 [Information interfaces and presentation]: User Interfaces. - Graphical user interfaces.

General terms
Design, Human Factors.

INTRODUCTION
Touch input is often considered intuitive and effective [7]. It is becoming a major input modality, especially on mobile devices. Recently, manufacturers have started producing laptops equipped with touch-screens, allowing users to use their fingers to directly interact with their applications. However, legacy applications typically utilize a ribbon or tool palette, consisting of small tiled icons, and research has shown that such targets are difficult to select with the finger due to occlusion [25] and accuracy [19] problems.

While there is an abundance of work in creating new UI paradigms specifically for touch [17, 26], it is unlikely that the legacy applications used most often by users would ever go through such a transformation. Very limited work has looked at making general purpose UIs more touch friendly, without impacting their non-touch experience.

Ideally, software interfaces should seamlessly adapt to the input modality [4, 8]. With the use of proximity based sensing [5, 10, 16, 22], UI components could transition to a touch-optimized variant only when the user's hand approaches, and thus be left unaltered for mouse input. We propose and study the benefit of this idea by introducing two new techniques: *TouchZoom* (Figure 1) and *TouchCuts*. Both techniques utilize target expansion as a basic UI enhancement to facilitate finger input on interfaces that host many small and tiled icons, such as ribbons. Both techniques only activate when a finger approaches, and therefore do not affect traditional cursor input.

In the following sections, we first perform a study investigating the benefits of touch input in a laptop configuration. Motivated by the high error rates found for small targets, we describe our new techniques, *TouchCuts*, a single target expansion technique, and *TouchZoom*, a multiple target expansion technique. A controlled study shows that our techniques improve performance in comparison to both the computer mouse and a baseline touch-based target acquisition technique, Shift [25]. We conclude by discussing other application scenarios that our techniques could support.

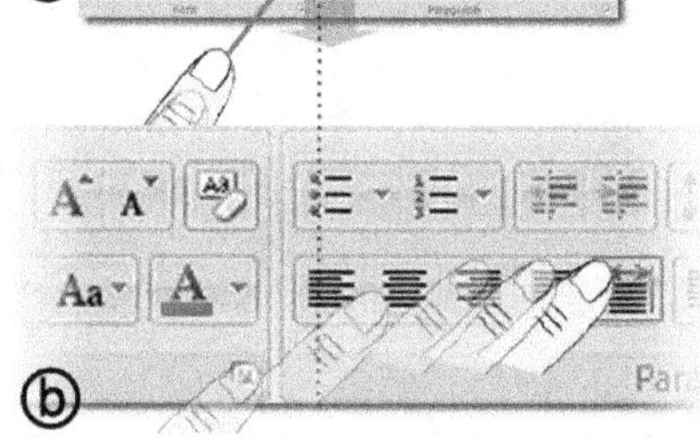

Figure 1 - *TouchZoom*. (a) The ribbon expands at the intersection of a finger's motion vector and the top edge of the ribbon. (b) After the expansion, finger movement is adjusted to acquire the new position of the highlighted goal target icon.

RELATED WORK

Selection with Touch

Having finger input available in tandem with the mouse in a shared UI environment allows these devices to complement each other, thus providing numerous benefits. Researchers have found that the finger can be faster than a mouse when selecting targets greater than 3.2mm [24]. Nevertheless users can perform better with a mouse than with a finger in tasks requiring fine movement and selection [15] as also confirmed by Forlines et al. [7].

Clearly, the size of a UI component will affect touch input. Established guidelines suggest that the target size for touch should be greater than 10mm [19]. However, smaller icons (e.g. 5mm) are still common in most of the current user interfaces. Finger based interactions also suffer from occlusion problems. Proposed solutions to alleviate this concern include the Offset Cursor [20], that relocates the cursor 0.5" above the finger; DTMouse, which presents the cursor between two fingers [6], Shift, which dynamically places a copy of the occluded area in a shifted callout [25], and Dual-Finger-Selections, which supports precise selections on multitouch displays [1].

In Shift, users slide the finger contact on the display, to fine tune a crosshair cursor position and select the target using a take-off gesture. Shift's callout was designed to be triggered only when necessary. However, in most cases, the selection can be separated into 2 steps – invoking the callout and adjusting the cursor to make a selection. Escape [26], allows selecting small and tiled targets by assigning a unique directional gesture for selection. An experimental study showed that Escape could perform 30% faster than Shift on targets smaller than 5mm while still maintaining a similar error rate. Similarly, Sliding widgets [17] require users to slide on a target in a particular direction for selection. These two techniques require changing the traditional UIs to visualize directional clues, which may not be suitable for an interface also shared with traditional cursor input.

Mouse-based Target Expansion

Target expansion techniques for the mouse have also been widely researched [3, 13, 27]. These techniques have been found helpful for selecting a single target, by expanding the target as the cursor approaches. However, in real-world situations, targets are often laid out in a tiled arrangement. The existing approaches for expanding tiled targets include expanding a single item that is predicted to be the desired target [27, 14] or expanding the predicted item as well as its immediate neighbors [23]. Obviously, one of the limitations of these methods is the lack of guaranteeing that the desired target will be magnified due to prediction errors. Note that when using a mouse the user can still make a precise selection on an unexpanded target [23]. However with finger input, the user's intended target may be too difficult to select if it is not expanded.

Zhai et al. [27] suggest that if space permits it, all the targets in the view should be expanded. However, it is typical for ribbons or toolbars to span the entire display space, so there would not be room to expand all targets. An alternative would be to use some form of fisheye distortion [2], but these have been shown to be harmful to pointing and selection tasks [9, 27].

Touch-Based Target Expansion

Despite its popularity in the target acquisition literature, target expansion has not been widely explored for touch. Olwal et al. [18] proposed using a rubbing gesture or a second finger tap to 'zoom into' a small target before attempting to make a selection. Similarly, Benko et al. [1]'s two-handed techniques also attempt to enlarge the target to ease selection. These techniques have been proven helpful for selecting small targets using bare fingers. However, they have a common limitation that users need to explicitly indicate a target of interest and then expand it manually.

The more traditional, automatic target expansion, has not been explored for touch. This is likely because target expansion relies on tracking the approach of the cursor, or in this case, the finger. This information is typically not available, as most touch devices today do not sense hover information. However, advanced sensing technology has pushed the detection of finger motion at a practical height above the surface [11, 22]. Major manufacturers (Mitsubishi, Primesense, and Cypress) have already announced such types of commercial systems or prototypes [5, 16, 21]. All of these have made target expansion feasible on small touch-screen devices, e.g. laptops.

In summary, target expansion for touch has not been investigated thoroughly, and is promising in that it may improve touch selection without impacting the user interface for traditional cursor input. However, even in the mouse-based research, there are challenges surrounding target expansion yet to be addressed, such as how to apply expansion in tiled-target environments. In the next section, we first demonstrate the added value of finger input in a keyboard/mouse setting. We then present our designs and studies of our techniques.

EXPERIMENT 1: EVLAUATION OF TOUCH

We believe touch input could be particular useful in a laptop configuration, since a mouse may not be available, and the hands, when in a resting state on the keyboard are already quite close to the display. However, despite the prevalence of touch-based laptops, the efficiency of using touch on such devices has not been investigated and is thus not fully understood. To better understand if and when target expansion techniques would be useful, we first study traditional target acquisition in a laptop configuration. While previous work has compared touch to other forms of input [7, 15, 24], here, on screen target acquisition is unique, since the hand would be moving from a horizontal plane of the keyboard to a vertical plane of the display. In addition, strictly following the KLM GOMS model, we would predict that such a task would require homing time (switching to the touch input device) and pointing time (acquiring the target). We postulate that one of the primary benefits of using touch for target selection tasks is allowing pointing and homing to take place in parallel. We are unaware of any investigation into this issue.

Motivated to answer these open questions, the goal of this experiment is to evaluate the performance of touch versus a mouse and touchpad in a task involving the use of a pointing device in conjunction with a keyboard.

Apparatus

Our study was conducted on a Dell SX2210 21.5" touchscreen monitor, as it provided more accurate touch input then current touch-enabled laptops. The display was used in conjunction with a standard desktop keyboard. To simulate a laptop configuration, we lowered the height of the touchscreen so that the button of the display is 4 cm above the keyboard, which is about the same distance that can be found on a Dell TouchSmart TX2 tablet PC. The display was tilted to a comfortable viewing angle (13° to the vertical plane). A USB touchpad (97 × 78 mm) from Ergonomic was placed below the space bar of the keyboard, and was raised to the same height as the keyboard (Figure 2).

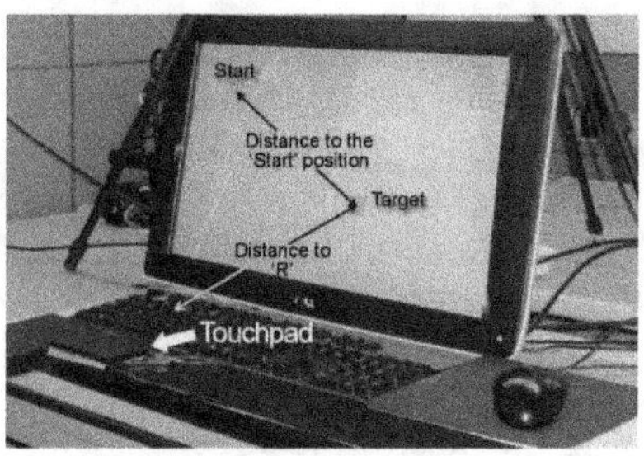

Figure 2 – Hardware setup for Experiment 1.

Participants

Twelve paid participants (7 males and 5 females) between the ages of 21 and 56 participated in this study. All participants were right-handed. They were all familiar with a computer mouse and touchpad, and had previous experience with mobile touch-screen devices.

Task and procedure

The task required participants to click a key on the keyboard and then using the same hand select a square target of various sizes in a random location on the screen. This task is analogous to that frequently employed by users of text editing programs, where the main task is typing on a keyboard but requires users to switch to a mouse or a touchpad to click an icon or other on-screen widget. The right hand was used for the mouse and touchpad. The left hand (non-dominant for all participants) was used for touch, since we felt testing touch with the dominant hand may be biased, since in some cases users may want to use the non-dominant hand (for example, if a target is on the left side, or if their right hand is on the mouse). Participants were told to only use their index finger during the touch conditions.

In the mouse and touchpad conditions, participants were asked to position a cursor inside a 0.5×0.5cm 'Start' square prior to the start of a trial. A trial started after participants pressed a keyboard key and finished after a target was successfully selected. Ideally, we would have like to use the 'F' key when using touch and the 'J' key when using the mouse and touchpad, as these are the typical resting keys for the left and right hands respectively. However, we used the 'R' key for touch and the '\' key for mouse, and the 'J' key for touchpad since the distance between these keys and their respective input devices more closely matched the distances on a Dell TouchSmart TX2 tablet PC.

Participants were asked to finish the task as fast and as accurately as possible. They were encouraged to take breaks during the experiment, which lasted about 40 minutes.

Design

The experiment employed a 3×4×3 within-subject factorial design. The independent variables were *Pointing Device* (*Finger, Mouse, and Touchpad*); *Target Distance* (*18, 24, 30*, and *36*cm); and *Target Size* (*0.5, 1*, and *2*cm).

The size of the target was chosen to be close to the size of the icons in real-world applications. For instance, 0.5cm is approximately the same size as the ***Bold*** button in Microsoft Word. Similarly, 1cm is approximately the same size as the *Paste* button. Target distance was measured from the center of the goal target to the center of the 'Start' position in the mouse and touchpad conditions. Distance was measured from the center of the 'R' key to the center of the goal target in the touch condition. Target locations were the same for all conditions. The 'Start' square was repositioned (in the mouse and touchpad conditions) according to the target position to ensure it satisfied the distance condition.

Windows cursor acceleration was turned on to facilitate pointing by using the cursor. If the user missed the target, they had to click again until successful. In each trial, participants performed tasks in one of each *Pointing Device* × *Target Distance* × *Target Size* combination. The experiment consisted of 5 blocks, each consisting of 3 repetitions of trials. The first block was used as practice trails, thus the data was not used in analysis. The *Pointing Device* was counter balanced among participants. The *Target Distance* and *Target Size* were randomized among trials.

Results and discussion

Dependent measures included the number of errors and the average task completion time. This data was analyzed using Repeated-measures ANOVA and Bonferroni corrections for pair-wise comparisons.

Task completion Time

ANOVA yielded a significant effect of *Pointing Device* ($F_{2,22}$ = 14.43, $p < 0.001$), *Target Distance* ($F_{3,33}$ = 3.61, $p < 0.05$), and *Target Size* ($F_{2,22}$ = 101.72, $p < 0.001$). There is also significant interaction effects on *Input Device* × *Target Distance* ($F_{6,66}$ = 8.68, $p < 0.001$), *Input Device* × *Target Width* ($F_{4,44}$ = 29.07, $p < 0.001$), and *Target Distance* × *Target Width* ($F_{6,66}$ = 5.53, $p < 0.001$). The interaction effects were mainly caused by the poor performance of finger touch on the target of 0.5cm (see Figure 3).

Overall (including trials with errors), the performance of finger (1528ms) was significantly faster than mouse (1639ms) ($p < 0.05$), which was significantly faster than touchpad (2242ms) ($p < 0.001$). As expected target size has more impact on finger than mouse or touchpad (Figure 3 left). Participants spent more time selecting the smallest target using finger than using mouse or touchpad.

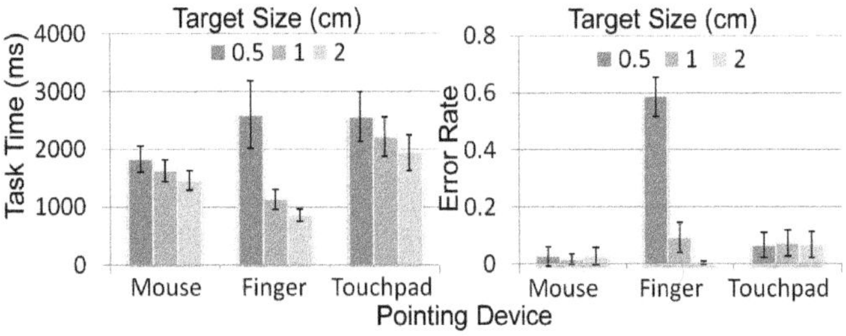

Figure 3 – Task time and error rate shown by Technique and Target Size. (Error Bars show 95% CI in all figures)

Number of errors

ANOVA yielded a significant effect of *Input Device* ($F_{2,22}$ = 57.46, $p < 0.001$), *Target Distance* ($F_{3,33}$ = 7.68, $p < 0.05$), and *Target Size* ($F_{2,22}$ = 202.36, $p < 0.001$). We also found significant interaction effects on *Input Device* × *Target Distance* ($F_{6,66}$ = 4.18, $p = 0.001$) and *Input Device* × *Target Width* ($F_{4,44}$ = 225.43, $p < 0.001$).

Overall, touch made significantly more errors (23%) than touchpad (7%) ($p < 0.001$), which made significantly more errors than mouse (2%) ($p < 0.001$). Figure 3 right shows that participants made closed to 60% errors using touch on target size 0.5cm but made less errors than mouse on target of size 2cm.

Fitts' Law Analysis

To perform a Fitts' Law analysis, we removed all trials in which errors occurred. Linear regression tests indicated that the task highly conformed to Fitts' Law, for all three conditions, showing that touch is constantly faster than mouse or touchpad across all index of difficulties (Figure 4). It can be seen that the main difference is due to the 'a' constant, which is typically reaction time, but for this study, encompasses the homing time as well. This is an interesting results, as it shows that touch does allow homing and pointing to be carried out concurrently. To repeat the analysis without homing time, we subtracted the elapsed time until the cursor began to move in the mouse and touchpad conditions. After doing so, we still see a 16% advantage of touch over the mouse ($p < 0.001$), and a 35% advantage over the touchpad ($p < 0.001$).

Summary

The study demonstrates certain benefits of using touch in a routine task, which requires users to switch from a keyboard to a pointing device prior to start acquiring a target. For targets that are at least 1cm large, touch was 36% faster than the mouse and 52% faster than the touchpad. Even without the homing time, touch was 8% faster than the mouse and 35% faster than the touchpad. However, as expected, the performance of touch decreased significantly with small targets. In particular, our study shows that touch completely fails for target sizes of 0.5×0.5cm. Unfortunately, many graphical user interfaces contain targets of this size, so further considerations must be made for touch to be practical on desktop applications.

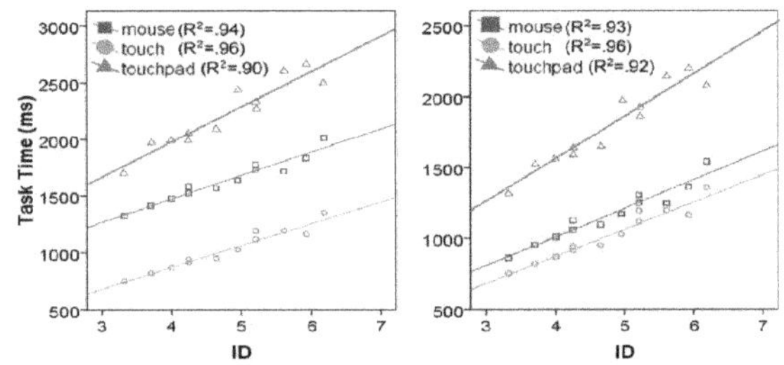

Figure 4 –Task completion time with homing time (left) and without homing time (right) by the index of difficulty.

EXPANDING TARGET TECHNIQUES FOR TOUCH

The results of Experiment 1 provide an important lesson: if targets are big enough, using touch to acquire them can have significant advantages. However, in desktop applications, increasing the size of the targets is not practical, as it would diminish the experience for users who never intend to use touch. It is also impractical to expect traditional legacy applications to be rewritten specifically for touch. Instead, we propose that **UI components transition to be optimized for touch *only* when the user intends to use touch**. Already, numerous technologies exist to detect the proximity of fingers [5, 11, 16, 21, 22]. Expanding the targets as a finger approaches the screen could be an efficient mechanism to overcome the challenges encountered in Experiment 1. In this section, we initiate the investigation of expanding targets for touch, through the design of two techniques: *TouchCuts* and *TouchZoom*.

TouchCuts

TouchCuts are a basic implementation of expanding targets for touch, where only certain targets within a UI palette, such as a toolbar or ribbon, expand when the finger approaches it. Only this subset of targets is accessible through touch, as surrounding targets may become occluded by them. As such, *TouchCuts* are akin to keyboard shortcuts, providing efficient access to some of an application's commands. However, they are not exhaustive or do not provide a replacement for other command access methods. *TouchCuts* use a visual gloss overlay, to indicate to the users which of the targets are accessible through touch. We also implemented a simple method to allow users to customize which targets are *TouchCuts*. The user taps close to a desired target using their finger, and drags the mouse to specify the size of a TouchCut (Figure 5). Similarly, tapping on a TouchCut, followed by a mouse click on the enlarged button can remove it. Using a transparent overlay window, we were able to prototype an application independent implementation of *TouchCuts*, that could be used to customize and access *TouchCuts* on any windows program.

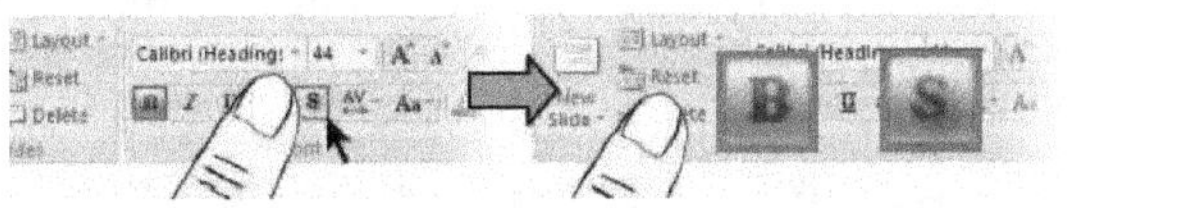

Figure 5 –Left: define a *TouchCuts*. Right: *TouchCuts* expands when a finger approaches.

The advantage of this technique is that it is a single target expansion, so no target prediction is required, and no targets are displaced. The limitation is that it cannot provide access to every target within a tool palette. Therefore, *TouchCuts* are most suitable for functions that are used frequently. In the case when a function is not available through *TouchCuts*, the user will have to use a mouse or re-customize the *TouchCuts*.

TouchZoom

We also wanted to develop a technique that could provide full access to a palette's icons. We focus our design on the ribbon, because it has become a common UI component for desktop applications, but the technique would work for any horizontal tool palette. Our approach is to magnify the entire ribbon, with a center of expansion at a predicted endpoint, similar to what Zhai et al. previously proposed [27]. This ensures expansion of the desired target, even if there is an error in the endpoint prediction. Thus, unlike *TouchCuts*, the *TouchZoom* makes every target within the ribbon accessible through touch. One concern, which will require investigation, is that the goal target may become offset from its original location, and in the worst case, the target may be displaced off-screen.

For prediction, a 2D motion vector is generated based on the projection of the finger movement on the screen. We use only the last 2 points of the sample to estimate the intended vector, as it tended to perform better than other regression algorithms we implemented. The intersection of the motion vector and the top of the ribbon determines the center of expansion (*CE*), and the ribbon expands once the index finger crosses an expansion point in a sufficient speed. If *CE* falls outside of the ribbon, it will be placed on the corresponding ribbon endpoint. The *CE* was fixed at the top of the ribbon in all cases. When the index finger crosses a certain distance threshold, the *CE* is calculated and the resulting ribbon expansion occurs (Figure 1). When the prediction is wrong, the goal target will be offset from its original location at a magnitude proportional to the prediction error. To recover from an off-screen error, users can either re-launch the expansion by moving below the distance threshold, or scrub the ribbon with a touch gesture to pan the target back into view.

We anticipated that the accuracy of the prediction would be dependent on the time when the ribbon expansion is triggered. Expanding late might lead to better prediction since the finger would be closer to its goal. However, considering that no prediction algorithm works perfectly [12, 13, 14], a user will need a certain amount of time to perceive target displacement, and to adjust his/her finger motion accordingly. Thus, it may be preferable to expand the ribbon early.

Another design option we considered is to group sets of ribbon icons together, and to set the *CE* to the center of the predicted group (For groups adjacent to the screen edge, the *CE* would be set to the edge) (Figure 6). This would allow a user to aim his/her finger movement at the group containing the desired icon, instead of aiming at a desired icon itself. Having this larger initial target would minimize prediction errors, and, once expanded, the user could adjust his/her finger movement to make the final selection. However, the target offset would be proportional to the distance between the target and the center of its group.

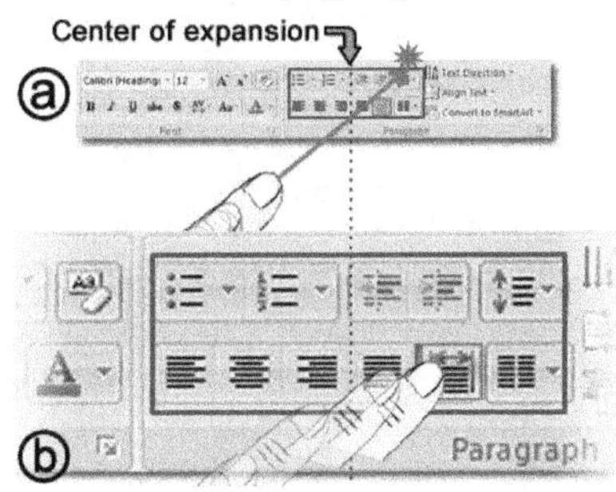

Figure 6 – (a) The ribbon expands at the center of a group of icons shown in the blue outline. (b) User adjusts finger movement to the new position of the highlighted target icon.

In the following section, we study the relevant parameters for our *TouchZoom* design. In Experiment 3 we will compare *TouchZoom* to *TouchCuts* and two baseline techniques.

EXPERIMENT 2: EVALUATION OF TOUCHZOOM

In this study, we were interested in measuring the impact of the pertinent design parameters for *TouchZoom*, to optimize the techniques efficiency. The parameters we investigated were group size, target position, and expansion point.

Apparatus

The hardware setup was the same as in Experiment 1. In addition, we used four OptiTrack motion capture cameras to capture the off-screen movement of the user's index finger. The cameras have 100Hz frame rates and millimeter accuracy. We put 3 reflective markers on a user's hand (Figure 7). The marker on the user's index finger was tilted to the right side to avoid occlusion. This should be considered enabling technology only, simulating the more practical technologies discussed earlier.

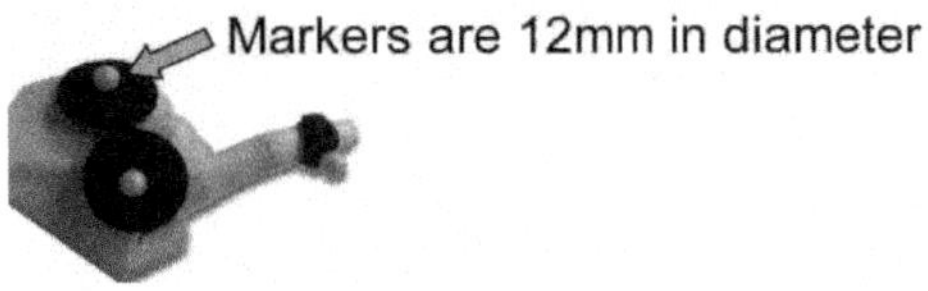

Figure 7 – Reflective marker placement.

Participants

Ten paid participants (5 males and 5 females) between the ages of 20 and 34 participated in this study. All participants were right-handed. They were all familiar with graphical user interfaces, and had previous experience with mobile touch-screen devices.

Task and Procedure

The task required participants to use their left index finger to press the 'O' key on a keyboard and then select a target button in our abstracted ribbon using the same finger. Upon pressing the 'O', the participants were instructed to select the target as fast and as accurately as possible. A trial started after the 'O' was pressed and finished after a target was successfully selected. Participants were encouraged to take breaks during the experiment. The entire experiment lasted about 45 minutes.

Design

The ribbon was 1.5cm high and 45cm width, and was rendered near the top of the screen in a window which has the same width as the ribbon and the same height as the screen. A 100ms animation was used for the Ribbon expansion. In each trial, a 0.5×0.5cm goal target was shown in the ribbon. An expansion magnification level of 3x, which was based on Experiment 1, was used to reduce the chance of errors. The ribbon had 90 icons across, and 3 icons in each column. The 'O' key was centered with the ribbon.

The experiment employed a 5×2×2×9 within-subject factorial design. The independent variables are *Group Size* (*1, 3, 9, 15,* and *30*); *Expansion Point* (*Late* and *Early*); *Target Y Position* (*Up* and *Down*), and *Target X Position* (*1* to *9*).

Group Size (GS) – Group size indicates the number of icons in a row that a group has. We chose to explore a range of groups size, that evenly divided into the 90 targets across: 1, 3, 9, 15, and 30.

Groups were visualized using vertical bars (Figure 8). For targets close to the screen edges, the participants were shown that by biasing their acquisition movement towards the edge of the screen, off-screen errors could be minimized.

Expansion Point (EP) – The distance to the goal target was measured as the distance from the 'O' key to the target in 3D space. Expansion Point took on the values 90% and 40%, representing the amount of distance travelled to the targets, before the expansion occurred. We chose 40% as a minimum value because our informal test showed that the distances below 40% could significantly impair the prediction. The value of 90% was chosen as it has been suggested by previous expanding target techniques [13].

Target Y Position (TY) –In the *Up* condition, the target was placed on the top row. In the Down condition, the target was placed in the bottom row.

Target X Position (TX) – In each trial, the target was placed in one of 9 different horizontal positions across the ribbon (see Figure 8). In addition to the 9 absolute positions, we were also interested in investigating the effects of 3 relative positions (left, middle, and right) of a target within a group of the ribbon. To ensure each group size had exactly 3 targets in each of these relative positions, we slightly shifted some of the X positions by ±1 icon

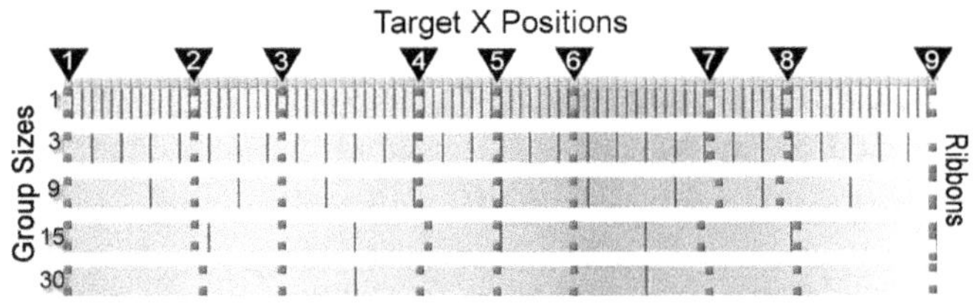

Figure 8 – Illustration of target positions (red dots) within each of the 5 group sizes. The gradient effect was added to provide spatial grounding. Blue bars indicate group borders.

The experiment consisted of 3 blocks, each consisting of 1 trial for each combination of *Group Size (GS)* × *Expansion Point (EP)* × *Target Y Position (TY)* × *Target X Position (TX)*. The order of *Group Size* was randomized between subjects. Within each group size, *Expansion Point* was randomized. Finally, target position was randomized in each *Group Size* × *Expansion Point* pair.

Dependent measures included the number of off-screen errors, the number of selection errors, and the average task completion time. An off-screen error was recorded when a target was pushed into off-screen space. A selection error was recorded when a participant missed a target. Task completion time was recorded as the time elapsed from the 'O' being pressed to a successful selection on the target.

Results and Discussion

The results were analyzed using Repeated-measures ANOVA and Bonferroni corrections for pair-wise comparisons. Before the analysis, we checked the ordering effects of group size on all the dependent measures, and found no significant effects.

Task completion time

ANOVA yielded a significant effect of *TX* ($F_{8,72} = 13.65$, $p < 0.001$). Interestingly, we found no significant effect of *GS* ($F_{4,36} = 1.16$, $p = 0.35$), *EP* ($F_{1,9} = 0.9$, $p = 0.37$), and *TY* ($F_{1,9} = 0.67$, $p = 0.44$). There were significant interaction effects on *GS* × *TX* ($F_{32,288} = 7.17$, $p < 0.001$), and *TY* × *EP* ($F_{1,9} = 6.1$, $p < 0.05$).

Post-hoc analysis showed that task time decreased significantly towards the center of the ribbon (Figure 9 left). In particular, task time at *TX* 1, 7, 8, and 9 were significantly longer than at 3, 4, 5, 6 (all $p < 0.05$).

Task completion time without off-screen error

There was a significant difference between trials when off-screen errors occurred (2700ms s.e. 119.74) and when off-screen errors did not occur (1094ms s.e. 20.82) ($F_{1,9}$ = 172.89, $p < 0.001$).

After removing these trials (7%), we found significant effects of *TX* ($F_{8,72}$ = 12.35, $p < 0.001$), *EP* ($F_{1,9}$ = 47.13, $p < 0.001$), and *TY* ($F_{1,9}$ = 14.22, $p < 0.005$). There was a weak effect of *GS* ($F_{4,36}$ = 2.88, p = 0.04), but pair-wise comparison showed no significant difference between group sizes. There was a significant interaction effect on *GS* × *TY* ($F_{4,36}$ = 0.67, $p < 0.05$). Figure 9 (left) shows the task time with and without off-screen errors.

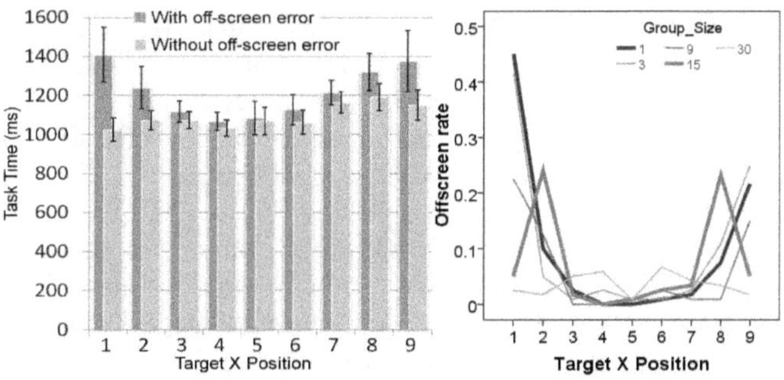

Figure 9 – Left: Task time shown by target position. Right: Off-screen rate shown by target position and group size.

The participants performed the task faster when the ribbon was expanded at 40% distance (1038ms s.e. 25.5ms) than when it was expanded at 90% distance (1147ms, s.e. 18.8). This is because the early expansion allowed users to adjust their initial movement path earlier, instead of following two separate acquisition paths (one for the group, and then one for the goal target position resulting from the expansion).

We also analyzed the effect of the relative position of the targets within their groups, excluding group size 1. We found a significant effect of target position ($F_{1,18}$ = 14.13, $p < 0.001$). Targets on the left (1116ms s.e. 24.23ms) and right side (1133ms s.e. 28.62ms) of a group took significantly longer than those on the center of a group (1046ms s.e. 23.68ms). This explains why we found only weak effect of group size. Although big groups (e.g. 15 and 30) have better prediction, their larger target displacements increase acquisition times.

Off-screen Errors

ANOVA yielded a significant effect of *TX* ($F_{8,72}$ = 22.72, $p < 0.001$), *GS* ($F_{4,36}$ = 10.68, $p < 0.001$), and *EP* ($F_{1,9}$ = 2.12, $p < 0.05$). There was no significant effect of *TY* ($F_{1,9}$ = 0.67, p = 0.44). There were also a significant interaction effect on *EP* × *TX* ($F_{8,72}$ = 2.58, $p < 0.05$).

The participants made more off-screen errors when the ribbon was expanded at 40% distance (0.09 s.e. 0.02) than when it was expanded at 90% distance (0.05 s.e. 0.01).

Figure 9 (right) shows that most off-screen errors were made on the targets on the left and right edge of the ribbon (*TX* 1 and 9). Post-hoc analysis showed that big groups (e.g. 15 and 30) introduced significantly less off-screen errors than the smaller groups ($p < 0.05$). It also shows that large group sizes can also cause off-screen errors. For instance, the participants made significantly more off-screen errors on the targets at position *TX* 2 and 8 with group size 15 than with other group sizes ($p < 0.05$). Going back to Figure 8 we see that these two target positions are at the edge of their respective groups. If a participant aimed at the target instead of the group, there was a chance the wrong group would be predicted, pushing the desired group off-screen.

Selection Error

Overall, the average selection error rate was 6.2%. No main effects or interaction effects were found on error rate.

HYBRID INTERPOLATION FOR TOUCHZOOM

Experiment 2 shows that reducing prediction error by increasing the size of the group does not improve the efficiency of the task, because of the larger target offsets. We also found that off-screen errors had an overwhelming effect on overall completion time. In this section we discuss a redesign of *TouchZoom* to prevent off-screen errors.

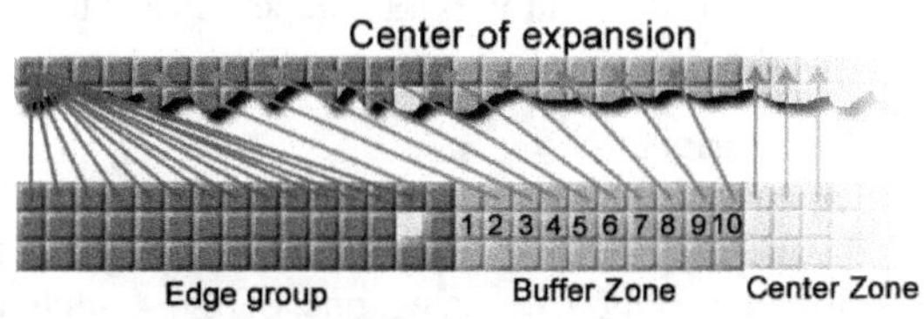

Figure 10 - Illustration of the left side of a ribbon with buffer zone. Red arrows associate the center of expansion for each of the icons in the 3 zones.

As suggested by Experiment 2, larger group sizes are effective in preventing off-screen errors on targets close to the left and right edges of the screen but can be error prone with targets closer to the center. The opposite was true for small group sizes. To leverage the benefits of both designs, we implemented a hybrid technique which uses a group size of 15 on the two edges, and individual ungrouped targets in between. To further reduce the chance of off-screen errors, we use a *buffer* zone between the group of 15 targets, and the center zone. The buffer zone consists of 10 individual targets, but their *CE* is based on a linear interpolation of the screen edge and the *CE* of the first target in the center zone (Figure 10). Having this buffer zone minimizes the impact of a prediction error when aiming at a target in the edge group. The exact sizes of the edge groups and buffer zones were chosen based on prediction error rates from Experiment 2, in an effort to minimize off-screen targets as much as possible.

EXPERIMENT 3

We have described two expanding target techniques for touch, *TouchCuts*, and *TouchZoom*. In study 2 we performed an evaluation of *TouchZoom*, which resulted in a resigned hybrid interpolation. In this study, we measured the performance of the redesigned *TouchZoom* and *TouchCuts*, in comparison to a baseline input device – the *Mouse* and a baseline touch technique – *Shift*.

While numerous techniques exist for aiding touch-based target acquisition, we used Shift as a baseline, since it does not have any visual impact on the user interface, unless the technique is used. Following previous guidelines, our implementation placed the callout window (16mm in diameter) 22mm on the right side of the initial touch point to facilitate the selection on a ribbon by using the left hand. The callout was placed on the opposite side if the touch point was within 30mm from the right end of the ribbon. We set the escalation time to zero so that the callout popped up as soon as a user touches the screen.

Apparatus

We used the same apparatus as in Experiment 2. Reflective markers were used in the target expansion techniques.

Participants

Twelve paid participants (6 males and 6 females) between the ages of 18 and 34 participated in this study. None of them had participated in the Experiment 1 and 2. All participants were right-handed. They were all familiar with graphical user interfaces. All but one had previous experience with mobile touch-screen devices.

Task and procedure

The participants were asked to press a keyboard key ('\' for the cursor and 'O' for the others), and to select a target (0.5×0.5cm) in a ribbon by using one of the 4 techniques. The task was required to be carried out by using the left hand for all the techniques except for the mouse. In the mouse condition, prior to pressing '\', the participants were asked to place the cursor in a start square (0.5×0.5cm) rendered in the center of the workspace. In the *TouchZoom* condition, we only showed the border between the edge groups and the buffer zone. The buffer zone and the groups of size 1 were invisible to the users. As in Experiment 2, for targets close to the screen edges, the participants were shown that by biasing their acquisition movement towards the edge of the screen, off-screen errors could be minimized. For both target expansion techniques, the expansion point was set to 60%.

Prior to the study, the participants were given a 3 minute training section for each technique. They were encouraged to take breaks during the experiment. The entire experiment lasted about 40 minutes. Participants filled out a post experiment questionnaire upon completion.

Design

The experiment employed a 4×3 within-subject factorial design. The independent variables are *Technique* (*TouchZoom*, *TouchCuts*, *Shift*, and *Mouse Cursor*) and *Target zone* (*Edge Group*, *Buffer Zone* and *Center Zone*).

In each trial, participants performed tasks in one of each *Technique* × *Target zone* combination. The experiment consisted of 3 blocks, each consisting of 30 trials, 10 for each target zone. In each trial, the position of the target was randomized for each target zone. The target was evenly distributed to the left and right side as well as the 3 rows of the ribbon. The order of the presentation of the techniques was counter balanced between participants.

Results

The data was analyzed using Repeated-measures ANOVA and Bonferroni corrections for pair-wise comparisons.

Task completion time

ANOVA yielded a significant effect of *Technique* ($F_{3,33}$ = 245.36, $p < 0.001$) and *Target Zone* ($F_{2,22}$ = 15.82, $p < 0.001$). There was a significant interaction effect on *Input Technique* × *Target Zone* ($F_{6,66}$ = 4.53, $p = 0.001$). Figure 11 left shows average time for *Target Zone* by *Technique*.

Performance with *TouchCuts* (768ms) was faster than *TouchZoom* (1130ms), which was faster than *Mouse cursor* (1280ms) and *Shift* (1883ms). Post-hoc analysis showed significant differences between all pairs of techniques. It is not surprising that *TouchCuts* performed the best overall, since it provides target expansion without any target offset. The difference between *TouchCuts* and *TouchZoom* (362 ms) is the added cost of the target offsets that *TouchZoom* introduces. It is worth reiterating that *TouchCuts* is slightly different from the other techniques, in that it only provides access to a predetermined subset of the ribbon icons.

What was more surprising was the difference between *TouchZoom* and *Shift*. Both techniques require initial and adjustment pointing phases. We believe that *TouchZoom* performed better because with *Shift* the two phases are explicitly sequential, while with the *TouchZoom* technique, the adjustment phase can be predicted and integrated into the end of the initial phase. In addition, *Shift* does not increase the motor activation size of the target.

Performance in the *Edge group* (1306ms) was slightly slower than *Center zone* (1249ms) and *Buffer zone* (1241ms) ($p = 0.001$), while no significant difference was found between *Buffer zone* and *Center zone* ($p = 1$). However, we found no significant effect of *Target Zone* ($F_{2,22}$ = 1.2, $p = 0.321$) in the *TouchZoom* condition, indicating that users can perform equally well across the ribbon.

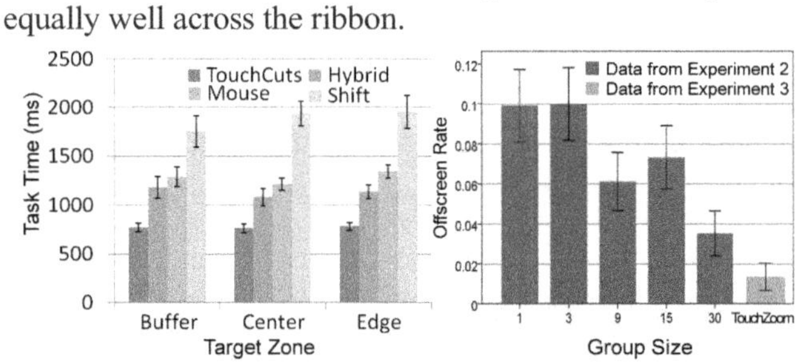

Figure 11 – Left: average task time shown for each target zone by technique. Right: off-screen rate shown by group sizes.

Selection Error

For selection errors, there was a significant effect of *Technique* ($F_{3,33}$ = 8.18, $p < 0.001$), but no significant effect of *Target Zone* ($F_{2,22}$ = 0.03, $p = 0.97$) or interaction effects.

TouchCuts had significantly less errors (0.02 s.e. 0.01) than the *TouchZoom* (0.11 s.e. 0.025), *Mouse cursor* (0.07 s.e. 0.01), and *Shift* (0.08 s.e. 0.02). We found no significant difference between *TouchZoom*, *Mouse cursor*, and *Shift*.

In the *TouchZoom* condition, we also found no significant effect of *Target zone* ($F_{2,22} = 0.07$, $p = 0.93$). This again confirms that users can perform equally well across the ribbon. Average off-screen error rate for the *TouchZoom* condition was 0.014(s.e. 0.006). We also found no significant effect of *Target zone* on off-screen error ($F_{2,22} = 0.836$, $p = 0.45$). This was an encouraging result, demonstrating that the hybrid interpolation we designed based on the results of Experiment 2 effectively minimized the chance of off-screen errors, in comparison to the static group sizes (shown in Figure 11 right). Application designers could color code ribbon or toolbar icons that indicate the zones utilized by the hybrid interpolation.

Subjective Preference

A short questionnaire was administered after the study. All scores reported below are based on a 7-point Likert scale, with 7 indicating highest preference.

The participants gave an average of 6.7 to *TouchCuts* and 5.2 to *TouchZoom* as the two most easy to use techniques. Whereas, *Shift* and *Mouse cursor* received an average of 3.7 and 4.6 respectively. Additionally, the participants gave an average of 6.9 to *TouchCuts* and 5.3 to *TouchZoom* as the two most enjoyable techniques. *Shift* and *Mouse cursor* received an average of 3.9 and 4 respectively. The mouse was rated lower because of both the switching between the keyboard and mouse, and also the small target sizes. Shift was rated lower because of the longer acquisition times. In addition, numerous users reported *Shift* as being fatiguing because it required careful movements of the finger while it was positioned on the screen. When shown a mockup of our techniques in an actual user interface (Microsof PowerPoint), feedback from users was gerneally encouraging. Overall, 83%, 67%, 67%, and 33% of all our participants expressed the desire to use *TouchCuts*, *TouchZoom*, *Mouse*, and *Shift* in the future.

DISCUSSION AND FUTURE WORK

In comparison to a mouse, *TouchCuts* reduced selection times by 40%, but does not provide access to every UI element. It will thus be important to study adoption and performance of TouchCuts in realistic settings, given the potential confusion caused by only some functionality being accessible. Our belief is that this may not be problematic, since traditional hotkeys are similarly only available and used for a subset of commands.

In contrast, *TouchZoom* gives the user access to an entire ribbon, and reduced selection times by 12% in comparison to a mouse. We also know from Experiment 1, that if the user does not have a mouse attached to their laptop, and has to use a touchpad, the levels of improvement would be even more substantial.

It is worth pointing out that we are not trying to replace the mouse. To the contrary, we made our design decisions carefully so that traditional cursor interaction would be unaffected. Note that our techniques are particularly beneficial when frequent mouse-keyboard switching is necessary. If the user is already performing mouse interactions close to the top of the screen, it may make more sense to acquire ribbon icons with the mouse. However, if the user is performing cursor intensive interactions, the non-dominant hand could be used to access UI elements in parallel, saving a round trip of the cursor (for example, changing colors while drawing). While our studies did show that touch can be effective with the non-dominant hand, future studies could explore this form of parallel, bimanual input.

Although the differences were not significant from the mouse or *Shift*, *TouchZoom* did exhibit a higher error rate (11%) in Experiment 3 than we expected. Our observations indicated that some of these errors were caused by users accidently touching the screen at the end of their first ballistic movements, just after the ribbon expanded. Since this error rate was higher than in Experiment 2 (6.2%), one potential explanation is that there were detrimental transfer effects from the *Shift* and *TouchCuts* techniques, where participants could touch the screen imprecisely after an initial ballistic movement.

Our work focused on a laptop configuration for three reasons: Most major manufactures have touch-enabled laptops; the hands are positioned close to the display; a mouse may not be available, and the track-pad is inefficient for pointing tasks. However, our work could generalize to desktop settings as well, but fatigue issues must be considered, since further reaching may be required. In addition, our work assumed proximity sensing was available, and for *TouchZoom*, the control being zoomed is horizontal. In the next section, we discuss several design variations to demonstrate how our techniques could generalize to other scenarios.

Further Design Alternatives

Functionality reduction controls – inspired by *TouchCuts*, we introduce functionality reduction controls to facilitate finger input. A functionality reduction control transitions to a preset touch-optimized component, that has the same screen footprint, but offers a subset of the functionality of its cursor-based counterpart. For example, we implemented a functionality reduction color palette, which replaces the color picker with 12 large color icons when the finger approaches. When users know they want to select one of these main colors, they can do so quickly with the non-dominant hand, saving a cursor round-trip.

Multi-level expansion – In this technique, the ribbon has 2 expansion points: 50% and 80%. It expands half-way if the finger crosses the 50% distance, and fully expands after the finger crosses the 80% distance. No discontinuity will be seen if the finger crosses the 2 expansion point at a sufficient speed. This technique was mainly designed to help users learn to use the *TouchZoom* technique.

Depth-based expansion – Depth-based expansion triggers the expansion when the finger is within a threshold distance to the screen, with the center of expansion equal to the on-screen projection of the current finger position. The finger is first positioned directly above the target of interest, and then the finger moves towards the screen to trigger the expansion. This could be particularly useful for implementing *TouchZoom* on vertical tool palettes, since endpoint prediction would be difficult. In addition, it could be useful on systems with a small proximity sensing range.

Touch activated expansion – To demonstrate the use of *TouchCuts* without proximity sensing, we delay expansion until the finger actually makes contact with the screen. This could also be used for *functionality reduction controls*, if the touch-optimized layout is predictable.

CONCLUSION

We have presented 3 studies to motivate and evaluate our design of *TouchCuts* and *TouchZoom*. We demonstrated that finger input has the benefit of allowing homing and pointing to be carried out concurrently, but suffers from extremely high error rates on icons in existing legacy applications. To support touch in such applications, our techniques trigger a transition of the user interface only when a finger approaches. Thus, controls can be effectively shared by both a traditional cursor and touch. Our study showed positive benefits of both techniques. Furthermore, the results of our studies show the hybrid interpolation used for *TouchZoom* effectively reduces the chance of off-screen errors. Finally, we present several alternative designs to show how our techniques could generalize to scenarios which we did not explicitly study. We believe with the continued increase in popularity of touch-based displays, our techniques may serve as important groundwork for integrating the benefits of touch into existing applications.

REFERENCES

1. Benko, H., Wilson, A., and Baudisch, P. (2006). Precise selection techniques for multi-touch screens. *CHI'06*, 1263-1272.
2. Carpendale, S., Ligh, J., and Pattison, E. (2004). Achieving higher magnification in context. *UIST'04*, 71-80.
3. Cockburn, A. and Brock, P. (2006). Human on-line response to visual and motor target expansion. *GI'06*, 81-87.
4. Carter, S., Hurst, A., Mankoff, J., and Li, J. (2006). Dynamically adapting GUIs to diverse input devices. *ACCESS'06*, 63-70.
5. Cypress Semiconductor Co., http://www.cypress.com/?rID=42793.
6. Esenther, A. and Ryall, K. (2006). Fluid DTMouse: better mouse support for touch-based interactions. *AVI'06*, 112-115.
7. Forlines, C., Wigdor, D., Shen, C., and Balakrishnan, R. (2007). Direct-touch vs. mouse input for tabletop displays. *CHI'07*, 647-656.
8. Gajos, K. and Weld, D. S. (2004). SUPPLE: automatically generating user interfaces. *IUI '04*, 93-100.
9. Gutwin, C. (2002). Improving focus targeting in interactive fisheye views. *CHI'02*, 267-274.
10. Hinckley, K. and Sinclair, M. (1999). Touch-sensing input devices. *CHI'99*, 223-230.
11. Hodges, S., Izadi, S., Butler, A., Rrustemi, A., and Buxton, B. (2007). ThinSight: Versatile Multi-touch Sensingfor Thin Form-factor Displays. *UIST'07*, 259-268.
12. Lank, E., Chun, Y., Cheng, N., and Ruiz, J. (2007). Endpoint prediction using motion kinematics. *CHI'07*, 637-646.
13. McGuffin, M. J. and Balakrishnan, R. (2002). Acquisition of Expanding Targets. *CHI'02*, 57-64.
14. McGuffin, M. J. and Balakrishnan, R. (2005). Fitts' Law and Expanding Targets: Experimental Studies and Designs for User Interfaces. *TOCHI*, 12(4) 388-422.
15. Meyer, S., Cohen, O., and Nilsen, E. (1994). Device comparisons for goal-directed drawing tasks. *Extended Abstracts of the CHI'94*, 251-252.
16. Mitsubishi 3D touch panel, http://techon.nikkeibp.co.jp/ english/NEWS_EN/20090310/166952/.
17. Moscovich, T. (2009). Contact Area Interaction with Sliding Widgets. *UIST'09* 13-22.
18. Olwal, A., Feiner, S., and Heyman, S. (2008). Rubbing and tapping for precise and rapid selection on touch-screen displays. *CHI'08*, 295-304.
19. Parhi, P. Karlson, A. K. and Bederson, B. B. (2006). Target size study for one-handed thumb use on small touch-screen devices. *MobileHci'06*, 203-210.
20. Potter, R., Weldon, L., Shneiderman, B. (1988). Improving the accuracy of touch screens: an experimental evaluation of three strategies. *CHI'*88, 27-32.
21. Primesense Ltd., http://www.primesense.com/?p=486.
22. Rekimoto, J. (2002). SmartSkin: An Infrastructure for Freehand Manipulation on Interactive Surfaces, *CHI'02*, 113 - 120.
23. Ruiz, J. and Lank, E. (2010). Speeding pointing in tiled widgets: understanding the effects of target expansion and misprediction. *IUI'10*, 229-238.
24. Sears, A. and Shneiderman, B. (1991). High precision touchscreens: design strategies and comparisons with a mouse. *IJMMS*, 34(4), 93–613.
25. Vogel, D. and Baudisch, P. (2007). Shift: a technique for operating pen-based interfaces using touch. *CHI'*07, 657-666.
26. Yatani, K., Partridge, K., Bern, M., and Newman, M. (2008). Escape: A target selection technique using visually-cued gestures. *CHI'08*, 285-294.
27. Zhai, S., Conversy, S., Beaudouin-Lafon, M., Guiard, Y. (2003). Human On-Line Response to Target Expansion. *CHI'03*, 177-184.

Of Passwords and People: Measuring the Effect of Password-Composition Policies

Saranga Komanduri[1], Richard Shay[1], Patrick Gage Kelley[1], Michelle L. Mazurek[1], Lujo Bauer[1], Nicolas Christin[1], Lorrie Faith Cranor[1], and Serge Egelman[2]

[1]Carnegie Mellon University
Pittsburgh, PA
{sarangak, rshay, pgage, mmazurek}@cmu.edu
{lbauer, nicolasc, lorrie}@cmu.edu

[2]National Institute of Standards and Technology
Gaithersburg, MD
serge.egelman@nist.gov

ABSTRACT

Text-based passwords are the most common mechanism for authenticating humans to computer systems. To prevent users from picking passwords that are too easy for an adversary to guess, system administrators adopt password-composition policies (e.g., requiring passwords to contain symbols and numbers). Unfortunately, little is known about the relationship between password-composition policies and the strength of the resulting passwords, or about the behavior of users (e.g., writing down passwords) in response to different policies. We present a large-scale study that investigates password strength, user behavior, and user sentiment across four password-composition policies. We characterize the predictability of passwords by calculating their entropy, and find that a number of commonly held beliefs about password composition and strength are inaccurate. We correlate our results with user behavior and sentiment to produce several recommendations for password-composition policies that result in strong passwords without unduly burdening users.

Author Keywords

Security, Usability, Passwords, Policy

ACM Classification Keywords

D.4.6 Security and Protection: Authentication; H.1.2 User/ Machine Systems: Human factors

General Terms

Experimentation, Human Factors, Measurement, Security

INTRODUCTION

To prevent attackers from predicting users' text-based passwords, and hence impersonating users, system administrators typically require that users select passwords according to a password-composition policy designed to make users' passwords harder to predict. Such a policy may require, for example, that passwords exceed a minimum length, that they contain uppercase letters and symbols, and that they do not contain dictionary words.

Unfortunately, it is difficult to define precisely the relationship between the components of a password-composition policy and the predictability of the resulting passwords, in large part because of a lack of empirical data on passwords and the policies under which they were created. Even the best current guidelines for designing password-composition policies, for instance, are based on theoretical estimates [4] or small-scale laboratory studies (e.g., [12, 20]).

What makes designing an appropriate password-composition policy even trickier is that such policies affect not only the passwords users create, but also users' behavior. For example, certain password-composition policies that lead to more-difficult-to-predict passwords may also lead users to write down their passwords more readily, or to become more averse to changing passwords because of the additional effort of memorizing the new ones. Such behavior may also affect an adversary's ability to predict passwords and should therefore be taken into account when selecting a policy.

With this paper, we take a significant step toward improving our understanding of how password-composition policies influence the predictability of passwords, as well as how they affect user behavior and sentiment. We describe the results of a two-part user study with more than 5,000 participants. In the first part we required each participant to create a password under one of four different password-composition policies. In the second part we asked participants to recall their passwords at least two days later. We also surveyed users to capture their sentiment toward a password-composition policy, as well as to to learn about their password-related behavior (e.g., whether and how they recorded the password).

Using the collected data, we characterize the predictability of passwords created under various password-composition policies by computing their entropy. Our results are the first entropy estimates derived from a large-scale empirical study that allow for comparison of entropy across different password-composition policies. Combining these results with our survey data, we compare the effects of different password-composition policies more comprehensively than was previously done, yielding a number of interesting findings. For instance, we compared two password-composition policies: one required only that passwords be at least 16 characters long; the other required at least eight characters but also an uppercase letter, a number, a symbol, and a dictionary check. According to the best available guidelines [4], these two policies should result in passwords of approximately the same entropy. We find, however, that the 16-character policy yields significantly less predictable passwords, and that it is, by several metrics, less onerous for users. We believe this and other findings will be useful both to security professionals seeking to establish or review password-composition policies, and to researchers examining how to make passwords more secure and usable.

In the next section, we provide background and survey related work. Next, we describe the methodology of our study, followed by the demographics of our participants and an explanation of how we analyzed our data. We then individually describe the results we derive for password entropy and for user behavior (including password-composition strategies, password storage and memorability, user sentiment, and ecological validity). We conclude with a discussion in which we weave together the individual results to give a more complete picture of the effects of different password-composition policies, and we also draw out the most significant findings.

BACKGROUND AND RELATED WORK

We evaluate tradeoffs between the empirical strength of passwords generated under a variety of password-composition policies and the pain those policies cause users. Others have examined similar tradeoffs. In a lab study, Proctor et al. measured creation time, memorability, and crackability of passwords under various composition policies, finding that stricter policies can make passwords harder to crack but also harder to create and remember. Overall, they found that increasing minimum length was more effective than applying content constraints [12]. We collected similar data for a much larger set of users, allowing us to estimate the entropy associated with various password-composition policies.

Several studies report that if password-composition policies are too demanding (e.g., when it is difficult to generate an acceptable password, or when passwords must be changed frequently), users will adopt coping strategies that can reduce both security and productivity [1, 7, 16, 18]. Vu et al. found that generating passwords from the first letter of each word in a sentence reduced vulnerability to cracking as compared to traditional rules about including numbers, symbols and capitals, but at some cost to memorability [20].

Florêncio and Herley report that stricter password-composition policies do not correlate with protection of high-value assets, but instead with how well insulated organizations are from customer service concerns [6]. Schechter et al. designed a popularity oracle to replace traditional password-composition policies with a tool that rejects passwords that have already been selected by too many other users [13].

Others have attempted to quantify password strength using real-world data, without examining the impact of policy restrictions. In 1989, 40% of 14,000 UNIX accounts were cracked using guesses derived from associated usernames or account numbers and dictionaries [2]. Florêncio and Herley, reporting in 2007 on data collected from half a million Windows Live users, calculated an average password strength of 40.54 bits, with stronger passwords associated with accounts with higher apparent importance [5]. In 2010, Zhang et al. found that 41% of passwords from a university system could be cracked in under three seconds each, given knowledge of expired passwords from the same account [22].

Similar studies have evaluated password characteristics using self-reported data. In a 1999 survey of military users, with no apparent compositional policies, Zviran and Haga found that most passwords contained four to seven characters. Eighty percent of participants claimed to use only alphabetic characters, with only 13% using alphanumeric passwords and less than a percent using symbols [23]. Ten years later, a survey of university users under a strict password-composition policy requiring at least eight characters, including at least one each of lowercase and uppercase letters, numbers, and symbols found an average password length of more than ten and almost three numbers per password [17]. These studies, along with our results, suggest that passwords have become more complex over time, whether due to increasingly strict policies, user education, or other factors.

While these empirical studies suggest an increase in password complexity over time, formally measuring password complexity, as we propose, requires defining a complexity metric. One possible metric is the information entropy of the password: a measure (in bits) of the expected value of information contained in the password. Shannon introduced the notion of information entropy, and subsequently developed a method to estimate entropy in printed English using n-grams [14]. Massey showed that entropy provides a lower bound on the expected number of guesses required to identify information; this result connects the entropy in passwords with an attacker's ability to guess them using a brute-force attack [9]. Miller showed that given good sampling but insufficient samples, entropy approximations always underestimate the true entropy; Paninski derived a threshold at which the sample size is sufficient, based on the number of observed categories [10, 11]. Paninski's method informed our choice of an appropriate sample size for our study.

Similar to previous work [17], we use a variation of Shannon's method for calculating entropy [15] that allows us to approximate the entropy of a password space from a much smaller dataset than traditional methods. Florêncio and Herley estimated entropy for a large set of real passwords they observed, calculating the theoretical maximum for each password given the set of character types used [5]. This calculation does not account for the actual distribution of passwords in use, because they were only able to collect transient information about passwords rather than store the passwords themselves. Our method calculates entropy more precisely, but we used passwords created for the study rather than passwords for real accounts; in the Discussion section we address how this affects our results. Weir et al. suggest that entropy by itself might not be the best metric for evaluating the security of a given password [21]. Along with computing entropy, we also briefly explore the resistance of passwords to guessing by a modern password-cracking algorithm.

METHODOLOGY

We conducted a two-part online study using Amazon's Mechanical Turk service.[1] We recruited 5,000 participants, each assigned randomly to one of five conditions. In the first part, we asked participants to create a password, complete an online survey, and then enter the password. Two days later we asked them to return to our website, login using their password, and complete a second survey.

Study Overview

We advertised our study on Mechanical Turk as a two-part "brief study" with a "bonus opportunity." We paid participants between 25 and 55 cents for the first part, and between 50 and 70 cents for the second part. The consent form informed participants that the study would survey users about their behavior visiting secure websites.

We gave participants a *scenario* and asked them to create a password that complied with a a *password-composition policy*. The scenarios and policy varied by condition, and are discussed below. We asked participants to create a password and enter it twice. We informed participants who entered passwords that failed to meet the requirements about which requirement they failed to meet and asked them to retry. After entering an acceptable password, we presented participants with a survey requesting demographic information, Likert questions about the password-creation process, and questions about the password-creation strategy employed.

We asked participants to enter the password they had just created. If a participant was unsuccessful in recalling her password in five attempts, the password was displayed. We then displayed a code for participants to enter into Mechanical Turk to receive payment. We told them they would be contacted to complete follow-up surveys, but not when we would contact them.

Two days after completing the first part, we sent participants emails asking them to return for the second part via an included URL. On return, we asked participants again to recall their passwords. The password-entry screen included an "I forgot my password" link to a page with an "Email password reset link" button and a note informing them that resetting a password "may take a few minutes." Participants who clicked the button were emailed a link to a page displaying their password. Participants who failed to recall their password after five tries were also shown their password on the screen. Participants were then presented with a second survey, which included additional questions about password creation, storage, and usage.

[1]Products are identified to specify the experimental procedure adequately. This is not intended to imply recommendation or endorsement by the National Institute of Standards and Technology.

Conditions

Our pilot studies informed our selection of five experimental conditions. These conditions allowed us to explore four sets of password composition requirements across two scenarios.

Instructions in the *survey scenario* read: "To link your survey responses, we will use a password that you create below; therefore it is important that you remember your password."

In the *email scenario*, we told participants, "Imagine that your main email service provider has been attacked, and your account became compromised. You need to create a new password for your email account, since your old password may be known by the attackers. Because of the attack, your email service provider is also changing its password rules. Please follow the instructions below to create a new password for your email account. We will ask you to use this password in a few days to log in again so it is important that you remember your new password. Please take the steps you would normally take to remember your email password and protect this password as you normally would protect the password for your email account. Please behave as you would if this were your real password!"

Condition basic8survey. We gave participants the survey scenario and the password-composition policy, "Password must have at least 8 characters." NIST predicts that such passwords would have 18 bits of entropy [4].

Condition basic8. We gave participants the email scenario and the password-composition policy, "Password must have at least 8 characters." This condition had the same password composition policy as the basic8survey condition, allowing us to observe the impact of framing on participant behavior.

Condition basic16. We gave participants the email scenario and the password-composition policy, "Password must have at least 16 characters." This condition required passwords twice as long as the basic8 condition, allowing us to observe the impact of increasing password length. NIST predicts that such passwords would have 30 bits of entropy [4].

Condition dictionary8. We gave participants the email scenario and the password-composition policy, "Password must have at least 8 characters. It may not contain a dictionary word." We performed a dictionary check consisting of removing all non-alphabetic characters from the password and looking up the remaining letters in a dictionary,[2] ignoring case. This method is known to be used in practice, including at CMU. According to NIST, adding the dictionary check raises the entropy of 8-character passwords to 24 bits [4].

Condition comprehensive8. We gave participants the email scenario and the password-composition policy, "Password must have at least 8 characters including an uppercase and lowercase letter, a symbol, and a digit. It may not contain a dictionary word." We performed the same type of dictionary check as in the dictionary8 condition. This condition was designed to reproduce NIST's comprehensive password

[2]http://download.openwall.net/pub/ wordlists

composition requirements [4]; NIST estimates that such 8-character passwords have 30 bits of entropy, similar to 16-character passwords with no composition requirements.

DEMOGRAPHICS AND ANALYSIS

A total of 6,212 participants began our study over a 48-day period from August to October 2010. 5,103 participants completed part one. We rejected four participants because their completion times were outside two standard deviations of the mean. We sent an email to participants two days after they completed part one inviting them to return for part two. 3,056 returned and 2,889 completed part two within three days of receiving the email. Any participant who returned more than three days after being emailed received payment, but we excluded their part two responses from our analysis.

Our entropy calculations require exactly the same number of passwords per condition to assure comparability across conditions. Therefore, we selected the first 1,000 participants in each condition who completed part one, regardless of whether they returned for part two. The remainder of this paper discusses the data from these 5,000 participants.

Fifty-one percent of our participants indicated they were male, 47% female, and 2% did not disclose gender. The mean age for our participants is 29.83 ($\sigma = 9.96$). Thirty-three percent reported studying or working in computer science, information technology, or a related field. We found no statistically significant difference in age, gender, or technical experience between conditions using a chi-square test.

In analyzing our data, we used Fisher's Exact Test (FET) to compare proportions when the sample size was tractable, and chi-square tests when it was not. Post-hoc comparisons were corrected for multiple-testing using the Bonferroni-Holm method when appropriate. Permutation testing was used to analyze differences between entropy estimates. No standard test exists for this purpose. The space of permutations, $\binom{2000}{1000}$ in most cases, was too large to perform an exact test, so random sampling of the permutation space was performed with 5,000 permutations per test.

PASSWORD COMPOSITION AND ENTROPY

In this section we explain our method for estimating entropy, then present and discuss our estimates for passwords created under the different conditions. We also interpret these results in light of using heuristics to guess passwords.

Entropy Calculation

We calculated entropy using a variation of Shannon's method [15] from earlier work [17]. More specifically, Shannon's formula for estimating entropy allows the entropy for a distribution of passwords (our final goal) to be calculated by summing the entropy values derived from each element of a password. Hence, we calculate individually the entropy contributed by password length; by number and placement of each class of character (lowercase, uppercase, numbers, symbols); and by the content of each character. The sum of these values is our estimate of the entropy of a password distribution.

Calculating an entropy estimate in this additive fashion gives us improved accuracy with smaller sample sizes than would be possible with traditional trigram methods. Traditional trigram methods, when applied to passwords, require thousands of samples to calculate an accurate estimate [11]. We confirmed empirically that the method we adopt results in useful approximations by applying both methods to multiple random samples (of 500, 1000, 10,000, 50,000, 100,000, and 500,000 passwords) of the RockYou password dataset [19]. The RockYou dataset was used because it is the only dataset large enough to support samples of this size. At the sample size of 1,000 that we use in our study, the numbers we show are significant underestimates of the true entropy, as determined by trigram methods. Hence, it is inappropriate to compare them directly to previously published results (e.g., [4]), and we use them chiefly to compare between conditions. The exception is when we find our *underestimates* to be significantly higher than previously reported estimates.

We show both the cumulative entropy and component entropies for each of the conditions in our study in Table 1.

Entropy Results

Our entropy calculations yield a number of interesting observations. Most notably, the entropy estimates for each condition are statistically significantly different ($p < 0.001$, permutation test, corrected), with the exception of dictionary8 and basic8, which do not differ significantly from each other ($p = 0.36$). This is notable partly because NIST estimates suggest that basic16 and comprehensive8 should result in passwords of the same entropy; we find, however, that basic16 (at 44.67 bits) has significantly more entropy than comprehensive8 (at 34.30 bits). Similarly, NIST estimates suggest that adding a dictionary check increases entropy (by an estimated 6 bits). Our basic8 and dictionary8 conditions were designed to verify that hypothesis. Surprisingly, we find adding the dictionary check actually resulted in a non-statistically-significant decrease in the observed entropy.

Adding numbers to passwords is thought to reduce predictability only slightly, due to the assumption the digits will occur in easily predictable locations within the passwords [4]. Our findings, however, are consistent with recent work [17], and show that a significant amount of the entropy of passwords is contributed by the portions of the passwords composed of numbers. This is a result of several factors. First, we find that the entropy per digit is higher than the entropy per lowercase letter (e.g., 2.82 vs 1.75 in the comprehensive8 condition), indicating that there is less consistency in which digits users choose than which letters they choose, despite the fact that there are 26 lowercase letters and only 10 digits. Second, participants used a larger than expected number of digits in their passwords. In all conditions, including the four that did not require a digit, participants' passwords had a mean of at least 2.20 digits (see Table 1). In particular, basic16 passwords used on average 3.76 numbers, significantly greater than in any other condition (corrected pairwise t-test, $p < 0.05$). Finally, there was greater than expected variability in where the users chose to put digits (see Figure 1).

		comprehensive8	basic16	dictionary8	basic8	basic8survey
Entropy in how many numbers		2.10	3.15	2.76	2.81	2.74
Entropy in where they are		1.61	1.92	1.80	1.84	1.62
Entropy in what they are		6.22	10.56	7.18	6.84	6.94
Total entropy in numbers		**9.94**	**15.63**	**11.74**	**11.49**	**11.30**
Entropy in how many symbols		0.67	0.58	0.56	0.51	0.30
Entropy in where they are		1.55	0.56	0.58	0.56	0.34
Entropy in what they are		3.52	0.37	0.43	0.30	0.13
Total entropy in symbols		**5.75**	**1.51**	**1.56**	**1.37**	**0.78**
Entropy in how many uppercase letters		1.30	0.99	0.90	1.02	0.68
Entropy in where they are		1.32	0.75	0.74	0.85	0.53
Entropy in what they are		2.62	0.89	0.64	0.73	0.48
Total entropy in uppercase letters		**5.24**	**2.63**	**2.29**	**2.60**	**1.69**
Total entropy in lowercase letters		**10.32**	**22.21**	**10.85**	**11.47**	**11.22**
Total entropy in length		**3.05**	**2.69**	**2.55**	**2.50**	**2.21**
Total entropy		**34.30**	**44.67**	**28.99**	**29.43**	**27.19**
Password composition						
Numbers	mean (median)	2.20 (2)	3.76 (2)	2.50 (2)	2.38 (2)	2.37 (2)
Symbols	mean (median)	1.13 (1)	0.16 (0)	0.16 (0)	0.12 (0)	0.06 (0)
Uppercase letters	mean (median)	1.50 (1)	0.54 (0)	0.40 (0)	0.43 (0)	0.28 (0)
Lowercase letters	mean (median)	5.90 (6)	13.46 (14)	6.65 (7)	6.74 (7)	6.54 (7)
Length	mean (median)	10.76 (10)	17.98 (17)	9.72 (9)	9.66 (9)	9.27 (9)
Entropy per usage	per number	2.82	2.81	2.87	2.88	2.93
	per symbol	3.11	2.36	2.65	2.59	2.29
	per letter	1.75	1.65	1.63	1.70	1.71

Table 1. Upper table shows entropy calculations across conditions, broken down by the entropy contributed by length and character categories. Lower table characterizes passwords by length and composition, across conditions.

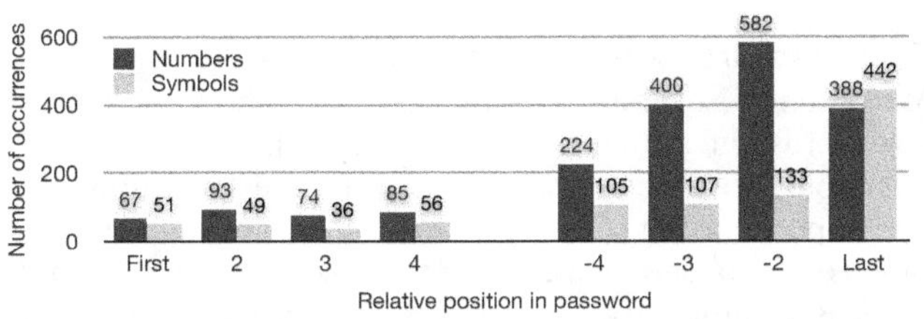

Figure 1. The distribution of digits and symbols in passwords in the comprehensive8 condition, relative to the start (left-most pair of bars) and end (right-most pair of bars) of the password. E.g., the pair of bars at '−3' shows the number of digits and symbols that occur as the third-to-last character of passwords. We omit digits and symbols more than four positions from either end of passwords to avoid duplicates, since many passwords are exactly eight characters long.

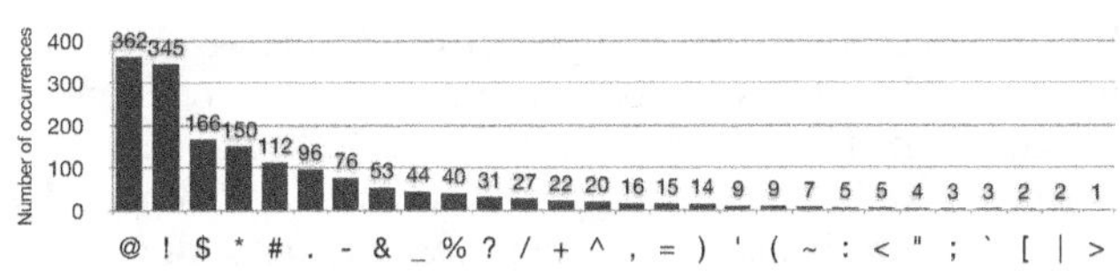

Figure 2. Frequency of occurrence of symbols in passwords created in the comprehensive8 condition.

As with numbers, participants used a variety of symbols; '@' and '!' were the most common, but many others were also used, causing the per-symbol entropy to exceed 2 in all conditions (see Figure 2 for a frequency distribution graph of symbols). However, symbols were used much less frequently than numbers. Only a small fraction of participants made use of symbols when they were not forced to do so by the password-composition policy (means of 0.06–0.16 symbols per password when not required by policy). Even when required by policy to use both symbols and numbers, participants favored numbers; in the comprehensive8 condition, which required both a symbol and a number, participants used a mean of 2.20 numbers but only 1.13 symbols. Hence, the overall entropy contributed by symbols is lower that that contributed by numbers, across all conditions.

Interestingly, median lengths consistently exceeded requirements (see Table 1), adding to entropy by making it harder to guess length. Participants in the comprehensive8 condition exceeded the length requirements by a mean of 2.76 characters, which is statistically significantly greater than the amount by which participants in other conditions exceeded the requirements (corrected pairwise t-test, $p < 0.001$).

	comp8	bas16	d8	bas8
Cracked	0/997	9/971	31/963	188/972
Cracked + passed dict. check	0/997	6/971	26/963	99/972
Cracked + not in large dict.	0/997	1/971	3/963	28/972

Table 2. Number of passwords cracked, cracked passwords that passed our dictionary check, and cracked passwords that would pass a dictionary check even against our largest dictionary; across all study conditions. Several users in each condition used identical passwords, which is why the number of unique passwords reported here is less than 1,000.

Dictionary Checks and Entropy

Including a dictionary check in the password-composition policy did not change the observed entropy significantly, but it still may strengthen passwords. Entropy is a good measure of the information-theoretic predictability of passwords, but it is possible even within a password distribution of high entropy to have a small set of passwords that are "easily" guessable. To evaluate this possibility, we used the popular password cracker John the Ripper[3] across conditions. We used the tool's heuristic mode, which transforms dictionary words into password guesses. We do not consider other types of guessing attacks, such as informed guessing based on knowledge of the user, in this discussion. The results are shown in Table 2. Comparing basic8 and dictionary8, it is notable that John the Ripper guessed 188 of 972 unique passwords in basic8, but only 31 of 963 in dictionary8. This difference is statistically significant (FET, $p < 0.0001$).

If we had performed a dictionary check on basic8, 89 of those 188 guessed passwords would have been rejected. Both these data points illustrate that dictionary checks, even if they do not increase entropy, help significantly in producing passwords more resistant to heuristic guessing.

Also notable is that the comprehensive8 and basic16 conditions produced passwords considerably more resilient to cracking, with 0 and 9 passwords successfully cracked. This appears to indicate that long passwords (as evidenced by basic16) are resistant to cracking even without a dictionary check, and that passwords that contain symbols and numbers in addition to a dictionary check (comprehensive8) are significantly harder to crack that those that contain a dictionary check (dictionary8). Unsurprisingly, the choice of dictionary used for the dictionary check also has an effect on the guessability of passwords. In our regular dictionary check, we used a comprehensive dictionary that contained about 3.9 million entries (words, common phrases, misspelled words, names and titles, etc.). As shown in Table 2, if we had instead used a larger dictionary with 24.7 million entries (also obtained from the Openwall Project), an overwhelming majority of the cracked passwords would have been caught by a dictionary check at password-creation time.

USERS AND THEIR BEHAVIOR

In this section, we discuss how variations in the password-composition policies affect users' behavior when creating and remembering passwords, as well as their impressions of the process. Overall, we find significant differences among the policies, with comprehensive8 proving least user-friendly on several measures, while unsurprisingly basic8 and basic8survey proved generally easiest for users to cope with. Less predictably, basic16 proved better than the comparable-strength comprehensive8 in several respects.

[3]http://www.openwall.com/john

	comp8	bas16	d8	bas8	surv
Average attempts to create a password					
Total	3.35	1.66	1.88	1.13	1.17
Among those who failed at least once	3.85	2.37	3.00	2.11	2.04
Password creation failures					
% failed confirmation	3.1	3.4	2.4	2.4	2.2
% failed policy	57.6	39.4	3.59	8.5	12.7
% failed both	21.6	4.5	5.1	0.5	0.3
Dropouts per condition					
% dropouts	25.0	15.0	18.3	14.7	16.5
Password reuse					
% exact reuse	3.3	2.3	19.7	25.6	34.6
% modified reuse	31.3	25.0	19.2	19.1	17.7
% created new	62.5	66.0	53.3	48.2	39.2

Table 3. Overview of password-creation data, across conditions. The average number of attempts required to successfully create a password, both among all participants and among only those who failed at least once. The percentage of participants who failed to create a valid password at least once; either because their initial and confirmation passwords did not match, because their password did not conform to requirements, or both. The percentage of potential participants who dropped out before completing part one. Finally, the percentage of participants who reused a password exactly, reused with modifications, and created an entirely new password.

Password Creation, Storage, and Memory

We obtained several interesting results on how users create passwords, including how often they fail to make a valid password, how they cope with such failures, and how often they report reusing passwords from other accounts. Most notably, our data demonstrate that successfully creating a password is significantly more difficult under stricter password policies, particularly those involving dictionary checks. Table 3 contains detailed data about these findings.

Failed creation attempts

We measured how many participants failed to create an acceptable password at least once, either because their "enter password" and "confirm password" entries failed to match or because the password they selected did not conform to the policy requirements. The comprehensive8 policy condition proved by far the most difficult, as only 17.7% of users in this condition could create a password in one try. By contrast, 52.7%, 56.6%, 88.6%, and 84.8% of participants in the basic16, dictionary8, basic8, and basic8survey conditions respectively created an acceptable password in one try.

As shown in Table 3, comprehensive8 participants required on average 3.35 attempts to create an acceptable password. This was significantly more attempts than in dictionary8 (mean 1.88), which was significantly more than in basic16 (mean 1.66). Those three, in turn, were significantly more failure-prone than basic8, with an average of 1.13 attempts per participant (all $p < 0.001$, pairwise-corrected t-tests).

Counting only participants with at least one failure, comprehensive8 participants also required the most attempts, averaging 3.85. Participants in the dictionary8 condition required significantly fewer attempts, at 3.00, than comprehensive8, but significantly more than any other condition ($p < 0.001$, pairwise corrected t-tests). These results suggest that the dictionary check was especially difficult for participants to deal with.

Coping with failure

Perhaps the dictionary checks gave our participants so much difficulty because they had trouble determining whether a password would be acceptable without trying it. Because our technique stripped non-alphabetic characters before testing against the dictionary, a participant who tried a password like "p1a1s1s1w1o1r1d" would be rejected, perhaps without understanding why. We have several examples of participants trying and failing to pass the dictionary check that seem to bolster this hypothesis. For example, one user made the following sequence of password attempts, first seemingly not aware that the dictionary check ignored digits, and on subsequent failures changing parts of the password (such as numbers and symbols) that were irrelevant to the dictionary check: "cheese" → "1cheese1" → "12#$asdf" → "12#$qwER" → "43@!reWQ".

This process may have been made more difficult because the error message indicated only that the password was not allowed to contain a dictionary word, rather than explaining the check mechanism in detail or highlighting the problem characters. In addition, our dictionary includes non-standard "words" based on common passwords that users might not expect to find in a dictionary.

Participants' strategies to cope with these apparently confusing failures fall into two broad categories: incrementally modifying the initial password attempt until a successful password is found, and changing directions entirely. Within the dictionary8 condition, 31% of participants who failed password creation used only incremental modifications, while the other 69% changed strategies entirely, including 16% who switched to an all-numeric password. Within comprehensive8, 38% of those who failed used incremental changes, with the other 62% changing direction.

Giving up on creating a password

Another indicator of the difficulty participants had creating passwords is the rate at which they dropped out before completing part one, possibly because they had given up on making an acceptable password. This data indicates that the comprehensive8 condition caused prospective users considerably more trouble than the other conditions.

Considering only users who began the study no earlier and no later than participants included in our final data (6,212 in total), we find that 25% in the comprehensive8 condition dropped out before completing part one, compared to less than 19% in each of the other conditions. Dropout rates for comprehensive8 were significantly higher than all other conditions, none of which differed significantly from each other ($p < 0.001$, pairwise corrected FET).

To test our theory that this greater dropout rate was motivated by difficulty creating acceptable passwords, we looked at how far participants progressed before quitting. Among 1,108 prospective participants who dropped out on the first day, 68% in the comprehensive8 condition dropped out while trying to create a password, along with 32% in dictionary8 and no more than 26% in any other condition. This is significantly higher for comprehensive8 than any other condition, and significantly higher for dictionary8 than either basic8 or basic8survey ($p < 0.002$, pairwise corrected FET).

Reusing passwords

We also examined how likely participants were to report reusing a password from another account, exactly or with modifications, when making a password for our study. Participants in the comprehensive8 and basic16 conditions were significantly less likely to report reusing a password exactly than those in the other conditions. By contrast, these participants were more likely than other participants to report reusing existing passwords with modification, though this difference was not always statistically significant.

Both of these practices can be dangerous; reusing passwords exactly is known to lead to security breaches [3, 8], and Zhang et al. found that modifications tend to be predictable, making the resulting passwords easy to crack [22]. We hypothesize that because comprehensive8 and basic16 are more stringent than the others, our participants were less likely to already have suitable passwords; as a result, they frequently modified an existing password instead. Nonetheless, when considering all participants who reused a password either exactly or with modifications, participants in the comprehensive8 and basic16 conditions still reported significantly less reuse than in other conditions.

Storing passwords

Overall, 31% of participants who returned for part two reported writing down the password they used for the study, either electronically or on paper. (See Figure 3 for details.) We found no significant difference in rates of reported storage on paper between our study passwords and real email passwords; however, reported electronic storage of study passwords is significantly lower than for real email passwords.

A significantly greater proportion (50%) of comprehensive8 participants stored their passwords than in all other conditions; and basic16 participants were significantly more likely to store (33%) than basic8 and basic8survey participants (26% and 17% respectively, $p < 0.03$, pairwise corrected FET).

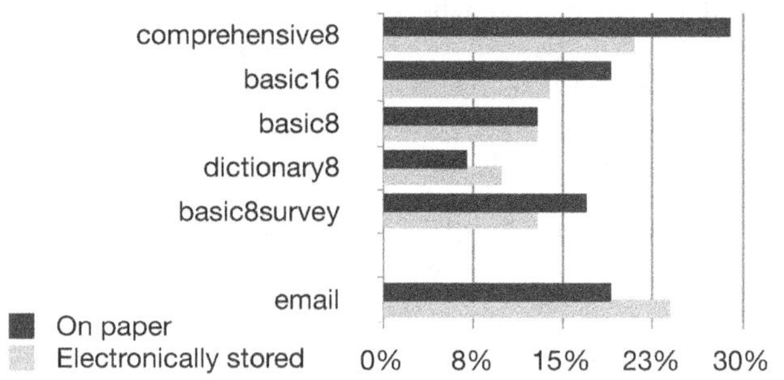

Figure 3. Percentage of users in each condition who stored their study password, either on paper or electronically. For reference, we also include the percentage of users storing their actual email password.

Remembering passwords

Overall, 11.1% of participants who returned for part two used the forgotten password email feature, and only 1.6% failed to log in after five attempts and were subsequently shown their password. Participants who did remember their password without being shown required on average 1.22 attempts to log in successfully. We found no significant differences in these rates across conditions, using an ANOVA.

Participants who did not think they would be able to remember their password tended to store it proactively, electronically or on paper. Considering only those participants who did not store their password, 13.0% used the forgotten password feature and 2.1% failed to login in five attempts, compared with 7.1% and 0.4% respectively for those who did store their password. These differences were significant ($p < 0.001$, FET). We found no significant differences in these rates across conditions; however, the fact that users wrote down comprehensive8 and basic16 passwords more frequently than others (as discussed above) suggests that participants perceive these passwords as harder to remember.

This idea is bolstered by results from a Likert question asking participants to respond to the statement "Remembering the password I used for this study was difficult." Thirty-five percent of comprehensive8 respondents agreed or strongly agreed, significantly more than in any other condition ($p < 0.001$, pairwise corrected FET). The next most difficult condition was basic16, with 23% reporting that their password was difficult to remember.

Finally, we measured how many attempts participants made to log in before resorting to the forgotten password e-mail feature. On average, participants made only 1.2 attempts, with 39% making zero attempts, suggesting they quickly determined they would not be able to remember. We found no significant difference in this rate across conditions.

User Sentiment

When we asked users their opinions of the password creation process, the results differed sharply by condition. Unsurprisingly, users generally found conditions with stricter requirements more onerous.

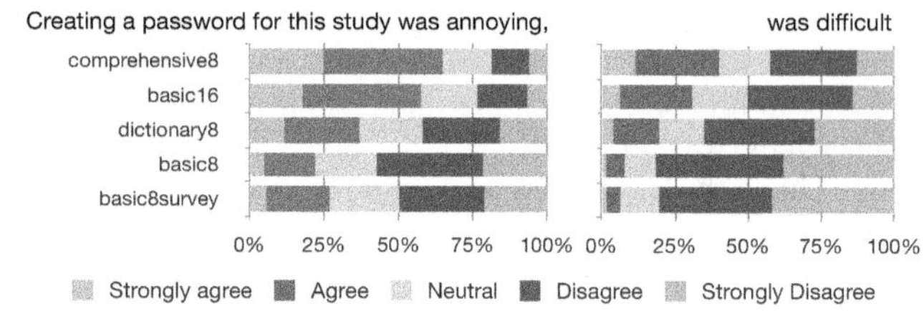

Figure 4. User responses to whether creating a password for this study was annoying or difficult. Answers were reported on a five-point Likert scale, from 1 (strongly agree) to 5 (strongly disagree).

Figure 4 shows user responses to the statement that creating a password for this study was annoying. User annoyance (agree or strongly agree) was significantly different between each condition (all $p < 0.02$, pairwise corrected FET). Responses to the statement "creating a password for this study was difficult" are shown in Figure 4. All pairs of conditions differ significantly in difficulty, except the pair of basic8 and basic8survey ($p < 0.001$, pairwise corrected FET).

We also considered user perceptions of password strength across conditions. Each participant was asked to agree or disagree with the statement "If my main email account required me to change my password using the same requirements as used in this study, it would make my email account more secure." Significantly more participants in the comprehensive8 condition (67%) agreed or strongly agreed with this statement than in the basic16 condition (57%); those participants in turn perceived added strength significantly more often than participants in the basic8 and dictionary8 conditions (43% and 49%), whose perceptions were also significantly different (all $p < 0.02$, pairwise corrected FET). Perceptions of password strength may affect users' willingness to "buy in" to new policies that they find annoying.

Ecological Validity

It is difficult to demonstrate ecological validity in any password study where participants are aware they are creating a password for a study, rather than for an account they value and expect to access repeatedly over time. Ideally, password studies would be conducted by collecting data on real passwords created by real users of a deployed system. However, due to the sensitivity of password data and the difficulty of partitioning real users into experimental conditions with different password-composition policies, it is difficult to collect the data we collected in this study from a deployed system.

We tested two approaches to approximate real-life password-composition scenarios. First, recall that in the basic8survey condition, we asked participants to create a password that they would use to complete follow-up surveys. This condition was designed to give us ecologically valid data on the password behavior users exhibit when they create passwords for low-value accounts they expect to use only on a short-term basis. However, this does not necessarily reflect user behavior when dealing with passwords for high-value accounts or accounts used on a long-term basis. Thus, we designed the other conditions to encourage participants to behave in the way they would when creating a password for one such account (an email account). Two indicators that participants may have answered honestly are that their self-reported password reuse was higher in the basic8survey condition than in the four other conditions, and that the computed entropy of passwords in these four conditions was significantly higher than the entropy of passwords in the basic8survey condition. Both findings are consistent with users picking better passwords to protect a hypothetical email account than to protect a real survey account. Despite this, we cannot conclude that our results completely approximate real-world behavior; because the hypothetical scenario was the same across the four conditions, however, we are confident that our comparisons among conditions are valid.

A further issue is that a significantly larger proportion of comprehensive8 participants than other participants dropped out before completing part one. While this creates a potential for selection bias, we have no evidence to believe one exists. We found no statistically significant difference in demographics between conditions. Furthermore, since entropy is logarithmic and the difference between the entropy of comprehensive8 and the other conditions is large, any bias is unlikely to affect the relative entropy differences we observed between conditions.

DISCUSSION

We have so far presented results that follow immediately from our data. In this section, we weave together results regarding entropy, user behavior, and user sentiment. Although many of these are noteworthy on their own, looking at them together reveals a number of interesting trends. Second, building on that discussion, we summarize the findings that are the main contribution of the paper.

Entropy Tradeoffs

Password-composition policies must strike a balance between maximizing security and minimizing user frustration. Our results indicate that, as might be expected, increases in entropy often correlate with decreases in usability. However, we provide hope for finding a desirable balance; a carefully chosen policy can "buy" as much or more entropy, at a similar or better level of usability, than less optimal policies.

At the low end of the entropy scale, we found that basic8 and dictionary8 do not provide significantly different levels of entropy, although the dictionary check provides extra protection against heuristic cracking. In terms of usability, however, the two conditions have important differences: dictionary8 participants had significantly more difficulty creating a valid password and found the process both more difficult and more annoying. The two conditions are similar, however, with respect to storing and remembering the password, as well as in terms of perceived security. An administrator choosing between these policies will make an explicit tradeoff between added protection from heuristic cracking and increased up-front frustration at creation time.

We also considered two stricter policies: comprehensive8 and basic16. From NIST calculations, we expected these policies to provide similar entropy levels; in reality, however, basic16 provided significantly more entropy. We did not observe a notable difference in resistance to heuristic cracking, but John the Ripper—like other similar tools—is optimized for short passwords. As a result, we cannot say confidently how the two conditions compare for cracking protection. In addition to providing more entropy, however, basic16 also proved as or more usable than comprehensive8 on every measure. We found that basic16 is easier to create, reportedly easier to remember, and less likely to be stored than comprehensive8; the two conditions were similarly annoying to participants. As a result, we consider basic16 clearly superior.

We expected, a priori, that our two strictest policies would provide strictly stronger passwords with strictly less usability than our two less demanding policies. In fact, both basic16 and comprehensive8 provide significantly more entropy than basic8 and dictionary8. But while comprehensive8 is worse on every usability measure than either basic8 or dictionary8, basic16 is not. The basic16 condition proved reasonably comparable to dictionary8 in terms of password creation, storage, and reported memorability, although it did perform worse in user sentiment. Overall, therefore, using basic16 rather than dictionary8 provides a strong gain in resistance to brute force attacks at only a small usability cost.

These results reflect the fact that dictionary checks appear to contribute heavily to reducing usability by making password creation difficult. To some extent, this may be a result of our harsh check that uses a cracking dictionary and matches words of any length, rather than ignoring words of less than three or four letters, as may be more typical. We believe, however, that what makes any dictionary check valuable—preventing the use of common or predictable letter strings in passwords—also makes it inherently more difficult for users to think of a valid password. An interface that more clearly explains to users why their passwords are being rejected and provides suggestions for avoiding future rejections might help to reduce frustration.

Except in basic8survey, we also noted differences between participants who claimed to have written down their password, and those who claimed they had not: writing down passwords produced, on average, an extra 1.9 bits of entropy (statistically significant across 10 pairs of random samples of 1,224 participants each, Bonferroni corrected $p < 0.015$). This seems to suggest that, when using memorability aids, users produce stronger passwords; and could make the case for encouraging the use of password managers.

All these tradeoffs should be considered within the scope of the conditions we tested; future work testing other minimum lengths and combinations of required character classes might find more subtle variations.

Summary of Major Findings

Among conditions we tested, a 16-character minimum with no additional requirements provides the most entropy while proving more usable on many measures than the strongest alternative. Dictionary checks rule out the majority of passwords that can be easily cracked using heuristics, but should use large cracking dictionaries if they are to eliminate almost all vulnerable passwords. Unfortunately, dictionary checks also significantly increase user frustration.

Most participants write down or otherwise store their passwords. Interestingly, however, we find that storage is correlated with use of higher-entropy passwords.

We identified several common misperceptions in how password entropy is thought to be affected by users' password-composition strategies. 1) Adding numbers to passwords is thought to add little entropy; we found, by contrast, a lot of entropy in numbers. 2) Dictionary checks, although otherwise useful, add much less entropy than expected. 3) Unexpectedly, users typically create passwords that exceed minimum requirements, thus increasing password entropy.

We believe our results are immediately actionable for system administrators considering how to balance security and usability in their password-composition policies. Future work collecting and analyzing additional empirical data could provide even more detailed information about these tradeoffs.

ACKNOWLEDGMENTS

This research was supported by NSF grants DGE-0903659 and CCF-0424422, by CyLab at Carnegie Mellon under grants DAAD19-02-1-0389 and W911NF-09-1-0273 from the Army Research Office, and by a gift from Microsoft Research. Serge Egelman was affiliated with Brown University when this research began.

REFERENCES

1. A. Adams, M. A. Sasse, and P. Lunt. Making passwords secure and usable. In *HCI 97*, 1997.
2. M. Bishop and D. V. Klein. Improving system security via proactive password checking. *Computers & Security*, 14(3):233–249, 1995.
3. J. Bonneau and S. Preibusch. The password thicket: technical and market failures in human authentication on the web. In *Proc. (online) of WEIS'10*, June 2010.
4. W. E. Burr, D. F. Dodson, and W. T. Polk. Electronic authentication guideline. Technical report, NIST, 2006.
5. D. Florêncio and C. Herley. A large-scale study of web password habits. In *Proc. WWW'07*, 2007.
6. D. Florêncio and C. Herley. Where do security policies come from? In *Proc. SOUPS '10*, 2010.
7. P. Inglesant and M. A. Sasse. The true cost of unusable password policies: password use in the wild. In *Proc. ACM CHI'10*, pages 383–392, 2010.
8. B. Ives, K. R. Walsh, and H. Schneider. The domino effect of password reuse. *C. ACM*, 47(4):75–78, 2004.
9. J. L. Massey. Guessing and entropy. In *Proc. IEEE ISIT'94*, page 204, 1994.
10. G. Miller. Note on the bias of information estimates. *Info. Th. Psych.: Problems and Methods*, 1955.
11. L. Paninski. Estimation of entropy and mutual information. *Neural Comp.*, 15(6):1191–1253, 2003.
12. R. W. Proctor, M.-C. Lien, K.-P. L. Vu, E. E. Schultz, and G. Salvendy. Improving computer security for authentication of users: Influence of proactive password restrictions. *Behavior Res. Methods, Instruments, & Computers*, 34(2):163–169, 2002.
13. S. Schechter, C. Herley, and M. Mitzenmacher. Popularity is everything: A new approach to protecting passwords from statistical-guessing attacks. In *Proc. HotSec'10*, 2010.
14. C. E. Shannon. A mathematical theory of communication. *ACM SIGMOBILE Mobile Comp. Comm. Rev.*, 5(1), 1949.
15. C. E. Shannon. Prediction and entropy of printed english. *Bell Systems Tech. J.*, 30:50–64, 1951.
16. R. Shay and E. Bertino. A comprehensive simulation tool for the analysis of password policies. *Int. J. Info. Sec.*, 8(4):275–289, 2009.
17. R. Shay, S. Komanduri, P. Kelley, P. Leon, M. Mazurek, L. Bauer, N. Christin, and L. Cranor. Encountering stronger password requirements: user attitudes and behaviors. In *Proc. SOUPS'10*, 2010.
18. J. M. Stanton, K. R. Stam, P. Mastrangelo, and J. Jolton. Analysis of end user security behaviors. *Comp. & Security*, 24(2):124 – 133, 2005.
19. A. Vance. If your password is 123456, just make it hackme. New York Times, `http://www.nytimes.com/2010/01/21/technology/21password.html`, January 2010, retrieved September 2010.
20. K.-P. L. Vu, R. W. Proctor, A. Bhargav-Spantzel, B.-L. B. Tai, and J. Cook. Improving password security and memorability to protect personal and organizational information. *Int. J. of Human-Comp. Studies*, 65(8):744–757, 2007.
21. M. Weir, S. Aggarwal, M. Collins, and H. Stern. Testing metrics for password creation policies by attacking large sets of revealed passwords. In *Proceedings of the 17th ACM conference on Computer and communications security*, CCS '10, pages 162–175, New York, NY, USA, 2010. ACM.
22. Y. Zhang, F. Monrose, and M. K. Reiter. The security of modern password expiration: An algorithmic framework and empirical analysis. In *Proc. ACM CCS'10*, 2010.
23. M. Zviran and W. J. Haga. Password security: an empirical study. *J. Mgt. Info. Sys.*, 15(4):161–185, 1999.

MARASIM: A Novel Jigsaw Based Authentication Scheme Using Tagging

Rohit Ashok Khot
IIIT-Hyderabad
Hyderabad, INDIA
rohit_a@research.iiit.ac.in

Kannan Srinathan
IIIT-Hyderabad
Hyderabad, INDIA
srinathan@iiit.ac.in

Ponnurangam Kumaraguru
IIIT-Delhi
Delhi, INDIA
pk@iiitd.ac.in

ABSTRACT
In this paper we propose and evaluate *Marasim*, a novel Jigsaw based graphical authentication mechanism using tagging. Marasim is aimed at achieving the security of random images with the memorability of personal images. Our scheme relies on the human ability to remember a personal image and later recognize the alternate visual representations (images) of the concepts occurred in the image. These concepts are retrieved from the tags assigned to the image. We illustrate how a Jigsaw based approach helps to create a portfolio of system-chosen random images to be used for authentication. The paper describes the complete design of Marasim along with the empirical studies of Marasim that provide evidences of increased memorability. Results show that 93% of all participants succeeded in the authentication tests using Marasim after three months while 71% succeeded in authentication tests using Marasim after nine months. Our findings indicate that Marasim has potential applications, especially where text input is hard (e.g., PDAs or ATMs), or in situations where passwords are infrequently used (e.g., web site passwords).

Author Keywords
User authentication, jigsaw, graphical passwords, tagging.

ACM Classification Keywords
H.5.2 [Information Interfaces and Presentations]: User Interfaces – Input devices and strategies; K.6.5 [Management of Computers and Information Systems]: Security and Protection – Authentication.

General Terms
Design, Experimentation, Human factors, Security.

INTRODUCTION
Usability is a significant concern in determining how authentication systems should be deployed and used in practice [6, 19]. If authentication systems are built without incorporating the knowledge of human strengths and limitations, then users will not use them or they will make errors in using them [1]. Their actions in turn, can compromise the security of entire system. This problem is evident in knowledge-based authentication systems like passwords. Today, static passwords are the most widely used authentication mechanism. Passwords are simple, easy to use, inexpensive and familiar to most users. They require no special hardware or training and can be distributed, maintained and updated by telephone, fax or email. But then, passwords are also the source of many security weaknesses, because they are often used inappropriately [4, 14]. For example, most users struggle to come up with strong and secure passwords that they can easily remember and recall without an external support. In effect, they choose simple dictionary words as passwords which are highly susceptible to guessing and theft [12, 14, 24]. On the other hand, when users are forced to use strong passwords, they either write passwords down or frequently forget them [1, 14]. Either outcome defeats the purpose of passwords which is to be secure and memorable at the same time.

Graphical passwords were introduced to overcome the drawback of text passwords. They are based on recall and recognition of visual information (images, in particular) instead of alphanumeric strings. The interest in graphical passwords is driven by the *Picture superiority effect* [25, 26]. According to this effect, humans have vast, almost limitless visual memory and images are better remembered than the text and for a longer time. Since images are easily remembered and can be chosen from a potentially large set of images, it was conceived that users would select and remember graphical passwords that are stronger than the text passwords they typically select [7]. However, this assumption is quickly falling apart as recent user studies on known graphical password schemes [7, 11, 29, 32] have shown predictable patterns in the user choices of graphical passwords. For example, users choose attractive, personal and semantically meaningful images as passwords which are easy to guess given some knowledge about the user [7, 29]. On the other hand, system generated random images are proven to be difficult to remember [9]. Therefore, designing a graphical password scheme involves the same tricky tradeoff between security and usability that affects the text passwords.

In this paper, we present, *Marasim*, a cued recognition based graphical authentication scheme, which blends together the security benefits of system chosen random images with the memorability gains of personal images using a unique semantic Jigsaw based authentication design. During enrollment, user provides tags for a personal image of her choice and then utilizes those tags to create a portfolio of random images. At the time of login, user recognizes those images amongst the set of decoy images and her identity is verified. The intuition behind Marasim is that a personal image and its associated tags will aid in the recognition of random images. In this paper, we describe the complete design of our scheme and discuss the potentials attacks on Marasim. We conducted a longitudinal user study with 30 participants for the period of nine months. Results show that, users had high success rates, with 93% of all participants succeeded in the authentication tests after three months while 71% of all participants were able to successfully login after nine months. Participants rated the system positively. A comparative laboratory study on Marasim shows that a tagging based approach helps users to remember their portfolio images better than otherwise. We also did an introductory laboratory study to study the effect of multiple passwords interference on recall. Results show that 71% the participants were able to successfully recall all their passwords after two weeks. Even though we found some positive results about Marasim in this study, there were some limitations in our research – our study methodology could have been better, study participants were not representative to the actual users of the system. We plan to address these in future studies that we are conducting around Marasim.

Before delving into the specifics of our approach, we catalogue the existing proposals on graphical passwords design focusing on the user choices of password images.

RELATED WORK

Based on the cognitive activity required to remember the password, we divide the graphical password schemes into four different categories [6]: Pure Recall, Cued Recall, Recognition and Cued Recognition.

Pure recall

Pure recall is considered to be the most difficult task for memory, since user must remember and reproduce the password from memory without any assistance or cues given by the system. Traditional text based passwords fall in this category. Notable example of recall based graphical authentication scheme is Draw-A-Secret (DAS) [17]. DAS scheme requires user to remember and repeat visual drawing on predefined grid cells. However, results indicate that users prefer to draw symmetric images with less number of strokes which reduces the overall password space [32]. Users often make mistakes in remembering the order and precise grid location, while repeating the drawing.

Cued recall

In a cued recall authentication scheme, user is given a cue that aids the recall of password from memory. Best example of cued recall scheme is PassPoints [36], where password is constructed with series of random clicks on predefined region of an image. To login, user must repeat clicking on the same location (within the system specified tolerance) and in correct order. However, PassPoints scheme is vulnerable against dictionary attack as users chose distinct and semantically meaningful regions of an image (known as hot spots) as click points [11]. InkBlot authentication is another cued recall based scheme [31]. It uses images as cue for text password entry. However, no longitudinal user study has been reported as yet, to measure the level of allowed abstractness and liability of the scheme. In cued recall schemes, the design of a cue becomes vital because an attacker can see what the user can see and can also understand what the user can understand. Ideally, the cue should only help the legitimate user and not the attacker.

Recognition

Recognition is an easier task than recall [21]. In a recognition based authentication scheme, the user typically memorizes a portfolio of images during enrollment and must distinguish those images from the presented decoy images to login. Some of the known recognition based graphical password schemes are: PassFaces [5], DejaVu [10] and VIP [8]. PassFaces scheme uses portfolio of faces while DejaVu scheme uses images of abstract art. VIP on the other hand, is based on the recognition of simple natural photographs. Although, initial memorability results for most of these schemes are encouraging, evaluations indicate common predictable patterns in user selected portfolio images [7, 29] which make them susceptible against dictionary attacks. For example, in PassFaces, users choose attractive faces over plain ones and the faces of the people of same gender and race [7]. Recognition based schemes discussed earlier, however do not allow the use of personal (self- chosen) images. The idea of using personal pictures as passwords was investigated in the work of Pering et al. [27], Tullis et al. [33] and Renaud [29]. Since these schemes do not employ any filtering on images, these images remain closely related to the person and thus are insecure in real life setting.

Cued recognition

A cued recognition is an interesting approach to graphical passwords design, where a cue helps the user in the recognition of portfolio images. An example of such a scheme is a Story scheme by Monrose et.al. [7], where the story or the semantic relationship between the images assists the user in the recognition of password images. Preliminary evaluations indicate that Story scheme offers better resilience against guessing attacks when compared to Faces (a scheme identical to PassFaces™ [5]). However, users had problems in remembering their story passwords correctly and they often forgot the order. The main reason was very few users actually chose stories, despite being suggested to do so. Instead, they picked images that looked attractive and tried to remember them [7]. ImageShield™ [16] is another cued recognition based authentication scheme. In ImageShield™, user memorizes a set of semantic image categories and recognizes images that belong to those categories from the set of presented images. The set of images changes with every login. However, no user study has been reported for this scheme.

MOTIVATION

The success of any graphical password scheme (recognition based, in particular) largely depends upon the type of images used for authentication [29]. The images can be of two types: Random images and Personal images.

Random images: These images are pieces of information created and used specifically for the purpose of authentication. Generally, they do not share any relation with the individual or events of her life, hence they are more secure. For example, randomly selected images from a public image database are more secure. However, since they are not related to user's life in any meaningful way, they are often difficult to remember [9, 29].

Personal images: These images on the other hand, are pieces of information that are intimately associated with the user and her life. Such images are highly meaningful and often unforgettable to their owners [29, 33]. Psychological studies confirm that self- generated or personal images are better recognized than those that are not [20]. However, such images are insecure in practical settings because of their vulnerability against guessing attacks [7, 29]. Another problem with them is of privacy, as most individuals do not wish to reveal their personal images to others (that includes even the authenticating system) [19].

In an ideal case, the authentication scheme should offer the best of both the worlds. That is, it should have the memorability of personal images as well as the security of random images. In order to achieve this ambitious goal, we looked into semantic jigsaw based design using tagging. Tagging [30] is an emerging approach of organizing information using keywords (called as tags) contributed by ordinary users. Tagging is popular because it is open ended and has nonhierarchical structure, which means that users can assign tags freely based on the cognitive connection they share with the tagged object. Tagging is used in photo sharing websites like Flickr [13] and in CAPTCHAs [22] to restrict automated bot (script) attacks. However, to the best of our knowledge, ours is the first attempt of leveraging tagging for the purpose of user authentication.

SEMANTIC JIGSAW BASED DESIGN

The intuition behind semantic jigsaw based design will be clear with a small cognitive experiment. Let us look at the twelve images shown in Figure 1 and try to find all possible relations that exist between these images.

Figure 1: Find out all the relations between the images shown

It appears that many images from the presented set can be related to each other. For example, images of *cute girl with rose in hand*, *birthday sticker*, *rose flower* and *toys* together form *a birthday theme*. Another relation can be of a *family* or *people* where the individual members are shown in the four corner images (Refer, Figure 1). Now, let us attempt to find the relation among the images shown in Figure 2.

Figure 2: Are these images related to each other?

On the first glance, images in Figure 2 do not seem to be related at all. However, after a careful examination, we can define a relation such as: *a mother and a daughter went to see an art exhibition* (the mirror symbolically represents the act of seeing). Notice that these images are also present in Figure 1. This relation however, is overshadowed by other superior relations like the ones described earlier. Let us try, if we can somehow make this relation to stand out amongst the existing relations with the help of an external image. So, let us turn our attention to the image in Figure 3 and try to describe its content in the form of tags.

Figure 3: Describe the image with four tags

Figure 3 is an image of a cute girl sitting in an art exhibition. We can also see the painting of an Indian actress *Nargis* and a mirror on the wall. Therefore, a possible set of tags for this image are: *cute girl*, *art exhibition*, *Nargis* and *mirror* (as marked in Figure 3). Notice that these tags are also valid for the four images we see in Figure 2. In fact, the images in Figure 2 recreate the scene we observe in Figure 3. Therefore, if we knew the image or the given tags for the image in Figure 3 earlier, then we could have easily described the relation between the images in Figure 2. The idea of semantic jigsaw based authentication design stuck to us with this cognitive experiment. Let us reverse the experiment to understand it better (as explained in following steps).

1. Start by describing the image in Figure 3. Let us say, we described it as: *cute girl*, *art exhibition*, *Nargis* and *mirror*. This step is analogous to breaking the image into pieces. However, unlike any typical jigsaw puzzle [18], we break the image into semantic concepts (tags) occurred in the image.
2. Find equivalent images for the entered tags from step 1. Assume that the found images were the ones shown in Figure 2.
3. Finally, mix the four images with decoy images as shown in Figure 1. Present the complete set to user and ask her to identify the correct four images that describe the predefined relation. It is like giving a Jigsaw puzzle to solve.

The above steps are summarized in Figure 4.

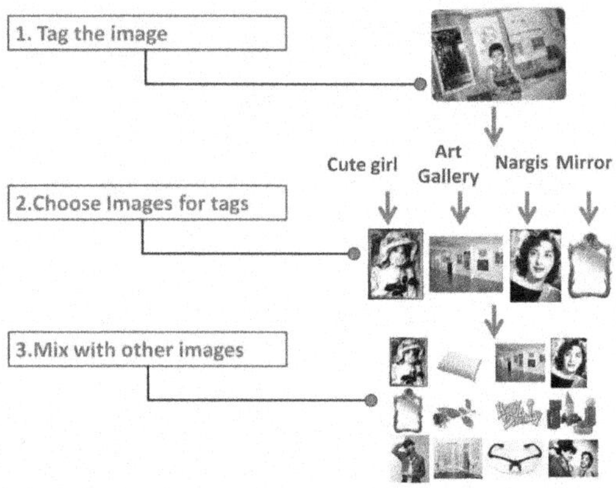

Figure 4: Steps in Semantic Jigsaw based design

The user who knows the original image and the assigned tags can solve the jigsaw by doing a visual search for the tags. Here the original image and the tags act a cue and aids in the assembly of correct images. However, for someone who has not seen the original image and the tags, finding the correct set of images is difficult in limited attempts, provided the set of decoy images is properly chosen to reflect multiple overlapping relations (as in Figure 1).

MARASIM: OUR PROPOSED SCHEME

Marasim is a novel Jigsaw based authentication scheme using tagging. Marasim is an Urdu word which means relations or affinity. Within our context, it denotes the association among the pictures. Our idea is to leverage memories associated with a personal image in creating a portfolio of random images. We call these random images as *Passimages* (in the same spirit of password). Doing so, will actively involve the user in the password creation process, thereby leveraging the action event memory, which is much stronger than the recognition memory [23].

System Architecture

During accounts setup, user provides p number of tags for a memorable image of her choice. These tags are then used to retrieve images that share the same tag from the image database. She then picks p number of images (one for each tag) from the set of retrieved images and registration is completed. During login, the same p images are presented along with n decoy images. User then must identify the correct p images in order to login. In the present prototype, the value of (n, p) is kept as $(21, 4)$ respectively. Figure 5 summarizes the sequence the operations.

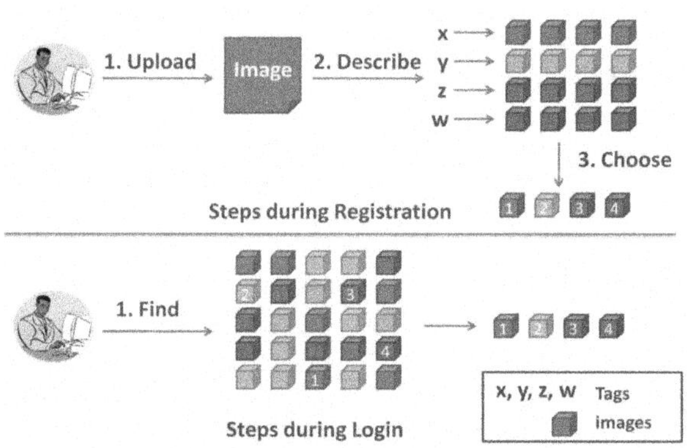

Figure 5: Steps followed during registration and login

Registration

Enrolling is a one-time event that involves two steps: 1) Tag an image and 2) Choose images for the entered tags

Step 1) Tag a personal image

In this step, user provides tags for a personal image of her choice as shown in Figure 6. The entered tags are then used to create the portfolio of passimages. In the present prototype, we ask the user to upload an image. However, instead of uploading, a set of images can also be presented to the user and she then picks an image from the presented set for tagging. The user is welcomed to describe the associated memories with the photo (For example, the event or place where the photo is taken). There is no restriction on the language or the words used to describe the concepts. Although, we encourage the use of simple English words of which specific pictorial representation is possible. For example, for the image shown in Figure 6, *apple tree* is better tag than a tag like *dark*.

Figure 6: Step 1) User describes the content of the image in the form four tags

Step 2) Choose images for the tags

We search Google Image Search engine [15] with the tags, user has entered in the last step. A representative set of returned images for each tag is then shown to the user as

(Refer Figure 7). User must select four images that correspond to the four tags. Each image carries a number with it. To select a particular image, user should enter the associated number in the textbox below. For example in Figure 7, to select first image from first three rows and third image from the fourth row, user should enter *1113* in the textbox. If the user is not satisfied with the presented set of images, she can ask for replacing them with a new set of images. User also has the option of going back and altering (improving) the entered tags. Once the user has submitted her choices of four passimages, a confirmation message is displayed about successful completion of registration.

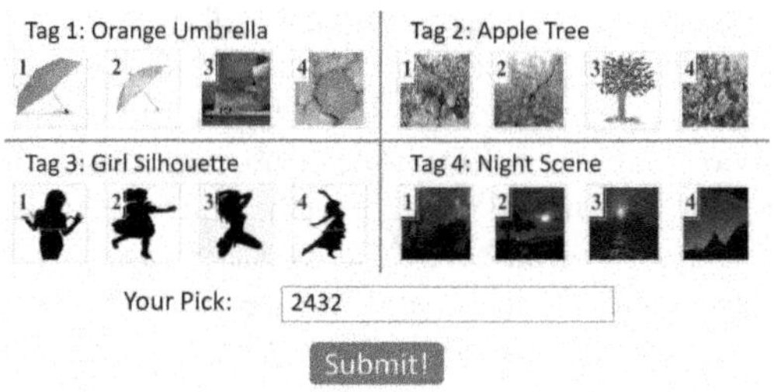

Figure 7: Step 2) User picks one image from each row as her password image

Post registration processing

Once the user is successfully registered to Marasim, post-processing begins in which we create a unique challenge set of images for the legitimate user. The challenge set consists of 4 passimages and 21 decoy images. In the current prototype, we have used images from Google Image search results [17] to build the image set. In future versions of Marasim, we are planning to use proprietary images.

In Marasim, the four passimages share a semantic relationship with respect to the original secret image (That is, each image depicts a concept from the original image). The passimages can be vulnerable if this relation is directly visible to the attacker. In order to avoid this, we add confusion by overriding this relation with other relations. There are two ways of doing it. One way is to find all the tags that are related to the entered tags and add images for each of them. For example, *raincoat* is a related tag to *umbrella*. Another way is to choose decoy images that already exhibit some relation. In the present prototype, we select the second option and add decoy images from the images chosen by other users. Once the Image challenge set for the particular user is created, it remains consistent for all login sessions (No new image is added or deleted).

Login

At the time of login, system presents the challenge set of 25 images randomly placed in a 5×5 grid as shown in Figure 8. Each image has a number (between 0-9) associated with it. To login, the user should not click on her passimages. Instead, she must identify her passimages and enter the corresponding number in the textbox below. User can enter those numbers in any order. The numbers associated with the images change with every session and thus become the *one time access code* for that particular login session.

Figure 8: Screenshot of a login session. User recognizes the password images and enter the corresponding number in the textbox provided below (Clicking on images is not allowed, the password images are highlighted with a border around them only to improve understandability)

A user can recognize her passimages in following three ways: 1) Recalling the secret memorable image used for tagging and doing a visual search for the tags from the original image. 2) Recalling the tags and doing a visual search for them. 3) Recognizing the four images which user saw and memorized during enrollment process.

SECURITY OF MARASIM

In this section, we discuss the possible attacks on Marasim and how we can defend them.

Brute force attack

Simplest of the attacks against any authentication scheme is to randomly guess the password. In Marasim, an attacker can try to randomly guess the one time access code. The access code is a combination of four digits (each digit can be a number between 0 and 9). Therefore, if the ordering constraint is kept, the one time access code will have 10,000 combinations. Without the ordering constraint, the overall combinations reduce by a factor of 24 (10,000/ 4!). However, brute force for one time access code is not economical, as it changes with every login session. Alternatively, the attacker can try to randomly guess the four passimages. In the current prototype, Marasim presents a challenge set of 25 images. There are 12,650 ($^{25}C_4$) possible combinations of choosing 4 images out of 25 images. Therefore, the probability that a single random guess will succeed is 1/12650. If ordering constraint is kept, the probability of a single random guess to succeed becomes 1/390625.

Marasim offers a password space comparable only with 4 digit PIN security. Therefore, Marasim is suitable for systems where PIN based security suffices and where usability is the main concern. We recommend that Marasim, should be implemented and deployed in systems where offline attacks are not possible or where number of guess attempts are limited per account in a given time period. Examples of such systems are ATMs, PDAs, and infrequently visited websites. We can also improve the security of Marasim by using larger image grid and by using a hardware token as a second factor.

Dictionary attack

In Dictionary based attacks, instead of random guessing, an attacker tries to crack the password using a dictionary of most commonly used passwords. Marasim presents a login image grid of 25 images that are unique per user. Therefore, the dictionary attack on Marasim needs to be dedicated one (No two users share the same set of 25 images). Secondly, the four passimages are related to each other with respect to one secret image, which is never revealed to the attacker. And as explained in the post registration processing step, the challenge set of images is carefully constructed with images of overlapping relationships to confuse the attacker. Therefore, without the prior knowledge of the image and the given tags, guessing the passimages is difficult (in limited attempts).

However, it is possible that users might define tags such as *dog, cat, puppy, kitten* that might have nothing to do with the secret image, but entered only in order to get related images as passimages. This is problematic because an attacker can easily build an image dictionary for such popular tags and use it to crack the passimages. Therefore, to address this problem, we plan to use a *password strength meter* (as a part of future work), which shows the relative strength of the password (based on the tags entered), at the time of the registration and which do not allow tags that are directly related to each other.

Social engineering attacks

Social engineering includes any technique used to trick people into divulging their credentials or private information to untrustworthy parties. Some of the popular social engineering techniques are: Shoulder surfing, phishing and malware attacks.

Most authentication schemes are vulnerable against social engineering attacks because user has to explicitly enter her password each time she wants to login and the password remains consistent (same) across all login sessions (unless and until user changes it herself). One solution to this problem is to generate a new password token every time the user logins without changing the actual password. In order to do that, we employ the probabilistic one time password scheme (POTP) [3]. It involves association of single number with multiple images to confuse the attacker. Explaining the theory behind POTP is beyond the scope of this paper. So, we illustrate the use of POTP in our scheme with a login example as shown in Figure 8. In Marasim, user never enters the password by clicking on her passimages. Instead, she must enter the four numbers that correspond to her passimages. These four numbers form the one time access code for that particular login session. For example, let's say, the one time access code for the image in Figure 8 is *3650*. We argue that even if the attacker is successful to capture the one time access code using any of the popular social engineering techniques (For example, by shoulder surfing or by using key-loggers or by phishing), she gains nothing about the actual passimages because of the following reasons.

- As numbers and their association with the images change with every login session, the one time access code is valid only for a session. Therefore, attacker cannot use the same code to login in next session.
- One time access code yields no direct information about the passimages, because the same numbers corresponds to multiple images in the grid. In such cases, the attacker must find all possible combinations and correlations among the numbers and the images in the grid to correctly identify the four passimages. To illustrate, the numbers *3*, *6* and *5* from the one time access code *3650* repeat thrice and the number 0 repeats twice in the grid (Refer Figure 8), which means the attacker would require $3 \times 3 \times 3 \times 2 = 54$ attempts to find the correct four passimages. In general, an attacker needs $a \times b \times c \times d$ attempts to find the actual password from the captured one time access code, where a, b, c, d denotes the frequency of occurrences of four numbers from the one time access code within the login grid.

The expected success probability of guessing, depending on the number of captured images per one time access code is 2.6% (1/38). The worst case occurs when all four numbers from the one time access code repeat twice, giving the success probability of 6.25% (1/16) while the best case occurs when all four numbers repeats thrice, giving success probability of 1.23% (1/81). However, if an attacker is able to record multiple login sessions then she can predict the passimages with little effort.

USER STUDY OF MARASIM

We conducted a longitudinal user study to evaluate the effectiveness of Marasim scheme in environments where users rarely login and from their point of view, the security is not a major concern (For example, infrequently visited websites). However, passwords used on these sites can become bottleneck and a source of security breaches [28, 35] if users start reusing them on high-security websites (For example, online banking websites). Ideally, there should be a clear separation between the passwords used for low-security websites and high-security websites [4]. If Marasim is found effective in situations where passwords are rarely used (That is, if users are able to recognize their passimages even after a long gap between logins) then our scheme can be used as a standard authentication mechanism for low-security websites, thereby helping to build the separation and avoiding attacks based on password reuse. Another goal of the study is to learn the characteristics of the user chosen passwords.

Procedure

We recruited 30 participants by sending invitation mails and posting flyers. All participants were students (graduate and undergraduate) from the university campus with their age ranging from 20 to 28. Twenty three participants were male while seven participants were female. None of the participants have used graphical password scheme before. Monetary incentives were kept to encourage participation. Our usability test consisted of six sessions that span nine months. A web based prototype of the Marasim was created and an email was sent to all the participants containing the URL of the site and instructions for the usage of the website. Table 1 shows the details of all the sessions.

Session No.	Date	Tasks
1	First day	Registration and Training
2	One day later	Authentication
3	One week later	Authentication
4	One month later	Authentication
5	Three months later	Authentication and Questionnaire
6	Nine months later	Authentication

Table 1: Details of each session of usability test

The first session (registration and training) happened in the lab where we introduced Marasim scheme to the participants. In this session, participants created a portfolio of password images using following three steps: 1) upload an image 2) provide four tags for the image 3) choose four passimages for the four tags from the presented set of images. Each participant required on average two minutes to register. The training involved two back to back login sessions to get the user familiar with the authentication process and image challenge set. We intentionally avoided the use of real accounts, because we wanted to test the memorability of Marasim in an isolated environment (without any external incentive to login). In the remaining five sessions (which happened over the web), we asked participants to login to Marasim by sending them a reminder mail. All participants received the study email in the morning (9 am) and they were given a maximum of 15 hours to respond to the mail (i.e. to login to Marasim before midnight on the same day). Most participants tried logging into Marasim within an hour of sending the email. We requested users not to login between sessions. If users fail to recall their password after three or more attempts, we revealed the password on request before the start of next session. At the end of the fifth session (after three months), we requested participants to fill out questionnaires for the sake of qualitative analysis.

Results

We report the viability of Marasim in terms of [6]: Accuracy (Number of successful Logins), Efficiency (Time required to login), Predictability (Password Strength) and User satisfaction.

Accuracy and Efficiency

We consider authentication to be successful, if the participant is able to login by correctly identifying her password images. Each participant was given a maximum of three attempts to login. Table 2 shows the numbers of successful logins along with the mean time needed to login. The numbers inside the parentheses are: *(m / n)* where *m* denotes the number of successful participants and *n* denotes the total number of participants.

Time interval	No. of Successful Logins	No. of users with more than one login attempt	Mean time to login (Std. Deviation) in seconds
Session 1	100% (30/30)	0	24.7 (3.9)
Session 2	100% (30/30)	0	18.1 (4.4)
Session 3	100% (30/30)	4	17.6 (4.1)
Session 4	97% (29/30)	6	21.3 (5.0)
Session 5	93% (28/30)	7	25.2 (4.7)
Session 6	71% (10/14)	7	23.7 (3.2)

Table 2: Login success rates

Results show that, all the participants were able to successfully login for the first four sessions. After three months, seven users made mistakes in login but eventually succeeded while two users failed to login within the given limit of three attempts. There were no dropouts till the fifth session (till three months). However, only fourteen participants took part in the last session of the study (after nine months)[1]. Ten out of these fourteen participants were able to successfully login to their accounts while seven participants required more than one attempt to login.

Table 2 also reports the details of the time required to login. The maximum delay occurred in the first session when participants were using the scheme for the first time and in the fifth session which was after three months gap. Although, the mean login time of more than 20 sec seems inappropriate for practical applications, we argue that following simple countermeasures can help in locating the password images faster in the login grid, thereby reducing

[1] Twenty out of the 30 students who participated in the study graduated after 6 months and only 4 out of the 20 graduated participants tried to login to Marasim by the deadline.

the login time. These countermeasures are: 1) use of properly annotated image database to avoid confusion among images and 2) uniform and small size images 3) static positioning of images in the login grid.

Comparison of Marasim with long term trials of some of the existing graphical password schemes[2] offers good evidences of increased memorability. For example, Valentine [36] did a five months user study on PassFaces scheme [4] and found 72% login success rate by third attempt. In comparison, Marasim reports a login success rate of 93% after three months and 71% after nine months. Zviran and Haga [39] report a 35% login success rate after three months at the first attempt, while, Marasim achieves 80% login success rate after three months by first attempt.

Predictability

We were interested in knowing the categories of the uploaded images and the relatedness of the assigned tags. These findings are important to determine the predictability of the passimages. We identified six different categories from which users choose their personal image as shown in Figure 9 a). None of the image categories was dominant in the password selection. The most frequent categories were Nature scenes and Everyday objects while the least frequent category was of abstract art images.

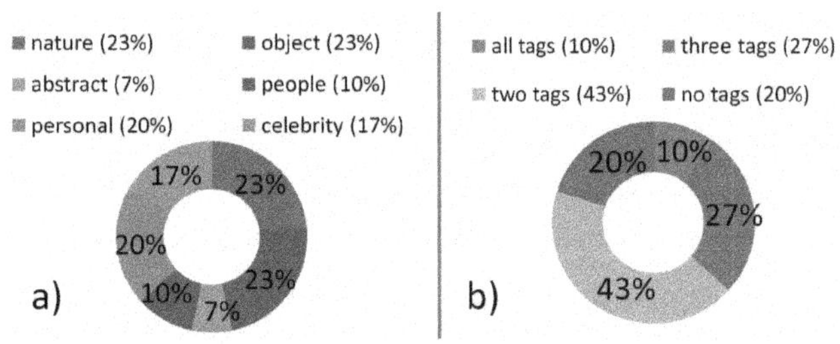

Figure 9: a) Common Categories of images b) Relatedness of the tags

We also tried to manually identify the relatedness of the tags used in creation of passimages. Results are shown in Figure 9 b). If the tags are closely related to each other, then the relation among the passimages is easy to predict. The knowledge of one tag can easily expose other tags since they are related. For example, tags like *cake, candles* and *balloons* can be tried along with the tag *birthday*. Therefore, related tags should strictly be avoided. Our study found that the majority of the passwords (43%) have at most two tags that are related to each other, whereas only 10% of passwords have all tags related to each other.

In the current prototype, users have tagged images that may not have a predefined set of tags. In next round of studies, we are asking participants to choose tags from the set of existing tags given to that image. This will help us to identify the likelihood of a tag being selected.

User satisfaction

At the end of three months, we requested users to answer a set of questionnaire providing feedback about the scheme and to write down any specific comments. The questionnaire had four multiple choice questions as follows: 1) *Marasim password is easy to remember.* 2) *No one can easily guess my password.* 3) *I can prefer Marasim based password over text password.* 4) *I can use Marasim effectively with practice.* Available responses to these questions were Yes, No and Neutral. Figure 10 shows the responses of the participants to these questions.

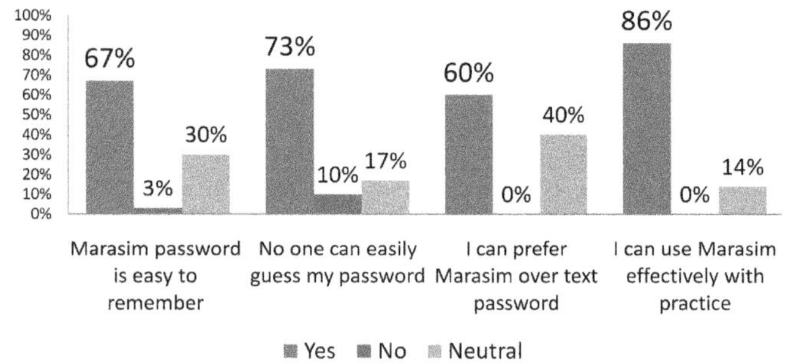

Figure 10: Questionnaire responses which show high levels of user satisfaction

As we can see in Figure 10, all questions had median value of neutral or higher, showing high levels of satisfaction. We also asked the users about how they were able to remember their passwords, Figure 11 summarizes their responses. Forty three percent of users said that the original image and the tags helped them to recognize their passimages. Twenty seven percent of users said they simply recognized the four passimages, while rest thirty percent users nodded for a combined effect of recalling the original image and recognition the four images. None of the participant said that they wrote their tags down or stored their passimages.

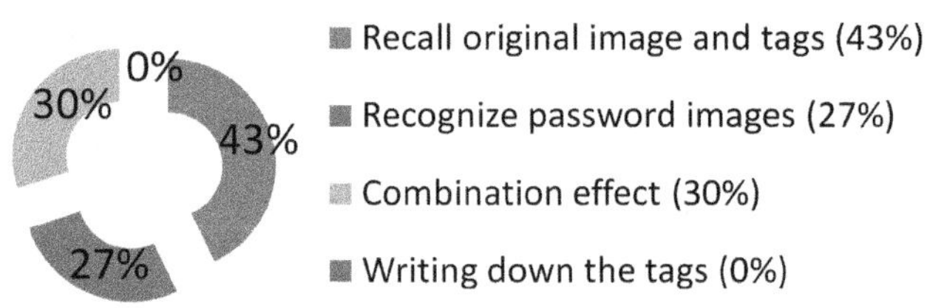

Figure 11: Most users remember their password by recalling original image and tags

To summarize, results of the user study show good improvements in terms of memorability with only 2 out of 30 participants (7%) failed to remember their password after three months and 10 out of 14 participants (71%) were able to successfully login to Marasim even after nine months. Users were satisfied with the scheme both in terms of usability: sixty seven percent of participants said they

[2] Long term trials of these schemes were performed with different number of subjects and under different settings.

can easily remember Marasim password and security: seventy three percent of participants were confident that their password is secure (refer Figure 10). We believe these evidences are good indications of the viability of the proposed scheme.

COMPARATIVE USER STUDY

We conducted a supervised laboratory study to test the hypothesis: *tagging aids in the recognition of password images*. We recruited 20 participants from the university campus by sending invitation mails. All the participants were students with their age in the range of 19 to 28 (14 male and 6 female). There was no overlap between participants from earlier studies. A simple recognition based scheme tVIP was built for the evaluation purpose. The tVIP scheme is similar to VIP [8] scheme where user directly creates and recognizes a portfolio of four images from the presented set of 25 images (without tagging).

Our usability test consisted of two sessions that span two weeks. In the first session, users created two passwords: one with the Marasim scheme (by uploading, tagging and then selecting the passimages) and another with tVIP scheme (by directly selecting the passimages). To counterbalance, we randomized the order in which the conditions (password schemes) are presented to the participants during both registration and login. Therefore, half of the participants learned and used Marasim before tVIP and vice versa. In the second session which happened after two weeks, we asked the participants to login to their accounts using both the schemes. Table 3 shows the login success rate for both the schemes along with the results of one tailed Chi-square test.

Condition	Marasim	tVIP	χ^2, df = 1
Within three attempts	95%	65%	$\chi^2 = 5.625$, $p < 0.02$
On first attempt	80%	45%	$\chi^2 = 5.227$, $p < 0.05$

Table 3: Comparisons of login success rates: Marasim had a higher success rate than tVIP after two weeks

Results show that, 19 of 20 participants were successful in login to Marasim while only 13 out of the 20 participants were able to login with the tVIP scheme after two weeks. In the one-tailed Chi-Square test, the differences in login success rates were in the predicted direction and were statistically significant.

MULTIPLE PASSWORD INTERFERENCE STUDY

We conducted a small-scale supervised laboratory study to examine the effects of multiple password interference on performance. We recruited 7 participants (6 male and 1 female) from the university campus with their age in the range of 24 to 28. We asked each participant to create three accounts (with different username-password pair) on Marasim and we tested whether the recall for all of their passwords after two weeks. Table 4 shows the login success rates after two weeks. The numbers inside the parentheses are: *(m / n)* where *m* denotes number of successful participants and *n* denotes the total number of participants.

Condition	Login success rate
On first Attempt	71% (5/7)
Within three attempts	100% (7/7)

Table 4: Login success rates after two weeks: Users were able to recall all three passwords after two weeks

Results show that, all the participants were able successfully recall all three passwords after two weeks and 71% of users recalled them in first attempt. However, in real life, users are unlikely to create three passwords simultaneously and to recall them one after the other. In fact, an average Internet user has about 25 accounts that require passwords [14]. Therefore, our findings should only be considered as an important starting step towards understanding the effects of multiple password interference on human memory.

ACKNOWLEDGEMENT

We sincerely thank everyone associated with this work.

CONCLUSION AND FUTURE WORK

In this paper, we presented Marasim, a simple-yet-strong authentication system, which is easy enough for users to grasp - but offering good security to keep the fraudsters at bay. Its strength lies in its simplicity and unique Jigsaw way of working. The novel contribution of this work is in the construction of image portfolio, bridging the security benefits of system-chosen image together with memorability gains of self-chosen images. We designed and tested a web based prototype of Marasim. Empirical studies of Marasim provide good evidences of increased memorability. We admit that, our participants are not representative of all users who could potentially use such a system, but since this was only an exploratory study, we used convenient sample. In future, we plan to do the study with a more representative sample (not just students). We also plan to remove some of the design flaws in data collecting that we had in this paper.

REFERENCES

1. Adams, A., and Sasse, M. A. Users are not the enemy. *Commun. ACM.* 42, 12 (1999), 40-46.
2. Ames, M. and Naaman, M. Why we tag: motivations for annotation in mobile and online media. In *Proc. CHI 2007*. ACM Press (2007), 971-980.
3. Bedworth, M. A. Theory of Probabilistic One-Time Passwords, *Proc. Security and Management 2008*, CSREA Press (2008) 113-118.

http://www.pinoptic.com/downloads/wp002_a_theory_of_potp.pdf. Last accessed August 2010.

4. Bonneau, J., and Preibusch, S. The password thicket: technical and market failures in human authentication on the web, In *Proc. WEIS 2010*.
5. Brostoff, S., and Sasse, M.A. Are Passfaces™ more usable than passwords? A field trial investigation. In *Proc.HCI 2000*, 405-424.
6. Cranor, L., and Garfinkel, S. *Security and Usability: Designing Systems that People can use.* O'reilly Media, 2005.
7. Davis, D., Monrose, F., and Reiter, M. K. On user choice in graphical password schemes. In *Proc. 13th USENIX Security Symposium* (2004).
8. De Angeli, A., Coventry, L., Johnson, G., and Renaud, K. Is a picture really worth a thousand words? Exploring the feasibility of graphical authentication systems. *International Journal of Human-Computer Studies*, 63(2005), 128-152.
9. Dhamija, R. Hash visualization in user authentication. In *Ext. Abstracts CHI 2000*, ACM Press (2000), 279-280.
10. Dhamija, R., and Perrig, A. Déjà Vu: a user study using images for authentication. In *Proc. USENIX Security Symposium* (2000).
11. Dirik, A. E., Memon, N., and Birget, J. Modeling user choice in the PassPoints graphical password scheme. In *Proc. SOUPS 2007*, ACM Press (2007), 20-28.
12. Feldmeier, D. C., and Karn, P. R. UNIX Password Security - Ten Years Later. In *Proc. 9th Cryptology Conference on Advances in Cryptology* (1989), 44-63.
13. Flickr. http://www.flickr.com.
14. Florencio, D., and Herley, C. A large-scale study of web password habits. In *Proc. WWW 2007*, ACM Press (2007), 657-666.
15. Google Images. http://images.google.com
16. ImageShield™. http://www.confidenttechnologies.com/products/confident-imageshield.
17. Jermyn, I., Mayer, A., Monrose, F., Reiter, M. K., and Rubin, A. D. The design and analysis of graphical passwords. In *Proc. 8th USENIX Security Symposium*, 1999.
18. Jigsaw puzzle. http://en.wikipedia.org/Jigsaw_puzzle.
19. Kent, S., and Millett, L. *Who goes there? Authentication through the lens of privacy*. The National academic press, 2003.
20. Kinjo, H., and Snodgrass, J. G. Does the generation effect occur for pictures? *Amer. J. of Psych.* 6(2000), 156-163.
21. Kintsch, W. Models for free recall and recognition. In *Models of human memory*, Academic Press, 1970.
22. Khot R.A., Srinathan K., iCAPTCHA:Image Tagging For Free, In the *Proc. Conference on Usable Software and Interface Design* (USID), 2009.
23. Knopf, M., Mack, A., Lenel, S., and Ferrante, S. Memory for action events: findings in neurological patients, *Scandinavian Journal of Psychology*. 46(2005), 11-19.
24. Morris, R., and Thompson, K. Password security: A case history. *Commun. ACM,* (1979), 594-497.
25. Nelson, D. L., Reed, U. S., & Walling, J. R. Pictorial superiority effect. *Journal of Experimental Psychology: Human Learning & Memory*, (1976), 523-528.
26. Paivio, A. *Mind and its evolution: a dual coding theoretical approach*. Lawrence Erlbaum, 2006.
27. Pering, T., Sundar, M., Light, J., and Want, R. Photographic Authentication through Untrusted Terminals. *IEEE Pervasive Computing* 2, (2003), 30-36.
28. Prince, B. Gawker Hack Leads to Twitter Spam Campaign, eWeek, December 2010.
29. Renaud, K. On user involvement in production of images used in visual authentication. *J. Vis. Lang. Comput.* 20, 1 (2009), 1-15.
30. Smith, G. *Tagging: People powered Metadata for the social web* (Voices that matter), New Riders Press, 2008.
31. Stubblefield, A., and Simon, D. Inkblot Authentication. Technical Report, MSR-TR-2004-85, Microsoft Research, 2004.
32. Thorpe, J., and van Oorschot, P. C. Human-seeded attacks and exploiting hot-spots in graphical passwords. In *Proc. 16th USENIX Security Symposium,* (2007), 1-16.
33. Tullis, T. S., and Tedesco, D. P. Using personal photos as pictorial passwords. In *Ext. Abstracts CHI 2005*, ACM Press (2005), 1841-1844.
34. Valentine, T. An evaluation of the Passface personal authentication system, Goldsmith College Univ. of London, Tech. Report. 1999.
35. Vance, A. If Your Password Is 123456, Just Make It HackMe. The New York Times, January 2010.
36. Wiedenbeck, S., Waters, J., Birget, J., Brodskiy, A., and Memon, N. PassPoints: design and longitudinal evaluation of a graphical password system. *Int. J. Hum.-Comput. Stud.* 63, 1-2 (2005), 102-127.
37. Zviran, M. and Haga, W. J. Cognitive passwords: the key to easy access control. *Comput. Secur.* 9, 9 (1991), 723-736.

Exploring Implicit Memory for Painless Password Recovery

Tamara Denning,[†*] Kevin Bowers,[†] Marten van Dijk,[†] and Ari Juels[†]
RSA Labs,[†] University of Washington[*]
tdenning@cs.washington.edu, {kevin.bowers, marten.vandijk, ari.juels}@rsa.com

ABSTRACT
Knowledge-based authentication systems generally rely upon users' explicit recollection of passwords, facts, or personal preferences. These systems impose a cognitive burden that often results in forgotten secrets or secrets with poor entropy. We propose an authentication system that instead draws on *implicit memory*–that is, the *unconscious* encoding and usage of information. In such a system, a user is initially presented with images of common objects in a casual familiarization task. When the user later authenticates, she is asked to perform a task involving a set of degraded images, some of which are based upon the images in the familiarization task. The prior exposure to those images influences the user's responses in the task, thereby eliciting authentication information. We ran a user study to investigate the plausibility of our system design. Our results suggest that implicit memory has potential as a basis for low-cognitive-overhead, high-stability, knowledge-based authentication.

Author Keywords
Authentication, implicit memory, password recovery, priming, security.

ACM Classification Keywords
H.5.m Information Interfaces and Presentation: Miscellaneous

General Terms
Human Factors, Security.

INTRODUCTION AND BACKGROUND
Explicit memory forms the basis of most "something-you-know" authentication systems in use today. Most commonly, password and PIN systems and password-recovery systems based on 'life' questions [7] set users the explicit task of recalling a piece of secret information. Most alternative systems, such as graphical passwords [2, 5, 10, 11] and preference-based authentication [3] rely on the same approach: the user enrolls by committing a secret to memory or presenting some personal secret, and authenticates by recalling or recognizing that secret. All of these systems are explicit in the sense that the user is consciously attempting to recall or recognize the authentication secret.

CHI 2011, May 7–12, 2011, Vancouver, BC, Canada.

Authentication schemes based upon explicit memory suffer from a tension between security and usability. User-generated passwords (visual or word-based) can be difficult to remember and are subject to reuse, having low entropy, and being written down for easy reference. Increasing the length or randomness of secrets increases the cognitive burden on the user. Life-history and preference questions avoid some of these pitfalls, but can be subject to low entropy, data-mining, or changing over time [7].

Implicit memory, in contrast to explicit memory, unconsciously influences or controls people's actions even when they are not attempting to retrieve the memory in question. Motor skills are one notable type of implicit memory; habituated physical actions—such as riding a bike—do not require explicit mental effort. Cognitive studies have shown that explicit and implicit memories have different biological mechanisms; patients with brain damage that makes them perform poorly when tested on their explicit memory may still perform well on motor and other implicit memory tasks [6].

One particular kind of implicit memory—priming—involves exposing a user to a particular set of stimuli in order to observe its effects in later testing. In short-term priming, a user unconsciously completes open-ended tasks with a bias towards recently viewed stimuli. Certain priming effects, however, have been shown to persist for weeks, months, and even years [1, 4]. We propose harnessing this priming effect for non-conscious, low-effort authentication.

In this paper, we devise a new implicit-memory approach to authentication with the following benefits: (1) Retention of secrets is potentially very long-lasting [1, 4]; (2) Registration and authentication effort by users does not require memorization; (3) Secrets are truly random and have precisely quantifiable entropy; and (4) Enrollment stimuli are distinctly different from authentication stimuli, thereby avoiding image set intersection attacks.

The protocol we explore here does not immediately yield a workable system: authentication would be intolerably slow for most users. But our experiments do suggest the potential of a novel approach—using implicit memory to authenticate a user—and point the way to more practical variants.[1]

[1]Previous work published in the community by Weinshall makes reference to the potential of implicit memory and priming for authentication; however, the systems and experiments described in the paper utilize explicit memory, not implicit memory [10].

SYSTEM CONCEPT

For our authentication system, we propose using pairs of images—complete images and their degraded counterparts—in a long-term visual priming activity. When the images are presented in their degraded form, it is difficult for a user to identify the content of the image. Exposure to a complete image makes identification of the counterpart degraded image easier—even after a substantial lapse of time [1]. Mitchell observed a priming effect lasting 17 years [4], even when the participants reported no conscious memory of participating in the original experiment.

In our design, a set of complete images is assigned to each user, she is exposed to the stimuli, and she is later authenticated based on her ability to identify the images' degraded counterparts. In the enrollment phase, we select a random subset of images from the corpus for each user. We expose the user to the complete variant of each image: we ask her to label each of these images by providing the word(s) that best describe the object. In keeping with terminology in the psychology literature, we refer to this exposure process as *priming*, and the presented images as *primed*.

Later, in the authentication phase, we present users with degraded versions of a combination of primed and random non-primed images, and again ask for labels. A user's *score* is the number of accurately identified primed images plus the number of incorrectly labeled (or skipped) non-primed images. Her score thus indicates the degree to which her identification of images aligns with the priming she received. To clarify, a user's score is not simply the number of degraded images that she is able to label: a user is scored on how well her labeling success aligns with her primed image set, meaning that she is penalized for correctly labeling non-primed images and rewarded for incorrectly labeling non-primed images. In an authentication system, a user's score would need to exceed a certain, predetermined threshold for the user to be accepted. Therefore, an adversary does not benefit from having complete knowledge of the image corpus and its labels. A primed stimulus is only used once in an authentication prompt. After this different primed stimuli must be used, otherwise the user would potentially be contaminated by previously viewed image fragments.

THEORETICAL ANALYSIS OF THE SYSTEM

Let p_i be the probability that a randomly selected user, who was primed on image i, is able to correctly label image i. Let n_i be the probability that a randomly selected user, who was not primed on image i, is able to correctly label image i. We assume that all images respond positively to priming and thus expect $p_i \geq n_i + \alpha$ where α is a measure of the priming effect and is ≥ 0.

If there are t images in a test corpus, users are primed on an arbitrary subset U of size $t/2$. During password recovery, the user is presented with all t images and attempts to correctly label them. The password recovery system counts the number c of images $i \in U$ that are correctly labeled plus the number of images $i \notin U$ that are not correctly labeled. If c is at least some threshold value τ, password recovery succeeds.

An image i is counted in c with probability p_i if $i \in U$ and with probability $1-n_i$ if $i \notin U$. For a user who is primed on U, c has mean $\mu = \sum_{i\in U} p_i + \sum_{i\notin U}(1-n_i)$ and standard deviation $\sigma = \sqrt{\sum_{i\in U} p_i(1-p_i) + \sum_{i\notin U} n_i(1-n_i)} \leq \sqrt{t}/2$.

The expectation of μ over all users, that is, over random choices of U, is equal to $\hat{\mu} = Exp[\mu] = \sum_i (p_i+1-n_i)/2 \geq t(1+\alpha)/2$. We may rewrite $\mu = \sum_i X_i(1-n_i)+(1-X_i)p_i$, where $X_i = 0$ for $i \in U$ and $X_i = 1$ for $i \notin U$. Since half of the images i have $X_i = 1$, we may approximate (for large enough t) μ as a sum of weighted binomial distributions by taking X_i to be a binary uniformly distributed random variable. Since $X_i(1-n_i) + (1-X_i)p_i$ has standard deviation $(1-n_i-p_i)/2$, μ has standard deviation $\hat{\sigma} = \sqrt{Exp[\mu^2] - Exp[\mu]^2} \approx \sqrt{\sum_i (1-n_i-p_i)^2}/2 \leq \sqrt{t}/2$.

Taken over all users, value c has mean μ and standard deviation $\sigma \leq \sqrt{t}/2$, where μ is distributed with mean $\hat{\mu} \geq t(1+\alpha)/2$ and standard deviation $\hat{\sigma} \leq \sqrt{t}/2$. By combining both distributions, we obtain that taken over all users, c has mean $\hat{\mu} \geq t(1+\alpha)/2$ and standard deviation $\sqrt{\hat{\sigma}^2+\sigma^2} \leq \sqrt{t}/\sqrt{2}$.

Adversarial Strategy: We now look at the optimal adversarial strategy given the strong assumption that an adversary knows the value of p_i and n_i for each image i, as well as the correct label for that image. The adversary then attempts to maximize his probability of password recovery without knowledge of the set U on which the user was primed. Without knowing U, his best strategy is to label each image correctly with probability $1/2$. The value c computed for the adversary then will have a binomial distribution with mean $t/2$ and standard deviation $\sqrt{t}/2$.

Suppose that an adversary is allowed to recover a user's password with probability at most 0.5% (false positive rate). This implies a threshold $\tau = t/2 + 3\sqrt{t}/2$. For valid password recovery to succeed at least 97.5% of the time (false negative rate of 2.5%), we need $\hat{\mu} - 2\sqrt{\hat{\sigma}^2+\sigma^2} \geq t(1+\alpha)/2 - 2\sqrt{t}/\sqrt{2} \geq \tau = t/2 + 3\sqrt{t}/2$, or, $\alpha \geq 5.8/\sqrt{t}$. If we assume $\alpha = 0.5$, this implies $t \geq 135$. A user would need to attempt to label 135 images to recover their password.

USER STUDY

We performed a user study in order to investigate the viability of our system design. Our implementation draws on an image corpus created by Snodgrass, Vanderwart, and Corwin (SVC) [8, 9] consisting of 150 line drawings of familiar objects (e.g., animals, vehicles, and tools). Each line drawing has two variants: a complete image and a degraded version (see Figure 1).

Experiment: Each subject was randomly assigned 75 of the 150 images from the SVC corpus on which to be primed,[2] with image assignments randomly and evenly distributed across the set. The priming task was distributed as a spreadsheet

[2]Not all of the primed images were used in the authentication tasks.

Figure 1. Complete and fragmented line drawing pairs from the SVC corpus. From left to right: a mushroom, a sandwich, and a roller skate.

via email. Two rounds of testing were administered via a web application that participants completed in situ on their computers. Participants were invited via email to complete test 1 approximately 14 days after priming and to complete test 2 approximately 21 days after completing test 1. Due to our sample size, the fact that participants varied in their completion times after receiving invites, and the exploratory nature of this study, we combined the results from the two tests in our analysis (min = 9 days, max = 49 days, average = 26.8 days, median = 28 days). Participants' image labels were coded as either correct or incorrect based upon both the original labels provided by Snodgrass and Corwin and the priming labels provided by participants.[3]

Participants: Participants were recruited from within RSA via email and an internal message board. 103 participants completed the priming task. Of those 103, 77 participants completed the first authentication test and 69 completed the second authentication test. 38 participants returned demographic surveys. The surveyed population is 21% female (79% male) and has the following age breakdown: 21–30 (24%), 31–40 (34%), 41–50 (21%), 51–60 (16%), 61+ (5%).[4] 89% of the population are employed in a technical profession (e.g. computer engineer). 68% of the survey respondents reported English as their primary language, with the remainder reporting predominantly dialects of India and China.

RESULTS

Looking at the experimental data from all images (treating them as a single image), we find that users correctly labeled images on which they were primed 984 out of 2149 times (45.8%). Users correctly labeled 831 out of 2143 images on which they were not primed (38.8%). This means primed users label images correctly 7% more often than non-primed users ($\alpha = 0.07 \pm 0.042$ at a 95% confidence interval, approximated using a normal distribution). This suggests that a priming effect does exist, even in the presence of a large number of images with negligible priming.

Figure 2 plots points (p_i, n_i) for each image as measured by our experimental set up. Each p_i and n_i is estimated by using the labels of approximately 14 users leading to wide confidence intervals. This potentially explains why for $\approx 1/3$ of all images the measured $p_i < n_i$. For example, if in truth $p_i \approx n_i$—meaning that the image demonstrates a negligible priming effect—then estimates for p_i and n_i have a standard deviation of $\sqrt{p_i(1-p_i)}/\sqrt{14}$. For $0.2 \leq p_i \approx n_i \leq 0.8$, this standard deviation is 0.1. Thus it is not surprising that 27 of the 150 images graphed above have $p_i \leq n_i \leq p_i + 0.1$.

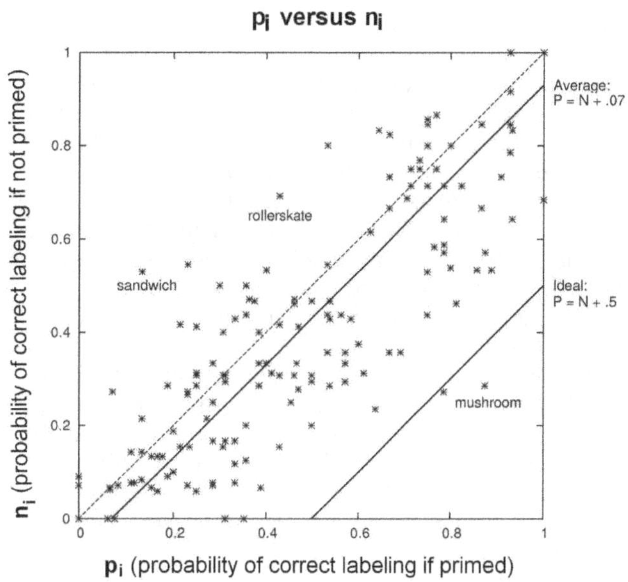

Figure 2. Priming effect as seen across all images.

As an example, Figure 1 depicts both a roller skate and a sandwich, which have a measured value $p_i < n_i$. The first was commonly mislabeled as a car, and the second as a fish. The later mislabeling can in part be attributed to cross-contamination (users who were primed on the fish).

Most of the images do show a positive priming effect, although only two images are measured to have $\alpha \geq 0.5$. Figure 1 shows one of these images (the mushroom). If 135 such images were created, then we would have a viable authentication system with a false positive rate of 0.5% and a false negative rate of 2.5%. Participants showed great variability in the amount of time that it took them to label an image; however, the median image labeling time of 3.9 seconds would result in a password recovery time of 8.8 minutes.

DISCUSSION

The results from the user study suggest that an authentication system based upon implicit memory might be viable; however, the system as implemented in the user study would take an impractical amount of time to authenticate and its images demonstrate an undesirably low priming effect (α). The viability of the system concept is dependent upon being able to systematically identify or create images with a sufficiently strong priming effect.

System Strengths: This system concept provides some usability and security improvements over current password,

[3]While some accommodations were made for mispellings, superlabels (e.g. "peregrine falcon" for "falcon"), and additional adjectives, codings were relatively literal comparisons. An actual implementation could use spell-checking (e.g. edit distance), synonyms, or adapt a database over time based on inputted labels.

[4]Due to an error, the actual survey listed 21–30, 30–40, 40–50, 50–60, and 60+.

life-question, or image-based alternatives. The usability advantage is fairly obvious: by not requiring the user to explicitly remember facts or passwords, the system removes a cognitive burden from the authentication process. Unless a user selects a random password (or creates a random answer to a question), it is difficult to accurately analyze or arbitrarily set the security of current authentication systems. In contrast, the core of our system consists of an arbitrarily set secret: the primed images assigned to the user. The entropy provided by this secret can be calculated and tuned according to the requirements of a particular system deployment.

System Weaknesses: The main problem with the current system design—and a strong obstacle to its being used in practice—is that effectively only one bit of entropy can be extracted per each image provided to the user at authentication. Since the priming effect is not overwhelmingly strong, it is necessary to show users a number of images before being able to authenticate them. As a result, this concept is most likely only suitable in an application such as password recovery, where authentication takes place seldom enough that the time required is not prohibitive. Ideally, we would want to modify the system design so that multiple bits of entropy can be extracted per image task.

CONCLUSIONS

We present the design of an authentication system that is based upon a user's implicit memory of images, which suggests the potential of an arbitrarily secure authentication scheme that does not burden the user with remembering explicit facts. We implemented a user study to perform a preliminary evaluation of such an authentication system and provide a formal evaluation of the properties of such a system. Results from the user study indicate that while such a system is plausible, there are two major obstacles to overcome before such a system could be deployed. First, the specific characteristics of images in the system's corpus affect how strongly they elicit a priming effect; a working authentication system would need a sufficient supply of complete and degraded image pairs that provide strong differentiation between primed and non-primed users. Second, the current system design only extracts one bit of entropy from every image provided to the user, which limits the amount of secret information that can be extracted from the user in a reasonable time frame. In order to produce a viable system with this concept, the design must be altered to collect additional information from the user for every displayed image.

FUTURE DIRECTIONS

There are a number of potential directions for future research relating to this system concept. One obvious goal would be to determine what image features or characteristics contribute to a strong priming effect; this information could then be used to auto-generate or select images for the authentication corpus. Crowdsourcing platforms such as Amazon's Mechanical Turk are potentially a useful mechanism for creating or collecting data on potential images, particularly for an automated degradation process.

Our current system design extracts a maximum of one bit of entropy per primed image: whether the user answers as expected (a correct label when primed or an incorrect label when unprimed) or not. Strong authentication thus requires the use of many images. Since the length of the registration and authentication tasks directly affects the usability of such a system, it would be preferable to change the system design so that more than one bit of entropy is extracted per image. One promising direction is to create multiple complete images that map to the *same* fragmented image. For example, we partition all complete images into groups of 16 images each, and for each group we map its 16 different complete images to one unique fragmented image. Priming each user on one random complete image within each group will give $\log 16 = 4$ bits of entropy per primed image.

There are also many opportunities to explore different registration and authentication tasks within the general system concept. Any task which familiarizes the user with an image set could potentially be used instead of the initial labeling task. Similarly, any task which successfully draws upon the user's implicit memory of the primed images can be used as an authentication task; while asking the user whether she recognizes an image or providing image label options via multiple choice most likely introduces too much noise into the authentication process, one might ask users to select an answer that indirectly demonstrates whether or not they can accurately identify the image (e.g., "Are you most likely to see this object in a bedroom, the kitchen, or the ocean?").

While we leverage users' visual memory in this scheme, priming and implicit memory can also be observed in other modalities (e.g. verbal, motor, and aural). An implicit-memory authentication system could potentially be built on top of one of these modalities if they show a sufficient long-term priming effect without requiring habituation.

REFERENCES

1. C. B. Cave. Very Long-Lasting Priming in Picture Naming. *Psychological Science*, 8:322–5, 1997.
2. E. Hayashi, R. Dhamija, N. Christin, and A. Perrig. Use Your Illusion: secure authentication usable anywhere. In *SOUPS '08*, 2008.
3. M. Jakobsson, E. Stolterman, S. Wetzel, and L. Yang. Love and authentication. In *CHI '08*, 2008.
4. D. B. Mitchell. Nonconscious Priming After 17 Years : Invulnerable Implicit Memory? *Psychological Science*, 17:925–9, November 2006.
5. Passfaces Corporation. Passfaces^{TM}. `http://www.realuser.com/`.
6. D. L. Schacter, C. Chiu, and K. N. Ochsner. Implicit Memory: A Selective Review. *Annu. Rev. Neurosci.*, 16:159–82, 1993.
7. S. Schechter, A. J. B. Brush, and S. Egelman. It's No Secret. Measuring the Security and Reliability of Authentication via "Secret" Questions. In *S&P '09*, 2009.
8. J. G. Snodgrass and J. Corwin. Perceptual Identification Thresholds for 150 Fragmented Pictures from the Snodgrass and Vanderwart Picture Set. *Perceptual and Motor Skills*, 67:3–36, 1988.
9. J. G. Snodgrass and M. Vanderwart. A Standardized Set of 260 Pictures: Norms for Name Agreement, Image Agreement, Familiarity, and Visual Complexity. *Journal of Experimental Psychology: Human Learning and Memory*, 6:174–215, 1980.
10. D. Weinshall and S. Kirkpatrick. Passwords you'll never forget, but can't recall. In *CHI '04*, 2004.
11. S. Wiedenbeck, J. Waters, J.-C. Birget, A. Brodskiy, and N. Memon. PassPoints: design and longitudinal evaluation of a graphical password system. *Int. J. Hum.-Comput. Stud.*, 63(1-2):102–127, 2005.

Self-reported Password Sharing Strategies

Joseph 'Jofish' Kaye
Nokia Research Center, Palo Alto
955 Page Mill Rd, Palo Alto CA 94304 USA
jofish.kaye at nokia.com

ABSTRACT
This paper contributes to the growing body of literature on privacy and security by looking at self-reported password sharing practices. 62 men and 60 women recruited through a combination of snowball sampling and small ads answered a series of open-ended questions about their password sharing strategies. One third of respondants shared their personal email password, and a quarter shared their Facebook password, both primarily with partners and close friends. Approximately 20 % of people who had work email passwords reported sharing them with colleagues. These results support understanding password sharing not as a deviant practice to be stamped out, but rather a nuanced practice engaged in with thought and care.

Author Keywords
passwords, sharing, security

ACM Classification Keywords
H.5.2 Information Interfaces and Presentation: Miscellaneous

General Terms
Design

INTRODUCTION
A recent study of Arab couples in long-distance relationships notes that most of the men interviewed knew the passwords of their girlfriends or wives, but it is unclear how culturally specific this is [1]. Similarly, I noticed a friend who used six different accounts to play Farmville, including her daughters', her husband's, and her son-in-law's. In this work I begin to characterize such practices of password sharing through a study of self-reported password-sharing habits of 126 password-users, 64 men and 62 women.

PREVIOUS WORK
Previous work on password sharing seems to generally fall into two categories. The first approach is to present password sharing as a deviant user behavior that must be stopped.

For example, Mandujano & Soto propose a system for tracking keystroke data as part of password entry to ensure that users cannot share their passwords, as the keystroke dynamics of entering a password, in addition to the characters themselves, must match the entry on record [4]. A similar attitude to limiting sharing can be found in a study of new password requirements implemented at CMU in January 2010 requiring passwords to have a minimum length, and inclusion of non-alphanumeric characters, and so on [5]. The authors report that of 470 users surveyed over a two week period soon after the new password policy was put into place, 397 had shared them with nobody and 58 (14%) reported they had shared their password with one or more people. When asked about their old password about 25% reported they had shared it with one or more people.

The second approach is to see password sharing as a tool used thoughtfully to manage the complexities of everday life. For example, Singh et al. studied of the banking practices of a wide variety of Australians, including indigenous people and people with disabilities [7]. They present the password sharing practices of their subjects as part of a set of methods for managing access, control, and distribution of money, rooted in practical realities that question the formalized approaches common in both theoretical security work in computer science and the explicit instructions provided by banks. They found that in remote Aboriginal and Torres Strait Islander communities, ATM cards and accompanying PINs are commonly shared with kin and members of a household cluster. The authors report one interviewee's description of how geographical distance results in sharing practices: "When one person goes into Thursday Island [which has the only banking facilities for miles] they [do] everybody's business and shopping" This means they have others' keycards with the PINs. 'You have to' says Sanna,'It's a matter of survival.'

Even outside of such isolated communities, the authors report (in a later study) that 43% of all Australians with a bank account share their banking passwords and PINs [6]. We see a similar approach in Inglesant & Sasse's week-long diary study of password use [2]. They looked at 32 people in two organizations, and found that password sharing, particularly passwords used for protecting shared files and shared web spaces, was extremely common. They observe that the current focus on password strength and change frequency that is common in contemporary organizational security misses the real problems, and ignores the significant costs to the user in return for an illusion of security by the organization.

METHODS

This paper presents the results of a primarily qualitative survey of 122 people, 62 men and 60 women, which asked about password sharing habits. I initially attempted to recruit people for this study through small advertisements on Facebook targeted at 18+ year old who lived in the United States, India, New Zealand, Canada, United Kingdom or Australia. This has previously proved to be a successful strategy for recruiting certain groups of subjects, but it turned out that that people were reluctant to click on advertisements that discussed passwords, perhaps, ironically, due to the very concerns about security we wished to study. Of the 443 people that clicked on the advertisement on Facebook, only around 30 actually filled out the survey. To augment these numbers, I recruited subjects by placing requests on my own personal Facebook and Twitter streams, which were in one or two cases copied by friends and placed on their personal Facebook and Twitter streams.

LIMITATIONS

By explicitly recruiting friends and family, I relinquished any claim regarding the representativeness of my subject pool. However, I realized that for people to answer these questions they needed to trust me and trust my motives. I therefor limit the quantitative analysis of this data, concentrating instead on the stories that the subjects reported about their experiences. Furthermore, this data is based on self-report rather than directly observed practices, from a potentially limited class of people. That being said, this work some insight into thoughtful practices of password sharing.

SURVEY DESIGN

The survey was designed to elucidate rich and detailed descriptions of peoples' experiences [3] with password sharing. I realized that many of our subjects would be familiar with injunctions not to share their passwords, and so wanted to reassure them that they would not be censured them for so doing, and reassure them as to our research group's intentions:

> Hi! You've probably seen the ads "Treat your password like your toothbrush: don't share it and change it often." But we think that people have good reasons for sharing passwords, and so we'd like to understand more about how and why people do it. [...]
>
> Also, we don't want to know what your passwords are. At all.

The survey then asked for their gender, age range, a description of their cultural background, and whether they were currently in a relationship or married, and, if so, for how long. We then asked a series of questions, each of the form "Who knows your [type] password?", where [type] was one of personal email, work email, Facebook, instant messaging, Amazon, eBay, smartphones, and computers. Each question had the same series of options: only me, partner/spouse, parent, son /daughter, colleague, friend, and "don't use". Each question also ended with a large text box labelled "Can you tell us more?". We then asked if there were other sites for which they shared their password, if they knew any of their friends' or families' passwords, and if they had different versions of their passwords for different sites. We asked what made them decide when it was alright to share their password, and for a case in which someone they knew had asked them for their password. Finally, we asked if there was anything else they would like to share with us.

RESULTS

Quantitative

The reported instances of sharing are summarized in Table 1, although it is hard to derive an overall picture of the practice. To produce a rough summary of the data, I added up each instance of sharing for each survey respondent to produce a single number that corresponded, in some way, to that person's willingness to share their passwords. This cannot be fully representative of a respondent's willingness to share, as it does not capture multiple instances of the same kinds of sharing. For example, someone who shared one password with their spouse and child would have a score of 2, whereas someone who shared one password with all of their friends would only have a score of 1. I tried alternate methods to summarize stories, such as counting each person with whom the password was shared, but there was simply not enough information in the responses to be able to reliably do so.

36 people reported no instances of sharing; one person reported 19 instances, many covering multiple people. On average, women described 2.75 instances of sharing (SD = 3.24), and men described 1.75 instances (SD = 2.54). I looked for effects of age on password sharing. An analysis of variance rejected the null hypothesis ($p = 0.0061$) between age groups in the men. Tukey's post-hoc analysis showed that instances of password sharing in men ages 46-49 were significantly higher than any of the age groups 13-39. There were no significant differences found in the women. Across both genders, there were marginally significant age effects ($p = 0.0547$). There were no significant effects of age on incidents of password sharing among women.

	only me	partner/ spouse	parent	son / daughter	friend	colleague	don't use
Personal Email	80	28	3	2	19	4	0
Work Email	78	10	1	1	2	17	20
Facebook	90	25	2	1	11	1	0
Instant Messaging	79	12	1	1	7	0	25
Amazon	74	19	0	1	1	0	31
eBay	64	9	2	1	3	0	48
Cellphone	24	20	6	1	6	11	67
Computer	36	19	6	4	3	14	23
Totals	525	142	21	12	52	47	214

Table 1. Reported instances of password sharing

Qualitative Results

There were a wide variety of personal stories told by survey respondents: on average they wrote a total of 318 words per survey in the free text fields. In this paper I present the results organized by the categories we used in the questionnaire, and includes sample stories for each of those categories. I include counts where possible to give an idea of scale, but reiterate that this is an analysis of self-reported free text of and so is of minimal statistical reliability.

Partners and Spouses

We saw 142 reports of people sharing their passwords with spouses and partners. Perhaps not surprisingly, having a partner had significant effect on password sharing: people in a relationship or married had on average 2.8 (SD=3.5) instances of password sharing, whereas people who weren't had on average 1.4 (SD=1.5) instances. It was most common to share email and Facebook passwords. However, this was not without nuance and care:

> I got burned early on in the sharing of passwords: my high school boyfriend had mine, we had a messy breakup, he sent a bunch of scary threatening emails and then went into the account later and deleted them. I was more careful throughout high school and college, but don't actually remember when I decided to share my passwords with my now-husband.

In the open ended responses, spouses pointed out they frequently shared bank account details and PIN codes. Some respondents pointed out that partners could guess or figure out passwords, even if they actually didn't know them.

Colleagues

Work situations produce particular demands on passwords and password sharing [2]. One respondent describes a common solution: ignoring any password limitations within a group:

> Stuff related to my work group (our group's website CMS, mailing list, shared accounts, etc.) are all shared within the group so everyone can update as needed. It's much easier than setting up individual accounts for everyone.

Others had personal passwords, but these were known within the company:

> I know my boss' password, for the same reasons he knows mine (though he forgets). We have a very small company and need to harbor no secrets from one another. We also trust one another implicitly.

This also extended to passwords for external services:

> My coworkers and I share common passwords for commercial sites we order from.

A particular case of colleagues seems to be in the sharing of passwords to academic journals and library services.

> *Are there other sites for which you share your passwords?* ...If a friend needs library access to things their library does not subscribe to I share it.

> *Do you know any of your friends' passwords?* I have access to 3 different friend's university library logins at 3 separate libraries for digital access to journals my university does not subscribe to.

> Lots of my friends have my University login details so they can access online journal articles.

Family

There were several themes in discussions of family use of passwords. One reoccurring theme was the need to remember passwords for other family members:

> *Do you know any of your friends' passwords?* my mom's, she would never remember it otherwise and i have to help her save it on new pcs, i also setup the account for her, my grandmother for the same reasons

> I know most of my parents' email passwords because I set them up!

Respondents also mentioned having shared, family-wide passwords:

> We have a standard password within my immediate family for things that don't need to be very secure, like the home wifi (the house/yard is big enough no one else can pick it up) or my mom's laptop.

People often turned to family members for temporary access to email when traveling:

> I once gave my brother my university email password because I had no email access and I needed to get a code to access my night's accommodation

Teenagers and parents negotiated password strategies:

> I know a couple of my oldest son's older passwords. I know the password for my youngest daughter's school-issued laptop. I'm deciding whether or not to demand other passwords for computers that are operated by the children still living in my house.

Finally, respondents frequently reported sharing passwords within the family for access to paid websites: Netflix (11 times), iTunes (7), but others discussed shared access to job sites (ladders.com) and travel sites (TripIt, Expedia) to avoid purchasing multiple or premium access.

Friends

Decisions to share passwords seemed to fall into two categories. We did see descriptions of temporary access to accounts to perform functions:

> Yes, I had to log into something for [a friend] recently, and she gave me her password.

However, others would share certain passwords with friends:

> Plenty of people have asked me for my Facebook profile. However, I have only given it to 3 or 4 of my close friends.

Friends would also share passwords to reduce the cost of paid sites. One young man (19-22) wrote:

> *Are there other sites for which you share your passwords?* Many Forums / Services sites , which I usually share with friends , may be some sites requires paid account so shared with friends by contributing money.

Other users gave specifics of such behaviors: one man (23-29) described a similar shared account among his friends for MegaUpload; a woman (23-29) described her friends' shared use of RapidShare. One common instance of sharing described in the open-ended responses was WiFi passwords: even people who shared no other passwords would share these with visiting friends and relatives.

Reflection

There was an impressive level of thoughtfulness and nuance exhibited by our survey respondents in their discussions of password sharing strategies in day-to-day life. Some of these expressed frustration at organizationally- imposed security measures:

> In my personal experience... people regularly share passwords... If organizations would stop making people change their passwords regularly I am sure that security would actually be enhanced. I think that the providers of digital security think that users care about it very much. But I think that users find the protective measures of many digital security providers to be over the top.

This was echoed by others:

> I pretty much never change my passwords, because I do not have the memory to handle that. If I am required to change them on some schedule, I actively attempt to work around it. Seriously, my brain is not designed for this... IT security community, FIND BETTER SOLUTIONS TO THIS PROBLEM!

Others reflected concern about the increasing complexity of password solutions.

> *Anything else?* I wish I didn't have so many passwords and that my husband didn't. If I lose my mind or he dies, I am locked out of my life. As the population ages this is a pending crisis.

Finally, it is important to recognize that not all of our respondents shared passwords, or were happy doing so:

> I refuse to use places that require frequent password changes. Since most sites have laughable security, I tend to not trust them with much.

> Sharing a work related password is a cardinal sin and I don't care if you're the CEO.

> I would not share my email or fb passwords with anyone. I can't believe people actually do it.

CONCLUSIONS

This paper paints a picture of the nuanced and careful decisions people make about what passwords to share and with whom. These stories lend support to an understanding of passwords and security that recognizes the care that many people take in their decisions to share passwords. These can reflect a sense that their decision is a morally right one that supersedes formal agreements, such as the decisions of some academics to allow others to use their passwords to access journals and academic resources. Several respondents expressed frustration at contemporary password policies, and we, and they, echo Inglesant & Sasse's call for password polices that better match human use: "Strength and Change Frequency is the *Wrong* Focus" [2].

CONCLUSIONS

Thanks to Tricia Wang for help preparing the survey, Tico Ballagas for statistical analysis, & everyone who took the time to answer the survey.

REFERENCES

1. T. G. Alsheikh. The use of Communication Technology by Arab Couples Who are in Long Distance Relationships. Master's thesis, University College London, 2009.
2. P. G. Inglesant and M. A. Sasse. The true cost of unusable password policies: password use in the wild. In *Proc. CHI 2010*, pages 383–392, 2010.
3. J. J. Kaye, M. K. Levitt, J. Nevins, J. Golden, and V. Schmidt. Communicating intimacy one bit at a time. In *Ext. Abs. CHI 2005*, pages 1529–1532, 2005.
4. S. Mandujano and R. Soto. Deterring password sharing: User authentication via fuzzy c-means clustering applied to keystroke biometric data. In *Proc. ENC'04*, pages 181–187, 2004.
5. R. Shay, S. Komanduri, P. G. Kelley, P. G. Leon, M. L. Mazurek, L. Bauer, N. Christin, and L. F. Cranor. Encountering stronger password requirements: user attitudes and behaviors. In *Proc. SOUPS 2010*, pages 1–20, 2010.
6. S. Singh. Secure shared passwords: the social and cultural centered design of banking. *J Fin. Transform.*, 23:110–114, 2008.
7. S. Singh, A. Cabraal, C. Demosthenous, G. Astbrink, and M. Furlong. Password sharing: implications for security design based on social practice. In *Proc. CHI'07*, pages 895–904, 2007.

On the Necessity of User-Friendly CAPTCHA

Christos A. Fidas and Nikolaos M. Avouris
Interactive Technologies Lab., HCI Group
Electrical and Computer Engineering Dept.
University of Patras, GR-26504, Patras, Greece
fidas@ece.upatras.gr, avouris@upatras.gr

Artemios G. Voyiatzis
Industrial Systems Institute/RC 'Athena'
Patras Science Park, GR-26504, Patras, Greece
bogart@isi.gr

ABSTRACT
A "Completely Automated Public Turing test to tell Computers and Humans Apart" (CAPTCHA) is a mechanism widely used nowadays for protection of web applications, interfaces, and services from malicious users. A questionnaire-based survey combined with a real usage scenario of a native-language CAPTCHA mechanism was conducted in order to investigate several aspects that affect end-user perceptions related to the quality of CAPTCHA. A total of 210 participants of age between 19 and 64 participated during May and July 2010. The survey results validate the common belief that CAPTCHAs are still difficult for humans to solve. They also provide insights that can be applied to improve users' experience on interacting with CAPTCHA systems.

Author Keywords
User Perceptions, CAPTCHA, Usable Security, Usability, Security, Native Language CAPTCHAs

ACM Classification Keywords
H.5.2. Information Interfaces and Presentation: User Interfaces.

General Terms
Human Factors, Design, Security

INTRODUCTION
The web has become gradually a platform for deployment of complex applications of increased interactivity. Within this highly dynamic and evolving context, security issues and concerns have shifted lately to the center of attention. Indeed, the consequences of a security breach can harm the credibility and legal liability of an organization, leading to loss of users' trust. In this context, a particularly important security concern is that malicious users or software agents try to automate the misuse of system resources having as a side effect the degradation of service quality for normal users.

Completely Automated Public Turing test to tell Computers and Humans Apart (CAPTCHA) is a type of a challenge-response test to defend against such threats. These tests try to ensure that it is a human interacting with a web system. CAPTCHA tests are commonly based on open problems of Artificial Intelligence like recognizing distorted text embedded in images. These open problems cannot yet be easily solved by computers but can be easily solved by a human [2].

Two important quality dimensions of a good CAPTCHA are its security and usability. The security level of a CAPTCHA determines its strength in resisting adversarial attacks. At the same time, a good CAPTCHA protecting a web application must also be user-friendly and transparent, aiming to minimize the added cognitive effort of a casual user interacting with the application.

Research on CAPTCHA has received lately significant attention. A lot of work focuses on the security of various CAPTCHA mechanisms, mainly on how to break and how to improve them [1,8,10,12,13]. Another direction of work focuses on evaluating widely-used implementations and proposing methods to improve their security or usability [4,5,9,14]. Lately, there is an increased interest on non-text CAPTCHA mechanisms, like audio and video [3,6,7,11]. In any case, it is acknowledged that the design of CAPTCHA mechanisms is still more an art than science [14].

The goals of this paper are to investigate the user views related to **perceptions, usage, and user preferences** related to CAPTCHA. Specifically, we investigate (i) users perceptions relating to the usability and security aspects of the CAPTCHA technology, (ii) usage statistics like frequency of solving a CAPTCHA and number of attempts needed to solve a CAPTCHA, and (iii) users experience and preferences relating to the usage of CAPTCHA consisting of characters in their native language (non-Latin alphabet) and conditions under which users would prefer it rather than a Latin-based alphabet one. To the best of our knowledge, this is among the first studies to report actual user views for CAPTCHA systems.

METHOD OF STUDY

Procedure
A survey was conducted to develop empirical evidence on the important of several quality factors relating with the usage of CAPTCHA. We formed an online questionnaire consisting of fifteen questions and statements. The

questions and statements were grouped in 4 categories: **Demographics** (gender; age group; and familiarity with computers, Internet, forum, blogs, and social networks), **CAPTCHA usage statistics** (importance of security and usability; frequency of solving a CAPTCHA; and number of attempts needed to solve a CAPTCHA), **Usage preferences of CAPTCHA** (fixed or random length and random characters or dictionary words), and **Perceptions related to the use of non-Latin CAPTCHA** (preference to Latin-based CAPTCHA; efficiency for protecting the system; perceived usability for the user; and comparison with Latin-based CAPTCHA) A five-point Likert scale was used to rank the level of importance from "Not Important" (1) up to "Most Important" (5).

The participants were recruited by using an invitation announced on the web site of the University and on social networking sites, by sending invitation through email at known mailing lists, and by lectures and invited talks at conferences and meetings. The aim of this selection process was to recruit a representative sample of participants of varying profiles and age, familiarized already with CAPTCHA challenges prior to the study. Given the subjective self-reporting character of the study, it was our intention to increase internal validity by involving rather experts and average users than novice users with respect to CAPTCHA challenges.

Initially, we asked the participants to visit a web page which entailed a short introduction about the CAPTCHA technology aiming to create a common ground among the participants relating to its usage. Next, we asked participants to solve a non-Latin CAPTCHA challenge (Figure 1). Then, we asked participants a set of questions related to the adequacy of utilizing a non-Latin CAPTCHA and their perceptions related to both drawbacks and benefits of using it. A limitation of the aforementioned self-reporting approach is that is actually measures perceptions of constructs rather than measuring them directly. The latter would be the case in a controlled experimental study which would lack ecological validity.

Demographics of Participants

A total of 210 people participated in the survey held between May and July 2010. Their age was between 19 and 64 years old. The distribution in age groups is depicted in Table 1. Males outnumbered females by 65.2%. Most people (N=192, f=91.4%) reported that they are not aware of having any kind of vision problem that hampered their effort to identify colors, shapes, or patterns.

	Male	Female	19-24	25-34	35-49	50-64
N	137	73	82	72	43	13
%	65.2	34.8	39.0	34.3	20.5	6.2

Table 1. Demographics of the sample.

Figure 1. A Latin-based CAPTCHA (left) and a native language CAPTCHA based on the Greek alphabet (right).

The participants consider themselves quite familiarized with computers (average rating 4.42 on a 5-point scale, 1 being "Very low" and 5 being "Very high"), Internet (4.47), forum (3.59), blogs (3.30), and social networks (3.36).

The participants are often exposed to CAPTCHA challenges: 65.7% once per week or more often; 33.8% once per day or more often (included); and 12% multiple times per day.

Hypotheses

The following null hypotheses were formulated for the purpose of this research: a) there is no significant difference in users' perception of the importance of security vs. usability relating to the usage of CAPTCHA, b) users consider CAPTCHA a hard problem that hampers usability and productivity, c) character distortion is the main obstacle on solving a CAPTCHA, and d) CAPTCHA containing non-Latin alphabet characters are acceptable by the users.

RESULTS AND DISCUSSION

We present and discuss the main findings of our study in the next. For our analysis, we separated users in two categories based on age: group O (adults) consisted of participants with age 25 or greater and group Y (teenagers) consisted of participants with age 24 or less. The first group contained mostly employees of some kind, while the second group consisted mostly of undergraduate students.

Security vs. usability

A common belief is that users will opt for usability when faced with the dilemma of usability versus security. We asked the participants: "*What is more important for you, security or usability?*" with possible answers "*Equally important*", "*Something else*", "*Security*", "*Usability*", and "*Depending on the system*". Nobody chose "*Something else*", which means that security and usability are the main concerns of the users. The majority of the participants take a neutral position by selecting "*Equally important*" (N=92) or "*Depending on the system*" (N=70). An interesting finding lies in answers "*Security*" (N=42) and "*Usability*" (N=6). Contrary to common belief, among participants selecting one of the two factors as most important (22.9% in total) the majority chooses "*Security*" (20%) over "*Usability*" (2.9%). A possible explanation could be that users come mainly from an academic background and are more aware of the various threats in the Internet. There is no significant association between age and the choice of the participants $x^2(3)=1.898$, $p>0.05$ or between gender and their choice $x^2(3)=8.065$, $p>0.05$. We seek to further explore and understand this rather interesting position in the future.

Number of tries needed to solve a CAPTCHA

The sample consists of users who consider themselves quite familiarized with Internet technologies and that are faced often with CAPTCHA challenges. Still, only a 48.5% reports that manages to solve a CAPTCHA challenge on first try, while the rest 51.5% require two or more tries on average. The findings indicate that users are already having a great difficulty in solving CAPTCHA challenges. There is a significant association between age and number of tries, since adults participants (Group O) are more likely to solve CAPTCHA at first try while teenager ones (Group Y) need two or more tries $x^2(1)=5.039$, $p<0.05$.

Main obstacle when solving a CAPTCHA

There are multiple techniques for hardening a CAPTCHA image, with varying difficulty. We asked participants to identify the main obstacle they face when trying to solve a CAPTCHA by choosing one of "*Character distortion*", "*Font size*", "*Font shape*", "*Character coloring*", "*Background patterns*", and "*Other, explain*" (open question). The majority of the users (61.4%) identified character distortion as the main obstacle. There is no statistically significant correlation between the two age groups, or gender, or number of tries needed to solve a CAPTCHA (grouped as "one try" and "two or more tries") with choosing either a character feature or the background as the main obstacle for solving a CAPTCHA $x^2(5)=4.528$, $x^2(5)=8.486$, $x^2(5)=3.309$, $p>0.05$ respectively. This indicates that the result is consistent across all users.

It is interesting to note that there is a significant percentage of 21.4% which considers the background patterns as the main obstacle. However, the background is known to offer little or no more additional security to a CAPTCHA, since it can be easily and automatically removed by cracking software [2]. Thus, users are exposed to a feature that hampers usability and their effort on solving CAPTCHA, which on the other hand offers little if any security value to the system. This is clearly an indication of bad design and an area for improvement of future CAPTCHAs.

A native language CAPTCHA

Finally, we tried to explore user views on solving a CAPTCHA composed by non-Latin characters. We asked participants two relevant questions. The first one was: "*Would you prefer to solve Native Language CAPTCHA challenges instead of Latin-based ones?*" with possible answers (and response percentage): "*Yes, everywhere*" (19%), "*Yes, only in Native Language content sites*" (11%), "*No, I prefer only Latin*" (18.1%), and "*No preference*" (51.9%). Again, the majority of the participants take a neutral position. Yet, there is a significant percentage (aggregate 30%) that clearly prefers Native Language CAPTCHA. A possible explanation could be that users are already having great difficulties solving Latin-based CAPTCHA and feel like a CAPTCHA in their native language would be easier to solve. This view is also supported by anecdotal evidence provided in [2]. Another interesting finding is that 18.1% of the participants prefer only Latin-based CAPTCHA challenges. These participants identified themselves as expert users in solving Latin-based CAPTCHA challenges. There is no significant correlation between the two age groups, gender, or number of tries needed to solve a CAPTCHA (grouped as one try and two or more tries) with the preference on solving Native Language CAPTCHA $x^2(5)=2.670$, $x^2(3)=3.408$, $x^2(5)=1.727$, $p>0.05$ respectively. This indicates that the result is consistent across all users.

The participants were required to use a research prototype of a Native Language CAPTCHA mechanism we developed. We asked participants to provide their early rating on "*How do you compare the Native Language CAPTCHA you solved with the other (Latin) CAPTCHA you are usually faced?*" (1="*definitely more usable*" up to 5="*definitely less usable*"). The answers (N=191, mean=2.31) indicate that users are positive to this option (definitely more usable: 31%, more usable: 20.3%) with only a small aggregate fraction of 9.7% evaluating it as less and definitely less usable. There is a significant correlation between gender and rating, since male participants rate the system higher (M=2.02, SE=0.142) than female participants (M=2.47, SE=0.090) $t(195)=2.775$, $p<0.05$. There is no significant correlation between the two age groups (M=2.19, SE=0.116) and (M=2.39, SE=0.104) respectively $t(195)=-1.234$, $p>0.05$.

In order to correlate with the previous question, we form two groups. The first group, A, consists of those participants that prefer Native Language CAPTCHA, either in every occasion or only on sites with content in their native language. The second group, B, consists of those participants that clearly prefer the Latin-based CAPTCHA. There is also a significant correlation between clearly preferring a Native Language CAPTCHA and grading positively our research prototype, since group A participants rate positively our research prototype (M=1.78, SE=0.126), while group B participants rate it more neutral (M=3.22, SE=0.183) $t(94)=-6.671$, $p<0.05$. The findings of the two last questions indicate that users consider a CAPTCHA composed of native language characters as a viable and probably usable alternative to a Latin-based one.

CONCLUSIONS AND FUTURE WORK

The findings of our study validate the common belief that CAPTCHAs are still difficult for humans to solve. We emphasize that the actual purpose of CAPTCHA existence is to protect the system and provider resources, like bandwidth and storage, or even its brand name, rather than to contribute to a positive user experience on interacting with the system.

We note that from a technology point of view, there are solutions albeit harder to implement that can achieve the same level of system resource protection. For example, rate limiting techniques (e.g., limiting the number of connections or queries per second or per IP address or both) can protect both a system and its users while not obligating the users to solve CAPTCHA challenges.

A second conclusion concerns the usability of the CAPTCHA mechanisms. Every other participant in our study needs on average two or more tries to solve one CAPTCHA challenge. This is even more worrying since study participants are challenged with CAPTCHA multiple times per week and consider themselves quite familiar with blogs and forums. These are the places where usually CAPTCHAs are installed. A user comment was: "*[...] if my post is not that important, I give up trying to post my [blog] comments if I don't solve CAPTCHA on first try*". This signifies that the usability problems caused by CAPTCHA can be deeper than a temporal user distraction and should be further examined.

A third conclusion relates to the background patterns found in CAPTCHA. It is known that these patterns offer little or no additional security to a CAPTCHA mechanism. Yet, one out of five participants ranks the background patterns as the main obstacle for solving a CAPTCHA. Clearly, this is an area of improvement and future CAPTCHA designs should not insert such patterns.

Our research underpins that the use of a native language CAPTCHA is a viable alternative, especially for users who are not proficient with English and the Latin alphabet. Also, in cases when they are using a web application in their native language. This is further supported by the fact that from a web design point of view, it is preferable to have a uniform presentation, including the actual site content and the CAPTCHA challenge. The native language CAPTCHA used in this study was based on the Greek alphabet and we plan to further explore and compare these findings with other native language mechanisms and participants aiming to increase external validity of the study.

Finally, from a usability point of view, our findings raise the question whether CAPTCHA mechanisms are still an acceptable trade-off solution between security and usability or whether we should work, in the short term, towards more user friendly CAPTCHAs and, in the long term, towards more sophisticated solutions.

REFERENCES

1. A. El Ahmad, J. Yan, and L. Marshall. The Robustness of a New CAPTCHA. In *Proc. of the Third European Workshop on System Security (EUROSEC '10)*. ACM, New York, NY, USA, 36-41.
2. L. von Ahn, M. Blum, and J. Langford. Telling humans and computers apart automatically. *Commun. ACM* 47, 2 (February 2004), 56-60.
3. S. Bohr, A. Shome, and J. Simon. Improving auditory CAPTCHA security. ISR Tech. rep., University of Maryland, College Park, MD 2008.
4. R. Chow, P. Gollé, M. Jakobsson, X. Wang, and L. Wang. Making CAPTCHAs clickable. In *Proc. of the 9th workshop on Mobile computing systems and applications* (HotMobile '08). ACM, New York, NY, USA, 91-94.
5. C.J. Hernandez-Castro and A. Ribagorda. Pitfalls in CAPTCHA design and implementation: The Math CAPTCHA, a case study. *Computers & Security*, 29, 1 (2010), 141–157.
6. J. Holman, J. Lazar, J. Feng, and J. d'Arcy. Developing Usable CAPTCHAs for Blind Users. In *Proc. of the 9th SIGACCESS conference on Computers and Accessibility* (Assets '07). ACM, New York, NY, USA, 245-246.
7. K.A. Kluever and R. Zanibbi. Balancing usability and security in a video CAPTCHA. In *Proc. of the 5th Symposium on Usable Privacy and Security* (SOUPS '09). ACM, New York, NY, USA, Article 14 , 11 pages.
8. S. Li, S.A.H. Shah, M.A.U. Khan, S.A. Khayam, A.-R. Sadeghi, and R. Schmitz. Breaking e-Banking CAPTCHAs. In *Proc. of 26th Annual Computer Security Applications Conference (ACSAC 2010)*, Austin, Texas, USA, December 6-10, 2010, 171-180.
9. M. Motoyama, K. Levchenko, C. Kanich, D. McCoy, G.M. Voelker, and S. Savage. Re: CAPTCHAs-Understanding CAPTCHA-solving services in an economic context. In *Proc. of the 19th USENIX Security Symposium*, USENIX Association, 435-462.
10. B. Pinkas and T. Sander. Securing Passwords Against Dictionary Attacks. In *Proc. of the 9th ACM conference on Computer and communications security* (CCS '02), ACM, New York, NY, USA, 161-170.
11. J. Tam, J. Simsa, S. Hyde, and L. Von Ahn. Breaking Audio CAPTCHAs. In *Proc. of the 22nd Annual Conference on Neural Information Processing Systems 2008*, MIT Press, 1625-1632.
12. J. Yan and A.S. El Ahmad. Breaking Visual CAPTCHAs with Naïve Pattern Recognition Algorithms. In *Proc. of. ACSAC 2007.* IEEE Computer Society, 279-291.
13. J. Yan and A.S. El Ahmad. The Robustness of CAPTCHAs: A Security Engineering Perspective. Newcastle Univ. Tech. rep. CS-TR-1180, Nov. 2009.
14. J. Yan and A.S. El Ahmad. Usability of CAPTCHAs or usability issues in CAPTCHA design. In Proc. of SOUPS '08. ACM, New York, NY, USA, 44-52.

A Diary Study of Password Usage in Daily Life

Eiji Hayashi
ehayashi@cs.cmu.edu

Jason I. Hong
jasonh@cs.cmu.edu

Carnegie Mellon University
5000 Forbes, Pittsburgh, PA 15213, USA

ABSTRACT
While past work has examined password usage on a specific computer, web site, or organization, there is little work examining overall password usage in daily life. Through a diary study, we examine all usage of passwords, and offer some new findings based on quantitative analyses regarding how often people log in, where they log in, and how frequently people use foreign computers. Our analysis also confirms or updates existing statistics about password usage patterns. We also discuss some implications for design as well as security education.

Author Keywords
Password, User Authentication, Diary Study

ACM Classification Keywords
H.5.2 Information Interfaces and Presentation: Miscellaneous

General Terms
Human Factors, Security

INTRODUCTION
Text-based passwords are the most commonly used authentication system today. There have been multiple studies investigating password usage, including people's selection of passwords [8], strength and memorability of user chosen passwords [9,11,12], and the number of passwords and accounts users have [3,4]. There are also studies investigating password usage in companies [5], as well as the effects of password policies on users' practices [6]. However, a relatively small amount of work [10] has investigated password usage in our daily lives.

In this paper, we present the results of a two-week diary study examining how participants used passwords in their everyday lives, spanning the entire day (as opposed to just work settings, as in [5]), as well as across all computers and services (as opposed to a single computer, as in [4]). This paper also contributes to our understanding of password usage by providing quantitative data on the number of logins and the number of accounts accessed. Finally, our analysis also includes aspects of password usage that have not been previously investigated, such as where people log into their accounts, what type of computer they used (e.g. users' computers or foreign computers), and what types of password aids they used to manage their passwords. These findings can help in the design of systems that facilitate password management.

RELATED WORK
Many studies have investigated how people use passwords. Adam and Sasse conducted a study focusing on people's attitudes towards password authentication systems. They found that if the authentication system did not mesh well with people's work practices, people tended to circumvent the authentication system, in effect undermining the security of the authentication system [1].

Inglesant and Sasse found that even if organizations enforced strict password policies on users, the policies did not guarantee security for certain attacks (such as key loggers) while also frustrating users [5]. Shay et al., through a survey of 470 students, showed that the students were annoyed when university adopted a new password policy requiring more complex passwords, but at the same time, the students felt more secure [6]. These studies imply that choosing appropriate password policies is crucial to making password authentication systems more secure and usable.

There have been other studies including password usage outside of organizations. Singh et al. conducted a qualitative study about how people shared banking passwords with spouses or significant others [7]. Gaw and Felten interviewed 49 undergraduate students and found that the students had 7.8 accounts on average, with three or less passwords [3]. Florencio and Herley deployed software to more than a half million clients over three months. They observed about 25 online accounts per *client*. [4].

In this paper, we present the results of a diary study investigating in what contexts people use passwords in their daily lives, examining password usage across all computers, services, and settings. Our analysis also provides novel data, such as where people log into their accounts and how frequently they use foreign computers. Furthermore, our analysis confirms or updates some password statistics, such as the number of accounts people have.

METHOD

We provided small diaries to participants and asked them to carry the diaries throughout their day. We asked participants to record each *password event* in their diaries when they log into their accounts using desktop computers or laptops. Password events included typing passwords to log into online accounts and computers, unlocking screensavers, and logging into applications (e.g., email clients). Even if an authentication system automatically filled passwords, we instructed the participants to record the password event, as long as the participants had to click some button (e.g., login or OK). In contrast, if a system automatically logged into an account, we asked them not to record the password event since some participants would have difficulty distinguishing if they actually went through an authentication process. On the first day of the study, we asked participants to clear cookies in their browsers to log out from all of their online accounts.

At the password events, the participants recorded contexts, including the participant's location, the purpose of the password event, type of computer they were using (e.g., personal or public computer), and whether they used a password aide (e.g., a sheet of paper with a list of passwords, or a piece of software to help with passwords).

The study lasted for two weeks from July 1st, 2010. At the end of the study, we asked participants to complete a post-survey. We compensated participants $20 USD.

PARTICIPANTS

We recruited 20 participants using a university recruitment web site. Nine participants were male and 11 participants were female. The participants consisted of 12 university students, three housewives, two university staffs, two self-employed and one unemployed. Their ages ranged from 21 to 59 with a median age of 29. In the survey, we examined the participants' expertise levels by asking whether participants agree or disagree with various statements (see Table 1). In general, the participants were comfortable using computers and estimated their expertise as average. Nine participants used computers at their workplaces, 15 participants used computers at their home, and 11 participants carried around mobile computers regularly.

Table 1 Self-reported level of computer expertise (1 = strongly disagree and 5 = strongly agree). For the bottom row, one stands for novice and five stands for expert.

Sentence	Mean (SD)
I'm comfortable with using email	4.6 (0.49)
I'm comfortable with using web browsers	4.6 (0.49)
I'm comfortable with purchasing products on-line	3.8 (1.09)
I'm comfortable with configuring computers	3.3 (1.00)
How do you estimate your computer expertise?	3.1 (0.89)

ANALYSIS

We start with a descriptive analysis of the data. We collected exactly 1,500 password events. Figure 1 shows the distribution of password events per participant observed in the study period. The numbers ranged from 11 to 169 password events, with a mean of 75 (σ=35.3). The most common purpose of these events was to log into online services (75.6%), followed by to log into computers (20.3%), to use applications on computers (7.4%), and to unlock screensavers (3.3%). The small ratio of "unlocking screensavers" implied that a small number of participants were using passwords to unlock screensavers. In our post-survey, we also found that only three participants had screensavers that required passwords to be unlocked. This data may imply that people do not need the screensavers with passwords because of their work practices or environments. However, there seem to be opportunities to design better user authentication systems for screensavers to facilitate its adoption.

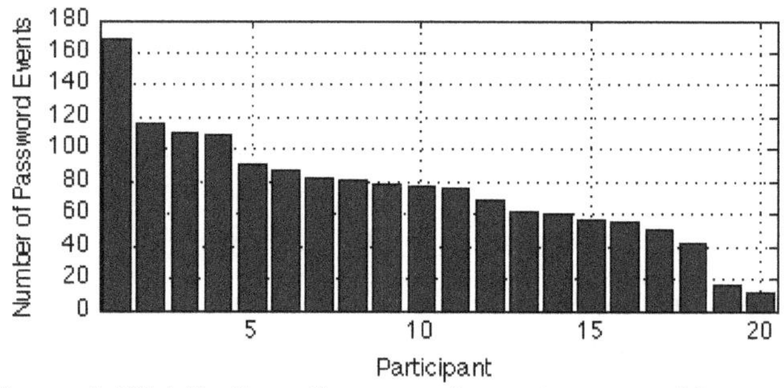

Figure 1 Distribution of password events across 20 users, sorted from most events to least. Most users accessed their accounts 40 to 110 times over a two-week study period.

ONLINE ACCOUNTS

In the study period, we observed 172 online accounts in total. The numbers ranged from 3 to 16 with a mean of 8.6 accounts (see Figure 2).

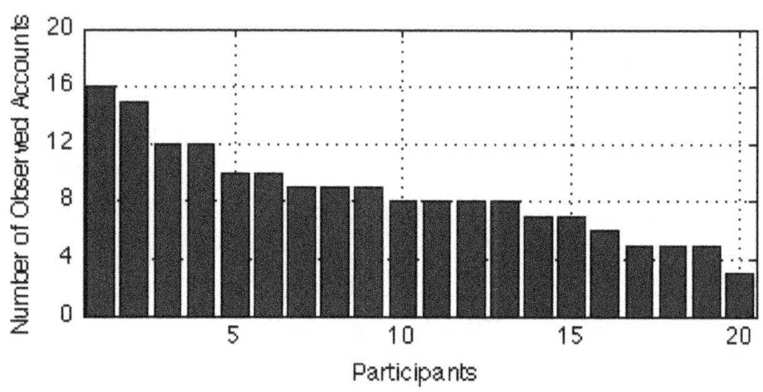

Figure 2 Distribution of the number of the observed accounts for each participant. The participants were sorted according to the number of the accounts, so this x-axis does not correspond to the x-axis in Figure 1.

Figure 3 shows the relationship between the number of days and the average number of accounts per participant observed. The dashed lines show one standard deviation. In the first two days, we observed five accounts. After that, the number steadily increased to 8.6. Florencio et al. [4] reported that it took 60 days for this number to be saturated. They also reported that they observed about 70% of the online accounts in the first 14 days. Thus, we estimated that participants had about 11.4 online accounts. This estimated number of online accounts is slightly larger than in Gaw et al.'s study conducted in 2006 (7.8 accounts per a user) [3].

One implication here is that, while password aids do need to scale for users with vastly more accounts, systems that can help people with about a dozen accounts would still be valuable. Another implication is that, for novel authentication systems, they should be tested for interference and memorability with roughly this number of accounts as an upper bound, rather than just for one (which is typically done).

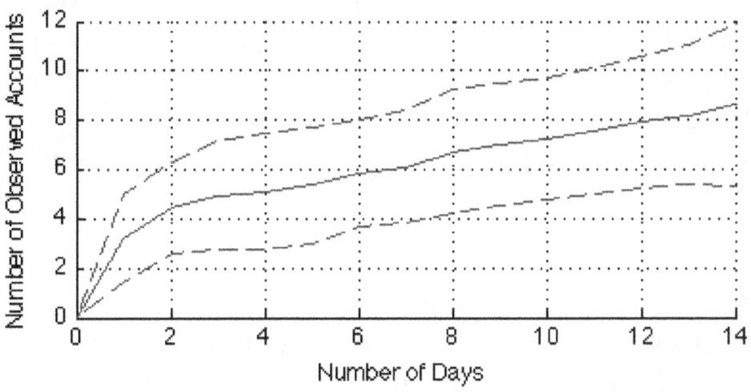

Figure 3 Cumulative number of the online accounts observed by day. The dashed lines stand for one standard deviation.

To facilitate analysis, we first categorized each account according to Google's categorization [13]. For the web sites not included in the Google's list, we manually categorized them using the same scheme. Then, we coded these categories into eight broader categories as shown in Table 2. "Email/Messaging" denotes webmail services, such as Gmail, or messaging services, such as Twitter. "Online Community" includes social networking sites or online forums. "University / Company" denotes web pages specific to universities or companies, such as online course registrations or work hour management system. "Portal" denotes pages such as MSN or Yahoo top pages. "Application" denotes online applications provided on web pages, such as Google Docs or Doodle.

Table 2. This table shows the number of accounts, number of password events, and mean number of events per account for each category. While email/messaging consisted of 19% of the accounts, it consisted of 40% of the password events.

Category	# of Events	# of Accounts	Events/Account
Email/Messaging	418 (40.4%)	33 (19.1%)	12.7
Online Community	165 (16.0%)	29 (16.7%)	5.7
University/Company	128 (12.4%)	17 (9.8%)	7.5
E-commerce	95 (9.2%)	35 (20.2%)	2.7
Portals	73 (7.1%)	10 (5.8%)	7.3
Applications	69 (6.7%)	16 (9.2%)	4.3
Finance	37 (3.6%)	14 (8.1%)	2.6
Others	49 (4.7%)	19 (11.0%)	2.6
Total	1034	173	6.0

Table 2 shows the number of password events in each category, as well as the number of accounts per category. Email and messaging had the largest number of password events, with 40% of all password events. Note that there were 33 accounts in this category, as some participants had multiple email/messaging accounts.

Email/messaging, online community, and university/ company were the three most frequently used categories, consisting of 68.4% of the total number of the password events while covering 45.6% of the accounts.

LOCATIONS AND COMPUTERS

We also asked participants to record their locations as well as the kind of computers used at password events. Table 3 shows the locations and the number of password events observed at those locations. 84.3% of the events were observed at either home or office. In contrast, only 6.9% of the events were observed in public places, such as libraries. Even if we include school as a public place, the total is 13.1%. Among the 20 participants, nine participants accessed their accounts only from home or office.

Table 3. Categorization of locations where participants accessed their accounts. 84.3% of the password events occurred either in home or office.

Place	# of Events
Home	889 (59.2%)
Office	377 (25.1%)
Public Places	104 (6.9%)
School	93 (6.2%)
Others	37 (2.4%)

Table 4. Categorization of computers that the participant used at password events. 93.9% of the time, the participant used either their personal computers or work computers.

Computer	# of Events
Personal	996 (66.4%)
Work	413 (27.5%)
Public	60 (4.0%)
Friends'	17 (0.9%)
Others	14 (0.9%)

Table 4 shows the type of computers that the participants used. We defined "personal computers" and "work computers" as computers primarily used by the participants for personal purposes or work purposes respectively. Public computers were computers that anyone can access, such as those in libraries. Friends' computers were computers owned by participants' friends.

We observe that 93.9% of password events occurred on either personal or work computers. There were 91 (5.8%) accesses from foreign computers (a public, a friend's, or other computer). Two participants accessed their accounts from foreign computers 45 times in total (accounting for half of the data) and nine participants never accessed their accounts from foreign computers. Naturally, those participants overlapped with those who accessed their accounts only from home or office.

Given that the vast majority of our participants only use their personal or work computers, and close to half of our participants do not login in public places at all, these findings suggest that if we can make the login process easier just for users' work and home computers, it can provide considerable benefit to a large number of users.

Furthermore, with the growing diffusion of location-based services, these findings suggest that we may be able to use one's current location at home or work as an additional factor in authentication. For instance, it is possible to build a screensaver that does not require a password to be unlocked when a laptop is at home or work, but would require a password or perhaps additional authentication in other places. Additionally, since many individuals access their accounts in similar contexts (e.g., the same locations, on the same computers, with the same printers and devices nearby), authentication systems could utilize these contexts to modulate the level of authentication required. These approaches could potentially improve the security of an authentication system without adding burden to users.

PASSWORD AIDS

In the post-survey, we asked participants what password aids they used to manage the accounts observed over the study period. We also asked them to self evaluate how concerned they would be if someone obtained access to that account. We missed three accounts due of lack of data in the survey. Thus, we only had 169 accounts in this analysis.

Surprisingly, Table 5 shows that for 60.3% of the accounts, participants did not use any password aids. This finding carries two implications. First, according to the survey, all participants except one reused their passwords for multiple accounts. Given that people chose not to use any passwords aids for important accounts, this suggests that people under-estimated the risk of reusing passwords compared to the risk of writing down passwords. Although we do not know which passwords were reused, (i.e., important vs. not important accounts), educating users about these risks seems prudent based on our data. Second, the low rate of adoption of password aids suggests that there is still a lot of room for helping people, and examining barriers to adoption may be a fruitful approach to improving security.

Table 5 The numbers denote the numbers of accounts in the categories. The rows denote types of password aids. The columns denote participants' self-evaluation of how concerned if someone obtains access to these account, 5 denotes *very concerned* and 1 denotes *not concerned at all*.

	5	4	3	2	1	Total
No using password aids	46	27	22	6	1	102 (60.3%)
Browsers' auto-fill features	21	5	12	10	2	50 (30.0%)
Writing down on paper	5	1	0	0	1	7 (4.1%)
Dedicated password manager	0	0	0	0	0	0 (0.0%)
Others	4	2	0	3	1	10 (5.9%)
Total	76	35	34	19	5	169

LIMITATIONS

One of the biggest limitations in our study was participants' demographics. Although our participants involved university staff and domestic residents, 60% of the participants were university students. Thus, our participants may not represent the general population.

Another limitation is that our study was based on participants' self-reports. Although we designed the diaries easy to record events to facilitate accurate reports, the participant may have under-reported.

Moreover, our study was limited to password events using computers. As other forms of computers, such as smart phones or tablet computers, people would have to use their passwords in wide variety of contexts. Further investigation would be necessary for password usages on these devices.

Finally, our study period could be short for some analyses. In the analysis of the number of accounts, the number did not saturate in the study period. Similarly, in the analysis of password aids, we may have observed larger number of infrequently used accounts, for which the participants might use different types of password aids.

CONCLUSION

Through a diary study, we collected 1,500 password events, which illustrated how participants used passwords in their everyday lives. The analyses of the data provided several implications about user authentication systems. We hope that this paper contributes to further investigation and development of user authentication systems.

ACKNOWLEDGEMENT

This research was supported by CyLab at Carnegie Mellon under grants DAAD19-02-1-0389 and W911NF-09-1-0273 from the Army Research Office.

REFERENCES

1. A. Adams, M. A. Sasse. Users are not the enemy. Comm. of the ACM (1999)
2. K.R. Walsh, B. Ives, H. Schneider. The Domino Effect of Password Reuse. Comm. of the ACM (2004)
3. S. Gaw, E. W. Felten. Password management strategies for online accounts. In Proc. of SOUPS (2006)
4. D. Florencio, C. Herley. A large-scale study of web password habits. In Proc. of WWW (2007)
5. P. Inglesant and M. A. Sasse. The true cost of unusable password policies: password use in the wild. CHI (2010)
6. R. Shay, S. Komanduri, P. G. Kelley, P.G. Leon, M. L. Mazurek, L. Bauer, N. Christin, L. F. Cranor Encountering stronger password requirements: user attitudes and behaviors. In Porc. of SOUPS (2010)
7. S. Singh, A. Cabraal, C. Demosthenous G. Astbrink M. Furlong. Password sharing: implications for security design based on social practice. In Proc. of CHI (2007)
8. E. F. Gehringer. Choosing passwords: security and human factors. In Proc. of ISTAS (2002)
9. J. Yan, A. Blackwell, R. Anderson, A. Grant. Password memorability and security: Empirical results. IEEE Security & Privacy (2004) vol. 2 (5) pp. 25-31
10. P. Dourish, E. Grinter, J. D. Flor, M. Joseph. Security in the wild: user strategies for managing security as an everyday, practical problem. Personal and Ubiquitous Computing (2004) vol. 8 (6)
11. C. Kuo, S. Romanosky, L. Cranor. Human selection of mnemonic phrase-based passwords. SOUPS (2006)
12. D. Florencio, C. Herley, B. Coskun. Do strong web passwords accomplish anything? In Proc. USENIX Hot Topics in Security (2007)
13. Google, http://google.com/adplanner/static/top1000

Understanding People and Animals: The Use of a Positioning System in Ordinary Human-Canine Interaction

Alexandra Weilenmann[i]
Department of Applied IT
University of Gothenburg
SE-412 96 Göteborg, Sweden
+46 703 032 953
alexandra.weilenmann@gu.se

Oskar Juhlin
Mobile Life @ Stockholm University
P.O. Box 1197
SE-164 26 Kista, Sweden
+46 703 793 964
oskarj@tii.se

ABSTRACT

Animals are increasingly integrated in interactive contexts depending on digital technologies. The current and future use of such technologies is a relevant topic for HCI research. However, the field is struggling with the inherent problem of 'interaction' in understanding interaction with animals. We argue for a way forward based on an ethnomethodological perspective on anthropomorphism, with a focus on manifest interaction. Drawing upon a field study of hunters' use of a GPS dog tracking-device, we discuss how interaction between dogs and humans is affected when new technology is introduced. The GPS data is situated and interpreted by the dog handler, and supports the hunter's work of dealing with the dogs' intentions. This opens up for new forms of interactions with the dog. When studying and designing for interaction between humans and animals we should move beyond merely looking at dyadic relationships, and also consider the social organization of the interaction.

Author Keywords
Dogs, human-canine interaction, GPS, mobile technology, social organization, ethnomethodology, anthropomorphism.

ACM Classification Keywords
H5.m. Information interfaces and presentation (e.g., HCI): Miscellaneous.

General Terms
Human factors.

INTRODUCTION

Digital technology is increasingly applied to support human-animal interaction, which is not so surprising given people's strong relation to pets and nature. There is a growing market for various types of digital technologies to support human-animal interaction. The commercial relevance of human-canine interaction can be seen in the many technologies marketed to dog owners. These consist of devices for *training* dogs (e.g. electric shocks to teach the dog to stay away from the sofa), *care-taking* of the dogs (e.g. remotely controlling feeding device from your laptop) as well as *surveillance* of dogs (e.g. GPS tracking of the pet's whereabouts). The social relevance is seen in such phenomenon as Dogbook, a popular Facebook application where dog owners can create profiles for their dogs.

However, the research in this area is limited, making it difficult to understand the experience of such new technologies and what to design next. Human-animal interaction is at best an emerging theme within HCI, with relatively few published studies [6;12;13;14;20]. The marginalization of this work, we suggest, might be because of a strong positioning of animals' similarities to humans, with limited theoretical articulation. We argue that the area should transcend the issue of assessing the 'appropriate' level of anthropomorphism, by applying an ethno-methodological perspective on human-animal interaction [4]. It implies that accounts of animals' mental states are seen as occurring in particular social situations for particular practical concerns. We should therefore analyze how such ordinary activities are conducted. Such investigations provide both a way of understanding how this type of activity, which includes animals, is pursued, and analytic resources informing the design of technology to support it.

In this paper we apply this approach to the case of hunting and the use of a mobile positioning technology for dogs. Technologies supporting human-animal interaction might seem like peripheral and odd, but in hunting they are already in everyday use. Dogs have long had a crucial role in the organization of many forms of hunting, and increasingly, technology has played an important role. By presenting material from a field study of how hunters use a GPS device aimed at monitoring the dogs, we show how the relationship between dogs and humans change when new technology is introduced. In order to do this, we rely upon another study of hunting, where this type of device was not used [8]. We show how the GPS allows the hunters to get a richer understanding of what the dog is doing and supports the interpretation of the dog's actions. The technology has the dual role of supporting the interaction between the dog and the hunter, and in adding to the role the dog has in the organization and experience of the hunt.

BACKGROUND

Our research is located in between the research community interested in human-animal interaction in general and a growing field of study focused on technological support for such interaction. Previous research on human-animal interaction of relevance for our study contains technical research on species-appropriate computer-mediated interaction, as well as studies on everyday interaction between humans and dogs. This research will be reviewed in the next section. After that, we outline the benefits of using an ethnomethodological perspective to understand and design for the interaction between humans and animals.

Studies of human-animal interaction

The relationship between human and non-human animals is a longstanding concern within anthropology and related disciplines [18]. Recently, Kirksey and Helmreich [9] have outlined the emergence of a multispecies ethnography, dealing with the study of "the host of organisms whose lives and deaths are linked to human social worlds" [ibid., p. 545]. Central to such approaches are to challenge distinctions between culture and nature, humans and non-humans. Haraway criticizes the common conception of human exceptionalism [5].

Within the HCI field, there are several technically oriented projects that investigate how to digitally enable interaction between humans and animals. Most of the early projects focus on establishing remote interaction over a distance, such as from a dog owner at an office to her pet at home. Mankoff et al. [13] present a paper on "supporting interspecies social awareness". They put forward a system where a remote dog owner gets notified when the animal is lying still in its bed. The owner can then remotely release tennis balls to play with the dog. The system is designed to support the dog's orientation to the humans and animals, as well as to stimulate and engage it. Similarly, Lee et al. [12] suggest a system through which a poultry owner can caress a bird remotely. The owner strokes a hen-like object equipped with touch sensors. The bird wears a jacket, which outputs the owner's strokes. Conversely, the jacket senses the movement of the bird's legs, transformed into low-level electrical currents in the user's shoes. The authors argue that this system could be useful also for interacting with dogs e.g. guiding them in rescue operations.

There are also other projects, which aims to support co-present human-animal interaction such as the serious gaming approach called "Canine amusement and training" [20]. MacGrath [14] provides an overview of technical research on these kinds of systems, which "enables a non-human to interact with a computer in a (species-specific) meaningful way." He identifies three critical research issues: designing the appropriate interaction mechanism, deciding on tasks, and the provision of translation mechanisms for inter-species communication. He concludes that the research shows that it is technically possible to design for human-animal interaction, but that the significance of the research lies in raising the questions and aims to "excite the imagination."

Here, we suggest that the issue of deciding on the appropriate approach to human-animal interaction is of specific importance. Human-animal interaction can be described as, at best, an emerging theme within HCI; related work in this area includes only a few academic publications. At worst, it can be described as a limited topic, which few researchers are taking serious. As it stands, the researchers in this field either diminishes the relevance of the area themselves [13;20] or motivate their research from an animals' right's position and pre-conceive their work as bound to be misunderstood and ridiculed [12].

We argue that both the political and the humorous approach suffer from under-articulated standpoints on the issue of anthropomorphism, that is, to what extent human characteristics should be ascribed to animal behavior. For example, the political concern in the research on "poultry internet" [12] is motivated by a critique of the mistreatment of chicken as objects of consumption. Lee et al. argue that "[p]oultry should have the same status as other pets such as cats and dogs because of their similar level of cognition and feelings". On the other hand, the humorous attempts are constructed by suggesting extended human abilities, such as authorship of research papers to animals [13]. Thus, the pun occurs through *maximizing* anthropomorphism. We argue that the area needs to articulate those anthropomorphic positions, and make them available for broader discussions within HCI.

Anthropomorphistic perspectives

When engaged in the study of human dog interaction we are facing an area where the most fundamental part of the unit of analysis, i.e. the *interaction*, is questionable. In what sense should we think about the activities we are studying as a form of interaction between the human dog handler and the dog? Already when conceptualizing something such as human-animal "interaction," we infer a form of anthropomorphism, where for example pets are thought of as being able to share our form of life. In order to interact with us, they and we must in some sense have some shared abilities and orientations.

Ethnomethodologist David Goode provides a thorough discussion on the topic in his book, "Playing with my dog Katie" [4], based on an autoethnographic account. He identifies two influential theoretical positions in this area. First, behaviorism has been a strong tradition within animal research. It sees interaction as a set of stimuli and responses, and discards any more ambitious ways of relating to animals. Goode argues that it is a theoretically guided research approach, making it difficult to account for the ubiquitous ways in which humans engage with animals. Second, symbolic interactionism argues that successful interaction depends on shared rules or mental states in order to be successful. What is at stake is the necessity of shared mental states to achieve mutual understanding, and whether that is present in human-animal interaction.

The latter idea, i.e. that dogs have mental states or psychological attributes, is referred to as "subjective anthropomorphism". The availability of such attributes is much discussed within animal science, according to Goode. In these discussions, two different errors are recurrently made. First, there is the categorical error that there are such mental states in general. Such understanding seems to be overly anthropomorphic. Second, there is the situational error of implying an incorrect attribute in a specific circumstance. To avoid the pitfalls described above, Goode adopts a perspective on anthropomorphism where "conventional interpretation of animal behavior that sensibly emerges within concrete situations of actions." In this approach, anthropomorphic accounts are seen as human representations of relevance in specific contexts. It is not necessary to know whether these attributes are correct or not in a theoretical sense. Instead, the topic is to account for interaction, as it is empirically available in concrete situations, and analyze how they are achieved as ongoing practical accomplishments including humans and animals. The ethnomethodological perspective on anthropomorphism avoids the perceived problem of whether sharing mental states with animals is actually possible. Thus, following Goode, we suggest that design oriented research on human-animal interaction should by-pass current politicization and irony by informing the research with (i) "A concern for the enacted nature of social settings": Goode argues that we should investigate members' accounts of e.g. human-dog interaction in specific situations, rather than taking such accounts as universal statements. (ii) "A respect for the indigenous": we should not preclude a priori any ontological statements on the human-canine interaction as being irrational or immoral.

In pursuing such a methodological approach, we need to recognize that there are several types of intersubjectivity that occurs between animals and humans. Goode argues that language interaction, where both the dog and the human, draw upon some form of codified or non-codified language, only account for part of the interaction. Instead the interaction depends on interpretation of non-gestural body postures. He also adds matters assumed but not communicated, or "concrete facticity", and communicated but not spoken, such as bodily gestures or exchanges.

The dependency on non-language interaction in human-animal interaction makes it important to choose methods, that give access to such communication as well as to the shared concrete facticity. Goode himself utilizes autoethnographic accounts, where he video records and analyzes his own interaction with his dog. Höök's study [6] of human-horse interaction is a recent example, within HCI, of an attempt to unpack the design-related benefits of incorporating analyses of embodied interaction into human-computer interaction. On the other hand, Laurier et al. [11] have shown how the interaction between a dog owner and a dog is publicly available for an outside observer. They suggest that we should study animals' "practical skills in the wildness of where ever it is that they inhabit", something that we have taken up on in this study.

The approach adopted in this paper, following Goode, is informed by ethnomethodology [3]. Ethnomethodology is particularly suitable for studying the relationship between animals and humans. This is because of its focus on manifest, observable actions, rather than inner, mental states. Further, ethnomethodology focuses on the analytic work of the members, making it useful when understanding how the hunters analyze, interpret and situate the GPS data. Goode argues that this approach is particularly suitable "for analyzing interaction between individuals with very different bodies and bodily potentialities" [4:12].

The aforementioned studies [4;6;11] investigate the interaction between a human-animal dyad. We expand that concern by looking at another type of activity consisting of many animals and many people. This case is described in the next section.

METHOD AND SETTING

In this paper, we focus on a particular form of human-canine interaction, i.e. that taking place during a hunt. In doing so, we are taking up the cue from previous ethnomethodological studies of how humans interact with dogs [4;11]. We have followed the dogs and their leaders during a hunt in the wild. In a previous study [8], we captured the hunting experienced through a field-study of all the different roles in the hunt. The current fieldwork focuses on the dog and its role in the hunt, as well as the interaction between the dog and the dog handler. Particularly, we investigate the ways in the dogs' role in the hunt transform with the advent of new technology.

In total, we have participated during five full days of hunting; including about eleven so-called drives. Previously we have studied all roles of the hunt, including the dog handlers, the rifles on stand and the leaders of the hunt [8]. In the current study, we focused primarily on the dog handlers' role. In both studies we have used ethnographic methods to capture the hunt, including video recordings and photography. Also, in this as in previous study, audio recordings of the radio communication have been made. We then matched the recordings with the video. This made it possible to get close to the participants' perspective, as the hunters had simultaneous access to both the local environment (as captured on video) and the remote sound environment (the radio talk as captured on audio recordings). The video clips chosen for analysis have been shown to the dog handler, enabling the discussion of analytic issues as well as clarifying misunderstandings.

In order to reveal more about the use of the GPS, the ethnographer would sometimes ask the dog handler to clarify his use of the GPS. There is particularly at one moment in our data, an instance where these instructional moments serve to reveal new information that the hunters might not have discovered otherwise. It could be argued that this disturbs the natural use of the GPS. However, we argue that of relevance here is how the positioning information, no matter on whose initiative it is accessed, is taken up and used as a resource in the interaction between the hunters and the dogs.

Figure 1: The GPS used by the dog handler studied in this paper.

The video and audio material collected in this study, was analyzed using an interaction analytic approach [7]. The data has been transcribed according to conventions in conversation analysis [17], see the appendix for details. The translations to English were made by the authors. Body movements, dogs barking, whistling and other non-verbal and verbal behavior difficult to render in writing are described within double parenthesis, and relevant events are illustrated with pictures from the video. Broadcasted radio talk is italicized.

Technology – the GPS

The device used by the dog handler we are following is a Garmin Astro. Every five seconds the dog's unit sends its position to the handheld unit (figure 1). The hunter can then see the dog's current position and a trace showing how it has moved is drawn on the map page of the GPS. The dog is represented by a small dog symbol. Shifting to another screen, there is a compass that shows the direction in which the dog is located, as well as the distance to it.

The hunter we followed, here called Ansgar, functions as a dog handler in this hunt. He has hunted together with his dog, here called Sam, for about ten years, and used a GPS for the last two years. It is important to mention that only Ansgar and one other dog handler used a GPS; all other participants in the hunt did not use this technology.

ANALYSIS

The dog is crucial to the organization of the hunt, since the dog can give the hunter information about where the prey is. Therefore, figuring out what the dog is up to is one of the most important tasks of the hunter. When looking at the material, we have been trying to pull out the resources the hunters have to make sense of what the dog is doing. In short, these resources are based on sounds and vision. The hunter relies upon what he[1] can see and hear in the close vicinity (e.g. a branch of a tree cracking behind him, a quick serendipitous movement captured in the corner of the eye), as well as sounds heard in the distance (e.g. shots or dogs barking). Besides this, there is also sound transported via radio, where other hunters share what they hear and see. So there is a complex web of sounds and visual impressions that the hunters map together to get a sense of the ongoing hunt. In fact, as was shown in our previous study, doing the work of puzzling these pieces together is a big part of the enjoyment of the hunting experience [8].

Now, with the advent of the GPS, appears a new form of information, a form of *remote vision*. It could be objected that this will take away the pleasure of the hunt, leaving no room for interpretation or need for skill on the part of the hunter. However, as we will show below, this new visual information needs to be interpreted and situated and combined with the previously existing resources. The GPS adds a new dimension but does not take away the challenge of the hunt. In the following, we will present examples of how the new GPS information provides an added resource in the hunt, and how it is interwoven with other resources.

In the analysis, we will present and discuss excerpts from one particular episode from the hunt. This sequence spans over about thirteen minutes. The reason why this particular case is chosen is that it highlights the multiplicity of ways in which the hunters are interpreting and articulating the information that the GPS provides them. This case will allow us to examine how the hunter construe of the dog's *intentions* based on the use of the GPS, and how that is used in the interaction with the dog, as well as interaction with other hunters, thereby affecting the hunt in general. Further, this case points out the *situatedness* of the GPS data; how the geographical information is used "in the wild". In order to get an understanding of what is going on in the hunt in this point in time, we begin with a short background and brief summary of the main points in this case. Then we will present the details with our analysis.

In this episode from the hunt the dog handler that we are focusing on, Ansgar, is dealing with mainly three different issues. First, he needs to figure out whether the animal that was just shot at (by another hunters) was the animal that his dog, Sam, was following. Second, he is trying to make sense of whether his dog is following a new lead, the traces of another animal, or whether the dog is backtracking, i.e. going in the same tracks as previously. Third and finally, he wants to get the dog back again, and leash it, in order to prepare for what might be a search for the presumably wounded deer that was shot in the beginning. In all these three activities he relies upon the GPS to provide him with information in various ways. This will be explored in more detail below.

[1] The hunting teams we have studied consisted of men only.

Part 1: What animal has been shot?

We begin when a shot has just been heard. It is initially unclear whether the animal has been killed or just wounded. Ansgar is trying to figure out if it was the animal that his dog, Sam, was following that was shot, or another animal.

Excerpt 1: Was it Sam's animal?

A=Ansgar, our dog handler, R= Researcher

001 R: Now there was a shot

002 A: Yes::: hhhhh

004 A: Yeah you see? ((shows GPS to R))

005 R: Yes

006 A: You see.

008 R: What is it I'm looking at

009 A: Yes: I don't know I check like if it was
010 (.) if it was shots e Sam's e: drive
011 animal that was shot

010 R: How do you see that then=

011 A: =Eh I should see that then he like
012 stops/stays there

013 R: =Yes

014 A: By the animal (.) but he's usually a
015 bit behind so ((laughs))

016 R: Right it takes some time

017 A: So it takes some time

...

018 A: It was maybe there right by the side path
019 that that it did sound like a bit far away

020 R: Yes

...

040 A: But it sounded as if it was like that so
041 (.) we'll see

042 ((Starts walking))

043 R: You mean the distance or

044 A: Yes: exactly

A shot echoes through the terrain, as commented by the researcher, and the hunter is looking at his GPS. The researcher asks for a clarification (line 8) "What is it I'm looking at". Ansgar explains that he checks if it was his dog's so called drive animal, i.e. the animal that his dog was following, that was shot. The researcher asks how he can see that on the GPS. The hunter explains that the dog stops/stays by the animal (line 11), but that the dog is usually a bit behind so it will take some time.

That means that there is a delay between the shot and the stopping of the dog. The hunter then is looking for the cessation of movement in the dog symbol representing his dog. If the symbol would stop moving, he could assume that it was his dog's animal that was shot. In this way, the GPS is used to try to answer the question that the hunter is currently struggling with (what animal has been shot?) by interpreting the dog's movement pattern as a *document* describing its motivation (following an animal) and a particular event (halting since the animal also stopped).

Summing up, here we have seen how the information that the GPS provides is used as a piece in the puzzle, trying to figure out what animal has been shot, and where that animal is located in relation to the dog. This information, that the new technology provides, is combined with other sound information (hearing the distance and the direction of the shot) as well as local knowledge of the terrain, and where the rifles at stand are located within this terrain. In order to know which animal has been shot, the hunter combines these different sources of information. In this way, the GPS adds to, rather than replaces, the interpretative material that the hunter has to work with in order to make sense of what's going on in the hunt and what the dog is doing.

While the issue dealt with in the first excerpt is still not completely resolved, a new concern arises; whether the dog has got a new trace. The dog, Sam, has returned to the hunter and then taken off again. Ansgar calls out to the rifles at stand close to where he can see that Sam is located:

Excerpt 2: That's not what Sam was hunting

A= Ansgar, our dog handler, F=Freddy rifle at stand, M= Micke, rifle at stand, X=unidentified speaker, G=Gitte, dog, S=Sam, our hunter's dog, R= Researcher.

001 A: *to the the rifles by the side path and h*
002 *the tongue then e (0.2) e .hh are the dogs*
003 *hunting still or is that animal down hh*
004 *(.) over h*

005 (4.0)

006 F: *the animal that Gitte hunted is shot but if*
007 *Sam is hunting go:d knows (.) cause he*
008 *came over and turned by me and there*
009 *hasn't been any animals here over*

010 A: *yea:h yeah there is something anyway hh*
011 *hhh*

012 R: how do you see that then

013 A: yes because he doesn't run this far without
014 having anything in front of him ((with
015 index finger, doing a quick lengthwise
016 movement from the bottom towards the top
017 of the screen))

018 (1.1)

019 M: *yeah Micke here (xxx)(.) I stand up by the*
020 *road (xxx) and shot a deer here but it*
021 *went in here (xxx) it's very dense here*
022 *(xxx)*

023 (6.1)

024 A: *yea::h that was good (.) but that's not*
025 *what Sam was hunting over*

026 (1.2)

027 M: *yea:::h (xxx)*

028 (0.9)

029 A: *okay that sorry*

030 R: but doesn't it seem to be moving now=

031 M: *=that animal came from the south*

032 X: *from Johan I think*

033 (3.1)

034 A: *°okay°*

035 (7.3) ((Dogs barking in the background))

036 A: *yeah both dogs are running around on that*
037 *old clear-felled area anyway wonder what*
038 *the hell it is (.) they are yelping after*

.hhh I take stand here so we'll see
what happens

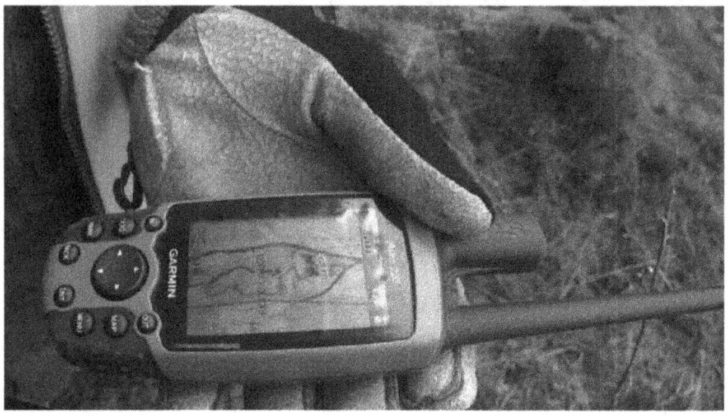

Figure 2: "Both dogs are running around on that old clear-felled area anyway wonder what the hell it is (.) they are yelping after".

Ansgar asks the rifles, over radio, if the dogs are still hunting (lines 2-3) or if the animal is down. Freddy, a rifle at stand in the area, reports that the animal is shot (not necessarily meaning that it is dead) but he does not know if the dog is hunting. He reports having seen the dog, without having seen any traces of an animal. In this way, Freddy shares his own local visual information with the dog handler over radio. We can also see that the GPS is used by the dog handler to know whom to address with questions, based on geographical proximity to the dog.

The hunter then adds to the discussion about whether the dog is hunting or not that "there is something anyway" (line 9). When asked by the researcher to clarify, he explains that the dog would not run that far without having something in front of him. In this way, the dog's movement and the distance it has run are taken to be signs that it is hunting.

Another hunter, a rifle on stand, reports in (lines 19-22), saying where he is located and that he has shot a deer. The deer has taken off, as they often do when shot. Ansgar is acknowledging this but adds that the animal that was shot was not what is dog was hunting.

Ansgar is standing still, listening to distant dog barking and watching his GPS. He notices that "both dogs are running around on that clear-felled area", "yelping", and decides to take stand. This means that Ansgar is shifting from being a dog handler to being a rifle at stand. The technology is providing him with added information about the dog's behavior, supporting this decision. He also explained, when being interviewed about this situation, that he knew that this area was well populated with deer, thus making it even more relevant to be prepared.

Part 2: Is the dog backtracking?

Excerpt 3: Sam you have already run there

A= Ansgar, our dog handler, R= Researcher.

((Dog barking heard continuously in the
background))

A: °yeah here comes Sam°

R: ° what°

A: °Sam is right down here° ((points in front
of them, into the forest))

A: °I think he has stopped°

A: >SAM SAM< ((whistles)) GOOD BOY >SAM SAM
SAM SAM< HERE I AM (.) >SAM SAM SAM SAM<
((whistles)) COME ON BOY GOOD BOY (.) HERE
I AM ((whistles))

R: when you checked last time did you see
that he was on his way back then or

A: yes

R: yeah

A: exactly but I don't know if he ((whistles))
has got something new now

((A is watching the GPS. Dog barking heard
in the background))

A: ((sighs)) yes: (.) no he goes in backtrack

A: SAM-SAM (.) YOU HAVE ALREADY RUN THERE
((laughs)) ((dog barking)) ((whistles))

R: what do you mean backtrack where he has
run before=

A: =yeah:: you see you see now he's running
exactly in the track back where he already
has been ((shows screen - see figure 3))

R: yes okay

A: eh (.) ((dog barking)) so that yes (.)
((puts down GPS)) YES: eh hh ((dog
barking, A brings GPS up again, watching
it)) eh h this is difficult (.) he
will notice that he's doing if after a
while but (.) (xxx)

In the beginning of this excerpt, Ansgar explains that he thinks that the dog has stopped hunting (line 7). This is based on the use of his GPS, as clarified in Ansgar's reply to the researcher's question (line 12.) He had seen on the GPS that the dog was on his way back, and that supported him in his decision to call on the dog. What follows then, is Ansgar trying to call his dog back. On lines 8-11 he calls out loud, and whistles, orienting to the dog. The GPS has informed Ansgar about the dog's action in a way that makes him communicate with the dog. Thus, the GPS affects the communication between dog and hunter.

The GPS is consulted again, and the hunter now makes the interpretation that the dog is "backtracking" – i.e. going in the same tracks as he has run before (line 20, see figure 3 below). This interpretation makes him call out to the dog (lines 21-22), telling the dog that he has already run there. When the researcher asks what backtracking means, Ansgar shows the screen of the GPS. The two tracks, the current track Sam is now running in, and the previous track, are now on top of each other (see figure 3). Ansgar explains that the dog is now "running exactly in the track back where he already has been" (lines 25-27).

In the next excerpt, new uncertainty is introduced. When showing the zoom feature to the researcher, the hunter notices that the dog is actually *not* going in his old tracks (see figure 4).

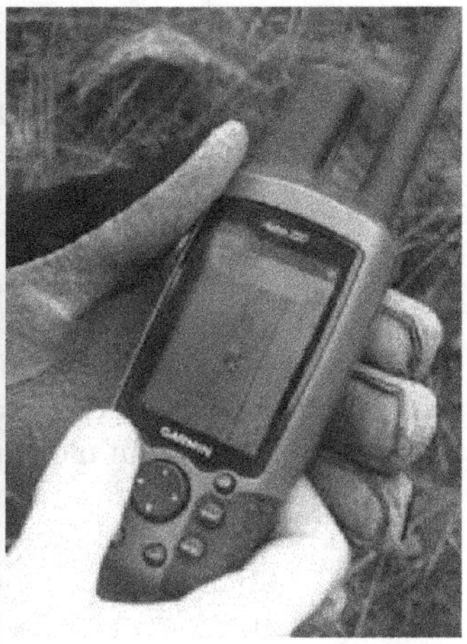

Figure 3: The hunter believes that the dog is backtracking – running in the same tracks as previously.

Figure 4: A bit later, he zooms in on the dog's tracks, and questions his previous assumption – maybe the dog is not backtracking, but instead following a new lead?

Excerpt 4: Zooming in

A= Ansgar, our dog handler, R= Researcher.

((A is standing still, watching the GPS))

A: oh stupid dog

R: shit it's slippery ((nearly falling over with video camera))

A: yes now it seems as if he got it- no okay ((sighs))

(2.0)

A: ((deep sigh)) well e: there's not much to do about this hhh

(9.6)

A: one can go and ((takes off glove with mouth)) follow the dog also if one wants (.) h ((changes to another screen on the GPS)) no (.) no it's possible to zoom in on the dog then even if he's far away he's not directly in backtrack actually but it's (.) very very similar (.) he h ((turns screen to R) isn't [it h

R: [yeah (.) if you zoom in you see that [it's not

A: [yes (.) yes but now it seems as if he's turning again (.) hope so (.) no maybe he's hunting something actually (.) what the hell could that be

In the beginning of this excerpt, the hunter is watching the GPS and says "stupid dog" (line 2). He believes that the dog is backtracking, thus not "understanding" that he is running in old tracks. Right after, the hunter displays a shift in this interpretation, based on the movement of the dog seen on the GPS ("yes now it seems as if he got it", line 5). But immediately, this is changed, again based on the dog's movements ("no okay", and a sigh, lines 5-6). The hunter expresses some frustration about the situation, sighing and saying that "there's not much to do about this" (lines 8-9).

He then explains to the observer that there is another view of the information, and zooms in on the traces from the dog. Interestingly enough, this explicative sequence results in his re-evaluation of what the dog is doing. He notices (on lines 15-17) that the dog is "not directly on backtrack" but something similar. In the previous view, zoomed out, the difference between the two tracks was not discernable. In the zoomed out view, the two traces representing the dog's movements (the previous and the current) seemed to be on top of each other. Zooming in, he notices that the traces are actually separated with a couple of meters. It then becomes an issue of how close to the previous tracks that the dog can be in order for it to be interpreted as "doing a backtrack".

Summing up, the practical concern here is whether the dog is backtracking or not. In excerpts 3 and 4, the dog handler shifts between these two interpretations of the information on the GPS. The challenge is that the GPS supports both interpretations. Further, this example shows how the dog handler is constantly revising his interpretation of the dog's actions and movements, and how the GPS supports that. It highlights the situated and accomplished character of GPS use. We have also seen how the dog's movements are interpreted by the hunter, and how those interpretations are played out in the interaction between the dog and the dog handler. In this way, the use of the GPS adds to the communicative environment made available to the dog.

Next, the leader of the hunt, Wolfgang, appears. He says that his radio is out of order, and he can only hear what the others are saying, but not talk himself. They discuss whether the dog is backtracking; note how they draw upon different locational recources to talk about the dog's movement (see also figure 5 below).

Excerpt 5: Sam was here before and turned

A= Ansgar, our dog handler, W= Wolfgang, the leader of the hunt, J=Johan, a rifle at stand.

W: eh:: there went a bastard snuck by there ((gestures into the forest))

A: yeah there was wasn't it that's probably what they are (going on about) ((points towards the dogs with the GPS))

W: yeah but eh is he going in backtracks (the dog) or ((points out in the forest))

A: he did that first I thought but now now there is something

W: otherwise it has turned ((makes a sweeping gestures with his arm into the forest, see figure 5 below)) but that seems a bit

A: ((looks at the GPS)) yeah yes but exactly because it's actually it's not precisely ((Ansgar points on the screen)) I just zoomed in and checked and it's not precisely backtrack he's sort of eh

W: but could it be the one that was shot ((points out in the forest))

A: well:: I'm hoping it's not (.) but on the other hand it's becoming ((points on the screen)) ((interrupted by radio traffic))

J: *Johan to Ansgar*

A: *Ansgar here over*

J: *now Sam is going in his old tracks*

A: noe: not not totally correct actually (.) so that's what I wonder what' it's all about

J: he was like here before and turned down towards Svarttorp when I called for Rickard

A: yes it was but I know i see but whatever but that (.) he is clearly in the vicinity i hope that he I will try to leash him then if there will be any search here later also

Figure 5: When discussing the dog's movement, the dog handler (left) is orienting to his GPS, while the leader of the hunt (right) gestures into the forest behind him.

The leader of the hunt asks whether Sam has been backtracking, and the dog handler says that Sam might be following a new lead. Ansgar explains what just happened, and also accounts for how he came to the conclusion that the dog is probably not backtracking. He refers to the GPS "I just zoomed in and checked and it's not precisely backtrack" (lines 14-17). In explaining this, he also points to the screen. Wolfgang, on the other hand, orients to the forest and the environment around them, when pointing out the movements of the deer he has just noticed and the dogs.

Another hunter, Johan, calls for Ansgar on the radio and says that Sam is going in his old tracks (line 25). Ansgar does not agree: "Not totally correct actually". The hunter insists, and also provides an account of how he came to the conclusion that the dog is backtracking - he mentions that he has seen the dog. Ansgar seems a bit hesitating "yes it was but I know I see but whatever but that he is clearly in the vicinity" (lines 31-32). For some reason, he does not provide an account of the analysis of the dog's movement; he does not refer to the GPS. Angar then says that he will leash the dog in case there will be a search. If anyone sees the dog, they shall leash it. Finally, and before moving on to the discussion, it should be noted that there is a happy ending to this: Ansgar finally finds Sam, and leashes him. The wounded animal is found and taken care of.

DISCUSSION

The detailed study of the use of positioning technologies to support collaborative hunting has implications for how new mobile technologies affect this type of leisure practices, as well as our understanding of human-animal relations in general. These issues will be discussed in the following.

Positioning technologies and the restructuring of uncertainties in hunting

We argue that the positioning system influences both the hunters practice as well as that of the dogs. First, with the advent of GPS technology, the hunters can obtain a new document of dog behaviour, i.e. the *position* of the dog as well as the history of the dog's movements, but not the *intention* of the dog. The GPS provides information about where the dog is and where it has been. It is in a sense a new window into the dog's actions, providing the hunter with a remote vision of the dog's action. We have seen how this information is used in the dog handler's analytic work trying to make sense of the dog's actions. Importantly, the intentions of the dog are still concealed for the hunter. The hunter gets more documents related to the wherabouts of the dog, but not what it is doing there or why. However, Goode [4] argues that most of the communication between canines and humans are non-language based where spatial attributes play a considerable role.

Second, the system also influences the ways in which dogs relate to the hunt. The dog's actions, visible on the GPS as well as made available through other resources, are oriented to by the dog handler as a turn in the interaction between him and the dog. Based on what the hunters see and hear they can adjust the communication with the dog. For example, the hunter calls out to the dog his interpretation, that the dog is back tracking – "you have already run there".

In all, the positioning technology does not provide such exhaustive information on the prey, or even the dogs, that it settles the discussions on what the animals are doing and where they are. Thus, the positioning technology is merely *restructuring the uncertainty* in the hunt, rather than dissolving it. This is probably a positive characteristics of the tracking system. Hunting [8] and other leisure activities [2] depend on balancing enjoyment and efficiency. Thus, the task of figuring out what the dog is doing is not a problem that should be removed from hunting. Finding out how to interpret the dogs' actions is part of the pleasure of the hunt. Getting more documents on the dogs actions seem not to ruin the hunting practice, rather the opposite.

Anthropomorphism, intentionality and human agency

We argue that it would be inappropriate to conduct research by theoretically, or politically, deciding on suitable levels of animal abilities a priori to empirical studies or design. For example Wingrave et al. [20] suggest that human-animal technologies should be designed to support the interaction between the participants symmetrically, providing interfaces to act on, both for humans and animals. However, in order to decide whether there is or is not a symmetrical relation, we need to figure out the attributes of both sides of the interfaces. Thus, we need to provide a position on the appropriate level of anthropomorhism for specific species. However, that is conceptually problematic. Therefore, we recommend avoiding design approaches that requires premature conceptions, but instead turn to approaches that open the area for investigation.

First, following Wingrave's interpretation [20], the system we studied was assymetrically designed since it only provided an interface to the hunter and not to the dog. However, from a situated perspective during the hunt, the system's influences is much less assymetrical. We have tried to show how the information is brought into the interaction between the dog handler and the dog. In various ways, the system influenced the dog handler's communication with the dog. Thus, from the perspective of the dog, it changes the way its tracking actions were supported and acted upon by the hunting organization.

Second, designing for symmetrical interaction depend on understanding the mental capabilities of animals and humans. Goode [4] argued that we could see two types of errors, i.e. *categorical* errors where we would completely misinterpret the possible mental attributes, as well as *situational* errors where the problem only had to do with what was working in a particular setting at a particular time. Again, we suggests that such preconceptualisations are premature when we have not yet understood dog handlers' ethnmethods of inquiring into this topic.

Further, we have seen how the hunters' ethnomethods of human-canine interaction draws on a multitude of contextual resources. It is not just a dyadic interaction between a dog and a human. The interaction is also informed by sound as well as interaction with other hunters. Thus, even though the GPS became much more of a topic in between the hunters, than between the dog handler and the dog, it still contributes to the overall experience of the hunt. And the dog becomes an even more central concern in their organizational endeavor. Thus, *we suggest that the design of HCI systems supporting interaction between human beings and animals, should account for complex interactions, which goes beyond dyadic relations between a person and an animal*. This is similar to the ways in which we have learnt to design for interaction that goes beyond a single person and a desktop computer, to considering computer support for various types of collaborative tasks.

We have seen how our dog handler, Ansgar, has treated the dog as a competent actor in the hunt, acting rationally upon different situations. Ansgar has claimed that the dog "will notice after some time" that he is running in his own tracks. Likewise, his statement "stupid dog", when he believed the dog to be backtracking, suggests that the dog is treated like a competent actor, who can make a mistake and do something stupid. The dog is treated as having the resources to discern the difference between backtracking and not backtracking (although failing to do so here, i.e. being stupid). However, we would not argue that the owner is taking a general stance on his dog's mental characteristics. Rather these statements are *contextually* dependent, visible in the ways that such statements are reinterpreted given new contextual cues and documents of actions. Thus, an ethnomethodological perspective on anthropomorphism reveals how 'situational errors' in understanding human dog interaction is a member's concern. In this case, the dog handler does not hold a fixed position as to what are the dog's abilities and intentions. Instead, we should see his anthropomorphic accounts as situated interpretations of relevance in the practical accomplishment of pursuing a hunt. The hunt, and the use of the GPS, is accomplished without taking stance on levels of anthropomorphism, and instead conducting an ongoing investigation of the relations to the animal along with other uncertainties. Similarly, *we argue that the research would benefit from focusing on instances of interaction, and practical accomplishments, rather than pushing particular anthropomorphical agendas.*

Our study has implications for morally or politically influenced research, as well as for the prevalent humorous and ironical style of writing. First, hunting per se is a practice which often evoke moral discussions. Here we do not take a stance on the moral appropriateness of hunting among humans or animals. It is not that we say that such moral positions are illegitimate. It is just that we argue that the research area, at this time, need to bracket such concerns, and instead attempt to formulate appropriate research agendas. Second, we have also shown how an ethnomethodological approach provides methodological tools to unpack the human-animal relation. Such a focus aligns it with other more accepted areas, such as the study of and design for work and leisure.

Figuring out the relation between humans and animals, and the way technology supports interaction between them, is as we have discussed a growing domain with its own relevance. However, understanding people and animals also have implications for broader areas of research within HCI. Here, the role of humans' anthropomorphism of personal computers per se has been a longstanding concern [16;19], and also in the attempt to design humanoid robots. The relevance to study technically mediated interaction with animals is made salient in Taylor's reformulation of how "machine intelligence" should be seen [18]. His starting point is people's ordinary ways of treating non-human things as intelligent in specific situations. He argues, along with much research in the area, that such relations occur when objects show some autonomy. Taylor further notes that the relations are engineered, and that the "intelligence" emerges in the relationships. He urges us to reflect on how assemblies of people and objects interact.

We argue that understanding technologically mediated human-animal interaction has a role to play here. This is not to say that animals and machines are the same thing, but that we can learn from the way people approach non-human "intelligence" in one area, by studying another domain. The 'assemblies' in hunting draw upon existing and historically established practices. Still, assessing the animals' abilities in the interaction is a constant concern, as well as the need to engineer the assemblies to make the interaction fit into social practices. Further, studying human-animal interaction makes it possible to understand how machine intelligence fits into wider social practices, beyond dyadic relationships between a person and e.g. a robot.

CONCLUSION

Animals are increasingly integrated in interactive contexts dependent on digital technologies. How such systems are used at present, and could be used in the future, is a relevant concern for design-oriented areas like HCI. But if we do not decide on how to handle the inherent problems in the interaction with animals, the area will struggle to expand. In this paper we have argued for a way forward based on an ethnomethodological perspective on anthropomorphism [4]. We suggest focusing on instances of interaction, rather than pushing particular anthropomorphical agendas.

By presenting material from an ethnographic study of how hunters use a new GPS device aimed at monitoring the dogs, we have shown how the relationship between dogs and humans change when new technology is introduced. The GPS allows the hunters to get a richer understanding of what the dog is doing and supports the interpretation of the dogs' actions. The technology has the dual role of supporting the interaction between the dog and hunter, and in adding to the role the dog has in the organization and experience of the hunt. When we design for interaction between humans and animals, we should consider the social organization of the activities, rather than looking primarily at dyadic relationships between one person and one animal.

APPENDIX: TRANSCRIPTION NOTATIONS

Based on Jefferson's transcript notation, as related in [1].

—	emphasis is indicated by underlining
e:hhh:	colon, indicates prolonged segment
(0.3)	a pause, timed in tenths of a second
(.)	pause shorter than one tenth of a second
Overlap []	simultaneous (overlapping) speech
-	interrupted speech
hhh	outbreath
.hh	inbreath
>what<	spoken faster
°yes°	'degree' signs enclose quieter speech
SAM	capitals are spoken louder than surrounding talk
Over	talk broadcasted on radio is italicized

ACKNOWLEDGEMENTS

We thank the hunting team; special thanks to Ottar Carlhem-Gyllensköld for negotiating access. Thanks to Gustav Lymer and to the anonymous reviewers for providing thorough and helpful comments. This research was partly made possible by a grant from the Swedish Governmental Agency for Innovation Systems to the Mobile Life VinnExcellence Center, in partnership with Ericsson, Microsoft Research, Nokia Research, TeliaSonera and the City of Stockholm.

REFERENCES

1. Atkinson, J. M., & Heritage, J. 1985. *Structures of social action: Studies in conversation analysis*. Cambridge, UK: Cambridge University Press.
2. Brown, B., & M. Chalmers. 2003. Tourism and mobile technology. In *Proc. from ECSCW* 2003: Kluwer.
3. Garfinkel, H. 1967. *Studies in Ethnomethodology*. Cambridge: Polity Press.
4. Goode, D., 2006. *Playing with my dog Katie: An ethnomethodological study of dog-human interaction*. Purdue University Press.
5. Haraway, D. 2008. *When species meet*. University of Minnesota Press.
6. Höök, K. 2010. Transferring qualities from horseback riding to design. In *Proc. of NordiCHI* 2010, Iceland.
7. Jordan, B., & Henderson, A. 1995. Interaction analysis: foundations and practice. *The Journal of the Learning Sciences*, 4, 1, 39-103.
8. Juhlin, O. & Weilenmann, A. 2008. Hunting for fun: solitude and attentiveness in collaboration. In *Proc. CSCW '08*. ACM, New York, NY, USA, 57-66.
9. Kirksey, S.E. & Helmreich, S. 2010. The Emergence of Multispecies Ethnography. *Cultural Anthropology*, 25 (4): 545-576.
10. Laurier, E. & B. Brown, 2008. Rotating maps and users: praxiological aspects of alignment and orientation. *Trans inst British Geographers*, 33 (201-21).
11. Laurier, E., Maze, R. & Lundin, J. 2006 Putting the dog back in the park: animal and human mind-in-action, *Mind, Culture & Activity*, 13, 2-24
12. Lee, S. P. Cheok A. D., James T. K. S. 2006. A mobile pet wearable computer and mixed reality system for human-poultry interaction through the internet. In *Personal and Ubiquitous Computing,* 10: 301-317
13. Mankoff, D. Dey, A., Mankoff J. et al. 2005. Supporting interspecies social awareness: using peripheral displays for distributed pack awareness. In *Proc. of UIST '05.*
14. McGrath, R. E. 2009. Species-appropriate computer mediated interaction. In *Proc. of CHI '09*, Boston, USA.
15. Mitchell, R., Thompson, S. & Miles, L. (eds.) 1997 *Anthropomorphism, Anecdotes, and Animals*. New York
16. Nass, C., Steuer, J. & Tauber E., 1994. Computers are social actors. In *Proc. CHI'94.*
17. Sacks, H., 1992/1995 *Lectures on Conversation*. Ed. G. Jefferson, Oxford: Blackwell.
18. Taylor, A.S. 2009. Machine intelligence. In *Proc. of* CHI '09. ACM, New York, 2109-2118.
19. Turkle, S. 1984. *The second self: computers and the human spirit*, Simon & Schuster, Inc., New York, NY,
20. Wingrave, C. A., Rose, J., Langston, T., & LaViola, J. J. 2010. Early explorations of CAT: canine amusement and training. In *Proc. of CHI EA '10*. ACM, New York.

[1] In reverse alphabetical order. The research was carried out while the first author was a VINNMER fellow at Mobile Life Centre.

Communication Technology for Human-Dog Interaction: Exploration of Dog Owners' Experiences and Expectations

Mikko Paldanius[1], Tuula Kärkkäinen[2], Kaisa Väänänen-Vainio-Mattila[2], Oskar Juhlin[3], Jonna Häkkilä[1]

Nokia Research Center[1]
Yrttipellontie 10
90230 Oulu, Finland
firstname.surname@nokia.com

Tampere University of Technology[2]
Korkeakoulunkatu 6
33720 Tampere, Finland
firstname.surname@tut.fi

Mobile Life[3]
Kistagången 16
16426 Kista, Sweden
oskarj@tii.se

ABSTRACT

Whereas communication technology to connect people has long been an integral part of our everyday lives, it has only recently expanded to offer applications for dogs and dog-owners. In this paper, we present two explorative studies to understand the experiences and expectations of dog owners for communication technology to support their interaction with dogs. These studies look at two different user groups, hunters and pet owners, charting the lessons learnt from the current technology and exploring the aspects that should be taken into account when designing future applications and services. Our findings reveal that usability problems are still the dominant issue with current applications. We also suggest key design implications which can be utilized in the development of future human-dog interaction systems.

Author Keywords

Dogs, user experience, communication technology.

ACM Classification Keywords

H5.m. Information interfaces and presentation (e.g., HCI): Miscellaneous.

General Terms

Design, human factors.

INTRODUCTION

Mobile communication technology has been used for a couple of decades for communicating between people, and more recently, for monitoring remote events or one's own health, activity and performance. Mobile technology is becoming omnipresent in all sectors of life. While the emphasis of research has been on the communication between people, trials of technology usage for interaction between people and animals are now emerging. In this paper, we investigate technology use between people and "extended family members" who are often regarded as companions, guards, or assistants–dogs.

A dog is typically an essential part of the everyday life of its owner, and in the urban world, the investment in both time and effort on it can be significant. There are an estimated 400 million dogs in the world [6] and more than 77 million pet dogs in the United States alone [1]. Despite the current economic pressures, pet-related products and service consumption seems to be growing. In 2009, approximately $45.5 billion was spent on pets in the U.S., and the basic annual expenses for a pet dog household was approximately $1000 for surgical vet visits, food and boarding kennels [1,2]. In addition, applications such as Dogbook [7], with hundreds of thousands of monthly users, and many discussion groups on the Internet have attracted lots of users seeking to share training experiences, explore nearby parks or find animal friends through social media. Technology is also slowly finding its way to the dog business, although thus far it has been limited to special target groups and rather scarce applications. Development of pet-related technology is still a new field, and many open questions remain–for instance, the technology's acceptability and the ability to design for true utility are issues that need to be considered.

In this paper, we explore dog owners' experiences with and expectations of technology intended to support the interaction between owners and their dogs. As human-dog interaction is an emerging field of study, there are no established traditions to study it. These studies take a user-research approach to the domain, where we assume the dog owners to be the users of the technology and experts in interacting with their dogs. Through two interview studies we aim to provide insight into what kind of contexts people are using–and willing to use–such technology, and what kind of features are appreciated. Thus, in addition to providing new insights to dog owners' requirements to communication technology, our contribution lies in exploring how applications should be designed for this specific domain. We conclude the paper by discussing what HCI approach would be appropriate to use when investigating human-dog interaction.

RELATED WORK

Earlier Research

Earlier HCI research on animal-human interaction or technology developed for animals has concentrated roughly on two areas–interacting with animals remotely [18,10,17],

CHI 2011, May 7–12, 2011, Vancouver, BC, Canada.

or monitoring the welfare and activities of the animal [24]. Both aspects usually have the same goal–to improve the quality of life of the animal, either by providing them stimuli they need (thereby creating a more intensive bond with their owner by providing more frequent contact), or deepening the owner's understanding of the pet. The related work includes developing a computer game where owners can interact remotely via the Internet with their pet hamsters [18], and a two-way tangible interface where a human can remotely touch a chicken wearing a special jacket by patting a chicken doll [19]. Dogs in particular are considered in studies such as one where remote control was used to throw a ball to a dog and then rewarding the dog with food [17, 10], and another where a dog played a chasing game while wearing a sensor harness [23]. In addition, in order to seek input for online and pervasive collaborative games, hunters and their dogs have been explored with an ethnographic approach [12]. Juhlin and Weilenmann found that while hunting is pursued and supported by technology, one must carefully consider where and how it is used, as task-solving and enjoyment have a fine-tuned relationship and can be either supportive or incompatible. Another loosely related area relates to robot animals and virtual pets [3,22], which already inhabit the physical and digital worlds. Although these are beyond the scope of our research, the popularity of these issues demonstrates the interest in the field of pets and technology.

Social networks are increasingly popular among pet owners wishing to share their experiments. Owners and kennels around the world are participating in pet-related discussions over the Internet. Due to the anonymous nature of pets, it is noteworthy that using a pet's identity encourages people to be more liberal in making friends than in cases where owners represent themselves [9]. After pet dog owners have shared data and their pets have become "friends" over the Internet, they may be interested in meeting other owners.

Existing Products

Our research concentrates particularly on the possibilities of communication technology. While HCI research has presented some case studies in providing game-type interaction between humans and dogs, there is already a selection of communication technology products on the market. Some Internet-based communication systems already exist: for example, with ISeePet [11], users can view the activity of their pets and feed them remotely. Webcams are also utilized for streamed pet monitoring [4]. Typically, however, off-the-shelf products relate to tracking technologies [15].

The tracking systems on the market are mainly based on Global Positioning System (GPS) navigation satellite information that is sent to the user via the Global System for Mobile Communications (GSM) network or a Very High Frequency (VHF) signal. The hardware used in hunting contains a GPS transmitter unit for the dog and a handheld GPS device that the user is carrying. The dog's GPS unit is attached to a collar or to a harness that the dog wears during the tracking. In the GSM-based systems [16,20,21] a mobile phone is used as the handheld device, and in systems using VHF there are special handheld GPS devices for this purpose [8]. GSM-based systems require a Subscriber Identity Module (SIM) in both the dog's unit and in the handheld device. VHF-based systems' maximum range is 3–10 km, depending on the surroundings. In the GSM-based systems, there is no limited operating range as long as the GSM network is available for both units. In addition, there are systems without GPS that use only radio frequency signals sent to a special hand-held receiver to show in what direction or how far away the dog is. These systems are no longer common in drive-oriented hunting, but are still used in fox hunting, for example, where dogs may go in caves underground.

POSITIONING AND OUTLINE OF OUR RESEARCH

The area of research looking at animals interacting with technology or human-animal interaction mediated by technology is relatively novel and unexplored. Moreover, the research area tends be somewhat politically slanted–on one hand, there are ethical or socio-economical aspects, such as animal rights and the animal's position and function in society, and on the other hand, building up things "for fun". The multifaceted approach within the topic can be easily recognized throughout the related work literature, where, as an example, the expression and style of [13] discussion about poultry welfare differs greatly from the lighter style of Mankoff et al. [14], where terms such as "pawticipatory" design are used and one of the authors is actually a dog.

Adopting communications technology in monitoring or interacting with dogs is still nascent–earlier work considering either narrow, specific design cases with early prototyping approach, or, with existing applications, targeting specific user groups, typically hunters or the like rather than the average pet owner. In the former case, the playful design aspect is strongly present, whereas tracking technology dominates in the latter case. In our research, we want to take pragmatic steps towards developing applications for large audiences. Moreover, we want to explore a suitable approach for designing dog-related technology for humans and, related to our goals, discuss the lessons learnt for methodological considerations.

In order to approach the problem, we organized two case studies. The first study, conducted with hunters and their dogs, concentrated on existing applications and aimed to chart the design indicators from the practices and barriers met with those. The second study focused on pet dog owners' needs and expectations for future technology and was arranged as focus groups, which included the evaluation of three concepts to facilitate the conversation.

STUDY 1 – HUNTER INTERVIEWS

Study Set-up

We conducted six semi-structured field interviews in two Finnish cities with hunters using dog-tracking systems.

Four of the interviews were conducted at the homes of the dog owners and two were held in a dog park. All of the hunters had one or more dogs and GPS trackers that they were asked to take with them to the interview (Figure 1). The interview started with charting background information about the user and the dogs they owned, and was followed by questions about the devices and services they had used. We explored the context of use with more detailed discussion about practices and asked the participants to show how the device was put on their dogs and used. The length of the interviews varied from 40 to 90 minutes. All the interviews were recorded and transcribed, and the transcriptions were analyzed qualitatively by two researchers.

Figure 1. Examples of dogs participating in the study.

Participants

Six participants (male, ages 28–67, avg. 45.5 years) were recruited via telephone with the help of their hunting club contact information on the Web. All the hunters had 2–7 years of experience using GPS tracking systems. Some of the hunters had additional radio-frequency collars (Figure 2) that had previously been used in hunting or were still for cave use. The dogs were actively used in hunting (Table 1). The participants were hunting, for example, elk, deer, rabbits, ducks and doves. The dogs played a big role in their owners' everyday lives and were also involved in many other activities, such as tracking competitions and tests for barking elk. About half of the 14 dogs were indoor dogs; the rest were kept outside in their own pounds. Only a few of the dogs could be kept unleashed when not hunting because of their strong drive orientation. Participants indicated that dogs with a strong drive orientation are not obedient after picking up the scent of game.

Sex/age	Occupation	Current Dogs
M67	Entrepreneur, pensioned	**2 Norwegian Elkhounds** Swedish Elkhound
M59	Machinist, part-time pensioned	**Finnish Spitz**
M52	Entrepreneur, Physiotherapist	**2 East Siberian Laikas**
M34	Engineer	**Beagle**
M28	Engineer	**Wire-haired Dachshund** German Pointer Bloodhound
M33	Programmer	**American Foxhound** Norwegian Elkhound Wire-haired Dachshund (Labrador) Retriever

Table 1. Hunter participants and their dogs. Dogs participating in the interviews are shown in bold in the table.

Figure 2. Radio-frequency collars for tracking.

Interview Results

Results reveal that the hunters were using the devices with their dogs mainly in the context of hunting in the fall. There were a few exceptions: e.g., when the owners released the dog free in familiar circumstances e.g. in the summer cabin or to test if the device is working properly.

Devices Used

The hunters used GSM- or VHF-based collars made by four different manufacturers. The cost of use varied and was based on the data transfer method and maps used. The advantage of a VHF-based system (Figure 3) is that it was completely free to use after purchasing. Even though the VHF system was not allowed in every country and it did not have an extremely wide operating range compared to GSM-based systems, it was arguably the most reliable and easiest to use. The missing features seemed to be a barking indicator and the ability to call to the collar, which were appreciated by the hunters using other devices. A barking indicator is a feature which detects barking and informs the user about it by visualizing it on the map or by sending a text message alert. Hunters reported that by calling to the collar they could listen and predict more accurately what is happening in a remote location.

Figure 3. Interview participant tracking his wire-haired Dachshund with a Garmin receiver.

The advantage of using a GSM-based Ultrapoint GPS tracker [21] was that it had replaceable batteries and unlimited use of maps. One participant (M33) reported that he replaced rechargeable batteries after every hunting season or even during the hunt in the forest in order to improve the device's performance. In addition, unlimited use of maps did not set any limitations to the place where the device was used, which was appreciated by several hunters. Although the application (software) was not always working properly and it was somewhat difficult to start using after a break, the Ultrapoint system was considered durable and easy to use compared to other systems. In the Pointer, Tracker and Benefon devices, maps are based on tiles. The need to purchase map tiles later on caused some confusion or worry about what might be needed in the future–though it was also known that it was not relevant if the device was used always on the same hunting grounds. The Pointer and Tracker users had quite similar user experiences to the Ultrapoint users, while Benefon suffered from slow operation, a poor display, outdated graphics on maps and a complicated user interface (according to two of the Benefon users). That is why one of the users, professionally software oriented, was developing his own application to improve the usability and to make the tracker more compatible with his own mobile phone.

Practices and preparations of use with tracking systems varied according to the device a hunter used. Some of the hunters had made their own fixes to assure the waterproofness and a good fit of the collar or harness. After putting the collar on, hunters checked the connection from their handheld device before the dog could be released. Some of the hunters also optimized the ability to get the signal as soon as possible by keeping the device on the roof of the car before putting the collar on.

To fit the collar to dogs with differences in physique, hunters made adjustments such as using a double collar to ensure a tight fit (M67, M33). The owner's phone number was also handwritten on the visible part of the collar/harness to secure that a lost dog would end up in the right place (M67, M59, M52, M34, M33). The most vulnerable features in cold and wet conditions were battery consumption and the reliability of the GPS signal/GSM network. Batteries were usually charged before every hunt. Users were hunting from 2 to 12 hours at a time, and sometimes devices were used up to 36 hours. All of the users agreed that there was no problem with their current GPS transmitter battery duration (approximately 12–36 h), but they were constantly worried about their mobile phones. Mobile phones ran out of batteries with continuous use and had frequent connection problems. The hunters using mobile phones in tracking carried at least two phones with them to secure functionality if the other phone crashed. Some of the hunters also said that they were using different mobile phones for speaking and for tracking because they did not want to be interrupted by phone calls while the tracking application was running. Answering the phone might crash the application and it would take time to start it over again.

Safety and Information Accessibility

According to the hunters, the dog's safety was strongly related to the awareness of the dog's context in real time. The most important feature was the location. Seeing live information on the map could speed up a rescue if the dog had fallen, e.g. into an icy river. Not knowing where the dog was could even lead to it being accidentally shot. The visibility–and thus safety–of the dog was improved using colorful materials such as bright orange or luminous tags in the collar or harness. A velocity indicator, a barking indicator and especially calling the collar provided useful information about what was happening in the dog's remote location, "whether the dog is barking at game or just digging an anthill" (M52). Calling to the collar and listening in particular were perceived as very useful. The dog's abnormal body temperature can also inform about overstrain and accidents.

Hunters benefitted from these systems with easier navigation, not only from knowing where the dog was, but also by having other hunting team members and their parked cars marked on the map. Data of the route was stored to the hand-held device [8,16,20] or to the Internet-mediated service [21]. In the Internet-mediated service, the hunt could be followed in real time on a PC. The data could prove useful also later on if a landowner was involved in a malicious prosecution or if a hunter wanted to make future hunting plans on the base of earlier routes, barking intensity and game behavior.

Communication Needs

The hunters were quite satisfied with the devices they were using. The number of suitable hunting dogs has also increased: "In the past good hunting dog backtracked to the owner while the long driving dog isn't nowadays necessarily bad with the help of these systems" (M33). Tracking systems are providing useful information for hunters exploring the hunt, but many of them still hoped that in the future the communication between the dog and the owner would improve. Hunters were excited about the possibility to command or guide their dogs remotely using the system, even though they wondered if that was possible. If the dog was losing the game, e.g. a rabbit, and kept on running in a small circle, it would be useful to somehow interrupt the action and send a command for it to make a bigger drive. The hunters also had difficulties in getting their drive-oriented dogs out of the forest after the hunt. Especially when the dogs could not hear the commands from the dog handlers, there was no easy way to command them to "come back" or "return to the car" when the hunt was over. As an extra option, the hunters were inspired by the feature that would allow picture or video stream retrieval from the collar, as a view to more precise real-time information.

The use of GPS-tracking devices for other purposes was not active. A few times the device had been used to secure human safety: when someone's wife was picking berries in the forest or a child taking part in the hunt. One user had also left the transmitter in the trunk when his son borrowed the car just to test how it worked. In general, hunters had real enthusiasm for tracking systems and many of them were ready to purchase the next, "better" version of the product, although the systems are quite expensive.

Hunters who used mobile phones for dog tracking ran into daily usability issues. The reliability of the system suffered from crashing software and lost connections. In addition, some users considered user interfaces (UIs) difficult to use after a break between hunting seasons because they had forgotten how to use the system. Urgent expectations of mobile phone software and hardware development, such as the reliability of the GSM network, a bigger display, waterproofness and better battery duration were revealed.

STUDY 2 – CONCEPT CREATION AND PET OWNER FOCUS GROUPS

Use Case Concept Creation

To facilitate Study 2, we created three use-case concepts in order to encourage innovative discussion in focus groups for pet dog owners. We used the gained background knowledge from the related work and Study 1, i.e. the current tracking possibilities, the most important features according to hunters, issues related to safety, information sharing, automated data input, social media, welfare and monitoring the dog. Each concept was presented as a picture accompanied by a short story. The aim of the material was to function as a stimulus for the discussion, i.e. not to present a fully designed solution.

Concept 1: Collar Concept (Figure 4) represents a scenario where the dog is away from the owner (Juha). Even though the dog is in their summer cottage with Juha's parents, he is a little bit concerned if the dog is doing all right. Through a collar system, Juha receives real-time data about the location, body temperature, amount of barking and the collar battery data. He can also call the collar and listen, order pictures or video and explore the dog's location on a map. The concept is based on the technology hunters are currently using, but it is enhanced with extended features that were inspired by the interviews.

Figure 4. Collar concept illustration. Dog owner is receiving collar data while the dog is in a remote location.

Concept 2: Activity Diary (Figure 5) represents a service that is related to health and leisure activities with the dog. In the scenario, Maria wants to secure an adequate amount of exercise for her dog and herself. Activity targets can be set for the dog, for a single user or for the whole family. Activity data is stored into the diary where users and families can easily explore their exercises. Data is collected through the user's own mobile phone, and the service can be used through a mobile phone or a PC. Some of the hunters were eager to save route and barking information in order to learn from their hunting activity, but also just for fun. In this concept users also share their information with their family, as some of the hunters do with their friends during a hunt.

Figure 5. Activity diary illustration. Data collected via a mobile device is used in family exercise diary on the Web.

Concept 3: Dog Blog Concept (Figure 6) presents a scenario where Tanja is away from home for quite long periods. Through the remote monitoring system she can check on her dog, checking if everything is fine and playing with the dog. Through the system she has also noticed that music helps her dog to relax while unfamiliar sounds are around. The system interacts with a little collar the dog wears and automatically updates the dog's own blog on the Web. There is also a feature sending posts to the blog while registering meetings with other dog friends outside the house. Hunters reported that their dogs are usually alone in their kennels during the daytime and there is a temporary need for monitoring the dog. Here it is suggested that interaction with the dog take place through social media.

Figure 6. Dog blog illustration. Home monitoring system is detecting and updating events to the blog.

Pet Owner Focus Groups

Study Set-up

In order to explore the user needs and expectations related to the created concepts as well as expected benefits of pet-related technology, two focus groups were conducted for pet-dog owners with five and six participants. The 90-minute focus groups started with an introduction of the study and background information questionnaire followed by general discussion about participants' experience in using dog-related technology, their needs for remote communication or monitoring of their dogs, and the need for collecting records about the dog's wellbeing.

Next, the three concepts were presented to the participants one at a time, each followed by discussion including the benefits, potential usage situations and value of the concept. How the concept could be improved to better fulfill one's needs was also discussed. Finally, the participants were asked about their favorite concepts and features, as well as in which contexts they consider technology useful and in which they would not want to use it. The focus groups were recorded and the discussions were transcribed. The data was organized by the discussion topics and analyzed qualitatively by two researchers.

Focus Group Participants

The participants (see Table 2) were recruited randomly from a local group of dog owners, from the local dog park, and via Facebook. There were altogether eleven participants (5 female, 6 male, aged 18–38 years) in the focus groups, five in the first one and six in the second. Their experience with dogs varied from 6 months up to 12 years, being on average 7 years and 2 months.

Sex/age	Occupation	Current Dogs
F38	Principal designer	2 Mongrels
M34	Coastguard	2 Parson Russell Terriers
M30a	UX team manager	Rottweiler
F28	Interaction designer	Australian Shepherd, 2 Shetland Sheepdogs
M30b	Graphic designer	East Siberian Laika, Hovawart
F24	Student	2 Collies
M38	Education & program service designer	Chihuahua, Irish Red Setter
F34	Journalist, photographer	Golden Retriever
M33a	Production planner	West Highland Terrie
M18	IT mechanic	Akita
F19	Student	Akita

Table 2. Focus group participants and their dogs. Same-aged male participants are distinguished by a or b.

Focus Group Results

The focus group participants had not used any consumer electronics designed for pets in taking care of their dogs. Many of them had, however, utilized technology to ensure or check that everything is alright with the pet when they had not been around themselves. The discussion indicated that owners wanted to make their dogs comfortable when leaving them alone at home, for example, by giving them treats or by leaving the radio on. These tricks were used by the participants and were said to be common in general. In addition, some of the participants had used consumer electronics for checking how their dogs were actually doing at home alone by recording video with mobile phone (M33a) or via webcam monitoring (F38, M30a, F28). The use of such video connection was particularly related to conditions like sickness, recovery from an operation or having pups alone.

In addition to wellbeing, owners wanted to know whether the dogs bark or make noise when left alone at home. Recorded barking logs could also work as evidence for neighbors complaining about noise coming from the apartment. Video recording the dog's activities at home could be useful with the dogs that behave badly while alone. Owners who had often found rubbish and belongings torn up around their flats wished for real-time video from home on the mobile phone. In situations like this, they would have also liked to command the dog remotely or to give a warning sound to make the dog stop doing harm.

When a dog was outside in the yard, the participants wanted information about the dog's location, how fast it was moving and whether it was running away. Yet another situation in which owners said they would especially like to get information about their dog was when the dog was temporarily left in a car.

Wellbeing-Related Information

The wellbeing of the dog was a predominant theme in the discussions of both focus groups. The participants were very interested and concerned about their dogs' wellbeing and physical condition: e.g., it was perceived that the heart rate monitoring would be valuable both when away from as well as with the dog. Similarly, information about how the dog was doing in a strange place, like a dog hotel, was seen valuable for the concerned owners.

For example, when the dog was recovering from an operation, it would be beneficial for the owner to be able to remotely follow the dog's physical condition (vital functions). Some participants reported that monitoring the barking and heart rate would also be useful in general. The information would tell much about the dog's stress level, and a system notifying the owner when the dog was experiencing stress would be appreciated among dog owners–for example, when an easily scared dog was at home alone during a thunderstorm, as mentioned by two participants (F38, M38). Getting information remotely about the dog's stress level would help the owners to decide whether they should go home to calm the dog.

In addition to this remote monitoring, the stress information would in some cases also be valuable when with the dog. One participant (F34) said that her dog became anxious during car trips, and now that the dog had got old, she would have liked to see how he was doing in the car–whether the anxiety was getting worse or better. She explained that one could not reliably determine the dog's condition from his appearance, so a system indicating when there was a need for a break and if the break actually improved the dog's condition would be very useful. Furthermore, storing information would enable her to follow the dog's progress.

Information about the dog's body temperature would be valuable in cases like illness, labor, and when the dog had been left in a car. For example, one participant (F24) reported that the onset of a dog's labor could be predicted from changes in body temperature and had frequently measured it when the time was near. Technology was considered to be beneficial after labor as well, as the progress of pups is often closely followed. Several focus group participants reported that they were documenting pups' growth extensively with videos, photos and dog diaries down the line. Owners were interested, for example, in whether they are feeding the dog correctly compared to the optimal growth curve. The possibility of daily monitoring of the pups via webcam was also considered valuable.

Collar Concept

The concept was considered to suit both professional (rescue) and consumer use and to be useful while hunting or if the dog got lost. Moreover, the participants saw benefits in it also in non hunting conditions. The tracking feature would make owners feel it was safer to unleash their dogs in unfamiliar places, as it would enable finding the dog even if it ran away. Furthermore, the collar would enable recording of training data, such as measuring the real length of the dog's track in agility and comparing it to the official length of the track. Recording certain data from both master and dog would enable analysis of how different guidance techniques and the master's behavior affected the dog's behavior.

The main strengths of the concept were considered to be the alerts about the significant changes in the dog's physical condition and barking, as these would inform the owner about changes in the dog's surroundings. Furthermore, calling the collar and hearing not only barking but other sounds like squeaking would provide useful information about the dog's condition and surroundings. Participants reported that real-time data of the speed and direction would add awareness and excitement in the woods, and the video stream would enable seeing the world through the dog's eyes.

The participants wished that the collar could provide information about the dog's stress level, happiness and hunger. They wanted the charging to be as effortless as possible, e.g., done wirelessly while the dog was sleeping. Furthermore, the concept inspired the idea of the collar working as a manual for the dog keeper, providing details about necessary nutrition and care.

The main concerns the participants had related to the concept were about the reliability of the collar itself and the data connection between the collar and the mobile phone. Participants also expressed doubts about the battery life and the durability of the collar. They stated that the battery should last at least five days on average. Furthermore, the participants anticipated that they were ready to pay about €100 for such a device, but expected that in reality the collar would be too expensive for a typical pet owner compared to the value it provides.

Activity Diary

The concept was considered suitable for both individual and collective use in sports by motivating people towards more active lifestyles. The system enables users to explore their own exercise data and data between family and friends, if wanted. Health monitoring based on heart rate and body temperature could produce useful information about dogs' physical condition in many outdoor activities. It would also allow the estimation of the birth of puppies while a dog is pregnant. By monitoring the physical condition of the dog, owners could keep their dogs' heart rates in the appropriate zone and feel safe to do sports with older dogs. According to users, the true benefit appears when optimal exercise, weight and recovery could be monitored. Exercise amounts and burnt calories are strongly related to a dog's nutritional needs, too.

In discussions about design features and usability, users preferred hardware that was easy to use. Automated functions with the service, e.g. recording, were considered easy, while there was no need for extra tagging or logging during activities. Pet-dog owners hoped that recorded data would be easy to understand through simple statistics, e.g. it could produce performance summaries for activities or skills such as agility. The system should enable users to log in and support activities remotely.

Focus groups expressed that the dog's obedience indicates successful interaction. Therefore, it would be very interesting if the dog's mental agility and the owner's behavior could be monitored simultaneously. Comparing the owner's actions with the dog's reactions could provide interesting data for obedience training. In the scope of seeking the most suitable techniques for dog control, it would facilitate discussions and comparison with other dog owners about the data, too. Even though focus groups were concerned about how the dogs' mental agility could be measured or how behavior or performance could be later analyzed based on numbers, they were hopeful about the value it could generate.

Home Monitoring via Dog Blog

The increased knowledge about the dog's behavior was considered valuable in general. On the other hand, monitoring dogs at home was expected to be boring, as participants supposed that their dogs were sleeping while they are away. According to the participants who had already monitored their dogs, in the beginning it was purely interesting to see something that they had never seen before, but this novelty value faded quickly. They also acknowledged that the ability to monitor the pet might also increase concerns and related stress–e.g., owners would not be happy about seeing that their dog is bored at home.

In situations such as the dog being pregnant or recovering from surgery, the ability to check the situation at home was appreciated, as it would ease the concerns participants had about the dogs' wellbeing. Related to this, the participants would have also liked to monitor the physical condition of the dog with the service. Notifications and logs about barking would be most useful in everyday life.

One of the appreciated features of the concept was the radio/music player that some of the participants had already used in practice for calming a lonely dog. In addition to easing separation anxiety by breaking the silence, music would drown out disturbing sounds like a postman or neighbors outside. Furthermore, timer-based activities were considered useful by several participants in eliminating extra energy and frustration during the day. There were, however, also doubts whether there is really a need for such features and how well they would actually work. The participants showed little interest in the remote feeding feature.

Web sites and blogs were considered natural environments to interact with other pet owners. Discussions and information sharing in the midst of breeds, secondary production, training and dog shows are getting more and more popular on the Web. In addition, breeders and kennels are very interested in browsing-related Web sites or blogs, and being able to find one specific dog. It is also used as a marketing channel for puppies by adding puppy weight, pictures and videos. The automated identification of a dog that friends met outside was considered to be valuable in situations such as infections, as one could track the dogs one has been in contact with lately.

SUMMARY OF THE RESULTS

The two studies presented above contributed to the understanding of what kind of communication technology could be offered to dog owners. In summary, the following expectations and requirements arose from the dog owner interviews.

In Study 1, the technology used in hunting with dogs was not used in any other contexts. Thus, the considered needs and benefits of systems were quite hunting-specific, such as navigation in the forest, locating the game and the dog, and monitoring the dog's safety. The needed improvements related mainly to the basic features of the devices–the reliability of the connection (network), picture quality and need for visual information in general, and the design and mechanical robustness of the systems. Many participants made adjustments themselves for protecting the devices and fastening the collar or harness. The battery duration of the mobile phone was perceived adequate during the hunting session itself, but it was considered a real challenge for continuous tracking use. Additionally, the question of monitoring the dog and its surroundings while being away arose–either in real time by request or recording to view after returning home. Here, barking and courses of events leading to (any general) damage were examples that were anticipated to trigger the owners' interest. The participants were also interested in statistics (e.g. on barking) with a view to more efficient or better-planned hunt later on.

In Study 2, the focus was on pet dog owners. The identified needs and interest areas were tracking (primarily to find a lost dog), activity and wellbeing of the dog, remote information access, and the communication and interaction with the dog; each topic included several refined areas of interest. A prevailing theme throughout the results was the owner's genuine interest in the dog, and often the discussed areas related to relieving the owner's own concern on the topic. Moreover, the owners' wish to better understand their dogs' needs and improve and intensify communication with their dogs was evident.

DISCUSSION

In this paper, we have investigated the dogs and technology theme through two case studies, which revealed different viewpoints in the needs and expectations of dog owners. While earlier studies have provided insight through designing proof-of-concept systems or applications, we believe our approach has value in expanding the knowledge in the domain in order to develop applications and service for wider audience. In the following, we discuss the salient themes rising from our findings per se as well as in relation to existing literature.

There are clear differences between the user groups of Studies 1 and 2 with respect to both needs and behavior. Hunting is very much task- and goal-orientated; the dog is not only a companion but also a "tool". Moreover, the use of the devices happens outdoors (tracking, monitoring), whereas with pet dogs, the indoors is at least as important a domain, and most of the dog's time is typically spent there. Even though the focus group participants' expectations were not significantly changed by the concept descriptions, the presented concepts broadened their views on the possible uses of technology in relation to pets. We looked at both types of users in order to gain essential insight into the domain as a whole, because hunters are especially early adopters of new technology.

There are also similarities between the two user groups which help support the findings. They both had a dog-oriented lifestyle, requiring time and effort invested in interacting with the dog, and training dogs, for instance, was a mutual interest. Both user groups saw possibilities in the technology and perceived it could bring something extra to their interaction with their dog(s). Both user groups also utilized the Web in seeking and browsing information. Although the discussions were accompanied by the fun that a product may bring, it seemed that pragmatic needs and benefits arose as more relevant factors in considering whether a product is desirable.

Designing for Dogs or Humans

While going through the earlier research as well as designing our own studies, the question of the target group surfaced frequently. Are we designing technology for dogs or for humans? Do we concentrate on dog-human interaction, or human-computer interaction with the technology used with dogs? We recognize that the goal in many cases can be mutual, and many design aspects overlap–for instance, ensuring the physical wellbeing of the dog is clearly of interest in both respects. However, while designing products and services, the focus of the work is essential. Thus, the framing of our approach is to design for the dog owners–without of course forgetting the wellbeing of the dog.

Current Products and Services

Prior to our first study concerning the existing technology used with the dogs, we presumed that barriers and lessons learnt related especially to the dog domain would arise. However, it turned out that most of the problems were rather general issues concerning the technical reliability and basic usability and interaction design with the applications. Improvement in this area can be addressed by improving the existing product creation process and taking a more extensive user-centric design approach–e.g. testing usability with target users and in situ. As the devices are used outdoors, mechanical robustness and durability obviously play a significant role, and this should be emphasized in the design. Technology was already bringing motivation for people in certain (hunting) activities involving dogs. We consider this as a sign that other user groups, i.e. pet dog owners, could find value in it. In addition, we suggest that products giving guidance, such as proposals concerning nutrition or amount of exercise for a pet, could become essential.

Overview to the Other Application Areas

It turned out that monitor the dog's wellbeing is one of the recurring themes interesting to owners, being on level of the current activity or the dog's physiology. This domain, however, is somewhat complicated, to say the least. Reliable monitoring of health and wellbeing is not a straightforward task, and interpreting the data correctly is also something requiring deep expertise. Here, the applications would probably be for a narrow, targeted user group and use cases. Moreover, it must be noticed that most of the feedback considering dogs is gained via their owners; and whereas physical activity level is easy to detect, mental strain or issues related to herd behavior are harder to assess.

Things that You Don't Want to Automate

It was evident throughout the studies that the people have pets because they are truly interested in them. The relation between the owner and the dog is typically perceived as personal and an integral part of everyday life, as discussed in previous research [17]. It is important to notice that the owners do want to spend time with their pets and care for them, and thus the technology developed should support this rather than attempt to automate such practices. It is important that the technology supports the feeling of interacting and communicating with the dog. Many of the aspects brought up in the focus groups indicated that owners also seek relief for their consciences–e.g. when away at work for a full day, or leaving a young or sick pet alone–and technology could provide means to ease this. It is important that the owner maintains the feeling of interacting with the dog as directly as possible; this technology merely provides a gateway for that without coming between the owner and the dog.

From the ethics point of view, there are few relevant concerns such as misuse of a product or service (e.g. wiretapping) and animal rights that should be resolved. To clarify, by animal rights we mean that technology should be developed in a way which supports animals' natural behavior, and does not cause them any stress or suffering.

Social Networks and Pet-Created Content

Another aspect appearing frequently during the studies was an interest in following up on a dog's activities both online and over a long time span.

The research on utilizing technology to motivate people to be more physically active has reported how the technology should offer an engaging experience, feedback and ideally evolve by providing new content or features over time in order to motivate people to use it in the long run [5]. This may apply to technologies relating to dogs as well. The question then is how to create an engaging user experience and design applications that owners would be interested in to follow in the long run. Pet-created content may be one interesting aspect to that, and automated content creation could be easily set up, e.g. with simple cameras and sensors attached either to the environment or as a wearable accessory. The updates would appeal to the owners' desire to communicate and understand the dog more, and the popularity of blogs and status updates in social media has demonstrates that there is an interest in this technology. Even though the idea is not novel and it has been implemented earlier [24], we believe that there is room for more, and this aspect provides an interesting topic for further investigations. Here, mobile communication technology can provide a good platform.

With this type of content creation there is, however, a threat that the surprises will become scarce when the familiarity with the dog's routines takes over. Here, being connected to a social network provides interesting possibilities. Again, in the area of wellness technologies, the ability to compare one's own data to that of friends and larger groups of peers has been noticed to increase the motivation to use the application [5].

CONCLUSION

In recent years there has been increasing interest around pets and technology. In this paper we have presented two case studies on dog owners–hunters and pet owners–on exploring people's needs and expectations towards technologies for dogs in order to gain insight into how communication technologies could be utilized for large audiences of dog owners.

Our findings reveal that the issues with current systems and applications designed for special groups of dog owners (hunters) suffer mainly from basic usability problems that can be improved through applying the standard methods of user-centric design methods more intensely. However, when designing for pet owners, there are several aspects that should be taken into account. Whereas technology can ease daily pet care practices and serve a whole new channel to widen our knowledge and understanding with our pet companions, it is important to retain the feeling that the actions are not automated but the technology supports the owner in building an intense and caring relationship with the dog. The expectations of owners regarding their pets can also be rather high–e.g. in activity monitoring, the owners easily wish there actually was activities happening, or in long-term monitoring, patterns or progress. Here, applications utilizing information not only of one's own dog, but also a larger network could help in providing more content and comparative data. We aim to address the aspects of designing engaging and usable technology for dog owners in more depth in the future.

The main contribution of this paper is to create insight about users' expectations of and experiences with human-animal communication technology. Our research differs from earlier research, which considers mainly narrow proof-of-concept design cases for human-dog interaction. We have sought to chart the barriers, expectations and needs of dog owners in order to develop applications for large audiences. While our study is limited by the sample size, we believe it offers insights to researchers and practitioners working with the topic of connecting people and dogs with the help of communication technology.

REFERENCES

1. American Pet Products Association. Industry Statistics and Trends. http://americanpetproducts.org/press_industrytrends.asp (accessed August 27, 2010).
2. American Veterinary Medical Association. U.S. Pet Ownership & Demographics Sourcebook 2007. http://www.avma.org/reference/marketstats/ownership.asp (accessed August 27, 2010).
3. Bartlett, B., Estivill-Castro, V., Seymon, S. Dogs or Robots: Why Do Children See Them as Robotic Pets Rather than Canine Machines? In *Proc. AUIC'04.* 2004, 7-14.
4. Camstreams for Pets. http://www.camstreams.com/petanimalwebcams.asp (accessed January 3, 2011).
5. Consolvo, S. Everitt, K., Smith, I. and Landay, J.A. Design Requirements for Technologies that Encourage Physical Activity. In *Proc. CHI 2006*, ACM Press, 2006, 457-466.
6. Coppinger, R. Dogs: A Startling New Understanding of Canine Origin, Behavior and Evolution; Scribner, 2001. 352.
7. Dogbook. http://itunes.apple.com/fi/app/dogbook/id337322846?mt=8 (accessed August 30, 2010).
8. Garmin astro. http://www8.garmin.com/astro/ (accessed July 23, 2010).
9. Golbeck, J. On the Internet, Everybody Knows You're a Dog: The Human-Pet Relationship in Online Social Networks. *In Proc. CHI '09*, ACM, 2009, 4495-4500.
10. Hu, F., Silver, D. and Trudel, A. LonelyDog@Home, Conf. on Web Int. and Int. Agent Tech, 2007, 333-337.
11. ISeePet. http://www.ehomeupgrade.com/2004/04/24/iseepet-webcamfeeder/ (accessed July 21, 2010).
12. Juhlin, O., and Weilenmann, A. Hunting for Fun: Solitude and Attentiveness in Collaboration. *In Proc. CSCW '08*, ACM Press, 2008, 57-66.
13. Lee, P., Cheok, D., James, S., Debra, L., Jie, W., Chuang, W., and Farbiz, F. A Mobile Pet Wearable Computer and Mixed Reality System for Human–Poultry Interaction through the Internet. *Personal Ubiquitous Comput.* 10, 5, Jul 2006, 301-317.
14. Mankoff, D., Dey, A., Mankoff, J. and Mankoff, K. Supporting Interspecies Social Awareness: Using Peripheral Displays for Distributed Pack Awareness. UIST, 2005, 253-258.
15. PetsCELL. http://www.petsmobility.com/ (accessed September 9, 2010).
16. Pointer Magnum. http://www.pointer.fi/tuotteet.php (accessed July 23, 2010).
17. Resnek, B.I. Rover@Home: Computer-Mediated Remote Interaction between Humans and Dogs. MSc Thesis, MIT, 2001.
18. Tan, T.T.K.C., Cheok, A.D., Peiris, R.L., Wijesena, I.J.P., Tan, D.B.S., Raveendran, K., Nguyen, K.D.T., Sen, Y.P., Yio, E.Z. Computer Game for Small Pets and Humans. *In Proc. ICEC 2007*, LNCS 4740, 2007, 28-38.
19. Teh, K.S., Lee, S.P., Cheok, A.D. Poultry Internet: A Remote Human-Pet Interaction System. Ext. Abstracts *CHI 2006*, ACM Press, 2006, 251-254.
20. Tracker G400. http://www.tracker.fi/webshop/index.php?pPath=2 (accessed July 23, 2010).
21. Ultrapoint Dog GPS. http://www.ultrapoint.fi/en/ultrapoint_dog_gps/ (accessed July 23, 2010).
22. Virtual Pet. http://www.virtualpet.com/vp/links/links.htm (accessed September 20, 2010).
23. Wingrave, C.A., Rose, J., Langston, T., and LaViola, J.J. Early Explorations of CAT: Canine Amusement and Training. In *Extended Abstracts on CHI 2010*, 2010, 2661-2670.
24. Yonezava, K., Miyaki, T. and Rekimoto, J. Cat@Log: Sensing Device Attachable to Pet Cats for Supporting Human-Pet Interaction. In *Proc. ACE '09*, 2009, 149-156.

Designing Sports: A Framework for Exertion Games

Florian 'Floyd' Mueller [1,2,3], Darren Edge [2], Frank Vetere [1], Martin R. Gibbs [1], Stefan Agamanolis [4], Bert Bongers [5], Jennifer G. Sheridan [6]

[1] Interaction Design Group, University of Melbourne, Australia
[2] Microsoft Research Beijing, People's Republic of China
[3] HCI Group, Stanford, USA
[4] Distance Lab, Forres, UK
[5] Interactivation Lab, University of Technology Sydney, Australia
[6] BigDog Interactive, London, UK

floyd@exertioninterfaces.com, darren.edge@microsoft.com, {f.vetere, martin.gibbs}@unimelb.edu.au, stefan@agamanolis.com, bertbon@xs4all.nl, jennifer@bigdoginteractive.com

ABSTRACT
Exertion games require investing physical effort. The fact that such games can support physical health is tempered by our limited understanding of how to design for engaging exertion experiences. This paper introduces the Exertion Framework as a way to think and talk about Exertion Games, both for their formative design and summative analysis. Our Exertion Framework is based on the ways in which we can conceive of the body investing in game-directed exertion, supported by four perspectives on the body (the Responding Body, Moving Body, Sensing Body and Relating Body) and three perspectives on gaming (rules, play and context). The paper illustrates how this framework was derived from prior systems and theory, and presents a case study of how it has been used to inspire novel exertion interactions.

Author Keywords
Exertion Interface, whole-body interaction, exergame, exergaming, bodily interaction, kinesthetic, sports.

ACM Classification Keywords: H5.2. Information Interfaces and presentation (e.g., HCI): User Interfaces.

General terms: Design, Human Factors

INTRODUCTION
Within the field of HCI, there is a trend towards interactions that place the human body at the center of the experience, fostering "exertion" interactions that require intense physical effort from users [35]. Computer games currently provide the most buoyant genre for exertion systems. The Nintendo Wii and Microsoft Kinect, along with research projects such as virtual reality stationary bikes [32], mobile games fueled by exercise [8, 26] and our own systems [35, 36, 38] have all contributed to a design space that highlights the value of such mediated exertion experiences. We define an Exertion Game (sometimes called exergame [52]) as a digital game where the outcome of the game is predominantly determined by physical effort.

Researching these exertion games is important, as they can offer physical health benefits [24, 29], which can contribute to weight loss and address the obesity epidemic. Research has also found that exertion facilitates social behavior in games, suggesting that we can create more engaging and social experiences if we know how to design for exertion [5, 27]. Unfortunately, at present we have a limited understanding of how to describe and design for compelling exertion experiences [11, 57].

Framing exertion games as "sports" helps illustrate why this understanding is difficult to attain. Sport is a highly complex social phenomenon centered on moving bodies [15] which engage in a wide spectrum of physical behaviors. These behaviors are often mediated by tools – both simple (e.g. a ball) and complex (e.g. a bike), and take place anywhere from small backyards to national stadiums. In addition, the complex cultural processes that shape our desire to engage in sport often focus on extreme experiences and emotions, ranging from delight and togetherness to violence and injury.

When designing for Exertion Games, we need to understand not only the bodily experience, but also the technological challenges of digitally capturing, interpreting, and communicating exertion. The goal of our Exertion Framework presented in this paper is therefore to encourage a systematic consideration of the ways in which the body engages in exertion experiences as well as the ways in which game design and technologies can support such experiences.

KEY EXPERIENCES

To address the challenges outlined in our introduction and to illustrate our Exertion Framework, we begin with a look at three of our own exertion systems – Table Tennis for Three [37], Jogging over a Distance [39] and Remote Impact [34] and draw on our rich history of designing for exertion [35, 36, 38]. The examples we illustrate here exploit the potential of networked computer games to allow players to communicate over long distances [45]. However, we illustrate how our framework is applicable in both distributed and non-distributed settings.

TABLE TENNIS FOR THREE

Table Tennis for Three is inspired by the game of table tennis, but accommodates three players at three different tables, rather than two players at one table.

Fig. 1. Table Tennis for Three.

Each player has an identical setup, which includes a ball, a paddle and a modified table tennis table. The table is set up so that the ball can be hit against a "backboard" – a vertically positioned opposite half of the table (Fig. 1). Digital bricks are projected onto the backboard so that the bricks exist in a virtual world shared by all three players. In addition, side-by-side video feeds of players' opponents are projected behind the bricks, thus creating a sense of "playing together" [37]. The goal of the game is for each player to break the bricks using their physical paddle and ball. The bricks crack a little, a lot, and then break after three strikes from any ball and any player. However, only the third striker receives the point. Play continues until all bricks are broken, and the player with the most points wins.

JOGGING OVER A DISTANCE

Jogging over a Distance is a jogging support system that uses heart rate data to control spatialized audio between geographically distant joggers. The aim of the system is to support "social" joggers, i.e. people who use exercise to socialize and socialize through the exercise [42].

Joggers run in pairs and each jogger wears a headset, a heart rate monitor, a mini computer and a mobile phone (Fig. 2). Before the run, users enter their target heart rate into the system. Each jogger hears the spatialized audio feed from their distant jogging partner. The spatialized audio appears to come from the front, side, or rear, according to whether the user's relative heart rate is lower than, equal to, or greater than that of their partner's. If both joggers diverge from their target heart rates by the same percentage, the spatialized audio remains "side by side". For example, if both joggers raise their heart rate to 110% of their target heart rate, the spatialized audio sounds as if it is "next" to the jogger. However, if their relative heart rates are at different levels, the audio will sound as if one person is in front and the other is behind. The spatialized audio therefore acts as a sign of relative effort and tells the joggers when they need to speed up or slow down to "stay" with their partner [40].

Fig. 2. Jogging over a Distance.

REMOTE IMPACT

Remote Impact is inspired by combat sports which encourage intense physical exertion (Fig. 3) [34].

Fig. 3. Remote Impact

In this game, each remote player interacts with a padded playing surface (mattresses). The shadow from both the remote and the physically present player are projected onto the surface. Each player tries to make forceful contact with their opponent's shadow without getting "hit" themselves. Any impact on the remote person's shadow with any body part is counted as a successful hit and an audiovisual effect is played (e.g. POW!). Points are awarded according to the force of the impact and the player who scores the most points within a set time limit wins the game.

Summary of the experiences

Despite the differences in type of exertion and technology used, our three systems share many common features: they support physical effort through gaming experiences; they engage players through physical as well as virtual spaces and objects; and they facilitate digitally mediated social play. In the next section, we integrate these concepts into our Exertion Framework and discuss how using different "lenses" to investigate the body can help us understand how these concepts support engaging game experiences both arising from and in spite of the effects of bodily exertion.

THE EXERTION FRAMEWORK

Understanding Exertion Games begins with an appreciation of the fundamental and central role that the body plays in such interactions. It is important to note that our intention is not to provide a framework which stresses optimizing health or fitness benefits to the body, but rather to describe how designers can use technology to create more engaging exertion experiences mediated by technology. We believe that more engaging experiences will lead to increased physical investment, and health benefits will follow naturally as a result.

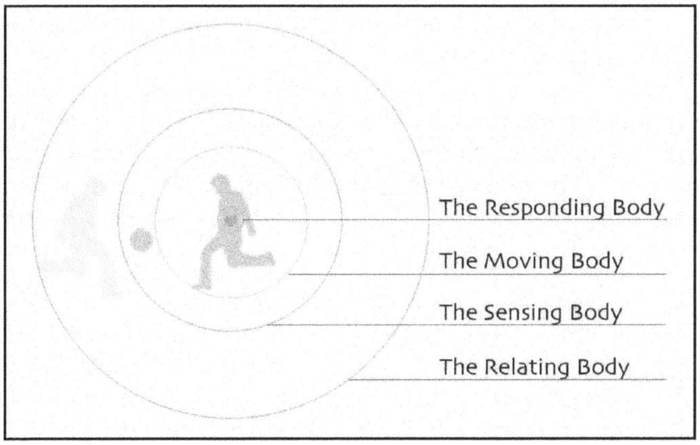

Fig. 4. The Four Lenses for Exertion Interactions

Four lenses

Our approach leans on Jacob et al.'s framework which describes the contextual factors arising from users' interactions with the environment as well as "social others" to explain bodily interaction with non-keyboard controlled devices [18, 19]. Jacob et al. suggest that a "four lens view" provides sufficient detail and abstraction to analyse new systems that feature the human body. As such, our perspective of the human body is similarly structured using four lenses: the Responding Body; the Moving Body; the Sensing Body; and the Relating Body (Fig. 4). Each lens is inspired by van Manen's phenomenological approach to the analysis of "lived" experience in terms of corporeality, temporality, spatiality and relationality [56]. While these lenses often overlap (for example, the moving and sensing body are often integrated [31]), our interest is in providing a simple structure for viewing the body and promoting creative design thinking when designing for exertion games.

Lens 1: The Responding Body

At the heart of the exertion experience is the *Responding Body*. The Responding Body is a view of the body "from the inside", or how the body's internal state changes over time as a result of the exertion - any activity from an outer layer necessitates a physiological response from the inner layer. The Responding Body emphasizes how both corporeality and temporality, or the body and change, are at the heart of people's experience of exertion [43].

The body reacts to physical activity by responding internally in a way that maintains balance, or "homeostasis" [43]: the user's heart rate typically increases, breathing becomes more frequent, and sweating occurs. These are consequences of exercise the user has not consciously initiated, but is usually aware of.

The body responds not just in anticipation of and during exertion, but also after such activities. For example, the body might lose weight, initiate the increase of muscle-mass, repair broken tissue, etc. These are all responses that continue to develop and persist beyond the "magic circle of play" [45] when the game ends. They can also affect how the body responds in subsequent exertion experiences: a participant might lift more weight on further exposures to the same exercise as a consequence of becoming stronger. The body's response is not always a positive experience however, for example, users might become aware of their bodies' response through muscle soreness or injury.

This lens of the Responding Body can be applied to each of the systems described in our Key Experiences section. In Table Tennis for Three, the external responses such as sweating and panting that are transmitted over the videoconference are in contrast to the internal responses of changing heart rates utilized as a core game mechanic in Jogging over a Distance. In Remote Impact, players became exhausted very quickly and needed resting breaks; as a consequence, games were played in several short sets that together made one full match.

Other games have used both heart rate [41] and EEG (electroencephalograph) feedback [23] from the Responding Body as control mechanisms. Smith notes that adjusting the game challenge based on participants' Responding Body could contribute to engagement [53] – something we exploited in Jogging Over a Distance.

Lens 2: The Moving Body

The *Moving Body* focuses on participants' muscular repositioning of body parts relative to one another during the course of physical activity. Temporality and spatiality are combined in the Moving Body – movement causes a body to respond (however, a Responding Body might not necessarily imply movement). This lens highlights movement characteristics such as intensity (movement can carry "weight"), continuousness (movement exhibits preparatory and follow-through phases) and variety (the richness of human movement) [31]. Loke et al. [28] has also found that space, weight, time and continuousness are useful in providing both constraints and resources for designing exertion experiences. Prior research concerning movement and dance has helped to identify these expressive characteristics [25, 28, 31].

The Moving Body also highlights the kinesthetic sense, or proprioception, an area that has been underexplored in HCI [13, 31, 48]. The kinesthetic sense governs users' awareness of the position of body parts [31]. Moen calls this a "bodily intelligence", a sense that allows humans to react intuitively without having to think about every single movement [31].

We can apply the Moving Body to each of the systems described in our Key Experiences section. In Table Tennis for Three, the preparatory and follow-through movements players made to hit the ball were secondary to the game and were communicated directly via videoconference, which enabled playful engagement such as "fake starts". In Jogging over a Distance, however, participants' jogging movements were primary to the experience but communicated only indirectly as spatialized audio in a virtual world. In Remote Impact, the need for both offensive and defensive movements led to players experimenting with tactics ranging from rapid, continuous arm and leg strikes to forcefully throwing the entire body at the surface.

Movements are related to the surrounding lens of the *Sensing Body*, or how the body perceives and acts within the hybrid physical and virtual Exertion Game environment and we discuss this in the next section.

Lens 3: The Sensing Body

The *Sensing Body* describes how the body is sensing and experiencing the world. In the world of sports, many popular games involve physical objects, which aid in shaping the exertion activity. Artifacts range from basic equipment such as balls to very specialized equipment (e.g. bicycles). The physical and technological environment also shapes the activity – playing in a big stadium is not the same as playing in the park [56], nor is running in a park the same as running on a treadmill. The Sensing Body therefore aims to offer a contextual perspective, highlighting the body and its interactions with the world. This perspective differentiates Exertion Games from conventional sports in that the world of Exertion Games consists of both physical and virtual objects and spaces. Previous research on tangible interfaces [16] has highlighted the potential of the body in relation to digitally augmented physical objects. Fogtman et al. have also speculated on the effects that physical objects can have on exertion actions [13]. Others suggest that adding virtual objects and spaces creates even more opportunities for exertion game design since participants must navigate the additional challenges of a hybrid space [4].

Adopting this lens of the Sensing Body, we can appreciate that Jogging over a Distance balances the risks of running outside with the reward of an ever-changing environment. Unlike in conventional jogging, this environment unfolds in a different way for each jogger, as jogging happens at different times of the day and joggers are separated by multiple time zones. In Table Tennis for Three, this lens highlights interactions with the physical ball (in contrast to a virtual one), while in Remote Impact it highlights the experiential correlation of the body physically hitting a mattress at the same time as the body is being hit via its digital shadow.

Lens 4: The Relating Body

The outer layer of the *Relating Body* is borrowed directly from van Manen [56], and encompasses the ways in which bodies and people relate to one another through digital technology. Such social interactions are highly diverse, mediated by a wide variety of roles such as co-players, opponents and audiences [48] and joint exertion can contribute positively to social outcomes [27, 54, 58]. A social view of exertion also helps us to understand the barriers and motivators for exercise [30]. Studies focused on physical activity participation have confirmed that "social interactions" are amongst the most common reasons for people being physically active [1, 55]. The ability to maintain existing relationships while also being able to develop new social networks are two of the key benefits of participating in physical activity [1]. Social facilitation theory suggests that social sportspeople will improve their athletic performance [15] and that athletes exhibit a higher tolerance to pain when exercising with others [7].

Using the lens of the Relating Body we see that the participants in Jogging over a Distance experienced their heart rate in relation to their partner's heart rate. In Table Tennis for Three, this lens illustrates how players relate to abstract virtual blocks that are shared amongst the players. In Remote Impact, this lens highlights that players relate to a virtual representation of their opponent.

EXERTION GAME SCHEMAS

As our exertion experiences center on digital games, we borrow gaming schemas from game literature: rules, play, and culture [45]. Each of these schemas helps us to explore: the formal structures of a game; the experiences of the people involved; and the larger context in which the game takes place (in this paper, we focus on the "immediate" context rather than the notion of culture). With these schemas, we can group the concepts we identified in our investigations of Exertion Games. These concepts can be considered from each of our four body lenses, offering a comprehensive breakdown of the ways in which we can think and talk about exertion experiences (Fig. 5).

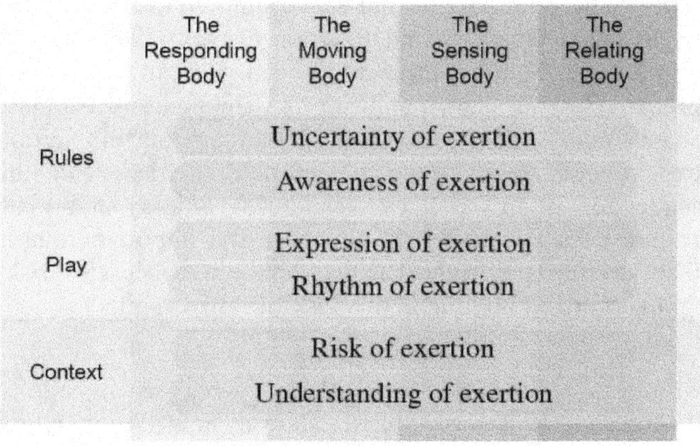

Fig. 5. The Exertion Framework

We now explain each concept in detail and show how they can be viewed using our body lenses by illustrating it through an example from one particular body lens.

RULES: Uncertainty of exertion

An important element of many games is uncertainty [45]: the ball dancing on the net before going over in a game of tennis, an adverse weather change in golf affecting some players but not others, and so on. Uncertainty contributes to an element of suspense and facilitates surprise in games through random or chance events, which can play an important part in what makes a game engaging.

In conventional button-press computer games, any chance encounters need to be artificially introduced through explicitly programmed code – simply pressing a key does not often offer a rich set of possibilities for uncertainty in terms of action and effect. For example, in a computer tennis game, the ball balancing on top of the net before dropping off either side might be controlled by a random function in the code that is not intuitively understandable to the players involved who might simply consider it a bug in the game [14]. In exertion games, on the other hand, uncertainty can also arise through the body. The body's response to exertion is hard to predict for player and technology alike ("how long can I keep up?"), and the variety of bodily movements can cause even simple actions to go wrong (e.g. missing a free-throw in basketball or a short putt in golf). Exertion as Uncertainty makes designers aware that they need to manage the relationship between the uncertainty arising from the body and the programmed uncertainty in the virtual world.

Uncertainty of exertion & the Sensing Body

The physicality of objects such as balls often amplifies the richness of bodily movement and draws on the nonlinearity between bodily actions and effects. This resulting uncertainty between bodies and objects has been exploited in sports [10] and mixed reality games [47]. In Table Tennis for Three, players react very emotionally when the ball hits the edge of the table and bounces off in unexpected ways as a result of "lucky" shots. With practice, players can achieve these shots intentionally, but even so these movements still carry an inherent risk and "fluke-factor" that heightens suspense for both players and audience.

RULES: Awareness of exertion

In Exertion Games, players aim to overcome the limitations of their bodies, for example wanting to run faster in Jogging over a Distance. The advantage of introducing computers to this bodily struggle is that digital technology can selectively hide bodily information from players as well as reveal it [44, 45] so that the player can then benefit from both increased and decreased awareness of their exertion. A person's awareness of the physical effort invested can entice participants to compare their energy expenditure over time and with others, fostering competition that motivates them to invest even more effort [8]. Alternatively, design can focus on distractions such as playing music, supporting anti-awareness that dissociates the user from the discomfort that comes with strenuous physical activity [20].

Awareness of exertion & the Responding Body

In Jogging over a Distance, participants noted that the social interaction with the other person distracted them from the discomfort of jogging, helping them to keep running. At the same time, participants reported that the audio enabled them to identify through their partner's breathing rate how much effort they invested, and whether they wanted to "push" their partner more.

PLAY: Expression of exertion

Exertion as a form of self-expression highlights the richness and expressive power of the human body beyond the merely pragmatic [5, 6, 25, 48], affording performative interactions [16, 48, 49]. Performative expression using the body is common in sports, often in the form of gestures such as "throwing fists" to oneself or to the opponent, and celebratory dances.

In Exertion Games, expression can be considered a form of "metagaming". Metagaming refers to "what happens during a game other than the game itself" [45]. Trash-talking is one example of metagaming in VoIP-supported computer gaming [45]. Exertion Game participants can draw on a wider range of metagaming strategies that leverage the expressive power of the body. Although such actions require the expenditure of bodily energy and hence one might come to the conclusion that they do not support making progress towards the goal of the game, they can significantly contribute towards the experience [5, 25].

The notion of exertion as a form of expression also resonates with work on interactive performances for an audience [3, 44, 48], but extends it by highlighting the various ways expression can be supported by the body. For example, participants could express themselves using their responding body by making heart rate visible to co-players, and variations could be rewarded through gameplay (e.g. the star-power points given for lifting up the guitar in Guitar Hero [5]).

Expression of exertion & the Relating Body

In Table Tennis for Three, participants hit balls not only to score points, but also to "send a message" to their remote partners, often smashing the ball at their heads. Such actions served a dual expressive role: that the players were "taunting" beaten opponents or "attacking" them after a loss, but only within the playful realm of the game in which the smasher of the ball would then have to retrieve the ball, watched by their two opponents through the video feed.

PLAY: Rhythm of exertion

Rhythm of exertion is about the ability of a system to support a uniform or patterned recurrence of a beat in bodily action. Rhythm in movement can exist within movement itself or without music, reflecting the inner pulse of the user [31]. It has been shown that the rhythm of music during exertion activities can regulate arousal, improve athletic performance, positively impact the acquisition of motor skills and dissociate from the discomfort of exercise [20]. Dance Dance Revolution is probably the most widespread example of an exertion game based on rhythm [2]. Players synchronize their movements to both the music and also to their partner, which makes for better performance and ultimately a better spectacle for the audience [2].

Rhythm of exertion & the Moving Body

From a Moving Body perspective, rhythm is supported by the continuousness of movement [48]. In Jogging over a Distance, participants tried to find a rhythm in their own jogging actions, but also used the rhythm they identified through their partner's footsteps and breathing in order to synchronize their movements with their partner's movements.

CONTEXT: Risk of exertion

Risk of exertion highlights the vulnerability of the body to overexertion and injury as a result of the exertion activity. Being injured, recovering from injury, and discussing injuries are prominent elements of the sports experience [17]. However, exposure of the body to risk in sport is different to risk-taking in computer games [45]. In computer games, risk is virtual, as most actions can be undone easily [21]. Dreyfus says that risk is a key differentiator between virtual and physical experiences [12]. With no real risk in virtual worlds, choice becomes meaningless. Risk-taking means committing to an act, and exertion is a commitment to physical actions as well as any potential consequences. Would choice in computer games become more meaningful if the physical risk was introduced to the experience?

When playing with a virtual game character, a player might experience an affective response when his/her avatar gets hurt, however, getting injured in an Exertion Game results in a different bodily response – the feeling of physical pain. This pain can obviously end the game, or worse, impact one's life well beyond gameplay. However, the feeling of putting the body at risk and succeeding contributes to the engagement of sports and Exertion Games alike. Dreyfus argues that bodily vulnerability can lead to a constant preparedness for danger and surprise, and that this readiness shapes one's life experience [12]. Participating in exertion experiences means exposing oneself to risk, and the realization of this risk can lead to a complex emotional response such as thrill [46]. However, it is important to note that striking the right balance between successful risk-taking "thrills" and the bodily risk of failed "spills" is non-trivial.

Risk of exertion & the Moving Body

The design of Remote Impact showed how designing for exertion can facilitate a reduction of risk in that the participant cannot be physically hurt by the distant partner, although it was still possible for players to hurt themselves.

CONTEXT: Understanding of exertion

Understanding of exertion refers to the potential of a system to support the development of knowledge about the body. For an understanding of the exerting body two key aspects come to the fore: knowledge and skill [22]. Knowledge about the exerting body is abstract and has an existence apart from the particular situation that it describes or explains. For example, participants in Jogging over a Distance expressed that knowledge about heart rate helps them understand their body better and therefore their effort investment, helping them to plan future runs. Skill allows people "to do things", and is gained predominantly through training and practice [22]. Skill can be facilitated by bodily exploration; for example, in Remote Impact participants explored the maximum intensity with which they could safely strike the surface with their fists, thus training their "hitting" skills.

Developing this bodily understanding has been described as acquiring kinaesthetic literacy [50, 51]. One design strategy to support such bodily understanding is through deliberate mapping between exertion actions and game actions that match players' abilities to the challenge ahead. This facilitates flow, putting the player "in the zone" in a manner thought to be conducive to learning [9]. We have identified four ways in which technology can support this matching, through the: 1) manual selection of difficulty level; 2) transformation of athletic abilities by "handicapping"; 3) pairing with similarly-skilled opponents in networked play; and 4) dynamic manipulation of game challenges in response to momentary and long-term changes in players' physical capabilities (e.g. detect when the player gets tired and adjust the difficulty accordingly).

Designers of exertion systems should also be aware of the dangers when mapping exertion actions: players who learn about their physical abilities through a non-uniform matching might overestimate the extent to which they can transfer their virtual skills to the physical world. As the involvement of the body can make these game experiences more emotional (when compared to button-press games)

[5], there is a danger of people over- or under-estimating their bodily powers, for example a player might believe that she/he is "superhero" strong after playing a superhero game.

Understanding of exertion & the Relating Body
In Jogging over a Distance, heart rate is mapped relative to the other person and is used as a game mechanic that contributes to social play. However, some study participants expressed that they would also like to access their individual heart rate in order to learn more about their bodies.

THE EXERTION FRAMEWORK IN ACTION

At its heart, the Exertion Framework is a **design vocabulary** – a tool for mediating discussions between designers. In the reverse of this process, the vocabulary can be used to set goals and aspirations for the design of new Exertion Games whose final forms are still unknown, using the body lenses and game concepts to systematically explore the space of possible exertion experiences. In this section, we describe how our framework was used to do just that.

Ideation using a Body Perspective

The central idea of "Hanging off a Bar" was inspired by considering how an Exertion Game could *not* have a **Moving Body**, unlike the majority of other Exertion Games.

Fig. 6. Hanging off a Bar

Hanging off a Bar is a game that plays with the idea of being a hero in an action movie who ends up hanging off a cliff, dangling over a wild river projected underneath the player (Fig. 6). The goal is for the player to hang on to the bar for as long as one can. From time to time, a raft slowly arrives, enticing the player to hang on just a little longer until the raft is close enough so that they can drop down onto it to rest and recover. They can't rest for too long, however, since they have to jump back up to the bar before the raft drifts into a waterfall behind the player. A projected timer shows the players how well they are doing. The longer the player hangs on to the bar, the less frequent and shorter the rafts become, resulting in decreasing opportunities for recovery which makes "hanging on" progressively harder.

Elaboration guided by the Exertion Framework

The core mechanic of Hanging off a Bar is based on the growing levels of pain and fatigue of the **Responding Body**. Conversely, the framework prompted a shift in focus from technological sensing based on the **Responding Body** (for example by measuring heart rate) to sensing based on the environment affected by the exertion. Since players naturally drop to the floor (both during opportunities to rest and when their grip fails) taking the view of the **Sensing Body** led to the decision to use a contact switch on the ground rather than strain sensors on the bar. A timer projected onto the floor provides **awareness** of the conflict between increasing pain and decreasing rest as the game progresses.

Although the game is only for solo-play at the moment, it has a strong element of the **Relating Body**. We noticed that observers quickly gather around a player, yelling motivational chants as the player faces **uncertainty** about the coming rafts (a typical game lasts only 30-50 seconds). Players also swing their legs to dissociate from the **awareness** of the increasing discomfort, which makes for a social experience by supporting a kind of **expression**. Players take away a new **understanding of exertion** about their physical response to hanging off a bar with only the slight **risk** of muscle strain.

Extensions suggested by the Exertion Framework

Possible extensions to the game inspired by the framework include a multi-player mode in which participants hang off the same bar over the same river, and share the same rafts. This would support a social **rhythm** of **moving bodies**, which could make for an interesting audience display. Furthermore, a multi-player system would allow for **Relating Bodies** to distract each other by, for example, slapping each other's hands or tickling the other person under the arm to steer the other player off the bar. This **Relating Body** notion could also occur in the virtual world: if one player does not need all the recovery time the raft offers and decides to get back on the bar early, the now lighter raft could drift off more quickly, thus affecting the other player.

A new game experience could also be created by shifting the scoring systems from the **Sensing Body** to the **Responding Body**: equipping players with heart rate monitors could create a challenging new play experience in which players have to hang on as long as they can while gaining bonus points for increasing their heart rate by swinging their legs, doing pull ups, etc. (increasing the **expression** of the **Moving Body**). Players will need to decide whether to "push their luck", as they try to find the right balance between energy conservation (to last longer) and expenditure (to get more points per unit time). This way, players could develop a greater **understanding of exertion** in terms of their **Responding Body** – what is the most effective way to raise heart rate without tiring the grip muscles: pulling up, swinging, or hanging loosely? Lastly, **risk** could be integrated into the reward system by having staggered bars of increasing height that the players can move between (the higher, the better), or by augmenting the bars or landing platform with light electrical shock capability.

Summary

We have presented a case study of how our Exertion Framework can be used to support the ideation, elaboration, and extension of novel Exertion Game concepts, but further work is needed to substantiate how the framework inspires creative design. Since the true value of such framework tools becomes evident within communities of design practice, our aim is to encourage interested designers and researchers to use the concepts and examples presented in this paper to perform their own analysis and design of Exertion Games, and to share the resulting ideas and experiences with the larger Exertion community.

DISCUSSION AND CONCLUSIONS

To understand what makes exertion experiences "tick" [4], and how and why they work, we have revisited and reflected on our experience designing, testing and evaluating Exertion Games. We propose a layered view of the human body, which provides designers with a "body perspective" for the design of exertion experiences. This perspective highlights that the body responds, moves, senses, and relates to other bodies in the context of exertion experiences. While such experiences can arise spontaneously, they typically benefit from determined goals in order to make the transition from action to activity. The special quality of games is that they offer goals that bring structure to such exertion experiences. Our body perspective and accompanying game schemas cut across all body lenses and provide a structure for exertion games.

Although our framework focused on games, our perspective on the human body helps us to see other interactive experiences that center on the body from an exertion perspective: for example, the nature of exertion in pervasive games, such as mobile phone games where players have to run across a city [33]. Furthermore, a view of exertion might also reveal insights into the design of interactive devices that support bodies exercising, such as computationally enhanced bikes and bodybuilding machines. We believe the Exertion Framework might also be useful in guiding studies of bodily labor, where it could contribute to design for a safer work environment. Additionally, the framework could be useful in learning environments where bodily skills are being taught and trained. As the use of exertion can affect trust and connectedness in mediated interactions [35], understanding exertion can also help us to create novel social experiences that expand our conventional view of CSCW applications: for example, networked exertion games could serve as trust-building activities for newly formed distributed teams. Our work also allows us to view embodied systems, such as tangible interfaces, from a body-centric, rather than device-centric, perspective.

In summary, our framework serves as a language for researchers to think and talk about exertion games, helps developers to identify opportunities for future interactive technologies and systems, and supports designers in creating new games that enable users to profit from the many benefits of exertion.

ACKNOWLEDGEMENTS

This work was partially supported by a Fulbright Scholarship and a Microsoft Research Asia Fellowship. Thanks to Nokia, Telstra, HCSNet and Scott Klemmer, Terry Winograd, Jeff Heer, Steven Dow, Ted Selker, Roz Picard and all the many helpers in the individual projects. Videos of the key experiences are at: http://exertioninterfaces.com

REFERENCES

1. Allender, S., Cowburn, G. and Foster, C. Understanding participation in sport and physical activity among children and adults: a review of qualitative studies. *Health Education Research*, *21* (6). (2006), 826.
2. Behrenshausen, B.G. Toward a (Kin) Aesthetic of Video Gaming: The Case of Dance Dance Revolution. *Games and Culture*, *2* (4). (2007), 335.
3. Benford, S., Crabtree, A., Reeves, S., Sheridan, J., Dix, A., Flintham, M. and Drozd, A. The Frame of the Game: Blurring the Boundary between Fiction and Reality in Mobile Experiences *Proceedings of the SIGCHI conference on Human Factors in computing systems*, ACM, Montreal, Quebec, Canada, 2006, 427-436.
4. Benford, S., Giannachi, G., Koleva, B. and Rodden, T. From interaction to trajectories: designing coherent journeys through user experiences *Proceedings of the 27th international conference on Human factors in computing systems*, ACM, Boston, MA, USA, 2009, 709-718.
5. Bianchi-Berthouze, N., Kim, W. and Patel, D. Does Body Movement Engage You More in Digital Game Play? and Why? in Paiva, A., Prada, R. and Picard, R. eds. *Affective Computing and Intelligent Interaction Conference*, Springer Berlin / Heidelberg, 2007, 102-113.
6. Bowers, J. and Hellstrom, S. Simple interfaces to complex sound in improvised music *CHI '00: Conference on Human Factors in Computing Systems, Extended Abstracts*, ACM, The Hague, The Netherlands, 2000, 125-126.

7. Cohen, E.E.A., Ejsmond-Frey, R., Knight, N. and Dunbar, R.I.M. Rowers' high: behavioural synchrony is correlated with elevated pain thresholds. *Biology Letters*, *6* (1). (2010), 106.
8. Consolvo, S., Everitt, K., Smith, I. and Landay, J.A. Design requirements for technologies that encourage physical activity *Proceedings of the SIGCHI conference on Human Factors in computing systems*, Montreal, Quebec, Canada, 2006, 457-466.
9. Csikszentmihalyi, M. *Flow: The psychology of optimal performance*. New York: Harper and Row, 1990.
10. Czajkowski, Z. The essence and importance of timing (sense of surprise) in fencing, n.d. Retrieved from http://www.mat-fencing.com/Akademia16.html.
11. de Kort, Y.A.W. and Ijsselsteijn, W.A. People, places, and play: player experience in a socio-spatial context. *Computers in Entertainment (CIE)*, *6* (2). (2008).
12. Dreyfus, H. *Being-in-the-world: A commentary on Heidegger's Being and Time, Division I*. The MIT Press, 1991.
13. Fogtmann, M.H., Fritsch, J. and Kortbek, K.J. Kinesthetic Interaction - Revealing the Bodily Potential in Interaction Design *OZCHI '08: Conference of the computer-human interaction special interest group (CHISIG) of Australia on Computer-Human Interaction*, ACM, Cairns, Australia, 2008.
14. Gaver, W.W. Affordances for Interaction: The Social Is Material for Design. *Ecological Psychology*, *8* (2). (1996), 111-129.
15. Hagger, M. and Chatzisarantis, N. *Social psychology of exercise and sport*. Open University Press, Bershire, England, 2005.
16. Hornecker, E. and Buur, J. Getting a grip on tangible interaction: a framework on physical space and social interaction *Proceedings of the SIGCHI Conference on Human Factors in Computing Systems*, Montreal, Quebec, Canada, 2006, 437-446.
17. Howe, P. *Sport, professionalism, and pain: ethnographies of injury and risk*. Routledge, New York, NY, USA, 2004.
18. Jacob, R., Girouard, A., Hirshfield, L., Horn, M., Shaer, O., Solovey, E. and Zigelbaum, J., Reality-based interaction: a framework for post-WIMP interfaces. in, (2008), ACM, 201-210.
19. Jacob, R., Girouard, A., Hirshfield, L., Horn, M., Shaer, O., Solovey, E. and Zigelbaum, J. Reality-based interaction: unifying the new generation of interaction styles *CHI '07 extended abstracts on Human factors in computing systems*, ACM Press, San Jose, CA, USA, 2007, 2465-2470.
20. Karageorghis, C. and Priest, D.-L. Music in Sport and Exercise : An Update on Research and Application. *The Sport Journal*, *11* (3). (2008).
21. Klemmer, S. and Hartmann, B. How Bodies Matter: Five Themes for Interaction Design *Proceedings of the 6th conference on Designing Interactive systems*, University Park, PA, USA, 2006, 140-149.
22. Kretchmar, R. *Practical philosophy of sport and physical activity*. Human Kinetics Publishers, Champaign, IL, USA, 2005.
23. Kuikkaniemi, K., Kosunen, I., Turpeinen, M., Saari, T., Laitinen, T. and Lievonen, P. Designing Biofeedback for Games and Playful Applications *CHI '10: Workshop at the SIGCHI conference on Human Factors in computing systems*, Atlanta, GA, USA, 2010.
24. Lanningham-Foster, L., Jensen, T.B., Foster, R.C., Redmond, A.B., Walker, B.A., Heinz, D. and Levine, J.A. Energy Expenditure of Sedentary Screen Time Compared With Active Screen Time for Children. *Pediatrics*, *118* (6). (2006), 1831-1835.
25. Larssen, A., Loke, L., Robertson, T., Edwards, J. and Sydney, A. Understanding Movement as Input for Interaction–A Study of Two Eyetoy Games *Proceedings of OzCHI '04*, Wollongong, Australia, 2004.
26. Lin, J., Mamykina, L., Lindtner, S., Delajoux, G. and Strub, H. Fish'n'Steps: Encouraging Physical Activity with an Interactive Computer Game *UbiComp 2006: Ubiquitous Computing*, 2006, 261-278.
27. Lindley, S.E., Le Couteur, J. and Berthouze, N.L. Stirring up experience through movement in game play: effects on engagement and social behaviour *Proceeding of the twenty-sixth annual SIGCHI conference on Human factors in computing systems*, ACM, Florence, Italy, 2008.
28. Loke, L., Larssen, A., Robertson, T. and Edwards, J. Understanding movement for interaction design: frameworks and approaches. *Personal and Ubiquitous Computing*, *11* (8 Special Issue Movement-Based Interaction). (2007), 691-701.
29. Maddison, R., Mhurchu, C., Jull, A., Jiang, Y., Prapavessis, H. and Rodgers, A. Energy expended playing video console games: an opportunity to increase children's physical activity? *Pediatric exercise science*, *19* (3). (2007), 334.
30. McElroy, M. *Resistance to exercise: A social analysis of inactivity*. Human Kinetics Publishers, Champaign, IL, USA, 2002.
31. Moen, J. KinAesthetic Movement Interaction: Designing for the Pleasure of Motion, Stockholm: KTH, Numerical Analysis and Computer Science, 2006.
32. Mokka, S., Väätänen, A., Heinilä, J. and Välkkynen, P. Fitness computer game with a bodily user interface *Proceedings of the second international conference on Entertainment computing*, Carnegie Mellon University Pittsburgh, PA, USA, Pittsburgh, Pennsylvania, 2003, 1-3.
33. Montola, M., Stenros, J. and Waern, A. *Pervasive Games: Theory and Design*. Morgan Kaufmann, Burlington, MA, USA, 2009.
34. Mueller, F., Agamanolis, S., Gibbs, M. and Vetere, F. Remote Impact: Shadowboxing over a Distance *CHI'09: Proceedings of the 27th International Conference on Human Factors in Computing Systems, Extended Abstracts*, ACM, Boston, MA, USA, 2009, 3531-3532.

35. Mueller, F., Agamanolis, S. and Picard, R. Exertion Interfaces: Sports over a Distance for Social Bonding and Fun *SIGCHI conference on Human factors in computing systems*, ACM, Ft. Lauderdale, Florida, USA, 2003, 561-568.
36. Mueller, F., Cole, L., O'Brien, S. and Walmink, W. Airhockey over a distance: a networked physical game to support social interactions *Proceedings of the 2006 ACM SIGCHI international conference on Advances in computer entertainment technology*, ACM, Hollywood, California, 2006, 70.
37. Mueller, F., Gibbs, M. and Vetere, F. Design Influence on Social Play in Distributed Exertion Games *CHI '09: Proceedings of the SIGCHI Conference on Human Factors in Computing Systems.*, ACM Press, Boston, MA, USA, 2009, 1539-1548.
38. Mueller, F., Gibbs, M.R. and Vetere, F. The Mousegrip *Proceedings of the 27th international conference on Human factors in Computing Systems, Extended Abstract*, ACM, Boston, MA, USA, 2009, 3199-3204.
39. Mueller, F., Vetere, F., Gibbs, M.R., Agamanolis, S. and Sheridan, J. Jogging over a Distance: The Influence of Design in Parallel Exertion Games *ACM SIGGRAPH 2010*, ACM, Los Angeles, USA, 2010.
40. Mueller, F., Vetere, F., Gibbs, M.R., Edge, D., Agamanolis, S. and Sheridan, J.G. Jogging over a distance between Europe and Australia *UIST '10. Proceedings of the 23nd annual ACM symposium on User interface software and technology*, ACM, New York, New York, USA, 2010, 189-198.
41. Nenonen, V., Lindblad, A., Häkkinen, V., Laitinen, T., Jouhtio, M. and Hämäläinen, P. Using heart rate to control an interactive game *Proceedings of the SIGCHI conference on Human factors in computing systems*, ACM Press New York, NY, USA, San Jose, California, USA, 2007, 853-856.
42. O'Brien, S. and Mueller, F. Jogging the distance *Proceedings of the SIGCHI conference on Human Factors in computing systems*, ACM, San Jose, California, USA, 2007, 523-526.
43. Plowman, S. and Smith, D. *Exercise physiology for health, fitness, and performance*. Lippincott Williams & Wilkins, Baltimore, MD, USA, 2007.
44. Reeves, S., Benford, S., O'Malley, C. and Fraser, M. Designing the spectator experience *Proceedings of the SIGCHI conference on Human factors in computing systems*, ACM New York, NY, USA, Portland, Oregon, USA, 2005, 741-750.
45. Salen, K. and Zimmerman, E. *Rules of Play: Game Design Fundamentals*. The MIT Press, Boston, MA, USA, 2003.
46. Schnaedelbach, H., Egglestone, S.R., Reeves, S., Benford, S., Walker, B. and Wright, M. Performing thrill: designing telemetry systems and spectator interfaces for amusement rides *Proceeding of the twenty-sixth annual SIGCHI conference on Human factors in computing systems*, ACM, Florence, Italy, 2008, 1167-1176.
47. Sharp, H., Rogers, Y. and Preece, J. *Interaction Design: Beyond Human Computer Interaction*. Wiley, West Sussex, England, 2007.
48. Sheridan, J. and Bryan-Kinns, N. Designing for Performative Tangible Interaction. *International Journal of Arts and Technology. Special Issue on Tangible and Embedded Interaction.*, *1* (3/4). (2008), 288-308.
49. Sheridan, J., Dix, A., Lock, S. and Bayliss, A. Understanding Interaction in Ubiquitous Guerrilla Performances in Playful Arenas. in Fincher, S., Markopoulos, P., Moore, D. and Ruddle, R. eds. *People and Computers XVIII — Design for Life*, Springer London, 2005, 3-17.
50. Sheridan, J. and Mueller, F. Fostering Kinesthetic Literacy Through Exertion Games *Workshop on Whole-Body Interactions at CHI'10: International Conference on Human Factors in Computing Systems*, ACM, Atlanta, USA, 2010.
51. Sheridan, J.G. When Clapping Data Speaks to Wii: Physical Creativity and Performative Interaction in Playground Games and Songs *Proceedings of 24th BCS Conference on Human Computer Interaction (BCS-HCI)*, Dundee, Scotland, 2010.
52. Sinclair, J., Hingston, P. and Masek, M. Considerations for the design of exergames *Proceedings of the 5th international conference on Computer graphics and interactive techniques in Australia and Southeast Asia*, Perth, Australia, 2007, 289-295.
53. Smith, B.K. Physical fitness in virtual worlds. *IEEE Computer*, *38* (10). (2005), 101-103.
54. Strömberg, H., Väätänen, A. and Räty, V.-P. A group game played in interactive virtual space: design and evaluation *4th Conference on Designing Interactive Systems*, ACM, London, England, 2002.
55. Trost, S., Owen, N., Bauman, A., Sallis, J. and Brown, W. Correlates of adults' participation in physical activity: review and update. *Medicine & Science in Sports & Exercise*, *34* (12). (2002), 1996.
56. Van Manen, M. *Researching lived experience: Human science for an action sensitive pedagogy*. State University of New York Press, London, Ontaria, Canada, 1990.
57. Voida, A. and Greenberg, S. Wii all play: The console game as a computational meeting place *Proceedings of the 27th international conference on Human factors in computing systems*, ACM, Boston, MA, USA, 2009, 1559-1568.
58. Wakkary, R., Hatala, M., Jiang, Y., Droumeva, M. and Hosseini, M. Making sense of group interaction in an ambient intelligent environment for physical play *Proceedings of the 2nd international conference on Tangible and embedded interaction*, ACM, Bonn, Germany, 2008, 179-186.

Cat Cat Revolution: An Interspecies Gaming Experience

Frank Noz
Carnegie Mellon University
University of Madeira
frank.noz@gmail.com

Jinsoo An
contact@jinsooan.com

ABSTRACT

Despite owners' desires to include pets in their everyday activities, pets have yet to be included in the digital gaming experience. The Cat Cat Revolution (CCR) is a digital game of cat and mouse that allows cats to participate in play through a species-appropriate interface. The game applies Human-Computer Interaction (HCI) principles to pets and casts pets as participants in the gaming experience. During the pilot study, pet owners characterized CCR as a mutually positive experience, describing the game as a "fun" way to play. CCR explores the effects of including pets in the digital gaming experience.

Author Keywords

Non-human interfaces, interspecies gaming, digital play

ACM Classification Keywords

H5.m. Information interfaces and presentation (e.g., HCI): Miscellaneous.

General Terms

Experimentation, Design, Theory.

Figure 1. User #1 watches his kitten track the mouse.

INTRODUCTION

In the U.S., felines are the largest group of pet companions with a population of 93.6 million [1]. Americans share their homes and lives with pets. Surveys, measuring attitudes and behavior towards pets, document how pet owners endow pets with human characteristics and needs. Owners consider pets as friends [3], extensions of self [2], and family [3]. Surveys also report the love, company, companionship, and affection enjoyed by owners [1]. Owners' attitudes and behaviors illustrate the significance of pets and their role in social interaction.

> "Whether animals have selves or not, what is more relevant to sociologists—and more verifiable—is that humans often act toward animals as if they have selves, and in ways that overlap with how they act toward humans" [11, p. 380].

RELATED WORK

Recent work acknowledges our desire to include pets in everyday activities. In the 1990's, virtual pets seduced consumers into nurturing their feelings and needs [14, 19]. The Tamagotchi digitized emotional engagement and illustrated human's capacity to attribute anthropomorphic characteristics to virtual pets. Other products such as the AIBO digitized the pet experience by introducing robotic pets into the home. Friedman, Kahn, and Hagman analyzed AIBO discussion boards and described how the robotic pets challenged traditional emotional boundaries, extended concepts of self, and replaced interaction with live pets [7].

Poultry.Internet also illustrates how pets can be included in HCI discourse [18]. The designers of the application digitized human-pet touch and explored various interaction methods by mediating remote petting. The system provided bi-directional communication using haptic and visual cues. Users touched pets via a tangible interface that mirrored the pet's position and orientation. The interface relayed touch through a specially designed vest, worn by the chicken. The vest simulated human touch and communicated the pet's movement back to the user, in turn enabling real-time touch interaction.

Despite these examples, digital interaction with pets remains understudied in HCI, so we turned to the fields of robotics and AI to better understand how to include pets in digital interaction. Suchman's theory of situated cognition caused us to rethink the constitutive nature of intelligence (human and cat) and machine [16]. Her theories highlighted the need to accommodate emergent play interactions and reframed the way we designed for intelligence. In addition, Brooks' "New AI" inspired us to build a relatively simple system, using minimal representations, centered on emergent intelligence [5].

Recent research provided actionable ways to translate lessons from the fields of robotics and AI into CCR's design. Leahu, Sengers, and Mateas highlighted a number of "New AI" strategies to create ubiquitous systems that "appeared to be intelligent" [12]. They use these strategies to address problems of "AI completeness," suggesting the development of systems that take advantage of highly-situated contexts. Influenced by Leahu's work, Taylor reflected on examples of "New AI" and suggested their potential application within HCI [17]. Taylor proposed HCI broaden its concepts of intelligence to expand the interactional possibilities between humans and machine. Taylor used the intersection of "New AI" and HCI to reposition the role of design in intelligent systems and create systems "where intelligence itself becomes the design focus" [17].

Sociological Study of Human-Pet Play

In the past 20 years, sociologists have begun to study human-pet play interactions. Alger's work suggests that owners actively assume the role of animals, and infer thoughts and feelings from the animal's perspective [2]. Sanders suggests that projecting human capabilities onto pets makes them legitimate participants in social interaction [15]. In addition, sociologists offer insights on how owners and pets use nonverbal communication to negotiate social order and interspecies interaction. Researchers suggests that humans and pets rely on their past play experiences, or a shared history of symbolic behavior, to non-verbally communicate [2, 4].

Ethnographic studies of human-animal play reflect on the intersubjectivity between participants [9, 11]. For example, Goode proposes that pets have an asymmetrical availability to interpret interaction [9]. Findings from Jerolmack's work suggest that human-pet play does not require shared meanings and/or intentions to coordinate interaction [11]. Other scholars [4, 11] do not view shared language as a prerequisite for intersubjectivity, instead, they view human-pet intersubjectivity along a continuum, ranging from shared understanding to a simple shared awareness of an object. The sociological study of human-pet play offers insights into the social interactions that allow owners and pets to negotiate and co-construct play experiences.

DESIGNING FOR INTERSPECIES INTERACTION

We conducted interviews with owners, reviewed online cat forums, and pet owner surveys [1, 3] to inform and inspire CCR's design. Our findings suggested chase as a common play theme and species appropriate activity. Next, we designed the interface to accommodate audio, visual, and touch interactions from human and cat participants. For example, we designed a *deictic* [12] mouse representation to communicate digital interactions in a species-appropriate, understandable, and actionable manner. We designed the mouse to entice cats to chase while catering to the human-centric model of the mouse as an input device. The interface appropriates a popular chase object, the mouse, and anchors the cat's interaction to natural chase behaviors, allowing felines to chase and paw during the game.

In addition, we designed the interface to support cat's color acuity. Cats are generally colorblind when it comes to red, but have excellent ability to distinguish blue and green. [13]. Early prototypes tested combinations of mouse color, size, brightness, and movement to bolster target discrimination and tracking on the display. The mouse squeaks when hit to provide audio feedback to participants. Audio testing ensured feedback did not frighten or discourage play.

System Description

Our system is comprised of two components, an iPad and an iPhone. The iPad application mediates cat-computer interaction through a combination of graphics, sound, and touch. The iPad interface uses a digital mouse representation entice cats by changing its orientation, velocity, and direction. The game has single and multi-player modes. In single-player mode, cats interact with the iPad by chasing the mouse as it randomly moves across the display. During multiplayer mode, owners wirelessly connect to the iPad using an iPhone. When connected, the iPhone mirrors the iPad's interface and allows owners to control the mouse's orientation, velocity, and direction. CCR uses iPads, iPhones, and game modes to support interspecies play.

RESEARCH APPROACH

Seven owners (five female and two males) and their cats participated in our pilot study. We recruited participants through our extended social network and none of the participants were involved in the study or development of CCR. The studies took place in participants' homes and lasted 60 to 90 minutes. During these sessions, we asked participants to perform four separate gaming tasks after familiarizing themselves with the game. Owners drove the play tasks and answered open-ended questions about their gaming experience and interactions with their pets.

We analyzed the data using grounded theory [8], borrowing themes from sociological studies of human-pet play [11] and surveys [1, 3]. We analyzed the audio, video, and subsequent transcriptions from the owner's responses, discussions, and think-alouds. The analysis used audio and transcripts from the sessions to interpret and encode the owners' interactions. The informal pilot study explored both owner and cat interaction during CCR.

Evalutating CCR

CCR is a game that allows pet owners to interact and potentially strengthen their relationship with their pets by playing a digital game. We feel that the novel experiences and interactions explored during our pilot tests may contribute knowledge to areas such as Human-Robot Interaction (HRI), design, and HCI. The following findings explore a number of play interactions to evaluate CCR's effect on human-pet play.

FINDINGS

General Findings

Our participants indicated that play was an important interaction with their cats and characterized CCR as a "fun" and mutually "beneficial" play experience. In addition, pet owners attributed a number of benefits to pet ownership including: mental well-being and therapeutic effects, freedom to be playful, feeling content, and felt play was good for the cat. Owners described a wide range of play interactions and gave detailed examples of "knowing" when their cat(s) wanted to play.

> The big guy is a tremendous rubber band fetcher. [W]hen we come out in the morning having coffee, he will go and find one and bring it to you, meaning he wants to play. {#7}

Participants also described their pet's dependence and reflected on their asymmetric relationship. For example:

> It's just nice to have something else to take care of, like something that needs you to take care of it, and feed it, help him, and play with him. {#1}

Despite owners' acknowledgments of interspecies boundaries, they all included cats as family members. Finally, another consistent theme in the data was that owners embraced digital gaming and the idea of engaging in digital play forms with their cats.

Pets as Viable Participants in Digital Gaming

Our findings suggest that some owners see pets as viable participants in social interaction. CCR appeared to create new opportunities for owners to socially construct and deconstruct interspecies boundaries with their pet. By endowing pets with human capacities, we suggest that owners may cast their pets as viable participants in the digital gaming experience. Moreover, the inclusion of pets in digital interaction satisfies owner's desire to include pets in everyday activities and may contribute to their physical health and mental well-being. For example:

> My God, she does actually learn how to play it... I have never seen her interact with the cat like this. I have never seen her and this cat this friendly. They love each other now. This is great! {#4}

> It actually has really has helped [sic] us bond with her. Cause even if she's not really interested in it, just us trying to get her interested in it is really a bonding experience. {#4}
> I like teaching her how to use technology, it's kind of cool. I feel like I am educating her. {#3}
> I feel like there is more of a reward system there for us than there is for her, because Wow! It looks like she is using the computer. {#4}

In the first quote, the owner expresses surprise when her cat begins to hit the mouse target during a game of CCR. The owner(s) describe the rewards of play interactions, which in turn strengthened and reinforced ownership bonds. These examples advance the viability, practical utility, and benefits of including pets in the gaming experience. In digital gaming, it is not important whether the pet has human capabilities; rather, what is important is whether owners act as if their pets have the capacity to do so [6, 11].

Evaluating the Design of CCR

CCR's design uses a number of strategies to engage participants in digital play. We used sociological studies of human-pet play to identify and design for existing emergent interactions that naturally occur during human-pet play. In addition, "New AI" strategies refocused the design to exploit the worldly contexts of play. The following examples highlight several important design considerations and their potential affect on play interactions, situated context, and emergence.

We designed CCR around existing human-pet play interactions to support play experiences. CCR accommodates asymmetrical relationships by coordinating interaction around a simple and species appropriate gaming experience. The analysis indicated the presence of existing play interactions in all owners including: role-play, projection of social identity, and use of symbolic behavior. In the excerpt below, the participants temporarily take-on the cat's role to describe the cat's multi-player preferences. This finding illustrates how some owners use role-play and projection of social identity during digital interaction.

> She likes it better when we control it. Uh huh. {#3}

> [S]eems like he likes it best when its not like directly under the holes, cause if I put it right here he doesn't . . . might be the reflection of the light off the top of the box cause he can see it easier. Maybe that makes it look more three-dimensional. {#1}

CCR's design was inspired by three "New AI" challenges including: placing participants "in the loop," allowing participants to interpret and interact with the system, and participating in the context of play. For example, the deictic mouse representation communicates state in actionable ways and elicited specific behavioral interactions from both participants. During each of the play-tasks, owners experimented with single and multi-player modes and reflected on their gaming experience.

> I like the single player one.... I think its more fun when I am interacting with him and the thing [CCR] at the same time.... One thing I do like about it though, I can play with him or be away and he can still play with it too. That feather thing [feather-on-a-stick] that I have, I have to manipulate that and if I am not there he is disinterested in it. {#1}

> Multi-player. She reacts to it better. Rather than it going randomly, sometimes she likes it better if it stays in one place for a while and then moves really fast. There are certain movement patterns that she reacts too. {#3}

> What is important for me in this experience is seeing her react to it and then engaging her. I was playing along with her. {#2}

The first example above demonstrates how the owner used single-player mode to interact with the iPad and the cat at the same time, a scenario we had not considered during the design of CCR. In the second quote, the owner elicits play behaviors by gauging the cat's interest. Using the iPhone, she experimented with mouse movements until finding a *pattern* that resulted in chase behaviors. In the third example above, we suggest the minimalist design accommodates unplanned play interactions by relying on the participants' ability to actively reconstitute play dynamics.

> They just have to learn to play. You just play with them. Trial and error a lot . . . but, part of it comes from the playing and observing. He just will learn. {#1}

> It makes you feel connected and it's like a conversation. They do not use words, so you use play. I think they contribute to our lives, so I think it is important to interact with them at their level. So, playing with them and seeing their natural play behaviors cause their play behaviors are attack and catch things. {#6}

In the first quote above, the participant describes the process of learning a new game as a constitutive process of trial and error, requiring both participants to actively interpret behavior to negotiate game play. In the second quote, the participant metaphorically describes play as a conversation. She redresses her pet's asymmetrical ability to share and interpret meaning by interacting with her pet at its level. She co-constructs play experiences by interpreting natural feline behaviors in the context of play. In addition, the second quote suggests an emotional component to digital pet play, which causes the participant to reflect on the emotional experience of CCR. These cases suggest that participants rely on context and extra-system knowledge to create meaningful play interactions.

CONCLUSION

Our findings suggest implications for future human-pet gaming systems. The examples above explore how participants actively negotiated play interactions, despite their asymmetrical ability to share or coordinate interaction, and reflect the constitutive nature of human-pet play. The game allows participants to co-construct play experiences by exploiting the contextual and social dynamics of human-pet play. In addition, the game uses *deictic representations* to communicate state in actionable ways and encourage specific behavioral interactions from both participants. These design considerations resulted in a novel opportunity to explore new ways to include pets in the digital gaming experience.

ACKNOWLEDGEMENTS

We are indebted to many friends who read and commented on the paper. We would like to thank the reviewers, Susan Wyche, Jofish Kaye, Daniel Ashbrook, Vas Kostakos, and Ian Oakley for their suggestions and feedback. We would like to thank Gavin Bowman and Daniel Yang for their help with testing and development. Thank-you Centro de Ciência e Tecnologia da Madeira.

REFERENCES

1. "2009-2010 National Pet Owners Survey." Survey. American Pet Products Association , 2010.
2. Alger, J. M. and S. F. Alger. *Cat Culture: The Social World of a Cat Shelter.* Temple University Press, 2003.
3. AP-Petside.com. "Pets and their owners." Conducted by GfK Roper Public Affairs & Media, 2009.
4. Arluke, A. and C. Sanders. *Regarding Animals.* Philadelphia: Temple University Press, 1996.
5. Brooks, R. A. Intelligence without representation. *Artificial Intelligence.* 42, (1991b).
6. Cerulo, K. A. "Nonhumans in Social Interaction." *Annu. Rev. Sociol.* 35 (2009), 531-552.
7. Friedman, B., Kahn, P.H., and Hagman, J. "Hardware Companions? – What Online AIBO Discussion Forums Reveal about the Human-Robotic Relationship." In *Proc. CHI '03*, ACM Press (2003), 273-280.
8. Glaser, B.G. and Strauss, A. *The Discovery of Grounded Theory: Strategies for Qualitative Research.* Aldine Transaction, 1967.
9. Goode, David. *Playing with My Dog, Kate: An Ethnomethodological Study of Canine-human Interaction.* Purdue University Press, 2007.
10. Irvine, Leslie. *If You Tame Me: Understanding Our Connection with Animals.* 2004.
11. Jerolmack, Colin. Humans, Animals, and Play: Theorizing Interaction When Intersubjectivity is Problematic. *Sociological Theory* 27.4 (2009).
12. Leahu, L., Sengers, P., & Mateas, M. "Interactionist AI and the promise of ubicomp, or, how to put your box in the world without putting the world in your box." In *Proc. Ubicomp '08*, ACM Press (2008), 134-143.
13. Loop, M.S., Millican, L.C., and Thomas, S.R. "Photopic spectral sensitivity of the cat." *J. Physiol.* 382 (1987).
14. Pettman, Dominic. "Love in the Time of Tamagotchi." *Theory, Culture & Society.* 26.2-3 (2009), 189-208.
15. Sanders, C. "Understanding dogs: caretakers attributions of mindedness in canine-human relationships." *J. Contemp. Ethnogr.* 22.2 (1993).
16. Suchman, L. A. *Human-machine reconfigurations: Plans and situated actions.* 2nd ed. 2007.
17. Taylor, Alex S. "Machine Intelligence." In *Proc. CHI '09*, ACM Press, 2109-2118.
18. Teh, K. S., Lee, S. P., and Cheok, A. D. "Poultry. Internet: a remote human-pet interaction system." In *Extended abstracts of CHI '06*, ACM Press, 251-254.
19. Turkle, Sherry. "Authenticity in the age of digital companions." *Interaction Studies* 8.3 (2007).

Antiquarian Answers: Book Restoration as a Resource for Design

Daniela K. Rosner
School of Information, UC Berkeley
Berkeley, CA 94720 USA
daniela@ischool.berkeley.edu

Alex S. Taylor
Microsoft Research Cambridge
Cambridge, CB3 0FB, UK
ast@microsoft.com

ABSTRACT
As technologies age, they experience wear and degradation, sometimes resulting in loss of functionality. In response, parts are replaced and software is updated. Yet *restoration*—the process of returning something to a previous condition, often regardless of its instrumental value—is a relatively rare practice with computational technologies. The aim of this paper is to enrich HCI design practices by considering the material qualities of restoration. We consider what makes a technology worth restoring and what constitutes the process of restoration by examining data collected from a three-month apprenticeship-based qualitative study of bookbinding. Building on relevant literatures, we offer antiquarian books—long-established information technologies—as a lens onto the ways values are enacted through material engagements. We conclude with a discussion of restoration's role in HCI.

Author Keywords
Handwork, skill, material, tool, handcraft, books, binding.

ACM Classification Keywords
K.4.0 Computers and Society: general.

General Terms
Design, Human Factors.

INTRODUCTION
From the rotary phone to the Walkman, technologies regularly undergo cycles of obsolescence. Given the recent proliferation of broken, outdated or discarded devices, HCI has examined ways of supporting repair practices, both through sustainable design [3] and Do-It-Yourself (DIY) processes of customization and reuse [11]. Yet, in this research on remaking, issues of obsolescence remain. What might it mean to restore old operating systems and software to their original condition, instead of, for example, simply upgrading them? Might there be value in how technologies wear, rather than how effectively they perform? How might HCI foster more *longstanding* relationships with digital technologies as they have developed with some traditional media—such as manuscripts, photographs or books?

CHI 2011, May 7–12, 2011, Vancouver, BC, Canada.

This work begins addressing these questions by examining appropriation and repair from a somewhat different angle: as enacted in the provenance of materials and their historical and social value. Drawing on social science literature [6,7,8,9,10], we examine *restoration*—the process of returning something to a previous condition—and consider how the material interactions may have some bearing on HCI. We focus on book restoration (for illustrative purposes) as a complex activity involving remaking longstanding, often quite intimate, media. For example, in restoring a family bible, the owner may want to preserve evocative traces of the book's past (creases on the spine, handwriting on the margins) while enabling the book to be read and handled by future generations. It is in the negotiation of a book's history and possibilities of its use—the careful balance of *authenticity* with *longevity*—that we find a sustainable design practice of an unusual sort, one that sheds some light on how digital technology might evolve over time. The aim of this paper is, then, to enrich HCI design practices by considering how the social and material qualities of restoration affect the life cycles of personal media.

METHOD
The first author visited seven bookbinding workshops—four in the UK and three in the US—and conducted semi-structured interviews with 10 key participants: five professional binders, five hobbyist binders, and three customers. Informed by previous HCI research on handwork [11], interview questions were designed to elicit reflections on binding practices (e.g. *What does it mean to use historical methods?*) and personal books (e.g. *What makes this object worth restoring?*). One of the UK workshops became a primary research site where the first author learned fine binding and book restoration over three months for an average of three days per week. This autoethnographic approach was informed by previous HCI research exploring naval tactical command and control systems [2] and anthropological work by Coy [4] that found apprenticeship provides valuable insights into technical and social behavior. During this period, the restoration work was documented through handwritten jottings, video and photos. The first author also collected bits of bound and unbound material and restored one personal book. Interviews and fieldwork observations were transcribed and reviewed by the authors—both meeting weekly to discuss the material and draw out relevant themes. These themes were subsequently developed and

organized alongside comparisons to analytic work from cultural studies scholars (such as anthropologist Tim Ingold's [7] description of "processional" tool use).

WHAT IS RESTORATION?

Restoration, as we experienced it, entailed a set of productive activities that transformed an existing information technology into something evocative of its former self. Asking Adam, a restoration binder, how he would describe his practice, he responded:

> *You know how these books can survive even when they're neglected for hundreds of years? I mean, it's an amazing—historically—it's an amazing technology. Isn't it really? As a way of passing on information. You know, a book can be so durable that leather can fall off, the spine can fall off, the headbands can go, the first two pages can get torn. But as long as those corners are on strong and those boards are good, and it doesn't get damp, you know? That can knock around even for a couple of hundred years just like that, can't it? It's great.*

This response illustrates how our participants appreciated the ways in which a book is made to last through its reconstruction. An awareness to durability is demonstrated in the language used ("square," "evenly coated," "flat"), binding activities, and aesthetic produced. In the workshop, books were observed passing through several stages of production, including *manual activities,* such as folding paper, *tooling activities,* such as sawing and sewing, *mechanical activities,* such as chopping (on the guillotine) and typesetting (on a blocking machine), and even *digital activities*, such as creating labels (using a laptop and printer). Each stage of restoration was readjusted based on several interwoven factors, such as the *age* of the book. For a 16th century manuscript with an elaborate but deteriorating gold leaf title, a binder might keep the remaining gold leaf or overlay additional gold leaf by hand. Whereas for a compilation of 19th century machine-bound books whose labels had fallen off, a binder might digitally design the label on a PC, print out several copies, and paste one on each book. A book's original binding informed the approach to rebinding. Other influential factors included: *cost* of the materials and labor, *time and effort* available to the binder or customer, *physical condition* of the book (deteriorating spine, pages falling out) and existing materials (brittleness of the paper, grain of the leather), *style of binding* (cloth case, half-leather, sewon chords, and so on), and—most importantly—the binder and customer's ideas of *authenticity.*

Making Authenticity

> *I asked Kate if she ever sawed into the spine of a book. She gasped. I thought something had gone terribly wrong, but she was reacting to my question. "No, we don't ever saw books." She explained that sawing the books was meant for putting cords in the books to keep the books flat, but that sawing is no longer necessary because flat tapes are now available. She let me feel the tapes, which were a distinctly modern material—flexible and strong. She would never do anything to harm the books if she didn't have to, she said.*

This fieldnote excerpt reveals the particular relationship Kate, a binder, has to her customers and to the books she rebinds. She is responding to a 19th century practice of sawing grooves into the spine of books for recessing cords in sewing, the subsequent stage of binding. While to one binder certain coated pages could not be bound without sawing, to another binder sawing books at the head (top) and tail (bottom) of the spine mitigated damage to the book while sewing. Kate disagreed with both claims. For her, restoration should be "reversible.". Having recently finished a set of catalogues for a customer who requested case-bindings (hardbound books), Kate and her co-workers proudly showed off their finished work: structurally supportive but removable dust jackets. To Kate, the jacket solved the customer's problem (increasing the book's longevity) while "respecting" the book (retaining its authenticity).

In working out how to balance authenticity and longevity we thus find contradictory ideas of appropriateness in restoration practice. Offering an informative parallel, anthropologist Christina Krebs [8] describes how some museum artifacts are understood not as artifacts behind glass cases, but through their interactions in the social world. Some Native Americans, for instance, felt conserving objects "*arrests the life cycle of the object*" [8]:93. Anthropologist Suzanne Küchler [9] has similarly shown how the process of destroying wooden sculptures—allowing them to rot and release an odor ("musung") [9]:633—allows those artifacts to continue to live on in Melanesian society. They are given a longer life not through their tangible features, but through their shifting materiality and the performance of that materiality in everyday life. These perspectives suggest that prolonging the life of an object by keeping it behind a case embodies just one concept of authenticity.

Kate's "reversible" restoration work—much like keeping a cultural artifact behind a case—might be seen as one construction of authenticity. While Kate's sense of authenticity does not, in itself, constitute an intervention, her production of the catalogues without case-bindings altered her customers' relationships to the catalogues and book. Her physically reversible work, thus, produced an *irreversible intervention.* This paradox in practice reveals a shared understanding of authenticity: one remade through binding.

PRODUCING A WELL-RESTORED BOOK

> *"When you close the book it should have a sense of weight about it. And that's the way it should be [...] So I made the decision that I'd like to see—about to the longevity of it, as you know—in my collection of books. If it had been for a customer than I would go along with what the customer wants."*

Throughout the binding process, binders sought to increase the longevity of the book. The language of "following what the customer wants" was frequently invoked when choices were justified after binding. However, in practice, things became part of a dialogue between the binder and materials, mediated by the binder's tools and her manual use of them.

"It shouldn't fall apart on the first reading. It shouldn't fall apart on the hundredth reading. It should look as good as it did the first time it was picked up. And most books now, obviously fail. [...] You walk into a bookshop and you couldn't preserve them if even if you wanted to. If you actually read them you'd destroy them on the first reading. And even the really big prestigious books - cloth covered, and hard boards, case bindings - they fall to pieces. You know, it's sad."

Such attitudes toward restoration have remained a contentious issue within the fields of Art History and Architecture over the last two centuries. Condemning restoration practices of the 19th century, notable Arts and Crafts scholar William Morris voiced legitimate concerns about the replacement of Medieval buildings with what he considered "*feeble and lifeless forgery*" [10]. His imagery of "*stripping [from] a building of some of its most interesting material features*" suggest some artifacts should not evolve with modernity but, instead, be protected from it through conservation. Yet, how might a building be protected from decay and degradation without help from modern hands? Such a view gives particular significance to the past while ignoring the inevitability of material and cultural change.

Choosing *What* to Restore

In our observations, reasons for restoration varied widely, from pragmatic goals (a book was unreadable in its current state) to emotive motivations (a book no longer felt as it once did). Pages of books and handprints on covers triggered memories of particular settings from childhood (reading behind a grandmother's rocking chair) or celebratory moments (graduation). One customer brought in a dictionary whose pages were beginning to unhinge from its spine, rendering the book unusable. As a child, the customer used the dictionary to solve crossword puzzles with his grandfather. Getting another copy cost only a few pounds, but the restoration would cost sixty. For the binders, such work meant balancing two distinct goals: preserving the physical qualities of the book that make it an evocative sentimental object (*preserving uniqueness*) and replacing materials that give the book a longer life in use (*increasing longevity*). Peter, a restoration binder, described this process simply:

There's a point at which you have to make a decision. Am I going to have that repaired before the damage gets any worse? And that's the decision you have to make. As a collector you can't always conserve things just by leaving them alone in a box or a safe or an archive because sooner or later they are going to deteriorate. After all, the sewing on most ancient books—15, 16, 1700s—they would've been sewing them with silk or cotton. You know, not like modern sewing threads. So, therefore, it's going to rot. Paper might be okay, but sewing will rot. Fall apart. You then have a book that's going to cost a great deal to repair. Better to have it done beforehand, stop the problem, and get the book back together.

This depiction of the decision of whether or not to restore a book rings true in abstract terms, but belies the nuances of the book's presence and use in a person's daily life.

"I remember when this [book] was falling apart and I started tossing [it] around. [...] I could have replaced it with another book. This book had already been with me for about 20 years so I thought well, you know, it's difficult to find."

This excerpt from an interview with Varnaz, a customer who had a music book repaired three years ago, highlights the difficulties of justifying restoration. While, notionally, his book was easy to find (Varnaz could have bought another copy online), in actuality it was difficult—indeed, impossible—to find again. As Varnaz played music from this book since childhood, it embodied multiple layers of his past. The particular mottling on the last five pages of the book indicated where Varnaz had spent the majority of his time: Bach's *III Concerto*, his favorite piece. The book's distinctive smell, which he called "sweet" as he breathed it in deeply, reminded him of the many years of learning to play piano through which the book had endured. The library label on the inside of the front cover revealed the book's origins: a school library, from which Varnaz stole the book when he was 13. These material traces created continuity with his past. Moving closer, the book revealed another layer of its history: a careful re-backing (replacement of the spine) by Sean, a restoration binder, three years ago. Varnaz's book illustrates the materially embedded nature of memory and personal history.

Creating Age

"My ideal is, if I bind a row of books, they look like that [points to restored 17th century book]. *And you think: are they old, are they new? [...]So if you have new materials that resist being eroded by time, then you could have something that would last almost indefinitely at certain levels."*

As we have seen, what it takes for a book to be worth restoring, and which aspects of the book one wants to restore, were carefully worked out in practice. However, how to perform the restoration was an equal part of this negotiation. Does restoring a 400-year-old book with a deteriorating spine entail re-binding the book as it would have been originally bound? Does it mean re-binding the book so that it *appears* in its original condition? Or does it mean creating a jacket and slipcase so that the book remains untouched? A previously restored book raises further questions. How these questions are answered in the process of binding is indicative of a well-restored book.

While working on a 19th century leather-bound book, we needed to replace the "red rot," the deteriorated leather that turns red over time. What was the original color? Peter saw green. Sean saw dark brown; and I saw black. The book was eventually covered in Nigerian goatskin, stained dark brown, and "sprinkled" with black paint (a 17th century technique for creating the "look of age").

These negotiations are reminiscent of how STS scholar Charles Goodwin described chemists' classification of color categories—working out what it means for something to be "*jet black*" [6]. Choosing how to make a book look old involved not only finding the appropriate balance between preserving what exists and extending the longevity of the book, but also *attending to the material elements of the book that exposed some seeable quality of its past*—grain, color and stain. If parts of a book were deteriorating, in need of repair or readjustment, some original materials might have been replaced while others might remain untouched. In this remaking of historical techniques ideas of age are enacted.

DISCUSSION AND CONCLUSIONS

Throughout our study, restoration bookbinding reveals itself as a set of complex and contested practices. Durability of the book and respect for the book's history are two central concerns, continually balanced through human-material interactions. In restoration work, books, as technologies, become agents of recovery—of fading techniques, of cultural traditions, and of intimate interactions. Using the practice of book restoration as a lens onto interaction design, we offer two central concerns aimed at sensitizing HCI design to issues of restoration.

Materiality of Authenticity. We found that it was materials that shaped the perception and performance of authenticity. Meaningful traces were left on artifacts, naturally shaping them over time. This arguably contrasts with many of our experiences with computational technology. During this field study, the first author exchanged her mobile phone for a newer model, even though it was not falling apart. Similarly, she had her laptop repaired when the screen unhinged, but did not care (or hope) to get the same laptop back; her hard drive was the thing of "material value." In addition to focusing on recycling, reuse, and repair [3], HCI might attend to the *making of authenticity* as a materially and situationally specific event. We argue that in valuing some materials over others, binders do not distinguish between form and function, content and container, or even digital bits and tangible atoms. Rather, they are attending to *how a technology's materiality enables certain constructions of authenticity*. It is through our continued interactions with material, and the impressions we leave on it, that deeper attachments evolve. How might we look at the interactional qualities of hardware (a mobile phone), software (tools for digital content generation) or digital content (images, videos or type), as a binder attends to those of paper, such as its grain, color, or thickness? Just as someone might cherish a leather-bound camera (http://emuu.net/camera-leather), might they also treasure a particular laptop, graphics card or digital photo if traces of use were left on it over time? By enabling continuous, multidimensional gestures among and within our technological practices, perhaps we can foster more historically and materially meaningful interactions.

Designing for Longevity. Following from research in cultural anthropology [7,8,9], we found that the longevity of an artifact was not only made through materials, but also through its integration in social practice. Here we stress the nuanced social configurations that enabled continued celebrations of ritual, not through static technologies but through (inter-)actions surrounding and remaking those technologies. As we consider the memory practices that carry us into the future [4], it becomes important to think about how we might design for and with the things that remain. Might we want to revisit an Apple IIe graphics program differently from a digital photograph of a deceased parent? Might different experiences of game play result from using an original game console rather than an emulator? Alongside online digital archives, such as the Wayback Machine [12], perhaps we can enable varying forms of interaction: ways of looking back through familiar mechanisms (rebound books, emulators) and novel reinventions (a 16th century book retrofitted as an e-reader, a relative's teleostereograph machine as a functioning input device). Our observations suggest such things should be seen as part of a process of actively constituting our connections to the past.

Looking forward, we offer this work as a different way of thinking about design in HCI—one sensitive to the ideas of longevity, authenticity and ways of the hand. What it is that makes a technology functional and evocative is invariably woven into how the technology wears and becomes remade over time. Our hope is that by describing how materials play into these processes of restoration, we inspire the design of more meaningful and enduring technologies in HCI.

REFERENCES

1. Akah, B., Bardzell, S. 2010. Empowering products: personal identity through the act of appropriation. EA from *Proc. CHI '10*, 4021-4026.
2. Aoki. P. M. 2007. Back stage on the front lines: perspectives and performance in the combat information center. In *Proc. CHI '07*, 717–726.
3. Blevis, E. 2007. Sustainable Interaction Design: Invention & Disposal, Renewal and Reuse. In *Proc. CHI '07*, 503-12.
4. Bowker, G. 2005. *Memory practices in the sciences*: MIT Press.
5. Coy, M. 1989. *Apprenticeship: From Theory to method and Back Again.* New York: State University of New York Press.
6. Goodwin, Charles. 1997. "The Blackness of Black: Color Categories as Situated Practice". In *Discourse, Tools and Reasonsing: Essays on Situated Cognition.* Lauren B. Resnick, et al., eds. 111-140. Berlin, Heidelberg, New York: Springer.
7. Ingold, T. 2006. "Walking the plank: meditations on a process of skill". In *Defining technological literacy: towards an epistemological framework*. J. R. Dakers ed. 65-80. New York: Palgrave Macmillan.
8. Krebs, Christina. 2003. *Liberating Culture: Cross-Cultural Perspectives on Museum Curation and Heritage Preservation*. London: Routledge.
9. Küchler, S. 1988. Malangan: objects, sacrifice and the production of memory. In *Am. Ethnol.* 15, 625-37.
10. Morris, W. "Manifesto of the Society for the Protection of Ancient Buildings". In: Price, Nicholas Stanley. *Historical and philosophical issues in the conservation cultural heritage*. Los Angeles: The Getty Conservation Institute, 1996, 319-21.
11. Rosner, D. and Bean, J. 2009. Learning from IKEA hacking: I'm not one to decoupage a tabletop and call it a day. In *Proc. CHI '09*. ACM Press, 419-422.
12. WayBack Machine http://www.archive.org/web/web.php

Which Version is This?: Improving the Desktop Experience within a Copy-Aware Computing Ecosystem

Amy K. Karlson, Greg Smith, Bongshin Lee
Microsoft Research
One Microsoft Way, Redmond, WA 98052
{karlson, gregsmi, bongshin}@microsoft.com

ABSTRACT
Computers today make it easy for people to scatter copies and versions of digital items across their file systems, but do little to help people manage the resulting mess. In this paper, we introduce the concept of a copy-aware computing ecosystem, inspired by a vision of computing when systems track and surface copy relationships between files. Based on two deployments of a copy-aware software prototype and in-depth interviews with individuals in collaborative relationships, we present our findings on the origins of copies and the barriers to eliminating them, but offer a promising solution based on the set of files that together represent a user's conceptual view of a document - the *versionset.* We show that the versionset is viable to infer, and we draw upon user activity logs and feedback on personalized views of versionsets to distill guidelines for the factors that define a versionset. We conclude by enumerating the many PIM user experiences that could be transformed as a result.

Author Keywords
File management, PIM, copy-aware computing, versioning.

ACM Classification Keywords
H5.m. Information interfaces and presentation (e.g., HCI): Miscellaneous.

General Terms
Human Factors, Design.

INTRODUCTION

"Computers are machines for copying data. A good computer is one that copies well, quickly and cheaply."

—Cory Doctorow, co-editor of BoingBoing [13]

While Doctorow's statement was made in the context of digital rights management and the proliferation of copyrighted materials, the insight is no less important for personal datasets. Backups, email attachments, synchronization services, collaboration spaces, clipboard operations, "Save As" dialogs, and many other mechanisms in common use today all result in a full or partial copy of a stream of digital content. The depth to which copying behaviors are built into today's computing systems means that a document that starts as a single file can very easily become two, or ten, or a hundred files with very little explicit effort—sometimes no effort—on the user's part. Indeed, people are filling their hard drives as quickly as storage capacity is increasing [1], and there is evidence that much of this data represents copies of other files, such as those originating from shared sources [1], intermediate versions of documents [27], and duplicates across multiple personal devices [22].

The role that these rampant copies play in supporting or undermining personal information management (PIM) strategies has received relatively little research attention. It is obvious that copies—in particular, potentially divergent copies—can lead to significant PIM confusion on a regular basis: "*Which copy of this document is the one that I submitted for review? Which one did I send to Alice? Is this the only copy I have of this picture?*" And basic human factors research informs us that the presence of additional files in a folder will increase the time it takes a person to scan and select the desired one [21]. Whether the content across various copies remains identical or diverges widely, there are a great number of scenarios in which the user considers them "versions" of the same document, and is negatively impacted when her documents' digital manifestations do not reflect this fundamental connection.

In this paper, we will use the term **versionset** to represent this set of digital items that users conceptualize as a single entity. Through our investigation of the content copy operations that lead to versionsets, we uncovered ample evidence of the problems they pose to effective PIM. But we will also show that these operations are integral to a number of different collaborative and organizational processes, and will never be engineered away. Indeed, over the course of our investigation, we became convinced of the *opportunities* that versionsets present in a **copy-aware computing ecosystem**—an ecosystem that can capture and make use of the semantics behind the copy operations its users so commonly perform. We set out to determine whether the versionset was computationally viable to infer in real time, and whether it could indeed serve as a point of leverage in improving the organizational user experience.

The contributions of this paper are threefold. First, we present a *vision* of the user experience enabled when copy-awareness is built deeply into the interface, incorporating

CHI 2011, May 7–12, 2011, Vancouver, BC, Canada.

several examples we have implemented in an early prototype form. Second, we *motivate* the need and desirability for such a system with insights gleaned from two phases of copy-aware software prototype deployment, combined with in-depth interviews and data collection. We offer a characterization of copies as "crucial clutter"—difficult to manage, but ultimately unavoidable, and even desirable in many circumstances. Finally, we distill *design guidelines* for copy-aware systems to infer the higher-level versionset abstraction from low-level inter-file relationships, and to use this abstraction in improving the user's PIM experience across a variety of strategies and tools.

BACKGROUND

Since the early days of the personal computer, there has been no shortage of research to classify and understand the organizational strategies involved in personal information management [3,16,20,24]. As observed by Dourish and others, information workers naturally use abstract concepts like "document" and "project" as organizational constructs in expressing their workflows. But the actual digital items (files, emails, web pages, etc.) in a user's content collection are computational artifacts with strict behaviors defined largely by their technical implementations [14].

The first possible solution to the problem of allowing digital "atoms" on a personal computer to be organized into "molecules" of related content arrived with the first personal computers themselves: the hierarchical file system. Users could freely define folders and subfolders as organizational structures into which to place their files. Although the size of the average user's aggregate content base and the number of constituent personal, shared, or online content repositories has increased dramatically over the last two decades, the primacy of this basic hierarchical storage and retrieval metaphor has yet to be seriously threatened [3,7,18].

Yet no one is under any illusions that the rigid hierarchical metaphor is the perfect solution. At any given moment, the proper mapping between the intuitive concepts of a user's workflow and the digital artifacts of their computing devices is difficult to define; and the inability of today's systems to address and support this complex, fluid, and contextual relationship is a source of ongoing user frustration [9,20, 24]. A wealth of research and commercial effort has gone toward better supporting PIM by allowing the aggregation of a user's digital items and activity into more flexible groupings across a variety of computing domains, and here we outline several important categories of approach.

Item Grouping

Keyword search as a PIM tool has received increasing scrutiny in recent years, but has not achieved the same pervasive utility on the desktop that it has on the web. Despite advances in speed and relevance, user preference for "orienteering" approaches in finding things and regaining context has served to reinforce usage of the venerable hierarchical grouping metaphor [5,28]. Some researchers have recognized the potential of file-to-file relationships to help users with PIM search tasks, and built systems to track and leverage such data [17,25]. Many have exploited groupings of items by clustering items with related content, or expanding the set of search results, e.g., by returning an item in search results that did not contain the actual keyword in question but was related in content to files that did [15].

Another, less keyword-centric approach to overcoming users' issues with strict hierarchical groupings involves elevating the role of a digital item's "attributes" to a prime organizational principle. In these systems, items are automatically grouped on attributes such as access time, file size, and content type [12,14,20]. In contrast to the standard hierarchy, where each item has a single path leading to it, such systems allow users the flexibility to intersect desired attribute values in any order when locating a digital resource. Several of these systems have extended the attribute types beyond standard file metadata to include associations with other items [11] or information about the user's activity with respect to the items [15].

The idea of leveraging a user's interaction activity in organization and retrieval has been explored extensively under the general rubric of "activity-based computing." Drawing on activity theory, a number of research systems have been proposed and built to give the abstract user concept of "project" an explicit manifestation and organizational role. In several of these, a user explicitly signals the beginning of an activity, and the system associates an activity tag with subsequently-accessed digital resources to group them or otherwise optimize their future accessibility [2,29]. To obviate the often-prohibitive overhead of manually specifying activity resumption, some systems attempt to infer an activity from the usage of the digital items themselves [23,26], although such efforts are prone to categorization errors.

Interestingly, less well-explored than groupings of heterogeneous items based on attributes or projects is the idea of creating or inferring a group of digital items that might collectively represent a single "document": the versionset. The most obvious reason for this is that the user concept of a document is already inherently much closer to the digital definition of a document—indeed, the digital manifestation was directly inspired by the user concept. But as pointed out in the Introduction, the widespread availability and use of copy operations on today's systems renders the simple one-to-one mapping between "document" and digital item untenable. Recognizing this, there are in fact several research efforts and commercial systems designed with explicit or implicit support for the versionset concept.

Versions

As part of an exploration into information flow between an individual's desktop files, Jensen *et al.* recently called attention to the frequency of inter-file "provenance" relationships (which include versioning relationships) created by today's information workers [17]. Interview data suggested the potential for provenance events to aid in context recall, but the authors point to difficulties posed by the sheer volume of relevant events in designing useful interfaces around such information. The Old'nGray design [4] proposes to

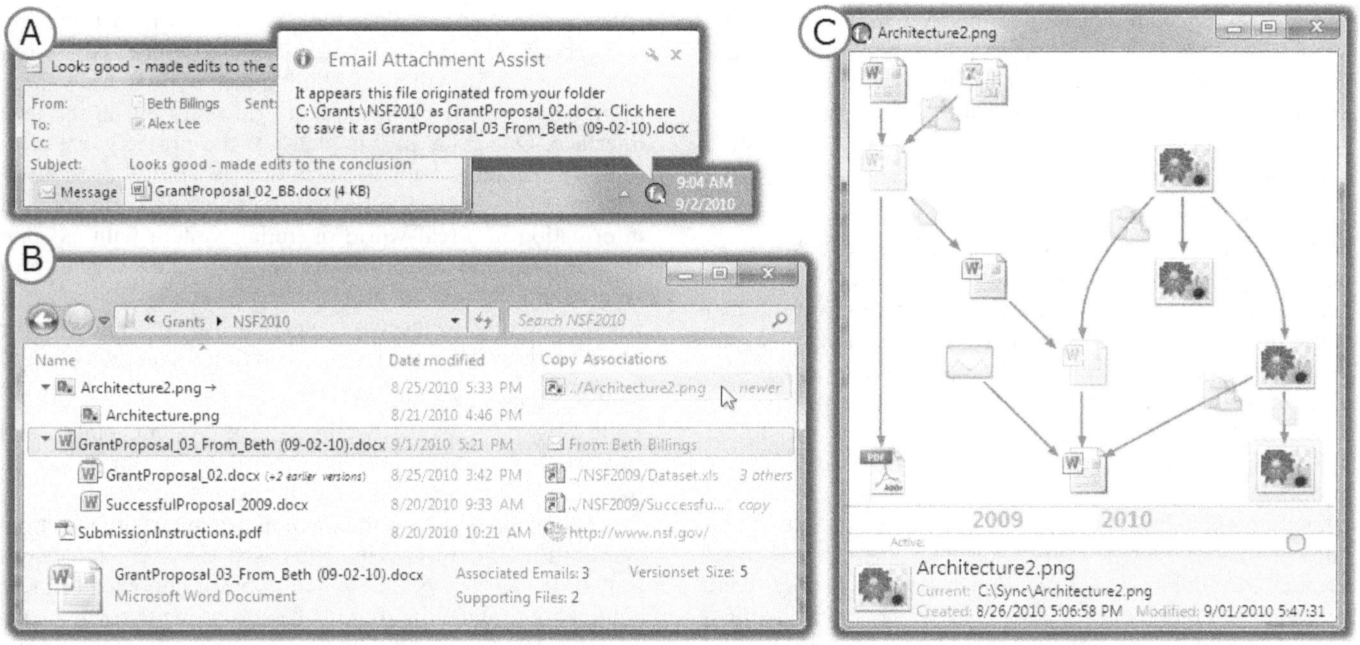

Figure 1. A copy-aware enhanced user experience. (A) Alex gets an email from his collaborator with the proposal revision attached; the system recognizes this and offers to save the attachment in the appropriate directory using his preferred naming scheme. (B) When Alex goes to edit an image file, he notices a small arrow, showing that a newer version is located elsewhere. Alex clicks on the Copy Associations metadata to investigate. (C) The graph view shows Alex the versionsets for the image and proposal, from which he sees that a newer version of the image is in his synced files folder (C:\Sync).

enhance the user's keyword search and hierarchical browse experience by automatically de-emphasizing older versions of documents in search results and explorer views to reduce clutter. This proposal, based on a "user-subjective approach," represents the most explicit acknowledgement to-date of the potential usefulness of the versionset in PIM literature, but again the authors stop short of defining what the versionset is or how to deduce it. Static analysis of the content duplication resulting from copy operations has also been directly leveraged in improving areas such as disk storage efficiency [8], quality of search result sets [10], and commonality-awareness among co-workers [27]. But none of these approaches propose to leverage the semantics of the copy operations themselves to enhance the user's organizational experience.

In areas such as software engineering and content sharing, several commercial systems exist entirely to implement support for document management and versioning (e.g., GIT, SharePoint, DropBox). These systems are usually centralized, and they dictate a single namespace within which all versioning activity must be reconciled. Unfortunately, from the point of view of a user struggling to organize and maintain a broad collection of content across a range of roles and devices, these systems simply serve to introduce yet another rigid hierarchy. Indeed, sometimes the act of creating a version (such as emailing a document to a home computer for further editing) is taken explicitly to work around an environmental limitation (such as lack of network access) that would render a version control or synchronization system useless. These systems have a number of desirable features, and their wide acceptance in certain environments is testament to the importance of managing document evolution carefully and rigorously. But we will demonstrate that a copy-aware computing ecosystem can provide similar benefits across a wider variety of content and use scenarios, without the overhead of centralized control or pre-meditated version-based structuring.

THE COPY-AWARE USER EXPERIENCE

If computing systems tracked and understood the flow of content across a person's devices, and used that understanding to reason about and reconcile related resources, what might the user experience look like? We use the following everyday scenario to introduce a vision of how deep system awareness of content copy relationships between files has the potential to improve the data management experience for today's information workers.

Scenario

Alex is a researcher who has been working with a small distributed group of collaborators on a project for several months. Alex, as the primary investigator, has been the one most active in pulling supporting resources together and maintaining a shared project folder. A few documents—such as the grant proposal, the system design specification, and milestone reports—periodically circulate through email among team members for edits. Alex tries to keep work at work, but he does subscribe to a commercial synchronization service that allows him to keep certain folders on his home and work machines in sync.

Organizational Assistance

Alex receives an email with the latest revision of the grant proposal as an attachment from Beth, one of his colleagues.

When Alex opens the document, his system asks him if he would like to save it in the project directory with the other versions, to identify which root version Beth was working from, and name the new file meaningfully with respect to this information (Figure 1a). Alex accepts the suggestion and heads home for the day.

Folder View

Returning to the grant proposal project the next day, Alex navigates to his project folder to orient himself for resuming his work. Several features of his copy-aware folder view make his sense-making easier (Figure 1b). First, the many prior versions of his grant proposal are indented with respect to the latest working copy from Beth, with only a few key intermediate versions showing. Because the folder holds many other files, several earlier versions of the grant proposal insignificant to his current browsing context are elided completely, to make more room for other items. In informational columns in his folder view, he can see copy-related metadata at a glance—such as which files were emailed to other collaborators, and which have identical copies in other folders or on other machines. Now that he has the proposal back, Alex wants to embed the updated system architecture diagram he's been working on, so he turns his attention to the PNGs in his project folder. These files are also indented to show a versioning relationship, but here Alex stops—he sees that the latest diagram file in the folder is decorated to indicate there is a newer version outside of his current view! He needs to explore the file's relationship history in more detail to resolve this mystery.

Graph View

Invoking an alternate view of the diagram file in his project folder, Alex is presented with his interaction history coalesced into a graph of relationships (Figure 1c). Here he can see other picture files from which he copied content, and the exact sequence of branching that went on as he iterated on the diagram. Most importantly, he can see that last week he copied the latest PNG into another local folder that was synchronized to his home machine. He now remembers making changes to the diagram from home, but he had not remembered to copy the new version from the sync folder back into his project folder. Correcting this oversight, assured now that he has the correct version, he embeds the latest diagram into the grant proposal.

This brief vision of a copy-aware desktop system has served multiple roles over the course of our project—as an inspiration for developing the necessary infrastructure, as a probe for soliciting end-user experiences about current data management practices and pitfalls, and as a reference point for designing novel representations of users' own data to elicit feedback. Next, we describe the process by which we first exposed end-users to various elements of this vision.

INITIAL EXPLORATION

For today's users, evidence suggests that much of the hierarchical approach to organization, and the orienteering approach to retrieval, are grounded in providing *context*: How does a given item or set of items relate to the rest of a user's collection? [28] To explore the question of whether copying and versioning events are potentially under-utilized as contextualizing information, we built a prototype to track these events and expose them explicitly in real-time in the user interface. Our goals in this phase of the project were two-fold: 1) to explore the basic technical feasibility of robustly tracking cross-application and cross-machine copy creation information in a real-world operating system with existing applications; and 2) to use the newly-tracked data to provide useful context to users of the prototype at moments where they might otherwise experience frustration with (or succumb to pitfalls in) their organizational schemes.

Prototype Implementation

Following prior work identifying file system, email, and web as three particularly important domains for PIM data [6,7,17,28], we identified the eight main applications across these domains that were in common use in our organization. We built a Microsoft Windows-based C# .Net Framework prototype that injects a C++ hook library into each of these applications (and Windows itself) at runtime to track a variety of otherwise un-tracked (and un-reconstructable) copy creation events. These events are recorded into a local SQL Compact Edition database in the form of a node/link graph: files, emails, and web URLs are the nodes, and various copy-creation relationships (Save As, SaveAttachment, etc.) are the links (Table 1). We built a visualization for this data, invoked by right-clicking a file in Windows Explorer and selecting "Show History..." from the resulting context menu. The visualization module queries the relationship database to perform an exhaustive graph traversal outward from the target file of all tracked content copy relationships. The results are presented in a graph view (Figure 1c).

During the course of prototype development, we solicited feedback at several events internal to our organization (all refereed to limit acceptance to potentially high-value or interesting technologies) as to the perceived utility of the prototype and the desired feature set. We used the earlier events to get individual feedback via one-on-one demonstrations of the system, and implemented the tracking and features deemed of highest interest to initial audiences. Responses to the system were very positive, quickly accruing 44 installations by users across the organization (who were not given any incentive or compensation for downloading and installing the software).

Ongoing bug reports from this set of users allowed us to iteratively refine our implementation over the ensuing months. After four months we followed up with 9 of the 16 people who were still running the original prototype to understand what was and was not working well for them with

SaveAs: Office, Notepad, Paint, Acrobat	**CopyFile:** Shell
Save: Office, Notepad, Paint	**Attach:** Outlook
SaveAttachment: Outlook	**Upload:** IE
Copy/Paste: Shell	**Download:** IE

Table 1. The file content copy events captured by our system.

respect to the tool itself, as well as in their own data management practices. We conducted semi-structured interviews at the participants' desks to elicit personal stories drawn from their own graphs and PIM structures. We brought with us a tool to identify interesting graphs to explore, and an early version of the file explorer (Figure 1c).

Users Need Integrated Assistance

Interestingly, almost none of the participants reported opening the prototype graph visualization after the initial installation. One possible explanation was that performing an explicit action to explore a graph was an act users would only think to take during "emergency" situations: P1, "*It's definitely a rare scenario that there are things I need to track down, but when it happens, this would save me a lot of time.*" Rare as such occasions may be, our system was unused in the opportunities that did occur, suggesting that despite its potential value, the assist was too hidden or too burdensome to invoke.

Yet during our joint interactive exploration, every interviewee discovered relationships that he or she found interesting and useful in the data we explored together, reinforcing findings by Jensen *et al.* [17]. Belying the hypothesis that this information would only be useful in rare cases, the explanations that our interviewees gave for why a particular piece of metadata was interesting often related to an everyday data management task, rather than a special occasion inquiry. A common theme that emerged was the need for assistance in determining the "correct" version of a file. For example, seven participants wanted more confidence that a file being accessed was the most recent version (e.g., that there wasn't a more recent version elsewhere). Four participants showed us folders with several similarly-named files and wanted easy ways to distinguish between them. Three others thought the copy metadata would help them understand which files were *un*important versions that could be deleted or moved. Thus, our lesson was not that users needed better reminders to open the graph view, but that they needed better integration of valuable file relationship information into their existing views and workflows.

While our interviews seemed to confirm that version and copy information could be useful if properly integrated into the existing user experience, we also needed to address the question of whether we were tackling the problem from the right perspective. That is, instead of surfacing information about the copies and versions that exist, perhaps we should be trying to eliminate the creation of copies in the first place? To answer the question of whether eliminating file copies was possible or desirable, we needed deeper insight into how copies manifest within a user's computing ecosystem, and what specific PIM problems they pose.

STUDY: THE HOW AND WHY OF COPIES

We designed a study that would provide us multiple perspectives from which to build a rich picture of the role, positive and negative, that copies play in users' file management practices. We wanted to: a) characterize the *origin* of copies, which would tell us whether the role of technology intervention should be to eliminate copies or to support users in managing them; and b) get users' perspectives on possible solutions to the PIM challenges that copies pose, to gauge the feasibility of using the versionset concept to provide such solutions. These goals dictated a field study involving real user data over a period of time.

Participants

We recruited 16 information workers (6 female) at our institution for the study. Since some of the copies we witnessed in our preliminary evaluation involved sharing files with others, we resolved to include in our study several sets of people who were in collaborative relationships with each other. Among our 16 people, 8 (4 female) were students visiting from academic institutions for a 12-week internship (I1-I8), and 8 (2 female) were full-time employees chosen from each intern's set of project collaborators to serve as mentors (M1-M8). This subject pool had several useful properties for our study. First, it ensured that a half of our participants (the interns) had information management habits originating from outside of our institution. Second, it allowed us to study a set of activities constituting a complete project lifecycle among the interns, yet still investigate organizational environments with multiple simultaneous, potentially long-lived projects among the mentors. Finally, it allowed us to explore the particular implications for copy-aware systems posed by collaborative relationships among information workers.

Approach

We employed multiple data collection methods to study copies simultaneously from three different perspectives:

The file system: We wrote a disk snapshot tool to gather information about the static state of the file system. This tool captured the file path, creation time, last access time, last modified time, and MD5 content hash value of each file on each local hard drive of the target system.

User behavior: We deployed an updated version of our copy-aware software prototype to log and examine user actions that lead to copies. This software logged the set of copy creation events shown in Table 1.

Social and organizational factors: We conducted semi-structured one-on-one interviews with each participant about their organizational and collaborative practices to catalogue the forces that cause users to create copies.

Procedure

Within one week of the start of each intern's internship we ran the disk snapshot tool on both the mentor and intern's primary work computers, and simultaneously installed our copy-aware activity logger. Two weeks prior to the end of each 12-week internship, we instructed each member of the intern/mentor pair to run the disk snapshot tool a second time. At the end of each internship, we instructed each intern/mentor pair to run a final disk snapshot. The snapshot software allowed participants to anonymize file names and URLs within the dataset if desired.

At the end of the internship, we separately interviewed the intern and the mentor about their data management practices. Interviews included questions along four dimensions: team structure and dynamics, including communication and sharing practices; file and data management strategies; archiving practices; and feedback on a design proposal for a copy-aware folder view. In this last phase of the interview, we pre-selected a folder from the participant's own file structure that had a large amount of file activity according to the pre-submitted log data. Using knowledge gathered from the participant's logged copy operations and file accesses, we hand-crafted a hypothetical copy-aware view of the folder using different visual elements to convey versionsets, duplicates, associated emails, and files (including URLs) related by copy/paste relationships. Because this representation was based on real data, not all participants saw all design elements.

RESULTS

As with many field studies, we encountered a number of issues—participant vacations, prototype bugs, machine reliability problems, etc.—that kept us from recording a full twelve weeks of data for each participant. Over the course of the study, we collected data representing 3,336 hours of logged user activity time across 820 unique person-days. Figure 2 shows the aggregate number of copy operations we captured by domain and direction of content movement. We wrote a visualization and analysis tool for exploring the logged data, and used an affinity diagramming approach to categorize the interview data. To address the question of whether copies could and should be eliminated, we turned to our interviews (N=14) to understand the origin of copies from the user's perspective. (One intern/mentor pair was unavailable for the final interview.) Our choice of highly technical, information-intensive study participants obviously dictates that care be taken in generalizing our results. But in the analysis that follows, hopefully the applicability to, say, a home computer user managing and sharing a collection of digital photographs, will be clear.

Crucial Copies

We identified three main categories of copy creation into which the logged copy operations fell among our study population: content preservation, sharing across a user's multiple content hierarchies, and sharing content with others. In each category, we found content copies to be crucial to achieving users' goals.

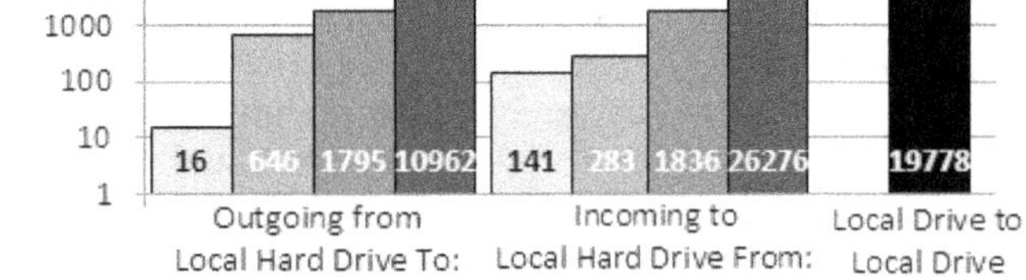

Figure 2. Number of copies logged from, to, and within participants' systems, by domain.

Copies for Content Preservation

To say that people are concerned about losing important digital content would be an understatement. Reinforcing findings by Jones *et al.* [18], participants unanimously kept volumes of data of questionable utility because of fear that a deleted item might someday become valuable. Almost as common was the habit of making deliberate copies of known-useful data for safety—nearly every participant had a nightmare story to relate about the catastrophic loss of useful data.

Participants used a variety of methods to ensure data preservation, including formal backups to servers (M5), manual backups to external drives or computers (M1, M7) data synchronization to other work or personal computers (M1, M4, M5), emailing oneself documents (M1, M3), server-backed source control (M1, M3, M6), and copying files and directories within the same computer to preserve a snapshot of work in progress (I4, I5).

All but three participants reported saving versions of documents to checkpoint those with contributions or comments from collaborators, and typically before sending documents out to collaborators for edit or review. Participants also created versions of documents before or after substantial changes to a document's content or formatting.

Despite their aversion to deletion, participants typically reported that they were "really never going to return to any of those old versions" (M1). Past versions often co-existed in folders alongside more recent versions and thus unavoidably contributed to folder clutter. But participants generally professed to be unfazed by the effect of this clutter because they used consistent manual naming schemes (e.g., incrementing numbers), albeit at the cost of cognitive overhead. Most participants relied on the system-maintained last modification timestamp to identify version relationships—although in one exceptional case, a participant used a script to auto generate version names with a date-time stamp because file modification dates had proven to be fallible.

Copies to Share Data across Devices

The information workers in our study all managed their work across multiple computers and expended considerable effort in making their content accessible from multiple locations—a goal they considered to be crucial to their work. All but one participant performed work activities from both a desktop and laptop. Each of the four mentors who synchronized data manually admitted occasional human error in keeping files up to date and keeping track of the canonical version of a file (M2, M3, M6, M7); both mentors who used email to transfer files admitted they sometimes forgot to email a file or save one they sent from another system. The two mentors who used a formal sync service were more confident in their strategies, but also keenly aware of its fragility. For example, M1 always keeps in mind that his sync software is peer-to-peer: "*It has yet to cause me problems but I do need to be cognizant of the state of the universe and which machine is 'on'*" and M5 falls back to email as insurance when data propagation is slow.

For five of the seven interns, the main challenge was keeping data synchronized between their development and deployment environments. Deployment machines included high performance clusters, web servers, and mobile devices. In all five cases, interns copied files manually between two or more systems and all encountered difficulties keeping changes synchronized between machines.

Copies to Share Data with Others

The need to collaborate and share data with others was a necessary part of all our participants' workflows, and yet was without question the largest contributor to unreconciled, ambiguous, and confusing data copies on their systems. Each intern-mentor pair chose a unique combination of tools and techniques for communicating, coordinating and sharing data during the project. Email attachments were the one sharing method used by every pair. Five pairs used a shared project folder, which was either synchronized automatically (three pairs) or hosted by the mentor (one pair) or intern (one pair). While four of the projects used a source control system, only one pair used it to actively share documents and code with one another during the internship.

All but one project pair used multiple methods to share data, which itself caused confusion about which files and versions were stored and shared in which locations. Although it is tempting to consider whether the solution to sharing-based copies lies in designing a single "perfect" sharing system, we developed two main insights from participants' reported behaviors that suggest little potential for converging on a single solution:

The Ownership Problem: Reinforcing prior PIM literature [19], we found users to be highly attached to their own local organizational practices. When people collaborate, they must either impose their organizational preferences on others, defer to someone else's preferences, or refuse to play—and we saw instances of all three in our study. The group that had the least confusion about collaborative versioning used an approach dictated by the mentor: "I3: *I found M3's process to be very stable. He's been using it a long time and once I learned his process it was easy to use...It just meant I didn't work outside work [because of the need for internal access] but it didn't turn into more artifacts.*"

Although some participants implied they would be willing to adopt a collaborator's version naming strategy (I1, M6), we also observed significant friction in groups trying to adopt a single sharing strategy. In one case, a synchronized folder was arranged between the intern and mentor, but was not taken up by new members of the team: M5: "*we also had a bunch of other people working on the project with us and not all of them were invested in getting up to date on the shared folder, so more stuff went back and forth through email than it might have needed to if only I5 and I were working on the project.*" Divergent naming schemes kept M4 from adopting the intern's sharing scheme: "*I completely ignored requests to put data [in the intern's directory], I emailed it to him. [...] I'm a neat freak when it comes to my file organization, so the idea of having two organizing schemes being applied to the same folder at the same time is disturbing to me. So I wouldn't do it. I'd email it to him and say: put it where you want it to be.*"

Distaste for the unruly state of a shared space was echoed by M5, referring to several collaboration spaces as "spaghetti." Yet there is also friction in taking responsibility to clean up a shared space: "*there's a tension between keeping the messy structure [in a shared project folder], because we know it. But there's also some concern that it would break the replication*" (M5). The perceived permanence of one's decisions when sharing data was also the source of some anxiety, as illustrated by M4's discomfort when sharing data out on a public directory: "*I'm traumatized by the fact that it means the filename is crystallized. Once you've shared the link, you'll break it if you change it.*"

The Tools Problem: Participants deemed certain tools to be more appropriate for some data types and work styles. Source control was useful for code but less appropriate for document collaborations because of the need for wide accessibility, which could not be fulfilled when outside the corporate network. Other synchronization methods were seen as too heavyweight or unreliable for time-constrained collaboration. Email was commonly used to circumvent these constraints, but had its own drawbacks. M4 recalled the synchronization problems he recently faced: "*There were so many people writing things all the time that it definitely happened that someone didn't follow the scheme, or, something that happens a lot is that something will get stuck in an outbox because it exceeds a file quota. Someone thinks it has been received or it gets junk-foldered. I think all of these things happened on that project. It was brutal.*" M2 had trouble using email to keep track of multiple documents at the same time: "*We were writing a bunch of papers so it did get a little confusing keeping track of it because, again, we were using email, and, you know, the classic 'use the email thread about the other paper' and so there was a bunch of that that happened.*"

Getting Feedback on Solutions

Our second study question was whether the versionset concept was useful and tractable as a leverage point in solving general copy-related PIM problems. To get useful feedback, we identified a specific PIM user experience for which to propose versionset-derived assistance. From our earlier investigation that folder clutter can be version-related, we hypothesized that visually demarcating a versionset in the standard Explorer folder view might serve to de-clutter the interface during folder browsing. This design was meant to probe the benefit, oft-cited in information management literature [14], of turning a cognitive task (in this case, identifying versions of a file) into a perceptual one.

For this exercise, we defined a versionset as the files related by logged SaveAs, CopyFile and Copy/Paste relationships. We understood this was overly simplistic, but the interview was designed to elicit a wider discussion of the factors involved in the versionset definition. We presented each participant with a paper prototype view of one of their own folders—a familiar organizational context, but with copy-aware enhancements. To get an idea of how the versionset definition might need to change according to context, we also solicited separate feedback from each mentor on their intern's prototype folder view—an unfamiliar organizational context, with the same copy-aware enhancements.

Versionsets were depicted in the view as collapsible sets of related files. In the collapsed view, a versionset was depicted as a single line showing the "canonical" current version; the expanded view showed all files in the versionset, using indentation to depict strict ancestry (SaveAs) relationships, and shortcut decorators on file icons to indicate "related" files as determined by CopyFile and Copy/Paste relationships. We also provided a metadata column showing the people that a file was emailed to or received from. The views were similar to Figure 1b, except that related documents were listed under, rather than next to, the versionset.

Context: My Organization

When looking at their own folders, participants were unanimously enthusiastic about the benefits of the view, especially the notion of the collapsible versionset, and its potential for reducing clutter. Although participants varied in their opinions about what aspects of the visual representation resonated the most, and under which scenarios the visual elements would be most useful, every element of the design was deemed "very useful" by at least several of the participants. Equally important was the finding that the precise versionset definition was an important factor in participants' satisfaction with the visuals. Participants were quick to point out examples of files in the indentation relationship that "didn't belong" in the collapsible set, such as milestone branches that were important in their own right ("submission branch" vs. "camera-ready branch"). It is clear that the correct determination of the versionset is a key factor in user satisfaction with copy-aware interfaces.

One surprise was the use that participants made of the email column, which we expected to be simply informational. However, participants were quite sensitive to the gaps and anomalies in the data that could signal an error in their data organization. As M4 explains: "*There are versions on my hard drive that I don't remember if I've sent them to the publisher or not, so it's happened a couple of times that I've sent two different versions, and the publisher says 'why are you sending us two different versions—which one is the right one?' So this would help. It would eliminate all of that. I could just say 'oh, well I haven't sent this yet.*'"

Context: Someone Else's Organization

When viewing their intern's folder view, mentors deemed the copy relationships equally or more useful than when viewing their own folder. Positive reactions to the resources related by Copy/Paste were explained as "*getting a sense of a file without having to open it*" (M2) and "*automatic annotation and referencing*" (M4). Mentors also appreciated how the indented view made it easy to pick out the "canonical" version of a file, as M1 points out, "*In [the copy-aware] view it is immediately evident which [file] is the most relevant. When I looked in the flat directory I would have been misled and grabbed the wrong one.*"

Overall, visually collapsing a versionset to a single canonical representative file appeared to represent a promising enhancement to the folder view in the existing PIM user experience. When browsing for a particular target version of a particular document, it was clear that the non-target versions of a file represented distracting clutter, and unsurprisingly, collapsing them away would be helpful. Our simple versionset definition for the user-feedback exercise was clearly not entirely sufficient for this task, but the study gave us the data we needed to produce a richer set of guidelines. The feedback taught us the factors that would allow us to create proper definitions and use cases for the versionset in a wider variety of user contexts.

INFERRING THE VERSIONSET

We analyzed the log data and the interviews to get a deeper understanding of what goes into the proper determination of versionset from a user-subjective perspective. Given the effects of context, we did not expect to be able to define a single set of characteristics that would suffice across all scenarios. But we attempted to comprehensively categorize all the factors surfaced to us in the interviews or visible in the logging data that appeared to have relevance in determining the versionset's proper membership.

Hierarchy co-location: Most participants went to great lengths to keep file versions in the same folder to the extent possible, and several reported confusion caused specifically by the issue of versions not being co-located.

File types: Most content copy operations we observed preserved the type of the content file, and thus it is no surprise that versionsets often consisted of a single file type. But there were notable exceptions, such as a .pdf file that represented a final version of a set of .docx files. Such exceptions often served to distinguish a particular file *within* the versionset, because a different operation led to its creation. Participants differed in their estimation of the relative importance different file types played within the versionset.

Naming patterns: In many examples we saw, versions consisted of a base name and a variety of semantic suffixes: numbers for establishing chronological order (e.g., "_09"), initials or person names for establishing ownership transfer (e.g., "_from_John"), and descriptors for representing milestones (e.g., "_final", "_uploaded"). Eleven participants made explicit reference to a "naming scheme", either theirs or someone else's, when discussing versions. It was clear that naming conventions were used both to visually establish versioning relationships and to call out semantic differences within the versionset. Many interviewees had strong attachment to their own personal conventions [19].

Timestamps: Versions often exhibited serial creation and modification dates, and users often depended on these attributes in determining the "correct" version within a versionset to use for a particular purpose. In other situations, a long gap between two clusters of timestamps among a set of files seemingly related by copy operations could be an indicator of a break in the versionset chain—for instance, when an old document with several prior revisions was branched to a new one simply to preserve formatting in kicking off a new document creation and revision process.

Access patterns: Users described accesses to the versionset that tended to be temporally clustered, because multiple versions in a versionset were associated with a particular user 'activity.' That is, multiple files in the same versionset were often open simultaneously, or sequentially, when a user was working on a task involving that document.

Content copy operations: Interviewees confirmed that SaveAs, file copy (CopyFile, Attach), and Copy/Paste operations were strong indicators of version relationships between files. SaveAs was often used to mark significant content changes or preserve earlier content that might otherwise be lost. File copy operations often bridged hierarchies (e.g., between an email attachment and a file system, or between a home and work system) for the purpose of content preservation, transmission to others, or improved accessibility. Depending on the context, the significance of a Copy/Paste operation as an indicator of a version ranged greatly: on one extreme, an entire document might be pasted into a new blank document and re-named in an act functionally equivalent to a SaveAs of a new version; on the other, a small portion of a completely unrelated document could be pasted simply to borrow formatting details; most commonly, Copy/Paste operations successfully identified *related* files, but not proper versionset members. The size and content of the pasted data serve as clues to differentiate the significance of such operations.

Content overlap: Even when specific copy operation history was unavailable, static metrics of content similarity were an indicator of version relationships. Large content overlaps between two files often suggested a common source file. This promises to be a particularly key feature to leverage in a real-world copy-aware system, because copy operations in legacy components or external namespaces that can't be recorded directly may sometimes be recoverable from static content analysis.

These categorizations make it clear that the versionset is not a simple set to define digitally, but each category reveals factors that have useful positive or negative correlations with version relationships in certain contexts.

USING THE VERSIONSET

Our investigation suggests that a wide variety of existing and proposed tools and systems used for personal information management have the potential to be enhanced by the versionset concept as part of a copy-aware ecosystem.

Applications or systems that allow digital items to cross organizational boundaries—such as email clients or synchronization services—are fertile ground for offering **integrated organizational assistance** using the versionset concept. Knowledge of the version correspondences across namespaces would allow these systems to suggest the correct course of action to the user just at the moment of potential confusion, as in Figure 1a. In-depth relationship views such as the graph view proposed in Figure 1c could be triggered by integrated assistance UI or other item-specific mechanisms. These views would have the ability to support complex sense-making with respect to a particular digital item, providing a rich history of user activity viewed through the lens of versionset-relevant operations.

During our investigation, we gained concrete insight on the use of versionsets for enhancing hierarchical navigation views with respect to two different information management contexts: exploring familiar data and exploring unfamiliar data. The difference in context had implications for the proper definition of the versionset, but in both cases the judicious de-emphasis of subordinate content, and the careful inclusion of related content normally not available in-view, showed promise (Figure 1b). Similar principles used in **keyword search** would allow the results view to either collapse items that were tightly related by version to allow more room for other relevant targets, or to include items related by version that might not otherwise match the query.

Attribute-based systems such as Presto [14] could benefit from the versionset by extending the application of properties meant to apply to the user concept of "document" to all the digital manifestations of the document. **Activity-based computing** systems attempting to group a user's digital items into activities could benefit from a particular definition of versionset by automatically extending project associations to all files within the versionset. For example, having associated a particular URL as a related resource to a particular document, they could automatically extend that association to later versions of the same document. In essence, any system that proposes new groupings for a user's organizational experience can benefit by using the versionset as a foundational building block.

CONCLUSION

At any given moment, the file is often the main unit of attention for the understanding, creating, and editing activities that make up the bulk of what an information worker considers to be her information work—whether that file is a web page, an email, or a spreadsheet. Yet the conceptual units of work natural for users to organize their overall workflow—e.g., project, task, or document—commonly span multiple file artifacts. Users today face a proliferation of these artifacts across their many devices but receive scant assistance from their systems in making sense of it.

In this paper we introduce the versionset—a context-sensitive aggregation of digital items defined as the set of files that, at a given moment, represent a single document to the user. We propose that a copy-aware computing ecosystem can leverage its understanding of the mechanisms and semantics of the ways copies and versions of content are created to define and exploit the versionset across a wide range of different PIM user experiences.

Through the deployment of copy-aware software prototypes, and interviews with real users about their data management challenges and practices, we gathered evidence that not only are copies unavoidable for a variety of personal, organizational, and contextual reasons, but they play a crucial role in achieving many specific user goals. At the same time, they cause confusion and inefficiency in users' data management strategies. Our observations allowed us to distill the factors that go into the proper determination of a versionset for a given user context. We also demonstrate that users perceive the versionset to be a valuable construct for managing clutter and reasoning about file versions. Finally, we enumerate the many PIM user experiences that could be transformed by leveraging the versionset. It is our hope that this approach points the way toward a PIM experience substantially less burdensome for tomorrow's users.

REFERENCES

1. Agrawal, N., Bolosky, W.J., Douceur, J.R. and Lorch, J.R. A five-year study of file-system metadata. *ACM Trans. Storage 3*, 3 (2007), 9:1-9:32.
2. Bardram, J., Bunde-Pedersen, J. and Soegaard, M. Support for activity-based computing in a personal computing operating system. *Proc. CHI '06*, ACM Press (2006), 211-220.
3. Barreau, D. and Nardi, B.A. 1995. Finding and reminding: file organization from the desktop. *ACM SIGCHI Bull. 27*, 3 (1995), 39-43.
4. Bergman, O., Beyth-Marom, R. and Nachmias, R. The user-subjective approach to personal information management. *JASIST 54*, 9 (2008). 872-878.
5. Bergman, O., Beyth-Marom, R., Nachmias, R., Gradovitch, N. and Whittaker, S. Improved search engines and navigation preference in personal information management. *ACM Trans. Inf. Syst. 26*, 4 (2008), 1-24.
6. Bergman, O., Tucker, S., Beyth-Marom, R., Cutrell, E. and Whittaker, S. It's not that important: demoting personal information of low subjective importance using GrayArea. *Proc. CHI '09*, ACM Press (2009), 269-278.
7. Boardman, R. and Sasse, M.A. "Stuff goes into the computer and doesn't come out": a cross-tool study of personal information management. *Proc. CHI '04*, ACM Press (2004), 583-590.
8. Bolosky, W.J., Corbin, S., Goebel, D. and John, R.D. Single instance storage in Windows 2000, *Proc. USENIX '00*, USENIX Association (2000), 2-2.
9. Bondarenko, O. and Janssen, R. Documents at hand: learning from paper to improve digital technologies. *Proc. CHI '05*, ACM Press (2005), 121-130.
10. Broder, A.Z., Glassman, S.C., Manasse, M.S. and Zweig, G. Syntactic clustering of the Web. *Compt. Networks ISDN 29*, 8-13 (1997), 1157-1166.
11. Chau, D., Myers, B. and Faulring, A. What to do when search fails: finding information by association. *Proc. CHI '08*, ACM Press (2008), 999-1008.
12. Cutrell, E., Robbins, D.C., Dumais, S.T. and Sarin, R. Fast, flexible filtering with Phlat-personal search and organization made easy. *Proc. CHI '06*, ACM Press (2006), 261-270.
13. Doctorow, C. Copy killers. The Guardian. July 31 2007. Accessed from http://www.guardian.co.uk/technology /2007/jul/31/comment.drm, September 23, 2010.
14. Dourish, P., Edwards, W.K., LaMarca, A. and Salisbury, M. Presto: an experimental architecture for fluid interactive document spaces. *ACM TOCHI 6*, 2 (1999), 133 -161.
15. Gyllstrom, K. and Soules, C. Seeing is retrieving: building information context from what the user sees. *Proc. IUI '08*, ACM Press (2008), 189-198.
16. Henderson, S. Personal document management strategies. *Proc. CHINZ '09*, ACM Press (2009), 69-76.
17. Jensen, C., Lonsdale, H., Wynn, E., Cao, J., Slater, M. and Dietterich, T.G. The life and times of files and information: a study of desktop provenance. *Proc. CHI '10*, ACM Press (2010), 767-776.
18. Jones. W. Finders, keepers? The present and future perfect in support of personal information management, *First Monday 9*, 3 (2004).
19. Jones, W., Phuwanartnurak, A.J., Gill, R. and Bruce, H. Don't take my folders away!: organizing personal information to get things done. *Ext. Abstracts CHI '05*, ACM Press (2005), 1505-1508.
20. Kaye, J., Vertesi, J., Avery, S., Dafoe, A., David, S., Onaga, L., Rosero, I. and Pinch, T. To have and to hold: exploring the personal archive. *Proc. CHI '06*, ACM Press (2006), 275-284.
21. Neisser, U. Visual search. *Scientific American 210*, 6 (1964). 94-102.
22. Oulasvirta, A. and Sumari, L. Mobile kits and laptop trays: managing multiple devices in mobile information work. *Proc. CHI '07*, ACM Press (2007), 1127-1136.
23. Rattenbury, T. and Canny, J. CAAD: an automatic task support system. *Proc. CHI '07*, ACM (2007), 687-696.
24. Ravasio, P., Schär, S.G. and Krueger, H. In pursuit of desktop evolution: User problems and practices with modern desktop systems. *ACM TOCHI 11*, 2 (2004), 156-180.
25. Shah, S., Soules, C.A., Ganger, G.R. and Noble, B.D. Using provenance to aid in personal file search. *Proc. USENIX '07*, (2007), 1-14.
26. Shen, J., Irvine, J., Bao, X., Goodman, M., Kolibaba, S., Tran, A., Carl, F., Kirschner, B., Stumpf, S. and Dietterich, T.G. Detecting and correcting user activity switches: algorithms and interfaces. *Proc. IUI '09*, ACM Press (2009), 117-126.
27. Tang, J. C., Drews, C., Smith, M., Wu, F., Sue, A. and Lau, T. Exploring patterns of social commonality among file directories at work. *Proc. CHI '07*, ACM (2007), 951-960.
28. Teevan, J., Alvarado, C., Ackerman, M.S. and Karger, D.R. The perfect search engine is not enough: a study of orienteering behavior in directed search. *Proc. CHI '04*, ACM Press (2004), 415-422.
29. Voida, S. and Mynatt, E.D. It feels better than filing: everyday work experiences in an activity-based computing system. *Proc. CHI '09*, ACM Press (2009), 221-230.

Enticing Consumers via Incomplete Product Experience: An Investigation of Online Product Interactivity Designs

Cheng Yi
Department of Information Systems
National University of Singapore
13 Computing Drive, Singapore
yicheng@comp.nus.edu.sg

Zhenhui Jiang
Department of Information Systems
National University of Singapore
13 Computing Drive, Singapore
jiang@comp.nus.edu.sg

Izak Benbasat
Sauder School of Business
University of British Columbia
2053 Main Mall, Vancouver,
BC, Canada
izak.benbasat@sauder.ubc.ca

ABSTRACT
This paper reports on two studies that investigate the design of online product interactivity. The first study compares three different presentation formats: a video presentation and two Virtual Product Experience (VPE) presentations, namely, triggered interaction and full interaction. The findings suggest that triggered interaction VPE is more effective in enticing users to attend to and further explore the featured products than both the non-interactive video presentation and the full interaction VPE. The second study builds upon the first and focuses on two specific VPE design factors. In particular, it investigates interaction constraint (high versus low constraint) in addition to the activation mode of interaction (process-based interaction versus event-based interaction). The results reveal interesting interaction patterns between the two design factors, i.e., providing less constrained interaction performs better when process-based interaction design is adopted, but performs worse when event-based interaction is employed.

Author Keywords
Virtual product experience (VPE), triggered interaction, full interaction, interaction constraint, product seductiveness.

ACM Classification Keywords
H5.m. Information interfaces and presentation (e.g., HCI): Miscellaneous.

General Terms
Design.

1 INTRODUCTION
Product advertisers have always tried to employ various tactics to grab their customers' attention, tug on their emotions, and entice them to react passionately to advertised products. Similarly, e-commerce website designers have utilized various innovative mechanisms, such as multimedia features, to attract online visitors' attention to and curiosity about their products. For example, www.landroverusa.com uses video clips to display cars in motion. Another example is www.sony-ericsson.com, which allows users to rotate and view a virtual cell phone as well as to try out its various functionalities via a mouse. This latter type of online experience which aims at simulating customers' feel, touch, and try of products is termed *virtual product experience* (VPE) [11].

Indeed, studies on online product displays have shown that designs incorporating motion and product interactivity are superior to static images in improving users' experience with products and their product understanding [11,21]. However, comparisons between videos and product interactivity designs have yielded equivocal results thus far. Specifically, studies suggest that while a certain amount of interactivity is desired, purely relying on interactivity may not necessarily benefit online consumers [14] as extensive and continuous user interactions may dilute the novelty and interest initially generated by the interactive features. This may not be beneficial for improving users' online experience or their interest in the displayed product. As such, instead of simulating a continuous process, designers may try to decompose a continuous flow into discrete events, i.e., single steps or actions users need to take, and embed product interactivity selectively.

For example, suppose you are on a cell phone website where new music phones are being promoted. One presentation to introduce "disc-to-phone music transfer" feature may let you directly act on the interface during every step of this functional process. You would first pick a disc and drag it into the drive. Next, you would click "add" to select the songs, and finally click "ok" to confirm. Alternatively, another form of presentation may start by showing a short introductory video, but at one point the video *suspends* and *prompts* you to drag a disc to a computer drive on the screen. Upon receiving your input, the presentation continues to reveal the subsequent steps of the feature, such as selecting and adding songs, in a fluent video form again. These two interactive designs convey the same product information, i.e., the working process of a

CHI 2011, May 7–12, 2011, Vancouver, BC, Canada.

particular product feature, but they differ in the extent to which user-product interaction is embedded. The former allows users to try out all the steps of the entire process in executing a product's functions on their own; hence is termed *full interaction*. The latter shows part of the process automatically but involves particular moments which the system prompts the user to act (i.e., dragging), and the user's action then triggers subsequent automatic demonstration; hence it is termed *triggered interaction*[1]. In essence, full interaction VPE provides users a complete interactive experience with the virtual product, whereas triggered interaction VPE engages users by using some interaction events but not a complete active experience.

As noted at the beginning of the paper, the major intention of merchants who feature products online is to engage and "seduce" potential consumers to the products, in order to increase the chances of product purchase. However, prior studies on online product presentation design have primarily focused on the facilitation of product understanding or evaluation [11]; the important impact of such online exposure on intriguing consumers has largely been ignored. This research thus designs and compares different product presentations – namely, video presentation, triggered interaction VPE and full interaction VPE – in terms of their impacts on *product seductiveness*, defined as the extent to which the displayed product arouses consumers' curiosity and desire to try it. While seduction may not ultimately result in a purchase since purchase can be largely shaped by users' need and the product quality per se, it nevertheless enhances the likelihood of a purchase [12]. Hence, in this paper, online product presentations are not treated as an instruction manual but are considered a "persuasive technology" [5,6] that can "seduce" people and "spur them on to further action" [22]. Indeed, although the idea of "persuasive" computing has been around for more than a decade, very little published work gives insights into the strategies used in persuasive technology or processes involved in users' behavior change [13]. This paper intends to demonstrate that designers can actually apply the findings from traditional consumer psychology research to the design of engaging and "persuasive" applications.

The paper is organized as follows. The next section presents a review of consumer psychology theories and their application to the online interactive design context. Hypotheses of Study One are then proposed, followed by the report of an experiment and its results. Built upon the theories and findings of Study One, hypotheses about more specific design factors are then developed in Study Two and the results of the second experiment are reported. Finally, the conclusions for the two studies are summarized.

[1] This term is also used in a working paper by Yi et al. [27], which addresses broader benefit of incomplete interactivity design and the moderating role of product class knowledge.

2 LITERATURE REVIEW

Many researchers and practitioners have noted that product marketing largely depends on "seduction" [7], i.e., whether the advertising encourages consumers' product exploration or product trial [9]. Seduction has also been the central concept in the growing field of "persuasive technology", which studies how technology intentionally changes users' attitudes or behaviors [5,6,12]. Researchers suggest that the design of persuasive technologies can actually benefit from the established body of research on behavioral psychology [13]. In the following sections, we will review relevant theories and studies in consumer psychology and describe how they can be applied to online interaction design to influence users' behavior in an intended way.

2.1 The Theoretical Foundation for Seduction-inducing Mechanisms

Research in marketing and consumer psychology has proposed that a seductive experience should be both open and engaging [3,8]. Specifically, seductiveness is enhanced when there is a gap in product knowledge or experience *and* when users are intrigued enough to attend to this gap, so that they are enticed into a forthcoming product experience. This is echoed in studies on persuasive technology [12], which suggest that the seductive qualities of product experience include intriguing users by attention-grabbing cues standing out from the environment and creating promises to be fulfilled to "hook" them into deeper discovery. The "promises" here imply an anticipation of further experience that is not provided at the moment. Hence, two *necessary* conditions to establish a seductive experience are (1) the incompleteness of product experience and (2) users' engagement in processing product information.

2.1.1 The Incompleteness of Interactive Product Experience

Since the early 1980s, marketing researchers have been investigating the different effects of a complete and clear product experience versus an incomplete or ambiguous product experience on consumers' responses and belief formation [9]. Many studies have suggested that a *premise* to "hook" users is the presence of a knowledge gap, or openness, in the advertising experiences [3,8,15,17]. The presence of the gap offers people a "promise" and induces them to hold their attention and energetically continue the exploration [3,7]. This is the psychological underpinning of human's curiosity and temptation and is thus the fundamental requirement in enhancing the alluring or seductive effect. The major theoretical base of such behavior is Gestalt psychology and its extensions [25,28], which refer to the form-shaping capability of the human senses and the fundamental human tendency to construct a closed and coherent knowledge structure [15,16]. For example, product advertisements which use incomplete visual cues have been found to intensify viewers' affective responses towards the product because of "the thrill of unsolved problems or undeciphered riddles" [19]. Studies in education also find that one way to entice learners is to present the right amount of information so that their existing knowledge seems incomplete [16]. The learners are then motivated to learn more, in order to make their cognitive structures better-formed.

2.1.2 Engagement in Product Information Processing

However, the presence of an experience gap does not always result in curiosity and further intentions to explore product information. Consider advertising for digital cameras in 1997, when they were first introduced. There was an ad which read "it changes the ways in which you capture, create, and communicate pictures" [17]. Although this advertisement intended to convey the promises offered by the product, yet did not convey all the information about the product, it might not have invoked users' curiosity or active exploration because users are not cued to *engage* in processing the information. Menon and Soman [17] term this case "no-cue curiosity", i.e., when users are presented with an information or experience gap but have no clue about how to interpret the presented information and thus little desire to elaborate it further. Indeed, studies have suggested that consumers should be actively engaged in the experience in order to be seduced [7,8]. The engaging cues of an experience attract the consumer's voluntary attention to the product information, intriguing focused and meaningful thoughts about the product [8,17]. In this way, users' awareness of the missing experience and their desire to resolve it can be reinforced. Fogg [4] has also contended that to change a person's attitudes or behavior in an intended way, a persuasive design should include a "trigger" or "cue" that the person can notice and associate with the target behavior. Specifically, theoretical and empirical work proposes that *surprising*, *suspenseful*, or *interesting* cues can trigger and maintain users' attention [2]. In computer interface design, these cues usually "differentiate from the surroundings", so that they can grab users' attention to the information conveyed [12].

3 STUDY ONE

3.1 Hypotheses on Product Seductiveness

Based on the marketing and persuasive technology literatures, seduction primarily concerns how to engage the consumers and invoke their curiosity and temptation for further action [3,8]. In this study, we use *product seductiveness* to address the tempting or enticing quality of users' online product experience, i.e., the extent to which the experience entices users to be curious about product features and to carry on further exploration. Seduction is the key to successful advertising as it attracts users' attention to the product and potentially increases store traffic.

As discussed earlier, Gestalt psychology implies that a seductive product experience should take users through part of the way and attract their attention to the information conveyed, so as to tantalize them into going the rest of way. *Triggered interaction* presentation prompts the user to interact with the virtual product only at particular steps during a functional demonstration process; the user's actions will then trigger the automatic display of subsequent product reactions. This form of presentation thus possesses the two necessary qualities of a seductive experience. First, by *suspending* the automatic demonstration at particular points and inviting users' active participation, it *engages* users in processing product information. Second, it allows direct interactions but does *not* offer users a *full experience*. More specifically, triggered interaction creates a change in interaction styles, from passive viewing to the new way of actively manipulating or experiencing a product. This prompts users to directly attend to the information presented, triggering their curiosity about the unrevealed steps and excitement about the new approach of experiencing the product, i.e., active exploration more than just watching and following. This desire can only be fulfilled by going beyond the current presentation.

Compared to triggered interaction, *video* does not let users experience a product actively at all. Since users are in a passive viewing mode and there is no engaging cue to trigger users' active and direct interpretation of the information being presented, a video presentation is similar to the case of "no-cue curiosity" in advertising, which conveys the information to users but may not be able to inspire them much. On the other hand, *full interaction* allows users to freely manipulate a product in its full detail and at their own pace. As implied in Gestalt theories, a complete sense-making experience is less likely to trigger users' curiosity due to a lack of tension or the need to explore beyond what has already been provided [7,26]. As Wilson et al. [26] have also stated, although "knowledge makes the world more predictable", it also makes it "less delicious" and "less exciting", as there is less curiosity and less anticipated pleasure from resolving it (p5). Therefore,

H1: Triggered interaction VPE leads to higher product seductiveness than both video presentation and full interaction VPE.

4 EXPERIMENT FOR STUDY ONE

4.1 Experimental Stimuli Design

We designed a cell phone with five applications: managing calls, managing contacts, setting alarm, setting shortcut key, and calculator. A hypothetical brand and model name was used, and the phone did not replicate any existing model in terms of the operating system and interface; hence it was completely new to the subjects. For every application, three different presentation formats were designed.

In the *video* condition, selected product applications can be previewed using pre-recorded videos loaded on the webpage; the whole process does not require any user participation. In the *full interaction* condition, users are able to launch a VPE simulator from the product homepage to sample the selected applications of the cell phone step-by-step using the mouse. For example, in the contact management application, the user is expected to press the menu button, enter the contact application, and perform functions like adding or searching for a contact. At each step, the cell phone reacts as a real product would by changing the display and emitting various sounds. In the *triggered interaction* condition, product interactivity is embedded in a video-based presentation such that participants interact with a product simulator at preset triggering points, and then the rest of the steps are performed automatically. For example, to demonstrate the contact management application, steps of accessing the contact application from the main screen are first shown in an automatic video flow. Then, the presentation suspends and prompts the user to press the *adding a new contact* button. After receiving the user's input, the presentation automatically completes the insertion of a preset name, phone number, and other contact information.

The factual product information is kept uniform across the different conditions. The Appendix (figure i and ii) shows the flow charts of the full and triggered interaction VPE during the initial steps of contact management application.

4.2 Experimental Procedure and Sample

Seventy-five students from various faculties of a major public university participated in the experiment. The average age of participants was 21.5 and 46% were female. Subjects were randomly assigned to the three conditions, with twenty-five in each. Subjects were asked to examine a cell phone using their assigned experimental websites as if they were considering a possible purchase. No time limit was imposed on the product inspection task. Subjects were guaranteed to receive $8 for participation. The measurement items for product seductiveness were developed based on [8, 17]: (1) I am curious about the features of the product; (2) I am eager to try these functions on the real product; (3) I am enticed to further explore the features of the product (measured using a 7-point scale).

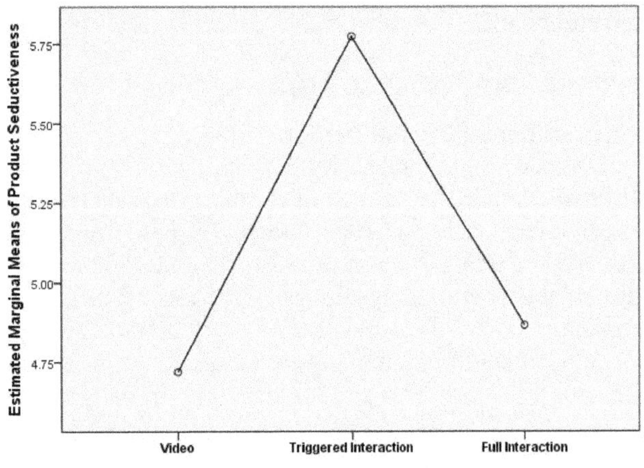

Figure 1. Mean Plot of Product Seductiveness in Study One

4.3 Results on Product Seductiveness

ANOVA on product seductiveness shows a significant effect of presentation forms ($F(2, 72) = 5.52$, $p<.01$) (See Figure 1). Post hoc analysis based on Scheffe test reveals that (1) triggered interaction ($M = 5.77$, $SD = 0.93$) is associated with significantly higher product seductiveness than video ($M = 4.72$, $SD = 1.45$) and full interaction ($M = 4.87$, $SD = 1.19$), thus supporting H1.

4.4 Supplementary Data Analysis

Thus far we have revealed the unique impact of incomplete product interactivity design, i.e., triggered interaction, on enticing online visitors to be curious and continue exploring the featured product. This is an important and interesting impact of online product presentations rarely examined before. However, people may question whether triggered interaction can perform as well in terms of users' overall experience on the websites, such as users' attitudes towards the websites, which represents their overall evaluation of the web interface and tightly relates to their tendency to visit the website again.

In fact, we adopted measurement items from prior studies [10] to measure users' attitudes towards the website[2]. The results show a significant effect of presentation forms ($F(2, 72) = 4.99$, $p<.01$). Post hoc analysis based on Scheffe test reveals that (1) both full interaction ($M=5.12$) and triggered interaction ($M=5.02$) are associated with significantly more positive attitudes towards the website than video presentation ($M=4.29$); (2) full interaction and triggered interaction do not differ from each other. Hence, in general, presentation designs with interactivity features exert more positive influence than a passive video design in users' overall evaluation of the website. It is important to note that triggered interaction, as a form of incomplete interaction design, performs as well as full interaction in this aspect. This may be attributed in part to the tension and engagement invoked by the interactive cues embedded in passive demonstrations, which may continuously arouse users' attention and make the experience appealing [1].

4.5 Discussion of Results of Study One

Consistent with our prediction, by engaging consumers in limited interactions with the virtual products, triggered interaction most effectively attracts consumers to the product and creates the highest level of willingness to further explore it. A full interaction experience with the product does not seem to entice consumers more than a passive experience with a video presentation. Also, both VPE presentations lead to more positive website evaluations than the video, whereas full interaction is no better than triggered interaction in this aspect. Hence, taking our main study and supplementary analysis together,

---

[2] The items are: (1) The website is good; (2) I have positive feelings about the website; (3) I have a favorable impression toward the website; (4) I like this website.

we conclude that incorporating interactivity into product presentations is generally beneficial, but providing maximum interactivity may not always be necessary, especially for seducing users to further action.

An in-depth look at the two VPE designs reveals that other than their difference in the mode of activating interaction (i.e., process-based interaction which completely activates user-product interaction from the inception throughout the process, or event-based interaction which activates interaction only at particular triggering events), they also differ in the level of interaction constraint, i.e., whether or not users have the complete freedom to choose an action among others at an interactive step. Specifically, in triggered interaction (i.e., event-based), users are invoked to perform a *specified* action at each interaction point. In other words, they act as "dummy controllers" since they only need to follow the preset product manipulation, e.g., to click on a certain button, but not to freely choose how to interact with the product, e.g., to choose which button to click on among all others. In contrast, in full interaction (i.e., process-based), users can decide which action to perform at each interaction point and thus determine the operations that followed. In Study One we have preliminarily attributed the effects of product presentations to the different activation modes of user-product interaction (i.e., event-based versus process-based), but prior studies have indeed paid much attention to the effects of interaction constraint as well. On the one hand, some suggest that learners prefer to have the freedom to choose learning strategies in an online interactive learning environment [23]. On the other hand, highly constrained design, as implemented by providing users with specific guidance concerning the most appropriate action to perform, was also found to be effective in many tasks because it helped users avoid potential disorientations and mistakes [20]. Hence, a second study is designed to investigate both design factors together, i.e., interaction activation mode and interaction constraint, in order to reveal more design possibilities and find out whether a particular activation mode fits a particular constraint level.

5. STUDY TWO

Study Two employs a 2×2 between subjects design, with two levels of interaction constraint design (low versus high) and two activation mode designs (event-based versus process-based). While the *high-constraint event-based* interaction and *low-constraint process-based* interaction correspond to the triggered interaction and full interaction in Study One, respectively, two new designs are introduced:

1) The *low-constraint event-based* interaction invokes user input only at particular events during the processes of product presentations and allows users to freely choose how to interact with the cell phone at these points. For example, in demonstrating a contact management application, the presentation shows the process of entering the main menu and selecting the contact application without user interaction. Then, a user can freely act on the phone, such as to choose to add a new contact, to search for an existing contact, or to return to the previous screen. They can trigger any of these paths to experience the corresponding functional process based on their own interest. This differs from the high-constraint event-based interaction where users are only allowed to perform a prescribed action at a particular step, i.e., only clicking on "adding a new contact", and the process of searching a contact will be experienced afterwards based on the predetermined presentation sequence.

2) The *high-constraint process-based* interaction needs user input at every step during the process and users are supposed to perform only the prescribed action at each step. For example, users will be asked to perform the predetermined actions step-by-step – entering main menu, selecting contact application, choosing to add a new contact, entering contact information by pressing the specific buttons and clicking save, and etc. This differs from the low-constraint process-based interaction, where users can interact with the product freely throughout the process[3].

The Appendix shows the flow charts of the four VPE designs during the initial steps of the contact management application.

6. HYPOTHESES DEVELOPMENT FOR STUDY TWO

6.1 Hypothesis on Product Seductiveness

In Study One, we demonstrate that the incompleteness of the product experience is an essential premise to enhance seductive effect as this is the psychological underpinning of intrinsic motivation for further exploration [15]. When the premise of incompleteness is achieved, how the design cues actually engage users in processing product information becomes influential on the level of product seductiveness. In the current context, this is largely determined by the level of constraint in user-product interactions.

Controlling information flow via the interface is different from evaluating product performance, and it consumes

[3] In highly constrained interaction design, users go through the sub-functions one by one following the defined sequence. In this example, users go through the steps for adding a contact first and then searching contact; whereas in the less constrained counterpart they can manage the sequence of accessing these sub-functions by manipulating the phone at this step. Nonetheless, the operational steps of various sub-functions users will go through in both low- and high-constraint conditions are the same. This applies to both event-based and process-based interaction design.

Also, the level of interaction constraint at a certain step is the same regardless of whether this interactive step is in an event-based or process-based interaction design.

users' attention and processing resources. As pointed out by research on dual-task, an additional task such as dealing with interface display designs or features usually distracts users from the primary task, e.g., information search and evaluation [24]. However, as mentioned in Study One, in order to seduce users to attend to the focal product, it is important to maintain users' engagement with product evaluation. Hence, if interface control activities distract users' engagement, users will not be able to consistently and fully focus on processing product information, which negatively influences the fostering of product curiosity and seductiveness. Similar ideas have been discussed in early studies on direct manipulation interfaces, which suggest that to achieve users' direct engagement with the objects of interest, the interface control should be "transparent", i.e., without intruding into users' ongoing thoughts and activities [18]. With the high-constraint event-based interaction design, users just follow the prescribed presentation flow and the interaction cues do not intervene in their product experience by imposing any extra information control task. Hence, users can preserve consistent and full engagement in the unveiling of product information at these points, such as the way a product responds to input. In contrast, if the interaction events allow free control (i.e., low-constraint), at these points users will have to proactively control the interface, which requires a switch from their ongoing focus of observing product performance to another task of managing the process of product examination. The abruptly added task of controlling the product inspection flow distracts users' engagement in product examination and leads to reduced product seductiveness.

With process-based interaction design, however, regardless of whether each action is pre-specified (i.e., highly constrained) or self-directed (i.e., less constrained), users are able to directly interact with the virtual product consistently at every step as the functional process unfolds. Without the premise of incompleteness which enhances product seductiveness, there is not much room to invoke users' curiosity and desire by varying the level of interaction constraint. Therefore,

H2: There is an interaction effect between activation mode and interaction constraint on product seductiveness: the high-constraint style leads to higher product seductiveness than the low-constraint style in the event-based interaction condition but not in the process-based interaction condition.

7. EXPERIMENT FOR STUDY TWO

7.1 Experimental Stimuli Design

Four different presentation formats were created for the experiment. The high-constraint event-based interaction and low-constraint process-based interaction conditions followed the same design used in Study One, i.e., triggered interaction and full interaction, respectively. The low-constraint event-based interaction and high-constraint process-based interaction designs are illustrated in Section 5. The factual product information (i.e., information about the operation steps of applications) is kept uniform across the different conditions.

7.2 Experimental Procedure and Sample

The hypotheses were tested through a lab experiment with a 2 (low versus high interaction constraint) * 2 (event-based versus process-based interaction activation mode) between-subject design. 188 students from various faculties in a major public university were recruited. Hence, there were forty-seven subjects each condition. The experimental procedure and measurement were similar to those in Study One.

7.3 Results on Product Seductiveness

There is a significant interaction effect between activation mode and interaction constraint on product seductiveness (F (1,184) = 4.29, p<.05) (See Figure 2). The results of simple main effect analysis confirm that in the event-based interaction conditions, the high-constraint version (M = 5.43, SD = 1.07) leads to significantly higher product seductiveness than the low-constraint version (M = 4.81, SD = 1.22) (F (1, 92) = 7.10, p<.05) and in the process-based interaction conditions, the low-constraint (M = 4.94, SD = 1.10) and high-constraint (M = 4.88, SD = 1.20) versions do not differ (F (1, 92) = .07, p>.05). Hence, H2 is supported.

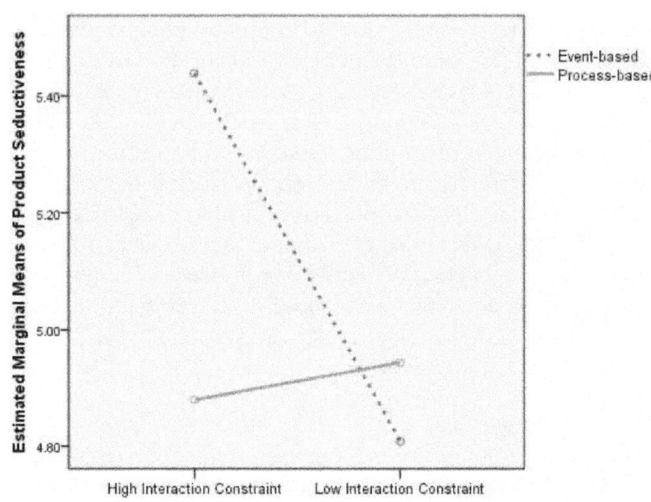

Figure 2. Plots of Interaction Effect in Study Two

7.4 Supplementary Analysis

We conducted ANOVA analysis on users' overall attitudes towards the websites in addition to product seductiveness. The result show that there is a significant interaction effect between activation mode and interaction constraint on users' attitudes towards websites (F (1,184) = 16.50, p<.01). For the process-based interaction conditions, the low-constraint version (M = 5.32) leads to significantly stronger positive attitudes than the high-constraint version (M = 4.88) (F (1, 92) = 5.28, p<.01). This is reasonable because less constrained control supports dynamic system responses to users' actions and thus leads to enhanced user fulfillment and pleasure. However, the reverse occurs for the event-based interaction conditions ($F(1, 92) = 11.31$, $p<.01$), i.e., high-constraint event-based interaction ($M = 4.95$) is better than low-constraint event-based interaction ($M = 4.14$) in terms of users' overall evaluation of the website. One possible explanation is that providing free control at the interaction points may have invoked users' intention to extend the active control over the subsequent processes, which, however, was not provided as it was an incomplete interaction design. This led to negative disconfirmation with the interaction experience and thus lower evaluation.

7.5 Discussion of Results of Study Two

The results of Study Two indicate that in the event-based interaction design, highly constrained interaction leads to both stronger product seductiveness and more positive attitudes towards websites than less constrained interaction design. In the process-based interaction design, less constrained interaction leads to more positive attitudes towards websites than highly constrained interaction design, though no significant difference is found in terms of product seductiveness. Hence, it seems that low interaction constraint design fits well with the process-based interaction mode whereas high interaction constraint design fits well with the event-based interaction mode.

It would also be important to find out which VPE design is indeed the best among the four. We have demonstrated that the high-constraint event-based interaction outperforms the low-constraint event-based interaction in both product seductiveness and attitudes towards websites. We then conducted pair-wise comparison tests between the high-constraint event-based interaction and the two process-based interaction designs. The results reveal that the high-constraint event-based interaction leads to significantly higher product seductiveness than both forms of process-based interaction ($p<.05$) without negative influence on users' attitudes towards websites. Indeed, it also requires less design effort than the other three[4]. Hence, high-constraint event-based interaction may be considered as a more attractive design option.

8. CONCLUSIONS

This research advocates the use of Gestalt psychology in guiding interaction design and promotes a brand-new design concept, namely *incomplete interactive design*. Past studies have mainly looked at the two contrasting ends of presentation design such as non-interactive video and full interaction VPE [11,21]. But we suggest that product interactivity design is a continuum rather than a dichotomy and there can be finer manipulations. Our purpose is to introduce new design possibilities and unveil the value of incomplete interactivity design in product presentations. This study provides important empirical evidence for the non-linear effect of interactivity design, i.e., the simpler and "smarter" interaction format such as triggered interaction VPE (i.e., a form of event-based design) may be more effective in achieving certain goals than both the non-interactive and the more "luxurious" full interaction VPE (i.e., a form of process-based design) format.

In particular, in view of the significant increase in web-influenced retail store sales and the importance of "persuasive technology" [5,6] nowadays, we focus on the ability of different online product presentation formats to entice or "allure" potential consumers into approaching the products. Indeed, a major goal of the vendors when promoting products online is to capture the attention of potential consumers and spur possible consumption by prolonging and furthering their desire. However, it is important to note that while seduction reflects the "alluring or tempting qualities" (Webster's Dictionary), it does not necessarily imply the "deceptive" side of marketing [5,12]. In fact, with seductive effect, consumers can be motivated to discover more product information that pertains to their needs before making purchase decisions.

Overall, understanding consumer psychology and interest-stimulating tactics is extremely helpful for web designers, who have long been seeking to "manipulate" the audience's attention and reaction to the exposed information. Our message to designers is that using the most complex technology may not necessarily imply the desired quality. When firms intend to advertise and promote new products or new features through the online channel, intelligently embedding some interaction events could be effective in invoking consumers' attention and desire to continue the learning and trial. Nonetheless, caution is needed when determining the extent of control given to users when embedding interactivity functions, as our results show that high control freedom may not be a universally embraced design. These findings may potentially be applied to other interaction design contexts as well, such as online gaming

[4] In our study, for each cell phone application, the low-constraint process-based interaction design involves more than 30 layers on average in the source Flash file, plus thousands of lines of code to implement the interaction logic. In contrast, the high-constraint event-based interaction design loads a video file, plus only 5-10 layers to implement user interaction (e.g., a button) at specific frames and a few lines of code at these frames to implement the logic. The low-constraint event-based interaction design, which requires more flexible interactions than the high-constraint counterpart, requires more efforts in designing the interaction options (such as different buttons) at specific frames. Similarly, high-constraint process-based interaction design requires implementing user interaction at many frames and thus needs more design efforts than the high-constraint event-based interaction design.

demo, educational software development, web services, etc., to increase users' involvement and usage.

REFERENCES

1. Alwitt, L.F., "Suspense and Advertising Response," *Journal of Consumer Psychology,* 12 (1), 2002.
2. Alwitt, L.F., "Maintaining Attention to a Narrative Event," In *Advances in Psychology Research*, S.P.Shohov and F. H. Columbus (ed.) New York: Nova Publishers, 2002
3. Deighton, J, and Grayson, K, "Marketing and Seduction: Building Exchange Relationships by Managing Social Consensus," *Journal of Consumer Research,* 21 (4), 1995, pp.660-676
4. Fogg, B. J., "A Behavior Model for Persuasive Design," in *Proc. Persuasive'09*, Article No. 40.
5. Fogg, B. J., "Persuasive Computers: Perspectives and Research Directions." In *Proc. CHI 1998*, ACM Press (1998), 225-232.
6. Fogg, B. J., *Persuasive Technology: Using Computers to Change What We Think and Do*, San Francisco: Morgan Kaufuenn, 2003.
7. Greene, Robert, *The Art of Seduction*, Sydney, NSW: Hodder, 2001.
8. Hoch, S. J., "Product Experience is Seductive," *Journal of Consumer Research,* 29 (December), 2002, pp.448-454
9. Hoch, S. J., and Ha, Y., "Consumer Learning: Advertising and the Ambiguity of Product Experience," *Journal of Consumer Research,* 13 (September), 1986, pp.221-233.
10. Jiang, Z., and Benbasat, I., "Investigating the Influence of the Functional Mechanisms of Online Product Presentations," *Information Systems Research,* 18 (4), 2007, pp.454-470
11. Jiang, Z., and Benbasat, I., "The Effects of Presentation Methods and Task Complexity on Online Consumers' Product Understanding," *MIS Quarterly,* 31 (3), 2007, pp.475-500
12. Khaslavsky, J., and Shedroff, N. , "Understanding the Seductive Experience," *Communications of the ACM,* 42 (5), 1999, pp.45-49
13. Kirman, B., Linehan, C., Lawson, S., Foster, D., and Doughty, M., "There's a Monster in my Kitchen: Using Aversive Feedback to Motivate Bahavior Change," In *Ext. Abstracts CHI 2010*, ACM Press (2010), 2685-2694.
14. Klein, L. R., "Creating Virtual Product Experiences: The Role of Telepresence," *Journal of Interactive Marketing,* 17 2003, pp.41-55
15. Loewenstein, G., "The Psychology of Curiosity: A Review and Reinterpretation," *Psychological Bulletin,* 116 (1), 1994, pp.75-98
16. Malone, T. W., "Toward a Theory of Intrinsically Motivating Instruction," *Cognitive Science,* 4 (333-369), 1981.
17. Menon, S., and Soman, D., "Managing the Power of Curiosity for Effective Web Advertising Strategies," *Journal of Advertising,* 31 (3), 2002, pp.1-14
18. Norman, D. A. (1986) "Cognitive Engineering," in D. A. Norman and S. W. Draper, eds., User Centered System Design: *New Perspectives on Human-Computer Interaction*, Lawrence Erlbaum Associates, Hillsdale, N.J., 31-61, 1986.
19. Peracchio, L. A., and Meyers-Levy, J., "How Ambiguous Cropped Objects in Ad Photos can Affect Product Evaluations," *Journal of Consumer Research,* 21 (1), 1994, pp.190-204
20. Sawicka, A. , "Dynamics of Cognitive Load Theory: A Model-based Approach," *Computers in Human Behavior,* 24 (3), 2008, pp.1041-1066
21. Schlosser, A.E. , "Experiencing Products in the Virtual World: The Role of Goal and Imagery in Influencing Attitudes Versus Purchase Intentions," *Journal of Consumer Research,* 30 (September), 2003, pp.184-198.
22. Sharp, H., Rogers, Y., and Preece, J., *Interaction Design: Beyond Human-Computer Interaction. 2nd Ed.*, San Francisco, CA: Wiley, 2007.
23. Sims, R., "Promises of Interactivity: Aligning Learner Perceptions and Expectations with Strategies for Flexible and Online Learning," *Distance Education,* 24 (1), 2003, pp.85-103
24. Somervell, J., Srinivasan, R., Woods, K., and Vasniak, O., "Measuring Distraction and Awareness Caused by Graphical and Textual Displays in the Periphery," In proceedings of *Proceedings of the 39th Annual ACM Southeast Conference*, Athens, GA, 2001.
25. Wertheimer, M., "Gestalt Theory," *Social Research,* 11 (1), 1944.
26. Wilson, T. D., Centerbar, D. B., Kermer, D. A., and Gilbert, D. T., "The Pleasure of Uncertainty: Prolonging Positive Moods in Ways People Do not Anticipate," *Journal of Personality and Social Psychology,* 88 (1), 2005, pp.5-21
27. Yi, C., Jiang, Z, and Benbasat, I., "From Online Inspection to Offline Trial: The Enticing Effect of Incomplete Product Interactivity Designs," working paper.
28. Zeigarnik, Bluma, "On the memory of completed and uncompleted actions," *Psychologische Forschung,* 9 1927, pp.1-85

APPENDIX: FLOW CHARTS OF THE FOUR VPE DESIGNS
(THE INITIAL STEPS OF THE CONTACT MANAGEMENT APPLICATION ARE ILLUSTRATED.)

Legend: ( ) explains the steps that are demonstrated automatically without user interaction; [ ] explains the steps that require user interaction. The small white circle represents the mouse at the moment of screen capture.

<table>
<tr>
<td>

(i) Low-constraint Process-based Interaction VPE (Full Interaction VPE in Study One)

<u>Descriptions</u>: Users can freely interact with the product at every step throughout a functional process.

For example, users can click on any key on the phone keypad, and thus choose among various sub-functions to continue, or to quit the current step.

</td>
<td>

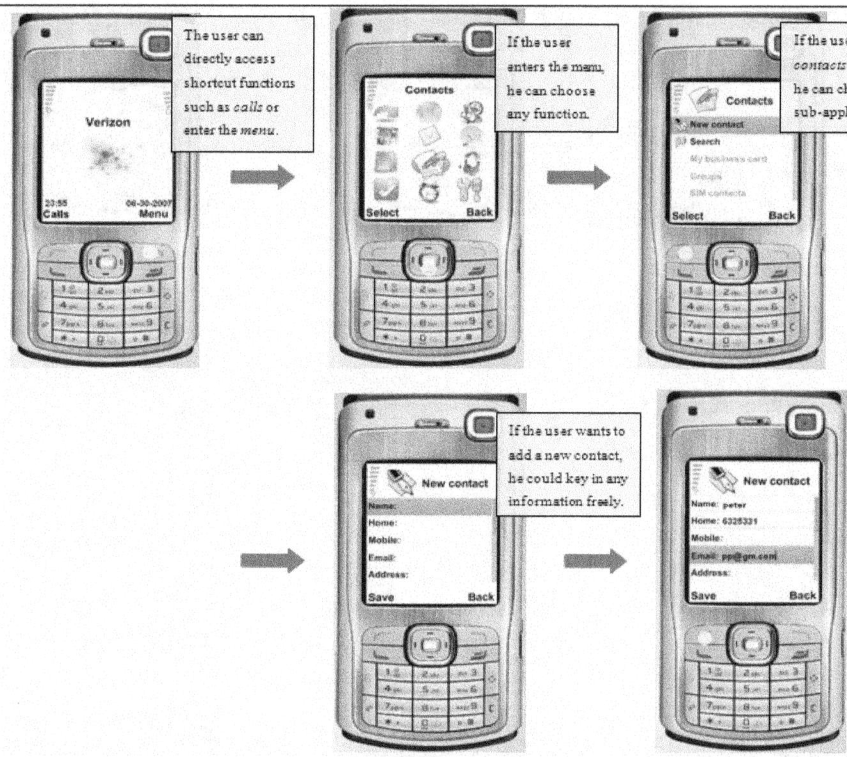

</td>
</tr>
<tr>
<td>

(ii) High-constraint Event-based Interaction VPE (Triggered Interaction VPE in Study One)

<u>Descriptions</u>: Users interact with the product only at particular triggering events, e.g., when a key is highlighted as clickable, as shown in the figure.

At such steps, users have to perform the system-specified action only, e.g., to click on the highlighted key and thus follow the instruction to enter *"add a contact"* sub-function.

</td>
<td>

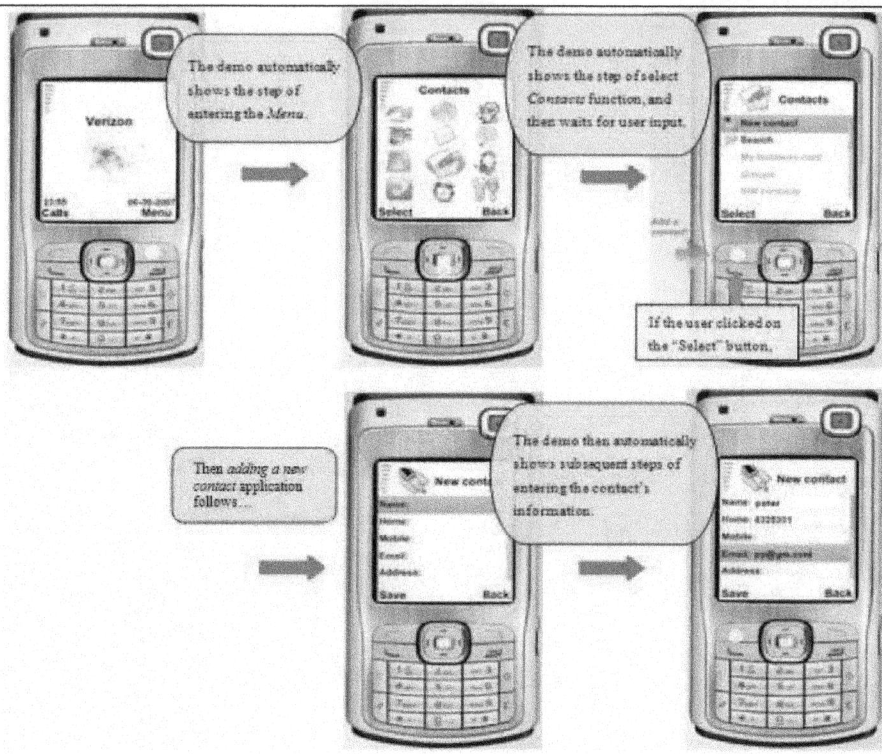

</td>
</tr>
</table>

(iii) Low-constraint Event-based Interaction VPE

Descriptions: Users interact with the product only at particular triggering events.

At such steps, users can freely act on the phone, e.g., to click on the left directional key and thus continue the function of "Add a Contact", or to click on the down directional key and thus continue the function of "Search Contacts", or to click on the right directional key to quit the current menu.

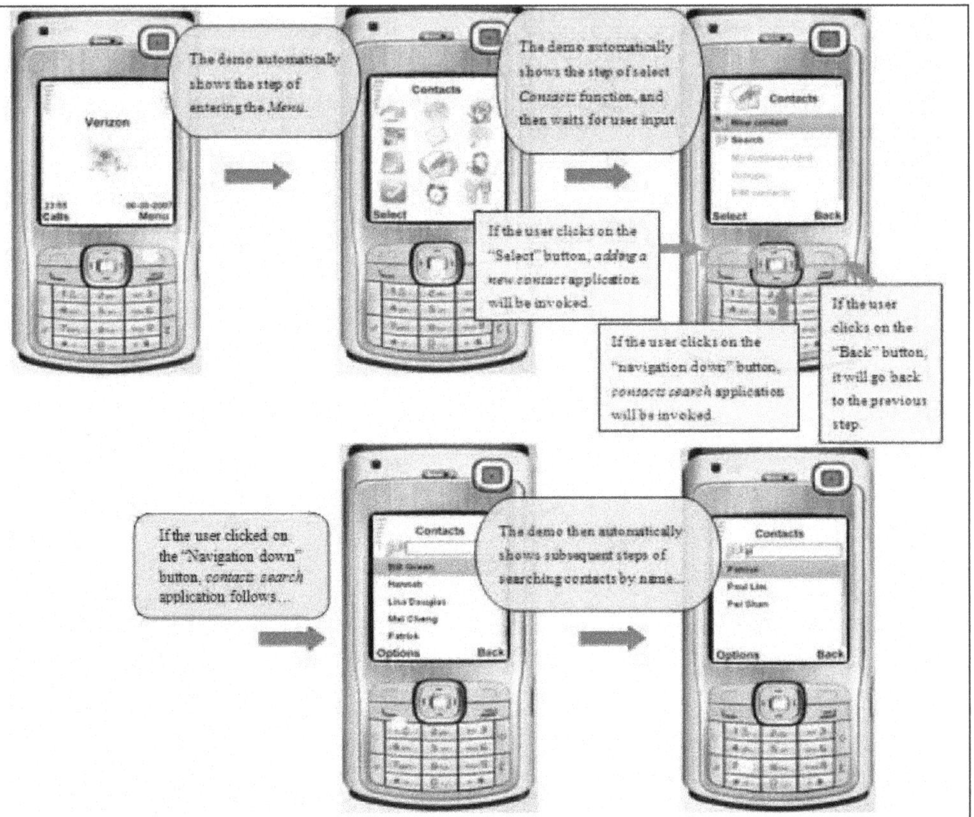

(iv) High-constraint Process-based Interaction VPE

Descriptions: Users interact with the product at every step throughout a functional process but they have to perform the specified action.

As shown in the figure, only one key on the phone keypad is highlighted as clickable at each step; users have to follow this guidance and click on that particular key in order to continue.

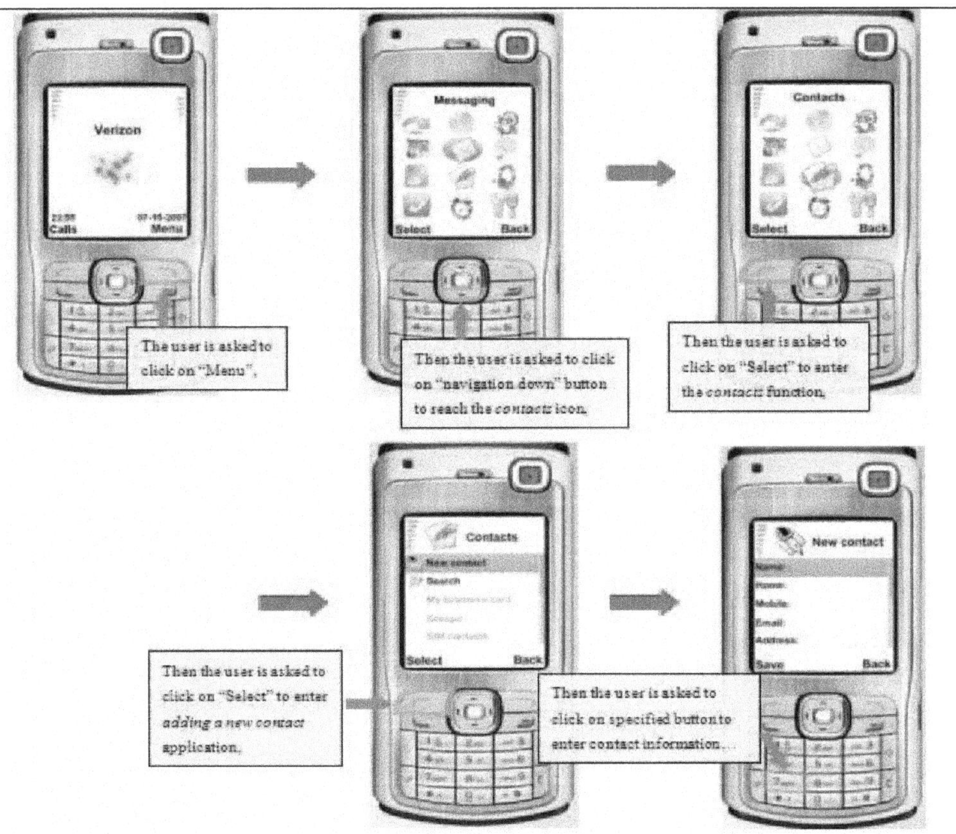

Old Wine in New Bottles or Novel Challenges? A Critical Analysis of Empirical Studies of User Experience

Javier A. Bargas-Avila
University of Basel, Dept. of Psychology,
Cognitive Psychology & Methodology
Missionsstr. 62a, 4055 Basel, Switzerland
javier.bargas@unibas.ch

Kasper Hornbæk
Department of Computer Science,
University of Copenhagen
Njalsgade 128, 2300 Copenhagen, Denmark
kash@diku.dk

ABSTRACT
This paper reviews how empirical research on User Experience (UX) is conducted. It integrates products, dimensions of experience, and methodologies across a systematically selected sample of 51 publications from 2005-2009, reporting a total of 66 empirical studies. Results show a shift in the products and use contexts that are studied, from work towards leisure, from controlled tasks towards open use situations, and from desktop computing towards consumer products and art. Context of use and anticipated use, often named key factors of UX, are rarely researched. Emotions, enjoyment and aesthetics are the most frequently assessed dimensions. The methodologies used are mostly qualitative, and known from traditional usability studies, though constructive methods with unclear validity are being developed and used. Many studies use self-developed questionnaires without providing items or statistical validations. We discuss underexplored research questions and potential improvements of UX research.

Author Keywords
User experience, UX, Usability, HCI, Review, Meta-Analysis

ACM Classification Keywords
H.5.2 User Interfaces: Evaluation/methodology

General Terms
Standardization

INTRODUCTION
User Experience (UX) has emerged as an umbrella phrase for new ways of understanding and studying the quality-in-use of interactive products. Research on UX began around the turn of the millennium, initially employing labels such as pleasurable products [40], hedonic quality [26], or engineering joy [23]. Early UX research argues that existing usability research is too focused on task efficiency and work, and that more encompassing notions of quality are needed. Later research aims at defining, conceptualizing, and designing for UX (see [29] for a review).

In contrast to an instrumental, task-oriented view of interactive products, UX research focuses also on hedonic qualities of use. Such qualities concern for instance aesthetics [77] or self-actualization [20]. Another frequently mentioned characteristic is a focus on the positive emotions and affect that people experience while interacting with products [66, 29]. UX research focuses on the dynamics of experience, and on modeling how interactive products, person characteristics, and context work together in shaping the experience of use [88]. Finally, UX research calls for new methods and approaches for designing and evaluating experience.

The motivation for the present paper is twofold. First, many authors in the field of UX claim that they methodologically or content-wise break new ground. We would like to understand if and how this happens in empirical studies. Second, taking stock of empirical studies may help clarify what UX is; survey approaches defining UX have advanced the field, but left many open questions [50].

This paper aims to provide an integrated review of UX. We look for similarities across products, dimensions of experience, and methodologies. For researchers, we aim to provide an overview, to point out under-explored research areas and potential improvements of methodology. For practitioners, our paper serves as a synopsis of current research on UX.

RELATED WORK
The phrase *user experience* is used in several ways in the HCI literature. One is to denote the design and use of user interfaces, in effect working as a synonym for interaction, usability, or even user-centered design. Such use occurs in early [73] and recent [80] HCI papers. Another use of the phrase is to denote an emerging movement in research – a new paradigm – that focuses on non-instrumental needs and experience in a more complex sense [22, 29, 51, 50]; this understanding of UX forms the focus of the present paper. Our goal is to take stock of the state of the art in the scientific UX literature. We therefore do not discuss the many companies that work with UX, practical resources for UX design, or the abundant discussions on UX on websites and blogs.

The key focus of the UX movement is on the experience of interaction with interactive products. In contrast to usability research, UX research represents "a turn to experience"

[91], and its motivation may be summarized as a search for "new approaches to the design of interactive products, which accommodate experiential qualities of technology use rather than product qualities" [24, p. 353]. A substantial body of research has analyzed the nature of this experience (e.g., [12, 13]). The tenets that this focus entails are as follows:

1. UX takes a holistic view of users' interaction with interactive products. Most definitions emphasize that all aspects of product use are in focus, and some include anticipated use of products (e.g., [59]) and experiences following the use situation (e.g., [50]). Some authors stress that the holistic view also implies that users' experience is indivisible and needs to be reasoned about and studied as such [59]. Others put a particular emphasis on emotions: "emotion is at the heart of any human experience" and "emotion affects how we plan to interact with products, how we actually interact with products, and the perceptions and outcomes that surround those interactions" [12, p. 264]. The holistic perspective for some writers implies an attention to user experience in social contexts of use, leading to a focus on co-experience; that is, the creation of meaning and emotion among users through product use [12].

2. UX focuses on positive aspects of users' interaction with interactive products. Initial UX research departed from a stated dissatisfaction with removing usability problems and improving task completion time [26, 40]. Instead, it was proposed to focus on positive aspects of interaction, in particular, on hedonic, non-instrumental aspects. The term non-instrumental usually refers to task-unrelated qualities that fulfill general human needs [23], contrasting instrumental aspects, where utilitarian task completion is the main focus [32]. Non-instrumental aspects include for instance visual aesthetics [19, 64, 78] and beauty [21], joy of use [32], stimulation, personal growth, or surprise [29]. For many researchers, the emphasis on positive aspects of UX leads to a focus on human values and needs [24], because they ultimately determine why something is positive to users.

3. UX emphasizes the situational and dynamic aspects of using interactive products [29, 50] and the importance of context [50, 69]. Karapanos and colleagues [42] studied how experiences with a smart phone developed over several weeks, and how anticipation shaped subsequent experiences. Other researchers discuss that retrospective summary assessments do not reflect a whole experiential episode, but rather its most recent incidents [27]. They propose the usage of additional measurement strategies, such as repeated measurements throughout the experiential episode.

4. UX views and models the quality of interactive products as multidimensional. Research does not focus exclusively on the value of a product to accomplish tasks; it focuses also on symbolic and aesthetic value [54, 86]. For instance, Diefenbach and Hassenzahl [11] showed that the beauty of products is valued but discounted when it comes to choosing between a beautiful or a usable mobile phone; or van Schaik and Ling [86] explored the relation between usability, hedonic value, beauty, and goodness for user experience with web sites.

5. UX entails a need for new methods and approaches for designing and evaluating experience: "In interactive systems the challenge is to understand the influence small experiences and emotional responses have on others, as well as the overall view ... emotional responses are hard to understand, let alone quantify. New research methods are needed to better articulate the relationship between what we feel and what we do" [12, p. 265]. Many researchers regard traditional methods as being inapt for UX research: "A common strategy ... is the reduction of experience into a number of factors or processes ... such approaches may be useful for experimental analysis but they can miss some of the insights available in accounts that resist such reduction ... qualitative data provides a richness and detail that may be absent from quantitative measures." [76, p. 91-92].

Despite the progress in understanding the use of interactive products, the UX movement has also raised several questions, in particular regarding the products used in UX research, the dimensions of experience that are relevant for UX, and the methodology to be used. Next, we describe these questions as they provide the motivation for this work.

The *products* studied in UX research are debated: On the one hand some researchers posit that the focus of UX research should be about "everyday life" [3], on the other hand many appear willing to apply UX methods to any domain.

The *dimensions* of UX research are unclear. Law and colleagues [50] surveyed the views of 275 researchers and practitioners working with user experience. They found varying opinions on the definition of UX and its key characteristics. The relation of UX research to usability research is also contested. Some researchers write of UX as an "alternative to traditional HCI" [29, p. 91] and that it is not just "old wine in new bottles" [22, p. 11]; whereas it is elsewhere maintained that usability criteria can be used to assess aspects of user experience [36].

The *methodologies* applied are also debated and reignite the discussion between qualitative and quantitative approaches. A key issue is whether UX may be measured and modeled, and if so how: "A current trend seems to ascribe higher signicance to qualitative data analysis methods. Conversely, a danger would be that lower importance, priority and attention may be given to statistical methods." [51, p. 320].

In sum, although many papers discuss UX, its definition and distinct characteristics as a research field are currently unclear. Moreover, empirical findings are rarely synthesized. These limitations may be addressed normatively, by some vision of what UX research should be (e.g., [12, 29, 51]). They may also be answered empirically, by taking stock of the products, dimensions and methodologies of existing UX research; the present paper purports to do just that.

METHOD

The goal of this study is to explore the products, dimensions, and methodological approaches used for UX research. To perform this analysis we followed an analytical approach, using a representative sample of published empirical works in this field, covering a broad range of disciplines and approaches. The selection of publications was conducted in four steps, adapted from the QUOROM statement [62] which defines a procedure for meta-analyses (see Figure 1).

Phase 1: Potentially relevant publications identified

Source selection. A search in Google Scholar for "user experience" showed that relevant publications are spread across multiple scientific journals and conferences. Thus a procedure similar to [33], where a set of venues are defined and searched through, would not be appropriate, because many relevant sources may be missed. Instead we chose three scientific repositories spanning more than 13000 publication venues: ACM Digital Library (DL), ISI Web of Knowledge (WoK) and ScienceDirect (ScD). We restricted the search to a timeframe of five years (2005 to 2009).

Search term. We used the exact query "user experience". Although variations describe the same or very similar topics (such as customer experience, use experience) or subareas in this field (e.g., game experience, product experience), we found this term to best represent the new movement within HCI. Also, key publications in UX such as Forlizzi & Batterbee's framework [12] or Hassenzahl & Tractinsky's research agenda [29] use this expression. This procedure has several implications: (1) We miss publications that cover relevant topics for the field of UX, but refrain from using the term "user experience". This restriction seems acceptable, because our main goal is to review works of authors that intentionally aim to contribute to the UX movement. (2) Regarding false positives, we include publications that do not use the term "user experience" to denote a new paradigm (the oldest entry in DL using this term stems from 1970). False positives were excluded in later phases.

Search procedure. In DL and ScD "user experience" was used to search the publication's title, abstract or keywords. In the search interface of WoK such a restriction is not possible, so we used the phrase within "all fields".

Search results. The search returned in total 1254 entries (DL = 879, WoK = 270, ScD = 105) that were used for phase 2.

Figure 1. Adapted QUOROM procedure for this study.

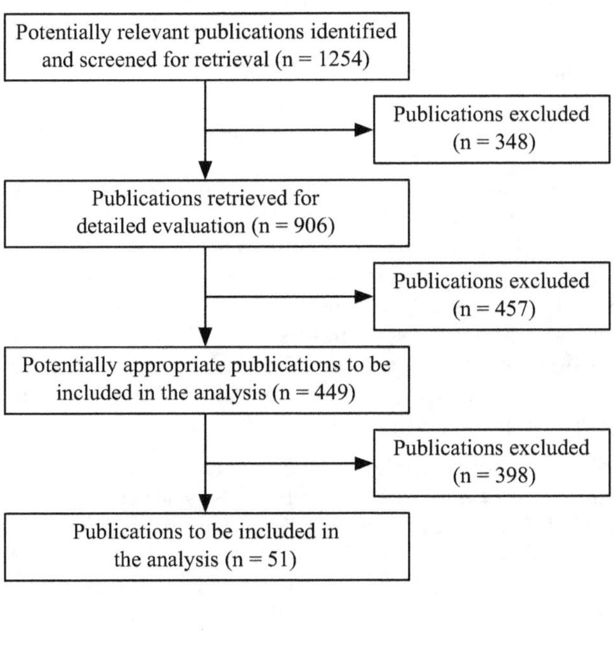

Phase 2: Publications retrieved for detailed evaluation

First exclusion. All search results from phase 1 were imported into the software "Papers" and duplicates (items that describe identical publication) were removed (296). We also excluded entries with wrong years, that despite having narrowed the search to 2005-2009 were included (2). Next, all corresponding PDFs were downloaded. In this procedure four entries were excluded, because they did not refer to a publication in paper form. 46 entries were not accessible to our academic institutions. Thus, 906 publications remained.

Phase 3: Potentially appropriate publications

Screening criteria. In this phase the goal was to narrow the entries down to (1) original full papers that are (2) written in English and (3) speak in a broad sense about interactions between users and some kind of product(s). The last criterion was used because UX is usually seen as resulting from interactions with systems, products or services [50].

Second exclusion. According to the three criteria we excluded 299 entries because they contained no original full paper (e.g., workshops, posters, speeches, unrefereed magazine articles). Eight entries were not written in English and 150 were out of scope, treating topics like construction, software development, network protocols, or nursery. Note that these categories are not mutually exclusive – as exclusion criteria the first obvious category was chosen. After the second exclusion, 449 publications remained for phase 4.

Interrater reliability. The exclusion in phase 3 was made by the first author. To control for interrater effects, the second author performed the same categorization using 20% of the entries. The interrater reliability was found to be Kappa = 0.851 ($p < .001$), 95% CI (0.773, 0.929). According to [46], Kappa values of .8 and higher can be regarded as *outstanding*. The set was therefore used for phase 4.

Phase 4: Publications to be included in the analysis

Screening criteria. In the last phase we wanted to narrow the publication pool to studies that (1) contain empirical user data and (2) speak about "User Experience" as a new movement. The first criterion (empirical user data) required a publication to report qualitative or quantitative data collected from users. Case studies – even of a single user – were also included, as long as user data were reported in a clear way. Studies that were based on author's self-reflections or introspection, without involving users, were excluded. The second criterion (UX as a new movement) required that the authors mentioned UX as a new movement, an extension of traditional HCI, a new paradigm or more than just performance measures. Alternatively, the authors must state that they assess UX or explicitly mention that the constructs they assess are dimensions of UX and not equivalent to traditional usability measures. To make sure that the authors speak about UX as new movement, at least one of the following authors that we consider key to UX research had to be cited: Blythe, Forlizzi, Gaver, Hassenzahl, Lavie, Law, Mahlke, McCarthy, Monk, Tractinsky, Ward, Wright.

Third exclusion. According to the criteria above we excluded 136 entries that reported no empirical user data. An example in this category is the UX research agenda [29]. We excluded 262 publications because they did not speak about UX as new movement (e.g., [79] where experience is researched as psychological perception), and/or did not mention one of the defined key authors (e.g., [16] where UX is used in the abstract but not defined as new movement nor are any key authors cited). Note that these categories are also not mutually exclusive. After the third exclusion a total of 51 publications remained for the final analysis.

Interrater reliability. The exclusion in phase 4 was also made by the first author. To control for interrater effects, the second author categorized 20% of the entries. The interrater reliability was again high, with Kappa = 0.821 ($p < .001$), 95% *CI* (0.652, 0.990).

A list with the 51 publications used for this review can be found on *http://bit.ly/gO2NQe*. For the analysis all descriptive data were entered into a database. Thus information such as results, measurements, measuring times, study types, study designs, participants, study setup, tasks, context, used products, was extracted for later anotation and analysis. Note that seven publications report two separate studies, and four report three. In the following sections, we often count and mark multiple studies as separate entities. In these cases, the number of studies sum up to N = 66.

RESULTS

In the following sections we report on products, dimensions and methodologies used in UX research.

Products, use situations and context in UX research

Table 1 shows an overview of the products in the sample. Among the most frequent products is art (21%). For instance, Blythe et al. [5] used an audio photography desk designed to challenge users' preconceptions about a city. Another example is van Boerdonk et al. [84], who developed an interactive canvas that aims to provide an alternative contact experience when meeting new people, while preventing visual prejudice.

The other products can be classified mostly as consumer or leisure products (e.g., mobile applications and phones, audio, video, TV applications). We categorized them into *leisure*, *work* or *mixed* (both leisure and work). In Table 1 it can be seen that leisure usage clearly dominates UX research (64%), whereas work or mixed are less frequent (each with 18%). It seems that the new movement of UX not only shifted the focus from usability to experience, but also changed the products researchers study.

Table 1. Products studied in UX research

Products used	e.g.	Total		Leisure		Work		Mixed	
		N	%	N	%	N	%	N	%
Art	[15]	14	21	14	100				
Mobile app/phone	[42]	14	21	5	36	4	29	5	36
Audio, video, TV	[55]	10	15	10	100				
Website	[86]	8	12			7	88	1	13
Imagined product	[31]	6	9	4	67			2	33
Interactive game	[56]	4	6	4	100				
No specific product	[67]	4	6	1	25			3	75
Other products		6	9	4	67	1	17	1	17

Notes. N = 66 studies; deviations from 100% due to rounding

Many researchers in the field of UX regard traditional measures such as task completion and performance as insufficient. We therefore looked at the use situations in which researchers study UX. We apply the term *use situation* to avoid possible confusion with tasks as used in usability research. We categorized them into three groups: (1) *Controlled tasks* stand for precisely defined assignments, which participants had to complete (e.g., find certain information on a website [86]); (2) *open use situations* stand for open instructions that explain the next steps, without providing detailed instructions or goals (e.g., instructions to play a game [56]); and (3) *user initiated use*, where users were free to choose if, when, and how they used the products (e.g., encourage users to use the product in their everyday life in tasks which they would be performing even when not evaluating a product [37]). The analysis shows that 61% of the studies use open use situations (n = 40), whereas 33% use controlled tasks (n = 22) and 20% leave the choice to participants (n = 13). Thus, UX focuses on more open use situations. Note that the total number of use situations surpass the number of studies, because some use multiple-use situation types.

Another frequently mentioned determinant of UX is *context* [29, 50]. We found that in almost half of the studies (45%, n = 30) researchers controlled the context by conducting their inquiry in a fixed setting. An example is [81], where UX of a multimodal media center is studied in a laboratory setting or [56], where UX of a game is measured in a psychophysiological lab. A third of the sample (33%, n = 22) used uncontrolled context and provided no descriptions of the physical or social setting. This is the case for most online studies conducted (e.g. [18, 11]). Only 21% (n = 14) described some parts of the context. This is often the case for studies using probes [39, 53] or methods similar to contextual inquiry [74, 70]. Considering that most researchers agree that UX is context dependent, it may be of interest to conduct more (field) studies exploring the role of context in UX.

Dimensions of Experience in UX research

A key question in UX is which experiential dimensions to assess. Table 2 shows all dimensions found in the sample.

The most frequent dimension is *Generic UX*. Here we summarize authors that do not further specify on which aspects of UX they focused. Common statements are "... it is possible to get a very rich view on the all-encompassing user experience" [44, p. 198] or "This paper reports on fieldwork, targeting user experiences of and with security technology" [57, p. 285]. *Generic UX* stems mostly from qualitative studies, where focus groups, interviews or probes are used (81% of *generic UX* dimensions originate from qualitative studies). In these cases, authors often do not report the dimensions that they focus on. Note that some of these studies do derive concrete conclusions about various product-specific dimensions of UX (e.g., [76, 53]).

The most frequent dimensions of UX that were assessed are *emotions and affect* (24%), followed by aspects of *enjoyment* (17%) and *aesthetics* (15%). This was unsurprising, as all three are often-mentioned core dimensions of UX. Although the dimension of aesthetics is often approached with experimental studies, the effect of emotion and enjoyment is

Table 2. Dimensions in UX research

UX dimension **	Examples and sources	N	%*
Generic UX	Interviews at the start and end of the trial [63]; Users made collages to express UX with mobile phones [61]	27	41
Affect, emotion ***	Affect measured with SAM [47] scale [28]; Emotional responses measured with psychophysiology [56]	16	24
Enjoyment, fun	Rate 13 play categories on a 5-point scale [8]; Pictures drawn after game experiences were coded e.g. for "fun" [92]	11	17
Aesthetics, appeal	Classical and expressive aesthetics [49] measured [87]; Website attractiveness [75] measured [19]	10	15
Hedonic quality	AttrakDiff [21] used to measure hedonic quality of websites [86]	9	14
Engagement, flow	FSS [38] used to measure flow [15]; Semi-structured interviews to understand engagement with technology [67]	8	12
Motivation	Probes used to understand motivation behind selecting a specific home [39]	5	8
Enchantment	Interview with a person to understand enchantment of technology [65]	4	6
Frustration	When people expressed aspects that they did not like (in semi-structured interviews) [4]	3	5
Other constructs	Values, spontaneity, ...	15	23

Notes. N = 66 studies * does not sum up to 100% because studies can measure several dimensions ** If authors mention exploring a certain dimension, it was counted as such without judging if the work really reports it *** We categorized *affect* and *emotion* in the same group, as they are treated mostly as synonyms in UX research. Many researchers in psychology, however, consider affect and emotions to be different (e.g., [72])

Table 3. UX data collection methods

Collection method	Examples and sources	N	%*
Questionnaires	Affect measured with SAM scale [30]; user feedback assessed with self-developed questionnaire [4]	35	53
Interviews (semi-structured)	Interview regarding interaction experience [84]; interview to elicit reactions regarding engagement [67]	13	20
User observation (live)	In-situ observation of PDA usage [70]; observation of people experiencing an artistic installation [8]	11	17
Videorecordings	Recordings of interactions with canvas [84]; videos to capture listening experiences on the move [52]	11	17
Focus groups	Focus group at end of trial to reflect PAD usage [70] ; group discussion to investigate preferences [19]	10	15
Interviews (open)	Interview to understand enchantment [65]; interviews regarding photo sharing experience [63]	8	12
Diaries	Emotions assessed with diaries [37]; diaries using day reconstruction & experience narration [42]	7	11
Probes	Participants were given a probe kit with a brief personal explanation and instruction [53]	6	9
Collage or drawings	From a list of topic areas participants chose an experience to articulate through collage [61]	5	8
Photographs	Encouraged users to take photographs related to attributes in their domestic environment [39]	5	8
Body movements	Choreography of interaction with canvas was evaluated by analysing the movements [84]	3	5
Psychophysiological measures	Psychopyhsiology (galvanic skin response, EMG, heart rate) of a game experience recorded [56]	3	5
Other methods	Think aloud, personal meaning maps, ...	18	27

Notes. N = 66 studies * data do not sum up to 100% because studies can use more than one method

never subject to experimental manipulation. An additional 14% of the studies focus on hedonic quality – all of them using AttrakDiff [21] or a modified version thereof (e.g., [83]).

We found many authors that propose new dimensions for understanding UX. These dimensions include enchantment [65], engagement [67], tangible magic [92], aesthetics of interaction [89], and relevance [76]. We will describe this phenomenon in the discussion section.

In addition, we looked at how many of these dimensions are usually assessed. Almost half of the studies (45%, n = 30) assessed only one, and 71% (n = 45) two or fewer dimensions. Half of the studies where only one dimension is assessed (n = 15) are categorized as "Generic UX"; in the other half, researchers focused on only one dimension (e.g., [65], where enchantment is the focus). Conversely, only 6% cover four or more dimensions (e.g., [56], where challenge, emotion, engagement, enjoyment and frustration are measured). It seems interesting that UX – despite being thought of as a multifaceted construct – is often approached in quite selective and restricted ways.

For Table 2, all assessments of usability were removed, even if the authors report them as being part of UX. A total of 45% (n = 30) of the studies also assessed usability metrics alongside UX (e.g., efficiency, effectiveness, satisfaction). Half of the studies that assessed both UX and usability (n = 15) looked into the relation between these two constructs (e.g., [55, 86]), whereas the other half refrained from doing so (e.g., [81, 90]). Studies with no usability metrics employed mainly qualitative or mixed study designs (90%, n = 27).

How are data on UX collected?

Half of the studies are qualitative (50%, n = 33), whereas 33% (n = 22) use quantitative methods, and 17% (n = 11) use both methodological approaches. These figures differ considerably from traditional HCI. Barkhuus and Rode analyzed 24 years of CHI publications [2]. For the year 2006 (the only reported year that falls within our sample), they found that only 14% of the studies were qualitative, whereas about 65% were quantitative (the rest used mixed designs or were not empirical). Thus the shift toward UX seems to be accompanied by a change in methodology.

Table 3 lists all UX data-collection methods found. Questionnaires are the dominant UX assessment method (53%). Others apply qualitative methods from HCI that involve talking directly with users, such as semi-structured interviews (20%), focus groups (15%) and open interviews (12%), as well as less intensive procedures such as user observation (17%), analysis of videorecordings (17%) and diaries (11%). We found an emerging group of constructive or projective methods such as probes, collage/drawings, or photographs. Objective measurement of UX via psychophysiology is used rarely. Thus data on UX are currently mostly collected with methods borrowed from traditional HCI.

More than half of the publications used questionnaires as a way of assessing UX. Table 4 shows an analysis of the surveys used for these 35 studies. Half of them (51%) use self-developed questionnaires but do not provide readers with the items used. Blythe et al., for example, conduct an online study with 563 users to analyze their experiences using a location-sensitive interactive play. The authors provide some selected conclusions, but refrain from reporting the content of the questionnaire [4]. A further example is Lankes et al., where a "standardized questionnaire, consisting of thirteen questions on the user experience factors fun, engagement and cognitive load" is used without providing any details about the items or the source [48, p. 255]. Another 29% also use selfmade questions, but provide them in the text (e.g., O'Brien et al. [67], where all items and their intended use are listed in the appendix), while 11% report them only partially (e.g., van Boerdonk et al. [84], where some selected items are reported as examples in the text). The finding that many researchers use selfmade items without providing them is not new and was also found for subjective satisfaction metrics in usability [33]. In terms of transparent study reporting, researchers as well as reviewers should aim at changing this in the future.

Table 4. Questionnaires in UX research

Used questionnaire	N	%*
Self-developed (items unknown)	18	51
Self-developed (items listed in the paper)	10	29
AttrakDiff [21]	7	20
Lavie & Traktinsky [49]	7	20
SAM [47]	7	20
Self-developed (items partly known)	4	11
Other surveys (e.g., FSS [38], IMI [58], Emocards [10])	11	35

Notes. n = 35 studies that used questionnaires * data do not sum up to 100% because some studies use more than one questionnaire

The most frequently used validated instruments cover Hassenzahl's hedonic quality [21] and Lavie & Tractinsky's aesthetics [49] with 20% each – a finding that is in line with frequently assessed UX dimensions (see Table 2). The most frequent tool for measuring emotions is Lang's SAM scale [47].

Note that 6 of the 11 studies that assessed "enjoyment" used self-developed items; not a single validated questionnaire was found in the sample. Remember that this dimension is one of the most frequently assessed in UX research (see Table 2). The reason why researchers who choose to use questionnaires stick to ad-hoc scales and refrain from using validated enjoyment scales remain unclear. There are validated scales with only 3 to 4 items (e.g., [85, 35]) and also instruments that were developed to measure more complex constructs like "Cognitive Absorption", where "heightened enjoyment" is assessed [1]. These are rich ressources mostly untapped by UX researchers.

When is UX assessed?

UX occurs before, during and after interaction [50]. Therefore we analyzed at which points in a study researchers chose to assess UX. We categorized the measuring points into *before*, *during*, and *after* interaction, as well as a fourth category labeled *imagined interaction*. In the latter studies, researchers did not look at real product interactions triggered by the study set-up, but used fictive products or retrospective techniques to analyze experiences from the past. Table 5 gives an overview of the temporal aspects of assessment.

Data show that frequencies increase over time, with *before* measurements being rare (20%) and *after* measurements being the most frequent (70%). Correspondingly, the most frequent pattern is the combination of *during* and *after* measurements – similar to traditional usability metrics, where users are observed when interacting and satisfaction is measured afterwards. Only 17% of the studies measure *before*, *during*, and *after* interaction.

Table 5. Temporal aspects of UX assessment

	before	during	after	imagined	N	%	Examples
		x	x		19	29	[39, 56]
			x		14	21	[92, 45]
	x	x	x		11	17	[76, 42]
		x			8	12	[70, 57]
	x		x		2	3	[81, 5]
				x	12	18	[67, 31]
N	13	38	46	12			
%*	20	58	70	18			

Notes. N = 66 studies * data do not sum up to 100% because studies can use multiple measurement times

Anticipated use assumes an important role in the field of UX, forms part of the ISO 9241-210 definition [36], and is a major difference to traditional HCI regarding temporal aspects. We therefore took a closer look at what researchers measure before interaction occurs. Thirteen studies used *before* assessments (see Table 5), of which only *expectations regarding the studied products* (36%, n = 5) was related to anticipated use. An example for this is the study of Turunen et al., where participants were asked about their expectations regarding multimodal media center applications [81]. The other assessed aspects were *prior experiences* with a similar product and *relevant habits* for the study (each with 36%, n = 5), as well as *open questions*, *attitudes* and *affective states* (each with 7%, n = 1). Thus, it seems that before measurements in UX are still widely disregarded.

The analysis of temporal aspects shows an additional phenomenon of current UX research: There are no truly longitudinal studies published. Some papers study experience over several weeks (e.g., [42, 52]), but projects that cover typical product life cycles of several months or even years are missing.

In addition to the reported analysis we grouped the papers by their main goal. This led to four groups: (1) *Basic research* (29%, n = 15) contains publications that investigate specific dimensions, the dynamics or the influencing factors to understand how UX works. (2) *Evaluation* (31%, n = 16) covers authors who developed a certain product or interface and conducted a study to evaluate its UX, such as an interactive canvas [84], a photo sharing service [63] or a tangible audio museum guide [89]. (3) *Methods* (29%, n = 15) consists of studies where a new method to design for, improve, measure, or explore UX is developed or applied. Finally a smaller group of publications covered (4) *requirements* (10%, n = 5), where authors aim at eliciting requirements for future products. In the following sections we will report on the groups *basic research*, *methods*, and *requirements*. Note that the papers in the group *evaluation* are too heterogenous to be discussed in detail.

Basic research

The group labeled as basic research contains publications that describe how UX is created, its core dimensions, and its development over time. There are two major subgroups consisting of four publications each: The first looks at the dimension of aesthetics, and its relation to usability [55, 86, 19, 87]. The other investigates how product judgements and choices are made and the factors influencing them [30, 18, 28, 11]. The remaining papers look at various dimensions of UX (e.g., engagement [67] or enchantment [65, 71]) or research how UX develops over time [42]. Surprisingly the authors within this group often do not relate to each other's work. Papers on basic research reference each other only six times, of which four are self-citations. It seems that for the time being, basic research in UX is quite heterogenous, going in various often unrelated directions.

Methods

Fifteen papers were mainly about the methodology of UX evaluation. The most prominent difference to mainstream HCI methods is that several papers present what may be called constructive or projective evaluation methods. Such methods ask participants to create one or more artifacts and use those to understand or assess UX. In four papers, the artifacts are visual representations, such as drawings [92] and collages [61]. Xu and colleagues [92] investigated how drawings may be used for interpreting children's experiences with technology. They developed a scheme for coding the drawings and showed how codes could differentiate three dimensions of UX: Fun, Goal Fit, and Tangible Magic. Others used video as the artifact produced to reflect experiences (e.g., [37]). Another constructive technique studied was Cultural Probes [14]. Lucero et al. [53] described how probes benefitted the design of new technologies for bathrooms, highlighting how probes help identify unexpected uses of the bathroom and look into participants' everyday lives.

Several papers presented evaluation techniques that did not rely on construction. These include papers using physiological measures of affect. For instance, Mandryk et al. [56] investigated heart rate, galvanic skin response and other measures, and showed how they could be used to distinguish gaming against a computer from against a friend. Others addressed UX methodology in ways resembling usability research: [82] described an expert evaluation method aimed at tapping UX and [83] adapted AttrakDiff to a work context.

The papers concerning methodology raise two open questions. First, papers in our sample rarely compare the new methods they propose to existing methods, or to alternative ways of gathering data on user experience (e.g., [7, 92, 53, 83], though see [37] for an exception). Thus, it is currently unknown whether the results obtained are valid or whether we could have, for instance, achieved the results obtained by probing in [53] by simply interviewing participants. Second, papers on constructive evaluation methods repeatedly discuss the difficulty of interpretation and data analysis. For instance, Xu et al. point out that the coding scheme is "open to evaluator's interpretation" [92, p. 224] and [37] discuss how interpretation of a diary method for expressing emotions and experiences is highly challenging.

Expectations and requirements

A considerable amount of studies (15%) report *expectations* or *requirements* for current or future products. Note that some researchers even report requirements and expectations within the same study and regard them as describing different things (e.g., [57]). Although it is important to look at what users expect from products, we would not consider these topics to be a dimension of UX (hence we did not code them in Table 2).

In most studies of expectations, users could not interact with a product – the research targets users' needs and imagined applications of these products (e.g., [74, 31]). Some publications treat requirements and expectations as one of many topics (e.g., Karapanos et al. [42] where expecations regarding the iPhone are treated), while others use it as main focus (e.g., Pyykkö et al. [41], where requirements regarding mobile 3D TV are elicited).

DISCUSSION

Next, we discuss what our findings mean to UX research, what to do (and perhaps do differently), and address the questions posed in the Related Work section.

Products, use situations, and goals

Our review suggests a heavy emphasis on art and consumer products. The phenomenon that art is often used in UX research is interesting, because the UX definition by Law et al. positions *Art* as being out of scope for UX [50, Figure 2]. Apparently the UX community disagrees on this point.

Further the turn to art and consumer products may preclude conclusions about experience with other types of products. The broadening of products studied is one of the purposes of UX research; it is fruitful, enriching, and an interesting expansion in scope. At the same time we find many studies in our sample that speak generally about UX, yet fail to reflect on the products used to study UX. The UX movement criticized traditional HCI for focussing only on work related products. Correspondingly we think that a narrow focus on consumer products and art only is comparably harmful to UX research, because the contribution to the understanding of a broad amplitude of products is largely ignored.

One common understanding is that non-instrumental, hedonic or non-task-oriented goals are associated with UX, whereas instrumental, pragmatic or task-oriented goals are associated with usability [29]. Initially, we aimed at categorizing the use situations into these two groups, but this proved difficult: Instrumental and non-instrumental goals were often interwoven and inseparable. For instance, one study even reported that users – not having received instrumental goals – started to invent such goals: "Although the designers did not deliberately structure goals or objectives for users, some imposed their own goals." [4, p. 132]. Recently, Law and van Schaik argued that the idea of applying type of goal as a differentiator between usability and UX is questionable [51]. Our data confirm this argument: While these concepts are certainly useful to reason about the influence of goals, they are not suited to serve as differentiators between traditional HCI and UX.

Dimensions of experience

As expected, affect and aesthetics are often used as indicators for quality of UX. With respect to affect, the most frequently used instrument is Lang's SAM scale [47]. With this scale, users provide ratings of emotion by selecting versions of a manikin that symbolizes different emotional states. This scale is well validated and widely used, but it is a relatively simplistic form of measuring emotions. We find it interesting that not a single UX study seeks to obtain more detailed measures of emotions, while at the same time many researchers agree that emotion is one of the key factors of UX [50]. In emotional psychology there are many established and validated ways of measuring emotions that provide more detailed and richer data – for an overview see [6]. Future research might benefit from these to do in depth studies of affective states in UX.

With respect to aesthetics, validated questionnaires are used [49, 21]. Recently, however, it was suggested that these questionnaires may be similar on subscales: "We argue that expressive aesthetics and hedonic quality are strongly overlapping constructs" [25, p. 254]. This phenomenon probably originates in the parallel development and publishing of these constructs and shows that a future consolidation may be beneficial to the field.

The studies reviewed also proposed many new dimensions of quality or variations of already known dimensions. We already mentioned enchantment [65], engagement [67], tangible magic [92], aesthetics of interaction [89], and relevance [76]. This variety in dimensions is inspiring to the field and supports new ways of thinking about experience. The main problem of this dimensionality explosion is that the relation to established constructs is rarely made clear. Let us briefly exemplify the problem using the notion of "enchantment". According to McCarthy and colleagues, enchantment is a "useful concept to facilitate closer relationships between people and technology" [60, p. 369], derived from a discussion of experiences of film and cell phones and used in many subsequent studies (e.g., [71, 65]). Although the notion of enchantment may be useful in many ways, one cannot help ponder how it relates to other constructs: Is enchantment a crucial and distinct component of UX? What is the difference between enchantment and established concepts such as for instance the experience of flow [9]? Is flow a condition for enchantment? Or a consequence? No studies in our sample report how enchantment can be measured and consequently help clarify its role within UX and the difference to other concepts. We argue that if new dimensions are needed and proposed, they should at some stage be accompanied by studies that clarify their difference to established constructs (see e.g. [68], where this step is partly taken for the dimension "engagement"). Else we risk ending up with an endless number of words that describe similar phenomena within UX, something from which the characterization of satisfaction in usability research has suffered [33].

Methodology

We have shown how research in UX draws on multiple methods. Although this in theory is attractive, in practice it leads to dichotomic research. On the one hand, some papers study very particular use situations, emphasizing richness of description and using mainly qualitative research methods (we call those *uniqueness studies*, e.g., [57, 65]). On the other hand, some studies model the dimensions of UX, emphasizing findings that generalize and using mostly quantitative research methods (we call those *dimension studies*, e.g., [11, 30, 87]). Settling the debate about the relative merits of these types of study is outside the scope of this review. Nevertheless, we argue that some studies overemphasize their methodological stance to the extent of damaging research quality. Many uniqueness papers do not report interview questions or protocols, rarely describe data analysis methods, focus mostly on generic UX, and contribute to the dimensionality explosion mentioned above. Many dimension papers do not attempt to study complex, ongoing interaction (often using screenshots or studying interaction lasting less than 30 minutes), and some say surprisingly little about experience and self-reports on UX. Unfortunately, few studies combine the methods of uniqueness and dimension studies (though see [42]) and our review shows a sad lack of reference between the groups.

The papers that contribute to method raise three points. First, the proposals for new methods are rarely validated. In work on usability evaluation, many papers have highlighted the difficulty of comparing methods [17, 34]. In work on UX methods, these difficulties receive scant attention: New methods are merely used without comparison to other methods, or the comparisons are weak. We see much opportunity here to improve our understanding of the relative merits of methods aimed at assessing or evaluating UX. Second, what we call constructive methods (e.g., sketches, probes) are not only rarely validated, they raise many issues about the process and validity of interpreting their results. Many authors use these methods as inspiration for design (as it may be argued is the purpose of cultural probes), but not all treat the methods this way. Third, some authors argue the need to rely on first-person methods for understanding experience. In contrast, much work on user centered design and usability research emphasize that we need to look at behavior, what people do, rather than merely listen to what they say and what they say they do. The tension between these approaches needs to be understood much better.

Limitations and future work

The aim of the present paper has been to critically discuss empirical studies of UX. Our approach has at least three shortcomings. First, we have focused on research studies and their treatment of UX, ignoring how practitioners work with UX. Although many of the publications we reviewed are from commercial research labs, additional work should review practice. Second, we have favored representativeness of studies through careful sampling. Although this has allowed us to broadly characterize the empirical studies that the UX movement has inspired, it means that the discussion of individual studies has been brief. Third, we have disregarded studies that explore UX through design, without empirical data. A review of design research could give an interesting and complementary view on UX research.

Our work has a number of implications for research in UX that should be clear from the above. Let us mention four additional areas in which more work is needed. First, rich descriptions of context were surprisingly absent in the studies reviewed. Even papers supposedly strong on capturing context reported not being able to reason about context sufficiently well [57]. Second, the basic research characterizing experience over time is meagre. Karapanos et al. [42] provided important insights, but their study nevertheless did not look at individual differences in use and the phases of use proposed were not clearly related to progression in time, neither for the individual participant nor across participants. Third, although multidimensionality is a key tenet of UX, surprisingly few studies describe several aspects of UX and their interrelation. Fourth, UX on desktop computers with productivity applications are rarely researched.

In sum, we have shown that UX research in several ways builds on existing research on HCI and usability. At the same time, the papers reviewed have helped identify novel challenges. We hope that our review helps take up and further develop existing solutions, while also addressing the distinct and pressing challenges in UX research.

REFERENCES

1. R. Agarwal and E. Karahanna. Time flies when you're having fun: Cognitive absorption and beliefs about information technology usage. *MIS Quarterly*, 24(4):665–694, 2000.
2. L. Barkhuus and J. Rode. From Mice to Men–24 years of Evaluation in CHI. *Proc. CHI '07*, 2007.
3. K. Battarbee and I. Koskinen. Co-experience: user experience as interaction. *CoDesign*, 1(1):5–18, 2005.
4. M. Blythe, J. Reid, P. Wright, and E. Geelhoed. Interdisciplinary criticism: analysing the experience of riot! *Behaviour & Information Technology*, 25(2):127–139, 2006 *.
5. M. Blythe, J. Robinson, and D. Frohlich. Interaction design and the critics: what to make of the weegie. In *Proc. NordiCHI '08*, 53–62. ACM, 2008 *.
6. J. Coan and J. Allen. *Handbook of emotion elicitation and assessment.* Oxford University Press, 2007.
7. B. Costello and E. Edmonds. A study in play, pleasure and interaction design. In *Proc. DPPI '07*, 76–91. ACM, 2007 *.
8. B. Costello and E. Edmonds. Directed and emergent play. In *Proc. C&C 09*, 107–116. ACM, 2009 *.
9. M. Csikszentmihalyi. Flow and the Psychology of Discovery and Invention. *HarperPerennial, New York*, 1997.
10. P. Desmet. *Designing Emotions*. PhD thesis, Delft University of Technology, 2002.
11. S. Diefenbach and M. Hassenzahl. The Beauty Dilemma: beauty is valued but discounted in product choice. In *Proc. CHI 2009*, 1419–1426. ACM, 2009 *.
12. J. Forlizzi and K. Battarbee. Understanding experience in interactive systems. In *Proc. DIS '04*, 261–268. ACM, 2004.
13. J. Forlizzi and S. Ford. The building blocks of experience: an early framework for interaction designers. In *Proc. DIS '00*, 419–423. ACM, 2000.
14. W. Gaver, T. Dunne, and E. Pacenti. Cultural probes. *Interactions*, 6(1):21–29, 1999.
15. S. Gilroy, M. Cavazza, and M. Benayoun. Using affective trajectories to describe states of flow in interactive art. In *Proc. ACE '09*, 165–172. ACM, 2009 *.
16. L. Gong. Is happy better than sad even if they are both non-adaptive? Effects of emotional expressions of talking-head interface agents. *Int. Journal of Human-Computer Studies*, 65(3):183–191, 2007.
17. W. Gray and M. Salzman. Damaged merchandise? A review of experiments that compare usability evaluation methods. *Human-Computer Interaction*, 13(3):203–261, 1998.
18. J. Hartmann, A. De Angeli, and A. Sutcliffe. Framing the user experience: information biases on website quality judgement. In *Proc. CHI '08*, 855–864. ACM, 2008 *.
19. J. Hartmann, A. Sutcliffe, and A. Angeli. Towards a theory of user judgment of aesthetics and user interface quality. *ACM TOCHI*, 15(4):1–30, 2008 *.
20. M. Hassenzahl. The thing and I: understanding the relationship between user and product. In M. Blythe, C. Overbeeke, A. Monk, and P. Wright, editors, *Funology: From Usability to Enjoyment*, 31–42. Dordrecht: Kluwer, 2003.
21. M. Hassenzahl. The interplay of beauty, goodness, and usability in interactive products. *Human-Computer Interaction*, 19(4):319–349, 2004.
22. M. Hassenzahl. User experience (UX): towards an experiential perspective on product quality. In *Proc. IHM '08*, 11–15. ACM, 2008.
23. M. Hassenzahl, A. Beu, and M. Burmester. Engineering joy. *IEEE Software*, 18(1):70–76, 2001.
24. M. Hassenzahl, S. Diefenbach, and A. Göritz. Needs, affect, and interactive products – facets of user experience. *Interacting with Computers*, 22(5):353–362, 2010.
25. M. Hassenzahl and A. Monk. The inference of perceived usability from beauty. *Human-Computer Interaction*, 25(3):235–260, 2010.
26. M. Hassenzahl, A. Platz, M. Burmester, and K. Lehner. Hedonic and ergonomic quality aspects determine a software's appeal. In *Proc. CHI '00*, 201–208. ACM, 2000.
27. M. Hassenzahl and N. Sandweg. From mental effort to perceived usability: transforming experiences into summary assessments. In *Proc. CHI '04*, 1283–1286. ACM, 2004.
28. M. Hassenzahl, M. Schöbel, and T. Trautmann. How motivational orientation influences the evaluation and choice of hedonic and pragmatic interactive products: The role of regulatory focus. *Interacting with Computers*, 20(4-5):473–479, 2008 *.
29. M. Hassenzahl and N. Tractinsky. User experience – a research agenda. *Behaviour & Information Technology*, 25(2):91–97, 2006.
30. M. Hassenzahl and D. Ullrich. To do or not to do: Differences in user experience and retrospective judgments depending on the presence or absence of instrumental goals. *Interacting with Computers*, 19(4):429–437, 2007 *.
31. J. Heikkinen, T. Olsson, and K. Väänänen-Vainio-Mattila. Expectations for user experience in haptic communication with mobile devices. In *Proc. MobileHCI '09*. ACM, 2009 *.
32. M. Hertzum. Images of Usability. *International Journal of Human-Computer Interaction*, 26(6):567–600, 2010.
33. K. Hornbæk. Current practice in measuring usability: Challenges to usability studies and research. *International Journal of Human-Computer Studies*, 64(2):79–102, 2006.
34. K. Hornbæk. Dogmas in the assessment of usability evaluation methods. *Behaviour & Information Technology*, 29(1):97–111, 2010.
35. M. Huang. Web performance scale. *Information & Management*, 42(6):841–852, 2005.
36. ISO. 9241-210: Ergonomics of human system interaction-Part 210: Human-centred design for interactive systems. *International Organization for Standardization*, 2008.
37. M. Isomursu, M. Tähti, S. Väinämö, and K. Kuutti. Experimental evaluation of five methods for collecting emotions in field settings with mobile applications. *International Journal of Human-Computer Studies*, 65(4):404–418, 2007 *.
38. S. Jackson and H. Marsh. Development and validation of a scale to measure optimal experience: The Flow State Scale. *Journal of Sport and Exercise Psychology*, 18:17–35, 1996.
39. S. Jacobson and A. Pirinen. Disabled persons as lead users in the domestic environment. In *Proc. DPPI '07*, 158–167. ACM, 2007 *.
40. P. Jordan. *Designing pleasurable products: An introduction to the new human factors*. CRC, 2002.
41. S. Jumisko-Pyykkö, M. Weitzel, and D. Strohmeier. Designing for user experience: what to expect from mobile 3d tv and video? In *Proc. UXTV '08*, 183–192. ACM, 2008 *.
42. E. Karapanos, J. Zimmerman, J. Forlizzi, and J. Martens. User experience over time: an initial framework. In *Proc. CHI '09*, 729–738. ACM, 2009 *.
43. E. Karapanos, J. Zimmerman, J. Forlizzi, and J. Martens. Measuring the Dynamics of Remembered Experience Over Time. *Interacting with Computers*, 22(5):328–335, 2010.
44. A. Koca, M. Funk, E. Karapanos, A. Rozinat, and N. van der Gaarden.

Grasping product pragmatics: a case with internet on tv. In *Proc. UXTV '08*, 193–202. ACM, 2008 *.
45. P. Kourouthanassis, G. Giaglis, and A. Vrechopoulos. Enhancing user experience through pervasive information systems: The case of pervasive retailing. *International Journal of Information Management*, 27(5):319–335, 2007 *.
46. J. Landis and G. Koch. The measurement of observer agreement for categorical data. *Biometrics*, 33(1):159–174, 1977.
47. P. J. Lang. Behavioral treatment and bio-behavioral assessment: Computer applications. In J. B. Sidowski, J. H. Johnson, and T. A. Williams, editors, *Technology in mental health care delivery systems*, 119–137. Ablex Publishing, Norwood, NJ, 1980.
48. M. Lankes, S. Riegler, A. Weiss, T. Mirlacher, M. Pirker, and M. Tscheligi. Facial expressions as game input with different emotional feedback conditions. In *Proc. ACE '08*, 253–256. ACM, 2008 *.
49. T. Lavie and N. Tractinsky. Assessing dimensions of perceived visual aesthetics of web sites. *International Journal of Human-Computer Studies*, 60(3):269–298, 2004.
50. E. Law, V. Roto, M. Hassenzahl, A. Vermeeren, and J. Kort. Understanding, scoping and defining user experience: a survey approach. In *Proc. CHI '09*, 719–728. ACM, 2009.
51. E. Law and P. van Schaik. Modelling user experience – an agenda for research and practice. *Interacting with Computers*, 22(5):313–322, 2010.
52. T. Leong, S. Howard, and F. Vetere. Choice: abidcating or exercising? In *Proc. CHI '08*, 715–724. ACM, 2008 *.
53. A. Lucero, T. Lashina, E. Diederiks, and T. Mattelmäki. How probes inform and influence the design process. In *Proc. DPPI '07*, 377–391. ACM, 2007 *.
54. S. Mahlke. Aesthetic and Symbolic Qualities as Antecedents of Overall Judgements of Interactive Products. *People and Computers XX – Engage*, 57–64, 2007.
55. S. Mahlke and M. Thüring. Studying antecedents of emotional experiences in interactive contexts. In *Proc. CHI '07*, 915–918. ACM, 2007 *.
56. R. Mandryk, K. Inkpen, and T. Calvert. Using psychophysiological techniques to measure user experience with entertainment technologies. *Behaviour & Information Technology*, 25(2):141–158, 2006 *.
57. N. Mathiasen and S. Bødker. Threats or threads: from usable security to secure experience? In *Proc. NordiCHI '08*, 283–289. ACM, 2008 *.
58. E. McAuley. Psychometric Properties of the Intrinsic Motivation Inventory in a Competitive Sport Setting. *Research Quarterly for Exercise and Sport*, 60(1):48–58, 1989.
59. J. McCarthy and P. Wright. Technology as experience. *Interactions*, 11(5):43, 2004.
60. J. McCarthy, P. Wright, J. Wallace, and A. Dearden. The experience of enchantment in human–computer interaction. *Personal and Ubiquitous Computing*, 10(6):369–378, 2006.
61. D. McKay, S. Cunningham, and K. Thomson. Exploring the user experience through collage. In *Proc. CHINZ '06*, 109–115. ACM, 2006 *.
62. D. Moher, D. Cook, S. Eastwood, I. Olkin, D. Rennie, and D. Stroup. Improving the quality of reports of meta-analyses of randomised controlled trials: the QUOROM statement. *The Lancet*, 354:1896–1900, 1999.
63. M. Montola, T. Nummenmaa, A. Lucero, M. Boberg, and H. Korhonen. Applying game achievement systems to enhance user experience in a photo sharing service. In *Proc. MindTrek '09*, 94–97. ACM, 2009 *.
64. M. Moshagen and M. Thielsch. Facets of visual aesthetics. *Int. Journal of Human-Computer Studies*, 68(10):689–709, 2010.
65. M. Ní Chonchúir and J. McCarthy. The enchanting potential of technology: a dialogical case study of enchantment and the internet. *Personal and Ubiquitous Computing*, 12(5):401–409, 2008 *.
66. D. Norman. *Emotional design*. Citeseer, 2004.
67. H. O'Brien and E. Toms. What is user engagement? A conceptual framework for defining user engagement with technology. *Journal of the American Society for Information Science and Technology*, 59(6):938–955, 2008 *.
68. H. O'Brien and E. Toms. The development and evaluation of a survey to measure user engagement. *Journal of the American Society for Information Science and Technology*, 61(1):50–69, 2010.
69. M. Obrist, A. Meschtscherjakov, and M. Tscheligi. User Experience Evaluation in the Mobile Context. *Mobile TV: Customizing Content and Experience*, 195–204, 2010.
70. Y. Rogers, K. Connelly, L. Tedesco, W. Hazlewood, A. Kurtz, R. Hall, J. Hursey, and T. Toscos. Why it's worth the hassle: the value of in-situ studies when designing Ubicomp. In *Proc. UbiComp '07*, 336–353. Springer-Verlag, 2007 *.
71. P. Ross, C. Overbeeke, S. Wensveen, and C. Hummels. A designerly critique on enchantment. *Personal and Ubiquitous Computing*, 12(5):359–371, 2008 *.
72. K. Scherer. What are emotions? And how can they be measured? *Social Science Information*, 44(4):695, 2005.
73. D. Smith, C. Irby, R. Kimball, and B. Verplank. Designing the Star user interface. *Byte*, 7(4):242–282, 1982.
74. X. Sun and A. May. The role of spatial contextual factors in mobile personalization at large sports events. *Personal and Ubiquitous Computing*, 13(4):293–302, 2009 *.
75. A. Sutcliffe. Assessing the reliability of heuristic evaluation for website attractiveness and usability. In *Proc. HICSS '02*, 1838–1847. IEEE Computer Society, 2002.
76. D. Swallow, M. Blythe, and P. Wright. Grounding experience: relating theory and method to evaluate the user experience of smartphones. In *Proc. EACE '05*, 91–98. ACM, 2005 *.
77. N. Tractinsky, A. Katz, and D. Ikar. What is beautiful is usable. *Interacting with Computers*, 13(2):127–145, 2000.
78. A. Tuch, J. Bargas-Avila, and K. Opwis. Symmetry and aesthetics in website design: It's a man's business. *Computers in Human Behavior*, 26(6):1831–1837, 2010.
79. A. Tuch, J. Bargas-Avila, K. Opwis, and F. Wilhelm. Visual complexity of websites: Effects on users' experience, physiology, performance, and memory. *International Journal of Human-Computer Studies*, 67(9):703–715, 2009.
80. T. Tullis and W. Albert. *Measuring The User Experience: collecting, analyzing, and presenting usability metrics*. Morgan Kaufmann, 2008.
81. M. Turunen, A. Kallinen, I. Sànchez, et al. Multimodal interaction with speech and physical touch interface in a media center application. In *Proc. ACE '09*, 19–26. ACM, 2009 *.
82. K. Väänänen-Vainio-Mattila and M. Wäljas. Developing an expert evaluation method for user eXperience of cross-platform web services. In *MindTrek '09*, 162–169. ACM, 2009 *.
83. H. Väätäjä, T. Koponen, and V. Roto. Developing practical tools for user experience evaluation: a case from mobile news journalism. In *Proc. ECCE '09*, 1–8. ACM, 2009 *.
84. K. van Boerdonk, R. Tieben, S. Klooster, and E. van den Hoven. Contact through canvas: an entertaining encounter. *Personal and Ubiquitous Computing*, 13(8):551–567, 2009 *.
85. H. Van der Heijden. User acceptance of hedonic information systems. *MIS Quarterly*, 28(4):695–704, 2004.
86. P. van Schaik and J. Ling. Modelling user experience with web sites: Usability, hedonic value, beauty and goodness. *Interacting with Computers*, 20(3):419–432, 2008 *.
87. P. van Schaik and J. Ling. The role of context in perceptions of the aesthetics of web pages over time. *International Journal of Human-Computer Studies*, 67(1):79–89, 2009 *.
88. P. van Schaik and J. Ling. An integrated model of interaction experience for information retrieval in a Web-based encyclopaedia. *Interacting with Computers*, [in press], 2010.
89. R. Wakkary and M. Hatala. ec (h) o: Situated Play in a Tangible and Audio Museum Guide. In *Proc. DIS '06*, page 290. ACM, 2006 *.
90. D. Wilfinger, M. Pirker, R. Bernhaupt, and M. Tscheligi. Evaluating and investigating an iTV interaction concept in the field. In *Proc. EuroITV '09*, 175–178. ACM, 2009 *.
91. P. Wright and M. Blythe. User experience research as an inter-discipline: Towards a UX Manifesto. In *Proc. BHCI '07*, 65–70, 2007.
92. D. Xu, J. Read, G. Sim, B. McManus, and P. Qualter. Children and 'smart' technologies: can children's experiences be interpreted and coded? In *Proc. BCS HCI '09*, 224–231. British Computer Society, 2009 *.

* Denotes a reference among the reviewed studies

Perceptual Analysis of Talking Avatar Head Movements: A Quantitative Perspective

Xiaohan Ma
Dept. of Computer Science
University of Houston
xiaohan@cs.uh.edu

Binh Huy Le
Dept. of Computer Science
University of Houston
bhle2@cs.uh.edu

Zhigang Deng
Dept. of Computer Science
University of Houston
zdeng@cs.uh.edu

ABSTRACT
Lifelike interface agents (e.g. talking avatars) have been increasingly used in human-computer interaction applications. In this work, we quantitatively analyze how human perception is affected by audio-head motion characteristics of talking avatars. Specifically, we quantify the correlation between perceptual user ratings (obtained via user study) and joint audio-head motion features as well as head motion patterns in the frequency-domain. Our quantitative analysis results clearly show that the correlation coefficient between the pitch of speech signals (but not the RMS energy of speech signals) and head motions is approximately linearly proportional to the perceptual user rating, and a larger proportion of high frequency signals in talking avatar head movements tends to degrade the user perception in terms of naturalness.

Author Keywords
Perceptual modeling, quantitative analysis, head motion, and audio-head motion features

ACM Classification Keywords
H.5.2 Information interfaces and presentation (e.g., HCI): User Interface—*Interaction styles*

General Terms
Human Factors

INTRODUCTION
Embodied interface agents (e.g., avatars) have been increasingly used in human-computer interfaces (HCI) [8]. In these HCI systems, perception of any human-like behaviors on avatars, such as facial expressions, hand gestures, lip movements, and head movements, can strongly influence user interaction experience. Among many human-like avatar behaviors [6], talking avatar head movement is considered as one of the crucial communication cues that can facilitate the social interaction between a human being and a humanoid avatar.

Previously, Wang *et al.* [6] studied human perception on head motion of a humanoid robot. They found that natural and appropriate robot head motions have a measurable positive effect on the social experience of users. Moreover, previous research studies [9, 5] show that head motion has a strong correlation with acoustic speech features. However, these studies were primarily focused on *qualitative* understanding of human perception on avatar head movements. The *quantitative* association between human perception and the audio-head motion characteristics of talking avatars remains to be uncovered, to the best of our knowledge.

Inspired by the above question, in this work we quantify how the characteristics of talking avatar head movements affect human perception (i.e. users' perceptual ratings). Specifically, it consists of the following steps: (1) Participants are asked to rate a number of constructed audio-head animation clips (as the visual stimuli); (2) joint features of speech signals and head motions are extracted from the audio-head animation clips; and (3) quantitative analysis is performed to study the association between the extracted features and the obtained subjective user ratings, including: a canonical correlation analysis based approach to model the correlation between joint audio-head motion features and subjective human ratings, and a frequency-domain analysis on the user-rated head movement patterns.

DATA ACQUISITION AND PROCESSING
The audio-head motion dataset used in this work was acquired from an actress using a VICON optical motion capture system. The actress was asked to speak a corpus (hundreds of sentences) while keeping her head movements as natural as possible. The original sampling frequency of the motion capture data was 120 Hz. The voice was recorded simultaneously using a close talking microphone at the sampling rate of 48 kHz. Based on the above acquired audio-motion data, three Euler angles of head rotation in each frame were computed using a Singular Value Decomposition (SVD) based technique [2]. Note that head translation is not the focus of this work. Meanwhile, we extracted the pitch (i.e. the fundamental frequency - F0) and RMS energy from the recorded acoustic speech signals. In this work, we used a Fourier analysis based cepstrum method to extract the F0 frequency from speech signals. The used window size of cepstrum sampling was 30 ms, and the output frame rate was set as 100 samples per second. RMS energy was extracted as the average squared intensity in a Hamming window (30 ms in our case). Finally, all the extracted Euler angles, pitches, and RMS energies were downsampled to the same 24 frames per second for our quantitative analysis.

SUBJECTIVE EVALUATION

We generated 60 audio-head animation clips as the visual stimuli in our perceptual study. Specifically, based on 15 speech clips randomly selected from the recorded dataset, we used the following four different audio-driven head animation generation techniques to produce 60 audio-head animation clips (i.e., each for 15 clips): (1) playing back the original captured head motions (called "original data"), (2) the HMMs-based head motion synthesis algorithm [2] (called "HMMs"), (3) the mood-swings head motion synthesis framework [3] (called "Mood-Swings"), and (4) randomly generated head motions (called "randomly generated"). The main consideration of choosing four different head motion generation approaches is that if all the animations were generated by a single technique, their user evaluations might fall into a narrow range, which will directly affect the generality of our quantitative analysis.

To suppress the potential influences of other visual/animation factors on user perception, we further postprocessed the audio-head animation clips as follows. (1) We used a 3D face model without photorealistic texture in order to remove the potential influence of photorealistic facial texture. (2) We only kept lip-sync motions and removed the motions at other facial regions (e.g., eyebrows), and the eye gazes stayed still (looking straight ahead). (3) Lastly, we intentionally applied an image mosaic filter to the mouth area so that participants only can see obscure lip movements. Its main consideration is that we attempted to minimize or even remove the influence of lip-sync quality on the participants' perception on head motions. Note that a similar face masking methodology was used in previous face recognition research [7]. The left-top and left-bottom panels of Figure 1 show an example frame of our generated audio-head animation clips.

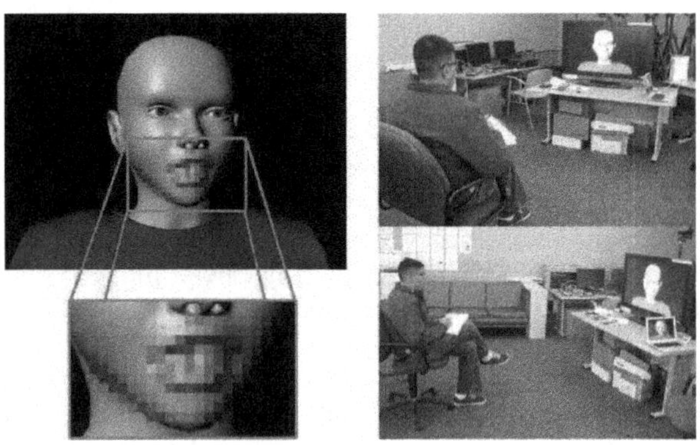

Figure 1. The left panels show an example frame of our generated audio-head animation clips. The right two panels show a snapshot of our user study.

We conducted a user study on the above 60 visual stimuli. A total of 18 student volunteers who were not informed the purpose of the study were invited to rate the naturalness of these clips individually. The demographics of the participants are: ages are from 23 to 28; 3 (16.67%) are female and 15 (83.33%) are male; and most of them are international students but all of them have been studying in the US for at least three years and can speak fluent English. It is noteworthy that although facial expression perception has been reported to be culture-dependent [10], it is still unclear whether a similar conclusion can be applied to the perception of head movements. The used rating scale was from 1 to 5 (1 represents "completely unnatural", and 5 represents "as natural as a real human's motion"). The participants viewed the clips in a 42 inches TV screen (approximately 3 meters away from them) and then wrote down their ratings (a snapshot is shown in Figure 1). For each participant, we first showed three example clips as test trials to allow him/her to get familiarized with the study procedure. The clip order for each participant was randomly generated to ensure the counter-balance of the experiment. Finally, we computed the average rating of each clip.

ANALYSIS OF RESULTS

For each audio-head animation clip, we obtained its average user rating, its 3D head rotation (Euler angles) sequence, and its speech pitch and RMS energy sequences. Our quantitative analysis is conducted in the following two ways. First, we analyze the quantitative correlation between the user rating and joint features of head motion and speech signals (in particular, the pitch and RMS energy). Second, we perform a frequency-domain analysis to study the association between the user ratings and head motion patterns.

Correlation between Speech-Head Motion Features and Human Perception

As reported in previous literature [5, 9], head motion has a strong correlation with the pitch (also known as the dominant frequency of repetition of speech signals) and the RMS energy of speech signals. Inspired by their work, we look into the quantitative association between human perception and joint audio-head motion feature. Specifically, we use Canonical Correlation Analysis (CCA) to measure the correlation between head motion and the two types of fundamental speech features: pitch and RMS energy.

For each used audio-head animation clip, we compute its CCA coefficient between its head rotation Euler angle sequence and its pitch sequence. Then, we plot the computed CCA coefficients versus their corresponding average user ratings (a total of 60) in Figure 2, where X axis represents the computed pitch and head motion CCA coefficients (i.e. between head motion Euler angles and pitch) and Y axis represents the average user ratings of these clips. As clearly shown in Figure 2, the highly rated animation clips (e.g., the audio-head animation clips generated by the original data approach) typically have high pitch and head motion CCA coefficients. Meanwhile, the lowly rated clips (e.g., those generated by the randomly generated approach) have low pitch and head motion CCA coefficients.

We also perform Pearson analysis to quantify the linear relationship between the computed pitch and head motion CCA coefficients and the subjective user ratings. The computed Pearson coefficient (in Figure 2), $r = 0.731$, which measurably proves the existence of a linear correlation between the pitch and head motion CCA coefficients and the perceptual user ratings.

The above validated tight coordination between avatar speech

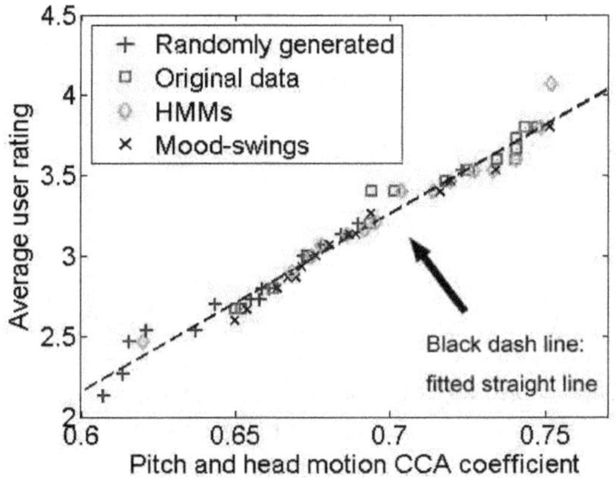

Figure 2. Plotting of the computed pitch and head motion CCA coefficients (X axis) and the obtained average user ratings (Y axis). The fitted line (the black dash line) shows the existence of an approximately linear correlation between the CCA coefficients and the user ratings.

and head motion implies the importance of precise timing in avatar head movement generation. Some previous head movement generation approaches (e.g. [1]) employ a delayed motion predictor for real-time applications. Our finding suggests that such delayed head movement generation strategy will potentially degrade human perception due to the importance of precise timing between head rotation and pitch, and for talking avatar head motion generation, designers need to heavily exploit vocal prosody timing (such as prosody-driven) in order to build a more perceptually believable head motion predictor. Also, our finding further gives a new and precise linear correlation between user ratings and the pitch and head motion CCA coefficients.

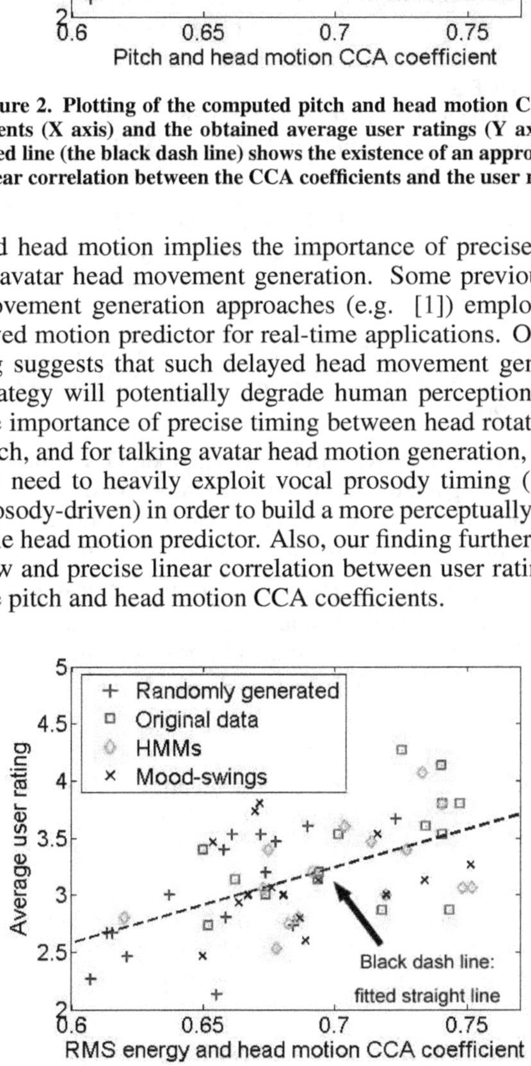

Figure 3. Plotting of the computed RMS energy and head motion CCA coefficients and the corresponding average user ratings. The fitted line (the black dash line) indicates that it is difficult to find a simple (e.g. linear) correlation between RMS-head motion CCA coefficients and the perceptual user ratings.

In a similar way, we also compute the CCA coefficients between head rotation Euler angles and the RMS energies of speech signals for all the 60 clips. Figure 3 plots the computed RMS energy and head motion CCA coefficients versus the obtained average user ratings. As shown in Figure 3, contrasting to the linear correlation between the user ratings and pitch-head motion CCA coefficients, we observe that such a linear correlation does not exist between the user ratings and RMS energy-head motion CCA coefficients. Our finding is contradicted with the previous results by Munhall et al. [5] that reported a strong correlation between RMS energy of speech signals and head movements helps to improve the auditory speech and non-verbal perception, and their evaluation experiment was limited to the case of a single sentence. Based on our finding, we argue that the quantitative relationship between RMS energy-head motion CCA correlation and human perception significantly varies, and it certainly does not fall into a simple correlation (e.g. linear), as in the case of the pitch and head motion CCA coefficients.

Frequency-Domain Analysis of Avatar Head Motion

As reported by Azuma and Bishop [1], human beings are more sensitive to the velocity and acceleration of head movements than static head poses. Thus, in this work, we use a frequency-domain analysis method to study the impacts of head motion spectrum patterns on human perception. Although frequency-domain analysis is not a new technique used in HCI community, previous frequency-domain analysis for head motion focused on analyzing the predicted results from linear head motion predictors [1], while our analysis intends to quantify the affects of frequency-domain head movements on human perception.

Our frequency-domain analysis of head motion (precisely, head rotation in our work) first separates 3D head motion Euler angles into three 1D signals inspired by the work of Azuma and Bishop [1]. This makes the analysis more accurate on each rotation axis. Then, we apply the Fourier and Z-transforms to the head rotation vector of each animation clip to derive its corresponding frequency spectrum. A classical Fast Fourier Transform (FFT) algorithm is used to compute the spectrum. The FFT point parameter is set as the smallest power of two that is greater than or equal to the absolute value of frame length of each animation clip. Figure 4 shows the frequency-domain analysis results of all the 60 clips, with an order from the highest user rating (4.2) to the lowest user rating (2.1). For a better illustration, in Figure 4, we only plot certain magnified part of head rotation spectrum with the squared magnitude less than 5 degree. Note that the degree unit (Y axis in Figure 4) is the squared magnitude of three Euler angles.

As shown in Figure 4, most of the highly rated audio-head animation clips have a low frequency pattern (i.e., most of the head motion frequencies are less than 12 Hz). We found that in the highly rated clips (i.e. the user rating is in the range of [3.5, 4.2]), 91.93% of their head motions are less than 10 Hz in the frequency domain, which suggests that natural head motions typically have low-frequency characteristics. By contrast, we also computed the frequency percentages of the lowly rated clips (i.e. the user rating is in the range of [2.1, 2.8]), and found that 19.39% of their head motions have are larger than 12 Hz in the frequency domain, which indicates that unnatural head motions usually enclose a significant portion of high-frequency movements (i.e. moving in a small range rapidly). For instance, in Figure 4, some of the lowly rated clips (<2.8 average user rat-

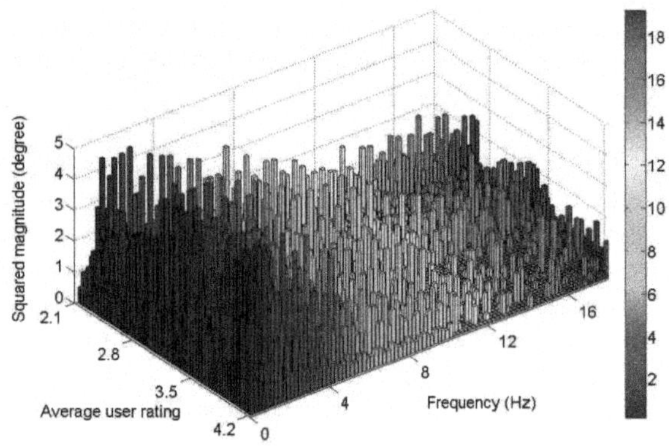

Figure 4. The frequency-domain analysis results of all the 60 clips. For a better illustration, we only plot certain magnified part of head motion spectrum with the squared magnitude less than 5 degree. The right color bar visualizes the head motion frequency range: from 0 Hz (blue) to 20 Hz(red).

ing) have a small range of head movements (<2.0 degree) with >14 Hz frequencies.

As pointed out by Grossman et al. [4], there is a critical instinctive mechanism that enables human beings to anchor their balance when the view is shifting, called Vestibulo Ocular Reflex (VOR). Therefore, during head rotations, if the maximum head velocity exceeds the range, the VOR mechanism will stabilize the motion spontaneously. Thus, our finding in this work is consistent with their results [4]. Furthermore, our quantitative analysis finding also suggests that 0~12 Hz is the comfortable zone in which VOR enables human beings to maintain natural head movements. This leads to one important implication for avatar-based human-computer interfaces, that is, since humans tend to give a lower rating to head motions with a larger portion of high frequencies, synthetic talking avatar head motions should be smoothed or simply cropped as a post-processing step. In this way, more natural avatar head movements can be obtained.

DISCUSSION AND CONCLUSIONS

Our quantitative analysis results clearly show that the coupling between the pitch of speech signals and head motion has a strong correlation with human perception. Generally, a higher coupling coefficient between pitch and head motion leads to a higher user rating on the audio-head animation. Moreover, our frequency-domain analysis results show that perceived-natural head motions mainly consist of low-frequency components (e.g. <10 Hz). By contrast, a measurable portion of high-frequency signals (e.g. >12 Hz) are found in unnatural head motions.

Animation clips used in current study only enclose a single avatar. However, we believe that our current findings can be soundly applied and generalized to more realistic scenarios due to two main reasons. First, although we only acquired the head movements of one female subject, she was participating in a natural two-party conversation (with another auxiliary subject that was not motion captured) during the data capture procedure. Second, in the user study, participants sat in front of the synthetic avatar clips (about 3 meters away from the screen, refer to Figure 1), which was approximately a natural face-to-face, two-party, human-avatar conversation scenario. In the future, we plan to further extend the proposed methodology to systematically study head movement patterns in multi-party conversations.

ACKNOWLEDGMENTS

This work is supported in part by NSF IIS-0914965, Texas NHARP 003652-0058-2007, and grants from Google and Nokia. Any opinions, findings, and conclusions or recommendations expressed in this material are those of the authors and do not necessarily reflect the views of the agencies.

REFERENCES

1. R. Azuma and G. Bishop. A frequency-domain analysis of head-motion prediction. In *Proc. of SIGGRAPH'95*, pages 401–408, 1995.
2. C. Busso, Z. Deng, U. Neumann, and S. Narayanan. Natural head motion synthesis driven by acoustic prosody features. *Journal of Computer Animation and Virtual Worlds*, 16(3-4):283–290, July 2005.
3. E. Chuang and C. Bregler. Mood swings: expressive speech animation. *ACM Trans. Graph.*, 24:331–347, April 2005.
4. G. E. Grossman, R. J. Leigh, L. A. Abel, D. J. Lanska, and S. E. Thurston. Frequency and velocity of rotational head perturbations during locomotion. *Experimental Brain Research*, 70(3):470–476, 1988.
5. K. G. Munhall, J. A. Jones, D. E. Callan, T. Kuratate, and E. Vatikiotis-Basteson. Visual prosody and speech intelligibility: Head movement improves auditory speech perception. *Psychological Science*, 15:133–137, 2004.
6. E. Wang, C. Lignos, A. Vatsal, and B. Scassellati. Effects of head movement on perceptions of humanoid robot behavior. In *HRI'06: Proc. of ACM SIGCHI/SIGART Conf. on Human-robot interaction*, pages 180–185, 2006.
7. M. Williams, S. Moss, and J. Bradshaw. A unique look at face processing: the impact of masked faces on the processing of facial features. *Cognition*, 91(2):155–172, 2004.
8. N. Yee, J. N. Bailenson, and K. Rickertsen. A meta-analysis of the impact of the inclusion and realism of human-like faces on user experiences in interfaces. In *CHI'07*, pages 1–10, 2007.
9. H. C. Yehia, T. Kuratate, and E. Vatikiotis-Basteson. Linking facial animation, head motion and speech acoustics. *Journal of Phonetics*, 30:555–568, 2002.
10. C. Yun, Z. Deng, and M. Hiscock. Can local avatars satisfy a global audience? a case study of high-fidelity 3d facial avatar animation in subject identification and emotion perception by us and international groups. *ACM Computer In Entertainment*, 7(2):1–26, 2009.

Diminishing Returns? Revisiting Perception of Computing Performance

Glen Anderson, PhD, Rina Doherty, MS, Eric Baugh, PhD
Intel
Hillsboro, OR
glen.j.anderson@intel.com

ABSTRACT

The computing performance literature offers guidelines and frameworks, but data on the limits of user appreciation for performance are scarce. This paper presents a study of user satisfaction with different levels of computing performance. Thirty-five participants performed common computing tasks such as creating email and Web surfing. They rated computing performance for specific task elements - such as application launching and menu responsiveness - that occurred during those tasks. They repeated the tasks under varying levels of computer performance. Results include user ratings as a function of computing performance for each of the task elements. The results have implications for system designers who create products that must meet user expectations for performance.

Author Keywords

Performance perception, time perception, usability

ACM Classification Keywords

H.5.2. Information interfaces and presentation (e.g., HCI): User Interfaces.

General Terms

Human Factors, Performance, Experimentation.

INTRODUCTION AND RELATED RESEARCH

The goal of this research is to help developers of computing systems better understand user satisfaction with specific levels of computing performance. Often the design of a computing system involves trade-offs between processing power and other factors such as cost of the hardware, size of the device, and battery usage. The existing research offers guidelines on performance, but some of the research is out of date, and research on what levels of computing performance users will notice or care about is limited.

Research on user perception of computing performance has a long history. In 1968 Miller [1] suggested guidelines on a range of system events, such as computer response to control activation and to simple queries. Much of the existing research was based on computing models of the past and on tasks that differ from current usage. For example, Shneiderman [2] described the way a user initiates an action from the computer as "usually by pressing an ENTER or RETURN key," which was typical of mainframe terminal interactions. While much of that work still applies to such tasks as queries over a client-server system, much of the current personal computing usage involves mouse clicks and menus. Various standards list duration requirements for computing events but without describing specific user interface elements [3, 4].

User expectations change over time, requiring fresh research to monitor trends. Recent research shows that under some conditions for e-commerce, user expectations have become more stringent, reporting even 4 seconds can be too long [5]. Previous studies have shown that under specific circumstances a slower response from the computer can allow more time for users to think about a task and thus perform the task with fewer failed attempts [6]. Again, this situation was more common in a mainframe usage model, when a user had to wait for faulty input to be processed. Generally, in modern computers, a well-designed user interface will be more efficient to use if computing performance is faster.

Many factors influence how satisfied users are with waiting for system response. Perhaps the greatest factor is previous experience with the task. Users are naturally more accepting of delays for task elements that they experience as delayed on an ongoing basis [2]. User attention to the task is also very important. Users judge short durations more accurately, and they judge the duration of events that hold their attention as longer than less attended events [7].

Seow [8] provided a practical discussion of performance guidelines for software developers and moved toward more specific recommendations on performance that users will notice. He suggested a "20% Rule" for system designers to ensure that users can perceive an improvement in duration of computing action. Using Weber's law [9] as a starting point, Seow determined that the minimum user-perceivable differences in duration range from 7% to 18% for durations

CHI 2011, May 7–12, 2011, Vancouver, BC, Canada.

up to 30 seconds. Thus a 20% improvement in performance in a new product would allow users to notice.

Based on a taxonomy by Card et al. [10] of duration periods, Seow suggested four duration ranges within a typical span of immediate attention:

Instantaneous (0.1 to 0.2 second): These are computer responses that simulate objects in the real world that respond instantaneously. Seow recommends less than 0.1 second for a key press and 0.2 second for a more complex action such as a menu drop-down. Dabrowski and Munson [11] tested thresholds of user perception performance delays, showing that users notice delays in typing at about 0.15 second and in menu appearance near 0.17 second. They provided an argument that the 0.1 second thresholds widely proposed in the literature were too stringent.

Immediate (0.5 to 1.0 second): The user perceives that the information is ready on the computer and simply needs to be displayed, for example, scrolling to part of a Web page that is not currently in view but is loaded in the browser.

Continuous (2 to 5 seconds): The user still experiences a continuous flow of "conversation" with the computer, but at the top of this range the user begins to expect feedback on progress since the event is not in the immediate response range.

Captive (7 to 10 seconds): Beyond this time period a user's attention wanders to other things. Even within the top of this range, users may abandon a Web site as unresponsive.

Seow's recommendations gave clear direction, but specific research on whether such durations are actually acceptable to users with modern user interfaces is needed.

RESEARCH QUESTIONS

The goal of this research was to understand:

1) At what levels of computing performance do users continue to appreciate performance improvement?

2) How does user satisfaction vary as a function of computer performance in a variety of computing tasks?

The focus was on sub-10 second tasks, those to which users will normally attend fully.

RESEARCH APPROACH

This study did not attempt to have participants evaluate computing performance relative to their current computing experience. Since many people use older computers that are slow compared to new computers, findings from such a study would quickly become obsolete. This study had users experience a range of computing performance and then gave their ratings, thus the participants had an internal (to the experiment) reference point for comparison.

Participants

Thirty-five residents of the Portland, Oregon area participated. They were a mix of employed, students, and retirees of various educational levels. All were 18 years or older and an approximately equal number of each gender. All had previous experience using a computer to store digital photos, to use Microsoft Office™ applications (including Microsoft Word™, Microsoft Outlook™, and Microsoft Power Point™), and to do photo editing.

Material

The stimuli were presented using an Intel Core 2 Duo™ 2.66 GHz processor, running Microsoft Windows Vista™, connected to a 22 inch computer display. Resume from sleep was simulated with a black form that filled the screen. When a participant pressed a keyboard key, the form disappeared after the allotted delay. Windows draw events (such as menu, dialog box, and application open) were delayed by altering the delivery of events to the application callback functions. Web page load was delayed by caching pages in a database on the hard drive, dividing the page components into chunks, and then sending the chunks so that the page was not loaded until the allotted delay transpired. Before each task the CPU was idled to limit varying performance.

Procedure

Sessions were run in a usability lab. Participants were told that the purpose of the research was to collect their perception of the performance of the computer they would be using. Participants were asked to pretend that they were in their natural environment such as at home, in the office, or at a coffee shop. A 5-point rating scale was used to rate the performance of the computers which had both a verbal anchor as well as a more descriptive explanation based on annoyance. Because of the possible ambiguity of the word "annoyance," it was defined as "the extent to which the performance bothers, disturbs, or disrupts you while carrying out these tasks in your natural environment."

5	Excellent	Usable with no annoyances
4	Good	Usable with minor annoyances
3	Fair	Usable but with multiple annoyances
2	Poor	Barely usable with many annoyances
1	Bad	Unusable – would not continue (would reboot, requires maintenance)

Table 1. Subjective rating scale.

Participants were instructed that the computer performance should include things like responsiveness or lag - how long the computer takes to open applications, display content, and process requests. Ratings were collected verbally and recorded by the facilitator, since participants made ratings while carrying out each task. Taking the time to stop and rate would have interrupted the natural flow of the task. Adequate training was provided to acclimate the participants to the tasks and rating procedures.

There were five levels of computer performance tested, which each participant experienced and rated. Participants were asked to carry out six different high-level tasks consisting of photo editing, word processing, video editing, and Internet usages (for example creating an email with an attachment or searching for and playing a YouTube™ video). Users rated 41 total task elements, including an overall rating for each level of performance. A complete, within-subjects design was used; performance levels and tasks were pseudo-randomized so as to control for order effects.

RESULTS

Table 2 shows the estimated task element durations at the mean participant rating of 4 (Good: Usable with minor annoyances), where users begin to notice performance decrements.

#	Task Element	Description *Time from click on…*	Time at "Good" (4) Rating
1	HTML page load via Internet Explorer™	Icon to page appears	5873 ms
2	Launch Outlook	Icon to application appears	6269 ms
3	Browser video load	Play button to playback begins	6071 ms
4	Wake from sleep	PC wake key to desktop appears	5235 ms
5	Open IrfanView™ file	Document name to document appears	5382 ms
6	Launch Word	Icon to application appears	3839 ms
7	Open new message window (in Outlook)	New button to message window appears	3692 ms
8	Open Microsoft Explorer™ window	Button to window appears	3601 ms
9	Application switch (from Internet Explorer to PowerPoint)	Task bar button to document opens	3773 ms
10	Office Menu (open)	Office button until list appears	2121 ms
11	Start Menu (open)	Start button until list appears	1345 ms
12	Dropdown menu (dropdown - IrfanView)	Image button until dropdown list appears	541 ms (4.5 rating)
13	Ribbon menu (ribbon style –Word '07)	Page layout button until ribbon appears	428 ms

Table 2. Task elements with corresponding performance times predicted for an average subjective rating of 4 (good).

Figures 1 through 4 show mean ratings as a function of the task element durations tested. Trend lines were fitted to the data using exponential equations because these resulted in strong correlation coefficients. It is unclear whether these trends will hold true if more than five levels of performance are used. The trend lines were used to estimate task element durations in Table 2. Error bars depicted in the figures are 95% confidence intervals.

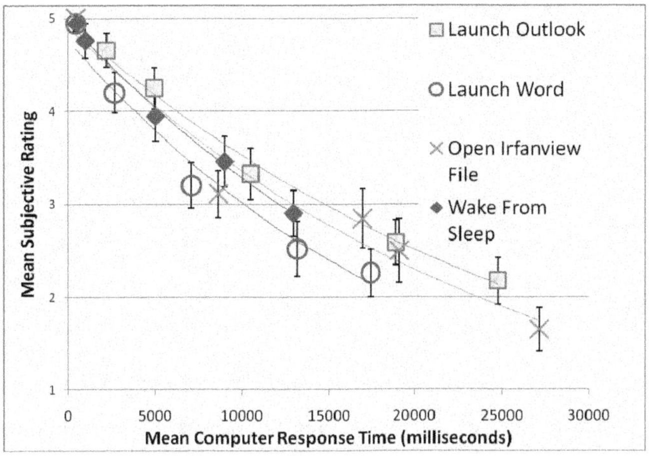

Figure 1. Mean rating by duration for launching Outlook, Word, an IrfanView file, and wake from sleep.

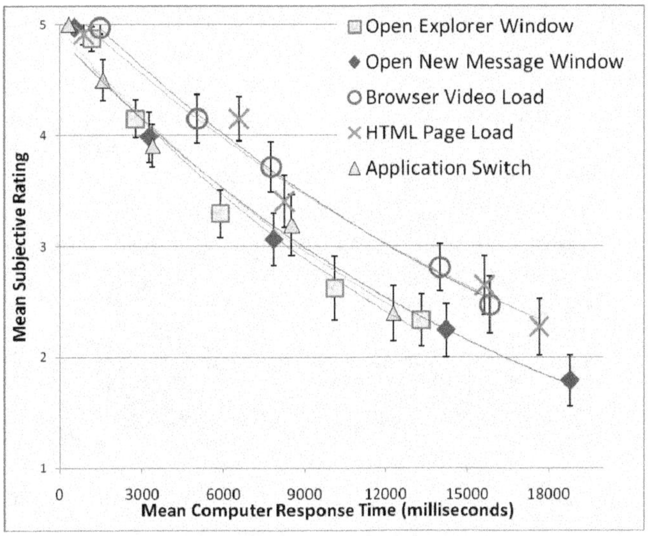

Figure 2. Mean rating by duration for opening an Explorer window, new email message, loading an online video, HTML page load, and switching applications.

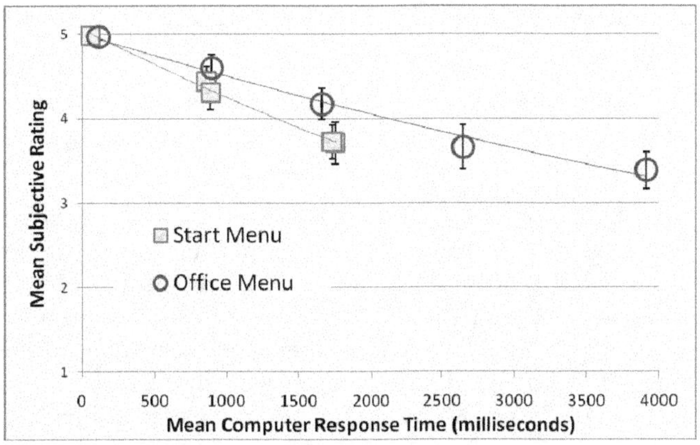

Figure 3. Mean rating by duration for the Start and Office menu to open.

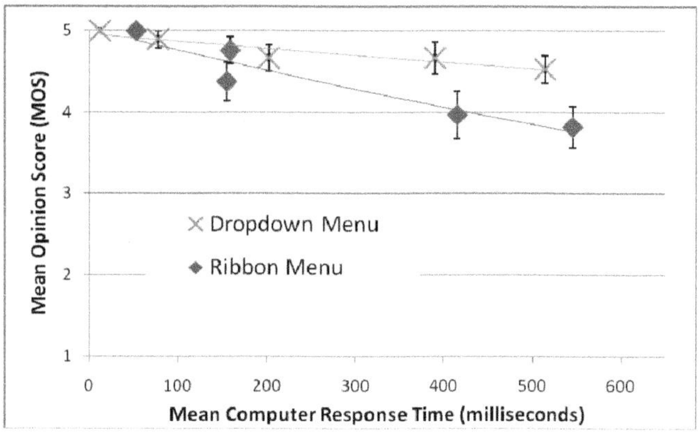

Figure 4. Mean rating by duration for an IrfanView dropdown and Word ribbon menu to appear.

CONCLUSION

These results show users continue to appreciate performance improvements to very fast levels across task events. Task events, such as application launch, that often occur in the Captive range in normal computing usage will have higher user satisfaction in the Continuous range. It is likewise true for task events going from Continuous to Immediate and Immediate to Instantaneous.

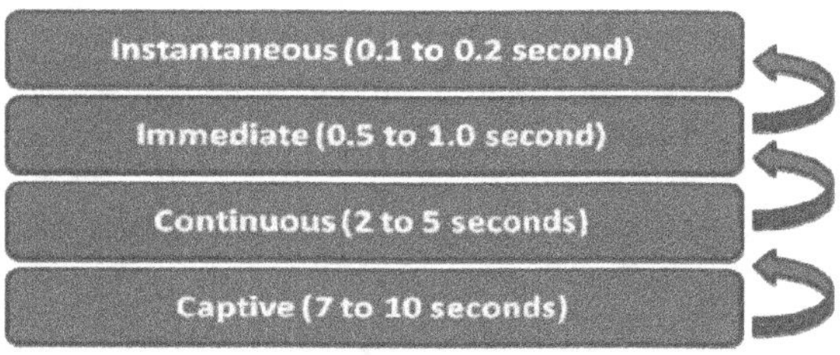

Figure 5. Duration ranges.

Seow's 20% rule holds up well in light of this data as a safe level where the designer can be fairly sure users will notice improvements. For task elements like launching applications and opening new windows, the steep curves at the shortest durations indicate users are more sensitive to percent of improvement in the Continuous and shorter ranges.

The participants appreciated a wake from sleep event up to very low delay. PCs can obviously benefit from an "instant on" capability.

For ribbon style menus (such as those in Microsoft Word 2007), up to 0.4 seconds may be acceptable. The apparatus did not allow long delay for drop-down menus. Users detected some delay at 0.2 seconds but still rated the task event highly at 0.5 second. The Start menu and Office menu are more global-level menus that require less frequency of use. Mean ratings of 4 appear at estimations of 1.4 and 2.0 seconds respectively.

Additional research could determine whether the same results occur using: a more realistic work context, post-task ratings instead of during task, performance measures for dependent variables, and subjects with various previous performance experiences.

As computers reach higher levels of performance in everyday use, task events in the Captive range will likely become unacceptable for those events that users must attend before pursuing the next step in a task. On the other hand, when designers can put task events into the Immediate and Instantaneous ranges, users will notice and appreciate the improvements. For many computing tasks, we have not met the point of diminishing returns.

REFERENCES

1. Miller, R. B. Response time in man-computer conversational transactions. *Proc. AFIPS Fall Joint Computer Conf,* Vol. 33 (1968), 267-277.
2. Shneiderman, B. Response Time and Display Rate in Human Performance with Computers. *ACM Computing Surveys,* 16, 4 (1984), 265-285.
3. Department of Defense. *Design Criteria Standard: Human Engineering; MIL-STD-1472F* (1999).
4. Smith, S. L. and Mosier, J. N. *Guidelines for Designing User Interface Software.* Report ESD-TR-86-278, The MITRE Corporation, Bedford, MA, 1986.
5. Forrester Consulting. *eCommerce Web Site Performance Today: An Updated Look At Consumer Reaction To A Poor Online Shopping Experience.* A commissioned study conducted by Forrester Consulting on behalf of Akamai Technologies, Inc., August, 2009.
6. Weinberg, S.M. Learning effectiveness: *The impact of response time.* Presentation at May 1981 Conference, Control Data Corporation, Minneapolis, MN., 1981 (as reported in Shneiderman, B., 1984).
7. Brown, S. W. Time and attention: Review of the literature. In S. Grondin (Ed.), *Psychology of time,* pp. 111-138. Bingley, U.K.: Emerald Group, 2008.
8. S.C. Seow. *Designing and Engineering Time: The Psychology of Time Perception in Software*, Addison-Wesley Professional, 2008.
9. Weber, E. H. *The sense of touch* (H. E. Ross & D. J. Murray, Trans.). London: Academic Press, 1978 (Original work published 1834).
10. Card, S. K., Robertson, G. G., and Mackinlay, J. D. The information visualizer: An information workspace. *Proc. CHI '91*, 1991, 181-188.
11. J. Dabrowski and E. V. Munson. Is 100 Milliseconds Too Fast? *Proc CHI 2001,* Extended Abstracts, (2001), 317-318.

ShadowPuppets: Supporting Collocated Interaction with Mobile Projector Phones Using Hand Shadows

Lisa G. Cowan
Computer Science and Engineering
University of California, San Diego
lgcowan@cs.ucsd.edu

Kevin A. Li
AT&T Labs – Research
Florham Park, NJ
kevinli@research.att.com

ABSTRACT
Pico projectors attached to mobile phones allow users to view phone content using a large display. However, to provide input to projector phones, users have to look at the device, diverting their attention from the projected image. Additionally, other collocated users have no way of interacting with the device.

We present ShadowPuppets, a system that supports collocated interaction with mobile projector phones. ShadowPuppets allows users to cast hand shadows as input to mobile projector phones. Most people understand how to cast hand shadows, which provide an easy input modality. Additionally, they implicitly support collocated usage, as nearby users can cast shadows as input and one user can see and understand another user's hand shadows.

We describe the results of three user studies. The first study examines what hand shadows users expect will cause various effects. The second study looks at how users perceive hand shadows, examining what effects they think various hand shadows will cause. Finally, we present qualitative results from a study with our functional prototype and discuss design implications for systems using shadows as input. Our findings suggest that shadow input can provide a natural and intuitive way of interacting with projected interfaces and can support collocated collaboration.

Author Keywords
Projector-camera system, mobile projector phone, shadow, gesture, interaction technique

ACM Classification Keywords
H5.2 [Information interfaces and presentation]: User Interfaces; B 4.2 Input Output devices

General Terms
Design, Experimentation, Human Factors

INTRODUCTION
Sharing information displayed on a mobile device's small screen with collocated people can be difficult. Pico projectors make it easier for mobile phone users to share visual information with those around them using a projected image, which can be much larger than the device's screen. However, current commodity projector phones only support input via the handset's user interface. As a result, users must look at the handset to interact with the phone's buttons or touch screen, dividing attention between the handset and the projected display. This context switching can distract presenters and viewers from ongoing conversations taking place around the projected display. Additionally, viewers may find it difficult to interpret what the presenter is doing as he interacts with the handset, and they have no way of interacting with the system themselves.

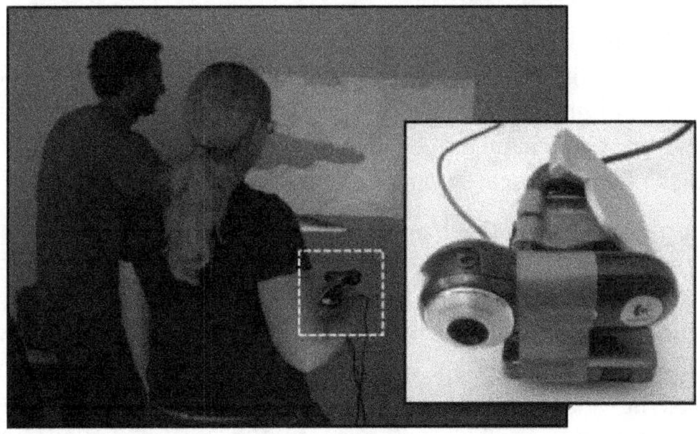

Figure 1: Interacting with ShadowPuppets prototype.

We present ShadowPuppets, a mobile projector phone system that allows users to provide input to the system by casting shadows (Figure 1). Users hold the mobile projector phone in one hand while casting shadows with the other hand, and shadows are detected using an attached camera. ShadowPuppets, like some previous research systems [3,4], precludes the need for visual attention to the device and supports ad hoc interaction with uninstrumented environments. Additionally, shadow interaction enables bystanders to provide input by casting hand shadows, without requiring additional equipment. Potentially, multiple collocated users could interact simultaneously.

We conducted a formative survey asking 19 smartphone users about the mobile phone applications they commonly use when collaborating with others in collocated settings. The maps and photo browsing applications were the most popular applications in these settings. These results formed the basis for guiding the design of shadows for our ShadowPuppets prototype.

Our first user study was focused on determining what types of shadows such a system should support, from the perspective of a user trying to interact with the system. In this study, we showed our participants video clips of different effects for both Maps and PhotoBrowser applications that would happen in response to a hypothetical user action (i.e. panning left on a map), though no shadow was shown. Participants were then asked to produce the shadow that they felt most appropriate for causing that effect. The shadows we observed provided an initial set of shadows to explore.

Since ShadowPuppets was motivated as a method for collocated collaboration, we were also interested in how observers would interpret shadows. Our second user study focused on this observer perspective. We presented participants with videos of hand shadows and then asked them to determine what kinds of effects the actor in the video was trying to cause.

In a final qualitative study, we documented how collocated users interacted with our functional ShadowPuppets prototype and reflected on their experiences. Our findings suggest that shadows can provide a natural and intuitive way of interacting with projected interfaces and can support collocated collaboration.

RELATED WORK

We build on related work on mobile projector camera systems and gestural computing. We also consider how shadows have been leveraged in interactive systems, and discuss relevant research on awareness in groupware.

Augmenting the Environment with Mobile Projectors

The seminal *Everywhere Displays* system [22] used steerable projectors to create multiple interactive surfaces within an environment. Researchers later investigated techniques for interacting with handheld projected displays: moving and pressing buttons on the device [1], touching the projection surface with fingers [29] or moving the projector like a "*spotlight*" within a virtual information space [23]. Cao et al. expanded on this metaphor, employing passively tracked pens and projectors to define and interact with information spaces and creating techniques for collocated collaboration with multiple projectors [3,4].

Researchers have also explored projector-device ensembles as a way of increasing interactive space. *Bonfire* [17] integrates projectors with a laptop to extend the interactive space to the table. Similarly, *PenLight* [27] and *MouseLight* [28] increase the interactive space for digital pens, providing visual feedback for interaction with paper.

Harrison et al. [12] analyzed vibrations to detect taps on the skin, and demonstrated using their technique to interact with an interface projected on the body, and Mistry et al. [19] relied on computer vision for interaction with a wearable camera-projector system. In the projector-phone space, Greaves and Rukzio [10] found that users preferred projector-based interaction over phone-based interaction. Cowan et al. documented commodity projector phone use "in the wild" [6], finding that, even without projection-specific input techniques, these devices afforded novel interaction modalities.

Gestural Interaction Techniques

Gestural interaction addresses many of the issues we examine. A mobile touchscreen, such as the *Touch Projector,* can be used to interact with distant displays but requires all users to have a handheld device [2]. Computer vision has been used for un-instrumented detection of gestures, such as pointing [5] and pinching [32]. Gustafson et al. [11] explore screenless, spatial, gestural interaction with *Imaginary Interfaces*, relying on users' memory in lieu of visual feedback. However, it can be difficult for observers to interpret a user's intent based on his gestures, without visual feedback, and interpretability is important for collaboration.

Usage of shadows in interactive computer systems

Shadows have been employed in interactive systems for both input and output because they are intuitively understood by users. Shoemaker et al. explored using real and virtual shadow representations of users to extend user's reach and enhance the interpretability of indirect interaction with large wall displays [25], and Snibbe and Raffle [26] analyzed the use of virtual shadow silhouettes to represent participants in interactive museum exhibits. Hilliges, et al. motivate the use of shadow feedback for 3D interaction above tabletops [13] and *ShadowGuides* [9] employed virtual shadows, visual representations of user's raw input, to guide users in learning tabletop gestures.

Computer vision techniques have been developed for robustly detecting shadows [14] and shadow detection has been leveraged for estimating 3D hand positions [24], detecting surface contacts [16], and tracking above-the-surface interactions with multi-touch tables [7].

Awareness and presence in groupware

Much work has focused on awareness and presence in groupware, to support anticipation and interpretation of others' intentions and actions [1]. The *VideoArms* system [30], which employed representations of users' arms, emphasized the role of embodiment for awareness in collocated and remote collaboration and Pinelle et al. [21] found that relative interaction and an arm-like virtual embodiment were preferred for tabletop groupware. Ishii et al. [15] emphasized the value of "*gaze awareness*," awareness of what one's partner is looking at and attending to. Also, several systems, including *VideoWhiteboard* [31] and *Distributed Designers' Outpost* [8], have used shadows superimposed on the work surface to provide awareness of remote collaborators' activities.

WHAT ACTIVITIES DO PEOPLE DO COLLABORATIVELY ON THEIR MOBILE PHONES?

We interviewed 19 volunteers (9 female), aged 21–56 (median 31.5) from within our institution about their smartphone usage habits. This survey was intended to guide the design of the ShadowPuppets system by highlighting potential usage scenarios. Interviews lasted 15 minutes. During the interviews, we asked users how often they perform various activities on their smartphones. We also asked how often they perform these activities collaboratively, in collocated settings. Finally, we asked participants to pick the top three activities that were most important to them in the context of collocated collaboration, and asked them to describe some recent scenarios.

Figure 2 plots the activities that were rated most important by respondents for collocated collaboration. Viewing photos, using maps, taking photos, and searching the web rated highest.

Since photo and map viewing were rated as the most important and most frequently performed collocated collaborative activities, we decided to study those applications further in the context of ShadowPuppets. It is less readily apparent how photo capture and web search (which requires extensive text entry) could benefit from gestural interaction with a projected display, even though these were highly rated as well.

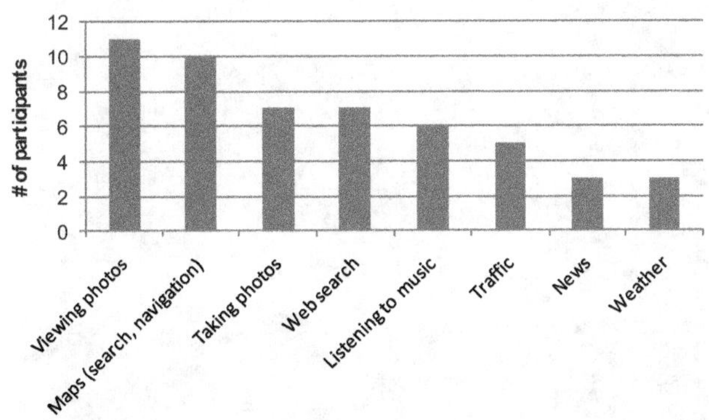

Figure 2. Number of participants out of 19 who rated the respective feature as "most important" for collocated collaboration on their mobile phone.

Current strategies for doing things together on phones

Respondents reported strategies for collocated collaboration on mobile phones varied widely. Their strategies fell into four categories: (1) one person controls the phone and verbalizes information for others, (2) one person holds up the phone for others to view, (3) the phone is passed around, and (4) someone shares a link or reference and others view the information their own phones. Strategies were selected based on group size, closeness of participants, availability of technology, the nature of the information, and other contextual factors. Respondents also varied in their perceptions of device control and privacy: some would physically pass around their handsets while others guarded their mobile phones closely.

USER STUDY 1: WHAT KIND OF HAND SHADOWS SHOULD BE USED?

One of the motivations for using hand shadows as a gestural input into our system was that users already know how to generate shadows with their hands. Although all users know *how* to cast different shadows, it was unclear *what* shadows users would expect to cause the different effects that an application might support.

The purpose of this study was to see what kinds of shadows users would expect to cause various effects in the interface. We structured our study based on Wobbrock et al.'s study of user generated gestures for surface computing [33]. In this study, participants were shown video clips of effects (e.g., a map panning left) for a *Maps* and a *PhotoBrowser* application and asked to generate hand shadows they felt would cause those effects.

Interfaces and Operations

Based on our survey results, we chose *Maps* and *PhotoBrowser* as our interface conditions. For each of these conditions, we considered 7 operations: 4 *Pan* operations (*Up, Down, Left, Right*), 2 *Zoom* operations (*In, Out*), and *Selection*. We chose these operations because they are commonly performed by users interacting with these applications, and because they could be readily conceptually mapped to spatial gestures.

For the *PhotoBrowser* application, *Pan Left* and *Pan Right* are used to view the previous and next photo, *Pan Up* and *Pan Down* are used to scroll through a list of thumbnails, *Zoom In* and *Zoom Out* are used to change the view of a photo, and *Select* may be used to choose a thumbnail or interact with a menu. Similarly, in the *Maps* application, users can *Pan* (we constrain the operation to 4 directions), *Zoom In* or *Out* on the map, and *Select* a marker or icon on the map or a menu option.

While shadow gestures could potentially support more numerous operations, we constrained the study to existing mobile applications, rather than exploring the breadth of possible interactions. Future work could unlock the potential of the ShadowPuppets approach. A primary challenge for scaling this technique to a larger number of gestures is to design gestures that the vision system can recognize and that users can readily learn, perform, and interpret.

Task

Participants were shown a video of an *effect* of what might happen in response to some user action. They were then prompted to cast the shadow that they felt would be most appropriate for causing that effect.

Immediately after casting the shadow, participants were asked to rate two statements on a 7-point Likert scale (1=disagree, 7=agree). The first read, *"The shadow I cast was a good match for causing this effect."* The second read, *"The shadow I cast was easy to make."*

Apparatus

A C# program was used to present videos of the effects of gestures to users. We used a *Microvision SHOWWX* laser pico projector to display the videos. The users and their shadows were video recorded.

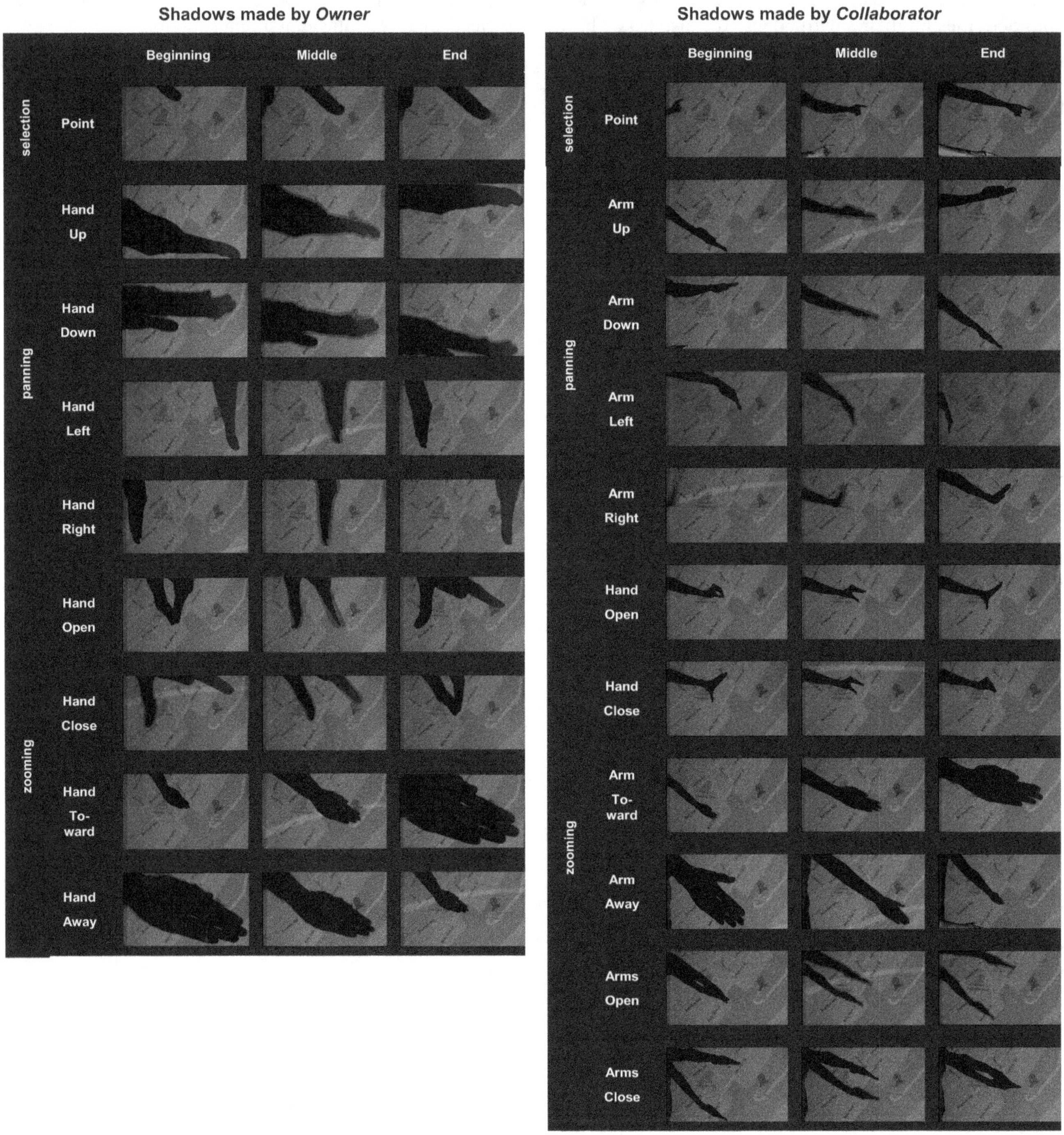

Table 1. The most common shadows generated by users for panning, zooming and selection. (Left) shows the shadows made in the *Owner* condition. (Right) shows the shadows made in the *Collaborator* condition. These are representative of shadows generated by users in Study 1 and formed the basis for the video clips used in Study 2.

Participants

Sixteen volunteers (9 female) ranging in age from 24 to 56 years (median 28.5) were recruited from within our institution. All participants were right-handed. We did not recruit left-handed participants because we expected that some of the tasks might be harder, depending on which hand was holding the projector. Half of our participants owned mobile phones with multitouch capabilities.

Hypothesis

We expected that most participants would cast similar shadows for any given effect. We also hypothesized that owners of multitouch phones would cast different types of shadows, given their experience with gestural interfaces.

Experimental Design

We used a within-participants factorial design. The independent variables were *Applications* (*Map* and *Photo-*

Browser), *Roles* (*Owner* and *Collaborator*), and *Effects* (*Pan Up, Pan Left, Pan Right, Pan Down, Zoom In, Zoom Out, and Select*).

Presentation of *Application* was counterbalanced across participants. We considered mixing tasks from the two *Application* conditions together. However, that might have caused users to converge on the same set of gestures for both contexts, a behavior that we were independently interested in.

For each application, we considered two *Role* conditions: *Owner* and *Collaborator*, with order of presentation counterbalanced across participants. In the *Owner* condition participants held the projector in their left hands and gestured with their right hands, standing 6 feet from the projection surface. In the *Collaborator* condition participants did not hold the projector and stood forward and to the left of the projector, 3 feet from the projection surface. Because *Collaborators* had both hands free, they could use either or both hands to cast shadows. Within each condition, the various *Effects* were presented in random order.

In summary, the experimental design was: 2 *Applications* (*Map* and *PhotoBrowser*) × 2 *Roles* (*Owner* and *Collaborator*) × 7 *Effects* (*Pan Up, Pan Down, Pan Left, Pan Right, Zoom In, Zoom Out* and *Select*). This resulted in 28 videos shown to 16 participants for a total of 448 shadows.

Goodness of Match and Ease of Making Gesture

We examined the participant ratings using the Mann-Whitney test. Participants rated their shadows in the *Collaborator* condition (*median* = 6) with significantly higher goodness ratings ($U = 21468.00$, $z = 2.74$, $p < .01$) than in the *Owner* condition (*median* = 6). They also rated their shadows in the *Collaborator* condition (*median* = 7) with significantly higher easiness ratings ($U = 21201.50$, $z = 2.944$, $p < .01$) than in the *Owner* condition (*median* = 6).

Owners of multitouch mobile phones rated their shadows significantly higher on the goodness rating (*median* = 6, $U = 21201.50$, $z = 2.944$, $p < .01$) than non-owners (*median* = 6). Owners of multitouch devices also rated their shadows significantly easier ($U = 20102.00$, $z = 3.821$, $p <.001$) than non-owners (*median* = 6).

Most Common Gestures

Here we highlight some of the more common shadows made in response to the different effects. The most popular gestures are highlighted in Table 1. In general, participants would perform similar gestures for a particular effect regardless of the role of *Owner* or *Collaborator*.

Collaborator

Pan: Participants would move their hand or arm across the projection in the direction they wanted to pan. Twelve of 16 participants performed this type of gesture. This is shown as *Arm Up/Down/Left/Right* in Table 1.

Zoom: Participants were split on their zooming technique when standing near the wall. Nine of 16 participants performed large opening and closing gestures with their arms (*Arms Open/Close*). Three participants performed an opening or closing of their hand (hand open/close). Four participants would move their hand toward or away from the wall (*Arm Toward/Away*).

Select: Fourteen participants performed some variant of pointing for selection (*Point*). Of these fourteen, ten would hold their finger near the marker and dwell, while others would wiggle or tap their finger to indicate selection.

Owner

Pan: Similar to the *Collaborator* condition, 12 participants moved their hand in the direction they wanted to pan (*Hand Up/Down/Left/Right*).

Zoom: Eleven participants performed some form of pinching (*Hand Open/Close*) to zoom in and out. Four participants moved their hand toward or away from the wall (*Hand Toward/Away*) to zoom.

Select: Participants used the same form of selection as in the *Collaborator* condition, with 14 participants performing some form of pointing (*Point*).

Discussion

The results of this study show that there was high agreement for many gestures, and similar shadows were cast for both the *Maps* and *PhotoBrowser* applications. Yet multiple gesture aliases may be helpful for supporting different usage scenarios (e.g. right or left-handed) when there is low agreement [33]. For example, there was some disagreement among users regarding pan direction, e.g. some users wanted to move their hands up to *Pan Up* while others wanted to move their hands down to cause the same action. Also, some users thought of zooming as expanding / contracting (performed with pinching gestures) while others thought of it as pushing / pulling (performed by moving hands or arms toward or away from the projector). In cases like this, the designer can either make an arbitrary choice or provide aliases from which users can choose.

Users typically wanted to perform symmetric gestures to perform inverse operations, but this was not always comfortable. Moving the right hand from left to right to *Pan Right* (*Owner* condition) was difficult when holding the projector in the left hand. Similarly, trying to move the arm right to left can be difficult when standing on the left side of the projection (*Collaborator* condition).

Most participants preferred the *Collaborator* condition (14 for *Maps* and 13 for *Photos*). They preferred *Collaborator* because their hand shadows were smaller relative to the display. As a result, they were able to control their shadows with finer granularity, and their shadows occluded less of the display. This was also reflected in significantly higher goodness and easiness ratings. Participants also described *Collaborator* as more "intuitive" since their shadows typically remained within the frame. In contrast, when they were holding the projector in the *Owner* condition, they had to first locate the projection frame and then position their hand appropriately. Participants also described *Col-*

laborator as more "familiar" and "comfortable." The participants who preferred *Owner* cited feeling more in control.

Even though we told participants that we were studying how to use shadow gestures for interaction, many of them described the experience as "*like using a touch screen*". They viewed shadows as a kind of virtual touch on the projection surface, i.e., the shadows were the contact points on a virtual, distant touchscreen.

Users typically mentioned familiar metaphors to describe their shadow gestures, which seemeed to provide some benefits of virtual reality. They drew on the direct manipulation GUI paradigm ("*using a trackball or mouse*", "*clicking*", "*using a scrollbar*") and on the physical world ("*grasping,*" "*pushing,*" "*pulling,*" "*pinching,*" "*tapping,*" "*clicking,*" and "*pointing*"). Only one user made a symbolic gesture (drawing a "z" with her finger to zoom).

In many cases, our participatory design approach resulted in direct translations of familiar multi-touch gestures, drawn from participants' prior knowledge and experiences. Direct translations, however, may sometimes be appropriate and are common starting points in new domains.

USER STUDY 2: DO USERS UNDERSTAND OUR LANGUAGE OF HAND SHADOWS

The previous study helped guide the set of shadows that our system should support. However, it remained to be seen whether casual observers would be able to determine the desired effect when shown a shadow gesture. As we alluded to earlier, this would be a potential benefit of using shadows for collocated interaction.

The purpose of this study was to see whether participants would be able to identify what action a user was trying to perform based on his hand shadow.

We also hoped to gain insight on an observation from the previous study regarding different shadows. For certain effects, multiple types of shadows were observed. Were some shadows more understandable than others?

In the previous user study we showed users an effect and elicited the gesture that would cause it. In this study, we did the inverse. We presented participants with a video clip of a shadow being cast and asked them what effect they thought it would cause. We were motivated to run this follow-up study, as suggested by Wobbrock, et al. [33], to gauge the intuitiveness of the gestures elicited in the previous study.

Task

We presented short video clips (about 2s in duration) of an actor making hand gestures that cast shadows on a static image of a map projected onto a wall. For each video of a shadow gesture, we asked the participant to describe what he thought the actor was trying to do with the map. In the video, the map did not actually respond to the shadow gestures (rendering this task harder than understanding interaction with a working system that provided immediate feedback). Rather than give users options of different effects to choose from, we left it as an open-ended response. This more closely reflected a real-world situation whereby one user has to determine what another user is trying to do based on their shadow.

Participants

We recruited 16 volunteers (8 female) aged 20–57 (median 28.5) from within our institution. Eleven were smartphone owners, and 5 were owners of multitouch mobile phones. No participants were reused from User Study 1, since prior experience could bias participants' understanding.

Gestures

Based on the results of our previous study, we selected a set of gestures for each effect to present to users. Participants in Study 1 performed many distinct gestures, and we aggregated them to create canonical gestures, trying to balance ease of recognition for users and for the system. Hence we recorded videos of an actor performing these canonical gestures, rather than using videos of participants' "raw" gestures captured during the previous study.

The set of gestures in the *Collaborator* condition include 4 panning gestures (*Arm Left*, *Arm Right*, *Arm Up*, *Arm Down*), 3 variations on zoom in and zoom out (*Hand Open* and *Hand Close*, *Arms Open* and *Arms Close*, *Arm Toward* and *Arm Away*), and selection (*Point*). The set of gestures in the *Owner* condition include 4 panning gestures (*Hand Left*, *Hand Right*, *Hand Up*, *Hand Down*), 2 variations on zoom in and zoom out (*Hand Open* and *Hand Close*, *Hand Toward* and *Hand Away*), and selection (*Point*) triggered by dwell.

Experimental Design

In our previous study, people used similar gestures for interacting in the *Maps* and *Photos* conditions, so in this study, we considered only one condition. We arbitrarily decided to use *Maps*. We presented the gesture videos using the same two role conditions as in User Study 1: *Collaborator* and *Owner*. Order of presentation was counterbalanced across participants. Within each condition, operations were presented in random order. Each participant observed 20 shadows: 11 shadows in the *Collaborator* condition, and 9 shadows in the *Owner* condition.

Results

Gender had an effect on goodness ratings with females rating (*median* = 6) the shadows significantly higher (U = 9675.50, $z = 3.914$, $p < .001$) than males (*median* = 6).

There were no significant differences in goodness ratings for the different zooming techniques.

We aggregated responses across participants, and found that participants rated the *Owner* condition (*median* = 6) significantly higher ($U = 10692.50$, $z = 2.492$, $p < .05$) than the *Collaborator* condition (*median* = 6).

gesture	pan up	pan down	pan left	pan right	zoom in	zoom out	select	other
hand up	15							draw path
hand down		15						move pin down
hand left			15					move pin left
hand right				16				
hand open					14	1		measure distance
hand toward					15		1	
hand away						14	2	
hand close					2	14		
point				1			15	

Table 2: Effects (column) perceived by participants for each of the different gestures (row) used in the *Owner* condition. Shaded boxes indicate effects we expected to see for each particular gesture.

In a post-study questionnaire, we asked each participant which role condition they preferred overall. Five users preferred *Collaborator*, citing the finer granularity (the hand shadow appears smaller, enabling more precise gestures) and the clarity from two handed usage. Eleven users preferred *Owner*, because the gestures were more clearly defined (framed by the projection area) and more similar to familiar touchscreen gestures.

gesture	pan up	pan down	pan left	pan right	zoom in	zoom out	select	other
arm up	15							rotate
arm down		14						rotate, move pin
arm left			16					
arm right				15				move pin
hand open					16			
arms open					15	1		
arms toward					15			go back to prev location
hand closed					1	15		
arms closed					2	14		
arm away					1	14	1	
point				1			15	pan right

Table 3: Effects (column) perceived by participants for each of the different gestures (row) used in the *Collaborator* condition. Shaded boxes indicate effects we expected to see for each particular gesture.

Table 2 and Table 3 tally the effects that our participants associated with different gestures. On the whole, the effects associated with the different hand shadows reflected similar findings to User Study 1. The outliers associated slightly different effects with certain hand shadows due to ambiguities arising from body mechanics. For example, one person thought the *Collaborator Arm Up* and *Collaborator Arm Down* gestures were intended to rotate the map because, in the video, the user's arm moves up or down relative to the shoulder's axis. Similarly, viewers expressed confusion when gestures for performing inverse operations were not symmetrical. For example, in the videos for *Owner Hand Left* and *Owner Hand Right*, the hand is facing different directions, which feels more natural.

Like in User Study 1, there was some confusion regarding gestures for *Zoom In* and *Zoom Out*. We believe that in an interactive system, this ambiguity will resolve itself.

SHADOWPUPPETS PROTOTYPE

We built a functional prototype to enable us to study the social implications of ShadowPuppets. The system consists of a Logitech 1.3 MP webcam attached to a *Microvision SHOWWX* laser pico projector (Figure 1). Due to low refresh rates associated with the video-out functionality of mobile phones, we used a laptop to drive the display of our prototype . This prototype is intended to simulate a future version running on a mobile phone. The camera and projector are 6cm apart, reasonable for a handheld device.

Gesture Recognition

Our ShadowPuppets prototype was written in C++ using OpenCV. At startup, a calibration step is performed to detect the outer edges of the projected image and the grayscale value of the projection surface. Each frame is thresholded to extract the shadow pixels—pixels with grayscale values close to that of the projection surface.

Connected components within the shadow pixels are detected and then filtered, keeping only the blobs with areas above a threshold, to reduce noise. The system detects a pan or zoom gesture when the average second derivative of the shadow pixels' centroid position or total area over a window of time is above a threshold, and it detects a select gesture when these metrics are below a threshold. We use the second derivatives to avoid the need for an explicit clutching mechanism. The system recognizes one gesture at a time, and a timeout is inserted after recognition to avoid falsely interpreting recoil actions as gestures.

Selection (Point)

To detect pointing shadows, we detect fingertips using an approach similar to Manresa et al. [18]; we look for points on the convex hull that are separated by defects, using the point separated by the deepest defects as our estimate of the fingertip.

When the location of this fingertip is stable over a window of time, we trigger a selection event. The projected map indicates selection by displaying a pop-up box with information about the selected point. The pop-up is removed when another form of input is detected.

Panning (Hand Up, Hand Down, Hand Left, Hand Right)

We track the acceleration of the shadow blob's centroid, taking the average over a sliding window (tuned empirically) of video frames to smooth the sensed data. If the average acceleration in the vertical or horizontal direction is above a threshold, then we fire a *Pan* event (*Up*, *Down*, *Left*, or *Right*), choosing the direction with highest average acceleration. The projected map provides visual feedback, panning in the indicated direction. Similar to existing map applications, we use high initial velocity with constant acceleration in the direction opposite of motion.

Zooming (Hand Toward, Hand Away, Pinching)

Our prototype supports two methods of zooming. Users can either move their shadow towards/away from the wall, or they can perform pinching.

To detect moving the shadow towards/away from the wall we track the second derivative of the change in area of the shadow blob. Again, we use the average over a sliding window for smoothing, and if this average is above a threshold we detect a *Zoom* input event.

Pinching was implemented by detecting finger points, similar to selection. When a transition from one fingertip to two fingertips was observed in close proximity, we fired a *Zoom* event. Unfortunately, in our pilot studies we found that the hand often occluded the shadow in the camera, making detection of this technique unreliable. Because of its unreliability, we left it out of our final user study. Increasing the distance between the camera and projector would reduce occlusion but would also increase the size of the device. A potential future approach could combine shadow and hand detection.

Implementation challenges

Pico projector-based shadow gesture recognition faces some general challenges. Shadow detection requires sufficient contrast between the shadow and the projected content, and may suffer if ambient light is bright.

USER STUDY 3: EXPERIENCES WITH THE SHADOWPUPPETS PROTOTYPE

We conducted a laboratory-based pairs study with our ShadowPuppets prototype to gain insight into users' experiences when using shadow gestures for collocated collaboration. We hoped to learn how it feels to perform the gestures with an interactive system, and what social and technical issues arise when two users interact with the system together. Our prototype supports a simple maps application, that responds to ShadowPuppets hand shadow gestures, and we observed pairs of participants using it.

Task

We first briefly demonstrated how to use each supported gesture to interact with the maps application. The prototype supports 7 different types of shadows (for both roles *Collaborator* and *Owner*): *Hand/Arm Right* to *Pan Right*, *Hand/Arm Left* to *Pan Left*, *Hand/Arm Up* to *Pan Up*, *Hand/Arm Down* to *Pan Down*, *Hand/Arm Toward* to *Zoom In*, and *Hand/Arm Away* to *Zoom Out*.

During the study, one participant performed gestures in the *Collaborator* conditions, while the other participant gestured in the *Owner* condition, as described previously. We asked the participants to interact with the map for 10 minutes using ShadowPuppets, then trade roles (*Collaborator / Owner*) and interact with the map for another 10 minutes. In a post-study interview, we asked participants to describe how it felt to perform each class of gesture: *Panning*, *Zooming*, and *Selection*. We also asked the participants to reflect on their preferences, between the *Collaborator* and *Owner* conditions, and their overall experiences using ShadowPuppets as a pair. We asked participants to think aloud during the task.

Participants

We recruited 8 volunteers (3 female), aged 24–30 (median 27) in 4 pairs of acquaintances, from within our institution. Five participants were reused from User Study 2. Seeing shadow gestures on video beforehand was not likely to bias participants' experiences performing them, since gestures would be demonstrated for training purposes.

Results

All participants learned the gestures quickly; they were able to remember them after viewing a single demonstration of each, and described them as "*intuitive*" and "*making sense*". 7 of 8 participants had positive overall impressions, describing shadow gestures as "*natural*", "*cool*", and "*useful*". The 8th participant explained that he does not like any gestural interfaces because they are imprecise.

Participants envisioned using shadow gestures to interact at-a-distance during presentations while teaching, while in a meeting, or while sharing photos or videos with friends. One participant, a projector-phone user, volunteered that she would want to use shadow gestures individually to get the full benefits of a large projected display, avoiding having to interact with it via the phone's screen.

Panning

All participants volunteered that panning felt *"comfortable," "natural,"* and *"intuitive."* One participant felt that the gestures were too large, and would prefer if a smaller physical movement would results in a larger movement of the map. Six participants wanted to have more control over how much or how fast to pan, suggesting that the distance and speed of the gesture should correspond to the distance and speed of the pan. Four participants suggested implementing a clutching mechanism, e.g. a hand gesture such as "*grabbing*", to control when a gesture should activate an input event. Four participants experimented with moving the projector relative to the shadow to pan.

Zooming

All the participants described zooming as intuitive and feeling good. One participant (who also participated in the inverse gesture study) commented that he had hated the *hand toward / away* gestures in the videos but that doing it was a lot more intuitive, "*like bringing the map closer to you or pushing it away from you*".

Selection

All the participants liked using pointing for selection. Two participants suggested making a "*tapping*" finger motion to activate selection (as suggested in Study 1). Another participant remarked that shadows are especially good for pointing because it's unambiguous what you are pointing at. He explained that "*when you're in a group and just pointing, the perspective is different for different people, but shadows make it much clearer since everyone sees the same shadow*".

Collaborator / Owner Conditions

Six participants preferred the *Collaborator* condition because they didn't have to hold the projector steady while gesturing. Four of the participants said that holding the projector and gesturing felt awkward, and one participant noted that the shadow was too large to control since a small movement had a big effect. Two participants preferred the *Owner* condition because they felt that the person holding the projector had priority to make gestures and had more control: "*I don't think you have as much control if you're not holding it*."

Social Aspects of Collaboration with ShadowPuppets

All the participants liked that more than one person could interact with and manipulate the map, and thought shadow gestures would be good for group interaction. All the participants said that while interacting, they primarily focused their attention on the shadows on the projected display, while attuning to their partners in their peripheral vision.

Because the prototype does not support multiple gestures simultaneously, pairs took turns, negotiating control verbally or by body language ("*if they look like they're going to do something*"). When the pair members both tried to gesture simultaneously, several strategies occurred for managing conflict: they verbally negotiated, both participants backed off and then tried again after an interval, or they "*went over the top of each other and the map did its own thing*". One pair of participants experimented with collaboratively coordinating their actions, with one moving the projector relative to the other's hand.

During the interaction task, one participant in the *Owner* condition intentionally thwarted his partner's gestures by pointing the projector away from her, and unintentionally caused the same problem in the *Collaborator* condition by standing in front of the projected display and occluding it. After the task, when asked how they would prevent the other person from doing something, participants said they would make a confounding gesture ("*making the opposite gesture*", "*waving my arms around*", or "*doing the chicken dance*"), move the projector to point in a different direction (as observed), or occlude the projector by covering it with a hand or standing in front of it.

REFLECTIONS ON SHADOW-BASED INPUT

Initial experiences with ShadowPuppets indicate that the system shows promise for collocated collaboration. Both participants in each pair were able to view and interact with the projected application, maintaining awareness of each other's actions while focusing on the shared display. Study 3 highlights the following issues.

Challenge of Designing for Performers and Observers

Supporting both performers and observers of shadow gestures presents a challenge, since they may have conflicting experiences and goals. To facilitate collocated collaboration shadows should be intuitive and comfortable to perform, and also easy to interpret. Yet these goals may be at odds with one another. For example, users in Study 1 found it easier to control their gestures in the *Collaborator* role, while users in Study 2 found shadows cast in the *Owner* role to be clearer. Similarly, in Study 1 users sometimes performed asymmetric gestures to perform inverse operations in a way that felt comfortable, while users in Study 2 found those gestures harder to interpret.

Need for Fine-Grained Interactions

As a first step toward understanding shadow gestures for interaction, we have examined coarse-grained interaction. Although, we explicitly focused on this part of the design space, users wanted more precision. For example, we selected a set of 7 relatively coarse operations to study and implement, and presented them to users in general terms (e.g., "pan left" rather than "pan left such that the marker on the map is centered"). Yet in Study 3, participants wanted their shadows to perform more precise operations (e.g., controlling the range and speed of panning and zooming), and in Study 2 they often interpreted gestures more precisely than we intended.

Most Popular Gestures May Not Be Best

We posit that the most popular gestures are not necessarily the best. For example, the gestures with highest agreement scores in User Study 1 may simply be the most familiar, since ShadowPuppets uses a new form of interaction. People are biased by what is familiar to them and new ways of interacting may not occur to them immediately. For example, many users drew on pinching gestures from iPhone interaction, while only 25% of users suggested motion in the *throw* dimension (toward or away from the projector). Users' prior expertise also led them to rate pinching gestures higher on the goodness and easiness ratings. Yet in User Studies 2 and 3, we found that *Hand Toward / Away* and *Arm Toward / Away* were intuitive to most users. If we had only considered the results of User Study 1, we might not have even explored those gestures at all. As Norman proposed, user-centered design may not always be the right approach [20].

CONCLUSION AND FUTURE WORK

In this paper we presented ShadowPuppets, a system that allows collocated users to provide input to a mobile projector based system by casting hand shadows.

We made four contributions. First we presented the results of a user study examining what types of shadows users expect to cause different effects. Second, we examined what kinds of effects users expect different hand shadows to cause. Third, we presented the design and implementation of the ShadowPuppets prototype, allowing collocated users to interact with a projected display. Finally, we presented the results of a user study of our prototype, suggesting issues that arise with using shadow-based input.

As future work, we plan to examine how to combine some of the coarse-grained interaction techniques described here with other techniques that provide fine-grained control.

ACKNOWLEDGEMENTS

This work has been funded by AT&T Labs, Microsoft Research ER&P, and UC MICRO 07-067.

REFERENCES

1. Beardsley, P., Forlines, C., Raskar, R., and VanBaar, J. Handheld Projectors for Mixing Physical and Digital Textures. In *Proc. CVPR 2005*, 112.
2. Boring, S., Baur, D., Butz, A., Gustafson, S., and Baudisch, P. Touch projector: mobile interaction through video. In *Proc. CHI 2010*, 2287–2296.
3. Cao, X. and Balakrishnan, R., Interacting with Dynamically Defined Information Spaces using a Handheld Projector and a Pen. In *Proc. UIST 2006*, 225–234.
4. Cao, X., Forlines, C., and Balakrishnan, R. Multi-user interaction using handheld projectors. In *Proc. UIST 2007*, 43–52.
5. Cheng, K. and Takatsuka, M. Initial evaluation of a bare-hand interaction technique for large displays using a webcam. In *Proc. EICS 2009*. 291–296.
6. Cowan, L., Weibel, N., Griswold, W. G., Pina, L., Hollan, J. D. Projector Phone Use: Practices and Social Implications. In *Journal of Personal and Ubiquitous Computing, theme issue on Personal Mobile Projection*, 2011.
7. Echtler, F., Huber, M., and Klinker, G. Shadow tracking on multi-touch tables. In *Proc. AVI 2008*, 388–391.
8. Everitt, K. M., Klemmer, S. R., Lee, R., and Landay, J. A. Two worlds apart: bridging the gap between physical and virtual media for distributed design collaboration. In *Proc. CHI 2003*, 553–560.
9. Freeman, D., Benko, H., Morris, M. R., and Wigdor, D. ShadowGuides: visualizations for in-situ learning of multi-touch and whole-hand gestures. In *Proc. ITS 2009*, 165–172.
10. Greaves, A. and Rukzio, E. Evaluation of picture browsing using a projector phone. In *Proc. MobileHCI 2008*, 351–354.
11. Gustafson, S., Bierwirth, D., Baudisch, P., Imaginary Interfaces: Spatial Interaction with Empty Hands and Without Visual Feedback. In *Proc. UIST 2010*.
12. Harrison, C., Tan, D., and Morris, D. Skinput: appropriating the body as an input surface. In *Proc. CHI 2010*, 453–462.
13. Hilliges, O., Izadi, S., Wilson, A. D., Hodges, S., Garcia-Mendoza, A., and Butz, A. Interactions in the air: adding further depth to interactive tabletops. In *Proc. UIST 2009*, 139–148.
14. Horprasert, T., Harwood D., Davis, L. S. A statistical approach for real-time robust background subtraction and shadow detection. In *Proc. ICCV 1999* Workshops.
15. Ishii, H., Kobayashi, M., and Arita, K. Iterative design of seamless collaboration media. *Commun. ACM* 37, 8 (Aug. 1994), 83–97.
16. Kale, A., Kwan, K., Jaynes, C., Epipolar Constrained User Pushbutton Selection in Projected Interfaces, In *Proc. CVPR 2004 Workshops*.
17. Kane, S. K., Avrahami, D., Wobbrock, J. O., Harrison, B., Rea, A. D., Philipose, M., and LaMarca, A. Bonfire: a nomadic system for hybrid laptop-tabletop interaction. In *Proc. UIST 2009*, 129–138.
18. Manresa, C., Varona, J., Mas, R. and Perales, F. (2005) Hand tracking and gesture recognition for human-computer interaction. *Electronic Letters on Computer Vision and Image Analysis, 5* (3), 96–104.
19. Mistry, P., Maes, P. and Chang, L., WUW - Wear Ur World - A Wearable Gestural Interface. In *Proc. CHI 2009*.
20. Norman, D. A., Human-centered Design Considered Harmful. *Interactions* 12, 4 (Jul./Aug. 2005) 14–19.
21. Pinelle, D., Nacenta, M., Gutwin, C., and Stach, T. The effects of co-present embodiments on awareness and collaboration in tabletop groupware. In *Proc. GI 2008*.
22. Pinhanez, C. S. The Everywhere Displays Projector: A Device to Create Ubiquitous Graphical Interfaces, In *Proc. Ubicomp 2001*, 315–331.
23. Rapp, S., Michelitsch, G., Osen, M., Williams, J., Barbisch, M., Bohan, R., Valsan, Z., and Emele, M. (2004). Spotlight navigation: Interaction with a handheld projection device. In *Proc. Pervasive 2004, Video Paper*.
24. Segen, J. and Kumar, S. Shadow gestures: 3D hand pose estimation using a single camera, In *Proc. CVPR 1999*, 479–485.
25. Shoemaker, G., Tang, A., and Booth, K. S. Shadow reaching: a new perspective on interaction for large displays. In *Proc. UIST 2007*, 53–56.
26. Snibbe, S. S. and Raffle, H. S. Social immersive media: pursuing best practices for multi-user interactive camera/projector exhibits. In *Proc. CHI 2009*, 1447–1456.
27. Song, H., Grossman, T., Fitzmaurice, G., Guimbretiere, F., Khan, A., Attar, R., Kurtenbach, G. PenLight: Combining a Mobile Projector and a Digital Pen for Dynamic Visual Overlay. In *Proc. CHI 2009*. 143–152.
28. Song, H., Guimbretiere, F., Grossman, T., and Fitzmaurice, G. MouseLight: bimanual interactions on digital paper using a pen and a spatially-aware mobile projector. In *Proc. CHI 2010*, 2451–2460.
29. Sugimoto, M., Miyahara, K., Inoue, H., and Tsunesada, Y. Hotaru: Intuitive Manipulation Techniques for Projected Displays of Mobile Devices. Proc. *INTERACT 2005*, 57–68.
30. Tang, A., Neustaedter, C., Greenberg, S.: Videoarms: embodiments in mixed presence groupware. In *Proc. BCS-HCI*, 2006.
31. Tang, J. C. and Minneman, S. VideoWhiteboard: video shadows to support remote collaboration. In *Proc. CHI 1991*, 315–322.
32. Wilson, A. D. Robust computer vision-based detection of pinching for one and two-handed gesture input. In *Proc. UIST 2006*, 255–258.
33. Wobbrock, J. O., Morris, M. R., and Wilson, A. D. User-defined gestures for surface computing. In *Proc. CHI 2009*, 1083–1092.

DoubleFlip: A Motion Gesture Delimiter for Mobile Interaction

Jaime Ruiz*
University of Waterloo
Waterloo, ON, Canada
jgruiz@cs.uwaterloo.ca

Yang Li
Google Research
Mountain View, CA, USA
yangli@acm.org

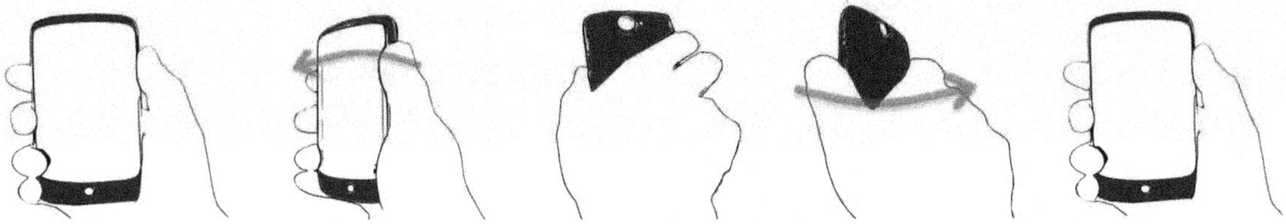

Figure 1: An illustration of the DoubleFlip gesture. In this figure, the user holds the phone right-handed. He rotates the phone along its long side so that the phone screen is away and then back.

ABSTRACT
To make motion gestures more widely adopted on mobile devices it is important that devices be able to distinguish between motion intended for mobile interaction and everyday motion. In this paper, we present DoubleFlip, a unique motion gesture designed as an input delimiter for mobile motion-based interaction. The DoubleFlip gesture is distinct from regular motion of a mobile device. Based on a collection of 2,100 hours of motion data captured from 99 users, we found that our DoubleFlip recognizer is extremely resistant to false positive conditions, while still achieving a high recognition rate. Since DoubleFlip is easy to perform and unlikely to be accidentally invoked, it provides an always-active input event for mobile interaction.

Author Keywords
Motion gestures, sensors, mobile interaction.

ACM Classification
H5.2. User Interfaces--Input devices and strategies.

General Terms
Design

INTRODUCTION
A major technical barrier for adopting motion-gesture-based interaction is the need for high recognition rates with low false positive conditions. This obstacle limits the potential of good interaction design since many proposed physical motions (e.g., flipping [3] and tilting [3,4,6,9]) are indistinguishable from everyday motions (i.e., walking). Hence, these gestures suffer from the inherent difficulty that they generate a large number of false positives. In addition, Rico and Brewster [10] reported that users rated motion gestures more socially acceptable when the gesture looks or feels similar to everyday motion, suggesting that distinctions between desired motion gestures and everyday motion may not necessarily exist.

While modeless interaction for motion gestures is ideal, it is difficult to achieve sufficient reliability to be practical for general interaction situations. The dilemma that we encounter is the same for other types of interactions, i.e., inking versus gesturing in pen-based user interfaces [5,7]. Previous work in delimiting normal motion from motion input has relied on hardware buttons [3,9] or additional sensors in order to determine the context of use [6]. Although successful, these mode-switching techniques require a designer to use interaction context (which is often hard to infer) or a user to switch input modalities (i.e. from motion input to pressing or touching a button).

We designed DoubleFlip to tackle the challenge of separating gestural input from normal motion. DoubleFlip is a unique motion gesture that acts as a delimiter for other motion gestures, and hence, separates normal mobile phone motion from a user's intended input. The gesture gives users the control to activate motion gestures without any hardware modifications to existing devices. The gesture is quick to perform and can be performed in a limited amount of physical space. We are unaware of any previous work that proposes the use of a distinct motion gesture to delimit motion gesture input.

As part of this work, we implemented a recognizer for the DoubleFlip gesture. Based on a collection of over 2,100 hours of motion data captured from the phones of 99 volunteers, we found that our DoubleFlip recognizer is extremely resistant to false positives (less than one false positive per eight hours of use). Thus, the DoubleFlip ges-

* The work was conducted during an internship at Google Research.

ture and recognizer can be used as a building block for other systems to provide motion-gesture-based interactions.

DESIGNING DOUBLEFLIP

Our goal for designing an input delimiter for motion gestures was inspired by an informative study conducted with 20 smartphone users on the potential uses of motion gestures. Although we instructed our participants to imagine a "magical" device capable of perfectly inferring their intention, participants preferred to have the explicit control over when motion input should be enabled. As one participant stated, "It's more of an assurance thing. If you said it worked perfect I still wouldn't trust you."

We considered two options for a motion input delimiter: a hardware button and a dedicated delimiter gesture. The use of a hardware button was ruled out for three reasons: 1) smartphones differ in the number and placement of buttons, thus, restricting motion gestures to smartphones with an available button; 2) there was no consensus among participants on where the button should be placed; and 3) requiring a user to activate mode on the device used for input increases the likelihood of mistaken activation [7].

As a result, we set out to design a delimiter that is not dependent on a touchscreen or buttons but instead relies on the sensors commonly available in current smartphones. From our study, we decided that the motion gesture delimiter should meet the following requirements: 1) the gesture should be resistant to false positives; 2) the screen must be visible to the user after completing the delimiter gesture so that they can continue to interact with the screen; 3) the physical space required to perform the gesture should be minimal to allow the gesture to be performed surreptitiously and in crowded spaces; 4) the gesture should be quick and easy to perform; and 5) the gesture should be distinct from any gestures that a user/developer would likely want to incorporate into an application.

Although the set of possible motion gestures a user can perform with a smartphone is large, our design requirements limit the number of suitable candidates for an input delimiter. Gestures that require multiple axes or complex movements were dismissed due to temporal and physical constraints imposed by our requirements. Simple gestures (e.g., shaking, flicking, and sudden impacts) were also dismissed because our participants often selected these gestures to interact with various applications. Using these gestures as an input delimiter would limit the ability of the designer to incorporate these gestures in their applications. In addition, these gestures are often indistinguishable from ambient motion which would result in a high number of false positives.

As shown in Figure 1, the DoubleFlip delimiter is performed by quickly rotating the wrist such that the phone's display is facing away from the user and back to the original position with the display of the phone facing the user. The design of DoubleFlip makes it resilient to false positives. During normal use, users commonly interact with the front of the device (due to the location of the display), which makes this gesture unlikely to be triggered accidently. The need to flip the phone back so the display is facing the user also allows us to fulfill our requirement that the display be visible to the user after performing the gesture. Finally, since the gesture can be performed with the simple rotation of the wrist and no arm movement, the gesture is compact and requires no more physical space than holding the phone for normal use. The gesture is also easy and quick to perform.

IMPLEMENTATION OF DOUBLEFLIP

The DoubleFlip gesture recognizer was developed in Java using the Android SDK [1] for use on the Nexus One phone with a Qualcomm QSD 8250 1 GHz processor, a three-axis accelerometer, and an orientation sensor.

Sensor input is matched to the DoubleFlip gesture using Dynamic Time Warping (DTW). DTW is a dynamic programming algorithm that measures the similarity of two time series with temporal dynamics [8] when given the function for calculating the distance between the two time samples. See [11] for more information.

Our implementation of the DoubleFlip gesture recognizer uses a weighted Euclidean distance function for calculating the distance between the quantized time series of acceleration and of orientation to the DTW templates. Since the display facing away from the user is an important characteristic of the gesture, we place a higher weight on the Euclidean distance for orientation values and a lower weight on the distance for acceleration. Giving a higher weight to the orientation values minimizes the probability that ambient motion will be recognized as a DoubleFlip gesture. If the calculated distance is less than a specified threshold, the recognizer reports a match for the DoubleFlip gesture.

Using data from an informal study benchmarking the number of DTW templates vs. computation time, we limited the number of DTW templates to 20 which were created from samples collected during a pilot study.

DETERMING OPTIMAL RECOGNITION THRESHOLDS

In this section, we present descriptions and results of our two experiments to find the optimal thresholds for our implementation. First, we describe an experiment to determine the appropriate threshold to minimize the number of false positives. This is followed by an experiment to find the balance between false negative and false positive conditions.

Methods

In both experiments data was collected using custom software written using the Android SDK to log the data stream received from a device's accelerometer and orientation sensors. The software periodically uploaded the recorded data to a secure server whenever the display was

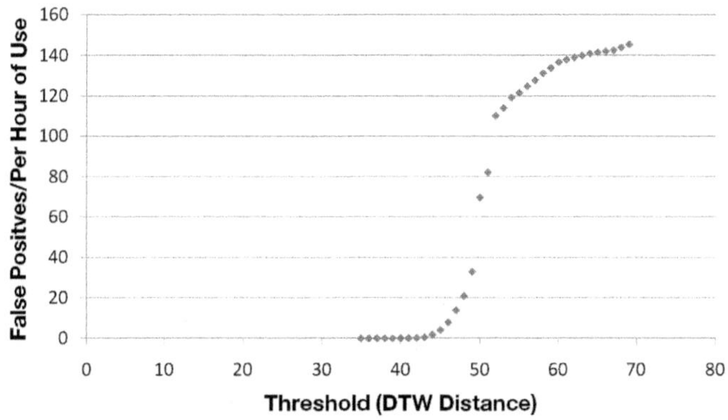

Figure 3: The DoubleFlip false positive rates versus distance threshold level.

off. The ability to remotely collect the data allowed us to recruit a large number of participants who do not have to be physically present.

To analyze the dataset, we developed a tool to replay the recorded sensor streams. As the sensor stream was replayed, gesture recognition was performed and each detection of the DoubleFlip gesture was flagged. To investigate the effect of varying the threshold of the recognizer, the program iterated through the complete dataset by incrementing the threshold distance for each iteration.

Experiment One: False Positives

The goal of our first experiment was to determine the appropriate threshold such that the number of false positives is minimized. Participants were recruited by sending an email to an internal list of employees at a high-tech company asking for volunteers. The email directed the employees to an internal webpage that provided information on the software and a link to download the application. Participants were required to use a Google Nexus One smartphone as their primary mobile device and were asked to run the software for at least 24 hours.

Ninety-nine participants installed and ran the software long enough so that at least one log was uploaded to our server. In total, 2,169 hours of sensor data was collected.

Results

Figure 3 illustrates the effect of varying the distance on the false positive rate. As the threshold increases, the number of false positive conditions increases dramatically. However, DoubleFlip benefits from a low false positive condition even at larger distance thresholds, which implies its inherent distinctiveness from normal use motion.

Experiment Two: True Positives

Our first experiment showed that a higher threshold distance will lead to more false positives. However, a lower distance threshold tends to result in more false negatives, which can result in user frustration. Therefore, our second experiment is designed to find a balance between false positive and false negative conditions.

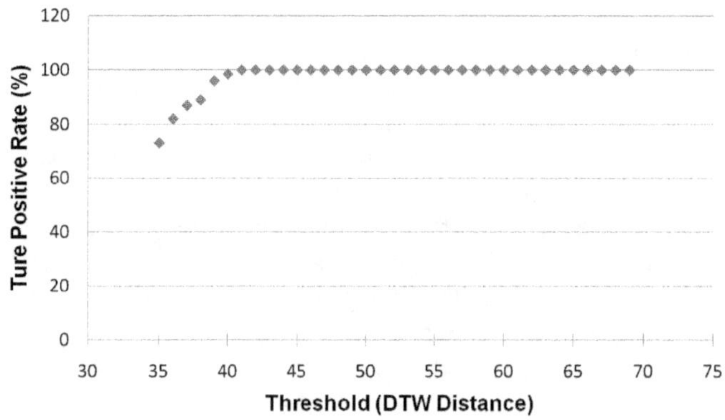

Figure 2: The DoubleFlip true positive rate versus distance threshold level.

Our second experiment required participants to be physically present during the experiment. Twenty volunteers were recruited via the same email list as the first experiment. At the beginning of the study, the researcher described the procedure and demonstrated the DoubleFlip gesture. The researcher then handed the participant a phone running the custom software and asked the participant to perform the DoubleFlip gesture twenty times, with approximately a five second pause after each gesture. Upon completion, the participants were asked to rate how easy the gesture was to perform using a five-point Likert. A trial took approximately five minutes to complete.

Results

The relationship between the true positive rate and the threshold level is shown in Figure 2. Based on the collected data, the true positive rate quickly converges to 100%. Using the ambient motion false positive rates form our first experiment and the recognition rates of our second experiment, we plotted the ROC curve to examine the relationship between false and true positives as the threshold is adjusted (see Figure 4). Based on the ROC curve, the optimal distance threshold achieved a 100% true positive rate with only one false positive per 8 hours of mobile phone use.

Our study participants highly rated the DoubleFlip gesture with an average rating of 4.6 (1 for difficult and 5 for easy). Only one participant rated the DoubleFlip gesture lower than "somewhat easy" and indicated that the gesture may cause fatigue if the gesture is performed frequently in succession for a long period of time.

DISCUSSION

Our goal was to develop a novel delimiter for motion-gesture-based interaction on mobile phones. Based on our interviews with smartphone users, we compiled a list of requirements that an effective delimiter gesture should meet. A delimiter gesture should be resilient to false positives and quick to perform, require limited physical space, and allow the screen to be visible to the user upon completing the gesture.

By testing our implementation of the DoubleFlip gesture recognizer against the sensor streams of naturally occurring motion, we found our DoubleFlip recognizer is resistant to false positives while still retaining a high true positive rate. Prior methods often rely on the current state (or context) of the system in order to reduce false positives (e.g., interpreting a shake as a shuffle gesture when playing music). In contrast, the DoubleFlip gesture and its detection are state-independent. Being state-independent is an important feature and it allows DoubleFlip to employ an "always on" listening strategy, which is a key requirement for any input delimiter.

The ability to distinguish the DoubleFlip gesture from normal motion also enables the gesture to be used as either the prefix or postfix to delimit an input motion gesture from everyday motion. For example, assume we want to use a shaking gesture to redial the last number called. Without the DoubeFlip gesture we are susceptible to high false positive conditions given the commonality of the motion. By incorporating the DoubleFlip gesture into the shake gesture we negate any false positives during normal usage. The user simply performs the DoubleFlip gesture and immediately performs the shake gesture, causing the phone to redial. When DoubleFlip is used as a postfix, the user would instead shake the phone and immediately perform the DoubleFlip gesture.

Appending the DoubleFlip gesture either before or after another gesture provides the user with a fluid method to enable motion gesture mode and perform the desired action. Similar to the benefits observed from using the Scriboli pigtail [5], the use of the DoubleFlip gesture may provide performance benefits over traditional mode switching techniques.

In addition to the quasi-mode switching[1] discussed in the previous example, the DoubleFlip gesture can be used to indicate the beginning and ending of gestural input. This approach allows the user to perform several sequential gestural commands. This approach is particularly useful in situations where the user would like to continuously pan or scroll content by tilting the phone, a common command in numerous contexts (e.g., navigating in a map application).

CONCLUSION & FUTURE WORK

In this paper, we presented DoubleFlip, a unique motion gesture that was designed as an input delimiter for mobile motion gestures. Our experiments showed that the DoubleFlip gesture is extremely resistant to false positive conditions, while still achieved a high recognition rate. Since DoubleFlip is easy to perform and unlikely to be

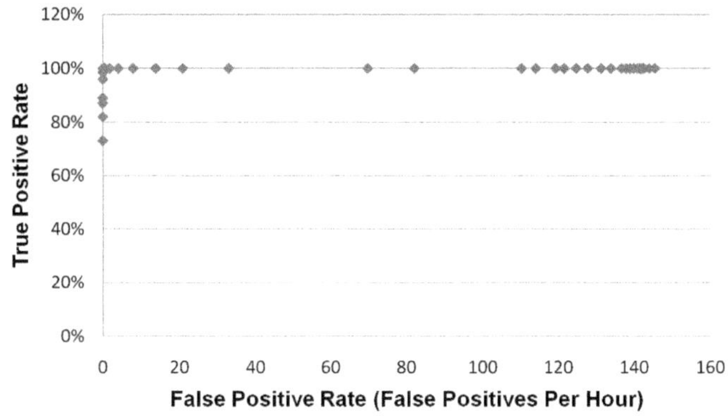

Figure 4: The ROC Curve of the DF recognizer.

accidentally invoked, it provides an always-active input event for mobile interaction.

Our future work will focus on more extensive evaluation of the DoubleFlip gesture as both a prefix and postfix gesture. We also plan on exploring and evaluating different methods to instruct and describe motion gestures to users. An implementation of the Double Flip gesture has been incorporated into Google Gesture Search [2] as an always-on activation method.

REFERENCES

1. *Android Open Source Project*. Google Inc.
2. *Google Gesture Search*. http://gesturesearch.googlelabs.com
3. Bartlett, J.F. Rock 'n' Scroll Is Here to Stay. *IEEE Comput. Graph. Appl. 20*, 3 (2000), 40–45.
4. Harrison, B.L., Fishkin, K.P., Gujar, A., Mochon, C., and Want, R. Squeeze me, hold me, tilt me! An exploration of manipulative user interfaces. *Proceedings of CHI '98*, ACM Press/Addison-Wesley Publishing Co. (1998), 17–24.
5. Hinckley, K., Baudisch, P., Ramos, G., and Guimbretiere, F. Design and analysis of delimiters for selection-action pen gesture phrases in scriboli. *Prococedings of CHI '05*, ACM (2005), 451–460.
6. Hinckley, K., Pierce, J., Sinclair, M., and Horvitz, E. Sensing techniques for mobile interaction. *Proceedings of UIST '00*, ACM (2000), 91–100.
7. Li, Y., Hinckley, K., Guan, Z., and Landay, J.A. Experimental analysis of mode switching techniques in pen-based user interfaces. *Proceedings of CHI '05*, ACM (2005), 461–470.
8. Myers, C. and Rabiner, L. A comparative study of several dynamic time-warping algorithms for connected word recognition. *The Bell System Tech Journal 60*, 7 (1981), 1389-1409.
9. Rekimoto, J. Tilting operations for small screen interfaces. *Proceedings of UIST '96*, ACM (1996), 167–168.
10. Rico, J. and Brewster, S. Usable gestures for mobile interfaces: evaluating social acceptability. *Proceedings of CHI 2010*, ACM (2010), 887–896.
11. Wobbrock, J.O., Wilson, A.D., and Li, Y. Gestures without libraries, toolkits or training: a $1 recognizer for user interface prototypes. *Proc. of UIST '07*, ACM (2007), 159–168.

[1] In quasi-mode switching techniques, the system state is automatically returned to the original state. Therefore, the user is not required to deactivate the mode by performing another mode switch.

Multi-User Interaction on Media Facades through Live Video on Mobile Devices

Sebastian Boring[1], Sven Gehring[2], Alexander Wiethoff[1], Magdalena Blöckner[1], Johannes Schöning[2], Andreas Butz[1]

[1]University of Munich, Munich, Germany
{sebastian.boring, alexander.wiethoff, andreas.butz}@ifi.lmu.de, bloeckner@cip.ifi.lmu.de

[2]German Research Center for Artificial Intelligence, Saarbrücken, Germany
{sven.gehring, johannes.schoening}@dfki.de

ABSTRACT
The increasing number of media facades in urban spaces offers great potential for new forms of interaction – especially for collaborative multi-user scenarios. In this paper, we present a way to directly interact with them *through live video* on mobile devices. We extend the *Touch Projector* interface to accommodate multiple users by showing individual content on the mobile display that would otherwise clutter the facade's canvas or distract other users. To demonstrate our concept, we built two collaborative multi-user applications: (1) painting on the facade and (2) solving a 15-puzzle. We gathered informal feedback during the ARS Electronica Festival in Linz, Austria and found that our interaction technique is (1) considered easy-to-learn, but (2) may leave users unaware of the actions of others.

Author Keywords
Mobile device, media facades, interaction techniques, input device, interface distribution, augmented reality.

ACM Classification Keywords
H5.2 [Information interfaces and presentation]: User Interfaces – Input devices and strategies, Interaction styles, Graphical user interfaces.

General Terms
Experimentation, Human Factors.

INTRODUCTION
More and more urban landscapes are equipped with media facades. The Beijing National Aquatics Center in Beijing, China and the ARS Electronica center in Linz, Austria are two prominent examples out of hundreds of such facades. However, due to their size and the required viewing distance, interacting with them directly (e.g., by touching them) is normally impossible. Recent advances in mobile computing allow users to interact with such facades in several ways. Current interaction approaches include controlling pointers on the facade's canvas [2] or pushing content to it through multimedia messages [8].

CHI 2011, May 7–12, 2011, Vancouver, BC, Canada.

The size, visibility, and large audience of media facades offer a great potential for collaborative interaction. Indirect pointing techniques, however, restrict the number of simultaneous users: (1) each pointer occludes a (small) portion of the facade, eventually leading to clutter and large content regions being invisible. (2) More pointers shown on the facade make finding one's own pointer rather difficult. In addition, facades showing pointers need reasonably high resolutions to provide enough pixels per pointer. One approach to solve these issues is to use an absolute and direct technique such as interaction *through live video* [3].

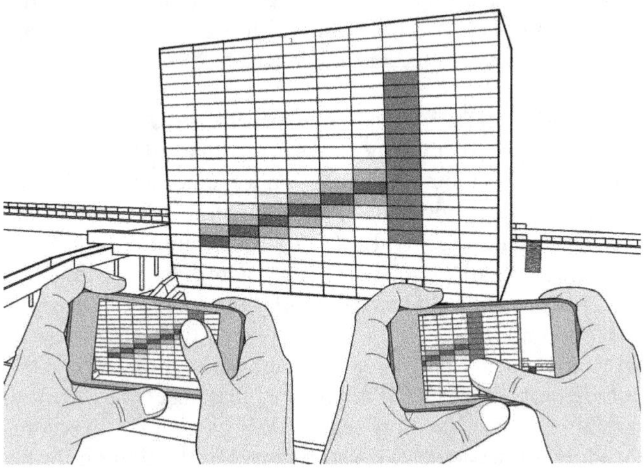

Figure 1. Interacting through live video allows multiple users to manipulate a media facade. Changes (also those of other users) are shown immediately on the facade and the mobile device. Colors denote actions from other users.

In this paper, we apply and extend the concept of *Touch Projector* [3] to media facades to avoid the limitations of current interaction techniques. With two applications, we demonstrate how multiple users can interact on a facade simultaneously. During the ARS Electronica Festival we found that our approach is (1) considered easy-to-learn, but (2) may leave users unaware of the actions of others.

RELATED WORK

The term "media facade" describes the idea of designing or modifying the architecture of buildings with the objective of using their surfaces as giant public screens [6,13]. In addition, urban public spaces are emerging more and more as prime locations for media facades that are embedded in the landscape of a city [11]. Researchers recently explored the social potential of such media facades as they can be seen or even designed by multiple persons simultaneously [10,12]. They further studied public participatory crowd experiences when porting popular games to media facades in combination with mobile devices [4]. Dalsgaard et al. described eight key challenges when designing such novel interactive systems and – most importantly – when offering users new, distributed interfaces [5].

Several techniques have been proposed to interact with distant displays. The most prominent techniques are relative and indirect pointing as well as augmented reality approaches. Relative and indirect pointing can be used to distant displays by turning a camera-equipped mobile device into a mouse-like device [1]. However, such input techniques may hinder multi-user scenarios due to the required virtual pointer. *MobiSpray* uses a world-in-miniature interface to allow for "spraying" color on various projected surfaces using the mobile device's accelerometers [9]. Recent advantages in mobile augmented reality allow absolute pointing on displays [7]. For tracking purposes, their system relies on a marker shown on the remote display. *Touch Projector* allows interaction with a distant display shown in the viewfinder using touch in real-time without relying on fiducial markers [3]. As this system follows a direct input approach, we decided to take it as the basis of our prototype.

DESIGNING INTERACTION ON MEDIA FACA

Our goal was to implement a system that allows multiple users to interact simultaneously on a media facade. As discussed in the previous section, relative and/or indirect approaches (e.g., *Sweep* [1]) may limit the number of users to the number of distinguishable (i.e., identifiable) pointers on the remote canvas. The low resolution facade of the ARS Electronica Center[1] (each window or pixel is about one by three meters in size) used for our prototypes lowers this number even more. Techniques that use a world-in-miniature representation (e.g., *MobiSpray* [9]) overcome this limitation at the expense of macro attention shifts between both the mobile and target display (here: facade).

To avoid the necessity of virtual pointers as well as the potential costs of macro attention shifts, we decided to use the concept of *Touch Projector* on media facades [3]. Users aim their device at the facade and observe it in live video, allowing them to point *through the display*. Touch input occurring on the mobile device is *projected* onto the facade, giving the impression that users directly touch the building (see Figure 1). Using this concept on large media facades in the wild, however, comes with several challenges.

Technical challenges of interacting with media facades

According to Dalsgaard et al., applications must consider potential shifts in lighting and weather conditions [5]. The facade of the ARS Electronica Center is only visible below a certain level of daylight. The original implementation of *Touch Projector* did not account for this, as it was built for regular computer screens with strong background lighting in controlled environments. Especially in the dark, reflections on wet ground are commonly caused by weather. As described in the IMPLEMENTATION section, we substantially changed the tracking algorithm to allow for outdoor use.

Another challenge is that media facades mostly have unique features (e.g., different sizes, resolutions, and optimal viewing distances). The ARS Electronica Center can easily be viewed at a distance of 300 meters. However, the distance influences the facade's apparent size in live video. To counter this, we used the zoom functionality of *Touch Projector*. Ideally, the building would fit exactly into the live video image. If this is not the case, the mobile device adjusts its zoom level. This ensures a practically constant control-display ratio for users independently of their distance.

Allowing multi-user interaction on media facades

The large size of such facades further allows multiple users to interact simultaneously on them. The original idea of *Touch Projector* only transforms input occurring on the mobile device to a facade's canvas. Thus, interactive controls or temporary feedback are shown on the facade. This is not always an optimal solution: (1) tool palettes waste screen real estate decreasing the size of the actual interaction canvas. (2) The resolution of the facade (in combination with the viewing distance) further limits the resolution of such controls. (3) Temporary feedback (e.g., highlighted regions) interferes with the interaction of others.

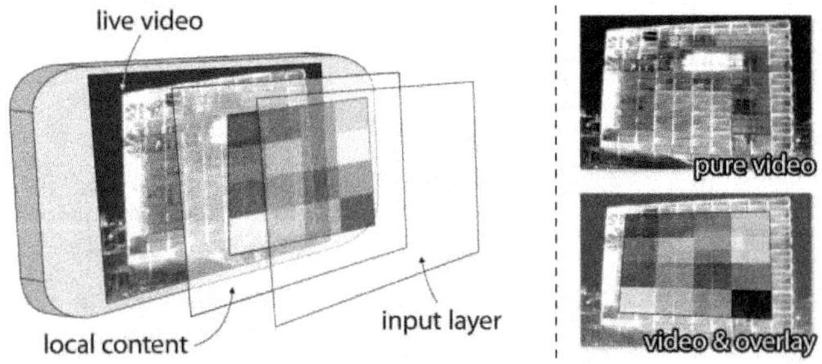

Figure 2. Inserting a local content layer (left) allows for showing pure or augmented live video for each user individually.

On the other hand, the live video on the mobile device shows the facade at all times. Thus, the facade's content can be augmented locally without introducing macro attention shifts. To allow for such feedback, the mobile screen superimposes a personal layer on the local live video (see Figure 2), leaving the shared view of the facade canvas unaffected.

[1] The facade of the ARS Electronica Center hosts about 40000 LEDs embedded into 1087 addressable windows.

IMPLEMENTATION AND DEPLOYMENT

Our prototype uses a dedicated server to (1) control the building's lighting through DMX and (2) communicate with mobile devices (here: three Apple iPhones). Similar to *Touch Projector*, the mobile devices send video frames over wireless LAN to this server, which calculates their spatial relationship to the building. The server further handles all touch events received from the mobile devices.

Addressing tracking challenges for outdoor use

To identify the facade, we chose to show a white frame around an entire side of the building by permanently lighting the outmost pixels. This frame can be detected using *Touch Projector's* image processing methods (i.e., contrast correction, edge detection, and corner identification). Our system then uses the detected perspective distortion of the building's outline (i.e., the frame), to calculate the spatial relationship between mobile device and building.

To avoid reflections on wet surfaces being falsely detected, we made two assumptions: (1) users point their devices at the building instead of the reflection, which causes the reflection to be shown only partly. (2) The reflection is slightly jittered resulting in less prominent lines of the building's outline. In early tests on the facade with real users and reflections caused by wet ground around the building, we found these assumptions to be sufficient.

Allowing for personal content on the mobile device

Aside from determining the spatial relationship of mobile devices, the server stores individual content for each user as image data which (on request) can be transferred to the mobile device. In some cases (i.e., directly superimposing individual content), the system also distorts the content for correct alignment with live video. This is done by using the inverted transformation matrix (i.e., homography) calculated during the detection process. Once the image is sent to the mobile device, it is overlaid on the live video image.

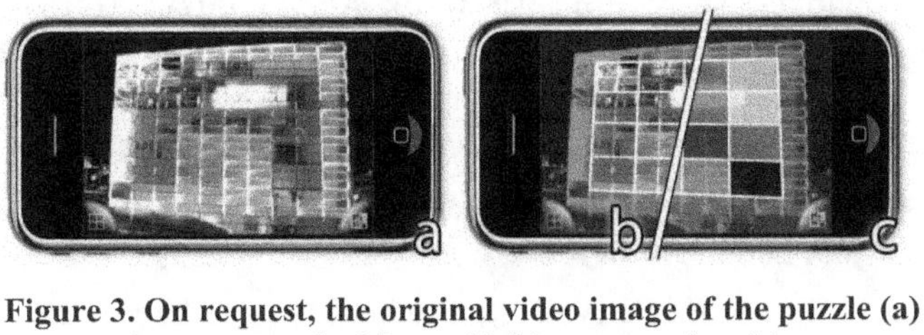

Figure 3. On request, the original video image of the puzzle (a) is augmented with a grid (b) or a preview (c).

All interaction events (i.e., touch inputs) are sent to the server regardless whether the user hit a "local" item or not. As the server knows the exact locations of all elements it can determine and execute the associated action. Thus, application developers only need to design the interface elements and their actions on the server. This type of implementation allows for greater flexibility in terms of the heterogeneity found in mobile device platforms. It limits scalability, however, since computation on the server linearly increases with the number of mobile devices.

Example applications at ARS Electronica

To demonstrate the use of (1) interacting through live video on media facades as well as (2) the distribution of public and personal content, we built two applications. These allowed users to paint freely on the facade or solve a 15-puzzle in a collaborative way.

Our first application allows users to solve a 15-puzzle on the facade. Eight pixels (i.e., 2 by 4 windows) are representing one tile of the puzzle. Tiles can be shifted by tapping on a tile next to the missing one. However, the facade's low resolution did not allow for clearly showing division lines that are important to identify tiles (see Figure 3a). We decided to allow users to superimpose these lines on the mobile device to allow for tile identification (see Figure 3b). As our tiles only have 8 pixels in total, it is hard to identify a tile's correct location. Users can peek at the solved puzzle by requesting a preview (see Figure 3c). We decided to show the preview locally so that others are not distracted.

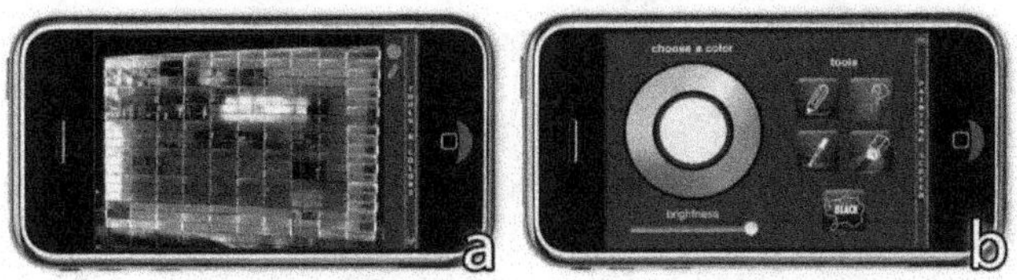

Figure 4. To keep the drawing canvas as large as possible (a), users can switch to the tool palette (b).

Our second application allows users to paint freely on the facade. Similar to common drawing applications, users (1) choose a color and (2) select a tool from a tool palette. To do so, users perform a slide gesture next to the live video image. The mobile device then shows a tool palette (see Figure 4b). After closing the palette (i.e., sliding in opposite direction), users can apply the selected color and tool to the building by touching (and dragging) on it in live video (see Figure 4a). Placing the controls on the mobile device was the only possible solution, as our facade does not offer a resolution high enough to display controls.

Initial user feedback

During the ARS Electronica Festival in Linz, Austria, we presented our applications to a broad audience. We handed phones with the application already running to users without any further instructions. By observing how others used the application, they immediately started to interact with the facade. Up to three persons were able to interact simultaneously, but we ensured that at least two did at all times. Downloading the application was not possible as (1) we used a restricted network and (2) it was not allowed in the AppStore at that time. Nevertheless, with three users interacting simultaneously, we were able to observe interesting scenarios including collaboration between them.

Out of the appr imately 50 users we asked 15 attendees (5 female; average age was 26.1) for feedback after interacting with the building. In informal interviews we found that this style of interaction is perceived as (1) easy-to-learn and (2) easy-to-use. Overall, the feedback we gained during the interviews was highly positive. The fact that they could directly change the facade in real time (e.g., a form of *digital graffiti*) was mentioned positively. However, users were sometimes annoyed by the parallel use of our application. The most important statement was: "It is good to interact in a parallel way if you know the person. But if you don't know the person, you are kind of fighting over pixels and space to draw. It's kind of annoying". While this user favored collaboration, another pair of users created a strobe-like effect, alternately filling the entire facade with white and black. Thus, interactions involving either collaboration or competition were supported by the painting application.

CONCLUSIONS & FUTURE WORK

In this paper, we presented an extension to the concept of *Touch Projector* to allow multiple users to interact collaboratively (or competitively) with media facades shown in live video on their mobile device. We described the technical realization that can be used under various weather conditions on any digital surface that has or can display a white frame. We further extended *Touch Projector* by superimposing individual content (i.e., UI elements that are not of interest for all users at a time) on the live video. While this was necessary for the low resolution facade in our deployment, it constitutes a very general mechanism when many users interact on larger digital surfaces with their mobile devices: When feedback only affects (or is intended for) a subset of these users, our approach does not distract or disturb others while they interact with the display.

We demonstrated our prototype during the ARS Electronica Festival in Linz, Austria with a large group of users. The feedback we gained informs future work in the area of multi-user interaction at-a-distance. In contrast to collocated scenarios in which users are next to or can see one another, larger facades may give rise to greater distances between users, so that they may not be aware of (1) *who* is interacting and (2) *where* others are. As this is a common problem of techniques that use interaction at-a-distance, we plan to develop solutions to the awareness problem, by, for example, visualizing the location and direction of others.

Another issue raised by our participants was the heavily parallel nature of interaction using our technique. The fact that users could simultaneously interact in the same region of the facade was only appreciated if users knew each other. Otherwise, they rather got frustrated if others interacted (and thus interfered) with them in "their" region. There will always be some tension between permitting desired interactions and preventing undesired ones on a large-scale, multi-user, public media facade. As this is an intrinsic property of the medium and not solvable in general, we hope to iteratively converge on a more appropriate balance, through partitioning time slots or sub-regions among users on the facade with the ultimate goal of maximizing enjoyment and minimizing frustrations for future users.

ACKNOWLEDGMENTS

This work has been funded by both the "Deutsche Forschungsgemeinschaft" (DFG) and the German State of Bavaria. We thank Antonio Krüger and Michael Rohs for their input in the initial design phase. We also thank Andreas Pramböck, Stefan Mittelböck and Horst Hörtner (AEC) for their technical support during preparation as well as the festival. We further thank Dominikus Baur and – especially – Joe McCarthy for their valuable comments and feedback.

REFERENCES

1. Ballagas, R., Borchers, J., Rohs, M., Sheridan, J.G. The Smart Phone: A Ubiquitous Input Device. *IEEE Pervasive Computing 5*, 1 (2006), 70-77.

Boring, S., Jurmu, M., Butz, A. Scroll, tilt or move it: using mobile phones to continuously control pointers on large public displays. *Proc. OzCHI 2009*, ACM Press (2009), 161-168.

3. Boring, S., Baur, D., Butz, A., Gustafson, S., Baudisch, P. Touch projector: mobile interaction through video. *Proc. CHI 2010*, ACM Press (2010), 2287-2296.
4. Borries, F., Walz, S., Böttger, M. Space Time Play: Computer Games, Architecture and Urbanism: The Next Level, *Birkhäuser, Basel,* 2007, 396-397.
5. Dalsgaard, P., Halskov, K. Designing Urban Media Facades: Cases and Challenges. *Proc. CHI '10*, ACM Press (2010), 2277-2286.
6. Häusler M.H. Media Facades: History, Technology, Content. *Av Edition*, Ludwigsburg, 2009.
7. Pears, N., Jackson, D.G., Olivier, P. Smart Phone Interaction with Registered Displays. *IEEE Pervasive Computing 8*, 2 (2009), 14-21.
8. Peltonen, P., Salovaara, A., Jacucci, G., Ilmonen, T., Ardito, C., Saarikko, P., Batra, V. Extending large-scale event participation with user-created mobile media on a public display. *Proc. MUM '07*, ACM (2007), 131-138.
9. Scheible, J., Ojala, T. MobiSpray: mobile phone as virtual spray can for painting BIG anytime anywhere on anything. *Proc. SIGGRAPH '09*, ACM Press, 332-341.
10. Schoch, O. My Building is my Display, *Proc. eCAADe '06*, 2006, 610-616.

. Seitinger, S., Perry, D.S., Mitchell, W.J., Urban Pixels: Painting the City with Light. *Proc. CHI 2009*, 839-848

12. Sommerer, C., Jain, L., Mignonneau, L. Media Facades as Architectural Interfaces. *The Art and Science of Interface and Interaction Design*, Springer, 2008, 93-104
13. Struppek, M. The social potential of Urban Screens, *Visual Communication 5*, 2, 2006; 173-188.
14. Tani, M., Yamashi, K., Tanikoshi, K., Futakawa, M., Tanifuji, S. Object-oriented video: interaction with real-world objects through live video. *Proc. CHI 1992*, ACM Press (1992), 593-598.

Interaction with Magic Lenses: Real-World Validation of a Fitts' Law Model

Michael Rohs[†*], **Antti Oulasvirta**[°], **Tiia Suomalainen**[°]

[†]Deutsche Telekom Laboratories, TU Berlin
[*]Ludwig-Maximilians-Universität München, Munich, Germany
[°]Helsinki Institute for Information Technology HIIT, Aalto University and University of Helsinki

ABSTRACT

Rohs and Oulasvirta (2008) proposed a two-component Fitts' law model for target acquisition with magic lenses in mobile augmented reality (AR) with 1) a physical pointing phase, in which the target can be directly observed on the background surface, and 2) a virtual pointing phase, in which the target can only be observed through the device display. The model provides a good fit (R^2=0.88) with laboratory data, but it is not known if it generalizes to *real-world* AR tasks. In the present outdoor study, subjects (N=12) did building-selection tasks in an urban area. The differences in task characteristics to the laboratory study are drastic: targets are three-dimensional and they vary in shape, size, z-distance, and visual context. Nevertheless, the model yielded an R^2 of 0.80, and when using effective target width an R^2 of 0.88 was achieved.

Author Keywords

Target acquisition, magic lens pointing, Fitts' law, human-performance modeling, field experiment, augmented reality.

ACM Classification Keywords

H.5.2 [Information Interfaces and Presentation]: User Interfaces – input devices and strategies, theory and methods.

General Terms

Experimentation, Human Factors.

INTRODUCTION

Mobile augmented reality (AR) improves information navigation on handheld devices by overcoming the limitations of display size. Particularly, *magic lens pointing,* or pointing through the movable camera-view of the device [6], is a promising kind of interaction, because it allows large-scale information presentation with private and up-to-date information on a personal display. While the early prototypes were marker-based and mainly used in close-range interaction, the present-day AR allows markerless recognition of objects and can therefore be utilized for a wider range of visual content, such as real-world scenes (Figure 1), as their background [8]. We use the term AR here in a broad way that encompasses real-world interactions using a camera-display unit to aim at targets in the environment.

Figure 1. Magic lens pointing over a real-world scene. The image illustrates target selection at one of the seven sites in the study with targets marked in red (not visible to the users).

In HCI, camera-based interaction with mobile AR interfaces has been analyzed as an instance of target acquisition performance that consists of rapid precise movements towards a point target or a spatially extended target. According to Fitts' law [1], the duration of such movements (t) is systematically dependent on the distance to the target (D) and the target's width (W) as follows:

$$t = a + b \log_2(D/W + 1) \quad (1)$$

Wang et al. [9] show that Fitts' law is applicable to target acquisition tasks in which the phone UI is controlled using optical flow motion sensing. Rohs and Oulasvirta [6] propose a modified Fitts' law model for target acquisition of external targets that fits data better than the standard model. The modified model supposes two phases in sensorimotor control: 1) a physical pointing phase, in which the target can be directly observed on the background surface, and 2) a virtual pointing phase, in which the target can only be observed through the display. Consequently, it needs a parameter for the size of the display (S):

$$t = a + b \log_2(D/S + 1) + c \log_2(S/2/W + 1) \quad (2)$$

Applied to the laboratory data of [6] this model achieves a fit of R^2=0.88, the original model (Eq. 1) only R^2=0.57.

However, these models, and all models of AR we know of, have been developed based on data acquired in rigorously controlled laboratory conditions where subjects are standing in front a surface (e.g., a large display) on which targets appear. It is an open question if the model generalizes to AR in the real world where targets 1) can be three-dimensional and 2) vary drastically in shape, size, z-distance, and visual context. Moreover, sequential selections can take place between targets with *different* characteristics. Because even seemingly small changes in task conditions can affect the performance of a Fitts' law task [1,2], the question of generalizability is best addressed empirically.

Therefore, to assess if the model of Eq. 2 generalizes to the abovementioned conditions, this paper presents an experiment using real-world targets. In the study, subjects were taken to balconies, bridges, parking lots, and streets to do reciprocal selection of buildings (see Figure 1). As we will show later, the model of Rohs and Oulasvirta [6] generalizes surprisingly well to this real-world task, achieving an R^2 of 0.80, but increasing to R^2 of 0.88 when effective target width [7] is used. We identified an "averaging behavior" that may explain this improvement.

MAGIC LENS POINTING: APPLYING THE MODEL OF ROHS AND OULASVIRTA TO REAL-WORLD SCENES

In the benchmark model [6], pointing consists of two phases. The first phase is denoted as *physical pointing*: The target can be directly observed in the physical world. At some point during the movement towards the target, the target falls below the display and can no longer be observed directly, but only through the magic lens. With a screen width of S, the split point is located at a distance of S/2. At this point, the second phase—*virtual pointing*—begins: The target can now only be observed through the display. As soon as a target falls below the lens, the characteristics of the *mediation* by the camera-display-unit come into play, such as delay and display update rate.

For the outdoor situation with buildings and landmarks as targets, the model has to be slightly adapted. The real sizes of the objects do not help in characterizing the situation, because objects can be located at a wide range of z-distances from the user. A smaller object might thus cover a wider field of view than a larger object if it is located closer to the user. The angular size of a target from the viewpoint of the user is more meaningful. Hence, we measure D and W in angular degrees, as proposed in earlier work [4].

Another complication lies in the fact that target shapes can be arbitrary polygons (see Figures 1-3) rather than squares as typical in Fitts' law studies. We defined the centers of the real-world targets as the centroid of the polygon area. Since the targets are arbitrary polygons, the target width is not constant, but depends on the direction from which the target is approached. To handle this case for rectangular targets, we follow MacKenzie [5] by considering the extent of the target along an approach vector through the center. But we extend this by defining the movement vector to lie on a line through the centers of the previous target and the next target as in Figure 2. The two intersection points of this line of movement and the next target's polygonal outline define the angular width of the target. Thus, in the real-world pointing case W of next target does not only depend on that target alone, but also on the movement vector from which the target is approached. Grossman et al. [3] derive a probabilistic model for rectangular targets that describes 2D pointing from different directions.

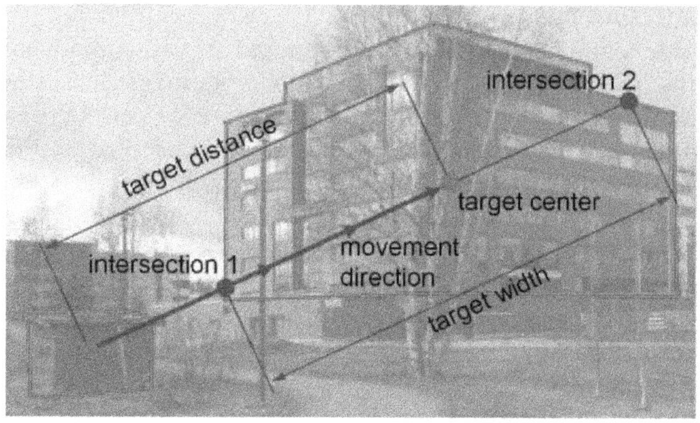

Figure 2. Target polygons are outlined in red. The movement axis goes through the target center points, from the left target to the right target. Target width depends on movement direction (intersection of movement vector and polygon).

EXPERIMENT

In the experiment, we utilized a non-conventional *reciprocal pointing task*, in which users have to move back and forth between two targets and the two targets have different properties (size, z-distance, shape, visual context). An interesting aspect of the experiment was to find out how users adapt to this situation. In particular because of widely differing widths, we wondered whether users would change their movement speed according to Fitts' law or whether they would apply some kind of averaging behavior. We therefore measured the effective target width W_e, which is computed as the width of the target based on the scatter of selection points around the target center point [7]. We also applied the model to averaged target widths, i.e., for each target pair we computed the average width and used this as the input to the model.

Participants

Twelve subjects (6 M, 6 F, age 21-26 years) were recruited from a local technical university. Seven were frequent users of the camera functionality on their phones. All subjects had normal or corrected-to-normal vision. Subjects were paid a small incentive for participation.

Experimental Platform

The experiment was conducted on a Nokia N95 8GB Symbian phone. The angular screen width of the phone camera is 42.5°. The test application shows a viewfinder image with a crosshair in the center of the screen to facilitate precise selection. The subject has to press the joystick button to make a selection. Since we dealt with arbitrary outdoor scenes and changing lighting conditions, no attempt was made to automatically recognize the image in real-time. This would have led to a noticeable processing delay with a detrimental effect on pointing performance [10]. Therefore, upon selection, the last visible frame is stored as a PGM image together with meta data.

Materials and Experimental Design

The main goal in choosing target stimuli was to have realistic variety in size, distance between target pairs. In terms of standard Fitts' law, we used index of difficulty (ID) values between 0.72 and 3.91 (ID = $\log_2(D/W+1)$).

Figure 3: Two scenes from the experiments' 7 sites. The four targets in each site are highlighted in red.

The route consisted of 7 *sites* (see Figure 3). It was short enough for the experiment to last about one hour including transitions. Each site consisted of 4 targets, yielding 6 target pairs. With 2 directions in each target pair this results in 84 directed target pairs. The angular target distances were between 6.8° and 74.8° and the target widths 2.3°-35.3°. Target borders were chosen to be clear and easily perceived, not blocked by other buildings or vegetation. Car traffic directly in front of a target was avoided to minimize distraction. Selection always started from the left target in the target pair (see Figure 2). Timekeeping started on the first selection and the next item had to be selected as quickly and accurately as possible. We did not give special instructions beyond that (e.g. how to deal with elongated targets) and did not explicitly check for systematic distortions of selection centers. Within each target pair, 24 selections were made (interleaved 12 left-to-right, 12 right-to-left).

Half of the male and half of the female participants walked the route in opposite direction. Target pairs were run in different random order for each participant. Standing position and orientation at each site were fixed. The total number of selections per subject was 24 selections for practice; and 7 sites × 6 target pairs × 24 selections = 1008 for the actual experiment.

Procedure

All subjects practiced selection of targets indoors before going outdoors. Before starting a selection of a target pair at a site, the current targets were pointed out to the subject as a photo on paper where their boundaries were highlighted with red. Moreover, they were pointed at in the real world by the experimenter. To select a target, the subjects had to move the crosshair (centered on the screen) on top of the target on the display and press the phone's joystick button.

Data Analysis

Each user selection resulted in capturing and storing an image on the device. Images were uploaded to a PC and analyzed off-line with a Java tool. We annotated the images, determining the distance between the target center and the point of selection, as well as whether the selection was successful. This data was used to compute the scatter around the target for W_e and the error rate.

To calculate the angular target distances and widths, a high-resolution image was taken with a DSLR camera at each site. The image was taken from the standing position of the participants and covered all four targets of a site. In addition, a calibration image of a brick wall from a known distance was taken, with the identical camera and lens configuration as with the high-resolution site images. The calibration image enabled us to compute the parameters to convert pixel coordinates in the image to angular coordinates in the real scene. Using this mapping, we computed the angles D between pairs of target center points. We verified the angular distances using a large-scale local map. To compute the target widths we entered the outlines of each target as polygons into the tool. From the outlines and the target center points, the tool computed the intersection points of the line of approach and the next target (Figure 2), which were then converted into the angular width W for that target pair.

RESULTS

The experiment yielded 11952 data points (one subject completed only 6 sites). The overall error rate (i.e., selection not on target) was low (2%), the mean selection time was 885ms. Preprocessing revealed that two targets (from two different sites) were problematic, because the participants had trouble distinguishing them from their backgrounds. Consequently, the two targets were excluded from further analysis. Including these targets leads to $R^2 = 0.71$ for our model, and $R^2 = 0.42$ for standard Fitts' law.

Without the outlier targets, the fit of the measured movement times and the movement times predicted by our model (Eq. 2) is $R^2 = 0.80$. The fit for standard Fitts' law (Eq. 1) is $R^2 = 0.47$. The results are shown in Figure 4 as predicted time against measured time. Typically ID is shown on the x-axis. With the extended model, ID cannot be used directly. The estimated parameters (all times in milliseconds) for our model were (S = 42.5°):

$$t = 185 + 727 \log_2(D/S + 1) + 62 \log_2(S/2/W + 1) \quad (3)$$

and for standard Fitts' law were:

$$t = 447 + 220 \log_2(D/W + 1). \quad (4)$$

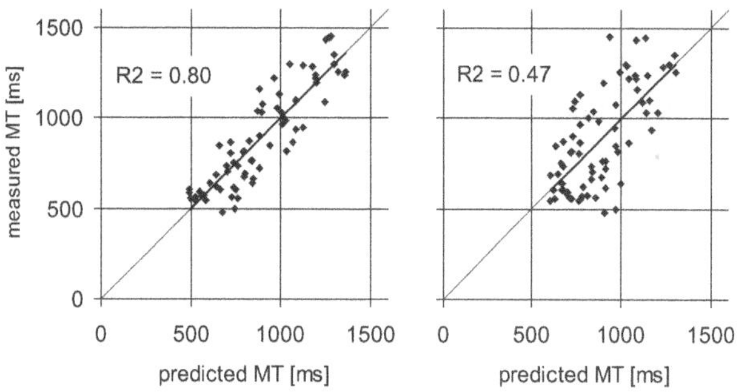

Figure 4: Movement time (MT) prediction by our model (left, $R^2 = 0.80$) and standard Fitts' law (right, $R^2 = 0.47$).

Even though Eq. 3 yields a better fit when compared to the standard Fitts' law, the fit (R^2=0.80) is still relatively low compared to lab studies in the literature. We therefore analyzed whether the large variation in target sizes within a single target pair might have an influence. To this end, we looked at the *actual* speed-accuracy tradeoff the participants chose within a target pair by computing the effective target width $W_e = 4.133\sigma$. Here, σ represents the standard deviation of the end-point positions, which here are angular deviations from the target center. Using the effective widths, fit raises to $R^2 = 0.88$ for our model and $R^2 = 0.72$ for the standard model. The parameters are now estimated to $t = -48+743\log_2(D/S+1)+144\log_2(S/2/W+1)$ for our model and $t = 184+266 \log_2(D/W+1)$ for standard Fitts' law.

The difference between actual and effective target width seems to be particularly large if the targets within a condition differ strongly in width. When selecting subsets of target pairs with restricted width ratio R^2 increases. However, also the number of D,W-pairs decreases, leading presumably to a better fit.

The results regarding effective target width let us suspect that participants performed an "*averaging behavior*" within the reciprocal task, i.e., adapting the task for the average of the width of a condition's two targets. We therefore re-evaluated the data using the average (across users) target width. This led to an extremely high fit of $R^2 = 0.96$ for our model and $R^2 = 0.88$ for the standard Fitts' law model. Hence we conclude that the users indeed employed an averaging behavior. The parameters for the averaged widths are $t = -69+750\log_2(D/S+1)+223\log_2(S/2/W+1)$ for our model and $t = 250+341\log_2(D/W+1)$ for the standard model.

SUMMARY AND OUTLOOK

The power of Fitts' law lies in its ability to simplify a complex phenomenon in a way that generalizes beyond immediate observations. The question is, whether models of performance in rigidly controlled laboratory conditions generalize to real-world conditions that may have different characteristics [2]. An essential part of research in this field should consist of validation of models in the real world. From this perspective, the results of the present study are highly promising. The laboratory model was found to generalize to a real-world task that is different in many respects, achieving an R^2 of 0.80. When using effective target widths W_e, a fit of 0.88 was achieved which is identical to that of the laboratory study [6]. This is remarkable, when considering that the real-world targets had much more complex shapes, were embedded in a rich visual context, and were selected from a wide range of z-distances. Moreover, sequential selections took place between targets with different characteristics.

As future work we intend to investigate the effects of visual saliency as well as the effects of z-distance and perspective on real-world AR pointing tasks. These challenges will require a metric for the visual saliency of a target relative to its background, and we expect that z-distance and in particular the effects of perspective distortion caused by the users position will have a strong influence on performance.

ACKNOWLEDGMENTS

We thank Antti Nurminen for help with image calibration. AO and TS were funded by the Tekes project Theseus2.

REFERENCES

1. Fitts, P.M. The information capacity of the human motor-system in controlling the amplitude of movement. *J. Exp. Psychol.* 47 (1954), 381-391.
2. Gillan, D.J., Holden, K., Adams, S., Rudisill, M., and Magee, L. How should Fitts' law be applied to human-computer interaction? *Int. w.Comp.*, 4, 3, 1992, 291-313.
3. Grossman, T. and Balakrishnan, R. A probabilistic approach to modeling two-dimensional pointing. *ACM Trans. Comput.-Hum. Interact.* 12, 3 (2005), 435-459.
4. Kondraske, G. An angular motion Fitt's law for human performance modeling and prediction. *Proc. Annual Int. Conf. of the IEEE, vol. 1. Engineering in Medicine and Biology Society*, 1994, 307-308.
5. MacKenzie, I.S. and Buxton, W. Extending Fitts' law to two-dimensional tasks. *Proc. CHI 1992*, 219-226.
6. Rohs, M. and Oulasvirta, A. Target acquisition with camera phones when used as magic lenses. *Proc. CHI 2008.* ACM Press (2008), 1409-1418.
7. Soukoreff, R.W. and MacKenzie, I.S. Towards a standard for pointing device evaluation, perspectives on 27 years of Fitts' law research in HCI. *Int. J. Hum.-Comput. Stud.* 61, 6 (Dec. 2004), 751-789.
8. Wagner, D., Reitmayr, G., Mulloni, A., Drummond, T., and Schmalstieg, D. Pose tracking from natural features on mobile phones. *Proc. ISMAR 2008.* IEEE, 125-134.
9. Wang, J., Zhai, S., and Canny, J. Camera phone based motion sensing: interaction techniques, applications and performance study. *Proc. UIST 2006.* ACM, 101-110.
10. Ware, C. and Balakrishnan, R. Reaching for objects in VR displays: lag and frame rate. *ACM Trans. Comput.-Hum. Interact.* 1, 4 (Dec. 1994), 331-356.

Xpaaand: Interaction Techniques for Rollable Displays

Mohammadreza Khalilbeigi, Roman Lissermann, Max Mühlhäuser, and Jürgen Steimle
Technische Universität Darmstadt
64289 Darmstadt, Germany
{khalilbeigi, lissermann, max, steimle}@tk.informatik.tu-darmstadt.de

ABSTRACT
We present a device concept and a prototype of a future mobile device. By featuring a rollable display, its display size and its form factor can be dynamically changed. Moreover, we investigate how physical resizing of the display can be used as an input technique for interacting with digital contents and present a set of novel interaction techniques. Evaluation results show that physical resizing of the display can improve the way we interact with digital contents on mobile devices.

Author Keywords
Tangible interaction, mobile device, rollable display, screen, scroll, resizing, input technique.

ACM Classification Keywords
H5.2. User interfaces: Graphical user interfaces (GUI), Input devices and strategies, Interaction styles.

General Terms
Human Factors

INTRODUCTION
The screen real estate of today's mobile and handheld devices is limited by the size of the device. Given the rapid advances in thin and flexible OLED displays [5] and flexible circuitry, it is very likely that this restriction can be overcome. In the near future, high-resolution electronic displays will be available that can be rolled in and out in a way very similar to ancient paper scrolls. This will enable the production of devices that have a very small form factor in a collapsed state yet can be expanded dynamically to feature a larger screen (Fig. 1).

Xpaaand is a prototypical realization of a handheld device in which the screen real estate can be dynamically adjusted. Employing a passive display approach, we introduce a set of novel interaction techniques for such devices and examine how dynamic display size changes can be used as an input technique for interacting with digital contents.

We start by briefly discussing related work. Next we present the device concept and our physical prototype. Then we introduce novel interaction techniques and conclude with results of a user study.

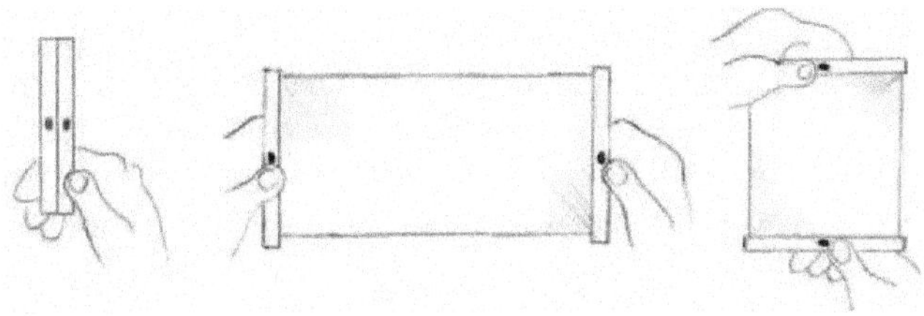

Figure 1. Xpaaand provides for dynamically resizing the mobile device and its display

RELATED WORK
Our work is situated in the area of embodied interactions for mobile and handheld devices. Small and Ishii [1] presented different concepts for scrolling through content on a mobile device by turning physical cylinders, tilting, and moving the display. Gummi [2] introduced a set of interaction techniques for bendable displays, which support scrolling and zooming. However, these devices have a fixed-size screen.

Chen et al. [3] introduced an e-book reader which features two displays. By folding and unfolding the device, the visible screen real estate can be decreased and increased by a factor of two. In contrast to this discrete resizing, rollable displays provide for continuous resizing.

Our work is particularly inspired by recent industrial prototypes of rollable OLED displays [5] and by the work of Lee et al. [4]. Lee et al. used a tracking and projection system similar to the approach taken by PaperWindows [6]. They demonstrated four types of foldable and resizable displays, including a rollable display. However, they examined resizing only as a means for altering the size and the aspect ratio of the viewport, similar to resizing a GUI window. Our goal is to improve upon this previous work by exploring the design space and proposing appropriate interaction techniques. Furthermore, the empirical results of a user study on deformable displays [8] influenced our design decisions.

DEVICE CONCEPT
We envision an ideal Xpaaand device (see Fig. 1) as a thin, lightweight appliance, equipped with on-board power supply. It features a high-resolution display that the user can (un)roll for dynamically resizing the display. Two handles on two opposing sides of the display provide for hold-

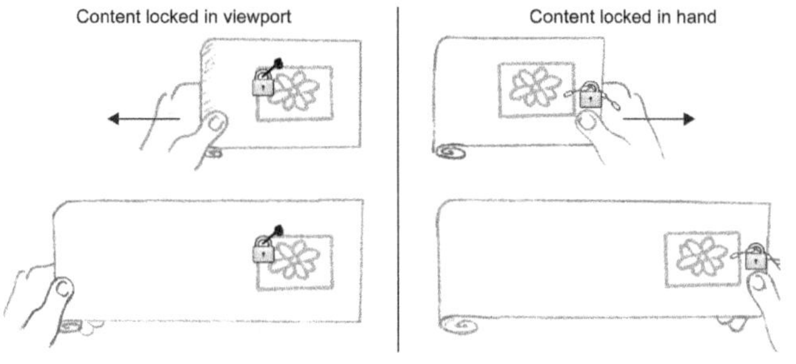

Figure 2. Metaphors for rollable displays

ing the device in a comfortable manner, either in landscape or in portrait mode, with one or two hands. The device, and hence the display, can be physically expanded in one dimension by pulling both handles apart. It can be collapsed by pushing them together. Once the device is resized it maintains its new size.

In this paper, we focus on the design space of dynamic resizing as a novel input technique. We advocate this interaction concept not to replace, but to complement the existing techniques (e.g. touch and pen input).

By embedding accelerometers in both handles, the device can sense which side is actuated. We distinguish three types of resizing: Pulling-out or pushing-in the left side of the display, the right side, or both sides (symmetric). These three types can be mapped to different functionality.

Inspired by the physical behavior of traditional paper scrolls and the work by Song et al. [7], we propose two metaphors for interacting with contents. These are depicted in Fig. 2. Considering a traditional scroll, the side at which it is pulled out or pushed in matters: either content remains at a fix position in the user's view (*content locked in viewport*) or it remains at a fix position with respect to the user's hand (*content locked in hand*). Interfaces for rollable displays can overcome this physical inconsistency and use either of these metaphors consistently for interactions on both sides.

We consider the *content locked in viewport* metaphor to be better suited in most cases, as it allows users to increase the display to the side on which they want to see more contents. In some specific cases which we will discuss below, *content locked in hand* is more adequate. For switching from the standard locked-in-viewport mode to locked-in-hand, the Xpaaand device offers a physical button on each handle. By pressing the button on either side, the user can lock the content, which is displayed at that side, in his hand.

XPAAAND PROTOTYPE

Despite the recent advances in flexible displays, the components required for realizing such a device are not available at the moment. Therefore, we followed a passive display approach and developed a prototype that emulates the most important properties of the envisioned device, i.e. the rollable display and physical resizing.

Our system tracks the physical position of the Xpaaand prototype with a 6-camera OptiTrack system using IR retro-

Figure 3. The Xpaaand prototype

reflective markers. A Full-HD overhead projector is used to display digital content on the device. This permits naturally moving the prototype in the high-resolution projection frustum of approximately 100 * 60 * 40 cm^3.

The Xpaaand prototype (Fig. 3) consists of a physical scroll made of white foil, where display content is projected. It can be resized to widths from 5 to 39 cm at a fix height of 18 cm. It is 4 cm thick and weights about 900g. A box is attached at each of the two ends. These boxes act as physical handles for easily grasping the device; they contain the scroll and electronic components. A physical button is positioned at the center of each of the boxes. As our current prototype does not support touch input and to support navigation on the display while it is held with two hands, a trackball is integrated into one box. It can be manipulated with the dominant hand (left-handers can rotate the device by 180 degrees). Wireless communication links the prototype to a nearby PC that hosts tracking software and applications. To keep the device stable, straight, and stiff at different display sizes, we fixed an expandable strut on the back of device.

INTERACTION TECHNIQUES

In this section, we introduce a set of interaction techniques that are based on resizing of the display. They enable users to accomplish common tasks for manipulating digital information. We explore expanding as a means for displaying more contents or more detailed contents. Moreover, we examine how additional screen real estate, created on-the-fly, can be used for exposing additional or different functionality. We developed and implemented the following interaction techniques. They are also demonstrated in the video figure accompanying this paper.

Viewport resizing Expanding or collapsing the display increases or decreases the viewport. In contrast to GUI windows, additional content appears or disappears either on the left, the right, or both sides of the current viewport, depending on which side is actuated (Fig. 4 a). This interaction facilitates common activities such as deeply focusing on a single item, comparing adjacent items, or getting a quick overview on many items. Moreover, scrolling can be performed by iteratively expanding the display on one side and collapsing it on the other side. For scrolling through longer lists, users can use the trackball. In order to examine this technique with different types of information we have

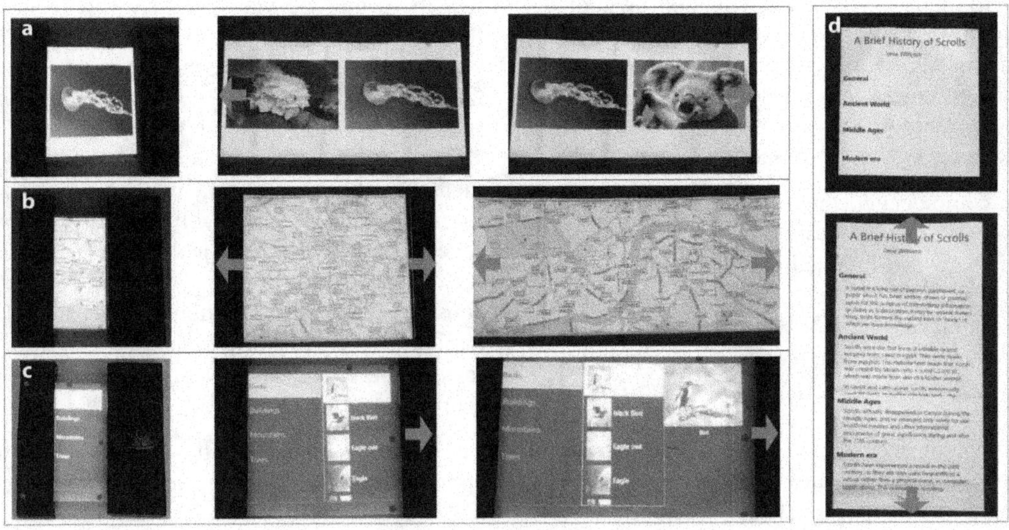

Figure 4. Selected interaction techniques: a) Viewport resizing, b) Geometric zooming, c) Menu navigation, d) Semantic Zooming

implemented it in a simple photo viewer (Fig. 4 a), a map viewer (4b) and a text viewer (using the scroll in portrait mode) (4d).

Zooming Zooming in or out is performed using the locked-in-hand metaphor. By pressing both buttons simultaneously, content gets locked-in-hand at both sides. While resizing the display, content on the viewport then gets "stretched" or "shrunk", which is mapped to zooming. This interaction is inspired by the findings of [7] on stretching gestures. For navigating to very deep zoom levels, which cannot be reached by pulling out the display once, the user can iterate over zooming and viewport resizing several times (similar to lifting a mouse to move the device but not the cursor).

This technique reduces a problem of zooming on fixed-size screens, where magnifying the view results in losing context information. In contrast, enlarging the viewport while zooming in enables seeing the detailed view *and* still having more context visible in one dimension. We have implemented applications for zooming in a 1D (semantic zoom within text, Fig. 4 d) and a 2D information space (geometric zoom within maps, Fig. 4 b).

Navigation in hierarchies This technique supports the physical navigation through hierarchical lists, e.g. menus and folders (see Fig. 4 c). In order to open a selected item, the user pulls the display out in the direction of the dominant hand. This selected item (e.g. the next menu level or contents of a folder) is displayed on the newly created display area, resulting in an overview + detail view. Going back in the hierarchy is performed in the reverse direction. As a further advantage in addition to the more direct experience of physically opening and closing items, the full navigation hierarchy is always visible.

Accessing additional information This technique provides for accessing additional information which is embedded within a document, e.g. a hyperlink within a web page. The user selects the hyperlink by pressing the button on the dominant hand's side and simultaneously expands the display. The link target is expanded in-place, within the context of the original document, leveraging the newly created display space. We have implemented an application for accessing additional images within a text.

Temporarily holding elements This technique leverages dynamically created additional display space for temporarily holding an information element. This allows the user to compare items and creating a *visual clipboard*. By locking one information element in hand (pressing button) while expanding, the element is moved to the clipboard region, which appears on the fly. Moving the item back (e.g. for pasting) is performed with the reverse action. Collapsing the display without pressing a button hides the visual clipboard (locked-in-viewport metaphor). We have implemented an application for cut and paste with photos.

Application switching Different applications require a different amount of screen real estate (e.g. phone app vs. web browser). This technique allows users to easily switch between a small number of frequently used applications by resizing the display to the size which is associated with a specific application. A similar approach can be taken for exposing or hiding functionality within one application.

EVALUATION AND DISCUSSION

To evaluate our concept, we conducted an explorative user study with 11 volunteer participants (5f, 6m) in single user sessions (each 1h, think-aloud protocol, videotaped). We were particularly interested to see how easy it is for novice users to understand the novel interaction style of Xpaaand. After 5 min. of introduction, participants explored the interaction techniques and were asked to perform the following tasks in the horizontal mode: searching and comparing photos using viewport resizing, finding certain photos in different albums using the navigation technique, performing multiple times the cut and paste operation with the aim of the visual clipboard, and performing application switching while thinking aloud. In the vertical mode, participants had to perform a reading task with and without the semantic zooming technique followed by revealing a hidden figure using the accessing additional information technique. The session ended with a semi-structured interview.

All 11 participants appreciated the possibility of changing the display size dynamically. Physical expanding and collapsing of the display for interacting with contents was found to be very *"intuitive"* and enjoyable. P3 commented that *"it is great and makes so much fun because it imitates something physical and has haptic feedback"*. P4 stated: *"I have just done it, without thinking, [...] it feels more active to me"*. Although *"it is really unusual to pull out"* (P2), all participants quickly got accustomed to the resizing technique and performed it with ease and confidence after a few minutes. The locked-in-viewport metaphor used for viewport resizing was appreciated by all participants. One participant (P2) commented: *"It is so intuitive because the contents remain entirely unchanged. The rest is just temporarily hidden in the scroll."*

Almost all users (10) reported that dynamic and continuous resizing helped them in searching and comparing items in a list. For a search task in the photo application, 7 users intuitively enlarged the viewport to gain a broader view before scrolling through the list. Moreover, 8 participants explicitly stated that the comparison of items was much easier in the flexible display size. 9 users enlarged the viewport before comparing adjacent items. This helped them to directly engage with more than one item while maintaining the full resolution of each item. P3 commented: *"I intuitively resized it to a size which allowed viewing two photos one besides the other."* Even though users had enough physical space for expanding the display to its full size, we observed some instances of collapsing the display to focus on a specific location of the viewport. Furthermore, during the interviews 3 users explicitly mentioned to envision that they can effectively use the device in restricted space very much like one handles physical maps or newspapers. These results indicate that intuitive resizing of the display eases search, comparison and serendipitous discovery of contents.

Besides simple viewport resizing, the techniques for zooming and hierarchy navigation were particularly well received. The participants appreciated the combination of resizing the display and basic interface operations (e.g. open, close, zoom) that provide for a rich physical experience of going in and out (7 users) and keeping the context visible (3 users). Participants reacted very positively to the technique for temporarily holding an element, which eased visual comparison. Application switching was found simple, but most participants needed 1-2 minutes for getting accustomed to this technique which does not use any of the metaphors of physical scrolls.

Most of the time users held the device easily with their two hands, their arms placed on the table. However, 7 users felt that the prototype was too heavy for comfort, particularly for holding in the vertical orientation when widely expanded. Five participants had concerns related to physical fatigue. Physical resizing *"is great but [it] might become a sport doing it too often or for a long time"* (P5). With one single exception in the photo application, all these comments were raised during navigation in hierarchies when users desired to repetitively and quickly switch between several folders. The physical effort of repeatedly collapsing the device for going up one level and expanding again was considered too high, particularly because the device eventually had the same size as before. Several users stated that in this specific case they prefer having alternatives to the proposed technique.

The issue of physical fatigue emphasizes the need for an appropriate trade-off between user experience, efficiency and physical effort. We believe that this limitation will become less severe with future devices that are more lightweight than our prototype and provide alternative input techniques.

Finally, as an unexpected advantage collaborative uses of the device were suggested. This comprised temporally enlarging the display for showing photos to other people (P2, P10) or games (P9) whereby each of two users holds the display at one side.

CONCLUSION AND FUTURE WORK

We have presented a device concept and a set of interaction techniques that leverage physical resizing of a rollable display. Our findings show that physical resizing of the screen real state creates a rich physical experience and can effectively improve interaction with handheld devices. Future work should compare this technique in more detail with existing input and navigation techniques for mobile devices with fixed-size displays, such as touch input, orientation sensitivity or peephole navigation. Future work should also investigate how resizing can be effectively integrated with these techniques.

REFERENCES

1. Small, D. and Ishii, H. Design of Spatially Aware Graspable Display. In *Proc. CHI 1997 Ext. Abstracts*, ACM Press (1997), 367-368.
2. Schwesig, C., Poupyrev, I. and Mori, E. Gummi: a bendable computer. In *Proc. CHI 2004*, ACM Press (2004), 263-270.
3. Chen, N., Guimbretière, F., Dixon, M., Lewis, C. and Agrawala, M. Navigation techniques for dual-display e-book readers. In *Proc. CHI 2008*, ACM Press (2008), 1779-1788.
4. Lee, J. C., Hudson, S. E. and Tse, E. Foldable interactive displays. In *Proc. UIST 2008*, ACM Press (2008), 287-290.
5. Sony Rollable Display. http://www.pcworld.com/article/197182/sony_shows_rollable_oled_display_video.html. Retrieved on 2011-01-13.
6. Holman, D., Vertegaal, R., Altosaar, M., Troje, N. and Johns, D. Paper windows: interaction techniques for digital paper. In *Proc. CHI 2005*, ACM Press (2005), 591-599.
7. Song, H., Grossman, T., Fitzmaurice, G., Guimbretière, F., Khan, A., Attar, R. and Kurtenbach, G. PenLight. Combining a Mobile Projector and a Digital Pen for Dynamic Visual Overlay. In *Proc. CHI 2009*, ACM Press (2009), 143-152.
8. Lee, S., Kim, S., Jin, B., Choi, E., Kim, B., Jia, X., Kim, D. and Lee, K. How users manipulate deformable displays as input devices. In *Proc. CHI 2010*, ACM Press (2010), 1647-1656.

TapBack: Towards Richer Mobile Interfaces in Impoverished Contexts

Simon Robinson[1], **Nitendra Rajput**[2], **Matt Jones**[1], **Anupam Jain**[2], **Shrey Sahay**[2], **Amit Nanavati**[2]

[1] Future Interaction Technology Lab
Swansea University, SA2 8PP, UK
{ s.n.w.robinson, matt.jones } @swan.ac.uk

[2] IBM India Research Laboratory
Vasant Kunj, New Delhi, 110070, India
{ rnitendra, anupamjain, shrsahay, namit } @in.ibm.com

ABSTRACT

Much of the mobile work by HCI researchers explores a future world populated by high-end devices and relatively affluent users. This paper turns to consider the hundreds of millions of people for whom such sophistication will not be realised for many years to come. In developing world contexts, people will continue to rely on voice-primary interactions due to both literacy and economic reasons. Here, we motivate research into how to accommodate advanced mobile interface techniques while overcoming the handset, data-connection and user limitations. As a first step we introduce TapBack: back-of-device taps to control a dialled-up, telephone-network-based voice service. We show how these *audio gestures* might be recognised over a standard telephone connection, via users' existing low-end devices. Further, in a longitudinal deployment, the techniques were made available on a live voice service used by rural Indian farmers. Data from the study illustrates the desire by users to adopt the approach and its potential extensions.

Author Keywords

Developing regions, mobile HCI, audio gestures, back-of-device interaction, spoken web.

ACM Classification Keywords

H.5.2 [User Interfaces]: Input devices and strategies; Interaction styles; H.5.1 [Multimedia Info. Systems]: Audio I/O.

General Terms

Design, Experimentation, Human Factors.

INTRODUCTION

For hundreds of millions of people in developing, rural regions, the mobile phone is the primary – if not only – interactive technology available. Already pervasively used for calling, these devices are increasingly set to become access terminals for remote information services.

Unlike the state-of-the-art, future-looking devices often studied by HCI researchers, though, a large proportion of these mobiles are likely to remain relatively dumb-phones with only a low proportion being routinely served by a data connection. Furthermore, the users themselves add additional challenges to the goal of universal access: many have a low level of textual literacy, and their prior exposure to computing technology is often very limited.

To meet these challenges, a class of network-level audio-based services have been proposed. These often combine automatic speech recognition (ASR) and touch tone dialling (DTMF) to allow people to create and browse through spoken content. The Spoken Web [4], for example, is a collection of interconnected *voice sites*. These interactive audio applications provide content on topics such as farming or health information over the public telecom network. Individual voice sites are accessed using any type of phone by dialling unique telephone numbers (analogous to URLs).

Although both ASR and DTMF allow a level of control and interaction with audio content, we believe there is still much work to be done in terms of improving the expressiveness and range of interactions. As a first step towards richer mobile voice interfaces, we present TapBack: an extended interaction method for voice sites that aims to allow callers to smoothly navigate through and control the content they are listening to without having to unnecessarily interrupt its playback. Our approach uses simple back-of-device interactions – *audio gestures* – on the phones users already own.

While there has been previous research on back-of-device and non-speech natural audio input (e.g. [5, 6]), this has involved state-of-the-art custom-built devices, and users with high levels of literacy and technology experience. In contrast, the majority of our target audience use relatively low-end mobile phones, so we have focused on providing these additional interaction features without requiring users to own a specialised device. The users themselves are also from very different backgrounds to those often studied by other researchers, bringing additional insights and challenges.

The contribution here, then, is an exploration of ways that impoverished platforms and their users can be afforded the sorts of advanced interactions being imagined for people living in the 'developed' world.

BACKGROUND

ASR & DTMF Interaction

Automatic speech recognition promises intuitive, low cognitive load interaction with audio content, with the benefit that no base level of literacy or numeracy is required. However, the pauses or cues that are needed to prompt speech input and detection can easily upset the interaction flow, especially for short inputs such as 'yes' or 'no' [7].

DTMF key tones are quick to enter on keypads, designed to be unambiguous when recognising, and offer many possible input sequences. However, because the tones generated are echoed in the phone speaker (confirming input, but drowning out incoming audio), interactions and responses are often fragmented, unlike in our design. A further key issue with DTMF is that it is often necessary for the caller to take the phone away from their ear to see the keypad and respond to any input cues. In our design we have concentrated on removing this disruption – instead we allow callers to interact on the back of their device during the normal call flow.

Back-of-Device Interaction

As mobile devices have continued to offer more features in increasingly-compact form factors, researchers have recognised the need for interactions beyond the screen and keypad. This has culminated, recently, in touch-based back-of-device interaction with almost no need for a device at all [1]. However, although these designs offer touch interaction anywhere, they also require users to own specialised hardware. We believe it is possible to offer a subset of these input methods to users who might not have the most modern devices.

Li et al. [5] noted the problems that can result when callers attempt to use a phone's keypad without taking the device away from their ear, addressing these issues by using a modified keypad on the back of a phone with audio cues to assist. However, this was aimed at allowing use of the phone's functions during a call, unlike our approach, which uses back-of-device interaction to control the call itself.

Tap and Scratch Interaction

We build upon previous research into interaction that appropriates a device's surface as an input channel. Murray-Smith et al. [6] used a custom-built sensor pack shell with exterior textures that produced distinct sounds when scratched. A microphone inside the device captured the sounds, allowing complex scratches to be recognised as distinct commands. Our approach, although not capable of the same diversity in inputs, affords similar interaction on a normal phone.

Harrison and Hudson [3] built on this work to allow scratches and taps to be used as inputs on any solid surface, capturing sounds using a modified stethoscope. They found that inputs were reliably recognised by a fast, lightweight recognition engine – an approach we adopt in our system.

Mobile possibilities for these interactions have recently been demonstrated as a commercial prototype[1] that can detect tapping locally on a dumb-phone. In contrast with these types of approaches, however, TapBack also separates the source of the audio gestures (the handset) and the system that interprets them (a server accessed over a normal telephone call).

[1] *TouchDevice* – www.inputdynamics.com

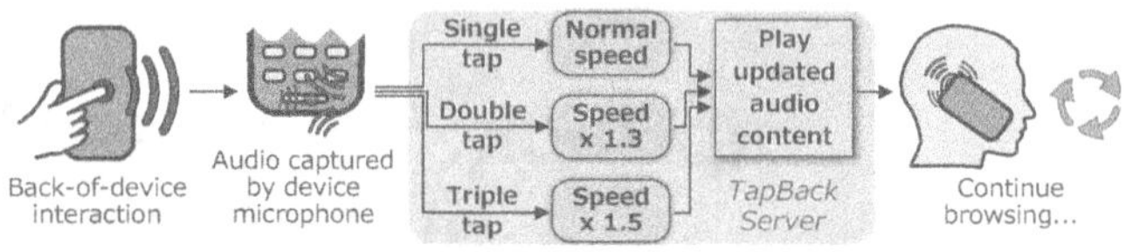

Figure 1. TapBack: Audio gestures are generated by the caller locally on the back of their handset, but analysed remotely (shaded region).

THE TAPBACK SYSTEM

The TapBack system allows callers a richer experience with interactive voice sites by enabling *audio gestures* to be used at any time during a call. By using the back of users' phones as an input surface while a call is in progress, we remove the interruptions of ASR/DTMF and allow users to keep the phone by their ear throughout the call. Unlike previous back-of-device methods, we use the phone's inbuilt microphone to pick up the sounds generated on the back of its case. These sounds are loud enough to be transferred to the other party in the call, but, unlike DTMF tones, are not so loud on the caller's end that they drown out the audio being played.

For a simple user introduction to audio gestures we chose to apply tapping recognition to the control of audio playback speed. Previous voice site analyses [2] have shown that callers would appreciate finer control of playback, so this was a natural application for our system. In our implementation, when users tap two or three times, the time compression is 25% and 35%, respectively, while still retaining intelligibility. Tapping once returns playback to its normal speed.

Implementation

The TapBack system is installed on a remote server, monitoring low-level network packets to track incoming phone calls to individual voice sites. When a call is established, real-time audio capturing, decoding and analysis is initialised. The audio is first filtered to remove frequencies below 3KHz, greatly reducing the problem of ambient noise. The stream is then windowed using a 512-sample Hamming window with an overlap of $\frac{7}{8}$. Tap recognition itself is very unsophisticated, simply searching each window for short, high-intensity, high-frequency sounds. Detected tap events are then fed to a higher-level audio gesture classifier which uses timeouts and basic heuristics to classify each tap type.

When an audio gesture is found, the system sends a command to the Spoken Web server, which adjusts the voice site playback speed in response to the request. Users are also free to control the speed of playback by using DTMF inputs instead of taps. In this case, keys 4, 5 and 6 correspond to single, double and triple taps, respectively.

EVALUATION

The TapBack system was evaluated in three ways, focusing primarily on the viability of the approach, rather than the sophistication of the recogniser. Recognition accuracy was measured and refined using a test voice site. A live deployment of the system over an extended period was used to assess the usefulness and usability of the approach. Finally, we explored alternative audio gestures with participants to understand the potential for extending such techniques.

RECOGNITION ACCURACY TEST

We conducted a user study to measure and improve the recogniser's accuracy over a standard telephone connection. 18 users of an existing, popular farming information voice site based in a rural region in India were recruited (see [7] for more detailed user population demographics). To ensure a cross-section of user expertise, participants included people who access the voice site very regularly and also those who are only casual users. All users were male, and the average age was 32. The set of phones used by the participants consisted of 14 different (low-end) handset types produced by four manufacturers. All participants had already used the DTMF speed control methods detailed in [2].

Each participant was called by phone to explain the study method and the concept of audio gestures. The calls were made to participants when they were at locations from which they usually interact with the voice site services. The participant was then connected to a test voice site, which asked them to tap the back of the phone while holding it to their ear, in response to four sets of cues. Each cue set asked users to tap once; twice; then, three times. Each participant, therefore, provided 12 tap commands.

Recognition rates were: 1-tap: 93%; 2-tap: 78%; and, 3-tap: 56%. High accuracy rates for single and double taps were encouraging given: the minimal explanation of the concept to users; this form of interaction with a service was entirely novel in users' experience; a diverse set of low-end phones were involved; the audio channel was of standard telephone quality; and, the study was in a live, not laboratory setting.

A large proportion of the errors in recognition were due to participants tapping slower than the recogniser expected. This led to 2-taps being recognised as 1+1 taps (accounting for 50% of the 2-tap errors) and 3-taps being recognised as 1+2, 2+1 or 1+1+1 taps (60% of 3-tap errors). To deal with these errors, the tap classifier was modified to employ simple correction heuristics so that, for example, a 2-tap shortly followed by a 1-tap was interpreted as a 3-tap instruction. The remaining errors were caused by taps not being distinct enough for the recogniser to extract from the input.

DEPLOYMENT

The TapBack system was made available on a live farming information voice site [7]. This exploratory study aimed at measuring the adoption of audio gestures by logging any tap interactions and responses during normal use of the service.

Method

The system was deployed for 12 days, during which any of the 110 registered active users could call at any time. These users are geographically dispersed over a wide area of India, and are all farmers living in rural settings. When calling, users were given a brief automated introduction to the new method that explained how they could tap the back of their phone to control the playback speed. The system logged call details and any input actions (both tap-based and DTMF).

We supplemented this data by conducting detailed telephone interviews with 15 users. Ten of these were selected at random from the set of those who had used TapBack during the deployment period; the remaining five were randomly selected from callers who did not attempt to use the tap interaction. The average age of participants was 31, and all except one were male. During the interviews these users were asked about their reactions to the approach; how usable it was; and, any issues they had encountered in its use. Interviews were conducted in the participants' native language (Gujarati).

Results

286 calls to the voice site were recorded over the study period, from 52 unique callers. 1293 tap interactions were recorded in total. 36 callers used the TapBack feature (166 calls; 7.8 taps per call, on average).

Of the 36 participants that used tap interaction, 25 used the feature on more than one call. Two others called more than once but only used tap interaction on their first call; the remaining 9 TapBack users called only once over the study period. The 16 participants who did not use tap interactions did not use DTMF for speed control, either.

Tap interactions consisted of 772 single, 301 double, and 220 triple taps. Few of the callers that wanted to control the speed of the call used the DTMF method – 52 speed control DTMF events were recorded in total.

Participant Interviews

Considering first the ten callers who had used the TapBack feature. Of these, the majority were positive in their comments about the approach. Benefits mentioned ranged from those related to utility to those concerning the less-tangible 'user experience'. Several respondents commented on the tapping being easier to use and quicker than DTMF. Another interviewee talked of the 'fun' of the new interaction. Interestingly, one participant said, *"This is like having a touch-screen, this is a modern thing to use – it's cool."*

Negative comments from these 10 adopters included the predictable, such as frustration when a tap-event was not recognised: one respondent said he would always use buttons because, *"they always work – end of story."* However, there were also issues related to the use-context. Two interviewees worried about using the system regularly as the tapping, to their mind, might damage the phone. For one of these interviewees this was particularly worrying as they often lent their phone to others to use (a practice quite common in rural areas). Another respondent said they tended to listen to the service with a group of people using the speakerphone.

There were two explanations for the non-use of the approach by the five other interviewees. For some, their environments (as witnessed during telephone interviews) were too noisy;

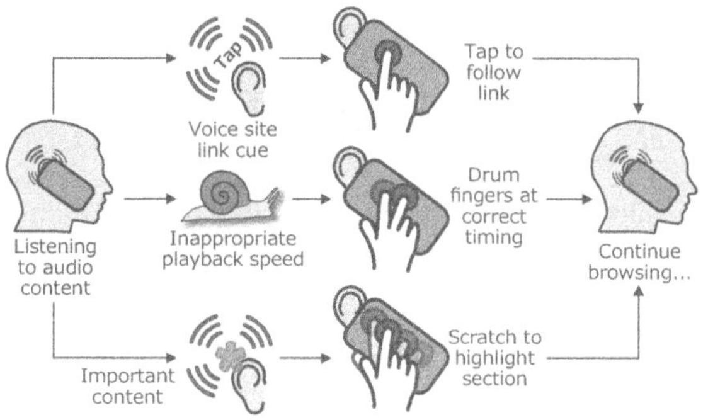

Figure 2. Potential future usage scenarios for audio gestures.

and, for others, they had not understood the new feature as explained by the voice site after call connection.

Discussion

The logged data provides evidence that callers are willing to adopt the tapping method, with the majority of callers using the approach. It should also be noted that the functions controlled by TapBack – speeding and slowing the audio – are optional: users are able to listen to and navigate through content without employing them. We would expect, then, that some calls during the study would not show tap interaction. Furthermore, 93% of callers who used TapBack during their first call also used it again in their subsequent calls. Callers that used TapBack did so several times in each call.

The comments about the system's utility value are, of course, encouraging, especially when considering the accuracy of our simple recogniser. However, of more note, perhaps, are the responses relating to the user experience – a fun, 'modern' interaction is something that is not usually associated with the low-end devices these users have access to. The negative comments are spurs to improve the recognition engine and explanation of its use. The social issues raised suggest extensions to our approach – we will need to ensure the tap-models used are tuned not just to individual phone numbers but the set of users that might use that phone; and, in speaker-mode use, we might be able to consider a wider set of audio gestures as suggested in [3].

ALTERNATIVE AUDIO GESTURES

In order to further understand the needs of the target users, we conducted a study to gather more potential audio gestures and corresponding actions. The 15 participants questioned during the deployment were also asked to suggest additional back-of-device interactions they were comfortable with, and to discuss what actions they felt these gestures might initiate.

The majority of interviewees identified the value of two single-handed, back-of-phone interactions: drumming fingers and scratching. Many users suggested finger-clicking (using the non-phone holding hand). Most users also raised the possibility of making non-verbal utterances – e.g., *"I could make the noise I make when shooing away cows."*

Interviewees found it hard to make mappings from their gestures to controls; unlike many participants, who have extensive computer experience, these respondents had no notion of interface metaphors. However, one commented on the use of drumming to skip through voice content; and many others wanted a fast way to jump to particular sections of the audio. Fig. 2 shows how we might widen the set of audio gestures in response to the studies.

CONCLUSIONS

We have introduced TapBack to illustrate the potential of audio gestures to complement voice-based interaction over the phone. While the technique might appear unsophisticated or less exciting compared to the methods proposed for high-end mobiles, we argue that it is far more likely to have impact in the sorts of context that concern us.

Of course, there is much work still to be done to improve our lightweight recogniser. Future work could focus on refinements to the recognition algorithms to improve accuracy. Alternatively, increased robustness might be achieved by simplifying the gesture set to allow only single taps. In the current speed control application, this could be applied as a toggle between options so each individual tap would change playback to the next speed preset.

We have shown how tapping can be used as input by rural Indian farmers via their basic mobile handsets. Further, these users' responses to the method, along with their suggestions for additional gestures, indicate the viability of the approach for groups of people with very low exposure to computing.

ACKNOWLEDGEMENTS

This work was supported by IBM Research India, IBM Faculty Award (Matt Jones) and EPSRC project EP/H042857/1.

REFERENCES

1. P. Baudisch and G. Chu. Back-of-device interaction allows creating very small touch devices. In *Proc. CHI '09*, pages 1923–1932. ACM, 2009.
2. K. A. Dhanesha, N. Rajput, and K. Srivastava. User driven audio content navigation for spoken web. In *Proc. Multimedia '10*, pages 1071–1074. ACM, 2010.
3. C. Harrison and S. E. Hudson. Scratch input: creating large, inexpensive, unpowered and mobile finger input surfaces. In *Proc. UIST '08*, pages 205–208. ACM, 2008.
4. A. Kumar, N. Rajput, D. Chakraborty, S. K. Agarwal, and A. A. Nanavati. WWTW: the world wide telecom web. In *Proc. NSDR '07: Workshop on Networked Systems for Developing Regions*, pages 1–6. ACM, 2007.
5. K. A. Li, P. Baudisch, and K. Hinckley. Blindsight: eyes-free access to mobile phones. In *Proc. CHI '08*, pages 1389–1398. ACM, 2008.
6. R. Murray-Smith, J. Williamson, S. Hughes, and T. Quaade. Stane: synthesized surfaces for tactile input. In *Proc. CHI '08*, pages 1299–1302. ACM, 2008.
7. N. Patel, D. Chittamuru, A. Jain, P. Dave, and T. S. Parikh. Avaaj Otalo: a field study of an interactive voice forum for small farmers in rural india. In *Proc. CHI '10*, pages 733–742. ACM, 2010.

"ClearPlate" for Capturing Printed Information: A Scanner and Viewfinder in One Optical Unit

Atsuhiko Maeda[1], Kenji Hara[2], Minoru Kobayashi[1] and Masanobu Abe[3]
[1]NTT Cyber Solutions Laboratories, NTT Corporation, Yokosuka-shi, Kanagawa, Japan
[2]NTT Communications Corporation, Minato-ku, Tokyo, Japan
[3]Okayama University, Okayama-shi, Okayama, Japan
maeda.atsuhiko@lab.ntt.co.jp, kenji.hara@ntt.com, minoru@acm.org, abe@cs.okayama-u.ac.jp

ABSTRACT
As it is becoming more common for various handheld devices to be equipped with a camera, applications that use image recognition are increasing. Therefore, improving the usability of these devices by enhancing their image capture characteristics is becoming more important. We present ClearPlate – a new optical unit for image capture. It has a physically transparent viewfinder through which the user can observe the target directly without offset; the framed image is captured by the built-in camera. We also present a user study that evaluates ClearPlate performance in the 2D barcode acquisition task. Results show that ClearPlate significantly outperforms the camera-phone-based approach with regard to 2D barcode acquisition.

Author Keywords
Image recognition, camera, target acquisition, 2D barcode, see-through interface, paper interface.

ACM Classification Keywords
H5.m. Information interfaces and presentation (e.g., HCI): Miscellaneous.

General Terms
Design, Experimentation, Human Factors.

INTRODUCTION
A recent trend is to add cameras to a wide variety of handheld devices such as mobile phones, portable game machines, and audio players. This functionality has stimulated the emergence of applications based on image recognition. For example, users can access web sites via the recognition of printed 2D barcodes, look up a printed word in an electronic dictionary via word recognition, access the online information of a real-world object via template matching, and create panoramic images by image mosaicing software [8]. Therefore, improving the usability of these devices by enhancing their image capture characteristics is becoming more important. Conventionally, these images are captured by a camera and confirmed by viewing an electronic display. However, the resulting user interface has the following problems.

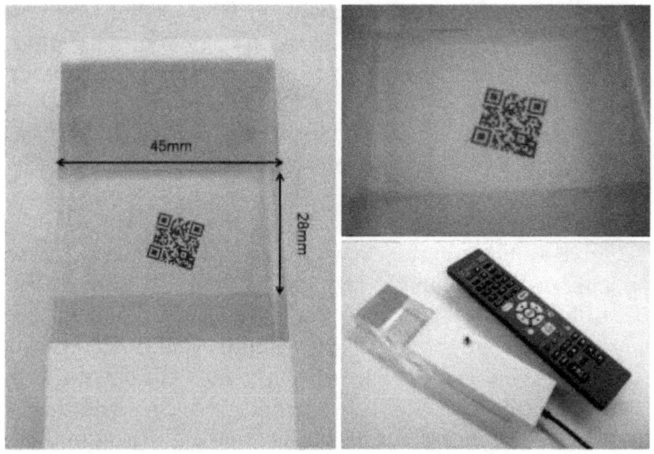

Figure 1. ClearPlate over a QR code (left) and the internal camera image (upper right). Basically what the user sees (left) is what the camera captures (upper right). The lower right is an external view (185 x 45 x 22 mm).

Parallax: The user experiences parallax between the view through the display and the direct observation. When changing from the direct observation to the observation via the display [6], the user may occlude the required information by hands or the device.

Delay: Delay is introduced by the display update rate when the target is observed through the electronic display rather than directly. This delay degrades interface usability [7].

Instability: The device is hand-held and must be positioned in three dimensions. Extra physical and mental burdens are created in operating the device [6].

To solve all these problems, we propose ClearPlate – a new optical unit for an image capture device. It has a transparent viewfinder through which the user can observe the target directly without lag and can capture the framed image by the built-in camera.

RELATED WORK
Given the parallax that exists between the view through the display and direct observation, the user may not be able to direct the device to the target correctly. If the location of the target is known to the device before the target is on the

display, advance cues to the location of the target, like techniques utilizing Halo [1], can significantly improve targeting performance. However, in many cases, the device does not know the location of the target in advance.

Laser sighting is used in some business-oriented 2D-barcode readers. This approach is effective in eliminating the problems caused by display lag and parallax because the user can position the camera without using the display. However, it fails to reduce the physical and mental burdens created in hand-holding the device in three dimensions.

It is troublesome for the user to stabilize the device in three dimensions and move the camera in front of the target in order to achieve successful image recognition. Therefore, software to correct perspective or blurred images has been proposed [2, 5]. However, these problems are difficult to solve with just image processing. Our proposal, in contrast, adopts a novel hardware-based approach.

CLEARPLATE

To solve all these problems, we propose ClearPlate – a new optical unit for image capture. Figure 1 shows the ClearPlate prototype, which has a transparent viewfinder that provides an optical light path to an image sensor (camera). As a result, when the user lays ClearPlate over the target (the left side of Figure 1), a well-focused and almost distortion-free image is automatically acquired by the camera (the upper right of Figure 1). ClearPlate prevents the user from experiencing parallax between the view through the viewfinder and the direct observation, eliminates the display lag, and eases the physical and mental burdens created by capturing the image.

Mechanism

ClearPlate is made of acrylic and the camera is set on the side. However, in an ordinary flat acrylic block, see Figure 2, though the target can be observed from the upper side (user's view yielded by ray (1)), it cannot be observed from the camera, ray (2). The reason for this is that when light reaches the acrylic/air boundary, all of it is reflected if the angle of incidence is greater than the critical angle (42.2 degrees for this setup) relative to the normal to the boundary. This phenomenon is known as total internal reflection. Actually, ray (2) traveling to the camera in Figure 2 touches boundary *BC* at more than the critical angle.

To solve the above problem, we add a very small diagonal air gap *BD* to the optical paths (see Figure 3). The air gap modifies the optical path so that the camera (ray 2) can observe the target simultaneously with the user (ray 1). The air gap folds ray 2 in block *BCD* so that light from the image surface reaches the camera.

In Figure 3, there are two internal reflections between *BD* and *BC*. While it is possible to increase the frequency of internal reflection, and use even sharper angles, this would

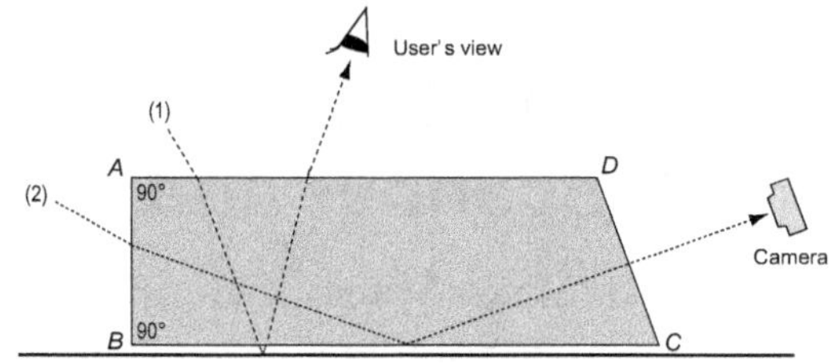

Figure 2. Optical light paths in a solid acrylic plate. Though the target can be observed from the upper side (user's view), it cannot be observed by the camera.

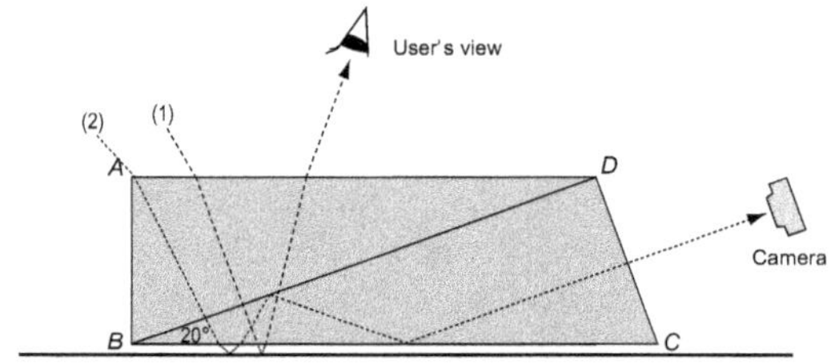

Figure 3. Optical light paths in ClearPlate. Diagonal air gap *BD* modifies the optical path so that the camera can observe the target simultaneously with the user.

increase block length. If the environmental lighting is not sufficient, it is possible to illuminate the target's surface by setting LEDs on the same face as the camera.

Limitation

We note that what the user sees through the viewfinder corresponds exactly with what the camera captures only when ClearPlate is laid on top of a flat surface. Therefore, ClearPlate is not so suitable for capturing 3D objects or far surfaces. As shown in Figure 4, as the target moves away from ClearPlate, the parallax between what the user sees and what the camera captures increases. The reason for this is that the user and the camera see the target via rays from slightly different directions unlike a single lens reflex camera, whose viewfinder and film (image sensor) get the same image.

Prototype

We developed the first ClearPlate prototype as a PC peripheral. It consists of a CMOS camera with a USB interface. The external size is 185 x 45 x 22 mm as shown in the lower right of Figure 1. It is possible to use the prototype by running image processing software on a PC.

The lower acrylic block, *BCD*, of the prototype is a 20-45-115-degree triangle. As a result, the camera can capture a 45 mm x 28 mm rectangle. Both acrylic blocks were set in an enclosure with a 2 mm thick transparent bottom plate. Because the air gap is effective regardless of how thin it is, the prototype simply places the upper and lower blocks in contact with each other, they are not bonded. The polishing level of the blocks is normal. Actually, after cutting the blocks, we polished them by hand using sandpaper and then a compound.

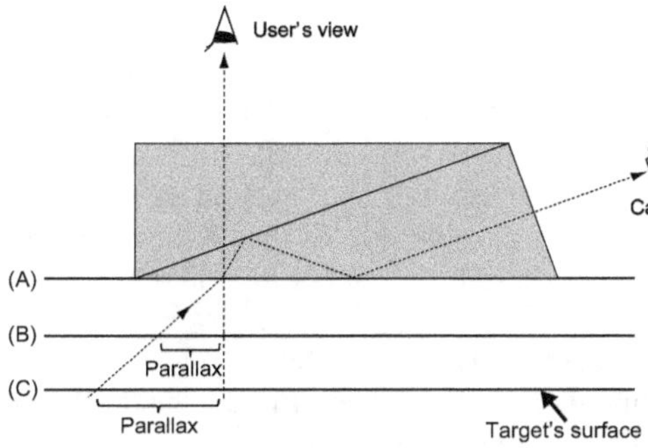

Figure 4. As the target moves away from (A) to (C), the parallax between what the user sees and what the camera captures increases.

Device examples equipped with ClearPlate

The prototype has only a camera, and so the results of image recognition are output on the support PC. ClearPlate makes it easy to scan name cards or handwritten memos by sliding operation. Because ClearPlate can capture an almost perspective-free image of the target as seen in the upper right of Figure 1, it is possible to get an easy-to-read image mosaic by using the image mosaicing technique [8].

The left of Figure 5 shows an electronic dictionary based on ClearPlate with a separate electronic display. The prototype has depth enough to cover one line height in books. As shown in the right of Figure 5, it is possible to overlay a see-through electronic display [3] on ClearPlate. This may improve the usability of augmented reality systems, which overlay digital information on real-world targets.

EVALUATION

Design

We evaluated whether ClearPlate facilitated the capture task. We used a camera phone as the baseline and QR codes as the targets. Within-subject design was used. The independent variables were reader type *RT* (camera phone, ClearPlate), distance from the starting point to the target *D* (150, 200, 250, 300 mm), and width of the target *W* (10, 12.5, 15, 17.5, 20 mm). The dependent variables were *operation time* and *error rate*. Eighteen subjects (8 male, 10 female) from a temporary staffing agency were recruited. Ages ranged from 24 to 34 years.

Apparatus

As the baseline, we used a commercial camera phone (NTT docomo N705i), which is popular in Japan; the camera is mounted near the hinge. The internal QR decoder with automatic code recognition used a 37 x 36 mm window in the display area, and its refresh rate was 5 FPS. The decoder has a perspective invariant function, which can read the QR codes used in this experiment at 30 degrees to the target's surface when the device is stable.

In the ClearPlate prototype, the viewfinder size was 45 x 28 mm (mean dimension is 36.5 mm matching that of the baseline). The camera's horizontal angle of view was 50

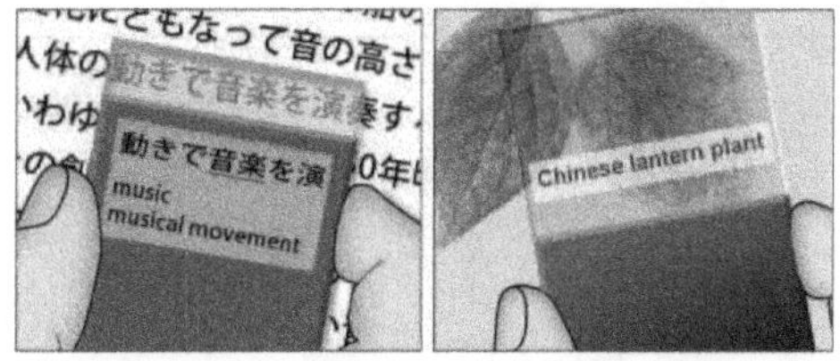

Figure 5. Envisioned device examples with a separate display (left) and an overlaid see-through display (right).

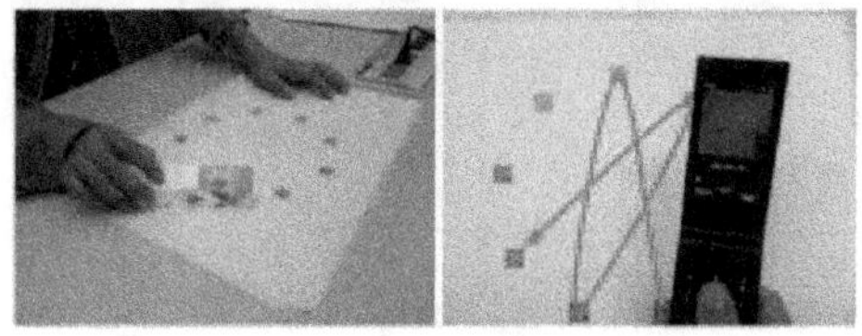

Figure 6. Cyclical target acquisition task with ClearPlate (left) and camera phone (right).

degrees matching that of the baseline. For fair comparison, we created a system that matched the conversion speed of the internal QR decoder of the baseline. However, automatic code recognition was unavailable due to system limitations, and the subjects had to push the recognition button.

Task

The experiments were carried out following the cyclical multi-direction pointing task of ISO 9241-9 [4]. Participants sat on a chair to read the targets on the desk, as shown in Figure 6. We prepared 20 papers (453 mm x 345 mm) on which nine numbered QR codes were printed in a circle; each paper replicated one of the *D* x *W* conditions. Given that the participant read the targets in numerical order, the next item was always opposite and slightly clockwise from the selected one (see the right of Figure 6). Participants were randomly divided into 2 groups of 9 each, with one group using ClearPlate first, and the other group using the camera phone first. Each participant was asked to complete 18 selections in each *D* x *W* condition (*i.e.*, 9 selections x 2 rounds). As practice, they also performed selections on three random *D* x *W* conditions using each reader before starting the actual reader trials. The presentation order of *D* x *W* conditions was randomized. The experiment yielded 12960 data points (18 participants x (2 x 4 x 5) conditions x 9 selections x 2 rounds). Sound effects were used as the signals of starting and reading. The time taken and error were automatically measured by the software in each reader.

Result

Figure 7 shows the mean operation time for reader type, distance, and width. We performed a within-subjects analysis of variance (ANOVA), the main significant effect was found for each *RT* ($F_{1,17}$=97.306, $p<0.001$), *D* ($F_{3,51}$=26.611, $p<0.001$), *W* ($F_{4,68}$=5.744, $p<0.001$), the interaction of *RT* x *W* ($F_{4,68}$=31.282, $p<0.001$), and the interaction of *RT* x *D* x *W* ($F_{12,204}$=2.013, $p<0.05$) on operation time. Shaffer's multiple comparison test showed

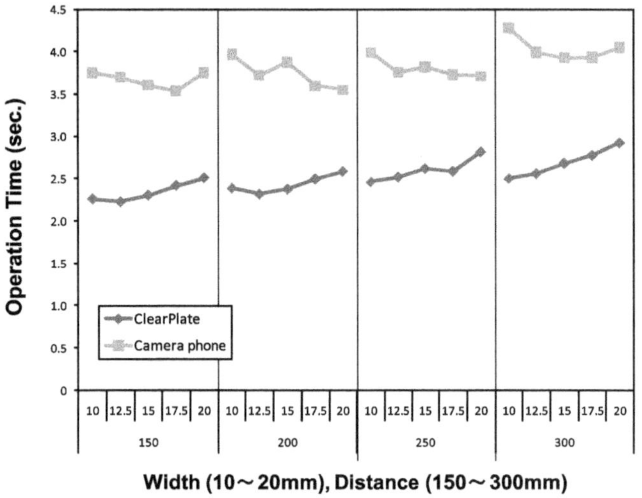

Figure 7. Operation time for reader type, distance, and width. For each of the 20 combinations, ClearPlate was significantly faster, all at the p<0.00001 level.

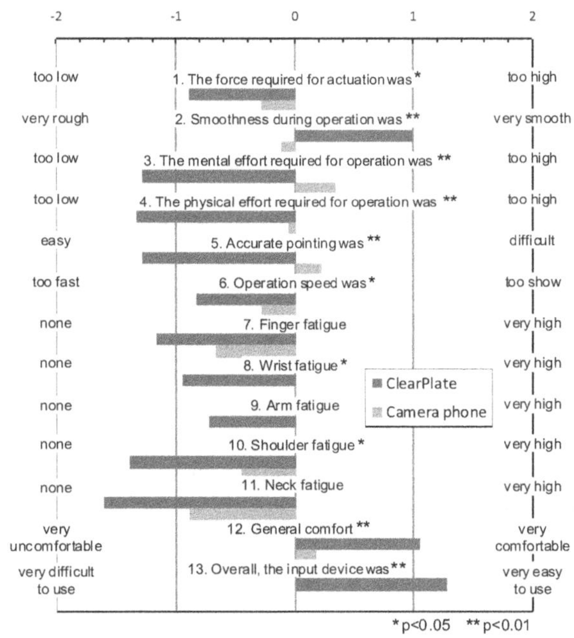

Figure 8. Subjective judgments. ClearPlate was significantly better than the camera phone in 10 of 13 items.

that for each of the 20 conditions, ClearPlate was significantly faster, all at the $p<0.00001$ level.

As errors, we classified the cases wherein a subject read a QR code that wasn't the next target, and the cases where, using ClearPlate, the subject pushed the recognition button when the target wasn't in the capture area. As a result, *error rate* was found to be not significantly impacted by *reader type*. Total *error rate* for the camera phone was 0.22%, and for ClearPlate, error in order was zero, and error in capture offset was 0.21%.

Figure 8 shows the results of subjective judgments based on questionnaires following ISO9241-9 [4]. Wilcoxon rank-sum tests showed that ClearPlate was significantly better than the camera phone in 10 of 13 items. From the 12th and the 13th questionnaires, we found that ClearPlate was more comfortable and easier-to-use for all participants; we asked them for their reasons. The responses indicated the advantages of non-parallax (14 of the 18 participants), rapid response (5), and stability in operating the device (9).

DISCUSSION AND CONCLUSION

Our experiments found that ClearPlate is faster than camera phones with no significant difference in error rate while automatic recognition was unavailable due to system limitation in ClearPlate, and the perspective invariant function of the decoder used in the experiment might have enhanced the usability of the camera phone. In addition, most participants judged that ClearPlate was better than the camera phone in 10 of 13 items. Therefore, we can conclude that ClearPlate outperforms camera phones in reading targets on paper. In this experiment, QR codes were used as the targets. Even if the targets are texts or pictures, the proposed technique is expected to yield the same results.

In the future, we plan to miniaturize ClearPlate and integrate it with see-through electronic display technologies such as [3] or more sophisticated image processing algorithms for capturing marker-less 2D content like text, pictures, and maps.

REFERENCES

1. Baudisch, P. and Rosenholtz, R. Halo: a technique for visualizing off-screen objects. In *Proc. CHI 2003*, ACM Press (2003), 481-488.
2. Chu, C., Yang, D., and Chen, M. Image stabilization for 2D barcode in handheld devices. In *Proc. MM 2007*, ACM Press (2007), 697-706.
3. http://abcnews.go.com/Technology/CES/samsung-demos-laptop-screen/story?id=9517223
4. International Organization for Standardization. *Ergonomic requirements for office work with visual display terminals (VDTs) - Requirements for non-keyboard input devices.* ISO/IEC 9241-9, 2000.
5. Ohbuchi, E., Hanaizumi, H., and Hock, L. A. Barcode readers using the camera device in mobile phones. In *Proc. CW 2004*, IEEE (2004), 260-265.
6. Rohs, M. and Oulasvirta, A. Target acquisition with camera phones when used as magic lenses. In *Proc. CHI 2008,* ACM Press (2008), 1409-1418.
7. Ware, C. and Balakrishnan, R. Reaching for objects in VR displays: lag and frame rate. *ACM Trans. Comput.-Hum. Interact.* 1, 4 (1994), 331-356.
8. Whichello, A.P., and Hong Yan. Document image mosaicing. In *Proc. ICPR 1998*, IEEE (1998), 1081-1083.

Dips and Ceilings: Understanding and Supporting Transitions to Expertise in User Interfaces

Joey Scarr[1], Andy Cockburn[1], Carl Gutwin[2], Philip Quinn[1]
[1]Computer Science, University of Canterbury, Christchurch, New Zealand,
{joey, andy}@cosc.canterbury.ac.nz, philip.quinn@canterbury.ac.nz
[2]Computer Science, University of Saskatchewan, Saskatoon, Canada, gutwin@cs.usask.ca

ABSTRACT
Interface guidelines encourage designers to include shortcut mechanisms that enable high levels of expert performance, but prior research has demonstrated that few users switch to using them. To help understand how interfaces can better support a transition to expert performance we develop a framework of the interface and human factors influencing expertise development. We then present a system called Blur that addresses three main problems in promoting the transition: prompting an initial switch to expert techniques, minimising the performance dip arising from the switch, and enabling a high performance ceiling. Blur observes the user's interaction with unaltered desktop applications and uses *calm notification* to support learning and promote awareness of an alternative *hot command* interface. An empirical study validates Blur's design, showing that users make an early and sustained switch to hot commands, and that doing so improves their performance and satisfaction.

Author Keywords
Expertise, novice-to-expert transition, command interfaces.

ACM Classification Keywords
H5.2. [User Interfaces]: Interaction Styles.

General Terms
Human Factors, Experimentation.

INTRODUCTION
Windows, Icons, Menus, Pointer (WIMP) interfaces mediate most communication between humans and computers. Their success is partly due to their natural support for novice users – the phrase 'see and point versus learn and remember' [38] describes how novices benefit from using visual search for salient controls, rather than retrieving command names from memory or manuals.

However, the very mechanisms that make WIMPs effective for novices fail to support users as they become more experienced, and they can trap users in a 'beginner mode' of interaction that has a low performance ceiling. The richness and power of human perception, cognition, and motor action is then constrained to relatively slow and laborious action. Conversely, interfaces designed for experts (e.g., keyboard shortcuts or command-lines) allow high performance ceilings, but only after extensive training.

Although it is clear that these expert interfaces *can* provide performance advantages [34], their success in practice has been limited, and several researchers have reported that users fail to switch to expert interface methods (e.g., [3, 7, 27]). Furthermore, while there has been considerable research into interfaces for either novices or experts, there has been relatively little on the transition to expertise.

We therefore form a framework encapsulating the factors influencing expertise development, with a focus on those affecting the switch to expert interface mechanisms. These factors include lack of knowledge about the availability or the performance benefits of the alternative UI; concern about the time or effort required to make the switch; the prevalence of satisficing [40], in which 'good enough' strategies are maintained; and fears about the drop in performance that can occur because the user must 'start from scratch' with the new interface. This drop in performance (called 'the dip') is particularly important, because it can deter switching in the first place, but also because it negatively affects the user's first impressions. The framework suggests that any system attempting to support a switch to expert interface mechanisms should have three goals: first, maximize the likelihood that the user will initiate a switch to the expert modality; second, minimize the cost of doing so; and third, enable a high performance ceiling to rapidly reward use.

To investigate supporting these goals, we have developed a new system (called *Blur*) that uses *calm notification* and *hot commands* to support a transition from WIMP interaction to a more efficient command-based interface. Through calm notifications, Blur provides an immediate and bidirectional translation between WIMP and command line (CLI) methods – WIMP inputs are immediately displayed as equivalent CLI outputs, promoting learning and awareness of the CLI. Through the hot commands mechanism, Blur enables CLI control of the interface without altering the underlying GUI, thereby supporting gradual exploration of the CLI without requiring users to completely abandon use of familiar WIMP interaction.

We carried out a study using repetitive tasks in PowerPoint to see how well Blur supports users' transition to the expert CLI. Results showed that Blur supported users' transition to the expert interface much better than standard shortcut keys – all 20 participants switched to Blur within the first three trials, whereas none switched to built-in Alt-shortcuts. The study also showed that Blur's performance dip was small and that its ultimate efficiency was faster than the WIMP and shortcut interfaces.

Blur demonstrates a general and reproducible strategy for supporting users' transition from a WIMP interface to a CLI-style interface. Blur provides both a mechanism for learning and promoting the expert interface while the user carries out WIMP actions, and a means for allowing gradual exploration and adoption of the higher-performance CLI interaction. Specifically, we make three contributions on expertise development:

- A framework of issues influencing expertise development within and across interface mechanisms.
- Design of Blur, which promotes the transition to expert interaction through calm notification and hot commands.
- Empirical evidence demonstrating Blur's success.

FRAMEWORK & REVIEW OF INTERFACE EXPERTISE

Learnability is consistently identified as a critical component of usability [13, 31, 37], but as Grossman *et al.* [18] observe, there is little agreement over how it can be defined or measured. Grossman *et al.* [18] provide a comprehensive review of definitions, metrics, and methodologies for assessing learnability, and they suggest a new protocol for measuring it. However, evaluation methodologies are applied after an interface has been designed, and current best-practice guidelines for supporting expertise are often high level generalisations, such as 'provide shortcuts' [31] that provide little direct guidance or insight into underlying design issues.

This section presents a framework of the interface and human factors influencing expertise development. Our focus is on issues of how interfaces can support users' transition to expertise, rather than on fundamental issues in human skill acquisition and strategic thinking; see [1] for a review of human skill acquisition and [3] for an analysis of the development of expert interaction strategies.

Intramodal and Intermodal expertise development

The framework adapts Newell and Rosenbloom's [30] power law of practice, using it as a qualitative guideline for characterisation, rather than a mathematical model. We use the power curve shown on the left side of Figure 1 to characterise *intramodal* expertise development: how user performance improves over time with a *single* interaction modality, subdividing the curve into three segments for *initial performance*, *extended learnability*, and *ultimate performance*. These three stages are suggestive of Anderson's [1] model of skill acquisition, which identifies *cognitive*, *associative*, and *autonomous* stages in which initial models are formed, followed by establishment of associations between concepts, finally leading to the development of autonomous skills.

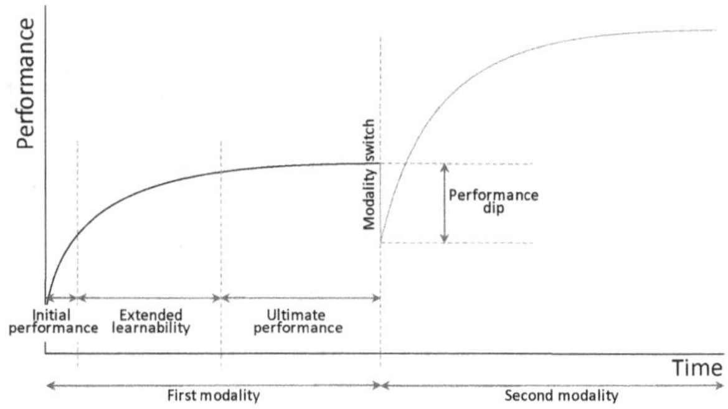

Figure 1. Performance curves characterising intra and intermodal performance improvement. Note the postulated performance dip when switching modalities.

Many interfaces, however, support more than one interaction mode for the same task. For our purposes modes are distinguished by the interaction mechanics used to control the interface. For example, menu items can be selected by direct clicking with the mouse, or by activating their associated hotkeys using the keyboard; similarly, files and file hierarchies can be manipulated via direct manipulation (e.g. using Windows Explorer or the Desktop) or through command line alternatives (such as the file path entry or a command window).

Our framework characterises *intermodal* expertise development by combining two power law curves (shown on the left and right sides of Figure 1). This characterisation postulates that users are likely to suffer a performance dip when switching to a new modality, even if it offers a higher ultimate performance ceiling. For example, a user who frequently uses the 'bulleted lists' toolbar item may decide to learn the keyboard shortcut, spending time to determine, memorise, and make autonomous its key sequence.

While the curve characterises the user's *actual* performance when switching modalities, the user's *perception* of future performance critically influences whether the modality switch is made – if users perceive that an interface will be hard to learn, temporarily slow, or ultimately inefficient they will ignore it, and thus never attain the high performance ceiling it actually enables.

Figure 2 summarises the properties of the intra and intermodal performance curves, and the interface and human factors affecting them, which are described in the following sections. The right hand side of Figure 2 also shows the techniques that our system, called Blur, uses to influence expertise development. We describe Blur and its relationship to the framework later in the paper.

Review of intramodal expertise development

Initial performance (intercept)

Interface design for the initial stages of learning is strongly promoted in most usability guidelines [13, 31, 32, 37]. At this stage, users are unfamiliar with the interface, and must

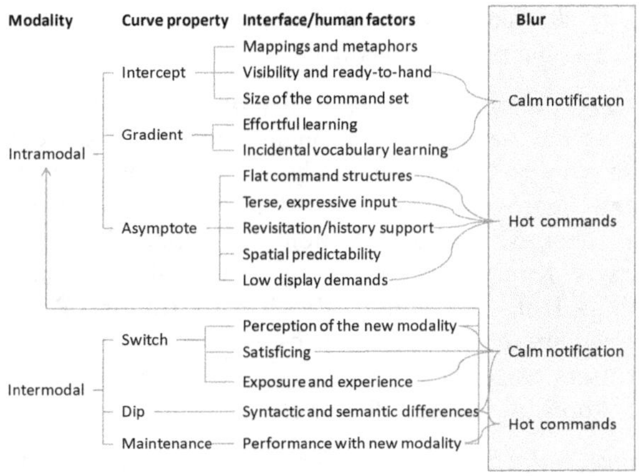

Figure 2. Summary facets of intra and intermodal expertise development, and the human and interface factors affecting them. Blur's mapping to the framework is described later.

rely on their prior experiences, visual search, and recognition to find the commands they need.

Mappings and metaphors [31, 33] promote initial interface familiarity, but supporting such mappings in command languages is difficult because of the variability in words used to describe actions [26]. Furnas *et al.* [15] describe how this vocabulary problem can be reduced through aliasing. In hotkey assignment creating meaningful mappings is further complicated by the limited expressive capacity of the input language: once 'P' is assigned to 'Print', for example, 'Paste', 'Previous', etc., must be assigned additional modifier keys or less symbolic letters.

Visibility and 'ready to hand'. The notion that controls should be visible to be learned is also well expressed in most usability guidelines, but the corollary of making novice things visible is that expert things are often suppressed, reducing the likelihood that they will be discovered. A related concept is that appropriate interface controls should be 'ready to hand' [23], where controls and feedback are available for use but not obstructing task completion. Dyck *et al.* [14] observe that many computer games achieve the dual objectives of availability without obstruction through '*calm messaging*', using transient text, animation, and audio.

Size of the command set. Large command vocabularies are likely to take longer to learn than small ones. Carroll and Carrithers [6] exploited this effect with their 'Training Wheels' interfaces, which intentionally reduced the vocabulary size to aid learning. Related ideas were recently pursued with 'multi-layer interfaces' [39].

Extended learning (gradient)

Several factors influence the rate at which performance increases after initial familiarisation. Our review focuses on interface techniques that improve the efficacy of *recall* and on assisting users in establishing a good vocabulary.

Effortful learning. Psychology researchers have proposed that "deeper" cognitions, which take longer to process, result in stronger memories [10, 35], and similar effects have been demonstrated with interfaces [8, 17]. However, explicitly manipulating the effort of interaction is risky as users are prone to frustration when training is too difficult and boredom when activities are mundane.

Incidental learning to extend vocabulary. Psychology literature also suggests that users should learn interface components as a side effect of their display while using other components. Shelton [36] showed that subjects' memory in a paired-associate learning task was improved simply by prior exposure to the stimuli. Jones [22] therefore hypothesised that hypertext browsing would result in greater incidental learning than indexed search (due to exposure to content), but experiments failed to find significant differences.

Ultimate performance (asymptote)

The final characteristic of the intramodal curve is the asymptote, or performance ceiling. There is extensive literature on supporting and understanding expert interface performance (although it is largely independent of the processes enabling its attainment). In particular, the seminal work of Card, Moran and Newell [5] provides strong predictive models and empirical evidence of 'expert performance of routine tasks', including analysis of one user who repeated the same editing task thousands of times to study progression to automaticity. Five interface characteristics for high performance ceilings follow:

Flat command structures. GUIs typically contain more controls than can be easily displayed at once, necessitating interface partitions such as windows, tabs, and menu hierarchies. Navigating through these partitions takes time, and consequently there are potential performance benefits in flattening the command structure to make more items accessible at once. Commands issued by CLIs and hotkeys are exemplars as they have global interface scope (e.g. <Ctrl>-C executes 'copy' regardless of the interface state). Several research and commercial systems have used CLIs to improve interface performance: e.g., Quicksilver[1], Spotlight[2], Enso[3], and GEKA [21]. Although empirical results for CLI benefits over GUIs have been mixed (e.g. [42]), it is widely accepted that CLIs enable higher efficiency, and power users are strong advocates (e.g. [2]).

Terse and expressive. Powerful interfaces communicate a lot of meaning in rapidly expressed actions. For example, a single alphabetic character can discriminate 26 commands, or 52 with case sensitivity; increasing to 2704 with two case-sensitive characters. However, there is often a tension between supporting terse, expressive power and meaningful mappings: for example, Alt-shortcuts in Office 2007 allow access to most controls, but they are abstract and hard to remember (e.g, '<Alt> n, nu, t' inserts a page number).

---

[1] http://www.blacktree.com
[2] http://support.apple.com/kb/HT2531
[3] http://humanized.com

Revisitation/history support. Users' interactive behaviour is often repetitive (e.g., command use [16] and web navigation [41]), and interfaces can aid efficiency by explicitly supporting repetition. For example, web browser URL address bars and the Google search box memorise previous activities and offer type-ahead shortcuts for them: e.g., the keystrokes 'cn↓<Ret>' become a shortcut for a user who frequently visits CNN's website.

Spatial predictability. Studies have demonstrated that spatial stability allows users to make rapid decisions about items' locations rather than relying on comparatively slow visual search (e.g. [19]). Despite the desirability of spatial stability it is often compromised due to display space constraints – interface controls are often elided and repositioned as window geometry is manipulated, and this is necessary because widgets typically do not scale. There are interesting design opportunities in spatially stable interfaces that dynamically scale widgets.

Low display demands. A final property of high performance interfaces is that they help the user focus on their primary activity, which typically involves their data. WIMPs rely on visual presentation, which consumes screen real-estate that might otherwise be used for data. This is critical on small devices, such as Netbook computers. For example, the window border, Ribbon, ruler and foot controls in Office 2007 applications consume approximately 195 vertical pixels, and the default Windows 7 Taskbar consumes another 30, for a sum of 225 pixels, which is 38% of a 600 pixel Netbook.

Review of intermodal expertise development

Compared to the extensive literature on intramodal expertise development, there has been much less on the factors influencing whether, how, and when users switch from novice to expert mechanisms. Note, our analysis does not review end-user programming (e.g., [11]) or interface customisation (see [4] for a good summary), which raise their own challenges (reviewed in [24] and [28]); although some of the factors identified below are applicable.

In the following analysis, we address three critical points on the *inter*modal performance curve shown in Figure 1: first, factors influencing the initial switch to a new interface modality; second, the performance dip that a user is likely to experience when switching from a familiar interface to an unfamiliar one; and third, factors influencing the maintenance of the new modality.

Making an initial switch

Perception of the new modality. As Figure 2 shows, the probability of switching to a new modality is likely to be influenced by how the user perceives any future interaction with the new modality, so all of the intramodal factors described above play a role. Importantly, though, several studies have demonstrated that perceived experience differs from actual (e.g. [12]), and that users can mistrust their abilities, leading to false assumptions of poor performance (e.g., [9] showed users predicted poor performance in a spatial task, but performed well).

Satisficing and optimising for immediate needs. The notion that users have a tendency to maintain existing strategies and use what is known and ready to hand in preference to new and improved ways of working is encapsulated by several theories, including Simon's 'satisficing' [40] and 'Maslow's hammer' [29] ('to a man with a hammer, everything looks like a nail'). In HCI, Carroll and Rossen [7] named the effect 'the paradox of the active user', in which users "are likely to stick with the procedures they already know, regardless of their efficacy".

Exposure and experience. Incidental learning, as described with the intramodal factors, can also be used to promote learning across modalities by exposing users to alternative ways of achieving their tasks as a side effect of their interactions. More forcefully, interfaces can demand that users experience the new modality by requiring that actions are completed through it.

Grossman [17] experimented with a variety of schemes for assisting hotkey learning. These included visual and audio schemes to expose users to the hotkeys, a delay-based technique to deter use of the GUI (i.e., making the system unresponsive for 2 seconds after each selection), and a technique that forced hotkey use following each menu selection. Their results showed that forced use and audio feedback worked well, with 72.8% and 66.6% of experimental selections being made with hotkeys. Subjective data showed no significant adverse response to the audio and forced use.

One concern for hotkey strategies, though, is that Grossman's results suggest that users may only be able to learn a small hotkey vocabulary. In their experiment 73% of selections could be completed using six hotkeys, and 83% with eight, yet the participants' mean use was less than 73%. Current desktop applications support hundreds of commands, and it is unclear how well audio feedback or enforced use can work in practice.

Performance dip after switching

Semantic and syntactic differences. The size of the performance dip that occurs after switching to a new interface modality will be influenced by the magnitude of the semantic and syntactic differences between the pre- and post-switch interfaces.

Interface semantics determine the interface and data states that can be attained with the interface. Frequently, these states differ across modalities, with one modality supporting a subset of the other. For example, it is common for only a subset of controls to be accessible via hotkeys. Semantic differences are likely to discourage users from investigating secondary modalities as the effort invested in seeking new facilities may go unrewarded (when it supports a subset) or require formation of a new model (when it supports a superset).

Interface syntax is determined by the mechanics of control and the manner in which control elements are combined. Marking menus [25] are an excellent example of promoting expertise by minimising the syntactic differences between novice and expert interaction modes. Their commands are arranged radially around the cursor, like segments of a pie. Novices attend the visual feedback and learn the drag-release movement directions for specific selections, such as 'print is East'. Experts, however, can use precisely the same interface syntax (a rapid directional drag and release) to select items without need for visual feedback.

Maintenance of the new modality

Whether users continue to use a new modality after making an initial switch depends on the magnitude of the performance dip they encounter and on their perception of their future performance with the modality, including how quickly they expect to outperform the original modality, and their estimation of their ultimate performance ceiling. These issues primarily depend on intramodal issues, described earlier, as shown in Figure 2.

BLUR: USAGE, RATIONALE, AND IMPLEMENTATION

The framework highlights three main challenges that Blur aims to address in assisting users to make a transition to expert interaction: *promote an initial switch, minimise the dip in performance*, and *enable a high performance ceiling*. Figure 2 shows how Blur's two main features of *calm notification* and *hot commands* (described below) are designed to map onto these components of the framework.

Overview of the user experience of Blur

Blur observes and controls interactions with unaltered desktop applications on Microsoft Windows platforms.

Blur's calm notification feedback during WIMP use. Figure 3 shows Blur's normal display state, with only a small translucent tab at the top of the screen displaying the text 'Press <Esc>'. When the user carries out an interface action by clicking on an interface control using the mouse, Blur provides *calm notification* of an alternative syntax for achieving the same action – the translucent tab expands

Figure 3. Blur's default state: a tab at the screen top.

Figure 4. Blur's calm notification: command name associated with a GUI action.

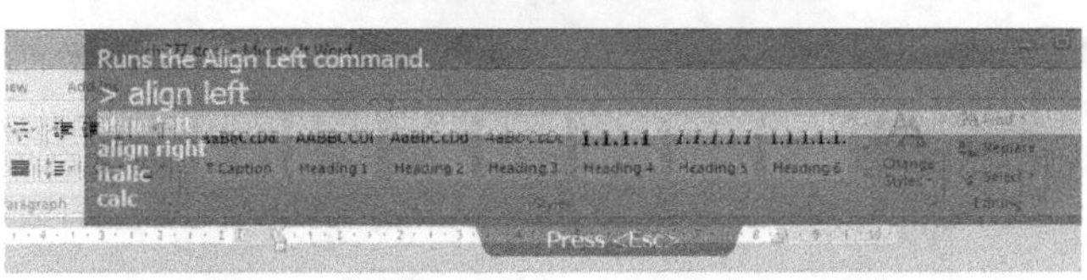

Figure 5. Blur's hot command suggestions.

displaying a command name. Figure 4 shows Blur's feedback ('Align Left') after clicking the button in Microsoft Word. After one second, the transparent window gradually contracts back to its tab state. Blur's window can be clicked through, allowing continued manipulation of the underlying GUI while Blur is visible.

Controlling interfaces with Blur's hot commands. Blur allows users to control the focal application, launch new applications, and manipulate windows using typed CLI *hot commands*. The user presses the Escape key to display Blur's translucent window, and command recommendations are shown in response to each successive typed letter. Figure 5 shows Blur's recommendations after typing *'<Esc>al'* when Microsoft Word is the focal application: the 'align left' command is recommended first and can be selected by pressing the Return key, but the arrow keys can be used to move through the recommendations (e.g. '*calc*').

Design rationale

Calm notification

Blur's calm notification provides transitory feedback revealing the command name that is equivalent to each mouse initiated action. Calm notification is primarily intended to reduce the tendency to satisfice and to promote an initial intermodal switch to Blur's *hot commands*. However as Figure 2 shows we also intend that it will provide a visually salient and continual reminder of the availability of the hot command alternative, as well as supporting incidental learning of the hot commands.

Importantly, we also intend that calm notification will help users identify that there is a one-to-one correspondence between each WIMP action and each *hot command*. This means that the user's mental model of interaction is largely unaffected by the transition between interface modalities. In other words, Blur's hot command interface does not change the structural decomposition of tasks into interface actions, and calm notification is the mechanism to communicate this absence of change to the user. This consistency is intended to minimise the performance dip associated with switching to Blur's hot commands.

Hot commands

As Figure 2 shows, Blur's hot commands are primarily designed to support a high performance asymptote, but as mentioned above they are also designed to provide a one-to-one mapping to WIMP commands to minimise the performance dip. This one-to-one relationship is unusual for CLIs, which normally require a different style of working typified by 'action-object' syntax, where data is identified through parameters following the command.

Blur's hot commands are symbolic (provided the original application designer has assigned meaningful names to controls), which should aid learning through appropriate mappings and metaphors. They support a flat command structure, allowing interface controls to be accessed with a single command, and eliminating the need to navigate through tab or menu hierarchies. They are terse and expressive, allowing unambiguous access to thousands of controls in a few keypresses. Hot commands also adapt to the user's interaction history by ordering command recommendations by frequency of use. Finally, Blur's interface consumes very little screen space.

Implementation[4]

Blur uses Microsoft's UI Automation API[5] to discover the GUI control elements that users interact with. All applications implementing this interface can therefore be observed and controlled by Blur. When the user clicks an interface widget Blur intercepts the event to determine the control under the cursor, retrieving the command name and the shortcut key sequence that can be used to activate the control. The action can then be performed by typing the command into Blur, which automatically translates the command into corresponding keyboard shortcuts and sends them to the application, controlling the GUI.

Blur orders command recommendations according to three candidate classes: exact matches, prefix matches and substring matches. Within each class, commands are sorted by frequency of use, and are displayed to the user. Typo correction is provided by remembering the most likely candidate at each keypress. If, at any point, the user's input matches an empty set of candidates, the most likely candidate from the previous keypress is suggested.

Blur's command recommendations are also context sensitive to the focal application. Consequently, the characters "se" may match "Send" while using an email system and "select all" when using a word processor. Context sensitivity has several advantages including fewer matching commands for any typed string, and reduced probability of illegal commands (e.g., "Send" is illegal unless an email composition window is open). Blur also supports 'global' interface controls such as window management and application launching. For example, window focus can be manipulated by typing any substring of the window title, (e.g., "in" for "email inbox"). Global commands are not context sensitive.

Summary of Blur

Blur is primarily designed to encourage an early and sustained switch to a command line interface. Blur's main mechanisms for supporting this are *calm notification* and *hot commands*, and importantly the hot command interface provides a one-to-one mapping to the WIMP interface. Although many previous research and commercial systems have supported CLIs (e.g., [21]), none have explicitly investigated the mechanisms used to initiate the modality switch. Grossman *et al.* [17] did investigate transitionary mechanisms, but the end modality was hotkeys, and their results suggest that hotkey vocabularies may be limited.

---

[4] Blur is available at: www.cosc.canterbury.ac.nz/blur

[5] http://msdn.microsoft.com/en-us/library/ms747327.aspx

EXPERIMENT: BLUR'S IMPACT ON USERS

We conducted an experiment to answer four key questions about Blur's performance, focusing on the point of modality transition rather than long term maintenance.

Q1. Do users switch to Blur's expert modality?
Q2. How does performance with Blur compare to performance without it and with other methods?
Q3. How large is the performance dip with Blur?
Q4. What is the subjective response to Blur?

The experiment involved a repetitive series of tasks using an unaltered version of Microsoft PowerPoint 2007, with and without Blur running. Participants also completed the tasks using the Office 2007 <Alt> shortcuts, which allows comparison between Blur and existing shortcut facilities. Repetitive tasks were used to compress long term interaction experiences into the short duration of a lab study, similar to Grossman's [17] study of hotkey learning.

Participants and Apparatus

The 20 participants aged 21 to 36 (mean 25, s.d. 4.4) were recruited from a local university. They reported using computers for a mean of 46.7 (s.d. 18.1) hours per week.

The experiment ran on a Windows 7 computer with a 1680×1050, 21" display. The target state for each task was shown on a sheet of paper placed alongside the computer.

Tasks

Five different PowerPoint slides were created, each containing five drawn objects of varying sizes and shading as shown in Table 1. The target state was shown on a sheet of paper at the side of the keyboard. All target states could be attained in a minimum of four commands, such as 'Select All', 'Align Left', 'Group', 'Flip Vertical'. Participants were instructed to complete tasks as quickly and accurately as possible. Automatic logs recorded all user interactions, including task time data.

Procedure

At the start of the experiment participants were given a two minute introduction to Blur using a PowerPoint slide containing a single text field. They were instructed to make the text Bold, Italic, Bulleted and Numbered using the GUI and to observe Blur's feedback, and then repeat the same actions by typing Blur commands.

The experiment proceeded through five stages, with each stage using one of Tasks 1-5 shown in Table 1, as follows:

1. familiarisation and training with PowerPoint
2. optional use of Blur (*blur*) ⎤ *counterbalanced*
3. normal PowerPoint (*wimp*) ⎦
4. instruction to maximise use of Blur (*blur-max*)
5. instruction to use <Alt> shortcuts (*alt*)

Participants repeated the manipulations to move from the initial to target states five times with Task 1 and twelve times each in Tasks 2-5. Participants completed NASA-TLX worksheets [20] and gave comments after Tasks 2-5.

Task 1 was used to familiarise participants with PowerPoint's alignment, rotation, grouping and flipping controls, with instruction as necessary. Participants then repeatedly moved from initial to target states five times.

Tasks 2 and 3 were completed with the WIMP and with Blur (counterbalanced). Before using Blur, participants were instructed to "*complete the tasks as you please.*"

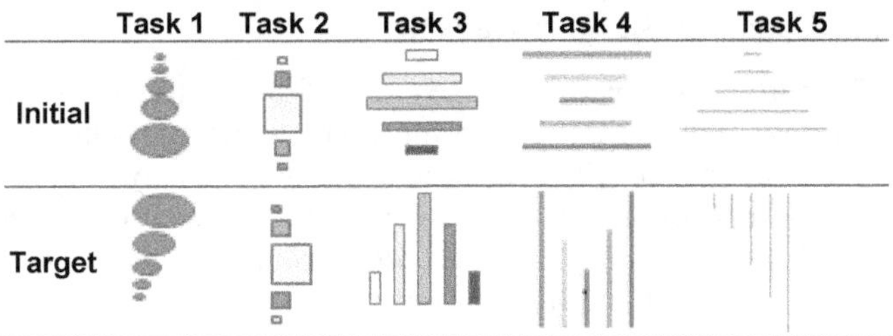

Table 1: Initial and target states for the five tasks.

Task 4 was completed following explicit instruction to "*use Blur's facilities as much as possible*". This condition was included because we wanted to be certain to obtain measurements of Blur's performance. We could not rely on Tasks 2/3 to produce this data because participants had the option to ignore Blur entirely.

Task 5 was used to analyse user performance with Microsoft Office's built in <Alt> shortcut navigation controls. This task was included because it was possible that the existing shortcut facilities would outperform Blur. Prior to completing these tasks participants received two minutes instruction on <Alt> shortcuts and practiced with the same text tasks used for familiarisation with Blur.

Results

Q1. Do users switch to Blur's expert modality?

In Task 2/3, where participants were instructed to complete tasks however they liked, *all* chose to use Blur. The mean trial number at which participants switched to Blur was 1.65 (s.d. 1.0), with 55% of participants using Blur in the first trial, increasing to 90% in the second, 95% in the third, and 100% by the fifth. Two of the participants briefly returned to using the WIMP after their first use of Blur, but switched back and continued using Blur through the final trials (we suspect that these participants were confirming that Blur was faster than the WIMP). In contrast to the successful switch to Blur, none of the participants tried to use <Alt> shortcuts. Several used prior knowledge of Ctrl-a for 'select all', and nearly half used Ctrl-g for 'group', but many expressed surprise similar to the statement "*there's no shortcut for group*" after visually inspecting the menu (there is, but it's not shown in the UI).

Q2. How does performance with Blur compare to performance without it and with other methods?

Trial times in Tasks 2-5 were analysed in a 4×3 repeated measures ANOVA for within-subjects factors *interface* (*wimp*, *blur*, *blur-max*, and *alt*) and *block* (repetitions 1-3, 4-7, and 8-11, with trial 0 discarded as preparation).

Results show a significant effect of *interface* ($F_{3,57}=97.9$, $p<.001$), with means of 9.72, 9.92, 7.54, and 19.97 seconds for *wimp*, *blur*, *blur-max* and *alt* respectively (see Figure 6). There is also a significant effect of *block* ($F_{2,38}=77.9$, $p<.001$), with participants' mean performance improving from 15.2 seconds in the first three trials to 10.7 seconds in trials 4-7 and 9.5 seconds in trials 8-11. Finally, as Figure 6 suggests, there is a significant *interface* × *block* interaction ($F_{6,114}=15.3$, $p<.001$), which is best explained by the relatively small cross block performance improvement with *blur-max* (due to prior experience to Blur) contrasting with the large improvement with *alt*.

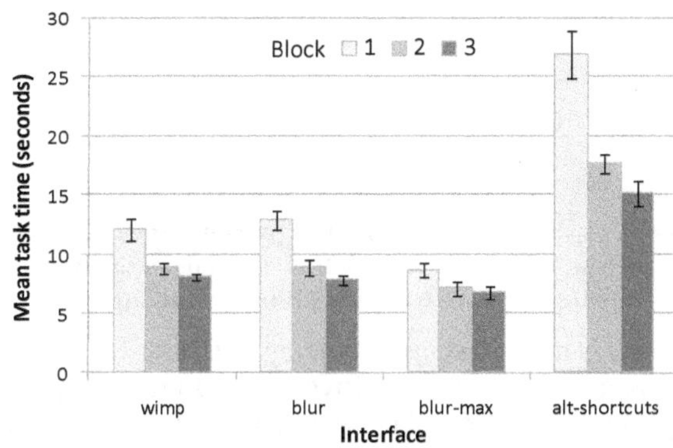

Figure 6. Mean task times with the four interfaces across the three blocks (1, 2, 3). Error bars ±1 s.e.m.

A planned comparison between *wimp* and *blur-max* in the final block (repetitions 8-11, where participants are reaching their maximum level of performance) shows a significant difference ($F_{1,19}=7.6$, $p<.05$) with *blur-max* 17% faster (6.77 seconds, s.d. 2.4) than the normal GUI controls (*wimp*, 8.14 seconds, s.d. 1.45). A final data point indicating that Blur enabled higher levels of performance is that 90% of the participants had their fastest task completion time when using Blur.

Performance with *Alt-shortcuts* was particularly slow, and participants commented that they were *'painful'* and *'awful'*. Participants also commented about the difficulty of learning the shortcuts due to their lack of symbolism (e.g. '<alt> h, g, a, l' for 'align left'). 35% of the participants stated that they were aware of Alt-shortcuts before the experiment, but none attempted to use them except during their enforced use in Task 5.

Q3. How large is the performance dip with Blur?

Our framework postulates that changing modality causes a performance dip, so we analysed performance data at the point that users switched to using Blur. Mean trial completion times are shown in Figure 7, with the solid line showing times immediately preceding and following the switch in the *blur* condition, and the dashed line showing data for the first four trials in the *wimp* condition for comparison. The figure shows that Blur caused a small performance dip in the first post-switch trial (from 20.5 sec to 20.9 sec), but that this loss was quickly recovered with performance matching that of the *wimp* condition by the third post-switch trial and eventually outperforming it.

Importantly, Blur's performance dip was relatively small, and consequently the participants were not discouraged from continuing to use it. The performance dip with *alt*, in contrast, was large (Figure 6), and participants would have immediately discontinued use if not required to do so.

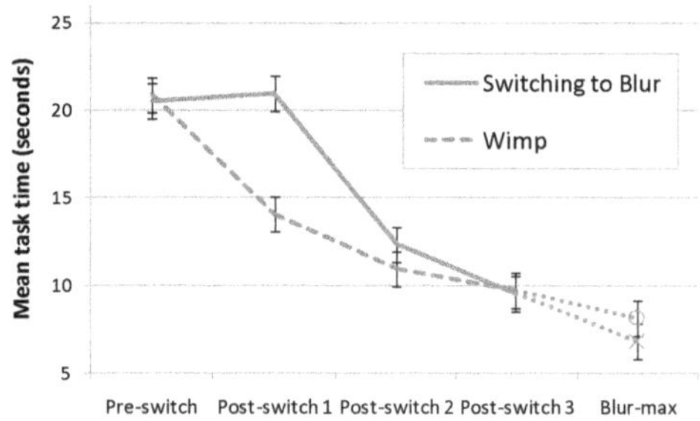

Figure 7. Evidence of Blur's small 'performance dip', shown by the slight increase in task time in trials preceding and following the switch to using Blur (including trial 0).

Q4. What is the subjective response to Blur?

Participants responded positively to Blur, and provided many suggestions for improvements. At the end of the experiment they ranked the three interfaces (*blur*, *wimp* and *alt*) in order of preference, with 1 most preferred, and 3 least. Twelve ranked *blur* first, 6 *wimp* first, and 1 *Alt-shortcuts*, giving a significant rankings difference (Friedman χ_r^2=18.9, p<.001), with means of 1.37 (s.d. 0.5), 1.84 (0.69) and 2.79 (0.54) for *blur*, *wimp* and *alt*.

We measured how intrusive participants found Blur's calm notification. One participant stated that it was "*annoying*", and another that it was "*distracting, but easily ignored*". The mean response to the question "Blur's feedback was distracting" (1 disagree, 5 agree) was 2.45 (1.4).

	Wimp	Blur	Alt	χ_r^2	Sig
Mental Demand	2.45 (1.1)	2.85 (0.9)	4.45 (0.8)	23.5	<.001
Physical Demand	3.15 (1.3)	2.5 (1.1)	3.1 (1.1)	3.8	=0.15
Hurried	2.85 (1.0)	2.8 (1.1)	3.5 (1.1)	3.7	=0.16
Successful	3.95 (0.7)	4.1 (0.4)	2.9 (0.9)	14.8	<.001
Hard work	2.85 (1.3)	3.2 (0.8)	4.3 (0.7)	16.1	<.001
Insecure	2.3 (1.4)	2.2 (0.7)	4.2 (1.0)	19.2	<.001
Efficient	2.9 (1.3)	4.3 (0.7)	2.1 (1.2)	20.1	<.001
Easy to learn	4.1 (1.1)	4.1 (0.8)	2.6 (1.2)	13.7	<.005
Error prone	2.5 (1.1)	2.8 (1.0)	4.35 (0.9)	19.1	<.001

Table 2. Mean responses (sd) to 5 point Likert-scale questions.

NASA-TLX worksheet responses, summarised in Table 2, show significant interface differences for mental demand, perceived success, amount of work, and insecurity, but the main cause is the poor performance of Alt-shortcuts, rather than differences between *wimp* and *blur* conditions. Table 2 also shows higher efficiency ratings for Blur's (mean 4.3) than *wimp* (2.9) or *alt* (2.1). Mean ratings for Blur's ease of learning were the same as the normal interface (4.1), despite their brief exposure to it; their rating of Alt-shortcuts learnability was much worse (2.6).

The final stage of the experiment involved asking participants to switch between windows and launch applications, performing minor operations in each: conducting an image search in Firefox, copying one of the resultant images to Paint, cropping the image, pasting it into a Microsoft Word document, checking their email inbox, then repeating the process with a different image search. They were instructed to complete the tasks in any way they liked, and that Blur was available.

The participants made extensive use of Blur throughout the task. We noted a tendency for users to persist with the mouse after using it to complete a task (e.g. cropping an image), and one user commented that "*it's easy to forget that Blur's available, but the fading window reminds you*" (referring to calm notification). Participants commented that "*I especially like it opening and running programs instead of the start menu*" and that "*I liked fast switching*".

Finally, two participants stated a desire for recency ordering in command recommendations: "*The ranking system should give higher precedence to the last used command*" and "*Items should be promoted faster*".

DISCUSSION

Blur's *calm notification* and *hot commands* interface was designed to promote an initial modality switch, to minimise the performance dip associated with doing so, and to offer a high performance ceiling (perceived and actual). The experiment validated the design, showing an early switch to hot commands, that the performance dip was small, that users continued to use Blur, that it enabled higher levels of performance than the normal UI and Alt-shortcuts, and that users preferred it.

Why did Blur succeed?

Blur is a realistic system that works with unaltered desktop applications. We designed calm notification and hot commands as generalisable and scalable transitionary mechanisms that could work in real work settings. Furthermore, our framework suggests that modality switches depend on many factors, including perception of the efficiency of expert modalities. Consequently, it is difficult to isolate the independent contribution of Blur's design elements in supporting the modality switch – while the gestalt design succeeds, we do not know whether this is due to the perceived efficiency of hot commands, the ready-to-hand reminder provided by calm notification, the one-to-one semantic relationship of hot commands, and so on. The participants' comments similarly highlight different aspects of Blur's perceived and actual utility. We believe that calm notification and hot commands are useful and generalisable approaches for interfaces wishing to support a transition to expertise, but further work is needed to tease out their independent and interacting value.

Does Blur work in the real world?

The experiment used repetitive tasks to compress long term command use into the short duration of a lab study. This is a common strategy for examining interface learning (e.g. [5,

17]), but it raises concerns that the findings may not generalise to real use, discussed below.

Limited vocabulary. The study used a small command vocabulary, so there are risks that Blur may not generalise to larger command sets (in the same way that Grossman's results suggest that hotkey vocabularies may be limited [17]). Two issues encourage us to believe that Blur's approach is robust to large vocabularies. First, the final stage of the experiment involved relatively unconstrained interaction within and across applications. The participants continued to use Blur throughout these activities, and were enthusiastic about its support for window switching and application launching, which were not heavily repeated. Second, we believe that the strategies of one-to-one Blur/GUI command relationship and of populating command names from the GUI create a strong and symbolic mapping that helps users anticipate commands. For example, Blur's command for X_2 is 'subscript' (or 'sub'), and the Zoom control is 'zoom' (or 'zo'), but the built-in hotkeys are much less symbolic and (we believe) harder to remember: 'Ctrl+=' (or 'Alt+h5') and 'Alt+wq'.

Novelty bias. Participants in the experiment will have inferred that we were interested in their performance with Blur, which may have drawn them to use it. We counter this concern in two ways. First, Alt-shortcuts were also novel to most of our participants, but their response was strongly negative. Second, any user who installs a system like Blur is also likely to be curious about its behavior.

Not real work. Real work has different engagement and time pressure than experimental tasks. This is true of nearly all controlled experiments, but is particularly important in our experiment where we are concerned about reducing the tendency to satisfice. We believe that our participants were genuinely trying to optimize their performance, but understand that this may have artificially eliminated some of the tendency to satisfice. We will examine Blur's logs of real use in the coming year.

Our own experiences. Our concerns about real-world use are eased by our own experiences in using Blur over the last few months. Two of the authors are enthusiastic users (the other two use Macs and cannot run it), particularly for two activities and settings. First, application launching and window switching is extremely rapid (e.g., 'Esc+in' to check the email inbox and 'Esc+fi' to launch Firefox). Second, Blur's control of applications is invaluable when using a laptop computer without a mouse (e.g., on planes, in waiting rooms, etc.) We have found that the threshold for using Blur is influenced by the pointing device. When using a mouse, the threshold often favours Blur, but not when tasks predominantly involve direct manipulation (e.g., drawing). However, when using a less precise device, like a trackpad, Blur's benefits are substantial.

How can Blur be improved and generalised?

Improvements to Blur's CLI trigger. Four participants stated that using the Escape key was awkward, and that they would prefer to assign their own key, such as Alt. One also stated that Blur's hot command window should remain open until explicitly dismissed, allowing multiple commands with a single Escape keypress.

Alternative implementations of calm notification and hot commands. Many tasks are predominantly mouse driven (e.g. CAD drawing), so hot commands would require a homing action away from the mouse. Blur could be adapted to support other expert modalities such as a ListMap [19], which provides a spatially stable miniaturized representation of UI controls (flattening the interface hierarchy). Calm notification could alert users to the location of selected controls within the ListMap. We are currently implementing this approach.

Removing limitations of the platform. Blur's support is limited by the capabilities of the UI Automation API and by how applications implement it. Many applications do not fully or properly implement the API, which requires Blur to implement work-arounds, such as parsing the control tree when an application is launched and dynamically detecting shortcuts for applications that do not properly connect the control tree. These issues increase implementation complexity and constrain functionality, but software vendors like Microsoft and Apple could ease the limitations by refining their scripting and automation technologies, and by promoting their use in applications.

Despite these limitations, Blur is a useful tool in its current implementation, and we have been using it successfully in unaltered Windows environments for several months.

CONCLUSIONS

Many office workers use their desktop applications for hundreds of hours each year, yet there is tendency to resist making the transition to expert strategies that could dramatically improve their performance.

This paper provided a framework for understanding the human and interface factors influencing the transition to expert interface modalities. We also described the design and evaluation of Blur, which uses *calm notification* of *hot commands* to prompt an initial switch to its expert modality, to minimise the performance dip associated with doing so, and to enable a high performance ceiling. Experimental participants made an early and sustained switch to Blur's hot commands, they benefited from doing so, and they preferred it to the normal interface.

There are several directions for further work. We will experiment with ListMap strategies for mouse-driven expert interaction, and with associated spatial means for calm notification. We will also refine and extend Blur's capabilities to assure that it is robust and functionally rich both within and across a wide range of applications. We will continue to empirically assess how its design features contribute to the initial modality switch, and finally, we will deploy Blur and assess its real-world use through field studies and log analyses.

REFERENCES

1. Anderson, J. Learning and Memory. Wiley, NY, 1995.
2. Barrett, R., Kandogan, E., Maglio, P., Haber, E., Takayama, L. and Prabaker, M. Field studies of computer system administrators. in *Proc. CSCW'04*, ACM, (2004), 388-395.
3. Bhavnani, S. and John, B. The Strategic Use of Complex Computer Systems. *HCIJ 15* (2000), 107-137.
4. Bunt, A., Conati, C. and McGrenere, J. Supporting Interface Customization using a Mixed-Initiative Approach. in *Proc. IUI '07*, ACM, (2007), 92-101.
5. Card, S.K., Moran, T.P. and Newell, A. *The Psychology of HCI.* Lawrence Erlbaum, 1983.
6. Carroll, J. and Carrithers, C. Training Wheels in a User Interface. *Comms. ACM* 27, 8 (1984), 800-806.
7. Carroll, J. and Rossen, M. Paradox of the active user. in Carroll, J. ed. *Interfacing Thought: Cognitive Aspects of HCI*, MIT Press, 1987, 80-111.
8. Cockburn, A., Kristensson, P., Alexander, J. and Zhai, S. Hard Lessons: Effort-Inducing Interfaces Benefit Spatial Learning. in *Proc. CHI*, (2007), 1571-1580.
9. Cockburn, A. and McKenzie, B. Evaluating the Effectiveness of Spatial Memory in 2D and 3D Physical and Virtual Environments. in *Proc. CHI'02*, ACM, (2002), 203-210.
10. Craik, F. and Lockhart, R. Levels of processing: A framework for memory research. *Journal of Verbal Learning and Verbal Behavior* 11 (1972), 671-684.
11. Cypher, A., Dontcheva, M., Lau, T. and Nichols, J. *No Code Required.* Morgan Kaufmann, 2010.
12. Czerwinski, M., Horvitz, E. and Cuttrell, E. Subjective Duration Assessment: An Impicit Probe for Software Usability. in *Proc. IHM-HCI*, (2001).
13. Dix, A., Finlay, J., Abowd, G. and Beale, R. *Human-Computer Interaction*, Prentice Hall. (1993).
14. Dyck, J., Pienelle, D., Brown, B. and Gutwin, C. Learning from Games: HCI Innovations in Entertainment Software. in *Proc. GI*, (2003).
15. Furnas, G.W., Landauer, T.K., Gomez, L.M. and Dumais, S.T. The vocabulary problem in human-system communication. *CACM 30*, 11 (1987), 964-971.
16. Greenberg, S. and Witten, I. Supporting Command Reuse. *IJMMS. 39* (1993), 353-390.
17. Grossman, T., Dragicevic, P. and Balakrishnan, R. Strategies for Accelearating On-line Learning of Hotkeys. in *Proc. CHI'07*, ACM, (2007). 1591-1600.
18. Grossman, T., Fitzmaurice, G. and Attar, R. A survey of software learnability. in *Proc. CHI*, (2009). 649-658.
19. Gutwin, C. and Cockburn, A. Improving List Revistation with ListMaps. in *Proc. AVI'06*, ACM, (2006), 396-403.
20. Hart, S. and Staveland, L. Development of NASA-TLX. in Hancock, P. and Meshkati, N. eds. *Human Mental Workload*, 1988, 139-183.
21. Hendy, J., Booth, K. and McGrenere, J. Graphically Enhanced Keyboard Accelerators for GUIs. in *Proc. Graphics Interface*, (2010).
22. Jones, T. Incidental learning during information retrieval: a hypertext experiment. in Maurer, H. ed. *Computer Assisted Learning*, Springer, 1989, 235-251.
23. Karat, J., Karat, C. and Ukelson, J. Affordances, motivation and the design of user interfaces. *CACM 43*, 8 (2000), 49-51.
24. Ko, A., Myers, B. and Aung, H. Six Learning Barriers in End-User Programming Systems. in *Proc. VL HCC'04*, IEEE, (2004), 199-206.
25. Kurtenbach, G. and Buxton, B. The Limits of Expert Performance Using Hierarchic Marking Menus. in *Proc. InterCHI'93*, (1993), 482-487.
26. Landauer, T.K., Galotti, K.M. and Hartwell, S. Natural command names and initial learning: a study of text-editing terms. *Comms. ACM 26*, 7 (1983), 495-503.
27. Lane, D.M., Napier, H.A., Peres, S.C. and Sandor, A. Hidden costs of graphical user interfaces. *I. J. HCI 18*, 2 (2005), 133-144.
28. Mackay, W. Triggers and barriers to customizing software. in *Proc. CHI'91*, ACM, (1991), 153-160.
29. Maslow, A. The Psychology of Science: A Reconnaissance. Harper & Row, New York, 1966.
30. Newell, A. and Rosenbloom, P.S. Mechanisms of Skill Acquisition and the Law of Practice. in Anderson, J. ed. *Cog. Skills & Acquisition*, Erlbaum,, 1981, 1-55.
31. Nielsen, J. *Usability Engineering*. Morgan Kaufmann, San Francisco, 1993.
32. Norman, D. Design principles for Human-Computer Interfaces. in *Proc. 'CHI 83*, 1983, 1-10.
33. Norman, D. The Psych. of Everyday Things (1988).
34. Odell, D., L., Davis, R., C., Smith, A. and Wright, P., K. Toolglasses, marking menus, and hotkeys: a comparison of one and two-handed command selection techniques. in *Proc. Graphics Interface*, (2004), 17-24.
35. Schmidt, R. and Bjork, R. The Conceptualizations of Practice. *Psychological Science 3*, 4 (1992), 207-217.
36. Shelton, D. and Newhouse, R.C. Incidental Learning in a Paired-Associate Task. *Journal of Experimental Education 50*, 1 (1981), 36-38.
37. Shneiderman, B. Designing the User Interface, Addison Wesley, 1992.
38. Shneiderman, B. Direct Manipulation: A Step Beyond Programming Languages (excerpt). in Baecker, *et al.*. *Readings in HCI*, 1987, 461-467.
39. Shneiderman, B. Promoting universal usability with multi-layer interface design. in *Proc. Universal Usability*, ACM, (2003), 1-8.
40. Simon, H. Theories of Decision-Making in Economics and Behavioral Science. *American Economic Review 49*, 3 (1959), 252-283.
41. Tauscher, L. and Greenberg, S. How People Revisit Web Pages. *IJHCS. 47*, 1 (1997), 97-138.
42. Whiteside, J., Jones, S., Levy, P. and Wixon, D. User Performance with Command, Menu, and Iconic Interfaces. in *Proc. CHI'85*, ACM, (1985), 185-191.

Ambient Help

Justin Matejka, Tovi Grossman, George Fitzmaurice
Autodesk Research
210 King St. E., Toronto, Ontario, Canada
{firstname.lastname}@autodesk.com

ABSTRACT
In this paper we present Ambient Help, a system that supports opportunistic learning by providing automatic, context-sensitive learning resources while a user works. Multiple videos and textual help resources are presented ambiently on a secondary display. We define and examine a collection of design consideration for this type of interface. After describing our implementation details, we report on an experiment which shows that Ambient Help supports finding more helpful information, while not having a negative impact on the user's productivity, as compared to a traditional help condition.

Author Keywords
Help, Learnability, Understanding, Ambient System

ACM Classification Keywords
H5.m. Information interfaces and presentation (e.g., HCI)

General Terms
Design, Human Factors

INTRODUCTION
Despite advancements in research making complex applications easier to operate, learning how to use these programs can still be a problem. There are often thousands of commands or functions to choose from, and many more ways to combine them into workflows. When using an unfamiliar area of the program, even expert users may require assistance [21].

For most large applications, many hours are spent creating an exhaustive set of documentation for the program's features. These references can sometimes be helpful for finding information about a particular command, but material on how the commands work together or how to perform higher level tasks are often lacking. Even though these standard help systems have improved in recent years, many people are reluctant to use them [37]. Some have found past help systems ineffective and refuse to give the new version a chance, while others would rather continue working and attempt to figure out what they need on their own [13].

Seeing other people work can sometimes be more valuable than traditional help resources [45]. Videos can serve as a reasonable approximation of watching another person's screen, and at the time of writing there are over 350,000 videos on YouTube for the query "Adobe Tutorial" alone. However, all of these videos run the risk of being underutilized since they are not available within the application so users are unaware of their existence or have difficulty finding them. ToolClips [20] show videos in application tooltips, but they are only available for help at the tool-level and don't always show higher level taskflows which utilize the tool. Also, users are still required to explicitly access the videos by calling up the tooltip.

Opposite to the traditional "pull" model where a user explicitly asks for help resources, an implicit "push" model for help has been explored [26]. These systems potentially provide help in situations where the user didn't even know they needed it, such as awareness of unknown functionality or transitioning from a novice workflow to a more expert one. Such learning could be referred to as "unintentional" learning [42] since the user has learnt something without even knowing there was something they needed to know. Previous attempts such as Microsoft's Clippy [26] and "Tip of the Day" have not been ambient, requiring user input on the system's terms, not the user's, and as such have been considered frustrating and ineffective.

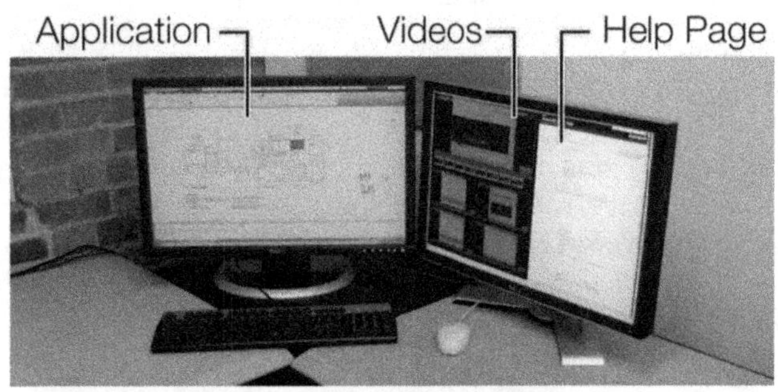

Figure 1. Structure of Ambient Help system. Main application monitor on the left, dynamically updating ambient help display on the right containing 5 videos and a web help page.

In the paper we present Ambient Help, a system that supports opportunistic learning by providing automatic, context-sensitive learning resources while a user works. Multiple videos and textual help resources are presented ambiently on a secondary display [Figure 1]. Opportunistic learning is supported during natural breaks in the user's workflow since the information is preloaded for convenient viewing. This design reduces the transaction cost traditionally associated with obtaining help information.

After reviewing related work, we discuss design considerations for an ambient help system, present our implementation, and report on a study that shows our system supports finding more useful information, while not having a negative impact on the user's productivity, compared to a traditional help system.

RELATED WORK

Contextual and Video Based Help

Since the outset of on-line help, there have been explorations into contextual [2,12,29] and video-based [5, 27,29] delivery, with less research exploring both [20,1]. Shneiderman [44] argues that graphical demonstrations can be the most direct way for novices to learn procedural knowledge. However, its implementation was expensive and time consuming when the ideas were first proposed in the early 90's [27], and in general, on-line documentation was "crippled" by hardware and software limitations [15]. The evolution of CPU power and video hosting services has made video documentation a viable possibility [31].

In terms of publishing, it is often easier to record a 5 minute tutorial video than it is to take the necessary screenshots and write up an easy to follow and useful tutorial [39]. However, with text based help a quick glance might provide the needed assistance, where a video may require a longer viewing period to get the same information [16]. It has also been found that some users naturally prefer videos while other prefer text-based help [20].

Despite psychology research which exposes the benefits of contextual assistance [3], help systems are generally offered through completely separate components. This discontinuity can result in delayed, disruptive, inconsistent, and obtrusive help systems [2,30].

Previous research in animated assistance [23,38,1] has explored contextual demonstrations. One good example is Google Sketchup which has an "instructor" panel providing tool-based contextual animated assistance whose content changes as the user switches tools. While their assistance consists of very basic animations which only illustrate how the tools function, we use full motion videos which show how the tools can be used in a workflow.

Ambient Information Systems and Displays

Ambient and peripheral displays [8,35,40,46] support the monitoring of noncritical information with the intent of not distracting or burdening the user. One typical example of an ambient display is Portholes [10] which periodically takes a video snapshot of members of a community and presents them as a grid of images for each user to view and have an awareness of who is in and available for communication.

Pousman and Stasko [41] describe four dimensions of consideration when designing an ambient display: information capacity, notification level, representational fidelity, and aesthetic emphasis. In our approach, we wish to present contextual learning resources in an ambient display where the information capacity and representational fidelity is high and always available to be absorbed by the user during breaks of work activity. Also, we do not interrupt the user, so the notification level is low.

Evaluation of the usefulness of ambient displays is often challenging [24,33,35,43]. The evaluation criteria typically centers around noticeability, comprehension, relevance, division of attention, and engagement. While these are all important, we are particularly interested in increasing the temptation to learn something new, perhaps serendipitously. This is similar to over the shoulder learning [45] where users can see how other users work.

One concern with an information rich ambient display is that it may induce information overload [28]. While this could be true, the very nature of our ambient display is that it contains optional information that can be ignored during intense work or during high levels of information processing in the main display.

Buxton describes a framework for modeling systems which factor in not only human-human and human-computer interaction but a second dimension of foreground and background activity [7]. Here, foreground activities are in the "fore of human consciousness – intentional activities" such as typing in a computer. Background activities take place "in the periphery 'behind' those in the foreground" such as being aware of someone in the next office typing. Our intent is that Ambient Help easily transitions between background and foreground activity.

Interruptability and Notification

A great deal of research has studied technology-mediated interruptions and notification of system or application events [1,17,22,36]. The concern is that interruptions can be an annoyance, adversely affect a user's task completion time, and make them vulnerable to mistakes. Thus, researchers have explored ways to mitigate the problems by deferring interruption until users are more open to the information during their work. Attentive user interfaces attempt to recognize some basic user states (presence, head position, mouse activity) and act differently according to user behavior [14]. Our goal is not to interrupt the user, particularly during their intense work.

Transaction cost

A key goal for our system is to reduce the transaction cost of a user accessing help and learning resources while working. Research has explored the dynamics of switching between work and help [4] and shown that small interaction improvements can cause categorical behavior changes that far exceed the benefits of decreased task times [6,18].

The Cocoa Buzz system [11] runs on a user's extra display, or a large shared display, and automatically cycles through different information sources (such as news sites) customized by the user. About every minute it updates and generates a new information collage. Our system differs in that the learning resources are contextually retrieved.

Instead of a user explicitly entering in search terms, implicit and activity based web searching is being researched. Maekawa et al. [32] have explored *query free* web searching based on activity detected by sensors and internet-connected domestic appliances. For example, while washing a coffee maker, a web page is automatically retrieved on how to clean it using vinegar. Henzinger et al. [25] automatically select web pages that a user might want to see which are relevant to a TV program they are currently watching. This implicit style of searching system matches our approach but differs in that we focus on software learnability [21].

DESIGN CONSIDERATIONS

In the following we look at a number of design goals we considered while creating the Ambient Help system to be as useful as possible, while not being disturbing or distracting.

Ambient Nature

A primary consideration is for the help content to be displayed ambiently; that is, in an always-on display which does not require user input to function. In this way, the time-cost to access the help content is reduced since user interaction is not required to call up the information. Since the display is persistent, the user can look over for help information at any time, and it should be designed in a way so there is no cost associated with *not* using the display; i.e., it can be easily ignored. Similarly, to minimize distraction the system should never interrupt the user.

Relevance of Content

For an ambient system to be useful, it must be able to find and display content which is relevant to the user. This is different from Tip of the Day where you have small pieces of help information, or standard help systems which give access to more content, neither of which use any knowledge of the user's context. Besides attempting to show help content which is a good match for what the user is looking for, it is also useful to present generally useful or interesting content to enhance the variety of the system and provide the opportunity for exploration and serendipitous learning [34].

Transition Between Ambient and Interactive

Ideally there should be no explicit switch required to move between ambient and interactive modes of operation. Users should be able to move between the main and help windows freely without concern for the state of the help system.

Multiple Forms of Information

Traditionally, product support materials have been delivered in mostly text, with some diagrams mixed in. A limited number of help videos are now being published by the software manufacturers, but with the recent advancements in the ease of posting videos to the internet (YouTube, etc.) many individuals and small third-party companies have started posting their own tutorial videos.

Videos have the benefit of being able to demonstrate the concept being described. Textual resources on the other hand have the benefit of being more easily skimmed or consumed quickly. Besides official product documentation, there are also significant web-based textual resources such as discussion boards and tutorial web pages which many users turn to for information.

With their being benefits to both video and textual help information, we recommend supporting both.

Channels of Information

Ambient display systems can range from displaying a single stream of information up to a great number simultaneously. By displaying only one channel, that single item takes up the entire information bandwidth of the display, and as such, when the user looks over they are assured to see it. With many channels on the same display, each individual channel must be of smaller size and possibly lower fidelity. With more channels the chances are greater that useful content will be displayed. However, if too many things are going on, that useful content might be missed. In the end, designers should ensure a balance between the extremes of too little and too much information.

Location

An ambient help system could be implemented on a secondary monitor or within the primary monitor. In our experience we have found that users are quicker to dismiss items which take space away from their primary application. Instead of using a secondary display on the same computer, the system could also run on a secondary system, such as an Apple iPad or similar device.

Content Variance

If the content of the ambient display never changes, users will stop looking over because they have already seen the information. On the other hand, if the content changes too often it could be a distraction, or relevant information could be swapped out while the user is trying to view it. As such, there should be a balance between updating too slowly leaving the information stagnant, and updating so frequently that the content doesn't have time to be used.

SYSTEM DESCRIPTION

Overview

Given these design considerations we now present our exploration into offering ambient help. The Ambient Help system is displayed on a secondary monitor placed beside the main monitor [Figure 1]. The user sits directly in front of the main application monitor with the secondary monitor angled off to the side, keeping the application in the center of focus while the ambient display is visible in the periphery. The system automatically presents help content relevant to the commands the user is working with.

Ambient and Interactive Modes

On the left side of the screen are relevant help videos, and on the right side is a web page [Figure 2]. We display closed captioning information as an overlay for videos with the information available making it possible to follow along without the audio playing. We choose to use the command reference pages as the source for the web pages since there is a page for each command with consistent formatting, making it easier for users to find information, and making for a smoother transition between pages.

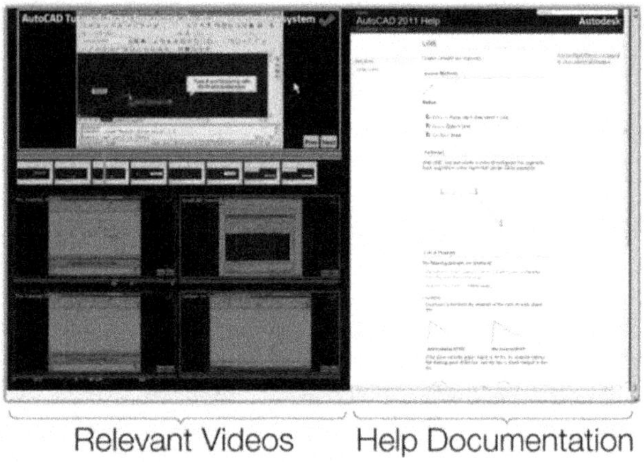

Figure 2. Ambient Help interface.

Our system reduces potential distractions by muting the audio and dimming the videos while the cursor is over the main application. We also reduce the frame rate at which videos are shown (only changing frames once every 5 seconds, with a 1 second smooth fade between frames). Being connected to the main application allows the system to use the application context to show relevant help content without specific input from the user.

When the cursor is within the help window, the video with cursor focus is shown at full brightness while the others remained dimmed. By default, when the cursor returns to the application window, the videos return to being dimmed and muted at the reduced frame rate. However, there is the option to "check" a video [Figure 3] which will keep the video playing at a reduced volume when the focus returns to the main application. This allows the user to keep listening to the video while working, and also ensures that the video will play to completion without being replaced.

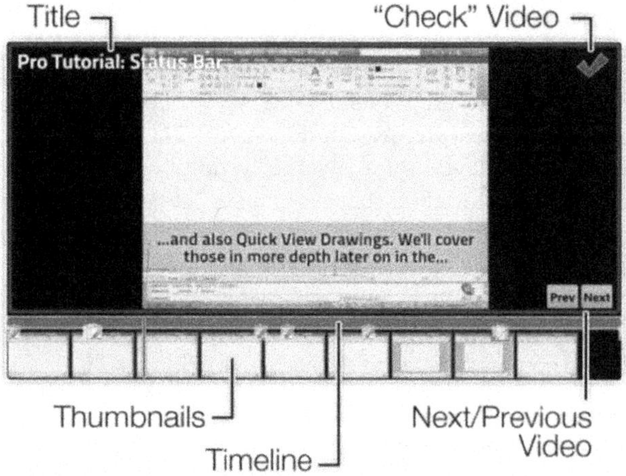

Figure 3. Elements of the Ambient Help video player.

In our system, the display may only change at the beginning of a new command, and even then, it may remain stable if the same command has been issued multiple times in succession, or the currently playing videos are sufficiently relevant. Between command issuances the content remains constant so users are able to read the help page or watch the videos without fear of them being replaced.

Based on the channels of information design consideration, we chose to show 5 videos. One video resides in the top "primary" position (at 970 by 536 resolution) and 4 smaller videos (at 490 by 278) below [Figure 2]. At this size we feel even the small videos are large enough for the user to get a sense of what is going on in the video while still allowing us to display a number of different clips to increase the chances of presenting a useful one. While the user is working and the display is updating, the video determined to be the most relevant is automatically transitioned up to the primary position, in theory placing the most useful video in the top, largest, position. The user can also manually promote a smaller video to the top by clicking on it, making it larger and easier to see the details.

If a video the user did want to watch happens to be replaced, it can be retrieved by clicking the "Prev" button in the video player. The interface also includes a timeline and thumbnails which allow navigation to different points in the video, and a button to move to the next video selected by the relevance algorithm described later.

AutoCAD Plug-in

The Ambient Help system was implemented as an AutoCAD plug-in using the ObjectARX framework. The system hooked into the `CommandStarted` messages from AutoCAD to get a notification whenever a user clicked on, or otherwise started to use a command. With these notifications the plug-in tracked which commands the user had recently used and was currently using. The videos came from two sources: a local cache of videos obtained from a YouTube search for "AutoCAD Tutorial" (1,379 videos), and an AutoCAD training DVD (107 videos) [Figure 2].

Automatic Video Analysis

Ideally, all tutorial videos ever created would be marked up with Chronicle-like [19] metadata indicating where in the video commands occurred, settings were changed, layers were modified, etc. Hopefully applications will someday allow users to record videos with this type of metadata, but for now, nearly all video help content is untagged.

Knowing which commands happened where allows us to find more germane videos. Additionally, we can seek directly to positions in the video to display relevant content, thus overcoming the need to manually scrub the video looking for command invocations. In the video timeline we display markers for the commands [Figure 4] that make it easier for users to navigate to parts of the video where commands of interest were used.

As a proof-of-concept to show one way in which this command scraping process could be automated, we created a program to analyze our collection of 107 professionally produced AutoCAD tutorial videos and generate the command stream tags for each. Limiting our source material for this process allowed us to make the simplifying assumptions that all videos would have the UI at the same scale, and the elements would be in the same positions. A system such as Sikuli [47] or Prefab [9] could be used to improve the algorithm to locate and recognize UI elements.

Figure 4. Video timeline showing command markers.

Possible Approaches for Detecting Commands

Different applications support unique ways of visually determining which tool is active or which command has just been issued. For example, in Adobe Photoshop you can tell the active tool by looking at which tool button is rendered darker than the others [Figure 5a]. This information is persistent and available for the entire time the tool is active. The buttons of many products become highlighted to one colour when the mouse if over, and another darker colour when they are clicked [Figure 5b]. Some products such as Autodesk Maya have a status bar indicating which tool or menu item the cursor is over [Figure 5c]. By combining this information with when the mouse button was clicked (perhaps from the audio track), one could determine which tools and menu items were used.

Figure 5. Example avenues for determining tool and command usage in: (A) Adobe Photoshop, (B) Microsoft Office, (C) Autodesk Maya, (d) Autodesk AutoCAD.

Commands in AutoCAD can be entered in multiple ways: clicking on a button, typing into the command line, issuing a shortcut, entering a command alias, or issued from an automated script. However, regardless of how the command is issued, all command history shows up in the command line window [Figure 5d] creating a good option for tracking command usage. It is possible to close the command line window in AutoCAD, but most users leave it open, and it is open in all of the videos in our sample collection.

Optical Character Recognition (OCR)

In the AutoCAD command line history, a line of the format `Command:name` indicates that the command "name" has been issued. We started by capturing individual image frames with the OpenCV toolkit. We cut out areas of the image for each of the 4 visible text lines and attempted to run some standard OCR packages (ABBYY FineReader, SimpleOCR, ocropus, and others) to extract the text. Since most OCR packages are tuned to recognize printed and then scanned text, they performed quite poorly on the text in our video frames—generally recognizing less than 50% of the characters correctly. This is consistent with previous work [47] where it appears that most of the text was not recognized correctly. To improve on this, we rendered the alphabet of characters using the same font and anti-aliasing settings as a default installation of AutoCAD, scaled to the same amount as the text in the video. Then, we were able to step along the line comparing each character in the image to our dictionary of rendered characters. Enlarging the source image and moving it around slightly to account for sub-pixel rounding, then using a squared difference comparison of the pixel values let us find the matching character with greater than 99% accuracy. This, combined with a dictionary of the commands in AutoCAD let us achieve 100% accuracy in command recognition.

Video Relevance

At the beginning of each command, a relevance score, R, was calculated for all available videos weighting the current command most highly and weighting the previous five commands with a decreasing power function:

$$R(v) = \sum_{i=1}^{5} S(v, c_i) \times (6 - i)^2$$

Each video v's relevance score for a given command c, $S(v, c)$ was calculated using the following formula:

$$\begin{aligned} S(v,c) = {} & v.title(c) \times 10 \\ & + v.keywords(c) \times 8 \\ & + v.description(c) \times 7 \\ & + \textstyle\sum(v.comment(c) \times 6 + 0.02) \\ & + v.commands(c) \times 12 \end{aligned}$$

where $v.title(c)$ is 1 if the title of the video contained the command name c, otherwise it is 0. Similarly, $v.keywords(c)$, $v.description(c)$, $v.comment(c)$ and $v.commands(c)$ operate on the keywords, description, comments and command stream (if available) respectively. For each user comment the video had, 0.02 points were added to account for generally popular videos. In this model, having the command used in the command stream is worth more than having the command name in the title, which is in turn more valuable than having the command mentioned in the keywords, description or comments. If a video is already playing in the display, its score is multiplied by a factor starting at 1.2 which decreases linearly down to 0.0 after 5 minutes. This gives videos that have just started playing priority, and then makes it easier for videos to be replaced after they have been playing for some time. Videos among the most recent 50 to be viewed are excluded from the calculations to support variation in the selections. The videos with the highest relevance scores are selected to be played when a new command is started.

This is just one rating scheme, which we have found works well with our mixed collection of YouTube and professionally authored tutorial videos.

EXPERIMENT

We wanted to evaluate Ambient Help to see if users, in work-like situations, could derive some instructional value from the system. In addition, the study allowed us to look at distraction and productivity compared to traditional help.

Participants

Twelve paid volunteer participants (8 male, 4 female) between the ages of 23 and 30 were recruited through an email list of AutoCAD users. To be eligible the users were required to be proficient with AutoCAD and were asked how long they had been using the program and how often they typically use it, with results ranging from 4 to 10 years, and 3 to 7 days/week respectively. All participants had used AutoCAD in a professional setting as well as receiving formal classroom training with the software.

Apparatus

The experiment was conducted in an enclosed office using a 3.16GHz quad-core desktop computer running Windows 7 64-bit Edition. The graphics card was a NVIDIA Quadro FX 5600 and was running two 24" Dell monitors each at a resolution of 1920 by 1200. Participants were seated with their chair and keyboard directly in front of the main monitor with the second monitor angled and positioned to the right [Figure 1].

Design

A repeated measures within-participant design was used with the independent variables being *task* (*intense*, *casual*) and *help system* (*ambient*, *manual*). The ordering of *task* and *help system* were counterbalanced. Each of the four trial conditions lasted 15 minutes. During each trial the statistics the experimenter judged and counted were: number of videos watched, number of help pages viewed, the number of useful/interesting items found, and in which data stream they were found in.

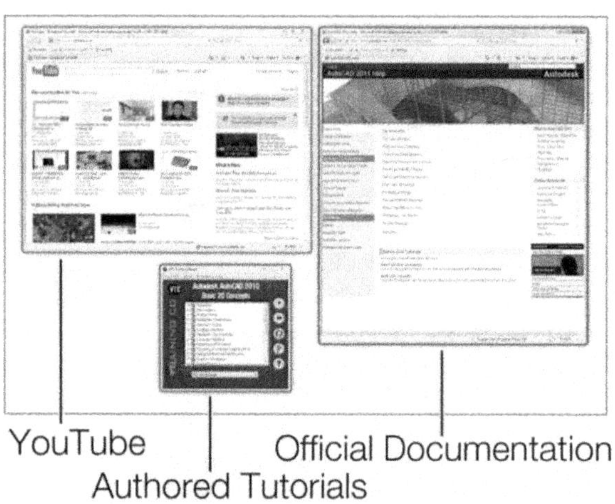

Figure 6. Setup of manual help condition.

Help Systems

The system described in this paper was used as the *ambient* condition. As a baseline comparison, the *manual* help system consisted of three windows: YouTube and the AutoCAD 2011 online documentation webpages, and the interface to an AutoCAD professional training DVD [Figure 6]. In this way the manual condition had all of the same material as the ambient help system, but was not integrated into AutoCAD and the content would need to be manually found by the participants.

Tasks

The *intense* and *casual* tasks were created to simulate two types of working conditions: those where the user is very focused on the task and cannot afford to be distracted (for instance, they are working towards a very tight deadline), and those where the user is working, but not in any particular rush (for example, they might spend some extra time browsing the internet or talking to colleagues).

For the *intense* task, users were given an AutoCAD document with a graphic underlay of 14 kitchen cabinet designs [Figure 7]. They were instructed to recreate these cabinets as quickly and accurately as possible. As motivation, the participant who completed the most cabinets was to be awarded an extra $100 gift card.

The task was designed to be simple enough that most experienced AutoCAD users would be able to draw the cabinets without much trouble. The cabinets themselves were also designed to each be of similar complexity so we could count and compare the user's cabinet drawing performance in both help system conditions.

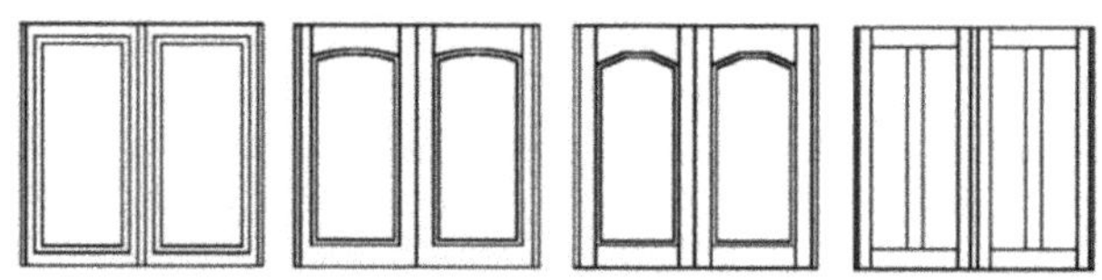

Figure 7. Portion of the intense task document.

For the *casual* task, participants were given a set of blueprints for a house and told to modify or extend the drawings in any manner they chose. Some examples given were to add a patio or some landscaping elements. The only requirement was that they use 3 commands from each of two command lists: *basic* commands, and *rare* commands. The *basic* list contained 20 of the most frequently used AutoCAD commands such as LINE, ERASE, and RECTANG, which are commands that all AutoCAD users would know. The *rare* list contained a collection of 10 commands which are among the 100 most frequently used commands, but are used by a small (<5%) percentage of the user population. The idea being that these would be useful commands that the participants were not familiar with. To ensure the commands selected from this list were new to the user, they were instructed to only choose commands from this list they had not used before. This allowed us to test the help systems when users may explicitly need help and also when they are doing exploratory learning.

Procedure

Upon arrival the participants were told that we were testing to see if *"a secondary display of information could be helpful to people while using AutoCAD"*. It was also explained that we would be presenting the help content in two different ways and we would be looking to see if they found any information that was useful or interesting to them. They were encouraged to *"glance at, or interact with, the content on the secondary monitor"* as much as they wanted to, and if they found anything useful or interesting, to let us know so we could keep a record. If during the study the examiner saw the participant looking at the secondary monitor for 10 seconds, he would prompt the user to explain what they were looking at and if they found anything useful.

Results

Because the two tasks were so different, separate analysis was performed for each of the *task* conditions.

Useful Items Found

To assess the effectiveness of the Ambient Help system for providing useful information to the user, we looked at the number of useful or interesting items found in each condition [Figure 8]. For the *casual* task, repeated measure analysis of variance showed a main effect for *help system* ($F_{1,11}$ = 12.6, p < .005) with means of 3.25 items for *ambient* and 1.25 items for *manual*, a 2.6 times increase. In the *intense* task the means were 0.92 items for *ambient* and 0.17 for *manual*. This difference however did not reach significance ($F_{1,11}$ = 2.83, p = .121).

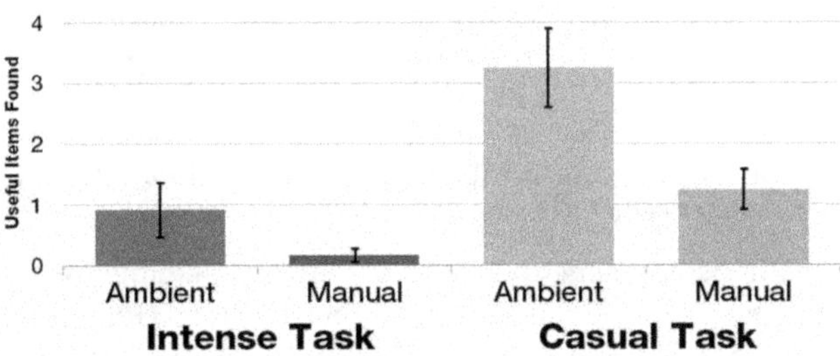

Figure 8. Average number of useful items found in each of the four task/help system conditions. (Note: Error bars report standard error).

With the cursor tracking data we can also look at how much time the users spent on average in AutoCAD and on the second monitor for each condition [Figure 9]. It is interesting to note that users found 2.6 times as many useful items while using the Ambient Help system in the *casual* task although they spent about the same amount of time on the second display for both help system conditions (17.7% and 18.4%). This result is consistent with the goal of the Ambient Help system to have users find more useful items, and they are able to do that without spending any more time than they would in a traditional manual help situation.

Impact on Performance

As a measure of performance in the *intense* task, we looked at the number of cabinets completed with each help system [Figure 10]. The mean results were 7.88 for *ambient* and 8.63 for *manual* with standard deviations of 4.54 and 3.73 respectively. The analysis of variance did not show the difference to be significant ($F_{1,12}$ = 0.974, ns) supporting our belief that Ambient Help would not have a negative impact when the user is immersed in an intensive task.

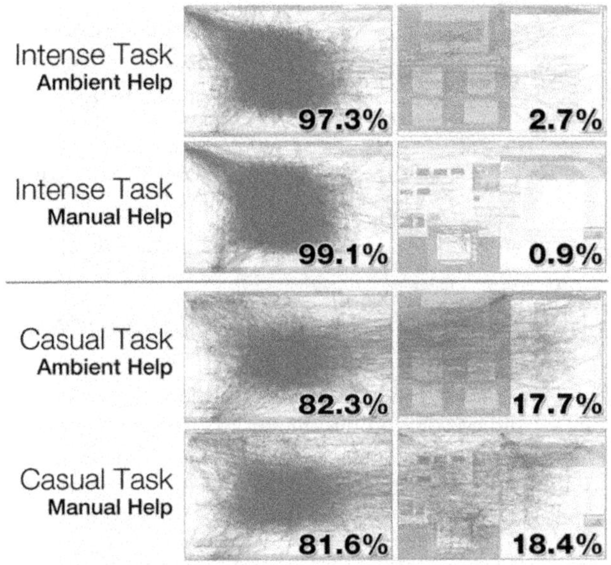

Figure 9. Cursor movement for each condition of all participants. Percentages show fraction of time spent on each monitor.

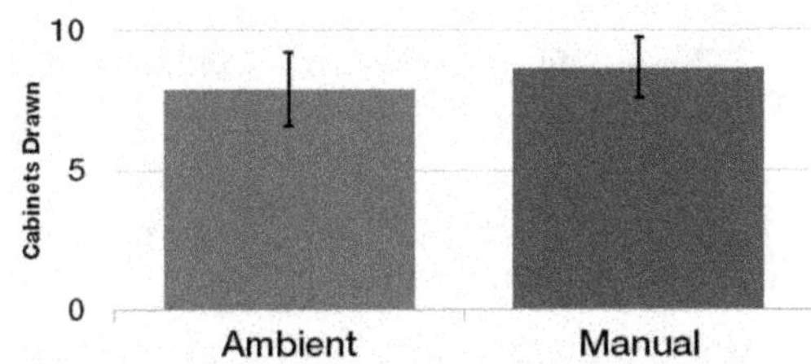

Figure 10. Number of cabinets drawn in the intense task. (Note: error bars report standard error)

After each condition the participants were asked to rate some statements on a Likert scale (between 1-Strongly Disagree, and 7-Strongly Agree). One of the statements was *"The content of the extra monitor was helpful"* [Figure 11]. The results have been aggregated into three categories: Disagree (1, 2), Neither (3, 4, 5) and Agree (6, 7). The majority of users (8 of 12) said they found the *ambient* system helpful in the *casual* task compared to only 1 user who found the *manual* system helpful.

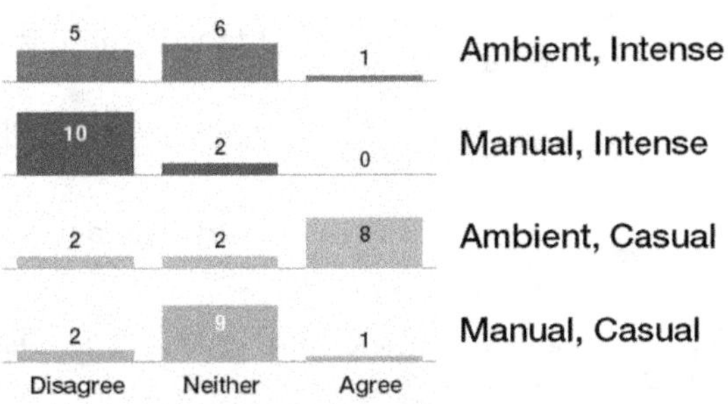

Figure 11. Results for *"The content of the extra monitor was helpful"*.

Participants were also asked if they *"found the content of the extra monitor distracting"*. In both the *intense* and *casual* tasks, 3 of 12 users agreed this was the case for the ambient help system [Figure 12].

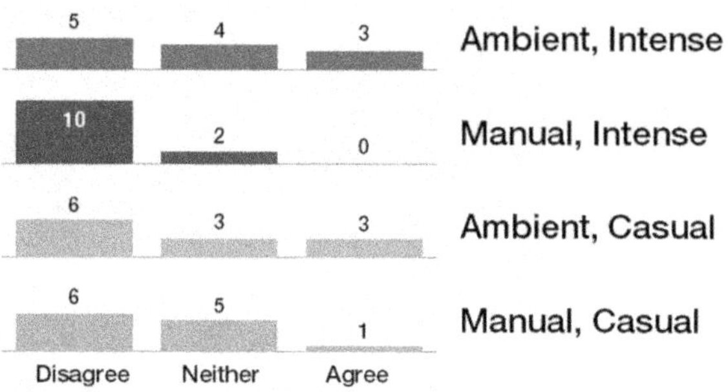

Figure 12. Results for *"The content of the extra monitor was distracting"*.

While not a longitudinal study, if we look at each user's rating of the distraction during the first task they used the ambient help interface compared with their second, 5 users said the interface was distracting during their first task, compared to only 1 during the second task [Figure 13].

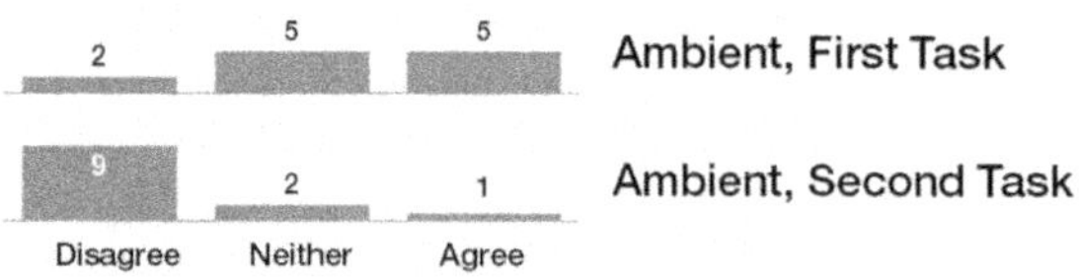

Figure 13. Results for *"The content of the extra monitor was distracting"* during the ambient help condition in first vs. second task.

With these results, we believe that many users would not find the interface distracting given time to get used to it.

Besides distraction, participants were also asked if the *"content of the extra monitor hindered their productivity"* [Figure 14]. Few users felt that either help system hindered their productivity in either task. This is of particular importance in the *intense* task where the participants were trying to be as productive as possible. It is promising that for this task the *ambient* and *manual* systems had essentially the same subjective rating, suggesting that even when not in use, the ambient display is no more of a hindrance to a user than a monitor showing static content.

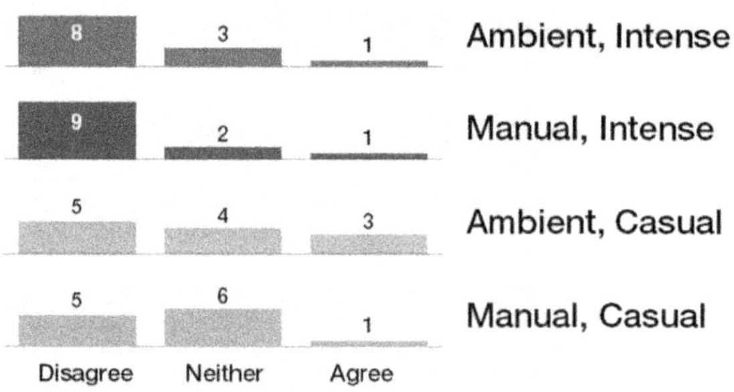

Figure 14. Results for *"The content of the extra monitor hindered my productivity"*.

Content Sources

For each of the two content sources (*videos*, and *help pages*), the number of items viewed was significantly higher in the *ambient* than the *manual* help condition [Figure 15]. For *videos* the means were 4.08 and 1.67 for *ambient* and *manual* respectively ($F_{1,11} = 5.04, p < .05$) and for *help pages* the means were 4.83 and 2.83 ($F_{1,11} = 8.25, p < .05$). It is important to note that here "viewed" means that the participant spent some amount of time actually looking at the content, not that it was simply shown on the screen.

The number of useful items found was also higher using the ambient help system for both *videos* (1.0 vs. 0.5) and *help pages* (3.17 vs. 0.92), however only the difference with *help pages* reached significance ($F_{1,11} = 7.44, p < .05$). Overall the ratio of useful items found to items viewed is significantly higher for *help pages* than for *videos* (0.448 vs. 0.184: $F_{1,11} = 7.56, p < .05$) as well as for *ambient* help compared to *manual* help (0.425 vs. 0.203: $F_{1,11} = 8.17, p < .05$). We believe this ratio is higher for help pages than videos since the static pages are easier to consume quickly. Several times we saw participants look at a video for 10 to 20 seconds and then move on to the help page because the "video was taking too long". The time it takes to get useful information from a video can hopefully be reduced by more complete tagging of the video content allowing the system to play the video at the point of the relevant information.

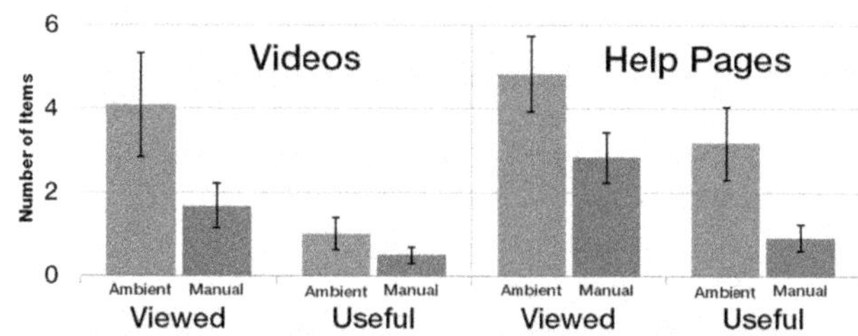

Figure 15. Number of videos and help pages viewed and found useful in each of the help system conditions. (Note: error bars report standard error)

Overall when users were asked if they felt either system could be useful, 7 of 12 agreed the Ambient Help system could be useful compared to 0 for *manual.* [Figure 16]. In fact, one user during the manual help condition remarked *"Oh no, my videos are gone now. I wish I had them back, they would be really useful right now"*.

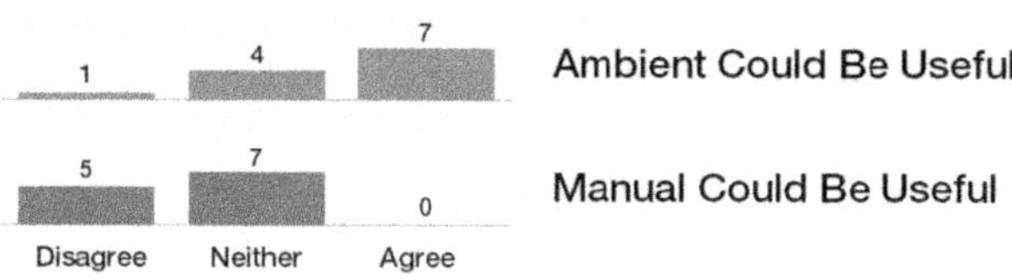

Figure 16. Results for *"A system like <Ambient/Manual> could be useful"*.

DISCUSSION & FUTURE WORK

Our study has shown that the Ambient Help system significantly improved the ability of the user to find useful information during casual work, while generally not objectively, or subjectively, hindering performance during intense tasks. A longer term study, or one performed on the users' own machine in their standard environment would be useful to see how these results hold over a longer period of time and explore the impact of the system on higher-level performance and learning. Given the often negative reactions users have to new help systems and interface designs, it would be interesting to see in what scenarios users would choose to keep the ambient display open.

We measured the number of useful or interesting items that the participants found with the system. It would be valuable to explore the relationship between information that is *interesting* to the user now and the potential it has to become *useful* in the future.

A potential concern with such an active help system is that it may be distracting to users. We found that after their second 15-minute exposure to our system most users did not find it distracting. However, we believe the system could be even less distracting if we choose not to animate the position changes of the videos from the bottom to the primary position while in the ambient mode. There may be other ideas such as pausing the videos completely while over the main application, or updating less frequently in general which would be interesting to explore.

We chose to show five videos and one web-based help page but a study to examine how many channels of information supports the best mix of providing information without the user becoming overloaded would be valuable. We suspect this might come to the finding that different users would like to see different volumes of information and would lead to the question of how to design the interface to support varying amounts of channels.

While we only used two sources of videos and one source of text-based help for this prototype, future work could explore using more sources and how to best integrate them into a single system. Along with more sources a more sophisticated algorithm could be developed for finding relevant content. Additional pieces of context which could be used to improve context matching include: which Ribbon tab is active, which dialogs are open, and the actual content of the document. Although not accessible through the public API, YouTube has the ability to automatically generate closed captioning data for their videos. This text might be a valuable resource for trying to automatically determine what is going on in each of the clips.

By virtue of being an always-on display, the transaction cost to access the help information is already very low. We could decrease the cost of interacting with the content by introducing keyboard shortcuts to perform some of the more common actions such as listening to a video. It would also be nice to reduce the amount of time required for a user to scan a video for useful content. We have thought of introducing some graphic overlays to the videos to more obviously show which commands are being used, and a longer selection of the closed captioning text to serve as a "glanceable summary" so they can be more quickly scanned for useful information.

CONCLUSION

Design considerations for an ambient system that provides help content using a push rather than pull delivery model were discussed. The resulting Ambient Help system offers the potential to increase the user's learning in multiple ways: both "intentional" learning, where the user knew they needed help, and perhaps as importantly, "unintentional" learning, where the push model presents information the user wouldn't even know to look for. In the casual task, which simulates what we envision to be the primary environment for using this type of system, Ambient Help led to 2.6 times as many useful insights as the control. Besides being helpful during casual tasks, users generally agreed that the system did not negatively impact their productivity during intense work and this result was supported by the quantitative data. Although implemented in AutoCAD, we believe Ambient Help is a general solution which could be made to work with almost any software application where learning is an important issue.

ACKNOWLEDGEMENTS

We thank Ramtin Attar for designing the AutoCAD tasks.

REFERENCES

1. Adamczyk, P. D., Iqbal, S. T., and Bailey, B. P. (2005). A method, system, and tools for intelligent interruption management. In *Proceedings of the 4th International Workshop on Task Models and Diagrams*. 123-126.
2. Ames, A. L. (2001). Just what they need, just when they need it: an introduction to embedded assistance. *ACM SIGDOC*. 111-115.
3. Anderson, J. R., Boyle, C. F., Farrell, R. and Reisner, B. J. (1984). Cognitive principles in the design of computer tutors. *Cognitive Science Society*. 2-9.
4. Andrade, O., Bean, N., and Novick, D. (2009). The macro-structure of help. *ACM SIGDOC 2009*. 143-150.
5. Baecker, R. (2002). Showing instead of telling. *ACM SIGDOC*. 10-16.
6. Brandt, J., Dontcheva, M., Weskamp, M., and Klemmer, S. R. (2010). Example-centric programming: integrating web search into the development environment. *CHI*, 513-522.
7. Buxton, W. (1995). Integrating the periphery and context: A new taxonomy of telematics. *GI*, 239-246.
8. Cadiz, J. J., Venolia, G., Jancke, G., and Gupta, A. (2002). Designing and deploying an information awareness interface. *ACM CSCW '02*, 314-323.
9. Dixon, M. and Fogarty, J. (2010). Prefab: implementing advanced behaviors using pixel-based reverse engineering of interface structure. *ACM CHI*, 1525-1534.
10. Dourish, P. and Bly, S. (1992). Portholes: supporting awareness in a distributed work group. *CHI*, 541-547.
11. Eagan, J. R. and Stasko, J. T. (2008). The buzz: supporting user tailorability in awareness applications. *ACM CHI*. 1729-1738.
12. Farkas, D. K. (1993). The role of balloon help. *Journal of Computer Documentation*. 17(2):3-19.
13. Fitzmaurice, G., Matejka, J., Mordatch, I., Khan, A., and Kurtenbach, G. (2008). Safe 3D navigation. *I3D*, 7-15.

14. Fosso, F. and Porta, M. (2009). A vision-based attentive user interface with (semi-)automatic parameter calibration. *Proceedings CompSysTech '09*, vol. 433. 1-6

15. Goodall, S. D. (1992). Online help: a part of documentation. *Systems Documentation*. 169-174.

16. Grabler, F., Agrawala, M., Li, W., Dontcheva, M. and Igarashi, T. (2009). Generating photo manipulation tutorials by demonstration. *ACM SIGGRAPH*. 66.

17. Grandhi, S. and Jones, Q. (2010). Technology-mediated interruption management. *Int. J. Hum.-Comput. Stud.* 68, 5 (May. 2010), 288-306.

18. Gray, W. D. and Boehm-Davis, D. A. (2000). Milliseconds Matter: An Introduction to Microstrategies and to Their Use in Describing and Predicting Interactive Behavior. *Journal of Experimental Psychology: Applied*, 6 (4), 322-335.

19. Grossman, T., Matejka, J., and Fitzmaurice, G. (2010). Chronicle: Capture, Exploration, and Playback of Document Workflow Histories. *ACM UIST'10*.

20. Grossman, T. and Fitzmaurice, G. (2010). ToolClips: an investigation of contextual video assistance for functionality understanding. *ACM CHI '10*. 1515-1524.

21. Grossman, T., Fitzmaurice, G., and Attar, R. (2009). A survey of software learnability: metrics, methodologies and guidelines. *ACM CHI*, 649-658.

22. Hameed, S., Ferris, T., Jayaraman, S. and Sarter, N. (2009). Using Informative Peripheral Visual and Tactile Cues to Support Task and Interruption Management. *Human Factors*, 51 (2). 126-135.

23. Harrison, S. M. (1995). A comparison of still, animated, or nonillustrated on-line help with written or spoken instructions in a graphical user interface. *CHI*. 82-89.

24. Hazlewood, W. R., Connelly, K., Makice, K., and Lim, Y. (2008). Exploring evaluation methods for ambient information systems.*CHI Ext. Abstracts*, 2973-2978.

25. Henzinger, M., Chang, B., Milch, B., and Brin, S. (2005). Query-Free News Search. *ACM WWW*, 101-126.

26. Horvitz, E. (1999). Principles of mixed-initiative user interfaces. *ACM SIGCHI*. 159-166.

27. Jackson, S. (2001). Editing computer hardware procedures for multimedia presentation. *SIGDOC*. 68-72.

28. Karr-Wisniewski, P. and Lu, Y. (2010). When more is too much: Operationalizing technology overload and exploring its impact on knowledge worker productivity. *Comput. Hum. Behav*. 26, 5 (Sep. 2010), 1061-1072.

29. Kelleher, C. and Pausch, R. (2005). Stencils-based tutorials: design and evaluation. *ACM CHI*. 541-550.

30. Knabe, K. (1995). Apple guide: a case study in user-aided design of online help. *ACM CHI*. 286-287.

31. Liu, T.-Y., Huang, Y.-C. and Chen, W.-C. (2001). A novel algorithm for real-time full screen capture system. *Multimedia Signal Processing*. 395-400.

32. Maekawa, T., Yanagisawa, Y., Sakurai, Y., Kishino, Y., Kamei, K., and Okadome, T. (2009). Web searching for daily living. *ACM SIGIR'09*, 27-34.

33. Mankoff, J., Dey, A. K., Hsieh, G., Kientz, J., Lederer, S., and Ames, M. (2003). Heuristic evaluation of ambient displays. In *ACM CHI '03*, 169-176.

34. Matejka, J., Li, W., Grossman, T., and Fitzmaurice, G. (2009). CommunityCommands: command recommendations for software applications. *UIST* 193-202.

35. Matthews, T. (2006). Designing and evaluating glanceable peripheral displays. *DIS '06*. ACM, 343-345.

36. McFarlane, D. C. and Latorella, K. A. (2002). The scope and importance of human interruption in human-computer interaction design. *Hum.-Comput. Interact.* 17, 1 (Mar. 2002), 1-61.

37. Novick, D. G. and Ward, K. (2006). Why don't people read the manual? *ACM international Conference on Design of Communication*. 11-18

38. Palmiter, S. and Elkerton, J. (1993). Animated demonstrations for learning procedural computer-based tasks. *Human.-Computer Interaction*. 8(3):193-216.

39. Plaisant, C. and Shneiderman, B. (2005). Show Me! Guidelines for Producing Recorded Demonstrations. *Visual Languages and Human-Centric Comp.* 171-178.

40. Plaue, C. and Stasko, J. (2007). Animation in a peripheral display: distraction, appeal, and information conveyance in varying display configurations. *GI*, 135-142.

41. Pousman, Z. and Stasko, J. (2006). A taxonomy of ambient information systems: four patterns of design. In *ACM AVI '06*, 67-74.

42. Sawyer, R.K. (Ed.), The Cambridge Handbook of the Learning Sciences. Cambridge University Press, 2006.

43. Shen, X., Moere, A. V., Eades, P., and Hong, S. (2008). The long-term evaluation of Fisherman in a partial-attention environment. In *ACM Beyond Time and Errors: Novel Evaluation Methods For information Visualization, BELIV '08*, 1-6.

44. Shneiderman, B. (1983). Direct Manipulation: A Step Beyond Programming Languages. *Computer*. 16(8):57-69.

45. Twidale, M. B. (2005). Over the Shoulder Learning: Supporting Brief Informal Learning. *CSCW*, 505-547.

46. Vogel, D. and Balakrishnan, R. (2004). Interactive public ambient displays: transitioning from implicit to explicit, public to personal, interaction with multiple users. *ACM UIST 2004*, 137-146.

47. Yeh, T., Chang, T., and Miller, R. C. (2009). Sikuli: using GUI screenshots for search and automation. *ACM UIST*. 183-192.

48. Zeleznik, R. C., Bragdon, A., Liu, C.-C. and Forsberg, A. (2008). Lineogrammer: creating diagrams by drawing. *ACM UIST*. 161-170.

Parameter Selection in Keyboard-Based Dialog Boxes

Jeff Hendy, Juliette Link, Kellogg S. Booth & Joanna McGrenere
Department of Computer Science, University of British Columbia, Vancouver, BC, V6T 1Z4, Canada
{jchendy, jlink, joanna, ksbooth}@cs.ubc.ca

ABSTRACT
Recent keyboard-based alternatives to WIMP interfaces do not have good support for commands that require multiple parameters. We remedy this by extending a previous design and mimicking dialog boxes to provide good visual feedback while still keeping the advantages of keyboard input. A laboratory study showed the new technique to be competitive with dialog boxes on speed and error rate, but strongly preferred over dialog boxes by experienced command line users. This is a marked improvement over the previous design, which was also preferred by the target user group but did not compete with dialog boxes in terms of performance.

Author Keywords
Command-line interfaces, dialog boxes, WIMP

ACM Classification Keywords
H52 [Information interfaces and presentation]: User Interfaces – Graphical user interfaces.

General Terms
Design

INTRODUCTION
Many systems allow keyboard input to augment or replace standard WIMP interfaces. The goal of these keyboard-based systems is to increase satisfaction and performance for experienced command line users. Examples include Quicksilver [1], Enso [3], Inky [4], GEKA [2], and Ubiquity [5]. They provide well thought out ways to specify commands. Not as much has gone into how parameters are specified, especially for commands with multiple parameters. In WIMP interfaces, parameters are often specified through dialog boxes, especially multiple parameters. Evidence suggests experienced computer users strongly dislike dialog boxes [2]. Quicksilver and Enso support only one parameter. Ubiquity and Inky support multiple parameters, but use imprecise syntaxes that can make parameter entry confusing. They are designed specifically for web-based commands with smaller, simpler sets of parameters. In contrast, GEKA has a keyword-based parameter system in which any number of parameters can be precisely input in any order, but it showed lower performance compared to existing WIMP dialog boxes [2].

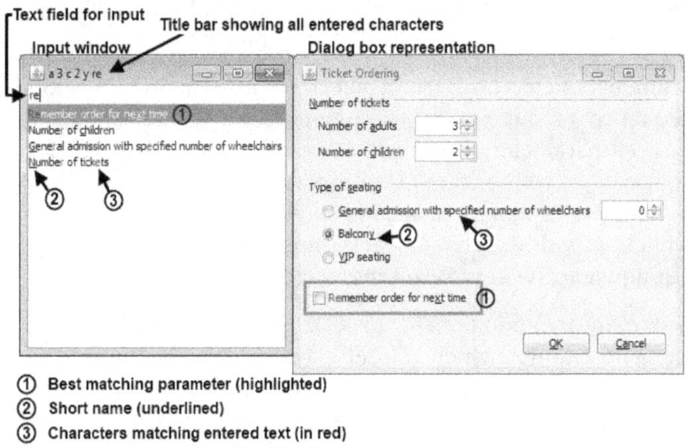

Figure 1: KDB graphical feedback. The characters "a 3 c 2 y re" have been entered. This sets the values of Number of adults (3), Number of children (2), and Type of seating (Balcony). The final input, "re", is selecting which parameter will be set next.

We describe a new method for specifying parameters, keyboard-based dialog boxes (KDB), that allows input of any number of parameters in any order. Our goal is to increase performance, improve experience, and minimize cognitive load. To accomplish this, KDB provides graphical feedback that looks and behaves very much like the dialog boxes users are familiar with, but with the speed of a command line interface. A lab experiment with experienced command line users showed our new method is preferred to and performs competitively with WIMP dialog boxes.

KDB DESIGN
KDB is based on GEKA. It makes minor changes to the GEKA command language but replaces its graphical feedback with a modified version of each command's existing dialog box. These changes should give KDB a strong performance advantage over GEKA and make it competitive with WIMP dialog boxes.

Multiple parameter entry utilizes auto-completion to quickly specify parameter name and value pairs. Example parameter specifications for the `print` command include:

`pages 2`
set the value of `pages` *to* `2`
`printer downstairs`
set the value of `printer` *to* `downstairs`
`downstairs`
because `downstairs` *can only be a value for* `printer`*, this sets* `printer` *to* `downstairs`

For parameter name selection, a ranked list of possible

matches is generated after each character is typed. Typing more characters refines the list. Pressing **SPACE** accepts the top-ranked match and moves on to value entry. If a parameter has a discrete set of possible values, the value is selected using the same auto-complete mechanism. Otherwise, the value is typed in its entirety. Again pressing **SPACE** accepts the value and allows the user to specify another parameter. If the top-ranked parameter name has a Boolean value, pressing **SPACE** toggles the value and immediately moves on to another parameter.

Each parameter also has a short name, which is a short sequence of characters that unambiguously identifies the desired parameter name. Auto-completion uses our GEKA four-category algorithm [2] to order possible matches: *exact match, prefix match, substring match, subsequence match*. Matches within each category are sorted alphabetically. Up/down arrow keys scroll the ranked list.

There are two components to KDB graphical feedback, the input window, which closely resembles the graphical feedback in GEKA, and a new dialog box representation, which provides additional visual feedback. Figure 1 shows these two components. The input window has a text box where input is typed and a list of possible matches to the input is shown. The best match is highlighted and appears first. For all entries, the matching characters are in red. The short name is underlined. The dialog box representation provides graphical feedback identical to a command's WIMP dialog box. Because users are already familiar with this dialog box, we expect that displaying it will allow users to quickly identify parameter names they want to use.

The best matching parameter highlighted in the input window is shown with a blue box in the dialog box. The dialog box also has the short name for each parameter underlined and the characters that match the entered text are in red. This gives users the same information whether they look for feedback in the parameter list or the dialog box. Highlighting also allows users to quickly verify that the parameter they want is selected. If the best matching parameter is located in a sub-dialog box or a different tab within the dialog box, the feedback is automatically updated to show the location with that parameter.

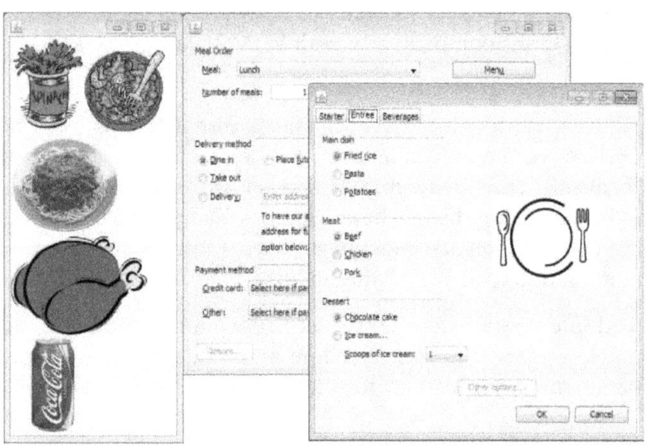

Figure 2: The dialog box condition showing the long task for order food. The user has already clicked "menu" to open a sub-dialog. The left window shows that "spinach salad," "pasta," "chicken," and "coke" must be selected. Salad and drink options are in different tabs. Parameters not listed in the left window use default values and are not set by participants.

LABORATORY EXPERIMENT

We conducted a laboratory experiment to evaluate KDB against the goals of high performance and preference over dialog boxes (DBs) by experienced command line users. We also included a GEKA condition to compare KDB to an existing keyboard-based interface.

The tasks were to specify parameters for one of four commands. This was done in three conditions: KDB, GEKA as implemented by Hendy et al. [2], and DBs. With DBs, participants could use any combination of mouse clicks, **TAB** key navigation, or keyboard mnemonics.

The experiment tested familiar commands from a standard application and unfamiliar commands that we invented. It also tested simple commands, specified in a single DB, and complex commands, which involved multiple tabs and sub-dialog boxes. The four commands are listed below.

	Familiar	Unfamiliar
Simple	**Insert table**	**Order tickets**
Complex	**Print**	**Order food**

For the two familiar commands we implemented replicas of Word 2003 DBs (including parameter names). All of our participants reported using these DBs in Word 2003. **Order tickets** was created for this experiment; it has the same number of parameters and a similar DB layout to **insert table**. **Order food** was similarly analogous to **print**. The two invented DBs are shown in Figures 1 & 2.

For each command in the experiment, we created a short task, in which only one parameter value was to be specified, and a long task, in which four values were to be specified. Thus, there were eight different task combinations. For the complex commands, both the short and long tasks required the use of at least one sub-dialog box. As in an earlier study of GEKA [2], all tasks were prompted using image-based descriptions to avoid biases introduced by using text descriptions. Figure 2 shows the prompts for the long **order food** task. For each task, the command was pre-selected in the interface, meaning that the dialog box or GEKA parameter pane was already open. The participant needed only to select the specified parameter values. This was done to isolate parameter selection times.

Participants

There were 12 participants (3 females). In a pre-screening questionnaire all reported command line experience and correctly answered at least two of three command line knowledge questions. Participants received $20. The top third fastest participants got a $5 bonus to motivate quick and accurate performance.

Procedure

Each participant completed a single two-hour session. A session began with an introduction. Participants then completed all trials in a particular condition before moving on to the next condition. Presentation order of the three conditions was counterbalanced. Each condition began with an introduction to the method used and a practice block in which the eights tasks were each completed once. During a practice block, participants could ask questions and refer to printouts of the task images that referred to each parameter. No aids were permitted during experimental blocks.

Presentation order of the four commands was randomized across participants but remained constant across the three conditions for each participant. The order of the two task lengths was similarly randomized across participants. During each condition, participants completed one trial for each of the two task lengths for a command and then repeated this pair four more times before moving on to the next command. Completion time was recorded for each trial from when the participant dismissed a begin-task prompt (by clicking the mouse or pressing a keyboard button) to when the task was successfully completed.

An error occurred if a participant selected `OK` in the DB condition or pressed `ENTER` in the GEKA or KDB conditions with an incorrect set of parameter values selected. If a participant made an error during a trial, a pop up notified the participant that an error was made and the task had to be repeated until it was successfully completed. After all trials for a command, participants took a 30 second break. Between conditions, participants took a 2 minute break. A questionnaire and interview completed the study.

Design

The experiment used a mixed factor design: 3 (interface) x 2 (command complexity) x 2 (command familiarity) x 2 (task length) x 5 (repetition) x 6 (presentation order). All factors were within-participant except for presentation order, which was a between-participant control variable. Bonferroni corrections were used for all pairwise comparisons. Greenhouse-Geisser corrections, identified by non-integer df, were used when sphericity was an issue.

Note on experimental design and participants

The focus of the KDB design and evaluation was on experienced command line users, but we were also interested in exploring how KDB would be received by users lacking command-line experience. Our initial experimental design thus included experience as a factor and we had 12 additional participants with no command line experience. We saw potential trends due to experience level, but there was very high variance in the data from inexperienced users. We would have needed to run many more participants to expose any significant differences that existed. We thus only report data from experienced users.

RESULTS

Most participants used both the keyboard and mouse (11/12), choosing the keyboard for different combinations of: inputting numbers (10/12), using a few mnemonics (4/12) and/or tabbing between adjacent parameters (7/12), and used the mouse for everything else.

Completion Time

A RM ANOVA indicated no main effect or interactions of presentation order, so it was dropped as a factor. Figure 3 shows that participants got faster over time: a main effect of repetition ($F(1.51, 16.58)=77.812$, $p<.000$, $\eta^2=.876$) with significant differences ($p<.05$) between all pairs of repetitions, except repetitions 4 and 5 ($p=.20$), indicating performance was plateauing. The RM ANOVA we report dropped repetition as a factor and used mean times for only repetitions 4 and 5 to eliminate the obvious learning affect.

Overall, KDB and DBs are not significantly different. There was a main effect of interface ($F(2, 22)=20.476$, $p<.001$, $\eta^2=.654$) with mean times for DBs, KDB, and GEKA being 5.76s, 6.19s, and 9.69s. Pairwise comparisons showed no significant difference between KDB and DBs ($p=1.0$). All other pairs had significant differences ($p<.05$).

For simple commands, DBs are fastest. The interfaces were impacted differently by command complexity (an interaction effect between interface and complexity, $F(2,22)=5.969$, $p=.008$, $\eta^2=.352$). For simple commands, a trend ($p=.072$) suggested DBs (4.09s) were faster than KDB (5.73s), but there was no difference for complex commands ($p=1.0$). GEKA was slower than DBs for both ($p<.003$).

For short tasks, KDB is fastest. An interaction between interface and task length ($F(2,22)=30.88$, $p=.000$, $\eta^2=.737$)

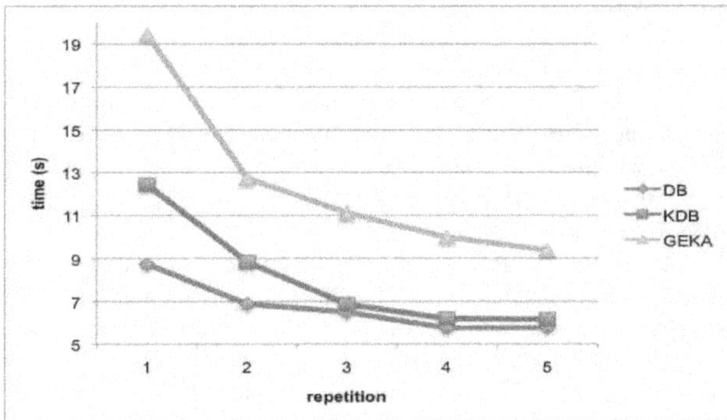

Figure 3: Mean completion times (N=12)

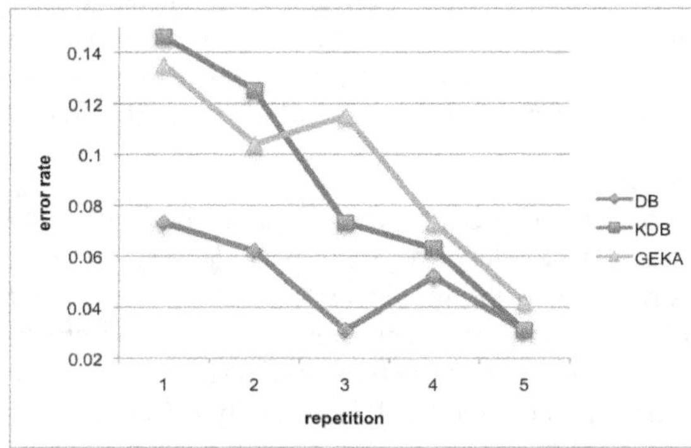

Figure 4: Error rates for interfaces in each repetition (N=12)

indicated that for short tasks, KDB (2.64s) was faster (p=.007) than DBs (3.74s). There was no difference between the two for long tasks (p=.355). GEKA was slower than KDB for both task lengths (p <.007).

There was no interaction between interface and command familiarity ($F(2,2)$=.867, p=.434, η^2=.073).

Errors

Figure 4 shows that participants made fewer errors as the study progressed. While there was a trend of interface ($F(2,22)$=3.01, p=.07, η^2=.215) across all repetitions, by repetition 5, errors had nearly disappeared for all three interfaces. In repetition 5, out of the 96 total trials for each interface DBs, KDB, and GEKA had 3, 3, and 4 errors, respectively, across all participants.

Questionnaire and interview

Overall, participants rated KDB the highest, with a mean of 17.00 on a scale of 0 ("I really dislike it") to 20 ("I really like it") vs. 10.50 for DBs and 12.25 for GEKA. A RM ANOVA showed no significant difference between DBs and GEKA (p=.392); all other pairs were significant (p<.004). When asked to explain why they preferred KDB, the most common reasons cited were being able to set parameter values without first having to specify the parameter name (7/12), liking the graphical feedback from the dialog box representation (6/12) (especially for verifying that the correct parameters were set (4/12)), and being able to only use the keyboard (5/12).

Participants said they were faster with KDB, with a mean of 18.17 on a scale of 0 ("very slow") to 20 ("very fast") vs. 11.75 for DBs and 13.25 for GEKA. There was no significant difference between DBs and GEKA (p=1.0); all other pairs were significant (p<.03). Participants explained they sometimes were able to skip specifying the parameter name (4/12) or that typing was faster than a mouse (3/12).

Participants said they made fewer errors with DBs, with a mean of 2.17 on a scale of 0 ("very few errors") to 20 ("many errors") vs. 6.58 for KDB and 9.08 for GEKA. The only significant difference was between DBs and GEKA (p=.002). While they did not necessarily like the mouse, they felt that using a mouse made errors less likely (5/12).

Ten of 12 participants said KDB was easier to learn than GEKA and gave reasons similar to why they had preferred KDB overall. However, DBs were felt to be the easiest to learn because participants were already familiar with them.

LIMITATIONS

Because we made improvements to both the command language (the changes only ever decrease the required keystrokes) and the graphical feedback, it is not clear how much of the improvement over GEKA can be attributed to each. Because the reduction in keystrokes is fairly small and the graphical feedback is radically different, we believe that most of the gains are a result of the graphical feedback.

While we made an effort to evaluate diverse tasks by using simple, complex, familiar, and unfamiliar commands with short and long tasks, our experiment still used only a small number of commands and tasks compared to what users experience in actual scenarios. Furthermore, while we saw performance appear to plateau by the end of our experiment, we cannot know how performance would change with prolonged usage. A longitudinal field study would help address these issues. Additional future work includes a study with more focus on non-experienced users and one that examines cognitive load.

DISCUSSION AND CONCLUSIONS

KDB showed speed and error rates in the final repetitions nearly identical to DBs. Participants reported a very strong preference for KDB. This suggests KDB should be an option for parameter specification: it makes experienced users more satisfied without impeding performance.

Despite the very similar speeds between dialog boxes and KDB, participants felt that they were much faster with KDB. We found a similar contradiction while evaluating GEKA [2]. This is an interesting finding about users' perceptions that bears further investigation.

KDB significantly outperforms GEKA in speed under almost all conditions. This suggests that the dialog box-like graphical feedback of KDB is a major improvement over the feedback in GEKA. Another major improvement over GEKA is that KDB can support a wide variety of parameter types. Earlier work [2] lists several types of commands that GEKA is not able to accommodate because of its restrictive graphical feedback. KDB overcomes most limitations.

We previously showed GEKA to be an effective general interaction method for specifying many types of commands, but it fell short compared to dialog boxes. We have now shown that KDB outperforms GEKA for parameter selection and is highly competitive with dialog boxes. Application designers looking to improve interfaces for experienced command line users could incorporate KDB-style parameter selection into any keyboard-based command selection scheme, including but not limited to GEKA. This would give users a well-liked way to select all commands and parameters using only a keyboard.

REFERENCES

[1] Blacktree (2009). Retrieved March 31. http://www.blacktree.com

[2] Hendy, J., Booth, K.S., McGrenere, J. (2010). Graphically Enhanced Keyboard Accelerators for GUIs. In *Proc. Graphics Interface 2010*, 3-10.

[3] Humanized (2009). Retrieved March 31. http://humanized.com

[4] Miller, R. C., Chou, V. H., Bernstein, M., Little, G., Van Kleek, M., Karger, D., and schraefel, m. (2008). Inky: a sloppy command line for the web with rich visual feedback. In *Proc. UIST 2008*, 131-140.

[5] Mozilla Labs. (2009). Ubiquity. Retrieved December 12. https://mozillalabs.com/ubiquity/

Categorization Costs for Hierarchical Keyboard Commands

Craig S. Miller
DePaul University
Chicago, IL
cmiller@cs.depaul.edu

Svetlin Denkov
DePaul University
Chicago, IL
svetlin.denkov@gmail.com

Richard C. Omanson
User Centric
Oakbrook Terrace, IL
romanson@usercentric.com

ABSTRACT
Previous research comparing methods of issuing commands found that selecting a toolbar item is faster than selecting an item from two menus with either a mouse or keyboard shortcut. Over the course of 90 trials, however, the keyboard method showed the most improvement, nearing the toolbar response time. The study presented in this paper compared the response time of the keyboard method across 240 trials when items were drawn from a single versus two menus. Throughout the trials, the 1-menu condition produced selection times that were on average 600 ms to 800 ms faster than the 2-menu condition suggesting users in the 2-menu condition were not able to bypass the menu decision by chunking the 3-key sequence into one cognitive unit. Models are presented to describe performance at various stages of learning. Practical implications are that hierarchical, category-based keyboard commands do not provide a clear advantage to toolbar-based selection and that theory-based evaluation methods may need to reflect this result.

Author Keywords
Keyboard shortcuts, toolbar, performance models, practice effects, command entry

ACM Classification Keywords
H.5.2 Information Interfaces and Presentation: User Interfaces—*Interaction styles*

General Terms
Experimentation, Human Factors, Theory

INTRODUCTION
Previous studies have shown that practiced users can select a command faster using a simple key sequence than by using the mouse to select the menu from a toolbar or menu [6, 7, 9]. In these studies, the simple keyboard command typically includes a control-key followed by a single key press for choosing the command. In contrast, a more recent study [10] suggests that more complex key sequences do not have such a clear advantage over toolbar selection. In that study, the keyboard command requires a control character followed by two keys: a key indicating a categorical selection and a key for selecting an item from the category. The study revealed faster selection times using a mouse-based toolbar than the two-level key sequence, at least throughout three blocks of practice consisting of 30 trials each (90 trials total). While the need for a categorical selection ostensibly contributed to the slower selection time for the keyboard command, it is not clear if additional practice would reduce the cost of categorical selection. Perhaps with more practice, users would eventually chunk the whole key sequence as one unit for selecting a command. For example, Lane et al. [8] report a result that suggests that hierchical key sequences can be chunked with enough experience. In their study, dedicated spreadsheet users were able to execute a 3-key command averaging 0.2 seconds per key. If the mental time cost of categorical selection can be similarly avoided, the two-level key sequence would provide the most efficient means for selecting a command or item for a practiced user.

This paper explores the cost of using two-level key sequences for selecting a command or item. Using a mock application in an experiment, participants were asked to select a window frame by issuing a three-key sequence. After issuing a control key (Window ALT key), the participant then pressed a key indicating a category (i.e., Business Lines or Regions) followed by a key indicating the selection from the category (e.g., Checking or Florida). To determine the mental cost of category selection, one condition required participants to select items from both categories and a second condition that avoided category selection by requiring participants to select items from one of the categories. By repeatedly asking participants to complete the task over 8 blocks of 30 trials (240 total trials), we investigate the the cost of categorical decision with user practice.

METHOD

Participants
This study was conducted with 20 participants between the ages of 21 and 42 with an average age of approximately 27. Eight of the participants were male and 12 were female. Fourteen of the participants were graduate university students, while the remaining six were professionals from various business environments (e.g., lawyer, project manager, user experience architect, web developer). Twelve of the participants used Windows as their primary computer plat-

form, seven used an Apple system, and one indicated both as a primary platform.

Materials

The experiment was conducted on Windows computers: fourteen sessions took place on university lab computers, four at the participants' homes, and two at the participants' work places. All computers had their monitors set to a resolution of at least 1280 X 1024 to accommodate the experiment application, which logged successful and failed selection events and selection times from each trial to a text file.

The application contained 20 different windows that were accessible from two domain menus: Regions (listing a collection of U.S. states) and Business Lines (listing financial lines of business). The application began with 10 randomly selected windows already open. The ratio of Regions to Business Lines items in the 10 windows varied from one experiment session to another.

To open or bring into focus the appropriate window, participants selected the correct item from two drop-down menus containing 10 alphabetized items for the Region (e.g., Alaska, Colorado) and Business Line (e.g., Accounts, Brokerage) domains. Each domain menu was opened by entering an Alt key sequence: Alt+R for Regions and Alt+B for Business Lines, where all letter selections were lowercase. Menu items were selected by adding the item's first letter to the Alt sequence used to open the menu. For example, selecting the Regions item Illinois required the sequence Alt+R+I.

Design and Procedure

The experiment used a 2 (menu condition) x 8 (trial blocks) mixed design with the participants assigned to either a 1-menu or 2-menu condition. Half of the participants in the 1-menu condition used the Regions menu while the other half used the Business Lines menu. Conditions were assigned by alternating conditions as each participant was tested.

Participants were shown how to use their assigned method of command entry on the test application during one block of five practice trials, where a single trial was bringing the correct window into focus. By the time the five trials were completed, all participants had learned to start each trial with their fingers on the appropriate key sequence.

Participants were then asked to complete eight blocks with 30 trials each. To prevent mental and physical fatigue, participants were encouraged to take a 20-second break between individual blocks. For each of the eight blocks of trials, a prompt dialog was displayed in the center of the screen. Clicking the OK button in the dialog started the current block of trials. At the end of the last trial in the eighth block, a prompt dialog was displayed asking the user to close the application.

For each trial within all eight blocks, the program displayed the name of the target window (e.g., Georgia) and the method used to find it (Select from menu using ALT sequences) at the bottom of the screen. When the target window was

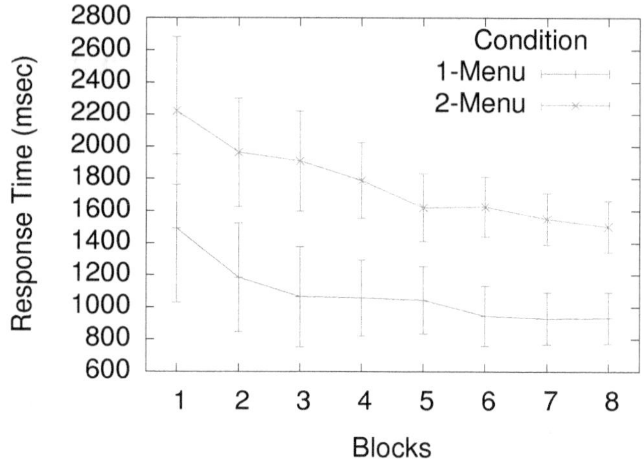

Figure 1. Response Time for Condition X Trial Block

opened, the next trial in the block began and the message at the bottom of the screen updated accordingly. Selection events and trial times were automatically recorded. The measure for selection was the time (in milliseconds) taken to bring the target window into focus. At the end of the experiment, participants were given $10 cash as compensation for their time and effort.

RESULTS

To examine the effects of the 1- versus 2-menu conditions and trial on selection time, means for each block of trials were computed for each participant. To ensure that the times reflected only the time needed to select a window, trials on which participants initially selected the wrong item were excluded. To see if participants in the two conditions differed in their likelihood to make a selection error, the number of correct trials in each block was tallied and analyzed using a 2 (Condition) X 8 (Block) mixed ANOVA. Fewer than 6% of the trials were excluded and none of the effects were significant, including the main effects of Condition, $F(1, 18) = 3.449$, $p = .080$, Block, $F(7, 126) = 0.827$, $p = .566$, and the Condition X Block interaction, $F(7,126) = 0.911$, $p = .500$.

The mean times of valid trials for each block of the two conditions are presented in Figure 1 with 95% confidence intervals. The selection time data were analyzed using a 2 (Condition) X 8 (Block) mixed ANOVA. The main effect of Condition, $F(1,18) = 17.983$, $p < .001$, was significant, indicating that the 2-menu condition was slower than the 1-menu condition. The main effect of Block, $F(7,126) = 20.20$, $p < .001$, was also significant, indicating that later blocks were faster than earlier blocks. The Condition X Block interaction, $F(7,126) = 1.061$, $p = .393$, was not significant.

To test the hypothesis that performance leveled off in the later blocks, tests of within-subject contrasts were performed to examine the overall trend. These contrasts indicated that the quadratic trend $F(1,18) = 13.\ 33$, $p = .002$, was significant, while the cubic trend $F(1,19) = 3.97$, $p = .062$, was not significant. Inspection of the means in Figure 1 suggests that performance leveled off after the sixth block. In a 2 (Condition) X 3 (Block) mixed ANOVA performed on the last three blocks, the block effect only approached significance $F(2, 36) = 3.22$, $p = .052$, suggesting that near asymptotic performance had been attained.

DISCUSSION

Throughout the trials, the 1-menu condition produced selection times that were on average 600 ms to 800 ms faster than the 2-menu condition. Since both conditions required participants to type the same key presses, this difference in time indicates the mental cost of category selection. Moreover, with both conditions at or near asymptotic performance, it appears that the cost of categorical selection will persist, at least for the training environment of this study.

Theoretically, the results indicate that participants in the 2-menu condition were not able to chunk the 3-key sequence into one cognitive unit. It is possible that the meaningful category names and their obvious mapping to keys hindered learning in the long term. While the categories and their key assignments were easy to learn, the reliance on this mapping appears to be an impediment to associating a target with a procedurally automated key sequence.

While participants in the 2-menu condition were not able to chunk the 3-key presses into one cognitive unit, it is clear that some learning occurred, even after the initial few blocks. Figure 2 provides accounts of human performance at two stages of practice, not unlike previous work where different models are used to represent novice users and expert users [2, 3]. The time constants are based on previous studies and theoretical work [1, 3], which were further developed in Omanson et al. [10]. No new time constants were needed for the models presented here.

The first model (2 Menus—Sequential Steps) provides a response time account of selecting from 2 menus based on a serial sequence of operations. This model is the same as presented in Omanson et al. for their account of user performance after three blocks of trials (90 trials total). Note that the model's predicted time matches the observed block-3 time for the study presented here.

The second model (2 Menus—Parallel Steps) suggests where learning occurs for the 2-menu condition. Consistent with previous efforts for modeling time costs [5], this model assumes that practiced users learn to perform cognitive and motor operations simultaneously. For example, a user can press the Alt key while deciding which menu needs to be selected. As the menu letter is being selected, the user can recall which letter key needs to be pressed to select the item from the menu. This model predicts a selection time of 1.5 seconds, which is consistent with performance in the final blocks of the study for the 2-menu condition.

As a point of comparison, a third model (1 Menu—Parallel Steps) shows an idealized performance where the user knows the menu in advance. Unlike the previous two models, no time is needed to categorize the intended item. Without this expense, the response time mainly comprises of the time

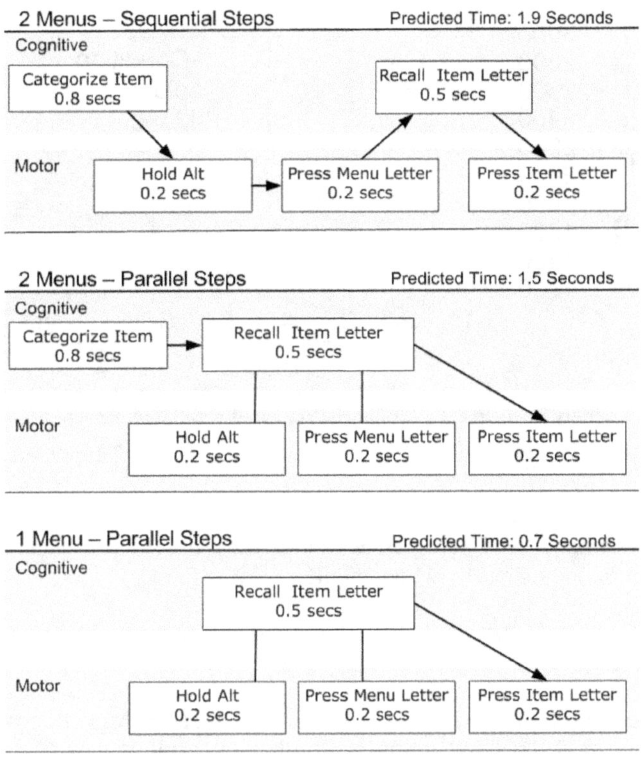

Figure 2. Models Explaining Response Times

needed to recall the item letter and then press its key, assuming that the user can automatically perform the Alt press and Menu press while recalling the needed item letter. While the predicted time of this model is .2 seconds faster than the observed time of our participants, the model is still helpful for making a qualitative comparison to the other models.

Our parallel-step models contrast with previous observations of dedicated spreadsheet users [8]. These dedicated users were able to execute a 3-key hierarchical sequence averaging approximately 0.2 seconds per key. While our parallel-step models (for both conditions) also depict users executing a a hierarchical sequence at 0.2 seconds per key, our analysis predicts a delay before a categorical selection. Relating to the 3-key sequence for a spreadsheet command, our analysis would indicate a delay between the first and second key, which was not observed in the spreadsheet study.

Two interpretations reconcile our analysis with the observations from the spreadsheet study. First, it is possible that additional trials would close the gap between performances requiring a categorical decision. While the 2-menu condition is ostensibly nearing asymptotic performance in the last few blocks, it is possible that small, incremental improvements in performance would continue across many more blocks to ultimately achieve a level of expertise consistent with the dedicated spreadsheet users. A second possibility is that our analysis only applies to categorical selections. The second key for the analyzed spreadsheet commands either indicates the command itself (e.g. I for insert) or qualifies the command (e.g. C for column). With this interpretation, it would

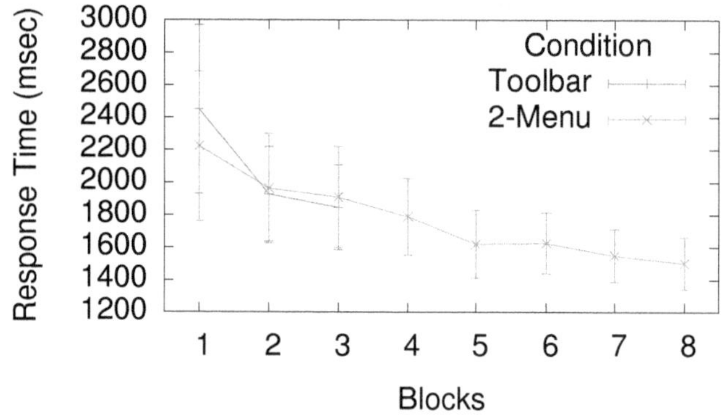

Figure 3. Toolbar Performance Compared with Menu Selection

be useful to distinguish between key presses that qualify commands and key presses that select a category in a taxonomic hieararchy where the item can be found.

The study's practical implications for design suggest that hierarchical, category-based keyboard commands do not provide a clear advantage when compared to toolbar-based selection. Figure 3 presents Toolbar performance from Omanson et al. [10] and contrasts it with the 2-menu results from our study. After 3 blocks, participants were able to select an item from the toolbar at 1.9 seconds on average. At most, the keyboard sequence produces a selection time that is 300 ms faster. However, this difference is likely to be much smaller. Compared to our results, the time of 1.9 seconds is a conservative upper bound for toolbar performance since the toolbar analysis did not remove trials where users had to recover from selection errors. It is also possible toolbar performance would continue to improve after three blocks.

For both our study and the Omanson et al. study, human participants could place their hands to best prepare for the mode of selection. However, other contexts of use can affect the relative benefits of key sequences and mouse-based toolbar selections. If the hands of the user is at the keyboard, an additional 0.4 seconds is required to move the hand to the mouse before selection at the toolbar can be made [1]. Likewise, a key sequence would require an additional 0.4 seconds if the needed hand is currently at the mouse.

Even considering small adjustments depending on context, toolbar-based command selection appears to provide the best benefit for a range of users, from novices to all but the most practiced users. Of course, multi-level keyboard selection permits a much larger choice of commands or items, but our results indicate that it may not produce meaningfully faster access than a mouse-based toolbar and, if it does produce faster access, the difference is small and only comes after substantial practice.

Finally, the findings may have implications for engineering tools such as CogTool [4], which predicts performance time given an interface design and task. CogTool automatically places "Think" operations before key sequences in order to account for mental preparation. Consistent with spreadsheet study [8], CogTool assumes that expert users can execute hierarchical key selections without any Think operations between the keys. Our analysis suggests possible cases where even practiced users might have delays within key sequences, particularly where a category selection is required. However, we recommend further study and analysis of how users learn categorical selections before proposing new rules for engineering tools.

ACKNOWLEDGMENTS

We would like to thank June Cline and Bonnie John for their comments on the manuscript.

REFERENCES

1. S. K. Card, T. P. Moran, and A. Newell. *The Psychology of Human-Computer Interaction*. Hillsdale, NJ: Lawrence Erlbaum Associates, 1983.
2. A. Cockburn and C. Gutwin. A model of novice and expert navigation performance in constrained-input interfaces. *ACM Transactions on Computer-Human Interaction (TOCHI)*, 17(3):1–38, 2010.
3. A. Cockburn, C. Gutwin, and S. Greenberg. A predictive model of menu performance. In *CHI '07: Proceedings of the SIGCHI conference on Human factors in computing systems*, pages 627–636, New York, NY, USA, 2007. ACM.
4. B. E. John. Cogtool user guide version 1.1. `http://cogtool.hcii.cs.cmu.edu/sites/default/files/CogToolUserGuide_1_1.pdf`, 2009. Accessed January 5, 2011.
5. B. E. John and D. E. Kieras. The GOMS family of user interface analysis techniques: comparison and contrast. *ACM Trans. Comput.-Hum. Interact.*, 3(4):320–351, 1996.
6. A. H. Jorgensen, B. Laursen, and B. R. Jensen. Using mouse and keyboard under time pressure: preference, strategies, and learning. *Behavioral and Brain Sciences*, 21:317–319, 2002.
7. J. Karat, J. E. McDonald, and M. Anderson. A comparison of menu selection techniques: Touch panel, mouse and keyboard. *International Journal of Man-Machine Studies*, 25:73–88, 1986.
8. D. Lane, H. Napier, R. Batsell, and J. Naman. Predicting the skilled use of hierarchical menus with the keystroke-level model. *Human-Computer Interaction*, 8(2):185–192, 1993.
9. D. M. Lane, H. A. Napier, S. C. Peres, and A. Sandor. Hidden costs of graphical user interfaces: Failure to make the transition from menus and icon toolbars to keyboard shortcuts. *International Journal of Human-Computer Interaction*, 18:133–144, 2005.
10. R. C. Omanson, C. S. Miller, E. Young, and D. Schwantes. Comparison of mouse and keyboard efficiency. In *Human Factors and Ergonomics Society Annual Meeting Proceedings*. HFES, Santa Monica, CA, 2010.

Sasayaki: Voice Augmented Web Browsing Experience

Daisuke Sato Shaojian Zhu[†] Masatomo Kobayashi Hironobu Takagi Chieko Asakawa

IBM Research – Tokyo
1623-14 Shimo-tsuruma, Yamato, Kanagawa, Japan
{dsato, mstm, takagih, chie}@jp.ibm.com
+81 46 215 {4793, 4679, 4557, 4633}

[†] UMBC
Baltimore MD 21250, United States of America
szhu1@umbc.edu
+1 410 455 3883

ABSTRACT
Auditory user interfaces have great Web-access potential for billions of people with visual impairments, with limited literacy, who are driving, or who are otherwise unable to use a visual interface. However a sequential speech-based representation can only convey a limited amount of information. In addition, typical auditory user interfaces lose the visual cues such as text styles and page structures, and lack effective feedback about the current focus. To address these limitations, we created *Sasayaki* (from 'whisper' in Japanese), which augments the primary voice output with a secondary whisper of contextually relevant information, automatically or in response to user requests. It also offers new ways to jump to semantically meaningful locations. A prototype was implemented as a plug-in for an auditory Web browser. Our experimental results show that the *Sasayaki* can reduce the task completion times for finding elements in webpages and increase satisfaction and confidence.

Author Keywords
Voice Augmentation, Voice Browser, Accessibility.

ACM Classification Keywords
H.5.2 [**Information Interfaces and Presentation**]: User Interfaces; K.4.2 [**Computers and Society**]: Social Issues – *Assistive Technologies for Persons with Disabilities.*

General Terms
Experimentation, Human Factors

INTRODUCTION
The Web represents one of the largest paradigm shifts in history. One out of every four people uses the Web [1] with great benefits. At the same time many people are unable to access the Web with standard visual browsers because they have visual or reading limitations, have only a basic and screenless mobile phone, or have constraints while moving or are otherwise unable to read a display. Given that an estimated one billion people have visual or reading limitations (est. 700 million with limited literacy [2] and 300 million with visual impairments [3]) and that about 4.6 billion mobile phones are in use [4], auditory interfaces could greatly expand access to the Web.

The current capabilities of auditory interfaces are quite limited and the Web is still rapidly evolving, making many webpages too complicated to access with vocal interfaces such as screen reading software. There is a central limitation in the current model of Web navigation. An auditory user interface is sequential, so it provides only a limited amount of information each time, which makes it hard for the users to get an overview of the webpage. Most webpages have highly visual layouts that are hard to understand by ear. Due to these limitations, people who use auditory interfaces to browse webpages find it slow and also tend to lose their places, making their browsing experience less reliable and less satisfying [5].

Therefore, we devised a new system called *Sasayaki* (which means 'whisper' in Japanese) to improve the Web experience of people who are using auditory interfaces rather than visual presentations. *Sasayaki* aims to simulate a friend of the user who is standing nearby with whispered tips for navigating the webpages. This virtual friend is watching the display and observing the behavior of the user to provide context-based hints and guidance. Computers cannot simulate complicated human behaviors, but even partial assistance can be helpful. Various kinds of information that cannot be produced by straightforward text-to-speech technologies can be provided by using heuristics and data analysis techniques with the data from the webpages and records of user behaviors.

As the first proof-of-concept prototype, the *Sasayaki* browser we developed presents the output of a standard auditory browser and the supporting information about the webpages in parallel through separate voice channels. The main voice provides raw text and some structured information from the webpages. In contrast, the secondary voice is for contextual navigation guidance based on the user's position and overviews of the webpages from content analysis and the metadata for the webpages. A user listens to these two different voices from two physically separated speakers. *Sasayaki* helps users dynamically switch their focus depending on the context, so they can focus on relevant information while moving and jumping quickly, but without losing track of their location within the webpage.

This paper summarizes related work and describes the concept and a prototype of the *Sasayaki* along with a user study involving nine blind participants. Although the prototype and the initial evaluation focus on the auditory Web browser for people who are blind, the insights obtained will be helpful for developing broader types of auditory user interfaces.

RELATED WORK

Our work was initially inspired by observing the urgent needs of screen reader users to overcome problems as they were surfing the Web. Barnicle [6] evaluated screen reader users' experiences with thirteen visually impaired people and identified 58 unique obstacles that are not problematic to the same degree for sighted people. Lazar et al. [7] collected users' reports of the causes of frustration when using screen readers, with confusing page layout being ranked as the leading problem. They also found that a user generally spends more time recovering from an incident than the time it took to create the problem.

User Interface Agent

Sasayaki was also guided by the concepts of user interface agents, which unobtrusively provide users with needed help. Maes [8] talked about the concepts of interface agents to help users save work and avoid information overload. Among the various types of user agents, we focused on two categories.

Voice Augmentation

Bederson [9] created an automated tour guide prototype that uses audio to guide tourists. Sawhney and Schmandt [10] worked on 'Nomadic Radio', a wearable system which allows users to access information by using voices and textual information in a nomadic environment. This agent system could decide how to most effectively present information to the user based on the context, interruption settings, and automatic text understanding. Eckel [11] created the Listen project, which augments everyday environments with interactive soundscapes. Depending on the location and other context data, the system can suggest the most effective options for users. Other voice-based agent systems seek to provide users an impression of reality. Kalantari et al. [12] and Miyashita et al. [13] wrote about their voice-based augmented reality systems for visitors at museums. Voice-based agents were also used for navigation. Shoval et al. [14] introduced NAVBELT and GUIDECANE, which are voice and touch-based tools that can use a stereo earphone with a tactile stimulator to help blind people navigate in real environments. Jones et al. [15] described the ONTRACK system which uses adaptive music playback to support navigation in a 3D virtual space.

Browser Agents

Web surfing is one of the important tasks for screen reader users when they interact with computers. Stylos et al. [16] introduced an intelligent clipboard monitoring agent that helps to identify formatted data (such as addresses or appointments) for smart pasting into webforms. Wagner and Lieberman [17] introduced Woodstein, which predicts and assists the next user action based on analysis of a collected sequence of previous actions on the webpages. Roth et al. [18] created an agent to provide audio feedback for the user's cursor location. Yu et al. [19] created context-aware Web agents to provide audio and haptic feedback for the user's cursor location in the screen reader. Dontcheva et al. [20] created a Web agent that can help record and organize user sessions for comparison and analysis. The authors reduced the users' memory load and simplified tasks. Hartmann et al. [21] described Augur, a context-based smart agent that can do three things for users: highlight, suggest, and automate by analyzing context data and using pre-defined rules. Parente [22] introduced Clique, an auditory interface with four assistants and distinct voices. Each assistant has a role involving tasks or events on a desktop including email, calendar, and browser applications. Although sometimes the assistants speak simultaneously, it is a different type of synchronicity from *Sasayaki* concepts.

Context Awareness

Context has also received attention for more intelligently improving accessibility. Most user agents systems [10, 14] make good use of context for decisions. Mahmud et al. [23] introduced their CSurf system that finds the most relevant information based on user behaviors and other contextual clues using a statistical machine-learning model. Borodin et al. [24] reported on the problem-causing lack of awareness of visual changes in dynamic webpages. This led to an algorithm to detect changes in dynamic webpages, allowing the system to collect useful context information. As in Web browsing scenarios, they found that user behavior, cursor location, and webpage layout were the most important contextual clues for analysis [17, 19, 21, 23].

Assistive Technologies

Sasayaki was guided by the previous work on adding intelligence to screen readers. Various approaches have been tried to help screen reader users have better browsing experiences by adding more powerful functions to the software. Yesilada et al. [25] introduced DANTE, a semantic transcoding system for webpages visited by blind people. DANTE can transform a typical webpage into a screen-reader-friendly format. Harper and Patel [26] described the effects when visually impaired people are unable to scan webpages. They created a system to summarize webpages for blind Web surfers. Miyashita et al. [27] created a multimedia voice browser that handles the multimedia objects on webpages by adding scripts to give visually impaired users full control over the objects. Lunn et al. [28] introduced SADIe, which uses semantic annotations in a CSS (Cascading Style Sheet) to transform webpages for better accessibility in a screen reader.

There are also studies focusing on employing the power of social networking to add smart tagging information to existing webpages to improve their accessibility. Takagi et al. [29] created Social Accessibility to enable third-party volunteers to effectively assign layout tags to webpages. The screen reader users have special tools to retrieve and use this metadata to improve their surfing experience. Chen and Ramen [30] created AxsJAX, which lets programmers dynamically insert ARIA statements into webpage content so that screen reader users can handle dynamic pages.

These technologies try to improve Web accessibility by transcoding content and also to provide better experience for the users based on the current single voice browsing interface. *Sasayaki* can coexist without conflict with these technologies and can further improve the Web experience by working with them.

SASAYAKI

We regard *Sasayaki* as an example of a general concept of a user interface that provides supplemental information for many kinds of people via an audio channel. From the users' various viewpoints, ideally they would have a non-intrusive audio-based augmented environment. *Sasayaki* tries to act in a supportive role to help the users as would a sighted person in assisting the visually impaired user (Figure 1). It provides apparently intelligent feedback by analyzing user behavior, status, and other related contextual evidence. *Sasayaki* then provides bits of verbal information and advice with a synthesized voice. *Sasayaki* can also provide other kinds of audio-based hints, such as sound effects, background music, or background noises. One simple example is that a car navigation system could provide extra information about popular restaurants near the anticipated location of the user's car based on the planned route, in parallel with the main voice that provides driving directions. Another example would help a blind user shopping for gifts on an e-commerce site. In this situation, the agent could suggest popular gifts while helping to orient and guide the user around the webpages. Given that people who have visual impairments are supposed to be the main population who must depend on the auditory interface and often experience various difficulties in using it, we focused on them in the initial design and development of *Sasayaki*.

Categories of Sasayaki Information

The following four categories of information are expected to be useful for blind users navigating webpages. This includes information that is hard to obtain from non-visual user interfaces as well as some information that is useful for sighted people.

Spatial: For the blind users, it is very hard to be aware of the position of their cursors or to know the position where the screen reader is currently reading. Although this is very fundamental and easy for sighted people, the blind users cannot get an overview of their context without special help. There are Braille blocks, Braille maps, and audio signals for crossing streets or climbing stairs in our physical world, and these give blind people some awareness of their locations and the context. Webpages need similar signals for easier navigation [31].

Figure 1. Concept of Sasayaki User Interface Agent

Contextual: *Sasayaki* changes behavior according to the context of the users. For example, the *Sasayaki* system can detect when a user seems to be lost and then provide appropriate support to recover. As described in the related work section, there are many forms of contextual support. For example, when a user is shopping, the *Sasayaki* provides prices and user reviews for achieving the goals of the user's tasks.

Social: *Sasayaki* provides a kind of extra intelligence for blind users. The intelligence can be socially generated by volunteers or users. Many studies tried to improve accessibility by using external metadata [27, 28, 29, 30]. Such metadata can provide an outline of a webpage, locating a header, the main content, advertisements, related information, and a footer.

Analysis: The intelligence also can be generated by the computer automatically. Analyzing many user reviews to summarize the users' positive and negative reactions to a restaurant is a typical example. Another example from an e-Commerce page would be to suggest popular links or buttons in webpages by analyzing clickstreams, which would allow them to be aware of which webpages other people tend to navigate to without any visual cues..

IMPLEMENTATION OF PROTOTYPE SYSTEM

We have implemented a prototype of the *Sasayaki* system. Our prototype helps users to retain awareness of their current position while providing overviews of the webpages. This supportive information becomes available to the users through the whispering channel, either automatically or as requested. *Sasayaki* comes from a different sound device physically separated from the main speaker and uses a different speech synthesizer engine to simulate the "whispering" scenario. In this way, *Sasayaki* efficiently and simultaneously presents both voices to the users, making

Sasayaki less intrusive but still noticeable. The *Sasayaki* system is designed as a plug-in component for our voice browser called aiBrowser [32]. The behaviors and functions of aiBrowser are similar to popular screen readers. Since *Sasayaki* system needs an API to obtain the context of the Web browsing, aiBrowser was extended to provide it. *Sasayaki* could work with other screen readers by adding a corresponding API as a plug-in or extension.

Role-based Notifications and Jumps

To provide users with contextual support, the *Sasayaki* plug-in retrieves pre-defined role-based data about a webpage from an Accessibility Commons [33] server. The typical roles for content include main content, header, advertisement, and so on. The *Sasayaki* plug-in also monitors the position of the current focus of the voice browser and tracks key events linked to user behaviors. This allows the plug-in to generate the most appropriate advice for each user. For example, when a user reaches the defined main content body for the first time, the system will decide that "Entering main" is a good contextual prompt. We call this *Sasayaki* whispering. It may also include more advanced help for the users such as "Skipped the main content". The *Sasayaki* whispering is provided at several role-tagged parts of the webpage. *Sasayaki* also allows users to freely change the focus of the screen reader between role-based parts using a 'jump' function. We decided to add this feature as jump functions are very common in modern screen reading software. For example, many users already use jumps between heading elements (H1-H6), table elements, list items, form elements, and so on. Hence users should benefit from the *Sasayaki* jump functions without changing their interaction model for browsing webpages.

Page Overview and Text Analysis

In addition, for webpages that belong to the same category, the important information tends to be similar. For example, for product pages from an online shopping website, each page has the same kinds of important information, including price, in-stock information, shipping rules, and so on. On complex webpages, non-visual users may have difficulties in simply finding that basic information. *Sasayaki* can collect the basic information for the page category and output it in an efficient format as requested by using metadata, so that the users can quickly get an overview of the crucial content in each page.

Another problem is when voice browser users want the useful information in a large body of user reviews. Some online shopping webpages collect such reviews, and in this case *Sasayaki* can extract and analyze a large number of user reviews by using its sentiment-based text mining component [34]. *Sasayaki* does this by retrieving the original user reviews as text from the related webpages and passing it internally to the text-mining component that generates statistics about the user comments, covering various product aspects such as price, quality, or texture.

EVALUATION

An empirical study was conducted to evaluate the user performance and behaviors in navigating webpages using our *Sasayaki*, comparing it to typical screen reader software. The primary foci of the evaluations were the role-based notifications and jump functions. Each participant was familiarized with *Sasayaki* and then asked to perform 5 tasks. After observing their performance, we also asked for their subjective ratings of the agent system.

Pilot Study

A pilot study [35] was done before the main experiment with three blind people (2 males and 1 female from 37 to 44 years old). Two of them are completely blind and one has limited vision. Four tasks and a survey were given to each participant. In this pilot study, we tried to explore differences between the same system with and without *Sasayaki* functions. We compared the original aiBrowser system and aiBrowser with all of the *Sasayaki* functions. We found that *Sasayaki* effectively supported the users' navigation. The users working with *Sasayaki* spent much less time navigating to the required page elements for each task. They also showed high confidence in their abilities to do Web browsing with *Sasayaki* functions. This study supported our belief that *Sasayaki* could be a useful aid to improve user experience. This led us to focus on the differences between *Sasayaki* whispering functions and the *Sasayaki* jump functions in the main experiment.

User Experiment

Nine native Japanese blind people (8 males and 1 female, from 30 to 53 years old), none of whom were involved in the pilot study, participated in the experiment as paid volunteers. They are referred to as P1 to P9 in the following sections. All of them were completely blind and all had experience with Web navigation using screen reading software. Eight of the participants were expert users with Web experience going back to the '90s. The participant P9 became blind a few years ago and also has less experience with the Web. Most of the participants had little or no exposure to the webpages used in this experiment, though one participant was already familiar with the Amazon.co.jp site. None of them had experience with aiBrowser.

Equipment

A ThinkPad T400 laptop with a 2.40-GHz Core 2 Duo CPU running Windows XP was used as the experimental computer. This laptop has a build-in stereo speaker which was used for the main voice output. A Yamaha USB-powered stereo speaker (NX-U10) was placed next to the laptop for the *Sasayaki* voice. A standard Japanese 109-key USB keyboard was used instead of the laptop keyboard, because keyboards differ among laptops and using a standard Japanese keyboard helped avoid confusion.

Sasayaki Conditions

We compared two types of differences, whether or not the system has the *Sasayaki* whispering function and whether or not the system has the *Sasayaki* jump function. There were four test conditions for the *Sasayaki* settings to evaluate how the *Sasayaki* whispering and the *Sasayaki* jump functions affected the participants' performance of typical navigation tasks.

The first condition was the original aiBrowser (**NS-NJ**). The second was aiBrowser with *Sasayaki* whispering but without *Sasayaki* jump (**S-NJ**). The third was aiBrowser with the *Sasayaki* jump function but without *Sasayaki* whispering (**NS-J**). The fourth was aiBrowser with both *Sasayaki* whispering and *Sasayaki* jump (**S-J**).

Tasks

We used a within-participant design, so for each webpage each participant was asked to perform the same set of tasks within each of the four *Sasayaki* conditions. The independent variables were whispering (with or without *Sasayaki* whispering) and jump (with or without *Sasayaki* jump). There were four sets of five target webpages (news article on Asahi[1] and Nikkei[2], product page on Amazon[3] and Yahoo[4], and product search result page on Amazon[3]). Each participant performed one trial for each combination. The presentation order of *Sasayaki* whispering was counterbalanced and the order of *Sasayaki* jump was fixed because *Sasayaki* jump was observed to be able to significantly reduce the task completion time in our pilot study leading us to focus primarily on the *Sasayaki* whispering conditions. Also, if the jump function was not fixed, then the number of samples for each condition became too small. Recruiting more blind participants for larger samples is also difficult.

The participants were first familiarized with the functions of aiBrowser and *Sasayaki*, including how to adjust the volumes and speech speeds of both voices. This involved a different and special webpage. They were then asked to attempt each task with a time limit or until they had failed three times. We prepared four different webpages with similar test problems for each category of webpage. For all of the tasks, each participant was asked to find specified information on the webpages and to report out loud with a phrase such as "Here it is." The observer would then look at the focus of aiBrowser to determine whether or not it was the correct position. We measured the task completion time from when we asked them to start to when they successfully reported finding the desired information. The keyboard events were recorded by the test system.

Tasks 1 and 2: Reading a news article

These two tasks were performed for article pages on two news websites, **Asahi** and **Nikkei**. The participants were asked to find the first paragraph of the article on the page within three minutes. This task assesses their navigation to the main content of a webpage.

Tasks 3 and 4: Shopping for a product

These two tasks were performed at product pages on two e-commerce Web sites, **Amazon** and **Yahoo**. They were asked to first find the price of the product and then find the button to purchase the product. The total time limit for each pair of tasks was five minutes. This task assessed navigation for the important information on the webpages.

Task 5: Searching for a price in a list of search results

The last task involved product search result pages on an e-commerce Web site, Amazon (referred as **A-search**). This kind of webpage has a list of more than twenty products. The participants were asked to find the product with the highest price among the first ten items in the list. This task tested navigation for a more sophisticated task and was timed up to seven minutes.

Questionnaire and Interview

After the experiment, we used a survey with seven-point Likert items from -3/definitely disagree to +3/definitely agree to compare the test conditions in pairs, NS-NJ against S-NJ and NS-J against S-J. This produced subjective scores for the Web experiences with the *Sasayaki* functions. The following list translates the items from the questionnaire. **NS** means NS-NJ or NS-J and **S** means S-NJ or S-J.

- Compared to **NS**, I found **S** to be easier to use
- Compared to **NS**, I found **S** to be useful
- Compared to **NS**, I had more control using **S**
- Compared to **NS**, I found **S** to be more pleasant
- Compared to **NS**, I felt more sure I would finish with **S**
- Compared to **NS**, I rated **S** output quality as better
- I would use **S** if I had access to it

The page overview functions, the text analysis functions, and the *Sasayaki* whispering voice setting features were all explained before we interviewed the participants about these three *Sasayaki* functions, about ideas for improving the system, and about some other questions.

RESULTS

Task Completion Time

Figure 2 shows the average task completion times with standard errors. The average values were 112 seconds for NS-NJ, 126 seconds for S-NJ, 71 seconds for NS-J, and 65 seconds for S-J. Analysis of variance showed significant primary effects for the *Sasayaki* jump ($F_{1,130} = 65.23$, $p < .001$) and the target website ($F_{4,130} = 51.05$, $p < .001$). There were interaction effects for the jump × the target website ($F_{4,130} = 5.06$, $p < .005$), whispering × the target website ($F_{4,130} = 3.33$, $p < .05$). A post hoc analysis indicated that *Sasayaki* jump function significantly decreased the task completion time and the impact of the

[1] Asahi newspaper: http://www.asahi.com/

[2] Nikkei newspaper: http://www.nikkei.com/

[3] Amazon.co.jp: http://www.amazon.co.jp

[4] Yahoo Japan Shopping: http://shopping.yahoo.co.jp/

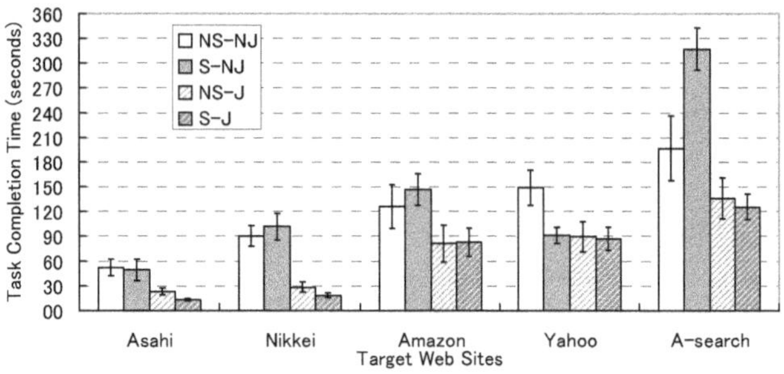

Figure 2. The average task completion times

	Asahi	Nikkei	Amazon	Yahoo	A-search
NS-NJ	0	1	7	2	4
S-NJ	0	0	4	0	3
NS-J	0	0	0	1	0
S-J	0	0	0	0	0

Table 1. Numbers of participants who failed to complete a task within the time limit

	Asahi	Nikkei	Amazon	Yahoo	A-search
NS-NJ	0	0	2	3	1
S-NJ	0	0	0	0	0
NS-J	0	0	0	1	0
S-J	0	0	0	0	0

Table 2. Number of participants had incorrect answers during a test

Sasayaki whispering function depended on the task. The data for the trials that were stopped because of the time limits are not included in this graph. Seven participants ran out of time in the Amazon webpage with NS-NJ and some participants were out of time for Nikkei, Yahoo, and A-search with the NS-NJ condition, for Amazon and A-search with the S-NJ condition and for Yahoo with the NS-J condition. With the S-J condition, there were no time out problems.

Error Rates

Table 1 shows the number of participants who failed to complete tasks due to the time limits. The reason many people failed on the Amazon webpages was that these webpages have a difficult structure. Table 2 shows the number of participants who had incorrect answers during the task. No participant had more than two mistakes and no participant made any mistakes with the S-NJ or S-J conditions.

Subjective Scores

Figures 3 and 4 show the average subjective ratings with standard errors for the seven questions comparing conditions without jump (NS-NJ vs. S-NJ) and conditions with jump (NS-J vs. S-J). All of the participants except P4

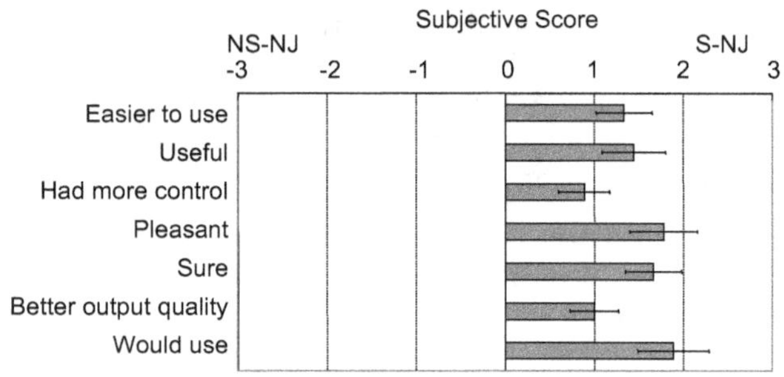

Figure 3. The average subjective scores for NS-NJ vs. S-NJ

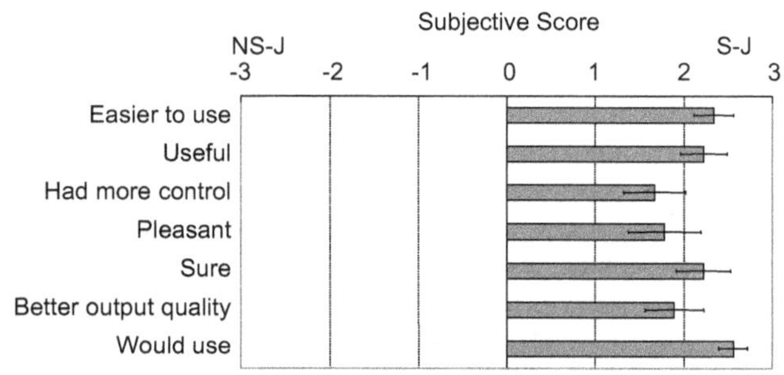

Figure 4. The average subjective scores for NS-J vs. S-J

gave positive ratings. The average score is 1.43 for NS-NJ vs. S-NJ and 2.10 for NS-J vs. S-J. All of the scores of NS-J vs. S-J are equal to or higher than those of NS-NJ vs. S-NJ. "Would use" received the highest score in both, with or without jump comparisons. For conditions without the *Sasayaki* jump feature, the "pleasant" and "sure" questionnaire items received higher scores. For conditions with jump, the "easy to use", "useful", and "sure" items received higher scores.

Navigation Behavior Analysis

The participants finished all of the tasks within 30 to 50 minutes. While working on the tasks they made from 1,800 to 3,500 keystrokes in navigating the webpages. Figure 5 shows the average numbers of keystrokes for each condition, including all of the trials with data. The average values were 194 keystrokes for NS-NJ, 175 for S-NJ, 77 for NS-J, and 69 keystrokes for S-J. Analysis of variance showed significant primary effects for the *Sasayaki* jump ($F_{1,152}$ = 80.090, $p < .001$) and for the target website ($F_{4,152}$ = 38.098, $p < .001$). There were interaction effects for the jump × the target website ($F_{4,152}$ = 10.85, $p < .001$). A post hoc analysis indicated that the *Sasayaki* jump function decreased the numbers of keystrokes. Table 3 shows the average ratios for using the navigation commands. More than 60% of the navigation commands were "Next element" and about 20% of the navigation commands were "Previous element". The rest of navigation commands were mostly for jumps.

Type	NS-NJ	S-NJ	NS-J	S-J
Next element	64.6%	66.7%	61.3%	60.0%
Previous element	21.8%	18.6%	21.1%	19.4%
Next heading	4.0%	6.0%	1.0%	1.5%
Previous heading	1.4%	2.0%	0.5%	0.3%
Next link	3.3%	3.2%	0.3%	1.1%
Previous link	3.1%	2.2%	0.0%	0.4%
Sasayaki jump (next)	0.0%	0.0%	9.4%	10.5%
Sasayaki jump (prev)	0.0%	0.0%	3.9%	5.3%
Others	1.8%	1.3%	2.4%	1.5%

Table 3. The average ratios of navigation command usage

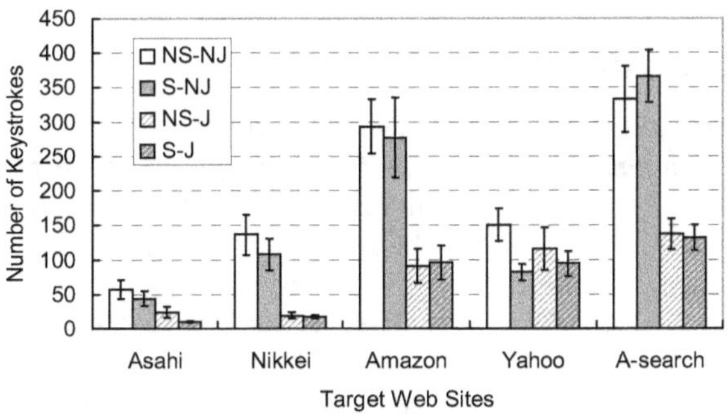

Figure 5. The average number of keystrokes

Navigation Trace Analysis

Each blind user has a strategy for Web navigation and may change that strategy based on the type of webpage or the purpose of navigation. Based on their different strategies, the nine participants can be categorized into three groups. In the first group, five participants (P1, P2, P3, P4, P5) mainly used the heading jump and page search as their second choice. In the second group, three participants (P6, P7, P9) mainly used page searching functions and heading jumps as second choice. There was only one participant in group three who mainly used the cursor keys, usually with the tab key, to explore elements linearly or to jump between links (P8).

Figure 6 shows the traces for P4 with the NS-NJ and S-NJ conditions in the Nikkei webpage. The vertical axis is the time spent on each task and the horizontal axis is the focus position in the page. The black line shows how the participant moved on the page and the vertical gray line indicates the area with the target element for that task. The dashed gray lines are for heading elements. In both the traces for NS-NJ and for S-NJ, by using heading jump functions the participants' focus arrived at the same location, which was just ahead of the target area. For NS-NJ, the participant accidentally passed the target area and came back to it. For S-NJ, the *Sasayaki* whispers such as "close to main" and "entering main" would be helpful for the participant in finding the target content. Figure 7 shows another trace of P6 with NS-NJ and S-NJ. This user's navigation strategy was mostly based on page search. For

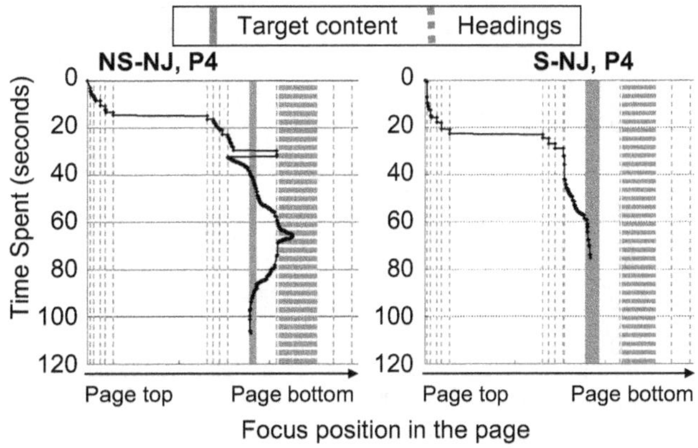

Figure 6. Navigation traces on Nikkei newspaper with NS-NJ and S-NJ by P4.

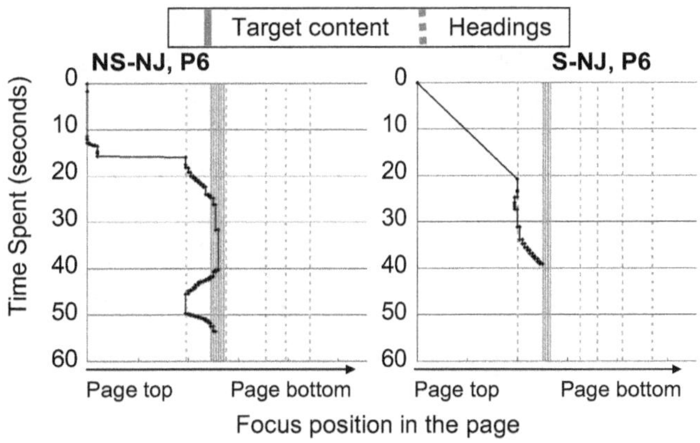

Figure 7. Navigation traces on Asahi newspaper with NS-NJ and S-NJ by P6.

NS-NJ, P6 failed in the search because of a typing mistake. He then used the heading jump function and found the main content. However P6 checked the previous content again to make sure about the goal of the task (in the period from 40 to 50 seconds). This kind of pattern was observed 11 times without *Sasayaki* whispering and only 5 times with *Sasayaki* whispering, indicating that the *Sasayaki* whispering improved users' confidence that they had found the desired webpage elements.

There were also cases in which the *Sasayaki* functions didn't work well. Figure 8 shows the traces for the Asahi newspaper with S-NJ by P3 and P9. P3 heard "close to main" as a *Sasayaki* whisper but P3 could not navigate step by step before passing the target area and then skipped the main content by using heading jump. Unfortunately the *Sasayaki* system basically tries to convey information about the current position rather than about the content the user has already passed. This design was chosen to reduce the amount of information whispered by *Sasayaki* so that the two voices could be heard more easily. P9 was confused by the *Sasayaki* whispering and said "the structure of the page from the *Sasayaki* whispers was not easy to understand" and "'close to main' should mean within two or three items of the position". This case suggests that we need either a

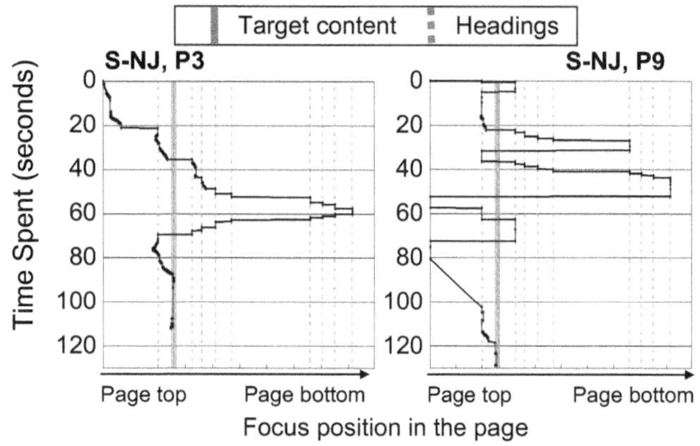

Figure 8. Navigation traces on Asahi newspaper with S-NJ by P3 and P9.

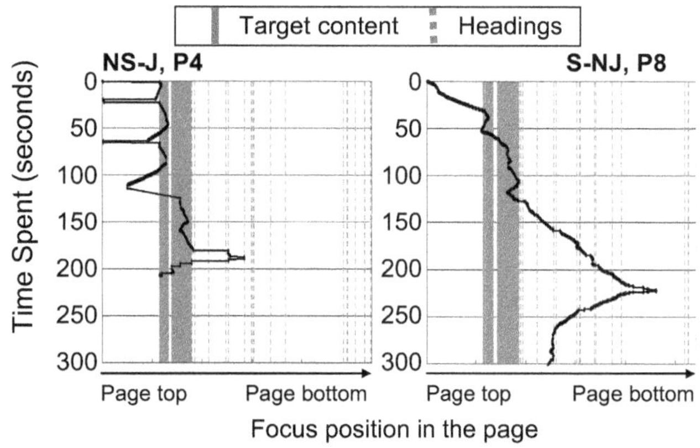

Figure 9. Navigation traces on Amazon product pages with NS-J by P4 and S-NJ by P8.

personalized control for the *Sasayaki* content details, or better training so that users would be more familiar with our *Sasayaki* system.

Another problem involved incorrect assumptions about the structure of the webpage, especially for the Amazon product page. In this page, the "add to cart" button, the product title as the first heading element, and the price appeared in that order. However, most participants thought that the "add to cart" button must be below the price. Figure 9 shows the traces of Amazon webpages for NS-J by P4 and for S-NJ by P9. There are two target areas in this task. The first area contains the "add to cart" button and the other contains the price information. P4 found the "add to cart" button by using the *Sasayaki* jump function, and then tried to search for the price in front of the button three times. Finally P4 used the page search function to get the price. In contrast, P8's strategy is to explore the webpage elements one by one, so P8 was aware of the position of the "add to cart" button when the *Sasayaki* whisper said "often used button" to emphasize it. P8, however, searched for the "add to cart" button after the price and thus could not finish.

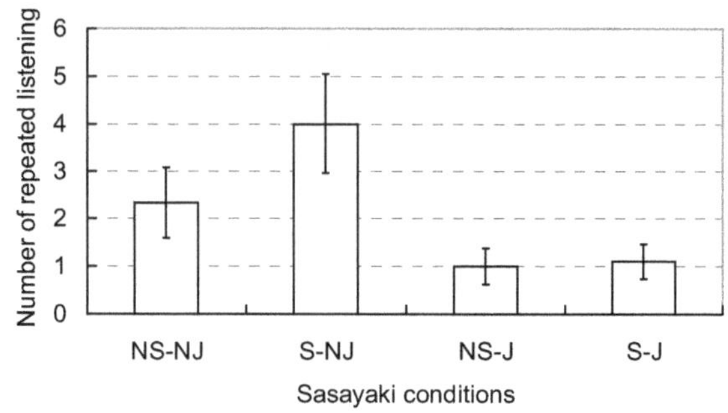

Figure 10. The average number of repetitions on Amazon search result pages.

DISCUSSION

Navigation Improvements with Sasayaki

Even though most of the participants gave positive ratings for the test conditions with *Sasayaki* whispers compared to those without *Sasayaki*, the quantitative results showed no significant difference between the conditions with and without *Sasayaki* whispers regarding the task completion time or number of keystrokes. The navigation traces also suggest improvements of the navigation behaviors. One of interpretations of the results is that assisted voice (*Sasayaki*) gave participants "feeling of confidence", but the processes of mental model building was not enhanced enough to improve the performance in the tasks.

The participants' comments support this interpretation. Typical positive comments include "I feel confident with *Sasayaki* compared to without *Sasayaki*" (P7), "A *Sasayaki* whisper, e.g. 'close to main' is so nice, making me feel comfortable" (P6) and "It is useful for exploring the structure of unfamiliar webpages" (P8). Those comments suggested that the *Sasayaki* system reduced the stresses of unaided navigation and the strain of sustained listening.

We also see evidence in the traces of navigation behaviors. As shown in Figure 6, the browsing pattern of passing the target and coming back to increase their confidence were frequently recognized in the conditions without *Sasayaki* whispering. Blind users concentrated on the synthesized voices to track their positions in the page. This indicates that unaided navigation is a very hard task that lowers the user's confidence. A *Sasayaki* system can help to increase their confidence with relatively little concentration on the second voice. The fact that the number of incorrect answers by the participants was reduced by *Sasayaki* whispering is evidence that supports this finding.

Based on the extracted approaches from the less successful patterns, we also got hints on how to improve the design of *Sasayaki* voices to enhance the mental model building processes. The cases shown in Figures 8 and 9 could be addressed by presenting a structure map for the users to study before they start to navigate on the page. In fact, some participants requested such a function in the interview session and one participant suggested that providing a tree view would be useful for him to form a basic idea of the webpage structure before exploring.

Are Two Simultaneous Voices Distinguishable?

Although we didn't explicitly experiment with the effects of the two simultaneous voices, we recognized repeated listening as a noticeable behavior of the participants in the Amazon search result pages. Figure 10 shows the average numbers of repetitions within each *Sasayaki* condition. For the webpages where they were asked to report the index of the item with the highest price among the top ten items, the *Sasayaki* whisper was available for the first element of each result item and the first element was the index number. In the S-NJ condition, seven participants did listen to the rank repeatedly. In contrast, we observed a smaller number of repeated listening in the S-J condition, as shown in Figure 10. In the test conditions with *Sasayaki* jump features (NS-J and S-J), the participants seem to be able to recognize the two voices simultaneously and properly interpret the *Sasayaki* whispering. This result would be caused by some learning effects as in the experiment all participants tested the conditions without *Sasayaki* jump features first.

The participants did not complain about audibility of the secondary voice and felt confident about it. Two participants commented about the two parallel voices, "the two physically separated voices were sufficiently distinguishable" (P2, P8), and "it could be improved by adjusting the volumes and combinations of the types of voices" (P6). This result might be due to the fact that blind people have good listening skills to compensate for their loss of visual perception. However even sighted people can recognize multiple voices near them. Further studies on improving the listenability of the secondary voice might be necessary, for example by adjusting the voice output timing and choosing more distinguishable combinations of the two voices. The information density of the auditory user interface could be increased by the *Sasayaki* approach. This would be a paradigm shift for the auditory interface.

Potential Applications

As we noted, *Sasayaki* is a general concept for a user interface that provides supplemental information for various kinds of people via an audio channel. This concept could be applied to many real world environments. One example might be navigation for blind pedestrians. This kind of system could be enhanced with a secondary voice to augment the primary voice that provides walking directions, for example to provide user-generated information about nearby restaurants. The creation of supplemental audio information to provide situational support has been already introduced in some emerging technologies (e.g., [36]). Telephony applications could also be enhanced to increase information density. For example, when a user is trying to access a telephony application for the first time, the user could hear the main voice, and, at the same time, if the system detects the user status to be "needs help" by analyzing the user's behavior and contextual information, then a second voice could provide situational instructions or tips on how to navigate or interact with the application more easily.

CONCLUSION

This paper describes a concept called *Sasayaki* which augments a primary voice output with a secondary voice that whispers contextually relevant information automatically or in response to user requests. A prototype system was implemented as a plug-in system for a voice-based Web browser with a small API for the *Sasayaki* controls. An empirical evaluation with nine visually impaired users showed that the *Sasayaki* system significantly improved their navigation behaviors and increased their confidence levels. The jump function based on *Sasayaki* significantly increased the navigation performance. The results also show the possibilities of the *Sasayaki* approach, with two simultaneous voices increasing the information density of the auditory user interface. For future work we will do more studies to explore the advantages of simultaneous voices, study the emotional effects of the *Sasayaki* functions, and also test *Sasayaki* for applications for other population groups.

REFERENCES

1. Internet World Stats, World Internet Users and Population Stats, http://www.internetworldstats.com/stats.htm.
2. UNESCO, International Literacy Statistics: A Review of Concepts, Methodology and Current Data, http://www.uis.unesco.org/template/pdf/Literacy/LiteracyReport2008.pdf.
3. WHO, Fact sheet of visual impairment and blindness, http://www.who.int/mediacentre/factsheets/fs282/en/.
4. ITU. Measuring the Information Society 2010. http://www.itu.int/ITU-D/ict/publications/idi/2010/.
5. Takagi, H., Saito, S., Fukuda, K. and Asakawa, C. Analysis of navigability of Web applications for improving blind usability. *ACM Trans. Comp.-Hum. Interact* 14:3 (2007), 13.
6. Barnicle, K. Usability testing with screen reading technology in a Windows environment. In *Proc. CUU 2000*, ACM Press (2000), 102-109.
7. Lazar, J., Allen, A.and Kleinman, J. and Malarkey, C. What Frustrates Screen Reader Users on the Web: A Study of 100 Blind Users. *International Journal of Human-Computer Interaction* 22:3 (2007), 247-269.
8. Maes, P. 1994. Agents that reduce work and information overload. *Communications of. ACM* 37, 7 (1994), 30-40.
9. Bederson, B. B. Audio augmented reality: a prototype automated tour guide.,In *Proc. CHI 1995*, ACM Press, (1995), 210-211.

10. Sawhney, N. and Schmandt, C. Nomadic radio: speech and audio interaction for contextual messaging in nomadic environments. *ACM Trans. Comput.-Hum. Interact.* (7:3), (2000), 353-383.

11. Eckel, G. Immersive Audio-Augmented Environments: The LISTEN Project, *Fifth Framework Programme, Creating a user-friendly information society* (IST), (2001), 571.

12. Kalantari, L., Hatala, M. and Willms, J. Using semantic web approach in augmented audio reality system for museum visitors. In *Proc. WWW 2004*, ACM Press, (2004), 386-387.

13. Miyashita, T., Meier, P., Tachikawa, T., Orlic, S., Eble, T., Scholz, V., Gapel, A., Gerl, O., Arnaudov, S. and Lieberknecht, S. An Augmented Reality museum guide. In *Proc. ISMAR 2008*, IEEE Computer Society (2008),103-106.

14. Shoval, S., Borenstein, J. and Koren, Y. The Navbelt - A Computerized Travel Aid for the Blind Based on Mobile Robotics Technology. *IEEE Trans. on Biomedical Engineering* (45:11) (1998), 1376-1386.

15. Jones, M., Jones, S., Bradley, G., Warren, N., Bainbridge, D. and Holmes, G. ONTRACK: Dynamically adapting music playback to support navigation. *Personal and Ubiquitous Computing* (12:7), (2008), 513-525.

16. Stylos, J., Myers, B. A. and Faulring, A. Citrine: providing intelligent copy-and-paste. In *Proc. UIST 2004,* ACM Press (2004), 185-188.

17. Wagner, E. J. and Lieberman, H. Supporting user hypotheses in problem diagnosis. In *Proc. IUI 2004,* ACM Press (2004), 30-37.

18. Roth, P., Petrucci, L., Pun, T., and Assimacopouls, A. Auditory browser for blind and visually impaired users, In *Proc. CHI 1999.* ACM Press (1999), 218-219.

19. Yu, W., McAllister, G., Strain, P., Kuber, R. and Murphy, E. Improving web accessibility using content-aware plug-ins. In *Proc. CHI 2005,* ACM Press (2005), 1893-1896.

20. Dontcheva, M., Drucker, S. M., Wade, G., Salesin, D., and Cohen, M. F. Summarizing personal web browsing sessions. In *Proc. UIST 2006.* ACM Press (2006), 115-124.

21. Hartmann, M., Schreiber, D. and Mühlhдuser, M. AUGUR: providing context-aware interaction support. In Proc. of symposium on Engineering interactive computing systems, ACM Press (2009), 123-132.

22. Parente, P.. Clique: a conversant, task-based audio display for GUI applications. SIGACCESS Access. Comput. 84 (2006), 34-37.

23. Mahmud, J. U., Borodin, Y., and Ramakrishnan, I. V. Csurf: a context-driven non-visual web-browser. In *Proc. WWW 2007.* ACM Press (2007), 31-40.

24. Borodin, Y., Bigham, J. P., Raman, R. and Ramakrishnan, I. V. What's new? Making web page updates accessible. In *Proc. ASSETS 2008,* ACM Press (2008), 145-152.

25. Yesilada, Y., Stevens, R., Harper, S. and Goble, C. Evaluating DANTE: Semantic transcoding for visually disabled users. *ACM Trans. Comput.-Hum. Interact.* (14:3), (2007), 14.

26. Harper, S. and Patel, N. Gist summaries for visually impaired surfers. In *Proc. ASSETS 2005,* ACM Press (2005), 90-97.

27. Miyashita, H., Sato, D., Takagi, H. and Asakawa, C. aiBrowser for multimedia: introducing multimedia content accessibility for visually impaired users. In *Proc.ASSETS 2007,* ACM Press (2007), 91-98.

28. Lunn, D., Bechhofer, S. and Harper, S. The SADIe transcoding platform. In Proceedings of the 2008 international cross-disciplinary conference on Web accessibility (W4A), ACM Press (2008), 128-129.

29. Takagi, H., Kawanaka, S., Kobayashi, M., Itoh, T., and Asakawa, C. Social accessibility: achieving accessibility through collaborative metadata authoring. In *Proc. ASSETS 2008.* ACM Press (2008), 193-200.

30. Chen, C. L. and Raman, T. V. AxsJAX: a talking translation bot using google IM: bringing web-2.0 applications to life. In *Proc. the 2008 international cross-disciplinary conference on Web accessibility (W4A),* ACM Press (2008), 54-56.

31. Goble, C., Harper, S., and Stevens, R. The travails of visually impaired web travellers. In *Proceedings of the Eleventh ACM on Hypertext and Hypermedia.* ACM Press (2000), 1-10.

32. Eclipse ACTF Accessibility Internet Browser, http://www.eclipse.org/actf/downloads/tools/aiBrowser/.

33. Kawanaka, S., Borodin, Y., Bigham, J. P., Lunn, D., Takagi, H. and Asakawa, C. Accessibility commons: a metadata infrastructure for web accessibility. In *Proc. ASSETS 2008,* ACM Press (2008), 153-160.

34. Kanayama, H., Nasukawa, T. and Watanabe, H. Deeper sentiment analysis using machine translation technology. In *Proc. of the 20th international conference on Computational Linguistic',* Association for Computational Linguistics (2004), 494.

35. Shaojian Zhu, Daisuke Sato, Hironobu Takagi, and Chieko Asakawa. Sasayaki: an augmented voice-based web browsing experience. In *Proc. ASSETS 2010.* ACM Press (2008), 279-280.

36. Wilson, J., Walker, B. N., Lindsay, J., Cambias, C., and Dellaert, F. SWAN: System for Wearable Audio Navigation. In *Proc. ISWC 2007.* IEEE Computer Society (2007), 1-8.

On the Audio Representation of Radial Direction

Susumu Harada, Hironobu Takagi, Chieko Asakawa
IBM Research – Tokyo
1623-14 Shimotsuruma, Yamato, Kanagawa, 242-8502 Japan
{ey05096, takagih, chie}@jp.ibm.com
+81-(46)-276-1111

ABSTRACT
We present and evaluate an approach towards eyes-free auditory display of spatial information that considers radial direction as a fundamental type of value primitive. There are many benefits to being able to sonify radial directions, such as indicating the heading towards a point of interest in a direct and dynamic manner, rendering a path or shape outline by sonifying a continual sequence of tangent directions as the path is traced, and providing direct feedback of the direction of motion of the user in a physical space or a pointer in a virtual space. We propose a concrete mapping of vowel-like sounds to radial directions as one potential method to enable sonification of such information. We conducted a longitudinal study with five sighted and two blind participants to evaluate the learnability and effectiveness of this method. Results suggest that our directional sound mapping can be learned within a few hours and be used to aurally perceive spatial information such as shape outlines and path contours.

Author Keywords
Audio display, sonification, non-verbal, non-speech, navigation, radial direction, visual impairment.

ACM Classification Keywords
H5.2. User Interfaces: Auditory (non-speech) feedback.

General Terms
Design, Experimentation, Human Factors, Performance.

INTRODUCTION
Visual modality continues to be the primary mode through which computers present information to their users ever since the graphical user interface superseded the command-line interface. The graphical user interface vastly expanded the types of information that can be presented to the user beyond textual information to include visual and spatial information. On the other hand, as computers continue to become more integrated into our daily lives, millions of people who are blind or have low vision are increasingly in need of ways to gain access to such information through non-visual means. While screen reading technology has been around for some time, its primary function has been to read out textual information to the user, requiring visual or spatial information to be first converted into textual descriptions. The need for an effective non-visual display method that can aurally present non-textual information will only continue to grow. Such demand will also be shared by the general population, as mobile devices continue to proliferate and are used under scenarios in which the user may temporarily be in an eyes-busy situation.

Recent research efforts in the area of *auditory displays* [16] offer promise towards the realization of an audio equivalent of the graphical user interface revolution. An auditory display system maps *data dimensions* of some information onto *auditory display dimensions*, and generates the output sound based on the mapping. In the case of spatial or visual information, examples of data dimensions include properties such as brightness, hue, size, and coordinate values such as *x*-axis and *y*-axis values. Examples of commonly used auditory display dimensions include sound properties such as pitch, volume, tempo, pan, and vibrato rate. As these examples suggest, the sound properties that are typically considered for use in auditory displays tend to be continuous but linearly-valued properties. As a result, much of the focus of auditory displays has been on the sonification of such linearly-valued data as well.

While the sonification of linearly-valued data has many useful applications, there is a different class of data—namely radially-valued data—that we believe is especially important in the context of auditory displays but has so far remained largely unexplored. A representative example of radially-valued data is angular data such as compass direction or heading. In a non-visual world, being able to perceive directional information—whether it be towards some destination relative to the user in a real-world setting or towards some target on a touch-screen device relative to the user's touch point—can be indispensable. Given the temporal and serial nature of auditory displays, certain types of spatial information, such as vector-based figures and path-like information, may also be more concisely and intuitively sonified as a sequence of tangent directions as the outline is traced dynamically.

We present a systematic approach for considering radial direction as a new type of auditory display value primitive, and define a mapping between directions and continuous sound properties to enable them to be sonified. Under this approach, a particular sound is directly mapped to a corresponding radial direction. We have developed a prototype auditory display system that is capable of sonifying such radial directions dynamically and in real time. We have selected vowel-like sounds as our initial choice for the auditory display dimension due to a number of favorable properties they possess. To determine the feasibility of having users learn to interpret such radially-mapped sounds, we conducted a longitudinal study with five sighted and two blind participants. We present the findings and observations from our study that indicate the viability of our directional sound mapping, and identify topics for further exploration towards the realization of richer and more effective auditory display systems.

RELATED WORK

Most of the prior work on the auditory display of spatial information can be categorized into one of the following three groups: sonification of graph-like information, sonification of image-like information, and sonification of physical-world spatial information. A common theme appears across many of the works: the use of linearly-valued auditory display dimensions. While in certain contexts such an application may be appropriate, in other cases, the potential benefit of being able to sonify radial directions become apparent.

Sonification of Graph-Like Information

One of the earlier works on sonification of graph-like information is the Sound Graphs system [19]. It set the precedent for sonification of line graphs, in which the *y* coordinate value is mapped to pitch and the *x* axis is presented serially over time in a monotonically increasing fashion, resulting in a sound whose pitch rises and falls in accordance with the shape of the graph. This style of sonification is also referred to as *passive* sonification, since the user simply listens to the information and does not take an active roll in how it is sonified. Most of the subsequent research on sonification of graph-like information have continued to use a similar metaphor of mapping pitch to some linearly-valued data [3,22,26]. For simple line graphs, such mapping may provide the benefit of being intuitive and sufficiently expressive.

Dealing with a different kind of graph composed of nodes and edges, PLUMB [6] is a system which enables a user to identify nodes and follow edges between them using digital stylus as input and sonified feedback as output. This style of sonification is referred to as *active* sonification since the user controls what aspect of the information to sonify. In this case, the user supplies the system with the Cartesian coordinate of the point of interest through the digital stylus, and the system speaks the name of the node if the point is on a node or plays a musical tone if the point is on an edge. The loudness of the latter tone increases as the stylus point moves closer to the central axis of the edge, and the amount of vibrato on the tone also increases as the stylus point approaches a node. In this manner, the user is expected to explore the graph by tracing the edges from node to node.

This latter example illustrates the case in which the ability to sonify radial directions may be beneficial, as the user can be guided towards the node via sounds indicating the direction towards which the user should move instead of arbitrarily "scanning" the surrounding region..

Sonification of Image-Like Information

Another class of auditory display methods attempt to aurally render image-like information, typically a bitmap grid of pixels or cells. Devices that attempt to directly convert visual images into aural renditions are referred to as optophones [4], and one specific implementation of such a device is the vOICe system [20]. The vOICe system aurally displays grayscale images by sweeping a vertical scan line across the image at a fixed rate, sonifying the column of pixels along the scan line as a mixture of sinusoidal waves, each of whose frequency is proportional to the *y* coordinate value of the corresponding pixel and whose amplitude is proportional to the pixel intensity. A similar system that supports active sonification is SoundView [8]. It allows the user to use a pointing device to move the pointer across a digital image, and each pixel traversed by the pointer is sonified with the hue, saturation, brightness, and pointer velocity all mapping to a set of filter parameters that transform an underlying white noise source.

Another work that employs a similar raster metaphor is the AudioGraph system [23]. AudioGraph presents a 1-bit, 40-by-40 grid on which various shapes could be drawn and rendered aurally. The horizontal and vertical grids are assigned piano and organ notes, respectively, of increasing pitch starting from the origin at the lower left. A particular grid cell coordinate is sonified as first a sequence of piano notes from the origin to its *x* coordinate, followed by a similar sequence of organ notes for the *y* coordinate.

In a sense, these auditory display systems that sonify image-like information are the aural analog of raster display systems. Our proposed approach—the aural analog of vector display systems—complements such systems by enabling shapes such as vector-based paths to be more concisely sonified as a sequence of tangent directions along the outline. For each point, instead of two linearly-valued properties (*x* and *y* coordinates), only one radially-valued property (direction angle) will need to be sonified.

Sonification of Physical-World Spatial Information

There have been a number of navigation-oriented systems developed for the physical world that employ stereophonic spatialized audio to present directional information to the user [13,17,25]. Various spatialized audio rendering techniques exist that can emulate a sound emanating from some spatial direction relative to the listener [1], making it an intuitive method for presenting such information, particularly in the physical world. However, they present the directional information in an inherently egocentric perspective, making it less suitable for allocentric contexts such as tracing out an outline of some shape. There is also the need for careful calibration to achieve good precision, and even then, vertical resolution is known to be significantly lower than the horizontal resolution [2].

The Value of Being Able to Sonify Radial Vectors

There are many benefits to having a well-defined, generalizable mapping of radial directions to sounds and the ability to sonify them dynamically. In active sonification systems, sonification of direction information at any particular point in the spatial input allows the user not only to probe the properties of that particular point, but also to be guided towards some other target, enabling a more directed exploration rather than an ad-hoc exploration. With the addition of aural encoding of magnitude along with the radial direction (e.g., by mapping to volume or pitch), we can represent a full radial vector which can provide the user with both a sense of direction as well as the distance to some target. Certain scenarios may benefit from simply having such information presented statically, but a key factor for such mapping to be successful would be its ability to be sonified continuously and dynamically as the direction or the magnitude, or both, change rapidly over time.

Static direction-only contexts are relatively simple cases in which verbal descriptions of the direction may be sufficient, as it does not have to be repeatedly presented over a short period of time. However, even in such cases, the ability to recognize non-verbal sonification of direction may have advantages over processing the linguistic meaning behind the verbal cue. For instance, such a sonification might alert a driver to the direction of some obstacle or a pedestrian, possibly more quickly and precisely than a verbal alert.

Dynamic direction-only information is also interesting, as the information may change rapidly over a short period of time, making verbal presentation less ideal. Such scenarios may arise in contexts such as getting a homing beacon signal towards some target relative to oneself, in scenarios including pedestrian navigation or spatial games such as blind soccer. Dynamic direction-only information may also be presented during an active exploration of some spatial information, such as in "playing back" a path or shape outline and getting the directional tangent information along the path as the control point is moved along the path.

With the ability to sonify full dynamic direction-and-magnitude information, many interesting applications become possible. For example, a system could be developed to aid a blind user in actively tracing some path (say, a handwritten letter or even an outline of some drawing) with a digital stylus, where a virtual guide point on the path can continuously "pull" the user's stylus point along by sonifying the vector cue representing the direction and distance between them. This is akin to what has been done using haptic pen interfaces to guide blind users along some virtual path [21,22], but without the need for expensive haptic devices.

OUR DIRECTION SONIFICATION SYSTEM

We have developed a prototype system to investigate one potential method for sonifying radial direction. While most prior use of sound properties for representing spatial information has focused on sonifying linearly continuous quantities in the Cartesian coordinate system, our system utilizes a mapping of sound properties to radial continuous quantity in the polar coordinate system. In particular, we investigated the use of vowel-like sounds as one of the potential methods for sonifying radial directions.

While there have been prior investigations into the use of vowel-like sounds for sonification [5,9,12,14,15], their use has been either for sonification of non-spatial data [5,12], or for sonification of physical motion within particular contexts [9,14,15]. There has not been a generalizable approach towards enabling sonification of radial directions in both static and dynamic contexts in computer interfaces.

The systematic mapping of vowel-like sounds to directions and its use as a fundamental auditory display dimension was primarily inspired by the Vocal Joystick project [18], in which radially-assigned vowel sounds were used to control a mouse pointer hands-free by vocalizing the sound corresponding to the direction of desired movement (Figure 1c). A longitudinal evaluation of their system [11] showed that people were able to learn to vocalize and memorize the directional mappings of the vowel sounds within few hours of training, and that it could also be used to create fluid, lifelike artwork using only one's voice [10]. Our own experience with the Vocal Joystick system also led us to hypothesize that perhaps it could be used as an output modality as well, and that with comparable training, people can learn to interpret a sequence of vowel sounds as two-dimensional paths.

The space of vowel sounds holds an interesting property that makes it especially appealing for serving as a representation of a closed-loop value of radial directions. Most basic sound properties such as loudness, pitch, and vibrato rate are inherently linear and one dimensional. However, vowel quality maps naturally to a two-dimensional representation, as evidenced by the International Phonetic Association vowel chart (Figure 1a). By vocalizing and moving the tongue (and the lips) continuously in such a way that the tongue position traces a loop around the perimeter of the chart, a smoothly-varying sequence of vowel sounds will be produced that correspond to the sequence of vowels along the perimeter of the chart, eventually looping back to the starting vowel. Such a "sound loop" we claim is well suited for mapping to radial directions. Another promising property of vowel sounds is its familiarity to human users. As cited by many of the prior investigations into vowel-based sonification [5,12,14,15], a

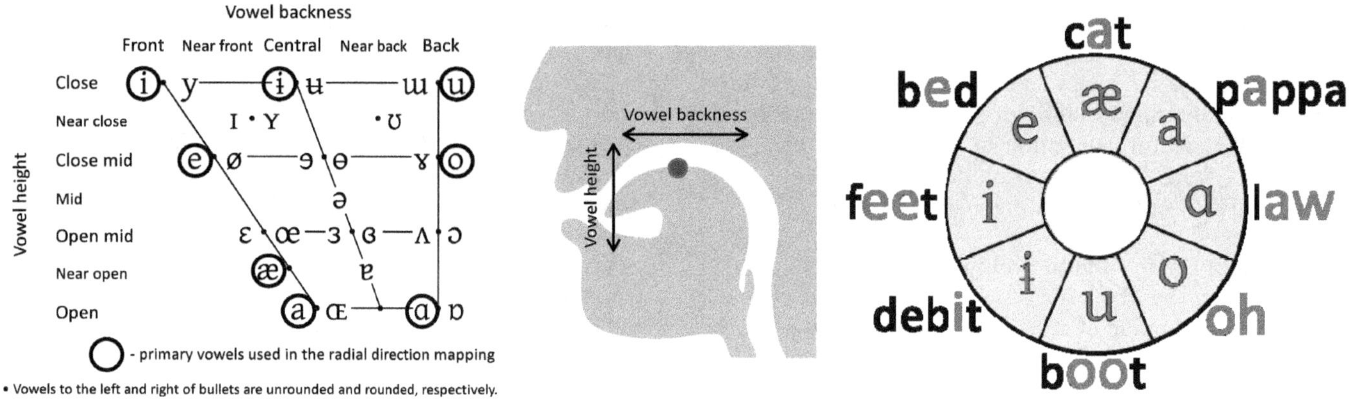

(a) (b) (c)

Figure 1: (a) IPA (International Phonetic Association) vowel chart showing the relative arrangement of vowel sounds and the primary sounds that are used in our system for the eight cardinal and ordinal directions. (b) The mid-sagittal plane view of the mouth and the tongue showing the corresponding dimensions of the IPA vowel chart. (c) Directional mapping of vowel sounds used in our system. The words in the periphery are provided as rough approximations of the corresponding vowel sounds. The mapping is adapted from the Vocal Joystick project [18], which had successfully trained people to memorize and vocalize the sounds.

human listener is particularly attuned to distinguishing between vowel sounds due to their essential role in speech.

It is worth noting that we are not claiming that vowel sounds are the most ideal sounds for aurally representing radial direction. We in fact believe that there are many other categories of sounds that can be considered multiparametric and offer multidimensional mapping, such as sounds of different musical instruments. Since very little prior work had investigated such mapping of sounds to radial directions—particularly in the context of having users learn it over an extended period of time—we decided to focus on vowel sounds for our investigation given our experience with and knowledge of the promising properties of vowel sounds as mentioned above.

We also do not claim that vowel sounds are necessarily "intuitively" mapped to radial directions from an untrained user's point of view. In fact, we believe that any choice from the variety of possible sound categories for mapping to radial directions will require the user to spend non-trivial amount of time learning the mapping before becoming able to respond instinctively towards the corresponding direction or "hear" the shape of some outline.

We have chosen to use the same vowel-to-direction mapping as the Vocal Joystick system (Figure 1c) as they had been chosen for their acoustically distinct nature in majority of the languages and had also been studied in the context of a longitudinal study, albeit for vocalization rather than perception.

Our system can produce sonification output given a directional input that can be dynamically changed over time. The system uses the MIDI protocol to communicate with a MIDI software synthesizer, controlling the sound onset, offset, and parameters such as volume and pitch using MIDI control signals. We created our own custom MIDI instrument in which pre-recorded vowel sounds for the eight directions were mapped to different keys, and the attack-sustain-decay-release points defined to enable sustained looping of the vowel sound when played.

While the current MIDI implementation limits us to having a discrete set of directional vowel sounds (in the current case, eight), in the ideal scenario we would utilize a sonification engine that would allow us to generate a gradual blend of all intermediary sounds seamlessly.

LONGITUDINAL USER STUDY

We conducted a longitudinal user study with five sighted participants and two blind participants to assess the initial potential of the proposed vowel-based directional sonification system. Our goal was to determine whether it was possible for a user to learn the directional mapping of the sounds and become able to interpret such sonification as directions and shapes.

We divided the experiment into three stages. In the first stage which we call "sound mapping," the goal was to get the users accustomed to the different vowel sounds and their corresponding directions. We first introduced the participants to just the four cardinal directional sounds, and after learning those mappings, introduced the other four ordinal directional sounds. In the second stage which we call "sound following," after the users were familiarized with all eight directional sounds, we sought to get the users accustomed to continuously tracking the sound as it varied over time and accurately interpreting the change in direction. In the final stage which we call "shape recognition," we presented users with some path-based shape, and provided an active control for letting the user control the playback of the path. Further details of each stage are presented in the Procedure section below.

ID	Age	Gender	Vision	Language experience (years)	Musical experience (years)
P1	29	M	Sighted	Spanish (native), English (10)	None
P2	30	M	Sighted	Dutch (native), French (24), English (18), German (16), Japanese (4)	Piano (18)
P3	33	M	Sighted	Indonesian (native), English (20), Japanese (14), German (3), Arabic (3) , French (2)	None
P4	35	M	Sighted	Japanese (native), English (13), French (2)	None
P5	38	M	Sighted	Japanese (native), English (25), German (5)	Guitar (5), Piano (5), Choir (3)
P6	23	F	Blind	Japanese (native), English (6)	Piano (3)
P7	23	F	Blind	Japanese (native), English (4), German (2)	Piano (3), Trumpet (2)

Table 1: Summary of demographic information of the participants who took part in the longitudinal study.

Participants

We recruited five sighted participants (P1 through P5) and two blind participants (P6 and P7) to try out our prototype system (Table 1). None of the participants had any auditory impairment, and none had previously used the Vocal Joystick system and therefore were unfamiliar with the notion of the directional vowel mappings. All had been using computers for over 10 years.

P6 and P7 were both born with low vision which has degenerated over the years. Currently they both have the ability to detect light changes in the environment, but are legally blind. Both have been using computers with a screen reader, and have also been familiarized with the written forms of the English alphabets and numerical digits.

Procedure

We had each participant come in for a series of eight sessions. Attempt was made to keep the sessions separated by at least 2 hours and no more than 48 hours.

First stage: sound mapping

During the first sound mapping stage, the participants were repeatedly presented with a block of 24 trials in which the computer generated a random directional audio cue, to which the participant responded using one of two devices: a joystick or a numeric keypad. The joystick was a dual-stick USB game controller. The keypad was a USB numeric keypad with all keycaps removed except for the peripheral numeric buttons (1,2,3,4,6,7,8,9) and the enter key. Upon hearing a directional audio cue, the participants responded by tilting the joystick in the corresponding direction or pressing a key in the corresponding direction on the numeric keypad. We let the participants choose the device they preferred and found most comfortable to use.

During each trial, the directional audio cue was sonified for one second. Participants were told that they can respond as soon as they recognized the corresponding direction, even while the cue was still being sonified. Upon a correct response, a short earcon was played representing a wine glass being flicked. Upon an incorrect response, a cat meow sound of falling pitch was played, and the participant was given as many chances to keep trying to respond with the correct direction. Each subsequent target cue was not sonified until one second after the correct user response was registered for the preceding cue.

At the end of each block, a synthesized voice reported the percentage of correct responses and the average response time, and a random encouragement phrase. During the beginning of the stage, the participants were instructed not to worry about the response time but to try to recognize the direction accurately. As their accuracy increased, they were free to try responding faster but were encouraged to keep the error rate below 5% (one error per block of 24 trials).

Second stage: sound following

During the sound following stage, participants were presented with a series of directional sounds, in which each direction was continually sonified for randomized durations and any change in direction was made smooth by interpolating incremental direction changes in between at a rate that was fixed for a given condition. There were three speed levels for the rate of direction change: 1Hz, 1.5Hz, and 2Hz. The participants used the joystick control to try to follow the sound as closely as possible, keeping the joystick tilted towards the direction of the sonification at each moment.

Third stage: shape recognition

During the third stage of shape recognition, participants were presented with three different types of path-based representations (Figure 2). The first was a random path, which was composed of connected segments of random lengths and directions (directions fell within one of the eight main directions). The second type was single numerical digit, and third was a set of alphabet letters. All shape paths were defined as a single stroke, so shapes such as the letter "k" had portions of the path which backtracked and overlapped itself. Since the primary target of evaluation for this study was the sonification of direction, we left out most of the shapes that were ambiguous without a distinct sense of path length, such as the lower-case letters "n"

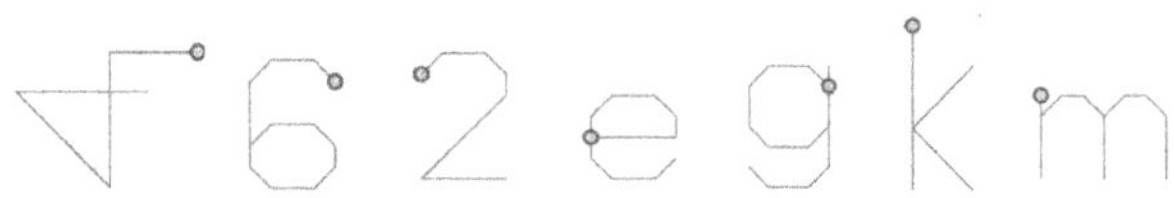

Figure 2: Examples of shapes (random paths, alphabet letters, and numerical digits) that participants actively sonified in the shape recognition stage of the user study.

versus “h”. We did leave in a few shapes such as the lowercase letter “g” that could be tricky to perceive if the relative duration of the long portion of the shape was completely ignored.

The participants were able to control the playback of the path using the numeric keypad. Two keys were assigned to move the virtual pointer forward and backward along the path at a constant rate as long as they were held down. While the virtual pointer was tracing the path, the tangent direction at the virtual pointer location on the path was continually sonified. When backward movement was specified, the sonification correspondingly reflected the tangent direction in the opposite direction as during the forward movement. This enabled the participant to backtrack along any segment whose direction they felt uncertain about to hear the opposite direction which hopefully would be more certain. Five traversal speeds were available ranging from 30 pixels per second to 150 pixels per second which the user could switch between using two keys designated as speed up and down keys. Total length of each shape varied between 300 and 600 pixels.

For alphabet letters and numerical digits, we measured the time it took the participants to correctly recognize the corresponding shape via verbal response. For random paths, the participants used a digital stylus to draw the perceived path shape, and the trial was considered completed when the drawn shape contained the correct sequence of segment directions (segment lengths were ignored).

RESULTS

We first present the quantitative results from the longitudinal study below, grouped by the three learning stages. The key objective of this section is to illustrate how directional vowel sonification can indeed be learned, and how easily people can follow it, and how well some people were able to use it to aurally “see” path-based shapes.

Sound Mapping Stage

For the four-directional mapping, every participant was able to achieve stable performance of greater than 95% accuracy (i.e., at most one error per block of 24 trials) within the first session. Furthermore, in all cases, the errors that were made were all “off by one” errors, meaning that the incorrect response direction was adjacent to the correct direction. The average response time for the four-directional mapping across all participants was 0.85 seconds, with the average best time of 0.68 seconds.

Session	P1	P2	P3	P4	P5	P6	P7
1	Map-4	Map-4	Map-4	Map-4	Map-4	Map-4	Map-4
2	Map-8	Map-8	Map-8	Map-8	Map-4	Map-8	Map-8
3	Map-8	Map-8	Map-8	Map-8	Map-8	Map-8	Map-8
4	Map-8	Map-8	Map-8	Map-8	Map-8	Follow	Follow
5	Follow	Follow	Follow	Follow	Map-8	Follow	Follow
6	Follow	Follow	Follow	Follow	Map-8	Reco	Reco
7	Reco	Follow	Reco	Reco	Follow	Reco	Reco
8	Reco	Reco	Reco	Reco	Follow	Reco	Reco
9	Reco	Reco		Reco	Reco		
10	Reco	Reco					

Table 2: Summary of the sessions at which each participant progressed to the subsequent stage in the user study. “Map-4” represents the sound mapping stage with only 4 cardinal directions, “Map-8” represents the sound mapping stage with all 8 directions, “Follow” is the sound following stage and “Reco” is the shape recognition stage.

When four additional directions were introduced for the eight-directional mapping, the time to stable performance varied across participants. P1, P6 and P7 showed stable performance by the 3rd session, while P2 and P4 did not stabilize until the 9th and 6th session, respectively. P3 and P5 performance did not seem to stabilize even into the last session. We suspect that the primary reason for this may be due to their over-optimization for response time. We observed that these participants seemed to be highly motivated by the response time feedback more than the accuracy feedback at the end of each block, at times commenting that they wish to “beat” their previous best time. The average response time for the eight-directional mapping across all participants was 1.26 seconds, with the average best time of 0.93 seconds.

Sound Following Stage

While the stabilization point for the eight-directional vowel-mapping varied widely across participants, when they switched to the sound following stage, all participants were able to follow the sounds and were able to reach stable performance. P1, P6 and P7 (the participants whose sound mapping stage performance stabilized early) as well as P2 and P4 (those whose sound mapping stage performance stabilized later) were able to attain stable performance across all three speed levels within the first two sessions of the sound following stage. Even P3 and P5, whose sound mapping stage performance did not stabilize throughout all the sessions, did well in the sound following stage, attaining over 90 percent match for all three speed levels.

Furthermore, even though the average response time during the sound mapping stage settled to different values for each participant, during the sound following stage, the average response delay for each new cue was 0.77 seconds regardless of the speed level, with the average best time of 0.56 seconds. This suggests that users can respond to and

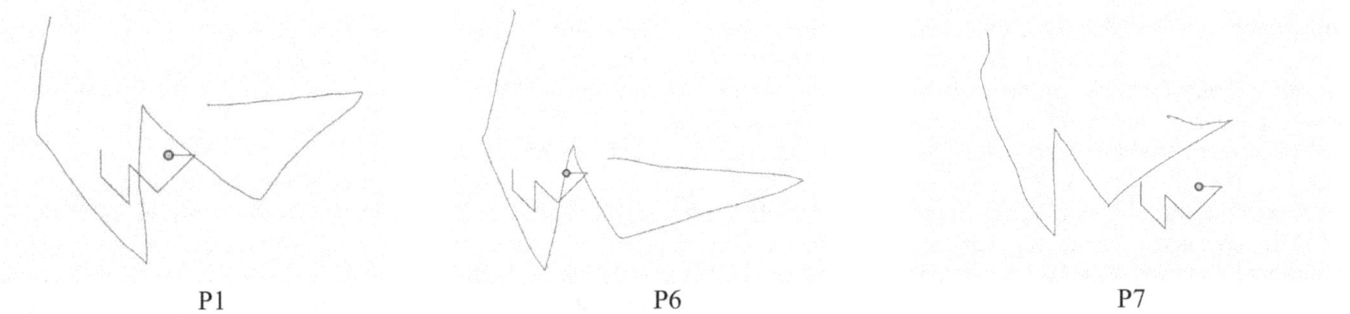

Figure 3: Three participants' drawings (in gray) of a random target path (in red) from the shape recognition stage of the user study. The participants actively sonified the target paths and used a digital stylus to draw the path based solely on the audio feedback.

track dynamic changes in aurally-presented directional cues at a rate of 0.5 seconds per change.

Shape Recognition Stage

Due to the difference in the rate at which each participant was able to progress through the first two stages, the amount of exposure to the shape recognition task varied across participants, from one full session up to four sessions.

Participants were able to determine almost all of the shapes presented to them, and in total, there were only two instances of letter shape unable to be recognized ("m" by P2 and "s" by P1) and two instances of numerical digit not being recognized ("5" by P6 and "9" by P5) within the time limit of five minutes. On average, letter shapes were recognized after 66 seconds of exploration, numerical digits after 107 seconds, and random shapes were traced accurately after 89 seconds. The fastest times for each type of shape were 17.2 seconds for letter shapes, 13.4 seconds for numerical digits, and 18.2 seconds for random shapes.

P1 in particular excelled towards the end of the series of sessions, exhibiting the fastest times for identifying numerical digits and letter shapes as mentioned above as well as tracing random paths correctly in as little as 26 seconds. He mentioned that he was able to "hear the shapes" of the paths, and to recognize various patterns representing curved sequences.

OBSERVATIONS

Beyond the quantified metrics, there were a number of intriguing observations made throughout the study for each individual participant that shed some light on the nature of the results obtained, as well as provide helpful insight for further exploration of this area. For brevity, we represent the radial directions using corresponding compass heading abbreviations (e.g., "NW" for the upper-right direction).

Sound Mapping

Interestingly, during the sound mapping stage, a number of participants expressed particular feelings about where a sound "should" be. For example, P2 mentioned that the SW sound "doesn't belong there," that it should be in the NW direction. P3 also mentioned that for the SW direction, he does not expect [ɨ] there, and wanted a sound closer to [u]. For P4, "[æ] sounded upper-right." P4 also mentioned that due to the fact that in Japanese the vowel order begins with the sequence [a][i][u], he expected [i] to come in clockwise order after [a], and because his initial perception of the sound for the E direction was closer to [a], he expected [i] at S and [u] at W. P4 also further stated that he expected the main cardinal directions to contain the main Japanese vowels, such as [e] and [o]. P7 also expressed her expectation of the vowels being arranged in Japanese order clockwise, starting with [a] at N.

There was also an interesting comment by P5 regarding the "brightness" and "progressiveness" of the sounds, with [æ] and [a] sounding "bright" and "forward" for him, and [u] sounding backward, closed, and dark. P4 also expressed [æ] as a sound that is more "frictional than [ɑ]."

All of these intriguing ways in which participants, especially initially, had perceived and held expectations about the sounds and their corresponding directions, opens up the question of how much we can leverage such preconceived notions, and how much they can simply be "overridden" through training using a fixed mapping. Our study seems to suggest that learning a predefined mapping is possible with just a few hours, although it would be ideal if we could customize the mapping to best take advantage of what the user expects in order to minimize the learning time and increase retention. Based on this observation, we are working on an interactive interface that allows users to explore a two-dimensional vowel space similar to the IPA vowel chart and selectively choose the most distinct set of vowel sounds on their own.

Input Device

From the very first sound mapping stage, input device preference varied widely across participants, with some feeling more comfortable with the joystick while others preferred the numeric pad. For example, P2, who played piano, initially showed preference for using the numeric pad since he could then position his fingers on the keys as if he was playing a piano and try to memorize the mapping of sounds to those keys and fingers. As this approach seemed to be inhibiting the directional association, he switched to the joystick in later sessions. P3 also preferred the numeric pad—even during the sound following stage—due to its consistent input and feel. One of the blind participants P7 also preferred the numeric pad since she had difficulty getting the feel for the alignment of the joystick axes. P6, however, seemed not to have problems with the joystick and used it throughout the study. Joystick was also the preferred device for P1 and P4. Such variance in preference for the input device highlights the need for offering a reliable, consistent input mechanism that can process directional input for the purposes of training.

The digital tablet and stylus also turned out to be quite difficult for the blind participants. While it was somewhat expected, we initially expected the tactile feedback of the tablet edges to be sufficient for alignment and reference. However, this did not seem enough for the blind participants to feel confident enough about the path they were drawing. This raises an important question of how much we can rely on proprioception in such tasks, especially for blind users. Furthermore, this could be seen as an opportunity to use directional sound output as an active form of assistive *feedback* for blind users as they draw some path, enabling them to compare it with the *expected* sonification of some correct path shape or their previously drawn path shape. In fact, Crossan and Brewster [7] suggests that adding such direct sound feedback can aid blind users in learning to draw various shapes.

Eyes Closed

Among the sighted participants, some preferred to keep their eyes closed during the tasks. For example, P3 mentioned that with his eyes closed, he felt that he can "see" the directional mapping better. P2 also preferred closing his eyes, citing the distraction he felt from seeing the numbers on the numeric keypad. On the other hand, P5 for instance preferred to keep his eyes open so that he could visually map the numeric keypad location to the sounds he was hearing. Such variance also suggests the need for further investigation on the role of visual stimulus in the formation of the mental model used in learning directional sound mappings, especially between users with or without vision and between blind users born with or without sight.

Sound Following

One of the main reasons why the sound following stage yielded positive results even for those who were struggling in the sound mapping stage seems to be the fact that the change in direction at any time was limited to being towards one of two adjacent directions, thereby reducing the required cognitive processing. While this may seem trivial, it implies that a system which dynamically presents changing directions aurally should interpolate the change via smooth transitions in order not to lose the user.

It also seemed to be the case that for most people, the transition from the sound mapping stage to the sound following stage could have been made easier if they were exposed more to smoothly varying sounds, i.e., in quadrants in both rotational directions. Several participants expressed explicitly that when they were able to hear a sequence of adjacent directional sounds consecutively, it helped them remember the "shape" of the curve as a sound pattern.

Shape Recognition

During the shape recognition stage, we observed a variety of strategies employed by the participants in listening to and inspecting the shape sounds. One group of participants (P1, P4, and also P7 to some extent) adopted the approach of first listening to the entire path at one of the faster speed settings to get an overview of the shape, and then retracing at a slower speed to determine or confirm the directions for each segment. This strategy seemed to work well, as reflected by the fact that these three participants had the best average shape recognition times.

P2, P3 and P5, on the other hand, tended to almost always start at one of the slower speeds, listening to each segment one at a time to incrementally build up the image of the path. This is most likely due to the fact that these participants were not yet comfortable with their sound mappings, as reflected in the fact that their sound mapping performance stabilized late or not at all.

P3 and P4 also made extensive use of the reverse traversal functionality to backtrack along parts of the path which they did felt uncertain about. The participants expressed their satisfaction with being able to hear the sound opposite in direction to the sound they were uncertain about, as it usually was the case that the uncertainty was isolated to a particular quadrant of the radial directions.

Another interesting observation was that several participants (P1, P2, P4) reported being able to remember what the shape sounded like after hearing it played through once, and be able to replay it in their minds while they traced out the shape at their own pace. We feel that this ability to retain and reproduce the sound sequence with relative ease to be a particularly useful and advantageous property of the directional vowel sound mapping. Even when the participant could not yet vocalize certain vowel sounds accurately, they seemed to retain their own perception of the actual sound they heard and correctly map them to the corresponding directions. We suspect that such a recall would be much more difficult with sounds that are not naturally meant to be vocalized, such as musical instrument sounds or other abstract tones.

On a related note, many of the participants were able to retain the sound sequences of common path features in their memory across trials, recognizing such patterns as circular paths and semicircles. For example, upon hearing the sonification of the numeral "9", P1 noticed that "there was a lot of curving" and "knew that there was a circle, followed by a long straight line." P4 was able to pick up from the sonification of the letter "k" the "presence of overlapped, backtracking portions, and combined with the fact that the shape was mostly linear," was able to quickly recognize the shape.

There were a number of challenges and obstacles that were observed as well. As expected, shapes that included features that were ambiguous without some length information proved to be challenging for a number of participants. For example, shapes such as the letter "g" and the number "6" were difficult, especially for those participants who tended to start at the lowest speed setting and incrementally building up the overall path. A more active interaction method may alleviate some of this uncertainty, as speculated in the Future Directions section.

For the blind participants, the transition from the sound following stage to the shape recognition stage—in particular the shift from the joystick to the digital tablet—seemed to have led to some initial confusion about the interpretation of the sonification produced in the latter stage. Specifically, it became clear shortly into the shape recognition stage that P6's interpretation of the path directions tended to be off by 90 degrees. Upon inquiry, it was discovered that she had been visualizing the motion of the joystick from the sound following stage, such that for example when the sequence N, NW, W was sonified, instead of visualizing a path which was being drawn upwards then gradually leftwards, she was imagining the arc described by the joystick tip, starting at the top and moving towards the left and eventually downwards.

Synesthesia

One of the highlight moments during the study was when participants reported synesthetic experiences in which they "saw" or "felt" the sounds sonified from the paths. For instance, at the end of the final session, P1 stated:

> It's happening to me, what you mentioned in the beginning, I'm "seeing" the curves now. Before, I was trying to decipher each segment, but now I just "feel." I heard the two repeating curves [referring to a shape recognition trial he just finished] and "saw" it was a "3".

P5 also commented in his last session upon hearing the letter "m" shape that he "first thought it seemed like an 'h', but then as I kept listening I saw the image of the clockwise turns repeating and knew it was an 'm'." Even in the case of random shapes, P4 reported that he was able to grasp the overall shape after the first pass through the entire path. The captured trace from the digital tablet indeed confirms that he had correctly interpreted the direction of each segment.

These comments indicate that with only a few hours of training, it is possible to learn to interpret the directional sound mappings to a point where both arbitrary and known shapes can be perceived via their sonified representations.

FUTURE DIRECTIONS

The findings and observations from our longitudinal study suggest a wide array of new questions and research directions that warrant further investigation.

Now that we know that it is indeed possible for people to learn the directional vowel sound mapping and for it to be used to aurally perceive path-like information, more in-depth investigations are needed to better understand the fundamental information capacity of vowel-like sounds as well as the users' perceptual abilities. For instance, what is the limit of the resolution at which people can be trained to discern vowel-like sounds, both statically and dynamically, and how does that compare to the discriminability of other aural properties such as pitch and loudness? At what level of precision can people develop "absolute vowel" akin to absolute pitch, in which given a particular directional vowel stimulus, the user can pinpoint the corresponding direction?

Further research is needed to understand the capabilities of our sonification method in light of other alternatives. For instance, how does the use of vowel sounds compare to using different musical instrument sounds for the principal directions and morphing them to create sounds for the intermediate directions? Our user participants have also raised a number of suggestions during the study, such as the use of animal sounds and voiced fricatives. There needs to be a systematic evaluation of the properties of such sounds in the context of continuous radial directional sonification.

Furthermore, as mentioned in the related work section, the next significant step towards an even more expressive sonification method would be to investigate ways to effectively encode magnitude information in parallel with the directional information such that a full polar vector can be aurally displayed. The questions that need to be answered include, which of the various aural representation of magnitude such as pitch, loudness, and Geiger-counter-like ticks, are best suited to be used in combination with the directional sound mapping? Talbot and Cowan [24] conducted a thorough investigation into the alternate ways of representing distance for blind users, although their study dealt with the notion of an egocentric distance as opposed to a more general allocentric notion of length or magnitude.

CONCLUSION

We presented a novel approach towards auditory display of spatial information by introducing the notion of radial direction as one of the data primitives to be sonified, and a mapping between radial direction and vowel-like sounds as a concrete example. Such a mapping enables a variety of useful information to be conveyed aurally, such as rapidly changing direction to some target and contour of a shape as it is traced. Our longitudinal study with five sighted participants and two blind participants revealed that our directional sound mapping was quickly learned by most participants, and was able to be used to successfully perceive various path shapes using only monaural non-speech audio. Of particular note was that towards the end of the study, several participants were able to "see" and "feel" the shapes described by the sounds. Such observations offer promising evidence towards the viability and applicability of our proposed method.

We are continuing to investigate other types of sounds to identify those that can be learned faster, offer finer resolution in terms of angular discrimination by the listeners, as well as those that have greater pleasantness or familiarity. We are encouraged by our initial findings, and are excited by the possibilities that this new approach to auditory display of spatial information could open up.

ACKNOWLEDGMENTS

We thank all the user study participants for taking part in the longitudinal study, and the members of the Barrie-Free Division and the Division of Human Information Engineering in the Research Center for Advanced Science and Technology at the University of Tokyo for helping us with participant recruitment and logistics.

REFERENCES

1. Begault, D.R. *3-D sound for virtual reality and multimedia*. Academic Press Professional, Inc., 1994.
2. Blauert, J. *Spatial hearing: the psychophysics of human sound localization*. MIT Press, 1997.
3. Brown, L.M. and Brewster, S.A. Drawing by ear: interpreting sonified line graphs. *Proc. ICAD 2003*, (2003).
4. Capp, M. and Picton, P. The optophone: an electronic blind aid. *Engineering Science and Education Journal 9*, 3 (2000), 137 -143.
5. Cassidy, R.J., Berger, J., Lee, K., Maggioni, M., and Coifman, R.R. Auditory display of hyperspectral colon tissue images using vocal synthesis models. *Proc. ICAD 2004*, (2004).
6. Cohen, R.F., Haven, V., Lanzoni, J.A., Meacham, A., Skaff, J., and Wissell, M. Using an audio interface to assist users who are visually impaired with steering tasks. *Proc. ASSETS 2006*, ACM (2006), 119-124.
7. Crossan, A. and Brewster, S. Multimodal trajectory playback for teaching shape information and trajectories to visually impaired computer users. *ACM Transactions on Accessible Computing 1*, 2 (2008), 1-34.
8. van den Doel, K. SoundView: sensing color images by kinesthetic audio. *Proc. ICAD 2003*, (2003), 303-306.
9. Fox, J., Carlile, J., and Berger, J. SoniMime: sonification of fine motor skills. *Proc. ICAD 2005*, (2005).
10. Harada, S., Wobbrock, J.O., and Landay, J.A. VoiceDraw: a hands-free voice-driven drawing application for people with motor impairments. *Proc. ASSETS 2007*, ACM (2007), 27-34.
11. Harada, S., Wobbrock, J.O., Malkin, J., Bilmes, J.A., and Landay, J.A. Longitudinal study of people learning to use continuous voice-based cursor control. *Proc. CHI 2009*, ACM (2009), 347-356.
12. Hermann, T., Baier, G., Stephani, U., and Ritter, H. Kernel regression mapping for vocal EEG sonification. *Proc. ICAD 2008*, (2008).
13. Holland, S., Morse, D.R., and Gedenryd, H. AudioGPS: spatial audio navigation with a minimal attention interface. *Personal Ubiq. Comp. 6*, 4 (2002), 253-259.
14. Hummel, J., Hermann, T., Frauenberger, C., and Stockman, T. Interactive sonification of German wheel sports movement. *Proc. ISon 2010*, (2010), 17-22.
15. Kleiman-Weiner, M. and Berger, J. The sound of one arm swinging: a model for multidimensional auditory display of physical motion. *Proc. ICAD 2006*, (2006), 278-280.
16. Kramer, G. *An introduction to auditory display*. Addison Wesley Longman, 1992.
17. Loomis, J.M., Golledge, R.G., and Klatzky, R.L. Navigation system for the blind: auditory display modes and guidance. *Presence: Teleoperators and Virtual Environments 7*, 2 (1998), 193-203.
18. Malkin, J., Li, X., Harada, S., Landay, J., and Bilmes, J. The Vocal Joystick Engine v1.0. *Computer Speech & Language in press*, (2010).
19. Mansur, D.L., Blattner, M.M., and Joy, K.I. Sound Graphs: a numerical data analysis method for the blind. *Journal of Medical Systems 9*, 3 (1985), 163-174.
20. Meijer, P. An experimental system for auditory image representations. *IEEE Transactions on Biomedical Engineering 39*, 2 (1992), 112-121.
21. Plimmer, B., Crossan, A., Brewster, S.A., and Blagojevic, R. Multimodal collaborative handwriting training for visually-impaired people. *Proc. CHI 2008*, ACM (2008), 393-402.
22. Ramloll, R., Yu, W., Brewster, S., Riedel, B., Burton, M., and Dimigen, G. Constructing sonified haptic line graphs for the blind student: first steps. *Proc. ASSETS 2000*, ACM (2000), 17-25.
23. Rigas, D. and Alty, J. The rising pitch metaphor: an empirical study. *International Journal of Human-Computer Studies 62*, 1 (2005), 1-20.
24. Talbot, M. and Cowan, W. On the audio representation of distance for blind users. *Proc. CHI 2009*, ACM (2009), 1839-1848.
25. Wilson, J., Walker, B.N., Lindsay, J., Cambias, C., and Dellaert, F. SWAN: system for wearable audio navigation. *Proc. ISWC 2007*, (2007), 1-8.
26. Zhao, H., Plaisant, C., and Shneiderman, B. "I hear the pattern": interactive sonification of geographical data patterns. *Ext. Abtract CHI 2005*, ACM (2005), 1905-1908.

Multidimensional Gesture Sensing at the Piano Keyboard

Andrew P. McPherson
Drexel University
Electrical & Computer Engineering
apm@drexel.edu

Youngmoo E. Kim
Drexel University
Electrical & Computer Engineering
ykim@drexel.edu

ABSTRACT
In this paper we present a new keyboard interface for computer music applications. Where traditional keyboard controllers report the velocity of each key-press, our interface senses up to five separate dimensions: velocity, percussiveness, rigidity, weight, and depth. These dimensions, which we identified based on the pedagogical piano literature and pilot studies with professional pianists, together present a rich picture of physical gestures at the keyboard, including information on the performer's motion before, during, and after a note is played. User studies confirm that the sensed dimensions are intuitive and controllable and that mappings between gesture and sound produce novel, playable musical instruments, even for users without prior keyboard experience. The multidimensional sensing capability demonstrated in this paper is also potentially applicable to button interfaces outside the musical domain.

Author Keywords
Piano, keyboard, gesture sensing, multidimensional input, musical interfaces.

ACM Classification Keywords
H.5.5 Sound and Music Computing: Systems; H.5.2 User Interfaces: Input devices and strategies

General Terms
Design, Human Factors

INTRODUCTION
A great many computer music interfaces have been developed over the past decades, but the piano keyboard remains the interface of choice for most digital music tasks. Most interactions between human performer and computer instrument continue to be governed by the MIDI (Musical Instrument Digital Interface) standard [19], now more than 25 years old. MIDI specifies that motion on the keyboard be described as a series of discrete press and release events, with accompanying information on the velocity of each key-press. In this way, the complex mechanical system of the piano keyboard was reduced to a low-bandwidth information stream suitable for processing by 1980s-era computers.

Despite continual efforts by manufacturers to produce controllers closely emulating the sound and feel of the piano keyboard, pianists frequently express dissatisfaction with current interfaces, feeling them to be insufficiently "expressive." In their view, MIDI keyboards inadequately capture the nuances of fine piano playing, failing to replicate the subtle mapping between physical action at the keyboard and musical sound.[1] Since current keyboard technology reduces complex physical gestures to simple velocity metrics, even the most sophisticated synthesizer designer is restricted to an over-simplified picture of the performer's actions.

This paper presents an alternative approach to keyboard controller design, beginning not with the mechanics of the piano but with piano *technique*. Drawing on the extensive pedagogical literature and pilot studies with professional pianists, we have developed a new keyboard interface which measures five distinct gestural dimensions that pianists feel are important. In addition to capturing the subtlety of advanced piano performance, we seek to build an interface playable by a wide community of users, even those without prior piano training. A trio of user studies demonstrate this playability. Specifically, we show our interface possesses three important properties:

1. **Intuition:** The interface makes use of gestures familiar even to untrained users with no keyboard experience.
2. **Controllability:** Users can consciously control the new dimensions with high accuracy.
3. **Mappability:** Gestural parameters can be mapped to sound production in ways that are novel and musically useful.

After presenting the results of our user studies, we discuss applications of the multidimensional keyboard interface to both musical and non-musical tasks.

BACKGROUND

Mechanical Tactile Interfaces
With the recent interest in multi-touch interfaces and virtual on-screen controls, the venerable mechanical button is sometimes overlooked as a platform for future development. Yet mechanical buttons retain certain advantages: they offer natural tactile feedback and are particularly well-suited to

[1] Pianist Boris Berman's advice to students is typical: "Often overlooked is the need to work on an instrument that responds sufficiently to the nuances of touch. (No electronic keyboard will do, I'm afraid.)" [1]

vision-free interaction [11]. These qualities can be particularly advantageous in musical performance, where the user's visual attention is often focused on reading sheet music or interacting with other musicians.

Within the mechanical realm, interest has been growing in adopting pressure sensitivity as an additional input dimension, with recent studies examining finger pressure in the context of mobile phones [23], mice [2], and computer keyboards [3]. Certain MIDI keyboards have long featured "aftertouch" pressure sensitivity [19].

An oft-cited drawback to the mechanical button is its static nature, but this need not be limiting. Harrison [11] has developed a pneumatic interface generating dynamically configurable buttons. The Monome [15] computer music controller consists of a square grid of identical lighted buttons whose function can be dynamically assigned by the user. Even MIDI keyboard instruments, though they make assumptions about musical pitch structure, offer a certain degree of flexibility through patch (sound-set) changes.

Several researchers have developed music keyboards reporting additional information for each key-press. Freed and Avizienis [6] developed a keyboard with continuous key position sensing; Moog [16] presents a keyboard whose keys move in two dimensions and feature touch sensitivity on the surface. The Haken Continuum [10] erases the mechanical distinction between keys, allowing independent horizontal, vertical, and depth control of multiple presses.

The Piano "Touch" Controversy

The current state of the keyboard interface partly reflects a longstanding debate between pianists and acousticians. At the heart of the disagreement is whether, for identical key velocities, the type of "touch" (the quality of a physical key-press gesture) affects the tone of the piano. Acousticians dismiss this notion, arguing that the piano hammer is in free ballistic motion when it strikes the strings, putting it outside the control of the player [5]. Hence, the argument goes, the only meaningful effect of a key-press can be to impart an initial velocity to the hammer. By contrast, pianists continue to swear by a rich variety of keyboard gestures. From the earliest days of the instrument, pianists have been concerned with finding ways to attenuate the instrument's percussive nature in favor of pure, long-lasting tones [1, 7, 21].

In the 1920s, Ortmann showed that piano key motion could be classified into two types of touch: percussive (in which a moving finger strikes the key) and non-percussive (in which the finger begins at rest on the surface) [17, 18]. More recently, Goebl et al. [8] demonstrated that the percussive touch produces a characteristic noise when the finger strikes the key; when this noise was removed from recordings, listeners were unable to distinguish between piano notes with the same velocity, regardless of the touch used.

Since experiments have put to rest the notion that touch affects the timbre of the acoustic piano, computer music researchers have largely lost interest in the expressive nuances of key motion, content to model only the timing and velocity of key-presses. (On the other hand, interest in the broader biomechanical process of piano playing remains strong [9].) Pianists, however, continue to perform and teach using a rich vocabulary of gestures to which they ascribe expressive meaning. Regardless of whether different types of key-press gestures have an effect on the piano sound, they may be resolvable from the key motion itself. If so, then we could build an interface which measures and responds to the touch qualities pianists value, producing a multi-dimensional controller with both musical and pedagogical applications.

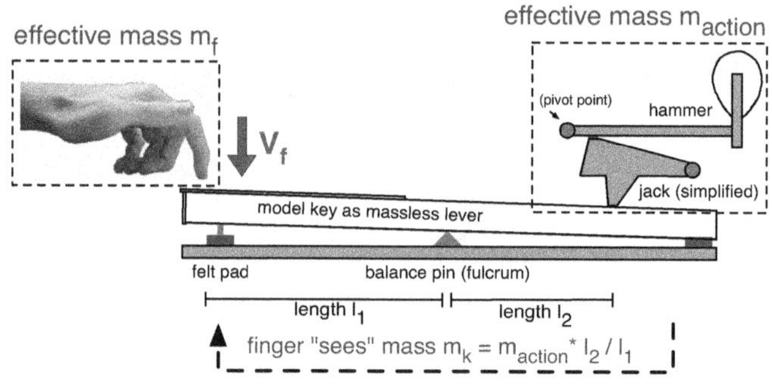

Figure 1. Simplified model of the piano action, approximating the interaction of finger and key as a collision between two simple masses.

DESIGN PRINCIPLES: MODELING THE PIANO KEYBOARD

To obtain the richest possible picture of performer-keyboard interaction, we will examine both the mechanics of the piano and the basic physiological techniques of human players.

Mechanics

Figure 1 shows a simplified diagram of the acoustic grand piano action. The key forms one end of a lever, the opposite end of which operates a series of additional levers culminating in a felt-covered wooden hammer. When the key is pressed, the hammer is thrown upward against the strings. A detailed discussion of piano action can be found in [5]; it is sufficient here to model the key as a massless lever, with the mass of the performer's finger and the hammer action acting on opposite sides. The key travels approximately 9 mm between its resting position and the key-bed, where it impacts a felt disc. Additional force on the key will compress the felt, allowing additional travel of approximately 1 mm. The instantaneous position of the key will thus be somewhere between 0 (resting) and 1 cm (depressed with maximum force).

Suppose that a constant force is exerted on the key, beginning from its resting position. We expect to see a linear increase in velocity (constant acceleration) throughout the stroke. Suppose, on the other hand, that the performer's finger is already in motion when it strikes the key surface. Let us model the finger (plus hand and arm) as a mass m_f with initial velocity v_f. If the collision is perfectly elastic, conservation of momentum tells us that the resulting key velocity will be $v_k = \frac{2m_f}{m_f+m_k} v_f$. In other words, an immediate spike in key velocity will occur, proportional to the momentum of the performer's finger.

After the collision, key and finger will tend to separate, and the key will lose velocity due to the weight of the action. If the performer continues to exert force, the finger will catch up with the key, causing a steady increase in velocity until it reaches the key-bed. The interval between initial impact and "catch-up" depends on a combination of elasticity of collision, force exerted by the performer, and weight of the muscles used (since a loose finger has a smaller effective mass than the whole arm, and thus will be repelled more strongly by the collision [22]).

Elements of Performance Technique

In summarizing his historical survey of pianists and their techniques, Gerig writes, "the pianist with the perfect technique is also a singer, a first-rate vocalist! The singing voice is the ideal tonal model and aid to phrasing, breathing, and interpretation." [7] (p. 520). Gerig divides historical techniques into two schools, those based primarily on the muscular action of rigid fingers and those based on applying the weight of relaxed larger muscles, advocating balance between these approaches. Sandor [21] makes a distinction between notes played by "free fall" versus "thrust" and places particular emphasis on maintaining "resilient" joints: "The essential quality in a singing tone is intensity, and this is true for soft as well as for loud sounds. The sound should carry; it should have body, it should be expressive, and it should have lasting quality. The playing mechanism, therefore, should be neither too hard nor too soft; the joints of the fingers, wrist, and hand must be supple, resilient, and elastic."

Berman [1] identifies five variables of piano touch: weight, mass, speed, perception of depth, and the shape of the fingers (pp. 10-12). He further distinguishes between two approaches to the keyboard: "in" (pouring weight into each note) and "out" (pulling the fingers away from the keys, "as if ... 'grabbing' the sound from the keyboard and bringing it out"). Schultz [22], departing from Ortmann's mechanical models [17, 18], classifies keyboard touch by the use of weight, pressure, or (muscular) fixation. Schultz analyzes the mechanics of the percussive key-press in detail, noting the effects of mass (finger vs. whole arm) and applied force after the collision (p. 42).

Though these authors (and indeed, every pianist) differ somewhat on the ideal technique, they share a goal of transcending the percussive mechanics of the instrument and a sense that musical expression and physical gesture are inextricably linked. Their writings reflect the collected knowledge of millions of pianists, developed over more than a century. For the designer of keyboard-based computer interfaces, it is hard to imagine a richer trove of data on human interaction. To identify the quantitative signatures of each type of playing, we next conducted pilot studies to isolate the important numerical factors of piano key motion.

SENSOR SETUP: QUANTIFYING KEY MOTION

In our previous work [13, 14], we developed a sensor to record the continuous position of each key (rather than traditional MIDI velocity). LEDs and photodiodes mounted above each key measure the amount of light reflected off the key surface, which is inversely related to the distance between key and sensor (Figure 2). Each photodiode is sampled at a rate of 600Hz with a resolution of 12 bits (8-10 bits in practice, given limited signal range). Samples are transmitted by USB to a host computer.

The system is calibrated by measuring the minimum and maximum light values for each key; key positions are subsequently normalized to a range of 0 (resting) to 1 (fully depressed). Continuous key velocity is calculated from the first difference of position. The sample rate is sufficient to capture anywhere from 10 to over 100 samples during the interval that the key is in motion, creating a detailed picture of each press. In our user studies, the sensor is installed on an acoustic grand piano; however, similar sensors could be integrated into an electronic keyboard or indeed any mechanical button interface.

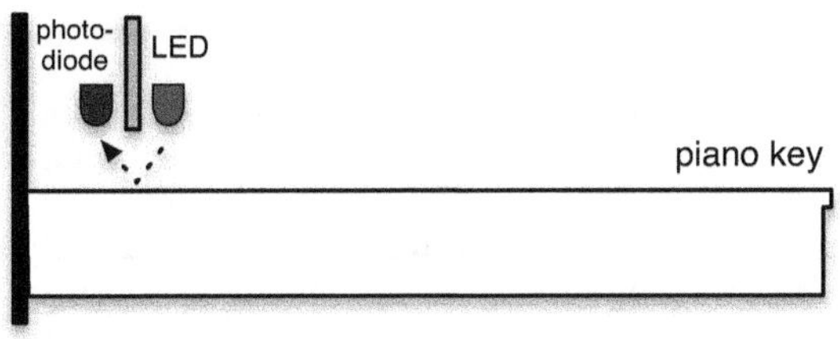

Figure 2. Optical reflectance sensors record the continuous position of each piano key, sampled 600 times per second.

Pilot Study: Identifying Dimensions of a Key-Press

We conducted pilot studies with four professional pianists, who played on a Steinway L grand piano equipped with our key position sensor. Subjects were given excerpts from the piano literature (Mozart, Beethoven, Schubert and Debussy) and asked to play each excerpt with several expressive affects. Subjects were also interviewed about their personal technique. Our goal was to identify the dimensions of a key-press that commonly varied with different expressive modes of playing. Our results identified four principal variables which closely align with the literature:

- **Velocity:** Key velocity controls the speed of the hammer and hence the volume of the tone. Naturally, it was the most important variable in all modes of playing.
- **Percussiveness:** The momentum of the hand in striking the key can vary from near-zero (finger begins resting on the key) to very high (large preparatory motions). The latter was often used in loud, forceful passages and to emphasize musical accents.
- **Rigidity:** For percussively-played notes, the hand muscles could be held loose or tight, and the principal force could come from the finger joints, the wrist, or the whole arm. We designate these low, medium, and high rigidity. For non-percussive notes, the difference was indistinguishable from key motion alone.
- **Weight:** Once the key impacts the key bed, weight on the key can range from just enough to hold it down to an exaggeratedly heavy touch. The latter was often seen in slow but intense music.

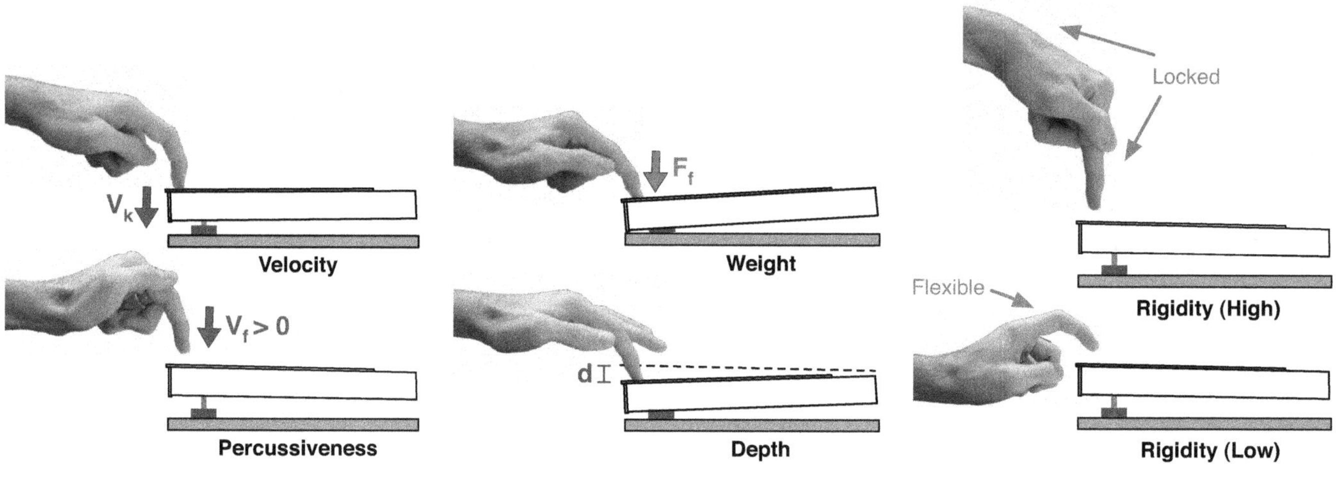

Figure 3. Five dimensions of a piano key press.

To this list we add one additional dimension not found in traditional piano playing, but easily controlled and measured:

- **Depth:** A key can be pressed completely or partially, stopping midway through its range of motion.

Figure 3 illustrates these five dimensions, by which every key-press can be measured.

Feature Extraction: Evaluating Each Dimension

Figure 4 shows position and velocity for two example key-presses. From each press we extract 12 features:

- Group A (1 feature): Overall velocity, measured at "escapement", where hammer flies free of the action (measured to be approximately key position 0.65).
- Group B (6 features): Magnitude, duration, and area under the velocity curve for the first velocity peak and trough.
- Group C (1 feature): Position at time of key-bed impact.
- Group D (4 features): Average positions and velocities for two brief post-impact intervals.

Group A (*velocity*) is self-explanatory. The features in Group B reflect our mechanical model, and can together be used to evaluate the *percussiveness* and *rigidity* of a press: a strongly percussive press will show a large initial velocity spike, where a non-percussive press will show none at all. Rigidity is evaluated by comparing the spike magnitude to its rebound. The features in Groups C and D reflect the reaction of the felt pad to varying key force. Group C directly measures the *depth* of press, where Groups C and D together assess its *weight*: a heavy press will hold the key deeply into the felt, where for a light press, the key will show a slight rebound after impact.

These features together present a detailed view of performer-keyboard interaction, from the preparation before the finger contacts the key to the way the performer responds after the key reaches the key-bed. The features can be used together or in specific combinations, either as continuous variables or as inputs to a discrete classifier system. Our user studies demonstrate the viability of both approaches.

USER STUDIES: OVERVIEW

We conducted three user studies to evaluate whether our interface is intuitive, controllable, and capable of useful musical mappings. Each study included 10 subjects (3 female, mean age 23.8), most of whom had little or no prior piano background. None of our subjects were professional performers or full-time music students; 3 of 10 subjects reported two or more years of piano training, with 5 subjects reporting no formal training at all. Asked to rate their piano familiarity on a scale of 1 (neophyte) to 10 (professional), subjects reported a mean of 3.4 (median 3, range 1-7).

All studies were conducted on a Steinway B grand piano which, like all pianos, provides auditory feedback proportional to key velocity. Subjects were presented each study in the order presented below. The order was chosen because the first study assumes no knowledge of the techniques under investigation, the second teaches and tests a few basic skills, and the third applies the skills to selected musical problems.

USER STUDY 1: GESTURE AND INTUITION

The purpose of this study is to evaluate the *intuitiveness* of the gestures used in our enhanced keyboard. Specifically, we want to resolve between the following hypotheses:

- **Hypothesis 1:** For a naive user, all key-presses differ only by velocity. Percussiveness, rigidity, weight, and depth relate linearly to velocity.
- **Hypothesis 2:** Naive users exhibit a range of values for each parameter, but the additional features can be considered as noise, having no correlation with expressive or gestural intent.
- **Hypothesis 3:** Even without knowledge of the system, naive users naturally demonstrate resolvable patterns along multiple dimensions.

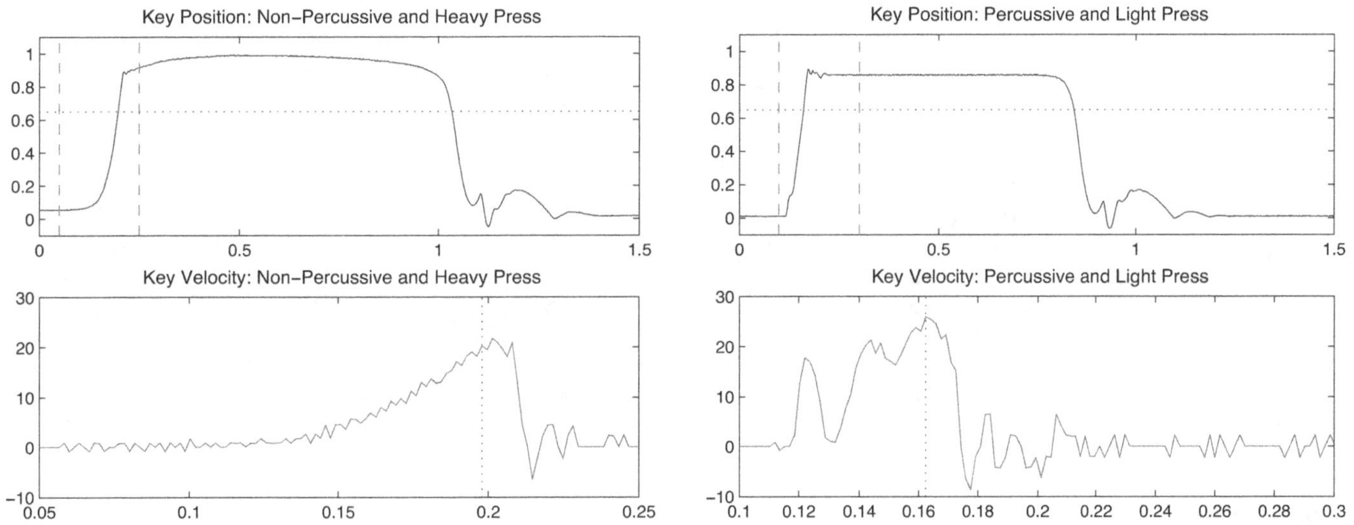

Figure 4. Key position and velocity measurements for two types of key-press. Velocity plots (bottom row) focus on the brief period of key motion (vertical dashed lines). Dotted lines show estimated position of hammer escapement. Times are in seconds, key position normalized 0-1.

Design

Subjects were taught to play a simple melody (Figure 5) consisting of 18 notes (5 distinct). Subjects were free to choose the most comfortable fingering. Once each subject felt comfortable with the melody, he or she was asked to play it in nine different whimsical styles: *normal (no cue)*; *very delicate, as if afraid of being heard*; *like Frankenstein*; *like flowing water*; *as if the keys are extremely hot to the touch*; *as if you're angry at the piano*; *like a bird pecking at the keys*; *as if the keys are very heavy and hard to press*; and *as if there are no bones in your hand*. The descriptions are deliberately chosen not to align with common musical terminology (*espressivo*, *legato*, etc.) so responses reflect intuition rather than acquired training. Although subjects were expected to have varying interpretations, the styles were designed to collectively elicit a broad range of physical behavior at the keyboard. Subjects were not told the purpose of the exercise so as not to bias their responses.

Each key-press was labeled by subject and style and scored according to the 12 aforementioned features. The complete data set thus consisted of $\approx 18 \times 9 \times 10 = 1620$ presses (performance mistakes slightly altered the exact number).

To accept or reject Hypothesis 1, principal component analysis was applied to the aggregate data set (with features normalized to zero mean, unit variance). Hypothesis 1, if correct, implies that most dataset variance should be attributable to a single component. Subsequently, to choose between Hypotheses 2 and 3, classifier learning systems were trained using the features as inputs and the style as output (i.e. a 9-class problem). Classifier performance was compared using 1 feature (Group A, velocity), 3 features (Group A and part of B), 8 features (Groups A-C), and all 12 features. If Hypothesis 3 is correct, the addition of extra features should improve classifier accuracy. All tests were performed both on the aggregate dataset and individually for each subject.

Figure 5. Melody used in User Studies 1 and 3.

Comp.	Score	Total Var.	Feature Group Weights
1	3.06	25.5%	D (.70), B (.70), A (.14)
2	2.21	44.0%	D (.71), B (.70), A (.11)
3	1.81	59.1%	C (.68), B (.68), A (.26)
4	1.74	73.6%	D (.71), B (.65), A (.27)
5	1.30	84.4%	C (.71), B (.60), A (.33)
6	1.00	92.8%	D (.70), B (.66), A (.25)
7	.46	96.5%	B (.90), A (.42), C (.10)
8	.22	98.5%	D (.71), B (.52), A (.48)

Table 1. Principal component analysis of Study 1 aggregate data. 6 components are required to explain 90% of the dataset variance.

Results

Table 1 shows the principal component strengths of the aggregate dataset, as well as the relative contribution of each feature group to each component. To account for 90% of the total variance, 6 components are required. Examining the eigenvectors of the covariance matrix shows that the first six components are heavily dependent on *weight* (Group D) and *percussiveness* (Group B) features, with secondary emphasis on *depth* (Group C). Surprisingly, though *velocity* (Group A) appears in each of the first 8 components, it never appears as the primary contributor to any of them. The high number of components required to explain the dataset variance suggests a rejection of Hypothesis 1.

Three types of classifiers were tested to evaluate Hypotheses 2 and 3: decision tree (with pruning), naive Bayes, and k-nearest neighbor ($k = 10$).[2] The 10-fold cross-validation

[2] Three types were used to minimize bias from any particular classifier on this relatively small dataset.

Aggregate Data				
# Features	1 (A)	3 (A,B)	8 (A-C)	12 (A-D)
Decision Tree	.327	.364	.383	.409
Naive Bayes	.322	.345	.309	.387
10-NN	.308	.359	.352	.399
Improvement	—	11.7%	9.1%	24.9%
Mean of Individual Subjects				
# Features	1 (A)	3 (A,B)	8 (A-C)	12 (A-D)
Decision Tree	.378	.437	.459	.491
Naive Bayes	.377	.441	.421	.461
10-NN	.394	.433	.412	.480
Improvement	—	14.4%	12.6 %	25.3%

Table 2. Study 1 cross-validation accuracy for varying numbers of features. Chance = .11. Letters specify feature groups used by classifier.

accuracy of each classifier is shown in Table 2. Chance accuracy for this problem is 11.1%. The superior classifier performance on per-subject versus aggregate data may reflect either different stylistic interpretations among subjects or an artifact of the small datasets. For both aggregate data and the mean of individual subjects, the inclusion of all 12 features creates a 25% relative improvement in accuracy versus velocity alone. Pairwise t-tests on the per-subject results demonstrate statistically significant differences ($p < .001$) for every pair except 3 and 8 features (p = .28).

Discussion

From these results we conclude that Hypothesis 3 is best: the intuitive keyboard actions of naive users vary independently along multiple dimensions in a way that meaningfully correlates with intent. This conclusion may indicate an easier learning curve for new players since multidimensional gestures are already part of their natural vocabulary.

USER STUDY 2: PERFORMANCE ACCURACY

The purpose of this study is to evaluate the *controllability* of the interface. In this study, each dimension is discretized into two or three classes; the performance of subjects in hitting target classes is evaluated in 5 unidimensional and 3 multidimensional tests:

1. Velocity (3 classes): *low*, *medium*, *high* (corresponding to the musical dynamics *piano*, *mezzo-forte*, *fortissimo*).
2. Percussiveness (2 classes): *non-percussive* (finger begins on key), *percussive* (finger in motion when it strikes key).
3. Rigidity (3 classes): *low* (loose finger), *medium* (rigid finger, loose wrist), *high* (muscles locked).
4. Weight (2 classes): *light*, *heavy* (force into key-bed).
5. Depth (2 classes): *full* (key reaches key-bed), *partial*.
6. Velocity + Percussiveness (2 classes each, 4 total): velocity divided into to only *low* and *high*.
7. Velocity + Weight (2 each, 4 total).
8. Velocity + Percussiveness + Weight (2 each, 8 total).

Because the classifiers are trained with the key-presses of one investigator, this study also evaluates the universality of the interface. In other words, do key-press feature patterns generated by one user generalize to other users, without user-specific training?

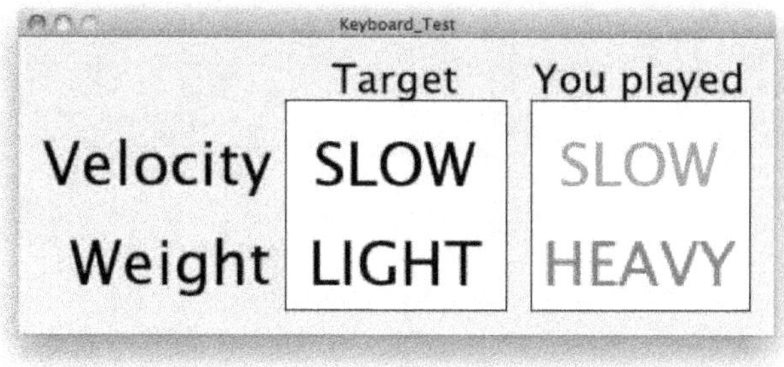

Figure 6. User Study 2 testing environment.

Design

Decision tree classifiers (with pruning) were trained in the Wekinator real-time machine learning environment [4] using 100 key-presses for each target class or combination of classes. All training and testing was performed on a single key (C4). Decision trees were chosen for their high performance with small training sets and for the minimal computational resources needed to evaluate each press in a real-time environment. A test tool was developed using the Processing graphical environment [20] which displayed the target class(es) and the user's actual input (Figure 6).

Each test consisted of 24 presses balanced across the possible targets, with target order randomized within each test. The eight tests were consistently presented in the sequence listed above. Though it is possible that greater familiarity with the piano may improve performance on later tests, several tests have prerequisites: for example, rigidity can only be evaluated in the context of a percussive press, and evaluating multidimensional problems only makes sense after each dimension has been introduced.

At the beginning of each test, the relevant dimension(s) were explained verbally and each target demonstrated by the investigator. Subjects were given up to five minutes to practice, receiving visual feedback on how each press was classified; during practice time, subjects were allowed to request suggestions on how to perform each gesture. Most subjects took 60 seconds or less to practice before each test.

Results

Figure 7 shows mean subject performance for each test. Note that chance accuracy varies with the number of classes. For multidimensional tests, an answer is considered "correct" only if it is correctly classified in every dimension. Subjects performed each unidimensional test except rigidity with better than 75% accuracy. Percussiveness and depth accuracies were above 90%, and we expect that a 2-class velocity problem would show similar results. (Because velocity uniquely provides aural feedback on the piano, and because it is familiar to everyone with even minimal keyboard experience, we chose to evaluate a more challenging problem.)

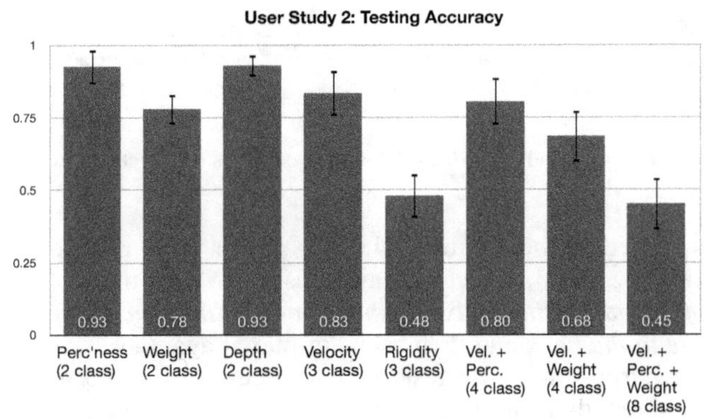

Figure 7. Proportion of key-presses correctly classified, with 95% confidence intervals.

	Velocity + Percussiveness		Velocity + Weight	
	Non-Perc.	Perc.	Light	Heavy
Slow	90.0%	**53.3%**	71.7%	**56.6%**
Fast	83.3%	95.0%	63.3%	81.7%

	Velocity + Percussiveness + Weight			
	Non-Perc.		Perc.	
	Light	Heavy	Light	Heavy
Slow	56.7%	76.7%	36.7%	**13.3%**
Fast	**6.7%**	66.7%	53.3%	50.0%

Table 3. Breakdown of testing accuracy for multidimensional models. Certain combinations of parameters proved difficult to execute.

Subjects performed better in the velocity-percussiveness test than in the velocity-weight test. Average performance was only 45% in the three-dimension problem, though 86% of presses were correctly classified in two or more dimensions. A look at the internals (Table 3) shows that certain combinations were especially difficult. For example, *slow-percussive* presses were correctly classified significantly less often than other types; *slow-heavy* and *fast-light* presses were also less accurate. *Slow-percussive-heavy* and *fast-nonpercussive-light* combinations were almost never classified correctly.

Mechanics and muscular control may explain these results. Certain groupings naturally correlate: *slow-nonpercussive-light* strokes are easily executed together as a careful, controlled motion; *fast-percussive-heavy* strokes can be played by bringing the weight of the whole arm down on the key from above. By contrast, combining slow velocity with a percussive stroke and heavy weight requires the finger to be in motion when it strikes the key, to slow down once the key is set in motion, then to follow through with significant force once the key reaches the key bed. This requires independent awareness of three separate phases of key motion, a non-trivial task for non-expert players.

Discussion

The results of this study show that velocity, percussiveness, weight, and depth are all viable modes of input, since users with only a few minutes of training can accurately control each dimension. Rigidity was much more difficult to control, particularly low rigidity, which was almost never classified correctly (16%). Perhaps this dimension depends on the specific mechanics of an individual player's hand.

Select combinations of dimensions can be used together in discrete classifiers; however, systems with three or more dimensions should be avoided in situations with a high cost of misclassifying a single dimension. We do not attempt to answer whether users with more piano training test better. Evaluating only the three subjects with 2+ years of piano experience shows no trend (better performance in 3 tests, worse in 4, identical in 1), but a larger study would be needed.

This study shows that the interface is consciously controllable and that classifiers trained on one player can accurately respond to another. Like Ortmann [17] and Goebl et al. [8], Study 2 focuses on single key strokes. Our results show that even if the sound of an individual piano note depends solely on key velocity, players are capable of controlling key motion in several independent dimensions. The next study explores selected musical applications, mapping continuous measurements of each dimension to sound production and evaluating user performance playing complete melodies.

USER STUDY 3: SELECTED MUSICAL MAPPINGS

This purpose of this study is to evaluate the *mappability* of the interface: can a deterministic relationship between gestural dimensions and sonic parameters produce a playable musical instrument? On the acoustic piano, the mapping is embedded in the mechanical action: choice of key affects the frequency of a note, and key velocity affects its amplitude and spectrum. There are innumerable possible choices of mapping, and choosing one that is "expressive" is a challenge involving both art and engineering [24]. In this study we demonstrate the usability of two selected mappings.

Study 3A: Keyboard Percussion

Our first musical application generates a ride cymbal sound alongside each piano note. (Pitched instruments are commonly doubled with percussion in many musical styles to add a distinctive attack.) We map the percussiveness of each key-press, measured by the magnitude of the initial velocity spike, to cymbal volume. Below a certain threshold (12 position units per second), the cymbal is muted. In this way, the piano can be played with or without cymbal by choosing percussive or non-percussive presses, and the cymbal can be played alone by tapping firmly on a key without pressing it all the way down.[3] The cymbal is generated by synthesizer and played through speakers atop the piano.

Each subject was explained the mapping and allowed up to three minutes to practice. Subjects were asked to play the melody from Study 1 (Figure 5) in three modes, twice per mode: piano alone, piano and cymbal, and cymbal alone. Subjects were instructed to play the melody using a single finger to eliminate variability from different fingerings.

Controlling the cymbal is arguably more difficult than the

[3]Some MIDI keyboards offer built-in doubling of pitched instruments and percussion; unlike our system, the two are not independently controllable since both relate to key velocity.

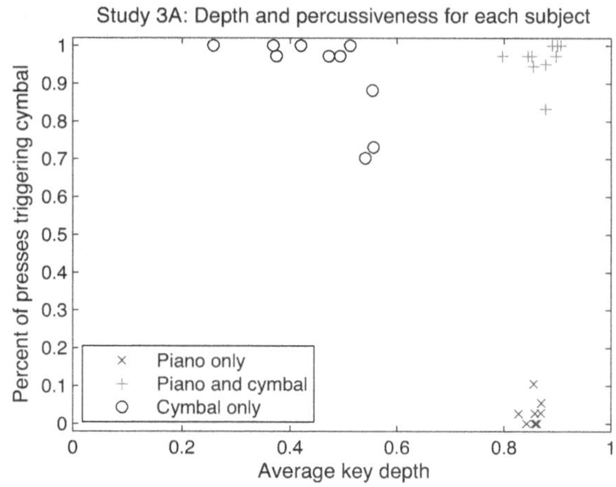

Figure 8. User performance in playing melody with piano alone, piano and cymbal together, and cymbal alone.

percussiveness classifier in Study 2 since multiple keys are played in rapid succession. However, accuracy in percussive versus non-percussive playing was higher than Study 2, with 96% of piano-and-cymbal notes exceeding the percussiveness threshold versus only 2.4% of piano-only notes (Figure 8). Cymbal-only notes were played above the threshold 92% of the time. In the cymbal-only test, 11% of key-presses reached the depth of hammer escapement, a rough estimate of how many notes contained a spurious piano sound.

Our results suggest that aural feedback is an asset to percussive versus non-percussive playing, though greater user familiarity in this study may contribute. Most importantly, this study establishes that percussive playing can add a useful new musical dimension to the traditional keyboard. One subject commented on the fast response time of the cymbal; another subject, an experienced drummer, remarked on the appropriateness of the mapping between percussive playing and cymbal sounds.

Study 3B: Continuous Control of the Acoustic Piano

Our second musical application makes use of our prior work augmenting the acoustic piano with electromagnetic string actuation [12]. Electromagnets placed above the piano strings induce the strings to vibration, allowing continuous modulation of the amplitude and spectrum of each note. In this study, key position is mapped to note volume, where resting position is silent and a fully depressed key produces the loudest tone. The conventional mode of piano playing is unimpeded, but hammer strokes are no longer necessary to initiate sound.

Design

Before the electromagnetic system was enabled, subjects were asked to play the Figure 5 melody in two modes: *softly and continuously, making smooth transitions from one note to the next*; and *lightly and soundlessly, still very connected.* This established a baseline performance against which the electromagnetic mapping could be evaluated.

The electromagnetic mapping was subsequently enabled and

Figure 9. Melody for Study 3B with crescendos on selected notes.

explained to the subject, who was given three minutes to practice. Each subject was again asked to play the melody *softly and continuously, making smooth transitions from one note to the next*, and then asked to play it again *even softer*. The purpose of these tests was to ascertain whether users could readily adapt to an unfamiliar mode of playing by accurately controlling key depth.

Subjects were next asked to practice making a crescendo on a single note (a technique impossible on the traditional piano). Once comfortable, they were asked to play the melody with a crescendo on the long notes (Figure 9). This experiment was repeated twice.

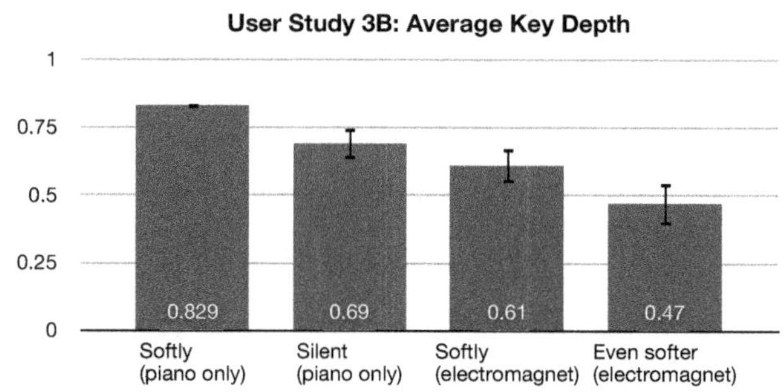

Figure 10. Average key-press depth for four modes of melodic playing, with and without electromagnetic mapping.

Results

Figure 10 compares the average key-press depth for the first four modes of playing (two piano only, two with electromagnets). A one-way, repeated measures ANOVA across subjects confirms these differences to be statistically significant ($p < .001$). A post-hoc pairwise t-test between the "soft" and "even softer" electromagnetic cases confirms the latter to exhibit significantly lower average depth ($p < .001$), which for this mapping indicates softer overall volume.

To evaluate the crescendo performances, we apply a linear regression to key depth versus time for the duration of each note (Figure 11). Notes played with crescendo should exhibit positive slope (increasing volume), where other notes should exhibit slope close to zero (constant volume). Table 4 shows the results. Both trials show significant differences ($p < .01$) in pairwise t-tests, but the second shows greater differentiation between crescendo and non-crescendo notes.

Our results show that a previously unused aspect of keyboard performance (key depth) can be successfully mapped to a musical result (volume). Subjects adjusted immediately to the new mapping when asked to play softly and consistently but required a longer learning period to execute the more

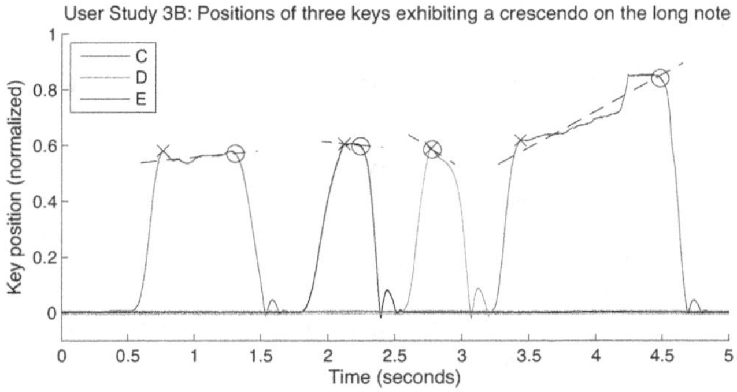

Figure 11. Key depth versus time in Study 3B, with best-fit lines to evaluate the slope of each key-press. (First measure of crescendo test shown.)

Mean slope of key-presses (Δdepth/Δtime)			
	Non-crescendo	Crescendo	Significance
Trial 1	-.015	.169	$p = .004$
Trial 2	-.088	.282	$p = .0013$

Table 4. Study 3B, slope of key depth versus time for crescendo and non-crescendo notes, mean of 10 subjects.

complex effect of shaping volume within a single note.

APPLICATIONS

User Study 3 demonstrated two simple mappings among a broad array of musical applications. We can classify these applications into three categories:

- **Augmented Piano:** One class of musical mappings focuses on the *subtlety* of piano technique, where the goal is to enhance the expressivity of the acoustic piano. Key velocity may remain the primary determinant of sound, but other dimensions map to subtle modulations of tone and timbre. With a synthesizer based on an adjustable physical model of the piano, for example, percussive strokes could be played with firmer felt hammers, enhancing an intuitive correlation between percussive gestures and "bright" sound. The electromagnetic resonator system of Study 3B [12] offers still greater potential by physically manipulating the vibrations of acoustic strings. Mappings between key motion and electromagnetic control can add dimensions to the piano while retaining its acoustic character.
- **Novel Keyboard Instruments:** A second class of applications assigns key-press dimensions to distinctive, independent musical results. Study 3A demonstrates a compound instrument where two classes of sounds can be played from the same controller. This mapping could be expanded to a complete drum kit using multi-finger taps and swipes across the keyboard, allowing a single performer to play both piano and drums without removing her hands from the keyboard. Unusual remappings of each key-press dimension are also possible; for example, key weight could modulate the pitch of the instrument like the 18th-century clavichord.
- **Pedagogy:** The dimensions of each key-press reveal a great deal about a pianist's physical technique. This information could be used in teaching contexts to identify improper motions, excessive stiffness or weight, or imbalanced force among the fingers. Hadjakos [9] has developed a pedagogical piano system based on arm-mounted accelerometers; our work would be a natural complement to produce a comprehensive piano training system.

Implementation Beyond the Piano Keyboard

The interaction techniques in this paper have been demonstrated on a piano keyboard, but they are applicable to any mechanical button interface. The implementation requirements are as follows:

1. Continuous position sensing at 500Hz or higher sampling rate. Sensor can be of any type (optical, resistive, etc.) as long as it provides approximately linear measurements of key position with 8 bits of resolution or more.
2. Buttons should have a non-trivial travel distance, so they are capable of accumulating velocity over the course of their throw.
3. For sensing *weight*, a compressible material (e.g. felt) should be mounted underneath the button so that pressure effects a change in its position.
4. For *depth* to be controllable, the button should be capable of being held steady at any point in its throw. A counter-example is the computer keyboard designed for a "click" feel, where after an initial activation force, the key travels immediately to the bottom of its throw.

An interface meeting these requirements will possess a superset of the capabilities of pressure-sensitive button interfaces, and in comparison to force-sensing resistors, buttons equipped with a compressible base may exhibit superior tactile feedback since finger pressure will produce a perceptible change in button position.

An exploration of the technology's extra-musical possibilities is a topic for another paper, but we point to studies with the Pressure Sensitive Keyboard [3] as a brief survey. Possible applications include:

- **Gaming:** Weight or depth can be mapped to the speed of movement or height of jump. Percussiveness could have particular application in sports games such as golf or baseball where precise control of a collision is required.
- **Editing and CAD:** Low-depth (incomplete) button presses could be used to preview the results of an action (image filter, etc.) before committing to it. Where Apple has introduced momentum-based scrolling on its trackpads, button velocity could be used to scrub through a video or navigate a 3D design with a simulation of momentum, with faster presses traveling greater distances.
- **Affective computing:** Users often express their frustration through excessively heavy, percussive impacts on the keyboard or mouse. The velocity, weight, and percussiveness of keyboard interactions could be revealing of emotional state, and used to either alter the response of a UI

or to transmit emotional information to another human via stylized text communication [3].

- **Computing for the disabled:** Our interface allows a single finger to control multiple simultaneous dimensions of a button-press. For users with the use of only a few muscles, multidimensional button input could enable faster, richer interactions.

Next Steps

We have demonstrated that users with no specialized training can accurately control the interface, a necessary step to its wider adoption. Future work will focus specifically on experienced pianists, for whom multidimensional control of key motion is part of developing a personal technique. In addition to investigating whether experienced pianists exhibit greater accuracy in the classification tasks of User Study 2, we will study the relationship between expressive intention and physical gesture at the piano keyboard. For example, pianists sometimes talk about emulating the sound of orchestral instruments from the keyboard [1]. What can we learn about these types of playing and other subjective musical qualities by studying a rich picture of key motion?

CONCLUSION

We have presented a new approach to a classic interface, demonstrating a musical keyboard which captures not only key velocity, but multiple dimensions of every gesture, including key-press percussiveness, rigidity, weight and depth. These dimensions were identified as important based on the piano pedagogical literature and pilot studies with professional pianists. User studies demonstrate that the new dimensions are intuitive to an untrained user, consciously controllable with limited practice, and have novel musical applications. This work lays a foundation for a new generation of intelligent musical keyboards, and the underlying mechanical principles can be applied to a broad range of button-based interfaces outside the musical realm.

ACKNOWLEDGMENTS

This material is based upon work supported by the National Science Foundation under Grant # 0937060 to the Computing Research Association for the CIFellows Project.

REFERENCES

1. B. Berman. *Notes from the Pianist's Bench*. Yale University Press, New Haven and London, 2000.
2. J. Cechanowicz, P. Irani, and S. Subramanian. Augmenting the mouse with pressure sensitive input. In *Proc. CHI 2007*.
3. P. Dietz, B. Eidelson, J. Westhues, and S. Bathiche. A practical pressure sensitive computer keyboard. In *Proc. UIST 2009*.
4. R. Fiebrink. Real-time interaction with supervised learning. In *Proc. CHI 2010 Extended Abstracts*.
5. N. Fletcher and T. Rossing. *The Physics of Musical Instruments*. Springer-Verlag, New York, 1998.
6. A. Freed and R. Avizienis. A new music keyboard featuring continuous key-position sensing and high-speed communication options. In *Proc. ICMC 2000*.
7. R. Gerig. *Famous Pianists & Their Technique*. Indiana University Press, Bloomington, IN, 2007.
8. W. Goebl, R. Bresin, and A. Galembo. Once again: The perception of piano touch and tone. Can touch audibly change piano sound independently of intensity? In *Proc. ISMA 2004*.
9. A. Hadjakos, E. Aitenbichler, and M. Mühlhauser. Probabilistic model of pianists' arm touch movements. In *Proc. NIME 2009*.
10. Haken Continuum Fingerboard. http://www.cerlsoundgroup.org/Continuum/.
11. C. Harrison and S. Hudson. Providing dynamically changeable physical buttons on a visual display. In *Proc. CHI 2009*.
12. A. McPherson. The magnetic resonator piano: Electronic augmentation of an acoustic grand piano. *Journal of New Music Research*, 39(3):189–202, 2010.
13. A. McPherson and Y. Kim. Augmenting the acoustic piano with electromagnetic string actuation and continuous key position sensing. In *Proc. NIME 2010*.
14. A. McPherson and Y. Kim. Toward a computationally-enhanced acoustic grand piano. In *Proc. CHI 2010 Extended Abstracts*.
15. Monome. http://monome.org.
16. R. A. Moog and T. L. Rhea. Evolution of the keyboard interface: The Bösendorfer 290 SE recording piano and the Moog multiply-touch-sensitive keyboards. *Computer Music Journal*, 14(2):52–60, Summer 1990.
17. O. Ortmann. *The Physical Basis of Piano Touch and Tone*. Kegan Paul, Trenc, Trubner & Co., 1925.
18. O. Ortmann. *The Physiological Mechanics of Piano Technique*. Kegan Paul, Trenc, Trubner & Co., 1929.
19. J. A. Paradiso. Electronic music: new ways to play. *IEEE Spectrum*, 34(12), 1997.
20. Processing. http://processing.org.
21. G. Sandor. *On Piano Playing*. Macmillan Publishing Co., 1981.
22. A. Schultz. *The Riddle of the Pianist's Finger and its Relationship to a Touch-Scheme*. University of Chicago Press, Chicago, 1936.
23. C. Stewart, M. Rohs, S. Kratz, and G. Essl. Characteristics of pressure-based input for mobile devices. In *Proc. CHI 2010*.
24. M. Wanderley and P. Depalle. Gestural control of sound synthesis. *Proceedings of the IEEE*, 92(4):632–644, 2004.

Spatialized Sound Enhances Biomechanically-Induced Self-Motion Illusion (Vection)

Bernhard E. Riecke, Daniel Feuereissen
Simon Fraser University, Canada
{ber1, dfeuerei}@sfu.ca

John J. Rieser, Timothy P. McNamara
Vanderbilt University, USA
{j.rieser, t.mcnamara}@vanderbilt.edu

ABSTRACT

The use of vection, the illusion of self-movement, has recently been explored as a novel way to immerse observers in mediated environments through illusory yet compelling self-motion without physically moving. This provides advantages over existing systems that employ costly, cumbersome, and potentially hazardous motion platforms, which are often surprisingly inadequate to provide life-like motion experiences. This study investigates whether spatialized sound rotating around the stationary, blindfolded listener can facilitate biomechanical vection, the illusion of self-rotation induced by stepping along a rotating floor plate. For the first time, integrating simple auditory and biomechanical cues for turning in place evoked convincing circular vection. In an auditory baseline condition, participants experienced only spatialized auditory cues. In a purely biomechanical condition, seated participants stepped along sideways on a rotating plate while listening to mono masking sounds. Scores of the bi-modal condition (binaural+biomechanical cues) exceeded the sum of both single cue conditions, which may imply super-additive or synergistic effects.

Author Keywords

Self-motion illusions, bio-mechanical and auditory circular vection, cognitive science, cue-integration, human factors, psychology, self-motion perception, virtual reality

ACM Classification Keywords

H.5.1 Information Interfaces and Presentation, HCI: Multimedia Information Systems – Artificial, augmented, and virtual realities; H 1.2 Information Systems: Models and Principles – User/Machine Systems; J.4 Social and Behavioral Sciences: Psychology.

General Terms

Experimentation, Human Factors, Measurement

INTRODUCTION

Although self-motion illusions have been known and investigated for more than a century by psychologists (see [2,8,12] for reviews), they have only recently received increasing attention in the context of virtual environments and embodied human-computer interaction (see [8,4] for reviews). While modern computer graphics allow for stunning photo-realistic sceneries as evidenced by recent computer games and computer-animated movies, they nevertheless often lack a compelling embodied sensation of being in and moving through the depicted environment. That is, while visually depicted observer movements can be photo-realistic, they are not necessarily perceptually realistic and often do not evoke a life-like sensation of self-motion. This might limit overall perceived realism, immersion or user acceptance. We propose that investigating and utilizing self-motion illusions might be an affordable yet effective way of addressing this challenge.

The most prominent and well-researched method of inducing compelling self-motion illusions ("vection") is through large-field visual motion (see reviews in [2,4,8,12]). This can lead to compelling embodied self-motion illusions which can be indistinguishable from actual self-motion. Similarly, compelling biomechanical vection can be induced in blindfolded participants by stepping along a rotating floor plate while being stationary [1]. Although moving sound cues have long been known to induce vection in blindfolded listeners [3,6], the attention auditory vection received pales in comparison to the efforts invested in studying visual vection. Whereas visual and biomechanical vection can be quite compelling, auditory vection is much weaker, less compelling, and occurs only in 20-75% of participants (for reviews see [10,11]). Nevertheless, as high-quality sound can be provided at small cost using reliable and affordable off-the-shelf hardware, even a small benefit of adding sound could be easily justified. Indeed, recent studies showed that adding spatialized sound can significantly improve visually induced vection [10,11]. Surprisingly, however, it has to the best of our knowledge never been investigated if or to what degree auditory cues might benefit biomechanical vection. To close this gap, we investigated circular vection in stationary blindfolded participants induced by

(1) Rotating sound fields alone presented via binaural recordings through headphones (**auditory vection** condition)

(2) Stepping along a rotating floor plate and listening to mono masking sounds (**biomechanical vection** condition)

(3) Combined auditory and biomechanical stimulation (**bi-modal vection** condition)

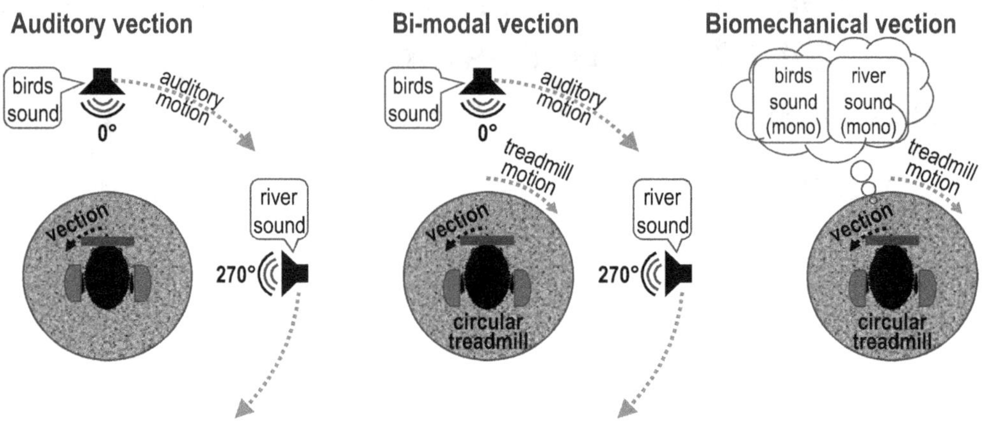

Figure 2: Top-down schematic view of the different vection conditions.

Based on previous findings, we hypothesized that

H1: Auditory vection is weaker than biomechanical vection

H2: Bi-modal vection is stronger than biomechanical vection. In addition, we were interesting in the degree of cross-modal facilitation and potential synergistic effects.

METHODS

A total of 19 participants (7 female) completed the experiment in exchange for monetary compensation at standard rates of $10 per hour. Participants were pre-screened for vestibular dysfunction using the Romberg test [5] and we asked them to rate how often they experience motion sickness in their daily lives on a scale between 0 (never) and 100 (very frequently). However, no participant was excluded because of motion sickness or vestibular dysfunction pre-screening. Due to the design of this experiment, we limited the scope to participants who were actually able to perceive auditory vection. Auditory vection occurs in only 25-75% of participants and thus, a auditory vection pre-screening method was used to select appropriate participants. All qualified participants had previously participated in an auditory vection experiment [9] and were thus familiar with the setup and overall procedure.

Stimuli and Apparatus

Throughout the experiment, participants were blindfolded and seated in a hammock chair mounted above a circular treadmill (Fig. 1a). Although fixed, the hammock chair allowed for minimal swaying movements, thus providing a cognitive-perceptual framework of movability, which has previously been shown to potentially facilitate vection (see reviews in [8,7]).

Biomechanical Cues

The biomechanical and bi-modal vection condition exploited proprioceptive cues from stepping along sideways on a rotating platter to evoke vection. To that end, participants were asked to comfortably step along sideways

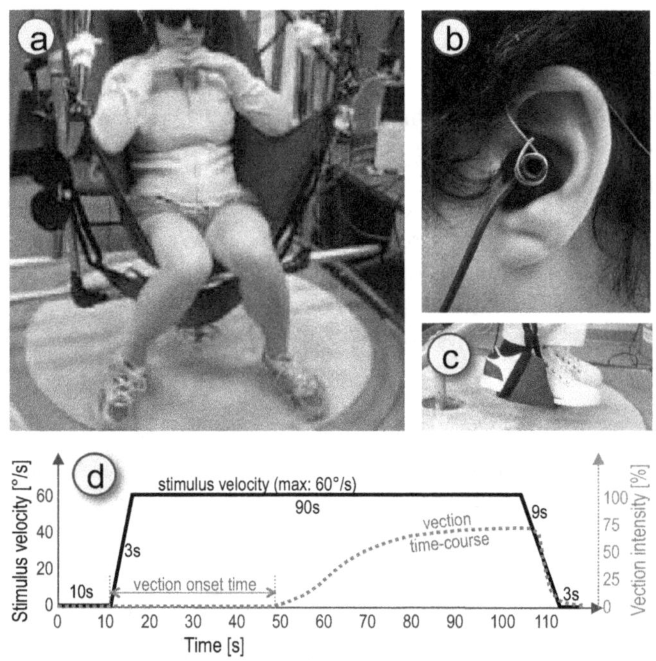

Figure 1: (a) Experimental setup showing a participant blindfolded and seated in the hammock chair mounted above the circular treadmill. (b) In-ear microphones used to create the binaural recordings that were later used to induce auditory vection. (c) For the auditory vection condition, participants' feet rested on a footrest and did not touch the rotating platform. (d) Stimulus velocity (platform and/or auditory rotation velocity) and sketch of vection time-course (red).

with the platform (Fig. 1a) which rotated according to the velocity profile depicted in Figure 1d.

Auditory Cues: Recordings

Auditory vection was induced by individualized binaural recordings of a rotating sound field presented through noise-cancelling headphones. Binaural recordings were obtained by placing miniature microphones (Core Sound Binaural Microphones) at the entrance of the ear canal (Fig.

	ANOVA main effect			Contrast auditory vection vs. biomechanical vection			Contrast biomech. vection vs. auditory+biom. vection		
	FF(2,36)	p	η_p^2	F(1,18)	p	η_p^2	F(1,18)	p	η_p^2
Realism	**60.41**	**<.0005*****	**.770**	**41.35**	**<.0005*****	**.697**	**22.84**	**<.0005*****	**.559**
Intensity	**69.64**	**<.0005*****	**.795**	**44.36**	**<.0005*****	**.711**	**33.95**	**<.0005*****	**.654**

Table 1: ANOVA and pair-wise contrasts results. The effect strengths expressed as η^2 indicate the percentage of variance explained by a given factor. Effect sizes exceeded 50%, indicating large effect sizes.

1b). Two easily localizable and distinguishable sound sources (bird and river sound mixes) were positioned at 0° and 270°, respectively, around the observer seated above the circular treadmill (see [9] for details). For the recordings only, participants were then physically rotated using the velocity profile depicted in Figure 1d. Note that auditory and biomechanical rotation velocities were matched at 60°/s (Fig. 1d).

Auditory Cues: Use in Conditions

During the auditory vection condition, participants were comfortably seated in the hammock chair and listened to rotating sound fields through noise cancelling headphones. Because participants were required to solely rely on auditory vection cues in this condition, we asked them to suspend their feet in a footrest to maximize the possibility of inducing purely auditory vection (Figure 1b). Auditory vection is commonly perceived as weak, so having the feet suspended should make self-motion more plausible [7,8].

During the biomechanical vection condition, a non-spatialized mono recording of the birds, river and platform sounds served as a masking sound. This ensured that participants did not perceive background noise from the lab that may conflict with the illusion of rotating. A mono recording was chosen to avoid any spatialization cues that might have affected biomechanical vection. A control experiment (unpublished) showed that monaural cues do not interfere with biomechanical vection Stimulus and perceived motion direction for each condition are illustrated in Fig. 2.

Experimental Design

As with all introspective measures, response bias cannot be excluded. However, within-subjects design has traditionally been used in vection research to reduce the typically large between-subject variability. The authors are not aware of any research showing systematic differences between within- and between-subject designs.

Participants completed 12 trials, consisting of a factorial combination of 3 vection conditions (auditory, biomechanical, and bi-modal) × 2 turning directions (left/right alternating) × 2 repetitions. Conditions were balanced among participants to avoid order effects. After each trial, participants verbally rated their vection experience using two dependent measures:

Perceived realism of rotation: "Did you feel like you were rotating in the physical room on a scale between 0-100%?"

Perceived vection intensity: "How intense was the sensation of self motion on a scale between 0-100%?"

RESULTS AND DISCUSSION

As predicted in hypothesis 1, auditory vection was overall fairly weak and only reported by 43% of the trials on average, whereas biomechanical and bi-modal vection was reported in 91% and 93% of the trials, respectively. Similarly, the perceived realism and intensity of auditory vection alone was significantly lower than in the biomechanical vection condition (see statistical results summarized in Table 1 and data plots in Fig. 3).

Although auditory cues themselves could not reliably induce compelling vection, adding rotating sound fields enhanced both the realism and intensity of biomechanical vection significantly, confirming hypothesis 2: Adding binaural rotating sound increased the perceived realism of rotating in the actual lab by 39% (effect size η^2 of 56%), and perceived vection intensity was increased by 37% (effect size η^2 of 65%).

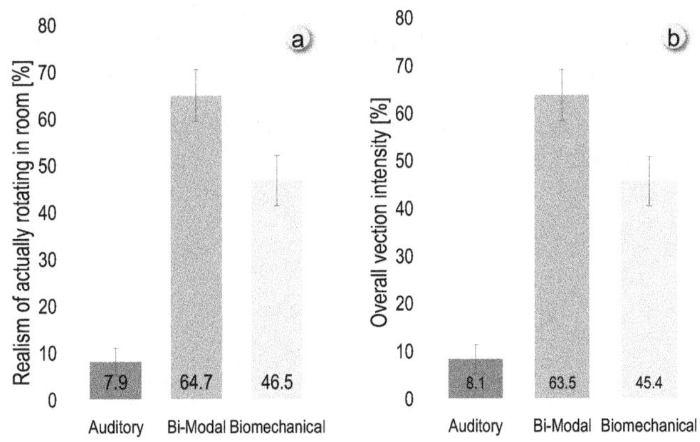

Figure 3: Means and standard error bars for the vection measures.

Interestingly, combining auditory and biomechanical vection showed a "super-additive", synergistic effect, in that the perceived realism and intensity of bi-modal vection was higher than the sum of the values observed for the pure auditory and biomechanical vection. This highlights the potential power of including high-quality spatialized sound for self-motion perception and cross-modal integration.

CONCLUSIONS

Apart from its theoretical relevance, the current findings have important implications for applications in, e.g., entertainment, gaming, and motion simulation: While spatialized sound seems not by itself sufficient to reliably induce compelling self-motion illusions, it can clearly support and facilitate biomechanical vection and has earlier been shown to also facilitate visually induced circular vection [2] and thus support information from other modalities. Furthermore, high-fidelity, headphone-based sound simulation is not only reliable and affordable, but also offers an amount of realism that is yet unachievable for visual simulations: While even the best existing visual display setups will hardly be confused with "seeing the real thing", headphone-based auralization can be virtually indistinguishable from listening to the real sound and thus can provide a true "virtual reality".

ACKNOWLEDGMENTS

Support: NIMH Grant 2-R01-MH57868, NSF Grant 0705863, NSERC, Vanderbilt University, & Simon Fraser University.

REFERENCES

1. Bles, W. Stepping around: circular vection and Coriolis effects. In J. Long and A. Baddeley, eds., *Attention and performance IX*. Erlbaum, Hillsdale, NJ, 1981, 47–61.

2. Dichgans, J. and Brandt, T. Visual-Vestibular Interaction: Effects on Self-Motion Perception and Postural Control. In *Perception*. Springer, 1978, 756 - 804.

3. Dodge, R. Thresholds of rotation. *J. Exp. Psychol. 6*, 2 (1923), 107-137.

4. Hettinger, L.J. Illusory Self-motion in Virtual Environments. In K.M. Stanney, ed., *Handbook of Virtual Environments*. Lawrence Erlbaum, 2002, 471-492.

5. Khasnis, A. and Gokula, R.M. Romberg's test. *J Postgrad Med 49*, 2 (2003), 169–172.

6. Lackner, J.R. Induction of Illusory Self-Rotation and Nystagmus by a Rotating Sound-Field. *Aviation Space and Environmental Medicine 48*, 2 (1977), 129-131.

7. Riecke, B.E. Cognitive and higher-level contributions to illusory self-motion perception ("vection"): does the possibility of actual motion affect vection? *Japanese Journal of Psychonomic Science 28*, 1 (2009), 135-139.

8. Riecke, B.E. Compelling Self-Motion Through Virtual Environments Without Actual Self-Motion – Using Self-Motion Illusions ("Vection") to Improve User Experience in VR. In *Virtual Reality*. Intech, 2011, 27 pages (book chapter in print).

9. Riecke, B.E., Feuereissen, D., and Rieser, J.J. Auditory self-motion simulation is facilitated by haptic and vibrational cues suggesting the possibility of actual motion. *ACM Trans. Appl. Percept. 6*, 3 (2009), 1-22.

10. Riecke, B.E., Väljamäe, A., and Schulte-Pelkum, J. Moving sounds enhance the visually-induced self-motion illusion (circular vection) in virtual reality. *ACM Trans. Appl. Percept. 6*, 2 (2009), 1-27.

11. Väljamäe, A. Auditorily-induced illusory self-motion: A review. *Brain Research Reviews 61*, 2 (2009), 240-255.

12. Warren, R. and Wertheim, A.H., eds. *Perception & Control of Self-Motion*. Erlbaum, New Jersey, London, 1990.

Name That Tune: Musicons as Reminders in the Home

Marilyn McGee-Lennon[1], Maria K. Wolters[2], Ross McLachlan[1], Stephen Brewster[1], Cordy Hall[1]

[1]Glasgow Interactive Systems Group, School of Computing Science, University of Glasgow, UK
(mcgeemr, stephen, cordy, mclachrd)@dcs.gla.ac.uk

[2]School of Informatics, University of Edinburgh
Edinburgh, UK
maria.wolters@ed.ac.uk

ABSTRACT

In this paper we argue that Musicons, short samples from pieces of music are a useful way to present private but memorable reminder messages. We investigated accuracy, memorability and response times for short, medium, and long Musicons. User performance on the Musicons was also compared to short spoken reminders. The study consisted of two sessions a week apart. Quantitative measures were augmented with qualitative questions about associations and memories. Overall, participants achieved a high level of accuracy (89%) on the Musicons. Recognition was stable at 90% or better across sessions for users who were able to construct meaningful links between Musicons and the associated tasks. Optimal response times were achieved for medium-length 0.5 sec. Musicons. We conclude that Musicons are a viable option for alarms and notifications that combine the high learnability of Auditory Icons with the more private nature of Earcons.

Author Keywords

Auditory reminders, Earcons, Musicons, memory.

ACM Classification Keywords

H5.2. [User Interfaces]: Auditory (non-speech) feedback.

General Terms

Human factors

INTRODUCTION

Prospective memory, the ability to remember to do something, is affected by factors such as age [11] or brain injury [10]. Reminder systems play an important role in allowing people with prospective memory loss to remain in their own homes. For example, reminders to lock the door at night greatly increase safety and reminders to take medication help people manage their own care.

User preferences for reminder delivery are highly varied [7]. It is even more crucial in the home than in the workplace to accommodate these preferences since the home is a private space that intimately reflects the owner's personality and habits. People who receive care at home often find it difficult to perceive themselves as "in need of care". Therefore, it is important for home care solutions to be as unobtrusive as possible.

Even though hearing acuity declines with age, auditory reminders are still a key interface modality, because they do not require the user to attend to a screen and are effective if eyesight is poor. The design space for auditory reminders is vast. It ranges from simple beeps to explicit spoken messages, and from Auditory Icons to Earcons. Auditory Icons are familiar sounds of everyday events with an intuitive mapping between sound and meaning [5], while Earcons are musical sounds that only bear an abstract relation to their meaning [1].

When creating reminder systems for the home, designers need to balance ease of comprehension and privacy. Privacy issues arise when there are others in the home who can overhear reminders that are easy for anyone to understand. While Earcons ensure privacy, some users may find them more difficult to learn than Auditory Icons [5].

We propose to address this gap in the design space between Earcons and Auditory Icons with Musicons, extremely brief samples of well-known music. We argue that recall, recognition and emotive memories for music can be exploited to create reminders that are both sufficiently abstract to ensure privacy and sufficiently memorable to be easy to learn.

In this study, we compared the accuracy and learnability of Musicons to synthetic speech, which requires no learning and yields perfect performance. We also systematically varied a particular design parameter, Musicon length, hypothesising that accuracy would be higher for longer Musicons, while response time would be lower for shorter ones. Through interviews and questionnaires, we also investigated how users associate the different Musicons with different task-based reminders.

MUSICONS

People tend to have strong musical memories. Music imagery in the brain is uniquely powerful – it can be highly repetitive, resulting in strong associations with the original stimulus. Music can help people remember by triggering context-dependent memories. Smith [9] found that people performed best in a word recall task when they heard the same background music during training and testing.

Musical cues can be implemented in a way that causes minimal disruption to others. Jung [6] successfully embedded musical cues into ambient soundscapes to

CHI 2011, May 7–12, 2011, Vancouver, BC, Canada.

provide multi-user auditory notifications that were more discreet and less disruptive than traditional auditory cues.

While music is certainly a promising method for implementing reminders, using long thematic clips may not be feasible. Fortunately, people can recognise extremely short clips of popular songs. This ability is demonstrated by game shows such as "Name that Tune" where contestants recognise and name a piece of music from a very short sample. Musicians are often trained to recognize extremely short samples from pieces of music. 'Drop the needle' tests are used in graduate musicology classes to test the ability of the student to recognise a piece of music from an extremely short snippet created by dropping the needle of a record player onto the record at a random point. Listeners can become very accurate at this task. But what is the minimum useful length of such a short sample?

Schellenberg *et al.* have shown that participants can identify popular chart songs from various different, very short snippets lasting 0.1 or 0.2 seconds [8]. Before being asked to identify the short snippets, participants underwent a short training phase where they listened to short, 30-second clips of the songs they had to identify.

Since the snippets that Schellenberg *et al.* used were too short to contain any substantial melodic and rhythmic information, the information that the participants used to identify the songs was timbral. The timbre of a piece of music refers to the overall sound of the elements that make up the melody, rhythm and pitch. The instruments used provide unique timbres and the accompanying harmonies add overtone combinations that can give the snippet of music a unique timbral signature.

We define Musicons as shorts clips of instrumental music used for information presentation. The key property of Musicons is that they are long enough to allow listeners to identify the original piece of music but too short to sound like a clip from the piece when played on their own without any context.

EXPERIMENTAL DESIGN

To discover if Musicons are a successful display technique, an experiment was conducted to compare them to speech and test their memorability over time. The study was a two-phase within-subjects repeated-measures design. The independent variable was the reminder type (Musicons Vs Speech) and the dependant variables were accuracy, as measured by the number of correct responses, and response time in seconds. Participants were invited back a week later to test memorability.

Qualitative data were gathered through a short questionnaire and interview after each session. These were analysed to explore the associations people had with the Musicons and the strategies they used for remembering the connection between Musicons and tasks.

Twelve university students participated in the study, 4 female and 8 male. All 12 participated in the first session, 11 returned for the second. Those who returned were paid £10.

Reminder Design

Four tasks were selected based on previous focus group work. For each task, speech and Musicon reminders were generated (available at www.multimemohome.com). Musicons were taken from popular and easily recognizable pieces of music. Tasks are listed in Table 1 together with their associated speech reminders and pieces of music.

Task	Speech	Music
Bins	"Take out the bin"	Johan Pachelbel: Canon
Door	"Lock the door"	Rembrandts "I'll be there for you " (Theme from Friends)
Keys	"Take your keys"	Ray Parker: Ghostbusters
Medicine	"Take your medicine"	John Williams: Theme from Jurassic Park

Table 1: Overview of reminders used in the experiment.

The pieces of music selected for the Musicons were chosen because they had strong thematic associations with UK popular culture and because they contained instrumental parts that could be recognisable by our sample of westernised younger adults.

For the training phase, a 20-30 second clip was used containing the part of the original piece that was deemed to be most recognizable by the researchers. For the testing phase, three Musicons were generated from a prominent musical phrase that strongly resembled the original training clip. Long Musicons (1-2s) consisted of the entire phrase; medium and short Musicons consisted of the first 0.5s (medium) and 0.2s (short) of the long version.

Spoken reminders were synthesized using the 2007 version of the HTS HMM-based synthesis toolkit [13] using a UK English male voice. Reminders were designed to be as succinct as possible to ensure their duration was similar to the long Musicons (1-2 secs).

Procedure

The first session consisted of a training and a testing phase. In the training phase, participants were given time to familiarize themselves with the mappings between tasks and the training clips. On average, people listened twice to each clip. In the testing phase, participants heard 64 auditory reminders (4 tasks (door, bin, keys, medicine) x 4 types of audio cue (long, medium, short, speech) x 4 presentations of each cue). Reminders were presented in a randomised order. On hearing a reminder, participants were asked to press the button corresponding to the correct task on the experiment user interface. Response times were measured from the start of the reminder, and participants were instructed to react as quickly as possible.

In the second session (a week later) the testing phase was repeated but no further training given. The only change was the order in which the buttons appeared on the user interface to test if participants remembered the mapping between song and task and not just the position of the button on the screen.

Data were discarded if participants pressed the response button before the reminder had started playing. This was the case for 3 responses in Session 1 and 4 in Session 2. The remaining data set contained at least three repetitions of each combination of task and audio cue for all sessions and participants for a total of 764 data points from 12 participants in Session 1 and 695 responses from 11 participants in Session 2. The person who failed to return did not give a reason for missing the session.

RESULTS

Accuracy and Memorability

As expected, participants recognized all speech reminders correctly, while Musicons were recognized correctly around 95% of the time in Session 1 and 84% in Session 2 (Table 2). We found no effects of gender, age and musical ability on performance. This level of accuracy is very promising.

Reminder Type		Session 1	Session 2
Speech		100%	100%
Musicon	Short	94%	82%
	Medium	96%	85%
	Long	94%	84%

Table 2: Accuracy by Session and Reminder Type.

All but one participant scored above 90% in Session 1. The participant with the lowest score, 75%, recognized none of the songs except for the Friends theme. He answered all of the reminders associated with this song correctly, but consistently confused the reminder for "keys" with the reminder for "bin". This could be due to a location-based recognition strategy, because the buttons for "keys" and "bin" were next to each other in the middle of the screen.

All of the 11 participants who scored highly in Session 1 returned in Session 2. The decrease in accuracy seen in Table 2 is mainly due to three participants, who scored 43%, 63%, and 64% on their return. The person with the lowest score commented that he had used the position of the buttons in the user interface to remember the task in the first round. The other two lower scoring participants found it hard to distinguish between the reminders for "door" and "keys" (Friends and Ghostbusters).

Response times

Response times for all reminder types were very similar (see Table 3). Participants responded faster in the second session (Wilcoxon test, $p<0.001$). The reaction time for accurate responses was significantly shorter in Session 1 (wrong: M=3.9s, SD=2.5, correct: M=2.5s, SD=1.8). In Session 2, reaction times for both accurate and inaccurate responses were similar (wrong: M=2.2s, SD=1.2; correct: M=2.2s, SD=1.8).

Reminder Type		M S1	SD S1	M S2	SD S2
Speech		2.5s	1.1	2.2s	1.4
Musicon	Short	2.8s	2.5	2.4s	2.0
	Medium	2.4s	2.0	2.1s	1.9
	Long	2.5s	1.5	2.1s	1.6

Table 3: Response Times by Reminder Type and Session (M=Mean, S=Session number, SD=Standard Deviation).

We compared response times for the three musicon lengths using pairwise Wilcoxon tests with Bonferroni correction on a fully balanced subset of the complete data set, which was obtained by taking the first three reminders for each combination of conditions. Since the point at which the speech reminders could be uniquely identified varied depending on the phrase, they were excluded from this analysis. For Session 1, the differences between medium and long Musicons ($p=0.05$) and short and medium Musicons ($p=0.07$) were weakly significant; for Session 2, none of the pairwise tests reached significance.

Qualitative Results

Most people recognised the four original clips, and most stated that they could recognise all of the clips from all three Musicon versions. The long Musicons were perceived as being too long and the short Musicons were seen as being too short and difficult to recognise. This suggests that 0.5s (medium) is an optimal length for Musicons in terms of preference, accuracy and response time.

For each of the songs, participants who performed well used remarkably similar strategies for remembering the link between Musicon and task. Users with highly accurate recall used existing associations they had with the original piece of music to help them remember. The most common association was between the television show Friends, and the action "Lock your door". Whenever characters in that show enter or exit a scene, they do so through a door. Seven out of 12 participants said they used this image to remember the reminder for "Lock your door". Some users relied on the associations between Jurassic Park and science or the fact that some of the characters in the film are doctors to remember "medicine". People also used the famous tag line from the film Ghostbusters, "Who you gonna call?", to imply "Who you gonna call if you forget your keys?".

After Session 2, participants were asked if they had

remembered the associations over the course of the week. While most people said that they never thought about it, some users mentioned that they heard one of the songs and thought of the reminder. For the most part, people were able to recall the associations between reminders and tasks easily by using the same strategies used in the first session.

DISCUSSION

We have shown that Musicons can be successfully used to present private but memorable reminder messages. If users can create strong, meaningful links between music and task, Musicons can be as effective as speech, as memorable as Auditory Icons and as abstract as Earcons. Our data suggests that optimum Musicon length is 0.5 seconds.

Since the Musicons used here were too short to contain any real melodic or rhythmic information, participants may have differentiated them based mainly on timbre, which is also one of the most effective parameters in Earcon design [3]. Thus, our results confirm that a rich timbre can be extremely effective in creating unique auditory cues.

The strategies people used to remember the meaning of Musicons are similar to those used for Earcons, where users construct meanings for abstract sounds to help them remember [2]. As we showed in our qualitative analysis, the high similarity of strategies across participants and the high recognition of the music confirmed our assumption that the original clips were musical 'memes' that contain a large amount of shared cultural knowledge. While we intended to create a completely arbitrary mapping between tasks and reminders, existing semantic associations clearly need to be carefully considered in Musicon design.

CONCLUSIONS AND FUTURE WORK

Musicons, very short clips of familiar music, can be highly memorable and robust auditory reminders. Since they can exploit highly personal associations and memories for music, Musicons are easy to recall, yet private as they contain no direct relation to the reminder they represent.

We are currently investigating the generation and personalisation of Musicons. Our aim is to let users choose their own music and then automatically identify clips from these pieces that are sufficiently memorable and distinctive to make a good Musicon. We will also examine the complexity of messages that can be delivered via Musicons, looking in particular at indicating meta-information such as urgency using properties like length, volume, or spectral shape.

In addition, we plan to compare Musicons to other auditory cues like Earcons, Auditory Icons, and Spearcons (radically time-compressed speech [12]). In order to ensure comparability of reaction times, care will be taken that all cues can be uniquely identified within 0.2s. Finally, we will extend our pilot work to include older people and people with care needs.

In conclusion, we suggest that interaction designers who want to create usable and acceptable reminders should consider Musicons for their ability to combine the memorability of Auditory Icons with the privacy of Earcons.

ACKNOWLEDGEMENTS

This work was funded by the EPSRC (EP/G069387/1 and EP/G060614/1) and the SFC (HR04016, MATCH).

REFERENCES

1. Blattner, M. and Sumikawa, D. Earcons and icons: Their structure and common design principles. *Human-Computer Interaction*, 4(1), 1989.
2. Brewster, S. Using nonspeech sounds to provide navigation cues. *ACM TOCHI*, *5* (3), 2002.
3. Brewster, S., Wright, P. and Edwards, A. Experimentally derived guidelines for the creation of earcons. *Adjunct Proc. HCI*, 1995.
4. Garzonis, S., Jones, S., Jay, T., O'Neill, E. Auditory Icon and Earcon Mobile Notifications: Intuitiveness, Learnability, Memorability and Preference. *Proc. CHI*, 1513-1522, 2009.
5. Gaver, W. The SonicFinder: An interface that uses auditory icons. *Human-Computer Interaction*, *4*(1), 1989.
6. Jung, R. Ambience for Auditory Displays: Embedded Musical Instruments as Peripheral Audio Cues *Proc. ICAD*, 2008.
7. McGee-Lennon, M., Wolters, M. and McBryan, T. Auditory Reminders in the Home Environment *Proc. ICAD*, 2007.
8. Schellenberg, E., Iverson, P. and McKinnon, M.C. Name that tune: Identifying popular recordings from brief excerpts. *Psychon Bull Rev*, 6 (4), 641-646, 1999.
9. Smith, S. Background music and context-dependent memory. *Am J Psych*, 98(4), 591-603, 1985.
10. Uttl, B. Transparent Meta-Analysis of Prospective Memory and Aging. *PLoS One*, *3* (2), 2008.
11. Walker, B., Nance, A. and Lindsay, J. Spearcons: Speech-based earcons improve navigation performance in auditory menus *Proc. ICAD*, 2006.
12. Zen, H., Nose, T., Yamagishi, J., Sako, S., Masuko, T., Black, A. and Tokuda, K. The HMM-based speech synthesis system (HTS) version 2.0 *Proc. SSW 6*, 2007.

Prototyping Dynamics: Sharing Multiple Designs Improves Exploration, Group Rapport, and Results

Steven P. Dow, Julie Fortuna, Dan Schwartz, Beth Altringer*, Daniel L. Schwartz, Scott R. Klemmer

Stanford HCI Group
Stanford, CA USA
[spdow, jfortuna, dschwartz13, danls, srk]@stanford.edu

Harvard School of Engineering and Applied Sciences*
Cambridge, MA USA
bethalt@seas.harvard.edu

ABSTRACT

Prototypes ground group communication and facilitate decision making. However, overly investing in a single design idea can lead to fixation and impede the collaborative process. Does sharing multiple designs improve collaboration? In a study, participants created advertisements individually and then met with a partner. In the *Share Multiple* condition, participants designed and shared three ads. In the *Share Best* condition, participants designed three ads and selected one to share. In the *Share One* condition, participants designed and shared one ad. Sharing multiple designs improved outcome, exploration, sharing, and group rapport. These participants integrated more of their partner's ideas into their own subsequent designs, explored a more divergent set of ideas, and provided more productive critiques of their partner's designs. Furthermore, their ads were rated more highly and garnered a higher click-through rate when hosted online.

Author Keywords

Prototyping, critique, design teams, creativity, exploration

ACM Classification Keywords

H.1.m. [Information Systems]: Models and Principles

General Terms

Experimentation, Design

INTRODUCTION

Many designers live by the principle, "never go to a client meeting without a prototype" [51]. Prototypes help people summarize their ideas, demonstrate progress and expertise, surface implicit design vocabulary, and ground group communication and decision making [9,44,45]. Creating a prototype—sketching a possible future—helps people see the entailments and interactions of their design ideas and communicates those to other stakeholders [15,23].

Rapid iteration provides value, but it does not guarantee broad exploration [16]. People systematically overestimate the predictability of the future, especially in complex situations [34]. For example, when financial experts estimate the range of possible futures, they consistently underestimate the variance [6]. In prediction and decision-making tasks, people can improve the quality of their estimates by broadening the frame and generating multiple guesses under different assumptions [26,34].

We hypothesize that creating and sharing *multiple* alternatives has more benefits than people may realize. Both cognitive and social factors motivate this hypothesis. First, the presence of a concrete prototype may (for better and for worse) focus the discussion on refining *that* idea rather than thinking more broadly [10,30]. Without exploration, people often interpret the frame of the design problem too narrowly [31]. Second, people presenting designs often believe their status to be on the line [9]. This risk encourages over-investing time, labor, psychological energy, and social momentum into a single concept [8,16]. In this single-prototype strategy, individuals may seek validation for their ideas and disregard or fear the critique and feedback necessary for exploration and revision [40]. Compounding this, collaborative work is often susceptible to *groupthink*, where members reinforce each other's belief in the current direction at the expense of other options [29].

Creating multiple prototypes in parallel can help individuals more effectively understand underlying design principles, enumerate more diverse solutions, and react less negatively to feedback [16,41]. Distributing one's psychological investment across multiple designs can reduce fixation and sunk-cost reasoning [1,30]. Individuals may be more candid and critical of their own and others' ideas [13,53], resulting in more fluid and effective collaboration.

However, creating multiple alternatives leaves less time to polish each one and may be perceived as wasting effort [45]. Focusing on fewer endeavors can help people focus, contemplate, relax, and be more productive [28,37]. Increasing options can cause analysis paralysis—a "paradox" of choice [46] — and may jeopardize a group's ability to achieve consensus [4].

This paper investigates whether sharing multiple prototypes increases design performance, improves group interaction, and leads to more effective idea sharing. In a between-subjects experiment, 84 participants working in pairs designed Web banner advertisements for a non-profit organization. The study comprised three steps. First, participants prototyped designs individually. Second, they worked with a partner to critique each other's ideas. Third, each individual created a final ad. Participants answered survey questions at several points and open-ended questions at the end. Pairs were randomly assigned to one of three conditions: creating and sharing multiple ads; creating multiple ads and

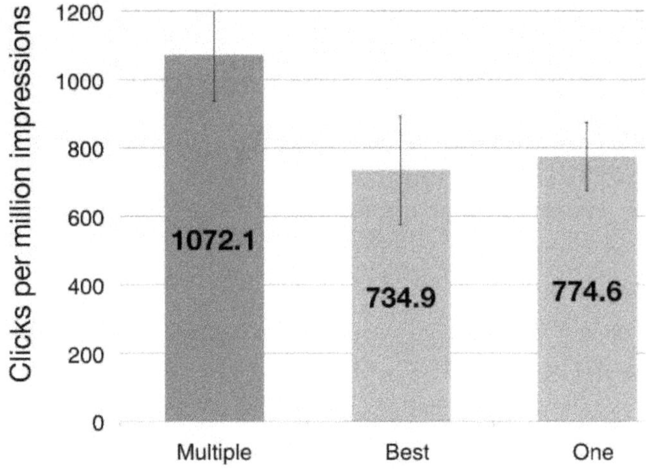

Figure 1 Online ad performance (clicks per million impressions): *Share Multiple* ads outperformed the other conditions.

sharing the best; and creating and sharing one ad. Comparing these three conditions separates the effects of *producing* multiple designs and *sharing* multiple designs. Each condition was allotted the same time for design.

Ads in the *Share Multiple* condition generated significantly more clicks per impression than the other conditions (see Figure 1). Independent (and blind-to-condition) judges rated ads from the *Share Multiple* condition significantly higher. Judges also rated *Share Multiple* ads as significantly more divergent. Participants in the *Share Multiple* condition shared significantly more ideas and moved more towards consensus than pairs who shared only one design. Group members in the *Share Multiple* condition reported a greater increase in rapport over the course of the experiment, while rapport in the other two conditions dropped. Moreover, *Share Multiple* participants exchanged speaking turns significantly more often.

In short, sharing multiple designs improves outcome, exploration, sharing, and group rapport. These results suggest that encouraging group members to share multiple ideas will pay dividends in both design outcomes and interpersonal dynamics. The following subsections elaborate the study's rationale and hypotheses.

Exposure to examples enhances individual exploration

Exposing people to examples increases the likelihood they will integrate similar features into their own designs [43], even when they are asked to create vastly different ideas [21]. Furthermore, borrowing increases with the number of examples people see [38]. Smith *et al.* hypothesized that people often take the path of least resistance, and that this conformity constrains creativity [43]. However, using Smith *et al.*'s task, Marsh *et al.* found that participants who saw many examples created equally novel work [38]. In other words, participants borrowed from examples when they lacked a better idea, but viewing examples did not "push out" or inhibit people's novel ideas. Furthermore, when viewed from a *quality* perspective, people perform better when examples are readily available [7,35]. In all of this prior work, examples were presented anonymously. Collaborative work is importantly different in this regard because the examples are produced by a known and co-present peer.

This paper hypothesizes that producing multiple designs and being exposed to multiple examples produced by other group members leads individuals to create a more divergent set of concepts.

Hypothesis 1: *Creating and viewing multiple designs leads to more individual exploration.*

This study measured individual design exploration by having independent raters judge the diversity/similarity of each participant's designs.

Sharing multiple designs improves collaboration

Designers often work collaboratively to generate, critique, and revise ideas, and to build consensus [23,44,54]. Under controlled conditions, individuals working separately often collectively produce a greater volume of ideas than group brainstorming [14,50]. Group members may block each other from sharing ideas [48], get frustrated with bad apples in the group [20], and "free ride" by deferentially following others' ideas [29]. However, measuring only the sheer volume of ideas is misleading: group brainstorming supports organizational memory of design solutions, recognizes skill variety among team members, and builds shared ownership of ideas—crucial for selecting and refining concepts [49]. To some extent, the debate over whether to design individually or collectively presents a false choice; creative work typically involves both [5,49].

Sharing ideas with a group can be an anxiety-laden experience, and this anxiety can negatively affect performance [12]. Individuals who know they will be judged by experts produce less novel ideas [14]. Many critique providers are aware that public feedback can be emotionally fraught; consequently they take care to temper criticism [53] and supplement critique with praise [27]. Anxiety may increase when people believe their worth as a person is part of what's being assessed [12,33]. For this reason, many educators and parents use language that critiques the *work* and the *behavior*, rather than the *person* [17].

Creating multiple designs may help both critiquers and creators separate egos from artifacts. When asked for feedback, people provide more substantive critique when presented with multiple design alternatives [53]. People react less negatively when they receive critique on multiple alternatives in parallel [16]. This prior work studied individual behavior; this paper analyzes the social effects.

This paper hypothesizes that sharing multiple designs—rather than one—improves group rapport and increases the rate at which people exchange ideas.

Hypothesis 2: *Sharing multiple designs leads to more productive dialogue and better group rapport.*

This study measured peer interaction by counting speech turns by each partner [42]. Also, five questions posed before and after the group discussion assessed individual views of their group's rapport.

Sharing multiple ideas facilitates conceptual blending

When collaborating, groups often merge properties of different concepts [19]. Sometimes, these blends directly inherit properties [24], other times blends spawn new emergent features [21,47]. Blending can be highly structured, as in morphological design [56], but is more commonly ad hoc. When concepts are dissimilar, blending them yields a more ambiguous artifact [55].

Conceptual ambiguity can beneficially provide a generative resource [22,36]. Sharing multiple designs may help collaborators blend ideas. The process of comparing and contrasting alternatives helps people create higher-level structures [52]; these structures help collaborators understand and communicate the rationale behind design decisions [39].

This paper hypothesizes that sharing multiple design concepts facilitates conceptual blending and that collaborators will use more surface-level and thematic features from their partner's work.

> **Hypothesis 3:** *Sharing multiple designs leads to more effective conceptual blending.*

This study measures conceptual blending by counting features that migrate from one partner's preliminary designs to the other's final design. Independent raters also judged the similarity of partner's designs before and after the pair shared their work.

Finally, this paper hypothesizes that sharing multiple designs leads to better performance due to a confluence of three factors: individuals explore more divergent ideas; groups have stronger dialogue and rapport; and the final design exhibit more effective conceptual blending.

> **Hypothesis 4:** *Sharing multiple designs produces better results.*

This study measures design quality by gathering click-through performance metrics on advertisement designs and by recruiting professionals, clients, and other independent judges to rate ads.

METHOD

A between-subjects study manipulated the prototyping process prior to a group critique. Web advertising was chosen as the design task because it fulfills key criteria:

- Quality can be measured objectively and subjectively;
- Participants need minimal artistic or engineering ability to either create or critique ads;
- Individuals can complete tasks within a single lab session;
- Solutions demonstrate creative diversity and a range of performance quality.

Study Design

Participants all created Web ads for the same client, *FaceAIDS.org*. The study allocated equal time for individual design and group discussions across three conditions. In the *Share Multiple* condition, participants created three preliminary advertisements and shared all three during the group discussion. In the *Share Best* condition, participants created three preliminary ads and chose one to share during the group discussion. In the *Share One* condition, participants spent the entire individual design time on a single ad to share during the group discussion.

Participants

We recruited 84 participants through papers fliers, online advertisements, and email lists. Two individuals arrived concurrently to form study pairs. Each pair was assigned to one of three conditions using a stratified randomization approach; the study balanced for gender (41 females) and graphic design knowledge across pairs and conditions. Ten true-or-false questions assessed graphic design knowledge (see Appendix A); participants were deemed *experienced* if they correctly answered eight or more (36 did). Participants who scored below eight were deemed *novices*. Participants' average age was 26.5; three-fourths were students.

Procedure

The experiment comprised the following steps: consent form, icebreaker, tool training, practice ad, design brief, individual design, group discussion, final individual design, group interview, and final debriefing. Questionnaires collected demographic and self-report assessments. The icebreaker, group discussion, and group interview were co-located and video-recorded. All other procedures took place in separate rooms at individual workstations with no video recording. For 120 minutes of participation, subjects received $20 USD cash.

Icebreaker activities

Partners collaborated on three icebreaker activities for three minutes each. They built a tower with toy blocks, played the game Operation, and generated a list of animal names beginning with 'M' (*e.g.*, monkey).

Graphic design tool training

At separate workstations, partners viewed a five-minute video about the Web-based graphic design tool (http://flashimageeditor.com). Then, using the tool, participants replicated a graphic unrelated to the main task. All participants replicated the graphic in less than ten minutes. None had used the tool before. Selecting a novel tool avoids confounds from participant's tool-specific expertise.

Design brief

A five-minute video described participants' main design activity: to create an ad for *FaceAIDS*, a non-profit organization dedicated to global health equity and social justice (http://faceaids.org). In the video, the organization's executive director outlined four goals: reach out to students interested in starting local chapters of *FaceAIDS*, increase traffic to the *FaceAIDS* Web site, impress three judges from the *FaceAIDS* organization, and create ads with effective graphic design. A paper version of the design brief was available for the group discussion (see Appendix A).

Individual Design Period

All participants had 30 minutes for individual design. In the *Share Multiple* and *Share Best* conditions, participants started a fresh design every 10 minutes. This was typically adequate, even for novices. At the end of this period, *Share Best* participants were prompted to select one design to be critiqued by the study partner. After the design period, a study proctor printed ads for the group discussion.

Group discussion

Participants sat together and viewed a print out of their partner's design(s). The study proctor set a timer for five minutes and then instructed the pair: "Examine your peer's design concept(s) and then provide a critique. What advice would you provide? Please speak aloud." After this, the proctor set another five-minute timer and instructed: "Now spend another 5 minutes discussing what you think is the most effective way to satisfy the design brief." After that, participants were instructed to return to their individual workstations to create a final ad design.

Final design period

Participants individually created another advertisement and were instructed that this final ad would be rated by judges and hosted in a live ad campaign.

Group interview

The study concluded with an open-ended group interview. A study proctor used an interview guide and followed up with related questions. These questions provided guidance for the final interview; the exact order and phrasing varied.

- Describe how you arrived at your final design.
- Explain the difference between your two final ads.
- How much did the group discussion affect what you did in your final ad design?
- How did your peer's critique affect your ad design?
- To what extent were you able to reach agreement on the final design concept?

Dependent Measures

Performance

After the experiment, the final graphic ads were hosted on Google AdWords (http://adwords.google.com) for a 12-day campaign. Design performance was determined through two objective measures:

- Click-through rates (CTR): number of clicks divided by the number of impressions, and
- Google Analytics (http://www.google.com/analytics) on the target client Website: total time spent and number of pages visited from each ad.

Ads were also independently judged by 30 individuals: three clients from *FaceAIDS*, six ad professionals, and twenty-one people recruited from Mechanical Turk, an online crowdsourcing system for paying workers for short tasks (http://mturk.com/mturk/welcome). This collection of raters provided important—and different—audience perspectives. Each judge read the *FaceAIDS* design brief and viewed ads in random order. For each ad, they estimated

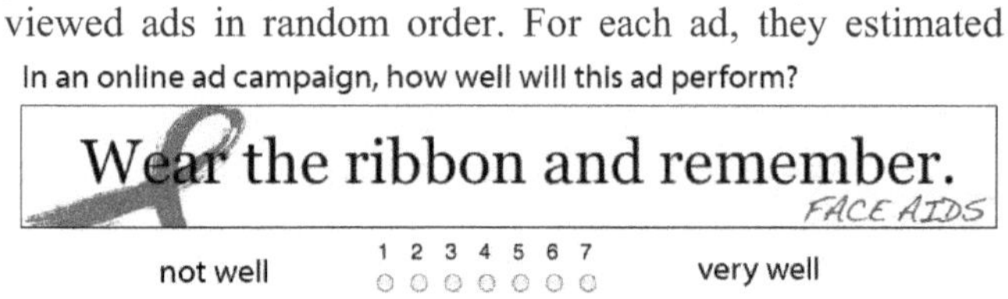

Figure 2 Quality rating: Judges rated (on a 1-7 scale) how well each ad will perform in an online campaign.

Figure 3 Similarity rating: Judges viewed a pair of ads and rated their similarity on a seven-point scale. This pair's average similarity rating was 5.7. (The overall average was 3.6.)

(on a 7-point scale) each ad's performance in an online campaign (see Figure 2).

Individual design exploration

Exploring a diverse set of ideas can help people examine the space of designs and their relative merits [9]. To obtain a measure of idea diversity, ten independent raters assessed pair-wise similarity of all combinations of individual participant's ads (see Figure 3). Raters recruited from Amazon Mechanical Turk assessed similarity on a scale from 1 to 7 (*not similar* to *very similar*).

Change in group rapport

At two points—after the icebreakers and after the discussion—five questions asked individuals to assess their group rapport. The change between these two points measures the discussion's impact on group rapport. Four questions originate from the Subjective Value Inventory (SVI), an assessment of viewpoints on negotiation [11]. The relationship questions from the SVI provide a systematic measure of a group rapport; they assess partners' feelings about the relationship in terms of overall impressions, satisfaction, trust, and foundations for future interaction. The fifth question derives from the Inclusion of Self in Others Scale (see Figure 4), a measure of someone's sense of connectedness with another [2]. The questions asked:

- What kind of overall impression did your peer make on you?
- How satisfied are you with your relationship with your peer as a result of the interaction?
- Did the interaction make you trust your peer?
- Did the interaction build a foundation for future interactions with your peer?
- Please check the picture below which best describes your relationship with your peer:

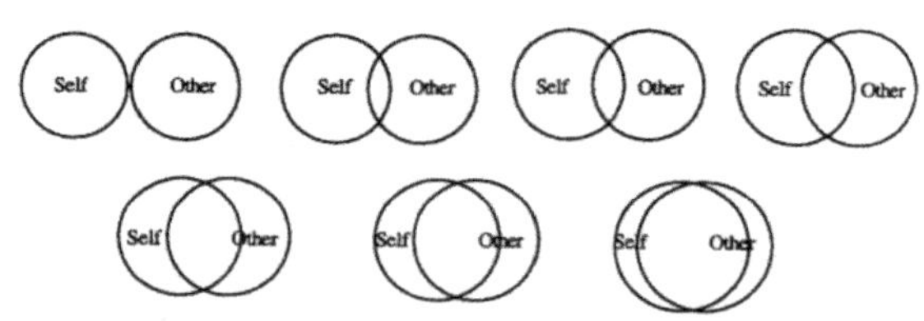

Figure 4 Inclusion of Self in Others Scale: Illustration reprinted from Aron *et al.* [7]

Conversational turn taking

In the group discussion, partners exchanged ideas. A coder recorded the start time and duration of each group member's utterances. This provided the overall number of

Figure 5 Design feature sharing: The two partner ads above have **three** commonalities: images, phrasing, and background color

speech turns by each partner, the total amount of speaking, the ratio of time spent by the more conversationally-dominant partner (high and low talkers), and the frequency of turns per minute of interaction.

Design feature sharing

For each final ad, we counted cross-pollinated features in five categories: word phrases, background color, images, layout, and styles (*i.e.*, fonts, rotations, *etc.*). Cross-pollination was a binary value for each category. A category received a mark if a participant's final ad exhibited a feature that was present in their partner's shared provisional ad, but *not* in their own provisional ad(s) (see Figure 5).

Group consensus

As an aggregate measure of group consensus, independent raters assessed pair-wise similarity between partner ads. The similarity assessment contrasted ads created before and after the discussion. Ten raters recruited from Mechanical Turk assessed similarity on a scale from 1 to 7 (not similar to very similar) (see Figure 3). If the designs are more similar after the discussion, it suggests that partners converge around similar concepts.

RESULTS

Participants created a wide variety of ad designs, demonstrating a range of quality. The highest-rated ads tended to be original, visually appealing, and cleverly touched on themes relevant to *FaceAIDS* (see Figure 6, left column). Ads with high click-through rates grabbed the attention of web users by employing more unconventional color palettes, layouts, and rhetorical hooks (see Figure 6, right column). Highly rated ads did not correlate with high performing ads ($R^2 = 0.018$, $F(1,79) = 2.445$, $p > 0.05$, $b = 0.174$). The third highest performing ad, for example, was the second lowest rated ad. This paper considers different meanings of quality by examining various outcomes.

FaceAIDS reviewed the ads before they appeared online. The client found four of the ads to have inappropriate negative imagery, and requested they not be shown. Three of these were from *Share Best;* one was from *Share Multiple.* In total, the ad campaign generated 239 clicks on 274,539 impressions (ad appearances). The total advertising costs were $362 USD (an average of $1.51 per click).

The results supported all four hypotheses. Participants in the *Share Multiple* condition produced higher-quality designs (better click-through rates and higher ratings) and created more diverse designs. Pairs in the *Share Multiple* condition reported a greater increase in rapport, exchanged more verbal information, and shared more ideas. Moreover, ads by more experienced participants received higher ratings than novices; the designs created by experienced participants were less diverse than novices.

Sharing multiple led to higher quality designs

Ad campaign results

A chi-squared analysis examined ad campaign performance for all 12 days. *Share Multiple* ads had 98,867 impressions with 106 clicks, *Share Best* ads had 77,558 impressions with 57 clicks, and *Share One* ads had 98,038 impressions with 76 clicks (Figure 1 summarizes the average clicks per million impressions). *Share Multiple* ads had a significantly higher click-through rate ($\chi2= 4.72$, $p<0.05$).

An analysis of variances was performed with condition (*Share Multiple*, *Share Best*, and *Share One*) and graphic design score (*experienced* or *novice*) as factors and total time spent and pages visited as dependent variables. Between conditions, there were no differences for total time spent ($F(5,202)=0.808$, $p>0.05$) or number of pages visited from each ad ($F(5,202)=0.461$, $p>0.05$).

Graphic design experience did not effect campaign results

Ads created by participants who scored high on the graphic design exam garnered 110 clicks on 128,783 impressions; novice ads had 129 clicks on 145,756 impressions. This was not a significant difference ($\chi2= 0.08$, $p>0.05$). Experienced participants benefited more from the manipulation

Figure 6 Top five highest-rated ads (left); ads with top five click-through rates (right)

than novices did (see Table 1). Experienced participants in the *Share Multiple* condition outperformed experienced participants in the *Share Best* ($\chi 2$= 3.95, p<0.05) and *Share One* conditions ($\chi 2$= 8.33, p<0.05). There were no ad performance differences between conditions for novices.

	Experienced	Novice
Share Multiple	1125.3 (818.0)	991.7 (482.2)
Share Best	704.3 (422.2)	758.9 (888.5)
Share One	540.3 (500.0)	905.5 (371.7)

Table 1 Online performance in clicks per million impressions for condition and experience (std dev in parentheses). Experienced participants created better ads and were more affected by condition.

An ANOVA showed that experience did not significantly affect total time spent (F(5,202)=0.091, p>0.05) or number of pages visited from each ad (F(5,202)=0.076, p>0.05).

Quality ratings

Thirty raters judged all final ads on a 7-point scale (1=poor and 7=excellent). An analysis of variances was performed with condition (*Share Multiple, Share Best,* and *Share One*) and graphic design score (*experienced* or *novice*) as factors and performance rating as the dependent variable. The *Share Multiple* condition (μ=3.89, SD=1.82) outperformed the other conditions (F(2,2519)=5.075, p<0.05). The difference between the *Share Best* (μ=3.63, SD=1.78) and *Share One* (μ=3.71, SD=1.71) conditions was not significant (p>0.05; Tukey's test).

Professionals, clients, and turkers (workers on Amazon Mechanical Turk) all rated *Share Multiple* ads higher than the other conditions (see Table 2). Clients (μ=3.77, SD=1.73) and turkers (μ=3.99, SD=1.74) ratings were higher on average than those by ad professionals (μ=2.85, SD=1.60) (F(2,2519)=86.961, p<0.05). This differential between advertising professionals and other stakeholders is consistent with prior work [16].

	Clients	Ad pros	Turkers
Share Multiple	4.06 (1.70)	2.95 (1.63)	4.14 (1.80)
Share Best	3.45 (1.77)	2.76 (1.63)	3.90 (1.74)
Share One	3.79 (1.69)	2.85 (1.55)	3.94 (1.68)

Table 2 Average ratings (std dev in parentheses). All rater types (clients, ad pros, and turkers) rated *Share Multiple* ads higher.

Graphic design experience led to better ratings

Participants who scored highly on the graphic design exam (μ=4.10, SD=1.709) significantly outperformed those who scored poorly (μ=3.48, SD=1.773), (F(1,2519)=74.613, p<0.05). The ANOVA shows that novices benefited more from the manipulation than experienced participants did (F(2,2519)=3.536, p<0.05) (see Table 3). This differential gain is the opposite from the click-through rate, where experienced participants benefited more from sharing multiple designs.

	Experienced	Novice
Share Multiple	4.11 (1.71)	3.68 (1.90)
Share Best	4.19 (1.71)	3.31 (1.74)
Share One	4.01 (1.71)	3.48 (1.67)

Table 3 Average ratings by condition and experience (std dev in parentheses). Experienced created higher-rated ads; novices were more affected by condition.

Sharing multiple led to more individual exploration

Raters from Amazon Mechanical Turk deemed *Share Multiple* ads to be most divergent. An analysis of variances was performed with condition (*Share Multiple, Share Best,* and *Share One*) and graphic design score (*experienced* or *novice*) as factors and pair-wise similarity rating as the dependent variable. The similarity rating differed significantly across conditions (F(2,3640)=82.07, p<0.05). Tukey post-hoc comparisons of the three conditions indicate that *Share Multiple* ads (μ=3.85, SD=1.93) were more diverse than *Share Best* ads (μ=3.99, SD=1.96) (p<0.05) and *Share Best* ads were more diverse than *Share One* ads (μ=5.45, SD=1.86) (p<0.05).

Experienced participants created ads that were deemed significantly more similar (μ=4.20, SD=1.96) than those who scored poorly (μ=3.91, SD=1.99) (F(1,3640)=7.692, p<0.05). There was no interaction effect between condition and prior experience.

Group rapport rose for partners who shared multiple

A one-way ANOVA showed the group rapport differed significantly across conditions (F(2,83)=4.147, p<0.05). Tukey post-hoc comparisons of the three conditions indicate that group rapport increased in the *Share Multiple* condition (μ = 0.89, SD 3.06) compared to the others (p<0.05). In absolute terms, rapport *only* increased in the Share Multiple condition (see Table 4).

	Before design critique	After design critique	Group rapport shift
Share Multiple	μ=24.6 (4.35)	μ=25.5 (4.66)	+0.89
Share Best	μ=24.0 (5.24)	μ=22.3 (4.79)	-1.75
Share One	μ=24.9 (5.18)	μ=22.8 (5.86)	-2.11

Table 4 Individual views of group rapport rose in the *Share Multiple* condition; it dropped in other conditions (std dev in parentheses)

Share Multiple partners took more conversational turns

An video analysis of speech duration during the group discussion showed that participants in the *Share Multiple* condition had significantly more frequent verbal exchanges (a higher number of speaker turns per minute of speaking time) than other conditions (F(2,39)=3.506, p<0.05). *Share Multiple* pairs averaged 12.1 (SD=4.99) turns per minute, compared to 9.1 (SD=2.62) and 8.6 (SD=2.86) turns per minute, for *Share Best* and *Share One*, respectively. There were no significant between-condition differences for total number of speaker turns (F(2,39)=0.695, p>0.05), total speaking time (F(2,39)=1.057, p>0.05), or the ratio of high and low talkers (F(2,39)=0.092, p>0.05).

Share Multiple pairs borrowed more features

In total, *Share Multiple* partners borrowed 32 features, *Share Best* 18, and *Share One* 19 (see Table 5). (The theoretical maximum for each condition is 140: 28 participants, 5 categories.) Participants in the *Share Multiple* condition borrowed significantly more features overall ($\chi2=4.05$, $p<0.05$).

	Share Multiple	*Share Best*	*Share One*
Word phrases	15	9	6
Background color	3	0	2
Images	10	6	7
Layout	3	2	3
Surface patterns	1	1	1
Total	**32**	**18**	**19**

Table 5 Participants in the *Share Multiple* condition borrowed more features from their partners than other conditions

Share Multiple pairs reached a better consensus

Independent judges rated the partner ad similarity before and after the discussion. The similarity change provides a measure of shared perspective. Overall, final ads were more similar ($\mu=3.40$, SD=1.91) than initial ads ($\mu=2.68$, SD=1.64) ($t(3078)=8.107$, $p<0.05$). Tukey post-hoc comparisons of shifts by each pair show that similarity increased more for the *Share Multiple* condition (0.91) than the *Share Best* (0.55) or *Share One* conditions (0.52) ($p<0.05$) (see Table 6).

	Before design critique	After design critique	Similarity shift
Share Multiple	2.59 (1.55)	3.50 (1.91)	0.91
Share Best	2.75 (1.71)	3.30 (1.97)	0.55
Share One	2.87 (1.81)	3.39 (1.85)	0.52

Table 6 Pairs designs in the *Share Multiple* condition increased in similarity more than other conditions (st. dev. in parentheses)

DISCUSSION

Sharing *multiple* designs led to several kinds of better outcomes. Simply *creating* multiple designs (without feedback) led to broader exploration, but not better results. The benefits were only realized if participants *shared* multiple designs. It's important to remember that participants worked on the same task for the same amount of time. The only variable was how many designs they created and shared. This section suggests reasons for why this simple act yielded differential outcomes, illustrating these with interview excerpts.

Hypotheses revisited

Creating and viewing multiple designs leads to more individual exploration.

The *Share Multiple* and *Share Best* participants explored significantly more broadly than the *Share One* participants. Creative work often benefits from broadly exploring possibilities before choosing a direction to refine [9]. As this study and prior work found [16,41], rapidly producing alternatives and getting feedback on them yields higher-quality, more-diverse results. As one *Share Multiple* participant described after seeing her partner's designs: "they were completely different from mine and I was like holy hell, that's pretty good. I didn't think about that." Another participant claimed that "getting a different perspective helped and also seeing different ideas—not flaws in mine, but different ideas in his that I'd like to borrow."

Experienced participants created less diverse designs than novices; their ads were also rated higher. Expert designers can rapidly construct entailments, mentally simulating design moves and their consequences [44]. Drawing on their many prior experiences, experts can often ignore or disregard the obviously bad options [18]. This foresight enables experts to strategically explore highly-promising subsets of the design space.

Sharing multiple designs leads to more productive dialogue and better group rapport.

Across all conditions, there was a small but statistically significant decline in reported group rapport after the discussion ($t(83)=2.050$, $p<0.05$). While critique obviously provides a valuable channel for feedback and learning new information, negative critique can also degrade group relations and performance. Individuals' self efficacy may decrease in reaction to negative critique, which in turn lowers their performance [12]. Furthermore, people receiving negative critique may resent the critique provider, poisoning team dynamics. In an understatement, one crest-fallen *Share Best* participant demurred, "she didn't make me feel like a total failure." Clearly the critique damaged her estimation of her abilities. Would this participant have felt better about herself and her team if she had shared multiple designs? In this study, group rapport actually increased when participants shared multiple designs. And prior work has shown that when teams generate lots of ideas, people feel more shared ownership and stronger team cohesiveness [23,49].

Pairs in the *Share Multiple* condition exchanged speaking turns significantly more often. As one *Share Multiple* participants said, "being able to see the other person's designs and actually bounce ideas back and forth... that helped clarify what was good design and what wasn't." Frequent exchanges helped participants discuss design tradeoffs and consider changes that address fundamental issues. As one participant said, "it got me thinking about who would click on an ad and why someone would click on an ad."

Sharing multiple designs increases conceptual blending.

Participants in the *Share Multiple* condition integrated more features and modified their designs to be more like their partner's. Participants often talked about the process of merging designs. One *Share Multiple* participant said, "we agreed we like elements of mine and I really like some elements of one of his and we just kind of did a mash-up and combined them." In contrast, a *Share Best* participant said, "we thought about some ideas, but we didn't really get to a consensus of what we were going to design." Likewise, a *Share One* participant said, "I didn't really get a lot of things to change on mine, so I just stuck with what I had."

This notion of "sticking" with an idea did not surface in the *Share Multiple* condition.

Seeing multiple of a partner's designs provides more raw material for comparison. This was beneficial because comparison helps people understand underlying principles better than just one [52]. One participant in the *Share Multiple* condition said "(our) ads look different, but I feel like in general it's the same message that's getting across." Forming a stronger understanding of their partner's design rationale may be one reason *Share Multiple* participants reached more consensus and produced better results. Consensus is importantly different than groupthink, where a group blindly follows along one path without considering alternatives. In this study, convergence between Share Multiple pairs occurred *after* participants had explored many concepts.

Applying a *Share Multiple* Approach

Several interesting questions emerge about applying these results.

What are this study's implications for teaching and practice?
Design organizations and educators can structure group work around creating and sharing alternative designs. For example, Stanford's introductory HCI course revised its curriculum to more strongly emphasize creating and comparing alternatives (http://cs147.stanford.edu). For designers and educators who already employ a "share multiple" approach, this result provides them empirical support.

(How) can the share multiple strategy help with more complex design work?
In this study, participants were able to create complete designs in a short amount of time. In many domains, sketches can be produced quickly, but creating *complete* designs is costly and time consuming. Does that mean for complex domains, a share multiple strategy can only be employed early in the design process? When creating multiple comprehensive designs is impractical, designers can still prototype and share alternatives to sub-problems. For example, in Web design it may be infeasible to produce three very different functional sites, but invaluable to create and test strategically selected elements. In fact, some of the world's best sites do so every day [32].

Considerations for Using Ad Analytics in Experiments

This paper's advertising paradigm provides experimenters leverage when studying creative work. It offers strong quantitative benchmarks through its Web analytics, captures the views of many stakeholders, and provides measures of several different types of outcomes. While using advertising analytics is appealing for its ecological validity, this section shares three practical challenges.

Ensure ads are shown evenly
To maximize profit, many advertisers show ads differentially. If an ad performs well, it is shown more. If initial performance is poor, it is shown less (or not at all). Some platforms provide a setting to show ads more evenly; use this when available. Even with this setting, rotation may not be completely even; monitor this daily. It is important to run a pilot test with a few ads to determine effective keywords, budget (cost per click and daily maximums). Specifying geographical regions and time of day can also help generate a sufficient volume of impression and clicks.

Be mindful of ad market capacity
While it may appear that—given a sufficient budget—advertising platforms have unlimited capacity, this is not the case. Web adverting succeeds because it shows ads relevant to a user's current interests (http://en.wikipedia.org/wiki/Online_advertising). Showing irrelevant ads yields few clicks and little revenue for the host. On a given day, a finite number of people search for a particular topic like AIDS, design, or real-estate. That's the upper bound of relevant ads that can be served.

It's preferable to show all ads simultaneously to factor out differential effects of external variables, such as day of week, time of year, current events, *etc*. Furthermore, one needs a sufficient number of impressions and clicks to make meaningful statistical distinctions. For this paper's study, 80 ads pushed the limits of how many alternate ads can be simultaneously shown. Circulating more ads would have sliced the market of available impressions too thin.

Gather multiple outcome measures
Which measure is "best"? In our study, online click performance did not correlate with overall rating. Some unattractive ads receive many clicks; the Web has a preponderance of such examples. Is an advertisement's success defined by its click-through performance or by expert ratings? Each tells a valuable story.

CONCLUSIONS AND FUTURE WORK

This paper found that when people produce and share multiple alternatives with peers, they explore more diverse ideas, integrate more of their partner's features, engage in more productive design conversations, and ultimately, create higher-quality work. Many designers already practice this approach. These results suggest that more practitioners and teachers might beneficially adopt a "share multiple" strategy. More broadly, this work raises several important questions.

First, (how) do these results generalize to different types of groups? In this study, participants were independently recruited with no prior collaboration. In most professional work, collaboration is longitudinal, and power relationships and social dynamics are more complex. In this study, all group members performed the same role. Often for a variety of reasons, different team members perform different functions. Cross-functional teams can add value in both professional and learning contexts, such as jigsaw learning where different students are responsible for complementary parts of a topic [3]. What does sharing multiple designs mean for cross-functional teams and how does the outcome change depending on who does the creating and sharing?

Second, recent research on "the crowd within" suggests that at least some of the benefits of aggregating many people's perspectives can be accomplished by providing individuals with a structured approach to considering alternatives [26]. This study witnessed several benefits of group discussion; can structured reflection help individuals benefit similarly?

Third, we hypothesize the share multiple condition benefited in two ways. *Creating* several alternatives spread participants' investment and discouraged fixation. *Seeing* others' designs gave participants a larger palette to work from. An important step for future work is to separate these two effects. One strategy would be to have designers supplement their own creations with previously created examples. An alternative would be for software to synthesize design alternatives [25,35].

Forth, the benefits of rapidly creating and sharing multiple alternatives are myriad. How might software tools help designers explore more broadly? Initial results are promising [25,35]; more exciting work remains.

REFERENCES

1. Arkes, H.R. and Blumer, C. The psychology of sunk cost. *Organizational Behavior and Human Decision Processes 35*, 1 (1985), 124-140.
2. Aron, A., Aron, E.N., and Smollan, D. Inclusion of Other in the Self Scale and the Structure of Interpersonal Closeness. *Journal of Personality and Social Psychology 63*, 4 (1992), 596-612.
3. Aronson, E., Bridgeman, D., and Geffner, R. Interdependent Interactions and Prosocial Behavior. *Journal of Research and Development in Education 12*, 1 (1978), 16-27.
4. Ball, L.J. and Ormerod, T.C. Structured and opportunistic processing in design: a critical discussion. *International Journal Human-Computer Studies 43*, 1 (1995), 131-151.
5. Bao, P., Gerber, E., Gergle, D., and Hoffman, D. Momentum: getting and staying on topic during a brainstorm. *Proc of conf on Human factors in computing systems*, ACM (2010), 1233-1236.
6. Ben-David, I., Graham, J.R., and Harvey, C.R. Managerial Overconfidence and Corporate Policies. *National Bureau of Economic Research Working Paper Series No. 13711*, (2007).
7. Brandt, J., Dontcheva, M., Weskamp, M., and Klemmer, S.R. Example-centric programming: integrating web search into the development environment. *Proc of conf on Human factors in computing systems*, ACM (2010), 513-522.
8. Brereton, M., Cannon, M., Mabogunje, A., and Leifer, L. Collaboration in Design Teams: How Social Interaction Shapes the Product. In *Analyzing Design Activity*. Wiley, 1996.
9. Buxton, B. *Sketching User Experiences: Getting the Design Right and the Right Design.* Morgan Kaufmann, 2007.
10. Cross, N. Expertise in design: an overview. *Design Studies 25*, 5 (2004), 427-441.
11. Curhan, J.R., Elfenbein, H.A., and Xu, H. What Do People Value When They Negotiate? Mapping the Domain of Subjective Value in Negotiation. *Journal of Personality and Social Psychology 91*, 3 (2006), 493-512.
12. Dannels, D.P. and Martin, K.N. Critiquing Critiques: A Genre Analysis of Feedback Across Novice to Expert Design Studios. *Journal of Business and Technical Communication 22*, 2 (2008), 135-159.
13. Davidoff, S., Lee, M.K., Dey, A.K., and Zimmerman, J. Rapidly Exploring Application Design Through Speed Dating. *Proc. of Conf on Ubiquitou Computing*, (2007).
14. Diehl, M. and Stroebe, W. Productivity Loss In Brainstorming Groups: Toward the Solution of a Riddle. *Journal of Personality and Social Psychology 53*, 3 (1987), 497-509.
15. Dow, S.P., Heddleston, K., and Klemmer, S.R. The Efficacy of Prototyping Under Time Constraints. *Proceeding of ACM Conf. on Creativity and Cognition*, ACM (2009), 165-174.
16. Dow, S., Glassco, A., Kass, J., Schwarz, M., Schwartz, D.L., and Klemmer, S.R. Parallel Prototyping Leads to Better Design Results, More Divergence, and Increased Self-Efficacy. *Transactions on Computer-Human Interaction 4*, (2010).
17. Dweck, C. *Mindset: The New Psychology of Success.* Ballantine Books, 2007.
18. Ericsson, K.A. and Smith, J. *Toward a General Theory of Expertise: Prospects and Limits.* Cambridge University Press, 1991.
19. Fauconnier, G. and Turner, M. *The Way We Think: Conceptual Blending and the Mind□s Hidden Complexities.* Basic Books, 2003.
20. Felps, W., Mitchell, T., and Byington, E. How, When, and Why Bad Apples Spoil the Barrel: Negative Group Members and Dysfunctional Groups. *Research in Organizational Behavior 27*, (2006), 175-222.
21. Finke, R.A., Ward, T.B., and Smith, S.M. *Creative Cognition: Theory, Research, and Applications.* The MIT Press, 1996.
22. Gaver, W.W., Beaver, J., and Benford, S. Ambiguity as a resource for design. *Proceedings of the SIGCHI conference on Human factors in computing systems*, ACM (2003), 233-240.
23. Gerber, E. Prototyping Practice in Context: The Psychological Experience in a High Tech Firm. *Journal of Design Studies*, (2010).
24. Hampton, J.A. Inheritance of attributes in natural concept conjunctions. *Memory & Cognition 15*, 1 (1987), 55-71.
25. Hartmann, B., Yu, L., Allison, A., Yang, Y., and Klemmer, S.R. Design as exploration: creating interface alternatives through parallel authoring and runtime tuning. *Proc of the conf on User interface software and technology*, ACM (2008), 91-100.
26. Herzog, S.M. and Hertwig, R. The Wisdom of Many in One Mind. *Psychological Science 20*, 2 (2009), 231 -237.
27. Hyland, F. and Hyland, K. Sugaring the pill: Praise and criticism in written feedback. *Journal of Second Language Writing 10*, 3 (2001), 185-212.
28. Iyengar, S.S. and Lepper, M.R. When choice is demotivating: can one desire too much of a good thing? *Journal of Personality and Social Psychology 79*, 6 (2000), 995-1006.
29. Janis, I.L. *Groupthink: Psychological Studies of Policy Decisions and Fiascoes.* Wadsworth Publishing, 1982.
30. Jansson, D. and Smith, S. Design Fixation. *Design Studies 12*, 1 (1991), 3-11.
31. Kershaw, T.C. and Ohlsson, S. Multiple causes of difficulty in insight: the case of the nine-dot problem. *Journal of Experimental Psychology. Learning, Memory, and Cognition 30*, 1 (2004), 3-13.
32. Kohavi, R. and Longbotham, R. Online Experiments: Lessons Learned. *Computer 40*, 2007, 103-105.
33. Kosara, R. Visualization Criticism - The Missing Link Between Information Visualization and Art. *Proc of the Conf on Information Visualization*, IEEE Computer Society (2007), 631-636.
34. Larrick, R.P. Broaden the decision frame to make effective decisions. In *Handbook of Principles of Organizational Behavior.* Wiley and Sons, 2009.
35. Lee, B., Srivastava, S., Kumar, R., Brafman, R., and Klemmer, S.R. Designing with interactive example galleries.

Proc of the conf on Human factors in computing systems, ACM (2010), 2257-2266.
36. Leifer, L. Dancing with Ambiguity: design thinking in theory and practice. 2010.
37. Mark, G., Gonzalez, V.M., and Harris, J. No task left behind?: examining the nature of fragmented work. *Proc of the conf on Human factors in computing systems*, (2005), 321-330.
38. Marsh, R.L., Landau, J.D., and Hicks, J.L. How examples may (and may not) constrain creativity. *Memory & Cognition 24*, 5 (1996), 669-680.
39. Moran, T.P. and Carroll, J.M. *Design Rationale: Concepts, Techniques, and Use*. CRC Press, 1996.
40. Nickerson, R.S. Confirmation Bias: A Ubiquitous Phenomenon in Many Guises. *Review of General Psychology 2*, (1998), 175-220.
41. Nielsen, J. and Faber, J.M. Improving System Usability Through Parallel Design. *Computer 29*, 2 (1996), 29-35.
42. Ranganath, R., Jurafsky, D., and McFarland, D. It□s not you, it's me: detecting flirting and its misperception in speed-dates. *Proc of Conf on Empirical Methods in Natural Language Processing*, Association for Computational Linguistics (2009), 334-342.
43. S. Smith. Constraining effects of examples in a creative generation task. *Memory & Cognition 21*, (1993), 837-845.
44. Schon, D.A. *The Reflective Practitioner: How Professionals Think in Action*. Ashgate Publishing, 1995.
45. Schrage, M. *Serious Play: How the World□s Best Companies Simulate to Innovate*. Harvard Business School Press, 1999.
46. Schwartz, B. *The Paradox of Choice: Why More Is Less*. Ecco, 2004.
47. Schwartz, D.L. The Emergence of Abstract Representations in Dyad Problem Solving. *Journal of the Learning Sciences 4*, 3 (1995), 321.
48. Stroebe, W. and Diehl, M. Why Groups are less Effective than their Members: On Productivity Losses in Idea-generating Groups. *European Review of Social Psychology 5*, (1994), 271.
49. Sutton, R. and Hargadon, A. Brainstorming groups in context: effectiveness in a product design firm. *Administrative Science Quarterly*, (1996).
50. Taylor, D., Berry, P., and Block, C. Does Group Participation When Using Brainstorming Facilitate or Inhibit Creative Thinking? *Administrative Science Quarterly 3*, 1 (1958), 23-47.
51. Thomke, S. and Nimgade, A. IDEO Product Development. *Harvard Business School Case*, (2000).
52. Thompson, L., Gentner, D., and Loewenstein, J. Avoiding Missed Opportunities in Managerial Life: Analogical Training More Powerful Than Individual Case Training. *Organizational Behavior and Human Decision Processes 82*, 1 (2000), 60-75.
53. Tohidi, M., Buxton, W., Baecker, R., and Sellen, A. Getting the right design and the design right. *Proceedings of the SIGCHI conference on Human Factors in computing systems*, ACM (2006), 1243-1252.
54. Warr, A. and O□Neill, E. Understanding design as a social creative process. *Proc of the conf on Creativity & Cognition*, ACM (2005), 118-127.
55. Wisniewski, E. and Gentner, D. On the combinatorial semantics of noun pairs: {Minor} and major adjustments to meaning. In *Understanding word and sentence*. Amsterdam: North Holland, 1991, 241-284.
56. Zwicky, F. *Discovery, Invention, Research Through the Morphological Approach*. MacMillan, 1969.

APPENDIX A: Graphic Design Assessment

Instructions: For each of the statements below, indicate (True or False) whether or not the statement is a rule of graphic design.

1	Mix serif and sans serif fonts in order to give variety to the ad.	F
2	To help balance the ad, leave slightly more space at the top relative to the bottom of the ad.	F
3	Create a visual separation between the text and the background.	T
4	Angle the text in order to contrast different parts of the ad.	F
5	Keep all elements in the ad aligned to one side.	F
6	Create multiple visual focal points in order to attract attention to the ad as a whole.	F
7	Use borders or white around text and images to help frame the content.	T
8	You may use repetition to create a consistent and balanced look.	T
9	You may break alignment to draw the viewer's attention to important elements in the ad.	T
10	Draw the viewer's attention to important elements by	T

APPENDIX B: Advertising Design Brief

Assignment

You have been hired to design a graphic advertisement for FACEAIDS.org. You will learn to use a new graphic design tool, design provisional ads, and create a final ad to be posted through the Google ad network.

Goals

Keep in mind the following goals as you create your ads:

a) Increase traffic to the *FaceAIDS* website: http://faceaids.org/
b) Reach out to the target audience: students interested in improving global healthcare equality and making a difference in the AIDS epidemic in Africa.
c) Impress the clients from *FaceAIDS*, who will rate your ads. The client wants an ad that fits their overall aesthetic and theme (see below).
d) Create ads with effective graphic design. Ad prpreceiofessionals will rate your ads.

What is FaceAIDS?

FaceAIDS is a nonprofit organization dedicated to mobilizing and inspiring students to fight AIDS in Africa. *FaceAIDS* aims to build a broad-based movement of students seeking to increase global health equality. The organization raises awareness and funds, with the goal of increasing global health equality starting with the AIDS epidemic in Africa.

Theme and Aesthetic for the FaceAids Ad

FaceAIDS would like an advertisement that embodies the theme and general aesthetic of the organization. In particular, they are looking to encourage high school and college students interested in getting involved in service or social justice work to start *FaceAIDS* chapters on their campuses, as a leadership development opportunity and a way to join a vibrant, impactful community of like-minded, driven peers. In general they are looking for an ad that is tasteful, creative, professional, visually appealing, and conveys a clear message about the organization.

Rules/Requirements

- You may download and use graphics & images as you see fit.
- You may not use another company's logo, copyrighted images, profanity, obscenity or nudity. Unacceptable ads will be rejected by the research team.
- Do not include the magazine's URL on the ad. Clicking the ad will direct the user to the site.

CHI 2011 Author Index

CHI 2011 Author Index

CHI 2011 Author Index

CHI 2011 Author Index

CHI 2011 Author Index

CHI 2011 Author Index

CHI 2011 Author Index

CHI 2011 Author Index

CHI 2011 Author Index

CHI 2011 Author Index

CHI 2011 Author Index

CHI 2011 Author Index

CHI 2011 Author Index

CHI 2011 Author Index

CHI 2011 Author Index

CHI 2011 Author Index

CHI 2011 Author Index

www.ingramcontent.com/pod-product-compliance
Lightning Source LLC
LaVergne TN
LVHW080101011026
849160LV00013B/1008